ELEMENTS OF
Literature
FIFTH COURSE
LITERATURE OF
THE UNITED STATES
WITH LITERATURE OF THE AMERICAS

For we must consider that
we shall be as a city
upon a hill . . .

— John Winthrop, 1630

HOLT, RINEHART AND WINSTON
Harcourt Brace & Company
Austin • New York • Orlando • Atlanta • San Francisco • Boston • Dallas • Toronto • London

Credits

EDITORIAL

Project Director:	Kathleen Daniel
Managing Editors:	Richard Sime, Bill Wahlgren
Project Editor:	Hester Weeden
Book Editor:	Ian Lague
Editorial Staff:	Steven Fechter, Abigail Winograd, Susan Kent Cakars, Dorothy M. Coe, Edward S. Cohen, Lanie Lee, Christine de Ligniéres, and Ron Ottaviano; David Knaggs and Sharon Churchin; Vicky Aeschbacher, Jane Archer-Feinstein, Roger Boylan, James Decker, Eric Estlund, Peggy Ferrin, Emily Gavin, Mikki Gibson, Annie Hartnett, Sean Henry, Julie Hoover, Eileen Joyce, Marcia Kelley, Linda Miller, Chi Nguyen, Carla Robinson, Deanna Roy, Tressa Sanders, Errol Smith, Suzanne Thompson, and Stephen Wesson
Editorial Support Staff:	Dan Hunter, Laurie Muir, Su Gordon, Leila Jamal, David Smith, Elizabeth Butler, Ruth Hooker, Kelly Keeley, Marie Price, Margaret Sanchez
Permissions:	Ann B. Farrar, Sacha Frey, Mark Hughs
Research and Development:	Joan Burditt

PRODUCTION AND DESIGN

Text Design:	Preface, Inc.
Design Coordinator:	Fariba Hajahmadi
Electronic Files:	GGS Information Services, Banta Digital
Production and Manufacturing:	Athena Blackorby
Marketing Design:	Bob Bretz

COVER

Cover Artist:	Greg Geisler
Photo Credits:	City skyscrapers, New York, Rafael Macia/Photo Researchers, Inc.; Chicago, Walter Bibikow/FPG International and Nathan Benn/Woodfin Camp & Assoc.; Dallas, Dan Budnik/Woodfin Camp & Assoc.; San Francisco, David L. Brown/Nawrocki Stock Photo; Seattle, Porterfield/Chickering/Photo Researchers, Inc.; Tampa, Ken Biggs/Tony Stone Images; Providence, Joseph Sohm/Tony Stone Images; mountain forest, J. Robert Stottlemyer/International Stock; mountain range, Toyohiro Yamada/FPG International; sky, Xefa/Index Stock Imagery; yellow foliage, Chad Ehlers/International Stock; red foliage, H. Okamoto/Photonica; (back cover) nautilus, Kathleen Campbell/Tony Stone Images.
Quotation on Cover:	From a sermon delivered delivered by John Winthrop, 1630. For a longer extract, see page T2.

Printed in the United States of America

ISBN 0-03-052117-3

3 4 5 6 048 03 02 01 00

Program Authors

Robert E. Probst established the pedagogical framework for the 1997 and 2000 editions of *Elements of Literature.* Dr. Probst is Professor of English Education at Georgia State University. For several years he was an English Teacher in Maryland and Supervisor of English for the Norfolk, Virginia, Public Schools. He is the author of *Response and Analysis: Teaching Literature in Junior and Senior High School.* He has also contributed chapters to such books as *Literature Instruction: A Focus on Student Response; Reader Response in the Classroom: Evoking and Interpreting Meaning in Literature; Handbook of Research on Teaching the English Language Arts; Transactions with Literature: A Fifty-Year Perspective;* and *For Louise M. Rosenblatt.* Dr. Probst is a member of the National Council of Teachers of English and has worked on the council's Committee on Research, the Commission on Reading, and the Commission on Curriculum. Dr. Probst has also served on the board of directors of the Adolescent Literature Assembly and is a member of the National Conference on Research in Language and Literacy.

Robert Anderson wrote the introduction to "American Drama," the biography of Arthur Miller, and the instructional material on *The Crucible.* Mr. Anderson is a playwright, novelist, screenwriter, and teacher. His plays include *Tea and Sympathy; Silent Night, Lonely Night; You Know I Can't Hear You When the Water's Running;* and *I Never Sang for My Father.* His screenplays include *The Nun's Story* and *The Sand Pebbles.* Mr. Anderson has taught at the Writer's Workshop at the University of Iowa, the American Theater Wing Professional Training Program, and the Salzburg Seminar in American Studies. He is a past president of the Dramatists' Guild, a past vice president of the Authors' League of America, and a member of the Theater Hall of Fame.

John Malcolm Brinnin wrote the introductions to "A New American Poetry: Whitman and Dickinson," "The Harlem Renaissance," and "Symbolism, Imagism, and Beyond." He co-authored the introductions to "The Moderns" and "Contemporary Literature." Mr. Brinnin wrote the biographies of poets and instructional material on poetry, including Critical Comments. He wrote all the Elements of Literature features on poetry. Mr. Brinnin is the author of six volumes of poetry that have received many prizes and awards. He was a member of the American Academy and Institute of Arts and Letters. He was also a critic of poetry and a biographer of poets and was for a number of years director of New York's famous Poetry Center. His teaching career, begun at Vassar College, included long terms at the University of Connecticut and Boston University, where he succeeded Robert Lowell as Professor of Creative Writing and Contemporary Letters. Mr. Brinnin wrote *Dylan Thomas in America: An Intimate Journal* and *Sextet: T.S. Eliot & Truman Capote & Others.*

John Leggett co-authored the introductions to "The Moderns" and "Contemporary Literature." He wrote biographies of the fiction writers, the instructional material on fiction, including Critical Comments, and the Elements of Literature features on fiction. Mr. Leggett is a novelist, a biographer, and a former teacher. He went to the Writer's Workshop at the University of Iowa in the spring of 1969, expecting to work there for a single semester. In 1970, he assumed temporary charge of the program, and for the next seventeen years he was its director. Mr. Leggett's novels include *Wilder Stone; The Gloucester Branch; Who Took the Gold Away?; Gulliver House;* and *Making Believe.* He also wrote the highly acclaimed biography *Ross and Tom: Two American Tragedies.*

Richard Vacca established the conceptual basis for the reading strand in Grades 9 through 12 for the 2000 edition of *Elements of Literature.* Dr. Vacca is Professor of Education at Kent State University. He has also taught at Northern Illinois University and the University of Connecticut and at the middle school and high school levels. Dr. Vacca is co-author of *Content Area Reading; Reading and Learning to Read; Whole Language in Middle and Secondary Classrooms;* and *Case Studies in Whole Language.* For several years he served as the project director of the Cleveland Writing Project, a collaborative effort of Kent State University and the Cleveland Public Schools. In 1989, he was the College Reading Association's recipient of the A. B. Herr Award for Outstanding Contributions to Reading Education. Dr. Vacca served as a member of the board of directors of the International Reading Association and recently completed a term as the association's forty-second president. As this book goes to press, he is co-chair of the IRA's Commission on Adolescent Literacy.

Special Contributors

Gary Q. Arpin wrote the introductions to "Beginnings," "American Romanticism," "The American Renaissance," and "The Rise of Realism." He wrote the essays called "The American Language" and biographies of nonfiction writers in the early collections. Dr. Arpin received his doctorate from the University of Virginia, where he taught for several years before taking a position with Western Illinois University at Macomb. He has written articles on John Berryman and other American poets and has published a book, *John Berryman: A Reference Guide.*

Joseph Bruchac wrote the essay "The Sun Still Rises in the Same Sky: Native American Literatures." Mr. Bruchac is a professional storyteller and author inspired by his American Indian heritage and the Adirondack region where he lives. His work has appeared in more than five hundred publications, including the *American Poetry Review* and *National Geographic*. He has written more than sixty books for adults and children. His awards include the Cherokee Nation Prose Award, the Hope S. Dean Award for Notable Achievement in Children's Literature, and the Benjamin Franklin Award as "Person of the Year" by the Publisher's Marketing Association.

Thomas Hernacki co-authored the introduction to "Contemporary Literature" and wrote instructional material for some fiction and poetry. Dr. Hernacki is an educational writer specializing in modern and contemporary literature, particularly American poetry. A native of Chicago, he holds a doctorate in English from Columbia University. His dissertation explores "the poetics of place" in the works of Wallace Stevens. In the 1970s, he contributed to Northrop Frye's archetype-based literatures series, *Uses of the Imagination*. Over the past two decades Dr. Hernacki has directed the editorial development of numerous literature and composition textbooks for secondary schools.

Susan Allen Toth co-authored the introduction to "Contemporary Literature" and wrote biographies and instructional material for contemporary nonfiction writers. Dr. Toth has written *Blooming: A Small-Town Girlhood,* about her childhood in Ames, Iowa; *Ivy Days: Making My Way Out East,* about her experiences at Smith College in Northampton, Massachusetts; and *How to Prepare for Your High-School Reunion and Other Mid-Life Musings*. She studied at the University of California at Berkeley and received her doctorate from the University of Minnesota. She is an adjunct professor and writer-in-residence at Macalester College in St. Paul, Minnesota. She contributes articles to many periodicals, including *Harper's, Redbook, McCall's,* and *The New York Times*.

Writers

The writers prepared instructional materials for the text under the supervision of Dr. Probst and the editorial staff.

Richard Cohen
Former Teacher
Novelist
Educational Writer and Editor
Austin, Texas

Jan Freeman
Poet
Educational Writer and Editor
Williamsburg, Massachusetts

Phyllis Goldenberg
Educational Writer and Editor
North Miami Beach, Florida

Lynn Hovland
Former Teacher
Educational Writer and Editor
Berkeley, California

Rose Sallberg Kam
Former Teacher
Educational Writer and Editor
Sacramento, California

Carol Moulton
Former Teacher
Educational Writer and Editor
Southampton, New York

Susanna Nied
Former Teacher
Educational Writer and Editor
San Diego, California

Eileen Hillary Oshinsky
Educational Writer and Editor
Rhinebeck, New York

Mary Elizabeth Podhaizer
Former Teacher
Educational Writer and Editor
Colchester, Vermont

Gerry Tomlinson
Educational Writer and Editor
Lake Hopatcong, New Jersey

Joan Clark Tornow
Teacher
Austin, Texas

Sarah Wolbach
Educational Writer and Editor
Austin, Texas

Acknowledgments

For permission to reprint copyrighted material, grateful acknowledgment is made to the following sources:

Adams Media Corporation: From *What Every American Should Know About Women's History* by Christine Lunardini. Copyright © 1992 by Christine Lunardini.

African American Review, Indiana State University: From "The Blues Poetry of Langston Hughes" by Edward Waldron from *Negro American Literature Forum* (currently *African American Review*), vol. 5, no. 4 (1971). Copyright © 1971 by African American Review.

The Antioch Review, Inc.: From "Richard Wright's Blues" by Ralph Ellison from *Antioch Review*, vol. 5, no. 1, March 1945. Copyright 1945 by The Antioch Review, Inc.

Roger Asselineau: From *The Evolution of Walt Whitman: The Creation of a Book* by Roger Asselineau. Copyright © 1962 by Roger Asselineau.

Atheneum Books for Young Readers, an imprint of Simon & Schuster Children's Publishing Division: From *Empires Lost and Won* by Albert Marrin. Copyright © 1997 by Albert Marrin.

Capricorn Books, a division of Penguin Putnam Inc.: From Introduction by Kenneth Eble from *The Awakening* by Kate Chopin. Copyright © 1964 by Capricorn Books.

The Condé Nast Publications, Inc.: From "Hersey and History" by Roger Angell from *The New Yorker,* July 31, 1995. Copyright © 1995 by Roger Angell. All rights reserved.

Doubleday, a division of Random House, Inc.: From interviews with Jimmy Santiago Baca and Garrett Hongo from *The Language of Life: A Festival of Poets* by Bill Moyers. Copyright © 1995 by Public Affairs Television, Inc., and David Grubin Productions, Inc.

Encyclopaedia Britannica: Quote by Upton Sinclair from *Encyclopaedia Britannica CD-ROM.* Copyright © 1994, 1998 by Encyclopaedia Britannica.

Farrar, Straus & Giroux, Inc.: From "The Social Function of Poetry" from *On Poetry and Poets* by T. S. Eliot. Copyright © 1957 by T. S. Eliot; copyright renewed © 1985 by Valerie Eliot. From footnote from "Writing Short Stories" from *Mystery and Manners: Occasional Prose* by Flannery O'Connor, edited by Sally and Robert Fitzgerald. Copyright © 1969 by the Estate of Mary Flannery O'Connor. From "Hemingway: Gauge of Morale" from *The Wound and the Bow: Seven Studies in Literature* by Edmund Wilson. Copyright © 1941 and renewed © 1970 by Edmund Wilson.

Harcourt, Inc.: From "Herman Melville" by Richard Chase and from "Edgar Allan Poe" by Richard Wilbur from *Major Writers of America,* vol. 1, edited by Perry Miller. Copyright © 1962 by Harcourt Brace & Company. From "The Dry Salvages" from *Four Quartets* by T. S. Eliot. Copyright 1941 by T. S. Eliot; copyright renewed © 1969 by Esme Valerie Eliot. From "Notes for a Preface" from *The Complete Poems of Carl Sandburg.* Copyright 1950 by Carl Sandburg; copyright renewed © 1978 by Margaret Sandburg, Helga Sandburg Crile, and Janet Sandburg.

Harvard University Press: From *The Given and the Made: Strategies of Poetic Redefinition* by Helen Vendler. Copyright © 1995 by Helen Vendler. Published by Harvard University Press, Cambridge, Mass.

Harvard University Press and the Trustees of Amherst College: "This is my letter to the World" from *The Poems of Emily Dickinson,* edited by Thomas H. Johnson. Copyright © 1951, 1955, 1979, 1983 by the President and Fellows of Harvard College. Published by The Belknap Press of Harvard University Press, Cambridge, Mass.

Henry Holt and Company: From *Eight Men Out* by Eliot Asinof. Copyright © 1963 by Eliot Asinof. From Introduction from *Selected Poems of Robert Frost,* with Introduction by Robert Graves. Introduction copyright © 1963 by Robert Graves.

Alfred A. Knopf, Inc.: From "Gathering Around the Welcome Table" from *James Baldwin: A Biography* by David Leeming. Copyright © 1994 by David Leeming.

Yusef Komunyakaa: From "Monsoon Season" from *Toys in a Field* by Yusef Komunyakaa. Copyright © 1986 by Yusef Komunyakaa.

Estate of Robert N. Linscott: From *Selected Poems and Letters of Emily Dickinson: Together with Thomas Wentworth Higginson's Account of his Correspondence with the Poet and his Visit to her in Amherst,* edited by Robert N. Linscott. Copyright © 1959 by Robert N. Linscott.

The Modern Language Association of America: From "Chinese American Women Writers" by Amy Ling from *Redefining American Literary History,* edited by A. LaVonne Brown Ruoff and Jerry W. Ward, Jr. Copyright © 1990 by The Modern Language Association of America.

New Directions Publishing Corporation: From *Gaudier-Brzeska: A Memoir* by Ezra Pound. Copyright © 1970 by Ezra Pound. From Foreword from *Selected Essays of William Carlos Williams.* Copyright 1931, 1936, 1938, 1939, 1940, 1942, 1944, 1946, 1948, 1951, 1954 by William Carlos Williams.

The New York Times Company: From a review (of *Black Boy* by Richard Wright) by Orville Prescott from *The New York Times,* February 28, 1945, p. 21. Copyright © 1945 by The New York Times Company.

W. W. Norton & Company, Inc.: From "An Introduction to *The Sound and the Fury*" by William Faulkner from *Mississippi Quarterly* 26, Summer 1973. Copyright © 1973 by Mrs. Jill Faulkner Summers, Executrix for the Estate of William Faulkner.

The Oakland Tribune/Alameda Newspaper Group: Quote by Amy Tan from "Biographic: In the Arts" from *Oakland Tribune,* November 26, 1989. Copyright © 1989 by Alameda Newspaper Group.

Harold Ober Associates Incorporated: From *Yankee from Olympus* by Catherine Drinker Bowen. Copyright © 1944 by Catherine Drinker Bowen.

Pantheon Books, a division of Random House, Inc.: Quote by John Hersey from the cover of *Unforgettable Fire,* edited by Japan Broadcasting Corporation (NHK). Copyright © 1977 by NHK.

Penguin Books Ltd.: From letter by Ezra Pound to Harriet Monroe, January 1915, from *Imagist Poetry,* edited by Peter Jones. Copyright © 1972 by Peter Jones.

Publishers Weekly®: From "Raymond Carver" by Sybil Steinberg from *Publishers Weekly,* vol. 233, no. 21, May 27, 1988. Copyright © 1988 by Publishers Weekly®.

Random House, Inc.: From Introduction from *The Complete Essays and Other Writings of Ralph Waldo Emerson,* edited by Brooks Atkinson. Copyright 1940 by Random House, Inc. From Introduction from *Rock and Hawk: A Selection of Shorter Poems by Robinson Jeffers,* edited by Robert Hass. Introduction copyright © 1987 by Robert Hass.

San Quentin News: From "San Francisco Group Leaves S. Q. Audience Waiting for Godot" from *San Quentin News,* November 28, 1957. Copyright © 1957 by San Quentin News.

The Saturday Review: From "*The Crucible* in Production: Comments and Reviews in New York" by Henry Hewes from *Saturday Review,* XXXVI, January 31, 1953. Copyright © 1979 by General Media Communications, Inc.

Mark Shechner: From "Sad Music" by Mark Shechner, a review of *The Stories of Bernard Malamud,* from *The Partisan Review,* vol. 51, no. 3, 1984. Copyright © 1984 by Mark Shechner.

Southern Illinois University: From "Flannery O'Connor: Backwoods Prophet in the Secular City" by Michael D. True from *PLL: Papers on Language and Litera-* ture, Southern Illinois University, vol. 5, no. 2, Spring 1969. Copyright © 1969 by the Board of Trustees, Southern Illinois University.

U.S. Capitol Historical Society: From "Grant and Lee: A Study in Contrasts" by Bruce Catton. Copyright © by U.S. Capitol Historical Society. All rights reserved.

University of Nebraska Press: From *Ancestral Voice: Conversations with N. Scott Momaday* by Charles L. Woodard. Copyright © 1989 by the University of Nebraska Press.

University of South Carolina Press: From *Understanding Tim O'Brien* by Steven Kaplan. Copyright © 1995 by University of South Carolina.

John Updike: From *Conversations with John Updike,* edited by James Plath. Copyright © 1994 by John Updike.

Vintage Books, a division of Random House, Inc.: Quote by Wallace Stevens from Introduction from *Poems by Wallace Stevens,* Selected, and with an Introduction by, Samuel French Morse. Copyright 1947, 1954 by Wallace Stevens; copyright © 1957, 1959 by Elsie Stevens and Holly Stevens; Introduction copyright © 1959 by Samuel French Morse.

SOURCES CITED:

From *Borges: A Life* by James Woodall. Published by Basic Books, New York, 1996.

From *Men Seen: Twenty-Four Modern Authors* by Paul Rosenfeld. Published by The Dial Press, New York, 1925.

From letters from James Thurber to Frank Gibney, October 31, 1956, and to Herman Miller, May 24, 1943, from *Thurber: A Biography* by Burton Bernstein. Copyright © 1975 by Burton Bernstein. Published by Dodd, Mead & Company, New York, 1975.

From *The Complete Tales of Washington Irving,* edited, with an Introduction, by Charles Neider. Published by Doubleday, New York, 1975.

From "Notes on the Next Way: A Serious Topical Letter" by Ernest Hemingway from *Esquire,* September 1935.

From "The Road Taken" by Derek Walcott from *Homage to Robert Frost.* Published by Farrar, Straus & Giroux, Inc., New York, 1996.

From Introduction from *Great Short Works of Mark Twain,* edited, with an Introduction, by Justin Kaplan. Published by HarperCollins Publishers, New York, 1967.

From "I Learn to Be a President's Wife" from *The Autobiography of Eleanor Roosevelt.* Published by HarperCollins Publishers, New York, 1958.

From *Edgar A. Poe: Mournful and Never-Ending Remembrance* by Kenneth Silverman. Published by HarperCollins Publishers, New York, 1991.

From *One Writer's Beginnings* by Eudora Welty. Published by Harvard University Press, Cambridge, 1984.

From Introduction by W. H. Auden and quote by D. H. Lawrence from *Edgar Allan Poe: Selected Prose, Poetry, and Eureka,* edited by W. H. Auden. Published by Holt, Rinehart and Winston, Inc., New York, 1950.

Quote by John Buckler from *A History of Western Society.* Published by Houghton Mifflin Company, Boston, 1995.

From letter from T. S. Eliot to I. A. Richards, November 11, 1931. Courtesy of the Library of Magdalene College, Cambridge.

Quote about Emily Dickinson from *Final Harvest: Emily Dickinson's Poems,* selection and introduction by Thomas H. Johnson. Published by Little, Brown and Company, Boston, 1961.

From Introduction from *The Poetry of Randall Jarrell* by Suzanne Ferguson. Published by Louisiana State University Press, Baton Rouge, 1971.

From *Zen and the Art of Motorcycle Maintenance* by Robert M. Pirsig. Published by William Morrow and Company, Inc., New York, 1974.

From *America's Humor: From Poor Richard to Doonesbury* by Walter Blair and Hamlin Hill. Published by Oxford University Press, New York, 1978.

From "Metafiction: Introduction" from *Elements of Literature,* vol. 5, edited by Robert Scholes. Published by Oxford University Press, Inc., New York, 1982.

Quote by Julia Alvarez from *Writing for Your Life #3,* edited by Sybil Steinberg and Jonathan Bing. Published by Pushcart Press, Wainscott, NY, 1997.

From Introduction from *American Indian Prose and Poetry* by Margot Astrov. Published by Putnam Publishing Group Inc., New York, 1962.

From "The Story of a Novel" from *Thomas Wolfe: Short Stories.* Published by Charles Scribner's Sons, a division of Simon & Schuster, New York, 1933.

From *Eudora Welty: A Study of the Short Fiction* by Carol Ann Johnston. Published by Twayne Publishers, an imprint of Simon & Schuster Macmillan, New York, 1997.

Quote from *E. E. Cummings* by Barry A. Marks. Published by Twayne Publishers, an imprint of Simon & Schuster Macmillan, New York, 1964.

Quote from *John Steinbeck* by Paul McCarthy. Published by Frederick Ungar Publishing Co., Inc., New York, 1980.

From *I Hear America Talking* by Stuart Berg Flexner. Published by Van Nostrand Reinhold Company, New York, 1976.

From Introduction from *Collected Plays* by Arthur Miller. Published by Viking Penguin, New York, 1957.

Quote by Alice Walker from *Current Biography Yearbook 1984,* page 433, edited by Charles Moritz. Published by The H. W. Wilson Company, New York, 1984.

CONTENTS

Beginnings to 1800

Collection 1

Visions and Voyages

American Romanticism
1800–1860

Collection 4

The Transforming Imagination

COLLECTION PLANNING GUIDE T150A–150D

The American Renaissance
A Literary Coming of Age
1840–1860

Collection 5

The Life Worth Living

COLLECTION PLANNING GUIDE T214A–214D

Collection 6

The Realms of Darkness

COLLECTION PLANNING GUIDE T258A-258D

COMMUNICATIONS WORKSHOPS

A New American Poetry
Whitman and Dickinson

A New American Poetry: Whitman and Dickinson *by* John Malcolm Brinnin 342

COMMUNICATIONS WORKSHOPS

The Rise of Realism
The Civil War and Postwar Period 1850–1900

Collection 9

Shackles

Collection 10

From Innocence to Experience

COLLECTION PLANNING GUIDE T448A–448D

COMMUNICATIONS WORKSHOPS

The Moderns 1900–1950

The Moderns by John Leggett and John Malcolm Brinnin 524

Time Line 526

■ **A Closer Look**
The Best of Times, the Worst of Times 528

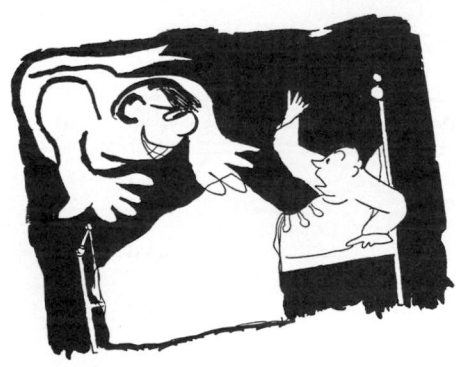

Collection 13

No Time for Heroes

COLLECTION PLANNING GUIDE T642A–642D

COMMUNICATIONS WORKSHOPS

Collection 14

Shadows of the Past

COLLECTION PLANNING GUIDE T690A–690D

Collection 15

I, Too, Sing America
The Harlem Renaissance
COLLECTION PLANNING GUIDE T732A–732D

Collection 16

Make It New!
COLLECTION PLANNING GUIDE T768A–768D

American Drama

American Drama by Robert Anderson 812

Collection 17

The Breaking of Charity

COLLECTION PLANNING GUIDE T824A–824D

Contemporary Literature
1950 to Present

Contemporary Literature *by* John Leggett, Susan Allen Toth,
John Malcolm Brinnin, *and* Thomas Hernacki 904

Time Line 906

■ **A Closer Look**
Atomic Anxiety 908

Collection 18
The Wages of War

Collection 21

The Created Self

COLLECTION PLANNING GUIDE T1126A–1126F

COMMUNICATIONS WORKSHOPS

Resource Center

ELEMENTS OF *Literature*

OVER THE YEARS, *Elements of Literature* has earned the trust of teachers across the country and generated tremendous enthusiasm in the literature and language arts classroom. The success of this unique program is due in large part to the authentic authorship team that shaped it. In no other literature textbook can you find the expertise of professional writers who have made the instruction focused and connected. These authors have given *Elements of Literature* its unique voice—a voice that speaks to students and gets them excited about reading and writing.

CREATED BY LEADING EDUCATORS AND AUTHORS

Robert Anderson, John Malcolm Brinnin, and John Leggett, program authors since the inception of **Elements of Literature,** have been determined to involve students in the experience of literature, reflected in the program's respectful tone to students. The authors' motivational approach to instruction, through the use of anecdotes, story, and media, has helped establish the literary framework of this outstanding literature series. Dr. Robert Probst, respected nationally for his response approach, has been instrumental in shaping the student-centered pedagogy of the program. His commitment to making literature meaningful to students and relevant to their lives and experiences is the central focus of *Elements of Literature.*

AN INCREASED EMPHASIS ON READING SKILLS

With this edition of **Elements of Literature,** Dr. Richard Vacca, national reading and literacy expert, joins the authorship team. As special advisor, Dr. Vacca assisted in developing the conceptual framework for the reading strand in the *Pupil's Editions* for grades nine through twelve. Dr. Kylene Beers, well known for her expertise in the area of reading, brings to the program the classroom experiences necessary to answer an increasingly urgent need in today's classrooms—reaching struggling and reluctant readers. Dr. Beers helped to integrate the strong reading development strand in the *Pupil's* and *Annotated Teacher's Editions* with a major new program component, *Reading Skills and Strategies: Reaching Struggling Readers.* This invaluable resource binder includes model lessons, instructional transparencies, and easy readings that help teach students the strategies needed to develop good reading skills.

The lessons in *Reading Skills and Strategies: Reaching Struggling Readers* correlate directly to the *Pupil's Edition* and provide a more thorough and detailed approach for students who are having difficulty. The binder includes the following resources:

- **MiniRead Skill Lessons** are based on short, easy selections enabling students to practice the reading strategies in a less-challenging situation. A complete lesson plan models instruction for the teacher.

- **Selection Skill Lessons** provide opportunities for students to apply the reading strategies they've learned to the literature selections in their textbook.

- The **Reading Strategies Handbook** includes explanations of how the strategies actually worked in classrooms where they were tested with struggling and reluctant readers.

- The **QuickGuide** provides a concise, convenient reference guide for using the instructional materials effectively.

Expanding the Role

THIS EDITION OF *Elements of Literature* expands the role of technology, bringing students face-to-face with the media that will shape their understanding of the role of language in their world.

INTERNET RESOURCES ENCOURAGE INVOLVEMENT

The *Elements of Literature* Web resources extend, enhance, and support the series by linking students to carefully researched resources.

When students use the **go.hrw.com** logo and keyword from their textbook, they will be instantly linked to specific resources ranging from biographical information about authors, to extensions of in-text activities and writing assignments, to cross-curricular support for selections. These Internet connections provide a fun and easy way to reach relevant sites without spending valuable time surfing the Web.

INTERACTIVE CD-ROMS MAKE GRAMMAR AND WRITING PRACTICE FUN

The **Language Workshop Interactive Multimedia CD-ROMs** offer a complete course of study in grammar, usage, and mechanics. Sound effects, animation, fine art, and other visuals complement interactive exercises so that students actually enjoy honing their grammar skills.

The **Writer's Workshop Interactive Multimedia CD-ROMs** guide students step-by-step through eight different writing assignments, such as writing a personal narrative, an informative report, or a persuasive essay.

MULTIMEDIA RESOURCES MAKE LITERATURE COME ALIVE

The **Audio CD Library** includes professional readings of nearly every selection in the textbook and reflects a wide range of genres, periods, and cultures.

The **Visual Connections Videocassette Program** features video segments directly related to course content. Author biographies, interviews, historical summaries, and cross-curricular connections enrich and extend instruction.

# of Technology

THE ALL-IN-ONE RESOURCE TOOL

The new **One-Stop Planner CD-ROM with Test Generator** is an all-in-one, comprehensive management tool that makes planning your lessons easier and more efficient. Two CD-ROMs for each grade level include all your teaching resources—organized in easy-to-understand, point-and-click menus.

Here are just a few of the teaching resources you can access on the **One-Stop Planner:**

- Editable lesson plans, importable into several word-processing formats
- Video previews of the *Visual Connections Videocassette Program*
- *Viewing and Representing* Transparencies and Worksheets
- Selection Tests and Answer Keys

LESSON PLANS FOR EVERY CLASSROOM NEED

Lesson Plans Including Strategies for English-Language Learners are designed to help make literature more accessible to students whose first language is not English.

Block Scheduling Lesson Plans help you manage instruction and activities for each day of the 90-day block.

ASSESSMENT TOOLS MATCHED TO THE WAY YOU TEACH

Elements of Literature provides a rich variety of assessment tools—including traditional, alternative, and standardized—that allows you to evaluate students' performance according to your teaching methods.

- *Formal Assessment*
- *Portfolio Management System with Rubrics for Assignments*
- *Standardized Test Preparation* and *Preparation for College Admission Exams*
- *Test Generator* (included on the *One-Stop Planner CD-ROM*)

ADDITIONAL TEACHING RESOURCES

Elements of Literature includes an array of flexible resources correlated to the *Pupil's Edition*.

- *Workshop Resources Transparencies and Worksheets*
- *Literary Elements Transparencies and Worksheets*
- *Daily Oral Grammar Transparencies and Worksheets*
- *Viewing and Representing* (Fine Art Transparencies and Worksheets, and the HRW Multimedia Presentation Maker)
- *Language Handbook Worksheets*
- *Grammar and Language Links Worksheets*
- *Cross-Curricular Activities*
- *Words to Own Worksheets*
- *Graphic Organizers for Active Readers*
- *Spelling and Decoding Worksheets (for grades 6–8)*

Literature

AN INVITATION TO A DIALOGUE

Dr. Robert Probst, *Georgia State University*

The classroom is the place for students to learn to read and reflect on visions of human possibilities offered them by the great literature and to begin to tell their own visions and stories.

Literature and Life

Surely, of all the arts, literature is most immediately implicated with life itself. The very medium through which the author shapes the text—language—is grounded in the shared lives of human beings. Language is the bloodstream of a common culture, a common history.

— LOUISE ROSENBLATT

Mathematicians, scientists, and engineers build bridges and send people to the moon, statisticians calculate our insurance premiums and life expectancies, and accountants figure our taxes and amortize our house payments, but the poets, dramatists, novelists, and story writers have nonetheless remained at the center of life. They bind us together as a society, and they define us as individuals within that society.

When we're very young we need stories almost as much as we need food and protection. Stories entertain us and help us sleep, but they also teach us how to get through the world. They tell us there are pots of gold waiting for us at the end of the rainbow, and they warn us about the trolls hiding under the bridges. They teach us about hope, fear,

courage, and all the other elements of our lives. As we grow out of childhood, the great stories, poems, and plays of the world's literature encourage us to reflect on the issues that have intrigued men and women for centuries, inviting us into a continuing dialogue about human experience. When we're older, our own stories represent what we've done, capturing for us what we've made of our lives. Some we'll tell happily, some we'll tell with great pain, and some we may not tell at all, but they're all important because they are a way of making sense of our lives.

If literature is the ongoing dialogue about what it means to be human, then the language arts classroom is society's invitation to students to join that conversation. The texts we use represent the reflections of the world's cultures on the nature of human experience, and the writings we elicit from our students are their first efforts to join in that reflection. The classroom is the place for students to learn to read and reflect on visions of human possibilities offered them by the

great literature and to begin to tell their own stories.

Literature offers an invitation to reflect, but it doesn't offer formulas to memorize or answers to write dutifully in notes so that later on, when life presents us with problems, we can pull out our tattered old notebooks and find our path sketched out for us. Literature is an invitation to a dialogue.

That, perhaps more than any other reason, is why it's so important that we teach literature and writing well. It's too easy to avoid the responsible thought demanded by the significant issues, too tempting to accept someone else's formulation of the truth. "Life imitates art," Richard Peck said in a speech in New Orleans in 1974, "especially bad art." By that he meant, I think, that we may too often give in to tempting laziness and allow our lives to be governed by visions of human possibilities that we take from film, television, or graffiti. The problem for teachers, of course, is to lead students not simply to absorb unthinkingly what art offers, but to reflect on it.

This textbook series tries to support teachers' efforts to lead students to think, to feel, and to take responsibility for themselves. It will have much in common with other textbooks. After all, we'd miss "The Raven" if he didn't land croaking on our window sill one morning just before homeroom, and twelfth grade wouldn't be the same without an evening or two around the hearth with Beowulf. But if this series has much in common with other textbooks, it will also have much that differs—including new authors, perhaps authors we haven't met before, exploring lives and circumstances that previously may not have been well represented in the pages of school texts. And similarly, there will be familiar approaches to teaching—perhaps specific activities—that we've all come to rely upon, but there will be other suggestions that emphasize aspects of literary experience, writing, and discussion that may not have been prominent in other books.

Principles of the Program

❶ First among the principles of the program is that *the subject matter of the language arts classroom is human experience comprehended and expressed in language.* The classroom invites the student into the dialogue about the big issues of human experience. The content of literature is the content of our days, and we think and feel about these issues before we enter the classroom and open the text.

When we do finally come to the text, it offers students an opportunity to begin to make sense of experience and to see it captured in the literature.

❷ Implicit in this vision of the language arts is a second principle, *that learning in the English classroom is a creative act,* requiring students to make things with language. Reading literature is a process of engaging the text, weighing it against the experiences readers bring to it.

Similarly, writing isn't simply a matter of learning and applying the rules of grammar and usage or of memorizing the structure and strategies of narratives, descriptions, and arguments.

Literature offers us access to hidden experiences and perceptions.

❸ *The third principle focuses on the encounter between student and content.* It doesn't focus exclusively on the information and skills that have at times provided the framework for our instruction.

Nor, on the other hand, is teaching planned with thought only for the student's interests, needs and desires, and thus organized around whatever concerns happen to predominate at the moment. It is, to borrow Rosenblatt's term, transactional.

❹ For this series, *the integration of the several aspects of the English language arts program* is the fourth governing principle. Literature can't be taught effectively without work in composition. Writing, without the inspiration offered by good literature, remains shallow and undeveloped. Oral language has to be acquired in the context of groups working collaboratively. And so, these texts will suggest ways of interrelating instruction in literature, writing, and language.

Working With the Series

You will find, as you work with selections in this textbook, that students have immediate responses to what they've read. That may be the place to start. The students' responses are very likely to lead you back to the issues you would have wanted to discuss anyway, and so the questions we've suggested might be addressed naturally during the flow of the discussion. Look for the potential in students' reactions and their questions even before turning to the questions in the "First Thoughts" section. Then, the questions in the text can extend or expand the discussion.

The same might be said about the writing. The series has been designed so that experiences with literature, with writing, and with group processes will often be interconnected. We hope that the literature will inspire and shape the students' writing, that their writing will lead back to further reading, and that the discussions and group activities suggested will build a supportive community in which all this work can take place.

The objective in all of this is for students to be able to draw upon their literary heritage and their developing skill with written and spoken language so that, as humane and reasoning people, they may be responsibly engaged with the world around them. If the language arts class helps to achieve that goal, we should be well satisfied with our labors. ✲

Reading Matters

Dr. Richard T. Vacca, *Kent State University*

As is the case with many teachers, I have had my fair share of unforgettable students, the "usual suspects," who have made a difference in the way I think about teaching and learning literature. Two such students quickly come to mind.

Tommy was an English teacher's dream; Johnny, a saboteur-in-training. They were contemporaries, but I'm sure their paths never crossed in school. One was a high achiever; the other, a low achiever. The classroom lessons I learned from each of them changed the way I think about reading and literature in English classrooms.

A Tale of Two Students

Johnny was just three years younger than I when I began teaching in a high school just outside Albany, New York. He was one of the forgotten students at school who went unnoticed until he got into trouble. Johnny couldn't read well, but he knew how to take apart a carburetor and replace a timing belt with his eyes closed. (As it turned out, he dropped out of school on his nineteenth birthday and went to work at his uncle's garage.) He and his cohorts tried to sabotage my teaching plans whenever I initiated the study of literature, no matter how relevant the text was to their lives. If the literature study required reading, Johnny could dismantle the lesson as skillfully as he could dismantle a car engine. I held my ground the best I could, but often to little avail. The more I urged him and others in the class to learn about what it means to be human through literature, the more they resisted.

I was tough on Johnny, always challenging him to do better, and I believe there was a measure of respect between the two of us. Even though it's been more than three decades since I saw him, I won't soon forget our last encounter. I remember running into Johnny at his uncle's garage and telling him that I had resigned my teaching position to go back to school to be a reading specialist. "Man," he said, "you read good already." Then he added somewhat wistfully, somewhat defiantly, "Reading robbed me of my manhood."

I had never heard the inability to read put in such human terms. Johnny helped me to understand how much reading matters, not only in students' literate lives but also in their human lives outside of school. What I learned from Johnny, and from other students who struggle with reading literature, is this: Reading gets in the way of too many students' understanding, enjoyment, and appreciation of literary texts. I made assumptions about Johnny's ability to use reading to learn that, in hindsight, were ill-informed. I assumed, for example, that by the time he reached high school he should be using reading to make meaning with literary texts. Because reading was second nature to me, I often assigned literary texts as if reading were second nature to my students. But I couldn't reach Johnny with literature because he didn't have the skills and strategies of an accomplished reader. I, on the other hand, didn't have the instructional know-how to bridge the gap between potentially difficult texts and the literacy capital that Johnny brought to the classroom and the study of literature.

Tommy, on the other hand, made teaching literature smooth sailing. He was tracked in an above-average class with others who knew how to do school well. I recall that his class was in the midst of reading Thornton Wilder's *Our Town* during the birth of my first (and only) child. I shared with the class every heartfelt moment of my ascent into fatherhood and connected the experience to Wilder's play. Unbeknownst to me, Tommy took it upon himself to write a letter to Thornton Wilder, which he mailed to Wilder's publisher. In the letter he shared how much the play (and my journey into fatherhood) had changed the way he thought about life and about relationships that he would have taken for granted. Several weeks later, Tommy received a letter from Wilder's sister explaining that her brother, who was nearly blind at the time and quite ill, enjoyed having the letter read to him. She went on to say that he insisted that she write to Tommy and apologized for not being able to do so directly. Wilder wanted Tommy to know that the letter brightened his spirits and reaffirmed his reasons for writing *Our Town*. Wilder's sister concluded by telling Tommy that her brother was especially grateful for readers such as Tommy who made writing well worth the effort. I remember Tommy saying, "I'll treasure this letter forever."

Reading matters to accomplished students such as Tommy who know how to use literary texts to explore the significance of what they are reading. Often, they are high achievers who are skillful and thoughtful in their approach to reading. But not all average and above-average students are accomplished readers. What I learned early on as a literature teacher is that many academically oriented students—adolescents who were most like me in high school, promising students who sometimes worked hard and sometimes didn't—struggle with reading literature as much as low-achieving students. In between the Johnnys and the Tommys are students who often go through the motions of reading literary texts but are likely to conceal some of their difficulties. These students have developed the ability to read print smoothly and accurately, but they don't know what to do with texts beyond just reading the words. They appear *skillful* in the mechanics of reading, but they aren't *strategic* in their ability to explore and interpret meaning.

Bringing Literature and Reading Together

Technologically advanced societies like ours value literate behavior and demand that citizens acquire literacy for personal, social, academic, and economic success. The pressure to hold teachers accountable for students' reading development is greater today than at any time in our nation's history. To the extent that texts are an integral part of learning in all content areas, *every* teacher has a role to play in helping students become readers, writers, and oral communicators. Yet the responsibility for teaching literacy usually lies with English teachers and with reading specialists in middle and high schools. English teachers, however, are not reading specialists and shouldn't view their roles as such. Showing students how to use reading strategies in the literature classroom doesn't require the specialized training of a reading specialist. Nor does the development of reading skills and strategies in the context of the literature classroom diminish the teacher's role as a subject matter specialist. It is far more realistic and effective to integrate the skills and strategies that readers actually need. The real value of reading lies in the way it is used. To be literate in literature classrooms, students must learn how to use reading to construct meaning from literary texts. Because literacy use is situational, the most meaningful way for students to develop reading skills and strategies is in the context in which they must be used. A student using reading to find meaning in literature gains confidence in his or her ability to read and to interpret texts.

Scaffolding reading experiences is the key to bringing literature and reading together in the literature classroom. The term *scaffolding* is a metaphor used in teaching and learning to suggest a means by which you help students do what they cannot do at first. In other words, scaffolding reading experiences allows teachers to provide the instructional support and guidance that students need to be successful. Instructional scaffolding allows teachers to support students' efforts to think clearly, critically, and creatively about literary texts *while* showing them how to use skills and strategies that will allow them to read more effectively than if left to their own devices.

Developing Skills and Strategies

Because skills and strategies are best learned through meaningful use, the lesson organization for the literary selections in **Elements of Literature** provides numerous opportunities to scaffold students' exploration and interpretation of literary texts. Each lesson creates an instructional framework that respects the nature of the literary experience while making provisions to scaffold students' use of reading skills and strategies. Instructional scaffolding before reading, for example, demonstrates to students the importance of anticipation, making predictions, raising questions, and other strategies that connect their world to the world of the text.

Students are in a strategic position to learn with literature whenever they use their prior knowledge to construct meaning. Prior knowledge includes the experiences, conceptual understandings, attitudes, values, skills, and strategies the reader brings to a text situation. How readers *activate* prior knowledge is the mechanism by which they connect their world to the world of the text. Prior knowledge, when activated, allows readers to seek, organize, retain, and elaborate meaning. In **Elements of Literature**, features such as *Make the Connection* and *Quickwrites* activate prior knowledge in relation to the issues, problems, conflicts, or themes to be studied through the literary experience. These scaffolds provide students with an imaginative entry into the text by raising expectations, arousing curiosity, and anticipating what is ahead in the literature selection.

Making students aware of *why, how,* and *when* they should use strategies to activate prior knowledge and anticipate content is as important as understanding *what* the strategies are. For example: Why is activating what students already know about a topic through a quickwrite (or any prereading strategy) important? How can students connect what they know to what they are about to read? When should a technique such as quickwrite be used and when shouldn't it? From a strategy-learning perspective, these discussions provide students with a rationale for skill and strategy use and build *procedural knowledge*, which is knowledge about why, how, and what skill and strategy to use.

Providing instructional support during and after reading also encourages struggling readers to develop and use skills and strategies as they explore, clarify, and extend their understandings of the text. A skilled reader recognizes the important parts of a text. A struggling reader doesn't. Instead, the student who struggles with text tends to read each word, each sentence, each paragraph with equal emphasis and reverence.

While readers explore meaning before and during reading, they often need to engage in clarification and elaboration after reading. Postreading questions and activities at the end of each literary selection in **Elements of Literature** create another type of instructional support for students. They help students extend their thinking and evaluate the significance of the literary experience.

In addition to scaffolding reading experiences at the point of use, there are other features of **Elements of Literature** that will help you support and guide students' reading development. For example, the MiniRead lessons in the reading binder, *Reading Skills and Strategies: Reaching Struggling Readers,* are instructional resources that provide *explicit instruction* for students who need additional guidance and support. The MiniRead lessons allow students to share insights and knowledge that they might otherwise never discover. These explicit lessons create a framework that unifies skill and strategy development. They provide methods for struggling readers to become aware of, to use, and to develop control over skills and strategies that can make a difference in their literate lives. ❋

Reaching Struggling Readers

AN INTERVIEW WITH

DR. KYLENE BEERS

Dr. Kylene Beers

from the Editor's Desk

As we have listened to teachers over the past few years, one dominant issue has emerged: How do we teach literature to struggling readers? In our search for an answer, we read the research, attended workshops, and interviewed teachers and students. It was obvious that fill-in-the-blank drill worksheets weren't the answer. It was time for a change, but nothing we encountered seemed to offer a real solution to the problem of teaching literature to struggling readers.

Finally, one day Dr. Robert Probst suggested we contact Dr. Kylene Beers. He told us she knew a great deal about reading and might be the person with the answers. During our first meeting with Dr. Beers, she explained the link between reading skills and strategies and discussed the difference she had seen strategies make in the lives of struggling readers. She made a lot of sense to those of us who can recite whole sections of the *Iliad* but had never heard the words *reading* and *strategy* in the same sentence. A year and a half later we see the results of that first meeting: the *Reading Skills and Strategies: Reaching Struggling Readers* binder. This wasn't the easiest project in the history of publishing. Drill worksheets would have been easier to produce, but it was time for a change—time to turn struggling readers into successful ones.

Here are some of the questions we asked Dr. Beers during the course of this project.

The curriculum demands on English teachers are enormous. Teachers often ask us why they should add reading skills and strategies to an already loaded course.

❝ I used to ask myself the same thing. Twenty years ago, when I began teaching, I expected that I'd carefully guide excited students through the prose and poetry of literary giants like Whitman, Emerson, Dickinson, Thoreau, Kipling, Joyce, Márquez, Angelou, and well, you know the names. I expected that students would arrive early for literature class and leave late for their next class. I expected I'd never have to worry about teaching someone to read—that was for the elementary teachers. I was going to teach *Literature*. Those expectations changed quickly. First, I didn't have students who loved literature. Most of my students didn't even like literature. Second, I didn't have students who could already read. When I didn't get the students I expected, I didn't know what to do.

Twenty years later, I'm still not getting what I expected when it comes to teaching. But I've learned that if I understand students' strengths and have some ideas about how to address their weaknesses, then they'll often give me more than I ever expected.

I've spent the past twenty years learning how to help these secondary students who can't read and don't like to read become better readers. I've worked with students at all grade levels and all ability levels. I've gone back to school to study how to teach reading, and now I see myself as a reading/literature teacher. The teaching of literature and the teaching of reading are integral to one another, so interconnected that separating them seems an abomination. ❞

How can a teacher use a literature anthology with the increasing numbers of students who have serious difficulty reading any text?

❝ After many years of working with all types of readers, but especially struggling and reluctant readers, I've learned some things that have helped me reach those students. I've found that struggling readers have difficulty reading for a myriad of reasons. Often they don't know a lot of words, so limited vocabulary keeps them from understanding what they've read. Sometimes they lack decoding ability, so they don't know how to get through big words. Other times, they can call words well, but they don't know how to make sense of what they've read. And sometimes, their distaste for reading makes them think reading is meaningless, so they see no reason for putting any effort into it. As I work with students and address those issues, I keep what I call the ABCDE rules in mind. A look at the diagram below will quickly show you what these rules are. ❞

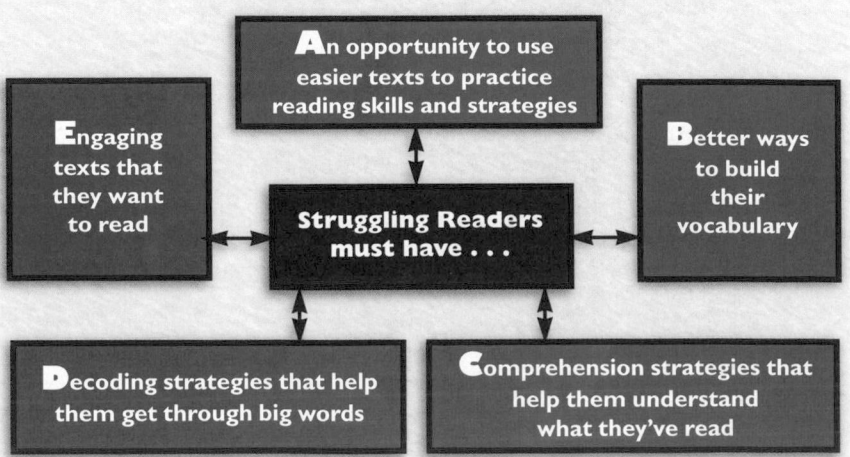

To help provide this ABCDE rule for struggling readers, what should a literature program include?

"" A literature program should help teachers with each of those areas, particularly A, B, C, and E. If publishers want to help, they will have to develop specialized materials that complement the basal text. Here's what we did with the *Reading Skills and Strategies* binder for *Elements of Literature*:

❶ Easier Selections Provide Practice for Skills and Strategies.

We hired a group of professional writers to write easy fiction and nonfiction pieces. These selections, or MiniReads, are short texts written at an easier level than the selections in the literature book. The purpose of the MiniReads is to give students the opportunity to practice decoding skills, comprehension strategies, and vocabulary strategies with a text that is not only easier but engaging as well.

❷ Our MiniRead Lessons Include Modeling.

Each MiniRead includes a complete lesson plan that provides modeling of the skill and strategy. Transparencies help teachers focus students on the strategies. Blackline masters give students a chance to practice the strategies before applying them to selections in the Pupil's Edition.

❸ Reading Skills and Strategies Are Connected to the Selections in *Elements of Literature*.

All skills and strategies are *applied* to selections in the anthology. The detailed lesson plans can be used not only with struggling readers, but with all readers.

❹ The *Handbook* Provides a Thorough Explanation of the Research.

Without research to back them up, the lessons would have no foundation. The *Reading Strategies Handbook* includes transcripts from actual classrooms in which the strategies have been tested with struggling readers. The handbook *shows* rather than just *tells* how to initiate specific strategies, what pitfalls to avoid, and how to document progress. Articles about each of the strategies help teachers become more comfortable with using the strategies with any selection. ""

DR. KYLENE BEERS

HRW LIBRARY

WITH CONNECTIONS THAT MATTER

Attractive hardcover editions with contemporary art that captures students' imaginations

Readings from a variety of authors and genres—poems, short stories, essays, memoirs, biographical sketches, interviews, and many more—that complement the theme

Study guides with support for both the novel and the Connections:

• Pacing suggestions, vocabulary activities, inclusion strategies, and cross-curricular and multimedia projects

• Reproducible masters for reading skills, vocabulary, literary elements, and assessments

• One-page news sheets, Novel Notes, that provide high-interest background information relating to historical, cultural, or literary elements of the novel

Elements of Literature on the Internet

TO THE STUDENT

Discover more about the stories, poems, and essays in *Elements of Literature* by logging on to the Internet. At **go.hrw.com** we help you complete your homework assignments, learn more about your favorite writers, and find facts that support your ideas and inspire you with new ones. Here's how to log on:

1. Start your Web browser and enter **go.hrw.com** in the location field.

| Back | Forward | Reload | Home | Search |

Location: http://go.hrw.com

2. Note the keyword in your textbook.

go.hrw.com
LE0 11-1

3. In your web browser, enter the keyword and click on GO.

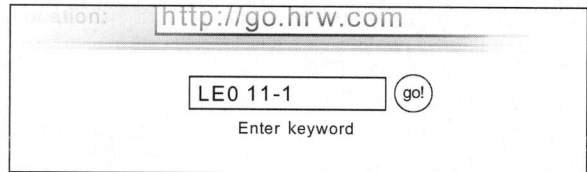

Location: http://go.hrw.com

LE0 11-1 go!
Enter keyword

Now that you've arrived, you can peek into the palaces and museums of the world, listen to stories of exploration and discovery, or view fires burning on the ocean floor. As you move through *Elements of Literature,* use the best on-line resources at **go.hrw.com.**

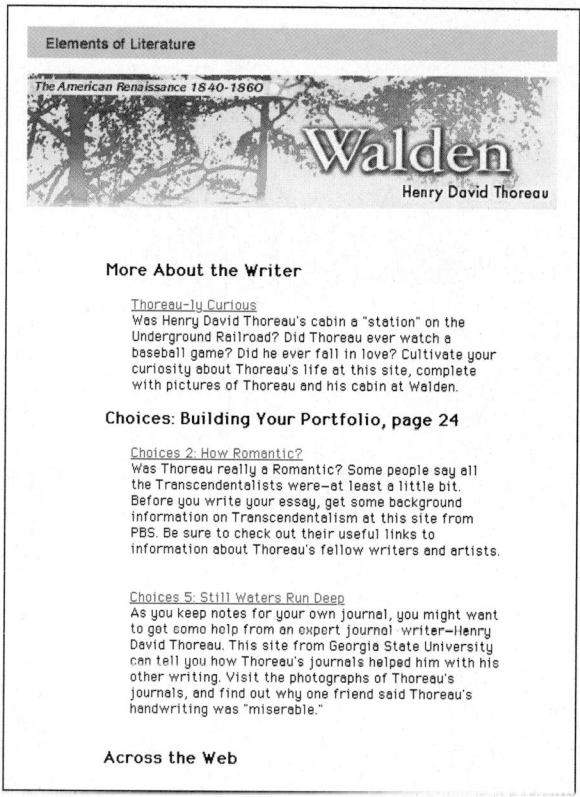

Elements of Literature

The American Renaissance 1840-1860

Walden
Henry David Thoreau

More About the Writer

Thoreau-ly Curious
Was Henry David Thoreau's cabin a "station" on the Underground Railroad? Did Thoreau ever watch a baseball game? Did he ever fall in love? Cultivate your curiosity about Thoreau's life at this site, complete with pictures of Thoreau and his cabin at Walden.

Choices: Building Your Portfolio, page 24

Choices 2: How Romantic?
Was Thoreau really a Romantic? Some people say all the Transcendentalists were—at least a little bit. Before you write your essay, get some background information on Transcendentalism at this site from PBS. Be sure to check out their useful links to information about Thoreau's fellow writers and artists.

Choices 5: Still Waters Run Deep
As you keep notes for your own journal, you might want to get some help from an expert journal writer—Henry David Thoreau. This site from Georgia State University can tell you how Thoreau's journals helped him with his other writing. Visit the photographs of Thoreau's journals, and find out why one friend said Thoreau's handwriting was "miserable."

Across the Web

Enjoy the Internet, but be critical of the information you find there. Always evaluate your sources for credibility, accuracy, timeliness, and possible bias.

Web sites accessed through **go.hrw.com** are reviewed regularly. However, on-line materials change continually and without notice. Holt, Rinehart and Winston cannot ensure the accuracy or appropriateness of materials other than our own. Students, teachers, and guardians should assume responsibility for checking all on-line materials. A full description of Terms of Use can be found at **go.hrw.com.**

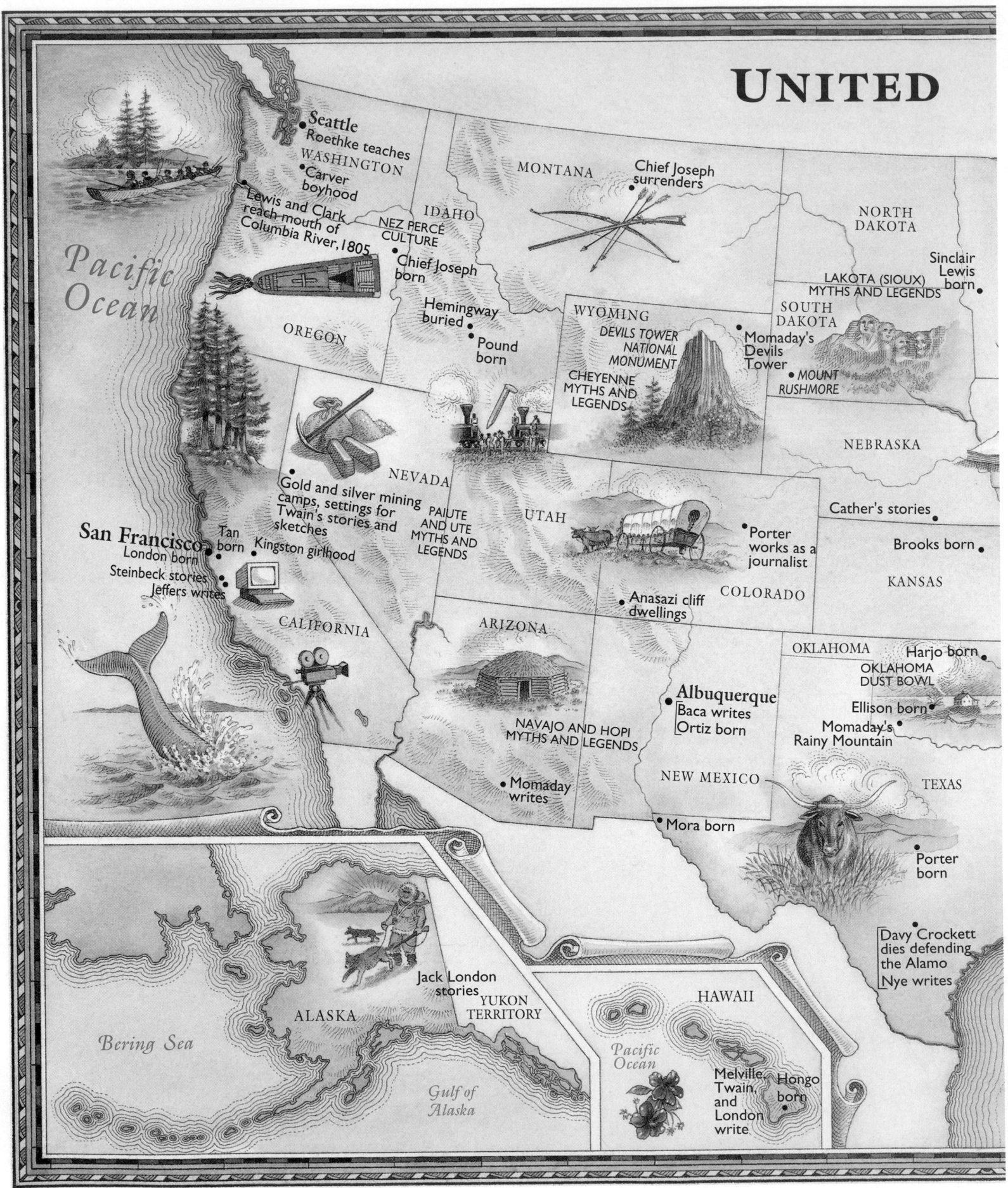

UNITED

Seattle
Roethke teaches
WASHINGTON
Carver boyhood
Lewis and Clark reach mouth of Columbia River, 1805

MONTANA
Chief Joseph surrenders

IDAHO
NEZ PERCÉ CULTURE
Chief Joseph born

NORTH DAKOTA
Sinclair Lewis born

Pacific Ocean

Hemingway buried
Pound born

OREGON

WYOMING
DEVILS TOWER NATIONAL MONUMENT
CHEYENNE MYTHS AND LEGENDS

LAKOTA (SIOUX) MYTHS AND LEGENDS
SOUTH DAKOTA
Momaday's Devils Tower
MOUNT RUSHMORE

NEBRASKA

NEVADA
Gold and silver mining camps, settings for Twain's stories and sketches

PAIUTE AND UTE MYTHS AND LEGENDS

UTAH

Porter works as a journalist

Cather's stories

Brooks born

KANSAS

San Francisco
Tan born
London born
Steinbeck stories
Jeffers writes
Kingston girlhood

CALIFORNIA

Anasazi cliff dwellings
COLORADO

ARIZONA

OKLAHOMA
OKLAHOMA DUST BOWL
Harjo born

NAVAJO AND HOPI MYTHS AND LEGENDS

Momaday writes

Albuquerque
Baca writes
Ortiz born

NEW MEXICO

Mora born

Ellison born
Momaday's Rainy Mountain

TEXAS

Porter born

Jack London stories
YUKON TERRITORY

ALASKA

Bering Sea

Gulf of Alaska

HAWAII

Pacific Ocean

Melville, Twain, and London write
Hongo born

Davy Crockett dies defending the Alamo
Nye writes

STATES

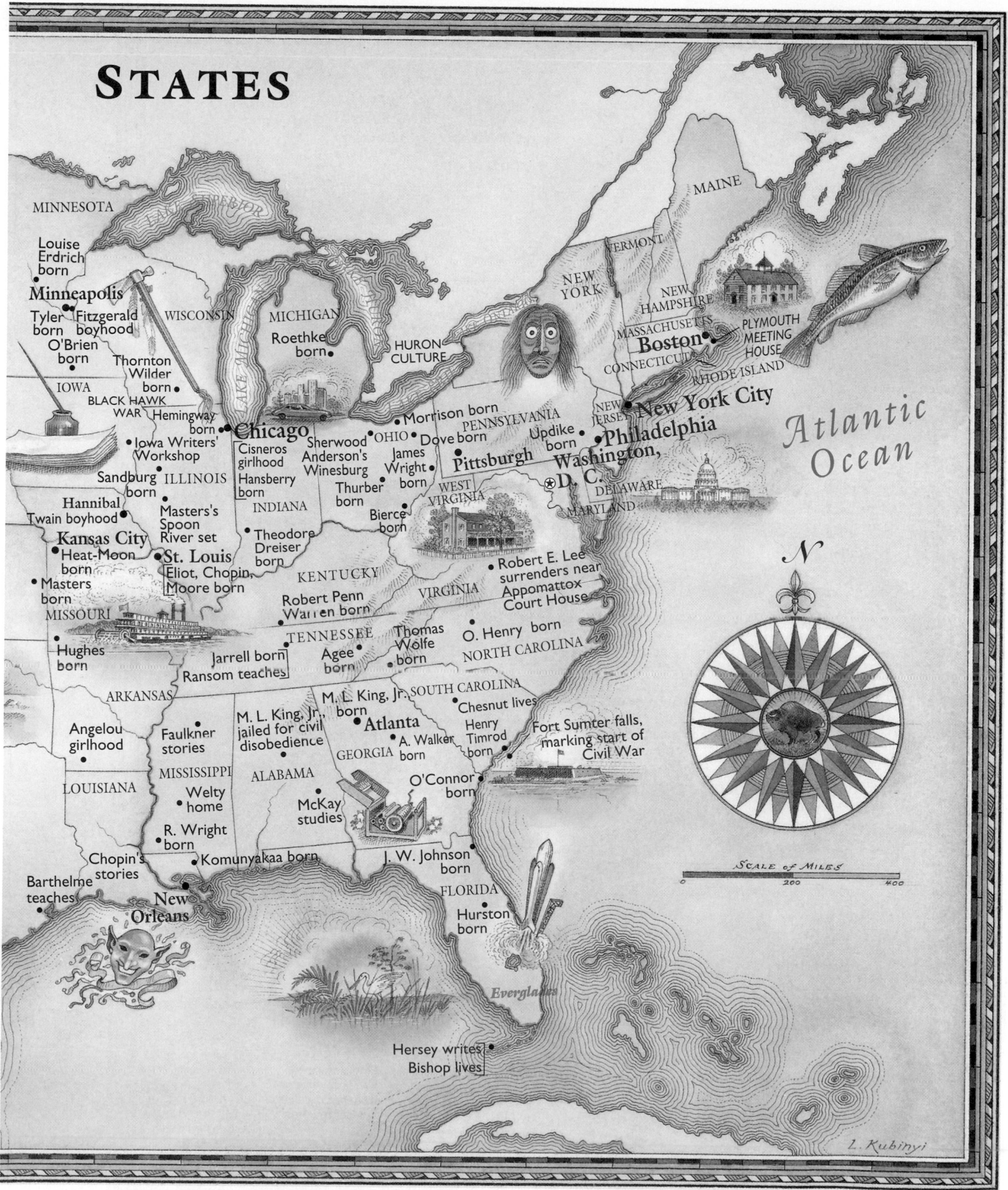

MINNESOTA

Louise Erdrich born

Minneapolis

Tyler born · Fitzgerald boyhood

O'Brien born

Thornton Wilder born

IOWA

BLACK HAWK WAR

Hemingway born

Iowa Writers' Workshop

Sandburg born · ILLINOIS

Hannibal Twain boyhood

Master's Spoon River set

Kansas City

Heat-Moon born

St. Louis

Eliot, Chopin, Moore born

Masters born

MISSOURI

Hughes born

WISCONSIN

MICHIGAN

Roethke born

Chicago

Cisneros girlhood

Hansberry born

Sherwood Anderson's Winesburg · OHIO

James Wright born

Thurber born

Bierce born

INDIANA

Theodore Dreiser born

KENTUCKY

Robert Penn Warren born

TENNESSEE

Jarrell born

Ransom teaches

Agee born

HURON CULTURE

Morrison born · PENNSYLVANIA

Dove born

Updike born

Pittsburgh

WEST VIRGINIA

VIRGINIA

Robert E. Lee surrenders near Appomattox Court House

Thomas Wolfe born

O. Henry born

NORTH CAROLINA

MAINE

NEW YORK

VERMONT

NEW HAMPSHIRE

MASSACHUSETTS

Boston

CONNECTICUT

PLYMOUTH MEETING HOUSE

RHODE ISLAND

NEW JERSEY

New York City

Philadelphia

Washington, D. C.

DELAWARE

MARYLAND

Atlantic Ocean

N

ARKANSAS

Angelou girlhood

Faulkner stories

M. L. King, Jr. jailed for civil disobedience

MISSISSIPPI

LOUISIANA

Welty home

R. Wright born

Chopin's stories

Barthelme teaches

New Orleans

Komunyakaa born

M. L. King, Jr. born · SOUTH CAROLINA

Atlanta

A. Walker born

GEORGIA

ALABAMA

McKay studies

O'Connor born

Chesnut lives

Henry Timrod born

Fort Sumter falls, marking start of Civil War

J. W. Johnson born

FLORIDA

Hurston born

Everglades

Hersey writes

Bishop lives

SCALE OF MILES

0   200   400

L. Kubinyi

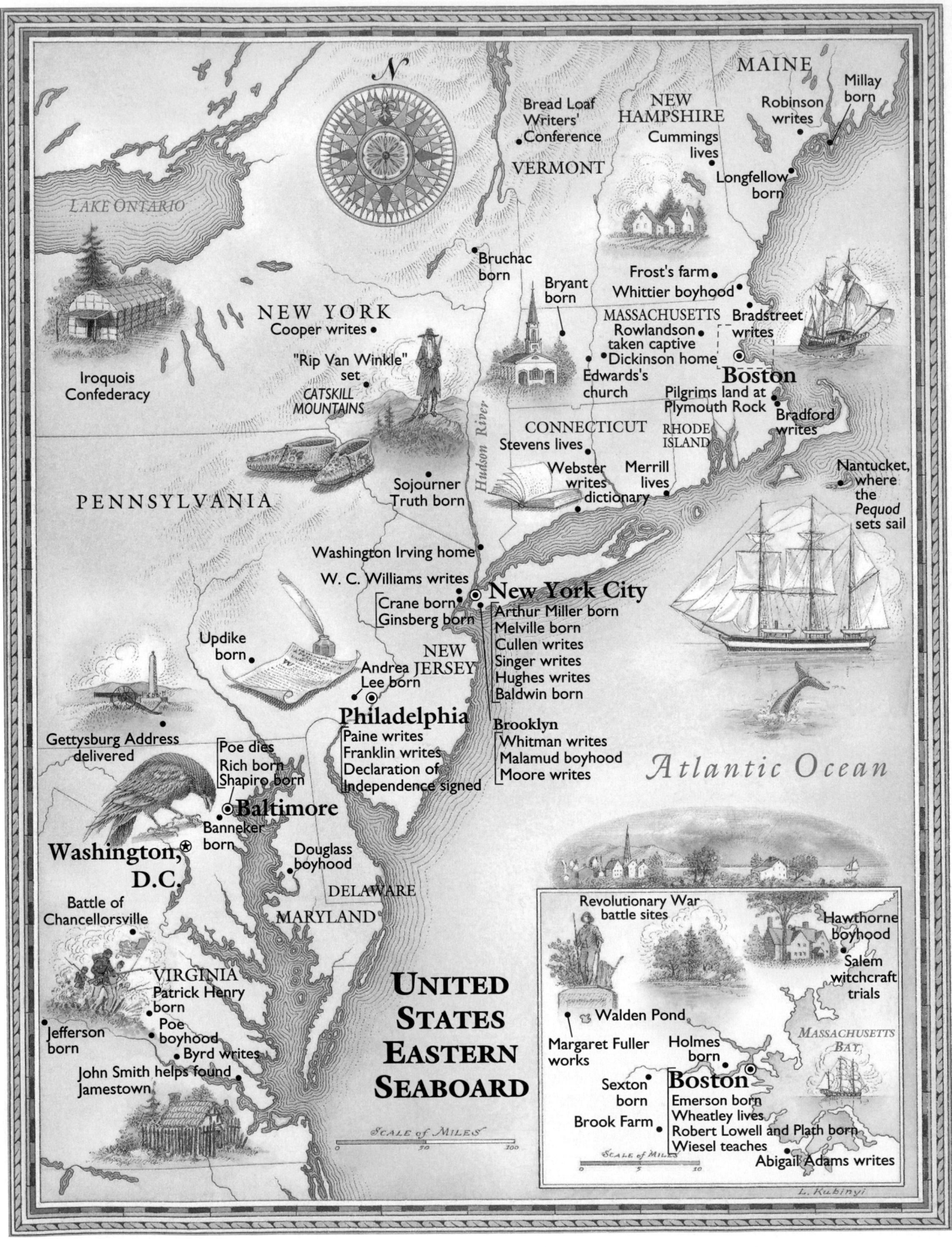

N

Bread Loaf
Writers'
Conference

MAINE

Millay
born

Robinson
writes

NEW
HAMPSHIRE

Cummings
lives

Longfellow
born

VERMONT

LAKE ONTARIO

Bruchac
born

Frost's farm

Whittier boyhood

Bryant
born

MASSACHUSETTS
Rowlandson
taken captive

Bradstreet
writes

Iroquois
Confederacy

NEW YORK
Cooper writes

"Rip Van Winkle"
set

CATSKILL
MOUNTAINS

Dickinson home

Boston

Edwards's
church

Pilgrims land at
Plymouth Rock

Bradford
writes

Hudson River

CONNECTICUT
Stevens lives

RHODE
ISLAND

PENNSYLVANIA

Sojourner
Truth born

Webster
writes
dictionary

Merrill
lives

Nantucket,
where
the
Pequod
sets sail

Washington Irving home

W. C. Williams writes

Crane born
Ginsberg born

New York City
Arthur Miller born
Melville born
Cullen writes
Singer writes
Hughes writes
Baldwin born

Updike
born

NEW
JERSEY
Andrea
Lee born

Gettysburg Address
delivered

Philadelphia
Paine writes
Franklin writes
Declaration of
Independence signed

Brooklyn
Whitman writes
Malamud boyhood
Moore writes

Atlantic Ocean

Poe dies
Rich born
Shapiro born

Baltimore

Banneker
born

Douglass
boyhood

Washington,
D.C.

DELAWARE

MARYLAND

Battle of
Chancellorsville

UNITED
STATES
EASTERN
SEABOARD

Revolutionary War
battle sites

Hawthorne
boyhood

Salem
witchcraft
trials

VIRGINIA
Patrick Henry
born

Poe
boyhood

Jefferson
born

Byrd writes

Walden Pond

Margaret Fuller
works

Holmes
born

MASSACHUSETTS
BAY

John Smith helps found
Jamestown

Sexton
born

Boston
Emerson born
Wheatley lives
Robert Lowell and Plath born
Wiesel teaches

Brook Farm

SCALE OF MILES
0   50   100

SCALE OF MILES
0   5   10

Abigail Adams writes

L. Rubinyi

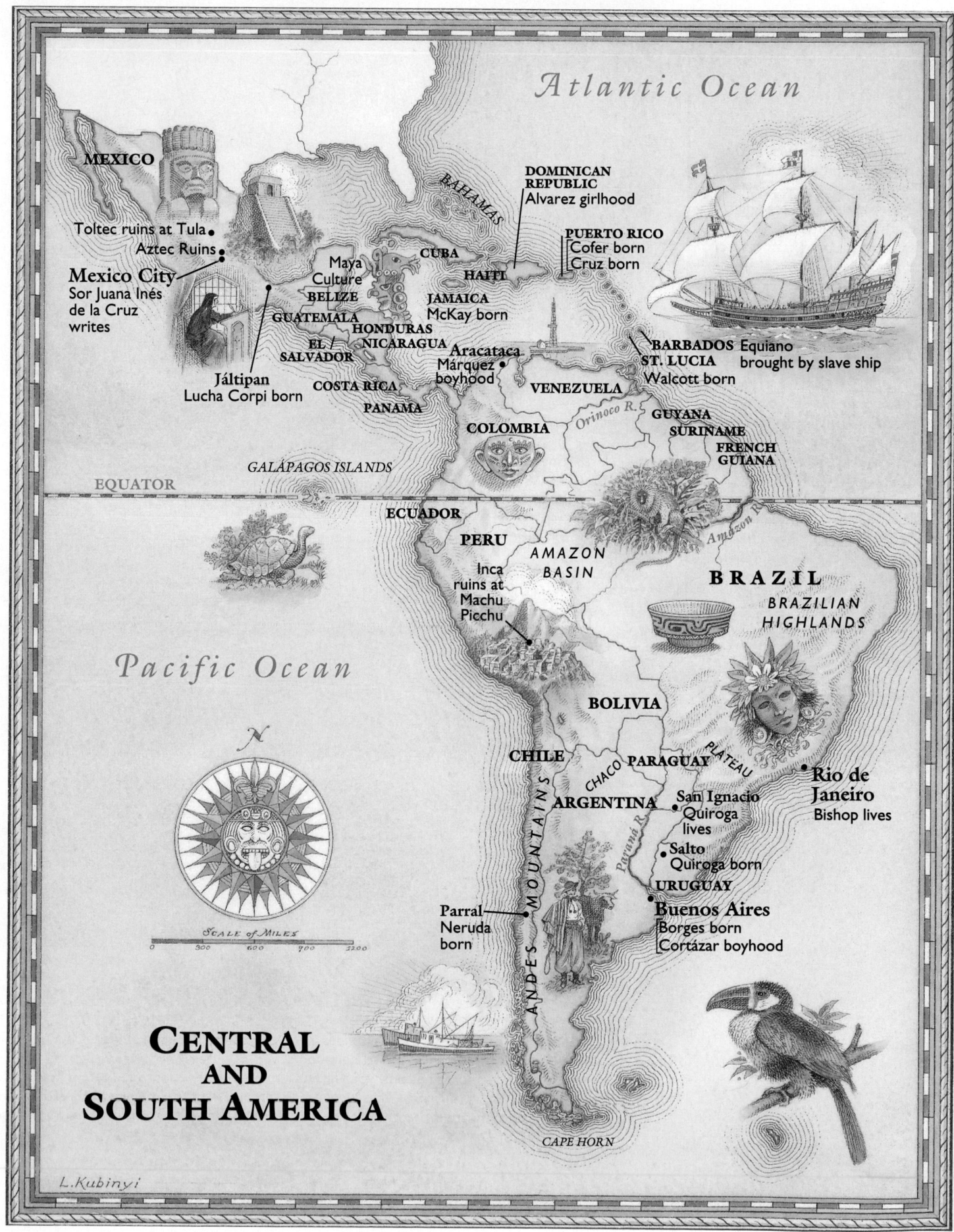

Atlantic Ocean

MEXICO

Toltec ruins at Tula •
Aztec Ruins •

Mexico City
Sor Juana Inés
de la Cruz
writes

Jáltipan
Lucha Corpi born

BAHAMAS

Maya
Culture

BELIZE

GUATEMALA

**EL
SALVADOR**

HONDURAS
NICARAGUA

COSTA RICA

PANAMA

CUBA

HAITI

JAMAICA
McKay born

Aracataca
Márquez •
boyhood

**DOMINICAN
REPUBLIC**
Alvarez girlhood

PUERTO RICO
Cofer born
Cruz born

VENEZUELA

Orinoco R.

COLOMBIA

BARBADOS
ST. LUCIA
Walcott born

Equiano
brought by slave ship

GUYANA
SURINAME
**FRENCH
GUIANA**

GALÁPAGOS ISLANDS

EQUATOR

ECUADOR

PERU

Inca
ruins at
Machu
Picchu

*AMAZON
BASIN*

Amazon R.

BRAZIL

*BRAZILIAN
HIGHLANDS*

Pacific Ocean

BOLIVIA

CHILE

CHACO

PARAGUAY

ARGENTINA

San Ignacio
Quiroga
lives

Salto
Quiroga born

URUGUAY

Parral
Neruda
born

Buenos Aires
Borges born
Cortázar boyhood

PLATEAU

Rio de
Janeiro
Bishop lives

N

SCALE of MILES

0   300   600   900   1200

ANDES MOUNTAINS

Paraná R.

CAPE HORN

CENTRAL
AND
SOUTH AMERICA

L. Kubinyi

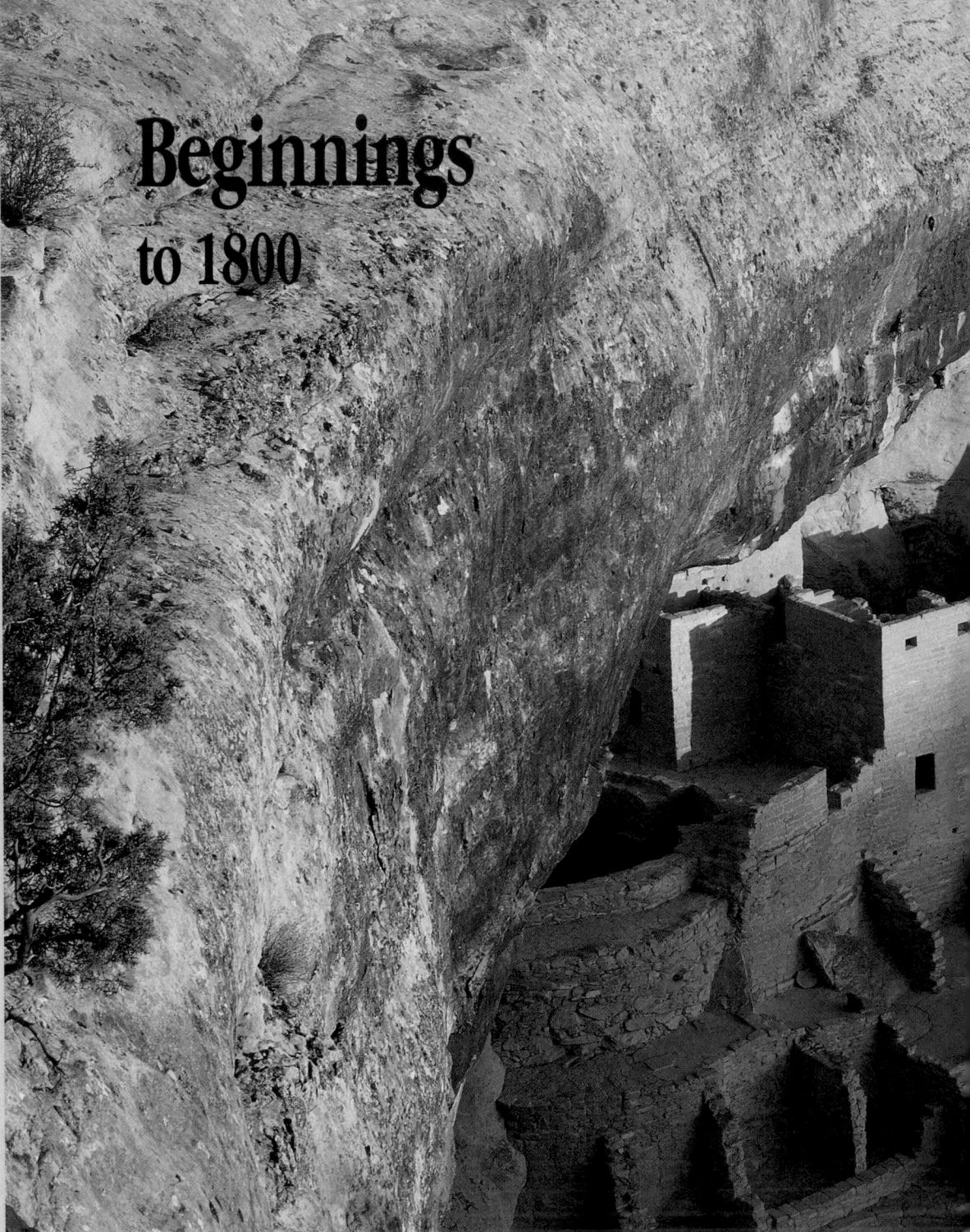

Beginnings
to 1800

Selection Readability

This Annotated Teacher's Edition provides a summary of each selection in the student book. Following each Summary heading, you will find one, two, or three small icons. These icons indicate, in an approximate sense, the reading level of the selection.

■ One icon indicates that the selection is easy.

■ ■ Two icons indicate that the selection is on an intermediate reading level.

■ ■ ■ Three icons indicate that the selection is challenging.

This ancient city was built about A.D. 1100 by a pueblo people known as Anasazi ("the old ones"). By 1300, three hundred years before the Pilgrims landed on Plymouth Rock, this beautiful city had been mysteriously abandoned.

Cliff Palace at Mesa Verde National Park, Colorado. © David Muench Photography.

RESPONDING TO THE ART

Before A.D. 550, when the Anasazi settled in Mesa Verde (now part of Colorado), they had been a nomadic people. At Mesa Verde, they became farmers, growing corn, beans, squash, and cotton. They also raised turkeys and hunted deer and mountain sheep.

Cliff Palace is the name given to the largest dwelling from the ancient city, part of which is shown at the left. At one time, Cliff Palace was home to 250–300 people. It included apartment-like dwellings as well as underground rooms called kivas. The kivas may have been used for religious ceremonies; they also served as gathering places and weaving rooms.

No one knows why the Anasazi abandoned their city—it remains as great a mystery as the disappearance of the dinosaurs or the engineering methods used to build Stonehenge. However, historians believe that the droughts and crop failures of the last quarter of the 1200s may have had something to do with the city's abandonment.

Activity. Have students compile a list of inferences they can make about the Anasazi based on the ruins of their city. [Possible answers: They were skilled builders; they made effective and imaginative use of the natural resources; they built with an eye to protection from their enemies—the walls are strong and intruders can only approach from one direction; their social organization seems quite complex and sophisticated.]

Reaching All Students

Struggling Readers

The large amount of expository text in this introduction has been organized with subheads and charts of major points. Main ideas are set in boldface type. For lessons tied to this introduction that will help students understand the text, see the *Reading Skills and Strategies* binder:

- MiniRead Skill Lesson, p. 1
- Selection Skill Lesson, p. 9

OBJECTIVES

1. To understand historical and social forces that shaped culture and society in North America before 1800
2. To identify the influence of history on the literary works of the Early American period
3. To examine the influence of Puritanism and rationalism in contemporary American life
4. To read a time line

Beginnings

by **Gary Q. Arpin**

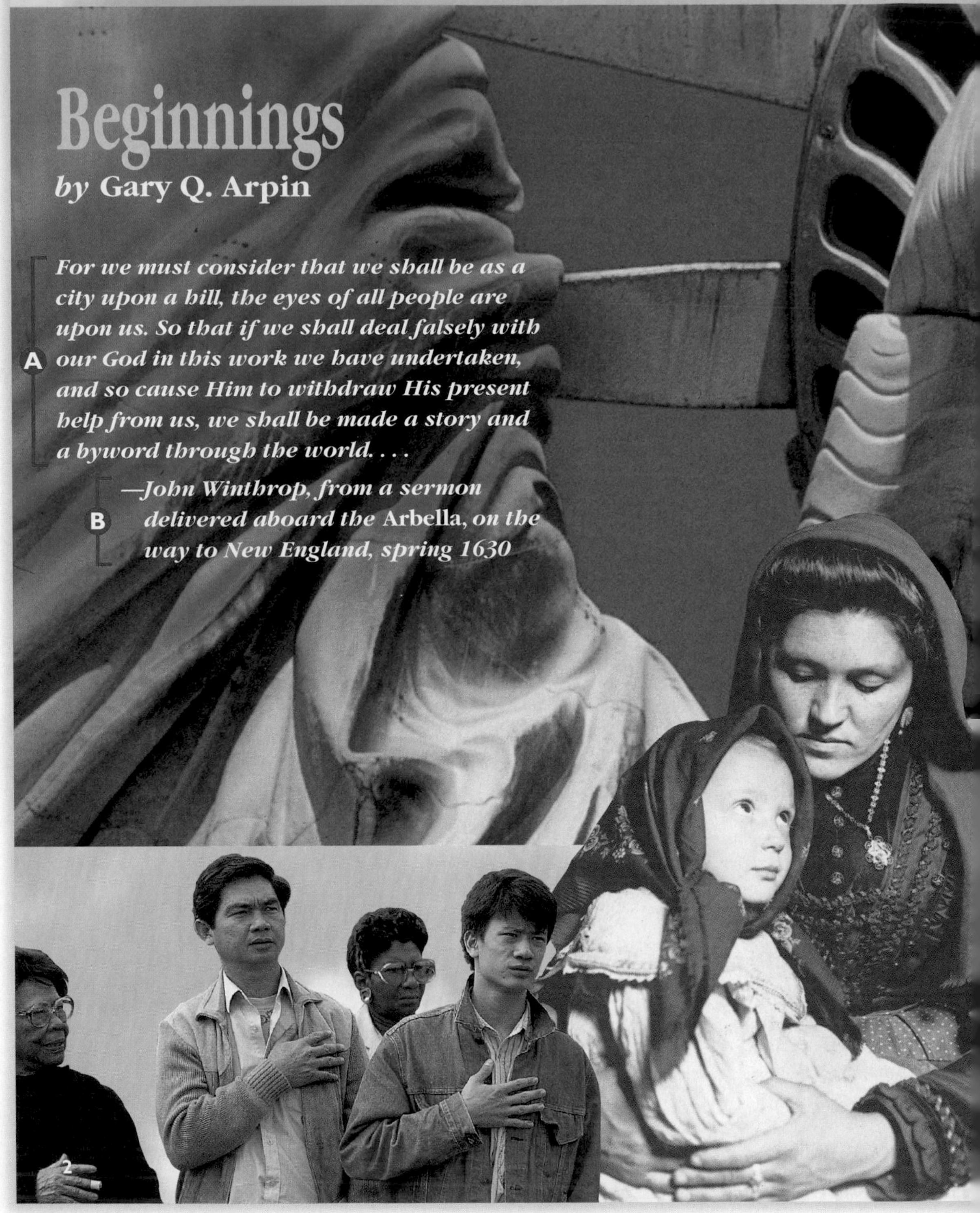

A *For we must consider that we shall be as a city upon a hill, the eyes of all people are upon us. So that if we shall deal falsely with our God in this work we have undertaken, and so cause Him to withdraw His present help from us, we shall be made a story and a byword through the world. . . .*

B *—John Winthrop, from a sermon delivered aboard the* Arbella*, on the way to New England, spring 1630*

Ⓐ Cultural Connections

Biblical References

Puritan John Winthrop was the first governor of the Massachusetts Bay Colony and the founder of the city of Boston. Tell students that this quote is an allusion to Jesus Christ's Sermon on the Mount (Matthew 5:14). Jesus urges his listeners to let their good deeds show forth to the world. He says, "You are the light of the world. A city built on a hill cannot be hid. No one after lighting a lamp puts it under the bushel basket, but on the lampstand, and it gives light to all in the house." Ask students what can they gather about the Puritans from Winthrop's quotation. [Possible responses: They feel they must set an example; they think that their behavior is important and that there will be serious consequences if they do not live up to their beliefs.]

Ⓑ Historical Connections

John Winthrop and his fellow Puritans believed they had a covenant, or contract, with God to create a society governed by the Scriptures in which everyone worked together for the common good. These Puritans, however, demanded strict conformity. Dissenters were often flogged, banished, or on occasion even put to death.

Resources

Viewing and Representing

Videocassette A, Segment 3

This segment "The Puritan Experience" is available in Spanish and English. For full lesson plans and worksheets, see the *Visual Connections Teacher's Manual.*

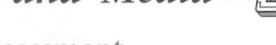

Resources: Print and Media

Viewing and Representing

- *Visual Connections*
  Videocassette A, Segment 3

Assessment

- *Formal Assessment,* p. 1
- *Test Generator (One-Stop Planner CD-ROM)*

Internet

- go.hrw.com (keyword: LE0 11-1)

The United States is a land of immigrants. The first people began entering North America on foot many thousands of years ago. Then came people in wooden sailing ships. Later, millions came against their will in the stifling holds of slave ships. Millions of others, lacking money for better accommodations, endured weeks of discomfort in cramped, uncomfortable steerage sections of ships. The latest immigrants probably are arriving by plane or even on flimsy rafts as you read these words. Most likely you, your relatives, or some of your classmates immigrated to this country.

HRW go.hrw.com
LEO 11-Beginnings

BEGINNINGS **3**

Using Students' Strengths

Verbal Learners

Emma Lazarus wrote a sonnet called "The New Colossus" in 1883. In the poem, Lazarus compares Lady Liberty to the Colossus of Rhodes, a giant bronze statue that was one of the seven wonders of the ancient world. Read aloud the final lines of the poem, which appear below:

Give me your tired, your poor,
Your huddled masses yearning to breathe
   free,

The wretched refuse of your teeming shore.
Send these, the homeless, tempest-tost
   to me,
I lift my lamp beside the golden door!
Tell students that these words are inscribed in the base of the Statue of Liberty. Ask how these words affect students, and discuss why the statue has become a symbol of freedom around the world.

Visual Learners

Have students locate photographs of the Statue of Liberty that show more complete views. If any students have visited the Statue of Liberty, have them share their experiences. If your school is in the New York City area, urge students to visit the statue, if possible, and share their impressions with the class.

Time Line

This time line provides a historical overview of events on the North American continent from 1450 to 1800 and places them in the context of other historical, literary, and cultural happenings around the world. The annotations below either expand on an event listed or add other key facts that students will find interesting.

• 1450–1615

In 1517, Martin Luther posts a list of criticisms against the Catholic Church on the door of the cathedral in Wittenberg, Germany. The Ninety-five Theses, as the list comes to be known, suggests that the way to salvation lies through faith, not through good works, and protests what he sees as the avarice and corruption of the papacy. Luther paves the way for the Reformation and the spread of Protestantism. Not long after this, England permanently breaks away from the Catholic Church, in part because King Henry VIII wants to divorce his queen and remarry. When the Pope refuses Henry's request, the king founds the Anglican Church, naming himself as its supreme head. Although Henry breaks from the Church for purely personal reasons, many of his subjects are disillusioned enough with the Catholic Church to follow his lead without protest.

• 1615–1699

In 1635, Roger Williams is banished from the restrictive Massachusetts Bay Colony and "exposed to winter miseries in a howling wilderness after criticizing the Colony's Puritan doctrine." The next year he establishes a colony in Providence, Rhode Island, known for its religious freedom and the separation of church and state.

• 1730–1749

In 1748, French philosopher and jurist Charles de Montesquieu suggests in *The Spirit of Laws* that there are three types of governments: the republic based on virtue, the monarchy based on honor, and the tyranny based on fear. He also proposes the system of checks and balances that has come to characterize the United States government: that three powers, the executive, judiciary, and legislative, operate independently of one another and curb one another's powers.

Beginnings to 1800

Reverend Jonathan Edwards (1750–1755) by Joseph Badger. Oil on canvas.
Yale University Art Gallery. Bequest of Eugene Phelps Edwards (1938.74).

LITERARY EVENTS

Mary Rowlandson's captivity narrative is published, 1682

Anne Bradstreet's *The Tenth Muse Lately Sprung Up in America* is published in England, 1650

William Bradford writes *Of Plymouth Plantation*, 1630–1647

Spain's Miguel de Cervantes publishes his novel *Don Quixote*, in two parts, 1605, 1615

England's William Shakespeare writes *King Lear* and *Macbeth*, 1605–1606

William Byrd writes *The History of the Dividing Line*, 1728

England's Jonathan Swift publishes the satiric novel *Gulliver's Travels*, 1726

England's Daniel Defoe publishes *Robinson Crusoe*, considered one of the first English novels, 1719

England's Henry Fielding publishes the novel *The History of Tom Jones*, 1749

Jonathan Edwards delivers his vivid sermon, "Sinners in the Hands of an Angry God," 1741

1450–1615	1615–1699	1700–1729	1730–1749

CULTURAL/HISTORICAL EVENTS

Christopher Columbus lands on an island in the Bahamas, 1492

Songhai Empire in West Africa reaches peak, c. 1493–1528

Protestant Reformation starts in Germany, 1517

Aztec Empire falls to Spanish army, 1521

Spanish explorer Álvar Núñez Cabeza de Vaca lands in Florida and spends eight years walking through Texas, New Mexico, and Arizona, 1528–1536

Settlement founded at Jamestown, Virginia, 1607

Mayflower Pilgrims land at Plymouth, 1620

Great Migration of Puritans to New England begins, c. 1630

Mughal emperor Shah Jahan builds Taj Mahal, in northern India, 1632–1638

Metacomet's war on Massachusetts Colonies begins, 1675

England's Isaac Newton explains laws of motion and gravity in *Principia Mathematica*, 1687

Slavery exists in all English colonies in North America, 1690

Twenty people executed in witch trials in Salem, Massachusetts, 1692

About 251,000 European settlers live in what is now the United States, 1700

Smallpox epidemic hits Boston, 1721

German composer Johann Sebastian Bach completes the oratorio *St. Matthew Passion*, 1729

The Great Awakening is touched off by a traveling English preacher, 1740–1745

George Frideric Handel's *Messiah* is first performed, in Dublin, Ireland, 1742

France's Charles de Montesquieu publishes *The Spirit of Laws*, a study of government later reflected in the U.S. Constitution, 1748

Arresting a witch in the streets of Salem.
The Granger Collection, New York.

4 BEGINNINGS

Skill Link

Building a Time Line

The ability to create graphic organizers that reflect the structure of a text or its important points is a critical comprehension skill. Have students review the introductory essay on pp. 3–18 and then place the following events in the appropriate spot on the time line.

- The Pilgrims sign the *Mayflower Compact*. [1620]
- The first printing press in America is set up. [1639]

- The *New England Primer* is published. [1690] Next, have students research the following events and add them to the time line.
- The English colony at Roanoke disappears without a trace. [1586]
- The war against the Pequots of Connecticut ends in a bloody massacre. [1637]
- Cotton Mather explains his support for the Salem witch trials in *Wonders of the Invisible World*. [1693]

Benjamin Franklin's sister-in-law Anne Franklin becomes first woman printer in New England, 1762

•

England's Samuel Johnson publishes his monumental *Dictionary of the English Language,* 1755

•

John Woolman publishes two antislavery essays, 1754, 1763

Thomas Paine publishes *Common Sense,* 1776

•

Patrick Henry demands liberty from British rule, at the Virginia Convention, 1775

•

Phillis Wheatley publishes *Poems on Various Subjects, Religious and Moral,* 1773

•

Benjamin Franklin begins to write his *Autobiography,* 1771

The Federalist, a series of essays by Alexander Hamilton, James Madison, and John Jay, urges voters to approve the U.S. Constitution, 1787–1788

•

Thomas Jefferson publishes *Notes on the State of Virginia,* 1785

•

France's Michel-Guillaume Jean de Crèvecoeur publishes *Letters from an American Farmer,* 1782

Phillis Wheatley.
The Granger Collection, New York.

England's Samuel Taylor Coleridge publishes *The Rime of the Ancient Mariner,* a long Romantic poem, 1798

1750–1769	1770–1779	1780–1789	1790–1800

Benjamin Franklin's experiments with a kite and a key prove that lightning is a manifestation of electricity, 1752

•

French and Indian War officially ends as British gain control of most French North American territory, 1763

•

American colonists hold Stamp Act Congress to protest a direct British tax, 1765; British repeal tax, 1766

Boston Tea Party.
Culver Pictures.

Boston Tea Party occurs in Boston Harbor, 1773

•

First shots of American Revolution fired at Lexington and Concord, Massachusetts, April 19, 1775

•

Second Continental Congress adopts Declaration of Independence, July 4, 1776

U.S. governed under Articles of Confederation, 1781–1788

•

American Revolutionary War ends as British surrender at Yorktown, Virginia, October 1781; peace treaty signed, 1783

•

Austrian composer Wolfgang Amadeus Mozart finishes the opera *Don Giovanni,* 1787

•

George Washington inaugurated as first president under U.S. Constitution, 1789

•

French Revolution begins, 1789

First census in America sets population at about 3.9 million, 1790

•

New York Stock Exchange organized, 1792

•

Invention of cotton gin leads to increase in slave labor, 1793

•

English physician Edward Jenner develops smallpox vaccine, 1796

•

Napoleon Bonaparte becomes dictator of France, 1799

•

Library of Congress established, 1800

•

Washington, D.C., named capital of U.S., 1800

Stamp from Stamp Act, 1765.
© Collection of The New-York Historical Society.

Skill Link

Reading a Time Line

Tell students that a time line can help them see the relationships between events. Model how to glean information from this time line by posing the following questions:

• What cause and effect relationship exists between the adoption of the Declaration of Independence in 1776 and the French Revolution in 1789? [Some of the egalitarian ideals of the Declaration of Independence were echoed by supporters of the French Revolution including Mirabeau.]

• When did the first major epidemic of smallpox occur among the settlers? [1721] How was the problem of smallpox eventually solved? [Edward Jenner developed a safe vaccine in 1796.] Now urge students to study the time line in order to create similar questions about events.

• **1770–1779**
In 1771, Benjamin Franklin begins his *Autobiography,* the first American example of a "rags-to-riches" story.

• **1780–1789**
During the Revolutionary War (1775–1783) twenty-two-year-old Deborah Sampson, an unknown schoolteacher, strikes a blow for equal rights when she becomes the first American woman to serve as a combat soldier. She disguises herself as a man and enlists in the 4th Massachusetts regiment in 1782, using the name Robert Shurtleff. She fights in a number of battles and is wounded at least twice. In order to protect her identity, she conceals a serious leg wound; but when she is hospitalized for a high fever, her disguise is discovered. General George Washington grants her an honorable discharge.

• **1780–1789**
The eighty-five essays collectively known as *The Federalist Papers* or *The Federalist* appear in New York newspapers over a six-month period. Alexander Hamilton writes fifty-one of the essays, James Madison twenty-nine, and John Jay five. All appear under the name "Publius" (in the eighteenth-century fashion of publishing editorials under Latin pseudonyms). As delegates to the Constitutional Convention, the three writers are well aware of the strife and dissension among its members. The essays of *The Federalist Papers* are the medium through which they take their case to the public.

Many congressional delegates argue that a unified republican government cannot work in a country as large as the United States. In *Federalist 10,* the most famous of the essays, Madison argues that a large population will inevitably break up into many factions or special interests, ensuring that no one faction can grow powerful enough to control the government. Ask students whether they think Madison has been proved right or wrong in the long run.

• **1780–1789**
In 1789, the African Olaudah Equiano (see p. T56) publishes his account of his life, first as a slave and then as a free man.

A **Cultural Connections**

Native American Cultures

For purposes of comparison, scholars often organize the Native American populations at the arrival of the Europeans into eight geographic groups:

- *Northeast Coast:* coastal dwellers; fishers; developed complex culture
- *Plateau:* river valley dwellers; primarily fishers; relatively small population
- *Great Plains:* grassland dwellers; nomadic buffalo hunters after introduction of the horse
- *Northeast:* forest dwellers; primarily hunter-gatherers, but also farmers and fishers
- *Great Basin:* desert basin dwellers; primarily gatherers because of barren surroundings; small population
- *California:* desert, mountain, river, or coastal dwellers depending on location; primarily gatherers and fishers
- *Southwest:* canyon, mountain, and desert dwellers; either farmers or nomadic hunters
- *Southeast:* river valley dwellers; primarily farmers, but also hunter-gatherers and fishers

B **Historical Connections**

The Pequot War

In 1636, friction between the Pequots and the Puritans led to the Pequot War. After the Pequots' defeat in a massacre in 1637, survivors were beheaded or sent into slavery. The Puritan leader of the raid rejoiced at his victory: "We had sufficient light from the word of God for our proceedings."

The First Migration: Ice Age Travelers

Archaeological evidence tells us that anywhere from twenty to over forty thousand years ago, Ice Age hunters traveling with dogs crossed the Bering land bridge (now submerged under the Bering Strait) from Siberia to what is now Alaska. Slowly, these people and their descendants migrated south. Over the centuries, other migrants followed that route across the strait (some adventurers possibly used other means to reach the shores of North America). By the 1490s, **A** when the great wave of European exploration of the Americas started, numerous groups of American Indians were living all over North America. These societies were diverse, and each had its own long history. (The Aztec Empire in present-day Mexico was the largest Native American civilization in the fifteenth century, with millions of people living within its borders.)

What's important to remember is that there were people here when the Europeans arrived in the fifteenth century; descendants of those people are still here, and their traditions remain. In 1994, for example, the Pequots, whom the English met when they arrived in what is now Connecticut, Rhode Island, and Massachusetts, **B** donated ten million dollars to the new National Museum of the American Indian in Washington, D.C., to promote and save native cultures.

People first migrated to North America from twenty to over forty thousand years ago. When the first Europeans arrived in the fifteenth century, American Indians were living in diverse societies spread across the continent.

The Europeans Arrive: The Explorers

The first detailed European observations of life in this vast continent were recorded in Spanish and French by explorers of the fifteenth and sixteenth centuries. These writings open a window to a tumultuous time when the so-called New World was the heady focus of the dreams and desires of an entire era. Christopher Columbus (1451–1506), Francisco Vásquez de Coronado (1510–1554), and many others described the Americas in a flurry of eagerly read letters, journals, and books. Hoping to fund further expeditions, the explorers emphasized the Americas' abundant resources, the peacefulness and hospitality of the inhabitants, and the promise of the unlimited wealth to be gained from fantastic treasuries of gold.

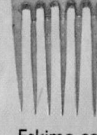

Black Coat, a Cherokee chief (1836) by George Catlin. Oil on canvas.
The Granger Collection, New York.

Eskimo comb.
Breton Littlehales/ National Geographic Image Collection.

> Columbus did not discover a new world; he established contact between two worlds, both already old.
>
> —J. H. Parry,
> *The Spanish Seaborne Empire* (1966)

Turtle and *Flamingo* (1585–1587) by John White. Watercolor.
Copyright British Museum, London. Courtesy of Lee Boltin.

6 BEGINNINGS

Jacques Cartier's Discovery of the St. Lawrence River (1957) by Thomas H. Benton. Tempera on canvas (7' × 6').

In 1528, only thirty-six years after Columbus first sighted that flickering fire on the beach of San Salvador, a Spaniard named Álvar Núñez Cabeza de Vaca (c. 1490–1557) landed with an expedition (he was its treasurer) on the west coast of what is now Florida. Cabeza de Vaca and others left the ship and marched inland. They did not return. Their fleet waited an entire year for them, then departed for Mexico, giving up the explorers for dead. Lost in the Texas Gulf area, Cabeza de Vaca and his companions wandered for the next eight years in search of other Europeans who would help them to get home. Cabeza de Vaca's narrative of his journeys through what is now Texas is a gripping adventure story. It is also

Europeans did not find a wilderness here; rather, however involuntarily, they made one. Jamestown, Plymouth, Salem, Boston, Providence, New Amsterdam, Philadelphia—all grew upon sites previously occupied by Indian communities. So did Quebec and Montreal and Detroit and Chicago. The so-called settlement of America was a resettlement, a reoccupation of a land made waste by the diseases and demoralization introduced by the newcomers.

—Francis Jennings,
The Invasion of America (1975)

© Historical Connections

Encomienda

Christopher Columbus introduced the *encomienda* system to the Americas. In this system, colonists had the right to require Indians to mine gold, grow food, and build homes for them without being given significant compensation. Although some critics, including Bartolomé de Las Casas (see p. T8), tried to halt this virtual enslavement, the system did not disappear until after decades of suffering, malnutrition, and death.

Professional Notes

Critical Comment: Cabeza de Vaca

In *Empires Lost and Won: The Spanish Heritage in the Southwest,* historian Albert Marrin finishes the account of Álvar Núñez Cabeza de Vaca's life after his eight-year trek.

"Cabeza de Vaca returned to Spain in 1537. We do not know whether he rejoined his wife, or, for that matter, if she was still alive. What is certain is that his fame preceded him and that His Majesty promised him high office as a reward for his achievements. After three

years of waiting, he was named governor of the province of Río de la Plata in South America. From 1540 to 1543, he explored the jungles south of the equator. His humane treatment of the Indians, however, made enemies among the colonists. They had him arrested on false charges and sent back to Spain in chains. For six years he lay in a dungeon with scarcely enough light to see his hand in front of his face. Upon his release, he

vanished from history. It is believed that Álvar Núñez Cabeza de Vaca spent his last years in loneliness and poverty. The date of his death is unknown. He never knew that his travels had opened a new chapter in American history."

Critical Thinking

Evaluating the Credibility of Sources

❓ As a colonist with the right to have natives work for him in virtual slavery, Bartolomé de Las Casas had firsthand contact with the Spanish rule in the Americas. He became a Dominican priest in 1512 and apparently rethought his role, for he gave up his *encomienda*. Given his experience, how might you evaluate the statement by de Las Casas? [Possible responses: His words are persuasive, because he has seen how the system works; he is not persuasive because as a priest, he is no longer responsible for the administration and survival of the colony.]

Ⓑ **Background**

Cabeza de Vaca

Cabeza de Vaca's eight-year journey through the New World was a remarkable feat of endurance. However, his account is more than a chronicle of his travels. In his work, he also undertakes an inward journey, transforming himself from a competent conquistador and Spanish gentleman into a new American who sympathizes with and appreciates the native peoples he encounters. He spent much of the rest of his time in America fighting for their just treatment.

Ⓑ a firsthand account of the habits of some of the indigenous people in what is now the United States: what they ate (very little), how they housed themselves, and what their religious beliefs were. De Vaca also provides the first account of some animals and plants that the Europeans had never known existed.

Cabeza de Vaca and his shipmates were alternately captives or companions of the various Native American peoples they encountered on their long trek. Here is part of de Vaca's account of the expedition's experiences with a tribal group in the Gulf Coast area, struggling to survive a famine.

Ⓐ The reason why the [Europeans] have killed and destroyed such infinite numbers of souls is solely because they have made gold their ultimate aim, seeking to load themselves with riches in the shortest time. . . . These lands, being so happy and so rich, and the people so humble, so patient, and so easily subjugated, they have . . . taken no more account of them . . . than—I will not say of animals, for would to God they had considered and treated them as animals—but as even less than the dung in the streets.

—Bartolomé de Las Casas,
Very Brief Account of the Destruction of the Indies (1542)

Their support is principally roots, of two or three kinds, and they look for them over the face of all the country. The food is poor and gripes the persons who eat it. The roots require roasting two days: Many are very bitter, and withal difficult to be dug. They are sought the distance of two or three leagues, and so great is the want these people experience, that they cannot get through the year without them. Occasionally they kill deer, and at times take fish; but the quantity is so small and the famine so great, that they eat spiders and the eggs of ants, worms, lizards, salamanders, snakes, and vipers that kill whom they strike; and they eat earth and wood, and all that there is, the dung of deer, and other things that I omit to mention; and I honestly believe that were there stones in that land they would eat them. They save the bones of the fishes they consume, of snakes and other animals, that they may afterward beat them together and eat the powder.

—Álvar Núñez Cabeza de Vaca

The first Europeans to visit the Americas were the explorers. Their enthusiastic accounts of the beauty and wealth of the Americas led to increased expeditions to what Renaissance Europeans saw as the New World.

Making the Connections

Cultural Connections:
Colonial Conscience

In his *Apologetic History of the Indies,* published in 1566, Bartolomé de Las Casas argued that the native people were the equal of Europeans:

"Not only have the Indians shown themselves to be very wise peoples and possessed of lively and marked understanding . . . governing and providing for their nations . . . but they have equaled many diverse nations of

the . . . past and present . . . and exceed by no small measure the wisest of these."

However, the voices of de Las Casas and other dissenters were not strong enough to counteract the colonists' desire for gold, glory, and converts to Catholicism. Encourage students to research the culture of the Taino and other Caribbean tribes that were destroyed in their encounters with Europeans.

The Puritan Legacy

Interesting and valuable as the explorers' writings are, they were not central to the development of the American literary tradition in the way the writings of the Puritans of New England were. In many respects, the American character has been shaped by the moral, ethical, and religious convictions of the Puritans.

The first and most famous group of these English Puritans landed, in 1620, on the tip of Cape Cod, just before Christmas. They were followed, ten years later, by seven hundred more Puritan settlers. By 1640, as many as twenty thousand English Puritans had sailed to what they called New England.

Although the real commerce of the Puritans was with heaven, they were competent in the business of the world as well: The founding of a new society in North America was a business venture as well as a spiritual one. For the Puritans, the everyday world and the spiritual world were closely intertwined.

(Left) Page from *The Day of Doom* by Michael Wigglesworth.

Seal on meeting notice.

Who Were These Puritans?

Puritan is a broad term, referring to a number of Protestant groups that, beginning about 1560, sought to "purify" the Church of England, which since the time of Henry VIII (who reigned from 1509 to 1547) had been virtually inseparable from the country's government. Like other Protestant reformers on the European continent, English Puritans wished to return to the simpler forms of worship and church organization described in the New Testament. For them, religion was first of all a personal, inner experience. They did not believe that the clergy or the government should or could act as an intermediary between the individual and God.

Many Puritans suffered persecution in England. Some were put in jail and whipped, their noses slit and their ears lopped off. Some fled England for Holland. But fearing that in Holland they would lose their identity as English Protestants, a small group led by William Bradford (page 26) and others set sail in 1620 for what was advertised as the New World. There they hoped to build a new society patterned after God's word.

> The Puritans were single-minded visionaries convinced of the rightness of their beliefs, but they were also practical and businesslike. They felt that Christian worship and church organization should be simplified in order to more closely resemble Biblical models. Many Puritans were persecuted for their beliefs and fled England for Holland and, ultimately, for North America.

The Puritan Deacon Samuel Chapin (1899) by Augustus Saint-Gaudens. Bronze model.
James Graham & Sons, Inc., New York.

C Additional Background
The Rise of Capitalism
Many historians feel that the Puritan ethic of thrift, hard work, and self-sufficiency contributed to the success of capitalism in the New World. Because the Puritans believed wealth was a sign of God's favor, they strove to attain it.

D Humanities Connections
Protestant Denominations
Make sure students understand the difference between Anglicans (called Episcopalians in the United States) and Presbyterians, Methodists, and Lutherans. These latter three denominations were born out of protest against both Catholicism and Anglicanism, which maintained many of the practices and doctrines that early Protestants had criticized in Catholicism. The three denominations share a belief in a literalistic interpretation of the Bible and an insistence on plain, spare churches without the statues, candles, elaborate vestments, and other pageantry typical of Catholicism and Episcopalianism.

RESPONDING TO THE ART
Augustus Saint-Gaudens (1848–1907), was born in Dublin, Ireland, but raised in New York City. His most highly regarded works include the expressive figure of *Abraham Lincoln* in Chicago's Lincoln Park; the shrouded, seated woman of the *Adam's Memorial* in Rock Creek Cemetery, Washington, D.C.; and the equestrian statue of General William Tecumseh Sherman in New York City's Central Park.
Activity. Have students generate a list of adjectives which capture the Puritan spirit by examining the stance and bearing of Deacon Chapin. [Possible response: sternness, dignity, pride, steadfastness, faith, religious fervor.]

THE SALEM WITCHCRAFT TRIALS

The Trial for Witchcraft of George Jacobs, August 5, 1692
(1855) by T. H. Matteson. Oil on canvas.
Courtesy Peabody Essex Museum, Salem, Massachusetts.
Photograph by Mark Sexton.

During the cold, dreary winter of 1691–1692, the daughter and the niece of Samuel Parris, a minister in Salem Village, Massachusetts, began to dabble in magic. By February the two girls started having fits. Lesions appeared on their skin, and it seemed as though they were being choked by invisible hands. A doctor diagnosed the girls as being the victims of malicious witchcraft.

Urged to name those responsible for bewitching them, the girls accused Sarah Good and Sarah Osborne, two unpopular women from the village, and Tituba, a slave whom Samuel Parris had brought back from Barbados. During the subsequent trial, the girls writhed and moaned and behaved as though they were being choked. Based on this "evidence," Sarah Good was condemned. In an attempt to save her own life, Tituba confessed to being a witch. She claimed that there was a coven of witches in Massachusetts and testified that she had seen several names written in blood in the Devil's book. The witch hunt had begun.

Puritan Beliefs: Sinners All?

In Adam's Fall
We sinned all.
—*The New England
Primer* (c. 1690)

For a people who were so convinced they were right, the Puritans had to grapple with complex uncertainties. At the center of Puritan theology was an uneasy mixture of certainty and doubt. The certainty was that because of Adam and Eve's sin of disobedience, most of humanity would be damned for all eternity. But the Puritans were also certain that God in his mercy had sent his son Jesus Christ to earth to save particular people.

The doubt centered on whether a particular individual was one of the saved (the "elect") or one of the damned (the "unregenerate"). How did you know if you were saved or damned?

As it turns out, you did not know. A theology that was so clear-cut in its division of the world between saints and sinners was fuzzy when it came to determining which were which. There were two principal indications of the state of your soul, neither of them completely certain. You were saved by the grace of God, and you could *feel* this grace arriving, in an intensely emotional fashion. The inner arrival of God's grace was demonstrated by your outward

Warrant for the arrest of Ann Pudeator (1692).
Courtesy Peabody Essex Museum, Salem, Massachusetts.

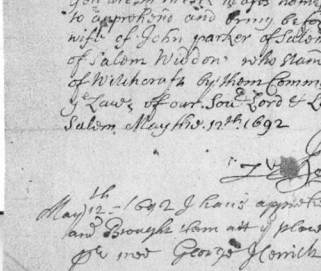

Tompkins Harrison Matteson (1813–1884) was a New York genre and portrait painter who took his subjects from American history and rural life. This painting depicts the witch trial of George Jacobs (kneeling at right), who was hanged following his conviction.

Activity. Ask students how they would characterize the mood of this witch trial. [Possible answers: dramatic; traumatic; emotional.] How does Matteson's composition capture this mood? [Possible response: The tableau of bright colors, stylized features, and dramatic gestures helps communicate the drama and intensity of the scene.]

Ⓐ Critical Thinking

Speculating

❓ What do you think might explain the girls' symptoms? [Possible answers: The girls were playacting (while coincidentally suffering from a skin infection); the girls had come to believe themselves possessed and their convulsions and hallucinations were psychosomatic symptoms brought about by fear and hysteria.]

Ⓑ Background

The Youngest Witch

Dorcas Good was four years old when she was accused and convicted of being a witch. Although her mother and baby sister died in prison, she survived but suffered severe emotional difficulty for the rest of her life.

Ⓒ Literary Connections

The *New England Primer*

Generations of colonial children learned to read from the *New England Primer*. This work included a brief rhymed couplet for each letter of the alphabet. The couplet for the letter *A* is shown here. Most couplets preached a simple Biblical lesson so that children could absorb moral lessons along with the alphabet. Here is the couplet for the letter *T*.

Time cuts down all
Both great and small.

Listening to Music ♪♫

"Jordan" by William Billings,
    performed by His Majesties Clerkes

While the Puritans frowned on instrumental music in church, New England developed a musical tradition centered around mobile "singing schools" with traveling masters who taught people to read and sing church music. The best-known singing master was William Billings (1746–1800), whom a contemporary called "the father of our New England music."

Composing before, during, and after the Revolution, Billings created patriotic anthems as well as hymns. In the 1800s, his vibrant style fell out of favor in New England, replaced by more formal organ-accompanied music.

Activity

Listen to the hymn "Jordan," in which "Jordan" refers to the Biblical Promised Land, in turn associated with heaven. Then, discuss which Puritan values the hymn represents.

Zealous ministers like Cotton Mather argued that the epidemic of witchcraft proved beyond a doubt that New England was a holy place, since the Devil was so interested in it. Mather and others demanded that all witches be rooted out and severely punished. Hundreds of people from Salem and other eastern Massachusetts towns came forward to testify that they were victims of witchcraft.

Before long the prisons were overcrowded, and a special court was established in Salem Village. Within the next ten months, about 150 people in this small community were accused of witchcraft. Neighbors, especially those with long-standing quarrels, turned on each other. Between June and September, nineteen people were hanged, and one man, Giles Corey, who had refused to plead either innocent or guilty, was crushed to death under a pile of stones.

What really happened at Salem? Many historians believe that Salem experienced a mass hysteria, a sort of shared delusion. Still others have suggested that a more restrictive form of government recently imposed on the Massachusetts Bay Colony, in addition to new economic pressures in the Colony's towns, may have led to bitterness, aggression, and outright paranoia. Perhaps the strict society of Puritan New England finally erupted under the strain of its repression. A recent theory proposes that fear of unusual or powerful "nonconformists"—particularly women—may have led to an attempt to constrain their behavior. Statistics show that the majority of the "witches" were unmarried women between the ages of forty and sixty: eccentric and independent loners with abrasive personalities. Some of them may have been "cunning folk," that is, midwives or people with unusual healing abilities and knowledge of herbal remedies. They were often women who could potentially come into their fathers' inheritances and therefore be seen as a threat to male power.

The Salem trials fascinate to this day. They are the subject of one of the great contemporary American plays, Arthur Miller's *The Crucible* (1953), which is printed in Collection 17 of this text (see page 829).

D Historical Connections
Salem's Society
Another theory proposed by some historians to explain the Salem hysteria is that it grew out of mutual hostilities between the wealthy residents of Salem seaport, who had made money in trade, and the poorer farmers who lived outside the town in Salem Village. They contend that many of the accusers were villagers and the accused were largely townsfolk.

E Historical Connections
McCarthyism
Conviction by accusation did not end with the Salem witchcraft trials. From 1950 to 1954, Senator Joseph McCarthy of Wisconsin seized the political spotlight by charging that communists had infiltrated the State Department. His accusations were backed up by almost no hard evidence, but they gained credence at the height of the Cold War. As chairman of the Senate Permanent Investigations Subcommittee, McCarthy summoned hundreds of Americans to testify and threatened to brand them as communists if they refused to cooperate. As in Salem, mere accusations were enough to ruin a person's career and social life—and hundreds of those McCarthy accused were "blacklisted" or unofficially prohibited from working in their chosen professions. McCarthy was ultimately condemned by the Senate in 1954 for his misconduct and abuse of power.

F Historical Connections
Salem's Aftermath
In 1696, after the wave of hysteria in Salem had passed, a judge repented; then twelve of the jurors repented. Eventually, Ann Putnam, one of the chief accusers, apologized. In 1711, the state reimbursed heirs of most of the victims with up to 150 pounds sterling.

behavior. After receiving grace, you were "reborn" as a member of the community of saints, and you behaved like a saint. People hoping to be among the saved examined their inner lives closely for signs of grace, and they tried to live exemplary lives. So American Puritans came to value self-reliance, industriousness, temperance, and simplicity. These were, coincidentally, the ideal qualities needed to carve out a new society in a strange land.

> God's altar needs not our polishing.
> —The Bay Psalm Book (1610)

Puritans believed that Adam and Eve's sin had damned most people for all eternity. They also believed that Jesus Christ had been sent to earth to save particular people, known as the "elect." It was difficult to know for certain if one was saved or damned, so the Puritans tried to behave in as exemplary a manner as possible.

Puritan Politics: Government by Contract

In the Puritan view, a covenant, or contract, existed between God and humanity. This spiritual covenant was a useful model for worldly social organization as well: Puritans believed that people should enter freely into agreements concerning their government. On the *Mayflower,* for example,

---

Crossing the Curriculum

Social Studies
What were the Puritans' values and beliefs? Review with students the following tenets of the Puritan credo:
- Human beings are sinful by nature.
- Salvation belongs to the elect, or God's chosen, who can be identified by their virtue.
- Hard work and worldly success are signs of God's grace.
- Education is essential in order to read the Word of God.

- A person should be thrifty, modest, and simple.
- Society should be ruled by covenants that parallel God's covenant with His people.

Then, ask students to consider these values in light of what is often seen as the materialistic, celebrity-crazed culture of America at the beginning of the twenty-first century. How many of these Puritan beliefs are still valued in America? Do Americans admire self-made people who have built careers through hard work, or do they consider get-rich-quick investment schemes a better route to financial security? Is modesty still a virtue, or has the art of self-promotion knocked it off its pedestal? Throughout this discussion about Puritan values in American culture, be sure students back up their opinions with logical arguments and specific examples.

Pilgrims Signing the Compact Aboard the Mayflower, *November 11, 1620,* depicts the signing of the first governmental constitution in America. This rendering was done in mezzotint. Mezzotint, from the Italian *mezzatinta,* or "half-tone," was a laborious printing technique used from the seventeenth through nineteenth centuries. The process was designed to imitate the shades of color in oil paintings. An etcher first incised the entire surface of a metal plate with hundreds of tiny pricks, and then scraped at various depths to create areas that would print in gradations of light and shadow. Color could be added after the print was made. (The portrait of Cotton Mather on p. 15 is a noncolorized mezzotint.)

Activity. Ask the students whether or not they feel this mezzotint idealizes the signers of the Mayflower Compact. [Possible responses: Yes, the etcher produced an assembly of unrealistic and sentimental figures with contrived poses or with their eyes uplifted to heaven; no, the Pilgrims were religious people and quite possibly assumed these very positions.]

Pilgrims Signing the Compact Aboard the Mayflower, *November 11, 1620* (19th century). Colored mezzotint.

The Granger Collection, New York.

the Puritans composed and signed the Mayflower Compact, outlining how they would be governed once they landed. In this use of a contractual agreement, they prepared the ground for American constitutional democracy.

On the other hand, because the Puritans believed the saintly "elect" should exert great influence on government, their political views tended to be undemocratic. There was little room for compromise. The witchcraft hysteria in Salem, Massachusetts, in 1692 (pages 10–11), resulted in part from fear that the community's moral foundation was threatened, and therefore its political cohesion was also in danger.

The Bible in America

The Puritans read the Bible as the story of the creation, fall, wanderings, and rescue of the human race. Within this long and complex narrative, each Puritan could see connections to events in his or her own life or to events in the life of the community. Each Puritan was trained to see life as a pilgrimage, or journey, to salvation. Each Puritan learned to read his or her life the way a literary critic reads a book.

The Puritans believed that the Bible was the literal word of God. Reading the Bible was

Characteristics of Puritan Writing

- The Bible provided a model for Puritan writing: a conception of each individual life as a journey to salvation. Puritans saw direct connections between Biblical events and their own lives.

- Puritans used writing to explore their inner and outer lives for signs of the workings of God.

- Diaries and histories were the most common forms of expression in Puritan society; in them writers described the workings of God.

- Puritans favored a plain style, similar to that of the Geneva Bible. They stressed clarity of expression and avoided complicated figures of speech.

Professional Notes

Primary Sources:
The Mayflower Compact

Here is the first voluntary compact of government written in the New World:

"We, whose names are underwritten . . . Having undertaken for the Glory of God, and Advancement of the Christian Faith, and the Honour of our King and Country, a Voyage to plant the first colony in the northern Parts of Virginia; Do by these Presents [this document], solemnly and mutually in the Presence of God and one another, covenant and combine ourselves together into a civil Body Politick, for our better Ordering and Preservation, and Furtherance of the Ends aforesaid; And by Virtue hereof do enact, constitute, and frame, such just and equal Laws, Ordinances, Acts, Constitutions, and Offices, from time to time, as shall be thought most meet and convenient for the general Good of the Colony; unto which we promise all due Submission and Obedience."

a necessity for all Puritans, as was the ability to understand theological debates. For these reasons, the Puritans placed great emphasis on education. Thus, Harvard College, originally intended to train Puritan ministers for the rapidly expanding Colony, was founded in 1636, only sixteen years after the first Pilgrims had landed. And, just three years later, the first printing press in the American Colonies was set up.

Their beliefs required the Puritans to keep a close watch on both the inner and outer events of their lives. This central aspect of the Puritan mind greatly affected their writings. Diaries and histories were important forms of Puritan literature, because they were used to record the workings of God.

Puritan belief in a spiritual compact between God and humanity paved the way for American constitutional democracy. The Puritans emphasized education so that people could read and understand the Bible and follow religious debates. Diaries and histories were important forms of Puritan literature.

The Age of Reason: Tinkerers and Experimenters

By the end of the seventeenth century, new ideas that had been fermenting in Europe began to present a challenge to the unshakable faith of the Puritans.

The Age of Reason, or the Enlightenment, began in Europe with the philosophers and scientists of the seventeenth and eighteenth centuries who called themselves rationalists. **Rationalism** is the belief that human beings can arrive at truth by using reason, rather than by relying on the authority of the past, on religious faith, or on intuition.

The Puritans saw God as actively and mysteriously involved in the workings of the universe; the rationalists saw God differently. The great English rationalist Sir Isaac Newton (1642–1727), who formulated the laws of gravity and motion, compared God to a clockmaker. Having created the perfect mechanism of this universe, God then left his creation to run on its own, like a clock. The rationalists believed that God's special gift to humanity was reason—the ability to think in an ordered, logical manner. This gift of reason enabled people to discover both scientific and spiritual truth. Everyone, then, had the capacity to regulate and improve his or her own life.

While the theoretical background for the Age of Reason took shape in Europe, a home-grown practicality and interest in scientific tinkering or experimenting already thrived in the American Colonies. From the earliest Colonial days, Americans had to be generalists and tinkerers; they had to make do with what they had, and they had to achieve results.

Title page of the *Bay Psalm Book* (1640).

The Granger Collection, New York.

Sir Isaac Newton, President of the Royal Society (1802). Engraving, after a painting by Vanderbank.

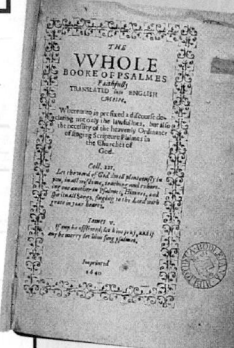

The Granger Collection, New York.

Hornbook for children.
Rare Book Department, Free Library of Philadelphia.

BEGINNINGS 13

A Historical Connections
Higher Education
Harvard was followed by Yale College (1701) and Princeton College (1746). Although these were the first colleges in North America, it was not until the mid-twentieth century that they began to offer female students the same privileges and opportunities as male students. By contrast, Oberlin College in northeastern Ohio opened its doors to female students as soon as it was founded, in 1833.

B Humanities Connections
Deism
The view that God created a well-ordered universe, controlled by immutable laws and operating without divine intervention, is the central belief of deism. Deists generally accepted naturalistic explanations for miracles in the Bible and allegorical interpretations of Biblical prophecies. Adherents saw deism as a philosophy that could reconcile religion and science. Their beliefs, however, clashed with the Puritan emphasis on revelation, divine providence, and the final judgment.

C Additional Background
Enlightenment Metaphors
Congressional delegate John Adams of Massachusetts (who would eventually become our second president) picked up on Newton's idea of the universe as a finely tuned clock when he referred to the unanimous vote by the Second Continental Congress to adopt Virginia's resolution on independence as "thirteen clocks striking at the same moment." Ask students to consider how difficult it would be to cause thirteen clocks to strike at the same moment. [Students should realize that such an exact synchronization would have been almost impossible.] What is Adams saying about the thirteen colonies' unanimity about independence? [It was difficult to achieve.]

Making the Connections

Cultural Connections: Hornbooks

A hornbook was a type of children's primer used from the fifteenth to eighteenth centuries. A lesson was printed on a sheet of parchment or paper and covered for protection with a thin, transparent sheet of animal horn, both of which were then fastened to a board. The board usually featured a perforated handle that could be attached to a child's belt or a cord worn around the neck. Lessons included the alphabet in capitals and lower case and a variety of other topics, such as Roman numerals or the Lord's Prayer. The contents of hornbooks and early primers reflect the fact that the curricula of the earliest schools in the North American colonies centered on religion. You might ask how this approach contrasts with the teaching of letters today. [Students usually learn the alphabet from their parents or from television shows such as *Sesame Street* that have no religious content.]

Cotton Mather

Cotton Mather (1663–1728) was a child prodigy who went to Harvard at age twelve. He came from a prominent New England family of theologians and thinkers; his grandfather Richard and his father, Increase, were both well-known ministers, writers, and orators. Beginning in the 1680s, Mather and his father both preached at Boston's Second Church. There (in spite of a bad stutter) he became famous for his rousing sermons and his interest in science, witchcraft, and prophesies about the end of the world. Although Mather is now praised for his attempts to prevent smallpox through inoculations, some historians have criticized him for his views supporting the Salem witch trials, which he expressed in his *Wonders of the Invisible World.*

RESPONDING TO THE ART

Boston Landmarks. The photographic collage on pp. 14–15 includes the Revolutionary War monuments of Paul Revere's home, a statue of Revere, and the Old State House. Revere (1735–1818) was a Boston-born silversmith who became famous for his ride on April 18, 1775, to warn his fellow revolutionaries of the impending approach of the British army on Lexington and Concord, Massachusetts (see p. T15). Tell students that the Old State House, which was the home of the British governor, came to symbolize English tyranny. Consequently, after the Revolution, a new State House was built on Beacon Hill, and Revere joined Samuel Adams in laying its cornerstone (1795).

Activity. You might ask students to research a presentation on Boston's Freedom Trail walking tour, which features many of these historical points of interest from the Revolutionary period.

The Smallpox Plague

The unlikely hero of America's first foray into scientific exploration was the strict Puritan minister Cotton Mather (1663–1728), who was interested in natural science and medicine.

In April 1721, a ship from the West Indies docked in Boston Harbor. This was not unusual, for trade with the West Indies was one of the foundations of New England economic life. This ship was different, though. For in addition to its cargo of sugar and molasses, this ship carried smallpox.

In the seventeenth and eighteenth centuries, smallpox was one of the scourges of life, as the AIDS virus is today. The disease spread rapidly, disfigured its victims, and was often fatal. The outbreak in Boston in 1721 was a major public-health problem. What was to be done?

Horrible outbreaks of smallpox had ravaged Native Americans ever since the white settlers first landed. Smallpox had been unknown in North America, and the native people had no immunity to the virus. Nearly a century before Boston's smallpox outbreak, Bradford described the horrors of the disease:

For want of bedding and linen and other helps . . . they fall into a lamentable condition as they lie on their hard mats, the pox breaking and mattering and running one into another, their skin cleaving by reason thereof to the mats they lie on. When they turn them, a whole side will flay off at once as it were, and they will be all of a gore blood, most fearful to behold. And then being very sore, what with cold and other distempers, they die like rotten sheep.

—William Bradford

Paul Revere's house, Boston.

Professional Notes

Smallpox: A Contemporary View

Smallpox outbreaks continued throughout the seventeenth century. "In 1736," wrote Benjamin Franklin in his *Autobiography,* "I lost one of my sons, a fine boy of four years old, by the smallpox, taken in the common way. I long regretted bitterly, and still regret that I had not given it to him by inoculation. This I mention for the sake of parents who omit that operation, on the supposition that they should never forgive themselves if a child died under it, my example showing that the regret may be the same either way, and that, therefore, the safer should be chosen."

At the time of the smallpox epidemic, Cotton Mather was working on what would be the first scholarly essay on medicine written in America. In his opening sentences he reveals his Puritan perspective: "Let us look upon sin as the cause of sickness." His religious point of view did not, however, prevent Mather from seeking cures for specific diseases. He had heard of a method for dealing with smallpox devised by a Turkish physician. The method seemed illogical, but it apparently worked. It was called inoculation. In June 1721, as the smallpox epidemic spread throughout Boston, Mather began a public campaign for inoculation.

Boston's medical community was violently opposed to such an experiment, especially one borrowed from the Muslims. The debate was vigorous, raging all the summer and into the fall. Controversy developed into violence: In November, Mather's house was bombed.

Despite such fierce opposition, Mather succeeded in inoculating nearly three hundred people. By the time the epidemic was over, in March of the following year, only six of these had died. Of the almost six thousand other people who contracted the disease (nearly half of Boston's population),

B

Cotton Mather (1727) by Peter Pelham. Mezzotint.

The Granger Collection, New York.

(Left) Paul Revere statue, Boston.
(Right) Old State House, Boston. **C**

BEGINNINGS 15

Crossing the Curriculum

Drama

Have a volunteer give a dramatic reading of "Paul Revere's Ride." Ask students to discuss such aspects of the poem as rhythm, rhyme, alliteration, sound, diction, and tone. What devices does Longfellow use to make the story dramatic and interesting? Might it have been equally gripping if Longfellow had included William Dawes in his narrative?

Science

Have students locate and read John Adams's 1764 letters describing the experience of smallpox inoculation. (Adams's correspondence is readily available in most academic libraries.) Have them share with their classmates what they learn about 1760s medical practice. What was inoculation like? How long did it take? How was Adams's experience of inoculation different from inoculation students may have undergone for measles or other diseases?

The Battle Against Smallpox

Variolus inoculation, the name for the method Cotton Mather advocated in 1721, was controversial because it involved deliberate infection with the disease. The doctor would inject the patient with serum containing a mild smallpox virus. The theory was that the patient would survive the mild sickness and thenceforth be immune to smallpox; the human immune system will not succumb twice to the same disease. As we have seen from Franklin's comments (see p. T14), many people were alarmed at the idea of infecting themselves with smallpox. Even a mild case of smallpox was unpleasant and dangerous, making people's hesitation to undergo the procedure understandable. Not until the end of the century did Edward Jenner (see p. 5) discover that the injection of a much milder disease, cowpox, would immunize people from smallpox.

C Historical Connections

Paul Revere's Ride

If you ask any school child about the start of the Revolutionary War, you will probably hear about Paul Revere's ride. Along with numerous friends and fellow artisans, silversmith Revere had been keeping watch on the British army that had been occupying Boston since 1768. On the night of April 18, 1775, the British redcoats tried to slip out of the city to seize supplies stored in the countryside by rebel colonists. William Dawes rode to the neighboring town of Lexington to warn the Patriot leaders John Hancock and Samuel Adams of the approach of the enemy. Revere rowed across the Charles River, borrowed a horse, and set out for Lexington, too. Along the way, he sounded the alarm at every house he passed. Revere met Dawes in Lexington; on the way to Concord, the two men narrowly escaped being shot by the British. For some reason, retellings of this story rarely mention Dawes. Henry Wadsworth Longfellow (see p. 175) recorded Revere's heroism for posterity in perhaps his most famous narrative poem, "Paul Revere's Ride."

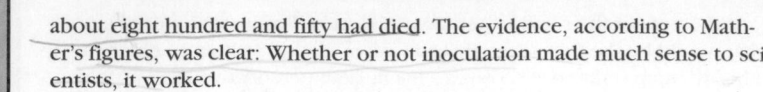

A Critical Thinking
Evaluating

? What prediction does Crèvecoeur make about America's future? Has that prediction come true? [Possible answer: He predicts that Americans will develop a culture free from the prejudices and manners of Europe, and that this "new race" of men living in new ways will revolutionize the world. Although many students will question whether America is truly free from the prejudices and formalities, most will agree that Crèvecoeur was right to predict that America's Constitution, economy, and foreign policy have had an enormous impact on world history.]

B Additional Background
Deists

American deists included prominent revolutionaries such as Benjamin Franklin, Thomas Jefferson, George Washington, and Thomas Paine.

about eight hundred and fifty had died. The evidence, according to Mather's figures, was clear: Whether or not inoculation made much sense to scientists, it worked.

The smallpox controversy illustrates two interesting points about American life in the early eighteenth century. First, it shows that contradictory qualities of the American character often existed side by side. Puritan thinking was not limited to a rigid and narrow interpretation of the Bible; a devout Puritan like Mather could also be a practical scientist.

Mather's experiment also reveals that a practical approach to social change and scientific research was necessary in America. The frontier farmer with little access to tools shared a problem with the scientist who had few books and a whole new world of plants and animals to catalog. American thought had to be thought in action: an urge to improve the public welfare by being willing to experiment, to try things out, no matter what the authorities might say.

> What then is . . . this new man? . . . He is an American, who, leaving behind him all his ancient prejudices and manners, receives new ones from the new mode of life he has embraced, the new government he obeys, and the new rank he holds. . . . [In America] individuals of all nations are melted into a new race of men, whose labors . . . will one day cause great changes in the world.
>
> —Michel-Guillaume Jean de Crèvecoeur, *Letters from an American Farmer* (1782)

Thomas Jefferson (1805) by Rembrandt Peale. Oil on canvas. Accession number 1867.306.

© Collection of The New-York Historical Society.

Deism: Are People Basically Good?

Like the Puritans, the rationalists discovered God through the medium of the natural world, but in a different way. Rationalists thought it unlikely that God would choose to reveal himself only at particular times to particular people. It seemed much more reasonable to believe that God had made it possible for *all* people at *all* times to discover natural laws through their God-given power of reason.

This outlook, called **deism** (dē′iz′əm), was shared by many eighteenth-century thinkers, including many founders of the American nation. American deists came from different religious backgrounds. But the deists avoided supporting specific religious groups. They sought, instead, the principles that united all religions.

Deists believed that the universe was orderly and good. In contrast to the Puritans, deists stressed humanity's goodness. They believed in the perfectibility of every individual through the use of reason. God's objective, in the deist view, was the happiness of his creatures. Therefore, the best form of worship was to do good for others. There already existed in America an impulse to improve people's lives, as Cotton Mather's struggle to save Boston from small-

16 BEGINNINGS

The Battle of Bunker Hill (detail) (1776) by Winthrop Chandler (1747–1790). United States. Oil on canvas (34½" × 53⅝").
Museum of Fine Arts, Boston/Gift of Mr. and Mrs. Gardner Richardson (1982.281).

Ⓐ

pox illustrates. Deism elevated this impulse to one of the nation's highest goals. To this day, social welfare is still a political priority and still the subject of fierce debate.

The American struggle for independence was justified largely by appeals to rationalist principles. The Declaration of Independence bases its arguments on rationalist assumptions about the relations between people, God, and natural law.

In contrast to Puritans, deists believed that God was available to all people all of the time. Deists believed that people were inherently good, that every individual had the gift of reason and with that gift could perfect himself or herself and society.

Ⓑ Reason and free inquiry . . . are the natural enemies of error, and of error only. **Ⓒ**
—Thomas Jefferson, *Notes on the State of Virginia* (1785)

Crossing the Curriculum

Social Studies

The expression "the smoke of battle" originated because the black powder that soldiers used to fire their muskets created a fog of white smoke. This smoke made it difficult to see what was going on in the heat of hand-to-hand combat. Because swords were reserved for gentlemen, bayonets inflicted eighty percent of all casualties. Thus, seeing the enemy as he attacked was critical to survival. As Chandler's painting of the Battle of Bunker Hill shows, cannons and other artillery played a large part in laying siege to fortifications and forts. Cannons shot cast-iron balls and grapeshot, a cluster of small iron balls in the shaft of a wooden disk. If students are interested, they might read primary sources that convey the atmosphere of Revolutionary War battles.

A Critical Thinking

Analyzing Cause and Effect

❓ **How did the rationalist idea that people are basically good help to incite revolution?** [Enlightenment thinkers argued that if the will of the people was basically rational and good, then government should take its authority from them, and not the will of a single monarch. Furthermore, it implied that a government that failed to respect the popular will could legitimately be overthrown.]

B Reading Skills and Strategies

Connecting with the Text

❓ **What contemporary autobiographies do you know by self-made Americans?** [Sample responses: Sam Walton's *Sam Walton: Made in America*; Bill Gates's *The Road Ahead*.]

RESPONDING TO THE ART

The wood carving *E Pluribus Unum* adopts elements from the Great Seal of the United States, first approved by the Continental Congress in 1782. The seal shows an American bald eagle bearing in its beak a ribbon reading *E Pluribus Unum*—Latin for "Out of many, one." The reverse side of the seal shows an unfinished, thirteen-step pyramid topped by the eye of Providence within a triangle. **Activity.** Students may wish to research the additional symbols of the seal which can be found on the back of a one-dollar bill. [The front of the seal includes a shield with thirteen stripes on the eagle's breast, a constellation of thirteen stars (for the original colonies), an olive branch (for peace) in the eagle's right talon, and a bundle of thirteen arrows in its left. The back of the seal includes the words *Annuit coeptis* ("He has favored our undertakings") above the pyramid, the Roman numeral MDCCLXXVI (1776) on its base, and the words *Novus ordo seclorum* ("A new order of the ages") on a scroll below the pyramid.]

Self-Made Americans

Most of the literature written in the American Colonies during the Age of Reason was, understandably, rooted in reality. This was an age of pamphlets, since most literature was intended to serve practical or political ends. Following the Revolutionary War (1775–1783), the problems of organizing and governing the new nation were of the highest importance. The unquestioned masterpiece of the American Age of Reason is Benjamin Franklin's *Autobiography* (page 86). Franklin used the autobiographical narrative, a form common in Puritan writing, and took out its religious justification. Written in clear, witty prose, this account of the development of the self-made American provided the model for a story that would be told again and again. In the twentieth century, it appears in F. Scott Fitzgerald's novel *The Great Gatsby* (1925), as well as in the countless biographies and autobiographies of self-made men and women on the best-seller lists today.

E Pluribus Unum. Wood-carving.

Shelburne Museum, Shelburne, Vermont. Photograph by Ken Burris.

> *The masterpiece of the Revolutionary era is Franklin's* **Autobiography.** *Franklin took the Puritan impulse toward self-examination and molded it into the classic American rags-to-riches story—the triumph of the self-made person.*

Benjamin Franklin.

Drawing by David Levine. Reprinted with permission from *The New York Review of Books.* Copyright © 1967 NYREV, Inc.

The Rationalist Worldview

- People arrive at truth by using reason rather than by relying on the authority of the past, on religion, or on nonrational mental processes like intuition.
- God created the universe but does not interfere in its workings.
- The world operates according to God's rules, and through the use of reason we can discover those rules.
- People are basically good and perfectible.
- Since God wants people to be happy, they worship God best by helping other people.
- Human history is marked by progress toward a more perfect existence.

Quickwrite

Legacies of the Puritans and Rationalists

Do you see evidence of the worldviews of the Puritans and rationalists around you today? Think especially of debates about government, social welfare, and self-improvement. Write down a few of your observations about Puritanism and rationalism in American public life today. Give some examples.

Assessing Learning

Check Test: Multiple Choice

1. Puritans believed that they could be saved by (a) prayer. (b) good deeds. (c) God's grace. [c]
2. Puritans saw the hand of God in (a) American Indian ceremonies. (b) stained-glass windows. (c) everyday events. [c]
3. Cotton Mather proposed combating the smallpox epidemic by (a) rounding up witches. (b) inoculation. (c) continuous prayer. [b]
4. Deists believed that people were (a) inherently sinful. (b) inherently good. (c) not responsible for their actions. [b]
5. Most of the literature written in America during the Age of Reason consisted of (a) political tracts. (b) epic poetry. (c) religious tracts. [a]

Collection 1

Visions and Voyages

Theme

Who Are We? *The identity of any nation can be found in the early oral traditions and documents that define its values and its vision of its future. Here are Native American origin myths; political, social, and personal histories of the early English settlers; and the personal account of an African brought here by force. The dreams that unite Americans and the clashes that sometimes separate us are evident even in these very early documents of our nation's story.*

Reading the Anthology

Reaching Struggling Readers

The *Reading Skills and Strategies: Reaching Struggling Readers* binder provides materials coordinated with the Pupil's Edition (see the Collection Planner, p. T18B) to help students who have difficulty reading and comprehending text, or students who are reluctant readers. The binder for eleventh grade is organized around ten individual skill areas and offers the following options:

- **MiniRead** MiniReads are short, easy texts that give students a chance to practice a particular skill and strategy before reading selections in the Pupil's Edition. Each MiniRead Skill Lesson can be taught independently or used in conjunction with a Selection Skill Lesson.

- **Selection Skill Lessons** Selection Skill Lessons allow students to apply skills introduced in the MiniReads. Each Selection Skill Lesson provides reading instruction and practice specific to a particular piece of literature in the Pupil's Edition.

Reading Beyond the Anthology

Read On

At the end of the Beginnings to 1800 collections, the grade eleven book includes an annotated bibliography of books suitable for extended reading. The suggested books are related to works in these collections by theme, by author, or by subject. To preview the Read On for the Beginnings to 1800 period, please turn to p. T126.

Collection 1 Visions and Voyages

Resources for this Collection

Note: All resources for this collection are available for preview on the *One-Stop Planner CD-ROM 1 with Test Generator.* All worksheets and blackline masters may be printed from the CD-ROM.

Internet Resources
go.hrw.com LE0 11-1

Selection or Feature	Reading and Literary Skills	Vocabulary, Language, and Grammar
Literature of the Americas: North America **The Sun Still Rises in the Same Sky: Native American Literature** (p. 20) Huron Eastern *by* Joseph Bruchac • **The Sky Tree** (p. 22) Woodland Traditional *told by* Joseph Bruchac • **The Earth Only** (p. 23) Teton Sioux Traditional *retold by* Used-As-A-Shield • *from* **The House Made of Dawn** *from* **The Night Chant** (p. 23) Navajo Traditional *translated by* Washington Matthews • **Coyote Finishes His Work** (p. 24) Nez Percé Traditional *retold by* Barry Lopez	The Literature of the Americas feature offers selections from a variety of American cultures representing North, Central, and South America. These selections connect to the collection theme, and students explore the thematic links through structured group discussions called Finding Common Ground.	• *Daily Oral Grammar,* Transparency 1
from **Of Plymouth Plantation** William Bradford (p. 27) **Connections: An American Story** Anthony Lewis (p. 34)	• *Graphic Organizers for Active Reading,* Worksheet p. 1 • *Literary Elements:* Transparency 1 Worksheet p. 4	• *Words to Own,* Worksheet p. 1 • *Grammar and Language Links:* Reviewing Nouns, Worksheet p. 1 • *Language Workshop CD-ROM,* Nouns • *Daily Oral Grammar,* Transparency 2
from **A Narrative of the Captivity** Mary Rowlandson (p. 39)	• *Reading Skills and Strategies: Reaching Struggling Readers* • MiniRead Skill Lesson, p. 13 • Selection Skill Lesson, p. 19 • *Graphic Organizers for Active Reading,* Worksheet p. 2	• *Words to Own,* Worksheet p. 3 • *Grammar and Language Links:* Reviewing Pronouns, Worksheet p. 3 • *Language Workshop CD-ROM,* Pronouns • *Daily Oral Grammar,* Transparency 3
The Southern Planters (p. 48) • *from* **The History of the Dividing Line** (p. 50) William Byrd	• *Graphic Organizers for Active Reading,* Worksheet p. 3	• *Words to Own,* Worksheet p. 4 • *Grammar and Language Links:* Reviewing Verbs, Worksheet p. 5 • *Language Workshop CD-ROM,* Verbs • *Daily Oral Grammar,* Transparency 4
from **The Interesting Narrative of the Life of Olaudah Equiano** (p. 57) Olaudah Equiano	• *Graphic Organizers for Active Reading,* Worksheet p. 4	• *Words to Own,* Worksheet p. 5 • *Grammar and Language Links:* Reviewing Adjectives, Worksheet p. 7 • *Language Workshop CD-ROM,* Adjectives • *Daily Oral Grammar,* Transparency 5

Other Resources for this Collection

- *Cross-Curricular Activities*, p. 1
- *Portfolio Management System*, Introduction to Portfolio Assessment, p. 1
- *Formal Assessment*, Literary Period Introduction Test, p. 1
- *Test Generator*, Collection Test

Writing	Listening and Speaking Viewing and Representing	Assessment
	• *Audio CD Library*, Disc 1, Tracks 2, 3, 4 	
• *Portfolio Management System*, Rubrics for Choices, p. 89	• *Audio CD Library*, Disc 1, Track 5  • *Viewing and Representing:* Fine Art Transparency 1 Worksheet p. 4  • *Portfolio Management System*, Rubrics for Choices, p. 89	• *Formal Assessment*, Selection Test, p. 3 • *Test Generator (One-Stop Planner CD-ROM)* 
• *Portfolio Management System*, Rubrics for Choices, p. 90	• *Audio CD Library*, Disc 2, Track 2  • *Portfolio Management System*, Rubrics for Choices, p. 90	• *Formal Assessment*, Selection Test, p. 5 • *Test Generator (One-Stop Planner CD-ROM)*  • *Preparation for College Admission Exams*, p. 1
• *Portfolio Management System*, Rubrics for Choices, p. 91	• *Audio CD Library*, Disc 2, Track 3  • *Portfolio Management System*, Rubrics for Choices, p. 91	• *Formal Assessment*, Selection Test, p. 7 • *Test Generator (One-Stop Planner CD-ROM)* 
• *Portfolio Management System*, Rubrics for Choices, p. 92	• *Audio CD Library*, Disc 2, Track 4  • *Portfolio Management System*, Rubrics for Choices, p. 92	• *Formal Assessment*, Selection Test, p. 9 • *Test Generator (One-Stop Planner CD-ROM)*  • *Preparation for College Admission Exams*, p. 3

 Transparency    CD-ROM    Video    Audio CD

Selection or Feature	Reading Skills and Strategies	Elements of Literature and Language	Writing	Listening and Speaking	Viewing and Representing
Literature of the Americas: North America **The Sun Still Rises in the Same Sky: Native American Literature** (p. 20) Joseph Bruchac • **The Sky Tree** (p. 22) Woodland Traditional *retold by* Joseph Bruchac • **The Earth Only** (p. 23) Teton Sioux Traditional *retold by* Used-As-A-Shield • *from* **The House Made of Dawn from The Night Chant** (p. 23) Navajo Traditional *translated by* Washington Matthews • **Coyote Finishes His Work** (p. 24) Nez Percé Traditional *retold by* Barry Lopez	Use a KWL Chart, pp. 21, 25	The Oral Tradition, p. 20 Moral Lessons, p. 20 Metaphor, p. 21 Simile, p. 21	The Literature of the Americas feature offers selections from a variety of American cultures representing North, Central, and South America. These selections connect to the collection theme, and students explore these thematic links through structured group discussions called Finding Common Ground.		
from **Of Plymouth Plantation** (p. 26) William Bradford	Use Study Strategies, pp. 27, 35 • Note Taking • Time Lines • Event Chains	The Plain Style, pp. 27, 35 Quotations and Allusions, p. 35 Archaic Syntax and Vocabulary, p. 35 Purpose, p. 36 Audience, p. 36 Motivation, p. 36	Collect Ideas for Writing an Autobiographical Incident, p. 36 Write an Essay Contrasting Two Writers' Purposes and Audiences, p. 36	Organize and Participate in a Panel Discussion, p. 36	
Reading Skills and Strategies: Vocabulary (p. 37)	Archaisms, p. 37 Use a Dictionary, p. 37				
from **A Narrative of the Captivity** (p. 38) Mary Rowlandson	Analyze Text Structures: Chronological Order, pp. 39, 46	Allusions, pp. 39, 46–47 Captivity Narratives, p. 42 Subjective Reporting, p. 46 Connotations, p. 46	Reflect on Personal Experiences, p. 47 Write an Essay Comparing Texts, p. 47 Research and Write a Journal Entry from a Specified Point of View, p. 47		
The Southern Planters (p. 48) • *from* **The History of the Dividing Line** (p. 49) William Byrd	Identify the Writer's Tone, pp. 50, 55	Satire, pp. 50, 55 Purpose, p. 55 Tone, p. 55 Style, p. 55	Make a List of Descriptive Phrases Associated with an Experience, p. 55 Write an Essay Comparing and Contrasting Two Writers, p. 55 Write a Journal Entry from a Specified Point of View, p. 55		
from **The Interesting Narrative of the Life of Olaudah Equiano** (p. 57) Olaudah Equiano	Use a KWL Chart, pp. 57, 66	Autobiography, pp. 57, 66 Images, p. 66	Write an Autobiographical Incident, p. 66 Write an Essay Comparing and Contrasting Two Authors' Experiences, p. 66 Write a Children's Book About the African American Experience, p. 66		Use a Venn Diagram, p. 66 Illustrate a Children's Book, p. 66

Skills Focus

The Journey

One day you finally knew
what you had to do, and began,
though the voices around you
kept shouting
their bad advice—
though the whole house
began to tremble
and you felt the old tug
at your ankles.
"Mend my life!"
each voice cried.
But you didn't stop.
You knew what you had to do,
though the wind pried
with its stiff fingers
at the very foundations—
though their melancholy
was terrible.
It was already late
enough, and a wild night,
and the road full of fallen
branches and stones.
But little by little,
as you left their voices behind,
the stars began to burn
through the sheets of clouds,
and there was a new voice,
which you slowly
recognized as your own,
that kept you company
as you strode deeper and deeper
into the world,
determined to do
the only thing you could do—
determined to save
the only life you could save.

—Mary Oliver (1935–   )

OBJECTIVES

1. Read literature of the Colonial period on the theme, "Visions and Voyages"
2. Interpret literary elements used in the literature, with special emphasis on plain style
3. Apply a variety of reading strategies, with emphasis on using a dictionary
4. Respond to the literature in a variety of modes
5. Learn and use new words

Responding to the Poem

Mary Oliver is a contemporary American poet, whose work has earned both a Pulitzer Prize and an American Book Award. Her restrained lyric poems often focus on the intricacies of nature and the experience of a self-conscious human being, confronted by nature's laws. To help students connect with the poem, have them answer the following questions. **Where is the speaker going?** [Possible responses: into the future; to begin or search for a different life; toward a specific goal.] **What do you think the branches and stones on the road symbolize?** [obstacles or challenges the speaker had to overcome] **Do you agree with the poem's conclusion?** [Possible answers: Yes, people must help themselves, not rely on others; no, refusing to help people in need is selfish.] **How does the poem reflect any attitudes of the Puritans?** [Possible answer: It reflects Puritan views in that it advocates taking personal responsibility for yourself and leaving an old life behind to make your way in a new world.]

Writing Focus: Autobiographical Incident

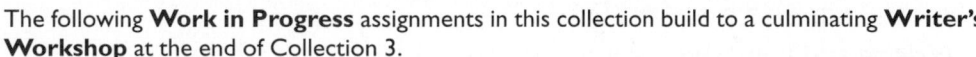

The following **Work in Progress** assignments in this collection build to a culminating **Writer's Workshop** at the end of Collection 3.

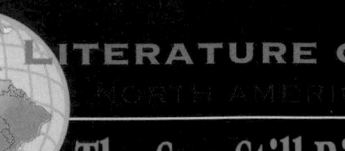
Planning

- **Block Schedule**
  Block Scheduling Lesson Plans with Pacing Guide

- **Traditional Schedule**
  Lesson Plans Including Strategies for English-Language Learners

- **One-Stop Planner**
  CD-ROM with Test Generator

BROWSING IN THE FILES

About the Author. The grandson of an Abenaki Indian, Joseph Bruchac draws on his Native American heritage for much of his writing. He urges readers to remember that "the earth lasts longer than our footprints do. . . . If we treat it well, it will treat us well in return."

 Ⓐ Literary Connections

The Song of Hiawatha

Romantic adventures featuring Indians were popular in the nineteenth century. Longfellow's *The Song of Hiawatha* (1855) was a phenomenal bestseller in spite of the fact that Longfellow had no firsthand knowledge of Native American customs or beliefs.

Ⓑ Historical Connections

Native American Languages

Researchers estimate that when Columbus arrived in the New World, some 2,000 independent tribes speaking more than 500 languages in 50 language groups were spread across the North American continent. Since writing did not exist, it is not surprising that many treasures in the oral tradition went undiscovered for years.

The Sun Still Rises in the Same Sky: Native American Literature

by Joseph Bruchac

Background

Few peoples have been as appreciated and, at the same time, as misrepresented as the many different cultures today called "American Indian" or "Native American." Images of "Indians" are central to mainstream America, from Longfellow's misnamed epic poem
Ⓐ *The Song of Hiawatha* (which actually tells the story of the Chippewa hero Manabozho, not the Iroquois Hiawatha) to the "cowboys and Indians" tradition of movies about the Old West. Yet it's only recently that the authentic literary voices of Native Americans have received serious attention. Native American literature has been a living oral tradition, but it was never treated with the same respect as European, or Western, literature. But Western literature itself has its roots firmly planted in the oral tradition—such ancient classics as the *Odyssey* and *Beowulf,* long before they were written down, were stories kept alive by word of mouth. The vast body of American Indian oral literature, encompassing dozens of epic narratives and countless thousands of stories, poems, songs, oratory, and chants, was not even recognized by Western scholars until the late 1800s. Until then, it was assumed that Native Americans had no literature.

Part of the problem scholars had in recognizing the rich traditions of American Indian literature was translating the texts from hundreds
Ⓑ of different languages—a task often best done by Native Americans themselves. Over the decades, various American Indian writers— N. Scott Momaday, Louise Erdrich, Simon J. Ortiz, and Leslie Marmon Silko, among others—have revitalized Native American literature by combining their fluency in English with a deep understanding of their own languages and traditions.

We can make some important generalizations about American Indian oral traditions. First of all, Native American cultures use stories to teach moral lessons and convey practical information about the natural world. A story from the Abenaki people of Maine, for example, tells how Gluskabe catches all of the game animals. He is then told by

 go.hrw.com
LEO 11-1

  — *Resources: Print and Media* —

Reading
- *Audio CD Library*
  Disc 1, Tracks 2, 3, 4

Writing and Language
- *Daily Oral Grammar*
  Transparency 1

Internet
- go.hrw.com (keyword: LEO 11-1)

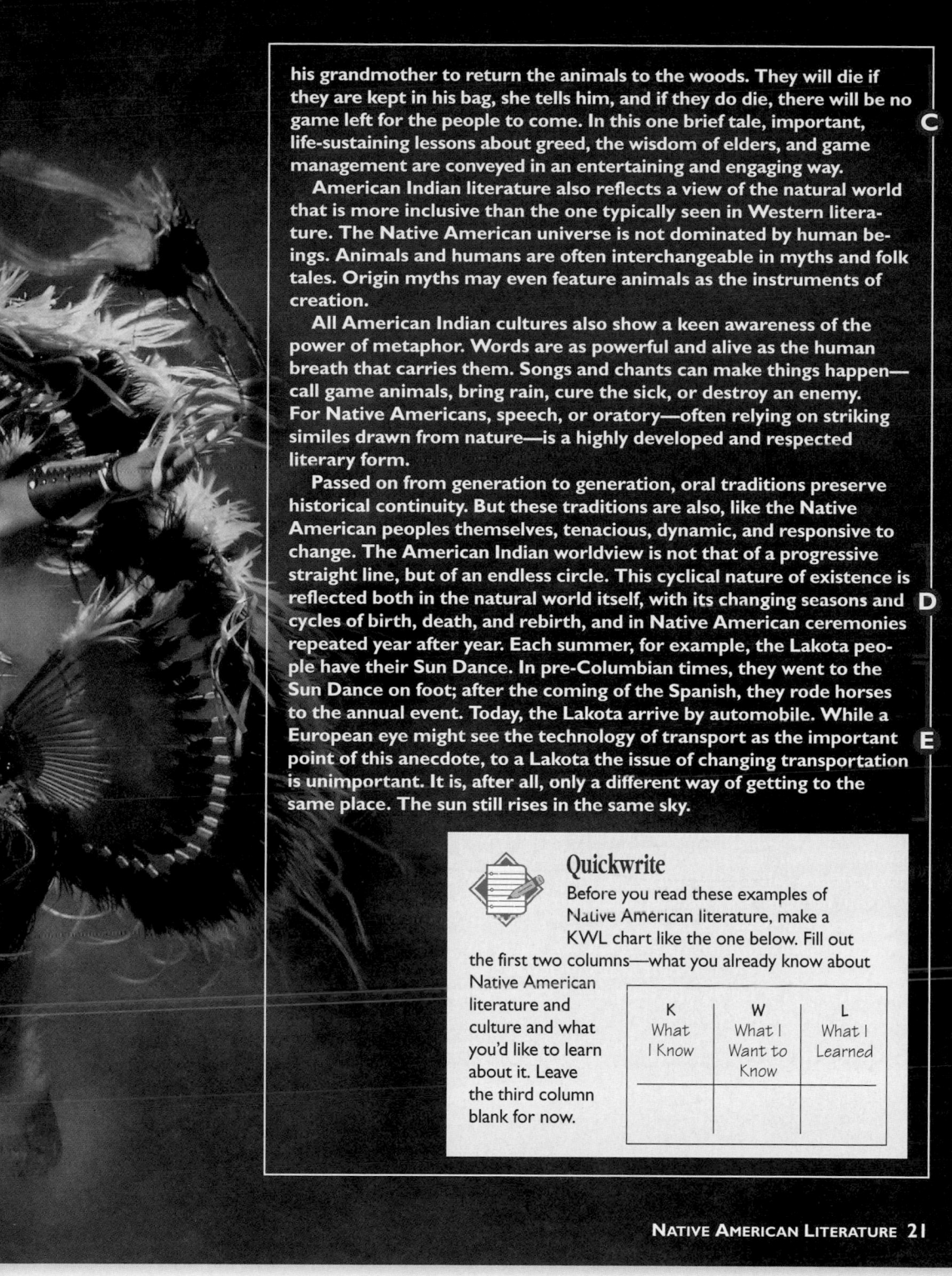

his grandmother to return the animals to the woods. They will die if they are kept in his bag, she tells him, and if they do die, there will be no game left for the people to come. In this one brief tale, important, life-sustaining lessons about greed, the wisdom of elders, and game management are conveyed in an entertaining and engaging way. **C**

American Indian literature also reflects a view of the natural world that is more inclusive than the one typically seen in Western literature. The Native American universe is not dominated by human beings. Animals and humans are often interchangeable in myths and folk tales. Origin myths may even feature animals as the instruments of creation.

All American Indian cultures also show a keen awareness of the power of metaphor. Words are as powerful and alive as the human breath that carries them. Songs and chants can make things happen—call game animals, bring rain, cure the sick, or destroy an enemy. For Native Americans, speech, or oratory—often relying on striking similes drawn from nature—is a highly developed and respected literary form.

Passed on from generation to generation, oral traditions preserve historical continuity. But these traditions are also, like the Native American peoples themselves, tenacious, dynamic, and responsive to change. The American Indian worldview is not that of a progressive straight line, but of an endless circle. This cyclical nature of existence is reflected both in the natural world itself, with its changing seasons and **D** cycles of birth, death, and rebirth, and in Native American ceremonies repeated year after year. Each summer, for example, the Lakota people have their Sun Dance. In pre-Columbian times, they went to the Sun Dance on foot; after the coming of the Spanish, they rode horses to the annual event. Today, the Lakota arrive by automobile. While a European eye might see the technology of transport as the important **E** point of this anecdote, to a Lakota the issue of changing transportation is unimportant. It is, after all, only a different way of getting to the same place. The sun still rises in the same sky.

Quickwrite

Before you read these examples of Native American literature, make a KWL chart like the one below. Fill out the first two columns—what you already know about Native American literature and what you'd like to learn about it. Leave the third column blank for now.

K What I Know	W What I Want to Know	L What I Learned

C Cultural Connections
Gluskabe
Explain that Gluskabe, according to Abenaki legend, was a giant who came from across the sea in a stone canoe. He created people by splitting open an ash tree and allowing the human beings to step out.

D Literary Connections
Time in Native American Storytelling
Native American storytelling is characterized by its sense of a ceaseless or circular movement of time. As an example, point out that the Abenaki creation myth referred to above espouses the idea of preserving a balance in nature so that the earth can renew itself eternally.

E Cultural Connections
The Sun Dance
The Sun Dance is a yearly ceremony of the Plains Indians. For three to four days, dancers gather around a central pole with a buffalo skull on top of it. This pole represents the east/west axis of the world. The ceremony celebrates the concept of sacrifice by having dancers endure a ritual ordeal. In the 1800s, this ordeal required putting skewers tied to the central pole through the chest muscles of the dancers, who then danced until the skewers pulled loose. Today the ceremonial sacrifice is fasting. Despite the change of ordeal, the principles of the sacrificial rite are timeless and are the highest expression of the Plains Indians' religion.

Professional Notes

Critical Comment:
Native American Voices

Scholars attest to the stereotypes and misrepresentations of American Indian cultures in mainstream culture in the United States and suggest remedies for the harm done. According to the critic Margot Atrov, "Until recently . . . the popular concept of Indian literature was shaped not by the Indian and not even by his translator but by the white American writer or moviemaker. . . . There is no better way to correct the misrepresentations that have ingrained themselves in our folklore than to listen to the genuine voices of the Indian peoples. Since their poems are really songs meant to be chanted or sung as part of various rituals, it is indeed the voices of the Indians, ancient and authentic, despite the drawbacks of translation, that we hear when we read them."

Summary ■

In this Huron creation myth, the Sky Tree provides food for the people of Sky Land. To cure the ailing chief of Sky Land, his wife, Aataentsic, cuts down the Sky Tree, which falls through a hole in the sky. Because the tree is the source of life, Aataentsic jumps after it. Looking up at the falling woman, the animals on the water-covered earth hurry to create an island on Turtle's back, where Aataentsic and the tree come to rest. Eventually the Sky Tree takes root in the new earth.

Ⓐ Struggling Readers

Setting a Purpose

Orient students by pointing out that this story offers an explanation of how the world came to be. As in many creation myths, the account begins with a water-filled void. Read the first paragraph aloud, and then encourage students to predict what role the Sky Tree plays in the story. Then, have them read the rest of the story and determine whether their predictions were correct.

Ⓑ Critical Thinking

Making Connections

❓ What creation story from another culture also features a tree with fruit? [Possible answer: the Judeo-Christian story of Adam and Eve, in Genesis 3:1–6.] Why might this motif repeat itself in different cultures? [Sample response: The fruit-bearing tree is a symbol of life and abundance across the planet, since it offers an easy food source.]

Ⓒ Literary Connections

The Earth Diver Myth

In the earth diver myth, common among Northeast Native American cultures, the Earth is covered by water, and some creature—usually an otter, loon, or beaver—dives down to bring up a piece of it. That clump is placed on the back of a great turtle—which is why some Native American tribes refer to North America as Turtle Island.

Ⓓ Elements of Literature

Symbol

❓ What does the rooting of the tree symbolize? [Possible answer: It symbolizes rebirth in that the tree will grow again and life will not end.]

T22

The Sky Tree

Navajo sand painter at Hubbell Trading Post, Ganado, Arizona.

Jerry Jacka Photography.

Ⓐ In the beginning, Earth was covered with water. In Sky Land, there were people living as they do now on Earth. In the middle of that land was the great Sky Tree. All of the food which the people in that Sky Land ate came from the great tree.

The old chief of that land lived with his wife, whose name was Aataentsic,[1] meaning "Ancient Woman," in their long house near the great tree. It came to be that the old chief became sick, and nothing could cure him. He grew weaker and weaker until it seemed he would die. Then a dream came to him, and he called Aataentsic to him.

Ⓑ "I have dreamed," he said, "and in my dream I saw how I can be healed. I must be given the fruit which grows at the very top of Sky Tree. You must cut it down and bring that fruit to me."

Aataentsic took her husband's stone ax and went to the great tree. As soon as she struck it, it split in half and toppled over. As it fell, a hole opened in Sky Land, and the tree fell through the hole. Aataentsic returned to the place where the old chief waited.

"My husband," she said, "when I cut the tree, it split in half and then fell through a great hole. Without the tree, there can be no life. I must follow it."

Then, leaving her husband, she went back to the hole in Sky Land and threw herself after the great tree.

As Aataentsic fell, Turtle looked up and saw her. Immediately Turtle called together all the water animals and told them what she had seen.

"What should be done?" Turtle said.

Beaver answered her. "You are the one who saw this happen. Tell us what to do."

"All of you must dive down," Turtle said. "Bring up soil from the bottom, and place it on my back."

Ⓒ Immediately all of the water animals began to dive down and bring up soil. Beaver, Mink, Muskrat, and Otter each brought up pawfuls of wet soil and placed the soil on Turtle's back until they had made an island of great size. When they were through, Aataentsic settled down Ⓓ gently on the new Earth, and the pieces of the great tree fell beside her and took root.

—*from* the Huron–Eastern Woodland tradition, *as retold by* Joseph Bruchac

1. Aataentsic (ä′tä·ent′sik).

22 BEGINNINGS

Skill Link

Interpreting Stories for an Audience

Ask students to imagine that on a bitter cold night they are in a Huron long house or a Nez Percé tepee surrounded by many family groups. As the storytellers for the evening, they must create a version of "The Sky Tree" or "Coyote Finishes His Work" (see p. 24) that has never been heard before. Encourage them to think about whether they will emphasize moral values, traditional tribal ways, or the entertainment value of the tale.

After students have read both tales, have them form small groups and select one of the stories for an oral interpretation. Discuss vocal techniques, such as raising or lowering pitch and volume and changing tone and accent. Remind them also to use gestures, facial expressions, and movements to achieve desired effects.

The Earth Only

Wica'hcala kin	The old men
heya'pelo'	say
maka' kin	the earth
lece'la	only
tehan yunke'lo	endures
eha' pelo'	You spoke
ehan'kecon	truly
wica' yaka pelo'	You are right.

E

—composed by Used-As-A-Shield
(Teton Sioux), *translated in 1918*

Storyteller figurine by Helen
Cordero. Pottery. Cochiti Pueblo,
New Mexico.
Courtesy of The Heard Museum, Phoenix,
Arizona/Jerry Jacka Photography.

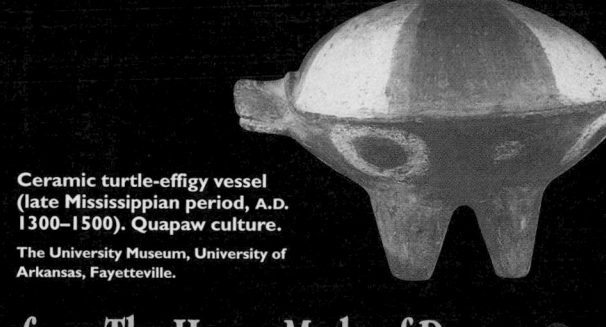

Ceramic turtle-effigy vessel
(late Mississippian period, A.D.
1300–1500). Quapaw culture.
The University Museum, University of
Arkansas, Fayetteville.

from The House Made of Dawn **F**
from The Night Chant **G**

In Tsegihi,
In the house made of dawn,
In the house made of evening twilight,
In the house made of dark cloud,
5 In the house made of male rain,
In the house made of dark mist,
In the house made of female rain,
In the house made of pollen,
In the house made of grasshoppers,
10 Where the dark mist curtains the doorway,
The path to which is on the rainbow,
Where the zigzag lightning stands on top,
Where the he-rain stands high on top,
Oh, male divinity!
15 With your moccasins of dark cloud, come to us. . . .

I have made your sacrifice.
I have prepared a smoke for you.
My feet restore for me.
My limbs restore for me.
20 My body restore for me.
My mind restore for me.
My voice restore for me. . . .

Happily I recover.
Happily my interior grows cool.
25 Happily my limbs regain their power.
Happily my head becomes cool.
Happily I hear again.
Happily I walk.
Impervious to pain, I walk.
30 Feeling light within, I walk.
With lively feelings, I walk. . . .

—*from* the Navajo tradition,
translated by Washington Matthews

NATIVE AMERICAN LITERATURE 23

Summary ▪

"The Earth Only" and "The Night Chant" are traditional poems of praise. "The Earth Only" celebrates the permanence of the natural world. "The Night Chant" is a poem of healing that affirms the divinity of nature.

E **Critical Thinking**
Interpreting
❓ What do the old men mean? [Possible responses: They may be commenting on individual human mortality; they may be warning that all life is transient and that the only stability lies in the natural cycles of the earth.]

F **Literary Connections**
House Made of Dawn
The protagonist of N. Scott Momaday's 1968 novel *House Made of Dawn* is "healed" through reconciliation with his Native American heritage. (For more on Momaday, see p. 1092.)

G **Cultural Connections**
The Night Chant
The Night Chant is part of a Diné (Navajo) ceremony performed to lend support to a sick person. Among the Diné, good health is regarded as the natural state and ill health as an imbalance. The Night Chant ceremony is performed to restore the balance to the sick person. The Diné word *hozhoni*, translated here as "happily," also includes the concepts of beauty, peace, and harmony.

RESPONDING TO THE ART
Activity. Have students analyze the color, texture, composition, and design of the two sculptures and then write a brief interpretation in which they explore what these artifacts reveal about the cultures they come from. [Both objects are painted in striking, earthlike hues and rely on the natural tones and textures of the clay itself. They suggest a culture that emphasizes community and the natural world. The Pueblo children are crawling all over the unseeing storyteller, soaking up his tales and songs. This turtle vessel shows the importance of the turtle, associated in numerous Native American cultures with long life.]

Professional Notes

Critical Comment:
Native American Songs

The poet Orpingalik defines *songs* as follows: "Songs are thoughts, sung out with the breath when people are moved by great forces and ordinary speech no longer suffices. Man is moved just like the ice floe sailing here and there out in the current. His thoughts are driven by a flowing force when he feels joy, when he feels sorrow. Thoughts can wash over him like a flood, making blood come in gasps and his heart throb. Something like an abatement in the weather will keep him thawed up, and then it will happen that we, who always think we are small, will feel still smaller. And we will fear to use words. But it will happen that the words we need will come of themselves. When the words we want to use shoot up by themselves—we get a new song."

Summary ■

"Coyote Finishes His Work" is a Nez Percé myth that tells of how the trickster Coyote creates the Indians and teaches them how to live but also plays tricks on them. When the Great Spirit decides Coyote's work on earth is completed, he sends him to a resting place but tells the people that one day he and Coyote will return to make the world right.

Ⓐ Elements of Literature
Character

❓ How would you characterize Coyote? [He has many human qualities. He is creative, nurturing, generous, imaginative, wise, fallible, self-centered, mischievous.]

Ⓑ Literary Connections
The Trickster

The trickster, a favorite character of Native American tales, often takes the form of an animal. Tricksters live by their wits. Because they symbolize the dual nature of human beings, trickster tales usually present their protagonists as complex characters, mixing humor and seriousness, earthiness and spirituality.

Ⓒ Critical Thinking
Making Inferences

❓ In this passage, Coyote, the great imitator, is trying to pretend that he is as powerful as the Great Spirit. Ask students how Coyote's test works out. What lessons can be drawn from this incident? [Possible response: Coyote's attempt fails. To prove that he is more powerful, the Great Spirit tests Coyote by asking him to move a lake back and forth. Coyote is able to complete only half the job, so the Great Spirit finishes it. Students might say that this shows that the Great Spirit sees through our pretenses and schemes.]

Coyote Finishes His Work

From the very beginning, Coyote was traveling around all over the earth. He did many wonderful things when he went along. He killed the monsters and the evil spirits that preyed on the people. He made the Indians, and put them out in tribes all over the world because Old Man Above wanted the earth to be inhabited all over, not just in one or two places.

He gave all the people different names and taught them different languages. This is why Indians live all over the country now and speak in different ways.

He taught the people how to eat and how to hunt the buffalo and catch eagles. He taught them what roots to eat and how to make a good lodge and what to wear. He taught them how to dance. Sometimes he made mistakes, and even though he was wise and powerful, he did many foolish things. But that was his way.

Coyote liked to play tricks. He thought about himself all the time, and told everyone he was a great warrior, but he was not. Sometimes he would go too far with some trick and get someone killed. Other times, he would have a trick played on himself by someone else. He got killed this way so many times that Fox and the birds got tired of bringing him back to life. Another way he got in trouble was trying to do what someone else did. This is how he came to be called Imitator.

Coyote was ugly too. The girls did not like him. But he was smart. He could change himself around and trick the women. Coyote got the girls when he wanted.

One time, Coyote had done everything he could think of and was traveling from one place to another place, looking for other things that needed to be done. Old Man saw him going along and said to himself, "Coyote has now done almost everything he is capable of doing. His work is almost done. It is time to bring him back to the place where he started."

So Great Spirit came down and traveled in the shape of an old man. He met Coyote.

Coyote said, "I am Coyote. Who are you?"

Old Man said, "I am Chief of the earth. It was I who sent you to set the world right."

"No," Coyote said, "you never sent me. I don't know you. If you are the Chief, take that lake over there and move it to the side of that mountain."

"No. If you are Coyote, let me see you do it."

Coyote did it.

"Now, move it back."

Coyote tried, but he could not do it. He thought this was strange. He tried again, but he could not do it.

Chief moved the lake back.

Coyote said, "Now I know you are the Chief."

Old Man said, "Your work is finished, Coyote. You have traveled far and done much good. Now you will go to where I have prepared a home for you."

Then Coyote disappeared. Now no one knows where he is anymore.

Old Man got ready to leave, too. He said to the Indians, "I will send messages to the earth by the spirits of the people who reach me but whose time to die has not yet come. They will carry messages to you from time to time. When their spirits come back into their bodies, they will revive and tell you their experiences.

"Coyote and myself, we will not be seen again until Earthwoman is very old. Then we shall return to earth, for it will require a change by that time. Coyote will come along first, and when you see him you will know I am coming. When I come along, all the spirits of the dead will be with me. There will be no more Other Side Camp. All the people will live together. Earthmother will go back to her first shape and live as a mother among her children. Then things will be made right."

Now they are waiting for Coyote.

—from the Nez Percé tradition, retold by Barry Lopez

Making the Connections

Cultural Connections: Coyote's Careers

Coyote is by far the most popular trickster character in the stories of Native Americans in North America. According to the author Bernard Haile, these tales show Coyote in roles as diverse as a corpse, fool, gambler, evil trickster, wise trickster, hero, savior, and god. Have students discuss the roles Coyote fulfills in this tale. [Possible responses: fool, evil trickster, hero, and savior.]

Troupe of Tricksters

Have students find tales about other trickster characters such as the Native American Raven, the African trickster Anansi the Spider, and the African American trickster Br'er Rabbit. Have students compare the characters of these tricksters and their abilities to affect the world around them. Some students might enjoy role-playing these figures in a trickster talk-show.

Sand painting, which represents storm, lightning, and the four seasons, by Michael Tsosie.

Courtesy of Fifth Generation Trading Company/Jerry Jacka Photography.

Coyote Crooner by Rosemary "Apple Blossom" Lonewolf. Pottery (3½″ × 4½″). Santa Clara Pueblo, New Mexico.

Courtesy Gallery 10, Scottsdale/Jerry Jacka Photography.

Coyote-Effigy Platform Pipe (Middle Woodland period, 200 B.C.–A.D. 100). Pipestone; Temper mound (6.4″ × 7″). Scioto County, Ohio. Ohio Hopewell culture.

Photograph © The Detroit Institute of Arts, 1995. Collection of Ohio Historical Society, Columbus. Photo courtesy © The Detroit Institute of Arts, Dirk Bakker, photographer (WL-117).

FINDING COMMON GROUND

Now that you've read these examples of Native American literature, meet in small groups to share your questions, comments, and discoveries.

- **Each person in the group should review the KWL chart in his or her Quickwrite and fill in the third column, "What I Learned."**

- **As a group, discuss what members learned from reading these selections. Then go back to the "What I Want to Know" column, and decide if there are any other topics you'd like to discuss and learn more about. Be sure someone in the group records the suggested topics and any group responses.**

- **Choose some aspect of Native American culture you'd like to learn more about: storytelling, ceremonies, healing, symbols, dances, myths, historical figures, language, art, environmental issues, or whatever else you like. Choose something that grabs your interest, and, by yourself or with a partner, develop your own avenue of exploration. Share your newfound knowledge with the rest of the class.**

NATIVE AMERICAN LITERATURE **25**

FINDING COMMON GROUND

This feature requires students to discover areas of agreement on a topic related to the theme.

- Tell students to consider not just the literary selections but also the art and artifacts pictured on pp. 22–25. What do the artifacts tell about the people who made them? Are any of these objects similar to items students see or use every day? What materials were used to make these objects and artwork? Encourage interested students to consider Native American arts as a research topic.

- Invite students to research the Native American cultures of their area. They could begin by contacting local cultural organizations and museums or the archives department of the local government or library.

- Students who are interested in learning more about Native American stories could choose to research a type of tale, such as creation myths, trickster tales, hero stories, or tales about animal husbands and wives. They could consult the work of Stith Thompson or Joseph Campbell to gain a basic understanding of the genres they are investigating.

Encourage all students to pursue their chosen topics via keyword searches on the Internet. To complement the oral tradition represented in the text, you might want to ask students to present their findings orally. For example, students doing a report on storytelling could tell some of their own original stories. For a report on ceremonies, they could locate pictures or video clips to show the class.

Crossing the Curriculum

Geography

Have interested students find out which tribes lived in which areas of North America before European settlers forced their migration. Students can trace the migration routes and compare and contrast the climates where the tribes had to move with those where they had lived before the European settlement. Students should then consider what the tribes had to do to adapt to the different climates.

History

As students read the next two selections, have them think about relations between Native Americans and European immigrants. What did the two peoples have in common? How were they different? What were the sources of disagreement? If students could write an "alternate history" (a popular category of science fiction and historical fiction), what would they change about the encounter between Native Americans and European immigrants?

Health

Sand paintings are part of Navajo healing ceremonies, which also include songs and blessings. Students may be surprised to learn that many American Indians do not see disease as an individual problem but as a social problem manifested in the individual. Have small groups choose a Native American culture and research its concepts of health and illness and its healing practices, and then put together an oral presentation for the class.

William Bradford

(1590–1657)

William Bradford's life displayed a mixture of the commonplace and the extraordinary that was characteristic of the Puritan experience. Bradford was the son of a prosperous farmer in Yorkshire, England. He received no higher education but instead was taught the practical arts of farming. Despite his lack of formal training (or perhaps because of it), Bradford was to become a successful, longstanding Colonial governor in America, dealing out justice and settling disputes.

Growing up in England, Bradford took a radical step when he was twelve years old. Inspired by his reading of the Bible and by the sermons of a Puritan minister, Bradford began attending the meetings of a small group of Nonconformists, despite the vehement objections of his family and friends. It was illegal for Nonconformists to worship publicly, so the group met furtively in a private house in the nearby town of Scrooby. In 1606, when the group organized as a separate Congregational church, Bradford joined them. In 1608, under increasing pressure of persecution and fearful that they would be imprisoned, the Scrooby group crossed the North Sea to Holland. In 1620, after twelve years in Holland, the group was aided by London profiteers and merchants, who lent them a ship and crew as an investment. In September the Nonconformists sailed for America in order to found a community where they would be free to worship and live according to their beliefs.

For Bradford the hardships of the long ocean voyage did not end with the landing at Plymouth. In December, while the *Mayflower* was anchored in Provincetown Harbor, Bradford and other men took a small boat ashore to scout for a place to land and build shelter. When they returned, Bradford learned that his young wife had fallen or jumped from the ship. Perhaps Dorothy Bradford was in despair when land was finally sighted and she did not see the hoped-for green hills of an earthly paradise. Beyond the ship lay only the bleak sand dunes of Cape Cod. That bitter winter, half the settlers were to die of cold, disease, and malnutrition.

The following year, Bradford was elected governor of the plantation. "If he had not been a person of more than ordinary piety, wisdom, and courage," the Puritan preacher Cotton Mather later recorded, Bradford would "have sunk" under the difficulties of governing such a shaky settlement. Bradford proved to be an exemplary leader, and he went on to be elected governor of the Colony no fewer than thirty times.

As the Plymouth Colony prospered and grew, it also gradually disintegrated as a religious community, despite Bradford's efforts to hold it together. The ideal of the "city on the hill," the Pilgrims' dream of an ideal society founded on religious principles, gradually gave way to the realities of life in the new land. Bradford's record of this grand experiment ends in disappointment. When more fertile areas for settlement were found and when Boston became a more convenient port to England, Plymouth lost much of its population. "Thus was this poor church left," Bradford wrote in 1644, "like an ancient mother grown old and forsaken of her children. . . . Thus, she that had made many rich became herself poor."

Page from *Of Plimoth Plantation* by William Bradford.

Courtesy of the State Library of Massachusetts.

go.hrw.com
LEO 11-1

 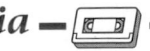

Before You Read

FROM OF PLYMOUTH PLANTATION

Make the Connection

Journey to Salvation

Every age has at least one figure or heroic type that seems to embody its ideals and aspirations. The Puritans who came to America identified so powerfully with one figure that they called themselves by that name: "Pilgrim." A pilgrim is someone who makes a pilgrimage, or a journey to a holy place. But for the Puritans, the word *pilgrimage* took on a wider meaning—it was a journey to salvation.

For the Pilgrims, the outward journey of their lives and the specific voyage to America were also inner, spiritual journeys. "A Christian is sailing through this world unto his heavenly country," the poet Anne Bradstreet (page 68) wrote some years after sailing across the Atlantic to America. "We must, therefore, be here as strangers and pilgrims, that we may plainly declare that we seek a city above."

Elements of Literature

The Plain Style

In their style of writing, as well as in their manner of worship, the Puritans favored the plain and unornamented. Though the style used by Puritan writers now seems hard to read, in the 1600s it was considered simple and direct. This **plain style** emphasized uncomplicated sentences and the use of everyday words from common speech, and it steered clear of elaborate figures of speech and imagery.

Reading Skills and Strategies

Using Study Strategies

When you encounter texts as challenging as Bradford's, two study strategies will help you: **note taking** and compiling a **time line of main events.**

As you read, jot down questions you have about the text, along with any of your personal responses to Bradford's ideas. For this text, be sure especially to note places where Bradford tries to link the Pilgrims' experience with God's plan for their salvation.

When you have finished reading, go back over the text and make a time line of the main events. You can include both main and subsidiary events by using a series-of-events chain like the one below. Put main events in the large boxes and subsidiary events in the smaller ones.

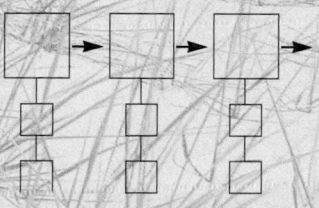

The **plain style** is a way of writing that stresses simplicity and clarity of expression.

For more on the Plain Style, see page 35 and the Handbook of Literary Terms.

Background

In 1630, Bradford began to write this account of the Plymouth settlement, and he continued to write an annual account until 1647. Unlike many other early Colonial histories, it was not composed for immediate publication or to attract more colonists, but was intended to inspire future generations to carry on the Pilgrims' ideals. The first nine chapters of Bradford's history were copied into the Plymouth church records, but the entire manuscript was lost when British troops plundered the church during the Revolutionary War. Almost a century later, Governor Bradford's vellum-bound volume was discovered in the library of the bishop of London. *Of Plymouth Plantation* was first published in 1856 by the Massachusetts Historical Society. The manuscript was finally returned to the United States in 1897, and it can be seen today in Boston.

Summary ■■■

Chapter 9 of William Bradford's historical narrative of the Pilgrims opens in 1620 during the voyage of the *Mayflower*. One of the *Mayflower's* crew jeers at the Pilgrims, certain they will not survive the voyage. When this sailor dies, Bradford insists God has punished him. After some fierce storms, the ship's main beam cracks, but the sailors and passengers repair it. Finally, in early November, the *Mayflower* lands at Cape Cod. Chapter 11 describes the Pilgrims' first winter in North America, during which half of the colonists succumb to disease and starvation. In early spring, local Wampanoag Indians befriend the English settlers, and both groups agree to a peace treaty. Squanto, a Pawtuxet tribesman living with the Wampanoag, teaches the settlers how to grow corn and where to fish. In the fall of 1621, the Pilgrims and the Wampanoag gather together to celebrate a rich harvest. Throughout this account, Bradford's plain style and religious purpose impart the Puritan vision that guided this early American journey.

Background

Before it was lost, the manuscript for *Of Plymouth Plantation* was borrowed from a series of Bradford heirs by well-known figures such as Increase Mather, his son Cotton Mather, and the Reverend Thomas Prence. When Bradford's manuscript was first printed, his archaic spelling and punctuation were reproduced exactly as written. In 1952, the first modern edition (used in this textbook) was published. It was edited by Early American history scholar Samuel Eliot Morison, who explains his editorial approach as follows: "[T]o spell out all . . . abbreviations . . ., to adopt modern . . . capitalization, punctuation, and spelling, but *scrupulously to respect Bradford's language.* . . . I have omitted nothing. Every word that Bradford wrote . . . is here." The head at the beginning of each section is Morison's creation, designed to break up Bradford's long chapters.

Preteaching Vocabulary

Words to Own

Give students one night to study the Words to Own. Then, hold a spelling/vocabulary bee—a popular pastime in colonial America. Form two teams and give a word to the first student on one team to spell and define correctly. If the student misses, he or she sits down and the first student on the other team tries the same word. After the game, use the following exercise to review. Beside each word on the left, write the letter of its synonym from the right column.

1. sundry [c]	**a.** included
2. profane [h]	**b.** soften
3. discourse [i]	**c.** various
4. reproved [j]	**d.** curses
5. relent [b]	**e.** proud
6. confederates [g]	**f.** meeting
7. haughty [e]	**g.** allies
8. execrations [d]	**h.** irreligious
9. consultation [f]	**i.** discussion
10. comprised [a]	**j.** scolded

Resources

Viewing and Representing

Videocassette A, Segment 3
This segment, "The Puritan Experience," provides historical background on the first Anglo-Americans. Available in English and Spanish. For full lesson plans and worksheets, see the *Visual Connections Teacher's Manual.*

Fine Art Transparency
A fine art transparency of Joan Landis's *The First Thanksgiving* will prove a helpful source on the culture of both the Wampanoag and the Pilgrims.

- Transparency 1
- Worksheet, p. 4

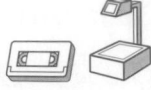

Responding to the Art

Michel Felice Corné (1752–1845) was an American painter famous for his dramatic maritime scenes. Here he depicts Pilgrim leaders in a small skiff landing at Plymouth Rock in December 1620.

Activities

1. Point out the elaborate headdresses and the bare arms and legs of the Wampanoag. Also point out the roof line of the dwellings in the background of the painting. Then, ask students to research the clothing, artifacts, and wigwams of the Wampanoag to check Corné's historical accuracy.
2. After students have read the selection, ask how Corné's depiction of the Plymouth landing differs from Bradford's depiction of the Provincetown one. [Possible answers: Bradford describes the landing as a moment of profound religious gratitude and tends to see the Native American population as potential antagonists; Corné depicts the landing in a more neutral fashion and presents the encounter with Native Americans as one of mutual curiosity.]

from Of Plymouth Plantation

William Bradford

They fell upon their knees and blessed the God of Heaven who had brought them over the vast and furious ocean . . .

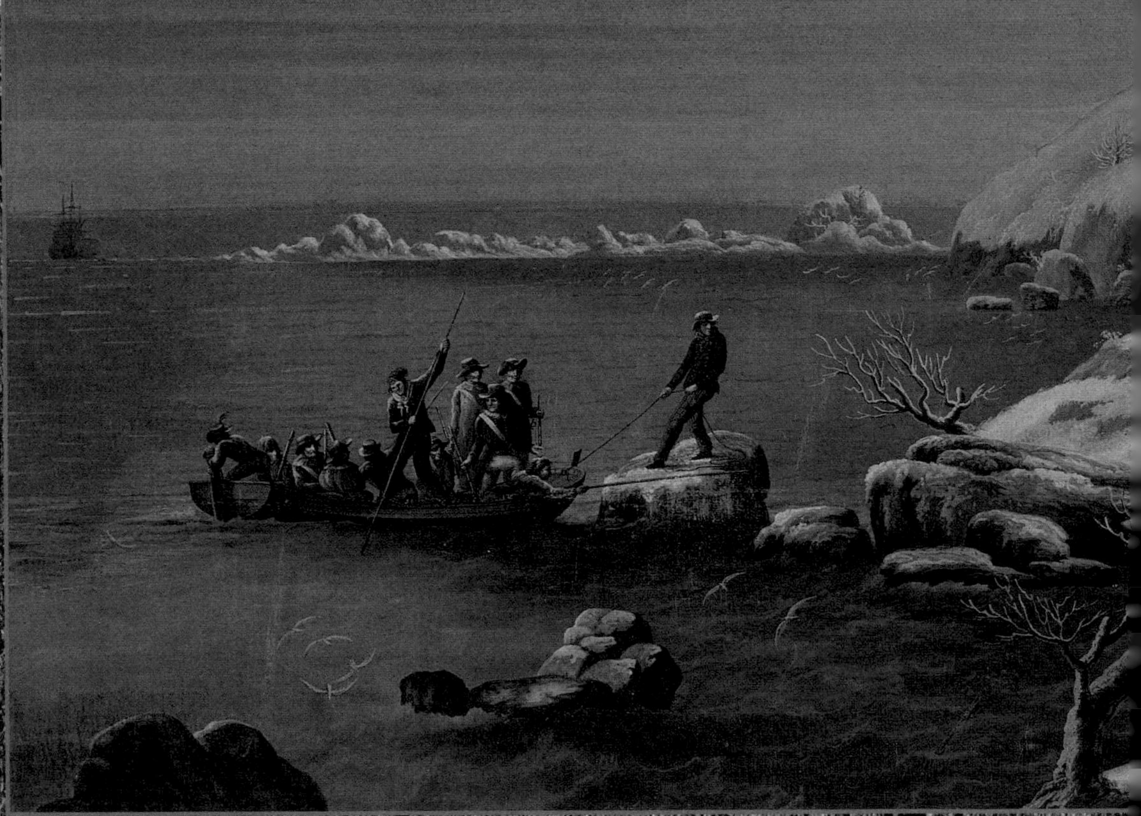

Reaching All Students

Struggling Readers

Encourage students to be patient with this selection: slow and careful reading is the best approach. Tell students that when they get lost in one of Bradford's long, complex sentences, they should eliminate the subordinate clause(s) and look for the main subject and verb. Once they have identified the main clause, they can then "tack on" the information in the subordinate clause(s).

English Language Learners

Students may have trouble with pronouns in this selection. Although Bradford was himself a Pilgrim, he writes about the Pilgrims in the third person, using *they, their,* and *them.* To help students with this unusual use of pronouns, review the cases of third-person pronouns. Then, have students read in pairs, using common sense and agreement clues to figure out the antecedents of the various pronouns.

from Chapter 9

Of their Voyage, and how they Passed the Sea; and of their Safe Arrival at Cape Cod

September 6 [1620]. These troubles[1] being blown over, and now all being compact together in one ship, they put to sea again with a prosperous wind, which continued divers[2] days together, which was some encouragement unto them; yet, according to the usual manner, many were afflicted with seasickness. And I may not omit here a special work of God's providence. There was a proud and very <u>profane</u> young man, one of the seamen, of a lusty,[3] able body, which made him the more <u>haughty</u>; he would always be condemning the poor people in their sickness and cursing them daily with grievous <u>execrations</u>; and did not let to tell them that he hoped to help to cast half of them overboard before they came to their journey's end, and to make merry with what they had; and if he were by any gently <u>reproved</u>, he would curse and swear most bitterly. But it pleased God before they came half seas over, to smite this young man with a grievous disease, of which he died in a desperate manner, and so was himself the first that was thrown overboard. Thus his curses light on his own head, and it was an astonishment to all his fellows for they noted it to be the just hand of God upon him.

1. **troubles:** the return of the *Speedwell* to England and the transfer of her passengers to the *Mayflower*
2. **divers** (dī′vərz): many.
3. **lusty:** energetic; robust.

WORDS TO OWN

profane (prō·fān′) *adj.:* irreverent.
haughty (hôt′ē) *adj.:* proud; disdainful of something or someone.
execrations (ek′si·krā′shənz) *n.:* angry words; curses.
reproved (ri·prōōvd′) *v.:* reprimanded.

Ear of corn (1535), pages 29, 31, 32, 33.
The Granger Collection, New York.

WILLIAM BRADFORD **29**

Landing of the Pilgrims at Plymouth (1803) by Michel Felice Corné. Oil on canvas.

A **Elements of Literature**
The Plain Style
Read the opening sentence aloud and ask the class what they notice about the writer's style. [Possible response: He uses simple diction and literal language to provide factual information. However, the sentence is long and complex by today's standards.]

B **Advanced Learners**
Determining Author's Purpose
? Why do you think Bradford chose to refer to the passengers as "they" instead of "we"? [Possible answers: because he wants to make his history sound more objective; because he wants to report the facts rather than reflect on how he felt about those facts; because he wants to praise the Pilgrims and doesn't want to appear boastful.]

C **Reading Skills and Strategies**
Compiling a Time Line
? When does the sailor die? ["before they came half seas over" or less than halfway across the ocean] How could you determine the approximate date of his death? [by noting the starting date above (Sept. 6, 1620) and watching for the landing date]

D **Critical Thinking**
Analyzing Anecdotes
? The Puritans believed that the will of God directs and guides the universe. This belief is demonstrated in the moral anecdotes Bradford includes in his history. What spiritual lesson does the anecdote of the haughty seaman teach? [Possible answers: Those who break God's laws will be punished; pride goes before a fall.]

Getting Students Involved

Cooperative Learning
Pack Your Bags. Ask students to imagine that they are on the *Mayflower,* setting out in 1620 on a journey of more than two months to a country they know little about. Then, ask the following questions: What will you need for the journey? What will you need once you get to the New World? What dangers should you provide for, both on the journey and once you arrive? Have small groups of students draw up a list of supplies, tools, medicines, and other items they would pack.

Now ask students to imagine they have been at sea a month. Squalls and violent storms have stalked the creaking ship across the ocean. There are no toilets and little fresh water, so no one can wash. Maggots, grubs, and vermin wriggle in the pork and the stale biscuits that they eat every day, and people are constantly seasick. Ask students how they would revise their list.

Professional Notes

Separatists
The Pilgrims were part of a radical group called Separatists who believed that churches should be independent of any government. According to historian Perry Miller, this was "an act equivalent in the legal system to high treason. The great body of Puritans were horrified by the Separatists. Separatists endangered the Puritan cause by seeming to prove that Puritanism was really what the government said it was—subversive, anarchical, disloyal."

A **Reading Skills and Strategies**

Using a Dictionary

Have students use a dictionary to find the derivation of the word *shroudly*.

B **English Language Learners**

Identifying Pronoun Antecedents

? To whom or what does the pronoun *her* refer? [the ship] Explain that in English a ship is usually referred to as "she" or "her" rather than "it."

C **Struggling Readers**

Finding the Main Idea

? The passengers and crew fear that the main beam will buckle, causing the ship to take on water and sink. How do they solve this problem? [They install a great screw, prop up the beam with a post, and caulk the upper decks.]

D **Critical Thinking**

Analyzing

? The Pilgrims' response to the problem with the main beam shows that they are practical as well as pious. Why would practicality be vital to their success? [In America, they would need to be self-sufficient, providing for their own shelter, food, clothes, and medicine.]

E **Historical Connections**

The Mayflower Compact

The Pilgrims and other passengers expected to settle within the grant area of the London company in Virginia, but the rough weather forced them to land on Cape Cod. Because they were uncertain of their legal status outside of Virginia, the passengers drew up the Mayflower Compact, which established majority rule by male church members.

F **Reading Skills and Strategies**

Compiling a Time Line

? The text does not include the date of landing. How can you determine that date? [By using footnotes 11 and 13.] Now estimate on your time line when the profane seaman died. [sometime before October 8]

After they had enjoyed fair winds and weather for a season, they were encountered many times with crosswinds and met with many fierce storms with which the ship was shroudly[4] shaken, and her upper works made very leaky; and one of the main beams in the midships was bowed and cracked, which put them in some fear that the ship could not be able to perform the voyage. So some of the chief of the company, perceiving the mariners to fear the sufficiency of the ship as appeared by their mutterings, they entered into serious <u>consultation</u> with the master and other officers of the ship, to consider in time of the danger, and rather to return than to cast themselves into a desperate and inevitable peril. And truly there was great distraction and difference of opinion amongst the mariners themselves; fain[5] would they do what could be done for their wages' sake (being now near half the seas over) and on the other hand they were loath[6] to hazard their lives too desperately. But in examining of all opinions, the master and others affirmed they knew the ship to be strong and firm underwater; and for the buckling of the main beam, there was a great iron screw the passengers brought out of Holland, which would raise the beam into his place; the which being done, the carpenter and master affirmed that with a post put under it, set firm in the lower deck and otherways bound, he would make it sufficient. And as for the decks and upper works, they would caulk them as well as they could, and though with the working of the ship they would not long keep staunch,[7] yet there would otherwise be no great danger, if they did not overpress her with sails. So they committed themselves to the will of God and resolved to proceed.

In <u>sundry</u> of these storms the winds were so fierce and the seas so high, as they could not bear a knot of sail, but were forced to hull[8] for divers days together. And in one of them, as they thus lay at hull in a mighty storm, a lusty young man called John Howland, coming upon some occasion above the gratings was, with a seele[9] of the ship, thrown into sea; but it pleased God that he caught

hold of the topsail halyards[10] which hung overboard and ran out at length. Yet he held his hold (though he was sundry fathoms underwater) till he was hauled up by the same rope to the brim of the water, and then with a boathook and other means got into the ship again and his life saved. And though he was something ill with it, yet he lived many years after and became a profitable member both in church and commonwealth. In all this voyage there died but one of the passengers, which was William Butten, a youth, servant to Samuel Fuller, when they drew near the coast.

But to omit other things (that I may be brief) after long beating at sea they fell with that land which is called Cape Cod;[11] the which being made and certainly known to be it, they were not a little joyful. After some deliberation had amongst themselves and with the master of the ship, they tacked about and resolved to stand for the southward (the wind and weather being fair) to find some place about Hudson's River[12] for their habitation. But after they had sailed that course about half the day, they fell amongst dangerous shoals and roaring breakers, and they were so far entangled therewith as they conceived themselves in great danger; and the wind shrinking upon them withal, they resolved to bear up again for the Cape and thought themselves happy to get out of those dangers before night overtook them, as by God's good providence they did. And the next day they got into the Cape Harbor[13] where they rid in safety. . . .

Being thus arrived in a good harbor, and brought safe to land, they fell upon their knees and blessed the God of Heaven who had brought them over the vast and furious ocean, and

10. **halyards** (hal′yərdz): ropes for raising a sail.
11. **Cape Cod:** They sighted Cape Cod at daybreak on November 9, 1620.
12. **Hudson's River:** They were trying for Manhattan Island. Henry Hudson had made his voyage in 1609 and had claimed the area for the Dutch, but the English did not recognize the Dutch claim.
13. **Cape Harbor:** now called Provincetown Harbor. The sea voyage from England had taken sixty-five days.

4. **shroudly** (shrōōd′lē): shrewdly, used here in its archaic sense of "wickedly."
5. **fain** (fān): archaic for "gladly."
6. **loath** (lōth): reluctant.
7. **staunch** (stônch): watertight.
8. **hull:** to float without using the sails.
9. **seele:** sudden lurch to one side.

WORDS TO OWN

consultation (kän·səl·tā′shən) *n.:* meeting to discuss or plan.
sundry (sun′drē) *adj.:* some.

Professional Notes

Critical Comment: Plymouth

Perceptive readers will notice that Cape Cod was named before the Pilgrims landed. European explorers, fishermen, and traders had been visiting the area since the 1500s. In 1614, Captain John Smith (see p. T36) had mapped the coast from Maine to Cape Cod. He renamed the Cape Cod village of Pawtuxet "Plymouth." In 1616, an epidemic—possibly smallpox—decimated the coastal population, and Plymouth was deserted.

When the Pilgrims landed in Plymouth in 1620, according to historian William Brandon, they found a "ghost town, the population dead in the houses, or fled from the plague....The colonists made the village and the fields their own, fields so handsomely cleared, said a delighted colonist later, there was 'scarce a bush or bramble, or any cumbersome underwood to be seen in the more champion ground...'"

delivered them from all the perils and miseries thereof, again to set their feet on the firm and stable earth, their proper element. . . .

But here I cannot but stay and make a pause, and stand half amazed at this poor people's present condition; and so I think will the reader, too, when he well considers the same. Being thus passed the vast ocean, and a sea of troubles before in their preparation (as may be remembered by that which went before), they had now no friends to welcome them nor inns to entertain or refresh their weather-beaten bodies; no houses or much less towns to repair to, to seek for succor.[14] It is recorded in Scripture[15] as a mercy to the Apostle and his shipwrecked company, that the barbarians showed them no small kindness in refreshing them, but these savage barbarians, when they met with them (as after will appear) were readier to fill their sides full of arrows than otherwise. And for the season it was winter, and they that know the winters of that country know them to be sharp and violent, and subject to cruel and fierce storms, dangerous to travel to known places, much more to search an unknown coast. Besides, what could they see but a hideous and desolate wilderness, full of wild beasts and wild men—and what multitudes there might be of them they knew not. Neither could they, as it were, go up to the top of Pisgah[16] to view from this wilderness a more goodly country to feed their hopes; for which way soever they turned their eyes (save upward to the heavens) they could have little solace or content in respect of any outward objects. For summer being done, all things stand upon them with a weather-beaten face, and the whole country, full of woods and thickets, represented a wild and savage hue. If they looked behind them, there was the mighty ocean which they had passed and was now as a main bar and gulf to separate them from all the civil parts of the world. . . .

What could now sustain them but the Spirit of God and His grace? May not and ought not the children of these fathers rightly say: "Our fathers

14. **succor** (suk′ər): aid.
15. **Scripture:** In the Acts of the Apostles (Chapter 28), Paul tells how the shipwrecked Christians were helped by the "barbarous people" of Malta.
16. **Pisgah** (piz′gə): mountain from which Moses first viewed the Promised Land.

were Englishmen which came over this great ocean, and were ready to perish in this wilderness; but they cried unto the Lord, and He heard their voice and looked on their adversity,"[17] etc.? "Let them therefore praise the Lord, because He is good: And His mercies endure forever." "Yea, let them which have been redeemed of the Lord, show how He hath delivered them from the hand of the oppressor. When they wandered in the desert wilderness out of the way, and found no city to dwell in, both hungry and thirsty, their soul was overwhelmed in them. Let them confess before the Lord His lovingkindness and His wonderful works before the sons of men."[18]

from Chapter 11

The Starving Time

[1620–1621] But that which was most sad and lamentable was, that in two or three months' time half of their company died, especially in January and February, being the depth of winter, and wanting houses and other comforts; being infected with the scurvy and other diseases which this long voyage and their inaccommodate condition had brought upon them. So as there died sometimes two or three of a day in the foresaid time, that of 100 and odd persons, scarce fifty remained. And of these, in the time of most distress, there was but six or seven sound persons who to their great commendations, be it spoken, spared no pains night nor day, but with abundance of toil and hazard of their own health, fetched them wood, made them fires, dressed them meat, made their beds, washed their loathsome clothes, clothed and unclothed them. In a word, did all the homely and necessary offices for them which dainty and queasy stomachs cannot endure to hear named; and all this willingly and cheerfully, without any grudging in the least, showing herein their true love unto their friends and brethren; a rare example and worthy to be remembered. Two of these seven were Mr. William Brewster, their

17. **they cried . . . their adversity:** paraphrase of Deuteronomy 26:7.
18. **Let them . . . the sons of men:** paraphrase of Psalm 107.

ⓖ Critical Thinking
Making Inferences
❓ Who are "these savage barbarians" that Bradford refers to in this passage? [American Indians] How does he contrast their behavior with the barbarians the Apostle Paul met? [The American Indians shoot arrows at the Pilgrims rather than help them.]

ⓗ Elements of Literature
Setting
❓ Setting is the time and place of an event. How does Bradford dramatically evoke the setting of the wintry Cape Cod seacoast? [Possible answer: He calls it a "hideous and desolate wilderness full of wild beasts and wild men."]

ⓘ Reading Skills and Strategies
Taking Notes
Encourage students to look up (in an encyclopedia or dictionary) the Biblical allusions cited in the footnotes. Ask them to take notes on how Bradford identifies the Pilgrims with the Hebrews who, after being led out of Egypt by Moses, dwelt in the wilderness before reaching the Promised Land. What purpose does Bradford have in making this comparison? [He wants to make the point that God acts to save the Pilgrims in the same way He acted to save the Hebrews, because both peoples are "chosen by Him."]

ⓙ Elements of Literature
The Plain Style
❓ This passage is an excellent example of the Puritan plain style. How does Bradford describe the starving time? [with two adjectives, *sad* and *lamentable*, and with plain, grim facts] What effect might this matter-of-fact style have on readers? [Possible response: The understated style can move readers because it lets them imagine the survivors' sorrow at the death of half their companions.]

ⓚ Struggling Readers
Identifying the Main Clause
Help students through these two long sentences by asking what the subject of the first sentence is. [six or seven sound persons] What did the subject do? [care for the sick]

Skill Link

Interpreting the Influence of Historical Context on Literary Works
Works of literature are marked by the time and place in which they were written. Writers' views are affected by their circumstances, their country, and their political and religious beliefs.
Activity
Have students consult an encyclopedia to obtain information about one of the following topics. Then, have them analyze how these influences help to explain the attitude and values Bradford expresses.
1. The religious changes that took place in England in the sixteenth and seventeenth centuries, especially the control of the church by the Crown and the position of the Calvinists
2. The efforts of the Virginia Company to explore and settle North America, especially their dealings with the Pilgrims

A. Literary Connections
Myles Standish

Henry Wadsworth Longfellow (p. T175) immortalized the captain in a long narrative poem called "The Courtship of Miles [Myles] Standish." In Longfellow's poem, Standish is portrayed as a gentle soul, too bashful to propose to the woman he loves.

B. Reading Skills and Strategies
Using a Dictionary

Have students use a dictionary to define the word *carriage* as Bradford uses it. [behavior] Then, have them paraphrase Bradford's sentence. [During this miserable time, the sailors behaved differently from the passengers.]

C. Reading Skills and Strategies
Comparing and Contrasting

[?] What specific contrast does Bradford point out between the Pilgrims' and the sailors' behavior toward their sick? [The sailors are selfish and refuse to care for the sick, while the Pilgrims are merciful, not only to their own company but even to those who were unkind to them. Bradford depicts the Pilgrims as model Christians.]

D. Vocabulary Note
Connotations

[?] What impression of the Indians does Bradford convey? [He portrays them as sneaky and cowardly.] Which words convey this impression? [skulking, run away, stole away]

E. Historical Connections
What Goes Around Comes Around?

In an earlier part of his narrative not included in this selection, Bradford tells how the Pilgrims had several times taken corn and beans from the Native Americans' stores without permission, although he says they planned to and did repay them six months later. This fact might help to explain the Indians' suspicious behavior.

F. Reading Skills and Strategies
Compiling a Time Line

[?] At this point, how long have the Pilgrims been in North America? [just over four months]

A reverend Elder, and Myles Standish,[19] their Captain and military commander, unto whom myself and many others were much beholden in our low and sick condition. And yet the Lord so upheld these persons as in this general calamity they were not at all infected either with sickness or lameness. And what I have said of these I may say of many others who died in this general visitation, and others yet living; that whilst they had health, yea, or any strength continuing, they were not wanting to any that had need of them. And I doubt not but their recompense is with the Lord.

But I may not here pass by another remarkable passage not to be forgotten. As this calamity fell among the passengers that were to be left here to plant, and were hasted ashore and made to drink water that the seamen might have the more beer, and one[20] in his sickness desiring but a small can of beer, it was answered that if he were their own father he should have none. The disease began to fall amongst them also, so as almost half of their company died before they went away, and many of their officers and lustiest men, as the boatswain, gunner, three quartermasters, the cook and others. At which the Master was something strucken and sent to the sick ashore and told the Governor he should send for beer for them that had need of it, though he drunk water homeward bound.

B But now amongst his company there was far another kind of carriage in this misery than amongst the passengers. For they that before had been boon companions in drinking and jollity in the time of their health and welfare, began now to desert one another in this calamity, saying they would not hazard their lives for them, they should be infected by coming to help them in their cabins; and so, after they came to lie by it, would do little or nothing for them but, "if they died, let them die." But such of the passengers as were yet aboard showed them what mercy they could, **C** which made some of their hearts <u>relent</u>, as the boatswain (and some others) who was a proud young man and would often curse and scoff at the passengers. But when he grew weak, they had compassion on him and helped him; then he confessed he did not deserve it at their hands, he had abused them in word and deed. "Oh!" (saith he) "you, I now see, show your love like Christians indeed one to another, but we let one another lie and die like dogs." Another lay cursing his wife, saying if it had not been for her he had never come this unlucky voyage, and anon cursing his fellows, saying he had done this and that for some of them; he had spent so much and so much amongst them, and they were now weary of him and did not help him, having need. Another gave his companion all he had, if he died, to help him in his weakness; he went and got a little spice and made him a mess of meat once or twice. And because he died not so soon as he expected, he went amongst his fellows and swore the rogue would cozen[21] him, he would see him choked before he made him any more meat; and yet the poor fellow died before morning.

Indian Relations

D **E** All this while the Indians came skulking about them, and would sometimes show themselves aloof off, but when any approached near them, they would run away; and once they stole away **F** their tools where they had been at work and were gone to dinner. But about the 16th of March, a certain Indian came boldly amongst them and spoke to them in broken English, which they could well understand but marveled at it. At length they understood by <u>discourse</u> with him, that he was not of these parts, but belonged to the eastern parts where some English ships came to fish, with whom he was acquainted and could name sundry of them by their names, amongst whom he had got his language. He became profitable to them in acquainting them with many things concerning the state of the country in the east parts where he lived, which was afterward profitable unto them; as also of the people here, of their names, number

21. **cozen** (kuz′ən): cheat.

WORDS TO OWN
relent (ri·lent′) *v.*: soften.
discourse (dis′kôrs′) *n.*: conversation.

19. **Myles Standish** (c. 1584–1656): a soldier who had been hired to handle the colonists' military affairs. Not a member of the Puritan congregation, he still became a most steadfast ally.
20. **one:** Bradford himself.

Crossing the Curriculum

History

After students finish reading the selection, ask them to compare and contrast Bradford's account to other accounts of colonial settlements. Students could read the section on the settling of Jamestown from *A True Relation of Such Occurrences and Accidents of Noate as Hath Hapned in Virginia* and Captain John Smith's rescue by Pocahontas in *The Generall Historie of Virginia,* both by Smith himself.

Science

The Master's unwillingness to share the beer may not have stemmed from pure selfishness—it is possible that he was concerned about the quality of the drinking water that he and his men would have on the return voyage. Ask students to research the logistics of supplying ship crews with fresh water and food during this period. What did sailors generally drink and eat at sea? Why? How was it kept fresh?

and strength, of their situation and distance from this place, and who was chief amongst them. His name was Samoset.[22] He told them also of another Indian whose name was Squanto,[23] a native of this place, who had been in England and could speak better English than himself.

Being, after some time of entertainment and gifts dismissed, a while after he came again, and five more with him, and they brought again all the tools that were stolen away before, and made way for the coming of their great Sachem, called Massasoit.[24] Who, about four or five days after, came with the chief of his friends and other attendance, with the aforesaid Squanto. With whom, after friendly entertainment and some gifts given him, they made a peace with him (which hath now continued this 24 years)[25] in these terms:

1. That neither he nor any of his should injure or do hurt to any of their people.

2. That if any of his did hurt to any of theirs, he should send the offender, that they might punish him.

3. That if anything were taken away from any of theirs, he should cause it to be restored; and they should do the like to his.

4. If any did unjustly war against him, they would aid him; if any did war against them, he should aid them.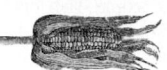

5. He should send to his neighbors <u>confederates</u> to certify them of this, that they might not wrong them, but might be likewise <u>comprised</u> in the conditions of peace.

6. That when their men came to them, they should leave their bows and arrows behind them.

After these things he returned to his place called Sowams, some 40 miles from this place, but Squanto continued with them and was their interpreter and was a special instrument sent of God

22. **Samoset** (sam′ə·set′) (1590?–1655): a Pemaquid from Maine.
23. **Squanto** (skwän′tō) (1585?–1622): one of the few survivors of the Pawtuxet, an Algonquian people. He later joined Massasoit's Wampanoags.
24. **Massasoit** (mas′ə·soit′) (c. 1580–1661): sachem (chief) of the Wampanoags, who lived in the area which became Rhode Island and southern Massachusetts.
25. **With whom . . . this 24 years:** The treaty was kept faithfully until the reign of Massasoit's younger son, Metacomet (1639?–1676), also known to the colonists as King Philip. (See Mary Rowlandson's narrative on page 40.)

for their good beyond their expectation. He directed them how to set their corn, where to take fish, and to procure other commodities, and was also their pilot to bring them to unknown places for their profit, and never left them till he died. He was a native of this place, and scarce any left alive besides himself. He was carried away with divers others by one Hunt, a master of a ship, who thought to sell them for slaves in Spain. But he got away for England and was entertained by a merchant in London, and employed to Newfoundland and other parts, and lastly brought hither into these parts by one Mr. Dermer, a gentleman employed by Sir Ferdinando Gorges and others for discovery and other designs in these parts. . . .

First Thanksgiving

They began now to gather in the small harvest they had, and to fit up their houses and dwellings against winter, being all well recovered in health and strength and had all things in good plenty. For as some were thus employed in affairs abroad, others were exercised in fishing, about cod and bass and other fish, of which they took good store, of which every family had their portion. All the summer there was no want; and now began to come in store of fowl, as winter approached, of which this place did abound when they came first (but afterward decreased by degrees). And besides waterfowl there was great store of wild turkeys, of which they took many, besides venison, etc. Besides they had about a peck of meal a week to a person, or now since harvest, Indian corn to that proportion. Which made many afterward write so largely of their plenty here to their friends in England, which were not feigned but true reports.[26]

26. **Which made . . . true reports:** Although the specific day of the Plymouth colonists' first Thanksgiving is not known, it occurred in the fall of 1621. For three days, Massasoit and almost a hundred of his men joined the Pilgrims, feasting and playing games.

WORDS TO OWN

confederates (kən·fed′ər·its) *n.:* allies; persons who share a common purpose.
comprised (kəm·prīzd′) *v.:* included.

G Struggling Readers
Identifying Pronoun Antecedents
Tell students that the Pilgrims and Massasoit agreed to a treaty with these six terms. As students review the terms, make sure they can identify which group is meant by each use of *he/his/him* and *they/their/them*. [In general *he/his/him* refers to Massasoit and the Wampanoag and *they/their/them* to the Pilgrims. The exceptions are clause 5, in which the first *them* refers to other tribes, and clause 6, which should be read as follows: That when the Indians visit the Pilgrims, the warriors should leave their bows and arrows behind them.]

H Reading Skills and Strategies
Taking Notes
Review the instructions on taking notes on the Before You Read page. Then, have students notice the way Bradford sees Squanto as part of God's plan for the Pilgrims' salvation. Be sure students note that Squanto taught the Pilgrims how to plant corn, fish, and where to trade.

I Reading Skills and Strategies
Noticing Shifts in Tone
Ask students to trace the tone of Bradford's references to Native Americans throughout the selection. [First he calls them "savage barbarians", next he accuses them of "skulking" and running away. However, when he meets Samoset, he is impressed with his knowledge and friendliness, and he calls Massasoit "great." Finally, he honors Squanto with a detailed biography and calls him "a special instrument sent of God." The final footnote in this selection shows Massasoit and his warriors feasting and playing with the Pilgrims at the first Thanksgiving.]

Assessing Learning

Check Test: Questions and Answers
1. What became of the sailor who scoffed at the sick passengers? [He died at sea.]
2. How many people died during the starving time? [half the settlers (about fifty people)]
3. What does Bradford say about Standish? [He identifies him as the Pilgrims' military commander and praises him for caring for the sick.]
4. What agreement did Massasoit make with the Pilgrims? [to be friends and allies]

Professional Notes

Critical Comment: Our Spiritual Ancestors
The American historian Samuel Eliot Morison wrote that *Of Plymouth Plantation* "is a story of a simple people inspired by an ardent faith to a dauntless courage in danger, a resourcefulness in dealing with new problems, an impregnable fortitude in adversity that exalts and heartens one. . . . It is this story . . . that has made the Pilgrim Fathers in a sense the spiritual ancestors of all Americans, all pioneers."

Journalist Anthony Lewis writes about the Dinh family's escape from Communist Vietnam and their efforts to reunite the entire family in Portland, Oregon. Lewis then goes on to describe the careers of the various family members, culminating with the news that Viet Dinh had graduated from Harvard Law School and would be a clerk for Justice Sandra Day O'Connor at the Supreme Court. Using the Dinhs as a model, Lewis argues that America is enriched by immigrants and urges Americans to continue accepting them.

Ⓐ Historical Connections
The Vietnam War
The United States and the former South Vietnam fought together in the Vietnam War (1957-1975) to prevent the Communists of North Vietnam from taking over South Vietnam. After intense fighting, from 1966 to 1972, the United States began withdrawing ground troops and in 1974 signed a cease-fire agreement. However, fighting and bombing continued, and gradually South Vietnam abandoned outposts it could no longer protect. The North began an offensive in 1974, and the Southern capital, Saigon (now called Ho Chi Minh City), fell in 1975. As a result, many South Vietnamese sought asylum in the United States.

Ⓑ Reading Skills and Strategies

Compiling a Time Line
Have students identify references to time in this paragraph and throughout the article. For additional practice of this study strategy, the class can collaborate on an illustrated time line of events in the Dinh family's story.

Ⓒ Reading Skills and Strategies
Comparing/Contrasting
❓ How are the Dinh family's reasons for emigrating to America similar to those of the *Mayflower* passengers? [Both seek political freedom and financial opportunity, and both are fleeing potential persecution at home.] How are they different? [The Dinh family is escaping a war-torn nation with a Communist government; the Pilgrims are seeking a place where they can practice their religious beliefs.]

An American Story

ANTHONY LEWIS

Ⓐ Fifteen years ago this Thanksgiving weekend, a ten-year-old Vietnamese boy named Viet Dinh arrived in this country as a refugee. He was with his mother, four sisters, and a brother. They had two hundred dollars, which they spent on used winter coats.

Ⓑ They were boat people. They had left Vietnam on a small fishing boat, which lost its engine in a storm. They drifted for days until they made it to Malaysia—swimming in at night to avoid patrol boats that had fired at them. After months in a refugee camp, they were cleared for admission to the United States and flown to Portland, Oregon.

Two members of the family were left behind in Vietnam: Viet Dinh's father, Phong Dinh, and his older sister Van Dinh, who was twenty then. She stayed behind to help their father.

Ⓒ Phong Dinh had been a city councilman in Vung Tau during the Saigon regime. When the Communists took over in 1975, he was sent to a reeducation camp. He escaped from the camp on June 12, 1978, and was on the run when his wife and six children left.

Over the next five years, Phong Dinh tried unsuccessfully twenty-five times to get out of Vietnam by boat. He paid boatmen who never turned up or who were arrested. Finally, in 1983, he made it to the Philippines, and then to the United States.

That left the oldest child, Van Dinh. She had helped her father pay the boatmen. But it was six years before she managed to leave herself: on a boat that reached Hong Kong in August 1989.

The family here knew that she had left Vietnam because they got a message to that effect. But for a year they did not know she was in a Hong Kong refugee camp; indeed, they did not know whether she had landed anywhere or had gone down at sea, as many boat people had.

Van Dinh was kept in the locked Hong Kong camp for three years, waiting for clearance as a refugee. With her was her five-year-old son, Quan, who had a congenital heart condition. That made her desperate to reach the United States, but for years she could not even get an interview with those in charge of the refugee process in Hong Kong.

At the end of 1991, Viet Dinh, then twenty-three years old, sent me an essay he had written about his sister Van's plight in Hong Kong. I forwarded it to *The New York Times* Op-Ed page, and the editors published it in January 1992.

Last month I had another letter from Viet Dinh. It had good news about his sister. After his Op-Ed piece was published, other papers picked up the story. The Hong Kong authorities, feeling the pressure, finally interviewed Van Dinh—and found that she was entitled to refugee status. In September 1992, she made it to Portland. The family was reunited after fifteen years.

There is more to tell about the Dinh family, as I learned when I interviewed Viet. His parents are running a small grocery in Salem, Oregon. A sister, Anh, helps them. Another sister, Thu, is an accountant. Kathleen and Leanne are computer programmers. Viet's one brother, Bao, is an architect.

The child with the heart condition, Van's son Quan, has been treated in Portland. He is doing fine.

Van herself, after fourteen months in the United States, is studying at a community college in Salem and working as an assembler in an electronics plant. "After she gets her English and cultural skills together," Viet said, "I think she'd like to open a business."

It is an American story, and one that I wish members of Congress and their constituents who are fulminating these days about "the immigrant threat" would think about. The Dinh family is doing exactly what immigrants on the Lower East Side and so many other places did in past years: struggling for themselves and making this country better.

There is no other country that has taken in so many people from so many places and cultures, and gained so much in the process. To turn away from that tradition now would do the United States great damage.

One more thing about Viet Dinh. His recent letter ended: "I graduated from the Harvard Law School in June and am now a law clerk for Judge Laurence H. Silberman of the U.S. Court of Appeals in Washington. Next year I clerk for Justice Sandra Day O'Connor at the Supreme Court."

—*from The New York Times,* November 26, 1993

Vietnamese boat people rescued by the cargo ship *Medecins du Monde.*

Connecting Across Texts

Connecting with *Of Plymouth Plantation*
Although they were written in different centuries, Bradford's narrative and "An American Story" are both about immigrants coming to the United States. From Bradford's narrative, students know that the Pilgrims had to endure hardships and earn the trust of the Wampanoag in order to survive. The Dinhs had to struggle against linguistic and financial barriers. In addition, they had to contend with residents who perceived them as "the immigrant threat." While the Pilgrims displaced the indigenous culture with their own way of life, the Dinhs had to adjust to a powerful, strongly rooted American culture.

MAKING MEANINGS

First Thoughts

1. What qualities or beliefs of the Puritans do you think enabled them to deal with the hardships they faced both on their voyage and in America?

Reading Check

With several classmates, compare the **time lines** you compiled. Discuss any differences, and try to agree on a common set of main and subsidiary events.

Shaping Interpretations

2. At what points in his history does Bradford give inner, spiritual significance to outward events?

3. Consider the treaty drawn up with Massasoit (Chapter 11), and explain whether or not you feel its terms were equally favorable to both parties. What seems to be Bradford's attitude toward the Wampanoag?

4. One event that Bradford does not describe is the death of his wife, who either fell or jumped overboard in Provincetown Harbor. What reasons can you propose for his having omitted it? How would his history have been different if he had included this tragedy?

Extending the Text

5. In what ways might the Pilgrims' experiences be relevant to contemporary pioneers or refugees? In your response, take into account the experiences of the Dinh family in "An American Story" (see **Connections** on page 34).

ELEMENTS OF LITERATURE

The Plain Style

At the beginning of his history, Bradford says he will try to unfold his story "in a plain style, with singular regard unto the simple truth in all things." He means that he will not imitate the ornate "high style" that was in fashion in England at the time—a style that used classical allusions, Latin quotations, and elaborate figures of speech, as in this 1629 example from the poet and Anglican clergyman John Donne:

> First, for the incomprehensibleness of God, the understanding of man hath a limited, a determined latitude; it is an intelligence able to move that sphere which it is fixed to, but could not move a greater: I can comprehend *naturam naturatam,* created nature, but for that *natura naturans,* God himself, the understanding of man cannot comprehend.

In a sense, Bradford's stylistic preference reflected the division between the Puritans and the Anglicans in matters of worship. A plain writing style was in keeping with the Puritans' preference for plainness in all other things, especially in church ritual. They thought that a "plain style" was much more effective than an elevated or "high style" in revealing God's truth. The **plain style** imitated the style of the Bible the Puritans used: the Geneva Bible, published in 1560. (Other English Protestants of the time used the elegant King James translation, published in 1611.) Simple sentences, everyday language, and direct, unembellished statements—without such figures of speech as similes and metaphors—were the chief characteristics of the plain style.

Bradford's style may seem far from "plain" to a modern reader because it abounds in **Biblical quotations** and **allusions**. Also, his **syntax** and **vocabulary** are now **archaic,** or no longer in common use.

1. Identify and write down three of Bradford's sentences that contain elements of the plain style.

2. Recast the sentences into straightforward modern prose. In doing this, how has the "Biblical" sound been affected?

Reading Check

Main events: *Mayflower* embarks; *Mayflower* lands on Cape Cod; disease and starvation kill half the colonists and sailors; Indians introduce themselves and sign peace treaty; first Thanksgiving is celebrated. Subsidiary events: death of profane sailor; rescue of Howland; quarrel over beer.

MAKING MEANINGS

First Thoughts [Respond]

1. Possible responses: courage, perseverance, endurance, belief in their cause, belief in God's wisdom

Shaping Interpretations [Interpret]

2. Bradford assumes that the profane seaman's death and John Howland's rescue are signs from God. Other outward events he interprets as spiritual signs are the safe completion of the journey, the continued health of those who serve the sick during the starving time, and Squanto's arrival.

3. The conditions favor the Pilgrims; only clauses 3 and 4 mention an even exchange of favors. Bradford is grateful for the Wampanoag's help, but sees it as a sign of God's protection of the pilgrims.

4. Bradford tries to be as impersonal and objective as possible, even using *they* rather than *we* in the narrative. The inclusion of his wife's death would have made the narrative more personal and less a tribute to the Pilgrims' success and the benign hand of God.

Extending the Text [Synthesize]

5. Both may have fears of starting out with nothing. Both have to struggle at first with different languages, their lack of knowledge of the new land, and the need to acquire new skills. Both run from oppression. Both have high hopes that the new land will be freer and better than their native countries.

ELEMENTS OF LITERATURE

1. Check students' choices for simple vocabulary, factual statements, and absence of figurative language.

2. Students should notice that the Biblical sound disappears. Sample paraphrase of opening sentence: When everything was taken care of, they all boarded one ship and sailed. The weather was good, so many passengers were optimistic. Some, however, were seasick.

Grading Timesaver

Rubrics for each Choices assignment appear on p. 89 in the *Portfolio Management System.*

CHOICES: Building Your Portfolio

1. **Writer's Notebook**   Ask students to consider whether they might like to present a detached view of the incidents they choose, as Bradford does, or whether they want to write more personally.

2. **Comparing Writers' Purposes** Before they begin writing, have students share what they know about Smith. Essays might contrast the bright promise of Smith's account with the hardships of Bradford's.

3. **Speaking and Listening**   Students representing the Native American point of view may want to review the selections on pp. 22–24.

CHOICES: Building Your Portfolio

Writer's Notebook

1. Collecting Ideas for an Autobiographical Incident

According to Murphy's Law, if anything can go wrong, it will. Most of us learn the hard way that when we try to do something—take a trip, for example, or reach a particular goal—the best-laid plans can often go awry. Make a list of challenges, setbacks, or hardships you've overcome on your "life's journey." Keep your notes for possible use in the Writer's Workshop on page 130.

Comparing Writers' Purposes

2. Come to America!

Captain John Smith (c. 1580–1631) led the first permanent English settlement in America at Jamestown, Virginia, in 1607. He hoped to establish another colony in New England, and in order to attract settlers, he wrote a pamphlet. In the following excerpt, Smith, somewhat like a contemporary travel agent, attempts to persuade people to join him in the new land. Write a brief essay in which you contrast Smith's rosy promises with Bradford's actual experiences in America. Contrast the **purposes** of the two writers and their intended **audiences.** Note how each writer's **motivation** may affect his credibility.

Here nature and liberty afford us that freely which in England we want, or it costs us dearly. What pleasure can be more than (being tired with any occasion ashore) in planting vines, fruits, or herbs, in contriving their own grounds to the pleasure of their own minds, their fields, gardens, orchards, buildings, ships, and other works, etc.; to re-create themselves before their own doors, in their own boats upon the sea, where man, woman, and child, with a small hook and line, by angling may take divers sorts of excellent fish at their pleasures? . . . He is a very bad fisher [who] cannot kill in one day with his hook and line one, two, or three hundred cods, which dressed and dried, if they be sold there for ten shillings the hundred [pounds], though in England they will give more than twenty, may not both the servant, the master, and merchant be well content with this gain? If a man work but three days in seven, he may get more than he can spend, unless he will be excessive. . . .

For hunting, also, the woods, lakes, and rivers afford not only chase sufficient for any that delight in that kind of toil or pleasure, but such beasts to hunt that besides the delicacy of their bodies for food, their skins are so rich as may well recompense thy daily labor with a captain's pay.

—John Smith,
from "A Description of New England," 1616

Speaking and Listening

3. When Cultures Clash

As a class, divide into two groups, one representing the Pilgrims and the other the American Indians. Each of the two groups should further divide into smaller groups to discuss problems, conflicts, and grievances that have arisen, or may arise in the future, between the two cultures. Afterward, each small group should choose a person to represent the group's viewpoint in a panel discussion. Start with a brief statement by each panelist, followed by questions from all class members.

Making the Connections

Cultural Connections

Students representing the Wampanoag position in Choice 3 could write to Nanepashemet, a Wampanoag educator at the Hobbamock Homesite at Plymouth Plantation, for more information about Native American grievances against the Pilgrims. Students could also gain information about this culture by researching the annual Fourth of July gathering of the Mashpee Wampanoag on Cape Cod.

Reading Skills and Strategies

VOCABULARY: WHEN A DICTIONARY CAN HELP

English speakers from long ago used words that we no longer use or that have changed meaning over time. These obsolete words and meanings are called **archaisms.** No matter how carefully we read, we cannot always find the appropriate definition by using clues in the text. We need outside help—a dictionary.

Most of the time, when you want to look up a word you don't know, a collegiate or abridged dictionary will be all you need. However, when you are reading a work of early American literature, you may need to use an unabridged dictionary, such as *Webster's Third New International Dictionary* or the *Oxford English Dictionary* (called *OED* for short). These dictionaries define numerous archaisms.

Bradford uses the archaic word *fain* in his history (page 30). He uses it to describe the mariners' dilemma of whether to continue on in the damaged *Mayflower* or to return to England—"fain would they do what could be done for their wages' sake . . . and on the other hand they were loath to hazard their lives too desperately." *Fain* is a common archaism,

so an abridged dictionary ably covers its meaning, both as an adjective and an adverb:

> **fain** (fān) *adj.* [ME joyful, joyfully < OE *fægen,* glad, akin to ON *feginn* < IE base **pek-,* to be satisfied > FAIR¹] [Archaic] **1** glad; ready **2** reluctantly willing **3** eager —**adv.** [Archaic] with eagerness; gladly: used with *would* [*he would fain stay]*

Because you don't encounter archaisms that frequently, you'll probably want to keep a careful record of these words in a vocabulary notebook so that you can review them. You may want to make a chart like the one below.

Word _____	
Word's etymology	
Meaning in this context	
Is meaning still in use?	
Is word still in use?	
Other common meanings	
Does the word imply a value judgment? If so, what evidence supports it?	
Dictionary (or dictionaries) used	

Of Plimoth Plantation by William Bradford. *Mayflower II,* a re-creation of the *Mayflower.*

Ms. courtesy of the State Library of Massachusetts. Mayflower photo courtesy of Plimoth Plantation.

Try It Out

Use a good dictionary—unabridged if necessary—to help you determine the meanings and parts of speech of the following underlined words as they are used in Bradford's history.

1. "These troubles being blown over, and now all being <u>compact</u> together in one ship . . ." (page 29)

2. ". . . and on the other hand they were loath to <u>hazard</u> their lives too desperately." (page 30)

3. ". . .they had now. . . no houses or much less towns to <u>repair</u> to, to seek for succor." (page 31)

Reading Skills and Strategies
Mini-Lesson:
Using a Dictionary to Define Archaisms

Remind students that they should always try to figure out new words from the context in which they appear. This challenge to their wits is always fun for verbal learners, and guessing definitions can be a good word game for the whole class. Unabridged dictionaries (and good college-level dictionaries) always give origins and derivations of words. Explain to students that this information can be fascinating and of great help in remembering new words. For instance, *hazard* (Try It Out, example 2) comes from the Arabic *al-zahr,* which means "the die." Dice are used for games of chance, or risk; hence *hazard* means "risk." Encourage students to look at derivations as well as definitions when they use a dictionary.

Try It Out

You might extend this exercise by dividing the class into four groups and having each group list unfamiliar words from one of the four full pages of text of this selection. Each group can look up their words in a dictionary. After the groups have shared their results, hold a spelling bee (see Preteaching Vocabulary activity on p. T27).

Answers
1. packed closely; adjective
2. risk; verb
3. return; verb

OBJECTIVES

1. Read and interpret the autobiographical narrative
2. Identify allusions
3. Analyze text structures including chronological order
4. Express understanding through creative and critical writing
5. Understand and use new words

SKILLS

Literary
- Identify allusions

Reading
- Analyze text structures including chronological order

Writing
- Write about a time when your perception of someone or something changed
- Explore allusions in two texts
- Write a journal entry

Vocabulary
- Use new words

Viewing/Representing
- Analyze a portrait (ATE)
- Analyze Native American artifacts (ATE)

Planning

- **Block Schedule**
  Block Scheduling Lesson Plans with Pacing Guide
- **Traditional Schedule**
  Lesson Plans Including Strategies for English-Language Learners
- **One-Stop Planner**
  CD-ROM with Test Generator

Mary Rowlandson

(c. 1636–c. 1678)

Courtesy of American Antiquarian Society.

From June 1675 to August 1676, the Wampanoag chief, Metacomet, called King Philip by the colonists, carried out a series of bloody raids on Colonial settlements in what is now called King Philip's War. The Puritans viewed the war as a sign of God's punishment for the sins of their young people (who had taken to dancing and wearing their hair long), but a conflict between colonists and American Indians was probably inevitable. It was the natural result of growing encroachments by the settlers on American Indian land. The native people of New England had been forced into ever more restricted areas, and, although they had sold the land, they rejected conditions stipulating that they could no longer hunt on it. To them, "selling" meant selling the right to share the land with the buyers, not selling its exclusive ownership.

Matters came to a head when Metacomet's former assistant, who had given information to the colonists, was killed by his own people. His killers were tried and hanged by the Puritans. This was too much for Metacomet to bear, and two weeks later the most severe war in the history of New England began. Its tragic result was the virtual extinction of the indigenous way of life in the region. Among the war's victims was Mary Rowlandson, the wife of the Congregational minister of Lancaster, a frontier town of about fifty families that was located thirty miles west of Boston. On a February morning, she and her three children were carried away by a Wampanoag raiding party that wanted to trade hostages for money. After eleven weeks and five days of captivity, Rowlandson's ransom was paid.

She was to survive for only two more years.

Rowlandson's captors, it is important to realize, were only slightly better off than their prisoners. Virtually without food, they were chased from camp to camp by Colonial soldiers. Their captives, they thought, were the only currency with which to buy supplies and food. In a graphic passage, Rowlandson describes the lengths to which the Wampanoag were driven by their hunger, eating horses, dogs, frogs, skunks, rattlesnakes, and even tree bark. "They would pick up old bones," she wrote, "and cut them to pieces at the joints, and if they were full of worms and maggots, they would scald them over the fire to make the vermin come out, and then boil them, and drink up the liquor. . . . They would eat horse's guts, and ears, and all sorts of wild birds which they could catch. . . . I can but stand in admiration," she concluded, "to see the wonderful power of God in providing for such a vast number of our enemies in the wilderness, where there was nothing to be seen."

Rowlandson's narrative not only presents a terrifying and moving tale of frontier life but also provides insight into how the Puritans viewed their lives with a characteristic double vision. For Rowlandson, as for other Puritans, events had both a physical and a spiritual significance. She did not want merely to record her horrifying experience; she wished to demonstrate how it revealed God's purpose. The full title of her narrative (when first published in 1682) illustrates this intention: *The Sovereignty and Goodness of God, Together with the Faithfulness of His Promises Displayed: Being a Narrative of the Captivity and Restauration of Mrs. Mary Rowlandson.*

T38

 Resources: Print and Media

Reading
- *Reading Skills and Strategies*
  MiniRead Skill Lesson, p. 13
  Selection Skill Lesson, p. 19
- *Graphic Organizers for Active Reading*, p. 2
- *Words to Own*, p. 3
- *Audio CD Library*
  Disc 2, Track 2

Writing and Language
- *Daily Oral Grammar*
  Transparency 3

- *Grammar and Language Links*
  Worksheet, p. 3

Assessment
- *Formal Assessment*, p. 5
- *Portfolio Management System*, p. 90
- *Preparation for College Admission Exams*, p. 1
- *Test Generator (One-Stop Planner CD-ROM)*

Internet
- go.hrw.com (keyword: LE0 11-1)

Before You Read

FROM **A NARRATIVE OF THE CAPTIVITY**

Make the Connection

Survival Skills

Who hasn't listened with rapt attention to stories of people enduring life-threatening circumstances—a flood, a plane crash on a snowy mountain, an earthquake, a wartime siege, or captivity as a hostage or prisoner of war? Perhaps our fascination with such stories comes from wondering how we would survive if we were put to the same test—instead of just sitting in safe surroundings reading about it.

Reading Skills and Strategies

Analyzing Text Structures: Chronological Order

As you read, keep track of events and how they affect Rowlandson by taking notes in three columns. Use the first column to list events in **chronological order** (also called time or sequential order). Use the second column to note where Rowlandson links her sufferings with those of people in the Bible. Use the third column to record her comments about her captors regarding some of the events. You will have more entries in the first column than in either of the other two.

Events in chronological order	References to Bible	Comments about captors

Portrait of Ninigret II, Chief of the Niantic Indians (c. 1681). Anonymous. American. Oil on canvas (33⅛" × 30⅛").

Museum of Art, Rhode Island School of Design. Gift of Mr. Robert Winthrop (48.246).

Elements of Literature

Allusions

The Puritans regarded Biblical captivity narratives, such as the enslavement of Moses and the Israelites by the Egyptians, as allegories representing the Christians' liberation from sin through the intervention of God's grace. Rowlandson views her experiences as a repetition of the same Biblical pattern and uses **allusions** to reflect her own situation. Through apt quotations from the Bible, Rowlandson places her experiences in the context of the ancient Biblical captivities.

> An **allusion** is a reference to someone or something that is known from history, literature, religion, politics, sports, science, or some other branch of culture.
>
> *For more on Allusion, see the Handbook of Literary Terms.*

MARY ROWLANDSON 39

Summary ■ ■

Mary Rowlandson chronicles her experience as a captive of the Wampanoag during King Philip's War in 1675. After being kidnapped by the retreating tribe, she tries to take care of her daughter Sarah, who has been wounded in the raid. The weather, however, is cold, and they have no food and little water, and Sarah soon dies. Rowlandson visits briefly with her son and her other daughter, also captives, and accepts the gift of a Bible from a Native American warrior. Throughout her captivity, the Wampanoag are on the run from the English. Although food is scarce, Rowlandson earns money and tidbits of meat by sewing—some of it for the Wampanoag leader Metacomet, or King Philip. Many of her captors treat her kindly, but what ultimately sustains her is reading the Bible and trusting in God.

RESPONDING TO THE ART

Portrait of Ninigret II shows a chief who was a contemporary of Rowlandson. Colonial portrait painters found Indians fascinating subjects because of their colorful costumes and, to the European eye, exotic features.

Activity. Explore these questions with students:

1. What impression do you have of Ninigret's character? [Possible answers: strong; decisive; youthful.]

2. If you were Mary Rowlandson, would you think such a captor might be kind or sympathetic? [Possible answers: He does not look mean or malicious; it looks as if he has a club and a knife, which makes him seem intimidating.]

Preteaching Vocabulary

Words to Own

Have students read the Words to Own and their definitions listed at the bottom of the selection pages. Then, have them use each word correctly in a sentence about the Native American tales and songs or *Of Plymouth Plantation*. Finally, have students use the words to complete the following sentences.

1. The sad story of Rowlandson's children makes the reader feel [melancholy].

2. The [bewitching] song of the whales lured the Wampanoag to the water's edge.

3. The Puritans stole corn from the Indians and shared this [plunder] among themselves.

4. Because the wigwam was old and [decrepit], she wanted a seat by the fire.

5. Rowlandson [entreated] King Philip to set her and her children free.

6. She was lame, but this [affliction] did not prevent her from succeeding.

7. Were those first Thanksgiving turkeys as [savory] as ours?

8. You will regret those [lamentable] words!

9-10. The [wearisome], [tedious] task bored and fatigued us.

RESPONDING TO THE ART

Native American artifacts, like this sash and belt (pp. 40, 45), were often decorated with feathers, precious metals, shells, or beads. Wampum (pp. 45, 46), consisted of belts and strings of polished shell beads, used as decoration, a currency of exchange, and a symbolic record of important events. The shell beads on wampum were mostly from the shells of the quahog clam and came in two colors: white and purple. Basketry (pp. 46–47) techniques included weaving, twining, and coiling.

Activity. Have students research the history of Native Americans in their state or region. Have them focus on the arts and craftwork of the tribes in the area. Students can share their research with the class, and bring in samples or photographs of regional Native American art.

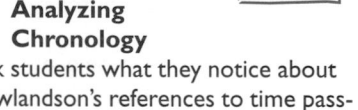

A Reading Skills and Strategies

Analyzing Chronology

Ask students what they notice about Rowlandson's references to time passing. [She keeps track of the hours and the days, using the sun to tell time.]

B Reading Skills and Strategies

Analyzing Chronology

Ask students how these remarks concerning her wounded child might explain Rowlandson's early opinion of her captors. Tell students to record their answers on their charts.

from A Narrative of the Captivity

Mary Rowlandson

The Move to an Indian Village on the Ware River, Near Braintree (February 12–27)

The morning being come, they prepared to go on their way. One of the Indians got up upon a horse, and they set me up behind him, with my poor sick babe in my lap. A very <u>wearisome</u> and <u>tedious</u> day I had of it; what with my own wound, and my child's being so exceeding sick, and in a <u>lamentable</u> condition with her wound. It may be easily judged what a poor feeble condition we were in, there being not the least crumb of refreshing that came within either of our mouths from Wednesday night to Saturday night, except only a little cold water. This day in the afternoon, about an hour by sun, we came to the place where they intended, *viz.*[1] an Indian town, called Wenimesset, norward of Quabaug. . . . I sat much alone with a poor wounded child in my lap, which moaned night and day, having nothing to revive the body, or cheer the spirits of her, but instead of that, sometimes one Indian would come and tell me one hour, that your master will knock your child in the head, and then a second, and then a third, your master will quickly knock your child in the head.

1. **viz.:** Latin for "namely."

WORDS TO OWN

wearisome (wir′i·səm) *adj.:* fatiguing; exhausting.
tedious (tē′dē·əs) *adj.:* tiring; dreary.
lamentable (lam′ən·tə·bəl) *adj.:* regrettable; distressing.

King Philip's sash, ornamented with glass beads (late 1600s). Wampanoag.

Peabody Museum, Harvard University. Photo by Hillel Burger.

40 BEGINNINGS

Reaching All Students

Struggling Readers

Analyzing Text Structures: Chronological Order was introduced on p. 39. For lessons directly tied to this selection that teach students to analyze this text structure with a strategy called Retelling, see the *Reading Skills and Strategies* binder:
• MiniRead Skill Lesson, p. 13
• Selection Skill Lesson, p. 19

English Language Learners

Make up two comprehension questions for every page of text. Have students individually jot down notes in response. Then, in a small group, have students take turns answering the questions orally. Students can help each other express ideas, and you can clarify confusing points. For other strategies, see
• *Lesson Plans Including Strategies for English-Language Learners*

Advanced Learners

As students read, have them look up each of Rowlandson's allusions to Bible verses and stories. By alluding to Biblical figures such as Job, whose faith is tested by a series of tragedies, Rowlandson suggests that she too is being tested by God. After students have read these stories, ask them to share the parallels between the Biblical stories and Rowlandson's fate.

This was the comfort I had from them, miserable comforters are ye all, as he said.[2] Thus nine days I sat upon my knees, with my babe in my lap, till my flesh was raw again; my child being even ready to depart this sorrowful world, they bade me carry it out to another wigwam (I suppose because they would not be troubled with such spectacles) whither I went with a very heavy heart, and down I sat with the picture of death in my lap. About two hours in the night, my sweet babe like a lamb departed this life, on February 18, 1675. It being about six years and five months old. It was nine days from the first wounding, in this miserable condition, without any refreshing of one nature or another, except a little cold water. I cannot but take notice, how at another time I could not bear to be in the room where any dead person was, but now the case is changed; I must and could lie down by my dead babe, side by side all the night after. I have thought since of the wonderful goodness of God to me, in preserving me in the use of my reason and senses, in that distressed time, that I did not use wicked and violent means to end my own miserable life. In the morning, when they understood that my child was dead they sent for me home to my master's wigwam: (by my master in this writing, must be understood Quanopin, who was a Sagamore,[3] and married King Philip's[4] wife's sister; not that he first took me, but I was sold to him by another Narragansett Indian, who took me when first I came out of the garrison). I went to take up my dead child in my arms to carry it with me, but they bid me let it alone: There was no resisting, but go I must and leave it. When I had been at my master's wigwam, I took the first opportunity I could get, to go look after my dead child: When I came I asked them what they had done with it. Then they told me it was upon the hill: Then they went and showed me where it was, where I saw the ground was newly digged, and there they told me they had buried it: There I left that child in the wilderness, and must commit it, and myself also in this wilderness condition, to him who is above all. God having taken away this dear child, I went to see my daughter Mary, who was at this same Indian town, at a wigwam not very far off, though we had little liberty or opportunity to see one another. She was about ten years old, and taken from the door at first by a Praying Ind.[5] and afterward sold for a gun. When I came in sight, she would fall aweeping; at which they were provoked, and would not let me come near her, but bade me be gone; which was a heart-cutting word to me. I had one child dead, another in the wilderness, I knew not where, the third they would not let me come near to: "Me (as he said) have ye bereaved of my Children, Joseph is not, and Simeon is not, and ye will take Benjamin also, all these things are against me."[6] I could not sit still in this condition, but kept walking from one place to another. And as I was going along, my heart was even overwhelmed with the thoughts of my condition, and that I should have children, and a nation which I knew not ruled over them. Whereupon I earnestly entreated the Lord, that He would consider my low estate, and show me a token for good, and if it were His blessed will, some sign and hope of some relief. And indeed quickly the Lord answered, in some measure, my poor prayers: For as I was going up and down mourning and lamenting my condition, my son came to me, and asked me how I did; I had not seen him before, since the destruction of the

2. **he said:** The Biblical allusion is to Job 16:2. In the passage cited, Job addresses those who try to console him in his afflictions. God had severely tested Job's faith by causing Job to lose his children and his money, and to break out in boils all over his body.

3. **Sagamore** (sag′ə·môr′): a secondary chief in the hierarchy of several Native American peoples.

4. **King Philip's:** Metacomet (1639?–1676), son of Massasoit (c. 1580–1661) and chief of the Wampanoag from 1661 to 1676, was called King Philip by the colonists. In 1675, Metacomet led the Wampanoag and other American Indians in an attempt to end settlements in New England. The colonists retaliated, and both sides sustained heavy losses of life in the resulting massacres, which came to be known as King Philip's War. Mary Rowlandson's captivity was part of this conflict. (See William Bradford's narrative *Of Plymouth Plantation*, page 33.)

5. **Praying Ind.:** Native Americans who converted to Christianity were known as "praying Indians." The Colonial assemblies allowed these converts to live in self-governing towns.

6. **Me . . . against me:** Rowlandson quotes Jacob's lament in Genesis 42:36. Jacob had only his youngest son, Benjamin, at home.

WORDS TO OWN

entreated (en·trēt′ed) v.: asked sincerely; prayed to.

MARY ROWLANDSON 41

LITERATURE AND HISTORY

To help students understand the captivity experience, ask them in groups of three to research various Native American groups—such as the Iroquois, Abenaki, Mohawks, Hurons, Penobscots, Cherokees, Shawnees, and Comanches—who took captives or were in contact with captives. Students should explore why these groups took such actions. How were Native Americans who were taken prisoner by settlers treated? [Students might note that those taken prisoner by settlers during King Philip's War were put to death or sold into slavery.] Have each group elect one student to sit on a panel that relates the group's findings to the rest of the class.

Ⓐ Reading Skills and Strategies
Making Inferences
? Why is Rowlandson so grateful to have the Bible? (Encourage students to use prior knowledge about the Puritans as well as details from this selection.) [Possible responses: She regards the Bible as a holy book; the Bible is full of stories and prayers that comfort her; it is a familiar object.]

Captivity Narratives

Mary Rowlandson's *A Narrative of the Captivity* was one of the most widely read prose works of the seventeenth century. It was especially popular in England, where people were eager for lurid tales of native inhabitants in the Americas. Rowlandson's story went through at least thirty editions, and it inspired a mass of imitations that were often partially faked or purely fictional. These "captivity" stories became one of the most widely produced forms of entertainment in America, but they had a tragic side effect: They contributed to the further deterioration of relations between American Indians and colonists.

Between the seventeenth and nineteenth centuries, as settlers moved westward and occupied American Indian lands, tensions between the two groups increased. American Indians, in retaliation for various injustices, raided settlements and took captives to ransom, to enslave, or to sell to the French or even to other native peoples. These captives didn't necessarily suffer grim fates: Some captives actually chose to remain with their captors and were adopted by them; a few married American Indians and never expressed any desire to return to their original homes. Many of those who escaped or were ransomed recorded their experiences when they returned home. Eventually, thousands of captivity tales—of varying quality and accuracy—sprouted up all over the country. Scarcely any first editions of these books remain, as they were literally read and re-read to shreds by an eager public.

From Providence to propaganda. Because early captivity narratives were almost all told from the limited first-person point of view, they didn't provide much context for settlers' actions that may have provoked American Indian aggression. Typically, seventeenth-century captivity narratives begin with a brief description of a raid and the rounding up of hostages; they then focus on the gritty details of the day-to-day struggle for survival. The captives in these early narratives generally accept their condition as a

town, and I knew not where he was, till I was informed by himself, that he was amongst a smaller parcel of Indians, whose place was about six miles off; with tears in his eyes, he asked me whether his sister Sarah was dead; and told me he had seen his sister Mary; and prayed me, that I would not be troubled in reference to himself. . . .

Ⓐ I cannot but take notice of the wonderful mercy of God to me in those afflictions, in sending me a Bible. One of the Indians that came from Medfield fight, had brought some plunder, came to me, and asked me, if I would have a Bible, he had got one in his basket. I was glad of it, and asked him, whether he thought the Indians would let me read. He answered, yes: So I took the Bible, and in that melancholy time, it came into my mind to read first the 28th chapter of Deuteronomy,[7] which I did, and when I had read it, my dark heart wrought on this manner, that there was no mercy for me, that the blessings were gone, and the curses come in their room, and that I had lost my opportunity. But the Lord helped me still to go on reading till I came to Chapter 30 the seven first

7. 28th chapter of Deuteronomy: In Deuteronomy 28, Moses warns that God will bless those who obey Him and curse those who do not.

WORDS TO OWN
plunder (plun'dər) *n.*: goods seized, especially during wartime.
melancholy (mel'ən·käl'ē) *adj.*: sad; sorrowful.

Professional Notes

The Last of the Mohicans

The captivity narrative probably reached its literary high point in 1826 with the publication of *The Last of the Mohicans* by James Fenimore Cooper. Although a work of fiction, it includes all the ingredients that made captivity narratives so popular—the clash between "natural" and "civilized" man, clearcut heroes and villains, danger, battle, and hairbreadth escapes. *The Last of the Mohicans* is set in 1757, during the French and Indian wars. Two English girls, Alice and Cora Munro, are captured by Delaware and Huron tribes. Cora is eventually killed during the battle between the Indians and the rescue party. Cooper portrays a variety of Indian personalities. Several of them are heroic, and even Magua, the Huron villain, wins the reader's sympathy as he speaks of the white man's greed and cruelty. Although his characters often seem clichéd to modern readers, Cooper marks a turning point in the literary depiction of the Native American.

punishment sent by God to test their faith, and any relief from their suffering is always evidence of Divine Providence, not sympathy from their captors. But by the eighteenth century, continuing animosity between settlers and American Indians, aggravated by the French and Indian War, led to a different kind of captivity narrative, one that was an undisguised expression of hatred toward Native Americans. No longer were captivity narratives instructive tales of physical and spiritual survival in the wilderness; now they were inflammatory propaganda, smugly asserting the superiority of Europeans.

Sensationalism and stereotypes. By the early nineteenth century, propaganda had turned into pure sensationalism. Journalists and authors of lurid fiction, gifted at manipulating the fantasies and prejudices of the reading public, revised the original narratives. They pulled out all the stops, using melodramatic plot devices and long passages of grisly detail. The public eagerly read these "penny dreadfuls" (the popular term for cheap magazines with tales of horror and crime), shuddering with mixed fascination and horror at fictional tales of American Indian atrocities and the suffering of innocent captives. The tawdriness of these publications didn't go unnoticed by more educated readers. Many actual nineteenth-century captives were reluctant to publish their stories, afraid that, by association with sleazy popular magazines, their experiences would not be taken seriously.

Some historians have argued that captivity narratives, by advancing the stereotype of the "savage Indian," made it easier for settlers to justify occupation of American Indian lands. By the late nineteenth century, with the "Indian threat" a thing of the past, captivity narratives gradually became less popular. But, unfortunately, stereotypes of the "bad" Indian and the "virtuous" European settler remained in the popular imagination well into the twentieth century, appearing in countless Western novels, Hollywood movies, and television programs.

(B)

verses, where I found, there was mercy promised again, if we would return to Him by repentance; and though we were scattered from one end of the earth to the other, yet the Lord would gather us together, and turn all those curses upon our enemies. I do not desire to live to forget this Scripture, and what comfort it was to me. . . .

(C)

The Fifth Remove

The occasion (as I thought) of their moving at this time, was, the English Army, it being near and following them: For they went, as if they had gone for their lives, for some considerable way, and then they made a stop, and chose some of their stoutest men, and sent them back to hold the English Army in play while the rest escaped: And then, like Jehu,[8] they marched on furiously, with their old, and with their young: Some carried their old decrepit mothers, some carried one, and some another. Four of them carried a great Indian upon a bier; but going through a thick wood with him, they were hindered, and could make no

(D)

(E)

8. **Jehu** (jē′hōō′): ninth century B.C. Israelite king. Jehu was said to be a "furious driver" (2 Kings 9:20), and Rowlandson's allusion here is to the speed and fury with which her captors moved away from the English Army.

- -

WORDS TO OWN

decrepit (dē·krep′it) *adj.*: run down; worn out by age or use.

- -

MARY ROWLANDSON 43

Getting Students Involved

Cooperative Learning

The King and I. King Philip, the son of Massasoit, the sachem or chief who negotiated the treaty with William Bradford (see p. 33), was angry at the settlers' use of alcohol to entice Wampanoags to sell their land. He said "only a small part of the land of my ancestors remains and I am determined not to live until I have no country." In fact, King Philip did not live to see this catastrophe, as he was defeated and killed within a year. His head was displayed on a spike in Plymouth for twenty years after his death. Given this background information, have students choose partners and role-play the conversation between Rowlandson and King Philip (p. 44). Partners should discuss why Rowlandson wanted to see the chief, why he agreed to see her, and what they might have discussed. Students can enact the conversation for the class.

A Film Festival. Students may want to get together for a screening of the 1992 film version of *The Last of the Mohicans,* starring Daniel Day-Lewis (R rated). You might share the information about Cooper on p. T42 before students see the film. Watching it should help students understand the enormous appeal of captivity narratives to eighteenth- and nineteenth-century readers. Encourage students who like the film to read the novel.

A. English Language Learners
Multiple Meanings

Ask students to define *meal*. [something to eat; breakfast, lunch, or dinner] Help them see that in this context, *meal* refers to any coarsely ground, edible grain—for example, wheat, rye, corn, barley, or rice.

B. Critical Thinking
Analyzing Motivation

? After favoring Rowlandson by giving her a light load, her captor refuses to give her a spoonful of meal. How do you explain this paradoxical behavior? [Possible responses: Her captor may think she has already given her enough privileges when others are hungry, too; her captor might think that a lighter load is a less obvious favor than feeding her precious food, which everyone would notice.]

C. Critical Thinking
Making Inferences

? What are the living conditions of the Indians at this point? [Conditions are very bad; they have almost no food.] How do you know? [They are reduced to making soup from an old horse leg and refilling the pot with more water to reuse the leg.]

D. Reading Skills and Strategies
Making Inferences

? When Rowlandson wants to comfort herself, she turns to the Bible. The Wampanoag try to comfort her by giving her food. Why do you think they do this? [Possible answers: Since food is life-sustaining, it would show her they do not mean to hurt her; it is tangible proof of their good will—and food is the only thing they have that Rowlandson wants.]

E. Cultural Connection
Tobacco

The Wampanoag believe that tobacco is a sacred substance that comes from the bones of the First Mother. To them, smoking tobacco signifies commitment and a request for support. Ask students why Rowlandson refuses Philip's offer of a smoke, and ask them to speculate on his reactions. [She viewed tobacco as a temptation of the devil; to him, on the other hand, it was a way to make contact with the spiritual world, and he was probably insulted at her refusal.]

---

haste; whereupon they took him upon their backs, and carried him, one at a time, till they came to Bacquaug River. Upon a Friday, a little after noon we came to this river. When all the company was come up, and were gathered together, I thought to count the number of them, but they were so many, and being somewhat in motion, it was beyond my skill. In this travel, because of my wound, I was somewhat favored in my load; I carried only my knitting work and two quarts of parched **A** meal: Being very faint I asked **B** my mistress to give me one spoonful of the meal, but she would not give me a taste. They quickly fell to cutting dry trees, to make rafts to carry them over the river: and soon my turn came to go over: By the advantage of some brush which they had laid upon the raft to sit upon, I did not wet my foot (which many of themselves at the other end were mid-leg deep) which cannot but be acknowledged as a favor of God to my weakened body, it being a very cold time. I was not before acquainted with such kind of doings or dangers. "When thou passeth through the waters I will be with thee, and through the Rivers they shall not overflow thee," Isaiah, 43:2. A certain number of us got over the river that night, but it was the night after the Sabbath before all the company **C** was got over. On the Saturday they boiled an old horse's leg which they had got, and so we drank of the broth, as soon as they thought it was ready, and when it was almost gone, they filled it up again.

The first week of my being among them, I hardly ate anything; the second week, I found my stomach grow very faint for want of something; and yet it was very hard to get down their filthy trash: but the third week, though I could think how formerly my stomach would turn against this or that, and I could starve and die before I could eat such things, yet they were sweet and <u>savory</u> to my taste. . . .

The Sixth Remove

We traveled on till night; and in the morning, we must go over the river to Philip's crew. When I was in the canoe, I could not but be amazed at the numerous crew of <u>pagans</u> that were on the bank on the other side. When I came ashore, they gathered all about me, I sitting alone in the midst: I observed they asked one another questions, and laughed, and rejoiced over their gains and victories. Then my heart began to fail: And I fell aweeping which was the first time to my remembrance, that I wept before them. Although I had met with so much <u>affliction</u>, and my heart was many times ready to break, yet could I not shed one tear in their sight: but rather had been all this while in a maze, and like one astonished: But now I may say as, Psalm 137:1, "By the rivers of Babylon, there **D** we sat down: yea, we wept when we remembered Zion." There one of them asked me, why I wept, I could hardly tell what to say: Yet I answered, they would kill me: "No," said he, "none will hurt you." Then came one of them and gave me two spoonfuls of meal to comfort me, and another gave me half a pint of peas; which was more worth than many bushels at another time. Then I went to see King Philip, he bade me come in and sit down, and asked me whether I would smoke it **E** (a usual compliment nowadays amongst saints and sinners) but this no way suited me. For though I had formerly used tobacco, yet I had left it ever since I was first taken. It seems to be a bait, the devil lays to make men lose their precious time: I remember with shame, how formerly, when I had taken two or three pipes, I was presently ready for another, such a <u>bewitching</u> thing it is: But I thank God, He has now given me power over it; surely there are many who may be better employed than to lie sucking a stinking tobacco pipe.

Now the Indians gather their forces to go against North Hampton: Overnight one went about yelling and hooting to give notice of the design. Whereupon they fell to boiling of groundnuts, and parching of corn (as many as had it) for their provision: And in the morning away they went. During my abode in this place, Philip spoke to me to make a shirt for his boy, which I did, for which he gave me a shilling: I offered the money to my master, but he bade me keep it: And with it I bought a piece of horseflesh. Afterward he

---

WORDS TO OWN

savory (sā′vər·ē) *adj.*: appetizing; agreeable.
affliction (ə·flik′shən) *n.*: pain; hardship.
bewitching (bē·wich′iŋ) *adj.*: enticing; irresistible.

---

smoking

Listening to Music

Third Movement (Scherzo) of *From the New World* (Symphony No. 9) by Antonín Dvořák

Bohemian composer Antonín Dvořák (1841–1904) was already internationally famous when he came to America. Because living in New York City made him homesick, he spent summers in the small Bohemian-American community of Spillville, Iowa. There he composed his most famous symphony, *From the New World,* which draws on Native American, African American, and other American musical traditions.

Activity

After students read the selections by Bradford, Rowlandson, and Byrd, have them listen to the scherzo, or lively third movement, from the symphony. Then, they can draw, paint, or describe in words the impression of the New World that the music makes.

Wampum belt. Iroquois.
Peabody Essex Museum, Salem, Massachusetts/Peabody Museum Collections. Photo by Mark Sexton.

asked me to make a cap for his boy, for which he invited me to dinner. I went, and he gave me a pancake, about as big as two fingers; it was made of parched wheat, beaten, and fried in bear's grease, but I thought I never tasted pleasanter meat in my life. There was a squaw who spoke to me to make a shirt for her *sannup*,[9] for which she gave me a piece of bear. Another asked me to knit a pair of stockings, for which she gave me a quart of peas: I boiled my peas and bear together, and invited my master and mistress to dinner, but the proud gossip, because I served them both in one dish, would eat nothing, except one bit that he gave her upon the point of his knife. . . .

The Move to the Ashuelot Valley, New Hampshire

But instead of going either to Albany or homeward, we must go five miles up the river, and then go over it. Here we abode[10] awhile. Here lived a sorry Indian, who spoke to me to make him a shirt. When I had done it, he would pay me nothing. But he living by the riverside, where I often went to fetch water, I would often be putting of him in mind, and calling for my pay: At last he told me if I would make another shirt, for a papoose not yet born, he would give me a knife, which he did when I had done it. I carried the knife in, and my master asked me to give it him, and I was not a little glad that I had anything that they would accept of, and be pleased with. When we were at this place, my master's maid came home, she had been gone three weeks into the Narragansett country, to fetch corn, where they had stored up some in the ground: She brought home about a

9. **sannup** (san'up): husband.
10. **abode** (ə·bōd'): stayed.

peck and half of corn. This was about the time that their great captain, Naananto,[11] was killed in the Narragansett country. My son being now about a mile from me, I asked liberty to go and see him, they bade me go, and away I went: but quickly lost myself, traveling over hills and through swamps, and could not find the way to him. And I cannot but admire at the wonderful power and goodness of God to me, in that, though I was gone from home, and met with all sorts of Indians, and those I had no knowledge of, and there being no Christian soul near me; yet not one of them offered the least imaginable miscarriage to me. I turned homeward again, and met with my master, he showed me the way to my son. . . .

But I was fain to go and look after something to satisfy my hunger, and going among the wigwams, I went into one, and there found a squaw who showed herself very kind to me, and gave me a piece of bear. I put it into my pocket, and came home, but could not find an opportunity to broil it, for fear they would get it from me, and there it lay all that day and night in my stinking pocket. In the morning I went to the same squaw, who had a kettle of groundnuts boiling; I asked her to let me boil my piece of bear in her kettle, which she did, and gave me some groundnuts to eat with it: And I cannot but think how pleasant it was to me. I have sometime seen bear baked very handsomely among the English, and some like it, but the thoughts that it was bear, made me tremble: But now that was savory to me that one would think was enough to turn the stomach of a brute creature.

One bitter cold day, I could find no room to sit down before the fire: I went out, and could not tell what to do, but I went in to another wigwam, where they were also sitting round the fire, but the squaw laid a skin for me, and bid me sit down, and gave me some groundnuts, and bade me come again: and told me they would buy me, if they were able, and yet these were strangers to me that I never saw before. . . .

11. **Naananto:** Naananto, or Canonchet (d. April 3, 1676), was a Narragansett leader who was the driving force behind the American Indians' wish to exterminate the New England colonists that resulted in King Philip's War. After his death, the conflict soon ended.

MARY ROWLANDSON 45

Assessing Learning

First Thoughts [Respond]

1. Possible answers: prayer; reading the Bible; trusting in God; seeing her children; her ability to do useful work; her courage.

Shaping Interpretations [Interpret]

2. At first, Rowlandson shrinks from her captors and dislikes them for not being "troubled with such spectacles" as seeing her daughter die. However, as her account progresses, she begins to see them more as individuals capable of kindness and generosity.

3. Possible responses: Like Job, she endures hardships and is not comforted by her companions when her child dies; like the Hebrews wandering the wilderness, she feels she is being tested spiritually by God; later, she compares herself to Jacob, who laments his lost children.

4. Possible responses: Rowlandson's story is exciting and suspenseful; the British could be excited by the horrors she describes from a safe distance; it has a plot with good versus evil; it tells of a culture and situation that would be considered exotic; it is true; it is spiritually uplifting. The account might have promoted negative stereotypes because it is one-sided: it does not relate the colonists' mistreatment of Native Americans and represents the view of a captive who has not personally injured anyone, making her captors appear particularly cruel. The journal depicts the Indians as desperately hungry savages, eating bear meat, grubs, and a horse-leg broth.

5. Possible answers: Rowlandson believed that God's will ruled the universe and that she should put her faith in Him; she believed that her trials were meant to test and strengthen her faith and prepare her for heaven.

Challenging the Text [Evaluate]

6. Possible responses: On p. 40, she describes Sarah as being "in a lamentable condition" and "there being not the least crumb of refreshing"; on p. 41, she calls her captors "miserable comforters"; on p. 44, she refers to the Wampanoag food as "filthy trash" and to some of King Philip's men as "a numerous crew of pagans."

MAKING MEANINGS

First Thoughts

1. What do you think helped Mary Rowlandson survive and maintain her sanity?

Shaping Interpretations

2. What conflicting attitudes, if any, does Rowlandson reveal toward her captors? Do you think her attitude toward her captors changes as the narrative progresses? Explain.

3. The Puritans' habit of seeing specific meaning in their experiences helped them find significance in even very minor events. Describe at least two **allusions** to Biblical stories that Rowlandson makes during her captivity. In what specific ways does each of these Biblical stories resemble Rowlandson's?

4. Rowlandson's narrative was enormously popular in England. What reasons can you propose for its popularity? What aspects of Rowlandson's journal might have promoted stereotyped and hostile views toward American Indians?

> ### Reading Check
>
> a. List in **chronological order** the main events described in Rowlandson's *Narrative*.
>
> b. What does Rowlandson tell us about how she was treated by her captors?
>
> c. What jobs does Rowlandson do to earn her food? How does her attitude toward food change while she is a captive?
>
> d. Find details that reveal that Rowlandson's captors themselves are desperate to find food.

Three American Indian baskets and a string of wampum.

Baskets: Peabody Museum, Harvard University, Cambridge, Massachusetts. Photo by Hillel Burger. Wampum: Peabody Essex Museum, Salem, Massachusetts/Peabody Museum Collections. Photo by Mark Sexton.

46 BEGINNINGS

5. In his classic work of psychology, *Man's Search for Meaning*, Dr. Viktor Frankl, a survivor of the Nazi concentration camps of World War II, tells how the best chance for survival in the camps was not physical endurance or general health but an internal sense that the experience, no matter how horrifying, had some ultimate meaning for the prisoner. Those who had strong religious faith, committed political views, or even just a strong love of family were far more likely to survive, both physically and mentally. In your view, what was Mary Rowlandson's ultimate source of meaning?

Challenging the Text

6. Despite her efforts to be accurate, Rowlandson's journal is full of **subjective reporting**. Instead of using neutral language (words with neither positive nor negative **connotations**), subjective reporting relies on "emotionally loaded" words—words with strongly positive or negative connotations. Select any extract from Rowlandson's journal, and find the emotionally loaded words or phrases that reveal her attitude toward her captors. What words or phrases does Rowlandson use that a detached, objective historian would *not* use?

> ### Reading Check
>
> a. Possible answer: Native Americans move to a village on Ware River. Sarah dies. Rowlandson speaks with her son and daughter. Rowlandson is given a Bible. The tribe retreats across the Bacquaug River. Rowlandson speaks with King Philip. She earns money by sewing.
>
> b. She mentions some cruelty but also mentions being given a Bible and food. She is paid fairly for her sewing.
>
> c. She sews and knits; she finds she can eat anything when she is truly hungry.
>
> d. Details include the boiling of the horse's leg and the rationing of meat.

CHOICES: Building Your Portfolio

Writer's Notebook

1. Collecting Ideas for an Autobiographical Incident

WORK IN PROGRESS

You've probably had the experience of changing your perception of someone or something. A negative viewpoint can soften over time and become more positive. But the reverse is also true: A good opinion or feeling can go sour. Write down your recollections of an instance in your life when your perception or opinion of something or someone changed as a result of a specific incident. Save your notes for possible use in the Writer's Workshop on page 130.

Comparing Texts

2. Sustained by Memories

On page 44, Mary Rowlandson makes an **allusion** to Psalm 137, which is a well-known "captivity" psalm. It was composed when the Israelites were held captive in Babylon by King Nebuchadnezzar. Read Psalm 137 below, and in a brief essay explain why Rowlandson thought of this psalm at a certain point in her sufferings. What parallel would she see between her experience and that of the psalmist? In her mind, what would "Babylon" be?

Creative Writing / Research

3. The Other Side of the Story

Write a journal entry from the point of view of a Wampanoag. Explain the position of your people, giving your reasons for the attack on the settlement and an explanation for the desperate conditions you have been enduring. Use history texts or encyclopedias as your sources. (You will find information under "King Philip's War" and "Metacomet.")

> By the rivers of Babylon, there we sat down, yea, we wept, when we remembered Zion.
>
> We hanged our harps upon the willows in the midst thereof.
>
> For there they that carried us away captive required of us a song; and they that wasted us required of us mirth, saying, Sing us one of the songs of Zion.
>
> How shall we sing the Lord's song in a strange land?
>
> If I forget thee, O Jerusalem, let my right hand forget her cunning.
>
> If I do not remember thee, let my tongue cleave to the roof of my mouth; if I prefer not Jerusalem above my chief joy.
>
> Remember, O Lord, the children of Edom in the day of Jerusalem; who said, Raze it, raze it, even to the foundation thereof.
>
> O daughter of Babylon, who art to be destroyed; happy shall he be, that rewardeth thee as thou hast served us.
>
> Happy shall he be, that taketh and dasheth thy little ones against the stones.
>
> —Psalm 137

Rubrics for each Choices assignment appear on p. 90 in the *Portfolio Management System.*

CHOICES
Building Your Portfolio

WORK IN PROGRESS

1. **Writer's Notebook**   Ask students to consider whether they will want to use "loaded language" like Rowlandson or whether they think objective language or understatement might be more effective.

2. **Comparing Texts**   Share with students this story of the psalm's origins: In the late seventh century B.C., the Babylonians became the dominant power in the Middle East. The Babylonian king Nebuchadnezzar conquered Jerusalem around 597 B.C. and exiled Judean nobles, artisans, and warriors to Babylon. The Israelites who remained in Judea revolted unsuccessfully a number of times. Nebuchadnezzar's forces finally laid siege to Jerusalem, which fell in 586 B.C. after nineteen months. The city was destroyed, the temple burned, and the inhabitants carried off to Babylon. You might also refer students to the music activity on Psalm 137 in Crossing the Curriculum on this page.

3. **Creative Writing**   Remind students to ask themselves what questions they need to answer before they begin to investigate source materials. Encourage them to outline their journal entries before they begin writing. Make sure students understand that they may want to write a series of entries covering several days. They may enjoy sharing their finished entries with classmates.

Crossing the Curriculum

Music

The song "On the Willows," from the 1970 Steven Schwartz musical *Godspell,* is adapted from Psalm 137, to which Rowlandson alludes. Have a volunteer read the psalm aloud (the full text is on p. 47); then, play the song for the class. Have students compare the reading to the song. Which do they prefer and why? Which has a greater emotional impact? How does the song enrich their understanding of Rowlandson's allusion?

The Southern Planters

Ⓐ In addition to the Puritan tradition of New England, there was another literary tradition in the American Colonies. This literature came from the Southern planters, also known as the Cavaliers, a group of people whose background and social views varied considerably from those of the Puritans.

There were many possible reasons for the differences. One factor may have been climate. The Southern climate was kind; it was warm and mild, and the land was enormously fertile. The Northern climate was harsher; springs and summers were brief, and winters were long and cold. Even the land in New England was hard. Its outcroppings of granite and bedrock broke plows and made farming difficult.

But economic and religious factors were even more important. The landholdings in New England were small for the most part; many colonists were small farmers or tradespeople who lived in villages and owned very little land. But the Southern planter was an aristocrat, the virtual ruler of a huge territory that was maintained by plentiful slave labor (though slavery was common in New England in those days, too).

Opposing Worldviews

Ⓑ Most Southerners belonged to the Church of England. In general, they were much more interested in the outside world—literature, music, art, politics, and the world of nature—than they were in the scrupulous examination of their own souls. Where the Puritan feared that the world's beauties were lures and sources of temptation, the Southerner saw the world as something to be conquered and enjoyed.

The Southern planters shared the worldview of the English Renaissance, with its emphasis on classical literature and scientific inquiry. Thus, when the Southerners wrote about life in America, they were apt to write about it in traditional ways. Even a work as original as *The Sot-Weed Factor* (1708), Ebenezer Cook's humorous tale of a tobacco merchant, was written in the bouncy couplets popular for satire in England.

A Renaissance Man

In many ways, William Byrd is a representative figure for the Southern writers of the Colonial period. He was truly a Renaissance man. He translated Greek and Latin works, composed original poetry (mostly satiric verse), and wrote about mathematics and medicine. Writing a generation before Thomas Jefferson (page 114), Byrd displayed the same intellectual curiosity that his fellow Virginian would so strongly exemplify later.

Byrd described the pleasures of the Southern planter's life: "I have a large family of my own, and my doors are open to everybody, yet I have no bills to pay. . . . I live in a kind of independence of everyone but Providence. . . . I must take care to keep all my people to their duty. . . . But then 'tis an amusement in this silent country."

William Byrd

(1674–1744)

It is worth remembering that Jamestown, Virginia, was named for James I, the king who vowed to harry the Puritans out of England. Virginia itself was named for Elizabeth I, the "Virgin Queen." These place names—and many others in the South—remind us of an important difference between Virginia and the Colonies of New England. New England was settled largely by those in conflict with British intellectual, theological, and social life; Virginia was settled by those in harmony with that life. By and large, the fervent, short-haired puritanical Round-heads went to New England; the aristocratic, long-haired, worldly Cavaliers went to Virginia.

William Byrd was a thorough Cavalier—worldly, sophisticated, and gentlemanly. Byrd was born in Virginia, the son of a wealthy landowner and merchant, but he was educated in England, where he spent half his life. In London, he acquired a passion for the theater, which the Puritans had once outlawed as immoral. Byrd had many scientific interests: He was even a member of the Royal Society, that pillar of the British scientific establishment.

Byrd alternated between living in England and living in Virginia. He preferred London, with its elegant homes, witty conversation, and gambling tables. During his visits to Westover, his 2,000-acre home in Virginia, he tried to keep alive both his social and intellectual life. Westover's gardens are still renowned, and its library of almost 4,000 volumes was rivaled in Byrd's time only by Cotton Mather's library in New England.

William Byrd (1704) by the Studio of Sir Godfrey Kneller. Oil on canvas.

Colonial Williamsburg Foundation, Williamsburg, Virginia (D583.1087).

Byrd had little in common with the New Englanders. He kept a diary, as many Puritans did. But the Puritans' diaries are primarily records of spiritual examination. Byrd's diary records the pleasures and practical concerns of a man of the world. Dinners, flirtations with women, literature, and natural science were of greater interest to him than matters of the spirit. In London in 1719, for example, he recorded a typical day:

> May 28. I rose about 7 o'clock and read a chapter in Hebrew and some Greek. I neglected my prayers, but had milk for breakfast. The weather was still warm and clear and very dry, the wind north. About eleven came Annie Wilkinson but I would not speak with her. I was disappointed in the [absence] of Mrs. B—s who wrote me word she would come and breakfast with me, so I read some English and ate some bread and butter because I was to dine late and about 3 o'clock went to dine with Sir Wilfred Lawson and ate some mutton. After dinner we talked a little and about 6 o'clock went to Kensington in Sir Wilfred's coach where there was a ball in the gardens and several ladies and among the rest Miss Perry whom I stuck most to and she complained I squeezed her hand. Here I stayed until 1 o'clock and then came home and neglected my prayers.

In 1728, Byrd joined a survey expedition of the disputed boundary line between Virginia and North Carolina. *The History of the Dividing Line* is far more than a simple record of that expedition. Witty and elegantly written, it is filled with philosophical observations and barbed comments on American Colonial life.

go.hrw.com
LEO 11-1

OBJECTIVES

1. Read and interpret the historical narrative
2. Identify and evaluate satire
3. Identify tone
4. Express understanding through critical and creative writing
5. Understand and use new words

SKILLS

Literary
- Identify and evaluate satire

Reading
- Identify tone

Writing
- Craft phrases that help vividly describe a significant experience
- Compare purpose, tone, and style of two historical narratives
- Write a journal entry

Vocabulary
- Use new words

Viewing/Representing
- Analyze a landscape painting (ATE)

Planning

- **Block Schedule**
  Block Scheduling Lesson Plans with Pacing Guide
- **Traditional Schedule**
  Lesson Plans Including Strategies for English-Language Learners
- **One-Stop Planner**
  CD-ROM with Test Generator

BROWSING IN THE FILES

About the Author. *The History of the Dividing Line* is only one of the histories Byrd wrote about the survey of the disputed boundary. The other was his private journal, written in code, and often referred to as *The Secret History.* Here he recorded private thoughts, applied unflattering nicknames to some members of the expedition, and revealed information that would have caused a scandal had it become generally known. Byrd used *The Secret History* to write *The History of the Dividing Line,* a formal account intended for publication.

Resources: Print and Media

Reading
- *Graphic Organizers for Active Reading,* p. 3
- *Words to Own,* p. 4
- *Audio CD Library*
  Disc 2, Track 3

Writing and Language
- *Daily Oral Grammar*
  Transparency 4
- *Grammar and Language Links*
  Worksheet, p. 5

Viewing and Representing
- *Visual Connections*
  Videocassette A, Segment 3

Assessment
- *Formal Assessment,* p. 7
- *Portfolio Management System,* p. 91
- *Test Generator (One-Stop Planner CD-ROM)*

Internet
- go.hrw.com (keyword: LEO 11-1)

T/

Summary ■ ■

William Byrd satirizes the aims, character, and practices of the earliest settlers of Virginia, dismissing them as idle adventurers. He argues that the English would have better relations with the Indians if they intermarried with them as the French did. He compares his guide's Native American religion with Christianity and notes three major tenets they share.

Resources

Videocassette A, Segment 3
This segment explores the American dream through our literary heritage, from its beginnings through the rise of Realism. Available in English and Spanish. For full lesson plans, see the *Visual Connections Teacher's Manual.*

Ⓐ Elements of Literature
Satire
❓ What does a "saunter to the Holy Land" allude to? [the Crusades of the Middle Ages] **Why is the phrase satirical?** [A saunter is a casual stroll, but Crusaders did not saunter to a holy war. They moved with the militant purpose of fierce conquerors, and this irony makes the phrase satirical.]

Ⓑ Literary Connections
Remind students of the rosy picture John Smith gave of America (p. 36).

Before You Read
FROM THE HISTORY OF THE DIVIDING LINE

Make the Connection
The Observer's Eye
Byrd's *History of the Dividing Line* is a record of personal experience, written while Byrd was helping out on a survey expedition. Byrd must have realized the value of his experience, understanding that a journey of any kind is an opportunity to observe and learn. By paying close attention—by seeing clearly, not merely looking—any traveler can learn about people, places, and practices that are different from those with which he or she is familiar.

Reading Skills and Strategies

Identifying Tone
In the first extract from the *History,* Byrd ironically describes the "modish frenzy" of early travelers to America, a fashionable craze that he compares to a "distemper" or illness. As you read each section of Byrd's journal, pay attention to Byrd's **tone.** Jot down any words, phrases, or expressions that make Byrd seem very "modern"—and funny.

Elements of Literature
Satire
The ironic, barbed approach Byrd takes in his *History* is in sharp contrast to the straightforward style of a Puritan such as William Bradford (page 26). Like many British writers of his time, Byrd excels at **satire,** the use of ridicule to expose the shortcomings of things he observes.

Background
William Byrd began his *History* in 1728. By then, more than a century had passed since the first English settlers reached Virginia. Byrd's journal was found among his personal papers after his death and wasn't published until 1841.

> **S**atire is a type of writing that ridicules the shortcomings of people or institutions, usually in an attempt to bring about some change.
>
> *For more on Satire, see the Handbook of Literary Terms.*

from
The History of the Dividing Line
William Byrd

Early Virginia Colonies

Ⓐ ⎡ **A**s it happened some ages before to be the fashion to saunter to the Holy Land and go upon other Quixote adventures,[1] so it was now grown the humor to take a trip to America. The Spaniards had lately discovered rich mines in their part of the West Indies, which made their maritime ⎣ neighbors eager to do so too. This modish frenzy,

Ⓑ ⎡ being still more inflamed by the charming account given of Virginia by the first adventurers, made ⎣ many fond of removing to such a Paradise.

Happy was he, and still happier she, that could

1. **Quixote** (kē·hōt′ē) **adventures:** foolish adventures, like those taken by the mad hero of Miguel de Cervantes's novel *The Ingenious Gentleman Don Quixote de la Mancha.*

Preteaching Vocabulary

Words to Own
Have students read the Words to Own and their definitions listed at the bottom of the selection pages. Then, have them choose partners and use the pronunciation guides to sound out each word correctly. After pronouncing, they can take turns giving one another words to define until each student can define them all. Afterwards, individual students should complete the following exercise by matching each word with its synonym.

1. disdained [e]	**a.** crowded
2. venerable [g]	**b.** relieve
3. propagated [h]	**c.** cautious
4. prudent [c]	**d.** get
5. populous [a]	**e.** scorned
6. eminent [i]	**f.** scoundrels
7. allay [b]	**g.** respected
8. procure [d]	**h.** spread
9. reprobates [f]	**i.** important
10. squeamish [j]	**j.** oversensitive

get themselves transported, fondly expecting their coarsest utensils in that happy place would be of massy[2] silver.

This made it easy for the Company to procure as many volunteers as they wanted for their new colony, but, like most other undertakers who have no assistance from the public, they starved the design by too much frugality; for, unwilling to launch out at first into too much expense, they shipped off but few people at a time, and those but scantily provided. The adventurers were, besides, idle and extravagant and expected they might live without work in so plentiful a country.

These wretches were set ashore not far from Roanoke Inlet, but by some fatal disagreement or laziness were either starved or cut to pieces by the Indians.

Several repeated misadventures of this kind did for some time allay the itch of sailing to this new world, but the distemper broke out again about the year 1606. Then it happened that the Earl of Southampton and several other persons eminent for their quality and estates were invited into the Company, who applied themselves once more to people the then almost abandoned colony. For this purpose they embarked about an hundred men, most of them reprobates of good families and related to some of the Company who were men of quality and fortune.

The ships that carried them made a shift to find a more direct way to Virginia and ventured

2. **massy:** weighty.

WORDS TO OWN

procure (prō·kyoor′) v.: to gain; obtain; acquire.
allay (ə·lā′) v.: lessen; relieve.
eminent (em′ə·nənt) adj.: well known for excellence; important; outstanding.
reprobates (rep′rə·bāts′) n. pl.: people without any sense of duty or decency.

The Plantation (c. 1825). Unknown American artist. Oil on wood (19⅛″ × 29½″).

The Metropolitan Museum of Art, Gift of Edgar William and Bernice Chrysler Garbisch, 1963 (63.201.3). Photograph © 1984 The Metropolitan Museum of Art.

WILLIAM BYRD 51

A Elements of Literature
Style
? Compare this passage to a passage in *Of Plymouth Plantation*. Which style seems more modern? Why? [Byrd's; Students may identify shorter sentence length, less convoluted syntax and punctuation, colloquial diction, lively rhythm, and relatively brief paragraphs as stylistic elements that make Byrd's text seem more modern.]

B Elements of Literature
Satire
? What are the satirical elements in this sentence? [It is ironic that the leaders spend their time arguing instead of administering the colony. Byrd also satirizes the laziness of the settlers in the phrase "detested work more than famine."]

C Reading Skills and Strategies

Identifying Tone
? How would you describe the tone of this sentence? Explain. [Possible answers: sarcastic, humorous; Byrd exaggerates for effect.] **What does he suggest about the colonists' priorities?** [They value drink more than religion.]

D Critical Thinking
Expressing an Opinion
? Do you agree with Byrd? [Most students will agree with Byrd. The English welcoming Indians into their families would have been a sign of respect and racial equality.] **Is Byrd serious?** [Possible answers: Given the general tone of the piece, Byrd is probably not serious; Byrd is serious—he respects Indians and finds the English settlers hypocritical.]

E Appreciating Language
Connotations
? In Byrd's day, lewdness meant sexual promiscuity and luxury was viewed as moral decay. What is Byrd implying about the Indians in this statement? [He is favorably contrasting Native Americans with the English. Having already accused the English people of laziness and drunkenness, he now accuses them of lechery and suggests that the Indians are morally superior.]

A through the capes into the Bay of Chesapeake. The same night they came to an anchor at the mouth of Powhatan, the same as James River, where they built a small fort at a place called Point Comfort.

B This settlement stood its ground from that time forward, in spite of all the blunders and disagreement of the first adventurers and the many calamities that befell the colony afterward. The six gentlemen who were first named of the Company by the Crown and who were empowered to choose an annual president from among themselves were always engaged in factions and quarrels, while the rest detested work more than famine. At this rate the colony must have come to nothing had it not been for the vigilance and bravery of Captain Smith,[3] who struck a terror into all the Indians round about. This gentleman took some pains to persuade the men to plant Indian corn, but they looked upon all labor as a curse. They chose rather to depend upon the musty provisions that were sent from England; and when they failed they were forced to take more pains to seek for wild fruits in the woods than they would have taken in tilling the ground. Besides, this exposed them to be knocked in the head by the Indians and gave them fluxes[4] into the bargain, which thinned the plantation very much. To supply this mortality, they were reinforced the year following with a greater number of people, amongst which were fewer gentlemen and more laborers, who, however, took care not to kill themselves with work. These found the first adventurers in a very starving condition but relieved their wants with the fresh supply they brought with them. From Kecoughtan[5] they extended themselves as far as Jamestown, **C** where, like true Englishmen, they built a church that cost no more than fifty pounds and a tavern that cost five hundred.

3. **Captain Smith:** John Smith (c. 1580–1631) helped found Jamestown, Virginia, the first permanent English settlement in America.
4. **fluxes** (fluks′iz): dysentery; severe diarrhea.
5. **Kecoughtan** (kē′kō′tan): present-day site of Hampton, Virginia.

> As the Colony grew, violence frequently erupted between the settlers and the American Indians. Byrd offers his solution to the conflicts between the two cultures.

Intermarriage

They had now made peace with the Indians, but there was one thing wanting to make that peace **D** lasting. The natives could by no means persuade themselves that the English were heartily their friends so long as they disdained to intermarry with them. And, in earnest, had the English consulted their own security and the good of the colony, had they intended either to civilize or convert these gentiles,[6] they would have brought their stomachs to embrace this prudent alliance.

The Indians are generally tall and well proportioned, which may make full amends for the darkness of their complexions. Add to this that **E** they are healthy and strong, with constitutions untainted by lewdness and not enfeebled by luxury. Besides, morals and all considered, I cannot think the Indians were much greater heathens than the first adventurers, who, had they been good Christians, would have had the charity to take this only method of converting the natives to Christianity. For, after all that can

6. **gentiles** (jen′tīlz′): here, nonbelievers. Historically, among Christians, *gentile* meant a pagan or nonbeliever. (*Gentile* comes from a Latin word meaning "foreigner.") The term is more commonly used by Jews to refer to those who are not Jewish.

WORDS TO OWN
disdained (dis·dānd′) *v.*: refused; disapproved; scorned.
prudent (prōōd′'nt) *adj.*: well thought out; cautious.

Using Students' Strengths

Visual Learners
Ask students if they ever look at satirical cartoons in the weekly newsmagazines. Point out that these cartoons make fun of our government officials the way Byrd makes fun of the Virginia aristocrats. Have students choose a public figure they want to poke fun at and sketch a quick satirical cartoon.

Naturalist Learners
Encourage students to find out about the life and work of John Bartram (1699–1777), considered the father of American botany. Just a few years after Byrd's work, Bartram was exploring the same part of the world, hunting for American plants. He established a botanical garden at his home near Philadelphia, which has since been revived.

be said, a sprightly lover is the most prevailing[7] missionary that can be sent amongst these or any other infidels.

Besides, the poor Indians would have had less reason to complain that the English took away their land if they had received it by way of a portion with their daughters. Had such affinities been contracted in the beginning, how much bloodshed had been prevented and how <u>populous</u> would the country have been, and, consequently, how considerable! Nor would the shade of the skin have been any reproach at this day, for if a Moor may be washed white in three generations, surely an Indian might have been blanched in two.

The French, for their parts, have not been so <u>squeamish</u> in Canada, who upon trial find abundance of attraction in the Indians. Their late grand monarch thought it not below even the dignity of a Frenchman to become one flesh with this people and therefore ordered 100 livres[8] for any of his subjects, man or woman, that would intermarry with a native.

By this piece of policy we find the French interest very much strengthened amongst the savages and their religion, such as it is, <u>propagated</u> just as far as their love. And I heartily wish this well-concerted scheme don't hereafter give the French an advantage over His Majesty's good subjects on the northern continent of America.

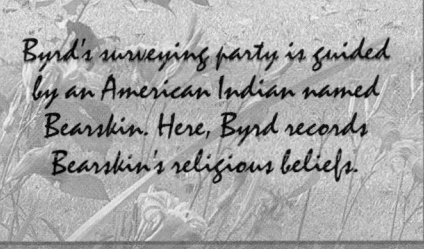

Byrd's surveying party is guided by an American Indian named Bearskin. Here, Byrd records Bearskin's religious beliefs.

7. **prevailing** (prē·vāl'iŋ): convincing.
8. **livres** (lē'vərz): former French monetary unit worth about a pound of silver each.

The Native Religion

In the evening we examined our friend Bearskin concerning the religion of his country, and he explained it to us without any of that reserve to which his nation is subject. He told us he believed there was one supreme god, who had several subaltern[9] deities under him. And that this master god made the world a long time ago. That he told the sun, the moon, and stars their business in the beginning, which they, with good looking-after, have faithfully performed ever since. That the same power that made all things at first has taken care to keep them in the same method and motion ever since. He believed that God had formed many worlds before he formed this, but that those worlds either grew old and ruinous or were destroyed for the dishonesty of the inhabitants. That God is very just and very good, ever well pleased with those men who possess those godlike qualities. That he takes good people into his safe protection, makes them very rich, fills their bellies plentifully, preserves them from sickness and from being surprised or overcome by their enemies. But all such as tell lies and cheat those they have dealings with he never fails to punish with sickness, poverty, and hunger and, after all that, suffers them to be knocked on the head and scalped by those that fight against them.

He believed that after death both good and bad people are conducted by a strong guard into a great road, in which departed souls travel together for some time till at a certain distance this road forks into two paths, the one extremely level and the other stony and mountainous. Here the good are parted from the bad

9. **subaltern** (səb·ôl'tərn): subordinate; of inferior rank or position.

WORDS TO OWN
populous (päp'yoo·ləs) *adj.*: crowded with people.
squeamish (skwēm'ish) *adj.*: easily offended.
propagated (präp'ə·gāt'id) *v.*: transmitted or spread.

WILLIAM BYRD **53**

Skill Link

Evaluating the Credibility of Information
Review the difference between fact and opinion using a current news story and a related editorial cartoon. Point out the value of verifying the facts and their sources. Remind students that satire calls for readers to be familiar enough with circumstances to know when a writer is exaggerating or understating the facts. Then, have students complete the following activities.

1. Have students evaluate whether Byrd's statements about the early English colonists are credible. Does Byrd state facts or opinions? Does he provide evidence?
2. Once students have finished reading, have the class discuss Byrd's motivation for writing. Does Byrd expect his reader to take his statements at face value? Does his exaggeration make him less credible? Why or why not?

A Critical Thinking

Analyzing

❓ What strikes you about this description of the place good Indians go after death? [The place is exactly like the one they live in now, but without any of its hardships. It has all the same animals and crops and the weather the Indians enjoy in May.]

B Reading Skills and Strategies

Making Inferences

❓ Note the reference to the "crystal gate." Do you think Byrd is embellishing Bearskin's story? [Possible responses: Yes, Native Americans probably didn't say "crystal"; no, he is probably trying to give a clear description to English readers.]

C Literary Connections

Greek Freaks

The Furies are three sisters, each with a dog's head, bat's wings, and snakes for hair. Harpies are birds with women's heads. The woman with hair of writhing snakes reminds the reader of another figure from Greek mythology— Medusa, the Gorgon who turned her victims into stone. The link Byrd points out between Native American and ancient Greek religions suggests that religions from all times and places share certain images and symbols.

D Reading Skills and Strategies

Identifying Tone

To be in a "state of nature" is to be untouched by civilization. The use of the word *mere* is probably condescending, but points to a degree of respect for people who had not entered John Locke's "social contract" and gained the "advantages" of religion and philosophy.

E Humanities Connections

Deism

The phrase "natural religion" is an allusion to deism. Popular during the Enlightenment, deism is a religion founded on reason rather than on faith or revelation. A deist believes in God because the natural world and its wonders are evidence of God's existence. Prominent American deists included Benjamin Franklin, Thomas Jefferson, and George Washington.

A by a flash of lightning, the first being hurried away to the right, the other to the left. The right-hand road leads to a charming, warm country, where the spring is everlasting and every month is May; and as the year is always in its youth, so are the people, and particularly the women are bright as stars and never scold. That in this happy climate there are deer, turkeys, elks, and buffaloes innumerable, perpetually fat and gentle, while the trees are loaded with delicious fruit quite throughout the four seasons. That the soil brings forth corn spontaneously, without the curse of labor, and so very wholesome that none who have the happiness to eat of it are ever sick, grow old, or die. Near the entrance into this blessed land sits a <u>venerable</u> old man on a mat richly woven, who examines strictly all that are brought before him, and if they have behaved well, the **B** guards are ordered to open the crystal gate and let them enter into the land of delight.

The left-hand path is very rugged and uneven, leading to a dark and barren country where it is always winter. The ground is the whole year round covered with snow, and nothing is to be seen upon the trees but icicles. All the people are hungry yet have not a morsel of anything to eat except a bitter kind of potato, that gives them the dry gripes[10] and fills their whole body with loathsome ulcers that stink and are insupportably painful. Here all the women are old and ugly, having claws like a panther with which they fly upon the men that slight their passion. For it seems these haggard old furies[11] are intolerably fond and expect a vast deal of cherishing. They talk much and exceedingly shrill, giving exquisite pain to the drum of the **C** ear, which in that place of the torment is so tender that every sharp note wounds it to the quick. At the end of this path sits a dreadful old woman on a monstrous toadstool, whose head is covered with rattlesnakes instead of tresses, with glaring white eyes that strike a terror un-

---

10. dry gripes: stomach cramps.
11. furies (fyoor′ēz): violent, vengeful women. In Greek and Roman mythology, the Furies are fierce avenging spirits.

---

speakable into all that behold her. This hag pronounces sentence of woe upon all the miserable wretches that hold up their hands at her tribunal. After this they are delivered over to huge turkey buzzards, like harpies,[12] that fly away with them to the place above mentioned. Here, after they have been tormented a certain number of years according to their several degrees of guilt, they are again driven back into this world to try if they will mend their manners and merit a place the next time in the regions of bliss.

D This was the substance of Bearskin's religion and was as much to the purpose as could be expected from a mere state of nature, without one glimpse of revelation or philosophy. It contained, however, the three great articles of natural religion: the belief of a god, the moral **E** distinction between good and evil, and the expectation of rewards and punishments in another world.

---

12. harpies (här′pēz): evil mythological creatures with women's heads and birds' wings and legs.

WORDS TO OWN

venerable (ven′ər·ə·bəl) *adj.*: respected; esteemed for age or distinguished character.

Making the Connections

Connecting to the Theme: "Visions and Voyages"

After students have finished reading the history, discuss the collection theme. What does Byrd think about the vision of the first English settlers in Virginia? Would he have gone with them if he had been born and raised in England? List students' ideas and reactions on the board, and have a class discussion about them.

First Thoughts

1. Did 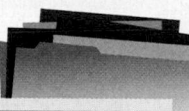 you find Byrd more or less interesting than the other Colonial writers you've read? What passages did you record in your reading notes because they struck you as funny or "modern"?

Shaping Interpretations

2. Describe Byrd's **tone**—his attitude toward his subject, the people he mentions, and his intended audience. Does the tone remain consistent throughout, or does it change? Cite passages to support your analysis.

3. What examples of **satire** did you find in Byrd's account of the early settlers of Virginia? Based on this scathing portrait, what personal qualities do you think Byrd admired?

4. Why might Byrd's observations on the first settlements in Virginia be less reliable than Bradford's on the Plymouth Colony (page 28)?

5. According to his description of Bearskin's religious beliefs, what "articles," or elements, of religion does Byrd consider most important? How closely do his views agree with those expressed by Mary Rowlandson (page 40)?

Extending the Text

6. What issues, events, or attitudes in American society today would be good topics for **satire?**

Reading Check

a. What reasons does Byrd suggest for the failure of the first Virginia settlements?

b. Explain Byrd's point of view about the first colonists and their expectations of life in North America.

c. Why does Byrd favor intermarriage with American Indians?

d. What, according to Byrd, are the three basic religious beliefs of Bearskin, the American Indian guide?

CHOICES:
Building Your Portfolio

Writer's Notebook

1. Collecting Ideas for an Autobiographical Incident

Byrd's keen perceptions and mastery of the language resulted in phrases such as this: ". . . their coarsest utensils . . . would be of massy silver" (page 51). Make a list of phrases that describe vividly an experience you have had that was significant in some way. Keep your notes; you may find them useful in the Writer's Workshop on page 130.

Comparing Texts

2. Different as Night and Day

In a brief essay, compare and contrast the excerpts from Byrd's *History* with William Bradford's account of the Puritan landing at Plymouth (pages 28–33). Consider specifically how the two accounts differ in **purpose, tone,** and **style.**

Creative Writing

3. Puritans and Planters

Imagine that you are a Puritan who has just returned from a visit to Jamestown. In a journal entry, describe the Southern planters, their approach to life, their physical appearance, and their interests, contrasting them with members of your own Puritan society.

Reading Check

a. lack of provisions, laziness, ignorance, and conflict with Native Americans

b. According to Byrd, the English expected to become rich quickly without work.

c. Byrd suggests that intermarriage would promote good relations.

d. Bearskin believes in one supreme God, in the moral distinction between good and evil, and in an afterlife that rewards good and punishes evil.

First Thoughts [Respond]

1. Students will almost certainly have found Byrd easier and more entertaining reading than Bradford or Rowlandson. Examples of both humor and a modern sensibility include comments about the Englishmen's laziness and the money they spent on the tavern.

Shaping Interpretations [Interpret]

2. Byrd is sarcastic toward the English throughout. He draws the reader in to laugh with him at their pretensions. Passages include "reprobates of good families" (p. 51), "detested work more than famine" (p. 52), and "tavern that cost five hundred" (p. 52).

3. Byrd repeatedly exaggerates the laziness, drunkenness, and ignorance of the English; Byrd seems to admire practical industry and common sense.

4. Possible answers: Bradford was an eyewitness to the events he describes, while Byrd was not; Bradford's plain style shows a concern with reporting facts, whereas Byrd's tone suggests a greater concern with style than with accuracy.

5. Byrd mentions belief in a god, the distinction between good and evil, and the concept of an afterlife in which sins will be punished and virtue rewarded. Rowlandson shares these beliefs, but would consider even the most mundane event as evidence of God's will.

Extending the Text [Synthesize]

6. Possible answers: fans' obsession with TV series; news media coverage of celebrities' personal lives.

Grading Timesaver

Rubrics for each Choices assignment appear on p. 91 in the *Portfolio Management System.*

OBJECTIVES

1. Read and interpret the autobiography
2. Analyze autobiography
3. Express understanding through creative writing, critical writing, and illustration
4. Understand and use new words

SKILLS

Literary
- Analyze an autobiography

Writing
- Write about a time you defended your rights
- Compare and contrast two texts that recount related events

Art
- Write and illustrate a children's book

Vocabulary
- Use new words

Viewing/Representing
- Compare the impact of images to the impact of verbal description (ATE)

Planning

- **Block Schedule**
  Block Scheduling Lesson Plans with Pacing Guide
- **Traditional Schedule**
  Lesson Plans Including Strategies for English-Language Learners
- **One-Stop Planner**
  CD-ROM with Test Generator

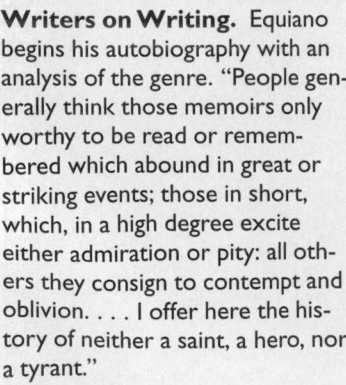

BROWSING IN THE FILES

Writers on Writing. Equiano begins his autobiography with an analysis of the genre. "People generally think those memoirs only worthy to be read or remembered which abound in great or striking events; those in short, which, in a high degree excite either admiration or pity: all others they consign to contempt and oblivion. . . . I offer here the history of neither a saint, a hero, nor a tyrant."

Olaudah Equiano

(c. 1745–1797)

Portrait of a Negro Man, Olaudah Equiano in 1780s, by English School (eighteenth century), previously attributed to Joshua Reynolds. Oil on canvas.

Royal Albert Memorial Museum, Exeter/Bridgeman Art Library, London/New York.

Olaudah Equiano (ō·lōō′dä ek′wē·än′o) was the first African writer to reach a sizable audience of American readers. A member of the Ibo people, Equiano was born in a part of West Africa that is now Nigeria. When he was only eleven years old, Equiano, along with his sister, was kidnapped from his home by African raiders involved in the slave trade. Over a period of six or seven months, during which he and his sister were separated, the slave traders took Equiano to a series of way stations. When he reached the coast, Equiano was put aboard one of the infamous slave ships bound for Barbados, an island in the West Indies, in the Caribbean. Slave labor was in demand to work on the sugar plantations in the Caribbean. In his narrative, Equiano vividly describes this cruel and horrifying part of the slave route, which was known as "the Middle Passage."

After a short stay in Barbados, Equiano was sold to a British military officer, who gave him the name Gustavus Vassa, after a Swedish king. Equiano served with this officer during the Seven Years' War between England and France and gained great skill as a seaman. In time, a Quaker merchant from Philadelphia purchased Equiano. From his own profitable business ventures while managing his master's business, Equiano saved enough money to purchase his freedom in 1766, after having been enslaved for almost ten years. He was about twenty-one years old.

After buying his freedom, Equiano worked as a sailor and led an exciting and adventurous life, sailing on exploratory expeditions to the Arctic and Central America. He finally settled in England, where he made his living as a free servant, a musician, and a barber. He also became active in the antislavery movement. In 1781, the captain of the *Zong,* which was transporting more than four hundred Africans to Jamaica, threw overboard a third of the shackled captives in order to collect the insurance. In 1783, Equiano was instrumental in bringing this atrocity to the attention of the public and the British naval authorities. When the abolition of the slave trade became a hotly debated issue in the English Parliament, Equiano actively campaigned against slavery, writing letters to officials and newspapers and visiting abolitionist leaders.

Equiano's autobiography, published in England in 1789, was titled *The Interesting Narrative of the Life of Olaudah Equiano, or Gustavus Vassa, the African.* Reprinted in New York in 1791, the book—considered the first great black autobiography—proved popular with readers in the United States as well as abroad. The author's account of the horrors he suffered struck a responsive chord with northern abolitionists, but by then Equiano had settled in London. In 1792, he married an Englishwoman, Susanna Cullen.

Though Equiano traveled widely, he never returned to the United States. Nor did he ever again see his native Africa, to which he dreamed of returning. He defined himself, to the end of his life, simply as "the African."

go.hrw.com
LE0 11-1

Resources: Print and Media

Reading
- *Graphic Organizers for Active Reading,* p. 4
- *Words to Own,* p. 5
- *Audio CD Library*
  Disc 2, Track 4

Writing and Language
- *Daily Oral Grammar*
  Transparency 5
- *Grammar and Language Links*
  Worksheet, p. 7

Assessment
- *Formal Assessment,* p. 9
- *Portfolio Management System,* p. 92
- *Preparation for College Admission Exams,* p. 3
- *Test Generator (One-Stop Planner CD-ROM)*

Internet
- go.hrw.com (keyword: LE0 11-1)

Before You Read

Make the Connection
Against Their Will
The first Africans in the Americas were unwilling immigrants who arrived on slave ships before 1600. Between the seventeenth and nineteenth centuries, about ten million people were captured in Africa and shipped to North and South America and the islands of the West Indies, where they were enslaved. People were literally seized from their homes and sold as commodities, with no thought for their human rights.

Quickwrite
Before you read Equiano's account, make a KWL chart like the one below. Fill out the first two columns—what you already know about slavery and the slave trade in the eighteenth century and what you'd like to learn about it. Leave the third column blank.

K What I Know	W What I Want to Know	L What I Learned

Elements of Literature
Autobiography
Equiano's **autobiography** is one of the first slave narratives by a black African to be published. Many accounts of the horrors of slavery were firsthand accounts used by abolitionists in the nineteenth century to fuel the crusade against slavery.

An **autobiography** is a firsthand account of a writer's own life.

For more on Autobiography, see the Handbook of Literary Terms.

---

from The Interesting Narrative of the Life of Olaudah Equiano

Olaudah Equiano

Kidnapped

My father, besides many slaves, had a numerous family of which seven lived to grow up, including myself and a sister who was the only daughter. As I was the youngest of the sons I became, of course, the greatest favorite with my mother and was always with her; and she used to take particular pains to form my mind. I was trained up from my earliest years in the art of war, my daily exercise was shooting and throwing javelins, and my mother adorned me with emblems after the manner of our greatest warriors. In this way I grew up till I was turned the age of 11, when an end was put to my happiness in the following manner. Generally when the grown people in the neighborhood were gone far in the

OLAUDAH EQUIANO **57**

Summary ■■

Equiano's autobiography opens with a brief description of his life as the pampered youngest son of an Ibo warrior. When he is eleven, he and his sister are kidnapped and separated. Equiano is sold to a series of African slave owners who treat him humanely, but he eventually ends up on a slave ship heading for the West Indies. His first sight of the white crew frightens him badly; in fact, he is afraid they will eat him. Equiano is put in the ship's hold, where the terrible stench and miserable overcrowding cause a few of his fellow captives to attempt suicide by jumping into the sea. Two, still chained together, succeed. When the ship docks in Barbados, the Africans are auctioned off with no regard to family members' desire to be kept together. Equiano ends with a persuasive meditation on the hypocrisy of so-called Christians who forget God's instruction to "do unto others as you would have them do unto you."

Ⓐ Historical Connections
Slave Narratives
Marion Wilson Starling reports that of the estimated sixty thousand slaves who escaped to freedom, more than six thousand wrote down or told their stories to interviewers between 1703 and 1944—an enormous accomplishment of testimony from people coming out of slavery.

Ⓑ Reading Skills and Strategies
Responding to the Text
❓ What is your reaction to the opening sentence? [Students may be surprised to learn that Africans enslaved one another or that Equiano was from a wealthy family.]

Preteaching Vocabulary

Words to Own
Have students read the Words to Own and their definitions listed at the bottom of the text on the selection pages. Have them look up the etymology of each word and search for ways to remember the word's meaning. Then, have students match each of the following words with its opposite, or antonym.

1. assailant [f]	a. extreme
2. distraction [j]	b. careful
3. commodious [d]	c. separate
4. dejection [g]	d. cramped
5. copious [i]	e. aggravate
6. improvident [b]	f. defender
7. moderate [a]	g. joy
8. countenances [h]	h. backs
9. alleviate [e]	i. few
10. interspersed [c]	j. calmness

Background

As early as 1517, sugar cane plantations in the Caribbean began using Africans as slaves. The first slaves in the colonies arrived in 1619 to work in the tobacco fields of Virginia. Over the next three centuries, ten to twelve million slaves were shipped to the New World. On the Middle Passage between Africa and the Americas, approximately two million captives died because of inhuman conditions and abuse.

Ⓐ Elements of Literature
Autobiography
❓ Why does Equiano provide this information? [Possible answers: to set up his own kidnapping; to establish that he grew up under the threat of enslavement.]

Ⓑ Struggling Readers
Finding the Sequence of Events
Point out time phrases such as "the next morning." Ask students to use these to create a time line of the events in the autobiography. This device will help them track Equiano's movements west. Students may want to work on time lines with partners.

RESPONDING TO THE ART
The pictures and diagrams of slave ships shown on pp. 58 and 61–63 reflect conditions at the height of the African slave trade in the seventeenth to nineteenth centuries. **Activity.** Have students read on until they reach the passages from Equiano's narrative that describe the conditions of the captives in the hold (p. 63). How do these illustrations compare with Equiano's description? [Possible answer: All these works depict inhumanely crowded conditions. In the watercolor, the slaves are uncomfortable and confined but, unlike Equiano's description, apparently able to move around. The drawing on pp. 62–63, however, reflects Equiano's horrifying account of people crammed together like cargo.]

---

fields to labor, the children assembled together in some of the neighbors' premises to play, and commonly some of us used to get up a tree to look for any assailant or kidnapper that might come upon us, for they sometimes took those opportunities of our parents' absence to attack and carry off as many as they could seize. One day, as I was watching at the top of a tree in our yard, I saw one of those people come into the yard of our next neighbor but one to kidnap, there being many stout young people in it. Immediately on this I gave the alarm of the rogue and he was surrounded by the stoutest of them, who entangled him with cords so that he could not escape till some of the grown people came and secured him.

But alas! ere long it was my fate to be thus attacked and to be carried off when none of the grown people were nigh. One day, when all our people were gone out to their works as usual and only I and my dear sister were left to mind the house, two men and a woman got over our walls, and in a moment seized us both, and without giving us time to cry out or make resistance they stopped our mouths and ran off with us into the nearest wood. Here they tied our hands and continued to carry us as far as they could till night came on, when we reached a small house where the robbers halted for refreshment and spent the night. We were then unbound but were unable to take any food, and being quite overpowered by fatigue and grief, our only relief was some sleep, which allayed our misfortune for a short time. The next morning we left the house and continued traveling all the day. For a long time we had kept to the woods, but at last we came into a road which I believed I knew. I had now some hopes of being delivered, for we had advanced but a little way before I discovered some people at a distance,

WORDS TO OWN
assailant (ə·sāl′ənt) *n.*: attacker.

Slave Deck of the Albanoz (1843–1847) by Lt. Francis Meynell. Watercolor on paper.
National Maritime Museum, Greenwich, England.

58 BEGINNINGS

Reaching All Students

Struggling Readers
Equiano uses words in unusual, often outdated ways. Explain the following to students:
- (p. 59) "anxiety after her fate" means "anxiety about her fate";
- (p. 60) "slaves to attend her" means "slaves to wait upon her";
- (p. 62) "eatables" means "things to eat";
- (p. 64) "They put us in separate parcels" means "they put us into different lots"

English Language Learners
Point out that English was not Equiano's first language. He heard it first when he was eleven or twelve—and yet his autobiography is written in a fluent and effective English prose style. You might use this example of second-language acquisition to encourage students.

on which I began to cry out for assistance: But my cries had no other effect than to make them tie me faster and stop my mouth, and then they put me into a large sack. They also stopped my sister's mouth and tied her hands, and in this manner we proceeded till we were out of the sight of these people.

When we went to rest the following night they offered us some victuals, but we refused it, and the only comfort we had was in being in one another's arms all that night and bathing each other with our tears. But alas! we were soon deprived of even the small comfort of weeping together. The next day proved a day of greater sorrow than I had yet experienced, for my sister and I were then separated while we lay clasped in each other's arms. It was in vain that we besought them not to part us; she was torn from me and immediately carried away, while I was left in a state of distraction not to be described. I cried and grieved continually, and for several days I did not eat anything but what they forced into my mouth. At length, after many days' traveling, during which I had often changed masters, I got into the hands of a chieftain in a very pleasant country. This man had two wives and some children, and they all used me extremely well and did all they could to comfort me, particularly the first wife, who was something like my mother. Although I was a great many days' journey from my father's house, yet these people spoke exactly the same language with us. This first master of mine, as I may call him, was a smith, and my principal employment was working his bellows, which were the same kind as I had seen in my vicinity. They were in some respects not unlike the stoves here in gentlemen's kitchens, and were covered over with leather; and in the middle of that leather a stick was fixed, and a person stood up and worked it in the same manner as is done to pump water out of a cask with a hand pump. I believe it was gold he worked, for it was of a lovely bright yellow color and was worn by the women on their wrists and ankles. . . .

Soon after this my master's only daughter and child by his first wife sickened and died, which affected him so much that for some time he was almost frantic, and really would have killed himself had he not been watched and prevented. However, in a small time afterward he recovered and I was again sold. I was now carried to the left of the sun's rising, through many different countries and a number of large woods. The people I was sold to used to carry me very often when I was tired either on their shoulders or on their backs. I saw many convenient well-built sheds along the roads at proper distances, to accommodate the merchants and travelers who lay in those buildings along with their wives, who often accompany them; and they always go well armed.

From the time I left my own nation I always found somebody that understood me till I came to the seacoast. The languages of different nations did not totally differ, nor were they so copious as those of the Europeans, particularly the English. They were therefore easily learned, and while I was journeying thus through Africa I acquired two or three different tongues. In this manner I had been traveling for a considerable time, when one evening, to my great surprise, whom should I see brought to the house where I was but my dear sister! As soon as she saw me she gave a loud shriek and ran into my arms—I was quite overpowered: Neither of us could speak, but for a considerable time clung to each other in mutual embraces, unable to do anything but weep. Our meeting affected all who saw us, and indeed I must acknowledge, in honor of those sable destroyers of human rights, that I never met with any ill-treatment or saw any offered to their slaves except tying them, when necessary, to keep them from running away.

When these people knew we were brother and sister they indulged us to be together, and the man to whom I supposed we belonged lay with us, he in the middle while she and I held one another by the hands across his breast all night; and thus for a while we forgot our misfortunes in the joy of being together: But even this small comfort was soon to have an end, for scarcely had the fatal morning appeared when she was again torn from me forever! I was now more miserable, if possible, than before. The small relief which her presence gave me from pain was gone, and the wretchedness of my situation was redoubled by my anxiety after her fate and my apprehensions

---

WORDS TO OWN

distraction (di·strak'shən) *n.:* mental disturbance or distress.

OLAUDAH EQUIANO 59

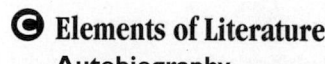

Crossing the Curriculum

lest her sufferings should be greater than mine, when I could not be with her to alleviate them. . . .

I did not long remain after my sister. I was again sold and carried through a number of places till, after traveling a considerable time, I came to a town called Tinmah in the most beautiful country I had yet seen in Africa. It was extremely rich, and there were many rivulets which flowed through it and supplied a large pond in the center of town, where the people washed. Here I first saw and tasted coconuts, which I thought superior to any nuts I had ever tasted before; and the trees, which were loaded, were also interspersed amongst the houses, which had commodious shades adjoining and were in the same manner as ours, the insides being neatly plastered and whitewashed. Here I also saw and tasted for the first time sugar cane. Their money consisted of little white shells the size of the fingernail. I was sold here for 172 of them by a merchant who lived and brought me there. I had been about two or three days at his house when a wealthy widow, a neighbor of his, came there one evening, and brought with her an only son, a young gentleman about my own age and size. Here they saw me; and, having taken a fancy to me, I was bought of the merchant, and went home with them. Her house and premises were situated close to one of those rivulets I have mentioned, and were the finest I ever saw in Africa: They were very extensive, and she had a number of slaves to attend her. The next day I was washed and perfumed, and when mealtime came I was led into the presence of my mistress, and ate and drank before her with her son. This filled me with astonishment; and I could scarce help expressing my surprise that the young gentleman should suffer me, who was bound, to eat with him who was free; and not only so, but that he would not at any time either eat or drink till I had taken first, because I was the eldest, which was agreeable to our custom. Indeed everything here, and all their treatment of me, made me forget that I was a slave. The language of these people resembled ours so nearly that we understood each other perfectly. They had also the very same customs as we. There were likewise slaves daily to attend us, while my young master and I with other boys sported with our darts and bows and arrows, as I had been used to do at home. In this resemblance to my former happy state I passed about two

months; and I now began to think I was to be adopted into the family, and was beginning to be reconciled to my situation, and to forget by degrees my misfortunes, when all at once the delusion vanished; for without the least previous knowledge, one morning early, while my dear master and companion was still asleep, I was wakened out of my reverie to fresh sorrow, and hurried away even amongst the uncircumcised.

Thus at the very moment I dreamed of the greatest happiness, I found myself most miserable; and it seemed as if fortune wished to give me this taste of joy only to render the reverse more poignant. The change I now experienced was as painful as it was sudden and unexpected. It was a change indeed from a state of bliss to a scene which is inexpressible by me, as it discovered to me an element I had never before beheld and till then had no idea of, and wherein such instances of hardship and cruelty continually occurred as I can never reflect on but with horror. . . .

The Slave Ship

The first object which saluted[1] my eyes when I arrived on the coast was the sea, and a slave ship which was then riding at anchor and waiting for its cargo. These filled me with astonishment, which was soon converted into terror when I was carried on board. I was immediately handled and tossed up to see if I were sound by some of the crew, and I was now persuaded that I had gotten into a world of bad spirits and that they were going to kill me. Their complexions too differing so much from ours, their long hair and the language they spoke (which was very different from any I had ever heard) united to confirm me in this belief. Indeed such were the horrors of my views and fears at the moment that, if ten thousand worlds had been my own, I would have freely parted with them all to have exchanged my condition with that of the meanest[2] slave in my own

1. **saluted:** met.
2. **meanest:** lowest.

WORDS TO OWN

alleviate (ə·lē′vē·āt′) v.: to relieve; reduce.
interspersed (in′tər·spʉrsd′) v.: placed at intervals.
commodious (kə·mō′dē·əs) adj.: spacious.

Connecting Across Texts

Connecting with Slave Narratives

The name *Olaudah* means "one favored," especially with the ability to speak well. Equiano spoke out through his autobiography, which is one of the classic slave narratives of all times. A slave narrative is an autobiographical account of the life of a slave. The first example of a slave narrative appeared in 1760 under the title *A Narrative of the Uncommon Sufferings and Surprising Deliverance of Briton Hammom.* Others, like Equiano's work in 1789, soon followed. Slave

narratives were filled with accounts of inhuman cruelty, unendurable suffering, the intense desire for freedom, successful and unsuccessful escape attempts, and, often, religious meditations. During the 1800s, many narratives were written specifically to support the cause of abolishing slavery. However, the slave trade in America was not outlawed until 1808, and slavery continued until Lincoln's Emancipation Proclamation in 1863.

Activities

1. Have students discuss the importance of slave narratives in American literature.
2. Have students compare this account to the slave narrative by Frederick Douglass on p. 426.

country. When I looked round the ship too and saw a large furnace or copper boiling and a multitude of black people of every description chained together, every one of their <u>countenances</u> expressing <u>dejection</u> and sorrow, I no longer doubted of my fate; and quite overpowered with horror and anguish, I fell motionless on the deck and fainted. When I recovered a little I found some black people about me, who I believed were some of those who had brought me on board and had been receiving their pay; they talked to me in order to cheer me, but all in vain. I asked them if we were not to be eaten by those white

men with horrible looks, red faces, and loose hair. They told me I was not, and one of the crew brought me a small portion of spirituous liquor in a wineglass, but being afraid of him I would not take it out of his hand. One of the blacks therefore took it from him and gave it to me, and I took a little down my palate, which instead of reviving me, as they thought it would, threw me into the greatest consternation at the strange feeling it

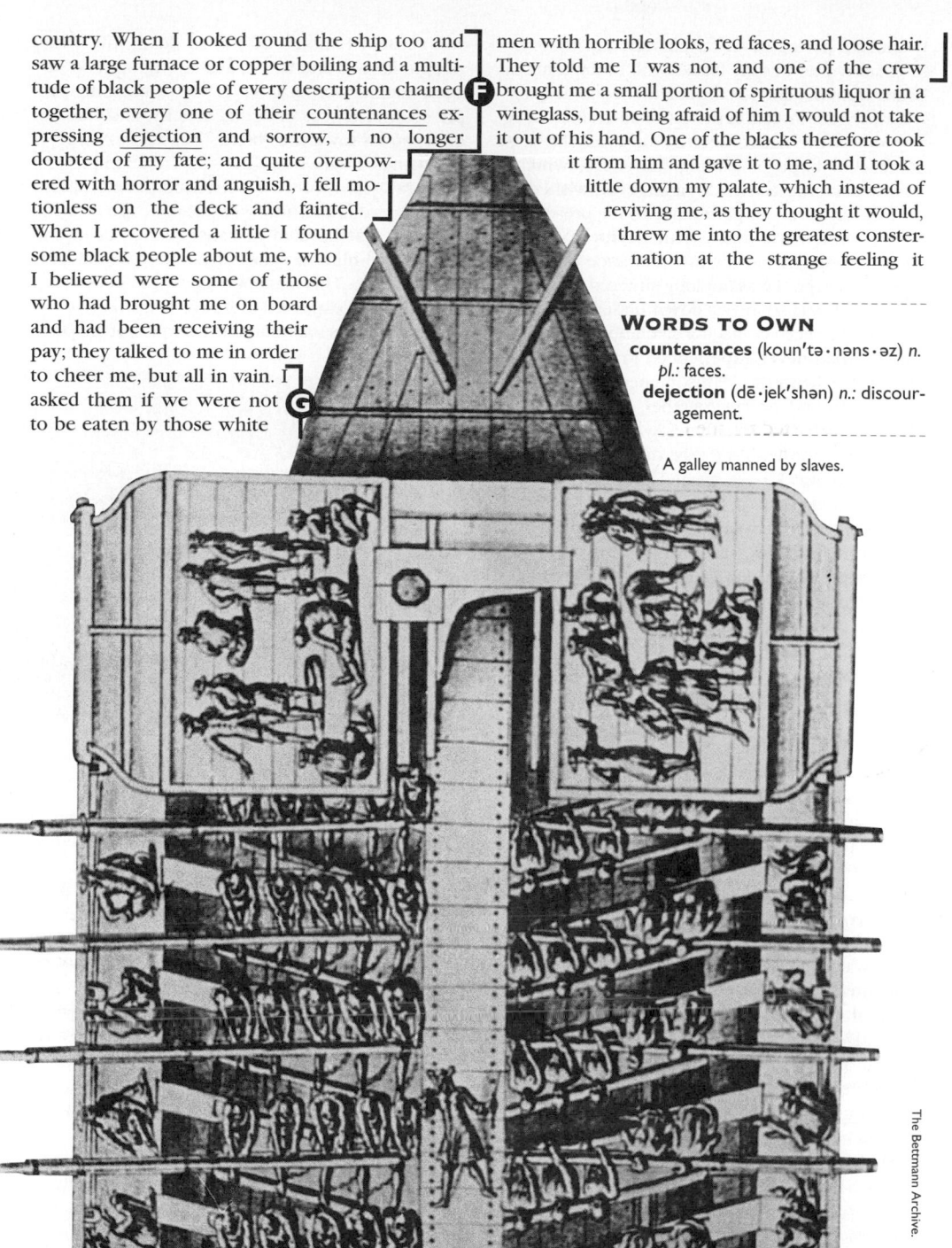

A galley manned by slaves.

The Bettmann Archive.

WORDS TO OWN

countenances (koun′tə·nəns·əz) *n. pl.*: faces.
dejection (dē·jek′shən) *n.*: discouragement.

F Critical Thinking
Analyzing
? Why does Equiano faint? [Possible answers: He is a child, and everything is strange to him; he has never seen a ship before; whites do not look like normal people to him, and they speak an incomprehensible language; Equiano could only conclude something terrible is about to happen to him.]

G Reading Skills and Strategies
Making Inferences
? What heightens Equiano's suffering when he first sees the slave ship? [His ignorance of what to expect fuels his imagination: he imagines horrors of every kind, like being boiled in the furnace and eaten, some of which are worse than what actually happens to him.]

RESPONDING TO THE ART
The galley was the basic seagoing vessel from the sixth century B.C. through the sixteenth century and continued in use into the nineteenth century. Early galleys included the small Phoenician bireme (bī·rēm′), which had two rows of oars on each side, and the fast two- and three-tiered battle cruisers of the Romans. By the mid-sixteenth century, the standard merchant galley measured up to 165 feet in length and 18 feet in width, with 150 oarsmen — several men working each long oar, as shown here.
Activity. Have students look into Equiano's experiences as a merchant and naval seaman. What type of ships did he serve on? How did life as a free sailor compare with the shipboard life of a slave?

Skill Link

Generating Questions for Research
Remind students that a work of nonfiction, such as Equiano's, gives information about particular places, people, and events, offering topics for research. Then, have them complete the following activity.

1. Have students begin filling in the third column of their KWL charts for the Quickwrite activity on p. 57. As they read, they should also list additional topics (such as the practice of slavery among native African peoples on pp. 56–60) that they come across and want to know more about.
2. After students have finished reading and taking notes, have them frame these notes into a

list of possible questions for research, considering exactly what it is they want to find out. They may need to do preliminary reading in reference books.
3. Tell students to choose one question and to narrow it if necessary. They should then use library resources and the Internet to find answers and write up their findings in short reports.

produced, having never tasted such any liquor before. Soon after this the blacks who brought me on board went off, and left me abandoned to despair.

I now saw myself deprived of all chance of returning to my native country or even the least glimpse of hope of gaining the shore, which I now considered as friendly; and I even wished for my former slavery in preference to my present situation, which was filled with horrors of every kind, still heightened by my ignorance of what I was to undergo. I was not long suffered to indulge my grief; I was soon put down under the decks, and there I received such a salutation in my nostrils as I had never experienced in my life: So that with the loathsomeness of the stench and crying together, I became so sick and low that I was not able to eat, nor had I the least desire to taste anything. I now wished for the last friend, death, to relieve me; but soon, to my grief, two of the white men offered me eatables, and on my refusing to eat, one of them held me fast by the hands and laid me across, I think, the windlass,[3] and tied my feet while the other flogged me severely. I had never experienced anything of this kind before, and although, not being used to the water, I naturally feared that element the first time I saw it, yet nevertheless could I have got over the nettings I would have jumped over the side, but I could not; and besides, the crew used to watch us very closely who were not chained down to the decks, lest we should leap into the water: And I have seen some of these poor African prisoners most severely cut for attempting to do so, and hourly whipped for not eating. This indeed was often the case with myself. In a little time after, amongst the poor chained men I found some of my own nation, which in a small degree gave ease to my mind. I inquired of these what was to be done with us; they gave me to understand we were to be carried to these white people's country to work for them. I then was a little revived, and thought if it were no worse than working, my situation was not so desperate: But

3. **windlass** (wind′ləs): device used to raise and lower heavy objects, like a ship's anchor.

still I feared I should be put to death, the white people looked and acted, as I thought, in so savage a manner; for I had never seen among my people such instances of brutal cruelty, and this not only shown toward us blacks but also to some of the whites themselves. One white man in particular I saw, when we were permitted to be on deck, flogged so unmercifully with a large rope near the foremast that he died in consequence of it; and they tossed him over the side as they would have done a brute. This made me fear these people the more, and I expected nothing less than to be treated in the same manner. I could not help ex-

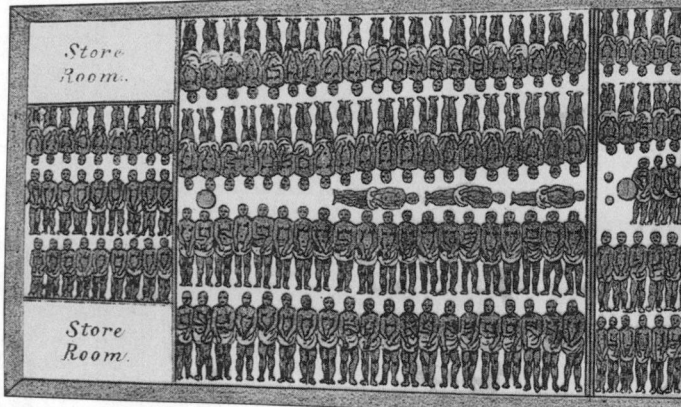

Drawing showing people squeezed together on the lower deck of a slave ship.

pressing my fears and apprehensions to some of my countrymen: I asked them if these people had no country but lived in this hollow place (the ship): They told me they did not, but came from a distant one. "Then," said I, "how comes it in all our country we never heard of them?" They told me because they lived so very far off. I then asked where were their women? Had they any like themselves? I was told they had: "And why," said I, "do we not see them?" They answered, because they were left behind. I asked how the vessel could go? They told me they could not tell, but that there were cloths put upon the masts by the help of the ropes I saw, and then the vessel went on; and the white men had some spell or magic they put in the water when they liked in order to stop the vessel. I was exceedingly amazed at this account and really thought they were spirits. I therefore wished much to be from amongst them for I expected they would sacrifice me: But my wishes were vain, for we were so quartered that it was impossible for any of us to make our escape.

While we stayed on the coast I was mostly on deck, and one day, to my great astonishment, I saw one of these vessels coming in with the sails up. As soon as the whites saw it they gave a great shout, at which we were amazed; and the more so as the vessel appeared larger by approaching nearer. At last she came to an anchor in my sight, and when the anchor was let go I and my countrymen who saw it were lost in astonishment to ob-

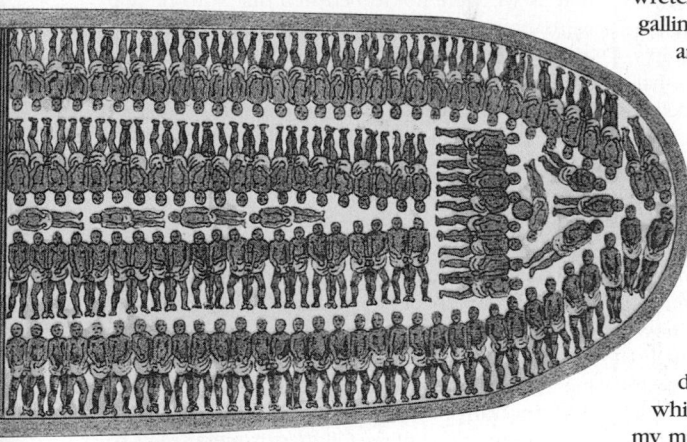

The Bettmann Archive.

serve the vessel stop, and were now convinced it was done by magic. Soon after this the other ship got her boats out, and they came on board of us, and the people of both ships seemed very glad to see each other. Several of the strangers also shook hands with us black people, and made motions with their hands, signifying I suppose we were to go to their country; but we did not understand them. At last, when the ship we were in had got in all her cargo, they made ready with many fearful noises, and we were all put under deck so that we could not see how they managed the vessel.

But this disappointment was the least of my sorrow. The stench of the hold[4] while we were on the coast was so intolerably loathsome that it was dan-

4. **hold:** enclosed area below a ship's deck, where cargo is usually stored.

gerous to remain there for any time, and some of us had been permitted to stay on the deck for the fresh air; but now that the whole ship's cargo were confined together it became absolutely pestilential. The closeness of the place and the heat of the climate, added to the number in the ship, which was so crowded that each had scarcely room to turn himself, almost suffocated us. This produced copious perspirations, so that the air soon became unfit for respiration from a variety of loathsome smells, and brought on a sickness among the slaves, of which many died, thus falling victims to the improvident avarice, as I may call it, of their purchasers. This wretched situation was again aggravated by the galling of the chains, now become insupportable, and the filth of the necessary tubs,[5] into which the children often fell and were almost suffocated. The shrieks of the women and the groans of the dying rendered the whole a scene of horror almost inconceivable. Happily perhaps for myself I was soon reduced so low here that it was thought necessary to keep me almost always on deck, and from my extreme youth I was not put in fetters. In this situation I expected every hour to share the fate of my companions, some of whom were almost daily brought upon deck at the point of death, which I began to hope would soon put an end to my miseries. Often did I think many of the inhabitants of the deep much more happy than myself, I envied them the freedom they enjoyed, and as often wished I could change my condition for theirs. Every circumstance I met with served only to render my state more painful, and heighten my apprehensions and my opinion of the cruelty of the whites. One day they had taken a number of fishes, and when they had killed and satisfied themselves with as many as they thought fit, to our astonishment who were on the deck, rather than give any of them to us to eat as we expected, they tossed the remaining fish into the sea again, although we

5. **necessary tubs:** toilets.

WORDS TO OWN

copious (kō′pē·əs) *adj.:* great amounts of.
improvident (im·präv′ə·dənt) *adj.:* careless; not providing for the future.

OLAUDAH EQUIANO **63**

Taking a Second Look

begged and prayed for some as well as we could, but in vain; and some of my countrymen, being pressed by hunger, took an opportunity when they thought no one saw them of trying to get a little privately; but they were discovered, and the attempt procured them some very severe floggings.

One day, when we had a smooth sea and moderate wind, two of my wearied countrymen who were chained together (I was near them at the time), preferring death to such a life of misery, somehow made through the nettings and jumped into the sea: Immediately another quite dejected fellow, who on account of his illness was suffered to be out of irons, also followed their example; and I believe many more would very soon have done the same if they had not been prevented by the ship's crew, who were instantly alarmed. Those of us that were the most active were in a moment put down under the deck, and there was such a noise and confusion amongst the people of the ship as I never heard before, to stop her and get the boat out to go after the slaves. However two of the wretches were drowned, but they got the other and afterward flogged him unmercifully for thus attempting to prefer death to slavery. In this manner we continued to undergo more hardships than I can now relate, hardships which are inseparable from this accursed trade. Many a time we were near suffocation from the want of fresh air, which we were often without for whole days together. This and the stench of the necessary tubs carried off many.

During our passage I first saw flying fishes, which surprised me very much: They used frequently to fly across the ship and many of them fell on the deck. I also now first saw the use of the quadrant; I had often with astonishment seen the mariners make observations with it, and I could not think what it meant. They at last took notice of my surprise, and one of them, willing to increase it as well as to gratify my curiosity, made me one day look through it. The clouds appeared to me to be land, which disappeared as they passed along. This heightened my wonder, and I was now more persuaded than ever that I was in another world and that everything about me was magic. At last we came in sight of the island of Barbados, at which the whites on board gave a great shout and made many signs of joy to us. We did not know what to think of this, but as the vessel drew nearer we plainly saw the harbor and other ships of different kinds and sizes, and we soon anchored amongst them off Bridgetown. Many merchants and planters now came on board, though it was in the evening. They put us in separate parcels and examined us attentively. They also made us jump, and pointed to the land, signifying we were to go there. We thought by this we should be eaten by these ugly men, as they appeared to us; and when soon after we were all put down under the deck again, there was much dread and trembling among us, and nothing but bitter cries to be heard all the night from these apprehensions, insomuch that at last the white people got some old slaves from the land to pacify us. They told us we were not to be eaten but to work, and were soon to go on land where we should see many of our countrypeople. This report eased us much; and sure enough soon after we were landed there came to us Africans of all languages.

We were conducted immediately to the merchant's yard, where we were all pent up together like so many sheep in a fold without regard to sex or age. As every object was new to me everything I saw filled me with surprise. What struck me first was that the houses were built with stories, and in every other respect different from those in Africa: But I was still more astonished on seeing people on horseback. I did not know what this could mean, and indeed I thought these people were full of nothing but magical arts. While I was in this astonishment one of my fellow prisoners spoke to a countryman of his about the horses, who said they were the same kind they had in their country. I understood them though they were from a distant part of Africa, and I thought it odd I had not seen any horses there; but afterward when I came to converse with different Africans I found they had many horses amongst them, and much larger than those I then saw.

We were not many days in the merchant's custody before we were sold after their usual manner, which is this: On a signal given (as the beat of a drum) the buyers rush at once into the yard where the slaves are confined, and make choice of that parcel they like best. The noise and clamor with which this is attended and the eagerness visible in the countenances of the buyers serve not a little to

WORDS TO OWN
moderate (mäd′ər·it) *adj.*: gentle.

Assessing Learning

Check Test: True-False
1. Equiano and his sister are kidnapped when he is eleven. [True]
2. Equiano is treated brutally by his African master and mistress. [False]
3. Equiano is frightened by the crew's pale skin, long hair, and language. [True]
4. The crew members make no attempt to prevent the captives from committing suicide. [False]

5. Equiano is horrified when one crew member flogs another. [True]

Standardized Test Preparation
For practice with ACT and SAT formats, see
- *Preparation for College Admission Exams,* p. 3

For practice in proofreading and editing, see
- *Daily Oral Grammar,* Transparency 5

increase the apprehensions of the terrified Africans, who may well be supposed to consider them as the ministers of that destruction to which they think themselves devoted. In this manner, without scruple, are relations and friends separated, most of them never to see each other again. I remember in the vessel in which I was brought over, in the men's apartment there were several brothers who, in the sale, were sold in different lots; and it was very moving on this occasion to see and hear their cries at parting. O, ye nominal Christians! might not an African ask you, Learned you this from your God who says unto you, Do unto all men as you would men should do unto you? Is it not enough that we are torn from our country and friends to toil for your luxury and lust of gain? Must every tender feeling be likewise sacrificed to your avarice? Are the dearest friends and relations, now rendered more dear by their separation from their kindred, still to be parted from each other and thus prevented from cheering the gloom of slavery with the small comfort of being together and mingling their sufferings and sorrows? Why are parents to lose their children, brothers their sisters, or husbands their wives? Surely this is a new refinement in cruelty which, while it has no advantage to atone for it, thus aggravates distress and adds fresh horrors even to the wretchedness of slavery.

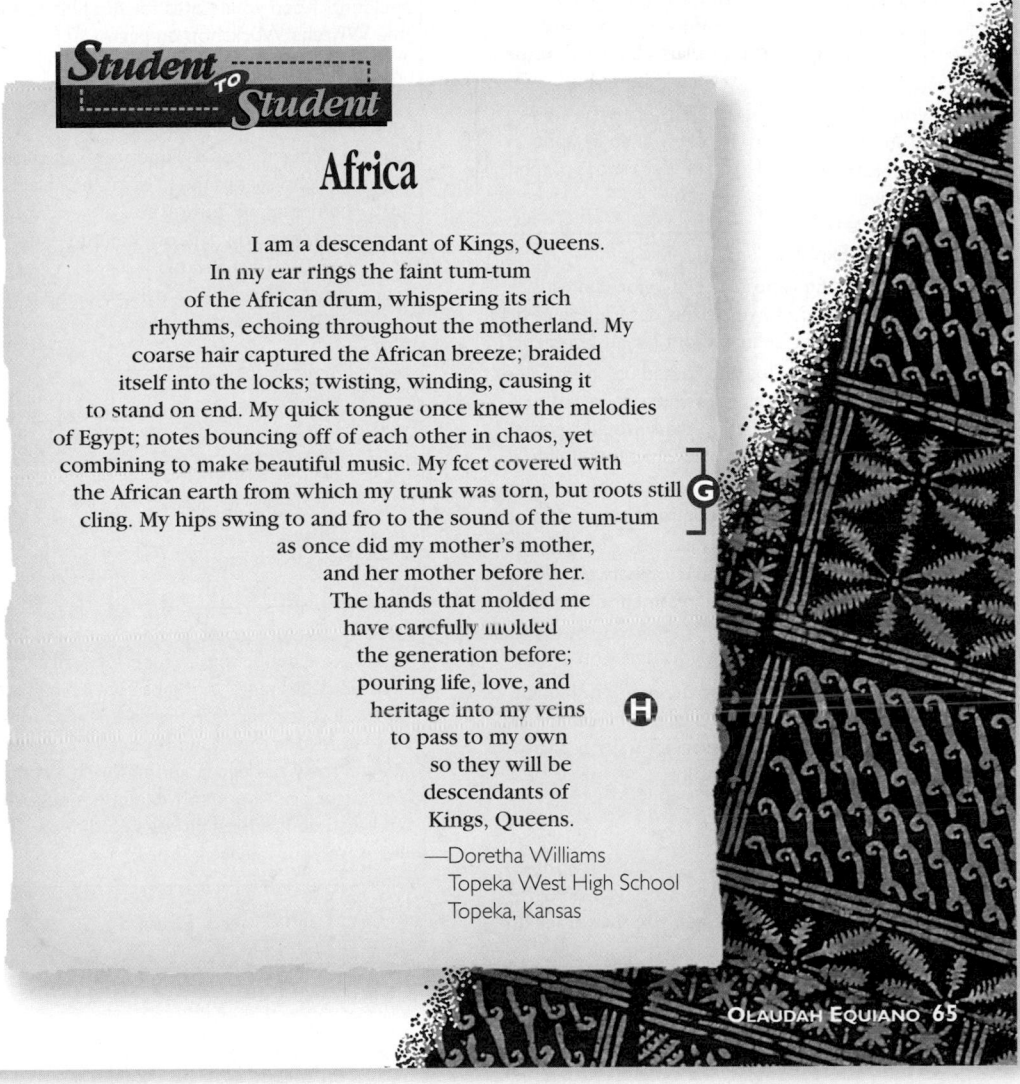

Student to Student

Africa

I am a descendant of Kings, Queens.
In my ear rings the faint tum-tum
of the African drum, whispering its rich
rhythms, echoing throughout the motherland. My
coarse hair captured the African breeze; braided
itself into the locks; twisting, winding, causing it
to stand on end. My quick tongue once knew the melodies
of Egypt; notes bouncing off of each other in chaos, yet
combining to make beautiful music. My feet covered with
the African earth from which my trunk was torn, but roots still
cling. My hips swing to and fro to the sound of the tum-tum
as once did my mother's mother,
and her mother before her.
The hands that molded me
have carefully molded
the generation before;
pouring life, love, and
heritage into my veins
to pass to my own
so they will be
descendants of
Kings, Queens.

—Doretha Williams
Topeka West High School
Topeka, Kansas

OLAUDAH EQUIANO 65

Connecting Across Texts

Connecting with *The Interesting Narrative of the Life of Olaudah Equiano*
Use these questions as a springboard to a class discussion of the two texts: What do Doretha Williams and Olaudah Equiano have in common? What voyages has Williams taken? What visions does she have? If Equiano could read Williams's poem, what might his reaction be? [He would probably be pleased that people were still embracing their African roots.]

Making the Connections

Connecting to the Theme: "Visions and Voyages"
Discuss the collection theme with students. How is Equiano's voyage as a slave different from Mary Rowlandson's trek as a hostage? How are their journeys alike? What kinds of visions does Equiano have on board ship? What does he dread about the white men's country? What visions inspire Mary Rowlandson?

E **Elements of Literature**
Autobiography
? Equiano writes not just to record his experiences for posterity but to raise people's consciousness about the horrors of slavery. How does this section reveal his purpose? [The direct address to "ye nominal Christians," followed by a series of rhetorical questions, shows his intent to change the opinions of the Christian whites reading his narrative.]

F **Elements of Literature**
Autobiography
This selection provides a rich opportunity for all students to reach a better understanding of the human cost of slavery. Have students discuss how autobiography works as both history and literature. Talk about how Equiano's narrative helps reveal the attitudes of the people of the time yet also functions as a powerful piece of persuasion.

Student to Student

The speaker claims to be a descendant of kings and queens in Africa and celebrates her heritage through references to the enticing rhythms of the African drum, Egyptian songs, and her foremothers. She plans to pass on her regal heritage to her own descendants.

G **Elements of Literature**
Metaphor
? A **metaphor** is a comparison between two unlike things. What comparison is this author making? [The speaker compares herself to a tree that has been torn out or cut down but still has roots in the soil. She is referring to her own cultural and familial ties to Africa.]

H **Elements of Literature**
Poetry
? This is an example of **concrete poetry,** in which the line lengths are planned to achieve an overall shape. What shape does this poem take? [the continent of Africa]

First Thoughts [Respond]

1. Possible responses: the images of the hold on the slave ship; the forced parting of Equiano and his sister; the floggings; or the chained slaves jumping into the sea.

Shaping Interpretations [Interpret]

2. Many students may say they did not know that Africans took an active part in the slave trade.

3. Equiano led a happy, pampered life with his family, shooting birds, playing with his friends and siblings, and training to be a warrior. Possible response: The fact that his family owned slaves makes his enslavement somewhat ironic.

4. They probably want to see if he is fit for travel and for sale; if he were not fit for sale, they might have killed him or let him go.

5. He wants to show the sailors' brutality even to their own people and to contrast their behavior with that of African slaveholders like his father.

6. The crew's main goal is to deliver as many healthy slaves as possible, which would yield the greatest profit to the investors for whom they work. When crew members starve and beat the slaves, they go against that financial interest.

Extending the Text [Synthesize]

7. Possible answers: Greed, as well as fear and ignorance of those who appear or behave differently from oneself, often leads to cruelty; without laws and enforcement of these laws, some people become barbaric. Brutish acts today take place during genocidal wars, terrorist campaigns, and gang warfare.

Challenging the Text [Evaluate]

8. Autobiographies may not be objective because they may recount events so as to put the writer and the writer's cause in the best light; however, they are eyewitness accounts of events, and they can reveal feelings and private details that could only be guessed at by a biographer or historian.

Grading Timesaver

Rubrics for each Choices assignment appear on p. 92 in the *Portfolio Management System.*

First Thoughts

1. What **images** from Equiano's account are most memorable or horrifying to you?

Shaping Interpretations

2. Fill in the third column in the KWL chart you made in your Quickwrite. Did your understanding of slavery and the slave trade change? Explain.

3. What was Equiano's life like before he was taken captive? How does his description of his life affect your feelings about his enslavement?

4. Equiano is "handled and tossed up" by some of the crew as soon as he is taken on board the ship. Why? What do you think would have happened to him if the crew had found him unsatisfactory?

5. Why does Equiano include the flogging of a crew member in his account?

6. What is the basic contradiction between the crew's main goal and the treatment of its captives?

Extending the Text

7. How do you account for the depth of human cruelty described in parts of this autobiography? What current events reveal a similar capacity for brutishness in human nature?

Challenging the Text

8. How reliable do you think **autobiographies** are? On the other hand, what can autobiographies, such as Equiano's, tell you that other historical documents cannot?

Reading Check

a. How is Equiano treated by his captors and owners while he is still enslaved in West Africa?

b. Under what circumstances is Equiano twice parted from his sister?

c. How do some Africans on board the ship try to escape life in bondage?

d. Why does the ship's crew keep Equiano on deck most of the time?

Reading Check

a. Most of his captors are humane. One family treats him like their own son.

b. They are separated a few days after the kidnapping. Some time later they meet again but are parted the next morning.

c. They attempt suicide by refusing food or leaping overboard.

d. He is on deck because the atmosphere in the hold makes him sick and because he is no threat to the crew.

CHOICES:
Building Your Portfolio

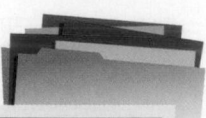

Writer's Notebook

1. Collecting Ideas for an Autobiographical Incident

Write down your memories of an incident in your life when you felt that one of your rights was being restricted or otherwise jeopardized. What kind of action, if any, were you able to take to protect that right? What did you learn about yourself as a result of the incident? Keep your notes for possible use in the Writer's Workshop on page 130.

Comparing Texts

2. Immigration Experiences

Equiano's journey to the Americas was quite different from that of the Pilgrims. In a brief essay, compare and contrast his experience with that of the voyagers on the *Mayflower* (see page 28). To generate ideas, you might want to use a Venn diagram like the one below:

Equiano   Pilgrims

came against his will | difficult journey | came freely

Creative Writing / Art

3. Teach Your Children Well

Create a picture book for children that will teach them about some aspect of African American heritage—perhaps something that you've just learned from Equiano's account. Research your topic, and report your findings in clear, easy-to-read language for children. You might even want to write in poetic form, as the student writer on page 65 did. Illustrate your children's book.

Collection 2

The Examined Life

Theme

How Shall We Live? *One of the most persistent qualities of the American character has its origins in our earliest writers. The Puritan habit of introspection—of self-evaluation, of reading one's life as if reading a book—can be found in the sermons of the Great Awakening, in the pragmatism of Ben Franklin, and in the newest titles in bookstores all over the nation today. Benjamin Franklin's* Autobiography *is the major work of this period.*

Reading the Anthology

Reaching Struggling Readers

The *Reading Skills and Strategies: Reaching Struggling Readers* binder provides materials coordinated with the Pupil's Edition (see the Collection Planner, p. T66B) to help students who have difficulty reading and comprehending text, or students who are reluctant readers. The binder for eleventh grade is organized around ten individual skill areas and offers the following options:

- **MiniRead** MiniReads are short, easy texts that give students a chance to practice a particular skill and strategy before reading selections in the Pupil's Edition. Each MiniRead Skill Lesson can be taught independently or used in conjunction with a Selection Skill Lesson.

- **Selection Skill Lessons** Selection Skill Lessons allow students to apply skills introduced in the MiniReads. Each Selection Skill Lesson provides reading instruction and practice specific to a particular piece of literature in the Pupil's Edition.

Reading Beyond the Anthology

Read On

At the end of the Beginnings to 1800 collections, the grade eleven book includes an annotated bibliography of books suitable for extended reading. The suggested books are related to works in these collections by theme, by author, or by subject. To preview the Read On for the Beginnings to 1800 period, please turn to p. T126.

Collection 2 **The Examined Life**

Resources for this Collection

Note: All resources for this collection are available for preview on the *One-Stop Planner CD-ROM 1 with Test Generator.* All worksheets and blackline masters may be printed from the CD-ROM.

Internet Resources
go.hrw.com LE0 11-2

Selection or Feature	Reading and Literary Skills	Vocabulary, Language, and Grammar
Here Follow Some Verses upon the Burning of Our House, July 10, 1666 (p. 69) Anne Bradstreet	• *Graphic Organizers for Active Reading,* Worksheet p. 5 • *Literary Elements:* Transparency 2 Worksheet p. 7	• *Grammar and Language Links:* Prepositions, Conjunctions, and Interjections, Worksheet p. 9 • *Language Workshop CD-ROM,* Prepositions, Conjunctions and Interjections • *Daily Oral Grammar,* Transparency 6
Huswifery (p. 73) Edward Taylor	• *Reading Skills and Strategies: Reaching Struggling Readers* • MiniRead Skill Lesson, p. 23 • Selection Skill Lesson, p. 29 • *Graphic Organizers for Active Reading,* Worksheet p. 6 • *Literary Elements:* Transparency 3 Worksheet p. 10	
Literature of the Americas: Mexico • **World, in Hounding Me…** • **En perseguirme, mundo…** (p. 76) Sor Juana Inés de la Cruz *translated by* Alan S. Trueblood	The Literature of the Americas feature offers selections from a variety of American cultures representing North, Central, and South America. These selections connect to the collection theme, and students explore the thematic links through structured group discussions called Finding Common Ground.	
from **Sinners in the Hands of an Angry God** (p. 78) Jonathan Edwards **Primary Sources:** • **Sarah Pierrepont** • **My Sense of Divine Things** (p. 82) Jonathan Edwards	• *Graphic Organizers for Active Reading,* Worksheet p. 7 • *Literary Elements:* Transparency 4 Worksheet p. 13	• *Words to Own,* Worksheet p. 6 • *Grammar and Language Links:* Subject, Predicate, and Complement, Worksheet p. 11 • *Language Workshop CD-ROM,* Parts of Sentences • *Daily Oral Grammar,* Transparency 7
from **The Autobiography** (p. 85) Benjamin Franklin **Spotlight On: Sayings of Poor Richard** (p. 95) Benjamin Franklin **Connections:** *from* **All I Really Need to Know I Learned in Kindergarten** (p. 96) Robert Fulghum	• *Graphic Organizers for Active Reading,* Worksheet p. 8	• *Words to Own,* Worksheet p. 7 • *Grammar and Language Links:* Compound Subject and Compound Verb, Worksheet p. 13; Revision Worksheet p. 15 • *Language Workshop CD-ROM,* The Subject and the Predicate • *Daily Oral Grammar,* Transparency 8

Other Resources for this Collection

- *Cross-Curricular Activities,* p. 2
- *Portfolio Management System,* Introduction to Portfolio Assessment, p. 1
- *Test Generator,* Collection Test

Writing	Listening and Speaking Viewing and Representing	Assessment
• *Portfolio Management System,* Rubrics for Choices, p. 93	• *Audio CD Library,* Disc 3, Track 2 • *Portfolio Management System,* Rubrics for Choices, p. 93	• *Formal Assessment,* Selection Test, p. 11 • *Test Generator (One-Stop Planner CD-ROM)*
• *Portfolio Management System,* Rubrics for Choices, p. 94	• *Audio CD Library,* Disc 3, Track 3 • *Portfolio Management System,* Rubrics for Choices, p. 94	• *Formal Assessment,* Selection Test, p. 11 • *Test Generator (One-Stop Planner CD-ROM)*
	• *Audio CD Library,* Disc 3, Tracks 4, 5	
• *Portfolio Management System,* Rubrics for Choices, p. 95	• *Audio CD Library,* Disc 3, Track 6 • *Portfolio Management System,* Rubrics for Choices, p. 95	• *Formal Assessment,* Selection Test, p. 13 • *Test Generator (One-Stop Planner CD-ROM)* • *Preparation for College Admission Exams,* p. 5
• *Portfolio Management System,* Rubrics for Choices, p. 96	• *Audio CD Library,* Disc 3, Track 7 • *Viewing and Representing:* Fine Art Transparency 2 Worksheet p. 8 • *Portfolio Management System,* Rubrics for Choices, p. 96	• *Formal Assessment,* Selection Test, p. 15 • *Test Generator (One-Stop Planner CD-ROM)* • *Preparation for College Admission Exams,* p. 7

 Transparency    CD-ROM   ▭ Video   🎧 Audio CD

Collection 2 The Examined Life

Skills Focus

Selection or Feature	Reading Skills and Strategies	Elements of Literature and Language	Writing	Listening and Speaking	Viewing and Representing
Here Follow Some Verses upon the Burning of Our House, July 10, 1666 Anne Bradstreet (p. 68)	Analyzing Text Structures: Inversion, pp. 69, 71 Paraphrase, p. 71	Extended Metaphor, p. 71 Aphorism, p. 71	Write About a "Baptism by Fire," p. 71 Write an Essay Discussing an Author's Attitude, p. 71 Create an Aphorism, p. 71		
Huswifery Edward Taylor (p. 73)	Analyzing Text Structures: Extended Metaphors, pp. 73–74	Extended Metaphor, pp. 73–74 Conceit, pp. 73–74 Figure of Speech, p. 74	Write a Conceit, p. 74 Identify Incidents that Define Identity, p. 74 Write an Essay Comparing Two Extended Metaphors, p. 74		
Literature of the Americas: Mexico World, in Hounding Me… En perseguirme, mundo… (p. 76) Sor Juana Inés de la Cruz *translated by* Alan S. Trueblood	Respond to a Poem, p. 76 Compare and Contrast Poems, p. 76	The Literature of the Americas feature offers selections from a variety of American cultures representing North, Central, and South America. These selections connect to the collection theme, and students explore the thematic links through structured group discussions called Finding Common Ground.			
from **Sinners in the Hands of an Angry God** (p. 78) Jonathan Edwards	Analyzing Literary Language: Figures of Speech, pp. 78, 83	Figures of Speech, pp. 78, 83 Allusions, p. 83 Images, p. 83 Metaphors, p. 83	Freewrite About an Autobiographical Incident, p. 83 Write an Essay Comparing Texts, p. 83 Write a Script of a Conversation, p. 83	Participate in a Panel Discussion, p. 83	
from **The Autobiography** (p. 85) Benjamin Franklin		Almanac, p. 95 Aphorism, pp. 95, 98 Character, p. 97 Tone, p. 97 Autobiography, p. 97 Biography, p. 97	Freewrite About a Character Trait, p. 98 Write an Essay Comparing and Contrasting Two Authors, p. 98 Create a Personal Book of Virtues, p. 98 Write a Proposal to a Publisher, p. 98 Create an Almanac, p. 98	Research and Report on the Scientific Achievements of Banneker or Franklin, p. 98	Illustrate a Book of Aphorisms, p. 98

Collection 2

THE EXAMINED LIFE

Bradstreet

Taylor

Sor Juana

Edwards

Franklin

All my life I had been looking for something, and everywhere I turned someone tried to tell me what it was. I accepted their answers too, though they were often in contradiction and even self-contradictory. I was naïve. I was looking for myself and asking everyone except myself questions which I, and only I, could answer. It took me a long time and much painful boomeranging of my expectations to achieve a realization everyone else appears to have been born with: That I am nobody but myself.

—**Ralph Ellison,**
from Invisible Man

Writing Focus: Autobiographical Incident

The following **Work in Progress** assignments in this collection build to a culminating **Writer's Workshop** at the end of Collection 3.

- Here Follow Some Verses upon the Burning of Our House, July 10, 1666
- Huswifery
- Sinners in the Hands of an Angry God
- The Autobiography

Write about a challenge (p. 71)

Recall key incidents (p. 74)
Write about emotions as motivators (p. 83)
Write about an important character trait (p. 98)

Writer's Workshop: Narrative Writing / Autobiographical Incident (p. 130)

OBJECTIVES

1. Read the literature of the colonial American period on the theme "The Examined Life"
2. Interpret literary elements used in the literature with special emphasis on the conceit
3. Apply a variety of reading strategies to the literature
4. Respond to the literature in a variety of modes
5. Learn and use new words

Resources

Viewing and Representing
Videocassette A Segment 3
Available in English and Spanish. This segment explores the historical background of Puritan society. For full lesson plans and worksheets, see *Visual Connections Teacher's Manual.*

Responding to the Quotation

? What does the quotation reveal about seeking an "examined life"? [You can search for meaning and identity all over, but ultimately you must look inside yourself.] **Ask students whether people can find themselves only by looking inward.** [Possible responses: Yes, people must look only within themselves to find out who they are—everything else is extraneous. No, people can also find out who they are by listening to others and learning from their experience.]

RESPONDING TO THE ART

Quill and ledger. The photograph shows a quill pen and inkwell, a box, a ledger, and the temples of a pair of glasses. Point out that these articles fit the time period and the theme "The Examined Life." Have students analyze the mood of this photograph and discuss its links with the collection theme. [Possible response: The mood is reflective and introspective, which is appropriate for a collection that examines the question of how to live life.]

Anne Bradstreet

(1612–1672)

Anne Bradstreet (detail) (1948) by Harry Grylls. Stained glass.

Reproduced by kind permission of the vicar and church wardens of St. Botolph's Church, Boston, England.

Who could have guessed that the writer who would begin the history of American poetry would be an immigrant, teenage bride? This fact seems less far-fetched when we know something about the life of the young woman who came from England to America when the Colonies were no more than a few villages precariously perched between the ocean and the wilderness.

Shakespeare was still alive when Anne Bradstreet was born, and like many budding poets, she found in Shakespeare, and in other great English poets, sources of inspiration and technique that would one day run like threads of gold through the fabric of her own work. However, what most determined the course of Anne Bradstreet's life was not a poetic influence but a religious one.

Anne Bradstreet was born into a family of Puritans. She accepted their reformist views as naturally as most children accept the religious teachings of a parent. When she was about sixteen, she married a well-educated and zealous young Puritan by the name of Simon Bradstreet. Two years later, in 1630, Simon, Anne, and Anne's father journeyed across the Atlantic to the part of New England around Salem that would become known as the Massachusetts Bay Colony. There her father and then her husband rose to prominence, each serving as governor of the colony, while Anne kept house first in Cambridge, then in Ipswich, and finally in Andover. She raised four boys and four girls and, without seeking an audience or publication, found time to write poems.

Bradstreet's poems might never have come to light had it not been for John Woodbridge, her brother-in-law and a minister in Andover. In 1648, he went to England and, in 1650, without consulting the author herself, published Bradstreet's poems in London under the title *The Tenth Muse Lately Sprung Up in America . . . By a Gentlewoman in those Parts.*

In one stroke, an obscure wife and mother from the meadows of New England was placed among the nine Muses of art and learning sacred to the ancient Greeks. In itself, this was embarrassing enough. But in the middle of the seventeenth century, the real arrogance was that a woman would aspire to a place among the august company of established male poets. *The Tenth Muse* fared better with critics and the public than Anne expected (later, even the learned Puritan minister Cotton Mather praised her work), and she felt encouraged to write for the rest of her life.

Today, Anne Bradstreet is remembered not for her elaborate earlier poems that focus on public events, but for a few simple, personal lyrics about such things as the birth of children, the death of grandchildren, her love for her husband, her son's departure for England, and her own illnesses and adversities. In a letter to her children just before she died, she wrote: "Among all my experiences of God's gracious dealings with me I have constantly observed this, that He hath never suffered me long to sit loose from Him, but by one affliction or other hath made me look home, and search what was amiss."

 go.hrw.com
LEO 11-2

Before You Read

HERE FOLLOW SOME VERSES UPON THE BURNING OF OUR HOUSE, JULY 10, 1666

Make the Connection
Tests of Strength
How we deal with losses in life is perhaps the greatest test of our inner strength. Some losses are so enormous that they shake us to our core and challenge our very sense of self. Response to such a loss is the topic of this poem: It portrays an internal debate, a kind of dialogue between self and soul.

Reading Skills and Strategies

Analyzing Text Structures: Inversion
Anne Bradstreet's poem is filled with **inversions**. In an inversion, the words of a sentence or phrase are wrenched out of our normal English syntax, or word order: "In silent night when rest I took," instead of "In silent night when I took rest." In English poetry of the previous centuries, poets used inversion frequently to accommodate the demands of **meter** or **rhyme**. As you read Bradstreet's poem, pay close attention to her use of inversion. Then, go through the poem line by line, and rewrite it so that these words appear in normal order. Read the new poem aloud. Jot down some notes on how this "noninverted version" changes the meter and emphases of the poem.

Here Follow Some Verses upon the Burning of Our House, July 10, 1666

Anne Bradstreet

In silent night when rest I took
For sorrow near I did not look   **A**
I wakened was with thund'ring noise
And piteous shrieks of dreadful voice.
5 That fearful sound of "Fire!" and "Fire!"
Let no man know is my desire.
I, starting up, the light did spy,
And to my God my heart did cry
To strengthen me in my distress
10 And not to leave me succorless.°
Then, coming out, beheld a space
The flame consume my dwelling place.
And when I could no longer look,
I blest His name that gave and took,°
15 That laid my goods now in the dust.
Yea, so it was, and so 'twas just.
It was His own, it was not mine,
Far be it that I should repine;
He might of all justly bereft

10. **succorless** (suk′ər·lis): without aid or assistance; helpless.
14. **that gave and took:** allusion to Job 1:21, "The Lord gave, and the Lord hath taken away; blessed be the name of the Lord."

Summary ■■

Awakened by shouts of "Fire!" the speaker escapes from her burning house and then watches flames consume it. When she later passes the ruins, she scolds herself for mourning the loss of her worldly goods and reminds herself that God gave her those goods and has justly taken them away. She concludes by affirming that her true house, hope, and treasure lie in heaven.

Background

Although the Puritans were industrious and often acquired material goods (the Bradstreets lost eight hundred books in this fire), they considered it sinful to place too much value on personal possessions. Bradstreet's emotional conflict between the loss of a comfortable, memory-filled home and her Puritan belief that such a loss should not matter is what gives this poem its emotional and philosophical power. Despite the Puritan emphasis on the hereafter, the critic Wendy Martin observes that Bradstreet "writes of her intense love for her husband and children, her grief at the loss of parents and grandchildren, her joy in nature. . . . The emphasis is on *this* life."

Ⓐ Reading Skills and Strategies

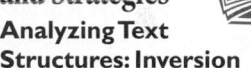

Analyzing Text Structures: Inversion

❓ Have students identify the inversion in l. 1. ["In silent night when rest I took"/ I took rest] Then, ask students to identify the inversions in l. 2 and then paraphrase the line. ["For sorrow near I did not look"/I did not look near for sorrow. I did not expect a tragedy to strike me.] **Why does the poet use inversion in this couplet?** [to create rhyme (*took/ look*) and to establish the meter (iambic tetrameter)]

Reaching All Students

Struggling Readers
Help students determine the meanings of archaic words, such as *oft* [often], *e'er* [ever], *'gin* [begin], and high-level vocabulary, such as that in ll. 18 and 19, i.e., *repine* [complain] and *bereft* [taken away].

Advanced Learners
Discuss how different religious faiths approach the question of personal possessions and mate-

rial things. For instance, the Buddhist faith greatly values a detached attitude toward worldly possessions as a means to inner tranquility. Then, review the Background material on this page that discusses the Puritan attitude toward possessions. Encourage students to keep these Puritan values in mind as they read the poem.

A **Elements of Literature**

Allusion

Help students understand that the phrase *all's vanity* in l. 36 is a Biblical allusion to Ecclesiastes 1:2 and 12:8: "Vanity of vanities; all is vanity."

B **Elements of Literature**

Rhetorical Question

Point out Bradstreet's effective use of rhetorical questions—questions asked for effect, with no expectation of an answer. For her, the obvious answer is "no." Ask students if they agree with Bradstreet.

C **Elements of Literature**

Allusion

The last verse of Psalm 23 is one of many Biblical references to a home in heaven: "Surely goodness and mercy shall follow me all the days of my life: and I will dwell in the house of the Lord for ever." Help students understand how Bradstreet alludes to this Biblical home through the extended metaphor of the "house on high," with its divine architect, furnishings, and purchasing price.

D **Reading Skills and Strategies**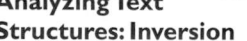

Analyzing Text Structures: Inversion

❓ How does the inversion in this couplet emphasize the poem's theme? [By putting *the world* before *no longer let me love*, Bradstreet rhymes *love* and *above*, emphasizing that she is not to love the world, but rather God and heaven.]

RESPONDING TO THE ART

This embroidered seat cover, designed by members of Bradstreet's family, is marked by vivid colors and religious symbols: the Biblical tree of life and the peacock (symbol of resurrection).

Activity. Have students make (1) a list of reasons that craft work such as this would be valued by colonial Puritans, and (2) a list of reasons that it is valued today. [Possible response: For the first list, students may note the practical value of homemade art and its personal religious significance; for the second list, they may emphasize the unique value of a homemade item in an era of mass–produced goods.]

20 But yet sufficient for us left.
When by the ruins oft I past
My sorrowing eyes aside did cast,
And here and there the places spy
Where oft I sat and long did lie:
25 Here stood that trunk, and there that chest,
There lay that store I counted best.
My pleasant things in ashes lie,
And them behold no more shall I.
Under thy roof no guest shall sit,
30 Nor at thy table eat a bit.
No pleasant tale shall e'er be told,
Nor things recounted done of old.
No candle e'er shall shine in thee,
Nor bridegroom's voice e'er heard shall be.
35 In silence ever shall thou lie,
Adieu, Adieu,° all's vanity.
Then straight I 'gin my heart to chide,

And did thy wealth on earth abide?
Didst fix thy hope on mold'ring dust?
40 The arm of flesh didst make thy trust?
Raise up thy thoughts above the sky
That dunghill mists away may fly.
Thou hast an house on high erect,
Framed by that mighty Architect,
45 With glory richly furnished,
Stands permanent though this be fled.
It's purchased and paid for too
By Him who hath enough to do.
A price so vast as is unknown
50 Yet by His gift is made thine own;
There's wealth enough, I need no more,
Farewell, my pelf,° farewell my store.
The world no longer let me love,
My hope and treasure lies above.

36. Adieu (à·dyö′): French for "goodbye."

52. pelf: wealth or worldly goods. Sometimes used as a term of contempt.

Museum of Fine Arts, Boston, Gift of Samuel Bradstreet (19.602).

Embroidered chair seat cover (1725–1750) by the Bradstreet family. American, New England, Boston area. Colored wool embroidered on cotton and linen twill (44 cm × 54 cm).

70 BEGINNINGS

Using Students' Strengths

Auditory/Musical Learners

Have students read through the poem for meaning and then read it aloud so they can hear the iambic tetrameter. Challenge students to find the two places at the end of the poem in which the *-ed* word ending must be pronounced as a separate syllable for the line to scan correctly. [ll. 45, 47] Students can copy the poem as running prose to help them with the meter.

Visual Learners

Have students create visual flash cards for the most important images of the poem. On one side of the card, they should draw an image (the flames consuming Bradstreet's home, scenes from the domestic life she lost, her heavenly home, etc.). On the other side, they should write down the line or lines their drawings represent. Each student should then present his or her drawings and have the class figure out the corresponding lines in the poem.

First Thoughts

1. Sometimes bad things happen to good people. Do you think any good can come from difficulties in life? Explain.

Shaping Interpretations

2. What are some of the specific losses that Bradstreet dwells on in the first half of the poem?

3. Bradstreet speaks of another "house" in an **extended metaphor** at the end of the poem. What is this house, who is its architect, and how is it better than the house she has lost? (For more information about extended metaphor, see page 188.)

4. *Pelf*—a word designating riches or worldly goods—is usually used only when the riches or goods are considered to be slightly tainted, ill-gotten, or stolen. Why do you suppose Bradstreet uses such a bitter word in line 52 to describe her own cherished treasures?

5. Using your "noninverted" version of the poem as a starting point, write a paraphrase of the entire poem. A **paraphrase** is a restatement of a text in your own words. Paraphrasing a text can help you clarify and interpret difficult or ambiguous passages.

Challenging the Text

6. Some readers have felt that, by so lovingly enumerating her losses, Bradstreet is "crying out to heaven" in a way that unconsciously reveals more attachment to her earthly possessions than she would admit to. On the other hand, what Bradstreet does *not* reveal in this poem is significant: Hundreds of books, as well as her papers and all her unpublished poems, were also lost in the fire. Using specific examples from the text, explain whether or not, by the end of the poem, you are convinced that the speaker means what she says.

Cradle of Peregrine White, first English child born in New England.
Courtesy of the Pilgrim Society, Plymouth, Massachusetts.

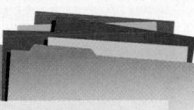

CHOICES:
Building Your Portfolio

Writer's Notebook
1. Collecting Ideas for an Autobiographical Incident

Write a few sentences about a time in your own life that seemed to you like a "baptism of fire"—a time when you were tested by challenges, such as peer pressure. Keep your notes for possible use in the Writer's Workshop on page 130.

Interpreting a Poem
2. Trials and Tribulations

In the Book of Job in the Bible, Job endures great misery, yet he is still able to say, "The Lord gave, and the Lord hath taken away; blessed be the name of the Lord" (Job 1:21). Bradstreet expresses a similar attitude in her poem; twice she checks herself from mourning over the loss of her beloved possessions. The first instance is in lines 14–20; the second begins with line 37. In a brief essay, discuss Bradstreet's attitude toward earthly suffering and the providence of God.

Creative Writing
3. The Taste of Adversity

An **aphorism** is a brief, cleverly worded statement that makes a wise observation about life. In Anne Bradstreet's book of aphorisms, *Meditations Divine and Moral,* she writes: "If we had no winter, the spring would not be so pleasant; if we did not sometimes taste of adversity, prosperity would not be so welcome." Using this observation and Bradstreet's poem as starting points, compose your own aphorism about adversity in life.

ANNE BRADSTREET 71

First Thoughts [Respond]

1. Possible answers: Some students may say that a person can become stronger by experiencing misfortune. Others may feel it is foolish to look for the silver lining in every cloud or tragedy.

Shaping Interpretations [Interpret]

2. She mourns the loss of her home, places where she used to sit and lie, a trunk, a chest, and the gatherings with friends and family that will never occur there.

3. The house is heaven, whose architect is God (l. 44). It is better than the poet's earthly home because it is richly furnished with spiritual glory. It has been paid for with a price "so vast as is unknown" (l. 49), an allusion to Jesus Christ's sacrifice on the cross.

4. She uses this surprisingly negative term because she feels her earthly treasures have corrupted her and caused her to forget the treasure of eternal life.

5. Answers should at least cover the following basic progression: "When I heard the roar of the flames and someone screaming 'Fire!' I cried out to God and ran from my burning house. I stared at the fire and blessed God. When I pass the ruins, I think about my lost goods, my memories, and the events that will now never take place in my house. Then I chide myself, remembering I have a better 'house' in heaven."

Challenging the Text [Evaluate]

6. Answers will vary. Most students will sympathize with Bradstreet about her losses. Some students will feel that within the context of the poem, there is little reason to doubt Bradstreet's sincerity or religious beliefs; her faith does seem to console her and help her to overcome the human impulse to lament her misfortune. Other students will feel that by writing the poem itself, she is trying to stifle a great attachment to personal possessions.

Grading Timesaver

Rubrics for each Choices assignment appear on p. 93 in the *Portfolio Management System*.

CHOICES:
Building Your Portfolio

1. **Writer's Notebook**
   Remind students to choose a situation they would not mind sharing with classmates.
2. **Interpreting a Poem** Be sure students realize Bradford believes God makes her suffer for a reason. God's will is always righteous.
3. **Creative Writing** Be sure to allow students the option of writing aphorisms about the more petty annoyances of life, such as having to do the dishes, if they wish.

Planning

- **Traditional Schedule**
  Lesson Plans Including Strategies for English-Language Learners
- **One-Stop Planner**
  CD-ROM with Test Generator

Edward Taylor

(1642?–1729)

To Puritans, the universe of God's Creation was sublime and magnificent. But to Edward Taylor, the universe could also be—*a bowling alley,* with God the bowler and the sun his bowling ball. This is the kind of imaginative surprise that made Taylor unique among American Puritan writers.

The publication in 1939 of *The Poetical Works of Edward Taylor* was the third important instance in American literature when buried poetic treasure was discovered. The first discovery occurred when Anne Bradstreet's brother-in-law carried her "private" poems to England and had them printed without her consent. The second occurred in 1890, when the heirs of Emily Dickinson (page 372) ignored her wishes and published the poems she had saved carefully in little packets that were to be destroyed after her death.

Headstone on Reverend Silas Bigelow's grave in Paxton, Massachusetts (1769). Carved by William Young.

Of these discoveries, the case of Edward Taylor is perhaps the most remarkable. Taylor wrote an enormous amount of poetry, but he allowed only a portion of one poem to be published during his lifetime. For many years, his brilliant poems moldered in the archives of Yale Library, to which Taylor's grandson had donated them. Then, once again, a body of work that an author had expected to remain unpublished came to light—in this case, with such compelling force as to cause the history of early poetry in America to be rewritten.

Edward Taylor was born in Leicestershire, England, near the town of Coventry. Like Anne Bradstreet, he was raised in a family that held dissenting views about many of the practices of the Church of England. Taylor lost a teaching position in England because he refused to take an oath—required by the royal Act of Uniformity—that conflicted with his religious beliefs. Feeling more and more uncomfortable in the religious climate of his country, where the Act of Uniformity was contributing to the persecution of Puritans, he determined to seek the freedom that other Nonconformists had found in Colonial America. In 1668, Taylor sailed for Boston.

Friends had equipped Taylor with letters of introduction to some of the established Colonial leaders, among them the great Puritan minister Increase Mather (1639–1723). Impressed with the young man's credentials and charmed by his personality, Mather and other influential people eased Taylor's way into Harvard College.

After training for the ministry, Taylor accepted a call in 1671 to become pastor of a church in Westfield, Massachusetts. Taylor stayed in Westfield for the rest of his life. During his fifty-eight years in this frontier town, he faithfully tended the spiritual needs of his flock. Taylor himself increased the flock by fourteen members—he had eight children by his first wife and six by his second. By the time he died in 1729, Taylor had outlived a number of his children.

After Taylor's death, only one book of poetry was found in his personal library—Anne Bradstreet's *The Tenth Muse Lately Sprung Up in America.* Like Bradstreet, Taylor could have had little notion that his poems, which he had scrupulously put away, would outlive him with a radiance bright enough to penetrate the darkness of two centuries of obscurity.

go.hrw.com
LE0 11-2

Resources: Print and Media

Make the Connection
By the Grace of God
Today many people believe that individual identity is shaped by numerous factors, such as family, friends, education, geography, and personal beliefs. The Puritans believed that each aspect of their identity was shaped by God and that all their emotions, thoughts, desires, and behavior should be directed toward God's service and glorification. The Puritans endlessly examined their lives for evidence of God's grace.

Reading Skills and Strategies

Analyzing Text Structures: Extended Metaphors
This poem contains a startling **extended metaphor**—a comparison between two very different things: making cloth and experiencing God's grace. This unusual type of comparison is known as a **conceit** (see page 74). As you read the poem, keep a double-entry journal. In the first column, list the implements and materials used in spinning cloth. In the second column, next to each item, list the spiritual experience that Taylor compares to the act of spinning.

Background
Huswifery (huz′wif′ər·ē) is an archaic spelling of *housewifery*, which means "the care and management of a household." It suggests the whole range of domestic responsibilities, as well as the qualities of thrift and orderliness. A *housewife* (huz′if) also came to be the name for a small sewing kit.

Huswifery

Edward Taylor

Make me, O Lord, thy Spinning Wheel complete.
    Thy Holy Word my Distaff° make for me.
Make mine Affections thy Swift Flyers neat
    And make my Soul thy holy Spool to be.
5   My Conversation make to be thy Reel
    And reel the yarn thereon spun of thy Wheel. **Ⓐ**

Make me thy Loom then, knit therein this Twine:
    And make thy Holy Spirit, Lord, wind quills:°
Then weave the Web thyself. The yarn is fine.
10   Thine Ordinances° make my Fulling Mills.°
    Then dye the same in Heavenly Colors Choice,
    All pinked° with Varnished° Flowers of Paradise. **Ⓑ**

Then clothe therewith mine Understanding, Will,
    Affections, Judgment, Conscience, Memory,
15 My Words, and Actions, that their shine may fill
    My ways with glory and thee glorify.
    Then mine apparel shall display before ye
    That I am Clothed in Holy robes for glory. **Ⓒ**

2. distaff (dis′taf′): On spinning wheels, the distaff is a stick around which fibers are wound before they are spun into thread. Flyers help govern the rate of spinning. The finished thread is wound upon a reel, or spool.

8. quills: a loom's spools or bobbins, on which thread is wound before weaving.

10. ordinances: religious rules and laws. **Fulling Mills:** Fulling, or milling, is the term used for the processing of raw wool cloth through a combination of washing, heating, and compressing. The cloth is processed in fulling mills to preshrink and treat the individual fibers, thereby enhancing its appearance in finished fabrics.
12. pinked: decorated. **varnished:** embellished.

EDWARD TAYLOR 73

Summary ■■■

This poem develops an extended metaphor that compares the granting of God's grace to three different stages in the making of cloth: the spinning of thread on a spinning wheel, the weaving of fabric on a loom, and the sewing and dyeing of clothes. The speaker asks God to serve as the actual weaver, guiding the speaker as an artisan guides his instruments, ultimately clothing the speaker in robes of glory and granting him eternal life.

Ⓐ Critical Thinking
Interpreting
❓ Whom is the speaker addressing? [God] What request is the speaker making of God? [to make him His spinning wheel—an instrument or tool in His hands]

Ⓑ Reading Skills and Strategies
The Conceit
Have students review their double-entry journals and then write a short paragraph discussing how, in Taylor's view, God is like a weaver, a fuller, and a dyer. [Like a weaver, God turns the quills of the loom to create the cloth of salvation. Similarly, God cleans the cloth through the "ordinances" of baptism and communion; He also dyes it with images of salvation and colors the heart and mind of a person seeking grace.]

Ⓒ Reading Skills and Strategies
Analyzing Text Structures: Extended Metaphor
❓ How do the final two lines, in which the speaker is clothed in "Holy robes," convey the Puritan belief that salvation is a gift from God that cannot be earned? [These robes are made by God and given to the speaker to "display" as a sign that he is one of the elect.]

Reaching All Students

Struggling Readers
Analyzing Text Structures: Extended Metaphors was introduced on p. 73. For a lesson directly tied to this selection that teaches students to analyze this text structure, see the *Reading Skills and Strategies* binder:
• MiniRead Skill Lesson, p. 23
• Selection Skill Lesson, p. 29

Making the Connections

Cultural Connections
Making Cloth. In Puritan New England, spinning and weaving were done by the mistress of the house, often by the fireside after it had gotten too dark to do any fine needlework. Dyeing was also a household art. Common dyes came from nature, including marigolds for the color gold, walnut husks for brown, cuprous oxide for green, and soot for black.

The Holy Word. Every major religion around the globe has its sacred writings, or holy word. The Puritan settlers in New England cherished the Geneva Bible. The Koran (c. A.D. 651–652) is the holy word of the Muslims, the followers of the prophet Muhammad. The *Tao Te Ching* consists of the sacred writings of Lao Tzu (c. 571 B.C.) and others, who are credited with inspiring Taoism. Have students research why the followers of these religions hold these works sacred.

First Thoughts [Respond]

1. Possible responses: Some students may respond emotionally, because of the religious content; others may respond intellectually, because of the complexity of the extended metaphor.

Shaping Interpretations [Interpret]

2. He asks God to make him His spinning wheel; His instrument.

3. Students should list specific parts of a spinning wheel and how the speaker applies them to his life. As examples, students may say that l. 2 asks that the Scriptures be like the distaff, the central core on which he, like the fibers, would be bound; l. 5 asks that the speaker's conversation be like the reel, the place where God's word, like the yarn, is kept.

4. The speaker is both familiar and reverent with God. If the speaker centers his life on God, he will radiate God's glory.

5. The speaker is transformed from a sinner to one of the saved. The garment woven by his holy life will be a sign that he has been chosen for heaven.

6. God is practicing huswifery by transforming the lowly speaker from a sinner into a person in a state of grace.

ELEMENTS OF LITERATURE

Encourage students to list points of similarity in their comparisons before they try to extend them in a conceit.

Grading Timesaver

Rubrics for each Choices assignment appear on p. 94 in the *Portfolio Management System*.

CHOICES: Building Your Portfolio

1. **Writer's Notebook** Caution students to choose a situation they would not mind sharing with others.

2. **Comparing Extended Metaphors** Suggest that students prewrite by completing a chart like this one. Then students can meet in small groups to evaluate the effectiveness of the metaphors.

MAKING MEANINGS

First Thoughts

1. Did you respond emotionally or intellectually to Taylor's extended comparison? Did you feel involved with the poem or distant from it? Why?

Shaping Interpretations

2. The poet states his main **metaphor** in the first line. What does he ask the Lord to make him?

3. Using your reading notes to help you review the poem, describe the specific ways that Taylor extends this central comparison.

4. Describe the relationship between this speaker and God. What does the speaker say will make him a complete and fulfilled person?

5. What transformation does the poet describe in the last two lines?

6. *Huswifery* can mean "thrift," or making the most of what one has. Who is practicing the art of huswifery in this poem?

ELEMENTS OF LITERATURE

The Conceit

In poetry, the term **conceit** refers to a startling **extended metaphor** or other **figure of speech** that makes a surprising, even shocking, connection between two different things. The connection may be witty, strange, exaggerated, or cleverly elaborate. When Emily Dickinson (page 372) compared the setting sun to a housewife sweeping up the sky with multicolored brooms and carelessly dropping shreds behind her, she created more than a metaphor: She created a conceit.

Conceits, then, are startling figures of speech that are extended as far as the poet wants to take them. They are exercises of imagination, devices for making us see sometimes profound connections between vastly different things in the world.

Making up a conceit. Devise your own original conceit. Begin by thinking of ordinary comparisons. Then try to match one half of a comparison with something no one is likely to have thought of before. Begin your conceit: _____ is like _____.

CHOICES: Building Your Portfolio

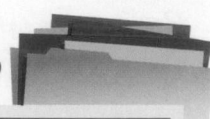

Writer's Notebook

1. Collecting Ideas for an Autobiographical Incident

Write down two or three incidents in your own life that helped define your identity. Keep your notes for possible use in the Writer's Workshop on page 130.

Comparing Extended Metaphors

2. Special Fabrics

In the excerpt below from the Reverend Jesse Jackson's speech to the Democratic National Convention in 1988, Jackson develops an interesting **extended metaphor.** Although Jackson and Taylor are comparing different things, look for similarities in their metaphors. In a brief essay, examine these questions: Does each speaker conclude the metaphor with a kind of transformation? How is each metaphor visual—what does each help you see? In general, how effective do you find each extended metaphor to be?

> America's not a blanket, woven from one thread, one color, one cloth. When I was a child growing up in Greenville, South Carolina, and Grandmother could not afford a blanket, she didn't complain, and we did not freeze. Instead she took pieces of old cloth—patches, wool, silk, gabardine, crockersack on the patches— barely good enough to wipe off your shoes with.
>
> But they didn't stay that way very long. With sturdy hands and a strong cord, she sewed them together into a quilt, a thing of beauty and power and culture.
>
> Now . . . we must build such a quilt.
>
> —Jesse Jackson

Taylor	Jackson
[Uses physical objects: spinning wheel, etc.]	[Uses physical objects: blanket, cord, etc.]
[Uses metaphor as a call for action or change by God.]	[Uses metaphor as a call for action or change by Americans.]

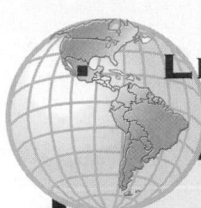

LITERATURE OF THE AMERICAS
MEXICO

Sor Juana Inés de la Cruz
(1648–1695)

Juana Ramírez de Asbaje was born in a village located between two volcanoes southeast of Mexico City. A solitary child with unusual intellectual curiosity, Juana learned to read and write by the age of six or seven. At age six, she heard of the university in Mexico City and pleaded with her mother to send her there dressed like a man. Her request denied, she threw herself into reading and study in her grandfather's library—a world of books and learning that, in the seventeenth century, was still a man's world. As a child she continued to learn Latin after taking only twenty lessons. She was a harsh taskmaster, cutting off her hair if she failed to learn her Latin grammar according to the schedule she had set for herself. "It didn't seem right to me," she wrote, "that a head so naked of knowledge should be dressed up with hair." She also stopped eating cheese, one of her favorite foods, because she had heard that it dulled the mind.

At sixteen, Juana was presented at the court of the Spanish viceroy in Mexico City, where she charmed everyone with her wit, beauty, and brilliance. She served as a lady-in-waiting for four years, then abruptly decided to enter a convent at the age of twenty, taking the name Sor (Sister) Juana Inés de la Cruz. For the next twenty-five years, she lived in a small apartment where she studied and wrote, amassing a huge library of about four thousand volumes and collecting musical and scientific instruments. She also proved to be a shrewd businesswoman, accruing a fortune, making investments, and serving as the convent's bookkeeper and archivist.

Sor Juana Inés de la Cruz (1750) by Miguel Cabrera (1695–1768). Oil on canvas.

Courtesy of Schalkwijk/Art Resource, New York.

Sor Juana's superiors in the Catholic Church continually criticized her for her intellectual pursuits and justifications of secular learning. Most controversial was her long autobiographical letter to a Catholic bishop, in which she defended the rights of women to be educated and intellectually independent—even to undertake public careers. For reasons that are unclear, Sor Juana suddenly abandoned her studies and sold her library, giving the money to the poor and devoting herself exclusively to her religious duties. She wrote nothing during the last two years of her life. In 1695, while nursing her sisters who had been stricken with the plague, Sor Juana became ill and died.

go.hrw.com
LEO 11-2

The speaker of this poem declares her independence from material treasures, which do not bring her pleasure. Instead of setting her mind on the attainment of wealth and comeliness, she chooses to stock her mind with things of beauty—a type of treasure that will outlast all worldly vanities.

Ⓐ Critical Thinking
Expressing an Opinion
❓ What is the speaker saying here? [Time takes away beauty; wealth is not lasting.] **Do you agree with her point? Why or why not?** [Some students will agree, noting that our spiritual, moral, and cultural achievements are the only things that last. Others may insist that we should enjoy life's fleeting pleasures.]

Ⓑ Appreciating Language
Rhyme Schemes
If possible, have someone read the poem in Spanish. Have students scan the English and Spanish versions to discover the rhyme scheme of each. [English: *abba cddc efg egf;* Spanish: *abba abba cdc dcd.* The g rhyme in English is approximate.] **Challenge students to explain the difference between the rhyme schemes.** [Possible answer: The translator was faithful to the spirit of the original yet altered the rhyme to accommodate the demands of English.]

FINDING COMMON GROUND

This feature asks students to discover areas of agreement about something related to the theme or to a controversial issue in the works. Do students agree that everything except mental and spiritual gain is "vanity"? Be sure students see the common thread of renouncing material treasures that runs throughout Bradstreet's and Sor Juana's poems. They should also note how Sor Juana's Catholic, Latin American cultural context distinguishes her poem from Bradstreet's, which arises from a Protestant, Puritan, and North American context.

Before You Read
WORLD, IN HOUNDING ME . . .

Background
At about the same time the Puritan poets Anne Bradstreet and Edward Taylor were in New England writing poems in praise of God, the brilliant Catholic nun Sor Juana Inés de la Cruz was writing poems, plays, songs, and essays in a convent in New Spain (in present-day Mexico). The contemporary Mexican poet Octavio Paz (1914–1998) considered Sor Juana's poems to be among "the most elegant and refined in Spanish. Few poets in our language equal her, and those who surpass her can be counted on the fingers of one hand." In her own time, Sor Juana was called "the tenth muse from Mexico," and her visitors spent evenings in an atmosphere similar to one of Europe's most cultivated salons, discussing ideas and reciting poems over biscuits, fruit, and cups of chocolate.

Reading Skills and Strategies

Responding to a Poem
As you read the following poem by Sor Juana, write down your thoughts, feelings, and questions. In particular, note the similarities or differences between this poem and those you have read by Bradstreet and Taylor.

World, in Hounding Me . . .
Sor Juana Inés de la Cruz
translated from the Spanish
by **Alan S. Trueblood**

   World, in hounding me, what do you gain?
How can it harm you if I choose, astutely,
rather to stock my mind with things of beauty,
than waste its stock on every beauty's claim?
5   Costliness and wealth bring me no pleasure;
the only happiness I care to find
derives from setting treasure in my mind,
and not from mind that's set on winning treasure.
   I prize no comeliness.° All fair things pay
10 to time, the victor, their appointed fee
and treasure cheats even the practiced eye.
   Mine is the better and the truer way:
to leave the vanities of life aside,
not throw my life away on vanity.

9. **comeliness:** beauty.

En perseguirme, mundo . . .
Sor Juana Inés de la Cruz

   En perseguirme, mundo, ¿qué interesas?
¿En qué te ofendo, cuando sólo intento
poner bellezas en mi entendimiento
y no mi entendimiento en las bellezas?
5   Yo no estimo tesoros ni riquezas;
y así, siempre me causa más contento
poner riquezas en mi pensamiento
que no mi pensamiento en las riquezas.
   Y no estimo hermosura que, vencida,
10 es despojo civil de las edades,
ni riqueza me agrada fementida,
   teniendo por mejor, en mis verdades,
consumir vanidades de la vida
que consumir la vida en vanidades.

FINDING COMMON GROUND

Using the notes you wrote while reading, meet in small groups to hold your own "salon," in which you discuss your questions about and responses to this poem.

  As a group, agree on the topics you want to talk about that are suggested by this poem: how you feel about Sor Juana's message, how the poem is similar to or different from the poetry of the Puritan writers you have read, or whatever else you want to discuss.

Making the Connections

Connecting to the Theme: "The Examined Life"
Sor Juana's poem elevates the life of the mind and spirit over material values. The speaker presents both sides of the question and her own deliberate choice. Have groups of students compare the way this poem advocates "The Examined Life" with other works they have read thus far in this collection. In particular, have students compare Sor Juana's concept of *vanity* with Bradstreet's.

Assessing Learning

Informal Assessment
Observation Assessment. As students debate the question of material versus spiritual values, appoint one person from each group to provide a written observation about the participation of each member, the time on-task, and the group's focus on chosen topics. In addition to writing comments, the observer could rate the group's performance on a scale of one (low) to three (high).

Jonathan Edwards

(1703–1758)

Reverend Jonathan Edwards (1750–1755) by Joseph Badger (1708–1765). Oil on canvas (28½″ × 22″).

Despite his fire-and-brimstone imagery, Jonathan Edwards was not merely a stern, zealous preacher. He was a brilliant, thoughtful, and complicated man. Science, reason, and observation of the physical world confirmed Edwards's deeply spiritual vision of a universe filled with the presence of God.

Edwards's abilities were recognized early. Groomed to succeed his grandfather as pastor of the Congregational Church in Northampton, Massachusetts, Edwards entered Yale when he was only thirteen. When his grandfather died in 1729, Edwards mounted the pulpit and quickly established himself as a strong-willed and charismatic pastor.

Edwards's formidable presence and vivid sermons helped to bring about the religious revival known as the Great Awakening. This revival began in Northampton in the 1730s and during the next fifteen years spread throughout the eastern seaboard. The Great Awakening was marked by waves of conversions that were so intensely emotional as to amount at times to mass hysteria.

The Great Awakening began at a time when enthusiasm for the old Puritan religion was declining. To offset the losses in their congregations, churches had been accepting growing numbers of "unregenerate" Christians—people who accepted church doctrine and lived upright lives but who had not confessed to being born again in God's grace, and so were not considered to be saved.

Edwards became known for his extremism as a pastor. In his sermons he didn't hesitate to accuse prominent church members, by name, of relapsing into sin. Edwards's strictness eventually proved to be too much for his congregation, and in 1750 he was dismissed from his prestigious position as pastor of Northampton. After rejecting a number of pastorships offered to him, Edwards relocated to the raw and remote Mohican community of Stockbridge,

Massachusetts. After eight years of missionary work in virtual exile, shared with his wife Sarah, Edwards was named president of the College of New Jersey (later called Princeton University). Three months after assuming this position, he died of a smallpox inoculation—a modern medical procedure that, ironically, had been promoted by the fierce Puritan minister Cotton Mather.

Intellectually, Edwards straddled two ages: the modern, secular world exemplified by such men as Benjamin Franklin (page 84), and the religious world of his zealous Puritan ancestors. He believed (like Franklin) in reason and learning, the value of independent intellect, and the power of the human will. On the other hand, he believed (like Mather) in the lowliness of human beings in relation to God's majesty and the ultimate futility of merely human efforts to achieve salvation. Edwards, as "the last Puritan," stood between Puritan America and modern America. Tragically, he fit into neither world.

go.hrw.com
LE0 11-2

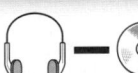 *Resources: Print and Media*

Reading
- *Graphic Organizers for Active Reading*, p. 7
- *Words to Own*, p. 6
- *Audio CD Library* Disc 3, Track 6

Elements of Literature
- *Literary Elements*
  Transparency 4, Worksheet, p. 13

Writing and Language
- *Daily Oral Grammar*, Transparency 7
- *Grammar and Language Links*
  Worksheet, p. 11

Viewing and Representing
- *Visual Connections*
  Videocassette A, Segment 3

Assessment
- *Formal Assessment*, p. 13
- *Portfolio Management System*, p. 95
- *Preparation for College Admission Exams*, p. 5
- *Test Generator (One-Stop Planner CD-ROM)*

Internet
- go.hrw.com (keyword: LE0 11-2)

OBJECTIVES
1. Read and interpret the sermon
2. Identify and explain figures of speech
3. Analyze literary language
4. Express understanding through writing and speaking
5. Understand and use new words

SKILLS
Literary
- Identify and explain figures of speech

Reading
- Analyze literary language

Writing
- Collect ideas for an autobiographical essay
- Compare texts
- Write a script

Speaking/Listening
- Hold a panel discussion

Vocabulary
- Use new words

Viewing/Representing
- Analyze paintings (ATE)

Planning

- **Block Schedule**
  Block Scheduling Lesson Plans with Pacing Guide
- **Traditional Schedule**
  Lesson Plans Including Strategies for English-Language Learners
- **One-Stop Planner**
  CD-ROM with Test Generator

RESPONDING TO THE ART

Joseph Badger (1708–1765) was a Massachusetts-born glazier, sign painter, and portraitist. Although appreciated for his charming portraits of children, his work today is rarely exhibited.
Activity. Ask students what impression they get of Jonathan Edwards from this portrait. [Possible responses: He is serious, even dour; forthright; determined.]

Summary ■ ■ ■

In this fire-and-brimstone sermon, Edwards uses extended metaphors to argue that those who have not accepted Christ as their Savior live on the brink of damnation and the torments of hell. Edwards believes that these people's only chance for salvation is to have a transforming religious experience. He wants those not "born again" to know that God could drop them into the gaping pit of hell at any moment. By emphasizing the tenuousness of their daily lives, Edwards hopes these "natural men" will throw themselves on God's mercy and ask to be saved.

RESPONDING TO THE ART

Benjamin Keach (1640–1704), the Baptist theologian and artist, captures the stakes of moral failure in the woodcut on pp. 78–81, *The Progress of Sin* (1744). In this detail, we can see "Beelzelbub" (the prince of devils), "Turks" (a generic term for infidels or unbelievers), and "Sion" (a Jerusalem hill), all popular motifs of the mid-1700s.

Before You Read

FROM SINNERS IN THE HANDS OF AN ANGRY GOD

Make the Connection

The Great Motivator

Ralph Waldo Emerson (page 216) wrote that "Fear is an instructor of great sagacity and the herald of all revolutions." Many people would agree that fear is one of the most powerful motivators of human behavior. Fear of injury makes us buckle our seat belts. Fear of failure makes some of us study or work harder. Edwards and other pastors used harsh warnings in their sermons to make "sinners" understand the precariousness of their situation by actually *feeling* the fear and horror of their sinful state.

Reading Skills and Strategies

Analyzing Literary Language

As you read Edwards's sermon, write down the phrases or details that you find particularly vivid or frightening. Make special note of the three central **figures of speech** in paragraphs 4–7 on pages 80–81.

Elements of Literature

Figures of Speech

Figures of speech describe one thing in terms of another, very different thing. Although Edwards's belief in eternal damnation is literal, he uses figures of speech to compare God's wrath to ordinary, everyday things that his listeners could relate to and understand.

Background

This is Edwards's most famous sermon, which he delivered on a visit to the congregation at Enfield, Connecticut, in 1741. The "natural men" he is trying to awaken and persuade are those people in the congregation who have not been "born again," meaning they have not accepted Christ as their savior. Edwards's methods in the sermon were influenced by the work of the English philosopher John Locke (1632–1704). Locke believed that everything we know comes from experience, and he emphasized that understanding and feeling were two distinct kinds of knowledge. (To Edwards, the difference between these two kinds of knowledge was like the difference between reading the word *fire* and actually being burned.) Edwards's sermon had a powerful effect on the congregation; several times he had to ask his shrieking and swooning audience for quiet.

> **F**igures of speech are words or phrases that compare one thing to another, unlike thing.
>
> *For more on Figures of Speech, see the Handbook of Literary Terms.*

The Progress of Sin (detail) (1744) by Benjamin Keach. Woodcut.

Sinclair Hamilton Collection no. 21. Graphic Arts Collections. Visual Materials Division. Department of Rare Books and Special Collections. Princeton University Libraries.

Preteaching Vocabulary

Words to Own

Have students work in pairs to read the Words to Own and their definitions and to write them on three-by-five cards. Then, have them play Password. The first player generates synonyms for each word; the second tries to guess the word from the synonyms. Have partners change places and play another round. To review, students can do the following exercises by matching the synonym in the left column with the correct Word to Own in the right.

1. enraged [c]	**a.** abhors
2. satisfy [f]	**b.** induce
3. physical condition [e]	**c.** provoked
4. plan [j]	**d.** ascribed
5. unimaginable [g]	**e.** constitution
6. all-powerful [i]	**f.** appease
7. hates [a]	**g.** inconceivable
8. hateful [h]	**h.** abominable
9. attributed [d]	**i.** omnipotent
10. persuade [b]	**j.** contrivance

from Sinners in the Hands of an Angry God

Jonathan Edwards

So that, thus it is that natural men are held in the hand of God, over the pit of hell; they have deserved the fiery pit, and are already sentenced to it; and God is dreadfully <u>provoked</u>, His anger is as great toward them as to those that are actually suffering the executions of the fierceness of His wrath in hell, and they have done nothing in the least to <u>appease</u> or abate that anger, neither is God in the least bound by any promise to hold them up one moment: The devil is waiting for them, hell is gaping for them, the flames gather and flash about them, and would fain lay hold on them, and swallow them up; the fire pent up in their own hearts is struggling to break out: And they have no interest in any Mediator, there are no means within reach that can be any security to them.

WORDS TO OWN
provoked (prō·vōkt') *adj.*: enraged; angered.
appease (ə·pēz') *v.*: to calm; satisfy.

JONATHAN EDWARDS **79**

Resources ────── 🔲

Viewing and Representing
Videocassette A, Segment 3
Available in English and Spanish. The segment "The Puritan Experience" provides an effective way to spark students' interest in this sermon by providing background material on Puritan society. For full lesson plans and worksheets, see the *Visual Connections Teacher's Manual.*

Ⓐ Cultural Connections
Predestination
Point out that Jonathan Edwards was a Calvinist who believed in predestination—the teaching that one's salvation or damnation was decided by God at the beginning of time. However, Edwards also believed people were responsible for their actions. Therefore, he argued that people could demonstrate and honor their salvation by accepting Christ as their savior and throwing themselves on God's mercy.

Ⓑ Elements of Literature
Parallelism
❓ Point out to students that some of the power of Edwards's sermon derives from his use of parallel constructions: "The devil is waiting for them, hell is gaping for them, the flames gather and flash about them." How does the parallel structure help to build a sense of horror? [The parallel structure hammers home the concept that sinners live on the brink of hell and enumerates some of the torment that awaits them there.]

BROWSING IN THE FILES
About the Author. Edwards was also the loving, affectionate, and thoughtful father of eleven children. When his daughter Esther was nine years old, she wrote movingly about a ride in the woods they took together: "Though father is usually taciturn or preoccupied . . . today he discoursed to me of the awful sweetness of walking with God in nature. He seems to feel God in the woods, the sky, and the grand sweep of the river. . . ."

Reaching All Students

Struggling Readers
To help struggling readers with this selection, use the Think-Aloud strategy. For specific step-by-step help in applying this strategy, see the *Reading Strategies Handbook,* p. 135 in the *Reading Skills and Strategies* binder.

Advanced Learners
Since Edwards's fire-and-brimstone sermon is based on the Bible, have students compare and contrast the content and style of the passages on God's wrath and hellfire from the New Testament with the sermon itself. For example, students could read and study Luke 3:4–9 (John the Baptist's preaching about the wrath of God) and Revelation 6:9–17 (the breaking of the fifth and sixth seals on the day of judgment).

Ⓐ Reading Skills and Strategies

Determining Author's Purpose

❓ What does Edwards hope his sermon will accomplish? [He wants to persuade members of his congregation who have not been "born again" to accept Christ as their savior.]

Ⓑ Reading Skills and Strategies

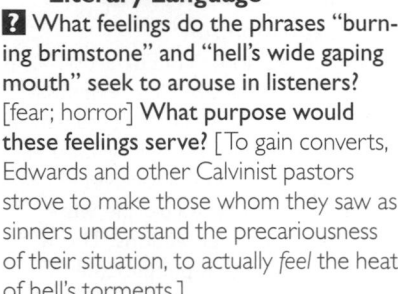

Analyzing Literary Language

❓ What feelings do the phrases "burning brimstone" and "hell's wide gaping mouth" seek to arouse in listeners? [fear; horror] **What purpose would these feelings serve?** [To gain converts, Edwards and other Calvinist pastors strove to make those whom they saw as sinners understand the precariousness of their situation, to actually *feel* the heat of hell's torments.]

Ⓒ Elements of Literature

Figures of Speech

❓ What is the meaning of the metaphor Edwards uses here? [People who depend on themselves rather than on God to keep them from the pit of hell are like people expecting to be held up by thin air.]

Ⓓ Elements of Literature

Figures of Speech

❓ What two figures of speech does Edwards use to describe God's wrath? [He uses the simile of dammed waters and the metaphor of a bow and arrow.] **Which comparison do you find more frightening?** [Possible answer: Many students will say the metaphor of God's anger as a lethal weapon is more disturbing.]

Ⓐ In short, they have no refuge, nothing to take hold of; all that preserves them every moment is the mere arbitrary will, and uncovenanted, unobliged forbearance of an incensed God.

The use of this awful subject may be for awakening unconverted persons in this congregation. This that you have heard is the case of every one of you that are out of Christ. That world of misery, that lake of burning brimstone, is extended abroad under you.

Ⓑ There is the dreadful pit of the glowing flames of the wrath of God; there is hell's wide gaping mouth open; and you have nothing to stand upon, nor anything to take hold of; there is nothing between you and hell but the air; it is only the power and mere pleasure of God that holds you up.

You probably are not sensible of this; you find you are kept out of hell, but do not see the hand of God in it; but look at other things, as the good state of your bodily <u>constitution</u>, your care of your own life, and the means you use for your own preservation. But indeed these things are nothing; if God should withdraw His hand, they would avail no more to keep you from falling, than the thin air to hold up a person that is suspended in it.

Your wickedness makes you as it were heavy as lead, and to tend downward with great weight and pressure toward hell; and if God should let you go, you would immediately sink and swiftly descend and plunge into the bottomless gulf, and your healthy constitution, and your own care and prudence, and best <u>contrivance</u>, and all your righteousness, would have no more influence to uphold you and keep you out of hell, than a spider's web would have to stop a fallen rock. . . .

Ⓓ The wrath of God is like great waters that are dammed for the present; they

increase more and more, and rise higher and higher, till an outlet is given; and the longer the stream is stopped, the more rapid and mighty is its course, when once it is let loose. It is true, that judgment against your evil works has not been executed hitherto; the floods of God's vengeance have been withheld; but your <u>guilt in</u> the meantime is constantly increasing, and you are every day treasuring up more wrath; the waters are constantly rising, and waxing more and more mighty; and there is nothing but the mere pleasure of God that holds the waters back, that are unwilling to be stopped, and press hard to go forward. If God should only withdraw His hand from the floodgate, it would immediately fly open, and the fiery floods of the fierceness and wrath of God, would rush forth with <u>inconceivable</u> fury, and would come upon you with <u>omnipotent</u> power; and if your strength were ten thousand times greater than it is, yea, ten thousand times greater than the strength of the stoutest, sturdiest devil in hell, it would be nothing to withstand or endure it.

The bow of God's wrath is bent, and the arrow made ready on the string, and justice bends the arrow at your heart, and strains the bow, and it is nothing but the mere pleasure of God, and that of an angry God, without any promise or obligation at all, that keeps

WORDS TO OWN

constitution (kän′stə·to͞o′shən) *n.:* physical condition.
contrivance (kən·trī′vəns) *n.:* scheme; plan.
inconceivable (in′kən·sēv′ə·bəl) *adj.:* unimaginable; beyond understanding.
omnipotent (äm·nip′ə·tənt) *adj.:* all-powerful.

Crossing the Curriculum

Social Studies

The Great Awakening. This movement, a series of religious revivals from about 1734 to 1750, aroused tremendous enthusiasm for Puritanism. When Edwards delivered this sermon in 1741, the revival movement was at its peak. As you can gather from his sermon, Edwards promoted a return to the original Covenant of Grace, which had been popular in early Puritan times, in which individuals had to experience an emotional public conversion in order to be admitted to the church. Although The Great Awakening did not restore Puritanism to the glory of its early colonial days, it did have far-reaching effects: It led to increased missionary work among American Indians (as demonstrated in Edwards's own biography), early anti-slavery activity, and the founding of a number of colleges, including Princeton, Rutgers, and Dartmouth.

the arrow one moment from being made drunk with your blood. Thus all you that never passed under a great change of heart, by the mighty power of the Spirit of God upon your souls; all you that were never born again, and made new creatures, and raised from being dead in sin, to a state of new, and before altogether unexperienced light and life, are in the hands of an angry God. However you may have reformed your life in many things, and may have had religious affections,[1] and may keep up a form of religion in your families and closets,[2] and in the house of God, it is nothing but His mere pleasure that keeps you from being this moment swallowed up in everlasting destruction. However unconvinced you may now be of the truth of what you hear, by and by you will be fully convinced of it. Those that are gone from being in the like circumstances with you, see that it was so with them; for destruction came suddenly upon most of them; when they expected nothing of it, and while they were saying, peace and safety: Now they see, that those things on which they depended for peace and safety, were nothing but thin air and empty shadows.

The God that holds you over the pit of hell, much as one holds a spider, or some loathsome insect over the fire, abhors you, and is dreadfully provoked: His wrath toward you burns like fire; He looks upon you as worthy of nothing else but to be cast into the fire; He is of purer eyes than to bear to have you in His sight; you are ten thousand times more abominable in His eyes than the most hateful venomous serpent is in ours. You have offended Him infinitely more than ever a stub

1. **affections:** feelings.
2. **closets:** rooms for prayer and meditation.

born rebel did his prince; and yet it is nothing but His hand that holds you from falling into the fire every moment. It is to be ascribed to nothing else, that you did not go to hell the last night; that you was suffered to awake again in this world, after you closed your eyes to sleep. And there is no other reason to be given, why you have not dropped into hell since you arose in the morning, but that God's hand has held you up. There is no other reason to be given why you have not gone to hell, since you have sat here in the house of God, provoking His pure eyes by your sinful wicked manner of attending His solemn worship. Yea, there is nothing else that is to be given as a reason why you do not this very moment drop down into hell.

O sinner! Consider the fearful danger you are in: It is a great furnace of wrath, a wide and bottomless pit, full of the fire of wrath, that you are held over in the hand of that God, whose wrath is provoked and incensed as much against you, as against many of the damned in hell. You hang by a slender thread, with the flames of divine wrath flashing about it, and ready every moment to singe it, and burn it asunder; and you have no interest in any Mediator, and nothing to lay hold of to save yourself, nothing to keep off the flames of wrath, nothing of your own, nothing that you ever have done, nothing that you can do, to induce God to spare you one moment. . . .

WORDS TO OWN

abhors (ab·hôrz′) *v.*: scorns; hates.
abominable (ə·bäm′ə·nə·bəl) *adj*: disgusting; loathsome.
ascribed (ə·skrībd′) *v.*: attributed to a certain cause.
induce (in·do͞os′) *v.*: to persuade; force; cause.

E **Struggling Readers**
Getting the Main Idea
❓ What point about their fate does Edwards want his listeners to understand? [He wants them to realize that their fate is in God's hands and that none of their efforts to lead a good life matter unless they experience a profound spiritual transformation.]

F **Elements of Literature**
Figures of Speech
❓ What two creatures does Edwards compare sinners to in this passage? [a spider; a serpent] Why did he choose these creatures? [Possible answers: Many people have a visceral repugnance for these creatures; the spider in Christianity often symbolizes the Devil snaring sinners in his web, and the serpent traditionally symbolizes original sin and betrayal.]

G **Elements of Literature**
Interpreting Analogies
Edwards compares God holding a sinner over the open pit of hell to a person holding a spider by its thread over an open flame. Ask students to describe the kind of God that this analogy depicts. [Possible responses: God is cruel, unyielding, vengeful, and easily angered.]

H **Reading Skills and Strategies**
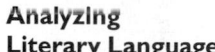
Analyzing Literary Language
❓ How does Edwards use repetition to heighten the effect of his sermon? [Repeating the word *nothing*, especially in the construction "nothing that you have ever done, nothing that you can do," emphasizes his belief that people cannot be saved by their actions, but only through acceptance of grace. Edwards uses this literary device to persuade his audience to repent.]

Making the Connections

Connecting to the Theme:
"The Examined Life"
Point out that the "sinners" Edwards is addressing are respectable, church-going people. Have students speculate about why he wants them to feel that they are "abominable" in God's sight and how Edwards's motivation may affect his credibility. [He wants his audience to examine their consciences and beg for God's mercy. He might exaggerate his own view of the dangers of damnation in order to sway his audience.]

Cultural Connections:
Evangelism
Remind students that Edwards's sermons prompted screams and fainting fits. Students who are familiar with modern evangelism, either from television or personal experience, might discuss the intense emotions that can accompany evangelical sermons. If your class has no experience with evangelism, have students do research on current movements that follow in the tradition of Edwards.

Assessing Learning

Check Test: True-False
1. Edwards says that God's forbearance is all that keeps sinners from going directly to hell. [True]
2. Edwards speaks chiefly about God's love and mercy. [False]
3. Edwards compares humanity to a spider and a serpent. [True]
4. Edwards says that God is holding humanity over the pit of hell. [True]

Primary Sources

This feature contains an entry from Edwards's journal extolling the virtues of his future wife, Sarah Pierrepont, and a short excerpt from Edwards's autobiography describing a religious epiphany in which he sees God's sweetness and majesty in everything in nature.

Ⓐ Critical Thinking

Speculating

❓ After reading these excerpts, students may find that they have a better understanding of Edwards. Ask students to speculate about how a man who could see so much evil in ordinary people could so idealize a girl he had never seen. How does Sarah relate to God in Edwards's view? [Students may say that he imagines her to perceive God everywhere, much as he does.] Why do they think Sarah's relationship to God would be important to Edwards? [To be happily married, she would probably need to share his beliefs.]

Ⓑ Reading Skills and Strategies

Analyzing Literary Language

❓ Compare the language of the sermon with that of the journal. Why are they different? [Possible answers: The images in the sermon are vivid and frightening. Edwards's language is equally vivid here, but not frightening. Here his purpose is entirely different. Here he describes a woman he loves.] Based on the journal entry, what do you think of Sarah?

Ⓒ Vocabulary Note

Shifts in Meaning

❓ Today, we use the word *awful* to mean "terrible; horrible." In Edwards's day, however, the word meant "full of awe" or "awe-inspiring." What would the phrase "awful sweetness" mean to Edwards? [something that fills one with the majesty of God and gives one a sweet or serene feeling]

Ⓓ Reading Skills and Strategies

Responding to the Text

❓ What do you think of Edwards's view of nature? [Some students will share this theological view of nature, in which God appears in all things.] You might suggest a comparison with Wilbur's "The Beautiful Changes" on p. 1006.

T82

Ⓐ When Jonathan Edwards was twenty years old, he wrote a journal entry describing thirteen-year-old Sarah Pierrepont of New Haven. Edwards idealized Sarah and viewed her as a source of great spiritual strength. He wrote this tribute before he had even seen her. They were married four years later. In the second entry, from his unfinished autobiography, Edwards records a spiritual experience.

Sarah Pierrepont

They say there is a young lady in [New Haven] who is beloved of that Great Being who made and rules the world, and that there are certain seasons in which this Great Being, in some way or another invisible, comes to her and fills her mind with exceeding sweet delight, and that she hardly cares for anything, except to meditate on Him—that she expects after a while to be received up where He is, to be raised up out of the world and caught up into heaven; being assured that He loves her too well to let her remain at a distance from Him always. There she is to dwell with Him, and to be ravished with His love and delight forever. Therefore, if you present all the world before her, with the richest of its treasures, she disregards it and cares not for it, and is unmindful of any pain or affliction. She has a strange sweetness in her mind, and singular purity in her affections; is most just and conscientious in all her conduct; and you could not persuade her to do anything wrong or sinful, if you would give her all the world, lest she should Ⓑ offend this Great Being. She is of a wonderful sweetness, calmness, and universal benevolence of mind; especially after this Great God had manifested Himself to her mind. She will sometimes go about from place to place, singing sweetly; and seems to be always full of joy and pleasure; and no one knows for what. She loves to be alone, walking in the fields and groves, and seems to have someone invisible always conversing with her.

—Jonathan Edwards

My Sense of Divine Things

. . . And as I was walking there, and looking up on the sky and clouds, there came into my mind so sweet a sense of the glorious *majesty* and *grace* of God, that I know not how to express. I seemed to see them both in a sweet conjunction; majesty and meekness joined together; it was a sweet, and gentle, and holy majesty; and also a majestic meekness; an Ⓒ awful sweetness; a high, and great, and holy gentleness.

After this my sense of divine things gradually increased, and became more and more lively, and had more of that inward sweetness. The appearance of everything was altered; there seemed to be, as it were, a calm, sweet cast, or appearance of divine glory, in almost everything. God's excellency, his wisdom, his purity, and love, seemed to appear in everything; in the sun, and moon, and stars; in the clouds and blue sky; in the grass, flowers, trees; in the water, and all nature; which used greatly to fix my mind. I often used to sit and view the moon for continuance; and in the day spent much time in viewing the clouds and sky, to behold the sweet glory of God in these things; in the meantime, singing forth, with a low voice, my contemplations of the Creator and Redeemer. And scarce anything, among all Ⓓ the works of nature, was so sweet to me as thunder and lightning; formerly, nothing had been so terrible to me. Before, I used to be uncommonly terrified with thunder, and to be struck with terror when I saw a thunderstorm rising; but now, on the contrary, it rejoiced me. I felt God, so to speak, at the first appearance of a thunderstorm; and used to take the opportunity, at such times, to fix myself in order to view the clouds and see the lightning's play, and hear the majestic and awful voice of God's thunder, which oftentimes was exceedingly entertaining, leading me to sweet contemplations of my great and glorious God.

—Jonathan Edwards

Connecting Across Texts

To help students compare and contrast this primary source with "Sinners in the Hands of an Angry God," you may wish to have them complete a chart like the one that follows. Guide students in analyzing Edwards's use of language, imagery, and figures of speech as they compare and contrast the two selections. Then lead a discussion in which you explore Edwards's true character and beliefs by citing both the public sermons and the private writings. Have students save their notes for use in Choice 2.

	Sermon	**Journal**
God nature love	fierceness, wrath spider, serpent . . .	grace, majesty grass, flowers . . .

First Thoughts

1. If you had been a member of the congregation listening to Edwards's sermon, what do you think your reaction would have been?

> **Reading Check**
>
> Identify the three famous **figures of speech** that Edwards develops in paragraphs 4–7 of the sermon. What things is he comparing in each one? How does Edwards extend each figure of speech?

Shaping Interpretations

2. What references in the sermon might be interpreted as **allusions** to divine mercy?

3. Edwards is directing his sermon to what he calls "natural men," those members of his congregation who have not been "reborn." Review your reading notes. What **images** and **figures of speech** do you think helped Edwards's listeners to *feel* the peril of their sinful condition?

4. Edwards strikes fear into the hearts of his listeners in order to persuade them to act to avoid everlasting torment. Which specific **metaphors** and **similes** in the sermon do you think were probably the most persuasive?

Challenging the Text

5. If you had a chance to respond to Edwards, what would you say?

CHOICES:
Building Your Portfolio

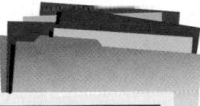

> **Writer's Notebook**
>
>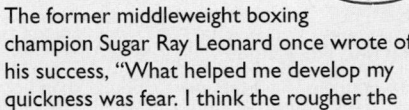
>
> #### 1. Collecting Ideas for an Autobiographical Incident
>
> The former middleweight boxing champion Sugar Ray Leonard once wrote of his success, "What helped me develop my quickness was fear. I think the rougher the

opponent, the quicker I am." Freewrite about an incident in your own life when fear or anxiety motivated you to take action, make a change, or try harder at something. Save your notes for possible use in the Writer's Workshop on page 130.

Comparing Texts
2. The Other Edwards

In a brief essay, compare the ideas about God that Edwards expresses in his sermon with those he expresses in Primary Sources (page 82). How do you explain the apparent differences between the "two" Edwardses?

Speaking and Listening
3. Fire and Fervor

Today's fiery religious orators are successors to Jonathan Edwards and other preachers of the Great Awakening. With four or five other students, form a panel to discuss the following questions in class: (a) Are "fire-and-brimstone" sermons still effective today, or are other methods used to motivate congregations? (b) What aspects of Edwards's sermon would be effective today? (c) Would modern telecommunications enhance or detract from Edwards's sermon?

Creative Writing
4. What the Parishioners Said

You and your family have just returned to your home in Enfield after listening to Pastor Edwards's sermon. Write a script of a conversation between the members of your family, including the reactions of both adults and children.

Mrs. Jonathan Edwards (1750–1755) by Joseph Badger (1708–1765). Oil on canvas (30⅜″ × 25½″).

Yale University Art Gallery. Bequest of Eugene Phelps Edwards (1938.75).

JONATHAN EDWARDS 83

> **Reading Check**
>
> 1. The wrath of God is compared to dammed waters, with God's hands on the floodgate, holding back the "fiery floods."
> 2. God's wrath is compared to a bent bow, whose tension is increasing as justice prepares to loose the arrow of God's vengeance.
> 3. Sinners are compared to "loathsome" spiders held over the fire, threatened with being dropped into the flames.

First Thoughts [Respond]

1. Possible responses: fear; terror; outrage; anger.

Shaping Interpretations [Interpret]

2. His references to the "mediator" (Christ) and to God's hand holding his listeners out of hell (for the moment) might be allusions to divine mercy.

3. Edwards's use of sensory images, such as flames in the first paragraph, "thin air" in the fourth, and the description of singeing and burning in the ninth, make listeners *feel* the danger. Also effective are Edwards's references to the "bodily constitution," blood, and heart of the listener.

4. Possible response: Any of the images cited above or the simile of God looking at sinners the way one looks at a spider or a serpent may have been the most persuasive.

Challenging the Text [Evaluate]

5. Responses will vary. Some students may say they believe God is more merciful than Edwards believes.

Grading Timesaver

Rubrics for each Choices assignment appear on p. 95 in the *Portfolio Management System*.

CHOICES:
Building Your Portfolio

1. **Writer's Notebook** Caution students to choose a situation they would not mind sharing with others.

2. **Comparing Texts** Remind students to keep in mind the era in which each piece was written.

3. **Speaking and Listening** To help panelists prepare, play tapes of modern evangelists. Have students analyze the speakers' techniques, including pauses, rising pitch, tremors, and stress.

4. **Creative Writing** To motivate students, read aloud selections from Arthur Miller's *The Crucible*, especially the speeches of Salem's Puritan judges.

Benjamin Franklin

(1706–1790)

Few people have been so energetically devoted to improvement—both self-improvement and the improvement of society—as Benjamin Franklin. Franklin's many accomplishments can only be summarized. Born in Boston, one of seventeen children, he rose from poverty to eminence even though he had to leave school early in order to work. By the time he was twenty-four, he was a prosperous merchant, owner of a successful print shop, and publisher of *The Pennsylvania Gazette*. He helped found the Academy of Philadelphia (which became the University of Pennsylvania), the American Philosophical Society, and the first public library in America. He promoted numerous municipal projects in Philadelphia: paved streets, sewer lines, improved street lighting, and a fire brigade. He was a scientist and an important inventor: His research, especially on electricity, resulted in his election to England's Royal Society. In addition, he invented an open heating stove (called a Franklin stove), bifocal eyeglasses, a type of harmonica, and a rocking chair that could swat flies. Like Thomas Jefferson (page 114), Franklin was a tinkerer, constantly looking for ways to make things work a little better or more efficiently.

Scientist, Socialite, and "Snake"

At forty-one, Franklin had made enough money to retire from business. He hoped to devote the rest of his life to study and scientific research, but this was not to be. Franklin possessed uncommon talents as a diplomat and negotiator, and for the rest of his life he used these skills in the service of his state and his country. Franklin lived in London in the 1750s and '60s, representing the interests of Pennsylvania as an agent of the Pennsylvania Assembly. A decade later he was back in London lobbying for the Colonies in their dispute with Britain, hoping to bring about a reconciliation that would prevent war. Franklin's wit and charm made him enormously popular in London for

Benjamin Franklin (1777) after Jean-Baptiste Greuze. Oil on canvas (28⅝″ × 22⅝″).

© 1998 Board of Trustees, National Gallery of Art, Washington, D.C. Gift of Adele Lewisohn Lehman.

many years; he once said that he was invited out to dinner there six nights a week. But by 1774, when he was sixty-eight, the stress between Britain and the Colonies had become too great for even this shrewd diplomat to control. The King's Privy Council publicly attacked him for his policies; the British press called him an "old snake." Franklin finally relinquished his hopes for peace and sailed for America in 1775.

When Franklin arrived home, he was greeted with news that the first battles of the Revolutionary War had been fought at Lexington and Concord, Massachusetts. The "shot heard round the world" had been fired. After helping to draft the Declaration of Independence in 1776, Franklin left for Paris to negotiate the treaty that brought the French into the war on America's side. When Franklin landed in France, Lord Stormont, the British ambassador, caustically remarked: "I look upon him as a dangerous engine, and am very sorry that some English frigate did not meet with him by the way."

The Jack of All Trades

In Paris, Franklin was even more popular than he had once been in England. Playing the role of the

go.hrw.com
LEO 11-2

sophisticated but homespun American, Franklin described himself as "an old man, with gray hair appearing under a marten fur cap, among the powdered heads of Paris." When the Revolution was over, he helped negotiate the peace, and he was a member of the Constitutional Convention in 1787. His death three years later was cause for international mourning.

Franklin's practicality, like the success story of his life, is typically American, but it has not been universally admired throughout the nation's history. The American novelist Herman Melville (page 311) gave this picture of Franklin: "Jack of all trades, master of each and mastered by none— the type and genius of his land. Franklin was everything but a poet." Franklin did lack a poet's depth of imagination and emotion, but his literary talents and accomplishments were substantial. He was especially gifted as a wit, as the lightly ironic tone of his *Autobiography* testifies.

> **F**ranklin's practicality is typically American.

Franklin's talents were so great that he could have left his mark on many areas of intellectual accomplishment. As the biographer Carl Van Doren wrote of him, "Mind and will, talent and art, strength and ease, wit and grace met in him as if nature had been lavish and happy when he was shaped."

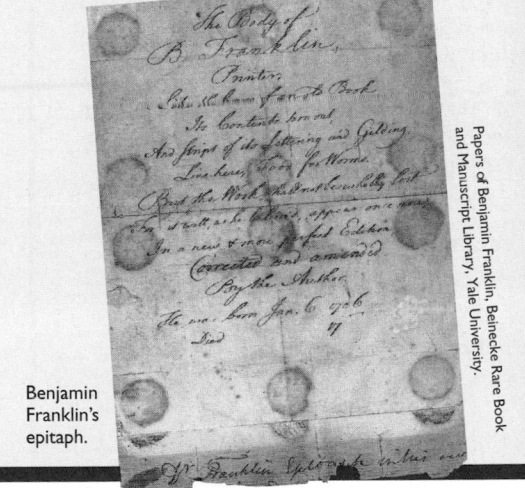

Benjamin Franklin's epitaph.

Papers of Benjamin Franklin, Beinecke Rare Book and Manuscript Library, Yale University.

Before You Read
FROM **THE AUTOBIOGRAPHY**

Make the Connection
The Road to Success
"Rags-to-riches" is the Cinderella-like success story at the core of American life and culture. The slew of once-popular novels by Horatio Alger (1832–1899) chronicle just such success stories— the meteoric rise from humble beginnings to wealth. Rags-to-riches is the story of many Hollywood movie stars and producers (such as Charles Chaplin) and of this country's early business and industrial giants (such as Andrew Carnegie), some of whom were immigrants from other lands. It is still the story of numerous people today, from well-known athletes, performers, and other celebrities to unsung people you might even know yourself.

Quickwrite
Using a chart like the one below, make a list of qualities that you think are necessary for success. Can these qualities be acquired, or do people have to be born with them? Do you think that the same basic qualities are required to be successful at anything?

A Successful Person		
IS decisive	HAS goals	PLANS ahead

Background
Franklin began his *Autobiography* when he was sixty-five and continued it intermittently for years, although he never finished it and it was not published during his lifetime. When Franklin was a teenager, he was apprenticed to his older brother James, who printed a Boston newspaper. As an apprentice, Franklin felt he was treated harshly, and disputes arose between the brothers. This selection begins with Franklin's escape from a second, secret "indenture," or contract of service, that his brother had forced him to sign.

BENJAMIN FRANKLIN 85

Summary ■■

In "Leaving Boston," the first excerpt from his autobiography, young Franklin leaves his apprenticeship in his brother's print shop to seek work in New York. Finding nothing there, Franklin hears of a job in Philadelphia. He sets sail for that city, gets caught in a storm, and suffers several mishaps. Once on land, he walks fifty miles to Burlington, New Jersey, where, after more adventures, he finds a boat to Philadelphia. In "Arrival in Philadelphia," Franklin narrates his first day in the city and describes his impressions. The chapter entitled "Arriving at Moral Perfection" describes Franklin's plan for achieving an ethical and disciplined life. He lists thirteen important virtues, their definitions, and his plans for mastering them.

Background

Students are probably unfamiliar with the system of apprenticeship in the eighteenth century. A youth, often between the ages of fourteen and sixteen, signed a contract, called an *indenture*, obligating him to work for a skilled craftsman for a given number of years in exchange for room, board, and training in his craft. Usually, the boys lived in the shop, lit the fires in the morning, chopped wood, and ran errands until they became old enough to start learning their trade. Those who completed their apprenticeship were free to work wherever they wished.

Preteaching Vocabulary

Words to Own
Have students read the Words to Own and their definitions and create rhymes as memory aids. Students should share their best mnemonics with the class. Then students can use the following exercise to review, choosing the vocabulary word that best completes each sentence.

1. [Assert] your independence!
2. His decision seemed unfounded and [arbitrary].
3. What a thoughtless, [indiscreet] move!
4. This balm helped the pain to [abate].
5. The [itinerant] salesman passed through town.
6. It was a long, [arduous] task.
7. His moral [rectitude] prevented him from lying.
8. She used her uncle's influence to [facilitate] her promotion.
9. His [subsequent] actions showed how much he had learned.
10. Good deeds can't [eradicate] past mistakes.

RESPONDING TO THE ART

David Levine (1926–) is noted for his witty caricatures of literary and political figures, which also appear on pp. 18, 166, 212, 343, and 493.

Activity. Caricature achieves its effect through exaggeration. In comparison with the portrait on p. 84, which of Franklin's features are exaggerated here? [his double chin, long hair, and intellectual expression]

Ⓐ Vocabulary Note

Technical Vocabulary
Because of his professional expertise in a print shop, Franklin often drew figures of speech from printing. Here he uses the technical word *errata* ("errors in print") to refer to mistakes in life.

Ⓑ Elements of Literature

Character
❓ What character flaws does Franklin admit to here? [He suggests that he may have been rude to his brother and too outspoken and opinionated for the governing party and Assembly.] How might these factors have contributed to his decision to leave Boston? [He might have wanted to be free from his reputation and to make a fresh start.]

---

from The Autobiography
Benjamin Franklin

Leaving Boston

At length, a fresh difference arising between my brother and me, I took upon me to assert my freedom, presuming that he would not venture to produce the new indentures. It was not fair in me to take this advantage, and this I therefore Ⓐ reckon one of the first errata[1] of my life; but the unfairness of it weighed little with me, when under the impressions of resentment for the blows his passion too often urged him to be-

Benjamin Franklin.
Drawing by David Levine. Reprinted with permission from *The New York Review of Books.* Copyright © 1973 NYREV, Inc.

stow upon me, though he was otherwise not an ill-natured man: Perhaps I was too saucy and provoking.

When he found I would leave him, he took care to prevent my getting employment in any other printing house of the town, by going round and speaking to every master, who accordingly refused to give me work. I Ⓑ then thought of going to New York, as the nearest place where there was a printer; and I was rather inclined to leave Boston when I reflected that I had already made myself a little obnoxious to the governing party, and, from the arbitrary proceedings of the Assem-

1. **errata** (er·rät′ə): Latin for "errors"; a printer's term.

bly in my brother's case, it was likely I might, if I stayed, soon bring myself into scrapes; and farther, that my indiscreet disputations about religion began to make me pointed at with horror by good people as an infidel or atheist. I determined on the point, but my father now siding with my brother, I was sensible that, if I attempted to go openly, means would be used to prevent me. My friend Collins, therefore, undertook to manage a little for me. He agreed with the captain of a New York sloop for my passage, under the notion of my being a young acquaintance of his, that had got a naughty girl with child, whose friends would compel me to marry

I wished to live without committing any fault at any time.

her, and therefore I could not appear or come away publicly. So I sold some of my books to raise a little money, was taken on board privately, and as we had a fair wind, in three days I found myself in New York, near 300 miles from home, a boy of but 17, without the least recommendation to, or knowledge of any person in the place, and with very little money in my pocket.

- -

WORDS TO OWN

assert (ə·surt′) *v.*: to declare; claim.
arbitrary (är′bə·trer′ē) *adj.*: based on whims or individual preferences.
indiscreet (in′di·skrēt′) *adj.*: careless in speech or action.

- -

86 BEGINNINGS

Reaching All Students

Struggling Readers

Encourage students to become more active readers by questioning the text as they read. Students can use a K-W-L chart like this one:

To help struggling readers further engage with a text as they read, you may want to use a strategy called Anticipation Guides. For step-by-step help in applying this strategy, see the *Reading Struggling Readers Handbook,* p. 17 in the *Reading Skills and Strategies* binder.

What I Know	What I Want to Know	What I Learned
Franklin did not get along with many people in Boston.	How will he get to New York and then to Philadelphia without money or friends?	He found kind people who helped him, and he schooled himself in behaving properly.

Benjamin Franklin Drawing Electricity from the Sky (c. 1805) by Benjamin West (1738–1820). Oil on paper on canvas (13¼″ × 10″).

Philadelphia Museum of Art: Mr. and Mrs. Wharton Sinkler Collection (P1984:23).

Professional Notes

Autobiographical Comment: Franklin's Influences

Franklin believed that imitation of good models was an effective way of learning to write. In *The Autobiography,* he describes how he learned from imitating the *Spectator* papers of the British writers Joseph Addison and Richard Steele: "I thought the writing excellent, and wished, if possible, to imitate it. With this view, I took some of the papers, and making short hints of the sentiment in each sentence, laid them by a few days, and then without looking at the book, tried to complete the papers again. . . . Then I compared my *Spectator* with the original, discovered some of my faults, and corrected them."

My inclinations for the sea were by this time worn out, or I might now have gratified them. But, having a trade, and supposing myself a pretty good workman, I offered my service to the printer in the place, old Mr. William Bradford,[2] who had been the first printer in Pennsylvania, but removed from thence upon the quarrel of George Keith. He could give me no employment, having little to do, and help enough already; but says he, "My son at Philadelphia has lately lost his principal hand,[3] Aquila Rose, by death; if you go thither, I believe he may employ you." Philadelphia was 100 miles further; I set out, however, in a boat for Amboy,[4] leaving my chest and things to follow me round by sea.

In crossing the bay, we met with a squall that tore our rotten sails to pieces, prevented our getting into the Kill,[5] and drove us upon Long Island. In our way, a drunken Dutchman, who was a passenger too, fell overboard; when he was sinking, I reached through the water to his shock pate,[6] and drew him up, so that we got him in again. His ducking sobered him a little, and he went to sleep, taking first out of his pocket a book, which he desired I would dry for him. It proved to be my old favorite author, Bunyan's *Pilgrim's Progress,*[7] in Dutch, finely printed on good paper, with copper cuts,[8] a

2. **William Bradford:** one of the first American printers; not to be confused with *Of Plymouth Plantation* author William Bradford (page 26). Bradford (1663-1752) set up the first printing presses in Philadelphia (1685) and New York (1693).
3. **principal hand:** best employee.
4. **Amboy:** Perth Amboy, New Jersey.
5. **Kill:** channel (from the Dutch *kil*). Based on the explorations of Henry Hudson in 1609, the Dutch claimed land in the Middle Colonies and gave Dutch names to some of its geographic features.
6. **shock pate** (pāt): shaggy head.
7. ***Pilgrim's Progress:*** religious allegory by the Puritan writer John Bunyan (1628–1688), first published in 1678. It tells how the hero, Christian, makes his journey to salvation. Notice that Franklin admires the book for literary and historical, rather than religious, reasons.
8. **copper cuts:** engravings.

dress better than I had ever seen it wear in its own language. I have since found that it has been translated into most of the languages of Europe, and suppose it has been more generally read than any other book, except perhaps the Bible. Honest John was the first that I know of who mixed narration and dialogue; a method of writing very engaging to the reader, who in the most interesting parts finds himself, as it were, brought into the company and present at the discourse. . . .

When we drew near the island, we found it was at a place where there could be no landing, there being a great surf on the stony beach. So we dropped anchor, and swung round toward the shore. Some people came down to the water edge and hallooed to us, as we did to them; but the wind was so high, and the surf so loud, that we could not hear so as to understand each other. There were canoes on the shore, and we made signs, and hallooed that they should fetch us; but they either did not understand us, or thought it impracticable, so they went away, and night coming on, we had no remedy but to wait till the wind should <u>abate</u>; and, in the meantime, the boatman and I concluded to sleep, if we could; and so crowded into the scuttle,[9] with the Dutchman, who was still wet, and the spray beating over the head of our boat, leaked through to us, so that we were soon almost as wet as he. In this manner we lay all night, with very little rest; but, the wind abating the next day, we made a shift to reach Amboy before night, having been thirty hours on the water, without victuals,[10] or any drink but a bottle of filthy rum, and the water we sailed on being salt.

9. **scuttle:** covered opening in hull or deck of a ship.
10. **victuals** (vit′′lz): food; sometimes spelled "vittles."

WORDS TO OWN

abate (ə·bāt′) *v.:* lessen.

Crossing the Curriculum

Geography

Have students trace the circuitous route Franklin follows from Boston to New York to Philadelphia. Then on the same map, ask students to show how Franklin would travel from Boston to Philadelphia today, using a car, train, or an airplane. Then estimate how much time it would take to make the journey today.

Mathematics

Have students calculate how much money someone would need today to make the journey from Boston to New York and then from New York to Philadelphia as inexpensively as possible. Students should include funds for travel, food, lodging, clothing, and miscellaneous expenses.

Social Studies

Students can work in groups to research printing methods from the eighteenth century to the present. They can compare and contrast hand-set type with electronic page composition and etched printed plates with computerized illustrations. Students will be astonished to discover how much labor was needed to print a page in Franklin's day.

In the evening I found myself very feverish, and went in to bed; but, having read somewhere that cold water drank plentifully was good for a fever, I followed the prescription, sweat plentiful most of the night, my fever left me, and in the morning, crossing the ferry, I proceeded on my journey on foot, having fifty miles to Burlington,[11] where I was told I should find boats that would carry me the rest of the way to Philadelphia.

It rained very hard all the day; I was thoroughly soaked, and by noon a good deal tired; so I stopped at a poor inn, where I stayed all night, beginning now to wish that I had never left home. I cut so miserable a figure, too, that I found, by the questions asked me, I was suspected to be some runaway servant, and in danger of being taken up on that suspicion. However, I proceeded the next day, and got in the evening to an

Speak not but what may benefit others or yourself; avoid trifling conversation.

Drawing by David Levine. Reprinted with permission from *The New York Review of Books*. Copyright © 1973 NYREV, Inc.

inn, within eight or ten miles of Burlington, kept by one Dr. Brown. He entered into conversation with me while I took some refreshment, and, finding I had read a little, became very sociable and friendly. Our acquaintance continued as long as he lived. He had been, I imagine, an <u>itinerant</u> doctor, for there was no town in England, or country in Europe, of which he could not give a very particular account. He had some letters,[12] and was ingenious, but much of an unbeliever, and wickedly undertook, some years after, to travesty the Bible in doggerel verse, as Cot-

ton had done Virgil.[13] By this means he set many of the facts in a very ridiculous light, and might have hurt weak minds if his work had been published; but it never was.

At his house I lay that night, and the next morning reached Burlington, but had the mortification to find that the regular boats were gone a little before my coming, and no other expected to go before Tuesday, this being Saturday; wherefore I returned to an old woman in the town, of whom I had bought gingerbread to eat on the water, and asked her advice. She invited me to lodge at her house till a passage by water should offer; and being tired with my foot traveling, I accepted the invitation. She understanding I was a printer, would have had me stay at that town and follow my business, being ignorant of the stock necessary to begin with. She was very hospitable, gave me a dinner of oxcheek with great goodwill, accepting only of a pot of ale in return; and I thought myself fixed till Tuesday should come. However, walking in the evening by the side of the river, a boat came by, which I found was going toward Philadelphia, with several people in her. They took me in, and, as there was no wind, we rowed all the way; and about midnight, not having yet seen the city, some of the company were confident we must have passed it, and would row no farther; the others knew not where we were; so we put toward the shore, got into a creek, landed near an old fence, with the rails of which we made a fire, the night being cold, in October, and

13. **doggerel . . . Virgil:** Doggerel is irregularly constructed comical verse, often used for satirical purposes. In 1664, Charles Cotton (1630–1687) published a doggerel version, or a parody, of the *Aeneid,* an epic poem by the Roman poet Virgil (70–19 B.C.).

- -

WORDS TO OWN
itinerant (ī·tin′ər·ənt) *adj.:* traveling.

- -

11. **Burlington:** Burlington, New Jersey; about eighteen miles from Philadelphia.
12. **letters:** education.

D Elements of Literature
Character
❓ **How would you describe Franklin's character at this point?** [Sample responses: He is brave, hearty, humorous, resourceful, or foolhardy.] **Do you admire him? Why or why not?** [Students who see him as courageous will admire him; those who consider him impetuous may not.]

E Historical Connections
Runaway Servants
Students may not understand why a runaway servant might be "taken up," that is, arrested. This happened because many servants were *bondsmen* or *bondswomen,* indentured to their employers for passage to the colony or for payment of debts. Servants who tried to escape from this condition of near-slavery could be forcibly returned to their employers.

F English Language Learners
Using Context Clues
❓ **How can you use context clues to figure out the meaning of the phrase "the stock necessary to begin with"?** [Students can infer from the clues "printer" and "follow my business" that the "stock" a person would need to start in the printing trade would include such large and expensive items as a press, type, and paper.]

G Struggling Readers
Understanding Sequence of Events
On his journey from Perth Amboy to Philadelphia, many events occur. Have students reread this page and list what happens at the following places: (1) the **first inn** [People suspect him of being a runaway servant]; (2) **Dr. Brown's inn** [Franklin makes friends with the irreverent Dr. Brown]; (3) **Burlington** [Franklin charms an old woman into inviting him to stay for a few days and then unexpectedly hops a boat for Philadelphia]; (4) **Cooper's Creek** [Franklin and the other travelers camp out for the night in the cold]

Taking a Second Look

Review: Chronological Order
Remind students that **chronological order** is the sequence in which events in a story happen. Authors of autobiographies use their life stories to explain why they became a certain way, why they hold certain opinions, or what they have learned about the world. To help readers keep track of events, writers use transitions—single words like *beforehand,* phrases like *that morning,* and clauses like *as I walked through the door.*

1. Have pairs of students look for a passage from *The Autobiography* with five transitions and then rewrite the passage without them. Ask whether the sequence of events is as clear as before.

2. Have students create a time line with eight events from one of the first two sections of Franklin's work. Discuss the sequence of events, and ask students what impression Franklin is trying to convey about himself.

Explain that almanacs were one of the earliest publications in history. The word comes from the Arabic *al-manakh,* meaning "the calendar." The earliest almanacs were carved on wood or on tablets made of stone. Banneker's and Franklin's almanacs were, of course, printed on paper. Tell students that in addition to publishing almanacs and coming up with inventions, such as his famous clock, Banneker was appointed in 1790 to the District of Columbia Commission by President George Washington and, with that group, surveyed Washington, D.C.

As a follow-up, students could research a number of inventors of the time—Banneker, Franklin himself, Thomas Jefferson, and Robert Fulton—and organize an "Invention Convention" to display information about their accomplishments.

Time on His Side: Benjamin Banneker

Poor Richard's Almanack (page 95) was a best-seller in its time, but Benjamin Franklin is not the only important figure in the history of the American almanac. Between 1792 and 1797, six remarkable almanacs were published by Benjamin Banneker (1731–1806), a Maryland farmer, astronomer, mathematician, and the first African American to have calculated almanacs. Banneker's almanacs, published in twenty-eight editions, were among the most successful almanacs of his era.

Self-taught scientist . . . Benjamin Banneker was the son of free African Americans. His grandmother was an Englishwoman, and his grandfather, who claimed to be an African prince, had the name Bannke or Bannaka. His grandmother taught him to read and write, and for a while he attended a one-room, interracial school where, recalled an African American classmate, "all his delight was to dive into his books." Banneker was mostly self-taught, and throughout his life he acquired considerable computational skill. For enjoyment he devised mathematical puzzles, some of them in verse. At twenty-two, using only a borrowed pocket watch and a picture of a clock as models, Banneker built a functioning wooden clock, each gear carved by hand, which struck the hours for over fifty years. Later in life, Banneker developed a passionate interest in the stars, and, in 1788, he calculated a solar eclipse using nothing but books as a guide.

A Reading Skills and Strategies
Making Predictions
? Based on his appearance, how do you think Franklin will be received by the residents of Philadelphia? [Possible response: It is likely that Franklin will have a difficult time, since he is dirty and disheveled.]

B Elements of Literature
Character
? Franklin has almost no money and is very hungry. Why, then, does he insist on paying for his passage on the boat? What does this reveal about his character? [Possible responses: Wary of being thought poor, he wants to pay his way and not be indebted to others. This shows that he is honest, upright, and proud.]

there we remained till daylight. Then one of the company knew the place to be Cooper's Creek, a little above Philadelphia, which we saw as soon as we got out of the creek, and arrived there about eight or nine o'clock on the Sunday morning, and landed at the Market Street wharf.

Arrival in Philadelphia

I have been the more particular in this description of my journey, and shall be so of my first entry into that city, that you may in your mind compare such unlikely beginnings with the figure I have since made there. I was in my working dress, my best clothes being to come round by sea. I was dirty from my journey; my pockets were stuffed out with shirts and stockings, and I knew no soul nor where to look for lodging. I was fatigued with travel-ing, rowing, and want of rest, I was very hungry; and my whole stock of cash consisted of a Dutch dollar, and about a shilling in copper. The latter I gave the people of the boat for my passage, who at first refused it, on account of my rowing; but I insisted on their taking it. A man being sometimes more generous when he has but a little money than when he has plenty, perhaps through fear of being thought to have but little.

Then I walked up the street, gazing about till near the market house I met a boy with bread. I had made many a meal on bread, and, inquiring where he got it, I went immediately to the baker's he directed me to, in Second Street, and asked for biscuit, intending such as we had in Boston; but they, it seems, were not made in Philadelphia. Then I asked for a three-penny loaf, and was told

Banneker published his almanacs to advance not only the cause of science, but also the cause of African Americans. In 1791, Banneker sent a manuscript copy of his first almanac to Secretary of State Thomas Jefferson, along with a famous letter in which he urges Jefferson to recognize the equality of all people and calls for the abolition of slavery. Jefferson in turn sent the almanac to the Academy of Sciences in Paris, the foremost body of scientific learning in France. Thus, Banneker achieved transatlantic fame through his almanacs, as Franklin did through his writings and diplomatic career.

. . . and star-gazing sage. Banneker was described by those who knew him as having the thoughtful demeanor of a sage as he leaned on the long staff that he always carried with him. Toward the end of his life, living alone in a small log house on his farm, Banneker continued to watch the stars, putter in his garden, study bees and locusts, play the violin and flute, and record his observations in a journal that became a unique record of an eighteenth-century almanac maker's method. His lifelong preoccupation with the measurement of time assured him a prominent place in the early history of science in America. Appropriately, the wooden clock Banneker had constructed kept excellent time until two days after his death: As Banneker's body was being lowered into his grave, his house a few yards away caught fire, destroying the clock he had made more than fifty years before.

Benjamin Banneker, from one of his almanacs, c. 1795, by an unknown artist. Woodcut.

Maryland Historical Society.

C Critical Thinking

Making Inferences

? What does Franklin's trip to the bakery suggest about travel and currency in the eighteenth century? [There were significant cultural differences between colonies, since even common items, such as bread, were so different in Boston and Philadelphia. In addition, Franklin's experiences suggest that the colonies functioned as relatively isolated economies, so the value of money differed slightly between them. Pennsylvania was one of the most prosperous colonies.]

D Elements of Literature

Character

? Franklin appears here in tattered clothes, with his pockets stuffed with stockings, a roll under each arm, and his mouth full of the roll he is eating. This description has become very famous. Why do you think it appeals to people? [Possible response: The scene is memorable because it is vivid and humorous and reveals the ability of a great man to laugh at himself. It also dramatizes the contrast between the great man's success and his humble beginnings.]

E Elements of Literature

Character

? What does the act of giving away the rolls tell you about Franklin? [Possible responses: He is generous, considerate, and self-confident.]

---

they had none such. So not considering or knowing the difference of money, and the greater cheapness nor the names of his bread, I bade him give me three-penny worth of any sort. He gave me, accordingly, three great puffy rolls. I was surprised at the quantity, but took it, and,

Tolerate no uncleanliness in body, clothes, or habitation.

Drawing by David Levine. Reprinted with permission from *The New York Review of Books.* Copyright © 1973 NYREV, Inc.

having no room in my pockets, walked off with a roll under each arm, and eating the other. Thus I went up Market Street as far as Fourth Street, passing by the door of Mr.

Read, my future wife's father; when she, standing at the door, saw me, and thought I made, as I certainly did, a most awkward, ridiculous appearance. Then I turned and went down Chestnut Street and part of Walnut Street, eating my roll all the way, and, coming round, found myself again at Market Street wharf, near the boat I came in, to which I went for a draft of the river water; and, being filled with one of my rolls, gave the other two to a woman and her child that came down the river in the boat with us, and were waiting to go farther.

Thus refreshed, I walked again up the street, which by this time had many clean-dressed people in it, who were all walking the same way. I joined them, and thereby was led into the great meetinghouse of the

BENJAMIN FRANKLIN **91**

Skill Link

Literary Interpretation

Point out how Franklin's depiction of other people helps create the impression he wishes to give of himself. Discuss how his interactions with his brother, the drunken Dutchman, Dr. Brown, and the mother and child at the wharf all highlight specific qualities about Franklin.

- How do the others act toward Franklin?
- How does Franklin act toward them?
- What observations does Franklin make about each incident?

Activity

Have small groups of students select a single incident from the *Autobiography* and interpret it as a pantomime or skit. Groups may need to write appropriate dialogue for their performance. After each presentation, let the performers discuss why they chose to interpret the incident as they did. Remind students to focus on each person's **motivation,** or the basic reason for his or her behavior.

Professional Notes

Franklin's Epitaph

Franklin wrote the following epitaph for himself in 1728. What does it reveal about Franklin's self-perception, humor, and faith? "The body of Benjamin Franklin, Printer (like the cover of an old book, its contents torn out and stripped of its lettering and gilding), lies here food for worms; but the work shall not be wholly lost, for it will . . . appear once more in a new and more elegant edition, revised and corrected by the Author."

Ⓐ Cultural Connections

Quaker Meetings

A Quaker meeting has no predetermined form. Any member may speak out in prayer, praise, or commentary. If no one speaks, the entire congregation may sit in silent prayer and contemplation. It was during such a period of silent communion that the exhausted Franklin fell asleep.

Ⓑ Elements of Literature

Irony

❓ Franklin is writing this passage with the wisdom of age. What irony does he see in his youthful project? [Possible response: Franklin probably realizes that it is impossible "to live without committing any fault at any time." He is gently mocking his youthful self here.]

Ⓒ Historical Connections

Tell students that when Franklin undertook this project, he had just returned from two years in Europe, where he was a social and political celebrity.

Ⓐ Quakers near the market. I sat down among them, and, after looking round awhile and hearing nothing said, being very drowsy through labor and want of rest the preceding night, I fell fast asleep, and continued so till the meeting broke up, when one was kind enough to rouse me. This was, therefore, the first house I was in, or slept in, in Philadelphia. . . .

Arriving at Moral Perfection

Ⓑ It was about this time I conceived the bold and arduous project of arriving at moral perfection. I wished to live without committing any fault at any time; I would conquer all that either natural inclination, custom, or company might lead me into. As I knew, or thought I knew, what was right and wrong, I did not see why I might not always do the one and avoid the other. But I soon found I had undertaken a task of more difficulty than I had imagined. While my care was employed in guarding against one fault, I was often surprised by another; habit took the advantage of inattention; inclination was sometimes too strong for reason. Ⓒ I concluded, at length, that the mere speculative conviction that it was our interest to be completely virtuous, was not sufficient to prevent our slipping; and that the contrary habits must be broken, and good ones acquired and established, before we can have any dependence on a steady, uniform rectitude of conduct. For this purpose I therefore contrived the following method.

WORDS TO OWN

arduous (är'joo·əs) *adj.:* difficult.
rectitude (rek'tə·tood') *n.:* correctness.

Second Street, North from Market Street, with Christ Church, Philadelphia (1799) by W. Birch & Son. Colored line engraving.

The Granger Collection, New York.

Using Students' Strengths

Interpersonal Learners

After students have finished the selection, have them imitate Franklin's example by trying to follow two of his resolutions. Ask students to track their progress once a week for a month. Based on what they have learned, students can collaborate to write an advice column for their school paper, which describes their experiment in "arriving at moral perfection."

Visual Learners

Have students create an illustrated time line or large-scale map depicting Franklin's adventures on his way to Philadelphia. If you prefer, you can have students finish the selection and then create a collage illustrating the thirteen virtues or the disastrous consequences of ignoring these virtues.

Getting Students Involved

Cooperative Learning

Achieving Moral Perfection. Like Franklin, Jonathan Edwards was determined to perfect himself. He resolved to "never lose one moment of time, but to improve it in the most profitable way." He awoke at 4:00 A.M., studied thirteen hours a day, and took a brisk walk daily. Have groups of five students do research and stage a debate about which man came closer to achieving his goal and why.

In the various enumerations of the moral virtues I had met with in my reading, I found the catalog more or less numerous, as different writers included more or fewer ideas under the same name. Temperance, for example, was by some confined to eating and drinking, while by others it was extended to mean the moderating every other pleasure, appetite, inclination, or passion, bodily or mental, even to our avarice and ambition. I proposed to myself, for the sake of clearness, to use rather more names, with fewer ideas annexed to each, than a few names with more ideas; and I included under thirteen names of virtues all that at that time occurred to me as necessary or desirable, and annexed to each a short precept, which fully expressed the extent I gave to its meaning.

These names of virtues, with their precepts, were:

1. *Temperance. Eat not to dullness; drink not to elevation.*

2. *Silence. Speak not but what may benefit others or yourself; avoid trifling conversation.*

3. *Order. Let all your things have their places; let each part of your business have its time.*

4. *Resolution. Resolve to perform what you ought; perform without fail what you resolve.*

5. *Frugality. Make no expense but to do good to others or yourself; i.e., waste nothing.*

6. *Industry. Lose no time; be always employed in something useful; cut off all unnecessary actions.*

7. *Sincerity. Use no hurtful deceit; think innocently and justly, and, if you speak, speak accordingly.*

8. *Justice. Wrong none by doing injuries, or omitting the benefits that are your duty.*

9. *Moderation. Avoid extremes; forbear resenting injuries so much as you think they deserve.*

10. *Cleanliness. Tolerate no uncleanliness in body, clothes, or habitation.*

11. *Tranquility. Be not disturbed at trifles, or at accidents common or unavoidable.*

12. *Chastity. Rarely use venery[14] but for health or offspring, never to dullness, weakness, or the injury of your own or another's peace or reputation.*

13. *Humility. Imitate Jesus and Socrates.[15]*

My intention being to acquire the *habitude* of all these virtues, I judged it would be well not to distract my attention by attempting the whole at once, but to fix it on one of them at a time; and, when I should be master of that, then to proceed to another, and so on, till I should have gone through the thirteen; and, as the previous acquisition of some might facilitate the acquisition of certain others, I arranged them with that view, as they stand above. *Temperance* first, as it tends to procure that coolness and clearness of head, which is so necessary where constant vigilance was to be kept up, and guard maintained against the unremitting attraction of ancient habits, and the force of perpetual temptations. This being acquired and established, *silence* would be more easy; and my desire being to gain knowledge at the same time that I improved in virtue, and considering that in conversation it was obtained rather by the use of the ears than of the tongue, and therefore wishing to break a habit I was getting into of prattling, punning, and joking, which only made me acceptable to trifling company, I gave *silence*

14. venery (ven′ər·ē): sex.
15. Socrates (säk′rə·tēz′) (470–399 B.C.): Greek philosopher. He is said to have lived a simple, virtuous life.

WORDS TO OWN
facilitate (fə·sil′ə·tāt′) v.: make easier.

Skill Link

Denotation and Connotation

Franklin, of course, was consciously defining virtues in his list. Remind students, however, that while the denotation, or dictionary definition, of words can be similar, their connotation, or emotional loading, can be very different. To be *slim*, for example, is often considered desirable; to be *skinny* is not. To *dine* is an elegant experience; to *chow down*, just the opposite.

To demonstrate the power of connotation, discuss with students the difference between *temperance* and *self-denial*, *silence* and *taciturnity*, *order* and *persnicketiness*, *resolution* and *stubbornness*, *frugality* and *cheapness*, *industry* and *obsessiveness*, *sincerity* and *bluntness*, *justice* and *righteousness*, *moderation* and *halfheartedness*, *cleanliness* and *sterility*, *tranquility* and *lethargy*, *chastity* and *prudishness*, and *humility* and *meekness*. Have students write pairs of sentences that demonstrate the different shades of meaning.

D English Language Learners
Understanding Key Words
Preteach key vocabulary before non-native speakers read this page. Possible words to explain include *virtues*, *temperance*, *avarice*, *precept*, *resolution*, *frugality*, *industry*, *moderation*, *tranquility*, *chastity*, and *humility*. List each word and its definition on the board. Then pronounce the words, and invite volunteers to use each one in a sentence.

E Struggling Readers
Getting the Main Idea
Have students define the virtues individually and provide an example of each from present-day life. [Students' definitions can vary, but should at least be based on the standard dictionary entries for these terms. Students' examples will also vary, and may include references to the exemplary behavior of classmates, local heroes, famous leaders, or characters in books, film, and television.]

F Elements of Literature
Irony
? Elsewhere in his *Autobiography*, Franklin says he tacked on the thirteenth virtue after someone accused him of being smug. What irony can you find in this addition? [Possible response: It may be presumptuous (and hardly humble) of Franklin to think that he can imitate Jesus and Socrates.]

G Elements of Literature
Character
? What do you learn about Franklin from his plan for moral development? [He is diligent, orderly, organized, and logical. He attempts to control emotional behavior with reason.]

H Cultural Connections
Enlightenment Values
Point out that Franklin's famous thirteen values were deeply rooted in Puritanism but were offered by him as a practical formula to perfect himself and his society and not as a way to win God's approval. Discuss how Franklin's "virtues" promote individualism, self-sufficiency, and success in *this* world rather than the next. Ask students to compare Franklin's Enlightenment values with their own spiritual or cultural values. What value do they consider most important, and why? [Answers will vary.]

A Advanced Learners

Making Connections

Explain that Pythagoras attracted a number of disciples who followed his rigorous ascetic practices intended to perfect the soul. Advanced learners can research Pythagoras's rules and compare them with Franklin's ideas.

B Vocabulary Note

Transition Words

? Franklin often connects his ideas with *thus*, meaning "as a result." What other words could he use to show the same relationship between ideas? [Possible responses: *hence; so; therefore; consequently; accordingly.*] What does his use of these transitions reveal about Franklin's thinking? [He presents his ideas logically and respects rational thinking.]

C Elements of Literature

Figures of Speech

? What metaphor does Franklin use to describe the process of eliminating the black dots on his virtue chart? [He compares it to eliminating weeds from a garden.] What point does he make with this metaphor? [If you try to get rid of all your faults at once, you will get frustrated and tired.]

D Critical Thinking

Making Connections

? How do you think Jonathan Edwards would feel about Franklin's plan for moral success? [Edwards would probably think it was pointless because it depended on human effort alone rather than on seeking God's grace. Edwards believed in the moral depravity of humanity, due to original sin, while Franklin seems to believe in humanity's perfectibility.]

---

the second place. This and the next, *order,* I expected would allow me more time for attending to my project and my studies. *Resolution,* once become habitual, would keep me firm in my endeavors to obtain all the subsequent virtues; *frugality* and *industry* freeing me from my remaining debt, and producing affluence and independence, would make more easy the practice of *sincerity* and *justice,* etc., etc. Conceiving then, that, agreeably **A** to the advice of Pythagoras[16] in his Golden Verses, daily examination would be necessary, I contrived the following method for conducting that examination.

I made a little book, in which I allotted a page for each of the virtues. I ruled each page with red ink, so as to have seven columns, one for each day of the week, marking each column with a letter for the day. I crossed these columns with thirteen red lines, marking the beginning of each line with the first letter of one of the virtues, on which line, and in its proper column, I might mark, by a little black spot, every fault I found upon examination to have been committed respecting that virtue upon that day.

I determined to give a week's strict attention to each of the virtues successively. Thus, **B** in the first week, my great guard was to avoid every[17] the least offense against *temperance,* leaving the other virtues to their ordinary chance, only marking every evening the faults of the day. Thus, if in the first week I could keep my first line, marked T, clear of spots, I supposed the habit of that virtue so much strengthened, and its opposite weakened, that I might venture extending my attention to include the next, and for the following week keep both lines clear of spots. Proceeding thus to the last, I could go through a course complete in thirteen weeks, and four courses in a year. And like **C** him who, having a garden to weed, does not attempt to eradicate all the bad herbs at

16. **Pythagoras** (pi·thag′ə·rəs): Greek philosopher and mathematician of the sixth century B.C.
17. **every:** archaic for "even."

Form of the Pages

Temperance							
Eat not to dullness. *Drink not to elevation.*							
	S	M	T	W	T	F	S
T							
S							
O							
R							
F							
I							
S							
J							
M							
Cl							
T							
Ch							
H							

once, which would exceed his reach and his strength, but works on one of the beds at a time, and, having accomplished the first, proceeds to a second, so I should have, I hoped, **D** the encouraging pleasure of seeing on my pages the progress I made in virtue, by clearing successively my lines of their spots, till in the end, by a number of courses, I should be happy in viewing a clean book, after a thirteen weeks' daily examination. . . .

WORDS TO OWN

subsequent (sub′si·kwənt) *adj.:* following.
eradicate (i·rad′i·kāt′) *v.:* to eliminate.

-----

94 BEGINNINGS

Professional Notes

Cultural Connections: Franklin's Purpose

Franklin wrote his autobiography partly to instruct others. He says: "Having emerg'd from the Poverty & Obscurity in which I was born & bred, to a State of Affluence & some Degree of Reputation in the World, and having gone so far thro' Life with a considerable Share of Felicity, . . . my Posterity may like to know [the means I used], as they may find some of them suitable to their own Situations. . . ."

Critical Comment: Jack of All Trades

The great novelist Herman Melville (see pp. 311–312) accused Franklin of not being a poet (see p. 85) but admitted he was "printer, postmaster, almanac maker, essayist, chemist, tinker, statesman, humorist, philosopher, parlor man, political economist, professor of housewifery, ambassador, projector, maxim monger, herb doctor, and wit."

Assessing Learning

Check Test: True-False

1. Franklin was educated at Harvard College. [False]
2. Franklin lied to get passage to New York. [True]
3. Franklin saved a man's life aboard the ship by pulling him from the water. [True]
4. Franklin got work in New York as a printer. [False]
5. Franklin arrived in Philadelphia with a Dutch dollar and a shilling. [True]

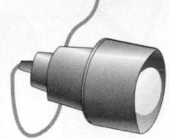

Sayings of Poor Richard

Panel from an engraving for Benjamin Franklin's *Poor Richard Illustrated* (c. 1800).

The Granger Collection, New York.

Poor *Richard's Almanack* was Franklin's biggest publishing success, and it continued to appear for over twenty-five years. Every house had an almanac. Almanacs calculated the tides and the phases of the moon, claimed to forecast the weather for the next year, and even provided astrological advice for those who believed in it. Many almanacs also supplied recipes, jokes, and **aphorisms**. "Poor Richard" was an imaginary astrologer, who had a critical wife named Bridget. One year Bridget wrote the maxims, to answer those her husband had written the year before on female idleness. Once, Bridget included "better" weather forecasts so that women would know the good days for drying their clothes.

Franklin took Poor Richard's wit and wisdom where he found it—from old sayings in other languages, from other writers, and from popular adages. He never hesitated to rework the texts to suit his own purposes. For example, for the 1758 almanac, Franklin skimmed all his previous editions to compose a single speech on economy. This speech, called "The Way to Wealth," has become one of the best known of Franklin's works. It has been mistakenly believed to be representative of Poor Richard's wisdom. Poor Richard often called for prudence and thrift, but he just as often favored extravagance.

1. Love your neighbor; yet don't pull down your hedge.
2. If a man empties his purse into his head, no man can take it away from him. An investment in knowledge always pays the best interest.
3. Three may keep a secret if two of them are dead.
4. Tart words make no friends; a spoonful of honey will catch more flies than a gallon of vinegar.
5. Glass, china, and reputation are easily cracked and never well mended.
6. Fish and visitors smell in three days.
7. He that lieth down with dogs shall rise up with fleas.
8. One today is worth two tomorrows.
9. A truly great man will neither trample on a worm nor sneak to an emperor.
10. A little neglect may breed mischief; for want of a nail the shoe was lost; for want of a shoe the horse was lost; for want of a horse the rider was lost; for want of the rider the battle was lost.
11. If you would know the value of money, go and try to borrow some; he that goes a-borrowing goes a-sorrowing.
12. He that composes himself is wiser than he that composes books.
13. He that is of the opinion that money will do everything may well be suspected of doing everything for money.
14. If a man could have half his wishes, he would double his troubles.
15. 'Tis hard for an empty bag to stand upright.
16. A small leak will sink a great ship.
17. A plowman on his legs is higher than a gentleman on his knees.
18. Keep your eyes wide open before marriage, half shut afterward.
19. Nothing brings more pain than too much pleasure; nothing more bondage than too much liberty.

Spotlight On

This feature provides some background about "Poor Richard" and offers nineteen aphorisms from the *Almanack*. These aphorisms give students a glimpse of Franklin's humor, insight, and philosophy.

A Literary Connections

To give students an idea of the personality Franklin originally created for Richard Saunders, read aloud the following selection from the preface to the first *Poor Richard's Almanack* in 1733:

> COURTEOUS READER, . . . The plain truth of the matter is, I am excessive poor, and my wife, good woman, is, I tell her, excessive proud; she cannot bear, she says, to sit spinning in her shift of tow, while I do nothing but gaze at the stars; and has threatened more than once to burn all my books and rattling-traps, (as she calls my instruments,) if I do not make some profitable use of them for the good of my family.

B Critical Thinking

Synthesizing

? Would Poor Richard agree or disagree with the following statements? Support your answer with reference to specific aphorisms. (1) Even close friends need some privacy from each other. [agree; 1] (2) Live for tomorrow. [disagree; 8] (3) May all your wishes come true. [disagree; 14] (4) There is dignity in hard work. [agree; 17] (5) A mind is a terrible thing to waste. [agree; 2]

Getting Students Involved

Cooperative Learning

Very Punny. Explain that part of the wittiness of these aphorisms lies in their clever use of multiple meanings, connotations, and associations.

1. Tell one student in each group to read aphorism 12. Have another student look up the word *compose* in a dictionary or thesaurus. After a brief period of discussion, have a third member write down the definitions that apply and an explanation for each. Then, as a class, discuss how *compose* is a metaphor for developing one's life as carefully as one would write a book and how it also means "to make oneself calm."

2. Have the groups repeat the exercise with aphorisms 1, 2, and 8. Tell them to identify the key words or images in each aphorism and explain how Franklin relies on connotation or multiple meanings to make his point. The groups should pass the dictionary and answer sheet around so that all can take turns.

T95

Connections

In this essay Robert Fulghum states that we learn the basic values of life in kindergarten. He then lists sixteen precepts, from "Share everything" to "LOOK," that he says we should follow as adults.

A Struggling Readers
Using Context Clues
? Remind students that they can often find the meaning of difficult words right in the text. For example, Fulghum provides the definition of *credo* in the first sentence. What is it? ["a personal statement of belief"]

B Vocabulary Note
Word Origins
When Fulghum uses the word *credo*, Latin for "I believe," he underscores his seriousness of purpose even if he expresses himself in a lighthearted tone.

C Reading Skills and Strategies
Finding the Main Idea
? What is Fulghum's main point? [Possible response: Although life is often complex and changeable, basic values don't have to be complicated. On the contrary, basic values are relatively simple and lasting.]

D Reading Skills and Strategies
Responding to the Text
? Which of these aphorisms do you agree with? Which ones do you disagree with?

E Appreciating Language
Word Choice
? Why does Fulghum use the word "blankies" here? What effect does he achieve? [Possible response: The childhood term conveys the comfort he found in cookies, milk, and the naps of childhood. It humorously suggests that the comforts of childhood are also valid in adulthood.]

Behind Ben Franklin's project for achieving moral perfection lies what seems to be a common human impulse—the need to simplify life, to get at the root of what's fundamental to us. In 1986, Robert Fulghum (fool'jum) published some thoughts of his own about how to live a full and happy life, in a best-selling book called *All I Really Need to Know I Learned in Kindergarten.*

from All I Really Need to Know I Learned in Kindergarten
Robert Fulghum

A Each spring, for many years, I have set myself the task of writing a personal statement of belief: a Credo. When I was younger, the statement ran for many pages, trying to cover every base, with no loose ends. It sounded like a Supreme Court brief, as if words could resolve all conflicts about the meaning of existence.

B The Credo has grown shorter in recent years—sometimes cynical, sometimes comical, sometimes bland—but I keep working at it. Recently I set out to get the statement of personal belief down to one page in simple terms, fully understanding the naïve idealism that implied. . . .

C I realized then that I already know most of what's necessary to live a meaningful life—that it isn't all that complicated. *I know it.* And have known it for a long, long time. Living it—well, that's another matter, yes? Here's my Credo:

All I really need to know about how to live and what to do and how to be I learned in kindergarten. Wisdom was not at the top of the graduate-school mountain, but there in the sandpile at Sunday School. These are the things I learned:

Share everything.
Play fair.
Don't hit people.
Put things back where you found them.
Clean up your own mess.
Don't take things that aren't yours.
Say you're sorry when you hurt somebody.
Wash your hands before you eat.
Flush.
Warm cookies and cold milk are good for you.
Live a balanced life—learn some and think some and draw and paint and sing and dance and play and work every day some.
D Take a nap every afternoon.
When you go out into the world, watch out for traffic, hold hands, and stick together.
Be aware of wonder. Remember the little seed in the Styrofoam cup: The roots go down and the plant goes up and nobody really knows how or why, but we are all like that.
Goldfish and hamsters and white mice and even the little seed in the Styrofoam cup—they all die. So do we.
And then remember the Dick-and-Jane books and the first word you learned—the biggest word of all—LOOK.

. . . Think what a better world it would be if we all—the whole world—had cookies and milk about three o'clock every afternoon and **E** then lay down with our blankies for a nap. Or if all governments had as a basic policy to always put things back where they found them and to clean up their own mess.

And it is still true, no matter how old you are—when you go out into the world, it is best to hold hands and stick together.

Connecting Across Texts

Connecting with *The Autobiography* and *Poor Richard's Almanack*
In *The Autobiography,* Franklin recounts his start in the world and his attempt to achieve moral perfection. In *Poor Richard's Almanack,* Franklin shares the wisdom he has learned over the years. Ask students how Franklin and Fulghum are similar. [Both look inside themselves and examine not only their own lives but also the world around them. They are both concerned with making the world a better place.]

Assessing Learning

Standardized Test Preparation
For practice with ACT and SAT formats, see
• *Preparation for College Admission Exams,* p. 7
For practice in proofreading and editing, see
• *Daily Oral Grammar,* Transparency 8

First Thoughts

1. If you had to name one character trait that you think made Franklin a success, what would it be? Review the chart you made in your Quickwrite to help you decide.

Shaping Interpretations

2. Franklin examines his actions and motives, discussing them at length throughout *The Autobiography.* Yet many of his personality traits are revealed through his actions, not through direct statements. What does the difficult journey from Boston to Philadelphia reveal about the **character** of young Franklin?

3. What does Franklin's project for moral perfection reveal about his views of human nature and his attitudes toward education? Do you agree or disagree with his views?

4. Franklin ends his list of virtues with "humility." Did you find evidence of pride—the opposite of humility—in his history? If so, where?

5. Which virtue on Franklin's list do you think is most important? least important? Why?

Connecting with the Text

6. Franklin resolves to acquire certain virtues through which he believes he will improve himself. Think of one of your own past resolutions, perhaps one you made on a New Year's Eve.

Reading Check

a. Why did Franklin decide to leave Boston secretly? How did he raise money for the journey from Boston to New York?

b. Today the trip from Boston to Philadelphia on a comfortable train takes five hours. On a map, trace the stages of Franklin's journey to Philadelphia.

c. What was Franklin's condition in life when he arrived in Philadelphia?

d. What virtue does Franklin place first on his list for achieving moral perfection? Why?

Were you able to keep it? Do you think making a resolution, as Franklin did, is a productive way of improving oneself? Explain.

Extending the Text

7. Compare Robert Fulghum's list of things learned in kindergarten (see **Connections,** page 96) to Franklin's list of virtues. Which list do you think would apply more broadly to people today? In general, how does Franklin's scheme for arriving at moral perfection compare with self-help books available today?

Challenging the Text

8. Reactions to Franklin's *Autobiography* have sometimes been negative. Read the following comment by Mark Twain. Based on Twain's **tone,** how does Twain feel about Franklin? Do you agree or disagree with Twain's assessment? Why?

> [Franklin had] a malevolence which is without parallel in history; he would work all day and then sit up nights and let on to be studying algebra by the light of a smoldering fire, so that all the boys might have to do that also, or else have Benjamin Franklin thrown upon them. Not satisfied with these proceedings, he had a fashion of living wholly on bread and water, and studying astronomy at mealtime—a thing which has brought affliction to millions of boys since, whose fathers had read Franklin's pernicious biography.
>
> —Mark Twain

9. As we read any **autobiography,** we have to ask ourselves if the writer is creating a character called "Myself," the same way that a novelist creates a fictional character. Has Franklin, the great inventor, invented an idealized version of himself in his autobiography? In other words, is he trying to make himself look good? Or do you think he is presenting himself just as he really was, warts and all? Explain and justify your opinion. (You might want to read a good **biography** of Franklin, such as the one by Ronald W. Clark [1989].)

Reading Check

a. He felt that his brother and father would prevent him from departing if he was open about his intentions. He sold some of his books.

b. It took him three days to get from Boston to New York and thirty hours to get from New York to Perth Amboy via ship. From Perth Amboy he took a ferry and then walked fifty miles, reaching Burlington three days later. That night he took a boat to Philadelphia and arrived in the morning.

c. He was dirty, tired, and hungry.

d. Temperance; it helps him to guard against other bad habits and perpetual temptations.

First Thoughts [Respond]

1. Possible responses: intelligence; self-discipline; sense of humor.

Shaping Interpretations [Interpret]

2. Possible responses: Undertaking the journey shows he is brave and determined; his rescue of the drowning man shows he is quick-thinking; curing himself of a fever shows he is self-reliant.

3. He believes people are capable of improving themselves and that education should be methodically organized. Students may disagree with Franklin's rationalist views.

4. Some students will agree that Franklin is proud, especially when he implies he can emulate Jesus and Socrates. Others will feel Franklin is disarmingly direct and often criticizes himself when he deserves it.

5. Possible responses: Justice is the most important because injustice directly hurts others, not just oneself. Moderation is the least important; there are times when one has to push oneself to extremes in order to succeed. Students should support their views.

Connecting with the Text [Evaluate]

6. Students will have had varying degrees of success keeping resolutions but will probably agree that resolutions are a productive way of improving oneself.

Extending the Text [Analyze]

7. Possible responses: Franklin's list is applicable in any age. Fulghum's list reflects today's emphasis on social relationships. Both share a concern for justice and order. Franklin's list emphasizes the goals of virtue and responsibility, while most self-help books emphasize goals like happiness or self-esteem.

Challenging the Text [Evaluate]

8. Some students will say Twain's ironic tone shows some admiration for Franklin; others will take his words at face value.

9. Possible response: Franklin presents himself favorably when he shows himself giving away his bread, but he reveals his warts when he describes his behavior in Boston.

CHOICES: Building Your Portfolio

1. **Writer's Notebook** Guide students to think of an achievement that made them feel proud of a specific character trait that enabled them to succeed.

2. **Comparing Texts** Help students set up a compare/contrast chart like this one:

	Edwards	Franklin
Goals		
Reasons		
Means		

3. **Creative Writing** Ask students to devise their own criteria for evaluating their progress. Have them include their criteria in their report.

4. **Crossing the Curriculum: Science** Suggest that students first decide on the format they will use. Let their choice guide their research as they consider their purpose and audience.

5. **Applying Ideas** Advise students that a proposal is a plan presented for consideration. Give them suggestions about appropriate formats. Also discuss the appropriate tone to use when writing to an editor-in-chief. Encourage students to keep their audience in mind when deciding what appeals to use.

6. **Creative Writing** Students may wish to develop a persona for their almanac, as Franklin did. If so, encourage them to decide first what tone they plan to employ so they can create the persona accordingly.

7. **Research/Art** Suggest that students also consider the traditional sayings used by family members and friends.

CHOICES: Building Your Portfolio

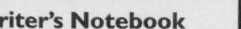

Writer's Notebook

1. Collecting Ideas for an Autobiographical Incident

A favorite question of job interviewers and college admissions officers is "What do you regard as your greatest strength?" Identify the character trait in yourself that you consider the most important or most valuable, and freewrite about an incident that demonstrated this trait in action. Did this aspect of your personality contribute to your success at something? Keep your notes for possible use in the Writer's Workshop on page 130.

Comparing Texts

2. Monuments of the American Tradition

Reread the selection by Jonathan Edwards (page 79), and write a brief essay in which you compare and contrast the Puritan preacher with Ben Franklin. When writing your essay, consider the following: (a) each man's goals in life; (b) his reasons for having these goals; and (c) the means by which he achieves his goals. Be sure to cite at least one way in which these two Americans are alike.

Creative Writing

3. Becoming Virtuous

Develop your own list of virtues and accompanying precepts. (You don't need as many as Franklin outlined, but you should have at least seven.) Then create your own "book of virtues," patterned after Franklin's (page 94). For one week, keep daily track of your "progress in virtue." (Unlike Franklin, you'll be keeping track of all the virtues simultaneously, not successively.) At the end of a week, write a brief report on how well the "book of virtues" worked for you. What did you learn? Is this a habit you'd like to continue?

Crossing the Curriculum: Science

4. Scientific Minds

Research either Benjamin Franklin's or Benjamin Banneker's (page 90) contributions to science and invention. What were their greatest accomplishments? What was the most surprising discovery each man made? Present your findings about either man's scientific interests, methods, and discoveries in one of the following forms: a written or oral report; a comic strip; a script for a documentary; or a story for children.

Applying Ideas

5. Franklin Today

Write a proposal to the editor-in-chief of a publishing company, suggesting that Franklin's *Autobiography* be published in a special new edition marketed as a self-help book. Using quotes from *The Autobiography,* give specific reasons why people today can still learn from Franklin.

Creative Writing

6. Our Almanac

As a class, create an almanac that covers a one-month period. Include weather forecasts, upcoming school and community events, and your own original maxims, jokes, and recipes.

Research / Art

7. Words from the Wise

Research **aphorisms** from Franklin and other sources (you might find some on bumper stickers and on the Internet) to find ones that you think would be especially helpful to high school students. Then, collect them in the form of a small booklet called "Words to Live By." You may use calligraphy, illustrations, or computer graphics to decorate your booklet.

Drawing by David Levine. Reprinted with permission from *The New York Review of Books.* Copyright © 1973 NYREV, Inc.

Justice

Resolution

Tranquility

Frugality

Cleanliness

Order

The American Dream

Theme

I Have a Dream *The words of the men and women who helped shape an emerging nation are the words that still define what is known as "the American dream." This powerful motif recurs in American literature even up to the present day. The core work here is the Declaration of Independence.*

Reading the Anthology

Reaching Struggling Readers

The *Reading Skills and Strategies: Reaching Struggling Readers* binder provides materials coordinated with the Pupil's Edition (see the Collection Planner, p. T98B) to help students who have difficulty reading and comprehending text, or students who are reluctant readers. The binder for eleventh grade is organized around ten individual skill areas and offers the following options:

- **MiniRead** MiniReads are short, easy texts that give students a chance to practice a particular skill and strategy before reading selections in the Pupil's Edition. Each MiniRead Skill Lesson can be taught independently or used in conjunction with a Selection Skill Lesson.

- **Selection Skill Lessons** Selection Skill Lessons allow students to apply skills introduced in the MiniReads. Each Selection Skill Lesson provides reading instruction and practice specific to a particular piece of literature in the Pupil's Edition.

Reading Beyond the Anthology

Read On

At the end of the Beginnings to 1800 collections, the grade eleven book includes an annotated bibliography of books suitable for extended reading. The suggested books are related to works in these collections by theme, by author, or by subject. To preview the Read On for the Beginnings to 1800 period, please turn to p. T126.

HRW Library

The *HRW Library* offers novels, plays, and short-story collections for extended reading. Each book in the Library includes one or more major works and thematically related Connections. The Connections are magazine articles, poems, or other pieces of literature. Each book in the *HRW Library* is also accompanied by a Study Guide that provides teaching suggestions and worksheets. For Collection 3, the following title is recommended.

A RAISIN IN THE SUN
Lorraine Hansberry
Hansberry's play, produced in 1959, has as its epigraph Langston Hughes's poem "A Dream Deferred." The play dramatizes the conflicts endured by a family trying to make the American dream their reality.

Collection 3 The American Dream

Resources for this Collection

Note: All resources for this collection are available for preview on the *One-Stop Planner CD-ROM 1 with Test Generator.* All worksheets and blackline masters may be printed from the CD-ROM.

Internet Resources
go.hrw.com LE0 11-3

Selection or Feature	Reading and Literary Skills	Vocabulary, Language, and Grammar
Speech to the Virginia Convention (p. 101) Patrick Henry	• *Reading Skills and Strategies: Reaching Struggling Readers* • MiniRead Skill Lesson, p. 43 • Selection Skill Lesson, p. 49 • *Graphic Organizers for Active Reading,* Worksheet p. 9 • *Literary Elements:* Transparency 5 Worksheet p. 16	• *Words to Own,* Worksheet p. 8 • *Grammar and Language Links:* Gerunds and Gerund Phrases, Worksheet, p. 17 • *Language Workshop CD-ROM,* Verbals and Verbal Phrases • *Daily Oral Grammar,* Transparency 9
from **The Crisis, No. 1** (p. 107) Thomas Paine **Spotlight On: Phillis Wheatley: A Revolutionary Woman** (p. 113)	• *Graphic Organizers for Active Reading,* Worksheet p. 10	• *Words to Own,* Worksheet p. 9 • *Daily Oral Grammar,* Transparency 10
from **The Autobiography: The Declaration of Independence** (p. 115) Thomas Jefferson **Primary Sources: A Letter from Jefferson to His Daughter** (p. 124) Thomas Jefferson	• *Reading Skills and Strategies: Reaching Struggling Readers* • MiniRead Skill Lesson, p. 53 • Selection Skill Lesson, p. 59 • *Graphic Organizers for Active Reading,* Worksheet p. 11	• *Words to Own,* Worksheet p. 10 • *Grammar and Language Links:* Infinitives and Infinitive Phrases, Worksheet, p. 19 • *Language Workshop CD-ROM,* Verbals and Verbal Phrases • *Daily Oral Grammar,* Transparency 11
The American Language: "Revolutionary" English (p. 127) Gary Q. Arpin		
Writer's Workshop: Autobiographical Incident (p. 130)		
Language Workshop: Coordinating Conjunctions (p. 133)		• *Workshop Resources,* p. 47 • *Language Workshop CD-ROM,* Connective Words and Phrases
Learning for Life: Researching the Immigrant Experience (p. 135)		

Collection Planner

Other Resources for this Collection

- *Cross-Curricular Activities*, p. 3
- *Portfolio Management System*, Introduction to Portfolio Assessment, p. 1
- *Formal Assessment*: Literary Period Test, p. 27; Literary Elements Test, p. 25
- *Test Generator*, Collection Test

Writing	Listening and Speaking Viewing and Representing	Assessment
• *Portfolio Management System*, Rubrics for Choices, p. 98	• *Audio CD Library*, Disc 4, Track 2 • *Viewing and Representing:* Fine Art Transparency 3 Worksheet p. 12 • *Portfolio Management System*, Rubrics for Choices, p. 98	• *Formal Assessment*, Selection Test, p. 17 • *Test Generator (One-Stop Planner CD-ROM)*
• *Portfolio Management System*, Rubrics for Choices, p. 99	• *Audio CD Library*, Disc 4, Tracks 3, 4 • *Portfolio Management System*, Rubrics for Choices, p. 99	• *Formal Assessment*, Selection Test, p. 19 • *Test Generator (One-Stop Planner CD-ROM)* • *Preparation for College Admission Exams*, p. 9
• *Portfolio Management System*, Rubrics for Choices, p. 100	• *Audio CD Library*, Disc 4, Track 5 • *Portfolio Management System*, Rubrics for Choices, p. 100	• *Formal Assessment*, Selection Test, p. 21 • *Test Generator (One-Stop Planner CD-ROM)* • *Preparation for College Admission Exams*, p. 11
		• *Formal Assessment*, The American Language Test, p. 23
• *Workshop Resources*, p. 1 • *Writer's Workshop 2 CD-ROM*, Autobiographical Incident	• *Viewing and Representing*, HRW Multimedia Presentation Maker	• *Portfolio Management System* • Prewriting, p. 101 • Peer Editing, p. 102 • Assessment Rubric, p. 103
		• *Portfolio Management System*, Rubrics, p. 104

 **Transparency**   **CD-ROM**   **Video**   **Audio CD**

Collection Planner

Collection 3 The American Dream

Skills Focus

Selection or Feature	Reading Skills and Strategies	Elements of Literature and Language	Writing	Listening and Speaking	Viewing and Representing
Speech to the Virginia Convention (p. 101) Patrick Henry	Recognizing Modes of Persuasion, pp. 101, 105 Identify the Main Idea, p. 105	Persuasion, pp. 101, 105 Logical Appeals, p. 105 Emotional Appeals, p. 105 Metaphor, p. 105 Rhetorical Question, p. 105 Allusion, p. 105	Write About a Personal Turning Point, p. 105 Compare and Contrast Two Speeches, p. 105	Prepare and Present a Recast Version of Henry's Speech, p. 105	
from **The Crisis, No. 1** (p. 107) Thomas Paine	Recognizing Modes of Persuasion, p. 107 • Logical Appeals • Emotional Appeals Identify the Main Idea, p. 112	Analogy, pp. 107, 112 Anecdote, pp. 107, 112 Style, pp. 107, 112 Diction, p. 107 Figurative Language, p. 107 Imagery, pp. 107, 112 Metaphor, p. 112 Argument, p. 112	Describe a Team Effort, p. 112 Write an Essay Evaluating an Author's Opinion, p. 112 Write a Response to Paine's Pamphlet, p. 112	Write a Song, p. 112	
from **The Autobiography: The Declaration of Independence** (p. 115) Thomas Jefferson	Identify the Main Idea, pp. 115, 125 Summarize, p. 125	Argument, p. 115 Parallelism, pp. 115, 125 Rhythm, p. 115 Image, p. 125 Theme, p. 125	Freewrite About the Benefits and Burdens of Freedom, p. 125 Write a Summary of the Theme, p. 125 Write an Essay Responding to a Text, p. 125	Participate in a Panel Discussion, p. 125	
The American Language: "Revolutionary" English (p. 127) Gary Q. Arpin		Americanisms, pp. 127, 129 Word Roots, p. 129 Pronunciation, p. 129		Participate in a Group Discussion, p. 129	
Writer's Workshop: Autobiographical Incident (p. 130)		Autobiographical Incident, p. 130	Write an Autobiographical Narrative, pp. 130–132		Create a Life "Road Map," p. 130
Language Workshop: Coordinating Conjunctions (p. 133)		Coordinating Conjunctions, p. 133	Revise Short, Choppy Sentences, p. 133		
Reading for Life: Monitoring Your Reading (p. 134)	Use Context Clues, p. 134 Adjust Reading Rate, p. 134	Context Clues, p. 134			
Learning for Life: Researching the Immigrant Experience (p. 135)			Research the Experiences of One or More Immigrant Groups, p. 135	Write and Present an Original Play, p. 135	Create a Time Line of Immigration, p. 135 Prepare a Multimedia Presentation, p. 135

Collection 3

Henry
Paine
Wheatley
Jefferson

OBJECTIVES

1. Read literature of the Revolutionary period on the theme "The American Dream"
2. Interpret literary elements used in the literature
3. Apply a variety of reading strategies
4. Respond to the literature in a variety of modes
5. Learn and use new words
6. Collect ideas for an autobiographical incident

Concord Hymn

By the rude bridge that arched the flood,
    Their flag to April's breeze unfurled,
Here once the embattled farmers stood
    And fired the shot heard round the world.

The foe long since in silence slept;
    Alike the conqueror silent sleeps;
And Time the ruined bridge has swept
    Down the dark stream which seaward creeps.

On this green bank, by this soft stream,
    We set today a votive stone;
That memory may their deed redeem,
    When, like our sires, our sons are gone.

Spirit, that made those heroes dare
    To die, and leave their children free,
Bid Time and Nature gently spare
    The shaft we raise to them and thee.

—Ralph Waldo Emerson (1803–1882)

Responding to the Poem

? "The Concord Hymn" is an example of occasional poetry, poetry written to commemorate an occasion of historical or local importance. This poem was written for the dedication, on July 4, 1837, of a monument to the Minutemen, the colonial farmers who, on April 19, 1775, routed the red-coated ranks of the British Militia and signaled the start of the Revolutionary War. Over the generations millions of Americans have made their pilgrimage to the monument at Concord. This poem was sung at the ceremonies to the tune of "Old Hundred" ("Praise God, from whom all blessings flow . . ,").

What role do deeds and heroes from the past play in your feelings about your civic duties, freedom, and the American dream? [Answers will vary, but students are likely to focus on inspirational deeds and unique accomplishments that enabled an individual to stand out from the crowd or that crystallized a social position or belief.]

Writing Focus: Autobiographical Incident

The following **Work in Progress** assignments in this collection build to a culminating **Writer's Workshop** at the end of Collection 3.

- Speech to the Virginia Convention
- The Crisis, No. 1
- The Autobiography: The Declaration of Independence

Write about a turning point (p. 105)
Describe a team effort (p. 112)
Write about freedom (p. 125)

Writer's Workshop: Narrative Writing / Autobiographical Incident (p. 130)

1. Read and interpret the speech
2. Analyze persuasive techniques
3. Recognize modes of persuasion
4. Express understanding through writing and speech
5. Understand and use new words

SKILLS

Literary
• Analyze persuasion

Reading
• Recognize modes of persuasion

Writing
• Collect ideas for an autobiographical incident
• Compare and contrast a sermon with a speech

Speaking/Listening
• Recast and deliver a speech

Vocabulary
• Use new words

Viewing/Representing
• Comparing and contrasting images (ATE)

Planning

• **Block Schedule**
  Block Scheduling Lesson Plans with Pacing Guide

• **Traditional Schedule**
  Lesson Plans Including Strategies for English-Language Learners

• **One-Stop Planner**
  CD-ROM with Test Generator

Patrick Henry

(1736–1799)

One fiery act can catapult someone from obscurity to fame. That is what happened to Patrick Henry, a young representative who stood up in the Virginia House of Burgesses one day in 1765. He delivered a dynamic, thundering speech against the hated Stamp Act, with which the British Parliament instituted taxes on all newspapers and public documents. For the ten years following his declaration of resistance, Henry—a tall, lank, somber-looking man who favored the kind of clothing a preacher might wear—was recognized as one of the most persuasive figures in Virginia politics.

Henry had not always been so successful. Born in a frontier region of Virginia, he was raised in a cultured but modest environment. During his youth the country was undergoing the religious revival known as the Great Awakening, and young Patrick often accompanied his mother to hear the sermons of the traveling preachers. Later, as a young man, he made several unsuccessful stabs at farming and merchant life before discovering his love of oratory and his true calling: the law.

In 1765, the twenty-nine-year-old lawyer was chosen to represent his region in the Virginia House of Burgesses. Henry's speech against the Stamp Act was the first of the two most famous speeches in American Colonial history. The second, his famous "liberty or death" speech, came ten years later in 1775 as the Colonies were nearing the breaking point with England. Following the Boston Tea Party in December 1773, the British had closed the port of Boston and inaugurated other harsh measures referred to by the colonists as the "Intolerable Acts." When the First Continental Congress protested these acts, the British Crown relieved the Colonies of taxation on a number of conditions. One condition was that the colonists fully support British rule and contribute toward the maintenance of British

Patrick Henry (1820–1830). Anonymous. Oil on canvas.
Shelburne Museum, Shelburne, Vermont. Photograph by Ken Burris.

troops in America, whose numbers were increasing greatly. On March 20, 1775, the Virginia House of Burgesses held a convention in St. John's Episcopal Church in Richmond to decide how to respond to the growing British military threat. George Washington and Thomas Jefferson (page 114) were both present.

On March 23, after several speeches in favor of compromise with the British, Patrick Henry rose to defend his resolution to take up arms. Later, a clergyman who was present recalled that during Henry's speech he felt "sick with excitement." As the speech reached its climax, Henry is said to have grabbed an ivory letter opener and plunged it toward his chest at the final word *death*.

Henry persuaded the delegation. The Virginia Convention voted to arm its people against England. On April 19, 1775, the Battle of Lexington, Massachusetts, ignited the Revolutionary War.

go.hrw.com
LEO 11-3

Resources: Print and Media

Reading
• *Reading Skills and Strategies*
    MiniRead Skill Lesson, p. 43
    Selection Skill Lesson, p. 49
• *Graphic Organizers for Active Reading*, p. 9
• *Words to Own*, p. 8
• *Audio CD Library*
    Disc 4, Track 2

Elements of Literature
• *Literary Elements*
    Transparency 5
    Worksheet, p. 16

Writing and Language
• *Daily Oral Grammar*
    Transparency 9
• *Grammar and Language Links*
    Worksheet, p. 17

Viewing and Representing
• *Viewing and Representing*

    Fine Art Transparency 3
    Fine Art Worksheet, p. 12
• *Visual Connections*
    Videocassette A, Segment 2

Assessment
• *Formal Assessment*, p. 17
• *Portfolio Management System*, p. 98
• *Test Generator (One-Stop Planner CD-ROM)*

Internet
• go.hrw.com (keyword: LEO 11-3)

Before You Read
SPEECH TO THE VIRGINIA CONVENTION

Make the Connection
Words into Actions
Words—acts of both thought and feeling—shape us; they are tools of self-making. We know now how much blood and suffering resulted from Henry's words "Give me liberty or give me death!" and what pride his impassioned cry continues to generate years after it was spoken. The "American dream," as we loosely call our aspirations toward freedom, self-

reliance, and self-creation, is defined in large part by the words of the men and women who helped to shape America in its early years.

Elements of Literature
Persuasion
Persuasion is a form of speaking or writing that aims to move an audience to take a specific action. A good persuasive speaker or writer uses both head and heart—reasons and feelings, or logic and emotion—to win over an audience. To be successful, a writer or speaker must provide reasons to support a particular opinion or course of action. In the final analysis, though, audiences are often won over not only by the force of the speaker's arguments but also by the power of his or her personality.

> **P**ersuasion is a form of discourse that uses reason and emotional appeals to convince another person to think or act in a certain way.
>
> *For more on Persuasion, see the Handbook of Literary Terms.*

Reading Skills and Strategies
Recognizing Modes of Persuasion
Patrick Henry uses two modes of **persuasion:** appeals to **logic** and appeals to **emotions** or values. As you read, track these two methods in a double-column chart. In the left column, list Henry's logical reasons for wanting war. In the right column, write down his emotional appeals. As you take notes, star (✶) those appeals that you find most effective. Place an "x" next to appeals that strike you as deceptive or faulty.

Background
The historian Garry Wills described Patrick Henry in this way: ". . . he had the actor's trick, in his oratory, of lifting his whole body up toward climaxes, along with his voice, as if he *could* add cubits by wanting to. . . . No one who beheld him incandescent with a Cause ever forgot the experience. . . ."

Although Henry's 1775 speech is one of the most famous in all American oratory, no manuscript of it exists. Henry's biographer, William Wirt, pieced together the traditionally accepted text forty years after it was delivered, using notes of people who were present at the speech. As you read Henry's speech, try to envision the physical surroundings of its delivery: a church in eighteenth-century Richmond, Virginia, on an early spring day. Try, also, to imagine the manner in which Henry delivered his speech.

Summary ■■

In this speech to the Virginia House of Burgesses, Patrick Henry advocates revolt against Britain by using imagery, hyperbole, and parallel structure to build to the climax: "Give me liberty, or give me death!" Henry pays respect to the speakers who have preceded him but criticizes their desire to avoid confrontation. He states that the decision to take up arms or not is a matter of freedom or slavery, and he presents a series of rhetorical questions which contrast British aggression with the colonists' repeated attempts at peaceful settlement. He argues that war is inevitable and ends with a call to rise and fight.

Background

Even after fighting broke out, many Americans still hoped for peace. Indeed, the following excerpt from a July 6, 1775, declaration by the First Continental Congress indicates that the colonial delegates still sought a negotiated settlement that did not include independence from Great Britain: "Lest this declaration should disquiet the minds of our friends and fellow-subjects in any part of the empire, we assure them that we mean not to dissolve that union which has so long and so happily subsisted between us, and which we sincerely wish to see restored. . . . We have not raised armies with ambitious designs of separating from Great Britain, and establishing Independent States."

Preteaching Vocabulary

Words to Own

Have students pronounce aloud all of the Words to Own. Then have volunteers pronounce each word again with a tone that corresponds to its meaning. Encourage students to exaggerate (adding a villainous sneer to *insidious*, for example) and to use appropriate gestures. Afterward, ask students to choose the vocabulary word that fits best in each of the following statements:

1. A letter from home can [solace] a soldier.
2. Henry knew that war was [inevitable].
3. Britain [spurned] the colonists' offers.
4. Americans have struggled to keep the principles of democracy [inviolate].
5. Washington was America's [martial] leader.
6. His heartfelt [supplication] was denied.
7. Spies must use [insidious] tactics.
8. England was the colonies' [adversary].
9. Guards on duty must remain [vigilant].
10. Could negotiation [avert] war?

(A) Historical Connections

Henry's Resolution
Henry spoke in support of his motion to form a militia, which previous speakers had argued would only provoke England. Thomas Jefferson supported Henry, but nevertheless the resolution passed by only five votes.

(B) Reading Skills and Strategies

Recognizing Modes of Persuasion
❓ What might be seen as a logical fallacy in Henry's declaration? [Possible response: He oversimplifies the issue by presenting only two extreme choices. This is often called the *either/or* fallacy.]

(C) Elements of Literature

Persuasion
❓ Figurative language is often used to support an emotional appeal. What metaphor does Henry use here and how does it illustrate his argument? [He calls the past experience of British oppression the only "lamp" that the colonists have to illuminate the future and implies that those who are hopeful about the conduct of the British are walking blindly in the dark.]

(D) English Language Learners

Syntax
Point out that the semicolon links the two clauses closely. Have students rephrase this sentence using simpler words and sentence structure. [These are preparations for war, which is the way kings ultimately settle arguments.]

Speech to the Virginia Convention
Patrick Henry

(A) Mr. President: No man thinks more highly than I do of the patriotism, as well as abilities, of the very worthy gentlemen who have just addressed the House. But different men often see the same subject in different lights; and, therefore, I hope that it will not be thought disrespectful to those gentlemen, if, entertaining as I do, opinions of a character very opposite to theirs, I shall speak forth my sentiments freely and without reserve. This is no time for ceremony. The question before the House is one of awful moment[1] to this country. (B) For my own part I consider it as nothing less than a question of freedom or slavery; and in proportion to the magnitude of the subject ought to be the freedom of the debate. It is only in this way that we can hope to arrive at truth, and fulfill the great responsibility which we hold to God and our country. Should I keep back my opinions at such a time, through fear of giving offense, I should consider myself as guilty of treason toward my country, and of an act of disloyalty toward the majesty of heaven, which I revere above all earthly kings.

Mr. President, it is natural to man to indulge in the illusions of hope. We are apt to shut our eyes against a painful truth, and listen to the song of that siren, till she transforms us into beasts.[2] Is this the part of wise men, engaged in a great and arduous struggle for liberty? Are we disposed to be of the number of those who, having eyes, see not, and having ears, hear not, the things which so nearly concern their temporal salvation? For my part, whatever anguish of spirit it may cost, I am willing to know the whole truth; to know the worst and to provide for it.

(C) I have but one lamp by which my feet are guided; and that is the lamp of experience. I know of no way of judging of the future but by the past. And judging by the past, I wish to know what there has been in the conduct of the British ministry for the last ten years, to justify those hopes with which gentlemen have been pleased to solace themselves and the House? Is it that insidious smile with which our petition[3] has been lately received? Trust it not, sir; it will prove a snare to your feet. Suffer not yourselves to be betrayed with a kiss. Ask yourselves how this gracious reception of our petition comports[4] with these warlike preparations which cover our waters and darken our land. Are fleets and armies necessary to a work of love and reconciliation? Have we shown ourselves so unwilling to be reconciled, that force must be called in to win back our love? Let us not deceive ourselves, sir. (D) These are the implements of war and subjugation; the last arguments to which kings resort.

1. **awful moment:** great importance.
2. **listen . . . beasts:** In Greek mythology, the sirens are sea-maidens whose seductive singing lures men to wreck their boats on coastal rocks. In the *Odyssey*, an epic by the Greek poet Homer (c. eighth century B.C.), Circe, an enchanter, transforms Odysseus' men into swine after they arrive at her island home. Henry's allusion combines these two stories.

3. **our petition:** The First Continental Congress had recently protested against new tax laws. King George III had withdrawn the laws conditionally, but the colonists were unwilling to accept his conditions.
4. **comports:** agrees.

WORDS TO OWN
solace (säl′is) *v.:* to comfort.
insidious (in·sid′ē·əs) *adj.:* sly; sneaky.

102 BEGINNINGS

Reaching All Students

Struggling Readers
Recognizing Modes of Persuasion was introduced on p. 101. For a lesson directly tied to this selection that teaches students to recognize modes of persuasion with a strategy called Save the Last Word for Me, see the *Reading Skills and Strategies* binder:
• MiniRead Skill Lesson, p. 43
• Selection Skill Lesson, p. 49

English Language Learners
Using the recording in the *Audio CD Library,* have students listen to the speech, noting the main idea (with supporting details) of each paragraph.

Advanced Learners
Ask students to choose a stirring speech by Franklin Delano Roosevelt, Martin Luther King, Jr., or John F. Kennedy. Have students listen to a recording of the speech and then compare and contrast it with Patrick Henry's.

Patrick Henry Arguing the Parson's Cause (c. 1830), attributed to George Cooke. Oil on canvas.

Virginia Historical Society, Richmond, Virginia.

RESPONDING TO THE ART

Patrick Henry Arguing the Parson's Cause is attributed to **George Cooke** (1793–1849), an American artist who painted portraits, landscapes, and historical subjects. Cooke is remembered primarily for his depictions of Native American dignitaries.

Activities

1. Ask students how this image of Patrick Henry (the central figure with upraised arm), depicting a scene from his early legal career, compares with the portrait on p. 100. [Possible responses: The faces are similar, especially the noses; p. 100 depicts him older, with gray sideburns. In this scene, he is shown in action; in the portrait, he is transformed into an icon of liberty.]

2. Discuss elements of the scene: Who are the men on the left? Why are the spectators' benches filled to the limit? [The men at left may be jurors. The courtroom may be filled because the issue was vital or sensational or because Henry had a reputation as a riveting speaker.]

Getting Students Involved

Cooperative Learning

Debate. Have students work in groups of six, each group divided into two teams, to debate the topic proposed in Henry's speech as if they were members of the Virginia Convention. Allow time for students to research the topic more fully. You may wish to ask the school librarian to set aside some useful sources. Some students could act as mediators and propose possible compromises.

Ethical Analysis. Explain to students that the third and often most powerful kind of persuasive appeal calls upon the audience's sense of what is just or morally right. Ethical appeals connect the speaker with the audience by stressing the values they share. Have students choose partners and then summarize together what they see as the core ethical argument in Henry's speech. Why does he feel it is the *right* thing to do?

Crossing the Curriculum

Mathematics

Have students do research and create a bar graph on a poster showing (1) how much money the Virginia Convention allotted to arming its people, (2) what this amount equals in today's dollars, (3) the amount of Virginia's contributions to the maintenance of British troops in the United States, and (4) a comparison of the size of Virginia's economy before and after the Revolution. Discuss whether the war was cost-effective.

A Elements of Literature

Persuasion

? One effective technique of persuasion is to anticipate and counter an opponent's arguments. What arguments does Henry forestall here? [He forestalls the claim that there is an innocent motive for England's accumulation of military force, by pointing out that there is no other enemy that England might be preparing to engage in the region. He answers those who will say that the colonies should try argument, or negotiation. He also answers those who will say that the colonies should try supplication.]

B Elements of Literature

Persuasion

? A **periodic** sentence is one in which the main clause is postponed until the end. What is the effect of this one? [The sentence builds to a conclusion, to a dramatic climax.] Ask students to recast the sentence, putting the main clause ("we must fight") first to compare the effect.

C Elements of Literature

Persuasion

? What technique is Henry using here? [repetition] Why? [To stress his main idea, "we must fight!" He even announces this intention—"I repeat it, sir"—to pound the point home.] Where does Henry use the same technique in the next paragraph? [in the last two sentences]

D Reading Skills and Strategies

Recognizing Modes of Persuasion

? What kind of appeal is Henry making here? [a highly emotional one] What two points is he making? [Without liberty, life and peace are worthless; he is willing to risk his own life for liberty.]

E Reading Skills and Strategies

Recognizing Modes of Persuasion

? An effective persuasive speech will usually have a memorable conclusion or *peroration*. Just as a piece of music might conclude with a loud and intense passage, so Henry's speech crests at the end. What makes Henry's conclusion so memorable? [He is willing to die for liberty. The direct choice he offers is stark and powerful.]

I ask gentlemen, sir, what means this <u>martial</u> array, if its purpose be not to force us to submission? Can gentlemen assign any other possible motives for it? Has Great Britain any enemy, in this quarter of the world, to call for all this accumulation of navies and armies? No, sir, she has none. They are meant for us; they can be meant for no other. They are sent over to bind and rivet upon us those chains which the British ministry have been so long forging. And what have we to oppose to them? Shall we try argument? Sir, we have been trying that for the last ten years. Have we anything new to offer on the subject? Nothing. We have held the subject up in every light of which it is capable; but it has been all in vain. Shall we resort to entreaty and humble <u>supplication</u>? What terms shall we find which have not been already exhausted? Let us not, I beseech you, sir, deceive ourselves longer. Sir, we have done everything that could be done, to <u>avert</u> the storm which is now coming on. We have petitioned; we have remonstrated; we have supplicated; we have prostrated ourselves before the throne, and have implored its interposition[5] to arrest the tyrannical hands of the ministry and Parliament. Our petitions have been slighted; our remonstrances have produced additional violence and insult; our supplications have been disregarded; and we have been <u>spurned</u>, with contempt, from the foot of the throne. In vain, after these things, may we indulge the fond[6] hope of peace and reconciliation. There is no longer any room for hope. If we wish to be free—if we mean to preserve <u>inviolate</u> those inestimable privileges for which we have been so long contending—if we mean not basely to abandon the noble struggle in which we have been so long engaged, and which we have pledged ourselves never to abandon until the glorious object of our contest shall be obtained, we must fight! I repeat it, sir, we must fight! An appeal to arms and to the God of Hosts is all that is left us!

They tell us, sir, that we are weak; unable to cope with so formidable an <u>adversary</u>. But when shall we be stronger? Will it be the next week, or the next year? Will it be when we are totally disarmed, and when a British guard shall be stationed in every house? Shall we gather strength by irresolution and inaction? Shall we acquire the means of effectual resistance, by lying supinely on our backs, and hugging the delusive phantom of hope, until our enemies shall have bound us hand and foot? Sir, we are not weak, if we make a proper use of the means which the God of nature hath placed in our power. Three millions of people, armed in the holy cause of liberty, and in such a country as that which we possess, are invincible by any force which our enemy can send against us. Besides, sir, we shall not fight our battles alone. There is a just God who presides over the destinies of nations; and who will raise up friends to fight our battles for us. The battle, sir, is not to the strong alone; it is to the <u>vigilant</u>, the active, the brave. Besides, sir, we have no election.[7] If we were base enough to desire it, it is now too late to retire from the contest. There is no retreat, but in submission and slavery! Our chains are forged! Their clanking may be heard on the plains of Boston! The war is <u>inevitable</u>—and let it come! I repeat it, sir, let it come!

It is in vain, sir, to extenuate the matter. Gentlemen may cry peace, peace—but there is no peace. The war is actually begun! The next gale that sweeps from the north will bring to our ears the clash of resounding arms! Our brethren are already in the field! Why stand we here idle? What is it that gentlemen wish? What would they have? Is life so dear, or peace so sweet, as to be purchased at the price of chains and slavery? Forbid it, Almighty God! I know not what course others may take; but as for me, give me liberty, or give me death!

7. **election:** choice.

WORDS TO OWN

martial (mär′shəl) *adj.*: warlike.
supplication (sup′lə·kā′shən) *n.*: earnest plea.
avert (ə·vʉrt′) *v.*: to prevent; turn away.
spurned (spʉrnd) *v.*: rejected.
inviolate (in·vī′ə·lit) *adj.*: uncorrupted.
adversary (ad′vər·ser′ē) *n.*: opponent.
vigilant (vij′ə·lənt) *adj.* used as *n.*: watchful.
inevitable (in·ev′i·tə·bəl) *adj.*: not avoidable.

---

5. **interposition:** intervention; stepping in to try to solve the problem.
6. **fond:** foolishly optimistic.

104 BEGINNINGS

Assessing Learning

Check Test: True-False
1. Henry says the British are preparing to make war against the colonists. [True]
2. At the time of the speech, the First Continental Congress had not yet assembled. [False]
3. Henry says that the only recourse for the colonists is to arm themselves. [True]
4. The purpose of Henry's speech is to win support for raising a local militia. [True]

Making the Connections

Connecting to the Theme: "The American Dream"
When contemporary Americans refer to the American dream, they often mean material prosperity. For Patrick Henry, however, the central issue was liberty. Freedom itself was (and is) the core of the American dream, the element that makes the other aspects possible. Ask students whether they think most Americans still have the intensity of feeling about freedom that Henry had.

First Thoughts

1. How did Henry's speech affect you?

> **Reading Check**
>
> What is the **main idea** of Henry's speech?

Shaping Interpretations

2. Review your double-column chart, noting especially the arguments you starred (★) and those you marked with an "x." What made these arguments powerful or weak? Were you more convinced by Henry's appeals to **logic** or by his appeals to **emotion**? What conclusions can you draw about the art of persuasion?

3. In paragraph four, what **metaphors** does Henry use to describe the coming war?

4. Henry makes use of the **rhetorical question**—a question that is asked for effect. Rhetorical questions, which are often used in **persuasion,** presume the audience agrees with the speaker on the answers, and so no answer is expected or required. Find a series of rhetorical questions in the fifth paragraph of this speech. Why do you think Henry uses this device, rather than straightforward statements of fact, to make his points? How does this technique make his speech more persuasive?

Extending the Text

5. Because Henry's audience knew the Bible, as well as classical mythology, the orator knew he could count on certain **allusions** producing emotional effects. Look up the classical or Biblical passages Henry alludes to in each of the following statements from his speech. How would each allusion relate to the conflict in Virginia in 1775? Could any of them relate to life today? Explain.

   a. "We are apt to . . . listen to the song of that siren, till she transforms us into beasts." (*Odyssey*, Books 10 and 12)

   b. "Are we disposed to be of the number of those who, having eyes, see not, and having ears, hear not the things which so nearly concern their temporal salvation?" (Ezekiel 12:2)

   c. "Suffer not yourselves to be betrayed with a kiss." (Luke 22:47–48)

CHOICES: Building Your Portfolio

Writer's Notebook

1. Collecting Ideas for an Autobiographical Incident

Write about an action you took or a particular time in your life that seems like a turning point—a decisive period that helped define the person you are today. Save your notes for possible use in the Writer's Workshop on page 130.

Comparing Orations

2. Politician and Preacher

In a brief essay, compare and contrast Henry's speech with Jonathan Edwards's sermon "Sinners in the Hands of an Angry God" (page 79). Consider the specific ways in which the speeches are alike and how they are different. Use the following chart to help organize your material.

Elements of the Oration	Edwards	Henry
Speaker's purpose and audience		
Main idea		
Appeals to reason and emotion		
Use of rhetorical questions and other literary devices		
Overall effectiveness		

Speaking and Listening

3. A Call to Action

Recast part or all of Henry's speech to pertain to some issue today that calls for action—poverty, drugs, crime, or military intervention to help end violent oppression in another country. Deliver the recast speech to the class.

First Thoughts [Respond]

1. Responses will vary. Some students might find any speech melodramatic or contrived; others may compare Henry's words favorably with today's political rhetoric.

Shaping Interpretations [Interpret]

2. Students are likely to admire the reasoning in the speech but be more viscerally affected by the rhythm and rhetoric. They might conclude that an effective persuasive speech appeals to both logic and emotion.

3. Henry compares the British threat to a coming storm and the colonists to the ancient Israelites.

4. Henry's rhetorical questions at the beginning of this paragraph allow him to attack his opponents' opinions indirectly, by reframing those opinions in a negative light, and then asking his audience if they still agree with them. By asking these questions, he elicits the audience's participation and engagement in his argument.

Extending the Text [Synthesize]

5. a. Illusory hopes are like the Sirens and Circe in Homer's *Odyssey*—attractive on the surface but destructive in reality. Henry urges his listeners not to surrender their freedom in exchange for false hopes of peace, advice as wise today as it was then.

   b. The allusion reminds listeners not to be like the heedless people in ancient Israel whom Ezekiel the prophet upbraided.

   c. The allusion to the apostle Judas, who betrayed Jesus, warns listeners not to be deceived by the apparently mild British reaction to the colonists' petitions against the tax laws.

Grading Timesaver

Rubrics for each Choices assignment appear on p. 98 in the *Portfolio Management System*.

> **Reading Check**
>
> The main idea of the speech is that if the colonists do not act immediately with military force to protect their freedoms, they will lose them completely, since the English are preparing to crack down on them.

CHOICES: Building Your Portfolio

1. **Writer's Notebook.** Encourage students to freewrite about childhood and adolescent memories.

2. **Comparing Orations.** Review some literary devices and logical fallacies beforehand.

3. **Speaking and Listening.** Remind students to use these persuasive techniques: logical and emotional appeals, countering opposing arguments, metaphors and allusions, rhetorical questions.

Thomas Paine

(1737–1809)

The most persuasive writer of the American Revolution came from an unlikely background. Thomas Paine, the poorly educated son of a corset maker, was born in England and spent his first thirty-seven years drifting through occupations—corset maker, grocer, tobacconist, schoolteacher, tax collector. In 1774, Paine was dismissed from his job as a tax collector for attempting to organize the employees in a demand for higher wages (an unusual activity in those days). Like many others at that time and since, he came to America to make a new start.

With a letter of introduction from Benjamin Franklin (page 84), whom he had met in London, Paine went to Philadelphia, where he worked as a journalist. In the conflict between England and the Colonies, he quickly identified with the underdog. In January 1776, he published the most important written work in support of American independence: *Common Sense,* a forty-seven-page pamphlet that denounced King George III as a "royal brute" and asserted that a continent should not remain tied to an island. The pamphlet sold a half million copies—in a country whose total population was roughly two and a quarter million.

After the Revolution, Paine lived peacefully in New York and New Jersey until 1787, when he returned to Europe. There he became involved once more in radical revolutionary politics, supporting the French Revolution. In 1791, he composed *The Rights of Man,* a reply to the English statesman Edmund Burke's condemnation of the French revolt. *The Rights of Man* was an impassioned defense of republican government and a call to the English people to overthrow their king. Although he was not living in England at the time, Paine was tried for treason there and banned from the country. Safe in France from English law, he was briefly celebrated as a hero of the French Revolution but was soon imprisoned in France for being a citizen of an enemy nation (England). James Monroe, the American minister to France at the time, gained his release in 1794 by insisting that Paine was an American citizen.

Paine's final notable work, *The Age of Reason,* was published in two parts, the first in 1794 and the second in 1796. Expounding the principles of deism (page 16), the book was controversial in America. Americans did not fully understand the book and thought Paine was an atheist—that he did not believe in God. When Paine returned to America in 1802, he was a virtual outcast, scorned as a dangerous radical and nonbeliever. He was stripped of his right to vote, had no money, and was continually harassed. When he died in New York in 1809, he was denied burial in consecrated ground. His body was buried on his farm in New Rochelle.

Even in death, though, Thomas Paine was not allowed to rest. In 1819, an English sympathizer dug up Paine's body and removed it and the coffin to England, intending to erect a memorial to the author of *The Rights of Man.* But no monument was ever built. The last record of Paine's remains shows that the coffin and the bones were acquired by a furniture dealer in England in 1844.

go.hrw.com
LEO 11-3

Reenactment of a redcoat musket firing, Trenton, New Jersey.

Joe Viesti/Viesti Associates.

Before You Read

FROM THE CRISIS, NO. 1

Make the Connection

A Common Cause

At various times in life, we have to put aside personal feelings and make sacrifices for a common cause or team effort. The early American colonists had to do just that, for much was being asked of them. At the time Thomas Paine wrote *The Crisis, No. 1,* the colonists had to make a crucial decision: Should they kneel as English subjects, or stand as Americans? As Benjamin Franklin (page 84) said, "We must all hang together, or assuredly we shall all hang separately."

Reading Skills and Strategies

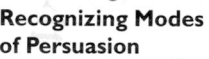

Recognizing Modes of Persuasion

A good writer of **persuasion** like Thomas Paine uses a variety of literary techniques that appeal to both **logic** and **emotions.** In

The Crisis, watch especially for these two—an **analogy** that compares the king with a thief, and an **anecdote** about a tavern keeper and his child. As you read, write down the extent to which each appeals to logic and to emotions.

Elements of Literature

Style

A writer's **style** is principally determined by sentence length, **diction,** and use of **figurative language** and **imagery.** Thomas Paine uses a combination of styles: Direct, common speech is mixed with heightened, impassioned expressions sharpened by dramatic rhetorical techniques. Paine says that he speaks "in language as plain as A, B, C," yet he also includes such lofty declarations as "What we obtain too cheap, we esteem too lightly."

> **S**tyle is the distinctive way in which a writer uses language.
>
> *For more on Style, see the Handbook of Literary Terms.*

Background

In 1776, Paine joined the Continental army as it retreated across New Jersey to Philadelphia. During the journey, he began writing a series of sixteen pamphlets called *The American Crisis,* commenting on the war and urging Americans not to give up the fight. The first of these pamphlets was read to Washington's troops in December 1776, a few days before the army recrossed the Delaware River to attack the British-held city of Trenton, New Jersey.

THOMAS PAINE **107**

Summary ■ ■

In this persuasive essay, Paine urges the colonists to renew their struggle against Britain. He argues that no prize worth fighting for is easily won and that the British objective is nothing less than the enslavement of the colonies. War for independence is inevitable, he insists, and only a selfish Tory father would leave it for his children to fight. Paine goes on to compare King George's actions to those of a common burglar and insists that the colonists refuse to accept any reconciliation with him. To do so would invite the destruction of their society at the hands of the Indians, the British army, and German mercenaries. Thus, the colonists must act now to ensure a "glorious issue" to the conflict.

Background

The excerpt below from *The Crisis, No. 13,* written after the war, offers a reflective contrast to the fiery rhetoric of *No. 1.*

> The times that tried men's souls are over—and the greatest and completest Revolution the world ever knew, gloriously and happily accomplished. . . .
>
> To see it in our power to make a world happy, to teach mankind the art of being so, to exhibit on the theatre of the universe a character hitherto unknown, and to have, as it were, a new creation entrusted in our hands, are honors that command reflection, and can neither be too highly estimated, nor too gratefully received.
>
> In this pause, then, of reflection, while the storm is ceasing, and the long-agitated mind vibrating to a rest, let us look back on the scenes we have passed, and learn from experience what is to be done.

Preteaching Vocabulary

Words to Own

Have students work in pairs. One student reads each vocabulary word and its definition aloud; the other student then provides a sentence that clearly illustrates that meaning. After five words and sentences, students should switch roles. Then have students choose the vocabulary word that means the *opposite* of each of the following expressions.

 1. giving up [perseverance]
 2. construction [ravage]
 3. genuineness [pretense]
 4. democracy [tyranny]
 5. incoherence [eloquence]
 6. retained [relinquished]
 7. aggravation [consolation]
 8. powerlessness [dominion]
 9. reverent [impious]
10. earthly [celestial]

A Vocabulary Note
Multiple Meanings

Point out that *dearness* is the opposite of *cheapness;* thus, here it means "costliness," and, hence, "difficulty of obtaining."

B Reading Skills and Strategies
Recognizing Modes of Persuasion

? What kind of appeal is Paine making here? [an emotional appeal] What is the substance of the appeal? [He claims God is on the side of the colonists.] Why, in his judgment, will God favor the colonists? [because they have, in his opinion, tried so hard to avoid war]

RESPONDING TO THE ART

Pewter, used to make the button shown here, is an alloy of tin. Boston became a global center for pewter production, even though England, hoping to retain a monopoly, refused to allow importation of English tin into the colonies.

Activity. Why is this button relevant to this essay? [Possible response: It is an early artifact of the independent industry and commerce in the United States and thus a symbol of the freedom Paine sought to achieve.]

from The Crisis, No. 1

Thomas Paine

These are the times that try men's souls. The summer soldier and the sunshine patriot will, in this crisis, shrink from the service of his country; but he that stands it NOW, deserves the love and thanks of man and woman. Tyranny, like hell, is not easily conquered; yet we have this consolation with us, that the harder the conflict, the more glorious the triumph. What we obtain too cheap, we esteem too lightly; 'tis dearness only that gives everything its value. Heaven knows how to put a proper price upon its goods; and it would be strange indeed, if so celestial an article as FREEDOM should not be highly rated. Britain, with an army to enforce her tyranny, has declared that she has a right (*not only to* TAX) but "to BIND *us in* ALL CASES WHATSOEVER,"[1] and if being *bound in that manner,* is not slavery, then is there not such a thing as slavery upon earth. Even the expression is impious, for so unlimited a power can belong only to God.

Whether the independence of the continent was declared too soon, or delayed too long, I will not now enter into as an argument; my own simple opinion is, that had it been eight months earlier, it would have been much better. We did not make a proper use of last winter, neither could we, while we were in a dependent state. However, the fault, if it were one, was all our own; we have none to blame but ourselves. But no great deal is lost yet; all that Howe[2] has been doing for this month past, is rather a ravage than a conquest, which the spirit of the Jerseys[3] a year ago

would have quickly repulsed, and which time and a little resolution will soon recover.

I have as little superstition in me as any man living, but my secret opinion has ever been, and still is, that God Almighty will not give up a people to military destruction, or leave them unsupportedly to perish, who have so earnestly and so repeatedly sought to avoid the calamities of war, by every decent method which wisdom could invent. Neither have I so much of the infidel in me, as to suppose that he has relinquished the government of the world, and given us up to the care of devils; and as I do not, I cannot see on what grounds the king of Britain can look up to heaven for help against us: A common murderer, a highwayman,[4] or a housebreaker, has as good a pretense as he....

I once felt all that kind of anger, which a man ought to feel, against the mean[5] principles that are held by the Tories:[6] A noted one, who kept a tavern at Amboy,[7] was standing at his door, with as pretty a child in his hand, about eight or nine years old, as I ever saw, and after speaking his mind as freely as he thought was prudent, finished with this unfatherly expression, *"Well! Give me peace in my day."* Not a man lives on the continent but fully believes that a separation must sometime or other

4. **highwayman:** thief who patrols the roads frequented by travelers, with the intent of stealing their valuables.
5. **mean:** low.
6. **Tories:** those who supported British rule in the American Colonies.
7. **Amboy:** Perth Amboy, New Jersey.

- -

WORDS TO OWN

tyranny (tirʹə·nē) *n.:* oppression.
consolation (känʹsə·lāʹshən) *n.:* comfort.
celestial (sə·lesʹchəl) *adj.:* divine; perfect.
impious (imʹpē·əs) *adj.:* irreverent.
ravage (ravʹij) *n.:* act of violent destruction.
relinquished (ri·liŋʹkwishd) *v.:* given up.
pretense (prē·tensʹ) *n.:* false claim.

- -

1. **to bind . . . whatsoever:** In response to Colonial protests over the Stamp Act (which taxed all commercial and legal documents in the Colonies), Parliament repealed the act on March 17, 1766. On the same day, it passed the Declaratory Act, which stated that Parliament had the right "to make laws . . . to bind the colonies and people of America . . . in all cases whatsoever."
2. **Howe:** Sir William Howe (1729–1814), commander in chief (1775–1778) of the British forces in America during the Revolution.
3. **Jerseys:** New Jersey was at this time divided into East Jersey and West Jersey.

108 BEGINNINGS

Reaching All Students

Struggling Readers
If students become confused by Paine's arguments, suggest they divide the pamphlet into the following categories: (1) emotional appeals; (2) criticism of Tories and exhortation to Whigs; (3) justification of military retreat; (4) warning against the dangers of surrender. Suggest that students break the pamphlet down to determine where each category applies.

English Language Learners
Point out some of Paine's sentences that sound like aphorisms. Students should see that Paine often connects two such clauses with a semicolon to create a compound sentence. Paragraph 1 has several of these, including the one that begins "Tyranny, like hell . . . " Ask students to find three examples of Paine's aphoristic compound sentences from different parts of the text and then to write three of their own.

Advanced Learners
Pamphlets and broadsides were common ways in which opinions were expressed and public communication kept open during Revolutionary times. Complete freedom of the press, however, was a right that had to be established over time. Have students research and report on the history of the free press in early America and the reasoning behind the subsequent Constitutional guarantee of a free press.

finally take place, and a generous parent should have said, *"If there must be trouble let it be in my day, that my child may have peace";* and this single reflection, well applied, is sufficient to awaken every man to duty. Not a place upon earth might be so happy as America. Her situation is remote from all the wrangling world, and she has nothing to do but to trade with them. A man can distinguish himself between temper and principle, and I am as confident, as I am that God governs the world, that America will never be happy till she gets clear of foreign <u>dominion</u>. Wars, without ceasing, will break out till that period arrives, and the continent must in the end be conqueror; for though the flame of liberty may sometimes cease to shine, the coal can never expire.

America did not, nor does not want[8] force; but she wanted a proper application of that force. Wisdom is not the purchase of a day, and it is no wonder that we should err at the first setting off. From an excess of tenderness, we were unwilling to raise an army, and trusted our cause to the temporary de-

8. **want:** lack.

fense of a well-meaning militia. A summer's experience has now taught us better; yet with those troops, while they were collected, we were able to set bounds to the progress of the enemy, and—thank God!—they are again assembling. I always consider militia as the best troops in the world for a sudden exertion, but they will not do for a long campaign. Howe, it is probable, will make an attempt on this city;[9] should he fail on this side the Delaware, he is ruined: If he succeeds, our cause is not ruined. He stakes all on his side against a part on ours; admitting he succeeds, the consequence will be, that armies from both ends of the continent will march to assist their suffering friends in the middle

9. **this city:** Philadelphia.

WORDS TO OWN

dominion (də·min′yən) *n*.: rule.

Colonial campfire reenactment, Valley Forge, Pennsylvania.

The Granger Collection, New York (swords).

THOMAS PAINE 109

Using Students' Strengths

Spatial/Visual Learners

Visual learners, especially those interested in history, might research and present a visual display of Washington and his troops crossing the Delaware or of the Battle of Trenton. Students might use maps showing troop positions and movements or create a three-dimensional model. Some students might use a computer to prepare a demonstration that displays graphics and information pertaining to these events.

Auditory/Musical Learners

Music played an important part in rousing and maintaining the spirits of the colonial soldiers. You might play library recordings of American Revolutionary fife-and-drum music or of some of the folk songs and ballads associated with the war, especially "Yankee Doodle." Then have students listen to the *Audio CD Library* recording of Paine's essay and compare the probable effects of the different works on different listeners.

A Elements of Literature
Style

? Note the length of this sentence—over nine lines. What is the point of the first independent clause? the second? [The first clause expresses hope for a reconciliation among the colonists, but the second advocates the expulsion from the country of all Tories and the seizure of Tory property if they assist or encourage the British.] Also note Paine's emphasis on the word *Christian;* he once again implies that to be a good Christian, one must follow his advice.

B Reading Skills and Strategies
Recognizing Modes of Persuasion

? Up to now Paine has used *we, us,* and *our* to refer to the colonists. Why does he switch to *you* and *your?* [Possible responses: Having finished his discussion of the Tories, Paine seeks to directly address those colonists he claims as his own, to make them feel personally committed to the cause, and to exhort them to redouble their efforts.]

C Reading Skills and Strategies
Recognizing Modes of Persuasion

? Ask students if they agree that Paine's argument is indeed "straight and clear as a ray of light" or if his appeal is based more on emotions than on logic. Keep in mind that for many colonists, events like the Boston Massacre (a 1770 incident in which British troops killed five unarmed colonists) and the passage of the so-called Intolerable Acts of 1774 (which included the provision that British troops could be quartered in private homes in Massachusetts) did indeed constitute "criminal" violations of their rights. [Possible response: Paine's "thief" metaphor is designed to elicit a strong emotional response, but it is also based on the logical point that a government's powers cannot be called "legal" if they don't in some way derive from the consent of the governed.]

D Critical Thinking
Analyzing

? Point out to students that Paine uses an *ad hominem,* or personal, attack in these sentences. Whom, by implication, is he calling an "individual villain"? [King George]

T110

---

states; for he cannot go everywhere; it is impossible. I consider Howe the greatest enemy the Tories have; he is bringing a war into their country, which, had it not been for him and partly for themselves, they had been clear of. Should he now be expelled, I wish with all the devotion of a *Christian,* that the names of Whig[10] and Tory may never more be mentioned; but should the Tories give him encouragement to come, or assistance if he come, I as sincerely wish that our next year's arms may expel them from the continent, and that congress appropriate their possessions to the relief of those who have suffered in well doing. A single successful battle next year will settle the whole. America could carry on a two years' war by the confiscation of the property of disaffected[11] persons; and be made happy by their expulsion. Say not that this is revenge, call it rather the soft resentment of a suffering people, who, having no object in view but the *good* of *all,* have staked their *own all* upon a seemingly doubtful event. Yet it is folly to argue against determined hardness; <u>eloquence</u> may strike the ear, and the language of sorrow draw forth the tear of compassion, but nothing can reach the heart that is steeled with prejudice.

Quitting this class of men, I turn with the warm ardor of a friend to those who have nobly stood, and are yet determined to stand the matter out: I call not upon a few, but upon all; not on *this* state or *that* state, but on *every* state; up and help us; lay your shoulders to the wheel; better have too much force than too little, when so great an object is at stake. Let it be told to the future world, that in the depth of winter, when nothing but hope and virtue could survive, that the city and the country, alarmed at one common danger, came forth to meet and to repulse it. Say not that thousands are gone, turn out your tens of thousands;[12] throw not the burden of the day upon Providence, but *"show your faith by your works,"*[13] that God may bless

Sentry and cannon reenactment, Valley Forge, Pennsylvania.

you. It matters not where you live, or what rank of life you hold, the evil or the blessing will reach you all. The far and the near, the home counties and the back, the rich and the poor, will suffer or rejoice alike. The heart that feels not now, is dead: The blood of his children will curse his cowardice, who shrinks back at a time when a little might have saved the whole, and made *them* happy. (I love the man that can smile at trouble; that can gather strength from distress; and grow brave by reflection.) 'Tis the business of little minds to shrink; but he whose heart is firm, and whose conscience approves his conduct, will pursue his principles unto death. My own line of reasoning is to myself as straight and clear as a ray of light. Not all the treasures of the world, so far as I believe, could have induced me to support an offensive war, for I think it murder; but if a thief breaks into my house, burns and destroys my property, and kills or threatens to kill me, or those that are in it, and to *"bind me in all cases whatsoever,"* to his absolute will, am I to suffer it? What signifies it to me, whether he who does it is a king or a common man; my countryman, or not my countryman; whether it be done by an individual villain or an army of them? If we reason to the root of things we shall find no difference; neither can any just

---

10. Whig: The Whigs were colonists who supported the Revolution.
11. disaffected: disloyal, especially toward the government.
12. thousands: "Saul hath slain his thousands, and David his ten thousands" (1 Samuel 18:7).
13. show . . . works: "Show me thy faith without thy works, and I will show thee my faith by my works" (James 2:18).

110 BEGINNINGS

WORDS TO OWN

eloquence (el′ə·kwəns) *n.:* well-articulated, persuasive speech.

Professional Notes

Critical Comment: A Literary Cannon

Paine's biographer John Keane explains the genesis of *The American Crisis:* "Paine had begun making notes for *The American Crisis* during the long retreat from Fort Lee to Trenton. He had been exhausted and alarmed by the realization that the American forces were heavily outnumbered, outgunned, and in utter disarray. . . .

"Upon returning to Philadelphia, he hurriedly drew together the manuscript, then offered it to the editor of the *Pennsylvania Journal,* who published it a week before Christmas, 1776. Several days later, it appeared as an eight-page pamphlet. . . . Paine emphasized that the overriding aim was to circulate its message among civilians at home and troops at the battlefront. . . . *The American Crisis* . . . proved to be a literary cannon on the battlefield of independence."

cause be assigned why we should punish in the one case and pardon in the other. Let them call me rebel, and welcome, I feel no concern from it; but I should suffer the misery of devils, were I to make a whore of my soul by swearing allegiance to one whose character is that of a sottish,[14] stupid, stubborn, worthless, brutish man. I conceive likewise a horrid idea in receiving mercy from a being, who at the last day shall be shrieking to the rocks and mountains to cover him, and fleeing with terror from the orphan, the widow, and the slain of America.

There are cases which cannot be overdone by language, and this is one. There are persons too who see not the full extent of the evil which threatens them; they solace themselves with hopes that the enemy, if he succeeds, will be merciful. Is this the madness of folly, to expect mercy from those who have refused to do justice; and even mercy, where conquest is the object, is only a trick of war; the cunning of the fox is as murderous as the violence of the wolf; and we ought to guard equally against both. Howe's first object is partly by threats and partly by promises, to terrify or seduce the people to deliver up their arms and to receive mercy. The ministry recommended the same plan to Gage,[15] and this is what the Tories call making their peace, *"a peace which passeth all understanding,"*[16] *indeed!* A peace which would be the immediate forerunner of a worse ruin than any we have yet thought of. Ye men of Pennsylvania, do reason upon these things! Were the back counties to give up their arms, they would fall an easy prey to the Indians, who are all armed; this perhaps is what some Tories would not be sorry for. Were the home counties to deliver up their arms, they would be exposed to the resentment of the back counties, who would then have it in their power to chastise their defection at pleasure. And were any one state to give up its arms, *that* state must be garrisoned by Howe's army of Britains and Hessians[17] to preserve it from the anger of the rest. Mutual fear is the

principal link in the chain of mutual love, and woe be to that state that breaks the compact. Howe is mercifully inviting you to barbarous destruction, and men must be either rogues or fools that will not see it. I dwell not upon the powers of imagination; I bring reason to your ears; and in language as plain as A, B, C, hold up truth to your eyes.

I thank God that I fear not. I see no real cause for fear. I know our situation well and can see the way out of it. While our army was collected, Howe dared not risk a battle, and it is no credit to him that he decamped from the White Plains, and waited a mean opportunity to ravage the defenseless Jerseys;[18] but it is great credit to us, that, with a handful of men, we sustained an orderly retreat for near an hundred miles, brought off our ammunition, all our field pieces, the greatest part of our stores, and had four rivers to pass. None can say that our retreat was precipitate,[19] for we were near three weeks in performing it, that the country[20] might have time to come in. Twice we marched back to meet the enemy, and remained out till dark. The sign of fear was not seen in our camp, and had not some of the cowardly and disaffected inhabitants spread false alarms through the country, the Jerseys had never been ravaged. Once more we are again collected and collecting, our new army at both ends of the continent is recruiting fast, and we shall be able to open the next campaign with sixty thousand men, well armed and clothed. This is our situation, and who will may know it. By perseverance and fortitude we have the prospect of a glorious issue; by cowardice and submission, the sad choice of a variety of evils—a ravaged country—a depopulated city—habitations without safety, and slavery without hope—our homes turned into barracks and bawdy-houses for Hessians, and a future race to provide for, whose fathers we shall doubt of. Look on this picture and weep over it! And if there yet remains one thoughtless wretch who believes it not, let him suffer it unlamented.

18. White Plains . . . Jerseys: Howe had defeated Washington at White Plains, New York, in 1776 but had failed to press his advantage.
19. precipitate (prē·sip′ə·tit): sudden; unexpected.
20. country: the local people. Paine uses the term to refer to local volunteers.

14. **sottish** (sät′ish): stupid or foolish from too much drinking.
15. **Gage:** General Thomas Gage (1721–1787), head of the British forces in America (1763–1775) before General Howe.
16. **a peace . . . understanding:** ironic echo of Paul's epistle to the Philippians (4:7).
17. **Hessians** (hesh′ənz): German troops, mostly from the region of Hesse, hired to fight on the British side.

WORDS TO OWN

perseverance (pʉr′sə·vir′əns) *n.*: persistence.

THOMAS PAINE 111

E Elements of Literature
Parallelism
? Remind students that writers can create **parallelism** in phrases, clauses, sentences, paragraphs, or even whole sections of a work. The parallelism may or may not include some verbatim repetition. What examples of parallelism occur here? [The three sentences beginning with *Were* are an example of parallelism.]

F Reading Skills and Strategies
Making Inferences
? Based on the evidence in this paragraph, as well as above, how would you characterize the author? [Possible responses: passionate, reflective, courageous, just, optimistic, eloquent.]

G Critical Thinking
Evaluating
Remind students that to evaluate a persuasive piece, they must first identify its thesis and purpose and then analyze the author's methods and credibility. How are key terms defined? On what assumptions are arguments based? What reasons and evidence are given? What appeals are used? How does the author try to win over the audience? What is his or her tone and style? Is the author believable? Have small groups answer the above questions about Paine's essay before discussing them as a class. [Student evaluations should be based on a thorough outline of Paine's argument and should cite specific examples from the text.]

Assessing Learning

Check Test: True-False
1. Paine believes that the American colonies should have taken military action against Britain eight months before they finally did. [True]
2. Paine compares the King of England to a thief who breaks into someone's house and threatens to murder the inhabitants. [True]
3. Paine describes the American forces' retreat to the Delaware River as disorganized but courageous. [False]

4. Paine believes that American isolation from Europe after gaining independence would lead to hardship and strife. [False]
5. Paine believes only those who have nothing or no one to lose should fight. [False]

Standardized Test Preparation
For practice with ACT and SAT formats, see
• *Preparation for College Admission Exams,* p. 9
For practice in proofreading and editing, see
• *Daily Oral Grammar,* Transparency 10

MAKING MEANINGS

First Thoughts [Respond]

1. Students are likely to focus on the first, third, and final paragraphs.

Shaping Interpretations [Interpret]

2. A summer soldier will not fight in the winter, or at any time when the fighting is especially difficult. Similarly, a sunshine patriot is not a patriot when times are rough. The images are appropriate for an army and a citizenry that faced early setbacks in their fight with the British and which were in danger of giving in to despair.

3. Self-interest in the form of mutual protection is the most compelling reason for standing united. Some students will criticize this idea as an overly cynical view of love, while others will agree that solidarity requires agreement on friends and enemies.

4. Paine argues that it is as just to rebel against England as it is to attack a thief who invades one's home, because England's abusive actions have overstepped any legal authority it had over the colonists. An opponent of this position might argue that England still has greater authority than any colonists taking the law into their own hands.

Extending the Text [Evaluate]

5. Possible response: Emerson would agree wholeheartedly with Paine's arguments and probably delight in his intense and highly rhetorical style. People today might agree with the arguments but would probably prefer a more informal style.

Grading Timesaver

Rubrics for each Choices assignment appear on p. 99 in the *Portfolio Management System*.

MAKING MEANINGS

First Thoughts

1. Which passages in this excerpt were especially stirring?

Shaping Interpretations

2. The pamphlet opens with two famous **images** (page 108). What kinds of people does Paine identify with summer and sunshine? Why are these images appropriate?

3. Explain the meaning of Paine's **metaphor** "Mutual fear is the principal link in the chain of mutual love" (page 111). Do you agree or disagree with this idea, and why?

4. An **analogy** is a comparison between two things that are alike in certain respects. Analogies are used often in **argument** and **persuasion** to demonstrate the logic of one idea by showing how it is similar to another, accepted idea. Analogies can be tricky, though, because few ideas or situations are completely alike in all aspects. What analogy does Paine draw when he talks about the thief (page 110)? What point is he making, and how might an opponent answer?

Extending the Text

5. How do you think Ralph Waldo Emerson, author of "Concord Hymn" (page 99), would respond to Paine's arguments and his writing **style**? How would people today react?

Reading Check

a. What reasons does Paine give for his confidence that God will favor the Americans?

b. Explain Paine's point in telling the **anecdote** about the Tory tavern keeper. Is he appealing more to reason or to emotions?

c. What powerful emotional appeal does Paine make at the end of his essay?

d. What is Paine's **main idea**? What details support it?

CHOICES:
Building Your Portfolio

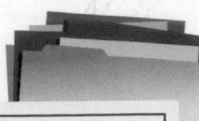

Writer's Notebook

1. Collecting Ideas for an Autobiographical Incident

Have you ever joined with others in a team effort for a common cause? Briefly describe the experience: What was the purpose of banding together? Did taking part in group action involve personal sacrifices on your part? Save your notes for possible use in the Writer's Workshop on page 130.

Evaluating Ideas

2. A Paine Prescription

"Not a place upon earth might be so happy as America. Her situation is remote from all the wrangling world, and she has nothing to do but to trade with them. . . . I am . . . confident . . . that America will never be happy till she gets clear of foreign dominion" (page 109). In a brief essay, evaluate these words from Paine's pamphlet. Considering the world as it is today, how would you reply to Paine?

Creative Writing

3. Crisis Zone

Imagine you are one of the volunteers who listened to this pamphlet being read a few days before Christmas, in 1776, just before you were to cross the Delaware River and attack General Howe and his troops in Trenton. In a paragraph, poem, or song lyrics, express how you felt while the pamphlet was being read, and describe the responses of the people around you.

Sir William Howe (1729–1814), British commander-in-chief in America during Revolutionary War.

The Granger Collection, New York.

Reading Check

a. The colonists have sought only peace; the English King, on the other hand, has claimed godlike authority for himself while behaving like a common criminal.

b. Allegiance to the king, based on selfish fear, merely defers the inevitable conflict. The anecdote appeals more to the emotions.

c. Paine appeals to fears of enslavement, a ravaged countryside, depopulated cities, and the corruption of colonial families by German mercenaries.

d. Paine's main idea is that the colonies have no choice but to stand together now and commit to defeating the British. Supporting details include the inevitability of independence, the threat of English, German, and Indian brutality, and the colonists' ultimate advantages with God and in battle.

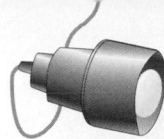

SPOTLIGHT ON

Phillis Wheatley: A Revolutionary Woman

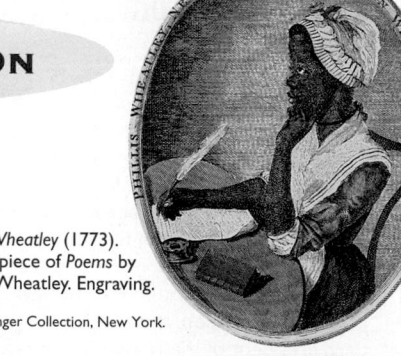

Phillis Wheatley (1773). Frontispiece of *Poems* by Phillis Wheatley. Engraving.

The Granger Collection, New York.

All the odds were stacked against her—she was an enslaved African, young, and female. But Phillis Wheatley (c. 1753–1784) published her first poem when she was barely thirteen, and by the time she was twenty years old she had developed a reputation as a poet whose work was praised by George Washington and Thomas Jefferson (page 114).

When Phillis Wheatley was about seven or eight years old, she, like Olaudah Equiano (page 56), was **A** stolen from her home in West Africa. She arrived in America on board a slave ship in 1761. At first, of course, she spoke no English. But she was purchased by the Wheatley family of Boston to assist Mrs. Susanna Wheatley and was treated kindly. Pleased to find this young woman intelligent and eager to learn, the Wheatleys provided her with an excellent education, equal to that of any free person **B** in Boston at the time.

Susanna Wheatley arranged the London publication of a volume of Phillis's poems in 1773; the book received generally encouraging reviews, and it was read widely in England, France, and the American Colonies. Around this time, Phillis was given her freedom, though she chose to remain with the Wheatleys. When they died, she married John Peters, a freeman, in 1778.

Wheatley's poems imitate the style popular in the poetry of her time: She uses a Latinate **C** vocabulary, inversions, and elevated diction. The following stanza is from her poem to the earl of Dartmouth, who had just been appointed secretary of state in charge of the American Colonies (1772). Dartmouth, she hopes, will be open to the colonists' grievances.

go.hrw.com
LEO 11-3

from **To the Right Honorable William, Earl of Dartmouth, His Majesty's Principal Secretary of State for North America, etc.**

Should you, my lord, while you peruse my song,
Wonder from whence my love of *Freedom* sprung,
Whence flow these wishes for the common good,
By feeling hearts alone best understood,
I, young in life, by seeming cruel fate
Was snatch'd from *Afric's* fancy'd happy seat:
What pangs excruciating must molest,
What sorrows labor in my parent's breast?
Steel'd was that soul and by no misery mov'd
That from a father seiz'd his babe belov'd:
Such, such my case. And can I then but pray
Others may never feel tyrannic sway?

—Phillis Wheatley

Wheatley's life ended on a tragic note. Her married life was filled with personal, financial, and familial hardships. Wheatley bore three children, but none of them survived. When she herself was sick and poor, the same society that lavished attention on her as a kind of "sideshow attraction"—an enslaved woman who could write lofty poetry—abandoned her to a position of powerlessness and anonymity. She died in her early thirties, destitute and grieving, without having published another book of poems. Since her death, however, her poems have been reprinted and, in the twentieth century, have again attracted lavish attention. Today Phillis Wheatley is praised as a true pioneer—the first African American poet in North America.

SPOTLIGHT ON 113

Spotlight On

This feature provides an overview of the life and career of Phillis Wheatley, who is generally regarded as the first African American poet. Students will also be introduced to a brief sample of Wheatley's work.

A Background

Phillis Wheatley was born in the area of present-day Senegal or Ghana. One source for her estimated age is the date when she lost her baby teeth.

B Literary Connections

Classical Allusions

Wheatley learned English in just sixteen months. She soon went on to master the highly rhetorical English poetic forms and conventions of her time. Like the poems of John Dryden and Alexander Pope, Wheatley's poems abound in classical allusions. Wheatley also wrote a lofty and formal poem called "To His Excellency, General Washington," praising Washington's military prowess and his virtue. Washington read the poem and invited Wheatley to meet him, which she did in Cambridge, Massachusetts, in 1776.

C Critical Thinking

Making Connections

❓ How does Wheatley's style compare with that of Anne Bradstreet (p. 68)? [Wheatley more obviously imitates elegant English neoclassical poetry.]

D Struggling Readers

Summarizing

Have students summarize Wheatley's explanation for her love of freedom. [She was captured and enslaved as a child; therefore, she has a passionate and compassionate desire that no one else be subjected to tyranny.]

Reaching All Students

Struggling Readers

To make the poem more accessible, have students

- Read the poem aloud three times
- Write a response to the poem
- Write down the most important line
- Share their response and selected line with a group
- Discuss the differences among the group's responses
- Write a response to the group's ideas

English Language Learners

To help students with the poem, have them

- Copy the poem, skipping a space between each line
- Mark unknown words and confusing phrases with colored markers
- Read the poem aloud in groups of three
- Help each other figure out troublesome passages
- Write a response to the poem, and share it with other groups

OBJECTIVES

1. Read and interpret the Declaration and the autobiographical excerpt
2. Identify and analyze parallelism
3. Identify the main idea and supporting details
4. Express understanding through writing and speaking
5. Understand and use new words

SKILLS

Literary
- Identify and analyze parallelism

Reading
- Identify the main idea

Writing
- Collect ideas for an autobiographical incident
- Summarize a document
- Respond to a text

Speaking/Listening
- Engage in a panel discussion

Vocabulary
- Use new words

Viewing/Representing
- Analyze historical paintings (ATE)

Planning

- **Block Schedule**
  Block Scheduling Lesson Plans with Pacing Guide
- **Traditional Schedule**
  Lesson Plans Including Strategies for English-Language Learners
- **One-Stop Planner**
  CD-ROM with Test Generator

RESPONDING TO THE ART

Charles Willson Peale (1741–1827) was a successful portraitist and student of Benjamin West (see p. 87) before the American Revolution catapulted him into fame. As a member of the civilian militia, he painted nearly every prominent figure on the American side, using a conventional, Neoclassical style. Peale went on to open the first truly American museum in 1786.

Activity. Have students research other Peale portraits.

T114

Thomas Jefferson

(1743–1826)

Thomas Jefferson (1791) by Charles Willson Peale. Oil on canvas.
Independence National Historical Park, Philadelphia, Pennsylvania.

At a White House dinner in 1962 honoring forty-nine Nobel Prize winners, President John F. Kennedy hailed his guests as "the most extraordinary collection of talent, of human knowledge, that has ever been gathered together at the White House, with the possible exception of when Thomas Jefferson dined alone." President Kennedy was exaggerating only slightly.

Thomas Jefferson, the brilliant and versatile third president of the United States, was an accomplished statesman, architect, botanist, paleontologist, linguist, and musician. He displayed the range of interests that we associate with the eighteenth-century mind at its best.

Jefferson was born in the red-clay country of what is now Albemarle County, Virginia. Jefferson's father, a surveyor and magistrate, died when Thomas was fourteen, but he had provided his son with an excellent classical education and a 5,000-acre estate. After attending the College of William and Mary, Jefferson became a lawyer, a member of the Virginia House of Burgesses, and a spokesperson for the rights of personal liberty and religious freedom. In 1774, he wrote a pamphlet called *A Summary View of the Rights of British America,* a call for the rejection of parliamentary authority. This pamphlet established his reputation, and two years later, the Second Continental Congress chose him to help draft the Declaration of Independence.

During the Revolution, Jefferson served for a time as governor of Virginia. When the British invaded Virginia, he retired to Monticello, the home he had designed, and devoted himself to his family and to scientific research. During this time he also composed most of his *Notes on the State of Virginia.* Shortly after Jefferson's beloved wife Martha died in 1782, he returned to public life, in part as an escape from his private grief. He served as minister to France, secretary of state, vice president, and president from 1801–1809.

A determined opponent of federal power, Jefferson embodied the principles of what would come to be called Jeffersonian democracy. He believed in the rights of individuals and states to govern themselves as much as possible. Politically and personally, he strove to keep power vested in the agrarian backbone of the country. He also expanded the country enormously in 1803: The Louisiana Purchase doubled the size of the United States, adding land that would later be divided into part or all of fifteen states. And as for Jefferson's presidential style, he avoided public displays and wore simple clothes: A president, he thought, should neither act nor look like a king. At state dinners, he eliminated seating by rank.

After his presidency, Jefferson retired once again to Monticello. He devoted his energy to establishing the University of Virginia, planning its courses of study and designing many of its buildings. In 1826, both Jefferson (at eighty-three) and the former president John Adams (at ninety) became gravely ill. Both hoped to live to see the fiftieth anniversary of the independence they had done so much to ensure. Jefferson died on the morning of July 4. several hours before Adams, whose last words were "Thomas Jefferson still survives."

 **go.hrw.com**
LE0 11-3

Resources: Print and Media

Reading
- *Reading Skills and Strategies*
  MiniRead Skill Lesson, p. 53
  Selection Skill Lesson, p. 59
- *Graphic Organizers for Active Reading,* p. 11
- *Words to Own,* p. 10
- *Audio CD Library*   Disc 4, Track 5

Writing and Language
- *Daily Oral Grammar,* Transparency 11
- *Grammar and Language Links*
  Worksheet, p. 19

Viewing and Representing
- *Visual Connections*
  Videocassette A, Segment 2

Assessment
- *Formal Assessment,* p. 21
- *Portfolio Management System,* p. 100
- *Preparation for College Admission Exams,* p. 11
- *Test Generator (One-Stop Planner CD-ROM)*

Internet
- go.hrw.com (keyword: LE0 11-3)

Before You Read

Make the Connection

The Burden of Freedom

Without a doubt, the cornerstone of the "American dream" is the ideal of freedom. The words of the Declaration of Independence are a ringing affirmation of freedom. Yet Jefferson knew well that freedom's twin is responsibility—every kind of liberty we enjoy has to be balanced by an equal amount of personal responsibility.

Reading Skills and Strategies

Identifying the Main Idea

Read the entire Declaration of Independence, and then write its **main idea** in your own words. Next, reread the text and locate the main arguments that support the idea you noted. Note also the details that underpin each argument. Arrange your notes in outline form or in a diagram like this:

- Main Idea
  - Argument 1
    - Supporting detail
    - Supporting detail
    - Supporting detail
  - Argument 2
  - Argument 3

Elements of Literature

Parallelism

Parallelism is the repeated use of sentences, clauses, or phrases with identical or similar structures. For example, when Jefferson cites the truths that are "self-evident," he begins each clause with *that*. He also begins a long series of paragraphs with the words "He has...." Jefferson's use of parallelism emphasizes his view that all the truths he presents are of equal importance. The parallel structure also creates a stately **rhythm** or cadence in the Declaration. Listen for this cadence as you read passages aloud.

> **P**arallelism, or parallel structure, is the repetition of grammatically similar words, phrases, clauses, or sentences to emphasize a point or stir the emotions of a reader or listener.
>
> *For more on Parallelism, see the Handbook of Literary Terms.*

Background

Four other writers worked with Jefferson on the draft of the Declaration that was submitted to Congress: John Adams of Massachusetts, Roger Sherman of Connecticut, Robert Livingston of New York, and Benjamin Franklin of Pennsylvania (page 84). Few changes were made by these other writers, but Congress insisted on several major alterations. Jefferson was upset by what he called "mutilations" of his document.

In this excerpt from his *Autobiography*, Jefferson offers a fascinating glimpse of how the most celebrated document in American history was put together. The underlined passages in the Declaration show the parts omitted by Congress from the original. The words added by Congress appear in the margins. Think about why Congress may have made the changes it did to the original draft.

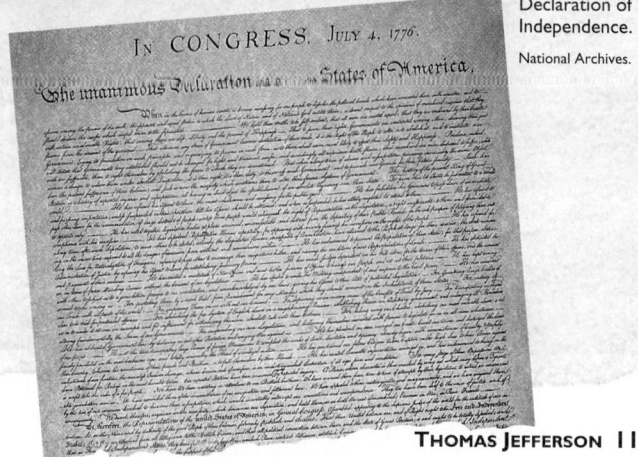

Declaration of Independence.
National Archives.

THOMAS JEFFERSON 115

Summary ■■

This selection from Jefferson's autobiography shows how the Second Continental Congress altered his original to produce the final draft of the Declaration of Independence. He recounts how Congress ruled out passages renouncing kinship with the English people, lest offense be given, and passages banning slavery, lest colonies with no intention of ending their slave trade oppose the Declaration. He presents his original draft in full, underlining the parts Congress deleted and including the phrases Congress added in the margins. The first paragraph of the Declaration states why independence is being declared. The second paragraph describes the ideal relationship between a people and its government, outlines the conditions that justify rebellion, and asserts that the actions of the British King create such conditions. The next twenty paragraphs, many of them composed of a single sentence, cite specific instances of the King's abuses. The final five paragraphs develop the ideas of the first two and solemnly declare the independence of the United States of America from allegiance to the British Crown.

Background

Explain to students that a committee was appointed to draft the Declaration. The members asked Jefferson to write the first draft, which he did in about two weeks. Other committee members then worked with him on minor revisions in the draft.

Preteaching Vocabulary

Words to Own

Have students read the definitions of the Words to Own listed at the bottom of the selection pages. Ask volunteers to use each of the words in a sentence that clearly demonstrates the meaning of the word. When you feel that students have grasped the definitions of all the words, use the following exercise for additional practice; students should choose the vocabulary word that fits best in each phrase.

1. offering a [candid] opinion
2. goods subject to [confiscation]
3. a responsibility that he [abdicated]
4. a [transient] man, just passing through
5. a generous display of [magnanimity]
6. when it [constrains] us to act
7. forced to [renounce] the throne
8. willing to [acquiesce] to the demands
9. wanting to [expunge] all errors
10. earned [censures] for his wrongdoing

F. Russell Bates, a painter active around 1900, depicts a military company whose title suggests continuity with Revolutionary times. Although the American colonial army did not wear the kind of helmets or armor shown here, the picture is a reminder of the "ancient and honorable" tradition of celebrating those who defend their country.

The painting hangs in Boston's Faneuil Hall, used today as a museum, meeting hall, and marketplace. The original building was presented to the city in 1742 by merchant Peter Faneuil. It became known as the "cradle of American Liberty" because patriots of the Revolutionary period so often met there.

Activity. Have students research the uniforms worn by the colonial army or the speakers connected with Faneuil Hall, including Revolutionary era patriots and later statesmen like Daniel Webster and Charles Sumner.

Resources

**Viewing and Representing
Videocassette A, Segment 2**
The segment explores the American dream through our literary heritage. Available in English and Spanish. For full lesson plans and worksheets, see the *Visual Connections Teacher's Manual.*

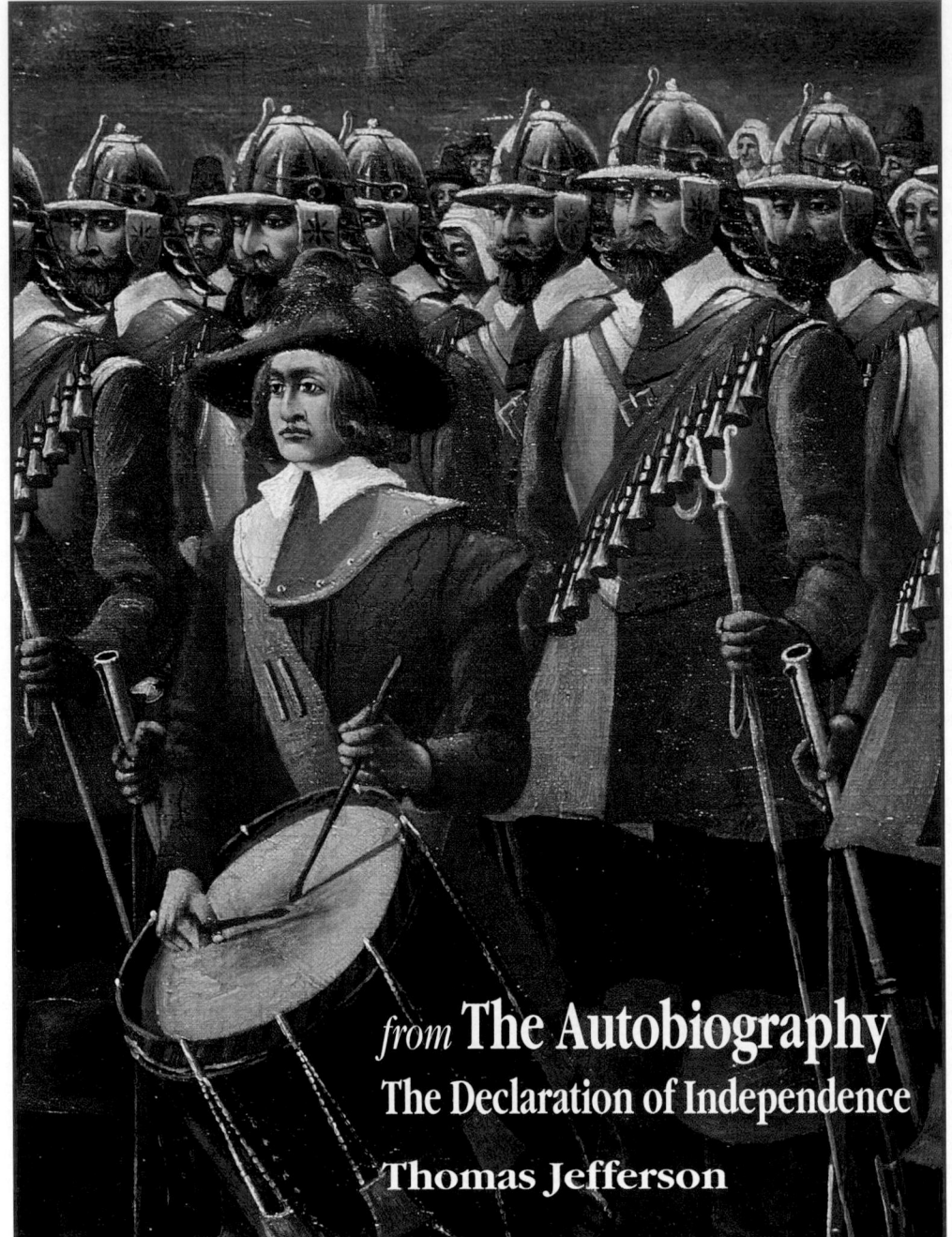

from **The Autobiography
The Declaration of Independence**

Thomas Jefferson

The First Muster of the Ancient and Honorable Artillery Company (detail) (1902) by F. Russell Bates. Oil on canvas (48" x 30"). Ancient and Honorable Artillery Company, Faneuil Hall, Boston.

Courtesy Richard Pasley/Viesti Associates.

116 BEGINNINGS

Reaching All Students

Struggling Readers

Identifying the Main Idea was introduced on p. 115. For a lesson directly tied to this selection that teaches students to identify the main idea with a strategy called The Most Important Word, see the *Reading Skills and Strategies* binder:
• MiniRead Skill Lesson, p. 53
• Selection Skill Lesson, p. 59

English Language Learners

Point out to students that the opening of the second paragraph of the Declaration is one of the most famous and important statements of basic American values. Be sure they understand the meanings of *self-evident* (obvious), *inherent* (innate), and *inalienable* (unable to be taken away).

Advanced Learners

Have students compare the tone of the Declaration to the tone of Patrick Henry's *Speech to the Virginia Convention* (p. 102) and to the tone of Thomas Paine's *The Crisis, No. 1* (p. 108). Ask students how they would characterize each document; they should support their opinions with quotations from the texts. Students might also discuss the tone used in contemporary political documents.

Congress proceeded the same day to consider the Declaration of Independence, which had been reported and lain on the table the Friday preceding, and on Monday referred to a committee of the whole. The pusillanimous[1] idea that we had friends in England worth keeping terms with, still haunted the minds of many. For this reason, those passages which conveyed <u>censures</u> on the people of England were struck out, lest they should give them offense. The clause too, reprobating the enslaving the inhabitants of Africa, was struck out in complaisance to South Carolina and Georgia, who had never attempted to restrain the importation of slaves, and who, on the contrary, still wished to continue it. Our northern brethren also, I believe, felt a little tender under those censures; for though their people had very few slaves themselves, yet they had been pretty considerable carriers of them to others. The debates, having taken up the greater parts of the 2d, 3d, and 4th days of July, were, on the evening of the last, closed; the Declaration was reported by the committee, agreed to by the House, and signed by every member present, except Mr. Dickinson.[2] As the sentiments of men are known not only by what they receive, but what they reject also, I will state the form of the Declaration as originally reported. The parts struck out by Congress shall be distinguished by a black line drawn under them; and those inserted by them shall be placed in the margin, or in a concurrent column.

1. **pusillanimous** (pyoo'si·lan'ə·məs): cowardly; lacking courage.

2. **Mr. Dickinson:** John Dickinson (1732–1808), one of Pennsylvania's representatives to the Second Continental Congress, led the conservative opposition to the Declaration and refused to sign the document.

WORDS TO OWN

censures (sen'shərz) n. pl.: strong, disapproving criticisms.

A Declaration by the Representatives of the United States of America, in General Congress Assembled 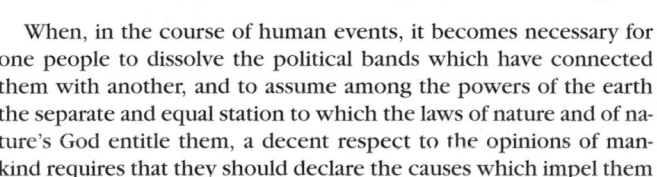 **A**

When, in the course of human events, it becomes necessary for one people to dissolve the political bands which have connected them with another, and to assume among the powers of the earth the separate and equal station to which the laws of nature and of nature's God entitle them, a decent respect to the opinions of mankind requires that they should declare the causes which impel them to the separation. **B**

We hold these truths to be self-evident: that all men are created equal; that they are endowed by their creator with <u>inherent and inalienable rights;</u>[3] that among these are life, liberty, and the pursuit of happiness; that to secure these rights, governments are instituted among men, deriving their just powers from the consent of the governed; that whenever any form of government becomes destructive of these ends, it is the right of the people to alter or to abolish it, and to institute new government, laying its foundation on such principles, and organizing its powers in such form, as to them shall seem most likely to effect their safety and happiness. Prudence, indeed, will dictate that governments long established should not be

certain **C**

D

3. **inalienable** (in·āl'yən·ə·bəl) **rights:** rights that cannot be taken away.

Thomas Jefferson (date and artist unknown). Fragment of white marble.
Maryland Historical Society.

THOMAS JEFFERSON 117

A **Cultural Connections**
The French Revolution
The Declaration of Independence was a source of strength and inspiration to the French during their revolution (which began in 1789) and continues to inspire people seeking liberty today. Ask students to compare the French revolutionary motto—"*Liberté! Egalité! Fraternité!*" ("Liberty! Equality! Brotherhood!")—with the ideas presented here.

B **Elements of Literature**
Persuasion
❓ What is the purpose of this paragraph? [to establish the Congress's credibility by showing that its members are conscious of the gravity of declaring independence and are prepared to justify this course of action]

C **Elements of Literature**
Parallelism
❓ Why does Jefferson use parallelism in the second paragraph? [to signal that the ideas listed are equally important] In terms of the overall argument, what is the purpose? [to establish the premises, or underlying assumptions, on which the argument is based]

D **Literary Connections**
Debt to European Thinkers
This paragraph draws on the ideas of thinkers like John Locke and Jean Jacques Rousseau, who theorized that in the state of nature all men are equal and have natural rights and that they choose to form governments, which they can then dissolve at will.

Using Students' Strengths

Spatial/Visual Learners
Visual learners, or those interested in musical theater or drama, might enjoy watching a videotape of *1776,* the film version of the Broadway musical by Peter Stone and Sherman Edwards about the writing of the Declaration of Independence. Have students compare the portrayal of Jefferson in the movie with the Jefferson revealed in his writings.

Kinesthetic Learners
Have pairs of students choose one or two of the examples of King George's injustices and make up a sketch illustrating them, along with their consequences for the colonists. Allow them to perform their sketches before the class, which should then identify the issues dramatized.

Auditory Learners
Use the recorded reading of the Declaration (*Audio CD Library,* Disc 4, Track 5) to help students engage with the tone and emotional energy of the Declaration. Have students listen to the recording in brief sections. After each section, invite responses to the Declaration's argument, tone, and style. At the end, invite students to draft summary statements.

A Critical Thinking

Evaluating

? The Continental Congress altered Jefferson's original Declaration to make it more diplomatic. They also cut words and phrases that seemed redundant. Which changes on this page strike you as diplomatic changes to soften the Declaration's impact, and which strike you as stylistic changes to make it stronger? [Responses will vary, but perceptive students will cite the shift from *expunge* to *alter* and *unremitting* to *repeated* as political compromises; other deletions seem to be stylistic choices that reduce redundancy.]

B English Language Learners

Identifying Pronoun Antecedents

Point out to students that the repeated pronoun *He* on this page and on the following four pages refers to "the present king of Great Britain" (George III), mentioned in the second paragraph of the Declaration.

C Reading Skills and Strategies

Identifying the Main Idea

? Ask students to identify the main idea of these paragraphs. How are all these actions by the King related? [Possible response: The main idea is that the King has obstructed the colonists' access to self-determination and democratic representation, and these facts justify rebellion against his rule.]

D Elements of Literature

Parallelism

To help students hear the cadences of **parallelism,** have one student read aloud the repeated phrases, while the others take turns reading the new words in each clause.

---

changed for light and <u>transient</u> causes; and accordingly all experience hath shown that mankind are more disposed to suffer while evils are sufferable, than to right themselves by abolishing the forms to which they are accustomed. But when a long train of abuses and usurpations,[4] begun at a distinguished[5] period and pursuing invariably the same object, evinces a design to reduce them under absolute despotism, it is their right, it is their duty to throw off such government, and to provide new guards for their future security. Such has been the patient sufferance of these colonies; and such is now the necessity which <u>constrains</u> them to <u>expunge</u> their former systems of government. The history of the present king of Great Britain is a history of <u>unremitting</u> injuries and usurpations, <u>among which appears no solitary fact to contradict the uniform tenor of the rest, but all have</u> in direct object the establishment of an absolute tyranny over these states. To prove this, let facts be submitted to a <u>candid</u> world <u>for the truth of which we pledge a faith yet unsullied by falsehood.</u>

alter

repeated

all having

  He has refused his assent to laws the most wholesome and necessary for the public good.

  He has forbidden his governors to pass laws of immediate and pressing importance, unless suspended in their operation till his assent should be obtained; and, when so suspended, he has utterly neglected to attend to them.

  He has refused to pass other laws for the accommodation of large districts of people, unless those people would relinquish the right of representation in the legislature, a right inestimable to them, and formidable to tyrants only.[6]

  He has called together legislative bodies at places unusual, uncomfortable, and distant from the depository of their public records, for the sole purpose of fatiguing them into compliance with his measures.

  He has dissolved representative houses repeatedly <u>and continually</u> for opposing with manly firmness his invasions on the rights of the people.

  He has refused for a long time after such dissolutions to cause others to be elected, whereby the legislative powers, incapable of annihilation, have returned to the people at large for their exercise, the state remaining, in the meantime, exposed to all the dangers of invasion from without and convulsions within.

4. **usurpations** (yōo′zər·pā′shənz): acts of unlawful or forceful seizure of property, power, rights, and the like.
5. **distinguished** (di·stiŋ′gwisht): clearly defined.
6. **formidable . . . only:** causing fear only to tyrants.

WORDS TO OWN
transient (tran′shənt) *adj.*: temporary; passing.
constrains (kən·strānz′) *v.*: forces.
expunge (ek·spunj′) *v.*: erase; remove.
candid (kan′did) *adj.*: unbiased; fair.

Professional Notes

John Adams Chooses Jefferson
Benjamin Franklin was too ill with gout to write the Declaration, and John Adams, the independence leader, refused. Adams (who wrote the Massachusetts constitution) told Jefferson to write it: "Reason 1st. You are a Virginian, and a Virginian ought to appear at the head of this business. Reason 2d. I am obnoxious, suspected, and unpopular. You are very much otherwise. Reason 3d. You can write ten times better than I can."

Skill Link

Recognizing Shared Cultural Characteristics
Have students work in groups of four to research the Declaration of the Rights of Man and of the Citizen, the Bill of Rights of the French Constitution. An article including all or most of the text may be found in major encyclopedias or at Internet sites specializing in historical documents. Ask students to compare the main idea and the principles set forth in the French document with those contained in the Declaration of Independence. Have groups present their findings and points of comparison on charts or other graphic displays and use them in oral presentations to the class.

He has endeavored to prevent the population of these states; for that purpose obstructing the laws for naturalization of foreigners, refusing to pass others to encourage their migrations hither, and raising the conditions of new appropriations of lands.

E

obstructed / by

He has <u>suffered</u> the administration of justice <u>totally to cease in some of these states</u> refusing his assent to laws for establishing judiciary powers.

He has made <u>our</u> judges dependent on his will alone for the tenure of their offices, and the amount and payment of their salaries.

G

He has erected a multitude of new offices, <u>by a self-assumed power</u> and sent hither swarms of new officers to harass our people and eat out their substance.

F

He has kept among us in times of peace standing armies <u>and ships of war</u> without the consent of our legislatures.

He has affected to render the military independent of, and superior to, the civil power.

He has combined with others[7] to subject us to a jurisdiction foreign to our constitutions and unacknowledged by our laws, giving

7. **others:** members of British Parliament and their supporters and agents.

The Declaration of Independence, July 4, 1776 by John Trumbull (1756–1843). Oil on canvas.

Yale University Art Gallery, Trumbull Collection.

THOMAS JEFFERSON 119

E **Historical Connections**

King Limits Settlement

After Ottawa chief Pontiac began a revolt against Britain, the Crown issued the Proclamation of 1763, prohibiting settlement west of the Appalachians. This angered prospective small and large colonial landowners.

F **Elements of Literature**

Persuasion

? What loaded words does Jefferson use here? [*swarms, harass, eat out their substance*] Why might he have used them? [Possible answers: to express the colonists' anger; to produce an emotional reaction.]

G **Elements of Literature**

Parallelism

? The Declaration presents a logical argument substantiated by parallel examples. What is the cumulative effect? [Possible responses: The examples emphasize the colonists' sense of injury; they make a conciliatory view seem naive; they build emotional intensity; they make the conclusion seem inevitable.]

RESPONDING TO THE ART

John Trumbull (1756–1843) was an American historical painter who spent more than twenty years painting this canvas, searching out thirty-six of the signers in order to paint them from life. The depiction of the Assembly Room of Philadelphia's State House (see p. 210) is based on a description by Thomas Jefferson.

Activity. Have students do research in order to match individual portraits with the names of the signers.

Skill Link

Using Text Organizers

1. Have students scan the table of contents of this book and any of the unit introductory essays to review graphic techniques that help readers effectively use the material: the arrangement of text on a page; different sizes, styles, and colors of type; quotations set apart and in different type; illustrations, both separate and in the background; and call-out boxes that summarize key points or highlight related information.

2. Now read students background information on Jefferson's involvement with the sciences: For instance, remind them that he investigated issues in meteorology, paleontology, archaeology, agriculture, geology, astronomy, chemistry, botany, and medicine. He also invented a number of practical devices, including an adjustable drafting desk, a threshing machine, and a dumbwaiter to bring wine up from his wine cellar.

3. Have students research some of Jefferson's scientific accomplishments in these fields and feature them in a graphic display: a full bulletin board, a series of posters, or an illustrated booklet. Students should consciously apply some of the text organizers discussed. Evaluate the results in terms of both content and effective use of these techniques.

LITERATURE AND POLITICS

Jefferson embodies the complex and ambiguous relationship between Native Americans and the early American federal government. In his biography of Jefferson, historian Joseph J. Ellis points out that Jefferson celebrated Native American culture in his 1787 book, *Notes on the State of Virginia,* and that he praised Native American oratory, encouraged study of Native American languages, and, as president, always treated Native American delegations with respect. Jefferson recognized that liberty is fundamental to Native American culture. Nevertheless, as Ellis puts it, "It was during Jefferson's presidency that the basic decisions were made that required the deportation of massive segments of the Indian population to land west of the Mississippi."

Ⓐ Reading Skills and Strategies

Identifying the Main Idea

❓ Finding the main idea sometimes involves generalizing from details. To what general sphere do all these actions refer? [law or politics] What is the main idea of the paragraph? [Possible response: The king has unfairly and illegally taken away the colonists' legal and political rights.]

Ⓑ Historical Connections

After the French and Indian War, Britain gained Quebec, which it extended to the Ohio River in 1774, permitting existing French laws to rule in this territory.

LITERATURE AND POLITICS

Legacy of Peace and Unity: The Iroquois Constitution

Before Revolutionary patriots put pen to paper to draft the U.S. Constitution in 1787, Colonial leaders such as Thomas Jefferson and Benjamin Franklin studied examples of government from Greek and Roman times, examples from the Bible, and an example flourishing closer to home: the Iroquois Confederacy.

The Iroquois Confederacy, also known as the League of Five Nations, was a union of the Senecas, Cayugas, Onondagas, Oneidas, and Mohawks (the Tuscaroras joined later). Around 1500, so the legend goes, a Mohawk visionary named Dekanawidah convinced the nations to unite in order to establish peace and to protect "life, property and liberty." Thanks to the constitution they created, called the Law of the Great Peace, the confederacy became a formidable power; by 1750, it numbered about fifteen thousand people, and Iroquois hunters and warriors ranged over one million square miles.

The oldest living constitution. The Iroquois Constitution, which still governs the Iroquois today, is regarded as the world's oldest living constitution. It gives member tribes equal voice in the nation's affairs, spells out a system of checks and balances, and guarantees political and religious freedom. Most amazing by European standards of the time, the Iroquois Constitution grants extensive political power to women, who hold the right to nominate and impeach chiefs. The constitution specifies that "Women shall be considered the progenitors of the Nation. They shall own the land and the soil. Men and women shall follow the status of the mother."

The Iroquois Confederacy had what Jefferson and Franklin were searching for: a constitution infused with basic principles of democracy and federalism. Franklin

---

his assent to their acts of pretended legislation for quartering large bodies of armed troops among us; for protecting them by a mock trial from punishment for any murders which they should commit on the inhabitants of these states; for cutting off our trade with all parts of the world; for imposing taxes on us without our consent; for depriving us [   ] of the benefits of trial by jury; for transporting us beyond seas to be tried for pretended offenses; for abolishing the free system of English laws in a neighboring province,[8] establishing therein an arbitrary government, and enlarging its boundaries, so as to render it at once an example and fit instrument for introducing the same absolute rule into these states; for taking away our charters, abolishing our most valuable laws, and altering fundamentally the forms of our governments; for suspending our own legislatures, and declaring themselves invested with power to legislate for us in all cases whatsoever.

in many cases

colonies

Ⓐ
Ⓑ

8. **neighboring province:** Québec in Canada.

Crossing the Curriculum

Architecture

Have pairs of students research Jefferson's work in architecture. Suggest that they bring to class blueprints for or photographs of Monticello, the University of Virginia buildings he designed, or the classical models he drew on. You might create a bulletin-board display of the pictures.

Social Studies

Jefferson had an excellent classical education and believed that educated voters would make good choices. Have students explore their own ideas about voting and education in small groups and then draw up a curriculum for the education of an ideal electorate.

F. Russell Bates, a painter active around 1900, depicts a military company whose title suggests continuity with Revolutionary times. Although the American colonial army did not wear the kind of helmets or armor shown here, the picture is a reminder of the "ancient and honorable" tradition of celebrating those who defend their country.

The painting hangs in Boston's Faneuil Hall, used today as a museum, meeting hall, and marketplace. The original building was presented to the city in 1742 by merchant Peter Faneuil. It became known as the "cradle of American Liberty" because patriots of the Revolutionary period so often met there.

Activity. Have students research the uniforms worn by the colonial army or the speakers connected with Faneuil Hall, including Revolutionary era patriots and later statesmen like Daniel Webster and Charles Sumner.

Resources

Viewing and Representing
Videocassette A, Segment 2
The segment explores the American dream through our literary heritage. Available in English and Spanish. For full lesson plans and worksheets, see the *Visual Connections Teacher's Manual.*

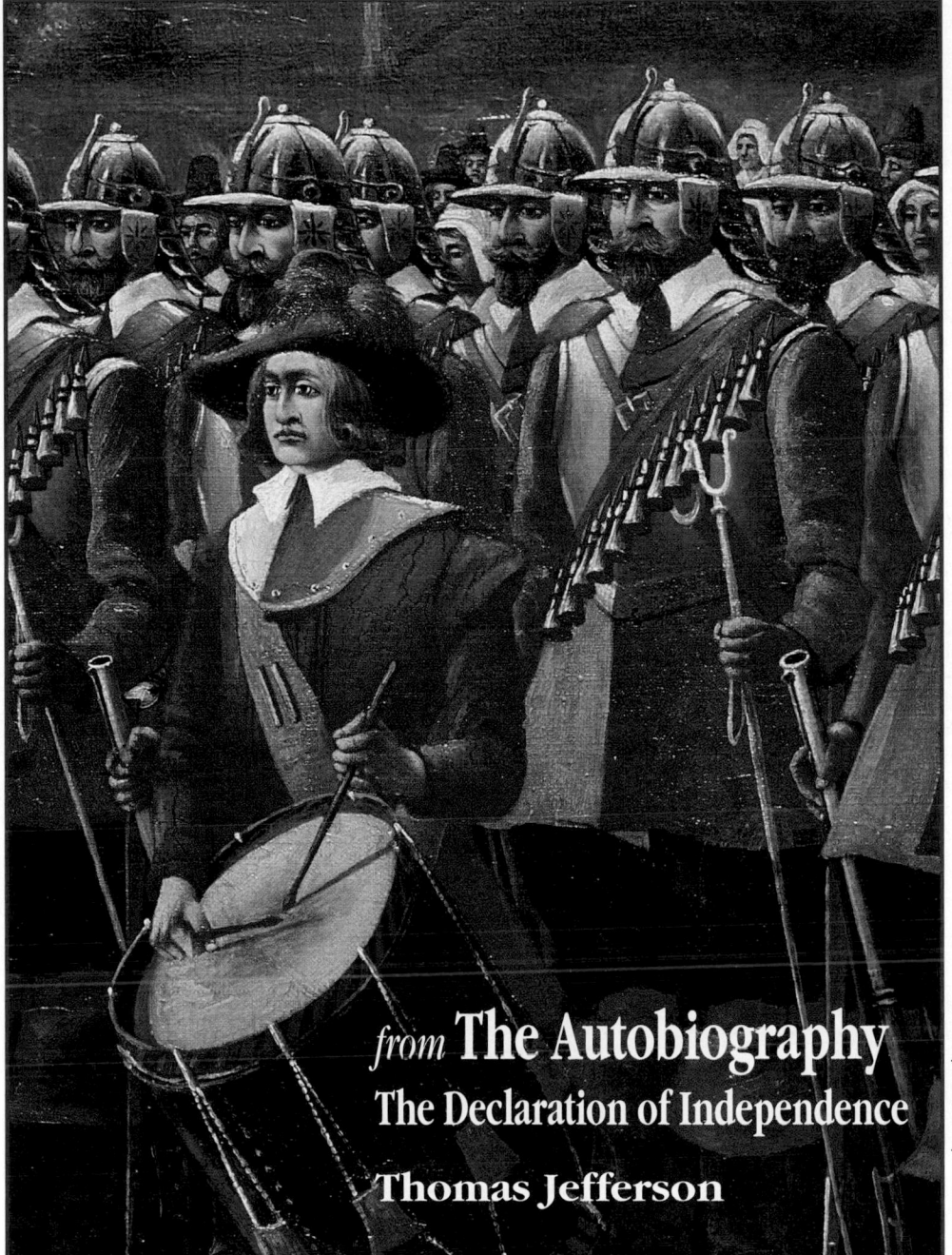

from **The Autobiography**
The Declaration of Independence

Thomas Jefferson

The First Muster of the Ancient and Honorable Artillery Company (detail) (1902) by F. Russell Bates. Oil on canvas (48" x 30"). Ancient and Honorable Artillery Company, Faneuil Hall, Boston.

116 BEGINNINGS

Courtesy Richard Pasley/Viesti Associates.

Reaching All Students

Struggling Readers
Identifying the Main Idea was introduced on p. 115. For a lesson directly tied to this selection that teaches students to identify the main idea with a strategy called The Most Important Word, see the *Reading Skills and Strategies* binder:
• MiniRead Skill Lesson, p. 53
• Selection Skill Lesson, p. 59

English Language Learners
Point out to students that the opening of the second paragraph of the Declaration is one of the most famous and important statements of basic American values. Be sure they understand the meanings of *self-evident* (obvious), *inherent* (innate), and *inalienable* (unable to be taken away).

Advanced Learners
Have students compare the tone of the Declaration to the tone of Patrick Henry's *Speech to the Virginia Convention* (p. 102) and to the tone of Thomas Paine's *The Crisis, No. 1* (p. 108). Ask students how they would characterize each document; they should support their opinions with quotations from the texts. Students might also discuss the tone used in contemporary political documents.

Before You Read

FROM THE AUTOBIOGRAPHY: THE DECLARATION OF INDEPENDENCE

Make the Connection

The Burden of Freedom
Without a doubt, the cornerstone of the "American dream" is the ideal of freedom. The words of the Declaration of Independence are a ringing affirmation of freedom. Yet Jefferson knew well that freedom's twin is responsibility—every kind of liberty we enjoy has to be balanced by an equal amount of personal responsibility.

Reading Skills and Strategies

Identifying the Main Idea
Read the entire Declaration of Independence, and then write its **main idea** in your own words. Next, reread the text and locate the main arguments that support the idea you noted. Note also the details that underpin each argument. Arrange your notes in outline form or in a diagram like this:

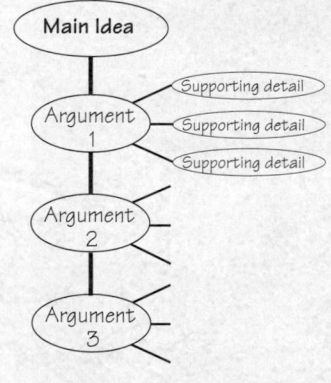

Elements of Literature

Parallelism
Parallelism is the repeated use of sentences, clauses, or phrases with identical or similar structures. For example, when Jefferson cites the truths that are "self-evident," he begins each clause with *that*. He also begins a long series of paragraphs with the words "He has...." Jefferson's use of parallelism emphasizes his view that all the truths he presents are of equal importance. The parallel structure also creates a stately **rhythm** or cadence in the Declaration. Listen for this cadence as you read passages aloud.

> **P**arallelism, or parallel structure, is the repetition of grammatically similar words, phrases, clauses, or sentences to emphasize a point or stir the emotions of a reader or listener.
>
> *For more on Parallelism, see the Handbook of Literary Terms.*

Background

Four other writers worked with Jefferson on the draft of the Declaration that was submitted to Congress: John Adams of Massachusetts, Roger Sherman of Connecticut, Robert Livingston of New York, and Benjamin Franklin of Pennsylvania (page 84). Few changes were made by these other writers, but Congress insisted on several major alterations. Jefferson was upset by what he called "mutilations" of his document.

In this excerpt from his *Autobiography*, Jefferson offers a fascinating glimpse of how the most celebrated document in American history was put together. The underlined passages in the Declaration show the parts omitted by Congress from the original. The words added by Congress appear in the margins. Think about why Congress may have made the changes it did to the original draft.

Declaration of Independence.

National Archives.

THOMAS JEFFERSON 115

Summary ■ ■

This selection from Jefferson's autobiography shows how the Second Continental Congress altered his original to produce the final draft of the Declaration of Independence. He recounts how Congress ruled out passages renouncing kinship with the English people, lest offense be given, and passages banning slavery, lest colonies with no intention of ending their slave trade oppose the Declaration. He presents his original draft in full, underlining the parts Congress deleted and including the phrases Congress added in the margins. The first paragraph of the Declaration states why independence is being declared. The second paragraph describes the ideal relationship between a people and its government, outlines the conditions that justify rebellion, and asserts that the actions of the British King create such conditions. The next twenty paragraphs, many of them composed of a single sentence, cite specific instances of the King's abuses. The final five paragraphs develop the ideas of the first two and solemnly declare the independence of the United States of America from allegiance to the British Crown.

Background

Explain to students that a committee was appointed to draft the Declaration. The members asked Jefferson to write the first draft, which he did in about two weeks. Other committee members then worked with him on minor revisions in the draft.

Preteaching Vocabulary

Words to Own
Have students read the definitions of the Words to Own listed at the bottom of the selection pages. Ask volunteers to use each of the words in a sentence that clearly demonstrates the meaning of the word. When you feel that students have grasped the definitions of all the words, use the following exercise for additional practice; students should choose the vocabulary word that fits best in each phrase.

1. offering a [candid] opinion
2. goods subject to [confiscation]
3. a responsibility that he [abdicated]
4. a [transient] man, just passing through
5. a generous display of [magnanimity]
6. when it [constrains] us to act
7. forced to [renounce] the throne
8. willing to [acquiesce] to the demands
9. wanting to [expunge] all errors
10. earned [censures] for his wrongdoing

Planning

- **Block Schedule**
  Block Scheduling Lesson Plans with Pacing Guide
- **Traditional Schedule**
  Lesson Plans Including Strategies for English-Language Learners
- **One-Stop Planner**
  CD-ROM with Test Generator

Thomas Jefferson

(1743–1826)

Thomas Jefferson (1791) by Charles Willson Peale. Oil on canvas.
Independence National Historical Park, Philadelphia, Pennsylvania.

At a White House dinner in 1962 honoring forty-nine Nobel Prize winners, President John F. Kennedy hailed his guests as "the most extraordinary collection of talent, of human knowledge, that has ever been gathered together at the White House, with the possible exception of when Thomas Jefferson dined alone." President Kennedy was exaggerating only slightly.

Thomas Jefferson, the brilliant and versatile third president of the United States, was an accomplished statesman, architect, botanist, paleontologist, linguist, and musician. He displayed the range of interests that we associate with the eighteenth-century mind at its best.

Jefferson was born in the red-clay country of what is now Albemarle County, Virginia. Jefferson's father, a surveyor and magistrate, died when Thomas was fourteen, but he had provided his son with an excellent classical education and a 5,000-acre estate. After attending the College of William and Mary, Jefferson became a lawyer, a member of the Virginia House of Burgesses, and a spokesperson for the rights of personal liberty and religious freedom. In 1774, he wrote a pamphlet called *A Summary View of the Rights of British America,* a call for the rejection of parliamentary authority. This pamphlet established his reputation, and two years later, the Second Continental Congress chose him to help draft the Declaration of Independence.

During the Revolution, Jefferson served for a time as governor of Virginia. When the British invaded Virginia, he retired to Monticello, the home he had designed, and devoted himself to his family and to scientific research. During this time he also composed most of his *Notes on the State of Virginia.* Shortly after Jefferson's beloved wife Martha died in 1782, he returned to public life, in part as an escape from his private grief. He served as minister to France, secretary of state, vice president, and president from 1801–1809.

A determined opponent of federal power, Jefferson embodied the principles of what would come to be called Jeffersonian democracy. He believed in the rights of individuals and states to govern themselves as much as possible. Politically and personally, he strove to keep power vested in the agrarian backbone of the country. He also expanded the country enormously in 1803: The Louisiana Purchase doubled the size of the United States, adding land that would later be divided into part or all of fifteen states. And as for Jefferson's presidential style, he avoided public displays and wore simple clothes: A president, he thought, should neither act nor look like a king. At state dinners, he eliminated seating by rank.

After his presidency, Jefferson retired once again to Monticello. He devoted his energy to establishing the University of Virginia, planning its courses of study and designing many of its buildings. In 1826, both Jefferson (at eighty-three) and the former president John Adams (at ninety) became gravely ill. Both hoped to live to see the fiftieth anniversary of the independence they had done so much to ensure. Jefferson died on the morning of July 4, several hours before Adams, whose last words were "Thomas Jefferson still survives."

 **go.hrw.com**
LE0 11-3

   *Resources: Print and Media*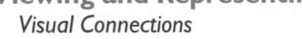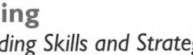

Reading
- *Reading Skills and Strategies*
  MiniRead Skill Lesson, p. 53
  Selection Skill Lesson, p. 59
- *Graphic Organizers for Active Reading,* p. 11
- *Words to Own,* p. 10
- *Audio CD Library* Disc 4, Track 5

Writing and Language
- *Daily Oral Grammar,* Transparency 11
- *Grammar and Language Links*
  Worksheet, p. 19

Viewing and Representing
- *Visual Connections*
  Videocassette A, Segment 2

Assessment
- *Formal Assessment,* p. 21
- *Portfolio Management System,* p. 100
- *Preparation for College Admission Exams,* p. 11
- *Test Generator (One-Stop Planner CD-ROM)*

Internet
- go.hrw.com (keyword: LE0 11-3)

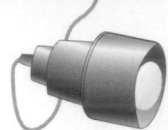

SPOTLIGHT ON

Phillis Wheatley: A Revolutionary Woman

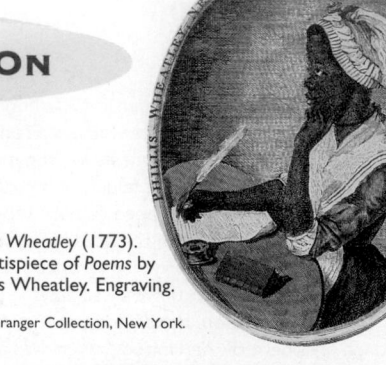

Phillis Wheatley (1773). Frontispiece of *Poems* by Phillis Wheatley. Engraving.

The Granger Collection, New York.

All the odds were stacked against her—she was an enslaved African, young, and female. But Phillis Wheatley (c. 1753–1784) published her first poem when she was barely thirteen, and by the time she was twenty years old she had developed a reputation as a poet whose work was praised by George Washington and Thomas Jefferson (page 114).

When Phillis Wheatley was about seven or eight years old, she, like Olaudah Equiano (page 56), was stolen from her home in West Africa. She arrived in America on board a slave ship in 1761. At first, of course, she spoke no English. But she was purchased by the Wheatley family of Boston to assist Mrs. Susanna Wheatley and was treated kindly. Pleased to find this young woman intelligent and eager to learn, the Wheatleys provided her with an excellent education, equal to that of any free person in Boston at the time.

Susanna Wheatley arranged the London publication of a volume of Phillis's poems in 1773; the book received generally encouraging reviews, and it was read widely in England, France, and the American Colonies. Around this time, Phillis was given her freedom, though she chose to remain with the Wheatleys. When they died, she married John Peters, a freeman, in 1778.

Wheatley's poems imitate the style popular in the poetry of her time: She uses a Latinate vocabulary, inversions, and elevated diction. The following stanza is from her poem to the earl of Dartmouth, who had just been appointed secretary of state in charge of the American Colonies (1772). Dartmouth, she hopes, will be open to the colonists' grievances.

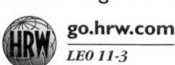
go.hrw.com
LEO 11-3

from **To the Right Honorable William, Earl of Dartmouth, His Majesty's Principal Secretary of State for North America, etc.**

Should you, my lord, while you peruse my song,
Wonder from whence my love of *Freedom* sprung,
Whence flow these wishes for the common good,
By feeling hearts alone best understood,
I, young in life, by seeming cruel fate
Was snatch'd from *Afric's* fancy'd happy seat:
What pangs excruciating must molest,
What sorrows labor in my parent's breast?
Steel'd was that soul and by no misery mov'd
That from a father seiz'd his babe belov'd:
Such, such my case. And can I then but pray
Others may never feel tyrannic sway?

—Phillis Wheatley

Wheatley's life ended on a tragic note. Her married life was filled with personal, financial, and familial hardships. Wheatley bore three children, but none of them survived. When she herself was sick and poor, the same society that lavished attention on her as a kind of "sideshow attraction"—an enslaved woman who could write lofty poetry—abandoned her to a position of powerlessness and anonymity. She died in her early thirties, destitute and grieving, without having published another book of poems. Since her death, however, her poems have been reprinted and, in the twentieth century, have again attracted lavish attention. Today Phillis Wheatley is praised as a true pioneer—the first African American poet in North America.

SPOTLIGHT ON 113

Reaching All Students

MAKING MEANINGS

First Thoughts [Respond]

1. Students are likely to focus on the first, third, and final paragraphs.

Shaping Interpretations [Interpret]

2. A summer soldier will not fight in the winter, or at any time when the fighting is especially difficult. Similarly, a sunshine patriot is not a patriot when times are rough. The images are appropriate for an army and a citizenry that faced early setbacks in their fight with the British and which were in danger of giving in to despair.

3. Self-interest in the form of mutual protection is the most compelling reason for standing united. Some students will criticize this idea as an overly cynical view of love, while others will agree that solidarity requires agreement on friends and enemies.

4. Paine argues that it is as just to rebel against England as it is to attack a thief who invades one's home, because England's abusive actions have overstepped any legal authority it had over the colonists. An opponent of this position might argue that England still has greater authority than any colonists taking the law into their own hands.

Extending the Text [Evaluate]

5. Possible response: Emerson would agree wholeheartedly with Paine's arguments and probably delight in his intense and highly rhetorical style. People today might agree with the arguments but would probably prefer a more informal style.

Grading Timesaver

Rubrics for each Choices assignment appear on p. 99 in the *Portfolio Management System*.

MAKING MEANINGS

First Thoughts

1. Which passages in this excerpt were especially stirring?

Shaping Interpretations

2. The pamphlet opens with two famous **images** (page 108). What kinds of people does Paine identify with summer and sunshine? Why are these images appropriate?

3. Explain the meaning of Paine's **metaphor** "Mutual fear is the principal link in the chain of mutual love" (page 111). Do you agree or disagree with this idea, and why?

4. An **analogy** is a comparison between two things that are alike in certain respects. Analogies are used often in **argument** and **persuasion** to demonstrate the logic of one idea by showing how it is similar to another, accepted idea. Analogies can be tricky, though, because few ideas or situations are completely alike in all aspects. What analogy does Paine draw when he talks about the thief (page 110)? What point is he making, and how might an opponent answer?

Extending the Text

5. How do you think Ralph Waldo Emerson, author of "Concord Hymn" (page 99), would respond to Paine's arguments and his writing **style**? How would people today react?

Reading Check

a. What reasons does Paine give for his confidence that God will favor the Americans?

b. Explain Paine's point in telling the **anecdote** about the Tory tavern keeper. Is he appealing more to reason or to emotions?

c. What powerful emotional appeal does Paine make at the end of his essay?

d. What is Paine's **main idea**? What details support it?

112 BEGINNINGS

CHOICES:
Building Your Portfolio

Writer's Notebook

1. Collecting Ideas for an Autobiographical Incident

Have you ever joined with others in a team effort for a common cause? Briefly describe the experience: What was the purpose of banding together? Did taking part in group action involve personal sacrifices on your part? Save your notes for possible use in the Writer's Workshop on page 130.

Evaluating Ideas

2. A Paine Prescription

"Not a place upon earth might be so happy as America. Her situation is remote from all the wrangling world, and she has nothing to do but to trade with them. . . . I am . . . confident . . . that America will never be happy till she gets clear of foreign dominion" (page 109). In a brief essay, evaluate these words from Paine's pamphlet. Considering the world as it is today, how would you reply to Paine?

Creative Writing

3. Crisis Zone

Imagine you are one of the volunteers who listened to this pamphlet being read a few days before Christmas, in 1776, just before you were to cross the Delaware River and attack General Howe and his troops in Trenton. In a paragraph, poem, or song lyrics, express how you felt while the pamphlet was being read, and describe the responses of the people around you.

Sir William Howe (1729–1814), British commander-in-chief in America during Revolutionary War.

Reading Check

a. The colonists have sought only peace; the English King, on the other hand, has claimed godlike authority for himself while behaving like a common criminal.

b. Allegiance to the king, based on selfish fear, merely defers the inevitable conflict. The anecdote appeals more to the emotions.

c. Paine appeals to fears of enslavement, a ravaged countryside, depopulated cities, and the corruption of colonial families by German mercenaries.

d. Paine's main idea is that the colonies have no choice but to stand together now and commit to defeating the British. Supporting details include the inevitability of independence, the threat of English, German, and Indian brutality, and the colonists' ultimate advantages with God and in battle.

cause be assigned why we should punish in the one case and pardon in the other. Let them call me rebel, and welcome, I feel no concern from it; but I should suffer the misery of devils, were I to make a whore of my soul by swearing allegiance to one whose character is that of a sottish,[14] stupid, stubborn, worthless, brutish man. I conceive likewise a horrid idea in receiving mercy from a being, who at the last day shall be shrieking to the rocks and mountains to cover him, and fleeing with terror from the orphan, the widow, and the slain of America.

There are cases which cannot be overdone by language, and this is one. There are persons too who see not the full extent of the evil which threatens them; they solace themselves with hopes that the enemy, if he succeeds, will be merciful. Is this the madness of folly, to expect mercy from those who have refused to do justice; and even mercy, where conquest is the object, is only a trick of war; the cunning of the fox is as murderous as the violence of the wolf; and we ought to guard equally against both. Howe's first object is partly by threats and partly by promises, to terrify or seduce the people to deliver up their arms and to receive mercy. The ministry recommended the same plan to Gage,[15] and this is what the Tories call making their peace, *"a peace which passeth all understanding,"*[16] *indeed!* A peace which would be the immediate forerunner of a worse ruin than any we have yet thought of. Ye men of Pennsylvania, do reason upon these things! Were the back counties to give up their arms, they would fall an easy prey to the Indians, who are all armed; this perhaps is what some Tories would not be sorry for. Were the home counties to deliver up their arms, they would be exposed to the resentment of the back counties, who would then have it in their power to chastise their defection at pleasure. And were any one state to give up its arms, *that* state must be garrisoned by Howe's army of Britains and Hessians[17] to preserve it from the anger of the rest. Mutual fear is the

E

principal link in the chain of mutual love, and woe be to that state that breaks the compact. Howe is mercifully inviting you to barbarous destruction, and men must be either rogues or fools that will not see it. I dwell not upon the powers of imagination; I bring reason to your ears; and in language as plain as A, B, C, hold up truth to your eyes.

I thank God that I fear not. I see no real cause for fear. I know our situation well and can see the way out of it. While our army was collected, Howe dared not risk a battle, and it is no credit to him that he decamped from the White Plains, and waited a mean opportunity to ravage the defenseless Jerseys;[18] but it is great credit to us, that, with a handful of men, we sustained an orderly retreat for near an hundred miles, brought off our ammunition, all our field pieces, the greatest part of our stores, and had four rivers to pass. None can say that our retreat was precipitate,[19] for we were near three weeks in performing it, that the country[20] might have time to come in. Twice we marched back to meet the enemy, and remained out till dark. The sign of fear was not seen in our camp, and had not some of the cowardly and disaffected inhabitants spread false alarms through the country, the Jerseys had never been ravaged. Once more we are again collected and collecting, our new army at both ends of the continent is recruiting fast, and we shall be able to open the next campaign with sixty thousand men, well armed and clothed. This is our situation, and who will may know it. By <u>perseverance</u> and fortitude we have the prospect of a glorious issue; by cowardice and submission, the sad choice of a variety of evils—a ravaged country—a depopulated city—habitations without safety, and slavery without hope—our homes turned into barracks and bawdy-houses for Hessians, and a future race to provide for, whose fathers we shall doubt of. Look on this picture and weep over it! And if there yet remains one thoughtless wretch who believes it not, let him suffer it unlamented.

F

G

---

18. White Plains . . . Jerseys: Howe had defeated Washington at White Plains, New York, in 1776 but had failed to press his advantage.
19. precipitate (prē·sip′ə·tit): sudden; unexpected.
20. country: the local people. Paine uses the term to refer to local volunteers.

WORDS TO OWN

perseverance (pʉr′sə·vir′əns) *n.:* persistence.

---

14. sottish (sät′ish): stupid or foolish from too much drinking.
15. Gage: General Thomas Gage (1721–1787), head of the British forces in America (1763–1775) before General Howe.
16. a peace . . . understanding: ironic echo of Paul's epistle to the Philippians (4:7).
17. Hessians (hesh′ənz): German troops, mostly from the region of Hesse, hired to fight on the British side.

THOMAS PAINE   111

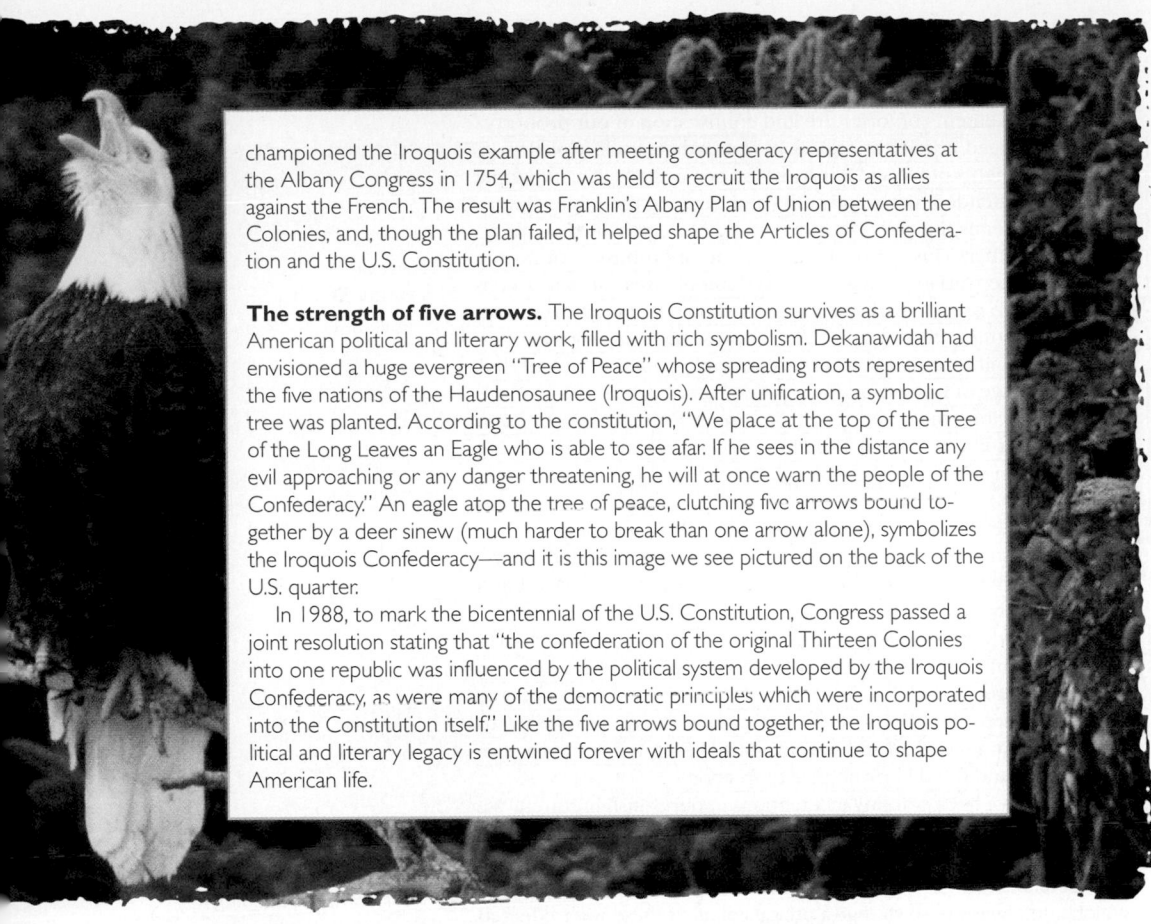

championed the Iroquois example after meeting confederacy representatives at the Albany Congress in 1754, which was held to recruit the Iroquois as allies against the French. The result was Franklin's Albany Plan of Union between the Colonies, and, though the plan failed, it helped shape the Articles of Confederation and the U.S. Constitution.

The strength of five arrows. The Iroquois Constitution survives as a brilliant American political and literary work, filled with rich symbolism. Dekanawidah had envisioned a huge evergreen "Tree of Peace" whose spreading roots represented the five nations of the Haudenosaunee (Iroquois). After unification, a symbolic tree was planted. According to the constitution, "We place at the top of the Tree of the Long Leaves an Eagle who is able to see afar. If he sees in the distance any evil approaching or any danger threatening, he will at once warn the people of the Confederacy." An eagle atop the tree of peace, clutching five arrows bound together by a deer sinew (much harder to break than one arrow alone), symbolizes the Iroquois Confederacy—and it is this image we see pictured on the back of the U.S. quarter.

In 1988, to mark the bicentennial of the U.S. Constitution, Congress passed a joint resolution stating that "the confederation of the original Thirteen Colonies into one republic was influenced by the political system developed by the Iroquois Confederacy, as were many of the democratic principles which were incorporated into the Constitution itself." Like the five arrows bound together, the Iroquois political and literary legacy is entwined forever with ideals that continue to shape American life.

C Critical Thinking
Speculating
Ask students why they think the Continental Congress chose to alter Jefferson's draft here and refer to the King's "waging war" against them. [Possible response: The statement that the King is waging war against the colonies is a greater justification for independence.]

D Elements of Literature
Parallelism
❓ What are the parallel structures within this sentence, and what parts of speech do they contain? [four predicates, each built around a verb plus a noun as a direct object]

E Historical Connections
Impressment
Jefferson is denouncing the Royal Navy's practice of "impressment," or forced conscription of British subjects at seaports. Inaugurated in the 1700s, this practice became particularly contentious in the years leading up to and during the American Revolution, since American colonists were considered British subjects by the Royal Navy.

He has <u>abdicated</u> government here <u>withdrawing his governors, and declaring us out of his allegiance and protection.</u> **C** / **D**   by declaring us out of his protection, and waging war against us.

He has plundered our seas, ravaged our coasts, burnt our towns, and destroyed the lives of our people.

He is at this time transporting large armies of foreign mercenaries to complete the works of death, desolation, and tyranny already begun with circumstances of cruelty and perfidy [ ] unworthy the head of a civilized nation.   scarcely paralleled in the most barbarous ages, and totally

He has constrained our fellow citizens taken captive on the high seas, to bear arms against their country, to become the executioners **E** of their friends and brethren, or to fall themselves by their hands.

He has [ ] endeavored to bring on the inhabitants of our frontiers, the merciless Indian savages, whose known rule of warfare is   excited domestic insurrection among us, and has

---

WORDS TO OWN
abdicated (ab′di·kāt′id) *v.*: given up responsibility for.

THOMAS JEFFERSON 121

Making the Connections

Cultural Connections
Have students work in small groups to research voters' rights in other countries. Challenge them to find one country that has long had universal suffrage, one that recently acquired it, and one that does not have it. Ask students to explore the political and educational systems in the three countries and to draw conclusions about the connections between education and voters' rights.

Connecting to the Theme: "The American Dream"
Allow students to explore these questions: How necessary is freedom to the American dream? Who was free in Jefferson's time? Who could vote? Challenge students to name the freedoms guaranteed in the Bill of Rights. Then have students determine which of the remaining amendments to the Constitution extend basic human rights.

an undistinguished destruction of all ages, sexes, and conditions of existence.

He has incited treasonable insurrections of our fellow citizens, with the allurements of forfeiture and confiscation of our property.

Ⓐ He has waged cruel war against human nature itself, violating its most sacred rights of life and liberty in the persons of a distant people who never offended him, captivating and carrying them into slavery in another hemisphere, or to incur miserable death in their transportation thither. This piratical warfare, the opprobrium[9] of INFIDEL powers, is the warfare of the CHRISTIAN king of Great Britain. Determined to keep open a market where MEN should be bought and sold, he has prostituted his negative[10] for suppressing every legislative attempt to prohibit or to restrain this execrable commerce. And that this assemblage of horrors might want no fact of distinguished die,[11] he is now exciting those very people to rise in arms among us, and to purchase that liberty of which he has deprived them, by murdering the people on whom he also obtruded them: thus paying off former crimes committed against the LIBERTIES of one people, with crimes which he urges them to commit against the LIVES of another.

In every stage of these oppressions we have petitioned for redress in the most humble terms: Our repeated petitions have been answered only by repeated injuries.

Ⓑ A prince whose character is thus marked by every act which may define a tyrant is unfit to be the ruler of a [ ] people who mean to be free. Future ages will scarcely believe that the hardiness of one man adventured, within the short compass of twelve years only, to lay a foundation so broad and so undisguised for tyranny over a people fostered and fixed in principles of freedom.

Ⓒ Nor have we been wanting in attentions to our British brethren. We have warned them from time to time of attempts by their legislature to extend a jurisdiction over these our states. We have reminded them of the circumstances of our emigration and settlement here, no one of which could warrant so strange a pretension: that these were effected at the expense of our own blood and treasure, unassisted by the wealth or the strength of Great Britain: that in constituting indeed our several forms of government, we had adopted one common king, thereby laying a foundation for perpetual league and amity with them: but that submission to their parliament was no part of our constitution, nor ever in idea, if history may be credited: and, we [ ] appealed to their native justice and magnanimity as well as to the ties of our

free

an unwarrantable / us

have
and we have conjured[12] them by

9. **opprobrium** (ə·prō′brē·əm): shameful conduct.
10. **negative:** veto.
11. **fact of distinguished die:** clear stamp or mark of distinction. Jefferson is being sarcastic here.
12. **conjured** (kən·jŏŏrd′): solemnly called upon.

WORDS TO OWN

confiscation (kän′fis·kā′shən) *n.*: seizure of property by authority.
magnanimity (mag′nə·nim′ə·tē) *n.*: nobility of spirit.

(Background) The Great Seal of the United States, original version; present seal reverse.
The Bettmann Archive.

122 BEGINNINGS

common kindred to disavow these usurpations which were likely to interrupt our connection and correspondence. They too have been deaf to the voice of justice and of consanguinity,[13] and when occasions have been given them, by the regular course of their laws, of removing from their councils the disturbers of our harmony, they have, by their free election, re-established them in power. At this very time too, they are permitting their chief magistrate to send over not only soldiers of our common blood, but Scotch and foreign mercenaries to invade and destroy us. These facts have given the last stab to agonizing affection, and manly spirit bids us to renounce forever these unfeeling brethren. We must endeavor to forget our former love for them, and hold them as we hold the rest of mankind, enemies in war, in peace friends. We might have been a free and a great people together; but a communication of grandeur and of freedom, it seems, is below their dignity. Be it so, since they will have it. The road to happiness and to glory is open to us too. We will tread it apart from them and acquiesce in the necessity which denounces[14] our eternal separation [ ]!

D We must therefore

and hold them as we hold the rest of mankind, enemies in war, in peace friends.

We, therefore, the representatives of the United States of America in General Congress assembled, [ ] do in the name, and by the authority of the good people of these states reject and renounce all allegiance and subjection to the kings of Great Britain and all others who may hereafter claim by, through or under them; we utterly dissolve all political connection which may heretofore have subsisted between us and the people or parliament of Great Britain: And finally we do assert and declare these colonies to be free and independent states, and that as free and independent states, they have full power to levy war, conclude peace, contract alliances, establish commerce, and to do all other acts and things which independent states may of right do.

E appealing to the supreme judge of the world for the rectitude of our intentions,

colonies, solemnly publish and declare, that these united colonies are, and of right ought to be free and independent states; that they are absolved from all allegiance to the British crown, and that all political connection between them and the state of Great Britain is, and ought to be, totally dissolved;

And for the support of this declaration, [ ] we mutually pledge to each other our lives, our fortunes, and our sacred honor.

F with a firm reliance on the protection of divine providence,

The Declaration thus signed on the 4th, on paper, was engrossed on parchment, and signed again on the 2d of August. **G**

---

13. **consanguinity** (kän′saŋ·gwin′ə·tē): kinship; family relationship.
14. **denounces** (dē·nouns′iz): archaic for "announces, proclaims."

WORDS TO OWN

renounce (ri·nouns′) v.: to give up.
acquiesce (ak′wē·es′) v.: agree or accept quietly.

Syng silver used at the signing of the Declaration of Independence, Independence Hall, Philadelphia, Pennsylvania.

Joe Viesti/Viesti Associates.

THOMAS JEFFERSON 123

D Critical Thinking
Interpreting
? What does the deleted passage mean? [Possible response: Jefferson denounces mercenaries in the British forces and regrets that they have made peaceful coexistence with the British people impossible.]

E Elements of Literature
Parallelism
This original passage uses parallelism subtly. Just as the list of charges against the king uses vivid verbs to identify his crimes—he has *refused, abdicated, plundered, constrained, incited,* etc.—so now, to create balance, the Americans announce what they will do. Have students identify the verbs that provide a parallel list of the Americans' actions. [*reject, renounce, dissolve, assert, declare*]

F Appreciating Language
Style
? How many sentences compose the next-to-last paragraph of the final draft? How would you describe the style? [One sentence. It is complex yet clear, straightforward yet sophisticated and elegant.]

G Historical Connections
The Original Parchment
The parchment copy of the Declaration was damaged in an 1823 attempt to make a copperplate facsimile and is now barely legible in parts. It is on display in the National Archives Building in Washington, D.C.

RESPONDING TO THE ART
Phillip Syng, Jr. (1703–1789), a distinguished Philadelphia craftsman and patriot, was a co-inventor with his friend Benjamin Franklin. He made the silver inkstand shown here, later used in Philadelphia's Independence Hall (see p. 210) for the signing of both the Declaration of Independence (1776) and the U.S. Constitution (1787).
Activity. Has our contemporary shift from print to electronic media made the tools we use to communicate less important and less meaningful?

Assessing Learning

Check Test: True-False
1. The Declaration of Independence explains the necessity and right of the colonies to declare independence. [True]
2. Jefferson did not care that Congress deleted passages of his draft. [False]
3. The Declaration blames the King and the British people for the war. [True]
4. The Declaration states that the colonies are not under the jurisdiction of the British Parliament. [True]

Standardized Test Preparation
For practice with ACT and SAT formats, see
• *Preparation for College Admission Exams,* p. 11
For practice in proofreading and editing, see
• *Daily Oral Grammar,* Transparency 11

Primary Sources

Jefferson's letter to his daughter Patsy fits into the long tradition of letters of advice from parents to children. In this letter, Jefferson gives his daughter the benefit of his advice on the importance of industry and self-reliance. The losses he refers to in the next-to-last paragraph include the death of his wife, the blow to his reputation resulting from the invasion of British forces in Virginia during his term as governor (1779–1781), and the childhood deaths of three of his children.

Background

Jefferson was also capable of giving advice in a much more informal way. In an 1825 letter to Thomas Jefferson Smith, the son of an old friend, he sent these ten precepts for living, a "little bundle of canons of conduct":

1. Never put off till tomorrow what you can do today.
2. Never trouble another for what you can do yourself.
3. Never spend your money before you have it.
4. Never buy what you don't want, because it is cheap: it will be dear to you.
5. Pride costs more than hunger, thirst and cold.
6. When at table, remember that we never repent of having eaten or drunk too little.
7. Nothing is troublesome that we do willingly.
8. How much pains have cost us the things which have never happened.
9. Take things always by their smooth handle.
10. When angry count 10 before you speak. If very angry 100.

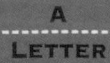

PRIMARY Sources A LETTER

A Letter from Jefferson to His Daughter

In 1784, Jefferson was sent to Paris to work out the treaty ending the Revolutionary War. Jefferson stayed in France for five years. His daughter Patsy was in a Catholic convent school in Paris when Jefferson wrote this letter from the south of France. The wrist Jefferson complains of in the letter had been injured a few months earlier.

Aix-en-Provence, March 28, 1787

I was happy, my dear Patsy, to receive, on my arrival here, your letter informing me of your health and occupations. I have not written to you sooner because I have been almost constantly on the road. My journey hitherto has been a very pleasing one. It was undertaken with the hope that the mineral waters of this place might restore strength to my wrist. Other considerations also concurred. Instruction, amusement, and abstraction from business, of which I had too much at Paris. I am glad to learn that you are employed in things new and good in your music and drawing. You know what have been my fears for some time past; that you do not employ yourself so closely as I could wish. You have promised me a more assiduous attention, and I have great confidence in what you promise. It is your future happiness which interests me, and nothing can contribute more to it (moral rectitude always excepted) than the contracting a habit of industry and activity. Of all the cankers of human happiness, none corrodes it with so silent, yet so baneful a tooth, as indolence. . . . It is while we are young that the habit of industry is formed. If not then, it never is afterward. The fortune of our lives therefore depends on employing well the short period of youth. If at any moment, my dear, you catch yourself in idleness, start from it as you would from the precipice of a gulf. You are not, however, to consider yourself as unemployed while taking exercise. That is necessary for your health, and health is the first of all objects. For this reason if you leave your dancing master for the summer, you must increase your other exercise. I do not like your saying that you are unable to read the ancient print of your Livy,[1] but with the aid of your master. We are always equal to what we undertake with resolution. A little degree of this will enable you to decipher your Livy. If you always lean on your master, you will never be able to proceed without him. It is a part of the American character to consider nothing as desperate; to surmount every difficulty by resolution and contrivance. In Europe there are shops for every want. Its inhabitants therefore have no idea that their wants can be furnished otherwise. Remote from all other aid, we are obliged to invent and to execute; to find means within ourselves, and not to lean on others. Consider therefore the conquering your Livy as an exercise in the habit of surmounting difficulties, a habit which will be necessary to you in the country where you are to live, and without which you will be thought a very helpless animal, and less esteemed. . . .

You ask me to write you long letters. I will do it, my dear, on condition you will read them from time to time, and practice what they will inculcate. Their precepts will be dictated by experience, by a perfect knowledge of the situation in which you will be placed, and by the fondest love for you. This it is which makes me wish to see you more qualified than common. My expectations from you are high: yet not higher than you may attain. Industry and resolution are all that are wanting. Nobody in this world can make me so happy, or so miserable, as you. Retirement from public life will ere long become necessary for me. To your sister and yourself I look to render the evening of my life serene and contented. Its morning has been clouded by loss after loss till I have nothing left but you. I do not doubt either your affection or dispositions. But great exertions are necessary, and you have little time left to make them. Be industrious then, my dear child. Think nothing unsurmountable by resolution and application, and you will be all that I wish you to be. . . .

Continue to love me with all the warmth with which you are beloved by, my dear Patsy, yours affectionately,

TH: JEFFERSON

1. **Livy:** Roman historian (59 B.C.–A.D. 17).

Listening to Music

"Liberty Bell" by John Philip Sousa, Performed by Major E. W. Jeanes
Philadelphia's Liberty Bell was rung when the Continental Congress adopted the Declaration of Independence in 1776; it received its famous crack in 1835. Celebrating the American independence that the bell represents is the march called "Liberty Bell," one of the best-known compositions of the great American "march king" John Philip Sousa (sōō′zə) (1854–1932).

Activity
After reading the Declaration of Independence, listen to Sousa's popular march celebrating the Liberty Bell's ringing at the signing of the document. Then, working in a small group, create an audiotape for young children that retells the legend of the Liberty Bell. Use portions of the march as background music, and also incorporate sound effects as well as lines from the Declaration of Independence.

First Thoughts

1. What word, phrase, or **image** struck you as most important? Why?

Shaping Interpretations

2. What changes show a desire not to make an absolute break with the English people? Why do you think it would be important that the new nation maintain its "consanguinity," or close kinship, with the English people?

3. Which changes seem to have been adopted primarily for stylistic reasons, such as clarity or greater impact, and which for political reasons?

4. Find at least two passages in the Declaration that use **parallelism**. What is the effect of the parallel structure on the *idea* of the passage?

Reading Check

a. What is the **main idea** of the Declaration of Independence?

b. List the truths that Jefferson considers self-evident.

c. List the offenses charged to the king of England.

d. What are some of the powers of the independent countries?

CHOICES:
Building Your Portfolio

Writer's Notebook

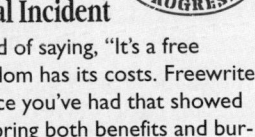

1. Collecting Ideas for an Autobiographical Incident

Americans are fond of saying, "It's a free country." But freedom has its costs. Freewrite about an experience you've had that showed that freedom can bring both benefits and burdens, gains and losses. Keep your notes; you may use them later in the Writer's Workshop on page 130.

Summarizing a Document
2. In the Course of Human Events

Review your reading notes on the **main idea** and supporting arguments of the Declaration of Independence. Then, write a one- or two-paragraph summary of the central **theme** of the document. Include some of the supporting arguments with relevant details.

Responding to a Text
3. A Voice for Women

On March 31, 1776, Abigail Adams (1744–1818) wrote to her husband John Adams, who was on the committee preparing the Declaration of Independence. In a brief essay, respond to this excerpt from her letter.

> … in the new Code of Laws which I suppose it will be necessary for you to make, I desire you would remember the ladies, and be more generous and favorable to them than your ancestors. Do not put such unlimited power into the hands of the husbands. Remember all men would be tyrants if they could. If particular care and attention is not paid to the ladies, we are determined to foment a rebellion, and will not hold ourselves bound by any laws in which we have no voice, or representation.
>
> —Abigail Adams

Speaking and Listening
4. Unequal Signs

In "Harrison Bergeron," a famous short story by Kurt Vonnegut, Jr. (1922–), Vonnegut imagines a future America in which "everybody was finally equal": "Nobody was smarter than anybody else. Nobody was better-looking than anybody else. Nobody was stronger or quicker than anybody else." In a panel discussion, explore what you and your classmates think the framers of the Declaration meant by the statement "all men are created equal." Then, discuss why some people believe that all Americans, in fact, are not yet equal.

THOMAS JEFFERSON 125

First Thoughts [Respond]

1. Possible response: The passage beginning "We hold these truths . . ." because it states the premises on which the Declaration is based.

Shaping Interpretations [Interpret]

2. The omission objecting to submission to the English Parliament (p. 122); the deletion of "renounce forever these unfeeling brethren" (p. 123); and the omission of the "people" of Great Britain in the last long paragraph. Most colonists still felt close personal ties to England and many had relatives there. Historically, the colonies had also depended on their close economic, political, and military ties to Britain.

3. Stylistic changes include the deletion of "begun at a distinguished period and" and the deletion of "and continually" (p. 118). Political changes include "expunge" to "alter" (p. 118), the deletion of the reference to slavery, and a shift from "a people who mean to be free" to "a free people" (both p. 122).

4. The paragraph beginning "He has combined with others . . ." (p. 119) contains a number of clauses beginning with the word *for* plus a present participle ("for protecting"). The repetition creates a catalogue of mounting offenses and contributes to a regular, almost poetic, rhythm. The last lines—"our lives, our fortunes, and our sacred honor"—repeat the word *our* in structurally balanced phrases. This parallelism emphasizes the personal commitment of the passage and provides a rhythmic and powerful conclusion.

Grading Timesaver

Rubrics for each Choices assignment appear on p. 100 in the *Portfolio Management System*.

Reading Check

a. The American colonies are separating from England.

b. "All men are created equal" and have "inalienable rights"; governments derive their "powers from the . . . governed," who have the right "to alter or to abolish" them.

c. Some involve refusal to assent to necessary laws; harassment and dissolution of legislative bodies; preventing states from being settled and populated; coercion of judges; maintenance of standing armies in the colonies; plunder of coasts and destruction of towns; coercion of citizens captured on the high seas; and inciting American Indians to war against the colonists.

d. the power to levy war, conclude peace, contract alliances, and establish commerce

READ ON

Coming to America

"It was 1906. I was six years old and we were on a train with some other immigrants. . . . When people on the train spoke to me in Russian, I said, 'Speak only English. I'm an Americanka now.'" Thus recalls Sonia Walinsky, just one of dozens of immigrants whose testimonials Joan Morrison and Charlotte Fox Zabusky gathered in *American Mosaic* (E. P. Dutton), a collection of vivid remembrances by Americans from many lands.

For a Captive Audience

In 1704, as part of the fighting during the War of the Spanish Succession, or Queen Anne's War, a French and American Indian raiding party captured a family of British Puritans in Deerfield, Massachusetts. Though the rest of the family was released, young Eunice Williams remained with the Mohawks, refusing to return home even when she could. The prize-winning historian John Demos tells Eunice's gripping story in *The Unredeemed Captive* (Alfred A. Knopf).

Puritan Principles

Puritan culture has had a profound impact on the American character. In *The Puritan Experiment* (St. Martin's), the historian Francis J. Bremer explores this culture, from its origins in sixteenth-century England to its role in colonial America.

A famous fictional account of the Puritan era is Nathaniel Hawthorne's powerful novel *The Scarlet Letter*, which examines the consequences of private sin and public penance. It touches on many familiar conflicts in literature—emotion vs. reason, love vs. hate, and the individual vs. society. It has also inspired several film adaptations. This title is available in the HRW Library.

Another Passage

In 1830, African American Rutherford Calhoun, newly freed from slavery, stows away on a ship without realizing it is bound for Africa and the slave trade. His trip is chronicled in Charles Johnson's National Book Award–winning novel *Middle Passage* (Atheneum).

Revolutionary Tales

What was it like to be there when "the shot heard round the world" was fired? In *April Morning* (Crown), Howard Fast describes the first battle of the Revolution from the viewpoint of young Adam Cooper of the Lexington militia. For another view of the time, try Fast's historical novel, *Citizen Tom Paine* (Grove Press), the story of the famous patriot from his early days in poverty to his last days in infamy.

The American Language

"Revolutionary" English

by Gary Q. Arpin

As American English began to develop in the years following the settlement of North America by Europeans, differences between British and American usage became more and more apparent. British travelers noticed that Americans spoke with a nasality that was disagreeable to their British ears. The visitors also noticed what they thought of as corruptions of the language: Words were being used in "barbarous" ways, and brand-new words were being coined at an alarming rate.

Effects of Physical Separation

The simple fact of physical separation caused some of the differences between British and American English. Differences in pronunciation, for example, became marked as the accents of speakers on both sides of the ocean gradually changed. Such differences are apparent even today; for example, British speakers omit the vowel before the second r in words like *secretary* and *laboratory*, but most Americans pronounce all the syllables in such words.

Physical separation also resulted in differences in usage. In the Colonies, for example, and especially in New England, it was common to hear someone speak of throwing a *rock*. In Britain, however, *rock* continued to refer only to a massive stone, such as Plymouth Rock. Throwing a rock would have seemed as odd to a British person as tossing a boulder would be to an American.

Sometimes the meaning or usage of a word would change in England while Americans retained its older meaning. The American usage of *guess* to mean "suppose" is an example of this. In the eighteenth and nineteenth centuries, "I guess" in this sense sounded odd to British visitors, who would have said, "I suppose." But these visitors were unaware that "I guess" had been common in England until the eighteenth century. (It even appears in the writings of Chaucer and Shakespeare.) The British also criticized Americans for saying *fall* instead of *autumn,* apparently unaware that *fall* had been used in England until around 1750.

Ugly Americanisms

The word *Americanism* came into use to describe a word or expression that originated in the United States or that was peculiar to the States. The word was first used in print in 1781 by the Reverend John Witherspoon, a Scottish clergyman who had come to this country in 1768 to become president of the College of New Jersey (now Princeton University). Witherspoon traveled a good deal and recorded words and phrases that were peculiar to the United States. Many of these words are so common today that it's hard to imagine a time when they might have been considered unusual. Among the Americanisms recorded by Witherspoon were *to notify,* meaning "to inform"; *mad,* in the sense of "angry"; *chunks,* to describe big pieces of wood; *spell,* meaning "a period of time" (as in "a spell of bad weather"); *once in a while,* meaning "occasionally"; and *tote,* meaning "to carry."

Some critics considered English to be a complete language that had evolved through the centuries to a state of perfection in the eighteenth century. Any change was horrendous to them, especially any change brought about by people thought to be unrefined. As one writer put it around 1800, "A language, arrived at its zenith, requires no introduction of new words."

Some years later, the same point was made by a British purist in response to a question posed by the American language

---

A Exploring the Culture
States' Names

Thomas Jefferson once said that "new circumstances . . . call for new words, new phrases, and the transfer of old words to new objects." Among the many new words used by Americans were the names of the states themselves. Looking at the entire roster of fifty states, linguist Stuart Berg Flexner has pointed out that the state names come from six basic sources:

(1) Twenty-eight come from native words, twenty-six of which come from American Indian words, one from an Eskimo word, and one from a Hawaiian word.
(2) Eleven are from English with some Latin mixtures.
(3) Six come from Spanish.
(4) Three come from French.
(5) One comes from Dutch.
(6) One comes from American history itself (Washington).

Have students research and identify the source of their own state's name.

B Struggling Readers
Finding the Main Idea

❓ In what three fundamental ways do British and American English differ? [pronunciation, usage, and vocabulary]

C Reading Skills and Strategies
Connecting with the Text

❓ What developments in the last decade of the twentieth century do you think will have a lasting effect on the English language? [Possible responses: computers, Internet communications, biotechnology, foreign relations, new immigrants.]

Reaching All Students

Struggling Readers

Have struggling readers write their responses to the following questions:
1. Read the title and the subheadings.
   a. What do you think the selection is about?
   b. Why do you think so?
2. Read until you can tell if your guess about the reading was correct.
   a. Were you right or wrong?
   b. How do you know?

English Language Learners

Encourage English language learners to contribute details and comments about changes in their original languages. You might stimulate discussion with questions such as these:
- How has your language changed in your lifetime?
- What developments caused these changes?
- What do you think is one of the easiest—or one of the most difficult—things to master in your language? Why?

❓ Why did scholars in the early nineteenth century think that there was little authority to support the constant changes Americans made in the English language? [At that time, America was a new country with little uniquely American literature.]

B Critical Thinking
Extending the Text

❓ Should literature be used as an authority for usage if American speech keeps changing? Explain. [Possible responses: yes—even though speech keeps changing, literature can represent accepted usage; no—speech is too dynamic to be bound by past usage.]

C Background
What Country Is This?

According to linguist Stuart Berg Flexner, the name of our country itself underwent change:

- Since *America* originally meant the continent, *American* was originally used (1578) to mean a native of it, an Indian.
- Beginning in 1697, however, our own Cotton Mather popularized the word *American* to mean an English colonist in America.
- The distinction between colonies and states confused many people, and throughout the Revolutionary War many called the new country the *United Colonies.*
- George Washington wrote the abbreviation *U.S.* in 1791, and the abbreviation *U.S.A.* was recorded in 1795.
- Even though *the United States of America* appeared in the Declaration of Independence, the new government used the official title *the United States of North America* until 1778, when the *North* was dropped from the name by act of the Continental Congress.

expert Noah Webster (page 195). Webster had asked, "If a word becomes universally current in America . . . why should it not take its station in the language?" The British purist, a certain Captain Basil Hall, replied, "Because there are words enough already."

> If, as many people thought, literature was an authority for usage, then there was little authority supporting American usage.

A Reinforcing the purist's position was the fact that until the early nineteenth century, there was little distinctly *American* literature. There was not much demonstration of the *power* of the American idiom, and little indication that American speech could lead to anything of lasting worth. If, as many people thought, literature was an authority for usage, then there was little authority supporting American usage.

B Many people on both sides of the question expected, or feared, that the two forms of English would eventually grow separate until the two groups would no longer understand each other. They predicted that Americans, completely cut off from their past, would have to read the works of Shakespeare and Milton in translation.

"What Language Should Americans Speak?"

C The conflict between purists and advocates of change was especially heated in America in the eighteenth and nineteenth centuries. On the American side, the rejection of English authority in language was for some an

aspect of America's rejection of English political authority. In 1788, a march in New York supporting the ratification of the U.S. Constitution contained a language contingent. This group carried a scroll advocating the use of something called "Federal English." A Federal English would establish the independence of American English and, at the same time, preserve the purity of the language in its new home.

The most radical political position on language argued for the establishment in America of a completely new language. At various times French, Greek, and Hebrew were suggested as alternatives. Each had as its principal virtue, apparently, the fact

that it was not English. Nor was it Spanish, the other main Colonial language, or one of the many Native American languages. (Though words like *raccoon* from Virginia Algonquian and *totem* from Ojibwa have been with us since the eighteenth century, English was only minimally influenced by the languages of American Indians, largely because political dominance was held by English-speaking settlers.)

Democratic Language

Some proponents of American English pointed to the humble, democratic character of the language as its greatest virtue: Class distinctions were not marked by accents in America, as they were in Britain, and geographical differences in speech were not nearly as important.

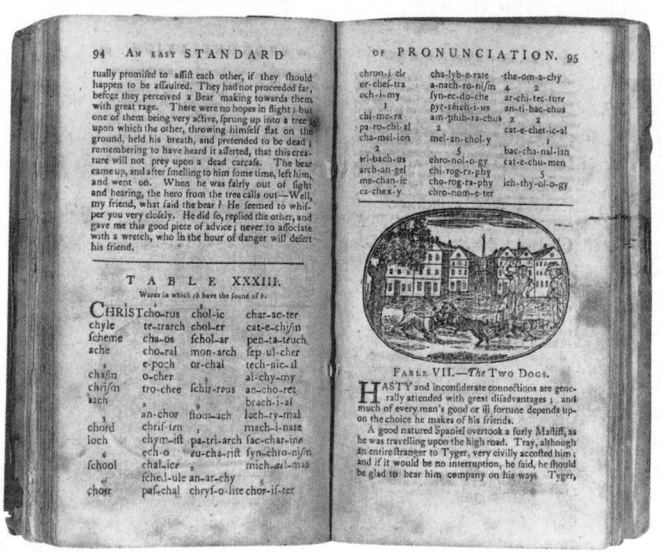

The American Spelling Book by Noah Webster.

Using Students' Strengths

Auditory Learners

Show students a British movie, such as *Passport to Pimlico* or any Sherlock Holmes film. Have students identify specific phrases, idioms, pronunciations, vocabulary, or grammar that they find difficult to understand. Use these examples to discuss how American and British English have diverged and how geography and class distinctions have influenced these changes.

Visual/Verbal Learners

Ask students to create cartoons based on their reading of The American Language feature. Encourage them to focus on topics that deal with regional or cultural differences in language, the American character, or ways that television and the movies have influenced the English language. To help students get started, bring to class examples of cartoons, from America and other countries, as models.

Because of this, an American would (in theory, at least) be immediately understood and accepted wherever he or she went in the country, which was not the case in England. Of course, there were still some regional differences in language. One writer's observation that "America has no dialects" was surely overstated.

John Adams (1735–1826) argued for the establishment of an American academy that would try to govern the usage of English in America and protect it against whatever changes might originate in England in the future. Having established its democratic purpose and its independence from the British, American English would thereafter remain stable or at least change only in approved ways.

Language Resists Rules

Language changes primarily according to the way it is used, not the way authorities say it should be used. Thomas Jefferson (page 114), perhaps the best American linguist of the Revolutionary period, took the most reasonable view. Speaking of the foundations of an American academy, he wrote:

Ⓓ

> If, like the French Academicians, it were proposed to *fix* our language, it would be fortunate that the step was not taken in the days of our Saxon ancestors, whose vocabulary would ill express the science of this day.

Thus, Jefferson found himself at odds with both British and American purists. And he was right. The move for an academy finally died, and the American language continued to develop in its own unpredictable and exuberant ways.

Try It Out

1. **Researching word origins.** Eighteenth-century British purists complained about the ways Americans adapted words to suit life in the Colonies. Their criticism was based on an assumption that words should develop historically from their roots, not in response to need and usage. Explain how the histories of the following words, all in common English usage, puncture the purists' argument. A good dictionary will give you the information you need.

   clue   precocious
   companion   steward
   daughter   town
   expedite

2. **Contrasting pronunciations.** Look up the following items in an American dictionary that includes British pronunciations (such as *Webster's New World Dictionary*) or in a British dictionary (like the *Oxford English Dictionary*). How is each pronounced in Great Britain? in the United States?

   ate   schedule
   been   lieutenant
   clerk   the letter z

3. **Analyzing Americanisms.** The following expressions are all Americanisms—they originated in America or have a usage peculiar to American speech. What do the words reveal about features and customs that were uniquely American? What other Americanisms can you add to the list?

   cold snap   potpie
   dude   ranch
   everglade   salt lick
   Indian summer snowshoe

4. **Debating language regulation.** In France and in Québec province in Canada, official or semiofficial organizations try to regulate the usage of language. Such organizations decide on proper spelling and whether a foreign word should be accepted into the language, among other things. Should such an organization oversee American English as John Adams suggested? Together with four or five other students, discuss this issue. The discussion should (1) begin by stating why the question is of interest to Americans; (2) present some reasons why an American-language regulatory commission would be a good idea; (3) offer some reasons why language regulation would *not* be a good idea; and (4) conclude by stating whether such an organization to regulate American English should or should not be established.

THE AMERICAN LANGUAGE 129

Ⓓ Exploring the Culture
A Language Controversy

Language scholars do not always agree on the acceptability of language changes. For example, while the word *author* is used by many Americans today as a verb as well as a noun, some language purists continue to resist such change. On the other hand, other experts would approve such usages as *host* as a verb ("He hosted the party") or *they* with the antecedent *everyone*.

Try It Out

1. The histories of these words prove that the British themselves had long since adapted their words in response to need and usage, often drawing on other languages for needed words.

2. *ate:* (et) in England
   been: (bēn) in England
   clerk: (klärk) in England
   schedule: (shed′ yōol) in England
   lieutenant: (lef·ten′ənt) in England
   the letter z: (zed) in England

3. Answers about what features and customs peculiar to American life the words reveal will vary. *Indian summer, cold snap,* and *snowshoe* originated in response to the American climate. *Everglade* is a word for the unique wetlands environment found in southern Florida. *Dude, ranch,* and *salt lick* all originated with the business of raising cattle on large tracts of land. *Potpie* is an American dish born out of the hardships of colonial and frontier life.

4. Students with a knowledge of French or Spanish may be familiar with the work of the French and Spanish Academies and be able to explain how those languages are regulated. Or perhaps you could invite a foreign-language teacher to speak to the class.

Resources

Assessment
Formal Assessment
• The American Language Test, p. 23

Assessing Learning

Check Test: Questions and Answers

1. In what three fundamental ways do British and American English differ? [pronunciation, usage, and vocabulary]

2. What was one cause for differences between British and American English? [physical separation]

3. What is an *Americanism*? [a word or expression that originated in or that is peculiar to the United States]

4. What was the purists' view in regard to American English? [They objected to changes originating in America.]

5. What was Thomas Jefferson's view regarding the English language? [He thought that the language should change with the times.]

Writer's Workshop

MAIN OBJECTIVE
Write an autobiographical incident

PROCESS OBJECTIVES
1. Use appropriate prewriting techniques to identify and develop a topic
2. Create a first draft
3. Use Evaluation Criteria as a basis for determining revision strategies
4. Revise the first draft, incorporating suggestions generated by self- or peer evaluation
5. Proofread and correct errors
6. Create a final draft
7. Choose an appropriate method of publication
8. Reflect on progress as a writer

Planning

- **Block Schedule**
  Block Scheduling Lesson Plans with Pacing Guide
- **One-Stop Planner**
  CD-ROM with Test Generator

See Writer's Workshop 2 CD-ROM. *Assignment: Autobiographical Incident.*

ASSIGNMENT
Write a narrative about a significant incident in your life that helped you to learn more about yourself.

AIM
To express yourself; to inform.

AUDIENCE
Your classmates, family, or general readers.

NARRATIVE WRITING

AUTOBIOGRAPHICAL INCIDENT

The ancient Greeks followed an important maxim: "Know thyself." The Greek philosopher Plato went even further and said, "The life which is unexamined is not worth living." Many of the early American writers you have studied in these collections struggled to make sense of themselves and their experiences. From the Puritan tendency to examine oneself for signs of salvation to Benjamin Franklin's inventory of methods for attaining moral perfection to the latest biographies, memoirs, and self-help books on the best-seller lists, self-examination has been an important feature of the American character. You can do a little of your own self-examination by writing about an **autobiographical incident:** an event from your life that taught you something, that contributed to your self-knowledge.

Prewriting

1. **Choosing an incident.** An incident is a specific occurrence—usually one that takes place over a short period of time. The incident you choose to narrate might be a moment of crisis or danger, but it might just as likely be a quiet, seemingly ordinary event that nevertheless had significance for you. If you've kept your Writer's Notebook notes from these collections, you may already have some ideas for an autobiographical incident you want to recount.

   If you still haven't decided what to write about, it might help to draw a "road map" of your life, an **overview** that starts at birth and extends to the present. As you draw the map, locate significant events with brief **headings.** At points where you think the course of your life changed in an important way, draw a turn in the road. Look over your road map, and select the topic that draws your interest the most and isn't too private to comfortably share with others.

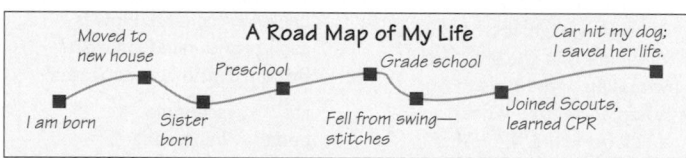

A Road Map of My Life

Moved to new house • Preschool • Grade school • Car hit my dog; I saved her life.
I am born • Sister born • Fell from swing—stitches • Joined Scouts, learned CPR

2. **Freewriting to remember details.** To recall specific details about your incident, freewrite your memories of it. Pay special attention to

130 BEGINNINGS

 — *Resources: Print and Media* —

Writing and Language
- *Portfolio Management System*
  Prewriting, p. 101
  Peer Editing, p. 102
  Assessment Rubric, p. 103

- *Workshop Resources*
  Revision Strategy Teaching Notes, p. 1
  Revision Strategy Transparencies 1, 2
- *Writer's Workshop 2 CD-ROM*
  Autobiographical Incident

The history of the written word is rich and
Once upon a time
Page 1

details that involve the senses: What smells, sounds, sights, tastes, and textures characterized your experience? If you have difficulty recalling details of the incident, here are some memory-prompting techniques you can try:

- **Visualizing.** Close your eyes and see the scene in your mind. Sketch the images as they occur to you.
- **Visiting.** If you can, go back to the location where the event took place. Note details, and give your memories time to emerge.
- **Interviewing.** Talk to people who were involved—family members, friends, neighbors, and teachers. Ask how they remember the incident.
- **Using memory "souvenirs."** Find objects and other artifacts you associate with the incident—a photo, a scarf, a song, a diary entry, even a smell—and focus on the memories they bring back.

3. **Discovering your meaning.** Most likely, the meaning of your incident will emerge in the process of writing. You might, however, want to write a brief, private statement of what the incident meant to you. Or, you may want to discuss it with a friend or relative. These steps can help you focus your ideas when you're shaping your initial draft.

Drafting

1. **Establishing the context.** Your readers may need some background, or context, in order to understand how and why the incident is significant in your life. Select necessary details about people, places, relationships, and prior events that put the incident in context.

2. **Conveying a tone.** Depending on the incident, its effects, and your own personality, your attitude toward the subject might be lighthearted, satirical, nostalgic, angry, rueful, or solemn. As you write, and as you re-read your first draft, make sure that this attitude, or **tone,** is deliberately chosen and is the one you wish to communicate to your readers.

3. **Ordering events.** Most narratives move forward chronologically, from the first event in a sequence to the last. To give yourself a basic framework for your narrative during this initial draft stage, try following the pattern of organization shown on the right. In revision stages, you can experiment with the order, perhaps beginning with the climax of the action and then using flashbacks to show what led up to the central incident.

4. **Using narrative devices:**
   - **Be specific: Show, don't simply tell.** Use specific names of people, places, and objects. Instead of "dog," write "Bobbi, my black Labrador

Strategies for Elaboration

Here are some effective ways to open an autobiographical incident.

1. **Use intriguing dialogue:** "Any reason there's a fish in the bathtub?" Janine asked me casually.
2. **Hint at things to come:** A box of old, musty books changed my life.
3. **Join events in progress:** This was it—my first vocal solo. So I opened my mouth and— squeaked.

Try It Out

Fill out the following to generate a framework for your essay.

Introduction

_____

Order of events

1. _____

2. _____

3. _____

Conclusion

_____

Bring several autobiographical books, magazine articles, or newspaper stories to class, and ask students to discuss ways in which they are similar to and different from the autobiographical writings of Bradstreet and Franklin. Point out that each work is in some way a self-examination. Explain to students that their assignment will be to write about an autobiographical incident in a way that examines some aspect of their own lives.

Teaching the Writer's Workshop

Prewriting
Remind students to choose an incident they would not mind sharing with others. Tell students that they may write about anything from passing moments that taught them simple truths to major events that changed their lives.

Drafting
- Ask students to focus on how the incident started. Have them write at least one alternative opening, using one of the Strategies for Elaboration.
- Before students complete their drafts, focus their attention on the model conclusion provided on p. 132. Have students discuss what features of this conclusion make it particularly satisfying.

Using Students' Strengths

Visual Learners
As students visualize the setting of their autobiographical incidents, they may want to sketch the scene or draw a map of the actual setting. Encourage them to refer back to prewriting notes as they prepare their drafts. During revision, ask students to develop their sketches into finished drawings to be included as part of their essay. Discuss the similarities between drafting an essay and sketching an image.

Evaluating and Revising

Ask students to use the Evaluation Criteria when reviewing each other's papers. Remind students to read each sentence carefully and to use connective words whenever appropriate. For help with coordinating conjunctions, refer students to the Language Workshop, p. 133.

Proofreading

Remind students to correct any errors in grammar, spelling, or mechanics before moving on to publish and reflect on their essays. Ask them to pay particular attention to the correct use of verb tenses, which will help the reader understand how events relate to one another. If students have included dialogue, they should be particularly careful to punctuate it correctly.

Publishing

Students should exchange essays and prepare brief critiques based on the Evaluation Criteria. Call on students to present their responses to their partners.

Reflection

Ask students to include in their portfolio a written response to one of the following topics:

- The method that I found most helpful for recalling the details of the incident was . . .
- The most rewarding part of writing this essay was . . . The most challenging part was . . .
- Some things I do well in my writing are . . . I need to improve on . . .

Resources

Peer Editing Forms and Rubrics
- *Portfolio Management System*, p. 102

Revision Transparencies
- *Workshop Resources*, p. 1

■ *Evaluation Criteria*

A good autobiographical incident
1. focuses on a single incident
2. includes enough background information for the reader to understand what happened
3. presents events in a logical, coherent order
4. includes sensory details and describes specific actions to bring the incident to life
5. makes the personal significance of the incident clear through either implication or direct statement

Communications Handbook HELP

See Proofreading.

Language Handbook HELP

Quotation Marks, page 1246.

---

retriever." Record specific gestures, movements, body language: "My heart pumped wildly as I ran from the front porch to the horrible scene." Describe sounds, smells, tastes, and physical sensations.

- **Use dramatic techniques.** Use flashbacks or foreshadowing if they increase suspense and help your pacing. Play on the element of surprise by withholding some important information from your readers until the crucial moment. Add tension and suspense.

- **Use realistic dialogue.** Record as accurately as you can what you and others said. Dialogue can effectively reveal character and move the events of your narrative forward.

5. **Writing a satisfying conclusion.** Your conclusion may simply reveal the final outcome of events, or it may be the place where you make clear how the incident you reported was significant for you. For example, your clearheaded response to an incident in which your dog was hit by a car might have been central to the development of your self-confidence.

Model: A Conclusion

All through my childhood I had felt a bit uncertain of myself. Anything new, even if it was something as simple as learning a new craft at camp or going to a party where I didn't know many people, always filled me with dread. What if I wasn't good enough? What if I failed? Those feelings of inadequacy were never quite as strong after the incident with my dog Bobbi. I had kept my head during a crisis and saved my dog's life. My love for my dog had made me brave, and my moment of bravery made me believe in myself to a degree I never had before.

Evaluating and Revising

1. **Peer review.** With a group of students, read and discuss one another's autobiographical narratives. Here are some focal points for discussion:

- Did the writer describe the experience in sufficient detail?
- Were any details out of place or unnecessary?
- What areas could the writer improve? Does the narrative need more details, better pacing, more dialogue, or more effective organization?
- How effective was the writer in getting you to care about the incident and the effect it had on his or her life? Did the writing seem honest and personal? Was the tone appropriate to the content?
- Did the narrative come to a satisfying conclusion? Could you understand why the incident was significant for the writer?

2. **Self-evaluation.** After you've listened to your peers' comments, look over the Evaluation Criteria, and see if your essay contains everything on the list. Identify three areas for improvement in your essay, and make appropriate revisions.

Grading Timesaver

Rubrics for this Writer's Workshop assignment appear on p. 103 of the *Portfolio Management System.*

Language Workshop

OBJECTIVES
1. Combine sentences by using coordinating conjunctions
2. Choose an appropriate conjunction to indicate the relationship between two joined sentences

LINKING IT UP: COORDINATING CONJUNCTIONS

Here's one way to describe Benjamin Franklin's plight when he first arrived in Philadelphia:

> Benjamin Franklin was practically penniless when he arrived in Philadelphia. He was able to buy some bread.

Here's a better way to express the same information:

> Benjamin Franklin was practically penniless when he arrived in Philadelphia, *yet* he was able to buy some bread.

In the second sentence, the writer combined two related thoughts into a single sentence by using a connective word—in this case, the **coordinating conjunction** *yet*. Separating two thoughts into two sentences is not incorrect; there are times when short, simple sentences sound best. However, using **coordinating conjunctions** to combine two thoughts into one sentence can result in more graceful **syntax,** or sentence structure.

Some Connective Words and What They Indicate

Conjunction	Indicates
and	similarity, addition
but	opposition, contrast
yet	opposition, contrast
or	choice
nor	negation
so	cause and effect, result
for	explanation

All the words in the chart above function as coordinating conjunctions, but some can also function as other parts of speech. For example, *for* is a preposition in this sentence: "We went to the store *for* apples." However, the word *for* is a conjunction in this sentence: "We went to a store downtown, *for* the store on our block was closed." To combine two related sentences into a single sentence, you will need to select an appropriate conjunction.

Writer's Workshop Follow-Up: Revising

Reread the autobiographical narrative you wrote for the Writer's Workshop (page 130). Are there any short, choppy sentences that have a clear relationship to one another? Where appropriate, use conjunctions to combine such sentences and make your writing flow more gracefully.

Technology HELP

See Language Workshop CD-ROM. *Key word entry: connective words and phrases.*

Language Handbook HELP

Combining by Coordinating Ideas, page 1238.

Try It Out

Combine each pair of sentences into one sentence, using the most appropriate conjunction from the chart. Make necessary revisions so that the resulting sentence reads smoothly.

1. Franklin wished to achieve moral perfection. He devised a book in which he could record his transgressions and his progress.
2. It is not easy to achieve moral perfection. One can still try.

Resources

Workshop Resources
• Worksheet, p. 47
Language Workshop CD-ROM
• Connective Words and Phrases

Try It Out
Possible Answers
1. Franklin wished to achieve moral perfection, so he devised a book in which he could record his transgressions and his progress.
2. It is not easy to achieve moral perfection, but one can still try.

Assessing Learning

Quick Check: Short Answers

Have students combine each pair of sentences into one sentence by using an appropriate coordinating conjunction. Sample answers are given.

1. William Brewster and Myles Standish tended the sick during the starving time. They were not infected with either sickness or lameness. [William Brewster and Myles Standish tended the sick during the starving time, yet they were not infected with either sickness or lameness.]

2. Anne Bradstreet did not seek an audience or publication for her writing. She did not seek notoriety. [Anne Bradstreet did not seek an audience or publication for her writing, nor did she seek notoriety.]

3. Franklin lacked a poet's depth. His literary talents were substantial. [Franklin lacked a poet's depth, but his literary talents were substantial.]

4. Thomas Jefferson was president of the United States. He wanted to be remembered for writing the Declaration of Independence. [Thomas Jefferson was president of the United States, but he wanted to be remembered for writing the Declaration of Independence.]

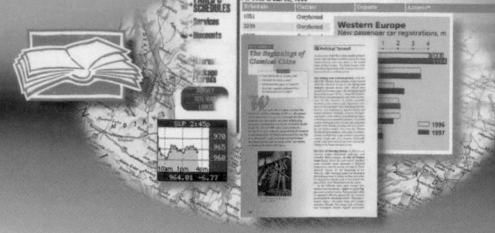

OBJECTIVES
1. Monitor and adjust reading
2. Break down difficult texts
3. Use context clues or dictionaries to define unknown words
4. Paraphrase ideas
5. Find the main idea or key passage of a document

Teaching the Lesson

You may wish to bring in such documents as a local voter's guide or a Supreme Court opinion. Have students practice the strategies in small groups, each with a different document.

Using the Strategies
Possible Answers
1. April 22, 1793
2. The president of the United States, George Washington, issued it. The title is simply "A Proclamation."
3. France is at war with Austria, Prussia, Sardinia, Great Britain, and the United Netherlands.
4. *aforesaid* ("spoken of before," using the similarity of *afore/before* and the root *said*); *exhort* ("to urge earnestly by advice or warning," using similarity to related word; *exhort to*, like *warn to*, must mean "to strongly tell someone to do something in a particular fashion"); *contravene* ("to go against; oppose; conflict with," by opposition to an earlier phrase, "to observe the conduct aforesaid"; thus, to not observe it must be to conflict with or oppose it); *forfeiture* ("a thing taken away as a penalty," by similarity to related word, *punishment*); *contraband* ("forbidden by law to be imported or exported," by using *carry to,* which could mean "export" or "import," and the negative context, which suggests what cannot be exported or imported).
5. The main idea is that it is in the interest of the United States to maintain friendly relations with both sides of the conflict in Europe and that any citizen who violates this neutrality will be punished.

Situation

Suppose a U.S. government document has been published in a newspaper or on the Internet and you have to evaluate it — either because it's part of your job or because the document is important to you as a voter. The strategies that follow will help you read such a document.

Strategies

Do background research.
- Use a textbook, an encyclopedia, or the Internet to review the historical or political context of the document.

Monitor and adjust your reading.
- Be aware of any difficulty you are having in understanding the document.
- Read more slowly if the material is complex.
- If necessary, adjust your purpose for reading the document. (Major purposes for reading include *enjoying, understanding, interpreting,* and *solving problems*.) As you read an official document, you may decide that you must interpret it as well as merely understand it on a literal level.

Break down difficult texts.
- Break down complicated sentences into shorter sentences; identify modifiers and the sentence elements they modify.

Address ▾ http://www.whitehouse.gov

BY THE PRESIDENT OF THE UNITED STATES OF AMERICA
A PROCLAMATION
  Whereas it appears that a state of war exists between Austria, Prussia, Sardinia, Great Britain, and the United Netherlands on the one part and France on the other, and the duty and interest of the United States require that they should with sincerity and good faith adopt and pursue a conduct friendly and impartial toward the belligerent powers:
  I have therefore thought fit by these presents to declare the disposition of the United States to observe the conduct aforesaid toward those powers respectively, and to exhort and warn the citizens of the United States carefully to avoid all acts and proceeding whatsoever which may in any manner tend to contravene such disposition.
  And I do hereby also make known that whosoever of the citizens of the United States shall render himself liable to punishment or forfeiture under the law of nations by committing, aiding, or abetting hostilities against any of the said powers, or by carrying to any of them those articles which are deemed contraband by the modern usage of nations, will not receive the protection of the United States against such punishment or forfeiture . . .
  Philadelphia, the 22d of April, 1793
  Geo. WASHINGTON

Use context clues or a dictionary to define unfamiliar words.
- If you are unsure of meaning, reread sentences. See if context clues help you understand the sentence. If not, consult a reference book or speak with a knowledgeable person.
- Ask yourself questions based on what you *do* understand. Ask, for example, "Does this familiar word mean something different in this context?"

Find the main idea, or key passage, of the document.

Using the Strategies
1. What is the date of the document reprinted on this page?
2. Who issued the document? What is its title?

3. What is the world situation described in the first paragraph?
4. Use context clues to see if you can define *aforesaid, exhort, contravene, forfeiture,* and *contraband.* Be sure to check your guesses in a dictionary.
5. What is the main idea of this document?

Extending the Strategies

In a library or on the Internet, find a law recently enacted by the U.S. government or your state government. Make a copy of the law. Then, apply these strategies to your reading and evaluation of the legislation. Be sure to share your understanding of the legislation with other readers.

134 BEGINNINGS

Using the Internet

HRW Internet Site. Documents suitable for the activity suggested in Extending the Strategies may be found on the HRW Internet site: go.hrw.com (keyword: LE0 11-3).

Learning for Life

Researching the Immigrant Experience

OBJECTIVES
1. Research the experiences of immigrant groups
2. Conduct supplemental primary research
3. Choose and complete a project presenting research information.

Problem
The three collections you've studied thus far tell the stories of some of the earliest immigrants to America. The experiences of each early immigrant group were unique.

Project
Use library and community resources to research the experiences of one or more immigrant groups, past or present.

Preparation
Form a small research team. Agree on responsibilities for each team member. Decide which aspect, or aspects, of the immigrant experience each member will focus on.

Procedure
1. Research the experiences of one or more of the following groups on their journeys to America:
   - Africans brought to the United States to be enslaved
   - Irish who immigrated as a result of the potato famine in the 1840s
   - Jews who fled persecution in Europe and Russia
   - Cubans who fled from the Communist revolution
   - Vietnamese who came after the Vietnam War ended in 1975
   - other groups currently immigrating to the United States in large numbers from countries in the Caribbean, the Middle East, Latin America, East Asia, Africa, Europe, and other parts of the world
2. Supplement library research by interviewing people in your own community who are recent immigrants or who remember stories about grandparents, parents, or other relatives who immigrated to the United States.
3. Keep a record of all your sources. Evaluate and organize your information. Then prepare your presentation. You may want to focus on the following topics for the group or groups you are researching:
   - how the circumstances of the immigration affected the subsequent adjustment of the group in the United States
   - particular obstacles encountered in this country
   - important achievements and accomplishments
   - contributions to U.S. society
   - noteworthy individuals

Presentation
Present your research in one of the following formats (or another format that your teacher approves):

1. **Original Play**
   Write and present a play in which your team presents the story of an immigrant group or groups in the United States. Use props, costumes, food, music, and other audio and visual support.

2. **Time Line**
   As a class, collaborate on a wall-sized time line that includes names of immigrant groups, dates of significant events in the history of U.S. immigration, quotations, illustrations and photographs, and other data.

3. **Multimedia Presentation**
   Write a script based on your findings, and read it to the class, supplementing it with audio and visual aids: recorded music, photos, slides, overhead transparencies, posters, video or audio interviews, and props (clothing, food, art objects).

   No matter which format you choose, consider sharing your presentation with an audience outside the class: school, library, newspaper, TV station, or a cultural or ethnic club or association.

Processing
What did you learn about the immigrant experience by doing this project? For your portfolio, write your reflections on this statement: "Every American is descended from immigrants."

Resources

Viewing and Representing
HRW Multimedia Presentation Maker
Students may wish to use the *Multimedia Presentation Maker* to visualize and coordinate their critical project deadlines.

Grading Timesaver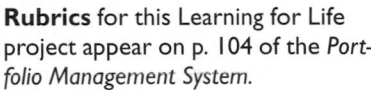

Rubrics for this Learning for Life project appear on p. 104 of the *Portfolio Management System*.

LEARNING FOR LIFE 135

Developing Workplace Competencies

Preparation	Procedure	Presentation
• Makes decisions • Works on teams • Demonstrates individual responsibility	• Acquires data • Evaluates data	• Thinks creatively • Exhibits self-esteem • Communicates ideas and information • Selects appropriate equipment

OBJECTIVES

1. Read nineteenth-century American literature on the theme of "The Transforming Imagination"
2. Interpret literary elements in American Romantic literature, with special emphasis on the sonnet
3. Apply a variety of reading strategies to the literature of American Romanticism, particularly using context clues to discover word meanings
4. Respond to the literature in a variety of modes
5. Learn and use new words
6. Learn about the history of Noah Webster's Dictionary
7. Plan, draft, revise, edit, proof, and publish a literary analysis
8. Insert modifiers effectively into sentences
9. Demonstrate the ability to read a map
10. Explore ways to move toward a lifestyle in harmony with nature

American Romanticism
1800–1860

Selection Readability

This Annotated Teacher's Edition provides a summary of each selection in the student book. Following each Summary heading, you will find one, two, or three small icons. These icons indicate, in an approximate sense, the reading level of the selection.

■ One icon indicates that the selection is easy.

■ ■ Two icons indicate that the selection is on an intermediate reading level.

■ ■ ■ Three icons indicate that the selection is challenging.

The Grand Canyon of the Yellowstone (1872) by Thomas Moran
(1837–1926). Oil on canvas (84" × 144¼").

Lent by the Department of the Interior Museum. National Museum of American Art,
Smithsonian Institution, Washington, DC, U.S.A./Art Resource, NY.

**RESPONDING TO
THE ART**

Thomas Moran (1837–1926)
was born in England to Irish parents who immigrated to the
United States in 1844. Entirely
self-taught, he was a member
of the second generation of the
Hudson River School, a group of
landscape painters united by a
Romantic approach to rendering
the spirit of the American landscape. The Hudson River School's
subject matter was not limited to
the Hudson River, as can be seen
in Moran's *The Grand Canyon of
the Yellowstone.*

On its completion, this vast
panoramic painting was shown to
President Grant, who, in March
1872, signed into law an act of
Congress protecting the whole
Yellowstone area forever. Moran's
landscape was then bought by
the U.S. government; it was the
first American landscape by an
American artist ever purchased by
the government. Displayed in the
Capitol alongside effigies of human
heroes, it became, as art historian
Robert Hughes notes, a painting of
the American landscape as hero.
Activity. Ask students to find
the human figures. What do they
add to the effect? [They provide
scale and emphasize the size of the
canyon.] Ask students to discuss
what this painting might tell us
about the American landscape in
the nineteenth century. [Possible
responses: It is vast, grand, wild,
open, and inspiring; it is populated
by both Native Americans and
European Americans.] **Also ask
why the landscape might be called
Romantic.** [Possible responses: It is
overwhelming in its scale and intensity; it appeals to the emotions; its
sublimity inspires awe.]

Resources: Print and Media

Reading
• *Reading Skills and Strategies*
    MiniRead Skill Lessons, pp. 63, 73
    Selection Skill Lessons, pp. 69, 79

Viewing and Representing
• *Visual Connections*
    Videocassette A, Segment 4

Assessment
• *Formal Assessment,* p. 30
• *Preparation for College Admission Exams,* p. 13
• *Test Generator* (One-Stop Planner CD-ROM)

Internet
• go.hrw.com (keyword: LE0 11-3)

Resources

**Viewing and Representing
Videocassette A, Segment 4**
The *Video Connections* segment
"The American Journey" explores
the American interpretation of the
Romantic journey. For full lesson plans
and worksheets, see *Video Connections
Teacher's Manual.*

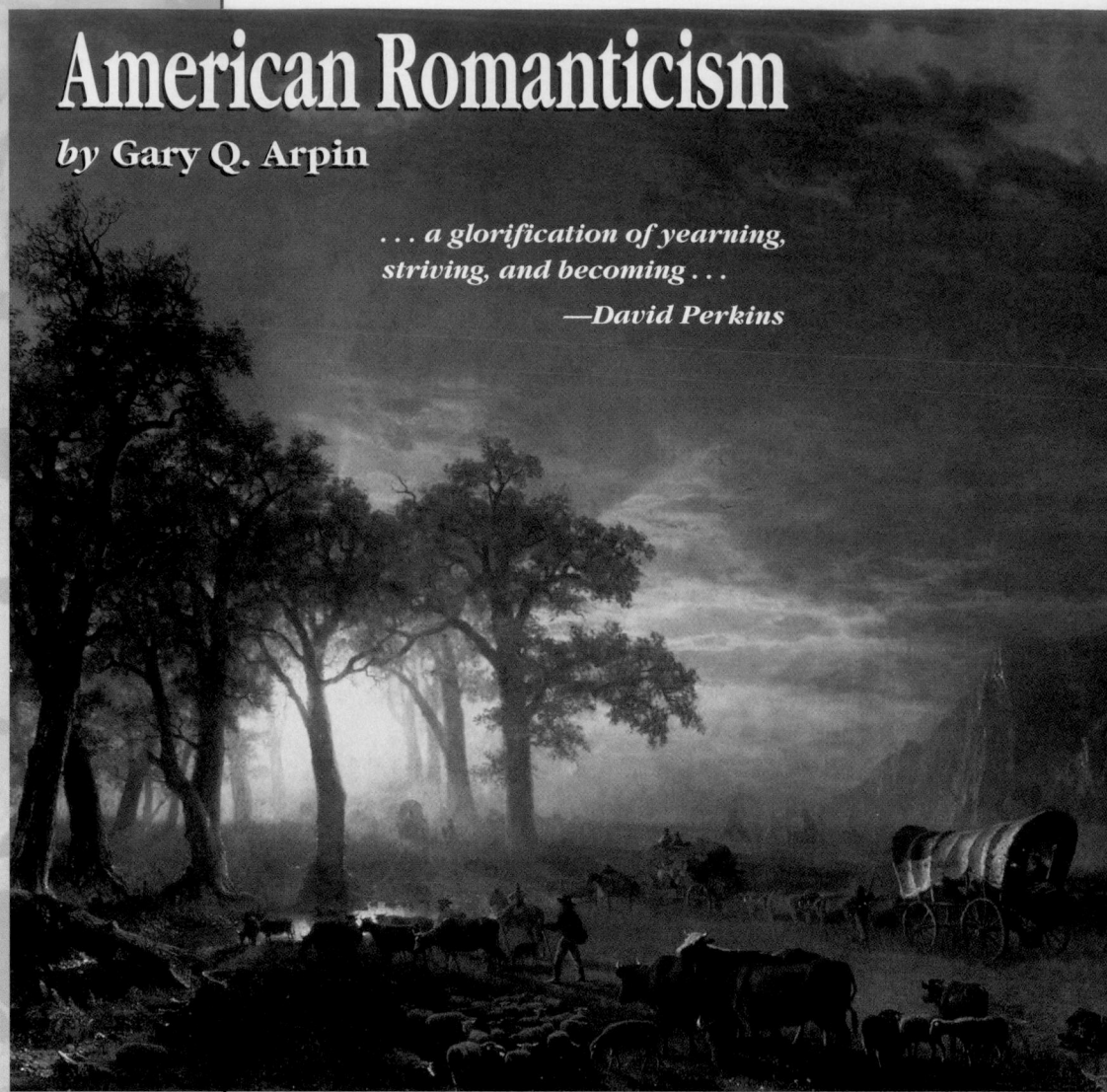

. . . a glorification of yearning, striving, and becoming . . .

—David Perkins

The Pattern of the Journey

The journey—there is probably no pattern so common in all of narrative literature, from the Bible, to the Greek epic the *Odyssey*, to modern films like *The Wizard of Oz* and *Forrest Gump*. Very early in his *Autobiography* (page 86), Benjamin Franklin describes in great detail an important American journey: a personal quest in which the young Ben leaves his home in Boston and travels to Philadelphia. The significance of Franklin's journey is clear: It is a declaration of independence, a move away from the constraints of his family and toward a city where he might prosper. It is, in other words, a quest for opportunity. Without stretching the metaphor too greatly, we can see in Franklin's journey an expression of both his personal goals and the goals of eighteenth-century America: a reaching out for independence, prosperity, commerce, and urbane civilization.

Franklin wrote about his journey to Philadelphia in 1771. In 1799, the American writer Charles Brockden Brown described a very different journey to Philadelphia in his Romantic novel *Arthur Mervyn*. In this tale a young farmboy hero leaves his home in the country for Philadelphia. Instead of finding a place of promise where he can make his dreams come true, however, the boy is plunged into a plague-ridden urban world of decay, corruption, and evil. The Philadelphia of this novel is no city of promise; it is an industrial hell that devours all hope and ambition.

The journeys described in Franklin's *Autobiography* and Brown's *Arthur Mervyn* make clear the differences between

Emigrants Crossing the Plains (detail) (1867) by Albert Bierstadt. Oil on canvas (67″ × 102″).

National Cowboy Hall of Fame and Western Heritage Center, Oklahoma City, Oklahoma.

> The long-distance journey is part of our history, both real and fictional: Lewis and Clark, the pioneers in their Conestogas, the Joads in their overloaded jalopy. Something about the nation—its breadth, its variety, its vastness—beckons the adventurer, the eccentric, the fame seeker, Balloonists, glider pilots, joggers, and bladers. People on pogo sticks and unicycles.
>
> —*The New York Times*
> April 24, 1995

Ⓐ Literary Connections
Charles Brockden Brown
Brown (1771–1810) is considered the first professional American novelist. Born and raised in Philadelphia, he completed a legal education but moved to New York to further his literary career. He wrote his best Gothic novels in a single two-year period: *Edgar Huntly* (1799), *Ormond* (1799), *Wieland* (1799), and *Arthur Mervyn* (1799–1800). His fiction was admired by such great Romantic authors as John Keats, Percy Bysshe Shelley, Sir Walter Scott, James Fenimore Cooper, Nathaniel Hawthorne, and Edgar Allan Poe. Critic Van Wyck Brooks sees Brown as an innovator in psychological horror and a strong influence upon Poe, Hawthorne, Herman Melville, and Henry James. After 1800, Brown dedicated himself to a career in business, but he remained active as a magazine editor and a writer of nonfiction.

Ⓑ Literary Connections
Steinbeck's Joads
"The Joads in their overloaded jalopy" refers to the main characters of John Steinbeck's great novel *The Grapes of Wrath* (1939) and the 1940 John Ford film adapted from it. The journey from Oklahoma to California that the Joads undertake in *The Grapes of Wrath* is based on the historical flight of impoverished farmers from the Oklahoma Dust Bowl of the 1930s

Time Line

This time line shows major cultural and political events in American history, and events in world history that had global impact, during the era of the American Romantics.

- **1790–1809**
  English Romantics
  The publication of *Lyrical Ballads* is generally considered the beginning of Romantic poetry in Britain. Wordsworth's preface to the second edition (1800) emphasizes the role of emotion in poetry and urges poets to draw inspiration from the everyday life and speech of ordinary people.

- **1810–1819**
  The National Anthem
  Francis Scott Key wrote "The Star-Spangled Banner" as a poem. It was later set to the music of "To Anacreon in Heaven," composed by John Stafford Smith, an Englishman. The song officially became the national anthem by an act of Congress in 1931.

- **1820–1829**
  Noah Webster
  In addition to his dictionaries, Noah Webster published a grammar book and a speller that sold sixty million copies and that distinguished American spelling from British. Webster also edited political journals and campaigned for a strong federal government.

- **1830–1839**
  Alexis de Tocqueville
  Tocqueville was sent to the United States by the French government in 1831 to study the penitentiary system, but he ultimately wrote the earliest, and most enduringly influential, analysis of American democracy. Besides studying government and administration, he evaluated social conditions—including American literature, which he found lacking.

American Romanticism 1800–1860

LITERARY EVENTS

James Fenimore Cooper. English. Engraving (4″ x 6″). The Granger Collection, New York.

William Wordsworth and Samuel Taylor Coleridge publish *Lyrical Ballads,* a landmark of English Romanticism, 1798

- England's Mary Wollstonecraft publishes *A Vindication of the Rights of Woman,* 1792

William Cullen Bryant publishes "Thanatopsis," 1817

Noah Webster publishes a landmark dictionary of American English, 1828

- James Fenimore Cooper publishes *The Pioneers,* 1823

Washington Irving publishes *The Sketch Book of Geoffrey Crayon, Gent.,* 1820

France's Alexis de Tocqueville publishes *Democracy in America,* a noted study of U.S. political and social institutions, 1835

- **John Greenleaf Whittier** publishes *Justice and Expediency,* in which he calls for the abolition of slavery, 1833

- **Oliver Wendell Holmes** publishes "Old Ironsides," 1830

1790–1809	1810–1819	1820–1829	1830–1839

CULTURAL/HISTORICAL EVENTS

First ten amendments, Bill of Rights, added to U.S. Constitution, 1791

- Eli Whitney's improved cotton gin increases U.S. cotton cultivation and expands demand for slave labor, 1794

Smithsonian Institution.

- U.S. population is 5.3 million, 1800

- Washington, D.C., becomes U.S. capital, 1800

- President Thomas Jefferson negotiates Louisiana Purchase from France, more than doubling U.S. territory, 1803

Miguel Hidalgo y Costilla launches the Mexican war of independence from Spain, 1810

- In War of 1812, British burn much of Washington, D.C., 1814

- Francis Scott Key, commemorating the War of 1812, writes "The Star-Spangled Banner," 1814

- Napoleon I of France is defeated at Waterloo and subsequently exiled, 1815

- Simón Bolívar, South American independence leader, becomes Greater Colombia's first president, 1819

Missouri admitted as a slave state, Maine as a free state, in Missouri Compromise, 1820–1821

- Liberia founded on west coast of Africa as a settlement for freed U.S. slaves, 1822

- Peru assures its independence by defeating Spain at Ayacucho, 1824

- Erie Canal opens, connecting Great Lakes and Atlantic Ocean, 1825

- Thomas Jefferson and John Adams die on same day, July 4, 1826

Underground Railroad, a secret system for helping fugitive slaves reach safety, is organized, c. 1830

- Thomas Cole completes *The Oxbow,* an early Hudson River School Romantic landscape painting, 1836

- Queen Victoria of England is crowned, 1837

- U.S. Army forces Cherokees out of Georgia on long Trail of Tears to Oklahoma, 1838

(Right) The flag that flew over Fort McHenry and inspired "The Star-Spangled Banner."

Using the Time Line

Assign two events from the lower half of the time line to pairs of students, and give the pairs three minutes to write down as much information as they know about the events. In some cases, students may not know much about the events they are assigned, but suggest they might make inferences based on what they can learn from examining the rest of the time line. For example, in 1803 Thomas Jefferson negotiated the Louisiana Purchase. Students can infer that this addition increased the international stature of the United States, promoted national identity, removed the threat of a French takeover, and gave the country access to more natural resources. Ask students to read their notes to the class. You might have other students verify and supplement information by using an encyclopedia or electronic database.

Margaret Fuller publishes *Woman in the Nineteenth Century*, the first full-length study of women's position in American society, 1845

•

Edgar Allan Poe publishes *The Raven and Other Poems*, 1845

•

Ralph Waldo Emerson publishes his first collection, *Essays*, including "Self-Reliance" and "The Over-Soul," 1841

Margaret Fuller. After a painting (c. 1872) by Alonzo Chappel.
The Granger Collection, New York.

James Russell Lowell publishes *The Biglow Papers*, satirical poems opposing the Mexican War and written in a Yankee dialect, 1848

Emily Dickinson begins to copy her poems into bound booklets, 1858

•

Henry David Thoreau publishes *Walden*, 1854

•

Herman Melville publishes *Moby-Dick; or, The Whale*, 1851

•

Nathaniel Hawthorne publishes *The Scarlet Letter*, 1850

Henry Wadsworth Longfellow (1871) by Theodore Wust. Watercolor on ivory.

Henry Wadsworth Longfellow publishes *The Courtship of Miles Standish*, 1858

•

Walt Whitman publishes the first edition of his book of poems, *Leaves of Grass*, 1855

National Portrait Gallery, Smithsonian Institution, Washington, DC/Art Resource, NY.

1840–1849

U.S. population is 17.1 million, 1840

•

Brook Farm undertakes experiment in cooperative living, 1841–1847

•

By Treaty of Nanking, China cedes Hong Kong to Great Britain and opens five ports to foreign trade, 1842

•

First baseball game under rules resembling the modern sport played at Hoboken, N.J.; the New York Club defeats the Knickerbockers 23 to 1, 1846

•

U.S. annexes Texas, 1845; leads to war with Mexico, 1846–1848

Famine in Ireland due to potato crop failure causes increased emigration from Ireland to U.S., 1846

•

Lucretia Mott and Elizabeth Cady Stanton organize first women's rights convention in the U.S. at Seneca Falls, N.Y., 1848

•

California gold rush begins as thousands of gold miners travel to Sacramento area, 1849

1850–1859

Oberlin College established as one of first coeducational colleges in the U.S., 1837

•

The New York Times founded, 1851

•

Modern Republican Party organized to oppose the extension of slavery, 1854

•

After Indian revolt against British East India Company rule, British government takes over administration of India, 1858

Commodore Matthew Perry opens two Japanese ports to U.S. trade, 1854

•

U.S. Supreme Court's *Dred Scott* decision antagonizes antislavery forces, 1857

•

The Granger Collection, New York.

Library of Congress.

Abraham Lincoln and Stephen A. Douglas stage a noted series of seven debates as candidates for the Illinois seat in the U.S. Senate, 1858

AMERICAN ROMANTICISM 141

Using the Time Line

Have students use an encyclopedia or other reference to place the following cultural events on the time line.

- John Isaac Hawkins invents the upright piano, which soon becomes a staple of middle-class households. [c. 1800]
- Elizabeth Blackwell becomes the first female physician in the United States. [1849]
- Sequoyah, a Cherokee, creates the first written Native American language and publishes parts of the Bible and a newspaper, *The Cherokee Phoenix*. [1820s]
- William Lloyd Garrison begins publication of *The Liberator*, an influential antislavery newspaper. [1831]
- American Samuel Morse devises the Morse Code. [1838]
- Sojourner Truth delivers her famous defense of the rights of women, "Ain't I a Woman?" [1851]

RESPONDING TO THE ART

The American painter **Hyppolite Sebron** (1801–1879) created this picture of the Manhattan neighborhood known today as SoHo, where five-story cast-iron buildings such as those on the right can still be seen.

Activity. Ask students what inferences they can make about Romantic-era New York, based on this picture. [Possible responses: The city had an active fire department; political picketers were familiar sights; there was a general bustle of activity; women walked in pairs without male chaperones; public transportation was popular.] Also have students compare and contrast the vision of New York in this painting with that conveyed by the text of A Closer Look. [Possible response: The text highlights social problems, such as the prevalence of disease and crime which the painting doesn't depict.]

A Closer Look

This feature explores everyday life in New York City in the first half of the nineteenth century.

Ⓐ Exploring the Historical Period

New Urban Centers

Aside from the major eastern seaboard cities named, several frontier towns were growing into urban centers by the 1850s: Buffalo, Pittsburgh, Cincinnati, Detroit, Milwaukee, and Chicago.

Broadway at Spring Street (1855) by Hyppolite Sebron (1801–1879). Oil on canvas (29¼″ × 42½″).

Courtesy Schweitzer Gallery, New York.

THE CITY, GRIM AND GRAY

Ⓐ In the first half of the nineteenth century, the largest American cities were Boston, Philadelphia, Baltimore, Charleston, and, largest of all, New York. The Romantic writers represented in this collection would have been very familiar with New York; some of them, like Washington Irving and William Cullen Bryant, even lived there. What was life like in the largest American city of the early 1800s?

Between 1820 and 1840, the population of New York more than doubled, from 124,000 to 312,000 people. In the 1830s, the first official tenements were built—buildings where a bathtub might be shared with four hundred people, where eight or more people might live in a single room without furniture, and where tenants might be ragpickers who kept their smelly stashes inside their homes. The soundtrack to the squalor and dinginess of life in one of these buildings might be provided by the bloodcurdling screeches of chickens being slaughtered indoors for the night's meal.

The city streets were fouled with droppings from the main source of transportation: horses. When a horse was injured in a collision or had collapsed from malnutrition or overwork, it was left to die on the curbside. Its body might remain on the street for days or weeks at a time. Given

the views of the rationalists and those of the Romantics. To Franklin and other rationalists, the city was a place to find success and self-realization. To the Romantic writers who came after Franklin, though, the city, far from being the seat of civilization, was often a place of moral ambiguity and, worse, of corruption and death.

The characteristic Romantic journey is to the countryside, which Romantics associated with independence, moral clarity, and healthful living. Sometimes, though, as in the works of Gothic-influenced writers like Edgar Allan Poe (page 260), the Romantic journey was a voyage to the country of the imagination. But whatever the destination of the Romantic journey, it was a flight both *from* something and *to* something. In fact, America's first truly popular professional writer is today known principally for an immortal story about an escape from civilization and responsibility. The writer was Washington Irving, and the escape was made by Rip Van Winkle (page 154).

> *American Romanticism can best be described as a journey away from the corruption of civilization and the limits of rational thought and toward the integrity of nature and the freedom of the imagination.*

Reaching All Students

Struggling Readers

Because large amounts of expository text are sometimes difficult for struggling readers, we organized this introduction with the use of subheads, charts of major points, and main ideas in boldface. For a lesson directly tied to this introduction that helps students understand this text, see the *Reading Skills and Strategies* binder:
- MiniRead Skill Lesson, p. 63
- Selection Skill Lesson, p. 69

English Language Learners

Have students research and give brief reports on the immigration history of a particular group. Also have students report on what this group added to the American cultural kaleidoscope. Encourage students to add key words they encounter to their personal vocabulary.

Advanced Students

You can enhance students' understanding of American Romanticism by linking it to European Romanticism. Encourage students to explore the poetry of British Romantics William Blake, William Wordsworth, Samuel Taylor Coleridge, John Keats, Percy Bysshe Shelley, and Lord Byron. Many students will also benefit from exposure to Romantic composers such as Beethoven, Schubert, Chopin, and Schumann.

such conditions, it's no surprise that disease was rampant. In Manhattan in the summer of 1832, one third of the city's population—those who could afford to leave—left the city to escape a cholera epidemic that killed an average of one hundred people a day.

There were 20,000 homeless children on the streets of New York. Some worked in sweatshops, some sold toothpicks or newspapers, others turned to petty crime. If they lived to be twenty, they were lucky; disease, accidents, exposure, violence, and starvation took most of them long before that time.

Crime and violence were no strangers to the city. Waterfront gangs often included "pirates" who would kill for next to nothing. On the infamous Cherry Street, 15,000 sailors were robbed in a single year. Throughout the city, buildings sometimes burned to the ground while various competing fire companies fought with each other over who had the right to put out the fire. There were even riots on the streets: In 1834, men opposed to the abolition of slavery burned down homes, churches, and a school, trying to destroy free African Americans and their supporters.

There was one bright spot in the picture of squalor and degradation, though: talk in the 1840s of constructing a huge and expensive city park, to be built for "health and recreation." It was the poet William Cullen Bryant's idea—a dream of bringing a taste of the blessed countryside to a city wracked with poverty, illness, and crime. But New Yorkers would have to wait until after the Civil War for their oasis: Central Park would not become a completed reality until 1876.

Culver Pictures.

A tenement-house alley gang.

The Romantic Sensibility: Celebrating the Imagination

In general, **Romanticism** is the name given to those schools of thought that value feeling and intuition over reason. The first rumblings of Romanticism were felt in Germany in the second half of the eighteenth century. Romanticism had a strong influence on literature, music, and painting in Europe and England well into the nineteenth century. But Romanticism came relatively late to America, and, as you will see in this collection and in the collections that follow, it took different forms.

Romanticism, especially in Europe, developed in part as a reaction against **rationalism.** In the sooty wake of the Industrial Revolution, with its squalid cities and wretched working conditions, people had come to realize the limits of reason. The Romantics came to believe that the imagination was able to apprehend truths that the rational mind could not reach. These truths were usually accompanied by powerful emotion and associated with natural, unspoiled beauty. To the Romantic sensibility the imagination, spontaneity, individual feelings, and wild nature were of greater value than reason, logic, planning, and cultivation. The Romantics did not flatly reject

> The question of common sense is always "What is it good for?"—a question which would abolish the rose and be answered triumphantly by the cabbage.
>
> —James Russell Lowell

The cholera epidemic was part of a worldwide outbreak. Cholera is a bacterial infection of the digestive system that causes diarrhea, vomiting, dehydration, and severe muscle cramps, sometimes ending in death from kidney failure or heart attack. It is contracted by ingesting contaminated food or water.

C Exploring the Historical Period
Riot Year

1834 was called the "riot year" in New York. Its disturbances included the "stonecutters' riot," in which stonecutters took to the streets to protest the city's planned use of convict labor to cut the marble for a New York University building. More than one riot began as a protest against stage appearances by British actors who were rumored to have insulted the United States. One such theater riot turned its rage on the members of the local abolition movement, fueled by the rumor that black freedmen would take Northern jobs; the violence lasted three days and required three thousand militia to quell.

D Exploring the Culture
Central Park

The park was designed by Frederick Law Olmsted and Calvert Vaux to turn an area of swamps, dumps, quarries, and pigsties into a peaceful refuge in the heart of the city. In addition to trees and rolling lawns, the park now includes a zoo, a skating rink, a medieval castle, a world-class art museum, and outdoor theaters.

E Exploring the Culture
European Romanticism

Romanticism grew out of the ideals of freedom and reason embodied in the Enlightenment and the French Revolution. German philosopher and literary critic Friedrich von Schlegel was the first to apply the term "romantic" to literature that opposed classicism. The great German thinkers Johann Wilhelm von Goethe, Immanuel Kant, and Friedrich von Schiller had an important influence on Romanticism, as did the French philosopher Jean Jacques Rousseau.

Getting Students Involved

Cooperative Learning

Formulating Questions. In order to help familiarize students with literary and philosophical ideas that are new to them, assign students different sections of the introduction and ask them to write two test questions about their individual sections. After students have finished reading the introduction and have written questions on their sections, have them turn to a partner who was an "expert" on another section. Ask students to quiz each other on their sections. Have students change partners until all students have been asked questions and given answers for all the sections in the introduction.

A Critical Thinking
Evaluating the Text

Both of these Romantic strategies for seeking beauty are based on the premise that the urban, industrial world does not offer beauty to the beholder. Ask students to evaluate that premise. [Sample responses: It is valid; cities are crowded, dirty, noisy places, and the industrial areas are an ugly blight on the environment. No, cities are vital, vibrant places, and industrial areas offer stirring proof of human ingenuity.]

B Literary Connections
Gothic Literature

The Gothic novel, or Gothic romance, was typified by Horace Walpole's novel *The Castle of Otranto,* by Mary Shelley's *Frankenstein,* and by the novels of Ann Radcliffe, Matthew Gregory Lewis, and Charles R. Maturin. The genre influenced such later English and American writers as Coleridge, Poe, and Emily and Charlotte Brontë. Jane Austen, primarily a realistic novelist, satirized the gothic genre in *Northanger Abbey.* The Gothic novel of the Romantic era was also a predecessor of the modern genre of the same name, represented by writers such as Daphne du Maurier, Catherine Cookson, Victoria Holt, and Mary Stewart.

RESPONDING TO THE ART

The French **Baroness Hyde de Neuville** (c. 1749–1849) made this charming and accomplished picture of a street in America's capital city, which was, in her time, a relatively small, quiet, Southern-style town with a rural feel.
Activity. Ask students to do research to find out what F Street in Washington looks like now.

logical thought as invalid for all purposes. But for the purpose of art, they placed a new premium on intuitive, "felt" experience.

To the Romantic mind, poetry was the highest and most sublime embodiment of the imagination. Romantic artists often contrasted poetry with science, which they saw as destroying the very truth it claimed to seek. Edgar Allan Poe, for example, called science a "vulture" with wings of "dull realities," preying on the hearts of poets.

Romanticism, originally a European movement, emphasized feeling and intuition over reason, sought wisdom in natural beauty, and valued poetry above all other works of the imagination.

Romantic Escapism: From Dull Realities to Higher Realms

The Romantics wanted to rise above "dull realities" to a realm of higher truth. They did this in two principal ways. First, the Romantics searched for exotic settings in the more "natural" past or in a world far removed from the grimy and noisy industrial age. Sometimes they found this world in the supernatural realm, or in old legends and folklore. Second, the Romantics tried to contemplate the natural world until dull reality fell away to reveal underlying beauty and truth.

We can most easily see the first Romantic approach in the development of the Gothic novel, with its wild, haunted landscapes, supernatural events, and mysterious medieval castles.

Characteristics of American Romanticism

- Values feeling and intuition over reason
- Places faith in inner experience and the power of the imagination
- Shuns the artificiality of civilization and seeks unspoiled nature
- Prefers youthful innocence to educated sophistication
- Champions individual freedom and the worth of the individual
- Contemplates nature's beauty as a path to spiritual and moral development
- Looks backward to the wisdom of the past and distrusts progress
- Finds beauty and truth in exotic locales, the supernatural realm, and the inner world of the imagination
- Sees poetry as the highest expression of the imagination
- Finds inspiration in myth, legend, and folk culture

F Street, Washington, D.C. (1821) by Baroness Hyde de Neuville (c. 1749–1849). Watercolor and pencil (7 1/2″ × 9 7/8″).
© Collection of the New-York Historical Society.

Using Students' Strengths

Auditory Learners

Have students assimilate the characteristics of Romanticism by offering them the following mnemonic device. Go over each of the terms in the device, making sure students understand their meaning and can explain their connection to the introduction. Tell students that the I in the device should also remind them that Romanticism was a fundamentally individualistic outlook on life.

5 I's of Romanticism:

Intuition
Imagination
Innocence
Inspiration from nature
Inner experience

Illustration by Wilfred Satty for Edgar Allan Poe's "The Fall of the House of Usher."

The Gothic, with its roots in French, German, and English literature, seemed an unlikely transplant to the new nation of America, where there were seemingly no places old enough to have accumulated a contingent of ghosts or to reek of the decay of ages. But even writers in America, notably Edgar Allan Poe, were attracted to the exotic, otherworldly trappings of the Gothic. In America, particularly in the works of Poe, the Gothic took a turn toward the psychological exploration of the human mind.

The second Romantic approach, the contemplation of the natural world, is evident in many lyric poems. In a typical Romantic poem, the speaker sees a commonplace object or event. A flower found by a stream or a waterfowl flying overhead brings the speaker to some important, deeply felt insight, which is then recorded in the poem. This contemplative process is similar to the way the Puritans drew moral lessons from nature. The difference is one of emphasis and goal. The Puritans' lessons were defined by their religion. In nature they found the God they knew from the Bible. The Romantics, on the other hand, found a far less clearly defined divinity in nature. Their contemplation of the natural world led to a more generalized emotional and intellectual awakening.

> **C** | They who dream by day are cognizant of many things which escape those who dream only by night. | **D**
> —Edgar Allan Poe

American Romanticism took two roads on the journey to understanding higher truths. One road led to the exploration of the past and of exotic, even supernatural, realms; the other road led to the contemplation of the natural world.

C Literary Connections
Transcendentalists
The direct contemplation of nature as a source of spiritual knowledge and inspiration became a central point in the doctrines of Ralph Waldo Emerson and other Transcendentalists (see pp. 210–225).

D Critical Thinking
Classifying
Ask students what Poe meant by distinguishing "those who dream by day" from "those who dream only by night." [Possible responses: Those who dream by day are imaginative, emotionally sensitive, otherworldly, distracted; those who dream only at night are pragmatic, unsentimental, unaffected by the darker side of their inner lives.]

Crossing the Curriculum

Art
Invite students to locate prints and photos of art by members of the Hudson River School of painting, such as Thomas Cole, Albert Bierstadt, and Frederick E. Church, and to bring the examples to class for display. (Make sure students understand that this kind of artistic "school" is not an academic institution, but a group of like-minded artists.) Interested students might also report on the photographic works of some members of the school. Add available photographs to the class display. Ask students to discuss the ways art and literature from the Romantic era are similar in content or style. To connect nineteenth-century Romanticism to the present day, you might ask students to find contemporary works of art (including advertising) that have a focus and technique that seems similar to the art of the Hudson River School.

Social Studies
In response to public demand, the government sold millions of acres of land in the Southeast and Middle West to settlers and speculators. (In some areas, this land was forcibly taken from the Native Americans, who were then forced to migrate west of the Mississippi.) Ask students to concentrate on a single region and to make maps showing how the area developed during this period and how the population densities of settlers and Native Americans shifted over time.

James Russell Lowell (1819–1891) was one of a distinguished family of Bostonians that later produced two other renowned American poets: Amy Lowell (1874–1925) and Robert Lowell (1917–1977; see p. 948). James Russell Lowell, along with John Greenleaf Whittier (p. 181), was a socially committed, antislavery Fireside Poet. He was the first editor of the magazine *The Atlantic Monthly* and often conveyed his progressive political opinions through essays, articles, and poems. Lowell's *A Fable for Critics* (1848) brought him considerable attention for its satirical criticism of the American literature of the time: Lowell felt that this literature was too dependent on European influences and not sufficiently American. He poked fun at Hawthorne, Poe, and himself, among others, saying

> There is Lowell, who's striving Parnassus to climb
> With a whole bale of *isms* tied together with rhyme.

Ⓑ Literary Connections
James Fenimore Cooper

Cooper wrote another novel in 1823, *The Pilot,* which has the distinction of being the first sea adventure in American letters. In addition to *The Pioneers,* the Leatherstocking tales include *The Last of the Mohicans, The Prairie, The Pathfinder,* and *The Deerslayer.*

Ⓒ Background
The Pioneers

In *The Pioneers* Natty Bumppo is imprisoned for shooting a deer out of season, reflecting the Romantic conflict between Bumppo's frontier ethics and the laws of the town. Eventually, Bumppo flees the town for the Western wilderness, where he remains an uncorrupted "natural" man throughout the series, embracing the moral code of the American Indian, who respects nature and tries to live in harmony with it. (Bumppo's nickname, "Leatherstocking," comes from the deerskin leggings he wears.)

The American Novel and the Wilderness Experience

During the Romantic period, the big question about American literature was: Would American writers continue to imitate the English and European models, or would they finally develop a distinctive literature of their own? While the Romantic poets of the period were still staying close to traditional forms, American novelists were discovering that the subject matter available to them was very different from the subjects available to European writers. America pro-

> Ⓐ You steal Englishmen's books and think Englishmen's thoughts,
> With their salt on her tail your wild eagle is caught;
> Your literature suits its each whisper and motion
> To what will be thought of it over the ocean.
>
> —James Russell Lowell, *from A Fable for Critics*

vided a sense of limitless frontiers that Europe, so long settled, simply did not possess. Thus, the development of the American novel coincided with westward expansion, with the growth of a nationalist spirit, and with the rapid spread of cities. All these factors tended to reinforce the idealization of frontier life. A "geography of the imagination" developed, in which town, country, and frontier would play a powerful role in American life and literature—as they continue to do today.

We can see how the novel developed in America by looking at the early career of James Fenimore Cooper (1789-1851). Cooper's first novel, *Precaution* (1820), describes life in an English country vicarage. His second novel, *The Spy* (1821), was influenced by the romances of the Scottish novelist Sir Walter Scott, though it is set during the American Revolution. It was in his third novel, *The Pioneers* (1823), that Cooper finally broke free of European constraints. In this novel, Cooper explored uniquely American set-Ⓑ tings and characters: frontier communities, American Indians, backwoodsmen, and the wilderness of western Ⓒ New York and Pennsylvania. Most of all, he created the first American heroic figure: Natty Bumppo (also known variously as Hawkeye, Deerslayer, and Leatherstocking), a heroic, virtuous, skillful frontiersman whose simple morality, love of nature, distrust of town life, and almost superhuman resourcefulness mark him as a true Romantic hero. It was this character who appeared in the rest of the Leatherstocking tales—a highly popular series of sequels that Cooper wrote over the next eighteen years.

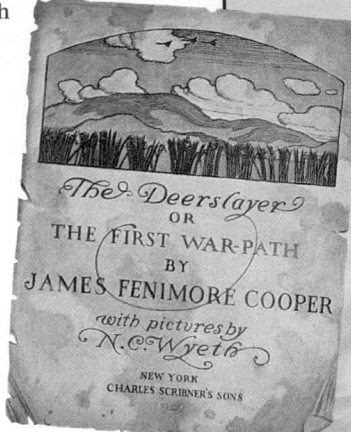

Title page of *The Deerslayer* (1925) illustrated by N. C. Wyeth (1882–1945).

American novelists looked to westward expansion and the development of the frontier for inspiration, creating subject matter that broke with European tradition.

Assessing Learning

Informal Assessment

As students consider the role of nature in Romantic writing, have them write short answers to the following reflective questions:

1. How often do I focus my attention on the natural world?
2. How often do I discuss aspects of nature with family and friends?
3. Overall, of what value is nature to me?
4. How much effort am I willing to give to help preserve nature?
5. Overall, do I judge myself a Romantic when it comes to nature?

The Deerslayer (detail) (1925) illustrated by N. C. Wyeth (1882–1945).

N. C. Wyeth (1882–1945) was perhaps the most respected illustrator of his generation, and the father of the famous naturalistic painter Andrew Wyeth. N. C. Wyeth illustrated many classics, such as *Treasure Island, Kidnapped, Robin Hood,* and *King Arthur.*

Activity. Ask students to discuss how the man in the picture exemplifies the "new" Romantic hero of early nineteenth-century America. [Possible response: The Deerslayer is a frontiersman; he exults in solitude and in nature.] Also ask which aspects of the picture seem realistic and which seem idealized or imaginary. [Possible response: The man's clothing and rifle and the forest setting appear realistic, but the spotlighting on the hero and his exuberant mood seem idealized.]

A New Kind of Hero

Most Europeans had an image of the American as unsophisticated and uncivilized. This was a stereotype that Ben Franklin, when he lived in France, took great pains to demonstrate was unfair and untrue. But Cooper and other Romantic novelists who followed him took no such pains. Instead, by creating such heroes as Natty Bumppo, they turned the insult on its head. Virtue, they implied, was in American innocence, not in European sophistication. Eternal truths were waiting to be discovered not in dusty libraries or crowded cities or glittering court life, but in the American wilderness that was unknown and unavailable to Europeans.

> It has been a matter of marvel to my European readers, that a man from the wilds of America should express himself in tolerable English. I was looked upon as something new and strange in American literature. . . .
>
> —Washington Irving

D

ⓓ Literary Connections

Washington Irving

Not only was Washington Irving (p. 152) widely read in Europe, but he lived on that side of the Atlantic for seventeen years, beginning in 1815. In England, he befriended Romantic novelist Sir Walter Scott, read German Romantic literature, studied European folklore, and wrote "The Legend of Sleepy Hollow" and "Rip Van Winkle." He believed that folklore revealed the inner dreams of a people and also offered fascinating glimpses of the supernatural.

Crossing the Curriculum

Art

Ask students to create their own visual version of the Romantic American hero, using a computer paintbrush program if available. If that medium is not available to your students, they may choose another convenient medium, such as collage, paint, or pen and ink.

Music

Encourage students to explore the work of Stephen Foster (1826–1864), whose songs have taken on the status of American folk songs. He wrote his first song at fourteen, published his first at eighteen, and had his first hit at twenty-two—"Oh! Susanna," a favorite among the forty-niners in the California gold rush. Students may want to prepare a tape with excerpts from Foster's most beloved songs—"Old Folks at Home," "Camptown Races," "My Old Kentucky Home," "Old Dog Tray," "Jeanie with the Light Brown Hair," and "Beautiful Dreamer." (Some of Foster's songs use black dialect and are criticized today for presenting stereotypical images of African Americans.) After listening to this tape, hold a class discussion about why Foster's songs captured the imagination of the growing nation.

Extending the Text

Explore with students whether these fictional heroes impact the culture at large, and if so, how. Ask students whether and how they inspire or provide role models for young people. Have students compare the qualities of this type of Romantic hero with those of a celebrity hero—say, a current music star, a famous athlete, or a business icon. Ask students if they can identify real-life examples of Romantic heroes, and if not, why.

RESPONDING TO THE ART

Activity. Have students imagine that they are screenwriters for the movies represented by these stills. Ask them to invent a scenario for each still and to include a few lines or a brief soliloquy that each hero would speak. The lines should reflect, in natural dialogue, the characteristics of a Romantic hero. Ask volunteers to read their lines expressively.

Cooper's Natty Bumppo is a triumph of American innocence and an example of one of the most important outgrowths of the early American novel: the American Romantic hero. Here at last was a new kind of heroic figure, one quite different from the hero of the Age of Reason. The rationalist hero—exemplified by a real-life figure such as Ben Franklin—was worldly, educated, sophisticated, and bent on making a place for himself in civilization. The typical hero of American Romantic fiction, on the other hand, was youthful, innocent, intuitive, and close to nature. He was also, by today's standards, hopelessly uneasy with women, who were usually seen (by male writers, at least) to represent civilization and the impulse to "domesticate."

Today, Americans still create Romantic heroes; the twentieth-century descendants of Natty Bumppo are all around us. They can be found in the guise of dozens of pop culture heroes: the Lone Ranger, Superman, Luke Skywalker, Indiana Jones, and any number of Western, detective, and fantasy heroes.

> His face would have had little to recommend it except youth, were it not for an expression that seldom failed to win upon those who had leisure to examine it, and to yield to the feeling of confidence it created. This expression was simply that of guileless truth, sustained by an earnestness of purpose, and a sincerity of feeling, that rendered it remarkable.
>
> —James Fenimore Cooper, describing Natty Bumppo, from *The Deerslayer*

20th Century Fox (Courtesy Kobal).

Daniel Day-Lewis as Natty Bumppo in the movie *The Last of the Mohicans* (1992).

Harrison Ford in the movie *Raiders of the Lost Ark* (1981).

Photofest.

148 AMERICAN ROMANTICISM

Crossing the Curriculum

Social Studies

Among real-life examples of Romantic heroes are the explorers Meriwether Lewis and William Clark as well as their Native American guides, particularly the Shoshone woman Sacajawea. Encourage students to find out more about their epic 1804–1806 journey from St. Louis to the west coast and back: what trials and tribulations they encountered, how they communicated with and avoided conflict with Indian tribes, what natural wonders they discovered and described in their journals and maps. (Among the plants they brought back for Thomas Jefferson, who commissioned the expedition, were two western flowers subsequently named for the explorers: *Lewisia* and *Clarkia*.) Students may enjoy historian Stephen Ambrose's 1996 book, *Undaunted Courage: Meriwether Lewis, Thomas Jefferson, and the Opening of the American West*.

> *The American Romantic hero possesses qualities of youthfulness, innocence, intuitiveness, and closeness to the natural world that set him solidly apart from the hero of the Age of Reason.*

American Romantic Poetry: Read at Every Fireside

The American Romantic novelists looked for new subject matter and innovative themes, but the opposite tendency appears in the works of the Romantic poets represented in this collection. Like Franklin, these Romantic poets wanted to prove that Americans were not unsophisticated hicks, and they attempted to prove this by working solidly within European literary traditions rather than by crafting a different and unique American voice. Even when they constructed poems with American settings and subject matter, the American Romantic poets used typically English themes, meter, and imagery. In a sense, they wrote in **(A)** a style that a cultivated person from England who had recently immigrated to America might be expected to use.

In many respects the American poets in this collection looked backward—over their shoulders, as it were—at established European literary models. Their poetry was limited by this slavish devotion to tradition and by their own allegiance to standard meter and diction, which resulted in poems with skillful but predictable "dum-de-dum" rhythms. Yet, for genera- **(B)** tions, many of their poems were staples of home and school reading.

In fact, the Fireside Poets, as the Boston group of Henry Wadsworth Longfellow (page 175), John Greenleaf Whittier (page 181), Oliver Wendell Holmes (page 187), and James Russell Lowell (1819–1891) was called, were, in their own time and for many decades afterward, the most popular **(C)** poets America had ever produced. In many ways their popularity has never been matched. They were called "Fireside Poets" because their poems were so often read aloud at the fireside as family entertainment. They were also sometimes called "Schoolroom Poets" because their poems were, for many years, memorized and recited in American classrooms.

Although the Fireside Poets' attempts to create a new American literature relied too reverently on the literature of the past, we should not view them only as backward-looking traditionalists. Certainly, they were not great innovators. Their choice of subject matter—love, patriotism, nature, family, God, and religion—was, for the most part, comforting rather than challenging to their audience. Their poetry could be preachy and didactic, their symbolism could be heavy and obvious, and they often wrote in a "pretty" or pleasing style that took the edge off their messages. (A well-

Characteristics of the American Romantic Hero

- Is young, or possesses youthful qualities
- Is innocent and pure of purpose
- Has a sense of honor based not on society's rules but on some higher principle
- Has a knowledge of people and of life based on deep, intuitive understanding, not on formal learning
- Loves nature and avoids town life
- Quests for some higher truth in the natural world

(A) Exploring the Culture
American Originality
Even though the American poets of the Romantic period imitated their English colleagues, their focus on American landscapes and American social conditions still represented a kind of literary innovation. The Puritans and other early American writers had written relatively little poetry, and the poetry they did write belonged to an older Neoclassical tradition. The American Romantics established the foundation for later American poets such as Walt Whitman and Emily Dickinson, who revolutionized poetry in America and beyond.

(B) Exploring the Culture
What They Learned in School
Not only was American Romantic poetry often studied in American schools, but Washington Irving's prose was used across the Western world, as a model for students of English. Irving's *Sketch Book* replaced Joseph Addison's *Spectator* as a first reader in the language. It was a source of national pride that an American author's work had usurped an Englishman's as a model of pure English prose style. (See Irving's boxed quote on p. 147.)

(C) Background
The Fireside Poets
The Fireside Poets published their work in many different formats in order to appeal to a wide audience. Expensive illustrated versions and inexpensive paperback versions of their works were sold widely, at prices to suit a range of incomes. While the subjects and sentiments of their poems had broad popular appeal, the Fireside Poets still demanded interpretation and attention from their readers. Their work contains many allusions to mythology, history, and the Bible, and their long, convoluted sentences are challenging. Consequently, many modern readers find the work of the Fireside Poets difficult. Their ideas, however, are not complex and are accessible to all readers.

Getting Students Involved

Isn't It Romantic?

Help students to see that contemporary America has many characteristics of a Romantic era. First have small groups of students review the list of traits of American Romanticism on p. 144 and the list of traits of the American Romantic hero on this page. Then, for each item on each list, have groups brainstorm examples from contemporary American culture that fit those traits. Examples might include famous people; modern customs, lifestyles, and fashions; creations of art or science; and modern events and public movements. Have one member in each group act as secretary to record the ideas. Then, hold a discussion with the whole class so that groups can compare their examples. You might close the discussion by noting that if the present is a Romantic era, it is partly because of the influence of nineteenth-century Romanticism.

A Responding to the Poem

This poem is addressed to a "psalmist," probably the writer of Ecclesiastes 3:20 or the writer of Psalm 103, whose outlook on life is ironic and sometimes despairing. A subtitle often used with the poem is "What the heart of the young man said to the psalmist." Longfellow's poem has been called "a small sermon." It is a call for action, not despair. The focus of life, says the poet, should be progress, not the grave. The poet urges his readers not to be like dumb cattle, but to be like heroes. He urges them to act in the present and not to dwell on the past. Our actions, the poet says, will inspire those who come after us. Perhaps the most famous verse is the seventh. You might have students memorize this poem—millions of Americans have already done so!

Ask students to compare and contrast this poem with Longfellow's "The Tide Rises, the Tide Falls," on p. 176.

You might also have them connect the sentiments in the poem to the quote that opens the introduction to the Romantic period (p. 138).

The message in the poem could be contrasted with Steinbeck's story "The Leader of the People" (p. 609).

B Quickwrite

Give students three options: they may call themselves Rationalists, Romantics, or some combination of both. If they are both, they might state a rough proportion. Have students support their answers with specific examples and anecdotes from their lives.

---

loved inspirational "Fireside" poem is on the right.) However, Whittier, for one, wrote powerful anti-slavery poems, and all of the Fireside Poets furthered the evolution of American poetry by introducing uniquely American subject matter in their choices of topics: American folk themes, descriptions of the American landscape, abolitionist issues, American Indian culture, and celebrations of American people, places, and events.

Limited by their essential literary conservatism, the Fireside Poets were unable to recognize the poetry of the future, which was being written right under their noses. Whittier's response in 1855 to reading the first volume of a certain poet's work was to throw the book into the fire. Ralph Waldo Emerson's response was much more far-sighted. "I greet you," Emerson wrote to this maverick new poet, Walt Whitman, "at the beginning of a great career."

The Fireside Poets, immensely popular in their time, created some poems of lasting merit, but their essential literary conservatism prevented them from being truly innovative. The first uniquely American poetry was yet to be created.

Quickwrite B
Rationalist or Romantic?

If you had to classify yourself as either a rationalist or a Romantic, which would you be? Would you be a practical, ambitious, worldly Benjamin Franklin or an intuitive, close-to-nature Romantic? Which traits—of either school of thought—do you truly value and think you would like to encourage in your own life? Freewrite an exploration of your thoughts on this issue.

A Psalm of Life A

Tell me not, in mournful numbers,
    Life is but an empty dream!
For the soul is dead that slumbers,
    And things are not what they seem.

Life is real—life is earnest—
    And the grave is not its goal:
Dust thou art, to dust returnest,
    Was not spoken of the soul.

Not enjoyment, and not sorrow,
    Is our destined end or way;
But to *act*, that each tomorrow
    Find us farther than today.

Art is long, and time is fleeting,
    And our hearts, though stout and brave,
Still, like muffled drums, are beating
    Funeral marches to the grave.

In the world's broad field of battle,
    In the bivouac of Life,
Be not like dumb, driven cattle!
    Be a hero in the strife!

Trust no Future, howe'er pleasant!
    Let the dead Past bury its dead!
Act—act in the glorious Present!
    Heart within, and God o'erhead!

Lives of great men all remind us
    We can make *our* lives sublime,
And, departing, leave behind us
    Footsteps on the sands of time.

Footsteps, that, perhaps another,
    Sailing o'er life's solemn main,
A forlorn and shipwrecked brother,
    Seeing, shall take heart again.

Let us then be up and doing,
    With a heart for any fate;
Still achieving, still pursuing,
    Learn to labor and to wait.

—Henry Wadsworth Longfellow

Reaching All Students

Struggling Readers
Because large amounts of expository text are sometimes difficult for struggling readers, we organized this introduction with the use of subheads, charts of major points, and main ideas in boldface. For a lesson directly tied to this introduction that helps students understand this text, see the *Reading Skills and Strategies* binder:
- MiniRead Skill Lesson, p. 73
- Selection Skill Lesson, p. 79

Assessing Learning

Check Test: Sentence Completion
1. Romantic literature is often about a journey from [the city] to [the country].
2. America's first popular professional writer was [Washington Irving].
3. Romanticism values feeling over [reason].
4. The typical Romantic hero is [young, innocent, nature-loving, adventurous].
5. The Fireside Poets were so called because [their poems were often read aloud at family firesides].

Collection 4

The Transforming Imagination

Theme

Striking Out on Our Own *For several years, American writers imitated European models. The earliest writers were deeply influenced by the Romantic movement, and so they looked for inspiration to unspoiled nature and to the past. They also celebrated imagination and intuition as the faculties that can reveal meaning. The novels of James Fenimore Cooper are key to this period, as are the writings of the first American to make a living as a writer, Washington Irving.*

Reading the Anthology

Reaching Struggling Readers

The *Reading Skills and Strategies: Reaching Struggling Readers* binder provides materials coordinated with the Pupil's Edition (see the Collection Planner, p. T150B) to help students who have difficulty reading and comprehending text, or students who are reluctant readers. The binder for eleventh grade is organized around ten individual skill areas and offers the following options:

- **MiniRead** MiniReads are short, easy texts that give students an opportunity to practice a particular skill and strategy before reading selections in the Pupil's Edition. Each MiniRead Skill Lesson can be taught independently or used in conjunction with a Selection Skill Lesson.

- **Selection Skill Lessons** Selection Skill Lessons allow students to apply skills introduced in the MiniReads. Each Selection Skill Lesson provides reading instruction and practice specific to a particular piece of literature in the Pupil's Edition.

Reading Beyond the Anthology

Read On Collection 4 includes an annotated bibliography of books suitable for extended reading. The suggested books are related to works in this collection by theme, by author, or by subject. To preview the Read On for Collection 4, please turn to p. T194.

Resources for this Collection

Note: All resources for this collection are available for preview on the *One-Stop Planner CD-ROM 1 with Test Generator.* All worksheets and blackline masters may be printed from the CD-ROM.

Internet Resources
go.hrw.com LE0 11-4

Collection Planner

Selection or Feature	Reading and Literary Skills	Vocabulary, Language, and Grammar
Rip Van Winkle (p. 153) Washington Irving	• *Reading Skills and Strategies: Reaching Struggling Readers* • MiniRead Skill Lesson, p. 83 • Selection Skill Lesson, p. 89 • *Graphic Organizers for Active Reading*, Worksheet p. 12 • *Literary Elements:* Transparency 6 Worksheet p. 19	• *Words to Own*, Worksheet p. 11 • *Grammar and Language Links:* Prepositional Phrases, Worksheet p. 21 • *Language Workshop CD-ROM,* Prepositional Phrases
Thanatopsis (p. 170) William Cullen Bryant **Connections: Sea Canes** (p. 173) Derek Walcott	• *Graphic Organizers for Active Reading*, Worksheet p. 13	• *Words to Own*, Worksheet p. 12 • *Daily Oral Grammar,* Transparency 12
• **The Tide Rises, the Tide Falls** (p. 176) • **The Cross of Snow** (p. 178) Henry Wadsworth Longfellow	• *Graphic Organizers for Active Reading,* Worksheets pp. 14, 15 • *Literary Elements:* Transparency 7 Worksheet p. 22	• *Words to Own*, Worksheet p. 12 • *Daily Oral Grammar,* Transparency 13
from **Snow-Bound: A Winter Idyll** (p. 182) John Greenleaf Whittier	• *Graphic Organizers for Active Reading*, Worksheet p. 16	• *Words to Own*, Worksheet p. 12 • *Daily Oral Grammar,* Transparency 14
• **The Chambered Nautilus** (p. 188) • **Old Ironsides** (p. 190) Oliver Wendell Holmes	• *Graphic Organizers for Active Reading*, Worksheet p. 17	• *Words to Own*, Worksheet p. 12 • *Daily Oral Grammar,* Transparency 15
The American Language: "Noah's Ark": Webster's Dictionary (p. 195) Gary Q. Arpin		
Writer's Workshop: Analyzing a Literary Work (p. 198)		
Language Workshop: Inserting Modifiers (p. 201)		• *Workshop Resources*, p. 49 • *Language Workshop CD-ROM,* Inserting Modifiers
Learning for Life: Environmental Concerns (p. 203)		

Other Resources for this Collection

- *Cross-Curricular Activities*, p. 4
- *Portfolio Management System*, Introduction to Portfolio Assessment, p. 1
- *Formal Assessment:* Literary Period Introduction Test, p. 30; Literary Period Test, p. 44; Literary Elements Test, p. 42
- *Test Generator*, Collection Test 💿

Writing	Listening and Speaking / Viewing and Representing	Assessment
• *Portfolio Management System*, Rubrics for Choices, p. 105	• *Audio CD Library*, Disc 5, Track 2 🎧 • *Portfolio Management System*, Rubrics for Choices, p. 105	• *Formal Assessment*, Selection Test, p. 32 • *Test Generator (One-Stop Planner CD-ROM)* 💿 • *Preparation for College Admission Exams*, p. 15
• *Portfolio Management System*, Rubrics for Choices, p. 107	• *Audio CD Library*, Disc 5, Track 3 🎧 • *Portfolio Management System*, Rubrics for Choices, p.107	• *Formal Assessment*, Selection Test, p. 34 • *Test Generator (One-Stop Planner CD-ROM)* 💿
• *Portfolio Management System*, Rubrics for Choices, p. 108	• *Audio CD Library*, Disc 5, Tracks 4, 5 🎧 • *Viewing and Representing:* Fine Art Transparency 4 Worksheet p. 16 • *Portfolio Management System*, Rubrics for Choices, p. 108	• *Formal Assessment*, Selection Test, p. 35 • *Test Generator (One-Stop Planner CD-ROM)* 💿
• *Portfolio Management System*, Rubrics for Choices, p. 109	• *Audio CD Library*, Disc 5, Track 6 🎧 • *Portfolio Management System*, Rubrics for Choices, p. 109	• *Formal Assessment*, Selection Test, p. 37 • *Test Generator (One-Stop Planner CD-ROM)* 💿
• *Portfolio Management System*, Rubrics for Choices, p. 110	• *Audio CD Library*, Disc 5, Tracks 7, 8 🎧 • *Portfolio Management System*, Rubrics for Choices, p. 110	• *Formal Assessment*, Selection Test, p. 38 • *Test Generator (One-Stop Planner CD-ROM)* 💿
		• *Formal Assessment*, The American Language Test, p. 40

• *Workshop Resources*, p. 5
• *Writer's Workshop 2 CD-ROM*, Interpretation 💿
	• *Viewing and Representing*, HRW Multimedia Presentation Maker	• *Portfolio Management System*
		  • Prewriting, p. 112
		  • Peer Editing, p. 113
		  • Assessment Rubric, p. 114

		• *Portfolio Management System*, Rubrics, p. 115

📽 Transparency   💿 CD-ROM   📼 Video   🎧 Audio CD

Collection 4 The Transforming Imagination

Skills Focus

Selection or Feature	Reading Skills and Strategies	Elements of Literature and Language	Writing	Listening and Speaking	Viewing and Representing
Rip Van Winkle (p. 153) Washington Irving	Draw Inferences and Make Predictions, pp. 153, 166 Reading Inflated Diction, p. 166	Foreshadow, p. 153 Setting, pp. 153, 166 Plot, pp. 153, 167 Tone, p. 166 Satire, p. 166 Theme, p. 166 Character, p. 166 Stereotypes, p. 166 Conflict, p. 167	Write an Essay Explaining an Analogy, p. 167 Write an Essay Analyzing Conflict, p. 167 Write an Epilogue to the Story, p. 167 Write a Futuristic News Article, p. 167 Compile a Missing-Person Dossier on Rip Van Winkle, p. 167		Make a Before-and-After Chart, p. 166 Use a Chart to Track Plot Pattern, p. 167 Make a "Missing Person" Sketch of Rip Van Winkle, p. 167
Reading Skills and Strategies: Using Context Clues (p. 168)		Context Clues, p. 168			Make a Word Map, p. 168
Thanatopsis (p. 170) William Cullen Bryant	Track Your Response, pp. 170, 174 Read Inverted Sentences, p. 174	Tone, p. 174 Image, p. 174 Theme, p. 174 Inversion, p. 174	State the Theme of the Poem, p. 174 Write a Letter of Response from the Point of View of Another Author, p. 174		Create Illustrations for Two Poems, p. 174
The Tide Rises, the Tide Falls (p. 176) **The Cross of Snow** (p. 178) Henry Wadsworth Longfellow		Meter, pp. 176, 179–180 Foot, p. 176 Iamb, pp. 176, 180 Spondee, p. 176 Image, p. 178–179 Metaphor, pp. 178–179 Onomatopoeia, pp. 179–180 Personify, p. 179 Sonnet, p. 180 Rhyme Scheme, p. 180 Refrain, p. 180 Mood, p. 180 Tone, p. 180 Alliteration, p. 180	Write an Essay Comparing and Contrasting Two Poems, p. 180	Read a Poem Aloud to Determine the Melodies of Language, p. 180 Perform a Musical Setting for a Poem, p. 180	Write an Essay Evaluating the Appropriateness of Images Used to Illustrate a Poem, p. 180
from **Snow-Bound: A Winter Idyll** (p. 182) John Greenleaf Whittier	Recognize Allusions, p. 186	Idyll, p. 182 Imagery, p. 186 Mood, p. 186 Allusion, p. 186	Identify Sensory Images, p. 186 Analyze a Poem's Appeal, p. 186	Participate in a Class Discussion of the Message of a Poem, p. 186	
The Chambered Nautilus (p. 188) **Old Ironsides** (p. 190) Oliver Wendell Holmes	Paraphrase, p. 193	Extended Metaphor, pp. 188, 192–193 Apostrophe, p. 188 Metaphor, p. 192 Images, p. 192 Irony, p. 192 Symbols, p. 193	Freewrite on the Use of Metaphor and Symbol in a Poem, p. 193 Write an Essay Discussing the Message of a Poem, p. 193 Write an Objective, Scientific Description, p. 193 Research and Write a Historical Story for Children, p. 193 Write a Meditative Poem, p. 193		Create a Scientific Illustration, p. 193 Illustrate a Children's Story, p. 193
The American Language: "Noah's Ark": Webster's Dictionary (p. 195) Gary Q. Arpin		American Spelling, p. 195 Webster's Dictionary, p. 196	Write a Passage in Simplified but Consistent Spelling, p. 197 List Homophones and Homographs, p. 197 Identify Nonstandard Spellings, p. 197		
Writer's Workshop: Analyzing a Literary Work (p. 198)	Primary and Secondary Sources, p. 199		Write an Essay Analyzing Key Elements of a Literary Work, pp. 198–200		Use a Graphic Organizer, p. 199
Language Workshop: Inserting Modifiers (p. 201)		Base Sentence, p. 201	Combine Sentences Using Modifiers, p. 201		
Reading for Life: Reading Maps (p. 202)	Types of Maps, p. 202 Map Features, p. 202				Use a Map to Plan a Trip, p. 202
Learning for Life: Environmental Concerns (p. 203)			Write a Proposal for an Environmentally Friendly Business, p. 203 Create an Advertising Campaign, p. 203		Make a Video Documentary, p. 203

OBJECTIVES

1. Read literature of the Romantic period on the theme of "The Transforming Imagination"
2. Interpret literary elements used in the literature, with special emphasis on the sonnet
3. Apply a variety of reading strategies, using context clues to discover word meanings
4. Respond to the literature in a variety of modes
5. Learn and use new words
6. Collect ideas for a literary analysis

Irving
Bryant
Longfellow
Whittier
Holmes

A Blessing

Just off the highway to Rochester, Minnesota,
Twilight bounds softly forth on the grass,
And the eyes of those two Indian ponies
Darken with kindness.
They have come gladly out of the willows
To welcome my friend and me.
We step over the barbed wire into the pasture
Where they have been grazing all day, alone.
They ripple tensely, they can hardly contain their happiness
That we have come.
They bow shyly as wet swans. They love each other.
There is no loneliness like theirs.
At home once more,
They begin munching the young tufts of spring in the darkness.
I would like to hold the slenderer one in my arms,
For she has walked over to me
And nuzzled my left hand.
She is black and white,
Her mane falls wild on her forehead,
And the light breeze moves me to caress her long ear
That is delicate as the skin over a girl's wrist.
Suddenly I realize
That if I stepped out of my body I would break
Into blossom.

—James Wright (1927–1980)

Responding to the Poem

❓ In what ways does James Wright's imagination transform the experience of seeing the two horses? [Possible responses: He has an inner, spiritual experience; he personifies the horses in their happiness, loneliness, and love for each other; he responds deeply to nature as "a blessing," feeling he is about to burst into blossom; he transforms his experience into poetry.]

Writing Focus: Analyzing a Literary Work

The following **Work in Progress** assignments in this collection build to a culminating **Writer's Workshop** at the end of Collection 6.

• Rip Van Winkle	Track story's plot line (p. 167)
• Thanatopsis	State poem's theme (p. 174)
• The Tide Rises, the Tide Falls; The Cross of Snow	Note examples of melodic language (p. 180)
• Snow-Bound: A Winter Idyll	Note powerful images (p. 186)
• The Chambered Nautilus; Old Ironsides	Note uses of metaphor and symbol (p. 193)

Writer's Workshop: Expository Writing / Analyzing a Literary Work (p. 198)

OBJECTIVES

1. Read and interpret the story
2. Identify and evaluate setting
3. Draw inferences and make predictions
4. Analyze inflated diction
5. Express understanding through writing or art
6. Understand and use new words

SKILLS

Literary
- Identify and evaluate setting

Reading
- Draw inferences and make predictions
- Analyze inflated diction

Writing
- Collect ideas for a literary analysis
- Explain an analogy
- Analyze a conflict
- Write an epilogue to the story
- Write an article for a newspaper of the future
- Compile a character profile

Art
- Draw a sketch of a character

Vocabulary
- Use new words

Viewing/Representing
- Use an illustration to make a prediction about a story (ATE)
- Compare and contrast details in an illustration and a story (ATE)

Planning

- **Block Schedule**
  Block Scheduling Lesson Plans with Pacing Guide

- **Traditional Schedule**
  Lesson Plans Including Strategies for English-Language Learners

- **One-Stop Planner**
  CD-ROM with Test Generator

Washington Irving

(1783–1859)

Many people in Europe and England felt that America would never develop a literary voice of its own. But then came Washington Irving, the youngest and not-too-well-educated son of a pious hardware importer and his amiable wife. Irving, who was from New York City, had a genius for inventing comic fictional narrators. (In fact, he did not sign his real name to his work until he was over fifty.) The first of these narrators Irving called Jonathan Oldstyle, Gent.—a caricature of those British writers who could not accept the simple values of the new nation.

Irving's second invented narrator was called Diedrich Knickerbocker. Irving pretended that Knickerbocker was the author of a book called *A History of New York, from the Beginning of the World to the End of the Dutch Dynasty.* The mysterious Knickerbocker is supposed to have left the manuscript to his landlord in payment of back rent. This fake and comical history, in which the entire American past is ridiculed, established Washington Irving as the foremost New York satirist.

All this time Irving was enjoying the literary societies that were popular then in New York. His interest in law, which he practiced halfheartedly, was lukewarm. In 1815, he was sent off by his father to Liverpool, England, to look after the failing overseas branch of the family business. Irving found the business beyond repair, but he loved the British literary scene and stayed abroad for seventeen years. He was particularly attracted to the works of the Romantic novelist Sir Walter Scott (1771–1832), who gave Irving advice that was to make his reputation. Scott told the younger writer to read the German Romantics and find inspiration in folklore and legends.

Now Irving made the decision he had previously lacked the courage to make. He decided against putting further energy into business and

its "sordid, dusty, soul-killing way of life." He would now give himself entirely to writing. In 1817, Irving began to write the first drafts of stories based on German folk tales. These were narrated by yet another of Irving's comic voices, Geoffrey Crayon, and the stories were collected under the title *The Sketch Book* (1819–1820). This book carried Irving to the summit of international success.

Washington Irving (1809) by John Wesley Jarvis (1780–1840). Oil on wood panel (33″ × 26″).

Something about Irving's comic narrators touched a responsive chord in the American public. Even though Irving borrowed openly from a European past, he brought to his material a droll new voice, as inflated as a preacher's or politician's at one moment, self-mocking the next. It was a voice the new nation recognized as its own.

Irving gave his country its first international literary celebrity. This was a role Irving enjoyed exploiting to the fullest. He had always loved parties and people and praise. Now he had access to the literary circles of the world. It was a remarkable achievement for the unpromising child of a middle-class American family.

Irving never again wrote anything that matched the success of the two great comic tales in *The Sketch Book*. Today we remember Irving for Rip Van Winkle who slept through the American Revolution, and the Headless Horseman who plagued the lovelorn Yankee schoolteacher Ichabod Crane in the dreamy glen of Sleepy Hollow, in New York's lush Hudson Valley.

go.hrw.com
LE0 11-4

Resources: Print and Media

Before You Read

RIP VAN WINKLE

Make the Connection

What if, instead of moving along with the rest of the world, you were placed in suspended animation for twenty years? When you woke from your "nap," your expectations and views would be the same as they were when you fell "asleep." The world, however, would be very different.

Reading Skills and Strategies

Drawing Inferences and Making Predictions

An **inference** is an educated guess based on clues in the text and your own knowledge and experience. A **prediction** is a special type of inference—an educated guess about what will happen later. Some predictions may not turn out to be accurate, and adjusting them is an essential part of active reading. As you read "Rip Van Winkle," take notes in chart form. First, identify a clue that suggests or **foreshadows** what might happen further into the story. (Pictures that illustrate the story can be the basis of your predictions too.) Make a prediction based on the clue. Later, note what actually happens. Repeat this process as you read.

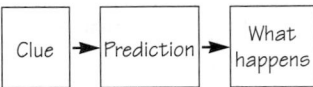

A good writer always surprises you. That is the pleasure of actively participating in a story—you are engaged with the writer in a game of wits.

Elements of Literature

Setting

Misty mountaintops, a mysterious forest, an old-fashioned village, a distant era—these are some details of **setting** that Irving uses in "Rip Van Winkle." Like many Romantic writers, Irving was fascinated by times past and by wild, natural landscapes. In this story it is setting that effects a magical change in the hero and sets the **plot** in motion.

> **S**etting is the physical, geographical, and historical environment in which a story takes place.
>
> *For more on Setting, see the Handbook of Literary Terms.*

Background

Even for its first readers in 1819, "Rip Van Winkle" was a story about times past. The story begins just before the Revolutionary War, which started in 1775—before Irving was even born. Irving draws on the history of the America he knew during his childhood, when George Washington was everyone's hero and the Democrats and Federalists were the young nation's two political parties.

"It was with some difficulty that he found the way to his own house." From *Rip Van Winkle* (New York: David McKay, 1921) illustrated by N. C. Wyeth (1882–1945). Oil on canvas (48″ × 38″).
Millport Conservancy and Museum.

153

Summary ▪ ▪

The narrator claims that the text is a manuscript by the scholar Diedrich Knickerbocker, who studied the Dutch history of New York. Knickerbocker relates the story of Rip Van Winkle, a congenial but lazy man who is loved by his fellow villagers but is in constant conflict with his overbearing wife. One day, on a ramble in the Catskill Mountains with his dog, Rip meets a mysterious little man in sixteenth-century Dutch garb who leads him to a remote glen, where the man and his companions bowl ninepins and drink liquor. Rip watches them, sneaks liquor from their keg, and falls asleep for twenty years. Returning to his village, he finds his house in ruins and the village tavern changed. The American Revolution has taken place, and his wife has died. (Freedom has been won on two fronts!) He moves in with his now-grown daughter and becomes a popular village eccentric. The story ends with a tongue-in-cheek note from Knickerbocker attesting to its veracity.

RESPONDING TO THE ART

N. C. Wyeth (1882–1945) illustrated many classics for young people by Mark Twain, Robert Louis Stevenson, Daniel Defoe, and others. (See also pp. 146, 147, and 155.)

Activity. Ask students to make a prediction about the story based on the illustration. [Possible response: It is about an old man's difficulties in returning home.]

Preteaching Vocabulary

Words to Own

Have students work in pairs, alternating as one student reads a Word to Own aloud and the partner pantomimes the word's meaning. Then have students choose the vocabulary word that best completes each phrase below.

1. an honest, [conscientious] cashier
2. the smiling, [amiable] friend
3. a quiet, [placid] surface
4. bent the [malleable] metal bar
5. the deep [torpor] of a hot summer afternoon
6. the [obsequious] servant bowed
7. to disagree [vehemently] and violently
8. he [reiterated] the same thing over and over
9. doubt the [fidelity] of an account
10. [scrupulous] in taking care of every detail

Resources ━━━━━

Viewing and Representing
Videocassette A, Segment 4
Available in English and Spanish. This segment explores the American interpretation of the Romantic journey. For full lesson plans and worksheets, see the *Visual Connections Teacher's Manual.*

Ⓐ Critical Thinking

Determining Author's Purpose

❷ The italicized opening of the story is a frame, purportedly explaining how the tale was found, and defending its credibility. What does it add to the story? [Since Knickerbocker is clearly an eccentric character of Irving's invention, the frame adds humorous touches of self-mockery.]

Ⓑ Vocabulary Note

Word Origins

The word *hobby* comes from "hobby-horse," or play horse—a child's favored toy or pastime—which is why Knickerbocker could "ride his hobby."

Ⓒ Elements of Literature

Irony

❷ Why might it be ironic to be imprinted on a Waterloo medal or a farthing? [Possible response: Both are worth very little. In addition, Napoleon Bonaparte's loss at the Battle of Waterloo is a famous symbol of defeat.]

Rip Van Winkle

A Posthumous Writing of Diedrich Knickerbocker

Washington Irving

Ⓐ *The following tale was found among the papers of the late Diedrich Knickerbocker, an old gentleman of New York, who was very curious in the Dutch history of the province, and the manners of the descendants from its primitive settlers. His historical researches, however, did not lie so much among books, as among men; for the former are lamentably scanty on his favorite topics; whereas he found the old burghers,[1] and still more, their wives, rich in that legendary lore so invaluable to true history. Whenever, therefore, he happened upon a genuine Dutch family, snugly shut up in its low roofed farmhouse, under a spreading sycamore, he looked upon it as a little clasped volume of black letter,[2] and studied it with the zeal of a bookworm.*

The result of all these researches was a history of the province, during the reign of the Dutch governors, which he published some years since. There have been various opinions as to the literary character of his work and, to tell the truth, it is not a whit better than it should be. Its chief Ⓒ *merit is its scrupulous accuracy, which indeed was a little questioned on its first appearance,*

but has since been completely established; and it is now admitted into all historical collections as a book of unquestionable authority.

Ⓑ *The old gentleman died shortly after the publication of his work, and now that he is dead and gone, it cannot do much harm to his memory to say that his time might have been much better employed in weightier labors. He, however, was apt to ride his hobby his own way; and though it did now and then kick up the dust a little in the eyes of his neighbors, and grieve the spirit of some friends for whom he felt the truest deference and affection; yet his errors and follies are remembered "more in sorrow than in anger," and it begins to be suspected that he never intended to injure or offend. But however his memory may be appreciated by critics, it is still held dear by many folk whose good opinion is well worth having; particularly by certain biscuit bakers, who have gone so far as to imprint his likeness on their New Year cakes, and have thus given him a chance for immortality, almost equal to being stamped on a Waterloo[3] medal, or a Queen Anne's farthing.[4]*

1. **burghers:** citizens.
2. **black letter:** ornamental printing font, now called Old English or Gothic.

3. **Waterloo:** Belgian town where the British and their allies finally defeated Napoleon I, emperor of France, on June 18, 1815.
4. **farthing:** former British coin worth one fourth of a British penny.

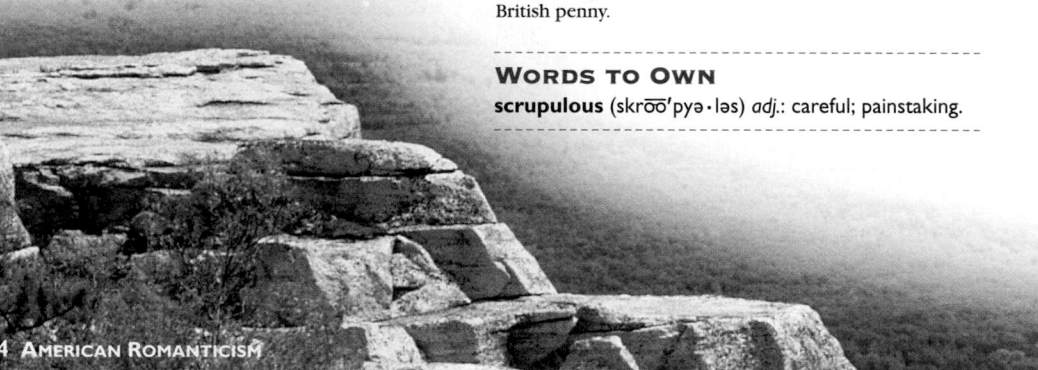

WORDS TO OWN
scrupulous (skrōō′pyə·ləs) *adj.*: careful; painstaking.

154 AMERICAN ROMANTICISM

Reaching All Students

Struggling Readers
Making Predictions was introduced on p. 153. For a lesson tied to this story that teaches students to make predictions by using a strategy called Anticipation Guide, see the *Reading Skills and Strategies* binder:
• MiniRead Skill Lesson, p. 83
• Selection Skill Lesson, p. 89

English Language Learners
As a Romantic, Irving presents the Catskill Mountains as both beautiful and mysterious. Use maps of the United States and New York to help students locate the Hudson River and the Catskill region. Point out the villages of Catskill and Palenville at the foot of Kaaterskill Clove, both of which claim to be Rip's "ancient village." Use photographs of the area to help students visualize the physical setting.

Advanced Learners
Encourage students to keep track of how Irving interweaves a realistic depiction of a Dutch colonial village and a fantastical folktale plot. Discuss why both of these elements might have struck a responsive chord with readers in a nation that had recently won independence. [Possible response: Americans sought to take stock of their historical origins and to understand the enormous change that they had experienced "overnight."]

Whoever has made a voyage up the Hudson must remember the Kaatskill[5] Mountains. They are a dismembered branch of the great Appalachian family, and are seen away to the west of the river swelling up to noble height and lording it over the surrounding country. Every change of season, every change of weather, indeed every hour of the day, produces some change in the magical hues and shapes of these mountains, and they are regarded by all the good wives far and near as perfect barometers. When the weather is fair and settled they are clothed in blue and purple, and print their bold outlines on the clear evening sky; but sometimes, when the rest of the landscape is cloudless, they will gather a hood of gray vapors about their summits, which, in the last rays of the setting sun, will glow and light up like a crown of glory.

At the foot of these fairy mountains the voyager may have descried the light smoke curling up from a village, whose shingle roofs gleam among the trees, just where the blue tints of the upland melt away into the fresh green of the nearer landscape. It is a little village of great antiquity, having been founded by some of the Dutch colonists in the early times of the province, just about the beginning of the government of the good Peter Stuyvesant[6] (may he rest in peace!), and there were some of the houses of the original settlers standing within a few years; built of small yellow bricks brought from Holland, having latticed windows and gable fronts, surmounted with weathercocks.

In that same village, and in one of these very houses (which to tell the precise truth was sadly timeworn and weather-beaten) there lived many years since, while the country was yet a province

of Great Britain, a simple good-natured fellow of the name of Rip Van Winkle. He was a descendant of the Van Winkles who figured so gallantly in the chivalrous days of Peter Stuyvesant, and accompanied him to the siege of Fort Christina.[7] He inherited, however, but little of the martial character of his ancestors. I have observed that he was a simple good-natured man; he was moreover a kind neighbor, and an obedient, henpecked husband. Indeed to the latter circumstance might be owing that meekness of spirit which gained him such universal popularity; for those men are most apt to be obsequious and conciliating abroad, who are under the discipline of shrews at home. Their tempers doubtless are rendered pliant and malleable in the fiery furnace of domestic tribulation, and a curtain lecture[8] is worth all the sermons in the world for teaching the virtues of patience and long-suffering. A termagant[9] wife may therefore in some respects be considered a tolerable blessing—and if so, Rip Van Winkle was thrice blessed.

Certain it is that he was a great favorite among all the good wives of the village, who as usual with the amiable sex, took his part in all family squabbles, and never failed, whenever they talked those matters over in their evening gossipings, to lay all the blame on Dame[10] Van Winkle. The

Title page of *Rip Van Winkle* (1921) illustrated by N. C. Wyeth. Lithograph.

---

7. Fort Christina: Delaware's first permanent settlement; founded by Swedish colonists on the Delaware River and captured by Stuyvesant from the Swedes in 1655. Present-day site of Wilmington, Delaware.
8. curtain lecture: scolding delivered by a wife to her husband, from behind the curtains of an old-fashioned bed.
9. termagant (tur′mə·gənt): abusive; scolding.
10. Dame: title formerly used for the woman in charge of a household.

WORDS TO OWN

obsequious (əb·sē′kwē·əs) *adj.*: overly obedient; submissive.
malleable (mal′ē·ə·bəl) *adj.*: capable of being shaped.
amiable (ā′mē·ə·bəl) *adj.*: agreeable; likable.

(footnotes, left column)

5. Kaatskill: original Dutch spelling of *Catskill.*
6. Peter Stuyvesant (stī′və·sənt): last Dutch governor of New Netherland (1647–1664), a Dutch colony in America. Irving is being ironic here. Stuyvesant was unpopular with the Dutch colonists, who considered him intolerant and harsh.

⓭ Reading Skills and Strategies

Drawing Inferences and Making Predictions

❓ What might the early, detailed description of the mountains suggest about their role in the story? [Possible response: A character in the story lives in these mountains or will have an adventure in them.]

ⓔ Elements of Literature

Setting

To help students appreciate the long descriptive paragraphs which introduce the story, have them read each paragraph aloud. Ask students to imagine the story as a movie, with each paragraph zooming in closer than the one before it: first an establishing shot of the Catskill Mountains, then a view of the village, then a close shot of the Van Winkle house, then a closeup of Rip.

ⓕ Elements of Literature

Stereotype

❓ What words and phrases help build a comically stereotyped portrait of Rip and his wife? [Possible responses: Rip—"simple good-natured man"; "a kind neighbor"; "obedient, henpecked husband"; his wife—"shrews"; "termagant."]

ⓖ Elements of Literature

Irony

❓ How is the word *amiable* ironic in this context? [The women are taking sides in the private affairs of another family instead of minding their own business and their blame of Dame Van Winkle hardly seems amiable.]

Using Students' Strengths

Verbal Learners

Ask students to rewrite their favorite passages to make them more accessible to a present-day audience. Encourage them to pinpoint passages where Irving's nineteenth-century style remains appealing and could be kept as is, in addition to passages that might be substantially altered or omitted.

Naturalist Learners

Encourage students to reread passages that describe the Catskill Mountains and their flora, fauna, weather, and topography. Some students may wish to sketch their impressions of that region based on the descriptions, perhaps aided by such field guides as *The Walking News Guide to the Catskills* or *The Audubon Society Field Guide to North American Birds*. (Remember Rip's gun is called a "fowling piece.")

Visual Learners

Suggest that students keep visualizing the unfolding tale as a movie (either live-action or animated). They may wish to clarify their understanding of the plot and characters by keeping a shot sequence list or drawing a storyboard, as might be done for a film production.

children of the village too would shout with joy whenever he approached. He assisted at their sports, made their playthings, taught them to fly kites and shoot marbles, and told them long stories of ghosts, witches, and Indians. Whenever he went dodging about the village he was sur- Ⓐ rounded by a troop of them hanging on his skirts, clambering on his back and playing a thousand tricks on him with impunity; and not a dog would bark at him throughout the neighborhood.

The great error in Rip's composition was an insuperable aversion to all kinds of profitable labor. It could not be from the want of assiduity[11] or perseverance; for he would sit on a wet rock, with a rod as long and heavy as a Tartar's lance,[12] and fish all day without a murmur, even though he should not be encouraged by a single nibble. He would carry a fowling piece[13] on his shoulder for hours Ⓑ together, trudging through woods, and swamps and up hill and down dale, to shoot a few squirrels or wild pigeons; he would never refuse to assist a neighbor even in the roughest toil, and was a foremost man at all country frolics for husking Indian corn, or building stone fences; the women of the village too used to employ him to run their errands and to do such little odd jobs as their less obliging husbands would not do for them—in a word Rip was ready to attend to anybody's business but his own; but as to doing family duty, and keeping his farm in order, he found it impossible.

In fact he declared it was of no use to work on his farm; it was the most pestilent little piece of ground in the whole country; everything about it went wrong and would go wrong in spite of him. His fences were continually falling to pieces; his cow would either go astray or get among the cabbages; weeds were sure to grow quicker in his fields than anywhere else; the rain always made a point of setting in just as he had some outdoor work to do. So that though his patrimonial estate had dwindled away under his management, acre by acre until there was little more left than a mere

11. **assiduity** (as'ə·dyoo̅'ə·tē): close and continuous application of effort.
12. **Tartar's lance:** Tartars, now usually spelled Tatars, are a Turkic-speaking people of Europe and Asia. When they invaded China and eastern Europe in the thirteenth century, each Tatar cavalryman carried a battle-ax, a sword, and a twelve-foot lance.
13. **fowling piece:** shotgun used in hunting wild birds.

patch of Indian corn and potatoes, yet it was the worst-conditioned farm in the neighborhood.

His children too were as ragged and wild as if they belonged to nobody. His son Rip, an urchin begotten in his own likeness, promised to inherit the habits with the old clothes of his father. He was generally seen trooping like a colt at his mother's heels, equipped in a pair of his father's castoff galligaskins,[14] which he had much ado to hold up with one hand, as a fine lady does her train in bad weather.

Rip Van Winkle, however, was one of those happy mortals of foolish, well-oiled dispositions, who take the world easy, eat white bread or brown, whichever can be got with least thought Ⓒ or trouble, and would rather starve on a penny than work for a pound. If left to himself, he would have whistled life away in perfect contentment, but his wife kept continually dinning in his ears about his idleness, his carelessness, and the ruin he was bringing on his family. Morning, noon, and night, her tongue was incessantly going, and everything he said or did was sure to produce a torrent of household eloquence. Rip had but one way of replying to all lectures of the kind, and that by frequent use had grown into a habit. He shrugged his shoulders, shook his head, cast up Ⓓ his eyes, but said nothing. This, however, always provoked a fresh volley from his wife, so that he was fain to draw off his forces and take to the outside of the house—the only side which in truth belongs to a henpecked husband.

Rip's sole domestic adherent was his dog Wolf who was as much henpecked as his master, for Dame Van Winkle regarded them as companions in idleness, and even looked upon Wolf with an evil eye as the cause of his master's going so often astray. True it is, in all points of spirit befitting an honorable dog, he was as courageous an animal as ever scoured the woods—but what courage can withstand the ever-during and all-besetting[15] terrors of a woman's tongue? The moment Wolf entered the house his crest fell, his tail drooped to the ground or curled between his legs, he sneaked about with a gallows air,[16] casting many a

14. **galligaskins** (gal'i·gas'kinz): loose, baggy pants.
15. **ever-during and all-besetting:** everlasting and continually attacking.
16. **with a gallows air:** like someone condemned to be hanged.

Making the Connections

Cross-Cultural Connections: Heroic Traditions

Most cultures have heroic traditions that share strikingly similar features. Traditional heroes possess remarkable strength, courage, and resourcefulness, which differentiate them from the average person. They often unify and empower their people and offer them hope while providing a role model. To do so, most heroes of legend and popular fiction can be seen to pass through six distinct stages of life called the heroic cycle: a mysterious yet noble birth, a youth fated for greatness, a challenge usually presented in the form of a quest, a long, arduous journey home, the collection of a reward, and a successful romantic relationship. As students read this tale, ask them to notice how Irving plays with these heroic conventions.

sidelong glance at Dame Van Winkle, and at the least flourish of a broomstick or ladle he would fly to the door with yelping precipitation.[17]

Times grew worse and worse with Rip Van Winkle as years of matrimony rolled on; a tart temper never mellows with age, and a sharp tongue is the only edged tool that grows keener with constant use. For a long while he used to console himself when driven from home, by frequenting a kind of perpetual club of the sages, philosophers, and other idle personages of the village which held its sessions on a bench before a small inn, designated by a rubicund portrait of his majesty George the Third. Here they used to sit in the shade, through a long lazy summer's day, talking listlessly over village gossip, or telling endless sleepy stories about nothing. But it would have been worth any statesman's money to have heard the profound discussions that sometimes took place, when by chance an old newspaper fell into their hands from some passing traveler. How solemnly they would listen to the contents as drawled out by Derrick Van Bummel the schoolmaster, a dapper, learned little man, who was not to be daunted by the most gigantic word in the dictionary; and how sagely they would deliberate upon public events some months after they had taken place.

The opinions of this junto[18] were completely controlled by Nicholaus Vedder, a patriarch of the village, and landlord of the inn, at the door of which he took his seat from morning till night, just moving sufficiently to avoid the sun and keep in the shade of a large tree; so that the neighbors could tell the hour by his movements as accurately as by a sundial. It is true he was rarely heard to speak, but smoked his pipe incessantly. His adherents, however (for every great man has his adherents), perfectly understood him and knew how to gather his opinions. When anything that was read or related displeased him, he was observed to smoke his pipe vehemently, and to send forth short, frequent, and angry puffs; but when pleased he would inhale the smoke slowly and tranquilly and emit it in light and placid clouds, and sometimes taking the pipe from his mouth

17. **precipitation:** haste; suddenness.
18. **junto** (jun'tō): council; group with a common purpose.

and letting the fragrant vapor curl about his nose, would gravely nod his head in token of perfect approbation.

From even this stronghold the unlucky Rip was at length routed by his termagant wife who would suddenly break in upon the tranquility of the assemblage and call the members all to naught; nor was that august personage Nicholaus Vedder himself sacred from the daring tongue of this terrible virago,[19] who charged him outright with encouraging her husband in habits of idleness.

Poor Rip was at last reduced almost to despair; and his only alternative to escape from the labor of the farm and the clamor of his wife, was to take gun in hand and stroll away into the woods. Here he would sometimes seat himself at the foot of a tree and share the contents of his wallet[20] with Wolf, with whom he sympathized as a fellow sufferer in persecution. "Poor Wolf," he would say, "thy mistress leads thee a dog's life of it, but never mind my lad, whilst I live thou shalt never want a friend to stand by thee!" Wolf would wag his tail, look wistfully in his master's face, and if dogs can feel pity I verily believe he reciprocated the sentiment with all his heart.

In a long ramble of the kind on a fine autumnal day, Rip had unconsciously scrambled to one of the highest parts of the Kaatskill Mountains. He was after his favorite sport of squirrel shooting and the still solitudes had echoed and reechoed with the reports of his gun. Panting and fatigued he threw himself, late in the afternoon, on a green knoll, covered with mountain herbage, that crowned the brow of a precipice. From an opening between the trees he could overlook all the lower country for many a mile of rich woodland. He saw at a distance the lordly Hudson, far, far below him, moving on its silent but majestic course, with the reflection of a purple cloud, or the sail of a lagging bark[21] here and there sleeping on its glassy bosom, and at last losing itself in the blue highlands.

19. **virago** (vi·rä'gō): quarrelsome, scolding woman.
20. **wallet:** knapsack.
21. **lagging bark:** slow-moving boat.

WORDS TO OWN

vehemently (vē'ə·mənt·le) *adv.:* emphatically.
placid (plas'id) *adj.:* calm; quiet.

E Elements of Literature
Setting
Have students describe in their own words the setting of the place where Rip consoles himself. [a bench outside a small village inn under a portrait of the British King George]

F Historical Connections
Dictionaries
Dictionaries were a hot topic in Irving's day. Samuel Johnson had published his great *A Dictionary of the English Language in England* in 1755. Noah Webster had published his first dictionary in 1806. "Rip Van Winkle" appeared ten years later.

G Struggling Readers
Finding Details
Have students reread the description of Vedder's pipe-smoking in order to discover how Vedder communicates. [When he disagrees with what has been said, he takes short, angry puffs; when he agrees, he inhales and exhales the smoke slowly and tranquilly.]

H Elements of Literature
Setting
? What change of setting occurs in this passage? [The village gives way to the mountains; society gives way to solitude.] Discuss the effects this shift of scene seems to have on Rip's spirits. (See the last paragraph on p. 157.) [Rip's domestic troubles are dwarfed by the beauty and majesty of nature. He now seems calm and contemplative.] For the Romantics, nature offered a chance to escape the conventions and doldrums of the town, to reinvigorate oneself, and perhaps to encounter the sublime. The sheer immensity of the natural world is evident in the paintings of the Hudson River School, in which human figures are either absent or dwarfed by vast panoramas.

Getting Students Involved

Writing Dialogue
Ask students to work in pairs to compose a dialogue for the men who spend their time philosophizing and discussing the newspaper in front of Nicholaus Vedder's inn. Tell them to note Irving's slightly satirical description of Vedder and the schoolmaster Derrick Van Bummel. Remind students to use quotation marks and to change paragraphs for each speaker. Invite willing students to enact or read aloud their dialogues.

Expressive Reading
Have pairs of students select a favorite passage from the story to divide between them and read aloud to one another. Ask students to practice individually at first, determining where they will pause for suspense, raise or lower their voices, or slow down for emphasis. As partners read to each other, have the listener note three specific lines that were read with special effectiveness and why.

Rip Chased from Home by His Wife (detail) (1880) by Albertus Del Orient Browere (1814–1887). Oil on canvas (36″ × 50″).

Courtesy of the Shelburne Museum, Shelburne, Vermont. Photograph by Ken Burris.

RESPONDING TO THE ART

Albertus Del Orient Browere (1814–1887) created large paintings to illustrate various scenes from "Rip Van Winkle." Details from two of them appear on pp. 158 and 161.

Activity. Have students create a two-column table in which they compare and contrast details in Browere's depiction of the incident and in Irving's description.

A Reading Skills and Strategies

Drawing Inferences and Making Predictions

? How might Rip's wife act when he returns home? [Possible response: She will be angry, yell, throw pans at him.]

B Critical Thinking

Determining Author's Purpose

? Why do you think Irving highlights Wolf's distress and Rip's sense of apprehension at the stranger's approach? [Possible response: Irving wishes to foreshadow the malevolent or supernatural power that the stranger will exercise in the story.]

C Elements of Literature

Character

? What aspect of Rip's character does this passage affirm? [It affirms his cheerful willingness to tend to the responsibilities of others rather than his own.] **Do you think this character trait might constitute a kind of "fatal flaw" in Rip as a hero?** [Possible responses: Yes, his good-natured complacency will get him into trouble. No, his generosity is admirable and will be rewarded.]

A On the other side he looked down into a deep mountain glen, wild, lonely, and shagged, the bottom filled with fragments from the impending cliffs and scarcely lighted by the reflected rays of the setting sun. For some time Rip lay musing on this scene, evening was gradually advancing, the mountains began to throw their long blue shadows over the valleys, he saw that it would be dark, long before he could reach the village, and he heaved a heavy sigh when he thought of encountering the terrors of Dame Van Winkle.

B As he was about to descend he heard a voice from a distance hallooing "Rip Van Winkle! Rip Van Winkle!" He looked around, but could see nothing but a crow winging its solitary flight across the mountain. He thought his fancy must have deceived him and turned again to descend, when he heard the same cry ring through the still evening air: "Rip Van Winkle! Rip Van Winkle!"— at the same time Wolf bristled up his back and giving a low growl, skulked to his master's side, looking fearfully down into the glen. Rip now felt a vague apprehension stealing over him; he looked anxiously in the same direction and perceived a strange figure slowly toiling up the rocks and bending under the weight of something he carried on his back.

C He was surprised to see any human being in this lonely and unfrequented place, but supposing it to be someone of the neighborhood in need of his assistance he hastened down to yield it.

On nearer approach he was still more surprised at the singularity of the stranger's appearance. He was a short, square-built old fellow, with thick bushy hair and a grizzled beard. His dress was of the antique Dutch fashion, a cloth jerkin[22] strapped round the waist, several pair of breeches, the outer one of ample volume decorated with rows of buttons down the sides and bunches at the knees. He bore on his shoulder a stout keg that seemed full of liquor, and made signs for Rip to approach and assist him with the load. Though rather shy and distrustful of this new acquaintance Rip complied with his usual alacrity, and mutually relieving each other they clambered up a narrow gully apparently the dry

22. **jerkin** (jur′kin): sleeveless jacket.

158 AMERICAN ROMANTICISM

Crossing the Curriculum

Art

Ask some students to draw or paint Rip before his long sleep and others to portray him after he wakes up. Have volunteers pair these pictures for display in the classroom. Interested students might want to study the early Romantic painter John Quidor (1801–1881), who became fascinated by the character of Rip Van Winkle and often drew imaginative but slightly grotesque depictions of him.

T158

bed of a mountain torrent. As they ascended, Rip every now and then heard long rolling peals like distant thunder, that seemed to issue out of a deep ravine or rather cleft between lofty rocks, toward which their rugged path conducted. He paused for an instant, but supposing it to be the muttering of one of those transient thundershowers which often take place in mountain heights, he proceeded. Passing through the ravine they came to a hollow like a small amphitheater, surrounded by perpendicular precipices, over the brinks of which impending trees shot their branches, so that you only caught glimpses of the azure sky and the bright evening cloud. During the whole time Rip and his companion had labored on in silence, for though the former marveled greatly what could be the object of carrying a keg of liquor up this wild mountain, yet there was something strange and incomprehensible about the unknown, that inspired awe and checked familiarity.

On entering the amphitheater new objects of wonder presented themselves. On a level spot in the center was a company of odd-looking personages playing at ninepins.[23] They were dressed in a quaint, outlandish fashion—some wore short doublets,[24] others jerkins with long knives in their belts and most of them had enormous breeches of similar style with that of the guide's. Their visages too were peculiar. One had a large head, broad face, and small piggish eyes. The face of another seemed to consist entirely of nose, and was surmounted by a white sugarloaf hat, set off with a little red cock's tail. They all had beards of various shapes and colors. There was one who seemed to be the commander. He was a stout old gentleman, with a weather-beaten countenance. He wore a laced doublet, broad belt and hanger,[25] high-crowned hat and feather, red stockings, and high-heeled shoes with roses[26] in them. The whole group reminded Rip of the figures in an old Flemish painting, in the parlor of Dominie Van Schaick the village parson, and which had been brought over from Holland at the time of the settlement.

What seemed particularly odd to Rip was, that though these folks were evidently amusing them-

selves, yet they maintained the gravest faces, the most mysterious silence, and were, withal, the most melancholy party of pleasure he had ever witnessed. Nothing interrupted the stillness of the scene, but the noise of the balls, which, whenever they were rolled, echoed along the mountains like rumbling peals of thunder.

As Rip and his companion approached them they suddenly desisted from their play and stared at him with such fixed statuelike gaze, and such strange uncouth, lackluster countenances, that his heart turned within him, and his knees smote together. His companion now emptied the contents of the keg into large flagons[27] and made signs to him to wait upon the company. He obeyed with fear and trembling; they quaffed the liquor in profound silence and then returned to their game.

By degrees Rip's awe and apprehension subsided. He even ventured, when no eye was fixed upon him, to taste the beverage, which he found had much of the flavor of excellent Hollands.[28] He was naturally a thirsty soul and was soon tempted to repeat the draft. One taste provoked another, and he reiterated his visits to the flagon so often that at length his senses were overpowered, his eyes swam in his head—his head gradually declined and he fell into a deep sleep.

On awaking he found himself on the green knoll from whence he had first seen the old man of the glen. He rubbed his eyes—it was a bright, sunny morning. The birds were hopping and twittering among the bushes, and the eagle was wheeling aloft and breasting the pure mountain breeze. "Surely," thought Rip, "I have not slept here all night." He recalled the occurrences before he fell asleep. The strange man with a keg of liquor—the mountain ravine—the wild retreat among the rocks—the woebegone party at ninepins—the flagon—"ah! that flagon! that wicked flagon!" thought Rip—"what excuse shall I make to Dame Van Winkle?"

He looked round for his gun, but in place of the clean well-oiled fowling piece he found an old

23. **ninepins:** a bowling game.
24. **doublets:** closefitting jackets.
25. **hanger:** short, curved sword hung from the belt.
26. **roses:** ornaments shaped like roses; often called rosettes.

27. **flagons:** bottlelike containers for liquids.
28. **Hollands:** Dutch gin.

WORDS TO OWN
reiterated (rē·it'ə·rāt'id) v.: repeated.

Making the Connections

Cultural Connections:
Scenes from a Marriage
Dame Van Winkle seems to dominate Rip and their family—at least as Rip and the narrator see it. Form heterogeneous student groups to discuss how family members relate to one another in various cultural traditions. Some topics to explore include how household chores are divided up, which adult handles family finances, who has the final word in rules for children to follow, and how major decisions are made within families. Students might also discuss the roles humor and stereotyping play in representing—and sometimes misrepresenting—family relationships. For instance, is a henpecked husband always powerless, and is a domineering wife always powerful, and vice versa?

D Elements of Literature
Setting
❓ Irving's descriptions of setting on this page are simultaneously mysterious, ominous, and comical. Have students take note of the strange and shadowy amphitheater, and the foreboding roar of thunder—and then ask them to read on to find the comic twist that Irving gives to these descriptions. What does Rip find in the amphitheater? [mysterious little men getting drunk and bowling] What does the thunder turn out to be? [the noise of the bowling balls]

E Reading Skills and Strategies
Using Context Clues
Have students use context clues to guess the meaning of *azure*. [blue] Ask students to specify which clues they used. ["glimpses of the . . . sky" and "bright evening cloud"]

F Reading Skills and Strategies

Drawing Inferences and Making Predictions
❓ What do you infer or predict about the bowlers? [Possible responses: They are friends of Rip's companion; they are leprechauns, or other supernatural beings; they are dangerous.]

G Struggling Readers
Paraphrasing
Ask volunteers to paraphrase the crucial events in this scene. [Rip gets drunk on the mysterious liquor and falls asleep. Waking up, he is surprised to see that it is morning and worries about what he will say to his wife.]

H Elements of Literature
Irony
Although he places his protagonist in a grand landscape, among mysterious, supernatural beings, Irving plays with Romantic and heroic conventions. Rip's quest in the woods is to help carry a keg of liquor and his achievement is to wake up after a night out drinking, wondering how he will explain it to his wife—a most unheroic predicament.

A Reading Skills and Strategies

Drawing Inferences and Making Predictions

As students proceed, encourage them to keep revising their inferences and predictions in light of new details, such as the rusting of the firelock, the absence of Wolf, and the creaking in Rip's joints.

B Critical Thinking

Hypothesizing

? What might have happened to close off the entrance to the amphitheater? [Possible responses: Erosion, landslides, and other natural phenomena might have closed it off; or, some supernatural force has made the amphitheater appear and disappear.]

C Elements of Literature

Setting

? What is familiar about this setting and what is unfamiliar about it? [It is Rip's old village, but it is larger and there are strange names over the doors. The people are new to Rip and the style of their clothing is unfamiliar.]

D Struggling Readers

Finding the Main Idea

? What two possibilities does Rip consider to explain the strange new scene he faces? [He wonders if he and the world are bewitched, or if his mind is still being influenced by the drink.]

---

firelock[29] lying by him, the barrel encrusted with rust; the lock falling off and the stock[30] worm-eaten. He now suspected that the grave roysters of the mountain had put a trick upon him, and having dosed him with liquor, had robbed him of his gun. Wolf too had disappeared, but he might have strayed away after a squirrel or partridge. He **A** whistled after him and shouted his name—but all in vain; the echoes repeated his whistle and shout, but no dog was to be seen.

He determined to revisit the scene of the last evening's gambol, and if he met with any of the party, to demand his dog and gun. As he arose to walk he found himself stiff in the joints and wanting in his usual activity. "These mountain beds do not agree with me," thought Rip, "and if this frolic should lay me up with a fit of the rheumatism, I shall have a blessed time with Dame Van Winkle." With some difficulty he got down into the glen; he found the gully up which he and his companion had ascended the preceding evening, but to his astonishment a mountain stream was now foaming down it; leaping from rock to rock, and filling the glen with babbling murmurs. He, however, made shift to scramble up its sides working his toilsome way through thickets of birch, sassafras, and witch hazel, and sometimes tripped up or entangled by the wild grapevines that twisted their coils and tendrils from tree to tree, and spread a kind of network in his path.

B At length he reached to where the ravine had opened through the cliffs, to the amphitheater—but no traces of such opening remained. The rocks presented a high impenetrable wall over which the torrent came tumbling in a sheet of feathery foam, and fell into a broad deep basin black from the shadows of the surrounding forest. Here then poor Rip was brought to a stand. He again called and whistled after his dog—he was only answered by the cawing of a flock of idle

29. **firelock:** early type of gun.
30. **stock:** wooden handle attached to metal gun barrel.

crows, sporting high in air about a dry tree that overhung a sunny precipice; and who, secure in their elevation seemed to look down and scoff at the poor man's perplexities.

What was to be done? The morning was passing away and Rip felt famished for want of his breakfast. He grieved to give up his dog and gun; he dreaded to meet his wife; but it would not do to starve among the mountains. He shook his head, shouldered the rusty firelock, and with a heart full of trouble and anxiety, turned his steps homeward.

As he approached the village he met a number of people, but none whom he knew, which somewhat surprised him, for he had thought himself acquainted with everyone in the country round. Their dress too was of a different fashion from that to which he was accustomed. They all stared at him with equal marks of surprise, and whenever they cast their eyes upon him, invariably stroked their chins. The constant recurrence of **C** this gesture induced Rip involuntarily to do the same, when to his astonishment he found his beard had grown a foot long!

He had now entered the skirts of the village. A troop of strange children ran at his heels, hooting after him and pointing at his gray beard. The dogs too, not one of which he recognized for an old acquaintance, barked at him as he passed. The very village was altered—it was larger and more populous. There were rows of houses which he had never seen before, and those which had been his familiar haunts had disappeared. Strange names were over the doors—strange faces at the windows—everything was strange. His mind now misgave him; he began to doubt whether both he and the world around him were not bewitched. Surely this was his native village which he had left but the day before. There stood the Kaatskill Mountains—there ran the silver Hudson at a dis-**D** tance—there was every hill and dale precisely as it had always been—Rip was sorely perplexed— "That flagon last night," thought he, "has addled my poor head sadly!"

It was with some difficulty that he found the way to his own house, which he approached with silent awe, expecting every moment to hear the

160 AMERICAN ROMANTICISM

Taking a Second Look

Review: Analyzing Text Structures: Compare and Contrast

Remind students that *comparing* means "seeing similarities" and *contrasting* means "seeing differences." Comparison and contrast is used to distinguish related objects or ideas by finding their similarities and differences. The reader looks for "points of comparison," or characteristics both have to see how they are alike or different.

Activity

Have students construct compare/contrast charts like the following, to show how Rip and his environment become different and remain similar during his twenty-year sleep. Then, have students construct a similar chart for similarities and differences between themselves and their world today, and themselves and their world ten years ago.

	Same	Different
Rip His Family His Village His Society		

Rip Van Winkle Asleep (detail) (1880) by Albertus Del Orient Browere (1814–1887). Oil on canvas.

RESPONDING TO THE ART

Albertus Del Orient Browere also painted the illustration on page 158.

Activity. Have students compare and contrast details in Browere's and Irving's descriptions of Rip asleep.

E Reading Skills and Strategies

Connecting with the Text

❓ To help students identify with Rip's feelings, ask them, "How would you feel if you woke up in a world you no longer knew and which no longer knew you?" [Possible responses: frightened, confused, curious, excited, lonely.]

F Elements of Literature

Setting

❓ How has the inn changed since Rip fell asleep? [It has become a hotel; the tree has been replaced by a flagpole flying the Stars and Stripes; the portrait of King George has been altered to represent George Washington.]

G Critical Thinking

Determining the Author's Purpose

❓ Why do you think Irving highlights this shift in the "character" of Rip's fellow villagers? What might he be saying about the American Revolution, and how might it relate to his Romantic ideals? [Possible responses: Irving wishes to satirize his contemporary post-revolutionary society, which he suggests may be too argumentative, rationalistic, and dogmatic. As a Romantic, he expresses nostalgia for the stability, calm, and natural beauty of the colonial village.]

shrill voice of Dame Van Winkle. He found the house gone to decay—the roof fallen in, the windows shattered, and the doors off the hinges. A half-starved dog that looked like Wolf was skulking about it. Rip called him by name but the cur snarled, showed his teeth, and passed on. This was an unkind cut indeed—"My very dog," sighed poor Rip, "has forgotten me!"

He entered the house, which, to tell the truth, Dame Van Winkle had always kept in neat order. It was empty, forlorn, and apparently abandoned. This desolateness overcame all his connubial[31] fears—he called loudly for his wife and children—the lonely chambers rung for a moment with his voice, and then all again was silence.

He now hurried forth and hastened to his old resort, the village inn—but it too was gone. A large, rickety wooden building stood in its place, with great gaping windows, some of them broken, and mended with old hats and petticoats, and over the door was printed "The Union Hotel, by Jonathan Doolittle." Instead of the great tree, that used to shelter the quiet little Dutch inn of yore, there now was reared a tall naked pole with something on top that looked like a red nightcap,[32] and from it was fluttering a flag on which was a singular assemblage of stars and stripes—all this was strange and incomprehensible. He recognized on the sign, however, the ruby face of King George under which he had smoked so many a peaceful pipe, but even this was singularly metamorphosed.[33] The red coat was changed for one of blue and buff; a sword was held in the hand instead of a scepter; the head was decorated with a cocked hat, and underneath was printed in large characters[34] GENERAL WASHINGTON.

There was as usual a crowd of folk about the door; but none that Rip recollected. The very character of people seemed changed. There was a busy, bustling disputatious tone about it, instead of the accustomed phlegm and drowsy tranquility.

---

32. red nightcap: "liberty cap"; worn as a symbol of independence during the French and American Revolutions.

33. metamorphosed (met′ə·môr′fōzd′): transformed.

34. characters: letters.

31. connubial (kə·nōō′bē·əl): related to marriage.

Skill Link

Recognizing Characteristics of Cultures

Tell students that they can learn about the eighteenth-century culture presented in the story by noticing such details as what material goods and technologies the characters use, what their clothing and dwellings are like, what occupations and recreations they pursue, and what their speech and behavior show about their values.

Have groups work together to brainstorm answers to the following questions:

1. What aspects of present-day American culture can you see in Rip's culture? [Possible responses: People still bowl, talk politics, own dogs.]

2. In what ways is Rip's America different from today's? [Possible responses: Fashions and political concerns are different today. Perhaps, also, people today are less politically involved. Would patrons in a bar be arguing something like citizens' rights today? (Maybe they would!)]

Explain to students that handbills were the eighteenth-century equivalent of leaflets and that this "bilious-looking fellow" is talking about the Revolutionary War. Bunker Hill was one of the first major battles to take place between Great Britain and the colonies in the year 1775, and the "heroes of Seventy-six" refer to the Minutemen who fought in that battle and others.

LITERATURE AND FOLKLORE

The motif of "enchanted sleep" can mean different things in different tales. Bruno Bettelheim, in *The Uses of Enchantment*, maintains that in the classic tale of "Sleeping Beauty," Sleeping Beauty's sleep is meant to symbolize the "period of quiescence, of contemplation" that precedes a period of personal growth. In the tale of Rip Van Winkle, however, it is American society itself, rather than the protagonist, which undergoes the most dramatic transformation during the period of enchanted slumber.

Have students collaborate on a short story about enchanted sleep. Students might generate their own ideas or use one of the following prompts: Sleeping Beauty awakens in modern times or in the age of cave dwellers; Han Solo, of the Star Wars movies, is released from frozen sleep to discover himself on Earth in the eighteenth century; a student who has fallen asleep while studying for a final exam awakens in the remote past or distant future.

He looked in vain for the sage Nicholaus Vedder with his broad face, double chin, and fair long pipe, uttering clouds of tobacco smoke instead of idle speeches. Or Van Bummel the schoolmaster doling forth the contents of an ancient newspaper. In place of these a lean bilious-looking fellow with his pockets full of handbills, was **A** haranguing vehemently about rights of citizens —elections—members of Congress—liberty— Bunker's hill—heroes of Seventy-six—and other

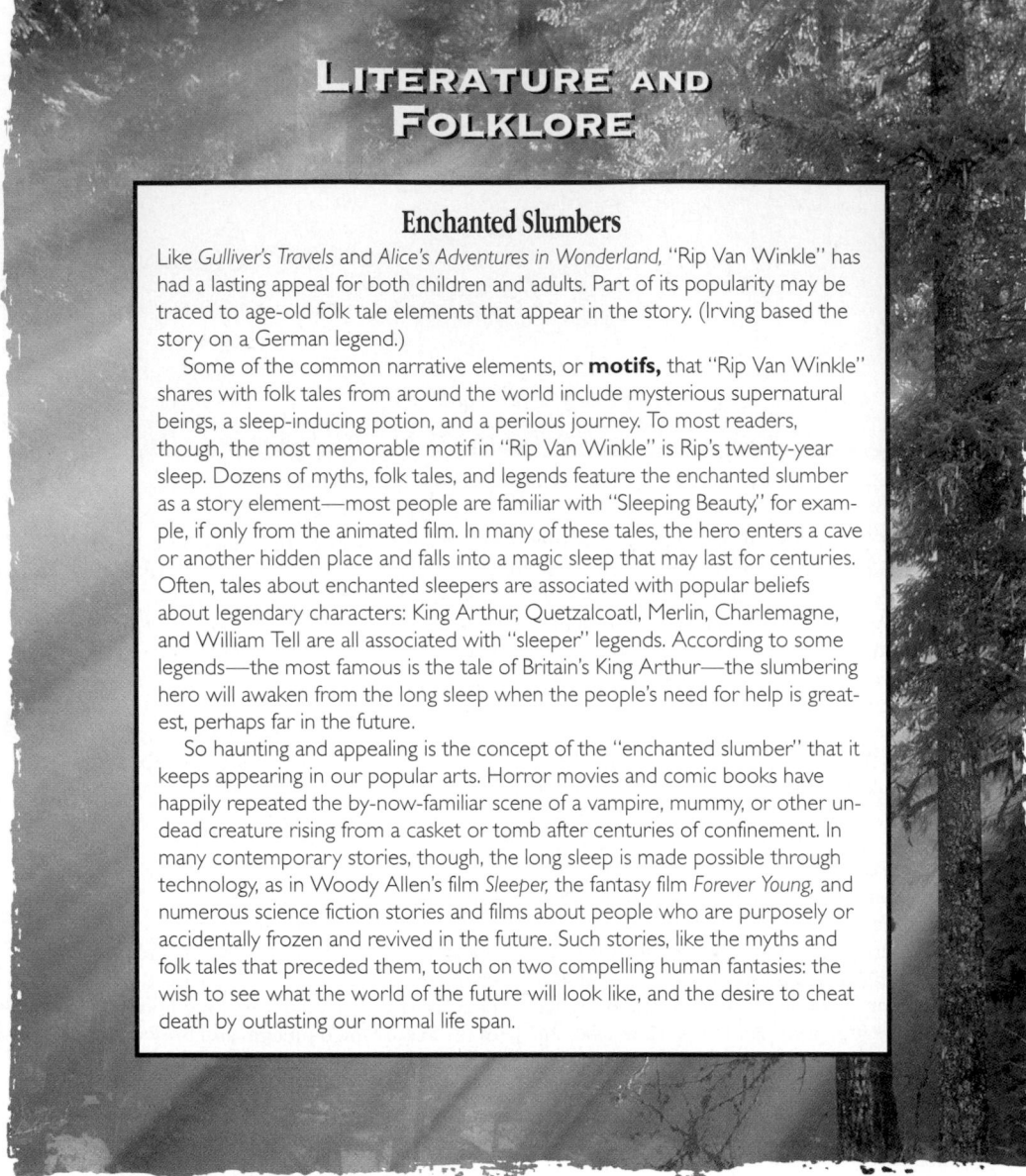

LITERATURE AND FOLKLORE

Enchanted Slumbers

Like *Gulliver's Travels* and *Alice's Adventures in Wonderland,* "Rip Van Winkle" has had a lasting appeal for both children and adults. Part of its popularity may be traced to age-old folk tale elements that appear in the story. (Irving based the story on a German legend.)

Some of the common narrative elements, or **motifs,** that "Rip Van Winkle" shares with folk tales from around the world include mysterious supernatural beings, a sleep-inducing potion, and a perilous journey. To most readers, though, the most memorable motif in "Rip Van Winkle" is Rip's twenty-year sleep. Dozens of myths, folk tales, and legends feature the enchanted slumber as a story element—most people are familiar with "Sleeping Beauty," for example, if only from the animated film. In many of these tales, the hero enters a cave or another hidden place and falls into a magic sleep that may last for centuries. Often, tales about enchanted sleepers are associated with popular beliefs about legendary characters: King Arthur, Quetzalcoatl, Merlin, Charlemagne, and William Tell are all associated with "sleeper" legends. According to some legends—the most famous is the tale of Britain's King Arthur—the slumbering hero will awaken from the long sleep when the people's need for help is greatest, perhaps far in the future.

So haunting and appealing is the concept of the "enchanted slumber" that it keeps appearing in our popular arts. Horror movies and comic books have happily repeated the by-now-familiar scene of a vampire, mummy, or other undead creature rising from a casket or tomb after centuries of confinement. In many contemporary stories, though, the long sleep is made possible through technology, as in Woody Allen's film *Sleeper,* the fantasy film *Forever Young,* and numerous science fiction stories and films about people who are purposely or accidentally frozen and revived in the future. Such stories, like the myths and folk tales that preceded them, touch on two compelling human fantasies: the wish to see what the world of the future will look like, and the desire to cheat death by outlasting our normal life span.

Professional Notes

Critical Comment:
Rip and the *Odyssey*

Like *Gulliver's Travels* and *Alice in Wonderland,* this story has perennial appeal to both children and adults. Part of its popularity may be traced to age-old folk tale elements: the perilous journey, the use of the supernatural, and disguise and recognition scenes.

Just as in Homer's *Odyssey,* this hero embarks on a journey which keeps him away from home for twenty years. When he returns, few people recognize him. The comic conclusion portrays an elaborate recognition scene and the hero's reintegration into society.

"Rip Van Winkle," of course, is essentially a light-hearted, comic narrative. Rip's "journey" is hardly a heroic expedition. Instead of the faithful wife Penelope, we have an ill-tempered shrew, whose passing from the scene is a great relief to the hero. When Rip returns, it is not as the long-awaited king, but as a fumbling, disoriented old man who must plead his case before suspicious townspeople.

A symbolic level to the story's meaning is unmistakable, however. Rip's domination by his wife parallels the country's colonial past; his awakening to a new life suggest the new condition of the United States. The happy ending hints at Irving's optimism about the future.

words which were a perfect Babylonish jargon[35] to the bewildered Van Winkle.

The appearance of Rip with his long grizzled beard, his rusty fowling piece, his uncouth dress, and an army of women and children at his heels soon attracted the attention of the tavern politicians. They crowded around him eyeing him from head to foot, with great curiosity. The orator bustled up to him, and drawing him partly aside, inquired "on which side he voted?"—Rip stared in vacant stupidity. Another short but busy little fellow, pulled him by the arm and rising on tiptoe, inquired in his ear "whether he was Federal or Democrat?"[36]—Rip was equally at a loss to comprehend the question—when a knowing, self-important old gentleman, in a sharp cocked hat, made his way through the crowd, putting them to the right and left with his elbows as he passed, and planting himself before Van Winkle, with one arm akimbo, the other resting on his cane, his keen eyes and sharp hat penetrating as it were into his very soul, demanded in an austere tone— "what brought him to the election with a gun on his shoulder and a mob at his heels, and whether he meant to breed a riot in the village?"—"Alas gentlemen," cried Rip, somewhat dismayed, "I am a poor quiet man, a native of the place, and a loyal subject of the King—God bless him!"

Here a general shout burst from the bystanders—"A Tory![37] a Tory! a spy! a Refugee![38] hustle him! away with him!"—It was with great difficulty that the self-important man in the cocked hat restored order; and having assumed a tenfold austerity of brow demanded again of the unknown culprit, what he came there for and whom he was seeking. The poor man humbly assured him that he meant no harm; but merely came there in search of some of his neighbors, who used to keep about the tavern.

"—Well—who are they?—name them."

Rip bethought himself a moment and inquired, "Where's Nicholaus Vedder?"

There was a silence for a little while, when an old man replied, in a thin, piping voice, "Nicholaus Vedder? Why he is dead and gone these eighteen years! There was a wooden tombstone in the churchyard that used to tell all about him, but that's rotted and gone too."

"Where's Brom Dutcher?"

"Oh he went off to the army in the beginning of the war; some say he was killed at the storming of Stoney Point—others say he was drowned in a squall at the foot of Antony's Nose[39]—I don't know—he never came back again."

"Where's Van Bummel the schoolmaster?"

"He went off to the wars too—was a great militia general, and is now in Congress."

Rip's heart died away at hearing of these sad changes in his home and friends, and finding himself thus alone in the world—every answer puzzled him too by treating of such enormous lapses of time and of matters which he could not understand—war—Congress, Stoney Point—he had no courage to ask after any more friends, but cried out in despair, "Does nobody here know Rip Van Winkle?"

"Oh, Rip Van Winkle?" exclaimed two or three—"oh to be sure!—that's Rip Van Winkle—yonder—leaning against the tree."

Rip looked and beheld a precise counterpart of himself, as he went up the mountain: apparently as lazy and certainly as ragged! The poor fellow was now completely confounded. He doubted his own identity, and whether he was himself or another man. In the midst of his bewilderment the man in the cocked hat demanded who he was—what was his name?

"God knows," exclaimed he, at his wit's end, "I'm not myself.—I'm somebody else—that's me yonder—no—that's somebody else got into my shoes—I was myself last night; but I fell asleep on the mountain—and they've changed my gun—and everything's changed—and I'm changed—and I can't tell what's my name, or who I am!"

---

35. **Babylonish jargon:** confusing language. According to Genesis 11:1–9, when the people of the earth tried to build a tower high enough to reach heaven, God caused the people to speak many different languages. Because they could no longer communicate, they abandoned the project, which is now known as the Tower of Babel.

36. **Federal or Democrat:** American political parties after the Revolution. Federals favored a strong centralized government; Democrats favored states' rights.

37. **Tory:** one who supported British rule in the American Colonies.

38. **Refugee:** member of a group of British sympathizers, especially in New York State, who attacked supporters of the American cause, during the Revolutionary period.

39. **Antony's Nose:** mountain near West Point in New York.

WASHINGTON IRVING 163

B **Critical Thinking**
Making Inferences
? Why didn't Rip understand the question about voting? [When Rip falls asleep on the mountain, he is still a colonial subject, with no voting rights, and no choice of political parties.]

C **Reading Skills and Strategies**
Drawing Inferences and Making Predictions
? What do you think will happen to Rip as a result of his admission that he is a loyal subject of King George? [He might be chased out of town, be lectured, or be put in jail.]

D **Reading Skills and Strategies**
Using Context Clues
? Using context clues, define *general* as it's used here. [widespread] What does it mean in the seventh paragraph in the next column? [a high ranking military officer] What else can it mean? [not restricted; not specific]

E **Advanced Learners**
Literary Connections
This comic tale has an undercurrent of anxiety, even terror. Rip is thrust into a strange world where his identity is suddenly questioned. He can be seen as a man at the end of his tether, isolated, alienated from a changing world, and face to face with a different self. Some students may wish to compare and contrast Irving's treatment of this theme with the development of similar themes in Edgar Allan Poe's "William Wilson," Franz Kafka's *The Metamorphosis,* or Joseph Conrad's *The Secret Sharer.*

Professional Notes

Critical Comment:
"Rip Van Winkle" and Time
According to literary scholar Charles Neider, "The tale, which itself often feels like a nightmare, is particularly important because it reveals so early in Irving's career . . . keen folklorist interest and his intense and marvelous sense of place. It also has a larger than folklorist meaning in that it emphasizes what a great revolution had occurred internally and externally in Rip's society during his twenty-year sleep. England had been successfully defied and rejected, and the Dutch influence in manners and architecture had been powerfully subordinated to the Anglo-American along the Hudson and especially in the city of New York. 'Rip Van Winkle' is a fairy tale of bewitchment and a story of the magical changes wrought by Time."

A Critical Thinking

Hypothesizing

? Why does Rip take some comfort in the news of his wife's death? [Possible responses: He is relieved to be free of her; he is comforted that he was not the only person who made her angry.]

B Elements of Literature

Stereotype

Dishonest Yankee peddlers and their gullible and pompous Dutch victims were stock figures of American folklore.

C Elements of Literature

Tone

? What is the tone of this passage? [Possible responses: impassioned, dramatic, moving, serious, poignant.] Also note that Irving is using a dramatic motif recognizable in many other works, from the *Odyssey* to *Star Wars*: the climactic scene of recognition between the hero and his family.

D Elements of Literature

Tone

? How does the tone change as the narrative progresses here? [It becomes less serious and dramatic, more genial and folklorish.] What specific words, phrases, and devices produce this change? [Words like *wonderful, satisfactory, snug, cheery* create a positive tone.] How does it mark a transition point in the story? [The dramatic dialogue of the scene gives way to the leisurely narrative of the denouement.]

The bystanders began now to look at each other, nod, wink significantly, and tap their fingers against their foreheads. There was a whisper also about securing the gun, and keeping the old fellow from doing mischief—at the very suggestion of which, the self-important man in the cocked hat retired with some precipitation. At this critical moment a fresh likely looking woman pressed through the throng to get a peep at the gray-bearded man. She had a chubby child in her arms, which frightened at his looks began to cry. "Hush Rip," cried she, "hush you little fool, the old man won't hurt you." The name of the child, the air of the mother, the tone of her voice all awakened a train of recollections in his mind. "What is your name my good woman?" asked he.

"Judith Gardenier."

"And your father's name?"

"Ah, poor man, Rip Van Winkle was his name, but it's twenty years since he went away from home with his gun and never has been heard of since—his dog came home without him—but whether he shot himself, or was carried away by the Indians nobody can tell. I was then but a little girl."

Rip had but one question more to ask, but he put it with a faltering voice—

"Where's your mother?"—

Oh she too had died but a short time since—she broke a blood vessel in a fit of passion at a New England peddler.—

There was a drop of comfort at least in this intelligence. The honest man could contain himself no longer—he caught his daughter and her child in his arms.—"I am your father!" cried he—"Young Rip Van Winkle once—old Rip Van Winkle now!—does nobody know poor Rip Van Winkle!"

All stood amazed, until an old woman tottering out from among the crowd put her hand to her brow and peering under it in his face for a moment

exclaimed—"Sure enough!—it is Rip Van Winkle—it is himself—welcome home again old neighbor—why, where have you been these twenty long years?"

Rip's story was soon told, for the whole twenty years had been to him but as one night. The neighbors stared when they heard it; some were seen to wink at each other and put their tongues in their cheeks, and the self-important man in the cocked hat, who when the alarm was over had returned to the field, screwed down the corners of his mouth and shook his head—upon which there was a general shaking of the head throughout the assemblage.

It was determined, however, to take the opinion of old Peter Vanderdonk, who was seen slowly advancing up the road. He was a descendant of the historian of that name, who wrote one of the earliest accounts of the province. Peter was the most ancient inhabitant of the village and well versed in all the wonderful events and traditions of the neighborhood. He recollected Rip at once, and corroborated his story in the most satisfactory manner. He assured the company that it was a fact handed down from his ancestor the historian, that the Kaatskill Mountains had always been haunted by strange beings. That it was affirmed that the great Hendrick Hudson,[40] the first discoverer of the river and country, kept a kind of vigil there every twenty years, with his crew of the *Half Moon*—being permitted in this way to revisit the scenes of his enterprise and keep a guardian eye upon the river and the great city called by his name.[41] That his father had once seen them in their old Dutch dresses playing at ninepins in a hollow of the mountain; and that he himself had heard one summer afternoon the sound of their balls, like distant peals of thunder.

To make a long story short—the company broke up, and returned to the more important concerns of the election. Rip's daughter took him home to live with her; she had a snug well-furnished house, and a stout cheery farmer for a husband whom Rip recollected for one of the

40. **Hendrick Hudson:** Henry Hudson (?–1611), an English navigator hired by the Dutch, explored the river later named for him, in his ship, the *Half Moon*. Hudson's explorations were the basis for early Dutch claims in North America.

41. **great . . . name:** Hudson, New York.

Assessing Learning

Check Test: Fill in the Blank

1. Rip Van Winkle is a young man in the [eighteenth] century.
2. His region of New York State had been settled by the [Dutch].
3. The "thunder" Rip hears is really [the little men bowling].
4. Rip falls asleep for [twenty years].
5. When Rip wakes up, the colonies have become [independent; the United States].

Standardized Test Preparation

For practice with ACT and SAT formats see
• *Preparation for College Admission Exams*, p. 15

urchins that used to climb upon his back. As to Rip's son and heir, who was the ditto of himself seen leaning against the tree; he was employed to work on the farm; but evinced an hereditary disposition to attend to anything else but his business.

Rip now resumed his old walks and habits; he soon found many of his former cronies, though all rather the worse for the wear and tear of time; and preferred making friends among the rising generation, with whom he soon grew into great favor. Having nothing to do at home, and being arrived at that happy age when a man can be idle, with impunity, he took his place once more on the bench at the inn door and was reverenced as one of the patriarchs of the village and a chronicle of the old times "before the war." It was some time before he could get into the regular track of gossip, or could be made to comprehend the strange events that had taken place during his torpor. How that there had been a revolutionary war—that the country had thrown off the yoke of Old England and that instead of being a subject of his majesty George the Third, he was now a free citizen of the United States. Rip in fact was no politician; the changes of states and empires made but little impression on him; but there was one species of despotism under which he had long groaned and that was petticoat government. Happily that was at an end—he had got his neck out of the yoke of matrimony, and could go in and out whenever he pleased without dreading the tyranny of Dame Van Winkle. Whenever her name was mentioned, however, he shook his head, shrugged his shoulders, and cast up his eyes; which might pass either for an expression of resignation to his fate or joy at his deliverance.

He used to tell his story to every stranger that arrived at Mr. Doolittle's Hotel. He was observed at first to vary on some points, every time he told it, which was doubtless owing to his having so recently awaked. It at last settled down precisely to the tale I have related and not a man, woman, or child in the neighborhood but knew it by heart. Some always pretended to doubt the reality of it, and insisted that Rip had been out of his head, and that this was one point on which he always remained flighty. The old Dutch inhabitants, however, almost universally gave it full credit—Even to this day they never hear a thunderstorm of a summer afternoon about the Kaatskill, but they say Hendrick Hudson and his crew are at their game of ninepins; and it is a common wish of all henpecked husbands in the neighborhood, when life hangs heavy on their hands, that they might have a quieting draft out of Rip Van Winkle's flagon.

Note

The foregoing tale one would suspect had been suggested to Mr. Knickerbocker by a little German superstition about the emperor Frederick *der Rothbart* and the Kypphäuser Mountain;[42] the subjoined note, however, which he had appended to the tale, shows that it is an absolute fact, narrated with his usual fidelity.—

"The story of Rip Van Winkle may seem incredible to many, but nevertheless I give it my full belief, for I know the vicinity of our old Dutch settlements to have been very subject to marvelous events and appearances. Indeed I have heard many stranger stories than this, in the villages along the Hudson; all of which were too well authenticated to admit of a doubt. I have even talked with Rip Van Winkle myself, who when last I saw him was a very venerable old man and so perfectly rational and consistent on every other point, that I think no conscientious person could refuse to take this into the bargain—nay I have seen a certificate on the subject taken before a country justice and signed with a cross in the justice's own handwriting. The story therefore is beyond the possibility of doubt.

D. K."

42. **emperor . . . Mountain:** Frederick I, emperor of the Holy Roman Empire (1152–1190); also called der Rothbart (German for "red beard") or Barbarossa. Although he died near the Mediterranean during the Crusades, according to folk legend he sleeps on Kypphäuser (now called Kyffhäuser) Mountain in Germany.

WORDS TO OWN

torpor (tôr′pər) *n.*: inactive period.
fidelity (fə·del′ə·tē) *n.*: accuracy.
conscientious (kän′shē·en′shəs) *adj.*: careful and honest.

E **Reading Skills and Strategies**
Reading Inflated Diction
? What is the effect of the inflated diction in this passage? [It prompts us to recall similar language used to describe Rip. Again the language creates a comic tone, causing us to laugh at both Rip and Rip's son.]

F **Reading Skills and Strategies**
Drawing Inferences and Making Predictions
? Has Rip become a different person for having had his experience in the mountains? Explain. [Sample responses: not really, since he reverts to his old ways and reclaims his habitual position in society; yes, since he is happier in his new situation; other people's view of him changes, a fact which may affect him inwardly.]

G **Critical Thinking**
Determining Author's Purpose
? What is the purpose of the note? [It returns to the frame that opened the story. It supposedly supports the authenticity of the tale but actually provides a final touch of humor.]

H **Literary Connections**
The source for "Rip Van Winkle" is more likely the German tale of "Peter Klaus," which takes place in the magical Kyffhäuser Hills.

Making the Connections

Connecting with the Theme: "The Transforming Imagination"

"Rip Van Winkle" transforms a German folktale into written literature, which eventually becomes an American legend. Rip himself is also transformed, for when he leaves town he is regarded as a layabout, but when he returns, he becomes a celebrity. As a Romantic, Irving seems to value Rip's rustic innocence and kindness over the sophistication and worldliness that threaten to replace those qualities in a transformed America.

Have students form small groups to consider how America's culture and collective "imagination" have changed during their own lifetimes. Do students embrace the general direction of this transformation as a positive development, or do they, like the Romantics, look towards the past and nature for a deeper truth? [Accept all reasonable responses, supported by specific references to contemporary culture and Romantic ideals.]

MAKING MEANINGS

First Thoughts [Respond]

1. Possible response: Rip escapes from his scolding wife and becomes a local celebrity.

Shaping Interpretations [Interpret]

2. The supposedly reliable Crayon relays a supposedly substantiated Knickerbocker account. The tone is lightly ironic.

3. The mountain adventure with the little men and the references to New York's Dutch past are Romantic. The early descriptions of the mountain reflects nature's power to inspire and enchant.

4. Satirical elements include the frame device, descriptions of Rip, interactions between Rip and his wife, Rip's son, the "junto," and the changes in the town. Irving pokes fun at folklorists, the Van Winkles, the townspeople, and politicians.

5. Possible themes: The world is full of wonders that cannot be explained. Wishes can come true for even the lowliest of mortals. We all wish that we could one day awake in a new, free world and be rid of all our troubles.

Connecting with the Text
[Evaluate]

6. Possible responses: The challenging writing style and antique setting make the humor harder to appreciate today; the basic story elements, characters, and satirical jibes are still humorous.

Extending the Text [Synthesize]

7. Franklin was involved in civic affairs and was committed to hard work. Rip flees even family involvement and is lazy. The contemporary entrepreneur might be following Franklin, while the typical "slacker" follows Rip.

Challenging the Text [Evaluate]

8. Sample response: Shakespeare's *The Taming of the Shrew* is an example from classic literature, and Thurber's "The Secret Life of Walter Mitty" (p. 625) is a modern example. Many may find this stereotype offensive.

9. Some predictions will be accurate owing to prior familiarity with the basic tale; others will be inaccurate because Irving was hardly a formulaic writer.

MAKING MEANINGS

First Thoughts

1. In what ways is this a classic story of wish fulfillment?

> ### Reading Check
> Make a before-and-after chart of what happened in the story before Rip's sleep and what happened after he woke up.

Shaping Interpretations

2. In his introductory note, the narrator (who is Geoffrey Crayon) explains that the manuscript of "Rip Van Winkle" was written by Diedrich Knickerbocker, the narrator of Irving's earlier *History of New York*. How does Irving use his two narrators—Geoffrey Crayon and Diedrich Knickerbocker—to defend the tale's credibility? How would you describe Irving's **tone** in these introductory passages?

3. What details in "Rip Van Winkle" do you think reveal a Romantic fascination with the past and nature? Find some descriptions of the **setting** that you think reflect a Romantic's point of view.

4. Irving was a Romantic, but he was also a satirist. What elements of this story—including the narrator's commentaries—are **satirical**? Who or what are Irving's targets?

5. How would you state the **theme** of this story?

Connecting with the Text

6. Do you find "Rip" humorous, or do you think it's too outdated to be funny to us today? Explain your response with examples from the story.

Extending the Text

7. How does the fictional **character** of Rip Van Winkle contrast with the historical character of Benjamin Franklin, the self-made man (page 84)? Where do you still see both character types in American life today?

Challenging the Text

8. Dame Van Winkle and Rip are **stereotyped characters** that have been found in literature throughout the ages—the nagging wife and the henpecked husband. Can you identify these character types in current literature and in popular movies and TV shows? What is your response to Irving's characterization of Dame Van Winkle?

9. Review the prediction chart you made while reading. Did Irving succeed in surprising you, or did you find his story predictable? Explain.

READING SKILLS AND STRATEGIES

Reading Inflated Diction

One of the hallmarks of Irving's humor is his use of **inflated diction** (pompous, high-flown language) to describe commonplace things. For example, rather than simply saying that Rip is "lazy," or that he "hates work," Irving states that Rip has "an insuperable aversion to all kinds of profitable labor."

1. Skim the story to find at least two other comically inflated descriptions of Rip's family life.

2. Rephrase each inflated description in plain English.

3. How did Irving's inflated diction affect your reading of the story?

Washington Irving.

Drawing by David Levine. Reprinted with permission from *The New York Review of Books.* Copyright ©1976 NYREV, Inc.

Reading Check

Before	After
Wife scolds Rip	Rip returns to changed village
Rip meets stranger	Rip finds daughter
Rip arrives at amphitheater with stranger	Rip learns wife has died
Rip sees odd Dutchmen playing ninepins	Rip tells story to townspeople and visitors
Rip drinks	
Rip sleeps	

READING SKILLS AND STRATEGIES

1. In paragraphs three through seven, most sentences contain inflated language. Students may choose from these or others.

2. Students should simplify each sentence.

3. Some students may say the inflated language made the story difficult. Others may recognize that once they get the hang of it, this style becomes rewarding and hilarious and even spellbinding.

CHOICES: Building Your Portfolio

Writer's Notebook

1. Collecting Ideas for a Literary Analysis

When you analyze a literary work, you might want to investigate the ways it follows or deviates from a conventional **plot** pattern. You can show how "Rip Van Winkle," for example, relates to the archetypal plot of a classic work like the *Odyssey*. Use a chart like the one below to track Irving's use of this particular plot line. You'll probably note very quickly how Irving alters this traditional pattern. Keep your notes for possible use in the Writer's Workshop on page 198.

Hero	Plot
Perilous journey	
Use of supernatural	
Disguises	
Recognition scene	
Wife	

Explaining an Analogy

2. Parallel Awakenings

Rip's awakening has been seen by many critics as an analogy to the awakening of the new American nation. In a short essay, cite the specific details that support the idea that Rip's emancipation from his wife is like America's emancipation from Great Britain. In your essay, discuss how each "story" is about winning independence from a tyrant.

Analyzing Conflict

3. The Battle of the Sexes

This story reflects a **conflict** that has been used by hundreds of other writers of comedy, before and after Irving. The conflict might be described as the battle of the sexes. In a brief essay, tell how Irving's story reflects this conflict; name other comedies (in books, on TV, and in the movies) that use the same conflict; and explain your own response to its continued use and popularity.

©Touchstone Pictures and Television, Inc.

Sparring partners. The TV show *Home Improvement* with Patricia Richardson and Tim Allen.

Creative Writing

4. Dame Van Winkle Has Her Say

Write an epilogue to this story called "Dame Van Winkle." Describe her response to Rip's disappearance. Was she also emancipated? Will you have Dame Van Winkle tell her own story or let Diedrich Knickerbocker continue?

Creative Writing

5. After Twenty Years

The world is always changing, often in unexpected and amazing ways. Think about the future: What will the world be like in twenty years? Then, write an article that could appear in a newspaper twenty years from today. Your article can be about a current event of the time; it can also be an editorial or even an advice column.

Creative Writing / Art

6. Missing Person

You're a private investigator trying to discover the whereabouts of the missing Rip Van Winkle. First, compile a profile or dossier on Rip: a list of his character traits, a list of possible motives he may have had for wanting to escape, and brief interviews with people who knew him. Include a "missing person" sketch of Rip as you visualize him.

Rubrics for each Choices assignment appear on p. 105 in the *Portfolio Management System*.

CHOICES: Building Your Portfolio

1. **Writer's Notebook**   Remind students to save their work. They may use it as prewriting for the Writer's Workshop on p. 198.
2. **Explaining an Analogy**   Have small groups brainstorm the major events of the American Revolutionary period before they begin trying to find parallels in the story. A graphic organizer such as the following might help students clarify the connections they make.

Story's events		
Parallels to history		

3. **Analyzing Conflict**   Many situation comedies are based on the battle of the sexes. Ask students who are having difficulty getting started to reflect on one sitcom and to apply their insights to the story.
4. **Creative Writing**   As a prewriting activity, allow students to work in pairs to conduct an interview, with one student taking the part of Dame Van Winkle and the other taking the part of the interviewer.
5. **Creative Writing**   Have students study sample newspaper articles, editorials, and advice columns before they begin.
6. **Creative Writing/Art**   Have students begin by doing research on what an actual missing person dossier pulled from a detective's file looks like.

Using Students' Strengths

Auditory Learners

Allow pairs of students to work on choice 1 together. Suggest that one student tell the other what aspects of the story pattern he or she finds in "Rip Van Winkle." Have the partner ask questions that help to elicit specific details. The first student can jot down the words as they come to mind. Have students take turns, then read their notes aloud and fill in gaps.

Intrapersonal Learners

Encourage students composing Dame Van Winkle's speech for choice 4 to jot down a series of brief diary entries, from the day Rip disappears to the morning she is visited by the New England peddler. After students have explored her reactions, have them condense their notes to complete the activity.

OBJECTIVES

1. Learn to use context clues to determine the meanings of words
2. Learn to use a word map for unfamiliar words

Reading Skills and Strategies

This feature focuses on the way in which successful readers determine the meaning of an unfamiliar word by looking at the word's *relationships* with other, more familiar words in the sentence.

Mini-Lesson:
Context Clues

Divide the class into several groups, and ask each group to locate five unfamiliar words in "Rip Van Winkle." Have groups determine which parts of the sentences surrounding each word can be considered context clues and which of the six types of clues they are. Ask groups to draw conclusions about the meanings of the words they have chosen and to have one student in the group verify meanings in a dictionary. Finally, ask groups to share their findings and to discuss which types of context clues seem to appear most often in Irving's work.

Try It Out

Remind students that two valuable boxes on the chart indicate the importance of checking context-clue guesses against reference materials: "Dictionary Definition" and "What Other Words Mean the Same Thing?" Encourage students to fill in these boxes *after* they have finished reading a selection.

VOCABULARY: USING CONTEXT CLUES

Using **context clues**—clues to meaning that are in the text—is the best way to figure out the meaning of a word without interrupting yourself to check the dictionary. A word's context includes the words and sentences that surround it. Washington Irving's "Rip Van Winkle" provides examples of six kinds of context clues (there are more) that you will commonly encounter in your reading.

1. Example

". . . they **quaffed** the liquor in profound silence. . . ." (page 159)

Liquor is an example of something you can *quaff.* You can infer that *quaff* means "to drink."

2. Restatement

"He even ventured . . . to taste the beverage . . . and was soon tempted to repeat the **draft.**" (page 159)

"Repeat the *draft*" seems to restate "taste the beverage," so you can infer that *draft* means "drinking."

3. Summary

". . . he was observed to smoke his pipe **vehemently,** and to send forth short, frequent, and angry puffs. . . ." (page 157)

The clause after the comma tells you the meaning of *vehemently.*

4. Contrast

". . . he was rarely heard to speak, but smoked his pipe **incessantly.**" (page 157)

The conjunction *but* sets up an opposition—it helps you know that *incessantly* is the opposite of "rarely." *Incessantly* means "without stopping."

5. Items in a Series

"They were dressed in a **quaint,** outlandish fashion. . . ." (page 159)

The comma between *quaint* and *outlandish* lets you know they may be close in meaning.

6. Cause and Effect

". . . Rip felt **famished** for want of his breakfast." (page 160)

"For want of" indicates that being *famished* is a result of not having eaten breakfast. *Famished* means "extremely hungry."

Try It Out

Mapping unfamiliar words. A word map like the one below can help you use context clues to figure out words or phrases you may not know. It can also help you to make further associations with the new word that will enable you to "own" the word—to make it an active part of your vocabulary.

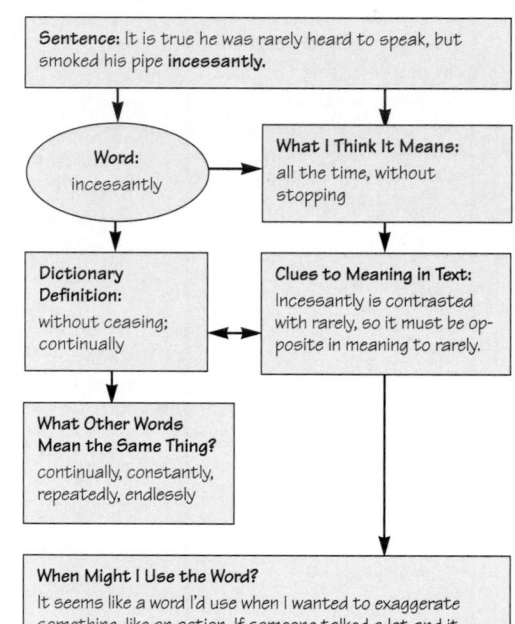

Using Students' Strengths

Auditory Learners

Let students choose a working partner. Have one student read aloud a sentence from "Rip Van Winkle" or another selection that contains a difficult word and a context clue. The other student can then define the meaning of the word and explain how he or she arrived at this definition. Students can alternate reading sentences and giving answers.

Kinesthetic Learners

On strips of heavy paper, write out sentences that employ the various context clues described in the Reading Skills and Strategies feature. Next, write out the types of context clues on separate strips of heavy paper, and, on the back, color-code the two sets of strips with felt-tip markers. Let students practice matching the sentences with the types of context clues. Students can check their accuracy by checking the color coding on the back of the strips.

Spatial Learners

Prepare a handout with a set of sentences that contain the kinds of context clues described in the Reading Skills and Strategies feature. Ask students to draw a line under the unfamiliar word and a circle or rectangle around the context clues. Then ask students to write a simple definition of the word based on the context clues. Have a volunteer check dictionary definitions for any word that remains unclear.

William Cullen Bryant

(1794–1878)

Poetry is a lonely occupation, but not a solitary one. Poets of any consequence rarely write in isolation from the influence of their predecessors or from the influence of other poets of their own time. When William Cullen Bryant was still an adolescent, he read a book of poems that would change his life: *Lyrical Ballads,* published in 1798 by his great English contemporaries William Wordsworth and Samuel Taylor Coleridge. This volume of poetry and theory focused the expression and much of the philosophy of the Romantic era. The book was a powerful source of inspiration for poets who wanted to replace conventional poetic diction with the common speech of their own time. Bryant was one of these poets—the first mature American Romantic, the country boy who translated the messages of English Romanticism into his native tongue.

William Cullen Bryant (1833) by James Frothingham (1786–1864). American. Oil on canvas (21″ × 17½″).

Courtesy Museum of Fine Arts, Boston. Gift of Maxim Karolik for the M. & M. Karolik Collection of American Paintings, 1815–1865 (62.271).

Two other important factors supported the influence of English Romanticism on Bryant's poetry. One factor was Bryant's own growing attraction to the philosophy of deism (page 16), which held that divinity could be found in nature. The other factor was the geography of his surroundings, which placed Bryant in immediate contact with everything that supported this philosophy.

By the time of Bryant's birth, western Massachusetts was no longer a Colonial frontier, but a widely settled countryside. Over the next hundred years and more, its farms, steepled towns, and mountain forests would be the homes of many poets. These writers would find in their surroundings metaphors to express their sense of correspondence between human life and the life of nature. After Bryant, the same New England seasons would turn for Herman Melville and Emily Dickinson, and later for Robert Frost and Richard Wilbur. All these poets were intimate with the shadows and whispers of the Berkshires and the adjacent Green Mountains. All would make their own small plot of ground part of the permanent landscape of American poetry.

Bryant was born in Cummington, Massachusetts. His father was a physician, and his mother came from a family of clergy. Bryant's literary gifts were evident from an early age: By the age of nine he was already writing poetry and had earned a reputation as a prodigy.

Bryant was tutored for a career as a lawyer, but with the publication of "Thanatopsis" his literary future was assured. In his late twenties he moved to New York City and for many years played the triple role of editor, critic, and poet.

Bryant became not only a famous literary figure, but also an influential voice in religion and politics. An outspoken liberal, Bryant supported social reform, free speech, and the growing movement for the abolition of slavery. He was also one of the founders of the Republican Party, which, in his lifetime, would produce one of America's great presidents, Abraham Lincoln. When Bryant died at the age of eighty-three, he was a millionaire and so widely honored at home and abroad that he had become a kind of national monument, the widely acknowledged "father of American poetry."

Today Bryant's poems are not read as the spiritual counsels they were meant to be; instead, they are read as period pieces that authentically reflect their time. Yet even when Bryant's poems seem more like moral fables than free expressions of the imagination, they ring with an air of piety and sincerity no one can doubt.

go.hrw.com
LE0 11-4

🎧 💿 — *Resources: Print and Media*

Reading
- *Graphic Organizers for Active Reading,* p. 13
- *Words to Own,* p. 12
- *Audio CD Library*
  Disc 5, Track 3

Writing and Language
- *Daily Oral Grammar*
  Transparency 12

Assessment
- *Formal Assessment,* p. 34
- *Portfolio Management System,* p. 107
- *Test Generator (One-Stop Planner CD-ROM)*

Internet
- go.hrw.com (keyword: LE0 11-4)

OBJECTIVES
1. Read and interpret the poem
2. Track responses
3. Understand inverted sentences
4. Express understanding through critical and creative writing
5. Interpret meaning through art

SKILLS
Reading
- Track responses
- Read and paraphrase inverted sentences

Writing
- Collect ideas for a literary analysis
- Write a letter from a Puritan perspective

Art
- Illustrate two poems

Viewing/Representing
- Write a caption for a painting (ATE)

Planning

- **Block Schedule**
  Block Scheduling Lesson Plans with Pacing Guide
- **Traditional Schedule**
  Lesson Plans Including Strategies for English-Language Learners
- **One-Stop Planner**
  CD-ROM with Test Generator

Background

Considering the period in which "Thanatopsis" was written and the background of its author, the position this famous poem takes is remarkable. Instead of heaven and immortality, the poem seems to suggest ways by which humankind may become resigned to an afterlife without the heaven that is promised in traditional religion. Some readers, however, may see indications of a more traditional faith in urgings to have "trust" (l. 79) (trust in whom?).

Bryant is recommending at the end of his poem a stoical, noble acceptance in the face of death. This is a result of his knowledge of classical Greece and Rome. It arises from the behavior of Socrates in the face of death in Plato's dialogue "Phaedo," and from the urgings of Marcus Aurelius.

Summary ■■■

The speaker celebrates and reflects upon Nature as a mirror that matches his happy moods and a comfort and balm for his dark thoughts—especially those of death. In death, our individual being intermingles with Nature's elements, and we join the company of all who have gone before. The speaker advises us to live in such a way that when our time comes to die, we can go to the grave sustained by trust, like a sleeper expecting pleasant dreams.

RESPONDING TO THE ART

John William Hill (1812–1879) was a London-born American artist known for his lithographs of city scenes and for his naturalistic landscapes, especially views in or near the Hudson River Valley.
Activity. Have students caption the painting with a phrase from "Thanatopsis." [Possible responses: "The hills/Rock-ribbed" (ll. 37–38); "rivers that move/ In majesty" (ll. 40–41).]

Fawn's Leap, Catskill, New York (detail) (1868) by John W. Hill (1812–1879). Oil on canvas (30″ × 38″).

Munson-Williams-Proctor Institute Museum of Art, Utica, New York.

Before You Read
THANATOPSIS

Make the Connection

The Endless Cycle
Romantic poets looked to nature for lessons—lessons that we too can see all around us. One of the ever-present lessons of nature is the organic cycle of birth, growth, death, and rebirth. Think of some of the ways that nature reminds us of this endless cycle of life, death, and rebirth. Do you find this aspect of nature disturbing or comforting?

Reading Skills and Strategies

Tracking Your Responses
As you read the poem, you may wish to keep a double-entry journal. In the left column, record a passage from the poem that particularly interests you. (It may remind you of something in your own experience or strike you with its vivid imagery; or it may be something you disagree with or don't quite understand.) In the right column, jot down your response to the passage. Pay special attention to Nature's "lesson," starting with line 17 and ending with line 72.

Background

Bryant composed the first version of this poem when he was only sixteen, during solitary rambles in the woods. In the poem, he draws moral lessons from nature, which was typical of the popular poetry of his time. *Thanatopsis* is a word Bryant coined by joining two Greek words, *thanatos* (death) and *opsis* (seeing). The word is defined by the poem: a way of looking at death and a way of thinking about it.

170

Reaching All Students

Struggling Readers
Tell students that Bryant wrote this poem when he was seventeen or eighteen years old while rambling through the woods on a day off. At Williams College, he had been reading eighteenth-century British poems, including Robert Blair's "The Grave," which might have inspired him to write this Romantic meditation on death. Students should realize that the human speaker is present in ll. 1–17 and 73–81, but a personified Nature speaks the rest of the poem.

English Language Learners
"Thanatopsis" contains poetic vocabulary, inverted word order, and omitted words, sometimes all in one sentence, as in "nor couldst thou wish / Couch more magnificent" (ll. 32–33). Translated, this line means "You could not wish [to have a] more magnificent couch." Have students work together in heterogeneous groups to decode the poem, following this model. As students work, move among the groups offering help where needed.

Advanced Learners
On first reading, have students notice the blank verse (unrhymed iambic pentameter) and the nature imagery. On later readings, focus attention on the speaker's philosophical views, which can be labeled Stoic in the tradition of Zeno, Seneca, and Marcus Aurelius. Have students discuss the kind of afterlife, if any, the speaker envisions and how consoling his view of death is.

Thanatopsis

William Cullen Bryant

To him who in the love of Nature holds
Communion with her visible forms, she speaks
A various language; for his gayer hours
She has a voice of gladness, and a smile
5 And eloquence of beauty, and she glides
Into his darker musings, with a mild
And healing sympathy, that steals away
Their sharpness, ere° he is aware. When thoughts
Of the last bitter hour come like a blight
10 Over thy spirit, and sad images
Of the stern agony, and shroud, and pall,°
And breathless darkness, and the narrow house,°
Make thee to shudder, and grow sick at heart;—
Go forth, under the open sky, and list°
15 To Nature's teachings, while from all around—
Earth and her waters, and the depths of air—
Comes a still voice.—

          Yet° a few days, and thee
The all-beholding sun shall see no more
In all his course; nor yet in the cold ground,
20 Where thy pale form was laid, with many tears,
Nor in the embrace of ocean, shall exist
Thy image. Earth, that nourished thee, shall claim
Thy growth, to be resolved to earth again,
And, lost each human trace, surrendering up
25 Thine individual being, shalt thou go
To mix forever with the elements,
To be a brother to the insensible rock
And to the sluggish clod, which the rude swain°
Turns with his share,° and treads upon. The oak
30 Shall send his roots abroad, and pierce thy mold.

          Yet not to thine eternal resting place
Shalt thou retire alone, nor couldst thou wish
Couch more magnificent. Thou shalt lie down
With patriarchs of the infant world—with kings,
35 The powerful of the earth—the wise, the good,
Fair forms, and hoary seers° of ages past,
All in one mighty sepulcher.° The hills
Rock-ribbed and ancient as the sun,—the vales
Stretching in pensive quietness between;
40 The venerable woods—rivers that move
In majesty, and the complaining brooks
That make the meadows green; and, poured round all,
Old Ocean's gray and melancholy waste,—

8. ere (er): before.

11. pall (pôl): coffin cover.
12. narrow house: grave.

14. list: listen.

17. Yet . . . : Here, the voice of
Nature begins to speak.

28. rude swain: uneducated
country youth.
29. share: short for "plow-
share."

36. hoary seers: white-haired
prophets.
37. sepulcher (sep′əl·kər):
burial place.

WILLIAM CULLEN BRYANT 171

Skill Link

Analyzing the Melody of Literary Language

Read several lines of "Thanatopsis" aloud, exaggerating the meter. Explain that the poem is written in blank verse, or unrhymed iambic pentameter. (Each line has five feet, composed of an unaccented syllable followed by an accented syllable.)

1. Discuss the role of meter in poetry. How does the regular rhythm affect the form of the poem? How does it affect the sound?

Read the last stanza aloud to demonstrate how Bryant moves the reader through the poem by breaking ideas across several lines.

2. Read ll. 31–37 and determine which syllables and words are connected. How does the emphasis help convey Bryant's meaning? Point out how important words fall on the accented feet. Then repeat the exercise with ll. 37–43.

A Elements of Literature
Metaphor
? What figure of speech is the speaker using in ll. 37–45? [a metaphor comparing the earth to a tomb] **What are the decorations on this tomb?** [the natural features of the earth—hills, vales, woods, rivers, brooks, oceans]

B Humanities Connections
The Living vs. the Dead
In Bryant's day, the number of people living was smaller than the number who had previously lived and died. In the late twentieth century that changed: with the explosion of the global population, there are more people now alive than all who lived before.

C Reading Skills and Strategies

Tracking Responses
? What particular human fear is Nature addressing here? [the fear of dying alone and being forgotten] **Is it consoling to think that everyone must die?** [Sample answers: Yes, because it makes you feel less lonely; no, because death can be, individually, a frightening experience.]

D Critical Thinking
Evaluating
? When "Thanatopsis" was first published in *The North American Review* in 1817, it did not contain the first seventeen or the last fifteen lines; these were added later. **Which version of the poem seems better?** [Sample response: The longer version is better because it provides a human frame for Nature's voice; it offers human consolation.]

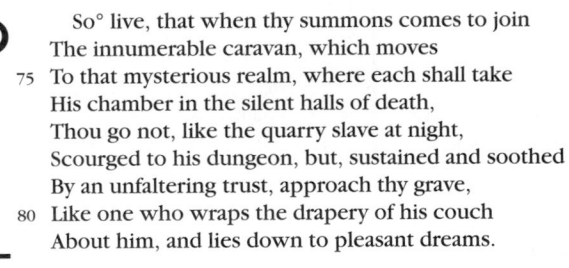

A
45 Are but the solemn decorations all
   Of the great tomb of man. The golden sun,
   The planets, all the infinite host of heaven,
   Are shining on the sad abodes of death,
B Through the still lapse of ages. All that tread
50 The globe are but a handful to the tribes
   That slumber in its bosom.—Take the wings
   Of morning,° pierce the Barcan wilderness,°
   Or lose thyself in the continuous woods
   Where rolls the Oregon,° and hears no sound,
   Save his own dashings—yet the dead are there:
55 And millions in those solitudes, since first
   The flight of years began, have laid them down
   In their last sleep—the dead reign there alone.
   So shalt thou rest, and what if thou withdraw
   In silence from the living, and no friend
C 60 Take note of thy departure? All that breathe
   Will share thy destiny. The gay will laugh
   When thou art gone, the solemn brood of care
   Plod on, and each one as before will chase
   His favorite phantom; yet all these shall leave
65 Their mirth and their employments, and shall come
   And make their bed with thee. As the long train
   Of ages glides away, the sons of men,
   The youth in life's fresh spring, and he who goes
   In the full strength of years, matron and maid,
70 The speechless babe, and the gray-headed man—
   Shall one by one be gathered to thy side,
   By those, who in their turn shall follow them.

D
    So° live, that when thy summons comes to join
   The innumerable caravan, which moves
75 To that mysterious realm, where each shall take
   His chamber in the silent halls of death,
   Thou go not, like the quarry slave at night,
   Scourged to his dungeon, but, sustained and soothed
   By an unfaltering trust, approach thy grave,
80 Like one who wraps the drapery of his couch
   About him, and lies down to pleasant dreams.

51. Take . . . morning: allusion to Psalm 139:9: "If I take the wings of the morning . . ." **Barcan wilderness:** desert near Barca (now al-Marj), Libya, in North Africa.
53. Oregon: early name for the Columbia River, which flows between Washington and Oregon.

73. So . . . : The speaker's voice resumes here.

172 AMERICAN ROMANTICISM

Assessing Learning

Check Test for "Thanatopsis": True-False
1. According to "Thanatopsis," nature can help us confront death. [True]
2. The still voice says we will keep our individuality after death. [False]
3. The speaker says kings and the reader shall be as one after death. [True]
4. Earth is compared to a large grave. [True]
5. The speaker indicates that nothing can lessen the pain of death. [False]

Making the Connections

Cross-Cultural Connections: Death
To the Greeks, Thanatos was Death personified, the son of Night and Darkness and the brother of Hypnos (Sleep). He was not portrayed as a frightening being, but as a winged man who lived in the underworld. Students may be aware that the concept of death varies among cultures. You might have students research the different ideas of death among Hindus, Muslims, American Indians, and others. Ask them to compare their findings with the implied ideas about death in "Thanatopsis."

Derek Walcott, who was born in 1930 on the island of St. Lucia in the Caribbean, won the 1992 Nobel Prize in literature. In "Sea Canes," Walcott, like Bryant, reflects on nature as he tries to come to his own understanding of loss and death. "Sea Canes" refers to wild canes—tall, slender, bamboo-like plants that grow near water.

Sea Canes

Derek Walcott

Half my friends are dead.
I will make you new ones, said earth.
No, give me them back, as they were, instead,
with faults and all, I cried.

5 Tonight I can snatch their talk
from the faint surf's drone
through the canes, but I cannot walk

on the moonlit leaves of ocean
down that white road alone,
10 or float with the dreaming motion

of owls leaving earth's load.
O earth, the number of friends you keep
exceeds those left to be loved.

The sea canes by the cliff flash green and silver;
15 they were the seraph lances of my faith,
but out of what is lost grows something
      stronger

that has the rational radiance of stone,
enduring moonlight, further than despair,
strong as the wind, that through dividing canes

20 brings those we love before us, as they were,
with faults and all, not nobler, just there.

WILLIAM CULLEN BRYANT 173

Connecting Across Texts

Connecting with "Thanatopsis"

Although "Thanatopsis" and "Sea Canes" are both about death and both use extensive nature imagery, Bryant's poem focuses on those concerned about their own death and "Sea Canes" on those mourning the deaths of loved ones. It is not surprising that the writer of "Thanatopsis" was much younger than the writer of "Sea Canes." Have students discuss what the speakers of these two poems might say to each other. Then ask pairs of students to write a script for a radio call-in show, with the two speakers answering anonymous callers' questions about death and related issues. Both students may brainstorm callers' questions. In writing answers, each student should focus on one of the two speakers' answers.

Connections

The speaker begs the earth to return his dead friends. He has lost too many to the grave, he can only faintly remember the sound of their voices, and he cannot follow them further. Yet at the end of the poem, he accepts his losses, and claims a stronger, more enduring beauty in recalling them, with honesty and love.

Ⓐ Reading Skills and Strategies

Tracking Responses

❓ Would you accept earth's offer to make you new friends or reject it, as the speaker does? [Possible answers: accept it, because life goes on and offers new experiences; reject it, because no one can replace them.]

Ⓑ Critical Thinking

Interpreting

❓ What emotions do these images convey? How does the speaker feel? [The speaker is lonely and is having trouble coping with the loss of loved ones.]

Ⓒ Critical Thinking

Interpreting

❓ How does the image of the sea canes which "flash" in the wind or surf relate to the speaker's sense of sorrow about his friends? [These "seraph lances" were supposed to stand straight in the wind, but instead the "dividing" canes flash and fall, just like the speaker's dead friends.]

Ⓓ Reading Skills and Strategies

Comparison and Contrast

❓ How does this "radiance" compare to the "faith" the speaker has before? [Possible response: The speaker claims the pure, wind-like force of objective memory, and gives up on longing for the immediate presence of lost friends. Like the canes, this presence is transitory, while the power of memory endures.]

MAKING MEANINGS

First Thoughts [Respond]

1. Sample responses: The speaker's view of the afterlife; the idea of Nature's personified voice; the speaker's positive attitude toward death.

Shaping Interpretations [Interpret]

2. In ll. 17–30, the dead become part of nature's rebirth. This thought comforts the speaker because it emphasizes the unity of the living and the dead.

3. The tone shifts from stern finality to consolation: We will not be alone in death; our resting place will be magnificent; we will lie down with the great of past generations; everyone alive will share this fate.

4. The speaker advises readers to live life so that they will be able to accept death peacefully. Opinions about this advice will vary.

5. "Rest" (l. 58), "unfaltering trust" (l. 79), "pleasant dreams" (l. 81), "lie down/With . . . the good" (ll. 33–35), and the image of sleep suggest more or less traditional views of the afterlife as a place of rest or of some kind of enduring consciousness. "Resolved to earth again" (l. 23), "surrendering up/Thine individual being" (ll. 24–25), and "mix forever with the elements" (l. 26) suggest an afterlife of unity with nature.

6. Sample responses: about death, because it tries to explain death as part of the natural cycle; about life, because it advises people to live more fully.

Extending the Text [Synthesize]

7. Answers will vary, but students should mention that "A Blessing" describes a personal, spiritual experience; "Thanatopsis" explores the human condition.

Challenging the Text [Synthesize]

8. The question of how to understand and face death is as important today as in Bryant's time; students' views on Bryant's advice will vary.

Grading Timesaver

Rubrics for each Choices assignment appear on p. 107 in the *Portfolio Management System*.

MAKING MEANINGS

First Thoughts

1. What thoughts or feelings expressed in "Thanatopsis" strike you as especially important or puzzling or controversial? Be sure to check your double-entry journal.

Shaping Interpretations

2. How does this poem reveal the Romantic conviction that the universe, far from operating like a machine, is really a living organism that undergoes constant cyclical changes? How is this "organic" view of the universe comforting to the speaker?

3. In line 31, what shift in the **tone** of the poem occurs? What comfort is offered in this section of the poem?

4. At the conclusion of the speech of the "still voice" (line 72), the speaker's voice resumes for the concluding section, or summing up. In your own words, state the main thrust of his advice. Do you find his advice wise and consoling, or disturbing? Or do you have some other reaction? Explain.

5. Some readers think this poem expresses a traditional notion of an afterlife in heaven, while others find in it a very untraditional view of an afterlife in which people rejoin the great chain of Nature instead of ascending to a heavenly realm. Which **images** in the poem support each of these interpretations?

6. Is this poem about death or about life? Explain.

Extending the Text

7. Read "A Blessing" by James Wright on page 151. Then, compare the ways in which Wright's and Bryant's imaginations work when they look at nature.

Challenging the Text

8. Many readers today read a poem like "Thanatopsis" simply as a period piece that has only historical interest, yet Bryant's intention was that his poem be taken seriously as spiritual counsel. In what ways does Bryant's poem still speak to us today, if at all?

READING SKILLS AND STRATEGIES

Answers

1. Possible responses: "while from all around— /. . . Comes a still voice" (ll. 15–17); "and thee/The all-beholding sun shall see no more" (ll. 17–18); "shall exist/Thy image" (ll. 21–22).

2. Possible responses: "While a still voice comes from all around"; "the all-beholding sun shall see thee no more"; "thy image shall exist."

READING SKILLS AND STRATEGIES

Reading Inverted Sentences

In order to maintain his meter and to create certain sound effects, Bryant often uses **inversion**—a reversal of the usual English word order. For example, "Yet not to thine eternal resting place / Shalt thou retire alone" is an inversion of "Yet thou shalt not retire alone to thine eternal resting place."

1. Find three examples of inversion in the first thirty lines of "Thanatopsis."

2. Revise each example to conform to usual English word order. How do your revisions change the meter and affect the clarity of the lines?

CHOICES: Building Your Portfolio

Writer's Notebook

1. Collecting Ideas for a Literary Analysis

If you were to write an analysis of "Thanatopsis," you might want to focus on its **theme.** Try now to state the poem's theme as precisely as you can. Then, jot down several passages of the poem that support this theme. Keep your notes for possible use in the Writer's Workshop on page 198.

Comparing Ideas

2. A Puritan Writes to a Romantic

How might Anne Bradstreet (page 68) or Jonathan Edwards (page 77) have reacted to Bryant's meditation on death? Write a letter from Bradstreet or Edwards to Bryant that conveys Puritan reactions to the poem.

Art

3. Picture This

You have been commissioned to provide illustrations for two poems: Bryant's "Thanatopsis" and Walcott's "Sea Canes" (see *Connections*, page 173). Create an image for each poem that communicates each poet's insights.

T174

Henry Wadsworth Longfellow

(1807–1882)

Longfellow was and still is the most popular poet America has ever produced. With the possible exception of Robert Frost (page 558), no twentieth-century poet has ever reached "household name" status, let alone achieved the kind of recognition suggested by the word *popular*.

Longfellow's immense popularity was based largely on his appeal to an audience hungry for sermons and lessons. That audience wanted assurances that their cherished values would prevail over the new forces of history—such as industrialization—that were threatening to destroy them. In themselves, the values Longfellow endorsed were positive forces in the making of the American character. But his tendency to leave these values unexamined led to poetry that often offered easy comfort at the expense of illumination.

Born in Portland, Maine, Longfellow was never far from the rocks and splashing waves of the Atlantic Coast, or from the cultural and religious influences of the well-to-do families who lived "north of Boston." Longfellow's early interest in foreign languages and literature led him naturally to an academic career. After attending Portland Academy, he continued his education at nearby Bowdoin College (where Nathaniel Hawthorne was one of his classmates), and then pursued three additional years of study in France, Spain, Italy, and Germany. When he returned, he joined the Bowdoin faculty, married, and began to write a series of prose sketches drawn from his experiences abroad.

During a second European trip in 1835, Longfellow's young wife died of a miscarriage. When he returned to America, still dealing with a "sorrow and a grief that almost killed," the young widower became a professor of French and Spanish at Harvard; seven years later he married Frances Appleton, whom he had met in Europe after his first wife's death. He settled into eighteen years of happily married life, living

Henry Wadsworth Longfellow (1871) by Theodore Wust (active 1860–1901). Watercolor on ivory ($3\frac{1}{2}'' \times 2\frac{3}{4}''$).

in the Cambridge mansion Craigie House (a gift from his new father-in-law), fathering six children, and producing some of his most celebrated poetry, much of it based on American legends: *Evangeline* (1847) and *The Song of Hiawatha* (1855).

By 1854, Longfellow had resigned from Harvard and devoted himself to writing full time. But seven years later a second tragedy struck: His wife Frances died in a fiery accident at home, when a lighted match or hot sealing wax she was using on a letter ignited her summer dress. Longfellow tried to save her, smothering the flames with a rug, and was badly burned himself.

Longfellow now devoted himself to his work with a religious and literary zeal. By the end of his long and productive life, he had become for Americans the symbolic figure of The Poet: wise, gray-bearded, haloed with goodness, and living in a world of still-untold romance. He was given honorary degrees by Cambridge and Oxford Universities in England and was received by Queen Victoria. Two years after his death, Longfellow's marble image was unveiled in the Poets' Corner in Westminster Abbey. He was the first American to be so honored.

go.hrw.com
LEO 11-4

OBJECTIVES

The Tide Rises . . . / The Cross of Snow

1. Read and interpret the poems
2. Analyze meter
3. Identify sonnet form
4. Express understanding through critical writing and music

SKILLS

Literary
- Analyze meter
- Identify sonnet form

Writing
- Collect ideas for a literary analysis
- Compare poems
- Analyze and evaluate fine art

Music/Performance
- Compose and perform a musical setting for a poem
- Recite a poem to music

Viewing/Representing
- Compare and contrast details in a poem and in a painting

Planning

- **Traditional Schedule**
  Lesson Plans Including Strategies for English-Language Learners

- **One-Stop Planner**
  CD-ROM with Test Generator

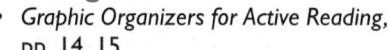 *Resources: Print and Media*

Reading
- *Graphic Organizers for Active Reading,* pp. 14, 15
- *Audio CD Library* Disc 5, Tracks 4, 5

Elements of Literature
- *Literary Elements*
    Transparency 7
    Worksheet, p. 22

Writing and Language
- *Daily Oral Grammar* Transparency 13

Viewing and Representing
- *Viewing and Representing*
    Fine Art Transparency 4
    Fine Art Worksheet, p. 16

Assessment
- *Formal Assessment,* p. 35
- *Portfolio Management System,* p. 108
- *Test Generator (One-Stop Planner CD-ROM)*

Internet
- go.hrw.com (keyword: LE0 11-4)

Summary ▪

At twilight a traveler hurries along the shore to the town. In the night, waves efface his footprints in the sand. At daybreak, normal activities in the town resume, but the traveler does not return to the shore. Through it all, the tides rises and the tide falls.

Background

Literary critic Cecil Williams says of this poem: "In 1879, when he was seventy-two and only three years from death, Longfellow wrote the lovely 'The Tide Rises, the Tide Falls'. . . . He returns again to his boyhood in Portland, where he had loved to listen to the sound of the waves and to the gentle rush of the tide coming in. As he visualized in old age the phenomena of water behavior, it became symbolic of life."

RESPONDING TO THE ART

Activity. Have students discuss how the painting, like the poem, might be seen to transform a "meditation" before the sea into a more symbolic commentary on human life in general. [Possible response: The expanse of the sea contrasted with the small silhouette of the man emphasizes the infinite power and endurance of nature, as opposed to the mortality and frailty of human life.]

Before You Read
THE TIDE RISES, THE TIDE FALLS

Make the Connection
Finite and Infinite
Nature repeats its cycles without foreseeable end. Summer turns to winter, day follows night, the tide rises and falls. In comparison, a person's lifetime is limited. There are no repeated cycles, just one journey from life's beginning to its end. Is there a lesson to be learned from the contrast between what we observe in the natural world and what we observe in our own existence?

Quickwrite
Write a few lines on how you see yourself in relation to nature. Are you an integral part of the natural world around you, or do you live in it without being part of it? Is nature your friend or your enemy?

Elements of Literature
Meter: A Pattern of Sounds
Meter is a pattern of stressed and unstressed syllables in poetry. **Scanning** a poem means marking the stressed syllables with the symbol (´) and the unstressed syllables with the symbol (˘).

A metrical unit of poetry is called a **foot,** which always contains at least one stressed syllable and usually one or more unstressed syllables. A common type of foot is the **iamb**—an unstressed syllable followed by a stressed syllable. The meter of "The Tide Rises, the Tide Falls"

Meditation by the Sea,
Anonymous, n.d. Oil on canvas (13¹/₂″ × 19¹/₂″; 34.3 cm x 49.5 cm).
Gift of Maxim Karolik for the M. and M. Karolik Collection of American Paintings, 1815–1865. Courtesy Museum of Fine Arts, Boston.

176 AMERICAN ROMANTICISM

Reaching All Students

Struggling Readers
Help students use *Meditation by the Sea* to visualize the major images of "The Tide Rises, the Tide Falls." Point out that the man gazing at the ocean seems dwarfed by the cliffs, the line of the horizon, and the swell of the surf, just as the traveler in the poem is dwarfed by the sea. Lead students to find other words and phrases in the poem that can be compared to or contrasted with details in the painting.

English Language Learners
The rising and falling of the tide is universal, crossing cultures and generations. Students who have lived by the shore can describe the tide as it ebbs and flows. They also may comment on how it feels to see their footprints in the sand wiped out by the sea. For other strategies for English language learners, see
• *Lesson Plans Including Strategies for English-Language Learners*

is essentially iambic. Read this line aloud giving special stress to syllables marked (′).

Ălóng / thĕ séa- / sănds dámp / ănd brówn

Poets usually include variations within a metrical pattern in order to avoid a mechanical, singsong effect. In the poem's first line, notice how Longfellow avoids a purely iambic meter by pairing two stressed syllables, which is a metrical foot called a **spondee.**

Read the entire poem aloud to feel the rise and fall of its rhythm, just like the rise and fall of the tide.

> **M**eter is a pattern of stressed and unstressed syllables in poetry.
>
> *For more on Meter, see the Handbook of Literary Terms.*

A ## Elements of Literature
Meter
Point out that in the middle of many of the metered lines in this poem, there is a pause, or caesura, which reinforces the steady, stately iambic beat. Encourage students to find the caesuras in the first stanza. [The tide rises,‖ the tide falls; The twilight darkens,‖ the curlew calls; And the tide rises,‖ the tide falls]

B ## Elements of Literature
Repetition
❓ What words in ll. 6–7 are repeated? [sea, darkness] Read the passage aloud to help students hear how the repetition and rhythm create a somber effect.

C ## Elements of Literature
Personification
❓ To what are the waves being compared? [a child's or a young woman's hands] Have students notice the delicacy of the image. Why are the hands "white"? [It suggests the color of the sea foam.]

D ## Elements of Literature
Alliteration
❓ What sound is used most for alliteration in lines 11–12? [st] Note that this, too, is a form of repetition. Also, because it is a complex sound to pronounce, it slows down the "beat," contributing to the poem's meditative effect and reinforcing the theme of nature's repeated cycles.

The Tide Rises, the Tide Falls

Henry Wadsworth Longfellow

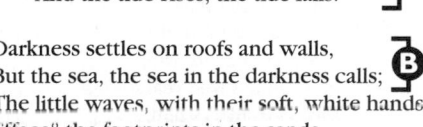

The tide rises, the tide falls,
The twilight darkens, the curlew° calls;
Along the sea-sands damp and brown
The traveller hastens toward the town,
5   And the tide rises, the tide falls.

Darkness settles on roofs and walls,
But the sea, the sea in the darkness calls;
The little waves, with their soft, white hands,
Efface° the footprints in the sands,
10   And the tide rises, the tide falls.

The morning breaks; the steeds in their stalls
Stamp and neigh, as the hostler° calls;
The day returns, but nevermore
Returns the traveller to the shore,
15   And the tide rises, the tide falls.

2. curlew (kur′lōō′): large, brownish shorebird with long legs.
9. Efface (ə·fās′): wipe out; erase.
12. hostler (häs′lər): person who takes care of horses.

HENRY WADSWORTH LONGFELLOW 177

Using Students' Strengths

Auditory/Musical Learners
Play a tape of the ocean with sounds of waves and birds as the class first reads the poem. Then have a group of interested students rehearse and tape-record a reading of the poem, complete with sound effects. Encourage students to use simple effects such as water in a bucket, sandpaper scraping against wood, and their own voices to simulate the sounds of the ocean, the traveler, the curlew, the horses, and the hostler. Have the group play their recording for the class.

Kinesthetic Learners
To help students understand iambic meter, write these phrases on the board: The day is hot; the marching feet. As students read these phrases in chorus, ask them to tap on their desks. Then tap again as they read the poem.

Naturalist Learners
Ask students to report on the physical phenomenon of tides: What causes them? What are the rhythms that result in high and low tides? What characterizes the ecosystem known as the intertidal zone? Where are the world's highest normal tides? What causes tides to run higher than usual? Historically, where have tidal waves caused destruction and death? What do environmentalists recommend about human use of tidal ecosystems?

T177

Summary ■■

In the octave of this sonnet, the speaker recounts how, during sleepless nights, the portrait of a woman who died long ago gazes at him. In the sestet, he makes an analogy between a frozen cross of snow in a Western mountain and the cross he has borne since she died.

Resources

Viewing and Representing
Fine Art Transparency
A fine art transparency of Thomas Moran's *Mount of the Holy Cross* can be used with this lesson. See the *Viewing and Representing Transparencies and Worksheets:*
• Transparency 4
• Worksheet, p. 16

Ⓐ Struggling Readers
Paraphrasing
Have students describe the scene in their own words. [Possible response: The speaker, sitting up sleepless at night, looks at the picture of his dead wife on the wall, where it is surrounded by a halo of lamplight.]

Ⓑ Elements of Literature
Meter
❓ What is the meter of the poem? [iambic pentameter] Which lines vary from the pattern? [Line 5 is apt to be read with the stress on *Here* instead of *in.* Line 6 opens with a stressed syllable followed by two unstressed syllables.]

Ⓒ Critical Thinking
Interpreting
❓ What is the meaning of the cross on the speaker's chest? [Sample responses: grief that does not disappear; remorse that he did not or could not save his wife; reverence for his wife.]

Ⓓ Elements of Literature
Sonnet
❓ Based on meaning, where could the poem be divided? [The first eight lines describe the speaker's wife; the last six describe the crosses on the mountain and on the speaker's chest.]

Before You Read
THE CROSS OF SNOW

Make the Connection
A Meaningful Image
Romantic poets often used aspects of nature to mirror or express emotions that might be too painful or personal to express directly. In this poem the poet has taken a dramatic sight from nature and transformed it through words into a powerful **image** that conveys several layers of intensely personal meaning.

Quickwrite
Of all human emotions, grief is one of the most difficult to express adequately. Think of an image from nature that could be used to describe a feeling of great sorrow. Set up your comparison like a **metaphor:** "Grief is _____." Then, explore in a few sentences some of the ways grief is like this image you have chosen.

Background
"I shall win this lady, or I shall die," Longfellow had written of Fanny Appleton, his second wife, who kept him waiting seven years before she agreed to marry him. Longfellow wrote this poem eighteen years after Fanny died in a fire. Three years later, Longfellow died without having shown it to anyone. Discovered among his papers, it was published four years later and immediately became one of his most famous poems. With a large audience waiting to read everything he wrote, why do you think Longfellow put this lyric aside?

Mount of the Holy Cross—Colorado (1873) by William Henry Jackson. Tinted photograph.
Historical Society of Colorado.

The Cross of Snow
Henry Wadsworth Longfellow

In the long, sleepless watches of the night,
    A gentle face—the face of one long dead—
    Looks at me from the wall, where round its head
    The night lamp casts a halo of pale light.
5 Here in this room she died; and soul more white
    Never through martyrdom of fire was led
    To its repose; nor can in books be read
    The legend of a life more benedight.°
There is a mountain in the distant West
10   That, sun-defying, in its deep ravines
    Displays a cross of snow upon its side.
Such is the cross I wear upon my breast
    These eighteen years, through all the changing scenes
    And seasons, changeless since the day she died.

8. benedight (ben′ə·dīt′) *adj.:* archaic for "blessed."

Making the Connections

Connecting to the Theme:
"The Transforming Imagination"
Longfellow's Romantic imagination transforms recognizable natural phenomena into symbols of philosophical thought and personal feeling. A traveler hurrying along a sandy beach, his footsteps erased by the tide, becomes a symbol of transient human life made trivial by contrast to eternal natural cycles. A mountain ravine that fills with snow, unreachable by the sunlight that might melt it, becomes a symbol of grief that cannot be assuaged, as well as a complex symbol of religious faith. Underlying Longfellow's symbol-making is his Romantic assumption that nature provides material for the human imagination.

The Tide Rises, the Tide Falls

First Thoughts

1. "Footprints on the sands of time" is a common expression referring to mortality and the passing of time. In the second stanza, what do you think is implied about the fate of the traveler when his footprints are washed away?

Shaping Interpretations

2. How does the division into stanzas reflect the passage of time in the poem?

3. What feeling is suggested by the stamping and neighing of the horses when morning comes? What contrasting feeling is suggested by what we are told about the traveler in this stanza?

4. **Onomatopoeia** is a poetic technique in which the sounds of words are used to echo their sense. If you have ever heard the call of a curlew, you know that the words "curlew calls" in line 2 echo the sound this shore bird itself makes. (Its cry is particularly mournful at dusk.) What sound do you think dominates this poem? What atmosphere does it suggest?

5. How does the **meter** of the poem reflect the movement of the tides?

6. Do you think this is a poem about one specific traveler? Or could it be seen as a "drama" about everyone's life? What do you think is suggested by the tide's continuing to rise and fall, despite the fact that the human traveler is gone?

Extending the Text

7. In your Quickwrite notes, how did you view yourself in relation to the natural world? Do you connect with the sentiments in this poem?

Challenging the Text

8. The waves are **personified** in stanza 2 as having "soft, white hands." This is an example of Longfellow's poetic style, which some readers think is too cute, or too sentimental, to be effective. Do you think the personification is justified here? Why or why not?

The Cross of Snow

First Thoughts

1. How did you respond to the strong personal emotion expressed in the poem? Were any of Longfellow's **images** of grief similar to the **metaphor** you explored in your Quickwrite? Explain.

Shaping Interpretations

2. The phrase "martyrdom of fire" in line 6 might confuse readers who did not know that Longfellow's wife had died in a fire. What is Longfellow suggesting about his wife's character when he uses such a powerful word to describe her death?

3. The phrase "watches of the night" usually refers to the rounds made by a watchman as he guards a house or a neighborhood. At certain hours the watch would call "All is well." What are Longfellow's figurative "watches of the night" (line 1)?

4. Explain how the phrase "sun-defying" (line 10) suggests conditions of weather and geology that might actually produce a permanent cross of snow on the side of a mountain. How does the poet relate the idea of a "sun-defying" formation of snow to his own feelings?

Extending the Text

5. What do you think about public expressions of personal grief? (Remember that Longfellow did not show "The Cross of Snow" to anyone during his lifetime.) How does the mass media—TV, radio, magazines, newspapers—affect our views of what's private and what's not? (Think of examples from news programs, talk shows, magazines, and documentaries.)

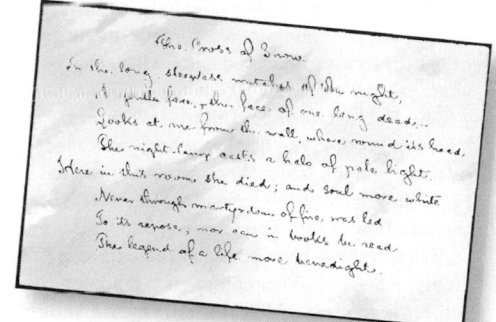

Portion of the original manuscript of "The Cross of Snow" by Henry Wadsworth Longfellow.
By permission of the Houghton Library, Harvard University.

The Tide Rises, the Tide Falls

First Thoughts [Respond]

1. Possible responses: The traveller's life and his actions are both transitory and temporary—they will be washed away by time. The traveller may have died before he got a chance to return across the beach.

Shaping Interpretations [Interpret]

2. The stanzas represent successive stages: twilight, night, and morning.

3. Possible response: The horses evoke a feeling of active life, while the traveler's absence suggests inactivity or death.

4. The poem is dominated by the "all" sound that begins and ends each stanza, following the rhyme scheme *aabba*. This and other repeated vowel sounds suggest a mournful atmosphere, and can be seen to evoke tolling bells, the calls of sea birds, or human cries of grief.

5. The meter, like the tides, is a steady rising and falling, a slow, continuous beat.

6. Sample response: The poem expresses a universal drama about the transience of human life, in contrast with the eternal cycles of nature.

Extending the Text [Respond]

7. Students may connect with the feelings in the poem because they think that nature endures but human life does not; or they may express little contact or connection with nature.

Challenging the Text [Evaluate]

8. Responses to the personification will vary.

The Cross of Snow

First Thoughts [Respond]

1. Accept all sincere attempts to answer the first question. In the second, make sure students cite specific lines from the poem when drawing parallels.

Shaping Interpretations [Interpret]

2. In the Christian tradition, martyrdom is usually associated with saints who die for their faith. By using this phrase, he emphasizes his wife's virtue and spirituality.

3. These are the times when, unable to sleep, the poet broods on the past and mourns his wife.

4. The sense is "untouched, or impenetrable by, sunlight." High altitudes and deep ravines might result in a permanent cross of snow on the mountain. Similarly, the poet's grief is too deep to be melted away by any ray of happiness.

Extending the Text [Apply]

5. Sample response: On the individual level, the expression of grief is natural and healthy. On the societal level, it can bring catharsis after, say, the death of an important person. Some students may note that both individuals and societies may allow grief to become exaggerated and even destructive.

Elements of Literature
The Sonnet
For additional instruction on the sonnet, see *Literary Elements:*
• Transparency 7
• Worksheet, p. 22

ELEMENTS OF LITERATURE

Mini-Lesson:
The Sonnet
In most Petrarchan sonnets, like "The Cross of Snow," the poet states a conflict or asks a question in the octave. In the sestet the poet offers a solution, a comment, or a resolution. Ask students to reread the first eight lines of "The Cross of Snow." What problem or conflict do they contain? [the poet's sleepless nights and his memories of his dead wife] In the sestet, what new comment does the poet make about his ordeal? [The changeless cross of snow has become a symbol of the grief he feels over his wife's death.] Students should also note that the rhyme is *abba, abba, cde, cde.*

Grading Timesaver

Rubrics for each Choices assignment appear on p. 108 in the *Portfolio Management System.*

CHOICES:
Building Your Portfolio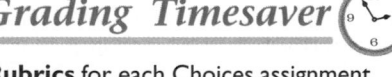

1. **Writer's Notebook** Tell students that the melodies of language often enhance meaning by first affecting our emotions. Suggest they take notes in a chart with four columns labeled Device, Quotation, Feeling Evoked, Meaning Conveyed.
2. **Comparing Poems** Ask students how they are affected by bad news heard on television versus bad news from a friend.
3. **Evaluating Visuals** Have students imagine what they would emphasize if they were illustrating the poem.
4. **Music/Performance** Remind student composers not only to think of melody but also to consider how different keys help create different moods.

ELEMENTS OF LITERATURE

The Sonnet

"The Cross of Snow" is a **sonnet,** a rhymed fourteen-line poem, usually written in **iambic pentameter.** *Iambic pentameter* describes verse in which each line is composed of five iambs. An **iamb** is a pair of syllables, an unstressed followed by a stressed syllable (ˇ′).

The sonnet is one of the oldest and most enduring poetic forms in world literature. Two of its early masters were the Italian poet Petrarch (1304–1374) and the English playwright William Shakespeare (1564–1616). In later periods, the sonnet was taken up by writers such as John Milton, William Wordsworth, John Keats, Elizabeth Barrett Browning, Edna St. Vincent Millay, John Berryman, Robert Frost, and Robert Lowell.

Two principal forms of the sonnet have been used in English. In the **Elizabethan,** or **Shakespearean,** sonnet, there are three four-line groups, called **quatrains,** followed by two final rhyming lines, called a **couplet.**

The **Petrarchan,** or **Italian,** sonnet, is divided into two groups: The first eight lines are called the **octave,** and the last six lines are called the **sestet.** Longfellow, who knew Italian literature well, used the Italian form for "The Cross of Snow."

What is the subject stated in the octave in "The Cross of Snow"? What comment is made on the subject in the sestet? What is the **rhyme scheme**?

What Is a Sonnet?

1. A sonnet has fourteen lines arranged in a specific pattern. It uses a set rhyme scheme.
2. The typical rhyme scheme in a Petrarchan, or Italian, sonnet is *abba, abba, cde, cde.*
3. The usual rhyme scheme in a Shakespearean sonnet is *abab, cdcd, efef, gg.*
4. The first part of a sonnet usually introduces a subject. The last group of lines makes a comment on the subject. When you read a sonnet, look for the subject and the comment on the subject.

CHOICES:
Building Your Portfolio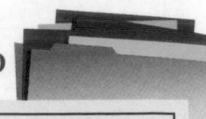

Writer's Notebook
1. Collecting Ideas for a Literary Analysis
When you write an analysis of a poem, you might concentrate on the **melodies of language**—on how the poem's language (sound) reinforces its meaning (sense). Read the Longfellow poems aloud to hear their music (or listen to them read aloud on audiotape). Then, jot down examples of the devices the poet uses to create his music—**meter, rhyme, refrain, onomatopoeia, alliteration.** Save your notes for possible use in the Writer's Workshop on page 198.

Comparing Poems
2. Complete and Incomplete
In a short essay, contrast the attitude toward death in "The Tide Rises, the Tide Falls" with that in "The Cross of Snow." Consider this question: Is it important that one poem is about an unnamed traveler while the other is about a specific person?

Evaluating Visuals
3. Visual and Verbal
In a brief essay, evaluate the fine art that accompanies "The Tide Rises, the Tide Falls." Is the image appropriate to the **mood** and **message** of the poem? Cite details from both the poem and the painting to support your position.

Music / Performance
4. A Traveler's Song
Compose and then perform for classmates a musical setting for "The Tide Rises, the Tide Falls." The setting should approximate the **tone** and **atmosphere** of the poem. Alternatively, choose an existing musical recording, an instrumental piece suitable in mood and tempo, and read or recite the poem while the music plays in the background.

Assessing Learning

Standardized Test Preparation
For practice in proofreading and editing, see
• *Daily Oral Grammar,* Transparency 13

John Greenleaf Whittier

(1807–1892)

John Greenleaf Whittier sent five dollars and this advice to a young man who had asked for help with his schooling: "I am sorry for the circumstance of thy condition for I have known what it is to be without money, and to live by hard labor. But, as to education, use thy leisure in educating thyself. Read and study a little every day, and before thee art twenty years of age, thee will find that a school is not needed."

Unlike the other Fireside Poets—Longfellow, Holmes, and Lowell—who were raised in privilege and enjoyed a distinguished education, Whittier was born into a poor Quaker family and had little formal schooling. Whittier started to write poetry when he was about fourteen years old, after his schoolmaster lent him a book by the popular Scottish poet Robert Burns (1759–1796), who had revived the Scottish literary heritage and written memorably of rural life.

At nineteen Whittier met the man whose influence would change the course of his life: the abolitionist William Lloyd Garrison (1805–1879). Garrison, then the editor of the local newspaper, had published a poem by the unknown young poet, and out of curiosity he journeyed out to the family farm to meet Whittier. He urged Whittier's father to give his son more schooling. "Poetry will not give him *bread*," was the father's terse reply.

With Garrison's help, the young Whittier found work in Boston as a newspaper editor. He soon immersed himself in current affairs, working side by side with Garrison, one of the most influential leaders in the antislavery movement. Whittier believed, as Garrison did, that slavery was not only unconstitutional, but also a sin against humanity—a conviction supported by his Quaker beliefs. At twenty-five Whittier paid for the publication of his own pamphlet, *Justice and Expediency* (1833), in which he called for an immediate end to slavery. As a result of

John Greenleaf Whittier (1833) by Robert Peckham (1785–1877). Oil on canvas (27" × 21½").

his stand against slavery, Whittier faced stone-throwing mobs, and magazines refused to print his poems.

In 1835, Whittier was elected to the Massachusetts state legislature. For the next quarter century, until the outbreak of the Civil War, Whittier worked tirelessly for the abolition of slavery. He contributed poems and articles to the *National Era*, which he also edited from 1847 to 1860. (It was this weekly newspaper that published Harriet Beecher Stowe's powerful antislavery novel, *Uncle Tom's Cabin*, in installments during 1851–1852.)

After the Civil War, Whittier retired to Amesbury, Massachusetts, where he wrote *Snow-Bound* (1866), a long poem of 759 lines that many critics consider his masterpiece. The poem made Whittier famous and, for the first time, financially comfortable.

Until he was well into his eighties, Whittier continued to publish poetry on homey incidents from rural life, episodes from Colonial history, and the humanitarian ideals of justice, religious faith, and tolerance. As much as his poetry, Whittier's humane convictions and moral example left a permanent mark on his era.

Summary ■ ■

The speaker tells of a December day in his youth when all the signs point to an approaching snowstorm. The family lives on a farm, far away from the nearest neighbors, so a heavy storm means isolation. After bringing in wood and bedding down the animals, the family goes to bed early, when it is already snowing. In the morning, the boys dig a path to the barn—tunneling where the drifts are deepest—and are welcomed by the animals. That evening the family gathers at the hearth, and sits around the roaring fire to enjoy warm cider, apples, and "nuts from brown October's wood."

Background

The full-length *Snow-Bound* introduces the household: the poet's mother and father, a brother, two sisters, an unmarried aunt and uncle, and the district schoolmaster. In the nearly six hundred lines remaining, the poet also narrates stories told by the characters.

Ⓐ Appreciating Language
  Word Choice
? How would your expectations of this poem change if the title were *Blizzard* or *Trapped?* [Possible response: These titles might suggest harsh, dangerous situations, while *Snow-Bound: A Winter Idyll* suggests a romantic, exciting, or homey interlude.]

Ⓑ Elements of Literature
  Rhythm and Rhyme
Whittier uses rhymed couplets in iambic tetrameter. Coach students to read the poem aloud using a natural, conversational style rather than a singsong one that stresses the four beats in each line.

Ⓒ Critical Thinking
  Determining Author's Purpose
? Why does the poet use this military image? [Possible responses: It suggests the boy is playing make-believe as he works; it conveys the personality of the rooster.]

Before You Read
FROM SNOW-BOUND: A WINTER IDYLL

Make the Connection
United We Stand
Sometimes hard times hold a blessing in disguise—they can draw us closer to other people. A warm bond of intimacy can develop even between total strangers who find themselves stranded, in trouble, or sharing unexpected pressures and hardships.

Quickwrite
Write a few sentences about a time when you experienced an unexpected sense of intimacy and even joy while sharing a difficult experience with other people. The experience could be a citywide blackout, a storm, or even a rush to meet a last-minute deadline on a project. What do you remember about the experience?

Background
An **idyll** is a nostalgic work describing a pleasant rural scene or homey setting. In *Snow-Bound,* Whittier looks back fondly on the life he spent as a boy in the farmhouse in Haverhill, Massachusetts, where his family had lived since 1688. Whittier remembers what we would call "an extended family," a gathering under one roof of eight or nine related people of varying ages, along with the male boarder who taught school nearby. Imprisoned by the storm, these people had to live for days without news of the outside world. Their rooms were dimly lighted by candles or perhaps by oil lamps. Their food, stored in crocks, barrels, and briny vats, was kept in the cellar. Water came from a pump in the kitchen or a well in the yard. A bathroom as we know it today did not exist. For heat and cooking, they burned wood. Life, in a word, was hard. But, like many people, Whittier found in his past a kind of benediction, or blessing.

Ⓐ *from* Snow-Bound: A Winter Idyll

John Greenleaf Whittier

To the memory of the household it describes, this poem is dedicated by the author

Ⓑ The sun that brief December day
Rose cheerless over hills of gray,
And, darkly circled, gave at noon
A sadder light than waning moon.
5 Slow tracing down the thickening sky
Its mute and ominous prophecy,
A portent seeming less than threat,
It sank from sight before it set.
A chill no coat, however stout,
10 Of homespun stuff could quite shut out,
A hard, dull bitterness of cold,
That checked, mid-vein, the circling race
Of lifeblood in the sharpened face,
The coming of the snowstorm told.
15 The wind blew east; we heard the roar
Of Ocean on his wintry shore,
And felt the strong pulse throbbing there
Beat with low rhythm our inland air.

Meanwhile we did our nightly chores,—
20 Brought in the wood from out of doors,
Littered° the stalls, and from the mows°
Raked down the herd's-grass for the cows;
Heard the horse whinnying for his corn;
And, sharply clashing horn on horn,
25 Impatient down the stanchion° rows
The cattle shake their walnut bows;°
While, peering from his early perch
Upon the scaffold's pole° of birch,
The cock his crested helmet bent
30 And down his querulous challenge sent.

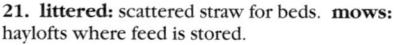

21. **littered:** scattered straw for beds. **mows:** haylofts where feed is stored.
25. **stanchion** (stan′chən): device placed around a cow's neck to keep the cow in its stall.
26. **walnut bows:** wooden yokes for harnessing cattle.
28. **scaffold's pole:** pole in the loft of a barn.

182 AMERICAN ROMANTICISM

Reaching All Students

Struggling Readers
Students may have trouble with the inverted syntax Whittier uses throughout the poem. Pull out three or more phrases from p. 182 that students cite as difficult, and go over them with students until they feel more confident. Then, encourage them to read the poem on their own or with partners, pausing to rephrase inverted sentences.

English Language Learners
There should not be difficulty for readers in following the narrative line of the poem. English language learners, however, may benefit from help with allusions and imagery. You might encourage them to work with a partner to sketch their interpretations of a few objects or scenes: for example, the "clothesline posts" (ll. 39–40); the tunnel (ll. 75–76); or the fire being laid (ll. 120–126).

The Cotters Saturday Night (detail) (c. 1815) by Eunice Pinney (1770–1849).
Pen and watercolor on paper.

Unwarmed by any sunset light
The gray day darkened into night,
A night made hoary° with the swarm
And whirl-dance of the blinding storm,
35 As zigzag, wavering to and fro,
Crossed and recrossed the wingèd snow:
And ere the early bedtime came
The white drift piled the window frame,
And through the glass the clothesline posts
40 Looked in like tall and sheeted ghosts.

So all night long the storm roared on:
The morning broke without a sun;
In tiny spherule° traced with lines
Of Nature's geometric signs,
45 In starry flake, and pellicle,°
All day the hoary meteor fell;
And, when the second morning shone,
We looked upon a world unknown,
On nothing we could call our own.

50 Around the glistening wonder bent
The blue walls of the firmament,
No cloud above, no earth below,—
A universe of sky and snow!
The old familiar sights of ours
55 Took marvelous shapes; strange domes and towers
Rose up where sty or corncrib stood,
Or garden wall, or belt of wood;
A smooth white mound the brush pile showed,
A fenceless drift what once was road;
60 The bridle post an old man sat
With loose-flung coat and high cocked hat;
The well curb° had a Chinese roof;
And even the long sweep,° high aloof,
In its slant splendor, seemed to tell
65 Of Pisa's leaning miracle.°

33. **hoary** (hôr′ē): white, as with age or frost.
43. **spherule** (sfer′ōōl): sphere.
45. **pellicle** (pel′i·kəl): thin film. Whittier is describing different kinds of falling snow.

62. **well curb:** frame over a well.
63. **sweep:** long pole with a bucket attached, used for getting water from a well.
65. **Pisa's leaning miracle:** Leaning Tower of Pisa in Italy. Whittier refers to it as a miracle because it looks as if it should fall over.

JOHN GREENLEAF WHITTIER 183

D **Reading Skills and Strategies**
Making Inferences
❓ What is "the hoary meteor"? [the snow]

E **Elements of Literature**
Imagery
Ask students to compare and contrast the imagery before and after ll. 48–49. What key difference do they see? [Lines 48–49 mark a transition from realistic description to metaphoric, fantastical imagery.]

F **Struggling Readers**
Using a Dictionary
Have students look up *firmament* in a dictionary and then paraphrase ll. 50–51. [Possible response: The blue sky curves around the glistening wonder of the snow.]

G **Reading Skills and Strategies**
Making Inferences
❓ What effect does the snowfall have? [It conceals familiar objects and transforms them into fantastic and wondrous shapes.]

H **Reading Skills and Strategies**
Recognizing Allusions
❓ Why does the speaker allude to the Leaning Tower of Pisa? [Possible answers: to help readers visualize the scene; to convey how familiar surroundings have become exotic and foreign.]

Using Students' Strengths

Naturalist Learners
People of Whittier's era depended on their immediate environment for many of the necessities of life. In *Snow-Bound,* the speaker's family uses natural resources from their region, such as oaken logs, apples, and nuts to sustain and comfort themselves during the harsh winter storm. Have interested students research how Native Americans and early European settlers "lived off the land" in your particular state or region. What native plants and animals did they use for food? How did they keep warm in the winter and cool in the summer? How did they use nature in their leisure time, in games and sports? Once students have completed this historical research, have them discuss whether it would still be possible in their state or region to depend on the natural environment for one's basic needs. Has development, extinction, or environmental degradation made some resources unavailable?

A

A prompt, decisive man, no breath
Our father wasted: "Boys, a path!"
Well pleased, (for when did farmer boy
Count such a summons less than joy?)
70 Our buskins° on our feet we drew;
With mittened hands, and caps drawn low,
To guard our necks and ears from snow,
We cut the solid whiteness through.
And, where the drift was deepest, made

B

75 A tunnel walled and overlaid
With dazzling crystal: We had read
Of rare Aladdin's° wondrous cave,
And to our own his name we gave,
With many a wish the luck were ours
80 To test his lamp's supernal powers.
We reached the barn with merry din,
And roused the prisoned brutes within.

C

The old horse thrust his long head out,
And grave with wonder gazed about;
85 The cock his lusty greeting said,
And forth his speckled harem led;
The oxen lashed their tails, and hooked,
And mild reproach of hunger looked;
The hornëd patriarch of the sheep,
90 Like Egypt's Amun° roused from sleep,
Shook his sage head with gesture mute,
And emphasized with stamp of foot.

D

All day the gusty north wind bore
The loosening drift its breath before;
95 Low circling round its southern zone,
The sun through dazzling snow mist shone.
No church bell lent its Christian tone
To the savage air, no social smoke
Curled over woods of snow-hung oak.
100 A solitude made more intense
By dreary-voicëd elements,
The shrieking of the mindless wind,
The moaning tree boughs swaying blind,
And on the glass the unmeaning beat
105 Of ghostly fingertips of sleet.
Beyond the circle of our hearth
No welcome sound of toil or mirth

E

Unbound the spell, and testified
Of human life and thought outside.
110 We minded° that the sharpest ear
The buried brooklet could not hear,
The music of whose liquid lip
Had been to us companionship,
And, in our lonely life, had grown
115 To have an almost human tone.

As night drew on, and, from the crest
Of wooded knolls that ridged the west,
The sun, a snow-blown traveler, sank
From sight beneath the smothering bank,

70. buskins (bus′kinz): calf- or knee-high leather boots.
77. Aladdin's: Aladdin is a young man in *The Arabian Nights* who finds a treasure in a cave.
90. Amun: god of ancient Egypt (also spelled Amon or Ammon). He is sometimes represented as a human with a ram's head.

110. minded: realized.

184 AMERICAN ROMANTICISM

Winter in the Country: A Cold Morning (1862)
by George Henry Durrie (1820–1863). Oil on canvas (26″ × 36″).

Crossing the Curriculum

Science
Ask students to find out the meteorological principles that govern the formation of snow and to report to the class as though they were meteorologists forecasting snow on the nightly news. Some students might also find out the average snowfall in Massachusetts and in your area, and report these facts as well.

Architecture/Geography
Ask students to draw an aerial map of the farm described in the poem. They should include the location and relative size of the farmhouse, the barn, and any other buildings they imagine the farm would include. They may also include such things as the sty, corncrib, garden wall, brush pile, and well in addition to topographical features such as the brook and the woods.

Taking a Second Look

Review: Analyzing Text Structures: Inversion
1. Have pairs of students identify two examples of inversion in *Snow-Bound* and write them in ordinary syntax. [Examples include: ll. 5–8, 29–30, 50–51, 104–105.]
2. Ask them to explain why Whittier might have chosen to invert those lines. [Possible answers: to maintain the meter; to create rhymes; to emphasize certain words by placing them in stressed syllables or at the end of lines.]

Courtesy of the Shelburne Museum, Shelburne, Vermont. Photograph by Ken Burris.

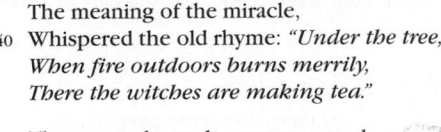

135 Our own warm hearth seemed blazing free.
     The crane and pendent trammels° showed,
     The Turks' heads° on the andirons° glowed;
     While childish fancy, prompt to tell
     The meaning of the miracle,
140 Whispered the old rhyme: *"Under the tree,*
     When fire outdoors burns merrily,
     There the witches are making tea."

     The moon above the eastern wood
     Shone at its full; the hill range stood
145 Transfigured in the silver flood,
     Its blown snows flashing cold and keen,
     Dead white, save where some sharp ravine
     Took shadow, or the somber green
     Of hemlocks turned to pitchy black
150 Against the whiteness at their back.
     For such a world and such a night
     Most fitting that unwarming light,
     Which only seemed where'er it fell
     To make the coldness visible.

155 Shut in from all the world without,
     We sat the clean-winged° hearth about,
     Content to let the north wind roar
     In baffled rage at pane and door,
     While the red logs before us beat
160 The frost line back with tropic heat;
     And ever, when a louder blast
     Shook beam and rafter as it passed,
     The merrier up its roaring draft
     The great throat of the chimney laughed;
165 The house dog on his paws outspread
     Laid to the fire his drowsy head,
     The cat's dark silhouette on the wall
     A couchant° tiger's seemed to fall;
     And, for the winter fireside meet,
170 Between the andirons' straddling feet,
     The mug of cider simmered slow,
     The apples sputtered in a row,
     And, close at hand, the basket stood
     With nuts from brown October's wood.

120 We piled, with care, our nightly stack
     Of wood against the chimney back,—
     The oaken log, green, huge, and thick,
     And on its top the stout backstick;
     The knotty forestick laid apart,
125 And filled between with curious art
     The ragged brush; then, hovering near,
     We watched the first red blaze appear,
     Heard the sharp crackle, caught the gleam
     On whitewashed wall and sagging beam,
130 Until the old, rude-furnished room
     Burst, flowerlike, into rosy bloom;
     While radiant with a mimic flame
     Outside the sparkling drift became,
     And through the bare-boughed lilac tree

136. crane . . . trammels: swinging arm (crane) attached to the fireplace, with iron hooks (trammels) from which cooking pots are hung.
137. Turks' heads: ornamental shapes resembling turbans. **andirons:** metal supports used to hold wood in a fireplace.
156. clean-winged: Turkey wings were used to brush ashes from the hearth.
168. couchant (kou′chənt): crouching.

JOHN GREENLEAF WHITTIER **185**

RESPONDING TO THE ART
George Henry Durrie (1820–1863) was a portrait and landscape painter known for his nostalgic seasonal views of his native Connecticut, many of them reproduced by Currier & Ives (see pp. 452–453).
Activity. Ask students what elements of the painting's subject matter convey the mood or atmosphere of the poem? [Possible responses: The snow and the bare trees convey cold; the farm buildings and farmhouse convey a sense of warmth and family life; the sky suggests an impending storm.]

F **Elements of Literature**
Imagery
❓ How does this image combine fire and snow? [The snowdrift outside the window reflects the firelight from inside.]

G **Reading Skills and Strategies**
Recognizing Allusions
❓ Explain how the speaker uses this allusion to a spooky nursery rhyme or fable. [It is used to explain the optical illusion of the fire in the snow.] Is the allusion dark and foreboding in this context, or is it more comforting and fanciful? [Possible response: It seems like a humorous and comforting piece of banter shared by the family.]

H **Elements of Literature**
Imagery
❓ Reread this stanza. How can "coldness" be visible? [Possible responses: The moonlight seems cold because it lights the winter landscape; shining on the white snow, the moonlight creates a silver and metallic quality with black shadows, all colors that seem cold.]

I **Critical Thinking**
Analyzing
❓ What characteristics of the poem make it a Romantic poem? [Be sure to send students back to the characteristics of Romanticism listed on p. 144. The poem emphasizes feelings over scientific facts and character dissection; places faith in imagination; celebrates nature; celebrates an innocent past; alludes to exotic stories and legends of the past.]

Making the Connections

Connecting to the Theme: "The Transforming Imagination"
Discuss with students how *Snow-Bound* exemplifies the collection theme. In the poem a farm boy's imagination transforms a New England snowstorm into a fairy-tale landscape. When the boy grows up, his adult imagination transforms the experience a second time by turning memory into poetry. Both transformations exemplify the imaginative spirit of American Romanticism.

Assessing Learning

Check Test: Fill-in-the-Blank
1. The family earns its living by [farming].
2. The blizzard takes place in [December].
3. The children imagine their snow tunnel is [Aladdin's] cave.
4. At night the family [sits by the fire].
5. How does the boy feel about the snow? [He is enchanted.]

MAKING MEANINGS

First Thoughts [Respond]

1. Sample responses: A world completely white with a crisp, blue sky; people huddled around a fireplace drinking hot apple cider.

Shaping Interpretations [Interpret]

2. Possible responses: "The sun . . . / Rose cheerless over hills of gray" (ll. 1–2); "darkly circled, gave at noon / A sadder light" (ll. 3–4); "the roar / Of Ocean on his wintry shore" (ll. 15–16); "the strong pulse throbbing." (l. 17).

3. Possible responses: The image of the "Chinese roof" (l. 62), the allusion to the Leaning Tower of Pisa (l. 65), the references to Aladdin's cave (ll. 77–80), and the "spell" (l. 108) cast by the storm.

4. They wish they could use Aladdin's lamp to grant wishes. Other details include the rhyme mentioning witches in ll. 140–142, the chimney seeming to laugh in l. 164, and the cat's shadow appearing to be that of a tiger in ll. 167–168.

Connecting with the Text [Apply]

5. Responses will vary.

READING SKILLS AND STRATEGIES

Possible Answers

(1) Architecture: Scaffold's pole in the barn (l. 28); Chinese roof on the well curb (l. 62); Leaning Tower of Pisa (l. 65). (2) Literature: Aladdin (ll. 77–80) is a character in *The Arabian Nights,* a collection of ancient folk tales. (3) History: Amun (l. 90) is an Egyptian god.

Student recognition of the allusions will vary; Aladdin is doubtless the most widely recognizable for contemporary Americans. The allusions reveal that Whittier assumes his readers have some knowledge of other cultures and eras.

Grading Timesaver

Rubrics for each Choices assignment appear on p. 109 in the *Portfolio Management System.*

MAKING MEANINGS

First Thoughts

1. What did you see as you read this part of *Snow-Bound*?

Shaping Interpretations

2. The first eighteen lines of the poem create a **mood** of foreboding and expectation. List the **images** that help build this mood.

3. The poet emphasizes the fabulous nature of the snowbound world. What specific **imagery** helps us see his farmyard as if it's an exotic sight from another world?

4. Another reference to folklore and the fabulous occurs in the lines describing the crystal cave. In line 80, what do the boys wish they could do? What other details in the poem connect the fabulous or the imaginary with the snowbound farmhouse?

Connecting with the Text

5. A few days spent locked up with family or friends would have some effect on your mood. How do you think you would feel if you were snowbound or otherwise confined with other people? Refer to your Quickwrite notes for ideas.

READING SKILLS AND STRATEGIES

Recognizing Allusions

Snow-Bound was an enormously popular poem, and until a few generations ago, parts of it could be recited by almost every schoolchild in America. However, the poem is not necessarily "easy"; what makes it difficult for some readers are its many **allusions**—references to people and events from history, literature, the arts, or other aspects of culture.

Skim the poem and find allusions to (1) architecture, (2) literature, and (3) history. Which of the references did you recognize? (Did you have to refer to the footnotes?) What do these allusions tell you about the kind of education Whittier assumed his readers would have?

CHOICES: Building Your Portfolio

1–2. To help students understand the appeal of the poem, have them recall special times they have spent with family and friends, such as holidays, and what made them special.

3. Encourage students to introduce each poem with a brief description of the historical context in which it was written, (such as a review of the Fugitive Slave Act of 1850 for "The Hunters of Men").

CHOICES: Building Your Portfolio
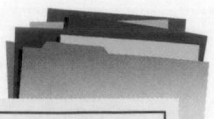

Writer's Notebook

1. Collecting Ideas for a Literary Analysis

Review the extract from *Snow-Bound,* and take notes on its most powerful **images**. Look for images that evoke sensations of sight, hearing, taste, smell, and even touch. What comparisons help to make the images particularly vivid? Save your notes for possible use in the Writer's Workshop on page 198.

Analyzing a Poem's Appeal

2. The Pull of the Past

When *Snow-Bound* was published, it was an immediate best-seller, and it continued to be reprinted well into the twentieth century. By then, the kind of life it pictures had all but vanished. In one paragraph or more, explain how you would account for the continuing appeal of this poem. Include in your analysis any similar appeals to the romantic past that you find in today's movies, TV shows, books, or popular songs.

Speaking and Listening / Analyzing Poetry's Persuasive Power

3. End Slavery!

In his own time Whittier considered himself an abolitionist first and a poet second. Find several of Whittier's antislavery poems—"The Hunters of Men" or "The Farewell," for example—and read them aloud to the class. Then, as a class, discuss the effectiveness of these poems as antislavery messages.

Oliver Wendell Holmes

(1809–1894)

Courtesy Boston Athenaeum (UR22.1936).

"Everybody wants to have a hand in a great discovery," Oliver Wendell Holmes wrote in 1846, when, for the first time, an American surgeon used gas to make a patient unconscious during surgery. Holmes, a physician himself, suggested the word *anesthesia* (without feeling), and the name stuck.

A descendant of Anne Bradstreet (page 68), Holmes was born into an already distinguished family in Cambridge, Massachusetts, and he graduated from Harvard College—just a short distance from home. Before turning to medicine, Holmes had studied law, a subject he found "cold and cheerless." He was a twenty-one-year-old law student when the United States government's plan to destroy the warship USS *Constitution* inspired him to write "Old Ironsides," a poem that aroused public sentiment to save the ship and made him famous.

In spite of this early taste of literary glory, Holmes became a physician, because he felt it could teach him about humanity. He was twenty-seven when he published his first book of poetry and, almost at the same time, was awarded a medical degree from Harvard. Combining poetry and medicine did not seem unusual to Dr. Holmes, who was said to hear poetic meter in the rhythm of the human heart.

One of the founders of *The Atlantic Monthly* magazine in 1857 (he also named it), Holmes gained a national reputation from a series of chatty, urbane, and sometimes irreverently witty essays that were eventually collected under the title *The Autocrat of the Breakfast Table* (1858). The leading character, recognizable as Holmes himself, presided over the lively table talk at an imaginary Boston boardinghouse.

Holmes's poetry is, for the most part, light and even comic. It comments on the social and intellectual shortcomings of his contemporaries, particularly those who aspired to higher forms of verse than he himself dared to write. But, on the evidence of his serious poems, such

Oliver Wendell Holmes (1858) by Thomas Hicks (1823–1890). Oil on canvas (53.4 cm × 43.1 cm).

as "The Chambered Nautilus," Holmes had earned the right to judge, not from an envious spirit but in the confidence of an equal talent.

Today, Holmes is perhaps remembered more as a phenomenon—an aristocrat with the common touch, an artist with a passion for science—than as a poet. The famous wit that made his books best-sellers in their day has long become outdated, but the benign figure of Oliver Wendell Holmes remains. It is impossible to forget the gentleness and humor of a man who, beginning his practice as a young physician, hung out a sign saying GRATEFUL FOR SMALL FEVERS.

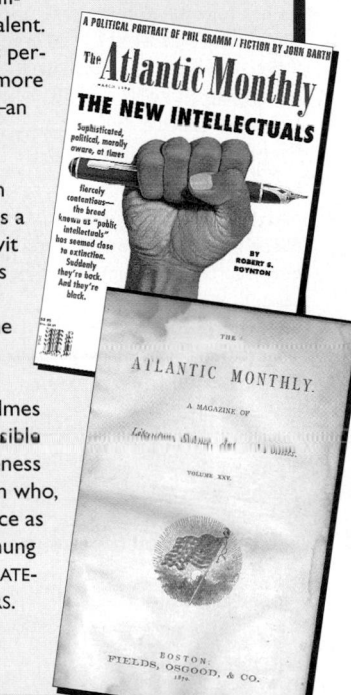

OBJECTIVES
The Chambered Nautilus / Old Ironsides
1. Read and interpret the poems
2. Analyze extended metaphor
3. Express understanding through critical and creative writing and art

SKILLS
Literary
- Analyze extended metaphor
Writing
- Collect ideas for a literary analysis
- Analyze a poem's message
- Write a scientific description
- Write a history for children
- Write a meditation
Art
- Illustrate a story for children
Viewing/Representing
- Responding to a photograph (ATE)

Planning

- **Block Schedule**
  Block Scheduling Lesson Plans with Pacing Guide
- **Traditional Schedule**
  Lesson Plans Including Strategies for English-Language Learners
- **One-Stop Planner**
  CD-ROM with Test Generator

— 🎧 💿 — *Resources: Print and Media* —

Reading
- *Graphic Organizers for Active Reading*, p. 17
- *Audio CD Library*
  Disc 5, Tracks 7, 8

Writing and Language
- *Daily Oral Grammar*
  Transparency 15

Assessment
- *Formal Assessment*, p. 38
- *Portfolio Management System*, p. 110
- *Test Generator (One-Stop Planner CD-ROM)*

Internet
- go.hrw.com (keyword: LEO 11-4)

Summary ■ ■

The first three stanzas of the poem celebrate the "lustrous coil" of the nautilus as a physical record of its inhabitant's steady progress into larger chambers. The last two stanzas use apostrophe, first to praise the nautilus and then hold it up as an example for the soul—to grow spiritually at every step, until the day that the body is cast aside like an "outgrown shell."

Background

The nautilus's chambers are connected to one another by a tube. The mollusk is able to force gases into the chambers through the tube, making the whole shell act as a float. When the animal wants to go deep into water, it absorbs gases from the chambers, and when it wants to rise to the surface, it fills the chambers with gases to enable it to float upward.

BROWSING IN THE FILES

About the Author. In February 1830, Holmes's poems began appearing anonymously in Harvard publications. Although his poetry was well-received, he maintained anonymity by signing later poems with only an H. Despite the success of "Old Ironsides," published in September 1830, he did not sign his name to a poem until 1833.

Dr. Holmes's son, Oliver Wendell Holmes, Jr., stuck to *his* legal studies and became a justice of the United States Supreme Court.

Before You Read
THE CHAMBERED NAUTILUS

Make the Connection
Things Change
Throughout our lives we outgrow old things and move on to new ones: clothes, attitudes, interests, jobs, types of entertainment—even friendships. As we learn more about ourselves and the world, we're often challenged to widen our perspectives and rethink our assumptions—and the process is not always comfortable.

Quickwrite
Read the Background that follows, and then look at the picture of the nautilus shell, at right. Write a few sentences reflecting on the shell and the creature that once lived in it. If the shell were "human," what would you say to it?

Elements of Literature
Extended Metaphor
A **metaphor** is a figure of speech that makes a comparison between two very unlike things. Sometimes writers extend a metaphor—that is, they take it as far it can logically be developed. An **extended metaphor** may continue for several lines, or it may be developed throughout an entire work.

> **A**n **extended metaphor** is a figure of speech developed throughout several lines or an entire work.
>
> *For more on Metaphor, see the Handbook of Literary Terms.*

188 AMERICAN ROMANTICISM

Background
A nautilus is a sea creature that lives in a shell, one of those mollusks that grow year by year from the size of a tiny bead to the size of a pumpkin. In Holmes's own description the nautilus shell is composed of a "series of enlarging compartments successively dwelt in by the animal that inhabits the shell, which is built in a widening spiral." The word *nautilus* comes from the Greek word for "sailor," reminding us that the Greeks thought this shell could actually move on the surface of the water, using a membrane as its sail. The nautilus is not only one of the most beautiful objects in nature; it is also one of the most fragile life-containing vessels.

The first three stanzas of this poem are a meditation upon the life and death of the nautilus. In the next-to-last stanza, the poet begins an **apostrophe** (a direct address to an object or to someone who is not present). The visual description here is like the scene in Shakespeare's *Hamlet* (Act V), in which a gravedigger unearths the skull of a man Hamlet knew. Hamlet holds the skull up to the light and speaks words about life and destiny that the skull evokes for him. We might picture the speaker in "The Chambered Nautilus" holding the shell before him and speaking.

Reaching All Students

Struggling Readers
Students may find it easier to read "The Chambered Nautilus" and "Old Ironsides" if they divide the poems into sentences. Have them read and paraphrase each sentence individually until they have grasped the sense of the lines. (Have them look carefully at the commas and dashes to see how clauses are set off.) Then have students write each poem as a prose paragraph.

English Language Learners
Studying the pictures on this page and on pp. 190–191 will help students visualize the extended metaphor in "The Chambered Nautilus" and the source of the appeal in "Old Ironsides." Before reading "Old Ironsides," help students place events from the USS *Constitution's* history on the time line on p. 140.

Advanced Learners
In turning to nature as a source of inspiration for self-improvement, Holmes was in tune with his slightly older contemporary Ralph Waldo Emerson (p. 216) and his younger contemporary Henry David Thoreau (p. 230). "The Chambered Nautilus," which first appeared in 1858 in *The Autocrat of the Breakfast Table,* can be discussed as a transitional work which foreshadows the exuberant and unconventional Transcendentalist thought of the American Renaissance.

The Chambered Nautilus Ⓐ

Oliver Wendell Holmes

This is the ship of pearl, which, poets feign,°
   Sails the unshadowed main,—
   The venturous bark that flings
On the sweet summer wind its purpled wings
5 In gulfs enchanted, where the siren° sings,
   And coral reefs lie bare,
Where the cold sea maids° rise to sun their streaming hair.

Its webs of living gauze no more unfurl;
   Wrecked is the ship of pearl!
10   And every chambered cell,
Where its dim dreaming life was wont to dwell,
As the frail tenant shaped his growing shell,
   Before thee lies revealed,—
Its irised° ceiling rent,° its sunless crypt unsealed!

15 Year after year beheld the silent toil
   That spread his lustrous coil;
   Still, as the spiral grew,
He left the past year's dwelling for the new,
Stole with soft step its shining archway through,
20   Built up its idle door,
Stretched in his last-found home, and knew the old no more.

Thanks for the heavenly message brought by thee,
   Child of the wandering sea,
   Cast from her lap, forlorn!
25 From thy dead lips a clearer note is born
Than ever Triton blew from wreathèd horn!°
   While on mine ear it rings,
Through the deep caves of thought I hear a voice that sings:—

Build thee more stately mansions, O my soul,
30   As the swift seasons roll!
   Leave thy low-vaulted past!
Let each new temple, nobler than the last,
Shut thee from heaven with a dome more vast,
   Till thou at length art free,
35 Leaving thine outgrown shell by life's unresting sea!

1. feign (fān): archaic for "imagine."

5. siren (sī′rən): in Greek mythology, one of a group of sea maidens whose seductive singing lures sailors to wreck their ships on coastal rocks.
7. sea maids: mermaids or sea nymphs.

14. irised (ī′risd): iridescent; rainbowlike. Iris is the Greek goddess of the rainbow. **rent:** torn.

26. than . . . wreathèd (rēth′id) **horn:** echoes a line from "The World Is Too Much with Us," a sonnet by English poet William Wordsworth (1770–1850): "Or hear old Triton blow his wreathèd horn." In Greek mythology, Triton is a sea god, often represented as blowing a trumpet made from a conch shell. *Wreathèd* means "coiled" or "spiral-shaped."

Ⓐ Reading Skills and Strategies
Poetic Melodies
Read the poem aloud and have students listen for its melody and rhythm. Discuss how alliteration softens the sounds, how punctuation slows the pace, and how lack of full stops at the end of some lines allows them to flow into each other.

Ⓑ Cultural Connections
Nautical Language
Explain that "the unshadowed main" refers to the sunlit sea. A "bark" is a sailing ship.

Ⓒ Elements of Literature
Extended Metaphor
❓ What is the general comparison that the metaphors in these lines make? [They compare the nautilus's shell to human dwellings—a prison cell, an apartment, and a tomb.]

Ⓓ Advanced Learners
Apostrophe
Ask students to speculate about why poets use apostrophe. [Possible answers: To convey an outburst of feeling; to make abstract ideas more immediate and emotional.]

Ⓔ Elements of Literature
Allusion
Ask students to summarize the lines with the Triton allusion. [The message of the nautilus is clearer and more powerful than the notes played by a god.] Why are this allusion and the one in l. 5 particularly apt? [Both allusions relate to the sea and sailing, and thus both underscore the metaphor in the nautilus's very name.]

Ⓕ Elements of Literature
Allusion
Line 29 suggests John 14:2 ("in my Father's house are many mansions"). As ll. 29–31 show, Holmes objected to the strict Calvinism of his background and expressed in this work his view that the soul should strive to achieve virtue and salvation.

Ⓖ Elements of Literature
Extended Metaphor
❓ What two things are compared in the extended metaphor? [the growth of the nautilus and the development of the human soul] What lesson does the speaker draw? [the importance of perpetually building a nobler, loftier, more spiritual existence until death]

Using Students' Strengths

Logical/Mathematical Learners
Students can apply the golden ratio, which will relate the shape of the shell to a series of nested rectangles. Have them draw rectangle ABDC, form square EBDF inside the rectangle, form square AEHG inside the new rectangle, and continue the process until they have formed five nested rectangles. Have them use a compass to make quarter-circles in each square. The resulting spiral will give them the growth pattern of the nautilus.

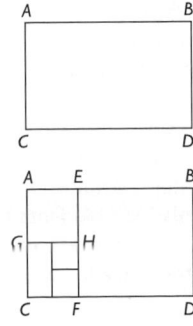
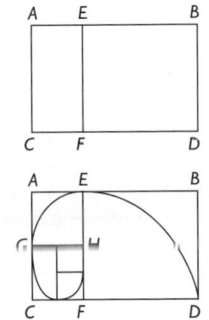

Summary ■

"Old Ironsides" uses vivid imagery and verbal irony to celebrate the patriotic value of the USS *Constitution* and to protest its proposed scrapping. In the first two stanzas, the speaker evokes the ship's battle history and parodies the cynical attitude of those who would have it destroyed. In the last stanza, he insists that a more fitting end for the noble hulk would be to let it sink into "the mighty deep."

Ⓐ Critical Thinking
Analyzing

❓ What is the tone that Holmes establishes in this first stanza? [one of bitter verbal irony] How do the connotations of the word "tattered" shift by the end of the first stanza? [At first, "tattered" seems to have negative connotations, since it emphasizes the dilapidated condition of the doomed ship. By the end of the stanza, it is clear that this condition has positive connotations for the speaker, underscoring the ship's glorious history.]

Ⓑ Elements of Literature
Metaphor

❓ How does the ship resemble a meteor? [It strikes quickly and causes destruction.]

Ⓒ Elements of Literature
Meter

❓ In what meter is the poem written? [one line of iambic tetrameter alternating with one line of iambic trimeter] What effect does the meter produce? [a driving, forceful beat that is emotionally intense]

Ⓓ Elements of Literature
Metaphor

❓ What qualities of the eagle make it a fitting metaphor? [Sample responses: the eagle rules the skies because of its swiftness, strength, and ability to strike. It is also a symbol of the United States, under whose flag the ship sailed.]

Ⓔ Reading Skills and Strategies
Drawing Conclusions

❓ How does this stanza contradict the first line? [It says nailing the ship's flag to the mast and sinking it would be preferable to tearing down its flag and then scrapping it.] Why is that an argument for preserving it? [Sinking the ship is unthinkable, and the speaker has ruled out the only other alternative—scrapping it—as a sacrilege.]

Before You Read
OLD IRONSIDES

Make the Connection
Word Power

As the old saying tells us, "The pen is mightier than the sword." Words can be powerful tools for resolving conflicts, righting wrongs, or otherwise influencing human actions and emotions. Words can preserve or destroy, praise or protest. They can change the world. The words in this poem saved an American legacy: a historic ship.

Quickwrite

Think of some historical object or place in your own state, city, town, or neighborhood that is being threatened with destruction—or could be one day. Jot down as many reasons as you can think of for why this piece of history should be preserved.

Background

In 1830, the forty-four-gun American warship USS *Constitution,* which had defeated the British warship *Guerrière* in the War of 1812, was scheduled to be scrapped. Holmes sent this poem to the Boston *Daily Advertiser* in protest. The poem aroused public sentiment and saved the ship, which you can still visit in Boston Harbor today.

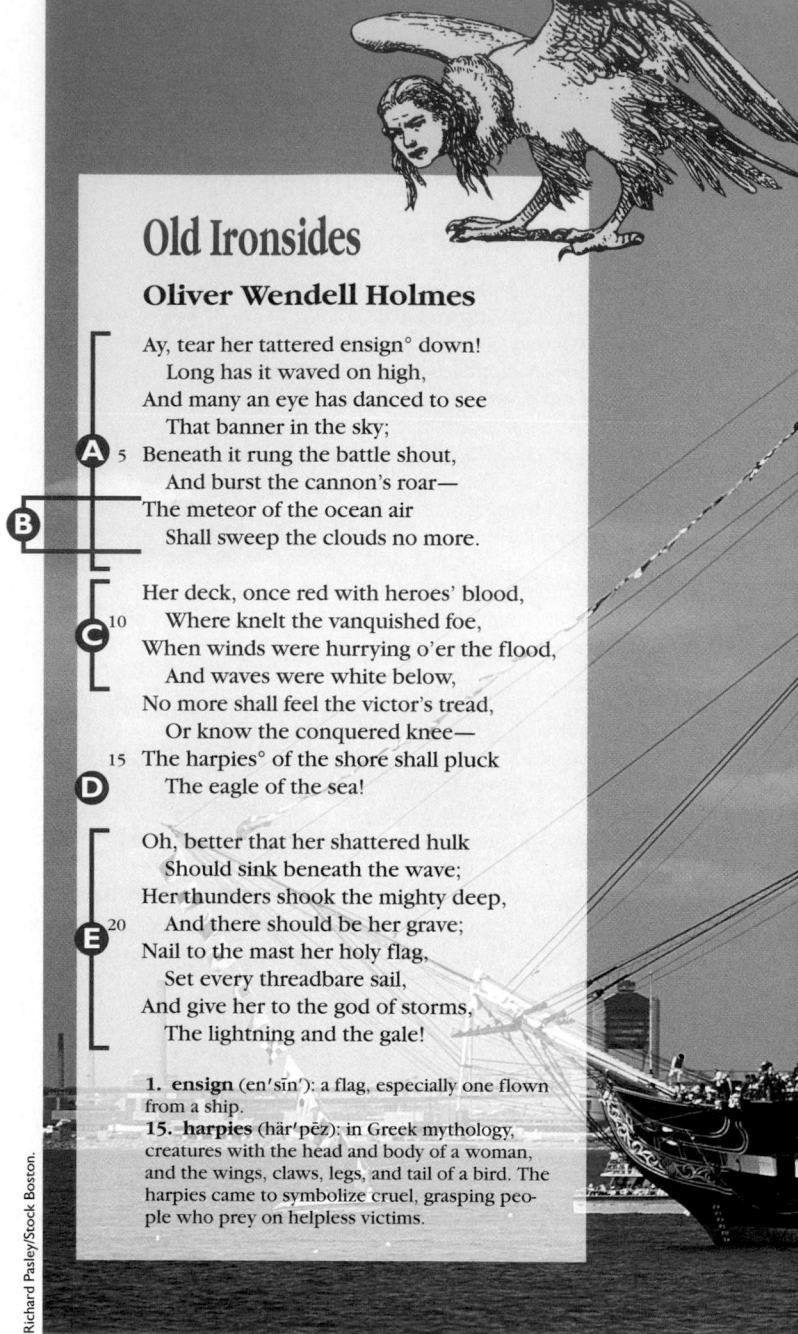

Old Ironsides
Oliver Wendell Holmes

Ay, tear her tattered ensign° down!
　　Long has it waved on high,
And many an eye has danced to see
　　That banner in the sky;
5　Beneath it rung the battle shout,
　　And burst the cannon's roar—
The meteor of the ocean air
　　Shall sweep the clouds no more.

Her deck, once red with heroes' blood,
10　　Where knelt the vanquished foe,
When winds were hurrying o'er the flood,
　　And waves were white below,
No more shall feel the victor's tread,
　　Or know the conquered knee—
15　The harpies° of the shore shall pluck
　　The eagle of the sea!

Oh, better that her shattered hulk
　　Should sink beneath the wave;
Her thunders shook the mighty deep,
20　　And there should be her grave;
Nail to the mast her holy flag,
　　Set every threadbare sail,
And give her to the god of storms,
　　The lightning and the gale!

1. ensign (en'sīn'): a flag, especially one flown from a ship.
15. harpies (här'pēz): in Greek mythology, creatures with the head and body of a woman, and the wings, claws, legs, and tail of a bird. The harpies came to symbolize cruel, grasping people who prey on helpless victims.

Richard Pasley/Stock Boston.

Crossing the Curriculum

Science/Mathematics/Art

In conjunction with "The Chambered Nautilus," have students find out about mathematical patterns that can be found in nature. (One source is *By Nature's Design,* with text by Pat Murphy and photographs by William Neill.) These include spirals, helixes, meanders, ripples, spheres, branches, and fractals. Ask students to show pictures and to discuss the places in art and nature where these patterns are found.

Social Sciences

In conjunction with "Old Ironsides," take students to a local history museum and show them what artifacts have been preserved in your community. Alternatively, invite a member of the local historic society to speak about buildings, ships, or vehicles that have been restored in your area and how they are significant. Have students discuss how local artifacts and people's feelings about them remain important today.

USS *Constitution* in Boston Harbor.

OLIVER WENDELL HOLMES 191

Professional Notes

The Poem's Genesis

In August 1830, the USS *Constitution* was almost thirty-three years old—more than twice the lifespan of the average wooden warship. A Navy report indicated it had a sound frame but needed "very extensive repairs." However, the *Boston Daily Advertiser,* on September 14, erroneously reported that the Navy had condemned the ship. What happened in the Holmes household that day or the next is dramatically recreated by historian Catherine Drinker Bowen in

Yankee From Olympus: ". . . Oliver, bursting in the door one afternoon, found [Abiel Holmes, his father] sitting moodily at his desk, trying to compose a letter to the *Boston Daily Advertiser.* . . . Oliver went upstairs and, sitting down by the western window, got out pen and paper. The lines poured from him, swept from him in a tide. It was as though he was writing someone else's poem, dictated carefully by its author and transcribed by Oliver Holmes. . . . It was late when

he took the poem downstairs. . . . His father was still at his desk. . . . Silently Oliver laid the poem on the desk and left the room. . . . A moment later his father called him in. When Oliver came in, Abiel Holmes was standing by the desk, the poem in his hand. He began to speak, and his voice choked. With enormous surprise, and a great lift to the heart, Oliver, looking up, saw tears in his father's eyes, saw that the hand holding the verses was trembling."

MAKING MEANINGS

The Chambered Nautilus

First Thoughts [Respond]

1. Accept all reasonable answers supported by specific references to the poem.

Shaping Interpretations [Interpret]

2. "Silent toil/That spread his lustrous coil" (ll. 15–16); "the spiral grew" (l. 17); "left the past year's dwelling for the new" (l. 18); moved through "its shining archway" (l. 19); "Built up its idle door" (l. 20).

3. The creature building its shell is a metaphor for the human soul striving toward virtue and ultimately heaven. The "stately mansions," or nautilus chambers, represent the spiritual achievements of the soul; the "low-vaulted past," or previous chambers, represent earlier, less spiritual states, of the soul; "each new temple," or chamber, represents each step of the soul toward its goals; the "outgrown shell" suggests the body discarded in death; the "unresting sea" represents life.

Extending the Text [Evaluate]

4. Possible responses: It endures because of its beauty and inspirational message about spiritual growth. Or it will not endure because its language and style are increasingly archaic, or because we look for different things in poetry today.

Challenging the Text [Evaluate]

5. Possible response: Both are optimistic. "Thanatopsis" may seem pessimistic since its subject is death, but it focuses on death as unity with nature.

Old Ironsides

First Thoughts [Respond]

1. Most students will accept the value of historic preservation, but some may say that humanitarian issues are more important. Most students will think that the public would try to save the ship.

Shaping Interpretations [Interpret]

2. *Old Ironsides* has too noble a history, and too much patriotic meaning, to be scrapped. The opening line is ironic, expressing the opposite of what Holmes wants.

Student to Student

The Sea

Shells and pebbles roll in
the mist of gentle waves.
    A mother cries, a daughter
    mourns.
    The ship went down in the
    storm.
Timber is tossed by the
mountains of the violent sea,
which churns against the cliffs.
    The captain's cry, the
    shipmate's tears.
As the angry waves scatter
their hope like sea spray
    against the wind.

—Elizabeth Enloe
Shades Valley Resource
Learning Center
Birmingham, Alabama

MAKING MEANINGS

The Chambered Nautilus

First Thoughts

1. Review your Quickwrite notes. Compare your thoughts with what the speaker of the poem thinks as *he* looks at the nautilus.

Reading Check

a. What **metaphor** describes the nautilus in line 1?

b. What **images** in the first stanza help you picture where the nautilus first sailed?

c. According to the second stanza, what has happened to the nautilus?

d. Why does the speaker thank the nautilus in the fourth stanza?

192 AMERICAN ROMANTICISM

3. Holmes is suggesting that those who are responsible for the decision to scrap the ship, and those who profit from it, are the harpies.

4. It symbolizes the nation's heroic past.

5. It appealed to the patriotic emotions of its readers. "Heroes' blood" (l. 9) and "her holy flag" (l. 21) are particularly persuasive.

Extending the Text [Evaluation]

6. Possible response: The arts can still sway public opinion; today, a persuasive lyric would probably be in a song rather than in print.

Shaping Interpretations

2. Stanza 3 describes the ways the nautilus grows. The poet uses a **metaphor** comparing the nautilus to a person who changes homes. What details describe how this happens year after year?

3. Step by step, describe the **extended metaphor.** What are the "stately mansions" (line 29), the "low-vaulted past" (line 31), "each new temple" (line 32), the "outgrown shell" (line 35), and the "unresting sea" (line 35)?

Extending the Text

4. "The Chambered Nautilus" is one of the most enduring poems in American literature. (Abraham Lincoln is said to have known it by heart.) Why do you think this poem has endured? Do you think it will still be read one hundred years from now? Be sure to give your reasons.

Challenging the Text

5. Did you find this poem more optimistic than Bryant's "Thanatopsis" (page 171)? Why or why not?

Old Ironsides

First Thoughts

1. Do you think that historical relics like *Old Ironsides* should be preserved? If, very soon, *Old Ironsides* were found to be in danger of sinking at its dock in Boston, do you think most Americans would let it go? Give reasons why or why not.

Shaping Interpretations

2. In simple terms, what message does the first stanza present? What is **ironic** about the way Holmes states his message?

3. When a ship is broken up in the dockyards, it is said to be *scrapped*—that is, stripped of everything valuable or reusable. Is Holmes comparing

Reading Check

a. The nautilus is compared to a "ship of pearl" sailing on the ocean.

b. The "main" (l. 2), or open sea; "gulfs enchanted" (l. 5); and "coral reefs" (l. 6).

c. The nautilus has been "wrecked" (l. 9)—taken from the sea and split open.

d. The speaker is grateful for the nautilus's example and the message he takes from it: to grow spiritually, mentally, and emotionally.

---

the directors of the scrapping business to harpies in stanza 2, or is his scorn directed at someone else? Explain.

4. What do you think the poet wants the ship to **symbolize**?

5. Why do you think this poem was successful in getting the public to save the ship? Point out specific words and phrases that you found particularly persuasive.

Extending the Text

6. Think about specific issues in today's world that have inspired public movements for preservation. Do you think a poem like "Old Ironsides" would be able to sway public opinion today? Why or why not?

Grading Timesaver

Rubrics for each Choices assignment appear on p. 110 in the *Portfolio Management System*.

CHOICES: Building Your Portfolio

Writer's Notebook

1. Collecting Ideas for a Literary Analysis

Think about the **extended metaphor**  in "The Chambered Nautilus" and the ship as **symbol** in "Old Ironsides." Sum up as clearly as you can what the metaphor is and what the ship symbolizes. Then, freewrite on how the metaphor and symbol are used in each poem. Save your notes for possible use in the Writer's Workshop on page 198.

Analyzing a Poem's Message

2. A Heavenly Message

In a brief essay, discuss the message of Holmes's poem "The Chambered Nautilus." First, discuss in what part of the poem the "heavenly message" of the shell is revealed. Then **paraphrase** this message—that is, state in your own words what the "voice that sings" says to the speaker. Finally, discuss whether you feel the poet has been successful in developing and leading up to the poem's message. Does the message seem tacked on to give the poem a moral, or is it a natural outgrowth of the poem? How can you relate the message of the poem to your own life?

Crossing the Curriculum: Technical Writing

3. A Scientific Stance

How would Holmes the scientist have described the chambered nautilus? Gather scientific data about the nautilus from other sources, and write an objective, accurate, scientific description of the creature. Include specific data on its vital statistics. What questions might a scientist ask of the nautilus? Present your findings in class. Include a scientific illustration, if you wish.

Creative Writing / Research / Art

4. The Story of a Ship

Research the history of the USS *Constitution,* from its days as a warship to its current use as a tourist attraction in Boston Harbor. Write a short story for children in which you describe the ship and tell its life story. Provide your own colorful illustrations.

Creative Writing

5. A Meditation

We might imagine that Holmes was inspired to write "The Chambered Nautilus" while he was looking at the beautiful nautilus shell. The student poem on page 192 might have been written while the writer was looking at or thinking about the sea. Write a meditation of your own, imitating one of these poems. (Check your Quickwrite notes.) Focus on some object or scene that brings memories, lessons, events, or stories to mind. Open with a line that tells what you are looking at.

OLIVER WENDELL HOLMES 193

Grading Timesaver

CHOICES: Building Your Portfolio

1. **Writer's Notebook** Remind students that an extended metaphor is developed over many lines. Review the meaning of symbol and discuss other national symbols such as the flag and the controversies that arise when people disagree on how they should be used.

2. **Analyzing a Poem's Message** Students might discuss the assignment in small groups before working on it independently. Ask students to spend up to five minutes on each of the three directives about the message of the poem. Remind them to take notes on others' ideas as well as their own.

3. **Crossing the Curriculum: Technical Writing** If students have difficulty getting started, prompt them with some of the following questions:
   • What shape does it have?
   • What other organisms does it resemble? In what ways? How does it differ from them?
   • Where does it live?
   • How does it grow?
   • What can you gather about its way of life from examining it?

4. **Creative Writing/Research/Art** After students complete their research and rough out an outline, discuss the age of the audience for whom they are writing, the vocabulary level they should use, and the appropriate sentence length and complexity.

5. **Creative Writing** Once students have chosen a subject, give them plenty of time to freewrite until they find what they want to say in connection with this subject.

Connecting Across Texts

Connecting with "The Chambered Nautilus" and "Old Ironsides"
Ask students to compare and contrast Elizabeth Enloe's view of the sea in "The Sea" with Holmes's in "The Chambered Nautilus" and "Old Ironsides." [Possible response: Enloe's vision is one of destruction and anger ("the angry waves," the shipwreck). Holmes finds the sea a source of optimistic, triumphal images.]

Assessing Learning

Standardized Test Preparation
For practice in proofreading and editing, see
• *Daily Oral Grammar,* Transparency 15

T193

READ ON

Women of Wonder

If "Rip Van Winkle" whetted your appetite for folk tales, consider *The Maid of the North* (Holt, Rinehart and Winston) by Ethel Johnston Phelps. The author collects and retells a variety of traditional folk tales with one thing in common—the heroes are all enterprising females! The twenty-one tales come from many parts of the world, including Africa, Japan, Scandinavia, and North America.

Past, Present, and Future

"If Albert Einstein is right once again . . . then hard as it may be to comprehend, the summer of 1894 *still exists*." Modern-day magazine photographer Si Morley proves Einstein's theory when he travels back to nineteenth-century New York City in Jack Finney's best-selling science fiction classic *Time and Again* (Simon and Schuster). Further time-travel adventures appear in Finney's recent sequel, *From Time to Time* (Simon and Schuster).

The Face of One Long Dead

"The Cross of Snow" is a poem of mourning for a lost love whose absence haunts the speaker years after her death. For an epic treatment of this theme, try reading Emily Brontë's classic *Wuthering Heights*. Inspired by many of the same Romantic poets that influenced Longfellow, Brontë's novel chronicles a tragic love of such intensity that it transcends even death. The novel has been adapted into several films, the most famous starring Laurence Olivier and Merle Oberon. This title is available in the HRW Library.

By the Seashore

"One never knows what chance treasures these easy unconscious rollers may toss up, on the smooth white sand of the conscious mind; what perfectly rounded stone, what rare shell from the ocean floor." In her acclaimed book *Gift from the Sea* (Random House), Anne Morrow Lindbergh describes a seaside vacation in which the shells she discovers on the beach prompt valuable inner discoveries about life.

The Rockets' Red Glare

If you liked Oliver Wendell Holmes's "Old Ironsides," then answers to questions like these might really interest you: Why was the Battle of New Orleans fought after the War of 1812 was officially over? Which battle scenes inspired "The Star-Spangled Banner"? Popular historian Walter Lord answers these and other questions in *The Dawn's Early Light* (W. W. Norton), a lively account of the conflict known in its day as the Second War of Independence.

The American Language

"Noah's Ark": Webster's Dictionary
by Gary Q. Arpin

By the nineteenth century, many Americans felt the need for some kind of authority to govern matters of usage. In England, the ultimate linguistic authority was royal—the King's English. In America, matters were very different.

In a relatively stable social structure, people of a particular class will speak the way their friends and associates speak, and questions of right and wrong speech patterns won't even be raised. In societies where social structure is fluid, though, the matter becomes more complex.

In eighteenth-century England, for instance, the rigid social structure began to give way as the middle class grew. People of humble origins had started to become successful in business. These newly well-to-do sent their children to recently founded schools that, among other things, taught the language habits of the aristocracy the middle class wanted to imitate. Written grammars dictating English usage became popular, and schoolmasters began to take over authority in matters of English language usage. *A New Guide to the English Tongue* (1747) by Thomas Dilworth was a popular grammar book in England.

In America the teaching of English arose for similar reasons. Before the Revolution it would have been difficult to find an "English School" in the Colonies—that is, a school that emphasized English grammar over Latin grammar. After the Revolution, though, regular instruction in English grammar became common in the public schools, as the Colonial social structure gave way to a more fluid and democratic society. However, the only available textbooks came from England. This was clearly an awkward situation for a new nation that wanted to establish linguistic independence.

An American Spelling Book

Enter Noah Webster (1758–1843), a schoolmaster from Connecticut. Webster was looking for a way to finance his legal education, and he was also passionately dedicated to the cause of American English. To help advance these two causes, Webster published a spelling book in 1783, when he was twenty-five. Even though it was based in important respects on English models—Dilworth's grammar and Samuel Johnson's great *Dictionary of the English Language* (1755)—the spelling book turned out to be a major force in the drive for American linguistic independence. Over the generations, *The American Spelling Book* (also known as the "Blue-Backed Speller") was issued in numerous editions, and more than sixty million copies were sold.

Webster prepared his speller and his later textbooks for a purpose:

> . . . to reform the abuses and corruption which . . . tincture the conversation of the polite part of Americans . . . and especially to render the pronunciation . . . accurate and uniform by demolishing those obvious distinctions of provincial dialects.

Webster reasoned that accurate and uniform American spelling would lead to uniform American speech, and that uniformity in speech would "reconcile the people of America to each other."

Consistency in Spelling

The whole idea of consistency in spelling was fairly new in Webster's time and was directly related to the increasing use of the printing press. Until the 1700s, people followed rather

---

A Historical Connections
The existence of written grammatical rules for a language, along with dictionaries and a body of literary works, are major indicators that a language has reached a standardized form. English achieved this status by the 1770s in England and by the mid-1800s in the United States.

B Background
Noah Webster (1758–1843) had an extremely varied and busy career. He fought beside his father in the Revolution, owned and edited a daily newspaper in New York City, wrote influential pamphlets In favor of the ratification of the Constitution, worked for the enactment of copyright laws, wrote and published a revised version of the Bible, and served in the General Assembly of Connecticut and the General Court of Massachusetts.

C Critical Thinking
Speculating
❓ How might Webster's dedication to the American Revolution and Constitution have influenced his commitment to the cause of American English? [Possible response: Webster may have wanted cultural, as well as political, independence from England, and may have believed that a distinctive language was one way to achieve this independence.]

D Historical Connections
While the idea of consistency in spelling was fairly new, Webster was not the first person to try to reform English spelling. As early as 1568, entrepreneur Sir Thomas Smythe called for consistency in spelling. In 1768, Benjamin Franklin even made up a new alphabet, eliminating some letters and adding others, in an attempt to bring about consistent spelling.

A Critical Thinking

Expressing an Opinion

❓ Given the pronunciations of words like *music* and *public,* did Webster really improve the spelling of those words by eliminating the *k*? [Possible response: No. The last sound of both words is /k/. The letter *c* is sometimes pronounced /k/ and sometimes /s/ (as in *certain*), so *c* is a more ambiguous choice; Yes, he simplified these unnecessary spellings, but Webster might have made a more simple and logical choice by spelling the words as *musik* and *publik*.]

B Cultural Connections

The Politics of Spelling

❓ Some people suggest that the word *women* should be spelled *womyn* to eliminate the dependence on *men* that they believe the traditional spelling implies. Do you think language, especially spelling, is as political as this controversy suggests it is? [Responses will vary. Some students may find this issue trivial and believe that the spelling of words does not really matter, while others may feel that language plays a strong role in shaping people's attitudes toward others and that changes in language can and should help build social harmony.]

C Background

Webster seems to reflect a *descriptivist* attitude toward language in this passage, which means that he feels he should describe the language as he finds it, rather than make value judgments about what is proper. When he tells people how words should be spelled, however, Webster reflects a *prescriptivist* attitude, which means that he feels correct language usage should be prescribed by some authority. Since the middle of the twentieth century, most linguists have regarded the two approaches as complementary.

---

flexible rules of spelling. In fact, some letters of the alphabet were not completely fixed: *i, j, y, u, v,* and *w* were not yet distinct letters. Sometimes a word would be written with an *e* at the end and sometimes not. Thus, *join* might be written *ioyn* or *joyne* or *ioyne.* The word *the* was frequently written *ye,* the *y* in this case being a form of an obsolete Middle English letter that stood for the sound *th.*

Early editions of Webster's American speller were quite conservative—that is, most of the spellings were consistent with Samuel Johnson's English spellings. The main exception was Webster's omission of *k* in words ending in *–ck.* Where Dr. Johnson's dictionary had *publick* and *musick,* Webster's speller had *public* and *music.* By 1789, though, Webster offered more radical ideas regarding spelling, and they aroused a great deal of mocking resistance, even in his own country.

Webster's first principle was the "omission of all superfluous or silent letters"—such as the k in *musick* and all silent vowels and consonants. *Bread, give, friend, programme, travelled,* and *built* thus became *bred, giv, frend, program, traveled,* and *bilt.*

Webster's second principle was to regularize spelling and sound. For example, *grieve* and *mean* contain the same vowel sounds spelled differently. Webster used *ee* for both as well as anywhere that sound occurred—*greev* and *meen,* and also *pleez* and *bleet.* Similarly, *laugh* and *draught* became *laf* and

draft, plough became *plow,* and *women* became *wimmin.*

Webster gradually yielded to public pressure and modified his more radical spellings. Still, virtually all of the present differences between British and American spelling were advocated by Webster.

Webster's First Dictionary (1806)

Readers were no doubt very surprised when they came across words spelled *tung, fether, soop,* and *definit* in Webster's first dictionary, *A Compendious Dictionary of the English Language,* published in 1806.

Many of Webster's recommended pronunciations must have been surprising as well. Webster disliked fashionable and urban people and manners almost as much as he disliked British ways. He hated any pronunciation that smacked of being affected or too fashionable. Webster rejected the *yu* sound in words such as *lecture, nature, figure,* and *tenure* as affectations. He recommended that they be pronounced *lecter, nater, figger,* and *tenor.*

Webster laid down stern rules regarding spelling and pronunciation, but he was often willing to bow to the practice of common people in matters of grammar and usage. The single thread running through these two contradictory attitudes was

Webster's democratic desire for a common, regular American language.

Many of Webster's spelling reforms and odd pronouncements make him appear to be a crackpot, and there is no question that there was something of the crackpot about him. He had a degree from Yale, but as a linguist he was self-taught. Like many self-taught people, he had odd gaps in his learning. As a result, his etymologies, or word histories, were frequently incorrect.

> Many of Webster's spelling reforms and odd pronouncements make him appear to be a crackpot, and there is no question that there was something of the crackpot about him.

Webster's American Dictionary (1828)

Even though his enthusiasms and spotty knowledge led him astray, Webster was no fool, and he was enormously energetic. His 1806 dictionary defined 37,000 words and indicated their pronunciation. The 1828 *American Dictionary of the English Language* was an incredible accomplishment for one person. It defined 70,000 words and provided etymologies as well as pronunciations. More than 12,000 definitions were published for the first time. Webster was the first lexicographer to include Americanisms such as *lot* ("a piece of land"), *to spell* ("to relieve someone at work"), and *clever* ("good-natured"). "Such local terms exist," Webster had written some years before, "in spite of lexicographers and critics. Is this *my* fault? And if local

---

Reaching All Students

Struggling Readers

To help students understand the progression toward standardization of the American language, draw the following time line on the chalkboard. Ask students to draw their own time lines and to place on them the specific dates and events mentioned in "Noah's Ark." In addition, have students draw on the time line pictures that represent the events noted. Such a time line might look like the following:

pre-1700s		contemporary times
flexible rules for spelling		Webster's New World Dictionary

English Language Learners

Let these students share their own frustrations about the spelling of English words. Have them explain spelling rules in their first languages and tell whether spelling in those languages is more or less phonetically based than English.

Advanced Learners

Have these students continue Webster's work by writing proposals to change the spelling of words to make them agree with their sounds. Have them each write a business letter to a dictionary editor that states the reason that a certain spelling should be changed and that includes a list of words that can be treated in the same fashion.

terms exist, why not explain them? . . . How are such words to be understood without the aid of a dictionary?"

The *American Dictionary* also included the new American meanings of older English words and settled for all time the changes in word endings that distinguish American from modern British usage: *–er* for *–re* (*center* rather than *centre*); *–or* for *–our* (*favor* rather than *favour*); *–c* for *–ck* (*music* rather than *musick*); *–ck* for *–que* (*check* rather than *cheque*); *–ize* for *–ise* (*legalize* rather than *legalise*); and *–ler* for *–ller* (*traveler* rather than *traveller*). We say *skedule* rather than *shedule* because Webster thought the pronunciation of *schedule* should follow the example of *school*.

Webster's Legacy

English purists shuddered to learn of Webster's determination to include American words and usages, and one critic suggested that the resulting volume of "foul and unclean" things be dubbed "Noah's Ark."

But Webster's pronouncements, even when they had little sound linguistic reasoning behind them, settled the uncertainties about authority in American English. Generations of Americans decided on the correctness of a word or a usage or a spelling by "looking it up in Webster's," and every household had to have a copy of Webster's dictionary next to the Bible.

By 1828, Webster's radical view of the development of American English had moder-

ated, though his patriotism had not diminished. "The body of the language is the same as in England," he wrote in the Preface to the *American Dictionary*, "and it is desirable to perpetuate that sameness." In the same Preface, though, he pointed proudly at the burgeoning American literature as a source of richness and at the growth of the language as a source of pride.

Over the years many of Noah Webster's etymologies have been corrected, and spelling has been regularized further. Old words have taken on new meanings, and thousands of new words have been added to American English. Yet Webster was a central figure in the evolution of American English, and his name continues to signify excellence in dictionaries. Two of the United States' biggest sellers, *Webster's New World Dictionary* and *Merriam-Webster's Collegiate Dictionary*, still proudly display his name in their titles. Webster would have been pleased to have seen the fruits of his labors.

Try It Out

1. **Using consistent spelling.** Consider this sentence written by Webster in his reformed spelling. "Every possible reezon that could ever be offered for altering the spelling of wurds, stil exists in full force; and if a gradual reform should not be made in our language, it wil proov that we are less under the influence of reezon than our ancestors." What incon-

sistencies do you see in Webster's reformed spelling? Find a brief prose passage of your choice and write it in your own simplified—but consistent—spelling. Accompany your passage with a brief explanation of the rules for your reformed spelling.

2. **Spelling sounds.** Make a list of words that are spelled in similar ways but are pronounced differently (such as *tough* and *bough*). Then, make a list of pairs of words that are spelled differently but have similar pronunciations (such as *dead* and *bed*). How would a consistent spelling rule help, for example, students for whom English is a second language? Would there be any drawbacks to consistent spelling?

3. **Inventing alternate spellings.** Nonstandard forms of simplified spellings have flourished in product names ("Tastee Treetz"); road signs ("Thruway North"); and even pop music groups ("Boyz II Men"). List five other examples of nonstandard spellings from your everyday experience. Then try inventing five original product or business names that use nonstandard spellings.

THE AMERICAN LANGUAGE **197**

ⓓ Critical Thinking
Extending the Text

❓ What advantages has the continuation of a common language between Great Britain and the United States produced for people in both countries? [Answers will vary. Most answers should focus on the fact that the common language has enabled people in both countries to easily share ideas, as well as many aspects of culture.]

Try It Out
Possible Answers

1. Inconsistencies in Webster's spelling: Unsounded double consonants are eliminated in some words (*stil* and *wil*) but not in others (*full*). Likewise, silent letters are eliminated in some words (*proov*), but not in others (*possible* and *influence*). Possible rewrite of a sample passage: "Webster gradually yielded to publik pressur and modified his mor radikal spellings." Explanation of rules: Substitute *k* for *c* and eliminate silent *e*.

2. Responses will vary. Words spelled similarly but pronounced differently include *tomb* and *comb* and *touch* and *couch*. Words that are spelled differently but have similar pronunciations include *tough* and *gruff* and *tight* and *bite*. Most students will probably feel that consistent spelling rules would help students for whom English is a second language and that there are few drawbacks to consistent spelling except, perhaps, in personal names that are spelled inconsistently to emphasize individuality.

3. Possible responses: Groups like INXS, Phish, and The Beatles, and phrases that include "2U," "lite," and "E-Z" are all examples.

Resources ━━━━━

Assessment
Formal Assessment
• The American Language Test, p. 40

Assessing Learning

Check Test: Fill-in-the-Blank

1. The English middle class felt that words should be used the way [the aristocracy] used them.
2. Webster felt that uniform American spelling and speech would [bring Americans together].
3. The new idea of consistency in spelling was directly related to the increasing use of the [printing press]

4. The two books of Webster's that had the biggest influence on American language were a [spelling book] and a [dictionary].
5. Webster had rules about spelling and pronunciation, but he would bow to the usage of the [common people].

T197

EXPOSITORY WRITING

ANALYZING A LITERARY WORK

When you read a literary work, your first response is often a strong feeling: "This poem really moved me," or "I thought this story was upsetting!" In a literary analysis, you go beyond this first response, to understand how and why the work produces these effects. Writing an analysis gives you a chance to take a work apart and explain how it creates meaning. You do this by looking at the literary elements that form its structure.

Prewriting

1. **Choose a literary work.** If you haven't been assigned a specific literary work to analyze, your first step will be to choose a work that you're interested in. Look over the notes you took for the Work in Progress assignments in this collection. Which selections caught your attention? What key literary elements make these works effective? Do your notes suggest a topic that would give you material for a sustained analysis?

2. **Focus your analysis.** You can discuss a wide range of literary elements in the work you choose, but your analysis will be stronger if you narrow your focus to one or two. Try to isolate the most prominent elements—those that distinguish the work, that contribute to its overall effect, and that help communicate its central theme or message. Here are some possible topics for a focused analysis:

   - The role of setting in "Rip Van Winkle"
   - Symbolism in "The Tide Rises, the Tide Falls"
   - Natural imagery in "Snow-Bound: A Winter Idyll"
   - The function of metaphor in "The Chambered Nautilus"

3. **Write a thesis statement.** Your thesis statement will be the controlling idea of your analysis. It will state a generalization about the work. A thesis statement is important because it will also determine the organizational structure of your essay. Experiment with a variety of thesis statements until you have crystallized your thoughts in a single strong sentence. Make sure your thesis statement isn't so broad that it could be the subject of an entire book, or so narrow that it can't be developed to much more than a paragraph.

   Example thesis statement: In "The Chambered Nautilus," the speaker uses an extended metaphor to compare the growth of the nautilus in its shell to the growth of a human soul.

 Resources: Print and Media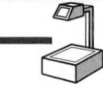

The history of the written word is rich and time
Once upon a time
Page 1

4. Gather Evidence. Reread the text at least twice as you negotiate your interpretation of the material. Then, list all the evidence you can find to support your thesis statement. While most of your evidence should come from the text itself (your **primary source**), you may also want to use citations from **secondary sources** if they are relevant to your main ideas. (Secondary sources are critical reviews, biographies, encyclopedia entries, and similar works.) Cite specific lines from your primary source; then, paraphrase their meaning in your own words. You may want to group your evidence into a **graphic organizer** like this:

Element	Examples	Support for Thesis
Metaphor	"ship of pearl," 1 "venturous bark," 3 "frail tenant," 12 "crypt unsealed," 14 "the silent toil," 15	In these first three stanzas, the speaker describes the life and death of a nautilus in human terms— comparing its shell to a variety of human dwellings: a ship, a building for a tenant, a tomb. These metaphors also suggest aspects of the human spirit: its dreamy thirst for adventure, its frailty, its experience of death.
	"heavenly message brought by thee," 22 "Build thee more stately mansions, O my soul," 29 "each new temple, nobler than the last," 32	In the last two stanzas, the speaker celebrates the growth and movement of the nautilus as a metaphor for the growth of his own soul, which expands into bigger and more noble dwellings until it is at last released from the body.

5. Organize your ideas. Before you begin to write your first draft, decide how you will present your ideas and then make an outline. Look at your graphic organizer to see how you grouped your main ideas and supporting details. You may want to organize your points in **chronological order,** the order in which the elements occur in the text. If your main ideas and supporting evidence focus on a particular theme, purpose, or effect, you might consider organizing your ideas in **order of importance:** emphasize your most powerful point first (or build up to it and place it at the end). As you make your outline, be sure that your main ideas and supporting details follow a logical progression. Be sure also to include in each paragraph details that directly support your thesis.

Strategies for Elaboration

To make the opening of your essay more interesting:

1. **Hook your reader's interest.** Open your introductory paragraph with an intriguing question, an anecdote, or a personal comment that relates to your thesis statement.
2. **Try for drama.** Open your essay with a dramatic quote from the piece, one that relates particularly well to your main idea.
3. **Make connections to theme.** Briefly refer to the theme of the text and describe how the elements you are analyzing relate to the theme.

Language Handbook HELP

See Using Modifiers, pages 1227-1228; Quotation Marks and Ellipsis Points, page 1247.

Prewriting

- Focus students' attention on the prewriting steps outlined on pp. 198–199. Emphasize that a good thesis statement includes ideas or opinions on the topic:

  Thesis statement = a subject + your ideas about the subject

- You may want students to create an organizer such as that shown on p. 199. This will help them to gather and organize information, identify weaknesses, and suggest a logical pattern of thought.

Reaching All Students

Struggling Writers

Students having difficulty with this assignment may need additional help selecting a topic and developing a thesis. Once these students have chosen a selection that interests them, it may be helpful to let them meet in groups, particularly those who have chosen the same selection. You may wish to give them some questions to guide the discussion:

- What is the author's main point?

- Are there special techniques the author uses to point the reader in the right direction? What are they?
- Are there figures of speech that seem to echo the same main idea? Are there words or ideas that are directly repeated? Why would the author do this?
- If you close your eyes and think about the piece, does some image or feeling come to mind? What?

Drafting

- Before students begin to write, discuss the Evaluation Criteria on this page with them. At the same time, it may be well to review also the Strategies for Elaboration on p. 199.
- Encourage students to continue to do research as they draft. Drafting may well focus an involved writer on a whole new line of inquiry.
- Encourage the sharing of drafts with other students familiar with the work. Have student reviewers use the Evaluation Criteria to comment and respond.

Evaluating and Revising

Many students writing about literature tend toward what they feel is a literary style—unnecessarily complex language, excessive use of adjectives, etc. Remind students that the best writing is often the simplest. Complex language may be nothing more than a mask for unresolved questions or unclear thoughts.

Proofreading and Publishing

Establish review groups of students working with the same piece or author. After working together to proof their papers, have them consider ways in which their collected essays might be published. For example, many Web sites are devoted to the authors covered in this collection. Perhaps the collected essays could be published on one of these.

Communications Handbook HELP

See Proofreading.

Revision STRATEGIES

Because a literary analysis can be subjective, you should aim for precise word choice, or diction. Replace vague words with specific ones; if necessary, refer to a thesaurus.

■ *Evaluation Criteria*

A good literary analysis
1. *opens with a striking quotation, anecdote, question, or personal comment*
2. *provides necessary background information on the work being studied*
3. *states the thesis concisely and directly, with main ideas presented in the order in which they will be discussed*
4. *provides ample supporting evidence from the text for each main idea*
5. *follows a clear and consistent pattern of organization*
6. *quotes accurately from primary and secondary sources, citing page and line numbers*
7. *closes with a summary that restates the main idea*

Drafting

1. **Introducing your ideas.** The main purpose of your introductory paragraph is to state your thesis, or main idea. Your thesis statement should be clear, concise, and direct. Avoid vagueness, ambiguity, and overstatement (claiming more than you can actually demonstrate). Your introductory paragraph should also identify the work you are writing about (by title and author) and provide whatever background information you think the reader will need (for example, dates, information on the author, literary history, and historical context).

2. **Analyzing and supporting.** Your outline and your graphic organizer will come in handy as you write the body of your essay. Follow the organization of your main ideas and supporting details set up in your outline. Use the entries on your graphic organizer to direct your analyses of the meaning, the purpose, and the effects of each element.

    While the main source of support for your argument will be citations and paraphrases from your primary source, you may want to bolster your claims with additional support. Here are some strategies to reinforce your analysis:

    - Make appeals to common sense and everyday experience.
    - Include references to other literary works. (Do other writers or works use literary elements in a similar way?)
    - Present relevant facts or details from the author's life. (Does the work reflect personal events in the writer's life or historical events that occurred during his or her lifetime?)
    - Use quotations from experts. (Have critics written about the work and said something interesting about these particular elements?)
    - Offer personal responses. (Do the responses have the potential to add authenticity and originality to your analysis?)

3. **Closing the essay.** Think of a way to summarize or restate your thesis at the end so that you pull all the threads of your analysis together. As you wrap up, you may want to note any questions you still have about the work. (Don't hesitate to admit that you don't have all the answers.)

Evaluating and Revising

1. **Peer review.** As a peer reviewer, comment on the following questions:
    - Is the thesis statement clear, concise, and direct?
    - Does the writer supply good supporting details from the text itself?
    - Is the essay organized clearly—in chronological order, in order of importance, or in some other logical order?
    - Does each paragraph make a clear point that supports the thesis?
    - Is the essay brought to a satisfying conclusion?

2. **Self-evaluation.** Read your peers' comments, be objective, and respond to them honestly. Try to reread your own essay as if you were not the author. Do you see places where you can improve the essay's organization, or make it clearer or stronger?

Grading Timesaver

Rubrics for this assignment appear on p. 114 of the *Portfolio Management System.*

Language Workshop

The history
of the written
word is rich and

Page 1

SMOOTHING IT OUT: INSERTING MODIFIERS

Imagine that Washington Irving had described Rip Van Winkle in this way:

> Rip Van Winkle was a simple fellow. He was also good-natured and helpful.

The description above is passable, but it's choppy and bland. (Try reading it aloud to catch its dull sound.) Here is a more vivid and readable description:

> Rip Van Winkle was a simple, good-natured, helpful fellow.

The following example provides information about where Rip Van Winkle lived. Once again, however, the sentences are short and choppy:

> Rip Van Winkle lived at the foot of the Kaatskill Mountains. He lived in a small house. It was timeworn and weather-beaten.

If the information were combined into one sentence, it would read much more smoothly:

> Rip Van Winkle lived in a small, timeworn, weather-beaten house at the foot of the Kaatskill Mountains.

Guidelines for Inserting Modifiers into Sentences

1. If your description is made up of several short, choppy sentences, look for the one that is your **base sentence**—the sentence that expresses the central idea. In the first example above, "Rip Van Winkle was a simple fellow" is the base sentence.
2. Look for modifiers in the other descriptive sentences. A modifier may be an adjective, adverb, prepositional phrase, or some other word or phrase that helps describe another word in the sentence.
3. Insert modifiers from the other sentences into the base sentence. Where necessary, change the word order and punctuation. For example, you might need to change a period to a comma.
4. When you transfer a modifier from one sentence to another, make sure it modifies the same word it used to.

Writer's Workshop Follow-Up: Revising

Reread the analysis you wrote for the Writer's Workshop (page 198). Does it contain any bland or choppy sentences that you could combine by using modifiers? Don't be overly eager to combine sentences; sometimes a short, unembellished sentence is exactly right for your purposes.

Technology HELP

See Language Workshop CD-ROM. *Key word entry: inserting modifiers.*

Language Handbook HELP

See Using Modifiers, pages 1227-1228.

Try It Out

Turn each of the following sentence pairs into a single sentence by inserting modifiers from the second sentence into the base sentence.

1. The children of the village shouted whenever Rip Van Winkle approached. They shouted with joy and expectancy.

2. Rip's daughter took him to her home. Her home was snug and well furnished.

LANGUAGE WORKSHOP 201

OBJECTIVES

1. Develop strategies for combining sentences
2. Identify the base sentence
3. Identify modifiers and the words that they describe
4. Insert modifiers in the base sentence, rewriting as necessary

Resources

Workshop Resources
• Worksheet, p. 49

Language Workshop CD-ROM
• Inserting Modifiers

Try It Out
Possible Answers
1. The children of the village shouted with joy and expectancy whenever Rip Van Winkle approached.
2. Rip's daughter took him to her snug, well-furnished home.

Assessing Learning

Quick Check: Sentence Combining

Turn the following sentence groups into single sentences by inserting modifiers.

1. Rip heard thunder. The thunder rolls were long. The thunder seemed distant. [Rip heard long, distant rolls of thunder.]

2. The people huddled inside the house. Outside the snow fell. The people sat close to the fire. The fire glowed brightly. [While the snow fell outside, the people inside the house huddled close to the brightly glowing fire.]

3. The face watched him from the wall. She had a gentle face. She had died eighteen years ago. She had been his wife. [The gentle face of his wife, who had died eighteen years ago, watched him from the wall.]

4. The ship had fought many a battle. Its tattered flag waved over the deck. The flag waved proudly. [The ship, with its tattered flag waving proudly over the deck, had fought many a battle.]

T201

Teaching the Lesson

You may wish to bring in examples of road maps, political maps, topographical maps, historical maps, or special-purpose maps for students to examine and discuss. Also, encourage students to bring in their own favorite maps, which they may have used for travel, outdoor recreation, hobbies, or historical research, and explain how to use them.

Using the Strategies:
Possible Answers
1. the Missouri River
2. approximately 200 miles
3. The route from Chamberlain west to Kennebec and then north to Pierre would be the fastest.
4. Fort Pierre Choteau, La Verendrye Monument, and the Oahe Chapel

Reading for Life
Reading Maps

Situation

Meriwether Lewis and William Clark's exploration of the American West (1804–1806) was a key event in the westward expansion of the United States and helped fuel the romantic imagination. Suppose you are planning a vacation in which you will retrace part of the route taken by these famous explorers.

Strategies
Select the right kind of map for your purposes.

- A U.S. road map shows the system of roadways currently linking cities, states, and geographical features. Most road maps also indicate campsites, parks, airports, and places of interest.

- A political map can show government divisions such as counties, congressional districts, and judicial jurisdictions.

- A physical or topographical map shows landforms, often with their elevation.

- A historical map shows the locations of important historical events, routes, and settlements.

- A special-purpose map may show such things as population density, agricultural products, and industrial zones.

Use map features.
- Map features include the map title, the compass rose, the distance scale (or scale bar), and the legend or key (explaining symbols used on the map).

Using the Strategies
1. Let's examine Lewis and Clark's route in present-day South Dakota, shown on the map above. What waterway did the expedition follow?

2. Approximately how many miles did Lewis and Clark travel between Chamberlain and Mobridge?

3. Traveling today by road, which of the two main routes from Chamberlain to Pierre is likely to be faster? In which two compass directions would you travel?

4. What three places of special interest could you visit in or near Pierre?

Extending the Strategies
- Use a historical map and a current road map to plan a sightseeing trip of New York's Lower Hudson Valley, made famous by Washington Irving.

- Use appropriate maps to plan a 10-mile bicycle ride or a 5-mile hike near where you live.

NOTE: Many maps are available on the Internet.

202 AMERICAN ROMANTICISM

Crossing the Curriculum

Local History
Mapping America.   Every area of the country was first mapped by explorers who followed Indian trails and often were guided by members of the tribes who lived there. Research the history of your area. What tribes lived there before European exploration? Who were the first European explorers? What were they seeking? How did they relate to the local people? Draw a map showing Indian tribal lands and the routes of the earliest European explorers. Use the names of individuals or tribes to mark the trails and the land. Be sure to include major landforms and rivers.

Learning for Life

Environmental Concerns

OBJECTIVES
1. Identify an important environmental issue
2. Explore solutions to environmental problems

Problem

American Romantic writers shared the belief that human beings can learn lessons from nature and that human activities should be conducted in harmony with the natural world. What are we doing today to ensure a better harmony with nature? What more can we do?

Project

Increase public consciousness of an important environmental issue. Explore specific ways that you, your family, your school, or your community can move toward a lifestyle that is in greater harmony with nature.

Preparation

1. Brainstorm with other students to identify various environmental groups in your community, and arrange to interview representatives from several of these groups. Consider as possible interviewees city planners, soil conservationists, organic farmers, wildlife biologists, and waste-disposal experts.

2. Contact environmental organizations, and request brochures, mission statements, and articles. Organizations to contact include the Sierra Club, the National Audubon Society, the World Wildlife Fund, and the U.S. Environmental Protection Agency.

3. Research some aspect of the history of the environmental movement. Look up information on key figures, such as John Muir, John James Audubon, Rachel Carson, and David Brower. Also consider writers and artists who have made the environment a central topic in their works—for example, Wendell Berry and Edward Abbey.

Procedure

1. If you are interviewing individuals, prepare a list of questions beforehand, but think of these questions as only a general guide. The person, or persons, being interviewed may introduce some interesting angle or a different topic.

2. Examine and evaluate your research, narrowing it down to a manageable topic that truly interests you.

3. If you are researching the history of the environmental movement, go beyond the library to other sources of information: city parks, environmental organizations, museums, and galleries.

Presentation

Present your information in one of the following formats (or another that your teacher approves):

1. **An Ecologically Sound Business**
   Write up a proposal for a business that would be environ-

ment-friendly. Include with your proposal a statement of your business philosophy, as well as a scrapbook that includes published materials (articles, brochures) that lend credibility to your idea for a business. You may also include quotations from environmental groups, transcripts of your interviews with people who work with the environment, and any visuals (artwork, photographs, diagrams, graphs) that support your proposal.

2. **An Advertising Campaign**
   With one or more other students, plan and develop an advertising campaign to make your school and community more environmentally aware. Make posters, design and create brochures and fliers, and come up with catchy slogans and logos that will get your message across.

3. **A Video Documentary**
   Make a short video documentary on some aspect of the environmental movement. Show the video to your class.

Processing

What did you learn about contemporary environmentalism by doing this project? What are some beliefs and policies you discovered that you agree with? Are there any ideas you disagree with? Write a reflection for your portfolio.

Resources

Viewing and Representing
HRW Multimedia Presentation Maker
Students may wish to use the *Multimedia Presentation Maker* to create their advertising campaigns.

Grading Timesaver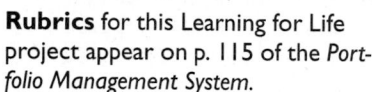

Rubrics for this Learning for Life project appear on p. 115 of the *Portfolio Management System*.

Developing Workplace Competencies

Preparation	Procedure	Presentation
• Makes decisions • Works well with people from diverse backgrounds • Acquires data	• Processes information • Thinks creatively • Evaluates data	• Communicates ideas and information • Applies technology to specific tasks

OBJECTIVES

1. Read literature of the American Renaissance, with focus on the themes "The Life Worth Living" and "The Realms of Darkness"
2. Interpret literary elements used in the literature, with special emphasis on Emerson's images and figures of speech and Poe's symbols and sound effects
3. Apply a variety of reading strategies to American literature, with special emphasis on tracing the origins of words
4. Respond to the literature in a variety of modes
5. Learn and use new words
6. Plan, draft, revise, edit, proof, and publish an essay about a controversial issue
7. Write sentences and paragraphs with parallel structure
8. Demonstrate the ability to evaluate the credibility of sources
9. Predict the effect of one social, cultural, or technological development on modern life

Resources

Viewing and Representing
Videocassette B, Segment 5
Use this segment to explore the popularization of American literature in the mid-nineteenth century.

Selection Readability

This Annotated Teacher's Edition provides a summary of each selection in the student book. Following each Summary heading, you will find one, two, or three small icons. These icons indicate, in an approximate sense, the reading level of the selection.

■ One icon indicates that the selection is easy.
■ ■ Two icons indicate that the selection is on an intermediate reading level.
■ ■ ■ Three icons indicate that the selection is challenging.

The American Renaissance
A Literary Coming of Age
1840–1860

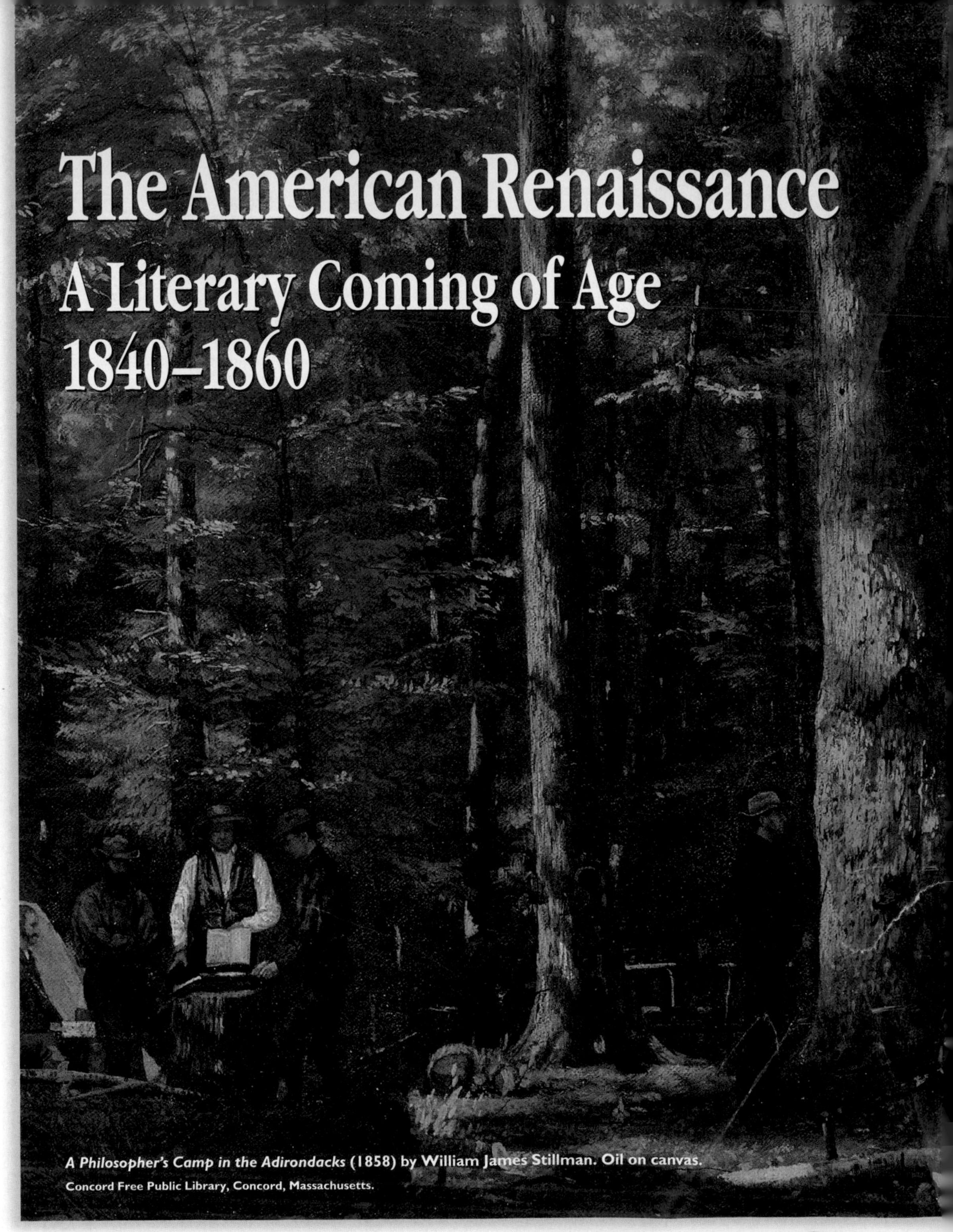

A Philosopher's Camp in the Adirondacks (1858) by William James Stillman. Oil on canvas.
Concord Free Public Library, Concord, Massachusetts.

 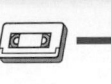 *Resources: Print and Media*

Viewing and Representing
- *Visual Connections*
  Videocassette B, Segment 5

Assessment
- *Formal Assessment*, p. 47
- *Test Generator (One-Stop Planner CD-ROM)*

Internet
- go.hrw.com (keyword: LE0 11-5)

205

RESPONDING TO THE ART

William James Stillman (1828–1901) was an American painter and journalist who was influenced by the British artists Dante Gabriel Rossetti and Sir John Everett Millais, two of the founders of the Pre-Raphaelite Brotherhood. The aims of the Brotherhood included the clear depiction of the natural world and the expression of moral ideals. *A Philosopher's Camp in the Adirondacks* demonstrates Stillman's attempt to depict an ideal relationship between people and nature.

Activities

1. Ask students to describe their reactions to the title of the painting. [Possible answer: The association of philosophy and the Adirondacks is unexpected and intriguing.]

2. Ask students how Stillman reinforces the idea that the campers are philosophers. [One man at the left has a book; the men at the right appear to be engaged in serious thought or observation; the atmosphere is contemplative and peaceful.]

3. Ask students what ideas the artist wishes to convey about the relationship between human beings and nature. [The artist portrays a harmonious relationship between human beings and nature. The forest dwarfs the philosophers in its beauty and grandeur, yet it serves as the source of their own mental and moral grandeur—as they study it and observe it.]

Reaching All Students

Struggling Readers

Knowing what's coming next aids some readers. To apply this principle to the upcoming historical introduction, suggest that students skim the boldfaced summary at the end of each section and take notes on the definitions and contexts of key words. Then, students should delve into each section and "flesh out" these key vocabulary words by taking additional notes in either list or cluster format.

English Language Learners

Hold up a photograph of a garden in the Neoclassical style, with its carefully planned paths and its clipped hedges, and then ask students to compare this garden with the wild forest in the Romantic Stillman painting. Help students understand that the literary coming of age in America occurs during the height of the Romantic movement.

Advanced Learners

After students have read the historical introduction, ask them to review the five tenets of Transcendentalism listed on p. 212 and to discuss these ideas in small groups.

OBJECTIVES

1. Understand the historical and social forces that shaped the American Renaissance
2. Interpret the way historical context influenced literary works in the pre–Civil War era
3. Read and understand a time line
4. Understand the relevance of the American Renaissance to contemporary culture
5. Take notes on and discuss Transcendentalist and Dark Romantic views of humanity

RESPONDING TO THE ART

In the early nineteenth century, young American women were expected to put marriage and raising children ahead of any personal achievements. By mid-century, however, reformers began to open separate all-female academies offering science, math, and other subjects deemed "unnecessary" for women. In 1833, Oberlin College was founded near Cleveland, Ohio, as the first coeducational college.

Activity. Ask students why these women might have sought education at this "Evening School." [Possible answers: Poverty forced them to support themselves. They wanted to make a greater contribution to society and culture. They were intellectually curious.]

Responding to the Quotation

American writers were well aware of the disdain of English critics, such as Sydney Smith. Edgar Allan Poe, who reviewed books and stories for literary magazines, lamented: "We have had no American tales of high merit. We have had no skillful compositions—nothing which could bear examination as works of art." His review, however, went on to praise Hawthorne's *Twice-Told Tales* as a collection "which would not do dishonor to the best of British essayists."

Girls' Evening School (c. 1840). American. Anonymous. Pencil and watercolor (13½″ × 18⅛″).

M. and M. Karolik Collection of American Watercolors and Drawings, 1800–1875. Courtesy, Museum of Fine Arts, Boston.

The American Renaissance
A Literary Coming of Age   *by* Gary Q. Arpin

Literature the Americans have none. . . . In the four quarters of the globe, who reads an American book?

—Sydney Smith, English critic, 1818

We have listened too long to the courtly muses of Europe. . . . The mind of this country, taught to aim at low objects, eats upon itself. . . . We will walk on our own feet; we will work with our own hands; we will speak our own minds. . . . A nation of men will for the first time exist, because each believes himself inspired by the Divine Soul which also inspires all men.

*—Ralph Waldo Emerson
from "The American Scholar," 1837*

206 THE AMERICAN RENAISSANCE

Professional Notes

**Critical Comment:
Democracy and Literature**

The French historian and politician Alexis de Tocqueville visited the United States in the 1830s and later made the following prediction about the direction American poetry would take: "[D]emocracy diverts the imagination from all that is external to man and fixes it on man alone. . . . The destinies of mankind, man himself taken aloof from his country and his age, and standing in the presence of Nature and of God, with his passions, his doubts, his rare prosperities and inconceivable wretchedness, will become the chief, if not the sole, theme of poetry." Return to this quotation at the end of the unit to discuss the accuracy of de Tocqueville's prediction.

A remarkable party took place on August 5, 1850, in Stockbridge, Massachusetts. Among those attending were a Boston publisher and two of his authors, Oliver Wendell Holmes (page 187) and Nathaniel Hawthorne (page 296), and a New York editor and two of *his* authors, Cornelius Mathews and Herman Melville (page 311). The party began in the morning with a climb in the Berkshire Mountains. The group was in good humor—in part, perhaps, because of a champagne picnic lunch. During the climb, Melville leaned out over the steep cliffs to demonstrate how sailors took in sail. Hawthorne, usually very restrained, loosened up enough to look wildly about for the great carbuncle (a deep-red gem), the subject of a tale, based on a local legend, that he had written many years before.

The hike in the Berkshires was followed in the evening by a long dinner. The table conversation turned to American literature. In response to a statement made by Holmes praising English writers, Melville vigorously defended American writers.

Would there ever be an American writer as great as England's William Shakespeare? This question started a heated discussion, with Melville again firmly supporting the American side. Hawthorne found himself agreeing with Melville, whom he had never met before.

> It is that blackness in Hawthorne that . . . fixes and fascinates me.
>
> —Herman Melville

By the mid–nineteenth century, learned people still debated whether America would ever produce great writing. At a celebrated gathering in 1850, Nathaniel Hawthorne and Herman Melville firmly agreed that it would.

Bandbox depicting Erie Canal. About 1830.
Cooper-Hewitt National Design Museum, Smithsonian Institution/Art Resource, NY. Gift of Sarah and Eleanor Hewitt (1918–19-12a, b).

Background

The Rise of Periodicals
The growth of literary culture in America was spurred on by a boom in periodical literature. *The Dial,* a magazine brought out by the Transcendentalists, began publication in 1840; *Harper's Magazine* was founded in 1850; and *The New York Times* first rolled off the press in 1851. Note the copy of *The Atlantic Monthly* (cofounded by Holmes) from 1857 among the illustrations.

Ⓐ Exploring the Culture
The Berkshires
The Berkshire Hills—called *Mountains* by their admirers—are a particularly beautiful area of western Massachusetts. Settled in the eighteenth century and dotted with small towns, the Berkshires became a resort area by the late nineteenth century. Today, the Berkshires continue to be a favorite destination for artists, hikers, and people simply seeking peaceful surroundings.

Ⓑ Literary Connections
The Story of the Stone
In Hawthorne's story "The Great Carbuncle," eight people search for a fabled garnet of great splendor. One dies in the search, another is blinded by the garnet, and yet another is impoverished. A husband and wife reject the jewel, which "would have dimmed all earthly things," and live happily the rest of their lives.

RESPONDING TO THE ART
A bandbox was usually cylindrical in shape. It was made of cardboard or thin wood and typically used to store light articles of clothing. The term *bandbox* may derive from the clergy's use of such boxes to store their clerical collars or "bands."
Activity. Have students consult *Brewer's Dictionary of Phrase and Fable* to learn about the expression "neat as a bandbox" and the historical "Bandbox Plot," which involved the British satirist Jonathan Swift.

Professional Notes

Critical Comment:
A Market for Writers
According to cultural historian Russel Blaine Nye: "Conditions were more favorable to the American writer during the middle decades of the nineteenth century than ever before. Not only was the population growing by millions annually, but it was an increasingly sophisticated and literate audience. The proliferation of colleges and public schools, the growth of lyceums, reading rooms, and libraries all contributed to the creation of a larger reading public. An expanding network of roads and railroads and canals meant swifter, cheaper, and wider distribution of newspapers, magazines, and books; improved oil lamps meant more reading hours per day. Ten thousand miles of new railroad, laid before 1860, carried books, authors and lecturers into places where few had been before."

Melville's first two novels, both adventure stories, were successful with the reading public. His third novel, *Mardi,* a blend of fantasy, romance, allegory, and metaphysics, was a commercial failure. Melville subsequently returned to the adventure genre in *Redburn* and *White Jacket.* In *Moby-Dick,* however, his sixth novel, Melville combined philosophical concerns and profound characterization with an exciting adventure at sea. The result was a unique and daring novel that would become a classic of American literature. (See also pp. 311–312.)

In this quotation, Melville is referring to *Typee,* one of his popular early novels. In this book, the cannibalistic Typee tribe is kinder and more humane than many self-professed Christians. Melville, however, is frustrated because he feels he will be remembered for this adventure novel rather than for his more philosophical later work.

When Hawthorne's novel of an adulterous Puritan woman first appeared, critics' reactions were mixed. Many were angered by Hawthorne's evident sympathy and admiration for his heroine. Some praised its complex moral vision; others denounced it as sacrilegious and pornographic. (See p. 297.)

RESPONDING TO THE ART

Scrimshaw—engraved ivory like the piece shown here—was a by-product of the thriving whaling industry of the nineteenth century. Ivory provided a beautiful smooth surface on which sailors could carve nautical scenes or other pictures. Ivory and whale bones were also used for piano keys, chess pieces, walking sticks, and even, in the case of *Moby-Dick's* Captain Ahab, an artificial leg.

Activity. Have students read and report on "the skimshandering business" as described on the first page of Chapter 57 in Melville's *Moby-Dick.*

Hawthorne and Melville: Opposites Attract

It seemed highly unlikely that these two writers would become friends. Herman Melville was an ex-sailor with little formal education. He had lived in the South Seas and had written a remarkable first novel, *Typee* (1846), about his adventures. At the time of the party, Melville was hard at work on his fifth novel, which, it appeared, would be very long.

Nathaniel Hawthorne, who was fifteen years older than Melville, was well educated, reserved, and a bit of a loner. He had written many short stories and had recently published *The Scarlet Letter* (1850), a novel about sin and hypocrisy in Puritan New England.

Despite their different backgrounds, a friendship sprang up between the two writers. "I met Melville the other day," Hawthorne wrote to a friend, "and liked him so much that I have asked him to spend a few days with me before leaving these parts." This was the beginning of an association that came at a critical point in Melville's life, when he was hard at work on his masterpiece, *Moby-Dick.*

After the meeting, Melville sat down and read Hawthorne's works—and was exposed for the first time to what he called the "power of blackness" in Hawthorne's writing.

Nathaniel Hawthorne and Herman Melville discovered a common bond: They both saw a dark side to human existence, and they sought to record this aspect of human nature in their works.

Puritan neighbors avoiding Hester Prynne. From *The Scarlet Letter* by Nathaniel Hawthorne. Lithograph after a painting by George H. Boughton.

The Granger Collection, New York.

Think of it. To go down to posterity as a "man who lived among the cannibals."
—Herman Melville, writing about himself to Hawthorne

MOBY-DICK;
OR,
THE WHALE.
BY
HERMAN MELVILLE,
AUTHOR OF
"TYPEE," "OMOO," "REDBURN," "MARDI," "WHITE-JACKET."

NEW YORK:
HARPER & BROTHERS, PUBLISHERS.
LONDON: RICHARD BENTLEY.

Peabody Essex Museum, Salem, Massachusetts.

208 THE AMERICAN RENAISSANCE

Crossing the Curriculum

Biology

In one sense, nineteenth-century whaling was a "conservative" business: All parts of the whale were put to use. Have students read those parts of *Moby-Dick* dedicated to this process; you might suggest Chapters 55–57, 74–78, 86, 90, and 92. Then have students compare Melville's account with a biology text on whales. Students should consider how our understanding of the behavior, life cycle, and anatomy of whales has changed since Melville's time.

Folk Art

The bandbox on p. 207 and the scrimshaw on p. 208 are examples of folk art. Ask students to locate other illustrations of folk art of the mid-nineteenth century to present to the class, and discuss how the folk art is indicative of the times.

First Flowering: A Declaration of Literary Independence

The immediate result of Melville's meeting with Hawthorne was a magazine essay in which Melville passionately defended American literature. Stating that England was in many ways "alien to us," Melville urged American readers to "prize and cherish" their own writers. In a burst of literary patriotism, Melville claimed that, in Hawthorne, America was very close to producing its own Shakespeare. **D**

Melville's horn blowing for American writing coincided with a vital period in American literature. It was a time when the American landscape and American culture would finally find their place in a literature distinct from European models. Writers were aware of this, and they sometimes used the word *renaissance* (ren′ə·säns′), meaning "rebirth," to describe this extraordinary explosion of American literary genius. When Americans referred to themselves as living in a renaissance, they were comparing their times to the European Renaissance, a period of extraordinary cultural vitality that lasted from about the fourteenth to the sixteenth century. A better term, however, for what happened in the still-raw America of the mid-1800s might be "coming of age." From 1849 to 1855, American writers produced a remarkable body of work, enough masterpieces for a national literature. **E**

> Nothing is at last sacred but the integrity of your own mind.
>
> —Ralph Waldo Emerson

In the mid–nineteenth century, writers such as Nathaniel Hawthorne, Ralph Waldo Emerson, Henry David Thoreau, and Herman Melville produced some of the early masterpieces of American literature.

Intellectual and Social Life in New England

This burst of American literature can be traced in large measure to the intellectual and social ferment in New England. New England had long been known for its interest in self-improvement and intellectual inquiry. This interest found expression in the Lyceum (lī·sē′əm) movement, begun in 1826 in Millbury, Massachusetts. Lyceum organizations, soon established in many communities, had a number of goals, including educating adults, training teachers, establishing museums, and instituting social reforms. A typical part of a Lyceum program was a course of lectures in winter. These became immensely popular in New England and the Midwest. One of the most popular speakers was Ralph Waldo Emerson (page 216). **F**

This was a time of social improvement in other ways too. New England was a center of many reform movements. Horace Mann dedicated

Lyceum Lecture by James Pollard Espy at Clinton Hall (1841) by an unknown artist. Pen and ink.

Museum of the City of New York.

D Literary Connections
Melville

Melville was noted for wild mood swings, alternating between grandiose exuberance and extreme dejection. His essay on Hawthorne was the fruit of the former. His claim that Hawthorne was close to being an American Shakespeare would have seemed exaggerated to most people even then, given Hawthorne's much more limited range.

E Cultural Connections
A British Evaluation

A century after Emerson and Thoreau, British poet W. H. Auden looked back at the American literary renaissance and pinpointed a difference between the American and British depictions of nature. Since Americans saw themselves as pioneers in an uncharted wilderness, they saw nature as tremendous, sweeping, grand, awe-inspiring, and often dangerous; the British, rooted in their ancestral homeland, saw it as essentially pastoral, tame, and beneficent.

F Exploring the Culture
The Lyceum

Josiah Holbrook founded the Lyceum movement in 1826. By 1835, fifteen states had Lyceums; by 1860, more than three thousand Lyceums existed. People went to Lyceum halls much as they go to movies today. They heard lectures about history, music, philosophy, famous people, and the latest discoveries in science. Many intellectuals spoke on the Lyceum circuit, including naturalist Louis Agassiz, politician Daniel Webster, and novelist Harriet Beecher Stowe.

RESPONDING TO THE ART

James Pollard Espy (1785–1860) was a pioneering meteorologist who laid the foundations for modern weather forecasting. He was called "Storm King" because of the theories he proposed in *Philosophy of Storms* (1841).
Activity. Have students identify today's sources of the kind of information people of the nineteenth century sought by going to Lyceums. [college courses, television, Internet]

Professional Notes

Critical Comment:
Abolition and Women's Rights

According to historian Christine Lunardi: "[M]any of the women who would become leaders of the women's movement met at abolitionist functions. . . .The antislavery societies were where many women learned the basic procedures of political mobilization: drawing up a constitution and bylaws, electing officers, speaking before groups, taking votes, organizing committees, and planning collective actions.

Similarly, in speaking out against slavery, they learned to speak out, period. The lesson was not forgotten when they confronted other injustices and their own grievances. Finally, their outrage against slavery made them conscious of other outrages— of the brutality of war, the debilitation of poverty, and the injustice of their own position in society."

T209

A Closer Look

This feature about everyday life in the 1840s discusses the average life span of men and women of the era and the devastating toll of tuberculosis, the number-one killer of the period. The feature also touches on the unhealthy conditions in the cities and the duties and pleasures of the average farm family. Finally, the feature closes with a discussion of the era's heroes—most notably George Washington.

Ⓐ Exploring the Historical Period

Three Influential Women

Elizabeth Peabody operated a bookstore in Boston, which became a gathering place for intellectuals and published works by Fuller and Hawthorne. (Peabody's sister Sophia married Nathaniel Hawthorne, and her sister Mary married Horace Mann.)

Margaret Fuller, a Transcendentalist, wrote reviews and collections of essays, edited *The Dial* for two years, and traveled abroad extensively. Determined to open up more options for women, for whom society expected nothing but marriage, she engaged female audiences in "Conversations" between 1839 and 1844 on topics ranging from poetry to ethics. Many of these "Conversations" were held at Peabody's bookstore and became so popular she was eventually pressed to admit men.

Emma Willard concluded from her experience as a teacher and a principal that the way to improve the education of women was through public funding of all-female schools. She failed to convince the Connecticut and New York legislatures, but the city of Troy, New York, offered $4,000 to found a girls' boarding school, today called the Emma Willard School.

Ⓑ Exploring the Culture

Urban Reformers

The early 1800s saw the beginning of the shift from agriculture to industry, from rural to urban life. Factories began to replace the shops of skilled artisans, and armies of Irish and German immigrants were hired at low wages to run machines. Several writers, including abolitionist Lydia Maria Child and novelist Rebecca Harding Davis, as well as Herman Melville and Margaret Fuller, addressed the worsening plight of factory workers.

THAT WAS THEN...

What would your life be like if you lived in the 1840s?

For one thing, it probably would be shorter. On average, you could expect to live only about forty years. A quarter of your friends would die relatively young, many of them victims of tuberculosis, the nineteenth-century plague.

Your world would be far less crowded than it is now. In 1840, there were about 17 million people living in the United States. (In contrast, by 1995 there were about 260 million Americans.) Some 3 million of them were of African heritage, and of those, only about half a million were not enslaved.

Back of the State House in Philadelphia by William Birch.
Library of Congress.

himself to improving public education; Dorothea Dix sought to relieve the horrible conditions in institutions for the mentally ill; William Lloyd Garrison and other abolitionists struggled to put an end to slavery; feminists like Elizabeth Peabody, Margaret Fuller, and Emma Willard campaigned to increase women's rights.

Social causes, both reasonable and crackpot, abounded during this time. Numerous utopian (yo͞o·tō′pē·ən) projects—plans for creating a more perfect society—were developed. In 1840, Emerson wryly remarked that every man who could read had plans in his pocket for a new community. Emerson was speaking from personal experience, for he was a member of one of the most influential of these utopian groups.

> *Ralph Waldo Emerson was a primary force behind the flowering of American culture. He helped inspire numerous reform movements that aimed to improve public education, end slavery, elevate the status of women, and generally smooth the edges off the rough social conditions of the time. Various utopian groups drew up comprehensive plans for a better society.*

The Transcendentalists: True Reality Is Spiritual

Emerson's utopian group quickly became known as "The Transcendental Club." The term *transcendental* comes from the eighteenth-century

Crossing the Curriculum

Social Studies

Have students form groups of two or three. Ask each group to choose, research, and report on a different topic mentioned in the unit introduction. Examples include Horace Mann and education, Dorothea Dix's work for mental hospitals, the women's rights movement, whaling, and the utopian projects. The groups should report their findings to the class.

Health

Thoreau died of tuberculosis, as did Emerson's father and wife. Have students report on what tuberculosis is, what causes it, what effects it had on the population at the time of the American Renaissance, and treatments used then. Students could also report on current incidence and control of the disease. Encourage students to present graphs or other visual aids with their reports.

Cities were rapidly expanding in the 1840s. The five largest were Boston, New York City, Philadelphia, Baltimore, and Charleston. Visitors to New York were stunned by the filth there. There was no citywide garbage collection, and pigs moved freely about the streets.

Chances are you'd live in the country, though, in a house heated by wood or coal fires and lit by oil lamps. Your father most likely would be a farmer, and your mother probably would concentrate on taking care of the home but would help out with the farm. You would probably have several brothers or sisters. If you went to school (many young people didn't), you'd likely walk to a one-room schoolhouse. There, side-by-side with students of varying ages, you'd be taught reading, writing, arithmetic, and proper behavior. It's possible

C

you'd already be married at your age. Both rich and poor married quite young—as early as thirteen or fourteen in the South.

What would you do for fun? In rural areas, you'd probably go dancing on weekend nights or attend cornhusking contests or quilting bees. You might start learning about a new pastime called baseball—the first game closely resembling the modern sport took place in 1846. You might read for entertainment. But wherever you lived, your main form of entertainment would probably be visiting friends and neighbors.

Who would be your heroes? Probably not athletes or entertainers. The main heroes were politicians, especially those with military backgrounds. Just about everyone's favorite hero was George Washington.

German philosopher Immanuel Kant. The word refers to the idea that in determining the ultimate reality of God, the universe, the self, and other important matters, one must transcend, or go beyond, everyday human experience in the physical world. Intuition is an important tool for discovering truth.

For Emerson, **Transcendentalism** was not a new philosophy but "the very oldest of thoughts cast into the mold of these new times." That "oldest of thoughts" was Idealism, which had already been articulated by the Greek philosopher Plato in the fourth century B.C. Idealists said that true reality involved ideas rather than the world as perceived by the senses. Idealists sought the permanent reality that underlay physical appearances. The Americans who called themselves Transcendentalists were idealists, but in a broader, more practical sense. Like many Americans today, they believed in human perfectibility, and they worked to achieve this goal.

D

To recall these village lyceums, these rude country halls, evening meetings in odd churches, barns, schools, and banquet rooms, tents spread in preparation for the idyllic summer's opening of the college year . . . is to imagine a time when people still looked to literary men for guidance. . . . Emerson made a thousand appearances, crossed the Mississippi on ice in dead winter to deliver a lecture in Iowa, was bumped, jostled, frozen in wagons, carriages, flatboats, steamboats, trains (where he felt so solitary that he vowed he would go over to any man reading a book and hug him).

—Alfred Kazin,
from An American Procession

C Literary Connections
Laura Ingalls Wilder
One of the best-loved records of the everyday life of ordinary nineteenth-century Americans is the eight-volume autobiography of Laura Ingalls Wilder. In these books, Wilder provides a wealth of detail about life in Wisconsin, Minnesota, and the Dakota territories during the 1870s and 1880s. Many students will have read some of Wilder's books; invite them to comment on what they have learned about the 1870s and 1880s from her work.

D Exploring the Culture
Transcendentalist Philosophy
Literary scholar Newton Arvin offers the following analysis of Emerson's philosophy: "Emerson for the first time in this country gave full and eloquent expression to the philosophy of romantic idealism—of what was soon known . . . as 'Transcendentalism.' . . . He felt that the spiritual and intellectual biases of the seventeenth and eighteenth centuries, of the Age of Reason, however creative they might have been in their prime, had ended in sterility. . . . The rationalistic mind seemed to him to have chilled and rigidified the whole of human existence, beginning with the life of the spirit on its profoundest levels. . . . [For him, religion] is a supernatural communication between the individual soul and what Emerson came to call the Over-Soul; its truth, as he said . . . 'is guarded by one stern condition; this, namely; it is an institution. It cannot be received at second hand.' . . . Divinity, as he says, is within as well as above: 'God in us worships God.' It is this divine principle that is the true self, not 'the biographical Ego.' What follows from such convictions is that the physical world, real as it is empirically, is dependent for its reality on Spirit, and that the ultimate nature of things is not to be found, as materialists have always held, in matter, but in mind."

Getting Students Involved

Cooperative Learning

Play Ball! Have students research the nineteenth-century origins of baseball. They may want to check out the numerous Internet sites available, as well as the extensive literature on this topic. One good source is *Baseball: An Illustrated History,* by Geoffrey C. Ward, the companion book to the PBS TV series by Ken Burns. Have students look up the original rules of baseball and, weather permitting, choose up sides and play a game with those rules. Aspects of the game that might interest students include these: What were the uniforms like? Who were the players? When did professional baseball begin? What are the greatest differences between baseball now and baseball when it began? Have each member of the class share what he or she learned about the origins of the game.

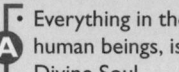 Cultural Connections

Hindu Influences

The Transcendentalists' view that everything in the world is a reflection of the Divine Soul may have been partly derived from the Hindu idea that the *atman,* the individual soul, is made of the same stuff as the *Atman,* the universal soul.

B Literary Connections

Emerson and Whitman

Whitman's great admiration for Emerson was returned in full measure. In 1855, Emerson wrote to thank Whitman for sending him a copy of *Leaves of Grass,* saying: "I find it the most extraordinary piece of wit and wisdom that America has yet contributed. . . . I give you joy of your free & brave thought. I have great joy in it. I find incomparable things said incomparably well, as they must be." Emerson passed the book on to others, noting that only Thoreau appeared to appreciate the gesture.

C Struggling Readers

Creating an Outline

Point out to students that this paragraph summarizes two sections of text: "The Transcendentalists: True Reality Is Spiritual" and "Emerson and Transcendentalism: The American Roots." Encourage students to use this summary to create an outline of Transcendental thought. For instance, the first sentence of the summary would correspond to the first main idea:

Transcendental Thought
I. Transcendentalism was based on Greek Idealism
   A. Plato advocated an Idealism
   B. Idealists say reality lies in rational ideas, not senses
   C. Idealists believe in human perfectibility
II. Transcendentalism was also based on Puritan thought

Have students continue to fill in the outline, using the summary for main ideas and then returning to the text to find supporting details.

A Transcendentalist's View of the World

A
- Everything in the world, including human beings, is a reflection of the Divine Soul.
- The physical facts of the natural world are a doorway to the spiritual or ideal world.
- People can use their intuition to behold God's spirit revealed in nature or in their own souls.
- Self-reliance and individualism must outweigh external authority and blind conformity to custom and tradition.
- Spontaneous feelings and intuition are superior to deliberate intellectualism and rationality.

Emerson and Transcendentalism: The American Roots

Though Emerson was skeptical of many of the Transcendentalists' ideas and projects, he was the most influential and best-known member of the group, largely because of his lectures and books. His writing and that of his friend Henry David Thoreau (page 230) clearly and forcefully expressed Transcendental ideas. As developed by Emerson, Transcendentalism grafted ideas from Europe and Asia onto a homegrown American philosophical stem. Its American roots included Puritan thought, the beliefs of the eighteenth-century religious revivalist Jonathan Edwards (page 77), and the Romantic tradition exemplified by William Cullen Bryant (page 169).

The Puritans believed that God revealed himself to people through the Bible and through the physical world. William Bradford (page 26), for example, saw the death of an abusive sailor on the *Mayflower* as the direct action of God in the human world. Anne Bradstreet (page 68) saw evidence of God in the grandeur of nature. Jonathan Edwards found God's wisdom, purity, and love in the sun, moon, and stars—in fact, in all of nature. This native mysticism—also typical of **Romanticism**—reappears in Emerson's thought. "Every natural fact," Emerson wrote, "is a symbol of some spiritual fact."

B
> I was simmering, simmering, simmering; Emerson brought me to a boil.
>
> —Walt Whitman

C
Transcendentalism was based partly on the philosophy of Idealism, which dated back to ancient Greece. It was based also on the ideas of American thinkers ranging from the Puritans to the nineteenth-century Romantics. Transcendentalists viewed nature as a doorway to a mystical world holding important truths.

Emerson's Optimistic Outlook

Emerson's mystical view of the world sprang not from logic but from intuition. Intuition is our capacity to know things spontaneously and immediately through our emotions rather than through our reasoning abilities. Intuitive thought—the

Ralph Waldo Emerson.
Drawing by David Levine.
Reprinted with permission from *The New York Review of Books.* Copyright ©1968 NYREV, Inc.

Cultural Connections

Mid–Nineteenth Century "Isms"

Romanticism is marked by these characteristics: (1) a conviction that intuition, imagination, and emotion provide a clearer route to truth than reason alone; (2) a conviction that poetry is superior to science; (3) a belief that contemplation of the natural world is a means of discovering the truth; (4) a distrust of industry and city life and an idealization of rural life and of the wilderness; (5) an interest in the supernatural.

Transcendentalism is marked by these beliefs: (1) God is in every aspect of nature, including every human being; (2) everyone is capable of apprehending God through intuition; (3) nature is a reflection of divine spirit.
Optimism holds that the existing world is the best possible one.
Abolitionism usually refers to the movement to end slavery.

kind Emerson believed in—contrasts with the rational thinking of someone like Benjamin Franklin (page 84). Franklin did not gaze on nature and feel the presence of a Divine Soul; Franklin looked at nature and saw something to be examined scientifically and used to help humanity.

An intense feeling of optimism was one product of Emerson's belief that we can find God directly in nature. God is good, and God works through nature, Emerson believed. Therefore, even the natural events that seem most tragic— disease, death, disaster—can be explained on a spiritual level. Death is simply a part of the cycle of life. We are capable of evil because we are separated from a direct, intuitive knowledge of God, according to Emerson. But if we simply trust ourselves—that is, trust in the power each of us has to know God directly—then we will realize that each of us is also part of the Divine Soul, the source of all good.

Emerson's sense of optimism and hope appealed to audiences who lived in a period of economic downturns, regional strife, and conflict over slavery. Your condition today, Emerson seemed to tell his readers and listeners, may seem dull and disheartening, but it need not be. If you discover the God within you, he suggested, your lives will partake of the grandeur of the universe.

Emerson believed in the power of intuition, our ability to learn directly without conscious use of reasoning. He emphasized the importance of each individual, and his outlook was optimistic.

"What do you think of the world to come?" an admirer asked the philosopher.
"One world at a time," Thoreau replied.

Old Manse in Concord, where first Emerson and then Hawthorne lived.

Steve Solum/ Bruce Coleman, Inc.

Melville, Hawthorne, and Poe: A Challenge to the Transcendentalists

Emerson's idealism was exciting for his audiences, but not all the writers and thinkers of the time agreed with Transcendentalist thought. "To one who has weathered Cape Horn as a common sailor," Herman Melville wrote of Emerson's ideas, "what stuff all this is."

Some people think of Nathaniel Hawthorne, Herman Melville, and Edgar Allan Poe (page 260) as anti-Transcendentalists, because their view of the world seems so profoundly opposed to the optimistic view of Emerson and his followers. But these Dark Romantics, as they are

D Humanities Connections
Deism
Franklin's view exemplifies deism, the idea that the universe was rationally designed by a divinity who endowed humanity with reason but who is not involved in the minute workings of the universe.

E Historical Connections
Optimism
Emerson's thinking has had a profound influence on the positive-thinking and self-realization trends of the twentieth century. Many of the social reformers and artists of the 1960s and 1970s saw themselves as renewing the Emersonian tradition. Indeed, it is no surprise that "Trust Yourself" is the title of a 1985 song by Bob Dylan.

F Literary Connections
Louisa May Alcott
During the 1970s, Louisa May Alcott was discovered to have been a writer solidly in the Dark Romantic tradition of Poe. As a woman, Alcott would have created a scandal if she had published her tales of mesmerism, murder, adultery, and the supernatural under her own name, so her stories appeared anonymously or under the pen name A. M. Barnard. By studying her journals and correspondence, scholars identified her as the author of *A Modern Mephistopheles* and a number of Gothic tales.

Clearly, however, Alcott regretted the need for anonymity: "Enjoyed [writing *A Modern Mephistopheles*], being tired of providing moral pap for the young," she wrote. "I think my natural ambition is for the lurid style. I indulge in gorgeous fancies and wish that I dared inscribe them upon my pages and set them before the public. . . . I shall always be a victim to the respectable traditions of Concord."

G Exploring the Culture
Hawthorne and the Transcendentalists
Hawthorne was one of the original members of the utopian project at Brook Farm and invested his savings in the community. All members shared in the work and intellectual life. Emerson, Fuller, and Bronson Alcott lectured at its school. Years later, Hawthorne based *The Blithedale Romance* on Brook Farm and its inhabitants.

Crossing the Curriculum

Science
Have students research mesmerism, a popular "science" of the mid-nineteenth century. Introduced by Franz Anton Mesmer, mesmerism was a form of hypnotism and supposedly based on magnetism. Poe, Emerson, Alcott, and Hawthorne were intrigued by the theory, and the Dark Romantics used it as a motif in their tales. Students should take notes to answer the following questions and then collaborate on a class presentation.

- Who was Franz Anton Mesmer?
- What was mesmerism, and did it have any scientific basis?
- Why were nineteenth-century Americans interested in mesmerism?
- What were the reactions of the Dark Romantic writers toward mesmerism, and how did they use it in their stories and novels?

Symbolism

The symbolism in Poe's work influenced an entire generation of French writers. The poet Charles Baudelaire (1821–1867) discovered Poe's stories in pirated French translations during the late 1840s and read them with "singular excitement" and "incredible sympathy." He published his own translations between 1856 and 1864 and thus gained a vast new audience for Poe's work. Among them were Symbolist poets Rimbaud, Verlaine, Mallarmé, and Claudel, who were all strongly influenced by Poe's symbols, motifs, images, and themes.

RESPONDING TO THE ART

Rick McCollum is a twentieth-century artist who incorporates a visual allusion to "The Raven" (p. 282) in his study of Poe.

Activities

1. Have students look at the daguerreotype of Poe on p. 260 of their textbooks. Which do they find more expressive and memorable, the portrait or the daguerreotype? Why? [Possible answers: portrait—image of raven is striking and dramatic; daguerreotype—facial expression is haunting; Poe seems more human than in the portrait.]
2. Ask students why McCollum included the raven, tree, quill, and papers. [The raven suggests both Poe's tragic life and his greatest poetic success; McCollum wanted the viewer to recall Poe's work, not just his personality.]

That blue-eyed darling Nathaniel knew disagreeable things in his inner soul. He was careful to send them out in disguise.
—D. H. Lawrence, on Hawthorne

known, had much in common with the Transcendentalists. Both groups valued intuition over logic and reason. Both groups, like the Puritans before them, saw signs and symbols in human events—as Anne Bradstreet found spiritual significance in the fire that destroyed her house (page 69). (Not surprisingly, the Dark Romantics used the literary technique of **symbolism** to great effect in their works.)

The Dark Romantics didn't disagree with Emerson's belief that spiritual facts lie behind the appearances of nature; they disagreed with the premise that those facts are necessarily good, or harmless. Emerson, they felt, had taken the ecstatic, mystical elements of Puritan thought and ignored its dark side—its emphasis on Original Sin, its sense of the innate depravity of human beings, and its Calvinistic notions of predestination. The Dark Romantics came along to redress the balance. Their view of existence developed from both the mystical and the melancholy aspects of Puritan thought. In their works, they explored the conflict between good and evil, the psychological effects of guilt and sin, and even madness and derangement in the human psyche. Behind the pasteboard masks of social respectability, the Dark Romantics saw the blankness and the horror of evil. From this imaginative, unflinching vision they shaped a uniquely American literature.

. . . in certain moods, no man can weigh this world without throwing in something, somehow like Original Sin, to strike the uneven balance.
—Herman Melville

Courtesy Rick McCollum.

Portrait of Edgar Allan Poe (1985) by Rick McCollum. Oil on linen board with oil pencil.

The works of writers such as Hawthorne, Melville, and Poe acknowledged the existence of sin, pain, and evil in human life and formed a counterpoint to the optimism of the Transcendentalists.

Quickwrite
How Do You See Yourself?

Do you agree with the Transcendentalists' optimistic views of human perfectibility? Or are you more like the Dark Romantics, believing that the world has a dark, irrational side that can't be ignored? Write down your own opinions about the ideas of the Transcendentalists and the Dark Romantics. How do you see yourself in relation to them?

Quickwrite

Ask students to refer to A Transcendentalist's View of the World on p. 212 and to draw up a similar list of characteristics for the Dark Romantics before responding to the Quickwrite questions.

Assessing Learning

Check Test: Multiple Choice

1. The "opposites" who became close friends were (a) Hawthorne and Poe (b) Emerson and Melville (c) Hawthorne and Melville [c]
2. The Lyceum movement refers to (a) the emergence of high schools (b) the formation of a writers' union (c) an organization that promoted lectures and museums [c]
3. Transcendentalists believed that (a) nature reveals spiritual truth (b) the dark side of human nature must be acknowledged (c) neither a nor b [a]
4. One American thinker who influenced the Transcendentalists was (a) Franklin (b) Edwards (c) Byrd [b]
5. Melville, Poe, and Hawthorne disagreed with the Transcendentalists about (a) nature (b) optimism (c) logic [b]

Collection 5

The Life Worth Living

Theme

Nothing Can Bring You Peace But Yourself *Two early giants of American writing—Emerson and Thoreau—echo the Romantic tradition and call on Americans to look to nature, to trust their own intuitions, and to declare their independence from the learning of other lands. The major thrust of these writings is a focus on the individual. The seminal work is Thoreau's* Walden, or Life in the Woods.

Reading the Anthology

Reaching Struggling Readers

The *Reading Skills and Strategies: Reaching Struggling Readers* binder provides materials coordinated with the Pupil's Edition (see the Collection Planner, p. T214B) to help students who have difficulty reading and comprehending text, or students who are reluctant readers. The binder for eleventh grade is organized around ten individual skill areas and offers the following options:

- **MiniRead** MiniReads are short, easy texts that give students a chance to practice a particular skill and strategy before reading selections in the Pupil's Edition. Each MiniRead Skill Lesson can be taught independently or used in conjunction with a Selection Skill Lesson.

- **Selection Skill Lessons** Selection Skill Lessons allow students to apply skills introduced in the MiniReads. Each Selection Skill Lesson provides reading instruction and practice specific to a particular piece of literature in the Pupil's Edition.

Reading Beyond the Anthology

Read On At the end of the American Renaissance collections, the grade eleven book includes an annotated bibliography of books suitable for extended reading. The suggested books are related to works in these collections by theme, by author, or by subject. To preview the Read On for the American Renaissance period, please turn to p. T330.

Collection 5 The Life Worth Living

Resources for this Collection

Note: All resources for this collection are available for preview on the *One-Stop Planner CD-ROM 1 with Test Generator.* All worksheets and blackline masters may be printed from the CD-ROM.

Internet Resources
go.hrw.com LE0 11-5

Selection or Feature	Reading and Literary Skills	Vocabulary, Language, and Grammar
• *from* **Nature** (p. 218) Ralph Waldo Emerson **Spotlight On: Emerson's Aphorisms** (p. 222) **Primary Sources: Hawthorne Talks About Emerson** (p. 223) Nathaniel Hawthorne • *from* **Self-Reliance** (p. 224) Ralph Waldo Emerson	• *Graphic Organizers for Active Reading,* Worksheet pp. 18, 19 • *Literary Elements:* Transparency 8 Worksheet p. 25	• *Words to Own,* Worksheet pp. 14, 15 • *Grammar and Language Links:* Appositives and Appositive Phrases, Worksheet p. 23 • *Language Workshop CD-ROM,* Appositives and Appositive Phrases • *Daily Oral Grammar,* Transparencies 16, 17
from **Walden, or Life in the Woods** (p. 232) Henry David Thoreau **Connections:** *from* **Heaven Is Under Our Feet** (p. 245) Don Henley	• *Reading Skills and Strategies: Reaching Struggling Readers* • MiniRead Skill Lesson, p. 103 • Selection Skill Lesson, p. 109 • *Graphic Organizers for Active Reading,* Worksheet p. 20	• *Words to Own,* Worksheet p. 16 • *Grammar and Language Links:* Common Usage Problems, Worksheet p. 25 • *Language Workshop CD-ROM,* Common Usage Problems • *Daily Oral Grammar,* Transparency 18
from **Resistance to Civil Government** (p. 248) Henry David Thoreau **Primary Sources: "A Healthy and Wholesome Man to Know"** (p. 255) Nathaniel Hawthorne and Sophia Peabody Hawthorne **Connections:** *from* **Letter from Birmingham City Jail** (p. 256) Martin Luther King, Jr.	• *Graphic Organizers for Active Reading,* Worksheet p. 21	• *Words to Own,* Worksheet p. 18 • *Daily Oral Grammar,* Transparency 19

Other Resources for this Collection

- *Cross-Curricular Activities*, p. 5
- *Portfolio Management System*, Introduction to Portfolio Assessment, p. 1
- *Formal Assessment*, Literary Introduction Period Test, p. 47

- *Test Generator*, Collection Test

Writing	Listening and Speaking / Viewing and Representing	Assessment
• *Portfolio Management System*, Rubrics for Choices, p. 116	• *Audio CD Library*, Disc 6, Tracks 2, 3 🎧 • *Viewing and Representing:* Fine Art Transparency 5 Worksheet p. 20 • *Portfolio Management System*, Rubrics for Choices, p. 116	• *Formal Assessment*, Selection Tests, pp. 49, 51 • *Test Generator (One-Stop Planner CD-ROM)* 💿 • *Preparation for College Admission Exams*, p. 17
• *Portfolio Management System*, Rubrics for Choices, p. 118	• *Audio CD Library*, Disc 7, Tracks 2, 3, 4, 5, 6, 7 🎧 • *Portfolio Management System*, Rubrics for Choices, p. 118	• *Formal Assessment*, Selection Test, p. 53 • *Test Generator (One-Stop Planner CD-ROM)* 💿 • *Preparation for College Admission Exams*, p. 19
• *Portfolio Management System*, Rubrics for Choices, p. 120	• *Audio CD Library*, Disc 7, Track 8 🎧 • *Portfolio Management System*, Rubrics for Choices, p. 120	• *Formal Assessment*, Selection Test, p. 55 • *Test Generator (One-Stop Planner CD-ROM)* 💿

Collection Planner

Transparency   💿 CD-ROM   ▭ Video   🎧 Audio CD

Collection 5 The Life Worth Living

Skills Focus

Skills Focus

Selection or Feature	Reading Skills and Strategies	Elements of Literature and Language	Writing	Listening and Speaking	Viewing and Representing
from **Nature** (p. 218) from **Self-Reliance** (p. 224) Ralph Waldo Emerson	Monitor Your Reading, p. 218 Identify Key Passages That State the Main Idea, pp. 218, 228 Paraphrase, pp. 218, 228 Understand Figures of Speech, p. 228 Context, p. 228	Imagery, p. 218 Aphorisms, pp. 222, 229 Figures of Speech, pp. 224, 228 Image, p. 228 Metaphor, p. 228 Paradox, p. 229	Write an Essay Responding to a Quotation, p. 229 Write an Explanation of a Paradox, p. 229 Write an Extended Definition, p. 229	Brainstorm Topics for Writing, p. 229 Identify and Discuss Aphorisms Drawn from Contemporary Sources, p. 229 Work with a Small Group to Create a Plan for a Utopia, p. 229	Draw a Map of a Utopia, p. 229
from **Walden, or Life in the Woods** (p. 232) Henry David Thoreau	Draw Inferences and Make Generalizations, pp. 232, 246 Paraphrase a Metaphor, p. 246	First-Person Point of View, p. 232 Parable, p. 246 Metaphor, p. 246	Identify Developmental Questions for Writing Topics, p. 247 Write an Essay Analyzing the Presence of Romantic Tenets in Walden, p. 247 Write an Essay Supporting a Topic Sentence, p. 247 Write a Journal for One Day, p. 247	Write and Read Aloud a Journal Entry Written from the Point of View of an Author, p. 247 Research and Report on Some Aspect of Nature Mentioned by Thoreau, p. 247	
from **Resistance to Civil Government** (p. 248) Henry David Thoreau	Determine the Precise Meanings of Words, p. 257	Paradox, pp. 248, 257	Define an Issue and Clarify Your Position, p. 258 Write a Brief Essay Supporting or Opposing an Opinion Statement, p. 258 Write an Essay Comparing and Contrasting Texts, p. 258	Write and Perform a One-Scene Play, p. 258 Research and Present an Oral Report on Some Aspect of Civil Disobedience, p. 258	

Skills Focus

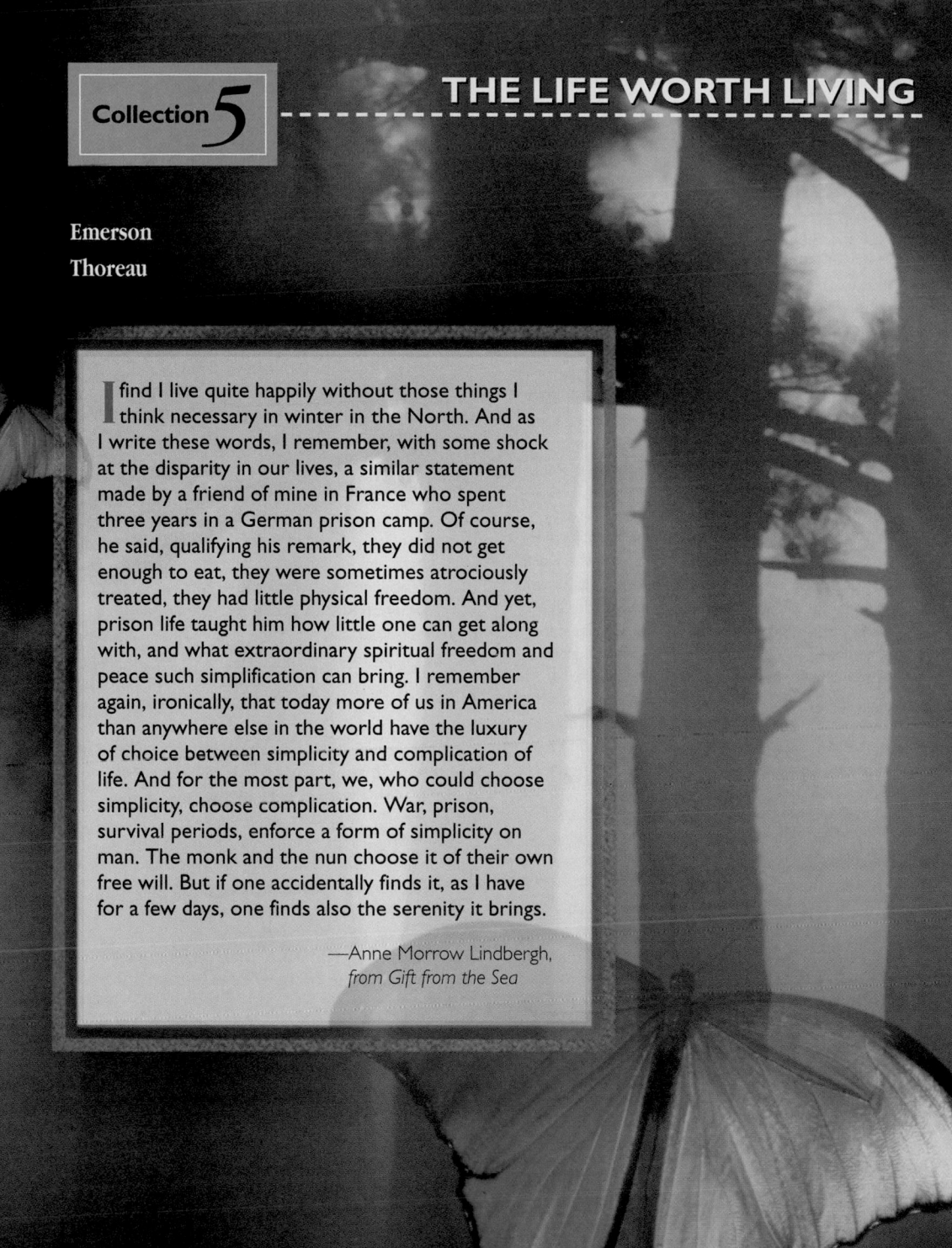

Emerson

Thoreau

I find I live quite happily without those things I think necessary in winter in the North. And as I write these words, I remember, with some shock at the disparity in our lives, a similar statement made by a friend of mine in France who spent three years in a German prison camp. Of course, he said, qualifying his remark, they did not get enough to eat, they were sometimes atrociously treated, they had little physical freedom. And yet, prison life taught him how little one can get along with, and what extraordinary spiritual freedom and peace such simplification can bring. I remember again, ironically, that today more of us in America than anywhere else in the world have the luxury of choice between simplicity and complication of life. And for the most part, we, who could choose simplicity, choose complication. War, prison, survival periods, enforce a form of simplicity on man. The monk and the nun choose it of their own free will. But if one accidentally finds it, as I have for a few days, one finds also the serenity it brings.

—Anne Morrow Lindbergh,
from Gift from the Sea

Responding to the Quotation

? Anne Morrow Lindbergh lived near Trenton, New Jersey, but was spending some time at the beach when she wrote *Gift from the Sea.* **What, according to Lindbergh and her friend, gives us freedom and peace?** [having few possessions or distractions; concentrating on one's thoughts or inner life] **Why do you think most people choose complication instead of simplicity?** [Possible responses: greed and compulsive consumerism; enjoyment of expensive things; the stimulation of a busy life; a desire to distract oneself from difficult or complex thoughts.] **What does Lindbergh think makes life worth living?** [simplicity; peace and quiet; inner freedom]

Writing Focus: Controversial Issue

WORK IN PROGRESS

The following **Work in Progress** assignments in this collection build to a culminating **Writer's Workshop** at the end of Collection 6.

- Nature; Self-Reliance   List controversial issues (p. 229)
- Walden   Pose questions on controversial issues (p. 247)
- Resistance to Civil Government   Define your position on one controversial issue (p. 258)

Writer's Workshop: Persuasive Writing / Controversial Issue (p. 331)

OBJECTIVES

from Nature / *from* Self-Reliance

1. Read and interpret the essays
2. Analyze imagery
3. Identify and interpret figures of speech
4. Monitor reading strategies
5. Express understanding through writing, speaking and listening, or conducting a project
6. Learn and use new words

SKILLS

Literary
- Analyze imagery
- Identify figures of speech

Reading
- Monitor reading strategies
- Understand and interpret figures of speech

Writing
- Collect ideas for an essay on a controversial topic
- Write a personal response
- Analyze paradoxes
- Define an abstract concept
- Plan a utopian community

Speaking/Listening
- Engage in a group discussion

Vocabulary
- Use new words

Viewing/Representing
- Compare verbal and visual responses to nature (ATE)

Planning

- **Block Schedule**
  Block Scheduling Lesson Plans with Pacing Guide

- **Traditional Schedule**
  Lesson Plans Including Strategies for English-Language Learners

- **One-Stop Planner**
  CD-ROM with Test Generator

Ralph Waldo Emerson

(1803–1882)

Shortly before the poet Walt Whitman died, he honored a man whose ideas had influenced him profoundly throughout his own long and controversial career. "America in the future," he wrote, "in her long train of poets and writers, while knowing more vehement and luxurious ones, will, I think, acknowledge nothing nearer [than] this man, the actual beginner of the whole procession."

"This man" was Ralph Waldo Emerson. Emerson expressed, better than anyone before him, the advantages of a young land—its freedom from the old, corrupt, and dying thought and customs of Europe; its access to higher laws directly through nature rather than indirectly through books and the teachings of the past; its energy; and its opportunity to reform the world.

Emerson was one of those rare writers who appealed both to intellectuals and to the general public. His influence on the popular mind—thanks to the thousands of lectures he gave throughout the United States—was strong. Although Emerson had something of a reputation for being hard to understand, his lectures were usually quite accessible. "I had heard of him as full of transcendentalisms, myths, and oracular gibberish," Herman Melville wrote a friend after hearing Emerson lecture. "To my surprise, I found him quite intelligible." Melville added wryly, "To say truth, they told me that that night he was unusually plain."

Despite his great influence, it is difficult even to classify what kind of writer Emerson was. *Essayist* is too limited, and *philosopher* is too broad. The best term, perhaps, is *poet*—a poet whose best work was not always in verse.

"I am born a poet," Emerson wrote to his fiancée, Lydia Jackson, in 1835, "of a low class without doubt, yet a poet. That is my nature and vocation. My singing, be sure, is very 'husky,' and is for the most part in prose. Still am I a poet in the sense of a perceiver and dear lover of the harmonies that are in the soul and in matter. . . ."

The Pennsylvania Academy of the Fine Arts, Philadelphia. Gift of Horace Howard Furness (1899.8).

Ralph Waldo Emerson (c. 1867) by William Henry Furness, Jr. (1828–1867). Oil on canvas (45¾" × 36³⁄₁₆").

The Burden of Expectation

Emerson was born in Boston in 1803 to a family that was cultured but poor. When he was only eight years old, his father, a Unitarian minister, died of tuberculosis. His mother, left with six growing children to care for, opened a boardinghouse.

The father's place in the lives of the Emerson children was taken by their aunt. Mary Moody Emerson was a strict Calvinist who emphasized self-sacrifice and whose enormous energy drove the Emerson boys to achievement. "She had the misfortune," Emerson later wrote, "of spinning with a greater velocity than any of the other tops."

Every step of Emerson's life had been laid out for him from an early age. He was to go to Harvard and become a minister like his father and the seven generations of Emersons before him. Emerson uncomfortably obeyed. His life was a series of attempts to establish his own identity against this background of expectation.

Young Rebel

Emerson entered Harvard at fourteen. He was an indifferent student, although he read widely in philosophy and theology. Upon graduation, Emerson took a job at a school run by his uncle and prepared himself, with many doubts, for the Unitarian ministry. In 1829, at the age of

go.hrw.com
LE0 11-5

Professional Notes

Critical Comment: Emerson's Politics

Literary scholar Brooks Atkinson explains that in spite of being actively involved in local affairs in Concord, regarding national politics, Emerson was reluctant: "From the first he had believed that the slaves should be freed. But he avoided as long as possible the radical societies that were promoting abolition. . . . But as the slavery clamor increased Emerson began to join in it. When the Fugitive Slave Law was passed, and Emerson believed his hero, Daniel Webster, had betrayed public trust, Emerson appeared at public meetings in Concord, Boston, and New York and spoke with a bitterness strange in so serene a person. In spite of the fact that all his instincts were against taking part in political action and in spite of his distrust of his own knowledge of practical affairs, he actively associated himself with the abolitionist cause after the passage of the Fugitive Slave Law. Once he observed to one of his children who had to write a school essay on building a house, that no house should be built without having in it a space to hide a runaway slave. He entertained John Brown in his house, contributed to the cause of abolition beyond his means and spoke in defense of John Brown after Harpers Ferry."

twenty-five, he accepted a post at Boston's Second Church; that same year, he married Ellen Tucker, a beautiful but fragile seventeen-year-old already in the early stages of tuberculosis. Seventeen months later, Ellen died.

Emerson's grief coincided with a growing disbelief in some of the central doctrines of his religion. In June 1832, he shocked his congregation by resigning the ministry and setting off on an extended tour of Europe. There he met and conversed with the Romantic poets William Wordsworth and Samuel Taylor Coleridge, as well as other influential writers.

Emerson's New Pulpit

Returning to the United States in late 1833, Emerson settled in Concord, Massachusetts, and soon married Lydia Jackson. He began to supplement his meager income by giving lectures and found in that occupation "a new pulpit," as he once wrote. Emerson's view was distinctively American in that he denied the importance of the past: "Let us unfetter ourselves of our historical associations and find a pure standard in the idea of man."

> "Let us . . . find a pure standard in the idea of man."

The last phrase points to Emerson's focus on humanity. Individual men and women were part of this "idea of man" in the same way that individual souls were part of a larger entity, which Emerson later called the "Over-Soul." The idea of nature also corresponded to the idea of man—both were part of a universal whole in which people could see their souls reflected.

Over the years, Emerson's influence grew. In 1837, he excited the student audience at Harvard with the lecture now known as "The American Scholar." In the speech, Emerson demanded that American scholars free themselves from the shackles of the past. "Our day of dependence," he declared, "our long apprenticeship to the learning of other lands, draws to a close."

A year later, Emerson was invited back to Harvard to speak to a group of divinity students. His speech, "The Divinity School Address," called for a rejection of institutional religion in favor of a personal relation with God. Religious truth, Emerson said, was "an intuition. It cannot be received at second hand." The lecture so outraged Harvard authorities (who heard in it a denial of the divinity of Christ) that three decades passed before Emerson was allowed to speak there again.

Twilight of an Idol

With the author's growing fame, Concord increasingly became a destination for truth-seeking young people who looked to Emerson as their guru. The young responded to Emerson's predictions that they were on the verge of a new age; intellectuals responded to his philosophical ideas about the relations among humanity, nature, and God; and society as a whole responded to his optimism.

That optimism was dealt a severe blow in 1842 when Emerson's son Waldo died of scarlet fever at the age of five. By nature a rather reserved man, Emerson had found in Waldo someone to whom he could show his love spontaneously. At the child's death, he shrank into an emotional shell from which he never emerged. "How can I hope for a friend," he wrote in his journal, "who have never been one?"

In later years, Emerson suffered from a severe loss of memory and had difficulty recalling the most ordinary words. This affliction resulted in his increasing public silence, and when he did appear in public, he read from notes.

In the autumn of 1881, Walt Whitman paid Emerson a visit of respect and was asked to dinner. Whitman wrote that Emerson "though a listener and apparently an alert one, remained silent through the whole talk and discussion. A lady friend [Louisa May Alcott] quietly took a seat next to him, to give special attention. A good color in his face, eyes clear, with the well-known expression of sweetness, and the old clear-peering aspect quite the same." Six months later, Emerson was dead.

BROWSING IN THE FILES

About the Author. At age twenty-one, Emerson took stock of himself in the following terms: "[M]y bearing in the world is the direct opposite of that good humoured independence & self esteem which should mark the gentleman. . . . I am unfortunate also . . . in a propensity to laugh & snicker. I am ill at ease therefore among men. I criticize with hardness; I lavishly applaud. I weakly argue; and I wonder with a foolish face of praise. . . . What is called a warm heart, I have not."

Writers on Writing. "No man can write well who thinks there is any choice of words for him," Emerson wrote in 1831. "The laws of composition are as strict as those of sculpture & architecture. There is always one line that ought to be drawn or one proportion that should be kept & every other line or proportion is wrong. . . . So in writing, there is always a right word, & every other than that is wrong. There is no beauty in words except in their collocation. The effect of a fanciful word misplaced, is like that of a horn . . . growing on a human head."

Resources: Print and Media

Reading
- *Graphic Organizers for Active Reading,* pp. 18, 19
- *Words to Own,* pp. 14, 15
- *Audio CD Library*
  Disc 6, Tracks 2, 3

Elements of Literature
- *Literary Elements*
  Transparency 8
  Worksheet, p. 25

Writing and Language
- *Daily Oral Grammar*
  Transparencies 16, 17
- *Grammar and Language Links*
  Worksheet, p. 23
- *Language Workshop CD-ROM*

Viewing and Representing
- *Viewing and Representing*
  Fine Art Transparency 5
  Fine Art Worksheet, p. 20

Assessment
- *Formal Assessment,* pp. 49, 51
- *Portfolio Management System,* p. 116
- *Preparation for College Admission Exams,* p. 17
- *Test Generator (One-Stop Planner CD-ROM)*

Internet
- go.hrw.com (keyword: LE0 11-5)

Summary ■ ■ ■

In *Nature*, Emerson uses striking imagery to discuss the exaltation human beings experience when they really look at the natural world around them. However, Emerson believes that most people lose this sense of wonder and delight in nature as they grow older. Those adults who never lose this sense remain youthful in spirit all their lives. Emerson explains that humans and plants are both part of the same natural world and that our delight in nature comes from this relationship. The beauty and grandeur are not only in nature but also in our perception of and response to it.

RESPONDING TO THE ART

This cartoon by the American painter, poet, and Unitarian minister **Christopher Pearce Cranch** (1813–1892) is the most famous of a number of lampoons of Emerson's phrase "I become a transparent eyeball" (p. 221). Although Cranch spoofed Emerson in *Illustrations of the New Philosophy,* he became friendly enough with the philosopher and his circle to have his poetry published in *The Dial* and to make extended visits to Brook Farm.

Activity. Have students review the context of the "eyeball" phrase (p. 221) and then evaluate the cartoon. [Possible responses: The cartoon is effective because the figure and the background reflect Emerson's ideas about seeing all nature and feeling a part of it; it is inappropriate—Cranch takes Emerson's ideas too lightly.]

Before You Read

FROM NATURE

"Standing on the bare ground, — my head bathed by the blithe air, & uplifted into infinite space, — all mean egotism vanishes. I become a transparent Eyeball." *Nature. p. 13.*

By permission of the Houghton Library, Harvard University, Cambridge, Massachusetts.

Caricature of Emerson by Christopher Pearce Cranch from *Illustrations of the New Philosophy.*

Make the Connection

Nature Nurtures
Exhilarated by nature's beauty and tranquility, Emerson felt he was in tune with his better self, in harmony with eternal things. If today we commune with nature in order to find ourselves, we may be taking up Emerson's search for "an original relation to the universe."

Reading Skills and Strategies

Monitoring Your Reading
As you study these essays, look for key passages that seem to state the **main idea** of a section. **Paraphrase** statements that seem difficult or puzzling to you. Check the footnotes, and use the glossary at the back of the book for definitions of difficult words. Above all, be sure to ask questions of the text.

Elements of Literature

Imagery
Emerson the poet helps out Emerson the philosopher in this essay, *showing* us scenes of nature that he loves rather than just *telling* us about his feelings in general. As you read, look for the **imagery**—descriptive language that appeals to one or more of our five senses—that Emerson uses.

> **I**magery is the use of language to evoke a picture or concrete sensation of a person, thing, place, or an experience.
>
> *For more on Imagery, see the Handbook of Literary Terms.*

Background

In his introduction to the book *Nature,* from which the following chapter is taken, Emerson offers a clue to the underlying purpose of his work when he encourages his contemporaries to look directly at nature:

"Our age is retrospective. It builds the sepulchers of the fathers. It writes biographies, histories, and criticism. The foregoing generations beheld God and nature face to face; we, through their eyes. Why should we not also enjoy an original relation to the universe? Why should we not have a poetry and philosophy of insight and not of tradition, and a religion by revelation to us, and not the history of theirs?"

Preteaching Vocabulary

Words to Own
Have students read the Words to Own and their definitions, listed at the bottom of the selection pages. Then, have each student use at least five of the words in a paragraph about nature. Afterward, have students find the vocabulary word that corresponds to each pair of synonyms that follows.

1. lasting, recurring [perennial]
2. various, numerous [manifold]
3. merry, carefree [blithe]
4. unify, combine [integrate]
5. magnificent, grand [sublime]
6. skin, covering [slough]
7. eternal, constant [perpetual]
8. doubtlessly, undeniably [indubitably]
9. hidden, secret [occult]
10. scolding, warning [admonishing]

Dover Plains, Dutchess County, New York (1848) by Asher Brown Durand.
Oil on canvas (42½″ × 60½″).

National Museum of American Art/Smithsonian Institution/Art Resource:
Gift of Thomas M. Evans and Museum Purchase through the Smithsonian
Collections Acquisition Program.

from Nature

Ralph Waldo Emerson

To go into solitude, a man needs to retire as much from his chamber[1] as from society. I am not solitary while I read and write, though nobody is with me. But if a man would be alone, let him look at the stars. The rays that come from those heavenly worlds, will separate between him and vulgar things. One might think the atmosphere was made transparent with this design, to give man, in the heavenly bodies, the <u>perpetual</u> presence of the <u>sublime</u>. Seen in the streets of cities, how great they are! If the stars should appear one night in a thousand years, how would men believe and adore; and preserve for many generations the remembrance of the city of God which had been shown! But every night come out these envoys of beauty, and light the universe with their <u>admonishing</u> smile.

1. **chamber:** room.

WORDS TO OWN

perpetual (pər·pech′oo·əl) *adj.:* constant; unchanging.
sublime (sə·blīm′) *adj.* used as *n.:* that which inspires awe.
admonishing (ad·män′ish·iŋ) *v.* used as *adj.:* mildly warning.

RALPH WALDO EMERSON **219**

Reaching All Students

Struggling Readers
Monitoring Your Reading was introduced on p. 218. Students were asked to paraphrase main ideas. One good strategy to use for this skill is Save the Last Word for Me. For information on using this strategy, see the *Reading Strategies Handbook*, p. 77 in the *Reading Skills and Strategies* binder.

English Language Learners
Even English-proficient students will have some difficulty with Emerson's philosophical concepts and antiquated diction. Guide the class in composing paraphrases of passages that prove troublesome. For the thornier sentences and words (such as *maugre*), paraphrases or definitions could be written on the board. Divide the essay into smaller passages, each of which can be analyzed by a group of students. (The opening paragraph itself can be divided among the groups.)

Resources

Viewing and Representing
Fine Art Transparency
A fine art transparency of Helen Hardin's *Recurrence of Spiritual Elements* allows students to compare different works about harmony.
- Transparency 5
- Worksheet, p. 20

RESPONDING TO THE ART
Asher Brown Durand (1796–1886) was one of the first American artists to paint outdoors, working directly from nature. His work emphasizes light in order to convey the idea that nature discloses God's design.
Activity. Ask students to compare Emerson's and Durand's views of nature. [Both depict the grandeur of nature. Both suggest that humanity has a unique place within nature.] Note that the painting seems especially relevant to the second-to-last paragraph of this excerpt.

A **Elements of Literature**
Paradox
❓ A paradox is a seemingly contradictory statement. How can Emerson be alone and not solitary? [When reading and writing, he is still wrapped up in society and human concerns.]

B **Elements of Literature**
Imagery
❓ Which of the five senses does Emerson appeal to? [sight] How does he feel when he looks at the stars? [awed; thrilled; reverent; admiring]

C **Literary Connections**
"Nightfall"
The sentence "If the stars should appear one night in a thousand years . . ." was used by Isaac Asimov as the premise and the epigraph for his science-fiction story "Nightfall" (1941), considered a classic of the genre. Have students read the story and discuss how Asimov supports and extends Emerson's ideas.

A Vocabulary Note

Multiple Meanings

Have students list definitions of the word *mean*. [cruel; average; stingy; shabby; ignoble] Then, have students determine what the word means in this sentence. ["ignoble" or "shabby"]

B Reading Skills and Strategies

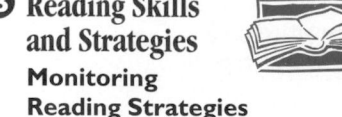

Monitoring Reading Strategies

Ask students to paraphrase this paragraph. [The poet looks at nature as an organic whole rather than a group of distinct objects or features. People own particular plots of land, but no one "owns the landscape."]

C Advanced Learners

Analyzing

❓ Why might adults not be able to see nature as well as children? [Possible answers: Adults tend to take nature for granted, as something that is either useful or destructive to their life projects. They don't have time to appreciate nature in itself, emotionally and aesthetically. Children can appreciate nature because to them it is surprising and new.]

D Critical Thinking

Challenging the Text

❓ Do you agree with Emerson's portrayal of the "lover of nature"? Do you think such a person would be consistently affected this way? [Some students will agree that nature consistently provides an appropriate, beneficial context for any emotional state. Others may feel that deep emotions are evoked only by human contact.]

E Elements of Literature

Imagery

❓ Identify the images in this line. [the bare common, snow puddles, twilight, a clouded sky] What effect does this description have on the reader? [The spare and simple images make readers feel as if they are crossing the common with Emerson. Emerson's direct language evokes the brisk exhilaration of the scene and calls on readers to imagine the treeless patch of ground and to feel the slush and cold.]

A The stars awaken a certain reverence, because though always present, they are always inaccessible; but all natural objects make a kindred impression, when the mind is open to their influence. Nature never wears a mean appearance. Neither does the wisest man extort all her secret, and lose his curiosity by finding out all her perfection. Nature never became a toy to a wise spirit. The flowers, the animals, the mountains, reflected all the wisdom of his best hour, as much as they had delighted the simplicity of his childhood.

B When we speak of nature in this manner, we have a distinct but most poetical sense in the mind. We mean the integrity of impression made by <u>manifold</u> natural objects. It is this which distinguishes the stick of timber of the woodcutter, from the tree of the poet. The charming landscape which I saw this morning, is <u>indubitably</u> made up of some twenty or thirty farms. Miller owns this field, Locke that, and Manning the woodland beyond. But none of them owns the landscape. There is a property in the horizon which no man has but he whose eye can <u>integrate</u> all the parts, that is, the poet. This is the best part of these men's farms, yet to this their warranty deeds[2] give no title.

C To speak truly, few adult persons can see nature. Most persons do not see the sun. At least they have a very superficial seeing. The sun illuminates only the eye of the man, but shines into the eye and the heart of the child. The lover of nature is he whose inward and outward senses are still truly adjusted to each other; who has retained the spirit of infancy even into the era of manhood. His intercourse with heaven and earth, becomes part of his daily food. In the presence of nature, a wild delight runs through the man, in spite of real sorrows. Nature says—he is my creature, and maugre[3] all his impertinent griefs, he shall D be glad with me. Not the sun or the summer alone, but every hour and season yields its tribute of delight; for every hour and change corresponds to and authorizes a different state of the mind, from breathless noon to grimmest midnight. Nature is a setting that fits equally well a comic or a mourning piece. In good health, the air is a cordial[4] of incredible virtue. Crossing a bare common, in snow puddles, at twilight, E under a clouded sky, without having in my thoughts any occurrence of special good fortune, I have enjoyed a perfect exhilaration. Almost I fear to think how glad I am. In the woods too, a man casts off his years,

2. **warranty deeds:** legal documents showing ownership of property.
3. **maugre** (mô′gər): archaic for "in spite of" or "despite."
4. **cordial** (kôr′jəl): a liquor that stimulates the heart.

WORDS TO OWN

manifold (man′ə·fōld′) *adj.*: many different.
indubitably (in·dōō′bi·tə·blē) *adv.*: without a doubt.
integrate (in′tə·grāt′) *v.*: unify.

Using Students' Strengths

Naturalist Learners

Ask students to research the natural history of their state or region. Have them find out what Emerson would have seen in their area around 1850. If they live in a city, they could determine how big it was then, what natural corners still existed, how far it was to the "country" or the woods. Outside cities, they should find out if the area was wilderness or settled, forest or prairie, swamp or farmland.

Auditory/Musical Learners

Students should note that Emerson does not discuss or describe the sounds of nature. Have students reread the nature descriptions and imagine the sounds they might hear, such as the caw of crows, the rush of a stream, or the whistling of wind through the trees. What effect do these sounds have on them? What would Emerson's essay have gained by including sound imagery? Do students feel that the sounds of nature are as powerful as its sights?

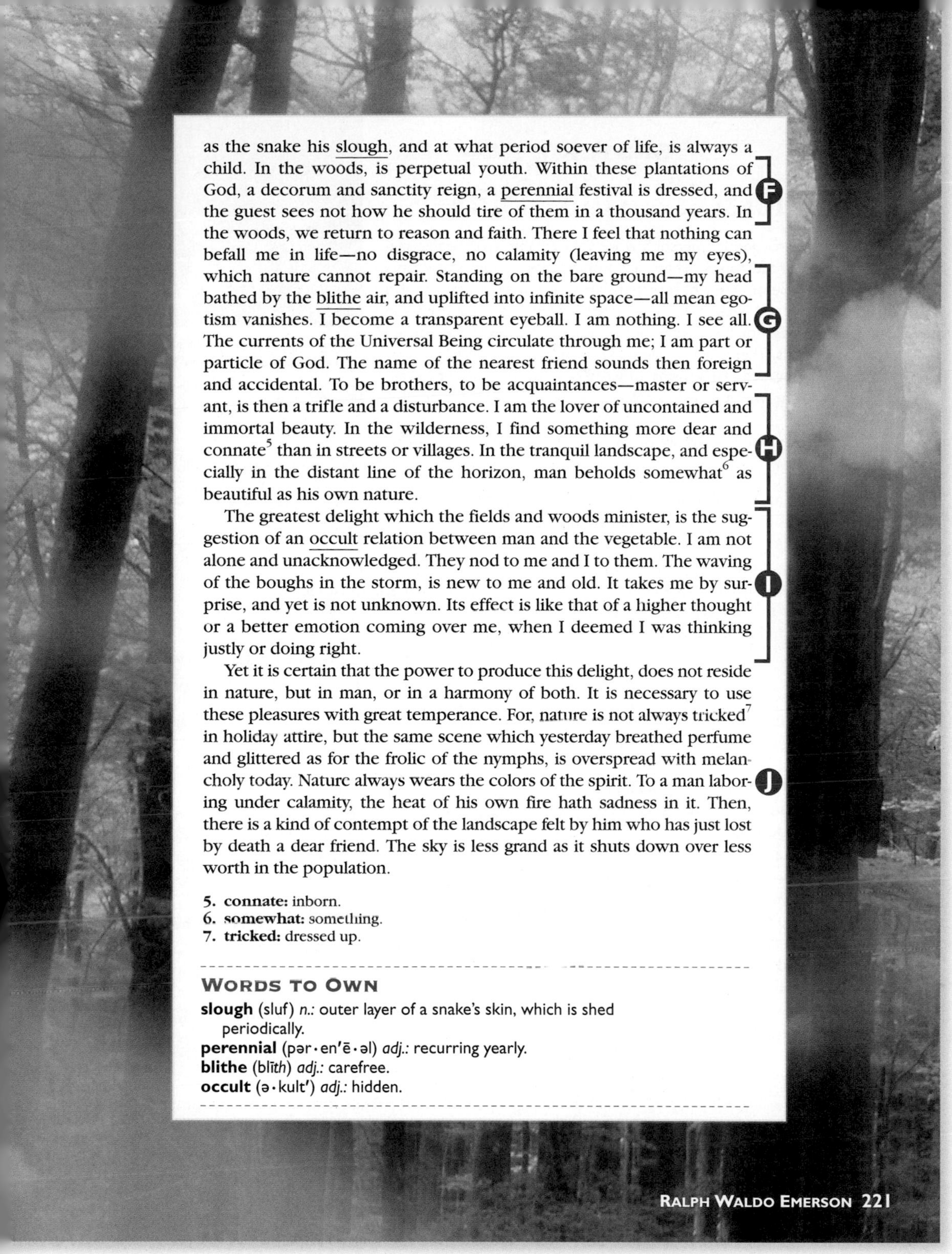

as the snake his <u>slough</u>, and at what period soever of life, is always a child. In the woods, is perpetual youth. Within these plantations of God, a decorum and sanctity reign, a <u>perennial</u> festival is dressed, and the guest sees not how he should tire of them in a thousand years. In the woods, we return to reason and faith. There I feel that nothing can befall me in life—no disgrace, no calamity (leaving me my eyes), which nature cannot repair. Standing on the bare ground—my head bathed by the <u>blithe</u> air, and uplifted into infinite space—all mean egotism vanishes. I become a transparent eyeball. I am nothing. I see all. The currents of the Universal Being circulate through me; I am part or particle of God. The name of the nearest friend sounds then foreign and accidental. To be brothers, to be acquaintances—master or servant, is then a trifle and a disturbance. I am the lover of uncontained and immortal beauty. In the wilderness, I find something more dear and connate[5] than in streets or villages. In the tranquil landscape, and especially in the distant line of the horizon, man beholds somewhat[6] as beautiful as his own nature.

The greatest delight which the fields and woods minister, is the suggestion of an <u>occult</u> relation between man and the vegetable. I am not alone and unacknowledged. They nod to me and I to them. The waving of the boughs in the storm, is new to me and old. It takes me by surprise, and yet is not unknown. Its effect is like that of a higher thought or a better emotion coming over me, when I deemed I was thinking justly or doing right.

Yet it is certain that the power to produce this delight, does not reside in nature, but in man, or in a harmony of both. It is necessary to use these pleasures with great temperance. For, nature is not always tricked[7] in holiday attire, but the same scene which yesterday breathed perfume and glittered as for the frolic of the nymphs, is overspread with melancholy today. Nature always wears the colors of the spirit. To a man laboring under calamity, the heat of his own fire hath sadness in it. Then, there is a kind of contempt of the landscape felt by him who has just lost by death a dear friend. The sky is less grand as it shuts down over less worth in the population.

5. **connate:** inborn.
6. **somewhat:** something.
7. **tricked:** dressed up.

WORDS TO OWN
slough (sluf) *n.:* outer layer of a snake's skin, which is shed periodically.
perennial (pər·en′ē·əl) *adj.:* recurring yearly.
blithe (blīth) *adj.:* carefree.
occult (ə·kult′) *adj.:* hidden.

RALPH WALDO EMERSON 221

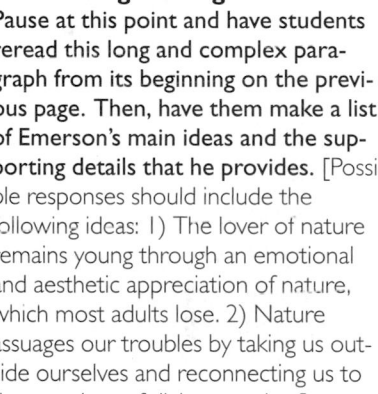

F Elements of Literature
Paradox
? According to Emerson, how can a place be both decorous and festive? [Evidence of the hand of God gives it sanctity, which inspires decorum; at the same time, nature is beautiful and colorful year round, "a perennial festival."]

G Critical Thinking
Making Judgments
? Do you find it contradictory that in the same passage Emerson says "all mean egotism vanishes" and "I see all. The currents of the Universal Being circulate through me"? [Possible responses: No, he means that he has become part of something far greater than himself; yes, claiming that he has the Universal Being circulating through him is egotism.]

H Reading Skills and Strategies
Monitoring Reading Strategies
Pause at this point and have students reread this long and complex paragraph from its beginning on the previous page. Then, have them make a list of Emerson's main ideas and the supporting details that he provides. [Possible responses should include the following ideas: 1) The lover of nature remains young through an emotional and aesthetic appreciation of nature, which most adults lose. 2) Nature assuages our troubles by taking us outside ourselves and reconnecting us to the grandeur of divine creation.]

I Elements of Literature
Imagery
? What images does Emerson conjure up here? [the "vegetable" world nodding and waving to him] What effect do these images have on him? [They carry him to a higher level of thought and emotion.]

J Struggling Readers
Interpreting Idioms
Ask students to explain the meaning of "Nature always wears the colors of the spirit." [A person's perception of nature depends on his or her mood.]

Taking a Second Look

Review:
Producing Summaries of Texts
Review the skill of summarizing a text. A summary should include the writer's main idea or ideas, plus the most important details the writer provides in support of those ideas. A summary is not a paraphrase of the text; it is a concise distillation of the author's ideas.

1. Students should summarize this excerpt, paragraph by paragraph, writing Emerson's main ideas in clear and concise language.

Remind them not to copy any part of the text word for word. After each main idea, students should note the most important supporting details or examples.

2. Give each student a different paragraph from other passages in *Nature*. Have students take their paragraphs home and produce a summary of the main ideas. Then, have students orally summarize their texts for the class.

T221

Spotlight On

This feature provides a general discussion of the aphorism as a literary element and contains a brief survey of Emerson's more famous aphorisms. These include Emerson's thoughts on patriotism, human fallibility, writing, wisdom, theology, and greed.

Ⓐ Critical Thinking
Extending the Text

❓ Do you think this aphorism still holds true today? [Most students will agree that this observation is more true than ever, especially in light of twentieth-century developments like nuclear weapons and global warming. Other students will point out the great achievements of responsible human power.]

Ⓑ Literary Connections
Chaos

❓ In Greek mythology, Chaos was one of the two original beings (the other was Gaea, the Earth) from which order and the universe sprang. Night was born from Chaos. What do Chaos and Night symbolize here? [the unknown, ignorance] What is "building a road" a metaphor for? [discovering something new and providing others with the means to reach it]

Ⓒ Critical Thinking
Challenging the Text

❓ Emerson believed that each individual soul is part of the Over-soul. Given such unity, why might Emerson feel that praying for oneself (personal benefit) might become "meanness and theft"? [Possible response: By praying for oneself, one separates oneself from others and nature and destroys the universal spirit Emerson felt to be at life's source.]

Ⓓ Critical Thinking
Interpreting

❓ What does this aphorism mean? [The people who live during a period make it good or bad.] From your study of history, do you agree that the people determine the times? [Possible response: Many students will feel the people of an era have some influence on the times but that other forces in history—such as natural disasters—are also influential.]

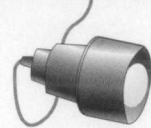

Emerson's Aphorisms

A Study Table (1882) by William Harnett.
Oil on canvas (39⅞" × 51⅜").
Munson-Williams-Proctor Institute Museum of Art, Utica, New York.

Studded throughout Emerson's work are quotable, memorable sayings on broad topics. These are **aphorisms**—short statements that express wise or clever observations about life. (Aphorisms are also called "maxims" or "adages.") Try paraphrasing Emerson's aphorisms in your own words: You'll see how much meaning the writer has packed into a few words. That is what makes an aphorism memorable.

Many of Emerson's aphorisms originated in the journal he began keeping when he was a junior in college; by the end of his life, it filled many volumes.

For more aphorisms, see those by the poet Wallace Stevens, page 786.

I confess I am a little cynical on some topics, and when a whole nation is roaring Patriotism at the top of its voice, I am fain[1] to explore the cleanness of its hands and purity of its heart. I have generally found the gravest and most useful citizens are not the easiest provoked to swell the noise, though they may be punctual at the polls.

—*Journals*, 1824

Ⓐ Don't trust children with edge tools. Don't trust man, great God, with more power than he has, until he has learned to use that little better. What a hell should we make of the world if we could do what we would! Put a button on the foil[2] till the young fencers have learned not to put each other's eyes out.

—*Journals*, 1832

Ⓑ The maker of a sentence, like the other artist, launches out into the infinite and builds a road into Chaos and old Night, and is followed by those who hear him with something of wild, creative delight.

—*Journals*, 1834

Poetry must be as new as foam and as old as the rock.

—*Journals*, 1844

1. **fain:** reluctantly willing. 2. **foil:** sword.

The invariable mark of wisdom is to see the miraculous in the common.

—*Nature*

A man is a god in ruins.

—*Nature*

Nothing can bring you peace but yourself. Nothing can bring you peace but the triumph of principles.

—"Self-Reliance"

Ⓒ Prayer as a means to effect a private end is meanness and theft. It supposes dualism and not a unity in nature and consciousness. As soon as the man is at one with God, he will not beg. He will then see prayer in all action.

—"Self-Reliance"

Ⓓ This time, like all times, is a very good one, if we but know what to do with it.

—"The American Scholar"

Books are the best of things, well used; abused, among the worst.

—"The American Scholar"

Public and private avarice make the air we breathe thick and fat.

—"The American Scholar"

Assessing Learning

Check Test: True-False
Answer according to Emerson's beliefs.
1. People look at the stars each night with the same wonder they would feel if they were seeing them for the first time. [False]
2. Adults do not appreciate nature as much as children do. [True]
3. Those who truly see nature remain young. [True]
4. There is a harmony between humanity and nature. [True]

Standardized Test Preparation
For practice with ACT and SAT formats, see
• *Preparation for College Admission Exams*, p. 17
For practice in proofreading and editing, see
• *Daily Oral Grammar*, Transparencies 16, 17

Hawthorne Talks About Emerson

Emerson, who thought of sin as merely a child's case of measles on the world, and Nathaniel Hawthorne, who plumbed the nature of evil, could never talk together. For a time, Hawthorne lived at Brook Farm, a self-governing, experimental community of Transcendentalists, founded by the minister George Ripley. But he left after a few months, finding the high-minded discussions stifling. Hawthorne then lived for a time in a house called the Old Manse in Concord, the same house where Emerson had written his first book, *Nature*. Here, in a passage from his essay called "The Old Manse," Hawthorne talks about Emerson and the "hobgoblins" who came to Concord seeking answers to the riddle of the world.

(A)

These hobgoblins of flesh and blood were attracted thither by the widespreading influence of a great original thinker, who had his earthly abode at the opposite extremity of our village. His mind acted upon other minds of a certain constitution with wonderful magnetism, and drew many men upon long pilgrimages to speak with him face to face. Young visionaries—to whom just so much of insight had been imparted as to make life all a labyrinth[1] around them—came to seek the clue that should guide them out of their self-involved bewilderment. Gray-headed theorists—whose systems, at first air, had finally imprisoned them in an iron framework—traveled painfully to his door, not to ask deliverance, but to invite the free spirit into their own thralldom.[2] People that had lighted on a new thought, or a thought that they fancied new, came to Emerson, as the finder of a glittering gem hastens to a lapidary,[3] to ascertain its quality and value. Uncertain,

1. **labyrinth:** maze.
2. **thralldom:** servitude.
3. **lapidary:** gem dealer.

troubled, earnest wanderers through the midnight of the moral world beheld his intellectual fire as a beacon burning on a hilltop, and, climbing the difficult ascent, looked forth into the surrounding obscurity more hopefully than hitherto. The light revealed objects unseen before—mountains, gleaming lakes, glimpses of a creation among the chaos; but also, as was unavoidable, it attracted bats and owls and the whole host of night birds, which flapped their dusky wings against the gazer's eyes, and sometimes were mistaken for fowls of angelic feather. Such delusions always hover nigh whenever a beacon-fire of truth is kindled.

(B) For myself, there had been epochs of my life when I, too, might have asked of this prophet the master word that should solve me the riddle of the universe; but now, being happy, I felt as if there were no question to be put, and therefore admired Emerson as a poet of deep beauty and austere tenderness, but sought nothing from him as a philosopher. It was good, nevertheless, to meet him in the wood paths, or sometimes in our avenue, with that pure, intellectual gleam diffused about his presence like the garment of a shining one; and he so quiet, so simple, so without pretension, encountering each man alive as if expecting to receive more than he could impart. And, in truth, the heart of many an ordinary man had, perchance, inscriptions which he could not read. But it was impossible to dwell in his vicinity without inhaling more or less the mountain atmosphere of his lofty thought, which, in the brains of some people, wrought a singular giddiness—new truth being as heady as new wine. Never was a poor little country village infested with such a variety of queer, strangely dressed, oddly behaved mortals, most of whom took upon themselves to be important agents of the world's destiny, yet were simply bores of **(C)** a very intense water. . . .

—Nathaniel Hawthorne,
from "The Old Manse"

RALPH WALDO EMERSON 223

RALPH WALDO EMERSON 223

Primary Sources

In this feature, Hawthorne comments on the quantity and quality of the "pilgrims" who traveled to Emerson's door in Concord, Massachusetts, to discuss ideas. While he insists that Emerson's thought revealed new, important truths, he also maintains that it inspired confusion, self-absorption, and zealotry in many of his readers. For his own part, Hawthorne is unimpressed with Emerson as a philosopher yet praises his poetry, his humility, and his lack of pretension.

Background

When Hawthorne died in 1864, Emerson was a pallbearer. He wrote in his journal of his regret that they never achieved an intimate friendship. "I thought him a greater man than any of his works betray. . . . I have felt sure . . . that I could well wait his time,—his unwillingness and caprice,—and might one day conquer a friendship. It would have been a happiness, doubtless to both of us, to have come into habits of unreserved intercourse. . . . Now it appears that I waited too long."

(A) Cultural Connections
Brook Farm
For more on Brook Farm, see p. 226.

For more on Brook Farm, see p. 226.

(B) Cultural Connections
The Old Manse
Now open to the public (see p. 213), the Old Manse was built in 1769 by the Reverend William Emerson. (*Manse* refers to the residence of a minister.) Reverend Emerson's descendants lived in the house for the next 169 years, except for the three-year period when Hawthorne rented it soon after marrying Sophia Peabody. Referring to the accidental nature of their courtship, Hawthorne used Sophia's ring to etch her words on a windowpane in the Manse: "Man's accidents are God's purposes."

Now open to the public (see p. 213),

(C) Vocabulary Note
Multiple Meanings
Explain that one fairly uncommon definition of *water* is "degree" or "quality," as in "a diamond of the first water."

Professional Notes

Concord Society

In the early 1800s, the small town of Concord, Massachusetts (only nineteen miles from Boston, the intellectual center of the country), contained an eclectic collection of minds and personalities that rivaled any in Boston. Concord had an athenaeum, or literary club and library, and a Lyceum where Emerson and Thoreau frequently lectured. The site of the first battle of the Revolution was later home to Ralph Waldo Emerson, Henry David Thoreau, Theodore Parker, Bronson Alcott (and daughter Louisa May Alcott), Nathaniel Hawthorne, poet William Ellery Channing, Judge E. R. Hoar, and Brooks Farm founder George Ripley. While these distinguished individuals were not all friends, many did share the same dinner table at times—which generated lively conversation and intellectual exchange.

Summary ■■■

In this essay, Emerson makes a persuasive argument for nonconformity and
self-sufficiency, finds sanctity in the
individual mind, and calls upon us to
express ourselves strongly. He asserts
that only we know the best course of
action for ourselves. Instead of allowing society to conspire against original
achievement, each individual must find
the divine presence at work within.
Only in nonconformity do people
become fully human.

RESPONDING TO THE ART

William Sidney Mount (1807–
1868) spent his life on Long Island.
He is best known for his warmly
lit rural genre paintings, which
emphasized the simplicity and
beauty of agrarian America.
Activity. Ask students the following questions:

1. Is the painting a realistic or a
   romantic vision of farm life?
   Explain. [Possible answer:
   romantic—the farmer is too
   well-dressed; the painting gives
   the impression of leisure and
   neglects the hard work and frequent disappointment involved
   in growing crops.]
2. Why would Mount depict the
   farmer this way? [Possible
   answers: to portray the ideal of
   the gentleman farmer—a man
   of the town and the country,
   both sophisticated and rustic; to
   represent Emerson's lover of
   nature—a man who retains a
   naive delight in the natural
   world despite his sophistication
   in the human world.]

Before You Read

FROM **SELF-RELIANCE**

Make the Connection
Rugged Individualism
For Americans in the early years of
the country's history, belonging to a
bold, young nation was a tremendous source of group pride. Perhaps
the greatest source of that pride
was the high value the group placed
on individual liberty. In 1841, Emerson nourished this creed of individualism with his essay "Self-Reliance."

Quickwrite
Write down the associa-
tions you make with the
word *self-reliance*: definitions, examples, and synonyms. How does
self-reliance differ from selfishness
or self-centeredness?

Elements of Literature
Figures of Speech
Emerson makes many of his points
through a series of **figures of
speech** that compare abstract ideas
with ordinary things or events, such
as "Society is a joint-stock company." Some of his figures of speech
are difficult and require rereading
before you can fully understand
Emerson's point.

> **A** **figure of speech** is a
> word or phrase that de-
> scribes one thing in terms of
> another and that is not
> meant to be taken literally.
>
> *For more on Figures of Speech, see
> page 78 and the Handbook of
> Literary Terms.*

Long Island Farmer Husking Corn (1833–1834) by William Sidney Mount.
Oil on canvas mounted on panel (20⅞″ × 16⅞″).
The Museums at Stony Brook, Stony Brook, New York. Gift of Mr. & Mrs. Ward Melville.

from Self-Reliance

Ralph Waldo Emerson

Preteaching Vocabulary

Words to Own
Point out to students that many of the difficult
words in this selection contain common prefixes and roots. Have students work in pairs
to look these up and use them as a study aid.
Then, ask students to complete the sentences
below with the correct Words to Own from
the excerpt.

1. The [benefactors] donated money to the
   library.

2. Hawthorne felt a strong [aversion] toward
   many of Emerson's disciples.
3. Emerson [imparted] wisdom to his audiences.
4. John Wilkes Booth and others formed a
   [conspiracy] to murder President Lincoln.
5. Thoreau spoke with [conviction]; he meant
   what he said.
6. The [predominating] color in this landscape
   is yellow.

7. George Washington's honesty and [integrity]
   were rarely questioned.
8. The corn stalks make [manifest] the arrival
   of summer.
9. Ideally, one's salary should be [proportion-
   ate] to the work one does.
10. Emerson could view a winter stroll as a
    [transcendent] experience, transporting him
    beyond petty egotism and worry.

There is a time in every man's education . . . when he arrives at the <u>conviction</u> that envy is ignorance; that imitation is suicide; that he must take himself for better, for worse, as his portion; that though the wide universe is full of good, no kernel of nourishing corn can come to him but through his toil bestowed on that plot of ground which is given to him to till. The power which resides in him is new in nature, and none but he knows what that is which he can do, nor does he know until he has tried. Not for nothing one face, one character, one fact makes much impression on him, and another none. This sculpture in the memory is not without preestablished harmony. The eye was placed where one ray should fall, that it might testify of that particular ray. We but half express ourselves, and are ashamed of that divine idea which each of us represents. It may be safely trusted as <u>proportionate</u> and of good issues, so it be faithfully <u>imparted</u>, but God will not have his work made <u>manifest</u> by cowards. A man is relieved and gay when he has put his heart into his work and done his best; but what he has said or done otherwise, shall give him no peace. It is a deliverance which does not deliver. In the attempt his genius deserts him; no muse befriends; no invention, no hope.

Trust thyself: Every heart vibrates to that iron string. Accept the place the divine Providence has found for you; the society of your contemporaries, the connection of events. Great men have always done so and confided themselves childlike to the genius of their age, betraying their perception that the absolutely trustworthy was seated at their heart, working through their hands, <u>predominating</u> in all their being. And we are now men, and must accept in the highest mind the same <u>transcendent</u> destiny; and not minors and invalids in a protected corner, not cowards fleeing before a revolution, but guides, redeemers, and <u>benefactors</u>, obeying the Almighty effort, and advancing on Chaos and the Dark. . . .

These are the voices which we hear in solitude, but they grow faint and inaudible as we enter into the world. Society everywhere is in <u>conspiracy</u> against the manhood of every one of its members. Society is a joint-stock company in which the members agree for the better securing of his bread to each shareholder, to surrender the liberty and culture of the eater. The virtue in most request is conformity. Self-reliance is its <u>aversion</u>. It loves not realities and creators, but names and customs.

Whoso would be a man must be a nonconformist. He who would gather immortal palms[1] must not be hindered by the name of goodness, but must explore if it be goodness. Nothing is at last sacred but the <u>integrity</u> of your own mind. Absolve you to yourself, and you shall have the suffrage of the world. . . .

A foolish consistency is the hobgoblin of little minds, adored by little statesmen and philosophers and divines. With consistency a great soul has simply nothing to do. He may as well concern himself with his shadow on the wall. Speak what you think now in hard words, and tomorrow speak what tomorrow thinks in hard words again, though it contradict everything you said today— "Ah, so you shall be sure to be misunderstood"— Is it so bad then to be misunderstood? Pythagoras was misunderstood, and Socrates, and Jesus, and Luther, and Copernicus, and Galileo, and Newton,[2] and every pure and wise spirit that ever took flesh. To be great is to be misunderstood. . . .

---

1. **he who . . . immortal palms:** he who would win fame. In ancient times, palm leaves were carried as a symbol of victory or triumph.
2. **Pythagoras . . . Newton:** people whose contributions to scientific, philosophical, and religious thought were ignored or suppressed during their lifetimes.

WORDS TO OWN

conviction (kən·vik′shən) *n.:* belief.
proportionate (prō·pôr′shən·it) *adj.:* having a correct relationship between parts; balanced.
imparted (im·pärt′əd) *v.:* revealed.
manifest (man′ə·fest′) *adj.:* plain; clear.
predominating (prē·däm′ə·nāt′iŋ) *v.* used as *adj.:* having influence.
transcendent (tran·sen′dənt) *adj.:* excelling; surpassing.
benefactors (ben′ə·fak′tərz) *n. pl.:* people who help others.
conspiracy (kən·spir′ə·sē) *n.:* secret plot with a harmful or illegal purpose.
aversion (ə·vʉr′zhən) *n.:* intense dislike.
integrity (in·teg′rə·tē) *n.:* sound moral principles; honesty.

Ⓐ Elements of Literature
Figures of Speech
? Elaborate on Emerson's idea that each of us has unique talents and passions that we can discover only on our own. What does Emerson mean by "This sculpture in the memory"? [Possible response: Different people, facts, places, etc., strike each of us as "right" or familiar when we first meet them, almost as if we had already known them. These "preestablished" differences hint at our unique purpose in life and at an overall design or harmony.]

Ⓑ Elements of Literature
Figures of Speech
? What does the eye represent? [one individual's perception] the ray? [a particular experience or aspect of creation] Paraphrase this sentence. [Each person has a unique perspective and a unique role to play in the world.]

Ⓒ Critical Thinking
Challenging the Text
? Emerson says that true satisfaction comes only by working hard on something one loves. Do you agree? [Possible answers: Yes, all of us share that goal; no, many of us do what we must to meet our obligations or to make a living.]

Ⓓ Critical Thinking
Challenging the Text
? Do you agree with this famous charge? Why or why not? [Possible answers: Yes, people should trust their instincts, although peer pressure discourages nonconformity; no, trusting oneself too much can lead to arrogance and ignorance; society cannot tolerate a situation in which every person does whatever he or she wishes.]

Ⓔ Elements of Literature
Figures of Speech
? What is a "hobgoblin"? [Possible answers: a frightening apparition; something spooky.] What comment is Emerson making about consistency through this figure of speech? [Possible response: He is saying that rigid consistency in thought and action can prevent people from growing, changing, and fulfilling their potential.]

Crossing the Curriculum

History

To elaborate on Emerson's point in the final paragraph of the excerpt from "Self-Reliance," you might first explain that Pythagoras was exiled for his religious and mathematical beliefs. Then, have students look up each of the great men Emerson lists. Have students research the personality behind each of these famous names, what these men accomplished, what new ideas they introduced to the world, and how the world responded to them during their lifetimes.

Students can share their research in class. Then, ask students to name a person they consider "great," either someone from history or someone still alive, and explain why the person is admirable. Does the person belong on Emerson's list? In what way is he or she self-reliant? Was the person misunderstood during his or her lifetime? Afterward, ask students if they agree that "to be great is to be misunderstood."

This feature discusses the origins of the utopian movement of the mid-nineteenth century and the various experimental communities that sprang up across America during those years.

Ⓐ Humanities Connections

Utopias

The word *Utopia* was coined by Thomas More as the title of a book (1516) and the name of a fictional island. The world More describes bears more than a passing resemblance to an ideal communist society, in which there is no private property, and the means of production are shared by all citizens. The citizens of Utopia work cheerfully for the state; there are no other occupations and, incidentally, no place for art. Other literary utopias include Eldorado in Voltaire's *Candide* (1759). Eldorado was based on what Voltaire knew of Pennsylvania, which William Penn had founded as an idealistic Quaker province in America in 1682. Voltaire greatly admired the Quakers for their pacifism and the simplicity of their lives.

Ⓑ Historical Connections

Brook Farm

The goal at Brook Farm was to create a simpler and more harmonious American community, composed of individuals who were both thinkers and workers. Thus, the seventy or eighty members—intellectuals, teachers, farmers, craftspeople—were paid a dollar a day for their contributions to the operation of the farm.

Ⓒ Cultural Connections

Other Utopian Groups

Although all three groups held property in common, they were significantly different. The Shakers believed that their leader, Ann Lee, had received God's revelation. They practiced celibacy and believed that men and women were equal. Unlike the majority of utopian groups, which were centered in the east, the Amana Society established itself in Iowa as a pacifist farming community.

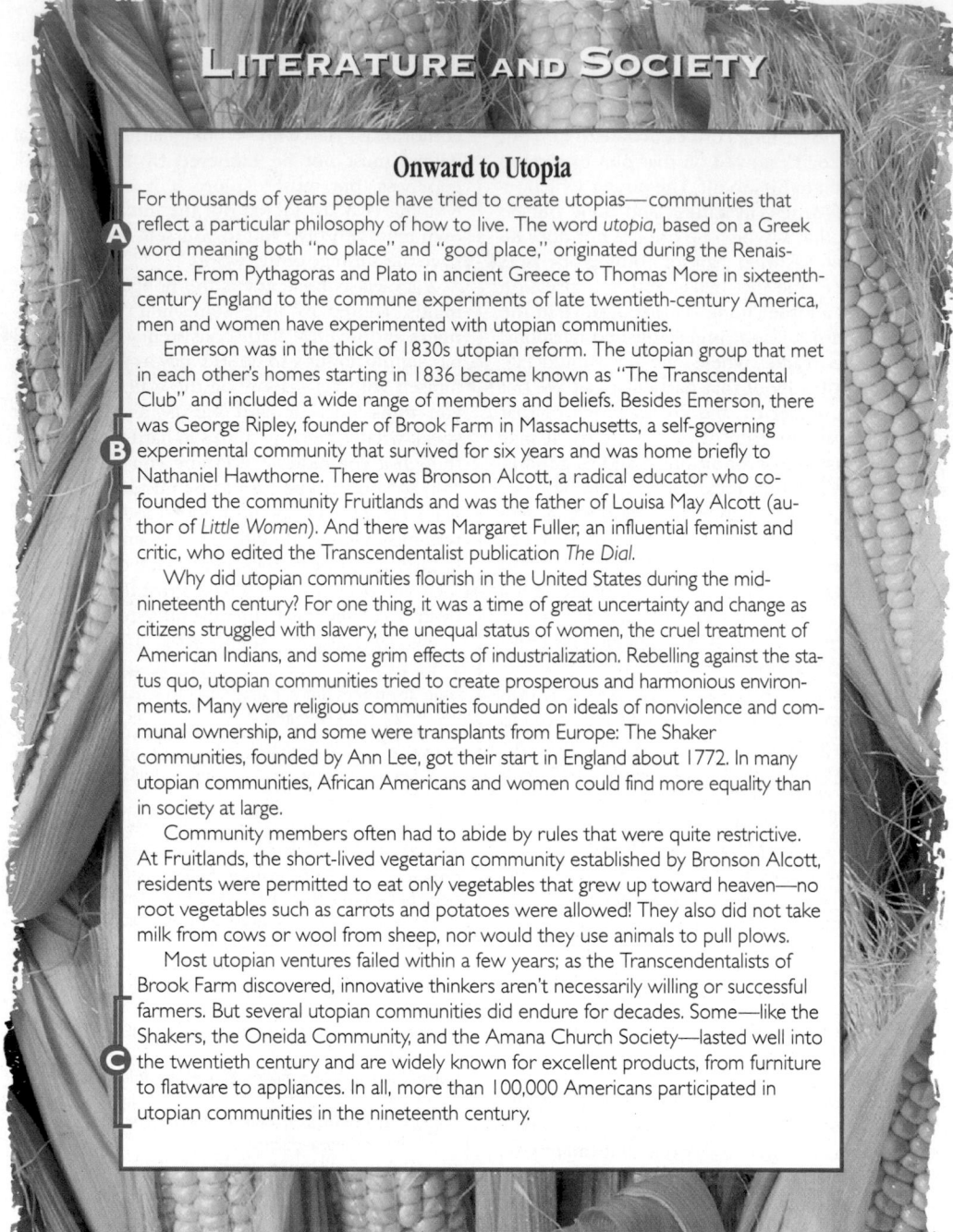

LITERATURE AND SOCIETY

Onward to Utopia

Ⓐ For thousands of years people have tried to create utopias—communities that reflect a particular philosophy of how to live. The word *utopia*, based on a Greek word meaning both "no place" and "good place," originated during the Renaissance. From Pythagoras and Plato in ancient Greece to Thomas More in sixteenth-century England to the commune experiments of late twentieth-century America, men and women have experimented with utopian communities.

Emerson was in the thick of 1830s utopian reform. The utopian group that met in each other's homes starting in 1836 became known as "The Transcendental Club" and included a wide range of members and beliefs. Besides Emerson, there **Ⓑ** was George Ripley, founder of Brook Farm in Massachusetts, a self-governing experimental community that survived for six years and was home briefly to Nathaniel Hawthorne. There was Bronson Alcott, a radical educator who co-founded the community Fruitlands and was the father of Louisa May Alcott (author of *Little Women*). And there was Margaret Fuller, an influential feminist and critic, who edited the Transcendentalist publication *The Dial*.

Why did utopian communities flourish in the United States during the mid-nineteenth century? For one thing, it was a time of great uncertainty and change as citizens struggled with slavery, the unequal status of women, the cruel treatment of American Indians, and some grim effects of industrialization. Rebelling against the status quo, utopian communities tried to create prosperous and harmonious environments. Many were religious communities founded on ideals of nonviolence and communal ownership, and some were transplants from Europe: The Shaker communities, founded by Ann Lee, got their start in England about 1772. In many utopian communities, African Americans and women could find more equality than in society at large.

Community members often had to abide by rules that were quite restrictive. At Fruitlands, the short-lived vegetarian community established by Bronson Alcott, residents were permitted to eat only vegetables that grew up toward heaven—no root vegetables such as carrots and potatoes were allowed! They also did not take milk from cows or wool from sheep, nor would they use animals to pull plows.

Most utopian ventures failed within a few years; as the Transcendentalists of Brook Farm discovered, innovative thinkers aren't necessarily willing or successful farmers. But several utopian communities did endure for decades. Some—like the Shakers, the Oneida Community, and the Amana Church Society—lasted well into **Ⓒ** the twentieth century and are widely known for excellent products, from furniture to flatware to appliances. In all, more than 100,000 Americans participated in utopian communities in the nineteenth century.

226 THE AMERICAN RENAISSANCE

Professional Notes

Primary Sources: Eyewitness at Fruitlands

Bronson Alcott's experimental vegetarian society, Fruitlands, lasted less than a year. Although Louisa May Alcott was only age twelve at the time, the experience stayed with her and she described it years later: "A new dress was invented, since cotton, silk, and wool were forbidden as the products of slave labor, worm slaughter, and sheep robbery. Tunics and trousers of brown linen were the only wear.

The women's skirts were longer and their straw hatbrims wider than the men's, and this was the only difference. . . . Money was abjured as the root of all evil. The produce of the land was to supply most of their wants or to be exchanged for the few things they could not grow. This idea had its inconveniences, but self-denial was the fashion, and it was surprising how many things one can do without."

Student to Student

Imagination

A personal response to Ralph Waldo Emerson's essay, "Self-Reliance"

Imagine a flower growing in a garden. Create the surroundings—perhaps a brook or a tree, possibly a butterfly nearby. Picture the tranquility of the scene. Now color the sky and the grasses. What color will your flower be? Red? White? Yellow? Did you choose that color because it was that of a flower you had seen somewhere in nature or in a painting? Did you color your flower according to accepted values—a red rose, a yellow daffodil, a white lily—laid down years ago by other artists or nature itself? Now close your eyes for a moment and visualize a brilliant purple rose in your garden. What do you think? Is that flower wrong? Many people would think a purple rose silly, the product of an ignorant child, perhaps. They would tell you that roses can't possibly be purple—everybody knows that! And yet, who can say that an idea is wrong? A purple rose. Think: If the world accepted only "normal" visions, nothing new would ever be created. No one would dare stray from the "luster of the firmaments laid down by bards and sages." There would be no imagination, no fantasy, no chimerical creatures.

Imagine a great arch, soaring into the heavens—a "firmament," if you will, of "bards and sages." People of long ago built this arch, strengthening it with their ideas, extending the graceful curve until it once again touched the ground. They cherished their arch and nurtured it with fancy and imagination. The keystone proclaimed in scripted letters: "Imagine! From a gleam in the darkness can a new world be created!" The arch shone in the sunlight, ethereal and majestic. Then, the imagination stopped—people condemned fanciful inventions and the people who imagined them. People closed their minds, determined to preserve the old way of thinking as the only correct way. Relinquishing their creativity, they discarded their visions in favor of "normality," the way things "should be." Slowly, the arch crumbled. With no imagination to sustain its graceful form, it grew weaker and weaker, eventually vanishing altogether. As it faded into people's memories, their universe, too, shrank quietly, until they realized that they had nothing left; every object had its "normal" shape, size, and color.

And so they sit, clutching their red roses, amidst the remains of their imagination.

—Shelby Pearl, James Madison High School, Vienna, Virginia

RALPH WALDO EMERSON 227

Student to Student

This personal essay encourages readers to nurture their unique imaginative resources, in spite of conventional standards.

Ⓐ Appreciating Language
Style
❓ In what ways does Pearl draw readers into the essay? [through the use of imperative verbs, such as "Imagine" and "Create"]

Ⓑ Elements of Literature
Figures of Speech
❓ What figurative comparison does the author make? [Creative ideas are compared to an arch in the sky.] **What connections make this an effective comparison?** [Possible answers: An arch, like an idea, has to be "built" or developed from the ground up; an arch soars, just as imagination does.] **Is there any word choice you might revise or quibble with?** [*Nurture* usually applies to living things. Imagination can be nurtured, but probably not an arch.]

Ⓒ Critical Thinking
Extending the Text
❓ Why do people sometimes cling to conventional ways of thinking, even in the face of worthy new ideas? [Possible responses: They fear new ways of thinking will discredit the older ways; they fear they may not be able to adapt to something new; they may wield power through tradition and convention and not wish to give it up.]

Ⓓ Critical Thinking
Making Connections
❓ Given Emerson's deep appreciation of nature, would he find red roses an effective image of conformity? [Possible answers: Yes, in the context in which Pearl presents it; no, because, like everything else in nature, each rose is unique, a little different in shape, size, and color from the others.]

Making the Connections

Connecting to the Theme: "The Life Worth Living"

After students have finished reading the excerpts, discuss the collection theme. What does Emerson feel makes a life worth living? Is such a life possible in today's world? Do "Nature" and "Self-Reliance" present the same life philosophy, or are there differences between the two? [Possible response: "Nature" champions the natural world as a means of transcending the egotistical self, for connection to the whole of creation; "Self-Reliance" stresses the primacy of the self vis-à-vis other people or society.] **Do the two excerpts contradict each other at all? If so, how?** [Possible response: "Nature" stresses the unity of individual souls in the Over-soul. "Self-Reliance" stresses the importance of following one's "inner voice," even if this leads to conflicts with others.]

from **Nature**

First Thoughts [Respond]

1. Possible strategies: rereading; reading more slowly; questioning the text; noting main ideas.

> **Reading Check**
>
> Sample paraphrase of the opening sentence: To be truly alone and at peace, one must not only leave the company of other people but also seek out undomesticated nature, free from human development.

Shaping Interpretations [Interpret]

2. Emerson believes people would value the stars more highly if they appeared rarely. He wishes to point out that nature is no less marvelous for being accessible to us at all times.
3. The "poetical sense" experiences nature emotionally and aesthetically, not as something to use. Emerson distinguishes the poetic image of the landscape's horizon from the practical image of the property lines that divide it. He distinguishes the poetic illumination of the heart from the pragmatic illumination of the eye alone.
4. By becoming "transparent," he submerges his individual identity in observation of and participation in the whole of divine creation.
5. God is to be found in humans and in nature or, more precisely, in the harmony of both. Nature achieves its full splendor when a human being appreciates its grandeur.

Connecting with the Text [Evaluate]

6. Agree; people lose their innocence and sense of wonder as they grow older. Disagree; a sense of wonder does not depend on a person's age.

from **Self-Reliance**

First Thoughts [Respond]

1. Students may have suggested financial independence, the ability to survive on their own, the ability to enjoy being alone, and faith in their own judgments.

T228

---

from **Nature**

First Thoughts

1. Look back over your reading notes, and discuss passages that struck you as difficult or puzzling. What reading strategies could you apply to figure out the meaning of each?

> **Reading Check**
>
> What three or four sentences from the essay do you think express Emerson's **main ideas**? Paraphrase each of the sentences you choose.

Shaping Interpretations

2. How would our attitude toward the stars change if they appeared only once every thousand years? What point is Emerson making about nature with this attention-getting example?
3. What do you think Emerson means by a "poetical sense" of looking at nature? What **images** illustrate the distinction between nature used for practical benefits and nature viewed in this poetic way?
4. Emerson's **image** of a "transparent eyeball" in the fourth paragraph is one of the most famous passages in all of his works. How is this image a description of a visionary experience of God?
5. Describe the relation presented, starting in the fourth paragraph, between people, nature, and God. According to Emerson, is God to be found only in nature, only in people, or in some elements they share?

Connecting with the Text

6. "To speak truly," Emerson says, "few adult persons can see nature." Emerson sees children as having the advantage over adults when it comes to having a direct experience of nature. Do you agree with Emerson? What do people seem to lose as they grow older?

> **Reading Check**
>
> a. to trust himself or herself
> b. reliance on convention or other people's opinions

Shaping Interpretations [Interpret]

2. Emerson believes that each of us has a unique place and purpose in God's vision.
3. He does not admire those who are consistent without reason or who distort their own truth for fear of being misunderstood.

---

from **Self-Reliance**

First Thoughts

1. Look at the associations you made with self-reliance before reading Emerson. How does your understanding of the term compare with Emerson's?

> **Reading Check**
>
> a. According to the second paragraph, what is the destiny of every human being?
> b. What is the opposite of self-reliance?

Shaping Interpretations

2. What do you think Emerson means by "that divine idea which each of us represents" (paragraph 1)?
3. What does Emerson think of people who call for consistency in thought and action and who fear being misunderstood?

Connecting with the Text

4. Do you think there's too little, too much, or just the right amount of emphasis on individualism in our society today? What might Emerson have thought about our focus on the individual?
5. If this essay were to be delivered as a political address during a presidential campaign today, how do you think people would respond?

READING SKILLS AND STRATEGIES

Understanding Figures of Speech

In "Self-Reliance," Emerson makes many of his points through a series of **figures of speech**—comparisons between two things that are basically unlike each other. **Context** can sometimes help you understand difficult figures of speech.

1. Describe what Emerson compares with these things and events: planting corn, an iron string, a joint-stock company, a shadow on the wall.
2. Explain what Emerson means by the famous **metaphor** that opens the final paragraph. What exactly is meant by a "hobgoblin," a "little mind," a "foolish consistency"? What do you think Emerson would consider a "wise" consistency?

Connecting with the Text [Evaluate]

4. Possible answers: The success of mass marketing and the mass media shows the high value Americans place on conformity; Emerson would likely disapprove. Yet America still provides some kind of forum for many different points of view, which would please him.
5. Some students may say that people would react enthusiastically. Others may feel Emerson's ideas are too impractical to be well received on a national level.

CHOICES: Building Your Portfolio

Grading Timesaver

Rubrics for each Choices assignment appear on p. 116 in the *Portfolio Management System*.

Writer's Notebook

1. Collecting Ideas for Writing About a Controversial Issue

Brainstorm a list of controversial issues that people debate and disagree about. Write down as many topics as you can possibly think of. Keep your notes; you may use them later in the Writer's Workshop on page 331.

Evaluating Ideas / Creative Writing

2. Trick or Truth?

On page 227, you'll find a student response to this statement from another portion of Emerson's "Self-Reliance": "A man should learn to detect and watch that gleam of light which flashes across his mind from within, more than the luster of the firmament of bards and sages." Write your own response in the form of an essay, fable, or poem (about one page long) to one of the following statements from Emerson:

a. "Envy is ignorance."

b. "Trust thyself: Every heart vibrates to that iron string."

c. "To be great is to be misunderstood."

d. "A foolish consistency is the hobgoblin of little minds."

Analyzing Paradoxes

3. Not Contradictory

Emerson was fond of using **paradox,** the linking of seemingly contradictory elements (as in the line from *Romeo and Juliet:* "Parting is such sweet sorrow"). Read the following sentences from *Nature,* and write a brief explanation of the meaning of each paradox. End your explanation with an expression of each statement in your own words.

a. "I am not solitary while I read and write, though nobody is with me."

b. "But every night come out these envoys of beauty, and light the universe with their admonishing smile."

c. "Most persons do not see the sun."

d. "Almost I fear to think how glad I am."

Developing an Idea

4. A Personal Definition

"Self-Reliance" is one long definition. But Emerson's definition of self-reliance is fuller, more thought-provoking, more poetic, more personal, and less exact than a dictionary definition. Write a one- or two-paragraph **extended definition** of a human quality that you feel is valuable or important. Like Emerson, you might want to begin with a hook, an attention-grabbing introduction.

Identifying Aphorisms / Speaking and Listening

5. Sage Sayings

With a small group of classmates, brainstorm a list of modern **aphorisms:** lines from popular songs or political speeches, things you've read, things you've heard in conversation, things you yourself have said or thought—even sayings from bumper stickers or T-shirts. Have one member of the group write down the sayings. As a group, interpret and briefly discuss each entry. What do these sayings tell you about the values of modern society? Compare and contrast them with Emerson's values.

Crossing the Curriculum: Social Studies

6. Inventing Utopia

With one or more partners, make a plan for a community based on the ideals you've found in Emerson. Give the community a name, and decide on a geographical setting for it. What kind of government would the community have? What would be its economic base? What would be the attractions of life in this community? What would the population be? What problems would the community face? Finally, draw a map of your fictional community, and write a description of its goals.

RALPH WALDO EMERSON **229**

CHOICES: Building Your Portfolio

1. **Writer's Notebook** Have students consider how Emerson's views on nature and self-reliance might relate to contemporary controversies, such as environmentalism, gun control, or school choice.

2. **Evaluating Ideas/Creative Writing** Students who write particularly original and thoughtful responses should consider submitting them to the school newspaper or literary magazine for publication.

3. **Analyzing Paradoxes** Remind students to reread the paragraph from which each paradox was taken to understand its context.

4. **Developing an Idea** Discuss possible strategies for defining, such as beginning with a negation (what the quality does not mean) or researching the origins of the word. Remind students that in defining, they must restrict the meaning of a word and address its connotations.

5. **Identifying Aphorisms/Speaking and Listening** Commercial slogans offer a fruitful source for aphorisms, but remind students that these usually have only one purpose—to sell a product.

6. **Crossing the Curriculum: Social Studies** Suggest that each student in the partnership be responsible for a particular concern, such as food, housing, health, or education. Then, partners should collaborate on fitting the pieces together.

READING SKILLS AND STRATEGIES

1. Planting corn is compared to nurturing one's inner potential. The iron string is compared to trust in oneself. A joint-stock company represents society because both provide benefits to members who willingly surrender their liberty and conform; both promote dependence, not self-reliance. A shadow on the wall represents mechanical consistency, imitative rather than creative living.

2. A hobgoblin is a frightening creature or a bugbear, an obsession; a little mind is not open to new ideas; and foolish consistency maintains the status quo at the expense of reason or progress. Being open to self-realization and true to one's inner potential might be considered a wise consistency.

Planning

T230

Henry David Thoreau

(1817–1862)

On July 4, 1845 (the date was apparently accidental), a young man ended a three-year stay at the house of a friend and moved to a cabin on the shores of Walden Pond in Massachusetts. He was almost twenty-eight years old and, to all appearances, a failure. He had lasted only two weeks as a schoolteacher (he refused to whip a child, then a mandatory form of punishment); his public lectures had been uninspiring; the woman to whom he had proposed marriage had turned him down; and he had little interest in the family business. Despite his impressive Harvard education, he had not realized his literary ambitions.

Henry David Thoreau (1856) by Benjamin D. Maxham. Photograph.

If ever a person looked like a self-*un*made man, a man who had squandered the advantages of intelligence, education, and the friendship of brilliant and successful people, it was Henry David Thoreau. On top of all his other problems, Thoreau was difficult to get along with. Three days before Thoreau went to Walden, Nathaniel Hawthorne (page 296) wrote to a New York publisher that Thoreau was "tedious, tiresome, and intolerable. And yet," Hawthorne added, "he has great qualities of intellect and character."

Even his closest friends had doubts about Thoreau. "He seemed born for great enterprise and for command," Emerson said years later at Thoreau's funeral, "and I so much regret the loss of his rare powers of action, that I cannot help counting it a fault in him that he had no ambition. Wanting this, instead of engineering for all America, he was the captain of a huckleberry party."

What Emerson failed to see, and what Thoreau knew (or hoped) all along, was that by leading a berry-picking party on a jaunt in the woods he could "engineer for all America" in the most profound way. This paradox is at the center of Thoreau's life and work.

The Student Who Wouldn't Wear Black

Thoreau was born in Concord, Massachusetts, in 1817. His father was a moderately successful manufacturer of pencils. His mother took in boarders, among them the sister of Emerson's wife, thus establishing the relationship between the two families. As a boy, Thoreau tramped the woods and fields around Concord, often with a fishing rod and seldom with a gun.

Thoreau entered Harvard in 1833 and graduated four years later. Independent and eccentric even then, he attended chapel in a green coat, "because," he wrote, "the rules required black." He never ranked higher than the middle of his class, but he was extremely well read. He became thoroughly familiar with English literature and with the German philosophers who provided many of the underpinnings of Transcendentalism.

After returning to Concord and teaching school, Thoreau went to New York in 1843, but he pined for his hometown. After six months of struggling, he gave up and returned to Concord. A friend proposed that Henry and he sail to Europe and work their way across the Continent, but Henry turned him down. He appeared to be floundering, but in fact he knew what he was doing; Thoreau's voyage would be inward, and it would depart from Walden Pond, where Emerson had offered him the use of some land.

National Portrait Gallery/Smithsonian Institution/Art Resource, NY.

go.hrw.com
LE0 11-5

 *Resources: Print and Media*

Walden: Life in Its Essence

The experiment at Walden Pond was an attempt to rediscover the grandeur of a simple life led close to nature. Though only two miles from town, Walden offered a focus for Thoreau's contemplative urge. "I wish to meet the facts of life," he wrote in his journal, "the vital facts, which are the phenomena or actuality the gods meant to show us . . . and so I came down here."

This private confrontation was to Thoreau's mind the truly heroic enterprise of his time. "I am glad to remember tonight as I sit by my door," he wrote on the evening of July 7, "that I too am at least a remote descendant of that heroic race of men of whom there is a tradition. I too sit here on the shore of my Ithaca, a fellow wanderer and survivor of Ulysses."

When he looked toward town, Thoreau saw his fellow citizens so caught up in making a living that they had become one-dimensional. "The mass of men," as one of the most famous sentences in *Walden* puts it, "lead lives of quiet desperation." He hoped to wake them up and show them that the heroic enterprise of confronting the "vital facts of life" lay literally in their own back yards.

Walden—one of the most well-known works ever produced in America—owes much of its artistic success to Thoreau's blending of style and content. He looked to nature, rather than to the stylists of the past, for a model. To Thoreau, a style that imitated nature would speak fundamental spiritual truths. Thoreau wished to build sentences "which lie like boulders on the page, up and down or across; which contain the seed of other sentences, not mere repetition, but creation; which a man might sell his grounds and castles to build."

> Thoreau's voyage would be inward, and it would depart from Walden Pond.

Thoreau the Protester

It was while he was at Walden that Thoreau's other famous act took place. As a protest against the Mexican War, which he and many others saw as an attempt to extend American slaveholding territory, Thoreau refused to pay his poll tax, and spent a night in jail as a result. While at Walden, and again in 1851 (after the Fugitive Slave Act had been passed), Thoreau helped fugitives escaping slavery make their way to Canada. In 1859, he was one of the first defenders of John Brown, the radical abolitionist who staged a famous raid on the Federal arsenal at Harpers Ferry in Virginia.

Thoreau remained at Walden for a little more than two years. In 1847, he left the cabin and moved back into the Emersons' house, in exchange for a few hours a day of odd jobs and gardening. During the next few years, he worked on *Walden* (which was published in 1854) and essays such as "Resistance to Civil Government." The latter, delivered as a lecture in 1848 and published as an essay in 1849, had little immediate influence, but few essays have had such an overwhelming, long-term effect on human history. It was especially important in helping to inspire the passive resistance used by Mohandas K. Gandhi in India and, later, by Martin Luther King, Jr., in the United States.

Thoreau moved back into his parents' house in 1848 and lived there the rest of his life. He supported himself by making pencils, taking odd jobs—he was an excellent carpenter, mason, and gardener—and doing survey work on the land around Concord. He became a kind of local recordkeeper, a fount of knowledge about the amount of rainfall and snowfall and the first days of frost. He could predict to the day when each wildflower in the area would bloom.

In 1860, Thoreau caught a cold, and it soon became clear that beneath the cold lay incurable tuberculosis. He faced his coming death with great calm. The town constable, Sam Staples (who had jailed Thoreau for refusing to pay his poll tax), told Emerson that he "never saw a man dying with so much pleasure and peace."

"Henry, have you made your peace with God?" his aunt is said to have asked him toward the end. "Why, Aunt," he replied, "I didn't know we had ever quarreled."

Professional Notes

Thoreau on Grammar and Mechanics

"When I hear the hypercritical quarreling about grammar and style, the position of the particles, etc., etc., stretching or contracting every speaker to certain rules . . . I see that they forget that the first requisite and rule is that expression shall be vital and natural," wrote Thoreau around 1859. "Essentially, your truest poetic sentence is as free and lawless as a lamb's bleat. The grammarian is often one who can neither cry nor laugh, yet thinks that he can express human emotions.

"When I read some of the rules for speaking and writing the English language correctly,—as that a sentence must never end with a particle,—and perceive how implicitly even the learned obey it, I think—

Any fool can make a rule
And every fool will mind it."

Summary ■ ■ ■

The narrative of Thoreau's two-year experiment in simple living, *Walden* is both philosophical and autobiographical. The excerpt from "Economy" relates how Thoreau constructs a cabin from used lumber and grows crops to earn a few dollars. "Where I Lived, and What I Lived For" explains his Transcendentalist intention to live simply and deliberately, in touch with the essential elements of life. In "Solitude," he insists that his physical isolation is nothing compared to the mental isolation of people in communities and that his immersion in nature is a truer communion with all life. "The Bean Field" describes planting beans and battling weeds, using metaphors from Greek myths. "Brute Neighbors" recounts an ant war, with allusions to epic human wars, and satirizes hunters' attempts to shoot loons. In "Conclusion," Thoreau urges each reader to follow the call of a "different drummer" and summarizes his own spontaneous, nonconformist approach to the creation of a life worth living.

Before You Read

FROM WALDEN, OR LIFE IN THE WOODS

Make the Connection

What's Necessary

Thoreau went to Walden Pond to find out what was necessary in life and what could be done without. He discovered that the key to making his life more fulfilling was to make it simpler.

Few people go off to the woods for a couple of years to find out how they really want to live. Every thinking person, however, stops at times to ask, "How do I really want to live? What do I need in order to feel fulfilled—and what am I doing now that's unnecessary?" Thoreau can be an inspiration for anyone who asks these questions.

Reading Skills and Strategies

Drawing Inferences: Generalizations

Active readers make generalizations based on information they get from their reading and on their own experiences. Such a **generalization** is a specific type of **inference**—a conclusion that extends the ideas in a text to a broader situation. Like all inferences, generalizations are reasonable guesses. For example, after reading Thoreau's call for "simplicity, simplicity!" you might reasonably guess that he believed people should lead lives focused on what matters most to them, while eliminating unnecessary complexity. You need not agree with the generalization; you are simply extending the implications of an idea into new territory. (You would probably need to do additional research before stating that Thoreau in fact agreed with your generalization.)

As you read *Walden*, take notes in the form of a double-entry journal. In the left column, list Thoreau's ideas. In the right column, examine some of the interesting generalizations that logically follow from his views.

Elements of Literature

Point of View

In the second paragraph of this excerpt, Thoreau justifies using the **first-person point of view** to narrate his experiences at Walden Pond. "[I]t is, after all, always the first person that is speaking," he writes. Think about what Thoreau might mean. As you read, look for passages in which you think the use of the first person makes a difference.

> In the **first-person point of view,** the narrative is told by a particular person who uses the personal pronoun *I* or *we* to describe experiences.
>
> *For more on Point of View, see the Handbook of Literary Terms.*

Thoreau's journals and a writing box.

The Pierpont Morgan Library / Art Resource, NY.

232 THE AMERICAN RENAISSANCE

Preteaching Vocabulary

Words to Own

Have students read the Words to Own and their definitions, listed at the bottom of the selection pages. Then, have each student write a paragraph addressing the topic "How do I really want to live?" in which he or she uses any five of the words correctly. Afterward, tell students to match each of the following words with its synonym.

1. effete [f]	**a.** scorn
2. tumultuous [c]	**b.** burden
3. ethereal [i]	**c.** turbulent
4. pertinent [e]	**d.** extra
5. derision [a]	**e.** relevant
6. incessantly [g]	**f.** sterile
7. impervious [j]	**g.** constantly
8. encumbrance [b]	**h.** worldly
9. superfluous [d]	**i.** spiritual
10. temporal [h]	**j.** resistant

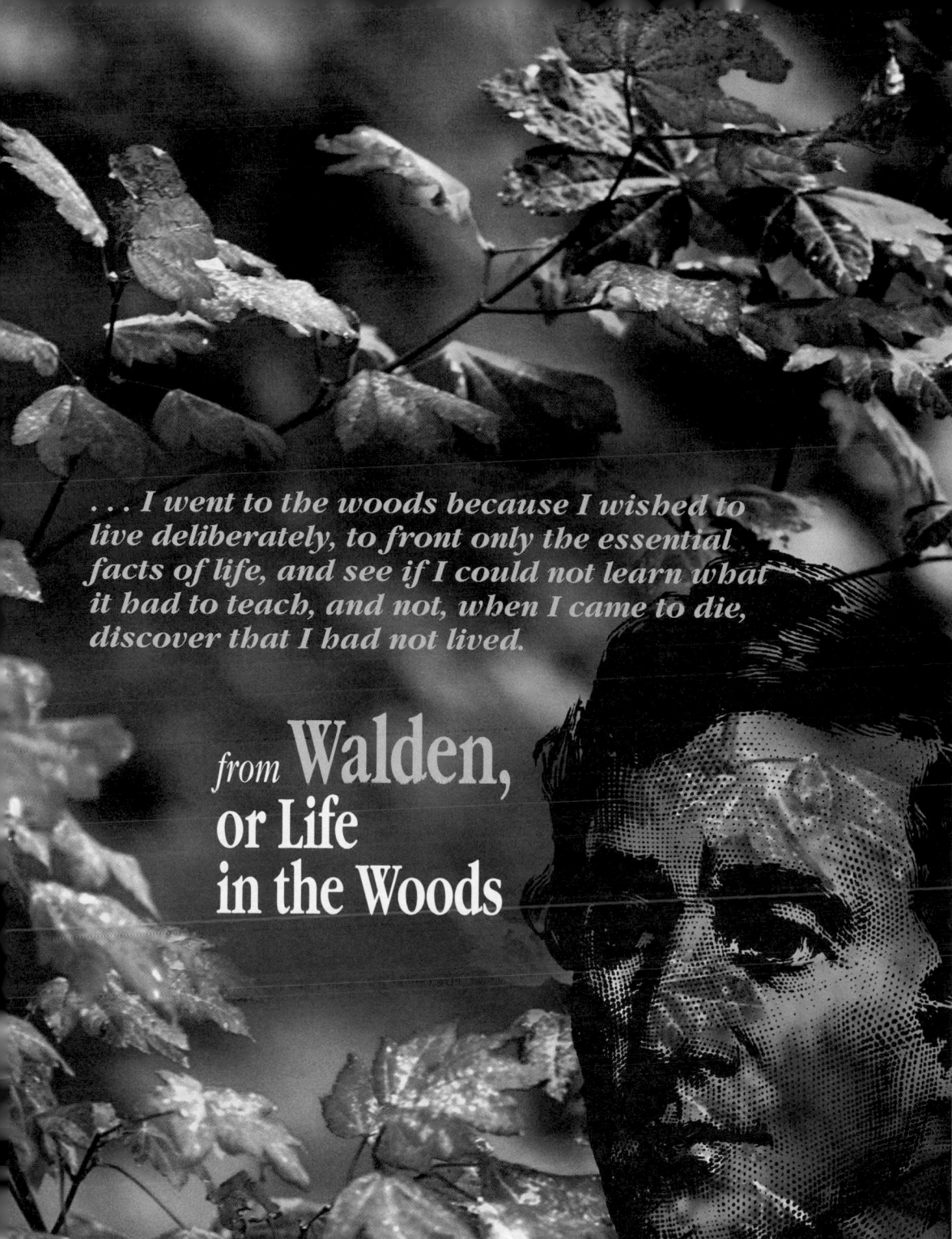

Responding to the Quotation

Have students consider this quotation and write personal responses to it. Questions they should ask themselves include these: What does "deliberately" mean in this context? How do students define "essential facts of life"? How might one die without having lived? Must one retreat from society in order to determine one's own destiny? Students may want to read more of "Where I Lived, and What I Lived For" (either the excerpt in their textbook or the complete section) to help put Thoreau's creed in context.

. . . I went to the woods because I wished to live deliberately, to front only the essential facts of life, and see if I could not learn what it had to teach, and not, when I came to die, discover that I had not lived.

from Walden, or Life in the Woods

Reaching All Students

Struggling Readers
Drawing Inferences: Generalizations was introduced on p. 232. For a lesson directly tied to this selection that teaches students to draw generalizations with a strategy called Sketch to Stretch, see the *Reading Skills and Strategies* binder:
• MiniRead Skill Lesson, p. 103
• Selection Skill Lesson, p. 109

English Language Learners
Much of Thoreau's vocabulary will challenge students acquiring English. Have students read *Walden* section by section, writing down unfamiliar words as they go. Partners can then compare word lists and work together to teach each other the new words, using context clues, root words, cognates, and dictionaries.

Advanced Learners
Have students read the entire text of one section of *Walden*. Have them discuss their reading in small groups and make a cluster diagram with the main idea in the center and the supporting arguments and evidence radiating from it. Then, tell students to determine what kind of appeal (logical, emotional, or ethical) each argument makes

A Critical Thinking

Recognizing Persuasive Techniques

❓ Why does Thoreau recount these objections and questions concerning his "impertinent" lifestyle? Why is this an effective persuasive technique? [By introducing his work as a simple response to his audience's questions, Thoreau lends credibility to his work and anticipates potential criticism.]

B Elements of Literature

Point of View

❓ What does Thoreau mean when he says that it is "always the first person" who speaks? [All writers express their own points of view, whether or not they write in the first person.] Do you agree? [Yes, writers cannot avoid expressing their own views; no, writers of fiction, for example, truly express the viewpoints of many different characters.]

C Critical Thinking

Speculating

❓ Why might Thoreau single out "poor students" as his intended audience? [Possible answer: Thoreau may feel that such students—whether they are "poor" financially or academically—might share his own nontraditional strain of intellectual curiosity.]

D Reading Skills and Strategies

Drawing Inferences: Generalizations

❓ Thoreau gives no direct opinion of the shanty. Does he agree with the local opinion that it is "uncommonly fine"? Why do you think so? [No, he presents this opinion ironically and later compares the shanty to a compost heap, mentions its dampness, and notes its unhealthy living conditions.]

---

from Economy

When I wrote the following pages, or rather the bulk of them, I lived alone, in the woods, a mile from any neighbor, in a house which I had built myself, on the shore of Walden Pond, in Concord, Massachusetts, and earned my living by the labor of my hands only. I lived there two years and two months. At present I am a sojourner in civilized life again.

I should not obtrude my affairs so much on the notice of my readers if very particular inquiries had not been made by my townsmen concerning my mode of life, which some would call impertinent, though they do not appear to me at all impertinent, but, considering the circumstances, very natural and <u>pertinent</u>. Some have asked what I got to eat; if I did not feel lonesome; if I was not afraid; and the like. Others have been curious to learn what portion of my income I devoted to charitable purposes; and some, who have large families, how many poor children I maintained. I will therefore ask those of my readers who feel no particular interest in me to pardon me if I undertake to answer some of these questions in this book. In most books, the *I*, or first person, is omitted; in this it will be retained; that, in respect to egotism, is the main difference. We commonly do not remember that it is, after all, always the first person that is speaking. I should not talk so much about myself if there were anybody else whom I knew as well. Unfortunately, I am confined to this theme by the narrowness of my experience. Moreover, I, on my side, require of every writer, first or last, a simple and sincere account of his own life, and not merely what he has heard of other men's lives; some such account as he would send to his kindred from a distant land; for if he has lived sincerely, it must have been in a distant land to me. Perhaps these pages are more particularly addressed to poor students. As for the rest of my readers, they will accept such portions as apply to them. I trust that none will stretch the seams in putting on the coat, for it may do good service to him whom it fits. . . .

By the middle of April, for I made no haste in my work, but rather made the most of it, my house was framed and ready for the raising. I had already bought the shanty of James Collins, an Irishman who worked on the Fitchburg Railroad, for boards. James Collins's shanty was considered an uncommonly fine one. When I called to see it he was not at home. I walked about the outside, at first unobserved from within, the window was so deep and high. It was of small dimensions, with a peaked cottage roof, and not much else to be seen, the dirt being raised five feet all around as if it were a compost heap. The roof was the soundest part, though a good deal warped and made brittle by the sun. Doorsill there was none, but a perennial passage for the hens under the door board. Mrs. C. came to the door and asked me to view it from the inside. The hens were driven in by my approach. It was dark, and had a dirt floor for the most part, dank, clammy, and aguish,[1] only here a board and there a board which would not bear removal. She lighted a lamp to show me the inside of the roof and the walls, and also that the board floor extended under the bed, warning me not to step into the cellar, a sort of dust hole two feet deep. In her own words, they were "good boards overhead, good boards all around, and a good window"—of two whole squares originally, only the cat had passed out that way lately. There was a stove, a bed, and a place to sit, an infant in the house where it was born, a silk parasol, gilt-framed looking glass, and a patent new coffee mill nailed to an oak sapling, all told. The bargain was soon concluded, for James had in the meanwhile returned. I to pay four dollars and twenty-five cents tonight, he to vacate at five tomorrow morning, selling to nobody else meanwhile: I to take possession at six. It were well, he said, to be there early, and anticipate certain indistinct but wholly unjust claims on the score of ground rent and fuel. This he assured me was the only <u>encumbrance</u>. At six I passed him and his family on the

---

1. **aguish** (ā′gyōō·ish): likely to cause ague, or fever and chills.

WORDS TO OWN

pertinent (pur′tə·nənt) *adj.*: to the point; applying to the situation.
encumbrance (en·kum′brəns) *n.*: burden; hindrance.

Skill Link

Analyzing Allusions

Remind students that an **allusion** is a reference a writer makes to an event, another text, a historical or fictional character, or any other significant cultural item. Mary Rowlandson's captivity narrative (p. 40), for instance, contains numerous allusions to biblical stories. Thoreau's *Walden* contains numerous allusions to the history and culture of ancient Greece, particularly to the Trojan War.

Activity

1. As they read, have students note references and allusions to the Trojan War and to other aspects of the classical age. Point out footnotes 2 and 5 on p. 235. Have students share any knowledge they have of the *Iliad*. Thoreau had read the *Iliad* many times in its original Greek; it was as familiar to him as the Bible was to Rowlandson or as the lyrics of popular music are to most students.

2. Have students list the allusions to the *Iliad* they find as they read. Once they finish the selection, have them discuss why Thoreau might have alluded to the ancient Greeks so often. What thematic importance does the classical age have to Thoreau's story? How might Thoreau have considered his experiment as a return to the classical ideals of simplicity, beauty, and harmony?

road. One large bundle held their all—bed, coffee mill, looking glass, hens—all but the cat; she took to the woods and became a wild cat, and, as I learned afterward, trod in a trap set for woodchucks, and so became a dead cat at last.

I took down this dwelling the same morning, drawing the nails, and removed it to the pond side by small cartloads, spreading the boards on the grass there to bleach and warp back again in the sun. One early thrush gave me a note or two as I drove along the woodland path. I was informed treacherously by a young Patrick that neighbor Seeley, an Irishman, in the intervals of the carting, transferred the still tolerable, straight, and drivable nails, staples, and spikes to his pocket, and then stood when I came back to pass the time of day, and look freshly up, unconcerned, with spring thoughts, at the devastation; there being a dearth of work, as he said. He was there to represent spectatordom, and help make this seemingly insignificant event one with the removal of the gods of Troy.[2]

I dug my cellar in the side of a hill sloping to the south, where a woodchuck had formerly dug his burrow, down through sumac and blackberry roots, and the lowest stain of vegetation, six feet square by seven deep, to a fine sand where potatoes would not freeze in any winter. The sides were left shelving, and not stoned; but the sun having never shone on them, the sand still keeps its place. It was but two hours' work. I took particular pleasure in this breaking of ground, for in almost all latitudes men dig into the earth for an equable temperature. Under the most splendid house in the city is still to be found the cellar where they store their roots as of old, and long after the superstructure has disappeared posterity remark its dent in the earth. The house is still but a sort of porch at the entrance of a burrow.

At length, in the beginning of May, with the help of some of my acquaintances, rather to improve so good an occasion for neighborliness than from any necessity, I set up the frame of my house. No man was ever more honored in the character of his raisers[3] than I. They are destined, I trust, to assist at the raising of loftier structures one day. I began to occupy my house on the 4th of July, as soon as it was boarded and roofed, for the boards were carefully featheredged and lapped,[4] so that it was perfectly <u>impervious</u> to rain, but before boarding I laid the foundation of a chimney at one end, bringing two cartloads of stones up the hill from the pond in my arms. I built the chimney after my hoeing in the fall, before a fire became necessary for warmth, doing my cooking in the meanwhile out of doors on the ground, early in the morning: which mode I still think is in some respects more convenient and agreeable than the usual one. When it stormed before my bread was baked, I fixed a few boards over the fire, and sat under them to watch my loaf, and passed some pleasant hours in that way. In those days, when my hands were much employed, I read but little, but the least scraps of paper which lay on the ground, my holder, or tablecloth, afforded me as much entertainment, in fact answered the same purpose as the *Iliad*.[5]

It would be worth the while to build still more deliberately than I did, considering, for instance, what foundation a door, a window, a cellar, a garret, have in the nature of man, and perchance never raising any superstructure until we found a better reason for it than our <u>temporal</u> necessities even. There is some of the same fitness in a man's building his own house that there is in a bird's building its own nest. Who knows but if men constructed their dwellings with their own hands, and provided food for themselves and families simply and honestly enough, the poetic faculty would be universally developed, as birds univer-

---

3. **raisers:** Thoreau's helpers included the Transcendentalist writers Ralph Waldo Emerson (page 216), Bronson Alcott (1799–1888), and William Ellery Channing (1780–1842), hence the reference in the next sentence to raising loftier structures one day.
4. **featheredged and lapped:** The edges were cut at an angle and overlapped.
5. **the *Iliad*:** Homer's epic about the Greek siege of Troy.

WORDS TO OWN

impervious (im·pʉr′vē·əs) *adj.*: resistant; impenetrable.

temporal (tem′pə·rəl) *adj.*: worldly.

---

2. **the gods of Troy:** Thoreau loved classical allusions. Here, he humorously compares taking down a little cabin with the destruction of the great ancient city of Troy. In the *Aeneid*, by Virgil (70–19 B.C.), the conquering Greeks carry off the images of the Trojan gods after the fall of Troy.

Listening to Music

"Emerson" and "Thoreau" from *Sonata for Piano No. 2* by Charles Ives, performed by Gilbert Kalish
Widely praised for his innovative approach to music, Charles Ives (1874–1954) drew on many aspects of American culture, from camp meeting songs to gospel tunes to historical events and the classics of American literature. The second of his two piano sonatas, subtitled *Concord,*

Mass., 1840–60, celebrates the New England literary renaissance of those decades. The sonata's four movements are subtitled with names of important writers of that renaissance: "Emerson," "Hawthorne," "The Alcotts," and "Thoreau."

Activity
After students have read the selections by Emerson and Thoreau, have them listen to the

first and last movements of Ives's sonata and try to guess which movements Ives subtitled "Emerson" and which, "Thoreau." Afterward, have students explain their guesses in a group discussion in which they cite details from the writings of both authors.

A Critical Thinking

Extending the Text

? Compare the size of Thoreau's house with your own. Could you live contentedly in a house this size? Why or why not? [Possible answers: Yes, Thoreau is not trapped in the house but goes out when he wants; no, there is no room to have friends come and stay or to store possessions.]

B Vocabulary Note

Prefixes/Suffixes

Ask a volunteer to define the word *unmerchantable.* Help students break it into its prefix *un-,* root *merchant,* and suffix *-able.* Students should understand that this word indicates that something cannot be sold and thus cannot be handled by a merchant.

C Appreciating Language

Denotations

Ask students to find the denotation of *outgoes,* by first providing the opposite of *out* [in] and then the opposite of *go* [come]. Given these antonyms, what is the meaning of *outgoes?* [It means the opposite of *income*—expenses.]

D Reading Skills and Strategies

Drawing Inferences: Generalizations

? Why does Thoreau believe that he did better with his small profit than any other farmer in Concord? [While the actual amount he earns is small, his percentage of profit is probably higher than the average farmer.] What generalization about earning a living can be drawn? [Possible answer: If your needs are simple, you can meet them, still be independent, and enjoy life.]

---

sally sing when they are so engaged? But alas! we do like cowbirds and cuckoos, which lay their eggs in nests which other birds have built, and cheer no traveler with their chattering and unmusical notes. Shall we forever resign the pleasure of construction to the carpenter? What does architecture amount to in the experience of the mass of men? I never in all my walks came across a man engaged in so simple and natural an occupation as building his house. . . .

Before winter I built a chimney, and shingled the sides of my house, which were already impervious to rain, with imperfect and sappy shingles made of the first slice of the log, whose edges I was obliged to straighten with a plane.

A ⎡ I have thus a tight shingled and plastered house, ten feet wide by fifteen long, and eight-foot posts, with a garret and a closet, a large window on each side, two trapdoors, one door at the ⎣ end, and a brick fireplace opposite. The exact cost of my house, paying the usual price for such materials as I used, but not counting the work, all of which was done by myself, was as follows; and I give the details because very few are able to tell exactly what their houses cost, and fewer still, if any, the separate cost of the various materials which compose them—

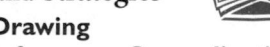

Boards,	$ 8 03 ½	mostly shanty boards
Refuse shingles for roof and sides,	4 00	
Laths,	1 25	
Two secondhand windows with glass,	2 43	
One thousand old brick,	4 00	
Two casks of lime,	2 40	That was high
Hair,	0 31	More than I needed
Mantle-tree iron,	0 15	
Nails,	3 90	
Hinges and screws,	0 14	
Latch,	0 10	
Chalk,	0 01	
Transportation,	1 40	I carried a good
In all,	$28 12 ½	part on my back

. . . Before I finished my house, wishing to earn ten or twelve dollars by some honest and agreeable method, in order to meet my unusual expenses, I planted about two acres and a half of light and sandy soil near it chiefly with beans, but also a small part with potatoes, corn, peas, and turnips. The whole lot contains eleven acres, mostly growing up to pines and hickories, and was sold the preceding season for eight dollars and eight cents an acre. One farmer said that it was "good for nothing but to raise cheeping squirrels on." I put no manure whatever on this land, not being the owner, but merely a squatter, and not expecting to cultivate so much again, and I did not quite hoe it all once. I got out several cords of stumps in plowing, which supplied me with fuel for a long time, and left small circles of virgin mold, easily distinguishable through the summer by the greater luxuriance of the beans

B ⎡ there. The dead and for the most part unmerchantable wood behind my house, and the driftwood from the pond, have supplied the remainder of my fuel. I was obliged to hire a team ⎣ and a man for the plowing, though I held the

C plow myself. My farm outgoes for the first season were, for implements, seed, work, etc., $14.72 ½. The seed corn was given me. This never costs anything to speak of, unless you plant more than enough. I got twelve bushels of beans, and eighteen bushels of potatoes, beside some peas and sweet corn. The yellow corn and turnips were too late to come to anything. My whole income from the farm was

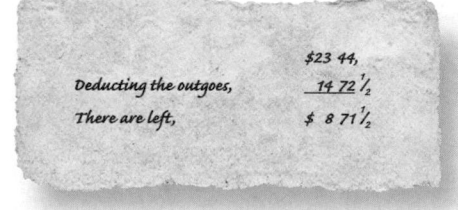

	$23 44,
Deducting the outgoes,	14 72 ½
There are left,	$ 8 71 ½

D

beside produce consumed and on hand at the time this estimate was made of the value of $4.50—the amount on hand much more than balancing a little grass which I did not raise. All things considered, that is, considering the importance of a man's soul and of today, notwithstanding the short time occupied by my experiment,

---

Using Students' Strengths

Mathematical Learners

Have students devise their own personal budgets for a month, listing their sources of income and their expenses. Using Thoreau's principle of simplification as a model, have students consider whether there are expenses in their budgets that they can reduce or eliminate through better planning, through more efficient use of resources, or by taking advantage of free or secondhand items. Have students make sure their budgets are balanced (that their incomes meet or exceed their expenses).

Intrapersonal Learners

After students have finished this excerpt, have them consider how Thoreau defines his place in the human community and in the natural world. Do students consider him arrogant or selfish in any way? Might Emerson have included Thoreau in his list of "great" and "misunderstood" men? Why does Thoreau feel that isolation from society is essential to living "deliberately"? Have students write a journal entry addressing these questions.

nay, partly even because of its transient character, I believe that that was doing better than any farmer in Concord did that year. . . .

from Where I Lived, and What I Lived For

. . . I went to the woods because I wished to live deliberately, to front only the essential facts of life, and see if I could not learn what it had to teach, and not, when I came to die, discover that I had not lived. I did not wish to live what was not life, living is so dear; nor did I wish to practice resignation, unless it was quite necessary. I wanted to live deep and suck out all the marrow of life, to live so sturdily and Spartan-like[6] as to put to rout all that was not life, to cut a broad swath and shave close, to drive life into a corner, and reduce it to its lowest terms, and, if it proved to be mean, why then to get the whole and genuine meanness of it, and publish its meanness to the world; or if it were sublime, to know it by experience, and be able to give a true account of it in my next excursion. For most men, it appears to me, are in a strange uncertainty about it, whether it is of the devil or of God, and have *somewhat hastily* concluded that it is the chief end of man here to "glorify God and enjoy him forever."[7]

Still we live meanly, like ants; though the fable tells us that we were long ago changed into men; like pygmies we fight with cranes;[8] it is error upon error, and clout upon clout, and our best virtue has for its occasion a <u>superfluous</u> and evitable wretchedness. Our life is frittered away by detail. An honest man has hardly need to count more than his ten fingers, or in extreme cases he may add his ten toes, and lump the rest. Simplic-

ity, simplicity, simplicity! I say, let your affairs be as two or three, and not a hundred or a thousand; instead of a million count half a dozen, and keep your accounts on your thumbnail. In the midst of this chopping sea of civilized life, such are the clouds and storms and quicksands and thousand-and-one items to be allowed for, that a man has to live, if he would not founder and go to the bottom and not make his port at all, by dead reckoning, and he must be a great calculator indeed who succeeds. Simplify, simplify. Instead of three meals a day, if it be necessary eat but one; instead of a hundred dishes, five; and reduce other things in proportion. Our life is like a German Confederacy,[9] made up of petty states with its boundary forever fluctuating, so that even a German cannot tell you how it is bounded at any moment. The nation itself, with all its so-called internal improvements, which, by the way are all external and superficial, is just such an unwieldy and overgrown establishment, cluttered with furniture and tripped up by its own traps, ruined by luxury and heedless expense, by want of calculation and a worthy aim, as the million households in the land; and the only cure for it, as for them, is in a rigid economy, a stern and more than Spartan simplicity of life and elevation of purpose. It lives too fast. Men think that it is essential that the *Nation* have commerce, and export ice, and talk through a telegraph, and ride thirty miles an hour, without a doubt, whether *they* do or not; but whether we should live like baboons or like men, is a little uncertain. If we do not get out sleepers,[10] and forge rails, and devote days and nights to the work, but go to tinkering upon our *lives* to improve *them,* who will build railroads? And if railroads are not built, how shall we get to heaven in season? But if we stay at home and mind our business, who will want railroads? We do not ride on the railroad; it rides upon us. Did you ever think what those sleepers are that underlie the railroad? Each one is

---

9. German Confederacy: At the time Thoreau was writing, Germany was not yet a unified nation.
10. sleepers: British usage for "railroad ties"; so called because they lie flat.

WORDS TO OWN
superfluous (sə·pûr′flŌŌ·əs) *adj.:* unnecessary.

---

6. **Spartan-like:** like the Spartans, the hardy, frugal, and highly disciplined citizens of the ancient Greek city-state Sparta.
7. **glorify . . . forever:** answer to catechism question, "What is the chief end of man?"
8. **the fable . . . cranes:** In a Greek fable, Zeus changes ants into men. In the *Iliad,* Homer compares the Trojans to cranes fighting with pygmies.

HENRY DAVID THOREAU 237

Professional Notes

Critical Comment:
Spartan Simplicity

To help students evaluate Thoreau's allusions to Spartan culture, have them consider the following analysis by historian Dr. John Buckler: "Suppression of the individual together with emphasis on military prowess led to a barracks state. . . . Once Spartan boys reached the age of twelve, they were enrolled in separate companies. . . . They slept outside on reed mats and underwent rugged physical and military training

until age twenty-four, when they became front-line soldiers. . . . The older men were expected to be models of endurance, frugality, and sturdiness. . . . Spartans were supposed to stand and die rather than retreat. . . . Spartan men were expected to train vigorously, disdain luxury and wealth, do with little, and like it." Ask students which aspects of Spartan culture Thoreau would embrace or reject.

a man, an Irishman, or a Yankee man. The rails are laid on them, and they are covered with sand, and the cars run smoothly over them. They are sound sleepers, I assure you. And every few years a new lot is laid down and run over; so that, if some have the pleasure of riding on a rail, others have the misfortune to be ridden upon. And when they run **(A)** over a man that is walking in his sleep, a supernumerary[11] sleeper in the wrong position, and wake him up, they suddenly stop the cars, and make a hue and cry about it, as if this were an exception. I am glad to know that it takes a gang of men for every five miles to keep the sleepers down and level in their beds as it is, for this is a sign that they may sometime get up again. . . .

from Solitude

. . . Some of my pleasantest hours were during the long rainstorms in the spring or fall, which confined me to the house for the afternoon as well as the forenoon, soothed by their ceaseless roar and pelting; when an early twilight ushered in a long evening in which many thoughts had time to take root and unfold themselves. In those driving northeast rains which tried the village houses so, when the maids stood ready with mop and pail in front entries to keep the deluge out, I sat behind my door in my little house, which was all entry, and thoroughly enjoyed its protection. In one heavy thundershower the lightning struck a large pitch pine across the pond, making a very conspicuous and perfectly regular spiral groove from top to bottom, an inch or more deep, and four or five inches wide, as you would groove a walking stick. I passed it again the other day, and was struck with awe on looking up and beholding that mark, now more distinct than ever, where a terrific and resistless bolt came down out of the harmless sky eight years ago. Men frequently say to me, "I should think you would feel lonesome down there, and want to be nearer to folks, rainy

and snowy days and nights especially." I am tempted to reply to such—This whole earth which we inhabit is but a point in space. How far apart, think you, dwell the two most distant inhabitants of yonder star, the breadth of whose disk cannot be appreciated by our instruments? **(B)** Why should I feel lonely? Is not our planet in the Milky Way? This which you put seems to me not to be the most important question. What sort of space is that which separates a man from his fellows and makes him solitary? I have found that no exertion of the legs can bring two minds much nearer to one another. What do we want most to **(C)** dwell near to? Not to many men surely, the depot, the post office, the barroom, the meetinghouse, the schoolhouse, the grocery, Beacon Hill, or the Five Points, where men most congregate, but to the perennial source of our life, whence in all our experience we have found that to issue, as the willow stands near the water and sends out its roots in that direction. This will vary with different natures, but this is the place where a wise man will dig his cellar. . . .

from The Bean Field

Meanwhile my beans, the length of whose rows, added together, was seven miles already planted, were impatient to be hoed, for the earliest had grown considerably before the latest were in the ground; indeed they were not easily to be put off. What was the meaning of this so steady and self-respecting, this small Herculean labor, I knew not. I came to love my rows, my beans, though so many more than I wanted. They attached me to the earth, and so I got strength like Antaeus.[12] But why should I raise them? Only Heaven knows. This was my curious labor all summer—to make this portion of the earth's surface, which had yielded only cinquefoil, blackberries, johnswort, and the like, before, sweet wild fruits and pleasant

---

11. **supernumerary** (soo′pər·noo′mə·rer′ē): additional; unnecessary.

12. **Antaeus** (an·tē′əs): in Greek mythology, the giant who draws strength from the earth, his mother.

238 THE AMERICAN RENAISSANCE

Taking a Second Look

Quaker Ladies (1956) by Andrew Wyeth. Watercolor and drypoint.

RESPONDING TO THE ART

Andrew Wyeth (1917–   ), son of N. C. Wyeth (see p. 147), belongs to a distinguished family of American painters. Best known for landscapes of the Brandywine River Valley and of rural Maine, Wyeth has been successful and popular, although critical opinion of his works is divided. (See p. 392.)

Activity. Ask students to speculate about what Thoreau might think of this painting. [Possible answer: He would admire Wyeth's close observation of nature.] **Ask students to compare Wyeth's attitude toward nature with Thoreau's.** [Possible answer: Both seem to believe that nature's smallest details have a great deal to teach human beings about themselves and their environment.]

flowers, produce instead this pulse.[13] What shall I learn of beans or beans of me? I cherish them, I hoe them, early and late I have an eye to them; and this is my day's work. It is a fine broad leaf to look on. My auxiliaries are the dews and rains which water this dry soil, and what fertility is in the soil itself, which for the most part is lean and effete. My enemies are worms, cool days, and most of all woodchucks. The last have nibbled for me a quarter of an acre clean. But what right had I to oust johnswort and the rest, and break up their ancient herb garden? Soon, however, the remaining beans will be too tough for them, and go forward to meet new foes. . . .

It was a singular experience that long acquaintance which I cultivated with beans, what with planting, and hoeing, and harvesting, and threshing, and picking over and selling them—the last was the hardest of all—I might add eating, for I did taste. I was determined to know beans. When they were growing, I used to hoe from five

o'clock in the morning till noon, and commonly spent the rest of the day about other affairs. Consider the intimate and curious acquaintance one makes with various kinds of weeds—it will bear some iteration in the account, for there was no little iteration in the labor—disturbing their delicate organizations so ruthlessly, and making such invidious distinctions with his hoe, leveling whole ranks of one species, and sedulously cultivating another. That's Roman wormwood—that's pigweed—that's sorrel—that's pipergrass—have at him, chop him up, turn his roots upward to the sun, don't let him have a fiber in the shade, if you do he'll turn himself t'other side up and be as green as a leek in two days. A long war, not with cranes, but with weeds, those Trojans who had sun and rain and dews on their side. Daily the beans saw me come to their rescue armed with a hoe, and thin the ranks of their enemies, filling up the trenches with weedy dead. Many a lusty

---

WORDS TO OWN
effete (e·fēt′) *adj.*: sterile; unproductive.

---

13. **pulse:** beans, peas, and other edible seeds of plants having pods.

HENRY DAVID THOREAU **239**

D **Elements of Literature**
Point of View
? How would removing the *I* affect this passage? [It would eliminate the personal touch; the passage would become a treatise on gardening.]

E **Appreciating Language**
Humor and Idiom
"I was determined to know beans" is a witticism that playfully compares the study of beans to the study of an academic subject, such as algebra or literature. It may also be a twist on the common expression "He doesn't know beans."

F **Reading Skills and Strategies**
Unlocking Metaphors
? What two things are being compared in this paragraph? [Weeding a bean field is compared to fighting a war.] **What is the effect of the military language?** [By comparing himself to a warrior fighting the Trojan weeds, Thoreau adds self-mocking humor to the essay; most weeds are tough and stubborn, and readers will identify with the comparison to a battle. Thoreau, however, also uses the comparison to point out the heroic qualities of daily labor.]

Using Students' Strengths

Kinesthetic Learners
Help students see how Thoreau organized his simplified life in a small living space. Using chalk or tape, have students lay out the dimensions of Thoreau's cabin in the classroom or on the school grounds. They can also indicate where the chimney, closet, windows, trapdoors, and furniture may have been placed. Have students pantomime the activities of a day in Thoreau's cabin, demonstrating how he managed to eat, work, and sleep in this small space.

Naturalist Learners
Quaker Ladies, the title of the Andrew Wyeth painting above, is another name for bluets (*Houstonia*), an American wildflower. Have students determine the genus of other native plants Thoreau mentions— such as cinquefoil, johnswort, and pigweed—and present sketches and/or verbal descriptions of each. Students can also choose an object from nature and explain how it teaches a lesson about life, using Thoreau's work as a model.

crest-waving Hector,[14] that towered a whole foot above his crowding comrades, fell before my weapon and rolled in the dust. . . .

from Brute Neighbors

. . . One day when I went out to my woodpile, or rather my pile of stumps, I observed two large ants, the one red, the other much larger, nearly half an inch long, and black, fiercely contending with one another. Having once got hold they never let go, but struggled and wrestled and rolled on the chips incessantly. Looking farther, I was surprised to find that the chips were covered with such combatants, that it was not a *duellum,* but a *bellum,*[15] a war between two races of ants, the red always pitted against the black, and frequently two red ones to one black. The legions of these Myrmidons[16] covered all the hills and vales in my wood yard, and the ground was already strewn with the dead and dying, both red and black. It was the only battle which I have ever witnessed, the only battlefield I ever trod while the battle was raging; internecine[17] war; the red republicans on the one hand, and the black imperialists on the other. On every side they were engaged in deadly combat, yet without any noise that I could hear, and human soldiers never fought so resolutely. I watched a couple that were fast locked in each other's embraces, in a little sunny valley amid the chips, now at noonday prepared to fight till the sun went down, or life went out. The smaller red champion had fastened himself like a vise to his adversary's front, and through all the tumblings on that field never for an instant ceased to gnaw at one of his feelers near the root, having already caused the other to go by the board; while the stronger black

14. **Hector:** In the *Iliad,* Hector is the Trojan prince killed by the Greek hero Achilles.
15. **not a *duellum,* but a *bellum:*** not a duel, but a war.
16. **Myrmidons:** Achilles' soldiers in the *Iliad. Myrmex* is Greek for "ant."
17. **internecine** (in´tər·nē´sin): harmful to both sides of the group.

one dashed him from side to side, and, as I saw on looking nearer, had already divested him of several of his members. They fought with more pertinacity than bulldogs. Neither manifested the least disposition to retreat. It was evident that their battle cry was "Conquer or die." In the meanwhile there came along a single red ant on the hillside of this valley, evidently full of excitement, who either had dispatched his foe, or had not yet taken part in the battle; probably the latter, for he had lost none of his limbs; whose mother had charged him to return with his shield or upon it.[18] Or perchance he was some Achilles, who had nourished his wrath apart, and had now come to avenge or rescue his Patroclus.[19] He saw this unequal combat from afar—for the blacks were nearly twice the size of the red—he drew near with rapid pace till he stood on his guard within half an inch of the combatants; then, watching his opportunity, he sprang upon the black warrior, and commenced his operations near the root of his right foreleg, leaving the foe to select among his own members; and so there were three united for life, as if a new kind of attraction had been invented which put all other locks and cements to shame. I should not have wondered by this time to find that they had their respective musical bands stationed on some eminent chip, and playing their national airs the while, to excite the slow and cheer the dying combatants. I was myself excited somewhat even as if they had been men. The more you think of it, the less the difference. And certainly there is not the fight recorded in Concord history, at least, if in the history of America, that will bear a moment's comparison with this, whether for the numbers engaged in it, or for the patriotism and heroism displayed. For numbers and for carnage it was an Austerlitz or Dresden.[20]

18. **return . . . upon it:** echoes the traditional charge of Spartan mothers to their warrior sons: return victorious or dead.
19. **Achilles . . . Patroclus** (pə·trō´kləs): In the *Iliad,* Achilles withdraws from the battle at Troy but rejoins the fight after his friend Patroclus is killed.
20. **Austerlitz or Dresden:** major battles of the Napoleonic Wars.

WORDS TO OWN

incessantly (in·ses´ənt·lē) *adv.:* without stopping.

Getting Students Involved

Cooperative Learning

Forward Into Battle. Organize students into three groups. One group can research the battles between Greeks and Trojans in the *Iliad;* another, the Napoleonic War battles of Austerlitz and Dresden; and the third, the Battle of Concord. Remind students that before the Civil War, battles for most soldiers involved hand-to-hand combat, as opposed to the mechanized weapons and mass destruction that affect civilians and infrastructure in modern war.

Have each group narrate the story of its assigned battle for the class. Encourage students to give as dramatic and compelling a presentation as they can devise. If students need help getting started, you might suggest a dramatic reading from the *Iliad,* an "eyewitness account" like Thoreau's narrative of the ant war, or a series of posters or drawings with captions. Students should work together as they research, design, and take part in the presentation.

Concord Fight! Two killed on the patriots' side, and Luther Blanchard wounded! Why here every ant was a Buttrick—"Fire! for God's sake fire!"—and thousands shared the fate of Davis and Hosmer.[21] There was not one hireling there. I have no doubt that it was a principle they fought for, as much as our ancestors, and not to avoid a three-penny tax on their tea; and the results of this battle will be as important and memorable to those whom it concerns as those of the Battle of Bunker Hill, at least.

I took up the chip on which the three I have particularly described were struggling, carried it into my house, and placed it under a tumbler on my windowsill, in order to see the issue. Holding a microscope to the first-mentioned red ant, I saw that, though he was assiduously gnawing at the near foreleg of his enemy, having severed his remaining feeler, his own breast was all torn away, exposing what vitals he had there to the jaws of the black warrior, whose breastplate was apparently too thick for him to pierce; and the dark carbuncles of the sufferer's eyes shone with ferocity such as war only could excite. They struggled half an hour longer under the tumbler, and when I looked again the black soldier had severed the heads of his foes from their bodies, and the still living heads were hanging on either side of him like ghastly trophies at his saddlebow, still apparently as firmly fastened as ever, and he was endeavoring with feeble struggles, being without feelers and with only the remnant of a leg, and I know not how many other wounds, to divest himself of them; which at length, after half an hour more, he accomplished. I raised the glass, and he went off over the windowsill in that crippled state. Whether he finally survived that combat, and spent the remainder of his days in some Hôtel des Invalides,[22] I do not know; but I thought that his industry would not be worth much thereafter. I never learned which party was victorious, nor the cause of the war; but I felt for the rest of that day as if I had had my feelings excited and harrowed by witnessing the struggle, the ferocity and carnage, of a human battle before my door. . . .

In the fall the loon (*Colymbus glacialis*) came, as usual, to molt and bathe in the pond, making the woods ring with his wild laughter before I had risen. At rumor of his arrival all the Mill-dam sportsmen are on the alert, in gigs and on foot, two by two and three by three, with patent rifles and conical balls and spyglasses. They come rustling through the woods like autumn leaves, at least ten men to one loon. Some station themselves on this side of the pond, some on that, for the poor bird cannot be omnipresent; if he dive here he must come up there. But now the kind October wind rises, rustling the leaves and rippling the surface of the water, so that no loon can be heard or seen, though his foes sweep the pond with spyglasses, and make the woods resound with their discharges. The waves generously rise and dash angrily, taking sides with all waterfowl, and our sportsmen must beat a retreat to town and shop and unfinished jobs. But they were too often successful. When I went to get a pail of water early in the morning I frequently saw this stately bird sailing out of my cove within a few rods.[23] If I endeavored to overtake him in a boat, in order to see how he would maneuver, he would dive and be completely lost, so that I did not discover him again, sometimes, till the latter part of the day. But I was more than a match for him on the surface. He commonly went off in a rain.

As I was paddling along the north shore one very calm October afternoon, for such days especially they settle onto the lakes, like the milkweed down, having looked in vain over the pond for a loon, suddenly one, sailing out from the shore toward the middle a few rods in front of me, set up his wild laugh and betrayed himself. I pursued with a paddle and he dived, but when he came up I was nearer than before. He dived again, but I miscalculated the direction he would take, and we were fifty rods apart when he came to the surface this time, for I had helped to widen the interval; and again he laughed long and loud, and with more reason than before. He maneuvered so cunningly that I could not get within half a dozen

21. **Luther . . . Hosmer:** All these men fought at the Battle of Concord, the first battle of the Revolutionary War. Major John Buttrick led the minutemen who defeated the British. Isaac Davis and Abner Hosmer were the two colonists killed.
22. **Hôtel des Invalides** (ō·tel′ dez ēn′vä·lēd′): Home for Disabled Soldiers, a veterans' hospital in Paris, France. Napoleon I (1769–1821) is buried there.

23. **rods:** One rod measures 16½ feet.

C Critical Thinking
Determining Author's Purpose
? What effect does Thoreau hope to achieve with the suggestion that the ants were fighting for a principle? [Possible responses: He wishes to add humor (since ants would probably fight only over food or territory), but he also wants to suggest that humans fight like ants—out of instinctive need. He also implies that the colonists' battle over a three-penny tax was more petty than principled.]

D Elements of Literature
Tone
? What tone does Thoreau take toward his subject in this passage? [He maintains a personal but satirical tone.]

E Elements of Literature
Point of View
? Look back over this section. What point of view does Thoreau use to describe the battle? [He speaks from the viewpoint of an observer or reporter; he is not involved in the battle but witnesses it.] What is the effect of this point of view? [The section reads like a war correspondent's report; Thoreau does not take sides yet is still caught up in the excitement of the battle.]

F Critical Thinking
Determining Author's Purpose
? This section, which contains Thoreau's description of the loon, is a digressive piece of nature writing. What might be the purpose of the section? [Possible answers: It is a philosophical metaphor about the relationship between people and nature—or between people and the elusive meaning of their own existence.]

Professional Notes

The Laughing Loons

Loons live in fresh and salt waters in northern climates. Clumsy on land, they fly and swim exceptionally well, however, and they can dive deeper than any other bird except penguins, reaching depths of up to two hundred feet in pursuit of fish. During mating, the only time they are on land, loons develop striking white dorsal plumage, which offsets their usually dull gray and white coat. Both male and female loons take care of the hatchlings, which often ride on their parents' backs for the first few weeks of life. Loons are famous for their distinctive call, often likened to wailing or insane shrieking.

Common Loon (1833) by John James Audubon. Watercolor, graphite, gouache, pastel.

© Collection of the New-York Historical Society.

rods of him. Each time, when he came to the surface, turning his head this way and that, he coolly surveyed the water and the land, and apparently chose his course so that he might come up where there was the widest expanse of water and at the greatest distance from the boat. It was surprising how quickly he made up his mind and put his resolve into execution. He led me at once to the widest part of the pond, and could not be driven from it. While he was thinking one thing in his brain, I was endeavoring to divine his thought in mine. It was a pretty game, played on the smooth surface of the pond, a man against a loon. Suddenly your adversary's checker disappears beneath the board, and the problem is to place yours nearest to where his will appear again. Sometimes he would come up unexpectedly on the opposite side of me, having apparently passed directly under the boat. So long-winded was he and so unweariable, that when he had swum farthest he would immediately plunge again, nevertheless; and then no wit could divine where in the deep pond, beneath the smooth surface, he might be speeding his way like a fish, for he had time and ability to visit the bottom of the pond in its deepest part. It is said that loons have been caught in the New York lakes eighty feet beneath the surface, with hooks set for trout—though Walden is deeper than that. How surprised must the fishes be to see this ungainly visitor from another sphere speeding his way amid their schools! Yet he appeared to know his course as surely underwater as on the surface, and swam much faster there. Once or twice I saw a ripple where **Ⓐ** he approached the surface, just put his head out to reconnoiter, and instantly dived again. I found that it was as well for me to rest on my oars and wait his reappearing as to endeavor to calculate where he would rise; for again and again, when I was straining my eyes over the surface one way, I would suddenly be startled by his unearthly laugh behind me. But why, after displaying so much cunning, did he invariably betray himself the moment he came up by that loud laugh? Did not his

Crossing the Curriculum

white breast enough betray him? He was indeed a silly loon, I thought. I could commonly hear the plash of the water when he came up, and so also detected him. But after an hour he seemed as fresh as ever, dived as willingly, and swam yet farther than at first. It was surprising to see how serenely he sailed off with unruffled breast when he came to the surface, doing all the work with his webbed feet beneath. His usual note was this demoniac laughter, yet somewhat like that of a waterfowl; but occasionally, when he had balked me most successfully and come up a long way off, he uttered a long-drawn unearthly howl, probably more like that of a wolf than any bird; as when a beast puts his muzzle to the ground and deliberately howls. This was his looning—perhaps the wildest sound that is ever heard here, making the woods ring far and wide. I concluded that he laughed in <u>derision</u> of my efforts confident of his own resources. Though the sky was by this time overcast, the pond was so smooth that I could see where he broke the surface when I did not hear him. His white breast, the stillness of the air, and the smoothness of the water were all against him. At length, having come up fifty rods off, he uttered one of those prolonged howls, as if calling on the god of loons to aid him, and immediately there came a wind from the east and rippled the surface, and filled the whole air with misty rain, and I was impressed as if it were the prayer of the loon answered, and his god was angry with me; and so I left him disappearing far away on the <u>tumultuous</u> surface. . . .

from Conclusion

. . . I left the woods for as good a reason as I went there. Perhaps it seemed to me that I had several more lives to live, and could not spare any more time for that one. It is remarkable how easily and insensibly we fall into a particular route, and make a beaten track for ourselves. I had not lived there a week before my feet wore a path from my door to the pond side; and though it is five or six years since I trod it, it is still quite distinct. It is true, I

fear, that others may have fallen into it, and so helped to keep it open. The surface of the earth is soft and impressible by the feet of men; and so with the paths which the mind travels. How worn and dusty, then, must be the highways of the world, how deep the ruts of tradition and conformity! I did not wish to take a cabin passage, but rather to go before the mast and on the deck of the world, for there I could best see the moonlight amid the mountains. I do not wish to go below now.

I learned this, at least, by my experiment: That if one advances confidently in the direction of his dreams, and endeavors to live the life which he has imagined, he will meet with a success unexpected in common hours. He will put some things behind, will pass an invisible boundary; new, universal, and more liberal laws will begin to establish themselves around and within him; or the old laws be expanded, and interpreted in his favor in a more liberal sense, and he will live with the license of a higher order of beings. In proportion as he simplifies his life, the laws of the universe will appear less complex, and solitude will not be solitude, nor poverty poverty, nor weakness weakness. If you have built castles in the air, your work need not be lost; that is where they should be. Now put the foundations under them. . . .

Some are dinning in our ears that we Americans, and moderns generally, are intellectual dwarfs compared with the ancients, or even the Elizabethan men. But what is that to the purpose? A living dog is better than a dead lion.[24] Shall a man go and hang himself because he belongs to the race of pygmies, and not be the biggest pygmy that he can? Let everyone mind his own business, and endeavor to be what he was made.

Why should we be in such desperate haste to succeed and in such desperate enterprises? If a man does not keep pace with his companions, perhaps it is because he hears a different drum-

24. **A living dog . . . lion:** Ecclesiastes 9:4.

WORDS TO OWN

derision (di·rizh′ən) *n.*: ridicule; contempt.
tumultuous (tōō·mul′chōō·əs) *adj.*: stormy; turbulent.

HENRY DAVID THOREAU **243**

Getting Students Involved

Nature Study
1. Take or assign students to visit a park or nature preserve. Tell them to sit quietly apart from one another and to notice their sensory impressions (sight, sound, smell, and touch). Have students freewrite for as long as they can about what their senses perceive. The following day, tell students to read over their material and find a preliminary thesis for an essay about their experience. Allow their essays to follow any direction that arises from reflection on the natural surroundings.

2. Have students read selected chapters or all of Annie Dillard's *Pilgrim at Tinker Creek*. They can compare the insights she draws from nature with Emerson's and Thoreau's or analyze the connections she sees between the natural and spiritual realms. Students could also use her work as a model for their essays.

A Reading Skills and Strategies

Drawing Inferences: Generalizations

? What generalization is Thoreau making in this sentence? [Any human being can discover his or her unique way of living life to the fullest, but we must recognize that this occurs for different people at different times.] **Do you agree with Thoreau?** [Possible answers: Yes, there are times when we live fully and others when by necessity we are caught up in routine; no, people either live fully, like Thoreau, or they live "meanly, like ants."]

B Reading Skills and Strategies

Unlocking Metaphors

? What two things are being compared in this passage? [The long-dormant bug is compared to a person who suddenly breaks free from his or her unthinking routine.] **What does Thoreau imply about most people's lives through this comparison?** [The idea of human life buried inside deadwood is a strong indictment of the way most people in society live.]

C Reading Skills and Strategies

Drawing Inferences: Generalizations

? The last five sentences are ringing and apocalyptic. What do they mean? [Possible responses: The mere passing of time will not help us grasp the significance of our lives. We can live fully only if we open our eyes and seek to live fully. There is always more to explore, more to learn.]

---

mer. Let him step to the music which he hears, however measured or far away. It is not important that he should mature as soon as an apple tree or an oak. Shall he turn his spring into summer? If the condition of things which we were made for is not yet, what were any reality which we can substitute? We will not be shipwrecked on a vain reality. Shall we with pains erect a heaven of blue glass over ourselves, though when it is done we shall be sure to gaze still at the true <u>ethereal</u> heaven far above, as if the former were not? . . .

The life in us is like the water in the river. It may rise this year higher than man has ever known it, and flood the parched uplands; even this may be the eventful year, which will drown out all our muskrats. It was not always dry land where we dwell. I see far inland the banks which the stream anciently washed, before science began to record its freshets. Everyone has heard the story which has gone the rounds of New England, of a strong and beautiful bug which came out of the dry leaf of an old table of apple-tree wood, which had stood in a farmer's kitchen for sixty years, first in Connecticut, and afterward in Massachusetts—from an egg deposited in the living tree many years earlier still, as appeared by counting the annual layers beyond it; which was heard gnawing out for several weeks, hatched perchance by the heat of an urn. Who does not feel his faith in a resurrection and immortality strengthened by hearing of this? Who knows what beautiful and winged life, whose egg has been buried for ages under many concentric

A journal page (1845) by Henry David Thoreau.

The Pierpont Morgan Library/ Art Resource, NY.

244

layers of woodenness in the dead dry life of society, deposited at first in the alburnum[25] of the green and living tree, which has been gradually converted into the semblance of its well-seasoned tomb—heard perchance gnawing out now for years by the astonished family of man, as they sat round the festive board—may unexpectedly come forth from amidst society's most trivial and handselled[26] furniture, to enjoy its perfect summer life at last!

I do not say that John or Jonathan[27] will realize all this; but such is the character of that morrow which mere lapse of time can never make to dawn. The light which puts out our eyes is darkness to us. Only that day dawns to which we are awake. There is more day to dawn. The sun is but a morning star.

25. alburnum: sapwood; soft wood between the inner bark and the hard core of a tree.
26. handselled: given as a mere token of good wishes; therefore, of no great value in itself.
27. John or Jonathan: John Bull and Brother Jonathan were traditional personifications of England and the United States respectively.

WORDS TO OWN

ethereal (ē·thir′ē·əl) adj.: not earthly; spiritual.

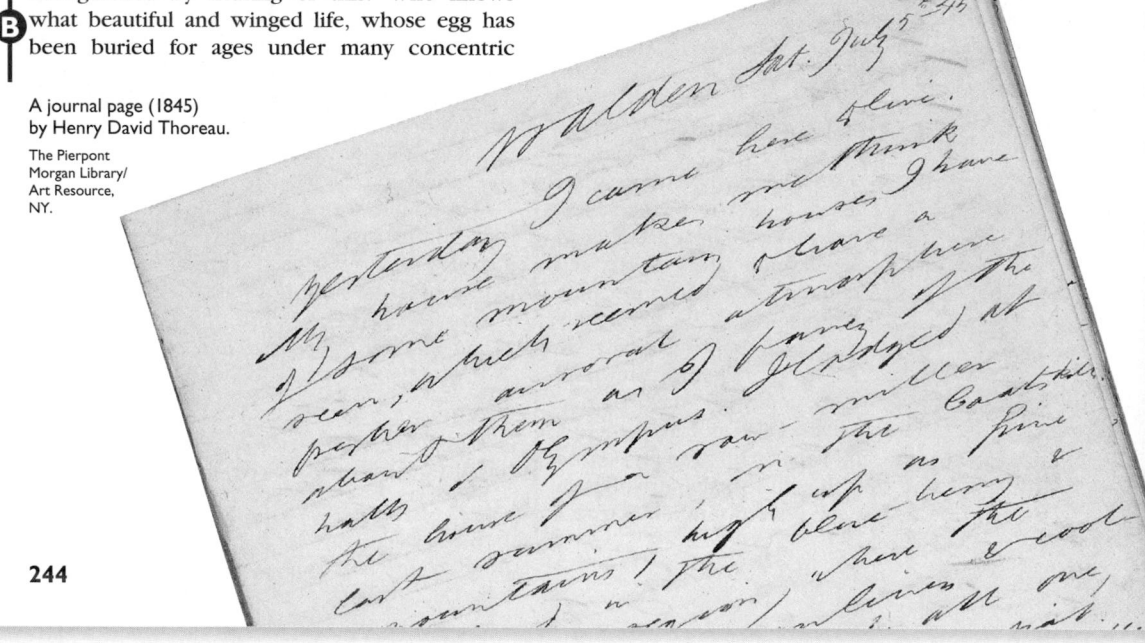

Assessing Learning

Check Test: True-False

1. Thoreau builds his house alone, with no help from his friends and neighbors. [False]
2. After selling his crops, Thoreau makes only enough money to cover the expenses of planting and seed. [False]
3. Thoreau plays a game of chase with a laughing loon, which easily eludes him. [True]
4. Thoreau leaves Walden Pond because he feels ready to move on to another adventure and does not want life on Walden to become an empty routine. [True]
5. Thoreau tells his readers they should all live as he has done, because only by withdrawing from society can people truly live. [False]

Standardized Test Preparation

For practice with ACT and SAT formats, see
• *Preparation for College Admission Exams,* p. 19
For practice in proofreading and editing, see
• *Daily Oral Grammar,* Transparency, 18

In 1990, the popular musician and songwriter Don Henley (of the rock group the Eagles) founded the Walden Woods Project to protect a part of Walden Woods under threat of real-estate development. Here Henley talks about how Thoreau and Emerson contributed to his "spiritual awakening" and his commitment to the preservation of Walden Woods.

from Heaven Is Under Our Feet

Don Henley

I honestly don't remember when I was first introduced to the works of Henry David Thoreau or by whom. It may have been my venerable high school English teacher, Margaret Lovelace, or it may have been one of my university professors. I was lucky enough to have a few exceptional ones and that is sometimes all a kid needs—just one or two really good teachers can make all the difference in the world. It can inspire and change a life. . . .

Thoreau's writing struck me like a thunderbolt. Like all great literature, it articulated something that I knew intuitively, but could not quite bring into focus for myself. I loved Emerson, too, and his essay, "Self-Reliance," was instrumental in giving me the courage to become a songwriter. The works of both men were part of a spiritual awakening in which I rediscovered my hometown and the beauty of the surrounding landscape, and, through that, some evidence of a "Higher Power," or God, if you like. This epiphany brought great comfort and relief. . . .

. . . [T]here has been a great deal of curiosity, speculation, and, in some quarters, skepticism bordering on cynicism, as to how and why I came to be involved in the movement to preserve the stomping grounds of Henry David Thoreau and his friend and mentor, Ralph Waldo Emerson. What, in other words, is California rock and roll trash doing meddling around in something as seemingly esoteric and high-minded as literature (pronounced "LIT-tra-chure"), philosophy, and history—the American Transcendentalist Movement and all its ascetic practitioners. Seems perfectly natural to me. American Literature, like the air we breathe, belongs—or should belong—to everybody. . . . The great halls of learning may keep Thoreau's literature and principles alive, but they will be of little help in fortifying the well from whence they sprang.

. . . Unfortunately, the focus of preservation efforts has come to rest on the pond and its immediate surroundings. That is all well and good, except that there remain approximately two thousand six hundred acres that are inside the historic boundaries of Walden Woods and deserve protection as well. Thoreau did not live *in* Walden Pond; he lived beside it. The man did not walk on water, he walked several miles a day through the woods, and his musings and writings therein figure at least as prominently in his literature as Walden Pond does. In other words, the width and breadth of his inspiration, the scope of his legacy is not limited to one sixty-two-acre pond, and it is absurd to think so. Walden Woods is not a pristine, grand tract of wilderness, but it is still, for the most part, exceedingly beautiful and inspiring. It is, for all intents and purposes, the cradle of the American environmental movement and should be preserved for its intrinsic, symbolic value or, as Ed Schofield, Thoreau Society president, so succinctly put it, "When Walden goes, all the issues radiating out from Walden go, too. If the prime place can be disposed of, how much easier to dispose of the issues it represents." Otherwise, we might just as well turn all our national parks, our monuments to freedom and independence, into theme parks and shopping malls.

Connecting Across Texts

Connecting to the Theme: "The Life Worth Living"
Have students consider the differences between Thoreau's and Henley's lives. Would Thoreau find Henley's life worthwhile? Is Henley living up to Thoreau's ideals, despite their different circumstances? Why does Henley admire Thoreau and Emerson? What about their lives does he consider the most worthwhile? [Possible response: With the help of Emerson and Thoreau, Henley has discovered for himself a kind of life worth living. He learned from Emerson to rely on himself, to listen to his own conscience, and to broaden his thinking. This helps him to speak out against what he sees as an injustice, the commercial development of Walden Woods. Henley also seems to have learned from Thoreau. He has come to appreciate his own hometown and its beauty and has acquired the courage to march to the beat of the drummer he hears.]

Connections

In this essay, Eagles' guitarist Don Henley recalls how the writings of Emerson and Thoreau gave him the courage to become a musician and inspired a spiritual awakening in him. He goes on to explain that because of its symbolic value to American literature and to the American environmental movement, Walden Pond, as well as the entire 2,600-acre tract of Walden Woods, where Thoreau roamed and wrote, should be preserved.

Ⓐ Cultural Connections
Walden Woods Project
The Walden Woods Project has raised more than thirteen million dollars and purchased almost one hundred acres abutting the 350-acre Walden State Pond Reservation. Included in the purchase was the historic Jacob Baker Farm, a locale frequented by Thoreau and now the home of the Thoreau Institute—dedicated to literary, environmental, and humanitarian research and education. The Walden Woods Project is also working on the creation of recreational and historic walking trails in the area.

Ⓑ Literary Connections
Heaven on Earth
Henley's essay is one of several included in *Heaven Is Under Our Feet,* a collection of essays by writers, entertainers, politicians, and environmentalists to help support the Walden Woods Project.

Ⓒ Reading Skills and Strategies
Responding to the Text
❓ Do Thoreau's and Emerson's ideas strike a chord with you? Are these ideas as inspirational to you as they were to Henley? Why or why not? Do they seem dated in any way? [Students' answers will vary.]

Ⓓ Critical Thinking
Making Judgments
❓ What is the symbolic value of Walden Pond and Walden Woods? To what degree does a place like Walden symbolize the American spirit? [Students may discuss the importance of individualism and self-sufficiency to Americans, as well as Thoreau's contribution to environmental awareness.]

First Thoughts [Respond]

1. Possible responses: The message is still valid; people can still find satisfaction in living simply despite the contemporary influence of conformity and consumerism.

Shaping Interpretations [Interpret]

2. He means that people should cut the clutter out of their lives so that they can live more spiritually. His message is more valid than ever because the complexity and stress of people's lives has only increased since Thoreau's day.

3. Thoreau distrusts technology and feels that it tends to control people rather than serve them. Disagree: Technology has no power until people consent to throw switches or push buttons to make it work. Agree: Once a particular technology has been discovered, everyone ends up being forced to use it to keep pace with others.

4. The full possibilities of life will open up to us only when we are committed to living fully.

5. People and nations carry the potential for dramatic and beautiful change inside them—even after years of thoughtless conformity.

Connecting with the Text [Apply]

6. Possible generalizations: People can achieve anything they truly want. People must believe in themselves and bypass the courses charted by others. Some students may feel that these ideas are too idealistic or individualistic.

7. Students might want to discuss peer pressure and nonconformity.

Extending the Text [Synthesize]

8. *Walden* got people to think about the greatness, majesty, and priceless value of the environment. This book gives the movement historical and philosophical credibility. Many students will agree that Walden Woods should be preserved.

Challenging the Text [Evaluate]

9. Agree: At times, Thoreau does regard himself as detached, or separate, from the society he criticizes, and he writes with mild contempt for those who disagree with him. Disagree: Thoreau barters with fellow citizens, visits them, entertains them in his cabin, and eventually rejoins them in society.

MAKING MEANINGS

First Thoughts

1. What do you think of Thoreau — as a writer and as a personality? Is his message still valid, or do you find it dated and irrelevant?

Shaping Interpretations

2. What does Thoreau mean when he says, "Simplify, simplify" (page 237)? Do you think he has a valid point here? Explain.

3. How would you summarize Thoreau's ideas on technological progress, judging from what he says about railroads and other inventions of his era? Do you agree with him? Why or why not?

4. What do you think Thoreau means in his final paragraph by the words "Only that day dawns to which we are awake"?

5. What do you think is the lesson of the **parable** involving the insect in the wood table at the conclusion of *Walden*?

Connecting with the Text

6. Review your double-entry journal. What **generalizations** did you make based on Thoreau's ideas? Did you find that some of his ideas, if extended, would prove to be unworkable? Did you disagree with any of these thoughts? Be sure to discuss your journal entries in class.

7. If it were possible, would you like to spend a day or two with Thoreau? What would you most like to discuss with him?

Reading Check

a. According to the second paragraph in "Economy," why has Thoreau decided to write about his life?

b. How does Thoreau answer the questions implied in the title "Where I Lived, and What I Lived For"?

c. What arguments does Thoreau present in "Solitude" to demonstrate that he is not lonely in his isolated situation?

d. What satisfactions does Thoreau find in the labor of raising beans in "The Bean Field"?

Reading Check

a. He wants to give "a simple and sincere account" of himself; he knows himself best.

b. He lived in a cabin in the woods; he lived as fully and "deliberately" as possible.

c. He is a part of the Milky Way; he is surrounded by countless living creatures; he feels close to the natural sources of life.

d. He learns all about them. They make him feel as if he is rooted to the earth.

Extending the Text

8. In *Connections* on page 245, the rock star Don Henley declares that Walden Woods is "the cradle of the American environmental movement and should be preserved for its intrinsic, symbolic value." In what ways do you think Thoreau's *Walden* has influenced the environmental movement in the United States? Do you agree with Henley that Walden Woods should be preserved because it has symbolic value to our society? Explain.

Challenging the Text

9. The Pulitzer Prize–winning author Wallace Stegner (1909–1993), who admired much of Thoreau's thought, once made this observation about Thoreau's message in *Walden:* "At times he sounds perilously like his spiritual descendants of the 1960s, who trusted no one over thirty and believed that they existed outside of, and were exempt from, the society they were protesting." Do you agree or disagree with Stegner's statement? Support or refute it with examples from *Walden*.

READING SKILLS AND STRATEGIES

Unlocking Meaning in Metaphors

Thoreau's **metaphors** are highly visual. Though they're clever and original, they aren't far-fetched. Thoreau takes his comparisons from nature and from other things he and his audience are familiar with, such as clothes and sailing. To be sure you understand Thoreau's figures of speech, **paraphrase** the following metaphors.

1. "As for the rest of my readers, they will accept such portions as apply to them. I trust that none will stretch the seams in putting on the coat, for it may do good service to him whom it fits." (page 234)

2. "I wanted to live deep and suck out all the marrow of life. . . ." (page 237)

3. "If a man does not keep pace with his companions, perhaps it is because he hears a different drummer. Let him step to the music which he hears, however measured or far away." (page 243)

READING SKILLS AND STRATEGIES

1. I hope my readers will take only what suits them personally in my work and not distort my philosophy.

2. I wanted to participate in and enjoy every experience that life offered.

3. If people live their own way, their destiny and their beliefs may be different from everyone else's. Let those people live according to their own convictions.

CHOICES: Building Your Portfolio

Writer's Notebook

1. Collecting Ideas for Writing About a Controversial Issue

In the Writer's Notebook on page 229, you drew up a list of controversial issues. By now you might have added to your list—especially after reading Thoreau. Review your topics. Under each, write questions that you would like to explore. For example, if one of your topics is preserving wilderness areas, you might pose the question "Should wilderness areas be preserved at the cost of new housing?" Save your notes for possible use in the Writer's Workshop on page 331.

Analyzing *Walden*

2. How Romantic?

In a brief essay, evaluate evidence of the Romantic point of view in *Walden*—for instance, the emphasis on intuition, the power of nature, and the importance of human emotion. Is Thoreau a Romantic, in your opinion? Or, can you identify strong anti-Romantic strains in his thinking? (Review the characteristics of Romanticism on page 144.) Be sure to quote details from *Walden* to support your evaluation.

Supporting a Topic Sentence

3. Everyday Miracles

"The invariable mark of wisdom," Emerson wrote, "is to find the miraculous in the common." Using Emerson's statement as your topic sentence, choose a scene from *Walden*, and in a brief essay use details from *Walden* to show how Thoreau finds "the miraculous in the common."

Creative Writing

4. Thoreau on Our Times

Thoreau would undoubtedly have strong, and probably controversial, opinions on many aspects of present-day technology and society. Write a paragraph or two as if you are Thoreau, expressing your opinion on an aspect of modern life. Use the **first-person point of view.** Find support in *Walden* for your position.

Creative Writing

5. Still Waters Run Deep

Walden does not record monumental events; it describes the ordinary events that most people would let pass unnoticed. Do the same for a day in your life. Take a few minutes at intervals throughout the day to write down your impressions of what is going on around you. At the end of the day, record in a journal what you saw, what you heard, and what you thought. Did any-

thing remind you of Thoreau's experiences? Did anything convey a lesson or seem to hold a message?

Creative Writing / Performance

6. In My Solitude

Suppose that a Puritan like Mary Rowlandson (page 38) or a rationalist like Benjamin Franklin (page 84) had done the "Walden experiment." Write a journal entry from the point of view of the Puritan or rationalist of your choice, recording the experience of solitude at Walden Pond. What lessons or morals does the person draw from the experience? How is the perspective different from Thoreau's? Read the journal entry aloud to the class, speaking like the person who might have written it.

Crossing the Curriculum: Science

7. Further Into Nature

Thoreau is remembered not only as a philosophical writer but as a keen observer of nature. Choose an aspect of nature that Thoreau mentions—an ant war, a loon, a bean field, or something less obvious—and do some research in a library or on the Internet. Find at least three facts about the subject that go beyond the information Thoreau provides. Report your findings to the class.

Rubrics for each Choices assignment appear on p. 118 in the *Portfolio Management System.*

CHOICES: Building Your Portfolio

1. **Writer's Notebook** Students may be interested to learn that because its preservation efforts displaced planned low-income housing, the Walden Woods Project pledged funds for construction of the housing elsewhere.
2. **Analyzing *Walden*** Students might consider Thoreau's practical approach toward the construction of his cabin and his keen observation of all aspects of nature—not just its beauty.
3. **Supporting a Topic Sentence** Have students consider the exact meanings of *miraculous* and *common* before they begin writing.
4. **Creative Writing** Students may enjoy writing not only from Thoreau's point of view, but in his style. Point out that Thoreau studied the classics and used many words derived from Greek and Latin. Suggest that students use allusions and metaphors from history and literature.
5. **Creative Writing** Remind students that even if their surroundings and everyday activities are widely different from Thoreau's, they can still observe, think, and write as he did.
6. **Creative Writing/Performance** Encourage students to reread previous selections as needed to refresh their memories about other writers' styles. Students may want to give their readings in appropriate costumes.
7. **Crossing the Curriculum: Science** Students may want to review the work they did in the Crossing the Curriculum activities on p. 242 for possible topics to investigate.

OBJECTIVES
1. Read and interpret the essay
2. Identify and interpret paradoxes
3. Determine the precise meanings of words
4. Express understanding through writing, drama, and research
5. Understand and use new words

SKILLS

Literary
• Identify and interpret paradoxes

Reading
• Determine the precise meanings of words

Writing
• Collect ideas for an essay on a controversial topic
• Support a position
• Compare and contrast two texts

Speaking/Listening
• Write and perform a play
• Present a research report

Vocabulary
• Use new words

Viewing/Representing
• Analyze a painting (ATE)

Planning

• **Traditional Schedule**
 Lesson Plans Including Strategies for English-Language Learners
• **One-Stop Planner**
 CD-ROM with Test Generator

Before You Read

FROM RESISTANCE TO CIVIL GOVERNMENT

Make the Connection

Civil Disobedience

The idea of civil disobedience is probably familiar to you if you know anything about the U.S. civil rights struggles of the 1960s or the struggle of Mohandas K. ("Mahatma") Gandhi and his followers to achieve independence for India in the first half of the twentieth century. Both movements were inspired by the essay that follows.

Some readers have concluded that this essay shows that Thoreau merely wanted to withdraw from life and all its difficult questions. Others see Thoreau's action as the logical outcome of his convictions. Decide for yourself if Thoreau's position is admirable or not.

Gandhi during the last months of his life in Birla House, New Delhi, India. He was assassinated in January 1948, shortly after India achieved independence.

Henri Cartier-Bresson/Magnum.

Quickwrite

Under what circumstances would you be willing to go to jail for a moral or political principle? Write a brief description of the principle and of your feelings about it. Alternatively, explain why you wouldn't be willing to commit civil disobedience under any circumstances.

Elements of Literature

Paradox

A **paradox** is a statement that expresses the complexity of life by showing how opposing ideas can be both contradictory and true, as in Emily Dickinson's famous line "Tell all the Truth but tell it slant—" (page 386). Paradox was one of Thoreau's favorite literary devices. The idea that a contradiction can contain a truth is in itself paradoxical—and truthful.

> **A paradox** is a statement that appears self-contradictory but that reveals a kind of truth.
>
> *For more on Paradox, see the Handbook of Literary Terms.*

Background

In July 1846, Thoreau's stay at Walden Pond was interrupted by a night in jail. Thoreau was arrested because he refused to pay a tax to the state—primarily because he was opposed to the government's support of slavery. The Concord police offered to pay the tax for Thoreau, but he refused that also. He was forced, therefore, to spend the night in jail, and he might have spent more time there, except that someone, probably his aunt, paid the tax for him. This night in jail inspired the essay known as "Resistance to Civil Government" or "Civil Disobedience."

248 THE AMERICAN RENAISSANCE

  Resources: Print and Media

Reading
• *Graphic Organizers for Active Reading,* p. 21
• *Words to Own,* p. 18
• *Audio CD Library*
 Disc 7, Track 8

Writing and Language
• *Daily Oral Grammar*
 Transparency 19

Assessment
• *Formal Assessment,* p. 55
• *Portfolio Management System,* p. 120
• *Test Generator (One-Stop Planner CD-ROM)*

Internet
• go.hrw.com (keyword: LE0 11-5)

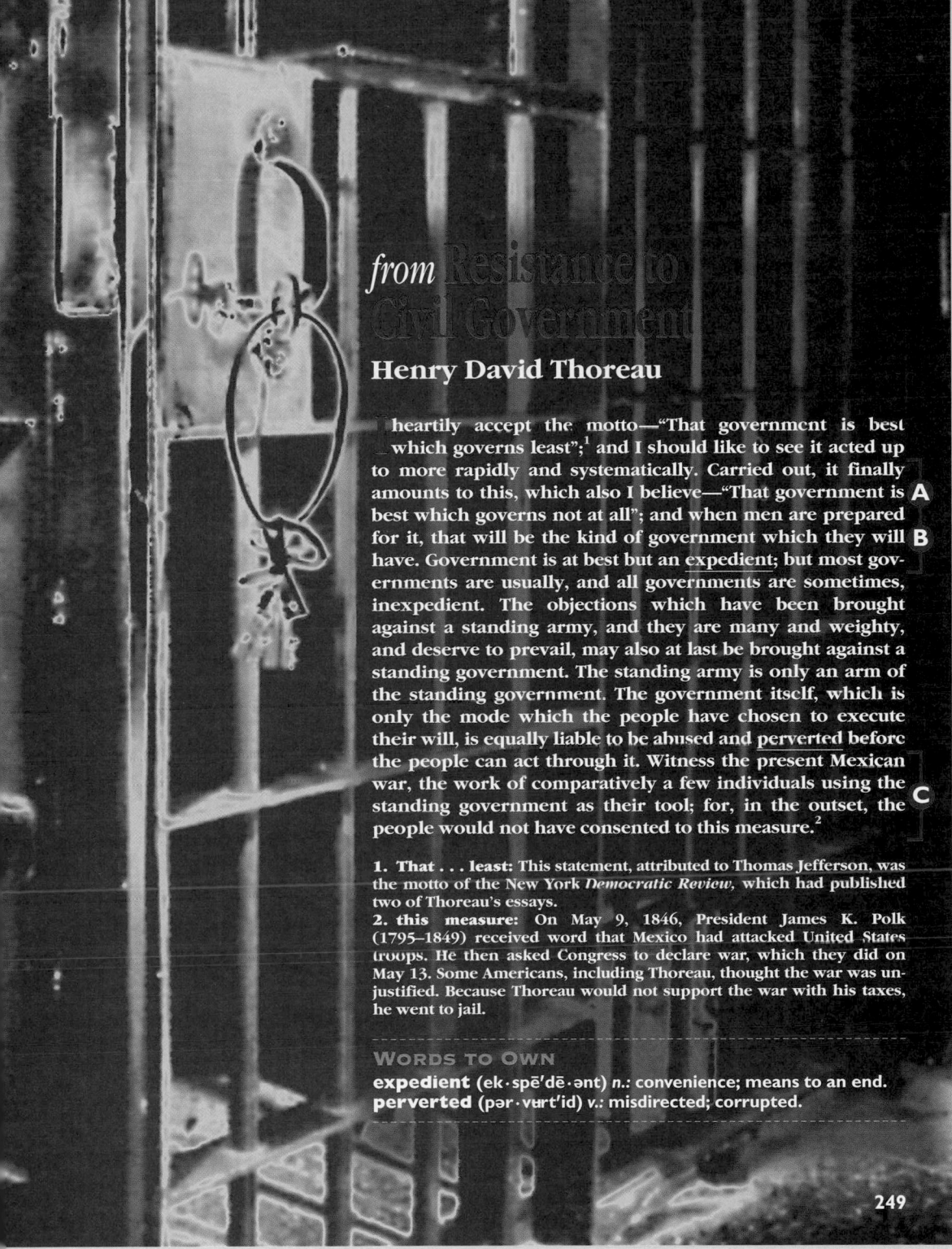

from Resistance to Civil Government

Henry David Thoreau

I heartily accept the motto—"That government is best which governs least";[1] and I should like to see it acted up to more rapidly and systematically. Carried out, it finally amounts to this, which also I believe—"That government is **A** best which governs not at all"; and when men are prepared for it, that will be the kind of government which they will **B** have. Government is at best but an <u>expedient</u>; but most governments are usually, and all governments are sometimes, inexpedient. The objections which have been brought against a standing army, and they are many and weighty, and deserve to prevail, may also at last be brought against a standing government. The standing army is only an arm of the standing government. The government itself, which is only the mode which the people have chosen to execute their will, is equally liable to be abused and <u>perverted</u> before the people can act through it. Witness the present Mexican war, the work of comparatively a few individuals using the **C** standing government as their tool; for, in the outset, the people would not have consented to this measure.[2]

1. **That . . . least:** This statement, attributed to Thomas Jefferson, was the motto of the New York *Democratic Review*, which had published two of Thoreau's essays.
2. **this measure:** On May 9, 1846, President James K. Polk (1795–1849) received word that Mexico had attacked United States troops. He then asked Congress to declare war, which they did on May 13. Some Americans, including Thoreau, thought the war was unjustified. Because Thoreau would not support the war with his taxes, he went to jail.

WORDS TO OWN
expedient (ek·spē′dē·ənt) *n.:* convenience; means to an end.
perverted (pər·vurt′id) *v.:* misdirected; corrupted.

249

Summary ■■

Thoreau argues that government should serve individuals, who are the real agents of change and progress. He criticizes people for passively accepting governmental actions with which they disagree; he says that if people defied the government in such a case, it would have to show more accountability to its citizens. He tests his theory of civil disobedience by serving a jail sentence rather than pay a tax he believes will help finance war with Mexico and the expansion of slavery. During his time in jail, Thoreau recognizes that few of his neighbors will have the courage to follow his example. He concludes with the hope that one day the state will be truly "free and enlightened."

Ⓐ Elements of Literature
Paradox
❓ This essay begins with a paradox. How can a government "govern not at all"? [Possible answers: It can respect the rights of the individual conscience. It can trust its citizens to do what they believe is right.]

Ⓑ Critical Thinking
Expressing an Opinion
❓ Would Thoreau's proposal work in a complex society? Explain. [Sample responses: Yes, many people today believe government should interfere far less than it presently does in individual lives and business; no, living in society requires that people sometimes compromise their principles and desires for the common good.]

Ⓒ Historical Connections
Mexican War
Explain that many Americans, including Thoreau, believed that the United States had provoked this war in order to expand its slaveholding territory.

Preteaching Vocabulary

Words to Own
Working with a partner, each student should look up five Words to Own in a dictionary and note their prefixes, suffixes, and roots (all the Words to Own in this selection are derived from Latin roots). Partners can then quiz each other on the Latin roots they have learned and create lists of other words with those roots that might prove useful. Next, have students match each of the following words with its synonym.

1. insurrection [c]
2. expedient [h]
3. penitent [f]
4. inherent [a]
5. alacrity [d]
6. effectual [i]
7. impetuous [b]
8. obstruction [g]
9. perverted [e]
10. posterity [j]

a. inborn
b. impulsive
c. rebellion
d. eagerness
e. corrupted
f. sorry
g. blockage
h. means
i. productive
j. descendants

A Elements of Literature

Parallelism

? What effect does the repetition of "*It does not . . .*" have on the reader? [Possible answers: The repetition reinforces the main point that people, not government, achieve these goals; the repetition impresses the people's power on the reader's mind.]

B Historical Connections

John Adams

Thoreau echoes John Adams on majority rule. As a delegate to both the First and Second Continental Congresses and as the first vice president and second president of the United States, Adams was a crucial figure in the formation of the U.S. Constitution. In 1815, Adams wrote, "Despotism . . . is the same in a Majority of a popular Assembly . . . and a single Emperor. Equally arbitrary cruel bloody and in every respect diabolical."

C Advanced Learners

Allusion

? What is the allusion in the phrase "wash his hands of it"? [Thoreau alludes to Pontius Pilate washing his hands before the crowd to claim that he was guiltless in the death of Jesus Christ.] **What is Thoreau saying through this allusion?** [Thoreau is saying that people do not have to solve all the world's problems, but they must make sure they are not providing de facto support for the immoral actions of their government.]

D Elements of Literature

Paradox

? What paradoxical behavior is Thoreau criticizing? [People in Concord disapprove of slavery and of America's war with Mexico; but when they purchase cotton or tobacco products, they add to the slavers' profits, and when they pay taxes, they support the war effort.]

This American government—what is it but a tradition, though a recent one, endeavoring to transmit itself unimpaired to <u>posterity</u>, but each instant losing some of its integrity? It has not the vitality and force of a single living man; for a single man can bend it to his will. It is a sort of wooden gun to the people themselves; and, if ever they should use it in earnest as a real one against each other, it will surely split. But it is not the less necessary for this; for the people must have some complicated machinery or other, and hear its din, to satisfy that idea of government which they have. Governments show thus how successfully men can be imposed on, even impose on themselves, for their own advantage. It is excellent, we must all allow; yet this government never of itself furthered any enterprise, but by the <u>alacrity</u> with which it got out of its way. **A** *It* does not keep the country free. *It* does not settle the West. *It* does not educate. The character <u>inherent</u> in the American people has done all that has been accomplished; and it would have done somewhat more, if the government had not sometimes got in its way. For government is an expedient by which men would fain[3] succeed in letting one another alone; and, as has been said, when it is most expedient, the governed are most let alone by it. Trade and commerce, if they were not made of India rubber, would never manage to bounce over the obstacles which legislators are continually putting in their way; and, if one were to judge these men wholly by the effects of their actions, and not partly by their intentions, they would deserve to be classed and punished with those mischievous persons who put obstructions on the railroads.

But, to speak practically and as a citizen, unlike those who call themselves no-government men, I ask for, not at once no government, but *at once* a better government. Let every man make known what kind of government would command his respect, and that will be one step toward obtaining it.

B After all, the practical reason why, when the power is once in the hands of the people, a majority are permitted, and for a long period continue, to rule, is not because they are most likely to be in the right, nor because this seems fairest to the minority, but because they are physically the strongest. But a government in which the majority rule in all cases cannot be based on justice, even as far as men understand it. Can there not be a government in which majorities do not virtually decide right and wrong, but conscience?—in which majorities decide only those questions to which the rule of expediency is applicable? Must the citizen ever for a moment, or in the least degree, resign his conscience to the legislator? Why has every man a conscience, then? I think that we should be men first, and subjects afterward. It is not desirable to cultivate a respect for the law, so much as for the right. The only obligation which I have a right to assume, is to do at any time what I think right. . . .

C It is not a man's duty, as a matter of course, to devote himself to the eradication of any, even the most enormous wrong; he may still properly have other concerns to engage him; but it is his duty, at least, to wash his hands of it, and, if he gives it no thought longer, not to give it practically his support. If I devote myself to other pursuits and contemplations, I must first see, at least, that I do not pursue them sitting upon another man's shoulders. I must get off him first, that he may pursue his contemplations too. See what gross inconsistency is tolerated. I have heard some of my townsmen say, "I should like to have them order me out to help put down an <u>insurrection</u> of the slaves, or **D** to march to Mexico—see if I would go"; and yet these very men have each, directly by their allegiance, and so indirectly, at least, by their money, furnished a substitute. The soldier is applauded who refuses to serve in an unjust war by those who do not refuse to sustain the unjust government which makes the war; is applauded by those whose own act and authority he disregards and sets at nought; as if the State were <u>penitent</u> to that degree that it hired one to scourge it while it sinned, but not to that degree that it left off sinning for a moment. Thus, under the name of order

---

3. **fain:** archaic for "gladly" or "willingly."

250 THE AMERICAN RENAISSANCE

WORDS TO OWN

posterity (päs·ter′ə·tē) *n.*: generations to come.
alacrity (ə·lak′rə·tē) *n.*: promptness in responding; eagerness.
inherent (in·hir′ənt) *adj.*: inborn.
insurrection (in′sə·rek′shən) *n.*: rebellion; revolt.
penitent (pen′i·tənt) *adj.*: sorry for doing wrong.

Reaching All Students

Struggling Readers

Explain that this essay is an argument for civil disobedience—the deliberate and responsible refusal to obey laws that violate personal conscience. Encourage students to note the various arguments that Thoreau offers to support this position. As they read, they should decide whether they agree or disagree with each supporting argument. This strategy will engage them in reading the selection.

English Language Learners

For student reference, here are some major points Thoreau makes in his essay:

- Government is a means to an end.
- The majority will inevitably, in some instances, harm the minority.
- People have an obligation not to support what they feel is wrong.
- The "free and enlightened state" is one that will "recognize the individual as a higher power."

and civil government, we are all made at last to pay homage to and support our own meanness. After the first blush of sin, comes its indifference and from immoral it becomes, as it were, *un-moral*, and not quite unnecessary to that life which we have made. . . .

I meet this American government, or its representative the State government, directly, and face to face, once a year, no more, in the person of its tax-gatherer; this is the only mode in which a man situated as I am necessarily meets it; and it then says distinctly, Recognize me; and the simplest, the most <u>effectual</u>, and, in the present posture of affairs, the indispensablest mode of treating with it on this head, of expressing your little satisfaction with and love for it, is to deny it then. My civil neighbor, the tax-gatherer, is the very man I have to deal with—for it is, after all, with men and not with parchment that I quarrel—and he has voluntarily chosen to be an agent of the government. How shall he ever know well what he is and does as an officer of the government, or as a man, until he is obliged to consider whether he shall treat me, his neighbor, for whom he has respect, as a neighbor and well-disposed man, or as a maniac and disturber of the peace, and see if he can get over this <u>obstruction</u> to his neighborliness without a ruder and more <u>impetuous</u> thought or speech corresponding with his action? I know this well, that if one thousand, if one hundred, if ten men whom I could name—if ten *honest* men only—aye, if *one* HONEST man, in this State of Massachusetts, *ceasing to hold slaves*, were actually to withdraw from this copartnership, and be locked up in the county jail therefor, it would be the abolition of slavery in America. For it matters not how small the beginning may seem to be: What is once well done is done forever. . . .

I have paid no poll tax[4] for six years. I was put into a jail once on this account, for one night; and, as I stood considering the walls of solid stone,

two or three feet thick, the door of wood and iron, a foot thick, and the iron grating which strained the light, I could not help being struck with the foolishness of that institution which treated me as if I were mere flesh and blood and bones, to be locked up. I wondered that it should have concluded at length that this was the best use it could put me to, and had never thought to avail itself of my services in some way. I saw that, if there was a wall of stone between me and my townsmen, there was a still more difficult one to climb or break through, before they could get to be as free as I was. I did not for a moment feel confined, and the walls seemed a great waste of stone and mortar. I felt as if I alone of all my townsmen had paid my tax. They plainly did not know how to treat me, but behaved like persons who are underbred. In every threat and in every compliment there was a blunder; for they thought that my chief desire was to stand the other side of that stone wall. I could not but smile to see how industriously they locked the door on my meditations, which followed them out again without let or hindrance, and *they* were really all that was dangerous. As they could not reach me, they had resolved to punish my body; just as boys, if they cannot come at some person against whom they have a spite, will abuse his dog. I saw that the State was half-witted, that it was timid as a lone woman with her silver spoons, and that it did not know its friends from its foes, and I lost all my remaining respect for it, and pitied it. . . .

The night in prison was novel and interesting enough. The prisoners in their shirt sleeves were enjoying a chat and the evening air in the doorway, when I entered. But the jailer said, "Come, boys, it is time to lock up"; and so they dispersed, and I heard the sound of their steps returning into the hollow apartments. My roommate was

> They plainly did not know how to treat me, but behaved like persons who are underbred.

WORDS TO OWN

effectual (e·fek′chŏŏ·əl) *adj.*: productive; efficient.
obstruction (əb·struk′shən) *n.*: blockage; hindrance.
impetuous (im·pech′ŏŏ·əs) *adj.*: impulsive.

---

4. **poll tax:** fee some states and localities required from each citizen as a qualification for voting. It is now considered unconstitutional in the United States to charge such a tax.

E 🅔 **English Language Learners**
Superlatives
Ask students what the suffix *-est* indicates. [most, as in *most simple* or *simplest*] Explain that this suffix is normally used only with one- or two-syllable words; longer words are usually preceded by the word *most* instead. Ask students why Thoreau might have broken this rule by writing "indispensablest." [Possible responses: for emphasis; to catch the reader's attention.]

F 🅕 **Reading Skills and Strategies**
Determining Precise Meanings
❓ Look up the word *maniac* in a dictionary. What does it mean? What is the origin of the word? [It means "lunatic" or "madman," from the Greek *maniakos*, or "mad."] Why would Thoreau choose this word? [The word provides an ironic commentary on the nature of Thoreau's crime.]

G 🅖 **Elements of Literature**
Parallelism
❓ What effect does the repetition in this sentence have on the reader? [Possible answers: It makes the point dramatically; it emphasizes the writer's strong feelings.]

H 🅗 **Elements of Literature**
Allusion
Thoreau is alluding to the Bible story in which the Lord offers to spare the city of Sodom if ten righteous residents can be found (Genesis 18:26–32).

I 🅘 **Elements of Literature**
Paradox
❓ Why does Thoreau not feel confined in prison? [His body is in prison, but his thoughts and imagination are free—unlike those of his fellow citizens; physical confinement does not worry him.]

J 🅙 **Elements of Literature**
Figurative Language
❓ What is the simile in this sentence? [The simile compares government to "a lone woman with silver spoons."] What does it tell the reader about the government? [The lone woman is scared not of actual thieves, but thieves she imagines; through this comparison, Thoreau emphasizes the government's cowardice and paranoia in the face of his peaceful defiance.]

Using Students' Strengths

Auditory Learners
Read aloud passages of Thoreau's essay or have students listen to the recording in the *Audio CD Library*. Have students explain in their journals why this treatise lends itself to being read aloud.

Logical/Mathematical Learners
Indicate a section of the text, such as Thoreau's critique of majority rule, and have students analyze the kinds of appeals Thoreau uses by category: logical, emotional, or ethical. Which type does he use most? Why do they think he favors it? (You might introduce Taking a Second Look on p. 253 before assigning this activity.)

A **Literary Connections**

Thoreau on John Brown

Thoreau wrote of his admiration for John Brown in his journal. Later, his essay "The Last Days of John Brown" was read at an 1860 service in Brown's memory: "It seemed to me, that John Brown . . . *had not died.* . . . I never hear of any particularly brave and earnest man, but my first thought is of John Brown. . . . I meet him at every turn. He is more alive than ever he was. He has earned immortality. . . . He works in public, and in the clearest light that shines on this land."

A *John Brown Going to His Hanging* (1942) by Horace Pippin. Oil on canvas (24 ⅛″ × 30 ¼″).

Crossing the Curriculum

History

Have students research John Brown. Who was he? What did he accomplish? How did he live up to, or fail to live up to, the ideals Thoreau expresses in this essay? You might start students off by sharing the Literary Connections information above. Why did Thoreau and Pippin admire Brown so much? Students can share what they learn about Brown in small-group discussions.

Fine Arts

Have students locate and view reproductions of Pippin's two other works on Brown—*John Brown Reading His Bible* and *The Trial of John Brown*—and analyze these works as they did the painting here. Ask students to bring the art books to class so that everyone can see the paintings. As an extension, encourage students to visit any museums in your area that have Pippin's works in their collections.

The Pennsylvania Academy of the Fine Arts, Philadelphia, John Lambert Fund (1943.11).

introduced to me by the jailer, as "a first-rate fellow and a clever man." When the door was locked, he showed me where to hang my hat, and how he managed matters there. The rooms were whitewashed once a month; and this one, at least, was the whitest, most simply furnished, and probably the neatest apartment in the town. He naturally wanted to know where I came from, and what brought me there; and, when I had told him, I asked him in my turn how he came there, presuming him to be an honest man, of course; and, as the world goes, I believe he was. "Why," said he, "they accuse me of burning a barn; but I never did it." As near as I could discover, he had probably gone to bed in a barn when drunk, and smoked his pipe there; and so a barn was burnt. He had the reputation of being a clever man, had been there some three months waiting for his trial to come on, and would have to wait as much longer; but he was quite domesticated and contented, since he got his board for nothing, and thought that he was well treated.

He occupied one window, and I the other; and I saw, that, if one stayed there long, his principal business would be to look out the window. I had soon read all the tracts that were left there, and examined where former prisoners had broken out, and where a grate had been sawed off, and heard the history of the various occupants of that room; for I found that even here there was a history and a gossip which never circulated beyond the walls of the jail. Probably this is the only house in the town where verses are composed, which are afterward printed in a circular form, but not published. I was shown quite a long list of verses which were composed by some young men who had been detected in an attempt to escape, who avenged themselves by singing them.

I pumped my fellow prisoner as dry as I could, for fear I should never see him again; but at length he showed me which was my bed, and left me to blow out the lamp.

It was like traveling into a far country, such as I had never expected to behold, to lie there for one night. It seemed to me that I never had heard the town-clock strike before, nor the evening sounds of the village; for we slept with the windows open, which were inside the grating. It was to see my native village in the light of the middle ages, and our Concord was turned into a Rhine stream, and visions of knights and castles passed before me. They were the voices of old burghers that I heard in the streets. I was an involuntary spectator and auditor of whatever was done and said in the kitchen of the adjacent village inn—a wholly new and rare experience to me. It was a closer view of my native town. I was fairly inside of it. I never had seen its institutions before. This is one of its peculiar institutions; for it is a shire town.[5] I began to comprehend what its inhabitants were about.

5. **shire town:** town where a court sits, like a county seat.

HENRY DAVID THOREAU **253**

Taking a Second Look

A Reading Skills and Strategies
Determining Precise Meanings
? Look up the denotation of the word *interfere*. [to meddle or intervene in the concerns of others] What does this word tell about Thoreau's reaction to his tax being paid? [He is annoyed; he feels it was his own business; he might have preferred to remain in jail to prove his point.]

B Critical Thinking
Analyzing
? Why does Thoreau criticize his neighbors so harshly? [He believes they go through their lives without thinking seriously about the morality of their everyday lives. He thinks they blindly follow rules and blindly condemn people like him who disrupt society's status quo. He is angry that his neighbors support the government that jailed him for an act of conscience.]

C Struggling Readers
Identifying the Main Idea
? How would Thoreau define a just government? [Possible response: a government with relatively narrow authority, limited by the consent of the governed.]

D Elements of Literature
Paradox
? How could citizens live "aloof" from government and still fulfill the duties of "neighbors and fellow men"? [Possible answer: People could refuse to pay certain taxes and thus not receive certain governmental benefits—but still be honest, kind, and patriotic citizens.]

In the morning, our breakfasts were put through the hole in the door, in small oblong-square tin pans, made to fit, and holding a pint of chocolate, with brown bread, and an iron spoon. When they called for the vessels again, I was green enough to return what bread I had left; but my comrade seized it, and said that I should lay that up for lunch or dinner. Soon after, he was let out to work at haying in a neighboring field, whither he went every day, and would not be back till noon; so he bade me good day, saying that he doubted if he should see me again.

When I came out of prison—for someone interfered, and paid the tax—I did not perceive that great changes had taken place on the common, such as he observed who went in a youth, and emerged a tottering and gray-headed man; and yet a change had to my eyes come over the scene—the town, and State, and country—greater than any that mere time could effect. I saw yet more distinctly the State in which I lived. I saw to what extent the people among whom I lived could be trusted as good neighbors and friends; that their friendship was for summer weather only; that they did not greatly purpose to do right; that they were a distinct race from me by their prejudices and superstitions, as the Chinamen and Malays are; that, in their sacrifices to humanity, they ran no risks, not even to their property; that, after all, they were not so noble but they treated the thief as he had treated them, and hoped, by a certain outward observance and a few prayers, and by walking in a particular straight though useless path from time to time, to save their souls. This may be to judge my neighbors harshly; for I believe that most of them are not aware that they have such an institution as the jail in their village.

It was formerly the custom in our village, when a poor debtor came out of jail, for his acquaintances to salute him, looking through their fingers, which were crossed to represent the grating of a jail window, "How do ye do?" My neighbors did not thus salute me, but first looked at me, and then at one another, as if I had returned from a long journey. I was put into jail as I was going to the shoemaker's to get a shoe which was mended. When I was let out the next morning, I proceeded to finish my errand, and, having put on my mended shoe, joined a huckleberry party, who were impatient to put themselves under my conduct; and in half an hour—for the horse was soon tackled[6]—was in the midst of a huckleberry field, on one of our highest hills, two miles off; and then the State was nowhere to be seen.

This is the whole history of "My Prisons." . . .

The authority of government, even such as I am willing to submit to—for I will cheerfully obey those who know and can do better than I, and in many things even those who neither know nor can do so well—is still an impure one: To be strictly just, it must have the sanction and consent of the governed. It can have no pure right over my person and property but what I concede to it. The progress from an absolute to a limited monarchy, from a limited monarchy to a democracy, is a progress toward a true respect for the individual. Is a democracy, such as we know it, the last improvement possible in government? Is it not possible to take a step further toward recognizing and organizing the rights of man? There will never be a really free and enlightened State, until the State comes to recognize the individual as a higher and independent power, from which all its own power and authority are derived, and treats him accordingly. I please myself with imagining a State at last which can afford to be just to all men, and to treat the individual with respect as a neighbor; which even would not think it inconsistent with its own repose, if a few were to live aloof from it, not meddling with it, nor embraced by it, who fulfilled all the duties of neighbors and fellow men. A State which bore this kind of fruit, and suffered it to drop off as fast as it ripened, would prepare the way for a still more perfect and glorious State, which also I have imagined, but not yet anywhere seen.

6. **tackled:** harnessed.

> *I please myself with imagining a State at last which can afford to be just to all men, and to treat the individual with respect as a neighbor...*

Assessing Learning

Check Test: Questions and Answers
1. Why is Thoreau freed? [His tax gets paid.]
2. Why does Thoreau criticize his neighbors? [They continue to support the government that pursues policies they know are immoral.]
3. What does Thoreau do when he is released? [He goes to pick up his shoe at the cobbler's and then leads a berry picking expedition.]
4. What is Thoreau's ideal government? [one that recognizes the ultimate authority of the individual conscience]

Professional Notes

Critical Comment:
Emerson on Thoreau

"If I knew only Thoreau, I should think cooperation of good men impossible," Emerson wrote. Yet he admired Thoreau's writing. In 1863, Emerson wrote: "In reading Henry Thoreau's journal, I am very sensible of the vigour of his constitution. That oaken strength which I noted whenever he walked, or worked, or surveyed woodlots, the same unhesitating hand with which a field-labourer accosts a piece of work, which I should shun as a waste of strength, Henry shows in his literary task. He has muscle, and ventures on and performs feats which I am forced to decline. In reading him, I find the same thought, the same spirit that is in me, but he takes a step beyond, and illustrates by excellent images that which I should have conveyed in a sleepy generality." Ask students if they feel Emerson's assessment of Thoreau is accurate.

"A Healthy and Wholesome Man to Know"

On August 31, 1842, the young Thoreau had dinner with Nathaniel Hawthorne (page 296). In his notebooks, Hawthorne gave this description of his guest (whose name he spells "Thorow").

Henry David Thoreau in his traveling outfit, at age 37 (c. 1854). Sketch.

The Bettmann Archive.

Mr. Thorow dined with us yesterday. He is a singular character—a young man with much of wild original nature still remaining in him; and so far as he is sophisticated, it is in a way and method of his own. He is as ugly as sin, long-nosed, queer-mouthed, and with uncouth and somewhat rustic, although courteous manners, corresponding very well with such an exterior. But his ugliness is of an honest and agreeable fashion, and becomes him much better than beauty. He was educated, I believe, at Cambridge, and formerly kept school in this town; but for two or three years back, he has repudiated all regular modes of getting a living, and seems inclined to lead a sort of Indian life. . . . He has been for some time an inmate of Mr. Emerson's family; and, in requital, he labors in the garden, and performs such other offices as may suit him—being entertained by Mr. Emerson for the sake of what true manhood there is in him. Mr. Thorow is a keen and delicate observer of nature—a genuine observer, which, I suspect, is almost as rare a character as even an original poet; and Nature, in return for his love, seems to adopt him as her especial child, and shows him secrets which few others are allowed to witness. He is familiar with beast, fish, fowl, and reptile, and has strange stories to tell of adventures, and friendly passages with these lower brethren of mortality. . . . With all this he has more than a tincture of literature—a deep and true taste for poetry, especially the elder poets. . . . On the whole, I find him a healthy and wholesome man to know.

—Nathaniel Hawthorne

• • • • •

Hawthorne's wife, Sophia, described a skating trio on the Concord River: Emerson, Thoreau, and Hawthorne are on the ice. (In ancient Greece, a *dithyramb* was a wild, emotional hymn. In Greek and Roman myth, Bacchus is the god of wine and merrymaking.)

One afternoon, Mr. Emerson and Mr. Thoreau went with him [Hawthorne] down the river. Henry Thoreau is an experienced skater, and was figuring dithyrambic dances and Bacchic leaps on the ice—very remarkable, but very ugly, methought. Next him followed Mr. Hawthorne who, wrapped in his cloak, moved like a self-impelled Greek statue, stately and grave. Mr. Emerson closed the line, evidently too weary to hold himself erect, pitching head-foremost, half lying on the air.

—Sophia Peabody Hawthorne

HENRY DAVID THOREAU **255**

Primary Sources

These two primary sources provide impressions of Thoreau from the Hawthorne family, who knew him as an acquaintance and friend of Emerson's. Both sources paint a portrait of Thoreau that is both admirable and comic, emphasizing his unique strength of character and relation to nature, as well as a certain un-self-conscious eccentricity.

A Background

The Concord Intellectuals
Only seven weeks before this dinner with Thoreau, Hawthorne had married Sophia Peabody of Salem, Massachusetts. The Bronson Alcotts, the Emersons, and Margaret Fuller were other visitors in the first weeks of the Hawthornes' residency at the Old Manse. Although they were warmly welcomed, the Hawthornes had interests that were somewhat different from those of the Transcendentalists, and they did not form deep friendships with their philosophical neighbors.

B Background

Second Thoughts
After knowing Thoreau for a while, Hawthorne found the "healthy and wholesome man" increasingly irritating. "He is the most unmalleable fellow alive," Hawthorne complained to a friend, "the most tedious, tiresome, and intolerable—the narrowest and most notional, and yet, true as all this is, he has great qualities of intellect and character." Hawthorne later wrote to a friend that Thoreau "despises the world, and all that it has to offer, and like other humorists, is an intolerable bore . . . I shall cause it to be known to him that you sat up till two o'clock reading his book; and he will pretend that it is of no consequence, but will never forget it . . . he is not an agreeable person, and in his presence one feels ashamed of having any money, or a house to live in, or so much as two coats to wear, or having written a book that the public will read—his own mode of life being so unsparing a criticism on all other modes, such as the world approves."

Professional Notes

**Primary Sources:
Haughty Henry**

After four and a half years of correspondence with Daniel Ricketson, Thoreau abruptly stopped writing—and offered the following chilly explanation after a year and a half of silence. "Why will you waste so many regards on me, and not know what to think of my silence? Infer from it what you might from the silence of a dense pine wood. . . . My silence is just as inhuman as that, and no more. You know that I never promised to correspond with you, and so, when I do, I do more than I promised. . . . Life is short, and there are other things also to be done. I admit that you are more social than I am, and far more attentive to 'the common courtesies of life,' but this is partly for the reason that you have fewer or less exacting private pursuits." Ask students what this letter indicates about Thoreau's personality.

Connections

In this famous open letter, King articulates the ethical and religious foundation of his theory of civil disobedience. He draws a distinction between just laws, which uphold the moral law of God, and those that violate it—such as the segregationist policies of the Alabama legislature. Such laws should not be defied or evaded for selfish reasons, but broken openly, with a willingness to pay the penalty for one's conscience. This, King concludes, is a moral act that upholds the highest principles of law itself.

Background

King was in Birmingham to lead a boycott of discriminatory stores. The goals of the boycott were to desegregate store facilities and establish fair hiring practices. On April 12, King defied an injunction against marching and led fifty protesters in a peaceful march toward City Hall. Four blocks into the march, he was arrested.

Ⓐ Critical Thinking
Extending the Text
Ask students to give examples of current laws they consider just and unjust. [Answers will be varied and controversial, ranging from local curfew laws to gun-control legislation. Be sure to encourage lively but respectful debate.]

Ⓑ Reading Skills and Strategies
Recognizing Persuasive Techniques
❓ What persuasive techniques does King use here? [logic, in his example concerning Alabama's laws; anecdote, in his account of his arrest for marching without a parade permit]

Ⓒ Reading Skills and Strategies
Recognizing Modes of Persuasion
❓ Does King's final sentence appeal to the reader's reason, emotions, or morals? [Such an appeal to conscience is an ethical or moral argument.]

Ⓓ Reading Skills and Strategies
Determining Precise Meaning
❓ In what two senses does King use the word *law* in this sentence? [The first use refers to actual laws enacted by governmental bodies. The second refers to law as a principle, an embodiment of justice and the good of society.]

T256

Connections — A LETTER

The Reverend Dr. Martin Luther King, Jr., was a leader of the U.S. civil rights movement in the 1960s. He wrote this open letter on April 16, 1963, while serving a sentence for participating in a civil rights demonstration.

from Letter from Birmingham City Jail
Martin Luther King, Jr.

You express a great deal of anxiety over our willingness to break laws. This is certainly a legitimate concern. Since we so diligently urge people to obey the Supreme Court's decision of 1954 outlawing segregation in the public schools, it is rather strange and paradoxical to find us consciously breaking laws. One may well ask, "How can you advocate breaking some laws and obeying others?" The answer is found in the fact that there are two types of laws: there are *just* and there are *unjust* laws. I would agree with Saint Augustine that "An unjust law is no law at all."

Now what is the difference between the two? How does one determine when a law is just or unjust? A just law is a man-made code that squares with the moral law or the law of God. An unjust law is a code that is out of harmony with the moral law. . . .

An unjust law is a code inflicted upon a minority which that minority had no part in enacting or creating because they did not have the unhampered right to vote. Who can say that the legislature of Alabama which set up the segregation laws was democratically elected? Throughout the state of Alabama all types of conniving methods are used to prevent Negroes from becoming registered voters and there are some counties without a single Negro registered to vote despite the fact that the Negro constitutes a majority of the population. Can any law set up in such a state be considered democratically structured?

These are just a few examples of unjust and just laws. There are some instances when a law is just on its face and unjust in its application. For instance, I was arrested Friday on a charge of parading without a permit. Now there is nothing wrong with an ordinance which requires a permit for a parade, but when the ordinance is used to preserve segregation and to deny citizens the First Amendment privilege of peaceful assembly and peaceful protest, then it becomes unjust.

I hope you can see the distinction I am trying to point out. In no sense do I advocate evading or defying the law as the rabid segregationist would do. This would lead to anarchy. One who breaks an unjust law must do it *openly, lovingly* (not hatefully as the white mothers did in New Orleans when they were seen on television screaming, "nigger, nigger, nigger"), and with a willingness to accept the penalty. I submit that an individual who breaks a law that conscience tells him is unjust, and willingly accepts the penalty by staying in jail to arouse the conscience of the community over its injustice, is in reality expressing the very highest respect for law.

Martin Luther King, Jr., being booked at a police station.
Charles Moore/Black Star.

Making the Connections

Connecting to the Theme:
"The Life Worth Living"
After students have finished reading the essay, discuss the collection theme. What makes life worth living for Thoreau? Why does he believe his neighbors are not living fully and justly? Would life be worth living if everyone behaved like Thoreau? Which of Thoreau's qualities do students admire? Which would they not want to emulate?

Connecting with
"Resistance to Civil Government"
Have students consider the differences between Thoreau and King's definitions of civil disobedience. How do the two men think and act alike? How do the two men think and act differently? Have students share outside knowledge they have of both Thoreau and King. Which of the two do students think lived the more worthy life? Why?

First Thoughts

1. Would you have spent the night in jail as Thoreau did? Explain.
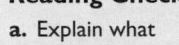

Shaping Interpretations

2. Explain the truth in each of these **paradoxes**.
   a. "I saw that, if there was a wall of stone between me and my townsmen, there was a still more difficult one to climb or break through, before they could get to be as free as I was." (page 251)
   b. "I felt as if I alone of all my townsmen had paid my tax." (page 251)
3. How are Thoreau's perceptions of his fellow citizens changed by his night in jail?
4. What idea is Thoreau stressing in telling us about getting his shoe fixed and leading the huckleberry party on the day he was released?
5. From what you know about American Romanticism (pages 138–150), would you say that Thoreau's assumptions and points in this essay are fundamentally Romantic? Explain.
6. What influences of Emerson's thought can you find in "Resistance to Civil Government"?

Connecting with the Text

7. Review your Quickwrite notes about civil disobedience. Which of Thoreau's arguments did you find convincing, and

Reading Check

a. Explain what Thoreau thinks is wrong with majority rule. What does he say is the only obligation he has a right to assume?
b. What does Thoreau predict about slavery in America?
c. Explain why Thoreau was put in jail. What were his feelings about the government when he was in jail?
d. At the end of the essay, what qualities does Thoreau envision in an ideal "perfect and glorious State"?

which did you disagree with? Could there be civil order if each person always followed his or her own conscience? Explain.

Extending the Text

8. Comment on how Thoreau's main points in this essay relate to the points Martin Luther King, Jr., makes in *Connections* on page 256. How do Thoreau's and Dr. King's views relate to American life today?

Challenging the Text

9. Imagine that someone has made the following observation: "When Thoreau let someone pay the tax for him, he betrayed his own principles. He became just like the people he criticized, who opposed the Mexican War but supported it with their tax money. If he had wanted to make a truly courageous and effective protest, he should have insisted on staying in jail." Do you agree with this statement? Why or why not?

READING SKILLS AND STRATEGIES

Determining the Precise Meanings of Words

1. "After the first blush of sin," writes Thoreau on page 251, "comes its indifference and from immoral it becomes, as it were, *unmoral* . . ."
   a. The word *indifference* can mean "neutrality" or "apathy." What is the difference between the two meanings? Which meaning does the word have here?
   b. How is *unmoral* different from *immoral*?

2. Thoreau was arrested because he did not pay "poll tax."
   a. The word *poll* comes from a Middle English word for "top of the head." Usage has added other meanings, including the sense of "individual" ("one head"). What do you think a "poll tax" is?
   b. What do the words *poll, pollster,* and *poll booth* mean today? How are they related to the sense of "head"?

Reading Check

a. It does not represent everyone's conscience; to do what he or she thinks right.
b. It will begin to erode when people are arrested for protesting it.
c. He refused to pay his poll tax. He lost respect for government.
d. The state recognizes the individual's authority and accepts the principled protests of nonconformists.

READING SKILLS AND STRATEGIES

1a. *Neutrality* implies a refusal to take sides. *Apathy* implies a lack of interest. Here, *indifference* means "moral apathy."
   b. *Unmoral* means that morality does not apply. *Immoral* means "corrupt."
2a. It is a tax on each voter
   b. A pollster takes people's "votes" in a non-electoral survey (a poll). A poll booth is where a person votes. Each involves a person's opinion or state of mind (head).

First Thoughts [Respond]

1. Yes, one should live according to one's beliefs. No, one night in jail accomplishes nothing.

Shaping Interpretations [Interpret]

2a. The townspeople are imprisoned by conformity. Thoreau is free even when he is in jail because he lives according to his own principles.
  b. By following his conscience and trying to improve the moral condition of his society, he feels he has figuratively paid his tax.
3. He sees that he has little in common with them because they do not act on their principles.
4. His point is that being jailed for one's conscience can be a normal part of life's duties and pleasures.
5. Like the Romantics, Thoreau believes in the importance of being true to oneself.
6. Thoreau heeds Emerson's call to "Trust thyself." Thoreau puts into practice and radicalizes Emerson's ideas of self-reliance, integrity, and shaping one's own destiny.

Connecting with the Text [Evaluate]

7. Many students will probably admire Thoreau's idea of fighting injustice through civil disobedience. Some students may feel that civil order would break down if each person followed his or her own conscience without respect for law and convention.

Extending the Text [Synthesize]

8. Thoreau and King agree that majority rule can be unjust; that individuals should do what they think is right and take responsibility for their actions; and that being jailed for a principle shows the highest kind of civic pride and patriotism.

Challenging the Text [Evaluate]

9. Possible answers: No, staying in jail would have accomplished nothing; yes, acceptance of that "interference" was a selfish compromise.

CHOICES: Building Your Portfolio

1. **Writer's Notebook** Point out that Thoreau writes from a personal and subjective viewpoint. Have students consider whether this is the best way to argue their controversial issue.

2. **Supporting a Position** Students should consider what they know about their local, state, and federal governments. How effective are they? Do they govern "not at all" or too much?

3. **Comparing Texts** Remind students that Thoreau, like most educated Americans of his day, was familiar with the text of the Declaration. He may have thought about or recalled it while he wrote his essay.

4. **Creative Writing/Drama** Encourage students to use their imagination; any number of characters might "visit" Thoreau in his thoughts. Students may want to collaborate on writing, directing, and performing their plays.

5. **Crossing the Curriculum: Social Studies** If several students are interested in researching the same person, encourage them to work together. Students may want to interview family members who lived through the civil rights movement or talk to history teachers about their projects.

CHOICES: Building Your Portfolio

Writer's Notebook
1. Collecting Ideas for Writing About a Controversial Issue

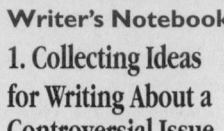

If you have already brainstormed a list of possible topics for an essay about a controversial issue and written questions about them, it's time to focus on the issue you want to write about and define it so that it can be argued effectively. At the top of a page, write your issue. Then, write your ideas defining the issue and clarifying your position on it. Save your notes for possible use in the Writer's Workshop on page 331.

Supporting a Position
2. Taking a Stand

Write a brief essay either in support of or in opposition to this statement from "Resistance to Civil Government": "That government is best which governs not at all." Include at least two emotional appeals in your essay.

Comparing Texts
3. Declarations of Independence

In a brief essay, compare and contrast Thoreau's ideas in his essay with the ideas in the Declaration of Independence (page 117). Cite specific passages from both documents to support your views.

Creative Writing/Drama
4. Thoreau's Night in Jail

Write and perform a one-scene play called "Thoreau's Night in Jail." Keep all the action within the setting of the Concord jail. In addition to Thoreau, you may want to use his jailer and his fellow prisoner as characters; feel free to add other characters, either real or fictional.

Crossing the Curriculum: Social Studies
5. Resisters All

Prepare and present a brief research report on some aspect of the history of nonviolent resistance or civil disobedience. You might focus on an event or movement, or report on a figure like Mohandas K. Gandhi, Martin Luther King, Jr., Cesar Chavez, Leo Tolstoy, Rosa Parks, Lech Walesa, Daw Aung San Suu Kyi, or Nelson Mandela.

Nelson Mandela, who became president of South Africa in 1994 after spending many years imprisoned for his political views.

AP/Wide World Photos.

Getting Students Involved

Cooperative Learning
Meeting of the Minds. Have two students stage a discussion of civil disobedience between King and Thoreau, in which the two men discuss how to end slavery in Thoreau's time and segregation in King's. Encourage students to consider how each man might have reacted to the social issues of the other man's century. Students can either prepare written scripts or present them as one-act plays.

The Realms of Darkness

Theme

On Every Visage a Black Veil *The Romantics' other side is epitomized in the writings of Edgar Allan Poe, Nathaniel Hawthorne, and Herman Melville. The Puritans' legacy of introspection and their conviction that a palpable evil inhabits the world is revealed in the great works of these three Americans.*

Reading the Anthology

Reaching Struggling Readers

The *Reading Skills and Strategies: Reaching Struggling Readers* binder provides materials coordinated with the Pupil's Edition (see the Collection Planner, p. T258B) to help students who have difficulty reading and comprehending text, or students who are reluctant readers. The binder for eleventh grade is organized around ten individual skill areas and offers the following options:

- **MiniRead** MiniReads are short, easy texts that give students a chance to practice a particular skill and strategy before reading selections in the Pupil's Edition. Each MiniRead Skill Lesson can be taught independently or used in conjunction with a Selection Skill Lesson.

- **Selection Skill Lessons** Selection Skill Lessons allow students to apply skills introduced in the MiniReads. Each Selection Skill Lesson provides reading instruction and practice specific to a particular piece of literature in the Pupil's Edition.

Reading Beyond the Anthology

Read On

At the end of the American Renaissance collections, the grade eleven book includes a Read On, an annotated bibliography of books suitable for extended reading. To preview the Read On for the American Renaissance period, please turn to p. T330.

HRW Library

The *HRW Library* offers novels, plays, and short-story collections for extended reading. Each book in the Library includes one or more major works and thematically related Connections. A Study Guide provides teaching suggestions and worksheets. For Collection 6, the following titles are recommended.

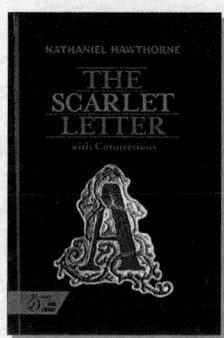

THE SCARLET LETTER
Nathaniel Hawthorne
Hawthorne's great novel is about hypocrisy that leads to public shame and death, and heroic endurance that leads to spiritual freedom.

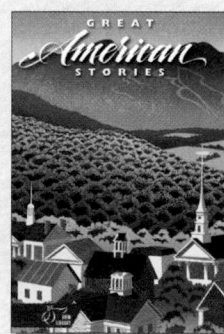

GREAT AMERICAN STORIES
This collection includes stories by Hawthorne and Poe which can be used to extend your study of these major American writers.

Collection Planner

Collection 6 The Realms of Darkness

Resources for this Collection

Note: All resources for this collection are available for preview on the *One-Stop Planner CD-ROM 1 with Test Generator.* All worksheets and blackline masters may be printed from the CD-ROM.

Internet Resources
go.hrw.com LE0 11-6

Selection or Feature	Reading and Literary Skills	Vocabulary, Language, and Grammar
The Fall of the House of Usher (p. 262) Edgar Allan Poe **Connections: The Fall of the House of Usher** (p. 279) Reed Whittemore	• *Graphic Organizers for Active Reading,* Worksheet p. 22 • *Literary Elements:* Transparency 9 Worksheet p. 28	• *Words to Own,* Worksheet p. 19 • *Grammar and Language Links:* Participles and Participle Phrases, Worksheet p. 27 • *Language Workshop CD-ROM,* Verbals and Verbal Phrases • *Daily Oral Grammar,* Transparency 20
The Raven (p. 282) Edgar Allan Poe **Primary Sources: Poe's Process: Writing "The Raven"** (p. 287) Edgar Allan Poe	• *Graphic Organizers for Active Reading,* Worksheet p. 23 • *Literary Elements:* Transparency 10 Worksheet p. 31 • *Literary Elements:* Poetry Transparencies 1–5 Teaching Notes, p. 111	• *Daily Oral Grammar,* Transparency 21
Literature of the Americas: Argentina **House Taken Over** (p. 290) Julio Cortázar *translated by* Paul Blackburn	The Literature of the Americas feature offers selections from a variety of American cultures representing North, Central, and South America. These selections connect to the collection theme, and students explore the thematic links through structured group discussions called Finding Common Ground.	
The Minister's Black Veil (p. 298) Nathaniel Hawthorne	• *Graphic Organizers for Active Reading,* Worksheet p. 24 • *Literary Elements:* Transparency 11 Worksheet p. 34	• *Words to Own,* Worksheet p. 20 • *Grammar and Language Links:* Common Usage Problems, Worksheet p. 29 • *Language Workshop CD-ROM,* Common Usage Problems • *Daily Oral Grammar,* Transparency 22
from **Moby-Dick** (p. 313) Herman Melville	• *Reading Skills and Strategies: Reaching Struggling Readers* • MiniRead Skill Lesson, p. 113 • Selection Skill Lesson, p. 119 • *Graphic Organizers for Active Reading,* Worksheet p. 25	• *Words to Own,* Worksheet p. 21 • *Daily Oral Grammar,* Transparency 23
Writer's Workshop: Controversial Issue (p. 331)		
Language Workshop: Parallel Structure (p. 337)		• *Workshop Resources,* p. 51 • *Language Workshop CD-ROM,* Parallel Structure
Learning for Life: A Model of Self-Reliance (p. 339)		

Other Resources for this Collection

- *Cross-Curricular Activities*, p. 6
- *Portfolio Management System*, Introduction to Portfolio Assessment, p. 1
- *Formal Assessment:* Literary Period Test, p. 69; Literary Elements Test, p. 67

- *Test Generator*, Collection Test

Writing	Listening and Speaking Viewing and Representing	Assessment
• *Portfolio Management System*, Rubrics for Choices, p. 122	• *Audio CD Library*, Disc 8, Track 2 • *Viewing and Representing:* Fine Art Transparency 6 Worksheet p. 24 • *Portfolio Management System*, Rubrics for Choices, p. 122	• *Formal Assessment*, Selection Test, p. 57 • *Test Generator (One-Stop Planner CD-ROM)* • *Preparation for College Admission Exams*, p. 21
• *Portfolio Management System*, Rubrics for Choices, p. 124	• *Audio CD Library*, Disc 8, Track 3 • *Portfolio Management System*, Rubrics for Choices, p. 124	• *Formal Assessment*, Selection Test, p. 59 • *Test Generator (One-Stop Planner CD-ROM)*
	• *Audio CD Library*, Disc 9, Track 2	
• *Portfolio Management System*, Rubrics for Choices, p. 125	• *Audio CD Library*, Disc 9, Track 3 • *Portfolio Management System*, Rubrics for Choices, p. 125	• *Formal Assessment*, Selection Test, p. 61 • *Test Generator (One-Stop Planner CD-ROM)* • *Preparation for College Admission Exams*, p. 23
• *Portfolio Management System*, Rubrics for Choices, p. 127	• *Audio CD Library*, Disc 9, Track 4 • *Portfolio Management System*, Rubrics for Choices, p. 127	• *Formal Assessment*, Selection Tests, pp. 63, 65 • *Test Generator (One-Stop Planner CD-ROM)*

• *Workshop Resources*, p. 11
 • *Writer's Workshop 2 CD-ROM*, Controversial Issue
	• *Viewing and Representing*, HRW Multimedia Presentation Maker	• *Portfolio Management System*
		  • Prewriting, p. 129
		  • Peer Editing, p. 130
		  • Assessment Rubric, p. 131

		• *Portfolio Management System*, Rubrics, p. 132

 Transparency    CD-ROM    Video    Audio CD

Skills Focus

Skills Focus

Selection or Feature	Reading Skills and Strategies	Elements of Literature and Language	Writing	Listening and Speaking	Viewing and Representing
The Fall of the House of Usher (p. 262) Edgar Allan Poe	Using Resources, pp. 262, 281 Make Predictions, p. 262 Identify the Main Events, p. 280 Support an Inference, p. 280 Connotations and Denotations, p. 281 Loaded Words, p. 281	Allusions, p. 262 Atmosphere, pp. 262, 280–281 Chronological Order, p. 280 Point of View, p. 280 Allegory, pp. 280, 281 Symbols, p. 280	Develop Emotional Appeals to Support a Position, p. 281 Defend a Literary Interpretation, p. 281 Retell the Story in Another Genre, p. 281	Select Music to Evoke an Atmosphere, p. 281 Discuss Reading Strategies, p. 281	Create an Image of the House of Usher, p. 281
The Raven (p. 282) Edgar Allan Poe	Analyze the Melodies of Language, pp. 282, 288	Sound Effects, pp. 282, 288–289 Atmosphere, p. 288 Images, p. 288 Symbol, p. 288 Internal Rhyme, p. 288 Refrain, p. 288 Rhyme Scheme, pp. 288–289 Alliteration, p. 288 Onomatopoeia, p. 288	Develop Details to Support a Persuasive Argument, p. 289 Interpret an Idea, p. 289 Write a Parody, p. 289		Make a Collage Portrait, p. 289
Literature of the Americas: Argentina **House Taken Over** (p. 290) Julio Cortázar *translated by* Paul Blackburn	Use Questions to Develop Understanding of a Text, pp. 290, 295	The Literature of the Americas feature offers selections from a variety of American cultures representing North, Central, and South America. These selections connect to the collection theme, and students explore the thematic links through structured group discussions called Finding Common Ground.			
The Minister's Black Veil (p. 298) Nathaniel Hawthorne	Draw Inferences, p. 298 Make Predictions, pp. 298, 308 Understand Archaisms, p. 308 Use Context Clues, p. 308	Symbol, pp. 298, 308 Theme, pp. 298, 308 Character, p. 308 Tone, p. 308 Connotative Words, p. 308 Atmosphere, p. 308 Parable, p. 308	Develop Topics for Writing, p. 309 Write an Essay Comparing and Contrasting Authors' Points of View, p. 309 Write an Autobiographical Sketch of a Character from the First-Person Point of View, p. 309 Write an Essay Interpreting the Story, p. 309	Participate in and Report on a Group Discussion, p. 309 Prepare and Perform a Reader's-Theater Version of the Story, p. 309	
Reading Skills and Strategies: Tracing the Origins of Words (p. 310)	Use Etymologies, p. 310				Use a Chart to Record Etymologies, p. 310
from **Moby-Dick** (p. 313) Herman Melville	Draw Inferences About Character, pp. 313, 328 Identify Major Events, p. 328	Characterization, pp. 313, 328 Image, p. 328 Epic, p. 328 Point of View, p. 329	Write an Essay Interpreting the Meaning of a Symbol, p. 329 Write an Essay Comparing Ideas, p. 329 Write from a Character's Point of View, p. 329	Take Part in a Panel Discussion, p. 329 Research and Present an Oral Report, p. 329	Select and Prepare Graphics to Accompany an Oral Report, p. 329
Writer's Workshop: Controversial Issue (p. 331)		Logical and Emotional Appeals, p. 334	Write an Essay Taking a Stand on a Controversial Issue, pp. 331–336		
Language Workshop: Parallel Structure (p. 337)		Parallel Structure, p. 337 Correlative Conjunctions, p. 337	Revise Sentences to Correct Lapses in Parallelism, p. 337		
Reading for Life: Evaluating Credibility of Sources (p. 338)	Evaluate Credibility, p. 338		Research and Report on Print and Electronic Sources, p. 338		
Learning for Life: A Model of Self-Reliance (p. 339)			Write an Encyclopedia Entry, p. 339 Write a Short Story, p. 339		Create a Brochure, p. 339

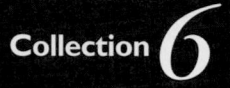

THE REALMS OF DARKNESS

Poe

Cortázar

Hawthorne

Melville

If you cannot bear the silence and the darkness, do not go there; if you dislike black night and yawning chasms, never make them your profession. If you fear the sound of water hurrying through crevices toward un- known and mysterious destina- tions, do not consider it. Seek out the sunshine. It is a simple prescription. Avoid the darkness.

It is a simple prescription, but you will not follow it. You will turn immediately to the darkness. You will be drawn to it by cords of fear and of longing. You will imagine that you are tired of the sun- light; the waters that unnerve you will tug in the ancient recesses of your mind; the midnight will seem rest- ful—you will end by going down.

—Loren Eiseley,
from The Night Country

The Granger Collection, New York.

OBJECTIVES

1. Read literature of the Ameri- can Renaissance on the theme "The Realms of Darkness"
2. Interpret literary elements used in the literature with spe- cial emphasis on symbols and sound effects
3. Apply a variety of reading strat- egies, particularly researching word origins
4. Respond to the literature in a variety of modes
5. Learn and use new words

Responding to the Quotation

Read the passage aloud and ask stu- dents to respond to it from their own experience. Prompt discussion with questions such as "Is it really simple to 'avoid the darkness'?" "Is it really inev- itable to be drawn toward darkness?" Then, ask students what predictions they can make about the selections in this collection based on this passage from *The Night Country*. [Possible response: The selections will be filled with fear, suspense, and darkness.]

Resources

Viewing and Representing
Videocassette B, Segment 8
Available in English and Spanish. This segment traces the progression of American Gothic fiction from Poe to the modern Southern Gothic. For full lesson plans and worksheets, see the *Visual Connections Teacher's Manual*.

Writing Focus: Controversial Issue

The following **Work in Progress** assignments in this collection build to a culminating **Writer's Workshop** at the end of Collection 6.

- The Fall of the House of Usher — List emotional appeals to support controversial issue (p. 281)
- The Raven — Use imagery and repetition to support position (p. 289)
- The Minister's Black Veil — Take notes on controversial topics (p. 309)
- Moby-Dick — Pick a passage to use in a persuasive essay (p. 329)

Writer's Workshop: Persuasive Writing / Controversial Issue (p. 331)

Edgar Allan Poe

(1809–1849)

Edgar Allan Poe.

"The want of parental affection," wrote Poe, "has been the heaviest of my trials." Edgar Poe was, indeed, most unfortunate in his parents. His father, David Poe, was a mediocre traveling actor who drank heavily. His mother, Elizabeth Arnold, was a talented actress who was deserted by her husband when Edgar was still a baby. She died on tour in Richmond, Virginia, leaving Edgar virtually an orphan before his third birthday.

The boy was taken in by John and Frances Allan, a charitable and childless couple in Richmond. John Allan, an ambitious and self-righteous merchant, became Edgar's guardian (and the source of the writer's middle name). He provided generously for Edgar's early education, but he never formally adopted the boy.

Although Frances Allan was kind to Edgar, the boy grew up feeling both the lack of a natural father and the disapproval of his foster father. John Allan made no secret of his disappointment in Edgar—in his idleness, in his indifference to business life, and in his literary ambitions. Surely Allan's criticism added to Edgar's growing moodiness.

Breaking Away

At seventeen, Edgar entered the University of Virginia. He did well in his studies but was resentful of the meager allowance Allan gave him. When he tried to earn extra money by gambling, he went deep into debt. On discovering this, Allan refused to help his foster son and instead withdrew him from college.

After an especially bitter quarrel with Allan, Poe ran off to Boston to make his own way in the world. There, in 1827, he published a small volume of poems, *Tamerlane.* The book did not attract much attention, and Poe could find no other work. In despair, he joined the army. He was promoted to the rank of sergeant major, but he disliked the enlisted man's life and appealed to Allan for help. At the request of his wife, who was dying, Allan interceded for Edgar

(for the last time) and agreed to help him enter the U.S. Military Academy at West Point. Poe's motive in going to the Academy was probably to please his foster father.

While waiting to get into the Academy, Poe published a second book of poems, *El Aaraaf,* in 1829 and received his first real recognition as a writer. The next year, while at West Point, Poe learned that Allan (now a widower) had remarried and that the woman was young enough to have children. Since this appeared to end all hope of becoming Allan's heir, Poe had himself dismissed from West Point.

Exploring the Darkness and the Depths

Poe moved in with an aunt, Maria Poe Clemm, in Baltimore, Maryland. In 1835, he married her thirteen-year-old daughter, Virginia. The difference in their ages and Virginia's poor health resulted in a very odd marriage. But need and a strong sense of family drew the three housemates together.

Poe supported his family by working as an editor at various magazines. He wrote when he could find the time, completing his only full-length novel, *The Narrative of Arthur Gordon Pym,* several years after his marriage. But it was his short stories that had the greatest effect on other writers.

go.hrw.com
LEO 11-6

In "The Gold Bug," and in the tales built around the intuitive sleuth C. Auguste Dupin, "The Purloined Letter" and "The Murders in the Rue Morgue," Poe laid the foundations for the modern detective story. In fact, he inspired Sir Arthur Conan Doyle to create Sherlock Holmes. In tales such as "The Tell-Tale Heart" and "The Cask of Amontillado," Poe inspired the Russian novelist Feodor Dostoevski (1821–1881) to explore the criminal mind.

Poe was a master of the psychological thriller. His tales of the ghastly and the grotesque are peopled with distraught narrators, deranged heroes, and doomed heroines. Yet his purpose in creating such characters was not to present readers with convincing likenesses of human beings—nor merely to shock and frighten. Instead, Poe wanted to take us behind the curtain that separates the everyday from the incredible. He wanted to leave behind the sunlit, tangible, rational world and discover the unsettling truth that lies in the dark, irrational depths of the human mind.

Small Triumphs and Great Tragedy

Poe produced a considerable body of work in spite of humiliating poverty and a serious drinking problem. The slightest amount of alcohol made him senseless; yet he drank to escape a reality he found agonizing. Publication of his poem "The Raven" in 1845 brought him some fame at last, but financial security still eluded him.

When Virginia died of tuberculosis in 1847, Poe and "Muddy" (Virginia's mother) were left alone. Poe grew more unstable and contracted illnesses, including a brain lesion that would leave him little time to live. But he pursued romance relentlessly, always looking for someone to "adopt" him. In 1849, during a visit to Virginia to a woman he hoped to marry, Poe disappeared. A week later, he was found in a Baltimore tavern—delirious, his clothing torn and wet from a raging storm. He regained enough consciousness to pray "Lord help my poor soul" before he died four days later. It was a tragic yet strangely appropriate end to the tortured life of a man obsessed by loss and death.

LITERATURE AND POPULAR CULTURE

Poe the Pop Icon

Can you guess what Edgar Allan Poe has in common with Elvis Presley, Marilyn Monroe, the Beatles, Michael Jordan, and the cast of *Star Trek*? Like all of the above, Poe is a legend of popular culture. Consider these facts:

- Poe's works have been translated into virtually every language.

- Such popular writers as Stephen King and Ray Bradbury point to Poe as their literary forefather.

- The Mystery Writers of America annually honors great achievements in mystery writing with the "Edgar"—the equivalent of an Oscar or an Emmy.

- Poe has been immortalized in the popular arts, on everything from posters, buttons, and coffee mugs to bumper stickers and T-shirts.

- Poe has been "ushered" into twentieth-century pop culture through dozens of film adaptations, including *The Masque of the Red Death, The Black Cat, The Tomb of Ligeia,* and *The Pit and the Pendulum.*

Keep your eye out for Poe. He may be closer than you think.

Vincent Price in *The Masque of the Red Death.*

Movie Still Archives.

Professional Notes

Critical Comment: The Gothic Novel

Anyone who hears an unexplained sound in the night has felt the prickly sensation of fear. Fear—bone-chilling, palm-sweating fear—is what the Gothic novel is all about. The Gothic novel, which emerged in England in the late eighteenth century, adopted the setting of the medieval Gothic castle, with its pointed arches and vaults, dark dungeons, sliding doors, subterranean passages, and rook-filled turrets, and used it to evoke fear. The term *Gothic novel* was later expanded to include any fiction that created a haunting atmosphere and included strange and macabre events, such as live burials, horrifying tortures, mesmerism (hypnotism), and resurrection of corpses. In America, Edgar Allan Poe was the master of the Gothic novel. Although he was criticized for using Gothic devices that were already clichéd by the 1830s, Poe used them as symbolic devices to make readers think about his real subject—the workings of the human mind.

Summary ■■■

In this suspenseful Gothic thriller, Poe explores the realms of darkness within the human mind. As the story opens, the narrator finds himself outside the decaying House of Usher, the ancestral home of his boyhood friend, Roderick Usher, who has sent him a desperate letter. The Ushers are an ancient and aristocratic family, now reduced to Roderick and his twin sister Madeline. Inside Usher's studio, the narrator finds Roderick in physical decline and agitated about his sister's cataleptic illness. The narrator makes futile efforts to relieve Roderick's distress by reading, painting, and playing music with him. But his condition only worsens, especially after the apparent death of his sister. Roderick and the narrator lock Madeline's body in a vault deep in the mansion, prior to final interment. For days, Usher's nerves continue to fray as he is terrified by sounds only he can hear. One night, during a violent storm, an emaciated, bloodied Madeline lurches into the room, falls on her brother, and dies. Realizing that what he has feared is true—he has buried his sister alive—Usher, too, dies in shock. As the narrator flees the dark realm of the Usher mansion, the house collapses in on itself.

Before You Read
THE FALL OF THE HOUSE OF USHER

Make the Connection
The Furnishings of Our Nightmares

Why do we watch movies like *Dracula, Psycho,* and *Jurassic Park?* Why do we make best-sellers of books by authors like Stephen King and Anne Rice?

In everyday life, we all feel fright from time to time: We tremble, sweat, get tense. Maybe those responses are designed to send us flying from danger to a less threatening place. Perhaps it's the need to periodically re-hearse those feelings in a safe place that draws us to those scary movies and terrifying tales. Although we each have different furnishings for our nightmares, we all respond in similar ways to images of crumbling houses, reeking swamps, lonely moors, and characters who are sick in mind and body, who speak little and never hum or whistle.

Reading Skills and Strategies

Using Resources

Poe's story, perhaps the most famous horror story in American literature, is written in the ornate style favored in the 1800s. If you have difficulty reading the story, you can use various strate-gies and resources:

- If a sentence is very complicat-ed, look for its **main subject and verb.** Then, look for words that the phrases modify.
- If you don't understand Poe's **allusions,** use the footnotes.
- If an unfamiliar word is not defined in a footnote, try the

glossary at the back of the book. Or use **context clues** to guess at the word's meaning and so continue with the story.
- Use the **question boxes** in the margins of the story. These questions will help you sum up important sections or note the **main ideas** of key passages.
- Make **predictions** and modify them as you read. It is the na-ture of a horror story to make you intensely anxious about what will happen next.

Elements of Literature
Atmosphere

A rotting mansion, mysterious illnesses, strange sounds at night, a person buried alive: Poe uses all of these Gothic details—and more (a list would stretch to the bottom of the page)—to create a single effect, a mood, or **atmos-phere,** of dread and menace. Notice how Poe begins to build his mood in the very first para-graph of this story, with its hissing s sounds and powerful sensory images. It's a good paragraph to read aloud—listen to its sounds and feel its effects. Which words and phrases in this paragraph make you aware that the narrator is leaving one region and entering another, uncertain one?

> **A**tmosphere is the mood or feeling created in a piece of writing.
>
> *For more on Atmosphere, see the Hand-book of Literary Terms.*

Preteaching Vocabulary

Words to Own

Tell students that all the Words to Own except *sojourn, inordinate,* and *pervade* relate to the themes that Poe is exploring in this story: men-tal illness versus health, and appearance versus reality. Based on the definitions of the words and their use in the story, have students catego-rize the words under those themes. Then, have students choose the vocabulary word that fits best in each of the following sentences.

1. Illness made his face [pallid].
2. My [sojourn] in England lasted a week.
3. The poem is juvenile and [insipid].
4. Don't be [obstinate]! Apologize!
5. Hunger left her [emaciated].
6. What is the drug's [potency]?
7. Cheer up! Stop being [morbid]!
8. She fell into a [stupor] and died.
9. We fled when smoke [pervaded] the room.
10. Her [vivacious] smile cheered us all.

11. Give one gift; two are [inordinate].
12. The hero had [prodigious] strength.
13. Her [demeanor] was shy and polite.
14. Your logic is [specious]; try again.
15. My [profuse] thanks for the gift!
16. What [similitude]! The copy is exact!
17. Police are [scrutinizing] every clue.
18. A change is [discernible] if you look.
19. A pulse is a [palpable] sign of life.
20. Don't be [equivocal]; speak plainly.

THE FALL OF THE HOUSE OF USHER

by Edgar Allan Poe

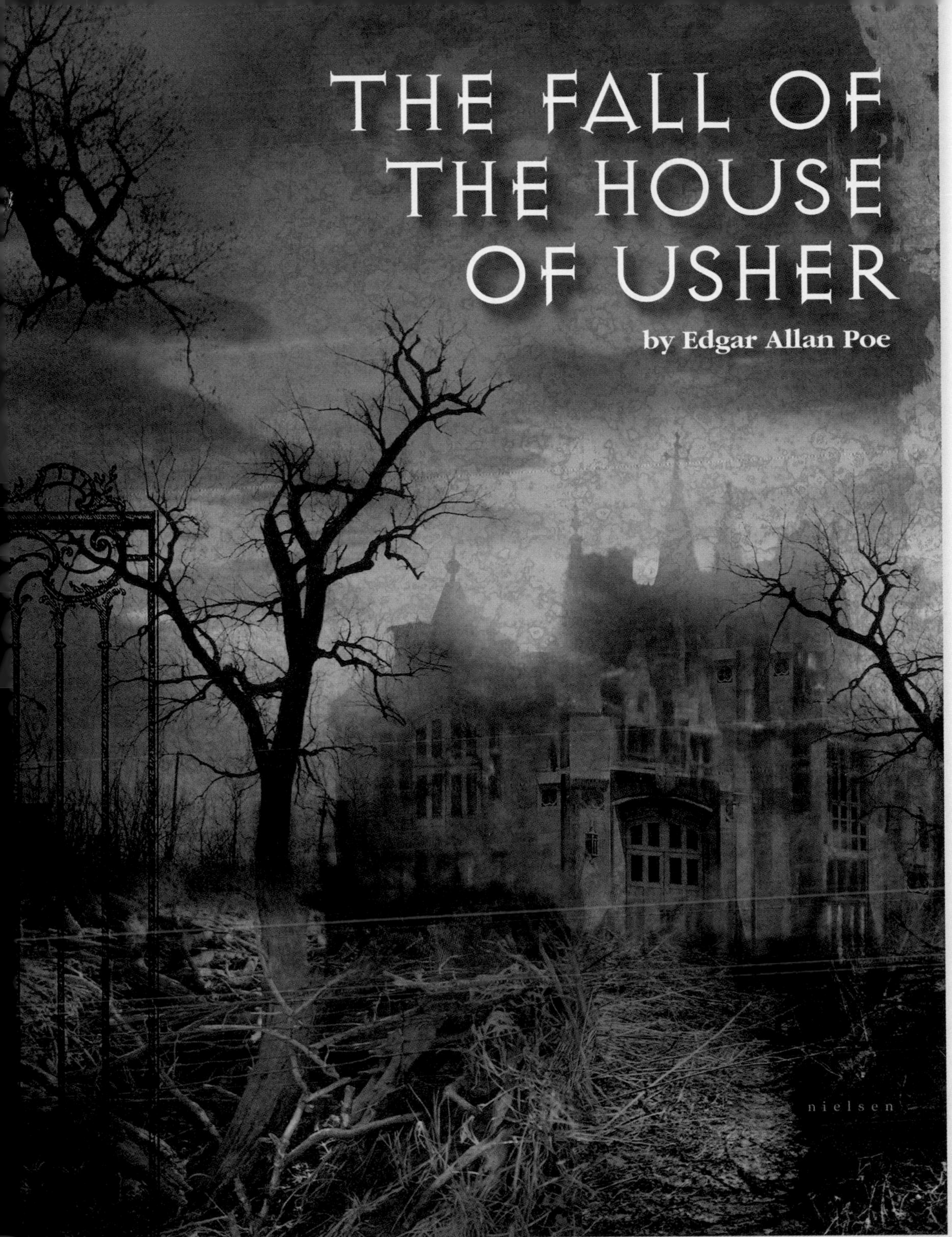

nielsen

Resources ———

Viewing and Representing
Fine Art Transparency
A fine art transparency of René Magritte's *L'Hirondelle des Faubourgs* can be used to discuss atmosphere and setting in both Poe selections (pp. 263–279 and 282–286). See the *Viewing and Representing Transparencies and Worksheets:*
• Transparency 6
• Worksheet, p. 24

RESPONDING TO THE ART

Poe said that the boarding school to which the Allans sent him in Stoke Newington, England, inspired the setting for "The Fall of the House of Usher."
Activity. Ask students to find Gothic elements in this illustration. [Possible responses: a rambling, decaying mansion with turrets and empty windows; skeletal, leafless trees; weeds; mist; an iron gate; a starless night]

Reaching All Students

Struggling Readers
To set the stage for this story, have students read "The Gothic Tradition" on p. 274. Next, supplement this information by sharing with students the Critical Comment on p. T261. Once you are sure they understand that this is a horror story, help them find the translation of the de Béranger quotation in the footnote on p. 264. Explain that the quotation stresses the sensitivity of the human mind and emotions, an important theme of the story.

English Language Learners
Encourage each student to join with a reader fluent in English and read the story aloud, page by page. Partners should take turns reading aloud. Advise students to pause to discuss the story content and to look up unfamiliar words in the glossary.

Advanced Learners
In a famous essay on his craft, Poe wrote that a story should achieve "a certain unique or single effect. . . . In the whole composition there should be no word written, of which the tendency, direct or indirect, is not to the one pre-established design." Have students keep in mind this purpose as they read the story, and discuss (a) whether Poe achieved that purpose, and (b) whether his rule should be followed by all writers.

T263

Son cœur est un luth suspendu;
Sitôt qu'on le touche il résonne.[1]

—*De Béranger*

A During the whole of a dull, dark, and soundless day in the autumn of the year, when the clouds hung oppressively low in the heavens, I had been passing alone, on horseback, through a singularly dreary tract of country; and at length found myself, as the shades of the evening drew on, within view of the melancholy House of Usher. I know not how it was—but, with the first glimpse of the building, a sense of insufferable gloom <u>pervaded</u> my spirit. I say insufferable; for the feeling was unrelieved by any of that half-pleasurable, because poetic, sentiment, with which the mind usually receives even the sternest **B** natural images of the desolate or terrible. I looked upon the scene before me—upon the mere[2] house, and the simple landscape features of the domain—upon the bleak walls—upon the vacant eyelike windows—upon a few rank sedges[3]—and **B** upon a few white trunks of decayed trees—with an utter depression of soul which I can compare to no earthly sensation more properly than to the afterdream of the reveler upon opium—the bitter lapse into everyday life—the hideous dropping off of the veil. There was an iciness, a sinking, a sickening of the heart—an unredeemed dreari-**C** ness of thought which no goading of the imagination could torture into aught[4] of the sublime. What was it—I paused to think—what was it that so unnerved me in the contemplation of the House of Usher? It was a mystery all insoluble; nor could I grapple with the shadowy fancies that crowded upon me as I pondered. I was forced to fall back upon the unsatisfactory conclusion, that **D** while, beyond doubt, there *are* combinations of very simple natural objects which have the power of thus affecting us, still the analysis of this power lies among considerations beyond our depth. It was possible, I reflected, that a mere different arrangement of the particulars of the scene, of the details of the picture, would be sufficient to

modify, or perhaps to annihilate its capacity for sorrowful impression; and, acting upon this idea, I reined my horse to the precipitous brink of a black and lurid tarn[5] that lay in unruffled luster by the dwelling, and gazed down—but with a shudder even more thrilling than before— upon the remodeled and inverted images of the gray sedge, and the ghastly tree stems, and the vacant and eyelike windows.

> The narrator is riding on horseback to visit the House of Usher. **E**
>
> **?** What are the narrator's first impressions as he draws near to the House of Usher?

Nevertheless, in this mansion of gloom I now proposed to myself a <u>sojourn</u> of some weeks. Its proprietor, Roderick Usher, had been one of my boon companions in boyhood; but many years had elapsed since our last meeting. A letter, however, had lately reached me in a distant part of the country—a letter from him—which, in its wildly importunate nature, had admitted of no other than a personal reply. The MS.[6] gave evidence of nervous agitation. The writer spoke of acute bodily illness—of a mental disorder which oppressed him—and of an earnest desire to see me, as his best, and indeed his only personal friend, with a view of attempting, by the cheerfulness of my society, some alleviation of his malady. It was the manner in which all this, and much more, was said—it was the apparent *heart* that went with his request—which allowed me no room for hesitation; and I accordingly obeyed forthwith what I still considered a very singular summons.

Although, as boys, we had been even intimate associates, yet I really knew little of my friend. His reserve had been always excessive and habitual. I was aware, however, that his very ancient family had been noted, time out of mind, for a peculiar sensibility of temperament, displaying itself,

---

1. *Son cœur . . . il résonne:* "His heart is a suspended lute; / Whenever one touches it, it resounds." From "Le Refus" ("The Refusal") by Pierre-Jean de Béranger (1780–1857).
2. **mere** (mir): lake.
3. **sedges:** grasslike plants that grow in watery ground.
4. **aught** (ôt): anything.

5. **tarn:** small but deep mountain lake. Its waters are dark from the decomposition of vegetation and because there is no circulation.
6. **MS.:** abbreviation for "manuscript."

- -

WORDS TO OWN
pervaded (pər·vād′id) *v.*: spread throughout.
sojourn (sō′jʉrn) *n.*: short stay.

- -

through long ages, in many works of exalted art, and manifested, of late, in repeated deeds of munificent yet unobtrusive charity, as well as in a passionate devotion to the intricacies, perhaps even more than to the orthodox and easily recognizable beauties, of musical science. I had learned, too, the very remarkable fact, that the stem of the Usher race, all time-honored as it was, had put forth, at no period, any enduring branch; in other words, that the entire family lay in the direct line of descent, and had always, with very trifling and very temporary variation, so lain. It was this deficiency, I considered, while running over in thought the perfect keeping of the character of the premises with the accredited character of the people, and while speculating upon the possible influence which the one, in the long lapse of centuries, might have exercised upon the other—it was this deficiency, perhaps, of collateral issue,[7] and the consequent undeviating transmission, from sire to son, of the patrimony with the name, which had, at length, so identified the two as to merge the original title of the estate in the quaint and equivocal appellation of the "House of Usher"—an appellation which seemed to include, in the minds of the peasantry who used it, both the family and the family mansion.

I have said that the sole effect of my somewhat childish experiment—that of looking down within the tarn—had been to deepen the first singular impression. There can be no doubt that the consciousness of the rapid increase of my superstition—for why should I not so term it?—served mainly to accelerate the increase itself. Such, I have long known, is the paradoxical law of all sentiments having terror as a basis. And it might have been for this reason only, that, when I again uplifted my eyes to the house itself, from its image in the pool, there grew in my mind a strange fancy—a fancy so ridiculous, indeed, that I but mention it to show the vivid force of the sensations which oppressed me. I had so worked upon my imagination as really to believe that about the whole mansion and domain there hung an atmosphere peculiar to themselves and their immediate vicinity—an atmosphere which had no affinity with the air

of heaven, but which had reeked up from the decayed trees, and the gray wall and the silent tarn—a pestilent and mystic vapor, dull, sluggish, faintly discernible, and leaden-hued.

> The mansion's atmosphere seems connected with the underworld, with decay and disease.

Shaking off from my spirit what *must* have been a dream, I scanned more narrowly the real aspect of the building. Its principal feature seemed to be that of an excessive antiquity. The discoloration of ages had been great. Minute fungi overspread the whole exterior, hanging in a fine tangled webwork from the eaves. Yet all this was apart from any extraordinary dilapidation. No portion of the masonry had fallen; and there appeared to be a wild inconsistency between its still perfect adaptation of parts, and the crumbling condition of the individual stones. In this there was much that reminded me of the specious totality of old woodwork which has rotted for long years in some neglected vault, with no disturbance from the breath of the external air. Beyond this indication of extensive decay, however, the fabric gave little token of instability. Perhaps the eye of a scrutinizing observer might have discovered a barely perceptible fissure, which, extending from the roof of the building in front, made its way down the wall in a zigzag direction, until it became lost in the sullen waters of the tarn.

> ❓ What details in this description of the house seem most significant?

Noticing these things, I rode over a short causeway to the house. A servant-in-waiting took my horse, and I entered the Gothic archway of the

---

7. **collateral issue:** relatives, such as cousins, who share the same ancestors but who are not in a direct line of descent.

WORDS TO OWN

equivocal (ē·kwiv'ə·kəl) *adj.:* having more than one meaning.
discernible (di·sʉrn'ə·bəl) *adj.:* noticeable.
specious (spē'shəs) *adj.:* seemingly sound, but not really so.
scrutinizing (skrōōt''n·īz'iŋ) *v.* used as *adj.:* carefully observant.

EDGAR ALLAN POE 265

Getting Students Involved

Giving an Oral Interpretation

Poe wrote lyrical prose that becomes easier to understand when it is read aloud. Encourage students to choose a section of the text that contains descriptive narrative, such as the opening paragraphs on pp. 264–268, or a section that is laced with urgency or emotional dialogue, such as the paragraph that begins, "Not hear it?" (p. 277). Have them focus on the dramatic effect Poe was trying to achieve in each instance. Have students study the passages,

looking closely at Poe's dashes and his inversions to see what he wanted to emphasize. Then, review with students elements of speech, such as pitch, tone, articulation, accent, and pace. Encourage students to pay particular attention to the pace, or speed, at which they read and to the pitch of their voices. Finally, urge volunteers to present their interpretations to the class.

RESPONDING TO THE ART

Activity. Ask students to point out the Gothic details in this illustration. [Possible responses: the crumbling wall; the skull motif of the fireplace; the unexplained light source on the subject's head; his inert pose.]

Getting Students Involved

Cooperative Learning

Writing a Radio Script. After students have read the story, have them meet in groups of three and assume appropriate responsibilities to adapt "The Fall of the House of Usher" to a fifteen-minute radio presentation. Ask them to write the script and to include directions for sound effects and background music that support the story's mood. If time permits, ask groups to perform their adaptations as though in a recording studio.

Skill Link

Analyzing Cultural Influences

Edgar Allan Poe lived during the height of the Romantic movement in England and America. How did this cultural influence affect his writing? To explore this question, urge small groups to complete the following:

1. Review the characteristics of Romantic literature as explained in the essay on American Romanticism, pp. 139–145.
2. Analyze the text of "Usher" to identify its Romantic characteristics, especially noting its setting and its focus on the theme of the imagination.
3. Determine the nature of the narrator's journey. Is it a Romantic quest? What are the conflicts and where does the plot take him?
4. Decide whether "Usher" is a Romantic work. Does it address Romantic concerns? Does it explore ideas from a Romantic perspective?

hall.[8] A valet, of stealthy step, thence conducted me, in silence, through many dark and intricate passages in my progress to the *studio* of his master. Much that I encountered on the way contributed, I know not how, to heighten the vague sentiments of which I have already spoken. While the objects around me—while the carvings of the ceilings, the somber tapestries of the walls, the ebon blackness of the floors, and the phantasmagoric[9] armorial trophies which rattled as I strode, were but matters to which, or to such as which, I had been accustomed from my infancy—while I hesitated not to acknowledge how familiar was all this—I still wondered to find how unfamiliar were the fancies which ordinary images were stirring up. On one of the staircases, I met the physician of the family. His countenance, I thought, wore a mingled expression of low cunning and perplexity. He accosted me with trepidation and passed on. The valet now threw open a door and ushered me into the presence of his master.

[B] [C] *What might the presence of a physician foreshadow?*

The room in which I found myself was very large and lofty. The windows were long, narrow, and pointed, and at so vast a distance from the black oaken floor as to be altogether inaccessible from within. Feeble gleams of encrimsoned light made their way through the trellised panes, and served to render sufficiently distinct the more prominent objects around; the eye, however, struggled in vain to reach the remoter angles of the chamber, or the recesses of the vaulted and fretted[10] ceiling. Dark draperies hung upon the walls. The general furniture was profuse, comfortless, antique, and tattered. Many books and musical instruments lay scattered about, but failed to give any vitality to the scene. I felt that I breathed an atmosphere of sorrow. An air of stern, deep, and irredeemable gloom hung over and pervaded all.

Upon my entrance, Usher arose from a sofa on which he had been lying at full length, and greeted me with a vivacious warmth which had

much in it, I at first thought, of an overdone cordiality—of the constrained effort of the *ennuyé*[11] man of the world. A glance, however, at his countenance, convinced me of his perfect sincerity. We sat down; and for some moments, while he spoke not, I gazed upon him with a feeling half of pity, half of awe. Surely, man had never before so terribly altered, in so brief a period, as had Roderick Usher! It was with difficulty that I could bring myself to admit the identity of the wan being before me with the companion of my early boyhood. Yet the character of his face had been at all times remarkable. A cadaverousness[12] of complexion; an eye large, liquid, and luminous beyond comparison; lips somewhat thin and very pallid, but of a surpassingly beautiful curve; a nose of a delicate Hebrew model, but with a breadth of nostril unusual in similar formations; a finely molded chin, speaking, in its want of prominence, of a want of moral energy; hair of a more than weblike softness and tenuity;[13] these features, with an inordinate expansion above the regions of the temple, made up altogether a countenance not easily to be forgotten. And now in the mere exaggeration of the prevailing character of these features, and of the expression they were wont to convey, lay so much of change that I doubted to whom I spoke. The now ghastly pallor of the skin, and the now miraculous luster of the eye, above all things startled and even awed me. The silken hair, too, had been suffered to grow all unheeded, and as, in its wild gossamer texture, it floated rather than fell about the face, I could not, even with effort, connect its arabesque[14] expression with any idea of simple humanity.

In the manner of my friend I was at once struck with an incoherence—an inconsistency; and I soon found this to arise from a series of feeble and futile struggles to overcome an habitual trepi-

11. **ennuyé** (än·nwē·ā'): French for "bored" or "jaded."
12. **cadaverousness:** paleness or gauntness, as a corpse.
13. **tenuity:** fineness; lack of substance.
14. **arabesque:** strangely mixed; fantastic.

8. **Gothic . . . hall:** The hallway looked like a Gothic arch—high, pointed, and elaborately carved.
9. **phantasmagoric** (fan·taz'mə·gôr'ik): images appearing to change rapidly, like the events in a dream.
10. **fretted:** carved in an ornamental architectural design.

WORDS TO OWN

profuse (prō·fyoos') *adj.*: abundant.
vivacious (vī·vā'shəs) *adj.*: cheerful; lively.
pallid (pal'id) *adj.*: pale.
inordinate (in·ôr'də·nit) *adj.*: excessive.

[A] Elements of Literature
Connotation
? What are some of the words in this description of the interior of the house that enhance the atmosphere of gloom and dread? [Possible responses: *stealthy; somber; ebon blackness; phantasmagoric; cunning; perplexity.*]

[B] Appreciating Language
Puns
? Which word in the last sentence of the paragraph is a pun? [*ushered*]

[C] Question Box
A physician often foreshadows illness or death.

[D] Elements of Literature
Atmosphere
? What is the atmosphere in Usher's study? [dark, depressing] What condition would it lead the narrator to expect Usher to be in? [depressed, troubled, confused]

[E] Advanced Learners
Interpreting Characterization
? What parallels can you see between this description of Usher and Poe's description of the house? [Possible responses: Like the white decayed tree trunks around the mansion, Usher's face is shaded by a "cadaverousness of complexion," and a "ghastly pallor." Usher's weblike hair has been allowed to grow untamed like the fungi on the walls of the mansion and the wild grasses that surround the tarn.]

Taking a Second Look

Review: Using Study Strategies
Discuss pre-reading strategies, such as reading the background information, analyzing illustrations and graphics, and studying vocabulary words. Suggest that students also create a study guide by copying the boxed questions and the Making Meanings questions ahead of time so they have a sense of what to look for as they read. Students should leave a space under each question for their answer. Have small groups complete the following activity.

Activity
Have group members review the study guide first and then take turns reading passages from the selection aloud. When they think they have an answer to one of the questions, the group can record their answer on the guide sheet. Once the group have finished reading the story, they can go over their answers and make revisions as necessary.

dancy—an excessive nervous agitation. For something of this nature I had indeed been prepared, no less by his letter, than by reminiscences of certain boyish traits, and by conclusions deduced from his peculiar physical conformation and temperament. His action was alternately vivacious and sullen. His voice varied rapidly from a tremulous indecision (when the animal spirits seemed utterly in abeyance) to that species of energetic concision—that abrupt, weighty, unhurried, and hollow-sounding enunciation—that leaden, self-balanced and perfectly modulated guttural utterance, which may be observed in the lost drunkard, or the irreclaimable eater of opium, during the periods of his most intense excitement.

It was thus that he spoke of the object of my visit, of his earnest desire to see me, and of the solace he expected me to afford him. He entered, at some length, into what he conceived to be the nature of his malady. It was, he said, a constitutional and a family evil, and one for which he despaired to find a remedy—a mere nervous affection,[15] he immediately added, which would undoubtedly soon pass. It displayed itself in a host of unnatural sensations. Some of these, as he detailed them, interested and bewildered me; although, perhaps, the terms, and the general manner of the narration had their weight. He suffered much from a morbid acuteness of the senses; the most insipid food was alone endurable; he could wear only garments of certain texture; the odors of all flowers were oppressive; his eyes were tortured by even a faint light; and there were but peculiar sounds, and these from stringed instruments, which did not inspire him with horror.

To an anomalous[16] species of terror I found him a bounden slave. "I shall perish," said he, "I *must* perish in this deplorable folly. Thus, thus, and not otherwise, shall I be lost. I dread the events of the future, not in themselves, but in their results. I

15. **affection:** ailment; disorder.
16. **anomalous:** abnormal.

shudder at the thought of any, even the most trivial, incident, which may operate upon this intolerable agitation of soul. I have, indeed, no abhorrence of danger, except in its absolute effect—in terror. In this unnerved—in this pitiable condition—I feel that the period will sooner or later arrive when I must abandon life and reason together, in some struggle with the grim phantasm, FEAR."

I learned, moreover, at intervals, and through broken and equivocal hints, another singular feature of his mental condition. He was enchained by certain superstitious impressions in regard to the dwelling which he tenanted, and whence, for many years, he had never ventured forth—in regard to an influence whose supposititious[17] force was conveyed in terms too shadowy here to be restated—an influence which some peculiarities in the mere form and substance of his family mansion, had, by dint of long sufferance, he said, obtained over his spirit—an effect which the *physique* of the gray walls and turrets, and of the dim tarn into which they all looked down, had, at length, brought about upon the *morale* of his existence.

He admitted, however, although with hesitation, that much of the peculiar gloom which thus afflicted him could be traced to a more natural and far more palpable origin—to the severe and long-continued illness—indeed to the evidently approaching dissolution—of a tenderly beloved sister—his sole companion for long years—his last and only relative on earth. "Her decease," he said, with a bitterness which I can never forget, "would leave him (him the hopeless and the frail) the last of the ancient race of the Ushers." While

17. **supposititious** (sə·päz′ə·tish′əs): supposed; assumed; hypothetical.

WORDS TO OWN
insipid (in·sip′id) *adj.:* bland; without flavor.
palpable (pal′pə·bəl) *adj.:* obvious; perceivable.

he spoke, the lady Madeline (for so was she called) passed slowly through a remote portion of the apartment, and, without having noticed my presence, disappeared. I regarded her with an utter astonishment not unmingled with dread—and yet I found it impossible to account for such feelings. A sensation of stupor oppressed me, as my eyes followed her retreating steps. When a door, at length, closed upon her, my glance sought instinctively and eagerly the countenance of the brother—but he had buried his face in his hands, and I could only perceive that a far more than ordinary wanness had overspread the emaciated fingers through which trickled many passionate tears.

The disease of the lady Madeline had long baffled the skill of her physicians. A settled apathy, a gradual wasting away of the person, and frequent although transient affections of a partially cataleptical[18] character, were the unusual diagnosis. Hitherto she had steadily borne up against the pressure of her malady, and had not betaken herself finally to bed; but, on the closing in of the evening of my arrival at the house, she succumbed (as her brother told me at night with inexpressible agitation) to the prostrating power of the destroyer; and I learned that the glimpse I had obtained of her person would thus probably be the last I should obtain—that the lady, at least while living, would be seen by me no more.

> Usher, who has not left his mansion in years, discloses a natural reason for his gloom: the strange illness of his sister Madeline.

For several days ensuing, her name was unmentioned by either Usher or myself: And during this period I was busied in earnest endeavors to alleviate the melancholy of my friend. We painted and read together; or I listened, as if in a dream, to the wild improvisations of his speaking guitar. And thus, as a closer and still closer intimacy admitted me more unreservedly into the recesses of his spirit, the more bitterly did I perceive the futility

18. **cataleptical** (kat'ə·lep'tik·əl): Catalepsy is an emotional condition, associated with disorders such as epilepsy and schizophrenia, which may cause the victim to lose sensation and the ability to move the limbs, or even the entire body. In a cataleptic attack, Madeline could be as stiff as a corpse.

of all attempt at cheering a mind from which darkness, as if an inherent positive quality, poured forth upon all objects of the moral and physical universe, in one unceasing radiation of gloom.

I shall ever bear about me a memory of the many solemn hours I thus spent alone with the master of the House of Usher. Yet I should fail in any attempt to convey an idea of the exact character of the studies, or of the occupations, in which he involved me, or led me the way. An excited and highly distempered ideality[19] threw a sulfureous[20] luster over all. His long improvised dirges will ring forever in my ears. Among other things, I hold painfully in mind a certain singular perversion and amplification of the wild air of the last waltz of Von Weber.[21] From the paintings over which his elaborate fancy brooded, and which grew, touch by touch, into vaguenesses at which I shuddered the more thrillingly, because I shuddered knowing not why—from these paintings (vivid as their images now are before me) I would in vain endeavor to educe more than a small portion which should lie within the compass of merely written words. By the utter simplicity, by the nakedness of his designs, he arrested and overawed attention. If ever mortal painted an idea, that mortal was Roderick Usher. For me at least—in the circumstances then surrounding me—there arose out of the pure abstractions which the hypochondriac contrived to throw upon his canvas, an intensity of intolerable awe, no shadow of which felt I ever yet in the contemplation of the certainly glowing yet too concrete reveries of Fuseli.[22]

> The narrator tries to cheer Usher by painting and reading with him and listening to him play the guitar.

19. **distempered ideality:** mental derangement.
20. **sulfureous** (sul·fyoor'ē·əs): hellish; infernal. Poe's description probably comes from the yellowish color of sulfur, which is associated with the fires of hell.
21. **Von Weber:** Carl Maria von Weber (1786–1826), German Romantic composer.
22. **Fuseli:** Johann Heinrich Füssli (1741–1825), Swiss painter who lived in England and is known for scenes of horror and the supernatural.

WORDS TO OWN

stupor (stōō'pər) *n.:* state of mental dullness; loss of the senses.

G Reading Skills and Strategies
Responding to the Text

? How did you respond to the Lady Madeline's wordless passage through the room? [Possible responses: Her strange actions make her seem ghostlike or supernatural; her appearance heightens suspense and fear.]

H Reading Skills and Strategies

Using Resources

? What do you learn about Madeline's illness from Footnote 18? [Possible response: She suffers from a disease that sometimes renders her as stiff as a corpse; this disease may be associated with epilepsy or schizophrenia.]

I Elements of Literature
Symbol

? The narrator attempts to divert Usher through the influence of art, literature, and music. What might the wild improvisations of Usher's guitar symbolize here? [The music might represent Roderick's inner turmoil, or his wild creative energies.]

J Cultural Connections
Carl Maria von Weber

Carl Maria von Weber ran the opera house in Dresden, Germany, and wrote two influential Romantic operas titled *Der Freischütz* (1821) and *Oberon* (1826).

K Elements of Literature
Atmosphere

? What atmosphere is created by these long descriptions of Roderick's reading, painting, and music? [an atmosphere of fevered intensity] What might these creations represent? [Possible response: They might represent the wildly Romantic, creative portion of Roderick's personality.]

L Reading Skills and Strategies

Using Resources

Ask students to look for the main subject and verb in this long complicated sentence and to then paraphrase it with the other phrases and clauses. [(subject) An intensity (verb) arose. Here is a paraphrase: *Under the circumstances I felt an intense awe for the abstractions the hypochondriac had painted, which I have never felt when looking at the concrete images of Fuseli.*]

Getting Students Involved

Cooperative Learning

Fine Arts Soothe the Savage Beast. Painting, playing a musical instrument, and reading soothe Roderick Usher's nerves. Divide the class into three groups: one for art, music, and literature. Tell each group to locate examples of their art form that the narrator might have used successfully to calm Usher's nerves. Examples may be anachronistic—that is, they may have been created after Usher's time. During their searches, students may wish to consult the school librarian or a teacher of fine arts. After locating several works, the groups should prepare to show, play, or read them to the class and to hold a panel discussion about their emotional effects.

One of the phantasmagoric conceptions of my friend, partaking not so rigidly of the spirit of abstraction, may be shadowed forth, although feebly, in words. A small picture presented the interior of an immensely long and rectangular vault or tunnel, with low walls, smooth, white, and without interruption or device. Certain accessory points of the design served well to convey the idea that this excavation lay at an exceeding depth below the surface of the earth. No outlet was observed in any portion of its vast extent, and no torch, or other artificial source of light was discernible; yet a flood of intense rays rolled throughout, and bathed the whole in a ghastly and inappropriate splendor.

I have just spoken of that morbid condition of the auditory nerve which rendered all music intolerable to the sufferer with the exception of certain effects of stringed instruments. It was, perhaps, the narrow limits to which he thus confined himself upon the guitar, which gave birth, in great measure, to the fantastic character of his performances. But the fervid *facility* of his *impromptus*[23] could not be so accounted for. They must have been, and were, in the notes, as well as in the words of his wild fantasias (for he not unfrequently accompanied himself with rhymed verbal improvisations), the result of that intense mental collectedness and concentration to which I have previously alluded as observable only in the moments of the highest artificial excitement. The words of one of these rhapsodies I have easily remembered. I was, perhaps, the more forcibly impressed with it, as he gave it, because, in the under or mystic current of its meaning, I fancied

> **?** Do you think the narrator is a reliable source of information about the Ushers and their house? Do the narrator's interpretations of Roderick's personality make sense to you? Would you analyze Roderick differently?

that I perceived, and for the first time, a full consciousness on the part of Usher, of the tottering of his lofty reason upon her throne. The verses, which were entitled "The Haunted Palace," ran very nearly, if not accurately, thus:

> **?** What are some of the characteristics of the works of art and musical compositions that Roderick produces? As you read the lyric "The Haunted Palace," ask yourself what it reveals about Roderick's frame of mind.

I

In the greenest of our valleys,
　　By good angels tenanted,
Once a fair and stately palace—
　　Radiant palace—reared its head.
In the monarch Thought's dominion—
　　It stood there!
Never seraph[24] spread a pinion[25]
　　Over fabric half so fair.

II

Banners yellow, glorious, golden,
　　On its roof did float and flow;
(This—all this—was in the olden
　　Time long ago)
And every gentle air that dallied,
　　In that sweet day,
Along the ramparts plumed and pallid,
　　A winged odor went away.

III

Wanderers in that happy valley
　　Through two luminous windows saw
Spirits moving musically
　　To a lute's well-tunéd law,
Round about a throne, where sitting
　　(Porphyrogene!)[26]
In state his glory well befitting,
　　The ruler of the realm was seen.

24. **seraph:** angel.
25. **pinion** (pin'yən): wing.
26. **porphyrogene** (pôr·fir'ə·jēn'): Poe coined this word from "porphyry," a purple dye reserved for royalty, to mean "one born to the purple," or "one of royal blood."

WORDS TO OWN

morbid (môr'bid) *adj.:* diseased; unhealthy.

23. **impromptus** (im·prämp'tōōz'): spontaneous performances.

Crossing the Curriculum

Health

Roderick Usher: A Case Study. Have students form a medical board to examine Usher's symptoms and determine a diagnosis and prognosis for his ailment. Have individual students consult medical references to help formulate their diagnosis. Students might also recommend a treatment plan, if appropriate. Ask the board to meet in front of the class to discuss their findings and reach a consensus about Usher's case.

Fine Art

Roderick Usher creates "abstract" paintings long before this style of art came into vogue. Ask students to bring in reproductions of abstract art; discuss why this style might appeal to Usher. Then, have them consider how Poe could have described abstract art before it was invented. [Possible answers: Abstract art was anticipated by some earlier non-Western art; what Poe had in mind was not exactly the abstract art we know.]

IV

And all with pearl and ruby glowing
    Was the fair palace door,
Through which came flowing, flowing, flowing,
    And sparkling evermore,
A troop of Echoes whose sweet duty
    Was but to sing,
In voices of surpassing beauty,
    The wit and wisdom of their king.

V

But evil things, in robes of sorrow,
    Assailed the monarch's high estate;
(Ah, let us mourn, for never morrow
    Shall dawn upon him, desolate!)
And, round about his home, the glory
    That blushed and bloomed
Is but a dim-remembered story
    Of the old time entombed.

VI

And travelers now within that valley,
    Through the red-litten[27] windows, see
Vast forms that move fantastically
    To a discordant melody;
While, like a rapid ghastly river,
    Through the pale door,
A hideous throng rush out forever,
    And laugh—but smile no more.

I well remember that suggestions arising from this ballad led us into a train of thought wherein there became manifest an opinion of Usher's which I mention not so much on account of its novelty (for other men have thought thus), as on account of the pertinacity with which he maintained it. This opinion, in its general form, was that of the sentience[28] of all vegetable things. But, in his disordered fancy, the idea had assumed a more daring character, and trespassed, under certain conditions, upon the kingdom of inorganization.[29] I lack words to express the full extent, or the earnest *abandon* of his persuasion. The be-

lief, however, was connected (as I have previously hinted) with the gray stones of the home of his forefathers. The conditions of the sentience had been here, he imagined, fulfilled in the method of collocation of these stones—in the order of their arrangement, as well as in that of the many *fungi* which overspread them, and of the decayed trees which stood around—above all, in the long undisturbed endurance of this arrangement, and in its reduplication in the still waters of the tarn. Its evidence—the evidence of the sentience—was to be seen, he said (and I here started as he spoke), in the gradual yet certain condensation of an atmosphere of their own about the waters and the walls. The result was discoverable, he added, in that silent, yet importunate and terrible influence which for centuries had molded the destinies of his family, and which made *him* what I now saw him—what he was. Such opinions need no comment, and I will make none.

> Usher expresses his belief that not only all living things but also all nonliving things are sentient, or conscious.
>
> **?** What specific details in the story thus far suggest that Usher's belief is reflected by his surroundings?

Our books—the books which, for years, had formed no small portion of the mental existence of the invalid—were, as might be supposed, in strict keeping with this character of phantasm. We pored together over such works as the *Ververt et Chartreuse* of Gresset; the *Belphegor* of Machiavelli; the *Heaven and Hell* of Swedenborg; *The Subterranean Voyage of Nicholas Klimm* by Holberg; the Chiromancy of Robert Flud, of Jean D'Indaginé, and of De la Chambre; the *Journey into the Blue Distance* of Tieck; and *The City of the Sun* of Campanella. One favorite volume was a small octavo edition of the *Directorium Inquisitorum,* by the Dominican Eymeric de Gironne; and there were passages in Pomponius Mela, about the old African Satyrs and Ægipans,[30] over which Usher would sit dreaming for hours. His

---

27. **red-litten:** red-lighted; Poe coined this archaic-sounding term.
28. **sentience** (sen'shəns): consciousness.
29. **kingdom of inorganization:** world of inorganic objects.

30. ***Ververt et Chartreuse . . . Satyrs and Ægipans:*** The books, authors, and subjects listed have to do with mysticism, magic, and horror.

EDGAR ALLAN POE 271

Professional Notes

Critical Comment:
"The Haunted Palace"

chief delight, however, was found in the perusal of an exceedingly rare and curious book in quarto Gothic—the manual of a forgotten church—the *Vigiliae Mortuorum*[31] *secundum Chorum Ecclesiae Maguntinae.*

I could not help thinking of the wild ritual of this work, and of its probable influence upon the hypochondriac, when, one evening, having informed me abruptly that the lady Madeline was no more, he stated his intention of preserving her corpse for a fortnight (previously to its final interment), in one of the numerous vaults within the main walls of the building. The worldly reason, however, assigned for this singular proceeding, was one which I did not feel at liberty to dispute. The brother had been led to his resolution (so he told me) by consideration of the unusual character of the malady of the deceased, of certain obtrusive and eager inquiries on the part of her medical men, and of the remote and exposed situation of the burial ground of the family. I will not deny that when I called to mind the sinister countenance of the person whom I met upon the staircase,[32] on the day of my arrival at the house, I had no desire to oppose what I regarded as at best but a harmless, and by no means an unnatural, precaution.[33]

> Usher suddenly announces that his sister Madeline has died. Before her final burial, Usher plans to inter Madeline temporarily in a vault within the house, to prevent doctors from stealing her body for an autopsy.

At the request of Usher, I personally aided him in the arrangements for the temporary entombment. The body having been encoffined, we two alone bore it to its rest. The vault in which we placed it (and which had been so long unopened that our torches, half smothered in its oppressive atmosphere, gave us little opportunity for investigation) was small, damp, and entirely without means of admission for light; lying, at great depth, immediately beneath that portion of the building in which was my own sleeping apartment. It had been used, apparently, in remote feudal times, for the worst purposes of a dungeon-keep,[34] and, in later days, as a place of deposit for powder, or some other highly combustible substance, as a portion of its floor, and the whole interior of a long archway through which we reached it, were carefully sheathed with copper. The door, of massive iron, had been, also, similarly protected. Its immense weight caused an unusually sharp grating sound, as it moved upon its hinges.

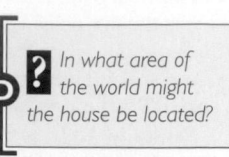

> **?** In what area of the world might the house be located?

Having deposited our mournful burden upon tressels within this region of horror, we partially turned aside the yet unscrewed lid of the coffin, and looked upon the face of the tenant. A striking similitude between the brother and sister now first arrested my attention; and Usher, divining, perhaps, my thoughts, murmured out some few words from which I learned that the deceased and himself had been twins, and that sympathies of a scarcely intelligible nature had always existed between them. Our glances, however, rested not long upon the dead—for we could not regard her unawed. The disease which had thus entombed the lady in the maturity of youth, had left, as usual in all maladies of a strictly cataleptical character, the mockery of a faint blush upon the bosom and the face, and that suspiciously lingering smile upon the lip which is so terrible in death. We replaced and screwed down the lid, and, having secured the door of iron, made our way, with toil, into the scarcely less gloomy apartments of the upper portion of the house.

> **?** What does the narrator notice about Madeline's appearance and condition after looking at her corpse?

And now, some days of bitter grief having elapsed, an observable change came over the

31. *Vigiliae Mortuorum:* Latin for "vigil of the dead."
32. **person . . . staircase:** the physician.
33. **precaution:** Usher wishes to be sure his sister's body will not be dissected by doctors. At the time, bodies were sometimes stolen and sold to medical students for dissection and study.

34. **dungeon-keep:** underground prison.

WORDS TO OWN

similitude (sə·mil′ə·tood′) *n.:* likeness.

Professional Notes

Critical Comment: Doubling

Biographer Kenneth Silverman writes: "Doubling is extensive in Poe's tales, many of whose heroes and heroines are hard to distinguish from each other and often have the physical and mental traits of Poe himself. It appears in many elements of the narrative. Roderick resembles his house, whose sentience has influenced and is duplicated in his own 'morbid acuteness of the senses': local peasants use the name 'The House of Usher' to mean 'both the family and the family mansion.' The house in turn is mirrored in the 'lurid tarn' outside: the narrator gazes into it hoping to escape the oppressive effect of the house, only to meet there its remodeled and inverted images. . . . Although such doubling is common in Romantic literature and essential to Gothic fiction, where criminals resemble victims, it has a special gravity in Poe's tales." Have students predict how this "doubling" motif might affect the outcome of the story.

FROM THE EDITOR'S DESK

As both readers and editors, we especially like Poe's extravagant use of language. His plots, characters, and ideas have often been transferred into other media, but only by reading the actual story can one appreciate the sheer wild joy of Poe's verbal imagination. His untranslated quotations from foreign languages, his invented titles of books by fictitious authors with comical names, his mock-erudite discourses on natural and psychological phenomena, his winks of irony in macabre passages, all testify to the fevered inner life of a man for whom language and literature were powerful, if ultimately doomed, ways of keeping the demons at bay.

RESPONDING TO THE ART

Activity. Have students discuss how well the illustration represents this pivotal scene in the story. Ask them how they imagine the scene without the illustration. Are some details in the illustration excessively dramatic, or does it accurately capture the tone of the scene? [Most students will feel that the illustration captures the classic Gothic elements of the scene, (the chains hanging from the dungeon ceiling, the corpse with folded hands, etc.), but many will also feel that the exaggerated grief of Roderick and some of the more grotesque aspects of the illustration go overboard, and miss the more subtle horror of Poe's narrative.]

Using Students' Strengths

Naturalist Learners

Have students reread the descriptions of nature on pp. 264–265 and 275 (column 2, paragraph 1). Ask them to visualize the two settings and imagine themselves in them. How might such surroundings affect a person? Ask students to describe their feelings, then evaluate the narrator's reactions. Are they believable? Is the narrator reacting to his surroundings or does the setting reflect his mental condition?

Kinesthetic Learners

The poet W. H. Auden believed that characters like Roderick Usher are symbolic of intense mental states. For purposes of the story, the characters must remain in that heightened state, thereby becoming "operatic." Have volunteers act out the events of Lady Madeline's entombment, putting special emphasis on Usher's emotions and reactions.

LITERATURE AND POPULAR CULTURE

Discuss the ways in which the Gothic tradition carries Romantic conventions to an extreme. How does it emphasize emotion over reason? Ask students to consider the degree to which the narrator of "The Fall of the House of Usher" gets swept up by the intensity of Romanticism. Had he depended more on his "sense" than on his "sensibility," would the plot be the same?

Then, have students research and write a report on one of the famous Gothic writers, such as the Brontë sisters or Mary Shelley. Ask them to include information about the historical context of the writing. Students might also consider whether the writer led a tragic life, as Poe did, or just had a fertile imagination.

The Gothic Tradition

What is Gothic? The word *Gothic* comes from an architectural style of the late Middle Ages in Europe. People later used the term *Gothic* to describe a kind of romantic, scary novel that sprang up in Germany in the late 1700s and early 1800s. These eerie Gothic novels summoned up the mysterious atmosphere suggested by all those old castles and cathedrals, whose dank dungeons and secret passageways might have witnessed any number of sinister or even supernatural events.

Real page-turners. One of the earliest and most successful Gothic novels in English was written by a woman. Ann Radcliffe's *The Mysteries of Udolpho* (1794) was only the first of many Gothics penned by women, who took up writing Gothic novels as a way to make a living. The public eagerly devoured these sensational stories, which sold the way Stephen King best-sellers do today. Gothic novels so saturated the popular culture of the time that, in 1818, *Northanger Abbey* was published—a novel by the English writer Jane Austen that parodies the Gothic. By the nineteenth century, several novels of high literary merit by women writers fell solidly within the Gothic framework: Mary Shelley's *Frankenstein, or the Modern Prometheus*, Charlotte Brontë's *Jane Eyre*, and Emily Brontë's *Wuthering Heights*. In our time, women writers such as Shirley Jackson, Daphne du Maurier, Barbara Michaels, and Anne Rice have kept the Gothic tradition alive and well.

Ⓐ **Critical Thinking**

Interpreting

❓ How has Roderick changed? [He looks sickly, like a corpse, and he seems deranged, unable to pursue even his artistic activities. He wanders from room to room in a daze, just as his sister has done in an earlier scene.] **What is the probable cause of the change?** [the loss of his sister] **What does this suggest about the relationship between brother and sister or about her role in the story?** [Possible responses: They were extremely close, they had enjoyed "sympathies of a scarcely intelligible nature"; she was his inspiration, his muse, and without her he feels lost; she represents part of his mind, or his other self.]

Ⓑ **Reading Skills and Strategies**

Using Resources

❓ What might Roderick's secret be? [He feels guilty about something involving his sister.]

Ⓒ **Reading Skills and Strategies**

Responding to the Text

❓ How has Roderick's behavior affected the narrator? [He, too, is frightened; he can't sleep.]

---

features of the mental disorder of my friend. His ordinary manner had vanished. His ordinary occupations were neglected or forgotten. He roamed from chamber to chamber with hurried, unequal, and objectless step. The pallor of his countenance had assumed, if possible, a more ghastly hue—but the luminousness of his eye had utterly gone out. The once occasional huskiness of his tone was heard no more; and a tremulous quaver, as if of extreme terror, habitually characterized his utterance. There were times, indeed, when I thought his unceasingly agitated mind was laboring with some oppressive secret, to divulge which he struggled for the necessary courage. At times, again, I was obliged to resolve all into the mere inexplicable vagaries[35] of madness, for I beheld him gazing upon vacancy for long hours, in an attitude of the profoundest attention, as if listening to some imaginary sound. It was no wonder that his condition terrified—that it infected me. I felt creeping upon me, by slow yet certain degrees, the wild influences of his own fantastic yet impressive superstitions.

It was, especially, upon retiring to bed late in the night of the seventh or eighth day after the placing of the lady Madeline within the dungeon, that I experienced the full power of such feelings. Sleep came not near my couch—while the hours waned and waned away. I struggled to reason off the nervousness which had dominion over me. I endeavored to believe that much, if not all of what I felt, was due to the bewildering influence of the gloomy furniture of the room—of the dark and tattered draperies, which, tortured into mo-

35. **vagaries** (vā′gər·ēz): whims.

274 THE AMERICAN RENAISSANCE

Making the Connections

Cultural Connections: Women's Writings

In the early nineteenth century, many women began writing Gothic novels because it was socially more acceptable for them to write in that genre than to write "high" literature or philosophical treatises. In different cultures and times, there have been varying views on what kinds of writing were "suitable" for women. In eleventh-century Japan, women wrote diaries and romances rather than the learned, Chinese-influenced poetry written by men. Ironically, the women's works not respected in those days, such as *The Pillow-Book of Sei Shōnagon*, have clearly stood the test of time. Ask students to choose a genre that interests them, to evaluate whether there are differences between men's and women's work, and to discuss what might cause these differences.

tion by the breath of a rising tempest, swayed fitfully to and fro upon the walls, and rustled uneasily about the decorations of the bed. But my efforts were fruitless. An irrepressible tremor gradually pervaded my frame; and, at length, there sat upon my very heart an incubus[36] of utterly causeless alarm. Shaking this off with a gasp and a struggle, I uplifted myself upon the pillows, and, peering earnestly within the intense darkness of the chamber, harkened—I know not why, except that an instinctive spirit prompted me—to certain low and indefinite sounds which came, through the pauses of the storm, at long intervals, I knew not whence. Overpowered by an intense sentiment of horror, unaccountable yet unendurable, I threw on my clothes with haste (for I felt that I should sleep no more during the night), and endeavored to arouse myself from the pitiable condition into which I had fallen, by pacing rapidly to and fro through the apartment.

I had taken but few turns in this manner, when a light step on an adjoining staircase arrested my attention. I presently recognized it as that of Usher. In an instant afterward he rapped, with a gentle touch, at my door, and entered, bearing a lamp. His countenance was, as usual, cadaverously wan—but, moreover, there was a species of mad hilarity in his eyes—an evidently restrained *hysteria* in his whole demeanor. His air appalled me—but anything was preferable to the solitude which I had so long endured, and I even welcomed his presence as a relief.

> About a week after Madeline's death, an agitated Usher wanders through the house. The narrator, unable to sleep, is overcome by the atmosphere of dread around him.
>
> **?** Describe the emotional states of the narrator and Roderick. In what ways are their reactions similar?

"And you have not seen it?" he said abruptly, after having stared about him for some moments in silence—"you have not then seen it?—but, stay! you shall." Thus speaking, and having carefully shaded his lamp, he hurried to one of the casements, and threw it freely open to the storm.

The impetuous fury of the entering gust nearly lifted us from our feet. It was, indeed, a tempestuous yet sternly beautiful night, and one wildly singular in its terror and its beauty. A whirlwind had apparently collected its force in our vicinity; for there were frequent and violent alterations in the direction of the wind; and the exceeding density of the clouds (which hung so low as to press upon the turrets of the house) did not prevent our perceiving the lifelike velocity with which they flew careering from all points against each other, without passing away into the distance. I say that even their exceeding density did not prevent our perceiving this—yet we had no glimpse of the moon or stars—nor was there any flashing forth of the lightning. But the under surfaces of the huge masses of agitated vapor, as well as all terrestrial objects immediately around us, were glowing in the unnatural light of a faintly luminous and distinctly visible gaseous exhalation which hung about and enshrouded the mansion.

"You must not—you shall not behold this!" said I, shudderingly, to Usher, as I led him, with a gentle violence, from the window to a seat. "These appearances, which bewilder you, are merely electrical phenomena not uncommon—or it may be that they have their ghastly origin in the rank miasma of the tarn.[37] Let us close this casement—the air is chilling and dangerous to your frame. Here is one of your favorite romances. I will read, and you shall listen;—and so we will pass away this terrible night together."

The antique volume which I had taken up was the *Mad Trist* of Sir Launcelot Canning;[38] but I had called it a favorite of Usher's more in sad jest than in earnest; for, in truth, there is little in its uncouth and unimaginative prolixity[39] which could have had interest for the lofty and spiritual ideality of my friend. It was, however, the only book

---

37. **rank miasma** (mī·az′mə) . . . **tarn:** The decomposing matter of the tarn could have given rise to swamp gas or electrical discharges, resulting in frightening optical illusions.
38. ***Mad Trist* of Sir Launcelot Canning:** a book invented by Poe for this story.
39. **prolixity** (prō·lik′sə·tē): wordiness.

Words to Own

demeanor (di·mēn′ər) *n.:* behavior; conduct.

----

36. **incubus** (in′kyo͞o·bəs): nightmare. In medieval times, it was believed that nightmares were caused by demons (incubi) who tormented the sleeping.

D ## Elements of Literature
Atmosphere
? What details heighten the atmosphere of the narrator's nighttime fears? [Possible answers: the gloomy furniture, the dark and tattered draperies that sway in an imperceptible breeze, a rising tempest.]

E ## Question Box
Both characters are seized by feelings of hysteria and horror. The narrator has begun to fall prey to Usher's delusions and agitation.

F ## Elements of Literature
Symbol
? What does this strange whirlwind symbolize? [Usher's conflicting emotions; the approaching climax of the story.]

G ## Elements of Literature
Connotation
? Poe uses the storm to create a mood. How would you describe this mood? [Possible responses: wild, turbulent, hysterical, mad, ominous.] What specific words and phrases produce it? [Possible answers: *impetuous fury; wildly singular in its terror and its beauty; violent alterations; careening from all points against each other; huge masses of agitated vapor; unnatural light; enshrouded.*]

H ## Appreciating Language
Diction
Even as the narrator attempts to dissuade Usher from his terrors, he still speaks with Poe's extravagant and ominous Gothic diction, with phrases like "their ghastly origin in the rank miasma of the tarn." Have students use a dictionary to look up unfamiliar denotations in this phrase, to better appreciate Poe's skillful use of language. [*ghastly* means "horrible, frightful" or "ghostlike; pale; haggard"; *rank* means "strong and offensive in smell or taste"; *miasma* is "a vapor rising as from marshes or decomposing matter."]

Professional Notes

Critical Comments:
Lawrence and Auden on Poe
Poe has engendered strong feelings among his fellow writers. According to D. H. Lawrence, "Poe had a pretty bitter doom. Doomed to seethe down his soul in a great continuous convulsion of disintegration, and doomed to register the process. And then doomed to be abused for it, when he had performed some of the bitterest tasks of human experience, that can be asked of a man. Necessary tasks too. For the human soul must suffer its own disintegration, consciously, if ever it is to survive." From a different perspective, W. H. Auden adds, " 'Abused?' No, a worse doom than that. Doomed to be used in school textbooks as a bait to interest the young in good literature, to be a respectable rival to the pulps."

A Question Box

He reads a romance called the *Mad Trist* to Usher.

B Literary Connections

Poe's Parody

? Poe is parodying the excesses of romances—popular tales of knights who undertake adventures, perform heroic deeds and, eventually, win a virtuous lady. Ask students to point out ways that Ethelred is not all a medieval knight should be. [Ethelred is supposed to be "doughty," yet requires wine for courage and strength; he is intimidated by a stubborn hermit and confronts him only to escape the weather.] **Why might Poe have inserted this parody into his story?** [Possible answer: It provides comic relief, yet also heightens the suspense by dramatizing the mysterious phenomena in the Usher mansion.]

C Reading Skills and Strategies

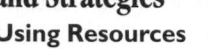

Using Resources

Have students make predictions based on the "coincidence" between the sound of cracking wood in the story of Ethelred, and the sound the narrator and Usher hear. [Possible responses: A door in the house is cracking; someone is ripping wood plankings; something terrible is about to happen.]

D Elements of Literature

Symbol

? What might the dragon symbolize? [Possible responses: a terrible secret; the source of the evil in the tarn; the spirit of Madeline Usher.]

E Question Box

There are parallels between the two tales, especially through sound linkages. The story-within-the-story can be seen as foreshadowing what is about to take place in the Usher mansion.

F Critical Thinking

Making Connections

? When was a grating sound first heard in the story? [Possible response: when Usher and the narrator place Madeline in the tomb.] **What effect does the sound have now?** [It heightens the suspense.]

---

immediately at hand; and I indulged a vague hope that the excitement which now agitated the hypochondriac, might find relief (for the history of mental disorder is full of similar anomalies) even in the extremeness of the folly which I should read. Could I have judged, indeed, by the wild overstrained air of vivacity with which he harkened, or apparently harkened, to the words of the tale, I might well have congratulated myself upon the success of my design.

> **A** **?** *What does the narrator do to try to calm Usher?*

I had arrived at that well-known portion of the story where Ethelred, the hero of the *Trist,* having sought in vain for peaceable admission into the dwelling of the hermit, proceeds to make good an entrance by force. Here, it will be remembered, the words of the narrative run thus:

B "And Ethelred, who was by nature of a doughty[40] heart, and who was now mighty withal, on account of the powerfulness of the wine which he had drunken, waited no longer to hold parley with the hermit, who, in sooth, was of an obstinate and maliceful turn, but, feeling the rain upon his shoulders, and fearing the rising of the tempest, uplifted his mace outright, and, with blows, made quickly room in the plankings of the door for his gauntleted hand; and now pulling therewith sturdily, he so cracked, and ripped, and tore all asunder, that the noise of the dry and hollow-sounding wood alarumed and reverberated throughout the forest."

At the termination of this sentence I started, and for a moment, paused; for it appeared to me (although I at once concluded that my excited fancy had deceived me)—it appeared to me that, from some very remote portion of the mansion, there came, indistinctly, to my ears, what might have been, in its exact similarity of character, the echo (but a stifled and dull one certainly) of the very cracking and ripping sound which Sir **C** Launcelot had so particularly described. It was, beyond doubt, the coincidence alone which had arrested my attention; for, amid the rattling of the sashes of the casements, and the ordinary commingled noises of the still increasing storm, the sound, in itself, had nothing, surely, which should

40. **doughty** (dout′ē): courageous.

have interested or disturbed me. I continued the story:

"But the good champion Ethelred, now entering within the door, was sore enraged and amazed to perceive no signal of the maliceful hermit; but, **D** in the stead thereof, a dragon of a scaly and prodigious demeanor, and of a fiery tongue, which sate in guard before a palace of gold, with a floor of silver; and upon the wall there hung a shield of shining brass with this legend enwritten—

Who entereth herein, a conqueror hath bin;
Who slayeth the dragon, the shield he shall win;

And Ethelred uplifted his mace, and struck upon the head of the dragon, which fell before him, and gave up his pesty breath, with a shriek so horrid and harsh, and withal so piercing, that Ethelred had fain to close his ears with his hands against the dreadful noise of it, the like whereof was never before heard."

> The narrator continues reading aloud from the book about a medieval knight.
>
> **E** **?** *How does the story-within-a-story about Ethelred relate to the main story about the narrator and Usher?*

Here again I paused abruptly, and now with a feeling of wild amazement—for there could be no doubt whatever that, in this instance, I did actually hear (although from what direction it proceeded I found it impossible to say) a low and apparently distant, but harsh, protracted, and **F** most unusual screaming or grating sound—the exact counterpart of what my fancy had already conjured up for the dragon's unnatural shriek as described by the romancer.

Oppressed, as I certainly was, upon the occurrence of this second and most extraordinary coincidence, by a thousand conflicting sensations, in which wonder and extreme terror were predominant, I still retained sufficient presence of mind to avoid exciting, by any observation, the sensitive nervousness of my companion. I was by

---

WORDS TO OWN

obstinate (äb′stə·nət) *adj.:* stubborn.
prodigious (prō·dij′əs) *adj.:* of great size and power.

Professional Notes

Critical Comment: The Protagonist's Mind

According to poet and critic Richard Wilbur, "The narrator's journey to Usher's domain is a dream-journey into his own mind, in the depths of which, and on the brink of sleep, he encounters in Roderick Usher his visionary soul . . . Usher is struggling to purge himself of waking and worldly consciousness, and Lady Madeline's 'wasting away' . . . enacts this process of purgation. Once dead and encoffined—once 'death-refined'—Lady Madeline can rise again . . . [and] 'bear him to the floor a corpse.' Grisly as their death-embrace may seem, it actually symbolizes the momentary reunion of a divided soul; and . . . the final restoration and purification of that soul in the life to come." Ask students if they, like the narrator, were drawn into Usher's world as they were reading. Have them explain their responses.

no means certain that he had noticed the sounds in question; although, assuredly, a strange alteration had, during the last few minutes, taken place in his demeanor. From a position fronting my own, he had gradually brought round his chair, so as to sit with his face to the door of the chamber; and thus I could but partially perceive his features, although I saw that his lips trembled as if he were murmuring inaudibly. His head had dropped upon his breast—yet I knew that he was not asleep, from the wide and rigid opening of the eye as I caught a glance of it in profile. The motion of his body, too, was at variance with this idea—for he rocked from side to side with a gentle yet constant and uniform sway. Having rapidly taken notice of all this, I resumed the narrative of Sir Launcelot, which thus proceeded:

"And now, the champion, having escaped from the terrible fury of the dragon, bethinking himself of the brazen shield, and of the breaking up of the enchantment which was upon it, removed the carcass from out of the way before him, and approached valorously over the silver pavement of the castle to where the shield was upon the wall; which in sooth tarried not for his full coming, but fell down at his feet upon the silver floor, with a mighty great and terrible ringing sound."

No sooner had these syllables passed my lips, than—as if a shield of brass had indeed, at the moment, fallen heavily upon a floor of silver—I became aware of a distinct, hollow, metallic, and clangorous, yet apparently muffled reverberation. Completely unnerved, I leaped to my feet; but the measured rocking movement of Usher was undisturbed. I rushed to the chair in which he sat. His eyes were bent fixedly before him, and throughout his whole countenance there reigned a stony rigidity. But, as I placed my hand upon his shoulder, there came a strong shudder over his whole person; a sickly smile quivered about his lips; and I saw that he spoke in a low, hurried, and gibbering murmur, as if unconscious of my presence. Bending closely over him, I at length drank in the hideous import of his words.

? *What coincidences unnerve the narrator during his reading of the book? How would you describe the atmosphere of the story at this point?*

"Not hear it?—yes, I hear it, and *have* heard it. Long—long—long—many minutes, many hours, many days, have I heard it—yet I dared not—oh, pity me, miserable wretch that I am!—I dared not—I *dared* not speak! *We have put her living in the tomb!* Said I not that my senses were acute? I *now* tell you that I heard her first feeble movements in the hollow coffin. I heard them—many, many days ago—yet I dared not—*I dared not speak!* And now—tonight—Ethelred—ha! ha!— the breaking of the hermit's door, and the death cry of the dragon, and the clangor of the shield!— say, rather, the rending of her coffin, and the grating of the iron hinges of her prison, and her struggles within the coppered archway of the vault! Oh whither shall I fly? Will she not be here anon? Is she not hurrying to upbraid me for my haste? Have I not heard her footstep on the stair? Do I not distinguish that heavy and horrible beating of her heart? *Madman!*"—here he sprang furiously to his feet, and shrieked out his syllables, as if in the effort he were giving up his soul—*"Madman! I tell you that she now stands without the door!"*

As if in the superhuman energy of his utterance there had been found the <u>potency</u> of a spell— the huge antique panels to which the speaker pointed, threw slowly back, upon the instant, their ponderous and ebony jaws. It was the work of the rushing gust—but then without those doors there *did* stand the lofty and enshrouded figure of the lady Madeline of Usher. There was blood upon her white robes, and the evidence of some bitter struggle upon every portion of her

Hearing the noises in the house, Usher has become increasingly distraught.

? *What horrible conjecture has Usher not dared to express until now? Locate the sentence that explains the exact connection between the three noises in the story of Ethelred and the three noises in the house of Usher.*

WORDS TO OWN
potency (pōt''n·sē) *n*.: strength; power.

EDGAR ALLAN POE 277

G **Critical Thinking**
Making the Connections
? Ask students to describe Usher at this point in the tale. Whom or what does he seem to resemble? [Possible response: Usher seems to have entered a trance, as indicated by his mumbling and compulsive rocking. His eyes are "wide and rigid" like the vacant windows on the House of Usher. His stony rigidity and sickly smile may remind students of his twin Madeline when she was entombed.]

H **Question Box**
He hears the same violent, nerve-wracking noises in the mansion that he has been reading about in the romance. The atmosphere is one of extreme tension, suspense and terror.

I **Appreciating Language**
Reading Aloud
In this speech Usher's terrible secret is revealed. You might want to read it aloud, or have a volunteer read the speech aloud. (Students may recognize that Usher's speech here echoes one in "The Tell-Tale Heart.")

J **Critical Thinking**
Making Judgments
Premature burial was one of Poe's favorite themes, figuring also in "The Premature Burial" and "The Cask of Amontillado." Ask students if they think Roderick buried Madeline alive on purpose, or at least with some subconscious awareness of what he was doing. Refer them to the burial scene, where it is suggested that she looks alive, and to Usher's strange, disoriented behavior after her death.

K **Question Box**
He has hidden the conjecture that his sister has been buried alive. The sentence beginning "And now—tonight—Ethelred—ha! ha! . . ." explains the exact connection between the noises in the two stories.

L **English Language Learners**
Archaic Words
Explain that the word *without* is used to mean "outside."

Skill Link

Comparing Text Events to Personal Experience

The events of "The Fall of the House of Usher" may seem remote to most students. Few if any readers will ever be invited to the home of a long-forgotten, deranged friend, whose castle is decaying around him, to assist at his twin sister's burial. However, this story line is an extreme extrapolation of a surprising number of common circumstances.

Activity

Ask students the following questions: Have you ever gone into a place that made you uneasy? Have you ever gotten back in touch with someone you hadn't heard from in a long time and discovered your friend had changed? Have you ever been so conflicted that you questioned your sanity? Invite students to frame more questions that parallel the story.

A **Struggling Readers**
Getting the Main Idea

❓ What happens in the climactic scene? [Madeline, barely alive and bloody after her escape from the vault, collapses on her brother, and they die together.]

B **Elements of Literature**
Symbol

❓ What might Madeline symbolize? [Madeline, Usher's double, comes to claim him, and nature—in the form of the wind—helps her out. She may symbolize a part of Usher's self or mind that he was trying to suppress. This might include some dark urge, his physical sensations, a family secret, or his terror itself—many interpretations are possible.]

RESPONDING TO THE ART

Activity. Have students draw their own versions of this climactic moment, using charcoal, pastels, watercolors, oil paints, or whatever medium they have access to. Ask students to sketch out and plan their composition before they begin the actual illustration. Have them select a particular motif or theme from the story to emphasize. Students should present their work to the class, explaining their artistic choices, and comparing and contrasting their illustration to the one on this page.

A emaciated frame. For a moment she remained trembling and reeling to and fro upon the threshold—then, with a low moaning cry, fell heavily inward upon the person of her brother, and in her **B** violent and now final death agonies, bore him to the floor a corpse, and a victim to the terrors he had anticipated.

From that chamber, and from that mansion, I fled aghast. The storm was still abroad in all its wrath as I found myself crossing the old causeway. Suddenly there shot along the path a wild light, and I turned to see whence a gleam so unusual could have issued; for the vast house and its shadows were alone behind me. The radiance

WORDS TO OWN

emaciated (ē·mā'shē·āt'id) v. used as *adj.:* unusually thin.

278 THE AMERICAN RENAISSANCE

Assessing Learning

Check Test: Questions and Answers
1. How does the narrator know Usher? [They were childhood friends.]
2. How does the narrator try to calm Usher on the night of the storm? [He reads to him.]
3. What three coincidental sounds occur on the night of the storm? [cracking or ripping; screaming or grating; clanging]
4. What is the source of the mysterious sounds? [Madeline, after being buried alive, has broken out of her vault.]

5. What happens to the mansion as the narrator flees from it? [It collapses.]

Standardized Test Preparation
For practice with ACT and SAT formats, see
• *Preparation for College Admission Exams,* p. 21
For practice in proofreading and editing, see
• *Daily Oral Grammar,* Transparency 20

was that of the full, setting, and blood-red moon, which now shone vividly through that once barely discernible fissure, of which I have before spoken as extending from the roof of the building, in a zigzag direction, to the base. While I gazed, this fissure rapidly widened—there came a fierce breath of the whirlwind—the entire orb of the satellite burst at once upon my sight— my brain reeled as I saw the mighty walls rushing asunder—there was a long tumultuous shouting sound like the voice of a thousand waters—and the deep and dank tarn at my feet closed sullenly and silently over the fragments of the *"House of Usher."*

? What happens to Roderick Usher? to the house of Usher? to the narrator? What image are you left with at the end of the story?

C

D

C Elements of Literature
Symbol
? What does the widening fissure, or crack, symbolize? [Possible response: It might symbolize a dark secret, fatal flaw, or inherited insanity that was always latent in the Usher family, and which ultimately widened into the tragic end of the Ushers' sanity, life, and ancestral line.]

D Question Box
Usher dies of shock and fright when his sister, dying, falls on him; the narrator flees as the house collapses into the lake. Possible lasting images include the red moon gleaming above the dark waters of the lake, and the collapse of the mansion.

Connections

A POEM

The Fall of the House of Usher

Reed Whittemore

It was a big boxy wreck of a house
Owned by a classmate of mine named Rod Usher,
Who lived in the thing with his twin sister.
He was a louse and she was a souse.

5 While I was visiting them one wet summer, she died.
We buried her,
Or rather we stuck her in a back room for a bit, meaning to bury her
When the graveyard dried.

But the weather got wetter.
10 One night we were both waked by a twister,
Plus a screeching and howling outside that turned out to be sister
Up and dying again, making it hard for Rod to forget her.
He didn't. He and she died in a heap, and I left quick,
Which was lucky since the house fell in right after,
　　　　　　Like a ton of brick.

EDGAR ALLAN POE 279

Connections

This poem is a lighthearted parody of Poe's tale in contemporary language. Far from being affected by his friend's malady, the narrator is the callous, indifferent, and flippant classmate of "Rod Usher," who narrates the Usher tragedy with an offhand banality that makes for a hilarious contrast to Poe's fevered narrative.

Connecting Across Texts

**Connecting with
"The Fall of the House of Usher"**
Invite students to compare the experience of reading the story with the experience of reading the poem. [Possible responses: The story is a detailed, engrossing, and frightening experience for the reader. The poem is a light, amusing, and intelligent satire. Both are effective in their respective genres.] How is the poem a satire of the story? What else does it satirize? [Possible response: The poem can be seen to satirize the melodramatic, exaggerated, and clichéd aspects of the story with its ridiculously matter-of-fact summary of the story's events. But it also satirizes any contemporary personality (or contemporary reader) who could be this callously insensitive to the emotions Poe tries to evoke.]

First Thoughts [Respond]

1. Student opinions of the story will vary; accept all reasonable reactions. Students who were not deterred by the story's difficult style will probably say that the Gothic devices such as the dungeon vault and the lake's miasma created a powerful, ominous atmosphere.

Shaping Interpretations [Interpret]

2. They reveal a tortured, disordered mind; they reveal a mind that questions its own soundness.

3. Possible response: Roderick and Madeline are, in some sense, two sides of the same personality—one agitated and lively, the other distracted and stupefied to the point of catalepsy.

4. The narrator admits, "I felt creeping upon me, by slow yet certain degrees, the wild influences of his own [Usher's] fantastic yet impressive superstitions." The narrator's reactions to certain events—such as burying Madeline—don't seem normal, either. Moreover, Usher addresses him twice in the closing scene as "Madman!" Some students may say his susceptibility to Usher's fantasy world makes them doubt his version of the events; others may say they trust his account.

5. Possible responses: Isolation from society drove them mad. They became trapped by their Romantic imaginations. They suffered from a congenital mental illness, perhaps aggravated by the family's "direct line of descent."

6. Some students may feel that the ending of the story demonstrates that the narrator has been pulled into Roderick's insanity, and is thus also "haunted" by Madeline. Others will read the narrative more literally, and will locate the insanity in Roderick's mind alone—prompting him to subconsciously plan and execute the murder of his sister.

7. Possible responses: Usher has shut out the outside world. His disordered imagination now dominates his life, and his world collapses because it has lost connection with reality. The fall of the house symbolizes the final collapse of Usher's mind and the end of the family line. Poe's symbolism may suggest that if undisciplined aesthetic impulses are given free rein, the mind may crack and disintegrate into insanity or death.

First Thoughts

1. Did you like "Usher"? How successful was Poe's use of Gothic devices in creating an **atmosphere** of dread?

> **Reading Check**
>
> Imagine that you are telling a friend about the story. List the **main events** in **chronological order.**

Shaping Interpretations

2. What do Roderick's artistic efforts—his guitar solo, his painting, and his poem "The Haunted Palace"—reveal about his state of mind?

3. Why do you think Poe made Roderick and Madeline *twins*—not just brother and sister?

4. The story is presented from the **point of view** of a typical Poe narrator—a character who claims to provide an objective view, but whose rationality becomes suspect during the course of the tale. What evidence can you find that the narrator's state of mind may be deteriorating? How does this uncertainty about the narrator's objectivity affect your response to the story?

5. What do you infer was basically wrong with the Ushers? What evidence do you find to support this **inference**?

6. What do you think is happening at the end of the story, when Madeline Usher appears? (Is she a hallucination, a ghost, or a real person who has been buried alive?) Support your response with evidence from the story.

7. Poe said that the poem "The Haunted Palace" is meant to suggest a disordered brain. How might the whole story be read as an allegory of a journey into the human mind? (An **allegory** is a story or poem that can be read on one level for its literal meaning and on a second level for its symbolic meaning.) What could the final *fall* of the house represent?

Challenging the Text [Evaluate]

8. Possible response: The premature burial of a comatose woman, her escape days later, her brother's immediate death from shock, and the coincidental, sudden collapse of the building, are all far-fetched.

(For Elements of Literature annotations, see bottom of p. T281.)

Challenging the Text

8. Which details in this story fail to make sense to you? For example, how could the narrator not have known his old friend had a twin? (Be sure to refer to your reading notes.) Discuss your challenges with other readers.

ELEMENTS OF LITERATURE

Poe's Symbols

What do these symbols mean to you?

⊘ ∞ ♥ π

The images above are sometimes called conventional, or public, symbols. This means that they are well known, at least in a particular culture, and that their meaning is agreed upon.

Writers and artists often create their own unique **symbols.** In this story, for example, Poe has Roderick mention his strange theory of the "sentience," or consciousness, of the mansion's stones. It could be that Poe is suggesting a relationship between the house and Roderick's mind. As we think about this, we might decide that the decaying house symbolizes Roderick's decaying sanity.

With a group, list details from Poe's story that might be symbolic. Next to each item, write your guess as to what it symbolizes.

> **Guidelines for Recognizing Symbols**
>
> 1. A symbol is a concrete object, a person, a place, or an action that works on at least two levels: It functions as itself and suggests a wider meaning.
> 2. Symbols are often visual.
> 3. The symbol is identified with something that is very different from it, yet the two things share a similar quality.
> 4. The writer gives the symbol a great deal of emphasis.
> 5. The symbol usually relates to the story's theme.

> **Reading Check**
>
> Narrator arrives at House of Usher; Roderick Usher and his sister Madeline are in physical and emotional decline; narrator is unable to relieve Usher; Madeline apparently dies; narrator and Usher place her in a dungeon vault; Madeline reappears days later, falls dead upon her brother; he dies of shock; narrator flees; house collapses and sinks into lake.

Sensing Connotations: Creating Atmosphere

All words have particular **denotations,** or specific dictionary definitions. Some words also have **connotations**—associations and emotional overtones that people have come to attach to them. For example, the word *puzzling* suggests that something is mildly confusing or confounding. The word *bewildering* goes a step further, suggesting that something is so puzzling as to be hopelessly confusing.

Words that have especially strong positive or negative connotations are called **loaded,** or

suggestive, words. Poe felt that a story's mood, or **atmosphere,** was of paramount importance, so it's no surprise that he often used suggestive words to manipulate our emotional responses.

1. Reread the famous first paragraph of Poe's story. Which words suggest decay, sterility, finality, and emptiness? List them.

2. Rewrite the first few sentences of the first paragraph. Change the time of day, the time of year, and the weather conditions to paint a cheerful or cozy picture of the house of Usher. How does your choice of words change the atmosphere of the paragraph?

CHOICES: Building Your Portfolio

Writer's Notebook

1. Collecting Ideas for a Controversial Issue

Using the topic you explored in an earlier Writer's Notebook (page 258), or another controversial topic of your choice, write down two or three emotional appeals. Use words with strong **connotative** meanings to persuade readers to accept your position on the issue. Save your notes for possible use in the Writer's Workshop on page 331.

Interpreting a Story

2. What's It All About?

Select one of these interpretations of "The Fall of the House

of Usher"—or develop a position of your own—and defend it in a brief essay.

- The house personifies the diseased, dying Usher family.
- The narrator is insane or dreaming. The entire story is a projection of his mind.
- The story is an **allegory** about an artist who is drawn on a journey through the dark side of the human mind.

Creative Writing

3. Changing Genres

Tell the story of the house of Usher in another genre: a poem, a newspaper article, a magazine interview, a script, a picture book, a comic strip— even a drawing or song. For inspiration, see Reed Whittemore's poem "The Fall of the House of Usher" (***Connections,*** page 279).

Music

4. A Little Night Music

Search for music—classical, jazz, contemporary instrumental, rock, movie soundtracks— that to you evokes the **atmosphere** and events of the story. Play the music for the class and explain why you chose it.

Art

5. House of Horrors

What does the house of Usher *look* like? Draw, paint, or even build your vision of this ghastly Gothic structure.

Monitoring Your Reading

6. Talk It Over

With a group, discuss the reading problems posed by Poe's story and share the strategies you used to work them out.

Sensing Connotations: Creating Atmosphere

1. *dull, dark, soundless, autumn, oppressively, dreary, evening, melancholy, insufferable gloom, unrelieved, desolate, terrible, bleak, vacant, rank, decayed, depression, hideous, iciness, sinking, sickening, unredeemed dreariness, unnerved, insoluble, shadowy fancies, annihilate, sorrowful, precipitous brink, black and lurid tarn, unruffled luster, gray sedge, ghastly tree stems, vacant and eyelike windows*

2. Possible response: "One bright, sunny, spring morning, birds singing in joy, white clouds floating benignly high in the heavens, I was riding alone, on horseback, through an unusually picturesque tract of country. At length I found myself, as noon approached, within view of the magnificent House of Usher." The mood becomes energetic and happy.

Grading Timesaver

Rubrics for each Choices assignment appear on p. 122 in the *Portfolio Management System.*

CHOICES: Building Your Portfolio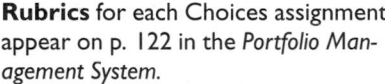

1–2. Suggest that partners brainstorm words with connotations. Suggest that students analyze the evidence in the story for a specific thesis.

3. Advise students to choose a genre they themselves read and with which they are familiar.

4–5. Tell students to imagine the sounds or look of the story before beginning.

6. Keep a list of the strategies.

ELEMENTS OF LITERATURE

Poe's Symbols

Ask students to identify each of the symbols on p. 280 and to describe what each means to them. Remind students that though they are surrounded by symbols in daily life, symbols within a literary work are usually open to a variety of interpretations and are not as clear cut as those shown here.

Examples from "Usher" include the following:
- the vacant, eyelike windows of the house,

symbolizing Roderick's lack of sensory feeling or his growing madness
- the gloomy, decaying house, symbolizing the condition of the family and Usher's mind
- Roderick's painting of a vault or tunnel, its tomblike appearance symbolizing Madeline's tomb or the condition of his mind
- the frequent and violent alterations in the direction of the wind during the tempest, symbolizing the split in Roderick's psyche

Before You Read

THE RAVEN

Make the Connection

Exploring the Dark Side
"The Raven" has the sound of a lyric, but, actually, it is a narrative poem with a plot that leads the reader from curiosity to horror. The poem explores one aspect of the dark side of human nature: what Poe himself called "that species of despair which delights in self-torture." In the jargon of psychology, the narrator "projects" onto the bird whatever his own wild imagination dredges up.

Reading Skills and Strategies

Analyzing the Melodies of Language
You'll enjoy "The Raven" more if you read it aloud. After you have read the poem aloud once, write down some lines and passages that strike you as being especially musical, clever, or memorable.

Elements of Literature

Sound Effects
One of the reasons "The Raven" became so popular was that it was catchy in the way a song can be. Like many songs, the poem uses evocative rhythms, clever rhymes, alliteration, and other sound effects. These elements make the poem cry out for oral interpretation. (For more on Sound Effects, see page 288 and the Handbook of Literary Terms.)

Background

It may be hard to imagine today, but when Poe's "The Raven" was first published in 1845, it was a hit—a popular success with the same kind of impact that the Beatles' first single had in 1962. It seemed as though everyone read "The Raven," recited it, and talked about it. Poe became a household name with this poem, but he received only about ten dollars for it.

The Raven

Edgar Allan Poe

Once upon a midnight dreary, while I pondered, weak and weary,
Over many a quaint and curious volume of forgotten lore—
While I nodded, nearly napping, suddenly there came a tapping,
As of someone gently rapping, rapping at my chamber door—
5 " 'Tis some visitor," I muttered, "tapping at my chamber door—
  Only this and nothing more."

Ah, distinctly I remember it was in the bleak December;
And each separate dying ember wrought its ghost upon the floor.
Eagerly I wished the morrow;—vainly I had sought to borrow
10 From my books surcease° of sorrow—sorrow for the lost Lenore—
For the rare and radiant maiden whom the angels name Lenore—
  Nameless *here* for evermore.

10. **surcease:** an end.

282 THE AMERICAN RENAISSANCE

Resources: Print and Media

And the silken, sad, uncertain rustling of each purple curtain
Thrilled me—filled me with fantastic terrors never felt before;
15　So that now, to still the beating of my heart, I stood repeating
" 'Tis some visitor entreating entrance at my chamber door—
Some late visitor entreating entrance at my chamber door;—
　　　This it is and nothing more."

Presently my soul grew stronger; hesitating then no longer,
20　"Sir," said I, "or Madam, truly your forgiveness I implore;
But the fact is I was napping, and so gently you came rapping,
And so faintly you came tapping, tapping at my chamber door,
That I scarce was sure I heard you"—here I opened wide the door;———
　　　Darkness there and nothing more.

25　Deep into that darkness peering, long I stood there wondering, fearing,
Doubting, dreaming dreams no mortal ever dared to dream before;
But the silence was unbroken, and the stillness gave no token,
And the only word there spoken was the whispered word, "Lenore?"
This I whispered, and an echo murmured back the word, "Lenore!"
30　　　Merely this and nothing more.

Back into the chamber turning, all my soul within me burning,
Soon again I heard a tapping somewhat louder than before.
"Surely," said I, "surely that is something at my window lattice;
Let me see, then, what thereat is, and this mystery explore—
35　Let my heart be still a moment and this mystery explore;—
　　　'Tis the wind and nothing more!"

Open here I flung the shutter, when, with many a flirt and flutter,
In there stepped a stately Raven of the saintly days of yore;°
Not the least obeisance° made he; not a minute stopped or stayed he;
40　But, with mien of lord or lady, perched above my chamber door—
Perched upon a bust of Pallas° just above my chamber door—
　　　Perched, and sat, and nothing more.

Then this ebony bird beguiling my sad fancy into smiling,
By the grave and stern decorum of the countenance it wore,
45　"Though thy crest be shorn and shaven, thou," I said, "art sure no craven,
Ghastly grim and ancient Raven wandering from the Nightly shore—
Tell me what thy lordly name is on the Night's Plutonian shore!"°
　　　Quoth the Raven "Nevermore."

D

38. **Raven . . . of yore:** "Of yore" is an obsolete way of saying "of time long past." Poe's allusion is to 1 Kings 17:1–6, which tells of the prophet Elijah being fed by ravens in the wilderness.
39. **obeisance** (ō·bā′səns): gesture of respect or subservience.
41. **Pallas:** Pallas Athena, the Greek goddess of wisdom.
47. **Plutonian shore:** Pluto is the Greek god of the underworld—the land of darkness—called Hades (hā′dēz′). Hades is separated from the world of the living by several rivers, hence the mention of a shore.

EDGAR ALLAN POE 283

Summary ■ ■

Studying at midnight, a weary student mourns his dead love, Lenore. He hears a tapping at his door and flings it open but sees nothing. Opening the shutter, he is greeted by a mysterious raven that enters the room. The talking bird amuses the speaker at first, but its refrain of "Nevermore," in answer to the speaker's pleading questions about meeting Lenore after death, drive him to despair and madness. As the poem closes, the bird still sits above the door, a brooding symbol and symptom of his mental distress.

A Reading Skills and Strategies
Analyzing the Melodies of Language
At first, students may read too quickly or in a singsong fashion. Consider playing the CD of the selection or beginning the reading yourself to set the mood.

B Elements of Literature
Sound Effects
? What is the poem's rhyme scheme? [abcbbb] The entire poem uses the same b end rhyme. What difficulties does this pose for the writer? [Possible response: The writer must come up with a lot of rhyming words for the or sound.]

C Elements of Literature
Refrain
? Examine how Poe used this second refrain of the poem to fill in crucial background information, and also to establish a central recurrent idea in the poem. Where is "here" and what is the significance of "evermore"? [Possible response: Lenore is without a name in this life ("here") because she has died. The speaker uses the word evermore to emphasize the eternity of her death, and to introduce this underlying theme of absolute eternity in the poem.]

D Reading Skills and Strategies
Making Inferences
? In Greek myth the Raven symbolizes both wisdom and prophecy. What does the raven's perching on the bust of Athena imply? [It twice suggests that the narrator will be offered wisdom. It suggests that the raven has the powers of an oracle.]

Reaching All Students

Struggling Readers
The rhyme and rhythm of the poem sometimes make it hard to follow the narrative. Suggest that students read the poem at least twice: first for the sound, then for the story.

English Language Learners
To help improve students' pronunciation and cadence, read the first two lines of the poem aloud and have students read after you. (For more proficient English language learners, you might read the entire first stanza.)

? Why does the speaker think at first that Nevermore is the bird's name? [The bird speaks that word in answer to the question, "Tell me what thy lordly name is" (l. 47).] Tell students that the word *Nevermore* becomes the new refrain in the poem. Challenge students to ask themselves, after each stanza, what specific comment or question the word *Nevermore* refers to.

B **Reading Skills and Strategies**
Getting the Main Idea

? What explanation does the speaker offer for why the Raven replies "Nevermore" to every question? [Possible response: Some unhappy master from the past taught the Raven only that word.] What do you think of this explanation? [Possible response: This explanation is possible, but it seems more likely that this imagined victim of "unmerciful Disaster" is, (like perhaps the voice of the raven itself) an external projection based on the narrator's own sorrows.]

C **Elements of Literature**
Sound Effects

? What sound effects does Poe employ in these three lines? [He uses repetition, alliteration, assonance and onomatopoeia.] What do these effects tell the reader about the speaker's mood and state of mind at this point in the poem? [Although the speaker starts out with a lighthearted tone in this stanza, his compulsive repetition of "ominous," along with the alliterative list of *grim, ungainly, ghastly, gaunt* suggest that he is feeling agitated by the bird, and beginning to see it as a symbol of his unending sorrow.]

D **Reading Skills and Strategies**
Analyzing the Melodies of Language

? Note the repetition of words and phrases in ll. 4–5 of every stanza as well as the use of internal rhyme and alliteration in these lines. What effect does Poe achieve with these techniques? [They usually emphasize the depressing "dark" idea in each stanza and pick up the rhythm leading to the refrain.]

Resources ————

Literary Elements
• Poetry Transparencies 1–5, p. 111

Much I marveled this ungainly fowl to hear discourse so plainly,
50 Though its answer little meaning—little relevancy bore;
For we cannot help agreeing that no living human being
Ever yet was blessed with seeing bird above his chamber door—
Bird or beast upon the sculptured bust above his chamber door,
   With such name as "Nevermore."

55 But the Raven, sitting lonely on the placid bust, spoke only
That one word, as if his soul in that one word he did outpour.
Nothing farther then he uttered—not a feather then he fluttered—
Till I scarcely more than muttered "Other friends have flown before—
On the morrow *he* will leave me, as my Hopes have flown before."
60   Then the bird said "Nevermore."

Startled at the stillness broken by reply so aptly spoken,
"Doubtless," said I, "what it utters is its only stock and store
Caught from some unhappy master whom unmerciful Disaster
Followed fast and followed faster till his songs one burden bore—
65 Till the dirges of his Hope that melancholy burden bore
   Of 'Never—nevermore.' "

But the Raven still beguiling my sad fancy into smiling,
Straight I wheeled a cushioned seat in front of bird, and bust and door;
Then, upon the velvet sinking, I betook myself to linking
70 Fancy unto fancy, thinking what this ominous bird of yore—
What this grim, ungainly, ghastly, gaunt, and ominous bird of yore
   Meant in croaking "Nevermore."

This I sat engaged in guessing, but no syllable expressing
To the fowl whose fiery eyes now burned into my bosom's core;
75 This and more I sat divining, with my head at ease reclining
On the cushion's velvet lining that the lamplight gloated o'er,
But whose velvet-violet lining with the lamplight gloating o'er,
   She shall press, ah, nevermore!

284 THE AMERICAN RENAISSANCE

Making the Connections

Cross-Cultural Connections

Poe's use of the raven in this poem draws on his wide reading about ancient and foreign cultures. As stated earlier, in Greek mythology the bird is a symbol of wisdom and prophecy. In Norse mythology, two ravens sit on the chief god Odin's shoulders, one raven symbolizing thought and the other memory. For some Native American groups, the raven is a god and a cunning trickster figure. In ancient Brazilian stories, the raven is associated with death. When someone dies, his or her soul leaves the body in the form of a raven. In Christian lore, the raven often is a symbol of sin, the devil, and death. As students read the poem, ask them to think about what symbolic meaning the raven might have.

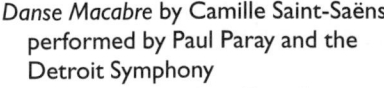

285

RESPONDING TO THE ART

These illustrations for "The Raven" feature a scratchboard technique which accounts for the distinctive style of the talon prints on p. 282, the menacing raven on pp. 284–285, and the raven perched on a bust on p. 286. A scratchboard is a cardboard coated with white chalk or clay and then covered with glossy black ink. Drawings are made by scratching through the ink to the white compound. **Activity.** Ask students to evaluate the mood created by the drawings of the raven. [Possible responses: frightening, foreboding, exciting.] Explore whether the mood would be the same if a more lifelike rendition of a raven had been used, perhaps like the raven in the Poe portrait on p. 214.

BROWSING IN THE FILES

A Critic's Comment. The poet Richard Wilbur explains "Poe's rhythmic regularity" as principally due to the poet's thinking "of the poem not as an object for contemplation but as a means of engendering 'sensations which bewilder while they enthrall—and which would *not* so enthrall if they did not so bewilder.' In short, he thought of the poem as casting a spell, and accordingly endowed it with the brevity, repetitiveness, sonority, and the impressive rhythmic monotony of a charm or incantation."

Listening to Music 🎵

Danse Macabre by Camille Saint-Saëns performed by Paul Paray and the Detroit Symphony

Unlike Edgar Allan Poe, French composer Camille Saint-Saëns (san säns') (1835–1921) never had to struggle for recognition. A prodigy who began playing the piano at age two-and-a-half, he began winning prizes for musical composition while still a student at the Paris Conservatory and at age twenty-two became the organist at Paris's famous church, Église de la Madeleine. The *Danse Macabre,* a "symphonic poem," tells of a wintry midnight when Death plays a tune on his violin that sets some skeletons dancing until the rooster's crow ushers in the dawn.

Activity

Listen to the *Danse Macabre,* and try to identify the sounds that signal the stroke of midnight and the crowing of the rooster at dawn. Then, working with other students, choreograph and perform a pantomime of "The Raven" or "The Fall of the House of Usher," or read either text aloud with Saint-Saëns's composition as background music.

Ⓐ Critical Thinking

Analyzing

? How does the speaker's attitude toward the bird change in the course of the first two stanzas on this page? [The speaker at first associates the Raven with the seraphim and God, but when the Raven continues to respond "Nevermore" to the speaker's urgent appeals for relief from his suffering, the speaker begins to revile the bird as an evil creature.]

Ⓑ Critical Thinking

Analyzing

? What is the effect of the multiple dashes in ll. 85–89? [The short, broken phrases emphasize the speaker's growing agitation.]

Ⓒ Elements of Literature

Sound Effects

? Line 91 repeats l. 85. In these lines, what slant rhyme does Poe use? [*evil* and *devil*] What does this repetition reveal about the speaker's state of mind? [Possible responses: The man sees the bird as an evil omen; he is becoming more obsessed, and his mind keeps running through the same phrases.]

Ⓓ Critical Thinking

Analyzing

? What makes this use of "Nevermore" possibly the most heart-rending in the poem? [Possible response: The bird seems to dash the speaker's last hopes that he will meet Lenore in an afterlife.]

Ⓔ Reading Skills and Strategies

Making Inferences

? How is the speaker behaving now? [He is jumping up and shrieking at the bird.] What seems to be happening to him? [Possible response: He seems to be losing control; he may be going mad with grief.]

Ⓕ Reading Skills and Strategies

Analyzing the Melodies of Language

? What is the emotional effect of repeating the phrase "still is sitting"? [It underscores the speaker's anguish at the continued traumatic presence of the raven in his room.]

Then, methought, the air grew denser, perfumed from an unseen censer
80   Swung by seraphim° whose footfalls tinkled on the tufted floor.
     "Wretch," I cried, "thy God hath lent thee—by these angels he hath sent thee
     Respite—respite and nepenthe° from thy memories of Lenore;
     Quaff, oh quaff this kind nepenthe and forget this lost Lenore!"
              Quoth the Raven "Nevermore."

85   "Prophet!" said I, "thing of evil!—prophet still, if bird or devil!—
         Whether Tempter sent, or whether tempest tossed thee here ashore,
     Desolate yet all undaunted, on this desert land enchanted—
     On this home by Horror haunted—tell me truly, I implore—
     Is there—*is* there balm in Gilead?°—tell me—tell me, I implore!"
90   Quoth the Raven "Nevermore."

     "Prophet!" said I, "thing of evil!—prophet still, if bird or devil!
     By that Heaven that bends above us—by that God we both adore—
     Tell this soul with sorrow laden if, within the distant Aidenn,°
     It shall clasp a sainted maiden whom the angels name Lenore—
95   Clasp a rare and radiant maiden whom the angels name Lenore."
              Quoth the Raven "Nevermore."

     "Be that word our sign of parting, bird or fiend!" I shrieked, upstarting—
     "Get thee back into the tempest and the Night's Plutonian shore!
     Leave no black plume as a token of that lie thy soul hath spoken!
100 Leave my loneliness unbroken!—quit the bust above my door!
     Take thy beak from out my heart, and take thy form from off my door!"
              Quoth the Raven "Nevermore."

     And the Raven, never flitting, still is sitting, *still* is sitting
     On the pallid bust of Pallas just above my chamber door;
105 And his eyes have all the seeming of a demon's that is dreaming,
     And the lamplight o'er him streaming throws his shadow on the floor;
     And my soul from out that shadow that lies floating on the floor
              Shall be lifted—nevermore!

80. seraphim: the highest of the nine ranks of angels; often pictured as having three sets of wings.
82. nepenthe (nē·pen'thē): a sleeping potion that people once believed would relieve pain and sorrow. Eventually it came to stand for anything that brought such relief.
89. Is . . . Gilead: literally, "Is there any relief from my sorrow?" Poe paraphrases a line from Jeremiah 8:22: "Is there no balm in Gilead?" Gilead was a region in ancient Palestine known for its healing herbs, such as balm. Balm has come to mean any healing ointment.
93. Aidenn: Arabic for "Eden" or "Heaven."

Making the Connections

Connecting to the Theme: "The Realms of Darkness"

The raven, a black bird who arrives from "Night's Plutonian shore," croaks a word of nihilism, and remains stubbornly in the speaker's home, is a symbol of the darkness within the human soul—a symbol so appropriate that it has become part of popular as well as literary culture.

Assessing Learning

Informal Assessment

Have peers assess each other's appreciation of the poem by rereading it aloud in groups of three or four. As the reading proceeds, have students pause to share their responses to these questions:

• Which passages make you laugh or smile?
• Which passages give you the chills?
• Which passages do you not understand?

PRIMARY Sources — AN ESSAY

Poe's Process: Writing "The Raven"

Several years after the hugely successful publication of "The Raven," Poe wrote an essay describing how he composed the poem. He described the writing of the poem as though he were solving a mathematical puzzle. Here are the first stages of Poe's writing process:

1. He decided he wanted to write a poem with a melancholy effect.

2. Then he decided that the melancholy would be reinforced by the refrain "Nevermore" (he liked its sound) and that a raven would utter the refrain. (Before he settled on a raven, though, he considered an owl and even a parrot.)

3. Finally, he decided his subject would be what he thought was the most melancholy subject in the world: a lover's mourning for a beautiful woman who has died.

Now Poe was ready to write. The first stanza he wrote, he claimed, was the climactic one, lines 85–90. From there he set about choosing his details: the interior space in which the lover, who is a student, and the Raven are brought together; the tapping that introduces the Raven; the fact that the night is stormy rather than calm; and the action of the Raven alighting on the bust of Pallas.

Then Poe goes on to describe his writing process:

> . . . The raven addressed, answers with its customary word, "Nevermore"—a word which finds immediate echo in the melancholy heart of the student, who, giving utterance aloud to certain thoughts suggested by the occasion, is again startled by the fowl's repetition of "Nevermore." The student now guesses the state of the case, but is impelled, as I have before explained, by the human thirst for self-torture, and in part by superstition, to propound such queries to the bird as will bring him, the lover, the most of the luxury of sorrow, through the anticipated answer "Nevermore." . . .

> It will be observed that the words "from out my heart," involve the first metaphorical expression in the poem. They, with the answer, "Nevermore," dispose the mind to seek a moral in all that has been previously narrated. The reader begins now to regard the Raven as emblematical [symbolic]—but it is not until the very last line of the very last stanza, that the intention of making him emblematical of *Mournful and never ending Remembrance* is permitted distinctly to be seen. . . .

—Edgar Allan Poe

Illustration by Wilfred Satty for "The Fall of the House of Usher."

EDGAR ALLAN POE 287

This feature contains excerpts from Edgar Allan Poe's essay on the composition of "The Raven." Starting with his formal goals in writing the poem, Poe recounts how he established the intended effect on the audience, then chose the bird's refrain to help produce that effect, and only then arrived at the speaker's painful personal history. After beginning with the speaker's dramatic confrontation with the bird in ll. 85–90, Poe insists that the exposition of the poem followed the logic of "the human thirst for self-torture," as the student aggravates his own sorrow by pursuing the "conversation" with the raven.

A Background

Critic Daniel Hoffman believes that Poe's analysis in *The Philosophy of Composition* of how he wrote "The Raven" is pure fiction. He thinks the essay is more a defense of Poe's theories of poetry than an actual account of writing "The Raven." Moreover, he thinks Poe realized this. He says "Poe . . . does warn us, at the very end of his essay, to look more deeply than his autopsy of 'The Raven' delved: look, he says, for 'some undercurrent, however indefinite, of meaning.' Even as he revels in having so dexterously performed a complete anatomy of his poem, he cannot stop his mouth from whispering 'This wonderful dissection has merely skinned my Raven, it hasn't exposed the vital organs of the soul.'"

B Critical Thinking

Making Judgments

After students have read Poe's explanation of his writing process, ask them to discuss his ideas, considering whether they think most writers begin with an inspiration to write about a theme or with a desire to produce a single effect, such as melancholy. Ask students how they themselves begin writing. Finally, ask students if they feel that the Raven is "emblematic of *Mournful and never ending Remembrance*," as Poe maintains.

Using Students' Strengths

Visual/Spatial Learners

Provide students with a copy of the poem. Ask them to cut it apart by stanzas and to then organize the stanzas as Poe claims he wrote the poem. (The climax, setting of the room, tapping, details of the night, and Raven's alighting on the bust.) Have students compare the two versions.

Verbal Learners

Have students consult a rhyming dictionary to find other words that rhyme with *nevermore*. Invite them to compose an additional stanza, in Poe's style, using those words. You might also ask them to suggest alternative refrains.

MAKING MEANINGS

First Thoughts [Respond]

1. Possible responses: It is a figment of the speaker's imagination, arising from mental and physical exhaustion; the raven is real, and encountering this symbol of Death after losing Lenore pushes the speaker into madness.

Shaping Interpretations [Interpret]

2. The atmosphere is mysterious and ominous. The narrator describes the time of the events as "bleak December." Dying embers in the fireplace produce "ghosts upon the floor." The curtains rustle sadly, and the narrator feels "fantastic terrors."

3. The bird's prophecy that the speaker will never forget his sorrow or see Lenore wounds him deeply.

4. Although the poem starts somberly, the first appearance of the raven evokes a kind of amusement in the speaker (ll. 37–54). The speaker's mood becomes more reflective in ll. 55–78. It is only in ll. 79–84 that the speaker decides that the visit of the raven may be intended as a message for him, and the tone becomes ever more desperate in ll. 85–102. In ll. 103–108, in a tone of quiet despair, the speaker says that the demon-eyed raven remains on the bust and that his own soul lies forever in the shadow of the raven. The exaggerated nature of both claims suggests that perhaps the speaker has gone mad.

5. Students should refer to the poem's rhyme scheme and meter and to Poe's use of devices such as internal rhyme, alliteration, and onomatopoeia.

6. The raven is an unending reminder of the speaker's loss and sorrow.

7. Possible symbolic meanings include death, the pain of loss, despair, or eternal remembrance. A chicken would be too humorous, a hawk too noble, a sparrow too small, a dove or nightingale too gentle. The raven's black color and squawking sound also make it appropriate for the mournful mood.

MAKING MEANINGS

First Thoughts

1. Do you think there really *was* a raven in the speaker's chambers? Why or why not? If not, what is your explanation for what happened on that "midnight dreary" in the speaker's room?

Shaping Interpretations

2. How would you describe the **atmosphere** created by the setting? Which **images** in the beginning of the poem create this atmosphere?

3. In line 101, what do you think the speaker might mean when he begs the bird, "Take thy beak from out my heart"?

4. The speaker's **tone** changes as the Raven gradually turns from a comic figure into a demonic figure. Trace these changes in tone. Is there evidence in the last stanza that the speaker goes mad? Explain.

5. How did the poem's **sound effects** affect your response to the poem? Go back to the text and the notes you made after reading the poem aloud. Then, cite passages that you'd especially like to read aloud.

6. By the end of the poem, what do you think it means that the Raven "*still* is sitting" in the speaker's chamber?

7. Many readers take the Raven as a **symbol**—it functions as a real raven in the poem, but it also has a broader, figurative meaning. What, in your opinion, does the Raven symbolize? Why do you suppose Poe chose a raven to carry this meaning rather than a chicken, hawk, sparrow, or other bird? (For more on symbols, see page 280. For Poe's thoughts on the Raven, see Primary Sources, page 287.)

Connecting with the Text

8. What do you make of the poem's speaker? Freewrite some thoughts that you imagine might be running through his head during or after the events of the poem. Then get together with a small group of other students, and take turns being the speaker, who has been put on the "hot seat" to answer questions.

Extending the Text

9. Compare "The Raven" with any other stories you know of in which a person is deeply moved by the loss of someone he or she loves. One such story is "The Jilting of Granny Weatherall" (page 704) by Katherine Anne Porter.

Challenging the Text

10. Suppose someone said to you that "The Raven" is not worth reading because it's unbelievable. How would you answer this challenge?

READING SKILLS AND STRATEGIES

Hearing Sound Effects

"The Raven" is a virtuoso performance in the use of **internal rhyme**—rhyme that occurs within the lines, or repetition of an end rhyme within a line. "Dreary" and "weary" in line 1 prepare us for a pattern of internal rhyming sounds. "Napping," "tapping," and "rapping" in lines 3 and 4 make us expect more. Some of Poe's rhymes are ingenious. Not many writers would think of rhyming "window lattice" with "what threat is" (lines 33–34).

Skillful use of repetition occurs with the **refrain** "Nevermore"; it is also an important element in the **rhyme scheme** of the poem. Poe keeps the sound of the word echoing in our ears through repetition combined with changes in tone.

Throughout the poem, Poe uses the technique of **alliteration** (the repetition of a consonant sound) to create **onomatopoeia**—the use of words with sounds that actually echo their sense. A good example of alliteration is in line 71, where the hard *g* is repeated four times, almost resulting in a tongue twister: "this grim, ungainly, ghastly, gaunt, and ominous bird of yore."

1. Locate the internal rhymes in lines 79–84 and 91–96. What other internal rhymes can you find?

2. What other word are you reminded of when you hear the refrain "Nevermore"? How does this echo affect you?

3. Where in lines 13–18 and 37–42 is alliteration used to create onomatopoeia?

Connecting with the Text [Apply]

8. Students should base their ideas on evidence in the poem and demonstrate the change in the speaker's tone as the narrative progresses.

Extending the Text [Extend]

9. Students should analyze points of comparison, such as the character of the lost love, character traits of the mourner, or the speaker's or another character's reaction to loss.

Challenging the Text [Evaluate]

10. Possible responses: The poem is an outstanding example of the creative use of poetic devices; the poem is a superb analysis of the effects of fixating on feelings of loss; the poem is a romantic tribute to the importance of remembering the dead.

(For Reading Skills and Strategies annotations, see the bottom of p. T289.)

CHOICES: Building Your Portfolio

Writer's Notebook

1. Collecting Ideas for a Controversial Issue

In the Writer's Workshop on page 331, you'll write about a controversial issue. You can use vivid images and even a repeated refrain—as Poe does in "The Raven"—to make your arguments more persuasive. Review your Writer's Notebook entries for topics, or choose a controversial issue you know something about. Write down at least three details supporting your position. Try to arouse your readers' feelings and persuade them to agree with you. Can you think of an effective refrain? Keep your notes for possible use in the Workshop.

Interpreting an Idea

2. What's His Problem?

In Primary Sources (page 287), Poe explains that the speaker in "The Raven" is impelled "by the human thirst for self-torture." In a paragraph, explain what you think this statement means, and tell whether or not you think the speaker in the poem exhibits this compulsion.

Creative Writing / Performance

3. A Poe-etic Parody

One of the best measures of a popular success is the number of times it has been parodied. "The Raven" has surely been one of the world's most successful poems, for it has been parodied countless times. In Poe's day, parodies with such titles as "The Craven," "The Turkey," and "The Mammoth Squash" abounded. One parodist used the poem as an inspiration for a political lampoon:

> Once upon an evening dreary, the Council pondered weak and weary,
> Over many a long petition which was voted down a bore.

Try your own hand at parody by writing at least two stanzas of a humorous version of "The Raven" that imitates Poe's **rhyme scheme** and use of **sound effects**. You may want to change the name Lenore to another name that has many possible rhymes. Perform your humorous poem for the class.

Art

4. A Portrait of Poe

Make a collage "portrait" of Edgar Allan Poe by putting together different visual items—colors, images, and even textures—that, to you, suggest Poe and his works. You might want to refer to Poe's typical settings and characters, as well as to his thematic concerns and actual events in his life. When you have completed your collage, write a "Note from the Artist" explaining what each element in the collage stands for.

Drawing by Chas. Addams; © 1983
The New Yorker Magazine, Inc.

"One more time."

EDGAR ALLAN POE 289

Grading Timesaver

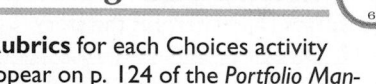

Rubrics for each Choices activity appear on p. 124 of the *Portfolio Management System*.

CHOICES: Building Your Portfolio

1. **Writer's Notebook** Encourage students to let their minds range freely and to jot down images or phrases next to their notes on ideas and details.
2. **Interpreting an Idea** Suggest that students prewrite by writing "The Human Thirst for Self-Torture" at the top of a sheet of paper and freewriting for two to five minutes, then circling their best ideas as they reread the freewriting.
3. **Creative Writing/Performance** Students may wish to do this activity in pairs or groups of three or four. Larger groups may be unwieldy.
4. **Art** Encourage students to look for collage items in sources they might not at first link with Poe, such as contemporary magazines.

READING SKILLS AND STRATEGIES

Have one student read aloud the first paragraph, on internal rhyme. Ask students to write a line using internal rhyme and to share it with the class. Have another student read the second paragraph and ll. 79–90 from the poem. Ask students to discuss the effect of the rhyme scheme in these two stanzas. Have a third student read the paragraph on alliteration, and have students compose two phrases that use alliteration and share the phrases with the class.

Possible Answers

1. Internal rhymes can be found in stanzas 14 (ll. 79, 81–83) and 16 (ll. 91, and 93–95). Other internal rhymes occur in the first line of each stanza and in the third and fourth lines of each stanza. In ll. 79–84, the rhyme in the third and fourth lines of the stanza is carried into the fifth line by repetition of the rhyming word in the fourth.

2. We are reminded of "Lenore." Students may say the echo leaves them with a feeling of finality or of the speaker's despair.

3. In ll. 13–18, onomatopoeia is created by the alliteration "silken, sad, uncertain rustling of each purple curtain." In ll. 37–42, it is created in "Open here I flung the shutter, when, with many a flirt and flutter." Each choice of words mimics the sounds described in the lines.

Planning

- **Block Schedule**
  Block Scheduling Lesson Plans with Pacing Guide

- **Traditional Schedule**
  Lesson Plans Including Strategies for English-Language Learners

- **One-Stop Planner**
  CD-ROM with Test Generator

Resources

Listening
Audio CD Library
A recording of this story is provided in the *Audio CD Library:*
- Disc 9, Track 2

Summary ■ ■ ■

In this disturbing example of magical realism, the first-person narrator explains how he and his sister Irene, both middle-aged and single, share their old family home, where they spend their days quietly performing household chores. One night the narrator hears muted sounds coming from the empty back rooms and informs Irene that an anonymous "they" have taken over the back of the house. The siblings agree to occupy only the front half, but eventually they hear the same presence moving into their domain. They flee, lock the house, and throw the key in the sewer.

Background

Like Poe, Cortázar writes about siblings in a large ancestral home, but he views this subject through the lens of magical realism. A major twentieth-century literary movement in Latin America, magic realism portrays a reality that is composed of religion, myth, magic, and dreams as well as factual events. The fabulous elements are incorporated into the story as ordinary parts of human experience—as realistically as the "real" events—thereby raising questions in the readers' mind about the nature of reality.

Julio Cortázar
(1914–1984)

Julio Cortázar was born in Brussels, Belgium, to Argentine parents. The family returned to Argentina when Cortázar was six, and he was educated there. As an adult, he first supported his writing career by teaching high school and university courses, then by managing a publishing association, and finally by working as a translator. A change in Argentina's political regime caused him to move to France in 1951. In Paris, he worked as a translator for the United Nations. He eventually became a French citizen, but he retained his Argentine citizenship, and he always thought of himself as both South American and European.

Because Cortázar believed that sober, objective reality masks a hidden dimension of the fantastic, he used his stories to awaken readers to that dimension. Like nightmares that begin with ordinary scenes that are distorted into something bizarre, his stories move seamlessly from reality to fantasy. As the critic Alexander Coleman observed, "Cortázar's stories start in a disarmingly conversational way, with plenty of local touches. . . . But something always seems to go awry just when we least expect it."

One of Cortázar's short stories was the basis for Michelangelo Antonioni's classic film *Blow Up* (1966).

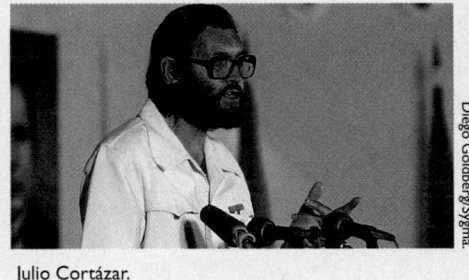

Julio Cortázar.

Diego Goldberg/Sygma.

Before You Read

Background

Julio Cortázar once explained the effects of first reading Edgar Allan Poe at the age of nine: "I stole the book . . . because my mother didn't want me to read it; she thought I was too young and she was right. The book scared me and I was ill for three months, because I believed in it."

Cortázar's fascination with Poe continued into his adult life. As a translator, he rendered four books of Poe into Spanish. As a writer, he echoed Poe in producing novels and stories in which nightmare intrudes into ordinary reality.

Cortázar's link with Poe is especially noticeable in "House Taken Over." As in Poe's "The Fall of the House of Usher," a house is occupied by the last members of a family line. In Cortázar's house, a brother and a sister experience a gradual, mysterious takeover of their ancestral home. They accept the takeover calmly . . . or do they?

Reading Skills and Strategies

Using Questions to Understand a Text
As you read "House Taken Over," write down notes in response to these questions:

- What humdrum routines mark the daily life of the narrator and his sister?

- At what point do you begin to think there is something strange about their house?

- How does the behavior of the brother and sister during sleep differ from their behavior during waking hours?

- Who—or what—do you think the narrator and his sister mean by "they"?

- How is this story similar to and different from Poe's "The Fall of the House of Usher"?

When you finish, sketch the layout of the interior of the house.

go.hrw.com
LEO 11-6

Reaching All Students

Struggling Readers
Despite its simple vocabulary and conversational tone, the story contains many long sentences. Have students read the opening sentence, first omitting everything between the first two commas and then omitting only the material in parentheses. Finally, have them reread the whole opening and write a paraphrase. Urge them to continue this process of breaking down long sentences into smaller chunks to make the story easier to read.

English Language Learners
Spanish-speaking students may wish to locate a copy of the story in Spanish and read both versions alternately, preferably with English-fluent classmates who are studying Spanish. Let other English language learners participate in the activity suggested for struggling readers. Have these students ask English-fluent classmates to explain difficult ideas, such as *unvoiced concept* and *indispensable end* (p. 291).

House Taken Over

Julio Cortázar

translated from the Spanish
by Paul Blackburn

We liked the house because, apart from its being old and spacious (in a day when old houses go down for a profitable auction of their construction materials), it kept the memories of great-grandparents, our paternal grandfather, our parents, and the whole of childhood.

Irene and I got used to staying in the house by ourselves, which was crazy, eight people could have lived in that place and not have gotten in each other's way. We rose at seven in the morning and got the cleaning done, and about eleven I left Irene to finish off whatever rooms and went to the kitchen. We lunched at noon precisely; then there was nothing left to do but a few dirty plates. It was pleasant to take lunch and commune with the great hollow, silent house, and it was enough for us just to keep it clean. We ended up thinking, at times, that that was what had kept us from marrying. Irene turned down two suitors for no particular reason, and María Esther went and died on me before we could manage to get engaged. We were easing into our forties with the unvoiced concept that the quiet, simple marriage of sister and brother was the indispensable end to a line established in this house by our grandparents. We would die here someday, obscure and distant cousins would inherit the place, have it torn down, sell the bricks, and get rich on the building plot; or more justly and better yet, we would topple it ourselves before it was too late.

JULIO CORTÁZAR 291

Professional Notes

Critical Comment: Metafiction

Literary theorist Robert Scholes calls the work of Cortázar and others *metafiction*. "A work of *meta*-fiction is a fictional experiment that either explores or questions the nature and conventions of fiction itself. The very elements of fiction—the relationship of the writer to the text or the text to the world, the concepts of plot, character, setting, and point-of-view—all these are taken not as givens but as questionable or problematic." When students have finished reading the story, return to this quotation to see if the story has raised questions for students about the nature and status of "realistic" fiction.

A Cultural Connections
Family Heritage

❓ The narrator and his sister belong to an affluent social class that owned large land holdings in Argentina in the 1940s. How does their devotion to their home and their family's past compare with attitudes today in the United States and other cultures with which you are familiar? [Possible response: The United States is often considered a culture that doesn't care about history, yet many Americans care deeply about genealogical research and historic preservation.]

B Elements of Literature
Point of View

❓ From what points of view is the story told? [first person singular and plural] **For whom does the narrator often speak?** [He speaks for himself and his sister Irene.] **Can he legitimately do so? Why or why not?** [Possible answers: Yes, he presumably knows her well enough to do so; no, because he may not be representing her feelings fairly.]

C Reading Skills and Strategies

Using Questions to Understand a Text

❓ What routines mark the daily life of the narrator and his sister? [Possible response: They have a rigid schedule of household chores. They rise at seven and lunch at noon. During the morning they clean house.] **How would you describe their lives?** [Possible answers: humdrum, repetitive, unimaginative, comfortable.]

D Critical Thinking
Making Connections

❓ What kind of relationship do the narrator and his sister enjoy? [They appear to be extremely close.] **What relationship do they have with their house?** [According to the narrator, they are completely tied to it. They intend to die there and would sooner destroy it themselves than have it torn down by "obscure and distant cousins."] Ask students to compare the siblings' relationship to each other and to their house with Roderick and Madeline Usher's.

T291

The Empire of Light (1954) by René Magritte. Oil on canvas (146 cm × 114 cm).

Royal Museum of Fine Arts, Brussels, Belgium. Courtesy Art Resource, NY. © 1998 C. Herscovici, Brussels/Artists Rights Society (ARS), New York.

292 THE AMERICAN RENAISSANCE

Using Students' Strengths

Irene never bothered anyone. Once the morning housework was finished, she spent the rest of the day on the sofa in her bedroom, knitting. I couldn't tell you why she knitted so much; I think women knit when they discover that it's a fat excuse to do nothing at all. But Irene was not like that, she always knitted necessities, sweaters for winter, socks for me, handy morning robes and bedjackets for herself. Sometimes she would do a jacket, then unravel it the next moment because there was something that didn't please her; it was pleasant to see a pile of tangled wool in her knitting basket fighting a losing battle for a few hours to retain its shape. Saturdays I went downtown to buy wool; Irene had faith in my good taste, was pleased with the colors and never a skein[1] had to be returned. I took advantage of these trips to make the rounds of the bookstores, uselessly asking if they had anything new in French literature. Nothing worthwhile had arrived in Argentina since 1939.

But it's the house I want to talk about, the house and Irene, I'm not very important. I wonder what Irene would have done without her knitting. One can reread a book, but once a pullover is finished you can't do it over again, it's some kind of disgrace. One day I found that the drawer at the bottom of the chiffonier, replete with mothballs, was filled with shawls, white, green, lilac. Stacked amid a great smell of camphor[2]—it was like a shop; I didn't have the nerve to ask her what she planned to do with them. We didn't have to earn our living, there was plenty coming in from the farms each month, even piling up. But Irene was only interested in the knitting and showed a wonderful dexterity, and for me the hours slipped away watching her, her hands like silver sea urchins, needles flashing, and one or two knitting baskets on the floor, the balls of yarn jumping about. It was lovely.

How not to remember the layout of that house. The dining room, a living room with tapestries, the library, and three large bed-

rooms in the section most recessed, the one that faced toward Rodríguez Peña.[3] Only a corridor with its massive oak door separated that part from the front wing, where there was a bath, the kitchen, our bedrooms, and the hall. One entered the house through a vestibule[4] with enameled tiles, and a wrought-iron grated door opened onto the living room. You had to come in through the vestibule and open the gate to go into the living room; the doors to our bedrooms were on either side of this, and opposite it was the corridor leading to the back section; going down the passage, one swung open the oak door beyond which was the other part of the house; or just before the door, one could turn to the left and go down a narrower passageway which led to the kitchen and the bath. When the door was open, you became aware of the size of the house; when it was closed, you had the impression of an apartment, like the ones they build today, with barely enough room to move around in. Irene and I always lived in this part of the house and hardly ever went beyond the oak door except to do the cleaning. Incredible how much dust collected on the furniture. It may be Buenos Aires is a clean city, but she owes it to her population and nothing else. There's too much dust in the air, the slightest breeze and it's back on the marble console tops and in the diamond patterns of the tooled-leather desk set. It's a lot of work to get it off with a feather duster; the motes rise and hang in the air, and settle again a minute later on the pianos and the furniture.

I'll always have a clear memory of it because it happened so simply and without fuss. Irene was knitting in her bedroom, it was eight at night, and I suddenly decided to put the water up for *maté*.[5] I went down the corridor as far as the oak door, which was ajar, then turned into the hall toward the kitchen, when I heard something in the library or the dining room. The sound came through muted

3. **Rodríguez Peña:** street in Buenos Aires, Argentina.
4. **vestibule:** small entrance hall.
5. **maté** (mä′tā′): tealike beverage made from dried leaves of a South American evergreen tree.

1. **skein** (skān): coiled length of thread or yarn.
2. **camphor:** chemical used as an insect repellent.

Connecting Across Texts

Connecting with Poe's Selections

Gothic fiction is a style of writing that evokes realms of darkness by the use of desolate or remote settings and macabre, mysterious, or violent incidents. As Cortázar found out during his childhood, Poe is one of the great Gothic writers. Once students have finished reading, ask them to list Gothic elements in "House Taken Over" in a chart like the following, and to compare those elements with ones they have found in the Poe selections

Element	Poe	Cortázar

A Historical Connections
Argentina in WWII
❓ What happened in 1939 that might have separated Argentina from Europe? [World War II began with Hitler's invasion of Poland.] Argentina was officially neutral but unofficially pro-Axis during most of the war when Hitler occupied Belgium and France. In March 1945, just before the end of the war, Argentina joined the Allies. Wartime French literature that the narrator may have missed out on included Albert Camus's essays in *The Myth of Sisyphus* (1942) and Camus's novel *The Stranger* (1942), Jean-Paul Sartre's plays *The Flics* (1943) and *No Exit* (1944), and Antoine de Saint-Exupéry's *The Little Prince* (1943).

B Critical Thinking
Analyzing
❓ What does Irene do when she is not cleaning house? [She knits.] What does she knit? [Possible responses: necessities—sweaters, socks, morning robes, bedjackets; unused shawls.] What do you think of this pastime? [Possible responses: Knitting is good because it involves creating beautiful things; knitting more things than you can use is unproductive.]

C Elements of Literature
Simile
❓ What simile does the author use to describe Irene's knitting? [Her hands are like silver sea urchins.] Sea urchins are round creatures covered with long spikes. How does this image help readers see the way Irene knits? [Possible response: The spikes of the sea urchins are the knitting needles and the creatures' bodies are Irene's hands.]

D Struggling Readers
Getting the Main Idea
Although the house is large, the story has a claustrophobic atmosphere. If your students have trouble following the story, urge them to sketch a floor plan of the house to indicate where the narrator and his sister live at various stages in the story.

E Cultural Connections
Maté
Explain that in Argentina it is traditional to drink *yerba maté* (yer′bä mätā′), tea made from an evergreen tree grown principally in Paraguay. The tea is sometimes brewed in fancily engraved silver cups and stirred with long silver stirrers.

T293

T294

---

and indistinct, a chair being knocked over
onto the carpet or the muffled buzzing of a
conversation. At the same time or a second
later, I heard it at the end of the passage
which led from those two rooms toward the
door. I hurled myself against the door before
it was too late and shut it, leaned on it with
the weight of my body; luckily, the key was
on our side; moreover, I ran the great bolt into
place, just to be safe.

I went down to the kitchen, heated the kettle, and when I got back with the tray of
maté, I told Irene:

A "I had to shut the door to the passage.
They've taken over the back part."

She let her knitting fall and looked at me
with her tired, serious eyes.

B "You're sure?"
I nodded.
"In that case," she said, picking up her nee-
dles again, "we'll have to live on this side."

I sipped at the *maté* very carefully, but she
took her time starting her work again. I remember it was a gray vest she was knitting. I
liked that vest.

C The first few days were painful, since we'd
both left so many things in the part that had
been taken over. My collection of French literature, for example, was still in the library.
Irene had left several folios of stationery and
a pair of slippers that she used a lot in the
winter. I missed my briar pipe, and Irene, I
think, regretted the loss of an ancient bottle
of Hesperidin.[6] It happened repeatedly (but
only in the first few days) that we would close
some drawer or cabinet and look at one another sadly.

"It's not here."

One thing more among the many lost on
the other side of the house.

But there were advantages, too. The cleaning was so much simplified that, even when
we got up late, nine-thirty for instance, by
eleven we were sitting around with our arms
folded. Irene got into the habit of coming to

the kitchen with me to help get lunch. We
thought about it and decided on this: while I
prepared the lunch, Irene would cook up
dishes that could be eaten cold in the evening.
We were happy with the arrangement because it was always such a bother to have to
leave our bedrooms in the evening and start
to cook. Now we made do with the table in
Irene's room and platters of cold supper.

Since it left her more time for knitting,
Irene was content. I was a little lost without
my books, but so as not to inflict myself on
my sister, I set about reordering papa's stamp
collection; that killed some time. We amused
ourselves sufficiently, each with his own
thing, almost always getting together in
Irene's bedroom, which was the more comfortable. Every once in a while, Irene might
say:

"Look at this pattern I just figured out,
doesn't it look like clover?"

After a bit it was I, pushing a small square
of paper in front of her so that she could see
the excellence of some stamp or another
D from Eupen-et-Malmédy.[7] We were fine, and
E little by little we stopped thinking. You can
live without thinking.

F (Whenever Irene talked in her sleep, I
woke up immediately and stayed awake. I
never could get used to this voice from a
statue or a parrot, a voice that came out of the
dreams, not from a throat. Irene said that in
my sleep I flailed about enormously and
shook the blankets off. We had the living
room between us, but at night you could hear
everything in the house. We heard each other
breathing, coughing, could even feel each
other reaching for the light switch when, as
happened frequently, neither of us could fall
asleep.

Aside from our nocturnal rumblings, everything was quiet in the house. During the day
there were the household sounds, the metallic click of knitting needles, the rustle of
stamp-album pages turning. The oak door was
massive, I think I said that. In the kitchen or

---

6. Hesperidin (hes·per'i·din): liquid made from
the rind of citrus fruits and used for various medicinal
purposes.

7. Eupen-et-Malmédy (ə·pen'ā·mäl'mä·dē'): district in eastern Belgium.

Assessing Learning

Check Test: Questions and Answers

1. How do the narrator and his sister spend
   their days? [They clean house; she knits;
   he reads and goes to bookstores but buys
   nothing.]

2. What is the first indication of trouble in the
   house? [The narrator hears noises in the
   library or dining room.]

3. What do the brother and sister miss most
   about the rooms they can no longer go into?
   [the personal items they have left there]

4. How does the narrator fill his time after he
   has lost his books? [working on his father's
   stamp collection]

5. What does the narrator do with the house
   key when he and his sister flee? [He tosses it
   down a sewer.]

the bath, which adjoined the part that was taken over, we managed to talk loudly, or Irene sang lullabies. In a kitchen there's always too much noise, the plates and glasses, for there to be interruptions from other sounds. We seldom allowed ourselves silence there, but when we went back to our rooms or to the living room, then the house grew quiet, half-lit, we ended by stepping around more slowly so as not to disturb one another. I think it was because of this that I woke up irremediably and at once when Irene began to talk in her sleep.)

Except for the consequences, it's nearly a matter of repeating the same scene over again. I was thirsty that night, and before we went to sleep, I told Irene that I was going to the kitchen for a glass of water. From the door of the bedroom (she was knitting) I heard the noise in the kitchen; if not the kitchen, then the bath, the passage off at that angle dulled the sound. Irene noticed how brusquely I had paused, and came up beside me without a word. We stood listening to the noises, growing more and more sure that they were on our side of the oak door, if not the kitchen then the bath, or in the hall itself at the turn, almost next to us.

We didn't wait to look at one another. I took Irene's arm and forced her to run with me to the wrought-iron door, not waiting to look back. You could hear the noises, still muffled but louder, just behind us. I slammed the grating and we stopped in the vestibule. Now there was nothing to be heard.

"They've taken over our section," Irene said. The knitting had reeled off from her hands and the yarn ran back toward the door and disappeared under it. When she saw that the balls of yarn were on the other side, she dropped the knitting without looking at it.

"Did you have time to bring anything?" I asked hopelessly.

"No, nothing."

We had what we had on. I remembered fifteen thousand pesos in the wardrobe in my bedroom. Too late now.

I still had my wristwatch on and saw that it was 11 P.M. I took Irene around the waist (I think she was crying) and that was how we went into the street. Before we left, I felt terrible; I locked the front door up tight and tossed the key down the sewer. It wouldn't do to have some poor devil decide to go in and rob the house, at that hour and with the house taken over.

FINDING COMMON GROUND

Meet in a small group to discuss your notes on the story. Have one member of the group record conclusions the group agrees upon.

- Take turns sharing what you wrote in response to the questions on page 290.
- Focus especially on Cortázar's huge omission—the identity of "they." What conclusion does the group reach about who "they" are? What evidence supports this conclusion?

- After you have compared Cortázar's story with Poe's "The Fall of the House of Usher," decide whether the main point of Cortázar's story is the end of a family line or something else. What evidence supports your conclusions?
- Agree on a sketch of the layout of the house's interior. Is the story unclear on any areas?
- Reconvene as a class, and listen to reports from all of the groups. Has class discussion changed your initial interpretation of the story?

JULIO CORTÁZAR 295

FINDING COMMON GROUND

This feature requires students, through lively discussion, to discover areas of agreement among their interpretations of the ambiguous elements in this text. As the discussion unfolds, be sure students consider the following possibilities about who "they" are:
(1) figments of the narrator's imagination
(2) projections of the character's own fears
(3) the spirit of other, more productive middle-class people who are replacing the older, less productive landowning aristocrats

(4) Nazi or other totalitarian leaders that encroach on people's individual freedoms and rights
(5) ghosts or other supernatural forces

Be sure, as well, that students consider these ideas about the main point of the story:
(1) disastrous results occur when people deliberately ignore encroachments on their property or freedoms
(2) passivity can lead to ruin and perhaps madness

(3) disastrous results can occur when people complacently withdraw from the world and produce nothing useful

Finally, be sure to point out that both Poe's "The Fall of the House of Usher" and Cortázar's "House Taken Over" illustrate the pitfalls of extreme behavior. The Ushers are cut off from the world and Roderick devotes his life to pursuing his wild romantic projects. The brother and sister in "House Taken Over" are removed from the world and passive.

T295

G Critical Thinking
Interpreting
❓ Why do the brother and sister make noise and sing lullabies in the kitchen and bath? [Possible response: They do not want to know what is happening on the other side of the door. They are afraid to know too much.]

H Struggling Readers
Getting the Main Idea
❓ What have the brother and sister lost at this point in the story? [Possible response: their beloved house; their habitual comforts, and all their possessions.]

I Critical Thinking
Interpreting
❓ How do you understand the siblings' resignation to having their property occupied, and later taken over entirely by this mysterious, anonymous group—accepting this event without even contacting the police or government? What might Cortázar be saying about his characters and the way they think? [Possible response: The narrator and his sister are affluent, insular people, who have avoided outside influences of any kind. In a certain sense, this "occupation" seems like a metaphoric confirmation of their deepest fears: that the comfortable, insulated sphere of their family cannot resist the demands of the outside world.]

J Critical Thinking
Evaluating
❓ Is the ending appropriate? Why or why not? [Sample responses: Yes, forcing the characters "outside" invites readers to speculate about what happens next; no, the ending is too open-ended and difficult to interpret.]

1. Read and interpret the story
2. Interpret symbols
3. Draw inferences
4. Understand archaisms
5. Express understanding through writing, speaking/listening, and performance
6. Understand and use new words

SKILLS

Literary
- Analyze symbols

Reading
- Draw inferences
- Understand archaisms

Writing
- Collect ideas for a persuasive essay on a controversial issue
- Compare ideas on human nature
- Compare religious beliefs
- Write an autobiographical sketch from the point of view of a character
- Write a theatrical version of the story
- Write an interpretive essay

Speaking/Listening
- Discuss two authors' works

Performance
- Perform a theatrical adaptation of the story

Vocabulary
- Use new words

Viewing/Representing
- Analyze illustrations (ATE)

Planning

- **Block Schedule**
  Block Scheduling Lesson Plans with Pacing Guide

- **Traditional Schedule**
  Lesson Plans Including Strategies for English-Language Learners

- **One-Stop Planner**
  CD-ROM with Test Generator

Nathaniel Hawthorne (1840) by Charles Osgood. Oil on canvas.

Peabody Essex Museum, Salem, Massachusetts. Photo by Mark Sexton (121.459).

Nathaniel Hawthorne

(1804–1864)

Nathaniel Hawthorne was an unusually handsome man, with a loving and beloved wife. By midlife he had earned recognition as a writer and won the admiration of his contemporaries. Nevertheless, he became increasingly dissatisfied, remote, and disappointing to his friends. It was as if his dark insights into the human heart had cast gloom into his own. His fiction, which has survived the changing tastes of many generations and is more admired today than when it was written, is fueled by an awareness of the guilt that accompanies a Puritan conscience. This shadow of guilt appears to have darkened Hawthorne's life.

The source of darkness is thought to lie in Hawthorne's illustrious ancestors. William Hathorne, a serious soldier and judge, came to the Massachusetts Colony in 1630. Hawthorne describes him in the preamble to *The Scarlet Letter* as the "bearded, sable-cloaked, and steeple-crowned progenitor." William Hathorne's son, John, was also a judge. During the Salem witch trials of 1692, he played a minor role in sentencing nineteen of the accused to death.

By 1804, however, the year of Hawthorne's birth in Salem, the family had lost its wealth and renown. His own father, a sea captain, died during a voyage and left his grief-stricken wife with three young children to raise and few resources beyond the charity of relatives.

Prisoner of the Dismal Chamber

Hawthorne (who added the *w* to the family name to ensure a broad *a* in its pronunciation) attended schools in Salem and college at Bowdoin in Maine. Here, by his own judgment, he was an idle student, "rather choosing to nurse my own fancies than to dig into Greek roots." He chewed tobacco, played cards, drank wine at the taverns, and avoided intellectual company in favor of pleasure. After graduation, Hawthorne wrote to his sister Elizabeth, "I shall never make a distinguished figure in the world, and all I hope or wish is to plod along with the multitude." There is good reason to believe that this was an ironic statement, concealing an ambition that burned intensely.

Returning to Salem, Hawthorne set himself up in what he called the "dismal chamber," a room on the third floor of the family house. He kept himself a virtual prisoner there for the next twelve years, until he had learned the craft of fiction. In 1837, Hawthorne emerged to publish a collection of stories, *Twice-Told Tales*. They offered a vision of the human heart as a lurking place for the secrets of past sins. The book won Hawthorne just enough success to encourage further work.

Over the next few years Hawthorne courted and became engaged to Sophia Peabody, and he briefly joined the utopian experiment in communal living at Brook Farm. Neither the shoveling of manure nor the endless, lofty discussions of the Transcendentalists appealed to him. After their marriage in 1842, the Hawthornes

go.hrw.com
LE0 11-6

 *Resources: Print and Media*

Reading
- *Graphic Organizers for Active Reading*, p. 24
- *Words to Own*, p. 20
- *Audio CD Library* Disc 9, Track 3

Elements of Literature
- *Literary Elements*
  Transparency 11
  Worksheet, p. 34

Writing and Language
- *Daily Oral Grammar* Transparency 22

- *Grammar and Language Links*
  Worksheet, p. 29
- *Language Workshop CD-ROM*

Assessment
- *Formal Assessment*, p. 61
- *Portfolio Management System*, p. 125
- *Preparation for College Admission Exams*, p. 23
- *Test Generator (One-Stop Planner CD-ROM)*

Internet
- go.hrw.com (keyword: LE0 11-6)

moved into the Old Manse in Concord, where Emerson had lived before them. Hawthorne often walked with Thoreau and Emerson, but neither creativity nor warm friendship resulted.

A Novel with No "Cheering Light"

Making only the barest living from his stories, Hawthorne had to accept a political appointment as surveyor to the Salem customhouse in 1846. The job freed him from financial worry, but he hated the work. In 1849, he lost the job. Despite this loss and the simultaneous death of his mother, he somehow found the energies for his masterwork, *The Scarlet Letter*. It was, he said, "positively a hell-fired story, into which I found it almost impossible to throw any cheering light."

The novel is set in Puritan Boston during the mid–seventeenth century. The title refers to a cloth letter *A* that the narrator finds in a customhouse, along with documents outlining the tragic story of Hester Prynne, who bore an illegitimate child. Refusing to name the baby's father, she was sentenced to wear the scarlet *A* (for adultery) on her breast. The tale is one of sin and redemption, and the tragic consequences of hypocrisy and concealed guilt.

The novel's publication in 1850 brought Hawthorne wide acclaim, some money, and the admiration and friendship of Herman Melville. Another great novel, *The House of the Seven Gables*, appeared the following year.

Out of Harmony with His Times

In 1853, President Franklin Pierce—Hawthorne's old friend from his days at Bowdoin—offered Hawthorne the post of United States consul at Liverpool. Hawthorne and his family lived in Europe for seven years. As an expatriate, however, he found his creativity dwindling, and he had become inexplicably dejected. Even his return to America in 1860 was oddly cheerless. After his years abroad, he was disenchanted with both the Europe where he had been and the America from which he now felt estranged. His old friend Pierce, for whom he had written a campaign biography in 1852, had been defeated for reelection. Abraham Lincoln was in the White House, and with the onset of the Civil War, Hawthorne felt out of harmony with his times.

Back in Concord, Hawthorne found himself unable to complete the several fiction projects he had promised his publisher. His health declined. On the night of May 18, 1864, while on a trip with Pierce, Hawthorne died in a New Hampshire hotel room.

Emerson felt that Hawthorne, no longer able to endure his solitude, "died of it." Emerson also noted in his journal, after attending Hawthorne's funeral, that he was sorry he hadn't known Hawthorne better. And he recorded this sadly ironic anecdote: "One day, when I found him on the top of his hill, in the woods, he paced back the path to his house, and said, '*This path is the only remembrance of me that will remain.*'"

The Scarlet Letter,
a
Romance.
By Nathaniel Hawthorne.

The Granger Collection, New York.

Nathaniel Hawthorne
THE SCARLET LETTER

BROWSING IN THE FILES

About the Author. Hawthorne may have in some way resembled Mr. Hooper of "The Minister's Black Veil." He wore black and wrapped himself in a large cloak, which, on occasion, obscured his face and gave him a mysterious appearance. Hawthorne may also have resembled his other guarded characters, the Reverend Arthur Dimmesdale of *The Scarlet Letter,* and Goodman Brown of "Young Goodman Brown," who hid their secrets beneath figurative, if not literal, veils.

NATHANIEL HAWTHORNE 297

Skill Link

The Short Story

Remind students that the short story is a fictional narrative that can usually be read in one sitting. It usually contains no more than two or three major characters, involved in a single conflict. The plot concentrates on a limited number of events—often the events leading up to and including the climax. Most short stories produce a single, overarching impression or effect.

Activities

1. Invite students to identify the main character and central conflict in "The Fall of the House of Usher," "House Taken Over," or "The Minister's Black Veil."

2. Have students identify the single, overarching effect of each story.

3. Ask students what would change if the story were presented as a movie, novel, television miniseries, or comic book.

Summary ■ ■ ■

This story begins as Mr. Hooper, a young Puritan clergyman, shocks his congregation by appearing in a black veil to preach his Sunday sermon. His subject is secret sin, and while he speaks as gently as ever, the veil gives his hearers the strong impression that somehow, perhaps because of his own guilt, he sees their secret iniquities. Gossip about the veil spreads among the parishioners, but no one dares ask Mr. Hooper why he wears it. When his fiancée confronts him, he hints that it represents the universality of sorrow and sin, and that he must wear it for the rest of his life. Although his fiancée begs him to remove it, he continues to wear it at the cost of his marriage and social acceptance. In the story's resolution, he is still isolated and unloved, although respected as a clergyman. On his deathbed, Hooper insists that the veil remain on his face, not because of his own private sin, but because of the black veil "on every visage" around him.

Background

Hawthorne may have been fascinated with Puritan New England because of the sense of guilt he felt about his ancestor Judge Hathorne's role in condemning people to death in the Salem Witch Trials of 1692 (see *The Crucible,* p. 829). Although much of Hawthorne's work reflects the austere sin-obsessed atmosphere of the Puritan era, Hawthorne intellectually and emotionally was not a Puritan and struggled to overcome some of the more damaging consequences of their rigid and often unforgiving view of humankind.

RESPONDING TO THE ART

Activity. After students have read the story, have them return to the illustration and explain the behavior of each person in it. [Possible responses: Mr. Hooper bows his head in thought, worry, or gloom; the little girl is frightened; the women seem to be trying to understand Mr. Hooper's behavior.]

Before You Read
THE MINISTER'S BLACK VEIL

Make the Connection
Secret Sin
The narrator of this story remarks that the "saddest of all prisons" is a person's "own heart." Hawthorne expertly imagined the sometimes fantastic ways in which people suffer guilt for secret sins they have committed in the past. He shows us that guilty secrets serve to isolate people from the world and from their relationships with others.

Reading Skills and Strategies

Drawing Inferences
When you come to Goodman Gray's line "Our parson has gone mad!" (page 300), stop and write down three possible reasons why the minister has draped his face with the black material ordinarily used by mourners.

Elements of Literature
Symbol
A **symbol** is something that has meaning in itself but also stands for something more than itself. Hawthorne—indeed, all the Dark Romantics—used symbolism as a technical strategy in his writing. As the title suggests, Hawthorne's central symbol in this story is a "horrible black veil," a "dismal shade" that separates its wearer from the world.

Illustration by Elenore Plaisted Abbott for "The Minister's Black Veil," from the 1900 edition of *Twice-Told Tales.*
Houghton Mifflin Company.

As you read, be aware of the ways this symbol directs your thoughts to the story's central **theme**.

> **A symbol** is a person, place, thing, or event that has meaning in itself and also stands for something more than itself.
>
> *For more on Symbol, see page 280 and the Handbook of Literary Terms.*

Background
This story, like much of Hawthorne's best work, is set in the times of his Puritan ancestors, an era he viewed as "characterized by . . . gloom and piety."

Hawthorne added the following note to the story: "Another clergyman in New England, Mr. Joseph Moody, of York, Maine, who died about eighty years since, made himself remarkable by the same eccentricity that is here related of the Reverend Mr. Hooper. In this case, however, the symbol had a different import. In early life he had accidentally killed a beloved friend; and from that day till the hour of his own death, he hid his face from men."

Preteaching Vocabulary

Words to Own
Have students look up synonyms and antonyms for the Words to Own. Then, ask the following:
1. If someone were *ostentatious,* would you notice her or not? [notice her]
2. Would someone acting *pensively* be likely to shout? [no]
3. If you felt *antipathy* toward someone, would you like or dislike him? [dislike]
4. Would a story's *plausibility* make you believe it or disbelieve it? [believe]
5. Does a *resolute* person have a strong will or a weak will? [strong]
6. Is a *semblance* something similar to or different from something else? [similar to]
7. Is *iniquity* good or wicked? [wicked]
8. Is a *sagacious* person foolish or wise? [wise]
9. If a symbol *portends* doom, does it prevent doom or foretell doom? [foretell]
10. Is an artist working in *obscurity* famous or unknown? [unknown]

> "He has changed himself into something awful, only by hiding his face."

The Minister's Black Veil

A Parable Ⓐ

Nathaniel Hawthorne

The sexton[1] stood in the porch of Milford meetinghouse, pulling lustily at the bell rope. The old people of the village came stooping along the street. Children, with bright faces, tripped merrily beside their parents, or mimicked a graver gait, in the conscious dignity of their Sunday clothes. Spruce bachelors looked sidelong at the pretty maidens, and fancied that the Sabbath sunshine made them prettier than on weekdays. When the throng had mostly streamed into the porch, the sexton began to toll the bell, keeping his eye on the Reverend Mr. Hooper's door. The first glimpse of the clergyman's figure was the signal for the bell to cease its summons.

1. **sexton:** church officer or employee whose duties may include maintenance, ringing the bells, and digging graves.

NATHANIEL HAWTHORNE **299**

Ⓐ **Elements of Literature**
Parable
Point out the story's subtitle. Remind students that parables are short tales that teach a moral. They often come from religious scriptures, such as the New Testament, which contains the parables of Jesus. The meaning of a parable is often ambiguous and elusive. Tell students that they must pay careful attention to the story's details to determine the meaning of this extended parable.

Ⓑ **Reading Skills and Strategies**
Drawing Inferences

❓ What is the mood in Milford? What is the villagers' attitude toward going to service? [People seem cheerful and happy. The Sabbath is a happy, social occasion.] As the story progresses, track the changes in the atmosphere of the village.

Ⓒ **Historical Connections**
Puritan Meetinghouse
Explain that in Puritan times church was held in a building called the meetinghouse, which had high boxed pews and seating around the outside walls. Dominating the pews was the parson's, or minister's, pulpit where he stood to preach. This pulpit was reached by a small flight of stairs.

Reaching All Students

Struggling Readers
Drawing Inferences was introduced on p. 298. One good strategy to use for drawing inferences is It Says . . . I Say. Students might use an It Says . . . I Say chart to answer questions on p. 308. For information on using this strategy, see the *Reading Strategies Handbook,* p. 25 in the *Reading Skills and Strategies* binder.

English Language Learners
To help students understand the story's premise, show photographs of people wearing veils in several contexts. Explain that until recent times in America, women wore black veils over their faces in mourning—especially at funerals. Point out that it was unusual for a Puritan minister to wear a veil.

Advanced Learners
As students read, and afterward, have them imagine what the story would have been like if Poe instead of Hawthorne had written it. What might have been gained, and what lost? Would they have enjoyed it more? Would they have gotten as much of a glimpse into human nature? Encourage discussion, and invite students to rewrite a passage in the style of Poe.

T299

"But what has good Parson Hooper got upon his face?" cried the sexton in astonishment.

All within hearing immediately turned about, and beheld the <u>semblance</u> of Mr. Hooper, pacing slowly his meditative way toward the meetinghouse. With one accord they started, expressing more wonder than if some strange minister were coming to dust the cushions of Mr. Hooper's pulpit.

"Are you sure it is our parson?" inquired Goodman[2] Gray of the sexton.

"Of a certainty it is good Mr. Hooper," replied the sexton. "He was to have exchanged pulpits with Parson Shute of Westbury; but Parson Shute sent to excuse himself yesterday, being to preach a funeral sermon."

The cause of so much amazement may appear sufficiently slight. Mr. Hooper, a gentlemanly person of about thirty, though still a bachelor, was dressed with due clerical neatness, as if a careful wife had starched his band, and brushed the weekly dust from his Sunday's garb. There was but one thing remarkable in his appearance. Swathed about his forehead, and hanging down over his face, so low as to be shaken by his breath, Mr. Hooper had on a black veil. On a nearer view, it seemed to consist of two folds of crape,[3] which entirely concealed his features, except the mouth and chin, but probably did not intercept his sight, farther than to give a darkened aspect to all living and inanimate things. With this gloomy shade before him, good Mr. Hooper walked onward, at a slow and quiet pace, stooping somewhat and looking on the ground, as is customary with abstracted men, yet nodding kindly to those of his parishioners who still waited on the meetinghouse steps. But so wonder-struck were they, that his greeting hardly met with a return.

"I can't really feel as if good Mr. Hooper's face was behind that piece of crape," said the sexton.

"I don't like it," muttered an old woman, as she hobbled into the meetinghouse. "He has changed himself into something awful, only by hiding his face."

"Our parson has gone mad!" cried Goodman Gray, following him across the threshold.

---

2. **Goodman:** form of polite address similar to *mister.*
3. **crape:** kind of black cloth worn as a sign of mourning; from the French word *crêpe.*

A rumor of some unaccountable phenomenon had preceded Mr. Hooper into the meetinghouse, and set all the congregation astir. Few could refrain from twisting their heads toward the door; many stood upright, and turned directly about; while several little boys clambered upon the seats, and came down again with a terrible racket. There was a general bustle, a rustling of the women's gowns and shuffling of the men's feet, greatly at variance with that hushed repose which should attend the entrance of the minister. But Mr. Hooper appeared not to notice the perturbation of his people. He entered with an almost noiseless step, bent his head mildly to the pews on each side, and bowed as he passed his oldest parishioner, a white-haired great-grandsire, who occupied an armchair in the center of the aisle. It was strange to observe, how slowly this venerable man became conscious of something singular in the appearance of his pastor. He seemed not fully to partake of the prevailing wonder, till Mr. Hooper had ascended the stairs, and showed himself in the pulpit, face to face with his congregation, except for the black veil. That mysterious emblem was never once withdrawn. It shook with his measured breath as he gave out the psalm; it threw its obscurity between him and the holy page, as he read the Scriptures; and while he prayed, the veil lay heavily on his uplifted countenance. Did he seek to hide it from the dread Being whom he was addressing?

Such was the effect of this simple piece of crape, that more than one woman of delicate nerves was forced to leave the meetinghouse. Yet perhaps the pale-faced congregation was almost as fearful a sight to the minister, as his black veil to them.

Mr. Hooper had the reputation of a good preacher, but not an energetic one: He strove to win his people heavenward, by mild persuasive influences, rather than to drive them thither, by the thunders of the Word. The sermon which he now delivered, was marked by the same characteristics of style and manner, as the general series of his pulpit oratory. But there was something, either in the sentiment of the discourse itself, or in

---

WORDS TO OWN

semblance (sem′bləns): *n.:* outward appearance.

Using Students' Strengths

Logical/Mathematical Learners

Have students speculate about Mr. Hooper's motivations by listing or charting possible reasons for his wearing the veil. For each possible motive students think of, have them jot down points in favor of, and against, believing that to be the motive. Finally, have students discuss or write about whether they feel Mr. Hooper has acted reasonably, and why.

Visual Learners

After students have finished the story, have them produce the visual design for a film version of "The Minister's Black Veil." Each student should choose a different aspect of production to illustrate. One student should design the cos_____ _____mit swatches of fabrics for _____ illustrate or build models _____ould draw storyboards of _____s' work in the class- _____y case.

the imagination of the auditors, which made it greatly the most powerful effort that they had ever heard from their pastor's lips. It was tinged, rather more darkly than usual, with the gentle gloom of Mr. Hooper's temperament. The subject had reference to secret sin, and those sad mysteries which we hide from our nearest and dearest, and would fain conceal from our own consciousness, even forgetting that the Omniscient[4] can detect them. A subtle power was breathed into his words. Each member of the congregation, the most innocent girl, and the man of hardened breast, felt as if the preacher had crept upon them, behind his awful veil, and discovered their hoarded iniquity of deed or thought. Many spread their clasped hands on their bosoms. There was nothing terrible in what Mr. Hooper said; at least, no violence; and yet, with every tremor of his melancholy voice, the hearers quaked. An unsought pathos came hand in hand with awe. So sensible were the audience of some unwonted attribute in their minister, that they longed for a breath of wind to blow aside the veil, almost believing that a stranger's visage would be discovered, though the form, gesture, and voice were those of Mr. Hooper.

At the close of the services, the people hurried out with indecorous confusion, eager to communicate their pent-up amazement, and conscious of lighter spirits, the moment they lost sight of the black veil. Some gathered in little circles, huddled closely together, with their mouths all whispering in the center; some went homeward alone, wrapped in silent meditation; some talked loudly, and profaned the Sabbath day with ostentatious laughter. A few shook their sagacious heads, intimating that they could penetrate the mystery; while one or two affirmed that there was no mystery at all, but only that Mr. Hooper's eyes were so weakened by the midnight lamp, as to require a shade. After a brief interval, forth came good Mr. Hooper also, in the rear of his flock. Turning his veiled face from one group to another, he paid due reverence to the hoary heads, saluted the middle-aged with kind dignity, as their friend and spiritual guide, greeted the young with mingled authority and love, and laid his hands on the little children's heads to bless them. Such was always

4. **the Omniscient:** the all-knowing God.

his custom on the Sabbath day. Strange and bewildered looks repaid him for his courtesy. None, as on former occasions, aspired to the honor of walking by their pastor's side. Old Squire Saunders, doubtless by an accidental lapse of memory, neglected to invite Mr. Hooper to his table, where the good clergyman had been wont to bless the food, almost every Sunday since his settlement. He returned, therefore, to the parsonage, and, at the moment of closing the door, was observed to look back upon the people, all of whom had their eyes fixed upon the minister. A sad smile gleamed faintly from beneath the black veil, and flickered about his mouth, glimmering as he disappeared.

"How strange," said a lady, "that a simple black veil, such as any woman might wear on her bonnet, should become such a terrible thing on Mr. Hooper's face!"

"Something must surely be amiss with Mr. Hooper's intellects," observed her husband, the physician of the village. "But the strangest part of the affair is the effect of this vagary, even on a sober-minded man like myself. The black veil, though it covers only our pastor's face, throws its influence over his whole person, and makes him ghostlike from head to foot. Do you not feel it so?"

"Truly do I," replied the lady; "and I would not be alone with him for the world. I wonder he is not afraid to be alone with himself!"

"Men sometimes are so," said her husband.

The afternoon service was attended with similar circumstances. At its conclusion, the bell tolled for the funeral of a young lady. The relatives and friends were assembled in the house, and the more distant acquaintances stood about the door, speaking of the good qualities of the deceased, when their talk was interrupted by the appearance of Mr. Hooper, still covered with his black veil. It was now an appropriate emblem. The clergyman stepped into the room where the corpse was laid, and bent over the coffin, to take a last farewell of his deceased parishioner. As he stooped, the veil hung straight down from his forehead, so that, if her eyelids had not been

---

WORDS TO OWN

iniquity (i·nik′wi·tē): *n.:* wickedness.
ostentatious (äs′tən·tā′shəs) *adj.:* conspicuous.
sagacious (sə·gā′shəs) *adj.:* wise; keenly perceptive.

NATHANIEL HAWTHORNE **301**

Making the Connections

**Cultural Connections:
Sin in Puritan Times**

In Puritan times, sin was a constant topic of conversation. (Refer students to Jonathan Edward's sermon "Sinners in the Hands of an Angry God," pp. 77–83). Sin, of course, can mean different things to different people. To the Puritans, sin often meant original sin, the belief that humans are born in a state of sin, a primary alienation from God, based on the sin of Adam and Eve. Calvinists of the Puritan era believed that people were predestined by God either to be saved from sin or damned. Additionally, sin could mean any violation of the Ten Commandments or even such minor offenses as speaking harshly to a neighbor.

F Struggling Readers
Getting the Main Idea
? How does Mr. Hooper define "secret sin"? [Possible response: A sin someone has committed that no one else knows about or that the sinner finds hard to admit.] **Why does the congregation tremble at the minister's words?** [This sermon forces people to consider their own sinful secrets, locked away from daily thought in the hope that they can be concealed from loved ones, and from God Himself.]

G Reading Skills and Strategies
Drawing Inferences

? Why might the veil lend power to Mr. Hooper's sermon? [Possible responses: It links Hooper personally to his sermon, and makes his audience feel it personally too—his talk of sin can no longer be heard comfortably as "someone else's issue." The mysterious symbolic shame of the veil makes Hooper seem to know and threaten all shameful secrets.]

H Critical Thinking
Making Generalizations
? How does Mr. Hooper behave toward his congregation after the sermon? [He treats them with the same kindness, reverence, and love he has always shown.] **How does the congregation behave toward him?** [They decline to walk with him or to invite him to Sunday dinner.]

I Elements of Literature
Irony
? What is Hawthorne's attitude toward the congregation's behavior? [He uses subtle irony to criticize their avoidance of Hooper as selfish and cowardly.] **Does Saunders really forget to invite Hooper?** [No, the narrator ironically implies that he too is threatened by the veil.]

J Critical Thinking
Extending the Text
? Why are we all sometimes afraid to be alone with ourselves? [Possible response: We don't want to think about some of the things we've done; we become lonely or slip into anxious patterns of thought.]

The Sermon (1886) by Julius Gari Melchers. Oil on canvas.

National Museum of American Art, Bequest of Henry Ward Ranger through The National Academy of Design. Courtesy Art Resource.

closed forever, the dead maiden might have seen his face. Could Mr. Hooper be fearful of her glance, that he so hastily caught back the black veil? A person, who watched the interview between the dead and living, scrupled[5] not to affirm, that, at the instant when the clergyman's features were disclosed, the corpse had slightly shuddered, rustling the shroud and muslin cap, though the countenance retained the composure of death. A superstitious old woman was the only witness of this prodigy.[6] From the coffin, Mr.

Hooper passed into the chamber of the mourners, and thence to the head of the staircase, to make the funeral prayer. It was a tender and heart-dissolving prayer, full of sorrow, yet so imbued with celestial hopes, that the music of a heavenly harp, swept by the fingers of the dead, seemed faintly to be heard among the saddest accents of the minister. The people trembled, though they but darkly understood him, when he prayed that they, and himself, and all of mortal race, might be ready, as he trusted this young maiden had been, for the dreadful hour that should snatch the veil from their faces. The bearers went heavily forth,

5. scrupled: hesitated.
6. prodigy: extraordinary act that foretells the future.

Taking a Second Look

Review:
Breaking Down Long Sentences
Review with students the process of finding the main subject and verb first and then adding subsidiary clauses one by one. In the case of the second sentence on this page, for example, the subject begins the sentence. Instruct students to omit the clause in commas and look for the verb "scrupled." With the base sentence in place, encourage students to add the other clauses one by one. This process would proceed as follows: (1) The person, who watched Mr. Hooper and the corpse, did not hesitate to state that the corpse had shuddered. (2) The person, who watched Mr. Hooper and the corpse, did not hesitate to affirm that, at the moment when the veil fell forward, the corpse had shuddered. (3) And so forth.
Activity. Have students select a difficult sentence and repeat this process on their own.

and the mourners followed, saddening all the street, with the dead before them, and Mr. Hooper in his black veil behind.

"Why do you look back?" said one in the procession to his partner.

"I had a fancy," replied she, "that the minister and the maiden's spirit were walking hand in hand."

"And so had I, at the same moment," said the other.

That night, the handsomest couple in Milford village were to be joined in wedlock. Though reckoned a melancholy man, Mr. Hooper had a placid cheerfulness for such occasions, which often excited a sympathetic smile, where livelier merriment would have been thrown away. There was no quality of his disposition which made him more beloved than this. The company at the wedding awaited his arrival with impatience, trusting that the strange awe, which had gathered over him throughout the day, would now be dispelled. But such was not the result. When Mr. Hooper came, the first thing that their eyes rested on was the same horrible black veil, which had added deeper gloom to the funeral, and could portend nothing but evil to the wedding. Such was its immediate effect on the guests, that a cloud seemed to have rolled duskily from beneath the black crape, and dimmed the light of the candles. The bridal pair stood up before the minister. But the bride's cold fingers quivered in the tremulous hand of the bridegroom, and her deathlike paleness caused a whisper, that the maiden who had been buried a few hours before, was come from her grave to be married. If ever another wedding were so dismal, it was that famous one, where they tolled the wedding knell.[7] After performing the ceremony, Mr. Hooper raised a glass of wine to his lips, wishing happiness to the new-married couple, in a strain of mild pleasantry that ought to have brightened the features of the guests, like a cheerful gleam from the hearth. At that instant, catching a glimpse of his figure in the looking glass, the black veil involved his own spirit in the horror with which it overwhelmed all others. His frame shuddered—his lips grew white—he spilt the untasted wine upon the carpet—and rushed

7. **If . . . wedding knell:** reference to Hawthorne's story "The Wedding Knell." A knell is the ringing of a bell.

forth into the darkness. For the Earth, too, had on her Black Veil.

The next day, the whole village of Milford talked of little else than Parson Hooper's black veil. That, and the mystery concealed behind it, supplied a topic for discussion between acquaintances meeting in the street, and good women gossiping at their open windows. It was the first item of news that the tavern keeper told to his guests. The children babbled of it on their way to school. One imitative little imp covered his face with an old black handkerchief, thereby so affrighting his playmates, that the panic seized himself, and he well nigh lost his wits by his own waggery.[8]

It was remarkable, that, of all the busybodies and impertinent people in the parish, not one ventured to put the plain question to Mr. Hooper, wherefore he did this thing. Hitherto, whenever there appeared the slightest call for such interference, he had never lacked advisers, nor shown himself averse to be guided by their judgment. If he erred at all, it was by so painful a degree of self-distrust, that even the mildest censure would lead him to consider an indifferent action as a crime. Yet, though so well acquainted with this amiable weakness, no individual among his parishioners chose to make the black veil a subject of friendly remonstrance. There was a feeling of dread, neither plainly confessed nor carefully concealed, which caused each to shift the responsibility upon another, till at length it was found expedient to send a deputation of the church, in order to deal with Mr. Hooper about the mystery, before it should grow into a scandal. Never did an embassy so ill discharge its duties. The minister received them with friendly courtesy, but became silent, after they were seated, leaving to his visitors the whole burden of introducing their important business. The topic, it might be supposed, was obvious enough. There was the black veil, swathed round Mr. Hooper's forehead, and concealing every feature above his placid mouth, on which, at times, they could perceive the glimmering of a melancholy smile. But that piece of crape, to their

8. **waggery:** joke.

WORDS TO OWN

portend (pôr·tend′) v.: signify.

E **Elements of Literature**

Symbol

❓ What might this vision of the minister and the maiden's spirit symbolize? [Possible answers: The veiled minister seems closer to the dead, whose veil God has removed, than to the living; the couple might imagine there to have been some secret, sinful connection between Hooper and the deceased.]

F **Reading Skills and Strategies**

Drawing Inferences

❓ Why does Mr. Hooper run away from the wedding reception? [Possible response: He, too, is affected by the sight of the veil because it reminds him of his own sinfulness.] **What does the narrator mean when he says, "For the Earth, too, had on her Black Veil"?** [On one level, he means it was night. On another, he means that the material world itself and all its inhabitants have sins to veil.]

G **Reading Skills and Strategies**

Drawing Inferences

❓ Why doesn't anyone ask Mr. Hooper directly why he wears the veil? [Possible responses: People are intimidated by the sight of it; they don't really want to learn the answer, since deep down they suspect it has to do with their own sins.]

Professional Notes

Critical Comment:
Poe on Hawthorne

In his review of *Twice-Told Tales,* Edgar Allan Poe concludes that Hawthorne "has the purest style, the finest taste, the most available scholarship, the most delicate humor, the most touching pathos, the most radiant imagination, the most consummate ingenuity"—but he "is infinitely too fond of allegory." Poe considers "The Minister's Black Veil" to be "a masterly composition of which the sole defect is that to

the rabble its exquisite skill will be *caviare*. The *obvious* meaning of this article will be found to smother the insinuated one. The *moral* put into the mouth of the dying minister will be supposed to convey the *true* import of the narrative; and that a crime of dark dye, (having reference to the 'young lady') has been committed, is a point which only mind congenial with that of the author will perceive."

> Her eyes were fixed insensibly on the black veil, when, like a sudden twilight in the air, its terrors fell around her.

imagination, seemed to hang down before his heart, the symbol of a fearful secret between him and them. Were the veil but cast aside, they might speak freely of it, but not till then. Thus they sat a considerable time, speechless, confused, and shrinking uneasily from **Ⓐ** Mr. Hooper's eye, which they felt to be fixed upon them with an invisible glance. Finally, the deputies returned abashed to their constituents, pronouncing the matter too weighty to be handled, except by a council of the churches, if, indeed, it might not require a general synod.[9]

But there was one person in the village, unappalled by the awe with which the black veil had impressed all beside herself. When the deputies returned without an explanation, or even venturing to demand one, she, with the calm energy of her character, determined to chase away the strange cloud that appeared to be settling round Mr. Hooper, every moment more darkly than before. As his plighted[10] wife, it should be her privilege to know what the black veil concealed. At the minister's first visit, therefore, she entered upon the subject, with a direct simplicity, which made the task easier both for him and her. After he had seated himself, she fixed her eyes steadfastly upon the veil, but could discern nothing of the dreadful gloom that had so overawed the multitude: It was but a double fold of crape, hanging down from his forehead to his mouth, and slightly stirring with his breath.

9. **synod** (sin'əd): governing body of a group of churches.
10. **plighted:** promised.

"No," said she aloud, and smiling, "there is nothing terrible in this piece of crape, except that it hides a face which I am always glad to look upon. Come, good sir, let the sun shine from behind the cloud. First lay aside your black veil: Then tell me why you put it on."

Mr. Hooper's smile glimmered faintly.

"There is an hour to come," said he, "when all of us shall cast aside our veils. Take it not amiss, beloved friend, if I wear this piece of crape till then."

"Your words are a mystery too," returned the young lady. "Take away the veil from them, at least."

"Elizabeth, I will," said he, "so far as my vow **Ⓑ** may suffer me. Know, then, this veil is a type and a symbol, and I am bound to wear it ever, both in light and darkness, in solitude and before the gaze of multitudes, and as with strangers, so with my familiar friends. No mortal eye will see it withdrawn. This dismal shade must separate me from **Ⓒ** the world: Even you, Elizabeth, can never come behind it!"

"What grievous affliction hath befallen you," she earnestly inquired, "that you should thus darken your eyes forever?"

"If it be a sign of mourning," replied Mr. **Ⓓ** Hooper, "I, perhaps, like most other mortals, have sorrows dark enough to be typified by a black veil."

"But what if the world will not believe that it is the type of an innocent sorrow?" urged Elizabeth. "Beloved and respected as you are, there may be whispers, that you hide your face under the con- **Ⓔ** sciousness of secret sin. For the sake of your holy office, do away this scandal!"

The color rose into her cheeks, as she intimated the nature of the rumors that were already

---

Crossing the Curriculum

Psychology

To help students understand what it might be like to be Mr. Hooper or a member of his community, have volunteers wear veils similar to the one in the story during class one day. Have students write in their journals their responses to wearing or seeing the veils. The following day, let students share their reactions with the class.

Social Studies

Have students report on the wearing of veils in many Moslem cultures. What is the purpose? What are the historical and religious origins of the custom? What arguments are raised for the wearing of a full veil? a modified veil? no veil at all? What countries have laws governing the wearing of veils? What are the penalties for violations? What is the reaction of women's and human rights groups to these penalties?

abroad in the village. But Mr. Hooper's mildness did not forsake him. He even smiled again—that same sad smile, which always appeared like a faint glimmering of light, proceeding from the obscurity beneath the veil.

"If I hide my face for sorrow, there is cause enough," he merely replied; "and if I cover it for secret sin, what mortal might not do the same?"

And with this gentle, but unconquerable obstinacy, did he resist all her entreaties. At length Elizabeth sat silent. For a few moments she appeared lost in thought, considering, probably, what new methods might be tried, to withdraw her lover from so dark a fantasy, which, if it had no other meaning, was perhaps a symptom of mental disease. Though of a firmer character than his own, the tears rolled down her cheeks. But, in an instant, as it were, a new feeling took the place of sorrow: Her eyes were fixed insensibly on the black veil, when, like a sudden twilight in the air, its terrors fell around her. She arose, and stood trembling before him.

"And do you feel it then at last?" said he mournfully.

She made no reply, but covered her eyes with her hand, and turned to leave the room. He rushed forward and caught her arm.

"Have patience with me, Elizabeth!" cried he passionately. "Do not desert me, though this veil must be between us here on earth. Be mine, and hereafter there shall be no veil over my face, no darkness between our souls! It is but a mortal veil—it is not for eternity! Oh! you know not how lonely I am, and how frightened to be alone behind my black veil. Do not leave me in this miserable obscurity forever!"

"Lift the veil but once, and look me in the face," said she.

"Never! It cannot be!" replied Mr. Hooper.

"Then, farewell!" said Elizabeth.

She withdrew her arm from his grasp, and slowly departed, pausing at the door, to give one long, shuddering gaze, that seemed almost to penetrate the mystery of the black veil. But, even amid his grief, Mr. Hooper smiled to think that only a material emblem had separated him from happiness, though the horrors which it shadowed forth, must be drawn darkly between the fondest of lovers.

From that time no attempts were made to re-

move Mr. Hooper's black veil, or, by a direct appeal, to discover the secret which it was supposed to hide. By persons who claimed a superiority to popular prejudice, it was reckoned merely an eccentric whim, such as often mingles with the sober actions of men otherwise rational, and tinges them all with its own semblance of insanity. But with the multitude, good Mr. Hooper was irreparably a bugbear.[11] He could not walk the streets with any peace of mind, so conscious was he that the gentle and timid would turn aside to avoid him, and that others would make it a point of hardihood to throw themselves in his way. The impertinence of the latter class compelled him to give up his customary walk, at sunset, to the burial ground; for when he leaned pensively over the gate, there would always be faces behind the gravestones, peeping at his black veil. A fable went the rounds, that the stare of the dead people drove him thence. It grieved him, to the very depth of his kind heart, to observe how the children fled from his approach, breaking up their merriest sports, while his melancholy figure was yet afar off. Their instinctive dread caused him to feel, more strongly than aught else, that a preternatural[12] horror was interwoven with the threads of the black crape. In truth, his own antipathy to the veil was known to be so great, that he never willingly passed before a mirror, nor stooped to drink at a still fountain, lest, in its peaceful bosom, he should be affrighted by himself. This was what gave plausibility to the whispers, that Mr. Hooper's conscience tortured him for some great crime, too horrible to be entirely concealed, or otherwise than so obscurely intimated. Thus, from beneath the black veil, there rolled a cloud into the sunshine, an ambiguity of sin or sorrow, which enveloped the poor minister, so that love or sympathy could never reach him. It

---

11. **bugbear:** source of irrational fears.
12. **preternatural:** abnormal; supernatural.

WORDS TO OWN

obscurity (əb·skyoor'ə·tē) *n.*: something hidden or concealed.
pensively (pen'siv·lē) *adv.*: thinking deeply or seriously.
antipathy (an·tip'ə·thē) *n.*: strong dislike.
plausibility (plô'zə·bil'i·tē) *n.*: believability.

NATHANIEL HAWTHORNE **305**

F **Reading Skills and Strategies**
Drawing Inferences
? How does Elizabeth feel? [Possible responses: rejected, stunned, puzzled, sad that he won't reveal himself to her; frightened and disturbed by his sense of inescapable guilt and sin] How does Mr. Hooper feel? Possible responses: torn between love for Elizabeth and a sense of duty to his vow; sad, lonely, frightened.]

G **Critical Thinking**
Making Judgments
? Is Mr. Hooper right to say, "Never!"? [Possible responses: Yes, for to lift the veil would be to deny the overwhelming sense of personal and universal shame that he feels; No, it is arrogant to think that one can atone for one's own sins, much less other peoples', without seeking confession, love, and forgiveness.] Is Elizabeth right to say, "Then, farewell!"? [Possible responses: Yes, for she recognizes that Hooper's awareness of sin in himself and others runs too deep for him to ever truly accept happiness with her; no, she should have the courage to share Hooper's somber reality, since it is a more honest vision of life.]

H **Struggling Readers**
Summarizing
Have students summarize Mr. Hooper's thoughts in this sentence. [Although he is distraught at the loss of Elizabeth, he takes comfort knowing that his material veil is nothing compared to the emotional and spiritual veil of misunderstanding, mistrust, and dishonesty that often separates even the closest confidantes.]

I **Elements of Literature**
Symbol
? How does the black veil affect his relationship with the villagers? [Possible responses: Some people say he is eccentric, but most people avoid him whenever possible; some say he is responsible for a great crime; he is cut off from love and sympathy.]

Getting Students Involved

Cooperative Learning

Off or On? Have students conduct a mock trial to decide the fate of Mr. Hooper's veil. Tell them to list reasons for Mr. Hooper to remove the veil or keep it on. At the end of the session, divide the class into three approximately equal groups as follows: (1) those who found more reasons to take the veil off, (2) those who found more reasons for keeping the veil on, and (3) those who found almost an equal number of

reasons for each. Group 3 will be the jury, while groups 1 and 2 will be the opposing sides. Allow Groups 1 and 2 to appoint a lead lawyer, assistants, and a recording secretary. Give these groups time to discuss and prepare their case. At the conclusion of the trial, "sequester" the jury in a corner of the room for deliberations and then have a foreperson announce and explain the verdict.

A Reading Skills and Strategies

Drawing Inferences

❓ Why do people come to deeply respect Mr. Hooper as a clergyman? [Possible answers: In personally taking on this mysterious emblem of sin and sorrow, Hooper makes people feel the moral and spiritual stakes of their own lives. Much more than a personal symbol of guilt, Hooper's veil comes to symbolize sin itself, and makes sinners feel that he, above all, understands their struggles and can lead them to goodness.]

B Struggling Readers

Paraphrasing

❓ How might this be paraphrased? [He had served at the church for so long that his deceased parishioners outnumbered his living ones; and having worked so hard, for so long, he deserved the peace of death.]

C Reading Skills and Strategies

Drawing Inferences

❓ What does Elizabeth's faithfulness—her secret, solitary lifelong affection for Mr. Hooper—reveal about her character? [Possible response: In maintaining yet restraining her feelings for Hooper, she has shown as much or more strength of character than the Reverend. For in doing so, she holds him to his vow to accept the weight of sin in himself and others, without a moment of denial or relief.]

D Elements of Literature

Symbol

❓ In what sense can the human heart be a prison? [Possible responses: For someone who harbors a sense of guilt, the heart (or soul or psyche) is a prison. A sense of sin can make people suffer and lose faith in themselves.]

E Reading Skills and Strategies

Noting Details

❓ What is Elizabeth's attitude toward the veil now? [She too now believes that it is a moral and spiritual imperative that he keep it in place.]

was said, that ghost and fiend consorted with him there. With self-shudderings and outward terrors, he walked continually in its shadow, groping darkly within his own soul, or gazing through a medium that saddened the whole world. Even the lawless wind, it was believed, respected his dreadful secret, and never blew aside the veil. But still good Mr. Hooper sadly smiled, at the pale visages of the worldly throng as he passed by.

Among all its bad influences, the black veil had the one desirable effect, of making its wearer a very efficient clergyman. By the aid of his mysterious emblem—for there was no other apparent cause—he became a man of awful power, over souls that were in agony for sin. His converts always regarded him with a dread peculiar to themselves, affirming, though but figuratively, that, before he brought them to celestial light, they had been with him behind the black veil. Its gloom, indeed, enabled him to sympathize with all dark affections. Dying sinners cried aloud for Mr. Hooper, and would not yield their breath till he appeared; though ever, as he stooped to whisper consolation, they shuddered at the veiled face so near their own. Such were the terrors of the black veil, even when Death had bared his visage! Strangers came long distances to attend service at his church, with the mere idle purpose of gazing at his figure, because it was forbidden them to behold his face. But many were made to quake ere they departed! Once, during Governor Belcher's[13] administration, Mr. Hooper was appointed to preach the election sermon. Covered with his black veil, he stood before the chief magistrate, the council, and the representatives, and wrought so deep an impression, that the legislative measures of that year, were characterized by all the gloom and piety of our earliest ancestral sway.

In this manner Mr. Hooper spent a long life, irreproachable in outward act, yet shrouded in dismal suspicions; kind and loving, though unloved, and dimly feared; a man apart from men, shunned in their health and joy, but ever summoned to their aid in mortal anguish. As years wore on, shedding their snows above his sable veil, he acquired a name throughout the New England

13. **Governor Belcher's:** Jonathan Belcher (1682–1757) was governor of the Massachusetts Bay Colony from 1730 to 1741.

churches, and they called him Father Hooper. Nearly all his parishioners, who were of mature age when he was settled, had been borne away by many a funeral: He had one congregation in the church, and a more crowded one in the churchyard; and having wrought so late into the evening, and done his work so well, it was now good Father Hooper's turn to rest.

Several persons were visible by the shaded candlelight, in the death chamber of the old clergyman. Natural connections he had none. But there was the decorously grave, though unmoved physician, seeking only to mitigate the last pangs of the patient whom he could not save. There were the deacons, and other eminently pious members of his church. There, also, was the Reverend Mr. Clark, of Westbury, a young and zealous divine, who had ridden in haste to pray by the bedside of the expiring minister. There was the nurse, no hired handmaiden of death, but one whose calm affection had endured thus long, in secrecy, in solitude, amid the chill of age, and would not perish, even at the dying hour. Who, but Elizabeth! And there lay the hoary head of good Father Hooper upon the death-pillow, with the black veil still swathed about his brow and reaching down over his face, so that each more difficult gasp of his faint breath caused it to stir. All through life that piece of crape had hung between him and the world: It had separated him from cheerful brotherhood and woman's love, and kept him in that saddest of all prisons, his own heart; and still it lay upon his face, as if to deepen the gloom of his darksome chamber, and shade him from the sunshine of eternity.

For some time previous, his mind had been confused, wavering doubtfully between the past and the present, and hovering forward, as it were, at intervals, into the indistinctness of the world to come. There had been feverish turns, which tossed him from side to side, and wore away what little strength he had. But in his most convulsive struggles, and in the wildest vagaries of his intellect, when no other thought retained its sober influence, he still showed an awful solicitude lest the black veil should slip aside. Even if his bewildered soul could have forgotten, there was a faithful woman at his pillow, who, with averted eyes, would have covered that aged face, which she had last beheld in the comeliness of manhood. At

Professional Notes

A Critical Comment

About a century before Hawthorne wrote this story, Jonathan Edwards had raged at his congregation that they were "Sinners in the Hands of an Angry God" (pp. 77–83). It did not take the people of Northampton, Massachusetts, long to decide that Edwards's theology was too harsh, and he was soon dismissed from his post. Mr. Hooper's action in "The Minister's Black Veil" inspires dread in his parishioners, as much as Edwards's words did in *his* congregation. But unlike Edwards, who denounced others as sinners, Hooper humbly wears a visual emblem of his own and all people's guilt. Nevertheless, Hooper's emblem upsets his congregation, which is unwilling to face whatever unpleasant truths reside in their own hearts. Rather than consider their own sins, they isolate and mock him. Hooper consequently pays a terrible price for his decision to wear the veil.

T306

> ... there he sat, shivering with the arms of death around him, while the black veil hung down ...

length the death-stricken old man lay quietly in the torpor of mental and bodily exhaustion, with an imperceptible pulse, and breath that grew fainter and fainter, except when a long, deep, and irregular inspiration seemed to prelude the flight of his spirit.

The minister of Westbury approached the bedside.

"Venerable Father Hooper," said he, "the moment of your release is at hand. Are you ready for the lifting of the veil, that shuts in time from eternity?"

Father Hooper at first replied merely by a feeble motion of his head; then, apprehensive, perhaps, that his meaning might be doubtful, he exerted himself to speak.

"Yea," said he, in faint accents, "my soul hath a patient weariness until that veil be lifted."

"And is it fitting," resumed the Reverend Mr. Clark, "that a man so given to prayer, of such a blameless example, holy in deed and thought, so far as mortal judgment may pronounce; is it fitting that a father in the church should leave a shadow on his memory, that may seem to blacken a life so pure? I pray you, my venerable brother, let not this thing be! Suffer us to be gladdened by your triumphant aspect, as you go to your reward. Before the veil of eternity be lifted, let me cast aside this black veil from your face!"

And thus speaking, the Reverend Mr. Clark bent forward to reveal the mystery of so many years. But, exerting a sudden energy, that made all the beholders stand aghast, Father Hooper snatched both his hands from beneath the bedclothes, and pressed them strongly on the black veil, resolute to struggle, if the minister of Westbury would contend with a dying man.

"Never!" cried the veiled clergyman. "On earth, never!"

"Dark old man!" exclaimed the affrighted minister, "with what horrible crime upon your soul are you now passing to the judgment?"

Father Hooper's breath heaved; it rattled in his throat; but, with a mighty effort, grasping forward with his hands, he caught hold of life, and held it back till he should speak. He even raised himself in bed; and there he sat, shivering with the arms of death around him, while the black veil hung down, awful, at that last moment, in the gathered terrors of a lifetime. And yet the faint, sad smile, so often there, now seemed to glimmer from its obscurity, and linger on Father Hooper's lips.

"Why do you tremble at me alone?" cried he, turning his veiled face round the circle of pale spectators. "Tremble also at each other! Have men avoided me, and women shown no pity, and children screamed and fled, only for my black veil? What, but the mystery which it obscurely typifies, has made this piece of crape so awful? When the friend shows his inmost heart to his friend; the lover to his best-beloved; when man does not vainly shrink from the eye of his Creator, loathsomely treasuring up the secret of his sin; then deem me a monster, for the symbol beneath which I have lived, and die! I look around me, and, lo! on every visage a Black Veil!"

While his auditors shrank from one another, in mutual affright, Father Hooper fell back upon his pillow, a veiled corpse, with a faint smile lingering on the lips. Still veiled, they laid him in his coffin, and a veiled corpse they bore him to the grave. The grass of many years has sprung up and withered on that grave, the burial-stone is moss-grown, and good Mr. Hooper's face is dust; but awful is still the thought, that it moldered beneath the Black Veil!

WORDS TO OWN

resolute (rez′ə·lōōt′) *adj.*: determined.

NATHANIEL HAWTHORNE 307

F **Critical Thinking**
Interpreting
? What does the minister of Westbury mean by "the lifting of the veil"? [the passage from life into death]

G **Reading Skills and Strategies**
Drawing Inferences
? Why does Mr. Hooper claim to see a black veil on every human face? What is he saying in this final argument? [Hooper points out that he has not been shunned and isolated for any "horrible crime" of his own, but because the mystery of his symbolic gesture reminded people of their own secret sins, their own "black veils." He insists that he is no monster, and that his only goal was to be honest before God and humanity about a truth that everyone else hides.]

H **Elements of Literature**
Symbol
? What does the onlookers' reaction to Hooper's statement reveal about the meaning of the minister's veil? [The fear and horror that Hooper's auditors feel when they look at each other suggest that they have always known on some level the truth that Mr. Hooper could never escape: that all humans are deeply marked by envy, dishonesty, hypocrisy and other sins, yet try to deny it in public life.]

I **Critical Thinking**
Evaluating
? Was Mr. Hooper a sympathetic or unsympathetic character, and how does Elizabeth's character help to define his? [Most people will say that Hooper was a sympathetic character for whom they felt sorry, and that Elizabeth's character was a foil that helped illuminate Hooper's conflict.] Discuss Hawthorne's purpose. Is he examining the destructive effect of guilt for some dark deed? the destructive effect of focusing only on humanity's alienation from God and not enough on human and divine love? the destructive effect of public hypocrisy (or the need for such hypocrisy)? The "veils" people hide behind? All of these? Something else? Does Hawthorne succeed in his purpose?

Assessing Learning

Check Test: True-False

1. The veil makes Mr. Hooper an effective minister. [True]
2. Mr. Hooper himself is horrified to see what he looks like with the veil on his face. [True]
3. No one besides his fiancée ever asks Mr. Hooper why he wears the veil. [True]
4. Governor Belcher orders him to remove the veil. [False]
5. Mr. Hooper draws back the veil before dying. [False]

Making the Connections

Connecting to the Theme:
"The Realms of Darkness"
Hawthorne explores realms of darkness akin to, but distinct from, those Poe unveils. Poe deals with primal terrors, not with the moral issues Hawthorne explores. Urge students to identify features that the works share. [Possible responses: deaths, secrets, troubled souls, burials, inexplicable events, the effects of isolation and guilt on the human heart.]

MAKING MEANINGS

First Thoughts [Respond]

1. Many students will have predicted that Hooper committed a crime, but by the end of the story, many may feel that was incorrect.

Shaping Interpretations [Interpret]

2. At first, Elizabeth is loving and full of common sense, but when Hooper resists her pleas to remove his veil, she becomes sad and then terrified. She may fear that he has committed a crime; she may fear his preoccupation with universal sin; she may fear for her own soul. At the end of the story, however, she seems to share the moral and spiritual conviction that Mr. Hooper must never remove the veil.

3. Anyone who cannot share his or her emotions with other people—especially emotions regarding shame and sin—is isolated and confined in a personal prison. This truth applies to everyone in the story.

4. His tone is neutral, presenting unusual events and strong emotions in a detached way, but he also adds to the story's tragic atmosphere with connotative language, using phrases such as "darkened aspect" and "gloomy shade."

5. The veil may represent Hooper's belief that everyone is a sinner, his mourning at people's denial of their state of sin, or his belief in a barrier between people and true self-awareness.

6. Although the veil inspires fear, it also makes Mr. Hooper an effective minister, especially with those who acknowledge sin.

7. Possible themes: We should all admit we are secret sinners. We should not be too quick to judge the actions of others. We must learn to acknowledge our sins but also see the love in people. It is a parable because it is short, ambiguous, and has a moral lesson.

8. Possible responses: They do so out of respect or fear or because they agree with his ideas about sin.

Connecting with the Text [Apply]

9. Sample responses: Guilt can help us do good and avoid evil, and it can spur confession. It can also lead to apathy and despair.

(Reading Skills and Strategies annotations appear on the bottom of p. T309.)

T308

MAKING MEANINGS

First Thoughts

1. What did you predict was the reason for the minister's veil? Why do you think your prediction was, or was not, correct?

Shaping Interpretations

2. Trace the progression of Elizabeth's response to the veil. How do you explain her changing attitudes?

3. Explain the narrator's remark on page 306 about the human heart being the "saddest of all prisons." Do you agree or disagree? Do you think this observation refers only to Hooper, or is it true of everyone in the story?

4. Would you describe the narrator's **tone** as neutral or emotional? (Think particularly of the words the narrator uses in referring to the veil.) Make a list of specific **connotative** words and phrases that contribute to the story's tone. How do the words the narrator uses affect the story's tone and **atmosphere**?

5. On his deathbed, Hooper says, "I look around me, and, lo! on every visage a Black Veil!" Explain that statement. In what ways is Hooper's veil a **symbol**? What do you think it symbolizes?

> ### Reading Check
>
> a. How does the congregation respond at first to Mr. Hooper's black veil? Why?
>
> b. Briefly describe Hooper's **character** as revealed in the story's opening paragraphs. What does the congregation's attitude toward him seem to have been up to this point?
>
> c. In a single afternoon, Hooper presides at both a funeral and a wedding. How do people react to the presence of the veil at each event?
>
> d. What explanation does Hooper give to Elizabeth, his fiancée, of why he wears the veil? What arguments against wearing the veil does she make?

---

6. Does Hooper's veil have any positive effects during his long life? Explain.

7. Hawthorne added the subtitle "A Parable" to this story, indicating the importance moral themes had for him. A **parable** is a short, simple story from which a moral or religious lesson can be drawn. Unlike many of the world's parables, which come from religious scriptures such as the Bible, this story is a literary parable with meanings that may be ambiguous and elusive rather than clear-cut. What would you say is the moral lesson of this story—its **theme,** or main idea? In what sense *is* it a parable?

8. Why do you think the villagers bury Hooper without removing the veil?

Connecting with the Text

9. Almost all people, at some point in life, have done things that made them feel guilty and that they have concealed from others. What do you think is useful and beneficial about having a sense of guilt, and what is harmful about it? In what ways can guilt isolate people, and in what ways can it bring people together?

READING SKILLS AND STRATEGIES

Understanding Archaisms

If modern readers have trouble with Hawthorne, it is with his **archaic,** or old-fashioned, language (see page 37). **Context clues** (page 168) should help you figure out any language that is strange. Which word or words in each of the following passages from the story are rarely used today? Rephrase each passage in a modern idiom. Are any of these words used today in different senses?

1. "So sensible were the audience of some unwonted attribute in their minister. . . ." (page 301)

2. "A superstitious old woman was the only witness of this prodigy." (page 302)

3. ". . . he well nigh lost his wits by his own waggery." (page 303)

4. ". . . having wrought so late into the evening. . . ." (page 306)

> ### Reading Check
>
> a. They are threatened by this sign of personal and universal sin.
>
> b. Hooper is neat, gentle, and kind. They seem to have been fond of him.
>
> c. At the funeral, the people find the veil appropriate. At the wedding, the guests regard the veil as an ominous portent.
>
> d. He says that the veil is a symbol of universal secret sin and that he is bound to wear it forever. Elizabeth says that the world may not believe that the veil is the sign of an innocent sorrow. She warns Hooper that people will gossip about him, whispering that he has been involved in some scandal, and that his ministry may be compromised. She appeals to their love and asks him to cast the veil aside once for her sake.

CHOICES: Building Your Portfolio

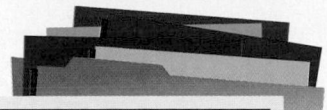

Writer's Notebook

1. Collecting Ideas for a Controversial Issue

You can find topics for persuasive essays in the literature you read. For example, you might find a specific passage in Hawthorne's famous story that you would like to support or argue with. Or, you might find an issue here that people disagree on—perhaps something on the nature of guilt or the psychological effects of isolation. Or, you might want to take a controversial stand on interpreting this story. Take notes on possible topics, jot down details to support your position, and save your work for possible use in the Writer's Workshop on page 331.

Comparing Ideas

2. On Human Nature

In *Nature*, on page 219, Emerson says that we are "part or particle of God," and that in the beauties of nature we can behold something "as beautiful as [our] own nature." In a brief essay, explain how Emerson's views of human nature compare or contrast with Hawthorne's. Cite specific passages from both writers to support what you say. Do you agree with either writer? Why or why not?

Comparing Religious Beliefs

3. Hawthorne and Puritanism

In a brief essay, compare and contrast the attitudes revealed in Hawthorne's story to attitudes held by Puritans such as Jonathan Edwards (see Edwards's sermon "Sinners in the Hands of an Angry God" on page 79). Consider especially attitudes toward sin, guilt, and the conditions necessary for salvation. How do you think Hawthorne felt about the tenets of Puritanism?

Creative Writing

4. Behind the Veil

Write a brief autobiographical sketch of Mr. Hooper, using the **first-person point of view**. Using clues from the text, and your own imagination, have Hooper explain the significance of the veil and how he first thought of wearing it. Let him describe how he feels wearing it all the time.

Critical Thinking/ Speaking and Listening

5. Rating the Prose

In a group of three or more students, discuss similarities and differences between Hawthorne and Poe, based on your reading of their works. Compare and contrast their literary styles, their choices of subject matter, their **themes**, and their use of **symbolism**. Discuss which author's work you prefer and why. Present your group's "verdict" to the rest of the class.

Creative Writing/ Performance

6. Theatrical Version

With one or more partners, write a condensed version of the story, to be spoken aloud. You'll need to create some dialogue on the basis of narrated scenes. The major characters will be Hooper, Elizabeth, and the narrator, who will summarize events and describe characters. Perform your reader's theater for the class.

Interpreting a Story

7. A Crime of Dark Dye

Edgar Allan Poe said that Hooper wore the veil because ". . . a crime of dark dye (having reference to the 'young lady') has been committed. . . ." What do you think Poe is referring to? Does this interpretation make sense to you, or do you think it is too literal? (Think about whether the story would have been more effective had Hawthorne revealed why Hooper wears the veil.) Write a brief essay expressing your views.

NATHANIEL HAWTHORNE 309

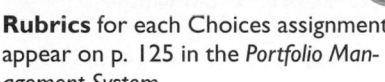

Grading Timesaver

Rubrics for each Choices assignment appear on p. 125 in the *Portfolio Management System*.

CHOICES: Building Your Portfolio

1. **Writer's Notebook** Encourage students to jot down at least one idea in response to each suggestion and at least one more of their own devising.

2–3. **Comparing Ideas/Beliefs** Have students work in groups of varying abilities. Suggest that they prewrite by making charts comparing and contrasting Hawthorne with Emerson or with the Puritans.

4. **Creative Writing** For students who need help getting started, suggest that they begin their sketch, "This is how I attempted to do right before my God and my congregation."

5–6. **Speaking and Listening/Performance.** After a group has made its presentation, give listeners the opportunity to ask questions and offer comments.

7. **Interpreting a Story.** Share with students the Professional Notes on p. T303. Some students may feel that Poe is projecting his own psyche onto Hawthorne's story, while others may see evidence of Mr. Hooper's guilt.

READING SKILLS AND STRATEGIES

Discuss how archaisms help to create the flavor of the historical period.

1. *sensible* and *unwonted.* The audience could sense something unusual in their minister. Today *sensible* means "reasonable" and *unwonted,* though seldom used, means "not common" or "rare."

2. *prodigy.* A superstitious woman was the only witness of this marvel. Today *prodigy* often refers to "a child genius."

3. *well nigh* and *waggery.* He almost lost his wits by joking. Both have the same meaning today, although they are not commonly used.

4. *wrought.* Having worked so late. Today *wrought* means "formed" or "made."

Reading Skills and Strategies

Mini-Lesson: Tracing the Origins of Words

Choose one of the words listed in the text and, with your students, work through the charting process shown in the Try It Out activity. Then, have students work in pairs to complete their charts. To help students to retain their new words, encourage them to use the words in conversation during the next week, and record in their notebooks the contexts in which the words come up.

Try It Out

The answers below are from *Webster's New World Dictionary Third College Edition.*

iniquity: from Latin *iniquus,* "unequal"; meaning "wickedness."

superstitious: from Latin *superstitio,* "excessive fear of the gods"; meaning "any belief, based on ignorance, that is inconsistent with known laws of science."

portend: from Latin *portendere,* "to stretch"; meaning "to be an omen."

ambiguity: from Latin *ambigere,* "to wander"; meaning "having two possible meanings."

vagaries: from Latin *vagari,* "to wander"; meaning "an odd or whimsical idea."

prelude: from Latin *praeludere,* "to play beforehand"; meaning "to serve as the introduction to an event or performance."

VOCABULARY: TRACING THE ORIGINS OF WORDS

While some languages have few imported words, English is a language full of borrowings. Many English words come originally from Latin by way of Germanic languages or Old English. Other words have Greek, French, Native American, or Spanish origins. And this is just the tip of the iceberg.

Since Latin words make up such a large part of our language, learning the meaning of an English word that comes from Latin may help you understand the meanings of other English words derived from Latin. Such words are considered members of the same word family. You can learn about word families by consulting a dictionary to discover a word's **etymology**—the history of its origins and development.

Hanging tales on words.
Learning the etymology of a word can help you to quickly recognize related words. It can also help you to remember a new word by giving you interesting and perhaps surprising information. For example, the noun *volcano*

Vulcan making a new armor for Achilles.

is derived from *Vulcan,* the Roman god of fire and forges. If you can use a word's etymology to "hang a tale" on a word—that is, associate an interesting fact or anecdote with it—you're more likely to remember the word.

Here are some words that come from Latin. All of them appear in Hawthorne's story. See if the etymologies help you to remember and use these words.

averted from *a-,* "from" + *vertere,* "to turn"
Meaning: turned away from; kept from happening

celestial from *caelestis,* "heaven"
Meaning: of the heavens

discern from *dis-,* "apart" + *cernere,* "to separate"
Meaning: to separate (a thing) mentally from another or others; to recognize as separate or different

obscurity from *obscurus,* "covered over"
Meaning: the condition of being unclear or indistinct; not easily understood

placid from *placidus,* "to please"
Meaning: undisturbed; tranquil; calm; quiet

preclude from *pre-,* "before" + *claudere,* "to close"
Meaning: to make impossible, especially in advance; to shut out; to prevent

sagacious from *sagax,* "wise; foreseeing"
Meaning: having or showing keen perception or discernment; having or showing sound judgment

Try It Out

Charting etymologies. When you find an unfamiliar word, looking it up in a dictionary and recording its etymology along with its meaning can both help you remember it *and* make it a permanent part of your vocabulary. Try using a chart like the one below to record etymologies for the following words from Hawthorne and for any other new words you want to own and use.

iniquity (page 301)   ambiguity (page 305)

superstitious (page 302)   vagaries (page 306)

portend (page 303)   prelude (page 307)

Word	
Etymology	
Meanings	
Where Found	

Using Students' Strengths

Spatial Learners

Have students create a visual representation for each word, in order to help them remember the word's meaning and etymology. Students may conceive and draw any image that helps their memories. They should then list the word, meaning, and etymology below the image. For example, for *ambiguity,* the image might be arrows pointing in two directions; for *prelude,* it might be a theater curtain.

Kinesthetic Learners

Ask students to list street names, business names, car models, advertising slogans, or other words found in their neighborhood that they think might have a Latin etymology. Then, have students look up the etymologies. You may want students to work in teams to see which group can come up with the most words. Students should present their words and etymologies to the class.

Herman Melville

(1819–1891)

Herman Melville (1870) by Joseph Eaton. Oil on canvas.
By permission of the Houghton Library, Harvard
University, Cambridge, Massachusetts (H585).

It is the central irony of Herman Melville's career that his triumphant achievement, now widely recognized as one of the greatest American novels, was almost wholly ignored while its author was alive. Melville's contemporaries—so absorbed with success; so eager to discover it, bestow it, reward it, celebrate it—passed by *Moby-Dick* without the barest recognition.

As a result, Melville spent the last third of his life in poverty and despair, thinking himself a failure. His disappointment was even more painful because he had known easy, early success with his adventure stories. With ambitious, serious work, he met only failure and humiliation.

It is a further irony that Melville became resigned to the contempt of the world; that in spite of the painfulness of the world's judgment, he deliberately decided in the world's favor. In a remark that was to be echoed by the twentieth-century novelist William Faulkner, Melville once remarked that "failure is the true test of greatness."

A Whale Ship Was His College

Herman Melville was born into a distinguished family—wealthy Boston merchants on his father's side, early New York landowners on his mother's, Revolutionary War heroes on both. But his father went bankrupt in 1830, suffered an emotional breakdown, and died when Melville was twelve. Melville's mother, an austere, God-fearing woman, moved with her eight children from New York City to Albany. Under the pressures of poverty, she became even more remote from her children.

The teenage Melville clerked in his brother's hat store and in his uncle's bank, taught school in Pittsfield, Massachusetts, and tried writing articles and stories. However, faced with a grim life in his family's house, he took to the sea in 1839 as cabin boy on a merchant ship.

A whaling expedition to the South Seas followed in 1841. A year and a half later, Melville jumped ship at the Marquesas Islands and stumbled upon the valley of the Typees, who were reputed to be cannibals but turned out to be gentle and hospitable. After a month, Melville signed on to an Australian ship, which he deserted in a semimutiny at Papeete. He roamed the islands of Tahiti and Moorea, working in the fields and studying island life, before joining a whaler to Honolulu, and then enlisting as a seaman on a U.S. Navy frigate. When his ship docked at Boston in October 1844, a career's worth of seagoing adventure had ended. Ishmael, the young narrator of *Moby-Dick,* surely voices Melville's own sentiments when he says, "A whale ship was my Yale College and my Harvard."

The Road to Success

In less than two years, Melville produced a book of slightly fictionalized travel memoirs, *Typee,* that became an immediate success. With the publication of four other semiautobiographical sea tales between 1847 and 1850, Melville became one of the most popular authors of the

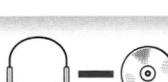 

day. He was now married to the former Elizabeth Shaw, daughter of an old family friend. In the course of their long and often troubled marriage, she bore four children and was never more loyal and devoted than at times of crisis.

In the fall of 1850, Melville bought a farm near Pittsfield, Massachusetts. Nathaniel Hawthorne, who lived in nearby Lenox, responded to Melville's admiration, and they saw much of each other. Hawthorne's example encouraged Melville, who was writing a book that would both exploit his whaling experience and, on a far more ambitious plane, seek the ultimate truth of human existence. That truth, and the mystery of whether it is benign or evil in nature, is embodied in Moby-Dick, the great white whale that gives the book its title and central symbol.

Melville found the perfect narrator for his whale story in a young character named Ishmael, who has a keen eye and a questioning voice. Moreover, Melville saw his other main character clearly: Captain Ahab, standing on the *Pequod*'s quarter-deck with his peg leg, his heart full of brooding vengeance. In Ahab, Melville created an obsessed, tragic, larger-than-life figure with few equals in American literature.

> **"I have written a wicked book. . . ."**

When he finished *Moby-Dick* in July 1851, Melville sensed that he had taken a great risk and won. He dedicated his great novel to Hawthorne and wrote him, "I have written a wicked book, and feel spotless as the lamb."

To Risk All—and Lose

Yet for all Melville's bright expectations, *Moby-Dick* was a failure. Critics and readers alike were either puzzled or indifferent, and Melville finally had to admit that his literary career had foundered. He wrote Hawthorne:

> The calm, the coolness, the silent grass-growing mood in which a man *ought* always to compose—that, I fear, can seldom be

mine. Dollars damn me; and the malicious Devil is forever grinning in upon me, holding the door ajar. My dear Sir, a presentiment [feeling of fear about the future] is on me —I shall at last be worn out and perish. . . . What I feel most moved to write, that is banned—it will not pay. Yet, altogether, write the *other* way I cannot. So the product is a final hash, and all my books are botches.

Melville was in debt, unable to meet the needs of his family, and in ill health. However, he continued to hope for a change in his fortunes. In the next six years, he published three poorly received novels.

In 1856, Melville scraped together enough money for a trip to Europe and the Middle East. He returned home with his emotions restored, but his literary and financial fortunes still low.

In 1866, Melville found a job, much as Hawthorne had, with the customhouse. But if the work gave him the financial security he yearned for, the "grass-growing" peace of mind was still denied him. A different kind of tragedy hit the following year when his son Malcolm took to his room and killed himself with a pistol.

True to the Dreams of Youth

Although Melville never stopped writing during this dark period, almost none of his work found a publisher, and he was obliged to bring it out in private editions of only a few copies. To end this period in Melville's life, there was further tragedy. In 1886, his son Stanwix, always an unstable wanderer, died in San Francisco.

At about the same time, Elizabeth, Melville's wife, came into a small inheritance which allowed her husband to retire from the customhouse and begin work on a book that would become another masterpiece. This was *Billy Budd*. When Melville died on September 28, 1891, the novella lay unwanted in his desk drawer. In 1924, thirty-three years later, it was published and acclaimed. Near the desk where Melville had composed it, a note was found. It read, "Keep true to the dreams of thy youth."

Professional Notes

Critical Comment: Melville's America

For critic Richard Chase, Melville's writing is "a kind of culmination . . . of the American imagination as it developed before the Civil War." Chase points to Calvinism's "sense of 'blackness' and of moral and psychological complexity" and "the pastoral idyll of the frontier" as the two most important forces in shaping the American imagination, and suggests that "Melville was the first great writer who was able to draw on both these forces."

Skill Link

Technical Vocabulary

You might have students learn the following nautical terms before they read:

quarterdeck—the part of the upperdeck of a ship reserved for officers and ceremonies
gangway—passageway
mainmast—principal mast of a vessel, generally the second from the bow in whaling ships, behind the foremast

masthead—top part of a ship's mast; sailor who works there
shroud—any rope set from the ship's side to the masthead
jib—triangular sail stretching in front of the mast or foremast
aft—the rear of the ship, the opposite of fore

Before You Read

FROM **MOBY-DICK**

Make the Connection

The Meaning of a White Whale

Moby-Dick is both a thrilling sea story about men who hunt whales in wooden boats and a search for the truth of human existence. The mystery of whether existence is benign, indifferent, or evil is embodied in Moby-Dick, the great white whale.

Elements of Literature

Characterization

To create the larger-than-life **characterization** of Captain Ahab, Melville uses all the tools at a writer's command: He tells us directly (through the narrator, Ishmael) what Ahab is like, he describes Ahab's appearance and clothing, he lets us overhear Ahab speaking and thinking, he shows Ahab in action, and he shows us how other characters feel about and behave toward Ahab.

> **C**haracterization is the process by which a writer reveals a character's personality.
>
> *For more on Characterization, see the Handbook of Literary Terms.*

Reading Skills and Strategies

Drawing Inferences about Character

By combining clues in the text with what experience has taught us about people, we can draw inferences, or conclusions, about the kind of people we meet in literature.

As you read these episodes from *Moby-Dick*, watch especially for clues to the characters of Captain Ahab and the first mate, Starbuck.

To take notes on these men as you read, divide a sheet of paper into two columns. In the left column, list details in the text that tell you something significant about each man. After you complete your reading, review the clues you've noted. Then, in the right column, write the inferences you can make about the characters of Ahab and Starbuck. What kind of people are they? What drives each man?

Summary ■■■

This selection from the novel establishes the sinister atmosphere of the *Pequod* and foreshadows Captain Ahab's momentous conflict with the great white whale. As the chapter opens, Captain Ahab paces the deck furiously, lost in thought. Just before sunset, he orders Starbuck, his first mate, to assemble the crew. He works them into a frenzy of anticipation about hunting the white whale, Moby-Dick, and nails a Spanish doubloon to the main mast for the man who first spots the whale. The men respond enthusiastically, except for the level-headed Starbuck, who objects to Ahab's seeking revenge on an animal that had, in his view, acted instinctively when it severed Ahab's leg years before. Nevertheless, the crew drinks to the pursuit of Moby-Dick in blasphemous mock communion.

from Moby-Dick

Herman Melville

Two chapters from Melville's great novel will give you only a taste of its characters, setting, plot, and themes. The novel opens with the famous line, "Call me Ishmael." The narrator who adopts this pseudonym is a moody young New Yorker who takes to sea to escape the "damp, drizzly November in my soul." First traveling to the Massachusetts seaport of New Bedford, he shares a room with a South Sea Islander named Queequeg. Becoming friends, the two go to the island of Nantucket, where they sign on for a three-year voyage on the whaling ship Pequod, under the command of the mysterious Captain Ahab. While still ashore, Ishmael receives warnings of disaster; but he ships out anyway, and the Pequod, weirdly decorated with whale bones, sets sail on an icy Christmas Day. The officers and crew are an assortment of men from all over the world: South Pacific islanders, Massachusetts Gay-Head Indians, inhabitants of the Isle of Man off the coast of Ireland, and more. The harpooners are Queequeg, Tashtego, and Daggoo; the first, second, and third mates are Starbuck, Stubb, and Flask, respectively.

Shortly before the chapter "The Quarter-Deck," Stubb and Ahab have quarreled violently, and an ominous dream has suggested to Stubb that he beware of his captain's anger. In this chapter, Ahab calls the men to assemble on the deck, where he will reveal the true nature of his quest.

Background illustration by Rockwell Kent from *Moby-Dick*.
Rockwell Kent Collection, Rare Book and Manuscript Library, Columbia University.

HERMAN MELVILLE 313

BROWSING IN THE FILES

Writers on Writing. In September 1851 Herman Melville wrote to an acquaintance: "Concerning my own forthcoming book—it is off my hands, but must cross the sea before publication here. Don't you buy it, don't you read it when it does come out, because it is by no means the sort of book for you. It is not a piece of fine feminine Spitalfield silk—but is of the horrible texture of a fabric that should be woven of ship's cables and hausers. A Polar wind blows through it, & birds of prey hover over it. Warn all gentle fastidious people from so much as peeping into the book—on risk of a lumbago & sciatic."

Preteaching Vocabulary

Words to Own

Have students page through the selection to find the Words to Own. Have volunteers read the words and their definitions aloud, find the sentences in the text in which the vocabulary words are underlined, and read aloud those sentences. Then, have students use the words in the phrases below. You may want to have students add subjects and verbs, as necessary, to create complete sentences.

1. enjoyed his witty [rejoinder]
2. did it of his own [volition]
3. [incapacitated] by ill health
4. attacked with great [ferocity]
5. gave a [tacit], not spoken, warning
6. an award for the [erudite] scholar
7. angered by the offensive [imprecations]
8. saw a ghostly [apparition]
9. the [ubiquitous] element of water
10. no clues on her [inscrutable] face

A Literary Connections

Shakespeare's Influence

As the stage direction *"Enter Ahab: Then all,"* shows, Melville uses touches of the dramatist's art, perhaps reflecting his love of Shakespeare (p. T318). Have students consider what effect such dramatic touches have in a novel. [They steer the novel away from simple realism, towards a mythical and allegorical approach.]

B Reading Skills and Strategies

Drawing Inferences about Character

? What inferences about Ahab can you make from the description of him walking on the deck? [Possible responses: He is a thoughtful, powerful person; when he wants to think things through, he paces; something is bothering him.] **What two clues suggest that he is driven man?** [His forehead is marked by "his one unsleeping, ever-pacing thought" and "you could almost see that thought . . . so completely possessing him, indeed, that it all but seemed the inward mold of every outer movement."]

C Elements of Literature

Simile

? Why does the author compare the planks upon which Ahab walks to geological stones? [The comparison magnifies Ahab's impact on the ship and emphasizes the symbolic nature of his quest.] **To what does he compare these dents on the planking?** [The dents of Ahab's one thought on his brow.]

D Reading Skills and Strategies

Responding to the Text

Encourage students to visualize this scene, perhaps pacing back and forth yourself as you read it aloud. Also note how the rhythm of the language, particularly in the third paragraph, mimics the rhythm of Ahab's pacing.

E Elements of Literature

Characterization

? In contrast to the descriptive passage before it, what technique does this passage use for characterizing Ahab? [It uses dialogue to show the opinions other characters have about Ahab.] **What do you think the crew members are saying about Ahab?** [Possible responses: that he is hatching a plan; that his thoughts are tormenting him.]

T314

The Quarter-Deck

A *(Enter Ahab: Then all.)*

It was not a great while after the affair of the pipe,[1] that one morning shortly after breakfast, Ahab, as was his wont, ascended the cabin gangway to the deck. There most sea captains usually walk at that hour, as country gentlemen, after the same meal, take a few turns in the garden.

B **C** Soon his steady, ivory stride was heard, as to and fro he paced his old rounds, upon planks so familiar to his tread, that they were all over dented, like geological stones, with the peculiar mark of his walk. Did you fixedly gaze, too, upon that ribbed and dented brow; there also, you would see still stranger footprints—the footprints of his one unsleeping, ever-pacing thought.

D But on the occasion in question, those dents looked deeper, even as his nervous step that morning left a deeper mark. And, so full of his thought was Ahab, that at every uniform turn that he made, now at the mainmast and now at the binnacle,[2] you could almost see that thought turn in him as he turned, and pace in him as he paced; so completely possessing him, indeed, that it all but seemed the inward mold of every outer movement.

E "D'ye mark him, Flask?" whispered Stubb; "the chick that's in him pecks the shell. 'Twill soon be out."

The hours wore on—Ahab now shut up within

---

1. affair of the pipe: Ahab had thrown his pipe overboard one evening when he realized that he had no business with "this thing that is meant for sereneness."

2. binnacle: upright stand holding the ship's compass.

314 THE AMERICAN RENAISSANCE

Reaching All Students

Struggling Readers

Drawing Inferences about Character was introduced on p. 313. For a lesson directly tied to this selection that teaches students to draw inferences with a strategy called It Says . . . I Say, see the *Reading Skills and Strategies* binder:
- MiniRead Skill Lesson, p. 113
- Selection Skill Lesson, p. 119

English Language Learners

Pair English language learners with English-fluent readers for an Echo Reading.

Advanced Learners

Encourage advanced students to read more of the novel, beginning with chapter 1, "Loomings." Memorable early excerpts include Ishmael's first encounter with Queequeg in the New Bedford Inn; the signing-on for the voyage; and the sermon heard by Ishmael before departure. Memorable events later in the book include the *Pequod*'s encounter with the *Rachel* and the climactic hunt for the whale.

his cabin; anon, pacing the deck, with the same intense bigotry of purpose in his aspect.

It drew near the close of day. Suddenly he came to a halt by the bulwarks,[3] and inserting his bone leg into the auger hole there, and with one hand grasping a shroud, he ordered Starbuck to send everybody aft.

"Sir!" said the mate, astonished at an order seldom or never given on shipboard except in some extraordinary case.

"Send everybody aft," repeated Ahab. "Mastheads, there! Come down!"

When the entire ship's company were assembled, and with curious and not wholly unapprehensive faces were eyeing him, for he looked not unlike the weather horizon when a storm is coming up, Ahab, after rapidly glancing over the bul-

3. **bulwarks** (bul′wərks): above-deck part of a ship's side.

warks, and then darting his eyes among the crew, started from his standpoint; and as though not a soul were nigh him resumed his heavy turns upon the deck. With bent head and half-slouched hat he continued to pace; unmindful of the wondering whispering among the men; till Stubb cautiously whispered to Flask, that Ahab must have summoned them there for the purpose of witnessing a pedestrian feat. But this did not last long. Vehemently pausing, he cried—

"What do ye do when ye see a whale, men?"

"Sing out for him!" was the impulsive rejoinder from a score of clubbed[4] voices.

4. **clubbed:** united.

WORDS TO OWN
rejoinder (ri·join′dər) *n.:* answer.

HERMAN MELVILLE **315**

Ⓕ Vocabulary Note
Technical Vocabulary
Some of the sailing terms in the selection, such as *bulwarks,* are footnoted; for others, such as *mastheads,* students may need to look up meanings in a dictionary. You may wish students to list technical terms and definitions as they read. You could also display in class an illustration from an encyclopedia or dictionary to show the parts of a ship.

Ⓖ English Language Learners
English Negatives
Point out that the usages "not . . . unapprehensive" and "not unlike the weather horizon" are grammatically correct; they are not double negatives, because each negative deliberately cancels the meaning of the other. "Not . . . unapprehensive" means "apprehensive" (although there is a shade of difference in connotation). "Not unlike the weather horizon when a storm is coming up" means "like the horizon when a storm is approaching."

Ⓗ Vocabulary Note
Multiple Meanings
The adjective *pedestrian* means "having to do with walking" and "commonplace, humdrum." Stubb's comment is a pun.

Ⓘ Reading Skills and Strategies
Responding to the Text
The dramatic scene in which Ahab addresses the men is a good passage to read aloud. Select volunteers to be Ahab and the other sailors and have them read only the dialogue, using the descriptions as stage directions.

Listening to Music

"Greenland Whale Fisheries," traditional, performed by Peter, Paul, and Mary.
In the nineteenth century, whaling was a huge and dangerous enterprise that attracted sailors from virtually all seafaring nations. Songs helped pass the time between whale sightings aboard ship; they also served as an oral record of whaler's adventures to be recounted back on land. The song "Greenland Whale Fisheries" tells of one such adventure in the cold Arctic waters of Greenland.

Activity
Before reading the excerpt from *Moby-Dick,* have students listen to "Greenland Whale Fisheries," noting its setting, characters, and plot as well as its ironies. Then, after reading, ask them to write the lyrics to a whaling song about the events in the selection. Suggest they set the lyrics to original music or a tune borrowed from another folk song, and perform their song live or on tape.

"Good!" cried Ahab, with a wild approval in his tones; observing the hearty animation into which his unexpected question had so magnetically thrown them.

"And what do ye next, men?"

"Lower away, and after him!"

"And what tune is it ye pull to, men?"

"A dead whale or a stove[5] boat!"

More and more strangely and fiercely glad and approving grew the countenance of the old man at every shout; while the mariners began to gaze curiously at each other, as if marveling how it was that they themselves became so excited at such seemingly purposeless questions.

But, they were all eagerness again, as Ahab, now half-revolving in his pivot hole, with one hand reaching high up a shroud, and tightly, almost convulsively grasping it, addressed them thus—

"All ye mastheaders have before now heard me give orders about a white whale. Look ye! d'ye see this Spanish ounce of gold?"—holding up a broad bright coin to the sun—"it is a sixteen-dollar piece, men. D'ye see it? Mr. Starbuck, hand me yon top-maul.[6]

While the mate was getting the hammer, Ahab, without speaking, was slowly rubbing the gold piece against the skirts of his jacket, as if to heighten its luster, and without using any words was meanwhile lowly humming to himself, producing a sound so strangely muffled and inarticulate that it seemed the mechanical humming of the wheels of his vitality in him.

Receiving the top-maul from Starbuck, he advanced toward the mainmast with the hammer uplifted in one hand, exhibiting the gold with the other, and with a high raised voice exclaiming: "Whosoever of ye raises me a white-headed whale with a wrinkled brow and a crooked jaw; whosoever of ye raises me that white-headed whale, with three holes punctured in his starboard fluke[7]—look ye, whosoever of ye raises me that same white whale, he shall have this gold ounce, my boys!"

"Huzza! huzza!" cried the seamen, as with swinging tarpaulins they hailed the act of nailing the gold to the mast.

"It's a white whale, I say," resumed Ahab, as he threw down the top-maul; "a white whale. Skin your eyes for him, men; look sharp for white water; if ye see but a bubble, sing out."

All this while Tashtego, Daggoo, and Queequeg had looked on with even more intense interest and surprise than the rest, and at the mention of the wrinkled brow and crooked jaw they had started as if each was separately touched by some specific recollection.

"Captain Ahab," said Tashtego, "that white whale must be the same that some call Moby-Dick."

"Moby-Dick?" shouted Ahab. "Do ye know the white whale then, Tash?"

"Does he fantail[8] a little curious, sir, before he goes down?" said the Gay-Header deliberately.

"And has he a curious spout, too," said Daggoo, "very bushy, even for a parmacety,[9] and mighty quick, Captain Ahab?"

"And he have one, two, tree—oh! good many iron in him hide, too, Captain," cried Queequeg disjointedly, "all twiske-tee be-twisk, like him—him——" faltering hard for a word, and screwing his hand round and round as though uncorking a bottle—"like him—him——"

"Corkscrew!" cried Ahab, "aye, Queequeg, the harpoons lie all twisted and wrenched in him; aye, Daggoo, his spout is a big one, like a whole shock of wheat, and white as a pile of our Nantucket wool after the great annual sheepshearing; aye, Tashtego, and he fantails like a split jib in a squall. Death and devils! men, it is Moby-Dick ye have seen—Moby-Dick—Moby-Dick!"

"Captain Ahab," said Starbuck, who, with Stubb and Flask, had thus far been eyeing his superior with increasing surprise, but at last seemed struck with a thought which somewhat explained all the wonder. "Captain Ahab, I have heard of Moby-Dick—but it was not Moby-Dick that took off thy leg?"

"Who told thee that?" cried Ahab; then pausing, "Aye, Starbuck; aye, my hearties all round; it was Moby-Dick that dismasted me; Moby-Dick that brought me to this dead stump I stand on now. Aye, Aye," he shouted, with a terrific, loud, animal

---

5. **stove:** with a hole smashed in it.
6. **top-maul:** heavy wooden hammer.
7. **starboard fluke:** right-hand side of the whale's tail.

8. **fantail:** spread the tail like a fan.
9. **parmacety** (pär′mə·sed′ē): slang for "spermaceti" (a sperm whale).

316 THE AMERICAN RENAISSANCE

Crossing the Curriculum

History

The History of Whaling in America.
Although whales have been hunted since the Stone Age by Inuit and other peoples of the Polar regions, whaling began in the United States in 1690 off the islands of Nantucket and Long Island. In the 1760s brick ovens for processing whale blubber were built on the ships and the industry began to spread around the globe. After 1800, most of the American whaleships sailed to the Pacific Arctic in search of sperm whales. Although the *Pequod* sailed out of Nantucket, by 1848 New Bedford had surpassed that port as the biggest whaling center in the country. Urge students to write whaling museums in Cold Spring Harbor, New York, and Nantucket and New Bedford, Massachusetts, for information on the early days of whaling. The museums also have Web sites.

sob, like that of a heart-stricken moose; "Aye, aye! it was that accursed white whale that razeed[10] me; made a poor pegging lubber[11] of me for ever and a day!" Then tossing both arms, with measureless imprecations he shouted out: "Aye, aye! and I'll chase him round Good Hope and round the Horn, and round the Norway Maelstrom, and round perdition's flames before I give him up. And this is what ye have shipped for, men! to chase that white whale on both sides of land, and over all sides of earth, till he spouts black blood and rolls fin out. What say ye, men, will ye splice[12] hands on it, now? I think ye do look brave."

"Aye, aye!" shouted the harpooners and seamen, running closer to the excited old man: "a sharp eye for the White Whale; a sharp lance for Moby-Dick!"

"God bless ye," he seemed to half sob and half shout. "God bless ye, men. Steward! Go draw the great measure of grog.[13] But what's this long face about, Mr. Starbuck; wilt thou not chase the White Whale? Art not game for Moby-Dick?"

"I am game for his crooked jaw, and for the jaws of Death too, Captain Ahab, if it fairly comes in the way of the business we follow; but I came here to hunt whales, not my commander's vengeance. How many barrels will thy vengeance yield thee even if thou gettest it, Captain Ahab? It will not fetch thee much in our Nantucket market."

"Nantucket market! Hoot! But come closer, Starbuck; thou requirest a little lower layer. If money's to be the measurer, man, and the accountants have computed their great countinghouse the globe, by girdling it with guineas, one to every three parts of an inch; then, let me tell thee, that my vengeance will fetch a great premium *here*!"

"He smites his chest," whispered Stubb, "what's that for? Methinks it rings most vast, but hollow."

"Vengeance on a dumb brute!" cried Starbuck, "that simply smote thee from blindest instinct! Madness! To be enraged with a dumb thing, Captain Ahab, seems blasphemous."

"Hark ye yet again—the little lower layer. All visible objects, man, are but as pasteboard masks.

But in each event—in the living act, the undoubted deed—there, some unknown but still reasoning thing puts forth the moldings of its features from behind the unreasoning mask. If man will strike, strike through the mask! How can the prisoner reach outside except by thrusting through the wall? To me, the White Whale is that wall, shoved near to me. Sometimes I think there's naught beyond. But 'tis enough. He tasks me; he heaps me; I see in him outrageous strength, with an inscrutable malice sinewing it. That inscrutable thing is chiefly what I hate; and be the White Whale agent, or be the White Whale principal, I will wreak that hate upon him. Talk not to me of blasphemy, man; I'd strike the sun if it insulted me. For could the sun do that, then could I do the other; since there is ever a sort of fair play herein, jealousy presiding over all creations. But not my master, man, is even that fair play. Who's over me? Truth hath no confines. Take off thine eye! More intolerable than fiends' glarings is a doltish stare! So, so; thou reddenest and palest; my heat has melted thee to anger-glow. But look ye, Starbuck, what is said in heat, that thing unsays itself. There are men from whom warm words are small indignity. I meant not to incense thee. Let it go. Look! see yonder Turkish cheeks of spotted tawn—living, breathing pictures painted by the sun. The pagan leopards—the unrecking and unworshipping things, that live; and seek, and give no reasons for the torrid life they feel! The crew, man, the crew! Are they not one and all with Ahab, in this matter of the whale? See Stubb! he laughs! See yonder Chilean! he snorts to think of it. Stand up amid the general hurricane, thy one tossed sapling cannot, Starbuck! And what is it? Reckon it. 'Tis but to help strike a fin; no wondrous feat for Starbuck. What is it more? From this one poor hunt, then, the best lance out of all Nantucket, surely he will not hang back, when every foremast-hand has clutched a whetstone? Ah! constrainings seize thee; I see! the billow lifts thee! Speak, but speak!—Aye, aye! thy silence, then, *that* voices thee. (*Aside*) Something shot from my dilated nostrils, he has inhaled it in his lungs.

WORDS TO OWN

imprecations (im′pri·kā′shənz) *n. pl.:* curses.
inscrutable (in·skrōōt′ə·bəl) *adj.:* mysterious.

---

10. **razeed** (rā·zēd′): to *razee* is to make a wooden warship lower by removing the upper deck.
11. **lubber:** big, slow, clumsy person.
12. **splice:** join.
13. **grog:** watered-down liquor drunk by sailors.

G Elements of Literature

Characterization

? How does Ahab speak when he describes what Moby-Dick did to him? [His tone is furious, vengeful, frenzied, savage.] Discuss what effect the near-comic simile of a "heart-stricken moose" has. [It makes Ahab seem more human—almost pathetic—yet all the more deranged.]

H Cultural Connections

Geographical Notes

The Maelstrom is a dangerous whirlpool formed by tides off the Lofoten Islands of Norway. The word *maelstrom* has come to be used for any whirlpool or, figuratively, for a dangerous situation that might draw a person down to destruction. The Cape of Good Hope is at the southern tip of Africa; Cape Horn is at the southern tip of South America.

I Historical Connections

The Economics of Whaling

Point out that each crewman on a whaler was paid a percentage of the profits at the end of the voyage. The captain received one-twelfth of the take, whereas the cabin boy might get only one thirty-five-hundredth. Therefore, the crew's inclination would be to hunt as many whales as possible. Given this fact, Starbuck and Ahab are debating whether it is wise to pursue only one whale for the sake of revenge.

J Elements of Literature

Characterization

? What does Stubb's comment imply about Captain Ahab? [Possible response: Stubb suggests that Ahab's fixation on Moby-Dick has killed his last vestiges of human emotion—that his pursuit of vengeance has become a heartless animal need.]

K Cultural Connections

Influence of Transcendentalism

Tell students that Ahab's speech conveys an inverse or negative transcendentalism. The transcendentalists believed that one should transcend or go beyond the senses to perceive an ennobling truth in Nature. Here, Ahab suggests that one should transcend the senses (pierce the mask) but that there may be no truth or meaning to be found.

Taking a Second Look

Review: Tracing the Origins of Words

Ishmael identifies Ahab's madness as *monomania,* or a fixation on one thing. The Greek roots *mania* and *phobia* have spawned a number of interesting words students may enjoy exploring.

1. Have students determine the roots and meaning of the words *pyromania, kleptomania, megalomania,* and *bibliomania.*

2. Have students determine the roots and meaning of the words *acrophobia, agoraphobia, claustrophobia,* and *xenophobia.*

3. The suffixes *-phobe* and *-phile* mean, respectively, "one who fears or dislikes" and "one who likes or loves." Ask students to find pairs of words that link these suffixes with countries. [Possible answers: *Anglophile* and *Anglophobe; Francophile* and *Francophobe*]

A Reading Skills and Strategies

Drawing Inference about Character

? Judging from Starbuck's comment and the description of his expression, what is his state of mind? [He has grave doubts about Ahab, but follows him out of a sense of duty; he realizes the crew supports Ahab and he doesn't want to be responsible for a mutiny.]

B Struggling Readers

Finding Details

In this paragraph Melville describes a number of omens or premonitions about the *Pequod*'s voyage. Discuss why Ahab does not pay attention to these signs. [Possible responses: He does not care about them; he can't see them because he can focus only on his obsession.]

C Elements of Literature

Characterization

? How is Ahab described in this paragraph? [He is described as an alpha male wolf leading his pack on a hunt—a savage, animalistic image.] What does Ishmael prophesy for Ahab, and what might the "Indian" in this metaphor represent? [He predicts that Ahab the "wolf" will fall into the snare of "the Indian," which could be Moby-Dick or fate itself.]

D Elements of Literature

Allusion

Guide students to recognize that this scene is a powerful inversion of the Christian sacrament of communion with Ahab officiating as a venomous "Pope."

E Critical Thinking

Interpreting

? What does the mates' reaction to Ahab's ceremony with the lances indicate? [They are uncomfortable with the ceremony, which is taking on blasphemous overtones.] What does Ahab's comment "In vain!" refer to? [It refers to his failure to inflame their passions as he did the harpooners.] How does Ahab rationalize and then dismiss their reluctance? [He rationalizes that the electrical force of his will would have killed them. He then decides that the mates don't need his prodding to do their duty: "Perchance ye need it not."]

Starbuck now is mine; cannot oppose me now, without rebellion."

"God keep me!—keep us all!" murmured Starbuck lowly.

(A) But in his joy at the enchanted, <u>tacit</u> acquiescence of the mate, Ahab did not hear his foreboding invocation; nor yet the low laugh from the hold; nor yet the presaging vibrations of the winds in the cordage; nor yet the hollow flap of the sails against the masts, as for a moment their hearts sank in. For again Starbuck's downcast eyes lighted up with the stubbornness of life; the subterranean laugh died away; the winds blew on; the sails filled out; the ship heaved and rolled as **(B)** before. Ah, ye admonitions and warnings! Why stay ye not when ye come? But rather are ye predictions than warnings, ye shadows! Yet not so much predictions from without, as verifications of the foregoing things within. For with little external to constrain us, the innermost necessities in our being, these still drive us on.

"The measure! the measure!" cried Ahab.

Receiving the brimming pewter, and turning to the harpooners, he ordered them to produce their weapons. Then ranging them before him near the capstan,[14] with their harpoons in their hands, while his three mates stood at his side with their lances, and the rest of the ship's company formed a circle round the group; he stood for an instant searchingly eyeing every man of his crew. **(C)** But those wild eyes met his, as the bloodshot eyes of the prairie wolves meet the eye of their leader, ere he rushes on at their head in the trail of the bison; but, alas! only to fall into the hidden snare of the Indian.

"Drink and pass!" he cried, handing the heavy charged flagon to the nearest seaman. "The crew alone now drink. Round with it, round! Short drafts—long swallows, men; 'tis hot as Satan's hoof. So, so; it goes round excellently. It spiralizes in ye; forks out at the serpent-snapping eye. Well **(D)** done; almost drained. That way it went, this way it comes. Hand it me—here's a hollow! Men, ye seem the years; so brimming life is gulped and gone. Steward, refill!

"Attend now, my braves. I have mustered ye all round this capstan; and ye, mates, flank me with

---

14. **capstan:** similar to a winch; a large cylinder, usually on a ship's deck, around which cables are wound to lift heavy objects such as anchors and weights.

318 THE AMERICAN RENAISSANCE

---

your lances; and ye, harpooneers, stand there with your irons; and ye, stout mariners, ring me in, that I may in some sort revive a noble custom of my fisherman fathers before me. O men, you will yet see that—— Ha! boy, come back? bad pennies come not sooner. Hand it me. Why, now, this pewter had run brimming again, wert not thou St. Vitus's imp[15]—away, thou ague!

"Advance, ye mates! Cross your lances full before me. Well done! Let me touch the axis." So saying, with extended arm, he grasped the three level, radiating lances at their crossed center; while so doing, suddenly and nervously twitched them; meanwhile, glancing intently from Starbuck to Stubb, from Stubb to Flask. It seemed as though, by some nameless, interior <u>volition</u>, he would fain have shocked into them the same fiery **(E)** emotion accumulated within the Leyden jar[16] of his own magnetic life. The three mates quailed before his strong, sustained, and mystic aspect. Stubb and Flask looked sideways from him; the honest eye of Starbuck fell downright.

"In vain!" cried Ahab; "but, maybe, 'tis well. For did ye three but once take the full-forced shock, then mine own electric thing, *that* had perhaps expired from out me. Perchance, too, it would have dropped ye dead. Perchance ye need it not. Down lances! And now, ye mates, I do appoint ye three cupbearers to my three pagan kinsmen there—yon three most honorable gentlemen and noblemen, my valiant harpooneers. Disdain the task? What, when the great Pope washes the feet of beggars, using his tiara for ewer?[17] Oh, my sweet cardinals! your own condescension, *that* shall bend ye to it. I do not order ye; ye will it. Cut

---

15. **St. Vitus's imp:** Saint Vitus is the patron saint of people ill with chorea, a nervous disorder characterized by irregular, jerking movements. An imp is a mischievous child or young demon. Ahab is complaining that the steward's clumsiness caused the pitcher of grog to be spilled.

16. **Leyden jar:** device for storing electrical charges.

17. **tiara for ewer:** literally, "crown for a pitcher"; a reference to the practice of the pope washing the feet of the poor on Holy Thursday, in imitation of Jesus' washing the feet of his disciples.

WORDS TO OWN

tacit (tas′it) *adj.:* implied but not expressed openly.
volition (vō·lish′ən) *n.:* will.

Making the Connections

Cultural Connections: Religious Imagery in *Moby-Dick*

Some students may be offended by the mock communion scene. Help them to see how Melville uses it to portray the depth to which Ahab has sunk into "the realms of darkness." You could list religious images in a two-column chart: mates as clergymen, grog rather than wine, maledictions in place of prayers, and "murderous chalices." Discuss how Ahab pulls his men to physical, moral, and spiritual destruction.

Cultural Connections: Melville's Debt to Shakespeare

Ahab's monologue demonstrates Melville's debt to Shakespeare. To help students hear the Shakespearean cadences, read them one of Hamlet's soliloquies (especially III.i.56 or IV.iv.32) when discussing the first half of Ahab's monologue. With the second half, read Iago's speech in *Othello*, II.iii.319. Students might enjoy seeing film clips of these speeches.

Sailors—Companion to the Tailors (mid–19th century). Unsigned, attributed to John Cranch. Oil on wood panel.

Peabody Essex Museum, Salem, Massachusetts (M16265).

RESPONDING TO THE ART

The ship on which these seamen climb the rigging is probably similar to the *Pequod* in that it is a masted, wooden sailing ship. Between 1835 and 1865, whaling voyages generally lasted two and one half to three years, but could last as long as four or five years. In fact, a cabin boy or young sailor could essentially grow up aboard ship.

Activity. Ask students what might be happening in the painting. [Sample response: The sailors are trying to spot whales, land, or other ships, or to prepare for a storm.] Have each student choose one of these scenarios and write an interior monologue from the viewpoint of either sailor, recording his thoughts.

Assessing Learning

Check Test: True-False

1. Captain Ahab calls every member of the crew to assemble for his commands. [True]
2. Ahab offers an extra week's wages to any sailor who spots the white whale. [False]
3. The harpooners are asked to take a drink as an oath to kill the white whale. [True]
4. The narrator calls himself Ishmael. [True]
5. Moby-Dick has a deformed jaw that makes him look malicious. [True]

First Thoughts [Respond]

1. Possible responses: obsessed, romantic, insane. Students might say they fear him but admire his force of will.

Shaping Interpretations [Interpret]

2. Starbuck says that Ahab's vengeance on a dumb brute seems blasphemous and a waste of time and money. These remarks suggest that he is religious and sensible.

3. He is a professional sailor and loyal to his captain. He doesn't want to incite the crew to mutiny.

4. People and things have no meaning in themselves. Meaning can only be found by acting to penetrate life's artificial appearances and by searching for what lies beyond—be it even evil or nothingness.

5. For Ahab, the whale symbolizes the "inscrutable malice" of the universe that Ahab feels he must confront and defeat.

6. The multiracial composition of the Pequod's crew suggests the ship might be a microcosm. If the ship represents the world, then Ahab assumes mythic proportions as the leader in search of triumph and meaning.

7. Ahab's comparison of himself to the Pope and the mates to cardinals; the allusion to the papal custom of washing the feet of beggars on Holy Thursday. The whole blasphemous scene reinforces the idea that Ahab sees his quest as a holy crusade of sorts.

8. The statement suggests Ahab's pride, determination, and ferocity. His goal to "wreak . . . hate" upon the "inscrutable thing" in nature suggests that he is challenging God Himself.

9. Possible response: The premonitions on p. 318 (the "low laugh from the hold"; the "presaging vibrations of the winds in the cordage"); the apostrophe beginning, "Ah, ye admonitions and warnings!"; the reference to the hunting wolves falling into the hidden snare of the Indian. Prediction: The whale will destroy Ahab, and perhaps the ship and the crew with him.

---

your seizings and draw the poles, ye harpooneers!"

Silently obeying the order, the three harpooneers now stood with the detached iron part of their harpoons, some three feet long, held, barbs up, before him.

"Stab me not with that keen steel! Cant[18] them; cant them over! know ye not the goblet end? Turn up the socket! So, so; now, ye cupbearers, advance. The irons! take them; hold them while I fill!" Forthwith, slowly going from one officer to the other, he brimmed the harpoon sockets with the fiery waters from the pewter.

"Now, three to three, ye stand. Commend the murderous chalices! Bestow them, ye who are now made parties to this indissoluble league. Ha! Starbuck! but the deed is done! Yon ratifying sun now waits to sit upon it. Drink, ye harpooneers! drink and swear, ye men that man the deathful whaleboat's bow—Death to Moby-Dick! God hunt us all, if we do not hunt Moby-Dick to his death!" The long, barbed steel goblets were lifted; and to cries and maledictions[19] against the White Whale, the spirits were simultaneously quaffed down with a hiss. Starbuck paled, and turned, and shivered. Once more, and finally, the replenished pewter went the rounds among the frantic crew; when, waving his free hand to them, they all dispersed; and Ahab retired within his cabin.

18. **cant:** overturn or tilt.

19. **maledictions** (mal'ə·dik'shənz): curses.

MAKING MEANINGS

First Thoughts

1. What words would you use to describe Captain Ahab? Do you pity him, fear him, or feel something else?

Shaping Interpretations

2. What are Starbuck's misgivings about Ahab's pursuit of the great white whale? What does this help us infer about Starbuck's **character**?

3. Why do you think Starbuck gives in to Ahab?

> **Reading Check**
>
> a. After his obsessive pacing of the deck, what command does Ahab issue to the crew? Why does Ahab meet with his crew?
>
> b. What do you learn about Moby-Dick's appearance from Ahab's dialogue with his crew?
>
> c. Toward the end of the chapter, what does Ahab order the mates to do with their lances?
>
> d. Where does the narrative shift from Ishmael's **point of view** to an **omniscient** point of view? What details in this chapter could only be known by an omniscient narrator?

4. Explain the idea Ahab expresses in his famous **metaphor** comparing visible objects to "pasteboard masks" (page 317). What do you think he means when he says "strike through the mask"?

5. What **symbolic** meaning might the white whale have? (Recall Ahab's comment that the white whale "is that wall. . . . Sometimes I think there's naught beyond.")

6. What might the ship and crew **symbolize**? Do they form a microcosm—a world in miniature? If you see them as symbols, do you read the text differently? Explain.

7. What details in the drinking scene suggest a **parody** or mockery of a religious ritual? What might the scene signify about Ahab's quest?

8. What inferences can you draw about Ahab's **character** when he says "Talk not to me of blasphemy, man; I'd strike the sun if it insulted me" (page 317)? What did he say prior to this that sounded like blasphemy—that is, mockery of God?

9. Identify the details in this chapter that **foreshadow** disaster for the *Pequod* and its crew. What do you think will happen next?

Extending the Text

10. Who are Ahab and Ishmael in the Bible? Look up Ahab's story in 1 Kings 16:29–22:40 and Ishmael's story in Genesis 21:9–21. Why do you think Melville chose these names?

Extending the Text [Analyze]

10. Ahab, king of Israel (c. 875–850 B.C.), reinstated the worship of idols under the influence of his wife, Jezebel. Similarly, Captain Ahab meets his destruction in his pursuit of a "false god," Moby-Dick. The Biblical Ishmael was the son of Abraham and the servant Hagar. When a son was born to Abraham and his wife Sarah, they cast out Hagar and Ishmael into the wilderness to protect their legitimate heir, Isaac. The name Ishmael has thus come to be associated with a wandering outcast.

> **Reading Check**
>
> a. He assembles the crew to convince them to kill the white whale.
>
> b. It has a white head, a wrinkled brow, a crooked jaw, three holes in one fluke, and many twisted harpoons embedded in its body.
>
> c. He orders them to raise and cross their lances before him.
>
> d. It shifts at "But in his joy. . . ." The low laugh, the vibrations in the cordage are also omniscient details.

Summary ■■■

Ishmael recounts the fear and superstition surrounding whales in general and Moby-Dick in particular. He also recounts the story of Ahab's monomaniacal obsession with the whale that dismembered him, and how the whale became a symbol for evil.

Ⓐ **Reading Skills and Strategies**

Drawing Inferences about Character

? What is Ishmael's attitude at this stage of the voyage? [He has been caught up in Ahab's passion and in the excitement of the chase.] What hint suggests that his enthusiasm is not altogether genuine? [He says he had to be loud and insistent to still the dread in his soul.]

Ⓑ **Struggling Readers**

Getting the Main Idea

? What happens, according to the narrator, when "a sperm whale of uncommon magnitude and malignity" destroys a sailing ship? [Often the whale is assumed to be Moby-Dick.]

Following the ritual on the quarter-deck, in which Ahab fills the harpoon-tips with liquor and reveals the object of his chase, we hear three characters privately reflect on their journey's goal. Ahab recognizes himself as a driven man; Starbuck reflects on what he sees as the captain's insanity; and Stubb fatalistically resigns himself to whatever destiny may bring. That night a squall threatens to strike the ship, and the crew become tense. At last we are about to meet the object of Ahab's obsession—the white whale, Moby-Dick.

from **Moby-Dick**

I, Ishmael, was one of that crew; my shouts had gone up with the rest; my oath had been welded with theirs; and stronger I shouted, and more did I hammer and clinch my oath, because of the dread in my soul. A wild, mystical, sympathetical feeling was in me; Ahab's quenchless feud seemed mine. With greedy ears I learned the history of that murderous monster against whom I and all the others had taken our oaths of violence and revenge.

For some time past, though at intervals only, the unaccompanied, secluded White Whale had haunted those uncivilized seas mostly frequented by the sperm whale fishermen. But not all of them knew of his existence; only a few of them, comparatively, had knowingly seen him; while the number who as yet had actually and knowingly given battle to him, was small indeed. For, owing to the large number of whale-cruisers; the disorderly way they were sprinkled over the entire watery circumference, many of them adventurously pushing their quest along solitary latitudes, so as seldom or never for a whole twelvemonth or more on a stretch, to encounter a single news-telling sail of any sort; the inordinate length of each separate voyage; the irregularity of the times of sailing from home; all these, with other circumstances, direct and indirect, long obstructed the spread through the whole worldwide whaling fleet of the special individualizing tidings concerning Moby-Dick. It was hardly to be doubted, that several vessels reported to have encountered, at such or such a time, or on such or such a meridian, a sperm whale of uncommon magnitude and malignity,[1] which whale, after doing great mischief to his assailants, had completely escaped them; to some minds it was not an unfair presumption, I say, that the whale in question must have been no other than Moby-Dick. Yet as of late

---

1. **malignity** (mə·lig′nə·tē): intense ill will.

HERMAN MELVILLE **321**

Reaching All Students

Struggling Readers

In this excerpt, readers learn what sailors say about Moby-Dick. Have students complete a chart like the following to distinguish between what may be true of Moby-Dick in the world of the story and what may be exaggeration. On the top half of the chart, have students list probable truths; on the bottom half, rumors and folklore. Ask students to put the source of each item in the column beside it.

Truths	
Item	Source
The whale took Ahab's leg	Ahab's testimony
Rumors/Folklore	
Item	Source
Moby-Dick is immortal	Whalers' superstition

Advanced Learners

Have students prepare a detailed presentation on varieties of whales. In their presentation, students should describe each major subspecies, giving its physical characteristics, habitat (ocean region and migration pattern), diet, and current (estimated) population. Students should consult at least three sources, including one Internet site.

A Historical Connections

First-Hand Accounts

The destructive power of whales was not exaggerated by Melville. Thomas Heffernan's book, *Stove by a Whale: Owen Chase and the Essex,* tells of an 1820 incident in which an eighty-five-foot sperm whale attacked and sank the whaling ship *Essex* in the Pacific Ocean. A survivor, Owen Chase, wrote a sixty-three-page account of the frightful ramming. Chase and several witnesses survived for three months on a smaller whaleboat until they were rescued off the coast of Chile. In an 1839 article, "Mocha Dick," J. N. Reynolds describes a ferocious white whale, sporting nineteen harpoons, that caused the death of thirty men by ramming several ships. Melville acknowledged reading both accounts, which he referred to as "fish documents."

B Critical Thinking

Analyzing

? How does Ishmael support his portrayal of the white whale? [He cites outside authorities, expert whalers who were skeptical of the rumors about Moby-Dick but who came to believe them after experiencing the whale's ferocity first-hand.]

C Reading Skills and Strategies

Getting the Main Idea

? Why are whalers especially superstitious? [They are especially superstitious because they come into contact with the most terrifying creatures of the sea; also, they spend a great deal of time alone away from home and civilization, which tends to increase their powers of imagination.]

D Reading Skills and Strategies

Noting Details

? What distinction between whalers does Ishmael draw? [He distinguishes between right whalers and sperm whalers.]

---

the sperm whale fishery had been marked by various and not unfrequent instances of great ferocity, cunning, and malice in the monster attacked; therefore it was, that those who by accident ignorantly gave battle to Moby-Dick; such hunters, perhaps, for the most part, were content to ascribe the peculiar terror he bred, more, as it were, to the perils of the sperm whale fishery at large, than to the individual cause. In that way, mostly, the disastrous encounter between Ahab and the whale had hitherto been popularly regarded.

And as for those who, previously hearing of the White Whale, by chance caught sight of him; in the beginning of the thing they had every one of them, almost, as boldly and fearlessly lowered for him, as for any other whale of that species. But at length, such calamities did ensue in these assaults—not restricted to sprained wrists and ankles, broken limbs, or devouring amputations—but fatal to the last degree of fatality; those repeated disastrous repulses, all accumulating and piling their terrors upon Moby-Dick; those things had gone far to shake the fortitude of many brave hunters, to whom the story of the White Whale had eventually come.

Nor did wild rumors of all sorts fail to exaggerate, and still the more horrify the true histories of these deadly encounters. For not only do fabulous rumors naturally grow out of the very body of all surprising terrible events—as the smitten tree gives birth to its fungi; but, in maritime life, far more than in that of terra firma, wild rumors abound, wherever there is any adequate reality for them to cling to. And as the sea surpasses the land in this matter, so the whale-fishery surpasses every other sort of maritime life, in the wonderfulness and fearfulness of the rumors which sometimes circulate there. For not only are whalemen as a body unexempt from that ignorance and superstitiousness hereditary to all sailors; but of all sailors, they are by all odds the most directly brought into contact with whatever is appallingly astonishing in the sea; face to face they not only eye its greatest marvels, but, hand to jaw, give battle to them. Alone, in such remotest waters, that though you sailed a thousand miles, and passed a thousand shores, you would not come to any chiseled hearthstone, or aught hospitable beneath that part of the sun; in such latitudes and longi-

tudes, pursuing too such a calling as he does, the whaleman is wrapped by influences all tending to make his fancy pregnant with many a mighty birth.

No wonder, then, that ever gathering volume from the mere transit over the wildest watery spaces, the outblown rumors of the White Whale did in the end incorporate with themselves all manner of morbid hints, and half-formed fetal suggestions of supernatural agencies, which eventually invested Moby-Dick with new terrors unborrowed from anything that visibly appears. So that in many cases such a panic did he finally strike, that few who by those rumors, at least, had heard of the White Whale, few of those hunters were willing to encounter the perils of his jaw.

But there were still other and more vital practical influences at work. Not even at the present day has the original prestige of the sperm whale, as fearfully distinguished from all other species of the leviathan,[2] died out of the minds of the whalemen as a body. There are those this day among them, who, though intelligent and courageous enough in offering battle to the Greenland or right whale, would perhaps, either from professional inexperience, or incompetency, or timidity, decline a contest with the sperm whale; at any rate, there are plenty of whalemen, especially among those whaling nations not sailing under the American flag, who have never hostilely encountered the sperm whale, but whose sole knowledge of the leviathan is restricted to the ignoble monster primitively pursued in the North; seated on their hatches, these men will hearken with a childish fireside interest and awe, to the wild, strange tales of Southern whaling. Nor is the preeminent tremendousness of the great sperm whale anywhere more feelingly comprehended, than on board of those prows which stem him. . . .

So that overawed by the rumors and portents concerning him, not a few of the fishermen recalled, in reference to Moby-Dick, the earlier days of the sperm whale fishery, when it was

2. **leviathan** (lə·vī′ə·thən): huge sea monster.

WORDS TO OWN
ferocity (fə·räs′ə·tē) *n.*: fierce cruelty.

---

322 THE AMERICAN RENAISSANCE

Crossing the Curriculum

Science

The sperm whale is a social animal that usually lives in groups called pods. These may be bachelor, female, or harem pods. The whales swim, dive, feed, and sleep together and communicate by means of sonar clicks. Sperm whales begin their migration from the Arctic and Antarctic every breeding season. The bulls try to create harem pods of up to thirty adult females and fiercely protect them and their young. They feed on bottom-dwelling organisms such as

squid and shark and swallow their prey whole. It is believed that a sperm whale can dive 560 feet per minute and reach depths of 10,000 feet. A large bull can dive deepest and stay underwater for up to forty-five minutes. After students finish reading this chapter, have them research further the rumors and legends recorded in the text. Are sperm whales really more dangerous than right or Greenland whales?

Painted sternboard from the ship *Mary and Susan*.

RESPONDING TO THE ART
This painted sternboard from the ship *Mary and Susan* depicts, in folk-art style, a harpooners' boat pursuing a whale.
Activity.
1. Have students describe all the details that show the dangers of the small boat's situation. [Possible responses: It is a very small, open boat; it is close to a large whale; there are other whales in the vicinity; the whaling ship is some distance away; the sun is going down.]
2. Ask students to speculate about what kinds of people would take the job of hunting whales. [Possible response: brave or reckless people in search of adventure; desperate people in need of money; people ignorant of the dangers they were getting into.]

oftentimes hard to induce long-practiced right whalemen to embark in the perils of this new and daring warfare; such men protesting that although other leviathans might be hopefully pursued, yet to chase and point lance at such an apparition as the sperm whale was not for mortal man. That to attempt it, would be inevitably to be torn into a quick eternity. On this head, there are some remarkable documents that may be consulted.

Nevertheless, some there were, who even in the face of these things were ready to give chase to Moby-Dick; and a still greater number who, chancing only to hear of him distantly and vaguely, without the specific details of any certain calamity, and without superstitious accompaniments, were sufficiently hardy not to flee from the battle it offered.

One of the wild suggestings referred to, as at last coming to be linked with the White Whale in the minds of the superstitiously inclined, was the unearthly conceit that Moby-Dick was ubiquitous; that he had actually been encountered in opposite latitudes at one and the same instant of time.

Nor, credulous as such minds must have been,

was this conceit altogether without some faint show of superstitious probability. For as the secrets of the currents in the seas have never yet been divulged, even to the most erudite research; so the hidden ways of the sperm whale when beneath the surface remain, in great part, unaccountable to his pursuers; and from time to time have originated the most curious and contradictory speculations regarding them, especially concerning the mystic modes whereby, after sounding to a great depth, he transports himself with such vast swiftness to the most widely distant points.

It is a thing well known to both American and English whale-ships, and as well a thing placed upon authoritative record years ago by Scoresby, that some whales have been captured far north in

---

WORDS TO OWN

apparition (ap′ə·rish′ən) *n.:* unexpected sight or ghostlike figure that appears suddenly.
ubiquitous (yoō·bik′wə·təs) *adj.:* everywhere at the same time.
erudite (er′yoō·dīt′) *adj.:* scholarly; well informed.

HERMAN MELVILLE 323

E **Elements of Literature**
Symbol
❓ How do these rumors that the white whale is ubiquitous relate to the symbolic value that Ahab attaches to Moby-Dick? [They extend Ahab's conception of Moby-Dick as more than a single whale, but as a supernatural, malevolent force in nature—a force of evil and meaninglessness that can be found wherever one attempts to break through the "pasteboard masks" of the sensory world.] How does Ishmael seem to feel about these rumors? [He seems to be tempted by their drama, but will only accept them with the qualification that there is some as yet unknown scientific explanation for the whale's travels.]

Getting Students Involved

Cooperative Learning
Read All About It. Have student groups create two newspaper articles based on the whale tales mentioned in Ishmael's account. Ask them to write their articles in the spirit of Melville's time and to include illustrations. The articles could be front-page stories, editorials, feature stories, or lengthy obituaries. Ask two students in each group to be writers and the others to be illustrator and editor.

Analyzing Literary Criticism
After discussing the excerpts, ask the school librarian to guide students in finding sources of literary criticism.
1. Ask small groups to choose Ahab or Ishmael. Students should list their chosen character's main characteristics and the supporting evidence in the text.
2. Have each group find and read three critical reviews that discuss the character they chose.

Skill Link

3. Tell groups to list characteristics and evidence cited by the critics.
4. Have groups compare their views with those of the critics. Do the critics agree with each other? with the group? How will the group modify its ideas after reading the sources?
5. Tell students to write a group essay, either using their readings in support of their thesis or analyzing their disagreements with the critics.

Ⓐ the Pacific, in whose bodies have been found the barbs of harpoons darted in the Greenland seas. Nor is it to be gainsaid, that in some of these instances it has been declared that the interval of time between the two assaults could not have exceeded very many days. Hence, by inference, it has been believed by some whalemen, that the Nor'west Passage,[3] so long a problem to man, was never a problem to the whale. . . .

Forced into familiarity, then, with such prodigies as these; and knowing that after repeated, intrepid assaults, the White Whale had escaped alive; it cannot be much matter of surprise that some whalemen should go still further in their superstitions; declaring Moby-Dick not only ubiquitous, but immortal (for immortality is but ubiquity in time); that though groves of spears should be planted in his flanks, he would still swim away unharmed; or if indeed he should ever be made to spout thick blood, such a sight would be but a ghastly deception; for again in unensanguined[4] billows hundreds of leagues away, his unsullied jet would once more be seen.

Ⓑ But even stripped of these supernatural surmisings, there was enough in the earthly make and incontestable character of the monster to strike the imagination with unwonted power. For, it was not so much his uncommon bulk that so much distinguished him from other sperm whales, but, as was elsewhere thrown out—a peculiar snow-white wrinkled forehead, and a high, pyramidical white hump. These were his prominent features; the tokens whereby, even in the limitless, uncharted seas, he revealed his identity, at a long distance, to those who knew him.

The rest of his body was so streaked, and spotted, and marbled with the same shrouded hue, that, in the end, he had gained his distinctive appellation of the White Whale; a name, indeed, literally justified by his vivid aspect, when seen gliding at high noon through a dark blue sea, leaving a milky-way wake of creamy foam, all spangled with golden gleamings.

Nor was it his unwonted magnitude, nor his remarkable hue, nor yet his deformed lower jaw,

3. **Nor'west Passage:** waterways that connect the Atlantic and Pacific Oceans, discovered in the mid-1800s.
4. **unensanguined** (un·en·saŋ′gwind): unbloodied.

A Whaling Scene (mid–19th century). Unsigned. Oil on canvas.

that so much invested the whale with natural terror, as that unexampled, intelligent malignity Ⓒ which, according to specific accounts, he had over and over again evinced in his assaults. More than all, his treacherous retreats struck more of dismay than perhaps aught else. For, when swimming before his exulting pursuers, with every apparent symptom of alarm, he had several times

324 THE AMERICAN RENAISSANCE

Crossing the Curriculum

History

The Process of Whaling. Whaling ships carried at least two boats, each manned by a mate, four oarsmen, and a harpooner. Once a whale was killed, the crew removed the blubber and cooked it in large pots on the ship to extract the oil. Not only did the blubber yield oil (used as a lamp fuel and in soaps and candles), but the skin was used for leather and the cartilage for glue. The meat, of course, was eaten. Sperm whales were particularly difficult to hunt, but a single whale could produce hundreds of gallons of spermaceti (or sperm oil)—a waxy substance used in making candles, ointments, and cosmetics—and ambergris, used in making perfume. Students should research ships and equipment used in a whale hunt, and the way whalers lived at sea. Have groups present the information in a five-minute oral report with visuals.

Peabody Essex Museum, Salem, Massachusetts. Photo by Mark Sexton (M17109).

bruited[6] ashore, were by no means unusual in the fishery; yet, in most instances, such seemed the White Whale's infernal aforethought of ferocity, that every dismembering or death that he caused, was not wholly regarded as having been inflicted by an unintelligent agent.

Judge, then, to what pitches of inflamed, distracted fury the minds of his more desperate hunters were impelled, when amid the chips of chewed boats, and the sinking limbs of torn comrades, they swam out of the white curds of the whale's direful wrath into the serene, exasperating sunlight, that smiled on, as if at a birth or a bridal.

His three boats stove around him, and oars and men both whirling in the eddies, one captain, seizing the line-knife from his broken prow, had dashed at the whale, as an Arkansas duelist at his foe, blindly seeking with a six-inch blade to reach the fathom-deep life of the whale. That captain was Ahab. And then it was, that suddenly sweeping his sickle-shaped lower jaw beneath him, Moby-Dick had reaped away Ahab's leg, as a mower a blade of grass in the field. No turbaned Turk, no hired Venetian or Malay, could have smote him with more seeming malice. Small reason was there to doubt, then, that ever since that almost fatal encounter, Ahab had cherished a wild vindictiveness against the whale, all the more fell for that in his frantic morbidness he at last came to identify with him, not only all his bodily woes, but all his intellectual and spiritual exasperations. The White Whale swam before him as the monomaniac incarnation of all those malicious agencies which some deep men feel eating in them, till they are left living on with half a heart and half a lung. That intangible malignity which has been from the beginning; to whose dominion even the modern Christians ascribe one-half of the worlds; which the ancient Ophites of the East reverenced in their statue devil—Ahab did not fall down and worship it like them; but deliriously transferring its idea to the abhorred White Whale, he pitted himself, all mutilated, against it. All that most maddens and torments; all that stirs up the lees of things; all truth with malice in it; all that cracks the sinews and cakes the brain; all the subtle

been known to turn round suddenly, and, bearing down upon them, either stave[5] their boats to splinters, or drive them back in consternation to their ship.

Already several fatalities had attended his chase. But though similar disasters, however little

5. **stave:** smash.

6. **bruited** (broot′id): reported; rumored.

HERMAN MELVILLE 325

D Critical Thinking

Interpreting

? How did the White Whale's reputation for "intelligent malignity" arise? [His tactic of fleeing and then turning to ram boats led sailors to believe he was deliberately malicious.]

E Critical Thinking

Speculating

? How do you think sailors caught in such a situation would react? [with horror, anger, desperation] How would they view the whale and, by extension, nature? [as the enemy] Why would emerging into calm waters and sunlight inflame rather than relieve them? [Possible responses: The contrast would underscore the horror; they might feel as if nature were mocking them.]

F Elements of Literature

Simile

? What simile describes the way Moby-Dick took Ahab's leg? [Moby-Dick's act is compared to a mower chopping a blade of grass.]

G Reading Skills and Strategies

Drawing Inferences about Character

? In what sense is Ahab one of these "deep men"? [Possible response: He is concerned about intellectual and spiritual matters and sees a dark side in himself and the world.] Discuss further how the anger people feel can become magnified into an obsession.

H Reading Skills and Strategies

Finding the Main Idea

? In Ishmael's view, what does Moby-Dick signify for Ahab? [original evil, and the necessity of destroying it]

I Cultural Connections

Geographical Note

Ophir was a region known in Old Testament times for its gold and precious stones (see, for example, I Kings 10:11). Different theories site it in Arabia, East Africa, or India.

T325

demonisms of life and thought; all evil, to crazy Ahab, were visibly personified, and made practically assailable in Moby-Dick. He piled upon the whale's white hump the sum of all the general rage and hate felt by his whole race from Adam down; and then, as if his chest had been a mortar, he burst his hot heart's shell upon it.

It is not probable that this monomania in him took its instant rise at the precise time of his bodily dismemberment. Then, in darting at the monster, knife in hand, he had but given loose to a sudden, passionate, corporal animosity; and when he received the stroke that tore him, he probably but felt the agonizing bodily laceration, but nothing more. Yet, when by this collision forced to turn toward home, and for long months of days and weeks, Ahab and anguish lay stretched together in one hammock, rounding in midwinter that dreary, howling Patagonian Cape; then it was, that his torn body and gashed soul bled into one another; and so interfusing, made him mad. That it was only then, on the homeward voyage, after the encounter, that the final monomania seized him, seems all but certain from the fact that, at intervals during the passage, he was a raving lunatic; and, though unlimbed of a leg, yet such vital strength yet lurked in his Egyptian chest, and was moreover intensified by his delirium, that his mates were forced to lace him fast, even there, as he sailed, raving in his hammock. In a straitjacket, he swung to the mad rockings of the gales. And, when running into more sufferable latitudes, the ship, with mild stunsails spread, floated across the tranquil tropics, and, to all appearances, the old man's delirium seemed left behind him with the Cape Horn swells, and he came forth from his dark den into the blessed light and air; even then, when he bore that firm, collected front, however pale, and issued his calm orders once again; and his mates thanked God the direful madness was now gone; even then, Ahab, in his hidden self, raved on. Human madness is oftentimes a cunning and most feline thing. When you think it fled, it may have but become transfigured into some still subtler form. Ahab's full lunacy subsided not, but deepeningly contracted; like the unabated Hudson, when that noble Northman flows narrowly, but unfathomably through the Highland gorge. But, as in his narrow-flowing monomania, not one jot of Ahab's broad madness had been left behind;

326 THE AMERICAN RENAISSANCE

Making the Connections

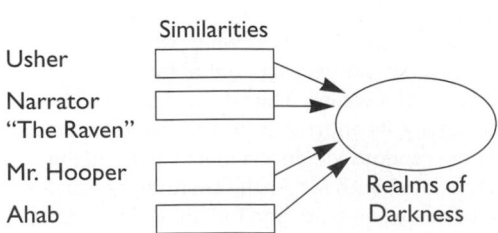

so in that broad madness, not one jot of his great natural intellect had perished. That before living agent, now became the living instrument. If such a furious trope[7] may stand, his special lunacy stormed his general sanity, and carried it, and turned all its concentrated cannon upon its own mad mark; so that far from having lost his strength, Ahab, to that one end, did now possess a thousandfold more potency than ever he had sanely brought to bear upon any one reasonable object. . . .

Now, in his heart, Ahab had some glimpse of this, namely: all my means are sane, my motive and my object mad. Yet without power to kill, or change, or shun the fact, he likewise knew that to mankind he did long dissemble; in some sort, did still. But that thing of his dissembling was only subject to his perceptibility, not to his will determinate. Nevertheless, so well did he succeed in that dissembling, that when with ivory leg he stepped ashore at last, no Nantucketer thought him otherwise than but naturally grieved, and that to the quick, with the terrible casualty which had overtaken him.

The report of his undeniable delirium at sea was likewise popularly ascribed to a kindred cause. And so too, all the added moodiness which always afterward, to the very day of sailing in the *Pequod* on the present voyage, sat brooding on his brow. Nor is it so very unlikely, that far from distrusting his fitness for another whaling voyage, on account of such dark symptoms, the calculating people of that prudent isle were inclined to harbor the conceit, that for those very reasons he was all the better qualified and set on edge, for a pursuit so full of rage and wildness as the bloody hunt of whales. Gnawed within and scorched without, with the unfixed, unrelenting fangs of some incurable idea; such an one, could he be found, would seem the very man to dart his iron and lift his lance against the most appalling of all brutes. Or, if for any reason thought to be corporeally incapacitated for that, yet such an one would seem superlatively competent to cheer and howl on his underlings to the attack. But be all this as it may, certain it is, that with the mad secret of his unabated rage bolted up and keyed in him, Ahab had purposely sailed upon the present

voyage with the one only and all-engrossing object of hunting the White Whale. Had any one of his old acquaintances on shore but half dreamed of what was lurking in him then, how soon would their aghast and righteous souls have wrenched the ship from such a fiendish man! They were bent on profitable cruises, the profit to be counted down in dollars from the mint. He was intent on an audacious, immitigable, and supernatural revenge.

Here, then, was this gray-headed, ungodly old man, chasing with curses a Job's whale[8] round the world, at the head of a crew, too, chiefly made up of mongrel renegades, and castaways, and cannibals—morally enfeebled, also, by the incompetence of mere unaided virtue or right-mindedness in Starbuck, the invulnerable jollity of indifference and recklessness in Stubb, and the pervading mediocrity in Flask. Such a crew, so officered, seemed specially picked and packed by some infernal fatality to help him to his monomaniac revenge. How it was that they so aboundingly responded to the old man's ire—by what evil magic their souls were possessed, that at times his hate seemed almost theirs; the White Whale as much their insufferable foe as his; how all this came to be—what the White Whale was to them, or how to their unconscious understandings, also, in some dim, unsuspected way, he might have seemed the gliding great demon of the seas of life—all this to explain, would be to dive deeper than Ishmael can go. The subterranean miner that works in us all, how can one tell whither leads his shaft by the ever shifting, muffled sound of his pick? Who does not feel the irresistible arm drag? What skiff in tow of a seventy-four[9] can stand still? For one, I gave myself up to the abandonment of the time and the place; but while yet all a-rush to encounter the whale, could see naught in that brute but the deadliest ill.

---

8. **Job's whale:** curse or affliction. In the Bible, Job was visited with grievous afflictions as a test of his faith in God.
9. **skiff . . . seventy-four:** small boat being pulled by a larger one.

WORDS TO OWN
incapacitated (in′kə·pas′ə·tāt′id) *adj.*: disabled.

---

7. **trope** (trōp): figure of speech.

HERMAN MELVILLE 327

Reading Skills and Strategies
Drawing Inferences about Character
? How does Ahab's great intellect give "more potency" to his monomania? [Possible responses: Ahab can analyze the problem of how to kill the whale in greater depth; he can see more aspects to the question of evil.]

Elements of Literature
Characterization
? What does Ahab realize about himself? [that he is obsessed and hiding it from others] Why does he "dissemble"? [He cannot help himself. It is not a question of will.]

Reading Skills and Strategies
Responding to the Text
? How can the narrator know what Ahab thinks and feels? [Possible responses: from reports from other sailors; from Ahab's subsequent words and actions; from Ishmael's knowledge of human nature.] Discuss how people analyze others without knowing them well. Ask students whether the possibility that Ishmael is speculating makes him less reliable. [Possible response: Most students will feel Ishmael's speculations are reliable, or that it doesn't matter in a novel this far removed from realist fiction.]

Advanced Learners
Analyzing Theme
In describing the owners' and mates' attitudes toward Ahab, Melville touches on the theme of the responsibility of people who acquiesce to evil. Note the irony in the reference to "righteous souls" who appear principally concerned about their investment.

Critical Thinking
Interpreting
? What are the problems with the crew and officers? [They are either too mediocre, indifferent, reckless, or weak to oppose Ahab's monomania.]

Reading Skills and Strategies
Responding to the Text
? What is "the subterranean miner that works in us all"? [Possible responses: fate, an attraction to evil.] Explore with students why people allow themselves to be carried away by emotion, even when they know it is a bad idea

---

Assessing Learning

Check Test: True-False
1. Ishmael's excitement about hunting for Moby-Dick is unclouded by dread. [False]
2. The white color is not the only distinctive feature of Moby-Dick. [True]
3. When the whale takes his leg, Ahab loses all will to live. [False]
4. The people of Nantucket know Ahab is demented. [False]
5. Ishmael secretly believes that nothing good can come of the search for Moby-Dick. [True]

Informal Assessment
Observe students while they read. As students write and discuss their responses to the chapter, use the following points to assess their performance.
   1 = Rarely   2 = Sometimes   3 = Often
_____ 1. Makes personal connections
_____ 2. Attends to lengthy narrative

MAKING MEANINGS

First Thoughts [Respond]

1. Possible responses: "The subterranean miner that works in us all" because it is frightening and convincing; "Human madness is oftentimes a cunning and most feline thing" because it seems true.

Shaping Interpretations [Interpret]

2. Ahab's rationality is deceptive in that, underneath, he is still monomaniacally obsessed with the whale. His surface rationality helps him by convincing others that he is fit to be the captain of a whaling ship. Possible inferences: He is clever and tricky; though mad, he has some self-control and self-awareness.

3. They suggest that he is ubiquitous, or present everywhere, and immortal. These suggestions heighten suspense and dread.

4. The narrator's attitude seems ambiguous. He calls Ahab an "ungodly old man" and refers to the crew as a collection of "mongrel renegades, and castaways, and cannibals." Yet, he says he is "all a-rush to encounter the whale." Ultimately Ishmael seems most comfortable relying on the idea of fate, referring to the "infernal fatality" of this particular crew turning up to help the captain in his "monomaniac revenge."

Extending the Text [Apply]

5. Possible responses: Melville combines terror and beauty in his description of the whale "leaving a milky-way wake of creamy foam, all spangled with golden gleamings." In literature, Poe combines the two qualities in his descriptions of Madeline. In nature, they can be found in volcanoes, storms, fires, predatory animals, and the immensity of outer space.

6. *Moby-Dick* is an epic in that it describes a quest; and although a madman, Ahab is a madman of heroic proportions who infects his society—the ship—with his ambition. Ahab may also embody the American values of grandiose individualism, conquest of wild territory (in this case, the sea), the subduing of nature, and the search for the truth.

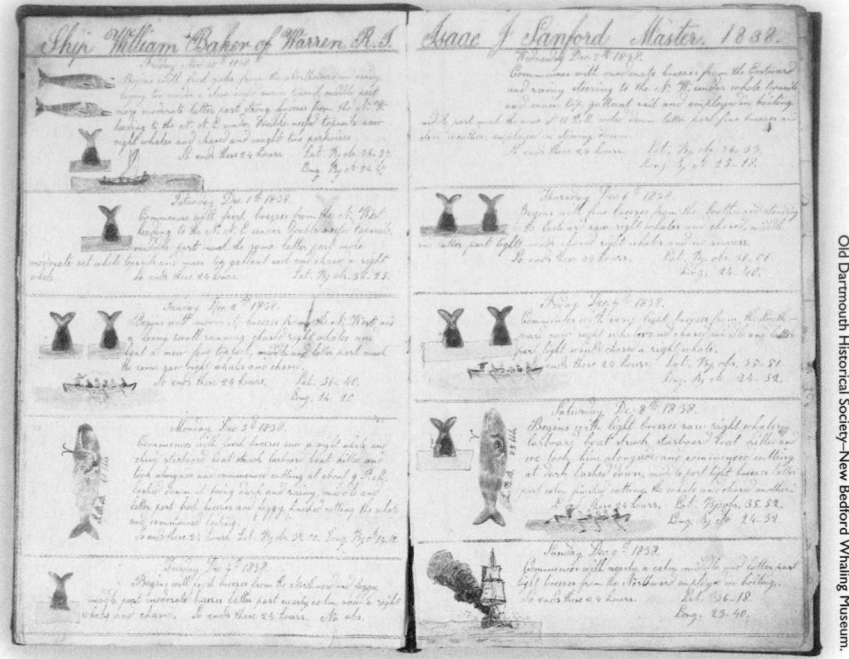

Page from whaling logbook.

Old Dartmouth Historical Society–New Bedford Whaling Museum.

MAKING MEANINGS

First Thoughts

1. What idea or statement in this chapter did you respond to most strongly? Explain.

> **Reading Check**
>
> With a partner or two, chart the **major events** in the development of Ahab's obsession with the white whale.

Shaping Interpretations

2. After Moby-Dick's attack, how is Ahab's rational behavior deceptive—but how does it also help him toward his goal? What does this tell you about Ahab's personality?

3. What supernatural qualities do the sailors attribute to Moby-Dick? What is the effect of turning Moby-Dick into a mythical monster?

4. The final paragraph draws a picture of the *Pequod*'s crew as they travel the world's oceans on Ahab's quest. What is the narrator's attitude here toward the ship's captain, the crew, and the quest?

Extending the Text

5. What **images** used to describe Moby-Dick in this chapter suggest beauty as well as horror? Can you think of any other instances (from life or literature) where these two qualities are combined in one person or event or thing?

6. An **epic** is a long narrative, written in heightened language, which recounts a quest undertaken by a heroic character who embodies the values of a particular society. (Homer's *Odyssey*, for example, is a famous epic of ancient Greece.) In what ways does *Moby-Dick* resemble an epic? What mid-nineteenth-century American values might Ahab embody?

328 THE AMERICAN RENAISSANCE

> **Reading Check**
> Allow students to use chart forms of their own choice, including simple lists. The major phases of Ahab's madness were the shock of the loss of his leg; his delirium while lying in the ship's hammock; and his later apparent calm, with madness lurking underneath.

CHOICES: Building Your Portfolio

Writer's Notebook

1. Collecting Ideas for a Controversial Issue

Melville's novel is full of ideas that you could use as the focus of a persuasive essay. Pick a passage that contains such an idea. How does the passage connect to life today? What do you think it means? Do you disagree with the passage? Save your notes for the Writer's Workshop on page 331.

Interpreting a Symbol

2. Who Knows, Exactly?

The British novelist and poet D. H. Lawrence wrote this about *Moby-Dick*:

> A hunt. The last great hunt.
> For what?
> For Moby-Dick, the huge white sperm whale: who is old, hoary, monstrous, and swims alone; who is unspeakably terrible in his wrath, having so often been attacked; and snow-white.
> Of course he is a symbol.
> Of what?
> I doubt that even Melville knew exactly. That's the best of it.
> —D. H. Lawrence

In a brief essay, explain what you think Moby-Dick **symbolizes**—insofar as you can tell from what you've read. Cite passages to support your interpretation.

Critical Thinking / Speaking and Listening

3. Analyzing Ahab

In a panel discussion with two or three classmates, analyze the **character** of Captain Ahab. To prepare your analysis, refer to your reading notes and gather your data in a chart like the following:

What we know about Ahab:	
From his speech	
From his actions	
From his appearance	
From his thoughts	

Comparing Ideas

4. Ahab and Transcendentalism

Write a brief essay comparing Ahab's **monologue** in "The Quarter-Deck" (beginning on page 317 with "Hark ye yet again . . .") to Transcendentalist ideas (see pages 210–212). In what ways does the speech reflect Transcendentalist thought, and in what ways does it reject it? In your essay, you might want to include quotations from Emerson or Thoreau.

Creative Writing

5. The Voice of Ahab

We hear most of the events of *Moby-Dick* from Ishmael's **point of view.** Now let Captain Ahab speak. In two or three paragraphs, write his thoughts on the night after the ritual on the quarter-deck. What does Ahab want? What does he fear? How does he feel about the crew?

Crossing the Curriculum: Science

6. Whales Today

Research and deliver a brief oral report to your class on some aspect of whales or whaling that interests you: for example, what the major types of whales are, how the whale population has changed since the 1850s, what whaling activities continue today, and what efforts have been made to preserve whales from extinction. Accompany your report with graphs, maps, or photographs. (The Internet should be a good source of information.)

Grading Timesaver

Rubrics for each Choices assignment appear on p. 127 in the *Portfolio Management System*.

CHOICES: Building Your Portfolio

1. **Writer's Notebook** Encourage students to practice skimming in order to search for ideas.
2. **Interpreting a Symbol** Encourage advanced students to find and use critical interpretations that challenge or bolster their own ideas.
3. **Critical Thinking/Speaking and Listening** Have students conduct their discussions in groups of varying abilities. Suggest that students begin by assigning these specific roles to group members: facilitator, questioner, clarifier.
4. **Comparing Ideas** Before students begin writing, suggest that they work in pairs to organize their ideas by noting on a Venn diagram differences and similarities between Ahab's monologue and Transcendentalist ideas.
5. **Creative Writing** Before students begin writing, have them work in pairs to review their reading notes and the questions in Making Meanings for the chapter "The Quarter-Deck" (p. 320).
6. **Crossing the Curriculum: Science** Encourage visual learners to view a documentary on whales or whaling, paying particular attention to how the documentary presents factual information. Suggest that students include this information in their reports. Invite them to use visual aids, such as pictures or charts, in their presentations.

Time Is But a Stream

In *The Survival of the Bark Canoe* (Farrar, Straus & Giroux), John McPhee explores the New England wilderness on a no-frills paddling trip in a hand-made birch-bark canoe, much as Henry David Thoreau once did. Thoreau's own journey is chronicled in *A Week on the Concord and Merrimack Rivers* (Ticknor and Fields).

Civil Disobedience

In the struggle for India's independence, Mohandas K. (Mahatma) Gandhi successfully put Thoreau's ideas on nonviolent resistance into action to effect change. Gandhi's successes helped inspire Martin Luther King, Jr., in the United States. Find out more about Gandhi's achievements in *An Autobiography: The Story of My Experiments with Truth* (Greenleaf Books) and in the award-winning film *Gandhi* (1982), directed by Richard Attenborough and featuring Ben Kingsley in the title role.

More Unwholesome Houses

Shirley Jackson's eerie fiction often focuses on houses that are not quite . . . normal. In *We Have Always Lived in the Castle* (Viking Press), two odd sisters live in the strangest house in town. In *The Haunting of Hill House* (Viking Penguin), a group of psychics tries to discover if Hill House really *is* haunted. The latter book was adapted into a classic horror film, *The Haunting* (1963), directed by Robert Wise and starring Julie Harris.

A Smorgasbord of Scares

The critic Alberto Manguel defines "fantastic literature"—including horror, fantasy, and magic realism—as "the impossible seeping into the possible." *Black Water* and *Black Water 2* (Clarkson N. Potter), edited by Manguel, are anthologies of short "fantastic literature" by an international list of authors including Edgar Allan Poe, Nathaniel Hawthorne, Julio Cortázar, Ursula K. Le Guin, and Ryunosuke Akutagawa.

Save the Whales

As a result of so much whaling, several species of whale are now endangered. The Canadian environmentalist Farley Mowat pleads for the preservation of these intelligent creatures in *A Whale for the Killing* (Little, Brown), his real-life account of a tormented whale trapped in a Newfoundland tide pool.

PERSUASIVE WRITING

CONTROVERSIAL ISSUE

In "Resistance to Civil Government," Thoreau tries to persuade people to look at government in a new way—a way that certainly not everyone would agree with. Disagreement is the essence of controversy, and a controversial issue is one that reasonable people can argue convincingly from two or more vantage points. Many current local, national, and world events qualify as controversial issues, since people may take sides on them. When you take up a controversial issue in writing, your primary goals are to communicate your views on the issue and to persuade your readers to take your position seriously—even to change their minds. To achieve these goals, you will draw on an arsenal of persuasive techniques to present and defend your point of view.

Prewriting

1. **Finding out what you care about.** If you've kept any of the Writer's Notebook activities from these collections, you might already have ideas for a controversial issue you'd like to write about. If not, one way to generate ideas for an issue worth writing about is to list topics. On a sheet of paper, draw a vertical line down the center. In the left-hand column, brainstorm a list of controversial topics. Your possible topics could relate to your town, your city, your state, or the nation, or they might be suggested by subjects you've been studying in school. (Controversy can even stem from a literary work: Did Madeline Usher really come back from the dead? Was there really a raven in the young scholar's room?) In the right-hand column, write ideas for possible issues connected with these topics. List the ideas in question form. For example, your list might include the topic "drinking among young people." A question suggested by this topic might be, "Should the drinking age be raised to twenty-three?" If you want to explore a controversial literary issue, your list could include relevant quotations from a story or poem you want to work with. Think of issues that have not only captured your intellectual interest but also stirred your emotions.

    Another way to discover current controversial issues is to read the editorial page in your local newspaper and to closely watch television news programs. Should your city have a teen curfew? Should your state require helmets for bicycle riders? Should the federal government set aside land to protect an endangered species? In each case, the issue is a matter of dispute about which reasonable people disagree.

Technology HELP

See Writer's Workshop 2 CD-ROM. *Assignment: Controversial Issue.*

ASSIGNMENT
Write an essay in which you take a stand on a controversial issue that you feel strongly about.

AIM
To shape your audience's opinions and feelings; to persuade them to take your position seriously; to urge an audience to take an action or change a stance on an issue.

AUDIENCE
Individuals or a group interested in your issue; your teacher; your classmates.

PROCESS OBJECTIVES
1. Use appropriate prewriting techniques to identify and develop a topic
2. Create a first draft
3. Use Evaluation Criteria as a basis for determining revision strategies
4. Revise the first draft, incorporating suggestions generated by self- or peer evaluation
5. Proofread and correct errors
6. Create a final draft
7. Reflect on progress as a writer (ATE)

Planning

- **Block Schedule**
  Block Scheduling Lesson Plans with Pacing Guide
- **One-Stop Planner**
  CD-ROM with Test Generator

Introducing the Writer's Workshop

Bring in editorial pages from local newspapers to give students some ideas about controversial Issues in their community. You might also provide samples of editorials and letters to the editor in national news, sports, or humanities magazines so that students can preview a broader range of possible issues. Students will also need to consider their potential audiences.

- Is there a logical target audience?
- Which issues are intended for specific interest groups?
- Which issues are of interest to the general population?
- Which issues are likely to spark an interest among students?

Resources: Print and Media

Writing and Language
- *Portfolio Management System*
  - Prewriting, p. 129
  - Peer Editing, p. 130
  - Assessment Rubric, p. 131
- *Workshop Resources*
  - Revision Strategy Teaching Notes, p. 11
  - Revision Strategy Transparencies 6, 7
- *Writer's Workshop 2 CD-ROM*
  - Controversial Issue

Teaching the Writer's Workshop

Prewriting

If students have difficulty thinking of controversial issues that interest them, suggest some of the following topics:

- requiring students to have passing grades before getting work permits
- requiring cyclists and motorcyclists to wear helmets
- building special lanes for cyclists
- raising or lowering the speed limit on expressways
- requiring all citizens to devote some hours each month to volunteer work in their communities

As students make their lists, remind them that for a topic to be controversial, it must have two defensible sides. For example, an argument can be made both for and against providing free medical service for all citizens.

Try It Out:
Possible Answers

1. driving while talking on the phone
2. the right to privacy
3. the age at which you're considered an adult
4. the cost of medical care

Try It Out

Find a possible topic for a controversial issue essay by completing one or more of these sentences:

1. There really ought to be a law against _____.

2. One right I think is in jeopardy today is _____.

3. If I could change anything about life in the United States today, I'd change _____.

4. I really think people need to get together and do something about _____.

Strategies for Elaboration: Finding a Topic

- Read the Letters to the Editor sections in your school and local newspapers.
- Watch local and national news programs on television.
- Discuss current controversial issues with family and friends.
- Go over your reading notes and other class notes to find a controversial literary issue you might want to argue.
- Consider both sides of the issues that interest you, and develop a point of view for each issue.

2. **Selecting and defining one issue.** Put an asterisk next to the issues about which you have the strongest feelings and have the most to say. Share these preferred issues with one or two classmates, explaining your positions. (Listen to the ideas of your peers, too, to help them clarify their thinking.) Use these questions to help you choose an issue:

- Is the issue important to you?
- Can the issue be argued, and can the arguments be supported with evidence? (For example, whether life in the city is better than life in the country is a matter of personal preference; it can't be supported with evidence.)
- Is there an audience that is interested in this topic and that you would like to convince?

3. **Trying out a position statement.** Write a brief, direct statement of where you stand on the issue. This is your **position statement,** or **proposition**—the thesis statement of your persuasive essay. If, for example, your question is "Should there be a teen curfew to curtail juvenile crime?" then your position statement might read, "The most effective way to cut down on juvenile crime in our city is to implement a teen curfew." Your position statement might be one, two, or three sentences long. In many cases, a position statement indicates one or two broad, fundamental reasons for a writer's position.

4. **Setting up a pro-con table.** It's important that you understand and anticipate all the arguments and counterarguments that your issue gives rise to. Make a two-column chart headed "Pro" on the left-hand side and "Con" on the right-hand side. In the Pro column, jot down all the reasons you can think of for the "in favor" side of the issue; in the Con column, list all the reasons you can think of for the "against" side. (See page 333 for an example.)

5. **Listing arguments and counterarguments.** Using your pro-con table as a basis, write a more extensive list of possible arguments to support your side and a list of possible objections, or counterarguments, for the other side. Once again, share your prewriting with a group of classmates. They might provide for your position support that you have overlooked, and they can comment upon the validity of your arguments.

332 THE AMERICAN RENAISSANCE

Using Students' Strengths

Logical/Mathematical Learners

Encourage students to use an informal poll as part of the evidence supporting their positions. For example, if students are writing in favor of the mandatory use of seat belts, they could poll their classmates to see how many agree. If they are writing in favor of exempting certain students from final exams, they could devise a questionnaire to find out the conditions students would propose.

What happens if, as you collect arguments for and against the issue, you come across an opposing argument that you can't refute? In fairness, you can't just ignore such an argument; you must acknowledge it and affirm its validity. This is called **conceding a point.** It's not a weakness to give the opposing side a nod; in fact, it's a sign of strength that shows you have thoroughly considered all sides and are being fair.

Model

Topic: Should there be a citywide teen curfew?

Pro	Con
controls gang violence	prohibits legitimate activities
minimizes auto accidents	requires expanded police force
reduces underage drinking	further overloads justice system with people who may have broken no other law
minimizes vandalism	takes away liberties from those not involved in criminal activities

6. **Searching for evidence.** You should do some research to find objective and reliable support for your position. This may include library research to find irrefutable facts—such as statistics, examples, and anecdotes. It may also include interviews with people who, as authorities on the issue, can offer expert opinions. Brainstorm a list of possible research sources you can consult for evidence in support of your issue. Then begin your search.

Drafting

1. **Your credibility is at stake.** To be truly effective, your essay will have to be well reasoned and feature plenty of support that no one could argue with (examples, expert opinions, quotations, statistics), that is, any sound evidence that makes a good case for your position. Be sure to deal thoroughly and fairly with possible arguments against your stance.

2. **Crafting an effective introduction.** In persuasive writing, it's important to make your readers care about the issue from the outset. Convince them that the issue affects them—even if they're on the other side. Begin with an attention-getting anecdote or example, a surprising statistic, or a rhetorical question. (A rhetorical question is a question asked to make people think; it is not a "real" question that actually requires an answer. See page 105.) Then, clearly identify the issue, and state your position on it.

3. **Organizing your work.** There are three major ways to organize a controversial-issue essay:

   • **Order of importance.** You can develop your argument according to order of importance, beginning with either the most important or the least important reason for supporting your position. If, for example, you

---

Drafting

Students might find the following graphic organizer helpful in organizing their essays:

Position Statement: _____

Supporting Evidence:

1. _____
2. _____
3. _____

Counterargument: _____

Rebuttal: _____

Restatement of Thesis: _____

Remind students to use only every other line when they write their drafts. They should also leave extra space in the right margin. These blank spaces will be used for comments and editing marks.

Getting Students Involved

Cooperative Learning

Informal Debate. Have an even-numbered small group of students work together on a controversial issue. Half of the students should take one position and the other half, the opposing stand. Each student should prepare part of the argument. Students also must anticipate the counterarguments. Each side should present its position to the class. Then, each side should give a two-minute rebuttal to the arguments presented by the opposing side.

Using Students' Strengths

Auditory Learners

To help students evaluate their essays before they revise them, suggest that they record their drafts on audiotape or have partners record them. Then, they may listen to their work, stopping the tape at places that do not flow well or that need strengthening. After students have made some written revisions, they may again record their essays and listen to judge the effectiveness of their revisions.

Strategies for Elaboration

When writing persuasively, students will need to have a good understanding of the connotative power of words. Before directing students' attention to the Strategies for Elaboration box, you may wish to review by asking students to provide as many synonyms as possible for the word *eat*. Then, go through the list and have the class identify each synonym as having a positive, neutral, or negative connotation. [positive: dine, feast. neutral: consume, feed, ingest. negative: stuff, cram, devour, gulp, gorge, gobble]

Communications Handbook HELP

See Recognizing Logical Fallacies.

Strategies for Elaboration

Here's how you might use connotative language if your goal is to argue *for* a teenage curfew:
- In your introduction, you might use words that have negative connotations, such as *reckless, delinquent,* and *hazard.*
- As you develop your points, you might want to use transition expressions with positive connotations, such as *It is clear that…* or *It is reasonable to assume that….*
- In your conclusion, you might use words or phrases with positive connotations such as *safe* or *family time.*

begin with the most important reason, then you would move methodically through your other reasons, ending with the least important. It can also be effective to save the heaviest ammunition for last, leading from the least to the most important reason.

- **Chronological order.** The order in which events occur in time is chronological order. Presenting your points in this order is especially helpful in making cause-and-effect relationships clear.
- **Logical order.** In logical order, you present your opponents' positions or arguments and then present your refutations of them through comparison and contrast. You may present all the objections first, followed by all your rebuttals; or you may move back and forth from each objection to its respective rebuttal.

4. **Using logical appeals.** Rather than merely listing abstract arguments to support your position, make your arguments concrete. Whenever possible, use your library research to add documented facts, anecdotes, quotations, and expert opinions. Provide real-life examples of the causes and effects of adopting the position you are arguing for or against. An extended example, or case study, can sometimes be sustained throughout an essay or even be used as an organizational device. Well-reasoned hypothetical cases, or scenarios, can sometimes be used for support as well, especially if you make the scenario believable. All of these are **logical appeals**—appeals that are made to the audience's reason. Logical appeals include both reasons and evidence, and they make your arguments more appealing to the audience because they engender trust. They also make it harder for the other side to challenge you and for your audience to reject your reasoning. But watch out for *overgeneralization* (broad statements that lack sufficient support), *oversimplification* (concentrating on only one or a few aspects of a complex issue), and other lapses in logic. Signs of sloppy thinking and a lack of objectivity can diminish your audience's trust in you.

5. **Appealing to emotions.** The power of persuasive writing resides not just in logical argument, but also in emotional appeals. To develop emotional appeals, think about the evidence you've collected that will speak to your readers' hearts: Examples, vivid details, anecdotes, and personal experiences can all be used effectively.

6. **The power of loaded words.** You are also using emotional appeals when you take advantage of the power of **connotative language.** Every word has a **denotative meaning**—its dictionary definition—as well as its **connotative meaning**—the feelings or attitudes the word suggests. Words like *integrity, honor,* and *steadfastness* have positive associations, or connotations, and if you used them in describing a political candidate, you would be giving him or her excellent "press." Words like *rigidity, self-interest,* and *stubbornness,* on the other hand, have negative connotations, and your candidate would appear less desirable if described with those words. Connotative words are "loaded" words that pack a punch. Used sparingly and carefully, they will cause readers to become not only intellectually involved, but emotionally involved as well. Consider the following example from Thoreau's "Resistance to Civil Government."

Reaching All Students

Advanced Learners
Students might want to take this assignment one step further by planning strategic advertising campaigns to get their positions across. They will need to determine what kind of media exposure would be most effective, how they would present their positions, and what kind of speakers could best represent their cause. They should display or present their campaigns by hanging visuals in the classroom or hall or by playing audiotapes or videotapes for their classmates.

> I saw that, if there was a *wall of stone* between me and my towns-men, there was a still more *difficult* one to climb or *break through,* before they could get to be as free as I was. I did not for a moment feel *confined,* and the walls seemed a great waste of *stone and mor-tar.* I felt as if I alone of all my townsmen had paid my tax. They plainly did not know how to treat me, but behaved like persons who are *underbred.* In every *threat* and in every compliment there was a *blunder;* for they thought that my chief desire was to stand the other side of that *stone wall.*
>
> —Henry David Thoreau

The italicized words and phrases have strong connotative meanings. In choosing these particular words, Thoreau is able to evoke an emotional re-sponse that extends beyond the literal meaning of the passage. His feelings about the restrictive nature of society come through loud and clear.

7. **Audience.** When writing about a controversial issue, it's crucial to con-sider your audience's response, since affecting their opinions is your pri-mary goal. Think about how much your audience already knows about your issue, and provide background information accordingly. Also, think about whether they are likely to agree or disagree with your position. If they are inclined to disagree, put yourself in their shoes: What counterarguments will be the most compelling? What points might you have to concede?

8. **Closing your essay.** The conclusion of your essay should leave the audi-ence feeling that an issue has been adequately and fairly explored. You might repeat your position statement at the end but in different words than those used at the beginning. Or, you might make a strong statement about what might happen if the course of action you recommend is not followed.

Evaluating and Revising

1. **Peer review.** Exchange essays with a classmate. As you read each other's essays, consider the following questions:
   - Is the issue well defined and interesting to you?
   - Is the writer's position clearly stated at the beginning of the essay?
   - Does the writer use both logical and emotional appeals effectively?
   - Which reasons are most persuasive? least persuasive? Which should be developed further?
   - Is the order in which reasons are presented effective? If not, what changes should the writer make?
   - Is the evidence relevant and credible?
   - Does the writer convincingly rebut arguments against his or her position?
   - Does the writer seem to have considered the intended audience?

Language Handbook HELP

See *Combining Sentences for Variety,* page 1238.

■ *Evaluation Criteria*

A good controversial issue essay

1. *defines the issue and the writer's stand on it*
2. *includes a strong and credible position state-ment (thesis)*
3. *develops a position clearly, in convincing and well-developed arguments*
4. *includes and answers important counterargu-ments, showing considera-tion of the audience's point of view*
5. *is organized logically*
6. *has a conclusion that shows that the writer is clear about the outcome he or she desires*

After students have studied Thoreau's model, ask them to look through their drafts and circle loaded words. Then ask them to evaluate their word choices by con-sidering the following questions:
- Do the loaded words give a fair presentation of the situation?
- Do the words create vivid images?
- Could more graphic words with more persuasive connotations be substituted?
- What type of audience reaction are the connotations likely to elicit?
- Will the word choices prejudice or persuade the audience?

Evaluating and Revising

Have students use the Evaluation Cri-teria provided here to review their drafts and determine needed revisions.
- To check for adequate development of supporting details in their essays, students may use highlighters of dif-ferent colors to mark each item of evidence.
- Have students check their writing for sentences that have parallel ideas. Remind students to link ideas in a sentence by placing them in the same grammatical form. Refer them to the Language Workshop on p. 337. Have students check their work to see if they can improve bal-ance in their sentences by using par-allel structure.

Reaching All Students

Struggling Writers

Suggest that students having difficulty read their rough drafts aloud to themselves. When they stumble over a phrase or have to reread a sen-tence, they should mark that place in their essays. Then, they can go back and determine whether or not that section needs revision. If a student has difficulty understanding his or her own argument, other readers are likely to have difficulty also.

English Language Learners

Students learning English may have difficulty with the connotative meaning of words in Eng-lish. Suggest that students brainstorm in their native languages lists of powerful, persuasive words they want to include. Then, students should write a basic translation of the words in English. Assign each student a partner who is proficient in English and can help to evaluate the connotative meaning of the translated words.

Proofreading

Have students proofread their own papers first and then exchange them with another student. For this persuasive writing assignment, remind students that careful use of mechanics, grammar, and usage will improve their credibility. If time permits, the final copy should be put aside for at least a day before it is proofread for the final time by the author.

Reflecting

Ask students to go through their papers and find two or more examples of their most effective use of persuasive language, especially the use of words with connotative meanings. Have each student list the examples on a separate paper and attach it to the essay before filing.

Resources

Peer Editing Forms and Rubrics
• *Portfolio Management System,* p. 130
Revision Transparencies
• *Workshop Resources,* p. 11

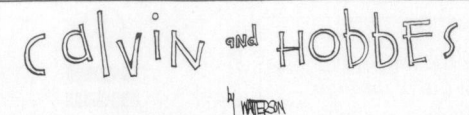

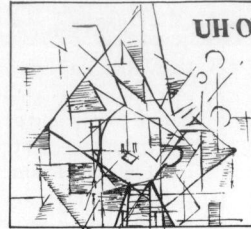

Revision STRATEGIES

Review your essay or speech for unclear writing. Make abstract ideas concrete. Use straightforward diction and clear syntax. If any sentences are convoluted, rewrite them.

Communications Handbook HELP

See Proofreading.

2. **Self-evaluation.** Pay especially close attention to the response you get from peers or others who read your draft and who disagree with your position. They can provide you with especially useful feedback as to the persuasive power of your essay. If you can win their respect with your arguments, then you may be able to influence their opinions, too. Have you listened to constructive criticism with an open mind?

Underline passages that seemed to make your readers puzzled, impatient, or bored, and revise them so that they are stronger, both in terms of logic and language. Varying your sentence structure can also help you retain your readers' interest. However, don't assume that disagreement on your audience's part means ineffectiveness on your part. People can disagree with even the most powerful persuasive writing.

Grading Timesaver

Rubrics for this Writer's Workshop assignment appear on p. 131 of the *Portfolio Management System.*

Language Workshop

The history of the written word is rich and

KEEPING IT IN BALANCE: PARALLEL STRUCTURE

When you link ideas within a sentence, be aware of balance in your writing. You can make your writing smoother and more balanced by using **parallel structure,** placing equivalent ideas in the same grammatical form.

In the following sentence, the boldface structures are *not* parallel:

> The professor said that **to read Emerson** is more useful than **watching television.**

"To read" is an infinitive form, but "watching" is a gerund. You can make the structures parallel by changing the sentence so that both forms are equivalent, as in the following example:

> The professor said that **reading Emerson** is more useful than **watching television.** [gerunds in both cases]

The key to parallel structure is balance: You use the same grammatical form to express equal, or parallel, ideas. If you use a gerund to express one idea, use another gerund to express the idea to which it is linked. Pair an infinitive with an infinitive, a clause with a clause, a noun with a noun, and so on.

Here are some situations when you would want to be certain that your sentences have parallel structure.

1. Use parallel structure when you link coordinate ideas.

    > Emerson believed **that people must be true to their unique capabilities** and **that they must practice self-reliance.** [noun clause paired with noun clause]

2. Use parallel structure to compare or contrast ideas.

    > Emerson's **lectures** were often more accessible than his **essays.** [noun contrasted with a noun]

3. Use parallel structure to link ideas when you are using **correlative conjunctions**—pairs of conjunctions such as *both . . . and, either . . . or, neither . . . nor,* or *not only . . . but also.*

    > Emerson was *not only* **a great lecturer** but also **a gifted poet.**

Writer's Workshop Follow-Up: Revising

Parallel structures are important in persuasive writing because they clearly organize ideas in a sentence and create a smooth, authoritative rhythm. Reread the persuasive essay you wrote on a controversial issue for the Writer's Workshop (page 331), and correct any lapses in parallelism.

Technology HELP

See Language Workshop CD-ROM. *Key word entry: parallel structure.*

Language Handbook HELP

See Using Parallel Structure, pages 1235–1236.

Try It Out

Rewrite the following sentences, making them parallel in structure.

1. To Emerson, it was important that people be nonconformists, true to themselves, and listen to their intuition.

2. Thoreau's writing style involves the use of paradox, imagery, and he also used many figures of speech.

3. Many students find it easier to read Thoreau's *Walden* than reading anything by Emerson.

LANGUAGE WORKSHOP 337

OBJECTIVES

1. Maintain balance within a sentence by using parallel structure
2. Use parallel structure to link coordinate ideas
3. Use parallel structure to compare or contrast ideas
4. Use parallel structure to link ideas using correlative conjunctions

Resources

Workshop Resources
• Worksheet, p. 51
***Language Workshop* CD-ROM**
• Parallel Structures

Try It Out
Possible Answers

1. To Emerson, it was important that people be nonconformists, be true to themselves, and listen to their intuition.
2. Thoreau's writing style involves using paradoxes, imagery, and figures of speech.
3. Many students find reading Thoreau's *Walden* easier than reading anything by Emerson.

Assessing Learning

Quick Check: Parallel Structure
Use parallel structure to link ideas in these sentences.

1. *Walden* was a book about Thoreau's philosophy and it helped expand his reputation. [*Walden* revealed Thoreau's philosophy and helped expand his reputation.]
2. Some people prefer Emerson's poetry to reading his prose. [Some people prefer Emerson's poetry to his prose.]

3. In Hawthorne's "The Minister's Black Veil," the minister does not remove the veil, and he and Elizabeth do not get married. [In Hawthorne's "The Minister's Black Veil," the minister neither removes the veil nor marries Elizabeth.]
4. Poe wrote fiction, and he was also a poet. [Poe wrote not only fiction but also poetry.]

Using the Strategies
Possible Answers

1. Jim Murphy and Margaret S. Creighton would probably provide the most reliable and relevant information. Murphy's book is the most recent, and has been brought out by a major and well-respected publishing house. Creighton has published multiple books on this subject, the most recent with a respected academic publisher, and another through a prestigious museum.

2. Students should select the New Bedford Whaling Museum site and the "History of Whaling" site associated with a Virginia university as top choices. Both institutions lend credibility to their Web sites. The first seems to be well organized, with an overview of the museum's history and mission, while the second promises to offer information on the specific subject of whaling.

3. Students should shy away from using *Free Willy 2,* since it doesn't even focus on nineteenth-century whaling, as does *Moby Dick.*

Situation
Suppose you share Herman Melville's interest in nineteenth-century American whaling and want to write a book for children about this subject. You should begin by identifying various sources of information that will help you plan your book. Then, evaluate the credibility of these sources.

Strategies
Evaluate the author's or director's credentials.
- Does the author have any special training in the field?
- Is the author associated with a respected organization, such as a university, museum, scientific institute, or professional organization?
- Has he or she produced other books, articles, or video material on the same or on a similar subject? If so, read a few reviews to get a sense of the person's reliability.
- Does the author have any ulterior motives or conflicts of interest that might affect his or her credibility?

For Internet sources, evaluate the quality of the Web site.
- Is the Web site well-planned and well-edited, without spelling and other errors?
- Does the Web site offer a comprehensive overview, or is it just bare-bones with few necessary details?

For video sources, evaluate the accuracy of the images.
- Are the images well researched and faithful to the facts? Is there distortion through clever editing?

Evaluate the timeliness.
- Has the information been eclipsed by more recent research?

Using the Strategies
Examine the material in the box on this page.
1. Which print authors would probably provide the most reliable and most relevant information? Why?
2. Which Internet sources would you use? Why?
3. Which sources would you not use? Why?

Extending the Strategies
- Think of another subject you would like to learn more about. Jot down questions you want answered. Then, do research in a library and on the Internet and make a list of three print and electronic sources you could refer to with confidence. If you like, write up your research findings. You might also suggest additional aspects of the subject that need to be investigated.

Sources on Nineteenth-Century American Whaling:

Books
Creighton, Margaret S. *Rites & Passages: The Experience of American Whaling, 1830–1870.* Cambridge: Cambridge University Press, 1995.
——. *Dogwatch and Liberty Days: Seafaring Life in the 19th Century.* Salem, MA: Peabody Museum Press, 1982.
Gourley, Catherine. *Hunting Neptune's Giants: True Stories of American Whaling.* Brookfield, Conn.: Millbrook Publishers, 1995.
Murphy, Jim. *Gone a Whaling: The Lure of the Sea & the Hunt for the Great Whale.* New York: Houghton Mifflin Company, 1998.

Films
Moby Dick (1956), directed by John Huston.
Free Willy 2: The Adventure Home (1995), directed by Dwight H. Little.

Internet
New Bedford Whaling Museum History and Mission, http://www.whalingmuseum.org/about.htm
History of Whaling, http://curry.edschool.virginia.edu/go/Whales/HisWhaling.HTML
Whales on the Net, http://whales.magna.com.au/HISTORY/index.html
Eden's Killer Whale Museum, http://www.acr.net.au/whales/history.html

Note: URLs for illustrative purposes only; may not be current.

Crossing the Curriculum

Science/Social Studies
Suggest that students' research and evaluations might serve a dual purpose. Have interested students discuss with their science or social studies teacher the possibility of using whaling research as the background for a project or paper.

Art
A children's book on nineteenth century whaling would include illustrations. Have students brainstorm a list of things they would need to know to create these illustrations. The list might include the physical dimensions of whales and whaling ships, of whaling ports and locales, and of the costumes of sailors and others in whaling ports. Have students use the strategies listed on p. 338 for evaluating sources on these topics.

Learning for Life
A Model of Self-Reliance

OBJECTIVES
1. Use research to identify a person who fulfills a particular set of criteria such as those for Thoreau's self-reliant individual
2. Choose a method and plan a presentation of research

Problem

Emerson's self-reliant individual is a nonconformist who finds strength and fulfillment in solitude and in being true to his or her unique nature. "Nothing is at last sacred but the integrity of your own mind," Emerson tells us. In *Walden,* Thoreau makes a similar observation: "If a man does not keep pace with his companions, perhaps it is because he hears a different drummer." Who is the self-reliant individual? What can we learn from the person who "hears a different drummer"?

Project

Research a living or dead person who you think fulfills Emerson's ideal of the self-reliant individual—someone who stands apart from the multitude and exemplifies integrity, nonconformity, and uniqueness. Demonstrate how that person can be a role model for us all.

Preparation

1. Reread the excerpt from Emerson's essay "Self-Reliance," and make notes on what qualities he identifies as being central to the self-reliant individual. If you disagree with any of his points, make note of your disagreements. Add any qualities that you think are necessary for a self-reliant person to possess.

2. You may already have some ideas about people, living or dead, who strike you as being models of self-reliance. If you don't, brainstorm with your teacher, family, or classmates. Look through magazines, newspapers, encyclopedias, and books for ideas. Perhaps someone you know fits your definition of a self-reliant person.

Procedure

1. List the criteria you've come up with for a truly self-reliant person. Your criteria may be based solely on Emerson's ideas, or you may introduce some of your own criteria.

2. Research and take notes on the person you have chosen as an example of a self-reliant person. If the person is someone in your community or someone you know well, tape-record an interview with him or her.

Presentation

Present what you have learned in one of the following formats (or another format your teacher approves):

1. **Encyclopedia Entry**
   Write an encyclopedia entry about the person. Instead of simply presenting a narrative of the events of the person's life, focus on his or her accomplishments and philosophy. Demonstrate how this person is, or was, truly self-reliant. Include visual images.

2. **Short Story**
   Write a short story about the self-reliant person you researched. Describe the person's daily life, thoughts and feelings, and the reactions of others to his or her individuality and accomplishments. Publish your story in your school newspaper, or read it to your class.

3. **School for Self-Reliance**
   Prepare a brochure advertising a private school founded by the person you researched. The school should be dedicated to building self-reliant individuals, and it should emphasize the virtues and knowledge considered most important by the founder. Include a statement of the school's philosophy and an outline of the course of study—what subjects will be taught, what extracurricular activities will be encouraged, how classes will be run, and so on. Illustrate your brochure.

Processing

What did you learn about Emerson's principles of self-reliance by completing this project? Is it really possible to live a self-reliant life? Is it desirable to be a nonconformist? Are there any drawbacks to being self-reliant? Write your reflections for your portfolio.

Publishing

Ask students who have written encyclopedia entries to compile and publish them using computer software. Suggest that they illustrate their entries with scanned sketches or with clip art. Students may wish to collect and merge their entries into a series arranged alphabetically or by area of expertise (scientists, writers, etc.). If possible, consider having students compile encyclopedia entries from all classes on one disk or CD-ROM. Have them donate a copy of their work to the school library.

Resources

Viewing and Representing
HRW Multimedia Presentation Maker
Students may wish to use the *Multimedia Presentation Maker* to create brochures.

Grading Timesaver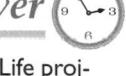

Rubrics for this Learning for Life project appear on p. 132 of the *Portfolio Management System.*

Developing Workplace Competencies

Preparation	Procedure	Presentation
• Processes information • Uses resources well • Makes decisions	• Processes information • Acquires data	• Communicates ideas and information • Exhibits self-esteem • Teaches others

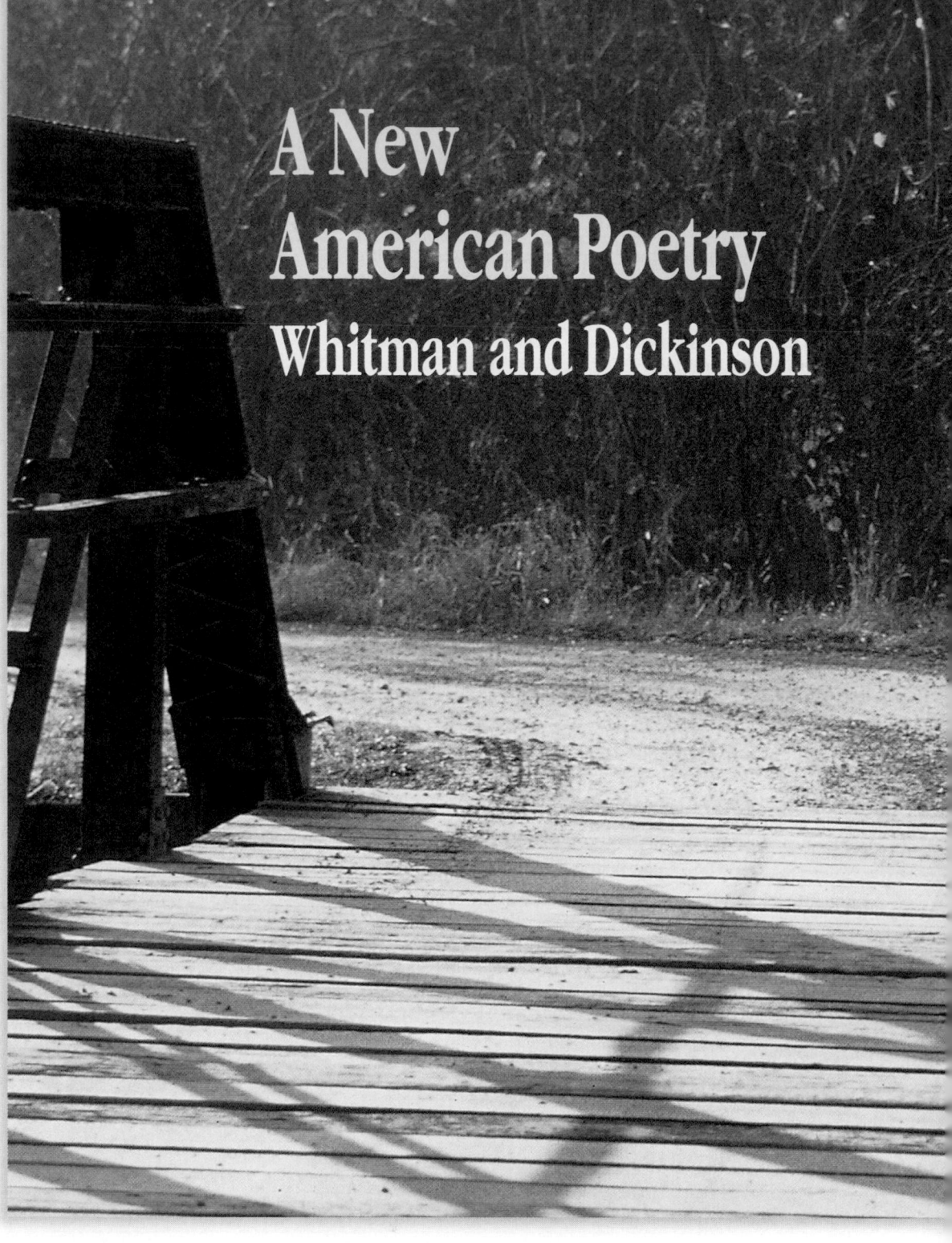

OBJECTIVES

1. Read nineteenth-century American poetry and prose by Walt Whitman and Emily Dickinson, on the subjects "The Large Hearts of Heroes" and "Tell it Slant"
2. Interpret literary elements in Whitman and Dickinson with special emphasis on free verse and slant rhyme
3. Apply a variety of reading strategies to the poetry of Whitman and Dickinson
4. Respond to literature in a variety of modes
5. Learn about the historical growth of the American vocabulary
6. Plan, draft, revise, edit, proof, and publish a comparison and contrast essay
7. Write sentences with varied beginnings
8. Demonstrate the ability to read a textbook
9. Examine the changing world of work

Resources

Viewing and Representing
Videocassette B, Segment 6
Available in English and Spanish.
Use this videocassette to introduce the reinvention of American poetry in the nineteenth century.

For full lesson plans and worksheets, see *Visual Connections Teacher's Manual.*

A New American Poetry
Whitman and Dickinson

Selection Readability

This Annotated Teacher's Edition provides a summary of each selection in the student book. Following each Summary heading, you will find one, two, or three small icons. These icons indicate, in an approximate sense, the reading level of the selection.

■ One icon indicates that the selection is easy.
■ ■ Two icons indicate that the selection is on an intermediate reading level.
■ ■ ■ Three icons indicate that the selection is challenging.

341

Responding to the Quotations

Ask students what Whitman is suggesting about himself in this quotation. [Possible responses: He thinks of himself as responsive to his audience and intertwined with their daily lives; he sees himself as part of the grass and dirt of the American soil.] Ask what the lines by Emily Dickinson suggest about the poet and her work. [Possible response: She sees her work as the document of a solitary, deeply personal realm, separate from any intended audience.] Read the entire poem to the class, and ask students if their opinions change:

> This is my letter to the World
> That never wrote to me—
> The simple News that Nature
>   told—
> With tender Majesty
>
> Her Message is committed
> To Hands I cannot see—
> For love of Her—Sweet—
>   Countrymen—
> Judge tenderly—of me

Ⓐ Literary Connections
Literary Isolation
Poet and Whitman biographer Paul Zweig sees a common feature between Whitman's pre–Civil War life and Dickinson's reclusiveness: both poets, Zweig claims, developed their poetic practice apart from the established literary world of their era. Whitman, for example, had no acquaintance of Herman Melville, who lived near him in New York City. While Zweig acknowledges that "[o]nly Emily Dickinson was as formidably alone," he maintains that the isolation of both poets from literary conventions helped them develop innovative and unique poetic styles.

A New American Poetry
Whitman and Dickinson
by John Malcolm Brinnin

If you want me again look for me under your boot-soles.
—*Walt Whitman*

This is my letter to the World
That never wrote to me—
—*Emily Dickinson*

The two greatest American poets of the nineteenth century were so different from one another, both as artists and as personalities, that only a nation as varied in character as the United States could possibly contain them.

Ⓐ Walt Whitman worked with bold strokes on a broad canvas; Emily Dickinson worked with the delicacy of a miniaturist. Whitman was sociable and gregarious, a traveler; Dickinson was private and shy, content to remain in one secluded spot through all of her lifetime.

While both poets were close observers of people and of life's daily activities, the emphasis they gave to what impressed them was so distinct as to make them opposites. Whitman was the public spokesman of the masses and the prophet of progress. "I hear America singing," he said, and he joined his eloquent voice to that chorus. Dickinson was the obscure homebody, peering through the curtains of her house in a country village, who found in nature metaphors for the spirit and recorded them with no thought of an audience. Whitman expected that his celebration of universal brotherhood and the bright destiny of democracy would be carried like a message into the future. Dickinson expected nothing but oblivion for the poetry that was her "letter to the World."

Whitman and Dickinson were true innovators who expressed themselves in poetic voices that broke with the established literary traditions of their time.

Skill Link

Analyzing the Language of Poetry
Discuss with students how the evocative and ambiguous language of poetry allows writers to express several different levels of thought and feeling in a single line. How does it differ from a prose expression of the same ideas and feelings? How does poetry allow for—even encourage—subjective perceptions? Have students read "This is my letter to the World" and answer the following questions:

1. What idea does Dickinson express about the world? [The world has been indifferent to her.]
2. What wishes and fears does she articulate? [She wants to speak to the world about the message she sees expressed in nature; she is afraid the world will dismiss or ignore her letter—her poems.]
3. What evocative word conveys how Dickinson hopes she will be treated by the world? [*tenderly*]

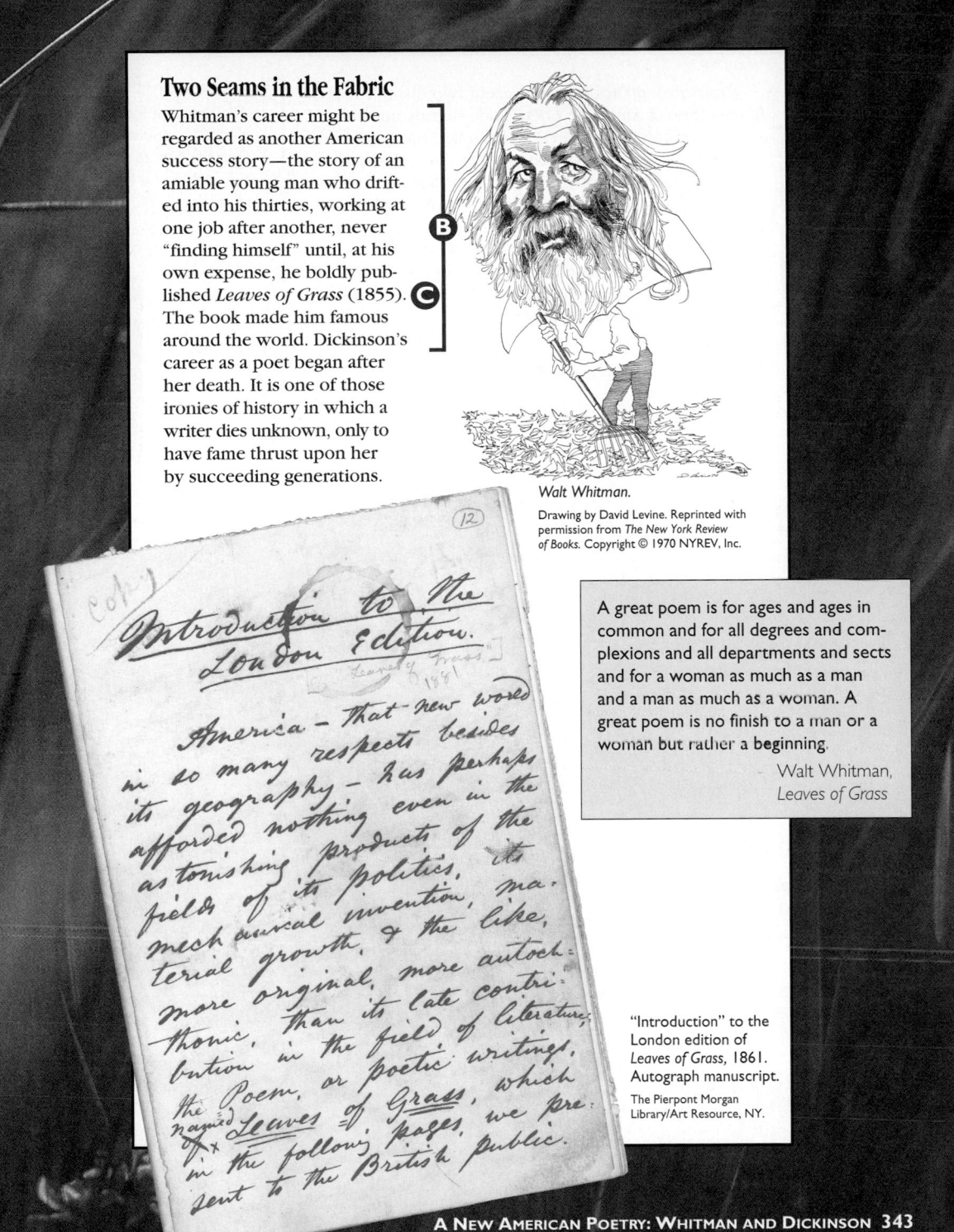

Two Seams in the Fabric

Whitman's career might be regarded as another American success story—the story of an amiable young man who drifted into his thirties, working at one job after another, never "finding himself" until, at his own expense, he boldly published *Leaves of Grass* (1855). The book made him famous around the world. Dickinson's career as a poet began after her death. It is one of those ironies of history in which a writer dies unknown, only to have fame thrust upon her by succeeding generations.

B

C

Walt Whitman.

Drawing by David Levine. Reprinted with permission from *The New York Review of Books.* Copyright © 1970 NYREV, Inc.

A great poem is for ages and ages in common and for all degrees and complexions and all departments and sects and for a woman as much as a man and a man as much as a woman. A great poem is no finish to a man or a woman but rather a beginning.

—Walt Whitman,
Leaves of Grass

"Introduction" to the London edition of *Leaves of Grass*, 1861. Autograph manuscript.

The Pierpont Morgan Library/Art Resource, NY.

A NEW AMERICAN POETRY: WHITMAN AND DICKINSON **343**

B Background

Leaves of Grass

When *Leaves of Grass* was published in 1855, it sparked a firestorm of negative criticism. In 1856, a critic for the *Saturday Review* suggested that "if the *Leaves of Grass* should come into anybody's possession, our advice is to throw them instantly behind the fire."

C Literary Connections

1850–1855

Other events in American literature during the early 1850s include the appearance of Hawthorne's *The Scarlet Letter*, Melville's *Moby-Dick*, and Thoreau's *Walden*. In England, Charles Dickens published three novels: *David Copperfield*, 1850; *Bleak House*, 1853; and *Hard Times*, 1854.

Reaching All Students

Struggling Readers

To help students predict main ideas, point out that the title and headings of an informational essay usually indicate the main ideas expressed. Ask students to page through this introductory essay and find the headings "A New American Poetry," "Two Seams in the Fabric," and "Models for Future Poets." Ask students to speculate on the precise meanings of these heads and to make predictions about the material that follows them.

English Language Learners

Remind students that Whitman wanted to develop a uniquely American poetic voice. Refer them to Whitman's quotation about the proof of a poet (p. 344). What are common objects that absorb? [Possible responses: sponge, towel, cloth.] How can a country absorb a poet? [by making that person's work part of its national consciousness] How can a poet absorb a country? [by capturing the character of the land and giving voice to its various peoples and cultures]

Advanced Students

Ask students what they can learn by examining the handwriting and corrections on these original manuscripts. Do they shed light on the writer's personality or method of working? If so, what do they reveal? Encourage students to examine these illustrations carefully and then find out more about these manuscript collections. Who has access to these documents and when?

A Critical Thinking

Analyzing

Invite discussion of the Whitman quotation. Is it an absolute truth, a partial truth, a falsehood, or perhaps an expression of an ideal rather than a reality? Then ask students to think of poets who have been absorbed by their countries and poets who haven't. [Possible responses: Longfellow was absorbed affectionately by his public, but Poe was not, at least not until after his death. Also, many poets in countries with authoritarian regimes have been forced into exile from their homelands. (One example is Pablo Neruda in Chile, see p. 367.)]

B Literary Connections

Influences on Whitman

According to biographer Paul Zweig, the young Whitman was influenced more by prose than by poetry, and much of the 1855 edition of *Leaves of Grass* was written originally as prose. "His achievement was to incorporate the advantages of prose—its flexibility, its ability to mold itself freely to an actual speaking voice—into a new line that was subtly accented, yet never far from the extended rhythms of prose." Whitman's prose influences included Emerson (and possibly Thoreau), British writers Thomas Carlyle and John Ruskin, and the King James Bible.

C Critical Thinking

Drawing Conclusions

? What can you conclude from the presence of handwritten revisions on Whitman's printed copy of his poem? [Possible response: He saw his work as a flexible document of his experiences and ideas—and wanted to incorporate new revisions even after publication. Nowhere is this more apparent than in the nine revised editions of *Leaves of Grass*.]

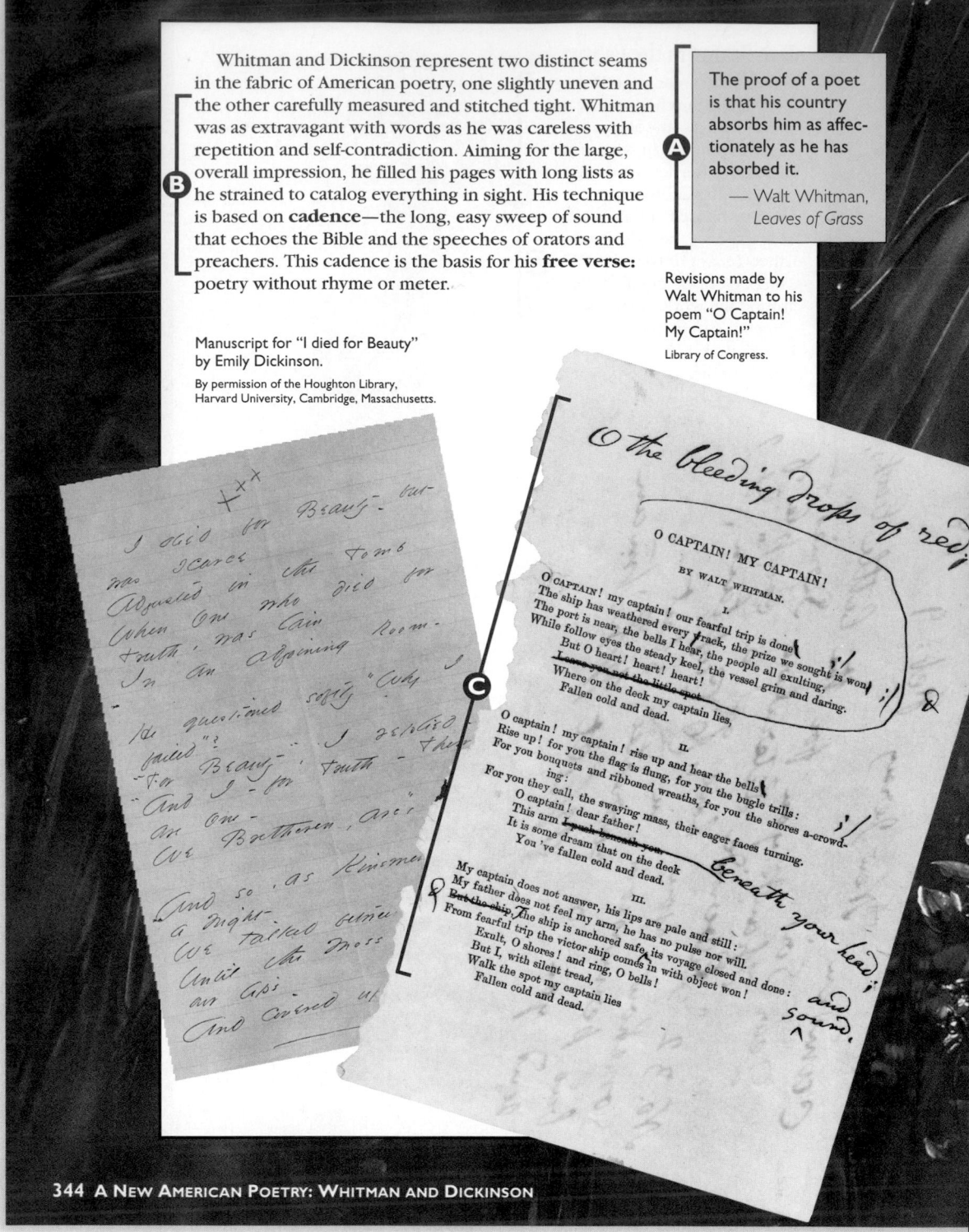

Whitman and Dickinson represent two distinct seams in the fabric of American poetry, one slightly uneven and the other carefully measured and stitched tight. Whitman was as extravagant with words as he was careless with repetition and self-contradiction. Aiming for the large, overall impression, he filled his pages with long lists as he strained to catalog everything in sight. His technique is based on **cadence**—the long, easy sweep of sound that echoes the Bible and the speeches of orators and preachers. This cadence is the basis for his **free verse:** poetry without rhyme or meter.

Manuscript for "I died for Beauty" by Emily Dickinson.

By permission of the Houghton Library, Harvard University, Cambridge, Massachusetts.

The proof of a poet is that his country absorbs him as affectionately as he has absorbed it.

— Walt Whitman,
Leaves of Grass

Revisions made by Walt Whitman to his poem "O Captain! My Captain!"

Library of Congress.

344 A NEW AMERICAN POETRY: WHITMAN AND DICKINSON

Crossing the Curriculum

Geography

Use a map of the United States to point out the wide range of Whitman's travels in an era without automobiles or airplanes. Ask students to discuss what role travel and varied experience play in the development of a poet, noting that Whitman and Dickinson differed greatly in this respect. Young writers are often advised "Write what you know." Ask students to discuss to what extent Whitman and Dickinson each followed this advice.

Social Studies

During the Civil War, Whitman worked in army hospitals, where he developed a passionate concern for public health and the economic improvement of working-class Americans. Ask students to research one or more of the political, social, and religious reform movements of the nineteenth century that focused on these goals. Students could share their findings with the class via oral reports or posters.

Art

Invite students to research the art of the period and to bring in pictures that exemplify nineteenth-century American artistic perspectives, particularly sweeping Romantic landscapes and fine miniaturist work, such as scrimshaw or needlework. As students become familiar with Whitman's and Dickinson's poetry, have them discuss how these works of visual art compare to the images evoked by the poetry.

Emily Dickinson's bedroom.

Dress that belonged to Emily Dickinson.

Dickinson, on the other hand, wrote with the precision of a diamond cutter. Meticulous in her choice of words, she aimed to evoke the feelings of things rather than simply to name them. She was always searching for the one right phrase that would fix a thought in the mind. Her technique is economical, and her neat stanzas are controlled by the demands of rhyme and the meters she found in her hymn book.

Dickinson used precise language and unique poetic forms to simultaneously reveal and conceal her private thoughts and feelings. Whitman, on the other hand, let loose his passion, philosophy, and observations in a torrent of language shaped by cadence rather than traditional meter.

Models for Future Poets

As the history of our poetry shows, both modes of expression have continued to be used by American writers. Both poets have served as models for twentieth-century poets who have been drawn to the visions they fulfilled and the techniques they mastered. Poetry as public speech written in the cadences of free verse remains a part of our literature; poetry as private observation, carefully crafted in rhyme and meter, still attracts young writers who tend to regard poems as experiences rather than as statements.

Walt Whitman
August 3 1884

Leaves

of

Grass.

Brooklyn, New York:
1855.

> **Emily Dickinson**
>
> Like you, I belong to yesterday,
> to the bays where
> day is anchored to
> wait for its hour.
>
> Like me, you belong to today,
> the progression of that hour
> when what is unborn
> begins to throb.
>
> We are cultivators of
> the unsayable, weavers
> of singulars, migrant
> workers in search of
> floating gardens as yet
> unsown, as yet unharvested.
>
> —Lucha Corpi, **E**
> *translated from the Spanish by
> Catherine Rodríguez-Nieto*

D

A NEW AMERICAN POETRY: WHITMAN AND DICKINSON **345**

Assessing Learning

Walt Whitman's birthplace, Long Island, N.Y.

Courtesy of the Walt Whitman Birthplace Association, South Huntington, Long Island, New York.

The coequal importance of the two poetic methods has never been more clearly affirmed than in the following words by Ezra Pound (see page 773). Pound speaks for himself here as a poet more attuned to the abbreviations of Dickinson than to the expansiveness of Whitman. Nevertheless, he offers in this poem a benediction that represents the feeling of every poet who has envied the gemlike artistry of Dickinson and the all-embracing power of Whitman:

B A Damascus blade gleaming and glancing in the sun was her wit. Her swift poetic rapture was like the long glistening note of a bird one hears in the June woods at high noon, but can never see. Like a magician she caught the shadowy apparitions of her brain and tossed them in startling picturesqueness to her friends, who, charmed with their simplicity and homeliness as well as profundity, fretted that she had so easily made palpable the tantalizing fancies forever eluding their bungling, fettered grasp.

C —*from* Susan Dickinson's obituary for Emily Dickinson, published in the *Springfield Republican*, May 18, 1886

A Pact

I make a pact with you, Walt Whitman—
I have detested you long enough.
I come to you as a grown child
Who has had a pig-headed father;
A I am old enough now to make friends.
It was you that broke the new wood,
Now is a time for carving.
We have one sap and one root—
Let there be commerce between us.

—Ezra Pound

Quickwrite

Whitman was a public poet; Dickinson, a private one. Yet both have had a lasting influence on American poets who have followed them. Write your thoughts and feelings about poetry. What do you think is the value of poetry? What roles can poets and poetry serve in contemporary life?

The Large Hearts of Heroes

Theme

An American Epic America has no oral epic tradition—no Beowulf, no Gilgamesh. Whitman gave America its first epic—a book of poems called Leaves of Grass that celebrated the poet as hero and that showed that the American voice could sing and speak of everything under the sun. Suddenly, American poetry was changed forever.

Reading the Anthology

Reaching Struggling Readers

The *Reading Skills and Strategies: Reaching Struggling Readers* binder provides materials coordinated with the Pupil's Edition (see the Collection Planner, p. T346B) to help students who have difficulty reading and comprehending text, or students who are reluctant readers. The binder for eleventh grade is organized around ten individual skill areas and offers the following options:

- **MiniRead** MiniReads are short, easy texts that give students a chance to practice a particular skill and strategy before reading selections in the Pupil's Edition. Each MiniRead Skill Lesson can be taught independently or used in conjunction with a Selection Skill Lesson.

- **Selection Skill Lessons** Selection Skill Lessons allow students to apply skills introduced in the MiniReads. Each Selection Skill Lesson provides reading instruction and practice specific to a particular piece of literature in the Pupil's Edition.

Reading Beyond the Anthology

Read On At the end of the New American Poetry collections, the grade eleven book includes an annotated bibliography of books suitable for extended reading. The suggested books are related to works in these collections by theme, by author, or by subject. To preview the Read On for the New American Poetry period, please turn to p. T397.

Collection 7 The Large Hearts of Heroes

Resources for this Collection

Note: All resources for this collection are available for preview on the *One-Stop Planner CD-ROM 2 with Test Generator.* All worksheets and blackline masters may be printed from the CD-ROM.

Internet Resources
go.hrw.com LE0 11-7

Selection or Feature	Reading and Literary Skills	Vocabulary, Language, and Grammar
I Hear America Singing (p. 351) *from* **Song of Myself** • **10. Alone far in the wilds...** (p. 353) • *from* **33. I understand the large hearts of heroes...** (p. 356) • **52. The spotted hawk swoops by...** (p. 359) Walt Whitman **Connections: Who Understands Me but Me** (p. 360) Jimmy Santiago Baca • **A Sight in Camp in the Day-break Gray and Dim** (p. 362) • **Primary Sources:** *from* **Specimen Days** (p. 363) Walt Whitman	• *Reading Skills and Strategies: Reaching Struggling Readers* • MiniRead Skill Lessons, pp. 33, 123 • Selection Skill Lessons, pp. 39, 129 • *Graphic Organizers for Active Reading,* Worksheet pp. 26, 27, 28, 29, 30 • *Literary Elements:* Transparency 12 Worksheet p. 37	• *Words to Own,* Worksheet p. 22 • *Grammar and Language Links:* Understanding Clauses, Worksheet p. 31 • *Language Workshop CD-ROM,* Independent and Subordinate Clauses • *Daily Oral Grammar,* Transparencies 24, 25
Literature of the Americas: Chile • **Plenos Poderes** (p. 368) • **Full Powers** (p. 368) Pablo Neruda *translated by* Ben Belitt and Alastair Reid	The Literature of the Americas feature offers selections from a variety of American cultures representing North, Central, and South America. These selections connect to the collection theme, and students explore the thematic links through structured group discussions called Finding Common Ground.	

Other Resources for this Collection

- *Cross-Curricular Activities*, p. 7
- *Portfolio Management System*, Introduction to Portfolio Assessment, p. 1
- *Formal Assessment*, Literary Period Introduction Test, p. 72

- *Test Generator*, Collection Test

Writing	Listening and Speaking Viewing and Representing	Assessment
• *Portfolio Management System*, Rubrics for Choices, p. 133	• *Audio CD Library*, Disc 10, Tracks 2, 3, 4, 5, 6, 7 • *Viewing and Representing:* Fine Art Transparency 7 Worksheet p. 28 • *Portfolio Management System*, Rubrics for Choices, p. 133	• *Formal Assessment*, Selection Test, p. 74 • *Test Generator (One-Stop Planner CD-ROM)* • *Preparation for College Admissions Exams*, p. 25
	• *Audio CD Library*, Disc 10, Track 8	

Transparency   CD-ROM   Video   Audio CD

Collection Planner

Skills Focus

Skills Focus

Selection or Feature	Reading Skills and Strategies	Elements of Literature and Language	Writing	Listening and Speaking	Viewing and Representing
I Hear America Singing (p. 351) *from* **Song of Myself** • **10. Alone far in the wilds ...** (p. 353) • *from* **33. I understand the large hearts of heroes ...** (p. 356) • **52. The spotted hawk swoops by ...** (p. 359) **A Sight in Camp in the Daybreak Gray and Dim** (p. 362) Walt Whitman	Summarizing a Text, p. 353 Support Inferences with Text Evidence, pp. 356 Compare Themes Across Texts, pp. 359, 361 Identify Sources, p. 362	Catalogs, pp. 351, 358 Images, pp. 355, 358, 364–365 Tone, pp. 355, 358, 364 Cadence, p. 355 Free Verse, p. 355 Meter, p. 355 Rhyme, p. 355 Alliteration, p. 355 Assonance, p. 355 Onomatopoeia, p. 355 Parallel Structure, p. 355 Repetition, p. 355 Rhythm, p. 355 First-Person Point of View, p. 358 Coda, p. 359 Theme, p. 361 Style, p. 361, 366 Message, pp. 361, 364 Setting, p. 364 Sound Effects, p. 365	Identify Points of Comparison and Contrast for Two Poets, p. 365 Write a Free-Verse Poem in the Tradition of Whitman, p. 365 Write an Essay Comparing and Contrasting Two Viewpoints of Nature, p. 365 Compare and Contrast an Author's Diction and Style in Two Genres, p. 366 Write Captions for Civil War Photographs, p. 366 Write an Essay Analyzing Whitman's Poems, p. 366	Read a Poem Aloud to Experience the Sound Structure, p. 355 Prepare and Present a Public Reading of Whitman's Poems, p. 365 Organize a Class Poetry Reading, p. 365 Play a Musical Tribute, p. 366	Design a New Cover for *Leaves of Grass*, p. 366 Create a Civil War Display, p. 366
Literature of the Americas: Chile • **Plenos Poderes** (p. 368) • **Full Powers** (p. 368) Pablo Neruda *translated by* Ben Belitt and Alastair Reid	Recognize Shared Characteristics of Cultures, pp. 368, 370	Images, p. 370	The Literature of the Americas feature offers selections from a variety of American cultures representing North, Central, and South America. These selections connect to the collection theme, and students explore the thematic links through structured group discussions called Finding Common Ground.		

Whitman
Neruda

from Song of Myself

1.

I celebrate myself, and sing myself,
And what I assume you shall assume,
For every atom belonging to me as good belongs to you.

I loaf and invite my soul,
I lean and loaf at my ease observing a spear of summer grass.

My tongue, every atom of my blood, form'd from this soil, this air,
Born here of parents born here from parents the same, and their
     parents the same,
I, now thirty-seven years old in perfect health begin,
Hoping to cease not till death.

Creeds and schools in abeyance,
Retiring back a while sufficed at what they are, but never forgotten,
I harbor for good or bad, I permit to speak at every hazard,
Nature without check with original energy.

—Walt Whitman, *from Leaves of Grass*

Writing Focus: Comparison-and-Contrast Essay

The following **Work in Progress** assignment in this collection builds to a culminating **Writer's Workshop** at the end of Collection 8.

- Poems of Walt Whitman   Take notes on how Whitman's poems differ from those of the Fireside Poets (p. 365)

Writer's Workshop: Expository Writing / Comparison-and-Contrast Essay (p. 401)

Walt Whitman

(1819–1892)

Less than a hundred years after the United States was founded, the new nation found its voice in a poet who spoke to all the world. His name was Walt Whitman, and he struck a note in literature that was as forthright, as original, and as deeply charged with democracy's energies as the land that produced him.

Student of the World

Whitman was born on May 31, 1819, to parents of Dutch and English descent. They kept a farm in West Hills, Long Island, in what is today the town of Huntington. His father's ancestors had come from England only twenty years after the landing of the *Mayflower* and had settled in Connecticut. On his mother's side, his ancestors were among the early immigrants from Holland who settled on Manhattan Island and along the Hudson River. Whitman and his seven brothers and sisters were able to assume their essential American-ness with an uncommon confidence. They knew their American grandparents, and they grew up in circumstances that allowed them both the communal experience of country life and the experience of Brooklyn, a new city on its way to becoming a metropolis.

Here young Walter went to school until he was eleven. He then worked as an office clerk and printer's assistant, and for a time he taught school. On weekends spent along the beaches and in the woods of Long Island, Whitman read Sir Walter Scott, the Bible, Shakespeare, Homer, Dante, and ancient Hindu poetry. He never became a scholar; he never went to college.

Before Whitman was twenty, his feeling for the written word and his fascination with the boomtown atmosphere of Brooklyn led him into journalism. After ten years of this, he took a kind of working vacation—a difficult overland trip by train, horse-drawn coach, and riverboat to New Orleans. There he put his journalistic talent to work for the *Crescent* and his own

talent for observation to work for himself. After a few months, he returned to New York by way of the Great Lakes and a side trip to Niagara Falls. By this time Whitman had added to his limited sense of America the experience of a wilderness surrendering its vastness to civilization. He also had become acquainted with the entirely alien culture that French Catholic New Orleans represented to him.

Back in Brooklyn, Whitman accepted an offer to become editor of the *Brooklyn Freeman*. For the next six or seven years, he supplemented his income as a part-time carpenter and building contractor. All this while, he was keeping notebooks and quietly putting together the sprawling collection of poems that would transform his life and change the course of American literature.

The Making of a Masterpiece

In 1855, Whitman published his collection at his own expense under the title *Leaves of Grass*. Since the book was too boldly new and strange to win the attention of reviewers or readers who had fixed ideas about poetry, its publication went all but unnoticed. To stir up interest in the book, he sent samples to people whose endorsement he thought might be useful. One of these samples reached Ralph Waldo Emerson, who at once wrote to Whitman the most important letter Whitman would ever receive:

> Concord, Massachusetts, 21 July, 1855
>
> Dear Sir—I am not blind to the worth of the wonderful gift of *Leaves of Grass*. I find it the most extraordinary piece of wit and wisdom that America has yet contributed. I am very happy in reading it, as great power makes us happy. It meets the demand I am always making of what seemed the sterile and stingy Nature, as if too much handiwork, or too much lymph in the temperament, were making our Western wits fat and mean.
>
> I give you joy of your free and brave thought. I have great joy in it. I find incomparable things said incomparably well, as they must be. I find the courage of treatment

go.hrw.com
LE0 11-7

Resources: Print and Media

Reading
- *Reading Skills and Strategies*
  MiniRead Skill Lessons, pp. 33, 123
  Selection Skill Lessons, pp. 39, 129
- *Graphic Organizers for Active Reading*, pp. 26, 27, 28, 29, 30
- *Audio CD Library*
  Disc 10, Tracks 2–7
- *Words to Own*, p. 22

Elements of Literature
- *Literary Elements*
  Transparency 12
  Worksheet, p. 37

Writing and Language
- *Daily Oral Grammar*
  Transparencies 24, 25
- *Grammar and Language Links*
  Worksheet, p. 31
- *Language Workshop CD-ROM*

Viewing and Representing
- *Viewing and Representing*
  Fine Art Transparency 7
  Fine Art Worksheet, p. 28

Assessment
- *Portfolio Management System*, p. 133
- *Test Generator (One-Stop Planner CD-ROM)*

Internet
- go.hrw.com (keyword: LE0 11-17)

which so delights us, and which large perception only can inspire.

I greet you at the beginning of a great career, which yet must have had a long foreground somewhere, for such a start. I rubbed my eyes a little, to see if this sunbeam were no illusion; but the solid sense of the book is a sober certainty. It has the best merits, namely, of fortifying and encouraging.

I did not know until I last night saw the book advertised in a newspaper that I could trust the name as real and available for a post-office. I wish to see my benefactor, and have felt much like striking my tasks and visiting New York to pay you my respects.

R. W. Emerson

The "long foreground" of which Emerson wrote had not been the careful, confident period of preparation to which many poets devote themselves before they are ready to publish. Instead, it had been a precarious existence. Journalism had kept Whitman going financially, but not even the editorials he wrote for the *Brooklyn Eagle* had brought him distinction. On the surface, at least, his "long foreground" of preparation had been a mixture of hack work and jack-of-all-trades ingenuity.

By the time he was ready to declare himself a poet and to publish the first version of his book, Walt Whitman was unique. *Leaves of Grass* is a masterpiece that Whitman was to expand and revise through many editions. Its process of growth did not end until the ninth, "deathbed" edition was published in 1891, thirty-six years after its first appearance. It is a spiritual autobiography that tells the story of an enchanted observer who says who he is at every opportunity and claims what he loves by naming it. "Camerado," he wrote, "this is no book / Who touches this touches a man."

In the Crowd, but Not of It

The figure we know today as Walt Whitman was conceived and created by the poet himself. Whitman endorsed his "image" and sold it to the public with a promoter's skill worthy of P. T. Barnum, the great show manager of the nineteenth century. At first glance that figure is a bundle of contradictions. Whitman seems to have had the theatrical flair of a con artist and the selfless dignity of a saint; the sensibility of an artist and the carefree spirit of a hobo; the blustery egotism of a braggart and the demure shyness of a shrinking violet. On second glance these contradictions disappear: Walt Whitman was everything he seemed to be. The figure he so carefully crafted and put on display was not a surrogate, but the man himself.

Walt Whitman.
Courtesy of Ohio Wesleyan University, Bayley-Whitman Collection, Delaware, Ohio.

Planning

- **Block Schedule**
  Block Scheduling Lesson Plans with Pacing Guide
- **Traditional Schedule**
  Lesson Plans Including Strategies for English-Language Learners
- **One-Stop Planner**
  CD-ROM with Test Generator

RESPONDING TO THE ART

This engraving, made from a contemporary photograph, decorated the first edition of *Leaves of Grass*. It was considered shocking in its day because of the poet's open-collared shirt, his work pants, and his casual posture.

Activity. Ask students to jot down answers to the following questions:

1. How would you characterize this man if you saw him in a shopping mall today? [Possible responses: He looks confident, casual, sure of himself, handsome; he looks like an aging hippie; he fits in, because he seems to be making a statement about his individuality, and today everyone does that.]

2. Why would Whitman choose to include this picture in his book? [Possible answers: to set himself apart from other poets; to emphasize his attempt to speak for all Americans, not just the upper class or the well educated.]

Professional Notes

Critical Comment:
The Common Man as Hero

According to literary critic Roger Asselineau, Whitman always maintained faith in the average American and in the strength of American democracy. He explains, "The civil war revealed to him the heroism and the spirit of sacrifice of the average American and confirmed his faith in man 'en-masse.' . . . When he happened to sing of Lincoln . . . he showed him . . . not as a great leader of men, but . . . as a magnificent example of the virtues of the average man whom power does not corrupt."

"One would see him afar off," wrote the great naturalist John Burroughs, "in the crowd but not of it—a large, slow-moving figure, clad in gray, with broad-brimmed hat and gray beard—or, quite as frequently, on the front platform of the street horse-cars with the driver. . . . Whitman was of large mold in every way, and of bold, far-reaching schemes, and is very sure to fare better at the hands of large men than of small. The first and last impression which his personal presence always made upon one was of a nature wonderfully gentle, tender, and benignant. . . . I was impressed by the fine grain and clean, fresh quality of the man. . . . He always had the look of a man who had just taken a bath."

If there is a side of Whitman that today we would associate with "image building," or self-promotion, there is nothing in his poetry to suggest that it was anything but the product of the kind of genius that permanently changes the history of art. He modified standard, "King's English" diction and abandoned traditional rhyme schemes and formal meters in favor of the rhythms and speech patterns of free verse.

Everything Under the Sun

The result was poetry that could sing and speak of everything under the sun. Its sweep was easy and its range was broad. Suddenly, poetry was no longer a matter of organized word structures that neatly clicked shut at the last line; instead, it was a series of open-ended units of rhythm that flowed one into the other and demanded to be read in their totality.

> The result was poetry that could sing and speak of everything under the sun.

"Whitman throws his chunky language at the reader," writes the critic Paul Zweig. "He cajoles and thunders; he chants, celebrates, chuckles, and caresses. He spills from his capacious American soul every dreg of un-Englishness, every street sound thumbing its nose at traditional subject matter and tone. Here is Samson pulling the house of literature down around his ears, yet singing in the ruins."

Walt Whitman had invented a way of writing poetry that perfectly accommodated his way of seeing. His form is loose enough to allow for long lists and catalogs abundant in detail; it is also flexible enough to include delicate moments of lyricism as well as stretches of blustering oratory. This form served Whitman as observer and prophet—as a private man tending the wounded in the hospital wards of the Civil War, and as the public man who gave voice to the grief of a nation in his great elegy for the slain Abraham Lincoln, "When Lilacs Last in the Dooryard Bloom'd."

An American Epic

When Whitman died in 1892, he had met a great personal goal. He had enlarged the possibilities of American poetry to include the lyricism of simple speech and the grand design of the epic.

How is *Leaves of Grass* like an epic? Who is its hero? What is its action? The hero is the poet, and he is a hero not of the ancient past but of the future. As in all epics, the action takes the form of a journey. In *Leaves of Grass,* the journey is the one the speaker takes as he becomes a poet:

> I am the poet of the Body and I am the poet of the Soul . . .
> I am the poet of the woman the same as the man . . .
> I am not the poet of goodness only, I do not decline to be the poet of wickedness also. . . .

By the end of his epic journey, which even takes him down into a kind of hell, the poet has also been transformed. The "I" has become identified with every element in the universe and has been reborn as something divine. The poet has become the saving force that Whitman believed was the true role of the American poet.

Nothing quite like it had ever been done in America before.

Professional Notes

Critical Comment: Whitman's Readers

American literature scholar Sculley Bradley suggests that Whitman was the only poet who was "persistently overrated and steadily underrated at the same time and for so long. . . . Yet men so diverse as Emerson, Lincoln, Burroughs, and Ingersoll were impressed by the man or his work, and even Tennyson, who lived in a totally different world, saw in Whitman 'a great big something' which he could not quite identify as a poet." Once students have finished reading Whitman's work, ask them to elaborate on Tennyson's comment about Whitman. What is that "great big something" that the English poet saw in the American?

Before You Read

I HEAR AMERICA SINGING

Make the Connection

Work of Their Own

This famous lyric appears in *Leaves of Grass* and serves to introduce one of the poet's major themes: America's cultural diversity. In this poem, Whitman celebrates work through the "varied carols" of men and women who take pride in their occupations.

Quickwrite

Why do you think a poet who celebrates American culture would focus on work songs rather than on love songs or some other kind of song? Write down the sorts of jobs you would expect to be celebrated in a truly American epic written today.

Elements of Literature

Catalog

One of the most obvious characteristics of Whitman's poetry is his frequent use of **catalogs**— long lists of related things, people, or events. Keep an eye out for catalogs in this poem and others by Whitman.

Summary ∎

In this lyric poem, Whitman's first-person, all-embracing "I" catalogs the unique "songs" expressed by the labors of mechanics, carpenters, masons, shoemakers, young wives, seamstresses, and other ordinary workers. The poem celebrates the spirit of candor and joy that infuses these Americans working for themselves and for their country.

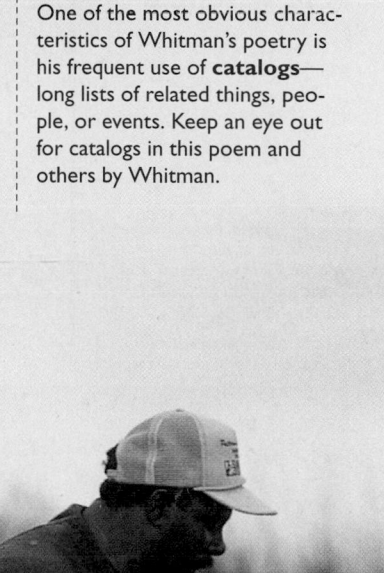

BROWSING IN THE FILES

Critical Comment. Critic Roger Asselineau explains Whitman's love of catalogs by saying that the poet felt "mysterious correspondences" existed between words and reality. He says that for Whitman it was often enough to put a word down on paper to evoke the object that it represented. The poet loved to draw up long lists of words, which sometimes seemed monotonous to those readers who did not lend credence to this mystical connection between words and reality. For Whitman, however, these lists were as rich and moving as reality itself. "They enabled him to become one with all the things he named in turn and mystically to annex the universe to himself."

WALT WHITMAN 351

Reaching All Students

Struggling Readers

One useful strategy for helping students understand and connect with this poem is called Sketch to Stretch. For information on using this strategy, see the *Reading Strategies Handbook*, p. 101 in the the *Reading Skills and Strategies* binder.

English Language Learners

Have students list nouns and verbs in the poem that are unfamiliar to them. Work with students by providing definitions of the words or displaying appropriate pictures. For instance, in "I Hear America Singing," you might explain that the word *carol* means a song of joyous praise as in a Christmas carol, or the word *fire-lock* in "Song, #10" refers to a rifle. Once you have answered students' questions, ask them to reread the poem and develop summary statements.

Advanced Learners

Encourage students to notice the rich connotations of Whitman's diction in this collection. For example, a blanket covering dead soldiers is called "ample"; the sun is described as "runaway"; shipwrecked infants are called "old-faced." Ask students to select and analyze examples of word choice they find especially evocative. Challenge them to offer and analyze possible alternative choices using a dictionary and thesaurus.

I Hear America Singing

Walt Whitman

I hear America singing, the varied carols I hear,

A Those of mechanics, each one singing his as it should be blithe and strong,

The carpenter singing his as he measures his plank or beam,

B The mason singing his as he makes ready for work, or leaves off work,

The boatman singing what belongs to him in his boat, the deckhand
5   singing on the steamboat deck,

The shoemaker singing as he sits on his bench, the hatter singing as he stands,

The wood-cutter's song, the plowboy's on his way in the morning, or at noon intermission or at sundown,

The delicious singing of the mother, or of the young wife at work, or of the girl sewing or washing,

Each singing what belongs to him or her and to none else,

C The day what belongs to the day—at night the party of young
10   fellows, robust, friendly,

Singing with open mouths their strong melodious songs.

Construction of the Dam (1937) by William Gropper. Mural study, Department of the Interior, National Park Service.

National Museum of American Art, Washington, D.C./Courtesy Art Resource, NY.

MAKING MEANINGS

First Thoughts

1. Imagine what kinds of singing Whitman might hear if he were alive today. In what ways might these "songs" be different from those he heard in his own time? In what ways would they be the same as what he heard? Before you answer, review your Quickwrite notes.

Shaping Interpretations

2. Perhaps what Whitman has in mind here are not the actual work songs associated with various trades, but something more subtle. What would you say this poem is really about?

3. A feeling of acceptance, even of contentment, runs throughout the sounds of these many voices. Considering the long hours and small pay of laborers in the nineteenth century, would you say Whitman is romanticizing or idealizing their lot? Or would you say the songs he hears are expressions of independence and joy in life? Support your response with specific references to the poem.

352 A NEW AMERICAN POETRY: WHITMAN AND DICKINSON

Side column (teacher notes)

A Critical Thinking
Hypothesizing

? Why does the speaker say that each person's singing *should be* "blithe and strong"? [He believes, like Emerson and Thoreau, that each should express his or her individuality, without fear.]

B Critical Thinking
Interpreting

? Look at Gropper's mural and the occupations Whitman mentions. Who does Whitman seem to feel is truly building America? [working-class men and women]

C Struggling Readers
Reading Elliptical Constructions

Tell students that **elliptical constructions** are sentences with words left out. Ask them what they think "The day what belongs to the day" might mean. [Possible response: "The day is singing what belongs to the day."]

D Elements of Literature
Catalog

? This whole poem can be viewed as a catalog. What is Whitman celebrating with this list? [the optimistic, energetic, joyous spirit of working Americans who take pride in their labors—each with a different task and a different personality]

RESPONDING TO THE ART

William Gropper (1897–1977) became a social-protest painter after he was dismissed from the *New York Tribune* for his radical political views.

Activity. Ask students to discuss how the mural relates to the poem. [Both idealize the heroism and beauty of the ordinary worker.]

MAKING MEANINGS

First Thoughts [Apply]

1. Possible response: Whitman might hear the songs of office and assembly-line workers, fast-food employees, and other service-industry workers. Because of the high-stress atmosphere of many contemporary work environments, Whitman might hear more sighing than singing.

Shaping Interpretations [Interpret]

2. Possible response: It is about the diversity of America and the value of each person's self-expression in work and culture.

3. Possible response: It is a romanticized view, considering these workers had little control over their lives and were often exploited; yet perhaps Whitman's point is deeper than this; perhaps he would find the same inspiration and independence even in the frustrations and struggles of these workers.

Crossing the Curriculum

Social Studies

How many people do students know who are hatters? How many people today make a living as wood cutters or lumberjacks? Ask students to research some of the common occupations people had during Whitman's lifetime and to create a poster that depicts occupations that no longer play an important role in society, those that have disappeared altogether, and those that are still important but have changed greatly.

Make the Connection

The Poet as Director

Here the speaker both observes and participates in the diversity of American experience. Whitman carefully juxtaposes different scenes and emotions in these movielike glimpses into the broad American scene. The speaker presents himself as though he were not only the cinematographer who shoots the pictures but also the director behind each scene who arranges just what each frame will look like.

Reading Skills and Strategies

Summarizing a Text

As you read this poem, pay attention to the arrangement of details and images. Then, as an aid in understanding the text, briefly summarize the scene presented in each stanza.

from Song of Myself

Walt Whitman

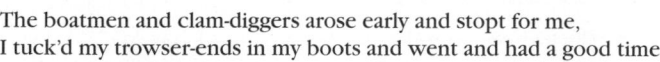

10.

Alone far in the wilds and mountains I hunt,
Wandering amazed at my own lightness and glee, **Ⓐ**
In the late afternoon choosing a safe spot to pass the night, **Ⓑ**
Kindling a fire and broiling the fresh-kill'd game,
5 Falling asleep on the gather'd leaves with my dog and gun by my side.

The Yankee clipper is under her sky-sails,° she cuts the sparkle and scud,° **Ⓒ**
My eyes settle the land, I bend at her prow or shout joyously from the deck.

The boatmen and clam-diggers arose early and stopt for me,
I tuck'd my trowser-ends in my boots and went and had a good time;
10 You should have been with us that day round the chowder-kettle.

I saw the marriage of the trapper in the open air in the far west, the bride was a red girl, **Ⓓ**
Her father and his friends sat near cross-legged and dumbly smoking, they had moccasins to
   their feet and large thick blankets hanging from their shoulders,
On a bank lounged the trapper, he was drest mostly in skins, his luxuriant beard and curls
   protected his neck, he held his bride by the hand,
She had long eyelashes, her head was bare, her coarse straight locks descended upon her
   voluptuous limbs and reach'd to her feet.

6. **sky-sails:** small sails atop a square-rigged mast. **scud:** windblown sea spray or foam.

WALT WHITMAN **353**

Reaching All Students

Struggling Readers

Summarizing was introduced on p. 353. For a lesson directly tied to this selection that teaches students to summarize with strategies called Text Reformulation and Most Important Word, see the *Reading Skills and Strategies* binder:
• MiniRead Skill Lesson, p. 123
• Selection Skill Lesson, p. 129

Using Students' Strengths

Naturalist Learners

Ask students to report on nineteenth-century trapping or hunting of beavers, buffalo, and wolves (the latter spurred by a federal bounty). Students should report on the purpose of these undertakings, the immediate results, and the long-term consequences. Students might also research the recent comeback of beaver or the attempts to reintroduce buffalo and wolves to selected areas in the West.

Summary ■■

In this excerpt from "Song of Myself," the speaker recounts his experiences hunting in the wilderness, sharing chowder with clam-diggers, witnessing a trapper's marriage into a Native American family, and sheltering a runaway slave. These vignettes convey Whitman's vision of a self that embraces nature, others, and the cosmos.

Resources

Viewing and Representing
Fine Art Transparency

The Fine Art Transparency of Miriam Schapiro's *I'm Dancin' as Fast as I Can* conveys the same energy and exuberance that is found in Whitman's poetry. See the *Viewing and Representing Transparencies and Worksheets:*
• Transparency 7
• Worksheet, p. 28

Ⓐ Struggling Readers

Deciphering Syntax

❓ Reread the first stanza as if it were a prose sentence. What is the simple subject? [I] What is the simple predicate? [hunt] Discuss the function of the participial phrases in the introductory stanza: "Wandering . . . ," "Kindling . . . ," "Falling . . ."

Ⓑ Elements of Literature

Free Verse

Read this stanza aloud or play the recording in the *Audio CD Library.* Ask what makes the stanza free verse. [the lack of regular rhyme and meter] Tell students that the poem does not sound like prose: cadenced lines add rhythm and melody, while words like *lightness, glee, asleep,* and *leaves* produce alliteration and assonance.

Ⓒ Cultural Connections

Yankee Clippers

Clipper ships were some of the fastest and most popular sailing vessels of the nineteenth century. Speed was a priority in shipping—to be first with tea from China or gold from California.

Ⓓ English Language Learners

Cultural Concepts and Idioms

Inform students that the adjective *red* was used (inaccurately) to refer to Native Americans.

A Reading Skills and Strategies

Summarizing a Text

To help students summarize ll. 16–24, point out that the stanza is a catalog of actions that the speaker did to help a runaway slave. Work with students to list the key verbs on the board. [*heard, saw, went, led, assured, brought, filled, gave, gave, remember, remember, stayed, was recuperated, pass'd, had (him) sit, lean'd*] Once all the verbs appear in order, students should be able to flesh out the summary.

B Historical Connections

Whitman as Free-Soiler

Historical context is important to an understanding of "Song of Myself," #10. By 1848, Whitman was a "Free-Soiler"—a member of a political party opposed to the acquisition of more territory in which slavery would be legal. That year he was a delegate to the party's New York convention, a sign of his strong feelings against slavery long before the Civil War.

C Elements of Literature

Theme

Have students recall the title of the poem from which this excerpt is taken and discuss how such varied images of America can represent one person.

RESPONDING TO THE ART

Alfred Jacob Miller (1810–1874) might never have become the first important painter of the American West had he not met a Scottish adventurer who wanted to decorate his family castle with paintings of American Indians. Previously a Baltimore portrait painter, Miller joined William Drummond Stewart's wagon train from Missouri to the Rockies in 1837, his only duty being to sketch what he liked.

Activity. Ask students what phrases from "Song of Myself," #10 could be used as titles for this painting. [Possible responses: "Alone far in the wilds" (l. 1); "choosing a safe spot to pass the night" (l. 3); "the trapper" (l. 11).]

T354

---

15 The runaway slave came to my house and stopt outside,
I heard his motions crackling the twigs of the woodpile,
Through the swung half-door of the kitchen I saw him limpsy° and weak,
And went where he sat on a log and led him in and assured him,
And brought water and fill'd a tub for his sweated body and bruis'd feet,
And gave him a room that enter'd from my own, and gave him some coarse clean
20   clothes,
And remember perfectly well his revolving eyes and his awkwardness,
And remember putting plasters on the galls° of his neck and ankles;
He stayed with me a week before he was recuperated and pass'd north,
I had him sit next me at table, my fire-lock lean'd in the corner.

17. limpsy: limp; exhausted.
22. galls: sores.

Lost on the Prairie (1837) by Alfred Jacob Miller. Watercolor on paper (9¼″ × 13½″).
Stark Museum of Art, Orange, Texas.

Skill Link

Understanding Point of View

Remind students that point of view is the vantage point from which a writer tells a story. In the first-person point of view, one of the characters tells the story, using first-person pronouns, such as *I* and *we*. In the omniscient point of view, an all-knowing narrator tells the story, using third-person pronouns, such as *he, she,* and *they*. Whitman puts his own characteristic twist on point of view. His first-person narrator is omniscient: a universal speaker who can enter any consciousness and yet remain *I*.

Activities

1. Ask students to find and list examples of the omniscient first-person point of view in the poems.
2. Have small groups of students write Whitmanesque catalogs using this point of view. Have each member contribute a line, with each line describing a different type of person who might be seen in the United States today.

First Thoughts

1. What **images** of sight, touch, and sound in this poem are most vivid to you?

Shaping Interpretations

2. In the five stanzas of this poem, the speaker observes and participates in five American scenes. Look at the summaries you made while reading, and describe the scene in each stanza. What feelings did each scene evoke?

3. Whitman changes the **tone** of this poem when he describes the fourth and fifth scenes. Identify the tone of the first three scenes. What is the tone of the last two scenes? What effect do you think the poet hoped to create by changing the tone?

4. When you read the poem aloud, what repetitions of sentence patterns help to create a **cadence**—a rhythmic rise and fall of your voice as the lines are spoken aloud? What feelings does the cadence create?

5. In the last scene, the "runaway slave" is one of thousands who entrusted their lives to those who would help them escape. What do you think the stanza—especially the last line—shows about the speaker's relationship with his guest?

Connecting with the Text

6. If you could drop yourself into one particular American setting today, which would you choose? Explain your response.

ELEMENTS OF LITERATURE

Free Verse

Today we are so used to poetry written in free verse that we take it for granted. But in Whitman's time, Americans preferred poetry that was like the poetry being written in England; they expected a poem to show the very strictest concern for **meter** and **rhyme**. Thus, Whitman's sprawling lines were revolutionary, as was his daring use of American slang, foreign words, and words he occasionally made up to suit his purpose.

Free verse is poetry that is written without concern for regular rhyme schemes and meter. But free verse is not really free at all. Whitman abandoned meter and regular rhyme schemes, but he made full use of these other literary elements:

- **Alliteration:** the repetition of similar consonant sounds
- **Assonance:** the repetition of similar vowel sounds
- **Imagery:** the use of language to evoke visual pictures, as well as sensations of smell, hearing, taste, and touch
- **Onomatopoeia:** the use of words whose sounds echo their meaning (such as *buzz*)
- **Parallel structure:** the repetition of the same or similar words, phrases, clauses, or sentences

When you read Whitman's lines aloud, you hear **cadence,** the run of words that rise and fall in emphasis when he has a particular point to make and measures his lines to emphasize it. As you can see from Whitman's poems, cadence does not depend on any strict count of stressed syllables.

Poets who, like Whitman, choose to write in cadence have nothing but their own sense of balance and proportion to tell them when a line should end and when it should continue. They must rely completely on their own sense of spacing and timing, and on their own feelings about what sounds right to them.

In the twentieth century, many poets have accepted the challenge of writing in free verse, trusting their own sense of balance and measure. A poem written in regular meter might be compared to a metronome, which keeps a predictable, mechanical beat. Free verse, on the other hand, might be compared to the style of a jazz drummer, who may vary the beat throughout a performance.

Reading aloud. To best hear Whitman's cadences, you should read his poems aloud. In the collection opener, "Song of Myself," Number 1 (page 347), you should hear no fewer than thirty-three occurrences of the same consonant sound. What sound do you hear? What other examples of **repetition** help create the **rhythms** and music in Whitman's supposedly "free" verse?

4. The cadence is created by a sequence of present participles in ll. 4–5 (kindling, broiling, falling) and the repetition of verbs connected by "and" in ll. 18–22. The cadence might be seen to create a feeling of passing time or to evoke the rhythms of physical labor.

5. Possible responses: The speaker sees the man as a guest; he treats the guest with kindness; it may suggest that the speaker and the guest trust each other or that the speaker is ready to defend the man from bounty hunters or slave holders.

Connecting with the Text [Apply]

6. Responses will vary. Students may choose settings such as rock concerts, sporting events, or city coffee shops.

ELEMENTS OF LITERATURE

Free Verse

To review these concepts, divide the class into groups of four; each group should make lists of examples of the literary elements in popular songs and in poetry they have read. Ideally, each student should contribute at least one example of each element. Groups should share their lists with the class. If possible, put at least one advanced student in each group.

Reading Aloud

The most-repeated consonant sound is *s*. Other examples of repetition include alliteration in words beginning with *b, p, n, h, l,* and *th*; assonance in words with long and short *a* and *e* sounds; repetition of key words such as *myself, loaf, my,* and *parents*; and parallel structure in, for example, "I celebrate myself, and sing myself."

Once students have finished looking at "Song of Myself," #1, have them practice analyzing the verse in another one of Whitman's poems.

MAKING MEANINGS

First Thoughts [Respond]

1. Students might mention any detail, from the Yankee clipper to the rifle in the corner.

Shaping Interpretations [Interpret]

2. (1) Hunting in uncharted wilderness—contentment; (2) sailing a Yankee clipper—joy, exhilaration; (3) clamming by the shore—camaraderie, humor; (4) witnessing a far West marriage—admiration, curiosity;

(5) helping a runaway slave—compassion, sorrow.

3. In the first three scenes, the speaker is joyous. In the fourth, his tone is more reverent and thoughtful. In the fifth, he describes the runaway slave with somber, emotional lyricism. The change of tone helps create a poignant and subtly ironic contrast with the optimistic patriotism of the first three stanzas.

Summary ■■

The speaker pays tribute to a group of unsung heroes, taking on their voices and perspectives: a skipper in a storm at sea, a mother burnt as a witch in front of her children, a runaway slave hunted by men on horseback, a fire-man crushed by a collapsing building, and a dying general under fire. The speaker identifies with each person and proclaims, "All these I feel or am."

Ⓐ Elements of Literature
Free Verse

Encourage students to point out examples of literary elements used in these lines of free verse, particularly parallel structure [the parallel lines beginning "How he" and "How the"] and cadence [the bounding, conversational rhythm of the linked clauses].

Ⓑ Reading Skills and Strategies
Making Inferences

❓ What does this passage imply about Whitman's *I*, this speaker who states "I am the man, I suffer'd, I was there"? [Possible answer: that Whitman's speaker is larger than any one person. It is both the omniscient voice of the nation or of the human condition and Whitman's own swaggering, empathetic persona.]

Ⓒ Reading Skills and Strategies

Supporting Inferences with Text Evidence

❓ What does the speaker admire about the "disdain and calmness of martyrs"? Use text evidence to explain how Whitman dramatizes these qualities. [In these portraits of the mother and the runaway, Whitman emphasizes their quiet dignity in moments of injustice and defeat, noting poignant details like the gaze of the children and the panting of the runaway by the fence.]

Make the Connection
"All these I feel or am"

Much of Whitman's work is distinguished by his attempt to erase the line between observer and object. The poet does this in order to—imaginatively speaking—*become* the thing or person he is talking about. Whitman is capable not only of sympathy, but also of *empathy*—the ability to share in another's thoughts or feelings. This excerpt from the thirty-third section of "Song of Myself" includes one of Whitman's most famous lines: "I am the man, I suffer'd, I was there." Through empathy, Whitman explores the greatness of heart that characterizes some unlikely heroes.

Reading Skills and Strategies

Supporting Inferences with Text Evidence

Throughout "Song of Myself," Whitman honors individuals whose hardships and courageous acts make them true heroes. As you read, write down words and phrases that reveal Whitman's ability to feel empathy for those quite different from himself.

from Song of Myself
Walt Whitman

from 33.

I understand the large hearts of heroes,
The courage of present times and all times,
How the skipper saw the crowded and rudderless wreck of
    the steam-ship, and Death chasing it up and down the
    storm,
How he knuckled tight and gave not back an inch, and was
    faithful of days and faithful of nights,
And chalk'd in large letters on a board, *Be of good cheer, we
    will not desert you;*
5 How he follow'd with them and tack'd with them three days
    and would not give it up,
How he saved the drifting company at last,
How the lank loose-gown'd women look'd when boated from
    the side of their prepared graves,
How the silent old-faced infants and the lifted sick, and the
    sharp-lipp'd unshaved men;
10 All this I swallow, it tastes good, I like it well, it becomes mine,
I am the man, I suffer'd, I was there.°

The disdain and calmness of martyrs,
The mother of old, condemn'd for a witch, burnt with dry
    wood, her children gazing on,
The hounded slave that flags in the race, leans by the fence,
    blowing, cover'd with sweat,
The twinges that sting like needles his legs and neck, the
15   murderous buckshot and the bullets,
All these I feel or am.

356 A NEW AMERICAN POETRY: WHITMAN AND DICKINSON

1–11. I understand . . . I was there: This stanza was inspired by an actual incident that occurred in 1853. According to reports in the New York *Weekly Tribune* of January 21, 1854, the ship *San Francisco* sailed from New York City on December 22, 1853, destined for South America. A violent storm hit the ship several hundred miles out of port, washing many passengers overboard. The captain of another ship helped rescue the survivors. A copy of the newspaper story was found among Whitman's papers after his death.

Taking a Second Look

Review:
Recognizing Modes of Persuasion

Remind students that telling an anecdote, or brief story, is an effective technique of persuasion. Anecdotes engage the audience's emotions as well as intellect and allow the author to explore shared values without didacticism. For example, Thoreau's anecdote about the ant war (pp. 240–241) contains an implicit message about the petty and senseless nature of human war.

Activity

Divide students into groups of five. Have each group identify the anecdotes in "Song of Myself," #33. Some are as brief as one line (l. 13); others are longer (ll. 3–9). Then have the group discuss what values and ideas each anecdote implies. Students should take turns jotting down the anecdotes, the implied values, and the persuasive elements in a three-column chart.

A Ride for Liberty—The Fugitive Slaves (c. 1862) by Eastman Johnson. Oil on board
(22" × 26¼").

I am the hounded slave, I wince at the bite of the dogs,
Hell and despair are upon me, crack and again crack the
   marksmen,
I clutch the rails of the fence, my gore dribs,° thinn'd with the
   ooze of my skin,
20 I fall on the weeds and stones,
The riders spur their unwilling horses, haul close,
Taunt my dizzy ears and beat me violently over the head with
   whip-stocks.

Agonies are one of my changes of garments,
I do not ask the wounded person how he feels, I myself
   become the wounded person,
25 My hurts turn livid upon me as I lean on a cane and observe.

I am the mash'd fireman with breast-bone broken,
Tumbling walls buried me in their debris,
Heat and smoke I inspired,° I heard the yelling shouts of my
   comrades,
I heard the distant click of their picks and shovels,
30 They have clear'd the beams away, they tenderly lift me forth.

19. **dribs:** dribbles.

28. **inspired:** breathed in.

 D
 E

WALT WHITMAN 357

Making the Connections

Connecting to the Subject:
"The Large Heart of Heroes"

Some of our most notable contemporary heroes have been participants in America's space program. These include Neil Armstrong, the first man to set foot on the moon, and John Glenn, the first American to orbit the earth. In 1998, Glenn, who first went into space in 1962, returned there, at age seventy-seven, aboard NASA's space shuttle. Whitman would have approved. In "Night on the Prairie," the poet writes: "Now while the great thoughts of space and eternity fill me I will measure myself by them, / And now touch'd with the lives of other globes arrived as far along as those of the earth, / Or waiting to arrive, or pass'd on farther than those of the earth, / I henceforth no more ignore them than I ignore my own life, . . ."

Ask students to discuss why Whitman would feel that it is heroic to explore "other globes."

RESPONDING TO THE ART

First a portraitist and then a painter of popular sentimental scenes, (Jonathan) Eastman Johnson (1824–1906) became skilled at communicating story and mood by juxtaposing human figures against atmospheric landscapes.

Activity. Although the painting does not literally illustrate Whitman's lines about the hounded runaway (ll. 14–22), its details help create a mood appropriate for that anecdote. Ask students to identify these details. [Possible responses: The eerie sky and blurred ground suggest a twilight or predawn escape; the child seems barely awake; the man focuses on the goal ahead; the woman looks over her shoulder for pursuers; the horse's flowing tail suggests desperate speed; all these details convey the same urgency, fear, and danger as Whitman's anecdote does.]

D Reading Skills and Strategies
Supporting Inferences with Text Evidence

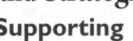

? What evidence of the speaker's omniscient empathy emerges in these lines? [Possible responses: He says he wears the agonies of others; he is able to "become" the wounded person; he evokes the slave's pain in excruciating detail ("my gore dribs", "beat me violently over the head . . .") and even identifies with the feelings of the "unwilling" horses.]

E Elements of Literature
Point of View

? What shift in point of view takes place in the third stanza? [Instead of describing the "hounded slave" in the third person, as he does the heroes in the first two stanzas, the speaker switches completely to the first-person point of view, in effect taking on the perspective of the slave.] What lines in stanzas one and two prepare the way for this shift? [lines 11 and 16]

T357

Ⓐ Reading Skills and Strategies

Supporting Inferences with Text Evidence

? What words, phrases, and details establish the speaker's identification with and empathy for the artillerist and his general? [Possible responses: "I am there again" (l. 38); "I take part, I see and hear the whole" (l. 42); "gasps through the clot *Mind not me*" (l. 49).]

Ⓑ Elements of Literature

Free Verse

? How does Whitman use literary elements to produce a dramatic, yet irregular, rhythm in these lines? How does it enhance the scene of the attack? [The repetition of the word *again* emphasizes the constant bombardment; the shorter lines might resemble the bursts of cannon fire; the alliterative use of the letter *r* helps to evoke the sounds of drums and artillery.]

MAKING MEANINGS

First Thoughts [Respond]

1. Students may be impressed by the diversity of heroes and heroines or moved by individual scenes, such as the burning of the mother.

Shaping Interpretations [Interpret]

2. Possible Answers: "I suffer'd, I was there"; "All these I feel or am." Students should cite details that appeal to the senses.

3. He makes restatements in ll. 16, 17, 26, 36, 37, 38, and 42. These restatements force the reader back into the immediacy and drama of the scenes. They also develop the character of Whitman's compassionate and flamboyant speaker.

4. The tone is empathetic, taking pride in the heroes' courage and mourning their suffering and loss.

5. Short lines are usually the most emphatic and personal; see ll. 11, 16, 38, and 42. They might be spoken slowly and forcefully.

6. Whitman's heroes are people who suffer or sacrifice themselves in the pursuit of justice, honor, or compassion. They are all martyrs or risk becoming martyrs.

I lie in the night air in my red shirt, the pervading hush is for
   my sake,
Painless after all I lie exhausted but not so unhappy,
White and beautiful are the faces around me, the heads are
   bared of their fire-caps,
The kneeling crowd fades with the light of the torches.

35 Distant and dead resuscitate,
They show as the dial or move as the hands of me, I am the
   clock myself.

I am an old artillerist, I tell of my fort's bombardment,
I am there again.

Ⓑ 40 Again the long roll of the drummers,
Again the attacking cannon, mortars,
Again to my listening ears the cannon responsive.

I take part, I see and hear the whole,
The cries, curses, roar, the plaudits for well-aim'd shots,
Ⓐ The ambulanza° slowly passing trailing its red drip,
Workmen searching after damages, making indispensable
45   repairs,
The fall of grenades through the rent roof, the fan-shaped
   explosion,
The whizz of limbs, heads, stone, wood, iron, high in the air.

Again gurgles the mouth of my dying general, he furiously
   waves with his hand,
He gasps through the clot *Mind not me—mind—the
   entrenchments.*

44. ambulanza (äm·boo·länt′sə): Italian for "ambulance."

MAKING MEANINGS

First Thoughts

1. How did you respond to Whitman's **catalog** of heroic individuals? Which details packed the strongest emotional punch?

Shaping Interpretations

2. Look back at your reading notes. What words and phrases indicate Whitman's empathy with heroic people? What **images** of sight and sound help us feel we also are there?

3. At what moments does the speaker restate the point that "I am the man, I suffer'd, I was there"? What is the effect of these restatements?

4. How would you describe the speaker's **tone**? What are his feelings for these heroes?

5. Notice the way Whitman alternates between groups of very long lines and groups of very short lines. What is the reason for each short line? How would you use your voice in reading each short line aloud?

6. What do the heroes Whitman describes suggest about the poet's concept of heroism?

Connecting with the Text

7. Whitman empathizes with people by using the pronoun *I*. How does his use of the **first-person point of view** affect you as you read this poem?

Extending the Text

8. If you could add a contemporary hero to this poem, whom would you choose, and why?

Connecting with the Text [Apply]

7. His use of the first-person helps readers to empathize with the heroes in the poem, just as the speaker does.

Extending the Text [Synthesize]

8. Possible response: Martin Luther King, Jr. and Nelson Mandela, because they stood up for what they believed in and suffered for it.

Before You Read

FROM SONG OF MYSELF, 52

Make the Connection

Highly Personal

In this final song, Whitman restates some of the **themes** that have run throughout "Song of Myself." The poet weaves these themes in and out of this final verse like a composer filling a song with familiar refrains. Since the most insistently present element throughout "Song of Myself" is the mind and spirit of the speaker himself, this passage is highly personal. True to his nature, Whitman mocks his own egotism. But, true to his confidence in himself, he also proclaims his importance—and his inescapability.

Reading Skills and Strategies

Comparing Themes Across Texts

The final section of "Song of Myself" is a coda—a summing up and restatement of the entire poem's themes. As you read this concluding section of the poem, write down your observations about how particular lines and phrases echo themes and concepts you've already encountered in the Whitman poems you've read.

from Song of Myself

Walt Whitman

52.

The spotted hawk swoops by and accuses me, he complains
    of my gab and my loitering.
A

I too am not a bit tamed, I too am untranslatable,
I sound my barbaric yawp over the roofs of the world.
B

The last scud° of day holds back for me,
It flings my likeness after the rest and true as any on the
5   shadow'd wilds,
It coaxes me to the vapor and the dusk.

I depart as air, I shake my white locks at the runaway sun,
I effuse° my flesh in eddies, and drift it in lacy jags.

I bequeath myself to the dirt to grow from the grass I love,
10 If you want me again look for me under your boot-soles.
C

You will hardly know who I am or what I mean,
But I shall be good health to you nevertheless,
And filter and fiber your blood.

Failing to fetch me at first keep encouraged,
15 Missing me one place search another,
I stop somewhere waiting for you.

---

4. scud: windblown mist and low clouds.
8. effuse: spread out.
D

WALT WHITMAN **359**

Summary ■ ■

In this dramatic monologue, Whitman's epic "I" declares his union with the soil and with nature, and he also claims his involvement in the lives of his audience—a "you" whom he addresses directly as a companion.

Ⓐ Elements of Literature

Metaphor

❓ In l. 1 the cry of a hawk is compared to a human complaint. In the second line the speaker compares himself to the hawk. What is the point of these metaphors? How is the speaker, as a man and as a poet, also untamed and "untranslatable"? [The speaker claims a poetic voice that is powerful like the hawk's cry, because it is natural and spontaneous—and can't be "translated" by conventional standards of beauty.]

Ⓑ Vocabulary Note

"Barbaric Yawp"

Yawp, meaning "rough, vigorous language" or "a sharp cry," is not one of Whitman's invented words. As a verb, it dates to fourteenth-century Middle English, perhaps related to *yelp.* The noun form is younger, dating to 1824.

Ⓒ Appreciating Language

Unusual Verbs

❓ Note the verbs Whitman uses in unusual ways ("I effuse my flesh," "I bequeath myself") or invents ("I shall . . . fiber your blood"). What is the effect of these verbs? [Possible responses: They are startling in their freshness; they establish a vigorous cadence; they maintain the energy of the poem by sustaining the active voice; they extend the omnipresent, epic presence of the speaker.]

Ⓓ Reading Skills and Strategies

Comparing Themes Across Texts

❓ What specific passages from #52 link thematically to specific passages in other excerpts from "Song of Myself"? [Possible responses: Lines 2–3 express the theme of wild and untamed nature that is found in the final line of #1. Lines 7–10 express Whitman's complete identification with nature, similar to #1, ll. 6 and 13; the themes of good health (ll. 12, 13 in #52 and l. 8 in #1) and loafing (l. 9 in #52 and ll. 4, 5 in #1) also appear in both; the theme of empathy appears in l. 16 of #52 and throughout #10 and #33.]

Reaching All Students

Struggling Readers

Comparing Themes Across Texts was introduced on p. 359. For a lesson directly tied to this selection that teaches students to compare themes with a strategy called Sketch to Stretch, see the *Reading Skills and Strategies* binder:
• MiniRead Skill Lesson, p. 33
• Selection Skill Lesson, p. 39

Getting Students Involved

Cooperative Learning

You're Allowed to Interrupt! To experiment with Whitman's line breaks and irregular line lengths, have students work in groups using a strategy called Interrupted Reading. One person begins reading aloud. When another notices a breakpoint, he or she picks up on the reading, and the previous reader stops. The first reader should also function as a monitor to ensure that interruptions occur at valid points.

In this free verse poem, the speaker catalogs the mental and physical deprivations that have been inflicted on him by an anonymous "they." Yet he insists on finding beauty and amazement in his own capacity for emotion, perseverance, and even failure.

BROWSING IN THE FILES

Writers on Writing. Jimmy Santiago Baca had a troubled childhood and ended up in prison. "I came out of my cell one day, and said 'I'm not going to work anymore. . . . I'm going to learn how to write. I want to know why ninety-five percent of the men in this prison . . . can't read or write, and why ninety-five percent are killing each other for smokes and coffee.' And they said to me, 'You're a coward, you're nothing.' That same day they threw scalding water on me. . . . And I was in ecstasy. I was joyous. Because it was the first time I had ever found my own thought, and the first time I had ever followed my own feeling."

Ⓐ Elements of Literature
Free Verse
❓ What Whitmanesque free-verse devices does Baca use extensively? [parallel structure, repetition, catalogs, cadence, alliteration] Encourage students to cite specific examples, which can be found in virtually every line. Note that, beginning with the second clause in l. 4, Baca varies the parallel structure (and thus the cadence) in order to avoid monotony and maintain rhythmic interest.

Ⓑ Reading Skills and Strategies
Comparing Themes Across Texts
❓ What Whitmanesque themes or ideas can you find in this stanza? [The speaker's amazement at, and acceptance of, himself as an imperfect, yet miraculous, creature.]

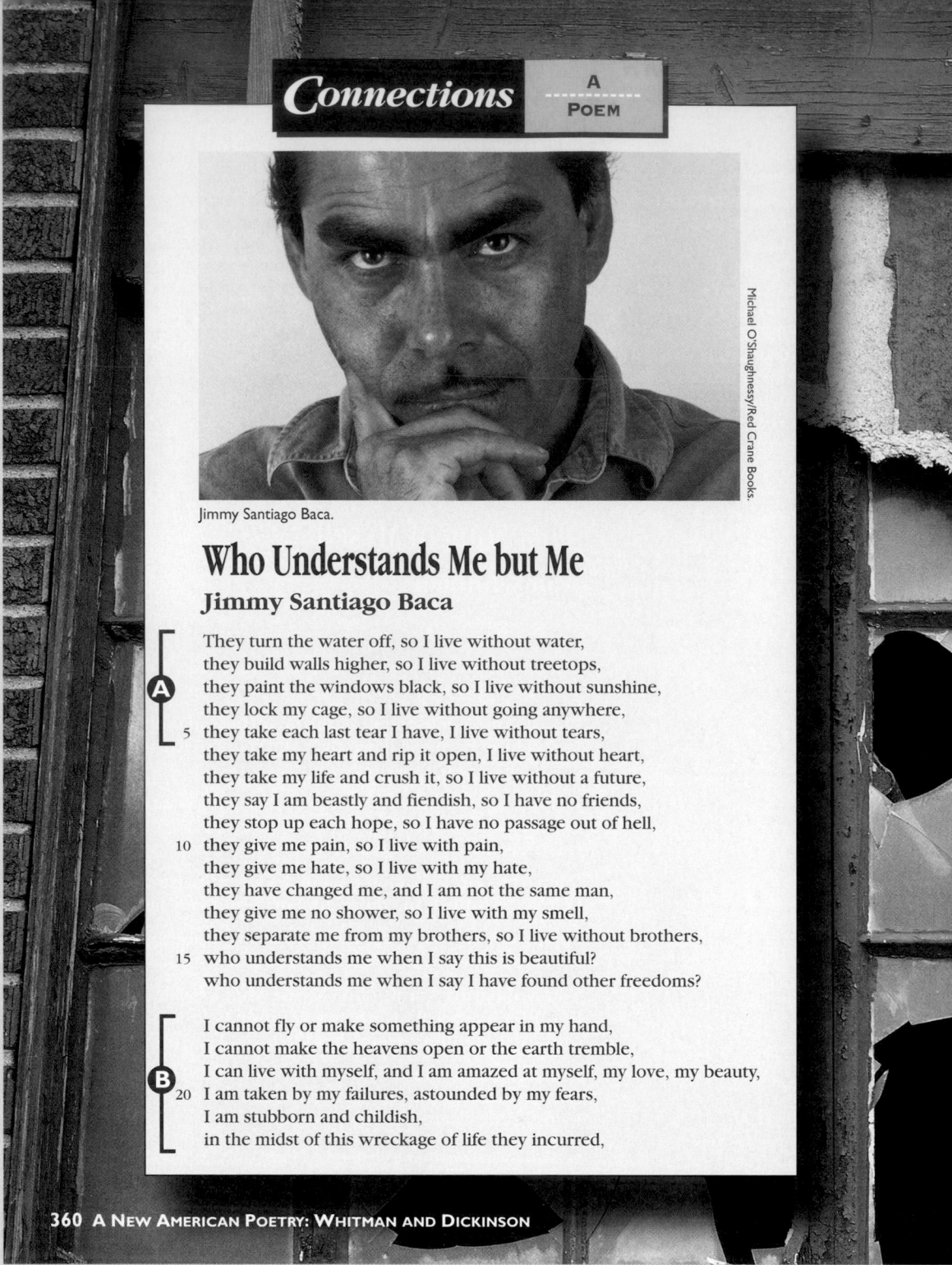

Michael O'Shaughnessy/Red Crane Books.

Jimmy Santiago Baca.

Who Understands Me but Me
Jimmy Santiago Baca

Ⓐ
They turn the water off, so I live without water,
they build walls higher, so I live without treetops,
they paint the windows black, so I live without sunshine,
they lock my cage, so I live without going anywhere,
5   they take each last tear I have, I live without tears,
they take my heart and rip it open, I live without heart,
they take my life and crush it, so I live without a future,
they say I am beastly and fiendish, so I have no friends,
they stop up each hope, so I have no passage out of hell,
10   they give me pain, so I live with pain,
they give me hate, so I live with my hate,
they have changed me, and I am not the same man,
they give me no shower, so I live with my smell,
they separate me from my brothers, so I live without brothers,
15   who understands me when I say this is beautiful?
who understands me when I say I have found other freedoms?

Ⓑ
I cannot fly or make something appear in my hand,
I cannot make the heavens open or the earth tremble,
I can live with myself, and I am amazed at myself, my love, my beauty,
20   I am taken by my failures, astounded by my fears,
I am stubborn and childish,
in the midst of this wreckage of life they incurred,

Professional Notes

Critical Comment:
A Sense of Inspiration

Both Whitman and Baca have expressed a feeling of transcendence in writing poetry. According to Roger Asselineau, Whitman felt "that he was 'divinely possessed, blind to all subordinate affairs and given up entirely to the surgings and utterances of the mighty tempestuous demon' that was in him. At such times, he can only 'scream electric' and deliver 'curious enveloped messages'; he has no will left; he is no longer conscious and he acts passively." Similarly, Baca has said, "When you work at a poem long enough . . . the imagery of verse line exudes a sparkling fountain of energy that fills your spirit. So in the most difficult of circumstances after working on a poem I walk out and I feel that, whatever there is in front of me, I will go right through it like the saxifrage flower that splits the rocks."

I practice being myself,
and I have found parts of myself never dreamed of by me,
25 they were goaded out from under rocks in my heart
    when the walls were built higher,
    when the water was turned off and the windows painted black.
    I followed these signs
    like an old tracker and followed the tracks deep into myself,
30 followed the blood-spotted path,
    deeper into dangerous regions, and found so many parts of my-
       self,
    who taught me water is not everything,
    and gave me new eyes to see through walls,
    and when they spoke, sunlight came out of their mouths,
35 and I was laughing at me with them,
    we laughed like children and made pacts to always be loyal,
    who understands me when I say this is beautiful? **C**

MAKING MEANINGS

First Thoughts

1. What, in your opinion, is the most important—
   or most interesting, or most puzzling—line in
   Whitman's poem?

Shaping Interpretations

2. How does Whitman show his connection to the
   natural world in this poem? For example, what
   qualities does he say he shares with the spotted
   hawk?

3. What verb tense does Whitman use in this
   poem and other selections from "Song of Myself"? How would the effect have been different
   if the speaker had spoken in a different tense?

4. What might Whitman mean by line 10: "If
   you want me again look for me under your
   boot-soles"?

5. The first line of "Song of Myself" is "I celebrate
   myself, and sing myself"; the last line is "I stop
   somewhere waiting for you." Taking into account
   all that you have learned of the poet's character
   and the range of his poetry, tell what you think
   the last words of poem Number 52 reveal about
   Whitman's purpose in writing "Song of Myself."

6. Reread the Whitman poems,
   including the collection opener
   (page 347), and review your
   reading notes. Then, sum up the **themes** re-
   stated in the coda to "Song of Myself."

7. Suppose you had to select a line or word from
   Whitman's works to characterize him. Which
   line(s) or word(s) from these excerpts from
   "Song of Myself" would you select, and why?

Extending the Text

8. What ties do you see between Baca's poem
   (**Connections**, page 360) and Whitman's poems?
   Consider each poet's **style** and **message**.

9. You've already studied some of the American
   poets who preceded Whitman—Poe (page
   260), Longfellow (page 175), Bryant (page 169),
   and other Romantics. Based on what you know
   about the work of these earlier poets, what do
   you think Whitman means when he describes
   his own poetry as his "barbaric yawp" (line 3)?

10. Some readers of this poem have further taken
    the meaning of "barbaric yawp" to refer to
    the way Europeans might have viewed the
    "American experiment" of democracy. What
    do you think?

WALT WHITMAN 361

Connecting Across Texts

Connecting with "Song of Myself"
After reading the excerpts from "Song of
Myself," students should recognize the influence
of Whitman in the style of Baca's poem and in
the heroism of his speaker's struggles with
poverty and isolation.

   Have students model Baca's structure in a
series of *They* _____, *so I* _____ statements,
substituting heroic actions from their own
experiences or imaginations, or from current
events. Hold a poetry reading with the results.

Assessing Learning

Informal Assessment
Self-Assessment. Ask students to respond to
the following questions: (1) How would I
describe Whitman's poetic technique in specific
terms? (2) What did I learn from studying Whitman's poetry? (3) What did I learn about myself
from this study? (4) What challenges or problems did I encounter? (5) How might I pursue
further study of Whitman, his work, or his
place in literary history? Ask students to share
their answers in small groups.

Summary ■■

Early one morning in an army camp, the speaker peers at the faces of three dead soldiers: an old man, a youth, and another young man whose face he sees as that of Christ himself. These anonymous soldiers thus come to represent not only the range of human tragedy in war but also, perhaps, the possibility of redemption and forgiveness.

RESPONDING TO THE ART

William Morris Hunt (1824–1879) was an American Romantic painter who was influenced by the French Barbizon School's insistence on naturalness in the use of light and color.

Activity. Ask students to list the lines of the poem that best fit the painting and explain why. [Possible response: lines 11–12, because of their reference to the youth or line 1, because of the twilight setting of the painting.]

A **Struggling Readers**
Rearranging Syntax

Ask students to rearrange the syntax in clauses, such as "Curious I halt and silent I stand" (l. 7), reading Whitman's phrasing aloud first and then experimenting with the effect of an alternative word order.

B **Reading Skills and Strategies**

Identifying Sources

❓ This line, like much of this poem, can be traced directly back to Whitman's prose notes, as quoted in the Before You Read feature. What might this connection indicate about Whitman's poetic technique? [Possible response: His poetic expression was grounded in the direct statements of prose.]

C **Critical Thinking**
Interpreting Symbolism

❓ In what sense is the dead soldier like Christ? [Possible responses: Both suffered and gave their lives for the good of others; both have a beatific air in death; for the believer, Christ is in everyone.]

T362

Before You Read
A SIGHT IN CAMP IN THE DAYBREAK GRAY AND DIM

Make the Connection
The Suffering of Thousands
In December 1862, Whitman traveled to Virginia to care for his brother George, who was wounded at the first battle of Fredericksburg. Though he discovered that George's injuries were minor, Whitman witnessed the terrible suffering of hundreds of other young men. Whitman volunteered to assist the staffs of several medical field units and hospitals. Comforting and feeding the injured and dying, bringing them treats, dressing their wounds, reading to them, and writing letters home to their families, Whitman helped to care for close to a hundred thousand soldiers by the end of the war. His experiences brought a wider dimension of tragedy into his poetry.

Reading Skills and Strategies

Identifying Sources
When Whitman was visiting his wounded brother in Virginia, he took these notes:

"*Sight at daybreak*—in camp in front of the hospital tent on a stretcher (three dead men lying), each with a blanket spread over him—I lift up one and look at the young man's face, calm and yellow—'tis strange!

(Young man: I think this face of yours the face of my dead Christ!)"

As you read the following poem, write down the **images** that Whitman has drawn from his wartime notes.

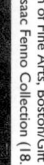

Wounded Drummer Boy (c. 1862–1865) by William Morris Hunt (1824–1879). American. Oil on canvas (14″ × 19¼″).

Museum of Fine Arts, Boston/Gift from the Isaac Fenno Collection (18.393).

A Sight in Camp in the Daybreak Gray and Dim

Walt Whitman

A sight in camp in the daybreak gray and dim,
As from my tent I emerge so early sleepless,
As slow I walk in the cool fresh air the path near by the hospital tent,
Three forms I see on stretchers lying, brought out there untended lying,
5 Over each the blanket spread, ample brownish woolen blanket,
Gray and heavy blanket, folding, covering all.

Curious I halt and silent stand,
Then with light fingers I from the face of the nearest the first just lift the blanket;
Who are you elderly man so gaunt and grim, with well-gray'd hair, and flesh all sunken about the eyes?
10 Who are you my dear comrade?

Then to the second I step—and who are you my child and darling?
Who are you sweet boy with cheeks yet blooming?

Then to the third—a face nor child nor old, very calm, as of beautiful yellow-white ivory;
Young man I think I know you—I think this face is the face of the Christ himself,
15 Dead and divine and brother of all, and here again he lies.

362 A NEW AMERICAN POETRY: WHITMAN AND DICKINSON

Making the Connections

Connecting to the Subject:
"The Large Hearts of Heroes"
Explore with students the attitude toward heroism Whitman celebrates in the poems in this collection: the heroism in performing the quiet, ordinary tasks of daily life, such as a ploughboy turning the fields in "I Hear America Singing"; the heroism of dramatically daring acts, like harboring a runaway slave in "Song of Myself," #10 or the rescue of drowning passengers in "Song of Myself," #33; the poignant heroism of the dead soldiers in "A Sight in Camp . . . ," whom Whitman portrays as beautiful and holy; the heroism of humanity and of nature itself, as shown in the behavior of ordinary workers in "I Hear America Singing" and in Whitman's empathy with others and his identification with the cosmos.

from Specimen Days

The following extracts are from Whitman's "memoranda book," which he called *Specimen Days*.

The Inauguration

March 4, 1865—The President[1] very quietly rode down to the Capitol in his own carriage, by himself, on a sharp trot, about noon, either because he wished to be on hand to sign bills, or to get rid of marching in line with the absurd procession, the muslin temple of liberty, and pasteboard monitor. I saw him on his return, at three o'clock, after the performance was over. He was in his plain two-horse barouche,[2] and looked very much worn and tired; the lines, indeed, of vast responsibilities, intricate questions, and demands of life and death, cut deeper than ever upon his dark brown face; yet all the old goodness, tenderness, sadness, and canny shrewdness, underneath the furrows. (I never see that man without feeling that he is one to become personally attached to, for his combination of purest, heartiest tenderness, and native western form of manliness.) By his side sat his little boy, of ten years. There were no soldiers, only a lot of civilians on horseback, with huge yellow scarves over their shoulders, riding around the carriage. (At the inauguration four years ago, he rode down and back again surrounded by a dense mass of armed cavalrymen eight deep, with drawn sabers; and there were sharpshooters stationed at every corner on the route.) I ought to make mention of the closing levee[3] of Saturday night last. Never before was such a compact jam in front of the White House—all the

1. **The President:** Abraham Lincoln. He would be assassinated in April, just a month after Whitman wrote this.
2. **barouche** (bə·rōōsh′): four-wheeled, horse-drawn carriage.
3. **levee:** reception.

grounds filled, and away out to the spacious sidewalks. I was there, as I took a notion to go—was in the rush inside with the crowd—surged along the passageways, the Blue and other rooms, and through the great East Room. Crowds of country people, some very funny. Fine music from the Marine band, off in a side place. I saw Mr. Lincoln, dressed all in black, with white kid gloves and a claw-hammer coat, receiving, as in duty bound, shaking hands, looking very disconsolate, and as if he would give anything to be somewhere else.

The Real War Will Never Get in the Books

And so goodbye to the war. I know not how it may have been, or may be, to others—to me the main interest I found (and still, on recollection, find) in the rank and file of the armies, both sides, and in those specimens amid the hospitals, and even the dead on the field. To me the points illustrating the latent personal character and eligibilities of these States, in the two or three millions of American young and middle-aged men, North and South, embodied in those armies—and especially the one-third or one fourth of their number, stricken by wounds or disease at some time in the course of the contest—were of more significance even than the political interests involved. (As so much of a race depends on how it faces death, and how it stands personal anguish and sickness. As, in the gusts of emotions under emergencies, and the indirect traits and asides in Plutarch, we get far profounder clues to the antique world than all its more formal history.)

Future years will never know the seething hell and the black infernal background of countless minor scenes and interiors, (not the

In the first excerpt from *Specimen Days*, Whitman sketches an admiring portrait of Abraham Lincoln on his inauguration day, emphasizing Lincoln's integrity, dignity, and weariness at the conclusion of the Civil War. The second excerpt explores the human tragedy of the war—in the fields, among ordinary soldiers, and in the makeshift hospitals where Whitman worked—the part of the story of the war that had not been told to the public.

Background

Whitman first published *Specimen Days* in 1882, when he was sixty-three and still convalescing from the stroke he had suffered nine years earlier. Notes for the Civil War sections of the book, however, had been jotted down at the time of the events themselves. Working as a government clerk and a war correspondent in Washington, D.C., Whitman had been able to devote a good deal of his time to helping wounded soldiers in the nearby military hospitals. He had visited the battle front as early as 1862, when his brother George was wounded in Virginia (see p. 413). Whitman called his book *Specimen Days* because these journal entries offered specimens of his life.

Ⓐ Literary Connections

In assuming that the "Real War" would escape American writers, Whitman perhaps was being premature, as can be seen by reading critic Edmund Wilson's masterpiece, *Patriotic Gore*. Among others, Stephen Crane was able to write convincingly about the Civil War in *The Red Badge of Courage* and in many short stories, even though he was not born until 1871. Have students compare Whitman's descriptions of the Civil War with Crane's in "A Mystery of Heroism" on p. 487.

Crossing the Curriculum

Social Studies/Media Studies

Have students work in small groups to compare and contrast outlooks on war in literature and popular media from the Civil War to the present. The Civil War photographs of Mathew Brady and journalists' and soldiers' writings of the time, including the memoirs of General Ulysses S. Grant, offer a sobering view of war. Successive American wars have each had their fictional and nonfictional chroniclers: Ernest Hemingway, Martha Gellhorn, Norman Mailer, and Tim O'Brien are notable for having written in both forms. Some students may wish to compare writers' views of war with those offered by movie directors, such as Steven Spielberg in *Saving Private Ryan* (about World War II). Suggest that groups narrow their topic by selecting two distinct outlooks on war and writing a comparison and contrast essay.

Assessing Learning

Standardized Test Preparation
For practice with ACT and SAT formats, see
• *Preparation for College Admission Exams,* p. 25

MAKING MEANINGS

First Thoughts [Respond]

1. Possible emotional responses include sympathy for the dead, sadness about the war, and wonder at the comparison of Christ and the soldier.

Shaping Interpretations [Interpret]

2. Whitman develops the setting by using images from his notes, such as the three dead men with blankets spread over them lying in front of the hospital tent. He then adds details such as the "ample brownish woolen" blankets and the day breaking "gray and dim."

3. Possible responses: The dead man was young and had sacrificed his life to preserve the Union and fight slavery. Whitman may be using the trio symbolically to represent the crucifixion of Christ and the two thieves on Golgotha or the Christian Trinity of Father, Son, and Holy Spirit.

4. The tone is somber. The speaker is sleepless and walks slowly as he spies the forms lying on stretchers. At the end, he invokes the memory of Christ's death.

5. Possible response: In war, human deaths are the ultimate tragedy, reminding us of other tragedies, such as the crucifixion of Christ.

6. Images include the camp (ll. 1–3); the three bodies from a distance (ll. 4–6); lifting the blanket from the first man's face (ll. 8–10); looking at the face of the second figure (ll. 11–12); and looking at the face of the third man (ll. 13–15).

Extending the Text [Evaluate]

7. Possible answers include Ken Burns's powerful PBS documentary on the Civil War.

---

official surface courteousness of the generals, not the few great battles) of the Secession war; and it is best they should not—the real war will never get in the books. In the mushy influences of current times, too, the fervid atmosphere and typical events of those years are in danger of being totally forgotten. I have at night watched by the side of a sick man in the hospital, one who could not live many hours. I have seen his eyes flash and burn as he raised himself and recurred to the cruelties on his surrendered brother, and mutilations of the corpse afterward. (See, in the preceding pages, the incident at Upperville—the seventeen killed as in the description, were left there on the ground. After they dropped dead, no one touched them—all were made sure of, however. The carcasses were left for the citizens to bury or not, as they chose.)

Such was the war. It was not a quadrille[4] in a ballroom. Its interior history will not only never be written—its practicality, minutiae of deeds and passions, will never be even suggested. The actual soldier of 1862-1865, North and South, with all his ways, his incredible dauntlessness, habits, practices, tastes, language, his fierce friendship, his appetite, rankness, his superb strength and animality, lawless gait, and a hundred unnamed lights and shades

4. **quadrille** (kwə·dril'): French dance for four couples.

of camp, I say, will never be written—perhaps must not and should not be.

The preceding notes may furnish a few stray glimpses into that life, and into those lurid interiors, never to be fully conveyed to the future. The hospital part of the drama from 1861 to 1865, deserves indeed to be recorded. Of that many-threaded drama, with its sudden and strange surprises, its confounding of prophecies, its moments of despair, the dread of foreign interference, the interminable campaigns, the bloody battles, the mighty and cumbrous and green armies, the drafts and bounties—the immense money expenditure, like a heavy-pouring constant rain—with, over the whole land, the last three years of the struggle, an unending, universal mourning wail of women, parents, orphans—the marrow of the tragedy concentrated in those Army Hospitals—(it seemed sometimes as if the whole interest of the land, North and South, was one vast central hospital, and all the rest of the affair but flanges)—those forming the untold and unwritten history of the war—infinitely greater (like life's) than the few scraps and distortions that are ever told or written. Think how much, and of importance, will be—how much, civic and military, has already been—buried in the grave, in eternal darkness.

—Walt Whitman

MAKING MEANINGS

First Thoughts

1. What was your emotional response to "A Sight in Camp"? What specific words or **images** affected your response?

Shaping Interpretations

2. Look back at the notes you took while reading. How did Whitman develop the **setting** from the notes that inspired the poem?

Which **images** in the poem spring directly from Whitman's own experiences?

3. Why, given the circumstances of the Civil War, might the poet have seen the face of Christ on one of the dead soldiers? What might be the significance of the fact that the "forms" are a trio?

4. In Whitman's poems, we seem to be overhearing a man's conversation with himself. How would you describe the **tone** of this poem? What main elements support your description?

5. The point of the poem is never openly stated. What do you think is the **message** behind the poem?

364 A NEW AMERICAN POETRY: WHITMAN AND DICKINSON

Listening to Music

Folksong Symphony (No. 4) by Roy Harris, performed by the American Festival Chorus
Like Whitman, Harris "heard America singing" and often incorporated indigenous American tunes and themes into his music. Among Harris's compositions for choral performance is the *Whitman Triptych,* based on some of Walt Whitman's poems.

Activity
After reading Whitman's poetry, play this portion of Harris's *Symphony No. 4,* better known

as the *Folksong Symphony.* Use the second part, with "Streets of Laredo" and "Oh, Bury Me Not on the Lone Prairie," followed by the instrumental interlude of dance tunes, to illustrate Whitman's catalog style. As students listen, have them jot down elements that Harris's music shares with Whitman's poetry and then have students hold a class discussion based on their notes.

6. Paul Zweig, one of Whitman's biographers, says that Whitman had a genius for the single line, "the verbal snapshot." Do you agree with this observation? Which **images** in this poem make particularly unusual and evocative "verbal snapshots"?

Extending the Text

7. Think of movies or television series you have seen set during the Civil War. Based on what you know about the Civil War, which media depictions strike you as best capturing the "real war" that Whitman describes in *Specimen Days* (page 363)?

CHOICES: Building Your Portfolio

Writer's Notebook

1. Collecting Ideas for a Comparison-Contrast Essay

In the Writer's Workshop on page 401, you'll write an essay comparing and contrasting two pieces of literature. You might find an interesting topic for your essay in comparing and contrasting Whitman with one or two of the Fireside Poets (see pages 149–150). Before you start taking notes, read this statement of Whitman's: "For grounds for Leaves of Grass, as a poem, I abandoned conventional themes, which do not appear in it: none of the stock ornamentation or choice plots of love or war, or high, exceptional personages of Old World song . . . no legend, or myth, or romance, nor euphemism, nor rhyme." Jot down notes now on the ways in which Whitman's poems differ from the poems of the

Fireside Poets. Focus on the poetic features mentioned by Whitman. Save your notes.

Performance

2. Barbaric Yawp

Prepare a public reading of Whitman's poems. You will have to decide when you will use solo readers and when you will use a chorus. For some poems, you might want to use musical accompaniment. Be sure to ask your audience to evaluate your performance.

Creative Writing / Speaking and Listening

3. My Walt Whitman

Write a free-verse poem in the tradition of Walt Whitman, using one of the poems in this collection as a model. (You could even begin your poem with one of Whitman's openers, such as "I hear America singing" or "I celebrate myself.") Before you start, make notes on the following to help you decide on subject matter:
• How would Whitman celebrate diversity today?

• Who would be his overlooked heroes?
• What landscapes would he cherish?
• With whom would he empathize?
• What "songs," or lives, would he pay tribute to?

When you write in free verse (see page 355), you are freeing yourself from the demands of a rhyme scheme and meter. However, you will want to use **imagery** and **sound effects** (alliteration, repetition, parallel structure), as well as one or more of Whitman's techniques: catalogs, rolling cadences, and modulations of voice that result in a specific tone.

When you finish your poem, organize a class poetry reading. As you and other students read your poems aloud, identify the images and tone that seem the most like those Whitman used.

Comparing Ideas

4. Reading Nature

You have seen that it was a habit of the Puritans to "read" nature for signs of divinity. You have also seen how the Transcendentalists "read" nature.

Rubrics for each Choices assignment appear on p. 133 in the *Portfolio Management System*.

CHOICES: Building Your Portfolio

1. **Writer's Notebook** You might conduct this activity as a class discussion. Suggest that students take notes on the discussion.
2. **Performance** Ask students to decide what audience they want to invite to the reading. For example, they might invite family members or another class.
3. **Creative Writing/Speaking and Listening** Encourage students to make lists of items to be included in their poems. Have them share these lists in small groups. After the poems are written, let students read them to each other in pairs; the listeners should give specific feedback and point out similarities to Whitman's poems.
4. **Comparing Ideas** Ask students to organize their thinking by using a three-column chart. Have students list at least three examples of how each writer "reads" nature.

Bradford	Emerson	Whitman
[North American wilderness not a Pisgah, from where Moses viewed the Promised Land (p. 31)]	[The Universal Being circulates through people who are close to nature (p. 221)]	

T365

5. **Comparing Diction and Style**
You might have students add a third column to their charts, titled "Reactions/Connections." Ask them to list their own reactions to and personal connections with Whitman's tone, democratic feelings, lists and catalogs, and vigorous language.

6. **Analyzing Poetry** Remind students that every point they make in their essays needs to be supported by a quotation from or reference to the text and an explanation of how the example supports the point.

7. **Music** Some students in the group may want to work on poetry rather than on music and help create a spoken-word performance with musical accompaniment.

8. **Art** Let students choose whether to work alone or in pairs for this project. Encourage them to make sketches and doodles as a form of brainstorming.

9. **Crossing the Curriculum: History** Have students work in small groups for this activity. Assign different aspects of the war, such as new recruits, wounded soldiers, formal group portraits, and so on, to each group so that displays are not duplicated.

In a brief essay, compare and contrast Whitman's "reading" of nature with that of the Puritan William Bradford (page 26) and the Transcendentalist Ralph Waldo Emerson (page 216).

Comparing Diction and Style

5. Whitman's Prose and Poetry

Read the sample of Whitman's prose writing in Primary Sources on page 363. In a brief essay, compare the **diction** and **style** of his prose with that of his poems. Before you write, collect your data in a chart like the following:

	Prose	Poetry
Tone		
Democratic feelings		
Use of lists and catalogs		
Use of vigorous language		

Analyzing Poetry

6. A Close Look

In an essay, analyze the poems by Whitman presented here (including the one on page 347). Focus on analyzing an aspect of his poems that interests you: perhaps his everyday American diction, his use of catalogs, his application of elements of free verse, his commonplace subject matter, his celebration of the ordinary person as hero, or his themes of identification with nature and with all of human existence. Open your essay with a thesis statement that clearly states the main idea of your analysis. Be sure to use evidence from the poems to support your main points.

Music

7. Whitman's Music

Music, singing, melody—Whitman's poetry resonates with references to music and sound. Find a recording of vocal or instrumental music that expresses the spirit of Walt Whitman's poetry, and play it for the class. Or, if you wish, compose and play your own musical tribute to Whitman.

Art

8. Design a Book Cover

In the first edition of *Leaves of Grass*, Whitman selected a green, pebbled cloth for the cover of his book. He stamped the title *Leaves of Grass* in gold paint, using simple letters with roots descending from the letters and leaves shooting up above them. The book was roughly the size of a piece of typewriter paper, about eight by eleven-and-a-quarter inches.

Design a new cover for Whitman's *Leaves of Grass*. Try to reflect the feeling or content of the poems in your design, but also reflect your personal response to Whitman's poetry. Hold an art show, and display your cover design with the designs of other students.

Crossing the Curriculum: History

9. Eyewitness to War

At your school or local library, find a book of pictures by a Civil War photographer (page 414). Make a chart comparing photographic depictions of soldiers with Whitman's poetic depiction in "A Sight in Camp in the Daybreak Gray and Dim." Set up a museum display using reproductions of Civil War photographs accompanied by captions written in Whitmanesque style.

Maria Stenzel/National Geographic Image Collection, Courtesy Walt Whitman House, Camden, New Jersey.

Using Students' Strengths

Naturalist Learners
When doing Choice 4, students might enjoy adding a fourth column to their charts, labeled with their own last name. They should then compare and contrast their own "reading" of nature with those of Bradford, Emerson, and Whitman. They can analyze their own interpretations of nature by giving examples and anecdotes both from their writing and from their lives.

Auditory Learners
Ask students to read Whitman's writings aloud for Choice 5. This may help them to identify the differences in tone and language more easily.

Pablo Neruda.

Sygma.

Pablo Neruda
(1904–1973)

Pablo Neruda was born and educated in Chile. Neruda wrote that he went out "hunting poems" as a child, and he received his first acclaim as a poet at the age of sixteen when he won first prize in a poetry competition. By the age of twenty he was already regarded as a young poet with great promise. In addition to enjoying an enormously full and diverse life as a writer, Neruda served as a diplomat and a member of the Chilean Senate for several years. He also lived in exile from his homeland when the Chilean right-wing government outlawed his socialistic political party and terminated his senatorial position. Before resettling on Isla Negra, in Chile, in 1953, Neruda lived in many countries around the world, including Burma (now called Myanmar), Italy, Spain, France, Mexico, Russia, and China. In 1971, he was awarded the Nobel Prize in literature. Known for his diverse range of poetic styles and voices, Neruda is celebrated for his humanism, his call for peace and equality, and his love and respect for the natural elements of the world. His poems are questions, riddles, political shouts, observations, homages, and introspective movements toward truth. Like Whitman, he has influenced and inspired many of the great poets of the twentieth century.

HRW go.hrw.com
LEO 11-7

PABLO NERUDA 367

Connecting Across Texts

Connecting with Whitman's Poetry
Like Walt Whitman, Pablo Neruda uses images from nature in his poetry. Ask students to make a cluster diagram like the following to help them compare Neruda's images of nature in "Full Powers" with Whitman's images of nature in the excerpts from "Song of Myself" on pp. 347, 353–354, and 356–359.

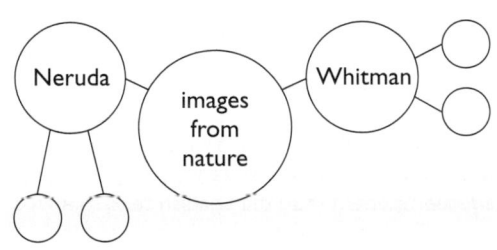

Summary ■■■

The speaker of this poem says he writes in the sun, in the street, at the sea. He is inhibited by night, yet in darkness he forges keys of understanding. The poem suggests that it is the ambiguity between "being" and "nonbeing," between silent death and defiant song, that makes both living and writing possible. Death is not an object of fear but evokes speculation about "origins" and a commitment to keep on singing. Several lines in the poem can be read as allusions to Whitman's "Song of Myself."

Background

In "Song of Myself," #52, Whitman bequeaths himself to the dirt in order to filter or nourish the blood of others. Neruda expresses a related sentiment in the closing line of his long poem *The Heights of Macchu Picchu.* The two poets share an elemental love of the earth and humanity. In different ways, both poets' lives also reflect a continuing devotion to civic life: Neruda as a professional diplomat, Whitman as a journalist and hospital volunteer.

Before You Read
FULL POWERS

Background

Like many great writers the world over, the Chilean poet Pablo Neruda was deeply inspired by Walt Whitman's *Leaves of Grass.* In fact, this Nobel laureate declared that Whitman was his most important literary influence. Neruda made the following remarks to a New York City audience a year before his death:

"I was barely fifteen when I discovered Walt Whitman, my primary creditor. I stand here among you today still owing this marvelous debt that has helped me live.

"To renegotiate this debt is to begin by making it public, by proclaiming myself the humble servant of the poet who measured the earth with long, slow strides, pausing everywhere to love and to examine, to learn, to teach, and to admire. . . . Clearly, he feared neither morality nor immorality, nor did he attempt to define the boundaries between pure and impure poetry. He is

the first absolute poet, and it was his intention not only to sing but to impart his vast vision of the relationships of men and of nations. In this sense, his obvious nationalism is part of an organic universality. He considers himself indebted to happiness and sorrow, to advanced cultures and primitive societies.

"Greatness has many faces, but I, a poet who writes in Spanish, learned more from Walt Whitman than from Cervantes [Spain's premier Renaissance novelist, poet, and playwright]. In Whitman's poetry the ignorant are never humbled, and the human condition is never derided.

"We are still living in a Whitmanesque epoch. . . . The bard complained of the all-powerful European influence that continued to dominate the literature of his time. In fact, it was he, Walt Whitman, in the persona of a specific geography, who for the first time in history brought honor to an American name."

Reading Skills and Strategies
Recognizing Shared Characteristics of Cultures
In many ways, Whitman and Neruda are two poets cut from the same cloth, even though they emerged from different cultures, years apart. As you read Neruda's poem, write down **images** and feelings that remind you of parts of "Song of Myself." Be especially aware of lines that seem actually to refer to Whitman's poetry.

Reaching All Students

Struggling Readers
After students read the poem once, focus their attention on ll. 1, 17, and 19–20. Then have them reread "I Hear America Singing" and the opening Whitman quote on p. 342. Once students see the parallels between Whitman and Neruda, they will have an easier time interpreting the poem.

English Language Learners
To help students appreciate the cadences and sounds of the two languages and connect sound to meaning, have one student read a line in Spanish, and then have another student read the same line in English, going back and forth until the entire poem has been read. Then, have another student read the Spanish text, followed by the English translation read by yet another student.

Advanced Learners
Encourage students who know some Spanish to attempt a new translation of the poem. They can use a Spanish-English dictionary, an English language dictionary, and an English language thesaurus. English-fluent and Spanish-fluent classmates can then discuss the challenges of capturing the connotations and feelings of one language in another, such as the willfulness of the speaker in ll. 19–20.

Plenos Poderes

Pablo Neruda

A puro sol escribo, a plena calle,
a pleno mar, en donde puedo canto,
sólo la noche errante me detiene
pero en su interrupción recojo espacio,
5   recojo sombra para mucho tiempo.

El trigo negro de la noche crece
mientras mis ojos miden la pradera
y así de sol a sol hago las llaves:
busco en la oscuridad las cerraduras
10   y voy abriendo al mar las puertas rotas
hasta llenar armarios con espuma.

Y no me canso de ir y de volver,
no me para la muerte con su piedra,
no me canso de ser y de no ser.

15   A veces me pregunto si de donde
si de padre o de madre o cordillera
heredé los deberes minerales,

los hilos de un océano encendido
y sé que sigo y sigo porque sigo
20   y canto porque canto y porque canto.

Full Powers

Pablo Neruda

translated from the Spanish by
Ben Belitt and Alastair Reid

I write in the clear sun, in the teeming street,
at full sea-tide, in a place where I can sing;
only the wayward night inhibits me,
but, interrupted by it, I recover space,
5   I gather shadows to last me a long time. **B**

The black crop of the night is growing
while my eyes meanwhile take measure of the meadows. **A**
So, from one sun to the next, I forge the keys.
In the darkness, I look for the locks
10   and keep on opening broken doors to the sea, **C**
for it to fill the wardrobes with its foam.

And I do not weary of going and returning.
Death, in its stone aspect, does not halt me.
I am weary neither of being nor of non-being.

15   Sometimes I puzzle over origins—
was it from my father, my mother, or the mountains
that I inherited debts to minerality, **D**

the fine threads spreading from a sea on fire?
And I know that I keep on going for the going's sake,
20   and I sing because I sing and because I sing.

PABLO NERUDA 369

Taking a Second Look

T369

A Critical Thinking

Interpreting

? What might the symbol of the sea mean? [Possible responses: It may symbolize death or nonbeing surrounding the speaker's consciousness; this death, however, may be life-affirming, since the awareness of death gives him a view onto life; the sea may also symbolize the ambiguity of life.]

B Reading Skills and Strategies

Drawing Conclusions

? Why do you think the poem is titled "Full Powers"? [Possible answers: Neruda is exploring multiple aspects of life and living, of existence and death, of emotion and physicality; he may be saying that the source of his full creative powers lies in this interplay of death and life.]

C Reading Skills and Strategies

Drawing Conclusions

? How are Neruda's and Whitman's poems similar and different? [Students may hear a similar songlike cadence in both poems. However, they may also note that Whitman's singing is usually a joyous celebration of life, with the poet embracing all that he encounters and finding himself in all people, while Neruda's song is a more somber search for meaning among the songs of life and the shadows of death.]

FINDING COMMON GROUND

As its name suggests, this feature encourages students to explore similar themes or points of view that cross cultures. To make sure that each student has a chance to participate in the discussion, instruct groups to select leaders, presenters, and note takers. The leader's job is to call on one student at a time to read his or her notes and observations. The note taker records the key images for the entire group to organize, and the presenter reports orally to the class.

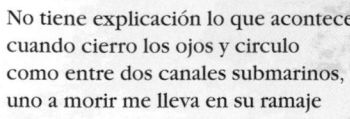

No tiene explicación lo que acontece
cuando cierro los ojos y circulo
como entre dos canales submarinos,
uno a morir me lleva en su ramaje
25 y el otro canta para que yo cante.

Así pues de no ser estoy compuesto
y como el mar asalta el arrecife
con cápsulas saladas de blancura
y retrata le piedra con la ola,
30 así lo que en la muerte me rodea
abre en mí la ventana de la vida
y en pleno paroxismo estoy durmiendo.
A plena luz camino por la sombra.

There is no way of explaining what does happen
when I close my eyes and waver
as between two lost channels under water.
One lifts me in its branches toward my dying,
25 and the other sings in order that I may sing.

And so I am made up of a non-being,
and, as the sea goes battering at a reef
in wave on wave of salty white-tops
and drags back stones in its retreating wash,
30 so what there is in death surrounding me
opens in me a window out to living,
and, in the spasm of being, I go on sleeping.
In the full light of day, I walk in the shade.

FINDING COMMON GROUND

Now that you've read Neruda's poem, meet in a small group, and share the comments you recorded while reading.

Read your notes aloud, and discuss each other's observations and thoughts.

- Identify the **images** and feelings that different members of your group jotted down.
- Discuss the elements in the poem that seem to refer directly to Whitman's "Song of Myself."

- List the qualities that Whitman and Neruda seem to share. For instance, how do they view themselves in relation to others? How do they view the natural world in relation to the world of people and industry?
- If possible, have a Spanish-speaker read «Plenos Poderes» to the class, followed by a reading of "Full Powers." Then, compare and contrast the sound and meter of the two poems. Was the translator faithful to the original?
- Share your observations and thoughts with the rest of the class.

Assessing Learning

Self-Assessment

Ask students to reflect on what they have gained by reading the poetry of Whitman and Neruda. Have them keep in mind the following questions: (1) What does looking through the "lenses" of Whitman or Neruda show me about life? (2) What does it show me about Whitman or Neruda? (3) What does it show me about myself?

Tell It Slant

Theme

The Universal in the Particular Another major American poet was contemporaneous with Walt Whitman, but they never met or exchanged letters. In fact, Whitman probably did not even know of Emily Dickinson's existence. Whitman wrote poems that swept over the whole country and spoke of everything under the sun. Dickinson wrote poems that explored the subtlest nuances of human experience as she observed them in a small New England village.

Reading the Anthology

Reaching Struggling Readers

The *Reading Skills and Strategies: Reaching Struggling Readers* binder includes a Reading Strategies Handbook that offers concrete suggestions to help students who have difficulty reading and comprehending text, or students who are reluctant readers. When a specific strategy is most appropriate for a selection, a correlation to the Handbook is provided at the bottom of the teacher's page under the head Reaching Struggling Readers. This head may also be used to introduce additional ideas for helping students read challenging texts.

Reading Beyond the Anthology

Read On At the end of the New American Poetry collections, the grade eleven book includes an annotated bibliography of books suitable for extended reading. The suggested books are related to works in these collections by theme, by author, or by subject. To preview the Read On for the New American Poetry period, please turn to p. T397.

Resources for this Collection

Note: All resources for this collection are available for preview on the *One-Stop Planner CD-ROM 2 with Test Generator.* All worksheets and blackline masters may be printed from the CD-ROM.

Internet Resources
go.hrw.com LE0 11-8

Collection Planner

Selection or Feature	Reading and Literary Skills	Vocabulary, Language, and Grammar
• **Heart! We will forget him!** (p. 374) • **If you were coming in the Fall** (p. 376) **Primary Sources: If you were coming in the Fall** (p. 377) • **The Soul selects her own Society** (p. 378) • **Some keep the Sabbath going to Church** (p. 381) • **I taste a liquor never brewed** (p. 382) • **Much Madness is divinest Sense** (p. 383) • **Apparently with no surprise** (p. 385) • **Tell all the Truth but tell it slant** (p. 386) • **Success is counted sweetest** (p. 388) **Connections: Emily Dickinson's Homestead** (p. 389) Anne Bernays • **Because I could not stop for Death** (p. 391) • **I heard a Fly buzz—when I died** (p. 392) • **I died for Beauty—but was scarce** (p. 393) Emily Dickinson **Primary Sources: "I sing... because I am afraid"** (p. 394) Thomas Wentworth Higginson	• *Graphic Organizers for Active Reading,* Worksheet pp. 31, 32, 33, 34, 35, 36, 37, 38, 39, 40, 41, 42 • *Literary Elements:* Transparency 13 Worksheet p. 40	• *Words to Own,* Worksheet p. 24 • *Grammar and Language Links:* Revision Worksheet p. 33 • *Daily Oral Grammar,* Transparencies 26, 27
The American Language: A Period of Vocabulary Growth (p. 398) Gary Q. Arpin		
Writer's Workshop: Comparison-and-Contrast Essay (p. 401)		
Language Workshop: Varying Sentence Beginnings (p. 403)		• *Workshop Resources,* p. 53 • *Language Workshop CD-ROM,* Sentences—Beginnings
Learning for Life: The Changing World of Work (p. 405)		

Other Resources for this Collection

- *Cross-Curricular Activities,* p. 8
- *Portfolio Management System,* Introduction to Portfolio Assessment, p. 1
- *Formal Assessment:* Literary Period Test, p. 82; Literary Elements Test, p. 80

- *Test Generator,* Collection Test

Writing	Listening and Speaking Viewing and Representing	Assessment
• *Portfolio Management System,* Rubrics for Choices, p. 136	• *Audio CD Library,* Disc 10, Tracks 11, 12, 13, 14, 15, 16, 17, 18, 19, 20, 21, 22 • *Viewing and Representing:* Fine Art Transparency 8 Worksheet p. 32 • *Portfolio Management System,* Rubrics for Choices, p. 136	• *Formal Assessment,* Selection Test, p. 76 • *Test Generator (One-Stop Planner CD-ROM)* • *Preparation for College Admission Exams,* p. 27
		• *Formal Assessment,* The American Language Test, p. 78
• *Workshop Resources,* p. 15	• *Viewing and Representing,* HRW Multimedia Presentation Maker	• *Portfolio Management System* • Prewriting, p. 138 • Peer Editing, p. 139 • Assessment Rubric, p. 140
		• *Portfolio Management System,* Rubrics, p. 141

 Transparency  CD-ROM  Video  Audio CD

Collection Planner

Skills Focus

Skills Focus

Selection or Feature	Reading Skills and Strategies	Elements of Literature and Language	Writing	Listening and Speaking	Viewing and Representing
• **Heart! We will forget him!** (p. 374) • **If you were coming in the Fall** (p. 376) • **The Soul selects her own Society** (p. 378) • **Some keep the Sabbath going to Church** (p. 381) • **I taste a liquor never brewed** (p. 382) • **Much Madness is divinest Sense** (p. 383) • **Apparently with no surprise** (p. 385) • **Tell all the Truth but tell it slant** (p. 386) • **Success is counted sweetest** (p. 388) • **Because I could not stop for Death** (p. 391) • **I heard a Fly buzz—when I died** (p. 392) • **I died for Beauty—but was scarce** (p. 393) Emily Dickinson	Multiple Meanings of Words, pp. 379, 390 Evaluate an Analogy, p. 384 Identify a Theme, p. 384 Paraphrase, p. 390 Define from Context, p. 390 Summarize a Text, p. 391	Imagery, p. 376 Figures of Speech, p. 376 Slant Rhyme (Off Rhyme, Half Rhyme, Approximate Rhyme), pp. 379–380, 395–396 Rhyme Scheme, p. 379 Irony, pp. 379, 395 Simile, pp. 379, 396 Metaphor, pp. 379, 384–385, 390–391, 395–396 Meter, pp. 379, 396 Title, p. 384 Analogy, p. 384 Tone, pp. 384, 391, 395 Paradox, p. 384 Theme, p. 384 Personification, pp. 390, 395 Pun, p. 390 Image, 390 Message, p. 395 Hymn Meter, p. 396	Evaluate Editorial Changes, p. 377 Take Notes Comparing Two Poems, p. 396 Write a Poem Based on One of Dickinson's Themes, p. 396 Write an Essay Analyzing the Use of Hymn Meter in Dickinson's Poetry, p. 396	Prepare and Present "An Evening with Emily Dickinson," p. 396	Create an Illustrated Book of Poems, p. 396
The American Language: A Period of Vocabulary Growth (p. 398) Gary Q. Arpin		American Vernacular, p. 398 Suffixes, p. 400 Specialized Vocabulary, p. 400 Loanwords, p. 400	Compile a Dictionary of Specialized Vocabulary, p. 400 Make a "Loanword Lexicon," p. 400		
Writer's Workshop: Comparison-and-Contrast Essay (p. 401)		Parallel Structure, p. 402	Write an Essay Comparing and Contrasting Two Poems, pp. 401–402		
Language Workshop: Varying Sentence Beginnings (p. 403)		Sentence Structure, p. 403	Revise Sentences to Vary Beginnings, p. 403		
Reading for Life: Reading a Textbook (p. 404)	Organization, p. 404 Special Features, p. 404				
Learning for Life: The Changing World of Work (p. 405)			Research and Report on Projected Changes in Career Fields, p. 405	Tape-Record a Radio Broadcast, p. 405 Conduct an Interview, p. 405	Create a Brochure, p. 405

TELL IT SLANT

Emily Dickinson

We think of her hidden in a white dress
among the folded linens and sachets
of well-kept cupboards, or just out of sight
sending jellies and notes with no address
to all the wondering Amherst neighbors.
Eccentric as New England weather
the stiff wind of her mind, stinging or gentle,
blew two half-imagined lovers off.
Yet legend won't explain the sheer sanity
of vision, the serious mischief
of language, the economy of pain.

—Linda Pastan (1932–   )

Responding to the Poem

? Read the poem to form initial impressions of Emily Dickinson as a person of legend and a poetic genius. **What picture of Dickinson do ll. 1–5 create?** [Students may picture a serious, pious woman in a white dress; a shy, reclusive woman; a person who feels vulnerable outside her domestic environment.] **What picture do you form from ll. 9–11?** [Sample responses: a strong, sincere person who looks at the world imaginatively; a poet who plays with words; a poet who compresses language to express difficult and complex feelings.]

RESPONDING TO THE ART

Activity. Have students brainstorm interpretations of the collection theme "Tell It Slant." [Sample responses: to tell from a biased point of view; to tell indirectly.] **Then ask what the illustration suggests.** [Possible responses: a look at the world from a special perspective; an oblique approach to a beautiful vision.]

Writing Focus: Comparison-and-Contrast Essay

WORK IN PROGRESS

The following **Work in Progress** assignment in this collection builds to a culminating **Writer's Workshop** at the end of Collection 8.

- Poems of Emily Dickinson

Take notes on how Dickinson's poems compare with poems by earlier poets (p. 396)

Writer's Workshop: Expository Writing / Comparison-and-Contrast Essay (p. 401)

Heart! . . . / If you were . . . /
The Soul selects . . . / Some
keep . . . / I taste a liquor . . . /
Much Madness . . . / Apparently . . . / Tell all the Truth . . .
Success is . . . / Because I could
not . . . / I heard a Fly . . . / I
died for Beauty . . .

1. Read and interpret the poems
2. Analyze slant rhyme
3. Summarize a text
4. Express understanding through
   writing, performance, and art

SKILLS

Literary
- Analyze slant rhyme

Reading
- Summarize a text

Writing
- Compare two poems
- Write a poem
- Write a script

Speaking/Listening
- Prepare and perform a script

Art
- Design a book of poems

Music
- Compare meters

Viewing/Representing
- Compare paintings with poems
  (ATE)

Planning

- **Block Schedule**
  *Block Scheduling Lesson Plans with Pac-
  ing Guide*

- **Traditional Schedule**
  *Lesson Plans Including Strategies for
  English-Language Learners*

- **One-Stop Planner**
  CD-ROM with Test Generator

Emily Dickinson

(1830–1886)

A brief outline of Emily Dickinson's life reads like the plot of a story destined to become a legend. Once upon a time there was born to a religious and well-to-do New England family a daughter, whom they named Emily. As a child, she was lively, well behaved, and obedient; she took pleasure in the busy household of which she was a part and in the seasonal games, parties, and outings of a village snowy cold in winter and brilliantly green and flowering in the summer.

At home she learned to cook and sew. When she was old enough, she was sent to a school where strict rules did not keep Emily and the other girls from displaying their high spirits as they enjoyed the entertainments of boarding school life. Emily took part in these, but not always with as much enthusiasm as she might have. As she said many years later, something sad and reserved in her nature made her "a mourner among the children."

To her family and friends, everything about the young Dickinson seemed normal. No one doubted that she would grow gracefully into womanhood, make a good marriage, and settle into a village life of churchgoing, holiday gatherings, and neighborly harmony. But something happened in her life that has been the subject of speculation for decades.

When Dickinson was twenty-four years old, her father, who had become a U.S. congressman, took her with him to Washington, D.C., and then on to Philadelphia. The journey seems to have marked the start of a turning point in her life. Her father may have taken her with him because she had fallen in love with someone she could never marry. This person might have been a married lawyer, older than Emily, a man who would die that year of tuberculosis.

Culver Pictures.

Whatever happened, it seems likely that in the course of the journey, Emily fell in love with someone else: Charles Wadsworth, who was also married and who was pastor of the Arch Street Presbyterian Church in Philadelphia. Letters to Wadsworth show that Dickinson saw him as a "muse," someone who could inspire her, someone she could love passionately in her imagination.

But, in 1862, Wadsworth took up a new assignment in San Francisco. His leaving seems to have caused a great crisis in Dickinson's life: "I sing," she wrote around this time, "as the boy does by the burying ground, because I am afraid."

The Recluse of Amherst
The young woman quietly and abruptly withdrew from all social life except that involving her immediate family. Within a few years, dressed always in white—like the bride she would never become—she had gone into a state of seclusion. Her only activities were household tasks and the writing of poems that she either kept to herself or sent out as valentines, birthday greetings, or notes to go with the gift of a cherry pie or a batch of cookies.

Around the time that Wadsworth was preparing to move to California, Dickinson sent a few of her poems to Thomas Wentworth Higginson (page 394). As editor of the *Atlantic Monthly*, Higginson had been encouraging the work of younger poets. Higginson never became a substitute for Wadsworth, but he did serve as a kindly, distant "teacher" and "mentor." Eventually, Dickinson gave up hope of ever finding a wider audience than her few friends and relatives. About 1861, she wrote "I'm Nobody! Who are you? / Are you—Nobody—too?"

During her lifetime, Emily Dickinson published no more than a handful of her typically

go.hrw.com
LE0 11-8

Resources: Print and Media

Reading
- *Graphic Organizers for Active Reading,*
  pp. 31–42
- *Words to Own,* p. 24
- *Audio CD Library*
  Disc 10, Tracks 11–22

Elements of Literature
- *Literary Elements*
  Transparency 13
  Worksheet, p. 40

Writing and Language
- *Daily Oral Grammar*
  Transparencies 26, 27
- *Grammar and Language Links*
  Worksheet, p. 33

Viewing and Representing
- *Viewing and Representing*
  Fine Art Transparency 8
  Fine Art Worksheet, p. 32
- *Visual Connections*
  Videocassette B, Segment 6

Assessment
- *Formal Assessment,* p. 76
- *Portfolio Management System,* p. 136
- *Preparation for College Admission Exams,* p. 27
- *Test Generator (One-Stop Planner CD-ROM)*

Internet
- go.hrw.com (keyword: LE0 11-8)

brief poems. She seemed to lack all concern for an audience, and she went so far as to instruct her family to destroy any poems she might leave behind after her death. Still, she saw to it that bundles of handwritten poems were carefully wrapped and put away in places where, after her death, friendly, appreciative, and, finally, astonished eyes would find them. The poems were assembled and edited by different family members and friends; they were then published in installments so frequent that readers began to wonder when they would ever end.

Then, in 1955, a collection called *The Poems of Emily Dickinson* was finally made available. This was the devoted work of Thomas H. Johnson, a scholar who, unlike Dickinson's earlier editors, refrained from making "presentable" entities of poems whose punctuation, rhyme schemes, syntax, and word choice were frequently baffling. Instead, he attempted to remain faithful to the original manuscript.

As a result of Johnson's research, whole generations of readers who had grown up on Dickinson poems were faced with new versions of those poems, versions that sometimes rescued Dickinson's originals from the tamperings of her first editors. Sometimes these originals made emphases, which, in the interest of "smoothness," those editors had overlooked.

Here is an example of how one stanza was changed by the original editors. Johnson's version is first:

> We passed the School, where Children
>   strove
> At Recess—in the Ring—
> We passed the Fields of Gazing Grain—
> We passed the Setting Sun—

And this is how the early editor changed it:

> We passed the school where children played
> Their lessons scarcely done;
> We passed the fields of gazing grain,
> We passed the setting sun.

The Secret of Genius

When Dickinson died at the age of fifty-five, hardly anyone knew that the strange, shy woman in their midst was a poet whose sharp and delicate voice would echo for generations to come. Some seventy years after her death, when the quarrels among her relatives who had inherited her manuscripts had died down and all her poems were finally published, she was recognized as one of the greatest poets America, and perhaps the world, had produced.

The self-imposed restrictions of Dickinson's actual life were more than matched by her ability to see the universal in the particular, and vice versa. She perceived the relationship between a drop of dew and a flood, between a grain of sand and a desert. These perceptions helped her make metaphors that embraced experiences far beyond the limited compass of Amherst village life.

> **S**he perceived the relationship between a drop of dew and a flood.

Yet, no matter how far her imagination ranged, Dickinson never denied those experiences their truth as aspects of a cycle of existence important in itself. When an Amherst neighbor's barn caught fire and lit up the sky, it was a real barn at the edge of a real pasture, and its loss became a matter of local anguish. But these local actualities did not prevent Dickinson from regarding the incident as a reminder of ultimate doom, of the Biblical prophecies of destruction of the earth by fire.

Behind the now famous legend of Emily Dickinson, and the plays and novels that have romanticized and sentimentalized her life, is a woman whose genius made its own rules, followed its own commands, and found its own fulfillment. Emily Dickinson's life as a recluse may have been richer, more varied, and—in the satisfactions that come with the exercise of natural talent—even happier than the lives of those around her. In the prospect of history, we can see that the untold secret of Emily Dickinson's emotional life is secondary to the great secret of her genius, the secret that destiny would not let her keep.

BROWSING IN THE FILES

Writers on Writing. In a letter to Thomas Wentworth Higginson, Dickinson described her standards for judging poetry: "If I read a book and it makes my whole body so cold no fire ever can warm me, I know *that* is poetry. If I feel physically as if the top of my head were taken off, I know *that* is poetry. These are the only ways I know it. Is there any other way?"

Resources

Viewing and Representing
Videocassette B, Segment 6
Available in English and Spanish. This segment explores the work of modern American poets. For full lesson plans and worksheets, see the *Visual Connections Teacher's Manual*.
Fine Art Transparency
A fine art transparency of Robert Helm's *November Lake* allows students to compare unconventional visual art with unconventional poetry. The transparency is specifically tied to "The Soul selects her own Society" (p. 378) and "If you were coming in the Fall" (p. 376).
- Transparency 8
- Worksheet, p. 32

Professional Notes

Critical Comment: An Original Voice

The essayist and editor Thomas Wentworth Higginson was the first person outside Dickinson's circle of family and friends to read her poetry. The poems and the poet impressed and bewildered him. Later, he wrote of the experience: "The impression of a wholly new and original poetic genius was as distinct on my mind at the first reading of these four poems as it is now, after half a century of further knowledge; and with it came the problem never yet solved, what place ought to be assigned in literature to what is so remarkable, yet so elusive of criticism. The bee himself did not evade the schoolboy more than she evaded me; and even at this day I still stand somewhat bewildered, like the boy." After students have read the poems in this collection, you may want to return to this statement by Higginson. Invite students to share their responses to his comments about her originality and her elusiveness.

Summary ■■

The speaker urges her heart to forget a lost love. She hopes that by "forgetting," first her emotional and then her intellectual loss, she will obliterate the pain of remembering her love.

Ⓐ Elements of Literature

Apostrophe

The poet uses **apostrophe**—a figure of speech in which an absent or dead person or something abstract or inanimate is addressed directly. Ask students to identify what the speaker is addressing. [Possible answers: her heart; her emotions.]

Ⓑ Critical Thinking

Analyzing

❓ How do the short sentences, exclamation points, and dashes help to convey the poet's ideas? [Possible answers: They create a sense of urgency, almost a panic, as the speaker tries to command her emotions; the abruptness of the short exclamatory sentences suggests that the speaker is trying to control her distress.]

Ⓒ Reading Skills and Strategies

Responding to the Text

Point out that the speaker is holding a dialogue with herself. Ask students if they sometimes "talk to themselves" in this way and how such a conversation might reveal an internal conflict. [Students may say that they talk to themselves when they are feeling uncertain or when parts of themselves are in conflict—one part wanting or believing one thing and another part, something else.]

Before You Read

HEART! WE WILL FORGET HIM!

Make the Connection

The Head and the Heart

Here we have Dickinson's version of the old story of unrequited love—or of love that is impossible because of the circumstances of the lovers. The substance of this poem is conflict—between will and emotion, between the thinking mind and the feeling heart.

Quickwrite

Are most people persuaded more by the promptings of intellect or of feeling? On a separate sheet, write examples from real life, literature, or films.

Ⓐ Heart! We will forget him!

Emily Dickinson

Ⓑ Heart! We will forget him!
You and I—tonight!
You may forget the warmth he gave—
I will forget the light!

Ⓒ When you have done, pray tell me
That I may straight begin!
Haste! lest while you're lagging
I remember him!

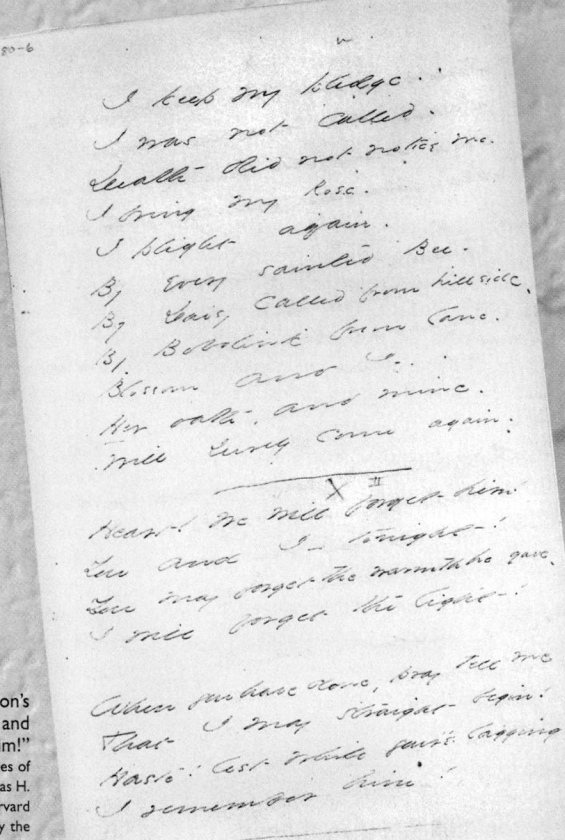

Original manuscript of Emily Dickinson's "I keep my pledge" and "Heart! We will forget him!"

Reaching All Students

Struggling Readers

Remind these students that in poetry many of the words are used figuratively to suggest comparisons that convey ideas or feelings. Also, explain that a poem is a kind of shorthand and that readers need to supply some of the missing connections. You might point out, for example, that in this poem Dickinson uses the single word *light* to express the idea that her love inspires and stimulates her intellectually and spiritually.

English Language Learners

Dickinson's unconventional punctuation may be especially confusing to students learning English. In many European languages, a dash is used to set off dialogue. Make sure students understand that in English a dash indicates a pause. You may want to read aloud a few of Dickinson's poems while students follow along in their books, so that they get a sense of her use of punctuation.

Advanced Learners

Have students concentrate on Dickinson's economy of style. Point out that the poems and the lines are short, and the vocabulary is for the most part simple and familiar. Have students consider how Dickinson uses each word and phrase to convey profound meaning, to suggest multiple interpretations, and to address universal themes.

T374

Memories (1885–1886) by William M. Chase. Oil on canvas (50½″ × 37″).

Listening to Music

"The Chariot" (No. 12) from *Twelve Poems of Emily Dickinson* by Aaron Copland

Brooklyn native Aaron Copland (kōp′lənd) (1900–1990) ranks high among twentieth-century composers. Sometimes called the "dean of American music," Copland infused his compositions with a sound that is distinctly American, and he passionately promoted the appreciation of music in America. His works often draw on American folk songs and other American tradi-tions. In his song cycle, *Twelve Poems of Emily Dickinson,* Copland respectfully gave a predominant role to the poet's words.

Activity
After students have read Dickinson's poems in the textbook, have them listen to this musical version of "Because I could not stop for Death," which Copland referred to as "The Chariot," its title in early editions of Dickinson's poems. Then, have them create their own song version of another of the poems. The style need not be classical or choral—it could be a pop, rap, or country song, whatever students wish.

Summary ■■■

The speaker of the poem longs for the return of an absent person and imagines that any amount of time (a summer, a year, a century) would go by quickly if the date of their reunion were known. The speaker would even give up her life if she knew they would meet in eternity. It is the uncertainty of the length of the separation, rather than the separation itself, that pains the speaker above all.

RESPONDING TO THE ART

George Inness (1825–1894) painted with a kind of poetic Impressionism, depicting the soft effects of early spring and the glowing hues of autumn.
Activity. Have students speculate about how the speaker might respond to *Pastoral Scene*. [Possible answer: The fall might look as idyllic as this scene to the speaker if the absent person addressed were to arrive.]

Ⓐ Appreciating Language
Diction
❓ How do the words "brush by" and "spurn" reveal the speaker's feelings? [Sample responses: The word "spurn" reveals that the speaker scorns the present, seeing it only as a time of waiting; the words "brush by" reveal the speaker's determination to rush past experiences, even pleasant ones, in order to see the beloved more quickly.]

Ⓑ Critical Thinking
Analyzing
❓ How does the speaker use understatement to make a point? [She speaks of "only Centuries," as though the passage of hundreds of years is a brief time.]

Ⓒ Elements of Literature
Metaphor
❓ To what does the speaker compare life? [to a rind of fruit] What do ll. 13–16 say about her feelings for the absent "you"? [Possible responses: She cares more for this person than for her own life; she will discard this life if she knows she will be with her love in the next.]

Make the Connection
From the Ordinary, the Extraordinary
Poetry becomes metaphysical when its **imagery** and **figures of speech** are intellectual and sometimes far-fetched and fantastic. In metaphysical poetry, ordinary things are often seen in relation to the universal. Private emotions, such as unfulfilled love, take on the importance of great and profound events. See if you think this poem meets these requirements.

Quickwrite

Think of a story, movie, or song that deals with the hope of romantic fulfillment—a hope so profound that it can be maintained almost forever. Jot down some notes on this question: Why do you think this topic interests so many people?

Pastoral Scene by George Inness (1825–1894). Oil on canvas (51 cm × 76 cm).
R. C. Love Gallery, Chicago. Courtesy Rosenthal Art Slides, Worcester, Massachusetts.

If you were coming in the Fall

Emily Dickinson

Ⓐ
   If you were coming in the Fall,
   I'd brush the Summer by
   With half a smile, and half a spurn,
   As Housewives do, a Fly.

5 If I could see you in a year,
   I'd wind the months in balls—
   And put them each in separate Drawers,
   For fear the numbers fuse—

Ⓑ
10 If only Centuries, delayed,
   I'd count them on my Hand,
   Subtracting, till my fingers dropped
   Into Van Dieman's Land,°

Ⓒ
   If certain, when this life was out—
   That yours and mine, should be
15 I'd toss it yonder, like a Rind,
   And take Eternity—

   But, now, uncertain of the length
   Of this, that is between,
   It goads me, like the Goblin Bee—
20 That will not state—its sting.

12. Van Dieman's (dē'mənz) **Land:** former name of Tasmania, an island that is a state of Australia.

Using Students' Strengths

Intrapersonal Learners
Have students select something about which they feel an inner conflict. Maybe a part of them wants to move ahead and make changes, but another part is holding them back; maybe they feel torn between striving for independence and needing others. Invite students to compose a dialogue between the parts of the self about this conflict. They may pattern it after the head speaking to the heart in Dickinson's "Heart! We will forget him!"

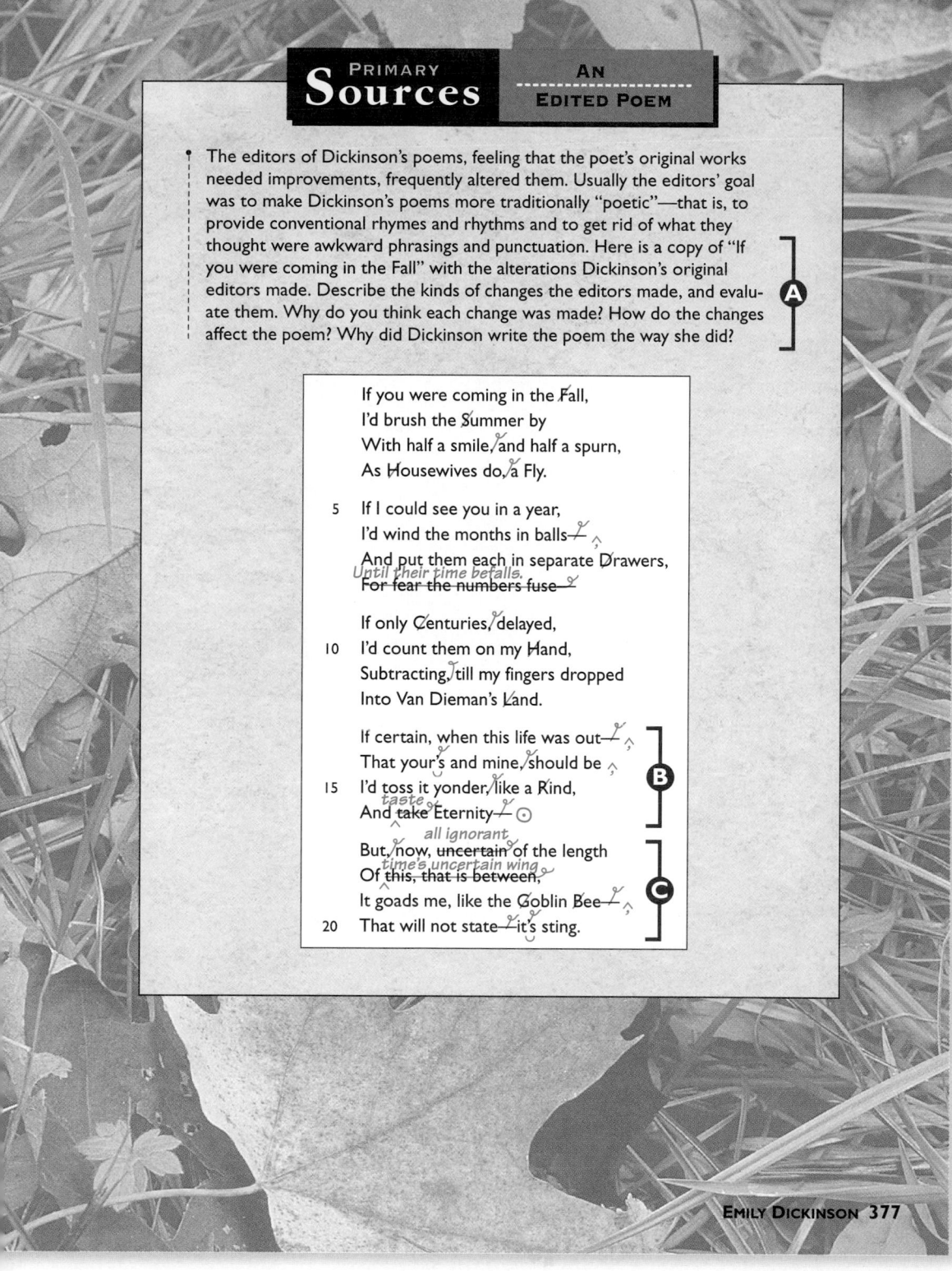

PRIMARY Sources — AN EDITED POEM

The editors of Dickinson's poems, feeling that the poet's original works needed improvements, frequently altered them. Usually the editors' goal was to make Dickinson's poems more traditionally "poetic"—that is, to provide conventional rhymes and rhythms and to get rid of what they thought were awkward phrasings and punctuation. Here is a copy of "If you were coming in the Fall" with the alterations Dickinson's original editors made. Describe the kinds of changes the editors made, and evaluate them. Why do you think each change was made? How do the changes affect the poem? Why did Dickinson write the poem the way she did?

A

> If you were coming in the Fall,
> I'd brush the Summer by
> With half a smile, and half a spurn,
> As Housewives do, a Fly.
>
> 5 If I could see you in a year,
> I'd wind the months in balls —
> And put them each in separate Drawers,
> Until their time befalls.
> For fear the numbers fuse —
>
> If only Centuries, delayed,
> 10 I'd count them on my Hand,
> Subtracting, till my fingers dropped
> Into Van Dieman's Land.
>
> If certain, when this life was out —
> That your's and mine, should be
> 15 I'd toss it yonder, like a Rind,
> And take Eternity —
> taste
> all ignorant
> But, now, uncertain of the length
> time's uncertain wing
> Of this, that is between,
> It goads me, like the Goblin Bee —
> 20 That will not state — it's sting.

B

C

EMILY DICKINSON 377

Professional Notes

Critical Comment:
Dickinson's Diction

Thomas H. Johnson, who compiled and edited the complete 1955 edition of Emily Dickinson's poems, believes that for her, choosing words was an intense and almost religious experience. "Emily Dickinson loved words ardently. Her feeling about them amounted to veneration and her selection of them was ritualistic. . . . 'A word that breathes distinctly / Has not the power to die' [she wrote]. . . . Near the end of her life she wrote a close friend, 'I hesitate which word to take, as I can take but few and each must be the chiefest. . . .'" Another critic, Joel Conarroe, also focused on Dickinson's love of words. "What mainly held her attention, year after year," Conarroe said, "was the mysterious power of words. 'We used to think,' she wrote a friend, 'that words were cheap & weak. Now I don't know of anything so mighty.'"

Primary Sources

This feature includes Dickinson's poem, "If you were coming in the Fall," complete with proofreaders' marks, which show the "corrections" to the manuscript made by Dickinson's earliest editors. It allows students to compare and contrast Dickinson's innovative phrasings and punctuation with the conventional poetic style imposed by her first editors.

A Background

Because Dickinson's early editors mistook originality for error, her poems did not appear as she wrote them until the 1950s. Dickinson's frequent use of dashes, capitalization, and elliptical phrasing were unconventional in her time, and the reasons behind many of her stylistic choices remain somewhat obscure today.

B Humanities Connections
Proofreaders' Marks

As students study the edited poem, make sure they all understand the proofreader's marks on the text. You might draw each mark on the board and explain that a slash through a capital letter means "change to lowercase," a slash with a loop at the top means "delete," a ∧ mark means "insert," and a ∪ mark means "close up space between characters."

C Critical Thinking
Evaluating

Ask students how they would define an editor's job. [Possible answers: fixing errors; helping a writer to express ideas more clearly.] Ask students if they think making changes in a writer's work without the writer's knowledge is acceptable. (Remind them that most of Dickinson's work was published only after her death.) Students might choose sides and debate the question of whether a text should be left exactly as a writer wrote it or whether certain changes are advisable or necessary.

Summary ■■■

The Soul is personified as a queen or goddess. She refuses to admit most of the people who come to see her and, after choosing one, shuts the door.

RESPONDING TO THE ART

Claude Monet (1840–1926) was the leading exponent of late-nineteenth-century French Impressionism. He repeatedly painted the same subject at different times of the day in order to catch the passing effects of natural light. With its strong brush strokes and patches of bright color, *Woman with Parasol* catches a moment that looks ready to dissolve the instant the light changes.

Activity. Have students discuss whose "society" Monet's subject has selected. [Possible answers: her own; nature's.]

Ⓐ Elements of Literature

Personification

❓ How would you explain Dickinson's use of the word *soul* here? [Possible responses: a person's spiritual nature; the inner self.] How does the poet personify the Soul? [Possible response: by having the Soul take human actions ("selects," "shuts the door")]

Ⓑ Appreciating Language

Diction

❓ What is the effect of the word "Stone"? [Possible answers: It sounds absolutely final; it demonstrates the obduracy of the Soul's standards and suggests that only one other person will be given intimate access to it.]

Ⓒ Critical Thinking

Challenging the Text

❓ Why does Dickinson leave the poem "unfinished," using a dash to suggest a pause or break in the speaker's thoughts? [Possible answers: Expression seems choked off; the sudden break echoes the image of the shut-off valves, as well as suggesting an abrupt end to the Soul's openness to others.]

Before You Read

THE SOUL SELECTS HER OWN SOCIETY

Make the Connection

Choices of the Soul

This poem is about choices and the mysterious instinct that leads each one of us to prefer certain things and cherish certain people above all others. In Dickinson's view, this instinct has less to do with the discriminations of the mind than with the yearnings of that spiritual part of us that some call the soul.

Quickwrite

How do you think most people select their friends, with their minds (thoughts), with their souls (feelings), or with a combination of the two? Write your responses to this question on a separate sheet. If you like, cite examples to support your viewpoint.

Musée d'Orsay, Paris. Courtesy Giraudon/Art Resource, NY.

Woman with Parasol—Turned to Left (1886) by Claude Monet. Oil on canvas.

The Soul selects her own Society

Emily Dickinson

Ⓐ The Soul selects her own Society—
Then—shuts the Door—
To her divine Majority—
Present no more—

5   Unmoved—she notes the Chariots—pausing—
At her low Gate—
Unmoved—an Emperor be kneeling
Upon her Mat—

I've known her—from an ample nation—
10 Choose One—
Ⓑ Then—close the Valves of her attention—
Ⓒ Like Stone—

Skill Link

Defending and Clarifying Responses and Interpretations

Dickinson's poems provide an opportunity for students to articulate and defend their responses and interpretations.

1. Have each student choose a poem that seems especially intriguing. Then, have them respond to the poem, making notes in a journal.

2. Tell students to reread the poems they have selected once a day for two weeks and write down any new ideas that occur to them. Then, have them write thoughtful interpretations of and responses to the poems. After sharing their work, have them defend and clarify their thoughts with details from the poems.

Heart! We will forget him!

First Thoughts

1. Review your Quickwrite notes. Whom do you identify with in this poem—the head or the heart? Why?

Shaping Interpretations

2. Why do you think the heart is asked to take the lead in this situation?

3. What do you think the speaker means by "warmth" and "light"? If you were trying to forget someone, which would you try to forget first?

4. Exclamation points punctuate this little poem, as if the speaker were saying, "Hurry up! We must get this over with!" Why do you suppose the speaker is in such a hurry?

5. Read the feature on **slant rhyme** on page 380. Then, describe the **rhyme scheme** of the poem, noting the instance of slant rhyme. What is the function of the end rhymes?

6. Some would say this poem is **ironic** to the core: The speaker doesn't really expect to—doesn't want to—forget the man. Do you agree? Why or why not?

If you were coming in the Fall

First Thoughts

1. Look over your Quickwrite notes. Do you think the hopes expressed in the poem are fairly common, or are they far-fetched? Explain.

Shaping Interpretations

2. How would you describe the speaker's situation? How does she feel about it?

3. What two things are being compared in the **simile** in the first stanza?

4. In the second stanza, what domestic articles are the months compared to? Why does the speaker put them in separate drawers?

5. Van Dieman's Land has come to mean places on the globe farthest away from us. Given this information, how would you paraphrase the third stanza?

6. How would you describe the speaker's **tone** in the first four stanzas? How does it change in the fifth stanza, where her exaggerations disappear? What goads, or pushes, her against her will?

7. In folklore, a goblin is a tormenting creature. What do you think Dickinson is suggesting when she says that the bee is a goblin and will not "state" its sting?

Challenging the Text

8. What changes, if any, would you suggest in capitalization and punctuation in this poem? Why?

The Soul selects her own Society

First Thoughts

1. What advantages and disadvantages may lie in a selection as strict as this soul makes? Do most people make choices like this? (Check your Quickwrite notes.)

Shaping Interpretations

2. *Majority* has at least two meanings: "having reached full legal age" (or "having come into one's own") and "the greater part of something." It could also mean "superiority" (an obsolete usage). What do you think it means in this poem? What kind of person does the adjective "divine" suggest?

3. Do you think the phrase "Valves of her attention" is derived from organic things (valves of a clamshell) or mechanical ones (valves of a faucet)? What do you picture happening here?

4. Dickinson's early editors changed the word *valves* to *lids.* How does this change the **metaphor**? How does it change what you *see*?

5. Look at the **meter** of lines 10 and 12. How does their rhythmical pattern differ from the corresponding lines in the first and second stanzas? What is the effect of this difference?

Challenging the Text

6. Dickinson did not give her poems titles. (The titles in this text are the first lines of the poems.) Her early editors called this poem "Exclusion." In what ways does this title apply? In what ways is it limiting?

EMILY DICKINSON 379

If you were coming in the Fall

First Thoughts [Respond]

1. Desperately wanting and waiting for something is common.

Shaping Interpretations [Interpret]

2. The speaker can only wait. The uncertainty tortures her.

3. Making the summer pass quickly is compared to brushing away a fly.

4. The months are compared to balls of yarn. She separates them to make sure she does not lose count.

5. If mere centuries delayed you, I could tick them off indefinitely.

6. Exaggerations in stanzas 1–4 create hope that changes to frustration in stanza 5. Uncertainty finally tortures her.

7. Possible answer: She would prefer concrete knowledge—the bee's sting—no matter how painful.

Challenging the Text [Evaluate]

8. Possible answers: Capitalize *year* and *months* to match other time words; eliminate dashes in ll. 8 and 16, since these lines end stanzas. Some students would make no changes.

The Soul selects her own Society

First Thoughts [Respond]

1. Advantages: Ability to focus one's attention; to be a committed companion. Disadvantages: narrowness; loneliness. Most do not.

Shaping Interpretations [Interpret]

2. Possible meanings: "the greater part," since the Soul's select few outweigh all others; "maturity," since the Soul has control over her life; "superiority," since the Soul finds few acceptable. "Divine" suggests one who is magnificent, godlike, and detached.

3. In shutting out people, she seems to be closing the valves of her heart (love).

4. *Lids* suggests eyelids. The metaphor suggests shutting out unwanted sights. It creates a more human image.

5. They have two rather than four syllables. This slows the rhythm and weights the lines.

Challenging the Text [Evaluate]

6. It applies to the Soul's excluding others but fails to convey the profound emotional affinity that the poet also describes.

Heart! We will forget him!

First Thoughts [Respond]

1. Possible responses: heart—love is hard to control; head—self-control can help us heal.

Shaping Interpretations [Interpret]

2. Possible responses: because emotions are what keep one person tied to another; because emotions can undermine one's decisions.

3. One might forget warmth (love, affection) first because its loss is more painful. One might forget light (inspiration) first because forgetting it may dim other memories.

4. She fears losing her resolve; she wants to stop suffering quickly.

5. Rhyme scheme: *abcb defe.* Slant rhyme: *begin/him.* End rhymes add emphasis.

6. Agree; she wants to hang on to valuable, albeit painful, memories. Disagree; she wants to forget—remembering makes her suffer.

ELEMENTS OF LITERATURE

This lesson explains why poets sometimes choose to use slant rather than exact rhyme and what effects they can achieve with it. You might give students this additional explanation: Rhyme and meter establish a pattern that sets up expectations in the reader or listener. The audience expects the poem to sound a certain way, to move a certain way, to resolve the questions and feelings it raises according to that established pattern. When the poet alters that pattern, he or she surprises the audience and forces it to think about what is being said.

Possible answers

1. One exact rhyme: *Door/more.* Four slant rhymes: *Society/Majority, Gate/Mat, nation/attention, One/Stone.* Students might also suggest *pausing/kneeling* as a slant rhyme.

2. Possible examples: In "If you were coming in the Fall," the slant rhyme of *between/sting* emphasizes the sharp, smarting pain. In "Success is counted sweetest" (see p. 388), the slant rhyme of *today/victory* suggests the hollowness and irony of achieving fame by dying for a lost cause.

Resources

Elements of Literature
Identifying Rhyme in a Poem
For additional instruction on slant rhyme, see *Literary Elements:*
• Transparency 13
• Worksheet, p. 40

Assessment
Formal Assessment
• Literary Elements Test, p. 80

Ⓐ Elements of Literature
Slant Rhyme
? What effect does the final slant rhyme have on the reader? [Possible answers: It provides an echo in sound of the image of breaking; it startles the reader.]

ELEMENTS OF LITERATURE

Slant Rhyme

Not long ago, **exact rhyme**—two or more words whose syllables share identical sounds, as in the words *free* and *bee*—was part of every poet's craft. Today it is still the most familiar aspect of sound in poetry. But rhyme has, over the years, fallen out of favor with many poets. One reason is that these poets feel almost all the exact rhymes in English have been used over and over again. Another reason is that imposed rhymes can act as a constraint and can limit expression. Some poets, as a solution, have abandoned rhyme altogether. Other poets, like Dickinson, use slant rhyme.

Slant rhyme is a close, but not exact, rhyming sound. (It is also called **off rhyme, half rhyme,** or **approximate rhyme.**) Word pairs like *society/majority* or *nerve/love* are examples of slant rhymes—"not quite, but almost" rhyming sounds. Part of the shock value of Dickinson's poems comes from her use of slant rhyme. Slant rhyme makes many readers uncomfortable—in the way that a sharp or flat note on a piano would disturb a listener who wasn't expecting it.

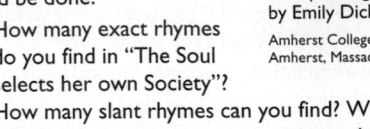

The Mirror Girl—stares back at me
(In the Style of Emily Dickinson)

The Mirror Girl—stares back at me—
With a Look that knows too much—
And a Skin that's never felt the Burn
Of a soft—caressing—Touch

She speaks with Lips that smile—and laugh—
But never have been—kissed—
And cries with careful—Countenance—
That never has been missed

The Mirror Girl is cold and crystal—
Hard enough to feel—
But who is to say, on the other Side,
She's not the One who's real?

The Mirror Girl is a stoic Thing—
Ⓐ That does not pain or ache—
But while I suffer and endure—
The Mirror Girl merely—breaks

—Brigid Spackman
James E. Taylor Senior High School
Katy, Texas

First appeared in *Merlyn's Pen: The National Magazines of Student Writing*

380 A NEW AMERICAN POETRY: WHITMAN AND DICKINSON

Analyzing slant rhyme. Slant rhyme is a subtle use of sound. It is often used to force our attention onto particular words. For example, the last word in "The Soul selects her own Society," *stone,* stands out because it doesn't match exactly in sound with the word *one.* Why is it important that the word *stone* be emphasized? To hear and understand the difference, imagine that Dickinson had ended her poem with the words, "And be done."

1. How many exact rhymes do you find in "The Soul selects her own Society"? How many slant rhymes can you find? What rhyming sounds were you expecting to hear in each case?

2. Look through Dickinson's other poems for slant rhymes. Read them aloud, and see if you can identify the purpose and effect of each rhyme.

First printing of *Poems* by Emily Dickinson.
Amherst College Library, Amherst, Massachusetts.

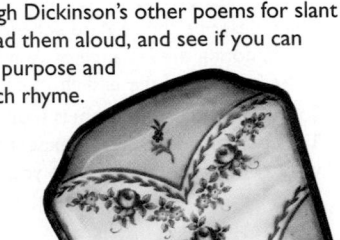

Professional Notes

Critical Comment
Scholar Joel Conarroe writes that Dickinson "employed off rhymes, or near rhymes, to ensure that the quatrains, couched in the language of surprise, were neither conventional nor predictable. . . . Rarely containing so much as an unnecessary syllable, the poems are almost all characterized by an epigrammatic precision. . . . A reader soon learns the pleasures of collaboration, filling in the missing keys she has deliberately left out."

Connecting Across Texts

Connecting with the Poems of Emily Dickinson
Have students consider how Spackman's poem is like and unlike Dickinson's poems in style. [Like: There is similar use of capitalization and dashes. Unlike: Each thought is complete, with a subject and verb. There are no fragments like the one in l. 14 of "If you were coming in the Fall."] Ask students how the concerns in Spackman's poem are like Dickinson's. [Possible response: Both poets are concerned with self-reflection and solitude.]

Summary ■ ■ ■

The speaker worships God by appreciating nature, not by attending church. Through her reverence for God's creations, she experiences a heaven on earth all the time.

Before You Read

SOME KEEP THE SABBATH GOING TO CHURCH

Make the Connection

Transcendence

Although she rejected the teachings of her family's Congregationalist church, Dickinson was a deeply spiritual poet who constantly reflected on the divine. The fifth of seven poems published in her lifetime appeared on March 12, 1864. It was titled "My Sabbath," and unlike this version, it used the word "going" instead of "getting" in line 11. Later called "A Service of Song," it was included in a collection published in 1890, after Dickinson's death.

Quickwrite

Does a church—or any place of worship—have to be a human-built construction made expressly for worship, or can there be a broader understanding of what a church is? Record your thoughts on a separate sheet of paper.

© Collection of The New-York Historical Society.

Bobolink (1822) by John J. Audubon. Watercolor, graphite, pastel, gouache, selective glazing.

Some keep the Sabbath going to Church

Emily Dickinson

Some keep the Sabbath going to Church—
I keep it, staying at Home—
With a Bobolink° for a Chorister°—
And an Orchard, for a Dome—

5   Some keep the Sabbath in Surplice°—
I just wear my Wings—
And instead of tolling the Bell, for Church,
Our little Sexton°—sings.

God preaches, a noted Clergyman—
10 And the sermon is never long,
So instead of getting to Heaven, at last—
I'm going, all along.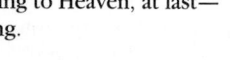

---

3. bobolink: small bird. **chorister:** choir member.
5. surplice (sur′plis): loose white vestment worn by clergy or choir members on top of longer robes.
8. sexton: church officer or employee whose various duties may include maintenance and ringing the bells.

EMILY DICKINSON 381

Ⓐ English Language Learners

Specialized Vocabulary

These students may be puzzled by the ecclesiastical vocabulary. Point out the footnotes, and encourage students to match the English with similar terms in their native language.

Ⓑ Struggling Readers

Rearranging Word Order

Make it clear to these students that in l. 9 Dickinson is referring to God as "a noted Clergyman." Have students rearrange the order of the words: "God, a noted Clergyman, preaches—." Point out that Dickinson is gently chiding churchgoers for paying more attention to preachers than to God. In l. 10, she is both praising God's creation and scolding preachers for their sometimes boring or oppressive sermons.

Ⓒ Critical Thinking

Determining the Author's Purpose

❓ How might you summarize Dickinson's message to readers? [Possible responses: Don't ignore the greatness of God's creation that is all around you. You don't have to wait to get to heaven; you can experience paradise right now.]

Professional Notes

The Religious Climate

A period of great religious fervor, called the Second Great Awakening, occurred during the first half of the nineteenth century. The belief that salvation was available to all supplanted the Calvinist idea of predestination. Revivalism, a movement that used emotional public sermons to move people to "convert" and accept salvation, swept the country. Transcendentalism and utopian philosophies flourished, and the Unitarian and African Methodist Episcopal churches were founded. All of these groups shared a belief that both individuals and society could be improved, and they were instrumental in the reform movements of the century—abolitionism, women's rights, prison reform, public education, and temperance.

Summary ■ ■ ■

The speaker confesses she is "drunk" on the glories of nature. She shocks the angels and saints in heaven with her giddiness.

RESPONDING TO THE ART

Martin Johnson Heade (1819–1904) painted luminous landscapes, seascapes, flowers, and birds in beautiful and meticulous detail. Hummingbirds were among his favorite subjects.

Activity. Ask students how the painting matches the mood of the speaker. [The painting suggests a fantastical and dizzying world, appropriate to the speaker's feeling of intoxication; like the poem's "drunken Bee" and butterflies, hummingbirds feed on nectar.]

A Elements of Literature

Conceit

? Identify the extended comparison in this poem. [The gorgeousness of nature is compared to strong liquor.] **Why is this metaphor so striking?** [Possible answers: Portraying nature as inebriating is unusual; drunkenness is generally viewed with disapproval, but here being drunk is depicted as a wonderfully inspiring, even exalted, feeling.]

B Literary Connections

Dickinson's Religion

The great critic Northrop Frye believed that Emily Dickinson "never felt that the path of social conformity and assent to doctrine was her path." Instead, she experienced religion as "a state of heightened consciousness . . . when the poet feels directly in communion with nature and in a state of 'identity' . . . with it." How might this stanza support Frye's assertion? [Possible response: The speaker's willingness to shock the Seraphs and Saints with her natural intoxication suggests an ironic distance from institutionalized religion.]

T382

Before You Read

I TASTE A LIQUOR NEVER BREWED

Make the Connection

Intoxicating Inspiration

Some critics believe that Dickinson is making fun of Emerson (page 216) in the following poem. Like Emerson's poem "Bacchus," this poem compares a poet's feeling of inspiration to the feeling of intoxication some get when drinking liquor. However, in contrast to Emerson's serious tone, Dickinson's is humorous.

Quickwrite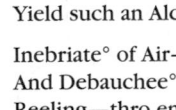

Record some of your own remembrances of what it feels like to be inspired, or describe some of the qualities you associate with inspiration or even with complete absorption in doing something you love.

Passion Flowers and Hummingbirds (c. 1865) by Martin Johnson Heade. Oil on canvas (15 ¼″ × 21 ½″).

Gift of Mrs. Maxim Karolik for the M. and M. Karolik Collection of American Paintings, 1815–1865. Courtesy of Museum of Fine Arts, Boston.

I taste a liquor never brewed

Emily Dickinson

I taste a liquor never brewed—
From Tankards scooped in Pearl—
Not all the Vats upon the Rhine°
Yield such an Alcohol!

5 Inebriate° of Air—am I—
And Debauchee° of Dew—
Reeling—thro endless summer days—
From inns of Molten Blue—

When "Landlords" turn the drunken Bee
10 Out of the Foxglove's° door—
When Butterflies—renounce their "drams"—
I shall but drink the more!

Till Seraphs° swing their snowy Hats—
And Saints—to windows run—
15 To see the little Tippler°
Leaning against the—Sun—

3. Rhine: an allusion to the Rhine River in Germany, an area that is noted for fine wine and beer.

5. inebriate: (in·ē′brē·it′): drunk.

6. debauchee (deb′ô·shē′): person who overindulges in pleasures.

10. foxglove's: A foxglove is a kind of plant with cuplike flowers.

13. seraphs: angels of the highest order.

15. tippler: drinker.

382 A NEW AMERICAN POETRY: WHITMAN AND DICKINSON

Getting Students Involved

Enrichment Activity: Picture a Poem

Remind students that a writer uses words to create pictures in the reader's mind. In the poem above, for instance, "inns of Molten Blue" (l. 8) suggests color and texture and "Saints— to windows run" (l. 14) paints a specific action taken by particular characters.

Invite students to choose a poem in this collection that has particularly vivid imagery. Ask them to analyze how Dickinson created those images using adjectives, action verbs, concrete nouns, and figures of speech. Then have students use paints and colors to create an artwork that captures similar images—the sights, textures, actions, and colors of the poem. Tell students to plan a way to arrange their artwork with the poem. For example, they might create their own version of an illuminated manuscript, wrapping images around words and phrases in the poem or placing art inside the lines of capital letters.

Before You Read

MUCH MADNESS IS DIVINEST SENSE

Make the Connection

The Solace of Solitude
Since her death, Dickinson has often been portrayed as the mad recluse of Amherst. In fact, Dickinson lived as many other great poets (and quite a few "ordinary" people) have lived —deliberately choosing solitude for contemplation, reading, and writing.

Quickwrite

Write down what you think the unusual title of this poem means.

Courtesy of the Trustees of Amherst College/The Emily Dickinson Homestead.

Garden at Emily Dickinson's house.

Much Madness is divinest Sense

Emily Dickinson

Much Madness is divinest Sense— **A**
To a discerning Eye—
Much Sense—the starkest Madness—
'Tis the Majority
In this, as All, prevail— **B**
Assent—and you are sane—
Demur—you're straightway dangerous—
And handled with a Chain— **C**

Summary ▪▪

This poem asserts that those judged mad by society are often the sane ones and that those deemed sensible are the truly mad. The poem warns the reader that those who do not conform to the majority's narrow standards of sanity will be ostracized or coerced.

Ⓐ Appreciating Language

Diction

❓ Why does Dickinson use the word "divinest" here? [Possible answers: to suggest that the "madness" the poem describes is in reality a gift from God; to suggest that the "madness" is the artist's urge to create, which is the human analogy to God's creation of the world.]

Ⓑ Critical Thinking

Interpreting

Ask students what the poet seems to say about madness and sanity in these lines. [Possible responses: Those people who go against the majority are often thought of as mad and are shunned. To the poet, such madness means divine inspiration, which she sees as a higher sense.]

Ⓒ Critical Thinking

Expressing an Opinion

❓ What does the image in the last line suggest? [Possible answers: that people who dissent from the majority will be punished; that dissenters will be treated as criminals or lunatics and will be locked up.] Why do you think the majority might at times view dissenters as dangerous? [Possible responses: because their ideas threaten the status quo; because their ideas shake up people's concepts of themselves and their world.]

Connecting Across Texts

Connecting with Emerson and Thoreau

Have students compare the feelings expressed in "Some keep the Sabbath" with those expressed in the excerpts from Emerson's *Nature* and Thoreau's *Walden* (pp. 219 and 233). Do these three writers view God, nature, and worship in the same way? If not, what are the differences? Remind students that Emerson was once a minister and that ministers played crucial roles in Dickinson's life. What might Emerson and Thoreau have thought of Dickinson's poem? How might they have reacted to "I taste a liquor" and "Much Madness"? Do the themes, ideas, and images in those poems remind students of Emerson's or Thoreau's works? Have students gather in pairs or groups of three to discuss these questions. Students can then write brief essays, setting forth and defending their opinions, or choose representatives for a panel discussion.

Some keep the Sabbath . . .

First Thoughts [Respond]

1. Possible answers: The poem broadens the idea of "church"; nature, God's creation, is just as majestic as any human-made church.

Shaping Interpretations [Interpret]

2. She glories in nature's wonders. She might lose this source of exaltation if cloistered in a church.

3. The speaker worships nature. She compares her wings (a possible metaphor for her roving spirit) to a surplice, an orchard to a church dome, and a bird to a choir member and a sexton.

4. She means that by worshipping God's creation, she experiences heaven every day.

Extending the Text [Analyze]

5. People who prefer solitude or independence or who see God in nature would agree. Those with orthodox religious views or who desire church fellowship and spiritual guidance might not.

Challenging the Text [Evaluate]

6. Possible responses: "My Sabbath," because it focuses on the speaker's personal choice; "A Service of Song," for its play on words.

I taste a liquor never brewed

First Thoughts [Respond]

1. Possible responses: Yes, because it expresses the intensity and headiness of the feeling; no, because the feeling of inspiration is usually a feeling of calm happiness.

Shaping Interpretations [Interpret]

2. The speaker is drinking in the gorgeousness of summer. It thrills her too much to stop.

3. Since a bee usually abandons a flower only when it is empty of pollen, the "Landlords" may be Time or nightfall. The speaker's insistence on drinking more (l. 12) and her tippling before the "Seraphs" and "Saints" suggest a defiance of sorts.

4. She may be in a garden or in heaven. *Sun* may be a pun on *Son,* suggesting that she is leaning on Christ.

Extending the Text [Connect]

5. Possible responses: love; a religious or musical experience.

Some keep the Sabbath going to Church

First Thoughts

1. Review your Quickwrite notes. What is your response to the speaker's "Church"?

Shaping Interpretations

2. In what ways does the speaker keep the Sabbath? How might keeping the Sabbath as others do affect her worship?

3. What is the speaker's relationship to nature? How is this revealed in the **metaphors** the speaker chooses?

4. What do you think the speaker means in the last line by saying "I'm going, all along"?

Extending the Text

5. What kinds of people might share the speaker's preference? Who would disagree with this way of keeping the Sabbath?

Challenging the Text

6. Which **title** do you feel better suits the poem: "My Sabbath" or "A Service of Song"? Or do you have a better title? Explain your answer.

I taste a liquor never brewed

First Thoughts

1. Review your Quickwrite notes, and explain whether you have ever felt what this speaker is feeling. Do you think the **analogy,** or comparison, of inspiration to intoxication works? Why or why not?

Shaping Interpretations

2. What is the speaker drinking in the poem? Why doesn't he or she want to stop?

3. Who would the "Landlords" in stanza 3 be? What details in the poem suggest a **tone** of defiance?

4. Where is the little "Tippler," or drinker, in the last stanza? Can you see any significance in the last word of the poem?

Much Madness is divinest Sense

First Thoughts [Respond]

1. Sample responses: independent thinkers; artists. Creative people may see reflections of themselves in the poem.

Shaping Interpretations [Interpret]

2. The paradoxes are that the mad make sense and much that is deemed sane is nonsense. They convey the poem's message that originality is often misunderstood and suppressed.

Extending the Text

5. Many readers see this poem, at least in part, as a description of the inspiration that drives artists to create. What other human activities or emotions could it pertain to?

Much Madness is divinest Sense

First Thoughts

1. What kinds of people might take this poem as a personal "anthem"? Does anything in this poem reflect ideas you have had about yourself?

Shaping Interpretations

2. What is the meaning of the two **paradoxes,** or apparent contradictions, in the first three lines? How do they affect the poem's meaning?

3. What do you think is the poem's **theme**? What does the speaker think about the individual's proper relationship to society?

4. Dickinson liked to use dashes—a mark of punctuation her first editors usually removed. How do dashes help emphasize certain ideas in this poem?

5. What would you say is Dickinson's **tone** in this poem? What similarities do you notice to other poems in this collection?

Extending the Text

6. The public has often said of creative and independent thinkers that they are "crazy." Name at least three people—writers, artists, inventors, or other creative types (besides Dickinson)—who are or have been considered "mad." In what ways is their "madness" a kind of "sense," at least in terms of their work? Are they really mad at all? (Did you mention these ideas in your Quickwrite?)

3. People should follow their own beliefs. Majority opinion should be questioned.

4. They suggest the speaker is spontaneous, "mad" and proud of it.

5. Possible tone: defiant; ironic. Other poems also cherish nonconformity.

Extending the Text [Synthesize]

6. Possible choices: Galileo, Poe, Joan of Arc. Their "divinest Sense" lay in creating or seeing things that others cannot.

Before You Read

APPARENTLY WITH NO SURPRISE

Make the Connection

Metaphor Metamorphosis
Dickinson had only to look out her window to see the ordinary—and extraordinary—powers of nature at work. In using **metaphors** built on images of birds, flies, and flowers, her deceptively innocent observations reveal deep and sometimes disturbing ideas.

Quickwrite

Do you think nature is essentially benign, or threatening and hostile? Create a double-column chart in which you write evidence of nature's benevolence in one column and evidence of nature's destructiveness in the other.

Jim Zipp/Photo Researchers.

Apparently with no surprise

Emily Dickinson

Apparently with no surprise
To any happy Flower
The Frost beheads it at its play—
In accidental power—
The blonde Assassin passes on—
The Sun proceeds unmoved
To measure off another Day
For an Approving God. **B**

EMILY DICKINSON 385

Summary ■ ■ ■

At the height of its beauty, a flower is indifferently killed by frost. But nevertheless God approves, as the sun rises and sets, following the beautiful yet merciless progress of the seasons.

Ⓐ Appreciating Language
Diction
❓ Why does Dickinson use the word "accidental" to describe the frost's power? [Possible answers: The frost cannot control its own power; the frost has no conscious intention to hurt or harm.]

Ⓑ Critical Thinking
Analyzing
❓ What is it that God approves of? [Possible answers: the actions of the frost and sun; the seasons and the cycles of nature.] **What does the speaker seem to be saying about God's attitude toward creation?** [Possible answer: The cycles in nature of light and dark, life and death, are part of God's plan.]

Getting Students Involved

Writing Activity:
Drawing Lessons from Nature
Though self-confined to a very narrow world through much of her life, Dickinson keenly observed the people and things around her and from these particulars expressed themes and feelings about life, love, nature, and immortality. Suggest that students reread the poems in this collection, focusing on how the poet evokes images of nature and subtly personifies such natural phenomena as flowers, frost, birds, and bees.

Ask students if they ever imagine that things in nature have personalities such as those Dickinson ascribes to them. Invite students to observe nature for a time in order to look for comparisons that will help them convey some aspect of their own experience. Ask them to write poems or essays in which they use personification to express their own feelings and views about the issues that matter most to them.

Summary ▪▪▪

The poet compares truth to a blinding light and suggests that truth can be fully comprehended only if it is revealed obliquely.

Ⓐ Reading Skills and Strategies

Finding the Main Idea

❓ What does the expression *slant the truth* mean? [Possible responses: to tell things in a biased way; to "put a spin" on the facts.] What might *tell all the truth slant* mean? [Possible answers: to tell the truth indirectly; to tell it through fables or figurative language.] What is a major difference between the two expressions? [To *slant the truth* means to mislead, but to *tell all the truth slant* means to tell the truth but partially, gradually, or indirectly.]

Ⓑ Struggling Readers

Breaking Down Difficult Text

Of all the poems in this collection, "Tell all the Truth . . ." may be the most fragmented in terms of normal sentence structure. Have students choose partners and go over the poem in pairs, breaking it down into a series of paraphrased thoughts and images.

Ⓒ Critical Thinking

Expressing an Opinion

❓ In your opinion, what kinds of truths might need to be revealed "slant" (indirectly) or "gradually"? [Possible responses: complex truths that resist easy explanation; truths that contradict people's established beliefs or core values; truths about life-and-death issues; personal truths that can damage someone's self-image; scientific findings that threaten people's visions of themselves and their world.]

Before You Read

TELL ALL THE TRUTH BUT TELL IT SLANT

Make the Connection

Forms of Truth

Dickinson's famous line "Tell all the Truth but tell it slant" may reveal her method of survival as well as the essence of her own poetry.

Quickwrite

What do you think it would mean to tell the truth "slant"? Write some examples of the truth "told slant."

Tell all the Truth but tell it slant

Emily Dickinson

Ⓐ Tell all the Truth but tell it slant—
Success in Circuit° lies
Ⓑ Too bright for our infirm Delight
The Truth's superb surprise
As Lightning to the Children eased
With explanation kind
Ⓒ The Truth must dazzle gradually
Or every man be blind—

2. **circuit:** an indirect path.

Reaching All Students

Advanced Learners

You might point out that this poem by Dickinson, unlike many of her others, contains no slant rhymes. Challenge students to come up with possible reasons why this is so and share their ideas with the class. [They may say that exact rhymes make the poem easier to read; they may suggest that the lack of slant rhymes is ironic since it contradicts the reader's expectation asso-ciated with the word *slant;* they may say that the word *slant* has different meanings in the phrases *tell all the truth but tell it slant* and *slant rhymes* and that one has nothing to do with the other. *Slant rhymes* means "almost rhymes," while *tell the truth slant* means "approaching the truth obliquely or from an angle."] Have these students suggest **what the rhymes in the poem contribute to the** meaning. [They may say that the rhymes add emphasis to key words: The word *lies* puts stress on the word *surprise;* the word *Delight,* on *bright;* and the word *kind,* on *blind.*] Finally, ask students to identify and explain examples from Dickinson's poems in which she tells the truth "slant."

Rooms by the Sea (1951) by Edward Hopper. Oil on canvas.

EMILY DICKINSON 387

Crossing the Curriculum

Drama

The Belle of Amherst is William Luce's 1976 play about Emily Dickinson. The famed actress Julie Harris played the poet in an award-winning one-woman stage performance on Broadway. A tape of this performance is available on video. You may want to obtain a copy for your students to view.

Before they view the play, tell students that both the playwright and actress did considerable research on Dickinson's writing to prepare for this production and that several of the poems and letters in this collection appear in the playscript. After students view the tape, have them discuss how successful they think the play is. Do they agree with Luce's and Harris's interpretation of Dickinson? Do they think a one-woman show is a good idea, or should other characters have appeared onstage? Students may want to use this activity as a spring board to Choices activity 4 (p. 396).

Art

Have student pairs explore further how *tell the truth slant* applies to modern painting, as well as poetry. Have them investigate such questions as these: Which artists present their subjects straightforwardly? Which present them "slant"? What elements of modern art are analogous to elements of modern poetry? What do both require of the viewer/reader? Ask students to report on this subject to the class, using art reproductions to illustrate their points.

Summary ■■

The speaker states that success is most valued by those who fail, just as victory in battle seems most precious to a soldier who is defeated and dying.

RESPONDING TO THE ART

Gilbert Gaul (1855–1919), who painted military and Western subjects, is noted for his accurate depictions of weapons and uniforms. He spent considerable time doing firsthand research on Western army posts and Indian reservations.

Activity. Explain to students that "Taps" is the military bugle call for "lights out" at close of day and by metaphoric extension is associated with death and is often played at funerals. Ask students what makes the painting *Taps* an appropriate illustration for "Success. . . ." [Possible answers: The final "lights out" has come for the soldier in the painting and is coming for the soldier in the poem; the title *Taps* suggests a somber sound that contrasts with the "strains of triumph" of the opponents of the agonized soldier in the poem.]

Ⓐ Elements of Literature
Analogy

❓ What analogy does Dickinson draw here? [She compares a thirsty person's appreciation of drink to a loser's appreciation of victory.] **Is this an effective comparison? Why?** [Possible answers: Yes, it expresses how those who have failed are "thirsty" for success; yes, it links the sweetness of victory to the drink of the gods.]

Before You Read
SUCCESS IS COUNTED SWEETEST

Make the Connection
The Taste of Fame
In 1862, Dickinson sent this poem along with three others to Thomas Wentworth Higginson, editor of the *Atlantic Monthly,* to ask his advice about the quality of her poems. It is one of several poems that show Dickinson's feelings about success and her struggles with the world.

Quickwrite

Write down some of your own thoughts about success. How do people feel who always encounter failure?

Background
Literary scholars debate Dickinson's lack of interest in publishing and recognition. This poem, included in *A Masque of Poets,* is one of the poems that Dickinson did publish during her lifetime. Ironically, many readers thought it was written by Ralph Waldo Emerson (page 216).

Taps (c. 1907–1909) by Gilbert Gaul. Oil on canvas (32¾″ × 43″).
Collection of the Birmingham Museum of Art, Birmingham, Alabama. Gift of John Meyer.

Success is counted sweetest

Emily Dickinson

Ⓐ
Success is counted sweetest
By those who ne'er succeed.
To comprehend a nectar°
Requires sorest° need.

5 Not one of all the purple Host°
Who took the Flag today
Can tell the definition
So clear of Victory

As he defeated—dying—
10 On whose forbidden ear
The distant strains of triumph
Burst agonized and clear!

3. nectar: a name for the drink of the Greek and Roman gods; also, a term applied to any delicious beverage.
4. sorest: deepest; most extreme.
5. purple host: royal army.

Professional Notes

Bittersweet Success:
A Poet's "Letter to the World"

In an introduction to a volume of Dickinson's poems, Robert N. Linscott writes: ". . . she lived a life, outwardly uneventful, inwardly dedicated to a secret and self-imposed assignment—the mission of writing a 'letter to the world' that would express, in poems of absolute truth and of the utmost economy, her concepts of life and death, of love and nature, and of what Henry James called 'the landscape of the soul.'

Unpublished in her lifetime, unknown at her death in 1886, her poems, by chance and good fortune, reached, at last, the world to which they had been addressed. 'If fame belonged to me,' she had written in 1861, 'I could not escape her; if she did not, the longest day would pass me on the chase, and the approbation of my dog would forsake me.' The long day passed and fame was finally hers. . . ."

The following excerpts describe a visit to the Dickinson house—called the Homestead—in Amherst, Massachusetts. (See photos on pages 345 and 383.)

Emily Dickinson's Homestead

The place today is decidedly light, airy, underfurnished. Even so, Emily Dickinson's singular presence is felt almost from the moment you step inside the front door and your guide begins to talk about "Emily" as if the two of them had recently had a tête-à-tête about fresh flowers or what sort of cake to bake for Sunday dinner. . . .

At the Homestead, as in a good many other "restored" writers' houses, most of the furniture, curtains, toys, saucepans, and God-knows-what-else have been gathered together decades after its owners have re-moved to a far less stressful existence. Very little of the actual stuff is there; most of it has been gathered by buying or begging from folks who happen to own pieces that fit the particular decorating bill. While the outside walls are intact, the domestic appa-ratus inside them is only an approximation of what was there when the famous writer lived in its midst. Yet we go out of our way to visit these temples to the Word, if only for a whiff of the Great One who once prowled the premises seeking the mot juste[1] or staring out the window, waiting for a nudge from the muse. . . .

Emily's bedroom contains the few things that almost certainly belonged to her: a Franklin stove, a sleigh bed adorned with a paisley shawl I was dying to touch but was not quick enough. The family cradle is here, too, an odd touch in a spinster's room. In the middle of the room, one of her dresses (it looks like a size eight) is draped on a headless dummy inside a Plexiglas case. The display destroys the illusion that she might return from her beloved garden at any moment. But the dress is irresistible—made of heavy white cotton with twelve nickel-sized buttons down the front, long sleeves, a custom-ordered patch pocket (to tuck scraps of paper into), and the trim look of a head nurse's uniform. On the windowsill is a basket with a cord attached to it, which she filled with cookies she baked and then lowered out the window to nephews and nieces.

We were told by our guide . . . that Emily was "lucky in a way—she never had to go out to work" and that she was "witty and funny." Pointing to pictures of three men in Emily's life, [the guide] said that the poet "only liked intellectual men. My pick [for Emily's true love] is Bowles," meaning Samuel Bowles, editor of the *Springfield Daily Republican,* who may have been the "Master" to whom Emily addressed a series of letters. Bowles was married. Personally, I think Emily tended to pick her men for their unavailability—what she didn't need was a husband.

—Anne Bernays, *from* "A Poet's Safe Haven in Amherst," *The New York Times Magazine,* October 1, 1989

1. **mot juste** (mō zhüst'): French for "right word."

Connecting Across Texts

Connecting with Dickinson's Poetry
Ask students which poems in this collection best connect with the image of Dickinson's life that Bernays provides in this piece. [Possible responses: "Some keep the Sabbath going to Church," "Heart! We will forget him!," and "The Soul selects her own Society."] Then, ask stu-dents how the article adds to the picture they have been forming of Emily Dickinson. [Possible responses: It establishes her as a real person who lived in an actual place, rather than just the voice of a dead poet from the distant past; it puts her in a domestic realm, outside the literary world; it adds to the picture of her eccentricity, particularly in the description of her dress and the incident of her lowering cookies to children below.]

Connections

In this article, Anne Bernays captures the flavor of a guided tour of the poet's home.

BROWSING IN THE FILES

About the Author. Scholar Joel Conarroe observes: "When we realize that [Dickinson] wrote scores of poems every year, any thought that her life was without drama quickly disappears. It is dif-ficult, in fact, to imagine a life lived more passionately, even if the pas-sion falls outside what we think of as erotic or romantic love. . . . Every now and then, Emerson said an individual exquisitely made can live alone. For a poet, as Marianne Moore put it, 'there is society in solitude.' 'I find ecstasy in living,' Dickinson wrote a friend. 'The mere sense of living is joy enough.'"

Ⓐ Literary Connections
A World Apart
The Dickinson home is an imposing two-story structure sitting behind a metal fence and a tall row of hemlocks. Huge trees border the front sidewalk. Gardens flank the sides and rear; these areas, plus an orchard and a field, com-prised much of Dickinson's world.

Ⓑ Critical Thinking
Speculating
❓ What do you think Anne Bernays means by "what she didn't need was a husband"? Why might Dickinson have sought out love that she knew would never be realized? [Possible responses: Dickinson wanted to maintain her inde-pendence in an age when many women were subjugated by their husbands and consumed by domestic responsibilities; she wanted to have the time and free-dom to pursue her writing; her inner world was so rich, she needed no spouse.]

MAKING MEANINGS

Apparently with no surprise

First Thoughts [Respond]

1. The message might be that death is part of nature and of God's law. Some students may say that the conjunction of the words "beheads" and "Assassin" with "an Approving God" shocked them; others may say that the constancy of life's cycles and seasons is reassuring.

Shaping Interpretations [Interpret]

2. the frost
3. The flower is like a happy child; the frost, like a heedless and accidental killer; the sun, like an uncaring surveyor.
4. The pun is a play on the double meaning of *unmoved,* which can mean either "unfeeling" or "stationary." Since *proceeds* means "moves ahead," the sun "moves unmoved."
5. God approves. The words "beheads" and "Assassin" and the shock of the last line suggest that the speaker feels disturbed by, yet resigned to, this reality.

Extending the Text [Compare]

6. Emerson focuses on nature's majesty; the speaker here focuses on the indifferent constancy of nature's laws. Students' charts will vary.

Tell all the Truth . . .

First Thoughts [Respond]

1. *Slant* is an indirect revelation of the truth; lying is a distortion or negation of the truth.

Shaping Interpretations [Interpret]

2. *Circuit* means "going around" the truth or reaching it in a roundabout way. "The Truth's superb surprise" is too bright.
3. Children's fears of lightning are eased when they are gently given an explanation of what it is.
4. The surprise of direct truth is too shocking. *Dazzle* may mean "enlighten." *Blind* may mean "uncomprehending."
5. Truth is compared to an intensely bright light.

Challenging the Text [Evaluate]

6. Poetry works by "telling the truth slant"—that is, through implication, metaphor, allusion, symbols, and so on.

T390

MAKING MEANINGS

Apparently with no surprise

First Thoughts

1. What is the message of this poem? Do you feel it is shocking, reassuring, or something else?

Shaping Interpretations

2. What is the "blonde Assassin"?
3. How are the flower, the frost, and the sun **personified** in this poem? What kind of person does each seem to be compared to?
4. A **pun** is a play on words based on multiple meanings of a single word or words that sound alike but mean different things. What pun is in line 6? How would you explain it?
5. According to the speaker, how does God feel about the flower's beheading? How do you think the speaker feels?

Extending the Text

6. How does the speaker's attitude toward nature differ from Emerson's attitude in the excerpt from his essay *Nature* (page 219)? Is either point of view supported by the chart you made before reading the poem? Explain.

Tell all the Truth but tell it slant

First Thoughts

1. Look back over your Quickwrite notes. How would you define the word *slant* as it is used in the poem? Is telling something "slant" different from lying?

Shaping Interpretations

2. Explain the meaning of "Circuit" (line 2) in the context of the poem. What is "Too bright for our infirm Delight" (line 3)?
3. Lines 5 and 6 provide an example to illustrate the poet's point about truth. As is typical of Dickinson's technique, she omits several words

in these lines. How would you rephrase the lines to make a full sentence?
4. According to the last two lines, why must the truth be told "slant"? How would you define *dazzle* and *blind* here?
5. What **metaphor** is implied in line 7? What is "Truth" being compared with?

Challenging the Text

6. Do you agree with the poet's message? In what way can this lyric be seen as a reference to the way poetry "works"?

Success is counted sweetest

First Thoughts

1. According to the speaker, who is likely to count success as sweetest? Review your Quickwrite notes. Do you think the poet is on target in describing the feelings of people who fail?

Shaping Interpretations

2. Purple is a color associated with blood shed in battle (the Purple Heart medal is given to those killed or wounded in battle). Purple is also a color associated with royalty or nobility. What is the "purple Host" in line 5?
3. Whose ear is mentioned in line 10? What is the ear "forbidden" to hear?
4. Describe the **image** you see in the last stanza.

Connecting with the Text

5. Do you agree with the idea expressed in lines 3–4? Why or why not? How would you **paraphrase** these lines?
6. Have you ever been like the soldier in the last stanza—in agony because someone else is being proclaimed winner? What other circumstances in life (other than a wartime battle) could this situation be applied to? Could it describe the feelings of a poet who could not publish her work?

390 A NEW AMERICAN POETRY: WHITMAN AND DICKINSON

Success is counted sweetest

First Thoughts [Respond]

1. The defeated cherish success most. Possible answers: Yes, what is out of one's reach seems most desirable; no, winning after a great effort or a close contest is the sweetest success.

Shaping Interpretations [Interpret]

2. It represents the victorious army, or wounded soldiers who fought hard and won.
3. The dying soldier's ear is forbidden to hear the sounds of victory.

4. Possible answer: a mortally wounded soldier in agony on the battlefield.

Connecting with the Text [Evaluate]

5. For possible answers, see 1. Possible paraphrase: To fully appreciate the taste of a beverage, you have to be extremely thirsty.
6. Possible parallel situations: losing a sports contest; failing an exam; not being cast in a play; not being accepted at a college. Most students will probably feel it describes the poet's situation.

Make the Connection

Drawn by Death

Like many other **metaphors** in Dickinson's poetry, the one in this poem imaginatively captures the most awesome and inevitable of human experiences—death—and does so with playfulness and wit. The literal elements of the metaphor are simple: Dying is compared to an unexpected ride in a horse-drawn carriage. But these are just about the only simple elements in a poem that depends for its effect on **irony**, on gradual comprehension, and on a blithe **tone** that is much at odds with the subject of the story being told.

Reading Skills and Strategies

Summarizing a Text

Dickinson uses time in an unusual way. As you read, sum up what is happening in each stanza, and note when the events occur.

Because I could not stop for Death

Emily Dickinson

Because I could not stop for Death—
He kindly stopped for me—
The Carriage held but just Ourselves—
And Immortality.

5   We slowly drove—He knew no haste
And I had put away
My labor and my leisure too,
For His Civility—

We passed the School, where Children strove
10 At Recess—in the Ring—
We passed the Fields of Gazing Grain—
We passed the Setting Sun—

Or rather—He passed Us—
The Dews drew quivering and chill—
15 For only Gossamer,° my Gown—
My Tippet—only Tulle°—

We paused before a House that seemed
A Swelling of the Ground—
The Roof was scarcely visible—
20 The Cornice°—in the Ground—

Since then—'tis Centuries—and yet
Feels shorter than the Day
I first surmised the Horses Heads
Were toward Eternity—

15. gossamer: thin, soft material.
16. tippet . . . tulle: shawl made of fine netting.
20. cornice: projecting horizontal molding at the top of a building.

EMILY DICKINSON 391

Death is personified as a carriage driver who politely stops to collect the speaker. On their drive, they pass a schoolyard, fields of grain, and a sunset. The passenger grows cold. The carriage pauses at her graveside. The speaker realizes that she is on a long ride to "Eternity."

Ⓐ Elements of Literature

Symbol

❓ What might the three things they pass symbolize? Why does Dickinson put them in this order? [Possible answer: Children at play symbolize youth; fields of grain ready for harvest signify maturity; the sunset symbolizes old age and death. The order shows the chronological progression of life's stages.]

Ⓑ Elements of Literature

Rhyme

❓ Note that Dickinson rhymes the word *ground* with itself. What effect does this repetition have? [Possible answers: It calls attention to the finality of death; it is like a death knell, adding a touch of horror to the poem; it suggests that the speaker is transfixed by the sight of the grave.]

Ⓒ Literary Connections

"Tragic Vision"

In the eyes of scholar Thomas H. Johnson, what makes Emily Dickinson a great poet "is her tragic vision. She knew that she could not pierce through to the unknowable, but she insisted on asking the questions." She had an "agonizing sense of ironic contrasts; of the weight of suffering; of the human predicament in which man is mocked, destroyed, and beckoned to some incomprehensible repose; of the limits of reason, order, and justice in human as well as divine relationships."

Reaching All Students

Struggling Readers

Suggest to these students that one way to approach the last three poems in this collection is to think of them as miniature short stories. As the students read each poem, have them identify elements that we usually associate with prose fiction: plot, characters, setting, and theme. Then, group students into pairs and have them tell each other the story of each poem.

English Language Learners

These students may be confused by the use of the verb *be* in ll. 8 and 10 of "I heard a Fly . . ." (p. 392). Explain that these uses of the verb are archaic and discuss which forms of the verb would be used today (in l. 8, *would be*; in l. 10, *was*). Ask students why the poet may have used the archaic *be* in these lines. [Possible answers: for the long e sound; to fit the rhythm; because she often condenses language, expecting readers to fill in missing words.]

Summary ■ ■

The speaker describes her own death. Others are gathered around, waiting for death to come to her. She is in the midst of giving away her last possessions. Then, a buzzing fly interposes itself between the speaker and the light, and her ability to perceive is swiftly extinguished as death overtakes her.

Ⓐ Elements of Literature
Mood

❓ What is the mood created in ll. 2–8? [Possible responses: solemnity; expectation; gravity.] **What changes the mood?** [Possible answers: the appearance of a fly; the introduction of an insignificant, everyday event.]

Ⓑ Elements of Literature
Alliteration

❓ What effect does the poet achieve by repeating the *s* and *z* sounds in l. 13? [The sounds mimic the buzzing of the fly.]

Ⓒ Appreciating Language
Denotation

❓ How could this line be paraphrased to denote the two senses in which the speaker is using the word *see*? [Possible answers: I did not have the faculty of sight to perceive or discern; I did not have the vision to comprehend or understand.]

RESPONDING TO THE ART

Andrew Wyeth (1917–   ) is a popular American artist known for his austere New England scenes and his spare, uncluttered style. (See the note on Wyeth's art on p. T239.)

Activity. What makes Wyeth's *Wind from the Sea* a suitable work to accompany Dickinson's "I heard a Fly buzz . . ."? [Sample responses: Both have images of light, air, and a window; the rush of air through the window might be taken to parallel the extinguishing of the speaker's consciousness.]

Before You Read

I HEARD A FLY BUZZ—WHEN I DIED

Make the Connection

Death Be Not Proud

This poem begins with such boldness and continues with such quick shifts of attention that we may not stop to think about what we are hearing—a voice from the dead.

Quickwrite

Write down what you would expect someone to sense at the time of death—that ultimate moment when we cannot "see to see."

I heard a Fly buzz—when I died

Emily Dickinson

> I heard a Fly buzz—when I died—
> The Stillness in the Room
> Was like the Stillness in the Air—
> Between the Heaves of Storm—
>
> 5 The Eyes around—had wrung them dry—
> And Breaths were gathering firm
> For that last Onset—when the King
> Be witnessed—in the Room—
>
> I willed my Keepsakes—Signed away
> 10 What portion of me be
> Assignable—and then it was
> There interposed a Fly—
>
> With Blue—uncertain stumbling Buzz—
> Between the light—and me—
> 15 And then the Windows failed—and then
> I could not see to see—

Wind from the Sea (1947) by Andrew Wyeth. Tempera (18½″ × 27½″).

Mead Art Museum, Amherst College. Gift of Charles and Janet Morgan.

392 A NEW AMERICAN POETRY: WHITMAN AND DICKINSON

Connecting Across Texts

Connecting with "The Jilting of Granny Weatherall"

After students have read Katherine Anne Porter's "The Jilting of Granny Weatherall" (p. 704), have them reread "I heard a Fly Buzz—when I died," and explore questions like these: What themes do the poem and story have in common? How are the two deaths alike? How are they different? Which writer's use of images is more striking? Why? Then, have students read Dickinson's other poems on death again to see whether any aspects of Porter's story are reminiscent of either "I died for Beauty . . ." (p. 393) or "Because I could not stop for Death" (p. 391). If so, what do the poem or poems and the story have in common? You might have students meet in pairs or in small groups to brainstorm comparisons between the story and the poems.

T392

Before You Read

I DIED FOR BEAUTY—BUT WAS SCARCE

Make the Connection

Beauty and Truth
The following lines, which conclude John Keats's "Ode on a Grecian Urn," are among the most famous lines in English poetry:

"Beauty is truth, truth
beauty"—that is all
Ye know on earth, and all ye
need to know.

Emily Dickinson knew these lines, and in this poem she presents her own version of the theme suggested by Keats.

Quickwrite

Beauty and Truth are two concepts that have been defined and debated for centuries. Write your own definitions of Beauty and Truth.

Michael Cornish.

I died for Beauty—but was scarce

Emily Dickinson

I died for Beauty—but was scarce
Adjusted in the Tomb
When One who died for Truth, was lain
In an adjoining Room—

5 He questioned softly "Why I failed"?
"For Beauty," I replied—
"And I—for Truth—Themself are One—
We Bretheren, are," He said—

And so, as Kinsmen, met a Night—
10 We talked between the Rooms—
Until the Moss had reached our lips—
And covered up—our names—

EMILY DICKINSON 393

Summary ■ ■ ■

In a tomb, a person who died for Beauty meets one who died for Truth. Recognizing their kinship, the dead talk together until moss obscures their lips and names.

D Critical Thinking

Analyzing
❓ What examples can you suggest of people who might be said to have died for Beauty? for Truth? Explain. [Possible answers: A composer who ignored ill health to finish a symphony might be said to have died for Beauty. A reporter who was killed while covering a war might be said to have died for Truth.]

E Struggling Readers

Rearranging Syntax
Point out that, as worded, this line is an indirect quotation, and, therefore, should not be enclosed in quotation marks. However, early-nineteenth-century usage allowed this punctuation. Explain that, as a direct quotation, the line would read, "Why did you fail?" Also, make sure students know that *fail* here means "die," a meaning that is more commonly used in an expression such as "She's failing."

F Advanced Learners

Compare and Contrast
Have students locate and read "Ode on a Grecian Urn." They can then get together for a small-group discussion of the ode and "I died for Beauty. . . ." Students should consider themes, images, and tone as they compare and contrast the poems.

Skill Link

The Speaker

Remind students that the **speaker** of a poem is the person who speaks the words. The speaker may claim to be the writer, as in Walt Whitman's *Leaves of Grass* poems, or he or she may be more clearly a character, like the heartbroken student in Edgar Allan Poe's "The Raven" (p. 282). Tell students that many readers automatically assume that the speaker of Dickinson's poems is the poet herself. However, this is not a safe generalization; too little is known of her life,

her feelings, or her nature to prove such an assumption. Nevertheless, by literary convention, a speaker is considered to be the same gender as the poet unless evidence in the poem suggests otherwise, as in Ezra Pound's "The River-Merchant's Wife" (p. 774).

1. Have students read through the twelve poems in this collection and take brief notes about the speaker of each poem. What clues are there to the speaker's age, gender, or

position in life? How would students describe the speaker's personality? What is the speaker's tone?

2. Ask students to compare the twelve speakers as they look back over their notes. Then, hold a class discussion in which students debate whether or not all twelve speakers might be the same person. Encourage students to defend their positions by citing details from the poems that support their arguments.

In this feature, the critic Thomas Wentworth Higginson introduces two brief samples of Emily Dickinson's correspondence with him. In the first letter, she eludes his questions regarding her experience as a poet, her education, her friends, and her family—claiming nature as her most constant companion and hinting at a vague "terror" she experienced in the past. She asks for Higginson's advice on her poetry and deflects his suggestion that she read Whitman. In a later letter, she responds to his request for a picture of her with a brief, evocative description of her appearance.

Ⓐ Reading Skills and Strategies
Connecting with the Text

After students have finished reading this account, you might ask them if they noticed any comments or feelings in the letters that are echoed in Dickinson's poetry. Have them point out these similarities. [Possible answers: Dickinson's comment about her "terror" (fourth paragraph of her letter) might suggest feelings in "Heart! We will forget him!" or in "Because I could not stop for Death"; her comment about a friend who "never returned" (fifth paragraph) might suggest "If you were coming in the Fall"; her comments about her companions (sixth paragraph) might suggest "The Soul selects her own Society"; her comments about religion (seventh paragraph) might suggest "Some keep the Sabbath. . . ."]

PRIMARY Sources | A LETTER

Ⓐ "I sing . . . because I am afraid"

In 1862, Emily Dickinson sent the critic Thomas Wentworth Higginson a letter and four poems, asking for critical help. Dickinson saw him as a mentor, and they corresponded for several years. Four years after Dickinson's death, Higginson assisted Mabel Loomis Todd in editing Dickinson's poems. The following year, Higginson wrote an article in *The Atlantic Monthly* about his experiences with Emily Dickinson.

I remember to have ventured on some criticism which she afterwards called "surgery," and on some questions, part of which she evaded, as will be seen, with a naive skill such as the most experienced and worldly coquette might envy. Her second letter (received April 26, 1862) was as follows:

Mr. Higginson,—Your kindness claimed earlier gratitude, but I was ill, and write today from my pillow.

Thank you for the surgery; it was not so painful as I supposed. I bring you others, as you ask. . . .

You asked how old I was? I made no verse, but one or two, until this winter, sir.

I had a terror since September, I could tell to none; and so I sing, as the boy does of the burying ground, because I am afraid.

You inquire my books. For poets, I have Keats, and Mr. and Mrs. Browning. For prose, Mr. Ruskin, Sir Thomas Browne, and the Revelations. I went to school, but in your manner of the phrase had no education. When a little girl, I had a friend who taught me Immortality; but venturing too near, himself, he never returned. Soon after my tutor died, and for several years my lexicon was my only companion. Then I found one more, but he was not contented I be his scholar, so he left the land.

You ask of my companions. Hills, sir, and the sundown, and a dog large as myself, that my father bought me. They are better than beings because they know, but do not tell; and the noise in the pool at noon excels my piano.

I have a brother and sister; my mother does not care for thought, and father, too busy with his briefs to notice what we do. He buys me many books, but begs me not to read them, because he fears they joggle the mind. They are religious, except me. . . .

But I fear my story fatigues you. I would like to learn. Could you tell me how to grow, or is it unconveyed, like melody or witchcraft?

You speak of Mr. Whitman. I never read his book, but was told that it was disgraceful. . . .

. . . I must soon have written to ask her for her picture, that I might form some impression of my enigmatical correspondent. To this came the following reply, in July 1862:

Could you believe me without? I had no portrait, now, but am small, like the wren; and my hair is bold, like the chestnut bur; and my eyes, like the sherry in the glass, that the guest leaves. Would this do just as well?

It often alarms father. He says death might occur, and he has molds [photographs] of all the rest, but has no mold of me. . . .

—Thomas Wentworth Higginson,
from "Emily Dickinson's Letters"

Making Connections

Connecting to the Theme
"Tell It Slant"

Invite students to identify ways in which Dickinson tells the truth "slant" in her letters. [Possible answers: She evades the question about her age; she refers obliquely to a terror she experienced and to those who influenced her; rather than send a photograph, she uses similes to describe herself indirectly; she allows her correspondent to form impressions but gives little direct information about herself.]

Assessing Learning

Standardized Test Preparation

For practice with ACT and SAT formats, see
• *Preparation for College Admission Exams*, p. 27
For practice in proofreading and editing, see
• *Daily Oral Grammar*, Transparencies 26, 27

Because I could not stop for Death

First Thoughts

1. If you were going to **personify** Death, would Death be like the person described in this poem? Why or why not?

Shaping Interpretations

2. Can you paraphrase the first two lines in a way that emphasizes their **irony**? What word in line 2 tells you that the tone is ironic?

3. In stanza 2, *civility* means "politeness." How does this kind of behavior on the part of Death and the speaker extend the **irony** of the first stanza?

4. What three things do the riders pass in stanza 3? What is significant about the fact that the sun passes the carriage in stanzas 4–5, and about the nature of the change in temperature? Be sure to review your reading notes.

5. Stanza 5 is a riddle in itself. What is the nearly buried house?

6. Do you think the concluding stanza introduces a **tone** of terror, because the speaker has suddenly realized she will ride on forever, conscious of being dead? Or is the poem really an expression of trust and even triumph? Explain your response.

Challenging the Text

7. The critic Alfred Kazin said of the last stanza of this poem: "What that famous Eternity is, we cannot say." Do you agree with Kazin? What do *you* think Dickinson meant by the "Eternity" the horses were going toward?

I heard a Fly buzz—when I died

First Thoughts

1. Do you find this poem grotesque, moving, humorous, or something else? Look back over your Quickwrite notes, and explain whether or not you were surprised by the poem's conclusion.

Shaping Interpretations

2. According to the second and third stanzas, how had the speaker and those around her prepared for death?

3. What are the dying person and those around her expecting to find in the room? What appears instead, and why is this **ironic**?

4. In line 4, Dickinson used the word "Heaves" to refer to the behavior of storms. Why is "Heaves" an appropriate word to describe what is happening in the poem?

5. How does the poet use pauses and specific words in lines 12–13 to make the appearance of the fly dramatic and lively?

6. In the third stanza, what portion of the speaker is "assignable"? What portion, by implication, is *not* assignable?

7. Who is the "King" (line 7)? What does the phrase "the Windows failed" (line 15) mean?

8. What **tone** do you hear in this poem? What feeling do you think the poet expresses by inserting the fly into this deathbed scene?

I died for Beauty—but was scarce

First Thoughts

1. What thoughts and feelings would you say are expressed in this poem? Are they similar to or different from those you recorded in your Quickwrite notes? Explain.

Shaping Interpretations

2. What is the situation described in the first stanza? What do the two speakers have in common that allows one of them to claim they are "Bretheren," or brothers?

3. In the third stanza the "Moss" is real, but it is also a **metaphor.** What do you think it represents? What is significant in the fact that it covers up the speakers' names?

4. **Slant rhyme** makes the last word stand out. Do you think this is an important word? Why or why not?

5. What do you think Dickinson's **message** is? Would you say it is optimistic or pessimistic?

EMILY DICKINSON **395**

Challenging the Text [Evaluate]

7. "Eternity" may mean permanent death, everlasting life, or something in between.

I heard a Fly buzz—when I died

First Thoughts [Respond]

1. Students may see humor in the contrast between the solemnity of death and the triviality of a buzzing fly.

Shaping Interpretations [Interpret]

2. The mourners cried until their tears dried up, and they caught their breath in expectation. The speaker wills away her possessions.

3. The contrast between what they expect to appear—God or Christ ("the King")—and what does appear—a fly—creates irony.

4. "Heaves" suggests the spasms of a dying person or a weeping mourner gasping for breath.

5. The dashes and the formal word "interposed" suggest drama. The pause in l. 13 sets a staccato rhythm that mirrors the flight of the fly. In l. 13, the poet uses alliteration, assonance, and onomatopoeia.

6. Material possessions are assignable, while her spirit is not.

7. "King"—God; Christ; Death. "Windows" that fail—the speaker's eyes fail; a lack of spiritual revelation.

8. Sample responses: The tone is first solemn, then sad or ironic. The poet is disappointed that a commonplace fly blocked a spiritual revelation; the poet is puncturing the portentousness of death.

I died for Beauty—but was scarce

First Thoughts [Respond]

1. Beauty and truth are the same. They are worth dying for, but those who do so will be forgotten.

MAKING MEANINGS

Because I could not stop for Death

First Thoughts [Respond]

1. Possible responses: Yes, because Death should not be frightening; no, because Death should be menacing.

Shaping Interpretations [Interpret]

2. Possible paraphrase: Because I could not stop my busy life, Death put a stop to it. *Kindly* is ironic.

3. Death's politeness is ironic in contrast to the usually ominous figure of the Grim Reaper. *Civility* extends the irony of *Kindly*.

4. They pass a school, fields of grain, and a sunset. The sun's passing brings nightfall. The cold suggests the body's temperature after death.

5. The house is the speaker's grave.

6. Possible responses: There is a tone of terror—the day of the speaker's realization seemed to last longer than centuries; there is a tone of acceptance—the centuries have passed quickly.

Shaping Interpretations [Interpret]

2. The speaker is in the tomb when another is brought in. One died for truth and one for beauty, which they agree are the same.

3. The "Moss" represents time's passage and the impermanence of human memory. Its covering the names signifies oblivion for the individuals.

4. Yes. One's name symbolizes identity. When it is covered, the person is forgotten.

5. Beauty and truth endure, but people die and are forgotten.

Rubrics for each Choices assignment appear on p. 136 in the *Portfolio Management System*.

CHOICES:
Building Your Portfolio

1. **Writer's Notebook** Students may also find a comparison of Dickinson's and Whitman's work interesting; both broke radically from tradition in different ways.

2. **Creative Writing** Students may want to consider using other poetry forms, such as concrete poetry, the sonnet, blank verse, or haiku. Encourage students to use their imagination and to write in whatever style they feel best expresses their ideas.

3. **Analyzing Meter/Music** You might invite a musician in the class to play "O God, Our Help in Ages Past" while students silently read "If you were coming in the Fall" to the meter of the tune. You might also ask students to discuss in their essays how Dickinson avoids the monotony of traditional hymnal meter while adhering to its form.

4. **Performance/Research** Point out to students that researching biographies may provide further insights into Dickinson's views. Suggest that group members all work together on shaping the script and performance but that each should take on a primary role, such as writer, director, or performer.

5. **Art** Have students think about whether and how to illustrate their books. They might consider anything from no illustrations to decorative borders to collages.

CHOICES: Building Your Portfolio

Writer's Notebook
1. Collecting Ideas for a Comparison-Contrast Essay

One interesting topic for a comparison-contrast essay would be an examination of how one of Emily Dickinson's poems compares with a poem by an earlier poet—perhaps "Huswifery" by Edward Taylor (page 73), "Upon the Burning of Our House" by Anne Bradstreet (page 69), or "Thanatopsis" by William Cullen Bryant (page 171). Take notes now on how one of these poems compares with one of Dickinson's poems. You might collect your notes in a chart like the one below.

	Dickinson Poem	Other Poem
Subject matter		
Theme		
Tone		
Figures of Speech		

Save your notes for the Writer's Workshop on page 401.

Creative Writing
2. Echoes of Dickinson

Write a poem that treats one of the themes that engaged Emily Dickinson: love and loss, the spiritual life, death and immortality, nature, or the power of the imagination. You might even use one of Dickinson's lines as your opener. Experiment with **metaphors, similes,** and **slant rhymes.** Try out Dickinson's style of punctuation and capitalization, or invent your own unique style. For inspiration, read the student poem on page 380.

Analyzing Meter / Music
3. Hymn to Her

Dickinson let the strict **meters** she found in her hymnbook provide the basic beat for her poems, but the variations she introduced gave her poems subtlety and prevented monotony. In a brief essay, analyze at least two of her poems to show how she uses this traditional hymn meter:

> 8 syllables in line 1
> 8 syllables in line 3
>
> 6 syllables in line 2
> 6 syllables in line 4

Then show how she also uses a short hymn meter of 6, 6, 8, and 6 syllables. To see how closely some of the poems conform to a hymn meter, you might try singing "If you were coming in the Fall" to the tune of "O God, Our Help in Ages Past."

Performance / Research
4. Dickinson Onstage

With a partner or a small group, prepare a script for a performance called "An Evening with Emily Dickinson." In the script, let Dickinson tell about her life, her views of poetry and language, and her feelings about nature, faith, and eternity. Include in your performance readings of selected poems. You might want to include Linda Pastan's poem "Emily Dickinson" (page 371). Present your performance for the class.

Art
5. Book of Poems

Dickinson sewed the final copies of her poems into the form of small booklets. To make your own small book, fold four pages of white paper in half. Then, gather them at the fold, which will give you sixteen pages. Select poems you would like to reproduce—either your own, or some favorite poems by Dickinson or by other poets. On the first page, design a book cover including a title. Then, copy one poem onto each of the remaining pages. Try to match your penmanship or calligraphy with the feelings conveyed in the poems. (You might also use a computer, choosing fonts appropriate to the poems.) Finally, sew your book along the fold.

Making the Connection

Connecting to the Theme:
"Tell It Slant"

Discuss the collection theme. How does Dickinson "tell it slant"? [Possible answers: She compresses language, making the reader supply missing words and ideas; she uses metaphors and personification, from which readers must infer meaning.] **What "truths" does the poet suggest?** [her beliefs about life and death, love and relationships, nature, creativity, and religion]

READ ON

Song of Himself

Around the turn of the twelfth century, the Persian scientist Omar Khayyám produced several well-known works in mathematics and astronomy, as well as a series of quatrains, or four-line poems, for which he is now even more famous. The brilliant 1850s English translation by Edward FitzGerald of *The Rubáiyát of Omar Khayyám* made Khayyám the rage of the Victorian era. This powerful expression of the Persian poet's personal vision and philosophy of life has remained in print for over a century.

Legacy in Latin America

Who's the most popular U.S. poet in Latin America? The answer is probably Walt Whitman. One of his greatest admirers was the Cuban poet José Martí, who introduced Whitman's work to Spanish-speaking audiences at the turn of the century. Whitman's influence on Martí's own verse is evident in *José Martí: Major Poems* (Holmes and Meier), a bilingual edition with English translation by Elinor Randall, edited by Philip Foner.

Beholder of Mysteries

"I am no scientist," Annie Dillard says of herself. "I am a wanderer with a background in theology and a penchant for quirky facts." In *Pilgrim at Tinker Creek* (Harper and Row), Dillard draws on her experiences in an isolated Virginia valley to create a memorable reflection on life, death, and the mysteries of nature.

The Country Way

Maxine Kumin has always drawn from nature in producing her vivid poetry. *In Deep* (Viking) is the Pulitzer Prize–winning poet's collection of essays on country living. Of special interest is the last essay, "A Sense of Place," which examines nature's role in inspiring the poetic imagination.

Before and After Dickinson

Did you know that the world's first known poet was a woman? Her name was Enheduanna, and she was born around 2300 B.C. She was the daughter of a king and served as a Sumerian moon priestess. She is just one of many women poets whose works appear in *A Book of Women Poets from Antiquity to Now* (Schocken Books), a collection edited by Aliki and Willis Barnstone.

A Period of Vocabulary Growth
by Gary Q. Arpin

OBJECTIVES

1. Understand the sources of Americanisms added to English in the early 1800s
2. Identify words in which suffixes are used to change the part of speech
3. Identify loanwords from other languages

A Background

Some colorful polysyllabic words of backwoods English remain in the American language. Ask students if they know the meanings of the following words: *discombobulate* (confuse), *hornswoggle* (swindle), *squablification* (quarreling), *lollapalooza* (extraordinary person or thing), and *absquatulate* (go away).

B Background

Davy Crockett (1786–1836) was an actual frontiersman, who quickly became a folk hero. After serving three terms in Congress, he left for Texas, where he died heroically at the Alamo. The *Crockett Almanacs* contained tall tales about Crockett, as well as about two other frontiersmen who became folk heroes: Daniel Boone and Kit Carson.

C Historical Connections

A number of frontier expressions still in existence derive from the game of poker, the French origins of which were quickly forgotten as its popularity spread. These include *you bet, call one's bluff, square deal, poker face, up the ante, throw in one's hand, ace up one's sleeve,* and *stacked deck.* The Gold Rush contributed *bonanza, pan out, stake a claim,* and *strike it rich.*

Languages are always changing and growing, adding new words and expressions and shading the meaning of terms that already exist. American English enjoyed a remarkable period of growth in the first half of the nineteenth century as a variety of sources contributed to its expanding vocabulary.

Backwoods English

The word *backwoods* was first recorded in 1709. Some sixty-five years later, the word *backwoodsman* appeared. John Pickering, a linguist in the nineteenth century, wrote that the word was applied "by the people of the commercial towns in the United States, to those who inhabit the territory westward of the Allegheny Mountains." Backwoodsmen themselves used more colorful terms. They called themselves *ring-tailed roarers* or *mollagausaugers* (courageous men). The exploits of the backwoodsmen during the War of 1812 made them famous, and when Davy Crockett came to Washington, D.C., in 1827 as a congressman from Tennessee, people stared at him in the street. The following year, another backwoodsman, Andrew Jackson, was elected president.

Backwoods English teems with exaggeration and exuberant bragging—language equal to the awesome task of surviving on a new frontier. Crockett almanacs, collections of speeches by Davy Crockett that were popular from the 1830s to the 1850s, brought this backwoods language into Eastern homes. Here's an example:

> Hosses, I am with you! and while the stars of Uncle Sam, and the stripes of his country wave triumphantly in the breeze, whar, whar, whar is the craven, low-lived, chicken-bred, toad-hoppin', red-mounted, bristle-headed mother's son of ye who will not raise the beacon light of triumph, smouse the citadel of the aggressor, and squeeze ahead for Liberty and Glory! Whoop! h-u-rah, hosses, come along—Crockett's with you—show us the enemy!

Courtesy American Antiquarian Society.

Woodcut from *Davy Crockett Almanac* (1835).

Most backwoods slang had a short life, though some words and phrases have survived. Phrases like *fly off the handle, pull up stakes, a knock-down-drag-out fight, up a tree,* and *doing a land-office business* all date from this period.

The American Vernacular in Literature

The first half of the nineteenth century resounded with calls to establish an independent national literature describing the American landscape and dealing with American manners and interests, and by midcentury American literature was in full flower. To describe American phenomena, writers began to turn to the **vernacular**—the common spoken language of a region. The Crockett almanacs were a kind of subliterature, but by the 1870s, Mark Twain (page 450) was recording the language of the American West in substantial books like *Adventures of Huckleberry Finn, Roughing It,* and *Life on the Mississippi.*

Walt Whitman (page 348) also used American vernacular to create literature of a high order. In *Leaves of Grass,* he proclaims the virtues of American English:

go.hrw.com
LE0 11-American Language

The English language be-friends the grand American expression. . . . It is the powerful language of resistance—it is the dialect of common sense. It is the speech of the proud and melancholy races and of all who aspire. It is the chosen tongue to express growth, faith, self-esteem, freedom, justice, equality, friendliness, amplitude, prudence, decision, and courage. It is the medium that shall well nigh express the inexpressible.

Whitman frequently tapped American vernacular in his verse. For instance, he quite pointedly employed an Americanism (*to loaf*) in the first lines of "Song of Myself" (page 347):

I loaf and invite my soul, I lean and loaf . . . observing a spear of summer grass.

 **D**

In *Two Years Before the Mast* (1840), Richard Henry Dana, Jr., called *loafer* "the newly invented Yankee word." Four years later, in *Martin Chuzzlewit,* part of which is set in America, the British novelist Charles Dickens put *loaf* in quotation marks to show that it was a peculiarly American term. Whitman's use of the verb *loaf* eleven years later proclaimed his Americanness just as surely as if he had called himself a ring-tailed roarer.

E

The Language of the Stump: Political Coinage

The American vernacular did not appear only in literature. It was also spoken on the political platform, or "stump." (Candidates for office would stand on tree stumps to deliver their speeches.) Here is part of a speech by a candidate for office in Oregon in 1858:

Fellow-citizens, you might as well try to dry up the Atlantic Ocean with a broomstraw, or draw this 'ere stump from under my feet with a harnessed gadfly, as to convince me that I ain't gwine to be elected this heat [race]. My opponent don't stand a chance; not a sniff. Why, he ain't as intellectual as a common sized shad. . . . If thar's anybody this side of whar the sun begins to blister the yea'th [heath] that can wallop me, let him show himself—I'm ready. Boys, I go in for the American Eagle, claws, stars, stripes, and all; and may I bust my everlastin' buttonholes ef I don't knock down, drag out, and gouge everybody as denies me!

This so-called stump style is long gone, but many phrases coined by politicians of the period are still used. For instance, the word *gerrymander* was

Whitman's use of the verb *loaf* proclaimed his Americanness just as surely as if he had called himself a ring-tailed roarer.

coined in 1812 after Massachusetts Governor Elbridge Gerry reorganized the state election districts in order to maintain control of the state senate. One of the resulting districts was absurdly long and serpentine. The artist Gilbert Stuart saw a map of the districts in the office of a local newspaper editor. Noting its resemblance to a salamander, Stuart gave the district a head, wings, and claws. The editor proclaimed it a "gerrymander," and thus the word was born. **F**

Stump Speaker (1853–1854). Drawing from *Stump Speaking* by George Caleb Bingham. Brush, black ink, and wash over pencil (11½″ × 9½″).

From the Art Collection of Nations Bank.

The Language of the Press

Newspapers began to flourish in America in the late 1830s, thanks to improved printing methods that made penny newspapers profitable. Papers tried to attract readers with colorful language. One of the ways they did this was to invent whimsical abbreviations. The most famous Americanism of

D **English Language Learners**
Colloquialisms
Make sure students are familiar with the word *loaf* from informal American speech, meaning "to be lazy" or "to pass the time idly."

E **Background**
According to etymologists, *loafer,* meaning "a lazy person," is an Americanism first recorded in 1830. It probably is derived from the German *Landläufer,* meaning "vagabond." The verb *loaf* seems to have been formed from the noun *loafer* rather than the other way around. This way of forming new words by dropping, rather than adding endings, is known as *back-formation.* Other common words that were formed this way include *enthuse* from *enthusiasm* and *emote* from *emotion.*

F **Cultural Connections**
Political Terms
Another political phrase that comes from this period is *slush fund. Slush* originally referred to the surplus fat from a ship's galley. When the ship was in port, the slush was sold, and the money was put into a fund to purchase luxuries for the crew. Later, *slush fund* took on its present meaning: "money accumulated for corrupt political purposes."

Using Students' Strengths

Verbal Learners
These students may enjoy reading aloud the excerpts from Davy Crockett's speech on p. 398, as well as the stump speech on p. 399. Encourage them to rehearse the speeches until they are ready to perform them for the class.

Visual Learners
Have these students create cartoons to illustrate such colorful backwoods words and expressions as *fly off the handle, ring-tailed roarers, discombobulate, hornswoggle,* and *lollapalooza.*

T399

A Historical Connections

Once the Chisholm Trail was established by Jesse Chisholm in 1866, cow- and ranch-related terms also entered the language: *broncobuster, wrangler, range rider, cattle baron*. Frontier settlers dealing with Native Americans and Spanish-speaking Mexicans contributed enduring pidgin (a simplified form of English), phrases such as *no can do* and *long time no see*.

Try It Out
Possible Answers

1. A sample answer for each suffix is given: *mythology*, from the Greek *mythos* and *logos*; *hucksterism*, from the Middle Dutch *hoekster* and the Greek *-ismos*; *weatherize* from the Old English *weder* and the Greek *-izein*; *devilish* from the Greek *diabolos* and the Old English *-isc*.

2. If students have trouble with this activity, encourage them to listen closely to medical and legal dramas on TV; study the sports pages of newspapers; read magazines devoted to special interests, such as music and computers; or interview workers, such as restaurant workers. Sample special vocabulary includes *stat* ("immediately" to doctors), *bull market* ("rising stock prices" to stockbrokers), *sound bite* ("a brief, quotable, and usually superficial remark" to TV news reporters), *gig* ("job" to musicians), and *whiskey down* ("rye toast" to restaurant workers).

3. Students will need to consult reference books in the library to complete this activity. Ask students to submit photocopies of their sources for loanwords.

Resources ———

Assessment
Formal Assessment
• American Language Test, p. 78

---

them all—*OK*—originated as a witty abbreviation. *OK* was first used to mean "oll korrect" (a deliberate misspelling of "all correct") in a Boston newspaper in 1839. *OK* might never have survived as an expression had the New York Democratic Club not dubbed itself "The OK Club" during the 1840 presidential election. The Democrats intended *OK* to stand for "Old Kinderhook," a nickname for their candidate, President Martin Van Buren, a native of the town of Kinderhook, New York. Their opponents, however, claimed that *OK* stood for "oll korrect" and that the expression had been coined by former president Andrew Jackson, who had misspelled "all correct." (This was to remind voters that Van Buren was Jackson's personal choice as successor and to make fun of Jackson's limited education.) "OK!" became a Democratic rallying cry during that boisterous election year and remained in widespread popular use.

The Influence of Immigrants

The late 1840s saw a tremendous increase in the number of immigrants to the United States. In 1845, about 100,000 immigrants arrived; by 1854, the number had grown to 500,000. A large number of immigrants during the mid-nineteenth century were Germans, many of whom sought haven from political disorder. The German influence on American English was

strong, especially in words for food (*sauerkraut, frankfurter, hamburger, noodle*). German also gave us *kindergarten* (children's garden); *bum* (probably from *bummler*, meaning "loafer"); *dumb,* in the sense of "stupid" (from *dumm*); and *fresh,* meaning "saucy" or "impertinent" (from *frech,* "impudent").

However, the greatest source of **loanwords**—words borrowed from other languages—in the nineteenth century was Spanish. As Americans moved westward into territory originally settled by the Spanish, they came upon a host of items that are still known by their Spanish names. *Mustang, lasso, ranch, fiesta, plaza, bronco, canyon,* and *patio* are just a few commonly used English words of Spanish origin.

Try It Out

1. **Using suffixes to change parts of speech.** Americans frequently change nouns into verbs or adjectives, and verbs into nouns or adjectives, often through the addition of a suffix. The first suffix popularly used in the United States to make new nouns was *–ery. Printery* was coined in 1638. Other common suffixes used to change a word's function are *–logy, –ism, –ize,* and *–ish.* Make a list of five words that have been formed by the addition of each of these suffixes. What information is given in the dictionary about each word's origin?

2. **Compiling specialized vocabulary.** Nearly every occupation coins its own special vocabulary, which may then find its way into general usage. Compile a brief dictionary of the special vocabulary of people in a business or industry you are familiar with (stockbrokers, doctors, lawyers, politicians, advertisers, news reporters, weather forecasters, restaurant workers, computer programmers, athletes, musicians, and so on). Explain the meaning of each word or phrase, and, if you can, explain its derivation. Which of these words or phrases have been picked up and used by people outside the occupation? How many have been added to American English in the last twenty years or less? (Think of terms like *compact disc, virtual reality,* and *fax.*)

3. **Identifying loanwords.** With a partner or small group, make a "Loanword Lexicon"—a dictionary of words used in American English that were originally borrowed from other languages. You might try making a dictionary of loanwords from a particular language—Spanish or Japanese, for example—or a dictionary of specialized words (names of animals, foods, or inventions, for example) that are actually loanwords.

Assessing Learning

Check Test: True-False

1. Backwoods English is formal and precise. [False]

2. Davy Crockett is a completely fictitious character from the days of the American frontier. [False]

3. The common spoken language of a region is called the vernacular. [True]

4. *OK* began as a shortened form of *okay*. [False]

5. The word *kindergarten* means "children's garden" in German. [True]

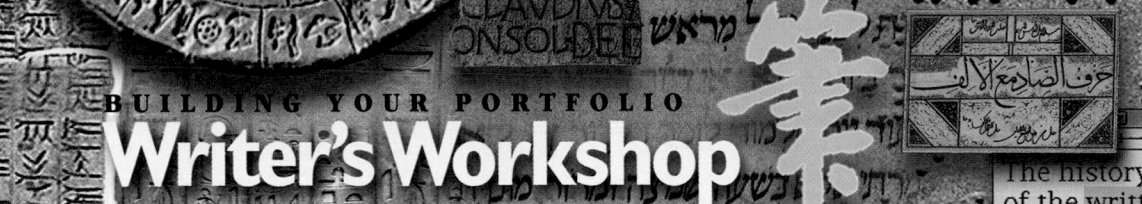

Writer's Workshop

The history
of the written
word is rich

Page 1

EXPOSITORY WRITING

COMPARISON-AND-CONTRAST ESSAY

Life is a continual series of decisions. Which movie will you see tonight—a drama starring your favorite actor, or a comedy with a cast of newcomers? By thinking in this way, you apply the strategy of comparison and contrast to everyday decisions. When you write a comparison-and-contrast essay, you examine the similarities and differences of two subjects. As a result, you understand the subjects better, and your evaluations and decisions become easier.

Prewriting

1. **Choosing topics.** Sometimes subjects to compare or contrast will be assigned to you—two novels, for example. When you need to choose two subjects on your own, be sure they have something obviously in common or have some significant differences. You might, for example, *compare* William Cullen Bryant and Emily Dickinson because they are both American poets; you might also *contrast* their poetic styles. Choose topics on which you know you can access relevant information, drawn from your own experience or from research.

2. **Developing a thesis statement.** As you explore your two subjects, you need to decide to what extent you will stress their similarities and to what extent you will stress their differences. Your thesis statement—the main idea of the essay—should reflect that decision and should be clear and straightforward: "William Cullen Bryant and Emily Dickinson both saw death as a solemn event, but their tones and images reveal profoundly different attitudes toward death."

3. **Organizing your essay.** You can help your readers understand the relationships between your subjects by using either the block method or the point-by-point method of organization. In the **block method,** you first discuss all the relevant elements of one subject and then all the relevant elements of the second subject. In the **point-by-point method,** you discuss one element at a time, as it relates to both subjects; then you go on to the next element. On the next page is a chart that shows how the two methods work.

ASSIGNMENT

Write an essay comparing and contrasting two poems, focusing on such elements as subject matter, theme, tone, and figures of speech.

AIM

To inform; to explain; to analyze.

AUDIENCE

Your classmates, family, and general readers.

Try It Out

Fill out an organization chart like this one to generate a possible framework for the body of your essay.

Subject 1 _____

Elements

1. _____
2. _____
3. _____

Subject 2 _____

Elements

1. _____
2. _____
3. _____

MAIN OBJECTIVE

Write a comparison-and-contrast essay

PROCESS OBJECTIVES

1. Use appropriate prewriting techniques to identify and develop a topic
2. Create a first draft
3. Use Evaluation Criteria as a basis for determining revision strategies
4. Revise the first draft, incorporating suggestions generated by self- or peer evaluation
5. Proofread and correct errors
6. Create a final draft
7. Choose an appropriate method of publication

Planning

- **Block Schedule**
  Block Scheduling Lesson Plans with Pacing Guide

- **One-Stop Planner**
  CD-ROM with Test Generator

Introducing the Workshop

Ask students to identify the courses they are taking that require them to compare and contrast different things. (For example, in history class, students might compare and contrast two Civil War generals; in biology, they might compare and contrast plants or animals.)

Point out that this workshop will show students how to gather and organize information in order to compare and contrast virtually any two topics, objects, or persons.

 *Resources: Print and Media*

Writing and Language
- *Portfolio Management System*
  Prewriting, p. 138
  Peer Editing, p. 139
  Assessment Rubric, p. 140

- *Workshop Resources*
  Revision Strategy Teaching Notes, p. 15
  Revision Strategy Transparencies 8, 9, 10

Teaching the Workshop

Prewriting
Students may read through the Prewriting suggestions by themselves, but it is a good idea to review the two types of organizational patterns in the Model on p. 402 with the class.

Drafting
Students are often reminded that anecdotes may be used effectively in an introduction, but many students have no idea how to find anecdotes related to a particular person or event. Before students begin drafting their introductions, you may wish to have the librarian come to class and show the variety of sources available and how to locate anecdotes and quotes systematically.

Evaluating and Revising
Have students use the Evaluation Criteria provided here to review their drafts and determine needed revisions.

Resources

Peer Editing Forms and Rubrics
• *Portfolio Management System*, p. 139
Revision Transparencies
• *Workshop Resources*, p. 15

Grading Timesaver

Rubrics for this Writer's Workshop assignment appear on p. 140 of the *Portfolio Management System*.

T402

Language Handbook HELP

See Comparison of Modifiers, pages 1227-1228; Using Parallel Structure, pages 1235-1236.

Communications Handbook HELP

See Proofreading.

■ *Evaluation Criteria*

A good comparison-and-contrast essay

1. *opens with an attention-getting statement*
2. *makes a clear thesis statement*
3. *uses the block method or the point-by-point method to present an argument*
4. *uses specific details to support the comparison-contrast*
5. *handles the features in the same order for both topics*
6. *closes with a summary*

Model

BLOCK METHOD	POINT-BY-POINT METHOD
Subject 1: "Because I could not stop for Death" 　Element 1: theme 　Element 2: tone 　Element 3: figures of speech Subject 2: "Thanatopsis" 　Element 1: theme 　Element 2: tone 　Element 3: figures of speech	Element 1: theme 　Subject 1: "Because I could not stop for Death" 　Subject 2: "Thanatopsis" Element 2: tone 　Subject 1: "Because I could not stop for Death" 　Subject 2: "Thanatopsis" Element 3: figures of speech 　Subject 1: "Because I could not stop for Death" 　Subject 2: "Thanatopsis"

Drafting

1. **Introduction.** Get your readers' attention with an amusing or dramatic anecdote, a surprising question, a powerful quotation, or a pointed detail. Then, clearly and carefully state your thesis.

   Remember that comparing two subjects does not mean that you must completely ignore their differences. Essays that explore similarities often begin by citing one or two differences and *then* focusing primarily on the similarities. The reverse is also true: Essays that contrast two subjects often begin by citing one or two similarities. You can build your introduction around such statements. By acknowledging both similarities and differences, you show your audience that you are aware of various aspects of your topic and that your perspective is not one-sided or simplistic.

2. **Body.** Use the block method or the point-by-point method to present the information you've gathered. Use facts, quotations, examples, and other kinds of information to elaborate the elements of each poem. Remain consistent throughout, maintaining your method of organization.

   Remember that your main goal is to understand or explain your subjects, the two poems you've selected; comparing and contrasting are simply methods to achieve that end. What light do the similarities and differences throw on your subjects? Ask yourself what new insights you have gained about the poems now that you have compared and contrasted them.

   To draw special attention to the comparisons and contrasts you make, you might want to use **parallel structure** in your sentences. Parallel structure is a natural way to express both similarities and differences. For example, you might say "While Bryant's tone is grand and romantic, Dickinson's tone is blithe and ironic."

3. **Conclusion.** Bring the essay to a satisfying close by summarizing or restating the main idea. You may wish to leave the reader with a final question or comment, perhaps indicating other topics or other features for comparison and contrast.

Language Workshop

OBJECTIVES
1. Vary sentence beginnings
2. Recognize the syntax of sentences

VARIETY IS THE SPICE: VARYING SENTENCE BEGINNINGS

The basic, no-frills English sentence begins with a subject that is closely followed by a verb: *Emily Dickinson wrote poems.* If every sentence followed that same pattern, however, readers would be unbearably bored. By using a variety of sentence beginnings, you can improve your style and hold your readers' interest. To vary sentences, you can use introductory words, phrases, or clauses.

1. Start a sentence with a modifier or modifiers.
   Private and *reclusive,* Emily Dickinson rarely tried to publish her poetry.

2. Start a sentence with a transitional word or phrase.
   Therefore, Dickinson's choice of subjects was bold and adventurous.

3. Start a sentence with a prepositional phrase.
   Throughout his writing career, Walt Whitman publicized himself frequently and enthusiastically.

4. Start a sentence with a verbal phrase.
   To understand a poem, read it at least twice.

5. Start a sentence with a dependent clause.
   After they died, Whitman and Dickinson took their places among the greatest nineteenth-century poets.

Writer's Workshop Follow-Up: Revising

Reread the comparison-and-contrast essay you wrote for the Writer's Workshop (page 401). Do too many of your sentences begin the same way? If so, revise them using strategies you've learned in this lesson. Remember to reword sentences for clarity, being careful to place phrase modifiers close to the words they modify. Don't feel that every sentence has to begin with a phrase or clause, however; sometimes a simple sentence will give you exactly the tone and emphasis you need.

Technology HELP

See Language Workshop CD-ROM. *Key word entry: sentences—beginnings.*

Language Handbook HELP

See Revising for Variety, page 1237.

Try It Out

With a partner, revise each of the following sentences by altering its beginning according to the strategy indicated in parentheses.

1. Walt Whitman never went to college, but he read widely. (transition)
2. Emily Dickinson was a reclusive person whose inner life was remarkably rich. (modifier)
3. Whitman's long poems are, in the opinion of many academics, as laboriously crafted as Dickinson's short poems. (dependent clause)
4. It is beside the point to attempt to rank Dickinson and Whitman in order of greatness. (verbal phrase)

Resources

Workshop Resources
• Worksheet, p. 53

Language Workshop CD-ROM
• Sentences — Beginnings

Try It Out
Possible Answers
1. Walt Whitman never went to college. However, he read widely.
2. Remarkably rich in her inner life, Emily Dickinson was a reclusive person.
3. Although Whitman's poems are long, they are, in the opinion of many academics, as laboriously crafted as Dickinson's short poems.
4. To attempt to rank Dickinson and Whitman in order of greatness is beside the point.

Assessing Learning

Quick Check:
Varying Sentence Beginnings
Revise these sentences by varying their beginnings. Use any strategy you prefer. (Sample answers are given.)

1. Dickinson became well known after her death. [After her death, Dickinson became well known.]
2. Whitman aimed for an epic tone by the use of long lists. [Using long lists, Whitman aimed for an epic tone.]

3. Whitman, sociable and gregarious, liked to travel. [Sociable and gregarious, Whitman liked to travel.]
4. Dickinson was a private person who requested that all her poems be destroyed after her death. [Since Dickinson was a private person, she requested that all her poems be destroyed after her death.]

T403

OBJECTIVES
1. Identify the basic parts of a textbook
2. Identify the special features of a textbook

Using the Strategies
Possible Answers

1. John Malcolm Brinnin wrote the introductory material on Whitman and Dickinson. He is the author of six volumes of award-winning poetry and several books of criticism. Mr. Brinnin was a member of the Academy and Institute of Arts and Letters and was director of New York's famous Poetry Center. He taught at universities for a number of years.

2. Special features include these: Primary Sources: "If you were coming in the Fall" (an edited poem); Elements of Literature: Slant Rhyme; Student to Student: "The Mirror Girl—stares back at me" (poem) by Brigid Spackman; Connections: "Emily Dickinson's Homestead" (article) by Anne Bernays; and Primary Sources: "I sing . . . because I am afraid" (a letter).

3. The textbook places Dickinson in the historical context of "The American Renaissance: A Literary Coming of Age (1840–1860)" and in the thematic grouping "A New American Poetry: Whitman and Dickinson."

4. Other special features include a biographical sketch; a picture of an original manuscript of Dickinson's "I keep my pledge" and "Heart! We will forget him!"; and a photograph of Dickinson's house.

5. It appears in the introductory essay "A New American Poetry: Whitman and Dickinson."

6. Features that might help students examine Dickinson's poetic structure include these: Primary Sources (an edited poem); Elements of Literature: Slant Rhyme; and the Making Meanings questions.

7. Possible features include the article "Emily Dickinson's Homestead" and the photograph of her house.

Situation

Suppose that you wish to do a special project on Emily Dickinson. Your first stop (before throwing yourself into extensive research in a library or on the Internet) might be to explore information available in this literature textbook. Here are strategies you can use to evaluate and read almost any textbook.

Strategies

Examine basic parts of the textbook.

- These basic parts include the book's Table of Contents, the author pages, the unit chapter overviews, and parts of the backmatter, including various indices.

Identify special features of the textbook.

- These might include time lines, statistical tables, unique images related to the book's content, firsthand sources, various types of commentary, lists of books for further reading, and special material in the back matter, such as the Glossary and, in this textbook, the Language Handbook.

Examine the book to see if it contains information relevant to your research needs.

- List questions you'd like answered. Then, examine the book to confirm that it contains information you're seeking.

Take notes on important passages.

- Take precise and complete notes on passages that focus on issues relevant to your topic.
- Outline key passages. You can use either of the following standard outline approaches.

I. Main idea
  A. Supporting point
    1. Detail
      a. Information or further detail

Main idea
- Supporting detail
- Supporting detail
- Supporting detail

Using the Strategies

Answer the following questions by examining this textbook:

1. Which author of this textbook wrote the introductory material on Whitman and Dickinson? What are the writer's qualifications?

2. According to the Table of Contents, what special features are included with the poems by Dickinson?

3. How does this textbook "place" Dickinson—in what historical context and under what thematic grouping?

4. Flip through the section on Dickinson. What other special features do you find?

5. Where in the textbook will you find an overview of Dickinson and her place as an American poet?

6. Suppose you are especially interested in Dickinson's poetic techniques. Which features in this book will help you to examine the structure of her poems?

7. If you wanted to travel to Amherst, Massachusetts, to visit the Dickinson house, which features might interest you? (Remember to look at pictures too.)

8. Find Dickinson's biography. Outline the main ideas and supporting details in this biography. What questions do you have that you want to do further research on?

9. Draw up a list of all the questions you have about Dickinson, based on information in this text. What further research would you like to undertake?

Extending the Strategies

Test Your Skill

Identify a topic or aspect of your everyday life about which you might want to consult a reference book or textbook. (Think of questions you might have about sports, automobile repair, or health.)

You might also use the strategies on this page to examine another textbook you use in school—in history, science, modern language, or math.

8. Outlines should mention Dickinson's childhood, her trip to Washington, D.C., her subsequent reclusiveness, her friendship with Higginson, and the eventual publication of her poems. Research questions will vary.

9. Responses will vary.

Reaching All Students

Advanced Learners

Have students formulate several additional questions about Emily Dickinson that can be answered by reading this textbook. Students can then trade questions and answer them in a game-show format.

Learning for Life

The Changing World of Work

OBJECTIVES
1. Research possible changes in a field of work over the next decade
2. Present research in a suitable format

Problem

In "I Hear America Singing," Walt Whitman presents a catalog of occupations that would have been familiar in his time. Since Whitman's time, however, the world of work has changed drastically, and it continues to change at a rapid rate. How will the world of work change for the average American in the next decade?

Project

Research one career field to discover how it may change over the next decade, what skills a person will need in order to work in that field, and what new occupations may emerge in that field.

Preparation

1. Decide what aspect of the broad topic *occupations* you'll focus on. Choose a field that you think you might be interested in pursuing one day. If you're interested in health care, for instance, you might want to research developing trends in health-care careers.

2. Use the *5W-How?* questions (*Who? What? When? Where? Why? How?*) to help you find the information you need. *How* will health care change? *Who* will be most affected by the changes? *When* are changes likely to occur?

3. Brainstorm a list of possible resources for your research.

Procedure

1. Start by getting an overview of your chosen occupation by consulting the government publications *Dictionary of Occupational Titles* and *Occupational Outlook Handbook*.

2. Cast your net wide for research information, but be sure you're using reliable and current sources.

   • Contact trade and professional organizations, and request publications from them.

   • Check with special-interest newsgroups on the Internet.

   • Consult local college or university career services offices.

   • Interview someone currently working in the field you're interested in.

3. Analyze your findings. Can you make some educated guesses about how the occupation you have researched will change in the next decade or so? How can people interested in that occupation prepare themselves for it?

Presentation

To present your findings, use one of the following formats (or another that your teacher approves):

1. **Radio Spot**
   Tape-record for possible broadcast a radio program in which you share your findings about coming changes in the occupation you researched.

2. **Brochure**
   Create a brochure that could be used by a student career-services office or a vocational-technical center ten years from now. The brochure should give specific information about education, training, and job skills necessary for the career you have researched. Make your brochure look as professional as possible; use desktop publishing, if you can, and provide illustrations.

3. **A Mock Interview**
   With another student, write and act out a scenario in which a person ten years from now is interviewing for a job in the field you researched. The dialogue of the interview should reveal what tasks and responsibilities the job will entail, what kind of education and skills are necessary, and what kind of career path the person being interviewed can expect.

Processing

What challenges await the American worker, and how do you think you and other students can better prepare yourselves for the future world of work? Write a reflection for your portfolio.

Resources

Viewing and Representing
HRW Multimedia Presentation Maker

Students may wish to use the *Multimedia Presentation Maker* to help prepare their brochures.

Grading Timesaver

Rubrics for this Learning for Life project appear on p. 140 of the *Portfolio Management System*.

Developing Workplace Competencies

Preparation	Procedure	Presentation
• Makes decisions • Reasons • Uses resources	• Acquires data • Applies technology to specific tasks • Processes information	• Communicates ideas and information • Thinks creatively • Works on teams

T405

OBJECTIVES

1. Read literature of the Civil War and postwar period on the themes "Shackles" and "From Innocence to Experience"
2. Interpret literary elements in nineteenth-century Realist literature
3. Apply a variety of reading strategies to nineteenth-century Realist literature, with special emphasis on affixes
4. Respond to literature in a variety of modes
5. Learn and use new words
6. Learn about American dialects
7. Plan, draft, revise, edit, proof, and publish a research paper
8. Write sentences with adverbial and adjectival clauses
9. Demonstrate the ability to read a college guide
10. Monitor the media

Resources ━━━━

Viewing and Representing
Videocassette B, Segment 7
Available in English and Spanish. This videocassette discusses the nineteenth-century movements of abolitionism and women's suffrage.

Prisoners from the Front (detail) by **Winslow Homer (1836–1910).** Oil on canvas (24″ x 38″).

The Metropolitan Museum of Art. Gift of Mrs. Frank B. Porter, 1922 (22.207). Photograph © 1995 The Metropolitan Museum of Art.

go.hrw.com
LE0 11-Realism

Selection Readability

This Annotated Teacher's Edition provides a summary of each selection in the student book. Following each Summary heading, you will find one, two, or three small icons. These icons indicate, in an approximate sense, the reading level of the selection.

■ One icon indicates that the selection is easy.

■ ■ Two icons indicate that the selection is on an intermediate reading level.

■ ■ ■ Three icons indicate that the selection is challenging.

The Rise of Realism
The Civil War and Postwar Period 1850–1900

RESPONDING TO THE ART

Winslow Homer (1836–1910) began his career as a lithographer and pictorial reporter, and gained fame through his illustrations of the Civil War for *Harper's Weekly*. He painted Realistic pictures, concentrating on composition, strong lines, and typically American scenes of farms, children at play, and fashionable young women. After the war, he began painting watercolors from nature, in which he captured the passing effects of light. In the final stage of his career, he sought to capture the battle of a human being and the sea and, finally, of the land and the sea.

Activity. This painting is famous for capturing the spirit of reconciliation that most Americans hoped for following the Civil War. Have students discuss what details in the depiction of the Southern soldiers and their Northern captors suggest this interpretation. [Possible responses: While the Southern captives are bedraggled and exhausted, they are shown as noble and dignified. The Northern soldiers seem calm and restrained, hardly triumphant in their victory. All four are presented side-by-side in a single line, as equals.]

The Rise of Realism
The Civil War and Postwar Period

by **Gary Q. Arpin**

A man said to the universe:
"Sir, I exist!"
"However," replied the universe,
"The fact has not created in me
A sense of obligation."
—Stephen Crane

Responding to the Quotation

Before the Civil War, America was essentially an idealistic, confident, and self-reliant republic. Ask students what Stephen Crane's poem from *War Is Kind* suggests happened to America after the Civil War. [Possible response: People's confidence about their purpose and place in the universe was shaken.]

RESPONDING TO THE ART

Mathew Brady (c.1823–1896) pioneered front-line photography during the Civil War. He and his staff traveled with the Union armies and took more than 3,500 photographs.
Activity. Have students discuss what the photograph reveals about the state of the Union soldiers. [Students may point to the unsanitary and makeshift conditions or the despair and exhaustion of the wounded man.]

Reaching All Students

Struggling Readers
Encourage students to create a graphic organizer, such as a map, chart, time line, or tree diagram, to reflect what they learn from this essay. Students could use the subheads, authors' names, or years in the essay as they organize information into the graphic. Then, invite students to assess how well this strategy helped them process information. Was the graphic they chose able to accommodate the information in the essay?

English Language Learners
Have students work in groups of three to review the essay. Each member of the group in turn should summarize a particular section. If the speaker omits a key event or cannot recall a particular word, the rest of the group can offer prompts. If a student relates incorrect information or uses the wrong word, other group members should correct the error.

Advanced Learners
Explain that the Confederacy had its own unofficial anthem and flag. Ask students to report to the class on the origin of "Dixie." [It was written in 1859 by Daniel Emmett for a minstrel show. The word *Dixie* is believed to come from the French word *dix*, "ten," which appeared on $10 notes issued by a bank in French-speaking New Orleans.]

Evening Gun Fort Sumter (detail) by John Gadsby Chapman. (Painted in Rome, 1864, after a sketch made by his son Conrad Wise Chapman). Oil on board.

The Museum of the Confederacy, Richmond, Virginia. Photography by Katherine Wetzel.

On the evening of April 12, 1861, Walt Whitman attended the opera at the Academy of Music in Manhattan. After the opera, he was walking down Broadway toward Brooklyn when, as he later wrote, "I heard in the distance the loud cries of the newsboys, who came presently tearing and yelling up the street, rushing from side to side even more furiously than usual. I bought an extra and crossed to the Metropolitan Hotel . . . where the great lamps were still brightly blazing, and, with a crowd of others, who gathered impromptu, read the news, which was evidently authentic."

The news that Whitman and the others read so avidly was of the Confederate attack on Fort Sumter, the opening shots of the Civil War. Thus solemnly

> War is at best barbarism. . . . Its glory is all moonshine. . . . War is hell.
>
> —Union General William Tecumseh Sherman

Quilt by Varina Davis.
The Museum of the Confederacy, Richmond, Virginia. Photograph by Katherine Wetzel.

THE RISE OF REALISM: THE CIVIL WAR AND POSTWAR PERIOD 409

RESPONDING TO THE ART

John Gadsby Chapman (1808–1889) depicts Fort Sumter in the harbor of Charleston, South Carolina, after the first decisive battle of the Civil War. Because South Carolina had seceded from the Union, the fort, a federal stronghold, was in a precarious position in March 1861. When President Lincoln commanded that the fort be sent supplies, Confederate General P. G. T. Beauregard responded by ordering the evacuation of the fort. When federal troops refused, Confederate forces fired on the fort on April 12, 1861, for thirty-four hours until the federal troops surrendered. The conflict over Fort Sumter led to the four-year war between the Northern and Southern states.

Activity. Have students analyze the details of Chapman's painting. What themes or message might Chapman be trying to convey? [Possible response: The raising of the Confederate flag, the dying light, and the title all suggest an end to the innocence of the prewar era, and the national trauma that lies ahead.]

Ⓐ Exploring the Historical Period

Causes of the Civil War

The Civil War was the culmination of four decades of intense sectional conflict. It reflected the deep-seated economic, social, and political differences between the North and the South. The agricultural South produced cash crops (sugarcane, tobacco, cotton) for export to the North and Europe. The South depended on the North for financial, manufacturing, and commercial services. One of the major differences between the regions was that the South included nearly four million enslaved blacks, who made up one third of its population. Although the slaveholding planter class was a small minority, it nonetheless dominated Southern politics. In addition, the North tended to regard the federal government as the primary authority over civil and economic life, while the South championed states' rights.

T409

Professional Notes

Southern Civilians and Fort Sumter

Mary Chesnut, a Southerner who supported the cause but was opposed to slavery, provides a telling description of the situation in Charleston on the day after the war began: "Fort Sumter has been on fire. He [Beauregard] has not yet silenced any of our guns. So the aides—still with swords and red sashes by way of uniforms—tell us.

But the sound of those guns makes regular meals impossible. None of us go to table. . . .

Not by one word or look can we detect any changes in the demeanor of these negro servants. . . . They carry it too far. You could not tell that they hear even the awful row that is going on in the bay, though it is dinning in their ears night and day. And people talk before them as if they were chairs and tables."

Time Line

This time line shows major events both in America and around the world from 1850 to 1900.

• 1850–1859
Sojourner Truth

Isabella Baumfree was born into slavery in New York State but was freed after the state abolished slavery in 1827. In 1843, she changed her name to "Sojourner Truth," to reflect her mission as an itinerant preacher, and travelled across the country, speaking in support of feminism, religion, and abolition. A powerful orator, she often shared the platform with Frederick Douglass. In her best-known speech, "Ain't I a Woman?," delivered in 1851 at a women's rights convention, Truth argued against those who used the Bible to claim that women could not have the same rights as men. She asked, "Where did your Christ come from? From God and a woman! Man had nothing to do with him." She argued that if Eve was strong enough to "turn the world upside down all alone, then women should be able to turn it right side up again." One account reports that during an 1858 speech, Truth was heckled by men claiming that she was too forceful to be a woman; in response, Truth bared her breasts and shamed her persecutors.

• 1850–1859
Harriet Jacobs

Harriet Jacobs (1813–1897), born into slavery in North Carolina, was sexually abused by her owner's father, Dr. James Norcom. To escape him, Jacobs went into hiding in 1835 and spent almost seven years in a crawl space in her grandmother's house. In 1842, Jacobs escaped to the North, but she was later pursued there by Norcom after the passage of the Fugitive Slave Act. Her narrative, *Incidents in the Life of a Slave Girl,* describes her life in bondage.

The Civil War and Postwar Period 1850–1900

LITERARY EVENTS

Sojourner Truth (1864) by an unidentified photographer.
National Portrait Gallery, Smithsonian Institution, Washington, D.C.

Sojourner Truth, abolitionist and women's rights advocate, dictates *Narrative of Sojourner Truth, c.* 1850

France's Gustave Flaubert publishes a classic realistic novel, *Madame Bovary,* 1856

•

Herman Melville publishes *The Piazza Tales,* short stories including "Bartleby the Scrivener," 1856

•

Harriet Beecher Stowe publishes an influential novel about slavery, *Uncle Tom's Cabin,* 1851–1852

Harriet Beecher Stowe (c. 1852). Daguerreotype.

Bret Harte publishes the short story "The Outcasts of Poker Flat," 1869

Russian author Leo Tolstoy completes his panoramic novel *War and Peace,* 1869

•

Louisa May Alcott publishes a popular novel about growing up, *Little Women,* 1868–1869

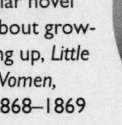

Louisa May Alcott. Oil over a photograph.
The Granger Collection, New York.

1850–1859 | 1860–1869

CULTURAL/HISTORICAL EVENTS

Fugitive Slave Act imposes stiff penalties on anyone helping a person escape enslavement, 1850

•

Susan B. Anthony and Elizabeth Cady Stanton become co-leaders of U.S. women's rights movement, early 1850s

The Sepoy Rebellion, a large-scale uprising against British rule in India, ends, 1858

•

England's Charles Darwin explains his groundbreaking theory of evolution in *Origin of Species,* 1859

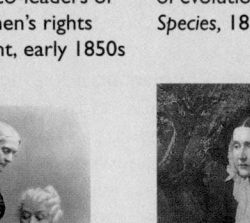

Susan B. Anthony and Elizabeth Cady Stanton.

Julia Ward Howe by John Elliott (c. 1910) and William H. Cotton (c. 1925). Oil on canvas.
National Portrait Gallery, Gift of Mrs. John Elliott 1933. Courtesy Art Resource.

First shots of Civil War fired, April 1861

•

Confederate troops defeat Union forces at Bull Run in Virginia, in the first major battle of the Civil War, July 1861

•

Julia Ward Howe publishes the song "The Battle Hymn of the Republic," 1862

•

President Abraham Lincoln delivers the Gettysburg Address at the dedication of a Civil War cemetery, November 1863

•

Confederate surrender at Appomattox Court House in Virginia ends Civil War, April 1865

President Lincoln is assassinated in Ford's Theater, Washington, D.C., April 14, 1865

•

The Thirteenth Amendment to the U.S. Constitution, outlawing slavery, is ratified, 1865

•

U.S. purchases Alaska from Russia, 1867

•

Restoration of Meiji emperor opens a period of modernization in Japan, 1867

Abraham Lincoln (1863). Photograph by Alexander Gardner.
Library of Congress.

Using the Time Line

1. Have students use an encyclopedia or other reference source to place the following major events on the time line:
   - John Brown, an abolitionist, leads a raid on Harpers Ferry, a federal arsenal, and is hanged for treason. [1859]
   - Charles Dickens publishes *A Tale of Two Cities.* [1859]
   - Abraham Lincoln is elected president. [1860]
   - Lincoln issues the Emancipation Proclamation. [1862]
   - Joseph Lister initiates antiseptic surgery by using carbolic acid on a wound. [1865]
   - First Impressionist art exhibition is held in Paris. [1874]
   - American Baseball Association is founded. [1882]
   - The French Lumière Brothers produce the first motion picture. [1895]
   - Max Planck formulates the quantum theory of physics. [1900]

Henry James.
Archive Photos.

William Dean Howells.
The Granger Collection, New York.

Henry James publishes the novel *Daisy Miller*, a study of European and American manners, 1879

•

Mark Twain publishes the popular novel *The Adventures of Tom Sawyer* and begins work on a famous sequel, *Adventures of Huckleberry Finn*, 1876

William Dean Howells publishes the realistic novel *The Rise of Silas Lapham*, 1885

•

José Martí, Cuban writer and independence leader, publishes his poetry collection *Ismaelillo*, 1882

•

Russian novelist Fyodor Dostoyevsky publishes *The Brothers Karamazov*, 1879–1880

Stephen Crane publishes *The Red Badge of Courage*, about a soldier's response to the Civil War, 1895

•

Kate Chopin publishes *Bayou Folk*, short stories about life in Louisiana, 1894

Russia's Anton Chekhov writes the realistic drama *Uncle Vanya*, 1899

•

African American writer Paul Laurence Dunbar publishes his poetry collection *Lyrics of Lowly Life*, 1896

•

Sarah Orne Jewett publishes *The Country of the Pointed Firs*, about life in a Maine seaport, 1896

1870–1879　1880–1889　1890–1900

John D. Rockefeller founds the Standard Oil Company of Ohio, 1870

•

Sioux soldiers defeat U.S. forces under Gen. George A. Custer on the Little Bighorn in Dakota Territory, 1876

•

Alexander Graham Bell patents the first telephone, 1876

•

Thomas Edison patents the first phonograph, 1878

Clara Barton organizes the American Red Cross, 1881

•

Booker T. Washington founds Tuskegee Institute, 1881

•

Statue of Liberty is dedicated, 1886

James Naismith invents game of basketball, at Springfield, Massachusetts, 1891

•

Naturalist John Muir publishes *The Mountains of California*, 1894

•

German physicist Wilhelm Roentgen discovers X-rays, 1895

Athens, Greece, is the site of the first modern Olympic Games, 1896

•

U.S. annexes Hawaii and wins Spanish-American War (gaining Puerto Rico, Guam, and the Philippines), 1898

•

U.S. population is about 76 million, 1900

•

Austrian physician Sigmund Freud advances the field of psychiatry by publishing *The Interpretation of Dreams*, 1900

Prisoners from the Front by Winslow Homer (1836–1910). Oil on canvas (24″ x 38″).
The Metropolitan Museum of Art. Gift of Mrs. Frank B. Porter, 1922 (22.207). Photograph © 1995 The Metropolitan Museum of Art.

411

Using the Time Line

2. What did Sojourner Truth, Susan B. Anthony, and Elizabeth Cady Stanton have in common? [They were advocates for women's rights.]

3. What three innovations occurred between 1876 and 1895? [the invention of the telephone and phonograph, and the discovery of X-rays] What generalization can you draw from this fact? [Possible response: The post-

war period was an age of scientific experimentation that inspired a number of new technologies.]

4. Have students look through the rest of this collection for illustrations that would complement any of the items in the time line. Be sure students can justify why an illustration should be included and designate where it should be placed in the graphic.

• **1870–1879**
General Custer
The battle at Little Bighorn in June 1876 marked the last major victory for the Lakota (Sioux) in the intense fight between Native Americans and white settlers for land in the West. The final defeat for the Lakota occurred on December 29, 1890, when the U.S. Army massacred men, women, and children at Wounded Knee, South Dakota, an atrocity which left an enduring stain on U.S. history.

• **1880–1889**
Booker T. Washington
Booker T. Washington's approach toward improving the quality of life for African Americans after the war sparked considerable controversy. He believed that blacks' interests were best served through vocational education, not through academic instruction or participation in politics. In spite of Washington's many critics, his Tuskegee Institute had about fifteen hundred students and an endowment of two million dollars at the time of Washington's death.

• **1890–1900**
John Muir
John Muir became a naturalist after he nearly lost an eye while working on mechanical inventions. He was influential in establishing Sequoia and Yosemite National Parks in California, in designating thirteen national forests, and in shaping Theodore Roosevelt's conservation program.
Anton Chekhov
Russian dramatist and short-story writer Anton Chekhov trained as a physician but rarely practiced medicine because he suffered from tuberculosis, incurable at that time. Highly successful in his day, Chekhov wrote a number of brilliant Naturalistic plays, including *The Sea Gull* (1896), *The Three Sisters* (1901), and *The Cherry Orchard* (1904). In addition, Chekhov is credited with creating the modern short story—dependent on mood and symbolism rather than on plot.

Ⓐ Background

A Clash of Ideals

Both the North and the South were motivated by a combination of ideology and economics. Northerners fought to end slavery and to preserve the constitutional Union of the founders. Southerners fought to uphold states' rights and to defend the Southern way of life from what they saw as the crass materialism of the industrial North. Both fought to protect their economic interests.

Ⓑ Exploring the Historical Period

First Battle of Bull Run

Since both sides were relatively untrained and disorganized, some historians think the war could have ended with this early battle. At the beginning of the battle, the Union nearly broke the left flank of the Confederate line. Had it done so, the Confederates would likely have lost the battle and the war. Late in the battle, the Union retreated. If the Confederates had pursued them, they might have captured Washington, D.C. But the war was to be long and painful, as the spectators from Washington, who had come to watch the battle with parasols, camp stools, and picnic lunches, soon learned.

RESPONDING TO THE ART

Winslow Homer (1836–1910) was the foremost painter of the Civil War. Here he captures the youth of the soldier and the exact details of his uniform.

Activity. Have students skim "Voices from the Civil War," pp. 476–483, and then write a letter home that this young man may be composing in his mind.

Young Soldier: Separate Study of a Soldier Giving Water to a Wounded Companion (1861) by Winslow Homer (1836–1910). Oil, gouache, black crayon on canvas (36 cm × 17.5 cm).

Cooper-Hewitt, National Design Museum, Smithsonian Institution; Gift of Charles Savage Homer, Jr./Courtesy Art Resource, NY.

began, for one of the few American poets or novelists who would witness it firsthand, the greatest cataclysm in United States history.

Responses to the War: Idealism . . .

In Concord, Massachusetts, home of Ralph Waldo Emerson, Henry David Thoreau, Nathaniel Hawthorne, and many other intellectual leaders of the nation, army volunteers met in 1861 at the bridge that Emerson had immortalized in "Concord Hymn" (page 99), his famous poem about the beginning of the American Revolution. Emerson had for decades warned that this day would come if slavery were not abolished. Now that the day had arrived, he was filled with patriotic fervor. He watched the Concord volunteers march to Boston, and he visited a navy yard, declaring that "sometimes gunpowder smells good."

Emerson had great respect for the Southern will to fight, however, and he suspected, quite rightly, that the war would not be over in a few months as some people had predicted. When the Concord volunteers returned a few months later from the First Battle of Bull Run (July 1861), defeated and disillusioned, many of them unwilling to reenlist, Emerson maintained his conviction that the war must be pursued.

Still, Northern disillusionment after the early defeat at Bull Run was strong. With a keen eye for the sad details, Whitman recorded the sense of gloomy defeat in Washington in late July when Northern troops returned from the disaster of Bull Run:

> The defeated troops commenced pouring into Washington over the Long Bridge at daylight on Monday, 22nd—day drizzling all through with rain. The Saturday and Sunday of the battle

> The war with its defeats and uncertainties is immensely better than what we lately called the integrity of the Republic, as amputation is better than cancer.
>
> —Ralph Waldo Emerson

412 THE RISE OF REALISM: THE CIVIL WAR AND POSTWAR PERIOD

Skill Link

Comparing Statistics

The rise of the textile industry in the Northeast and Europe created a sharp increase in the demand for cotton. By 1860, cotton made up half of all United States exports. Many Southerners hoped that the importance of cotton to the national economy would ensure the continuation of slavery.

Ask students to examine the following two graphs, and then answer these questions:

1. Note that both graphs show an increase during the period from 1820 to 1860. How might these two statistics be related? [Possible response: They might have a causal relationship.]

2. Would an increase in cotton production require more slaves? Would a growing slave population lead to increased production? Or could both be true? [Students should realize that both could be true.]

SLAVE POPULATION OF THE U.S.

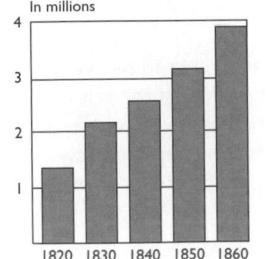

In millions

1820 1830 1840 1850 1860

COTTON PRODUCTION

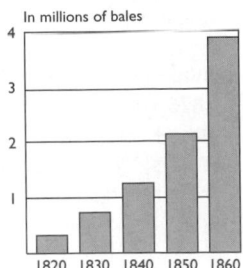

In millions of bales

1820 1830 1840 1850 1860

(20th, 21st) had been parched and hot to an extreme—the dust, the grime and smoke, in layers, sweated in followed by other layers again sweated in, absorbed by those excited souls—their clothes all saturated with the clay-powder filling the air—stirred up everywhere on the dry roads and trodden fields by the regiments, swarming wagons, artillery, etc.—all the men with this coating of murk and sweat and rain, now recoiling back, pouring over the Long Bridge—a horrible march of twenty miles, returning to Washington baffled, humiliated, panic-struck. Where are the vaunts, and the proud boasts with which you went forth? Where are your banners, and your bands of music, and your ropes to bring back your prisoners? Well, there isn't a band playing—and there isn't a flag but clings ashamed and lank to its staff.

—Walt Whitman

Civil War ambulance.
Culver Pictures.

Future years will never know the seething hell and the black infernal background of the countless minor scenes and interiors . . . and it is best they should not—the real war will never get in the books.

—Walt Whitman

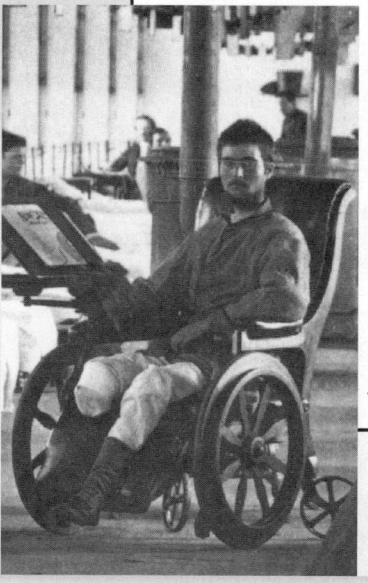

A patient in Armory Square Hospital, Washington, D.C., during the Civil War. Photograph (detail).

©Collection of The New-York Historical Society.

Late in 1862, Whitman traveled to Virginia to find his brother George, who had been wounded in battle. After George was nursed back to health, Whitman remained in Washington off and on, working part time and serving as a volunteer hospital visitor, comforting the wounded and writing to their loved ones. The condition of the wounded was appalling. Many of the injured had to remain on the battlefield for two or three days until the camp hospitals had room for them. Antiseptics were primitive, as were operating-room techniques. Anesthesia was virtually unknown. A major wound meant amputation or even death.

Whitman estimated that in three years as a camp hospital volunteer, he visited tens of thousands of wounded men. "I am the man," he had written in "Song of Myself," "I suffer'd, I was there," and now he *was* there, in the real heart of

THE RISE OF REALISM: THE CIVIL WAR AND POSTWAR PERIOD 413

C Critical Thinking

Expressing an Opinion

Ask students whether they agree with Whitman that perhaps citizens are better off not seeing "the real war" or whether they believe citizens have a right and a duty to learn as much as possible about the bloodshed their taxes help finance. Students may also want to explore the conflict between the principle of freedom of the press and the need of a government at war to maintain secrecy. This conflict was a hot topic during the Persian Gulf War of 1991, when an international force led by the United States attacked Iraqi forces, which had invaded Kuwait.

D Exploring the Culture

Military Nurses

Many women volunteered as nurses and worked side by side with the men. In the North, Dorothea Dix was in charge of the three thousand female Union nurses. "Dragon Dix," as she was called because she was so strict and demanding, would allow women to be nurses only if they were more than thirty years old, wore plain black or brown dresses, and were not interested in the attention of the male patients. With her no-nonsense attitude, Dix succeeded in improving the conditions for patients. In the South, Sally Tompkins worked with six other nurses to take care of 1,333 wounded men in Richmond, Virginia. Their record was unparalleled, for only twenty-three of these men died. As a result, Tompkins became the only recognized female officer in the Confederacy.

E Background

Because rifle balls often shattered bones, doctors were usually forced to amputate wounded soldiers' arms or legs, often piling the limbs up on a cart outside the surgeon's tent. Ignorant of hygienic science, surgeons frequently honed their scalpels on the soles of their boots, so infections in the field hospitals ran rampant. There were, of course, no antibiotics—Alexander Fleming did not discover penicillin until 1928—so even minor wounds could, and often did, prove deadly.

Professional Notes

Whitman's Search for His Brother

After Fredericksburg, George Whitman's name, garbled as "First Lieutenant G. W. Whitmore," appeared on the list of casualties. According to Whitman's biographer Justin Kaplan: ". . . Walt set out immediately for the front, had his money stolen while changing trains at Philadelphia, arrived in Washington without a dime for food or carfare. For a time of 'the greatest suffering I ever experienced in my life,' he hunted through the hospitals for George, 'walking all day and night, unable to ride, trying to get information, trying to get access to big people—I could not get the least clue to anything.' " Finally, Walt traveled to Falmouth, where George had relocated with his regiment, and found his brother alive and well, with just a nick on the cheek from a shell fragment.

A Closer Look

This feature describes the efforts of Mathew Brady and others to create a photographic history of the war.

A Exploring the Culture

Early Photography

The optical principle behind photography was known as far back as the ancient Greeks, and depended on a pinhole-sized opening in the wall of a darkened box or *camera obscura,* which focused the light and projected an image on the opposite wall. It wasn't until innovations in the production of glass lenses and light-sensitive chemicals, that modern photography became possible. The first image to be captured in a *camera obscura* and photochemically fixed was made in 1826 by a French military officer and inventor, Joseph-Nicéphore Niepce. But Niepce's process took hours to capture an image, which made it impractical. In 1851, British photographer Frederick Archer created a process that reduced the time it took to produce a picture to just a few seconds, but the picture had to be developed at once. This was the process Brady and his staff used during the Civil War—hence the need for mobile darkrooms.

B Critical Thinking

Making Inferences

? What do you think Whitman saw in the patients that he cared for that gave him such optimism? [Possible responses: The men were loyal to their cause; the men on each side developed strong bonds; the men were optimistic about winning the war and had hope for the future; the men had great courage in the face of death.]

EYES OF AN ERA

Television's close-up coverage of modern warfare has made the thick of battle a common sight on the nightly news. But during the American Civil War, photographs were the closest thing to newscasts. By the latter part of the 1800s, technical advances began to allow for truly mobile photographers. As a result, the Civil War became the first war to be fully documented in pictures. Cameras went on the march, up in observation balloons, and to sea on battleships. More than three hundred civilian photographers covered the Union's Army of the Potomac alone. But newspapers could not yet reproduce photos, so photographers did brisk business selling "war views" and portraits of soldiers directly to the public.

Cameras of the time could not capture motion; charging troops and thrusting bayonets came out as hazy blurs. But cameras richly recorded the preparations and the aftermath of war. After battles, photographers roamed the killing fields, shooting pictures while wearing handkerchiefs across their faces to block the stench of death. They captured the war's still lifes—fields and forests filled with dead soldiers, blasted cities and landscapes, and scenes taken inside prisons, hospitals, and camps.

Many of the pioneering Civil War photojournalists were probably motivated more by profit than by a sense of history. The most famous of these war photographers was Mathew Brady (c. 1823–1896). Brady was among the first photographers to think of moving mini-darkrooms into combat areas; usually, these darkrooms were customized delivery wagons, which soldiers nicknamed "what-is-it" wagons. Though Brady helped inspire Civil War photography with his views of the First Battle of Bull Run in 1861, more often he employed courageous photographers, such as Alexander Gardner and Timothy O'Sullivan, to take their cameras onto the battlefields. Brady helped guarantee the war's rich visual record, but

America. In his poems, he had presented a panoramic vision of America; now America passed through the hospital tents in the form of wounded men from every state in the Union and the Confederacy. Nevertheless, out of the horror that he viewed, Whitman was able to derive an optimistic vision of the American character, of "the actual soldier of 1862–65 . . . with all his ways, his incredible dauntlessness, habits, practices, tastes, language, his fierce friendship, his appetite, rankness, his superb strength—and a hundred unnamed lights and shades."

. . . and Disillusionment

The war that strengthened Whitman's optimism served at the same time to justify Herman Melville's pessimism. Melville's poems about the war, collected in *Battle-Pieces and Aspects of the War* (1866), were often dark and foreboding. Of the elation following the firing on Fort Sumter, Melville wrote:

Woman freed from slavery learning to read. Leib Image Archives, York, Pennsylvania.

Professional Notes

Critical Comment: Melville's War Writing

Richard Chase contends that *Battle-Pieces and Aspects of the War* is "the only volume of verse in the meager body of distinguished writing about the war that may be favorably compared with Whitman's *Drum Taps. . . .*" He says: "Melville does not write as a partisan. The war as he sees it is a catastrophe that has happened, not so much because of a Southern insurrection, but because of innate imperfections in man's very nature, because of historical forces no man or group could fully control, and because of certain weaknesses in American democracy that the war itself has made ominously apparent." How do Melville's views about the war confirm that Melville is one of the Dark Romantics? (See pp. 213–214.)

it was the skill and heroism of Gardner, O'Sullivan, and nameless others that actually produced the legacy of Civil War pictures.

Gardner came closer than anyone else to capturing an actual battle scene when he set his camera on a ridge overlooking the Battle of Antietam in Maryland in 1862. Gardner's genius at film processing and composition helped raise photographic coverage of the war to the level of art. He recognized that "verbal representations" of the war "may or may not have the merit of accuracy; but photographic presentments of them will be accepted by posterity with an undoubting faith."

O'Sullivan was one of the bravest and most brilliant of Brady's assistants. When bridge builders whom O'Sullivan was photographing were targeted by enemy sharpshooters, he calmly continued taking pictures while men screamed and fell. One of O'Sullivan's post-battle pictures shows corpses littering the quiet Gettysburg Cemetery; a sign hanging by the cemetery gatepost proclaims, with grim irony, that there is a five-dollar fine for discharging a firearm within cemetery limits.

Photographers fought heavy equipment, stray bullets, rain, mud, insects, foliage, wandering livestock, and frozen hands. Processing photographs in the field was complicated and messy: Many pictures were ruined when they were washed in streams where debris could stick to the gummy image.

Though about a million photos were taken, the photographic record of the war is incomplete. Neither Brady, Gardner, nor O'Sullivan arrived in time to capture the surrender at Appomattox in 1865. And lack of supplies made Confederate field photography virtually nonexistent after 1861.

Sadly, most Civil War photographers and their work fell into obscurity after the war. Hundreds of glass negatives were sold to gardeners for greenhouse windows, and, decades later, many of the glass plates ended up as eyepieces in gas masks worn by soldiers in World War I.

C

O, the rising of the People
   Came with the springing of the grass,
They rebounded from dejection
   After Easter came to pass.
And the young were all elation
   Hearing Sumter's cannon roar. . . .
But the elders with foreboding
   Mourned the days forever o'er,
And recalled the forest proverb,
   The Iroquois' old saw:
Grief to every graybeard
   When young Indians lead the war. **D**

—Herman Melville

Artist sketching the battlefield of Gettysburg, July, 1863. Photograph by T. H. O'Sullivan. Library of Congress.

Melville was fascinated by the war, but he never wrote a novel about it. The poems in *Battle-Pieces,* based on newspaper accounts of the battles as well as visits to battlefields, record the heroism and futility of the fighting on both sides and demonstrate respect for Southern soldiers as well as Northern troops. But in some of the best poems, there is a sense of human nature being stripped bare, revealing not the heroism and strength that Whitman found, but, rather, humanity's basic evil. **E**

THE RISE OF REALISM: THE CIVIL WAR AND POSTWAR PERIOD **415**

Crossing the Curriculum

Social Studies

Have students report on what was happening in your state during the Civil War. Who were its important spokespersons? How many troops did it provide—and lose? Were there battles or civilian losses? What memorials have been erected? If some of your students were born in other countries, they can make important cultural connections by finding out what was going on there during these years.

Statistics

About 623,000 American soldiers died in the Civil War. Ask students to prepare charts or graphs on the cost of the Civil War, both human and monetary. Students will discover that of 1.5 million Union troops, 360,000 were killed and 275,000 wounded; of 800,000 Confederate troops, about 258,000 died and 200,000 were injured. The financial cost is estimated at more than $15 *billion,* plus the physical and economic devastation of the South.

Challenging the Text

After the Civil War, Walt Whitman predicted that "a great literature will . . . arise out of the era of those four years." As the text states, there was little literary output during the war; since then, however, it has generated over sixty thousand books and articles written by scholars and historians, making it one of the most written-about wars in history. Discuss with students whether such works fulfill Whitman's prediction.

B Literary Connections

Where Were the Giants?

Some important American writers did not comment on the war. Washington Irving had died. Henry Wadsworth Longfellow was raising his children after his wife's death. Oliver Wendell Holmes was a professor at and later the dean of the Harvard Medical School. William Cullen Bryant was editor of the *New York Evening Post*.

C Literary Connections

William Dean Howells

William Dean Howells (1837–1920) was a novelist, playwright, critic, essayist, and editor. He championed both younger American writers, such as Edith Wharton, Emily Dickinson, Stephen Crane, Hamlin Garland, and Frank Norris, and the European writers Ivan Turgenev, Leo Tolstoy, Henrik Ibsen, Emile Zola, George Eliot, and Thomas Hardy.

D Literary Connections

Henry Adams

Henry Adams, the great-grandson of President John Adams, was a novelist and historian. He is famous for championing the social and political rights of women, and for his innovative philosophy of history. In *The Education of Henry Adams,* which won him a posthumous Pulitzer Prize, Adams traced the cultural shift away from tradition and custom toward the spontaneous exploration of life's myriad possibilities. He also wrote about the increasing importance of technology as a driving force.

E Background

Stephen Crane

Stephen Crane based his writing about the Civil War on stories told by veterans and on war photographs.

The American Civil War (1861–1865) resulted in terrible bloodshed as the national government sought to preserve the Union by ending the secession of Southern states. Despite his firsthand experience of the aftermath of battle, Walt Whitman retained an optimistic view of the American character. But the horrors of war merely reinforced the pessimism of Herman Melville.

The War in Literature

There was enough atrocity and heroism in the war to feed the views of both Melville and Whitman. What is odd, though, is that Melville's *Battle-Pieces* (which was ignored until the twentieth century) and Whitman's *Drum-Taps* (1865) and *Specimen Days and Collect* (1882) comprise the bulk of the war's immediate legacy of poetry and fiction. Although there were many works of historical interest—soldiers' letters and diaries, as well as journalistic writings—works of literary significance were rare, prompting the question: Why did an event of such magnitude result in such a scant literary output?

Modern readers think that one byproduct of a war is a literary account of it, largely in the form of novels and poems by people who participated in the war. Modern writers like Ernest Hemingway went to war intending to return with the material for novels. This was not the case with the Civil War. Few major American writers saw the Civil War firsthand. Emerson was in Concord during most of the war, "knitting socks and mittens for soldiers," as he wrote to his son, and "writing patriotic lectures." Thoreau, who had been a fervent abolitionist, died in 1862, and Hawthorne died two years later. Emily Dickinson remained in Amherst, Massachusetts, but the country's grief with the war seems to have informed her poetry. Of the younger generation of writers, William Dean Howells, Henry James, and Henry Adams were abroad. Perhaps most important, though, traditional literary forms of the time were inadequate to express the horrifying details of the Civil War. The literary form most appropriate for handling such strong material—the realistic novel—had not yet been fully developed in the United States. Thus, the great novel of the war, *The Red Badge of Courage,* had to wait to be written by a man who was not born until six years after the war had ended: Stephen Crane.

> With malice toward none; with charity for all; with firmness in the right, as God gives us to see the right, let us strive on to finish the work we are in; to bind up the nation's wounds; to care for him who shall have borne the battle, and for his widow, and his orphan—to do all which may achieve and cherish a just and lasting peace, among ourselves, and with all nations.
>
> —President Abraham Lincoln, Second Inaugural Address, March 4, 1865

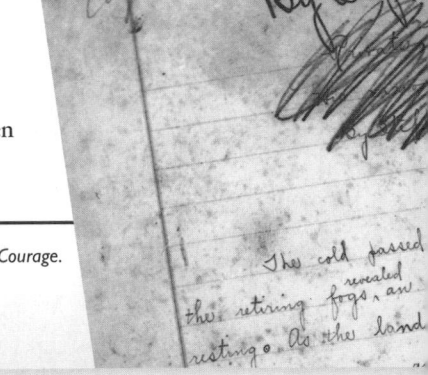

Detail from original manuscript of Stephen Crane's *The Red Badge of Courage.* University of Virginia Library.

Getting Students Involved

Creative Writing

Dear Diary. Invite students to write a diary entry from the point of view of someone who lived during the war and experienced it firsthand. Students can select one of the following perspectives or any other persona of their choosing: a Southern slave, a Northern free black, a Confederate soldier, a battlefield nurse, or a member of Lincoln's cabinet. In their entry, students should tell how the war is affecting their character's life.

Cooperative Learning

Award Night. Have students work in small groups to confer awards on the civilian heroes of the Civil War, such as Walt Whitman, writer and nurse; Clara Barton, army nurse; Mathew Brady and Alexander Gardner, photographers; or Belle Boyd, known as "La Belle Rebelle," a Confederate spy. Students should research their honorees and then devise appropriate awards. Students must also decide who will act as master of ceremonies and who will play the heroes.

Harriet Tubman Series No. 9 (1939–40) by Jacob Lawrence.
Hampton University Museum, Hampton, Virginia. Courtesy of the artist and the Francine Seders Gallery, Seattle, WA.

Very little important poetry and fiction issued directly from the Civil War, largely because few major American writers experienced the war firsthand. Direct accounts of the war found their way into other types of literature, however, including poignant letters and diaries. The "real war" would not find a place in American fiction until the development of the realistic novel. **F**

The Rise of Realism

One of the most enduring subjects for prose fiction has always been the exploits of larger-than-life heroes. Born of the chivalric romance, the **romantic novel** presents readers with lives lived idealistically—beyond the level of everyday life. The heroes and heroines of the novels of James Fenimore Cooper, for example, engage in romantic adventures

Look at me! Look at my arm! I have plowed and planted, and gathered into barns, and no man could head me! And ain't I a woman? I could work as much and eat as much as a man—when I could get it—and bear the lash as well! And ain't I a woman? I have borne thirteen children, and seen most sold off to slavery, and when I cried out with my mother's grief, none but Jesus heard me! And ain't I a woman?

—Sojourner Truth
(born in slavery in Ulster County, New York, c. 1797)

THE RISE OF REALISM: THE CIVIL WAR AND POSTWAR PERIOD **417**

F Literary Connections
Civil War Novelist
John William DeForest's *His First Time Under Fire,* published in *Harper's* magazine in 1864, is considered by some critics to be an underappreciated gem of "first hand" Civil War literature. DeForest recruited a company of volunteers at New Haven and served through the war as their captain. As a result, DeForest had few of the romanticized ideas about the war that many of the literary figures of the period had. He also wrote an account of his experiences entitled *A Volunteer's Adventures* (which went unpublished until 1946) and a novel that is considered among the best fictional accounts of the war, *Miss Ravenel's Conversion from Secession to Loyalty.*

Crossing the Curriculum

Social Studies
Beginning in the 1830s, thousands of American women joined the struggle for emancipation, voting rights, and educational and marital reform, among them Sarah and Angelina Grimké, Lucretia Mott, Susan B. Anthony, and Elizabeth Cady Stanton. Have students make a time line to track the growth of the women's movement from the 1848 Women's Rights Convention in Seneca Falls, New York, to the present.

Science and Technology
The decades after the Civil War also saw startling changes in science and technology. In 1864, Louis Pasteur invented the sterilization process that now bears his name; twelve years later, Alexander Graham Bell invented the telephone. Edison developed the phonograph and electric light; the Curies discovered radium and polonium. Invite students to select any one technological advance from the era, find out more about it, and possibly explain how it works.

Literary Connections

Decline of Romanticism

It's not easy to say when Americans first became disillusioned with Cooper's brand of Romanticism, but early on, Mark Twain pinpointed many of Cooper's "literary offenses" and satirized some of his formulaic literary techniques: "He prized his broken twig above all the rest of his effects, and worked it the hardest. It is a restful chapter in any book of his when somebody doesn't step on a dry twig and alarm all the reds and whites for two hundred yards about. Every time a Cooper person is in peril, and absolute silence is worth four dollars a minute, he is sure to step on a dry twig. There may be a hundred handier things to step on, but that wouldn't satisfy Cooper. Cooper requires him to turn out and find a dry twig; and if he can't do it, go and borrow one. In fact, the Leather Stocking Series ought to have been called the Broken Twig Series. . . ."

B **Critical Thinking**

Extending the Text

❓ What are some topics that contemporary realists could explore? [Possible responses: homelessness; discrimination; AIDS; toxic waste; the gulf between rich and poor.]

RESPONDING TO THE ART

Jacob Riis (1849–1914) was a reformer, journalist, and photographer who emigrated from Denmark to the United States at age twenty-one. His harshly Realistic photographs focused attention on the squalid living conditions of the city's poor, and his book *How the Other Half Lives* (1890) spurred many New Yorkers, including city Police Commissioner Theodore Roosevelt, to help effect change.

Activity. Riis's camera revealed urban blight: three families crammed into a single room, sweatshops turning out everything from clothes and cigars to furniture. Ask students what social problems they can deduce from this photograph. [Possible responses: bad sanitation; poor clothing; little sunlight.]

filled with courageous acts, daring chases, and exciting escapes. Cooper's Leatherstocking, or Hawkeye, like his modern-day heirs James Bond and Indiana Jones, has uncommon abilities that enable him to survive and prevail. His adventures are a far cry from the ordinary lives led by most of Cooper's readers. Such exciting exploits have always been a staple of prose fiction—and, before that, of epic poetry.

In America, the great fiction writers of the mid-nineteenth century, Edgar Allan Poe, Nathaniel Hawthorne, and Herman Melville, shared an aversion to simple realism. These writers used romance not simply to entertain readers, but to reveal truths that would be hidden in a realistic story that limited itself to what actually could happen.

After the Civil War, however, a new generation of writers came of age. They were known as **realists,** writers who aimed at a "very minute fidelity" to the common course of ordinary life. Their subjects were drawn from the slums of the rapidly growing cities, from the factories that were rapidly replacing farmlands, and from the lives of far from idealized characters: poor factory workers, corrupt politicians, even prostitutes.

Children in Mullen's Alley, off Cherry Street, New York City (c. 1888). Photograph by Jacob Riis.

The Granger Collection, New York.

418

Using Students' Strengths

Spatial/Visual Learners

Have students construct a photo essay showing the social problems that plague contemporary society. Students can take pictures from newspapers, magazines, or their own collections. Then, have students compare and contrast the topics they focused on with the topics selected by nineteenth-century realists. What problems have improved—and what problems have gotten worse?

Logical/Mathematical Learners

Ask students to create two pie charts that reflect the following information. From 1840 to 1860, about 4.2 million immigrants came to America. 93% were from Northern and Western Europe, especially Ireland, while 7% came from Eastern and Southern Europe. From 1880 to 1890, 61% came from Northern and Western Europe, 31% from Southern and Eastern Europe, 6% from the Americas, and 2% from all other areas.

Realism Takes Root in Europe

Realism was well entrenched in Europe by the time it began to flower in the United States. It developed in the work of such writers as Daniel Defoe, George Eliot, Anthony Trollope, Honoré de Balzac, Stendhal, Gustave Flaubert, and Leo Tolstoy. These writers tried to represent faithfully the environment and the manners of everyday life: the way ordinary people lived and dressed, and what they thought and felt and talked about.

But realism was not simply concerned with recording wallpaper patterns, hairstyles, or the subjects of conversations. It sought also to explain *why* ordinary people behave the way they do. Realistic novelists often relied on the emerging sciences of human and animal behavior—biology, psychology, and sociology—as well as on their own insights and observations.

> Language grows out of life, out of its needs and experiences. . . . Good work in language presupposes and depends on a real knowledge of things.
>
> —Annie Sullivan

> The only reason for the existence of a novel is that it does attempt to represent life.
>
> —Henry James

The literary movement known as realism dominated American fiction from the late nineteenth century to the middle of the twentieth. Realists sought to accurately portray real life, without filtering it through personal feelings, romanticism, or idealism.

American Regionalism: Brush Strokes of Local Color

In America, realism had its roots in **regionalism,** literature that emphasizes a specific geographic setting and that makes use of the speech and manners of the people who live in that region. Sarah Orne Jewett, Kate Chopin, Harriet Beecher Stowe, Bret Harte, and Charles W. Chesnutt are noted early regionalists who recorded the peculiarities of speech and temperament in their parts of a rapidly expanding nation. (Regionalism flourished again in the 1920s and 1930s, especially in the South, and is still today an important aspect of American literature.)

While regional writers strove to be realistic in their depiction of speech patterns and manners, they were often unrealistic—even sentimental—in their depiction of character and social environment. For example, the Southern writer Thomas Nelson Page, who wrote popular post–Civil War novels about the South before the war, stressed the romantic "moonlight and magnolia" environment at the expense of the realities of a social world that relied on slavery. Realism as a literary movement in the United States went far beyond regionalism in its concern for accuracy in portraying social conditions and human motivation.

Original edition of Mark Twain's *Adventures of Huckleberry Finn* (1885). The Granger Collection, New York.

THE RISE OF REALISM: THE CIVIL WAR AND POSTWAR PERIOD 419

C Literary Connections
European Realists

Although these writers are united by the strand of Realism, their novels have different subjects and different strengths. Defoe's *The Life and Strange Surprising Adventures of Robinson Crusoe of York, Mariner* (1719), sometimes regarded as the first English novel, describes how a shipwrecked sailor survives on a tropical island. Eliot's *The Mill on the Floss* (1860) and Trollope's *The Warden* (1855) are praised for their profound psychological insight. Balzac (1799–1850) helped develop the novel as a panoramic vision of society, through the finely-crafted Realism of his works, known collectively as *The Human Comedy*. Flaubert's *Madame Bovary* (1857) is the psychological study of a woman who longs for personal fulfillment. Tolstoy's *War and Peace* (1865–1869) is a complex interweaving of a large cast of characters and a commentary on the Napoleonic invasion of Russia that affects their lives.

D Humanities Connections
On the Origin of Species

Nearly every writer of the time had to come to terms with one of the key events of the age: the publication of Charles Darwin's *On the Origin of Species* (1859) and *The Descent of Man* (1871), in which he put forth the principles of evolution.

E Literary Connections
Regional Writers

Sarah Orne Jewett focused on the relationships between women in a rural Maine setting. Bret Harte was one of the first writers to shape the enduring myth of the "Wild West." Although Harte's novels often contained graphic violence, they were nevertheless awash in sentimentality. Beneath their tough exteriors, the denizens of the Wild West were really ladies and gentlemen—gamblers with a soft spot for orphans, dance-hall women with hearts of gold. Charles Chesnutt was a prolific writer whose work ranged from folk tales to short stories to novels to a biography of Frederick Douglass. Chesnutt's novelistic style was psychological realism, but he also incorporated and parodied other styles, especially the nostalgic, plantation-era pot-boiler. One of Chesnutt's most famous characters, Uncle Julius, seems to sentimentalize antebellum plantation life but actually provides an ironic commentary on it.

Taking a Second Look

Review: Analyzing Cause and Effect

Remind students that the causes are *why* something happens; the effects are *what* happens, the results. To find the cause of something, ask, "*Why* did this happen?" To find the result, ask, "*What* happened?" Warn students, however, to scrutinize the causal link a writer may be trying to establish. Remind them that the mere fact that one event follows another chronologically does not prove that the second was caused by the first.

Activities

1. Invite students to explain a simple cause-and-effect relationship, such as the reasons for and effects of passing or not passing an exam.
2. Point out that complex events often have multiple causes and effects. Have students trace the multiple causes and effects of the development of Realism including disillusionment with the war, the rise of photography, and developments in the social sciences.

Coming and Going of the Pony Express (1900) by Frederic Remington.
Oil on canvas (26" × 39").

The Thomas Gilcrease Institute of American History and Art, Tulsa, Oklahoma.

> Ⓐ All modern American literature comes from one book by Mark Twain called *Huckleberry Finn.*
> —Ernest Hemingway

Mark Twain is the best-known example of a regional writer whose realism far surpassed local bounds. Although he first established his reputation as a regional humorist, Twain evolved into a writer whose comic view of society became increasingly satiric. His best novel, *Adventures of Huckleberry Finn* (1884), describes the moral growth of a comic character in an environment that is at the same time physically beautiful and morally repugnant. *Huckleberry Finn* combines a biting picture of some of the injustices inherent in pre–Civil War life with a lyrical portrait of the American landscape.

American realism had its roots in regionalism, literature that focuses on a relatively small geographical area and attempts to accurately reproduce the speech and manners of that region.

420 THE RISE OF REALISM: THE CIVIL WAR AND POSTWAR PERIOD

Realism and Naturalism: A Lens on Everyday Life

The most active proponent of realism in American fiction was William Dean Howells, editor of the influential magazine *The Atlantic Monthly.* In both his fiction and his critical writings, Howells insisted that realism should deal with the lives of ordinary people, be faithful to the development of character even at the expense of action, and discuss the social questions perplexing Americans. Howells's "smiling realism" portrayed an America where people may act foolishly but where their good qualities eventually win out. "Ah! poor Real Life, which I love," Howells wrote in one of his many essays, "can I make others share the delight I find in thy foolish and insipid face?" For Howells, life *was,* even at its worst, merely "foolish and insipid," and this proved to be his greatest limitation as a novelist.

Other realistic novelists viewed life as a much rougher clash of contrary forces. The Californian Frank Norris, for example, agreed with Howells that the proper subject for fiction was the ordinary person, but he found Howells's fiction too strait-laced and narrow. It was, Norris said, "as respectable as a church and proper as a deacon." Norris was an earthier writer, interested in the impact of large social forces on individuals. His best-known novel, *The Octopus* (1901), is about the struggles between wheat farmers and the railroad monopoly in California. Norris was not the first to use the novel to examine social institutions with the aim of reforming them; Harriet Beecher Stowe's novel *Uncle Tom's Cabin* (1852) had been published before the Civil War and, according to Lincoln (and many historians), played a large part in helping to cause the war. But *Uncle Tom's Cabin* was more melodrama than realistic fiction.

Norris is generally considered to be a **naturalist.** Following the lead of the French novelist Emile Zola, naturalists relied heavily on the growing scientific disciplines of psychology and sociology. In their fiction, they attempted to dissect human behavior with as much objectivity as a scientist would dissect a frog or a cadaver. For naturalists, human behavior was determined by forces beyond the individual's power, especially by biology and environment. The naturalists tended to look at human life as a grim losing battle. Their characters often had only limited choices and motivations. In the eyes of some naturalist writers, human beings were totally subject to the natural laws of the universe; like animals, they lived crudely, by instinct, unable to control their own destinies.

Advertisement for Harriet Beecher Stowe's *Uncle Tom's Cabin* (1852). Culver Pictures.

135,000 SETS, 270,000 VOLUMES SOLD.

UNCLE TOM'S CABIN

FOR SALE HERE.

AN EDITION FOR THE MILLION, COMPLETE IN 1 Vol. PRICE 37 1-2 CENTS.
"   "   IN GERMAN, IN 1 Vol. PRICE 50 CENTS.
"   "   IN 2 Vols. CLOTH, 6 PLATES, PRICE $1.50.
SUPERB ILLUSTRATED EDITION, IN 1 Vol. WITH 153 ENGRAVINGS,
PRICES FROM $2.50 TO $5.00.

The Greatest Book of the Age.

B Literary Connections

Howells's Support of Realism
Before 1900, Howells spearheaded the battle for Realism in America. He used his position as the editor-in-chief of *The Atlantic Monthly* to proclaim his sympathies and to encourage young American writers who wanted to shake loose from convention and write what they saw and knew.

C Exploring the Culture

Norris's Changing Views
(Benjamin) Frank(lin) Norris scorned the pale and bloodless romances of his time—the "literature of chambermaids" he called them—and along with Theodore Dreiser and Jack London, fused Realism with Darwinism to create Naturalism. By the end of his life, however, Norris came to reject the brutally individualistic vision of Naturalism and to feel that, at root, people are interdependent. As the ranchman Annixter says in Norris's novel *The Octopus,* "I began to see that a fellow can't live *for* himself any more than he can live *by* himself. He's got to think of others."

D Literary Connections

Zola's Vision
Zola wrote a series of twenty novels he called *Les Rougon-Macquart: The Natural and Social History of a Family Under the Second Empire.* As shown in these books, Zola believed that heredity determined human nature and that few people could escape a dark fate if they were descended from a weak or evil family member. In Zola's view, these adverse qualities could be eliminated only through education and medicine.

Professional Notes

Uncle Tom's Cabin

Undoubtedly the most influential novel of the era, *Uncle Tom's Cabin* is the story of the hard life and cruel death of an enslaved man called Uncle Tom, who is devoted to Little Eva, the daughter of the plantation owner. Among the most famous scenes are the death of Little Eva, the escape of an enslaved woman named Eliza and her baby across the ice floes in the Ohio River, and the escape of her husband, George, via the Underground Railroad. Though Uncle Tom's name has come to be a pejorative term, he is, in fact, a character of immense human dignity. More polemical than literary, the novel strengthened the abolitionists' arguments against slavery. The first edition of five thousand copies sold out in forty-eight hours, and in the following two years the presses never caught up with the demand. Total book sales were in the millions, and soon after its publication the novel was adapted into a play that ran continuously from 1853 to 1930. Upon meeting the diminutive Mrs. Stowe for the first time, President Lincoln is reputed to have said, "So this is the little lady who started this big war."

Although Crane's ironic Naturalism has been most closely studied in his novels and short stories, it is also evident in his poems, as this excerpt from *War Is Kind* shows:

> The wayfarer
> Perceiving the pathway to truth
> Was struck with astonishment.
> It was thickly grown with weeds.
> "Ha," he said,
> "I see that none has passed here
> In a long time."
> Later he saw that each weed
> Was a singular knife.
> "Well," he mumbled at last,
> "Doubtless there are other roads."

Psychological Fiction: Inside the Human Mind

On the other hand, the New York–born Henry James, considered America's greatest writer of the **psychological novel,** concentrated principally on fine distinctions in character motivation. James was a realist, but no realist could be further from the blunt, naturalistic view that people were driven by animal-like instincts. In his finely tuned studies of human motivation, James opened the inner mind to the techniques of fiction. He was mainly interested in complex social and psychological situations. Many of his novels, including *Daisy Miller* (1879) and *The Portrait of a Lady* (1881), take place in Europe, because James considered European society to be both more complex and more sinister than American society. He frequently contrasts innocent, eager Americans with sophisticated, more reserved Europeans. In a typically "Jamesian" fiction, a straightforward American confronts the complexities of European society and either defeats or is defeated by them.

Stephen Crane was as profound a psychologist as James, but his principal interest was the human character at moments of stress. For James, the proper setting for an examination of human behavior under pressure was the drawing room; for Crane, it was the battlefield, the streets of a slum, or a lifeboat lost at sea. Although Crane is sometimes referred to as a naturalist, he is probably best thought of as an **ironist;** he was the first of many modern American writers—later including Ernest Hemingway and Kurt Vonnegut, Jr.—to juxtapose human pretensions with the indifference of the universe. Of all the nineteenth-century realists, only Crane could describe a stabbing death (in his story "The Blue Hotel") in this coolly cynical manner: "[The blade] shot forward, and a human body, this citadel of virtue, wisdom, power, was pierced as easily as if it had been a melon." It would take this sensibility to get the "real war" in the books at last.

Realism in American literature branched out in several directions, from the "smiling realism" of William Dean Howells to the gritty naturalism of Frank Norris, and from the psychological realism of Henry James to the ironic stance of Stephen Crane.

[Crane's] importance lies not only in those few works of his which completely come off, like "The Open Boat," but in his constantly seeking the primitive facts, the forbidden places, the dangerous people.
—Alfred Kazin

Reading Skills and Strategies
Establishing a Purpose for Reading

Think about what you already know about such topics as the Civil War, slavery, Reconstruction, the expansion and settlement of the frontier, and the rise of cities after the Civil War. Make a KWL chart (see page 431) in which you write down what you know about this period of American history and literature and what you want to know. Fill out what you have learned as you read the collections that follow.

Assessing Learning

Check Test: Questions and Answers
1. What type of novel idealizes people and their lives? [Romantic]
2. What type of novel tries to accurately mirror daily life and social issues? [Realistic]
3. Which writers respectively exemplify idealism and disillusionment about the Civil War? [Walt Whitman and Herman Melville]
4. Which humorous Regional writer expanded his vision to become a perceptive realist and social satirist? [Mark Twain]
5. What type of novel shows the effects of environment and heredity on people trapped in a cold, indifferent universe? [Naturalistic]

Collection 9

Shackles

Theme

Questions of Freedom *Two social problems are dealt with here: The first is the enormous horror of slavery; the second is a subtler kind of oppression. The rise of realism allowed Frederick Douglass to describe what it was like to be held in slavery, and it allowed Kate Chopin to abandon the romantic plots of "women's stories" and to tell what it is like to be regarded as another kind of property. These two strands of realistic writing are still popular today: the African American experience and the experience of women searching for an independent identity.*

Reading the Anthology

Reaching Struggling Readers The *Reading Skills and Strategies: Reaching Struggling Readers* binder includes a Reading Strategies Handbook that offers concrete suggestions to help students who have difficulty reading and comprehending text, or students who are reluctant readers. When a specific strategy is most appropriate for a selection, a correlation to the Handbook is provided at the bottom of the teacher's page under the head Reaching Struggling Readers. This head may also be used to introduce additional ideas for helping students read challenging texts.

Reading Beyond the Anthology

Read On At the end of the Rise of Realism collections, the grade eleven book includes an annotated bibliography of books suitable for extended reading. The suggested books are related to works in these collections by theme, by author, or by subject. To preview the Read On for the Rise of Realism period, please turn to p. T511.

HRW Library The *HRW Library* offers novels, plays, and short-story collections for extended reading. Each book in the Library includes one or more major works and thematically related Connections. A Study Guide provides teaching suggestions and worksheets. For Collection 9, the following titles are recommended.

THE NARRATIVE OF THE LIFE OF FREDERICK DOUGLASS

Here is Douglass's account of his own life, from his childhood in slavery to his escape from bondage and his work for the abolition of slavery. This autobiography is a must for any student of American literature.

ADVENTURES OF HUCKLEBERRY FINN
Mark Twain

Huck Finn and the escaped slave Jim take a raft down the Mississippi, floating out of reach of the small towns on the banks of the river, with all their bigotry and small-mindedness.

Collection 9 Shackles

Resources for this Collection

Note: All resources for this collection are available for preview on the *One-Stop Planner CD-ROM 2 with Test Generator.* All worksheets and blackline masters may be printed from the CD-ROM.

Internet Resources
go.hrw.com LE0 11-9

Collection Planner

Selection or Feature	Reading and Literary Skills	Vocabulary, Language, and Grammar
from **The Narrative of the Life of Frederick Douglass** (p. 425) Frederick Douglass **Spotlight On: Spirituals and Code Songs** (p. 432) Frederick Douglass	• *Graphic Organizers for Active Reading,* Worksheet p. 43	• *Words to Own,* Worksheet p. 26 • *Grammar and Language Links:* Noun Clauses, Worksheet p. 35 • *Language Workshop CD-ROM,* Types of Subordinate Clauses • *Daily Oral Grammar,* Transparency 28
A Pair of Silk Stockings (p. 436) Kate Chopin **Primary Sources:** *Vogue Stories* (p. 443) Emily Toth **Connections: Now and Then, America** (p. 444) Pat Mora **Spotlight On: American Indian Oratory** • **"For More Than a Hundred Winters . . ."** (p. 446) Black Hawk • **"I Will Fight No More Forever"** (p. 448) Chief Joseph	• *Graphic Organizers for Active Reading,* Worksheet p. 44	• *Words to Own,* Worksheet p. 27 • *Daily Oral Grammar,* Transparency 29

Other Resources for this Collection

- *Cross-Curricular Activities,* p. 9
- *Portfolio Management System,* Introduction to Portfolio Assessment, p. 1
- *Formal Assessment:* Literary Period Introduction Test, p. 86; Literary Elements Test, p. 102

- *Test Generator,* Collection Test

Writing	Listening and Speaking Viewing and Representing	Assessment
• *Portfolio Management System,* Rubrics for Choices, p. 142	• *Audio CD Library,* Disc 11, Tracks 2, 3 • *Viewing and Representing:* Fine Art Transparency 9 Worksheet p. 36 • *Portfolio Management System,* Rubrics for Choices, p. 142	• *Formal Assessment,* Selection Test, p. 88 • *Test Generator (One-Stop Planner CD-ROM)* • *Preparation for College Admission Exams,* p. 29
• *Portfolio Management System,* Rubrics for Choices, p. 143	• *Audio CD Library,* Disc 11, Tracks 4, 5, 6 • *Portfolio Management System,* Rubrics for Choices, p. 143	• *Formal Assessment,* Selection Test, p. 90 • *Test Generator (One-Stop Planner CD-ROM)* • *Preparation for College Admission Exams,* p. 31

Collection Planner

 Transparency    CD-ROM    Video   Audio CD

Collection 9 Shackles

Skills Focus

Selection or Feature	Reading Skills and Strategies	Elements of Literature and Language	Writing	Listening and Speaking	Viewing and Representing
from **The Narrative of the Life of Frederick Douglass** (p. 425) Frederick Douglass	Dialogue with the Text, pp. 425, 430 Make Predictions, pp. 425, 430 Use a KWL Chart, p. 431	Characterization, p. 430 Character, p. 430 Metaphor, p. 431 Image, p. 431 Spirituals and Code Songs, p. 432	Explore a Topic Suggested by Douglass's Narrative, p. 431 Write an Essay Comparing and Contrasting Ideas, p. 431 Write a Letter or Journal Entry from the Point of View of Frederick Douglass, p. 431	Participate in a Panel Discussion, p. 431	Use a Reading Organizer, p. 425 Use a KWL Chart, p. 431
A Pair of Silk Stockings (p. 436) Kate Chopin	Dialogue with the Text, pp. 436, 445 Make Predictions, pp. 436, 445	Character, p. 445 Motivation, p. 445 Symbol, p. 445 Theme, p. 445	Brainstorm a List of Topics, p. 445 Compare and Contrast Themes, p. 445 Write a Continuation of a Story, p. 445		

Skills Focus

Collection 9

Douglass
Spirituals and Code Songs
Chopin
American Indian Oratory

My Guilt

My guilt is "slavery's chains," too long
the clang of iron falls down the years.
This brother's sold. This sister's gone
is bitter wax, lining my ears.
My guilt made music with the tears.

My crime is "heroes, dead and gone"
dead Vesey, Turner, Gabriel,
dead Malcolm, Marcus, Martin King.
They fought too hard, they loved too well.
My crime is I'm alive to tell.

My sin is "hanging from a tree"
I do not scream, it makes me proud.
I take to dying like a man.
I do it to impress the crowd.
My sin lies in not screaming loud.

—Maya Angelou (1928–   )

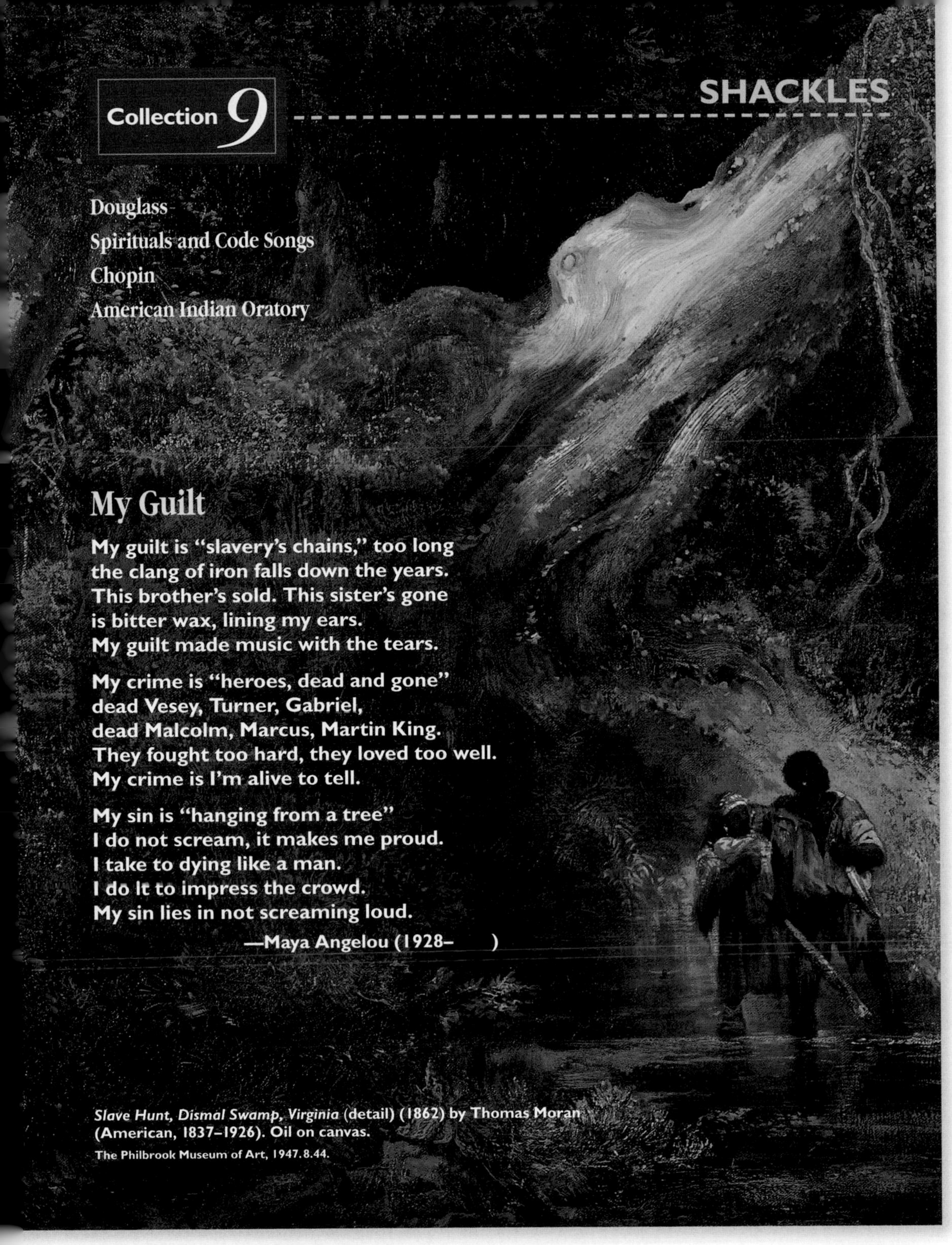

Slave Hunt, Dismal Swamp, Virginia (detail) (1862) by Thomas Moran
(American, 1837–1926). Oil on canvas.
The Philbrook Museum of Art, 1947.8.44.

Responding to the Poem

❓ Based on this poem, what do you predict the selections in Collection 9 will be about? [Possible response: Since "My Guilt" describes the guilt a person feels because he or she did not scream loud enough to protest injustice and persecution, it is likely that Collection 9 includes selections that describe persecution, endurance, and rebellion.]

RESPONDING TO THE ART

Thomas Moran (1837–1926) was an American Romantic artist famous for his majestic scenes of nature (see pp. 136–137). This painting exemplifies his focus on the wild and emotional aspects of the natural world.

Activity. Invite students to explain their reactions to the painting and why they think it is or is not an appropriate introduction to this collection. [Possible response: The huge tree and tiny human figures, set against the murky swamp, convey a mood of terror and vulnerability—both appropriate to the "Shackles" theme.]

Writing Focus: Research Paper

The following **Work in Progress** assignments in this collection build to a culminating **Writer's Workshop** at the end of Collection 10.

- The Narrative of the Life of Frederick Douglass
- A Pair of Silk Stockings

Explore a topic suggested by autobiography with a KWL chart (p. 431)

List topics suggested by story and methods of presentation (p. 445)

Writer's Workshop: Expository Writing / Research Paper (p. 515)

Planning

- **Block Schedule**
  Block Scheduling Lesson Plans with Pacing Guide

- **Traditional Schedule**
  Lesson Plans Including Strategies for English-Language Learners

- **One-Stop Planner**
  CD-ROM with Test Generator

Frederick Douglass

(1817?–1895)

Chester County Historical Society, West Chester, Pennsylvania.

Frederick Douglass was born into slavery in Talbot County, on the Eastern Shore of Maryland, and was separated from his mother soon after his birth. "The practice of separating children from their mothers," wrote Douglass years later, "and hiring the latter out at distances too great to admit of their meeting, except at long intervals, is a marked feature of the cruelty and barbarity of the slave system. But it is in harmony with the grand aim of slavery, which, always and everywhere, is to reduce man to a level with the brute. It is a successful method of obliterating from the mind and heart of the slave all just ideas of the sacredness of *the family. . . .*"

Since records were not kept of the birth of children born into slavery, Douglass was never sure of his exact age: "Genealogical trees do not flourish among slaves," he was to remark ironically later. Although Douglass received no formal education, he did teach himself to read with the help, at first, of members of the household he served. Later, these same people became furious when they saw Douglass reading a book or a newspaper; education, they decided, was incompatible with being enslaved.

When Douglass was about twenty-one, he satisfied his hunger for freedom by escaping to Massachusetts, where he married and soon started to make public speeches in support of the abolitionist cause. He changed his last name from Bailey to Douglass, after the hero of the romantic novel *The Lady of the Lake* by Sir Walter Scott.

In 1845, Douglass went to England, largely because of the danger he faced as a fugitive, especially after the publication that same year of his autobiography, *The Narrative of the Life of Frederick Douglass, an American Slave*. In England, he mobilized antislavery sentiment and became independent when British friends collected around $700 to purchase his freedom.

When he returned to the United States in 1847, Douglass founded a newspaper, the *North Star*. (The name was chosen because escapees used this star as a guide north.) In his newspaper, Douglass championed the abolition of slavery. In 1855, he published a revised version of his life's story, titled *My Bondage and My Freedom*. These "escape" narratives, like earlier "captivity" stories (page 40), were enormously popular, and Douglass's were widely read and very influential in the abolitionist cause.

When the Civil War began, Douglass worked ardently for the Underground Railroad, the secret network of abolitionists and their sympathizers that helped many people held in slavery escape to the North. He also energetically helped to recruit African American soldiers for the Union armies.

Continuing to write and lecture after the war, Douglass argued that the surest way to rehabilitate his tragically scarred people was through education. In 1881, he published yet another version of his autobiography, titled *The Life and Times of Frederick Douglass*. Today, Douglass is revered for the courage with which he insistently proclaimed his profoundly humane values, and admired for the quiet eloquence of his writing style.

424

Resources: Print and Media

Before You Read

FROM **THE NARRATIVE OF THE LIFE OF FREDERICK DOUGLASS**

Make the Connection

Fighting Back

While he was still enslaved, Frederick Douglass fought against society's shackles to assert his human rights and defend his dignity against a brutal, dehumanizing institution. His courageous action became a remarkable turning point in his life. Perhaps his actions will remind you of other heroic men and women who have taken stands against oppression.

Reading Skills and Strategies

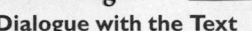

Dialogue with the Text

As you read, fill out an event-prediction-outcome chart like the one below. Each time Douglass acts to assert his human rights, write down your prediction—or fear—about what might happen to him as a result. As you continue reading, write down what actually happens. Do any of the outcomes surprise you?

Event in Story	Prediction About Outcome	Actual Outcome

go.hrw.com
LEO 11-9

Background

Douglass has been compared with Benjamin Franklin (page 84), another self-made man who struggled against tremendous odds to achieve distinction at a critical time in his nation's history. But Douglass's story, of course, is different from Franklin's. Franklin was never enslaved. He was never "owned" by another human being and considered to be of no more significance than a piece of personal property.

In the following selection from *The Narrative of the Life of Frederick Douglass*, Douglass provides a graphic account of a critical incident that occurred when he was sixteen years old. Earlier in his narrative, he explained to his readers "how a man was made a slave"; now he sets out to explain "how a slave was made a man." At the time, Douglass was owned by a man named Thomas who had rented Douglass for a year to a man named Covey.

425

Summary ■■

In this excerpt from his autobiography, Frederick Douglass recalls an incident during his enslavement, when a man named Mr. Covey had rented him from his owner for one year. One day, Douglass collapses while fanning wheat and is then kicked and beaten by Mr. Covey. Having sustained a head wound, and fearing he will be injured further, Douglass struggles through the woods to his master's farm, seven miles distant. Despite his explanations, his master refuses Douglass sanctuary and threatens to whip him himself if he fails to return to Covey. When Douglass returns, he manages to elude Covey for a day. That night a slave named Sandy Jenkins urges Douglass to carry a certain root as a talisman against whippings. Douglass accepts the root solely for Sandy's sake. The next day Covey treats Douglass decently, not because of the root, but because it is Sunday. On Monday, however, Covey and a hired hand try to beat Douglass and tie him up. Douglass fights back and gets the better of them, thus regaining some measure of dignity. For the remainder of the year, Covey treats Douglass with cautious respect.

Background

Frederick Douglass's personal sufferings led him to fight for human rights around the world. During his career as a writer and lecturer, Douglass spoke out for world peace, Irish independence, repeal of the Corn Laws oppressing English farm laborers, free speech, the abolition of capital punishment, prison reform, and women's rights. The day he died, Douglass had addressed a women's rights meeting with Susan B. Anthony.

Preteaching Vocabulary

Words to Own

Have students work in pairs. One partner reads aloud each word and its definition and waits while the other partner creates a sentence with the word. Have students repeat the activity, switching roles. When students fully demonstrate their understanding of the words and their meanings, have them test their knowledge by writing the vocabulary word that is the opposite of each word that follows.

1. proclaimed [intimated]
2. resist [comply]
3. gaiety [solemnity]
4. ordinary [singular]
5. living [expiring]
6. rumple [curry]
7. withdraw [interpose]
8. discredited [attributed]
9. fail to make [render]
10. withheld [afforded]

Resources

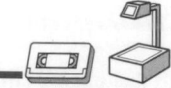

Viewing and Representing
Videocassette B, Segment 7
Available in Spanish and English. This segment explores several nineteenth-century protest movements and examines the connection between abolitionism and women's suffrage. For full lesson plans and worksheets, see *Visual Connections Teacher's Manual.*

Fine Art Transparency
Aaron Douglas's *Into Bondage* will help students imagine the horror of being enslaved and in shackles. See the *Viewing and Representing Transparencies and Worksheets:*
- Transparency 9
- Worksheet, p. 36

FROM THE EDITOR'S DESK

We selected this excerpt from Frederick Douglass's autobiography because it stresses the importance of dignity and self-respect.

A Reading Skills and Strategies

Dialogue with the Text

? Covey was nicknamed "the snake" because he used to sneak up on slaves to try to catch them doing something wrong. What role do you predict Covey will play in Douglass's life? [Students will probably predict that conflict with Mr. Covey will force Douglass to escape slavery.]

B Reading Skills and Strategies

Identifying Main Idea
Remind students that Collection 9 is called "Shackles." As students read, challenge them to analyze both the physical and psychological bonds of slavery. Then ask how "a man can be made a slave and a slave be made a man." [Possible response: People are enslaved both physically and psychologically through brutality; they become free through recognition of their human dignity.]

---

from The Narrative of the Life of Frederick Douglass

Frederick Douglass

The Battle with Mr. Covey

A I have already <u>intimated</u> that my condition was much worse, during the first six months of my stay at Mr. Covey's, than in the last six. The circumstances leading to the change in Mr. Covey's course toward me form an epoch in my humble history. **B** You have seen how a man was made a slave; you shall see how a slave was made a man. On one of the hottest days of the month of August, 1833, Bill Smith, William Hughes, a slave named Eli, and myself, were engaged in fanning wheat.[1] Hughes was clearing the fanned wheat from before the fan, Eli was turning, Smith was feeding, and I was carrying wheat to the fan. The work was simple, requiring strength rather than intellect; yet, to one entirely unused to such work, it came very hard.

About three o'clock of that day, I broke down; my strength failed me; I was seized with a violent aching of the head, attended with extreme dizziness; I trembled in every limb. Finding what was coming, I nerved myself up, feeling it would never do to stop work. I stood as long as I could stagger to the hopper with grain. When I could stand no longer, I fell, and felt as if held down by an immense weight. The fan of course stopped; everyone had his own work to do; and no one could do the work of the other, and have his own go on at the same time.

Mr. Covey was at the house, about one hundred yards from the treading yard where we were fanning. On hearing the fan stop, he left immediately, and came to the spot where we were. He hastily inquired what the matter was. Bill answered that I was sick, and there was no one to bring wheat to the fan. I had by this time crawled away under the side of the post-and-rail fence by which the yard was enclosed, hoping to find relief by getting out of the sun. He then asked where I was. He was told by one of the hands.

He came to the spot, and, after looking at me awhile, asked me what was the matter. I told him as

1. **fanning wheat:** separating usable grain.

well as I could, for I scarce had strength to speak. He then gave me a savage kick in the side, and told me to get up. I tried to do so, but fell back in the attempt. He gave me another kick, and again told me to rise. I again tried, and succeeded in gaining my feet; but, stooping to get the tub with which I was feeding the fan, I again staggered and fell. While down in this situation, Mr. Covey took up the hickory slat with which Hughes had been striking off the half-bushel measure, and with it gave me a heavy blow upon the head, making a large wound, and the blood ran freely; and with this again told me to get up. I made no effort to <u>comply</u>, having now made up my mind to let him do his worst. In a short time after receiving this blow, my head grew better. Mr. Covey had now left me to my fate.

At this moment I resolved, for the first time, to go to my master, enter a complaint, and ask his protection. In order to [do] this, I must that afternoon walk seven miles; and this, under the circumstances, was truly a severe undertaking. I was exceedingly feeble; made so as much by the kicks and blows which I received, as by the severe fit of sickness to which I had been subjected. I, however, watched my chance, while Covey was looking in an opposite direction, and started for St. Michael's. I succeeded in getting a considerable distance on my way to the woods, when Covey discovered me, and called after me to come back, threatening what he would do if I did not come. I disregarded both his calls and his threats, and made my way to the woods as fast as my feeble state would allow; and thinking I might be overhauled by him if I kept the road, I walked through the woods, keeping far enough from the road to

---

WORDS TO OWN
intimated (in'tə·māt'əd) *v.*: stated indirectly; hinted.
comply (kəm·plī') *v.*: to obey; to agree to a request.

Frederick Douglass Series No. 10 (1938–1939) by Jacob Lawrence. Casein tempera on gessoed hardboard (17 ⅞″ × 12″).

426 THE RISE OF REALISM: THE CIVIL WAR AND POSTWAR PERIOD

Reaching All Students

Struggling Readers
Help students interpret, analyze, and make generalizations about Douglass's narrative by using the strategy called Sketch to Stretch. For detailed instructions on how to apply this effective visual learning strategy, see the *Reading Strategies Handbook*, p. 101 in the *Reading Skills and Strategies* binder.

English Language Learners
Keep in mind that your class may have students whose family histories include the experience of slavery, as well as students whose families have experienced political, economic, or religious persecution. Encourage students to share their knowledge about these difficult experiences, if they feel comfortable doing so. For other strategies, see
- *Lesson Plans Including Strategies for English-Language Learners*

Hampton University Museum, Hampton, Virginia. Courtesy of the artist and the Francine Seders Gallery, Seattle, WA.

RESPONDING TO THE ART

Jacob Lawrence (1917–) is an African American painter who uses a spare, expressionistic style in his portrayals of black history. The paintings on this page and p. 428 come from his series on Frederick Douglass. He also painted a thirty-panel series on Harriet Tubman (see pp. 417 and 480) and a sixty-panel series on the African Americans who migrated north in huge numbers during the early decades of the twentieth century (see p. 735). Because Lawrence flattens compositions with blocks of basic colors and simplifies the forms of his subjects, his paintings often look like posters.
Activity. Ask students which painting—*Frederick Douglass Series No. 10*, shown here, or *No. 9* on p. 428—directly illustrates the excerpt from Douglass's autobiography. [No. 10 portrays Douglass's fight with Mr. Covey.] What strikes you most about this painting? [Some students will mention the red and yellow of Mr. Covey's shirt, suggesting anger, blood or cowardice.]

BROWSING IN THE FILES

About the Author. As a boy living in Baltimore, Frederick Douglass considered himself lucky to learn to read and write during a time when it was an "unpardonable offense to teach slaves to read." Douglass would carry a book with him on errands, finish early, and find a poor white boy to give him a lesson in exchange for bread. After he learned to write a few letters of the alphabet through his work at a shipyard, Douglass would boast to other boys that he could write as well as they. When the boys took the bait and rose to the challenge, Douglass used the contests to learn more letters.

Using Students' Strengths

Auditory/Musical Learners
Explain that Douglass was famous for his oratory as well as his writing. In fact, many opponents were so impressed with his speaking, they refused to believe he had ever been a slave. Invite students to find passages that show Douglass's skill with rhythm, alliteration, and other sound effects, such as pauses. For example, students might point out the pause in "You have seen how a man was made a slave; you shall see how a slave was made a man."

Spatial Learners
As students read, have them sketch a map of the route Douglass takes from Mr. Covey's farm to Master Thomas's store and back, and label the different places he stops along the way. Be sure to include Sandy Jenkins's cabin and Mr. Covey's barn. Then have students add a short description of what happens at each spot. Number these descriptions and place them in chronological order along the line of Douglass's journey.

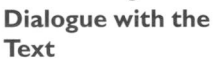

Frederick Douglass Series No. 9 (1938–1939) by Jacob Lawrence. Casein tempera on gessoed hardboard (12" × 17⅞"). Hampton University Museum, Hampton, Virginia. Courtesy of the artist and the Francine Seders Gallery, Seattle, WA.

avoid detection, and near enough to prevent losing my way.

A I had not gone far before my little strength again failed me. I could go no farther. I fell down, and lay for a considerable time. The blood was yet oozing from the wound on my head. For a time I thought I should bleed to death; and think now that I should have done so, but that the blood so matted my hair as to stop the wound. After lying there about three quarters of an hour, I nerved myself up again, and started on my way, through bogs and briers, barefooted and bareheaded, tearing my feet sometimes at nearly every step; and after a journey of about seven miles, occupying some five hours to perform it, I arrived at master's store. I then presented an appearance enough to affect any but a heart of iron. From the crown of my head to my feet, I was covered with blood. My hair was all clotted with dust and blood; my shirt was stiff with blood. My legs and feet were torn in sundry places with briers and thorns, and were also covered with blood. **B** I suppose I looked like a man who had escaped a den of wild beasts, and barely escaped them.

In this state I appeared before my master, humbly entreating him to <u>interpose</u> his authority for my protection. I told him all the circumstances as well as I could, and it seemed, as I spoke, at times to affect him. He would then walk the floor, and seek to justify Covey by saying he expected I deserved it. He asked me what I wanted. I told

him, to let me get a new home; that as sure as I lived with Mr. Covey again, I should live with but to die with him; that Covey would surely kill me; he was in a fair way for it. Master Thomas ridiculed the idea that there was any danger of Mr. Covey's killing me, and said that he knew Mr. Covey; that he was a good man, and that he could not think of taking me from him; that, should he do so, he would lose the whole year's wages; that **C** I belonged to Mr. Covey for one year, and that I must go back to him, come what might; and that I must not trouble him with any more stories, or that he would himself *get hold of me*. After threatening me thus, he gave me a very large dose of salts, telling me that I might remain in St. Michael's that night (it being quite late), but that I must be off back to Mr. Covey's early in the morning; and that if I did not, he would *get hold of me*, which meant that he would whip me.

D I remained all night, and, according to his orders, I started off to Covey's in the morning (Saturday morning), wearied in body and broken in spirit. I got no supper that night, or breakfast that morning. I reached Covey's about nine o'clock; and just as I was getting over the fence that divided Mrs. Kemp's fields from ours, out ran Covey

----

WORDS TO OWN

interpose (in′tər·pōz′) v.: to put forth in order to intervene.

Crossing the Curriculum

with his cowskin, to give me another whipping. Before he could reach me, I succeeded in getting to the cornfield; and as the corn was very high, it afforded me the means of hiding. He seemed very angry, and searched for me a long time. My behavior was altogether unaccountable. He finally gave up the chase, thinking, I suppose, that I must come home for something to eat; he would give himself no further trouble in looking for me. I spent that day mostly in the woods, having the alternative before me—to go home and be whipped to death, or stay in the woods and be starved to death.

That night, I fell in with Sandy Jenkins, a slave with whom I was somewhat acquainted. Sandy had a free wife who lived about four miles from Mr. Covey's; and it being Saturday, he was on his way to see her. I told him my circumstances, and he very kindly invited me to go home with him. I went home with him, and talked this whole matter over, and got his advice as to what course it was best for me to pursue. I found Sandy an old advisor.[2] He told me, with great solemnity, I must go back to Covey; but that before I went, I must go with him into another part of the woods, where there was a certain *root,* which, if I would take some of it with me, carrying it *always on my right side,* would render it impossible for Mr. Covey, or any other white man, to whip me. He said he had carried it for years; and since he had done so, he had never received a blow, and never expected to while he carried it. I at first rejected the idea, that the simple carrying of a root in my pocket would have any such effect as he had said, and was not disposed to take it; but Sandy impressed the necessity with much earnestness, telling me it could do no harm, if it did no good. To please him, I at length took the root, and, according to his direction, carried it upon my right side. This was Sunday morning.

I immediately started for home; and upon entering the yard gate, out came Mr. Covey on his way to meeting. He spoke to me very kindly, made me drive the pigs from a lot near by, and passed on toward the church. Now, this singular conduct of Mr. Covey really made me begin to think that there was something in the *root* which Sandy had given me; and had it been on any other

2. **an old advisor:** someone who can offer good advice.

day than Sunday, I could have attributed the conduct to no other cause than the influence of that root; and as it was, I was half inclined to think the *root* to be something more than I at first had taken it to be. All went well till Monday morning. On this morning, the virtue of the *root* was fully tested.

Long before daylight, I was called to go and rub, curry, and feed the horses. I obeyed, and was glad to obey. But while thus engaged, while in the act of throwing down some blades from the loft, Mr. Covey entered the stable with a long rope; and just as I was half out of the loft, he caught hold of my legs, and was about tying me. As soon as I found what he was up to, I gave a sudden spring, and as I did so, he holding to my legs, I was brought sprawling on the stable floor. Mr. Covey seemed now to think he had me, and could do what he pleased; but at this moment—from whence came the spirit I don't know—I resolved to fight; and, suiting my action to the resolution, I seized Covey hard by the throat; and as I did so, I rose. He held on to me, and I to him. My resistance was so entirely unexpected, that Covey seemed taken all aback. He trembled like a leaf. This gave me assurance, and I held him uneasy, causing the blood to run where I touched him with the ends of my fingers. Mr. Covey soon called out to Hughes for help. Hughes came, and, while Covey held me, attempted to tie my right hand. While he was in the act of doing so, I watched my chance, and gave him a heavy kick close under the ribs. This kick fairly sickened Hughes, so that he left me in the hands of Mr. Covey.

This kick had the effect of not only weakening Hughes, but Covey also. When he saw Hughes bending over with pain, his courage quailed.[3] He asked me if I meant to persist in my resistance. I told him I did, come what might; that he had used me like a brute for six months, and that I was determined to be used so no longer. With that, he

3. **quailed:** faltered.

WORDS TO OWN

solemnity (sə·lem′nə·tē) *n.*: seriousness.
render (ren′dər) *v.*: make.
singular (siŋ′gyə·lər) *adj.*: remarkable.
attributed (ə·trib′yoot·id) *v.*: believed to result from.
curry (kʉr′ē) *v.*: to groom.

E **Critical Thinking**

Hypothesizing

? What other options might Douglass pursue? [Possible responses: He could try to escape to the North or return to Covey and try to make Covey believe he has learned his lesson.]

F **Cultural Connections**

Talismans

Objects thought to bring good luck are called *talismans.* They include things like the familiar rabbit's foot and the four-leaf clover, as well as personal good luck charms. For example, Michael Jordan's personal talisman is his pair of Carolina blue shorts that he wore to every game.

G **Struggling Readers**

In order to help students understand Mr. Covey's altered behavior on Sunday, have them employ the strategy called Somebody Wanted But So. For step-by-step instructions on applying this strategy, see the *Reading Strategies Handbook,* p. 111 in the *Reading Skills and Strategies* binder. You can also use this strategy to help students summarize the entire narrative.

H **Reading Skills and Strategies**

Making Inferences

? What do you think makes Douglass rebel at this particular moment in his life? [Possible responses: Douglass has endured great suffering even when he was obedient, so he decides that he might as well defend himself now; he no longer feels psychologically bound by any loyalty to Master Thomas, who has refused his pleas for help.]

Assessing Learning

Check Test: True-False
1. Covey rents Douglass from Mr. Thomas. [True]
2. Covey beats Douglass for running away. [False]
3. Master Thomas won't take Douglass back before the rental period is over, and decides that Douglass deserved Covey's beating. [True]

4. Sandy Jenkins gives Douglass a root to ward off beatings. [True]
5. Covey wins his battle with Douglass and after that whips him severely. [False]

Informal Assessment
Have students work in groups to answer the Shaping Interpretations questions on p. 430,

and monitor their specific contributions. As you circulate around the room, make notes for future student/teacher conferences. Refer to these notes when you speak with students about their use of reading skills and strategies.

A Advanced Learners

Analyzing Motives

❓ What pretense does Mr. Covey try to maintain about the fight? [Possible responses: He pretends he has won the battle, in an attempt to preserve his authority. But Douglass knows Covey has lost, because he never tries to beat him again.]

B Reading Skills and Strategies

Identifying the Main Idea

❓ Why is Douglass's battle with Covey so important to him? [Although still enslaved, Douglass has asserted his humanity and dignity by resisting injustice.]

MAKING MEANINGS

First Thoughts [Respond]

1. Possible answers: Students may cite Douglass's early decision to let Covey do his worst, or his later decision to fight with Covey.

Shaping Interpretations

[Interpret]

2. Douglass discovers that a forceful assertion of his humanity and dignity is more powerful than any root.

3. Douglass's initial rejection of the root and Jenkins's insistence that he take it are humorous. So is Douglass's misapprehension that Covey's civilized behavior on Sunday can be attributed to the root.

4. He is loyal, hard-working, honest, proud, courageous, determined, and defiant.

5. Covey is cruel and cowardly. Like many bullies, he is deterred by firm resistance.

6. "A slave in form" refers to Douglass's legal designation as a slave. "A slave in fact" refers to a lack of pride and self-determination.

Extending the Text [Synthesize]

7. The only way most enslaved people could gain freedom at the time was either by escape or by force. Douglass's experience, while not unique, was shared by few. Douglass probably would recommend that people continue to fight the evils of racism today in order to feel "deep satisfaction." Today's battles, however, are likely to be fought nonviolently.

T430

---

strove to drag me to a stick that was lying just out of the stable door. He meant to knock me down. But just as he was leaning over to get the stick, I seized him with both hands by his collar, and brought him by a sudden snatch to the ground. By this time, Bill came. Covey called upon him for assistance. Bill wanted to know what he could do. Covey said, "Take hold of him, take hold of him!" Bill said his master hired him out to work, and not to help to whip me; so he left Covey and myself to fight our own battle out. We were at it for nearly two hours. Covey at length let me go, puffing and blowing at a great rate, saying that if I had not resisted, he would not have whipped me half so much. The truth was, that he had not whipped me at all. I considered him as getting entirely the worst end of the bargain; for he had drawn no blood from me, but I had from him. The whole six months afterward, that I spent with Mr. Covey, he never laid the weight of his finger upon me in anger. He would occasionally say, he didn't want to get hold of me again. "No," thought I, "you need not; for you will come off worse than you did before."

This battle with Mr. Covey was the turning point in my career as a slave. It rekindled the few <u>expiring</u> embers of freedom, and revived within me a sense of my own manhood. It recalled the departed self-confidence, and inspired me again with a determination to be free. The gratification <u>afforded</u> by the triumph was a full compensation for whatever else might follow, even death itself. He only can understand the deep satisfaction which I experienced, who has himself repelled by force the bloody arm of slavery. I felt as I never felt before. It was a glorious resurrection, from the tomb of slavery, to the heaven of freedom. My long-crushed spirit rose, cowardice departed, bold defiance took its place; and I now resolved that, however long I might remain a slave in form, the day had passed forever when I could be a slave in fact.

WORDS TO OWN

expiring (ek·spīr'iŋ) v. used as adj.: dying.
afforded (ə·fôrd'əd) v. used as adj.: given; provided.

MAKING MEANINGS

First Thoughts

1. Review the event-prediction-outcome chart you made as you read. Which details, events, or aspects of Douglass's account surprised you?

Shaping Interpretations

2. The root Sandy Jenkins gives to Douglass is a *talisman*, an object believed to possess supernatural powers. What does Douglass discover is even more powerful than the root?

3. What elements of humor do you find in the part of the story involving Sandy Jenkins? Explain.

4. Based on this account, how would you **characterize** the young Frederick Douglass?

5. What does the entire incident reveal about Covey's **character**?

6. At the end of the selection, Douglass distinguishes between being "a slave in form" and "a slave in fact." Explain the meaning of this distinction.

Extending the Text

7. "He only can understand the deep satisfaction which I experienced, who has himself repelled by force the bloody arm of slavery" (page 430). In what ways is Douglass's statement true? In what ways might it not be true? Discuss how Douglass's feelings might apply to the problems of racism today.

Reading Check

a. What action does Douglass take after Covey strikes him? What does Thomas order Douglass to do?

b. What is Covey's reaction when Douglass returns from his visit to Thomas?

c. Explain how Sandy Jenkins helps Douglass.

d. Describe what Douglass calls the turning point in his life as a slave.

Reading Check

a. He flees to his master, registers a complaint, and asks for protection. Thomas orders Douglass to return to Covey.

b. He is angry and searches for Douglass.

c. Jenkins gives Douglass shelter and a root which Jenkins believes will protect Douglass from harm.

d. The turning point is Douglass's battle with Covey and his decision to resist. This rebellion asserts his human dignity.

Douglass's Metaphors

At the end of the selection, Douglass uses **metaphors** that suggest resurrection and rebirth.

1. Explain the comparison implied in this line: "It [the battle] rekindled the few expiring embers of freedom." How are these **images** related to the idea of rebirth?

2. What is Douglass implicitly comparing slavery to when he refers to "the bloody arm of slavery"?

3. Find the passage that specifically compares Douglass's experience to a rebirth. In this comparison, what is being compared to what?

CHOICES:
Building Your Portfolio

Writer's Notebook
1. Collecting Ideas for a Research Paper

Douglass's narrative is a rich source of information, perspectives, and imagery on topics such as slavery, human rights, self-esteem, racism, and freedom. In a KWL chart like the one below, explore a topic suggested by Douglass's narrative that you would be interested in gathering more information about. Save your notes for possible use in the Writer's Workshop on page 515.

K What I Know	W What I Want to Know	L What I Learned

Comparing and Contrasting Ideas
2. Emerson Applied

Reread Emerson's essay "Self-Reliance" (page 224). Then, write a brief essay in which you (a) explain which of Emerson's ideas relate to

Douglass's experience and (b) identify any of Emerson's ideas that seem to be contradicted by Douglass's narrative.

Creative Writing
3. Responding to Other Voices

You have already read the work of other writers who have championed principles of freedom, such as Bradford, Jefferson, Paine, Franklin, Emerson, Thoreau, and Whitman. Write a letter or a journal entry in which Douglass responds to one of these writers, expressing his views of their writings, beliefs, actions, or achievements.

Crossing the Curriculum: History
4. Freedom Fighters

With two other students, research the lives of three people who have opposed racial discrimination. Among the people you might consider are the South African leaders Nelson Mandela, Helen Suzman, and Desmond Tutu; the American civil rights leaders W.E.B. Du Bois, Roy Wilkins, Malcolm X, and Martin Luther King, Jr.; Senator Daniel K. Inouye and others who have protested the internment of Japanese Americans in the United States during World War II; and Raoul Wallenberg, Janus Korczak, and Oskar Schindler, who worked to save Jewish lives during the Nazi Holocaust in Europe. Present a panel discussion in which each group member summarizes the life and career of a freedom fighter and explains how that person helped advance the cause of human rights.

Desmond Tutu.
UPI/Bettmann.

Douglass's Metaphors

1. A fading hope for freedom is compared to the embers of a dying fire; the battle is compared to a spark or puff of air that rekindles the fire. A fire offers a kind of rebirth through the warmth and light it gives. Fire is also central to the image of the mythical phoenix, said to die on a pyre and be reborn from the ashes.

2. The "bloody arm" personifies slavery as a cruel taskmaster who inflicts pain, wounds, or death. When part of something (the arm, in this case as part of the body) is used to represent the whole, the comparison is called a **synecdoche**. Here, "the bloody arm of slavery" represents the people (and the society) that condone such oppression.

3. "It was a glorious resurrection, from the tomb of slavery to the heaven of freedom" (p. 430). The metaphor compares Douglass's experience to that of Christ; slavery is a kind of crucifixion; freedom is a resurrection.

Grading Timesaver

Rubrics for each Choices assignment appear on p. 142 in the *Portfolio Management System*.

CHOICES:
Building Your Portfolio

1–4. Remind students to use both primary and secondary sources when they complete these activities. For instance, they might read the speeches of famous freedom fighters as well as their biographies.

Professional Notes

Oral History

During the Great Depression of the 1930s, one federal work project sent historians throughout the country to collect the stories of people who had once been enslaved. Invite the class to find and report information from interviews by historians of people who had been enslaved. Ahead of time, have the class prepare questions; then have the students performing the interview work together on the responses, using Douglass's narrative and other historical documents for details.

Critical Comment:
The Eye of Experience

Professor C. Vann Woodward comments that "Douglass does not stop at recording his sufferings and his protest, as most of the slave authors do. He analyzes perceptively what slavery did to children, mothers, and fathers of slave families, and what it did to drivers, overseers, masters, and their families." Have students discuss Douglass's analysis of the damage slavery inflicted on himself and others.

This feature explores the rich heritage of African American spirituals and code songs, through the eyes of Frederick Douglass and others. Douglass discusses the origins of spirituals in the pain and sorrow of slavery, and highlights their profound emotional and political power. The feature also explores the history of code songs—used to help people escape from slavery.

RESPONDING TO THE ART

Frederick Douglass is a somewhat stylized mid-nineteenth century portrait attributed to the painter **Elisha Hammond**.
Activity. Have students compare and contrast the portrait on this page with the photograph on p. 424. [Both works show the same clothing, facial features, and hairstyles. Douglass appears more stern and stately in the portrait; he appears more reflective in the photograph.] **Which picture better matches your mental image of Douglass?** [Some students may choose the photograph because it is more realistic; others may choose the portrait because Douglass looks more like the proud young adult they just finished reading about.]

Ⓐ Critical Thinking
Making Inferences
❓ Why do you think masters and overseers disliked a "silent slave"? [Possible answers: A noisy slave could be found easily; a silent slave might be lost in his or her own thoughts and could be plotting an escape.]

Ⓑ Historical Connections
Irish Potato Famine
Under British rule, Irish farmers were forced to export their grain to England and eat potatoes instead. In 1845–1846, a potato blight wiped out the yearly crop and close to one million people died of starvation or famine-related diseases.

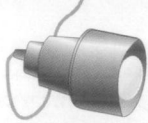

SPOTLIGHT ON
Spirituals and Code Songs

Frederick Douglass (detail) (c. 1844), attributed to Elisha Hammond. Oil on canvas (27½″ × 22½″).

National Portrait Gallery, Smithsonian Institution. Courtesy Art Resource, NY.

The moving and intensely emotional songs known as spirituals largely developed from the oral traditions of Africans held in slavery in the South before the Civil War. Spirituals, like other kinds of folk literature and music, were composed by anonymous artists and passed on orally. They were inevitably altered and refined, so numerous versions of a particular spiritual might exist. Many spirituals combine African melodies and rhythms with elements of white Southern religious music.

In this passage from *My Bondage and My Freedom*, Frederick Douglass writes eloquently about songs of slavery—called sorrow songs by the later African American writer W.E.B. Du Bois.

Ⓐ Slaves are generally expected to sing as well as to work. A silent slave is not liked by masters or overseers. *"Make a noise, make a noise,"* and *"bear a hand"* are the words usually addressed to the slaves when there is silence amongst them. This may account for the almost constant singing heard in the southern states. . . . On allowance day, those who visited the great house farm were peculiarly excited and noisy. While on their way, they would make the dense old woods, for miles around, reverberate with their wild notes. These were not always merry because they were wild. On the contrary, they were mostly of a plaintive cast, and told a tale of grief and sorrow. In the most boisterous outbursts of rapturous sentiment, there was ever a tinge of deep melancholy. I have never heard any songs like those anywhere since I left slavery, except when in Ireland. There I heard the same *wailing notes,* and was much affected by them. It was during the famine of 1845–1846. In all the songs of the slaves, there was ever some expression in praise of the great house farm; something which would flatter the pride of

go.hrw.com
LE0 11-9

Crossing the Curriculum

Art
Explain that many people worked to abolish slavery. These included people who had been enslaved—such as Frederick Douglass, Harriet Tubman, and Sojourner Truth—as well as whites—such as Angelina and Sarah Grimké, William Lloyd Garrison, John Brown, and Harriet Beecher Stowe. Invite students to paint a mural depicting this diverse group of freedom fighters. Encourage them to use symbolic objects associated with each person's biography.

For instance, Douglass might be represented with a lectern or Garrison with a printing press.

Social Studies
Have students give oral presentations analyzing code songs such as "Wade in the Water" (which Harriet Tubman used to explain how to elude bloodhounds), "Steal Away" (which Nat Turner used to call secret meetings), and "Good News, Member" (which indicated that a runaway slave had reached freedom).

the owner, and, possibly, draw a favorable glance from him.

. . . I cannot better express my sense of them now, than ten years ago, when, in sketching my life, I thus spoke of this feature of my plantation experience:

. . . The hearing of those wild notes always depressed my spirits, and filled my heart with ineffable sadness. The mere recurrence, even now, afflicts my spirit, and while I am writing these lines, my tears are falling. To those songs I trace my first **C** glimmering conceptions of the dehumanizing character of slavery. I can never get rid of that conception. Those songs still follow me, to deepen my hatred of slavery, and quicken my sympathies for my brethren in bonds. If any one wishes to be impressed with a sense of the soul-killing power of slavery, let him go to Colonel Lloyd's plantation, and, on allowance day, place himself in the deep, pine woods, and there let him, in silence, thoughtfully analyze the sounds that shall pass through the chambers of his soul, and if he is not thus impressed, it will only be because "there is no flesh in his obdurate heart."

—Frederick Douglass

Harriet Tubman and the Freedom Train (detail) (1989) by Barbara Olsen. Gouache, collage (22½″ × 30″).

© Barbara Olsen. Collection of Dr. and Mrs. J. S. Kahn.

Spirituals were concerned above all with issues of freedom: spiritual freedom in the form of salvation and literal freedom from the shackles of slavery. Many people during the time of slavery were called Moses by those looking for a deliverer to loose their chains. Harriet Tubman, for example, used Moses as her code name in her work with the Underground Railroad. A Methodist minister named Francis Asbury was also known as Moses, and according to some scholars, the spiritual "Go Down, Moses" really is a **D** plea for Asbury's help. Ultimately, of course, the name Moses refers to the man who, according to the Book of Exodus in the Bible, delivered the ancient Israelites from slavery in Egypt.

Some of the songs were code songs, or signal songs—that is, details in the songs provided runaways with directions, times, and meeting places for their escape. For example, the drinking gourd in "Follow the Drinking Gourd" is the Big Dipper, a group of stars; two stars in the bowl of the Big Dipper point to the North Star. A drinking gourd is actually the shell of a vegetable related to the squash or melon, dried and hollowed out for drinking.

Professional Notes

Critical Comment: Sorrow Songs

The African American scholar and activist W.E.B. DuBois (1868–1963) called spirituals "Sorrow Songs." However, he wrote, "Through all of the Sorrow Songs there breathes a hope—a faith in the ultimate justice of things. The minor cadences of despair change often to triumph and calm confidence. Sometimes it is faith in life, sometimes a faith in death, sometimes assurance of boundless justice in some fair world beyond. But whichever it is, the meaning is always clear: that sometimes, somewhere, men will judge men by their souls and not by their skins." DuBois described these songs "not simply as the sole American music, but as the most beautiful expression of human experience born on this side of the seas . . . the singular spiritual heritage of the nation and the greatest gift of the Negro people."

Assessing Learning

Check Test: True-False

1. Masters wanted slaves to make noise. [True]
2. Spirituals expressed the grief and sorrow of the slaves. [True]
3. The drinking gourd in "Follow the Drinking Gourd" is the North Star. [False]
4. Some code songs gave directions North. [True]

The Old Plantation (c. 1795) by an unknown artist (South Carolina). Watercolor on laid paper (11¹¹/₁₆″ × 17⅞″).

Abby Aldrich Rockefeller Folk Art Center, Williamsburg, Virginia.

Ⓐ Humanities Connections

The Bible Story

The events described in this song come from the Bible, Exodus 3–12. Moses asks the Pharaoh, probably Ramses II, to allow the Israelites to leave Egypt. Ramses refuses. Moses's staff turns into a serpent, the waters of the Nile River flow blood red, and Egypt is cursed with plagues of frogs, gnats, and flies. Next, an epidemic decimates the Egyptian flocks, and people and animals are tortured by boils. Fierce lightning and hail, locusts, and daytime darkness follow. When the firstborn sons of the Egyptians, including his own, are smitten by the plague, Ramses finally agrees to free the Israelites.

Ⓑ Elements of Literature

Symbol

❓ Whom does Israel symbolize? [people held in slavery] What does Egypt symbolize? [the South] Whom do Pharaoh and Moses symbolize? [Pharaoh represents slave holders. Moses is a leader who will rescue those who are enslaved.]

Resources

Listening

Audio CD Library

"Go Down Moses"
• Disk 11, Track 3

Go Down, Moses

Go down, Moses,
Way down in Egypt land
Tell old Pharaoh
To let my people go.

5 When Israel was in Egypt land
Let my people go
Oppressed so hard they could not stand
Let my people go.

Go down, Moses,
10 Way down in Egypt land
Tell old Pharaoh,
"Let my people go."

Ⓐ "Thus saith the Lord," bold Moses said,
"Let my people go;
15 If not I'll smite your firstborn dead
Let my people go."

Go down, Moses,
Way down in Egypt land,
Tell old Pharaoh,
Ⓑ 20 "Let my people go!"

Follow the Drinking Gourd

When the sun comes back and the first quail calls,
Follow the drinking gourd,
For the old man is a-waiting for to carry you to freedom
If you follow the drinking gourd.

[Refrain]
5 Follow the drinking gourd,
Follow the drinking gourd,
For the old man is a-waiting for to carry you to freedom
If you follow the drinking gourd.

The river bank will make a very good road,
10 The dead trees show you the way,
Left foot, peg foot traveling on
Follow the drinking gourd. [Refrain]

The river ends between two hills,
Follow the drinking gourd.
15 There's another river on the other side,
Following the drinking gourd. [Refrain]

Where the little river meets the great big river,
Follow the drinking gourd.
The old man is a-waiting for to carry you to freedom,
20 If you follow the drinking gourd. [Refrain]

Listening to Music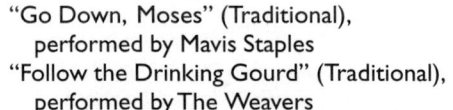

"Go Down, Moses" (Traditional), performed by Mavis Staples
"Follow the Drinking Gourd" (Traditional), performed by The Weavers

In contrast to the so-called "white spirituals" of the same era, African American spirituals have their roots in the music of Africa, with its distinctive rhythms and harmonies. They arose as an expression of a deeply felt religious faith but also became code songs against slavery.

Activity

Ask students to listen to the spirituals and think about the effect they would have had on the slaves who heard them. Take note of any differences between the lyrics in the versions you hear and the versions printed in your textbook. Then have students debate whether or not the chief attitude conveyed by the spirituals is one of hope or despair.

Kate Chopin

(1851–1904)

The Missouri Historical Society, St. Louis, Missouri.

Kate Chopin's work went unrecognized, and was even scorned, during her lifetime. Along with many other literary pioneers, Chopin never lived to see her work vindicated.

Kate Chopin was born Katherine O'Flaherty in St. Louis, Missouri, to an Irish immigrant father and a mother descended from French Creole aristocrats. (Creoles are people of French or Spanish descent who are born in the states bordering the Gulf of Mexico but who retain their European culture.) Kate's prosperous parents encouraged her early interest in music and reading; her mother invited such a flurry of stimulating visitors to their house that Kate sometimes escaped to the attic to read. She was given lessons in French and piano for a time by her worldly great-grandmother, who stirred the child's imagination with vivid tales of old St. Louis. Kate became a witty and popular young woman with a notably independent turn of mind.

At nineteen, Kate married Oscar Chopin, a French Creole from New Orleans, and they enjoyed a long European honeymoon, visiting art galleries and attending operas. The Chopins settled in Louisiana and reared a family of six children, but, when Kate was thirty-two, Oscar died suddenly from swamp fever. Kate returned to St. Louis, and it was then that she began to write. She published a poem when she was thirty-eight, followed by some short stories. In 1890, she published her first novel.

Chopin's short stories concern the life of French Creoles in Louisiana. Published in national magazines and collected in two volumes called *Bayou Folk* (1894) and *A Night in Acadie* (1897), the stories were praised for their accurate portrayal of the French Creole strand in American culture. Chopin's theme, however, was a much more controversial matter: the repression of women in Victorian America.

This theme was presented most dramatically in her novel *The Awakening* (1899). The novel portrays a dissatisfied New Orleans wife who breaks from the confines of her marriage and, in her quest for freedom, flagrantly defies the Victorian ideals of motherhood and domesticity. The novel was greeted with hostility by American critics, who condemned it as sordid and vulgar. Victorians, who looked to literature for moral lessons, saw only an immoral lesson in *The Awakening*. The novel was removed from circulation in St. Louis libraries, some of Chopin's friends shunned her, and the local arts club denied her membership. Chopin was disheartened enough by this rejection to allow her writing to languish, and she produced little more before her death in 1904. After her death, her work fell into obscurity, and often copies of her books couldn't even be obtained.

The Awakening and many of Chopin's other works were rediscovered decades after her death. With the help of discerning critics and the women's movement of the 1960s and 1970s, Kate Chopin is now recognized as a novelist of skill and perception, whose work appeared half a century before its time.

go.hrw.com
LEO 11-9

KATE CHOPIN **435**

Summary ■

When Mrs. Sommers unexpectedly finds herself with the large sum of fifteen dollars, she immediately thinks of the clothing she should buy for her four children. Once in the store, however, she feels faint from hunger and sits down at a counter to rest. Her hand strokes a luxurious pair of silk stockings, and a conflict arises between her obligations as a mother and her own desires. She buys herself not only the stockings, but also shoes, gloves, two high-priced magazines, a fancy meal, and a theater ticket. After a wonderful day, she boards a cable car for home, wishing in vain her dream would never end.

Background

Kate Chopin based her early stories on her experiences in Cloutierville, Louisiana, where her husband owned a plantation store. No doubt Chopin, as the wife of a store owner, met many women like poor Mrs. Sommers. Ironically, Chopin found herself plunged into similar circumstances when her husband Oscar died and she was left alone to raise six children.

RESPONDING TO THE ART

Mary Cassatt (1844–1926) was the only American artist of her day to have her works exhibited with the French Impressionists. **Activity.** After students have read the story, have them explore how the painting captures the elegance Mrs. Sommers craves. [The woman in the picture (Cassatt's sister Lydia) wears fine clothes and enjoys a moment of leisure.]

Before You Read

A PAIR OF SILK STOCKINGS

Make the Connection

Escaping the Humdrum
From time to time, everyone feels trapped by the humdrum duties of daily life. All of us—probably even rock stars and world travelers—fantasize about escape from routines that come to feel boring or confining. For a nineteenth-century woman of limited means trying to satisfy the needs of her family, even a brief reprieve from the demands of domestic life could be a life-changing bid for freedom and a temporary escape from day-to-day duties.

Reading Skills and Strategies

Dialogue with the Text
Read the story's first two paragraphs, and then stop. Write down your predictions of what Mrs. Sommers will do with her unexpected possession of money—a sum equivalent to a generous weekly salary in the 1890s.

Background

As you read, be aware that nylon had not yet been invented in the 1890s; most women wore long, thick, cotton stockings. Silk stockings ranked as pure luxury. Also, as you'll see in this story, fifteen dollars in the 1890s could buy far more than two meals at a fast-food restaurant.

The Cup of Tea (1879) by Mary Cassatt (1844–1926). Oil on canvas (36⅜″ × 25¾″).
The Metropolitan Museum of Art, New York. From the Collection of James Stillman. Gift of Dr. Ernest G. Stillman, 1922 (22.16.17). Photograph ©1983 The Metropolitan Museum of Art.

436 THE RISE OF REALISM: THE CIVIL WAR AND POSTWAR PERIOD

Preteaching Vocabulary

Words to Own

Point out that six of the ten vocabulary words end with either the suffix *-able,* "able to be," or *-ous,* "full of." Then, model how to break these words into roots and suffixes. For instance, *appreciable* is a combination of the suffix *—able* and the root word *appreciate,* which means "to note" or "to notice." An *appreciable* difference is one that can be noticed. Have students define the remaining five words using this technique and complete the following analogies.

1. memorable: forgettable:: facile: [laborious]
2. senses: vivid:: emotions: [poignant]
3. heartless: considerate:: reckless: [judicious]
4. knife: sharp:: pain: [acute]
5. peacock: vain:: cat: [fastidious]
6. common: unusual:: false: [veritable]
7. emotion: gushy:: jewelry: [gaudy]
8. mourners: weeping:: party goers: [reveling]
9. hilarity: funny:: incredulity: [preposterous]
10. achievement: notable:: effort: [appreciable]

A Pair of Silk Stockings

Kate Chopin

Little Mrs. Sommers one day found herself the unexpected possessor of fifteen dollars. It seemed to her a very large amount of money, and the way in which it stuffed and bulged her worn old *porte-monnaie*[1] gave her a feeling of importance such as she had not enjoyed for years.

The question of investment was one that occupied her greatly. For a day or two she walked about apparently in a dreamy state, but really absorbed in speculation and calculation. She did not wish to act hastily, to do anything she might afterward regret. But it was during the still hours of the night when she lay awake revolving plans in her mind that she seemed to see her way clearly toward a proper and judicious use of the money.

1. *porte-monnaie* (pôrt·mô·nā′): French for "purse."

A dollar or two should be added to the price usually paid for Janie's shoes, which would ensure their lasting an appreciable time longer than they usually did. She would buy so-and-so many yards of percale[2] for new shirtwaists for the boys and Janie and Mag. She had intended to make the old ones do by skillful patching. Mag should have another gown. She had seen some beautiful patterns, veritable bargains in the shop windows. And still there would be left enough for new stockings—two pairs apiece—and what darning that would save for a while!

2. **percale:** finely woven cotton cloth.

WORDS TO OWN
judicious (jōō·dish′əs) *adj.*: cautious; wise.
appreciable (ə·prē′shə·bəl) *adj.*: measurable.
veritable (ver′i·tə·bəl) *adj.*: genuine; true.

KATE CHOPIN **437**

FROM THE EDITOR'S DESK
We think students will relate to this story because most of us have at times wanted to buy something we can't afford, or longed for a more leisurely life.

A Reading Skills and Strategies
Dialogue with the Text
❓ What details in this passage suggest that Mrs. Sommers will spend the money on necessities? On luxuries? [Her "worn old *porte-monnaie*" and her preoccupation with how to spend the windfall suggest she will use the money for necessities; her "feeling of importance" suggests that she feels the money gives her a new freedom and hints that she might indulge in luxuries.]

B Critical Thinking
Interpreting
❓ What do these details suggest about Mrs. Sommers's life? [She is constantly worried about money and must often compromise on clothing and other necessities for the children. She spends a great deal of time mending, patching, and shopping for bargains. As a result, her life is often narrow and mundane.]

Resources

Listening
Audio CD Library
"A Pair of Silk Stockings"
• Disk 11, Track 4

Reaching All Students

Struggling Readers
Help students anticipate the story they are about to read by using a strategy called Story Impressions (see the *Reading Strategies Handbook*, p. 119 in the *Reading Skills and Strategies* binder.) Have students look at the following list of phrases. Then have them write how they think those phrases might be related to each other to make a story. They must use the items on the list in the order that they appear.

After they read, discuss how their Story Impressions compare to the actual text.

- little Mrs. Sommers
- fifteen dollars
- her little brood (children)
- wanted bargains
- luxurious things
- freed of her responsibility
- back to real life
- wishes and dreams

Advanced Learners
Chopin's early works, like this story, were tales of genteel Creole life. However, her masterpiece, *The Awakening*, explores a woman's growth toward financial, emotional, and intellectual independence. Characterized as "sad and mad and bad," the novel scandalized critics and readers alike. "Hardly the kind of book some people would look for from Kate Chopin," one critic sniffed. Challenge students to find the seeds of feminist rebellion in this story.

A Elements of Literature
Character
? What does Mrs. Sommers's "vision" reveal about her personality and concerns? [Possible answers: She is a good parent who worries about providing for her children; she puts others' needs before her own desires.]

B English Language Learners
Paradox
Non-native speakers may have difficulty interpreting the paradoxical expression "tomorrow never comes." Explain that the phrase means that one can live only in the present; the future is always just a vision. Have students analyze how Mrs. Sommers focuses on getting through one day at a time rather than longing for the "better days" of the past or looking too hard at the "gaunt monster" of the future.

C Critical Thinking
Interpreting
? What sentence in this passage signals that Mrs. Sommers is about to change her usual pattern of behavior? ["But that day she was a little faint and tired" suggests that she is not herself.]

D Appreciating Language
Word Choice
? How does Chopin's word choice make the stockings seem attractive—even seductive? [She uses sensory words and images. For example, *silk, soft,* and *glide* appeal to the sense of touch, *sheeny* and *glisten,* to the sense of sight. A "tiara of diamonds" suggests richness and luxury.]

She would get caps for the boys and sailor hats for the girls. The vision of her little brood looking fresh and dainty and new for once in their lives excited her and made her restless and wakeful with anticipation.

The neighbors sometimes talked of certain "better days" that little Mrs. Sommers had known before she had ever thought of being Mrs. Sommers. She herself indulged in no such morbid retrospection.[3] She had no time—no second of time to devote to the past. The needs of the present absorbed her every faculty. A vision of the future like some dim, gaunt monster sometimes appalled her, but luckily tomorrow never comes.

Mrs. Sommers was one who knew the value of bargains; who could stand for hours making her way inch by inch toward the desired object that was selling below cost. She could elbow her way if need be; she had learned to clutch a piece of goods and hold it and stick to it with persistence and determination till her turn came to be served, no matter when it came.

But that day she was a little faint and tired. She had swallowed a light luncheon—no! when she came to think of it, between getting the children fed and the place righted, and preparing herself for the shopping bout, she had actually forgotten to eat any luncheon at all!

She sat herself upon a revolving stool before a counter that was comparatively deserted, trying to gather strength and courage to charge through an eager multitude that was besieging breastworks[4] of shirting and figured lawn. An all-gone limp feeling had come over her and she rested her hand aimlessly upon the counter. She wore no gloves. By degrees she grew aware that her hand had encountered something very soothing, very pleasant to

3. **morbid retrospection:** brooding on things in the past.
4. **breastworks:** low walls put up as barricades. The bolts of shirting material and fine patterned cotton, or "figured lawn," are compared to barricades being stormed by shoppers.

touch. She looked down to see that her hand lay upon a pile of silk stockings. A placard nearby announced that they had been reduced in price from two dollars and fifty cents to one dollar and ninety-eight cents; and a young girl who stood behind the counter asked her if she wished to examine their line of silk hosiery. She smiled, just as if she had been asked to inspect a tiara of diamonds with the ultimate view of purchasing it. But she went on feeling the soft, sheeny luxurious things—with both hands now, holding them up to see them glisten, and to feel them glide serpentlike through her fingers.

Two hectic blotches came suddenly into her pale cheeks. She looked up at the girl.

"Do you think there are any eights-and-a-half among these?"

There were any number of eights-and-a-half. In fact, there were more of that size than any other. Here was a light blue pair; there were some lavender, some all black, and various shades of tan and gray. Mrs. Sommers selected a black pair and looked at them very long and closely. She pretended to be examining their texture, which the clerk assured her was excellent.

"A dollar and ninety-eight cents," she mused aloud. "Well, I'll take this pair." She handed the girl a five-dollar bill and waited for her change and for her parcel. What a very small parcel it was! It seemed lost in the depths of her shabby old shopping bag.

Mrs. Sommers after that did not move in the direction of the bargain counter. She took the elevator, which carried her to an upper floor into the region of the ladies' waiting rooms. Here, in a retired corner, she exchanged her cotton stockings for the new silk ones which she had just bought. She was not going through any <u>acute</u> mental process or reasoning with herself, nor was she

WORDS TO OWN
acute (ə·kyoot′) *adj.:* keen; sharp.

The Granger Collection, New York (coins).

Using Students' Strengths

Verbal Learners
Chopin uses specific words and phrases that evoke the style of Louisiana in the 1890s. Invite students to explain how words such as *porte-monnaie, percale, shirtwaists, figured lawn, blue-points,* and *crème-frappé* convey the ambience of the times. Then have students list words they might use to convey a sense of their own daily lives, such as *backpack, T-shirt, milkshake,* or *CD.*

Logical/Mathematical Learners
Fifteen dollars was a large sum in the 1890s. Invite students to discover what it was worth. Bring in periodicals from the era and history books to help students calculate buying power. Challenge students to find out what the stockings, a restaurant meal, and the other items in the story would cost in 1890 dollars. Then have students calculate what Mrs. Sommers's spree would cost in today's dollars.

Visual Learners
Kate Chopin loved to walk around both New Orleans and Cloutierville and, like Walt Whitman, often rode streetcars to observe city life. Help students imagine the world of the 1890s by bringing in some period pictures of cities—perhaps from a history textbook or your local historical society. If you can display local historical pictures, students will enjoy looking for buildings that still exist.

The Fitting (1891) by Mary Cassatt (1844–1926).
Color print with drypoint, softground, and aquatint (14¾″ × 10⅛″).

Rosenwald Collection. © 1998 Board of Trustees, National Gallery of Art, Washington, D.C.

Getting Students Involved

Speaking and Listening
One of this story's most notable characteristics is the richness of its descriptions. Invite students to read aloud their favorite passages and to use their voices to help convey the mood of each scene.

Writing the Prequel
Invite pairs or small groups of students to write a prequel to "A Pair of Silk Stockings." The stories should provide background about Mrs. Sommers's past, concentrating on the "better days" she once enjoyed and explaining what happened to change her life. A panel of student judges can select two stories to read to the class or all the stories can be displayed for the class to share.

LITERATURE AND HISTORY

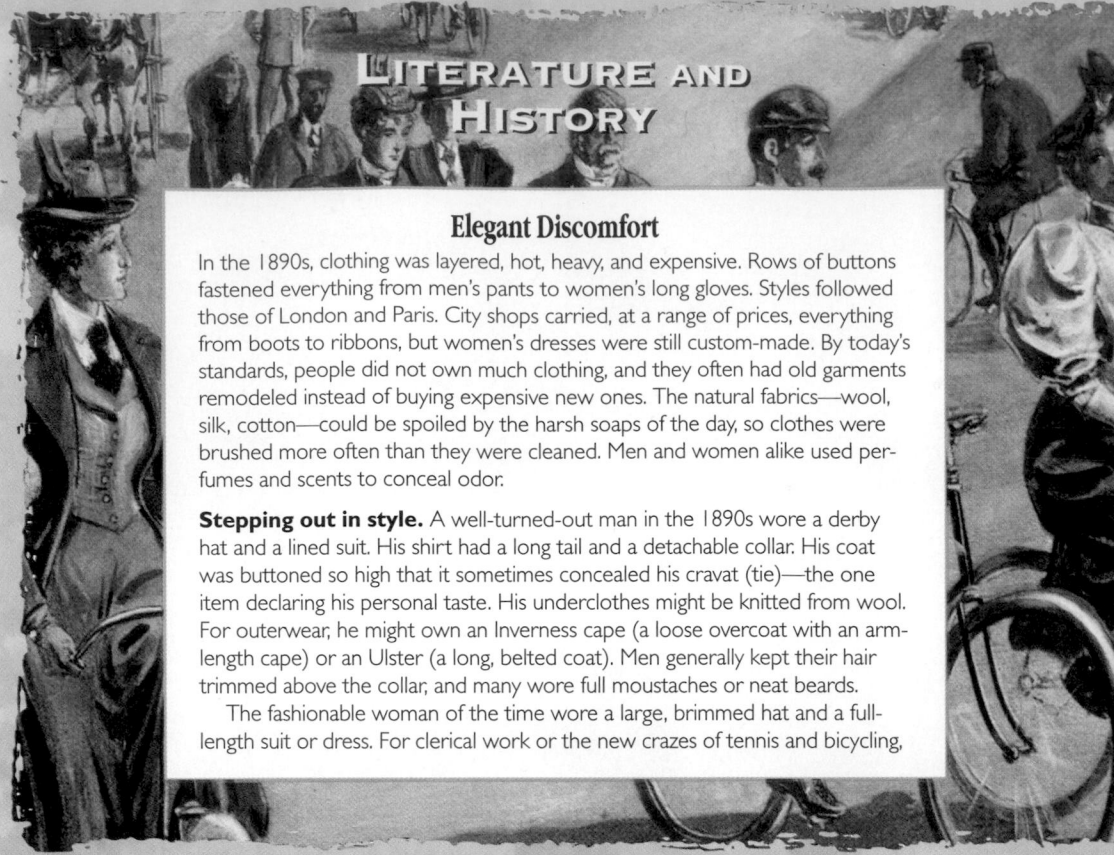

Have students read "Elegant Discomfort." Then ask them what fashions are popular today for men and women and for different age groups. Have them discuss what discomforts we suffer for fashion and the reasons for doing so. You might point out that hair straightening, body piercing, and tattooing are all fashions that require a certain amount of suffering.

Elegant Discomfort

In the 1890s, clothing was layered, hot, heavy, and expensive. Rows of buttons fastened everything from men's pants to women's long gloves. Styles followed those of London and Paris. City shops carried, at a range of prices, everything from boots to ribbons, but women's dresses were still custom-made. By today's standards, people did not own much clothing, and they often had old garments remodeled instead of buying expensive new ones. The natural fabrics—wool, silk, cotton—could be spoiled by the harsh soaps of the day, so clothes were brushed more often than they were cleaned. Men and women alike used perfumes and scents to conceal odor.

Stepping out in style. A well-turned-out man in the 1890s wore a derby hat and a lined suit. His shirt had a long tail and a detachable collar. His coat was buttoned so high that it sometimes concealed his cravat (tie)—the one item declaring his personal taste. His underclothes might be knitted from wool. For outerwear, he might own an Inverness cape (a loose overcoat with an arm-length cape) or an Ulster (a long, belted coat). Men generally kept their hair trimmed above the collar, and many wore full moustaches or neat beards.

The fashionable woman of the time wore a large, brimmed hat and a full-length suit or dress. For clerical work or the new crazes of tennis and bicycling,

---

A Reading Skills and Strategies
Dialogue with the Text

? Is Mrs. Sommers behaving the way you had predicted? Why or why not? How can you explain her actions? [Many students probably predicted that Mrs. Sommers would spend the money on her family. Her change of heart might be explained by her exhaustion from years of penny-pinching, or her need to escape her own life for a while.]

B Elements of Literature
Character

? How do your impressions of Mrs. Sommers start to change in this passage? Do you like her more now, or less? [Possible answers: Earlier, Mrs. Sommers seemed to be defined by her role as mother, but now she seems more individual and "human." Some students will like her more because she is fulfilling her own desires. Others may say she seems petty or snobbish now.]

A striving to explain to her satisfaction the motive of her action. She was not thinking at all. She seemed for the time to be taking a rest from that <u>laborious</u> and fatiguing function and to have abandoned herself to some mechanical impulse that directed her actions and freed her of responsibility.

How good was the touch of the raw silk to her flesh! She felt like lying back in the cushioned chair and <u>reveling</u> for a while in the luxury of it. She did for a little while. Then she replaced her shoes, rolled the cotton stockings together, and thrust them into her bag. After doing this she crossed straight over to the shoe department and took her seat to be fitted.

She was <u>fastidious</u>. The clerk could not make her out; he could not reconcile her shoes

B with her stockings, and she was not too easily pleased. She held back her skirts and turned her feet one way and her head another way as she glanced down at the polished, pointed-tipped boots. Her foot and ankle looked very pretty. She could not realize that they belonged to her and were a part of herself. She wanted an excellent and stylish fit, she

---

WORDS TO OWN
laborious (lə·bôr′ē·əs) *adj.:* difficult; involving much hard work.
reveling (rev′əl·iŋ) *v.:* taking pleasure.
fastidious (fas·tid′ē·əs) *adj.:* difficult to please; critical.

Professional Notes

Critical Comment: Story Structure

Kate Chopin's short stories are celebrated for their vivid descriptions of life among the Louisiana Creoles at the turn of the century. As literary critic Kenneth Eble notes, "Kate Chopin, almost from her first story, had the ability to capture character, to put the right word in the mouth, to impart the exact gesture, to select the characteristic action. Her deftness can be observed in the delineation of minor characters."

However, Chopin was perhaps not as deft a writer when it came to organization, plot, and the other conventional elements of the "well-made" short story. "Characterization was always Mrs. Chopin's talent," Eble continues. "Structure was not. Those who knew her working habits say that she seldom revised, and she herself mentions that she did not like reworking stories. Though her reputation rests upon her short narratives, her collected stories

themselves give abundant evidence of the sketch, the outline of stories which remain unformed. And when she attempted a tightly organized story, she often turned to Maupassant and was likely as not to effect a contrived symmetry." After students have finished reading the story, invite them to evaluate the characterization and structure of "A Pair of Silk Stockings" to see if they agree or disagree with Eble's assessment of Chopin's achievements.

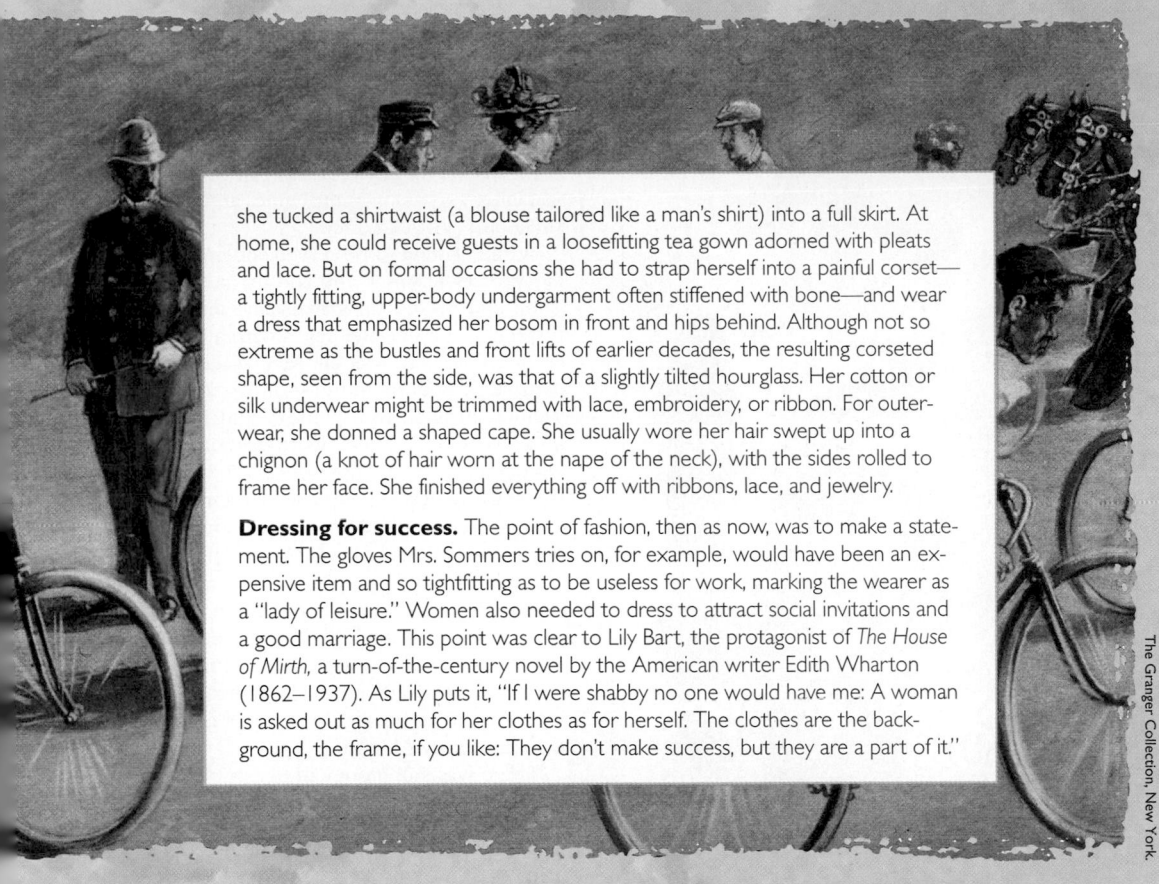

she tucked a shirtwaist (a blouse tailored like a man's shirt) into a full skirt. At home, she could receive guests in a loosefitting tea gown adorned with pleats and lace. But on formal occasions she had to strap herself into a painful corset—a tightly fitting, upper-body undergarment often stiffened with bone—and wear a dress that emphasized her bosom in front and hips behind. Although not so extreme as the bustles and front lifts of earlier decades, the resulting corseted shape, seen from the side, was that of a slightly tilted hourglass. Her cotton or silk underwear might be trimmed with lace, embroidery, or ribbon. For outerwear, she donned a shaped cape. She usually wore her hair swept up into a chignon (a knot of hair worn at the nape of the neck), with the sides rolled to frame her face. She finished everything off with ribbons, lace, and jewelry.

Dressing for success. The point of fashion, then as now, was to make a statement. The gloves Mrs. Sommers tries on, for example, would have been an expensive item and so tightfitting as to be useless for work, marking the wearer as a "lady of leisure." Women also needed to dress to attract social invitations and a good marriage. This point was clear to Lily Bart, the protagonist of *The House of Mirth*, a turn-of-the-century novel by the American writer Edith Wharton (1862–1937). As Lily puts it, "If I were shabby no one would have me: A woman is asked out as much for her clothes as for herself. The clothes are the background, the frame, if you like: They don't make success, but they are a part of it."

The Granger Collection, New York.

told the young fellow who served her, and she did not mind the difference of a dollar or two more in the price so long as she got what she desired.

It was a long time since Mrs. Sommers had been fitted with gloves. On rare occasions when she had bought a pair they were always "bargains," so cheap that it would have been preposterous and unreasonable to have expected them to be fitted to the hand.

Now she rested her elbow on the cushion of the glove counter, and a pretty, pleasant young creature, delicate and deft of touch, drew a long-wristed "kid" over Mrs. Sommers's hand. She smoothed it down over the wrist and buttoned it neatly, and both lost themselves for a second or two in admiring contemplation of the little symmetrical gloved hand. But there were other places where money might be spent.

There were books and magazines piled up in the window of a stall a few paces down the street. Mrs. Sommers bought two high-priced magazines such as she had been accustomed to read in the days when she had been accustomed to other pleasant things. She carried them without wrapping. As well as she could she lifted her skirts at the crossings. Her stockings and boots and well-fitting gloves had worked marvels in her bearing—had given her

WORDS TO OWN
preposterous (prē·päs′tər·əs) *adj.:* ridiculous.

KATE CHOPIN 441

Getting Students Involved

Making the Connections

Trade card of a glove manufacturer (c. 1890).

The Bettmann Archive.

a feeling of assurance, a sense of belonging to the well-dressed multitude.

Ⓐ She was very hungry. Another time she would have stilled the cravings for food until reaching her own home, where she would have brewed herself a cup of tea and taken a snack of anything that was available. But the impulse that was guiding her would not suffer her to entertain any such thought.

There was a restaurant at the corner. She had never entered its doors; from the outside she had sometimes caught glimpses of spotless damask and shining crystal, and soft-stepping waiters serving people of fashion.

When she entered, her appearance created no surprise, no consternation, as she had half feared it might. She seated herself at a small table alone, and an attentive waiter at once approached to take her order. She did not want a profusion; she craved a nice and tasty bite—a Ⓑ half dozen bluepoints,[5] a plump chop with cress, a something sweet—a crème-frappé,[6] for instance; a glass of Rhine wine, and after all a small cup of black coffee.

While waiting to be served she removed her gloves very leisurely and laid them beside her. Then she picked up a magazine and glanced through it, cutting the pages with a blunt edge of her knife.[7] It was all very agreeable. The damask was even more spotless than it had seemed through the window, and the crystal more sparkling. There were quiet ladies and gentlemen, who did not notice her, lunching at the small tables like her own. A soft, pleasing strain of music could be heard, and a gentle breeze was blowing through the window. She tasted a bite, and she read a word or two, and she sipped the amber wine and wiggled her toes in the silk stockings. The price of it made Ⓒ no difference. She counted the money out to the waiter and left an extra coin on his tray, whereupon he bowed before her as before a princess of royal blood.

There was still money in her purse, and her next temptation presented itself in the shape of a matinée poster.

It was a little later when she entered the theater, the play had begun, and the house seemed to her to be packed. But there were vacant seats here and there, and into one of them she was ushered, between brilliantly dressed women who had gone there to kill time and eat candy and display their <u>gaudy</u> attire. There were many others who were there solely for the play and acting. It is safe to say there was

5. **bluepoints:** small oysters.
6. **crème-frappé** (krĕm·fra·pā′): dessert similar to ice cream.
7. **cutting . . . knife:** At one time, magazines and books were often sold with folded, untrimmed pages. These outer edges had to be cut apart before one could read them.

WORDS TO OWN

gaudy (gôd′ē) *adj.:* showy, but lacking in good taste.

no one present who bore quite the attitude which Mrs. Sommers did to her surroundings. She gathered in the whole—stage and players and people in one wide impression, and absorbed it and enjoyed it. She laughed at the comedy and wept—she and the gaudy woman next to her wept over the tragedy. And they talked a little together over it. And the gaudy woman wiped her eyes and sniffled on a tiny square of filmy, perfumed lace and passed little Mrs. Sommers her box of candy.

The play was over, the music ceased, the crowd filed out. It was like a dream ended. Peo-

WORDS TO OWN
poignant (pɔin'yənt) *adj.:* emotionally moving.

ple scattered in all directions. Mrs. Sommers went to the corner and waited for the cable car.

A man with keen eyes, who sat opposite her, seemed to like the study of her small, pale face. It puzzled him to decipher what he saw there. In truth, he saw nothing—unless he were wizard enough to detect a <u>poignant</u> wish, a powerful longing that the cable car would never stop anywhere, but go on and on with her forever.

PRIMARY Sources — A BIOGRAPHY

Vogue Stories

Kate Chopin had trouble selling her stories. *Vogue* magazine, however, whose readership consisted mainly of young women from wealthy families, agreed to publish much of her work.

The title of Chopin's last *Vogue* story of the 1890s, "A Pair of Silk Stockings," suggests a tale for the rich—but it is really a message to *Vogue* readers about how the other half lives. Its central character, a struggling mother who once had "certain better days," must now scrimp to buy necessities for her children. But when Mrs. Sommers suddenly finds herself with fifteen dollars, she yields to temptation and spends all the money on herself: silk stockings, new boots, kid gloves, a tasty lunch, and a matinée. On the streetcar home, she feels "a poignant wish, a powerful longing that the cable car would never stop anywhere, but go on and on with her forever."

Mrs. Sommers was the kind of woman that *Vogue* readers might pass by on the street without noticing—but by the late 1890s, living frugally in St. Louis, Kate Chopin had seen the effects of poverty and urban strife on

The Bettmann Archive.

women. *Vogue,* unlike other magazines, did not expect her to write for "the young person" about domesticity and womanly self-sacrifice. *Vogue* allowed her to describe what she had seen, honestly and fearlessly.

Vogue moved with her; other magazines refused.

—Emily Toth, *from Kate Chopin*

KATE CHOPIN 443

Crossing the Curriculum

Art
Ask students to imagine that *Vogue* has asked them to illustrate "A Pair of Silk Stockings" for the next issue. To prepare for this work, students should first research the illustrations of the period in order to create drawings in the same style. You might suggest they look up the illustrations of Charles Dana Gibson, who created the Gibson Girl, the epitome of beauty in this era. Display students' work around the classroom.

Mathematics
In the 1890s, *Vogue* magazine was sold primarily to young, wealthy women. Have students find out the cost of the magazine in the 1890s and how much a comparable magazine costs today. Then have students find out how much *Vogue* paid for a short story such as "A Pair of Silk Stockings" and how much they pay for a similar story today. Students can consult *Literary Market Place* or *The Writer's Market* to find current payment schedules.

D Cultural Connections
According to this description, Mrs. Sommers attends a play that combined elements of comedy and tragedy. In the 1890s, this may well have meant a play about American life (as opposed to the prior generation's preference for European plays). When the story was written, comedies that exaggerated aspects of urban life were very popular, as were melodramas.

E Critical Thinking
Speculating
❓ Do you think Mrs. Sommers's experience has changed her outlook on life? How so? [Possible responses: Some students may argue that she will be completely dissatisfied from now on; others might say that the experience will have little effect, since it was "like a dream ended."]

F Reading Skills and Strategies

Dialogue with the Text
❓ How do you feel about what Mrs. Sommers does with the money? Are you sympathetic to her need to escape the bonds of her dreary, penny-pinching life, or do you feel she has simply neglected her children? Explain. [Most students will feel she probably deserves a day's respite from her life; some may feel that a mother should always put her children first.]

Primary Sources

This feature presents "A Pair of Silk Stockings" as a story with a frank social message for the upper-middle-class readers of *Vogue* magazine. It focuses on the plight of a woman living on the edge of poverty—a situation Chopin had experienced firsthand.

G Reading Skills and Strategies
Dialogue with the Text
❓ Do you agree that Chopin intended this story as a social message for affluent Vogue readers? Why or why not? [Some students may feel Chopin is trying to elicit support and concern for poor women; others may feel she is exploring universal feelings any person might have.]

Connections

In this poem, Pat Mora questions the cultural conformity of her fellow Americans—in life and in death—and refuses the stagnant "rot" of their uniform style. Instead, she champions her right to cultural difference—and claims its organic "blooms" both in her working life and in her burial.

A Reading Skills and Strategies

Dialogue with the Text

❓ What do you think this poem will be about, based on its title? What predictions can you make? [Possible responses: The poem will describe America in the past and the present, or on significant historical occasions.]

B Critical Thinking

Interpreting

❓ What do you think Mora is asking for in this line? [Possible responses: The speaker feels restricted by life in America and wants cultural freedom; the speaker doesn't want to conform but to allow her differences to show.]

C Advanced Learners

Word Choice

❓ How does the word *in* here contrast with the previous uses of the word? [In previous lines, *in* is repetitive and emphasizes confinement; here it emphasizes release, the speaker's request to be accepted for who she is.]

D Reading Skills and Strategies

Finding the Main Idea

❓ What does the speaker want? How does this stanza relate to the title of the poem and the predictions you made? [In her present life (now), she wants to be allowed to be herself, to dress and speak in keeping with her Latina heritage, even in formal business settings. After her death (then), she wants to have a burial site that expresses her individuality, her culture, and union with nature.]

Resources

Listening
Audio CD Library
"Now and Then America"
• Disc 11 Track 5

A Now and Then, America

Pat Mora

Who wants to rot
beneath dry, winter grass
in a numbered grave
in a numbered row
5 in a section labeled Eternal Peace
with neighbors plagued
by limp, plastic roses
springing from their toes?
B Grant me a little life now and then, America.

10 Who wants to rot
as she marches through life
in a pinstriped suit
neck chained in a soft, silk bow
in step, in style, insane.
C 15 Let me in
to boardrooms wearing hot
colors, my hair long and free,
maybe speaking Spanish.
Risk my difference, my surprises.
20 Grant me a little life, America.

And when I die, plant *zempasúchitl*,°
flowers of the dead, and at my head
plant organ cactus, green fleshy
fingers sprouting, like in Oaxaca.°
D 25 Let desert creatures hide
in the orange blooms.
Let birds nest in the cactus stems.
Let me go knowing life
    flower and song
30 will continue right above my bones.

21. *zempasúchitl* (sem·pä·soo'chē·t'l).
24. Oaxaca (wə·häk'ə).

Pat Mora.
Arte Publico Press.

444

Connecting Across Texts

Connecting with "A Pair of Silk Stockings"

Have students discuss how Mrs. Sommers in "A Pair of Silk Stockings" and the speaker in "Now and Then, America" may both feel restricted or chained. Ask students to identify each character's goals and desires. Students can use a cluster diagram such as the one here to help them organize their thoughts.

Mrs. Sommers feels constrained by lack of money.

Mrs. Sommers wants _____.

The speaker feels _____.

The speaker wants _____.

First Thoughts

1. What is Mrs. Sommers feeling as we leave her on the streetcar? Are you surprised or shocked by her "poignant wish"?

> **Reading Check**
> a. List the uses Mrs. Sommers plans to make of the fifteen dollars.
> b. List the items on which Mrs. Sommers actually spends the money.

Shaping Interpretations

2. The author describes her as "little Mrs. Sommers," and we learn that she has several children, lacks the time to recall "better days," and regards the future as a "dim, gaunt monster." No mention is made of her husband or source of income. How would you describe the **character** of Mrs. Sommers? How do you feel about what she does with the fifteen dollars?

3. Review the predictions you made after reading the first two paragraphs of the story. Can you explain why they were—or were not—on target? What details about Mrs. Sommers's earlier life might help explain the **motivation** for her shopping spree?

4. When Mrs. Sommers first feels the silk stockings, they "glide serpentlike through her fingers." What does a serpent often **symbolize** in Western culture? Explain whether or not you think Chopin's use of the word here is significant.

Extending the Text

5. This story is over a hundred years old. Do you think it is an old-fashioned story that could not happen today, or is the story still relevant? Could you see Mrs. Sommers in a TV sitcom? Could her conflict also be experienced by a man?

Challenging the Text

6. A feminist critic might say that this story is about a woman who strikes out to gain personal freedom and identity. A Marxist critic might say it is about the class struggle. The critic Barbara C. Ewell writes, "The power of money to enhance self-esteem and confidence is the core of this poignant tale." Which critic, if any, do you agree with? Why?

CHOICES:
Building Your Portfolio

Writer's Notebook

1. Collecting Ideas for a Research Paper

Brainstorm a list of topics suggested by Chopin's story that you would be interested in researching and reporting on, such as women's issues, the evolution of clothing, or city life in the 1890s. For each topic, list some effective ways to present the information that you gather for your report: interviews, descriptions, drawings, and tables or charts. Save your notes for possible use in the Writer's Workshop on page 515.

Comparing and Contrasting Themes

2. Breaking Bonds

Both Chopin and Pat Mora, in the **Connection** on page 444, write about escape, freedom, identity, and individuality. In a brief essay, compare and contrast the two writers' attitudes toward these **themes.** What kinds of images do they each use to convey their messages?

Creative Writing

3. The Untold Story

At the end of the story, Mrs. Sommers wishes the cable car would "go on and on" without ever stopping. What do you think the rest of Mrs. Sommers's life will be like? Will this day of indulgence mark a turning point in her life? Write one or more paragraphs telling the rest of Mrs. Sommers's story. Try to keep your version consistent with the character created in the story.

KATE CHOPIN 445

First Thoughts [Respond]

1. Mrs. Sommers regrets her day is over. Students may point out that many people want a different life; some may be shocked that Mrs. Sommers doesn't want to go home.

Shaping Interpretations [Interpret]

2. Some students may see her as a selfish person splurging at her children's expense; others, as a hard worker who deserves her escapism.

3. She was apparently much better off before her marriage and did not have to scrimp. Her behavior in the shoe store suggests she used to be very particular about style and fit, without concern for price.

4. A serpent often symbolizes sin, evil, and temptation—as in the book of Genesis. The word *serpentlike* signifies how the luxurious stockings tempt Mrs. Sommers away from buying clothing for her children and into self-indulgent spending.

Extending the Text [Evaluate]

5. Some students will say the story is still relevant because there are always people who want to escape their lives. Others will argue that it is out-of-date because people rarely feel guilt about selfish spending. Her story is too sad for a sitcom. Men could indeed act in the same way as Mrs. Sommers does.

Challenging the Text

[Express an Opinion]

6. Those who approach the text from a feminist perspective might note the conflict Mrs. Sommers suffers between her role as a "mother-woman" and her role as a person, and say she shouldn't have to choose between the two. Those who see the story from a Marxist perspective might say her poverty is a result of class oppression. Those who defend Ewell's view might say Mrs. Sommers's purchases enable her to find a new measure of self-esteem.

CHOICES:
Building Your Portfolio

1–3. Tell students to use the story as their starting point for each task.

T445

> **Reading Check**
> a. At first Mrs. Sommers intends to buy shoes, fabric, stockings, caps and hats—all for her children.
> b. She buys herself silk stockings, shoes, gloves, and magazines. She eats in a fine restaurant and attends a play.

Grading Timesaver

Rubrics for each Choices assignment appear on p. 143 in the *Portfolio Management System*.

Spotlight On

This section features powerful speeches by two great Native American leaders of the nineteenth century. In the first, Sauk Chief Black Hawk evokes the glory of his tribe's former stature and the expansive beauty of their lands. He mourns the loss of both—due to division of the tribe and their betrayal by white settlers. In the second speech, Nez Percé Chief Joseph surrenders to U.S. General Howard—recounting the human costs of the war for his land, and declaring that he will never fight again.

A Historical Connections

Black Hawk

Black Hawk was both a famous orator and a skilled warrior who had participated in battles by the age of fifteen. He steadfastly opposed leaving his home in Saukenuk and urged the Sauk to fight against the white settlers. He also opposed another Sauk chief, called Keokuk, who had agreed to divide the tribe by moving his followers west of the Mississippi.

B Critical Thinking

Recognizing Persuasive Techniques

? Why does Black Hawk present a long descriptive passage in a persuasive speech? [He hopes that this rich description of the tribe's former lands will inspire his listeners to try to recapture what they have lost.]

C Elements of Literature

Figures of Speech

? How does Black Hawk use *personification* and *metaphor* here? [He speaks of the former glory of the Sauk as if it were a living being who had run away. He compares the tribe's past stature to that of a bear and its present stature to that of a rabbit.]

SPOTLIGHT ON
American Indian Oratory

In the nineteenth century, American Indians felt keenly the shackles placed on them by the United States government. As the westward migration of European settlers increased, due in part to the California gold rush (1849) and the Civil War (1861–1865), Native Americans were forced to defend their land; more than two hundred fierce battles were fought between 1869 and 1878 alone.

For centuries, most American Indians have relied on spoken language for diplomacy, decision making, and preservation of their history and culture. In Native American cultures, spoken language mystically links the natural and spiritual worlds and has the power to shape and control events. Thus, American Indians have often chosen their leaders in part for their eloquence. Important speeches are even memorized exactly as spoken and passed on orally to future generations.

Faced with the destruction of their traditional way of life, Native Americans hoped that eloquent words might succeed where other weapons had failed. Their hopes were misplaced.

Black Hawk

Black Hawk (1767–1838) was born in what today is Illinois. He was leader of the Sauk—a group of Algonquian people native to present-day Michigan, Wisconsin, and Illinois. A proven warrior from his teens, Black Hawk earned renown for bravery and for oratory that roused his listeners to action. He spent much of his life battling the spread of European settlement. In the following excerpt from a speech he made in 1832, Black Hawk inspires his people to defend their land. However, in the ensuing conflict, the Black Hawk War, the Sauk were soundly defeated by U.S. forces.

"For More Than a Hundred Winters Our Nation Was a Powerful, Happy, and United People"

Headmen, Chiefs, Braves, and Warriors of the Sauks: For more than a hundred winters our nation was a powerful, happy, and united people. The Great Spirit gave to us a territory, seven hundred miles in length, along the Mississippi, reaching from Prairie du Chien[1] to the mouth of the Illinois River. This vast territory was composed of some of the finest and best land for the home and use of the Indian ever found in this country. The woods and prairies teemed with buffalo, moose, elk, bear, and deer, with other game suitable to our enjoyment, while its lakes, rivers, creeks, and ponds were alive with the very best kinds of fish, for our food. The islands in the Mississippi were our gardens, where the Great Spirit caused berries, plums, and other fruits to grow in great abundance, while the soil, when cultivated, produced corn, beans, pumpkins, and squash of the finest quality and largest quantities. Our children were never known to cry of hunger, and no stranger, red or white, was permitted to enter our lodges without finding food and rest. Our nation was respected by all who came in contact with it, for we had the ability as well as the courage to defend and maintain our rights of territory, person, and property against the world. Then, indeed, was it an honor to be called a Sauk, for that name was a passport to our people traveling in other territories and among other nations. But an evil day befell us when we became a divided nation, and with that division our glory deserted us, leaving us with the hearts and heels of the rabbit in place of the courage and strength of the bear.

All this was brought about by the long guns, who now claim all our territory east of the

1. **Prairie du Chien** (prer′ēd·ə·shēn): trading town at the junction of the Wisconsin and Mississippi Rivers; now a city in Wisconsin.

go.hrw.com
LE0 11-9

Taking a Second Look

Review: Using a Study Guide

Ask pairs of students to find out more about either Black Hawk or Chief Joseph. Have them use the questions that follow as a study guide and encourage them to take notes using words and phrases rather than complete sentences. Afterwards, each pair can work together to write a short report on their findings.

- What was the leader's major accomplishment?
- What were the high and low points of the leader's life?
- Did the speech presented here end a series of events or set new ones into motion, or both?
- How is the leader viewed today by both Native Americans and non-native Americans?

Making the Connections

Cultural Connections: Totems

Tell students that an Algonquin clan often adopted an animal as its symbolic *totem*—attributing the animal's characteristics to its clan members. Naturally, the bear was a symbol of great power and was always treated with the utmost respect. Tribal warriors or hunters often gathered the claws, skin, fur, etc., of their totem and put them in bags or *amulets* that they wore for protection. (Black Hawk's personal totem was the Sparrow Hawk.)

Black Hawk and Five Other Saukie Prisoners (1861–1869) by George Catlin. Oil on paperboard mounted on heavier paperboard (18⅝″ × 24¹⁵⁄₁₆″).

Paul Mellon Collection, ©1998 Board of Trustees, National Gallery of Art, Washington, D.C.

Black Hawk, Prominent Sauk Chief (detail) (1832) by George Catlin. Oil on canvas (29″ × 24″).

National Museum of American Art, Washington, D.C. Gift of Mrs. Joseph Harrison, Jr. Courtesy Art Resource, NY.

Mississippi, including Saukenuk,[2] our ancient village, where all of us were born, raised, lived, hunted, fished, and loved, and near which are our corn lands, which have yielded abundant harvests for a hundred winters, and where sleep the bones of our sacred dead, and around which cluster our fondest recollections of heroism and noble deeds of charity done by our fathers, who were Sauks, not only in name, but in courage and action. I thank the Great Spirit for making me a Sauk, and the son of a great Sauk chief, and a lineal descendant of Nanamakee, the founder of our nation.

The Great Spirit is the friend and protector of the Sauks, and has accompanied me as your War Chief upon the warpath against our enemies, and has given me skill to direct and you the courage to achieve a hundred victories over our enemies

2. **Saukenuk:** a village of the Sauk, located where the Rock River joins the Mississippi; present-day site of Rock Island, Illinois.

upon the warpath. . . . The Great Spirit created this country for the use and benefit of his red children, and placed them in full possession of it, and we were happy and contented. Why did he send the palefaces across the great ocean to take it from us? When they landed on our territory they were received as long-absent brothers whom the Great Spirit had returned to us. Food and rest were freely given them by our fathers, who treated them all the more kindly on account of their weak and helpless condition. Had our fathers the desire, they could have crushed the intruders out of existence with the same ease we kill the bloodsucking mosquitoes. Little did our fathers then think they were taking to their bosoms, and warming them to life, a lot of torpid, half-frozen, and starving vipers, which in a few winters would fix their deadly fangs upon the very bosoms that had nursed and cared for them when they needed help.

—Black Hawk

SPOTLIGHT ON 447

D Appreciating Language
Analogies
❓ How does the comparison of settlers to "bloodsucking mosquitoes" move Black Hawk's people to fight? [It dehumanizes the enemy, making them seem insignificant and bothersome. The analogy is designed to persuade Black Hawk's listeners that they could squash the enemy the way one swats a mosquito.]

E Elements of Literature
Figures of Speech
❓ Why does Black Hawk compare the whites to "torpid, half-frozen, and starving vipers"? [When the Europeans first settled in the New World, they needed the help of Native Americans to survive. The Native Americans gave that help, only to be bitten when the settlers grew strong.] What effect does this metaphor create? [The metaphor conveys Black Hawk's feeling of betrayal.]

Getting Students Involved

Conducting On-line Research
According to the current United States Census, there are 1,959,234 Native Americans and Native Alaskans living in the United States. (These figures reflect self-identification and are not based on any designation by federal or state government.) In October of 1993, the US Bureau of Indian Affairs published the *Federal Register,* a comprehensive listing of the 552 recognized Indian entities, tribes, bands, villages, groups, and pueblos in America. The states with the largest Native

American, Aleut, and Eskimo (Inuit) populations are Oklahoma (252,420), California (242,164), and Arizona (203,527). If current trends continue, the US will have 393.9 million people in 2050—forty-nine percent more than the population today. Nonetheless, the number of Native Americans (now at slightly under one percent of the population) is expected to increase only slightly

Activity
The Census Bureau home page, http://www.census.gov, is one of the "hottest" on the Web; on average, it gets 145,000 "hits" per day— more than 6,000 per hour, 100 per minute! Have students access this site to gather more data about Native Americans. Students can research a local tribe or do a comparative study. Encourage students to graph their findings.

In 1863, a group of Nez Percé led by Chief Joseph's father refused to sign a treaty that would send them to a reservation. In 1871, the old chief, now dying, urged his son, "You must stop your ears whenever you are asked to sign a treaty selling your home. . . . This country holds your father's body. Never sell the bones of your father and mother." After their 1877 flight, only 431 people of some 700 remained, mostly women and children. On October 5 of that year, Chief Joseph gave this speech of surrender to General Oliver O. Howard and Colonel Nelson A. Miles.

B **Elements of Literature**

Tone

❓ What word is repeated in this passage? [*dead*] How does this word affect the tone of the speech? [The word starkly names the tragedy befalling the tribe and establishes a mournful tone.]

C **Reading Skills and Strategies**

Drawing Conclusions

❓ After he and his people had fought so bravely, why do you think Chief Joseph surrendered? [Sample responses: He saw his people suffering and knew that they could not survive much longer; he knew that he and his people could never return to the life they had enjoyed in the past.]

Resources 🎧━━━━━

Listening
Audio CD Library
"I Will Fight No More Forever"
• Disc 11, Track 6

Chief Joseph

Born in what is now Oregon, Chief Joseph (c. 1840–1904) has become a symbol of the heroic fighting spirit of his people, the Nez Percé. In battles during 1877, he fought thirteen different U.S. military commands, defeating almost all of them. He then made a masterful one-thousand–mile retreat toward Canada through the mountainous country of the Pacific Northwest. His caravan, which included women and children, made it to within thirty miles of the border before exhaustion and near starvation forced them to surrender after eleven weeks of flight. Chief Joseph delivered the following speech upon his surrender to the U.S. Army in October 1877. He spent most of the rest of his life on a reservation in the present-day state of Washington.

"I Will Fight No More Forever"

Tell General Howard[1] I know his heart. What he told me before, I have in my heart. I am tired of fighting. Our chiefs are killed. Looking Glass[2] is dead. Toohoolhoolzote[3] is dead. The old men are all dead. It is the young men who say yes and no. He who led on the young men is dead. It is cold and we have no blankets. The little children are freezing to death. My people, some of them, have run away to the hills and have no blankets, no food; no one knows where they are—perhaps freezing to death. I want to have time to look for my children and see how many I can find. Maybe I shall find them among the dead. Hear me, my chiefs. I am tired; my heart is sick and sad. From where the sun now stands I will fight no more forever.

—Chief Joseph

1. **General Howard:** Oliver Otis Howard (1830–1909), Civil War general and founder of Howard University in Washington, D.C. (1867). Howard was the military commander who presented the Nez Percé with an ultimatum to give up their land in Idaho and move to a reservation.
2. **Looking Glass** (c. 1823–1877): ally of Chief Joseph. Looking Glass was killed in battle on the day this speech was delivered.
3. **Toohoolhoolzote** (c. 1810–1877): Nez Percé shaman and chief who argued against giving up Nez Percé lands.

Crossing the Curriculum

History

After his surrender, Chief Joseph said, "General Miles had promised that we might return to our country with what stock we had left. I thought we could start again. I believed General Miles, or I would never have surrendered." Chief Joseph was forced to live the rest of his life on the Colville Reservation in Washington State and died there, still longing for his homeland. Invite students to research Chief Joseph's speeches after the surrender.

Assessing Learning

Check Test: Questions and Answers

1. How were the Sauk regarded by others, according to Black Hawk? [They were respected for their courage and hospitality.]

2. How does Black Hawk want his people to respond to the wrongs committed against them? [He wants them to go to war.]

3. What changes does Black Hawk observe in his people? [They have become a divided nation and have lost their courage.]

4. Why does Chief Joseph stop fighting? [He is tired of war; his people are dead, dying, or lost, without food, shelter, or warm clothing.]

From Innocence to Experience

Theme

Coming of Age *America endured the crucible of the Civil War, and, with the country's awakening, realism was established as the dominant literary mode. Some writers now began to examine their characters with the detachment of a scientist looking at a specimen under a microscope. Others, like Crane, adopted the methods of impressionistic painters.*

Reading the Anthology

Reaching Struggling Readers

The *Reading Skills and Strategies: Reaching Struggling Readers* binder provides materials coordinated with the Pupil's Edition (see the Collection Planner, p. T448B) to help students who have difficulty reading and comprehending text, or students who are reluctant readers. The binder for eleventh grade is organized around ten individual skill areas and offers the following options:

- **MiniRead** MiniReads are short, easy texts that give students a chance to practice a particular skill and strategy before reading selections in the Pupil's Edition. Each MiniRead Skill Lesson can be taught independently or used in conjunction with a Selection Skill Lesson.

- **Selection Skill Lessons** Selection Skill Lessons allow students to apply skills introduced in the MiniReads. Each Selection Skill Lesson provides reading instruction and practice specific to a particular piece of literature in the Pupil's Edition.

Reading Beyond the Anthology

Read On

At the end of the Rise of Realism collections, the grade eleven book includes an annotated bibliography of books suitable for extended reading. To preview the Read On for the Rise of Realism period, please turn to p. T511.

HRW Library

The *HRW Library* offers novels, plays, and short-story collections for extended reading. A Study Guide provides teaching suggestions and worksheets. For Collection 10, the following titles are recommended.

THE RED BADGE OF COURAGE
Stephen Crane
Considered the definitive novel about the Civil War, this antiwar story is told with an impressionistic technique—through the sensations of a young soldier at the battle of Chancellorsville.

THE CALL OF THE WILD
Jack London
This naturalistic novel set in the Yukon explores the conflicts between civilization and primitive nature. London wants us to recognize "what a puppet thing life is."

Collection 10 From Innocence to Experience

Resources for this Collection

Note: All resources for this collection are available for preview on the *One-Stop Planner CD-ROM 2 with Test Generator.* All worksheets and blackline masters may be printed from the CD-ROM.

Internet Resources
go.hrw.com LE0 11-10

Collection Planner

Selection or Feature	Reading and Literary Skills	Vocabulary, Language, and Grammar
from **Life on the Mississippi** (p. 452) Mark Twain **Spotlight On: Mark Twain's Humor** (p. 465)	• *Graphic Organizers for Active Reading,* Worksheet p. 45 • *Literary Elements:* Transparency 14 Worksheet p. 43	• *Words to Own,* Worksheet p. 28 • *Grammar and Language Links:* Adjective Clauses, Worksheet p. 37 • *Language Workshop CD-ROM,* Types of Subordinate Clauses • *Daily Oral Grammar,* Transparency 30
An Occurrence at Owl Creek Bridge (p. 467) Ambrose Bierce **Spotlight On: Voices from the Civil War** (p. 476) Theodore Upson, Walt Whitman, Major Sullivan Ballou, Alexander Hunter, Abraham Lincoln, Susie King Taylor, Frederick Douglass, Mary Chesnut, and Seth M. Flint	• *Graphic Organizers for Active Reading,* Worksheet p. 46 • *Literary Elements:* Transparency 15 Worksheet p. 46	• *Words to Own,* Worksheet p. 30 • *Grammar and Language Links:* Misplaced and Dangling Modifiers, Worksheet p. 39 • *Language Workshop CD-ROM,* Misplaced or Dangling Modifiers • *Daily Oral Grammar,* Transparency 31
A Mystery of Heroism (p. 485) Stephen Crane **War Is Kind** (p. 494) Stephen Crane	• *Graphic Organizers for Active Reading,* Worksheet p. 47	• *Words to Own,* Worksheet p. 31 • *Grammar and Language Links:* Adverb Clauses, Worksheet p. 41 • *Language Workshop CD-ROM,* Types of Subordinate Clauses • *Daily Oral Grammar,* Transparency 32
To Build a Fire (p. 496) Jack London **Connections: Cold Kills: Hypothermia** (p. 508) Paul G. Gill, Jr., M.D.	• *Reading Skills and Strategies: Reaching Struggling Readers* • MiniRead Skill Lesson, p. 133 • Selection Skill Lesson, p. 139 • *Graphic Organizers for Active Reading,* Worksheet p. 48 • *Literary Elements:* Transparency 16 Worksheet p. 49	• *Words to Own,* Worksheet p. 32 • *Grammar and Language Links:* MLA Documentation, Worksheet p. 43 • *Language Workshop CD-ROM,* Research Paper • *Daily Oral Grammar,* Transparency 33
The American Language: American Dialects (p. 512) Gary Q. Arpin		
Writer's Workshop: Research Paper (p. 515)		
Language Workshop: Adverb and Adjective Clauses (p. 519)		• *Workshop Resources,* p. 55 • *Language Workshop CD-ROM,* Adverb Clauses and Adjective Clauses
Learning for Life: Monitoring the Media (p. 521)		

Other Resources for this Collection

- *Cross-Curricular Activities,* p. 10
- *Portfolio Management System,* Introduction to Portfolio Assessment, p. 1
- *Formal Assessment:* Literary Period Test, p. 104
- *Test Generator,* Collection Test

Writing	Listening and Speaking Viewing and Representing	Assessment
• *Portfolio Management System,* Rubrics for Choices, p. 144	• *Audio CD Library,* Disc 12, Track 2 • *Portfolio Management System,* Rubrics for Choices, p. 144	• *Formal Assessment,* Selection Test, p. 92 • *Test Generator (One-Stop Planner CD-ROM)*
• *Portfolio Management System,* Rubrics for Choices, p. 146	• *Audio CD Library,* Disc 12, Track 3, and Disc 13, Track 2 • *Portfolio Management System,* Rubrics for Choices, p. 146	• *Formal Assessment,* Selection Test, p. 94 • *Test Generator (One-Stop Planner CD-ROM)* • *Preparation for College Admission Exams,* p. 33
• *Portfolio Management System,* Rubrics for Choices, p. 147	• *Audio CD Library,* Disc 13, Tracks 3, 4 • *Viewing and Representing:* Fine Art Transparency 10 Worksheet p. 40 • *Portfolio Management System,* Rubrics for Choices, p. 147	• *Formal Assessment,* Selection Test, p. 96 • *Test Generator (One-Stop Planner CD-ROM)*
• *Portfolio Management System,* Rubrics for Choices, p. 148	• *Audio CD Library,* Disc 13, Track 5 • *Portfolio Management System,* Rubrics for Choices, p. 148	• *Formal Assessment,* Selection Test, p. 98 • *Test Generator (One-Stop Planner CD-ROM)* • *Preparation for College Admission Exams,* p. 35
		• *Formal Assessment,* The American Language Test, p. 100
• *Workshop Resources,* p. 21 • *Writer's Workshop 2 CD-ROM,* Informative Report	• *Viewing and Representing,* HRW Multimedia Presentation Maker	• *Portfolio Management System* • Prewriting, p. 150 • Peer Editing, p. 151 • Assessment Rubric, p. 152
		• *Portfolio Management System,* Rubrics, p. 153

 Transparency    CD-ROM    Video    Audio CD

Collection Planner

Skills Focus

Skills Focus

Selection or Feature	Reading Skills and Strategies	Elements of Literature and Language	Writing	Listening and Speaking	Viewing and Representing
from **Life on the Mississippi** (p. 452) Mark Twain	Identify Comic Devices, p. 463	Extended Metaphor, pp. 452, 463 Hyperbole, p. 463 Understatement, p. 463 Tall Tale, p. 463 Anecdote, p. 465 Proverbs, p. 465	Develop a Research Topic, p. 464 Write an Essay Analyzing Twain's Humor, p. 464 Write Captions to Accompany Photographs and Art, p. 464 Research and Write a Magazine Article, p. 464	Prepare and Perform an Oral Reading of Twain's Work, p. 464	Identify Art Work that Expresses a Theme, p. 464
An Occurrence at Owl Creek Bridge (p. 467) Ambrose Bierce	Clarify Responses to a Text, p. 467 List Events in Chronological Order, p. 474 Summarize, p. 474	Point of View, pp. 467, 474 • Omniscient • Objective • Third-Person Limited Chronology, p. 474 Theme, p. 474	Identify Sources of Information, p. 474 Write a Memorandum Proposing a Film Adaptation, p. 474 Write a Narrative, p. 474		
Reading Skills and Strategies: Affixes—The Long and Short of It (p. 475)		Affixes, p. 475 Prefixes, p. 475 Base or Root Word, p. 475 Suffixes, p. 475 Inflectional Suffixes, p. 475 Derivational Suffixes, p. 475			Make an Affix-Analysis Chart, p. 475
A Mystery of Heroism (p. 485) Stephen Crane		Naturalism, p. 484 Situational Irony, pp. 485, 493 Image, p. 493 Personify, p. 493 Motive, p. 493 Ambiguity, p. 493	Conduct and Summarize a Survey, p. 494 Write an Essay Summarizing Crane's Attitude Toward War, p. 494 Write a Poem Based on One of Crane's Themes, p. 494		
To Build a Fire (p. 496) Jack London	Analyze Text Structures: Cause and Effect, p. 496 Summarize a Plot Using a Cause-Effect String, p. 509	Naturalism, pp. 496, 509 Foreshadowing, p. 509 Sound Effects, p. 510 Conflict, p. 510 Dialogue, p. 510	Identify the Impact of Audience on Topic Development, p. 510 Research and Create a Survival Manual, p. 510 Write a Survival Story, p. 510 Write an Essay Identifying the Most Important Conflict in the Story, p. 510	Create and Role-Play a Dialogue, p. 510 Create a Recording Using Sound Effects and Music, p. 510	Illustrate a Survival Manual, p. 510
The American Language: American Dialects (p. 512) Gary Q. Arpin		Dialects, p. 513 Dialect Regions, p. 514	Identify Regional Dialects, p. 514		
Writer's Workshop: Research Paper (p. 515)			Write a Research Paper on a Factual Topic, pp. 515–518 Document Sources, p. 518		
Language Workshop: Adverb and Adjective Clauses (p. 519)		Adverb and Adjective Clauses, p. 519 Restrictive and Non-restrictive Clauses, p. 519	Combine Sentences Using Adverb and Adjective Clauses, p. 519		
Reading for Life: Reading a College Guide (p. 520)	Purpose, p. 520 Criteria, p. 520 Adjust Purpose and Priorities, p. 520				
Learning for Life: Monitoring the Media (p. 521)				Participate in a Panel Discussion, p. 521 Interview a Newscaster or Journalist, p. 521	Compare and Contrast Television and Print Media Coverage, p. 521 Rate the Media, p. 521

Skills Focus

Collection 10

FROM INNOCENCE TO EXPERIENCE

Twain

Bierce

Voices from the Civil War

Crane

London

OBJECTIVES

1. Read literature of the Civil War and Postwar period on the theme "From Innocence to Experience"
2. Interpret literary elements used in the literature
3. Apply a variety of reading strategies to the literature including using affixes to decode words
4. Respond to the literature in a variety of modes
5. Learn and use new words

Shiloh

A Requiem

(April, 1862)

Skimming lightly, wheeling still,
    The swallows fly low
Over the field in clouded days,
    The forest-field of Shiloh—
Over the field where April rain
Solaced the parched ones stretched in pain
Through the pause of night
That followed the Sunday fight
    Around the church of Shiloh—
The church so lone, the log-built one,
That echoed to many a parting groan
    And natural prayer
    Of dying foemen mingled there—
Foemen at morn, but friends at eve—
    Fame or country least their care:
(What like a bullet can undeceive!)
    But now they lie low,
While over them the swallows skim,
    And all is hushed at Shiloh.

—Herman Melville (1819–1891)

Shiloh National Battlefield, Tennessee.

Responding to the Poem

With a deceptive gentleness, Melville's poem mourns the physical, moral, and spiritual cost of war. Ask students what, according to the poem, is gained by the experience of battle. [Possible responses: Participants as well as bystanders may come to reflect on their common humanity or to appreciate the solace and beauty of nature. The experience of battle also teaches that the wartime journey from innocence to experience is brutal, cruel, and far from romantic.]

RESPONDING TO THE ART

Union troops were encamped around the small log building that was Shiloh Church in Pittsburg Landing, Tennessee. The battle of Shiloh was one of the bloodiest of the war. Of 42,000 Union troops, 13,000 were casualties. The Confederates counted 10,000 casualties out of 40,000 men.
Activity. Ask students how they think the photograph reflects the theme of the collection. [Possible response: The pastoral, peaceful scene belies the experience of the terrible battle fought there.]

Writing Focus: Research Paper

The following **Work in Progress** assignments in this collection build to a culminating **Writer's Workshop** at the end of Collection 10.

- Life on the Mississippi
- An Occurrence at Owl Creek Bridge
- A Mystery of Heroism
- To Build a Fire

Take notes on a place to research (p. 464)
List topics for research suggested by story (p. 474)
Survey people about attitudes (p. 494)
Note ways of presenting research to different audiences (p. 510)

Writer's Workshop: Expository Writing / Research Paper (p. 515)

Planning

Mark Twain

(1835–1910)

Mark Twain is the most celebrated humorist in American history. His ability to make us laugh has contributed to the singular popularity of his books, not just in Twain's own time but in following generations. Since humor is by nature very difficult to translate from language to language, it is even more surprising to find that Twain's appeal has traveled throughout the world.

The great humorist is also, ironically, our great realist. Behind the backwoods humor—especially in his novel *Adventures of Huckleberry Finn*—is a revelation of the illusions that exist in American life. Huck's journey on a raft with the escaped slave Jim is not a "hymn to boyhood." It is a dramatization of the grim realities of a slaveholding society.

Although Twain became remarkably successful, his later life was shadowed by disappointment and tragedy, and as he grew older he turned into a bitter man. He once told his friend William Dean Howells, the influential novelist and editor of *The Atlantic Monthly,* "Everyone is a moon and has a dark side which he never shows to anybody."

"Mark Twain!"

Twain was born Samuel Langhorne Clemens in the backwoods of Missouri. His father, John Clemens, a bright, ambitious, but impractical Virginian, had married Jane Lampton, a witty, dynamic woman who was also a great beauty. When John's store failed in 1839, he moved his hopes and his family to Hannibal, Missouri—the Mississippi River town that Sam, writing as Mark Twain, would later fashion into the setting of the most renowned boyhood in American literature, that of Tom Sawyer.

Sam's own carefree boyhood ended at twelve when his father died. Helping to support his mother and sister, he went to work setting type and editing copy for the newspaper started by his older brother Orion. At eighteen, Sam set

Mark Twain (1935) by Frank Edwin Larson (1895–1991). Oil on canvas (48″ × 36″).

National Portrait Gallery, Smithsonian Institution. Gift of the artist. Courtesy Art Resource, NY.

out on his own. Over the next fifteen years, he worked as a printer in various towns from Missouri to the East Coast. Smitten by a love for the magical steamboats that plied the Mississippi, he even apprenticed himself for a time to the greatest of the steamboat pilots, Horace Bixby. From Bixby, Sam Clemens learned the bends and shallows of the great river from Minnesota to the Louisiana delta. It was the leadsman's cry of "Mark twain!"—announcing a water depth of two fathoms (twelve feet)—that provided him with his celebrated pen name.

A Gold Mine of Humor

For a short time during the Civil War, Twain was a soldier with a company of Confederate irregulars. (He said he learned more about retreating than fighting.) But he soon abandoned the military life for that of a gold prospector in Nevada. While he found little gold there, he did discover the rich mine of storytelling within himself. With his Missouri drawl and relaxed manner, Twain captivated audiences. His secret lay in his deft use of a faintly pompous platform

T450

manner: In pretending not to recognize the coarseness or absurdity of his material, Twain's deadpan attitude added to his material's hilarity.

Twain soon turned his comic voice to prose, working as a journalist between 1862 and 1871. In 1865, he achieved wide recognition as a humorist with the publication of his hilarious version of an old tall tale, "The Celebrated Jumping Frog of Calaveras County." Four years later, Twain's dispatches from a Mediterranean tour were published as a book titled *The Innocents Abroad*. This satirical travelogue poked fun at the traditional American pilgrimage to the monuments of European civilization. Over five thousand copies were sold in the first month, and more than thirty-one thousand within the year. Twain had launched a prosperous literary career.

An American Masterpiece

At thirty-five, with a raffish, barroom air about him, Twain was a dubious candidate for marriage, but he courted Olivia Langdon, the daughter of an affluent family from Elmira, New York. She was a delicate, proper woman, but Twain overcame all resistance, and, in 1870, Livy's father gave the couple his consent and a lavish wedding. Twain embarked on a marriage of unceasing devotion.

In 1871, Twain moved to Hartford, Connecticut, where he built an enormous home that is still visited today by thousands of tourists. The next year he published *Roughing It*, which drew on his experiences as a tenderfoot in the West. Then William Dean Howells invited Twain to do a series for *The Atlantic Monthly* about his days as a riverboat pilot. Those reminiscences eventually were expanded into the book *Life on the Mississippi* (1883).

By the mid-1870s, Twain was also at work on *The Adventures of Tom Sawyer* (1876). This celebration of boyhood absorbed him but presented difficulties of voice and point of view. Twain could not be sure if he was writing a book for children or for adults. Nevertheless, in writing the book, he made an imaginative return to the Hannibal of his childhood and succeeded in transforming it into a compelling myth.

In *Adventures of Huckleberry Finn* (1884), Twain found the voice he had been seeking. Through Huck's natural, slangy, first-person narration, Twain forged a new relation between expression and content, causing a revolution in American literature. As Ernest Hemingway (page 650), speaking through a fictional character, later put it, "All modern American literature comes from one book by Mark Twain called *Huckleberry Finn*." T. S. Eliot (page 661), a fellow Missourian, added that Twain's was "a new way of writing . . . a literary language based on American colloquial speech."

> "**A**ll modern American literature comes from one book by Mark Twain. . . ."

Loss and Legacy

Twain was never able to duplicate the success of *Huckleberry Finn,* but he continued to produce popular books, including *A Connecticut Yankee in King Arthur's Court* (1889) and *Pudd'nhead Wilson* (1894). Twain's later years were marked by financial and professional disappointment as well as personal tragedy. His fascination with business and getting ahead financially, so typical of the new middle class, led him to invest disastrously in the Paige typesetting machine. The economic panic of 1893 bankrupted him.

Then illness overtook the close-knit Clemens family. Suzy, Twain's eldest daughter, died of meningitis in 1896. His wife, a permanent invalid during her last years, died in 1904. In a final blow, Jean, his youngest daughter, died in an epileptic seizure in 1909. "Possibly," said Twain after Jean's death, "I know now what the soldier feels when a bullet crashes through his heart." Four months later, he, too, was dead.

As loss followed loss, and as the whole country seemed to lose its vitality and become more complex, Twain had turned into an obsessive, embittered old man. In his final years, the subject matter of his work was his own disillusionment on a grand scale; the great comic writer appeared to be at war not only with the human race, but also with the God who had created it.

MARK TWAIN 451

BROWSING IN THE FILES

About the Author. Twain's work— audacious, original, and inspired by the spirit of both the old South and the freewheeling West—marked the end of the domination of American literature by New England writers. In doing so, it paved the way for the strong literary traditions of the West and, especially, the South—which would profoundly affect American literature in the twentieth century.

Writers on Writing. Twain's approach to storytelling was based on American oral traditions. He said, "I do not claim that I can tell a story as it ought to be told. I only claim to know how a story ought to be told, for I have been almost daily in the company of the most expert story-tellers for many years. . . . The humorous story is told gravely; the teller does his best to conceal the fact that he even dimly suspects that there is anything funny about it."

RESPONDING TO THE ART

The New England portraitist and landscape painter **Frank Edwin Larson** (1895–1991) composed this image of Mark Twain in 1935, based on photographs taken during the early 1900s by Frederick Bradley.

Activity. Have students quick-write their first impression of Twain, noting what his posture, expression, and appearance suggest about his character. [Possible answer: Twain appears serious, even stern, with the air of a statesman.]

Professional Notes

Literary Genres: The Memoir

Life on the Mississippi is a somewhat fictionalized memoir, a genre of literature little discussed in Twain's time and generally dismissed as minor history or biography. But because memoirs are written as firsthand history, they may, in fact, be more honest and accurate portrayals of life as it was than history written from secondhand research. In *Life on the Mississippi*, Twain presents a slice of a life long-lost. The memoir has become a highly popular genre, but today's versions are often filled with far more confessional revelations than Twain's gentle portrait of life on the river. As a result, some critics have dubbed contemporary memoirs "bibliotherapy."

T451

Summary ▪▪

Twain's humorous description of his apprenticeship piloting a Mississippi steamboat evokes the idiosyncrasies of the steamboat captains and the river they navigate. As he attempts to learn the river's exact shape, Twain is distressed to discover that the river constantly changes and that he must master a seemingly infinite number of details. Steering the ship alone, he fears he is about to run aground on a reef, but the reef turns out to be an illusion created by the wind. Ultimately, the young apprentice becomes a confident, competent pilot but feels a pang of grief because the river has lost its mystery and charm.

Background

In order to understand Twain's yearning to become a skilled riverboat pilot, students must understand that riverboats were a vital method of transportation before airplanes and trucks. The Mississippi River is the third-largest river in the world and still important to the transportation of industrial products. In the 1800s, it was crucial to the economy of half the country. Riverside plantations had private docks to facilitate the shipping of crops; towns prospered wherever goods were stored and steamboats serviced. During the Civil War, Union General Ulysses S. Grant initiated the siege of Vicksburg (in Mississippi) in order to gain control of this vital waterway.

Before You Read

FROM LIFE ON THE MISSISSIPPI

Make the Connection

Losing Its Luster
Sometimes, gaining something we've looked forward to isn't half as pleasurable as the anticipation of getting it. The person whose biggest wish is to be a movie actor might imagine all the glamorous trappings of that profession, but the reality of being an actor has more to do with hard work, discipline, and daily repetition than it does with adulation and fame. Experience brings its own rewards, but it can also make things seem too ordinary and familiar—lacking mystery and magic.

Quickwrite

Think about something you wished for—a skill or ability, or perhaps an honor or award—and then successfully gained. Were you in any way disappointed after achieving your goal? Write a few sentences describing how you felt before and after your wish came true.

Elements of Literature

Extended Metaphor
An **extended metaphor** is a **figure of speech** that makes a comparison between two unlike things and extends the comparison as far as the writer wants to take it. Much of Twain's humor comes from the surprise of two very unlike things joined to create an extended—and hilarious—comic metaphor.

> An **extended metaphor** is a figure of speech that makes a comparison between two unlike things and extends the comparison as far as the writer wants to take it.
>
> For more on Extended Metaphor, see page 188 and the Handbook of Literary Terms.

Background

As a youth, Twain was so fascinated by riverboats that he persuaded Horace Bixby, the locally famous pilot of the *Paul Jones,* to teach him how to navigate the river between New Orleans and St. Louis (a distance of about seven hundred miles) for five hundred dollars. Twain was not alone in his dream; every boy along the Mississippi, black or white, yearned to work on a steamboat. It didn't matter whether the job was clerk, engineer, mate, or pilot; life on the river meant adventure. "Once a day a cheap, gaudy packet [boat] arrived upward from St. Louis," Twain wrote, "and another downward from Keokuk. Before these events, the day was glorious with expectancy; after them, the day was a dead and empty thing."

Twain did succeed in becoming a steamboat pilot. These two chapters from *Life on the Mississippi* describe a time when he was still an apprentice, or "cub," pilot being trained by Horace Bixby.

Champions of the Mississippi by Currier & Ives. Lithograph.
Museum of the City of New York.
Scala/Art Resource, NY.

Preteaching Vocabulary

Words to Own

Have students study the Words to Own and their definitions listed at the bottom of the selection pages. Then, have them find a partner to play "Guess My Word." The first player gives his or her partner a synonym for the word, and the partner has to name the word. After they have used all the words, have partners change roles and play again. Then, have them match the numbered words at right with their synonyms.

1. serenely [g]	a. endless
2. complacency [i]	b. kindness
3. blandly [c]	c. mildly
4. interminable [a]	d. gloomy
5. subside [h]	e. lifeless
6. benevolence [b]	f. empty
7. misgivings [j]	g. calmly
8. inanimate [e]	h. diminish
9. void [f]	i. self-satisfaction
10. somber [d]	j. doubts

from Life on the Mississippi

Mark Twain

Perplexing Lessons

At the end of what seemed a tedious while, I had managed to pack my head full of islands, towns, bars, "points," and bends;[1] and a curiously <u>inanimate</u> mass of lumber it was, too. However, inasmuch as I could shut my eyes and reel off a **Ⓐ** good long string of these names without leaving out more than ten miles of river in every fifty, I began to feel that I could take a boat down to New Orleans if I could make her skip those little gaps. But of course my <u>complacency</u> could hardly **Ⓑ** get start enough to lift my nose a trifle into the air,

1. **islands . . . bends:** geographic features used in river navigation. Each numbered point was a landmark on a curve or bend in the river.

WORDS TO OWN

inanimate (in·an′ə·mit) *adj.*: lifeless.
complacency (kəm·plā′sən·sē) *n.*: self-satisfaction.

MARK TWAIN 453

Ⓐ Literary Connections
Twain's Notetaking
In an earlier section of his memoir, Twain describes the notes he took during his apprenticeship: "I had a notebook that fairly bristled with the names of towns, 'points,' bars, islands, bends, reaches, etc. but the information was to be found only in the notebook—none of it was in my head." At this point in the memoir, it *is* in his head.

Ⓑ Reading Skills and Strategies
Identifying Comic Devices
❓ How does the speaker create humor in this passage? [Possible answers: He uses a self-mocking tone coupled with sophisticated and precise diction; he uses a comic metaphor to describe the contents of his brain: "Inanimate mass of lumber." Note that this helps readers visualize the persona Twain has created: a cocky youth nonetheless well aware of his ignorance.]

RESPONDING TO THE ART
Nathaniel Currier (1813–1888) and **James Ives** (1824–1895) were nineteenth-century lithographers whose firm produced immensely popular illustrations of everything from news events and occupational scenes (such as these riverboats in action) to sentimental pictures of family life. Lithography was a sophisticated method of ink printing and, before photography, was the most common way to reproduce images. **Activity.** Have students make a list of adjectives that describe the impression the lithograph gives of riverboats. [Possible responses: majestic, colorful, powerful, patriotic, dangerous—note the fires.]

Reaching All Students

Struggling Readers
You can help students to make inferences as they read by having them use an It Says . . . I Say chart to answer three of the Reading Check questions and two of the Shaping Interpretations questions on p. 463. For detailed instructions on how to apply this strategy, see the *Reading Strategies Handbook,* p. 25 in the *Reading Skills and Strategies* binder.

English Language Learners
Twain's use of long sentences, elevated diction, and nautical terms may pose difficulties. Since Twain is essentially an oral storyteller, invite pairs of students to take turns reading passages aloud, using context clues and a dictionary to help them understand unfamiliar words.

Advanced Learners
Challenge students to read either William Shakespeare's Sonnet XVIII, "Shall I compare thee to a summer's day," or Emily Dickinson's poem "Because I could not stop for Death" (p. 391). Have students compare and contrast the use of the extended metaphors in the poem with those in the Twain excerpt, particularly the metaphor of the book on p. 461. Which is more effective? Why?

A Cultural Connections

Apprenticeship

Many tradespeople, such as electricians, plumbers, and mechanics, require apprenticeships as part of their training. An age-old strategy for passing on knowledge, apprenticeships provide direct hands-on experience to novices that a manual or a standardized test could never provide. Students can compare Twain's experiences as an apprentice with Ben Franklin's experiences as described in his *Autobiography* (p. 86).

B Elements of Literature

Extended Metaphor

? How does Twain create humor with this extended metaphor? [Possible response: The comparison of his volatile chief to a gun that continues firing until it is empty and useless is a humorous way of saying that Bixby's bark is worse than his bite.]

C Critical Thinking

Making Judgments

? Do you believe Bixby's assertion that Twain must learn the river better than he knows his own house, or is Bixby exaggerating? Explain. [Students should see that Bixby is deadly serious; lives and property depended on a riverboat pilot's knowledge of the Mississippi and its banks.]

D Reading Skills and Strategies

Identifying Comic Devices

? What comic device is Twain using here? [He is using a hyperbolic metaphor that compares the acquisition of knowledge to the acquisition of heavy cargo (such as in a steamboat).]

E Reading Skills and Strategies

Connecting with the Text

? What does Bixby mean in this passage? [Possible response: Bixby means that Twain must internalize the shape of the river so he can navigate from memory with absolute certainty—and ignore the variable impressions of his senses.] How might this strategy be seen as a metaphor for an approach to life in general? [Possible answer: It might be seen as a metaphor for steadfastly following a personal goal or doing what you know is right—in spite of confusing or negative feedback.]

A before Mr. Bixby would think of something to fetch it down again. One day he turned on me suddenly with this settler[2]—

"What is the shape of Walnut Bend?"

He might as well have asked me my grandmother's opinion of protoplasm.[3] I reflected respectfully, and then said I didn't know it had any particular shape. My gunpowdery chief went off with a bang, of course, and then went on loading and firing until he was out of adjectives.

B I had learned long ago that he only carried just so many rounds of ammunition, and was sure to subside into a very placable and even remorseful old smoothbore[4] as soon as they were all gone. That word "old" is merely affectionate; he was not more than thirty-four. I waited. By and by he said—

"My boy, you've got to know the *shape* of the river perfectly. It is all there is left to steer by on a very dark night. Everything else is blotted out and gone. But mind you, it hasn't the same shape in the night that it has in the daytime."

"How on earth am I ever going to learn it, then?"

"How do you follow a hall at home in the dark? Because you know the shape of it. You can't see it."

C "Do you mean to say that I've got to know all the million trifling variations of shape in the banks of this interminable river as well as I know the shape of the front hall at home?"

"On my honor, you've got to know them *better* than any man ever did know the shapes of the halls in his own house."

"I wish I was dead!"

"Now I don't want to discourage you, but"—

"Well, pile it on me; I might as well have it now as another time."

"You see, this has got to be learned; there isn't any getting around it. A clear starlight night throws such heavy shadows that if you didn't know the

---

"Have I got to learn the shape of the river according to all these five hundred thousand different ways? If I tried to carry all that cargo in my head it would make me stoop-shouldered."

---

shape of a shore perfectly you would claw away from every bunch of timber, because you would take the black shadow of it for a solid cape;[5] and you see you would be getting scared to death every fifteen minutes by the watch.[6] You would be fifty yards from shore all the time when you ought to be within fifty feet of it. You can't see a snag[7] in one of those shadows, but you know exactly where it is, and the shape of the river tells you when you are coming to it. Then there's your pitch-dark night; the river is a very different shape on a pitch-dark night from what it is on a starlight night. All shores seem to be straight lines, then, and mighty dim ones, too; and you'd *run* them for straight lines only you know better. You boldly drive your boat right into what seems to be a solid, straight wall (you knowing very well that in reality there is a curve there), and that wall falls back and makes way for you. Then there's your gray mist. You take a night when there's one of these grisly, drizzly, gray mists, and then there isn't *any* particular shape to a shore. A gray mist would tangle the head of the oldest man that ever lived. Well, then, different kinds of *moonlight* change the shape of the river in different ways. You see"—

D "Oh, don't say anymore, please! Have I got to learn the shape of the river according to all these five hundred thousand different ways? If I tried to carry all that cargo in my head it would make me stoop-shouldered."

E "*No!* you only learn *the* shape of the river; and you learn it with such absolute certainty that you can always steer by the shape that's *in your head*, and never mind the one that's before your eyes."

5. cape: land projecting into water.
6. by the watch: The workday on a steamboat was divided into three four-hour periods, or watches, every twelve hours: two watches for work and one off-watch for rest.
7. snag: tree trunk dangerous to navigation because it is partly or completely underwater.

WORDS TO OWN

subside (səb·sīd′) *v.*: to settle down.
interminable (in·tʉr′mi·nə·bəl) *adj.*: endless.

---

2. settler: colloquial for "something [such as Bixby's question] that does a person in."
3. protoplasm: living matter basic to all plant and animal cells.
4. smoothbore: gun with no grooves inside its barrel.

454 THE RISE OF REALISM: THE CIVIL WAR AND POSTWAR PERIOD

Getting Students Involved

Cooperative Learning

Role-Play. Have pairs of students role play a conversation between Twain and Mr. Bixby. Students can imagine that Twain did indeed run the riverboat aground or commit a relatively serious blunder. Students should focus on making sure the characters and their dialogue are consistent with Twain's narrative. After each group has rehearsed, students can present their skits to the class. Then, have all students discuss the insights gained by exploring the characters this way.

Comparing and Contrasting

Another Apprenticeship. Have students read chapters 28–30 of *Roughing It,* Twain's account of his experiences as a would-be miner in Nevada. Students can compare and contrast Twain's presentation of himself as an apprentice miner with his presentation of himself as an apprentice riverboat pilot and analyze his earlier observations about human nature and the world.

"Very well, I'll try it; but after I have learned it can I depend on it? Will it keep the same form and not go fooling around?"

Before Mr. Bixby could answer, Mr. W—— came in to take the watch, and he said—

"Bixby, you'll have to look out for President's Island and all that country clear away up above the Old Hen and Chickens. The banks are caving and the shape of the shores changing like everything. Why, you wouldn't know the point above 40.[8] You can go up inside the old sycamore snag,[9] now."

So that question was answered. Here were leagues[10] of shore changing shape. My spirits were down in the mud again. Two things seemed pretty apparent to me. One was, that in order to be a pilot a man had got to learn more than any one man ought to be allowed to know; and the other was, that he must learn it all over again in a different way every twenty-four hours.

That night we had the watch until twelve. Now it was an ancient river custom for the two pilots to chat a bit when the watch changed. While the relieving pilot put on his gloves and lit his cigar, his partner, the retiring pilot, would say something like this—

"I judge the upper bar is making down a little at Hale's Point; had quarter twain with the lower lead and mark twain[11] with the other."

"Yes, I thought it was making down a little, last trip. Meet any boats?"

"Met one abreast the head of 21,[12] but she was away over hugging the bar, and I couldn't make her out entirely. I took her for the 'Sunny South'—hadn't any skylights forward of the chimneys."

And so on. And as the relieving pilot took the wheel his partner[13] would mention that we were

---

8. **point above 40:** numbered navigational point on the river beyond the landmark numbered 40.
9. **inside . . . snag:** It may not be necessary but still can do no harm to explain that "inside" means between the snag and the shore. [Twain's note]
10. **leagues:** One league equals about 3 miles.
11. **quarter . . . mark twain:** Two fathoms. Quarter twain is 2¼ fathoms, [or] 13½ feet. Mark three is three fathoms. [Twain's note] These measures of water depth are calculated by using a lead weight attached to a rope. One fathom, or "mark one," equals 6 feet. Two fathoms, or "mark twain," equals 12 feet.
12. **abreast . . . 21:** beside landmark, or point, 21.
13. **partner:** "Partner" is technical for "the other pilot." [Twain's note]

---

in such and such a bend, and say we were abreast of such and such a man's woodyard or plantation. This was courtesy; I supposed it was *necessity.* But Mr. W—— came on watch full twelve minutes late on this particular night—a tremendous breach of etiquette; in fact, it is the unpardonable sin among pilots. So Mr. Bixby gave him no greeting whatever, but simply surrendered the wheel and marched out of the pilothouse without a word. I was appalled; it was a villainous night for blackness, we were in a particularly wide and blind part of the river, where there was no shape or substance to anything, and it seemed incredible that Mr. Bixby should have left that poor fellow to kill the boat trying to find out where he was. But I resolved that I would stand by him anyway. He should find that he was not wholly friendless. So I stood around, and waited to be asked where we were. But Mr. W—— plunged on serenely through the solid firmament of black cats that stood for an atmosphere, and never opened his mouth. Here is a proud devil, thought I; here is a limb of Satan that would rather send us all to destruction than put himself under obligations to me, because I am not yet one of the salt of the earth and privileged to snub captains and lord it over everything dead and alive in a steamboat. I presently climbed up on the bench; I did not think it was safe to go to sleep while this lunatic was on watch.

However, I must have gone to sleep in the course of time, because the next thing I was aware of was the fact that day was breaking, Mr. W—— gone, and Mr. Bixby at the wheel again. So it was four o'clock and all well—but me; I felt like a skinful of dry bones and all of them trying to ache at once.

Mr. Bixby asked me what I had stayed up there for. I confessed that it was to do Mr. W—— a benevolence—tell him where he was. It took five minutes for the entire preposterousness of the thing to filter into Mr. Bixby's system, and then I judge it filled him nearly up to the chin; because he paid me a compliment—and not much of a one either. He said—

WORDS TO OWN

serenely (sə·rēn′lē) *adv.*: calmly.
benevolence (bə·nev′ə·ləns) *n.*: kindness.

MARK TWAIN **455**

Crossing the Curriculum

History

Traffic on the Mississippi. Considering the traffic on the Mississippi during Twain's heyday as a pilot, it's no wonder the job carried such prestige. In 1814, twenty-one steamboats traveling down the "Great Muddy" (as it was called) stopped at New Orleans; four years later, the number had increased to nearly two hundred. By 1833, the number had swelled to more than 1,200 riverboats. During this period, the freight rate between Cincinnati and New Orleans dropped from nine cents a pound to less than half a cent, making it less expensive to ship goods east, sparking tremendous river traffic. Eventually, however, east-west canals and railroads diminished the usefulness of the Mississippi. Commercial traffic dwindled and was taken over by tow boats and barges.

A Reading Skills and Strategies

Identifying Comic Devices

Ask students to explain how Twain gets a comic effect here through a reversal of his reader's expectations. [Bixby's hyperbolic insult reverses the expectation that he was going to pay Twain a "compliment" and makes Twain's use of the word an ironic one.]

B Literary Connections

Expletive Deleted

Even realistic literature had boundaries it would not cross. To protect sensitive readers, *Damnation* could not be completely spelled out.

C Reading Skills and Strategies

Identifying Comic Devices

❓ Which comic technique does Twain draw on in this passage? Is this joke in keeping with Bixby's character? Why or why not? [Possible response: Twain draws on understatement—hence Bixby's focus on the trivial matter of the sash and his indifference to the injuries Twain might have sustained. The understatement matches Bixby's gruff nature.]

D Appreciating Language

Diction

❓ Twain, the narrator, uses a somewhat elevated diction while Bixby uses slang. What purposes does this difference serve? [Possible responses: The different styles create humor, differentiate characters, set the scene, and establish distance between Twain the raw apprentice and Twain the mature writer.]

E Appreciating Language

Diction

❓ What effect does the technical language have? [Possible responses: It demonstrates that time has passed and that Twain has gained some expertise; it helps the reader appreciate young Twain's difficulty in "learning" the river.]

A "Well, taking you by and large, you do seem to be more different kinds of an ass than any creature I ever saw before. What did you suppose he wanted to know for?"

I said I thought it might be a convenience to him.

B "Convenience! D-nation! Didn't I tell you that a man's got to know the river in the night the same as he'd know his own front hall?"

"Well, I can follow the front hall in the dark if I know it *is* the front hall; but suppose you set me down in the middle of it in the dark and not tell me which hall it is; how am *I* to know?"

"Well, you've *got* to, on the river!"

"All right. Then I'm glad I never said anything to Mr. W——"

C "I should say so. Why, he'd have slammed you through the window and utterly ruined a hundred dollars' worth of window sash[14] and stuff."

I was glad this damage had been saved, for it would have made me unpopular with the owners. They always hated anybody who had the name of being careless, and injuring things.

I went to work now to learn the shape of the river; and of all the eluding and ungraspable objects that ever I tried to get mind or hands on, that was the chief. I would fasten my eyes upon a sharp, wooded point that projected far into the river some miles ahead of me, and go to laboriously photographing its shape upon my brain; and just as I was beginning to succeed to my satisfaction, we would draw up toward it and the exasperating thing would begin to melt away and fold back into the bank! If there had been a conspicuous dead tree standing upon the very point of the **D** cape, I would find that tree inconspicuously merged into the general forest, and occupying the middle of a straight shore, when I got abreast of it! No prominent hill would stick to its shape long enough for me to make up my mind what its form really was, but it was as dissolving and changeful as if it had been a mountain of butter in the hottest corner of the tropics. Nothing ever had the same shape when I was coming downstream that it had borne when I went up. I mentioned these little difficulties to Mr. Bixby. He said—

"That's the very main virtue of the thing. If the shapes didn't change every three seconds they

14. **window sash:** frame that holds window glass.

wouldn't be of any use. Take this place where we are now, for instance. As long as that hill over yonder is only one hill, I can boom right along the way I'm going; but the moment it splits at the top and forms a V, I know I've got to scratch to starboard[15] in a hurry, or I'll bang this boat's brains out against a rock; and then the moment one of the prongs of the V swings behind the other, I've got to waltz to larboard[16] again, or I'll have a misunderstanding with a snag that would snatch the keelson[17] out of this steamboat as neatly as if it were a sliver in your hand. If that hill didn't change its shape on bad nights there would be an awful steamboat graveyard around here inside of a year."

It was plain that I had got to learn the shape of the river in all the different ways that could be thought of—upside down, wrong end first, inside out, fore-and-aft, and "thort-ships"[18]—and then know what to do on gray nights when it hadn't any shape at all. So I set about it. In the course of time I began to get the best of this knotty lesson, and my self-complacency moved to the front once more. Mr. Bixby was all fixed, and ready to start it to the rear again. He opened on me after this fashion—

E "How much water did we have in the middle crossing at Hole-in-the-Wall, trip before last?"

I considered this an outrage. I said—

"Every trip, down and up, the leadsmen[19] are singing through that tangled place for three quarters of an hour on a stretch. How do you reckon I can remember such a mess as that?"

"My boy, you've got to remember it. You've got to remember the exact spot and the exact marks the boat lay in when we had the shoalest[20] water, in every one of the five hundred shoal places between St. Louis and New Orleans; and you mustn't get the shoal soundings and marks[21] of

15. **scratch to starboard:** move quickly to the right side of the boat.
16. **larboard:** the left side of the boat.
17. **keelson:** wood or metal beams fastened along a boat's keel to strengthen it. The keel is the timber along the boat's bottom that supports the frame.
18. **fore-and-aft, and "thort-ships":** end to end and shore to shore.
19. **leadsmen:** workers who use a lead line to measure the water's depth.
20. **shoalest:** most shallow.
21. **soundings and marks:** measurements of water depth.

456 THE RISE OF REALISM: THE CIVIL WAR AND POSTWAR PERIOD

Using Students' Strengths

Naturalist Learners

Have students investigate the ecology of the Mississippi River (or of a river or lake in your area). What flora and fauna flourish in the water itself? on the banks? What portions have been protected through conservation laws? What human-made structures (bridges, dams, levees, etc.) control the water? What environmental problems does the river or lake face?

Logical/Mathematical Learners

Ask students to explore the present-day economic importance of the Mississippi River (or of a river or lake in your area). Does the water still yield fish or other edible products? Is it used as a water supply or for irrigation? Is it still important to transportation? What recreational or tourism industry does it support? Ask students to present their findings in a chart or graph.

one trip mixed up with the shoal soundings and marks of another, either, for they're not often twice alike. You must keep them separate."

When I came to myself again, I said—

"When I get so that I can do that, I'll be able to raise the dead, and then I won't have to pilot a steamboat to make a living. I want to retire from this business. I want a slush-bucket and a brush; I'm only fit for a roustabout.[22] I haven't got brains enough to be a pilot; and if I had I wouldn't have strength enough to carry them around, unless I went on crutches."

"Now drop that! When I say I'll learn[23] a man the river, I mean it. And you can depend on it, I'll learn him or kill him."

Continued Perplexities

There was no use in arguing with a person like this. I promptly put such a strain on my memory

22. **roustabout:** deckhand; laborer on a boat.
23. **learn:** "Teach" is not in the river vocabulary. [Twain's note]

that by and by even the shoal water and the countless crossing marks[24] began to stay with me. But the result was just the same. I never could more than get one knotty thing learned before another presented itself. Now I had often seen pilots gazing at the water and pretending to read it as if it were a book; but it was a book that told me nothing. A time came at last, however, when Mr. Bixby seemed to think me far enough advanced to bear a lesson on water-reading. So he began—

"Do you see that long slanting line on the face of the water? Now, that's a reef. Moreover, it's a bluff reef.[25] There is a solid sandbar under it that is nearly as straight up and down as the side of a house. There is plenty of water close up to it, but mighty little on top of it. If you were to hit it you would knock the boat's brains out. Do you see where the line fringes out at the upper end and begins to fade away?"

24. **crossing marks:** points on the river where a boat could cross safely.
25. **bluff reef:** hidden sandbar with a high, steep front. Its position is indicated by lines or ripples on the water.

The pilothouse of *The Great Republic*.

The Bettmann Archive.

MARK TWAIN **457**

Taking a Second Look

Ⓐ Historical Connections

Early Inhabitants

The Sioux had lived along the Mississippi before the arrival of Europeans. When they moved westward, numerous other peoples settled along its shores. The Fox, Sauk, Winnebago, and Ojibwa settled upriver. The Illinois Indians settled further down, and Choctaw, Chickasaw, Natchez, Alibamu, Biloxi, and others inhabited the lower valley.

Ⓑ Critical Thinking

Speculating

❓ The text explains that the local peoples saw the river as a trickster, a god, a devil, etc. Why might they have seen it in these different guises? [Possible response: The river might have been seen as a trickster with its deadly snags and undertows, as a god with its riches and power providing food and commerce, and as a devil with its ability to destroy through floods.]

Ⓒ Elements of Literature

Personification

❓ Here, Bixby talks about the boat as if it were a person. What is the effect of this personification? [It underscores the difficulty of Twain's task, guiding a craft that seems to have a mind of its own. Twain also shifts the focus from the river to the boat. Until this point in the narrative, the shape of the river has received most of the attention.] Point out that ships are traditionally referred to as female.

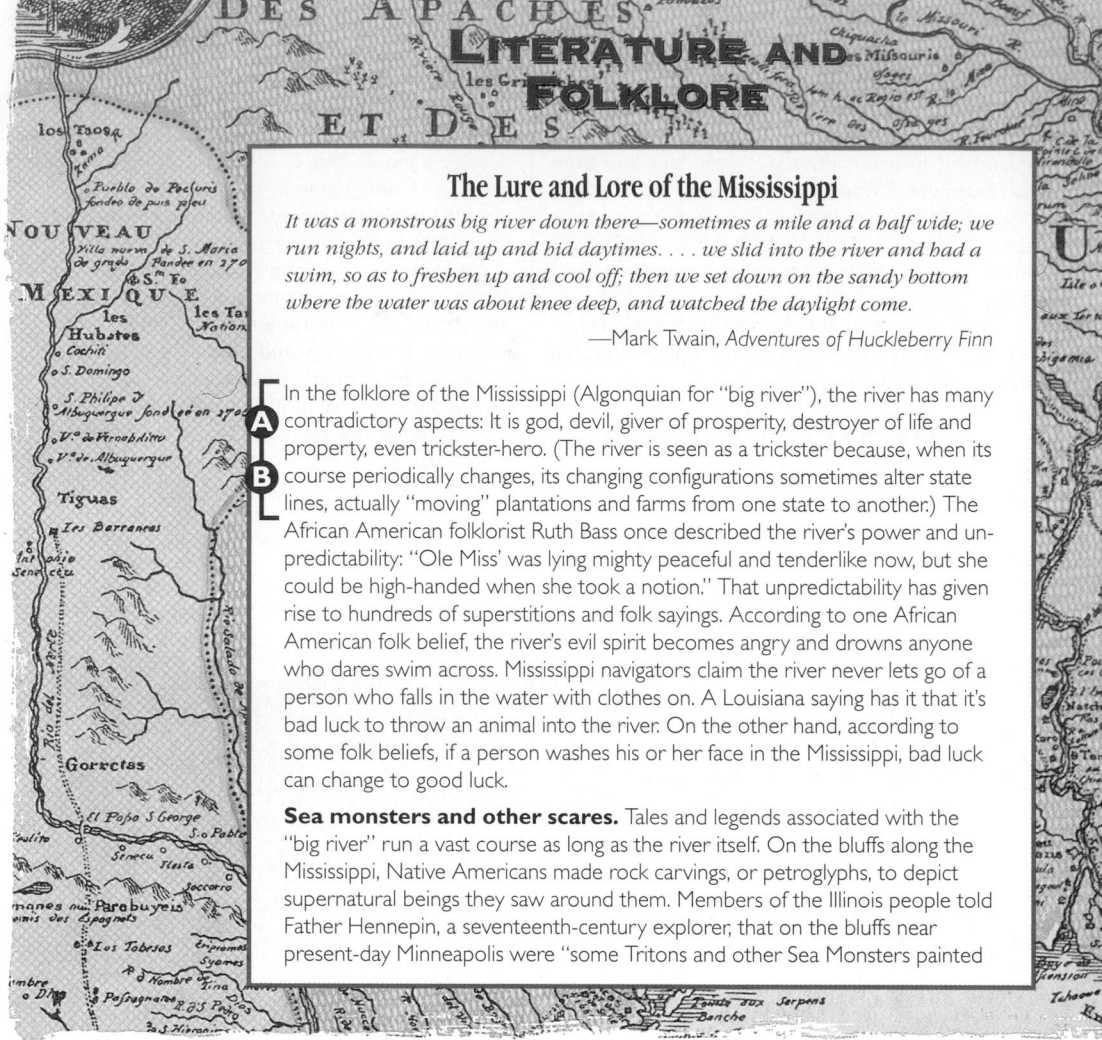

LITERATURE AND FOLKLORE

The Lure and Lore of the Mississippi

It was a monstrous big river down there—sometimes a mile and a half wide; we run nights, and laid up and hid daytimes. . . . we slid into the river and had a swim, so as to freshen up and cool off; then we set down on the sandy bottom where the water was about knee deep, and watched the daylight come.

—Mark Twain, *Adventures of Huckleberry Finn*

Ⓐ In the folklore of the Mississippi (Algonquian for "big river"), the river has many contradictory aspects: It is god, devil, giver of prosperity, destroyer of life and Ⓑ property, even trickster-hero. (The river is seen as a trickster because, when its course periodically changes, its changing configurations sometimes alter state lines, actually "moving" plantations and farms from one state to another.) The African American folklorist Ruth Bass once described the river's power and unpredictability: "Ole Miss' was lying mighty peaceful and tenderlike now, but she could be high-handed when she took a notion." That unpredictability has given rise to hundreds of superstitions and folk sayings. According to one African American folk belief, the river's evil spirit becomes angry and drowns anyone who dares swim across. Mississippi navigators claim the river never lets go of a person who falls in the water with clothes on. A Louisiana saying has it that it's bad luck to throw an animal into the river. On the other hand, according to some folk beliefs, if a person washes his or her face in the Mississippi, bad luck can change to good luck.

Sea monsters and other scares. Tales and legends associated with the "big river" run a vast course as long as the river itself. On the bluffs along the Mississippi, Native Americans made rock carvings, or petroglyphs, to depict supernatural beings they saw around them. Members of the Illinois people told Father Hennepin, a seventeenth-century explorer, that on the bluffs near present-day Minneapolis were "some Tritons and other Sea Monsters painted

"Yes, sir."

"Well, that is a low place; that is the head of the reef. You can climb over there, and not hurt anything. Cross over, now, and follow along close under the reef—easy water there—not much current."

I followed the reef along till I approached the fringed end. Then Mr. Bixby said—

Ⓒ "Now get ready. Wait till I give the word. She won't want to mount the reef: a boat hates shoal water. Stand by—wait—*wait*—keep her well in

hand. *Now* cramp her down![26] Snatch her![27] Snatch her!"

He seized the other side of the wheel and helped to spin it around until it was hard down, and then we held it so. The boat resisted, and refused to answer for a while, and next she came surging to starboard, mounted the reef, and sent a

26. **cramp her down:** turn the wheel sharply.
27. **Snatch her:** Act quickly.

Professional Notes

Critical Comment: The Mississippi in American Literature

Twain's fascination with the Mississippi culminated in his use of it as the central image of his masterpiece, *The Adventures of Huckleberry Finn*. According to critic Lionel Trilling, in *Huckleberry Finn* the Mississippi River becomes a god, "a power which seems to have a mind and will of its own, and which, to men of moral imagination, appears to embody a great moral idea." Trilling sees Huck as "the servant of the river-

god." Trilling notes that Twain is not alone in his worship of the Mississippi River. "T. S. Eliot's poem, 'The Dry Salvages,' the third of his *Four Quartets*, begins with a meditation on the Mississippi, which Mr. Eliot knew in his St. Louis boyhood. These are the opening lines:

I do not know much about gods, but I think that the river
Is a strong brown god . . ."

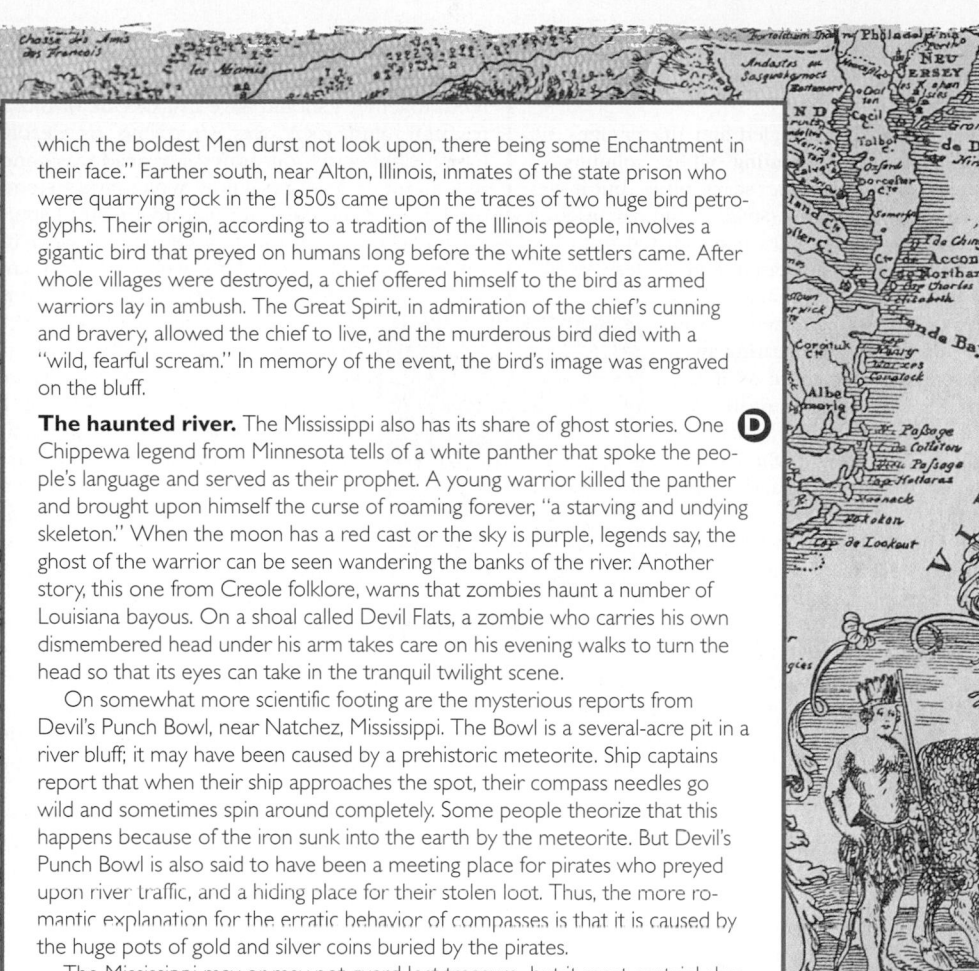

which the boldest Men durst not look upon, there being some Enchantment in their face." Farther south, near Alton, Illinois, inmates of the state prison who were quarrying rock in the 1850s came upon the traces of two huge bird petroglyphs. Their origin, according to a tradition of the Illinois people, involves a gigantic bird that preyed on humans long before the white settlers came. After whole villages were destroyed, a chief offered himself to the bird as armed warriors lay in ambush. The Great Spirit, in admiration of the chief's cunning and bravery, allowed the chief to live, and the murderous bird died with a "wild, fearful scream." In memory of the event, the bird's image was engraved on the bluff.

The haunted river. The Mississippi also has its share of ghost stories. One **D** Chippewa legend from Minnesota tells of a white panther that spoke the people's language and served as their prophet. A young warrior killed the panther and brought upon himself the curse of roaming forever, "a starving and undying skeleton." When the moon has a red cast or the sky is purple, legends say, the ghost of the warrior can be seen wandering the banks of the river. Another story, this one from Creole folklore, warns that zombies haunt a number of Louisiana bayous. On a shoal called Devil Flats, a zombie who carries his own dismembered head under his arm takes care on his evening walks to turn the head so that its eyes can take in the tranquil twilight scene.

On somewhat more scientific footing are the mysterious reports from Devil's Punch Bowl, near Natchez, Mississippi. The Bowl is a several-acre pit in a river bluff; it may have been caused by a prehistoric meteorite. Ship captains report that when their ship approaches the spot, their compass needles go wild and sometimes spin around completely. Some people theorize that this happens because of the iron sunk into the earth by the meteorite. But Devil's Punch Bowl is also said to have been a meeting place for pirates who preyed upon river traffic, and a hiding place for their stolen loot. Thus, the more romantic explanation for the erratic behavior of compasses is that it is caused by the huge pots of gold and silver coins buried by the pirates.

The Mississippi may or may not guard lost treasure, but it most certainly has riches in legend and lore.

The Granger Collection, New York.

Engraved map of Mississippi region and the Louisiana province (1687).

---

long, angry ridge of water foaming away from her bows.[28]

"Now watch her; watch her like a cat, or she'll get away from you. When she fights strong and the tiller slips a little, in a jerky, greasy sort of way, **E** let up on her a trifle; it is the way she tells you at night that the water is too shoal; but keep edging her up, little by little, toward the point. You are

well up on the bar, now; there is a bar under every point, because the water that comes down around it forms an eddy and allows the sediment to sink. Do you see those fine lines on the face of the water that branch out like the ribs of a fan? **E** Well, those are little reefs; you want to just miss the ends of them, but run them pretty close. Now look out—look out! Don't you crowd that slick, greasy-looking place; there ain't nine feet there; she won't stand it. She begins to smell it; look

28. **bows:** front part of a boat.

MARK TWAIN 459

LITERATURE AND FOLKLORE

Help students see how "The Lure and Lore of the Mississippi" relates to *Life on the Mississippi*. You may wish to use the following questions to spark discussion:
- In what ways does Twain see the Mississippi as a trickster, like the one described in "The Lure and Lore of the Mississippi"?
- How does the Mississippi's changing shape, as described in this essay, affect Twain's apprenticeship?

D **Cultural Connections**

The Mysterious Mississippi Steamboat navigation on the Mississippi generated its own share of mysteries and forbidding omens over the years. A case in point was the maiden voyage of the *New Orleans*, built in 1811 and the first steamboat to travel on the Mississippi River. Just as the *New Orleans* left port for the first time, the entire region was hit with the tremors of the massive New Madrid earthquake. This was seen as a terrifying omen for steam navigation because the earthquake resulted in huge floods and the shifting of parts of the river's main channel. The *New Orleans*, however, did complete a successful run.

E **Critical Thinking**

Evaluating

Have students analyze how Twain uses Bixby's dialogue not only to convey information but also to narrate an exciting action scene, as the young Twain navigates the reefs. [Students should point to the moments where Bixby interrupts his explanation in order to give Twain an urgent command.] Ask students to evaluate this style of narrating action. What are the advantages and disadvantages of this technique? How does it compare to the blow-by-blow third-person narrative employed in the action writing of Ambrose Bierce (pp. 466–473) or Jack London (pp. 495–507)? [By narrating action through dialogue, Twain adds color and variety to a scene that could be full of danger but rather bland to read about. On the other hand, he must sacrifice many of the gripping details of the action that Bierce and London both exploit.]

Professional Notes

Critical Comment: Twain and the New England Literati

The Atlantic Monthly was the most prestigious magazine in America during Twain's time. As critic Justin Kaplan points out, the *Atlantic's* readers were not surprised to find in the January 1875 issue poems by Henry Wadsworth Longfellow and an essay by Oliver Wendell Holmes, but they were astonished by the debut of one "Mark Twain." Kaplan suggests that Twain's voice dazzled readers just as Hanni-

bal was roused by the cry of "S-t-e-a-m-boat a-comin'!" Kaplan continues, "The gaudy packet . . . was Mark Twain's reasserting his arrival and declaring once and for all that his surge of power and spectacle derived not from such streams as the meandering Charles or the sweet Thames but from 'the great Mississippi, the majestic, the magnificent Mississippi, rolling its mile-wide tide along, shining in the sun.'"

A Elements of Literature
Personification
❓ How does the personification of the boat seem to diminish Twain's blame in this situation? [Possible response: When the boat is described as having a will of its own, the pilot—Twain—cannot be blamed for not being in control. The fault must lie with the willful boat.]

B Elements of Literature
Irony
❓ How does Twain use **dramatic irony** (which is derived from the protagonist's ignorance of information that the audience, or reader, knows) in order to satirize his youthful arrogance and ignorance? [The audience knows that Bixby is hiding behind the chimney while Twain, lost in his delusions of grandeur, loses control of the boat. Therefore they can laugh at the situation, like Bixby, instead of being terrified by it, like the young Twain.]

C Elements of Literature
Diction
❓ A deliberate craftsman, Twain famously insisted that the difference between the *nearly* right word and the right word was the difference between the lightning bug and lightning. How does Twain shift his diction in this passage to convey the drama and intensity of the situation? [Students should note Twain's use of evocative action verbs such as *gasped, spun,* and *fled,* and his sudden identification with the boat, as demonstrated in the shift in pronouns from the third-person feminine to the first person in phrases such as "I fled," "my bows," and "where I was going."]

D English Language Learners
Niagara Falls
Be sure that students understand Twain's reference to Niagara Falls and the hyperbole in it. Although it would be impossible to feel safe on the brink of the Falls, his remark makes clear how happy he is to see Mr. Bixby.

sharp, I tell you! Oh blazes, there you go! Stop the starboard wheel! Quick! Ship up to back! Set her back!"[29]

The engine bells jingled and the engines answered promptly, shooting white columns of steam far aloft out of the 'scape pipes, but it was too late. The boat had "smelt"[30] the bar in good earnest; the foamy ridges that radiated from her bows suddenly disappeared, a great dead swell[31] came rolling forward and swept ahead of her, she careened far over to larboard, and went tearing away toward the other shore as if she were about scared to death. We were a good mile from where we ought to have been, when we finally got the upper hand of her again.

During the afternoon watch the next day, Mr. Bixby asked me if I knew how to run the next few miles. I said—

"Go inside the first snag above the point, outside the next one, start out from the lower end of Higgins's woodyard, make a square crossing[32] and"—

"That's all right. I'll be back before you close up on the next point."

But he wasn't. He was still below when I rounded it and entered upon a piece of river which I had some misgivings about. I did not know that he was hiding behind a chimney to see how I would perform. I went gaily along, getting prouder and prouder, for he had never left the boat in my sole charge such a length of time before. I even got to "setting" her and letting the wheel go, entirely, while I vaingloriously turned my back and inspected the stern marks[33] and hummed a tune, a sort of easy indifference which I had prodigiously admired in Bixby and other great pilots. Once I inspected rather long, and

> *The engine bells jingled and the engines answered promptly, shooting white columns of steam far aloft out of the 'scape pipes, but it was too late.*

when I faced to the front again my heart flew into my mouth so suddenly that if I hadn't clapped my teeth together I should have lost it. One of those frightful bluff reefs was stretching its deadly length right across our bows! My head was gone in a moment; I did not know which end I stood on; I gasped and could not get my breath; I spun the wheel down with such rapidity that it wove itself together like a spider's web; the boat answered and turned square away from the reef, but the reef followed her! I fled, and still it followed still it kept—right across my bows! I never looked to see where I was going, I only fled. The awful crash was imminent—why didn't that villain come! If I committed the crime of ringing a bell, I might get thrown overboard. But better that than kill the boat. So in blind desperation I started such a rattling "shivaree"[34] down below as never had astounded an engineer in this world before, I fancy. Amidst the frenzy of the bells the engines began to back and fill in a furious way, and my reason forsook its throne—we were about to crash into the woods on the other side of the river. Just then Mr. Bixby stepped calmly into view on the hurricane deck.[35] My soul went out to him in gratitude. My distress vanished; I would have felt safe on the brink of Niagara, with Mr. Bixby on the hurricane deck. He blandly and sweetly took his toothpick out of his mouth between his fingers, as if it were a cigar— we were just in the act of climbing an overhanging big tree, and the passengers were scudding astern[36] like rats—and lifted up these commands to me ever so gently—

"Stop the starboard. Stop the larboard. Set her back on both."[37]

---

29. **Ship . . . back:** Put it in reverse.
30. **smelt:** dialect for "smelled." That is, the boat recognized water too shallow for safety.
31. **great dead swell:** huge wave.
32. **make a square crossing:** go directly between crossing marks.
33. **stern marks:** landmarks already passed and thus astern of, or behind, the boat.

34. **shivaree** (shiv′ə·rē′): noisy celebration.
35. **hurricane deck:** topmost deck of a steamboat.
36. **scudding astern:** running to the back of the boat.
37. **Stop . . . both:** Halt the forward motion of the boat by stopping both the right and left paddle wheels, and put both wheels in reverse.

WORDS TO OWN

misgivings (mis′giv′iŋz) *n. pl.:* doubts; worries.
blandly (bland′lē) *adv.:* mildly.

Crossing the Curriculum

Social Studies
Ask a small group of students to provide background information on steamboats, focusing on their role in American life, their importance in the development of transportation to the interior of the country, and on what "life on the Mississippi" was like during and after their heyday. Students could also report on the recent revival of steamboats as a tourist attraction.

Psychology
To help students understand how Twain memorized the shape of the river, have them discuss techniques for memorizing large masses of information. Students should share their own strategies, such as note-taking, mnemonic devices, visualization, repetition, and "muscle memory." Also have students discuss which techniques are best suited for memorizing specific types of information. Which techniques do students think Twain used? Why?

The boat hesitated, halted, pressed her nose among the boughs a critical instant, then reluctantly began to back away.

"Stop the larboard. Come ahead on it. Stop the starboard. Come ahead on it. Point her for the bar."

I sailed away as serenely as a summer's morning. Mr. Bixby came in and said, with mock simplicity—

"When you have a hail,[38] my boy, you ought to tap the big bell three times before you land, so that the engineers can get ready."

I blushed under the sarcasm, and said I hadn't had any hail.

"Ah! Then it was for wood, I suppose. The officer of the watch will tell you when he wants to wood up."

I went on consuming, and said I wasn't after wood.

"Indeed? Why, what could you want over here in the bend, then? Did you ever know of a boat following a bend upstream at this stage of the river?"

"No, sir—and I wasn't trying to follow it. I was getting away from a bluff reef."

"No, it wasn't a bluff reef; there isn't one within three miles of where you were."

"But I saw it. It was as bluff as that one yonder."

"Just about. Run over it!"

"Do you give it as an order?"

"Yes. Run over it."

"If I don't, I wish I may die."

"All right; I am taking the responsibility."

I was just as anxious to kill the boat, now, as I had been to save her before. I impressed my orders upon my memory, to be used at the inquest,[39] and made a straight break for the reef. As it disappeared under our bows I held my breath; but we slid over it like oil.

"Now don't you see the difference? It wasn't anything but a *wind* reef. The wind does that."

"So I see. But it is exactly like a bluff reef. How am I ever going to tell them apart?"

"I can't tell you. It is an instinct. By and by you

38. **hail:** call to land.
39. **inquest:** inquiry by a jury or panel investigating a crime.

will just naturally *know* one from the other, but you never will be able to explain why or how you know them apart."

It turned out to be true. The face of the water, in time, became a wonderful book—a book that was a dead language to the uneducated passenger, but which told its mind to me without reserve, delivering its most cherished secrets as clearly as if it uttered them with a voice. And it was not a book to be read once and thrown aside, for it had a new story to tell every day. Throughout the long twelve hundred miles there was never a page that was void of interest, never one that you could leave unread without loss, never one that you would want to skip, thinking you could find higher enjoyment in some other thing. There never was so wonderful a book written by man; never one whose interest was so absorbing, so unflagging, so sparklingly renewed with every reperusal. The passenger who could not read it was charmed with a peculiar sort of faint dimple on its surface (on the rare occasions when he did not overlook it altogether); but to the pilot that was an *italicized* passage; indeed, it was more than that, it was a legend[40] of the largest capitals, with a string of shouting exclamation points at the end of it; for it meant that a wreck or a rock was buried there that could tear the life out of the strongest vessel that ever floated. It is the faintest and simplest expression the water ever makes, and the most hideous to a pilot's eye. In truth, the passenger who could not read this book saw nothing but all manner of pretty pictures in it, painted by the sun and shaded by the clouds, whereas to the trained eye these were not pictures at all, but the grimmest and most dead earnest of reading matter.

Now when I had mastered the language of this water and had come to know every trifling feature that bordered the great river as familiarly as I

40. **legend:** inscription.

> *The face of the water, in time, became a wonderful book—a book that was a dead language to the uneducated passenger....*

WORDS TO OWN
void (void) *adj.:* empty.

MARK TWAIN **461**

E 🔵 **Reading Skills and Strategies**
Identifying Comic Devices
❓ What causes the humor in this ironic situation? [The humor stems from the irony: Bixby pretends to misunderstand Twain's motives in ringing the bell and so suggests various reasons for Twain's actions. For each reason, Twain is forced to explain himself and grows more and more embarrassed.]

F 🔵 **Critical Thinking**
Analyzing
❓ Does Twain really want to "kill the boat"? [Possible responses: No, this is another example of hyperbole. He knows Mr. Bixby would not allow the boat to be destroyed just to teach him a lesson, yet his senses tell him disaster is imminent; or yes, he is so ashamed by his previous mistake that he is eager to have someone else take blame for any disaster.]

G 🔵 **Critical Thinking**
Challenging the Text
❓ Does the idea that piloting is instinctual ring true? [Students who agree may refer to other activities that require skill and experience but that must be performed without conscious or deliberate decision-making, such as driving a car, dancing, playing a sport, or "throwing" a clay pot.]

H 🔵 **Elements of Literature**
Extended Metaphor
❓ What two unlike things is Twain comparing in this extended metaphor? [Possible response: He compares his understanding the face of the water to reading a book. The water, like a book in a dead language, is not understood by the uninitiated.] Why does he use it at this particular part of the narrative? [It clarifies one of his main ideas: that piloting a steamboat is a sophisticated pursuit, requiring the same discipline and subtlety that reading does. Just as reading skills improve with the experience of reading, so piloting skills become an "instinct" in one long-devoted to the river.] Note that Twain here has expanded on the book metaphor he introduced on p. 457.

Making the Connections

Connecting to the Theme:
"From Innocence to Experience"
After students finish reading, ask them to trace Twain's journey from innocence to experience as demonstrated in this excerpt from Life on the Mississippi. How might Twain's journey parallel the one that America would shortly take? [Possible responses: With the experience of knowing the river came a loss of innocence; the experience of the Civil War would bring a shattering loss of innocence.] Students may be interested to learn that the second half of Life on the Mississippi was written seven years after the first half was published. It describes Twain's return to the river in 1882, after life there had changed dramatically—yet another kind of innocence lost. Few contrasts are more moving than that between the kinetic energy and humor of the first part and the melancholy reminiscence of the second.

A Literary Connections

Zen and Piloting

? In his book *Zen and the Art of Motorcycle Maintenance*, Robert Pirsig comments on Twain's idea. "When analytic thought, the knife, is applied to experience, something is always killed in the process. . . . Mark Twain's experience comes to mind, in which, after he had mastered the analytic knowledge needed to pilot the Mississippi River, he discovered the river had lost its beauty. Something *is* always killed. But what is less noticed in the arts—something is always created too. And instead of just dwelling on what is killed it's important also to see what's created and to see the process as a kind of death-birth continuity that is neither good nor bad, but just *is*." Do you agree with Pirsig's perspective? Why or why not?

B Critical Thinking

Analyzing

? How has Twain changed from the beginning of the selection to the end? [Possible responses: He has been stripped of his romantic illusions. His ideas of the romantic life of pilots and their nonchalant approach to their work has changed.]

C Elements of Literature

Extended Metaphor

? Explain this extended metaphor. Is it suited to Twain's purpose? Why or why not? [Possible response: Twain compares a doctor's view of a beautiful patient to a riverboat pilot's view of a river: both must disregard the beauty of the subject in order to do their duty. The metaphor is very suitable because it points up the inevitable loss of wonder and innocence that comes with knowledge and experience.]

— DOWN THE — MISSISSIPPI.

The Bettmann Archive.

knew the letters of the alphabet, I had made a valuable acquisition. But I had lost something, too. I had lost something which could never be restored to me while I lived. All the grace, the beauty, the poetry had gone out of the majestic river! I still keep in mind a certain wonderful sunset which I witnessed when steamboating was new to me. A broad expanse of the river was turned to blood; in the middle distance the red hue brightened into gold, through which a solitary log came floating, black and conspicuous; in one place a long, slanting mark lay sparkling upon the water; in another the surface was broken by boiling, tumbling rings, that were as many-tinted as an opal; where the ruddy flush was faintest, was a smooth spot that was covered with graceful circles and radiating lines, ever so delicately traced; the shore on our left was densely wooded, and the <u>somber</u> shadow that fell from this forest was broken in one place by a long, ruffled trail that shone like silver; and high above the forest wall a clean-stemmed dead tree waved a single leafy bough that glowed like a flame in the unobstructed splendor that was flowing from the sun. There were graceful curves, reflected images, woody heights, soft distances; and over the whole scene, far and near, the dissolving lights drifted steadily, enriching it, every passing moment, with new marvels of coloring.

I stood like one bewitched. I drank it in, in a speechless rapture. The world was new to me, and I had never seen anything like this at home. But as I have said, a day came when I began to cease from noting the glories and the charms which the moon and the sun and the twilight wrought upon the river's face; another day came when I ceased altogether to note them. Then, if that sunset scene had been repeated, I should have looked upon it without rapture, and should have commented upon it, inwardly, after this fashion: This sun means that we are going to have wind tomorrow; that floating log means that the river is rising, small thanks to it; that slanting mark on the water refers to a bluff reef which is going to kill somebody's steamboat one of these nights, if it keeps on stretching out like that; those tumbling "boils" show a dissolving bar and a changing channel there; the lines and circles in the slick water over yonder are a warning that that troublesome place is shoaling up dangerously; that silver streak in the shadow of the forest is the "break" from a new snag,[41] and he has located himself in the very best place he could have found to fish for steamboats; that tall dead tree, with a single living branch, is not going to last long, and then how is a body ever going to get through this blind place at night without the friendly old landmark?

No, the romance and the beauty were all gone from the river. All the value any feature of it had for me now was the amount of usefulness it could furnish toward compassing the safe piloting of a steamboat. Since those days, I have pitied doctors from my heart. What does the lovely flush in a beauty's cheek mean to a doctor but a "break" that ripples above some deadly disease? Are not all her visible charms sown thick with what are to him the signs and symbols of hidden decay? Does he ever see her beauty at all, or doesn't he simply view her professionally, and comment upon her unwholesome condition all to himself? And doesn't he sometimes wonder whether he has gained most or lost most by learning his trade?

41. **"break" . . . snag:** ripple or line in the water indicating a newly fallen tree.

- - - - - - - - - - - - - - - -

WORDS TO OWN
somber (säm′bər) *adj.:* gloomy; dark.

- - - - - - - - - - - - - - - -

462 THE RISE OF REALISM: THE CIVIL WAR AND POSTWAR PERIOD

Assessing Learning

Check Test: True–False

1. A riverboat pilot steers by the shape of the river. [True]
2. Mr. W— yells at Twain for hitting a sandbar. [False]
3. Bixby gives Twain the wheel and watches his progress from a hiding place. [True]
4. The river becomes like a book that Twain learns to read. [True]
5. Twain doesn't learn the river well enough to become a pilot, so he becomes a doctor. [False]

Standardized Test Preparation

For practice with proofreading and editing, see
• *Daily Oral Grammar*, Transparency 30

MAKING MEANINGS

First Thoughts

1. Twain ruefully reports that "the romance and the beauty were all gone from the river." Do you think he is describing a common human reaction? Can you identify another example of this kind of experience?

Shaping Interpretations

2. In "Perplexing Lessons," what does Bixby mean when he says that Twain must learn the shape of the river?

3. In the chapter titled "Continued Perplexities," an **extended metaphor** compares the river with a book that "had a new story to tell every day" (page 461). Find three specific comparisons Twain makes between reading a book and "reading" the river.

4. Twain says that "All the grace, the beauty, the poetry had gone out of the majestic river!" (page 462). In what sense is he describing a loss of "innocence" that comes about as a result of increased experience?

Connecting with the Text

5. Think about the episode in which Bixby lets Twain get into trouble before giving him quiet guidance. On the basis of your own experience with a variety of teachers, do you rate Bixby as a good teacher or a poor one? Give the reasons for your answer.

Challenging the Text

6. Twain first wrote about his Mississippi experiences for *The Atlantic Monthly,* a magazine edited

> ### Reading Check
>
> a. What huge body of information is Twain told he must learn as well as he knows a hall in his own home?
>
> b. What happens the night Twain believes he is left at the wheel alone?
>
> c. Explain the factors that make "learning the river" a great challenge.
>
> d. What does Twain say he has lost when he finally learns the language of the river?

by William Dean Howells. Howells said of Twain's first installment, "It almost made the water in our ice pitcher muddy as I read it." Does Twain bring the river to life as vividly as Howells implies? Support your response with examples from the text.

READING SKILLS AND STRATEGIES

Identifying Comic Devices

Humor is hard to explain, but we do know that certain comic devices are used in humorous writings; and when they are used by a genius like Twain, they make us laugh.

- **Hyperbole:** outrageous exaggeration made for effect: ". . . when I faced to the front again my heart flew into my mouth so suddenly that if I hadn't clapped my teeth together I should have lost it" (page 460).

- **Comic metaphors:** comparisons between two unlike things that create colorful, hilarious images. Twain's metaphors often involve incongruity—two seemingly mismatched or even opposite images, events, or elements are unexpectedly joined: "My gunpowdery chief went off with a bang . . . and then went on loading and firing until he was out of adjectives" (page 454). Many of Twain's funniest comparisons are **extended metaphors.**

- **Understatement:** saying less than what is meant, usually for ironic purposes: "I was glad this damage had been saved, for it would have made me unpopular with the owners" (page 456).

1. Review the excerpt, and locate at least one more example of each of the three comic devices listed above. Read aloud the passages in which Twain uses each of these techniques.

2. Which of these comic devices is used most frequently in this excerpt from *Life on the Mississippi*? Overall, what adjectives would you use to describe Twain's humor?

3. Compare the comic devices in *Life on the Mississippi* with those in Twain's **tall tale** classic "The Celebrated Jumping Frog of Calaveras County." See if you can spot hyperbole, comic metaphors, and understatement in that tall tale about a jumping-frog contest held in a mining camp in California.

MARK TWAIN **463**

> ### Reading Check
>
> a. ". . . all the million trifling variations of shape in the banks of this interminable river . . ." (p. 454)
>
> b. He mistakes a wind reef for a bluff reef and, in trying to avoid it, almost runs the boat into the bank.
>
> c. The river looks different when the light and weather change; the appearance of the shore shifts from month to month.
>
> d. He says the "grace, the beauty, the poetry" and the "romance . . . were all gone from the river."

MAKING MEANINGS

First Thoughts [Respond]

1. Possible responses: Yes, Twain describes how the river becomes a source of factual information, not something to be enjoyed for its beauty. Some students may have had the opposite reaction, in which familiarity brings greater appreciation.

Shaping Interpretations [Interpret]

2. Bixby means that Twain must know the river's shape so completely that he can steer instinctively.

3. ". . . I had often seen pilots gazing at the water and pretending to read it as if it were a book; but it was a book that told me nothing" (p. 457); "The face of the water, in time, became a wonderful book . . ." (p. 461); "I had mastered the language of this water . . . as familiarly as I knew the letters of the alphabet . . ." (pp. 461–462).

4. In learning to "read" the river, Twain has lost the ability to view it purely as an aesthetic object.

Connecting with the Text [Evaluate]

5. Possible response: Since Twain does learn the intricate, complex task of navigating the river and says of Bixby's advice, "it turned out to be true," Bixby could be called an effective teacher.

Challenging the Text [Evaluate]

6. Possible response: Howells's assessment is sound. Twain is a great naturalistic writer who makes the river environment palpable.

READING SKILLS AND STRATEGIES

You may wish to tell students to watch for Twain's use of irony as well, which he frequently couples with one of the devices featured here.

1. Hyperbole: calling Mr. W— a "proud devil . . . a limb of Satan." (p. 455) Comic metaphor: a "skinful of dry bones." (p. 455) Understatement: the "little difficulties" he mentions to Bixby (p. 456)

2. Students may say hyperbole or understatement. His humor is dry, self-deprecating, and intelligent.

3. Students should find lots of examples of these devices, since the genre of the tall tale requires them.

T463

CHOICES:
Building Your Portfolio

1. **Writer's Notebook** Remind students to include oral histories and Internet resources in their research.
2. **Analyzing Humor** Caution students to select comedians whose language and topics are suitable for classroom discussion and written work.
3. **Creative Writing** Encourage students to select a specific example, but remind them that they do not have to share anything that makes them feel uncomfortable.
4. **Speaking and Listening** Students can also read Twain's essay "How to Tell a Story" to understand Twain's ideas about how humor should be read and written.
5. **Art/Research** Encourage students to locate art from nineteenth-century American masters, such as Nathaniel Currier, James Ives, and Thomas Eakins.
6. **Creative Writing/Research/Art** Students should read several articles in travel magazines to familiarize themselves with the structure, voice, and tone of this type of writing.

CHOICES: Building Your Portfolio

Writer's Notebook
1. Collecting Ideas for a Research Paper

Think of a place you would like to do research on—perhaps a historical place in your neighborhood or town, or a place that is threatened, such as a landmark slated for demolition. List some ideas of how you might approach your topic. You could focus your research on a question about the place, or how it has changed over time, or why it has meaning for you and others. You might also make some notes of ideas for drawings or maps you could use in your research paper. Save your notes for possible use in the Writer's Workshop on page 515.

Analyzing Humor
2. Does Twain Hold Up?

Twain's use of humorous devices is one of the strongest characteristics of his work. With reference to both *Life on the Mississippi* and Spotlight On Mark Twain's Humor (page 465), explore in a brief essay how Twain's use of humor is like or unlike the use of humor by today's humorists and comedians. How do contemporary comics appeal to their particular audiences? Would Twain hold up today as a stand-up comic or a humorous writer? Explain.

Creative Writing
3. Double Take

The last three paragraphs of this excerpt from *Life on the Mississippi* examine two very different ways of looking at the river. Try writing your own essay in which you compare and contrast two different views of something:

• your feelings before and after taking a particular action
• how you see some aspect of your life now and how you saw it in the past
• how a favorite place of yours looks in the daytime and at night

Be sure to check your Quickwrite notes.

Speaking and Listening
4. In Character

Alone or with a partner, rehearse an oral reading of Twain's writing—either from the excerpts in this text or from another book. To prepare for your reading, you might want to watch the video *Mark Twain Gives an Interview*, with the actor Hal Holbrook portraying Mark Twain. You might also want to use simple props—a hat or an object representing a pilot's wheel—to help keep you in character. Perform your reading for the class.

Art/Research
5. Big Muddy

Locate paintings, drawings, or engravings of the Mississippi River. Select three to five works that in your opinion best capture the Mississippi that Twain portrays in this excerpt. For each work, write a brief paragraph explaining why you chose it, and cite appropriate descriptions from Twain. Set up a display for your class, mounting your explanatory paragraph next to a photocopy or reproduction of each visual you've selected.

Creative Writing/ Research/Art
6. It Just Keeps Paddlin' Along

The editor of a travel magazine has asked you to write an article about the traditions and history of the Mississippi steamboat. Research the answers to such questions as these: When was the peak of the steamboat era? Did certain boats, captains, or pilots become famous? Where are the old steamboats now? How accurate are depictions like the musical *Show Boat* (available on video) in portraying the realities of the steamboat era? Write up your findings as a magazine story; include pictures for your article.

Taking a Second Look

Review: Understanding Figures of Speech

To review comic devices, have students identify each passage below as hyperbole, comic metaphor, or understatement.

1. When I pulled the slipper away from my neighbor's Chihuahua, it was as if a cloud passed over the dog's face. What I thought was a smile was actually a flash of lightning, and I heard from the back of its throat the thunder rolling in, threatening the region around my ankles with a storm of gnashing teeth. [comic metaphor]
2. William suspected that walking the plank would be a rather unpleasant experience. [understatement]
3. I saw a film so frightening that my hair stood on end and blocked the view of the people behind me until the theater lights finally came back on. [hyperbole]

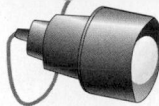

Mark Twain's Humor

During his lifetime, Mark Twain was better known as a lecturer than as a novelist, and he found considerable financial reward on the lecture circuit. Eyewitnesses reported that Twain had a genius for deadpan delivery, deliberately drawing out his remarks—and ending them with a perturbed expression. The **anecdotes** and maxims he delivered on stage would later be published in book form and sold by subscription in elaborate, illustrated volumes.

Twain's maxims have taken on the force of **proverbs,** a phenomenon securing his position as a pioneer of American humor. Here is a sampling of his many and varied one-liners.

Caricature of Mark Twain by Keppler. Lithograph.
The Bettmann Archive.

It's better to keep your mouth shut and appear stupid than to open it and remove all doubt.

By trying, we can easily learn to endure adversity. Another man's, I mean.

If the man doesn't believe as we do, we say he is a crank, and that settles it. I mean, it does nowadays, because now we can't burn him.

There are many humorous things in the world; among them, the white man's notion that he is less savage than the other savages.

There are several good protections against temptations, but the surest is cowardice.

If you pick up a starving dog and make him prosperous, he will not bite you. This is the principal difference between a dog and a man.

Few things are harder to put up with than the annoyance of a good example.

When I was a boy of fourteen, my father was so ignorant I could hardly stand to have the old man around. But when I got to be twenty-one, I was astonished at how much he had learned in seven years.

It takes your enemy and your friend, working together, to hurt you to the heart; the one to slander you and the other to get the news to you.

Nothing so needs reforming as other people's habits.

A sin takes on new and real terrors when there seems a chance that it is going to be found out.

Behold, the fool saith, "Put not all thine eggs in the one basket"—which is but a manner of saying, "Scatter your money and your attention"; but the wise man saith, "Put all your eggs in the one basket and—*watch that basket.*"

Connecting Across Texts

Connecting with *The Devil's Dictionary*
After students read the biography of Ambrose Bierce on p. 466, have them compare Twain's proverbs with the excerpts quoted from Bierce's *The Devil's Dictionary.* Is the tone similar? the type of humor? the probable purpose? Challenge students to read more of Twain's and Bierce's work to see if they can find comments by the two writers on similar subjects. Students could present their findings in a humorous poster.

Spotlight On

This feature describes Twain's successful career on the lecture circuit and provides a sampling of the colorful aphorisms and anecdotes he presented there. Many of the observations offered here focus on people's double standards and moral blind spots.

A Cultural Connections
Twain on Stage
Reviewing a lecture Twain gave in 1867, a *New York Tribune* critic wrote: "No other lecturer, of course excepting Artemus Ward, has so thoroughly succeeded in exciting the mirthful curiosity, and compelling the laughter of his hearers. Mark Twain's delivery is deliberate and measured to the last degree. He lounges comfortably around his platform, seldom referring to notes, and seeks to establish a sort of buttonhole relationship with his audience. . . . His style is his own and needs to be seen to be understood."

B Reading Skills and Strategies
Identifying Comic Devices
? What techniques does Twain use here to create humor? How do the methods Twain uses here compare with the ones he uses to create humor in *Life on the Mississippi?* [Possible responses: Although he uses hyperbole and understatement here, his principal methods are irony and caustic wit. In *Life on the Mississippi,* he creates humor mainly through comic metaphor, understatement, and hyperbole, with some use of irony. The humor Twain uses in the aphorisms is far more pointed and critical than the gentle, self-deprecating humor in *Life on the Mississippi.*]

RESPONDING TO THE ART
Joseph Keppler (1838–1894) founded *Puck,* the first successful humor weekly in America.
Activity. What details in the cartoon show that Twain is a humorist? [the audience's laughing faces, the speaker's absurdly contrived pose] Is Keppler's caricature an admiring portrayal of Twain or a satire of the satirist?

T465

Ambrose Bierce

(1842–1914?)

Courtesy of the Huntington Library, Art Collections, and Botanical Gardens, San Marino, California.

A mbrose Bierce infused his writing with an attitude of scorn for all the sentimental illusions human beings cling to. His dark vision of life centers on warfare and the cruel joke it plays on humanity. This bleak vision assures Bierce's place in our literary history.

Bierce was born in 1842, the tenth of thirteen children in the family of an eccentric and unsuccessful farmer named Marcus Aurelius Bierce. The Bierces lived in a log cabin in Meigs County, Ohio. Bierce was educated primarily through exploring his father's small library.

At nineteen, Bierce joined the Ninth Indiana Volunteers and saw action at the bloody Civil War battles of Shiloh and Chickamauga. He was also part of General Sherman's march to the sea in 1864. Bierce was once severely wounded and was cited for bravery no fewer than fifteen times.

At the war's end, Bierce reenlisted, but several years in the peacetime army left him discouraged about his prospects. He left the army and joined his brother Albert to work at the United States Mint in San Francisco. He began to contribute caustically witty, short pieces to the city's weeklies.

A growing reputation as a muckraking reporter brought Bierce the editorship of the San Francisco *News Letter* and the acquaintance of the literary community, including Mark Twain (page 450). When the financier Collis P. Huntington, head of the Southern Pacific Railroad, asked Bierce's price for silence on the railroad's tax fraud case, Bierce is said to have replied: "My price is about seventy-five million dollars, to be handed to the Treasurer of the United States." Bierce's disillusionment with the deceit and greed of his times continued to spur his pen and earned him the nickname "Bitter Bierce."

Bierce married in 1871 and moved to England, where he spent the next four years editing and contributing to humor magazines and making his first attempts at fiction. On his return to

Ambrose Bierce by J.H.E. Partington (1843–1899). Oil on canvas.

San Francisco in 1876, he wrote a regular column. This was the most active and fruitful time of Bierce's life. He became the witty scholar and literary dictator of the West Coast, but he never achieved wide recognition for his stories.

The Devil's Dictionary, first published in 1906 as *The Cynic's Word Book,* was more successful. In his dictionary, Bierce offered a collection of definitions filled with irony and sardonic humor. He defined war as a "by-product of the arts of peace," and peace as "a period of cheating between two periods of fighting." A cynic was a person who "sees things as they are, not as they ought to be. Hence the custom among the Scythians of plucking out a cynic's eyes to improve his vision."

In 1913, when Bierce was lonely and weary of his life, he asked his few friends to "forgive him in not perishing where he was." He set off for Mexico to report on, or join in, its revolution. "Goodbye," he wrote. "If you hear of my being stood up against a Mexican stone wall and shot to rags please know that I think it a pretty good way to depart this life. It beats old age, disease, or falling down the cellar stairs." No further word was ever heard from him.

 go.hrw.com
LEO 11-10

Before You Read

AN OCCURRENCE AT OWL CREEK BRIDGE

Make the Connection

All in the Mind
Can we ever really understand the complexities of the human mind? What's real? What's imaginary? When someone we love is long overdue, we can conjure up the details of disaster in a few seconds and make ourselves sick with worry. On the other hand, we can lift ourselves out of a blue mood by focusing on an event we can look forward to. Imagine, then, the extremes to which the human imagination might go in a time of severe, even life-threatening, stress. If a person were threatened with imminent death, what kinds of thoughts might pass through his or her mind? Would the mind provide a calming refuge or intensify the fear and horror?

Reading Skills and Strategies

Clarifying Responses to a Text
As you journey with Bierce's hero, pause three or four times to write down your own feelings, thoughts, or observations. What developments make you afraid for the hero? When do you feel relieved or even happy for him? What doubts, questions, or other reactions arise in your mind at other times?

Elements of Literature

Point of View
In the different sections of Bierce's story, watch for these variations in **point of view:** (1) **omniscient,** in which the narrator seems to know everything about all characters or events; (2) **objective,** in which the narrator reports without comment, much as a camera would record a scene; and (3) **third-person limited,** in which the narrator zooms in on the thoughts and feelings of a single character.

> **P**oint of view is the vantage point from which a writer tells the story.
>
> *For more on Point of View, see the Handbook of Literary Terms.*

Background

The belief that life will prove gratifying and will reward our virtues is so strong that it has become a main current in storytelling. But this romantic notion has its inevitable counterpart in realism and naturalism—fiction that conforms to the truth as it is experienced rather than as we would like it to be.

Bierce's no-punches-pulled story is set in the deep South during the Civil War (1861–1865). He invites us to sympathize with the hero, a Southerner who has tried to help the Confederate cause, and he portrays the Union side as brutal and treacherous. Yet the horrors of war may serve only as an external setting for the landscape that *really* interests the writer. That landscape is the inside of the mind of a man condemned to death.

Summary ▪▪▪

Bierce's psychological adventure story is set during the American Civil War. The protagonist, Peyton Farquhar, is a wealthy Confederate planter who has been lured by a Union spy into attempting to sabotage a bridge in enemy territory. As the story opens he has been captured after walking into the trap and is about to be hanged from a bridge. Instead of immediately witnessing his death, however, we first step into Farquhar's perspective and follow him on an incredible escape: the rope snaps, he falls into the river, and manages to elude the Union bullets long enough to run into the woods and ultimately back to his home in Confederate territory. At the end of this extended narrative, however, we learn that the escape has been a fantasy that Farquhar experienced in his last moments of life.

RESPONDING TO THE ART

In this portrait of Ambrose Bierce, artist **J. H. E. Partington** (1843–1899) captures Bierce's fascination with death and human physiology.
Activity. Before students read "An Occurrence at Owl Creek Bridge," ask them what they can infer about Bierce's character from his posture and facial expression, and from the prop depicted in this portrait. [Possible response: Bierce's expression and posture suggest a man who is intellectually serious yet socially casual. The skull suggests a fear of or fascination with death.]

Preteaching Vocabulary

Words to Own
Ask students to pair up with partners and read the Words to Own and their definitions listed at the bottom of the selection pages. Have a volunteer write the ten vocabulary words on the board. Then, have partners take turns reading the definitions of the words to each other and identifying the words that are being defined. Finally, to reinforce students' understanding of the words, have partners complete the following activity together.

1. Use your hands to demonstrate the difference between **oscillation** and **gyration.**
2. Use **malign** and **sentinel** to describe the threat of a natural disaster.
3. Explain how someone who **chafed** at a restriction could receive an **abrasion.**
4. Draw a compass; label its **pivotal** point.
5. Use **appalling** and **deference** to describe the behavior of people at a concert.
6. What word means "dangerous"? [**perilous**]

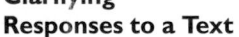
An Occurrence at Owl Creek Bridge

Ambrose Bierce

I

A man stood upon a railroad bridge in northern Alabama, looking down into the swift water twenty feet below. The man's hands were behind his back, the wrists bound with a cord. A rope closely encircled his neck. It was attached to a stout cross-timber above his head, and the slack fell to the level of his knees. Some loose boards laid upon the sleepers[1] supporting the metals of the railway supplied a footing for him and his executioners—two private soldiers of the Federal army, directed by a sergeant who in civil life may have been a deputy sheriff. At a short remove upon the same temporary platform was an officer in the uniform of his rank, armed. He was a captain. A sentinel at each end of the bridge stood with his rifle in the position known as "support," that is to say, vertical in front of the left shoulder, the hammer resting on the forearm thrown straight across the chest—a formal and unnatural position, enforcing an erect carriage of the body. It did not appear to be the duty of these two men to know what was occurring at the center of the bridge; they merely blockaded the two ends of the foot planking that traversed it.

Beyond one of the sentinels nobody was in sight; the railroad ran straight away into a forest for a hundred yards, then, curving, was lost to view. Doubtless there was an outpost farther along. The other bank of the stream was open ground —a gentle acclivity[2] topped with a stockade of vertical tree trunks, loopholed for rifles, with a single embrasure through which protruded the muzzle of a brass cannon commanding the bridge. Midway of the slope between bridge and fort were the spectators—a single company of infantry in line, at "parade rest," the butts of the rifles on the ground, the barrels inclining slightly backward against the right shoulder, the hands crossed upon the stock. A lieutenant stood at the right of the line, the point of his sword upon the ground, his left hand resting upon his right. Excepting the group of four at the center of the bridge, not a man moved. The company faced the bridge, staring stonily, motionless. The sentinels, facing the banks of the stream, might have been statues to adorn the bridge. The captain stood with folded arms, silent, observing the work of his subordinates, but making no sign. Death is a dignitary who when he comes announced is to be received with formal manifestations of respect,

----

WORDS TO OWN
sentinel (sen′ti·nəl) *n.:* guard; sentry.

----

1. **sleepers:** railroad ties.
2. **acclivity:** uphill slope.

even by those most familiar with him. In the code of military etiquette, silence and fixity are forms of deference.

The man who was engaged in being hanged was apparently about thirty-five years of age. He was a civilian, if one might judge from his habit, which was that of a planter. His features were good—a straight nose, firm mouth, broad forehead, from which his long, dark hair was combed straight back, falling behind his ears to the collar of his well-fitting frock coat. He wore a moustache and pointed beard, but no whiskers; his eyes were large and dark gray, and had a kindly expression which one would hardly have expected in one whose neck was in the hemp. Evidently this was no vulgar assassin. The liberal military code makes provision for hanging many kinds of persons, and gentlemen are not excluded.

The preparations being complete, the two private soldiers stepped aside and each drew away the plank upon which he had been standing. The sergeant turned to the captain, saluted, and placed himself immediately behind that officer, who in turn moved apart one pace. These movements left the condemned man and the sergeant standing on the two ends of the same plank, which spanned three of the crossties of the bridge. The end upon which the civilian stood almost, but not quite, reached a fourth. This plank had been held in place by the weight of the captain; it was now held by that of the sergeant. At a signal from the former, the latter would step aside, the plank would tilt and the condemned man go down between two ties. The arrangement commended itself to his judgment as simple and effective. His face had not been covered nor his eyes bandaged. He looked a moment at his "unsteadfast footing," then let his gaze wander to the swirling water of the stream racing madly beneath his feet. A piece of dancing driftwood caught his attention, and his eyes followed it down the current. How slowly it appeared to move! What a sluggish stream!

He closed his eyes in order to fix his last thoughts upon his wife and children. The water, touched to gold by the early sun, the brooding mists under the banks at some distance down the stream, the fort, the soldiers, the piece of drift—all had distracted him. And now he became conscious of a new disturbance. Striking through the thought of his dear ones was a sound which he could neither ignore nor understand, a sharp, distinct, metallic percussion like the stroke of a blacksmith's hammer upon the anvil; it had the same ringing quality. He wondered what it was, and whether immeasurably distant or nearby—it seemed both. Its recurrence was regular, but as slow as the tolling of a death knell. He awaited each stroke with impatience and—he knew not why—apprehension. The intervals of silence grew progressively longer; the delays became maddening. With their greater infrequency the sounds increased in strength and sharpness. They hurt his ear like the thrust of a knife; he feared he would shriek. What he heard was the ticking of his watch.

He unclosed his eyes and saw again the water below him. "If I could free my hands," he thought, "I might throw off the noose and spring into the stream. By diving I could evade the bullets and, swimming vigorously, reach the bank, take to the woods, and get away home. My home, thank God, is as yet outside their lines; my wife and little ones are still beyond the invader's farthest advance."

As these thoughts, which have here to be set down in words, were flashed into the doomed man's brain rather than evolved from it, the captain nodded to the sergeant. The sergeant stepped aside.

II

Peyton Farquhar was a well-to-do planter, of an old and highly respected Alabama family. Being a slave owner and, like other slave owners, a politician, he was naturally an original secessionist and ardently devoted to the Southern cause. Circumstances of an imperious nature, which it is unnecessary to relate here, had prevented him from taking service with the gallant army that had fought the disastrous campaigns ending with the fall of Corinth,[3] and he chafed under the inglorious

3. **Corinth:** Union forces under General William S. Rosecrans (1819–1898) took Corinth, Mississippi, on October 4, 1862.

WORDS TO OWN

deference (def′ər·əns) *n.:* respect.
chafed (chāft) *v.:* became impatient.

AMBROSE BIERCE 469

Ⓔ Appreciating Language
Diction
❓ Why does Bierce use the phrase "engaged in being hanged" rather than saying "was being hanged" or "was going to be hanged"? [Possible response: It is an understatement that emphasizes the violence and cruelty of the act.]

Ⓕ Critical Thinking
Determining Author's Purpose
❓ What effect do you think this description is designed to have on the reader? Why might this prove important later on in the story? [This description engenders sympathy for Farquhar and thus causes readers to hope that he manages to escape. If he were a villain, readers might be indifferent to his fate or eager to see him hanged.]

Ⓖ Elements of Literature
Point of View
❓ How does the point of view change? What effect does this have on the story? [The narration shifts from the objective or omniscient point of view to the third-person limited. This personalizes Farquhar and prompts readers to identify with him.]

Ⓗ Critical Thinking
Analyzing
❓ How do time and sound change in this passage? What effect does this create? [By slowing down time and amplifying sound, Bierce conveys Farquhar's mental state and moves the narrative wholly into Farquhar's internal perspective.]

Skill Link

Analyzing Chronological Order
Remind students that when stories are related in chronological order, the events proceed in sequence from first to last. Writers often include cue words such as *first, then, next, finally,* and *last* to help readers follow the chronological order of events. "An Occurrence at Owl Creek Bridge" begins in chronological order but then moves into a **flashback**, a scene that breaks into the story to show an earlier scene that preceded the rest of the narrative.

Activities
1. Have students list the events in the order in which they appear in the story. Then, divide the class into small groups and have them put the events in chronological order.
2. Have a group of students construct a time line to track the chronological order of events in the story.
3. Challenge students to explain why Bierce relates the story as he does.

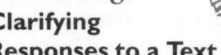

restraint, longing for the release of his energies, the larger life of the soldier, the opportunity for distinction. That opportunity, he felt, would come, as it comes to all in wartime. Meanwhile he did what he could. No service was too humble for him to perform in aid of the South, no adventure too _perilous_ for him to undertake if consistent with the character of a civilian who was at heart a soldier, and who in good faith and without too much qualification assented to at least a part of the frankly villainous dictum that all is fair in love and war.

One evening while Farquhar and his wife were sitting on a rustic bench near the entrance to his grounds, a gray-clad soldier rode up to the gate and asked for a drink of water. Mrs. Farquhar was only too happy to serve him with her own white hands. While she was fetching the water, her husband approached the dusty horseman and inquired eagerly for news from the front.

"The Yanks are repairing the railroads," said the man, "and are getting ready for another advance. They have reached the Owl Creek bridge, put it in order, and built a stockade on the north bank. The commandant has issued an order, which is posted everywhere, declaring that any civilian caught interfering with the railroad, its bridges, tunnels, or trains will be summarily hanged. I saw the order."

"How far is it to the Owl Creek bridge?" Farquhar asked.

"About thirty miles."

"Is there no force on this side the creek?"

"Only a picket post half a mile out, on the railroad, and a single sentinel at this end of the bridge."

"Suppose a man—a civilian and student of hanging—should elude the picket post and perhaps get the better of the sentinel," said Farquhar, smiling, "what could he accomplish?"

The soldier reflected. "I was there a month ago," he replied. "I observed that the flood of last winter had lodged a great quantity of driftwood against the wooden pier at this end of the bridge. It is now dry and would burn like tow."

The lady had now brought the water, which the soldier drank. He thanked her ceremoniously, bowed to her husband, and rode away. An hour later, after nightfall, he repassed the plantation, going northward in the direction from which he had come. He was a Federal scout.

III

As Peyton Farquhar fell straight downward through the bridge, he lost consciousness and was as one already dead. From this state he was awakened—ages later, it seemed to him—by the pain of a sharp pressure upon his throat, followed by a sense of suffocation. Keen, poignant agonies seemed to shoot from his neck downward through every fiber of his body and limbs. These pains appeared to flash along well-defined lines of ramification and to beat with an inconceivably rapid periodicity. They seemed like streams of pulsating fire heating him to an intolerable temperature. As to his head, he was conscious of nothing but a feeling of fullness—of congestion. These sensations were unaccompanied by thought. The intellectual part of his nature was already effaced; he had power only to feel, and feeling was torment. He was conscious of motion. Encompassed in a luminous cloud, of which he was now merely the fiery heart, without material

WORDS TO OWN

perilous (per'ə·ləs) _adj._: dangerous.

Crossing the Curriculum

Social Studies

During the Civil War, spies were engaged in acts of sabotage, as well as in collecting facts about the enemy and in spreading misinformation. Ask students to find out more about the role of spies. As students research, they should consider whether Bierce painted an accurate picture in his portrayal of the Union scout and of Peyton Farquhar. Did many wealthy planters become Confederate saboteurs? Invite students to share their research with the class.

Architecture

Ask students to research the railroads that were in use during the time of the Civil War. When were they built? What were they used for before the war? What role did they play during the war? What methods of engineering and construction were used in building them? Is Bierce's description of the railroad ties on the bridge over the river accurate? Interested students might want to build a model of a typical railroad bridge of the period.

substance, he swung through unthinkable arcs of oscillation, like a vast pendulum. Then all at once, with terrible suddenness, the light about him shot upward with the noise of a loud plash; a frightful roaring was in his ears, and all was cold and dark. The power of thought was restored; he knew that the rope had broken and he had fallen into the stream. There was no additional strangulation; the noose about his neck was already suffocating him and kept the water from his lungs. To die of hanging at the bottom of a river!—the idea seemed to him ludicrous. He opened his eyes in the darkness and saw above him a gleam of light, but how distant, how inaccessible! He was still sinking, for the light became fainter and fainter until it was a mere glimmer. Then it began to grow and brighten, and he knew that he was rising toward the surface—knew it with reluctance, for he was now very comfortable. "To be hanged and drowned," he thought, "that is not so bad; but I do not wish to be shot. No; I will not be shot; that is not fair."

He was not conscious of an effort, but a sharp pain in his wrist apprised him that he was trying to free his hands. He gave the struggle his attention, as an idler might observe the feat of a juggler, without interest in the outcome. What splendid effort!—what magnificent, what superhuman strength! Ah, that was a fine endeavor! Bravo! The cord fell away; his arms parted and floated upward, the hands dimly seen on each side in the growing light. He watched them with a new interest as first one and then the other pounced upon the noose at his neck. They tore it away and thrust it fiercely aside, its undulations resembling those of a water snake. "Put it back, put it back!" He thought he shouted these words to his hands, for the undoing of the noose had been succeeded by the direst pang that he had yet experienced. His neck ached horribly; his brain was on fire; his heart, which had been fluttering faintly, gave a great leap, trying to force itself out at his mouth. His whole body was racked and wrenched with an insupportable anguish! But his disobedient hands gave no heed to the command. They beat the water vigorously with quick, downward strokes, forcing him to the surface. He felt his head emerge; his eyes were blinded by the sunlight; his chest expanded convulsively, and with a supreme and crowning agony his lungs engulfed a great draft of air, which instantly he expelled in a shriek!

He was now in full possession of his physical senses. They were, indeed, preternaturally keen and alert. Something in the awful disturbance of his organic system had so exalted and refined them that they made record of things never before perceived. He felt the ripples upon his face and heard their separate sounds as they struck. He looked at the forest on the bank of the stream, saw the individual trees, the leaves, and the veining of each leaf—saw the very insects upon them: the locusts, the brilliant-bodied flies, the gray spiders stretching their webs from twig to twig. He noted the prismatic colors in all the dewdrops upon a million blades of grass. The humming of the gnats that danced above the eddies of the stream, the beating of the dragonflies' wings, the strokes of the water spiders' legs, like oars which had lifted their boat—all these made audible music. A fish slid along beneath his eyes, and he heard the rush of its body parting the water.

He had come to the surface facing down the stream; in a moment the visible world seemed to wheel slowly round, himself the pivotal point, and he saw the bridge, the fort, the soldiers upon the bridge, the captain, the sergeant, the two privates, his executioners. They were in silhouette against the blue sky. They shouted and gesticulated, pointing at him. The captain had drawn his pistol, but did not fire; the others were unarmed. Their movements were grotesque and horrible, their forms gigantic.

Suddenly he heard a sharp report and something struck the water smartly within a few inches of his head, spattering his face with spray. He heard a second report, and saw one of the sentinels with his rifle at his shoulder, a light cloud of blue smoke rising from the muzzle. The man in the water saw the eye of the man on the bridge gazing into his own through the sights of the rifle. He observed that it was a gray eye and remembered having read that gray eyes were keenest,

---

WORDS TO OWN

oscillation (äs′ə·lā′shən) *n.*: regular back-and-forth movement.
pivotal (piv′ə·təl) *adj.*: central; acting as a point around which other things turn.

AMBROSE BIERCE 471

D Elements of Literature
Point of View
❓ What two points of view does Bierce use here? How do these perspectives help convey Farquhar's altered state? [Possible response: Bierce alternates between a first-person and third-person limited perspective here— a technique that effectively conveys Farquhar's dreamlike disassociation from his own body.]

E Critical Thinking
Determining Author's Purpose
❓ How has Farquhar's vision changed? What purpose might this serve in the narrative? [Possible response: His senses have sharpened, and he now experiences the most minute details of nature with a strange intensity. Some readers might recall that a sharpening of the senses is sometimes said to occur at the moment of death, so this passage might be seen as a clue to Farquhar's true destiny.]

F Reading Skills and Strategies
Clarifying Responses to a Text
❓ Do you fear for Farquhar's life at this moment, or does the surreal, nightmarish quality of such images as the "grotesque and horrible movements" and the "gray eye" of the soldier diminish the urgency of Farquhar's plight? [Some students will say they still feel afraid for the protagonist; others may be less sympathetic now that they know his history; they may also note the dreamlike, almost slow-motion quality of the narrative.]

Using Students' Strengths

Logical/Mathematical Learners
Challenge students to design an escape plan for Farquhar, in which he uses his wits and any logical items or implements he might have access to. For example, Farquhar might try to bribe his captors to obtain his release. Students can share their plans with the class and calculate the odds of success for each stratagem.

Spatial/Visual Learners
After students have read the story, suggest that they draw rough sketches of the main events of the narrative, placing each event on a separate index card. Have them put the cards in order in two different ways. Ask them first to arrange the cards in the order in which the narrator tells the events. Next, have them arrange the cards in chronological order. These learners may also challenge other students in the class to place the cards in order.

and that all famous marksmen had them. Nevertheless, this one had missed.

A counterswirl had caught Farquhar and turned him half round; he was again looking into the forest on the bank opposite the fort. The sound of a clear, high voice in monotonous singsong now rang out behind him and came across the water with a distinctness that pierced and subdued all other sounds, even the beating of the ripples in his ears. Although no soldier, he had frequented camps enough to know the dread significance of that deliberate, drawling, aspirated chant; the lieutenant on shore was taking a part in the morning's work. How coldly and pitilessly—with what an even, calm intonation, presaging, and enforcing tranquility in the men—with what accurately measured intervals fell those cruel words:

"Attention, company! . . . Shoulder arms! . . . Ready! . . . Aim! . . . Fire!"

Farquhar dived—dived as deeply as he could. The water roared in his ears like the voice of Niagara, yet he heard the dulled thunder of the volley and, rising again toward the surface, met shining bits of metal, singularly flattened, oscillating slowly downward. Some of them touched him on the face and hands, then fell away, continuing their descent. One lodged between his collar and neck; it was uncomfortably warm and he snatched it out.

As he rose to the surface, gasping for breath, he saw that he had been a long time underwater; he was perceptibly farther downstream—nearer to safety. The soldiers had almost finished reloading; the metal ramrods flashed all at once in the sunshine as they were drawn from the barrels, turned in the air, and thrust into their sockets. The two sentinels fired again, independently and ineffectually.

The hunted man saw all this over his shoulder; he was now swimming vigorously with the current. His brain was as energetic as his arms and legs; he thought with the rapidity of lightning.

"The officer," he reasoned, "will not make that martinet's[4] error a second time. It is as easy to dodge a volley as a single shot. He has probably already given the command to fire at will. God help me, I cannot dodge them all!"

4. **martinet's:** A martinet is a disciplinarian of military rigidity.

An appalling plash within two yards of him was followed by a loud, rushing sound, *diminuendo,*[5] which seemed to travel back through the air to the fort and died in an explosion which stirred the very river to its deeps! A rising sheet of water curved over him, fell down upon him, blinded him, strangled him! The cannon had taken a hand in the game. As he shook his head free from the commotion of the smitten water, he heard the deflected shot humming through the air ahead, and in an instant it was cracking and smashing the branches in the forest beyond.

"They will not do that again," he thought; "the next time they will use a charge of grape.[6] I must keep my eye upon the gun; the smoke will apprise me—the report arrives too late; it lags behind the missile. That is a good gun."

Suddenly he felt himself whirled round and round—spinning like a top. The water, the banks, the forests, the now distant bridge, fort and men—all were commingled and blurred. Objects were represented by their colors only; circular horizontal streaks of color—that was all he saw. He had been caught in a vortex and was being whirled on with a velocity of advance and gyration that made him giddy and sick. In a few moments he was flung upon the gravel at the foot of the left bank of the stream—the southern bank—and behind a projecting point which concealed him from his enemies. The sudden arrest of his motion, the abrasion of one of his hands on the gravel, restored him, and he wept with delight. He dug his fingers into the sand, threw it over himself in handfuls, and audibly blessed it. It looked like diamonds, rubies, emeralds; he could think of nothing beautiful which it did not resemble. The trees upon the bank were giant garden plants; he noted a definite order in their arrangement, inhaled the fragrance of their blooms. A strange, roseate light shone through the spaces

5. *diminuendo* (də·min′yoo·en′dō): decreasing in loudness.
6. **charge of grape:** cannon charge of small iron balls, called grapeshot.

WORDS TO OWN

appalling (ə·pôl′iŋ) *adj.:* dismaying.
gyration (jī·rā′shən) *n.:* circular movement; whirling.
abrasion (ə·brā′zhən) *n.:* scrape.

---

472 THE RISE OF REALISM: THE CIVIL WAR AND POSTWAR PERIOD

among their trunks, and the wind made in their branches the music of aeolian harps.[7] He had no wish to perfect his escape—was content to remain in that enchanting spot until retaken.

A whiz and rattle of grapeshot among the branches high above his head roused him from his dream. The baffled cannoneer had fired him a random farewell. He sprang to his feet, rushed up the sloping bank, and plunged into the forest.

All that day he traveled, laying his course by the rounding sun. The forest seemed interminable; **D** nowhere did he discover a break in it, not even a woodsman's road. He had not known that he lived in so wild a region. There was something uncanny in the revelation.

By nightfall he was fatigued, footsore, famishing. The thought of his wife and children urged him on. At last he found a road which led him in what he knew to be the right direction. It was as wide and straight as a city street, yet it seemed untraveled. No fields bordered it, no dwelling anywhere. Not so much as the barking of a dog suggested human habitation. The black bodies of the trees formed a straight wall on both sides, terminating on the horizon in a point, like a diagram in a lesson in perspective. Overhead, as he looked **E** up through this rift in the wood, shone great golden stars looking unfamiliar and grouped in strange constellations. He was sure they were arranged in some order which had a secret and malign significance. The wood on either side was full of singular noises, among which—once, twice, and again—he distinctly heard whispers in an unknown tongue.

His neck was in pain and lifting his hand to it he found it horribly swollen. He knew that it had a circle of black where the rope had bruised it. His eyes felt congested; he could no longer close them. His tongue was swollen with thirst; he relieved its fever by thrusting it forward from between his teeth into the cold air. How softly the turf had carpeted the untraveled avenue—he could no longer feel the roadway beneath his feet!

7. **aeolian harps:** stringed instruments that are played by the wind. Aeolus is the god of the winds in Greek mythology.

Doubtless, despite his suffering, he had fallen asleep while walking, for now he sees another scene—perhaps he has merely recovered from a delirium. He stands at the gate of his own home. All is as he left it, and all bright and beautiful in the morning sunshine. He must have traveled the entire night. As he pushes open the gate and passes up the wide white walk, he sees a flutter of female garments; his wife, looking fresh and cool and sweet, steps down from the veranda to meet him. At the bottom of the steps she stands waiting, with a smile of ineffable joy, an attitude of matchless grace and dignity. Ah, how beautiful she is! He springs forward with extended arms. As he is about to clasp her he feels a stunning blow upon the back of the neck; a blinding white light **F** blazes all about him with a sound like the shock of a cannon—then all is darkness and silence!

Peyton Farquhar was dead; his body, with a broken neck, swung gently from side to side beneath the timbers of the Owl Creek bridge. **G**

WORDS TO OWN

malign (mə·līn′) *adj.:* harmful; evil.

AMBROSE BIERCE 473

D Reading Skills and Strategies
Understanding Prefixes, Roots, and Suffixes
? What prefix, suffix, and root are contained in the word *interminable*? How can you use these word parts to define the word? [*In-* means "not," *term* means "end," and *-able* means "capable"; therefore, *interminable* means "without end" or "unable to end."]

E Elements of Literature
Point of View
? How does the point of view add to the strangeness of this scene? [Since we see events through the third-person limited point of view (reflecting only Farquhar's thoughts and feelings), we would expect the landscape to be familiar, since he is not far from his home. Instead, the point of view gives the scene an eerie sense of unreality and disorientation, a nightmarish quality.]

F Reading Skills and Strategies

Clarifying Responses to the Text
? What has happened here? How does it relate to the rest of the story? [Farquhar is dead, hanged from the bridge as scheduled. His "escape" was all in his mind.] How do you feel about what has happened to Farquhar? [Possible responses: disappointed that he did not survive and reach home; surprised and upset by his death; satisfied, because his escape seemed implausible.]

G Elements of Literature
Theme
? How is the theme of illusion versus reality woven throughout this story? [Possible response: Farquhar's romantic illusions about the war end with his capture and execution. The reader's illusion of Farquhar's romantic escape from death ends with the conclusion of this story and this matter-of-fact final sentence.]

Assessing Learning

Check Test: True–False
1. Farquhar is a Confederate captain who has been captured on a sabotage attempt. [False]
2. Farquhar has been condemned to death by firing squad. [False]
3. Farquhar was entrapped by a Union scout into attempted sabotage of a bridge. [True]
4. Bierce uses a flashback to explain why Farquhar is being executed. [True]
5. At the end of the story, Farquhar is reunited with his wife. [False]

Standardized Test Preparation
For practice with ACT and SAT formats, see
• *Preparation for College Admission Exams*, p. 33
For practice in proofreading and editing, see
• *Daily Oral Grammar*, Transparency 31

BROWSING IN THE FILES
About the Author. The happy marriage between Mr. and Mrs. Farquhar that Bierce portrays in "An Occurrence at Owl Creek Bridge" is a far cry from the author's own tumultuous marriage, which ended in divorce in 1891.

MAKING MEANINGS

First Thoughts [Respond]

1. Possible responses: I was shocked to find out that he had not escaped; since his escape seemed so incredible, his actual fate made sense.

Shaping Interpretations [Interpret]

2. Bierce uses a third-person limited perspective to reveal the desperate flight of Farquhar's imagination. This limited perspective allows Bierce's narrative to maintain a realist approach—even as Farquhar's mind flees the reality of his death.

3. The Union soldier's trick may cause some readers to believe that Bierce wants readers to side with the Confederates. Other readers may think that Bierce exposes the naive complacency of white Southern aristocrats. Still other students may see the story as an examination of war's horror, waste, and futility.

4. Bierce gives the false hope that Farquhar has escaped but prepares readers for the ending by hinting at Farquhar's distortion of reality.

Extending the Text [Apply]

5. The story suggests that the terror of death heightens sense perceptions and distorts the passage of time. Many students are likely to find this psychology believable since it is part of popular mythology. The story also suggests that, when faced with a reality it cannot accept, the mind escapes into fantasy.

Challenging the Text [Evaluate]

6. Students who agree might argue that they felt tricked by the author and that the long fantasy section in Part III seems contrived and without profound meaning, given the rather shallow characterization of Farquhar. Those who disagree might argue that the story has a wider significance because it explores a universal human capacity for self-delusion and fantasy. They might argue that we are all a little like Farquhar, certain we will die someday yet pretending that day will never come.

CHOICES:
Building Your Portfolio

1–3. Encourage students to return to the story for ideas as they write.

T474

MAKING MEANINGS

First Thoughts

1. Did you feel that the outcome of this story was credible and powerful, or did you feel cheated by the surprise ending? What kind of ending had you been led to anticipate? Explain your response.

> **Reading Check**
> a. State the situation Peyton Farquhar faces in Part I.
> b. Part II of the story is a flashback. List its events in **chronological order.**
> c. **Summarize** in one sentence what Farquhar imagines in Part III.

Shaping Interpretations

2. What **point of view** does the writer use in the third part of the story, which occurs within the few seconds before Farquhar dies? Why is this point of view particularly appropriate?

3. Do you think Bierce tries to enlist your sympathies toward either the Union or the Confederate side? Or does the story seem to be focused on a more general **theme** about the nature of the war? Cite evidence from the story.

4. Review the notes you took on your responses to the story. How did Bierce manipulate your feelings? How did he prepare you for the ending?

Extending the Text

5. What does this story reveal about the psychology of a person in a life-or-death situation? Do you find this psychology believable or far-fetched? Explain.

Challenging the Text

6. The critics Cleanth Brooks and Robert Penn Warren have said that Bierce's story depends too much on a quirk of human psychology and is thus a mere "case study" that does not reveal anything important about human nature, as good fiction does. Do you agree? Why or why not?

CHOICES:
Building Your Portfolio

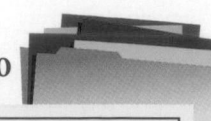

> **Writer's Notebook**
> ### 1. Collecting Ideas for a Research Paper
>
>
>
> Make some notes about interesting topics this story suggests (perhaps the use of spies during the Civil War or current psychological theories of stress). Then, write down a list of possible sources of information you could consult for your research: library resources, community sources (local museums or historical societies), and so on. Save your notes for possible use in the Writer's Workshop on page 515.
>
> **Adapting a Story to Another Medium**
> ### 2. Film Version
>
> Write a memorandum to a film producer outlining your plans for adapting "Occurrence" into a movie. Point out scenes where you would use each of the following techniques: (a) close-up shot; (b) panoramic shot; (c) moving-camera shot; (d) quick cut to new scene; (e) fast motion; (f) slow motion; (g) fuzzy image; (h) sound effects. Before you write your final draft of the memo, you might view the Academy Award®–winning short film (available on videocassette) of the story. It was made in 1962 in France and became a favorite episode of the old TV series *The Twilight Zone*. Compare your plans with the actual film, and then, if you choose, modify your memorandum.
>
> **Creative Writing**
> ### 3. Variations on Bierce
>
> Write a brief narrative in which you explore the inner workings of the mind of a character subjected to a moment of intense pressure or an extraordinary crisis. Try to imitate Bierce by shifting your narrative between external reality and internal thoughts.

> **Reading Check**
> a. He is about to be hanged.
> b. A soldier comes to Farquhar's house and tells him that Union soldiers have been working on the Owl Creek Bridge and will hang any civilian who interferes. At Farquhar's request, the soldier tells how one could burn the bridge. The soldier leaves but later returns, headed north because he is a Union spy.
> c. He imagines that the rope breaks, that he escapes, and that he makes it home.

Grading Timesaver

Rubrics for each Choices assignment appear on p. 146 in the *Portfolio Management System*.

Reading Skills and Strategies

OBJECTIVES
1. Recognize the function of prefixes and suffixes in changing the meanings of base words or roots
2. Identify and analyze affixes in order to understand the meanings of specific words

VOCABULARY: AFFIXES— THE LONG AND SHORT OF IT

Prefixes and suffixes are examples of **affixes,** word parts attached to the beginning or end of a base word or root to make a new word. Knowing some frequently used affixes can help you quickly unlock the meanings of words that seem long and inaccessible.

In fact, *inaccessible* is a good word to start with. Ambrose Bierce uses it in "An Occurrence at Owl Creek Bridge": "He opened his eyes in the darkness and saw above him a gleam of light, but how distant, how inaccessible!" (page 471). Context tells you that *inaccessible* has a similar meaning to *distant.* To fully understand the word, try affix analysis.

There are many prefixes and suffixes in English, but some are more commonly used than others. **Prefixes** are added to the beginning of a **base word** or **root** and always change its meaning. Some prefixes adjust their spelling so that the resulting word will be easier to say.

Prefixes	Meanings	Examples
co–, col–, com–	with, together	coexist, collide, compare
con–, cor–	with, together	convene, correspond
de–	away, from, off	defect, desert
dis–	away, off, opposing	dismount, dissent
em–, en–	cause to be, put into	empower, enrobe
ex–, e–, ef–	away from, out, up	excise, emigrate, efface
in–, im–, il–, ir–	not	incapable, impious, illegal, irregular
pro–	forward, in place of, favoring	proceed, pronoun, pro-American
re–	back, again	recede, recur
un–	not, reverse of	untrue, unfold

Suffixes are added to the end of a base word or root. **Inflectional suffixes,** like -ed and -ing, usually

just change the tense, person, or number of a word (generally a verb). **Derivational suffixes,** like the ones listed below, change the entire meaning of a root or base word.

Suffixes	Meanings	Examples
–able, –ible	able, likely	capable, flexible
–al	doer, pertaining to	rival, autumnal
–ant, –ent	doer, showing	servant, superintendent
–ate	having, characteristic of	collegiate
–ence	act, condition, fact	patience, evidence
–er, –or	doer	baker, director
–ic	dealing with, caused by, showing	classic, choleric, workaholic
–ion, –tion	action, result, state	union, fusion, selection
–ive	belonging or tending to	detective, native
–ous	marked by, given to	religious, furious
–y	quality, action	jealousy, inquiry

The chart below shows one way that you can use affixes to analyze the meaning of a word.

Word	Prefix	Base/Root	Suffix(es)	Meaning of Word
inaccessible	in– meaning: not	access meaning: to obtain	–ible meaning: able	not able to be obtained

Try It Out

Make your own affix-analysis chart for these words from "Occurrence."

1. inglorious
2. roseate
3. infrequency
4. commandant
5. manifestations
6. recurrence
7. deflected
8. disobedient
9. encircled
10. exalted

Reading Skills and Strategies

This feature focuses on the strategy of using affixes (prefixes and suffixes) to decode the meanings of words.

Mini-Lesson: Affixes

Call students' attention to the chart that shows the affixes in *inaccessible.* Point out the combined meaning of the affixes: "not able to be obtained." Ask students what synonyms they can think of for *inaccessible,* based on these clues. [Possible answers: *unreachable, unattainable, unapproachable, remote.*]

Try It Out

Answers will vary depending on the dictionary students use.

1. **inglorious** *in-* ("not") + *glory* ("renown") + *-ous* ("marked by") = "marked by a lack of renown."
2. **roseate** *rose* ("flower, pink") + *ate* ("having characteristic of") = "like a rose; pinkish."
3. **infrequency** *in-* ("not") + *frequent* ("often") + *-y* ("quality, condition") = "not occurring often."
4. **commandant** *com-* ("with") + *mand* ("order") + *-ant* ("actor, agent") = "agent entrusted with orders."
5. **manifestations** *manifest* ("evident") + *-ations* ("results, states") = "evident results."
6. **recurrence** *re-* ("again") + *cur* ("to run") + *-ence* ("condition") = "condition of happening again."
7. **deflected** *de-* ("away") + *flected* (bent) = "bent away."
8. **disobedient** *dis-* ("opposing") + *obedi* ("obey") + *-ent* ("showing") = "showing an opposition to obeying."
9. **encircled** *en-* ("caused to") + *circled* ("surrounded") = "caused to be surrounded."
10. **exalted** *ex-* ("out, away") + *alted* ("placed high") = "placed high and away."

Getting Students Involved

Root and Affix Roulette

On each of ten small strips of paper, write a different root or affix, and place the strips in a hat. Then, divide the class into groups of five. Draw a strip out of the hat at random, read the root or affix aloud, and then start a timer or stopwatch. Give each group two minutes to brainstorm and prepare (without dictionaries) a list of words that contain the selected root or affix. A member of each group should then read its list aloud.

Give one point to the group with the shortest list of correct words, two points to the group with the next shortest list, and so on. (Each group earns some points for its efforts.) The group with the longest correct list gets the highest number of points for the round. Continue with different roots and affixes until all the slips are drawn from the hat. The winning group is the one with the highest overall total.

Spotlight On

This feature contains excerpts from letters, diaries, speeches, newspaper columns, and memoirs of people who experienced the Civil War firsthand. The authors of these excerpts include everyone from an Indiana farm boy to the President of the United States. Students will find that the trauma of the war brought out a rare eloquence and emotional intensity in all these writers.

Ⓐ Exploring the Historical Period

Outcomes of War

Many people believed that the Civil War would be a quick conflict, easily resolved. They were tragically mistaken. The war lasted four years and resulted in about 623,000 dead and 470,000 wounded—the deadliest conflict in United States history, claiming more American lives than all other wars combined. Ironically, more men were killed by disease than in combat.

Ⓑ Reading Skills and Strategies

Making Predictions

❓ How does Upson's Grandmother think the South will suffer? [Possible response: She assumes that the South will lose the war and be punished (economically, politically, socially) for its insurrection.]

Ⓒ Exploring the Historical Period

Material Devastation

Upson's Grandmother's premonitions proved largely accurate. Not only did one quarter of Southern troops die, but the encroaching Northern armies destroyed everything that could be used to support the Southern cause, including crops, railroad tracks, bridges, livestock, homes, and businesses. The South lay in economic ruin for years after the war.

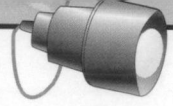

SPOTLIGHT ON
Voices from the Civil War

There are few literary records of the Civil War, but there are many personal testimonies in the form of letters, diaries, and memoirs. Some of these were written by well-known figures, but most were the work of ordinary people caught up in the most extraordinary and painful events of America's history.

The following excerpts provide a brief history of the war in the voices of those who experienced it, including an Indiana farm boy, President Lincoln, Frederick Douglass, a Southern gentlewoman, and a Union soldier who witnessed the surrender of General Robert E. Lee.

It is often said that any civil war is a war of brother against brother, but we must think a moment to realize what this meant in nineteenth-century America. The United States at the time was a mobile society, and many families, especially in the border states, had friends and relatives in both the North and the South. For such families, the Civil War was a profoundly personal conflict.

Ⓐ In April 1861, several months after seven Southern states had formally seceded from the Union, Confederate forces demanded the surrender of the Union garrison on Fort Sumter, located on an island in the harbor of Charleston, South Carolina. At dawn on the twelfth of April, fighting began. Here is the response of Theodore Upson, a teenage farm boy in Indiana, to the news of the attack on Fort Sumter.

The Granger Collection, New York (cannon).

Theodore Upson

APRIL 1861

Father and I were husking out some corn. We could not finish before it wintered up. When William Cory came across the field (he had been down after the mail) he was excited and said, "Jonathan, the Rebs have fired upon and taken Fort Sumter." Father got white and couldn't say a word.

William said, "The president will soon fix them. He has called for 75,000 men and is going to blockade their ports, and just as soon as those fellows find out that the North means business, they will get down off their high horse."

Father said little. We did not finish the corn and drove to the barn. Father left me to unload and put out the team and went to the house. After I had finished I went in to dinner. Mother said, "What is the matter with Father?" He had gone right upstairs. I told her what we had heard. She went to him. After a while they came down. Father looked ten years older. We sat down to the table. Grandma wanted to know what was the Ⓑ trouble. Father told her and she began to cry. "Oh, my poor children in the South! Now they Ⓒ will suffer! God knows how they will suffer! I knew it would come! Jonathan, I told you it would come!"

"They can come here and stay," said Father.

"No, they will not do that. There is their home. There they will stay. Oh, to think that I should have lived to see the day when brother should rise against brother. . . ."

Mother had a letter from the Hales. Charlie and his father are in their [that is, the Confederate] army and Dayton wanted to go but was too young. I wonder if I were in our army and they should meet me would they shoot me. I suppose they would.

—from *The Blue and the Gray: The Story of the Civil War as Told by Participants,* edited by Henry Steele Commager

476 THE RISE OF REALISM: THE CIVIL WAR AND POSTWAR PERIOD

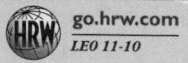 **go.hrw.com** *LEO 11-10*

Reaching All Students

English Language Learners

Some students may not be very familiar with the Civil War period of United States history. Before students read this feature, ask what they know about the war. Provide information as needed, such as when the war was fought and why. Point out that the war was the culmination of forty years of regional conflict over economic, social, and political policies between Northern and Southern states.

Advanced Students

Invite students to compare and contrast the usefulness of primary and secondary sources. What advantages—and disadvantages—does each type of source have? [Primary sources, for example, provide a fresh, immediate voice but lack the background information, balanced perspective, and analysis that secondary sources have.] Ask students to discuss how both kinds of sources are useful in understanding a historical period.

W alt Whitman (page 348) was too old to fight in the Civil War, but he did volunteer his services as a nurse in army hospitals. The following is an excerpt from his description of the wounded after the Battle of Chancellorsville, one of the bloodiest in the war, and one that Stephen Crane depicts in *The Red Badge of Courage*.

Walt Whitman

Then the camps of the wounded—O heavens, what scene is this?—is this indeed *humanity*—these butchers' shambles? There are several of them. There they lie, in the largest, in an open space in the woods, from 200 to 300 poor fellows—the groans and screams—the odor of blood, mixed with the fresh scent of the night, the grass, the trees—that slaughterhouse! O well is it their mothers, their sisters cannot see them—cannot conceive, and never conceived, these things. One man is shot by a shell, both in the arm and leg—both are amputated—there lie the rejected members. Some have their legs blown off—some bullets through the breast—some indescribably horrid wounds in the face or head, all mutilated, sickening, torn, gouged out—some in the abdomen—some mere boys—many rebels, badly hurt—they take their regular turns with the rest, just the same as any—the surgeons use them just the same. Such is the camp of the wounded—such a fragment, a reflection afar off of the bloody scene—while over all the clear, large moon comes out at times softly, quietly shining.

—Walt Whitman, *from Specimen Days*

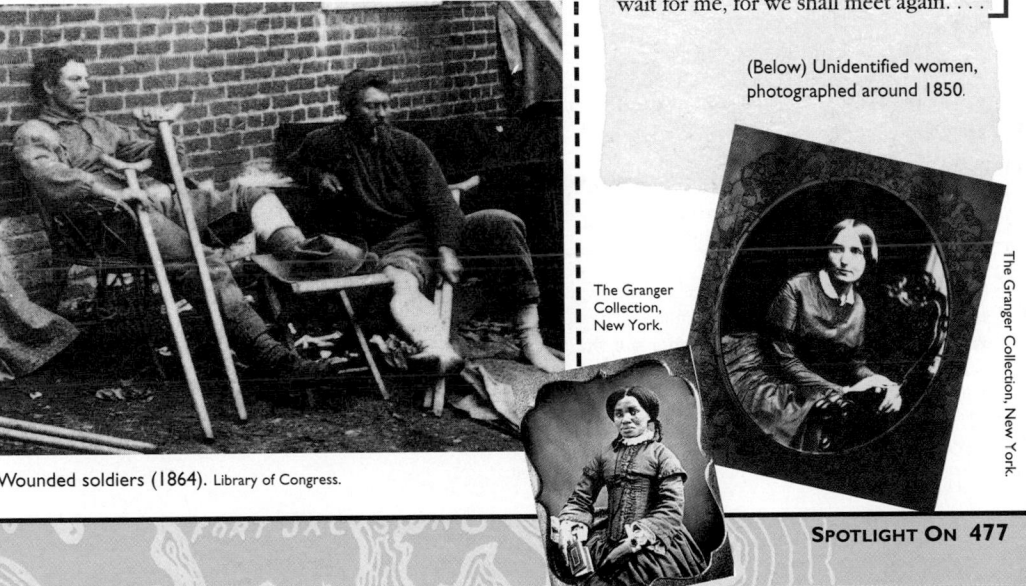
Wounded soldiers (1864). Library of Congress.

Major Sullivan Ballou

I n July 1861, Major Ballou wrote to his wife, Sarah, in Rhode Island. One week after he wrote this letter, Major Ballou was killed in the First Battle of Bull Run, Virginia.

. . . I know I have but few claims upon Divine Providence, but something whispers to me—perhaps it is the wafted prayer of my little Edgar, that I shall return to my loved ones unharmed. If I do not, my dear Sarah, never forget how much I love you, nor that when my last breath escapes me on the battlefield, it will whisper your name.

Forgive my many faults, and the many pains I have caused you. How thoughtless, how foolish I have sometimes been! How gladly would I wash out with my tears every little spot upon your happiness. . . .

But, O Sarah! If the dead can come back to this earth and flit unseen around those they love, I shall be always with you in the brightest day and the darkest night . . . *always, always,* and when the soft breeze fans your cheek, it shall be my breath, or the cool air your throbbing temple, it shall be my spirit passing by. Sarah, do not mourn me dead: Think I am gone and wait for me, for we shall meet again. . . .

(Below) Unidentified women, photographed around 1850.

The Granger Collection, New York.

The Granger Collection, New York.

D Literary Connections
Whitman as Nurse
Walt Whitman, the "good gray poet," made more than six hundred visits to hospitals and nursed many sick and wounded soldiers—both Union and Confederate. To amuse his patients, Whitman played "Twenty Questions" and recited his poetry. His prose account of his experiences, *Memoranda During the War,* was privately published many years later and was combined in 1882 with some of his other prose writings in a book called *Specimen Days.* (For more information on Whitman's experience of the war, see pp. 363–364.)

E Exploring the Historical Period
Writers and the War
Whitman was the only major American writer who experienced the consequences of the war firsthand. For Northern writers, the war was a distant event, and they had but a dim comprehension of its horror. When his son Charley ran away to join the Union Army, for example, Longfellow sent him a servant and two horses and could not understand why the packages he sent his son were delayed.

F Elements of Literature
Style
❓ What effect does Whitman create by contrasting the "clear, large moon" with the camp full of ravaged soldiers? [Possible response: The poignant contrast underscores the horror of war—nature's beauty persists in the face of humanity's greatest cruelties.]

G Cultural Connections
Love and Marriage
In the nineteenth century, the subdivision of large farms and the increasing opportunities for urban economic advancement resulted in a change in the incentives for marriage—from marriage as a way to increase family wealth (through acquiring property) to marriage based on love alone. Even the restrictive planter society of the South began to accept love as an integral part of marriage. In 1819, one planter wrote to his wife, "It is in the bosom of retirement all the sympathies of friendship and love are awakened. Then our souls commune and our hearts beat together." Numerous letters and diaries written during the Civil War testify to the intense devotion of American marriages.

Using Students' Strengths

Auditory/Kinesthetic Learners
Have students work in groups to create a tableau of some of the figures whose voices are represented here. Each figure can "come to life" and deliver part of his or her selection. As students perform their tableaux, encourage them to give their characters the appropriate voices, gestures, and postures. Invite the performers to explain how their interpretations added to their understanding of the selection.

Logical/Mathematical Learners
Invite students to prepare a bar graph or other visual to show the number of people killed in the Revolutionary War, the Civil War, World War I, World War II, and the Vietnam War. As students analyze their statistics, have them debate which more accurately reflects the devastation of war—charts showing the total number of people who lost their lives, or a small selection of individual accounts of personal losses.

A Cultural Connections

Epithets

? "Johnny Reb" and "Billy Yank" were generic terms for Confederate and Union soldiers, respectively. What names do we use today to refer to "Everyman" or "Everywoman"? [Possible responses: John Doe, Jane Doe, John Q. Public, Jane Smith.]

B Critical Thinking

Expressing an Opinion

? Would you trust an enemy soldier's word in this situation? Why or why not? [Possible responses: Yes, because the enemy is really a government, not a specific person with an intent to kill; no, because an enemy is an enemy.]

C Reading Skills and Strategies

Making Inferences

Explore the students' impressions of the soldiers and what the details (the paper boats, the Southerners' admiration of Yankee ingenuity, Joe Boteler's annoyance) suggest about their age, character, and attitudes. [These details suggest that all the soldiers are barely out of boyhood and share a basic innocence, enthusiasm, and honesty.]

D Reading Skills and Strategies

Making Inferences

? Why do you think the opposing sides trade supplies so readily? [Possible responses: More skeptical students may suggest the trade was self-serving; more idealistic students might argue that the trade reveals the essential goodness and humanity of both sides.] **How do you think Hunter felt the next day or the day after when he went into battle against these same Yankees?** [Possible answer: He was probably troubled and conflicted but probably carried out his orders without question.]

Resources

Audio CD Library

- A dramatic reading of Lincoln's Gettysburg Address is available in the *Audio CD Library:* Disc 13, Track 2

Alexander Hunter was a college boy who joined the Seventeenth Virginia Regiment at the outbreak of the war. His book, *Johnny Reb and Billy Yank,* provides a lively look at life in the Confederate Army. Here he describes a meeting between Union and Confederate soldiers.

Alexander Hunter

A Johnny Reb and Billy Yank

It was in the latter part of August [1863]; orders were given to be prepared to go on [guard duty] early in the morning; and until a late hour the men were busy cooking rations and cleaning equipment.

Before the mists had been chased by the rising sun, the company in close column of fours marched down the road. Men and animals were in perfect condition, brimful of mettle and in buoyant spirits.

The route lay along the banks of the river; upon the winding course of which, after several hours riding, the regiment reached its destination and relieved the various [guards]. A sergeant and squad of men were left at each post . . . to watch the enemy on the other side of the Rappahannock. . . .

The Rappahannock, which was at this place about two hundred yards wide, flowing slowly oceanward, its bosom reflecting the roseate-hued morn, was as lovely a body of water as the sun ever shone upon. The sound of the gentle ripple of its waves upon the sand was broken by a faint "halloo" which came from the other side.

"Johnny Reb; I say, J-o-h-n-n-y R-e-b, don't shoot!"

Joe Reid shouted back, "All right!"

"What command are you?"

The spoken words floated clear and distinct across the water, "The Black Horse Cavalry. Who are you?"

"The Second Michigan Cavalry."

"Come to the bank," said our spokesman, "and show yourselves; we won't fire."

"On your honor, Johnny Reb?"

"On our honor, Billy Yank."

In a second a large squad of blue-coats across the way advanced to the water's brink. The Southerners did the same; then the former put the query.

"Have you any tobacco?"

"Plenty of it," went out our reply.

"Any sugar and coffee?" they questioned.

"Not a taste nor a smell."

"Let's trade," was shouted with eagerness.

"Very well," was the reply, ". . . meet us here this evening."

"All right," they answered; then added, "Say, Johnny, want some newspapers?"

"Y-e-s!"

"Then look out, we are going to send you some."

"How are you going to do it?"

"Wait and see. . . ."

Eagerly he watched. . . . Presently he shouted: "Here they come!" and then in a tone of intense admiration, "I'll be doggoned if these Yanks are not the smartest people in the world."

On the other side were several miniature boats and ships—such as schoolboys delight in—with sails set; the gentle breeze impelled the little crafts across the river, each freighted with a couple of newspapers. . . .

Drawing lots, Joe Boteler, who found luck against him, started to town, with a muttered curse, to buy tobacco. . . .

Joe returned in the evening with a box of plug tobacco about a foot square; but how to get it across was the question. The miniature boats could not carry it, and we shouted over to the Yanks that we had about twenty pounds of cut plug, and asked them what we must do? They hallooed back to let one of us swim across, and declared that it was perfectly safe. . . . I volunteered. Having lived on the banks of the Potomac most of my life, I was necessarily a swimmer. . . .

As I approached the shore the news of my coming reached camp, and nearly all the Second Michigan were lined up along the bank.

I felt a little queer, but had perfect faith in their promise and kept on without missing a stroke. . . . The blue-coats crowded around me and gave me a hearty welcome, . . . and heaped the craft with offerings of sugar, coffee, lemons, and even candy.

Bidding my friends the enemy good-bye, I swam back with the precious cargo, and we had a feast that night.

—Alexander Hunter, *from Johnny Reb and Billy Yank*

478 THE RISE OF REALISM: THE CIVIL WAR AND POSTWAR PERIOD

Professional Notes

Civil War Hymns

The most important marching songs of the Civil War were "Dixie," for the South, and "The Battle Hymn of the Republic," for the North. Ironically, "Dixie" was written by a Northerner, Daniel Decatur Emmett, as a solo piece for several African American performers in minstrel shows. It had its first performance on Broadway in 1859 and became a hit throughout the country as other minstrel companies picked it up.

"The Battle Hymn of the Republic" was written by the famous reformer Julia Ward Howe in 1862. After watching Union soldiers singing "John Brown's Body" at a camp near Washington, D.C., Howe was inspired to write new words to the tune. Her hymn became the marching song of the Union Army and later of the United States Army through World War II. (See p. T494 for more on Civil War music.)

The Battle of Gettysburg: Pickett's Charge by Peter F. Rothermel.

On July 7, 1863, a few days after the Battle of Gettysburg, Lincoln noted in an informal address how important this battle had been, but concluded that he was "not prepared to make [a speech] worthy of the occasion."

Several months later, in November of that year, Lincoln in fact delivered a speech on this theme, perhaps the most memorable of his career, at the dedication of the cemetery in Gettysburg.

Abraham Lincoln
The Gettysburg Address

Fourscore and seven years ago our fathers brought forth on this continent a new nation, conceived in Liberty, and dedicated to the proposition that all men are created equal.

Now we are engaged in a great civil war, testing whether that nation, or any nation so conceived and so dedicated, can long endure. We are met on a great battlefield of that war. We have come to dedicate a portion of that field as a final resting place for those who here gave their lives that that nation might live. It is altogether fitting and proper that we should do this.

But, in a larger sense, we cannot dedicate—we cannot consecrate—we cannot hallow—this ground. The brave men, living and dead, who struggled here, have consecrated it far above our poor power to add or detract. The world will little note nor long remember what we say here, but it can never forget what they did here. It is for us the living, rather, to be dedicated here to the unfinished work which they who fought here have thus far so nobly advanced. It is rather for us to be here dedicated to the great task remaining before us—that from these honored dead we take increased devotion to that cause for which they gave the last full measure of devotion—that we here highly resolve that these dead shall not have died in vain—that this nation, under God, shall have a new birth of freedom—and that government of the people, by the people, for the people, shall not perish from the earth.

—Abraham Lincoln
November 19, 1863

Taking a Second Look

Review: Comparison and Contrast
Point out that the two subjects of a comparison-and-contrast essay must belong to the same category and possess parallel characteristics that serve as points of comparison. Remind students that essays can be organized in two ways: by subject (all the points about one subject are discussed, then all the points about the other are discussed) or by point (each characteristic is discussed first in relation to one subject then in relation to the other). Discuss how a clear thesis and parallel discussion of points keep the essay focused and how transitional words (such as *similarly* and *conversely*) add coherence.

Activity
Have students read Lincoln's Second Inaugural Address and compare it with the Gettysburg Address. Before students write individual essays, have small groups list points of comparison, such as purpose and style (diction, Biblical allusions, parallelism).

RESPONDING TO THE ART
Peter F. Rothermel (1817–1895) was an American painter known for his dramatic paintings of patriotic subjects. This detail, "Death of Reynolds," is a section of his colossal painting of the Battle of Gettysburg, commissioned by the Pennsylvania legislature.

E Exploring the Historical Period
Gettysburg
The Battle of Gettysburg, July 1–3, 1863, was the turning point of the war. Major General George Pickett led a force of 15,000 against the main body of Union troops. The assault did not succeed, and the Confederate Army—now one-third smaller—retreated. In all, the toll at Gettysburg was 5,660 dead, 27,000 wounded, and 10,500 missing.

F Appreciating Language
Diction
❓ Why do you think Lincoln started with the phrase "Fourscore and seven years ago" rather than "Eighty-seven years ago"? [Lincoln deliberately used Biblical diction to create a formal, elevated, and elegiac tone.]

G Appreciating Language
Parallelism / Repetition
❓ How does Lincoln use parallelism and repetition here and at the end of the paragraph to inspire his audience? [Possible response: Repetition creates emphasis on the inspiring sacrifice of the Gettysburg dead and the difficulty of fully honoring it. The parallelism at the end stresses the idea that American democracy itself is at stake.]

H Exploring the Historical Period
Everett's Reaction
The featured speaker on the day of Lincoln's address was Edward Everett, who spoke for nearly two hours. Lincoln was disappointed with his own speech, but Everett wrote, "I should be glad if I could flatter myself that I came as near to the central idea of the occasion, in two hours, as you did in two minutes."

A English Language Learners

Evolution of Language

Explain that language is a rich, living thing that changes as a result of immigration, cultural change, and inventions. For example, African Americans were called "colored" people during the nineteenth and much of the twentieth century. Today, the preferred terms are *black* or *African American*. You might use this as a springboard for a discussion of non-biased language in general.

B Critical Thinking

Expressing an Opinion

❓ Were the soldiers right to insist on full pay? Why or why not? [Most students will agree that the soldiers were correct, since they deserved equal pay for equal work. Some students may feel that the urgency of the war demanded that they accept less.]

C Cultural Connections

Clara Barton

Women on both sides of the conflict made numerous contributions during the Civil War. For example, Clara Barton (1821–1912), the "Angel of the Battlefield," ministered to the wounded even without official authorization. She was eventually appointed superintendent of nurses with the Union Army of the James. After the war, Barton founded the American branch of the International Association of the Red Cross.

Susie King Taylor was born in slavery near Savannah, Georgia, in 1848. In April 1862, when she was fourteen, her uncle took her and his own seven children behind the Union lines. Taylor found work as a launderer for an African American troop, and soon found herself doing emergency work tending the wounded.

In 1902, Taylor wrote down her memory of her experiences with an African American regiment at Camp Saxton in Georgia.

Sgt. Balldwin of Company G, Fifty-sixth U.S. Colored Infantry (1863). Tintype.

The Granger Collection, New York.

Susie King Taylor

A The first colored troops did not receive any pay for eighteen months, and the men had to depend wholly on what they received from the commissary established by General Saxton. A great many of these men had large families, and as they had no money to give them, their wives were obliged to support themselves and children by washing for the officers of the gunboats and the soldiers, and making cakes and pies which they sold to the boys in camp. Finally, **B** in 1863, the government decided to give them half pay, but the men would not accept this. They wanted "full pay" or nothing. They preferred rather to give their services to the state, which they did until 1864, when the government granted them full pay, with all the back pay due. . . .

About four o'clock, July 2, the charge [into battle] was made. . . . [The first] one [of the wounded] brought in was Samuel Anderson of our company. . . . Then others of our boys, some with their legs off, arm gone, foot off, and wounds of all kinds imaginable. They had to wade through creeks and marshes, as they were discovered by the enemy and shelled very badly. A number of the men were lost. . . .

My work now began. I gave my assistance to try to alleviate their sufferings. I asked the doctor at the hospital what I could get for them to eat. They wanted soup, but that I could not get; but I had a few cans of condensed milk and some turtle eggs, so I thought I **C** would try to make some custard. I had doubts as to my success, for cooking with turtle eggs was something new to me; but the adage has it, "Nothing ventured, nothing done," so I made a venture and the result was a very delicious custard. This I carried to the men, who enjoyed it very much.

—Susie King Taylor, *from Reminiscences of My Life in Camp*

Harriet Tubman Series No. 29 (1939–1940) by Jacob Lawrence. Casein tempera on gessoed hardboard (17⅞″ × 12″).

Hampton University Museum, Hampton, Virginia.

Courtesy of the artist and the Francine Seders Gallery, Seattle, WA.

Professional Notes

Personal Account: The Education of Susie King Taylor

One of the many jobs Susie King Taylor performed for the Union Army was teaching the many black soldiers eager to learn to read and write. But her account of how she herself obtained an education is remarkable: "My brother and I . . . were sent to a friend of my grandmother . . . to learn to read and write. . . . We went every day about nine o'clock, with our books wrapped in paper to prevent the police or white persons from seeing them. We went in, one at a time, through the gate, into the yard to the kitchen, which was the schoolroom. She had twenty-five or thirty children. . . .The neighbors would see us going in sometimes, but they supposed we were there learning trades, as it was the custom to give children a trade of some kind. After school we left the same way we entered, one by one. . . ."

The most famous African American spokesperson during the Civil War was Frederick Douglass (page 424). Douglass used all of his eloquence and passionate oratory to persuade African Americans in the North to enlist in the Union Army. Eventually, a number of all-black volunteer regiments were formed and trained. (The 1989 film *Glory* reenacts the tragic exploits of one such regiment.) About 180,000 African Americans enlisted, including two of Douglass's sons. The following call to action first appeared in Douglass's own newspaper in March 1863.

Frederick Douglass

When first the rebel cannon shattered the walls of Sumter and drove away its starving garrison, I predicted that the war then and there inaugurated would not be fought out entirely by white men. Every month's experience during these dreary years has confirmed that opinion. A war undertaken and brazenly carried on for the perpetual enslavement of colored men, calls logically and loudly for colored men to help suppress it. Only a moderate share of sagacity was needed to see that the arm of the slave was the best defense against the arm of the slaveholder. Hence with every reverse to the national arms, with every exulting shout of victory raised by the slaveholding rebels, I have implored the imperiled nation to unchain against her foes, her powerful black hand. Slowly and reluctantly that appeal is beginning to be heeded. Stop not now to complain that it was not heeded sooner. It may or it may not have been best that it should not. This is not the time to discuss that question. Leave it to the future. When the war is over, the country is saved, peace is established, and the black man's rights are secured, as they will be, history with an impartial hand will dispose of that and sundry other questions. Action! Action! not criticism, is the plain duty of this hour. Words are now useful only as they stimulate to blows. The office of speech now is only to point out when, where, and how to strike to the best advantage. There is no time to delay. The tide is at its flood that leads on to fortune. From East to West, from North to South, the sky is written all over, "Now or never." Liberty won by white men would lose half its luster. "Who would be free themselves must strike the blow." "Better even die free, than to live slaves." This is the sentiment of every brave colored man amongst us.

—from *The Life and Times of Frederick Douglass*

Unidentified Union Army soldier with his wife, around 1865.

The following is just a small sample of memorable quotations from Frederick Douglass's speeches and writings.

We are *Americans,* speaking the same language, adopting the same customs, holding the same general opinions . . . and shall rise and fall with Americans.

Once let the black man get upon his person the brass letters "U.S."; let him get an eagle on his button, and a musket on his shoulder, and bullets in his pocket, and there is no power on the earth or under the earth which can deny that he has earned the right of citizenship in the United States.

The day dawns; the morning star is bright upon the horizon! The iron gate of our prison stands half open. One gallant rush from the North will fling it wide open, while four millions of our brothers and sisters shall march out into liberty. The chance is now given you to end in a day the bondage of centuries, and to rise in one bound from social degradation to the plane of common equality with all other varieties of men.

—from *The Life and Times of Frederick Douglass*

The Granger Collection, New York.

D Historical Connections

Black Troops

Across the North, African Americans volunteered to serve in the army as soon as the war began. But they were told that it was "a white man's war." Historian James M. McPherson points out that "The Lincoln administration and the Republican press . . . declared emphatically that the purpose of the war was the restoration of the Union, and that the issues of slavery and the Negro had nothing to do with the conflict." A second objection was the charge that former slaves would not make good soldiers. Not until 1862, when the Union was meeting increasing difficulty in recruiting whites, did it begin to enlist blacks. The First South Carolina Volunteers were formed that year under the command of Thomas Wentworth Higginson, who wrote in his journal, "It needs but a few days to show the absurdity of doubting the equal military availability of these people, as compared with whites." The first Northern regiment of African Americans was the famous Fifty-fourth Massachusetts under Robert Gould Shaw.

E Critical Thinking

Expressing an Opinion

❓ Do you agree with Douglass's opinion here? Why or why not? [Possible responses: Some students may agree that the oppressed should lead the fight for their own freedom. Others may argue that accepting help from, or "liberation" by, the unoppressed is sometimes a better strategy.]

F Reading Skills and Strategies

Making Inferences

❓ A man did not have to go when he was drafted: Emily Dickinson's brother Austin was drafted in 1864 but paid $500 for a substitute. Why, then, were black men so eager to fight in the Civil War? [Possible response: because they had a much stronger stake in its outcome and valued the chance to prove their worth as citizens.]

Crossing the Curriculum

History

After the Civil War, black citizenship was established by the Thirteenth and Fourteenth Amendments. The Fifteenth Amendment, in 1870, established the right of formerly enslaved men to vote. Despite these laws, the rights of African Americans were far from guaranteed. Have students make a time line showing these and other civil rights landmarks, including *Brown* vs. *Board of Education of Topeka, Kansas,* the Twenty-fourth Amendment, the Civil Rights Act, and so on.

Art

In spite of pay inequities and other unfair conditions, African American soldiers were eager to serve their country in the Civil War. Unfortunately, black soldiers were not openly recruited and were often unaware that regiments were being organized. Invite students to create an advertising campaign to encourage African Americans to join the Union Army. Students can make posters and newspaper advertisements in the style of the 1860s.

T481

A Literary Connections
Biblical Allusion

Chesnut alludes to II Samuel 12: 20–23 in the Bible, where David weeps and prays for his sick child. After the child dies, "David arose from the earth, and washed, and anointed himself, and changed his apparel . . . he came to his own house; and they set bread before him, and he did eat." Asked why he cried before the child died and not after, David replied: "While the child was yet alive, I fasted and wept; for I said, Who can tell whether God will be gracious to me, that the child may live? But now he is dead, and wherefore should I fast? Can I bring him back again?"

B Critical Thinking
Interpreting

❓ How does this allusion apply to Chesnut's story? [Like David, she feels that prayer is no longer of any use in the Southern cause; it is time for life to go on.]

C Exploring the Historical Period
Jefferson Davis

Jefferson Davis (1808–1889) served as a United States Senator and as secretary of war under President Franklin Pierce. Elected president of the Confederacy in 1861, he showed able leadership and was partly responsible for the South's powerful showing against the more numerous Northern forces. Captured in Georgia in April 1865, Davis was imprisoned for two years and indicted for treason, but was never tried.

D Advanced Learners
Primary Sources

Have students choose important events of the period, such as specific battles, and read the entries in Chesnut's diary for those days. Then, have them report to the group or the class on Chesnut's reaction and those of the people around her. How objective does she seem? How reliable is she as a source?

Mary Boykin Chesnut was the wife of James Chesnut, ex-senator from South Carolina and aide to Jefferson Davis, president of the Confederacy. During the course of the war, Mary Chesnut traveled from city to city in the South as the capital of the Confederacy changed. She kept up with the latest war news through her husband and their wide circle of knowledgeable and influential friends. Mary Chesnut was sophisticated, witty, and sensitive. Her diaries present an invaluable firsthand view of the war.

In April 1861, Mary Chesnut had been in Charleston, South Carolina, when the attack on Fort Sumter took place, beginning the Civil War. As she had been present at the beginning of the war, Mary Chesnut was also present at its end. In Columbia, South Carolina, she received the news, increasingly depressing, from the field.

Mary Boykin Chesnut (1856) by Samuel Osgood (1801–1885). Oil on canvas adhered to masonite (48″ × 30″).

National Portrait Gallery, Smithsonian Institution; on loan from Serena Williams Miles Van Rensselaer. Courtesy Art Resource, NY.

Mary Chesnut

SEPTEMBER 1, 1864

The battle is raging at Atlanta, our fate hanging in the balance.

SEPTEMBER 2, 1864

Atlanta is gone. Well that agony is over. Like David, when the child was dead, I will get up from my knees, will wash my face and comb my hair. There is no hope, but we will try to have no fear. . . .

SEPTEMBER 21, 1864

The president [of the Confederacy] has gone West. He has sent for Mr. Chesnut.

I went with Mrs. Rhett to hear Dr. Palmer [a minister]. I did not know before how utterly hopeless was our situation. This man is so eloquent; it was hard to listen and not give way. Despair was his word, and martyrdom. He offered us nothing more in this world than the martyr's crown. He is not for slavery, he says; he is for freedom, the freedom to govern our own country as we see fit. He is against foreign interference in our state matters. That is what Mr. Palmer went to war for, it appears. Every day shows that slavery is doomed the world over. For that he thanked God. He spoke of this time of our agony; and then came the cry: "Help us, Oh God! Vain is the help of man." So we came away shaken to the depths. . . .

The end has come, no doubt of the fact. . . . We are going to be wiped off the face of the earth. Now what is there to prevent Sherman taking General Lee in the rear. We have but two armies, and Sherman is between them now.

SEPTEMBER 29, 1864

These stories of our defeats in the Valley fall like blows upon a dead body. Since Atlanta, I have felt as if all were dead within me, forever. Captain Ogden of General Chesnut's staff dined here today. Had ever a Brigadier with little or no brigade so magnificent a staff? The reserves, as somebody said, are gathered by robbing the cradle and the grave of men too old and boys too young. . . .

OCTOBER 30, 1864

Every man is being hurried to the front. Today Mr. Chesnut met a poor creature coming from the surgeon's with a radiant face and a certificate. "General, see! I am exempt from service; one leg utterly useless, the other not warranted to last three months."

—Mary Chesnut, from A Diary from Dixie

Skill Link

Using a Study Guide

Review how asking and answering their own study-guide questions can help readers maximize their chances for success on exams. This is especially important when a great deal of detailed material will be covered in the exam. Discuss the following strategies:

- skimming the readings to find main ideas
- making generalizations, drawing conclusions, and evaluating the material
- recognizing the author's point of view

- distinguishing between fact and opinion and fact and nonfact

Activities

1. Have each student prepare five study-guide questions for these selections, trade papers with a partner, and answer each other's questions.

2. Compile a class list of the ten best questions for students to use as study guides.

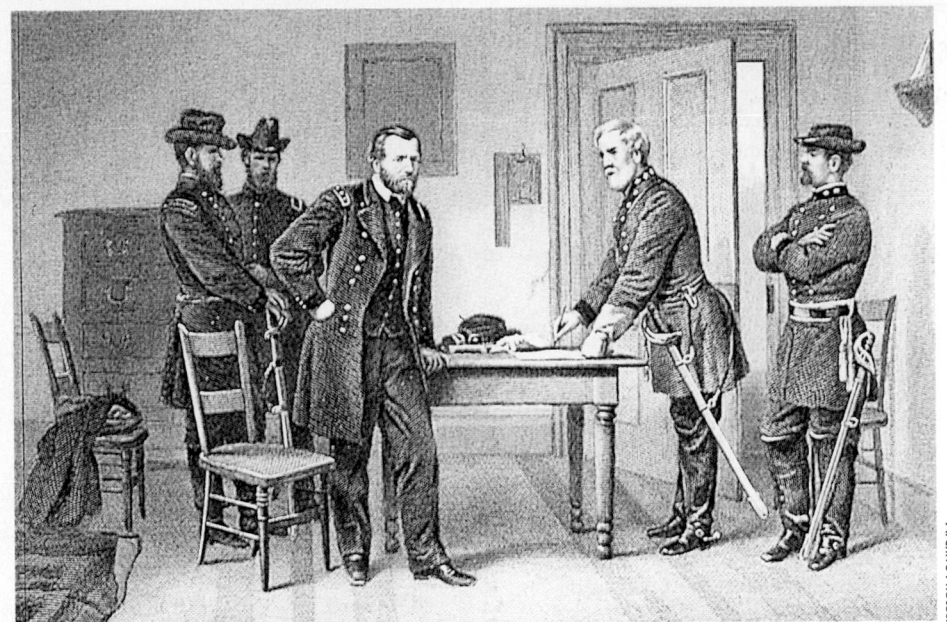

Surrender of General Lee.

On April 9, 1865, Lee surrendered to Grant at Appomattox Court House. Seth Flint, a Union soldier who witnessed the event, described the scene.

E

Seth M. Flint

I Saw Lee Surrender

Grant looked like an old and battered campaigner as he rode into the yard. His blue blouse was unbuttoned and underneath could be seen his undershirt. He was unlike Lee.

What a brave pair of thoroughbreds Lee and Traveler were. That horse would have attracted attention anywhere. General Lee's uniform was immaculate and he presented a superb martial figure. But it was the face beneath the gray felt hat that made the deepest impression on me. I have been trying to find a single word that describes it and I have concluded that "benign" is the adjective I'm after, because it means *kindly* and *gracious*. There was something else about him that aroused my deep pity that so great a warrior should be acknowledging defeat. . . .

Four o'clock—the door opened. Out came General Lee, his soldierly figure erect, even in defeat. We stiffened and gave him a salute, and the man in gray courteously returned it. At the moment his soul must have been heavy with sorrow—the years of desperate struggle fruitless—and yet he could return the salute of some Yankee troopers.

After the departure of General Lee, we quickly learned the happy news of the surrender and it spread like wildfire through the army. That night was one of the happiest I have ever known.

When I sounded taps, the sweetest of all bugle calls, the notes had scarcely died away when from the distance—it must have come from General Lee's headquarters—came, silvery clear, the same call. The boys on the other side welcomed peace.

Soldiers don't carry hatred.

—Seth M. Flint, *from* "I Saw Lee Surrender"

Assessing Learning

Check Test: Multiple Choice

1. Upson's story mainly shows that war (a) delayed harvest, (b) divided families, or (c) disrupted the mail. [b]
2. Whitman emphasizes the suffering of (a) the wounded, (b) entire families, or (c) animals. [a]
3. According to Lincoln, the cemetery at Gettysburg is consecrated by (a) his presence, (b) Congress, or (c) those who fought there. [c]
4. Douglass wanted African Americans to (a) join the Union army, (b) escape from slavery, (c) criticize the country's mistakes. [a]
5. Flint's description of the surrender at Appomattox concentrated on (a) the fine impression Traveler created, (b) General Grant's uncouth, sloppy dress, or (c) General Lee's demeanor in grief. [c]

E ## Historical Connections

Lee and Grant

Robert E. Lee (1807–1870) was offered command of the Union Army, but chose to stay with the Confederacy when his home state of Virginia seceded in 1861. He became commander of the Confederate Army in 1862 and made a number of daring and successful raids northward. After Gettysburg, however, he gradually fell back until he was forced to surrender at Appomattox. Like Lee, Ulysses S. Grant (1822–1885) was a West Point graduate who had served in the Mexican War. After he became commander of the Union forces in 1864, he planned to confront the enemy aggressively at every point so that the Confederate forces could not support each other. He personally led the main command against Lee, and their two armies engaged in a number of terrible battles before the surrender at Appomattox. In 1868, Grant was elected the eighteenth president of the United States and served two terms.

For American historian Bruce Catton, the two generals "were in complete contrast. . . . Grant was the modern man emerging; beyond him, ready to come on the stage was the great age of steel and machinery. . . . Lee might have ridden down from the old age of chivalry, lance in hand." But Catton also believes that they were very much alike: "Each man had, to begin with, the great virtue of utter tenacity and fidelity. . . . Daring and resourcefulness they had, too: the ability to think faster and move faster than the enemy." Finally, "and perhaps the greatest of all, there was the ability, at the end, to turn quickly from war to peace. . . . Out of the way these two men behaved at Appomattox came the possibility of a peace of reconciliation. It was a possibility not wholly realized . . . but which did, in the end, help the two sections to become one nation again."

F ## Reading Skills and Strategies

Making Inferences

? What does the writer mean when he says both Lee and his horse were "thoroughbreds"? [Both are noble and dignified in appearance.]

Planning

Stephen Crane

(1871–1900)

UPI/Bettmann.

Stephen Crane was the youngest of the fourteen children of a Methodist minister and his devout wife. Although frail as a child, Stephen grew up in upstate New York with a yearning to become a baseball star. He put in a year first at Lafayette College and then at Syracuse University (where he was captain of the baseball team) before he decided to try earning a living as a writer.

When Crane was about sixteen years old, he went to work for his brother Townley's news agency in Asbury Park, New Jersey. Later, struggling to make a living as a reporter in New York City, Crane was drawn to the city's underside. What he called his "artistic education" on the Bowery (Skid Row) kept him hungry and often ill.

Crane lived at the Art Students' League on East Twenty-third Street, writing his first significant fiction based on his explorations of the city's slums and saloons. This was *Maggie: A Girl of the Streets* (1893), a somber, somewhat shocking novel, whose plot involved brutality, alcoholism, prostitution, and suicide.

Maggie revealed Crane as a pioneer of **naturalism**—a literary movement that dissected human instincts and behavior and examined the social environment that "conditioned" people to turn out as they did. The novel was impossibly grim for popular magazines, and Crane borrowed $700 to have it printed. The copies of the little yellow paperback lay piled in his rented room for want of readers.

Crane's apparent failure with *Maggie* was followed by a triumph—a short novel titled *The Red Badge of Courage* (1895). Using an impressionistic technique, Crane filtered the events of the novel through the eyes of Henry Fleming, a young soldier at the Civil War battle of Chancellorsville. (In fiction, **impressionism** is a technique whereby the writer gives us not objective reality, but one character's impression of that reality.) As William Dean Howells observed, Crane's genius seemed to "spring to life fully armed" with this book. Crane had been born after the Civil War, but he had read about it and had seen the famous battlefield photographs (page 408) attributed to Mathew Brady. "I have never been in a battle, of course," wrote Crane later, "and I believe that I got my sense of the rage of conflict on the football field. The psychology is the same. The opposing team is an enemy tribe."

The Red Badge of Courage made Crane into a celebrity, a national expert on war, and he spent the rest of his short life writing about it for the newspapers. In fact, he became the prototype of the adventurous correspondent who not only writes about sensational events but also lives a sensational life, delighting in shocking conservative readers.

One of the fascinating elements of Crane's life was the degree to which he interwove his fiction and his real-life experiences. It was as if he had invented a war in his novels and then

go.hrw.com
LEO 11-10

 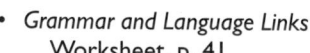 *Resources: Print and Media*

had to pursue the brush fires of his own times in order to confirm what he had written. Nor was experience wasted on him. When he sailed from Florida in late 1896 to cover a gunrunning operation to Cuba, he was shipwrecked off the Florida coast and endured a thirty-hour struggle against the sea. The result was his superb story "The Open Boat" (1898).

Before this ill-fated journey, Crane had stopped off at the Hotel de Dream in Jacksonville, Florida, and had taken up with the hostess, Cora Taylor. She soon decided that she would stay with him and become the first female war correspondent. This oddly matched couple later went off to Greece to cover a war. They settled eventually in England, renting a huge, dilapidated, medieval house in Sussex.

All of these adventures were taking their toll on Crane's always delicate health. Still, he continued to travel and write, desperate now to pay for Cora's extravagant domestic life. In 1899, he produced his second volume of poems, *War Is Kind* (page 494). But tuberculosis was sapping his strength. Crane died in June 1900, at a sanitarium in the Black Forest of Germany. He was only twenty-eight years old.

Detail from original manuscript page:
The Red Badge of Courage by Stephen Crane.
University of Virginia Library.

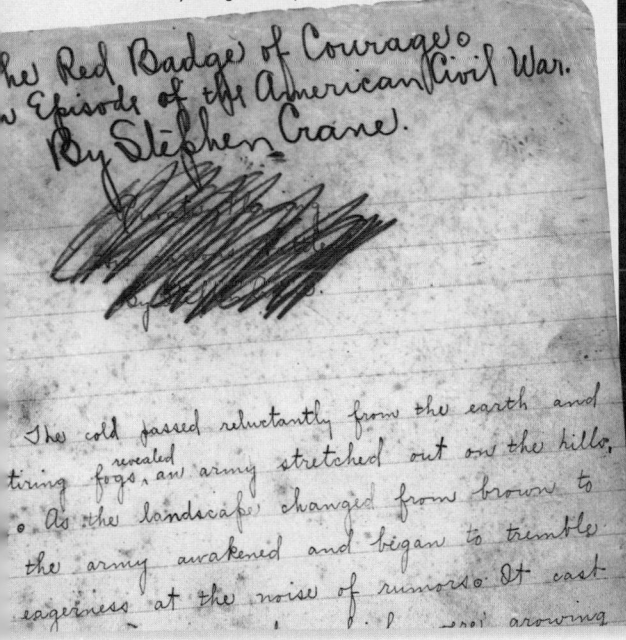

Before You Read
A MYSTERY OF HEROISM

Make the Connection
Fool or Hero?
What is heroism? Is it exceptional courage? fearlessness? If a person ignores normal human fear and risks his or her life for something others regard as trivial, is it an act of heroism or a deed of utmost foolishness?

Quickwrite
Imagine this scene, and then write down your thoughts about it: In the midst of all the frightful noise and bloody destruction of a Civil War battlefield, with death all around, a soldier suddenly has a mind to run straight into the battle on an impulse which, to his comrades, seems simply crazy. Right into the line of enemy fire—for *that*? Under what circumstances would such an action be regarded as heroic? When would such an action be considered foolhardy—even insane?

Elements of Literature
Situational Irony
Situational irony occurs when what actually happens differs from what one expects will happen. Such an irony is at the heart of this story.

> **S**ituational irony takes place when there is a discrepancy between what is expected to happen and what actually happens.
>
> For more on Irony, see the Handbook of Literary Terms.

Background
Firsthand accounts of Civil War battles speak of the stifling smoke and crashing noise of battle. Often, one soldier would escape death and another would die by the merest chance. Dazed by battle, soldiers could find it difficult later on to explain the reasons for their actions.

STEPHEN CRANE **485**

Summary ▪▪

In the midst of a heated Civil War battle, private Fred Collins decides he is willing to risk death to get some water. Egged on by his comrades, he sets out across a meadow that is being bombarded, fills an old bucket at a well, and with shells landing all about, makes his way back to his company's position. On the trip back, a dying officer asks for a drink. Collins initially refuses but then turns back to give the officer some water. Upon his safe return, two joking lieutenants get the bucket first and, in an ironic reversal of the story's climax, spill its contents on the ground.

Background

One reason for the wide popularity of Crane's Civil War stories was their novelty: they were told from a private's point of view. Wars in earlier fiction had been fought mainly by officers, noteworthy men who moved against a background of faceless troops. In Crane's war stories, the higher-ranked officers are relegated to the background.

Preteaching Vocabulary

Words to Own
Have students read the Words to Own and their definitions listed at the bottom of the selection pages. Next, have partners make flash cards, using all the vocabulary words. They can use the cards to help each other learn the words and their meanings. Then, hold a class Vocabulary Bee: read the words, and have teams alternate giving the definitions. Afterwards, tell students to complete the following matching exercise.

1. conflagration [e]	**a.** lying flat
2. stolidity [j]	**b.** gesturing
3. obliterated [d]	**c.** withdrawal
4. prostrate [a]	**d.** destroyed
5. ominous [h]	**e.** a huge fire
6. gesticulating [b]	**f.** drained of color
7. provisional [g]	**g.** temporary
8. retraction [c]	**h.** foreboding
9. indolent [i]	**i.** lazy
10. blanched [f]	**j.** lack of emotion

Viewing and Representing
Fine Art Transparency
A fine art transparency of Frederic Remington's "Through the Smoke Sprang the Daring Young Soldier" can be compared to Crane's presentation of war. See the *Viewing and Representing Transparencies and Worksheets:*
• Transparency 10
• Worksheet, p. 40

RESPONDING TO THE ART

Thomas Corwin Lindsay presents an anecdotal account of Civil War fighting in *The Hornet's Nest,* spread across these two pages. In the foreground, a Union officer gives orders from horseback while blue-clad gunnery soldiers are distracted by the deaths around them or work to reload their cannons. None of the foreground figures, except possibly the mounted officer, seems directly to notice the ghostly horde of gray-clad Confederate soldiers charging from the upper left.

Activity. Ask students to analyze the painting and speculate about why the artist called it *The Hornet's Nest.* [Possible responses: The title suggests the noise and sting of battle, the sting of bayonets, and the sheer danger of the situation. Perhaps the charging Confederate soldiers are the hornets, and the Union gunners have stumbled into their nest.]

The Hornet's Nest (1895) by Thomas Corwin Lindsay. Oil on canvas.
Courtesy Cincinnati Historical Society.

486 THE RISE OF REALISM: THE CIVIL WAR AND POSTWAR PERIOD

Reaching All Students

Struggling Readers
Some students may have trouble reading inverted sentences, such as "A glittering bugle swung clear of the rider's back as fell headlong the horse and the man" (p. 487). Preview such sentences before students read the story, making sure students understand which subjects go with the verbs. You may have students copy sentences in the inverted form and then rewrite them in ordinary syntax.

English Language Learners
These students may have difficulty with Crane's impressionistic technique of alternating between description and dialogue. To help these students, you may wish to have them read the plot portions of the story aloud with a native-speaking partner. To further help them follow the story line, have students create a storyboard with drawings and captions showing the most important actions.

Advanced Learners
Explore with these students how different people have disparate views of the military and dissimilar responses to military behavior. As a result, some readers react negatively to Crane's realistic depiction of war, while others believe that it is important to show that war is often frightening and inhuman rather than glorious. Remind students that they can debate this issue while still respecting each other's views.

A Mystery of Heroism

Stephen Crane

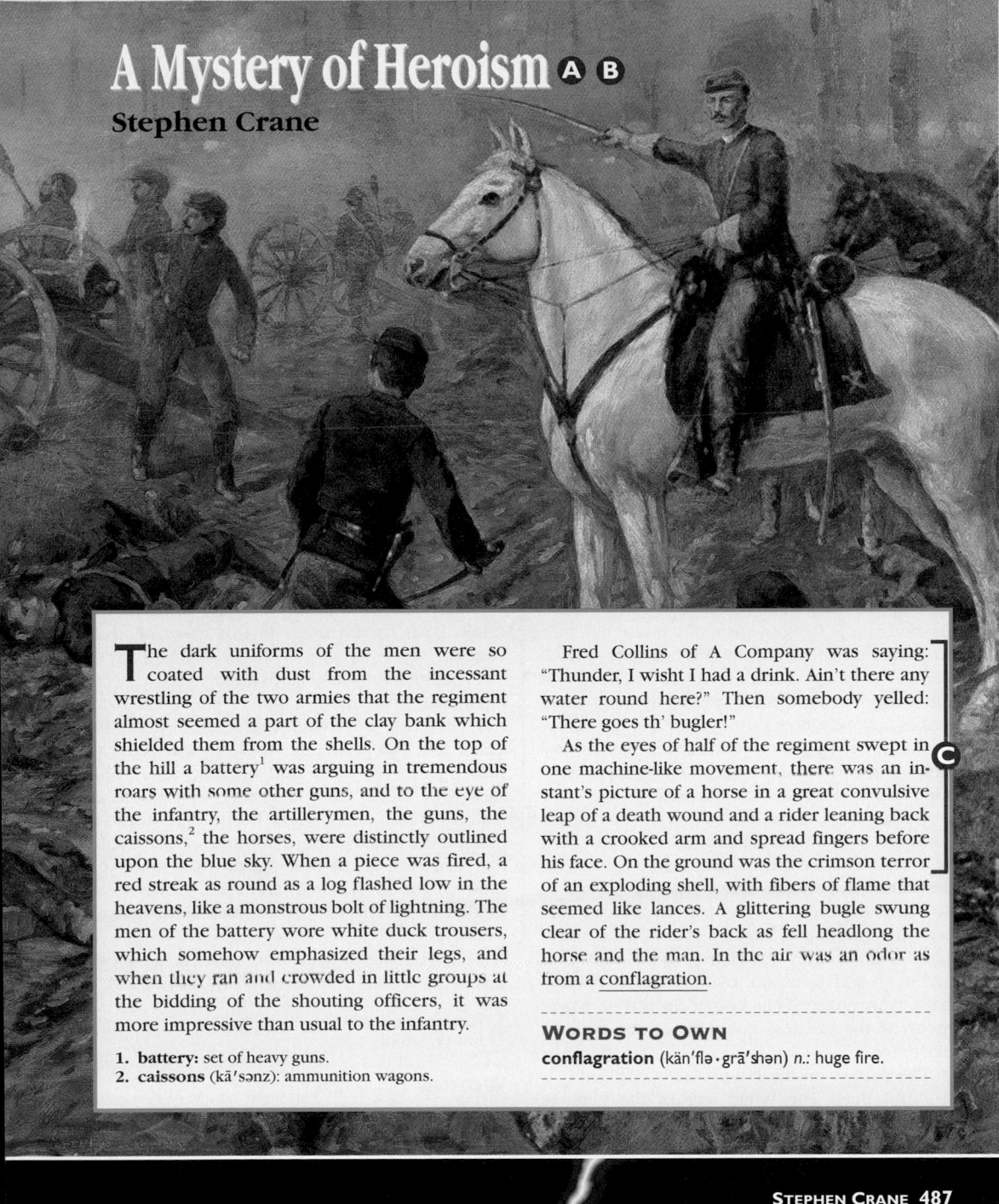

The dark uniforms of the men were so coated with dust from the incessant wrestling of the two armies that the regiment almost seemed a part of the clay bank which shielded them from the shells. On the top of the hill a battery[1] was arguing in tremendous roars with some other guns, and to the eye of the infantry, the artillerymen, the guns, the caissons,[2] the horses, were distinctly outlined upon the blue sky. When a piece was fired, a red streak as round as a log flashed low in the heavens, like a monstrous bolt of lightning. The men of the battery wore white duck trousers, which somehow emphasized their legs, and when they ran and crowded in little groups at the bidding of the shouting officers, it was more impressive than usual to the infantry.

1. **battery:** set of heavy guns.
2. **caissons** (kā'sənz): ammunition wagons.

Fred Collins of A Company was saying: "Thunder, I wisht I had a drink. Ain't there any water round here?" Then somebody yelled: "There goes th' bugler!"

As the eyes of half of the regiment swept in one machine-like movement, there was an instant's picture of a horse in a great convulsive leap of a death wound and a rider leaning back with a crooked arm and spread fingers before his face. On the ground was the crimson terror of an exploding shell, with fibers of flame that seemed like lances. A glittering bugle swung clear of the rider's back as fell headlong the horse and the man. In the air was an odor as from a conflagration.

WORDS TO OWN
conflagration (kän'flə·grā'shən) n.: huge fire.

STEPHEN CRANE 487

Ⓐ **Literary Connections**

Veterans' Response
Crane had interviewed Civil War veterans, but they told him only dry facts and seemed unable to recall—or at least articulate—their thoughts and feelings about the war. Crane drew upon his own imagination to fill in those thoughts and feelings. He succeeded so well that many veterans wrote to ask what regiment he had served in, and some others were even convinced that they had served with him.

Ⓑ **Critical Thinking**

Making Judgments
Before students read the story, have them discuss their personal definitions of the word *hero*. Help them reach consensus on a definition, and leave the result displayed on the board as they read and discuss the story. Tell students to keep asking themselves if Fred Collins, the main character, is indeed heroic.

Ⓒ **Elements of Literature**

Situational Irony
❓ What is the irony in this paragraph? [Collins is focused on a minor personal desire while all around him people are dying.] **How does Crane create this irony?** [He juxtaposes Collins's wish for a drink with the bugler's death. Further, Collins's earthy diction is juxtaposed with the elevated description of battle.]

Crossing the Curriculum

History
Have students locate and identify the war monuments in their region, especially any dedicated to the soldiers who fought in the Civil War. For each monument, students should find out when the monument was erected and research what the monument commemorates (such as a specific battle or hero). Students can pool their research and create a pamphlet for distribution through the local historical society or at the monuments themselves.

Science
Collins assumes the water in the well is safe to drink (p. 488), but this is not always the case. Further, it is often impossible to tell if water is safe to drink by merely looking at it. Have students find out how to test the safety of drinking water and how to treat unsafe water to make it potable. Invite volunteers to demonstrate the process for the class. Students can find information in a Scout handbook or from local health authorities.

Union soldier.

The Bettmann Archive.

Sometimes they of the infantry looked down at a fair little meadow which spread at their feet. Its long, green grass was rippling gently in a breeze. Beyond it was the gray form of a house half torn to pieces by shells and by the busy axes of soldiers who had pursued firewood. The line of an old fence was now dimly marked by long weeds and by an occasional post. A shell had blown the well house to fragments. Little lines of gray smoke ribboning upward from some embers indicated the place where had stood the barn.

From beyond a curtain of green woods there came the sound of some stupendous scuffle as if two animals of the size of islands were fighting. At a distance there were occasional appearances of swift-moving men, horses, batteries, flags, and, with the crashing of infantry, volleys were heard, often, wild and frenzied cheers. In the midst of it all, Smith and Ferguson, two privates of A Company, were engaged in a heated discussion, which involved the greatest questions of the national existence.

The battery on the hill presently engaged in a frightful duel. The white legs of the gunners scampered this way and that way and the officers redoubled their shouts. The guns, with their

demeanors of stolidity and courage, were typical of something infinitely self-possessed in this clamor of death that swirled around the hill.

One of a "swing" team was suddenly smitten quivering to the ground and his maddened brethren dragged his torn body in their struggle to escape from this turmoil and danger. A young soldier astride one of the leaders swore and fumed in his saddle and furiously jerked at the bridle. An officer screamed out an order so violently that his voice broke and ended the sentence in a falsetto[3] shriek.

The leading company of the infantry regiment was somewhat exposed and the colonel ordered it moved more fully under the shelter of the hill. There was the clank of steel against steel.

A lieutenant of the battery rode down and passed them, holding his right arm carefully in his left hand. And it was as if this arm was not at all a part of him, but belonged to another man. His sober and reflective charger went slowly. The officer's face was grimy and perspiring and his uniform was tousled as if he had been in direct grapple with an enemy. He smiled grimly when the men stared at him. He turned his horse toward the meadow.

Collins of A Company said: "I wisht I had a drink. I bet there's water in that there ol' well yonder!"

"Yes; but how you goin' to git it?"

For the little meadow which intervened was now suffering a terrible onslaught of shells. Its green and beautiful calm had vanished utterly. Brown earth was being flung in monstrous handfuls. And there was a massacre of the young blades of grass. They were being torn, burned, obliterated. Some curious fortune of the battle had made this gentle little meadow the object of the red hate of the shells and each one as it exploded seemed like an imprecation[4] in the face of a maiden.

The wounded officer who was riding across this expanse said to himself: "Why, they couldn't

3. **falsetto:** artificially high voice.
4. **imprecation:** curse.

WORDS TO OWN
stolidity (stə·lid′ə·tē) *n.:* showing no emotion.
obliterated (ə·blit′ər·āt′əd) *v.:* destroyed.

Professional Notes

Critical Comment: Crane's Style

Literary scholar R.W. Stallman describes Crane's writing as having the emotional intensity of poetry. He says Crane's "aim was to immerse the reader in the created experience so that its impact on him would occur simultaneously with the discovery of it by the characters themselves. Instead of panoramic views of a battlefield, Crane paints not the whole scene but disconnected segments of it—all that a participant in an action or a spectator of a scene can possibly take into his view at any one moment." Stallman continues, "Irony is Crane's chief technical instrument. . . . Crane is always dealing with the paradox of man, the paradox of his plight. . . . This . . . conflict, the conflict between ideals and realities, ruled Crane's struggle as artist and gave both his life and his art all their bitter ironies."

shoot any harder if the whole army was massed here!"

A shell struck the gray ruins of the house and as, after the roar, the shattered wall fell in fragments, there was a noise which resembled the flapping of shutters during a wild gale of winter. Indeed the infantry paused in the shelter of the bank, appeared as men standing upon a shore contemplating a madness of the sea. The angel of calamity had under its glance the battery upon the hill. Fewer white-legged men labored about the guns. A shell had smitten one of the pieces, and after the flare, the smoke, the dust, the wrath of this blow was gone, it was possible to see white legs stretched horizontally upon the ground. And at that interval to the rear, where it is the business of battery horses to stand with their noses to the fight awaiting the command to drag their guns out of the destruction or into it or wheresoever these incomprehensible humans demanded with whip and spur—in this line of passive and dumb spectators, whose fluttering hearts yet would not let them forget the iron laws of man's control of them—in this rank of brute soldiers there had been relentless and hideous carnage. From the ruck[5] of bleeding and prostrate horses, the men of the infantry could see one animal raising its stricken body with its forelegs and turning its nose with mystic and profound eloquence toward the sky.

Some comrades joked Collins about his thirst. "Well, if yeh want a drink so bad, why don't yeh go git it?"

"Well, I will in a minnet if yeh don't shut up."

A lieutenant of artillery floundered his horse straight down the hill with as great concern as if it were level ground. As he galloped past the colonel of the infantry, he threw up his hand in swift salute. "We've got to get out of that," he roared angrily. He was a black-bearded officer, and his eyes, which resembled beads, sparkled like those of an insane man. His jumping horse sped along the column of infantry.

The fat major standing carelessly with his sword held horizontally behind him and with his

> ... there was a noise which resembled the flapping of shutters during a wild gale of winter.

legs far apart, looked after the receding horseman and laughed. "He wants to get back with orders pretty quick or there'll be no batt'ry left," he observed.

The wise young captain of the second company hazarded[6] to the lieutenant colonel that the enemy's infantry would probably soon attack the hill, and the lieutenant colonel snubbed him.

A private in one of the rear companies looked out over the meadow and then turned to a companion and said: "Look there, Jim." It was the wounded officer from the battery, who some time before had started to ride across the meadow, supporting his right arm carefully with his left hand. This man had encountered a shell apparently at a time when no one perceived him and he could now be seen lying face downward with a stirruped foot stretched across the body of his dead horse. A leg of the charger extended slantingly upward precisely as stiff as a stake. Around this motionless pair the shells still howled.

There was a quarrel in A Company. Collins was shaking his fist in the faces of some laughing comrades. "Dern yeh! I ain't afraid t' go. If yeh say much, I will go!"

"Of course, yeh will! Yeh'll run through that there medder, won't yeh?"

Collins said, in a terrible voice: "You see, now!" At this ominous threat his comrades broke into renewed jeers.

Collins gave them a dark scowl and went to find his captain. The latter was conversing with the colonel of the regiment.

"Captain," said Collins, saluting and standing at attention. In those days all trousers bagged at the knees. "Captain, I want t' git permission to go git some water from that there well over yonder!"

The colonel and the captain swung about simultaneously and stared across the meadow.

6. **hazarded:** risked saying.

WORDS TO OWN

prostrate (präs′trāt′) *adj.:* lying flat on the ground.
ominous (äm′ə·nəs) *adj.:* sinister; foreboding.

---

5. **ruck:** mass; crowd.

STEPHEN CRANE **489**

Using Students' Strengths

The captain laughed. "You must be pretty thirsty, Collins?"

"Yes, sir; I am."

"Well—ah," said the captain. After a moment he asked: "Can't you wait?"

"No, sir."

A The colonel was watching Collins's face. "Look here, my lad," he said, in a pious sort of a voice. "Look here, my lad." Collins was not a lad. "Don't you think that's taking pretty big risks for a little drink of water?"

"I dunno," said Collins, uncomfortably. Some of the resentment toward his companions, which perhaps had forced him into this affair, was beginning to fade. "I dunno wether 'tis."

The colonel and the captain contemplated him for a time.

"Well," said the captain finally.

"Well," said the colonel, "if you want to go, why go."

Collins saluted. "Much obliged t' yeh."

As he moved away the colonel called after him. "Take some of the other boys' canteens with you an' hurry back now."

"Yes, sir. I will."

B The colonel and the captain looked at each other then, for it had suddenly occurred that they could not for the life of them tell whether Collins wanted to go or whether he did not.

They turned to regard Collins and as they perceived him surrounded by gesticulating comrades the colonel said: "Well, by thunder! I guess he's going."

Collins appeared as a man dreaming. In the midst of the questions, the advice, the warnings, all the excited talk of his company mates, he maintained a curious silence.

They were very busy in preparing him for his ordeal. When they inspected him carefully it was somewhat like the examination that grooms give a horse before a race; and they were amazed, staggered by the whole affair. Their astonishment found vent in strange repetitions.

"Are yeh sure a-goin'?" they demanded again and again.

"Certainly I am," cried Collins, at last furiously.

C He strode sullenly away from them. He was swinging five or six canteens by their cords. It seemed that his cap would not remain firmly on his head, and often he reached and pulled it down over his brow.

There was a general movement in the compact column. The long animal-like thing moved slightly. Its four hundred eyes were turned upon the figure of Collins.

"Well, sir, if that ain't th' derndest thing. I never thought Fred Collins had the blood in him for that kind of business."

"What's he goin' to do, anyhow?"

"He's goin' to that well there after water."

"We ain't dyin' of thirst, are we? That's foolishness."

"Well, somebody put him up to it an' he's doin' it."

"Say, he must be a desperate cuss."

D When Collins faced the meadow and walked away from the regiment, he was vaguely conscious that a chasm, the deep valley of all prides, was suddenly between him and his comrades. It was provisional, but the provision was that he return as a victor. He had blindly been led by quaint emotions and laid himself under an obligation to walk squarely up to the face of death.

E But he was not sure that he wished to make a retraction even if he could do so without shame. As a matter of truth he was sure of very little. He was mainly surprised.

F It seemed to him supernaturally strange that he had allowed his mind to maneuver his body into such a situation. He understood that it might be called dramatically great.

However, he had no full appreciation of anything excepting that he was actually conscious of being dazed. He could feel his dulled mind groping after the form and color of this incident.

Too, he wondered why he did not feel some keen agony of fear cutting his sense like a knife. He wondered at this because human expression had said loudly for centuries that men should feel

---

WORDS TO OWN

gesticulating (jes·tik′yoo·lāt′iŋ) *v.* used as *adj.:* gesturing, especially with the hands and arms, while speaking.

provisional (prō·vizh′ə·nəl) *adj.:* temporary; for the time being.

retraction (ri·trak′shən) *n.:* withdrawal.

Getting Students Involved

Cooperative Learning

Students can hold a mock trial to determine whether Collins is a hero or a fool. Have students assume roles, such as judge, attorney, witnesses, and the jury, as they debate the case. Guide the witnesses to read sections of the story as evidence of Collins's motivation and state of mind, as well as the danger of his actions. Students can also mention other works of literature they have read in this unit as they argue their side of the case.

Reading Activity

Invite students to read a war memoir or novel, such as Walt Whitman's *Specimen Days* (Civil War), John Dos Passos's *Three Soldiers* (World War I), Ernest Hemingway's *For Whom the Bell Tolls* (Spanish Civil War), James Michener's *Tales of the South Pacific* (World War II), or Tim O'Brien's *Going After Cacciato* (Vietnam War). Have students share their reactions in oral reports to the class.

afraid of certain things and that all men who did not feel this fear were phenomena, heroes.

He was then a hero. He suffered that disappointment which we would all have if we discovered that we were ourselves capable of those deeds which we most admire in history and legend. This, then, was a hero. After all, heroes were not much.

No, it could not be true. He was not a hero. Heroes had no shames in their lives and, as for him, he remembered borrowing fifteen dollars from a friend and promising to pay it back the next day, and then avoiding that friend for ten months. When at home his mother had aroused him for the early labor of his life on the farm, it had often been his fashion to be irritable, childish, diabolical, and his mother had died since he had come to the war.

He saw that in this matter of the well, the canteens, the shells, he was an intruder in the land of fine deeds.

He was now about thirty paces from his comrades. The regiment had just turned its many faces toward him.

From the forest of terrific noises there suddenly emerged a little uneven line of men. They fired fiercely and rapidly at distant foliage on which appeared little puffs of white smoke. The spatter of skirmish firing was added to the thunder of the guns on the hill. The little line of men ran forward. A color sergeant fell flat with his flag as if he had slipped on ice. There was hoarse cheering from this distant field.

Collins suddenly felt that two demon fingers were pressed into his ears. He could see nothing but flying arrows, flaming red. He lurched from the shock of this explosion, but he made a mad

Charge of VMI Cadets at New Market (1914) by Benjamin West Clinedinst. Oil on canvas (18″ × 23″).

Virginia Military Institute, Lexington, Virginia.

rush for the house, which he viewed as a man submerged to the neck in a boiling surf might view the shore. In the air, little pieces of shell howled and the earthquake explosions drove him insane with the menace of their roar. As he ran the canteens knocked together with a rhythmical tinkling.

As he neared the house, each detail of the scene became vivid to him. He was aware of some bricks of the vanished chimney lying on the sod. There was a door which hung by one hinge.

Rifle bullets called forth by the insistent skirmishers came from the far-off bank of foliage. They mingled with the shells and the pieces of shells until the air was torn in all directions by hootings, yells, howls. The sky was full of fiends who directed all their wild rage at his head.

When he came to the well he flung himself face downward and peered into its darkness. There were furtive silver glintings some feet from the surface. He grabbed one of the canteens and, unfastening its cap, swung it down by the cord. The water flowed slowly in with an indolent gurgle.

And now as he lay with his face turned away he was suddenly smitten with the terror. It came upon his heart like the grasp of claws. All the power faded from his muscles. For an instant he was no more than a dead man.

The canteen filled with a maddening slowness in the manner of all bottles. Presently he recovered his strength and addressed a screaming oath

- -

WORDS TO OWN
indolent (in′də·lənt) *adj.:* lazy.

- -

STEPHEN CRANE **491**

G Critical Thinking
Making Judgments
❓ Is Collins in fact an "intruder in the land of fine deeds"? Why or why not? [Possible responses: No, because he has tried his best to stare death in the face; yes, because his deed is selfish and foolish rather than noble and heroic.] Ask students if they wish to revise the class definition of heroism at this point.

H Elements of Literature
Figures of Speech
❓ How does Crane use figures of speech to make the battle seem even more menacing? [By personifying the rifle bullets, Crane seems to give them a will of their own. The battle becomes self-driven, beyond human control.]

I English Language Learners
Using Context Clues
❓ What are the "silver glintings"? Why are they "furtive"? Use context clues as you define the words. [Crane is describing the surface of the water. The sparkles of light are furtive because they are shifty and hard to see—but Crane also seems to suggest that even the water hides from the fierceness of this battle.]

Making the Connections

Connecting to the Theme:
"From Innocence to Experience"
Students can discuss whether Collins changes as a result of his experience and, if so, how. They are likely to begin by analyzing the story for clues that he has learned that accepting dares is foolish or dangerous. Guide the discussion toward Collins's reason for returning to the dying officer who had acted so bravely before, toward his thoughts about prior "shames" on p. 491, and toward how these are related to the idea of heroism. Explore the possibility that what begins as a rash, immature impulse ends as a mature, conscious, even noble, act of self-sacrifice, and that the other characters do not see all that is actually happening.

Ⓐ Literary Connections

Naturalism

❓ The naturalists believed, in part, that nature is indifferent to the human struggle for survival. How is a naturalist perspective upheld in this scene? [Possible response: Collins expects nature—the water—to cooperate with him, but it mocks his efforts.]

Ⓑ Critical Thinking

Analyzing

❓ How does the author create humor in this scene? [Possible response: The juxtaposition between the terrifying life-and-death battle and Collins's ridiculous gait is grimly amusing.]

Ⓒ Reading Skills and Strategies

Making Inferences

❓ The angel of death is usually considered to be a spiritual being that brings death. What is a "practical" angel of death? [a real projectile whose "flight" causes death, such as a cannonball or bullet]

Ⓓ Reading Skills and Strategies

Drawing Conclusions

❓ Why do you think Collins returns to give the dying officer a drink of water? [Possible responses: He is basically compassionate; he realizes that he could soon be in the same position as the dying officer; he does not want to carry another "shame."]

Ⓔ Elements of Literature

Situational Irony

Have students note the contrast between the "unspeakable noises of the swirling missiles" and the dying man's smile and childlike sigh. Have them discuss possible reasons why he smiles and why his sigh seems like that of a child. Is the situation believable? [Possible response: The officer may have smiled at the supreme irony of being bypassed in his dying wish by Collins and then seeing Collins return—too late. Or, he may simply be glad to be released from pain and the horror of war. His dying breath is weak, unburdened, and innocent, like a child's. Students may express various opinions regarding the scene's credibility.]

to it. He leaned over until it seemed as if he intended to try to push water into it with his hands. **Ⓐ** His eyes as he gazed down into the well shone like two pieces of metal and in their expression was a great appeal and a great curse. The stupid water derided him.

There was the blaring thunder of a shell. Crimson light shone through the swift-boiling smoke and made a pink reflection on part of the wall of the well. Collins jerked out his arm and canteen with the same motion that a man would use in withdrawing his head from a furnace.

He scrambled erect and glared and hesitated. On the ground near him lay the old well bucket, with a length of rusty chain. He lowered it swiftly into the well. The bucket struck the water and then turning lazily over, sank. When, with hand reaching tremblingly over hand, he hauled it out, it knocked often against the walls of the well and spilled some of its contents.

Ⓑ In running with a filled bucket, a man can adopt but one kind of gait. So through this terrible field over which screamed practical angels of **Ⓒ** death Collins ran in the manner of a farmer chased out of a dairy by a bull.

His face went staring white with anticipation—anticipation of a blow that would whirl him around and down. He would fall as he had seen other men fall, the life knocked out of them so suddenly that their knees were no more quick to touch the ground than their heads. He saw the long blue line of the regiment, but his comrades were standing looking at him from the edge of an impossible star. He was aware of some deep wheel ruts and hoof prints in the sod beneath his feet.

The artillery officer who had fallen in this meadow had been making groans in the teeth of the tempest of sound. These futile cries, wrenched from him by his agony, were heard only by shells, bullets. When wild-eyed Collins came running, this officer raised himself. His face contorted and <u>blanched</u> from pain, he was about to utter some great beseeching cry. But suddenly his face straightened and he called: "Say, young man, give me a drink of water, will you?"

Collins had no room amid his emotions for surprise. He was mad from the threats of destruction.

"I can't," he screamed, and in this reply was a full description of his quaking apprehension. His cap was gone and his hair was riotous. His clothes made it appear that he had been dragged over the ground by the heels. He ran on.

The officer's head sank down and one elbow crooked. His foot in its brass-bound stirrup still stretched over the body of his horse and the other leg was under the steed.

Ⓓ But Collins turned. He came dashing back. His face had now turned gray and in his eyes was all terror. "Here it is! Here it is!"

The officer was as a man gone in drink. His arm bended like a twig. His head drooped as if his neck was of willow. He was sinking to the ground, to lie face downward.

Collins grabbed him by the shoulder. "Here it is. Here's your drink. Turn over! Turn over, man, for God's sake!"

With Collins hauling at his shoulder, the officer twisted his body and fell with his face turned toward that region where lived the unspeakable **Ⓔ** noises of the swirling missiles. There was the faintest shadow of a smile on his lips as he looked at Collins. He gave a sigh, a little primitive breath like that from a child.

Collins tried to hold the bucket steadily, but his shaking hands caused the water to splash all over the face of the dying man. Then he jerked it away and ran on.

The regiment gave him a welcoming roar. The grimed faces were wrinkled in laughter.

His captain waved the bucket away. "Give it to the men!"

The two genial, skylarking young lieutenants were the first to gain possession of it. They played over it in their fashion.

When one tried to drink, the other teasingly knocked his elbow. "Don't, Billie! You'll make me spill it," said the one. The other laughed.

Suddenly there was an oath, the thud of wood on the ground, and a swift murmur of astonishment from the ranks. The two lieutenants glared at each other. The bucket lay on the ground empty.

WORDS TO OWN

blanched (blancht) *v.* used as *adj.*: drained of color.

Assessing Learning

Check Test: Multiple Choice

1. The occasion of the story is (a) a dress parade, (b) a furious battle, or (c) a military retreat. [b]
2. As they wait, the infantry witnesses (a) an artillery exchange, (b) an exchange of prisoners, or (c) a retreat across a river. [a]
3. Collins ventures into the fray in order to (a) save a wounded comrade, (b) spy on the enemy, (c) get some water. [c]
4. The wounded officer asks Collins to (a) give him shelter, (b) give him water, or (c) call for help. [b]
5. At the end, (a) the bucket lies on the ground, empty, (b) the officers drink all the water and toss away the bucket, or (c) Collins drinks all the water himself. [a]

Student to Student

What About Glory

Ask the child,
Who, without an answer,
Asks her brother,
"What is he like?"

Ask the brother,
Who, missing the memory,
Asks his mother,
"When will he be back?"

And ask the mother
Who, without a husband,
Asks herself, "Why'd
He have to be a hero?" Ⓐ

—Pindar VanArman
Gonzaga College High School
Washington, D.C.

MAKING MEANINGS

First Thoughts

1. What was your first reaction to the story? Did you consider Collins a hero or a fool? Why? Review your Quick-write notes before you answer.

Shaping Interpretations

2. There is a good deal of "rank" in this story—several lieutenants, a captain, a

Reading Check

a. What happens to the lieutenant who holds his wounded right arm carefully in his left hand?

b. Why is Collins disappointed when it occurs to him that he could be called a hero?

c. What does the maddened Collins do when the wounded lieutenant asks him for water?

d. How much of the water in the bucket does Collins get to drink?

major, a colonel, and a lieutenant colonel. But Collins is a private. Discuss whether or not you think his lowly rank is significant in any way.

3. When Crane "paints" the battle scene in colorful language, he draws our attention to the legs of certain men who are wearing white duck (linen) trousers. Why do you think Crane emphasizes the **image** of the men's white legs? What does the white contrast with?

4. In modern war, it has been said, machines resemble humans, and humans resemble machines. Find two or three examples from this story showing that Crane believes war **personifies** machines and dehumanizes people. What do you think of this idea about the dehumanizing effects of war and the glorification of its machines?

5. What **situational irony** occurs at the end of the story as a result of Collins's action?

Connecting with the Text

6. What do you think is Collins's **motive** for his daring act? Simple thirst? The reactions of his comrades? Some other force within him? In what sense might the "mystery" in the title of the story refer to Collins's motivation?

Challenging the Text

7. The ending of the story is **ambiguous**—that is, it is open to more than one interpretation. Do you think the lieutenants spilled the water, or was the bucket empty by the time Collins got back? Does the empty bucket mean something? Explain how you interpreted the final lines of the story, and comment on whether or not you think this is a good ending.

Stephen Crane.

Drawing by David Levine.
Reprinted with permission from
The New York Review of Books.
Copyright © 1968 NYREV, Inc.

STEPHEN CRANE 493

Connecting Across Texts

Connecting with "A Mystery of Heroism"

Discuss how the student's poem begins by looking at the consequences of heroism but ends by questioning its motives. What attitude does the speaker seem to have towards heroism? How does it compare to Collins's attitude? To the attitude of Crane's narrator?

Reading Check

a. He is hit by a shell; later he asks Collins for water.

b. He sees himself as ordinary; if he is heroic, then heroism is overrated.

c. He initially refuses and runs away but then runs back to bring him a drink.

d. none

Ⓐ **Reading Skills and Strategies**
Making Inferences
❓ What do you know about the character referred to as "he"? [He is a father and husband who has most likely died in a war somewhere.]

MAKING MEANINGS

First Thoughts [Respond]

1. Possible responses: He's a hero for giving the officer water; he's a fool for needlessly risking his life.

Shaping Interpretations [Interpret]

2. Collins's rank makes him "Everyman" and makes his rejection of his own heroism more poignant.

3. Associated with delicateness and innocence, white is ironic on a battlefield. It contrasts with the red of exploding shells and blood.

4. The artillery argues with the other guns; the guns are "stolid" and "courageous." The soldiers' eyes sweep in a "machine-like movement." Many students may think this idea captures well the grimness of war.

5. No one gets any water.

Connecting with the Text [Analyze]

6. Possible response: His motive seems more than thirst and his comrades' taunts. The "mystery" is what motivates his action and whether it is heroism at all.

Challenging the Text [Evaluate]

7. Students will have different explanations. The empty bucket may symbolize the vanished illusion that humans can control their destinies or fight the frequent absurdity of their lives.

RESPONDING TO THE ART

David Levine (1926–   ) is one of America's most esteemed caricaturists. For more on his distinctive approach, see pp. 86 and 343.

Activity. Have students compare and contrast Levine's caricature with the photograph of Crane on p. 484. What dominant impression does he suggest about Crane? [Possible answers: intensity, aestheticism.]

Rubrics for each Choices assignment appear on p. 147 in the *Portfolio Management System*.

CHOICES:
Building Your Portfolio

1. **Writer's Notebook**   Help students design an objective questionnaire that does not merely reflect their own views.
2. **Interpreting Texts**   Ask students to compare the speaker's attitude in the poem to the narrator's attitude in the story. Before they begin writing, encourage students to list the key points they will include in their summary.
3. **Creative Writing**   Suggest that students brainstorm ideas by using a cluster diagram or other graphic organizer. Then, remind students that poems do not have to rhyme but that both poetry and prose can be written in a rhythm that supports meaning.

CHOICES: Building Your Portfolio

Writer's Notebook
1. Collecting Ideas for a Research Paper

One approach to researching a topic might involve surveying people about their attitudes. To gather information about current attitudes toward war, you could distribute copies of Crane's "A Mystery of Heroism" or "War Is Kind" to ten people, together with a questionnaire that explores their feelings about war. Write up a summary of the responses you get, and keep your notes for possible use in the Writer's Workshop on page 515.

Interpreting Texts
2. The Outrage of War

Write a brief essay in which you summarize Stephen Crane's attitudes toward war, based on your reading of "A Mystery of Heroism" and the Crane poem, "War Is Kind," on this page. In your essay, respond to these questions: (a) Is anyone in the story or the poem a hero in the sense of being willing to risk his life for a high moral principle? (b) Does any scene in the poem remind you of a scene in the story? (c) Do you find **irony** in Crane's attitudes toward war? (d) Does Crane really show you that war is kind?

Creative Writing
3. War Is . . .

Write a poem or a short prose piece about war based on one of the subjects or **themes** in Crane's works. Your work should be clearly focused on the topic, and the content should be gritty and true to life. For an example, see the Student to Student poem "What About Glory" on page 493.

War Is Kind

Do not weep, maiden, for war is kind.
Because your lover threw wild hands toward the sky
And the affrighted steed ran on alone,
Do not weep.
5 War is kind.

Hoarse, booming drums of the regiment,
Little souls who thirst for fight,
These men were born to drill and die.
The unexplained glory flies above them,
10 Great is the Battle-God, great, and his Kingdom—
A field where a thousand corpses lie.

Do not weep, babe, for war is kind.
Because your father tumbled in the yellow trenches,
Raged at his breast, gulped and died,
15 Do not weep.
War is kind.

Swift blazing flag of the regiment,
Eagle with crest of red and gold,
These men were born to drill and die.
20 Point for them the virtue of slaughter,
Make plain to them the excellence of killing
And a field where a thousand corpses lie.

Mother whose heart hung humble as a button
On the bright splendid shroud of your son,
25 Do not weep.
War is kind.

—Stephen Crane, 1896

Listening to Music

"When Johnny Comes Marching Home" (Traditional), performed by Ronnie Gilbert
One of the most popular songs of the Civil War era, "When Johnny Comes Marching Home" is based on "Johnny, I Hardly Knew Ye," an eighteenth-century Scottish and Irish ballad about a soldier who has come home from the wars missing several body parts. Sung from the viewpoint of his wife or sweetheart, it is far more gruesome and ironic than the American Civil War version, which, in addition to changing the lyrics, slightly modifies the tune.

Activity
Listen to the song, and then write an imaginary addition to the "Voices from the Civil War" section (p. 476) in which one of the writers in this collection describes his or her reaction on first hearing the song.

Jack London
(1876–1916)

The Bettmann Archive.

In his teens and twenties, Jack London adventured on sea and ice. Then, in the sixteen remaining years of his life, he turned out nearly fifty volumes of essays and fiction. Known during his lifetime as a passionate socialist, London is remembered today not for his political convictions, but for his exciting, fast-paced adventure stories. Even his harshest critic, Ambrose Bierce (page 466), called London's novel *The Sea Wolf* a "rattling good story."

London was born into a poor family in San Francisco. As a boy, he was largely uncared for by his parents. He delivered newspapers, worked on an ice wagon, set up pins in a bowling alley, and worked in a cannery. "Almost the first thing I realized were responsibilities," he says. "I worked hard from my eighth year." He graduated from grammar school in Oakland, across the bay from San Francisco.

Meanwhile, London read everything he could find in the public library, especially stories of real-life adventure. In his teens, he plunged into danger. "I joined the oyster pirates in the bay; shipped as sailor on a schooner; took a turn at salmon fishing; shipped before the mast and sailed for the Japanese coast on a seal-hunting expedition. After sealing for seven months I came back to California, and took odd jobs. . . ."

London was still in his teens when he settled in Oakland again. He began to write, selling a few pieces to local papers. After attending high school for one year, he managed to pass the entrance exams for the University of California at Berkeley by cramming on his own. The combination of work, school, and writing proved to be too much, however, and he quit halfway through his freshman year. He submerged himself in writing for the next three months. But he earned practically nothing, so in 1897 he took off to prospect for gold in the Klondike—part of the Yukon Territory in northwestern Canada.

London became sick and had to leave the Klondike in less than a year, but the experience convinced him that life is a struggle in which the strong survive and the weak do not. London's short stories and novels dramatize his belief that "civilized" beings are either destroyed or re-created in savage environments.

London's first major success was a story collection, *The Son of the Wolf* (1900). Readers were thrilled by the shocking brutality of his stories, then hooked by the action and adventure. His most famous short story, "To Build a Fire" (1908), focuses on survival. His most famous novel, *The Call of the Wild* (1903), celebrates the escape to freedom of a sled dog named Buck.

London became a millionaire from his writings, and success greatly altered his life. In 1900, he married and had two daughters, but his wife sued him for divorce in 1905. He remarried and established his home at Glen Ellen in Sonoma County, north of San Francisco. There he intended to create a magnificent ranch estate, but he lost interest when Wolf House, his nearly completed mansion, burned down in 1913. London, for years an alcoholic, suffered in his later years from kidney disease and depression. One evening in November 1916, when the physical pain finally became unendurable, London took a lethal dose of narcotics and lapsed into a coma. He died the next evening; he was forty years old.

OBJECTIVES
1. Read and interpret the story
2. Identify and analyze naturalism
3. Analyze the text structure of cause and effect
4. Express understanding through critical and creative writing, science, and performance
5. Understand and use new words

SKILLS
Literary
- Identify and analyze naturalism

Reading
- Analyze the text structure of cause and effect

Writing
- Collect ideas for a research paper
- Analyze conflict
- Compose a dialogue
- Write a story

Speaking/Listening
- Role-play a dialogue
- Record a scene from the story

Science
- Make a survival manual

Music
- Select background music for the story

Vocabulary
- Use new words

Planning

- **Block Schedule**
  Block Scheduling Lesson Plans with Pacing Guide
- **Traditional Schedule**
  Lesson Plans Including Strategies for English-Language Learners
- **One-Stop Planner**
  CD-ROM with Test Generator

  Resources: Print and Media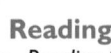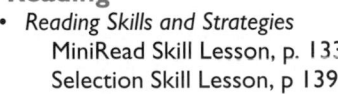

Reading
- *Reading Skills and Strategies*
  MiniRead Skill Lesson, p. 133
  Selection Skill Lesson, p 139
- *Graphic Organizers for Active Reading*, p. 48
- *Words to Own*, p. 32
- *Audio CD Library*
  Disc 13, Track 5

Elements of Literature
- *Literary Elements*
  Transparency 16
  Worksheet, p. 49

Writing and Language
- *Daily Oral Grammar*
  Transparency 33
- *Grammar and Language Links*
  Worksheet, p. 43

Assessment
- *Formal Assessment*, p. 98
- *Portfolio Management System*, p. 148
- *Preparation for College Admission Exams*, p. 35
- *Test Generator (One-Stop Planner CD-ROM)*

Internet
- go.hrw.com (keyword: LE0 11-10)

Summary ■■

Ignoring the advice of a more experienced man, a rookie prospector in the Yukon attempts a long journey on foot during an intense cold spell, with only his dog as a companion. When the man gets wet, he stops to build a fire to restore his circulation. He succeeds at first, but snow falls from a tree onto the fire and extinguishes it. He tries to get a new fire going, but he is too numb and clumsy. Panicked, the man starts running toward the camp where his partners are waiting for him, but he does not have the strength to go far. He collapses in the snow, falls asleep, and dies. The dog remains until the man is dead, then, seeking warmth, heads toward camp.

BROWSING IN THE FILES

About the Author. To London, life was a dog-eat-dog existence that came down to survival of the fittest. Beneath our veneer of civilization, London saw a prehistoric beast who fought and conquered through might and deceit. If the veneer were scratched, an inhuman beast would leap through. Our nature is fierce and cruel, London argued, tempered only by an equally spontaneous love. Although a socialist, London was heavily influenced by Friedrich Nietzsche's idea of a "superman," who, by force of will, rises above the masses.

Before You Read
TO BUILD A FIRE

Make the Connection
Cold, Cruel World
"To Build a Fire" must be the coldest story ever written. It is also one of the most effective examples of a conflict between a human being and the elements of nature. London draws on his own experience of prospecting for gold in the Yukon—a bleak, nearly sunless region of northwestern Canada—to give authenticity to the story.

But this is ultimately far more than a "person versus nature" story. It is a grimly realistic tale about a man who is "quick and alert in the things of life, but only in the things, and not in the significances"—an "innocent" who is not prepared for a cruel and unforgiving environment.

You may want to dress warmly before you read.

Reading Skills and Strategies
Analyzing Text Structures: Cause and Effect
Science tells us that for every action there is a reaction. In literature, we call this the relationship of **cause** and **effect**. A plot is made up of a string of causes and effects. As you read London's story, keep notes on each action the protagonist takes and note its effect. You will find that an action as small as a misstep or the lighting of a match can take on critical importance.

Elements of Literature
Naturalism
The naturalists were a group of nineteenth-century writers who went beyond realism in an attempt to portray life exactly as it is. Naturalist writers, influenced by the scientist Charles Darwin's (1809–1882) theories of natural selection and survival of the fittest, believed human behavior is determined by heredity and environment. Relying on new theories in sociology and psychology, the naturalists dissected human behavior with detachment and objectivity, like scientists dissecting laboratory specimens. **Naturalism** presents human beings as subject to natural forces beyond their control. This idea is at the center of "To Build a Fire."

> **N**aturalism was a nineteenth-century literary movement that claimed to portray life exactly as it is, with detachment and objectivity.
>
> *For more on Naturalism, see page 421 and the Handbook of Literary Terms.*

To Build

Day had broken cold and gray, exceedingly cold and

Preteaching Vocabulary

Words to Own
Ask students to read the Words to Own and their definitions listed at the bottom of the selection pages. Then, have pairs of students use the words to make word puzzles, such as crosswords and acrostics. Partners can trade papers with another pair and complete each other's puzzles. Then, tell students to match each of the numbered words at right with its antonym.

1. intangible [b]	a. pleasant
2. undulations [j]	b. solid
3. protruding [f]	c. visible
4. solidity [i]	d. preceded
5. imperative [h]	e. center
6. extremities [e]	f. indented
7. recoiled [g]	g. approached
8. imperceptible [c]	h. unnecessary
9. excruciating [a]	i. airiness
10. ensued [d]	j. flatness

a Fire
Jack London

...the man turned aside from the main Yukon trail and climbed the high earth bank . . .

Day had broken cold and gray, exceedingly cold and gray, when the man turned aside from the main Yukon trail and climbed the high earth bank, where a dim and little-traveled trail led eastward through the fat spruce timberland. It was a steep bank, and he paused for breath at the top, excusing the act to himself by looking at his watch. It was nine o'clock. There was no sun or hint of sun, though there was not a cloud in the sky. It was a clear day, and yet there seemed an intangible pall over the face of things, a subtle gloom that made the day dark, and that was due to the absence of sun. This fact did not worry the man. He was used to the lack of sun. It had been days since he had seen the sun, and he knew that a few more days must pass before that cheerful orb, due south, would just peep above the skyline and dip immediately from view.

The man flung a look back along the way he had come. The Yukon lay a mile wide and hidden under three feet of ice. On top of this ice were as many feet of snow. It was all pure white, rolling in gentle undulations where the ice jams of the freeze-up had formed. North and south, as far as his eye could see, it was unbroken white, save for a dark hairline that curved and twisted from around the spruce-covered island to the south, and that curved and twisted away into the north, where it disappeared behind another spruce-covered island.

WORDS TO OWN

intangible (in·tan′jə·bəl) *adj.*: difficult to define; vague.
undulations (un′dyōō·lā′shənz) *n. pl.*: wavelike motions.

JACK LONDON **497**

(A) Critical Thinking
Determining Author's Purpose
❓ Why do you think the protagonist does not have a name? [Possible responses: It makes him representative of all people, since we can all find ourselves unprepared; the author wants to show that people are insignificant in the greater scheme of nature.]

(B) Elements of Literature
Foreshadowing
❓ What does this passage suggest will happen later in the story? [It foreshadows both the weather and the man's death; the word *pall* suggests a funeral pall, a cloth draped over a coffin.]

(C) Reading Skills and Strategies
Analyzing Cause and Effect
❓ What are the possible effects of having this kind of attitude? [Overconfidence can lead to unnecessary risks or to carelessness.]

(D) Historical Connections
The Yukon
The Yukon is a powerful river that originates just north of the border between the Canadian provinces of British Columbia and the Yukon Territory. This territory remained an uninhabited wilderness until the Klondike gold strike of 1896. A gold rush ensued which, at its peak, brought the population of Dawson alone to about 30,000 people. One hundred million dollars worth of gold was mined in the Yukon between 1896 and 1904 and transported on the Yukon River. After the ore was exhausted, the population declined. Mining resumed in the 1960s, however, and the population began to grow again.

Reaching All Students

Struggling Readers
Analyzing Text Structures: Cause and Effect was introduced in Before You Read on p. 496. For a lesson directly tied to this selection that teaches students to analyze cause and effect with a strategy called Story Impressions, see the *Reading Skills and Strategies* binder
• MiniRead Skill Lesson, p. 133
• Selection Skill Lesson, p. 139

English Language Learners
The proper nouns and foreign words in the story are apt to pose challenges for some of these students. To help them along, you may wish to read the first three paragraphs of the story aloud and pronounce and define the words *Yukon, Chilkoot,* and *cheechako* (p. 498).

Advanced Learners
Invite students to analyze how the description of the environment affects the mood of the story. Guide students to do a close textual analysis, isolating specific words and phrases that create the mood. Then, have students explore how the description is naturalistic. What is London saying about the role of heredity and environment in our ability to survive?

This dark hairline was the trail—the main trail—that led south five hundred miles to the Chilkoot Pass, Dyea, and salt water; and that led north seventy miles to Dawson, and still on to the north a thousand miles to Nulato, and finally to St. Michael on the Bering Sea, a thousand miles and half a thousand more.

A But all this—the mysterious, far-reaching hairline trail, the absence of sun from the sky, the tremendous cold, and the strangeness and weirdness of it all—made no impression on the man. It was not because he was long used to it. He was a newcomer in the land, a *cheechako*,[1] and this was his first winter. The trouble with him was that he **B** was without imagination. He was quick and alert in the things of life, but only in the things, and not in the significances. Fifty degrees below zero meant eighty-odd degrees of frost. Such fact impressed him as being cold and uncomfortable, and that was all. It did not lead him to meditate upon his frailty as a creature of temperature, and upon man's frailty in general, able only to live within certain narrow limits of heat and cold, and from there on it did not lead him to the conjectural[2] field of immortality and man's place in the universe. Fifty degrees below zero stood for a bite of frost that hurt and that must be guarded against by the use of mittens, earflaps, warm moccasins, and thick socks. Fifty degrees below zero was to him just precisely fifty degrees below zero. That there should be anything more to it than that was a thought that never entered his head.

As he turned to go on, he spat speculatively. There was a sharp, explosive crackle that startled him. He spat again. And again, in the air, before it could fall to the snow, the spittle crackled. He knew that at fifty below, spittle crackled on the snow, but this spittle had crackled in the air. Undoubtedly it was colder than fifty below—how much colder he did not know. But the temperature did not matter. He was bound for the old claim on the left fork of Henderson Creek, where the boys were already. They had come over across the divide from the Indian Creek country, while he had come the roundabout way to take a look at the possibilities of getting out logs in the spring

1. *cheechako* (chē·chä′kō): Chinook jargon for "newcomer" or "tenderfoot."
2. *conjectural:* based on guesswork or uncertain evidence.

from the islands in the Yukon. He would be into camp by six o'clock; a bit after dark, it was true, but the boys would be there, a fire would be going, and a hot supper would be ready. As for lunch, he pressed his hand against the protruding bundle under his jacket. It was also under his shirt, wrapped up in a handkerchief and lying against the naked skin. It was the only way to keep the biscuits from freezing. He smiled agreeably to himself as he thought of those biscuits, each cut open and sopped in bacon grease, and each enclosing a generous slice of fried bacon.

C He plunged in among the big spruce trees. The trail was faint. A foot of snow had fallen since the last sled had passed over, and he was glad he was without a sled, traveling light. In fact, he carried nothing but the lunch wrapped in the handkerchief. He was surprised, however, at the cold. It certainly was cold, he concluded, as he rubbed his numb nose and cheekbones with his mittened hand. He was a warm-whiskered man, but the hair on his face did not protect the high cheekbones and the eager nose that thrust itself aggressively into the frosty air.

D At the man's heels trotted a dog, a big native husky, the proper wolf dog, gray-coated and without any visible or temperamental difference from its brother, the wild wolf. The animal was depressed by the tremendous cold. It knew that it was no time for traveling. Its instinct told it a truer tale than was told to the man by the man's judgment. In reality, it was not merely colder than fifty below zero; it was colder than sixty below, than seventy below. It was seventy-five below zero. Since the freezing point is thirty-two above zero, it meant that one hundred and seven degrees of frost obtained. The dog did not know anything about thermometers. Possibly in its brain there was no sharp consciousness of a condition of very cold such as was in the man's brain. But the brute had its instinct. It experienced a vague but menacing apprehension that subdued it and made it slink along at the man's heels, and that made it question eagerly every unwonted[3] movement of

3. **unwonted:** unusual.

- -

WORDS TO OWN
protruding (prō·trōōd′in) *v.* used as *adj.*: sticking out.

- -

the man, as if expecting him to go into camp or to seek shelter somewhere and build a fire. The dog had learned fire, and it wanted fire, or else to burrow under the snow and cuddle its warmth away from the air.

The frozen moisture of its breathing had settled on its fur in a fine powder of frost, and especially were its jowls, muzzle, and eyelashes whitened by its crystaled breath. The man's red beard and moustache were likewise frosted, but more solidly, the deposit taking the form of ice and increasing with every warm, moist breath he exhaled. Also, the man was chewing tobacco, and the muzzle of ice held his lips so rigidly that he was unable to clear his chin when he expelled the juice. The result was that a crystal beard of the color and solidity of amber was increasing its length on his chin. If he fell down it would shatter itself, like glass, into brittle fragments. But he did not mind the appendage. It was the penalty all tobacco chewers paid in that country, and he had been out before in two cold snaps. They had not been so cold as this, he knew, but by the spirit thermometer[4] at Sixty Mile he knew they had been registered at fifty below and at fifty-five.

He held on through the level stretch of woods for several miles, crossed a wide flat, and dropped down a bank to the frozen bed of a small stream. This was Henderson Creek, and he knew he was ten miles from the forks. He looked at his watch. It was ten o'clock. He was making four miles an hour, and he calculated that he would arrive at the forks at half past twelve. He decided to celebrate that event by eating his lunch there.

The dog dropped in again at his heels, with a tail drooping discouragement, as the man swung along the creek bed. The furrow of the old sled trail was plainly visible, but a dozen inches of snow covered the marks of the last runners. In a month no man had come up or down that silent creek. The man held steadily on. He was not much given to thinking, and just then particularly, he had nothing to think about save that he would eat lunch at the forks and that at six o'clock he would be in camp with the boys. There was nobody to talk to; and, had there been, speech

would have been impossible because of the ice muzzle on his mouth. So he continued monotonously to chew tobacco and to increase the length of his amber beard.

Once in a while the thought reiterated itself that it was very cold and that he had never experienced such cold. As he walked along he rubbed his cheekbones and nose with the back of his mittened hand. He did this automatically, now and again changing hands. But rub as he would, the instant he stopped his cheekbones went numb, and the following instant the end of his nose went numb. He was sure to frost his cheeks; he knew that, and experienced a pang of regret that he had not devised a nose strap of the sort Bud wore in the cold snaps. Such a strap passed across the cheeks, as well, and saved them. But it didn't matter much, after all. What were frosted cheeks? A bit painful, that was all; they were never serious.

Empty as the man's mind was of thought, he was keenly observant, and he noticed the changes in the creek, the curves and bends and timber jams, and always he sharply noted where he placed his feet. Once, coming around a bend, he shied abruptly, like a startled horse, curved away from the place where he had been walking, and retreated several paces back along the trail. The creek, he knew, was frozen clear to the bottom—no creek could contain water in that arctic winter—but he knew also that there were springs that bubbled out from the hillsides and ran along under the snow and on top of the ice of the creek. He knew that the coldest snaps never froze these springs, and he knew likewise their danger. They were traps. They hid pools of water under the snow that might be three inches deep, or three feet. Sometimes a skin of ice half an inch thick covered them, and in turn was covered by the snow. Sometimes there were alternate layers of water and ice skin, so that when one broke through he kept on breaking through for a while, sometimes wetting himself to the waist.

That was why he had shied in such panic. He had felt the give under his feet and heard the crackle of a snow-hidden ice skin. And to get his feet wet in such a temperature meant trouble and

4. **spirit thermometer:** alcohol thermometer. In places where the temperature often drops below the freezing point of mercury, alcohol is used in thermometers.

WORDS TO OWN
solidity (sə·lid′ə·tē) *n.:* firmness; solidness.

JACK LONDON 499

Professional Notes

Critical Comment: Naturalism

"Naturalism has been defined in two words as pessimistic determinism. . ." writes scholar Malcolm Cowley. "The naturalistic writers were all determinists in that they believed in the omnipotence of abstract forces. They were pessimists so far as they believed that men and women were absolutely incapable of shaping their own destinies. . . . [M]an was, in [Theodore] Dreiser's words, 'the victim of forces over which he has no control. . . .' For Jack London, the driv-

ing force behind human events was always biology—'I mean,' says his autobiographical hero, Martin Eden, 'the real interpretative biology, from the ground up, from the laboratory and the test tube and the vitalized inorganic right on up to the widest esthetic and social generalizations.' London believed that such biological principles as natural selection and the survival of the fittest were also the laws of human society."

E Reading Skills and Strategies
Analyzing Cause and Effect

❓ What causes the man to ignore the warnings of the extreme cold? [Since he has already been out in two cold snaps, he believes that he knows how to deal with the cold. As a result, he ignores all the warnings that this cold is far more extreme—and dangerous.]

F English Language Learners
Idioms

Explain that the phrase *was not much given to* means "did not ordinarily do much." Also point out that the context clues—the relationship between the two halves of the sentence—show that *save* means "except."

G Critical Thinking
Determining Author's Purpose

❓ Why do you think London keeps repeating the fact that it's cold? What do you predict this will mean in the story? [Possible responses: to show how out of touch the man is with nature and even his own physical reaction; to show that the man has ample warning of the likely consequences. The man may be overcome by the harsh conditions.]

H Elements of Literature
Foreshadowing

❓ What does the man's reaction to the frostbite on his cheeks suggest? [Possible responses: He continues to underestimate the force of nature; he thinks he is immune to the elements.]

I Elements of Literature
Naturalism

Point out that the one time the man might seem to be acting instinctually ("like a startled horse") he is actually acting from knowledge of springs running under thin ice. Lacking the instincts of the dog and the good judgment of the older man, he is still at the mercy of nature.

He did not expose his fingers more

than a minute, and was astonished at

the swift numbness that smote them.

A **Vocabulary Note**

Derivations

Have students look up the derivation of the word *footing*. Have them check its different meanings and trace how those meanings are related to the root *foot*. Then, tell students to make a chart of other words derived from *foot*.

B **Critical Thinking**

Making Judgments

? Is the man being fair by having the dog take the risk? Why or why not? [Possible response: Yes, because a human life is more valuable than an animal's; no, the man is being selfish and cruel.]

C **Critical Thinking**

Determining Author's Purpose

? Why does London point out that the dog acts from instinct? [to show that as part of nature, the dog acts in conjunction with nature and is thus protected in this situation; to contrast the dog and the man and to highlight how the man, who is detached from nature, misses every clue to his own survival]

danger. At the very least it meant delay, for he would be forced to stop and build a fire, and under its protection to bare his feet while he dried his socks and moccasins. He stood and studied the creek bed and its banks, and decided that the flow of water came from the right. He reflected awhile, rubbing his nose and cheeks, then skirted to the left, stepping gingerly and testing the footing for each step. Once clear of the danger, he took a fresh chew of tobacco and swung along at his four-mile gait.

In the course of the next two hours he came upon several similar traps. Usually the snow above the hidden pools had a sunken, candied appearance that advertised the danger. Once again, however, he had a close call; and once, suspecting danger, he compelled the dog to go on in front. The dog did not want to go. It hung back until the man shoved it forward, and then it went quickly across the white, unbroken surface. Suddenly it broke through, floundered to one side, and got away to firmer footing. It had wet its forefeet and legs, and almost immediately the water that clung to it turned to ice. It made quick efforts to lick the ice off its legs, then dropped down in the snow and began to bite out the ice that had formed between the toes. This was a matter of instinct. To permit the ice to remain would mean sore feet. It did not know this. It merely obeyed the mysterious prompting that arose from the deep crypts[5] of

5. **crypts:** hidden recesses.

Getting Students Involved

Cooperative Learning

A "Natural" Debate. Naturalism removed from literature the whole notion of human responsibility. If naturalistic stories such as "To Build a Fire" had tragic endings, these endings could not be explained by the traditional battles of human will. Instead, they were the result of conditions, forces, physical laws, or nature itself. In short, the outcome was out of human hands. Have groups of three students research, orga-nize, and present information on human efforts to gain control over natural phenomena such as extreme temperatures, floods, hurricanes, and earthquakes.

Research Activity

Fire It Up. A central image in this story is fire, and no wonder: it represents survival. The original source of fire was lightning, and such fortuitously ignited blazes remained the only source for centuries. Our ancestors first used fire around 500,000 B.C., but it wasn't until 7000 B.C. that they acquired reliable fire-making techniques. Invite students to find out more about fire: sacred fire rituals, signal fires and coding systems, fire's use in agriculture, and so on. Students might consider sharing their research in humorous skits.

its being. But the man knew, having achieved a judgment on the subject, and he removed the mitten from his right hand and helped tear out the ice particles. He did not expose his fingers more than a minute, and was astonished at the swift numbness that smote[6] them. It certainly was cold. He pulled on the mitten hastily, and beat the hand savagely across his chest.

At twelve o'clock the day was at its brightest. Yet the sun was too far south on its winter journey to clear the horizon. The bulge of the earth intervened between it and Henderson Creek, where the man walked under a clear sky at noon and cast no shadow. At half past twelve, to the minute, he arrived at the forks of the creek. He was pleased at the speed he had made. If he kept it up, he would certainly be with the boys by six. He unbuttoned his jacket and shirt and drew forth his lunch. The action consumed no more than a quarter of a minute, yet in that brief moment the numbness laid hold of the exposed fingers. He did not put the mitten on, but instead struck the fingers a dozen sharp smashes against his leg. Then he sat down on a snow-covered log to eat. The sting that followed upon the striking of his fingers against his leg ceased so quickly that he was startled. He had had no chance to take a bite of biscuit. He struck the fingers repeatedly and returned them to the mitten, baring the other hand for the purpose of eating. He tried to take a mouthful, but the ice muzzle prevented. He had forgotten to build a fire and thaw out. He chuckled at his foolishness, and as he chuckled he noted the numbness creeping into the exposed fingers. Also, he noted that the stinging which had first come to his toes when he sat down was already passing away. He wondered whether the toes were warm or numb. He moved them inside the moccasins and decided that they were numb.

He pulled the mitten on hurriedly and stood up. He was a bit frightened. He stamped up and down until the stinging returned into the feet. It certainly was cold, was his thought. That man from Sulfur Creek had spoken the truth when telling how cold it sometimes got in the country. And he had laughed at him at the time! That showed one must not be too sure of things. There was no mistake about it, it *was* cold. He strode up

6. **smote:** powerfully struck; past tense of *smite*.

and down, stamping his feet and threshing his arms, until reassured by the returning warmth. Then he got out matches and proceeded to make a fire. From the undergrowth, where high water of the previous spring had lodged a supply of seasoned twigs, he got his firewood. Working carefully from a small beginning, he soon had a roaring fire, over which he thawed the ice from his face and in the protection of which he ate his biscuits. For the moment the cold of space was outwitted. The dog took satisfaction in the fire, stretching out close enough for warmth and far enough away to escape being singed.

When the man had finished, he filled his pipe and took his comfortable time over a smoke. Then he pulled on his mittens, settled the earflaps of his cap firmly about his ears, and took the creek trail up the left fork. The dog was disappointed and yearned back toward the fire. This man did not know cold. Possibly all the generations of his ancestry had been ignorant of cold, of real cold, of cold one hundred and seven degrees below freezing point. But the dog knew; all its ancestry knew, and it had inherited the knowledge. And it knew that it was not good to walk abroad in such fearful cold. It was the time to lie snug in a hole in the snow and wait for a curtain of cloud to be drawn across the face of outer space whence this cold came. On the other hand, there was no keen intimacy between the dog and the man. The one was the toil slave of the other, and the only caresses it had ever received were the caresses of the whiplash and of harsh and menacing throat sounds that threatened the whiplash. So the dog made no effort to communicate its apprehension to the man. It was not concerned in the welfare of the man; it was for its own sake that it yearned back toward the fire. But the man whistled, and spoke to it with the sound of whiplashes, and the dog swung in at the man's heels and followed after.

The man took a chew of tobacco and proceeded to start a new amber beard. Also, his moist breath quickly powdered with white his moustache, eyebrows, and lashes. There did not seem to be so many springs on the left fork of the Henderson, and for half an hour the man saw no signs of any. And then it happened. At a place where there were no signs, where the soft, unbroken snow seemed to advertise solidity beneath, the

JACK LONDON 501

ⓓ Appreciating Language
Diction
❓ Why do you think London used the word *savagely* here? [Possible response: It suggests the effect of the bitter cold as well as the effect of the man's anger, panic, and desperation. Note that *savage* is not applied, as it usually is, to something inhuman or bestial—instead it refers here to the frustration and arrogance of the human will.]

ⓔ Reading Skills and Strategies
Analyzing Cause and Effect
❓ Why is the man startled? [In spite of having felt extreme cold earlier, he is cheered by the fulfillment of his expectations regarding his speed. The quick freezing of his fingers shakes his confidence.]

ⓕ Elements of Literature
Naturalism
❓ What is ironic about the man's response to his frostbite? [His casual chuckle shows that he continues to underestimate the force of nature and its cold indifference. The man's arrogance could cause his death.]

ⓖ Critical Thinking
Determining Author's Purpose
❓ Earlier on this page, it seemed as though the man was surely going to die, yet he manages to stay alive. How? [He is not totally unprepared: He does have matches; he locates a good supply of wood; he is careful; he starts small and builds slowly.] **Why does London reverse our expectations?** [Possible responses: London uses this scene to build suspense and keep us reading on; he is playing with us as nature or fate toys with humankind in a naturalistic universe.]

Crossing the Curriculum

Geography/Mathematics
Have students do research to discover what areas of Earth have temperatures cold enough to be immediately dangerous to people. After students identify the regions, have them figure out what percentage of Earth's surface this includes. Students can make a map or chart to illustrate their findings. Challenge students to explain how life, particularly human life, survives in these regions—if indeed it does.

Connecting Across Texts

Connecting with the New England Writers
Invite students to speculate whether some of the New England writers who rhapsodized about nature—like Emerson (p. 216), Thoreau (p. 230), or Dickinson (p. 372)—would have felt differently if they had lived in the Arctic. What quotations from these writers might be applied to the Arctic? Which describe a very different world? Do students believe people think differently, depending on whether they live in frigid, temperate, or tropical climates? What differences have students noted? Be sure students recognize that while nature does not wear the same face in all parts of the world, it can offer challenges everywhere.

man broke through. It was not deep. He wet
himself halfway to the knees before he floundered out to the firm crust.

A He was angry, and cursed his luck aloud. He
had hoped to get into camp with the boys at six
o'clock, and this would delay him an hour, for he
would have to build a fire and dry out his footgear.
This was imperative at that low temperature—he
knew that much; and he turned aside to the bank,
which he climbed. On top, tangled in the under-
brush about the trunks of several small spruce
trees, was a high-water deposit of dry firewood—
sticks and twigs, principally, but also larger portions of seasoned branches and fine, dry, last
year's grasses. He threw down several large pieces
B on top of the snow. This served for a foundation
and prevented the young flame from drowning itself in the snow it otherwise would melt. The
flame he got by touching a match to a small shred
of birch bark that he took from his pocket. This
burned even more readily than paper. Placing it
on the foundation, he fed the young flame with
wisps of dry grass and with the tiniest dry twigs.

He worked slowly and carefully, keenly aware
of his danger. Gradually, as the flame grew
stronger, he increased the size of the twigs with
which he fed it. He squatted in the snow, pulling
the twigs out from their entanglement in the
brush and feeding directly to the flame. He knew
there must be no failure. When it is seventy-five
below zero, a man must not fail in his first attempt
to build a fire—that is, if his feet are wet. If his
feet are dry, and he fails, he can run along the trail
for a half a mile and restore his circulation. But the
circulation of wet and freezing feet cannot be restored by running when it is seventy-five below.
No matter how fast he runs, the wet feet will
freeze the harder.

All this the man knew. The old-timer on Sulfur
Creek had told him about it the previous fall, and
now he was appreciating the advice. Already all
sensation had gone out of his feet. To build the
fire, he had been forced to remove his mittens,
and the fingers had quickly gone numb. His pace
of four miles an hour had kept his heart pumping
blood to the surface of his body and to all the
extremities. But the instant he stopped, the action
of the pump eased down. The cold of space
smote the unprotected tip of the planet, and he,
being on that unprotected tip, received the full

force of the blow. The blood of his body recoiled
before it. The blood was alive, like the dog, and
like the dog it wanted to hide away and cover itself
up from the fearful cold. So long as he walked four
miles an hour, he pumped that blood, willy-nilly, to
the surface; but now it ebbed away and sank down
into the recesses of his body. The extremities were
the first to feel its absence. His wet feet froze the
faster, and his exposed fingers numbed the faster,
though they had not yet begun to freeze. Nose and
cheeks were already freezing, while the skin of all
his body chilled as it lost its blood.

But he was safe. Toes and nose and cheeks
would be only touched by the frost, for the fire
was beginning to burn with strength. He was
feeding it twigs the size of his finger. In another
C minute he would be able to feed it with branches
the size of his wrist, and then he could remove his
wet footgear, and, while it dried, he could keep
his naked feet warm by the fire, rubbing them at
first, of course, with snow. The fire was a success.
He was safe. He remembered the advice of the
old-timer on Sulfur Creek, and smiled. The old-
timer had been very serious in laying down the
law that no man must travel alone in the Klondike
after fifty below. Well, here he was; he had had
the accident; he was alone; and he had saved himself. Those old-timers were rather womanish,
some of them, he thought. All a man had to do
was to keep his head and he was all right. Any
man who was a man could travel alone. But it was
D surprising, the rapidity with which his cheeks and
nose were freezing. And he had not thought his
fingers could go lifeless in so short a time. Lifeless
they were, for he could scarcely make them move
together to grip a twig, and they seemed remote
from his body and from him. When he touched a
twig, he had to look and see whether or not he
had hold of it. The wires were pretty well down
between him and his finger ends.

All of which counted for little. There was the
fire, snapping and crackling and promising life

WORDS TO OWN

imperative (im·per′ə·tiv) *adj.*: absolutely necessary;
compulsory.
extremities (ek·strem′ə·tēz) *n. pl.*: limbs of the
body, especially hands and feet.
recoiled (ri·koild′) *v.*: shrank away; drew back.

---

502 THE RISE OF REALISM: THE CIVIL WAR AND POSTWAR PERIOD

Even if he succeeded, he would most likely lose some toes. His feet must be badly frozen by now, and there would be some time before the second fire was ready.

with every dancing flame. He started to untie his moccasins. They were coated with ice; the thick German socks were like sheaths of iron halfway to the knees; and the moccasin strings were like rods of steel all twisted and knotted as by some conflagration. For a moment he tugged with his numb fingers, then, realizing the folly of it, he drew his sheath knife.

But before he could cut the strings it happened. It was his own fault, or, rather, his mistake. He should not have built the fire under the spruce tree. He should have built it in the open. But it had been easier to pull the twigs from the bush and drop them directly on the fire. Now the tree under which he had done this carried a weight of snow on its boughs. No wind had blown for weeks, and each bough was fully freighted. Each time he had pulled a twig he had communicated a slight agitation to the tree—an imperceptible agitation, so far as he was concerned, but an agitation sufficient to bring about the disaster. High up in the tree one bough capsized its load of snow. This fell on the boughs beneath, capsizing them. This process continued, spreading out and involving the whole tree. It grew like an avalanche, and it descended without warning upon the man and

the fire, and the fire was blotted out! Where it had burned was a mantle of fresh and disordered snow.

The man was shocked. It was as though he had just heard his own sentence of death. For a moment he sat and stared at the spot where the fire had been. Then he grew very calm. Perhaps the old-timer on Sulfur Creek was right. If he had only had a trail mate, he would have been in no danger now. The trail mate could have built the fire. Well, it was up to him to build the fire over again, and this second time there must be no failure. Even if he succeeded, he would most likely lose some toes. His feet must be badly frozen by now, and there would be some time before the second fire was ready.

Such were his thoughts, but he did not sit and think them. He was busy all the time they were passing through his mind. He made a new foundation for a fire, this time in the open, where no treacherous tree could blot it out. Next he

WORDS TO OWN

imperceptible (im′pər·sep′tə·bəl) *adj.:* not easily perceived.

JACK LONDON 503

A **Advanced Learners**

Analyzing

? Why is this development important? [This is the first mention of panic, which might significantly affect the man's ability to think about consequences and to save himself.]

B **Struggling Readers**

Interpreting

? Why does the man welcome the excruciating pain? [It means that his fingers still could be used to light a fire.]

C **Elements of Literature**

Naturalism

? How does this passage show London's belief that life is a struggle in which only the strong survive? [Possible response: The situation is deteriorating fast. The man lacks the means to survive by himself.]

D **Appreciating Language**

Connotation

? Note London's choice of words. What is implied by the fact that the man devotes his whole *soul* to his task? [It implies that he is taking his situation seriously and, when forced, is capable of drawing upon his entire being for strength.]

E **Reading Skills and Strategies**

Analyzing Cause and Effect

? What has caused the man to revise his opinion of the old-timer? What do you think will be the effect of this realization? [The man's panic and desperate situation make him realize that he was foolish to disregard the old-timer's advice. Some students might say the man will lose hope; others may feel he will continue as before.]

gathered dry grasses and tiny twigs from the high-water flotsam.[7] He could not bring his fingers together to pull them out, but he was able to gather them by the handful. In this way he got many rotten twigs and bits of green moss that were undesirable, but it was the best he could do. He worked methodically, even collecting an armful of the larger branches to be used later when the fire gathered strength. And all the while the dog sat and watched him, a certain yearning wistfulness in its eyes, for it looked upon him as the fire provider, and the fire was slow in coming.

When all was ready, the man reached in his pocket for a second piece of birch bark. He knew the bark was there, and, though he could not feel it with his fingers, he could hear its crisp rustling as he fumbled for it. Try as he would, he could not clutch hold of it. And all the time, in his consciousness, was the knowledge that each instant his feet were freezing. This thought tended to put him in a panic, but he fought against it and kept calm. He pulled on his mittens with his teeth, and threshed his arms back and forth, beating his hands with all his might against his sides. He did this sitting down, and he stood up to do it; and all the while the dog sat in the snow, its wolf brush of a tail curled around warmly over its forefeet, its sharp wolf ears pricked forward intently as it watched the man. And the man, as he beat and threshed with his arms and hands, felt a great surge of envy as he regarded the creature that was warm and secure in its natural covering.

After a time he was aware of the first faraway signals of sensation in his beaten fingers. The faint tingling grew stronger till it evolved into a stinging ache that was <u>excruciating</u>, but which the man hailed with satisfaction. He stripped the mitten from his right hand and fetched forth the birch bark. The exposed fingers were quickly going numb again. Next he brought out his bunch of sulfur matches. But the tremendous cold had already driven the life out of his fingers. In his effort to separate one match from the others, the whole bunch fell in the snow. He tried to pick it out of the snow, but failed. The dead fingers could neither touch nor clutch. He was very careful. He drove the thought of his freezing feet, and nose,

---

7. **high-water flotsam:** branches and debris washed ashore by a stream or river during the warm months when the water is high.

and cheeks, out of his mind, devoting his whole soul to the matches. He watched, using the sense of vision in place of that of touch, and when he saw his fingers on each side of the bunch, he closed them—that is, he willed to close them, for the wires were down, and the fingers did not obey. He pulled the mitten on the right hand, and beat it fiercely against his knee. Then, with both mittened hands, he scooped the bunch of matches, along with much snow, into his lap. Yet he was no better off.

After some manipulation he managed to get the bunch between the heels of his mittened hands. In this fashion he carried it to his mouth. The ice crackled and snapped when by a violent effort he opened his mouth. He drew the lower jaw in, curled the upper lip out of the way, and scraped the bunch with his upper teeth in order to separate a match. He succeeded in getting one, which he dropped on his lap. He was no better off. He could not pick it up. Then he devised a way. He picked it up in his teeth and scratched it on his leg. Twenty times he scratched before he succeeded in lighting it. As it flamed he held it with his teeth to the birch bark. But the burning brimstone went up his nostrils and into his lungs, causing him to cough spasmodically. The match fell into the snow and went out.

The old-timer on Sulfur Creek was right, he thought in the moment of controlled despair that <u>ensued</u>: After fifty below, a man should travel with a partner. He beat his hands, but failed in exciting any sensation. Suddenly he bared both hands, removing the mittens with his teeth. He caught the whole bunch between the heels of his hands. His arm muscles, not being frozen, enabled him to press the hand heels tightly against the matches. Then he scratched the bunch along his leg. It flared into flame, seventy sulfur matches at once! There was no wind to blow them out. He kept his head to one side to escape the strangling fumes, and held the blazing bunch to the birch bark. As he so held it, he became aware of sensation in his hand. His flesh was burning. He could smell it.

WORDS TO OWN

excruciating (eks·kroo′shē·āt′iŋ) *adj.*: extreme; intense.

ensued (en·sood′) *v.*: resulted.

Using Students' Strengths

Verbal Learners

The men who trek through London's stories are strange, savage, and remorseless. What about female characters in London's stories? This story is not unique in omitting them, although as the biography on p. 495 explains, London's life was not without a female presence: He was married twice. Have students theorize about why London wrote almost exclusively about men and consider relating it to his belief in naturalism.

Naturalist Learners

In "To Build a Fire," the Yukon is a frigid, forbidding place, a merciless frozen wasteland. But the Yukon is also a land of vast beauty, marked by the majestic ice-capped St. Elias Mountains and scenic alpine lakes. Caribou, moose, bear, sheep, and mountain goats roam freely; salmon run up the territory's rivers from the Pacific Ocean. Some students will be interested in researching the Yukon's geography.

Deep down below the surface he could feel it. The sensation developed into pain that grew acute. And still he endured it, holding the flame of matches clumsily to the bark that would not light readily because his own burning hands were in the way, absorbing most of the flame.

At last, when he could endure no more, he jerked his hands apart. The blazing matches fell sizzling into the snow, but the birch bark was alight. He began laying dry grass and the tiniest twigs on the flame. He could not pick and choose, for he had to lift the fuel between the heels of his hands. Small pieces of rotten wood and green moss clung to the twigs, and he bit them off as well as he could with his teeth. He cherished the flame carefully and awkwardly. It meant life, and it must not perish. The withdrawal of blood from the surface of his body now made him begin to shiver, and he grew more awkward. A large piece of green moss fell squarely on the little fire. He tried to poke it out with his fingers, but his shivering frame made him poke too far, and he disrupted the nucleus of the little fire, the burning grasses and tiny twigs separating and scattering. He tried to poke them together again, but in spite of the tenseness of the effort, his shivering got away with him, and the twigs were hopelessly scattered. Each twig gushed a puff of smoke and went out. The fire provider had failed. As he looked apathetically about him, his eyes chanced on the dog, sitting across the ruins of the fire from him, in the snow, making restless, hunching movements, slightly lifting one forefoot and then the other, shifting its weight back and forth on them with wistful eagerness.

The sight of the dog put a wild idea into his head. He remembered the tale of the man, caught in a blizzard, who killed a steer and crawled inside the carcass, and so was saved. He would kill the dog and bury his hands in the warm body until the numbness went out of them. Then he could build another fire. He spoke to the dog, calling it to him; but in his voice was a strange note of fear that frightened the animal, who had never known the man to speak in such a way before. Something was the matter, and its suspicious nature sensed danger—it knew not what danger, but somewhere, somehow, in its brain arose an apprehension of the man. It flattened its ears down at the sound of the man's voice, and its restless, hunch-ing movements and the liftings and shiftings of its forefeet became more pronounced; but it would not come to the man. He got on his hands and knees and crawled toward the dog. This unusual posture again excited suspicion, and the animal sidled mincingly away.

The man sat up in the snow for a moment and struggled for calmness. Then he pulled on his mittens, by means of his teeth, and got up on his feet. He glanced down at first in order to assure himself that he was really standing up, for the absence of sensation in his feet left him unrelated to the earth. His erect position in itself started to drive the webs of suspicion from the dog's mind; and when he spoke peremptorily,[8] with the sound of whiplashes in his voice, the dog rendered its customary allegiance and came to him. As it came within reaching distance, the man lost his control. His arms flashed out to the dog, and he experienced genuine surprise when he discovered that his hands could not clutch, that there was neither bend nor feeling in the fingers. He had forgotten for the moment that they were frozen and that they were freezing more and more. All this happened quickly, and before the animal could get away, he encircled its body with his arms. He sat down in the snow, and in this fashion held the dog, while it snarled and whined and struggled.

But it was all he could do, hold its body encircled in his arms and sit there. He realized that he could not kill the dog. There was no way to do it. With his helpless hands he could neither draw nor hold his sheath knife nor throttle the animal. He released it, and it plunged wildly away, its tail between its legs and still snarling. It halted forty feet away and surveyed him curiously, with ears sharply pricked forward. The man looked down at his hands in order to locate them, and found them hanging on the ends of his arms. It struck him as curious that one should have to use his eyes in order to find out where his hands were. He began threshing his arms back and forth, beating the mittened hands against his sides. He did this for five minutes, violently, and his heart pumped enough blood up to the surface to put a stop to his shivering. But no sensation was aroused in his hands. He had an impression that they hung like weights on

8. **peremptorily** (pər·emp′tə·ri·lē): in a commanding way.

JACK LONDON **505**

F ● **Appreciating Language**
Style
❓ What effect does the impersonal tone create here? [Possible responses: It implies that the man's pain and his fate do not matter in any larger scheme of things; the detached tone makes his suffering more disturbing and horrific.]

G ● **Elements of Literature**
Naturalism
❓ How does this scene exemplify the naturalistic philosophy? [Possible response: In a naturalistic world, the man is doomed to failure—since only the strong survive and he has clearly shown his weakness.] In a romantic tale, the man would have survived to learn from the hardships he endures.

H ● **Elements of Literature**
Naturalism
❓ Why is this brief scene even more bitterly naturalistic? [Possible response: His environment has reduced the man to an animal, but still he cannot survive because he lacks the dog's instincts.]

I ● **Critical Thinking**
Determining Author's Purpose
❓ In the beginning of the story, the narrator implied that the man was unrelated to the earth. How has that hint become all too true? [Now, he has lost a basic physical connection to the land: he cannot feel it even when he touches it.]

J ● **Historical Connections**
Dogs in the Arctic
Although students are likely to be appalled by the man's plan to kill the dog to save his life, it was actually a common practice among Arctic explorers. During their 1891 and 1893–1894 expeditions to the North Pole, for example, starvation forced Robert Peary and Matthew Henson to kill and eat their sled dogs.

the ends of his arms, but when he tried to run the impression down, he could not find it.

Ⓐ A certain fear of death, dull and oppressive, came to him. This fear quickly became poignant as he realized that it was no longer a mere matter of freezing his fingers and toes, or of losing his hands and feet, but that it was a matter of life and death, with the chances against him. This threw him into a panic, and he turned and ran up the creek bed along the old, dim trail. The dog joined in behind and kept up with him. He ran blindly, without intention, in fear such as he had never known in his life. Slowly, as he plowed and floundered through the snow, he began to see things again—the banks of the creek, the old timber jams, the leafless aspens, and the sky. The running made him feel better. He did not shiver. Maybe, if he ran on, his feet would thaw out; and, anyway, if he ran far enough, he would reach the camp and the boys. Without doubt he would lose some fingers and toes and some of his face; but the boys would take care of him, and save the rest of him when he got there. And, at the same time, there was another thought in his mind that said he would never get to the camp and the boys; that it was too many miles away, that the freezing had too great a start on him, and that he would soon be stiff and dead. This thought he kept in the background and refused to consider. Sometimes it pushed itself forward and demanded to be heard, but he thrust it back and strove to think of other things.

It struck him as curious that he could run at all on feet so frozen that he could not feel them when they struck the earth and took the weight of his body. He seemed to himself to skim along above the surface, and to have no connection with the earth. Ⓑ Somewhere he had once seen a winged Mercury,⁹ and he wondered if Mercury felt as he felt when skimming over the earth.

His theory of running until he reached camp and the boys had one flaw in it: He lacked the endurance. Several times he stumbled, and finally he tottered, crumpled up, and fell. When he tried to rise, he failed. He must sit and rest, he decided, and next time he would merely walk and keep on going. As he sat and regained his breath, he noted

9. **Mercury:** messenger of the gods in Roman mythology. He wears winged sandals and a winged hat.

that he was feeling quite warm and comfortable. He was not shivering, and it even seemed that a warm glow had come to his chest and trunk. And yet, when he touched his nose or cheeks, there was no sensation. Running would not thaw them out. Nor would it thaw out his hands and feet. Then the thought came to him that the frozen portions of his body must be extending. He tried to keep this thought down, to forget it, to think of something else; he was aware of the panicky feeling that it caused, and he was afraid of the panic. But the thought asserted itself, and persisted, until it produced a vision of his body totally frozen. This was too much, and he made another wild run along the trail. Once he slowed down to a walk, but the thought of the freezing extending itself made him run again.

And all the time the dog ran with him, at his heels. When he fell down a second time, it curled its tail over its forefeet and sat in front of him, facing him, curiously eager and intent. The warmth and security of the animal angered him, and he cursed it till it flattened down its ears appeasingly. Ⓒ This time the shivering came more quickly upon the man. He was losing in this battle with the frost. It was creeping into his body from all sides. The thought of it drove him on, but he ran no more than a hundred feet when he staggered and pitched headlong. It was his last panic. When he had recovered his breath and control, he sat up and entertained in his mind the conception of meeting death with dignity. However, the conception did not come to him in such terms. Ⓓ His idea of it was that he had been making a fool of himself, running around like a chicken with its head cut off—such was the simile that occurred to him. Well, he was bound to freeze anyway, and he might as well take it decently. With this newfound peace of mind came the first glimmerings of drowsiness. A good idea, he thought, to sleep off Ⓔ to death. It was like taking an anesthetic. Freezing was not so bad as people thought. There were lots worse ways to die.

Ⓕ He pictured the boys finding his body next day. Suddenly he found himself with them, coming along the trail and looking for himself. And, still with them, he came around a turn in the trail and found himself lying in the snow. He did not belong with himself anymore, for even then he was out of himself, standing with the boys and looking

Making the Connections

Connecting to the Theme: "From Innocence to Experience"

This story fits the theme in that it is set in the world of experience—a world dominated by cruel natural laws, where the characters are trapped, where the individual is nothing, where happy endings are not possible. The opposite of this kind of fiction is the romance; students can turn to Irving's "Rip Van Winkle" as a contrast. American fiction during this period became ironic, and that continues to be the dominant mode for the rest of the century.

. . . he came around a turn in the trail and found himself lying in the snow. He did not belong with himself anymore, for even then he was out of himself, standing with the boys and looking at himself in the snow.

F Critical Thinking
Making Judgments
❓ What is happening to the man? [Possible answers: His detachment from his frozen body is so great that he is having an out-of-body experience; he is fantasizing; he is—for one last time— denying the reality of his situation.]

G Elements of Literature
Naturalism
❓ The man's admission that the old-timer was correct comes too late to save his life. What message do you think London is conveying in this story? [Possible responses: Nature is colossally indifferent to human beings; humans lack the ability to survive in a harsh environment; the harmony of Romanticism is "unnatural."]

H Struggling Readers
Questioning
❓ What questions could you ask to clarify this text? [Possible responses: From whose point of view are we seeing events? Why do we shift from the man to the dog?] Encourage students to engage in a dialogue with the text to discover answers to their questions.

at himself in the snow. It certainly was cold, was his thought. When he got back to the States, he could tell the folks what real cold was. He drifted on from this to a vision of the old-timer on Sulfur Creek. He could see him quite clearly, warm and comfortable, and smoking a pipe.

"You were right, old hoss; you were right," the man mumbled to the old-timer of Sulfur Creek.

Then the man drowsed off into what seemed to him the most comfortable and satisfying sleep he had ever known. The dog sat facing him and waiting. The brief day drew to a close in a long, slow twilight. There were no signs of a fire to be made, and, besides, never in the dog's experience had it known a man to sit like that in the snow and make no fire. As the twilight drew on, its eager yearning for the fire mastered it, and with a great lifting and shifting of forefeet, it whined softly, then flattened its ears down in anticipation of being chidden[10] by the man. But the man remained silent. Later, the dog whined loudly. And still later it crept close to the man and caught the scent of death. This made the animal bristle and back away. A little longer it delayed, howling under the stars that leaped and danced and shone brightly in the cold sky. Then it turned and trotted up the trail in the direction of the camp it knew, where were the other food providers and fire providers.

10. **chidden:** scolded; past participle of *chide*.

JACK LONDON 507

Assessing Learning

Check Test: True–False
1. The man's trouble is that he lacks imagination. [True]
2. The air temperature is more than fifty degrees below zero. [True]
3. The man builds a fire as soon as he stops for lunch. [False]
4. The dog warns the man when they come near the springs. [False]
5. At the end, the man is rescued by his friends from the camp. [False]

Standardized Test Preparation
For practice with ACT and SAT formats, see
• *Preparation for College Admission Exams*, p. 35
For practice with proofreading and editing, see
• *Daily Oral Grammar*, Transparency 33

Connections

This article explains how extreme cold can cause different degrees of injury.

Ⓐ Critical Thinking

Determining Author's Purpose

❓ What effect is the article intended to have on the reader? [Possible response: The article is intended to educate people about the dangers of hypothermia. The author adopts an objective, matter-of-fact tone to convey the seriousness of the issue: the extreme danger that hypothermia presents.]

Ⓑ Vocabulary Note

Technical Terms

Have the budding scientists in the class define the technical terms in this article: *hypothermia, subcutaneous, arterioles,* and *capillaries.*

Ⓒ Reading Skills and Strategies

Analyzing Cause and Effect

Have students create a flow chart that depicts the stages of hypothermia.

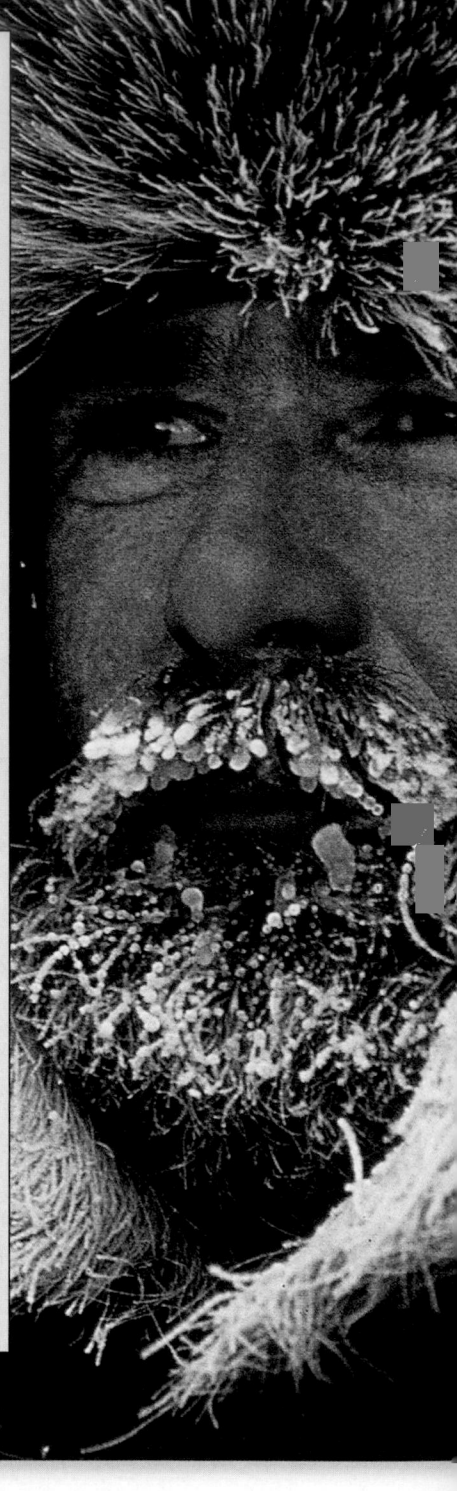

Connections — A MAGAZINE ARTICLE

Cold Kills: Hypothermia

Here's what happens when you develop frostbite. After sitting out in the cold for a few hours, you develop hypothermia. The blood vessels in your skin and extremities clamp down in order to minimize further heat loss. Standing on ice or cold ground draws the warmth out of your feet, and the skin and subcutaneous tissues of your toes freeze. Chilled arterioles beneath the frozen tissue constrict, and blood flow through the capillaries slows as the blood becomes thick and syrupy. Clots form and block the capillary bed, thus depriving the tissues of oxygen and nutrients. Blood running into the limb is then diverted away from the capillary beds by shunts that cyclically open and close, allowing waves of warm blood to surge into the hands and feet at intervals. When your core temperature drops further, these shunts remain open, and the tissues begin to freeze. The feet, hands, ears, and nose are most vulnerable to frostbite because they are more likely to be exposed to the cold, they are distant from the warm core, and their large surface-to-volume ratio causes them to cool rapidly.

Frostnip is the mildest form of cold injury. It causes stinging pain, then numbness and a small white patch on the cheeks, nose, or ears. Immediate rewarming is the treatment.

Frostnip that is ignored progresses to superficial frostbite involving the skin and the subcutaneous tissues. The skin remains bloodless, pale and cold to the touch, but the tissue beneath the surface remains soft and pliable. A day or so after the injury, large blisters develop. After a few more days, the blisters heal and a hard, dry eschar forms. This is a thick, black scar that separates from the underlying tissue in a few weeks and is replaced by new skin.

Deep frostbite is freezing of the superficial as well as deep structures, including nerve, muscle, tendon, and even bone. The affected part is hard as wood, purple or red in color, cool to the touch, and has no feeling. In contrast to superficial frostbite, in which the injured part is sensitive, warm, and pink after rewarming, the part remains cold and blue after thawing. Small blood blisters may form after one to three weeks, and the part may remain swollen for months. Eventually, it mummifies and falls off.

—Paul G. Gill, Jr., M.D., *from* "Winning the Cold War," *Outdoor Life,* February 1993

Connecting Across Texts

Connecting with "To Build a Fire"

After students have read the article by Dr. Gill, ask them to write a few ideas in their journals about the following topics:

• why campers, hikers, and travelers venture unprepared into brutally cold places such as the northern mountains in winter

• whether people in temperate climates take frostbite seriously enough

• what purpose frostbite serves in human anatomy

Discuss with students why the man in "To Build a Fire" underestimates the dangers of hypothermia. Then, ask students to create a profile of people like the man in "To Build a Fire" who refuse to take nature's dangers seriously. Students should list at least five characteristics of such people. Then, have them compare the average teenager to the profile. What dangers do teenagers ignore? How can teenagers be educated to take danger seriously?

First Thoughts

1. How did you feel about the way the story ended? Did you predict this kind of ending? Explain.

Shaping Interpretations

2. Several times in the story, the man recalls the old-timer from Sulfur Creek. What key advice did the old-timer give him? Why do you think the man did not follow his advice?

3. Early in the story, London writes, "The animal was depressed by the tremendous cold. It knew that it was no time for traveling" (page 498). This passage alerts you to possible trouble ahead. Locate four other passages that **foreshadow** later events. Explain the link between each passage and the later event.

4. London does not merely tell you that it is extremely cold. He gives details that make you *feel* the cold. For example, he notes the "sharp, explosive crackle" when the man spits into the frigid air. List five other details from the story that make the cold real to you.

5. In the story, a man who thinks is contrasted with a dog who reacts by instinct. How do the man and the dog differ in the ways they approach the intense cold? What point do you think London is making?

6. Reread the definition of **naturalism** that precedes this selection (page 496). How does this story reflect key naturalist beliefs? How do you feel about this philosophy's view of human beings?

> **Reading Check**
>
> Summarize the **plot** of the story by listing its string of major **causes** and **effects**. Start by identifying the man's mission. Then, review your reading notes and explain *why* the man builds two different fires, what happens to each fire, and what results from each of these events. Be sure to include what happens to the man and to the dog by the end of the story.

Connecting with the Text

7. The central character is not particularly likable. He's described as "without imagination," he ignores the advice of his elders, and he has no love for dogs. Would you have enjoyed the story more—or less—if the man were portrayed in a more sympathetic light? (For instance, suppose that he were a more humble and insightful man who loved animals.) Give specific reasons to support your opinion.

Challenging the Text

8. London wrote another, more commercially acceptable ending for an earlier version of "To Build a Fire." In the first version, the man survives, returns to camp, and learns an important lesson: Never travel alone. Do you think this ending improves the story or weakens it? Explain your opinion.

Then it turned and trotted up the trail in the direction of the camp it knew, where were the other food providers and fire providers.

JACK LONDON 509

> ## Reading Check
>
> Possible response: A man sets out toward an old claim with a dog, ignoring advice to travel with a partner when it gets colder than fifty below. He stops to eat lunch, then builds a fire to thaw out. He must build another fire after he falls into a spring and wets his legs and feet. A load of snow from a spruce tree falls on the second fire and puts it out. Try as he might, he is unable to build another fire because his hands are too frozen to move. As he realizes that he will freeze to death, the man decides to sleep rather than fight any more. After the man dies, the dog heads off toward camp.

First Thoughts [Respond]

1. While some students will find the ending disappointing, others will see it as inevitable, due to the author's purpose, the description of the main character, and the story's tone and setting.

Shaping Interpretations [Interpret]

2. The old-timer advised him not to travel alone in the extremely cold weather. The man did not follow the advice because he is arrogant, foolish, and sold on his own machismo.

3. Answers will vary, but several passages in paragraphs 2–5 on p. 498, for example, clearly foreshadow the fatal results.

4. Possible details: "the ice muzzle on his mouth" (p. 499), "the instant he stopped his cheekbones went numb" (p. 499), "The creek . . . was frozen clear to the bottom" (p. 499), "his moist breath quickly powdered with white his moustache, eyebrows, and lashes" (p. 501), "the moccasin strings were like rods of steel" (p. 503). Students should connect these details to the man's later accident, frostbite, and subsequent death.

5. The dog is sensitive to nature's signs of danger and follows his instinct. The man, in contrast, ignores the warnings and fails to apply logic or imagination. London shows that animal instinct is superior to human intellect in this situation.

6. This story shows that humans are subject to natural forces beyond their control. Nature is indifferent and only the strongest survive. Students are likely to feel that humans can still overcome nature through intelligence and ingenuity.

Connecting with the Text
[Evaluate]

7. Students are likely to say that they would feel more sympathy for a more likable protagonist but would not necessarily enjoy the story more.

Challenging the Text [Evaluate]

8. The earlier ending weakens the drama and danger in the story and does not convey as powerful a message because the man does not have to pay for his arrogance.

T509

CHOICES:
Building Your Portfolio

1. **Writer's Notebook** Guide students to consider diction, sentence length, and punctuation as they adjust their writing style.
2. **Analyzing Conflict** Be sure that students understand that conflict in literature is a struggle or fight. In an internal conflict, characters battle a force within themselves. In an external conflict, characters struggle against a force outside themselves.
3. **Creative Writing / Role-Playing** Encourage students to reread the story to help them keep the man in character and construct similar figures in keeping with London's style.
4. **Crossing the Curriculum: Science** Students can consult Boy Scout or Girl Scout manuals, their health-care provider, or The Sierra Club for information.
5. **Performance** Remind students to include a bibliography and give complete credit for any music they use.
6. **Creative Writing** Suggest that students construct a plot diagram to help them plan their story. The diagram should include the exposition, rising action, climax, and resolution.

CHOICES: Building Your Portfolio

Writer's Notebook
1. Collecting Ideas for a Research Paper

When you write a research paper, you will want to adjust your writing to suit your audience. For practice, think of a topic this story made you want to learn more about (for example, Jack London's life, the effects of cold on humans, the geography of the Yukon, or the naturalist literary movement). Imagine that you want to share the results of your research with three different audiences (for example, third-graders, a wilderness-exploration group, and a group of parents in your neighborhood). Make some notes about how you would tailor your coverage for each audience. Save your notes for possible use in the Writer's Workshop on page 515.

Analyzing Conflict
2. Opposing Forces

"To Build a Fire" contains both **internal** and **external conflict.** Identify what you consider the most important conflict of the story. In a brief essay, identify the opposing forces in this conflict. Use passages from the text to support your choice of this conflict as central to the story. Which force in the story wins?

Creative Writing / Role-Playing
3. Talk Before Leaving

Imagine that it's just before the story "To Build a Fire" begins. The man in the story is saying goodbye to his partners as he prepares to start out alone on the Yukon trail. Create a **dialogue** that occurs between the man and two of his partners. Then, with two classmates, role-play the dialogue for the class.

Crossing the Curriculum: Science
4. Survival Manual

You've been hired by a wilderness adventure company to create a "survival manual" for a group of people who will be traveling by foot in Yukon Territory during the winter, when the ground is covered by several feet of snow. Based on what you have learned from London's story, from reading about hypothermia in *Connections* (page 508), and from further research, work with a partner to make a list of the equipment and supplies these trekkers must assemble before they start out. After each item, write a sentence or two explaining its importance. To accompany the list of supplies, create a list of safety precautions. Illustrate your survival manual, if you wish.

Performance
5. Sound Matters

Consider how different sounds—or lack of all sound at some points—could enhance the drama if this story were recorded on audiocassette. With three or four other students, plan a recording of the story. First, break the story into small scenes. For each scene, list the **sound effects** you would use to heighten the tension. Be sure to include short, specific sounds, such as the matches that fall "sizzling into the snow." Also, select background music for various parts of the story. (Consider all kinds of music, from classical to rock to rap.) Finally, practice reading the story aloud, and record your reading together with sound effects and music. Play your recording for the class.

Creative Writing
6. Against All Odds

Write a survival story of your own, in which a character's life is threatened by a hostile environment: a weather condition, an isolated place, a terrain that poses difficulties. Like "To Build a Fire," your story should be built on realistic details that create suspense and a "you are there" feeling. For further inspiration, read *Into Thin Air* by Jon Krakauer, about the ill-fated Everest expeditions of 1996.

READ ON

Follow the Drinking Gourd

Henry Brown nailed himself into a box and had it shipped to Philadelphia. Harriet Tubman risked her own life many times to lead fugitives north and out of slavery. They are just two of the many daring "passengers" and "conductors" whose firsthand accounts describe the flight from slavery to freedom in *The Underground Railroad* (Prentice Hall), edited by Charles L. Blockson.

Where the Buffalo Roamed

What was the westward expansion like from the American Indian point of view? Dee Brown's *Bury My Heart at Wounded Knee* (Holt, Rinehart and Winston) is a powerful, well-documented American Indian history of the West. For an exploration of Native American culture, consider *Dee Brown's Folktales of the Native American: Retold for Our Times* (Henry Holt). In this book, Brown narrates thirty-six stories, which include examples of the rich mythology and spirituality that make up much of the Native American oral tradition.

The Great American Novel

Ernest Hemingway wrote, "All modern American literature comes from one book by Mark Twain called *Huckleberry Finn*." Widely regarded as Twain's masterpiece, *Adventures of Huckleberry Finn* is a wise and funny novel about a young boy coming of age on the Mississippi River. Several film adaptations are also available on video. This title is available in the HRW Library.

The War Between the States

Though Stephen Crane never fought in the Civil War, he carefully researched it for *The Red Badge of Courage,* his famous novel about a young Union soldier. On video are both *The Red Badge of Courage* and Crane's *Three Miraculous Soldiers,* based on his ironic story of a young girl's encounters with both Union and Confederate soldiers. For a nonfiction account of the war, consider *The Civil War: An Illustrated History* (Alfred A. Knopf), by Geoffrey C. Ward, et al., the companion volume to the popular PBS TV series, which is also available on video.

The Frozen North

If "To Build a Fire" piqued your interest in cold and desolate places, try *Arctic Dreams* (Scribner's), Barry Lopez's exciting account of a real-life journey through northern climes. For more outdoor adventure from Jack London, try *The Call of the Wild*—another "dog story" of undisputed literary merit, which is also available in a film adaptation. This title is available in the HRW Library.

READ ON

Portfolio Assessment Options
The following projects can help you evaluate and assess your students' reading accomplishments outside of class. Videotapes or audiotapes of completed projects may be included in students' portfolios.

- **Create a Folder Game**
  Have students work in groups of three to create a folder game that relates to the plot and the characters of the book they have read. (All three students need to have read the same book.) When other students in the class play the game, they should have a clear understanding of what the book is about. Group members must decide on directions for the game, invent rules, include game pieces, and design the game folder.

- **Design a Movie Poster**
  Have students design a poster to promote the movie of the book they have just read. The poster should include the main characters in the book as well as the title and author's name. Students could even cast famous actors and actresses in the parts if they choose. Tell students to be sure that the poster depicts a scene from the book and is persuasive enough to cause others to want to see the movie.

- **Write a Children's Book**
  Have students tell a story about the book they have read in the form of a children's book. Have them include pictures on each page, an attractive cover, and a new title appropriate for children. Remind students to use simple vocabulary and language that young children will understand.

(A) Background

Cooper actually lived in Europe from 1826–1833. His official position was American consul in France, but he traveled widely in Europe and, while abroad, wrote extensively about the contrasts he saw between European and American society.

(B) Critical Thinking

Extending the Theme

❓ Do you think that regional distinctions in speech could detract from the nation being unified? [Sample responses: Yes, because dialects are immediate reminders of the differences between people and can be used to identify insiders and outsiders to a particular region or subculture; no, because Americans have much more important things in common, such as their government and the popular culture spread by mass media.]

(C) Reading Skills and Strategies

Connecting with the Text

❓ If you had to describe the inhabitants of a region of America today, would dialect be part of your description, as it was in Twain's descriptions? [Possible responses: Yes, I would include dialect because it tells so much about the people—where they are from, their generation, what type of work they have been involved in; no, because dialects often prejudice different groups against one another, when, in fact, the things people have in common are much more important.]

Resources

Assessment
Formal Assessment
• The American Language Test, p. 100

The American Language

American Dialects

by Gary Q. Arpin

(A) James Fenimore Cooper, writing for a British audience in 1828, boasted about the absence of American dialects: "In America, while there are provincial or state peculiarities in tone, and even in the pronunciation and use of certain words, there is no patois [dialect]. An American may distinguish between the Georgian and the New England man, but you cannot." Americans, Cooper claimed, were too active and mobile for dialects to establish themselves—a point with which many other observers agreed.

Yet, a little over fifty years later, another American writer claimed to be using no less than seven dialects from a fairly small region in a single novel, *Adventures of Huckleberry Finn*. "In this book," Mark Twain wrote in an explanatory note, "a number of dialects are used, to wit: the Missouri Negro dialect; the extremest form of the backwoods South-Western dialect; the ordinary 'Pike-County' dialect; and four modified varieties of this last."

Unity or Variety?

Quite a bit had changed in America in that fifty years, but not enough to create a wholesale explosion of dialects where none had existed before. Even if Twain was exaggerating about his "four modified varieties" of the "'Pike-County' dialect," *Huckleberry Finn* depends for part of its effect on its use of dialect. Who was right about American dialects—Cooper or Twain?

Cooper was looking at an America that he was contrasting with England—a young, unified, mobile, democratic country, in which differences, if there were any, were kept within the family. Moreover, Cooper saw the country evolving toward even greater unity.

(B) Twain, on the other hand, was looking very closely at a particular region of America and at distinctions of ethnicity, education, upbringing, and geography, all of which had small but significant effects on speech. He was also looking at a country whose recent Civil War had underscored the disunity of its people.

The views of Cooper and Twain toward American dialects represent two ways of looking at America and American speech. The Cooper view saw America as a unified nation marked principally by its distinctness from England. Twain saw the nation in terms of regional distinctions.

The Cooper view was shared by people like Noah Webster. Webster's dream was to stamp out local dialects and further unify the country (see page 195). He stated his attitude in this comparison between American and British language: "We are less infected with various dialects, the remains of the different conquerors of the English nation, than the inhabitants of England." A dialect in Webster's view was a weakness, an infection to be cured by education and spelling reform.

(C) But Twain and other regional writers saw the local speech as one of the best ways of describing the inhabitants of a region. Dialect stories and poems, in fact, were very popular in the late nineteenth and early

"There wuz Maw and me, surrounded by screamin' Frenchmen, our Michelin-book lost and our faithful Cook's tour-guide nowhar in sight! . . ."

go.hrw.com
LE0 11-American Language

twentieth centuries. They were usually comic, and much of their humor derived from funny pronunciations and peculiar local words. At the same time, these stories and poems in regional dialect illustrated the wisdom of the common person.

A New Englander called Hosea Biglow was a famous "common-sense" character created by James Russell Lowell in his First Series of *The Biglow Papers,* a collection of dialect poems. In the following excerpt, Hosea's New England speech patterns are shown, as he addresses recruiting officers for the Mexican War—a conflict which Hosea, in his common sense, strongly disapproves of.

> Ez fer war, I call it murder—
>   There you hev it plain an' flat;
> I don't want to go no furder
>   Than my Testyment fer that;
> God hez sed so plump an' fairly,
>   It's ez long ez it is broad,
> An' you've gut to git up airly
>   Ef you want to take in God.

What Is a Dialect?

In his novel about the Great Depression of the 1930s, *The Grapes of Wrath,* John Steinbeck records a conversation between migrant workers from different parts of the country. Here, the Joads, from Oklahoma, meet Ivy Wilson, from Kansas:

> "We're Joads," said Pa. "We come from right near Sallisaw."
> "Well, we're proud to meet you folks," said Ivy Wilson. "Sairy, these is Joads."
> "I knowed you wasn't Oklahomy folks. You talk queer kinda—that ain't no blame, you understan'."
> "Ever'body says words different," said Ivy. "Arkansas folks says 'em different, and Oklahomy folks says 'em different. And we seen a lady from Massachusetts, an' she said 'em differentest of all. Couldn't hardly make out what she was sayin'."

What makes these Americans so different in speech is, of course, what linguists call dialect. A **dialect** can be defined as the characteristic language habits of a particular speech community. A speech community can be looked at in a very broad sense (as "American" versus "British"), or it can be subdivided almost endlessly. In fact, since no two people speak in exactly the same way, we might even say that each person speaks in his or her own dialect. (Linguists even have a term—*idiolect*—for the speech peculiar to one individual at one specific period of his or her life.) Though there are differences in the way the Joads, the Wilsons, and the puzzling lady from Massachusetts speak, they all are still clearly "American."

Dialects are distinguished from standard English and from each other in three principal ways:

1. In pronunciation: Pa Joad says "Oklahomy" and drops the final "d" in *understand.* ("Kinda" for *kind of* is a form of rapid speech, not dialect.)
2. In vocabulary: Pa Joad uses an expression typical of his region when he says they come from "right near" Sallisaw.
3. In grammar: Pa says "knowed" instead of *knew,* "you wasn't" instead of *you weren't,* and "that ain't no blame."

The grammar of a language is its most profound element—like the skeleton of an animal. Grammar is likely to be changed only superficially in a dialect. There can be an English dialect in which a person can say "Them was good peaches," but not one in which a person can say "Peaches good was them." When fundamental grammar rules are violated, the language becomes incoherent. Differences in vocabulary between dialects are more common, and most common are differences in pronunciation.

The main factors contributing to the formation of American dialects have been (1) settlement patterns—who settled in a region, where they came from, and how long they stayed there; (2) distance from a major cultural center; (3) influence of new immigrants; and (4) migration patterns.

English speakers settled first in the East, and the greatest profusion of dialects still exists

> Since no two people speak in exactly the same way, we might even say that each person speaks in his or her own dialect.

D Reading Skills and Strategies
Connecting with the Text
? What are some characteristics of the dialect in your community? [Responses should include specific words and pronunciations, expressions, phrases, grammar, or a particular accent that is common in the community.]

E Struggling Readers
Finding Details
? In what three ways are dialects different from standard English? [They can be different in grammar, vocabulary, and pronunciation.]

F Critical Thinking
Expressing an Opinion
? Do you think that immigrants want to retain their dialects? [Possible answers: No, because they come to America to start over and want to successfully assimilate into American society; yes, immigrants from a country often settle in the same area and try to maintain their distinctive ways of speaking for as long as possible in order to preserve a sense of ethnic and cultural identity.]

THE AMERICAN LANGUAGE 513

Reaching All Students

Struggling Readers
These students may find reading text in dialect difficult, even though they probably recognize different dialects when they hear them. Read aloud the examples of dialect from *The Biglow Papers* and *The Grapes of Wrath,* so students can hear the differences.

English Language Learners
These students bring a unique perspective to American dialects. Ask students who are learning English to describe differences they have noticed in the way various Americans speak. Do these differences make learning English more difficult for them?

Advanced Learners
Have students conduct a survey of dialects heard on television. Students could look at a TV program guide to analyze which programs use predominantly standard English and which feature speakers with regional or ethnic dialects. Ask students to categorize the shows and to draw conclusions about the kinds of programs in which dialect is found and the kinds in which a particular dialect may be unacceptable.

1. Answers will vary, according to the region in which students live and the way they speak.

2. **African American, New York City, 1980s**
Pronunciation: The narrator says "axin," "talkin" and "bout."
Vocabulary: The narrator uses an expression typical of her region when she says "run a hand over."
Grammar: The narrator says "you all" instead of "all of you" and "run a hand" and "stare" instead of "runs a hand" and "stares."

Kentucky, 1970s
Pronunciation: Edda says "law" instead of "Lord."
Vocabulary: Clausie says "while" for "awhile," "neither" for "either," and "little-bitty" for "itty-bitty."
Grammar: Clausie says "y'all" instead of "all of you" and "them Russians" instead of "the Russians."

there. As settlers moved westward, they mixed dialects in the new communities in the West, and their original dialects became less and less evident.

Three Major Dialect Regions

Scholars have divided eastern American speech into three basic types of English: Northern, Midland, and Southern. Western states, in general, have blended these dialects, since their English-speaking settlers originally came from all three areas.

As a rule, regional differences in vocabulary and pronunciation are the easiest to pinpoint. If you take a *pail of swill* out to feed the hogs, you're probably a Northern farmer. If you take out a *bucket of slops,* you're probably from the South. If you pronounce *greasy* to rhyme with *we see,* you're probably from the North. If you pronounce it to rhyme with *easy,* you're probably from the Midland or South. Speakers in the Midland usually sound the *r* in words like *barn* and *horse,* while older speakers in the Northern and Southern regions tend to eliminate it. Bostonians, as we know, "pahk the cah." Southerners say something like "pawk the caw." Bostonians sometimes add an *r* to the end of a word, as President John F. Kennedy did when he spoke of "Cuber" rather than "Cuba." Midlanders usually make no distinction between the pronunciations of *horse* and *hoarse* and *mourning* and *morning.* Older Northerners and Southerners usually distinguish

"hawss" from "hohse," and "mawnin'" from "mohnin'." Southerners pronounce the *u* sound in words like *duty* and *news* as "you": "dyuty" and "nyews." Most Northern and Midland speakers say "dooty" and "nooz."

In literature, the accurate portrayal of regional speech is an excellent way of creating both an individual character and a member of a class. The South, with its rich oral culture, is the region where dialect has been most effectively used in literature, in the works of such writers as William Faulkner (page 713), Flannery O'Connor (page 672), and Bobbie Ann Mason. All of these writers—and more—have made it clear that speech patterns are an essential aspect of both our character and our environment.

Try It Out

1. **Examining regional dialects.** The objects or activities named by the words in each group below are all the same, but people in different regions of the country give them different names. Which word do you use? Do all of your classmates agree?

   a. *couch, sofa,* or *divan?*
   b. *faucet, spigot,* or *tap?*
   c. *spider, skillet,* or *frying pan?*
   d. *stand in line* or *stand on line?*
   e. *soda* or *pop?*

   Draw up a list of five words that you think are used only in your region. Then, swap lists with two other stu-

dents. Do you all agree that the words are regional dialect?

2. **Identifying dialect.** For each of the following passages, list examples of dialect in (a) vocabulary, (b) pronunciation, and (c) grammar.

African American, New York City, 1980s

"I'm axin you all a simple question. You keep talkin bout what's proper for a woman my age. How old am I anyhow?" And Joe Lee slams his eyes shut and squinches up his face to figure. And Task run a hand over his ear and stare into his glass like the ice cubes goin calculate for him. And Elo just starin at the top of my head like she goin rip the wig off any minute now.

—Toni Cade Bambara,
from "My Man Bovanne"

Kentucky, 1970s

"Law, I wouldn't want to be cremated the way some of them are doing now," says Edda. "To save space."

"Me neither," says Clausie with a whoop. "Did y'all see one of them Russians on television while back? At his funeral there was this horse and buggy pulling the body, and instead of a casket there was this little-bitty vase propped up there. It was real odd looking."

—Bobbie Ann Mason,
from "The Rookers"

Assessing Learning

Check Test: True–False

1. Twain saw America in terms of regional distinctions. [True]
2. A dialect is the characteristic language habits of a particular speech community. [True]
3. An idiolect is the speech of one individual over the whole of his or her life. [False]
4. No two people speak in exactly the same way. [True]
5. There are four major dialect regions in the United States. [False]

Using Students' Strengths

Verbal Learners

These students may enjoy exploring volumes of the *Dictionary of American Regional English* (DARE), the official dictionary of the American Dialect Society. They may also report on how the information for the dictionary was collected by fieldworkers interviewing informants from different regions around the country.

The history of the written word is rich

Page 1

EXPOSITORY WRITING

RESEARCH PAPER

Informative writing is the kind of writing you'll do most often during your school career and, in most cases, during your working life. A vast amount of the writing you encounter every day—the textbook you hold in your hands, the liner notes for a music recording, or the articles in your print or electronic newspaper—serves to inform you of something. Your goal as the writer of a research paper—also known as an informative report—is to collect, organize, synthesize, and present facts in order to expand your readers' knowledge of a topic.

Prewriting

1. **Find a topic.** Whether the choice of a topic is up to you or whether you're required to focus on a narrow topic within a general subject area, begin by brainstorm-  ing a list of topics you are interested in. Write a brief list of potential subjects. If you kept any of your Writer's Notebook jottings from Collections 9 and 10, you may already have some potential subjects and notes on those subjects. Highlight a couple of the strongest possibilities, and decide which one most appeals to you and might be most interesting to readers. Any of these historical topics could in turn suggest contemporary topics that interest you: an aspect of current African American music, groups who stage reenactments of Civil War battles, or contemporary war-story writers, such as Tim O'Brien.

2. **Narrow your topic, and freewrite about it.** In most cases, the first topic you come up with will be too broad to effectively handle in a research paper. Your next step, then, will be to narrow the focus of the broad topic you're considering—to go from "the Civil War," for example, to the more specific topic "women's roles during the Civil War."

   Once you have narrowed your topic, freewrite on what you already know about it, and generate questions that you will want to find answers to.

3. **Be sure you have a topic that can be researched.** The questions you decide to explore should be ones for which answers exist in reliable research sources that you can obtain. For any topic you choose, you should be able to find five or six good sources that are readily available to you through a library, the Internet, or other research facilities.

go.hrw.com
LEO Research Paper

Technology HELP

See Writer's Workshop 2 CD-ROM. *Assignment: Informative Report.*

ASSIGNMENT
Write a research paper on a factual topic readers would be interested in learning more about.

AIM
To inform.

AUDIENCE
Your teacher; your classmates; other people interested in your topic.

Try It Out

With a partner or small group, review the introduction to "The Rise of Realism: The Civil War and Postwar Period" (pages 408–422). Then, brainstorm a list of possible subjects mentioned in the introduction that you think would make interesting topics to write about.

WRITER'S WORKSHOP 515

Resources: Print and Media

Introducing the Writer's Workshop

Bring to class examples of writing based on research. Examples may include extended newspaper or magazine articles, liner notes from a CD or cassette, papers from academic journals, and reports downloaded from the Internet. Have students working in pairs select a sample and examine it carefully, asking the following questions:

1. What is the writer's major thesis?
2. Are there at least five facts in the paper that are important to supporting this thesis? What are they?
3. Are sources given for these facts? Are the sources listed near each fact?

Have students write the thesis statements they have identified on the board. Then, have each pair present to the class the facts contained in their sample and the proof, if any, that was provided to substantiate the facts. Try to develop a list of sources organized by type on the board so that students can see the possibilities (previous publications, interviews, original research, surveys, historical records, etc.). Remind students that research is not just a skill, it is an attitude. Research requires a belief in the importance of the truth and a willingness to seek it out. You may wish to mention, for example, that most major newspapers require three independent sources to verify a news story before it can be published.

Teaching the Writer's Workshop

Prewriting
Many students will need to use a checklist to remind them of their incremental goals and progress. You may wish to create a Self-check Inventory, such as the one on p. T517, to help students remain organized and on schedule.

4. **Anticipate audience needs.** Before you start to write, it's important to think about the audience you'll be writing for. To anticipate your audience's needs, ask yourself the following questions:
   - What will my readers probably already know about the topic?
   - What will they need to know in order to understand the topic?
   - What will they be curious about? What will they be most interested in?

5. **Research your topic.** Though general reference books are often the first step in researching an informative paper, specialized reference books, such as biographical dictionaries and subject encyclopedias, are even more valuable once you begin digging into your topic. Check the card or on-line catalog of a library, the *Readers' Guide to Periodical Literature,* the indexes to major newspapers, and the library's vertical file. Also, look elsewhere for sources of information: Depending on your subject, you might contact government offices, museums, historical societies, newspapers, and experts.

   Throughout your research, you should be aware of striking a balance between primary and secondary sources. A **primary source** is original, firsthand information, such as a letter, a journal entry, a memorandum, an autobiography, or a historical document. A **secondary source** is information about, or derived from, primary sources: critical writings, reviews, encyclopedia entries, biographies, and so on. If primary sources are available, make use of them; secondary sources are usually plentiful, but try not to use them exclusively. Be sure to evaluate all sources carefully for accuracy and balance. Take notes from both primary and secondary sources on index cards, or use some other method that you find helpful.

6. **Examine your approach.** The nature of your subject, your sources, and your attitudes go into shaping your approach, or angle. Some research papers are concerned with presenting the newest findings about a subject. Others explore the development of the subject over time or its importance in a larger context. A research paper may show the causes and effects of a phenomenon or compare and contrast it to a related phenomenon.

7. **State a controlling idea.** Reread your notes, and summarize the **controlling idea,** or **thesis,** of your research paper in a brief statement. In informative writing, the controlling idea is an objective statement of the main concern of the paper; it defines the boundaries of the subject. Here are some examples of controlling ideas:
   - Harriet Beecher Stowe, though initially not an abolitionist herself, furthered the abolitionist cause and helped pave the way to the Civil War with her book *Uncle Tom's Cabin.*
   - The gambler with a heart of gold, the gentle farmer driven to a gunfight to defend his family, the tough-but-tender dance-hall girl—all of these familiar, stereotypical western characters owe their existence to one writer: Bret Harte.

8. **Organize.** Present your information in a logical sequence. You can create a framework for organizing a research paper using one of the following methods:
   - chronological order (usually, from earliest to latest)

Crossing the Curriculum

Library Science
Students may be unfamiliar with some of the research resources available in the school. Arrange with the school librarian to take your class on a research tour. Point out the encyclopedias, atlases, *Readers' Guide to Periodical Literature,* card catalog, vertical file, Internet access, and any other available resources. If your school is close to a major university or town library, you may wish to tell students how to avail themselves of these added resources.

- order of importance (from most to least important, or least to most important)
- block comparison and contrast (Examine a series of aspects of one subject, then the same aspects, in the same order, for a second subject.)
- point-by-point comparison and contrast (Examine one aspect for the first subject, then the same aspect for the second subject, and so on.)

9. **Outline.** List as main headings the major aspects of your topic in an order that reflects your approach to the subject. Your preliminary outline may change during the course of drafting and revising. For now, you might make separate piles of index cards—or computer documents—to represent your major headings. Within each pile or document, cluster information into subheadings. Look for holes in your outline—headings that haven't been fully explored, relevant questions that haven't been answered. Do additional research to fill in the holes.

Drafting

1. **Begin forcefully.** The introductory paragraph of a research paper has two purposes: to define the subject and to get the reader interested. Try to accomplish both purposes in one stroke by defining your subject in a memorable, engaging way. You might begin with a surprising fact or statistic that has a bearing on your thesis; a quotation from an expert on your subject; or a question that balances different views of the subject. Describing a scene or narrating an anecdote can also be effective ways to open your research paper.

2. **Develop your points.** Follow your outline, checking off each item as you cover it to make sure you don't omit any essential information. As you develop your draft, though, you can rework your outline to match your increased understanding of what is important about the subject, what can be left out, and where each subtopic naturally falls into place.

3. **Define terms.** Define the terms your intended audience probably hasn't encountered before. If you were writing an article on Civil War weaponry for a general audience, you would probably need to define *Gatling gun* and *Arkansas toothpick*. In an article for Civil War buffs, though, you could give specialized information about those weapons without first having to explain what they are.

4. **Support your points.** Back up generalizations with specific examples and, if space permits, anecdotes. Flesh out the subject with details. Try to use concrete words rather than abstract ones to ease the reader's understanding of new concepts. Use facts and figures to demonstrate the validity of your statements, and provide necessary background information.

5. **Use quotations as seasoning.** The exact words of expert sources can add interest and authority to a research paper, but you should avoid overusing direct quotations. In general, use quotations when they are memorable or when the wording of the statement makes a difference. Otherwise, summarize or paraphrase—but be sure to use your own wording and sentence structure, and to credit your source.

Outline Form

Title: _____

Thesis Statement: _____

I. Main point
  A. Supporting point
    1. Detail 1
    2. Detail 2
    3. Detail 3
  B. Supporting point
    1. Detail 1
    2. Detail 2
    3. Detail 3
II. Main point
  A. Supporting point
    1. Detail 1
    2. Detail 2
    3. Detail 3
(etc.)

Language Handbook HELP

See Quotation Marks, page 1246.

Self-check Inventory:

| Topic: |
| Areas to focus on: |
| 1. |
| 2. |
| 3. |

Rough thesis statement:
(Due date: _____)

Research
(Total number of sources needed: _____)
___ Encyclopedias
___ Almanacs and yearbooks
___ Atlas
___ Biographical references
___ Vertical file
___ Indexes
___ Card catalog
___ *Readers' Guide to Periodical Literature*
___ Internet
___ Other:
(Record all source information and any facts and ideas relevant to your report.)

Organize Your Material:
___ Take notes (total number of note cards required: _____)
___ Brainstorm
___ Use a diagram or chart
___ Make an outline
(due date: _____)
___ Other: _____

Drafting

Before they begin drafting their papers, have students read through the material on pp. 517–518. In particular, you may wish to review the boxed feature on Documenting Sources (p. 518). Be sure to refer students to the Communications Handbook in the back of their textbook, which contains additional information on citing and documenting sources.

Reaching All Students

Struggling Writers

Students who have not written a research paper before may feel overwhelmed. Ask more advanced students to help by acting as personal mentors. Have mentors set up a plan whereby they can check the progress of the writers and make suggestions. When the work is broken down into smaller parts, students may feel more confident about accomplishing the assignment. Have mentors use the Self-check Inventory and mark off each step in the writing process. Mentors will also benefit by focusing on the importance of each step of the process.

Evaluating and Revising

Have students use the Revision Strategies and Evaluation Criteria provided here as a guide for reviewing their drafts and determining needed revisions.

Proofreading

Have students proofread their own papers first and then exchange them with another student. For this assignment, remind students to be particularly careful about correct punctuation of direct and indirect quotes and the correct form for citing and documenting sources. If time permits, the final copy should be put aside for at least a day before it is proofread for the final time by the author. Remind students that proofreading is an opportunity to polish their work by correcting any errors in spelling, capitalization, punctuation, and usage.

Publishing

The primary form of publication will be handing in the report and sharing it with classmates. In addition, students may look for special-interest magazines, local publications, or Internet sites that accept contributions. *Be certain that students have the permission of their parents or guardians before publishing their papers, particularly on the Internet.*

Reflecting

Have students write a brief reflection on this writing experience, considering questions such as the following:

1. How effectively did I utilize research sources?
2. How could I have better tailored my report to my specific audience?
3. Do I find research reports easier or harder than more personal types of writing? Why or why not?
4. How might I be able to use these research and writing skills in the future?

Have students date their reflections and file them in their portfolios.

Resources ———

Peer Editing Forms and Rubrics
• *Portfolio Management System,* p. 151.
Revision Transparencies
• *Workshop Resources,* p. 21

Communications Handbook HELP

Taking Notes and Documenting Sources; Proofreading.

Revision STRATEGIES

Clear transitions smoothly guide your reader from subtopic to subtopic, from idea to idea. If you are dealing with the development of a subject over time, transitions such as first, then, next, last, *and* finally *will be important. For discussions of cause and effect, transitions such as* therefore, thus, so, *and because* come into play. *So do transitions that show exceptions or contrasts, such as* but, however, although, yet, rather, instead, *and* nevertheless.

▮ Evaluation Criteria

A good research paper
1. sets forth its subject clearly
2. has an identifiable controlling idea, or thesis
3. supports its points adequately, using a variety of strategies
4. is organized in a way that supports the writer's purpose and is suitable to the subject
5. presents facts objectively
6. uses formal language
7. includes a Works Cited list at the end of the paper

Documenting Sources: Parenthetical Citations and Works Cited

One crucial aspect of writing a research paper is deciding which information you must document. Use these guidelines to help determine whether you need to document a piece of information.

• In general, don't document basic information that appears in several reference works.
• Document unusual, little known facts, or facts and statistics your readers might question.
• Document the source of each direct quotation and paraphrase.
• Document theories or opinions that are not your own.
• Document any data from surveys, experiments, or research studies.

When you do document, you'll credit sources in two places—in parenthetical citations and in the Works Cited list at the end of your paper.

Parenthetical citations occur within the body of your essay. They are references that appear in parentheses after quoted or paraphrased material from a particular source. In many cases, all that you'll need in a parenthetical citation is the author's last name and a page number. For example, here's what a parenthetical citation might look like in a report on slave narratives:

> According to one critic, Equiano's story became "the prototype for the nineteenth-century slave narrative" (Gates xiv).

Your parenthetical citation tells the reader that you have picked up your quotation from a critical work by Gates that they will find documented in full in your Works Cited list at the end of your paper. (Note that the citation is placed before the final punctuation mark of the sentence, phrase, or clause you're documenting.)

Here's how your Works Cited entry for the same source will look:

> Gates, Henry Louis, Jr., ed. <u>The Classic Slave Narratives</u>. New York: New American Library, 1987.

The list of Works Cited contains all the works cited in your paper, with full bibliographic information that will enable readers to locate the sources you used. For more complete information on documenting sources in a research paper, be sure to consult the latest edition of the *MLA Handbook for Writers of Research Papers.*

---

6. Establish an authoritative stance. Your tone and point of view should consistently make your audience feel that you know what you are writing about. Depending on your intended audience, your paper may be either formal or somewhat informal in its level of language. Most research papers written as class assignments are relatively formal; they are serious and objective in tone and use the third-person point of view.

7. Wrap it up neatly. The ending of a research paper usually repeats the main point, or points, in a different way. It might also put the subject in a larger context or suggest topics for further exploration.

Grading Timesaver

Rubrics for this Writer's Workshop assignment appear on p. 152 of the *Portfolio Management System.*

Crossing the Curriculum

Depending on their topics, students may wish to talk to their social studies, science, physical education, foreign language, or math teacher about submitting their research paper for extra credit in another class.

Language Workshop

APPROPRIATE ADDITIONS: ADVERB AND ADJECTIVE CLAUSES

You can give your writing flavor, variety, and a smooth flow by using adjective and adverb clauses in your sentences. An **adjective clause** is a clause that modifies a noun or pronoun. Adjective clauses begin with the pronouns *who, whom, whose, which,* or *that.* An **adverb clause** is a clause that modifies a verb, an adjective, or another adverb. Adverb clauses begin with subordinating conjunctions such as *after, although, because, before, if, since, unless, until, when,* and *while.*

Use adverb and adjective clauses to combine two simple sentences into a single complex sentence.

EXAMPLE   Sojourner Truth wrote passionately for the abolition of slavery. Her first name means "visitor."

Joined by adjective clause:

Sojourner Truth, **whose first name means "visitor,"** wrote passionately for the abolition of slavery.

(**Note:** If an adjective clause is not essential to the meaning of a sentence, it is a **nonrestrictive clause** and needs to be set off from the rest of the sentence with a comma or commas, as in the example above. If the clause is essential to the meaning of the sentence, it is a **restrictive clause,** and no commas are necessary.)

EXAMPLE   Frederick Douglass fought with a slave-holder. Douglass was still enslaved then.

Joined by adverb clause:

While Frederick Douglass was still enslaved, he fought with a slaveholder.

(**Note:** When you place an adverb clause at the beginning of a sentence, separate it from the independent clause with a comma, as in the example above.)

Writer's Workshop Follow-Up: Revising

Look again at the research paper you wrote for the Writer's Workshop on page 515. Where can you improve your style by using adverb and adjective clauses to combine two simple sentences into a single complex sentence?

Technology HELP

See Language Workshop CD-ROM. *Key word entry: adverb clauses or adjective clauses.*

Language Handbook HELP

The subordinate clause: pages 1231–1232.

Try It Out
Combine each pair of sentences by using either an adjective clause or an adverb clause. State which kind of clause you have used.
1. Mark Twain's humor became caustic. It happened in his old age.
2. The hero of "To Build a Fire" is lost and alone in the snow. He fears dying from hypothermia.
3. Kate Chopin's fiction has been rediscovered in recent years. Her fiction shows women struggling against obstacles to their freedom.
4. Code songs often contained directions for enslaved people escaping to freedom. These songs were often sung in the presence of slaveholders.
5. Ambrose Bierce was nicknamed "Bitter Bierce." He was disillusioned by the greed and deceit of humanity.

LANGUAGE WORKSHOP 519

Resources
Workshop Resources
• Worksheet, p. 55
Language Workshop CD-ROM
• Adverb and Adjective Clauses

Try It Out
Possible Answers
1. When he was in his old age, Mark Twain's humor became caustic. (adverb clause)
2. Because he is lost and alone in the snow, the hero of "To Build a Fire" fears dying from hypothermia. (adverb clause)
3. Kate Chopin's fiction, which shows women struggling against obstacles to their freedom, has been rediscovered in recent years. (adjective clause)
4. Although code songs often contained directions for enslaved people escaping to freedom, they were often sung in the presence of slaveholders. (adverb clause)
5. Ambrose Bierce, who was disillusioned by the greed and deceit of humanity, was nicknamed "Bitter Bierce." (adjective clause)

Assessing Learning

Quick Check:
Adverb and Adjective Clauses
In each sentence, underline the clause. Then, identify it as an adjective clause or an adverb clause.
1. Because he had researched the Civil War, Crane was able to write *The Red Badge of Courage.* [adverb clause]
2. Everyone listened while our teacher read *Moby-Dick* by Herman Melville. [adverb clause]
3. Some of us have read *Leaves of Grass,* which was written by Walt Whitman. [adjective clause]
4. I have read nearly every book that Kate Chopin ever wrote. [adjective clause]
5. The writer was an American whom everyone admired. [adjective clause]

OBJECTIVES

1. Read a college guide
2. Establish a purpose for reading a college guide
3. Compare and contrast the information contained in college guides
4. Adjust purpose and criteria while reading

Using the Strategies

Be sure students examine the graphic before answering the questions.

Possible Answers

1. The Southwest college is more likely to have a strong biology department because it is a popular major. The Pacific Northwest college is rated 88 in academics, and the Southwest college is rated 75.
2. You are more apt to interact with professors at the Pacific Northwest college because the student-teacher ratio is 20:1 versus 21:1. Pacific Northwest
3. The Southwest college has a higher percentage of international students: 3% versus 1%. The Pacific Northwest school has more out-of-state students.
4. The Pacific Northwest school is located in a city.
5. The Pacific Northwest school seems best suited to your needs.

Situation

As you make crucial choices about your own life, good reading skills will prove to be important. For instance, if you plan to attend college after high school, you will probably want to examine a college guide in order to compare the academic programs, financial-aid options, location, student body, and social life of various colleges and universities.

Strategies

Establish your purpose.

Before you open the guide, establish your purpose: For example, you may decide that you need to select four public colleges to apply to for admission next fall. You lean toward staying in the Southwest but will also consider schools in the Pacific Northwest. These decisions have narrowed your college search considerably.

Establish your criteria.

What are your priorities when choosing a college? Are you looking for a strong academic program or a specialized research center? Are there other features of a college—such as a competitive sports team, a diverse student body, or a generous financial-aid program—that are especially important to you?

Compare and contrast.

As you read the information about each college or university,

	College in Southwest		College in Pacific Northwest	
Type of School	public		Type of School	public
Environment	suburban		Environment	city
Student Body			**Student Body**	
Total undergrad enrollment	14,000		Total undergrad enrollment	6,200
% male/female	48/52		% male/female	43/57
% from out of state	11		% from out of state	29
% transfers	32		% transfers	47
% live on campus	35		% live on campus	52
% international	3		% international	1
# of countries represented	100		% of countries represented	19
Academics			**Academics**	
Overall Rating	75		**Overall Rating**	88
Calendar	quarter		Calendar	quarter
Student/teacher ratio	21:1		Student/teacher ratio	20:1
Profs Interesting rating	66		Profs Interesting rating	89
% UG courses taught by profs	64		% UG courses taught by profs	100
Hours of study per day	2.90		Hours of study per day	3.32
Most Popular Majors			**Most Popular Majors**	
Biology			Education	
Psychology			Environmental studies	

check to see how well it meets each of your priorities. Then, compare it to the other schools in your narrowed search field.

Adjust your purpose and priorities.

Don't be afraid to alter your purpose and your priorities as you analyze data on colleges.

Using the Strategies

Suppose you are committed to finding an academically strong public school in the Southwest or in the Pacific Northwest. You intend to major in biology, and you hope to work closely with your professors during your first years of college. You'd also like, if possible, to go to a school located in a city, with a diverse student body. Review the information on this page. Then, answer the following questions:

1. Is one school more likely to have a stronger biology department? How are the schools rated for academics in general?
2. At which school are you likely to interact more with professors? At which school do students seem more enthusiastic about their professors?
3. Which school has a larger percentage of international students? Which school has more out-of-state students?
4. Which school is in a city?
5. Which school seems to best suit your needs?

Extending the Strategies

After looking through a college guide, make a list of additional pieces of information that you would like to find out about each college. Look for that information in other guide books, in college publications, in viewbooks, and on the Internet, where many colleges and universities offer details about themselves.

Crossing the Curriculum

Mathematics

Have students create a chart or graph showing their criteria and which colleges meet them. Display the charts in areas that other college-bound students have access to.

Reaching All Students

Struggling Learners

Many students may be uncertain whether or not they will be able to attend college. The information in this Reading for Life may be easily adapted to practice reading publications from technical or business schools, or career guides from the local employment office.

Learning for Life

Monitoring the Media

OBJECTIVES
1. Compare and contrast television and print-media coverage of an event
2. Evaluate the power of the media to shape the public's perceptions

Problem

For centuries, painters and sketch artists had recorded wars visually, but the new eye of the camera lens made the Civil War and its aftermath more immediate and horribly real to people than earlier conflicts had been. How do the different news media today (television, newspapers, magazines, the Internet) affect the messages we receive and the assumptions we make about events of consequence taking place in our world?

Project

Compare and contrast television and print media coverage of an important current event in order to evaluate the power of different media to shape perceptions.

Preparation

1. As a group, choose a current event to monitor: a war or other political situation; a disaster; or an ongoing social problem, such as gang violence or drug abuse. The event should be one that has been in the news for a while and that will probably have a high profile for a time.

2. Divide the group into halves, one to monitor television coverage of the event and one to monitor print coverage (newspapers, magazines).

Procedure

1. Monitor your medium for coverage of the current event. Examine such aspects as
   - how frequently the event or situation is reported
   - how prominently the event is featured in the coverage
   - the types of coverage that are most common (reports, interviews, news analyses, newsmagazine segments, Internet features, lengthy articles, editorials, polls, and so on)

2. You may want to address these questions:
   - Does the coverage seem to take sides, or is it neutral?
   - How does the medium use visual images?
   - How does *seeing* something on the news differ from *reading* about it?

3. Make notes about how your perceptions of the current event are shaped by the medium's coverage. What are the particular strengths and weaknesses of the medium you have monitored? Are there differences in coverage among TV networks or newspapers and magazines?

Presentation

Present your findings about media coverage in one of the following formats (or another that your teacher approves):

1. **Panel Discussion**
   As a group, conduct a panel discussion on differences in media coverage. Address issues you have focused on during your monitoring. Also, evaluate each medium's strengths and shortcomings, and recommend how coverage could be improved.

2. **The Medium and the Message**
   Create a *Consumer Reports*–style bulletin rating the media you monitored. Summarize characteristics that set each particular news medium apart from others—strengths and weaknesses in reporting, tendencies toward bias, the influence of personalities on news coverage, and so on.

3. **Interview with a Newscaster or Journalist**
   Arrange an in-class interview with a local television news reporter, a writer or editor for a local newspaper or magazine, or a freelance journalist. Prepare beforehand a list of questions on media coverage. Ask the interviewee to share his or her perceptions of news coverage.

Processing

What did you learn about the power of media to shape perceptions? How can you watch for possible media bias? Write a reflection for your portfolio.

Grading Timesaver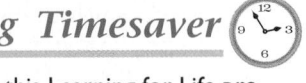

Rubrics for this Learning for Life project appear on p. 152 of the *Portfolio Management System*.

Developing Workplace Competencies

Preparation	Procedure	Presentation
• Acquires data • Organizes and maintains files for data • Applies technology to specific tasks • Exhibits sociability	• Evaluates data • Interprets information • Processes information • Makes decisions • Uses self-management skills • Reasons • Thinks creatively	• Demonstrates individual responsibility • Works on teams • Uses resources well • Teaches others • Communicates ideas and information

1. Read literature of the Modern period on the themes "Loss and Redemption"; "The Dream and the Reality"; "No Time for Heroes"; "Shadows of the Past"; "I, Too, Sing America"; and "Make It New!"
2. Interpret literary elements used in the literature, with special emphasis on blank verse, the four modes of fiction, and the objective correlative
3. Apply a variety of reading strategies to modern literature, with special emphasis on distinguishing the different connotations of synonyms
4. Respond to the literature in a variety of modes
5. Learn and use new words
6. Learn about the American language and American slang
7. Plan, draft, revise, edit, proof, and publish an analysis of causes and effects and an interpretive essay
8. Write sentences and paragraphs using subordinating conjunctions and the literary present tense
9. Demonstrate the ability to design a graphic organizer
10. Predict the effect of one modern social, cultural, or technological development on life

Responding to the Quotation

? How does the Willa Cather quotation frame the dilemma of the modern age? [Possible answer: Modern technology makes life easier and more efficient, but many people have allowed it to render worthwhile aspects of life, such as working with one's hands or simply taking time to reflect, obsolete.]

Resources ━━━━━

Assessment
- *Formal Assessment,* p. 109
- *Preparation for College Admission Exams,* p. 37

Selection Readability

This Annotated Teacher's Edition provides a summary of each selection in the student book. Following each Summary heading, you will find one, two, or three small icons. These icons indicate, in an approximate sense, the reading level of the selection.

- ■ One icon indicates that the selection is easy.
- ■ ■ Two icons indicate that the selection is on an intermediate reading level.
- ■ ■ ■ Three icons indicate that the selection is challenging.

The Moderns
1900–1950

Men travel faster now, but I do not know if they go to better things.

—Willa Cather, Death Comes for the Archbishop

Sixth Avenue Elevated at Third Street (1928) by John Sloan. Oil on canvas (30″ × 40″).
Collection of Whitney Museum of American Art, Purchase, 36.154. Photograph © 1998, Whitney Museum of American Art.

go.hrw.com
LEO 11-Moderns

523

Resources

Using Students' Strengths

Visual Learners
Have students examine works by The Eight: Arthur B. Davies, William Glackens, Robert Henri, Ernest Lawson, George Luks, Maurice Prendergast, Everett Shinn, and John Sloan. Then tell students to compare their work with that of nineteenth-century academic painters. In what way is the Ashcan School modern? As students read, have them think about what modern painters and writers have in common in terms of style, mood, and subject matter.

Kinesthetic Learners
Have students make a large map which includes the various locations associated with the authors mentioned in the text. After they read each section of the introduction, ask students to write a paragraph about each author on an index card. The students can attach their index cards to the appropriate places on the map. Display the map while studying Collections 11–16, and invite students to add to it as they learn about new authors.

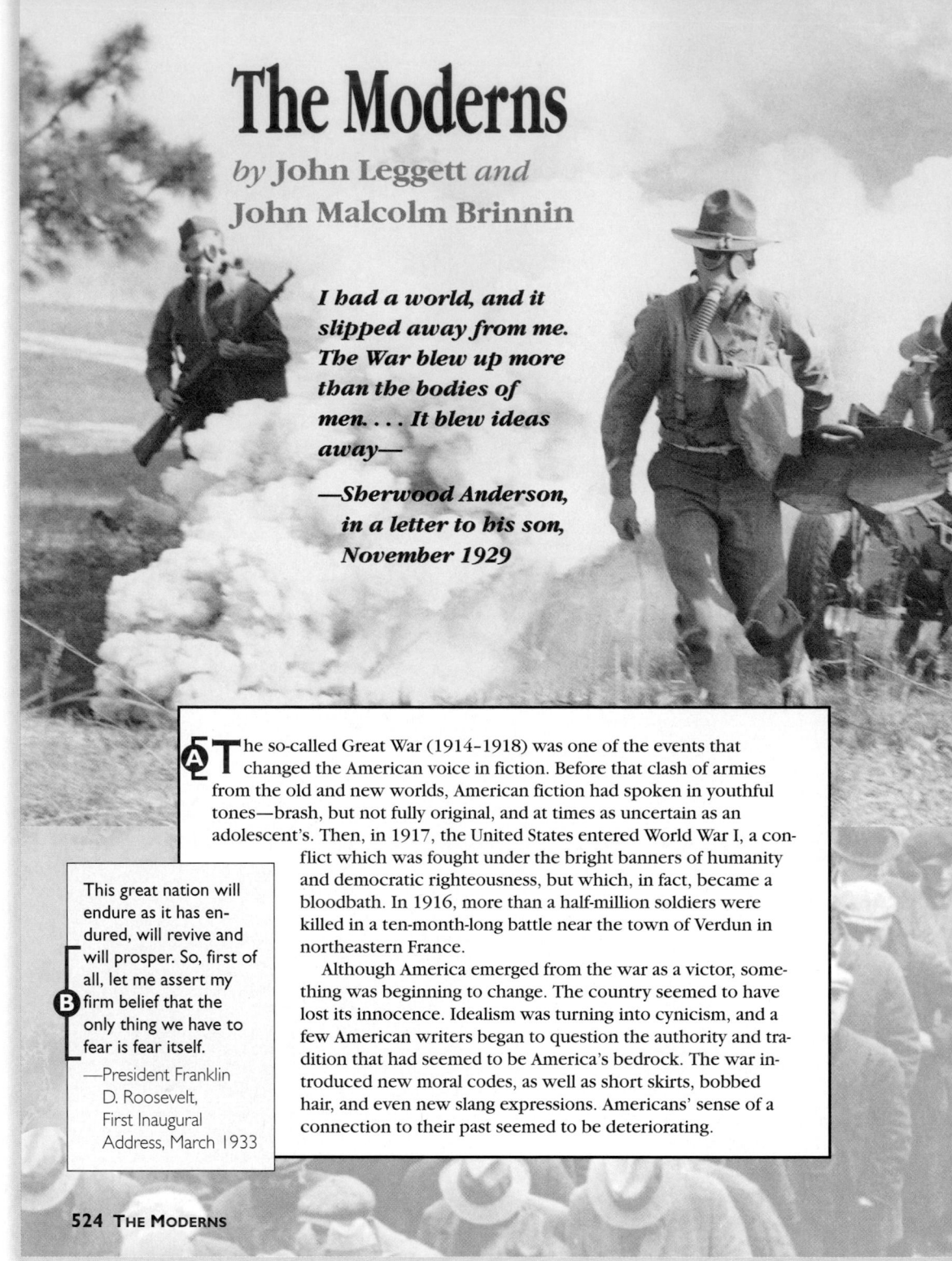

A Literary Connections

Although World War I marked the beginning of a new era in American literature, very little American literature of note deals directly with the war; most writers were noncombatants. In contrast, an entire generation of British writers gained immortality by turning their combat experiences into prose and poetry. Siegfried Sassoon, Robert Graves, Rupert Brooke, and most notably Wilfred Owen came of age in the trenches, and the horror of combat lives on in the pages of their work. Owen caught their feelings best with the foreword to his collected poems: "My subject is War, and the pity of War. The Poetry is in the pity." Probably the finest and most harrowing of all World War I novels was written by a German soldier. Erich Maria Remarque's *Im Westen nichts Neues* (*All Quiet on the Western Front,* 1929) went through nineteen printings in its first eight months of publication in the United States, despite the fact that the author had been an enemy soldier.

B Exploring the Historical Period

"I have never known a man who gave one a greater sense of security," wrote Eleanor Roosevelt of her husband. "I never heard him say there was a problem that he thought was impossible for human beings to solve. . . . I never knew him to face life or any problem that came up with fear, and . . . that courageous attitude was communicated to the people. . . . He believed in the courage and ability of men, and they responded."

The Moderns

by John Leggett *and* John Malcolm Brinnin

I had a world, and it slipped away from me. The War blew up more than the bodies of men. . . . It blew ideas away—

—Sherwood Anderson, in a letter to his son, November 1929

B This great nation will endure as it has endured, will revive and will prosper. So, first of all, let me assert my firm belief that the only thing we have to fear is fear itself.

—President Franklin D. Roosevelt, First Inaugural Address, March 1933

A The so-called Great War (1914–1918) was one of the events that changed the American voice in fiction. Before that clash of armies from the old and new worlds, American fiction had spoken in youthful tones—brash, but not fully original, and at times as uncertain as an adolescent's. Then, in 1917, the United States entered World War I, a conflict which was fought under the bright banners of humanity and democratic righteousness, but which, in fact, became a bloodbath. In 1916, more than a half-million soldiers were killed in a ten-month-long battle near the town of Verdun in northeastern France.

Although America emerged from the war as a victor, something was beginning to change. The country seemed to have lost its innocence. Idealism was turning into cynicism, and a few American writers began to question the authority and tradition that had seemed to be America's bedrock. The war introduced new moral codes, as well as short skirts, bobbed hair, and even new slang expressions. Americans' sense of a connection to their past seemed to be deteriorating.

Professional Notes

The Historian's View

Paul Fussell wrote in 1976 that World War I began "in what was, compared with ours, a static world, where the values appeared stable and where the meanings of abstractions seemed permanent and reliable. Everyone knew what Glory was, and what Honor meant. It was not until eleven years after the war that Hemingway could declare in *A Farewell to Arms* that 'abstract words such as glory, honor, courage, or hallow were obscene beside the concrete names of villages, the names and number of roads, the number of regiments and the dates.' In the summer of 1914 no one would have understood what on earth he was talking about."

The Soldier's View

Remarque's preface to *All Quiet on the Western Front* reads: "This book is to be neither an accusation nor a confession, and least of all an adventure, for death is not an adventure to those who stand face to face with it. It will try simply to tell of a generation of men who, even though they may have escaped its shells, were destroyed by the war."

There were other reasons for this change in outlook. The Great Depression that followed the crash of the New York stock market in 1929 brought suffering to millions of Americans—to those same hard-working people who had put their faith in the boundless capacity of America to provide them with jobs and their children with brighter futures.

American writers, like their European counterparts, were also being profoundly affected by the **modernist** movement. This movement in literature, painting, music, and the other arts—swept along by disillusionment with traditions that seemed to have become spiritually empty—called for bold experimentation and a wholesale rejection of traditional themes and styles.

World War I was a turning point in American life, marking a loss of innocence and a strong disillusionment with tradition.

The American Dream: Pursuit of a Promise

If we try to identify our uniquely American beliefs, we find three central ideas that we have come to call the **American dream.**

First, there is admiration for America as a new Eden: a land of beauty, bounty, and unlimited promise. Both the promise and the disappointment of this idea are reflected in one of the greatest American novels, *The Great Gatsby* (1925), by F. Scott Fitzgerald (page 584). This work appeared at a time when great wealth and the pursuit of pleasure had become ends in themselves for many people. The title character, Gatsby, is a self-made man whose wealth has mysterious and clearly illegal origins. Moving into a pretentious mansion near New York City, Gatsby tries to woo both society and the woman he loves with a series of lavish parties. His extravagant gestures are in pursuit of a dream. Unfortunately, Gatsby's capacity for dreaming is far greater than any opportunity offered by the Roaring Twenties, and he meets a grotesquely violent end. But Gatsby's greatness is bound up with his tragedy: He believes in an America that has virtually disappeared under the degradations of modern life.

It is left to Nick Carraway, the narrator, to reflect at the end of the novel on the original promise of the American dream:

> . . . gradually I became aware of the old island here that flowered once for Dutch sailors' eyes—a fresh, green breast of the new world. Its vanished trees, the trees that had made way for Gatsby's house, had once pandered in whispers to the last and greatest of all human dreams; for a transitory enchanted moment man must have held his breath in the presence of this continent, compelled into an aesthetic contemplation he neither understood nor desired, face to face for the last time in history with something commensurate to his capacity for wonder.

—F. Scott Fitzgerald, *from The Great Gatsby*

Eaton's Neck, Long Island (1872) by John Frederick Kensett. Oil on canvas (18″ × 36″).

The Metropolitan Museum of Art, gift of Thomas Kensett, 1874. (74.29) Photograph © 1979 The Metropolitan Museum of Art.

C **Humanities Connections**

The Armory Show

In 1913, the Modernist movement in art was introduced to the American public. Until that date, for Americans, The Eight (see Responding to the Art, p. 523) represented the avant-garde in painting. However, the 1913 show in New York's old 69th Regiment Armory made it plain that European painters had gone far beyond what their American counterparts were doing.

The Eight, who had been the first to break away from the juried system of major art exhibits, played a large part in organizing the Armory Show. Such European painters as Paul Cézanne, Edvard Munch, Henri Matisse, and Marcel Duchamp exhibited their work for the first time in the United States. For the first time, the general American public beheld Cubism, Fauvism, Post-Impressionism, and abstract art of a kind they had never seen before. Duchamp's *Nude Descending a Staircase* was a major focus of attention. Although one critic sneered at it as "an explosion in a shingle factory," the public was impressed. Americans would never look at art the same way again.

Skill Link

Locating Print and Nonprint Information

After reading the unit introduction, return to the quote at the top of p. 524. Discuss what kinds of ideas were "blown away" by the war. Students may suggest a loss of faith in military honor, the American dream, or in technology as a force for good. Ask students to research the opinions and sentiments of the people in their own state or local community during the period, using the following strategies.

1. Have them look up oral histories, photo essays, and news articles through databases and indexes in the library and on the Internet.
2. If possible, have students interview family members or neighbors who lived through this period.
3. Tell students to draw conclusions about why different people felt as they did and present their findings to the class in an oral report.

Time Line

• 1900–1909

Joseph Conrad (1857–1924) was born Konrad Korzeniowski in Poland. After twenty years as a sailor, he settled in England and began a career as a writer. In the years that followed, he wrote over fifteen novels, all in English. *Heart of Darkness* is a short novel in which the narrator, Marlow, travels far into the heart of Africa in search of his hero, Kurtz, only to find that he is a villain. *Heart of Darkness* is one of the first in a long line of twentieth-century novels to feature themes of disillusionment, the fallen hero, and the cynical realization that old standards are shot through with hypocrisy and moral ambiguity.

• 1910–1919

One of the greatest disillusionments in modern America concerned baseball. In 1919, professional gamblers bribed members of the Chicago White Sox to throw the World Series to the Cincinnati Reds. Because the White Sox were heavily favored to win, the gamblers stood to make a fortune by betting on the Reds. When the scandal broke in 1920, the public reeled from the shock. Baseball, invented in America and the only organized professional sport of its day, truly was the national pastime. In *The Great Gatsby,* Fitzgerald alluded to the fix as "play[ing] with the faith of fifty million people." Eight players were eventually banned from the game for life. It took the charisma and talent of young Babe Ruth to win back the fans.

• 1920–1950

Although African Americans had been playing baseball for years, they were excluded from the Major Leagues. In 1920, Rube Foster banded together eight Midwestern teams into the first official Negro National League. Negro League baseball was easily the most popular spectator sport for African Americans during this period and was a culturally important assertion of black identity. Suffering from poor funding and disorganization, the Negro Leagues eventually broke up after Jackie Robinson began the integration of the Majors in 1947.

The Moderns 1900–1950

LITERARY EVENTS			
England's Joseph Conrad publishes the psychological novel *Heart of Darkness,* 1902 • Frank Norris publishes *The Octopus,* a naturalistic novel about California wheat farmers fighting the railroad, 1901	William Carlos Williams's first collection of poems published, 1909 • W.E.B. Du Bois publishes an influential collection of essays, *The Souls of Black Folk,* 1903 • Jack London publishes *The Call of the Wild,* 1903	Carl Sandburg publishes *Chicago Poems,* 1916 • Edgar Lee Masters publishes *Spoon River Anthology,* 1915 • Willa Cather publishes *O Pioneers!,* 1913 • Robert Frost publishes his first poetry collection, 1913	Edna St. Vincent Millay wins Pulitzer Prize in poetry, 1923 • T. S. Eliot publishes *The Waste Land,* 1922 • Irish writer James Joyce publishes *Ulysses,* 1922 • Sinclair Lewis publishes *Main Street,* a novel about small-town Minnesota, 1920
	1900–1909	**1910–1919**	**1920–1929**
CULTURAL/HISTORICAL EVENTS	Queen Victoria of England dies, 1901 • South African (or Boer) War ends in costly British victory, 1902	Einstein formulates his theory of relativity, 1905 • Earthquake and fire ravage San Francisco, 1906 • Freud lectures on psychoanalysis in U.S., 1909	British ocean liner *Titanic* sinks after striking an iceberg off Newfoundland, 1912 • Armory Show in New York City introduces modern art to U.S., 1913 • Panama Canal opens, 1914 • World War I begins in Europe, 1914 • U.S. enters World War I, 1917 • Russian Revolution ends czarist regime, 1917	Harlem Renaissance begins, 1920 • 19th Amendment to Constitution grants U.S. women the right to vote, 1920 • Charles A. Lindbergh completes first transatlantic solo flight by airplane, 1927

Albert Einstein. The Granger Collection, New York.

Charles Lindbergh and the *Spirit of St. Louis.*

526

Professional Notes

The "Black" Sox Scandal in History

"The scandal was a betrayal of more than a set of ball games, even more than of the sport itself," writes historian Eliot Asinof of the World Series fix. "It was a crushing blow at American pride. . . . Baseball was our national game; its stars were national heroes, revered by kids and adults alike, in all classes of our society. In the public mind, the image was pure and patriotic. . . . Now, suddenly, that pride was shattered. The National Pastime was nothing more than another show of corruption. . . . If baseball was corrupt, then *anything* might be— and probably was. . . . There is no way to gauge the extent of the damage on the American psyche. It is impossible to add up bitterness like a batting average. How great was the layer of cynicism that settled over the nation? How many kids developed tolerance for a lie, for a betrayal, for corruption itself?"

Ernest Hemingway publishes noted World War I novel, *A Farewell to Arms,* 1929

•

Langston Hughes publishes his first poetry collection, *The Weary Blues,* 1926

•

The novels *An American Tragedy,* by Theodore Dreiser, and *The Great Gatsby,* by **F. Scott Fitzgerald,** are published, 1925

John Steinbeck publishes *The Grapes of Wrath,* 1939, and wins the Pulitzer Prize

•

Thornton Wilder's *Our Town* opens and wins Pulitzer Prize, 1938

•

Zora Neale Hurston publishes *Their Eyes Were Watching God,* 1937

•

Eugene O'Neill's dramatic trilogy *Mourning Becomes Electra* opens, 1931

Tennessee Williams's play *The Glass Menagerie* opens on Broadway, 1945

•

Richard Wright publishes *Native Son,* 1940

The play *Death of a Salesman,* by **Arthur Miller,** opens, 1949

•

William Faulkner publishes *Intruder in the Dust,* 1948

•

William Carlos Williams publishes first part of his long poem *Paterson,* 1946

THE GRAPES OF WRATH
DARRYL F. ZANUCK'S Production
BY John Steinbeck
HENRY FONDA

1920–1929	1930–1939	1940–1950

The Jazz Singer, one of the first sound films with dialogue, opens, 1927

•

U.S. stock market crashes, leading to Great Depression, 1929

Mohandas Gandhi leads protest against British salt tax in India, 1930

•

Franklin D. Roosevelt becomes U.S. president; New Deal program to counter Great Depression begins, 1933

Nazi leader Adolf Hitler comes to power in Germany, 1933

Nationalist forces of Francisco Franco win Spanish civil war, 1939

•

Germany invades Poland; World War II begins in Europe, 1939

U.S. enters World War II after Japan attacks Pearl Harbor in Hawaii, 1941

•

Oklahoma!, a groundbreaking musical play by Richard Rodgers and Oscar Hammerstein, opens, 1943

Allies begin final drive against German forces on D-day, June 6, 1944

Germany surrenders, 1945

•

U.S. explodes atom bombs over Hiroshima and Nagasaki, Japan; Japan surrenders, 1945

United Nations established, 1945

•

India gains independence from British rule, 1947

•

State of Israel established, 1948

Communist forces under Mao Zedong win control of mainland China, 1949

Korean War begins, 1950

•

U.S. population is about 151 million, 1950

Franklin D. Roosevelt.

Attack on Pearl Harbor.

United Nations Building, New York City.

Using the Time Line

Have students use encyclopedias or other reference sources to place the following major events in science and art on the time line:

- Tutankhamen's tomb is opened, revealing treasures. [1922]
- George Gershwin's *Porgy and Bess* opens. [1935]
- Roald Amundsen reaches the South Pole. [1911]
- Orson Welles directs the film *Citizen Kane.* [1941]

- Igor Stravinsky's *Rite of Spring* is first performed in Paris and causes a riot. [1913]
- New York City's Interborough Rapid Transit subway system opens. [1904]
- Immigrant Act excludes Japanese from immigrating to the United States. [1924]
- Bertolt Brecht and Kurt Weill's *Threepenny Opera* opens in Berlin. [1928]
- Max Planck proposes the quantum theory. [1900]

In 1921, the aspiring politician Franklin D. Roosevelt fell victim to polio. He recovered speedily but was never again able to walk more than a step or two, leaning heavily on crutches. Because of his relative immobility, during Roosevelt's four terms as president (from 1933 to 1945), First Lady Eleanor Roosevelt took on responsibilities and engagements unprecedented for a president's wife. Mrs. Roosevelt traveled as far as Guadalcanal in the South Pacific during the Second World War. She made numerous speeches and represented her husband in many places to which he was unable to travel. Although she was untrained as a public speaker and was painfully shy, Mrs. Roosevelt cared deeply enough about the issues of the day—widespread unemployment and poverty, the war, and civil rights—that she overcame her stage fright. After FDR's death, Eleanor became an ambassador to the United Nations. She was the first modern First Lady and one of the first modern professional women.

• 1930–1950

Martha Graham was already twenty-two when she began to study dance at the Denishawn School in Los Angeles in 1916. She began teaching and dancing professionally during World War I and even tried vaudeville. In 1927, Graham founded her own studio. Her style of dance was unconventional and completely modern, using dramatic gestures originating from the contraction and expansion of the torso. In her famous solo piece *Lamentation,* Graham attempted to embody grief: "the thing itself, not just a pretty picture of it." In the 1930s, Graham choreographed many American subjects. She explored American Indian dances in *Primitive Mysteries* (1931) and pioneer themes in *American Provincial* (1934) and *Frontier* (1935). Later, in 1944, Aaron Copland wrote *Appalachian Spring* for her.

In the 1940s, Graham turned to literary themes. Her *Letter to the World* (1940) is a dance that concerns Emily Dickinson, and her *Deaths and Entrances* (1943) is about the Brontë sisters. She also choreographed works based on the myths of Medea, the Minotaur, and Clytemnestra. Graham continued to dance, choreograph, and direct until her death in 1991.

A Closer Look

This feature examines the economic devastation of the Great Depression, along with breathtaking innovations in technology and popular entertainment during the 1930s.

Ⓐ Exploring the Historical Period

The Works Progress Administration (WPA) engineered a great number of public works projects. It was created in 1935 to provide paying jobs for those who had been thrown out of work by the Great Depression. Many of these jobs were in construction; WPA workers built bridges, post offices, roads, and public swimming pools. Many more were in the arts; actors, directors, and painters received WPA grants. WPA historians recorded the stories of hundreds of American towns, and one especially noteworthy project was a series of interviews with former slaves to record their memories. The WPA was disbanded in 1943.

RESPONDING TO THE ART

Diego Rivera (1886–1957) was one of the greatest twentieth-century muralists. Rivera studied art in Paris, but his art remained emphatically Mexican. Most of Rivera's great murals were commissioned for public buildings in Mexico City, but he also accepted a few commissions in the United States. Rivera's mural *Man at the Crossroads* for New York City's Rockefeller Center was destroyed because he included a portrait of Lenin. This incident was immortalized in E. B. White's poem "I Paint What I See." Rivera was a passionate patriot and socialist; he glorified working people in his murals. *Detroit Industry* had a strong influence on American artists, particularly muralists, such as Thomas Hart Benton.

Activity. Ask students how this detail from Rivera's mural reflects the modern age. [Possible answers: It magnifies machinery and industry; it emphasizes the change from farming society to manufacturing society.]

A CLOSER LOOK

THE BEST OF TIMES, THE WORST OF TIMES

The era of the 1930s in the United States was marked by triumph and tragedy, growth and hardship. Between 1890 and 1940, the U.S. population more than doubled, rising from 63 million to 132 million. African Americans made up about 10 percent of the population, and other ethnic groups about 0.5 percent. Families were slightly larger than they are today, but people died younger—on average, around age sixty.

By 1933, the United States was in the depths of the Great Depression. Anywhere from one fourth to one third of American workers were unemployed. People waited in bread lines, foraged for food in garbage dumps, and slept in sewer pipes. Homeless families lived in tents and shacks in camps called Hoovervilles, named for President Herbert Hoover. In 1933, the new president, Franklin Delano Roosevelt (FDR), ignited a spark of hope with his promise to help the "forgotten man." True to his word, FDR launched a blizzard of agencies, such as the Works Progress Administration and the Civilian Conservation Corps, that put millions of Americans back to work.

Despite hard times, human and technological marvels were a hallmark of the

FPG International.

The second element in the American dream is optimism, justified by the ever-expanding opportunity and abundance that many people have come to expect. Most of the time, Americans have believed in progress—that life keeps getting better and that we are moving toward an era of prosperity, justice, and joy that always seems just around the corner.

Finally, the third important element in the American dream has been the importance and ultimate triumph of the individual—the independent, self-reliant person. This ideal of the self-reliant individual was championed by Ralph Waldo Emerson (page 216), who probably deserves most of the credit for defining the essence of the American dream, including its roots in the promise of the "new Eden" and its faith that "things are getting better all the time." Trust the universe and trust yourself, Emerson wrote. "If the single man plant himself indomitable on his instincts, and there abide, the huge world will come round to him."

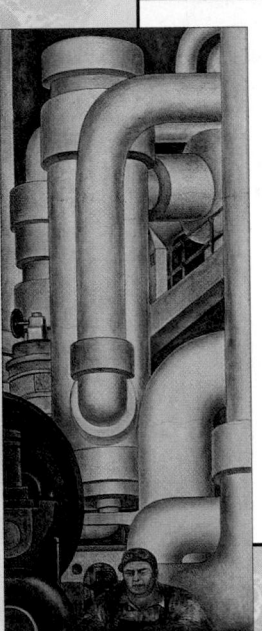

Detroit Industry, West Wall (detail) (1932–1933) by Diego M. Rivera. Fresco. Gift of Edsel B. Ford. Photograph ©1998 The Detroit Institute of Art.

Crossing the Curriculum

Film

Have students get together to view Steven Soderbergh's *King of the Hill* (1993), a story of the Depression. This film will show students some of the more harrowing aspects of the era, such as the Hoovervilles. Characters are locked out of their apartments and their possessions seized when they cannot pay their rent. Students are likely to identify with the hero of the story, a boy only a few years younger than themselves. After students see the film, have them discuss what they learned about the Depression and how the film might have brought home to them some issues they had read about but not fully understood.

era. Amelia Earhart became the first woman to fly solo across the Atlantic (1932). Three famous structures were built during this decade: the Empire State Building in New York City (1931), Boulder (now Hoover) Dam on the Arizona-Nevada border (1936), and the Golden Gate Bridge in San Francisco (1937).

Happily, during a decade of severe shortages, there was no shortage of entertainment. Mystery fans devoured whodunits featuring Dashiell Hammett's hard-boiled investigator, Sam Spade, while both young and old listened to the Dorseys' jazz orchestra and danced to the swing music of Count Basie.

By the late 1930s, the Depression had eased, and people could again afford one of the most popular entertainments: movies. The golden age of motion pictures had begun. Each week, over a hundred million Americans flocked to watch cartoons, newsreels, and feature films at elaborate movie palaces with names such as the Bijou, the Roxy, and the Ritz. Audiences loved slapstick comics like Laurel and Hardy or the Marx broth-

ers. Lines spoken by Mae West, such as "Come up and see me sometime," became household phrases. To top off the decade, audiences in 1939 thronged to behold the long-awaited blockbuster movie epic, *Gone with the Wind*. **B**

But perhaps the most popular form of entertainment during the 1930s was the radio. By 1933, two thirds of American households owned at least one radio, and families gathered together to listen to comedies like *Fibber McGee and Molly* and adventures like *The Shadow*. People also relied on radios for news, as was demonstrated by a famous Halloween broadcast of 1938. Six million listeners tuned in to Orson Welles's radio play "Invasion from Mars"—a series of convincing but fictional news bulletins about a Martian invasion near New York City, based on H. G. Wells's science fiction novel *War of the Worlds*. At the time, some people feared that the German dictator Adolf Hitler might actually invade the United States. Believing that the broadcast was describing a real invasion, hundreds of people clogged eastern highways, fleeing for their lives. **C**

> Fitzgerald's greatest work shows what happens to people who pursue illusory American dreams, and how society . . . fails to sustain them in their desperate hour.
>
> —Jeffrey Meyers, *Scott Fitzgerald: A Biography*, 1994

The three underpinnings of the American dream are a belief in the land as a bountiful new Eden, an unwavering faith in progress, and a confidence in the ultimate triumph of the individual.

A Crack in the World: Breakdown of Beliefs and Traditions

The cannonades of World War I and the economic crash a decade later severely damaged these inherited ideas of an Edenic land, an optimism in the future, and faith in individualism. Postwar writers became skeptical of the New England Puritan tradition and the gentility that had been central to the literary

The Tenets of the American Dream

- America is a new Eden, a "promised land" of beauty, unlimited resources, and endless opportunities.
- The American birthright is one of ever-expanding opportunity. Progress is a good thing, and we can optimistically expect life to keep getting better and better.
- The independent, self-reliant individual will triumph. Everything is possible for the person who places trust in his or her own powers and potential.

THE MODERNS **529**

A Exploring the Historical Period

Karl Marx argued that the economic structure of a society dictates every aspect of life in that society. He also believed that the poverty and brutality associated with the capitalist system could not be reformed from within; instead, capitalism had to be destroyed to make way for a classless society in which everything is owned communally and everyone receives equal benefits and rewards. His ideas greatly influenced Vladimir Ilyich Lenin, who became, in 1903, the head of the Bolshevik faction of the Social Democratic Party in Russia. In 1917, the Bolsheviks took control of the revolution that had deposed the czar and later established a Marxist government.

B Background

Ulysses

Joyce's famous novel is based on Homer's epic poem the *Odyssey*. *Ulysses* is the Latin form of the Greek name Odysseus. Although the protagonist's journey begins and ends in Dublin on one day, while Odysseus travels across the Mediterranean for ten years, the structure of the journey is the same. *Ulysses* has as many chapters as the *Odyssey* has books, and each event corresponds to one of Odysseus's adventures.

C Literary Connections

The Thin Man

Dashiell Hammett (see A Closer Look, p. 529) captured the era of Prohibition in his detective novel *The Thin Man* (1932). Nick and Nora Charles, a wealthy married couple spending the New Year's holiday in New York, move from speakeasy to cocktail party and back again as Nick sorts out a tangle of gangsters, liars, and cops to pin down a murderer. Prohibition was repealed in 1933.

Sigmund Freud looking at a manuscript in the office of his Vienna home (c. 1930).
The Bettmann Archive

William Faulkner.
The Granger Collection, New York.

ideal. In fact, the center of American literary life now finally started to shift away from New England, which had been the native region of America's most brilliant writers during the nineteenth century. Many of the modernist writers you will read in the collections that follow were born in the South, the Midwest, or the West.

In the postwar period, two new intellectual trends or movements, **Marxism** and **psychoanalysis,** combined to increase the pressure on traditional beliefs and values. In Russia during World War I, a Marxist revolution had toppled and even murdered an anointed ruler, the czar. The socialistic beliefs of Karl Marx (1818–1883) that had powered the Russian Revolution in 1917 were in direct opposition to the American system of capitalism and free enterprise, and Marxists threatened to export their revolution everywhere. After visiting Russia, American writer Lincoln Steffens reported: "I have seen the future and it works."

In Vienna, there was another unsettling movement. Sigmund Freud (1856–1939), the founder of psychoanalysis, had opened the workings of the unconscious mind to scrutiny and called for a new understanding of human sexuality and the role it plays in our unconscious thoughts. Throughout America, there was a growing interest in this new field of psychology, and a resultant anxiety about the amount of freedom an individual really had. If our actions were influenced by our subconscious, and if we had no control over our subconscious, there seemed to be little room left for "free will."

One literary result of this interest in the psyche was the narrative technique called **stream of consciousness.** This writing style abandoned chronology and attempted to imitate the moment-by-moment flow of a character's perceptions and memories. The Irish writer James Joyce (1882–1941) radically changed the very concept of the novel by using stream of consciousness in *Ulysses* (1922), his monumental "odyssey" set in Dublin. Soon afterward, the American writers Katherine Anne Porter (page 702) and William Faulkner (page 713) used the stream-of-consciousness technique in their works.

Two important trends, Marxism and psychoanalysis, were noteworthy factors in the breakdown of traditional beliefs and values. Psychoanalysis led to the literary technique of stream-of-consciousness narration.

At Home and Abroad: The Jazz Age

In 1919, the Constitution was amended to prohibit the manufacture and sale of alcohol, which was singled out as a central social evil. But far from shoring up traditional values, Prohibition ushered in an age characterized by the bootlegger, the speakeasy, the cocktail, the short-skirted flapper, the new rhythms of jazz, and the dangerous

Manuscript page, "A Rose for Emily" by William Faulkner.
William Faulkner Collection, Special Collections Department, Manuscripts Division, University of Virginia Library.

> The liberty of the individual is no gift of civilization. It was greatest before there was any civilization.
>
> —Sigmund Freud, *Civilization and Its Discontents*, 1930

Crossing the Curriculum

Psychology

Have students do some research on Sigmund Freud. Who was he? When did his teachings reach American readers? How did people react to his ideas? What are the titles of his major works? Have students share what they learn about Freud with their classmates. As they read the literature of the modern period, have them keep Freud's teachings in mind. How might his ideas have affected the American writers represented in this anthology?

Professional Notes

Freud on Writers

For Freud, the writer, like the daydreamer, taps into an egotistical desire for self-fulfillment. "The day-dreamer hid his phantasies carefully from other people because he had reason to be ashamed of them. . . . When we hear such phantasies they repel us, or at least leave us cold. But when a man of literary talent presents his plays, or relates what we take to be his personal day-dreams, we experience great pleasure. . . . The writer softens the egotistical character of the day-dream by changes and disguises, and he bribes us by the offer of a purely formal, that is, aesthetic, pleasure. . . . I am of the opinion that . . . the true enjoyment of literature proceeds from the release of tensions in our minds. Perhaps much that brings about this result consists in the writer's putting us into a position in which we can enjoy our own day-dreams without reproach or shame."

but lucrative profession of the gangster. Recording the Roaring Twenties and making the era a vivid chapter in our history, F. Scott Fitzgerald gave it its name: the Jazz Age. Other writers also became emblems of the era. The poet Edna St. Vincent Millay (page 697)—"Vincent" to her friends—became a symbol of the liberated woman of the era. Her bold, carefree public identity as a romantic, extravagant female Casanova made her a national celebrity while she was still in her twenties. In 1920, women had finally won the right to vote, and Millay's poems, as well as her public persona, assigned women social, intellectual, and romantic roles that society had previously reserved for men.

As energetic as the Roaring Twenties were in America, the pursuit of pleasure abroad was even more attractive to some than its enjoyment at home. F. Scott Fitzgerald was among the many American writers and artists who abandoned their own shores after the war for the expatriate life in France. After World War I, living was not only cheap in Paris and on the sunny French Riviera, but also somehow better; it was more exotic, more filled with grace and luxury, and there was no need to go down a cellar stairway to get a drink. This wave of expatriates was another signal that something had gone wrong with the American dream—with the idea that America was Eden, with our notion of inherent virtue, and especially with the conviction that America was a land of heroes.

The Jazz Age at home was racy and unconventional. The same decade of the 1920s witnessed the flight of many American authors to an expatriate life abroad, especially in France.

> The United States . . . is a country the right age to have been born in and the wrong age to live in.
>
> —Gertrude Stein, *transition* magazine, Fall 1928

Grace Under Pressure: The New American Hero

Disillusionment was a major theme in the fiction of the time. In 1920, Sinclair Lewis (1885–1951) lashed out satirically at the

Village Speakeasy, Closed for Violations (detail) (c. 1934) by Ben Shahn. Tempera on masonite (16½" × 48"). Museum of the City of New York. Permanent Deposit of the Public Art Project through the Whitney Museum.
© Estate of Ben Shahn/Licensed by VAGA, New York, NY.

F. Scott Fitzgerald (1896–1940) married Zelda Sayre of Alabama in 1920. In the years that followed, the couple epitomized the Jazz Age: wealthy, pleasure-seeking, spendthrift, beautiful, and talented. Fitzgerald's novel *Tender Is the Night* (1934) is based on their marriage. Zelda (1900–1948) was also a writer of considerable though undisciplined ability. Her one novel, *Save Me the Waltz* (1932), is based on her life with Fitzgerald. The novel failed with both critics and public, largely because of comparisons with her husband's work. Although their subject matter was similar, their writing styles were quite different. Zelda's prose is fragmented and full of brilliant and surrealistic images. It has never received the acclaim that her husband's has.

E Background

One of the most compelling images of this period was created by the poet T. S. Eliot (p. 661) in his masterpiece *The Waste Land*. In the opinion of some critics, the aridity and sterility of the landscape of this poem and of its characters' lives captured the mood of barrenness, pointlessness, and spiritual despair that many of these expatriates seemed to feel.

RESPONDING TO THE ART

Ben Shahn (1898–1969) was born in Lithuania and emigrated to the United States when he was eight. Shahn achieved fame in 1932 with a series of paintings titled *The Passion of Sacco and Vanzetti*, depicting the controversial trial and the 1927 execution for murder of Nicola Sacco and Bartolome Vanzetti. Shahn continued to address social issues throughout his career.

Activities

1. What is ironic about the shop on the corner? [It openly sells materials for making beer when such beverages are illegal.]

2. What impression do you have of the speakeasy's customers? [They seem unconcerned about the policemen. There are a lot of them; it must be a popular place.]

Making the Connections

Cultural Connections:
The Algonquin Round Table

The Algonquin Round Table was a celebrated group of wits who met for lunch at a round table in New York's Algonquin Hotel in the 1920s and 1930s. Among its members were Dorothy Parker, Robert Benchley, George S. Kaufman, Edna Ferber, Harpo Marx, and Alexander Woollcott. The group exemplified the sophistication of the Jazz Age: Its members extended the art of ironic conversation, trying to outdo each other at cleverness. Several of them were on the staff of *The New Yorker*, which had its offices down the block. Among them was Dorothy Parker, who was famous for her one liners, such as "Men seldom make passes at girls who wear glasses."

A Background

Sinclair Lewis and Theodore Dreiser focus on the lives of average Americans—on the misperceptions they have, the opportunities presented to them, the choices they make, and the consequences of those choices. In *Babbit,* Lewis satirizes the moral deficits of materialistic and conformist people who claim to be the pillars of society. His novels deal with the conflict between personal ethics and a corrupt or frivolous society. In novels like *Sister Carrie* and *The Financier,* Dreiser portrays the misplaced faith the poor have in the classic American success story. He explores their stoicism and shattered hopes as they follow ineffectual and unethical paths.

B Exploring the Culture

The American Hero

The Hemingway hero was a modern version of a type that had existed for decades. The American hero, always physically tough, a loner, self-reliant, answering only to his own authority, first captured the imagination of the reading public in the Leatherstocking Tales of James Fenimore Cooper. This type of hero can be traced from Cooper's Hawkeye through Ambrose Bierce's hard-edged heroes to Hemingway's Jake Barnes. American film was strongly influenced by this type of hero: Gary Cooper (right), Humphrey Bogart, and John Wayne had long and successful careers playing Hemingway-type heroes. They said little, they acted when necessary, they relied solely on their own judgment, and they were generally men of honor. Kevin Costner, Robert Redford, and Harrison Ford are contemporary heirs of this heroic tradition.

narrow-mindedness of small-town life in his immensely popular novel, *Main Street.* In 1925, Theodore Dreiser (1871–1945) produced a literary **A** landmark with his prototype of the realistic novel, *An American Tragedy,* the story of an ambitious but luckless man who takes a path that leads him not to the success he seeks, but to the execution chamber.

The most influential of all the post–World War I writers, however, was Ernest Hemingway (page 650). Hemingway is perhaps most famous for his literary style, which affected the style of American prose fiction for several generations. Like the Puritans who strove for a "plain style" centuries earlier, Hemingway reduced the flamboyance of literary language to a minimum, to the bare bones of the truth it must express.

Hemingway also introduced a new kind of hero to American fiction, a character type that many readers embraced as a protagonist and a role model. This Hemingway hero is a man of action, a warrior, and a tough competitor; he has a code of honor, courage, and endurance. He shows, in **B** Hemingway's own words, "grace under pressure." But the most important trait of this Hemingway hero is that he is thoroughly disillusioned, a quality that reflected the author's own outlook. For Hemingway feared, a little like Herman Melville (page 311), that at the inscrutable center of creation lay nothing at all.

Hemingway found his own "answer" to this crisis of faith in a belief in the self and in such qualities as decency, bravery, competence, and skill. He clung to this conviction in spite of what he saw as the absolutely unbeatable odds ranged against us all. A further part of the Hemingway code was the importance of recognizing and snatching up the rare, good, rich moments that life offers before those moments elude us.

Hemingway summed up the values of many post–World War I writers, both in his spare, plain style and in his creation of a new kind of hero, disillusioned but also honorable and courageous.

Modernist Voices in Poetry: A Dazzling Period

After the deaths of Emily Dickinson (page 372) and Walt Whitman (page 348), American poetry went into something of a decline. But time would show that the comparatively uneventful period between 1890 and 1910 was but the trough of a wave that was about to break. The force of this wave, when it arrived, would be strong enough to wash away the last traces of British influence on American poetry and to carry our poets into their most dazzling period of variety and experimentation.

During this period, many poets began to explore the artistic life of Europe, especially Paris. With other writers, artists, and composers from all over the world, they

Gary Cooper as Robert Jordan in the 1943 movie *For Whom the Bell Tolls,* based on Hemingway's novel.

Professional Notes

Critical Comment:
Wilson on Hemingway

In 1939, the great critic Edmund Wilson wrote: "[Hemingway's] whole work is a criticism of society: he has responded to every pressure of the moral atmosphere of the time, as it is felt at the roots of human relations, with a sensitivity almost unrivaled. Even his preoccupation with licking the gang in the next block and being known as the best basketball player in high school has its meaning in the present epoch.

After all, what ever is done in the world, political as well as athletic, depends on personal courage and strength. . . .

"But ideas, however correct, will never prevail by themselves: there must be people who are prepared to stand or fall with them, and the ability to act on principle is still subject to the same competitive laws which operate in sporting contests and sexual relations. Hemingway

has expressed with genius the terrors of the modern man at the danger of losing control of his world, and he has also, within his scope, provided his own kind of antidote. This antidote, paradoxically, is almost entirely moral. Despite Hemingway's preoccupation with physical contests, his heroes are almost always defeated physically, nervously, practically: their victories are moral ones."

Guernica (1937) by Pablo Picasso. Museo Nacional Centro de Arte Reina Sofía, Madrid. On permanent loan from the Museo del Prado, Madrid. © 2000 The Estate of Pablo Picasso/Artists Rights Society (ARS), New York.

absorbed the lessons of modernist painters like Henri Matisse and Pablo Picasso, who were exploring new ways to see and represent reality. In the same way, poets sought to create poems that invited new ways of seeing and thinking. Ezra Pound (page 773) and T. S. Eliot (page 661) used the suggestive techniques of **Symbolism** to fashion a new, modernist poetry (see page 770).

Pound also spearheaded a related poetic movement called **Imagism.** Exemplified by brilliant poets like William Carlos Williams (page 778), Marianne Moore (page 787), E. E. Cummings (page 796), and Wallace Stevens (page 783), the Imagist and Symbolist styles would prevail in poetry until midway into the twentieth century.

After an uneventful period between 1890 and 1910, an explosion of modernist poetry, heavily influenced by developments in Europe, began. Ezra Pound and T. S. Eliot, associated with the Symbolist and Imagist movements, were especially important in charting a modernist direction for American poetry.

The Elements of Modernism in American Literature

- Emphasis on bold experimentation in style and form, reflecting the fragmentation of society
- Rejection of traditional themes and subjects
- Sense of disillusionment and loss of faith in the American dream
- Rejection of the ideal of a hero as infallible in favor of a hero who is flawed and disillusioned but shows "grace under pressure"
- Interest in the inner workings of the human mind, sometimes expressed through new narrative techniques such as stream of consciousness

THE MODERNS **533**

◉ Literary Connections

Another important Imagist poet was H. D. (p. T772). H. D. was born Hilda Doolittle in Pennsylvania in 1886. She entered Bryn Mawr College, near Philadelphia, but left after a year, depressed by her poor grades. Confused by her up-and-down romance with Ezra Pound and unsure of her future, H. D. drifted to London, where she published her first volume of poems, *Sea Garden* (1916). Critics hailed it as "the most perfect exemplar of Imagism." H. D. wrote several autobiographical novels; she was already writing in the stream-of-consciousness technique by the time James Joyce published *Ulysses*. Because most of her novels were not published until after her death, her place in the prose canon has only recently been recognized. Her poetic output includes the epics *Trilogy* and *Helen in Egypt*. She died in 1961.

Getting Students Involved

Cooperative Learning

Spanish Civil War. Tell students that the Spanish Civil War has been considered a rehearsal for World War II. The opposing sides, Nationalists and Loyalists, were both coalitions of various smaller groups who were not always in agreement. As the war progressed, the two sides became increasingly polarized, and other nations began to provide arms, supplies, and even men. Many weapons used in World War II were first tested in Spain.

Have groups of students research an aspect of the Spanish Civil War that interests them. Permit them to work together on a dramatic presentation for the class. Have them imagine that they are war correspondents reporting for a major American news service. Students may want to give their report as a radio broadcast, a short play presenting the events, or a series of interviews.

Not all of the Modernist poets became expatriates like Pound and Eliot. William Carlos Williams (p. 778), for example, maintained a full-time medical practice in his native Rutherford, New Jersey. In fact, Williams, who has come to be one of the most influential poets of the twentieth century, scorned the decision of his friend Ezra Pound to leave the country.

B Literary Connections

Also prominent among the Midwesterners is Carl Sandburg (p. 792). Sandburg wrote in free verse; Walt Whitman's influence on his style, tone, subject, and attitude is very apparent. Like Whitman, Sandburg celebrated America and its working men and women. He found cause for wonder and admiration in the industrial city, in crowds of people, and on the lonely Midwestern plains. His freedom of expression and his celebratory tone contrast strongly with the work of his contemporary Robert Frost.

C Background

Other significant poets who were born in the Midwest include Vachel Lindsay (Springfield, Illinois); Archibald MacLeish (Glencoe, Illinois); Richard Eberhart (Austin, Minnesota); Sara Teasdale (St. Louis, Missouri); and Hart Crane (Garrettsville, Ohio).

Voices of American Character: Poetry in New England and the Midwest

A Meanwhile, other American poets rejected modernist trends. While their colleagues found inspiration in Paris, these poets stayed at home, ignoring or defying the revolution of modernism. These poets preferred to say what they had to say in plain American speech. Their individual accents reveal the regional diversity of American life and character.

Edwin Arlington Robinson (page 644) lightly disguised the people of his own "Down East" home—Gardiner, Maine—as characters representing American "types" whose fates were manifestations of their characters.

The greatest poetic voice in New England, however, was that of Robert Frost (page 558). Frost's independence was grounded in his ability to handle ordinary New England speech and in his surprising skill at taking the most conventional poetic forms and giving them a twist all his own. In an era when "good" was being equated by many artists with "new," the only new thing about Robert Frost was old: individual poetic genius. Using this gift to impose his own personality on the iambic line in verse, Frost created a poetic voice that was unique and impossible to imitate.

> Tell me what America is and I'll tell you what its poetry is.
> —Robert Frost

B **C** At the same time, poets of the Midwest brought the American heartland to life in slightly more adventuresome verse forms. They used rougher stanzas and looser lines. Best known of these poets is Edgar Lee Masters (page 692), who assembled a sort of town biography in his *Spoon River Anthology* (1915). Masters took the lid off sentimentalized small-town life—the *coffin* lid, to be exact—and allowed the dead of Spoon River to speak their own shocking litanies of greed, frustration, and spiritual poverty. His best-selling collection of poems received the same kind of interest Americans were beginning to give to Freudian case histories.

Poets like Edwin Arlington Robinson and Robert Frost from New England and Edgar Lee Masters from the Midwest continued to use traditional verse forms and offered penetrating insights into a variety of American character types.

The Harlem Renaissance: Voices of the African American Experience

African American culture found expression in poetry in two different ways. The works of black poets who wrote in conventional forms, like Paul Laurence Dunbar (1872–1906), were most quickly accepted by white readers. These metrically regular and rhymed verse forms tended to make even the most urgent and desperate of African American concerns seem undisturbing. A second

125th Street Apollo Theatre. Harlem, 1934. Many great African American artists performed here.

Getting Students Involved

Enrichment Activity

Silent Movies. Studying silent films of the 1920s as a way to understand Modernism can give students an enjoyable change of pace. Charlie Chaplin, Buster Keaton, and Harold Lloyd made numerous comedies—shorts as well as feature-length movies—set in what they saw as a bewildering modern world. Their heroes are either innocents or loners who find themselves in difficult circumstances ranging from assembly-line factories to high-rise buildings to Tin Pan Alley. Charlie Chaplin's tramp, with his expressive face and costume of bedraggled elegance, is absurd, yet noble and moral even in extreme circumstances. Buster Keaton's loner maintains his deadpan expression while going through a series of disasters (sight gags). Harold Lloyd always gets the girl, no matter how many physical obstacles he must overcome. Discuss with students how comedy can be used to explore serious subjects. Consider how an author or filmmaker can criticize political, social, or economic conditions while still leaving the audience feeling amused or uplifted. After watching one or more of Chaplin's, Keaton's, or Lloyd's films, have students choose one and write an essay analyzing how the film approaches a particular condition of modern life. Remind them to cite specific details from the film in support of their arguments.

group of black poets, however, focused directly on the unique contributions of African American culture to America. Their poetry based its rhythms on spirituals and jazz, its lyrics on songs known as the blues, and its diction on the street talk of the ghettos.

Foremost among African American lyric poets were James Weldon Johnson (page 736), Claude McKay (page 743), Langston Hughes (page 760), and Countee Cullen (page 746). These poets brought literary distinction to the broad movement of artists known as the **Harlem Renaissance** (page 734). The geographical center of the movement was Harlem, the section of New York City north of 110th Street in Manhattan. But its spiritual center was a place in the consciousness of African Americans—a people too long ignored, patronized, or otherwise shuffled to the margins of American art. When African American poetry, hand in hand with the music echoing from New Orleans, Memphis, and Chicago, became part of the Jazz Age, it was a catalyst for a new appreciation of the role of black talent in American culture.

The poets of the Harlem Renaissance revolutionized the African American contribution to American literature by introducing ghetto speech and the rhythms of jazz and blues into their verse.

Against the Grain: Poetic Voices of the West and South

The most distinctive poetic voice from the West in the early twentieth century was that of Robinson Jeffers (page 580), who carved out an isolated and almost hermitlike existence in a California town by the Pacific shore. Jeffers steered a wavering course between convention and experiment: Sometimes he worked in meter and rhyme, but more often he wrote in long lines of free verse. He became widely known less for his craftsmanship than for his unorthodox attitudes toward progress, religion, and the nature of humanity. While his contemporaries celebrated democracy and the rise of the common man, Jeffers took a very dim view of both. After his death, his poems became an inspiration to the Beats and other West Coast literary groups in the 1960s.

The South offered an equally distinctive literary voice in John Crowe Ransom (page 577). Ransom stood for wit, gentility, subtle intellect, and the manners of an earlier century. Ransom's formal grace and polish intimidated some readers, but others found in him a gentle nature and a passionate concern for the beauty and elegance of the English language.

Poetic voices of the West and the South included Robinson Jeffers, who was skeptical of social progress, and John Crowe Ransom, a Southerner who wrote with the courtly grace of an earlier age.

Paul Laurence Dunbar. Culver Pictures.

> . . . O, let America be America again— The land that never has been yet— And yet must be.
> —Langston Hughes

(Background) Museum of African Art/Smithsonian Institution/Courtesy Aldo Tutino/Art Resource, NY.

THE MODERNS **535**

D Exploring the Culture

In the words of David Levering Lewis, "The Harlem Renaissance was a somewhat forced phenomenon, . . . institutionally encouraged and directed by leaders of the national civil rights establishment for the paramount purpose of improving race relations in a time of extreme national backlash, caused in large part by economic gains won by Afro-Americans during the Great War." Moreover, whites feared that black GIs would demand more equitable treatment after taking part in the war effort. During this period between the wars, racist violence spread across the North and South. Black artists thus found themselves with the dual mission of following their own artistic visions while simultaneously trying to improve social conditions through their work.

E Background

Many African American writers contributed to the Harlem Renaissance. Prominent prose writers included Jessie Redmon Fauset, Nella Larsen, Arna Bontemps, Jean Toomer, and Zora Neale Hurston (p. 750). Langston Hughes called Fauset the "midwife" of the Harlem Renaissance because she published many young black writers in *The Crisis* magazine, where she was literary editor. She wrote four novels in which she addresses stereotypes of blacks and issues of class, as well as of race and gender. Larsen wrote two critically acclaimed novels, *Quicksand* (1928) and *Passing* (1929). In her novels, she explores the social restrictions and pressures that prevent women—especially black women—from defining their own identity and creating a satisfying life. She portrays a modern, fragmented individual with little hope for a better future. Bontemps wrote poetry, history, and fiction, including stories for children. In collaboration with Langston Hughes, he compiled several anthologies of black poetry and culture. He rounded out his career writing memoirs and critical essays about his time and its literary figures. In his influential novel *Cane*, Toomer wrote about the Southern black culture he believed was being lost to industrialization and the migration of African Americans to the North.

Professional Notes

Critical Comment

"Reading him again," writes critic Robert Haas about Robinson Jeffers, "I was struck by how much [his poems] seemed to say what anyone has thought who has ever stood on a height and contemplated a modern city. We have lived in a catastrophic time. The redundancy of violence and suffering, the sheer immensity of the danger, always threatens to wither the imagination, to make us turn back to the purely personal, as if it were somehow more real because the mind can, at least, compass it, whereas the effort to think about the fate of the planet, about what man is that he has done to himself all the terrible things that he has done in this century, comes to us mostly as dark and private musings. And it is just this that Jeffers sought in the verse of his short poems, an art to speak those musings largely, to claim for the clear mind that needs to compass the madness the central voice of poetry."

Gertrude Stein (1874–1946) was a central figure among the Modernist writers in Paris. Stein was born in Pennsylvania but spent her childhood in Vienna and Paris; in 1879, the family resettled in California. She studied psychology at Radcliffe and medicine at Johns Hopkins. In 1903, she moved to Paris, which became her permanent home. Stein's apartment at 27 rue des Fleurs became a modern version of the eighteenth-century salon. Many writers and artists who would become some of the most important cultural figures of the next half-century met, dined, and talked there. The apartment also featured one of the first collections of important modern art; Stein and her brother Leo were among the first to purchase paintings by Picasso, Matisse, Gaugin, and Cézanne.

Stein published her first book, *Three Lives,* in 1909. Her best-known work is *The Autobiography of Alice B. Toklas* (1933). In it, Stein takes the unique approach of writing her own biography from the point of view of another person; Toklas was her companion and domestic partner for years. Stein explored the lives of women, experimenting with the patterns of language, notably in the repetition of words and phrases.

Stein's recognition and encouragement of literary and artistic talents are as important as her innovations in prose. Her art collection gained recognition from Picasso and Matisse, who became her close friends. Picasso painted her portrait; when someone objected that it did not look like her, he replied, "It will." Stein was friendly with many American expatriate writers—the Fitzgeralds, Hemingway, John dos Passos—and famously identified them as belonging to "the lost generation."

The American Dream Revised

Even though the modernists rejected Emerson's optimism, a belief in self-reliance persisted, as did the old idea of America as Eden. Hemingway is really telling us about Eden in his *Up in Michigan* stories, where he describes the lakes and streams and woods he knew as a boy and where he extols the restorative power of nature in a way that Emerson might have recognized. This is the same Edenic America that has come down to us through Mark Twain's Mississippi, through Faulkner's Yoknapatawpha County, and through John Steinbeck's Salinas Valley.

As we explore this period of American writing—in some respects, the richest period since the flowering of New England in the first half of the nineteenth century—we stand at the threshold of our own time. Though this part of our own century has seen major changes in American attitudes, you'll recognize many concerns that are consistent with concerns of the past. These writers—some of the best that America has produced—experimented boldly with forms and subject matter. But they were also still trying to find the answers to the basic human questions: Who are we? Where are we going? And what values should guide us on that search for our human identity?

> I began to gather these impressions. There was a thing called happiness toward which men were striving. They never got to it. All of life was amazingly accidental. Love, moments of tenderness and despair, came to the poor and the miserable as to the rich and successful.
>
> It began to seem to me that what was most wanted by all people was love, understanding. Our writers, our storytellers, in wrapping life up into neat little packages, were only betraying life.
>
> —Sherwood Anderson, in a letter to George Freitag, August 27, 1938

American modernist writers both echoed and challenged the American dream. They constituted a broader, more resonant voice than ever before, resulting in a second American renaissance. With all the changes, however, writers continued to ask fundamental questions about the meaning and purpose of human existence.

Quickwrite
What Is Today's American Dream?

Ⓐ In 1929, Gertrude Stein, a leading modernist literary figure among the American expatriates in Paris, declared, "Everything is the same and everything is different." Apply her remark to the American dream today—and tomorrow. How do you define the American dream now? (Is there even an American dream anymore?) How has it remained the same? How has it changed? What forces might shape it in the future?

Assessing Learning

Check Test: True-False
1. World War I is often seen as the beginning of America's loss of innocence. [True]
2. Interest in psychoanalysis led to a general anxiety about the influence of the unconscious on people's actions. [True]
3. American writers were afraid to leave the country and live in Europe after World War I. [False]
4. Disillusionment was a major theme for many writers during the 1920s. [True]

5. Poets from New England maintained their dominant position in American literature after World War I. [False]

Interview Assessment
Have each student read a short work—a poem, review, letter, essay, or short story—by one of the authors mentioned in this essay. Remind them to choose something not included in this anthology. Students may want to find something by a writer they will not read in this unit, such as Dorothy Parker or Sherwood Anderson. Interview each student about how the piece he or she chose exemplifies the ideas discussed in this essay.

Collection 11

Loss and Redemption

Theme

Loss and Redemption: Questioning Values *Especially after the carnage of World War I, literature became more and more ironic. Writers reflected the widespread questioning of values that had once been taken for granted: How free is the individual? Do dreams drive us or are they merely illusions? Is life meaningful, or are we all driven by malignant forces beyond our control, even beyond our understanding?*

Reading the Anthology

Reaching Struggling Readers

The *Reading Skills and Strategies: Reaching Struggling Readers* binder includes a Reading Strategies Handbook that offers concrete suggestions to help students who have difficulty reading and comprehending text, or students who are reluctant readers. When a specific strategy is most appropriate for a selection, a correlation to the Handbook is provided at the bottom of the teacher's page under the head Reaching Struggling Readers. This head may also be used to introduce additional ideas for helping students read challenging texts.

Reading Beyond the Anthology

Read On

At the end of The Moderns collections, the grade eleven book includes an annotated bibliography of books suitable for extended reading. The suggested books are related to works in these collections by theme, by author, or by subject. To preview the Read On for The Moderns period, please turn to p. T800.

HRW Library

The *HRW Library* offers novels, plays, and short-story collections for extended reading. Each book in the Library includes one or more major works and thematically related Connections. The Connections are magazine articles, poems, or other pieces of literature. Each book in the *HRW Library* is also accompanied by a Study Guide that provides teaching suggestions and worksheets. For Collection 11, the following title is recommended.

ETHAN FROME Edith Wharton
Ethan Frome, married to a bitter, complaining woman, falls in love with a young woman who comes to help out on their bleak, lonesome farm. The young woman loves Ethan, but they are trapped in their isolated worlds. Written in 1911, the novel is a departure from Wharton's usual focus on high-society manners and intrigues.

Collection 11 Loss and Redemption

Resources for this Collection

Note: All resources for this collection are available for preview on the *One-Stop Planner CD-ROM 2 with Test Generator.* All worksheets and blackline masters may be printed from the CD-ROM.

Internet Resources
go.hrw.com LE0 11-11

Selection or Feature	Reading and Literary Skills	Vocabulary, Language, and Grammar
Wagner Matinée (p. 539) Willa Cather	• *Graphic Organizers for Active Reading,* Worksheet p. 49	• *Words to Own,* Worksheet p. 33 • *Grammar and Language Links:* Subject-Verb Agreement, Worksheet p. 45 • *Language Workshop CD-ROM,* Subject-Verb Agreement • *Daily Oral Grammar,* Transparency 34
His Father's Earth (p. 549) Thomas Wolfe	• *Graphic Organizers for Active Reading,* Worksheet p. 50	• *Words to Own,* Worksheet p. 34 • *Grammar and Language Links:* Active and Passive Voice, Worksheet p. 47; Common Usage Problems, Worksheet p. 49 • *Language Workshop CD-ROM,* Voice • *Daily Oral Grammar,* Transparency 35
Primary Sources: Frost on Frost's Diction (p. 559) • **Design** (p. 560) • **Nothing Gold Can Stay** (p. 562) **Connections: Trying to Name What Doesn't Change** (p. 563) Naomi Shihab Nye • **Once by the Pacific** (p. 564) • **Neither Out Far Nor In Deep** (p. 565) • **Birches** (p. 567) • **The Death of the Hired Man** (p. 569) Robert Frost **Primary Sources: "I must have the pulse beat of rhythm ..."** (p. 574) Robert Frost	• *Graphic Organizers for Active Reading,* Worksheet pp. 51, 52, 53, 54, 55, 56 • *Literary Elements:* Transparency 17 Worksheet p. 52	• *Daily Oral Grammar,* Transparency 36
Bells for John Whiteside's Daughter (p. 577) John Crowe Ransom	• *Graphic Organizers for Active Reading,* Worksheet p. 57	
Shine, Perishing Republic (p. 580) Robinson Jeffers	• *Graphic Organizers for Active Reading,* Worksheet p. 58	

Collection Planner

Other Resources for this Collection

- *Cross-Curricular Activities,* p. 11
- *Portfolio Management System,* Introduction to Portfolio Assessment, p. 1
- *Formal Assessment:* Literary Period Introduction Test, p. 109
- *Test Generator,* Collection Test

Writing	Listening and Speaking Viewing and Representing	Assessment
• *Portfolio Management System,* Rubrics for Choices, p. 154	• *Audio CD Library,* Disc 14, Track 2 • *Portfolio Management System,* Rubrics for Choices, p. 154	• *Formal Assessment,* Selection Test, p. 111 • *Test Generator (One-Stop Planner CD-ROM)* • *Preparation for College Admission Exams,* p. 39
• *Portfolio Management System,* Rubrics for Choices, p. 155	• *Audio CD Library,* Disc 14, Track 3 • *Viewing and Representing:* Fine Art Transparency 11 Worksheet p. 44 • *Portfolio Management System,* Rubrics for Choices, p. 155	• *Formal Assessment,* Selection Test, p. 113 • *Test Generator (One-Stop Planner CD-ROM)*
• *Portfolio Management System,* Rubrics for Choices, p. 156	• *Audio CD Library,* Disc 14, Tracks 4, 5, 6, 7, 8, 9, 10 • *Portfolio Management System,* Rubrics for Choices, p. 156	• *Formal Assessment,* Selection Test, p. 115 • *Test Generator (One-Stop Planner CD-ROM)*
• *Portfolio Management System,* Rubrics for Choices, p. 158	• *Audio CD Library,* Disc 14, Track 11 • *Portfolio Management System,* Rubrics for Choices, p. 158	• *Formal Assessment,* Selection Test, p. 117 • *Test Generator (One-Stop Planner CD-ROM)*
• *Portfolio Management System,* Rubrics for Choices, p. 159	• *Audio CD Library,* Disc 14, Track 12 • *Portfolio Management System,* Rubrics for Choices, p. 159	• *Formal Assessment,* Selection Test, p. 118 • *Test Generator (One-Stop Planner CD-ROM)*

 Transparency    CD-ROM    Video   Audio CD

Collection 11 Loss and Redemption

Skills Focus

Selection or Feature	Reading Skills and Strategies	Elements of Literature and Language	Writing	Listening and Speaking	Viewing and Representing
A Wagner Matinée (p. 539) Willa Cather		Setting, pp. 539, 547 Flashbacks, p. 547 Omniscient Narrator, p. 547 Theme, p. 547	Write an Essay Comparing Characters Across Texts, p. 547 Create Two Contrasting Settings, p. 547	Write an Interpretive Response to Music, p. 547	
His Father's Earth (p. 549) Thomas Wolfe	Clarify Responses to a Text, pp. 549, 557	Description, pp. 549, 557 Onomatopoeia, p. 557 Alliteration, p. 557 Catalogs, p. 557	Identify Interview Questions for an Author, p. 557 Write an Essay Comparing Whitman's Style with Wolfe's, p. 557 Write a Description Using a Catalog of Details, p. 557		Use a Graphic to Organize Information, p. 557
• **Design** (p. 560) • **Nothing Gold Can Stay** (p. 562) • **Once by the Pacific** (p. 564) • **Neither Out Far Nor In Deep** (p. 565) • **Birches** (p. 567) • **The Death of the Hired Man** (p. 569) Robert Frost	Compare the Tone and Message of Two Texts, p. 563 Reading Poetry, pp. 567–568 Drawing Inferences About Character, pp. 569, 575 Understanding Blank Verse, p. 575	Diction, p. 559 Sonnet, p. 560 Tone, pp. 561, 563, 566 Simile, pp. 561, 566, 568, 576 Rhyme Scheme, p. 561 Title, p. 562 Symbol, pp. 563, 566, 568 Rhyme, p. 563 Rhythm, p. 563 Alliteration, p. 563 Slant Rhyme, p. 563 Sound Effects, p. 563 Message, pp. 563, 566, 568, 575 Irony, p. 566 Parable, pp. 567–568 Blank Verse, pp. 567, 569, 575 Metaphor, pp. 568, 576 Moral, p. 568 Onomatopoeia, p. 568 Dialogue, pp. 569, 575–576 Setting, p. 575 Conflict, p. 576 Resolution, p. 576 Images, p. 576	Collect Ideas for an Analysis of Causes and Effects, p. 576 Write an Essay Exploring the "Dark Conflicts" in Frost's Poetry, p. 576 Write an Essay Comparing and Contrasting Two Poems by Different Authors, p. 576 Set the Poem in Contemporary Surroundings, p. 576	Participate in a Class Discussion of Frost's Links to the Puritans and the Romantics, p. 576	Use a Graphic to Organize Information, p. 576 Create a Collage Expressing Frost's Central Themes and Images, p. 576 Create a Multimedia Presentation of Frost's Poems, p. 576
Bells for John Whiteside's Daughter (p. 577) John Crowe Ransom	Identify Textual Support for an Interpretation, p. 579	Elegy, p. 577 Tone, pp. 577, 579 Theme, p. 579 Imagery, p. 579	Research a Topic Related to the New Criticism, p. 579 Write an Essay in Response to a Critical Comment, p. 579 Write an Essay Comparing Two Poems by Different Authors, p. 579		
Shine, Perishing Republic (p. 580) Robinson Jeffers		Implied Metaphor, p. 582	Brainstorm a List of Possible Topics for Writing, p. 582 Write an Essay Exploring the Validity of an Author's Viewpoint, p. 582		

Skills Focus

Cather

Wolfe

Frost

Ransom

Jeffers

On the rough wet grass of the back yard my father and mother have spread quilts. We all lie there, my mother, my father, my uncle, my aunt, and I too am lying there. First we were sitting up, then one of us lay down, and then we all lay down, on our stomachs, or on our sides, or on our backs, and they have kept on talking. They are not talking much, and the talk is quiet, of nothing in particular, or nothing at all in particular, of nothing at all. The stars are wide and alive, they seem each like a smile of great sweetness, and they seem very near. All my people are larger bodies than mine, quiet, with voices gentle and meaningless like the voices of sleeping birds. One is an artist, he is living at home. One is a musician, she is living at home. One is my mother who is good to me. One is my father who is good to me. By some chance, here they are, all on this earth; and who shall ever tell the sorrow of being on this earth, lying, on quilts, on the grass, in a summer evening, among the sounds of the night. May God bless my people, my uncle, my aunt, my mother, my good father, oh, remember them kindly in their time of trouble; and in the hour of their taking away.

—James Agee (1909–1955),
from "Knoxville: Summer 1915,"
from A Death in the Family

OBJECTIVES

1. Read literature of the Modern period on the theme "Loss and Redemption"
2. Interpret literary elements used in the literature
3. Apply a variety of reading strategies, including analysis of blank verse
4. Respond to the literature in a variety of modes
5. Learn and use new words
6. Collect ideas for an analysis of causes and effects

Responding to the Quotation

? **What impression do you have of the narrator? Why?** [Possible answer: The narrator is a child; he is the smallest person in the family; he is happy and secure; sentences like "One is an artist, he is living at home" suggest the simplicity of a child's picture book.] **Why might the family later be troubled?** [Possible answers: The title of the work suggests that someone has died—in the work itself, the boy's young father dies in an automobile accident; the year 1915 might suggest the family's involvement in World War I, a time of trouble for millions.]

Writing Focus: Analyzing Causes and Effects

WORK IN PROGRESS

The following **Work in Progress** assignments in this collection build to a culminating **Writer's Workshop** at the end of Collection 13.

- A Wagner Matinée — Take notes on how music affected character (p. 547)
- His Father's Earth — List cause/effect questions to ask subject of a biography (p. 557)
- Poems by Robert Frost — List speculative questions (p. 576)
- Bells for John Whiteside's Daughter — Research effects of New Criticism or of Fugitives (p. 579)
- Shine, Perishing Republic — List topics suggested by poem (p. 582)

Writer's Workshop: Expository Writing / Analyzing Causes and Effects (p. 685)

Planning

• **Block Schedule**
Block Scheduling Lesson Plans with Pacing Guide

• **Traditional Schedule**
Lesson Plans Including Strategies for English-Language Learners

• **One-Stop Planner**
CD-ROM with Test Generator

BROWSING IN THE FILES

Writers on Writing. "Art, it seems to me, should simplify," wrote Willa Cather in 1920. "Writing . . . should be an art, which is always a search for something for which there is no market demand, something new and untried, where the values are intrinsic and have nothing to do with standardized values. The courage to go on without compromise does not come to a writer all at once—nor, for that matter, does the ability. . . . In the beginning . . . [the artist's] vision is blurred by the memory of old delights he would like to recapture."

Willa Cather

(1873–1947)

Willa Cather, 1926 by Edward Steichen.
Courtesy George Eastman House. Reprinted with permission of Joanna T. Steichen.

Willa Cather was born in rural Virginia, the first of seven children. When she was nine, her father uprooted the family and headed for the untried lands of the West, settling in Webster County, Nebraska. She would later recall that this first encounter with the prairie was so striking that she felt "a kind of erasure of personality."

Nevertheless, Cather was stimulated by the hard life of the soil she saw around her, and she absorbed the stories of the immigrant families who were her neighbors. She read widely and became an outstanding student at the Red Cloud, Nebraska, school. In her boyish clothes and haircut, Willa was an unusual figure, and her teachers recognized in her an adolescent nonconformist.

While a freshman at the University of Nebraska, Cather published an essay in a Lincoln newspaper. She became a regular contributor to the newspaper and began to write poetry and stories. By the time Cather graduated in 1895, she had won a statewide reputation for brash, bright reviews. She moved to Pittsburgh and for a decade continued to work as a journalist. In 1903, she published her first book, a collection of verse entitled *April Twilights,* followed by *The Troll Garden,* a group of stories.

In 1906, the publisher S. S. McClure persuaded Cather to move to New York and join the staff of his dynamic, muckraking magazine, *McClure's.* For six years she served as a writer and editor, immersed in the social and political currents of the time; in 1912, she resigned from the magazine to give herself completely to writing fiction.

In 1908, Cather had met the Maine writer Sarah Orne Jewett (1849–1909), who had encouraged Cather to write about the themes and settings she knew best: the moral values of the hard-working immigrant families on the Midwestern prairie. Cather believed that these pioneers, who had sought to bring the wild, new land under cultivation, were heroic and that their era was the heart of the so-called American dream. She saw these immigrant settlers as contributing a cultural richness and an earthy love of life that were lacking in the pale, self-satisfied inhabitants of Eastern Seaboard cities. Cather developed these themes in *O Pioneers!* (1913), a novel whose title she borrowed from Walt Whitman, and in her novel *My Ántonia* (1918).

As Cather witnessed the decline of the agrarian ideal, her work became increasingly elegiac about the past and disillusioned with the present. *One of Ours* (1922), which was far from Cather's best novel but which won her the Pulitzer Prize, reflects Cather's dissatisfaction with the new people and machines who were betraying the pioneer ideal. "The world broke in two in 1922 or thereabout," Cather wrote, explaining that no one born in the twentieth century could grasp her own vision of America. She had seen her beloved Nebraska devastated by the machine, and she lamented the end of her epic vision of a noble society.

Cather reminds us of the novelist's duty to keep a wary eye on our relation to scientific progress. It was her profound intuition that a science that offers us new comfort, new speed, new security, and longer life will almost surely demand something of our spirit in return.

go.hrw.com
LE0 11-11

 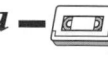

Before You Read

A Wagner Matinée

Make the Connection

Lost Pleasures

Most people can name at least one thing they enjoy that's a source of personal "bliss"—something they'd rather see, do, own, or listen to than anything else in the world. Sometimes circumstances in life force people to give up that beloved source of pleasure. Here is a story of a woman who has had to go without something important to her. As you will see, although Cather believed that Midwestern farm life fostered essential values, she was hardly a romantic who underestimated the hardships of that life, or the lost opportunities for some of the people who lived that life.

Quickwrite

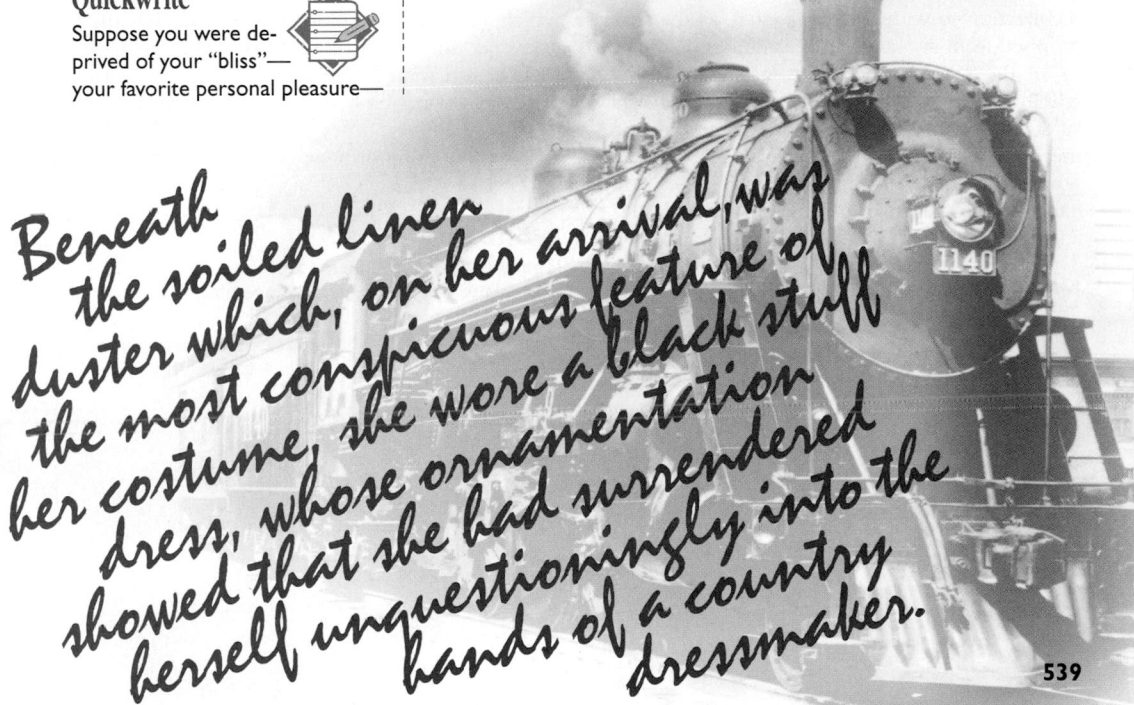

Suppose you were deprived of your "bliss"— your favorite personal pleasure— for many years, and then you had the opportunity to experience it again, but only briefly. Write your ideas about how you would respond. Would you seize the opportunity or pass up the chance for fear that it would be too painful to realize what you had been missing?

Elements of Literature

Setting

As in most of Cather's works, **setting** plays a central role in this story. Here, however, there are really two settings: Rural Nebraska—in which the narrator, like Cather, spent his formative years—is contrasted with Boston and its thriving cultural life.

> **S**etting is the time and location in which a story takes place.
>
> For more on Setting, see the Handbook of Literary Terms.

Background

Willa Cather loved music and was herself an accomplished musician. The story's title refers to the German composer Richard Wagner (rish'ärt väg'nər) (1813–1883), an outstanding Romantic composer of the nineteenth century. A matinée is an afternoon performance of a play or concert.

Beneath the soiled linen duster which, on her arrival, was the most conspicuous feature of her costume, she wore a black stuff dress, whose ornamentation showed that she had surrendered herself unquestioningly into the hands of a country dressmaker.

539

Summary ■■

The story opens in Boston, where the narrator, Clark, receives a letter from his uncle Howard asking him to look after his wife, Georgiana, during her forthcoming visit to the city from Nebraska. Clark recalls the unlikely marriage of Georgiana, then a thirty-year-old music teacher from Boston, and twenty-one-year-old Howard, an idle country boy. Clark remembers his first exposure to music, Shakespeare, and Classical culture at Aunt Georgiana's hands. With gratitude and affection, he takes her to a concert the next afternoon. Georgiana is spellbound by the music and musicians, which cause her to recall her youthful career. At the end of the concert, she breaks down, because she will once again have to abandon music and return to the desolate Nebraska farm.

Background

Make sure students understand that this story deals with an era in which there were no radios or recorded music. Any music one heard had to be performed live. In Boston, people could attend classical concerts and recitals, but on the remote Nebraska plains, there would be no such opportunities.

From the 1850s until after World War I, the majority of classical conductors and musicians in the United States were German or Austrian. This is why Richard Wagner was so well represented on concert programs. Because Germany became an enemy of the United States during both world wars, audiences began losing their taste for German music, and the composers of other countries began to balance concert programs.

Preteaching Vocabulary

Words to Own

Have students read the Words to Own and their definitions, listed at the bottom of the selection pages. Then, have students choose partners. The first student gives his or her partner a word. The second student has to use it correctly in a sentence. Have partners alternate roles until both have used all the words correctly. Then, have students complete the following exercise, filling in the blank with the correct word.

1. Dimitri Karamazov argues with his father over the _____ he inherits from his mother. [legacy]
2. Dorothy felt _____ as she approached the Witch. [trepidation]
3. Elizabeth Bennet found Mr. Collins too _____ and self-righteous. [pious]
4. Jean Valjean spent many years on the run, _____ the pursuing Javert. [eluding]

A Wagner Matinée

Willa Cather

A Elements of Literature

Setting

? What do these details reveal about the place that the letter comes from? [It is rustic and isolated.] What do the details suggest about Uncle Howard? [He is somewhat irresponsible about his wife's well-being.]

B Elements of Literature

Setting

? What does Clark's feeling suggest about the two settings of the city and the farm? [They are different as can be; people who live in one would not be comfortable in the other.] How do you think Georgiana will react to the city? [She may find it overwhelming or frightening.]

C Elements of Literature

Characterization

? What impression do you have of Georgiana? How has Cather created this impression? [She is timid and dazed; she is not self-reliant; she is feeble. Cather says Georgiana does not seem to recognize Clark and is covered with dust.]

D Elements of Literature

Simile

After students have read this entire paragraph, ask what the effect of Clark's comparison is. [Possible answers: It underlines the difference between Nebraska and the city; it suggests that Georgiana's choice to marry and leave Boston was as much a sacrifice as an explorer's injuries.]

A Wagner Matinée

Willa Cather

I received one morning a letter, written in pale ink on glassy, blue-lined note paper, and bearing the postmark of a little Nebraska village. This communication, worn and rubbed, looking as though it had been carried for some days in a coat pocket that was none too clean, was from my Uncle Howard and informed me that his wife had been left a small legacy by a bachelor relative who had recently died, and that it would be necessary for her to go to Boston to attend to the settling of the estate. He requested me to meet her at the station and render her whatever services might be necessary. On examining the date indicated as that of her arrival, I found it no later than tomorrow. He had characteristically delayed writing until, had I been away from home for a day, I must have missed the good woman altogether.

The name of Aunt Georgiana called up not alone her own figure, at once pathetic and grotesque, but opened before my feet a gulf of recollection so wide and deep, that, as the letter dropped from my hand, I felt suddenly a stranger to all the present conditions of my existence, wholly ill at ease and out of place amid the familiar surroundings of my study. I became, in short, the gangling farmer-boy my aunt had known, scourged with chilblains[1] and bashfulness, my hands cracked and sore from the cornhusking. I felt the knuckles of my thumb tentatively, as

1. **chilblains** (chil'blāns'): inflammation of the hands and feet, caused by exposure to cold.

though they were raw again. I sat again before her parlor organ, fumbling the scales with my stiff, red hands, while she, beside me, made canvas mittens for the huskers.

The next morning, after preparing my landlady somewhat, I set out for the station. When the train arrived I had some difficulty in finding my aunt. She was the last of the passengers to alight, and it was not until I got her into the carriage that she seemed really to recognize me. She had come all the way in a day coach; her linen duster had become black with soot and her black bonnet gray with dust during the journey. When we arrived at my boardinghouse the landlady put her to bed at once and I did not see her again until the next morning.

Whatever shock Mrs. Springer experienced at my aunt's appearance, she considerately concealed. As for myself, I saw my aunt's misshapen figure with that feeling of awe and respect with which we behold explorers who have left their ears and fingers north of Franz Josef Land,[2] or their health somewhere along the upper Congo. My Aunt Georgiana had been a music teacher at

2. **Franz Josef Land:** group of islands in the Arctic Ocean.

WORDS TO OWN
legacy (leg'ə·sē) *n.*: inheritance.
grotesque (grō·tesk') *adj.*: strange; absurd.

Reaching All Students

Struggling Readers

You can help students summarize Georgiana's motivations and actions in the story by introducing the strategy called Somebody Wanted But So. For thorough instructions on how to apply this strategy, see the *Reading Strategies Handbook*, p. 111 in the *Reading Skills and Strategies* binder.

English Language Learners

Students who are not familiar with U.S. geography and history may not understand the differences between a Nebraska village and Boston. Most students, however, will know the differences between country life and city life. Discuss these differences. Show students a map of the United States, and show pictures of Nebraska and Boston. Talk about the distance between the two locales and common means of travel at the time of the story.

Advanced Learners

Suggest to students that "A Wagner Matinée" might be read as an ironic or tragic fairy tale. Have them read it a second time with this idea in mind, looking for motifs and allusions that suggest such stories as "Cinderella" and "Sleeping Beauty." Ask students to note how Cather alters the traditional fairy tale to make her story ironic. Students can write brief essays exploring this idea.

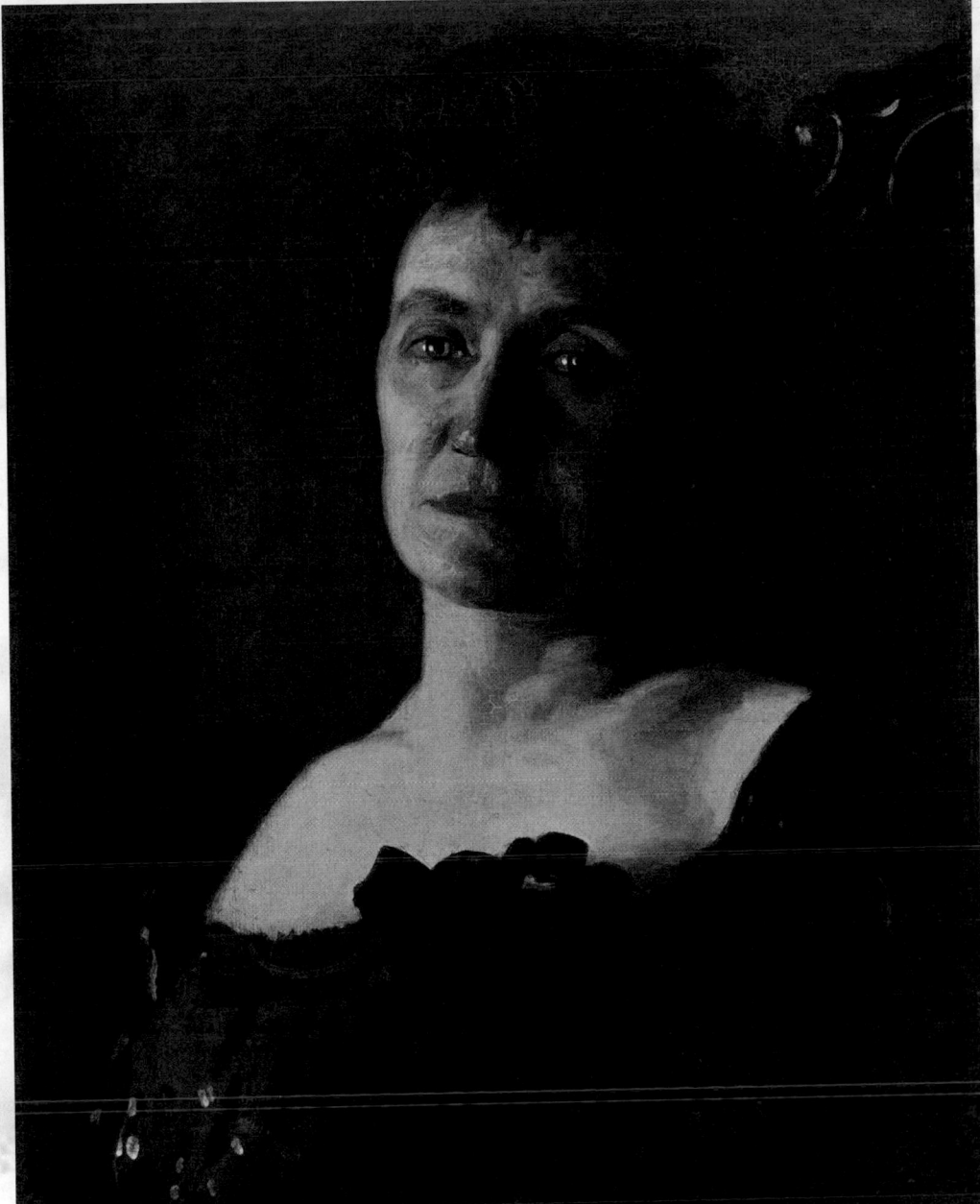

Edith Mahon (1904) by Thomas Eakins. Oil on canvas (20″ x 16″).
Smith College Museum of Art, Northampton, Massachusetts. Purchased Drayton Hillyer Fund, 1931.

Professional Notes

Critical Comment: Henri's Homage to Eakins

"I consider [Eakins] the greatest portrait painter America has produced," wrote American painter Robert Henri to his students in 1917. "Being a great portrait painter, he was, as usual, commissioned to paint only a very few. But he had friends and he painted his friends. Look at these portraits well. . . . You will find yourself, through the works, in close contact with a man who was strong, profound, and hon-

est, and, above all, one who had attained the reality of beauty in nature as it is; who was in love with the great mysterious nature as manifested in man and things, who had no need to falsify to make romantic, or to sentimentalize to make beautiful. Look, if you will, at the great Gross clinic picture for the real stupendous romance in real life. . . . Eakins's pictures and his sculptures are the recordings of a man who

lived and studied and loved with a strong heart."

Have students examine *Edith Mahon* in light of this comment. Then, have them locate and study more reproductions of Eakins's work (or originals, if possible). Have students agree or disagree with Henri's assessment of Eakins and explain why. Then, have students consider whether Henri's comments might apply to Cather and her story.

the Boston Conservatory, somewhere back in the latter sixties. One summer, while visiting in the little village among the Green Mountains where her ancestors had dwelt for generations, she had kindled the callow fancy of the most idle and shiftless of all the village lads, and had conceived for this Howard Carpenter one of those extravagant passions which a handsome country boy of twenty-one sometimes inspires in an angular, spectacled woman of thirty. When she returned to her duties in Boston, Howard followed her, and the upshot of this inexplicable infatuation was that she eloped with him, eluding the reproaches of her family and the criticisms of her friends by going with him to the Nebraska frontier. Carpenter, who, of course, had no money, had taken a homestead in Red Willow County, fifty miles from the railroad. There they had measured off their quarter section themselves by driving across the prairie in a wagon, to the wheel of which they had tied a red cotton handkerchief, and counting off its revolutions. They built a dugout in the red hillside, one of those cave dwellings whose inmates so often reverted to primitive conditions. Their water they got from the lagoons where the buffalo drank, and their slender stock of provisions was always at the mercy of bands of roving Indians. For thirty years my aunt had not been further than fifty miles from the homestead.

But Mrs. Springer knew nothing of all this, and must have been considerably shocked at what was left of my kinswoman. Beneath the soiled linen duster which, on her arrival, was the most conspicuous feature of her costume, she wore a black stuff[3] dress, whose ornamentation showed that she had surrendered herself unquestioningly into the hands of a country dressmaker. My poor aunt's figure, however, would have presented astonishing difficulties to any dressmaker. Originally stooped, her shoulders were now almost bent together over her sunken chest. She wore no stays,[4] and her gown, which trailed unevenly behind, rose in a sort of peak over her abdomen. She wore ill-fitting false teeth, and her skin was as yellow as a Mongolian's from constant exposure to a pitiless wind and to the alkaline water which hardens the most transparent cuticle into a sort of flexible leather.

I owed to this woman most of the good that ever came my way in my boyhood, and had a reverential affection for her. During the years when I was riding herd for my uncle, my aunt, after cooking the three meals—the first of which was ready at six o'clock in the morning—and putting the six children to bed, would often stand until midnight at her ironing board, with me at the kitchen table beside her, hearing me recite Latin declensions and conjugations, gently shaking me when my drowsy head sank down over a page of irregular verbs. It was to her, at her ironing or mending, that I read my first Shakespeare, and her old textbook on mythology was the first that ever came into my empty hands. She taught me my scales and exercises, too—on the little parlor organ, which her husband had bought her after fifteen years, during which she had not so much as seen any instrument, but an accordion that belonged to one of the Norwegian farmhands. She would sit beside me by the hour, darning and counting while I struggled with the "Joyous Farmer," but she seldom talked to me about music, and I understood why. She was a pious woman; she had the consolations of religion and, to her at least, her martyrdom was not wholly sordid. Once when I had been doggedly beating out some easy passages from an old score of *Euryanthe* I had found among her music books, she came up to me and, putting her hands over my eyes, gently drew my head back upon her shoulder, saying tremulously, "Don't love it so well, Clark, or it may be taken from you. Oh! dear boy, pray that whatever your sacrifice may be, it be not that."

When my aunt appeared on the morning after her arrival, she was still in a semisomnambulant[5] state. She seemed not to realize that she was in the city where she had spent her youth, the place longed for hungrily half a lifetime. She had been so wretchedly trainsick throughout the journey

5. **semisomnambulant** (sem'ē·säm·nam'byo͞o·lənt): confused and unperceiving, as if sleepwalking.

- -

WORDS TO OWN
eluding (ē·lo͞od'iŋ) *v.* used as *adj.*: escaping.
reverential (rev'ə·ren'shəl) *adj.*: deeply respectful.
pious (pī'əs) *adj.*: devoted to one's religion.

- -

3. **stuff:** cloth, usually woolen.
4. **stays:** a corset, or figure-enhancing women's undergarment, stiffened as with whalebone.

542 THE MODERNS

that she had no recollection of anything but her discomfort, and, to all intents and purposes, there were but a few hours of nightmare between the farm in Red Willow County and my study on Newbury Street. I had planned a little pleasure for her that afternoon, to repay her for some of the glorious moments she had given me when we used to milk together in the straw-thatched cowshed and she, because I was more than usually tired, or because her husband had spoken sharply to me, would tell me of the splendid performance of the *Huguenots*[6] she had seen in Paris, in her youth. At two o'clock the Symphony Orchestra was to give a Wagner program, and I intended to take my aunt; though, as I conversed with her, I grew doubtful about her enjoyment of it. Indeed, for her own sake, I could only wish her taste for such things quite dead, and the long struggle mercifully ended at last. I suggested our visiting the Conservatory and the Common before lunch, but she seemed altogether too timid to wish to venture out. She questioned me absently about various changes in the city, but she was chiefly concerned that she had forgotten to leave instructions about feeding half-skimmed milk to a certain weakling calf, "old Maggie's calf, you know, Clark," she explained, evidently having forgotten how long I had been away. She was further troubled because she had neglected to tell her daughter about the freshly opened kit of mackerel in the cellar, which would spoil if it were not used directly.

I asked her whether she had ever heard any of the Wagnerian operas, and found that she had not, though she was perfectly familiar with their respective situations, and had once possessed the piano score of *The Flying Dutchman*. I began to think it would have been best to get her back to Red Willow County without waking her, and regretted having suggested the concert.

From the time we entered the concert hall, however, she was a trifle less passive and inert, and for the first time seemed to perceive her surroundings. I had felt some trepidation lest she might become aware of the absurdities of her attire, or might experience some painful embarrassment at stepping suddenly into the world to

6. *Huguenots* (hyōō′gə·näts): opera by Giacomo Meyerbeer about the violent struggle between Catholics and Protestants in sixteenth-century France.

which she had been dead for a quarter of a century. But, again, I found how superficially I had judged her. She sat looking about her with eyes as impersonal, almost as stony, as those with which the granite Ramses[7] in a museum watches the froth and fret[8] that ebbs and flows about his pedestal—separated from it by the lonely stretch of centuries. I have seen this same aloofness in old miners who drift into the Brown Hotel at Denver, their pockets full of bullion, their linen soiled, their haggard faces unshaven; standing in the thronged corridors as solitary as though they were still in a frozen camp on the Yukon, conscious that certain experiences have isolated them from their fellows by a gulf no haberdasher[9] could bridge.

We sat at the extreme left of the first balcony, facing the arc of our own and the balcony above us, veritable hanging gardens, brilliant as tulip beds. The matinée audience was made up chiefly of women. One lost the contour of faces and figures, indeed any effect of line whatever, and there was only the color of bodices past counting, the shimmer of fabrics soft and firm, silky and sheer; red, mauve, pink, blue, lilac, purple, ecru, rose, yellow, cream, and white, all the colors that an impressionist finds in a sunlit landscape, with here and there the dead shadow of a frock coat. My Aunt Georgiana regarded them as though they had been so many daubs of tube paint on a palette.

When the musicians came out and took their places, she gave a little stir of anticipation and looked with quickening interest down over the rail at that invariable grouping, perhaps the first wholly familiar thing that had greeted her eye since she had left old Maggie and her weakling calf. I could feel how all those details sank into her soul, for I had not forgotten how they had

7. **Ramses** (ram′sēz′): one of the kings of ancient Egypt.
8. **froth and fret:** agitated waters moving around obstacles.
9. **haberdasher** (hab′ər·dash′ər): one who sells men's clothing. A men's clothing store is sometimes called a haberdashery.

WORDS TO OWN

inert (in·urt′) *adj.*: inactive; dull.
trepidation (trep′ə·dā′shən) *n.*: anxious uncertainty.

WILLA CATHER 543

G **Elements of Literature**
  Characterization
? What does this information reveal about Aunt Georgiana? [She is unselfish; to comfort another person, she revisits the rich memories that make her suffer because they remind her of the music and culture she left behind.]

H **Elements of Literature**
  Setting
? Why does Cather provide these details about the farm? What do they reveal about Aunt Georgiana? [They show how far she has traveled: from high culture to agriculture; from wealth and comfort (Paris) to poverty and hardship (not wasting the mackerel). She is now thoroughly absorbed in the life of the farm.]

I **Advanced Learners**
  Motif
Explore the recurring motif of sleep that is associated with Aunt Georgiana. On p. 540, she is put to bed for an entire day by the landlady. On p. 542, she is described as "semisomnambulant," and here Clark is afraid of "waking" her. Discuss the ways Georgiana could be said to be sleeping. Students could also look up the plot of Wagner's *The Twilight of the Gods,* the last part of the *Ring* cycle, in which sleep is a recurring theme.

J **Elements of Literature**
  Simile
? What aspects of Aunt Georgiana does this simile capture? [It captures her lack of motion, her distance from the contemporary age, and her ostensible detachment from everything but the mundane operation of the farm.]

K **Cultural Connection**
  Impressionism
Impressionism was a late-nineteenth-century movement in painting developed by Monet, Renoir, and Degas and extended by Seurat and Signac. It was characterized by the use of small strokes of unmixed primary colors to depict the subject through the play of reflected light. Ask students how Cather uses this comparison with Impressionism to convey Aunt Georgiana's experience. [Possible response: Her experience of these unfamiliar surroundings is a fleeting play of hazy impressions—only the musicians are sharp and distinct.]

Skill Link

Analyzing the Melodies of Language

Explain that writers use punctuation and phrasing to create rhythm in prose, as well as in poetry. Point out that they use sound effects, such as onomatopoeia and alliteration, to underscore meaning and bring out imagery.

1. Read aloud the paragraph that begins "We sat at the extreme left . . ." on p. 543. Discuss the rhythms created by the lists of phrases and words and those created by longer phrases and clauses. How do they

contribute to the effect of the passage? Discuss the use of onomatopoeia and alliteration. How do they extend these images?

2. Tell students to read the paragraph on p. 544 beginning "The first number was the *Tannhäuser* overture." Have them determine the effect Cather creates in this passage and analyze how rhythm and sound effects reinforce the images.

sunk into mine when I came fresh from plowing forever and forever between green aisles of corn, where, as in a treadmill, one might walk from daybreak to dusk without perceiving a shadow of change. The clean profiles of the musicians, the gloss of their linen, the dull black of their coats, the beloved shapes of the instruments, the patches of yellow light thrown by the green shaded lamps on the smooth, varnished bellies of the cellos and the bass viols in the rear, the restless, wind-tossed forest of fiddle necks and bows—I recalled how, in the first orchestra I had ever heard, those long bow strokes seemed to draw the heart out of me, as a conjurer's stick reels out yards of paper ribbon from a hat.

The first number was the *Tannhäuser*[10] overture. When the horns drew out the first strain of the Pilgrim's chorus, my Aunt Georgiana clutched my coat sleeve. Then it was I first realized that for her this broke a silence of thirty years; the inconceivable silence of the plains. With the battle between the two motives, with the frenzy of the Venusberg theme and its ripping of strings, there came to me an overwhelming sense of the waste and wear we are so powerless to combat; and I saw again the tall, naked house on the prairie, black and grim as a wooden fortress; the black pond where I had learned to swim, its margin pitted with sun-dried cattle tracks; the rain-gullied clay banks about the naked house, the four dwarf ash seedlings where the dishcloths were always hung to dry before the kitchen door. The world there was the flat world of the ancients; to the east, a cornfield that stretched to daybreak; to the west, a corral that reached to sunset; between, the conquests of peace, dearer bought than those of war.

The overture closed, my aunt released my coat sleeve, but she said nothing. She sat staring at the orchestra through a dullness of thirty years, through the films made little by little by each of the three hundred and sixty-five days in every one of them. What, I wondered, did she get from it? She had been a good pianist in her day I knew, and her musical education had been broader than that of most music teachers of a quarter of a century ago. She had often told me of Mozart's operas

---

10. *Tannhäuser* (tän′hoi′zər): Wagner's opera about German minstrels in the thirteenth century.

544 THE MODERNS

and Meyerbeer's, and I could remember hearing her sing, years ago, certain melodies of Verdi's. When I had fallen ill with a fever in her house she used to sit by my cot in the evening—when the cool, night wind blew in through the faded mosquito netting tacked over the window and I lay watching a certain bright star that burned red above the cornfield—and sing "Home to our mountains, O, let us return!" in a way fit to break the heart of a Vermont boy near dead of homesickness already.

I watched her closely through the prelude to *Tristan and Isolde*, trying vainly to conjecture what that seething turmoil of strings and winds might mean to her, but she sat mutely staring at the violin bows that drove obliquely downward, like the pelting streaks of rain in a summer shower. Had this music any message for her? Had she enough left to at all comprehend this power which had kindled the world since she had left it? I was in a fever of curiosity, but Aunt Georgiana sat silent upon her peak in Darien.[11] She preserved this utter immobility throughout the number from *The Flying Dutchman*, though her fingers worked mechanically upon her black dress, as though, of themselves, they were recalling the piano score they had once played. Poor old hands! They had been stretched and twisted into mere tentacles to hold and lift and knead with; the palms unduly swollen, the fingers bent and knotted—on one of them a thin, worn band that had once been a wedding ring. As I pressed and gently quieted one of those groping hands, I remembered with quivering eyelids their services for me in other days.

Soon after the tenor began the "Prize Song,"[12] I heard a quick drawn breath and turned to my aunt. Her eyes were closed, but the tears were glistening on her cheeks, and I think, in a moment more, they were in my eyes as well. It never really died, then—the soul that can suffer so excruciatingly

---

11. silent . . . Darien: allusion to John Keats's "On First Looking into Chapman's Homer," a poem about Keats's awe in the presence of a literary work of art.
12. "Prize Song": aria from the third act of Wagner's opera *Die Meistersinger von Nürnberg*.

WORDS TO OWN
obliquely (ō·blēk′lē) *adv.*: at a slant.

Crossing the Curriculum

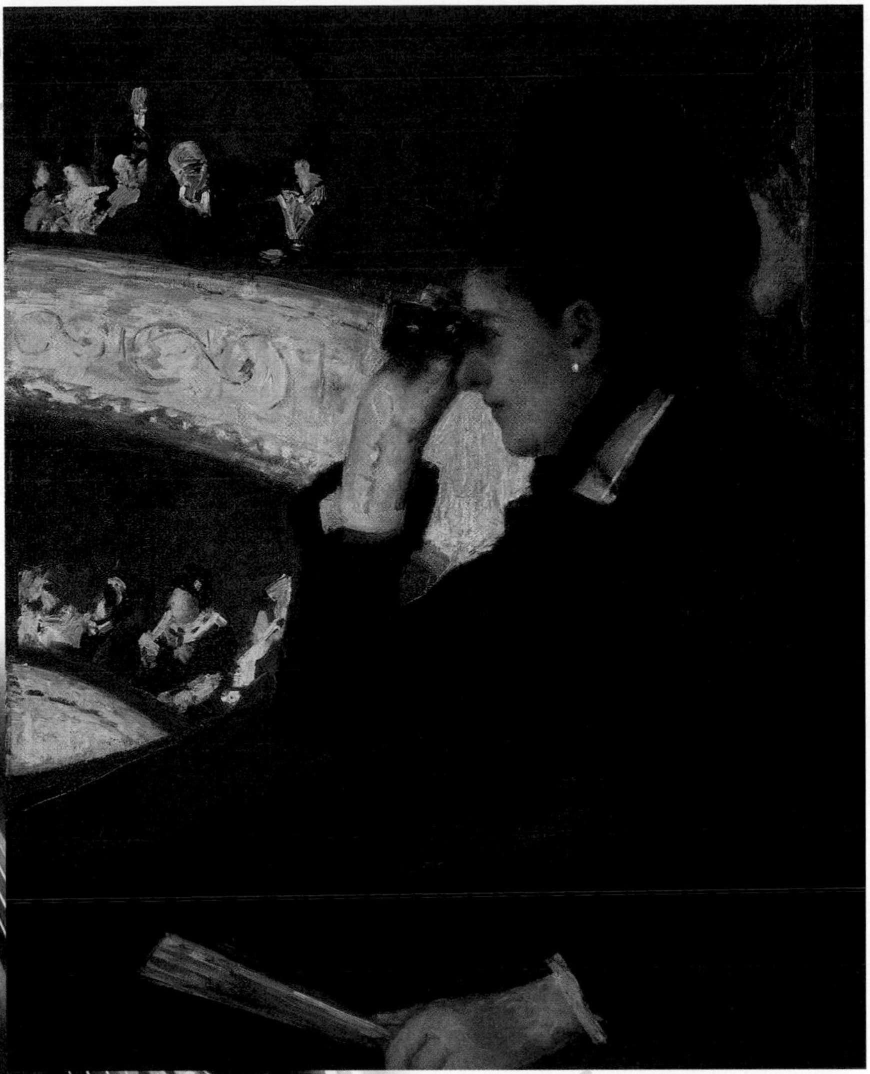

Museum of Fine Arts, Boston. Charles Henry Hayden Fund (10.35). Photograph courtesy of Museum of Fine Arts, Boston.

At the Opera (1879) by Mary Cassatt.
Oil on canvas (31½″ × 25½″).

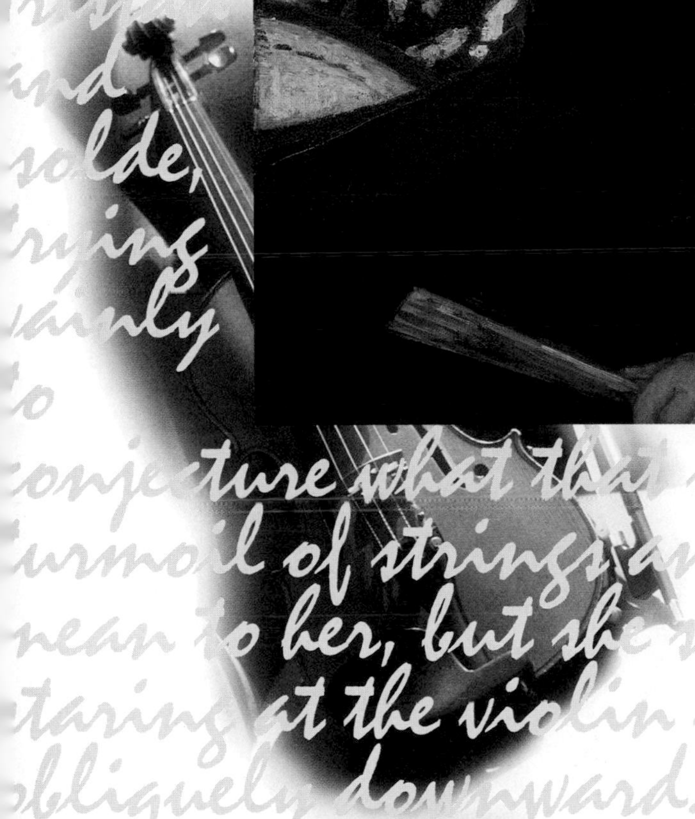

RESPONDING TO THE ART

Mary Cassatt (1844–1926) is considered one of the most important American artists of the nineteenth century. She left her native Philadelphia to study art in Paris and remained in France for the rest of her long career. She became one of the circle of French Impressionists, among whom her first and closest friend was Edgar Degas. She was represented in the Impressionist exhibits, and her male colleagues, such as Degas and Manet, greatly admired and respected her work. Toward the end of her life, Cassatt's eyesight began to fail, and she had all but stopped painting by 1915.

Cassatt painted many portraits of women: mothers with children, sisters, and society women like the one shown here. In *At the Opera,* Cassatt carefully modulates detail, color, and line to capture the unique play of light and perspective in the theater box, just as a spectator might see it. Have students take note of the man in the upper left, who watches the woman in the foreground as intently as she watches the stage.

Activity. Ask how this painting helps students appreciate Cather's description of the concert hall. [Possible answers: It shows the bright gowns and black frock coats Cather describes; it depicts an intent listener who shares Georgiana's silent awe at the music.]

Listening to Music

"Siegfried Idyll," performed by the New York Philharmonic Orchestra.

"Ride of the Valkyries," "*Gotterdammerung:* Siegfried's Funeral Music," "*Tannhaüser:* Overture," all performed by the Slovak State Philharmonic Orchestra.

Share the information about Wagner in the annotations in this teacher's edition on p. T544. Explain to students that when this story was written, Wagner's grandiose Romantic music was new to American ears; it was revolutionary.

Activities

1. Have students listen to some of the pieces on the concert program. "The Ride of the Valkyries" is probably Wagner's most accessible composition, and it may sound familiar to students; it is often used in movies, cartoons, and commercials. Students might also listen to the *Tannhaüser* overture (which may also sound familiar), the "Siegfried Idyll," and Siegfried's funeral march.
2. Suggest that students listen to each piece two or three times; none is long, but all are dense and cannot be fully comprehended on one hearing. After listening, students should discuss their impressions of the music. Have them explain how this activity enriched Cather's story for them.

? Consider the relationships Georgiana has with Clark and with the German cow-puncher. How are they alike? What can you infer about her relationship with Howard? [Possible answers: She loved to teach and share her love of music with both young men, who came into her life like surrogate children, and she was deeply hurt by the loss of those bonds. She may have tried to interest Howard in music, but failed.]

B Humanities Connection

Giuseppe Verdi and Wagner were born in the same year. *Il Trovatore* and the first part of the *Ring* were written at the same time—when Georgiana would have been in her early twenties. *Trovatore* is a traditional opera of arias and choruses strung together with recitatives (explanatory passages sung in a declamatory manner). Although it has many popular melodies, *Trovatore* is considered far from Giuseppe Verdi's best opera.

C Cultural Connections

? In the last part of the *Ring* cycle, Hagen plots against the hero, Siegfried, giving him a potion that makes him forget his bride, Brünnhilde. Brünnhilde believes herself to be betrayed by Siegfried. Hagen then gives Siegfried a second potion that restores his memory of Brünnhilde and his love for her before stabbing Siegfried in the back. Brünnhilde sacrifices herself on Siegfried's funeral pyre. Why do you think Cather chose to close the program that Georgiana and Clark hear with Siegfried's funeral march? [Possible answer: Georgiana expects to return to her farm soon, and leaving the music behind a second time represents the death of something vital inside her. Like Siegfried, she "awakens" from forgetfulness, only to experience the loss again.]

D Elements of Literature
Setting

? What strikes you most about this comparison? [Possible answer: For the first time, the city is likened to the plains—a sign that Georgiana must now face her return to Nebraska.] What is the effect of this image? [Possible answer: It underlines the desolation of life without music.]

and so interminably; it withers to the outward eye only; like that strange moss which can lie on a dusty shelf half a century and yet, if placed in water, grows green again. She wept so throughout the development and elaboration of the melody.

During the intermission before the second half of the concert, I questioned my aunt and found that the "Prize Song" was not new to her. Some years before there had drifted to the farm in Red Willow County a young German, a tramp cow-puncher, who had sung the chorus at Bayreuth,[13] when he was a boy, along with the other peasant boys and girls. Of a Sunday morning he used to sit on his gingham-sheeted bed in the hands' bedroom which opened off the kitchen, cleaning the leather of his boots and saddle, singing the "Prize Song," while my aunt went about her work in the kitchen. She had hovered about him until she had prevailed upon him to join the country church, though his sole fitness for this step, in so far as I could gather, lay in his boyish face and his possession of this divine melody. Shortly afterward he had gone to town on the Fourth of July, been drunk for several days, lost his money at a faro[14] table, ridden a saddled Texan steer on a bet, and disappeared with a fractured collarbone. All this my aunt told me huskily, wanderingly, as though she were talking in the weak lapses of illness.

"Well, we have come to better things than the old *Trovatore*[15] at any rate, Aunt Georgie?" I queried, with a well-meant effort at jocularity.

Her lip quivered and she hastily put her handkerchief up to her mouth. From behind it she murmured, "And you have been hearing this ever since you left me, Clark?" Her question was the gentlest and saddest of reproaches.

The second half of the program consisted of four numbers from the *Ring*,[16] and closed with Siegfried's funeral march. My aunt wept quietly, but almost continuously, as a shallow vessel

13. **Bayreuth** (bī·roit′): Bavarian city that hosts an annual festival of Wagnerian music.
14. **faro** (fer′ō): gambling game played with cards.
15. *Trovatore* (trô′vä·tô′rä): opera by the Italian composer Giuseppe Verdi.
16. *Ring:* Wagner's *Der Ring des Nibelungen,* a cycle of four operas based on traditional Germanic, Scandinavian, and Icelandic myths and legends.

overflows in a rainstorm. From time to time her dim eyes looked up at the lights which studded the ceiling, burning softly under their dull glass globes; doubtless they were stars in truth to her. I was still perplexed as to what measure of musical comprehension was left to her, she who had heard nothing but the singing of gospel hymns at Methodist services in the square frame schoolhouse on Section Thirteen for so many years. I was wholly unable to gauge how much of it had been dissolved in soapsuds, or worked into bread, or milked into the bottom of a pail.

The deluge of sound poured on and on; I never knew what she found in the shining current of it; I never knew how far it bore her, or past what happy islands. From the trembling of her face I could well believe that before the last numbers she had been carried out where the myriad graves are, into the gray, nameless burying grounds of the sea; or into some world of death vaster yet, where, from the beginning of the world, hope has lain down with hope and dream with dream and, renouncing, slept.

The concert was over; the people filed out of the hall chattering and laughing, glad to relax and find the living level again, but my kinswoman made no effort to rise. The harpist slipped its green felt cover over his instrument; the flute players shook the water from their mouthpieces; the men of the orchestra went out one by one, leaving the stage to the chairs and music stands, empty as a winter cornfield.

I spoke to my aunt. She burst into tears and sobbed pleadingly. "I don't want to go, Clark, I don't want to go!"

I understood. For her, just outside the door of the concert hall, lay the black pond with the cattle-tracked bluffs; the tall, unpainted house, with weather-curled boards; naked as a tower, the crook-backed ash seedlings where the dishcloths hung to dry; the gaunt, molting turkeys picking up refuse about the kitchen door.

Assessing Learning

Check Test: True-False
1. Clark lives in Boston. [True]
2. When Clark was young, Georgiana taught him to play the cello. [False]
3. Although Georgiana always loved music, she was not a trained musician. [False]
4. Verdi and Wagner composed all the pieces on the concert program. [False]
5. Clark invites Georgiana to stay with him in Boston instead of returning to Nebraska. [False]

Making the Connections

Connecting to the Theme: "Loss and Redemption"
After students have finished reading the story, discuss the collection theme. Has Georgiana lost anything by going to the concert? If so, what? Has the concert helped her redeem a loss? If so, how? How will she cope with this experience in the future? Students can share their ideas and responses in a class discussion.

First Thoughts

1. Georgiana says about music, "Don't love it so well, Clark, or it may be taken from you." How do you feel about her attitude?

Shaping Interpretations

2. Locate passages in which Clark, the first-person narrator, actually acts as an **omniscient narrator.** How would you characterize Clark? Why do you think Cather didn't use a woman's voice to tell this story?

3. In contrast to the music and the concert hall is the emotional effect of the Nebraska frontier—the **setting** we hear about over and over again in the story. How does Cather want you to feel about the Nebraska setting? What specific images create this "feeling"?

4. Summarize in your own words what you think Clark "understands" at the end of the story.

5. What seems to be Cather's **theme** in the story? How would you say the central episode of the concert contributes to this theme?

Connecting with the Text

6. Would you have attended the concert or avoided it? Why? (Refer to your Quick-write notes in your answer.)

Extending the Text

7. If this story were told by a Romantic, how would Aunt Georgiana's visit to Boston have turned

Reading Check

a. Numerous **flash-backs** in the story provide information about Aunt Georgiana's life after her move to Nebraska. Describe some of her hardships and disappointments.

b. Explain why the narrator feels he owes a great debt to Aunt Georgiana. What special treat has he planned for Aunt Georgiana in Boston? How does she react to this opportunity?

out? How do you think a Romantic writer would have described the Nebraska farm setting?

CHOICES: Building Your Portfolio

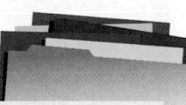

Writer's Notebook

1. Collecting Ideas for an Analysis of Causes and Effects

The powerful attraction of music is a **theme** that often recurs in Cather's fiction. Find recordings of some of the works of Richard Wagner. As you listen, write down your feelings about the emotional effects of this music. Speculate on the effect Wagner's music might have had on Georgiana's imagination and feelings. Do you think Cather succeeded in conveying the emotional effects anyone might experience in listening to any kind of music? Save your notes for possible use in the Writer's Workshop on page 685.

Comparing Characters Across Texts

2. Linked Lives

In what ways is Aunt Georgiana's experience like the experience of Mrs. Sommers in Kate Chopin's story "A Pair of Silk Stockings" (page 437)? Write a brief essay comparing the two women and their afternoons of escape. For each character, consider her life at the beginning of the story, her past life, her wants and needs, and her reactions to her "escape."

Creative Writing

3. The Power of a Setting

Cather's imagery creates a striking contrast between two very different **settings**—a bustling city with its rich cultural life and an isolated, windswept farm. Write a description of two very different settings that you might use in a short story. Create clear images and details to convey the distinct emotional impact of each setting.

WILLA CATHER **547**

First Thoughts [Respond]

1. Possible responses: Agree; it is better to guard against the pain of loss. Disagree; the joy of loving is worth the risk of suffering.

Shaping Interpretations [Interpret]

2. During the concert, Clark interprets Georgiana's thoughts for the reader. Clark seems sensitive, affectionate, and kind. Possible answer: Cather wanted to contrast the effects of Georgiana's character on three men: Howard, Clark, and the German cow-puncher.

3. Cather emphasizes the bleakness and isolation of the Nebraska setting with phrases like "black and grim," "silence of the plains," "flat," and "naked house."

4. Possible answer: He understands exactly how bleak and barren Georgiana finds her life.

5. Possible answers: It is not worth the sacrifice of one's soul (music) for security and affection (marriage to young Howard). Life's passions can be stifled and silenced but never entirely extinguished.

Connecting with the Text [Apply]

6. Possible answers: Attended; the first opportunity in many years to hear such a performance should not be squandered. Avoided; the memories aroused by a concert might be terribly painful.

Extending the Text [Synthesize]

7. Possible answer: A Romantic writer like Whittier might have glorified the Nebraska farm and had Georgiana be spiritually renewed by the concert; a dark Romantic might have had Georgiana die of heartbreak after the concert.

Grading Timesaver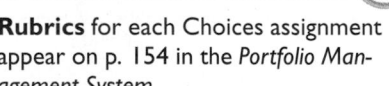

Rubrics for each Choices assignment appear on p. 154 in the *Portfolio Management System.*

Reading Check

a. She hears no music for fifteen years and very little for the next fifteen; having six children and working hard at cooking, cleaning, and so forth deplete her strength and health.

b. Clark owes Georgiana his early introduction to music and literature. He plans to take her to a concert. She is initially subdued but ultimately deeply moved by hearing great music again.

CHOICES: Building Your Portfolio

1. **Writer's Notebook** Students who completed the Listening to Music activity on p. T545 can apply their work to this essay.

2–3. **Comparing Characters/Creative Writing** Students may want to make two-column tables listing qualities of both characters and settings before they begin writing.

Planning

Thomas Wolfe

(1900–1938)

Thomas Wolfe is among the most autobiographical of all American writers. His fiction actually chronicles the events of his Southern upbringing and his later life in New York and Europe.

The youngest of eight children, Wolfe was born in the Smoky Mountains of Asheville, North Carolina. Much of his fiction centers on a character named Eugene Gant, who is the youngest child in a large Southern family and whose life parallels Wolfe's own. When Wolfe was six years old, his parents separated. His mother ran a boardinghouse, which she called The Old Kentucky Home; Wolfe's father, given to bouts of violent drinking, lived a few blocks away behind his stonecutting shop. The boy, very unhappy with the new situation, lived with his mother. Her boardinghouse appears repeatedly in Wolfe's fiction, usually depicted in an unpleasant light.

Wolfe entered the University of North Carolina when he was sixteen. His extraordinary height, six feet six inches, was one reason he was so self-conscious all his life. After graduating in 1920, Wolfe studied playwriting at Harvard. In 1924, he moved to New York City, where he taught at New York University and tried, without success, to have his plays produced. That same year he made the first of seven trips to Europe that he would make during his lifetime.

In 1925, Wolfe became involved with Aline Bernstein, a woman much older than he was; he later wrote extensively about this affair in *The Web and the Rock.* Bernstein and Wolfe spent five years together, in England and in New York, where Wolfe continued to teach and to work on his first and best novel, *Look Homeward, Angel.*

Wolfe completed *Look Homeward, Angel* in 1928; the first draft is said to have filled up more than one suitcase. After several publishers rejected it, Scribner's showed interest. As a result, Wolfe began what would become a remarkable association with Maxwell Perkins, the famous editor who persuaded Wolfe to cut three hundred pages, or about one third, from his enormous story and saw the novel through to publication in 1929.

Wolfe eventually ended his association with Perkins and Scribner's. Before his sudden death in 1938 from an illness, Wolfe had signed up with another publisher, Harper's, and had delivered to them enormous chunks of a new manuscript. Another editor labored over the mass of material and, after Wolfe's death, published several posthumous books, including *You Can't Go Home Again* (1940).

Some readers believe that Wolfe's editors did Wolfe a disservice by reducing his manuscripts to the size of manageable novels. They think that Wolfe wanted to create one huge epic work of fiction based on his own life, just as Walt Whitman had crafted an American epic in "Song of Myself" (page 353). In many ways, Wolfe's greatness can be measured by the magnitude of what he tried, and failed, to accomplish. As William Faulkner (page 713) noted, Thomas Wolfe was "the best failure," a writer who dared "to throw away style, coherence, all the rules of preciseness, to try to put all the experience of the human heart on the head of a pin."

Culver Pictures.

 go.hrw.com
LEO 11-11

Before You Read

HIS FATHER'S EARTH

Make the Connection

When the Circus Comes to Town

In the past, when much of the United States was made up of small towns and rural areas, the most exciting annual event was the coming of the circus. It began with a parade—colorfully dressed band members, a calliope piping its shrill steam-whistle notes, wild animals roaring in rolling cages, elephants lumbering along in single file, bareback riders on prancing ponies, and a wild array of clowns, acrobats, and jugglers. No wonder many young observers harbored the secret dream of running away to join the circus—it was the embodiment of fantasy and adventure.

Reading Skills and Strategies

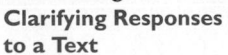

Clarifying Responses to a Text

The young dreamer in this story—perhaps Wolfe himself—imagines himself joining the circus to sell tickets, put up posters, and barter with farmers for fresh food. As you read, take notes on the effects his fantasy has on you. In what ways is it like a fairy tale? Do you feel pleasantly swept along in his fantasy, or does it create another response in you? As you read through to the end of the story, write your ideas about what "magic congruence" is shared by his "father's earth" and the circus as Wolfe describes it.

Elements of Literature

Description

Just as Napoleon realized the importance of food for his troops ("An army marches on its stomach"), so Wolfe in this story envisions a circus troupe eating its way through forty states. Wolfe's daydream, an exuberant **description** of the states' geographical features and abundant crops, coincides with the daydream of arriving at his father's house—a place that is not real but is pure fantasy. As you read, look for Wolfe's long descriptive lists of foods, people, and places.

> **D**escription is a form of writing that uses sensory language to create images and to convey moods or emotions.
>
> *For more on Description, see the Handbook of Literary Terms.*

American circus posters from the 1920s and 1930s.
The Granger Collection, New York.

549

Summary ■ ■ ■

As a child stands in a circus crowd with his brother, he lapses into an extended daydream. He imagines that he is traveling with the circus—taking tickets, sweeping up, and procuring colossal quantities of fresh food for the performers. In this extravagant vision of health, strength, and travel, the boy grows to love each region of America for its abundance, for its richness and diversity, and even for its childish intolerance and violence. Ultimately, however, the boy ends this epic circus journey in order to find "his father's earth," a land where he feels an immediate sense of belonging, nurturance, and maturity—and is welcomed by a fantastically large and powerful old man whom he recognizes as his father. The narrator explains that these symbolic images of exuberant exploration and mature arrival at "the father's land" will always haunt the imagination of the child—just as they haunt the imagination of every child who has ever lived.

RESPONDING TO THE ART

The circus was first introduced to America in 1792. In 1919, Ringling Brothers, one of the most famous circuses, merged with Barnum & Bailey to create what is still known today as "the greatest show on earth." It became famous not only for its spell-binding performances but also for its colorful, whimsical posters, which captured the imaginations of generations of American children.

Preteaching Vocabulary

Words to Own

Have students read the Words to Own and their definitions, listed at the bottom of the selection pages. Have them write sentences about trips they have taken to a circus or an amusement park, using at least seven of the words correctly. Then, have them find a synonym on the right for each word on the left.

prodigal [j]	**a.** small	
opulent [i]	**b.** topped	
nominal [a]	**c.** rejoiced	
vistas [g]	**d.** weak	
frugal [e]	**e.** thrifty	
garnished [b]	**f.** guess	
exulted [c]	**g.** views	
languid [d]	**h.** occasional	
surmise [f]	**i.** rich	
intermittent [h]	**j.** plentiful	

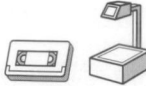
RESPONDING TO THE ART

Grant Wood (1892–1942) is best known for his stylized and often ironic views of ordinary American characters and landscapes. (See longer notes on pp. 647 and 681.)
Activity. Have students describe how Wood distorts and stylizes the landscape of Stone City. [Possible response: He simplifies the shapes of buildings and hills with smooth, almost geometric lines.]

A Struggling Readers
Finding the Main Idea
Have a volunteer read this paragraph aloud. Ask another student to identify its main idea. [The boy is captivated by two universally powerful images: the circus and his father's earth.] Make sure students understand that the rest of the story takes place in the boy's imagination.

B Critical Thinking
Classifying
❓ How would you classify the boy's "vision" at this point, based on this paragraph? Is it merely a daydream, or does it signify something more about the boy's life or the human condition? [Possible response: This "blazing real" vision is more detailed and powerful than any daydream. It suggests a moment of epiphany so powerful that it rivals "life itself" in its intensity.]

T550

Stone City, Iowa (1930) by Grant Wood. Oil on wood panel (30¼″ x 40″).
Joslyn Art Museum, Omaha, Nebraska (1930.35). © Estate of Grant Wood/Licensed by VAGA, New York, NY.

His Father's Earth

Thomas Wolfe

A s the boy stood looking at the circus with his brother, there came to him two images, which had haunted his childhood and the life of every boy who ever lived, but were now for the first time seen together with an instant and magic congruence.[1] And these two images were the images of the circus and his father's earth.

He thought then that he had joined a circus and started on the great tour of the nation with it. It was spring: The circus had started in New England and worked westward and then southward as the summer and autumn came on. His <u>nominal</u>

duties—for, in his vision, every incident, each face and voice and circumstance were blazing real as life itself—were those of ticket seller, but in this tiny show, everyone did several things: The performers helped put up and take down the tents, load and unload the wagons, and the roustabouts[2] and business people worked wherever they were needed.

The boy sold tickets, but he also posted bills and bartered with tradesmen and farmers in new places for fresh food. He became very shrewd and clever at this work, and loved to do it—some old,

2. **roustabouts** (roust′ə·bouts′): circus workers who handle various duties, including setting up and taking down tents.

- - - - - - - - - - - - - - - - - - - -

WORDS TO OWN
nominal (näm′ə·nəl) *adj.*: very small.

- - - - - - - - - - - - - - - - - - - -

1. **congruence** (käŋ′grōō·əns): harmony.

550 THE MODERNS

Reaching All Students

Struggling Readers
Help students to understand that this story contains four sections: the expository opening paragraph, the description of the circus, the arrival at the father's homeland, and the last two paragraphs, which place the boy's dream in a broader context. Have students identify where each section begins and ends. As they come to the end of each section, students should discuss it with a partner, each making sure that the other has understood it. Then

have students read the story again to appreciate Wolfe's sensory detail and rich descriptions.

Advanced Learners
As students read this story, they will notice a paradox: The boy has never seen his father's homeland, yet he recognizes it immediately when the circus stops there. Have students consider how the boy might recognize a place he has never seen and know the way there.

sharp, buried talent for shrewd trading, that had come to him from his mountain blood, now aided him. He could get the finest, freshest meats and vegetables at the lowest prices. The circus people were tough and hard, they always had a fierce and ravenous hunger, they would not accept bad food and cooking, they fed stupendously, and they always had the best of everything.

Usually the circus would arrive at a new town very early in the morning, before daybreak. He would go into town immediately: He would go to the markets, or with farmers who had come in for the circus. He felt and saw the purity of first light, he heard the sweet and sudden lutings of first birds, and suddenly he was filled with the earth and morning in new towns, among new men: He walked among the farmers' wagons, and he dealt with them on the spot for the prodigal plenty of their wares—the country melons bedded in sweet hay of wagons, the cool sweet prints of butter wrapped in clean wet cloths, with dew and starlight still on them, the enormous battered cans foaming with fresh milk, the new laid eggs which he bought by the gross and hundred dozens, the tender limy pullets by the score, the rude country wagons laden to the rim with heaped abundancies—with delicate bunches of green scallions, the heavy red ripeness of huge tomatoes, the sweet-leaved lettuces crisp as celery, the fresh podded peas and the succulent young beans, as well as the potatoes spotted with the loamy earth, the powerful winey odor of the apples, the peaches, and the cherries, the juicy corn stacked up in shocks of living green, and the heavy blackened rinds of home-cured hams and bacons.

As the market opened, he would begin to trade and dicker with the butchers for their finest cuts of meat: They would hold great roasts up in their gouted[3] fingers, they would roll up tubs of fresh ground sausage, they would smack with their long palms the flanks of beeves[4] and porks: He would drive back to the circus with a wagon full of meat and vegetables.

At the circus ground the people were already in full activity. He could hear the wonderful timed tattoo[5] of sledges on driven stakes, the shouts of men riding animals down to water, the slow clank and pull of mighty horses, the heavy rumble of the wagons as they rolled down off the circus flatcars. By now the eating table would be erected, and as he arrived, he could see the cooks already busy at their ranges, the long tables set up underneath the canvas with their rows of benches, their tin plates and cups, their strong readiness. There would be the amber indescribable pungency of strong coffee, and the smell of buckwheat batter.

And the circus people would come in for their breakfast: Hard and tough, for the most part decent and serious people, the performers, the men and women, the acrobats, the riders, the tumblers, the clowns, the jugglers, the contortionists, and the balancers would come in quietly and eat with a savage and inspired intentness.

The food they ate was as masculine and fragrant as the world they dwelt in: It belonged to the stained world of mellow sun-warmed canvas, the clean and healthful odor of the animals, and the mild sweet lyric nature of the land in which they lived as wanderers, and it was there for the asking with a fabulous and stupefying plenty, golden and embrowned: They ate stacks of buckwheat cakes, smoking hot, soaked in hunks of yellow butter which they carved at will with a wide free gesture from the piled prints on the table, and which they garnished (if they pleased) with ropes of heavy black molasses, or with the lighter, freer maple syrup.

They ate big steaks for breakfast, hot from the pan and lashed with onions, they ate whole melons, crammed with the ripeness of the deep pink meat, rashers of bacon, and great platters of fried eggs, or eggs scrambled with calves' brains, they helped themselves from pyramids of fruit piled up at intervals on the table—plums, peaches, apples, cherries, grapes, oranges, and bananas—they had great pitchers of thick cream to pour on everything, and they washed their hunger down with pint mugs of strong deep-savored coffee.

5. **tattoo:** pounding.

WORDS TO OWN

prodigal (präd′i·gəl) *adj.*: extremely abundant.
garnished (gär′nisht) *v.*: topped.

---

3. **gouted** (gout′id): swollen from gout, a kind of arthritis that usually affects the joints in the fingers or toes.
4. **beeves:** alternate plural of *beef*.

THOMAS WOLFE 551

C Reading Skills and Strategies
Clarifying Responses to a Text
? What is the boy's life like as he travels from town to town? [His life is rich and vibrant: He meets people, procures savory foods, and lives in harmony with nature.] What pictures come to your mind? Can you see yourself going out before dawn with the protagonist? What would it be like? [Responses will vary. Some students might refer to summer camp experiences; others might talk about a paper route or sports practice.]

D Elements of Literature
Description
? How does Wolfe make the market come alive for the reader? [He uses specific adjectives, such as "battered," "succulent," and "loamy"; and concrete nouns, such as "wagons," "apples," and "hams." He includes a great many details that appeal directly to the senses.]

E English Language Learners
Specialized Vocabulary
Go over this list of circus performers with students. Make sure they understand how each performer looks and what he or she does. Students may find the fine art transparency and the illustrations on p. 549 helpful in identifying the performers.

F Elements of Literature
Description
? In what ways is this catalogue reminiscent of Walt Whitman? [The description glories in the variety in the land, the people, and the food; it portrays an overwhelming abundance of life.]

G Critical Thinking
Interpreting
? What does this description imply about how hard the circus performers work? [They work very hard; it takes a great effort to build up such an appetite.] Discuss how all the details in the story are "epic" in scope. [Mundane activities like shopping and eating become heroic.]

Getting Students Involved

Cooperative Learning
Ask groups of three students to write their own catalogues to describe an event or a place. Tell each group to choose a recorder, an illustrator, and a timer (to keep students on track). All students must contribute to the contents of the catalogue. Have them compose orally while the recorder writes down their thoughts and the illustrator draws. Then, allow the timer to read the catalogue aloud to the class and display the finished drawings.

Enrichment Activity
Have students form a small reading group to read and discuss Wolfe's short story "Circus at Dawn." Ask them to consider it in the nature of a prelude to this story. What do students learn about the two boys? What do they learn about the circus? Why does each boy think that life with the circus would be so wonderful?

For their midday meal they would eat fiercely, hungrily, with wolfish gusts, mightily, with knit brows and convulsive movements of their corded throats. They would eat great roasts of beef with crackled hides, browned in their juices, rare and tender, hot chunks of delicate pork with hems of fragrant fat, delicate young boiled chickens, only a mouthful for these ravenous jaws, twelve-pound pot roasts cooked for hours in an iron pot with new carrots, onions, sprouts, and young potatoes, together with every vegetable that the season yielded: huge roasting ears of corn, smoking hot, stacked like cordwood on two-foot platters, tomatoes cut in slabs with wedges of okra and succotash, and raw onion, mashed potatoes whipped to a creamy smother, boats swimming with pure beef gravy, new carrots, turnips, fresh peas cooked in butter, and fat string beans seasoned with the flavor of big chunks of cooking-pork. In addition, they had every fruit that the place and time afforded: hot crusty apple, peach and cherry pies, encrusted with cinnamon, puddings and cakes of every sort, and blobbering cobblers inches deep.

Thus the circus moved across America, from town to town, from state to state, eating its way from Maine into the great plains of the West, eating its way along the Hudson and the Mississippi Rivers, eating its way across the prairies and from the North into the South, eating its way across the flat farmlands of the Pennsylvania Dutch colony, the eastern shore of Maryland and back again across the states of Virginia, North Carolina, Tennessee, and Florida—eating all good things that this enormous, this inevitably bountiful and abundant cornucopia[6] of a continent yielded.

They ate the cod, bass, mackerel, halibut, clams, and oysters of the New England coast, the terrapin[7] of Maryland, the fat beeves, porks, and cereals of the Middle West, and they had, as well, the heavy juicy peaches, watermelons, cantaloupes of Georgia, the fat sweet shad of the Carolina coasts, and the rounded and exotic citrus fruits of the tropics: the oranges, tangerines, bananas, kumquats, lemons, guavas down in Florida, together with a hundred other fruits and meats—the Vermont turkeys, the mountain trout, the bunched heaviness of the Concord grapes, the red winey bulk of the Oregon apples, as well as the clawed, shelled, and crusted dainties, the crabs, the clams, the pink-meated lobsters that grope their way along the sea floors of America.

The boy awoke at morning in three hundred towns with the glimmer of starlight on his face; he was the moon's man; then he saw light quicken in the east, he saw the pale stars drown, he saw the birth of light, he heard the lark's wing, the bird tree, the first liquorous liquefied lutings, the ripe-aired trillings, the plumskinned birdnotes, and he heard the hoof and wheel come down the streets of the nation. He exulted in his work as food-producer for the circus people, and they loved him for it. They said there had never been anyone like him—they banqueted exultantly, with hoarse gulpings and with joy, and they loved him.

Slowly, day by day, the circus worked its way across America, through forty states and through a dozen weathers. It was a little world that moved across the enormous loneliness of the earth, a little world that each day began a new life in new cities, and that left nothing to betray where it had been save a litter of beaten papers, the droppings of the camel and the elephant in Illinois, a patch of trampled grass, and a magical memory.

The circus men knew no other earth but this; the earth came to them with the smell of the canvas and the lion's roar. They saw the world behind the lights of the carnival, and everything beyond these lights was phantasmal and unreal to them; it lived for them within the circle of the tent as men and women who sat on benches, as the posts they came to, and sometimes as the enemy.

Their life was filled with the strong joy of food, with the love of traveling, and with danger and hard labor. Always there was the swift violence of change and movement, of putting up and tearing down, and sometimes there was the misery of rain and sleet, and mud above the ankles, of wind that shook their flimsy residence, that ripped the tent stakes from their moorings in the earth and

---

6. **cornucopia** (kôr′nyo͞o·kō′pē·ə): Also called a horn of plenty, a cornucopia is a symbol of fullness and abundance.
7. **terrapin** (ter′ə·pin): turtles.

552 THE MODERNS

WORDS TO OWN
exulted (eg·zult′id) *v.*: rejoiced greatly.

Crossing the Curriculum

lifted out the great center pole as if it were a match. Now they must wrestle with the wind and hold their dwelling to the earth; now they must fight the weariness of mud and push their heavy wagons through the slime; now, cold and wet and wretched, they must sleep on piles of canvas, upon the flatcars in a driving rain, and sometimes they must fight the enemy—the drunk, the savage, the violent enemy, the bloody man, who dwelt in every place. Sometimes it was the city thug, sometimes the mill hands of the South, sometimes the miners in a Pennsylvania town— the circus people cried, "Hey, rube!"[8] and fought them with fist and foot, with pike and stake, and the boy saw and knew it all.

8. **rube:** unsophisticated person, usually from the country. The term is used as a taunt.

When the men in a little town barricaded the street against their parade, they charged the barricade with their animals, and once the sheriff tried to stop the elephant by saying: "Now, damn ye, if you stick your . . . damned trunk another inch, I'll shoot."

The circus moved across America foot by foot, mile by mile. He came to know the land. It was rooted in his blood and his brain forever—its food, its fruit, its fields and forests, its deserts, and its mountains, its savage lawlessness. He saw the crimes and the violence of the people with pity, with mercy, and with tenderness: He thought of them as if they were children. They smashed their neighbors' brains out with an ax, they disemboweled one another with knives, they were murderous and lost upon this earth they dwelt upon as strangers.

Fall Plowing (1931) by Grant Wood. Oil on canvas.
From the Deere & Company Art Collection, Moline, Illinois.

THOMAS WOLFE 553

F **Elements of Literature**
Description
? How does this description modify your idea of circus life? [Possible answers: It makes circus life seem more dangerous and daring, given the hostility it seems to bring out in local residents; like the descriptions of the performers' eating habits, this paragraph makes the circus seem like the epitome of earthy, hearty living, filled with intense physicality and energy.]

G **Reading Skills and Strategies**

Clarifying Responses to a Text
? How does the boy respond to average people? [with compassion and forgiveness] What does the language of the last sentence sound like? [The last sentence sounds Biblical.] Point out how the boy's attitude is like a prophet's (or perhaps even Christlike) in this passage. Note that in this section (from the last paragraph of p. 552 to the first of p. 554), the boy witnesses the evil of the world but does not participate in it.

RESPONDING TO THE ART
Grant Wood is considered one of three major American Regionalists, along with John Curry and Thomas Hart Benton. They painted Midwestern types and scenes during the 1930s. Wood depicted his native Iowa, Curry painted Kansas, and Benton painted the Ozarks.
Activity. Ask students how this painting reflects Wolfe's descriptions of America. [Possible answers: It depicts the loneliness and vastness Wolfe refers to. The expansive green hillsides and the haystacks evoke the abundance and fertility that the whole story celebrates.]

Using Students' Strengths

Visual/Spatial Learners
Tell students to create a collage based on the vision of America Wolfe presents in this story. Remind them to portray the abundance, creative energy, and beauty of the land, as well as the ugly towns and pointless violence.

Naturalist Learners
Have students read the description of dawn on p. 554. Discuss whether they have ever watched daybreak and whether this description

rings true. What did they see, hear, and smell? What emotions did they feel?

Kinesthetic Learners
Have students pantomime what the boy sees in his two visions. Suggest that they play the parts of the boy, circus performers, cooks, roustabouts, townspeople, father, and brothers. Encourage them to concentrate on three or four important scenes and to convey the impression Wolfe tries to create.

T553

A Critical Thinking

Interpreting

? What is the relationship of the townspeople with the earth? [The people are scattered on the earth but are not part of it. The earth is "indifferent" to them, and they dwell upon it as "strangers."] Point out how the townspeople build ugliness, fight with each other, and live disconnected from nature—in contrast to the circus people, who confront the intolerance of the townspeople with exuberance and joy, wrestle with the forces of nature, and savor its bounties (food).

B Critical Thinking

Interpreting

? What is Wolfe implying about the father's land, with his assertion that the boy can remember it "with every atom of his life" without ever having seen it? [Possible answer: He is implying that the father's land is an archetype, or collective human image, that is present as an inherited memory in everyone yet accessed by only a few.]

C Elements of Literature

Description

Discuss how this passage appeals to all five senses. Explore how the description prepares the reader for a wonderful experience.

D Cultural Connections

? Like Odysseus at the end of his famous journey, the boy awakens at dawn to find that he has reached home. Analyze why this earth has "fences" that fit "a man's heart" but not his "desire." [Possible answer: Its boundaries reflect the contented heart of "fulfilled desire," and not the ever-broadening field of unsatisfied wants.] Why does home have boundaries? [Possible responses: to be protective, familiar, and comfortable.]

The tongueless blood of the murdered men ran down into the earth, and the earth received it. Upon this enormous and indifferent earth the little trains rattled on over ill-joined rails that loosely bound the sprawling little towns together. Lost and lonely, brief sawings of wood and plaster and cheap brick ugliness, the little towns were scattered like encampments through the wilderness. Only the earth remained, which all these people had barely touched, which all these people dwelt upon but could not possess.

Only the earth remained, the savage and lyrical earth with its rude potency, its thousand vistas, its heights and slopes and levels, with all its violence and delicacy, the terrible fecundity,[9] decay, and growth, its fierce colors, its vital bite and sparkle, its exultancy of space and wandering. And the memory of this earth, the memory of all this universe of sight and sense, was rooted in this boy's heart and brain forever. It fed the hungers of desire and wandering, it breached the walls of his secret and withdrawn spirit. And for every memory of place and continent, of enormous coffee-colored rivers and eight hundred miles of bending wheat, of Atlantic coast and midland prairie, of raw red Piedmont[10] and tropic flatness, there was always the small, fecund, perfect memory of his father's land, the dark side of his soul and his heart's desire, which he had never seen, but which he knew with every atom of his life, the strange phantasmal haunting of man's memory. It was a fertile, nobly swelling land, and it was large enough to live in, walled with fulfilled desire.

Abroad in this ocean of earth and vision he thought of his father's land, of its great red barns and nobly swelling earth, its clear familiarity and its haunting strangeness, and its dark and secret heart, its magnificent, its lovely and tragic beauty. He thought of its smell of harbors and its rumors of the seas, the city, and the ships, its wine-red apples and its brown-red soil, its snug weathered houses, and its lyric unutterable ecstasy.

A wonderful thing happened. One morning he awoke suddenly to find himself staring straight up at the pulsing splendor of the stars. At first he did not know where he was, but he knew instantly,

even before he looked about him, that he had visited this place before. The circus train had stopped in the heart of the country, for what reason he did not know. He could hear the languid and intermittent breathing of the engine, the strangeness of men's voices in the dark, the casual stamp of the horses in their cars, and all around him the attentive and vital silence of the earth.

Suddenly he raised himself from the pile of canvas on which he slept. It was the moment just before dawn: Against the east, the sky had already begun to whiten with the first faint luminosity of day, the invading tides of light crept up the sky, drowning the stars out as they went. The train had halted by a little river which ran swift and deep next to the tracks, and now he knew that what at first had been the sound of silence was the swift and ceaseless music of the river.

There had been rain the night before, and now the river was filled with the sweet clean rain-drenched smell of earthy deposits. He could see the delicate white glimmer of young birch trees leaning from the banks, and on the other side he saw the winding whiteness of the road. Beyond the road, and bordering it, there was an orchard with a wall of lichened stone: A row of apple trees, gnarled and sweet, spread their squat twisted branches out across the road, and in the faint light he saw that they were dense with blossoms: The cool intoxication of their fragrance overpowered him.

As the wan light grew, the earth and all its contours emerged sharply, and he saw again the spare, gaunt loneliness of the earth at dawn, with all its sweet and sudden cries of spring. He saw the worn and ancient design of lichened rocks, the fertile soil of the baked fields, he saw the kept order, the frugal cleanliness, with its springtime overgrowth, the mild tang of opulent greenery. There was an earth with fences, as big as a man's heart, but not so great as his desire, and after his

---

9. fecundity (fē·kun′də·tē): fertility.
10. Piedmont (pēd′mänt): hilly land east of the Appalachian Mountains.

WORDS TO OWN

vistas (vis′təz) *n. pl.:* views.
languid (laŋ′gwid) *adj.:* weak, as from exhaustion.
intermittent (in′tər·mit′'nt) *adj.:* pausing occasionally.
frugal (froo′gəl) *adj.:* thrifty; economical.
opulent (äp′yoo·lənt) *adj.:* abundant; plentiful.

Taking a Second Look

Review: Comparing and Contrasting

Help students compare and contrast the two settings in the story (the circus and the father's earth) and the boy's role in each. Have them also analyze how the settings contribute to an understanding of the story's thematic emphases. To prepare for the discussion, guide students through the following activity.

1. Draw a Venn diagram on the board. Have students list the characteristics of both settings. [Students may list the constant travel, the regional abundance, and the physical struggle with people and the elements that characterize the circus life, versus the fenced-in contentment, sweet calm of nature, and the exuberant familial warmth that greet the boy in his father's land.]

2. Draw a second Venn diagram on the board and have students use it to characterize the boy's role in each setting. [Students should note that the boy's circus dream features nurturance of others, pity for fellow creatures, and an endless desire to find America and himself. In his father's land, the boy receives nurturance, feels pity for himself, and arrives at a stable sense of adult identity and fulfilled desire.]

Spring Turning (1936) by Grant Wood. Oil on Masonite panel (18⅛″ x 40″).

Reynolda House, Museum of American Art, Winston-Salem, North Carolina. © Estate of Grant Wood/Licensed by VAGA, New York, NY.

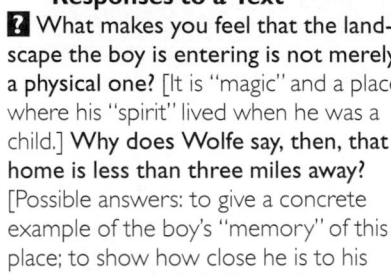

E **Reading Skills and Strategies**

Clarifying Responses to a Text

? What makes you feel that the landscape the boy is entering is not merely a physical one? [It is "magic" and a place where his "spirit" lived when he was a child.] Why does Wolfe say, then, that home is less than three miles away? [Possible answers: to give a concrete example of the boy's "memory" of this place; to show how close he is to his destination and his fulfillment.]

F **Advanced Learners**

Symbol

? What does the movement of the train away from the boy symbolize? [Possible answers: that his circus adventure is over; that he is about to enter a different stage in his life; that childhood is over and maturity is beginning.]

G **Elements of Literature**

Description

? Discuss how this descriptive passage (which culminates in the line "His steps grew slow, he sat upon a wall, he waited") contrasts with the descriptions of circus life on pp. 551–552. How does Wolfe's descriptive strategy change here? [Possible answers: Unlike the circus descriptions, which evoke months of travel through catalogs of food and places, this passage describes a single moment in the boy's life. The fact that the boy "waited" also contrasts with his constant motion and activity in the circus.] Are there any thematic reasons that Wolfe might use this strategy here? [Possible answer: to emphasize the sense of identity, arrival, and fulfillment that the boy finds in his father's land.]

giant wanderings over the prodigal fecundity of the continent, this earth was like a room he once had lived in. He returned to it as a sailor to a small closed harbor, as a man, spent with the hunger of his wandering, comes home.

Instantly he recognized the scene. He knew that he had come at last into his father's land. It was a magic that he knew but could not speak; he stood upon the lip of time, and all of his life now seemed the mirage of some wizard's spell—the spell of canvas and the circus ring, the spell of the tented world which had possessed him. Here was **E** his home, brought back to him while he slept, like a forgotten dream. Here was the dark side of his soul, his heart's desire, his father's country, the earth his spirit dwelt on as a child. He knew every inch of the landscape, and he knew, past reason, doubt, or argument, that home was not three miles away.

He got up at once and leaped down to the earth; he knew where he would go. Along the track there was the slow swing and dance of the brakemen's lamps, that moving, mournful, and beautiful cloud of light along the rails of the earth, that he had seen so many times. Already the train was in motion; its **F** bell tolled and its heavy trucks rumbled away from him. He began to walk back along the tracks, for

less than a mile away, he knew, where the stream boiled over the lip of a dam, there was a bridge. When he reached the bridge, a deeper light had come: The old red brick of the mill emerged sharply and with the tone and temper of deep joy fell sheer into bright shining waters.

He crossed the bridge and turned left along the road: Here it moved away from the river, among fields and through dark woods—dark woods bordered with stark poignancy of fir and pine, with the noble spread of maples, shot with the naked whiteness of birch. Here was the woodland maze: **G** the sweet density of the brake[11] and growth. Sharp thrummings, woodland flitters broke the silence. His steps grew slow, he sat upon a wall, he waited.

Now rose the birdsong in first light, and suddenly he heard each sound the birdsong made. Like a flight of shot the sharp fast skaps of sound arose. With chittering bicker, fast-fluttering skirrs of sound, the palmy honeyed bird-cries came. Smooth drops and nuggets of bright gold they were. Now sang the birdtrees filled with lutings in bright air: The thrums, the lark's wing, and tongue-trilling chirrs arose now. The little name-

11. **brake:** thicket; marshy, overgrown area.

THOMAS WOLFE 555

Assessing Learning

Check Test: Fill in the Blank

[Possible answers are given.]

1. The two images that come into the boy's head as he looks at the circus are _____. [his life in the circus and his return to his father's earth]

2. The boy imagines that his duties with the circus are _____. [to sell tickets, post bills, and barter for food]

3. The circus travels through _____ [the United States; all weathers; small towns]

4. The boy leaves the circus to go _____. [to his father's land]

5. At the end of the story, the boy is greeted by _____. [his father and brothers]

A **Appreciating Language**

Sound Effects

❓ How does Wolfe capture the atmosphere of the early morning in this paragraph and the previous one? [Onomatopoeia, neologisms (coined words), and alliteration help the reader hear the birds singing.]

B **Elements of Literature**

Description

Explore with students the richness in this description of the father. After the suggestion that the boy's quest is a spiritual one, the father he finds is Biblical in stature: enormous, powerful, prophetic, and roaring. Note how all emotional suffering is dissolved when they embrace. The experience is more than a physical hug from a physical father. Wolfe seems to suggest the boy has also returned to his Father, God.

C **Critical Thinking**

Interpreting

❓ What has the boy lost? What has been regained, and what cannot be regained? [Possible answers: He has lost time with the father; he regains his place in the home and in his father's heart; he cannot regain innocence or ignorance of the world he has seen; he cannot make up for past mistakes.]

D **Critical Thinking**

Interpreting

❓ What do you think this passage means? [Possible answer: The boy has reached the end of his quest and attained his reward: self-identity, fulfillment, and maturity. He has achieved this through a transcendence of selfish pain and desire and a compassionate celebration of humanity itself.]

E **Reading Skills and Strategies**

Clarifying

Responses to a Text

❓ Discuss the significance of the title. Why does Wolfe use "earth" rather than "home"? [Possible answer: The boy does not find his personal homeland, but the place where he, as a human being, originates and belongs. The boy does not find a humanly created spot, like a town or a farm, but the place in the world where he is in harmony with nature, the stars, the birds' songs, the smell of flowers, and the earth itself. Ultimately, Wolfe seems to suggest that the boy finds a place within himself that nurtures him, defines him, and brings him peace.]

less cries arose and fell with liquorous liquefied lutings, with lirruping chirp, plumbellied smoothness, sweet lucidity.

And now there was the rapid kweet kweet kweet kweet kweet of homing birds and their pwee pwee pwee: others with sharp cricketing stitch, a mosquito buzz with thin metallic tongues, while some with rusty creakings, high shrew's caws, with eerie rasp, with harsh far calls—all birds that are awake in the sweet woodland tangles: And above, there passed the whirr of hidden wings, the strange lost cry of the unknown birds, in full flight now; in which the sweet confusion of their cries was mingled.

Then he got up and went along that road where, he knew, like the prophetic surmise of a dream, the house of his father's blood and kin lay hidden. At length, he came around a bending in the road, he left the wooded land, he passed by hedges and saw the old white house, set in the shoulder of the hill, worn like care and habit in the earth; clean and cool, it sat below the clean dark shelter of its trees: A twist of morning smoke coiled through its chimney.

Then he turned in to the rutted road that led up to the house, and at this moment the enormous figure of a powerful old man appeared around the corner prophetically bearing a smoked ham in one huge hand. And when the boy saw the old man, a cry of greeting burst from his throat, and the old man answered with a roar of welcome that shook the earth.

Then the old man dropped his ham, and waddled forward to meet the boy: They met half down the road, and the old man crushed him in his hug; they tried to speak but could not; they embraced again and in an instant all the years of wandering, the pain of loneliness and the fierce hungers of desire, were scoured away like a scum of frost from a bright glass.

He was a child again, he was a child that had stood upon the lip and leaf of time and heard the quiet tides that move us to our death, and he knew that the child could not be born again, the book of the days could never be turned back, old errors and confusions never righted. And he wept with sorrow for all that was lost and could never be regained, and with joy for all that had been recovered.

Suddenly he saw his youth as men on hilltops might look at the whole winding course of rivers to the sea, he saw the blind confusions of his wanderings across the earth, the horror of man's little stricken mote of earth against immensity, and he remembered the proud exultancy of his childhood when all the world lay like a coin between his palms, when he could have touched the horned rim of the moon, when heroes and great actions bent before him.

And he wept, not for himself, but out of love and pity for every youth that ever hoped and wandered and was alone. He had become a man, and he had in him unique glory that belongs to men alone, and that makes them great, and from which they shape their mightiest songs and legends. For out of their pain they utter first a cry for wounded self, then, as their vision deepens, widens, the universe of their marvelous sense leaps out and grips the universe; they feel contempt for gods, respect for men alone, and with the indifference of a selfless passion, enact earth out of a lyric cry.

At this moment, also, two young men burst from the house and came running down the road to greet him. They were powerful and heavy young men, already beginning to show signs of that epic and sensual grossness that distinguished their father. Like their father, they recognized the boy instantly, and in a moment he was engulfed in their mighty energies, borne up among them to the house. And they understood all he wanted to say, but could not speak, and they surrounded him with love and lavish heapings of his plate. And the boy knew the strange miracle of return to the dark land of his heart's desire, the father's land which haunts men like a dream they never knew.

Such were the twin images of the circus and his father's land which were to haunt his dreams and waking memory and which now, as he stood there with his brother looking at the circus, fused instantly to a living whole and came to him in a blaze of light.

And in this way, before he had ever set foot upon it, he came for the first time to his father's earth.

WORDS TO OWN

surmise (sər·mīz') *n.*: guess.

Professional Notes

Home Is Where the Heart Isn't

Thomas Wolfe had no trouble finding a title for his novel *You Can't Go Home Again*. This novel deals with George Webber's return to his hometown and is based on Wolfe's return to a somewhat hostile Asheville after the publication of *Look Homeward, Angel*. Wolfe told the story of his less-than-inspiring experience to a dinner companion, who remarked, "But don't you know you can't go home again?" Thus, the title for his last book was born.

Making the Connections

Connecting to the Theme: "Loss and Redemption"

What has the boy in the story lost? In what way is he redeemed? How would you contrast his trip home after living with the circus with Georgiana's trip home after her visit to Clark? [Some students will feel the boy loses the circus's exhilarating sense of motion, but most will agree that his arrival at a mature identity is a worthwhile redemption. By contrast, Georgiana's return home is a journey of capitulation and despair.]

First Thoughts

1. Look back over the notes you made while reading. What words would you use to describe your response to this story?

Reading Check

a. Which words or passages tell you that Wolfe is describing a fantasy and not reality?

b. What examples of **onomatopoeia, alliteration,** and other poetic devices give Wolfe's story the "sound" of poetry?

Shaping Interpretations

2. Wolfe depicts the father as a nurturer—a male version of the "earth mother." What details help create that picture?

3. How does the world of the circus differ from "his father's earth"? What similarities are there in what the boy does and what the father represents?

4. How do **descriptions** of birdsong bring together descriptions of circus life and of home?

5. Wolfe is famous for evocative descriptions that are presented like the **catalogs** of Walt Whitman (page 348). Select one passage of description in Wolfe's story, and identify the sense or senses to which each image appeals: sight, taste, smell, hearing, or touch.

Extending the Text

6. Scenes in this story resemble other famous "reunion" scenes in literature. In Homer's *Odyssey,* Odysseus returns home after a twenty-year absence and is reunited with his aged father, who is tending vines. If you are familiar with the parable of the Prodigal Son in the New Testament (Luke 15:11–32), explain whether you think Wolfe's father-son reunion bears any resemblance to the reunion described there. Is the boy in this story a prodigal son? Why or why not?

CHOICES: Building Your Portfolio

Writer's Notebook

1. Collecting Ideas for an Analysis of Causes and Effects

Imagine that you are writing a biography of a writer. Brainstorm a list of questions you would ask your subject about what had influenced him or her. Influences might include family, friends, ideas, and the work of other writers. Save your notes for possible use in the Writer's Workshop on page 685.

Comparing Prose and Poetry

2. Two Grand Styles

Reread Walt Whitman's poetry (pages 352–362), especially the verses from "Song of Myself." In a brief essay, compare Whitman's style with Wolfe's. Gather details in a chart like the one below.

	Whitman	Wolfe
1. Use of catalogs		
2. Celebration of everyday people		
3. Celebration of America		
4. Emotional effect		

Creative Writing

3. Details, Details

Write a Wolfe-like description of a place you know well. Include a wide variety of people or items, and build up a **catalog** of details that capture the atmosphere of the place. Use rich, sensory details to imitate Wolfe's exuberant style.

THOMAS WOLFE 557

Reading Check

a. Sample answers: "... there came to him two images. ...."; "He thought then he had joined a circus. ...."; "Such were the twin images of the circus and his father's land. ...."; "... before he had ever set foot upon it, he came for the first time to his father's earth."

b. Sample answers: alliteration: "sweet and sudden cries of spring" (p. 554); onomatopoeia: "lirruping chirp" (p. 556).

First Thoughts [Respond]

1. Possible responses: dazed; exhilarated; hungry; impressed.

Shaping Interpretations [Interpret]

2. Possible answers: his appearance with the ham; the embrace and tears of his welcome; the boy's feeling of childlike contentment.

3. The circus moves constantly; the father's earth is at rest. The son brings people food and compassion in the circus; the father represents an ultimate nurturance and acceptance.

4. Each dawn, on the road or near home, the boy hears birds whose song he recognizes.

5. Sample answer: final paragraph, p. 551, sight: "deep pink meat," "pyramids of fruit"; taste and smell: all food words.

Extending the Text [Analyze]

6. Tell students that *prodigal* in the parable means "extravagant" or "wasteful." Similarities: After long journeys, Wolfe's boy and the Prodigal Son are warmly welcomed and fed. Differences: The Prodigal Son was a wastrel; Wolfe's boy, a hard worker. The Prodigal Son goes home when his money runs out; Wolfe's boy returns because home calls to his soul.

Grading Timesaver

Rubrics for each Choices assignment appear on p. 155 in the *Portfolio Management System.*

CHOICES: Building Your Portfolio

1. **Writer's Notebook** Have students look at the biographies in their textbooks for ideas about what questions to ask.

2. **Comparing Prose and Poetry** Suggest that students consider rhythm, alliteration, sensory detail, and figurative language, as well as the categories shown in the chart.

3. **Creative Writing** Encourage students to choose settings that made strong impressions on them.

OBJECTIVES

Design / Nothing Gold Can Stay / Once by the Pacific / Neither Out Far Nor In Deep / Birches / Death of the Hired Man

1. Read and interpret the poems
2. Interpret dialogue in verse
3. Use punctuation to read poetry for meaning
4. Draw inferences about characters
5. Identify and analyze blank verse
6. Express understanding through creative writing, critical writing, discussion, art, and music

SKILLS

Literary
- Interpret dialogue in verse

Reading
- Use punctuation to read poetry for meaning
- Draw inferences about characters

Writing
- Collect ideas for an essay on causes and effects
- Explore conflicts in poetry
- Compare and contrast two poems
- Place a narrative poem in a contemporary setting

Speaking/Listening
- Discuss whether poems belong to a particular literary tradition

Art
- Create a collage
- Illustrate poems

Music
- Choose music to accompany poems

Viewing/Representing
- Discuss the appropriateness of illustrations (ATE)
- Compare paintings with poems (ATE)

Robert Frost

(1874–1963)

Although Robert Frost is the poet whom Americans most closely identify with New England, he was born in San Francisco, California. Frost was about ten years old before he first saw the New England landscapes and knew the changing seasons that he would later describe with the familiarity of a native son. The boy's move across the country was the result of his father's early death and his mother's decision to settle in the industrial town of Lawrence, Massachusetts. After high school in Lawrence, Frost entered Dartmouth College in New Hampshire. He decided after a few months that he was not yet ready for higher education, and he returned to Lawrence to work in the cotton mills and to write. His verse, however, found little favor with magazine editors.

Married and with a growing family, Frost in his early twenties finally began to feel the need for a more formal education than his random reading could provide. He took his family to Cambridge, Massachusetts, where he entered Harvard and stayed for less than two years. He later wrote of his decision to leave: "Harvard had taken me away from the question of whether I could write or not."

Frost earned a living as a schoolteacher and as an editor before deciding to try farming. For ten years, Frost tilled the stony New Hampshire soil on thirty acres that his grandfather had bought for him. But he decided that the concentration necessary for writing poetry did not mix with the round-the-clock physical effort of working the land. Discouraged, he returned to teaching full time for a few years; then, in 1912, he sought a complete change of scene by taking his family to England.

From Scribbler to Scribe

The move turned out to be a wise one. Stimulated by meeting English poets, Frost continued to write poetry, though he found his subjects in

The Bettmann Archive.

New England. In the three years he spent in England, he completed the two volumes that would make him famous—*A Boy's Will* (1913) and *North of Boston* (1914). These collections included several poems that would stand among Frost's best-known works: "The Tuft of Flowers," "In Hardwood Groves," "Mending Wall," "The Death of the Hired Man," and "After Apple-Picking." These poems were marked by a flinty realism and an impressive mastery of iambic rhythm, narrative dialogue, and the dramatic monologue.

When Frost returned to New Hampshire in 1915, he was no longer an obscure scribbler intent on turning New England folkways into poetry; he was an accomplished writer who had already extended the scope and character of

go.hrw.com
LE0 11-11

Planning

- **Block Schedule**
  Block Scheduling Lesson Plans with Pacing Guide
- **Traditional Schedule**
  Lesson Plans Including Strategies for English-Language Learners
- **One-Stop Planner**
  CD-ROM with Test Generator

  — *Resources: Print and Media* —

Reading
- *Graphic Organizers for Active Reading,* p. 51, 52, 53, 54, 55, 56
- *Audio CD Library*
  Disc 14, Tracks 4, 5, 6, 7, 8, 9, 10

Elements of Literature
- *Literary Elements*
  Transparency 17
  Worksheet, p. 52

Writing and Language
- *Daily Oral Grammar*
  Transparency 36

Assessment
- *Formal Assessment,* p. 115
- *Portfolio Management System,* p. 156
- *Test Generator (One-Stop Planner CD-ROM)*

Internet
- go.hrw.com (keyword: LE0 11-11)

American literature into the twentieth century. In 1916, the publication of *Mountain Interval*—a collection that included such favorites as "The Road Not Taken," "'Out, Out—'," and "Birches"—solidified his fame. Rewarded with many prizes (including four Pulitzer Prizes and a Congressional Medal), numerous honorary degrees, and the faithful attention of a wide readership, Frost spent the rest of his life as a lecturer at a number of colleges and as a public performer who, as he put it, liked to "say" rather than to recite his poetry.

Poet of the People

On stage, Frost in his later years became a character of his own creation—a lovable, fumbling old gent who could nevertheless pierce the minds and hearts of those able to see beyond his playacting. In private, he was apt to put aside this guileless character and become a sometimes wicked commentator on the pretensions of rival poets; and he could be just as cutting to gushing devotees, who were unaware that he held in contempt the very flattery he demanded.

On Inauguration Day, 1961, standing bareheaded in a bright, cold wind beside President John F. Kennedy on the Capitol steps in Washington, D.C., Frost recited "The Gift Outright." His art with words had brought him not only the friendship of a president (who was half his age) but also, by means of radio and television, the largest single audience in history for a poet up until that time.

In a period when poetry was being changed by verbal experiment and by exotic influences from abroad, Frost remained devoted to traditional forms and firmly rooted in American soil. If, at the time of his death, he seemed to belong more to the past than to the present, his reputation today is secure. Neither the cranky realism nor the homely philosophy of self-reliance and spiritual independence that mark his work have been forgotten. He was an artist who developed his talents with stubborn persistence, and he created a unique voice that remained unaffected by the clamor of modernism.

Frost on Frost's Diction

It has been a long time since I used any word not common in everyday speech. For example, I would never think of using the word "casement" for window in general. Whenever I have used that word, which I have occasionally, it was because I was writing about *that* kind of a window—never for window as such. In this, perhaps, I have unconsciously tried to do just what Chaucer did when the language was young and untried and virile. I have sought only those words I have met up with as a boy in New Hampshire, working on farms during the summer vacations. I listened to the men with whom I worked, and found that I could make out their conversation as they talked together out of ear-shot, even when I had not plainly heard the words they spoke. When I started to carry their conversation over into poetry, I could hear their voices, and the sound posture differentiated between one and the other. It was the sense of sound I have been talking about. In some sort of way like this I have been able to write poetry, where characters talk, and, though not without infinite pains, to make it plain to the reader which character is saying the lines, without having to place his name before it, as is done in the drama.

—Robert Frost, quoted in *Robert Frost: Life and Talks—Walking* (1965) by Louis Mertins

In this quotation from Louis Mertins's *Robert Frost: Life and Talks—Walking,* Frost explains why and how he came to almost always use common, everyday vocabulary in his poetry. He traces this choice to the language of the men he worked with in New Hampshire as a boy and his attempt to capture the poetry of their colloquial speech. While this diction might seem unsophisticated, Frost points out how it can be so finely adjusted that readers can instantly recognize the shift from one speaker to another, without it being spelled out for them.

Background

Explain to students that in Chaucer's time, Latin was the language of educated Englishmen. Books were written in Latin; religious services were held in Latin. English was considered the vernacular or "vulgar" language, the language spoken by the common people. Chaucer was influenced by French medieval romances and the poetry and tales of Dante, Petrarch, and Boccaccio—all of which were written in the vernacular. In his own work—notably *The Canterbury Tales*—Chaucer has his characters speak in a way that reveals what they are like, and he writes about ordinary people, as well as nobles.

Reaching All Students

Struggling Readers

Have students choose partners. Both students should read aloud and listen to the first five Frost poems. Then tell partners to produce line-by-line paraphrases of the poems together.

English Language Learners

To help students hear Frost's conversational tone, have them listen to the recordings of his poems in the *Audio CD Library.* Then, have them listen a second time for meaning while following along in their books.

Advanced Learners

Have students read additional poems by Frost. Encourage them to present poems they especially like in class. Students may want to recite the poems they like, illustrate them, or write essays comparing and contrasting them with some of the poems in this collection.

Summary

The speaker of this poem sees a white spider on a white flower catch a white moth. The speaker muses on whether the disturbing convergence of these three pale creatures was chance or design.

Background

Students will recall that the sonnet form dates from the fourteenth century; they may be surprised to learn that Frost is only one of many modern and contemporary poets to use this very old form. Edward Arlington Robinson (p. 644), Chilean poet Pablo Neruda (p. 367) and Langston Hughes (p. 760), among others, have all focused on this form.

RESPONDING TO THE ART

Maurits Cornelis Escher (1898–1972), a Dutch graphic artist, based many of his richly imaginative compositions on geometry and optical illusions. In *Butterflies,* the detailed and realistic butterflies have metamorphosed from purely geometric forms.
Activity. Have students look up the noun *design* and discuss which meanings apply to Frost's poem and which to Escher's engraving. [Frost: intention; plan; purpose; plot. Escher: sketch; pattern; arrangement.]

Ⓐ Elements of Literature
Meter
Have a volunteer read the poem aloud. Ask students to name the meter. [iambic pentameter] Is the meter regular or irregular? [almost entirely regular] How do the meter and rhythm affect the tone of the poem? [Possible answer: Regular meter and long lines give it a grave, serious tone.]

Ⓑ Elements of Literature
Irony
❓ Why do you think Frost chose a heal-all rather than some other white flower? [Possible answer: for the irony of having a medicinal plant be an accessory to the moth's death.]

Before You Read
DESIGN

Make the Connection
Design of Darkness
Anyone who has had a direct experience of nature knows that sudden violence and grisly death are facts of life: The strong eat the weak; the slow are overcome by the quick; the healthy ultimately die and decay. By human standards, nature can be cold and merciless. To paraphrase Frost in this poem, nature can be "appalling."

Quickwrite

Read the first line of the poem, and write down your prediction about what the tone of the poem will be. What words lead you to that conclusion?

Background
Frost was particularly proud of his **sonnets,** which are considered among the finest in the English language. He often expressed regret that more of them were not reprinted in the hundreds of anthologies in which his work appeared. "Design" reveals how densely packed with ideas his sonnets can be. (For more about sonnets, see page 180 and the Handbook of Literary Terms.)

Butterflies (1950) by M. C. Escher. Wood engraving (28 cm × 26 cm).

Ⓐ Design

Robert Frost

I found a dimpled spider, fat and white,
On a white heal-all,° holding up a moth
Like a white piece of rigid satin cloth—
Assorted characters of death and blight
5 Mixed ready to begin the morning right,
Like the ingredients of a witches' broth—
A snowdrop spider, a flower like a froth,°
And dead wings carried like a paper kite.

Ⓑ What had that flower to do with being white,
10 The wayside blue and innocent heal-all?
What brought the kindred spider to that height,
Then steered the white moth thither° in the night?
What but design of darkness to appall?—
If design govern in a thing so small.

  2. heal-all: flowering plant of the mint family. The flowers, leaves, and stems are used in folk medicine to treat sore throats and other minor ailments.
  7. froth: foam.
  12. thither: archaic for "there."

Using Students' Strengths

Visual Learners
Have students locate and look at more of M. C. Escher's work. As an extension, students may enjoy dipping into *Gödel, Escher, Bach* (1979), Douglas Hofstadter's prize-winning study of recurrent and complementary patterns in the work of these three men. Then have them try illustrating this sonnet in Escher's style. Suggest that they limit the number of objects in their illustration.

Logical/Mathematical Learners
Discuss how a sonnet is like a puzzle or math problem because of the many restrictions the form has. Review the characteristics of an Italian sonnet in English (fourteen lines; the octave often poses a problem, and the sestet resolves it; *abbaabba, cdccdc* or *abbaabba, cdecde* rhyme scheme; iambic pentameter), and then ask pairs of students to compose a sonnet. Encourage them to choose a single event or dominant metaphor to convey their idea.

First Thoughts

1. Did your prediction in the Quickwrite about the **tone** of the poem prove correct, or did the poem surprise you? Explain.

Shaping Interpretations

2. What **similes** occur in the octave (first eight lines) of this sonnet? How do they affect the **tone** of the poem?

3. Identify the three "characters" of the poem, and tell what is happening to each one. What color is each character? What justifies the poet's description of these things as "characters of death and blight"?

4. Look up the word *character* in a dictionary. Explain which definitions of the word Frost might be applying in line 4. How does each definition affect the meaning of the line?

5. Describe the **rhyme scheme** of the poem. In your view, what key words or concepts do the limited rhyming sounds focus on?

6. In line 13, the poet answers his own questions with another question. Explain how his final question answers the previous ones. How would you define a "design of darkness"?

7. In line 14, Frost qualifies his answer with a reservation, beginning with a crucial "If." What is the reservation that remains in his mind?

8. How does the last line affect the whole **tone** and meaning of the poem?

Extending the Text

9. How do you think a Puritan (page 9) writer would have answered the questions Frost asks in this poem? How do you think a rationalist (page 13), or deist (page 16), would answer them?

Challenging the Text

10. The critic Laurence Perrine made this comment about "Design":

> Frost's brief poem, like the wayside blue or white heal-all, seems from the outside innocent enough. But within its fourteen innocent-seeming lines, Frost chillingly poses the problem of evil.
>
> —Laurence Perrine

Do you agree or disagree with this comment? Give reasons for your response. If you disagree, state what *you* think is the poem's central issue.

4. Definitions: personality; role in a story or play; signifying mark. Frost suggests that the moth, spider, and flower all play roles in this grim pageant.

5. Rhyme scheme: *abbaabba acaacc.* Frost emphasizes the word "white" by using it twice as an end rhyme and repeating it elsewhere.

6. The rhetorical question in l. 13 finds a sinister design in the deadly convergence of the white flower, spider, and moth. The "design of darkness" could be seen as a force of evil or malevolence.

7. The speaker questions whether one can claim purpose at all in the death of one small moth.

8. It suggests that evil may be random, not part of any plan. The poem ultimately allows the possibility that life and death may lack intrinsic meaning.

Extending the Text [Apply]

9. Possible answers: A Puritan would say that human beings should not try to fathom the mind of God; a rationalist or deist would say that insects and the plant are all part of the perfect mechanism of God's good design.

Challenging the Text [Evaluate]

10. Agree: Frost suggests that an appalling evil is woven into the fabric of nature—whether by design or by accident. Disagree: The poem is primarily about nature, not about evil.

MAKING MEANINGS

First Thoughts [Respond]

1. Possible answer: "Dimpled" suggested humor and cuteness and later seemed ironic, given the serious and disturbing tone of the poem.

Shaping Interpretations [Interpret]

2. The moth is compared to white cloth; spider, flower, and moth are compared to a witches' soup; the flower is like a froth; the moth's wings are like a kite. The tone is unsettling; all these similes suggest death or malignity.

3. The characters are the white flower, which camouflages the white spider, which captures the white moth, which lights on the flower. Each has the paleness of death and sickness, and each participates in the "play" of the moth's death.

Summary ■■■

The speaker suggests that beauty and goodness in nature and in human life are temporary and transient. All things in God's creation fall from a state of perfection.

Ⓐ English Language Learners

Paraphrasing

Have students rewrite the poem in their own words. Then, have them choose partners to discuss and answer the Making Meanings questions.

Ⓑ Critical Thinking

Analyzing

Remind students that Adam and Eve were expelled from the Garden of Eden for eating the fruit of the tree of knowledge. Ask students whether they think knowledge is better than beauty and innocence. Might it be just as well that "nothing gold can stay"? [Possible answer: Even if innocence or beauty (gold) represents a more perfect state of being, knowledge gives people more choices and greater power to alleviate suffering.]

RESPONDING TO THE ART

Thomas Cole (1801–1848) was a founder of the Hudson River School, a group of landscape painters known for their sweeping vistas of New York State. Later in his career, Cole turned increasingly away from landscapes and toward historical and allegorical themes like the one shown here.

Activity. Ask students whether this painting is an appropriate illustration for this poem and why or why not. [Yes, it depicts the expulsion from Eden that Frost alludes to. No, it is grandiose and romanticized, while Frost's poem is more modest and realistic.]

Before You Read
NOTHING GOLD CAN STAY

Make the Connection

Good as Gold

"Gold," whether it refers to the metal or to the color, conjures up a myriad of images and meanings. Over the centuries, writers and artists have used gold as a symbol of perfection.

Quickwrite

Briefly write what you predict the poem is going to be about, based on its title.

Background

To understand this little lyric, you need to know about two other literary accounts: the Biblical account of Adam and Eve's loss of innocence and their expulsion from the Garden of Eden; and, in Greek mythology, the loss of the Golden Age, a time of innocent happiness that was an image of paradise for the ancient Greeks and Romans.

Ⓐ Nothing Gold Can Stay

Robert Frost

Nature's first green is gold,
Her hardest hue to hold.
Her early leaf's a flower;
But only so an hour.
Then leaf subsides to leaf.
Ⓑ So Eden sank to grief,
So dawn goes down to day.
Nothing gold can stay.

Expulsion from the Garden of Eden (detail) (1828) by Thomas Cole.

Gift of Mrs. Maxim Karolik for the M. and M. Karolik Collection of American Paintings, 1815–1856. Courtesy, Museum of Fine Arts, Boston.

MAKING MEANINGS

First Thoughts

1. Review your Quickwrite, and explain whether the **title** of the poem helped you predict its message.

562 THE MODERNS

Shaping Interpretations

2. Identify four specific things that the poem says cannot, or did not, "stay."
3. Think what the first buds of leaves look like in spring, and explain what line 1 means.

Making the Connections

Cultural Connections

Adam and Eve's expulsion from the Garden of Eden represents both the loss of innocence as one passes from childhood to adulthood and the loss of innocence of all humanity. According to Greek and Roman mythology, the Golden Age was a time of innocent happiness. The Titans lived in a world of great abundance, where there was no sickness or war. When Zeus dethroned the Titan ruler, Cronus, the Golden Age ended.

MAKING MEANINGS

First Thoughts [Respond]

1. Possible answers: Yes, the title suggested a poem about loss. No, the title did not suggest a poem about nature.

Shaping Interpretations [Interpret]

2. Possible response: the first leaves of spring; Adam and Eve's innocence; dawn; everything gold.
3. Buds have a bright luster like gold and are valuable as harbingers of spring.

4. Explain the natural process described in line 5.
5. What Biblical event is alluded to in line 6? What state of mind or situation might "Eden" **symbolize** here?
6. What different ideas might "gold" symbolize in the poem? Why can't gold stay—or do you disagree?
7. Show how **rhyme** and **rhythm** contribute to this poem's compactness and completeness. How do **alliteration, slant rhyme,** and echo-ing **sound effects** contribute to the poem's tightly woven unity?

Extending the Text

8. In *Connections* below, Naomi Shihab Nye tries to name things that don't change. How are her poem and Frost's poem alike and different in **tone** and **message**? Identify the central point you think each poet is trying to convey about change and loss.

Connections A POEM

Trying to Name What Doesn't Change

Naomi Shihab Nye

Roselva says the only thing that doesn't change
is train tracks. She's sure of it.
The train changes, or the weeds that grow up spidery
by the side, but not the tracks.
5 I've watched one for three years, she says,
and it doesn't curve, doesn't break, doesn't grow.

Peter isn't sure. He saw an abandoned track
near Sabinas, Mexico, and says a track without a train
is a changed track. The metal wasn't shiny anymore.
10 The wood was split and some of the ties were gone.

Every Tuesday on Morales Street
butchers crack the necks of a hundred hens.
The widow in the tilted house
spices her soup with cinnamon.
15 Ask her what doesn't change.

Stars explode.
The rose curls up as if there is fire in the petals.
The cat who knew me is buried under the bush.

The train whistle still wails its ancient sound
20 but when it goes away, shrinking back
from the walls of the brain,
it takes something different with it every time.

ROBERT FROST 563

Connections

In this poem, Nye offers a number of different perspectives on what does and doesn't change in the world. While some people may see train tracks or neighborhood routines of cooking and work as unchanging, others may find constant change in these things—depending on their different perspectives and personalities. Even the predictable wail of the train whistle sounds different every time to the speaker, depending on the time, the mood, and the context.

A **Reading Skills and Strategies**
Connecting with the Text
❓ With whom do you agree, Roselva or Peter? Why? [Roselva: Train tracks don't change the way living things like weeds do. Peter: Tracks rust, split, or otherwise decay if not maintained. Both characters make accurate observations based on their own concerns.]

B **Critical Thinking**
Challenging the Text
❓ Why does Nye include the images of the butchers and the widow in her poem? [Possible answer: The speaker imagines that for these people, their daily routines are as unchanging as Roselva's train tracks.]

C **Critical Thinking**
Interpreting
❓ Why does the speaker include these images? [Possible responses: They show that enormous objects change; that things that seem stable and eternal to us change; that things change whether humans pay attention or not.]

---

4. The first young shoots become mature leaves.
5. "Eden sank to grief" when Adam and Eve disobeyed God and ate fruit from the tree of knowledge. It might symbolize any loss of innocence and disillusionment.
6. Possible answers: beauty; youth; happiness; love; innocence; goodness. Agree: Nature and emotions cannot remain static; they must develop and change. Disagree: Humanly created beauty, such as great works of art, represents a kind of gold that can stay.

7. The first and last lines depart from the otherwise regular meter (iambic trimeter), so they stand out. The rhymed couplets emphasize the poem's theme. The repetition, alliteration, and slant rhyme (*flower* and *hour*) connect the lines of the poem.

Extending the Text [Analyze]

8. Frost suggests that everything changes and that this is a cause for regret. Nye observes that change is largely dependent on patterns of human perception and activity.

Connecting Across Texts

Connecting with "Nothing Gold Can Stay"
Have students consider how Nye's poem relates to Frost's. Do the two poems share a common theme, or do they present opposing viewpoints? In what way does Nye's poem reflect the collection theme "Loss and Redemption"? Students can consider these questions in comparison-and-contrast essays.

Summary ▪▪

The speaker in this sonnet personifies great waves crashing on a beach at the foot of a cliff and imagines them carrying out an apocalyptic destruction of creation.

Ⓐ Reading Skills and Strategies
Making Inferences

❓ What are the "hairy" clouds? [storm clouds with descending trails of rain] **Whose eyes and hair might Frost be alluding to here? Why do you think so?** [Possible answers: God's, because of the allusion in the final line; a classical god's, perhaps Neptune's or Jupiter's (because the view is from the sky toward the earth).]

Ⓑ Appreciating Language
Parallelism and Connotation

❓ What is the effect of the parallellism in these lines? [Possible answer: The parallelism of "in being backed by" emphasizes the bulwark that the land is "lucky" to have against the sea, and by contrast this makes the encroaching force of the waves seem all the more threatening.] **How does the word "lucky" also undercut the sense of security?** [It suggests that other less lucky places will not fare as well.]

Ⓒ Humanities Connections

Here Frost reverses God's command in Genesis 1:3, "Let there be light," and imagines God destroying the world He created. Have students think of other examples from literature and popular culture in which light comes to represent creation or life.

With this phrase, Frost also echoes a famous line from the final act of Shakespeare's *Othello*. As he steels himself to murder Desdemona, Othello murmurs, "Put out the light; and then put out the light." He refers first to extinguishing a candle by the bed, and then putting out the flame of Desdemona's life.

Before You Read
ONCE BY THE PACIFIC

Make the Connection
The End of All Things

In the Bible, when God creates the universe, he says, "Let there be light." After each stage of creation, the Bible says, "And God saw that it was good." Keep these ideas in mind as you read Frost's vision of an event that is the opposite of creation.

Quickwrite

You've seen waves pounding against the shore, in person or on film. In a few sentences, describe your thoughts as you watched the watery assault.

Once by the Pacific

Robert Frost

> The shattered water made a misty din.
> Great waves looked over others coming in,
> And thought of doing something to the shore
> That water never did to land before.
> Ⓐ 5 The clouds were low and hairy in the skies,
> Like locks blown forward in the gleam of eyes.
> You could not tell, and yet it looked as if
> Ⓑ The shore was lucky in being backed by cliff,
> The cliff in being backed by continent;
> 10 It looked as if a night of dark intent
> Was coming, and not only a night, an age.
> Someone had better be prepared for rage.
> Ⓒ There would be more than ocean-water broken
> Before God's last *Put out the Light* was spoken.

564 THE MODERNS

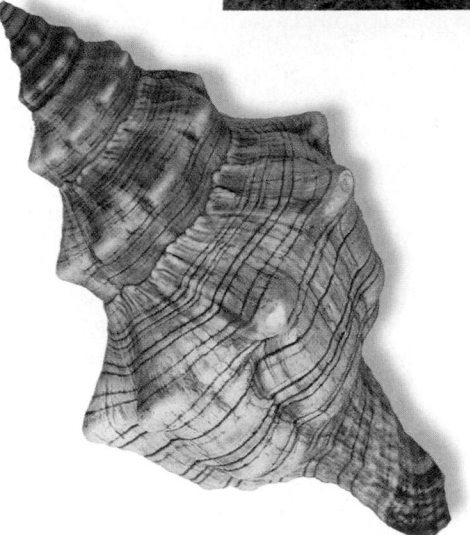

Using Students' Strengths

Verbal Learners

Students who know a second language well can read sonnets in that other language. Organize students into small reading groups. Tell them to read five sonnets in the second language. Possible sources include *Il Canzoniere* by Petrarch (Italian); *Sonnets pour Hélène* by Pierre de Ronsard (French); Rainer Maria Rilke's *Die Sonette an Orpheus* (German); and Pablo Neruda's *Cien sonetos de amor* (Spanish). Students who know only English can read sonnets by Shakespeare.

Reading groups should read the poems aloud and compare the poems with Frost's sonnets for content, language, and structure.

Naturalist Learners

Tell students to examine Frost's descriptions of and attitudes toward the natural world: insects, flowers, the sea, birch trees, an ice storm, and so on. Have them write brief essays on how effectively Frost uses language to evoke nature. Do students get the sense that Frost is a detailed observer and genuine lover of nature?

Rocks and Breakers, California (1913) by William Ritschel. Oil on canvas.

Make the Connection

Ocean Reveries

For some, the sea is an object of reverie, inspiring a sense of peace and oneness with the world. For others, the sea represents a powerful, mysterious force of nature. What other things might the sea symbolize?

Quickwrite

Before you read the poem, write down your guess as to the meaning of Frost's puzzling title.

Neither Out Far Nor In Deep

Robert Frost

The people along the sand
All turn and look one way.
They turn their back on the land.
They look at the sea all day.

 A

5 As long as it takes to pass
A ship keeps raising its hull;
The wetter ground like glass
Reflects a standing gull.

The land may vary more;
10 But wherever the truth may be—
The water comes ashore,
And the people look at the sea.

They cannot look out far.
They cannot look in deep.
15 But when was that ever a bar°
To any watch they keep?

B

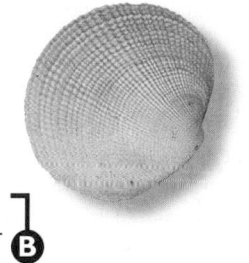

15. **bar:** barrier; obstruction.

ROBERT FROST **565**

Summary ■

In this poem, the speaker examines the limitation and conformity of human perception through the metaphor of people staring at the sea. Despite the greater variety of the land, despite the fact that they can see only a small piece of the ocean's expanse, and despite the fact that the truth may lie elsewhere, people keep watch on the sea, transfixed in their ignorance.

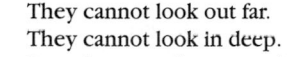

RESPONDING TO THE ART

William Ritschel (1864–1949) was born in Germany. He moved to the United States in 1895 and settled in California, where he soon won recognition as a painter of seascapes like the one pictured here.

Activity. Ask students whether the mood of this painting is more like that of "Once by the Pacific" or more like "Neither Out Far . . ." and why. [Possible responses: "Once by the Pacific," because of the violence of the waves crashing over the rocks; "Neither Out Far . . . ," because the painting emphasizes the contrast between the land and the sea.]

A Critical Thinking

Interpreting

❓ What do ll. 2–4 suggest or symbolize about the people the speaker refers to? [Line 2 suggests conformity and lack of creativity in the people who all "look one way." Lines 3–4 suggest that the same people turn their backs on substance and stability in favor of glossy and superficial surfaces.]

B Critical Thinking

Interpreting

❓ How do you interpret the reference to truth in this stanza? What is the speaker implying? [Possible answers: People are more interested in seeking than in finding, or people do not really want to know the truth. Even if the truth were on land and therefore accessible, people would rather reach for an intangible surface that is beyond their grasp.]

Professional Notes

Critical Comment:
Walcott on Frost's Characters

"Frost is an autocratic poet rather than a democratic poet," observed poet and critic Derek Walcott in 1996. "His invitations are close-lipped, wry, quiet; neither the voice nor the metrical line has the open-armed municipal mural expansion of the other democratic poet, Whitman. The people in Frost's dramas occupy a tight and taciturn locale. They are not part of Whitman's parade of blacksmiths, wheelwrights made communal by work. Besieged and threatened, their virtues are as cautious and measured as the scansion by which they are portrayed."

As students read through the poems in this collection, have them think about this assessment. Do students agree or disagree with Walcott?

Once by the Pacific

First Thoughts [Respond]

1. Students may have thought of the overwhelming power and beauty of nature, or perhaps they experienced a heightened sense of their own mortality.

Shaping Interpretations [Interpret]

2. The scene is high tide against the cliffs before an approaching storm. Possible responses: The scene puts the speaker in mind of Noah's flood or the apocalypse.
3. The speaker suggests that God intends to destroy his creation and that it will not recover for ages.
4. Humanity, or possibly only sinners, ought to be prepared to face God's rage.
5. All life on earth may be "broken" or destroyed.
6. The contrast between the everyday phrase and the apocalypse is chilling. Possible message: The world may end as it began, with God's simple command.
7. Possible answers: the end of the world; Noah's flood.

Connecting with the Text [Analyze]

8. Possible answers: The speaker warns us that the world may come to an end at any time. Or he may simply voice the philosophy that the power of nature is reminiscent of the God's power in the Bible or that nature has a cycle of creation and destruction.

Neither Out Far Nor In Deep

First Thoughts [Respond]

1. Possible response: These words emphasize the safe distance people maintain between themselves and the sea.

Shaping Interpretations [Interpret]

2. The wet sand is compared to glass. The simile adds a clear, concrete detail about the land amidst a vague picture of the sea.
3. These lines highlight the ironic detail that even the water is drawn to the land (of truth and stability), while people, in ignorant escapism, still look seaward.
4. The land may symbolize truth, stability, and what is known; the sea may symbolize danger and the unknown. "Watch" might mean waiting, or

MAKING MEANINGS

Once by the Pacific

First Thoughts

1. Review the notes you made in your Quickwrite. How do the speaker's thoughts in the poem compare to the thoughts you had while watching crashing waves?

Shaping Interpretations

2. Describe the scene presented in the poem. What does the scene remind the speaker of?
3. Explain what you think the speaker means by "a night of dark intent /. . . not only a night, an age" (lines 10–11). Whose "intent" is he referring to?
4. Who do you think is the "someone" who "had better be prepared for rage" (line 12)? Whose "rage"?
5. Besides ocean water, what else might be "broken" during that rage?
6. "Put out the light" is something anyone might say on an ordinary evening at home. How does the use of this casual, domestic phrase make the poem's **message** even more chilling? What would you say that message is?
7. The poem's title suggests that Frost is describing a scene he once saw as he gazed at the Pacific Ocean. What larger event might this scene **symbolize**?

566 THE MODERNS

Connecting with the Text

8. Do you view this poem as a warning? Or, do you think Frost is just expressing a certain philosophy of life? Explain what the warning might be, or discuss the philosophy revealed in the poem.

Neither Out Far Nor In Deep

First Thoughts

1. Review your Quickwrite. Why do you think Frost included the words *out far* and *in deep* in the poem's title?

Shaping Interpretations

2. What is the one **simile** that Frost uses in the poem? How does it affect the scene described?
3. In what way are lines 11–12 tinged with **irony**?
4. What might the sea and the land **symbolize** in this poem? What larger meaning might the "watch" (line 16) take on?
5. Comment on the poet's **tone** in the last line. Does he admire the watchers for keeping their vigil, or does he feel scorn or pity for their failure to recognize their limitations? Do you have another interpretation? Explain.
6. On a literal level, why is it that the people in the poem can look neither "out far" nor "in deep"? What more general human limitations might be symbolized by our inability to probe the distance and depth of the sea?

suggest that people look for something better without first recognizing what is around them.
5. The speaker is scornful or pitying in the face of human limitation and ignorance.
6. Possible response: The human eye cannot see far enough to observe the bounds of the ocean or the depths of the sea. Students might suggest that humans can never understand the larger picture of existence because they are always bound by their own experiences or that they follow the same patterns of behavior without considering alternatives.

Make the Connection

Life Lessons

A **parable** is a short story in which an ordinary event from everyday life is used to teach a much wider moral or religious lesson. In this poem, Frost draws a lesson from nature—from the sight of the bent branches of birch trees.

Reading Skills and Strategies

Reading Poetry

Frost's poems are written in a form that is very close to conversational English. (See Primary Sources, page 559, and **blank verse,** page 575.) Read the poem aloud to hear the rise and fall of the speaker's voice. When you come to a period, whether at the end of a line or in the middle of a line, make a full stop. When you come to a comma, semicolon, or dash, pause slightly. If there is no mark of punctuation at the end of a line, read right on to the next without pausing.

Background

As spindly and awkward as a giraffe's legs, the birch trees of Robert Frost's New England have white bark ringed with black. Their trunks are remarkably pliable—a fact that gives this poem its realistic base. Children do, in fact, climb and swing on birch trees.

Birches

Robert Frost

When I see birches bend to left and right
Across the lines of straighter darker trees,
I like to think some boy's been swinging them.
But swinging doesn't bend them down to stay
5   As ice storms do. Often you must have seen them   **A**
Loaded with ice a sunny winter morning
After a rain. They click upon themselves
As the breeze rises, and turn many-colored
As the stir cracks and crazes their enamel.
10 Soon the sun's warmth makes them shed crystal shells
Shattering and avalanching on the snow crust—
Such heaps of broken glass to sweep away
You'd think the inner dome of heaven had fallen.
They are dragged to the withered bracken° by the load,
15 And they seem not to break; though once they are bowed
So low for long, they never right themselves:
You may see their trunks arching in the woods
Years afterwards, trailing their leaves on the ground
Like girls on hands and knees that throw their hair
20 Before them over their heads to dry in the sun.
But I was going to say when Truth broke in
With all her matter of fact about the ice storm,
I should prefer to have some boy bend them
As he went out and in to fetch the cows—
25 Some boy too far from town to learn baseball,
Whose only play was what he found himself,
Summer or winter, and could play alone.
One by one he subdued his father's trees
By riding them down over and over again
30 Until he took the stiffness out of them,
And not one but hung limp, not one was left
For him to conquer. He learned all there was
To learn about not launching out too soon
And so not carrying the tree away   **C**

14. bracken: large, coarse fern.

ROBERT FROST 567

Summary ∎

When the speaker contemplates a row of birches, bent to the ground, he imagines the different ways they may have gotten that way, personifying the trees through metaphor and simile. When nature itself bends them, during ice storms, they stay bowed over permanently. But when, as the speaker prefers, they are bent by a young boy climbing them and swinging them down, they can be "subdued" only through the repeated play of the child, a process the speaker describes on a literal and symbolic level. As a boy, he learned to climb birches, carefully ascending toward the glory of heaven, but also cherishing his descent to earthly reality when the trees bent under his weight. The speaker remembers this compromise between heaven and earth in troubled times, and longs again to be a "swinger of birches."

A **Reading Skills and Strategies**

Reading Poetry

Have a volunteer read ll. 1–9 aloud. Ask students where the pauses occur. [ends of ll. 2 and 3; middle of ll. 5, 7, and 8; end of l. 9] Remind students to analyze these pauses as clues to the thematic emphasis of the poem.

B **Reading Skills and Strategies**

Making Inferences

❓ What does the speaker admire in the boy? [independence; ambition; creativity; self-sufficiency; perseverance] What is the speaker suggesting about the way people should be? What would he "prefer"? [People should have the boy's qualities, his enjoyment of the world, his ambition to climb high and to conquer the trees.]

C **Appreciating Language**

Symbol

Discuss the lessons for living that one learns from swinging on birches. Explore the meaning of "not launching out too soon," not carrying the tree "Clear to the ground," keeping one's "poise," and "climbing carefully." Have students consider how the subsequent comparison to the overfull cup attaches a metaphor to a symbol. Point out how Frost packs a tremendous amount of meaning into a few lines.

Crossing the Curriculum

Science

Have students do some research on birch trees. What do they look like? How fast do they grow? How long do they live? In what climate do they thrive? Are they native to America? If not, when were they first planted here? Students can look in botanical reference books or do research on the Internet. Have them share the information they find with their classmates, so that everyone can better understand the subject of Frost's poem.

Music

Have students listen to the score for the ballet *Appalachian Spring,* composed by Aaron Copland for the Martha Graham dance company. Like Frost's poems, the ballet tells a simple story of ordinary rural America. Students may recognize the famous Shaker tune that ends the ballet. Have them compare and contrast Copland's and Frost's means of depicting nature, the country, and the dreams of ordinary Americans.

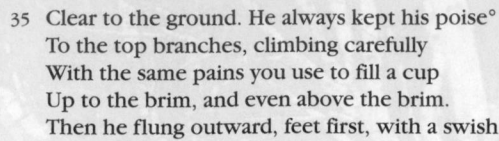

 A Elements of Literature
Simile

Ask students why this simile is especially effective. [Possible answers: It is an image of trees, so it underscores the poem's subject matter; it evokes an experience that many readers will identify with.]

B Reading Skills and Strategies
Reading Poetry

Ask a volunteer to read ll. 50–53 aloud, accenting the syllables in strict iambic pentameter. Have someone else read them naturally, as if they were prose. What do you hear? [Lines 51 and 52 tend to frustrate reading in strict iambic rhythm, while ll. 50 and 53 are more naturally iambic—thereby framing the complete idea between two smooth lines.]

MAKING MEANINGS

First Thoughts [Respond]

1. Possible answers: the affirmation of earth as the place for love; the portrait of a lonely child swinging in trees.

Shaping Interpretations [Interpret]

2. He imagines that a boy has been swinging on the trees. He realizes that the trees would not still be bent over if this were the case and that the trees were probably bent during an ice storm.

3. Metaphors: ice as "enamel," "crystal shells," and "broken glass" (ll. 9–12). Onomatopoeia: "click" (l. 7), "cracks" (l. 9), "swish" (l. 39), "lashed" (l. 47).

4. Bent birches are compared to girls bending forward to dry their hair (ll. 19–20). Life is compared to a pathless wood with cobwebs and sharp twigs (ll. 44–47).

5. Possible answers: It symbolizes a reasonable approach to the human pursuit of heavenly glory, fulfillment, greatness, or virtue.

6. Possible answer: People use the birches to climb toward heaven, to reach for something greater or accomplish something special, but the speaker reminds himself that he ultimately wishes to humbly descend to earth, where love—our greatest joy and satisfaction—is found. On the other hand, he recognizes that the attempt to ascend is part of human nature.

T568

---

35 Clear to the ground. He always kept his poise°
    To the top branches, climbing carefully
    With the same pains you use to fill a cup
    Up to the brim, and even above the brim.
    Then he flung outward, feet first, with a swish,
40 Kicking his way down through the air to the ground.
    So was I once myself a swinger of birches.
    And so I dream of going back to be.
    It's when I'm weary of considerations,
    And life is too much like a pathless wood
45 Where your face burns and tickles with the cobwebs
    Broken across it, and one eye is weeping
    From a twig's having lashed across it open.
    I'd like to get away from earth awhile
    And then come back to it and begin over.
50 May no fate willfully misunderstand me
    And half grant what I wish and snatch me away
    Not to return. Earth's the right place for love:
    I don't know where it's likely to go better.
    I'd like to go by climbing a birch tree,
55 And climb black branches up a snow-white trunk
    Toward heaven, till the tree could bear no more,
    But dipped its top and set me down again.
    That would be good both going and coming back.
    One could do worse than be a swinger of birches.

35. **poise:** balance.

MAKING MEANINGS

First Thoughts

1. Which passages of this poem do you think are especially interesting or true to life?

Shaping Interpretations

2. Describe the scenario that the speaker imagines when he sees birch trees. What realistic objection to his idea does he recognize in lines 4–5? What "matter of fact" does "Truth" break in with in lines 5–10?

3. Find at least three examples of **metaphor** and **onomatopoeia** in the poem.

4. Two strong **similes** give the poem a richness that is both imaginative and the result of close observation. What are these similes?

5. What does the playful activity of birch swinging seem to **symbolize** in the poem?

568 THE MODERNS

6. Summarize in your own words what you think is the **moral** or **message** of Frost's **parable** about birch swinging. What complex, conflicting attitudes toward life does it reveal?

7. How does the sound of Frost's poem differ from the sound of any of Whitman's poems (pages 352–362)?

Extending the Text

8. If a Puritan writer were to come upon the bent birches, what response do you think he or she would have to the natural scene? What response would a Transcendentalist like Ralph Waldo Emerson (page 216) have had?

Challenging the Text

9. In a famous remark about the nature of poetry, Frost said that a poem "begins in delight and ends in wisdom." Do you agree or disagree that this applies to "Birches"? Explain your view, including what you think *delight* and *wisdom* mean.

---

7. "Birches" has a conversational tone and regular meter that make it sound quieter, more intimate, and more private than Whitman's boisterous, forceful, and emphatic poems.

Extending the Text [Apply]

8. A Puritan might be thankful for God's gift of birches and draw a moral lesson, such as how one must bend to the will of God. Emerson might appreciate the beauty of the birches and see in them the immediate presence of God.

Challenging the Text [Evaluate]

9. Possible answer: "Birches" begins with an image of childhood pleasure and ends with a serious statement about life. *Delight* refers to the pleasure that comes from the artistry of the poem. *Wisdom* refers to the serious questions the poem makes the reader think about.

Make the Connection

Home Is Where the Heart Is
Embedded in this poem is one of Frost's most famous sayings, one often quoted by many people who probably have no idea where it comes from: "'Home is the place where, when you have to go there, / They have to take you in.'" Another definition of home is also offered in the poem: "'Something you somehow haven't to deserve.'" To some people, "home" is a definite place; to others, it is a state of mind, a sense of connectedness and belonging.

Reading Skills and Strategies

Drawing Inferences About Characters
Read this poem as if it were a short story. As you read, make notes about the feelings that you sense operate between Warren and Mary. What complex feelings do you think each of them has toward Silas, the hired man? Also, note your own feelings or impressions about each of these three characters. Do your feelings change as the poem goes on?

Elements of Literature

Dialogue in Verse
Most of this poem is a **dialogue** in **blank verse** (see page 575). The poem's main character never speaks for himself, yet his presence dominates the poem through the dialogue of the other characters. By the last line, we have heard enough about the hired man to understand his background, habits, and attitudes. In gradually coming to know him, we also come to know the personalities of the husband and wife whose dialogue carries the drama.

The Death of the Hired Man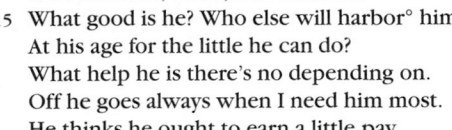

Robert Frost

Mary sat musing on the lamp-flame at the table,
Waiting for Warren. When she heard his step,
She ran on tiptoe down the darkened passage
To meet him in the doorway with the news
5 And put him on his guard. "Silas is back."
She pushed him outward with her through the door
And shut it after her. "Be kind," she said.
She took the market things from Warren's arms
And set them on the porch, then drew him down
10 To sit beside her on the wooden steps.

"When was I ever anything but kind to him?
But I'll not have the fellow back," he said.
"I told him so last haying, didn't I?
If he left then, I said, that ended it.
15 What good is he? Who else will harbor° him
At his age for the little he can do?
What help he is there's no depending on.
Off he goes always when I need him most.
He thinks he ought to earn a little pay,
20 Enough at least to buy tobacco with,
So he won't have to beg and be beholden.°
'All right,' I say, 'I can't afford to pay

15. **harbor:** provide safe shelter for.

21. **beholden:** indebted.

ROBERT FROST 569

Summary ◾

Mary and Warren, a farm couple, discuss Silas, a deteriorating old man who used to work for them. Silas has now returned after a lengthy absence. Warren does not want to take him in, but Mary insists that Silas has come "home" to die, and the couple speculate further about what his intentions might be, what "home" really means, and what redemption it might offer. When Warren goes inside to see Silas, he finds him dead.

Ⓐ Elements of Literature

Dialogue in Verse
To help students follow the conversation, point out that there is a line or stanza break each time a different character speaks.

Ⓑ Reading Skills and Strategies

Drawing Inferences About Characters
❓ What can you infer about Warren from Mary's warning him to be kind? [Possible answers: He is habitually impatient or harsh; there is some problem between him and Silas.]

Ⓒ Elements of Literature

Dialogue in Verse
Have a volunteer read the first four lines of Warren's speech aloud (omitting "he said"). What do students notice about the meter? [When the lines are spoken naturally and in character, they are not strictly iambic.] Why is this looseness appropriate? [Possible answers: because human beings don't speak in strict meter; because Warren is irritated.]

Ⓓ Reading Skills and Strategies

Drawing Inferences About Characters
❓ What does this statement reveal about Silas? [He is too proud to beg; he does not want the humiliation of being financially dependent on other people.]

Reaching All Students

Struggling Readers
One good strategy to use with this poem is Say Something. For information on using this strategy, see p. 85 in the *Reading Strategies Handbook,* in the *Reading Skills and Strategies* binder.

English Language Learners
Students may find this long, thoughtful poem easier to follow as a play than as a silent-reading assignment. Assign the roles of narrator, Mary, and Warren, and have students give a dramatic reading for the class.

Advanced Learners
Ask students to work in a group to write the scene of Silas's return. Have them write the dialogue between Silas and Mary in blank verse. They should use all the information they can glean from Mary and Warren's conversation, such as Silas's changed looks and Mary's trying to get him to talk about where he has been.

Winslow Homer (1836–1910) is best known for the solid and unsentimental realism of his depictions of fishermen, sailors, farmers, and seascapes. In *The Veteran in a New Field,* for example, he simultaneously communicates a realistic moment in the swinging of a scythe, an impression of peace, and Biblical symbols of war and reconciliation (Isaiah 2:4, "swords into plowshares").

Activities

1. Ask students how Homer's and Frost's works are similar in style. [Possible answer: Both portray the dignity of ordinary country people.]

2. Ask what this painting reveals about farm life. [This man's life is rustic and hard; farm work is solitary and demanding.]

The Veteran in a New Field (1865) by Winslow Homer. Oil on canvas.
The Metropolitan Museum of Art. Bequest of Miss Adelaide Milton de Groot, 1967 (67.187.131). Photograph © The Metropolitan Museum of Art.

 Elements of Literature
Dialogue in Verse
Explain to students that in this passage Warren is relating a conversation he had with Silas. The single quotation marks differentiate when Warren speaks and when Silas speaks.

B **Struggling Readers**
Paraphrasing
Have students explain what Warren's grudge against Silas is. [Silas deserted Warren during the busy season because he got a better offer; he came back in the slow season, when Warren doesn't need his help.]

 Reading Skills and Strategies
Drawing Inferences About Characters
❓ What does this exchange reveal about Mary and Warren? [She is kinder and more considerate than he is; he is more impatient and blunt than she is.]

A
Any fixed wages, though I wish I could.'
'Someone else can.' 'Then someone else will have to.'
25 I shouldn't mind his bettering himself
If that was what it was. You can be certain,
When he begins like that, there's someone at him
B
Trying to coax him off with pocket money—
In haying time, when any help is scarce.
30 In winter he comes back to us. I'm done."

C
"Sh! not so loud: He'll hear you," Mary said.

"I want him to: He'll have to soon or late."

"He's worn out. He's asleep beside the stove.
When I came up from Rowe's I found him here,
35 Huddled against the barn door fast asleep,
A miserable sight, and frightening, too—
You needn't smile—I didn't recognize him—
I wasn't looking for him—and he's changed.
Wait till you see."

                    "Where did you say he'd been?"

40 "He didn't say. I dragged him to the house,
And gave him tea and tried to make him smoke.
I tried to make him talk about his travels.

570 THE MODERNS

Getting Students Involved

Cooperative Learning

Role-Play. Have students choose partners to role-play a conversation between two of the characters. Offer the following three scenarios:
- Mary and Silas talk together before Warren comes home.
- Warren informs Silas's brother of Silas's death.
- Silas and Harold talk while they work on the farm together.

Encourage students to look at the poem for clues about how their characters might carry themselves and what they might say in these situations. How do the two characters feel about each other? What do they want from each other? Have students work together beforehand and then present their conversations to the class.

Nothing would do: He just kept nodding off."

"What did he say? Did he say anything?"

"But little."

45   "Anything? Mary, confess
He said he'd come to ditch° the meadow for me."

"Warren!"

    "But did he? I just want to know."

"Of course he did. What would you have him say?
Surely you wouldn't grudge the poor old man
50 Some humble way to save his self-respect.
He added, if you really care to know,
He meant to clear the upper pasture, too.
That sounds like something you have heard before?
Warren, I wish you could have heard the way
55 He jumbled everything. I stopped to look
Two or three times—he made me feel so queer°—
To see if he was talking in his sleep.
He ran on° Harold Wilson—you remember—
The boy you had in haying four years since.
60 He's finished school, and teaching in his college.
Silas declares you'll have to get him back.
He says they two will make a team for work:
Between them they will lay this farm as smooth!
The way he mixed that in with other things.
65 He thinks young Wilson a likely lad, though daft
On education—you know how they fought
All through July under the blazing sun,
Silas up on the cart to build the load,
Harold along beside to pitch it on."

70 "Yes, I took care to keep well out of earshot."

"Well, those days trouble Silas like a dream.
You wouldn't think they would. How some things linger!
Harold's young college-boy's assurance piqued° him.
After so many years he still keeps finding
75 Good arguments he sees he might have used.
I sympathize. I know just how it feels
To think of the right thing to say too late.
Harold's associated in his mind with Latin.
He asked me what I thought of Harold's saying
80 He studied Latin, like the violin,
Because he liked it—that an argument!
He said he couldn't make the boy believe
He could find water with a hazel prong°—
Which showed how much good school had ever done him.
85 He wanted to go over that. But most of all
He thinks if he could have another chance

46. **ditch:** dig drainage channels in.

56. **queer:** uncomfortable; ill at ease.

58. **ran on:** kept talking in a rambling way about.

73. **piqued:** provoked.

83. **hazel prong:** forked branch used to find water underground.

ROBERT FROST 571

D Reading Skills and Strategies

Drawing Inferences About Characters

? Is Warren justified in being suspicious of or angry at Silas? [Possible answer: Yes, Silas had not been a dependable worker; he left Warren shorthanded in the middle of the busy season and only returned in winter, when no one else would give him work. Warren does not want to be taken advantage of.]

E Critical Thinking

Interpreting

? Why does Mary feel uncomfortable? [Possible answer: because Silas is rambling, and does not even seem to be fully conscious.]

F Reading Skills and Strategies

Drawing Inferences About Characters

? Why didn't Silas get along with Harold Wilson? [Silas was envious of Harold. Harold was getting an education and building a future for himself; he was studying subjects he liked; and he was strutting about with pride. As Mary says in ll.100–101, Silas was an old man who had little to be proud of in his past and no hope for a better future. Harold represented everything Silas could never be.]

G Elements of Literature

Dialogue in Verse

? What does Silas's comment reveal about his life? [He has had little formal education. He has worked on the land, where formal education would not have been a useful asset, all his life. He was insecure and wanted to make Harold respect him.]

Using Students' Strengths

Intrapersonal Learners

Have each student write a letter from one character to another. If students have trouble getting started, you might suggest a letter from Harold to a friend, reminiscing about Silas, or a letter from Silas's brother, telling his parents of Silas's death. Remind students to write in language appropriate to each character. Collect the letters in a book, and share them with the class.

Auditory/Musical Learners

Review different types of meter with students. Working with partners, have them choose one of the characters in the poem. Tell pairs to take notes on the ideas that one of the characters expresses and on his or her tone or attitude. Then, have them write a ten- to fifteen-line speech expressing those ideas and feelings, using a different meter.

A **Reading Skills and Strategies**

Drawing Inferences About Characters

? What does this stanza suggest about Silas? What does it suggest about Warren? [Silas has a legitimate skill to offer; Warren is both observant and fair.]

B **Elements of Literature**

Imagery

? What is striking about these lines? [It is the first fanciful image in the poem.] What does Frost suggest about Mary? [Possible answers: The image of playing the harp suggests that she exerts a soothing, angelic influence on those around her; the phrase "wrought on him" suggests that her compassion casts a kind of spell over Warren.]

C **Reading Skills and Strategies**

Drawing Inferences About Characters

? What do Warren's and Mary's definitions of home suggest about their feelings toward Silas? [Possible answers: Warren believes that Silas is taking advantage of their decency, making a claim on them when they don't have a clear obligation to take him in. Mary believes Silas comes because he trusts their kindness and has no other home (a place he doesn't have to deserve) to return to.]

D **Appreciating Language**

Connotations

? Why might Frost have chosen to make the distance thirteen miles? [The number thirteen suggests bad luck, possibly that Silas is unlikely to fare well with his brother.]

To teach him how to build a load of hay——"

"I know, that's Silas' one accomplishment.
He bundles every forkful in its place,
90   And tags and numbers it for future reference,
So he can find and easily dislodge it
In the unloading. Silas does that well.
He takes it out in bunches like big birds' nests.
You never see him standing on the hay
95   He's trying to lift, straining to lift himself."

"He thinks if he could teach him that, he'd be
Some good perhaps to someone in the world.
He hates to see a boy the fool of books.
Poor Silas, so concerned for other folk,
100   And nothing to look backward to with pride,
And nothing to look forward to with hope,
So now and never any different."

Part of a moon was falling down the west,
Dragging the whole sky with it to the hills.
105   Its light poured softly in her lap. She saw it
And spread her apron to it. She put out her hand
Among the harplike morning-glory strings,
Taut with the dew from garden bed to eaves,
As if she played unheard some tenderness
110   That wrought° on him beside her in the night.
"Warren," she said, "he has come home to die:
You needn't be afraid he'll leave you this time."

"Home," he mocked gently.

                    "Yes, what else but home?
It all depends on what you mean by home.
115   Of course he's nothing to us, any more
Than was the hound that came a stranger to us
Out of the woods, worn out upon the trail."

"Home is the place where, when you have to go there,
They have to take you in."

                    "I should have called it
120   Something you somehow haven't to deserve."

Warren leaned out and took a step or two,
Picked up a little stick, and brought it back
And broke it in his hand and tossed it by.
"Silas has better claim on us you think
125   Than on his brother? Thirteen little miles
As the road winds would bring him to his door.
Silas has walked that far no doubt today.
Why doesn't he go there? His brother's rich,
A somebody—director in the bank."

110. **wrought:** worked.

Skill Link

Describing Plot and Identifying Conflicts

Remind students that **conflicts** are the struggles at the heart of narratives. They can occur between characters; between one character and nature or society; between feelings or wishes within a character; or between forces or human conditions (good and evil, innocence and experience). Explain that conflicts are usually addressed through the plot of a narrative. The **exposition** introduces the problem;

complications develop as characters try to deal with the conflict, leading to the point of greatest intensity, the **climax**; the **resolution** brings an end to the conflict, which need not be a satisfactory solution for the characters.

Have students chart the different conflicts between the characters in "The Death of a Hired Man." Tell them to describe how the conflicts are addressed and how they are resolved.

Characters	Conflict	Complication	Climax and Resolution
[Silas, Mary, and Warren]	[Warren does not trust Silas.]	[Warren must decide whether to take Silas in.]	[Mary convinces Warren, but Silas dies.]

"He never told us that."

130   "We know it, though."

"I think his brother ought to help, of course.
I'll see to that if there is need. He ought of right
To take him in, and might be willing to—
He may be better than appearances.
135 But have some pity on Silas. Do you think
If he had any pride in claiming kin
Or anything he looked for from his brother,
He'd keep so still about him all this time?"

"I wonder what's between them."

                                    "I can tell you.
140 Silas is what he is—we wouldn't mind him—
But just the kind that kinsfolk can't abide.
He never did a thing so very bad.
He don't know why he isn't quite as good
As anybody. Worthless though he is,
145 He won't be made ashamed to please his brother."

"*I* can't think Si ever hurt anyone." **F**

"No, but he hurt my heart the way he lay
And rolled his old head on that sharp-edged chair-back.
He wouldn't let me put him on the lounge.
150 You must go in and see what you can do.
I made the bed up for him there tonight.
You'll be surprised at him—how much he's broken.
His working days are done; I'm sure of it." **G**

"I'd not be in a hurry to say that."

155 "I haven't been. Go, look, see for yourself.
But, Warren, please remember how it is:
He's come to help you ditch the meadow.
He has a plan. You mustn't laugh at him.
He may not speak of it, and then he may.
160 I'll sit and see if that small sailing cloud
Will hit or miss the moon."

                           It hit the moon.
Then there were three there, making a dim row,
The moon, the little silver cloud, and she.

Warren returned—too soon, it seemed to her—
165 Slipped to her side, caught up her hand and waited. **H**

"Warren?" she questioned.

                       "Dead," was all he answered.

ROBERT FROST 573

Making the Connections

Primary Sources

In this excerpt from a 1923 interview, Frost explains his preference for blank over free verse and offers some of his objections to the practitioners of Modernist free verse. Frost suggests that many of his own contemporaries go far beyond Whitman's style of free verse to create work that is striking but not eternally beautiful.

Background

Students may be startled at Frost's scorn for free verse as a poetic form. Explain to students that *versification* is the art of expressing ideas in poetic structure. It includes the use of rhythm, meter, rhyme, diction, and phrasing. For this reason, the expression *free verse* is almost a contradiction in terms. For free verse to be *verse,* the poet must exercise a fine control over the few structural elements he or she reserves in composition, such as phrasing and rhythm. In unskilled hands, free verse can sound like chopped up prose.

Have students look back over Walt Whitman's poems in Collection 7. Do students think Whitman's poems are beautiful? Is that beauty "lasting"? Do students think Frost's poems are more beautiful simply because of their form?

PRIMARY
Sources
AN
INTERVIEW

"I must have the pulse beat of rhythm . . ."

These comments are from an interview held on October 21, 1923, with *New York Times* reporter Rose C. Feld. Not long after the interview, Frost won his first Pulitzer Prize. Here, Frost has been talking about American poetry.

. . . We're still a bit afraid. America, for instance, was afraid to accept Walt Whitman when he first sang the songs of democracy. His influence on American poetry began to be felt only after the French had hailed him as a great writer, a literary revolutionist. Our own poet had to be imported from France before we were sure of his strength.

Today almost every man who writes poetry confesses his debt to Whitman. Many have gone very much further than Whitman would have traveled with them. They are the people who believe in wide straddling.

I, myself, as I said before, don't like it for myself. I do not write free verse; I write blank verse. I must have the pulse beat of rhythm, I like to hear it beating under the things I write.

That doesn't mean I do not like to read a bit of free verse occasionally. I do. It sometimes succeeds in painting a picture that is very clear and startling. It's good as something created momentarily for its sudden startling effect; it hasn't the qualities, however, of something lastingly beautiful.

And sometimes my objection to it is that it's a pose. It's not honest. When a man sets out consciously to tear up forms and rhythms and measures, then he is not interested in giving you poetry. He just wants to perform; he wants

Robert Frost at John F. Kennedy's inauguration, January 20, 1961.
Jim Brown/Black Star.

to show you his tricks. He will get an effect; nobody will deny that, but it is not a harmonious effect.

Sometimes it strikes me that the free-verse people got their idea from incorrect proof sheets. I have had stuff come from the printers with lines half left out or positions changed about. I read the poems as they stood, distorted and half finished, and I confess I get a rather pleasant sensation from them. They make a sort of nightmarish half-sense. . . .

—Robert Frost

Professional Notes

Critical Comment: Frost's Defense

The British poet Robert Graves tells us: "Frost has always respected meter. When, during the *Vers Libre* period of the Nineteen Twenties and Thirties his poems were disdained as old-fashioned, he remarked disdainfully that writing free verse was like playing tennis without a net. The *Vers Librists,* it should be explained, had rebelled against a degenerate sort of poetry in which nothing mattered except getting the ball neatly over the net. Few games are so wearisome to watch as a methodical ping-pong, ping-pong tennis match in which each player allows his opponent an easy forehand return from the same court. The *Vers Librists,* therefore, abandoned the tennis-net of metre altogether, and concentrated on rhythm. But though metre is boring without rhythm, the reverse is equally true. A rhythmic manipulation of metre means . . . so placing your shots that you force the other fellow to dart all round his territory, using backhand, forehand, volley or half-volley as the play demands. Only the 'strain of rhythm upon metre' (Frost's own phrase), makes a poem worth reading, or a long rally in tennis worth watching. That you can't achieve much in poetry without, so to speak, a taut net and straight whitewashed lines, is shown by the difficulty of memorizing free verse; it does not fix itself firmly enough in the imagination."

MAKING MEANINGS

First Thoughts

1. Look back over your reading notes. How did you feel about each of the three characters in this poem?

Shaping Interpretations

2. Based on their **dialogue**, what inferences can you make about the relationship between Warren and Mary, and about how each relates to Silas?

3. Describe the basic problem facing Warren, Mary, and Silas. Some might say that Mary sees Silas as a hired man in an emotional sense, Warren in a work sense. Do you agree? Explain.

4. Identify the details in lines 103–110 that create a vivid image of the **setting**. What does this passage tell us about Mary's character?

5. Does the conclusion of this poem strike you as inevitable? Why or why not? What would your feelings have been if Warren, instead of answering "Dead" to Mary's question, had answered "Asleep," or "Sharpening his scythe"?

6. Find the two definitions of "home" offered in the poem. One critic has said that one definition is based on law and duty, the other definition on mercy. Identify each. Do you agree with the critic's observation? Which definition do you favor?

7. In Primary Sources on page 559, Frost says he aimed to give the speech of each character in his poetry a distinct sound, just as people's voices sound different in real life. Does he successfully differentiate Warren's and Mary's speech? Explain.

Extending the Text

8. State in your own words the poem's **message**. How would the message apply to the problem of homelessness in our society today?

READING SKILLS AND STRATEGIES

Understanding Blank Verse

"The poet goes in like a rope skipper to make the most of his opportunities," said Frost in an essay called "The Constant Symbol." "If he trips himself he stops the rope. He is of our stock and has been brought up by ear to choice of two meters, strict iambic and loose iambic (not to count varieties of the latter)." "The Death of the Hired Man" is written in **blank verse,** which is unrhymed iambic pentameter. It is called *blank* verse because the lines do not have end rhymes. Iambic pentameter means that there are five iambs to each line; an *iamb* is an unaccented syllable followed by an accented syllable: da DUM ($\smile$ $\prime$).

1. Scan the first ten lines, and recite them aloud to hear the meter.

2. Look over the poem, and find examples of strict iambic and loose iambic meter.

3. Do you think Frost ever "trips" himself in this poem?

4. Take ten lines from this poem, and rewrite them in the free-verse style of Walt Whitman (page 348). Where will you break the lines? What rearrangement of words will have to be made to break the iambic meter?

5. Look at Frost's comments on free verse in Primary Sources (page 574). What is *your* opinion of Frost's ideas?

C. Bradley Simmons/Bruce Coleman, Inc.

ROBERT FROST 575

READING SKILLS AND STRATEGIES

1–2. Lines 4 and 6–10 are in strict iambic pentameter. Lines 2 and 5 are in iambic pentameter with one instance each of "wrong" stress. Line 3 is in iambic pentameter with one extra unstressed syllable at the end of the line. Line 1 has thirteen syllables and an irregular rhythm.

3. Possible answer: No; the occasional looseness of the rhythm suits the subject matter and diction.

4. Students' rewrites will vary. Remind students to emphasize cadence, parallelism, and repetition of phrases, syntax, and images.

5. Students may prefer the strength and straightforwardness of free verse, or they may prefer the discipline that regular rhyme and rhythm impose on poetry. Some students may feel that appreciating free verse is simply a question of personal taste.

MAKING MEANINGS

First Thoughts [Respond]

1. Possible responses: liked Mary's kindness; admired Silas's endurance; disliked Warren's cynicism.

Shaping Interpretations [Interpret]

2. Warren and Mary are open, honest, and tender with each other. Warren is clearly in charge of business decisions, but Mary is not afraid to say what she thinks, and she influences the way he deals with other people. Mary pities Silas and is fond of him; Warren shows less emotion for him at first.

3. Hiring Silas would be bad for business, but refusing would be cruel. Warren is willing to help Silas, but not at the expense of the harvest. Ostensibly, the problem is financial, but Mary makes Warren see that Silas only wants to die among people who respect him as a human being, who don't make excuses for his shortcomings or shame and shun him for them.

4. The lines describe the moon, hills, morning-glories, and dew. The implied comparison to an angel underlines her ethics, pity, and compassion.

5. Possible answer: The central problem of the poem would not be resolved with either of the other answers. We would still be left with a sense of uncertainty about Silas's true motivations and about the conflict between Warren and Mary.

6. Warren's definition, based on law and duty: ll. 118–119; Mary's merciful definition: ll. 119–120. Most students will accept these characterizations and favor Mary's definition to a certain extent.

7. The difference in their speech is effectively achieved through the tone rather than the level of diction. Warren's tone is blunt, practical, and defensive, and Mary's is kind and compassionate.

Extending the Text [Apply]

8. Possible answers: All people have value and feelings and shouldn't have to earn compassion and mercy. No one in need should be turned away. If more people believed and acted on this, fewer people would be homeless.

Grading Timesaver

Rubrics for each Choices assignment appear on p. 156 in the *Portfolio Management System.*

CHOICES: Building Your Portfolio

1. **Writer's Notebook** Remind students that many effects have multiple causes and many causes have multiple effects.
2. **Interpreting a Poem** Remind students to support their arguments with specific evidence from the text of any poems they refer to.
3. **Comparing Poems** Diction is another aspect students should consider. Both poets use simple vocabulary, but do they achieve the same effect?
4. **Creative Writing** Suggest that students maintain the relationships among the characters: husband, wife, hired man, college boy, and rich brother. Students may want to present Harold, Silas, and the brother directly rather than keep them "offstage," as Frost does.
5. **Speaking and Listening** Students may want to review the textbook's essays on the Puritans and the Romantics before beginning the discussion.
6. **Art** Encourage students to look at and think about the illustrations in their textbooks. These illustrations may spark ideas for students' collages.
7. **Music/Art** Students could listen to *Frostiana,* a choral setting of seven Frost poems by Randall Thompson, to get ideas.

CHOICES: Building Your Portfolio

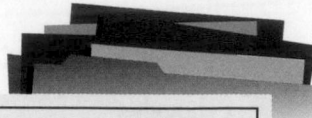

Writer's Notebook
1. Collecting Ideas for an Analysis of Causes and Effects

Jot down your own list of speculative questions suggested by the Frost poems you have read. Why is the speaker so appalled at the sight he sees in "Design"? Why are the people in "Neither Out Far Nor In Deep" looking out to sea? What motivated Silas in "The Death of the Hired Man" to come back to Warren and Mary? Keep your notes for possible use in the Writer's Workshop on page 685.

Interpreting a Poem
2. Frost Bites

The critic Louise Bogan pointed out the "tensions, dark conflicts, and passionate involvements" that appear in Frost's poetry and "pervade certain poems with almost nightmare intensity." In a brief essay, explore examples of the "dark conflicts" in Frost's poetry. What does Frost share with the Dark Romantics (page 213)? In what sense do Frost's poems have "bite"?

Comparing Poems
3. Accident or Design?

In a brief essay, compare and contrast "Design" and Emily Dickinson's poem "Apparently with no surprise" (page 385). Before you write, gather your data in a chart like the one below:

	Dickinson	Frost
Message in poem		
Use of symbols		
Tone		
Use of rhymes and rhythms		
Use of imagery		

Creative Writing
4. Updated "Hired Man"

In a poem, narrative, or screenplay, set "The Death of the Hired Man" in contemporary surroundings with up-to-date characters. You might set the story in a city, in a rural area, in a suburb, on a modern-day farm, or in a migrant worker camp. Be sure to include **dialogue, conflict,** and **resolution** in your story.

Speaking and Listening
5. Reading Nature

The Puritans and later the Romantics "read" lessons into nature. Lead a class discussion about whether or not Frost's poems "Design" and "Birches" are part of this same tradition. Discuss whether Frost is more like the Puritans or the Romantics in his attitude.

Art
6. Dark Design

Create a collage that captures some of the central themes and images that you feel sum up Frost's poetry. In choosing appropriate visuals, consider **similes, metaphors,** and **images** from the Frost poems you have read. Write a brief explanation of the thought that went behind each image you chose.

Music / Art
7. Frost Three Ways

With a partner or a team, choose several Frost poems from this collection or from a book of Frost's poetry, and select music and works of art that relate to the poems' **themes, images,** and **tones.** Prepare slides, video, or overhead transparencies to show your accompanying visuals, and play recorded music (or perform your own compositions) as you read aloud Frost's poems, creating your own multimedia presentation.

576 THE MODERNS

John Crowe Ransom

(1888–1974)

UPI/Bettmann.

He was the son of a minister and perhaps the most intellectually elegant conservative of twentieth-century American writers, but John Crowe Ransom—poet, teacher, editor, and critic—was nevertheless an innovator in his own way. He was the founder of a group of renegade Southern poets. He helped form a new and innovative school of critical thought called New Criticism. He was also mentor to some of the most important young poets and critics of the time. His students—among them Randall Jarrell (page 932), Robert Lowell (page 948), Robert Penn Warren, and James Wright (page 151)—found a larger audience than their teacher ever did, but Ransom did more than any of them to keep alive the delicacy, beauty, and endless resources of the English language.

Ransom was born in Pulaski, Tennessee. His illustrious teaching career at his alma mater, Vanderbilt University in Tennessee, lasted for more than twenty years, and it was during this stage of his life that he became a leader of the group of Southern writers called the "Fugitives." The Fugitives were determined to assert Southern cultural values, and they idealized a genteel, agrarian way of life that seemed to offer a more stable environment than Northern industrialism could. Their poetry was known for a combination of intellectual wit and the fatalism associated with Greek tragedy.

Changing times made Ransom's work—with its tone of wit, ironic detachment, and almost classical elegance of expression—seem like the echo of another age. Yet, today Ransom is appreciated not only for his considerable influence on some of the best poets of the modern era, but also for the shining perfection of his small but memorable body of work.

Before You Read

BELLS FOR JOHN WHITESIDE'S DAUGHTER

Make the Connection

Preserved in Memory
Everyone experiences losses in life; but poets, through their art, try to redeem what we have lost.

Quickwrite

The following poem is an **elegy**, written to mark a young girl's death. In a few sentences, list some aspects of the girl's life that you would expect the poet to mention.

Elements of Literature

Tone

Tone is the attitude a writer takes toward the subject of a work, the characters in it, or the audience. Ransom often combines two different tones—tenderness and detachment, for example—in one poem.

go.hrw.com

LEO 11-11

Frank Weston Benson (1862–1951) painted many women and children, often in outdoor settings. *Eleanor* is one of his best-known paintings. (See also p. 709.)

Activity. Compare *Eleanor* with John Whiteside's daughter. Ask students whether they seem alike or different and how. [They seem alike; they are young, strong, energetic, and determined.]

Ⓐ English Language Learners

Multiple Meanings

Ask students to explain what the girl is doing. [fighting with her shadow in play] Explain that in this sentence, *arms* denotes "weapons."

Ⓑ Elements of Literature

Simile

❓ What are the geese being compared to? [giant snowflakes falling on the grass] What is the effect of this comparison? [It makes the reader see feathers flying; it creates a comic picture of great activity.]

Ⓒ Elements of Literature

Tone

❓ What does the tone of the first and fourth stanzas suggest about the girl? [The warm and admiring tone suggests she was not only full of mischief but also full of vitality.] What is the speaker's attitude toward the girl? [He sees her as a complex person, at times admirable and at others more of a comic nuisance.]

Ⓓ Elements of Literature

Tone

Have students note the understatement of "vexed." It suggests something other than sadness; it implies a sense of injustice at the death of a child, especially one so full of life. Point out the title, and explore the speaker's relationship to the girl. He mentions her by her father's name, not her own, implying that he did not know her personally, but from a distance ("our high window"), as an adult might look at a neighbor's child.

Eleanor (1901) by Frank Benson. Oil on canvas (29½″ × 25″).
Museum of Art, Rhode Island School of Design; Gift of the Estate of Mrs. Gustav Radeke.

Bells for John Whiteside's Daughter

John Crowe Ransom

There was such speed in her little body,
And such lightness in her footfall,
It is no wonder that her brown study°
Astonishes us all.

5 Her wars were bruited° in our high window.
We looked among orchard trees and beyond.
Where she took arms against her shadow
Or harried° unto the pond

The lazy geese, like a snow cloud
10 Dripping their snow on the green grass,

Tricking and stopping, sleepy and proud,
Who cried in goose, Alas,

For the tireless heart within the little
Lady with rod that made them rise
15 From their noon apple-dreams, and scuttle
Goose-fashion under the skies!

But now go the bells, and we are ready;
In one house we are sternly stopped
To say we are vexed° at her brown study,
20 Lying so primly propped.

3. **brown study:** state of being lost in deep thought.
5. **bruited** (bro̅o̅t′id): reported.
8. **harried** (har′ēd): forced; pushed along.

19. **vexed:** disturbed; annoyed.

578 THE MODERNS

Reaching All Students

Struggling Readers

Have students choose partners to read and discuss the poem. Have them concentrate on the character of the girl. What was she like? What details in the poem tell them this? Would they have liked to be friends with her? Why or why not? Partners can then share their ideas with the class.

Advanced Learners

Have students listen to the song cycle *Kindertotenlieder* ("Songs on the Death of Children"), settings by Gustav Mahler of five Friedrich Rückert poems. Have students compare and contrast the songs with Ransom's poem. Students should consider tone, poetic structure, and how the addition of the music affects the mood.

First Thoughts

1. How does the speaker feel about the little girl who died? How did the poet make *you* feel about the Whitesides' daughter and about death itself?

Shaping Interpretations

2. What characteristics of the girl make the speaker astonished at her "brown study"?

3. What action of the little girl caused the geese to cry "Alas"? What additional overtones does this cry take on, given the poem's subject?

4. What details in the last stanza make it clear what the speaker is looking at?

5. What do you associate with the verb *vexed* in the next to last line of the poem? What verb would you expect the speaker to use to describe his reaction to the dead child?

Challenging the Text

6. The critic Babette Deutsch once said of Ransom:

> [W]hatever his subject . . . his tone is right. The glint of irony is there, deepened as well as softened by a sensitiveness without a grain of sentimentality.
>
> —Babette Deutsch

Do you think Ransom's **tone** is appropriate, given the highly emotional nature of the subject? Do you think he should also have covered other aspects of the girl's life? Explain.

CHOICES:
Building Your Portfolio

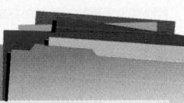

Writer's Notebook

1. Collecting Ideas for an Analysis of Causes and Effects

If you are interested in literature and in the ways it is studied in school, you might find a topic for investigation in the work of John Crowe Ransom. Do some preliminary research on one of these topics: New Criticism (or New Critics) or the Fugitives. What effect did the New Criticism have on the way literature was (and still is) studied in schools and colleges? What effect did the Fugitives have on Southern writing? Save your notes for possible use in the Writer's Workshop on page 685.

Interpreting a Poem

2. The Human Condition

A critic wrote that Ransom's poems emphasize **themes** like the following:

> mortality and the fleetingness of youthful vigor and grace . . . [and] the disparity between the world as man would have it and as it actually is, between what [people] want and need emotionally and what is available for them. . . .
>
> —Thomas Daniel Young

In a brief essay, explain whether or not you believe this comment is supported by the poem. Use specific references to the poem.

Comparing Poems

3. Remembrances

Write a brief essay comparing "Bells for John Whiteside's Daughter" with Henry Wadsworth Longfellow's "The Cross of Snow" (page 178). Compare the poems' **tone, imagery,** and views of death. Support your comparison with lines from the poems.

First Thoughts [Respond]

1. Possible answer: He was fond of her, but mildly critical of her rambunctiousness. She seemed lively, strong, and aggressive. Ransom makes us feel the injustice and the magnitude of such a loss.

Shaping Interpretations [Interpret]

2. It contrasts with her liveliness; her fighting spirit.

3. She chased them with a stick in her hand. "Alas" also implies sorrow for the death of the child.

4. The bells suggest a church; "propped" implies that he looks at her in the unnatural stillness of death, lying in her coffin.

5. *Vexed* means "irritated" or "annoyed." A more obvious (but probably less effective) choice might have been *distressed* or *grieved*.

Challenging the Text [Evaluate]

6. Possible answer: Ransom's blend of sad affection and comic criticism is appropriate and realistic; most people are a blend of good and bad qualities. His limited focus makes sense, given the speaker's indirect connection to the child.

CHOICES:
Building Your Portfolio

1. **Writer's Notebook** Tell students that the Fugitives took their name from the magazine they published from 1922 to 1925. *Fugitive Anthology* (1928) is a collection of pieces from the magazine.

2. **Interpreting a Poem** Remind students to support their arguments with specific evidence from the text.

3. **Comparing Poems** Students could also consider the effects of poetic form and structure.

Making the Connections

Connecting to the Theme: "Loss and Redemption"

After students have read the poem, discuss the collection theme. What has the speaker of this poem lost? Do his memories help him redeem that loss? Compare and contrast this speaker's feeling about the girl's death with Mary's and Warren's feelings about Silas's death.

Grading Timesaver

Rubrics for each Choices assignment appear on p. 158 in the *Portfolio Management System*.

Planning

- **Traditional Schedule**
  Lesson Plans Including Strategies for English-Language Learners
- **One-Stop Planner**
  CD-ROM with Test Generator

BROWSING IN THE FILES

About the Author. Robinson Jeffers formally studied a number of disciplines. After graduating from Occidental College, he studied literature at the University of Southern California. In 1906, he returned to Switzerland and studied philosophy, Old English, French literary history, and the history of the Roman Empire. He returned to USC to study medicine; he also studied forestry and taught physiology.

Robinson Jeffers

(1887–1962)

Robinson Jeffers by Edward Weston.
© 1981 Arizona Board of Regents, Center for Creative Photography. Courtesy Richard A. Gleeson. University of San Francisco Library.

The son of a theology teacher, Robinson Jeffers was born in Pittsburgh. His parents moved from place to place, and, by the time he was fifteen, he had already spent several years in Europe before the family settled in California. There Jeffers earned a degree from Occidental College and went on to do postgraduate work, including a term at medical school. But Jeffers did not pursue any of the careers he studied for. Fascinated with poetry, he found he could make no serious commitment to anything else.

In 1912 Jeffers inherited money from an uncle. This allowed him the freedom to live on his own terms and to provide for his wife and two sons without ever holding a job. Asserting his sudden independence, Jeffers bought property in the coastal village of Carmel, California. With his own hands he built a stone tower that would serve as a retreat and working studio for the rest of his life. As in the case of the Irish poet William Butler Yeats, the tower became symbolic for Jeffers of his worldview and his way of life; he lived a monklike existence apart from neighborly society and the literary world, marked by a lonely devotion to nature.

A man against the American grain, Jeffers had little confidence in the virtues of religion or democracy; he also kept a skeptical eye fixed on scientific progress and social advances. His philosophical outlook, combining fatalism with pessimism, was closer to that of the ancient Greeks than to that of the common American. For wayward humankind, aware of everything but its insignificance, he had little hope. He regarded awareness itself as a kind of disease to which natural forces are immune.

Much of Jeffers's poetic inspiration came from nature's power to endure and silently witness the absurdities of civilization. Rocks and the sea, hawks in the wind, sea creatures thrown upon the sea-washed ledges of the Pacific shore—these are Jeffers's recurring images and emblems. Although humorless, grandly isolated, and nourished by disgust, Jeffers was able to attract readers who were impressed by the integrity of his single-minded convictions and by his dark vision of the limited life of human beings.

Before You Read

SHINE, PERISHING REPUBLIC

Make the Connection

Self-Sufficiency

This poem was written in the Big Sur region in California, where great mountains emerge like dripping shoulders out of the Pacific Ocean. The circumstance is that of a remote homestead built with the speaker's own hands. The speaker is a father determined to live apart from civilization and to have his children learn the lessons of nature rather than those of schoolbooks.

Quickwrite

Quickwrite your own feelings about America today. Do you consider it a "perishing republic" that has lost its positive qualities, or do you think the nation's values and strengths are still intact?

go.hrw.com
LE0 11-11

  *Resources: Print and Media*

Reading
- *Graphic Organizers for Active Reading*, p. 58
- *Audio CD Library*
  Disc 14, Track 12

Assessment
- *Formal Assessment*, p. 118
- *Portfolio Management System*, p. 159
- *Test Generator (One-Stop Planner CD-ROM)*

Internet
- go.hrw.com (keyword: LE0 11-11)

Old Mill, Big Sur (1933) by Millard Sheets. Watercolor on paper.
The E. Gene Crain Collection, Laguna Beach, California.

Shine, Perishing Republic

Robinson Jeffers

While this America settles in the mold of its vulgarity, heavily
    thickening to empire,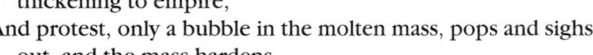
And protest, only a bubble in the molten mass, pops and sighs
    out, and the mass hardens,

I sadly smiling remember that the flower fades to make fruit,
    the fruit rots to make earth.
Out of the mother; and through the spring exultances,
    ripeness and decadence; and home to the mother.

ROBINSON JEFFERS 581

Reaching All Students

Struggling Readers

Because this poem's phrasing is fluid and complex, it may prove very difficult for students to comprehend. Have them write the poem out as prose, expressing each thought in a separate sentence. Then, have students read it again as written.

Advanced Learners

Have students compare and contrast this poem's view of America with the views expressed in Walt Whitman's "I Hear America Singing" (p. 352) and in Carl Sandburg's "Chicago" (p. 793). How are these views alike? How do they differ? Which poet most closely expresses students' views about America today? Which poet makes the most convincing case for his view? Why?

Summary ■ ■ ■

The speaker of this poem views America as a republic sinking into a decadent empire. He compares society's development to the natural cycle of a plant, whose flowers give way to fruit and whose fruit rots and becomes earth again. Thus, he wishes good health to the dying republic but hopes his children will avoid its corruption and be reserved in their love of humanity. For the speaker, this love is a trap, which leads the best spirits (like the crucified Jesus Christ) into ruin and death.

RESPONDING TO THE ART

Millard Sheets (1907–1989) was a native Californian. His work ranges from watercolors to murals and magazine illustrations. He also worked as an architectural and movie production designer.

Activity. Ask students to compare and contrast the poem and the painting. [Possible answer: Both convey a sense of lurking danger. The mill towers over the people, as Jeffers's corrupt society seems to tower over individual voices of protest.]

Ⓐ Historical Connections

Jeffers's description of America evokes the final days of the Roman republic. Students are probably familiar with the story of Julius Caesar's assassination; the assassins were motivated by their fears that Caesar would become a dictator. The ensuing civil wars brought about the end of the republic and the rise to power of the emperor Augustus. Under his successors (Tiberius, Caligula, Claudius, and Nero), Rome suffered from corruption and decadence. Ultimately, the Roman Empire collapsed.

Ⓑ English Language Learners
Cultural Concepts

Explain to students that "mother" refers to the earth because it gives birth to plants and—by extension— to all living things.

T581

You making haste, haste on decay: not blameworthy; life is
     good, be it stubbornly long or suddenly
Ⓐ A mortal splendor: meteors are not needed less than
     mountains: shine, perishing republic.

But for my children, I would have them keep their distance
     from the thickening center; corruption
Never has been compulsory, when the cities lie at the
Ⓑ   monster's feet there are left the mountains.

And boys, be in nothing so moderate as in love of man, a
     clever servant, insufferable master.
There is the trap that catches noblest spirits, that caught—
     they say—God, when he walked on earth.

MAKING MEANINGS

First Thoughts

1. What thoughts or feelings did you have about the speaker's advice in the last stanza? In what ways is this advice quite the opposite of "love thy neighbor"?

Shaping Interpretations

2. The first stanza contains an **implied metaphor.** What is America compared to? What does "vulgarity" mean here, and why does the republic thicken to *empire*?

3. What attitude toward America does the second stanza express?

4. What is the speaker's attitude in the last stanza? Do you think he really means what he says in line 9?

5. What does the speaker seem to think is the cause of the republic's condition?

Connecting with the Text

6. Review the Quickwrite you wrote before reading the poem. Did the poem make you rethink any of your responses? Explain.

7. If it were possible, would you like to take the speaker aside and instill a little optimism in him or her? What would you tell the speaker?

582 THE MODERNS

CHOICES:
Building Your Portfolio

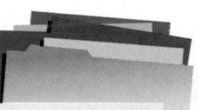

Writer's Notebook

1. Collecting Ideas for an Analysis of Causes and Effects

Brainstorm a list of possible topics suggested by Jeffers's poem: why a civilization might decay, why someone would choose to live apart from society, why someone would feel as Jeffers does about America. Save your notes for possible use in the Writer's Workshop on page 685.

WORK IN PROGRESS

Critical Writing

2. Taking Stock

This poem was published in 1925. In a brief essay, explain why you think Jeffers's view of the condition of American society is or is not still valid. Summarize the view expressed in the poem. Then tell whether or not you think this view applies to contemporary America. Support your position with specific references to the poem and to contemporary life.

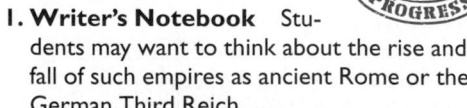

The Dream and the Reality

Theme

The American Dream *American literature questions our dreams and asks if the loss of the frontier and of this once pristine land has made the American dream impossible—that dream of an Edenic world, of freedom of movement, of expansion, of seeking new experiences and new opportunities. Has the new focus on money replaced the old dream of forging a new society? The work that epitomizes the period is Fitzgerald's* The Great Gatsby.

Reading the Anthology

Reaching Struggling Readers

The *Reading Skills and Strategies: Reaching Struggling Readers* binder includes a Reading Strategies Handbook that offers concrete suggestions to help students who have difficulty reading and comprehending text, or students who are reluctant readers. When a specific strategy is most appropriate for a selection, a correlation to the Handbook is provided at the bottom of the teacher's page under the head Reaching Struggling Readers. This head may also be used to introduce additional ideas for helping students read challenging texts.

Reading Beyond the Anthology

Read On At the end of The Moderns collections, the grade eleven book includes an annotated bibliography of books suitable for extended reading. The suggested books are related to works in these collections by theme, by author, or by subject. To preview the Read On for The Moderns period, please turn to p. T800.

Collection 12 The Dream and the Reality

Resources for this Collection

Note: All resources for this collection are available for preview on the *One-Stop Planner CD-ROM 2 with Test Generator*. All worksheets and blackline masters may be printed from the CD-ROM.

Selection or Feature	Reading and Literary Skills	Vocabulary, Language, and Grammar
Winter Dreams (p. 586) F. Scott Fitzgerald **Primary Sources: A Letter to His Daughter** (p. 603) F. Scott Fitzgerald	• *Graphic Organizers for Active Reading,* Worksheet p. 59 • *Literary Elements:* Transparency 18 Worksheet p. 55	• *Words to Own,* Worksheet p. 35 • *Grammar and Language Links:* Pronouns and Antecedents, Worksheet p. 51 • *Language Workshop CD-ROM,* Pronoun-Antecedent Agreement • *Daily Oral Grammar,* Transparency 37
The Leader of the People (p. 607) John Steinbeck **Primary Sources: Nobel Prize Acceptance Speech, 1962** (p. 620) John Steinbeck	• *Graphic Organizers for Active Reading,* Worksheet p. 60 • *Literary Elements:* Transparency 19 Worksheet p. 58	• *Words to Own,* Worksheet p. 36 • *Grammar and Language Links:* Personal Pronouns, Worksheet p. 53 • *Language Workshop CD-ROM,* Nominative and Objective Case • *Daily Oral Grammar,* Transparency 38
The Secret Life of Walter Mitty (p. 624) James Thurber **Primary Sources: *The New Yorker's* Farewell** (p. 629) E. B. White **Connections: Peanuts** (p. 630) Charles M. Schulz	• *Graphic Organizers for Active Reading,* Worksheet p. 61 • *Literary Elements:* Transparency 20 Worksheet p. 61	• *Words to Own,* Worksheet p. 37 • *Daily Oral Grammar,* Transparency 39
A Worn Path (p. 634) Eudora Welty **Primary Sources: "Is Phoenix Jackson's Grandson Really Dead?"** (p. 640) Eudora Welty	• *Graphic Organizers for Active Reading,* Worksheet p. 62 • *Literary Elements:* Transparency 21 Worksheet p. 64	• *Words to Own,* Worksheet p. 38 • *Grammar and Language Links:* Clear Pronoun Reference, Worksheet p. 55 • *Language Workshop CD-ROM,* Clear Pronoun Reference • *Daily Oral Grammar,* Transparency 40

Collection Planner

Other Resources for this Collection

- *Cross-Curricular Activities,* p. 12
- *Portfolio Management System,* Introduction to Portfolio Assessment, p. 1
- *Test Generator,* Collection Test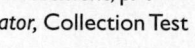

Writing	Listening and Speaking Viewing and Representing	Assessment
• *Portfolio Management System,* Rubrics for Choices, p. 160	• *Audio CD Library,* Disc 15, Track 2 • *Viewing and Representing:* Fine Art Transparency 12 Worksheet p. 48 • *Portfolio Management System,* Rubrics for Choices, p. 160	• *Formal Assessment,* Selection Test, p. 119 • *Test Generator (One-Stop Planner CD-ROM)* • *Preparation for College Admission Exams,* p. 41
• *Portfolio Management System,* Rubrics for Choices, p. 162	• *Audio CD Library,* Disc 16, Track 2 • *Portfolio Management System,* Rubrics for Choices, p. 162	• *Formal Assessment,* Selection Test, p. 121 • *Test Generator (One-Stop Planner CD-ROM)*
• *Portfolio Management System,* Rubrics for Choices, p. 163	• *Audio CD Library,* Disc 16, Track 3 • *Portfolio Management System,* Rubrics for Choices, p. 163	• *Formal Assessment,* Selection Test, p. 123 • *Test Generator (One-Stop Planner CD-ROM)*
• *Portfolio Management System,* Rubrics for Choices, p. 165	• *Audio CD Library,* Disc 17, Track 1 • *Portfolio Management System,* Rubrics for Choices, p. 165	• *Formal Assessment,* Selection Test, p. 125 • *Test Generator (One-Stop Planner CD-ROM)* • *Preparation for College Admission Exams,* p. 43

Collection Planner

 Transparency   CD-ROM   Video   Audio CD

T582C

Skills Focus

Selection or Feature	Reading Skills and Strategies	Elements of Literature and Language	Writing	Listening and Speaking	Viewing and Representing
Winter Dreams (p. 586) F. Scott Fitzgerald	Drawing Inferences About Character, pp. 586, 604 Understanding Paradoxes, p. 604	Motivation, pp. 586, 604–605 Theme, p. 604 Paradox, p. 604 Plot, p. 605 Atmosphere, p. 605 Tone, p. 605 Characterization, p. 605	Write an Essay Interpreting a Story, p. 605	Improvise a Scene Based on Characters and Situations in a Story, p. 605 Research and Report on Some Aspect of Jazz Age Music, p. 605	
The Leader of the People (p. 607) John Steinbeck	Interpreting Figures of Speech, p. 622	Conflict: External and Internal, pp. 607, 621 Irony, p. 621 Theme, pp. 621–622 Plot, p. 622 Character, p. 622 Setting, p. 622 Tone, p. 622 Simile, p. 622 Metaphor, p. 622 Personification, p. 622 Oxymoron, p. 622 Hyperbole, p. 622	Write an Extension of the Story, p. 622 Write an Essay Comparing and Contrasting the Development of Theme in Two Stories, p. 622	Participate in a Panel Discussion on Heroes in Today's World, p. 622	
The Secret Life of Walter Mitty (p. 624) James Thurber	Analyzing Text Structures: Cause and Effect, pp. 624, 631	Parody, pp. 624, 631 Irony, p. 631 Stock Character, p. 631	Freewrite About the Causes of Walter Mitty's Daydreaming, p. 632 Write an Essay Comparing and Contrasting Female Characters in Two Stories, p. 632 Write an Episode in "The Secret Life of Mrs. Mitty," p. 632	Create a Short Play or Video Drama Based on the Story, p. 632	Create a Cartoon of a Contemporary Walter Mitty, p. 632
A Worn Path (p. 634) Eudora Welty		Theme, pp. 634, 642 Description, p. 642 Character, p. 642 Irony, p. 642 Metaphor, p. 642	Take Notes Based on an Analysis of a Situation in the Story, p. 642 Write an Essay Analyzing a Story, p. 642 Write a Story on a Similar Theme, p. 642		

Skills Focus

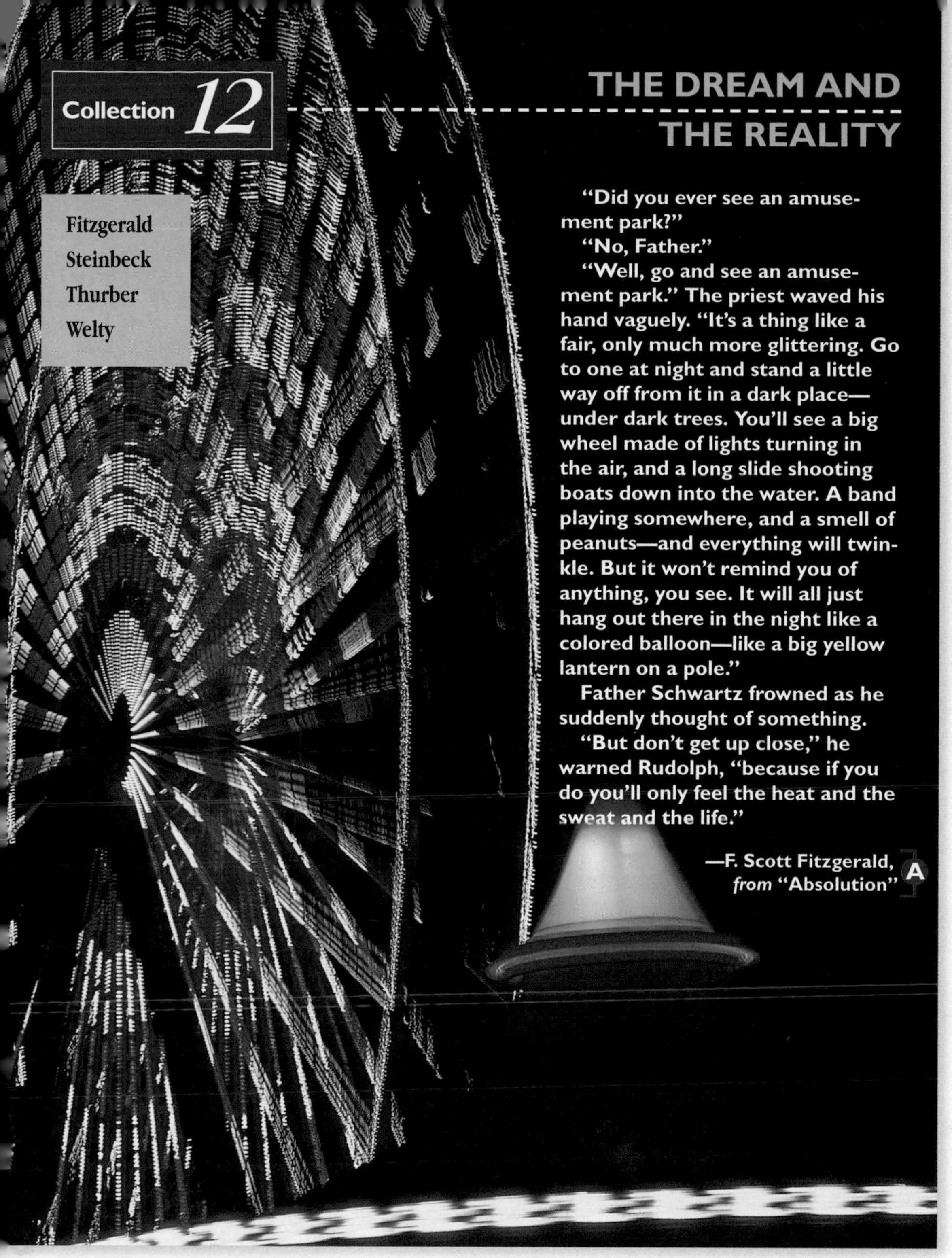

Collection 12

THE DREAM AND THE REALITY

Fitzgerald
Steinbeck
Thurber
Welty

"Did you ever see an amusement park?"

"No, Father."

"Well, go and see an amusement park." The priest waved his hand vaguely. "It's a thing like a fair, only much more glittering. Go to one at night and stand a little way off from it in a dark place—under dark trees. You'll see a big wheel made of lights turning in the air, and a long slide shooting boats down into the water. A band playing somewhere, and a smell of peanuts—and everything will twinkle. But it won't remind you of anything, you see. It will all just hang out there in the night like a colored balloon—like a big yellow lantern on a pole."

Father Schwartz frowned as he suddenly thought of something.

"But don't get up close," he warned Rudolph, "because if you do you'll only feel the heat and the sweat and the life."

—F. Scott Fitzgerald, *from* "Absolution"

Responding to the Quotation

? What does Father Schwartz's warning about getting too close to the amusement park reveal about the role that distance plays in the relationship between dream and reality? [Possible response: It suggests that a dream must be held at a distance in order to sustain its enchantment. Up close, a dream dissipates into the banal imperfections of real life and loses its magic.]

Ⓐ Background

The short story "Absolution" was written in June 1923. Fitzgerald planned it as the prologue to *The Great Gatsby* but found it marred the unity of that novel.

RESPONDING TO THE ART

Activity. Have students discuss how this photograph complements the collection theme. [Possible responses: The wondrous blur of light captures the illusion of a dream; in the cold light of day, a Ferris wheel loses its magic.]

Writing Focus: Analyzing Causes and Effects

The following **Work in Progress** assignments in this collection build to a culminating **Writer's Workshop** at the end of Collection 13.

F. Scott Fitzgerald

(1896–1940)

If ever there was a writer whose life and fiction were one, it was F. Scott Fitzgerald. Fitzgerald—handsome, charming, and uncommonly gifted—was not only part of the crazy, wonderful, irresponsible era of the 1920s; he helped to name it the Jazz Age. He made a literary legend of it and, with his wife Zelda, lived it out in all of its excesses. He also almost certainly died of it.

Early Failures—and a Smash Hit

Fitzgerald was born in 1896 in St. Paul, Minnesota, the son of a father with claims to an aristocratic Maryland family. Scott was named for an ancestor, Francis Scott Key, the composer of "The Star-Spangled Banner." His mother was the daughter of a rich Irish immigrant. The young Scott was a spoiled boy, a failure at schoolwork and—to his own great disappointment—at sports. But he was a success at daydreaming and, while still in his teens, at writing stories and plays.

At Princeton University, which he entered in 1913, he wrote one of the Triangle Club musical shows, contributed to the *Nassau Literary Magazine,* and befriended the serious writers Edmund Wilson and John Peale Bishop. When the United States entered the First World War in 1917, Fitzgerald left college for officers' training school, yearning for heroic adventure on the battlefields of France. He was never sent overseas, but in camp he began to work on a novel, *The Romantic Egoist,* which was twice turned down by Scribner's.

While he was stationed at Camp Sheridan in Alabama, romance of a different sort overtook him. He fell deeply in love with Zelda Sayre, a high-spirited and gorgeous woman whose escapades had scandalized her hometown of Montgomery. Like Scott, Zelda hungered for new experiences. She was sure of her appeal and felt it was bound to bring her a full measure of luxury and gaiety. Although Scott courted her persistently, he had not nearly enough money to offer her the kind of marriage she wanted, and at first she turned him down.

Now out of the army, Fitzgerald took a low-paying job he hated; he sent his novel, rewritten and retitled *This Side of Paradise,* off to Scribner's for the third time. In 1919, they agreed to publish it.

"I was an empty bucket," he said of the experience, "so mentally blunted by the summer's writing that I'd taken a job repairing car roofs at the Northern Pacific shops. Then the postman rang, and that day I quit work and ran along the streets, stopping automobiles to tell friends and acquaintances about it—my novel *This Side of Paradise* was accepted for publication. That week the postman rang and rang, and I paid off my terrible small debts, bought a suit, and woke up every morning with a world of ineffable toploftiness and promise."

When it was published in 1920, *This Side of Paradise* was a sensation. The old, prewar world with its Victorian code of behavior had been dumped in favor of a great, gaudy spree of new

The Bettmann Archive.

go.hrw.com
LE0 11-12

freedoms. Girls bobbed their hair and shortened their skirts, while boys filled their flasks with bootleg gin. To the wail of saxophones, couples danced the Charleston across the nation's dance floors. In young Fitzgerald's novel, the Jazz Age had found its definition.

> The Jazz Age had found its definition.

Taking Aim at the American Dream

Zelda married Scott in April of that year. The newlyweds moved to New York and became the center of a round of parties, while Scott turned out scores of stories. In the first years of the decade, he published two collections of stories and a second novel. After a stay in France, the Fitzgeralds returned to St. Paul, where their only child, a daughter named Frances, was born.

Scott announced to Maxwell Perkins, his editor at Scribner's, that he was going to write "something *new*—something extraordinary and beautiful and simple and intricately patterned." He fulfilled that ambition in *The Great Gatsby,* his nearly flawless masterpiece, which was published in 1925. It tells the story of James Gatz, a poor boy from the Middle West who dreams of success and elegance and finds their incarnation in a Louisville girl named Daisy Fay. When Gatz returns from the war, he learns that she has become Daisy Buchanan, married to a rich Chicagoan and leading a careless, sumptuous life on Long Island. The hero, now a successful bootlegger known as Jay Gatsby, hopes to win Daisy from what he believes is a loveless, unhappy marriage. The story ends in Gatsby's death, but we can see that his dreams and his feelings are admirable. The Buchanans, on the other hand, are insulated from life's possibilities by their wealth and self-indulgence.

The central triumph of *The Great Gatsby* was its revelation of the rich in all their seductive luxury and heedlessness, accompanied by an implicit condemnation of their way of life. In a remarkably concise work, Fitzgerald probed deeply the ambiguities of the American dream.

An Epitaph for the Jazz Age

The Great Gatsby won some critical praise, but it was a financial disappointment. Fitzgerald had to work even harder to keep up with the high cost of his and Zelda's international life. He turned out more potboiling short stories (mediocre in quality and written for money) and went to Hollywood to write movie scripts. In 1930, the tenth year of their marriage, Zelda suffered a mental breakdown and spent the rest of her life in and out of asylums. Hers was a search for both sanity and identity, an identity that seemed to have been devoured by Scott's productiveness. She aspired to be a dancer and a writer, and in 1932 produced her own novel, *Save Me the Waltz.* This was her thinly disguised account of her troubled marriage.

Scott's novel *Tender Is the Night,* published in 1934, was his rebuttal to Zelda's novel. Its hero, Dick Diver, is the protector and healer of the mad heroine, Nicole. However, the stock market crash of 1929 had put an end to Fitzgerald's era, and readers had lost interest in the problems of expatriates like Dick Diver. Still, the book displays Fitzgerald's hard-won experience of life, the commitment to early dreams, the self-destructiveness of charm, and a whole generation's craving for endless youth and irresponsibility. In its despair, *Tender Is the Night* is an epitaph for the Jazz Age.

It was Fitzgerald's epitaph as well. After its publication, he struggled with mounting debts, failing health, drinking, and depression. Zelda was hospitalized, and although Scott suffered under the drudgery of the Hollywood studios, he was bound to them. When he could, he continued to do serious work. Through his love affair with Sheilah Graham, a British journalist, he grew interested in the work of Hollywood producer Irving Thalberg and began to write a novel about him. He was at work on this novel, *The Last Tycoon,* in 1940 when he died of heart failure. *The Last Tycoon* was compiled and edited by his friend Edmund Wilson and was published to wide critical praise after Fitzgerald's death.

BROWSING IN THE FILES

A Critic's Comment. In an essay entitled "F. Scott Fitzgerald 1896–1940 The Poet of Borrowed Time," critic Arthur Mizener claimed: "Fitzgerald's great accomplishment is to have realized in completely American terms the developed romantic attitude, in the end at least in that most responsible form in which all the romantic's sensuous and emotional responses are disciplined by his awareness of the goodness and evilness of human experience. He had a kind of instinct for the tragic view of life and remarked himself how even at the beginning of his career, 'all the stories that came into my head had a touch of disaster in them—the lovely young creatures in my novels went to ruin, the diamond mountains of my stories blew up, and my millionaires were as beautiful and damned as Thomas Hardy's peasants.'"

Writers on Writing. Fitzgerald rarely addressed his ideas or gave advice about writing. However, his fiction offers some insights into his thoughts. In *The Last Tycoon,* he wrote, "Writers aren't people exactly. Or if they're any good, they're a whole lot of people trying so hard to be one person." In "The Crack-Up," Fitzgerald complained: "When the first-rate author wants an exquisite heroine or a lovely morning, he finds that all the superlatives have been worn shoddy by his inferiors. It should be a rule that bad writers must start with plain heroines and ordinary mornings, and, if they are able, work up to something better."

Professional Notes

Critical Comment: Green and Gatsby

Fitzgerald published "Winter Dreams" in 1922, three years before his masterpiece, *The Great Gatsby.* Critic Rose Adrienne Gallo points out that Fitzgerald saw "Winter Dreams" as "a sort of first draft of the *Gatsby* idea." While the two works share the same theme—"the pursuit of romantic illusions at the bitter price of inevitable disenchantment"—they are different in significant ways. Although Dexter and Gatsby both acquire great fortunes and fall in love with beautiful but shallow women, Dexter is accepted into the Joneses' social class because he acquires education along with wealth. More significantly, Dexter loses hope of ever winning Judy and becomes engaged to Irene Scheerer, a girl who has both sensitivity and intellect; Gatsby, in contrast, never untangles his dream from the allure of Daisy's beauty. His downfall comes in part from his inability to see Daisy's innate selfishness.

Summary ■■

Fourteen-year-old Dexter Green abruptly quits his caddying job when told that he must caddy for eleven-year-old Judy Jones, a rich girl whose smug, petulant behavior both frustrates and fascinates him. Judy becomes part of Dexter's "winter dreams" of achieving wealth and glamour. After graduating from college in the East, Dexter returns to Minnesota and makes his fortune in the laundry business. While playing golf, Dexter again encounters Judy Jones, now grown up and gorgeous, and falls in love. Judy, however, toys with Dexter; he is merely one of the many men who worship her. After a year and a half, Dexter gives up on Judy and proposes to Irene Scheerer. A week before the engagement, Judy proposes to Dexter. Dexter accepts, but their engagement lasts only a month. Dexter joins the army to fight in World War I. Seven years later, now a successful businessman in New York City, Dexter learns that Judy, bereft of spirit and beauty, is married to a man who treats her badly. Dexter weeps as he realizes that the dream he has cherished for years is irretrievably lost.

Background

Many of the settings and events of "Winter Dreams" mirror those in Fitzgerald's own life. In his daughter's view, what made Fitzgerald's stories so successful was his "identification" with the Jazz Age. "He was like a surgeon performing an operation upon himself, hurting terribly but watching the process with a fascinated detachment."

Before You Read
WINTER DREAMS

Make the Connection
You Can't Always Get What You Want

Have you ever met someone and thought, "That's the person I want to marry"? If you have had this thought—or if you ever do someday—you might find yourself facing the same kinds of problems that Dexter Green faces. In fiction, as well as in life, what individuals hope and long for is not always what they get.

Reading Skills and Strategies

Drawing Inferences About Characters

As you read this story, jot down your responses to these questions: How are Dexter's two ambitions—achieving material success and winning Judy's hand—tied together? What picture of Judy do you put together from what you learn about her? Why can't Dexter fully escape from Judy's magnetic charms?

Elements of Literature
Motivation

Motivation refers to the reasons for a character's behavior. Motivation can come from internal sources (ambition, insecurity, shyness) or from external factors (poverty, an ambitious parent, the crash of the stock market). In one-dimensional literature, motivation comes from a single cause. But in more sophisticated fiction, as in the complexity of life itself, motivation may come from many sources and is sometimes hard to pin down. In many stories, characters aren't even aware of their own motivation.

> **M**otivation refers to the reasons for a character's behavior.
>
> *For more on Motivation, see the Handbook of Literary Terms.*

Background

This story is one of several that Fitzgerald wrote about the dreams and illusions that marked the Jazz Age. "Winter Dreams" was written in 1922, when Fitzgerald's stories were commanding top prices from the *Saturday Evening Post* and other popular magazines. The story opens around 1911, when fourteen-year-old Dexter is caddying for wealthy golfers, and spans eighteen years of Dexter's life.

Preteaching Vocabulary

Words to Own

Have students read the definitions of the Words to Own listed at the bottom of the selection pages. Then, pair students to play "Opposites Attract." The first player gives his or her partner antonyms for the word, and the partner has to name the word. Have partners switch roles after they have used all the words and play another round. Then, have them complete the following activity, matching each word with its definition.

1. malicious [e]
2. petulance [i]
3. mirth [h]
4. turbulence [a]
5. ludicrous [g]
6. elation [b]
7. reserve [j]
8. plaintive [c]
9. divergence [f]
10. perturbation [d]

a. irregular behavior
b. celebration
c. expressing suffering
d. feeling of alarm
e. intentionally hurtful
f. variance; difference
g. laughable; absurd
h. joyfulness
i. irritability; impatience
j. self-restraint

Winter Dreams

F. Scott Fitzgerald

Some of the caddies were poor as sin and lived in one-room houses with a neurasthenic[1] cow in the front yard, but Dexter Green's father owned the second best grocery-store in Black Bear—the best one was "The Hub," patronized by the wealthy people from Sherry Island— and Dexter caddied only for pocket-money.

---

1. **neurasthenic** (n$\overline{oo}$′ras·then′ik): thin and weak, as though suffering from a nervous disorder.

Reaching All Students

Struggling Readers
Lead struggling readers to question each character's motives. Partners can hold question-and-answer sessions, taking turns asking questions and scanning the text to find the answers. For example, if the first partner questions why Dexter abruptly quits his job caddying, the second partner can find the answer on p. 589: "But he had received a strong emotional shock, and his perturbation required a violent and immediate outlet."

English Language Learners
Fitzgerald's long sentences and elevated diction may be challenging. Have pairs take turns reading passages aloud. Guide them to vary their reading rate to reflect the difficulty of the passage.

Advanced Learners
Fitzgerald is commonly called the "laureate of the Jazz Age" because he captured its unique spirit. Invite students to chronicle their age in a short story, poem, or song. What are the "winter dreams" of their generation?

Resources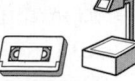

Viewing and Representing
Videocassette A, Segment 2
Available in English and Spanish. This segment explores the development of the American dream. For full lesson plans and worksheets, see the *Visual Connections Teacher's Manual.*
Fine Art Transparency
A transparency of an Arrow shirt advertisement by J. C. Leyendecker can be used to introduce the fashionable life Fitzgerald describes. See the *Viewing and Representing Transparencies and Worksheets:*
- Transparency 12
- Worksheet, p. 48

Ⓐ Historical Connections
Fitzgerald's story was written at the end of the Progressive Era—a period when many laws were passed to protect public health and factory workers; to increase educational opportunities; and to improve housing. Ironically, it was also the period when Jim Crow laws were passed to segregate blacks and whites.

The 1920s in America was a period of prosperity. It took only a small amount of money to be considered "well-off" because prices and taxes were low. A person earning $6,000 or more a year was in the upper five percent of the population.

Ⓑ Elements of Literature
Motivation
❓ What does the simile in the expression "poor as sin" suggest about characters' possible motivations in this society? [Possible responses: The simile suggests that being poor is viewed as a sin, a moral transgression. It suggests that people will be motivated to act for financial rather than altruistic or spiritual reasons.]

Ⓒ Critical Thinking
Analyzing
❓ Fitzgerald sketches three social classes in Black Bear, Minnesota. What classes does he describe, and what are their lives like? [Possible responses: The poor live in shacks and often supplement their income with livestock; the rich live on Sherry Island; the middle class includes shopkeepers, such as Dexter's father, who owns the town's second-most successful grocery store.]

T587

A Reading Skills and Strategies

Drawing Inferences About Characters

? What effect do the seasons have on Dexter's mood? [Possible responses: Winter makes him feel melancholy; spring, dismal; fall, elated.] Note how these moods suggest he is sensitive, moody, and romantic. What do these moods suggest will happen to his dreams? [They hint that his "winter dreams" are doomed to failure.]

B Elements of Literature

Motivation

? What do Dexter's dreams suggest he wants in the future? [Possible responses: He wants to be a golf champion, wealthy and admired; he wants to be a great athlete. His dreams suggest that he is motivated to stand out from the crowd.]

C Reading Skills and Strategies

Drawing Inferences About Characters

? What kind of woman do you think eleven-year-old Judy Jones will become? Why? [Possible responses: She will become beautiful and tantalizing, or she will be cruel and wild. Her "spark" and the "almost passionate quality in her eyes" suggest the former; her "general ungodliness" suggests the latter.]

D Vocabulary Note

Multiple Meanings of Words

Point out to students that Judy's "nurse" is what we today would call a *nanny,* a companion hired to take care of a child. The term *nurse* does not indicate that Judy is ill.

(A) In the fall when the days became crisp and gray, and the long Minnesota winter shut down like the white lid of a box, Dexter's skis moved over the snow that hid the fairways[2] of the golf course. At these times the country gave him a feeling of profound melancholy—it offended him that the links should lie in enforced fallowness, haunted by ragged sparrows for the long season. It was dreary, too, that on the tees where the gay colors fluttered in summer there were now only the desolate sand-boxes knee-deep in crusted ice. When he crossed the hills the wind blew cold as misery, and if the sun was out he tramped with his eyes squinted up against the hard dimensionless glare.

In April the winter ceased abruptly. The snow ran down into Black Bear Lake scarcely tarrying[3] for the early golfers to brave the season with red and black balls. Without <u>elation</u>, without an interval of moist glory, the cold was gone.

Dexter knew that there was something dismal about this Northern spring, just as he knew there was something gorgeous about the fall. Fall made him clinch his hands and tremble and repeat idiotic sentences to himself, and make brisk abrupt gestures of command to imaginary audiences and armies. October filled him with hope which November raised to a sort of ecstatic triumph, and in this mood the fleeting brilliant impressions of the summer at Sherry Island were ready grist to his mill.[4] **(B)** He became a golf champion and defeated Mr. T. A. Hedrick in a marvellous match played a hundred times over the fairways of his imagination, a match each detail of which he changed about untiringly—sometimes he won with almost laughable ease, sometimes he came up magnificently from behind. Again, stepping from a Pierce-Arrow automobile, like Mr. Mortimer Jones, he strolled frigidly into the lounge of the Sherry Island Golf Club—or perhaps, surrounded by an admiring crowd, he gave an exhibition of fancy diving from the spring-board of the club raft. . . . Among those who watched him in open-mouthed wonder was Mr. Mortimer Jones.

And one day it came to pass that Mr. Jones—himself and not his ghost—came up to Dexter with tears in his eyes and said that Dexter was the ——best caddy in the club, and wouldn't he decide not to quit if Mr. Jones made it worth his while, because every other——caddy in the club lost one ball a hole for him—regularly——

"No, sir," said Dexter decisively, "I don't want to caddy any more." Then, after a pause: "I'm too old."

"You're not more than fourteen. Why the devil did you decide just this morning that you wanted to quit? You promised that next week you'd go over to the State tournament with me."

"I decided I was too old."

Dexter handed in his "A Class" badge, collected what money was due him from the caddy master, and walked home to Black Bear Village.

"The best——caddy I ever saw," shouted Mr. Mortimer Jones over a drink that afternoon. "Never lost a ball! Willing! Intelligent! Quiet! Honest! Grateful!"

(C) The little girl who had done this was eleven—beautifully ugly as little girls are apt to be who are destined after a few years to be inexpressibly lovely and bring no end of misery to a great number of men. The spark, however, was perceptible. There was a general ungodliness in the way her lips twisted down at the corners when she smiled, and in the—Heaven help us!—in the almost passionate quality of her eyes. Vitality is born early in such women. It was utterly in evidence now, shining through her thin frame in a sort of glow.

She had come eagerly out on to the course at nine o'clock with a white linen nurse and five small new golf-clubs in a white canvas bag which **(D)** the nurse was carrying. When Dexter first saw her she was standing by the caddy house, rather ill at ease and trying to conceal the fact by engaging her nurse in an obviously unnatural conversation graced by startling and irrelevant grimaces from herself.

"Well, it's certainly a nice day, Hilda," Dexter heard her say. She drew down the corners of her

---

2. **fairways:** mowed parts of a golf course. The fairway of most holes starts at the tee and ends near the green.
3. **tarrying:** waiting.
4. **grist to his mill:** something that can be used to advantage.

WORDS TO OWN

elation (ē·lā′shən) *n.*: celebration.

Skill Link

Establishing and Adjusting a Purpose for Reading

Remind students that a work of fiction may be read for a number of different purposes, such as to enjoy, to find out, to interpret, and to understand. A single reader may have more than one purpose in reading a work; moreover, the purpose for reading a specific work may vary with the context.

Lead students in discussing what their purpose might be for reading "Winter Dreams" in the different contexts listed below. For each context, have students state what aspects of the story they might pay most attention to.

1. Context: *Metropolitan Magazine,* 1922. [Purpose: to enjoy a love story; you might pay attention to plot and characters.]

2. Context: a course in American studies. [Purpose: to understand the Jazz Age; you might pay attention to details of social life.]

3. Context: a course in psychology. [Purpose: to understand American ideas of love; you might pay attention to interpreting the characters.]

4. Context: a course in composition. [Purpose: to find out how to write; you might pay attention to plot, characterization, and style.]

5. Context: a reading group. [Purposes: to enjoy a story and share interpretations with friends; you might pay attention to themes and motifs.]

mouth, smiled, and glanced furtively around, her eyes in transit falling for an instant on Dexter.

Then to the nurse:

"Well, I guess there aren't very many people out here this morning, are there?"

The smile again—radiant, blatantly artificial—convincing.

"I don't know what we're supposed to do now," said the nurse, looking nowhere in particular.

"Oh, that's all right. I'll fix it up."

Dexter stood perfectly still, his mouth slightly ajar. He knew that if he moved forward a step his stare would be in her line of vision—if he moved backward he would lose his full view of her face. For a moment he had not realized how young she was. Now he remembered having seen her several times the year before—in bloomers.

Suddenly, involuntarily, he laughed, a short abrupt laugh—then, startled by himself, he turned and began to walk quickly away.

"Boy!"

Dexter stopped.

"Boy——"

Beyond question he was addressed. Not only that, but he was treated to that absurd smile, that preposterous smile—the memory of which at least a dozen men were to carry into middle age.

"Boy, do you know where the golf teacher is?"

"He's giving a lesson."

"Well, do you know where the caddy-master is?"

"He isn't here yet this morning."

"Oh." For a moment this baffled her. She stood alternately on her right and left foot.

"We'd like to get a caddy," said the nurse. "Mrs. Mortimer Jones sent us out to play golf, and we don't know how without we get a caddy."

Here she was stopped by an ominous glance from Miss Jones, followed immediately by the smile.

"There aren't any caddies here except me," said Dexter to the nurse, "and I got to stay here in charge until the caddy-master gets here."

"Oh."

Miss Jones and her retinue[5] now withdrew, and at a proper distance from Dexter became involved in a heated conversation, which was concluded

5. **retinue** (ret′'n·yōō′): group of followers or servants attending to a person of rank.

by Miss Jones taking one of the clubs and hitting it on the ground with violence. For further emphasis she raised it again and was about to bring it down smartly upon the nurse's bosom, when the nurse seized the club and twisted it from her hands.

"You damn little mean old *thing!*" cried Miss Jones wildly.

Another argument ensued. Realizing that the elements of the comedy were implied in the scene, Dexter several times began to laugh, but each time restrained the laugh before it reached audibility. He could not resist the monstrous conviction that the little girl was justified in beating the nurse.

The situation was resolved by the fortuitous[6] appearance of the caddy-master, who was appealed to immediately by the nurse.

"Miss Jones is to have a little caddy, and this one says he can't go."

"Mr. McKenna said I was to wait here till you came," said Dexter quickly.

"Well, he's here now." Miss Jones smiled cheerfully at the caddy-master. Then she dropped her bag and set off at a haughty mince[7] toward the first tee.

"Well?" the caddy-master turned to Dexter. "What you standing there like a dummy for? Go pick up the young lady's clubs."

"I don't think I'll go out to-day," said Dexter.

"You don't——"

"I think I'll quit."

The enormity of his decision frightened him. He was a favorite caddy, and the thirty dollars a month he earned through the summer were not to be made elsewhere around the lake. But he had received a strong emotional shock, and his perturbation required a violent and immediate outlet.

It is not so simple as that, either. As so frequently would be the case in the future, Dexter was unconsciously dictated to by his winter dreams.

6. **fortuitous** (fôr·tōō′ə·təs): fortunate.
7. **mince:** prim, affected walk.

WORDS TO OWN

perturbation (pur'tər·bā'shən) n.: feeling of alarm or agitation.

F. SCOTT FITZGERALD **589**

ⓔ Cultural Connections

Bloomers were full, loose pants gathered at the knees, formerly worn by women for athletics. They were named after nineteenth-century American social reformer Amelia Bloomer.

ⓕ Elements of Literature
Motivation

❓ Why do you think Dexter is so captivated by Judy Jones? [Possible response: Judy is not only radiant and charming but also uniquely self-confident and daring for her age.]

ⓖ Critical Thinking
Making Judgments

❓ Is it appropriate for Judy to call Dexter "Boy"? [Possible responses: No, by being a responsible caddy, Dexter has shown he is more mature than his years. Further, Judy is herself a child, three years younger than Dexter. On the other hand, Dexter is a boy—and not a wealthy one, as the demeaning term reminds him.]

ⓗ Elements of Literature
Irony

❓ How is Fitzgerald being ironic here? What does the irony suggest about Judy's character? [A "retinue" includes more than one servant. The word suggests that Judy considers royal treatment her due, a natural result of her beauty and wealth.]

ⓘ Reading Skills and Strategies

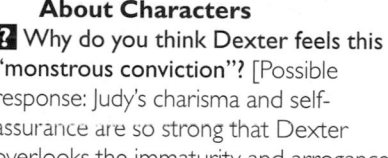

Making Inferences About Characters

❓ Why do you think Dexter feels this "monstrous conviction"? [Possible response: Judy's charisma and self-assurance are so strong that Dexter overlooks the immaturity and arrogance of her behavior.]

ⓙ Elements of Literature
Motivation

❓ Why does Dexter quit his job? [Possible responses: Meeting Judy has been a shock; he refuses to serve her because he is both repelled by and drawn to her; he doesn't want to wait on her like a servant.]

Using Students' Strengths

Kinesthetic Learners

Fitzgerald's characters often reflect aspects of himself and his wife, Zelda, especially their love of possessions. With the $30 he received for his first story, Fitzgerald bought himself a pair of white flannel slacks and Zelda a magenta feather fan. Students can show their grasp of Judy's and Dexter's personalities by creating collages featuring the things that they feel were important to each character. Invite students to share their collages with the class.

Verbal Learners

As students read the story, have them jot down memorable words and phrases. When everyone has finished reading, have students pool their lists and select eight words or phrases (not sentences) that they feel best communicate the theme. Then, have them narrow their lists to the top three words or phrases. After selections are made, have each student write one word or phrase on the chalkboard to create a "found poem."

II

Now, of course, the quality and the seasonability of these winter dreams varied, but the stuff of them remained. They persuaded Dexter several years later to pass up a business course at the State university—his father, prospering now, would have paid his way—for the precarious[8] advantage of attending an older and more famous university in the East, where he was bothered by his scanty funds. But do not get the impression, because his winter dreams happened to be concerned at first with musings on the rich, that there was anything merely snobbish in the boy. He wanted not association with glittering things and glittering people—he wanted the glittering things themselves. Often he reached out for the best without knowing why he wanted it—and sometimes he ran up against the mysterious denials and prohibitions in which life indulges. It is with one of those denials and not with his career as a whole that this story deals.

He made money. It was rather amazing. After college he went to the city from which Black Bear Lake draws its wealthy patrons. When he was only twenty-three and had been there not quite two years, there were already people who liked to say: "Now *there's* a boy—" All about him rich men's sons were peddling bonds precariously, or investing patrimonies[9] precariously, or plodding through the two dozen volumes of the "George Washington Commercial Course," but Dexter borrowed a thousand dollars on his college degree and his confident mouth, and bought a partnership in a laundry.

It was a small laundry when he went into it but Dexter made a specialty of learning how the English washed fine woolen golf-stockings without shrinking them, and within a year he was catering to the trade that wore knickerbockers. Men were insisting that their Shetland hose and sweaters go to his laundry just as they had insisted on a caddy who could find golf-balls. A little later he was doing their wives' lingerie as well—and running five branches in different parts of the city. Before he was twenty-seven he owned the largest string of laundries in his section of the country. It was

then that he sold out and went to New York. But the part of his story that concerns us goes back to the days when he was making his first big success.

When he was twenty-three Mr. Hart—one of the gray-haired men who like to say "Now there's a boy"—gave him a guest card to the Sherry Island Golf Club for a week-end. So he signed his name one day on the register, and that afternoon played golf in a foursome with Mr. Hart and Mr. Sandwood and Mr. T. A. Hedrick. He did not consider it necessary to remark that he had once carried Mr. Hart's bag over this same links, and that he knew every trap and gully with his eyes shut—but he found himself glancing at the four caddies who trailed them, trying to catch a gleam or gesture that would remind him of himself, that would lessen the gap which lay between his present and his past.

It was a curious day, slashed abruptly with fleeting, familiar impressions. One minute he had the sense of being a trespasser—in the next he was impressed by the tremendous superiority he felt toward Mr. T. A. Hedrick, who was a bore and not even a good golfer any more.

Then, because of a ball Mr. Hart lost near the fifteenth green, an enormous thing happened. While they were searching the stiff grasses of the rough there was a clear call of "Fore!"[10] from behind a hill in their rear. And as they all turned abruptly from their search a bright new ball sliced abruptly over the hill and caught Mr. T. A. Hedrick in the abdomen.

"By Gad!" cried Mr. T. A. Hedrick, "they ought to put some of these crazy women off the course. It's getting to be outrageous."

A head and a voice came up together over the hill:

"Do you mind if we go through?"

"You hit me in the stomach!" declared Mr. Hedrick wildly.

"Did I?" The girl approached the group of men. "I'm sorry. I yelled 'Fore!'"

Her glance fell casually on each of the men—then scanned the fairway for her ball.

"Did I bounce into the rough?"

It was impossible to determine whether this

---

8. **precarious** (prē·ker′ē·əs): uncertain.
9. **patrimonies** (pa′trə·mō′nēz): inheritances.

10. **fore:** warning cry that a golfer gives before hitting a ball down the fairway.

Crossing the Curriculum

question was ingenuous[11] or <u>malicious</u>. In a moment, however, she left no doubt, for as her partner came up over the hill she called cheerfully:

"Here I am! I'd have gone on the green except that I hit something."

As she took her stance for a short mashie[12] shot, Dexter looked at her closely. She wore a blue gingham dress, rimmed at throat and shoulders with a white edging that accentuated her tan. The quality of exaggeration, of thinness, which had made her passionate eyes and down-turning mouth absurd at eleven, was gone now. She was arrestingly beautiful. The color in her cheeks was centered like the color in a picture—it was not a "high" color, but a sort of fluctuating and feverish warmth, so shaded that it seemed at any moment it would recede and disappear. This color and the mobility of her mouth gave a continual impression of flux, of intense life, of passionate vitality—balanced only partially by the sad luxury of her eyes.

She swung her mashie impatiently and without interest, pitching the ball into a sand-pit on the other side of the green. With a quick, insincere smile and a careless "Thank you!" she went on after it.

"That Judy Jones!" remarked Mr. Hedrick on the next tee, as they waited—some moments—for her to play on ahead. "All she needs is to be turned up and spanked for six months and then to be married off to an old-fashioned cavalry captain."

"My God, she's good-looking!" said Mr. Sandwood, who was just over thirty.

"Good-looking!" cried Mr. Hedrick contemptuously, "she always looks as if she wanted to be kissed! Turning those big cow-eyes on every calf in town!"

It was doubtful if Mr. Hedrick intended a reference to the maternal instinct.

"She'd play pretty good golf if she'd try," said Mr. Sandwood.

"She has no form," said Mr. Hedrick solemnly.

---

11. **ingenuous** (in·jen′yo̅o̅·əs): innocent; without guile.
12. **mashie:** a number 5 iron golf club.

> *She was arrestingly beautiful. The color in her cheeks was centered like the color in a picture —*

"She has a nice figure," said Mr. Sandwood.

"Better thank the Lord she doesn't drive a swifter ball," said Mr. Hart, winking at Dexter.

Later in the afternoon the sun went down with a riotous swirl of gold and varying blues and scarlets, and left the dry, rustling night of Western summer. Dexter watched from the veranda of the Golf Club, watched the even overlap of the waters in the little wind, silver molasses under the harvest-moon. Then the moon held a finger to her lips and the lake became a clear pool, pale and quiet. Dexter put on his bathing-suit and swam out to the farthest raft, where he stretched dripping on the wet canvas of the springboard.

There was a fish jumping and a star shining and the lights around the lake were gleaming. Over on a dark peninsula a piano was playing the songs of last summer and of summers before that—songs from "Chin-Chin" and "The Count of Luxemburg" and "The Chocolate Soldier"—and because the sound of a piano over a stretch of water had always seemed beautiful to Dexter he lay perfectly quiet and listened.

The tune the piano was playing at that moment had been gay and new five years before when Dexter was a sophomore at college. They had played it at a prom once when he could not afford the luxury of proms, and he had stood outside the gymnasium and listened. The sound of the tune precipitated in him a sort of ecstasy and it was with that ecstasy he viewed what happened to him now. It was a mood of intense appreciation, a sense that, for once, he was magnificently attuned to life and that everything about him was radiating a brightness and a glamour he might never know again.

A low, pale oblong detached itself suddenly from the darkness of the Island, spitting forth the reverberate sound of a racing motor-boat. Two white streamers of cleft water rolled themselves out behind it and almost immediately the boat

---

WORDS TO OWN
malicious (mə·lish′əs) *adj.:* intentionally hurtful.

E **Reading Skills and Strategies**
Drawing Inferences About Characters

❓ What does Judy's behavior here suggest about her character? [She is selfish. Students are likely to judge her as arrogant, self-absorbed, and careless.]

F **Elements of Literature**
Connotation

Discuss the contradictory connotations of the phrase "sad luxury," such as unusual beauty, sophistication, wealth, dissatisfaction, unhappiness, and vulnerability.

G **Critical Thinking**
Analyzing

❓ How do the men feel about Judy? Why doesn't Dexter add his opinion to the conversation? [Possible responses: While Mr. Sandwood finds Judy attractive, Mr. Hedrick seems immune to Judy's charms, which suggests that Judy's appeal is not universal or that he is older and more experienced. Dexter does not speak up because he is afraid of revealing how attracted he is to Judy.]

H **Appreciating Language**
Style

❓ How does the style of this passage reflect Dexter's feelings for Judy? [Possible responses: The rich imagery and personification suggest the beauty and depth of Dexter's feelings; love makes the world intensely beautiful.]

I **Cultural Connections**

Chin-Chin, The Count of Luxembourg, and *The Chocolate Soldier* were all popular musicals of the time.

J **Reading Skills and Strategies**
Drawing Inferences About Characters

❓ How does the song help awaken Dexter's "winter dreams"? [Possible answer: Dexter is already experiencing the glow of falling in love. Hearing a song that he connected with the life he once longed for under such different circumstances makes him feel that his dream can come true. Judy's arrival on the scene in the next moment seems to confirm his hopes.]

Getting Students Involved

Cooperative Learning
Author Frederick J. Hoffman, in his book *The 20s: American Writing in the Postwar Decade,* says that Fitzgerald's characters suffer from "a fundamental lack of a clear moral sense . . . which had caused men in the very beginning to have the wrong dreams, and which gave them no proper way of judging them." Hold a panel discussion to discuss Hoffman's points. What is "a clear moral sense"? In what ways do Dexter and Judy lack one?

Enrichment Activity
The Jazz Age was a time of great gaiety and merriment. Nonetheless, a small but influential group of writers expressed their disillusionment. Fitzgerald described American society as "beautiful and damned." The intellectuals attacked the hypocrisy, conformity, and standardization of American life. Have groups of students critique contemporary society, focusing on these elements and drawing up lists of what is good and bad.

A Elements of Literature
Motivation

? Why does Judy leave the man waiting at her house? [Possible responses: She is motivated by revulsion at his fawning; an urge to taunt him; or a desire to save him pain since she knows that she is not what he thinks.]

B Reading Skills and Strategies

Drawing
Inferences About Characters

? Why does Judy invite Dexter to dinner the following evening? [Possible responses: She is genuinely interested in him; she is teasing him; she wants to add another man to her pool of admirers; she thinks he has good prospects and might be a suitable husband.]

C Critical Thinking
Analyzing

? In what way is Dexter not really going in a new direction? [Possible response: He has been intrigued by Judy and sought the glamour she represents for many years.]

D Reading Skills and Strategies

Drawing
Inferences About Characters

? According to this passage, what kind of man does Dexter represent? [Possible response: He represents the new American, the self-reliant, self-made man, vigorous but rough-edged.]

E Appreciating Language
Repetition

? What word does Fitzgerald repeat for emphasis? What effect does this repetition have on the story's theme? [He repeats the word *care* in *careless* and *careful*. Because he was not born into the upper class, he cannot disregard the rules of conduct the way Judy does. The phrase suggests the need for him to be careful in love as well.]

F Cultural Connections

Explain that Krimslich is an Eastern European name and that Dexter's mother speaks broken English because she is an immigrant. The implication is that in order to move in higher social circles, Dexter must be careful about his clothes, looks, and mannerisms.

---

was beside him, drowning out the hot tinkle of the piano in the drone of its spray. Dexter raising himself on his arms was aware of a figure standing at the wheel, of two dark eyes regarding him over the lengthening space of water—then the boat had gone by and was sweeping in an immense and purposeless circle of spray round and round in the middle of the lake. With equal eccentricity one of the circles flattened out and headed back toward the raft.

"Who's that?" she called, shutting off her motor. She was so near now that Dexter could see her bathing-suit, which consisted apparently of pink rompers.

The nose of the boat bumped the raft, and as the latter tilted rakishly, he was precipitated[13] toward her. With different degrees of interest they recognized each other.

"Aren't you one of those men we played through this afternoon?" she demanded.

He was.

"Well, do you know how to drive a motor-boat? Because if you do I wish you'd drive this one so I can ride on the surf-board behind. My name is Judy Jones"—she favored him with an absurd smirk—rather, what tried to be a smirk, for, twist her mouth as she might, it was not grotesque, it was merely beautiful—"and I live in a house over there on the Island, and in that house there is a man waiting for me. When he drove up at the door I drove out of the dock because he says I'm his ideal."

There was a fish jumping and a star shining and the lights around the lake were gleaming. Dexter sat beside Judy Jones and she explained how her boat was driven. Then she was in the water, swimming to the floating surf-board with a sinuous[14] crawl. Watching her was without effort to the eye, watching a branch waving or a sea-gull flying. Her arms, burned to butternut, moved sinuously among the dull platinum ripples, elbow appearing first, casting the forearm back with a cadence of falling water, then reaching out and down, stabbing a path ahead.

They moved out into the lake; turning, Dexter saw that she was kneeling on the low rear of the now uptilted surf-board.

"Go faster," she called, "fast as it'll go."

13. **precipitated:** thrown headlong.
14. **sinuous:** curving back and forth; snakelike.

592 THE MODERNS

Obediently he jammed the lever forward and the white spray mounted at the bow. When he looked around again the girl was standing up on the rushing board, her arms spread wide, her eyes lifted toward the moon.

"It's awful cold," she shouted. "What's your name?"

He told her.

"Well, why don't you come to dinner to-morrow night?"

His heart turned over like the fly-wheel[15] of the boat, and, for the second time, her casual whim gave a new direction to his life.

III

Next evening while he waited for her to come down-stairs, Dexter peopled the soft deep summer room and the sun-porch that opened from it with the men who had already loved Judy Jones. He knew the sort of men they were—the men who when he first went to college had entered from the great prep schools with graceful clothes and the deep tan of healthy summers. He had seen that, in one sense, he was better than these men. He was newer and stronger. Yet in acknowledging to himself that he wished his children to be like them he was admitting that he was but the rough, strong stuff from which they eternally sprang.

When the time had come for him to wear good clothes, he had known who were the best tailors in America, and the best tailors in America had made him the suit he wore this evening. He had acquired that particular <u>reserve</u> peculiar to his university, that set it off from other universities. He recognized the value to him of such a mannerism and he had adopted it; he knew that to be careless in dress and manner required more confidence than to be careful. But carelessness was for his children. His mother's name had been Krimslich. She was a Bohemian of the peasant class and she had talked broken English to the end of her days. Her son must keep to the set patterns.

15. **fly-wheel:** wheel that regulates the speed of a machine.

WORDS TO OWN
reserve (ri·zʉrv′) *n.*: self-restraint.

Getting Students Involved

Enrichment Activity
Sentences à la Fitzgerald. To enhance students' sentence-composing skills, ask them to write imitations of several sentences by Fitzgerald. Here are two sample sentences from the story, followed by models of imitative writing.

1. "Dexter stood perfectly still, his mouth slightly ajar." *The new truck idled softly, its power momentarily caged.*

2. "Perhaps from so much youthful love, so many youthful lovers, she had come, in self-defense, to nourish herself solely from within." *Doubtless in response to so many homework assignments, so little free time, they had asked, in desperation, to postpone the date of the test.*

After explaining the process, let students choose five sentences they particularly admire as models for imitation.

At a little after seven Judy Jones came downstairs. She wore a blue silk afternoon dress, and he was disappointed at first that she had not put on something more elaborate. This feeling was accentuated when, after a brief greeting, she went to the door of a butler's pantry and pushing it open called: "You can serve dinner, Martha." He had rather expected that a butler would announce dinner, that there would be a cocktail. Then he put these thoughts behind him as they sat down side by side on a lounge and looked at each other.

"Father and mother won't be here," she said thoughtfully.

He remembered the last time he had seen her father, and he was glad the parents were not to be here to-night—they might wonder who he was. He had been born in Keeble, a Minnesota village fifty miles farther north, and he always gave Keeble as his home instead of Black Bear Village. Country towns were well enough to come from if they weren't inconveniently in sight and used as footstools by fashionable lakes.

They talked of his university, which she had visited frequently during the past two years, and of the near-by city which supplied Sherry Island with its patrons, and whither Dexter would return next day to his prospering laundries.

During dinner she slipped into a moody depression which gave Dexter a feeling of uneasiness. Whatever petulance she uttered in her throaty voice worried him. Whatever she smiled at—at him, at a chicken liver, at nothing—it disturbed him that her smile could have no root in mirth, or even in amusement. When the scarlet corners of her lips curved down, it was less a smile than an invitation to a kiss.

Then, after dinner, she led him out on the dark sun-porch and deliberately changed the atmosphere.

"Do you mind if I weep a little?" she said.

"I'm afraid I'm boring you," he responded quickly.

"You're not. I like you. But I've just had a terrible afternoon. There was a man I cared about, and

During dinner she slipped into a moody depression which gave Dexter a feeling of uneasiness.

this afternoon he told me out of a clear sky that he was poor as a church-mouse. He'd never even hinted it before. Does this sound horribly mundane?"[16]

"Perhaps he was afraid to tell you."

"Suppose he was," she answered. "He didn't start right. You see, if I'd thought of him as poor—well, I've been mad about loads of poor men, and fully intended to marry them all. But in this case, I hadn't thought of him that way, and my interest in him wasn't strong enough to survive the shock. As if a girl calmly informed her fiancé that she was a widow. He might not object to widows, but——

"Let's start right," she interrupted herself suddenly. "Who are you, anyhow?"

For a moment Dexter hesitated. Then:

"I'm nobody," he announced. "My career is largely a matter of futures."

"Are you poor?"

"No," he said frankly, "I'm probably making more money than any man my age in the Northwest. I know that's an obnoxious remark, but you advised me to start right."

There was a pause. Then she smiled and the corners of her mouth drooped and an almost imperceptible sway brought her closer to him, looking up into his eyes. A lump rose in Dexter's throat, and he waited breathless for the experiment, facing the unpredictable compound that would form mysteriously from the elements of their lips. Then he saw—she communicated her excitement to him, lavishly, deeply, with kisses that were not a promise but a fulfillment. They aroused in him not hunger demanding renewal but surfeit that would demand more surfeit . . . kisses that were like charity, creating want by holding back nothing at all.

It did not take him many hours to decide that he had wanted Judy Jones ever since he was a proud, desirous little boy.

16. **mundane:** ordinary; everyday.

Words to Own

petulance (pech'ə·ləns) *n.:* irritability; impatience.
mirth (murth) *n.:* joyfulness.

F. SCOTT FITZGERALD **593**

Listening to Music

Rhapsody in Blue and *An American in Paris* performed by the Philharmonia Slavonica
Jazz flourished during the Twenties. Developed by African Americans from West African folk music, jazz is characterized by improvisation, repeated chord progressions, subtle modulations of pitch, and tonal effects, such as growls and wails. Near the end of the decade, George Gershwin composed two significant works that blended jazz with European classical music:

Rhapsody in Blue (1924) and *An American in Paris* (1928).
Activity
As students read the story, play an excerpt from *Rhapsody in Blue* or *An American in Paris*. Ask students to discuss how the freedom and improvisation of jazz reflects the lifestyle of the characters in "Winter Dreams." Have students comment on what they think today's musical styles reveal about contemporary Americans.

G **Elements of Literature**
Motivation
❓ Why does Dexter lie about his hometown? [Admitting to living in middle-class Black Bear Village would emphasize the social distance between himself and the wealthy lake residents.]

H **Reading Skills and Strategies**
Drawing Inferences About Characters
❓ If Judy had cared about the other man, she might have been troubled to learn he was poor, but she would not have stopped caring from the "shock" of finding out. Why does Judy paint such a frivolous picture of herself to Dexter? [Possible answers: to emphasize her control of their relationship by showing Dexter she can throw one man away in the afternoon and pick up another by dinner; to warn him that she is not serious about him; to make him jealous; because she is shallow.]

I **Critical Thinking**
Analyzing
❓ What does Dexter mean when he says that his career is "a matter of futures"? [Possible responses: He doesn't work in a family business or have family money, but he does have a promising future that he is creating himself.]

J **Reading Skills and Strategies**
Drawing Inferences About Characters
❓ What does the kiss symbolize for Dexter? [Possible responses: the fulfillment of his winter dreams; the start of their romance.]

K **Literary Connections**
This kiss prefigures the crucial kiss in *The Great Gatsby:* "[Gatsby knew] that when he kissed this girl [Daisy], and forever wed his unutterable visions to her perishable breath, his mind would never romp again like the mind of God. So he waited, listening for a moment longer to the tuning-fork that had been struck upon a star. Then he kissed her. At his lips' touch she blossomed for him like a flower and the incarnation was complete."

A Elements of Literature
Motivation
? Fitzgerald says that Judy goes directly after whatever she wants, but he leaves open the question of what exactly it is she wants. What do you think she wants? [Possible responses: love; respect; power; the fulfillment of romantic illusions; her problem is that she herself doesn't know.]

B Reading Skills and Strategies
Drawing Inferences About Characters
? There are elements of Judy's character that Dexter does not like, yet he doesn't want to change her. How do you explain his feelings? [Possible responses: It is Judy's very inconsistency that appeals to Dexter. He admires the way she lives in the moment, without regard for what others may think. Her beauty and vitality are so important to him that her faults don't matter.]

C Critical Thinking
Evaluating
? Does Judy's character seem realistic to you? Why or why not? [Possible responses: No, she is two-dimensional or stereotypical; yes, she is realistic, because some people are indeed that capricious, fickle, and insensitive.]

IV

It began like that—and continued, with varying shades of intensity, on such a note right up to the dénouement.[17] Dexter surrendered a part of himself to the most direct and unprincipled personality with which he had ever come in contact. Whatever Judy wanted, she went after with the full pressure of her charm. There was no <u>divergence</u> of method, no jockeying for position or

17. **dénouement** (dā′nōō·mä*n*′): final outcome.

594 THE MODERNS

premeditation of effects—there was a very little mental side to any of her affairs. She simply made men conscious to the highest degree of her physical loveliness. Dexter had no desire to change her. Her deficiencies were knit up with a passionate energy that transcended and justified them.

When, as Judy's head lay against his shoulder that first night, she whispered, "I don't know what's the matter with me. Last night I thought I was in love with a man and to-night I think I'm in love with you——" —it seemed to him a beautiful and romantic thing to say. It was the exquisite excitability that for the moment he controlled and owned. But a week later he was compelled to view this same quality in a different light. She took him in her roadster to a picnic supper, and after supper she disappeared, likewise in her roadster, with another man. Dexter became enormously upset and was scarcely able to be decently civil to the other people present. When she assured him that she had not kissed the other man, he knew she was lying—yet he was glad that she had taken the trouble to lie to him.

He was, as he found before the summer ended, one of a varying dozen who circulated about her. Each of them had at one time been favored above all others—about half of them still basked in the solace of occasional sentimental revivals. Whenever one showed signs of dropping out through long neglect, she granted him a brief honeyed hour, which encouraged him to tag along for a year or so longer. Judy made these forays[18] upon the helpless and defeated without malice, indeed half unconscious that there was anything mischievous in what she did.

When a new man came to town every one dropped out—dates were automatically cancelled.

The helpless part of trying to do anything about it was that she did it all herself. She was not a girl who could be "won" in the kinetic[19] sense—she was proof against[20] cleverness, she was proof

18. **forays** (fôr′āz): raids.
19. **kinetic** (ki·net′ik): coming about through action or energy.
20. **proof against:** able to withstand.

WORDS TO OWN
divergence (dī·vʉr′jəns) *n.:* variance; difference.

Taking a Second Look

Review: Point of View
Point of view is the vantage point from which the writer tells a story. In the *first-person point of view,* the narrator is one of the characters in the story and explains the events through his or her own eyes. In the *third-person omniscient point of view,* the narrator looks through the eyes of all the characters and so is "all-knowing." In the *third-person limited point of view,* the narrator tells the story through the eyes of only one character, and reports only what he or she

experiences. Sometimes the narrative voice changes to allow the author to control the immediacy or objectivity with which the story is told.

Activities
1. "Winter Dreams" is written in the third-person limited point of view, with occasional shifts to omniscient commentary. Find at least two of these shifts, and explain their purpose in the story.

2. All the action is seen through Dexter's eyes; all the feeling, through his emotions. As a result, we perceive all the nostalgia toward youth from his mature vantage point. How do the shifts to an omniscient point of view suggest that "Winter Dreams" is a cautionary tale, a moral lesson?

against charm; if any of these assailed her too strongly she would immediately resolve the affair to a physical basis, and under the magic of her physical splendor the strong as well as the brilliant played her game and not their own. She was entertained only by the gratification of her desires and by the direct exercise of her own charm. Perhaps from so much youthful love, so many youthful lovers, she had come, in self-defense, to nourish herself wholly from within.

Succeeding Dexter's first exhilaration came restlessness and dissatisfaction. The helpless ecstasy of losing himself in her was opiate rather than tonic.[21] It was fortunate for his work during the winter that those moments of ecstasy came in-

21. **opiate . . . tonic:** calming rather than stimulating.

frequently. Early in their acquaintance it had seemed for a while that there was a deep and spontaneous mutual attraction—that first August, for example—three days of long evenings on her dusky veranda, of strange wan kisses through the late afternoon, in shadowy alcoves or behind the protecting trellises of the garden arbors, of mornings when she was fresh as a dream and almost shy at meeting him in the clarity of the rising day. There was all the ecstasy of an engagement about it, sharpened by his realization that there was no engagement. It was during those three days that, for the first time, he had asked her to marry him. She said "maybe some day," she said "kiss me," she said "I'd like to marry you," she said "I love you"—she said—nothing.

F. SCOTT FITZGERALD **595**

The three days were interrupted by the arrival of a New York man who visited at her house for half September. To Dexter's agony, rumor engaged them. The man was the son of the president of a great trust company. But at the end of a month it was reported that Judy was yawning. At a dance one night she sat all evening in a motorboat with a local beau, while the New Yorker searched the club for her frantically. She told the local beau that she was bored with her visitor, and two days later he left. She was seen with him at the station, and it was reported that he looked very mournful indeed.

On this note the summer ended. Dexter was twenty-four, and he found himself increasingly in a position to do as he wished. He joined two clubs in the city and lived at one of them. Though he was by no means an integral part of the stag-lines[22] at these clubs, he managed to be on hand at dances where Judy Jones was likely to appear. He could have gone out socially as much as he liked—he was an eligible young man, now, and popular with down-town fathers. His confessed devotion to Judy Jones had rather solidified his position. But he had no social aspirations and rather despised the dancing men who were always on tap for the Thursday or Saturday parties and who filled in at dinners with the younger married set. Already he was playing with the idea of going East to New York. He wanted to take Judy Jones with him. No disillusion as to the world in which she had grown up could cure his illusion as to her desirability.

Remember that—for only in the light of it can what he did for her be understood.

Eighteen months after he first met Judy Jones he became engaged to another girl. Her name was Irene Scheerer, and her father was one of the men who had always believed in Dexter. Irene was light-haired and sweet and honorable, and a little stout, and she had two suitors whom she pleasantly relinquished when Dexter formally asked her to marry him.

Summer, fall, winter, spring, another summer, another fall—so much he had given of his active life to the incorrigible[23] lips of Judy Jones. She had treated him with interest, with encouragement, with malice, with indifference, with contempt. She had inflicted on him the innumerable little slights and indignities possible in such a case—as if in revenge for having ever cared for him at all. She had beckoned him and yawned at him and beckoned him again and he had responded often with bitterness and narrowed eyes. She had brought him ecstatic happiness and intolerable agony of spirit. She had caused him untold inconvenience and not a little trouble. She had insulted him, and she had ridden over him, and she had played his interest in her against his interest in his work—for fun. She had done everything to him except to criticize him—this she had not done—it seemed to him only because it might have sullied the utter indifference she manifested and sincerely felt toward him.

When autumn had come and gone again it occurred to him that he could not have Judy Jones. He had to beat this into his mind but he convinced himself at last. He lay awake at night for a while and argued it over. He told himself the trouble and the pain she had caused him, he enumerated her glaring deficiences as a wife. Then he said to himself that he loved her, and after a while he fell asleep. For a week, lest he imagined her husky voice over the telephone or her eyes opposite him at lunch, he worked hard and late, and at night he went to his office and plotted out his years.

At the end of a week he went to a dance and cut in on her once. For almost the first time since they had met he did not ask her to sit out with him or tell her that she was lovely. It hurt him that she did not miss these things—that was all. He was not jealous when he saw that there was a new man to-night. He had been hardened against jealousy long before.

He stayed late at the dance. He sat for an hour with Irene Scheerer and talked about books and about music. He knew very little about either. But he was beginning to be master of his own time now, and he had a rather priggish[24] notion that he—the young and already fabulously successful Dexter Green—should know more about such things.

That was in October, when he was twenty-five. In January, Dexter and Irene became engaged. It

22. **stag-lines:** lines of unaccompanied men at a dance, waiting for available dance partners.
23. **incorrigible:** incapable of correction or reform.
24. **priggish:** annoyingly precise and proper.

Getting Students Involved

Cooperative Learning

The 1920s was the age in which machines entered the home and began to affect daily life. In addition to the automobile and airplane, the 1920s saw the increased use of the radio, vacuum cleaner, and washing machine. Silent movies gave people a lens on the world; the "talkies" opened the audio domain. Have groups of students select one machine that was invented or refined during the 1920s and report on its impact.

Enrichment Activity

Culture Vulture. Dexter seeks the "finer things" in life: books, music, the arts. What do people have to know to be considered "well-educated"? Invite students to make a set of cards listing the top one hundred facts a person should know. The facts should be drawn from history, literature, math, art, music, and science. Students can then form teams and hold a "Knowledge Bowl" to learn their facts.

was to be announced in June, and they were to be married three months later.

The Minnesota winter prolonged itself interminably, and it was almost May when the winds came soft and the snow ran down into Black Bear Lake at last. For the first time in over a year Dexter was enjoying a certain tranquility of spirit. Judy Jones had been in Florida, and afterward in Hot Springs, and somewhere she had been engaged, and somewhere she had broken it off. At first, when Dexter had definitely given her up, it had made him sad that people still linked them together and asked for news of her, but when he began to be placed at dinner next to Irene Scheerer people didn't ask him about her any more—they told him about her. He ceased to be an authority on her.

May at last. Dexter walked the streets at night when the darkness was damp as rain, wondering that so soon, with so little done, so much of ecstasy had gone from him. May one year back had been marked by Judy's poignant, unforgivable, yet forgiven turbulence—it had been one of those rare times when he fancied she had grown to care for him. That old penny's worth of happiness he had spent for this bushel of content. He knew that Irene would be no more than a curtain spread behind him, a hand moving among gleaming tea-cups, a voice calling to children . . . fire and loveliness were gone, the magic of nights and the wonder of the varying hours and seasons . . . slender lips, down-turning, dropping to his lips and bearing him up into a heaven of eyes. . . . The thing was deep in him. He was too strong and alive for it to die lightly.

In the middle of May when the weather balanced for a few days on the thin bridge that led to deep summer he turned in one night at Irene's house. Their engagement was to be announced in a week now—no one would be surprised at it. And to-night they would sit together on the lounge at the University Club and look on for an hour at the dancers. It gave him a sense of solidity to go with her—she was so sturdily popular, so intensely "great."

He mounted the steps of the brownstone house and stepped inside.

"Irene," he called.

Mrs. Scheerer came out of the living-room to meet him.

"Dexter," she said, "Irene's gone up-stairs with a splitting headache. She wanted to go with you but I made her go to bed."

"Nothing serious, I——"

"Oh, no. She's going to play golf with you in the morning. You can spare her for just one night, can't you, Dexter?"

Her smile was kind. She and Dexter liked each other. In the living-room he talked for a moment before he said good-night.

Returning to the University Club, where he had rooms, he stood in the doorway for a moment and watched the dancers. He leaned against the door-post, nodded at a man or two—yawned.

"Hello, darling."

The familiar voice at his elbow startled him. Judy Jones had left a man and crossed the room to him—Judy Jones, a slender enamelled doll in cloth of gold: gold in a band at her head, gold in two slipper points at her dress's hem. The fragile glow of her face seemed to blossom as she smiled at him. A breeze of warmth and light blew through the room. His hands in the pockets of his dinner-jacket tightened spasmodically. He was filled with a sudden excitement.

"When did you get back?" he asked casually.

"Come here and I'll tell you about it."

She turned and he followed her. She had been away—he could have wept at the wonder of her return. She had passed through enchanted streets, doing things that were like provocative music. All mysterious happenings, all fresh and quickening hopes, had gone away with her, come back with her now.

She turned in the doorway.

"Have you a car here? If you haven't, I have."

"I have a coupé."

In then, with a rustle of golden cloth. He slammed the door. Into so many cars she had stepped—like this—like that—her back against the leather, so—her elbow resting on the door—waiting. She would have been soiled long since had there been anything to soil her—except herself—but this was her own self outpouring.

With an effort he forced himself to start the car and back into the street. This was nothing, he

---

WORDS TO OWN

turbulence (tʉr′byo͞o·ləns) n.: wild disorder.

F. SCOTT FITZGERALD **597**

Professional Notes

Critical Comment: Fitzgerald's Follies

In an article entitled "Fitzgerald Before *The Great Gatsby*," critic Paul Rosenfeld says: "The utmost that can be charged against F. Scott Fitzgerald is that too oftentimes his good material eludes him. Of the ultimate value of said material there is no dispute. Certain racehorses run for the pure joy of running, and the author of *The Beautiful and Damned* and *Tales of the Jazz Age* is such an animal. He is a born writer, amusing himself with tales and pictures, and eventually nothing is interesting except the natural bent. Salty and insipid, exaggeratedly poetical and bitterly parodistic, his writing pours exuberantly out of him. Flat paragraphs are redeemed by brilliant metaphors, and conventional descriptions by witty, penetrating turns. Ideas of diamond are somewhat indiscriminately mixed with ideas of rhinestone and ideas of window glass; yet purest rays serene are present in veritable abundance."

G **Reading Skills and Strategies**

Drawing Inferences About Characters

❓ What causes the fluctuations in Dexter's mood in this scene? What do you think will be the result of his feelings? [Possible responses: Dexter's mood swings are caused by his relationship to Judy, which is mirrored in the changing seasons. Dexter is trying to get over Judy and move on with his life, but the phrase "a certain tranquility of spirit" caused by her physical absence suggests that she still holds sway over him.]

H **English Language Learners**

Interpreting Idioms

❓ What does the aphorism mean? Did Dexter make the right decision? Why or why not? [Dexter has traded the small amount of passion and exhilaration he felt when he imagined Judy loved him for a lifetime of comfort with Irene. Students may or may not agree with Dexter's decision to give up happiness for contentment.]

I **Elements of Literature**

Symbol

❓ Why is Judy pictured in gold? [Possible responses: The color symbolizes Dexter's dreams, his own Golden Fleece—the wealth he longed for, achieved, and found wanting. It also symbolizes his still-elusive goal of claiming Judy herself and the glamour and elegance she represents.]

J **Elements of Literature**

Motivation

❓ Why is Dexter so overcome with emotion here? [Possible responses: He still regards Judy as the living embodiment of his dreams. She represents everything that he desires in life.]

K **Struggling Readers**

Breaking Down Difficult Text

❓ What is the narrator saying about Judy's character in the description of her entering "so many cars"? [Possible response: She has ridden in so many men's cars that it could have ruined her reputation, except for the fact that she was in control in every case and never let any of her suitors touch her emotionally.]

A

B must remember. She had done this before, and he had put her behind him, as he would have crossed a bad account from his books.

He drove slowly down-town and, affecting abstraction, traversed the deserted streets of the business section, peopled here and there where a movie was giving out its crowd or where consumptive[25] or pugilistic[26] youth lounged in front **C** of pool halls. The clink of glasses and the slap of hands on the bars issued from saloons, cloisters of glazed glass and dirty yellow light.

She was watching him closely and the silence was embarrassing, yet in this crisis he could find no casual word with which to profane the hour. At a convenient turning he began to zigzag back toward the University Club.

D "Have you missed me?" she asked suddenly.

"Everybody missed you."

25. **consumptive:** destructive; wasteful.
26. **pugilistic** (pyo͞o′jil·is′tik): eager to fight.

598 THE MODERNS

Making the Connections

Cultural Connections: Flappers and Other Teens

The country-club culture of the 1910s and 1920s will be unfamiliar to most students. Introduce the term *flapper,* which describes the young women of the Twenties who were breaking down conventions by cutting their hair short, wearing form-fitting dresses, and dancing the Charleston. Judy's aggressive allure and coy, flirtatious manner make her an ideal flapper, although she lacks the typical flapper's zaniness and seems calculating instead. To enable students to understand Judy (and Dexter), ask the class to name other unconventional types that have dominated later decades (the jitterbugger of the Forties; the beatnik of the Fifties; the hippie of the Sixties; the disco dancer of the Seventies; the punk, grunge, and hip-hop fans of more recent eras). How would Dexter and Judy have behaved in these eras?

He wondered if she knew of Irene Scheerer. She had been back only a day—her absence had been almost contemporaneous with his engagement.

"What a remark!" Judy laughed sadly—without sadness. She looked at him searchingly. He became absorbed in the dashboard.

"You're handsomer than you used to be," she said thoughtfully. "Dexter, you have the most rememberable eyes."

He could have laughed at this, but he did not laugh. It was the sort of thing that was said to sophomores. Yet it stabbed at him.

"I'm awfully tired of everything, darling." She called every one darling, endowing the endearment with careless, individual comraderie. "I wish you'd marry me."

The directness of this confused him. He should have told her now that he was going to marry another girl, but he could not tell her. He could as easily have sworn that he had never loved her.

"I think we'd get along," she continued, on the same note, "unless probably you've forgotten me and fallen in love with another girl."

Her confidence was obviously enormous. She had said, in effect, that she found such a thing impossible to believe, that if it were true he had merely committed a childish indiscretion—and probably to show off. She would forgive him, because it was not a matter of any moment but rather something to be brushed aside lightly.

"Of course you could never love anybody but me," she continued. "I like the way you love me. Oh, Dexter, have you forgotten last year?"

"No, I haven't forgotten."

"Neither have I!"

Was she sincerely moved—or was she carried along by the wave of her own acting?

"I wish we could be like that again," she said, and he forced himself to answer:

"I don't think we can."

"I suppose not. . . . I hear you're giving Irene Scheerer a violent rush."

There was not the faintest emphasis on the name, yet Dexter was suddenly ashamed.

"Oh, take me home," cried Judy suddenly; "I don't want to go back to that idiotic dance—with those children."

Then, as he turned up the street that led to the residence district, Judy began to cry quietly to herself. He had never seen her cry before.

The dark street lightened, the dwellings of the rich loomed up around them, he stopped his coupé in front of the great white bulk of the Mortimer Joneses house, somnolent,[27] gorgeous, drenched with the splendor of the damp moonlight. Its solidity startled him. The strong walls, the steel of the girders, the breadth and beam and pomp of it were there only to bring out the

27. **somnolent:** sleepy.

F. SCOTT FITZGERALD **599**

contrast with the young beauty beside him. It was sturdy to accentuate her slightness—as if to show what a breeze could be generated by a butterfly's wing.

He sat perfectly quiet, his nerves in wild clamor, afraid that if he moved he would find her irresistibly in his arms. Two tears had rolled down her wet face and trembled on her upper lip.

"I'm more beautiful than anybody else," she said brokenly, "why can't I be happy?" Her moist eyes tore at his stability—her mouth turned slowly downward with an exquisite sadness: "I'd like to marry you if you'll have me, Dexter. I suppose you think I'm not worth having, but I'll be so beautiful for you, Dexter."

A million phrases of anger, pride, passion, hatred, tenderness fought on his lips. Then a perfect wave of emotion washed over him, carrying off with it a sediment of wisdom, of convention,[28] of doubt, of honor. This was his girl who was speaking, his own, his beautiful, his pride.

"Won't you come in?" He heard her draw in her breath sharply.

Waiting.

"All right," his voice was trembling, "I'll come in."

"I'm more beautiful than anybody else . . . why can't I be happy?"

V

It was strange that neither when it was over nor a long time afterward did he regret that night. Looking at it from the perspective of ten years, the fact that Judy's flare for him endured just one month seemed of little importance. Nor did it matter that by his yielding he subjected himself to a deeper agony in the end and gave serious hurt to Irene Sheerer and to Irene's parents, who had befriended him. There was nothing sufficiently pictorial about Irene's grief to stamp itself on his mind.

28. **convention:** accepted practices of social behavior.

600 THE MODERNS

Dexter was at bottom hard-minded. The attitude of the city on his action was of no importance to him, not because he was going to leave the city, but because any outside attitude on the situation seemed superficial. He was completely indifferent to popular opinion. Nor, when he had seen that it was no use, that he did not possess in himself the power to move fundamentally or to hold Judy Jones, did he bear any malice toward her. He loved her, and he would love her until the day he was too old for loving— but he could not have her. So he tasted the deep pain that is reserved only for the strong, just as he had tasted for a little while the deep happiness.

Even the ultimate falsity of the grounds upon which Judy terminated the engagement, that she did not want to "take him away" from Irene—Judy, who had wanted nothing else—did not revolt him. He was beyond any revulsion or any amusement.

He went East in February with the intention of selling out his laundries and settling in New York—but the war came to America in March and changed his plans. He returned to the West, handed over the management of the business to his partner, and went into the first officers' training-camp in late April. He was one of those young thousands who greeted the war with a certain amount of relief, welcoming the liberation from webs of tangled emotion.

VI

This story is not his biography, remember, although things creep into it which have nothing to do with those dreams he had when he was young. We are almost done with them and with him now. There is only one more incident to be related here, and it happens seven years farther on.

Skill Link

Performance Techniques

Motion pictures were tremendously popular in the 1920s. Invite students to create a short videotape from "Winter Dreams" in the style of the era. One small group can write the script, and other groups can perform, direct, videotape, gather props and costumes, find background music, and create publicity posters.

1. Have the class discuss what they want the final project to be like.

2. As each group finishes its task, have the members gather to review how they completed it and why they chose as they did. For example, how did the writers portray the characters? Did they use lines from the story? What new lines did they write? Why?

3. Have each group write a brief rationale. Compile these as "The Making of Winter Dreams."

It took place in New York, where he had done well—so well that there were no barriers too high for him. He was thirty-two years old, and, except for one flying trip immediately after the war, he had not been West in seven years. A man named Devlin from Detroit came into his office to see him in a business way, and then and there this incident occurred, and closed out, so to speak, this particular side of his life.

"So you're from the Middle West," said the man Devlin with careless curiosity. "That's funny—I thought men like you were probably born and raised on Wall Street. You know—wife of one of my best friends in Detroit came from your city. I was an usher at the wedding."

Dexter waited with no apprehension of what was coming.

"Judy Simms," said Devlin with no particular interest; "Judy Jones she was once."

"Yes, I knew her." A dull impatience spread over him. He had heard, of course, that she was married—perhaps deliberately he had heard no more.

"Awfully nice girl," brooded Devlin meaninglessly, "I'm sort of sorry for her."

"Why?" Something in Dexter was alert, receptive, at once.

"Oh, Lud Simms has gone to pieces in a way. I don't mean he ill-uses her, but he drinks and runs around——"

"Doesn't she run around?"

"No. Stays at home with her kids."

"Oh."

"She's a little too old for him," said Devlin.

"Too old!" cried Dexter. "Why, man, she's only twenty-seven."

He was possessed with a wild notion of rushing out into the streets and taking a train to Detroit. He rose to his feet spasmodically.

"I guess you're busy," Devlin apologized quickly. "I didn't realize——"

"No, I'm not busy," said Dexter, steadying his voice. "I'm not busy at all. Not busy at all. Did you say she was—twenty-seven? No, I said she was twenty-seven."

"Yes, you did," agreed Devlin dryly.

"Go on, then. Go on."

"What do you mean?"

"About Judy Jones."

Devlin looked at him helplessly.

"Well, that's—I told you all there is to it. He treats her like the devil. Oh, they're not going to get divorced or anything. When he's particularly outrageous she forgives him. In fact, I'm inclined to think she loves him. She was a pretty girl when she first came to Detroit."

A pretty girl! The phrase struck Dexter as ludicrous.

"Isn't she—a pretty girl, any more?"

"Oh, she's all right."

"Look here," said Dexter, sitting down suddenly, "I don't understand. You say she was a 'pretty girl' and now you say she's 'all right.' I don't understand what you mean—Judy Jones wasn't a pretty girl, at all. She was a great beauty. Why, I knew her, I knew her. She was——"

Devlin laughed pleasantly.

"I'm not trying to start a row," he said. "I think Judy's a nice girl and I like her. I can't understand how a man like Lud Simms could fall madly in love with her, but he did." Then he added: "Most of the women like her."

Dexter looked closely at Devlin, thinking wildly that there must be a reason for this, some insensitivity in the man or some private malice.

"Lots of women fade just like *that*," Devlin snapped his fingers. "You must have seen it happen. Perhaps I've forgotten how pretty she was at her wedding. I've seen her so much since then, you see. She has nice eyes."

A sort of dullness settled down upon Dexter. For the first time in his life he felt like getting very drunk. He knew that he was laughing loudly at something Devlin had said, but he did not know what it was or why it was funny. When, in a few minutes, Devlin went, he lay down on his lounge and looked out the window at the New York skyline into which the sun was sinking in dull lovely shades of pink and gold.

He had thought that having nothing else to lose he was invulnerable at last—but he knew that he had just lost something more, as surely as if he had married Judy Jones and seen her fade away before his eyes.

The dream was gone. Something had been taken from him. In a sort of panic he pushed the

------

WORDS TO OWN

ludicrous (loo′di·krəs) *adj.*: laughable; absurd.

F. SCOTT FITZGERALD **601**

ⓔ Elements of Literature
Irony
❓ What is ironic about Devlin's comment? [Possible response: It is ironic that Dexter sees himself as a trespasser in the world of the rich, yet someone else sees him as a natural part of this world.] Point out that Wall Street is the home of the New York Stock Exchange and the financial capital of the country. To succeed there means manipulating great sums of money and moving among a sophisticated, international set. Dexter has moved far beyond Judy, who, in the Midwest, is wealthy but provincial.

ⓕ Elements of Literature
Motivation
❓ Why does Dexter want to rush into the street and take a train to Detroit? [Possible responses: He wants to save Judy from her husband; he can't believe that Devlin is telling the truth, so he wants to assess the situation himself; he still has a fantasy of being with her.]

ⓖ Reading Skills and Strategies

Drawing Inferences About Characters
❓ What makes this comment so bitterly ironic for Dexter? [Judy's *character* is completely changed, as well as her looks. Instead of being desired by men, she is now liked by women—who never before figured in her life, except perhaps when she tried to prove that she had power over their boyfriends.]

ⓗ Reading Skills and Strategies

Drawing Inferences About Characters
❓ What brought about the changes in Judy? Are they believable? Why or why not? [Possible responses: The changes in her appearance could be the result of her disappointment in a sour marriage; or the results of childbearing or aging. Yes; people can change dramatically if they are miserable. No; she would probably not retain her beauty as she aged, but she is still young.]

ⓘ Elements of Literature
Symbol
❓ What does the sunset represent? Why does Fitzgerald place it here? [Possible responses: The sunset symbolizes the death of Dexter's dream. The pink, like a rose, represents Judy's beauty; the gold, her glamour.]

Assessing Learning

Check Test: Multiple Choice

1. Dexter first sees Judy at (a) the lake, (b) the golf course, (c) a dance. [b]
2. Dexter becomes wealthy from (a) stocks and bonds, (b) a boat-rental shop, (c) laundries. [c]
3. When Dexter gets engaged to Irene, Judy (a) does not care, (b) lures him back, (c) loves him forever. [b]
4. Dexter's courtship of Judy ends when (a) she drops him, (b) he drops her, (c) they get married. [a]
5. When Dexter hears of Judy again, she is (a) playing golf, (b) in college, (c) married with children. [c]

The dream was gone. Something had been taken from him.

palms of his hands into his eyes and tried to bring up a picture of the waters lapping on Sherry Island and the moonlit veranda, and gingham on the golf-links and the dry sun and the gold color of her neck's soft down. And her mouth damp to his kisses and her eyes plaintive with melancholy and her freshness like new fine linen in the morning. Why, these things were no longer in the world! They had existed and they existed no longer.

For the first time in years the tears were streaming down his face. But they were for himself now. He did not care about mouth and eyes and moving hands. He wanted to care, and he could not care. For he had gone away and he could never go back any more. The gates were closed, the sun was gone down, and there was no beauty but the gray beauty of steel that withstands all time. Even the grief he could have borne was left behind in the country of illusion, of youth, of the richness of life, where his winter dreams had flourished.

"Long ago," he said, "long ago, there was something in me, but now that thing is gone. Now that thing is gone, that thing is gone. I cannot cry. I cannot care. That thing will come back no more."

WORDS TO OWN

plaintive (plān′tiv) *adj.:* expressing sadness.

---

602 THE MODERNS

Making the Connections

Connecting to the Theme: "The Dream and the Reality"

Fitzgerald made the contrast between dream and reality his life's work. The juxtaposition of the words *dreams* and *winter* in the story's title suggests that these are dreams that are fated to die or are consolations in a chilly landscape. This story deals with how a longtime dreamer wakes up—or perhaps only tells himself he's waking up. It deals, too, with the question of whether or not dreams can and should, in every

case, be attained. Have students make a comparison-and-contrast chart showing Dexter's dream and his reality, as shown in "Winter Dreams." Their charts might look like this:

Dream	Reality
1. Judy Jones's perfection	"She has nice eyes."
2.	
3.	

PRIMARY Sources — A LETTER

A Letter to His Daughter

La Paix, Rodgers' Forge,
Towson, Maryland,
August 8, 1933

Dear Pie:

I feel very strongly about you doing duty. Would you give me a little more documentation about your reading in French? I am glad you are happy—but I never believe much in happiness. I never believe in misery either. Those are things you see on the stage or the screen or the printed page, they never really happen to you in life.

All I believe in in life is the rewards for virtue (according to your talents) and the *punishments* for not fulfilling your duties, which are doubly costly. If there is such a volume in the camp library, will you ask Mrs. Tyson to let you look up a sonnet of Shakespeare's in which the line occurs *"Lilies that fester smell far worse than weeds."*

Have had no thoughts today, life seems composed of getting up a *Saturday Evening Post* story. I think of you, and always pleasantly; but if you call me "Pappy" again I am going to take the White Cat out and beat his bottom *hard, six times for every time you are impertinent.* Do you react to that?

I will arrange the camp bill.

Halfwit, I will conclude. Things to worry about:

    Worry about courage
    Worry about cleanliness
    Worry about efficiency
    Worry about horsemanship . . .
  Things not to worry about:
    Don't worry about popular opinion
    Don't worry about dolls
    Don't worry about the past
    Don't worry about the future
    Don't worry about growing up

F. Scott Fitzgerald with his daughter, Scottie.

Culver Pictures.

    Don't worry about anybody getting ahead of you
    Don't worry about triumph
    Don't worry about failure unless it comes through your own fault
    Don't worry about mosquitoes
    Don't worry about flies
    Don't worry about insects in general
    Don't worry about parents
    Don't worry about boys
    Don't worry about disappointments
    Don't worry about pleasures
    Don't worry about satisfactions
  Things to think about:
    What am I really aiming at?
    How good am I really in comparison to my contemporaries in regard to:
      (a) Scholarship
      (b) Do I really understand about people and am I able to get along with them?
      (c) Am I trying to make my body a useful instrument or am I neglecting it?

                With dearest love,

F. SCOTT FITZGERALD 603

Fitzgerald was always keen on giving self-improvement advice to others, and his only daughter, Scottie, was a natural recipient. The litany of things to worry about that ends this letter to Scottie at camp is mostly serious advice with a few pieces of jocular counsel thrown in.

Ⓓ Elements of Literature
Motivation
❓ According to this letter, what motivates Fitzgerald? Are these the same things that motivate Dexter? Explain. [Possible responses: Fitzgerald claims that he is motivated by rewards for his virtue and punishment for not fulfilling his duties. Dexter seems motivated only by his youthful dreams to achieve wealth, power and the love of the woman he idealizes.]

Ⓔ Critical Thinking
Challenging the Text
❓ Which suggestions do you think are sound? What additional advice would you add? [Possible responses: Students might disagree with Fitzgerald's advice to not worry about popular opinion, the future, triumph, and parents. They might add worries about popularity, grades, or money.]

Connecting Across the Texts

Connecting with "Winter Dreams"
Guide students in explaining how Fitzgerald's letter to his daughter relates to "Winter Dreams." You may wish to use the following questions to spark discussion:

- As this letter shows, Fitzgerald strongly believed in self-improvement. Do you think Dexter would agree or disagree with Fitzgerald's belief in self-improvement? Why or why not?

- If Dexter did give advice to others, what suggestions would he make? Support your contention with specific examples from the story.

- Based on this letter, how do you think Fitzgerald would have felt about Judy Jones? How would his feelings compare to Dexter's?

MAKING MEANINGS

First Thoughts [Respond]

1. Possible responses: Students who have been drawn to unattainable people will likely identify with Dexter; others might have less compassion.

Shaping Interpretations [Interpret]

2. Dexter's ambition is shown through his dreams and his efforts at achieving them. Although poor, Dexter attends a famous Eastern university, takes risks to buy a laundry, learns the business, and expands it. He is motivated by dreams of success and glamour. While Dexter's dreams seem unrealistic, his actions reveal his strength and determination.

3. Dexter's dreams reveal his longing for the magical, golden life he believes the wealthy live. Wealth doesn't satisfy him, because he wants the symbol of that life—Judy.

4. Judy represents the beauty, glamour, carelessness, and confidence of the wealthy. Dexter may love her or only what she represents.

5. The urgency of his ambitions and his working-class background make Dexter less complacent and more energetic, but he wants his children to feel they belong to the upper class. Those born into wealth are regarded more highly than the newly rich.

6. Fitzgerald saw the dream as success, wealth, and elegance (symbolized by Judy), achieved through self-reliance, ambition, and opportunity. Students may feel that he omitted moral and spiritual elements.

7. Judy's loss of beauty symbolizes the loss of Dexter's youth and idealism.

Connecting with the Text [Analyze]

8. Students might advise Judy to consider Dexter's feelings, abilities, ambition, and romantic nature; Dexter, Judy's indifference, selfishness, and shallowness.

9. No, because Judy would have corrupted his idealism; yes, because he would have won the woman he loves, who symbolizes membership in the upper classes.

Challenging the Text [Evaluate]

10. Students should see that the themes are timeless and universal.

MAKING MEANINGS

First Thoughts

1. Did you sympathize with Dexter Green in his tangled feelings for Judy Jones? Explain why or why not.

Shaping Interpretations

2. What details does Fitzgerald use to persuade us that Dexter is an ambitious young man? What does the story suggest are Dexter's **motivations**? Explain how Dexter's actions reveal his deepest motivations and conform to what the narrator and the other characters say about him.

3. In *Richard III,* Shakespeare refers to "the winter of our discontent." How do Dexter's "winter dreams" reflect his discontent? Does his sense of deprivation subside when he fulfills his ambition to become rich? Explain.

4. When they meet again as adults, Dexter decides that he has "wanted Judy Jones ever since he was a proud, desirous little boy" (page 593). What does Judy represent to Dexter? (Refer to the notes you made while reading.) Explain why you think he really does—or does not—love her.

5. What makes Dexter "newer and stronger" (page 592) than the wealthy people he meets? Why, then, does he want his children to be like those people?

6. A recurring **theme** of Fitzgerald's work is the pursuit of the American dream. Based on this story, explain what you think Fitzgerald saw as the American dream. (Be sure to include Dexter's quest for Judy as part of your answer.) What, if anything, do you think is left out of his vision?

604 THE MODERNS

Reading Check

a. How does his first meeting with Judy Jones lead Dexter to quit his job?

b. How does Dexter encounter Judy again after nearly a decade?

c. Why does Dexter break his engagement to Irene? Is he sorry later?

d. At the end of the story, what has happened to Judy?

---

7. Why do you think Dexter feels a profound sense of loss when he hears about Judy at the end of the story?

Connecting with the Text

8. According to the story, Dexter and Judy did not know each other during their high school years. Imagine that they did and that they asked you for advice. What would you tell Judy about Dexter's crush on her? What would you advise Dexter to do about Judy's coolness?

9. Do you think Dexter would have been happier in the end if Judy had married him? Why or why not?

Challenging the Text

10. Do you think the **themes** of this story are universal and timeless, or is this a story that could only have happened in its specific time and place? Explain.

READING SKILLS AND STRATEGIES

Understanding Paradoxes

A **paradox** is a seemingly contradictory statement which may, upon closer inspection, prove to illuminate a deeper truth. F. Scott Fitzgerald uses paradox frequently in "Winter Dreams," particularly in his descriptions of Judy Jones. For example:

"The smile again—radiant, blatantly artificial—convincing." (page 589)

". . . kisses that were like charity, creating want by holding back nothing at all." (page 593)

Find three more paradoxical descriptions of Judy's behavior. How does this method of phrasing help convey the enigmatic complexity Dexter perceives in her?

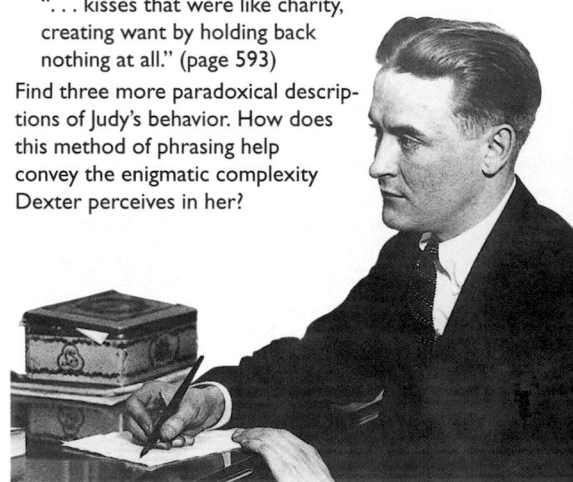

F. Scott Fitzgerald.
The Bettmann Archive.

Reading Check

a. Dexter won't caddy for the wealthy, arrogant little girl who rudely calls him "Boy."

b. While Dexter is playing golf with men he once caddied for, Judy plays through.

c. During another chance encounter, Judy proposes to him. Dexter succumbs, but he never regrets his decision.

d. Judy has married Lud Simms, who treats her badly, and her beauty and spirit have vanished.

READING SKILLS AND STRATEGIES

Paradox emphasizes the depth and complexity of people and life by highlighting the contradictions inherent in them. Paradoxes generally need to be concise—with the density of oxymorons or epigrams—to be effective. Three additional paradoxes include "beautifully ugly"; "Judy laughed sadly—without sadness."; and ". . . it was not grotesque, it was merely beautiful." Judy's enigmatic complexity is illustrated through the conflicting aspects of her nature.

CHOICES: Building Your Portfolio

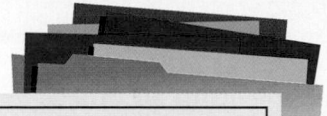

Writer's Notebook

1. Collecting Ideas for an Analysis of Causes and Effects

In the Writer's Workshop on page 685, you'll write an essay that speculates about causes and effects. One of your choices will be to analyze the **motivations** of a fictional character that interests you. Record a series of questions you'd like to ask either Judy Jones or Dexter Green. (For example, you could ask Judy questions like these: "Were you in love with all, some, or none of your suitors? Was your main goal to be the center of attention, or was it something else? Did you enjoy making your boyfriends jealous? Did you intend to hurt anyone?") Then, record the answers you'd expect to receive from the character. Keep your notes for possible use in the Writer's Workshop.

Interpreting a Story

2. A Dreamy Fairy Tale?

In a book review of Fitzgerald's stories, the novelist Jay McInerney wrote the following:

> . . . the young (poor) boy's quest for the hand of the beautiful, rich princess is undoubtedly Fitzgerald's best plot, the fairy-tale skeleton of his jazz age tales. One supposes that magazine editors preferred the stories in which the quest is successful, but in the better ones, like "Winter Dreams" (1922) and "The Sensible Thing" (1924), the success is qualified or the quest ends in failure.
>
> —Jay McInerney

In a brief essay, analyze the ways in which "Winter Dreams" is like and unlike a fairy tale. Consider the story's **plot, atmosphere, tone,** and **characterization.**

Performance/Improvising

3. Dexter and Judy, Talking

Imagine that it is a year after the end of "Winter Dreams." Dexter and Judy meet by chance in a railroad station, where they are waiting for different trains. In their few minutes together, they discuss their past and present feelings and what they have learned about life. With a partner, briefly plan the content and direction of their conversation, based on your understanding of the characters. Then, improvise the conversation in front of the class.

Music

4. Jazz Age

"Winter Dreams" mentions three musical works: *Chin-Chin, The Count of Luxemburg,* and *The Chocolate Soldier.* Learn about the "soundtrack" of Dexter's and Judy's life by listening to music composed from about 1920 to 1930. Try the jazz, blues, operetta, symphonic, and popular vocals sections of a library or music store. Report your findings to the class. Your report might focus on a particular aspect—for example, how jazz influences abound in George Gershwin's wonderful *Rhapsody in Blue* (1924). Bring recordings to share.

Louis Armstrong.
Culver Pictures.

F. SCOTT FITZGERALD **605**

Grading Timesaver

Rubrics for each Choices assignment appear on p. 160 in the *Portfolio Management System.*

CHOICES: Building Your Portfolio

1. **Writer's Notebook** Students may wish to have a "Q and A" session with a partner to help them generate and answer probing questions. Remind students to save their work.
2. **Interpreting a Story** To help students compare and contrast "Winter Dreams" with a fairy tale, suggest they complete a prewriting chart, such as the following:

Fairy Tale

	Like	Unlike
Setting		
Characters		
Plot		
Atmosphere		
Tone		

3. **Performance/Improvising** Before students write their dialogues, have them create a series of journal entries in the persona of each character. Students should describe the situation, the character's feelings, and what he or she has learned from the experience. Students can share their journal entries with their partner and use them as the basis for their role-play.
4. **Music** Stage a "Jazz Day" after students complete the assignment. Invite students to bring music to share with the class, give brief reports, and demonstrate popular dances of the time, such as the Charleston, the black bottom, and the fox trot.

Using Students' Strengths

Kinesthetic Learners

When students pursue Choice 3, also have them dramatize key sections of the story. Lead them to choose parts that reveal the characters' actions and motivations. If the sections do not include dialogue, have students improvise. Then, have them compare and contrast performances to decide which elements in each one best captured their impression of the characters. Finally, discuss how these characters might react to each other if they were to meet in the future.

Verbal Learners

Students may find it useful to consult a written history of jazz as a starting point in pursuing Choice 4. Once they have read about different styles of jazz, they can select recordings and proceed with the assignment.

Planning

• **Block Schedule**
  Block Scheduling Lesson Plans with Pacing Guide

• **Traditional Schedule**
  Lesson Plans Including Strategies for English-Language Learners

• **One-Stop Planner**
  CD-ROM with Test Generator

John Steinbeck
(1902–1968)

Most writers would probably agree that fiction that delivers a political message may be effective propaganda, but it is unlikely to be art. John Steinbeck would *not* have agreed with this precept, and he is a notable exception to it.

During the 1930s, the Great Depression cost millions of people their jobs and shook their faith in the American dream. But big business and the corporate farm seemed untouched by hard times; they were angrily perceived by many as impersonal and indifferent to human hardship.

Many novelists of the time were moved by this sense of injustice and turned their pens to a by-product of the Depression known as "the protest novel." Among these writers, John Steinbeck was the most widely praised and successful.

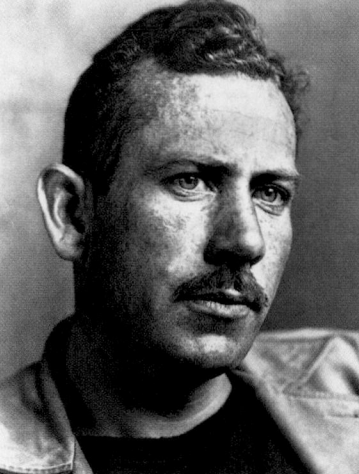

UPI/Bettmann.

Steinbeck was born in California's Salinas Valley in 1902, the son of a county treasurer and a schoolteacher. Although he graduated from high school and spent some time at Stanford University, he took more pride in the many jobs he held as a young man than in his formal education. He worked as a hod carrier, fruit picker, apprentice painter, laboratory assistant, caretaker, surveyor, and journalist. He also wrote seventeen novels, in addition to stories, plays, and screenplays.

Steinbeck's first major success came in 1937 with *Of Mice and Men,* a short, best-selling novel that Steinbeck himself adapted into a Broadway play. It is a tale of two itinerant farmhands: George and the powerful but simple-minded Lennie. Steinbeck took a pathetic situation and transformed it into an affirmative acceptance of life's brutal conflicts, along with life's possibilities for fellowship and courage.

He followed this success by living and working with some Oklahoma farmers—known as "Okies"—over the next two years. The result was his strongest and most enduring novel, *The Grapes of Wrath* (1939). It tells of the Joad family and their forced migration from the Dust Bowl of Oklahoma to California, the region that promised work at decent wages and a chance to buy land. Once in California, however, the Joads find only the exploitation and poverty of labor camps. Gradually they learn what "Okies" really means—people who never even had a chance.

The Grapes of Wrath was an angry book that spoke out on behalf of the migrant workers. Steinbeck sharply criticized a system that bankrupted thousands of farmers and turned them from their own land, making them into paid help for the big growers. When the novel appeared, it was greeted with outbursts of praise and condemnation, and it became the most widely read of all the protest novels of the 1930s.

The Grapes of Wrath won a Pulitzer Prize in 1940. After this major success, however, Steinbeck's eminence waned. Toward the end of his life, Steinbeck achieved a gratifying success with the award of the Nobel Prize in literature in 1962 and with the publication in that year of *Travels with Charley,* a nostalgic account of his odyssey across America with his aged poodle Charley. But Steinbeck's reputation is grounded on those earlier novels that portray California as the real and symbolic land of American promise.

go.hrw.com
LE0 11-12

   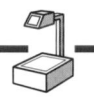

Make the Connection

The Golden Age

It seems that in every generation older people say to younger people, "It was different in my day." Most people feel nostalgic about the past, dreaming of it as a "golden age" that was somehow cleaner or more heroic or happier than the present. In fact, some people end up living mainly in memories of a past that might never have existed.

Quickwrite

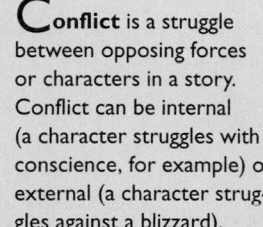

There's a jaded point of view that holds that the time of heroes is long past. Who are our heroes today (or are there none)? Would you consider them role models? What opportunities do you see for heroism today? Quickwrite your thoughts.

Elements of Literature

Conflict

"The Leader of the People" shows three generations of a family in conflict because of differences in age, gender, personal histories, and the roles they play on the family ranch. Some conflicts in the story are **external conflicts:** They occur between two or more people. Others are **internal conflicts,** occurring inside one person's mind. One conflict involves a close look at that recurring dream of a more heroic American past.

> **C**onflict is a struggle between opposing forces or characters in a story. Conflict can be internal (a character struggles with conscience, for example) or external (a character struggles against a blizzard).
>
> *For more about Conflict, see the Handbook of Literary Terms.*

Background

In "The Leader of the People," John Steinbeck explores the conflict between dream and reality at the heart of so much American fiction. This story appears as the fourth and final part of Steinbeck's novel *The Red Pony* (1945). Each part of this novel was published as a complete short story. The stories, all connected by their characters and settings, are "The Gift," "The Great Mountains," "The Promise," and "The Leader of the People."

JOHN STEINBECK **607**

Summary ∎

When Jody Tiflin's grandfather visits the family, Jody eagerly anticipates hearing again the old man's stories of leading a wagon train west to California. Jody's father, Carl, is impatient with Grandfather's stories but grudgingly allows him to tell them at dinner. However, the next morning, Grandfather overhears Carl complaining about the tedious stories. Carl apologizes, but Grandfather realizes that the heroism he hoped to evoke with his stories has died, along with the dream of "westering"—a hunger for the frontier. Grasping his grandfather's despair, Jody tries to comfort him with a lemonade.

Background

In "The Gift," Jody is thrilled to receive a red pony for his tenth birthday. Although Jody and the hired hand, Billy Buck, take good care of the pony, it dies. In "The Great Mountains," an old Mexican stranger named Gitano returns to his birthplace, in a house that was once part of the ranch, to die. Mrs. Tiflin and Jody want him to stay, but Mr. Tiflin makes him leave the next day. In "The Promise," Jody pays a stud fee and works all summer to get another colt. When the colt is being born, Billy realizes he must kill the mare to save the colt. Although terrified, Jody stays and watches.

The Red Pony was first published in 1937. That edition did not include "The Leader of the People." In 1938, *The Red Pony,* with "The Leader of the People," was included in Steinbeck's volume of stories *The Long Valley.* The full text of *The Red Pony* was reprinted separately as a novel in 1945.

Preteaching Vocabulary

Words to Own

Ask students to read the definitions of the Words to Own listed at the bottom of the selection pages. Then, pair students to write a brief dialogue, using all the vocabulary words. Partners can perform their dialogues for the class.

Then have them choose the vocabulary word that best completes each analogy below.

1. emotion : hardened :: disease : [immune]
2. food : tasteless :: behavior : [unseemly]
3. quickly : rapidly :: unhappily : [disconsolately]
4. energetically : lethargically :: admiringly : [contemptuously]
5. marriage : love :: revenge : [rancor]
6. maestro : conducting :: commander : [marshaling]
7. humble : modest :: proud : [arrogant]
8. students : assembled :: jury : [convened]
9. hole : opening :: cave : [cleft]
10. walking : strolling :: indulging : [humoring]

Philip Herschel Paradise (1905–) is a California painter, sculptor, illustrator, graphic artist, and teacher. During the 1940s, he also served as a film art director for Paramount Studios. He is known for Western subjects. San Luis Obispo lies about 140 miles south of Salinas, California.

Activity. Ask students to comment on how the shapes, colors, and action of the painting help them determine the time of day. [Possible responses: Contrasts of light and dark suggest early evening; the men in the center seem to be transferring the day's last load of hay into a loft.] **Ask students to describe the painting's mood.** [Possible response: The mood is peaceful and idyllic.]

BROWSING IN THE FILES

A Critic's Comment. Literary critic Paul McCarthy notes: "Steinbeck's accounts of Jody's life and survival show a . . . graceful and detailed realism. We gain a firm impression of the outward boy, his playing with Doubletree Mutt, deference to his parents, and a close relationship with Buck. The sensitive language and point of view create a sense also of the inner Jody. . . ."

Ranch Near San Luis Obispo, Evening Light (c. 1935) by Phil Paradise. Oil on canvas (28″ × 34″).

608 THE MODERNS

Reaching All Students

Struggling Readers
Since there is a great deal of dialogue in this story, you may wish to assign roles (narrator included) and have students read the story aloud. The other students can listen and jot down plot summaries after each page. Lead students to include at least five comments on the story's events, a question about the action, or a personal reaction to the action. Rotate roles so that everyone gets a chance to read and to create plot summaries.

English Language Learners
Encourage students to discuss situations in which people they know have taken a risk to move to a different place in order to create a better life. What hardships did they face? For strategies for engaging students learning English, see
- *Lesson Plans Including Strategies for English-Language Learners*

Advanced Learners
Invite students to read the other three stories in *The Red Pony* and explain in writing how they relate to "The Leader of the People." Students should consider plot, theme, setting, characters, and tone in their analysis. Then, invite volunteers to share their findings with the class.

The Leader of the People

John Steinbeck

The Buck Collection, Laguna Hills, California.

On Saturday afternoon Billy Buck, the ranch-hand, raked together the last of the old year's haystack and pitched small forkfuls over the wire fence to a few mildly interested cattle. High in the air small clouds like puffs of cannon smoke were driven eastward by the March wind. The wind could be heard whishing in the brush on the ridge crests, but no breath of it penetrated down into the ranch-cup.

The little boy, Jody, emerged from the house eating a thick piece of buttered bread. He saw Billy working on the last of the haystack. Jody tramped down scuffing his shoes in a way he had been told was destructive to good shoe-leather. A flock of white pigeons flew out of the black cypress tree as Jody passed, and circled the tree and landed again. A half-grown tortoise-shell[1] cat leaped from the bunkhouse porch, galloped on stiff legs across the road, whirled and galloped back again. Jody picked up a stone to help the game along, but he was too late, for the cat was under the porch before the stone could be discharged. He threw the stone into the cypress tree and started the white pigeons on another whirling flight.

Arriving at the used-up haystack, the boy leaned against the barbed wire fence. "Will that be all of it, do you think?" he asked.

The middle-aged ranch-hand stopped his careful raking and stuck his fork[2] into the ground. He took off his black hat and smoothed down his hair. "Nothing left of it that isn't soggy from ground moisture," he said. He replaced his hat and rubbed his dry leathery hands together.

"Ought to be plenty mice," Jody suggested.

"Lousy with them," said Billy. "Just crawling with mice."

"Well, maybe, when you get all through, I could call the dogs and hunt the mice."

"Sure, I guess you could," said Billy Buck. He lifted a forkful of the damp ground-hay and threw it into the air. Instantly three mice leaped out and burrowed frantically under the hay again.

Jody sighed with satisfaction. Those plump, sleek, <u>arrogant</u> mice were doomed. For eight months they had lived and multiplied in the haystack. They had been <u>immune</u> from cats, from traps, from poison and from Jody. They had grown smug in their security, overbearing and fat. Now the time of disaster had come; they would not survive another day.

---

1. **tortoise-shell:** having a pattern of brown and yellow markings, as commonly seen on the shell of a tortoise.
2. **fork:** pitchfork.

WORDS TO OWN

arrogant (ar′ə·gənt) *adj.:* proud and overly confident.
immune (im·myo͞on′) *adj.:* protected.

JOHN STEINBECK 609

A Elements of Literature

Conflict

? How does this conversation suggest that there is a conflict between Jody and his father? [Possible responses: Jody responds that his father doesn't care about the mice. The words "ominously" and "You know how he is" hint at a problem between Jody and his father.]

B Elements of Literature

Characterization

? What clues to the character of Carl Tiflin does the narrator provide here? [Possible responses: The dog's fear suggests that Tiflin has a dominant, unpredictable, and possibly violent personality. His silhouette against the sky suggests his independence and authority.]

C English Language Learners

Idioms

? Based on the context, what do you think *Big-Britches* means? Is it something you would like to be called? Why or why not? [Possible response: Literally, it means someone who is too big for his or her pants. Figuratively, it mocks people whose ambition outstrips their experience and abilities. Most students would not like to be called this.]

D Elements of Literature

Conflict

? What is the conflict in this scene? Who do you think has the upper hand? Why? [Possible responses: Mr. Tiflin doesn't want Grandfather to visit; Mrs. Tiflin does. The couple seems evenly matched, since Mr. Tiflin, normally stern and inflexible, backs away from his wife's anger.] What do the conversations on this page suggest about Jody's family? [They love one another but treat one another harshly.]

Billy looked up at the top of the hills that surrounded the ranch. "Maybe you better ask your father before you do it," he suggested.

"Well, where is he? I'll ask him now."

"He rode up to the ridge ranch after dinner. He'll be back pretty soon."

Jody slumped against the fence post. "I don't think he'd care."

As Billy went back to his work he said ominously, "You'd better ask him anyway. You know how he is."

Jody did know. His father, Carl Tiflin, insisted upon giving permission for anything that was done on the ranch, whether it was important or not. Jody sagged farther against the post until he was sitting on the ground. He looked up at the little puffs of wind-driven cloud. "Is it like to rain, Billy?"

"It might. The wind's good for it, but not strong enough."

"Well, I hope it don't rain until after I kill those damn mice." He looked over his shoulder to see whether Billy had noticed the mature profanity. Billy worked on without comment.

Jody turned back and looked at the side-hill where the road from the outside world came down. The hill was washed with lean March sunshine. Silver thistles, blue lupins[3] and a few poppies bloomed among the sage bushes. Halfway up the hill Jody could see Doubletree Mutt, the black dog, digging in a squirrel hole. He paddled for a while and then paused to kick bursts of dirt out between his hind legs, and he dug with an earnestness which belied the knowledge he must have had that no dog had ever caught a squirrel by digging in a hole.

Suddenly, while Jody watched, the black dog stiffened, and backed out of the hole and looked up the hill toward the cleft in the ridge where the road came through. Jody looked up too. For a moment Carl Tiflin on horseback stood out against the pale sky and then he moved down the road toward the house. He carried something white in his hand.

The boy started to his feet. "He's got a letter," Jody cried. He trotted away toward the ranch house, for the letter would probably be read aloud

and he wanted to be there. He reached the house before his father did, and ran in. He heard Carl dismount from his creaking saddle and slap the horse on the side to send it to the barn where Billy would unsaddle it and turn it out.

Jody ran into the kitchen. "We got a letter!" he cried.

His mother looked up from a pan of beans. "Who has?"

"Father has. I saw it in his hand."

Carl strode into the kitchen then, and Jody's mother asked, "Who's the letter from, Carl?"

He frowned quickly. "How did you know there was a letter?"

She nodded her head in the boy's direction. "Big-Britches Jody told me."

Jody was embarrassed.

His father looked down at him contemptuously. "He *is* getting to be a Big-Britches," Carl said. "He's minding everybody's business but his own. Got his big nose into everything."

Mrs. Tiflin relented a little. "Well, he hasn't enough to keep him busy. Who's the letter from?"

Carl still frowned on Jody. "I'll keep him busy if he isn't careful." He held out a sealed letter. "I guess it's from your father."

Mrs. Tiflin took a hairpin from her head and slit open the flap. Her lips pursed judiciously. Jody saw her eyes snap back and forth over the lines. "He says," she translated, "he says he's going to drive out Saturday to stay for a little while. Why, this is Saturday. The letter must have been delayed." She looked at the postmark. "This was mailed day before yesterday. It should have been here yesterday." She looked up questioningly at her husband, and then her face darkened angrily. "Now what have you got that look on you for? He doesn't come often."

Carl turned his eyes away from her anger. He could be stern with her most of the time, but when occasionally her temper arose, he could not combat it.

"What's the matter with you?" she demanded again.

---

3. **lupins** (lo͞o'pinz): flowering plants of the bean family; more often spelled *lupines*.

WORDS TO OWN

cleft (kleft) *n.*: opening.
contemptuously (kən·temp'cho͞o·əs·lē) *adv.*: scornfully.

Getting Students Involved

Cooperative Learning

1. Pair students to read the story together. At the end of each page, partners should independently write a prediction about what will happen next. Have partners trade papers and jot down their reactions to the predictions. As students read, have them check and revise their predictions. At the end, students should calculate the number of successful predictions they made to see how well they use

story clues and prior knowledge to make predictions.

2. Discuss how Steinbeck uses the third-person limited point of view to tell the story. Readers see events unfold through Jody's eyes. While this perspective allows readers to share Jody's thoughts and feelings, it also affects the narrative voice. If Jody were narrating, he would use different vocabulary and

syntax. Rewrite the opening paragraph of the story with the class, using a different point of view. Then, invite small groups to recast part of the story into the first-person point of view, using Jody's voice and vocabulary. How does the story change?

In his explanation there was a tone of apology Jody himself might have used. "It's just that he talks," Carl said lamely. "Just talks."

"Well, what of it? You talk yourself."

"Sure I do. But your father only talks about one thing."

"Indians!" Jody broke in excitedly. "Indians and crossing the plains!"

Carl turned fiercely on him. "You get out, Mr. Big-Britches! Go on, now! Get out!"

Jody went miserably out the back door and closed the screen with elaborate quietness. Under the kitchen window his shamed, downcast eyes fell upon a curiously shaped stone, a stone of such fascination that he squatted down and picked it up and turned it over in his hands.

The voices came clearly to him through the open kitchen window. "Jody's damn well right," he heard his father say. "Just Indians and crossing the plains. I've heard that story about how the horses got driven off about a thousand times. He just goes on and on, and he never changes a word in the things he tells."

When Mrs. Tiflin answered her tone was so changed that Jody, outside the window, looked up from his study of the stone. Her voice had become soft and explanatory. Jody knew how her face would have changed to match the tone. She said quietly, "Look at it this way, Carl. That was the big thing in my father's life. He led a wagon train clear across the plains to the coast, and when it was finished, his life was done. It was a big thing to do, but it didn't last long enough. Look!" she continued, "it's as though he was born to do that, and after he finished it, there wasn't anything more for him to do but think about it and talk about it. If there'd been any farther west to go, he'd have gone. He's told me so himself. But at last there was the ocean. He lives right by the ocean where he had to stop."

She had caught Carl, caught him and entangled him in her soft tone.

"I've seen him," he agreed quietly. "He goes down and stares off west over the ocean." His voice sharpened a little. "And then he goes up to the Horseshoe Club in Pacific Grove, and he tells people how the Indians drove off the horses."

She tried to catch him again. "Well, it's everything to him. You might be patient with him and pretend to listen."

Carl turned impatiently away. "Well, if it gets too bad, I can always go down to the bunkhouse and sit with Billy," he said irritably. He walked through the house and slammed the front door after him.

Jody ran to his chores. He dumped the grain to the chickens without chasing any of them. He gathered the eggs from the nests. He trotted into the house with the wood and interlaced it so carefully in the wood-box that two armloads seemed to fill it to overflowing.

His mother had finished the beans by now. She stirred up the fire and brushed off the stove-top with a turkey wing. Jody peered cautiously at her to see whether any rancor toward him remained. "Is he coming today?" Jody asked.

"That's what his letter said."

"Maybe I better walk up the road to meet him."

Mrs. Tiflin clanged the stove-lid shut. "That would be nice," she said. "He'd probably like to be met."

"I guess I'll just do it then."

Outside, Jody whistled shrilly to the dogs. "Come on up the hill," he commanded. The two dogs waved their tails and ran ahead. Along the roadside the sage had tender new tips. Jody tore off some pieces and rubbed them on his hands until the air was filled with the sharp wild smell. With a rush the dogs leaped from the road and yapped into the brush after a rabbit. That was the last Jody saw of them, for when they failed to catch the rabbit, they went back home.

Jody plodded on up the hill toward the ridge top. When he reached the little cleft where the road came through, the afternoon wind struck him and blew up his hair and ruffled his shirt. He looked down on the little hills and ridges below and then out at the huge green Salinas Valley. He could see the white town of Salinas far out in the flat and the flash of its windows under the waning sun. Directly below him, in an oak tree, a crow congress had convened. The tree was black with crows all cawing at once.

Then Jody's eyes followed the wagon road down from the ridge where he stood, and lost it

---

WORDS TO OWN

rancor (raŋ′kər) *n.:* anger.
convened (kən·vēnd′) *v.:* assembled.

Getting Students Involved

B Elements of Literature
Characterization

[?] What does this description reveal about Grandfather's character? [Possible responses: His giant shadow symbolizes his reputation, flickering darkly behind him. This suggests that his greatest achievements are in the past or that his "granite dignity" and purposefulness make him unable or unwilling to adapt to change.]

C Elements of Literature
Conflict

[?] What does Grandfather's reaction suggest about his relationship to the people of this new generation? [Possible response: Grandfather's contempt for the mouse hunt suggests that he has little respect for the next generation, believing them lacking in strength and courage.]

D Historical Connections

In 1829, after President Andrew Jackson had tried to persuade the Creeks to move westward beyond the Mississippi River, Chief Speckled Snake of the Creek ended a short but pointed speech to his tribe by saying: "Brothers! I have listened to a great many talks from our Great Father [Jackson]. But they always began and ended in this—'Get a little farther, you are too near me. I have spoken.'" In 1841, the first pioneers traveled in covered wagons across the plains. By 1843, more than a thousand whites had risked their lives trekking across America. Within two decades, eight million settlers had moved West.

E Elements of Literature
Conflict

[?] What internal conflict does Jody feel when his grandfather teases him? [Possible responses: He isn't sure how to interpret the teasing and whether to resent it; it may remind him of how his father berates him; it may threaten his adoration of his grandfather.]

---

behind a hill, and picked it up again on the other side. On that distant stretch he saw a cart slowly pulled by a bay[4] horse. It disappeared behind the hill. Jody sat down on the ground and watched the place where the cart would reappear again. The wind sang on the hilltops and the puff-ball clouds hurried eastward.

Then the cart came into sight and stopped. A man dressed in black dismounted from the seat and walked to the horse's head. Although it was so far away, Jody knew he had unhooked the check-rein, for the horse's head dropped forward. The horse moved on, and the man walked slowly up the hill beside it. Jody gave a glad cry and ran down the road toward them. The squirrels bumped along off the road, and a road-runner flirted its tail and raced over the edge of the hill and sailed out like a glider.

Jody tried to leap into the middle of his shadow at every step. A stone rolled under his foot and he went down. Around a little bend he raced, and there, a short distance ahead, were his grandfather and the cart. The boy dropped from his unseemly running and approached at a dignified walk.

The horse plodded stumble-footedly up the hill and the old man walked beside it. In the lowering sun their giant shadows flickered darkly behind them. The grandfather was dressed in a black broadcloth suit and he wore kid congress gaiters[5] and a black tie on a short, hard collar. He carried his black slouch hat in his hand. His white beard was cropped close and his white eyebrows overhung his eyes like mustaches. The blue eyes were sternly merry. About the whole face and figure there was a granite dignity, so that every motion seemed an impossible thing. Once at rest, it seemed the old man would be stone, would never move again. His steps were slow and certain. Once made, no step could ever be retraced; once headed in a direction, the path would never bend nor the pace increase nor slow.

When Jody appeared around the bend, Grandfather waved his hat slowly in welcome, and he called, "Why, Jody! Come down to meet me, have you?"

Jody sidled[6] near and turned and matched his step to the old man's step and stiffened his body and dragged his heels a little. "Yes, sir," he said. "We got your letter only today."

"Should have been here yesterday," said Grandfather. "It certainly should. How are all the folks?"

"They're fine, sir." He hesitated and then suggested shyly, "Would you like to come on a mouse hunt tomorrow, sir?"

"Mouse hunt, Jody?" Grandfather chuckled. "Have the people of this generation come down to hunting mice? They aren't very strong, the new people, but I hardly thought mice would be game for them."

"No, sir. It's just play. The haystack's gone. I'm going to drive out the mice to the dogs. And you can watch, or even beat the hay a little."

The stern, merry eyes turned down on him. "I see. You don't eat them, then. You haven't come to that yet."

Jody explained, "The dogs eat them, sir. It wouldn't be much like hunting Indians, I guess."

"No, not much—but then later, when the troops were hunting Indians and shooting children and burning teepees, it wasn't much different from your mouse hunt."

They topped the rise and started down into the ranch cup, and they lost the sun from their shoulders. "You've grown," Grandfather said. "Nearly an inch, I should say."

"More," Jody boasted. "Where they mark me on the door, I'm up more than an inch since Thanksgiving even."

Grandfather's rich throaty voice said, "Maybe you're getting too much water and turning to pith and stalk. Wait until you head out, and then we'll see."[7]

Jody looked quickly into the old man's face to see whether his feelings should be hurt, but there was no will to injure, no punishing nor putting-in-your-place light in the keen blue eyes. "We might kill a pig," Jody suggested.

---

6. **sidled** (sīd′'ld): approached sideways.
7. **Maybe . . . we'll see:** Like an overwatered plant, Jody may grow tall but not be very productive. Not until he "heads out" will anyone know what he is capable of.

WORDS TO OWN
unseemly (un·sēm′lē) *adj.*: improper.

4. **bay:** reddish brown.
5. **kid congress gaiters:** high leather boots with elastic inserts in each side.

612 THE MODERNS

Taking a Second Look

Review: Applying Prefixes, Roots, and Suffixes
Remind students that they can decode many unfamiliar words by knowing their parts.

1. Ask students to define these affixes: *ac-* [to], *hypo-* [under], *cata-* [down], *a-* [not], *com-* [with], *over-* [more than], *un-* [not], *andro-* [man], *gen-* [birth, kind], *polit-* [citizen], *thermo-* [heat], *zoo-* [animal], *dors-* [back], *multi-* [many], *alt-* [high], *ann-* [year], *-ness* [state of being], *-y* [full of], *-ly* [manner].

2. Have students define each of the following words from the story by using word parts:

Word	Affix	Meaning
overbearing	[over-]	[arrogant]
unsaddle	[un-]	[remove the saddle]
judiciously	[-ly]	[like a judge, in a serious way]
shrilly	[-ly]	[in a shrill manner]
listlessly	[-ly]	[in a lifeless manner]

Encourage students to add more unfamiliar words from the story.

"Oh, no! I couldn't let you do that. You're just humoring me. It isn't the time and you know it."

"You know Riley, the big boar, sir?"

"Yes. I remember Riley well."

"Well, Riley ate a hole into that same haystack, and it fell down on him and smothered him."

"Pigs do that when they can," said Grandfather.

"Riley was a nice pig, for a boar, sir. I rode him sometimes, and he didn't mind."

A door slammed at the house below them, and they saw Jody's mother standing on the porch waving her apron in welcome. And they saw Carl Tiflin walking up from the barn to be at the house for the arrival.

The sun had disappeared from the hills by now. The blue smoke from the house chimney hung in flat layers in the purpling ranch-cup. The puff-ball clouds, dropped by the falling wind, hung listlessly in the sky.

Billy Buck came out of the bunkhouse and flung a wash basin of soapy water on the ground. He had been shaving in mid-week, for Billy held Grandfather in reverence, and Grandfather said that Billy was one of the few men of the new generation who had not gone soft. Although Billy was in middle age, Grandfather considered him a boy. Now Billy was hurrying toward the house too.

When Jody and Grandfather arrived, the three were waiting for them in front of the yard gate.

Carl said, "Hello, sir. We've been looking for you."

Mrs. Tiflin kissed Grandfather on the side of his beard, and stood still while his big hand patted her shoulder. Billy shook hands solemnly, grinning under his straw mustache. "I'll put up your horse," said Billy, and he led the rig away.

Grandfather watched him go, and then, turning back to the group, he said as he had said a hundred times before, "There's a good boy. I knew his father, old Mule-tail Buck. I never knew why they called him Mule-tail except he packed mules."

Mrs. Tiflin turned and led the way into the house. "How long are you going to stay, Father? Your letter didn't say."

"Well, I don't know. I thought I'd stay about two weeks. But I never stay as long as I think I'm going to."

In a short while they were sitting at the white oilcloth table eating their supper. The lamp with the tin reflector hung over the table. Outside the dining-room windows the big moths battered softly against the glass.

Grandfather cut his steak into tiny pieces and chewed slowly. "I'm hungry," he said. "Driving out here got my appetite up. It's like when we were crossing. We all got so hungry every night we could hardly wait to let the meat get done. I could eat about five pounds of buffalo meat every night."

"It's moving around does it," said Billy. "My father was a government packer. I helped him when I was a kid. Just the two of us could about clean up a deer's ham."

"I knew your father, Billy," said Grandfather. "A fine man he was. They called him Mule-tail Buck. I don't know why except he packed mules."

"That was it," Billy agreed. "He packed mules."

Grandfather put down his knife and fork and looked around the table. "I remember one time we ran out of meat—" His voice dropped to a curious low sing-song, dropped into a tonal groove the story had worn for itself. "There was no buffalo, no antelope, not even rabbits. The hunters couldn't even shoot a coyote. That was the time for the leader to be on the watch. I was the leader, and I kept my eyes open. Know why? Well, just the minute the people began to get hungry they'd start slaughtering the team oxen. Do you believe that? I've heard of parties that just ate up their draft cattle. Started from the middle and worked toward the ends. Finally they'd eat the lead pair, and then the wheelers. The leader of a party had to keep them from doing that."

In some manner a big moth got into the room and circled the hanging kerosene lamp. Billy got up and tried to clap it between his hands. Carl struck with a cupped palm and caught the moth and broke it. He walked to the window and dropped it out.

"As I was saying," Grandfather began again, but Carl interrupted him. "You'd better eat some more meat. All the rest of us are ready for our pudding."

Jody saw a flash of anger in his mother's eyes. Grandfather picked up his knife and fork. "I'm pretty hungry, all right," he said. "I'll tell you about that later."

WORDS TO OWN

humoring (hyōō′mər·in) v.: indulging.

F **Critical Thinking**

Speculating

? Why do you think Billy and Jody's Grandfather feel this mutual admiration? [Possible response: Both seem to be independent men who have worked with animals, lived alone, and retained a sense of youthful adventure. It is no surprise that both get along well with Jody.]

G **Vocabulary Note**

Regional Words

Billy's father was a *mule packer*—that is, someone who transports goods and supplies by mule.

H **Elements of Literature**

Conflict

? What conflict is hinted at in Grandfather's comment about the length of his stay? [Possible response: Conflict between Carl and him may be one reason why he usually shortens his stay.]

I **Reading Skills and Strategies**

Interpreting Figures of Speech

? Do you think Grandfather is speaking literally or figuratively? [He is speaking figuratively; few people could eat five pounds of meat at one sitting.] What effect is created through his hyperbole? [Possible responses: It suggests that Grandfather is trying to impress the others; he is trying to make his story more interesting.]

J **Critical Thinking**

Determining Author's Purpose

? Why does Steinbeck have Grandfather tell his tales at such length? [Possible responses: Steinbeck, like Jody and unlike Carl, considers the tales interesting; the tales help characterize Grandfather as someone who lives in his memories and feels out of place in the present.]

K **Elements of Literature**

Conflict

? How does this incident symbolize the conflict between Grandfather and Carl? [Possible responses: Carl breaks the moth, as he will break Grandfather's spirit. The incident suggests that Grandfather's spirit has grown fragile and can be crushed by a simple action, as will prove to be the case.]

Crossing the Curriculum

Biology

Invite students to investigate the aging process. In what ways do some stereotypical views of aging reflect reality? [Possible responses: Many people do become more forgetful as they age. Alzheimer's disease really does have biological effects on memory.] **In what ways do they not?** [Possible response: Many elderly people remain alert and vigorous—even into their nineties.]

History

Ask students to research the westward movement in the mid-nineteenth century and the difficulties experienced by pioneers. Have students narrow their topic to a specific region: perhaps California, or another western region that students have connections to. Students may present their research either as a report to the rest of the class or as a research paper. Tell them to include illustrations, photographs, and maps.

A **Humanities Connections**

The Paiute are two different Native American groups. The Southern Paiute at one time lived in Utah, Arizona, and Nevada. They had relatively little conflict with the white settlers. The Northern Paiute lived in California, Nevada, and Oregon. After 1840, because the rush of settlers and prospectors had destroyed their already meager food supplies, the Northern Paiute armed themselves and fought the whites until 1874, when the federal government seized the last of their lands. Today, the remaining Paiute, who number fewer than 4,000, live on reservations.

B **Elements of Literature**

Conflict

? Why is Carl so cruel toward Grandfather? [Possible responses: He is cruel by nature; he is bored with the old man's stories; he is envious of the old man's heroism.]

C **Reading Skills and Strategies**

Making Inferences

? What internal conflict is Jody experiencing? [Possible response: He wants to make Grandfather feel better but is afraid to anger his father.]

D **Critical Thinking**

Determining Author's Purpose

? Do you think Grandfather isn't interested in his own stories? Why does he tell them? [Possible responses: Grandfather is interested, but he is affected by the audience's lack of response. He is depressed; he feels that his present life is so limited that he has nothing else to contribute; he needs to remind himself and others of his former glory.]

BROWSING IN THE FILES

Writers on Writing. About his motivation for writing, Steinbeck once said, "I instinctively recognized an opportunity to transcend some of my personal failings—things about myself I didn't particularly like and wanted to change but didn't know how."

When supper was over, when the family and Billy Buck sat in front of the fireplace in the other room, Jody anxiously watched Grandfather. He saw the signs he knew. The bearded head leaned forward; the eyes lost their sternness and looked wonderingly into the fire; the big lean fingers laced themselves on the black knees. "I wonder," he began, "I just wonder whether I ever told you how those thieving Piutes[8] drove off thirty-five of our horses."

"I think you did," Carl interrupted. "Wasn't it just before you went up into the Tahoe country?"

Grandfather turned quickly toward his son-in-law. "That's right. I guess I must have told you that story."

"Lots of times," Carl said cruelly, and he avoided his wife's eyes. But he felt the angry eyes on him, and he said, "'Course I'd like to hear it again."

Grandfather looked back at the fire. His fingers unlaced and laced again. Jody knew how he felt, how his insides were collapsed and empty. Hadn't Jody been called a Big-Britches that very afternoon? He arose to heroism and opened himself to the term Big-Britches again. "Tell about Indians," he said softly.

Grandfather's eyes grew stern again. "Boys always want to hear about Indians. It was a job for men, but boys want to hear about it. Well, let's see. Did I ever tell you how I wanted each wagon to carry a long iron plate?"

Everyone but Jody remained silent. Jody said, "No. You didn't."

"Well, when the Indians attacked, we always put the wagons in a circle and fought from between the wheels. I thought that if every wagon carried a long plate with rifle holes, the men could stand the plates on the outside of the wheels when the wagons were in the circle and they would be protected. It would save lives and that would make up for the extra weight of the iron. But of course the party wouldn't do it. No party had done it before and they couldn't see why they should go to the expense. They lived to regret it, too."

Jody looked at his mother, and knew from her expression that she was not listening at all. Carl picked at a callus on his thumb and Billy Buck watched a spider crawling up the wall.

Grandfather's tone dropped into its narrative groove again. Jody knew in advance exactly what words would fall. The story droned on, speeded up for the attack, grew sad over the wounds, struck a dirge[9] at the burials on the great plains. Jody sat quietly watching Grandfather. The stern blue eyes were detached. He looked as though he were not very interested in the story himself.

When it was finished, when the pause had been politely respected as the frontier of the story, Billy Buck stood up and stretched and hitched his trousers. "I guess I'll turn in," he said. Then he faced Grandfather. "I've got an old powder horn and a cap and ball pistol down to the bunkhouse. Did I ever show them to you?"

Grandfather nodded slowly. "Yes, I think you did, Billy. Reminds me of a pistol I had when I was leading the people across." Billy stood politely

---

8. **Piutes** (pī′yo͞ots′): usually spelled *Paiutes*. The Paiutes are an American Indian people who originally lived in Utah, Arizona, Nevada, and California.
9. **dirge** (dʉrj): sad song that accompanies a funeral or expresses grief.

614 THE MODERNS

National Museum of American Art, Washington D.C./Courtesy Art Resource, NY.

Listening to Music ♪

"Grandfather's Story" from *The Red Pony Suite* by Aaron Copland

The great twentieth-century American composer Aaron Copland (1900–1990) "talked with a Brooklyn accent and composed with a Western touch," music critic Fred Flaxman once observed. Among Copland's best-known works with a Western flavor are his ballets *Billy the Kid* and *Rodeo* and his score for two films based on novels by John Steinbeck, *The Red Pony* and *Of Mice and Men*. *The Red Pony Suite* has six parts, including "Morning on the Ranch," "Walk to the Bunkhouse," and "Grandfather's Story," the part that goes with "The Leader of the People."

Activity

Have students listen to Copland's music as they read "The Leader of the People," and consider how it captures the spirit of the tale. Then have them write or select their own background music for a film version of another selection in Collection 12—"Winter Dreams," for example, or "The Secret Life of Walter Mitty."

Pioneers of the West (1934) by Helen Lundeberg. Oil on canvas (40″ × 50¼″).

E

E Cultural Connections

The settlers portrayed in the painting were part of a population in the West in general and California in particular that was historically one of the most diverse in America. Starting with the Native Americans, then the Hispanic settlers who both preceded the "Anglo" or English-speaking settlers, the region has been home to a wide variety of cultural groups. These include the Portuguese Americans who can be glimpsed in Steinbeck's *Tortilla Flat,* the Armenian immigrants who inhabit William Saroyan's stories, and the Chinese Americans Maxine Hong Kingston (p. 1043) and Amy Tan (p. 1109) write about. Ask students to compare and contrast Jody's family's background and way of life with that of one other Californian ethnic group. How did each one make its own distinct use of California's rich opportunities, and yet how has each one become truly "Californian"? What does "Californian" mean?

Professional Notes

Critical Comment:
Jody and the Farm

In *John Steinbeck,* critic Paul McCarthy calls *The Red Pony* "an excellent short novel, which more fully than any other work except *The Grapes of Wrath* . . . examines the relationship of man and the land." McCarthy continues: "Jody Tiflin, a bright, imaginative ten-year-old, is keenly interested in most things and activities on the farm. . . . Jody grows up on good, fertile land, benefits from a secure family life, and survives his encounters with death and unpredictable nature. Steinbeck's accounts of Jody's life and survival show a similarly graceful and detailed realism. . . . Descriptions of farm activities, the countryside, and other people are inseparable from descriptions of a boy growing up. The descriptions, point of view, and concentration on the farm scenes and activities and on Jody in particular unify the four parts of the novel. . . ."

LITERATURE AND FILM

The classic Western genre was graced by some great directors, including John Ford (*Stagecoach, The Searchers*), Howard Hawks (*Red River, Rio Bravo*), Anthony Mann (*Winchester '73, Cimarron*), William Wellman (*Across the Wide Missouri*), and William Wyler (*The Westerner, The Big Country*). Revisionist directors of later years have included Robert Altman (*McCabe and Mrs. Miller**), Sam Peckinpah (*The Wild Bunch**), Arthur Penn (*Little Big Man*), and Kevin Costner (*Dances with Wolves*). Show, or reserve in the school library, videos or films that depict the myth of the West. After students have viewed them, have groups of five script their own. They can glorify the myth, revise history, or spoof the genre. Each group should write its script together but assign the roles of director, camera person, and set, lighting, and costume designers. Remind students to keep their videos short—ten to fifteen minutes, or about ten to fifteen pages of typed script. Groups should develop a rationale for their approach to the Western and prepare for a question-and-answer session.

*R-rated. Use discretion in recommending.

Ⓐ Cultural Connections

The Man Who Shot Liberty Valance is a 1962 film starring James Stewart, John Wayne, and Vera Miles. The story concerns a greenhorn lawyer (Stewart) who tries to bring order to the West with help from the more experienced Westerner played by Wayne.

Ⓑ Cultural Connections

High Noon is a legendary Western drama which concerns a crisis of conscience for a town marshal (Cooper) who learns that on the day of his wedding and retirement, a gang of vengeful outlaws is after him. The marshal feels it is his duty to face the gang—but no one is willing to help him. Directed by Fred Zinnemann, *High Noon* is a masterpiece of economy, pacing, and suspense that has influenced filmmakers around the world.

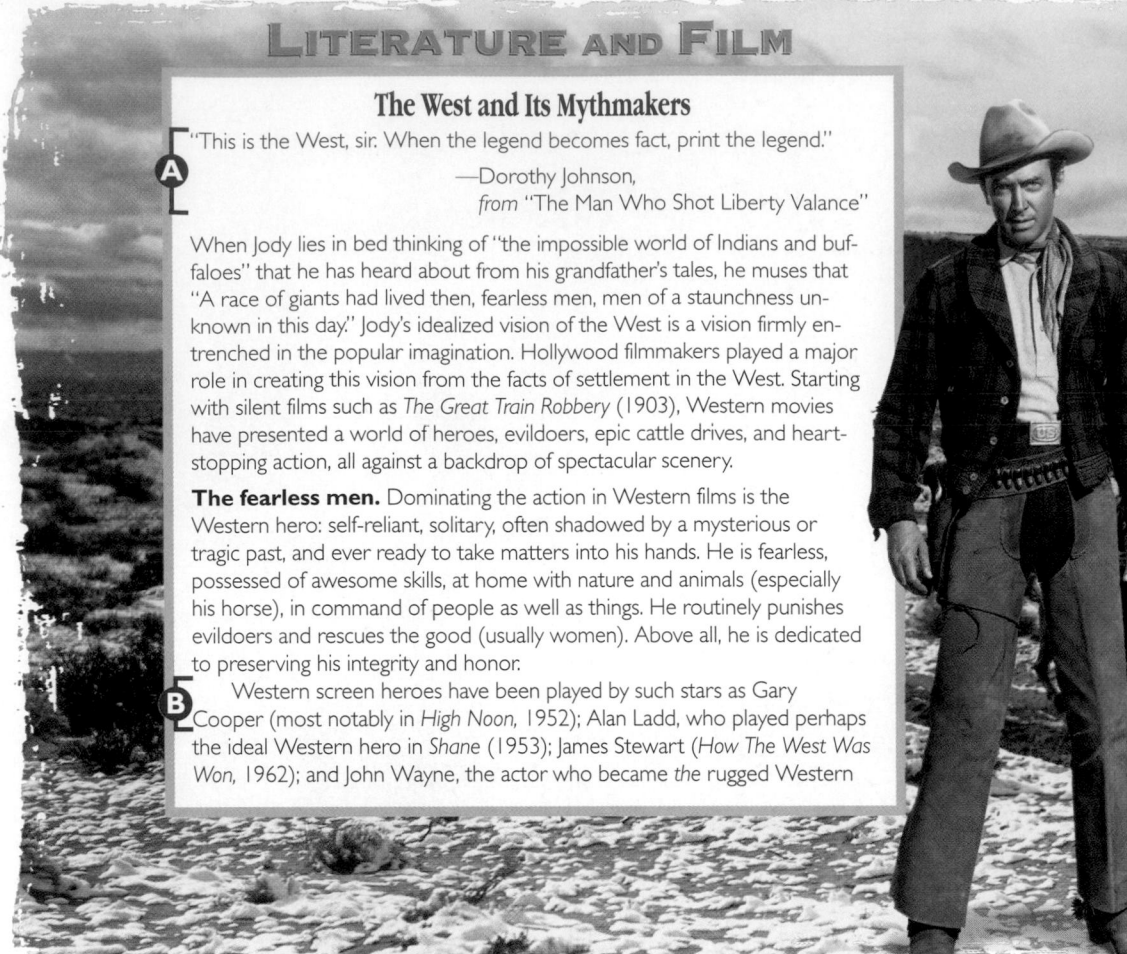

LITERATURE AND FILM

The West and Its Mythmakers

Ⓐ "This is the West, sir. When the legend becomes fact, print the legend."

—Dorothy Johnson,
from "The Man Who Shot Liberty Valance"

When Jody lies in bed thinking of "the impossible world of Indians and buffaloes" that he has heard about from his grandfather's tales, he muses that "A race of giants had lived then, fearless men, men of a staunchness unknown in this day." Jody's idealized vision of the West is a vision firmly entrenched in the popular imagination. Hollywood filmmakers played a major role in creating this vision from the facts of settlement in the West. Starting with silent films such as *The Great Train Robbery* (1903), Western movies have presented a world of heroes, evildoers, epic cattle drives, and heart-stopping action, all against a backdrop of spectacular scenery.

The fearless men. Dominating the action in Western films is the Western hero: self-reliant, solitary, often shadowed by a mysterious or tragic past, and ever ready to take matters into his hands. He is fearless, possessed of awesome skills, at home with nature and animals (especially his horse), in command of people as well as things. He routinely punishes evildoers and rescues the good (usually women). Above all, he is dedicated to preserving his integrity and honor.

Ⓑ Western screen heroes have been played by such stars as Gary Cooper (most notably in *High Noon,* 1952); Alan Ladd, who played perhaps the ideal Western hero in *Shane* (1953); James Stewart (*How The West Was Won,* 1962); and John Wayne, the actor who became *the* rugged Western

James Stewart in *The Naked Spur* (1953).

until the little story was done, and then he said, "Good night," and went out of the house.

Carl Tiflin tried to turn the conversation then. "How's the country between here and Monterey? I've heard it's pretty dry."

"It is dry," said Grandfather. "There's not a drop of water in the Laguna Seca. But it's a long pull from '87. The whole country was powder then, and in '61 I believe all the coyotes starved to death. We had fifteen inches of rain this year."

"Yes, but it all came too early. We could do with some now." Carl's eye fell on Jody. "Hadn't you better be getting to bed?"

Jody stood up obediently. "Can I kill the mice in the old haystack, sir?"

"Mice? Oh! Sure, kill them all off. Billy said there isn't any good hay left."

Jody exchanged a secret and satisfying look with Grandfather. "I'll kill every one tomorrow," he promised.

Jody lay in his bed and thought of the impossible world of Indians and buffaloes, a world that had ceased to be forever. He wished he could have been living in the heroic time, but he knew he was not of heroic timber.[10] No one living now,

10. **timber:** character.

Skill Link

Monitoring Reading Strategies

Remind students to vary their reading techniques to get at different levels of meaning. Readers often have to draw upon their own background to understand cultural, literary, and historical references, as well as why characters sometimes act as they do. Have students answer the following questions.

1. Which passages should be reread? Why?
2. What references could give you information about the movies mentioned on this page? about Native Americans and "westering"?
3. What questions could you ask to fully understand the inferential meaning of the exchange about the weather on p. 616?
4. How does knowledge of human nature help you understand the conflict between Grandfather and Carl?

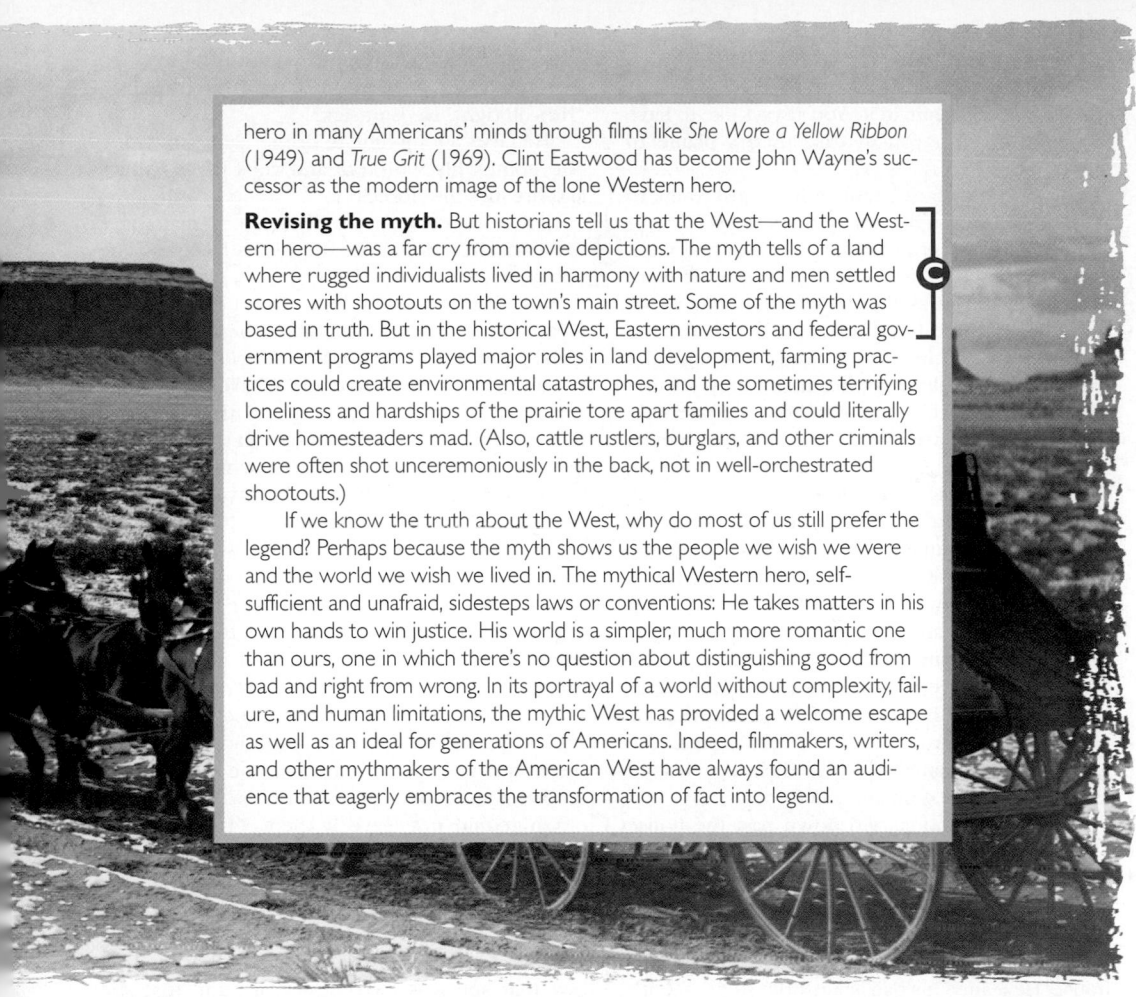

hero in many Americans' minds through films like *She Wore a Yellow Ribbon* (1949) and *True Grit* (1969). Clint Eastwood has become John Wayne's successor as the modern image of the lone Western hero.

Revising the myth. But historians tell us that the West—and the Western hero—was a far cry from movie depictions. The myth tells of a land where rugged individualists lived in harmony with nature and men settled scores with shootouts on the town's main street. Some of the myth was based in truth. But in the historical West, Eastern investors and federal government programs played major roles in land development, farming practices could create environmental catastrophes, and the sometimes terrifying loneliness and hardships of the prairie tore apart families and could literally drive homesteaders mad. (Also, cattle rustlers, burglars, and other criminals were often shot unceremoniously in the back, not in well-orchestrated shootouts.)

If we know the truth about the West, why do most of us still prefer the legend? Perhaps because the myth shows us the people we wish we were and the world we wish we lived in. The mythical Western hero, self-sufficient and unafraid, sidesteps laws or conventions: He takes matters in his own hands to win justice. His world is a simpler, much more romantic one than ours, one in which there's no question about distinguishing good from bad and right from wrong. In its portrayal of a world without complexity, failure, and human limitations, the mythic West has provided a welcome escape as well as an ideal for generations of Americans. Indeed, filmmakers, writers, and other mythmakers of the American West have always found an audience that eagerly embraces the transformation of fact into legend.

save possibly Billy Buck, was worthy to do the things that had been done. A race of giants had lived then, fearless men, men of a staunchness unknown in this day. Jody thought of the wide plains and of the wagons moving across like centipedes. He thought of Grandfather on a huge white horse, marshaling the people. Across his mind marched the great phantoms, and they marched off the earth and they were gone.

He came back to the ranch for a moment, then. He heard the dull rushing sound that space and silence make. He heard one of the dogs, out in the doghouse, scratching a flea and bumping his elbow against the floor with every stroke. Then the wind arose again and the black cypress groaned and Jody went to sleep.

He was up half an hour before the triangle sounded for breakfast. His mother was rattling the stove to make the flames roar when Jody went through the kitchen. "You're up early," she said. "Where are you going?"

"Out to get a good stick. We're going to kill the mice today."

WORDS TO OWN

marshaling (mär′shəl·iŋ) *v.* used as *adj.*: leading; guiding.

JOHN STEINBECK **617**

C Historical Connections

A guardian of law and order in the rugged West, Sheriff Bat Masterson provided a balanced, first-hand description of the peace officers who have since been mythologized in American culture. Masterson saw his colleagues as "just plain ordinary men who could shoot straight and had the most utter courage and perfect nerve—and, for the most part, a keen sense of right and wrong."

D Reading Skills and Strategies
Interpreting Figures of Speech
? What does this simile suggest about Jody's vision of "westering"? [Possible response: Jody's vision of the wagons as centipedes, like elements of nature themselves, and the image of Grandfather on the huge horse elevate "westering" to even more heroic heights. It is an ironic counterpoint to Carl's disregard for Grandfather and illustrates Jody's youth and innocence.]

E Elements of Literature
Characterization
Although in Grandfather's eyes the mouse hunt is symbolic of the triviality and inferiority of the next generation, it is an epic undertaking for Jody. Yet Jody is able to play his "heroic" game precisely because Grandfather's generation has endured the hardships of "westering" and frontier settlement.

Crossing the Curriculum

Art/Cinematography
Invite students to watch one of the classic Western movies mentioned on pp. 616–617. Then, have students write a critique of the movie, explaining how it glorifies the myth of the West through its characters, cinematographic techniques (camera angles, lighting, and so on), and dialogue. Students can compare the film to a contemporary heroic action movie to see if the same techniques are used to the same effect.

Health
Jody is excited about killing the mice for the thrill of the hunt, but mice and rats do pose a serious health risk. In addition to damaging food in storehouses, these rodents can transmit diseases, such as plague and typhus. They attack animals, poultry, and, occasionally, humans. Have students find out how mice and rats are controlled today. Which methods are the most successful? Why?

Mathematics
Have students survey their classmates to decide whom young people regard as role models. Students should prepare a list of twenty-five notable people, drawn from science, entertainment, technology, the humanities, sports, politics, business, and so forth. Finally, have students tabulate their findings and show their results in a bar graph or pie chart.

Interpreting Figures of Speech

[?] How does this simile foreshadow trouble? [Possible responses: The snake imagery suggests something evil will happen. Carl's cruel remarks will shatter Grandfather's self-confidence.]

B **Elements of Literature**

Irony

[?] How are Jody's actions ironic in light of Grandfather's past? [Possible response: Jody's great adventure is postponed for a meal, an ironic juxtaposition with Grandfather's determination to press on even though the pioneers are starving.]

C **Reading Skills and Strategies**

Making Inferences

[?] Why does Billy's statement "stagger" Jody? [Possible responses: It has never occurred to Jody that people can't always control their own destinies, that not everyone gets the opportunity to do great deeds. He might also be thinking of his grandfather, who has participated in a grand event but has lost his power and purpose.]

D **Elements of Literature**

Conflict

[?] In what tone of voice do you think Carl makes this remark? How does this reveal the conflict between the two men? [Possible response: Carl is probably using a sarcastic tone to show that he resents his father-in-law's glorifying the past and denigrating the present.]

E **Appreciating Language**

Style

[?] What grammatical, mechanical, and literary elements does Steinbeck use to convey emotion in this scene? [Possible responses: punctuation (dashes for pauses), action verbs ("jerked"), and diction ("sir," showing forced deference).]

F **Elements of Literature**

Conflict

[?] External conflict between Carl and Grandfather is avoided, but what internal conflicts remain? [Possible responses: Carl is conflicted between stubborn pride and the need to apologize; Grandfather is conflicted between clinging to his self-respect and acknowledging that his time is past.]

"Who is 'we'?"

"Why, Grandfather and I."

"So you've got him in it. You always like to have someone in with you in case there's blame to share."

"I'll be right back," said Jody. "I just want to have a good stick ready for after breakfast."

He closed the screen door after him and went out into the cool blue morning. The birds were noisy in the dawn and the ranch cats came down from the hill like blunt snakes. They had been hunting gophers in the dark, and although the four cats were full of gopher meat, they sat in a semi-circle at the back door and mewed piteously for milk. Doubletree Mutt and Smasher moved sniffing along the edge of the brush, performing the duty with rigid ceremony, but when Jody whistled, their heads jerked up and their tails waved. They plunged down to him, wriggling their skins and yawning. Jody patted their heads seriously, and moved on to the weathered scrap pile. He selected an old broom handle and a short piece of inch-square scrap wood. From his pocket he took a shoelace and tied the ends of the sticks loosely together to make a flail.[11] He whistled his new weapon through the air and struck the ground experimentally, while the dogs leaped aside and whined with apprehension.

Jody turned and started down past the house toward the old haystack ground to look over the field of slaughter, but Billy Buck, sitting patiently on the back steps, called to him, "You better come back. It's only a couple of minutes till breakfast."

Jody changed his course and moved toward the house. He leaned his flail against the steps. "That's to drive the mice out," he said. "I'll bet they're fat. I'll bet they don't know what's going to happen to them today."

"No, nor you either," Billy remarked philosophically, "nor me, nor anyone."

Jody was staggered by this thought. He knew it was true. His imagination twitched away from the mouse hunt. Then his mother came out on the back porch and struck the triangle, and all thoughts fell in a heap.

---

11. flail: farm tool for hand threshing grain. A flail is made of a short stick fastened with a leather strap to a longer handle. The user lets the short stick swing freely from the handle to knock the heads from the grain stalks.

Grandfather hadn't appeared at the table when they sat down. Billy nodded at his empty chair. "He's all right? He isn't sick?"

"He takes a long time to dress," said Mrs. Tiflin. "He combs his whiskers and rubs up his shoes and brushes his clothes."

Carl scattered sugar on his mush. "A man that's led a wagon train across the plains has got to be pretty careful how he dresses."

Mrs. Tiflin turned on him. "Don't do that, Carl! Please don't!" There was more of threat than of request in her tone. And the threat irritated Carl.

"Well, how many times do I have to listen to the story of the iron plates, and the thirty-five horses? That time's done. Why can't he forget it, now it's done?" He grew angrier while he talked, and his voice rose. "Why does he have to tell them over and over? He came across the plains. All right! Now it's finished. Nobody wants to hear about it over and over."

The door into the kitchen closed softly. The four at the table sat frozen. Carl laid his mush spoon on the table and touched his chin with his fingers.

Then the kitchen door opened and Grandfather walked in. His mouth smiled tightly and his eyes were squinted. "Good morning," he said, and he sat down and looked at his mush dish.

Carl could not leave it there. "Did—did you hear what I said?"

Grandfather jerked a little nod.

"I don't know what got into me, sir. I didn't mean it. I was just being funny."

Jody glanced in shame at his mother, and he saw that she was looking at Carl, and that she wasn't breathing. It was an awful thing that he was doing. He was tearing himself to pieces to talk like that. It was a terrible thing to him to retract a word, but to retract it in shame was infinitely worse.

Grandfather looked sidewise. "I'm trying to get right side up," he said gently. "I'm not being mad. I don't mind what you said, but it might be true, and I would mind that."

"It isn't true," said Carl. "I'm not feeling well this morning. I'm sorry I said it."

"Don't be sorry, Carl. An old man doesn't see things sometimes. Maybe you're right. The crossing is finished. Maybe it should be forgotten, now it's done."

Assessing Learning

Check Test: Fill-in-the-Blanks

1. Jody is looking forward to killing the [mice] that live under the haystack.
2. As a young man, Jody's grandfather was the leader of a [wagon train].
3. Billy Buck works as a(n) [ranch hand] on Jody's father's ranch.
4. The people on the wagon train refused to use [steel plates] to protect against Indians.
5. Jody offers his grandfather [lemonade] at the end of the story.

Carl got up from the table. "I've had enough to eat. I'm going to work. Take your time, Billy!" He walked quickly out of the dining-room. Billy gulped the rest of his food and followed soon after. But Jody could not leave his chair.

"Won't you tell any more stories?" Jody asked.

"Why, sure I'll tell them, but only when—I'm sure people want to hear them."

"I like to hear them, sir."

"Oh! Of course you do, but you're a little boy. It was a job for men, but only little boys like to hear about it."

Jody got up from his place. "I'll wait outside for you, sir. I've got a good stick for those mice."

He waited by the gate until the old man came out on the porch. "Let's go down and kill the mice now," Jody called.

"I think I'll just sit in the sun, Jody. You go kill the mice."

"You can use my stick if you like."

"No, I'll just sit here a while."

Jody turned disconsolately away, and walked down toward the old haystack. He tried to whip up his enthusiasm with thoughts of the fat juicy mice. He beat the ground with his flail. The dogs coaxed and whined about him, but he could not go. Back at the house he could see Grandfather sitting on the porch, looking small and thin and black.

Jody gave up and went to sit on the steps at the old man's feet.

"Back already? Did you kill the mice?"

"No, sir. I'll kill them some other day."

The morning flies buzzed close to the ground and the ants dashed about in front of the steps. The heavy smell of sage slipped down the hill. The porch boards grew warm in the sunshine.

Jody hardly knew when Grandfather started to talk. "I shouldn't stay here, feeling the way I do." He examined his strong old hands. "I feel as though the crossing wasn't worth doing." His eyes moved up the side-hill and stopped on a motionless hawk perched on a dead limb. "I tell those old stories, but they're not what I want to tell. I only know how I want people to feel when I tell them.

"It wasn't Indians that were important, nor adventures, nor even getting out here. It was a whole bunch of people made into one big crawling beast. And I was the head. It was westering and westering. Every man wanted something for himself, but the big beast that was all of them wanted only westering. I was the leader, but if I hadn't been there, someone else would have been the head. The thing had to have a head.

"Under the little bushes the shadows were black at white noonday. When we saw the mountains at last, we cried—all of us. But it wasn't getting here that mattered, it was movement and westering.

"We carried life out here and set it down the way those ants carry eggs. And I was the leader. The westering was as big as God, and the slow steps that made the movement piled up and piled up until the continent was crossed.

"Then we came down to the sea, and it was done." He stopped and wiped his eyes until the rims were red. "That's what I should be telling instead of stories."

When Jody spoke, Grandfather started and looked down at him. "Maybe I could lead the people some day," Jody said.

The old man smiled. "There's no place to go. There's the ocean to stop you. There's a line of old men along the shore hating the ocean because it stopped them."

"In boats I might, sir."

"No place to go, Jody. Every place is taken. But that's not the worst—no, not the worst. Westering has died out of the people. Westering isn't a hunger any more. It's all done. Your father is right. It is finished." He laced his fingers on his knee and looked at them.

Jody felt very sad. "If you'd like a glass of lemonade I could make it for you."

Grandfather was about to refuse, and then he saw Jody's face. "That would be nice," he said. "Yes, it would be nice to drink a lemonade."

Jody ran into the kitchen where his mother was wiping the last of the breakfast dishes. "Can I have a lemon to make a lemonade for Grandfather?"

His mother mimicked—"And another lemon to make a lemonade for you."

"No, ma'am. I don't want one."

"Jody! You're sick!" Then she stopped suddenly. "Take a lemon out of the cooler," she said softly. "Here, I'll reach the squeezer down to you."

WORDS TO OWN

disconsolately (dis·kän′sə·lit·lē) *adv.*: unhappily.

JOHN STEINBECK 619

G Struggling Readers
Questioning
? Why does Carl leave the table without finishing his meal? Why does Billy leave shortly thereafter? [Possible responses: Carl is embarrassed at his behavior and so wants to escape. Billy follows because he is the employee and believes he should follow Carl's lead; perhaps he is helping Carl save face; he may also be embarrassed.]

H Reading Skills and Strategies
Making Inferences
? Why doesn't Jody kill the mice? [Possible responses: The fun has gone out of the game without his grandfather to help; he wants to cheer up his grandfather.]

I Elements of Literature
Character
? Why does Grandfather tell the stories about westering? [Possible responses: He wants others to understand that he was once a hero; he recognizes that he was part of a great event, and he wants others to realize the significance of the event; he wants people to understand the dreams that urged people to move on.]

J Critical Thinking
Expressing an Opinion
? Do you agree with Grandfather's assessment? Why or why not? [Possible responses: Some students may argue that leaders are not interchangeable; others, that nearly anyone can lead if the need arises.]

K Elements of Literature
Conflict
? What causes Jody's mother to stop being critical? [Possible response: She recognizes that Jody has a mature, empathetic motive for wanting to get his grandfather lemonade and that she shouldn't tease him.]

Making the Connections

Connecting to the Theme:
"The Dream and The Reality"
Remind students of the title of this collection, and ask them how this story relates to this theme. Have them analyze every character, defining the difference between dream and reality for each one. Create a class chart such as this one:

Character	Dream	Reality
Grandfather	"westering"	The frontier is long closed.
Mr. Tiflin		
Mrs. Tiflin		
Jody		

At the conclusion of the discussion, explore the importance of dreams (imagination and vision) and reality (practicality and common sense) to a person's sense of completeness. Invite volunteers to share their own dreams.

Primary Sources

In this speech, Steinbeck discusses the responsibility of writers to try to allay people's fears and inspire them to greatness of the heart and spirit.

Ⓐ Historical Connections

The awarding of the Nobel Prize to Steinbeck was controversial. The day after the announcement, *The New York Times* ran an editorial questioning the selection. *Time, Newsweek,* and the *Washington Post* followed suit, and critic Arthur Mizener wrote a *Times* article criticizing Steinbeck's work for "sentimentality." Gore Vidal has defended Steinbeck, telling Steinbeck's biographer Jay Parini in 1993: "Critics . . . are always furious when a writer has voluntary readers. . . . Essentially, they believe that good literature is written for a small, elect group of people like themselves. They could never forgive Steinbeck for saying things that people wanted, or needed, to hear."

Ⓑ Reading Skills and Strategies

Interpreting Figures of Speech

❓ What effect does Steinbeck achieve through these similes? [He uses these comparisons to emphasize his pride in the writers of the past.]

Ⓒ Literary Connections

Five Americans won the Nobel Prize before Steinbeck: Sinclair Lewis (1930), Eugene O'Neill (1936), Pearl Buck (1938), William Faulkner (1949), and Ernest Hemingway (1954).

Ⓓ Reading Skills and Strategies

Making Inferences

❓ What does Steinbeck see as the function of the writer? [Possible response: Steinbeck sees literature as a medium of improvement and hope.]

Ⓔ Historical Connections

Alfred Nobel

Alfred Nobel (1833–1896) was a Swedish chemist, inventor, and philanthropist. He worked in St. Petersburg, developing explosives. After his brother and four others were killed in an explosion, Nobel set about devising a safe way of handling nitroglycerin. He achieved his goal in 1867 by creating dynamite. Nobel's will set up a fund of $9 million to be used for yearly awards in the sciences and humanities.

Nobel Prize Acceptance Speech, 1962

I thank the Swedish Academy for finding my work worthy of this highest honor.

Ⓐ In my heart there may be doubt that I deserve the Nobel award over other men of letters whom I hold in respect and reverence—but there is no question of my pleasure and pride in having it for myself.

It is customary for the recipient of this award to offer personal or scholarly comment on the nature and the direction of literature. At this particular time, however, I think it would be well to consider the high duties and the responsibilities of the makers of literature.

Ⓑ Such is the prestige of the Nobel award and of this place where I stand that I am impelled, not to squeak like a grateful and apologetic mouse, but to roar like a lion out of pride in my profession and in the great and good men who have practiced it through the ages.

Literature was not promulgated by a pale and emasculated critical priesthood singing their litanies in empty churches—nor is it a game for the cloistered elect, the tinhorn mendicants of low-calorie despair.

Literature is as old as speech. It grew out of human need for it, and it has not changed except to become more needed.

The skalds, the bards, the writers are not separate and exclusive. From the beginning, their functions, their duties, their responsibilities have been decreed by our species.

Ⓒ Humanity has been passing through a gray and desolate time of confusion. My great predecessor, William Faulkner, speaking here, referred to it as a tragedy of universal fear so long sustained that there were no longer problems of the spirit, so that only the human heart in conflict with itself seemed worth writing about [see page 723].

Faulkner, more than most men, was aware of human strength as well as of human weakness. He knew that the understanding and the resolution of fear are a large part of the writer's reason for being.

This is not new. The ancient commission of the writer has not changed. He is charged with exposing our many grievous faults and failures, with dredging up to the light our dark and dangerous dreams for the purpose of improvement.

Ⓓ Furthermore, the writer is delegated to declare and to celebrate man's proven capacity for greatness of heart and spirit—for gallantry in defeat—for courage, compassion, and love. In the endless war against weakness and despair, these are the bright rally-flags of hope and of emulation.

I hold that a writer who does not passionately believe in the perfectibility of man has no dedication nor any membership in literature.

The present universal fear has been the result of a forward surge in our knowledge and manipulation of certain dangerous factors in the physical world.

It is true that other phases of understanding have not yet caught up with this great step, but there is no reason to presume that they cannot or will not draw abreast. Indeed, it is a part of the writer's responsibility to make sure that they do.

With humanity's long, proud history of standing firm against natural enemies, sometimes in the face of almost certain defeat and extinction, we would be cowardly and stupid to leave the field on the eve of our greatest potential victory.

Ⓔ Understandably, I have been reading the life of Alfred Nobel—a solitary man, the books say, a thoughtful man. He perfected the release of explosive forces, capable of creative good or of destructive evil, but lacking choice, ungoverned by conscience or judgment.

Professional Notes

The Nobel "Jinx"

Steinbeck was thrilled by the award, but he was conscious of the fact that other American writers who had received the prize rarely ever produced as good work afterward. Hemingway and Faulkner were both cases in point. Steinbeck wrote to a friend that he had accepted the award because he thought he could "beat the rap." Like his fellow honorees, however, he did not. Fortunately, he didn't need to: *In Dubious Battle* (1936), *Of Mice and Men* (1937), and *The Grapes of Wrath* (1939) had sealed his reputation for craftsmanship, a concern for social and economic problems, and an enduring faith in humanity.

Nobel saw some of the cruel and bloody misuses of his inventions. He may even have foreseen the end result of his probing—access to ultimate violence—to final destruction. Some say that he became cynical, but I do not believe this. I think he strove to invent a control, a safety valve. I think he found it finally only in the human mind and the human spirit. To me, his thinking is clearly indicated in the categories of these awards.

They are offered for increased and continuing knowledge of man and of his world—for understanding and communication, which are the functions of literature. And they are offered for demonstrations of the capacity for peace—the culmination of all the others.

Less than fifty years after his death, the door of nature was unlocked and we were offered the dreadful burden of choice.

We have usurped many of the powers we once ascribed to God.

Fearful and unprepared, we have assumed lordship over the life or death of the whole world—of all living things.

The danger and the glory and the choice rest finally in man. The test of his perfectibility is at hand.

Having taken Godlike power, we must seek in ourselves for the responsibility and the wisdom we once prayed some deity might have.

Man himself has become our greatest hazard and our only hope.

So that today, Saint John the apostle may well be paraphrased: In the end is the Word, and the Word is Man—and the Word is with Men.

—John Steinbeck

F **Reading Skills and Strategies**
Making Inferences
? What is Steinbeck referring to here?
[He is referring to the atomic bomb.]

G **Literary Connections**
This is an allusion to the Gospel of John (1:1): "In the beginning was the Word, and the Word was with God, and the Word was God."

MAKING MEANINGS

First Thoughts [Respond]
1. Students might suggest that it makes Jody feel sad and sorry for his grandfather. It may make students look to new frontiers, such as space.

Shaping Interpretations [Interpret]
2. To Grandfather, "the crossing" symbolizes the heroic desire to push to the limits of human possibility.
3. Possible responses: Grandfather's visit causes the family conflict between Mr. and Mrs. Tiflin. Although Mrs. Tiflin ignores her father's stories, she insists that he be shown respect and compassion, which Carl gives only grudgingly. Carl's determination to control his son creates an intergenerational conflict between them. Jody's pleasure in his grandfather's company and his stories adds to this conflict. Carl's boredom with Grandfather's stories creates another generational conflict between them.
4. The mouse hunt contrasts with the wagon train's battle against Indians, suggesting, like Grandfather, that modern people have gone soft.
5. Possible responses: The story explores the clash between our spiritual hunger for heroism and the mundane realities of life. It demonstrates the power of following a dream, the necessity of facing reality, and the importance of creating a new heroic ideal.
6. Possible response: Jody is right, because he makes the old man feel needed and because the stories fuel Jody's own heroic spirit. Carl is also right, because Grandfather's obsession keeps him from finding his place in the modern world.

Extending the Text [Evaluate]
7. Students may suggest space, the ocean, or the human mind.

MAKING MEANINGS

First Thoughts
1. How does Grandfather's statement "Westering has died out of the people" make Jody feel? How did it make *you* feel?

Shaping Interpretations
2. What seems to have been the significance of "the crossing" for Jody's grandfather?
3. There are several **conflicts** in the story—between Carl Tiflin and his wife, between Jody and his father, and between Jody's father and his grandfather. Describe the source of each conflict. Would you say this story is more about family relationships or more about the changing attitudes of each new generation?
4. The story holds many **ironies**. How does Steinbeck ironically characterize the modern age with his use of the mouse hunt?
5. What would you say is the **theme** of the story? What does it say about the relation between dreams and reality and the loss of the heroic ideal?
6. Is Jody right to want to listen to the same stories over and over, or is Carl right in wanting the past to be forgotten? Or are these two characters both right *and* wrong? Give reasons to support your views.

Extending the Text
7. Look back at your Quickwrite. Do you believe, as Jody's grandfather does, that there are no longer any frontiers for young Americans—no opportunities for heroism? Where do you think young people today might look for frontiers?

Reading Check
a. Why does Jody look forward to his grandfather's visit, while his father dreads it? How does Jody feel about his grandfather?
b. What are Grandfather's stories about? In what way was he "the leader of the people"?

Reading Check
a. Jody enjoys his grandfather's company and his stories about Indians and crossing the plains. Jody's father dreads having to hear the same stories over and over again.
b. Grandfather tells about leading a wagon train across the plains to the West Coast. He was a leader of the pioneers in a literal sense. Metaphorically, he symbolizes the heroic age of American pioneering.

Help students understand that figures of speech are used often in everyday life. Give examples from clichés, advertisements, and ordinary conversation. For example, "it blew my mind" (metaphor, hyperbole); "took off like a rocket" (simile); "Mother Nature" and "Father Time" (personification). Then, ask students to give examples of their own. Paraphrases will vary. The figures of speech should be identified as follows:

1. personification
2. personification / metaphor
3. simile
4. oxymoron
5. metaphor
6. hyperbole
7. simile
8. hyperbole / metaphor

Grading Timesaver

Rubrics for each Choices assignment appear on p. 162 in the *Portfolio Management System.*

CHOICES: Building Your Portfolio

1. **Writer's Notebook** Remind students to maintain the integrity of the characters, matching their diction and actions to the story. Suggest that pairs of students first role-play the scene to help them capture Steinbeck's characterization.

2. **Comparing Texts** Be sure that students understand that the **theme** of a literary work is an idea, a conclusion, or a point about life or the world. The theme can be stated outright in the work or inferred from details of plot, characters, setting, and other elements of literature.

3. **Speaking and Listening** Have each group select a moderator who can keep the group on course and maintain balance among the panel members. To help students focus on the assignment, guide them to formulate the topic into a question: "Do heroes exist today, and if so, who are they, and what makes them heroic?"

READING SKILLS AND STRATEGIES

Interpreting Figures of Speech

Scholars have defined over three hundred different figures of speech, but most people are familiar with five types: **(1) simile,** which compares two unlike things by using words of specific comparison (such as *like, as,* or *resembles*); **(2) metaphor,** which identifies two unlike things directly without using a specific word of comparison; **(3) personification,** a type of metaphor that speaks of something non-human as if it were human; **(4) oxymoron,** a combination of words that seem to contradict each other (*wise fool, death in life, sweet sorrow*); and **(5) hyperbole,** which uses exaggeration for effect.

Read the following figures of speech from the story, and see if you can identify the type being used from the list above. Then, paraphrase the literal meaning of each phrase in your own words.

1. "plump, sleek, arrogant mice" (page 609)
2. "a crow congress had convened" (page 611)
3. "a road-runner . . . sailed out like a glider" (page 612)
4. "blue eyes were sternly merry" (page 612)
5. "a granite dignity" (page 612)
6. "a race of giants had lived then" (page 617)
7. "wagons moving across like centipedes" (page 617)
8. "a whole bunch of people made into one big crawling beast" (page 619)

CHOICES: Building Your Portfolio

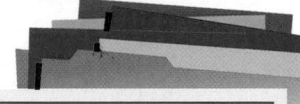

Writer's Notebook
1. Collecting Ideas for an Analysis of Causes and Effects

Reread the story's ending, this time thinking about what Jody and his mother are feeling and what their quiet words and actions signify. Then, write an extension of the ending, speculating on something Jody does afterward. You may continue the scene in the story, or skip to a new scene. In your scene, speculate on how Jody has been affected by his experiences with his grandfather and his father. Save your notes for possible use in the Writer's Workshop on page 685.

Comparing Texts
2. Variations on a Theme

Identify one of the basic **themes** of Steinbeck's story. It may have to do with the contrast between dream and reality, the loss of heroism, conflicts between generations, disillusionment, the limitations of the American dream, or some other subject. Choose another story from this textbook that deals with a similar theme. Write an essay comparing and contrasting the ways each story develops the theme. Focus on the stories' similarities and differences in **plot, character, setting,** and **tone.**

Speaking and Listening
3. Do Giants Walk the Earth?

With several students, organize a panel to discuss whether there are heroes today, and if so, who they are and what makes them heroic. As preparation for the panel, share your Quickwrite notes and exchange reactions to "The Leader of the People." In addition, try to obtain a video recording of Bill Moyers's interview of the anthropologist Joseph Campbell titled "The Hero's Adventure" (part of the PBS series *Joseph Campbell and the Power of Myth*). Play the interview as the opener of your presentation to the class or as a coda to it.

622 THE MODERNS

Using Students' Strengths

Kinesthetic Learners

For Choice 2, students might use note cards to collect details. They should take notes about theme, plot, characters, and setting, listing one detail for each literary element per card. Remind them to write which story the details refer to on the card. Then, ask students to place the cards for each literary element side by side to look for differences and similarities between stories and possible organizational patterns.

James Thurber
(1894–1961)

UPI/Bettmann.

James Thurber is generally acknowledged to be the foremost American humorist of the twentieth century. He was a supremely gifted cartoonist and a writer of essays, sketches, and stories. He once mocked the typical puffed-up biographies of literary figures by presenting this self-portrait:

> James Thurber was born in Columbus, Ohio, where so many awful things happened to him, on December 8, 1894. He was unable to keep anything on his stomach until he was seven years old, but grew to six feet one and a quarter inches tall and to weigh a hundred and fifty-four pounds fully dressed for winter. He began to write when he was ten years old . . . and to draw when he was fourteen. . . . Quick to arouse, he is very hard to quiet and people often just go away. . . . He never listens when anybody else is talking, preferring to keep his mind a blank until they get through, so he can talk. His favorite book is *The Great Gatsby*. His favorite author is Henry James. He wears excellent clothes very badly and can never find his hat. . . . He is Sagittarius with the moon in Aries and gets along fine with persons born between the 20th and 24th of August.

Thurber did grow up in Columbus, where he attended Ohio State University. He worked as a reporter in Columbus and Chicago for a number of years. He moved east, went to work for *The New Yorker* magazine in 1927, and remained on the staff for the rest of his life. Thurber's literary career peaked in the 1940s, even as his eyesight, damaged in a boyhood accident, worsened despite a series of operations. In addition to many collections of essays, stories, and children's books, he collaborated on a successful Broadway play.

His humor often turned on the chaos of contemporary American life. Thurber focused on the "little man," who cannot quite assert himself in a confusing world where women seem surer of their way. Walter Mitty, the antihero of Thurber's most famous story, seeks in fantasy a release from a wife who overwhelms him.

In many of his stories and cartoons, Thurber focused on relationships between men and women. While Thurber claimed to hope the feminist movement would seize power and prevent men from blowing the world to bits, he viewed women with a certain ambivalence—as intimidating to their mates, and as mother figures rather than partners. (His attitude toward women is comically revealed in the cartoons that illustrate his stories.)

Thurber defined humor as "a kind of emotional chaos told about calmly and quietly in retrospect." But humor is not subject to rational explanation. Perhaps this was in the mind of Thurber's friend, the writer Mark Van Doren, when he said of Thurber: "He was an extraordinary man . . . with so many quick changes: gentle and fierce, fascinating and boring, sophisticated and boorish, kind and cruel, broadminded and parochial. You can't explain Thurber."

go.hrw.com
LEO 11-12

Resources: Print and Media

Reading
- *Graphic Organizers for Active Reading*, p. 61
- *Words to Own*, p. 37
- *Audio CD Library*
  Disc 16, Track 3

Elements of Literature
- *Literary Elements*
  Transparency 20
  Worksheet, p. 61

Writing and Language
- *Daily Oral Grammar*
  Transparency 39

Assessment
- *Formal Assessment*, p. 123
- *Portfolio Management System*, p. 163
- *Test Generator (One-Stop Planner CD-ROM)*

Internet
- go.hrw.com (keyword: LEO 11-12)

Summary ■

Walter Mitty, a henpecked husband, goes on a mundane shopping trip with his wife, but he keeps escaping from reality into fantasies of drama and adventure that parody popular genres. Driving to town, he imagines himself piloting a Navy seaplane through a fierce storm. Passing a hospital triggers the fantasy that he is a famous surgeon who repairs a life-support system with a fountain pen. The rudeness of a parking-lot attendant and the effort to recall which item his wife asked him to buy send him into a courtroom where he is on trial for his life. He becomes a World War I flying ace after reading a magazine article on the subject. In his final daydream, the act of lighting a cigarette turns him into a prisoner, disdainfully facing a firing squad. Each fantasy is triggered by a trivial event and cut short by a rude summons back to reality.

Before You Read
THE SECRET LIFE OF WALTER MITTY

Make the Connection
Daydream Believer

The name "Walter Mitty" has entered our language as the epitome of the "little guy" who is dominated by an assertive wife. You might recognize Mitty and the formidable Mrs. Mitty—they are character types that have formed the basis of many TV situation comedies. Mitty is based on a stereotype of the henpecked husband, but Mitty himself is an original. In fact, the term "Walter Mitty" is found in *Webster's Third New International Dictionary*, where it is defined as "a commonplace unadventurous person who seeks escape from reality through daydreaming and typically imagines himself leading a glamorous life and becoming famous."

Reading Skills and Strategies

Analyzing Text Structures: Cause/Effect

In this famous story, James Thurber adapts the basic plot structure of **cause** and **effect** in a highly original way. He describes a pattern of free association, in which trivial details from real life cause grand adventures in Walter Mitty's daydreams. Thus, Mitty's daydream is the effect. As you read the story, jot down the decidedly unheroic event that triggers each daydream, as well as the subjects of the daydreams. Note also what snaps Mitty out of each fantasy.

Elements of Literature
Parody

A **parody** makes fun of another work by imitating aspects of its style or contents. You've probably encountered parodies of shows, songs, and movies in humor magazines, TV sitcoms, commercials, and movies.

After you've read the first paragraph of this story, ask yourself what kind of movie it parodies.

> **A** **parody** is a work that makes fun of another work by imitating some aspect of its style or content.
>
> *For more about Parody, see the Handbook of Literary Terms.*

"Why don't you let me know what it is, if it's so pleasant?"

From *Men, Women and Dogs.* Copyright © 1943 by James Thurber. Copyright © renewed 1971 by Helen Thurber and Rosemary A. Thurber. Reprinted by arrangement with Rosemary A. Thurber and the Barbara Hogenson Agency.

Preteaching Vocabulary

Words to Own

Have students read the definitions of the Words to Own listed at the bottom of the selection pages. Then, have students play "Catch Phrase," in which one player calls out synonyms or phrases and the other players have to name the vocabulary word. The first player to name the word gets a point and takes a turn. Then, have students unscramble each vocabulary word at right, so that it matches its definition.

1. asyhlkir—**dashingly** [rakishly]
2. stghutarid—**troubled** [distraught]
3. gagrahd—**worn-out** [haggard]
4. envcar—**cowardly** [craven]
5. entolsin—**arrogant** [insolent]
6. glyiiisnnnuat—**suggestively** [insinuatingly]
7. emumoindpna—**confusion** [pandemonium]
8. amdleb—**place of confusion** [bedlam]
9. gnidonnnaac—**artillery fire** [cannonading]
10. dngnier—**violently ripping apart** [rending]

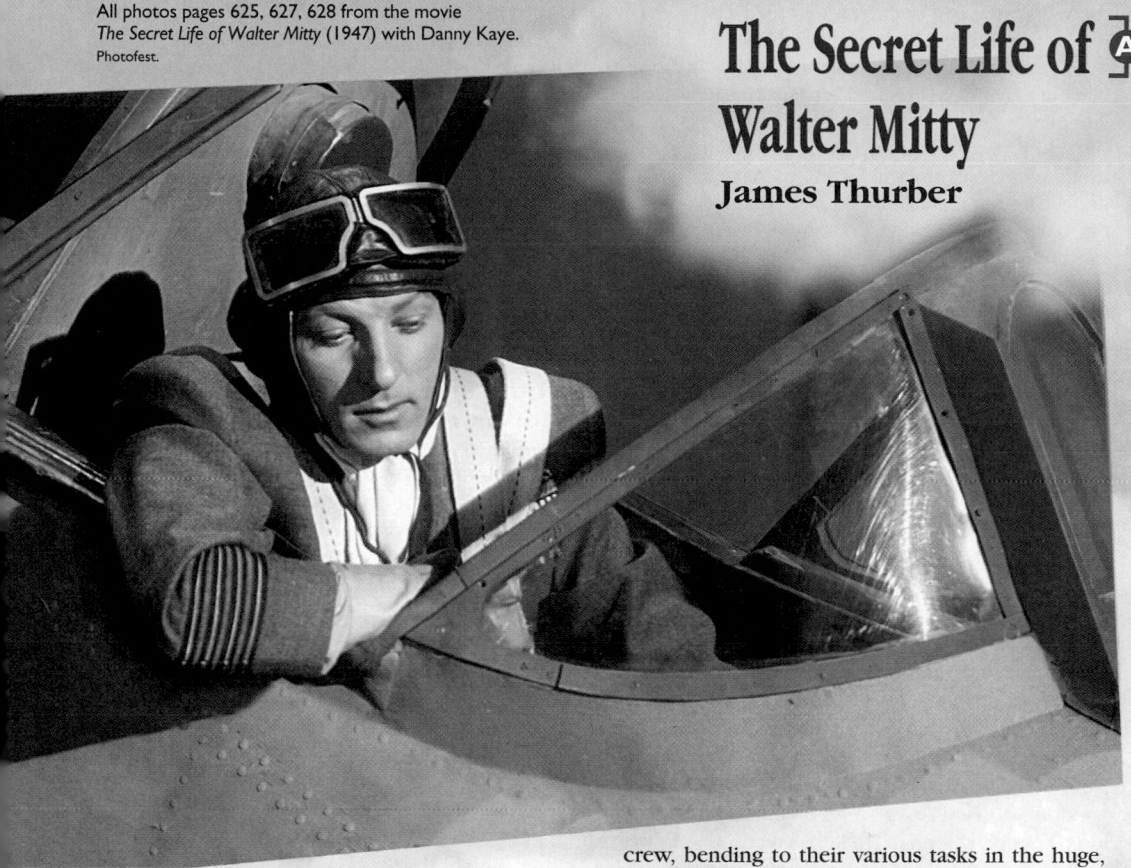

All photos pages 625, 627, 628 from the movie *The Secret Life of Walter Mitty* (1947) with Danny Kaye. Photofest.

The Secret Life of  Walter Mitty

James Thurber

"We're going through!" The commander's voice was like thin ice breaking. He wore his full-dress uniform, with the heavily braided white cap pulled down <u>rakishly</u> over one cold gray eye. "We can't make it, sir. It's spoiling for[1] a hurricane, if you ask me." "I'm not asking you, Lieutenant Berg," said the commander. "Throw on the power lights! Rev her up to 8,500! We're going through!" The pounding of the cylinders increased: ta-pocketa-pocketa-pocketa-*pocketa-pocketa*. The commander stared at the ice forming on the pilot window. He walked over and twisted a row of complicated dials. "Switch on No. 8 auxiliary!" he shouted. "Switch on No. 8 auxiliary!" repeated Lieutenant Berg. "Full strength in No. 3 turret!" shouted the commander. "Full strength in No. 3 turret!" The

crew, bending to their various tasks in the huge, hurtling eight-engined navy hydroplane, looked at each other and grinned. "The Old Man'll get us through," they said to one another. "The Old Man ain't afraid of Hell!" . . .

"Not so fast! You're driving too fast!" said Mrs. Mitty. "What are you driving so fast for?"

"Hmm?" said Walter Mitty. He looked at his wife, in the seat beside him, with shocked astonishment. She seemed grossly unfamiliar, like a strange woman who had yelled at him in a crowd. "You were up to fifty-five," she said. "You know I don't like to go more than forty. You were up to fifty-five." Walter Mitty drove on toward Waterbury in silence, the roaring of the SN202 through

------

WORDS TO OWN
rakishly (rāk′·ish·lē) *adv.*: dashingly; jauntily.

------

1. **it's spoiling for:** slang for "conditions are right for."

A Cultural Connections
The Hollywood Version
The filmed version is not very close to Thurber's story, but the daydream sequences are very funny. The movie is especially memorable for Danny Kaye's famous song "Anatole of Paris." In addition to Kaye, the movie stars Virginia Mayo and Boris Karloff.

B Elements of Literature
Parody
❓ What details of this scene reveal the parody? [Possible responses: An officer wouldn't wear a full-dress uniform while flying a plane; a hydroplane doesn't have eight engines or a turret—much less three turrets.]

C English Language Learners
Idioms
Explain that the phrase *Old Man* is often used as an affectionate term of respect for a leader.

D Reading Skills and Strategies

Analyzing Text Structures: Cause and Effect
❓ What causes Mitty to be shocked out of his daydream? What does this incident suggest about the relationship between Mr. and Mrs. Mitty? [Possible responses: Mrs. Mitty's rebuke brings Walter back to reality. Her rebuke and his response suggests that she is domineering and he is submissive. He daydreams often to escape her hectoring.]

Reaching All Students

Struggling Readers
The story consists of several daydreams or fantasies that are separated from each other by intrusions of reality. Have students keep track of the alternating sequence of fantasy and reality by noting the page and paragraph where each one begins and ends. Students may do this in conjunction with the charts they keep for Reading Skills and Strategies.

English Language Learners
The story contains colloquialisms that would have been found in the pulp entertainments of the 1930s, such as "The Old Man" on p. 625 and "Mac" on p. 626. Suggest newer alternatives. For additional strategies to supplement instruction for these students, see
• *Lesson Plans Including Strategies for English-Language Learners*

Advanced Learners
Thurber's fiction describes urban men beset by domineering women in a world they neither made nor understand. His illustrations show huge women menacing small men. The concept was funny in the 1940s, but the world has changed considerably in fifty years—or has it? Have students debate whether Thurber's fictional world still holds some truth or whether the "battle of the sexes" has been redefined and, if so, how and why.

A Reading Skills and Strategies

Analyzing Text Structures: Cause and Effect

? Why does Mitty race the engine—but just a little? [Possible responses: He is rebelling against his wife's domination by acting like a young man—up to a point. His relation to her is more like a teenager's to his mother than a husband's to a wife.]

B Elements of Literature

Parody

? What medical stereotypes does Thurber parody in this scene? [Possible responses: He parodies the melodramas about wealthy and well-connected medical patients who get preferential treatment and superhuman doctors who step in to save the day.]

C Appreciating Language

Jargon

Make sure students understand that the terms *obstreosis of the ductal tract* and *streptothricosis* are parodies of medical jargon, invented by Thurber.

D Reading Skills and Strategies

Comparing/Contrasting

? How does Mitty's performance in his operating-room fantasy contrast with his real performance in the parking lot? [Possible responses: In his fantasy, he saves the day by repairing a complicated machine and taking over difficult surgery; in the parking lot, he almost hits another car, and the attendant has to park his car.] Point out that not only his wife but the cop and the parking-lot attendant also yell at him.

---

the worst storm in twenty years of navy flying fading in the remote, intimate airways of his mind. "You're tensed up again," said Mrs. Mitty. "It's one of your days. I wish you'd let Dr. Renshaw look you over."

Walter Mitty stopped the car in front of the building where his wife went to have her hair done. **A** "Remember to get those overshoes while I'm having my hair done," she said. "I don't need overshoes," said Mitty. She put her mirror back into her bag. "We've been all through that," she said, getting out of the car. "You're not a young man any longer." He raced the engine a little. "Why don't you wear your gloves? Have you lost your gloves?" Walter Mitty reached in a pocket and brought out the gloves. He put them on, but after she had turned and gone into the building and he had driven on to a red light, he took them off again. "Pick it up, brother!" snapped a cop as the light changed, and Mitty hastily pulled on his gloves and lurched ahead. He drove around the streets aimlessly for a time, and then he drove past the hospital on his way to the parking lot.

. . . "It's the millionaire banker, Wellington McMillan," said the pretty nurse. "Yes?" said Walter Mitty, removing his gloves slowly. "Who has the case?" "Dr. Renshaw and Dr. Benbow, but there are two specialists here, Dr. Remington from New York and Mr. Pritchard-Mitford from London. He flew over." A door opened down a long, cool corridor and Dr. Renshaw came out. He looked <u>distraught</u> and <u>haggard</u>. "Hello, Mitty," he **B** said. "We're having the devil's own time with McMillan, the millionaire banker and close personal friend of Roosevelt. Obstreosis of the ductal tract. Tertiary. Wish you'd take a look at him." "Glad to," said Mitty.

In the operating room there were whispered **C** introductions: "Dr. Remington, Dr. Mitty. Mr. Pritchard-Mitford, Dr. Mitty." "I've read your book on streptothricosis," said Pritchard-Mitford, shaking hands. "A brilliant performance, sir." "Thank you," said Walter Mitty. "Didn't know you were in the States, Mitty," grumbled Remington. "Coals to Newcastle,[2] bringing Mitford and me up here for a tertiary." "You are very kind," said Mitty. A huge, complicated machine, connected to the operating

---

2. **coals to Newcastle:** an unnecessary effort. Newcastle, England, was a major coal-producing city.

---

table, with many tubes and wires, began at this moment to go pocketa-pocketa-pocketa. "The new anesthetizer is giving way!" shouted an intern. "There is no one in the East who knows how to fix it!" "Quiet, man!" said Mitty, in a low, cool voice. He sprang to the machine, which was now going pocketa-pocketa-queep-pocketa-queep. He began fingering delicately a row of glistening dials. "Give me a fountain pen!" he snapped. Someone handed him a fountain pen. He pulled a faulty piston out of the machine and inserted the pen in its place. "That will hold for ten minutes," he said. "Get on with the operation." A nurse hurried over and whispered to Renshaw, and Mitty saw the man turn pale. "Coreopsis has set in," said Renshaw nervously. "If you would take over, Mitty?" Mitty looked at him and at the <u>craven</u> figure of Benbow, who drank, and at the <u>grave</u>, uncertain faces of the two great specialists. "If you wish," he said. They slipped a white gown on him; he adjusted a mask and drew on thin gloves; nurses handed him shining . . .

"Back it up, Mac! Look out for that Buick!" Walter Mitty jammed on the brakes. "Wrong lane, Mac," said the parking-lot attendant, looking at Mitty closely. "Gee. Yeh," muttered Mitty. He **D** began cautiously to back out of the lane marked "Exit Only." "Leave her sit there," said the attendant. "I'll put her away." Mitty got out of the car. "Hey, better leave the key." "Oh," said Mitty, handing the man the ignition key. The attendant vaulted into the car, backed it up with <u>insolent</u> skill, and put it where it belonged.

They're so damn cocky, thought Walter Mitty, walking along Main Street; they think they know everything. Once he had tried to take his chains[3] off, outside New Milford, and he had got them wound around the axles. A man had had to come out in a wrecking car and unwind them, a young, grinning garageman. Since then Mrs. Mitty always made him drive to a garage to have the chains

---

3. **chains:** chains attached to automobile tires to increase traction in snow and ice.

WORDS TO OWN

distraught (di·strôt′) *adj.:* troubled.
haggard (hag′ərd) *adj.:* wasted or worn in appearance.
craven (krā′vən) *adj.:* very fearful; cowardly.
insolent (in′sə·lənt) *adj.:* arrogant.

Crossing the Curriculum

Mathematics

"You're not a young man any longer," Mrs. Mitty reminds her husband. How old is old? Invite students to use the Internet, an almanac, or another source to find the average life expectancy for men and women in 1939 (when the story was written) and today. Then, have students list five ways they can extend their life span, such as getting regular exercise, eating healthful foods, and refraining from smoking.

Health

Some students may be interested in forming an expert group to look up current theories on the causes and meanings of daydreams and fantasies. Others might want to research the causes and results of stress and low self-esteem. Both groups could join in a panel discussion as a means of reporting to the class.

Journalism

Have students research journalism as a career and make brief reports to the class. Students might focus on how the occupation has changed since Thurber's day. Encourage students to contact and interview journalists from local newspapers and magazines. If possible, invite a local journalist to speak to the class about conditions and opportunities in journalism.

taken off. The next time, he thought, I'll wear my right arm in a sling; they won't grin at me then. I'll have my right arm in a sling, and they'll see I couldn't possibly take the chains off myself. He kicked at the slush on the sidewalk. "Overshoes," he said to himself, and he began looking for a shoe store.

When he came out into the street again, with the overshoes in a box under his arm, Walter Mitty began to wonder what the other thing was his wife had told him to get. She had told him, twice, before they set out from their house for Waterbury. In a way he hated these weekly trips to town— he was always getting something wrong. Kleenex, he thought, Squibb's,[4] razor blades? No. Toothpaste, toothbrush, bicarbonate, carborundum, initiative and referendum? He gave it up. But she would remember it. "Where's the what's-its-name?" she would ask. "Don't tell me you forgot the what's-its-name." A newsboy went by shouting something about the Waterbury trial.

. . . "Perhaps this will refresh your memory." The district attorney suddenly thrust a heavy automatic at the quiet figure on the witness stand. "Have you ever seen this before?" Walter Mitty took the gun and examined it expertly. "This is my Webley-Vickers 50.80," he said calmly. An excited buzz ran around the courtroom. The judge rapped for order. "You are a crack shot with any sort of firearms, I believe?" said the district attorney, insinuatingly. "Objection!" shouted Mitty's attorney. "We have shown that the defendant could not have fired the shot. We have shown that he wore his right arm in a sling on the night of the fourteenth of July." Walter Mitty raised his hand briefly

"A brilliant performance, sir."
"Thank you," said Walter Mitty.

Photofest.

4. **Squibb's:** Squibb (now part of Bristol-Myers Squibb) was a U.S. pharmaceutical company, established in 1858, that manufactured a variety of prescription drugs and health-care products, such as cough and cold medicines and vitamins. It is not clear which product Mitty is thinking about.

and the bickering attorneys were stilled. "With any known make of gun," he said evenly, "I could have killed Gregory Fitzhurst at three hundred feet *with my left hand.*" Pandemonium broke loose in the courtroom. A woman's scream rose above the bedlam and suddenly a lovely, dark-haired girl was in Walter Mitty's arms. The district attorney struck at her savagely. Without rising from his chair, Mitty let the man have it on the point of the chin. "You miserable cur!"[5] . . .

"Puppy biscuit," said Walter Mitty. He stopped walking and the buildings of Waterbury rose up out of the misty courtroom and surrounded him again. A woman who was passing laughed. "He said 'Puppy biscuit,'" she said to her companion. "That man said 'Puppy biscuit' to himself." Walter Mitty hurried on. He went into an A & P, not the first one he came to but a smaller one farther up the street. "I want some biscuit for small, young dogs," he said to the clerk. "Any special brand, sir?" The greatest pistol shot in the world thought a moment. "It says 'Puppies Bark for It' on the box," said Walter Mitty.

His wife would be through at the hairdresser's in fifteen minutes, Mitty saw in looking at his watch, unless they had trouble drying it; sometimes they had trouble drying it. She didn't like to get to the hotel first; she would want him to be there waiting for her as usual. He found a big

5. **cur:** a cowardly or contemptible person; also, a mongrel dog.

WORDS TO OWN
insinuatingly (in·sin′yoo·āt′iŋ·lē) *adv.:* suggestively.
pandemonium (pan′də·mō′nē·əm) *n.:* wild confusion.
bedlam (bed′ləm) *n.:* place or condition of noise and confusion.

JAMES THURBER **627**

E **Struggling Readers**
Compound Words
❓ How could you figure out the meaning of *overshoes,* a compound word, by separating it into its two parts? [Possible response: *Overshoes* go *over* regular *shoes.* Therefore, they must be some type of boots.]

F **Appreciating Language**
Sound Effects
Note the list of four-syllable words: "*bicarbonate, carborundum, initiative* and *referendum.*" These are items that don't belong together, but Mitty associates them by their sound and rhyme.

G **Critical Thinking**
Determining Author's Purpose
❓ Why does Thurber follow Mitty's boring list of everyday drugstore items with his dramatic courtroom fantasy? [By juxtaposing Mitty's mundane world with his thrilling fantasy world, Thurber underscores the drabness of his existence and his need to enhance it.]

H **Literary Connections**
Under the Humor
Thurber was annoyed by readers who failed to grasp the sadness and even anger that laces his humor, giving it a tart, dry, ironic edge. Thurber once proposed to kick to death the next person who described him as "elfin."

I **Advanced Learners**
Parody
❓ What is Thurber making fun of? [advertising slogans] How is the slogan ironic? [In many ways, Mitty is like a puppy, obediently trailing after his wife. Although the image is humorous, it is also a poignant and savage comment on one type of modern American man.]

Skill Link

Responding to Aesthetic Elements in Texts

Explain that *aesthetics* is the study of beauty in art and that aesthetics derives its principles from cultural, social, religious, philosophical, and other values. Explore the purely aesthetic qualities of literature. Students may mention vivid imagery, mood, and musicality of language, appealing characters, and conflicts that are satisfactorily resolved. Discuss how rhythm, rhyme, and figures of speech contribute to the aes-

thetic effect of a work. Discuss whether language always has to be pleasing (or elevated or poetic or even logical) to be effective aesthetically. Delve into the roles of consistency and appropriateness in aesthetics. Then, have small groups complete the following activities.

1. Compare and contrast any two of Walter Mitty's fantasies. What similarities and differences do you see in tone, word choice,

details, and figurative language? in the character of the man Mitty imagines himself to be?

2. As the photographs show, Danny Kaye was cast as Mitty in the movie. Whom would you cast in the role today? Whom would you cast as Mrs. Mitty? Justify your choices.

3. You might ask advanced learners to report on the principles set forth in Aristotle's *Poetics,* a foundational study of aesthetics.

A Critical Thinking

Making the Connections

? How is Walter Mitty like the grandfather in "The Leader of the People"? [Possible response: Both men escape from the tedium of their daily lives by retreating into adventure narratives that restore their dignity—although the grandfather's stories are true and Mitty's are fantasy.]

B Elements of Literature

Parody

? What is the target of this parody? [Possible response: This scene parodies heroic war novels and movies that feature larger-than-life leaders who ignore threats to their personal safety. Students might also note the double meaning of Mitty's note about hell, which might refer to his real life, as well as to the fantasy war.]

C Critical Thinking

Determining Author's Purpose

? What does this story say about one of Thurber's key themes, the battle of the sexes? [Possible responses: that men and women cannot understand each other; that lack of communication and an inability or unwillingness to understand one's spouse can lead to unhappiness.]

D Reading Skills and Strategies

Responding to the Text

? Is the ending humorous or tragic? [Possible response: Mitty's imaginary escape from his wife to the firing squad is humorous; but the story is also tragic, because he lacks the courage to effect a real solution to his problems.]

"We only live once, Sergeant," said Mitty, with his faint, fleeting smile.

Photofest.

leather chair in the lobby, facing a window, and he put the overshoes and the puppy biscuit on the floor beside it. He picked up an old copy of *Liberty* and sank down into the chair. "Can Germany Conquer the World Through the Air?" Walter Mitty looked at the pictures of bombing planes and of ruined streets.

. . . "The <u>cannonading</u> has got the wind up in young Raleigh, sir," said the sergeant. Captain Mitty looked up at him through tousled hair. "Get him to bed," he said wearily. "With the others. I'll fly alone." "But you can't, sir," said the sergeant anxiously. "It takes two men to handle that bomber and the Archies[6] are pounding hell out of the air. Von Richtman's circus[7] is between here and Saulier." "Somebody's got to get to that ammunition dump," said Mitty. "I'm going over. Spot of brandy?" He poured a drink for the sergeant and one for himself. War thundered and whined around the dugout and battered at the door. There was a <u>rending</u> of wood and splinters flew through the room. "A bit of a near thing," said Captain Mitty carelessly. "The box barrage is closing in," said the sergeant. "We only live once, Sergeant," said Mitty, with his faint, fleeting smile. "Or do we?" He poured another brandy and

6. **Archies:** German antiaircraft guns or gunners in World War I.
7. **circus:** squadron of planes.

628 THE MODERNS

tossed it off. "I never see a man could hold his brandy like you, sir," said the sergeant. "Begging your pardon, sir." Captain Mitty stood up and strapped on his huge Webley-Vickers automatic. "It's forty kilometers through hell, sir," said the sergeant. Mitty finished one last brandy. "After all," he said softly, "what isn't?" The pounding of the cannon increased; there was the rat-tat-tatting of machine guns, and from somewhere came the menacing pocketa-pocketa-pocketa of the new flamethrowers. Walter Mitty walked to the door of the dugout humming "Auprès de Ma Blonde,"[8] He turned and waved to the sergeant. "Cheerio!" he said. . . .

Something struck his shoulder. "I've been looking all over this hotel for you," said Mrs. Mitty. "Why do you have to hide in this old chair? How did you expect me to find you?" "Things close in," said Walter Mitty vaguely. "What?" Mrs. Mitty said. "Did you get the what's-its-name? The puppy biscuit? What's in that box?" "Overshoes," said Mitty. "Couldn't you have put them on in the store?" "I was thinking," said Walter Mitty. "Does it ever occur to you that I am sometimes thinking?" She looked at him. "I'm going to take your temperature when I get you home," she said.

They went out through the revolving doors that made a faintly derisive whistling sound when you pushed them. It was two blocks to the parking lot. At the drugstore on the corner she said, "Wait here for me. I forgot something. I won't be a minute." She was more than a minute. Walter Mitty lighted a cigarette. It began to rain, rain with sleet in it. He stood up against the wall of the drugstore, smoking. . . . He put his shoulders back and his heels together. "To hell with the handkerchief," said Walter Mitty scornfully. He took one last drag on his cigarette and snapped it away. Then, with that faint, fleeting smile playing about his lips, he faced the firing squad; erect and motionless, proud and disdainful, Walter Mitty the Undefeated, inscrutable[9] to the last.

8. **Auprès de Ma Blonde** (ō·prä′ də mä blônd): French song. The title means "Near My Blonde."
9. **inscrutable** (in·skro͞ot′ə·bəl): mysterious.

WORDS TO OWN

cannonading (kan′ən·ād′iŋ) *v.* used as *n.:* artillery fire.
rending (rend′iŋ) *v.* used as *n.:* violent ripping apart.

Assessing Learning

Check Test: True–False

1. Mrs. Mitty reminds Walter to buy a snow shovel. [False]
2. As Dr. Mitty, Walter repairs a machine with a coat hanger. [False]
3. One item on Walter's shopping list is puppy biscuits. [True]
4. Walter imagines himself as a crusading district attorney. [False]
5. Walter dies by firing squad. [False]

Getting Students Involved

Enrichment Activity

Have pairs of students play a word-guessing game with the Words to Own. Partners alternate being word chooser and word guesser. The word chooser writes blank lines in place of the letters of the word. The guesser names a letter of the alphabet. If the word contains that letter, the word chooser fills in the appropriate line or lines with that letter. The guesser is allowed five wrong guesses. If the guesser guesses the word correctly before making five wrong guesses, he or she gets a point. Have pairs play a five-point game. Thurber loved word games, especially one in which players are given three or four letters from the middle of a difficult, and possibly imaginary, word and must guess the word.

Thurber's longtime associate on *The New Yorker,* E. B. White, wrote this parting tribute to his friend on November 11, 1961.

The New Yorker's Farewell

I am one of the lucky ones; I knew him before blindness hit him, before fame hit him, and I tend always to think of him as a young artist in a small office in a big city, with all the world still ahead. It was a fine thing to be young and at work in New York for a new magazine when Thurber was young and at work, and I will always be glad that this happened to me.

It was fortunate that we got on well; the office we shared was the size of a hall bedroom. There was just room enough for two men, two typewriters, and a stack of copy paper. The copy paper disappeared at a scandalous rate— not because our production was high (although it was) but because Thurber used copy paper as the natural receptacle for discarded sorrows, immediate joys, stale dreams, golden prophecies, and messages of good cheer to the outside world and to fellow workers. His mind was never at rest, and his pencil was connected to his mind by the best conductive tissue I have ever seen in action. The whole world knows what a funny man he was, but you had to sit next to him day after day to understand the extravagance of his clowning, the wildness and subtlety of his thinking, and the intensity of his interest in others and his sympathy for their dilemmas—dilemmas that he instantly enlarged, put in focus, and made immortal, just as he enlarged and made immortal the strange goings-on in the Ohio home of his boyhood. His waking dreams and his sleeping dreams commingled shamelessly and uproariously. Ohio was never far from his thoughts, and when he received a medal from his home state in 1953, he wrote, "The clocks that strike in my dreams are often the clocks of Columbus." It is a beautiful sentence and a revealing one.

From *The Owl In The Attic.* Copyright © 1931 by James Thurber. Copyright © renewed 1959 by James Thurber. Reprinted by arrangement with Rosemary A. Thurber and the Barbara Hogenson Agency.

He was both a practitioner of humor and a defender of it. The day he died, I came on a letter from him, dictated to a secretary and signed in pencil with his sightless and enormous "Jim." "Every time is a time for humor," he wrote. "I write humor the way a surgeon operates, because it is a livelihood, because I have a great urge to do it, because many interesting challenges are set up, and because I have the hope it may do some good." Once, I remember, he heard someone say that humor is a shield, not a sword, and it made him mad. He wasn't going to have anyone beating his sword into a shield. That "surgeon," incidentally, is pure Mitty. During his happiest years, Thurber did not write the way a surgeon operates, he wrote the way a child skips rope, the way a mouse waltzes.

Although he is best known for "Walter Mitty" and *The Male Animal,* the book of his I like best is *The Last Flower.* In it you will find his faith in the renewal of life, his feeling for the beauty and fragility of life on earth. Like all good writers, he fashioned his own best obituary notice. Nobody else can add to the record, much as he might like to. And of all the flowers, real and figurative, that will find their way to Thurber's last resting place, the one that will remain fresh and wiltproof is the little flower he himself drew, on the last page of that lovely book.

—E. B. White

E. B. White recalls James Thurber's dedication to humor, both in his daily life and in his writing.

E Background

E. B. White began contributing to *The New Yorker* in April 1925, just months after the magazine was founded, and became a staff member the following year. His elegant and witty style influenced not only every editorial feature of the magazine but American prose in general. Thurber and White first met at a party in 1927, shortly after Thurber had sold his first story to the magazine; they liked each other, and White encouraged Harold Ross, the magazine's founder, to hire Thurber. White became Thurber's literary mentor, and Thurber, in turn, always praised White highly. He once wrote: "Until I learned discipline in writing from studying Andy White's stuff, I was a careless, nervous, headlong writer. . . . The precision and clarity of White's writing helped me a lot, slowed me down from the dogtrot of newspaper tempo and made me realize a writer turns on his mind, not a faucet. . . ."

F Literary Connections

In addition to Thurber and White, the staff of *The New Yorker* included Robert Benchley (theater critic), Clifton Fadiman (book reviewer), and William Shawn (reporter and later editor-in-chief). Frank Sullivan, S. J. Perelman, Lewis Mumford, John O'Hara, Ogden Nash, Dorothy Parker, and Ring Lardner were frequent contributors.

G Struggling Readers

Finding the Main Idea

? What does White admire most about Thurber? [Possible response: his imaginativeness, sympathy for others, and connection to beauty and life.]

Using Students' Strengths

Visual/Spatial Learners

Invite students to draw cartoons to replace the photographs that now illustrate the story. Students can use their own techniques or parody Thurber's style. Have students include captions that add details or humor. Invite students to display the cartoons with a mock-up of the pages to which they belong.

Verbal Learners

Have students brainstorm a list of people they admire. Then, have students select one person and write a tribute to him or her. Guide students in using White's tribute as a model, mirroring the elegiac tone through carefully selected specific details and examples. Volunteers can deliver their tributes to the class as a speech.

Logical/Mathematical Learners

Have students create a flow chart tracing how each event in the story causes the next one.

Connections

In this cartoon, Snoopy's illusion that he is a world-famous commander in the French Foreign Legion poses a problem for Linus, who must pass by Snoopy's imaginary Fort Zinderneuf on his way to and from Charlie Brown's house.

Ⓐ Literary Connections

Beau Geste is Percival C. Wren's 1924 adventure story about three devoted brothers serving in the French Foreign Legion and battling a sadistic commander.

Ⓑ Elements of Literature

Parody

? What does this cartoon parody? [military and adventure novels and movies]

Ⓒ Elements of Literature

Humor

? Discuss how humor is often derived from an absurd or incongruous situation. The laughs are elicited through wordplay, irony, sarcasm, exaggeration, and understatement. How does Schulz create humor in this comic strip? [Possible responses: Schulz creates humor through incongruity and exaggeration. It's funny to see vulnerable little birds dressed as members of the French Foreign Legion and attacking Linus, who does not present a threat to them.]

One of the most familiar Walter Mitty–like characters in popular culture is Snoopy, Charles M. Schulz's (1922–) beloved creation from the famous "Peanuts" comic strip.

PEANUTS Reprinted by permission of United Feature Syndicate, Inc.

Connecting Across Texts

Connecting with "The Secret Life of Walter Mitty"

Have students discuss the following questions:

1. How is Snoopy like Walter Mitty? [Possible responses: Both escape drab, uneventful lives through fantasy. They both imagine themselves as great leaders and war heroes.]

2. How are Snoopy's relationship with Linus and Walter's with Mrs. Mitty the same and different? [Possible responses: Both are the butt of the joke, but Mrs. Mitty is oblivious to the fantasy swirling around her, while Linus is aware that Snoopy has constructed an alternate reality and can even identify it. Further, Mrs. Mitty's hectoring manner drives Walter to seek refuge in fantasy, while Linus is an innocent bystander.]

MAKING MEANINGS

First Thoughts

1. Do you think there's a little of Mitty in everyone? Explain.

Reading Check

a. List the errands Mitty is doing in real life.

b. In contrast, what deeds does Mitty perform in his fantasy life?

Shaping Interpretations

2. What is the central **irony** of Mitty's life? Is this irony humorous, serious, or partly both?

3. Thurber's story uses a technique called free association, in which words and sounds from real life become associated with elements of Mitty's daydreams. Review the notes you made while reading, and identify what causes Mitty to lapse into each daydream. What decidedly unheroic event snaps him out of each episode?

4. Where does Thurber use **parody** in the story? Who or what are the targets of his satire? (To help identify the targets, look especially at the jargon being bandied about in each daydream.)

5. Why do you think Mitty daydreams so much, and about these specific events? Do you think that his daydreaming enriches his life, or does it work as a handicap? Why?

He always half suspected that something would get him.

Some nights she threw them all.

Extending the Text

6. Walter Mitty could be seen as one of a line of archetypal American characters, beginning with Benjamin Franklin's "self-made man." What does Mitty's life reveal about the opportunities for heroism and "self making" today? Do you agree with Thurber's assessment of modern life?

7. Walter Mitty and the formidable Mrs. Mitty have become **stock character** types in American popular culture. Brainstorm a list of popular movies and TV sitcoms in which similar husbands and wives can be found. Why do these character types endure? Do you think changing views of gender roles will eventually make these stock characters obsolete? Explain.

From "The Night the Bed Fell" (top) and "The Night the Ghost Got In" (bottom) from *My Life and Hard Times*. Copyright © 1933 by James Thurber. Copyright © renewed 1961 by James Thurber. Reprinted by arrangement with Rosemary A. Thurber and the Barbara Hogenson Agency.

4. Thurber parodies military jargon in the war fantasies and technical jargon in the hospital fantasy. But the central targets are stereotypical movies, novels, and their stock characters—such as the heroic surgeon, sharpshooter, and flight commander.

5. In these standard types of fantasies, Mitty can be dashing, heroic, and admirable, all the elements missing from his daily life. The daydreaming offers an escape from daily life yet might also prevent him from honestly confronting his reality.

Extending the Text [Synthesize]

6. For Thurber, heroism exists primarily in the realm of fantasy; he sees little chance for the "ordinary" person to be outstanding in daily life. Some students may argue that even small achievements and common acts of bravery can be heroic; others, in contrast, will agree with Thurber's assessment.

7. Possible responses: *The Honeymooners* and *The Simpsons,* for example, use some stock characters, which endure because people are entertained by the way they exaggerate the differences between men and women, but it seems likely that new stock characters will evolve as the media portray more nontraditional families.

MAKING MEANINGS

First Thoughts [Respond]

1. Possible response: Most students will agree that many people enjoy rich fantasy lives in which they play heroic roles.

Shaping Interpretations [Interpret]

2. The central irony in Mitty's life is the contrast between his ineffectual life and his heroic daydreams. It is both humorous and sad.

3. Driving to town sparks Mitty's fantasy about piloting the Navy plane; Mrs. Mitty's rebuke about speeding ends it. Gloves send him into the operating-room fantasy; the parking-lot attendant's yell ends it. A newsboy's shout about the Waterbury trial sets off the courtroom fantasy; calling someone a "miserable cur" reminds him to buy puppy biscuits, which ends it. An article about the German air force leads into the bomber fantasy, which ends with Mrs. Mitty slapping his shoulder. Smoking a cigarette leads into the firing-squad fantasy.

Reading Check

a. His errands include buying overshoes and puppy biscuits.

b. He commands a warplane, performs a tricky surgical procedure, testifies at a murder trial, and executes a critical military mission.

Rubrics for each Choices assignment appear on p. 163 in the *Portfolio Management System.*

CHOICES: Building Your Portfolio

1. **Writer's Notebook**   If students choose to freewrite on a computer, suggest that they turn off the monitor. This will enable them to generate their thoughts without concern for grammar, usage, and mechanics. Students can turn the monitor back on when they have addressed all the questions and then read over their freewriting and add any additional ideas that come to them.

2. **Comparing Characters**   Suggest that students brainstorm ideas by using a Venn diagram. Have them describe Mr. and Mrs. Van Winkle in the left circle, Mr. and Mrs. Mitty in the right circle, and the couples' similarities in the intersection.

3. **Creative Writing**   Suggest that students first list incidents in the story that might spark Mrs. Mitty's daydreams, such as her visit to the hairdresser.

4. **Art/Creative Writing**   Students may wish to use a computer drawing program to create their cartoons.

5. **Drama**   Have each group select a director to guide the production, assign roles, and set a timetable. Allow students time to organize and rehearse, but establish dates and expectations.

6. **Creative Writing**   Remind students to use the correct form for a business letter, including the date, inside address, salutation, and complimentary close.

CHOICES: Building Your Portfolio

Writer's Notebook
1. Collecting Ideas for an Analysis of Causes and Effects

Imagine that you are a psychological counselor who has been assigned to the Walter Mitty case. Freewrite your speculations about the causes of Mitty's tendency to daydream and the possible effects if he continues to rely on fantasy. You'll want to consider these points:

- What is Mitty's problem? Is he a potential psychopath or merely a timid, disappointed romantic—or something else?
- What are some factors in Mitty's life that cause him to seek refuge in fantasy? What evidence or reasons make you think this?
- What will be the result(s) if Mitty continues his daydreaming?
- What's your recommendation? Should Mitty give up his daydreams, try to make some of them come true, or do something else?

Keep your notes for possible use in the Writer's Workshop on page 685.

Comparing Characters
2. The Gender Gap

Thurber has been accused of being "tough" on women, a criticism that has also been leveled against Washington Irving for his portrait of Dame Van Winkle (page 154). In a brief essay, compare and contrast these two famous American couples—Rip and Dame Van Winkle, and Walter and Mrs. Mitty. At the end of your essay, describe your response to the character types used in each story to make us laugh.

Creative Writing
3. The Secret Life of Mrs. Mitty

Everybody has fantasies in which they escape from their everyday lives. What do you think *Mrs.* Mitty daydreams about? Brainstorm a list of elements you would include in a story about Mrs. Mitty's everyday experiences and her contrasting daydreams. Use your list to write an episode in "The Secret Life of Mrs. Mitty."

Art / Creative Writing
4. Thoroughly Modern Mitty

Charles M. Schulz's character Snoopy (see *Connections* on page 630) is truly cast in the Walter Mitty mold. Try creating your own cartoon version of a contemporary Walter Mitty. What heroic fantasies might he or she escape to?

Drama / Performance
5. Dramatic Action

Because it contains five different fantasy settings and a recurring real-life setting, this story translates well into drama or film. (In fact, in 1947 the story was made into a movie starring Danny Kaye.) Work with a group of classmates to create a short play or video drama based on the story. Assign parts, and create costumes and props. Perform the scene for your class, or videotape it.

Creative Writing
6. Dear Mr. Thurber

In his lifetime, James Thurber sometimes complained that he received too many letters from students. Yet he answered such letters graciously and candidly. Write a letter in which you tell Thurber what you think of his story, giving reasons for your opinion.

From "The Dog That Bit People" from *My Life and Hard Times.* Copyright © 1933 by James Thurber. Copyright © renewed 1961 by James Thurber. Reprinted by arrangement with Rosemary A. Thurber and the Barbara Hogenson Agency.

Making the Connection

Connecting to the Theme: "The Dream and the Reality"

Mitty's dreams, unlike Dexter's in "Winter Dreams," pp. 587–602, are not the kind that can lead him to achieve a real, positive aspiration; they are merely useless, grandiose fantasies that shield him from a reality he hates. Ask students to discuss what might help Mitty improve his real life.

Eudora Welty

(1909–   )

© Rollie McKenna.

Eudora Welty was born in the quintessentially Southern city of Jackson, Mississippi, and she has lived in Jackson almost her whole life. As the daughter of an insurance man and a schoolteacher, she enjoyed a conventional girlhood. She recalls pleading with her brothers to teach her golf, sharing their enthusiasm for baseball, and bicycling to the library in *two* petticoats to forestall the librarian's caustic remark, "I can practically see through you."

Welty attended Mississippi State College for Women, graduated from the University of Wisconsin, and did graduate work at Columbia University, anticipating a career in advertising. However, the Depression sent her home to Jackson with a belief, which did not fail her, that she would succeed as a writer of fiction.

Welty's widely recognized triumph is a painstaking accuracy in colloquial speech. The exactly right word always matters to her. She has always been fascinated by words, by the *way* people say things, by snatches of overheard dialogue. She was once delighted to hear a country woman confess to "a gnawing and a craving" for something. Telling a friend about it, Welty added, "Wasn't that a wonderful way of putting it? A gnawing and a craving!"

She greatly admires the work of Katherine Anne Porter (page 702), who befriended her when she was sending out stories and getting back rejection slips. It was the literary agent Diarmuid Russell who shared Welty's belief in an ultimate success. He not only took her on as a client, but also said of a certain Welty story that if the editor didn't accept it, the two ought to "horsewhip the offending editor for his insult to literature." (The editor in question bought the story.)

Welty's first collections of stories, *A Curtain of Green* and *The Wide Net,* appeared in the 1940s. These were followed by *The Golden Apples* (1949), one of her best-known volumes of short stories. Then came a novella, *The Ponder Heart* (1954), which was made into a Broadway play. *Losing Battles,* Welty's fine comic novel about a family reunion in the rural South, was published in 1970. Two years later, Welty produced *The Optimist's Daughter,* a poignant short novel about family conflicts; this book won her the Pulitzer Prize. An autobiographical memoir entitled *One Writer's Beginnings,* based on lectures Welty gave at Harvard University, was published in 1983 to wide critical acclaim.

Welty admits to being blessed with a visual mind, and she says that this gift makes for "the best shorthand a writer can have." She once wrote, "To watch everything about me I regarded grimly and possessively as a *need.*" Clearly, that need became an enviable artistic vision.

 go.hrw.com
LE0 11-12

EUDORA WELTY **633**

 — *Resources: Print and Media* —

Reading
• *Graphic Organizers for Active Reading,* p. 62
• *Words to Own,* p. 38
• *Audio CD Library*   Disc 17, Track 1

Elements of Literature
• *Literary Elements*
    Transparency 21
    Worksheet, p. 64

Writing and Language
• *Daily Oral Grammar*   Transparency 40

• *Grammar and Language Links*
    Worksheet, p. 55

Assessment
• *Formal Assessment,* p. 125
• *Portfolio Management System,* p. 165
• *Preparation for College Admission Exams,* p. 43
• *Test Generator (One-Stop Planner CD-ROM)*

Internet
• go.hrw.com (keyword: LE0 11-12)

OBJECTIVES
1. Read and interpret the story
2. Analyze theme
3. Express understanding through critical and creative writing
4. Understand and use new words

SKILLS
Literary
• Analyze theme

Writing
• Collect ideas for an analysis of causes and effects
• Analyze the story as a mythic quest
• Write an original story

Vocabulary
• Use new words

Viewing/Representing
• Analyze a photograph (ATE)

Planning

• **Block Schedule**
  Block Scheduling Lesson Plans with Pacing Guide
• **Traditional Schedule**
  Lesson Plans Including Strategies for English-Language Learners
• **One-Stop Planner**
  CD-ROM with Test Generator

BROWSING IN THE FILES

In her autobiographical work *One Writer's Beginnings,* Eudora Welty emphasizes the importance of stories in her childhood: "Long before I wrote stories, I listened for stories. Listening for them is something more acute than listening to them. I suppose it's an early form of participation in what goes on. Listening children know stories are there. When their elders sit and begin, children are just waiting and hoping for one to come out, like a mouse from its hole."

Summary ■ ■

On a cold winter day, Phoenix Jackson, a poor, elderly African American woman, walks from her rural home to the city of Natchez, Mississippi. Along the way she overcomes obstacles in nature, comes upon a scarecrow and a dog, and encounters a hunter who both helps and threatens her. When she finally reaches her destination, she is patronized by a receptionist at a doctor's office. Only then do readers learn the ostensible reason for this perilous journey—to obtain medicine for her seriously ill grandson. It is a journey that Phoenix—whose name symbolizes regeneration—has made many times and will continue to make as long as she has the strength to walk the "worn path" of love.

Background

As Eudora Welty explains in the short essay that follows this story, she was inspired to write "A Worn Path" by the sight of an old woman walking slowly across a wintry landscape. Welty then invented the errand that would send the woman on her journey and the passing encounters that form the plot. Be sure to have students read this essay (pp. 640–641) when they finish reading "A Worn Path."

Before You Read
A WORN PATH

Make the Connection

The Perilous Journey

From earliest times, storytellers have used the perilous journey as a metaphor for life. When we think of a perilous journey, we might conjure up images of a steely, larger-than-life hero or heroine who endures incredible hardships and faces monstrous adversaries. But a perilous journey can be a much more ordinary—even everyday—affair, on a road as modest and simple as a worn path.

Quickwrite

The major character in this story is named Phoenix Jackson. Before you read, look up the word *phoenix* in a dictionary. Then, write down your prediction of what a character named Phoenix might be like.

Elements of Literature

Theme

The plot of the story you are about to read is very simple, but its **themes**—its main insights into life—are subtle and complex. You may need a second reading to be sure you have grasped what Eudora Welty is implying in her low-key narrative about Phoenix Jackson's walk down a worn path.

To get a handle on the theme, first visualize the story and characters in a literal sense: who they are, where they are, and what they are doing. Then, visualize people and circumstances that are very different—perhaps your own life or the lives of other people you know. Ask yourself how knowing about Phoenix Jackson's path might help you understand your own path or that of someone you know.

> The **theme** of a story is its main idea or insight into life.
>
> *For more on Theme, see the Handbook of Literary Terms.*

Background

Phoenix makes her journey in rural Mississippi, late in the Depression era of the 1930s. This story offers several clues to how a person's race determined his or her social status in that time and place.

Pages 634 and 640: A woman of the thirties, Hinds County (1935) by Eudora Welty. Photograph.

Eudora Welty Collection, Mississippi Department of Archives and History.

A Worn Path

Eudora Welty

Preteaching Vocabulary

Words to Own

Have small groups of students read the definitions of the Words to Own listed at the bottom of the selection pages. Then, have volunteers in each group act out the meanings of the adjectives: *persistent, meditative, intent, ceremonial,* and *solemn.*

Use the following exercise to deepen students' understanding of the words in context. Choose the vocabulary word that fits best:
1. repeated and [persistent] knocks
2. mail carriers on their [appointed] rounds
3. a child who was as [intent] as a judge
4. a farmer plowing a [furrow] in the field
5. the swinging [pendulum] marking out time
6. the professor's [ceremonial] robes
7. the glowing lamp that [illumined] her face
8. the [radiation] of spokes in the wheel
9. the [meditative] monk sitting by a stream
10. the [solemn] funeral procession

It was December—a bright frozen day in the early morning. Far out in the country there was an old Negro woman with her head tied in a red rag, coming along a path through the pinewoods. Her name was Phoenix Jackson. She was very old and small and she walked slowly in the dark pine shadows, moving a little from side to side in her steps, with the balanced heaviness and lightness of a pendulum in a grandfather clock. She carried a thin, small cane made from an umbrella, and with this she kept tapping the frozen earth in front of her. This made a grave and persistent noise in the still air, that seemed meditative like the chirping of a solitary little bird.

She wore a dark striped dress reaching down to her shoe tops, and an equally long apron of bleached sugar sacks, with a full pocket: all neat and tidy, but every time she took a step she might have fallen over her shoelaces, which dragged from her unlaced shoes. She looked straight ahead. Her eyes were blue with age. Her skin had a pattern all its own of numberless branching wrinkles and as though a whole little tree stood in the middle of her forehead, but a golden color ran underneath, and the two knobs of her cheeks were illumined by a yellow burning under the dark. Under the red rag her hair came down on her neck in the frailest of ringlets, still black, and with an odor like copper.

Now and then there was a quivering in the thicket. Old Phoenix said, "Out of my way, all you foxes, owls, beetles, jack rabbits, coons, and wild animals! . . . Keep out from under these feet, little bobwhites. . . . Keep the big wild hogs out of my path. Don't let none of those come running in my direction. I got a long way." Under her small black-freckled hand her cane, limber as a buggy whip, would switch at the brush as if to rouse up any hiding things.

Finally, trembling all over, she stood free, and after a moment dared to stoop for her cane.

On she went. The woods were deep and still. The sun made the pine needles almost too bright to look at, up where the wind rocked. The cones dropped as light as feathers. Down in the hollow was the mourning dove—it was not too late for him.

The path ran up a hill. "Seem like there is chains about my feet, time I get this far," she said, in the voice of argument old people keep to use with themselves. "Something always take a hold of me on this hill—pleads I should stay."

After she got to the top she turned and gave a full, severe look behind her where she had come. "Up through pines," she said at length. "Now down through oaks."

Her eyes opened their widest, and she started down gently. But before she got to the bottom of the hill a bush caught her dress.

Her fingers were busy and intent, but her skirts were full and long, so that before she could pull them free in one place they were caught in another. It was not possible to allow the dress to tear. "I in the thorny bush," she said. "Thorns, you doing your appointed work. Never want to let folks pass, no sir. Old eyes thought you was a pretty little *green* bush."

Finally, trembling all over, she stood free, and after a moment dared to stoop for her cane.

"Sun so high!" she cried, leaning back and

WORDS TO OWN

pendulum (pen′dyoo·ləm) *n.:* freely swinging weight suspended from a fixed point to regulate a clock's movement.
persistent (pər·sist′ənt) *adj.:* continuing.
meditative (med′ə·tāt′iv) *adj.:* deeply thoughtful; reflective.
illumined (i·loo′mənd) *v.:* lighted up.
intent (in·tent′) *adj.:* purposeful.
appointed (ə·point′id) *v.* used as *adj.:* assigned.

EUDORA WELTY 635

A Critical Thinking
Analyzing
? What is Phoenix doing as the story opens? [She is walking along a country path on an early December morning.] What does this opening imply about her journey? [Possible responses: She has been traveling for some time; her journey will be long.]

B Literary Connections
Remind students that storytellers often use journeys as metaphors for life: Odysseus's journey home and Huck Finn's raft trip on the Mississippi are examples. Ask students to consider as they read, in what ways Phoenix Jackson's journey may be symbolic.

C Elements of Literature
Imagery
Ask students to select one detail from this description that appeals to these senses: sight, smell, touch, hearing. [Possible responses: sight—the red rag; smell—the odor of copper; touch—light as a feather; hearing—the mourning dove.]

D Critical Thinking
Interpreting
? What do you think the thorny bush might symbolize? [Possible response: the unexpected difficulties one must overcome on the path of life.]

E Elements of Literature
Characterization
? Why does Phoenix talk to herself and to the plants? [Possible responses: to give herself courage; because she is thinking out loud; because she is elderly and is no longer bothered by what other people might think.]

Reaching All Students

Struggling Readers
As you read the first four paragraphs of p. 635 aloud, ask students to listen for clues about Phoenix Jackson's character. Then, call on volunteers to list details about Phoenix on the board. If students have trouble, ask questions such as "What do you learn about Phoenix by the way she talks to plants and wild animals?" Finally, encourage students to read on to see why she is making her journey and whether she succeeds.

English Language Learners
English language learners may find it difficult to "hear" the sound of dialect simply by reading it silently. Ask them to listen to the recording of the selection in the *Audio CD Library.* For additional strategies to supplement instruction for these students, see
• *Lesson Plans Including Strategies for English-Language Learners*

Advanced Learners
Ask students to choose another story that uses a journey as a metaphor for life—perhaps a fairy tale, Tolkien's *The Hobbit,* Homer's *Odyssey,* John Steinbeck's *The Grapes of Wrath,* or even a nonfiction work, such as William Least Heat-Moon's *Blue Highways* or Steinbeck's *Travels with Charley*—and compare and contrast it with "A Worn Path." Suggest that they begin by comparing heroes, types of obstacles, sources of help and strength, and finally, themes.

A Reading Skills and Strategies

Connecting with the Text

? Do you think most people talk to themselves—at least occasionally? If so, when are people most likely to do so? [Students may suggest that people talk to themselves during times of stress, loneliness, or intense concentration. All three conditions apply to Phoenix.]

B Reading Skills and Strategies

Visualizing

? What simile is used to describe Phoenix's progress across the log? ["like a festival figure in some parade"] Based on the simile, how do you visualize the character? [Possible responses: like a large puppet; like a stiff marionette.]

C Struggling Readers

Distinguishing Fantasy and Reality

Make sure students understand that Phoenix is dreaming when she sees the boy with the marble cake. Ask why they think she would imagine this particular scene. [Possible response: She is tired and hungry.] Ask students to look for similar incidents later in the story.

D English Language Learners

Understanding Dialect

Tell students that in Southern rural dialect, the word *nary* means "not one" or "not any." Help them paraphrase the dialogue in standard English: "Whose ghost are you? I haven't heard of any deaths near here." (See also Skill Link on p. T637.)

E Appreciating Language

Imagery

? What kind of setting do these images create? [The setting is magical, full of color and sound, and at this point quite comforting and hospitable.]

---

looking, while the thick tears went over her eyes. "The time getting all gone here."

At the foot of this hill was a place where a log was laid across the creek.

A "Now comes the trial," said Phoenix.

B Putting her right foot out, she mounted the log and shut her eyes. Lifting her skirt, leveling her cane fiercely before her, like a festival figure in some parade, she began to march across. Then she opened her eyes and she was safe on the other side.

"I wasn't as old as I thought," she said.

But she sat down to rest. She spread her skirts on the bank around her and folded her hands over her knees. Up above her was a tree in a pearly cloud of mistletoe. She did not dare to close her **C** eyes, and when a little boy brought her a plate with a slice of marble cake on it she spoke to him. "That would be acceptable," she said. But when she went to take it there was just her own hand in the air.

So she left that tree, and had to go through a barbed-wire fence. There she had to creep and crawl, spreading her knees and stretching her fingers like a baby trying to climb the steps. But she talked loudly to herself: She could not let her dress be torn now, so late in the day, and she could not pay for having her arm or her leg sawed off if she got caught fast where she was.

At last she was safe through the fence and risen up out in the clearing. Big dead trees, like black men with one arm, were standing in the purple stalks of the withered cotton field. There sat a buzzard.

"Who you watching?"

In the <u>furrow</u> she made her way along.

"Glad this not the season for bulls," she said, looking sideways, "and the good Lord made his snakes to curl up and sleep in the winter. A pleasure I don't see no two-headed snake coming around that tree, where it come once. It took a while to get by him, back in the summer."

She passed through the old cotton and went into a field of dead corn. It whispered and shook and was taller than her head. "Through the maze now," she said, for there was no path.

Then there was something tall, black, and skinny there, moving before her.

At first she took it for a man. It could have been a man dancing in the field. But she stood still and

636 THE MODERNS

---

listened, and it did not make a sound. It was as silent as a ghost.

D "Ghost," she said sharply, "who be you the ghost of? For I have heard of nary death close by."

But there was no answer—only the ragged dancing in the wind.

She shut her eyes, reached out her hand, and touched a sleeve. She found a coat and inside that an emptiness, cold as ice.

"You scarecrow," she said. Her face lighted. "I ought to be shut up for good," she said with laughter. "My senses is gone. I too old. I the oldest people I ever know. Dance, old scarecrow," she said, "while I dancing with you."

E She kicked her foot over the furrow, and with mouth drawn down, shook her head once or twice in a little strutting way. Some husks blew down and whirled in streamers about her skirts.

Then she went on, parting her way from side to side with the cane, through the whispering field. At last she came to the end, to a wagon track where the silver grass blew between the red ruts. The quail were walking around like pullets, seeming all dainty and unseen.

"Walk pretty," she said. "This the easy place. This the easy going."

She followed the track, swaying through the quiet bare fields, through the little strings of trees silver in their dead leaves, past cabins silver from weather, with the doors and windows boarded shut, all like old women under a spell sitting there. "I walking in their sleep," she said, nodding her head vigorously.

In a ravine she went where a spring was silently flowing through a hollow log. Old Phoenix bent and drank. "Sweet gum makes the water sweet," she said, and drank more. "Nobody know who made this well, for it was here when I was born."

The track crossed a swampy part where the moss hung as white as lace from every limb. "Sleep on, alligators, and blow your bubbles." Then the track went into the road.

Deep, deep the road went down between the high green-colored banks. Overhead the live oaks met, and it was as dark as a cave.

WORDS TO OWN

furrow (fur'ō) *n*.: groove in the land made by a plow.

Using Students' Strengths

Naturalist Learners

Use a guided-imagery exercise to help students picture Phoenix's trek through nature. Working in pairs, students should take turns reading passages from p. 636 aloud and sketching or describing Phoenix's struggles as she marches over the log, crawls through the barbed wire, passes through fields, dances with the scarecrow, drinks from the stream, and crosses the swamp. Have them list what Phoenix sees, hears, smells, tastes, and touches.

Interpersonal Learners

Jigsaw Reading. After students have read the story, form them into "home" groups of four students each. Have one member of each home group become expert on one of these elements: (1) setting, (2) motivation, (3) conflict, (4) suspense. Form "expert" groups for the literary elements. Each group will analyze the importance that its element has in "A Worn Path." Finally, have the "experts" present what they have learned to their home groups.

Logical/Mathematical Learners

The story's open ending leaves a puzzle students will enjoy trying to solve; in the process, they will need to review the story's details. Is Phoenix Jackson's grandson dead or alive? (See pp. 640–641.) Have a group of students review the story to find and list evidence for both possibilities. Have the group report its reasoning to the class.

A black dog with a lolling tongue came up out of the weeds by the ditch. She was meditating, and not ready, and when he came at her she only hit him a little with her cane. Over she went in the ditch, like a little puff of milkweed.

Down there, her senses drifted away. A dream visited her, and she reached her hand up, but nothing reached down and gave her a pull. So she lay there and presently went to talking. "Old woman," she said to herself, "that black dog come up out of the weeds to stall you off, and now there he sitting on his fine tail, smiling at you."

A white man finally came along and found her—a hunter, a young man, with his dog on a chain. "Well, Granny!" he laughed. "What are you doing there?"

"Lying on my back like a June bug waiting to be turned over, mister," she said, reaching up her hand.

He lifted her up, gave her a swing in the air, and set her down. "Anything broken, Granny?"

"No sir, them old dead weeds is springy enough," said Phoenix, when she had got her breath. "I thank you for your trouble."

"Where do you live, Granny?" he asked, while the two dogs were growling at each other.

"Away back yonder, sir, behind the ridge. You can't even see it from here."

"On your way home?"

"No sir, I going to town."

"Why, that's too far! That's as far as I walk when I come out myself, and I get something for my trouble." He patted the stuffed bag he carried, and there hung down a little closed claw. It was one of the bobwhites, with its beak hooked bitterly to show it was dead. "Now you go on home, Granny!"

"I bound to go to town, mister," said Phoenix. "The time come around."

He gave another laugh, filling the whole landscape. "I know you old colored people! Wouldn't miss going to town to see Santa Claus!"

But something held old Phoenix very still. The deep lines in her face went into a fierce and different radiation. Without warning, she had seen with her own eyes a flashing nickel fall out of the man's pocket onto the ground.

"How old are you, Granny?" he was saying.

"There is no telling, mister," she said, "no telling."

Then she gave a little cry and clapped her hands and said, "Git on away from here, dog! Look! Look at that dog!" She laughed as if in admiration. "He ain't scared of nobody. He a big black dog." She whispered, "Sic him!"

"Watch me get rid of that cur," said the man. "Sic him, Pete! Sic him!"

Phoenix heard the dogs fighting, and heard the man running and throwing sticks. She even heard a gunshot. But she was slowly bending forward by that time, further and further forward, the lids stretched down over her eyes, as if she were doing this in her sleep. Her chin was lowered almost to her knees. The yellow palm of her hand came out from the fold of her apron. Her fingers slid down and along the ground under the piece of money with the grace and care they would have in lifting an egg from under a setting hen. Then she slowly straightened up, she stood erect, and the nickel was in her apron pocket. A bird flew by. Her lips moved. "God watching me the whole time. I come to stealing."

The man came back, and his own dog panted about them. "Well, I scared him off that time," he said, and then he laughed and lifted his gun and pointed it at Phoenix.

She stood straight and faced him.

"Doesn't the gun scare you?" he said, still pointing it.

"No, sir, I seen plenty go off closer by, in my day, and for less than what I done," she said holding utterly still.

He smiled, and shouldered the gun. "Well, Granny," he said, "you must be a hundred years old, and scared of nothing. I'd give you a dime if I had any money with me. But you take my advice and stay home, and nothing will happen to you."

"I bound to go on my way, mister," said Phoenix. She inclined her head in the red rag. Then they went in different directions, but she could hear the gun shooting again and again over the hill.

She walked on. The shadows hung from the oak trees to the road like curtains. Then she smelled woodsmoke, and smelled the river, and she saw a steeple and the cabins on their steep

------

WORDS TO OWN

radiation (rā′dē·ā′shən) *n.*: pattern; arrangement.

EUDORA WELTY **637**

Skill Link

A Elements of Literature

Theme

❓ How does Phoenix's reliance on her feet emphasize the title and theme of the story? [Possible responses: Phoenix has made the trip so many times that her feet have worn a figurative path to her destination; Phoenix's journey is so important to her that her feet know the route "by heart."]

B Appreciating Language

Imagery

❓ What impression does the "tower of steps" produce? [Possible response: an endless climb, particularly difficult for an elderly person.]

C Reading Skills and Strategies

Making Inferences

❓ Considering the clue of the medical certificate, what dream do you think is in Phoenix's head? [Once students know the reason for Phoenix's trip, most will say her dream is to heal her grandson.]

D Critical Thinking

Analyzing

❓ Why is the reason for Phoenix's journey not revealed earlier? [Possible responses: Not knowing the reason makes us wonder why Phoenix goes on; it helps us see her journey as a symbol of the universal struggle through life; it adds suspense.]

E Critical Thinking

Interpreting

❓ How would you explain Phoenix's spell? [Possible responses: Some students will say that Phoenix is ill, because she loses touch with reality; others will say she has had only a short-term memory loss, as sometimes happens to old people; still others will see these spells as one of her sources of strength.]

F Historical Connections

Phoenix is referring to "the Surrender" that ended the Civil War. On April 9, 1865, the Confederate commander, Robert E. Lee, surrendered to the Union commander, Ulysses S. Grant, at the Appomattox Court House in Virginia. The war's end paved the way for the end of slavery. Phoenix's remark reveals that she was once a slave and that at the time of this story, in the 1930s, she is in her eighties.

---

steps. Dozens of little black children whirled around her. There ahead was Natchez shining. Bells were ringing. She walked on.

A In the paved city it was Christmas time. There were red and green electric lights strung and crisscrossed everywhere, and all turned on in the daytime. Old Phoenix would have been lost if she had not distrusted her eyesight and depended on her feet to know where to take her.

She paused quietly on the sidewalk where people were passing by. A lady came along in the crowd, carrying an armful of red-, green-, and silver-wrapped presents; she gave off perfume like the red roses in hot summer, and Phoenix stopped her.

"Please, missy, will you lace up my shoe?" She held up her foot.

"What do you want, Grandma?"

"See my shoe," said Phoenix. "Do all right for out in the country, but wouldn't look right to go in a big building."

"Stand still then, Grandma," said the lady. She put her packages down on the sidewalk beside her and laced and tied both shoes tightly.

"Can't lace 'em with a cane," said Phoenix. "Thank you, missy. I doesn't mind asking a nice lady to tie up my shoe, when I gets out on the street."

B Moving slowly and from side to side, she went into the big building, and into a tower of steps, where she walked up and around and around until her feet knew to stop.

C She entered a door, and there she saw nailed up on the wall the document that had been stamped with the gold seal and framed in the gold frame, which matched the dream that was hung up in her head.

"Here I be," she said. There was a fixed and ceremonial stiffness over her body.

"A charity case, I suppose," said an attendant who sat at the desk before her.

But Phoenix only looked above her head. There was sweat on her face, the wrinkles in her skin shone like a bright net.

"Speak up, Grandma," the woman said. "What's your name? We must have your history, you know. Have you been here before? What seems to be the trouble with you?"

Old Phoenix only gave a twitch to her face as if a fly were bothering her.

638 THE MODERNS

"Are you deaf?" cried the attendant.

But then the nurse came in.

D "Oh, that's just old Aunt Phoenix," she said. "She doesn't come for herself—she has a little grandson. She makes these trips just as regular as clockwork. She lives away back off the Old Natchez Trace." She bent down. "Well, Aunt Phoenix, why don't you just take a seat? We won't keep you standing after your long trip." She pointed.

The old woman sat down, bolt upright in the chair.

"Now, how is the boy?" asked the nurse.

Old Phoenix did not speak.

"I said, how is the boy?"

But Phoenix only waited and stared straight ahead, her face very solemn and withdrawn into rigidity.

"Is his throat any better?" asked the nurse. "Aunt Phoenix, don't you hear me? Is your grandson's throat any better since the last time you came for the medicine?"

E With her hands on her knees, the old woman waited, silent, erect and motionless, just as if she were in armor.

"You mustn't take up our time this way, Aunt Phoenix," the nurse said. "Tell us quickly about your grandson, and get it over. He isn't dead, is he?"

At last there came a flicker and then a flame of comprehension across her face, and she spoke.

"My grandson. It was my memory had left me. There I sat and forgot why I made my long trip."

"Forgot?" The nurse frowned. "After you came so far?"

F Then Phoenix was like an old woman begging a dignified forgiveness for waking up frightened in the night. "I never did go to school, I was too old at the Surrender," she said in a soft voice. "I'm an old woman without an education. It was my memory fail me. My little grandson, he is just the same, and I forgot it in the coming."

"Throat never heals, does it?" said the nurse, speaking in a loud, sure voice to old Phoenix. By

---

WORDS TO OWN

ceremonial (ser'ə·mō'nē·əl) *adj.*: formal.
solemn (säl'əm) *adj.*: serious.

Getting Students Involved

Cooperative Learning

Scenes and Snapshots. After students have read the story, share with them the Critical Comment on p. T640. Discuss how "The Worn Path" is like "a collection of scenes and snapshots." Then form students into four groups. Have each group brainstorm in order to decide on a visual technique to use to retell the story. They might create an album of "snapshots" or a storyboard for a film of the story by drawing the scenes.

They might pantomime the scenes, using props and costumes and acting out the roles of the human characters and the plants, animals, and scarecrow. Tell groups to draw on their members' strengths and assign them clearly defined tasks, such as researchers to find out information about the time period, resource people to collect materials or costumes and props, and artists to draw. Invite groups to present their works to the class.

Courthouse town, Grenada (1935), by Eudora Welty. Photograph. Eudora Welty Collection, Mississippi Department of Archives and History.

> *Old Phoenix held the bottle close to her eyes, and then carefully put it into her pocket.*

now she had a card with something written on it, a little list. "Yes. Swallowed lye. When was it?—January—two-three years ago—"

Phoenix spoke unasked now. "No, missy, he not dead, he just the same. Every little while his throat begin to close up again, and he not able to swallow. He not get his breath. He not able to help himself. So the time come around, and I go on another trip for the soothing medicine."

"All right. The doctor said as long as you came to get it, you could have it," said the nurse. "But it's an obstinate case."

"My little grandson, he sit up there in the house all wrapped up, waiting by himself," Phoenix went on. "We is the only two left in the world. He suffer and it don't seem to put him back at all. He got a sweet look. He going to last. He wear a little patch quilt and peep out holding his mouth open like a little bird. I remembers so plain now. I not going to forget him again, no, the whole enduring time. I could tell him from all the others in creation."

"All right." The nurse was trying to hush her now. She brought her a bottle of medicine. "Charity," she said, making a check mark in a book.

Old Phoenix held the bottle close to her eyes, and then carefully put it into her pocket.

"I thank you," she said.

"It's Christmas time, Grandma," said the attendant. "Could I give you a few pennies out of my purse?"

"Five pennies is a nickel," said Phoenix stiffly.

"Here's a nickel," said the attendant.

Phoenix rose carefully and held out her hand. She received the nickel and then fished the other nickel out of her pocket and laid it beside the new one. She stared at her palm closely, with her head on one side.

Then she gave a tap with her cane on the floor.

"This is what come to me to do," she said. "I going to the store and buy my child a little windmill they sells, made out of paper. He going to find it hard to believe there such a thing in the world. I'll march myself back where he waiting, holding it straight up in this hand."

She lifted her free hand, gave a little nod, turned around, and walked out of the doctor's office. Then her slow step began on the stairs, going down.

EUDORA WELTY 639

Eudora Welty (1909–) worked for the Works Progress Administration (WPA) during the 1930s. As part of her job, she traveled throughout Mississippi, writing news stories and taking photographs of people suffering from the effects of the Great Depression. During that time, she took hundreds of photographs and learned lessons she would apply to her writing. In *One Writer's Beginnings,* she says: "Life doesn't hold still. A good snapshot stopped a moment from running away. Photography taught me that to be able to capture transience, by being ready to click the shutter at the crucial moment, was the greatest need I had. Making pictures of people in all sorts of situations, I learned that every feeling waits upon its gesture; and I had to be prepared to recognize this moment when I saw it. These were things a story writer needed to know."

Activity. Ask students what feelings Eudora Welty may have hoped to capture in the portrait of the woman on this page. Ask them what qualities the facial expression and posture of the woman convey. [Possible responses: dignity; determination.] Ask students whether the woman resembles their image of Phoenix Jackson.

Fayette (1930s), by Eudora Welty. Photograph.
Eudora Welty Collection, Mississippi Department of Archives and History.

The path is the thing that matters.
— Eudora Welty

Primary Sources

Eudora Welty discusses a question she is frequently asked: Is Phoenix Jackson's grandson really *dead?* She answers this question by saying it doesn't really matter. It is the old woman's journey that counts.

PRIMARY Sources — AN ESSAY

"Is Phoenix Jackson's Grandson Really Dead?"

A story writer is more than happy to be read by students; the fact that these serious readers think and feel something in response to his work he finds life-giving. At the same time he may not always be able to reply to their specific questions in kind. I wondered if it might clarify something, for both the questioners and myself, if I set down a general reply to the question that comes to me most often in the mail,

from both students and their teachers, after some classroom discussion. The unrivaled favorite is this: "Is Phoenix Jackson's grandson really *dead?*"

. . . I had not meant to mystify readers by withholding any fact; it is not a writer's business to tease. The story is told through Phoenix's mind as she undertakes her errand. As the author at one with the character as I tell it, I must assume that the boy is alive. As the reader, you are free to think as you like, of course: The story invites you to believe that no matter what happens, Phoenix for as long as she is able to walk and can hold to her purpose

Professional Notes

Critical Comment: Visual Technique

Read this comment from Carol Ann Johnston, in *Eudora Welty: A Study of the Short Fiction,* aloud, and ask students to discuss it in light of the story: "Given Welty's visual mind, we should not be surprised to find that she uses a visual technique as the fundamental organizing principle in her stories. Individual stories often seem like a collection of scenes or snapshots rather than the sequential, causal telling of a plot. Early in her career, Welty often combined this . . . narrative strategy with a journey motif; the linear structures of the journey anchored her use of her visually grounded technique, giving a shape to the emotional revelation that an action-filled plot would otherwise provide a more traditional story."

Courthouse steps, Fayette (1930s), by Eudora Welty. Photograph.

Eudora Welty Collection, Mississippi Department of Archives and History.

will make her journey. The *possibility* that she would keep on even if he were dead is there in her devotion and its single-minded, single-track errand. Certainly the *artistic* truth, which should be good enough for the fact, lies in Phoenix's own answer to that question. When the nurse asks, "He isn't dead, is he?" she speaks for herself: "He still the same. He going to last."

The grandchild is the incentive. But it is the journey, the going of the errand, that is the story, and the question is not whether the grandchild is in reality alive or dead. It doesn't affect the outcome of the story or its meaning from start to finish. But it is not the question itself that has struck me as much as the idea, almost without exception implied in the asking, that for Phoenix's grandson to be dead would somehow make the story "better."

. . . The grandson's plight was real and it made the truth of the story, which is the story of an errand of love carried out. If the child no longer lived, the truth would persist in the "wornness" of the path. But his being dead can't increase the truth of the story, can't affect it one way or the other. I think I signal this, because the end of the story has been reached before old Phoenix gets home again:

she simply starts back. To the question "Is the grandson really dead?" I could reply that it doesn't make any difference. I could also say that I did not make him up in order to let him play a trick on Phoenix. But my best answer would be: "*Phoenix* is alive."

The origin of a story is sometimes a trustworthy clue to the author—or can provide him with the clue—to its key image; maybe in this case it will do the same for the reader. One day I saw a solitary old woman like Phoenix. She was walking; I saw her, at middle distance, in a winter country landscape, and watched her slowly make her way across my line of vision. That sight of her made me write the story. I invented an errand for her, but that only seemed a living part of the figure she was herself: What errand other than for someone else could be making her go? And her going was the first thing, her persisting in her landscape was the real thing, and the first and the real were what I wanted and worked to keep. I brought her up close enough, by imagination, to describe her face, make her present to the eyes, but the full-length figure moving across the winter fields was the indelible one and the image to keep, and the perspective extending into the vanishing distance the true one to hold in mind.

I invented for my character, as I wrote, some passing adventures—some dreams and harassments and a small triumph or two, some jolts to her pride, some flights of fancy to console her, one or two encounters to scare her, a moment that gave her cause to feel ashamed, a moment to dance and preen—for it had to be a *journey,* and all these things belonged to that, parts of life's uncertainty.

. . . What I hoped would come clear was that in the whole surround of this story, the world it threads through, the only certain thing at all is the worn path. The habit of love cuts through confusion and stumbles or contrives its way out of difficulty, it remembers the way even when it forgets, for a dumbfounded moment, its reason for being. The path is the thing that matters.

—Eudora Welty

A Literary Connections

You may want to tell students that some schools of literary criticism would not place importance on Welty's comments about her story. Some of these critics would say that a reader can independently analyze the elements of the story to derive a meaning different from Welty's. These critics believe that the experience of reading the text is unique for each reader and that these unique experiences are more important than what Welty intended. Have students discuss these viewpoints in light of their own responses to the story and their other experiences with literature.

Making the Connections

Connecting to the Theme: "The Dream and the Reality"

After students have discussed Welty's essay, talk about the theme. Point out that although the elderly heroine sometimes has trouble distinguishing fantasy and reality, she is firmly grounded in a vitally important reality of life—the "worn path" of love. According to Welty, devotion to others is what keeps a person going through life. Do students agree that it doesn't matter whether the grandson is dead or alive—that only the worn path matters?

Crossing the Curriculum

Geography

Ask students to go back to the story to find details of the countryside and then draw a map of the journey that Welty created for Phoenix. Then have them look up the geography of Mississippi, especially the area near Natchez. What is the terrain like? How big is Natchez? Compare it with how it was in the 1930s.

Science

Invite students to take a nature walk in their community, as a class or in supervised groups. Have them keep journal entries on the plants, insects, and animals they see. Have them compare their entries with the flora and fauna of Mississippi that Phoenix encounters.

MAKING MEANINGS

First Thoughts [Respond]

1. Possible response: The old woman's determination impressed me. Students may wonder why the story ends where it does or what will happen later.

Shaping Interpretations [Interpret]

2. Possible responses: The phoenix, a mythical bird that is periodically reborn from its own ashes, symbolizes renewal. The name is fitting because Phoenix renews her love for her grandson time after time—regardless of his actual condition.

3. Possible responses: Phoenix's kinship with plants and animals and the comparison of wrinkles on her forehead to a small tree identify her with nature. Her perseverance and her ability to "last" identify her with time.

4. Possible responses: With the boy, Phoenix is polite; with the buzzard, imaginative; with the scarecrow, humorous; with the bush, optimistic; with the hunter, courageous and sly. She is like traditional heroines, but unlike them in her age and physical strength.

5. The hunter's suggestion that Phoenix is on a frivolous and childish trip is ironic because she is on a mature and difficult errand of love. Racism, sexism, or ageism may explain the condescension.

6. Phoenix's act of charity for her grandson is performed at great sacrifice, whereas the nurse's self-congratulatory giving is anything but charitable.

7. "The habit of love" implies a steady, long-term commitment filled with daily loving acts. The other images suggest unused, transient, or glamorous pathways.

8. The title suggests the habitual path of love enables Phoenix to prevail. This suggests Welty's theme: The path of love—worn by sacrifice and repetition—is open to all.

Grading Timesaver

Rubrics for each Choices assignment appear on p. 165 in the *Portfolio Management System*.

1–2. Tell students to create a chart to organize their ideas.

3. Suggest they choose a symbolic name for the character.

MAKING MEANINGS

First Thoughts

1. What was your first reaction to the story: "Good story!" or "I don't get it"— or another response? What questions do you have about the story?

> ### Reading Check
>
> a. Describe the purpose of Phoenix Jackson's journey, and list the obstacles she overcomes.
>
> b. At the end of Phoenix's perilous journey, does she get what she wants? Explain.

Shaping Interpretations

2. Why is Phoenix an appropriate name for the main character? (Review your Quickwrite notes.)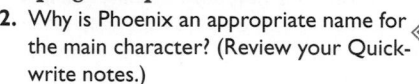

3. How do Welty's **descriptions** of Phoenix's appearance, speech, and behavior identify her with the world of nature and with time itself?

4. Describe what Phoenix's encounters with the little boy, the buzzard, the scarecrow, the thorny bush, and the hunter tell us about her **character.** Is she a heroine in the traditional sense of the word? Why or why not?

5. What is **ironic** about the reason the hunter suggests for Phoenix's long journey? Many people treat Phoenix in a condescending manner. Why would they do this?

6. When the nurse gives Phoenix the medicine, she says, "Charity," and makes a check mark in her book. Given the character of Phoenix, what is **ironic** about the nurse's statement and action?

7. Welty says that the worn path is a **metaphor** for the habit of love. Explain what Welty means by "the habit of love," and tell why this habit might be compared with a worn path (and not with a new road, or the shining path of a rocket, or a crystal stairway).

8. What do you consider Welty's major **theme** in "A Worn Path"? Put another way, what "worn path" is open to us all?

> ### Reading Check
>
> a. Phoenix's purpose: to get her grandson medicine. Obstacles: an uphill climb; crossing a creek on a log; getting through barbed wire; fending off a dog; standing up to a hunter's threat.
>
> b. She succeeds: She gets the medicine and prepares to buy her grandson a gift.

CHOICES:
Building Your Portfolio

> ### Writer's Notebook
>
> ### 1. Collecting Ideas for an Analysis of Causes and Effects
>
>
>
> This story reveals in an indirect way the effects of racism and segregation. Take notes on what you can infer about the effects of segregation on people like Phoenix—and on the white hunter. Or, you might want to approach the situation from another perspective: Take notes on what you infer to be the causes of segregation in Phoenix's community—why would people want to separate themselves from other people? Save your notes for the Writer's Workshop on page 685.
>
> ### Analyzing a Story
>
> ### 2. Stages of the Journey
>
> In her comment on the story (page 640), Welty summarizes the purposes of the adventures she invented for Phoenix. In an essay, identify the specific parts of the journey that can be characterized as **(a)** dreams, **(b)** harassments, **(c)** small triumphs, **(d)** some jolts to the traveler's pride, **(e)** some flights of fancy to console the traveler, **(f)** encounters to scare the traveler, **(g)** cause to be ashamed, and **(h)** a moment to dance and preen. In your essay, explain how Phoenix's journey takes on mythic significance. How is it like the quests of heroes like Odysseus or fairy-tale heroes and heroines?
>
> ### Creative Writing
>
> ### 3. Enduring a Worn Path
>
> Write a story of your own about a person who travels a worn path over and over again without complaint. Open your story with a description of your setting: the time and place of the action. Let us see your main traveler as clearly as Welty shows us Phoenix. Your story may be fiction, or it may be based on fact.

Collection 13

No Time for Heroes

Theme

A Lost Generation *As Sherwood Anderson said of World War I, "War blew up more than the bodies of men.... It blew ideas away." In the horror of modern warfare, is heroism possible? Writers now explore the antihero, the character who embodies qualities opposite of those once called heroic. Hemingway is the key writer here; the full-blown ironic hero is found in Flannery O'Connor's repellent Mr. Shiftlet.*

Reading the Anthology

Reaching Struggling Readers

The *Reading Skills and Strategies: Reaching Struggling Readers* binder provides materials coordinated with the Pupil's Edition (see the Collection Planner, p. T642B) to help students who have difficulty reading and comprehending text, or students who are reluctant readers. The binder for eleventh grade is organized around ten individual skill areas and offers the following options:

- **MiniRead** MiniReads are short, easy texts that give students a chance to practice a particular skill and strategy before reading selections in the Pupil's Edition. Each MiniRead Skill Lesson can be taught independently or used in conjunction with a Selection Skill Lesson.

- **Selection Skill Lessons** Selection Skill Lessons allow students to apply skills introduced in the MiniReads. Each Selection Skill Lesson provides reading instruction and practice specific to a particular piece of literature in the Pupil's Edition.

Reading Beyond the Anthology

Read On

At the end of The Moderns collections, the grade eleven book includes an annotated bibliography of books suitable for extended reading. The suggested books are related to works in these collections by theme, by author, or by subject. To preview the Read On for The Moderns period, please turn to p. T800.

Resources for this Collection

Note: All resources for this collection are available for preview on the *One-Stop Planner CD-ROM 2 with Test Generator.* All worksheets and blackline masters may be printed from the CD-ROM.

Internet Resources
go.hrw.com LE0 11-13

Selection or Feature	Reading and Literary Skills	Vocabulary, Language, and Grammar
• **Richard Cory** (p. 645) • **Miniver Cheevy** (p. 646) Edwin Arlington Robinson **Primary Sources: Robinson's Ruminations** (p. 648) Edwin Arlington Robinson	• *Graphic Organizers for Active Reading,* Worksheet pp. 63, 64	
Soldier's Home (p. 652) Ernest Hemingway **Primary Sources: Nobel Prize Acceptance Speech, 1954** (p. 659) Ernest Hemingway	• *Graphic Organizers for Active Reading,* Worksheet p. 65	• *Words to Own,* Worksheet p. 39 • *Grammar and Language Links:* Repetition and Wordiness, Worksheet p. 57 • *Language Workshop CD-ROM,* Revising to Reduce Wordiness • *Daily Oral Grammar,* Transparency 41
The Love Song of J. Alfred Prufrock (p. 663) T. S. Eliot **Critical Comment: The Oddest Love Song** (p. 667) **Connections:** *from* **Mr. Eliot, I Presume** (p. 668) John Malcolm Brinnin	• *Graphic Organizers for Active Reading,* Worksheet p. 66	• *Daily Oral Grammar,* Transparency 42

The Life You Save May Be Your Own (p. 673)
Flannery O'Connor
 	
Primary Sources: The Adventures of Mr. Shiftlet (p. 682)
Flannery O'Connor
 	
Elements of Literature: The Four "Modes" of Fiction (p. 683)
	• *Reading Skills and Strategies: Reaching Struggling Readers*
	  • MiniRead Skill Lesson, p. 93
	  • Selection Skill Lesson, p. 99
	• *Graphic Organizers for Active Reading,* Worksheet p. 67
	• *Literary Elements:* Transparency 22 Worksheet p. 67
		• *Words to Own,* Worksheet p. 40
		• *Daily Oral Grammar,* Transparency 43

Writer's Workshop: Analyzing Causes and Effects (p. 685)		
Language Workshop: Using Subordinating Conjunctions (p. 689)		• *Workshop Resources,* p. 58 • *Language Workshop CD-ROM,* Subordinating Conjunctions

Other Resources for this Collection

- *Cross-Curricular Activities*, p. 13
- *Portfolio Management System*, Introduction to Portfolio Assessment, p. 1
- *Test Generator*, Collection Test

Writing	Listening and Speaking / Viewing and Representing	Assessment
• *Portfolio Management System*, Rubrics for Choices, p. 166	• *Audio CD Library*, Disc 18, Tracks 2, 3 • *Portfolio Management System*, Rubrics for Choices, p. 166	• *Formal Assessment*, Selection Test, p. 127 • *Test Generator (One-Stop Planner CD-ROM)*
• *Portfolio Management System*, Rubrics for Choices, p. 167	• *Audio CD Library*, Disc 18, Track 4 • *Portfolio Management System*, Rubrics for Choices, p. 167	• *Formal Assessment*, Selection Test, p. 129 • *Test Generator (One-Stop Planner CD-ROM)* • *Preparation for College Admission Exams*, p. 45
• *Portfolio Management System*, Rubrics for Choices, p. 168	• *Viewing and Representing:* Fine Art Transparency 13 Worksheet p. 52 • *Portfolio Management System*, Rubrics for Choices, p. 168	• *Formal Assessment*, Selection Test, p. 131 • *Test Generator (One-Stop Planner CD-ROM)*
• *Portfolio Management System*, Rubrics for Choices, p. 170	• *Audio CD Library*, Disc 18, Track 5 • *Portfolio Management System*, Rubrics for Choices, p. 170	• *Formal Assessment*, Selection Test, p. 132 • *Test Generator (One-Stop Planner CD-ROM)* • *Preparation for College Admission Exams*, p. 47
• *Workshop Resources*, p. 27 • *Writer's Workshop 2 CD-ROM*, Cause and Effect	• *Viewing and Representing*, HRW Multimedia Presentation Maker	• *Portfolio Management System* • Prewriting, p. 172 • Peer Editing, p. 173 • Assessment, p. 174

Collection Planner

 Transparency    CD-ROM    Video    Audio CD

Skills Focus

Skills Focus

Selection or Feature	Reading Skills and Strategies	Elements of Literature and Language	Writing	Listening and Speaking	Viewing and Representing
• **Richard Cory** (p. 645) • **Miniver Cheevy** (p. 646) Edwin Arlington Robinson	Identify Words with a Specific Connotation, p. 649	Irony, p. 649 Contrast, p. 649 Personification, p. 649 Tone, p. 649	Brainstorm Possible Causes for a Character's Actions, p. 649 Write an Essay Comparing and Contrasting Values, p. 649	Write and Present the Story of Richard Cory as a Dramatic Monologue, p. 649	
Soldier's Home (p. 652) Ernest Hemingway	Read for Details, pp. 652, 660	Character Profile, p. 660 Conflict, p. 660 Theme, p. 660 Protagonist, p. 660	Freewrite a Speculation About a Character's Future, p. 660 Write an Essay Interpreting a Character, p. 660 Write an Essay Analyzing an Author's Style, p. 660	Write and Perform a Script of a Scene from the Story, p. 660	
The Love Song of J. Alfred Prufrock (p. 663) T. S. Eliot	Identify Main Ideas and Supporting Details, pp. 663 Understand Rhythms, Rhymes, Metaphors, and Allusions, p. 670 Paraphrase Lines from a Poem, p. 670 Determine Meaning from Context, p. 670	Dramatic Monologue, pp. 663, 671 Character, p. 669 Simile, p. 669 Image, pp. 669, 671 Metaphor, pp. 669–670 Extended Metaphor, p. 669 Setting, p. 669 Metrical Pattern, p. 670 Rhythm, p. 670 End Rhymes, p. 670 Internal Rhymes, p. 670 Allusion, p. 670 Resolution, p. 671	Write Speculations About the Causes of Prufrock's Isolation, p. 671 Write an Essay Comparing Characters in Two Poems, p. 671 Write a Critical Response to a Review, p. 671 Write a Dramatic Monologue, p. 671 Write an Essay Comparing and Contrasting Three Characters, p. 671	Write and Perform a Dialogue Between Prufrock and Another Person, p. 671	Draw a Cartoon Based on the Poem, p. 671
The Life You Save May Be Your Own (p. 673) Flannery O'Connor	Make Predictions, pp. 673 Identify Connotative Words and Figures of Speech, p. 683	Foreshadowing, pp. 673, 683 Suspense, p. 673 Irony, pp. 683–684 Figures of Speech, p. 683 Theme, p. 683 Modes of Fiction, pp. 683–684 • Tragedy • Comedy • Romance • Irony	Collect Ideas for an Analysis of Causes and Effects, p. 684 Write an Essay Analyzing a Story, p. 684 Write a Sequel to the Story, p. 684	Participate in a Class Discussion Based on the Author's Comments About the Story, p. 684	Design a Bumper Sticker Suitable for a Character in the Story, p. 684
Writer's Workshop: Analyzing Causes and Effects (p. 685)		Inductive Thinking, p. 687 Evidence, p. 687 Generalization, p. 687	Write an Essay Analyzing the Causes and/or the Effects of an Event, Situation, or Trend, pp. 685–688		Use a Graphic to Organize Information, p. 686
Language Workshop: Using Subordinating Conjunctions (p. 689)		Subordinating Conjunctions, p. 689	Revise Sentences Using Subordinating Conjunctions to Show Relationships, p. 689		
Reading for Life: Interpreting and Constructing a Graphic Organizer (p. 690)	Recognize the Types and Purposes of Graphic Organizers, p. 690				Determine the Type of Graphic Best Suited to a Particular Purpose, p. 690

Skills Focus

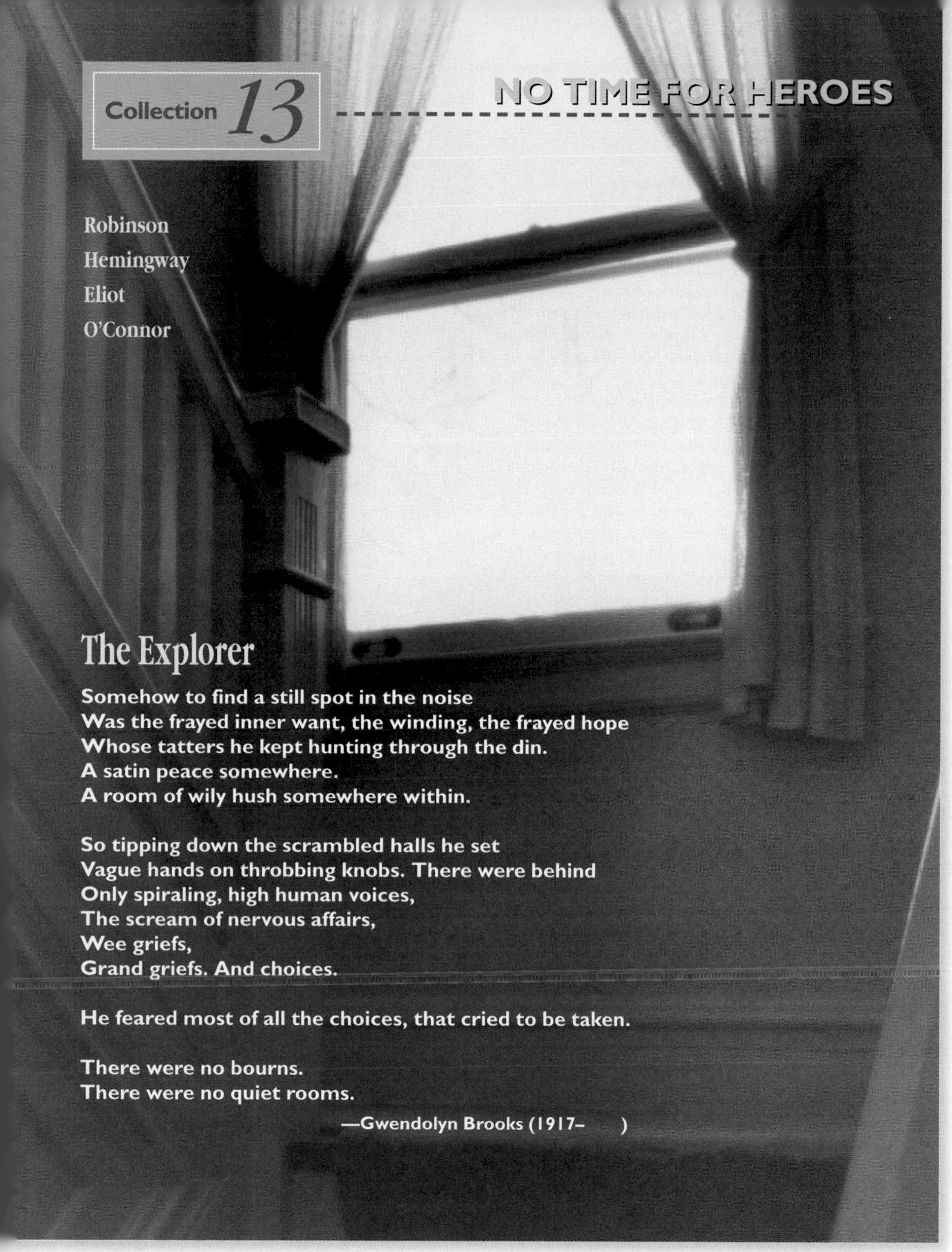

Robinson
Hemingway
Eliot
O'Connor

The Explorer

Somehow to find a still spot in the noise
Was the frayed inner want, the winding, the frayed hope
Whose tatters he kept hunting through the din.
A satin peace somewhere.
A room of wily hush somewhere within.

So tipping down the scrambled halls he set
Vague hands on throbbing knobs. There were behind
Only spiraling, high human voices,
The scream of nervous affairs,
Wee griefs,
Grand griefs. And choices.

He feared most of all the choices, that cried to be taken.

There were no bourns.
There were no quiet rooms.

—Gwendolyn Brooks (1917–   )

OBJECTIVES

1. Read literature of the Modern period on the theme "No Time for Heroes"
2. Interpret literary elements used in the literature, including dramatic monologue, foreshadowing, and the four modes of fiction
3. Apply a variety of reading strategies, including making predictions and reading for details
4. Respond to the literature in a variety of modes
5. Learn and use new words
6. Collect ideas for a cause-and-effect essay

Responding to the Poem

? A *bourn* is an archaic word for domain or home turf. **What is the explorer in this poem looking for?** [a quiet place; peace; escape from worry and anxiety] **What do you think the building symbolizes?** [Possible answers: society; the pressures of life; the explorer's inner self.] **What relationship do you see between this poem and the collection theme?** [Possible response: Modern protagonists are often tormented by indecision, anxiety, and social pressures and often fail as traditional heroes. There may be no heroes in modern life or *heroism* may need to be redefined.]

Resources ————

Viewing and Representing
Videocassette A, Segment 1
Available in Spanish and English.
This segment explores the American dream through our literary heritage. For full lesson plans and worksheets see, *Visual Connections Teacher's Manual.*

Writing Focus: Analyzing Causes and Effects

The following **Work in Progress** assignments in this collection build to a culminating **Writer's Workshop** at the end of Collection 13.

• Richard Cory; Miniver Cheevy	Brainstorm causes of characters' actions (p. 649)
• Soldier's Home	Speculate about effects of character's war experience (p. 660)
• The Love Song of J. Alfred Prufrock	Speculate on causes of Prufrock's condition (p. 671)
• The Life You Save May Be Your Own	Speculate about why irony is dominant mode (p. 684)

Writer's Workshop: Expository Writing / Analyzing Causes and Effects (p. 685)

Planning

Edwin Arlington Robinson

(1869–1935)

By the 1890s, the vitality of the nineteenth century seemed exhausted, and the gathering forces of modernism were still scattered and obscure. Between 1890 and 1910, many poets were churning out the same old rhymes and meters of Romanticism. But in those two decades, one voice spoke out in traditional forms enlivened with an authentic, contemporary American accent: the voice of Edwin Arlington Robinson.

The strengths that distinguish Robinson are his native voice and his wise and ironic view of human behavior. Robinson's bedrock realism informs even the most formal of his carefully wrought poems. In some of his poetic portraits of individuals, he anticipates by a decade the more loosely drawn portraits found in Edgar Lee Masters's *Spoon River Anthology* (page 692). In his skill with meter, Robinson foreshadows Robert Frost's gift for bending the strictly counted line to accommodate the ease and flow of vernacular speech.

Robinson was a Yankee from the rocky coast of Maine. Born at Head Tide in 1869, he lived for the next twenty-seven years in the town of Gardiner, except for the two years when he attended Harvard as a special student. Gardiner became the Tilbury Town of his poems, the home of some of his most famous characters. When he was in his late twenties, Robinson moved to New York City and published his first book. There he supported himself at various jobs, including one as a timekeeper at the construction site of the new subway system.

After a year of such work, Robinson's fortunes took a surprising turn for the better. Among the young poet's readers was none other than the president of the United States, Theodore Roosevelt. When Roosevelt learned that the poet he admired was barely scraping by on a laborer's salary, he arranged to have the

AP/Wide World Photos.

New York Custom House hire him as a clerk, a position Robinson held for almost five years. One year after Robinson resigned, he published *The Town Down the River* (1910) and dedicated the volume to Roosevelt.

Another form of assistance came in an invitation from the famous MacDowell Colony in Peterborough, New Hampshire. The colony is a center for composers, artists, and writers, established by the widow of the American composer Edward MacDowell. There Robinson spent long, working summers for the greater part of his life.

Robinson, a loner by temperament, became an increasingly popular poet. Even in a modernist age, Robinson's poetry, which was traditional in form, continued to be read and admired, and he was awarded a Pulitzer Prize three times. At the time of his death, Robinson's reputation had survived the tide of modernism that had once threatened to wash it away.

 **go.hrw.com**
LE0 11-13

 *Resources: Print and Media*

One of the persistent themes of early-twentieth-century American poetry is that the conventions of small-town life are a façade that often obscures unpleasant realities. (Some say similar façades still exist today, in cities as well as in small towns.) In this famous poem, which contains a harsh, surprise ending, an unidentified speaker tells what happened to a prominent citizen.

Quickwrite
Can we accurately determine the inner feelings of a person by observing his or her outward behavior? Write a few sentences stating your opinion, supported by specific reasons.

Winter Twilight (1930) by Charles Burchfield.
Oil on composition board (27¾" × 39½").

Collection of Whitney Museum of American Art (31.128).
Photograph © 1998 Whitney Museum of American Art.

Richard Cory

Edwin Arlington Robinson

Whenever Richard Cory went downtown,
    We people on the pavement looked at him:
He was a gentleman from sole to crown,
    Clean favored, and imperially slim.

5 And he was always quietly arrayed,
    And he was always human when he talked;
But still he fluttered pulses when he said,
    "Good morning," and he glittered when he walked.

And he was rich—yes, richer than a king—
10   And admirably schooled in every grace:
In fine, we thought that he was everything
    To make us wish that we were in his place.

So on we worked, and waited for the light,
    And went without the meat, and cursed the bread;
15 And Richard Cory, one calm summer night,
    Went home and put a bullet through his head. **C**

EDWIN ARLINGTON ROBINSON 645

Reaching All Students

Struggling Readers
Ask students to reformulate this narrative poem as a prose story. For information on using this strategy, see p. 127 of the *Reading Strategies Handbook* in the *Reading Skills and Strategies* binder. Who is the main character? How do other people feel about him? What happens to him? Tell them to be sure to include all the details of the poem.

English Language Learners
Several idioms in this poem should be explained. When the speaker says Cory was "always human," he means he acted like a regular person. In l. 7, "fluttered pulses" indicates that Cory's presence excited people. "In fine" (l. 11) simply means "in sum" or "all in all." For additional strategies to engage students with the literature, see
• *Lesson Plans Including Strategies for English Language Learners*

Summary ∎
In this ironic poem, a local resident describes Richard Cory—a wealthy, dapper, polite and sophisticated gentleman, who is envied by his less prosperous neighbors. They are shocked when he commits suicide.

RESPONDING TO THE ART
Charles Burchfield (1893–1967) specialized in scenes of rural and small-town America. *(For more biographical information, see p. T674.)*
Activity. Ask students how the mood of the painting suits the poem. [The dark colors, relieved only by a few spots of light, and the isolated human figures, suggest the dark mood of the poem and Cory's isolation.]

A **Reading Skills and Strategies**
  Making Inferences
❓ What can you infer about the speaker of the poem from the first stanza? [The speaker is one of the townspeople. Note that Cory goes "downtown" and the contrast between the people on the "pavement" and the "gentleman" who is "imperially" slim.]

B **Critical Thinking**
  Interpreting
❓ What assumptions do people make about Cory because he is rich? [Sample responses: They assume he is happy; they think he has everything; they wish they were "in his place."]

C **Elements of Literature**
  Irony
❓ Now that you know Cory's fate, why is it ironic that the townspeople envied him? [Possible responses: They had no idea that he was suffering; despite his wealth and good fortune, his troubles turn out to be harder to bear than theirs.]

Summary ■ ■

Miniver Cheevy wishes he lived in a more glorious past, among heroes, knights, and prancing steeds. He despises drab modern surroundings and the need to earn money. While cursing the fate that caused him to be born in the wrong century, he drinks to forget his misery.

Ⓐ Elements of Literature
Rhyme and Meter

❓ Would you describe the rhyme and meter of this poem as regular or irregular? [very regular] How does this singsong quality affect your expectations of the poem? [Possible answer: It sounds as if it's going to be funny.]

Ⓑ Struggling Readers
Listing Details

To get struggling readers into the poem, go through each stanza with them and ask them to list everything that Cheevy misses or mourns. You could be the scribe and put their lists on the chalkboard. At the end of this exercise, ask them to select what they think is the most important line, phrase or word from the poem. They should be able to explain their choices. (Be prepared for someone to choose the last line.)

Ⓒ Critical Thinking
Speculating

❓ How do you think Cheevy would react if he got his wish to live in the past? [Possible answer: He might find he still had to work—perhaps harder!—and wish to return to his own time.]

Ⓓ Advanced Learners

Have students expand on the historical allusions to Thebes, Camelot, and Priam in stanza three. For instance, some students may know that Oedipus answered the Sphinx's riddle outside Thebes or that King Arthur reigned in Camelot.

Make the Connection
Long Ago and Far Away
The glory and glamour of bygone days hold an irresistible charm for many of us. But sometimes a longing for the past leaves people sorely disappointed with the present.

Quickwrite
On a sheet of paper, write down some reasons why a person might be drawn to splendid times in the distant past.

Background
The title of this poem is not simply a man's name: It contains a clue to the poem's meaning. "Miniver" is the white fur trim, sometimes ermine, seen on the costumes of royalty in medieval and Renaissance portraits. The subjects of such portraits include rich and powerful members of the Medici family of Renaissance Italy. Other references in the poem also evoke heroic eras of the past.

Miniver Cheevy

Edwin Arlington Robinson

Miniver Cheevy, child of scorn,
   Grew lean while he assailed the seasons;
He wept that he was ever born,
   And he had reasons.

5 Miniver loved the days of old
   When swords were bright and steeds were prancing:
The vision of a warrior bold
   Would set him dancing.

Miniver sighed for what was not,
10   And dreamed, and rested from his labors;
He dreamed of Thebes° and Camelot,°
   And Priam's° neighbors.

Miniver mourned the ripe renown
   That made so many a name so fragrant;
15 He mourned Romance, now on the town,°
   And Art, a vagrant.

11. Thebes: city in ancient Greece associated with several myths.
Camelot: legendary site of King Arthur's court.
12. Priam's: In Homer's epic poem *The Iliad,* Priam (prī′əm) is the king of Troy during the Trojan War.
15. on the town: dependent on charity.

Using Students' Strengths

Auditory/Musical Learners
Have students prepare "Richard Cory" and "Miniver Cheevy" for performance. You might suggest that groups alternate choral readings with solo voices. Before they read, students should prepare scripts and indicate where lines run on, which lines need special emphasis, and where certain sound effects, such as alliteration, should be stressed.

Interpersonal Learners
Have students form small groups to discuss how Cory and Cheevy might have improved their situations. Start groups off by having them consider what each man's problems are and why each man seems isolated from his neighbors. Next, encourage students to suggest a wide range of solutions for the characters' problems. Students then can collaborate on a letter of advice to each character.

The Sentimental Yearner (1936) by Grant Wood. Pencil, black and white conté crayon, painted white around image.
The Minneapolis Institute of Arts; Gift of Alan Goldstein, 1980. © Estate of Grant Wood/Licensed by VAGA, New York, NY.

EDWIN ARLINGTON ROBINSON **647**

Crossing the Curriculum

History

Have students research small-town life in their own state during the early 1900s. Have them focus on the basic facts of existence: What existed in terms of schooling, transportation, access to cities, jobs, housing, health care? What was life like for women and minorities?

Music

Have students compare Robinson's "Richard Cory" to the Paul Simon and Art Garfunkel song of the same name. Pass around copies of the lyrics; then play a recording of the song for the class. Have students list the similarities and differences between the song and the poem. Then have them explain which they prefer and why.

A Elements of Literature
Irony
❓ How is the phrase "medieval grace of iron clothing" ironic? [This phrase is almost oxymoronic, or self-contradictory, because no one can be graceful in armor. It shows that the speaker is satirizing Cheevy's romantic illusions.]

B Appreciating Language
Word Choice
❓ Why do you think Robinson repeats the word "thought" four times? [Possible responses: to show the extent of Cheevy's brooding; to echo the repetitiousness of Cheevy's thoughts; to show that Cheevy does nothing about his "problem."]

C Reading Skills and Strategies
Responding to the Text
❓ Were you surprised by the ending of the poem? [Students might wonder what the coughing signifies—tuberculosis? Responses to the drinking will vary—some may see it as the key to Miniver's problem.]

Primary Sources

In these letters to Edith Brower, Robinson introduces the poem "Richard Cory," defends the poem after Brower's negative response, and discusses his poetic technique.

Ask students to speculate on what Edith Brower might have written to Robinson that prompted the second excerpt. Then have them write a letter from Brower to Robinson based on their guesses.

BROWSING IN THE FILES

A Critic's Comment. American literature scholar Stanley T. Williams writes, "These hard little poems are specimens of human experience in a world in which agony is real and happiness but a wish. . . ." Based on the excerpts from Robinson's letters, do you think he would agree with this critical assessment? Why or why not? [Most students will say the poet would agree, but some might comment on the surprising humor in Robinson's work and in his letters!]

Miniver loved the Medici,°
   Albeit° he had never seen one;
He would have sinned incessantly
20   Could he have been one.

Miniver cursed the commonplace
   And eyed a khaki suit with loathing;
He missed the medieval grace
   Of iron clothing.°

25 Miniver scorned the gold he sought,
   But sore annoyed was he without it;
Miniver thought, and thought, and thought,
   And thought about it.

Miniver Cheevy, born too late,
30   Scratched his head and kept on thinking;
Miniver coughed, and called it fate,
   And kept on drinking.

17. Medici (med′ə·chē′): members of a powerful Italian family of the fourteenth to sixteenth centuries. They were famous for their wealth, their sponsorship of the arts, and their control of the city of Florence.

18. albeit (ôl·bē′it): even though. The word combines and condenses "although it be."

24. iron clothing: armor worn by medieval knights.

PRIMARY Sources — LETTERS

Robinson's Ruminations

I've written a nice little thing called "Richard Cory"—"Whenever Richard Cory went downtown, we people on the pavement looked at him . . . And Richard Cory, one calm summer night, went home and put a bullet through his head." There isn't any idealism in it, but there's lots of something else—humanity, maybe.

. . .

Why don't you like "Richard Cory"? You say it makes you feel cold, but that statement doesn't seem to agree with my impression of your character. It can't be you are squeamish after all. If you are, don't read "Reuben Bright" or he will knock you down. I used to read about clearness, force, and elegance in the rhetoric books, but I'm afraid I go in chiefly for force. So you will not be offended if I'm not always elegant. There are too many elegant men in the world just now, and they seem to be increasing.

. . .

I don't have trances, furors, or ecstasies. My poetic spells are of the most prosaic sort. I just sit down and grind it out and use a trifle more tobacco than is good for me.

. . .

You may call me anything you like—anything but Eddie. I had an aunt who called me Eddie and now she doesn't call me at all.

—Edwin Arlington Robinson,
from Letters to Edith Brower

Making the Connections

Connecting to the Theme: "No Time for Heroes"

Cheevy "cops out" because he believes it is impossible to be a hero in the modern world. Do students agree? What qualities do they think make a hero? You might introduce or review the figure of the tragic hero—a noble, admirable character who falls from a position of prominence to death or disaster. In the process, the tragic hero recognizes a character flaw that helps precipitate the downfall (think of Shakespeare's heroes; see p. 683). Do students think Cory qualifies as a tragic hero? [Students should say no. In literary terms, Cory lives in an ironic world with severe limitations on freedom and no opportunity—it seems—for heroism. In contemporary psychological parlance, he might be diagnosed as clinically depressed.]

Richard Cory

First Thoughts

1. How did you respond to the ending of the poem?

Shaping Interpretations

2. What is **ironic** in the fact that Richard Cory takes his own life? What irony is there in the fact that the night was calm?

3. Find five words or phrases in "Richard Cory" that **connote** kingliness or royalty. How does the poet's choice of these words contribute to the **contrast** between the townspeople and Richard Cory?

4. Does the harsh surprise ending hint that the real story is the one that remains untold? What aspects of Richard Cory's life are *not* mentioned? How might these hidden or overlooked areas account for his fate?

5. Read Robinson's comments on "Richard Cory" (page 648). What do you think he means when he says there is a lot of "humanity" in the poem? Why do you think it made his correspondent feel "cold"? How did it make you feel?

Miniver Cheevy

First Thoughts

1. What were your thoughts or feelings about Cheevy and his attitude toward life?

Shaping Interpretations

2. What do you think "child of scorn" means?

3. Do Cheevy's problems really stem from his having been "born too late"? Explain. How does the disappointed Cheevy cope with his lot in life?

4. "Romance" and "Art" are **personified** in the fourth stanza. What does Cheevy think has happened to romance and art in his own time?

5. How would you describe the change of **tone** in the last stanza? How does this change affect the poem's meaning?

Extending the Texts

6. Explain whether or not you think the tales of Richard Cory and Miniver Cheevy have a moral or message for us today. Where can you find Corys and Cheevys in today's world?

7. Refer to your Quickwrite notes, and tell whether the poems indicate that appearances can be deceiving.

CHOICES:
Building Your Portfolio

Writer's Notebook

1. Collecting Ideas for an Analysis of Causes and Effects

Why does Richard Cory kill himself? Why does Miniver Cheevy suffer so much? Brainstorm a list of causes you could speculate on to answer these questions. With each cause, list details from the poem that might support your speculation. Save your notes for possible use in the Writer's Workshop on page 685.

Comparing and Contrasting Values

2. Rising Above or Mired Below?

In a brief essay, show how either Richard Cory or Miniver Cheevy demonstrates, or fails to demonstrate, the Transcendentalist ideals of self-reliance and individualism championed by Emerson (page 216) and Thoreau (page 230). As the focus of your essay, choose an appropriate quotation from either of these writers.

Creative Writing/Performance

3. From Page to Stage

In prose or verse, let Richard Cory tell his own story in the first person. Reveal the reasons for Cory's unhappiness and his true thoughts about the townspeople. Then, present his story to the class in a dramatic monologue. (For more on dramatic monologue, see page 663 and the Handbook of Literary Terms.)

EDWIN ARLINGTON ROBINSON 649

5. The poet might think that his portrayal of Cory is suffused with pity, and thus human. The speaker's bewilderment is certainly human. Brower may have found the statement about Cory's death cold and without feeling. She might have found Cory's isolation chilling. Students will probably pity Cory.

Miniver Cheevy

First Thoughts [Respond]

1. Students may think Cheevy is foolish, or they may sympathize with his wish to live in a more colorful era.

Shaping Interpretations [Analyze]

2. It may mean that Cheevy's parents scorned him, that he was an "illegitimate" child, or that he is a scornful person.

3. No, no matter when Cheevy lived, he would have longed for something else. Or, yes, some people indeed seem as if they would be better off in an earlier era. Cheevy copes by brooding and drinking.

4. He thinks they have been unappreciated and ignored.

5. The last stanza reveals Cheevy's drinking habit and hints at his ill health. The tone is one of satiric condemnation of Cheevy's unwillingness to deal with his own reality.

Extending the Text [Apply]

6. "Richard Cory": Appearances are deceiving. "Miniver Cheevy": Longing for the impossible leads to failure and unhappiness. Many students will feel that Corys and Cheevys can be found everywhere in today's unheroic, materialistic world.

7. Richard Cory deceives the townspeople, and the poet surprises his readers in this poem. Miniver Cheevy masks his drunken lethargy with longing for "days of old."

Grading Timesaver

Rubrics for each Choices assignment appear on p. 166 in the *Portfolio Management System*.

MAKING MEANINGS

Richard Cory

First Thoughts [Respond]

1. Students may have been shocked by or prepared for the end by the Before You Read page.

Shaping Interpretations [Interpret]

2. Cory seems to have every reason for happiness. The violent act belies the calm of the night.

3. Choices include *crown, imperially, arrayed, glittered, king, grace*. These words contrast with the commonplace words associated with the townspeople: *downtown, pavement, meat,* and *bread*.

4. We never hear of Cory's work, friends, or family. Any of these might have caused him to suffer.

Planning

- **Block Schedule**
  Block Scheduling Lesson Plans with Pacing Guide
- **Traditional Schedule**
  Lesson Plans Including Strategies for English-Language Learners
- **One-Stop Planner**
  CD-ROM with Test Generator

Ernest Hemingway

(1899–1961)

Karsh/Woodfin Camp and Associates.

Few American authors have offered as powerful a definition of the twentieth-century hero as Ernest Hemingway has. Hemingway's fiction presents a strict code of contemporary heroism. His vision centers on disillusionment with the conventions of an optimistic, patriotic society and a belief that the essence of life is violence, from which there is no refuge. As Hemingway saw it, the only victory that can be won from life lies in a graceful stoicism, a willingness to accept gratefully life's few moments of pleasure.

Although this ideal of rugged machismo may now seem superficial, it powerfully affected generations of American readers. Moreover, Hemingway launched a new style of writing so forceful in its simplicity that it became a measure of excellence around the world.

Hemingway's life, like F. Scott Fitzgerald's, bore a notable resemblance to the lives of his fictional characters. He was born in the Chicago suburb of Oak Park on July 21, 1899. His father, a doctor, initiated him early into a love for the Michigan woods and the hunting and fishing that could be found there. Growing up, Hemingway boxed and played football devotedly, but he also wrote poetry, short stories, and a column for the school newspaper. Graduating from high school just as the United States entered World War I in 1917, he yearned to enlist, but he was rejected by the army because of a boxing injury to his eye. He landed a job as a reporter for the *Kansas City Star*. Hemingway reached the war a year later as an ambulance driver for the Red Cross in Italy, but after six weeks he was wounded in the knee, seriously enough to require a dozen operations. This wound was a central episode in both Hemingway's real and creative life. During his long convalescence in an Italian hospital, he fell in love with a nurse who became the model for the heroine of his novel *A Farewell to Arms*.

After the armistice in 1918, Hemingway returned to Michigan. His experience of coming to terms with the war is reflected in his story "Big Two-Hearted River." In the story, Nick Adams, a war veteran, camps and fishes alone in the woods, escaping from the world in order to heal himself from both a physical and psychological shattering.

An American in Paris

In 1921, newly married and with a commission as a roving reporter for the *Toronto Star*, Hemingway set off for Paris. It was the era of the American expatriates, when writers and painters crowded the cafes of the Left Bank of the Seine. Here Hemingway worked at the craft of fiction and met other important writers, among them F. Scott Fitzgerald, James Joyce, and Ezra Pound. But most important, he met the American writer Gertrude Stein (1874–1946). She read all his work and advised him to prune his descriptions and to "concentrate." Hemingway took her advice and spoke fervently of writing "the truest sentence that you know," and of arriving through straight

go.hrw.com
LE0 11-13

presentation of unvarnished fact at a "true, simple declarative sentence."

Hemingway's first book, *Three Stories and Ten Poems* (1923), along with *The Torrents of Spring* (1926), a parody of his friend Sherwood Anderson's work, drew scant notice. Then, late in 1926, he published *The Sun Also Rises*, a novel based on his life in Paris but transplanted to Pamplona, the Spanish town famous for its annual running of the bulls through the streets. The novel brought Hemingway widespread critical attention. Gertrude Stein's remark, "You are all a lost generation," was the novel's epigraph, and the book did reveal the postwar epoch to itself. Many readers of Hemingway's age embraced it as a portrait of their shattered lives.

> "You are all a lost generation."

Hemingway, around thirty years old and married for the second time, went on to write an even more powerful and successful novel, *A Farewell to Arms* (1929). This is the beautifully told story of Frederic Henry, a wounded ambulance driver. Disillusioned with the war, he falls in love with Catherine Barkley, an English nurse, and flees with her to Switzerland, where she dies in childbirth. Frederic's farewell to the dying Catherine is one of the great love scenes in fiction.

Author and Adventurer

After the major success of *A Farewell to Arms,* Hemingway established himself as a worldwide adventurer, as though a heroic style was as important to his life as to his fiction. He fished and hunted wherever new seas and continents beckoned. And he periodically resumed his role as war correspondent, most notably during the Spanish civil war (1936–1939).

During the early 1930s, Hemingway brought out two nonfiction books that revealed his fascination with bullfighting and with big-game hunting—*Death in the Afternoon* (1932) and *Green Hills of Africa* (1935). Significantly, both books centered on the art of killing. In 1940,

just as the literary world was writing Hemingway off as a has-been novelist, he presented another triumph, *For Whom the Bell Tolls.*

The outbreak of World War II drew Hemingway back into uniform. Although officially a correspondent, he gathered around himself a small army of adventurers. During one battle, a First Army commander reported that Hemingway's band was sixty miles in front of the Americans' advancing line. When the Allies at last reached Paris in 1944, they found that Hemingway had already "liberated" the bar at the Ritz Hotel.

By 1952, Hemingway's celebrated literary accomplishments and his continuous pursuit of excitement and danger had made him as famous as any film star. In spite of his flamboyant exploits, he produced yet another widely acclaimed novel in that year, *The Old Man and the Sea,* which won the 1953 Pulitzer Prize. It tells of an old Cuban fisherman who hooks a giant marlin far out at sea and battles the fish for two days and nights. Although he finally succeeds in subduing the great fish and lashing it to the side of his boat, sharks tear at the carcass until the man is left with only the marlin's skeleton. The tale has been interpreted as Hemingway's metaphor for life: a vision of the hero, weighed down by the years, but still able to use his skill to taunt fate and so win a kind of victory from it.

In 1954, Hemingway won the Nobel Prize in literature. He now divided his time between his house in Ketchum, Idaho, and his restless travels all over the world: to Cuba, China, Venice, Spain, and Africa. His health deteriorated, and periods of elation alternated with episodes of severe depression. After a visit to the Mayo Clinic for treatment, he returned to Idaho. On the morning of July 2, 1961, he rose early, and with two charges of a double-barreled shotgun, he killed himself.

"He put life back on the page," wrote the critic Alfred Kazin, "made us see, feel, and taste the gift of life. . . . To read Hemingway was always to feel more alive."

BROWSING IN THE FILES

About the Author. The heroes in Hemingway's short stories are often wounded men—physically and psychologically. They carry with them the memory of violence. Facing a hypocritical world, they seek to find some code by which to live, some way to accept reality. When Hemingway was recuperating from his knee injury, he wrote his family from a Milan hospital: "Wounds don't matter. I wouldn't mind being wounded again so much because I know just what it is like . . . and it does give you an awfully satisfactory feeling to be wounded." During his lifetime Hemingway was repeatedly injured—in car crashes, airplane crashes, shooting accidents, and fires. Like many of the heroes in his novels, he, too, was a wounded man.

Writers on Writing. Hemingway's faith in what he called "the truest sentence" helped produce his distinctive style: "Sometimes when I was starting a new story and I could not get it going, I would sit in front of the fire and squeeze the peel of the little oranges into the edge of the flame and watch the sputter of the blue that they made. I would stand and look out over the roofs of Paris and think, 'Do not worry. You have always written before and you will write now. All you have to do is write one true sentence. Write the truest sentence that you know.' So finally I would write one true sentence, and then go on from there. It was easy then because there was always one true sentence that I knew or had seen or had heard someone say."

Professional Notes

Hemingway on War

Hemingway never forgot his combat experience. In 1935, as he watched Hitler prepare to launch World War II, he wrote, "They wrote in the old days that it is sweet and fitting to die for one's country. But in modern war there is nothing sweet or fitting in your dying. You will die like a dog for no good reason. . . . In a modern war there is no Victory. The allies won the war but the regiments that marched in triumph were not the men who fought the war. The men who fought the war were dead. More than seven million of them were dead and it is the murder of over seven million more that [Hitler and Mussolini] look forward hysterically to today."

Summary ▪️▪️

It is the summer of 1919 in a small Oklahoma town. Hemingway's protagonist, Harold Krebs, has just come home from war. He finds that he is too late for a hero's welcome and that he cannot speak honestly about his war experiences. He makes little effort to readjust to life with his parents and sisters and soon drifts into a passive routine of sleeping late, reading, and playing pool. He notices several pretty young women in town, but he can't make the effort to get to know them. The story's climax takes place when his worried mother confronts him about his future, and he decides to leave home for good.

Background

In order to understand Krebs's state of mind, students should know that the soldiers in France spent their days and nights in mud-filled trenches reeking of urine, poisonous gas, wet sandbags, and decomposing bodies. They fought rain, cold, lice, and rats, as well as diseases such as trench mouth, gangrene, and dysentery. The worst horror, however, was the constant threat of death from the enemy trenches. At any moment, a shell could be lobbed across the barren stretch of barbed wire called "no-man's-land."

RESPONDING TO THE ART

The photograph on the left of this page is of Ernest Hemingway and Agnes von Kurowsky, the twenty-six-year-old American nurse with whom the writer fell in love. This episode from Hemingway's life was fictionalized in the 1997 movie *In Love and War*.

Before You Read
SOLDIER'S HOME

Make the Connection
A Hero's Welcome
World War I was greeted as the "war to end all wars," and songs like "Over There" celebrated the heroism of hundreds of thousands of American soldiers who were shipped off to fight in the trenches of Europe. But advances in weaponry made the Great War devastating, both physically and psychologically. Returning soldiers sometimes couldn't readjust to life back home, which seemed to offer little they could relate to or believe in. As you can imagine, some became disillusioned, cynical, isolated, and overwhelmed by hopelessness. They became the most lost of Gertrude Stein's lost generation.

Reading Skills and Strategies
Reading for Details
As you read the story, try to piece together a **character profile** of the returned soldier Harold Krebs. Take notes on Krebs's feelings, attitudes, and views on the following: the war, his return home, his family, other people, his hometown, and his future.

Background
Soldiers who returned home from World War I were often described as shellshocked—suffering from a mental and emotional condition of confusion, exhaustion, anxiety, and depression. In the past, the condition—now termed *post-traumatic stress disorder*—was not well understood, and friends and relatives often found themselves at a loss. They expected returning soldiers to plunge directly back into civilian life and could not understand why some young men seemed unable to do so.

(Left and opposite page) Photos of Ernest Hemingway in Italy and France during World War I (1918).

Department of Rare Books and Special Collections/Princeton University Libraries.

Leib Image Archives.

Preteaching Vocabulary

Words to Own
Have students read the Words to Own and definitions listed at the bottom of the selection pages. Then have them choose partners. The first student gives his or her partner a word. The second student has to find one synonym and one antonym for it. Have partners alternate roles until they have both worked through all the words. Then have each group complete the following exercise, matching each word with its definition.

1. nauseated [g]	a. horror
2. hysteria [h]	b. false
3. consequences [f]	c. with great care
4. atrocity [a]	d. overstatement
5. elaborately [c]	e. partnerships
6. apocryphal [b]	f. results
7. engagements [j]	g. sickened
8. intrigue [i]	h. excitement
9. alliances [e]	i. plotting
10. exaggeration [d]	j. battles

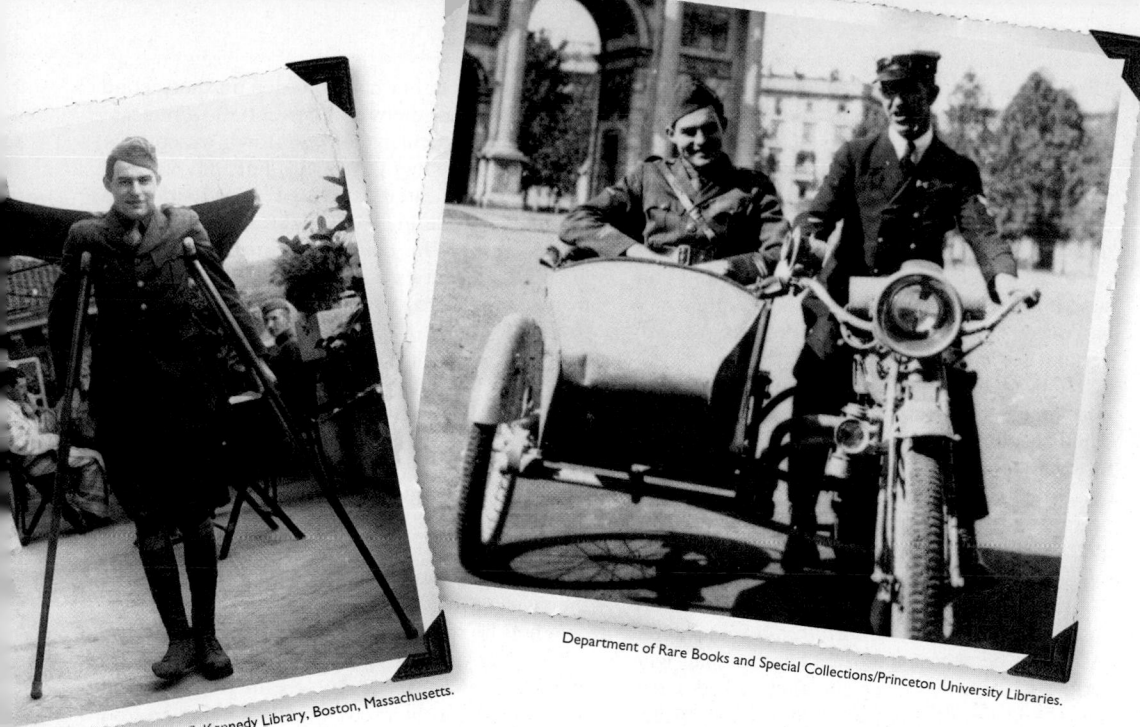

Department of Rare Books and Special Collections/Princeton University Libraries.

John F. Kennedy Library, Boston, Massachusetts.

Soldier's Home Ⓐ

Ernest Hemingway

Krebs went to the war from a Methodist college in Kansas. There is a picture which shows him among his fraternity brothers, all of them wearing exactly the same height and style collar. He enlisted in the Marines in 1917 and did not return to the United States until the second division returned from the Rhine[1] in the summer of 1919.

There is a picture which shows him on the Rhine with two German girls and another corporal. Krebs and the corporal look too big for their uniforms. The German girls are not beautiful. The Ⓑ Rhine does not show in the picture.

By the time Krebs returned to his home town in Oklahoma the greeting of heroes was over. He came back much too late. The men from the town who had been drafted had all been welcomed

1. **Rhine:** river that flows through Germany toward the North Sea.

elaborately on their return. There had been a great deal of hysteria. Now the reaction had set in. People seemed to think it was rather ridiculous for Krebs to be getting back so late, years after the Ⓒ war was over.

At first Krebs, who had been at Belleau Wood, Soissons, the Champagne, St. Mihiel and in the Argonne[2] did not want to talk about the war at all. Later he felt the need to talk but no one wanted to hear about it. His town had heard too many atrocity stories to be thrilled by actualities. Krebs found that to be listened to at all he had to lie, and Ⓓ after he had done this twice he, too, had a reaction against the war and against talking about it. A distaste for everything that had happened to him in the war set in because of the lies he had told.

2. **Belleau** (be·lō′) **Wood . . . Argonne** (är′gän′): sites of World War I battles that demonstrated the Allies' superior strength against the Germans.

WORDS TO OWN
elaborately (ē·lab′ə·rit·lē) *adv.*: with great care.
hysteria (hi·ster′ē·ə) *n.*: uncontrolled excitement.
atrocity (ə·träs′ə·tē) *n.* used as *adj.*: horrible; brutal.

ERNEST HEMINGWAY 653

All of the times that had been able to make him feel cool and clear inside himself when he thought of them; the times so long back when he had done the one thing, the only thing for a man to do, easily and naturally, when he might have done something else, now lost their cool, valuable quality and then were lost themselves.

His lies were quite unimportant lies and consisted in attributing to himself things other men had seen, done or heard of, and stating as facts certain apocryphal incidents familiar to all soldiers. Even his lies were not sensational at the pool room. His acquaintances, who had heard detailed accounts of German women found chained to machine guns in the Argonne forest and who could not comprehend, or were barred by their patriotism from interest in, any German machine gunners who were not chained, were not thrilled by his stories.

Krebs acquired the nausea in regard to experience that is the result of untruth or exaggeration, and when he occasionally met another man who had really been a soldier and they talked a few minutes in the dressing room at a dance he fell into the easy pose of the old soldier among other soldiers: that he had been badly, sickeningly frightened all the time. In this way he lost everything.

During this time, it was late summer, he was sleeping late in bed, getting up to walk down town to the library to get a book, eating lunch at home, reading on the front porch until he became bored and then walking down through the town to spend the hottest hours of the day in the cool dark of the pool room. He loved to play pool.

In the evening he practised on his clarinet, strolled down town, read and went to bed. He was still a hero to his two young sisters. His mother would have given him breakfast in bed if he had wanted it. She often came in when he was in bed and asked him to tell her about the war, but her attention always wandered. His father was non-committal.

Before Krebs went away to the war he had never been allowed to drive the family motor car. His father was in the real estate business and always wanted the car to be at his command when he required it to take clients out into the country to show them a piece of farm property. The car always stood outside the First National Bank building where his father had an office on the second floor. Now, after the war, it was still the same car.

Nothing was changed in the town except that the young girls had grown up. But they lived in such a complicated world of already defined alliances and shifting feuds that Krebs did not feel the energy or the courage to break into it. He liked to look at them, though. There were so many good-looking young girls. Most of them had their hair cut short. When he went away only little girls wore their hair like that or girls that were fast. They all wore sweaters and shirt waists with round Dutch collars. It was a pattern. He liked to look at them from the front porch as they walked on the other side of the street. He liked to watch them walking under the shade of the trees. He liked the round Dutch collars above their sweaters. He liked their silk stockings and flat shoes. He liked their bobbed hair and the way they walked.

When he was in town their appeal to him was not very strong. He did not like them when he saw them in the Greek's ice cream parlor. He did not want them themselves really. They were too complicated. There was something else. Vaguely he wanted a girl but he did not want to have to work to get her. He would have liked to have a girl but he did not want to have to spend a long time getting her. He did not want to get into the intrigue and the politics. He did not want to have to do any courting. He did not want to tell any more lies. It wasn't worth it.

He did not want any consequences. He did not want any consequences ever again. He wanted to live along without consequences. Besides he did not really need a girl. The army had taught him that. It was all right to pose as though you had to have a girl. Nearly everybody did that. But it

----

WORDS TO OWN
apocryphal (ə·päk′rə·fəl) *adj.*: of questionable authority; false.
exaggeration (eg·zaj′ər·ā·shən) *n.*: overstatement.
alliances (ə·lī′əns·iz) *n. pl.*: close associations for common objectives.
intrigue (in′trēg′) *n.*: scheming.
consequences (kän′si·kwens·iz) *n. pl.*: results of an action.

----

654 THE MODERNS

Crossing the Curriculum

History
Help students understand why World War I was considered such a tragedy that it would "end all wars." Military commanders sent boys armed with bayonets into the face of automatic machine gun fire, poisonous gas, and armored tanks. As a result of this colossal mismatch between old-fashioned military tactics and modern technology, casualties were greater than in any previous war. Russia lost 1,700,000 men, France 1,358,000, and Great Britain close to a million. In many cases these soldiers were literally blown to bits by grenades or choked to death after being exposed to chemical weapons. Interested students might compare casualty statistics from World War I with statistics from other wars and report their findings to the class.

wasn't true. You did not need a girl. That was the funny thing. First a fellow boasted how girls mean nothing to him, that he never thought of them, that they could not touch him. Then a fellow boasted that he could not get along without girls, that he had to have them all the time, that he could not go to sleep without them.

That was all a lie. It was all a lie both ways. You did not need a girl unless you thought about them. He learned that in the army. Then sooner or later you always got one. When you were really ripe for a girl you always got one. You did not have to think about it. Sooner or later it would come. He had learned that in the army.

Now he would have liked a girl if she had come to him and not wanted to talk. But here at home it was all too complicated. He knew he could never get through it all again. It was not worth the trouble. That was the thing about French girls and German girls. There was not all this talking. You couldn't talk much and you did not need to talk. It was simple and you were friends. He thought about France and then he began to think about Germany. On the whole he had liked Germany better. He did not want to leave Germany. He did not want to come home. Still, he had come home. He sat on the front porch.

He liked the girls that were walking along the other side of the street. He liked the look of them much better than the French girls or the German girls. But the world they were in was not the world he was in. He would like to have one of them. But it was not worth it. They were such a nice pattern. He liked the pattern. It was exciting. But he would not go through all the talking. He did not want one badly enough. He liked to look at them all, though. It was not worth it. Not now when things were getting good again.

He sat there on the porch reading a book on the war. It was a history and he was reading about all the engagements he had been in. It was the most interesting reading he had ever done. He wished there were more maps. He looked forward with a good feeling to reading all the really good histories when they would come out with good detail maps. Now he was really learning about the war. He had been a good soldier. That made a difference.

One morning after he had been home about a month his mother came into his bedroom and sat on the bed. She smoothed her apron.

"I had a talk with your father last night, Harold," she said, "and he is willing for you to take the car out in the evenings."

"Yeah?" said Krebs, who was not fully awake. "Take the car out? Yeah?"

"Yes. Your father has felt for some time that you should be able to take the car out in the evenings whenever you wished but we only talked it over last night."

"I'll bet you made him," Krebs said.

"No. It was your father's suggestion that we talk the matter over."

"Yeah. I'll bet you made him," Krebs sat up in bed.

"Will you come down to breakfast, Harold?" his mother said.

"As soon as I get my clothes on," Krebs said.

His mother went out of the room and he could hear her frying something downstairs while he washed, shaved and dressed to go down into the dining-room for breakfast. While he was eating breakfast his sister brought in the mail.

"Well, Hare," she said. "You old sleepy-head. What do you ever get up for?"

Krebs looked at her. He liked her. She was his best sister.

"Have you got the paper?" he asked.

She handed him *The Kansas City Star* and he shucked off its brown wrapper and opened it to the sporting page. He folded *The Star* open and propped it against the water pitcher with his cereal dish to steady it, so he could read while he ate.

"Harold," his mother stood in the kitchen doorway, "Harold, please don't muss up the paper. Your father can't read his *Star* if it's been mussed."

"I won't muss it," Krebs said.

His sister sat down at the table and watched him while he read.

"We're playing indoor over at school this afternoon," she said. "I'm going to pitch."

"Good," said Krebs. "How's the old wing?"[3]

"I can pitch better than lots of the boys. I tell them all you taught me. The other girls aren't much good."

3. **wing:** arm.

- -

WORDS TO OWN

engagements (en·gāj′mənts) *n. pl.*: battles.

- -

ERNEST HEMINGWAY 655

F Elements of Literature
Conflict

❓ What are some of the internal conflicts that Krebs seems to be struggling with in this passage? [Possible answers: His desire for a girlfriend conflicts with his sense that it would not be worth the effort; his attraction to the "nice pattern" of the American women conflicts with his wish to avoid the complications of real intimacy.]

G Critical Thinking
Analyzing Motivation

❓ Why do you think Krebs's father is now willing to allow Krebs to take out the car? [Possible responses: Krebs's father feels Krebs is now mature enough to drive after serving in the army; or his father is concerned about Krebs's lack of direction and hopes that driving the car will motivate Krebs to focus on the future.]

H Reading Skills and Strategies
Reading for Details

❓ Based on this brief interaction, why do you think this sister is Krebs's favorite? [Possible response: She is honest, unsentimental, and doesn't place any demands on Krebs, which contrasts with the "lies," "complications," and "consequences," which nauseate him in other relationships.]

I Elements of Literature
Conflict

❓ What does Mrs. Krebs's statement suggest about Harold's relationship with his father? [Possible response: Harold and Mr. Krebs do not communicate directly. Mr. Krebs values order, and Harold's life is disorganized.]

Listening to Music

"Over There" by George M. Cohan performed by Enrico Caruso.
The colorful life of songwriter-performer George M. Cohan (1878–1942) has been the subject of a 1942 movie, a Broadway musical, and numerous books. Cohan became associated with patriotic music from childhood, in part because his father recorded his birth date as July 4 (it was July 3). His songs include "Yankee Doodle Dandy" and "Over There," a popular anthem of World War I.

Activity
After they read Hemingway's story, have students listen to "Over There," and contrast Krebs's experiences with the impression of war conveyed in this rousing, positive song. What could the song suggest about the way the people at home *wanted* to think about the war? What does the song suggest about the feelings of Americans before World War I?

Have students read the material on the Roaring Twenties. Ask students to consider whether Krebs's behavior may have been, in part, a reaction to the frivolity and materialism of the postwar era. Invite students to discuss what other periods in United States history may have been similar to the Roaring Twenties and to compare and contrast that era with contemporary society.

RESPONDING TO THE ART

Rudolph Valentino (1895–1926), featured on the poster on p. 657, was the greatest idol of the silent screen, as popular in his decade as Leonardo Di Caprio and Madonna are in ours. Born in Italy as Rodolfo Guglielmi (the poster combines both spellings of his name), he arrived in New York City in 1913. *The Four Horsemen of the Apocalypse* (1921) catapulted him to fame as a smoldering, romantic hero. In *Blood and Sand* (1922, see poster) he played a naive *torero* torn between two women. He is best remembered, however, for his role in *Son of the Sheik* (1926), in which he played a masterful, turbaned Arab. After this film, the word *sheik* was commonly used to mean "boyfriend." The news of his sudden death at age thirty-one was greeted by mass hysteria and several suicides.

(A) Reading Skills and Strategies

Making Inferences

? What can you infer about Harold's mood from this conversation? [Possible response: His short answers imply that he is depressed, or more interested in the sports page than in his sister.]

Charleston endurance contest (1926).

UPI/Bettmann.

LITERATURE AND POPULAR CULTURE

The Decade That Roared

Harold Krebs finds his hometown much the same as he left it before the war, except for new styles in women's hair and clothing. He especially notices girls' short, bobbed hair—a style that marked a girl as "fast" only a few years earlier when he shipped out to the trenches of France.

The flap over flappers. Krebs was right on target. As the slick, sophisticated ads of the era show, nothing symbolized the decade after World War I so well as the "flapper"—a liberated young woman who cropped her hair into a caplike shape, wore half the amount of clothing of her Victorian-era counterpart, and boldly wore rouge and lipstick. The flapper abandoned the confines of the corset and opted instead for loose, long-waisted dresses that ended at or above the knee. She showed off her legs in the new silk or rayon stockings that were affordable at every income level. And she kicked, shimmied, and swayed in a wild, new dance called the Charleston.

An era of excess. Tired of war and disillusioned with political and social causes, city dwellers and even small-town residents yearned for fun and excitement in the Roaring Twenties. Millions of Americans purchased automobiles and took to the road on touring

"Yeah?" said Krebs.

"I tell them all you're my beau.[4] Aren't you my beau, Hare?"

"You bet."

"Couldn't your brother really be your beau just because he's your brother?"

"I don't know."

"Sure you know. Couldn't you be my beau, Hare, if I was old enough and if you wanted to?"

"Sure. You're my girl now."

"Am I really your girl?"

"Sure."

"Do you love me?"

4. **beau** (bō): boyfriend.

"Uh, huh."

"Will you love me always?"

"Sure."

"Will you come over and watch me play in-door?"

"Maybe."

"Aw, Hare, you don't love me. If you loved me, you'd want to come over and watch me play in-door."

Krebs's mother came into the dining-room from the kitchen. She carried a plate with two fried eggs and some crisp bacon on it and a plate of buckwheat cakes.

"You run along, Helen," she said. "I want to talk to Harold."

656 THE MODERNS

Taking a Second Look

Review: Analyzing Cause and Effect

Review cause and effect with students. They should remember that a cause answers "*Why* did something happen?" and that an effect answers "*What* happened?" A single cause can have any number of effects, and an effect may have multiple causes.

Activities

1. Have students read through the story and list main events and their causes. For example, one important effect of Krebs's delayed return home is that he does not receive a big welcome.

2. Have students speculate on the deeper causes of Krebs's behavior. What could his family do to change his state of mind?

3. After students have finished the story, have them predict the effect of Krebs's decision to leave home. They should consider the reactions of Mr. Krebs, Mrs. Krebs, and Helen.

vacations. Consumerism grew by leaps and bounds, fueled by abundant advertising and easy credit plans. Popular entertainment filled people's leisure time: Commercial radio and the movies changed American life by forming a national mass culture. People devoured the sensational stories of the day—vivid reports of scandals, crimes, freak disasters, and sports exploits. Young and old alike reveled in learning details of the private lives of movie stars like Rudolph Valentino, writers like Edna St. Vincent Millay (page 697), sports figures like Babe Ruth and the American Indian athlete Jim Thorpe, and celebrities like the pilot Charles Lindbergh. Crazes spread throughout the country—manias for the Chinese game of mahjong, six-day bicycle races, dance marathons, and even flagpole sitting. Jazz, one of the great African American contributions to popular culture, provided the exciting soundtrack to the era.

The young rebels. Women and men alike became more aware of modernist thought and the psychological theories of Sigmund Freud, calling for new social freedoms. Young people rebelled against the tight moral codes and even the good manners of the prewar years. They scoffed at the prohibition on alcohol by inventing the private cocktail party. With the new availability of motorcars, people roared off to dances in places where no one knew them, where they could feel free of their inhibitions. Couples danced closer together than ever before, tangoing and fox-trotting cheek to cheek to the sound of the saxophone.

The twenties' emphasis on youth and openness is recognizably "modern." At the time, many Americans were shocked and outraged by what they saw as the deterioration of culture and values. The 1920s were a rowdy, roisterous time—a decade that roared.

Archive Photos.

She put the eggs and bacon down in front of him and brought in a jug of maple syrup for the buckwheat cakes. Then she sat down across the table from Krebs.

"I wish you'd put down the paper a minute, Harold," she said.

Krebs took down the paper and folded it.

"Have you decided what you are going to do yet, Harold?" his mother said, taking off her glasses.

"No," said Krebs.

"Don't you think it's about time?" His mother did not say this in a mean way. She seemed worried.

"I hadn't thought about it," Krebs said.

"God has some work for every one to do," his mother said. "There can be no idle hands in His Kingdom."

"I'm not in His Kingdom," Krebs said.

"We are all of us in His Kingdom."

Krebs felt embarrassed and resentful as always.

"I've worried about you so much, Harold," his mother went on. "I know the temptations you must have been exposed to. I know how weak men are. I know what your own dear grandfather, my own father, told us about the Civil War and I have prayed for you. I pray for you all day long, Harold."

Krebs looked at the bacon fat hardening on his plate.

ERNEST HEMINGWAY 657

B Reading Skills and Strategies
Reading for Details
? What does this exchange reveal about Krebs's relations with his mother? [Possible answers: She does not really want to know what his problems are, but gently reproves him for not thinking about the future. He resents her criticism, because she doesn't understand the sources of his inertia.]

C Critical Thinking
Interpreting
? What is ironic about the concern Mrs. Krebs expresses for her son? [Possible response: Instead of worrying about the trauma of modern combat, she can only think about the temptations her father faced in the Civil War.]

D Elements of Literature
Symbol
Identify the hardening bacon fat as a possible symbol. Ask students to discuss what it might represent. [Possible responses: The feelings between Harold and his mother are "hardening." By preparing him a meal but not letting him eat it, Mrs. Krebs demonstrates both her love for and her displeasure with her son.]

Crossing the Curriculum

Psychology
Post-Traumatic Stress Disorder. This disorder, which psychologists have only begun to explore in the last thirty years, is a reaction to a trauma, or life-threatening event. Many aspects of this disorder are still poorly understood. Symptoms can include any of the following: recurrent nightmares or hallucinations, insomnia, amnesia, irritability, an inability to look to the future, feelings of detachment or estrangement from others, an inability to feel love, an inability to concentrate, and low energy and motivation. Treatments include encouraging patients to recall their experiences and make a story of the horrifying events, hypnosis, behavior modification, and antidepressant medications. Ask students to consider whether or not, in their opinion, Krebs suffers from this disorder.

Activity
Provide students with information on the experiences of Vietnam veterans when they returned home in the 1960s and 1970s and ask them to compare and contrast their reactions with Krebs's.

Edward Hopper (1882–1967) is the quintessentially American realist painter of the twentieth century. His images of solitary watchers in lonely Victorian houses, storefronts, empty theaters, and hotel rooms have come to symbolize modern alienation for many people. Weehawken, pictured here, is a town on the Palisades Cliffs of New Jersey, just across the Hudson River from New York City. (For more on Hopper, see note on p. T387.)

Activity. Compare this painting to what you know about Krebs's home town. Do you think this is what it looks like? [Possible answer: Yes, the homes seem very comfortable, unchanging, and old-fashioned, and many have front porches. The absence of people suggests Krebs's solitude and alienation.]

Ⓐ Reading Skills and Strategies

Connecting with the Text

❓ If you were Krebs, what might you say to your mother in this situation? [Possible responses: Krebs might explain that as a war veteran, he is still valuable to the community, or that after seeing so much death and destruction in combat, he finds the idea of a comfortable white-collar job irrelevant.]

Ⓑ Elements of Literature

Character

❓ Why does Krebs say that he does not love anybody? [Possible answers: His distaste for "lies" leaves him incapable of expressing emotion on command. Perhaps seeing the death of so many dulled his emotions, making him immune to feeling; or perhaps he is angry with his mother, who does not understand how he feels, and he is trying to hurt her.]

East Wind over Weehawken (1934) by Edward Hopper. Oil on canvas (34″ × 50¼″).

"Your father is worried, too," his mother went on. "He thinks you have lost your ambition, that you haven't got a definite aim in life. Charley Simmons, who is just your age, has a good job and is going to be married. The boys are all settling down; they're all determined to get somewhere; you can see that boys like Charley Simmons are on their way to being really a credit to the community."

Krebs said nothing.

"Don't look that way, Harold," his mother said. "You know we love you and I want to tell you for your own good how matters stand. Your father does not want to hamper your freedom. He thinks you should be allowed to drive the car. If you want to take some of the nice girls out riding with you, we are only too pleased. We want you to enjoy yourself. But you are going to have to settle down to work, Harold. Your father doesn't care what you start in at. All work is honorable as he says. But you've got to make a start at something. He asked me to speak to you this morning and then you can stop in and see him at his office."

"Is that all?" Krebs said.

"Yes. Don't you love your mother, dear boy?"

"No," Krebs said.

His mother looked at him across the table. Her eyes were shiny. She started crying.

"I don't love anybody," Krebs said.

It wasn't any good. He couldn't tell her, he couldn't make her see it. It was silly to have said it. He had only hurt her. He went over and took hold of her arm. She was crying with her head in her hands.

"I didn't mean it," he said. "I was just angry at something. I didn't mean I didn't love you."

His mother went on crying. Krebs put his arm on her shoulder.

"Can't you believe me, mother?"

His mother shook her head.

"Please, please, mother. Please believe me."

"All right," his mother said chokily. She looked up at him. "I believe you, Harold."

Krebs kissed her hair. She put her face up to him.

658 THE MODERNS

Getting Students Involved

"I'm your mother," she said. "I held you next to my heart when you were a tiny baby."

Krebs felt sick and vaguely <u>nauseated</u>.

"I know, Mummy," he said. "I'll try and be a good boy for you."

"Would you kneel and pray with me, Harold?" his mother asked.

They knelt down beside the dining-room table and Krebs's mother prayed.

"Now, you pray, Harold," she said.

"I can't," Krebs said.

"Try, Harold."

"I can't."

"Do you want me to pray for you?"

"Yes."

So his mother prayed for him and then they stood up and Krebs kissed his mother and went out of the house. He had tried so to keep his life from being complicated. Still, none of it had touched him. He had felt sorry for his mother and she had made him lie. He would go to Kansas City and get a job and she would feel all right about it. There would be one more scene maybe before he got away. He would not go down to his father's office. He would miss that one. He wanted his life to go smoothly. It had just gotten going that way. Well, that was all over now, anyway. He would go over to the schoolyard and watch Helen play indoor baseball.

C
D
E

WORDS TO OWN

nauseated (nô′zhē·āt′id) v. used as *adj.*: feeling sickness or discomfort in the stomach.

Nobel Prize Acceptance Speech, 1954

Having no facility for speech making and no command of oratory nor any domination of rhetoric, I wish to thank the administrators of the generosity of Alfred Nobel for this prize.

No writer who knows the great writers who did not receive the prize can accept it other than with humility. There is no need to list these writers. Everyone here may make his own list according to his knowledge and his conscience.

It would be impossible for me to ask the ambassador of my country to read a speech in which a writer said all of the things which are in his heart. Things may not be immediately discernible in what a man writes, and in this sometimes he is fortunate; but eventually they are quite clear and by these and the degree of alchemy[1] that he possesses he will endure or be forgotten.

1. **alchemy:** magical power to transform the ordinary into the extraordinary. Alchemy was a branch of medieval science in which one aim was to change common metals such as lead into gold.

Writing, at its best, is a lonely life. Organizations for writers palliate[2] the writer's loneliness, but I doubt if they improve his writing. He grows in public stature as he sheds his loneliness, and often his work deteriorates. For he does his work alone, and if he is a good enough writer he must face eternity, or the lack of it, each day.

For a true writer each book should be a new beginning where he tries again for something that is beyond attainment. He should always try for something that has never been done or that others have tried and failed. Then sometimes, with great luck, he will succeed.

How simple the writing of literature would be if it were only necessary to write in another way what has been well written. It is because we have had such great writers in the past that a writer is driven far out past where he can go, out to where no one can help him.

I have spoken too long for a writer. A writer should write what he has to say and not speak it. Again I thank you.

—Ernest Hemingway

2. **palliate** (pal′ē·āt′): ease; lessen.

Assessing Learning

MAKING MEANINGS

First Thoughts [Respond]

1. Possible responses: Krebs's desire that life have no complications or consequences is unrealistic and self-centered. What students would say to Krebs will vary, from suggesting he get a job and move away to recommending guidance, maybe therapy.

Shaping Interpretations [Interpret]

2. By the time Krebs returns, people have heard war stories and gone to many welcoming events. Now they want to forget the war. Krebs resorts to lies to hold their interest, but because of those lies his war experiences become distasteful and lose value.

3. Krebs's ambivalence toward the girls underlines his reluctance to make decisions or emotional commitments. This detachment may be caused by the horrors he experienced in combat.

4. Possible responses: Having seen the terrible consequences of war, Krebs wants to avoid pain, intimacy, and responsibility.

5. Mrs. Krebs wants Harold to settle down to the adult responsibilities of marriage and a job, but Harold wants to put off making such decisions. Harold has lost his faith, his ability to love, and his desire to participate fully in life.

6. Possible themes: Even survivors are damaged by war, but those on the home front may not understand that damage; or war disillusions young people, alienating them from the very values they fought to protect.

Extending the Text [Synthesize]

7. Possible response: Given this description, Krebs is an antihero. He may remind students of the characters in *The Pigman* and *The Outsiders,* or of Benjamin in *The Graduate* or Holden Caulfield in *Catcher in the Rye.*

Grading Timesaver

Rubrics for each Choices assignment appear on p. 167 in the *Portfolio Management System.*

MAKING MEANINGS

First Thoughts

1. Review your notes on Harold Krebs. What are your thoughts and feelings about Krebs's view of life? What advice would you give him?

Shaping Interpretations

2. By the time Krebs returns, his hometown has quit "the greeting of heroes" and "the reaction had set in." What is this reaction, and how does it affect Krebs?

3. What does Krebs's attitude toward the girls in town reveal about his state of mind?

4. What does Krebs mean by wanting "to live along without consequences"? Why do you suppose he feels that way?

5. Describe the **conflicts** expressed in the conversation between Mrs. Krebs and Harold at the end of the story. From this talk, what do we learn about the losses Harold has experienced?

6. How would you state the **theme** of "Soldier's Home"? What does the story reveal to you about the effects of war on the young?

Extending the Text

7. The "antihero" is a type of **protagonist** found in much modern literature. In contrast to the traditional hero, who responds to fate with strength and self-sacrifice, the antihero is generally disillusioned, passive, and defeated by life. Explain whether or not you consider Krebs to be an antihero. What does he have in common with antiheroes portrayed in contemporary books and movies? How is he different?

660 THE MODERNS

Reading Check

a. Describe the way Krebs spends his days.

b. What is Krebs's reaction to reading a history of all the battles he has been in?

c. How does Krebs's younger sister Helen feel about him?

d. What makes Krebs decide he should leave home?

Reading Check

a. He sleeps late, walks to the library, eats lunch, reads, plays pool, practices the clarinet, and takes walks.

b. He is proud of having been a good soldier; reading about the battles makes him feel he accomplished something.

c. He is her hero.

d. His conversation with his mother.

CHOICES:
Building Your Portfolio

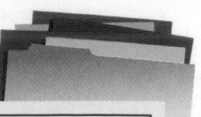

Writer's Notebook

1. Collecting Ideas for an Analysis of Causes and Effects

Freewrite your speculation about the effects that Krebs's war experience and homecoming might have on his future. Will he leave home after all? If so, where will he go, and what will he do? Will he maintain contact with his family? Save your notes for possible use in the Writer's Workshop on page 685.

Interpreting a Character

2. The Lost Generation

Gertrude Stein's remark "You are all a lost generation" summarized her perception of the pain and disillusionment experienced by many young people after World War I. In a brief essay, explain how Stein's quotation applies to Krebs. Is Krebs like or unlike someone you could meet today? Why or why not?

Analyzing a Writer's Style

3. The Tip of the Iceberg

Ernest Hemingway once remarked of his writing style: "I always try to write on the principle of the iceberg. There is seven-eighths of it under water for every part that shows." In a brief essay, explain what you think he means, and tell whether you feel that "Soldier's Home" illustrates the "iceberg principle."

Creative Writing / Performance

4. What Can We Do About Harold?

With another student, write and perform a script of the discussion between Krebs's parents that leads to Mrs. Krebs's talk with Harold. Why are Mr. and Mrs. Krebs worried about Harold? After your performance, tell how you think his parents should have dealt with Krebs's problems.

T. S. Eliot

(1888–1965)

At the time when he was regarded as America's most eminent living poet, T. S. Eliot announced that he was a "classicist in literature, royalist in politics, and Anglo-Catholic in religion." In 1927, Eliot gave up his U.S. citizenship and became a subject of the king of England. The same year he was received into the Church of England. By a kind of poetic justice, this loss to America was later to be made up for: W. H. Auden (1907–1973), the leading British poet of his time, became a naturalized American citizen in 1946. But residence in an adopted country does not necessarily change the philosophy or the style of a poet. Eliot continued to speak in a voice first heard in the Puritan pulpits of Massachusetts. And Auden retained a British sense of language unaffected by the inroads of American speech.

Thomas Stearns Eliot's family was rooted in New England, though he was born in St. Louis, Missouri, where his grandfather had been a founder and chancellor of Washington University. Eliot's childhood awareness of his native city would show itself in his poetry, but only after he had moved far away from St. Louis. He graduated from Harvard and went on to postgraduate work at the Sorbonne in Paris.

Just before the outbreak of World War I, Eliot took up residence in London, the city that would become his home for the rest of his life. There he worked for a time in a bank, suffered a nervous breakdown, married an emotionally troubled Englishwoman, and finally took up the business of literature. He became active as a publisher in the outstanding firm of Faber and Faber and, on his own, edited *The Criterion,* a literary magazine. As a critic, he was responsible for reviving interest in many neglected poets, notably the seventeenth-century English poet John Donne.

Complex Poetry for a Complex World

Long before he decided to live abroad permanently, Eliot had developed a taste for classical

UPI/Bettmann.

literature. He was as familiar with European and Eastern writings as he was with the masterpieces of English. But the most crucial influence upon his early work came from the late-nineteenth-century French poets who, as a group, came to be known as the Symbolists. (For more on the Symbolists, see page 770.) When he was nineteen, Eliot came upon a book by the British critic Arthur Symons titled *The Symbolist Movement in Literature.* "I myself owe Mr. Symons a great debt," wrote Eliot. "But for having read his book, I should not . . . have heard of Laforgue and Rimbaud; I should probably not have begun to read Verlaine; and but for reading Verlaine, I should not have heard of Corbière. So the Symons book is one of those which have affected the course of my life."

The poets Eliot mentions were men of distinctly different talents. Yet they all believed

OBJECTIVES

1. Read and interpret the poem
2. Identify and analyze elements of a dramatic monologue
3. Analyze rhythm, rhyme, metaphors, and allusions
4. Identify main idea and supporting details
5. Express understanding through writing, art, and performance

SKILLS

Literary
- Analyze elements of a dramatic monologue
- Analyze rhythm, rhyme, metaphors, and allusions

Reading
- Identify main idea and supporting details

Writing
- Collect ideas for an analysis of the causes of Prufrock's alienation
- Respond to a critical review
- Compare poems and their main characters
- Write a dramatic monologue

Speaking/Listening
- Perform a dialogue

Art
- Draw a cartoon

Planning

- **Block Schedule**
  Block Scheduling Lesson Plans with Pacing Guide

- **Traditional Schedule**
  Lesson Plans Including Strategies for English-Language Learners

- **One-Stop Planner**
  CD-ROM with Test Generator

— Resources: Print and Media —

Reading
- *Graphic Organizers for Active Reading,* p. 66

Writing and Language
- *Daily Oral Grammar* Transparency 42

Viewing and Representing
- *Viewing and Representing* Fine Art Transparency 13 Fine Art Worksheet, p. 52

Assessment
- *Formal Assessment,* p. 131
- *Portfolio Management System,* p. 168
- *Test Generator* (One-Stop Planner CD-ROM)

Internet
- go.hrw.com (keyword: LEO 11-13)

About the Author. I. A. Richards, a leading literary critic of his time, knew Eliot when the poet worked for Lloyd's Bank in London. Richards recalls meeting a senior banker who asked him what he thought of Eliot's poetry. When Richards praised it, the banker was pleased; he had debated whether banking and poetry mixed. He added that if Eliot continued doing well at the bank, he might aspire to a promotion—and might even become a branch manager some day! Richards loved to tease Eliot with the banker's prediction.

Writers on Writing. T. S. Eliot thought that poetry had a social function and wrote, "For I think it is important that every people should have its own poetry, not simply for those who enjoy poetry . . . but because it actually makes a difference to the society as a whole, and that means to people who do not enjoy poetry. . . . [Un]less [people] go on producing great authors, and especially great poets, their language will deteriorate, their culture will deteriorate and perhaps become absorbed in a stronger one."

Eliot once wrote that there were three things he would never allow in his published poetry: illustrations, notes of explanation, or musical settings. "I want my readers to get their impression from the words alone and from nothing else," he wrote. Despite that, the side notes in the text here have been enormously helpful to students as they read this famous—but difficult—text. (The prohibition on music went by the wayside when permission was granted to make the musical *Cats,* based on Eliot's *Old Possum's Book of Practical Cats.*)

in poetry as an art of suggestion rather than statement. They saw poetry as an art of re-creating states of mind and feeling, as opposed to reporting or confessing them. These beliefs became the basis of Eliot's own poetic methods. When people complained that this poetic method of suggestion was complex and difficult to understand, Eliot retorted that poetry had to be complex to express the complexities of modern life. More or less ignoring the still undervalued contribution of Walt Whitman, Eliot and other American poets also believed that, divorced from British antecedents, they would once and for all bring the rhythms of their native speech into the mainstream of world literature. Eliot and these other poets are often referred to as modernists.

> **E**liot retorted that poetry had to be complex to express the complexities of modern life.

Words for a Wasteland

Eliot had an austere view of poetic creativity; he disagreed with those who regarded a poem as a means of self-expression, as a source of comfort, or as a kind of spiritual pep talk. Practicing what he preached, Eliot startled his contemporaries with "The Love Song of J. Alfred Prufrock" in 1915 and "Portrait of a Lady" in 1917. Then, in 1922, with the editorial advice and encouragement of Ezra Pound, Eliot published *The Waste Land,* a long work considered the most significant poem of the early twentieth century. The poem describes a civilization that is spiritually empty and paralyzed by indecision.

Assembled in the manner of a painter's collage or a moviemaker's montage, *The Waste Land* proved that it was possible to write an epic poem of classical scope in the space of 434 lines. Critics pored over the poem's complex structure and its dense network of allusions to world literature, Oriental religion, and anthropology. A few years after *The Waste Land* appeared, Eliot published a series of notes identifying many of his key references. (He was dismayed to find that some of his more ardent admirers were more interested in the notes than in the poem itself.)

In 1925, Eliot published a kind of lyrical postscript to *The Waste Land* called "The Hollow Men," which predicted in its somber conclusion that the world would end not with a bang but with a whimper. In "The Hollow Men," Eliot repeats and expands some of the themes of his longer poem and arrives at that point of despair beyond which lie but two alternatives: renewal or annihilation.

A Submission to Peace

For critics surveying Eliot's career, it has become commonplace to say that, after the spiritual dead end of "The Hollow Men," Eliot chose hope over despair, and faith over the world-weary cynicism that marked his early years. But there is much evidence in his later poems to indicate that, for Eliot, hope and faith were not conscious choices. Instead, they were the consequences of a submission, even a surrender, to that "peace which passeth understanding" referred to in the last line of *The Waste Land.*

Eliot spent the remainder of his poetic career in an extended meditation upon the limits of individual will and the limitless power of faith in the presence of grace.

Cited for his work as a pioneer of modern poetry, Eliot was awarded the Nobel Prize in literature in 1948. In the decades that followed, he came frequently to the United States to lecture and to read his poems, sometimes to audiences so large that he had to appear in football stadiums. Some of those who fought to buy tickets on the fifty-yard line were probably unaware of the irony in all of this: that a man once regarded as the most difficult and obscure poet of his era had achieved the drawing power of a rock star.

Ezra Pound (who called Eliot "Possum") wrote a few final words on the death of his old friend, ending with this passage:

"Am I to write 'about' the poet Thomas Stearns Eliot? Or my friend 'the Possum'? Let him rest in peace, I can only repeat, but with the urgency of fifty years ago: READ HIM."

Make the Connection

Where Have All the Heroes Gone?

In the PBS television series *The Power of Myth*, the noted student of myths Joseph Campbell says, "The hero is today running up against a hard world that is in no way responsive to his spiritual need." Modern society has become a "stagnation of inauthentic lives and living . . . that evokes nothing of our spiritual life, our potentialities, or even our physical courage." According to Campbell, the times we live in are hostile to heroism. Heroes are people of action, but the drudgery of modern life has made many people observers rather than participants in life's adventures. See whether you agree that the protagonist of this poem is a person of profound self-absorption and passivity, who fits the profile of antihero, the disillusioned and ineffectual protagonist we find in much modern and contemporary literature.

Reading Skills and Strategies

Identifying Main Ideas and Supporting Details

Read the poem through twice. The first time, aim for a general sense of Prufrock's thoughts. As you read the poem again, write down examples of how his thoughts reflect the following ideas about his own time (the poem was published in 1915, during World War I), and perhaps about our time as well: (1) the idea that people are spiritually empty, and (2) the idea that contemporary life is unromantic and unheroic.

Elements of Literature

Dramatic Monologue

This poem is written as a **dramatic monologue**—a poem in which a character speaks directly to one or more listeners. The words are being spoken by a man named Prufrock.

In a dramatic monologue, we must learn everything about the setting, situation, other characters, and the personality of the speaker through what the speaker tells us. Sometimes Prufrock's line of reasoning is interrupted by an unexpected thought. You will often have to supply the missing connections in the speaker's stream of thoughts and associations.

> A dramatic monologue is a poem in which a character speaks directly to one or more listeners.
>
> *For more on Dramatic Monologue, see the Handbook of Literary Terms.*

The Love Song of J. Alfred Prufrock

T. S. Eliot

S'io credessi che mia risposta fosse
a persona che mai tornasse al mondo,
questa fiamma staria senza più scosse.
Ma per ciò che giammai di questo fondo
non tornò vivo alcun, s'i'odo il vero,
senza tema d'infamia ti rispondo.

Let us go then, you and I,
When the evening is spread out against the sky
Like a patient etherized upon a table;
Let us go, through certain half-deserted streets,
5   The muttering retreats

Epigraph: This quotation is from Dante's epic poem *The Divine Comedy* (1321). The speaker is Guido da Montefeltro, a man consigned to Hell for dispensing evil advice. He speaks from a flame that quivers when he talks: "If I thought my answer were to one who ever could return to the world, this flame should shake no more; but since none ever did return alive from this depth, if what I hear be true, without fear of infamy I answer this." (*Inferno*, Canto 27, lines 61–66) Think of Prufrock as speaking from his own personal hell.

? 3. *What is the evening compared with?*

T. S. ELIOT 663

A question trembles on the lips of J. Alfred Prufrock, but he cannot bring himself to ask it. He wanders, or recalls wandering, through deserted streets. He worries about his own appearance. He knows he is well dressed, but this cannot mask his weak, thin arms and legs or hide his bald spot. He longs to articulate a dramatic meaning and purpose in his life, and he longs for romantic love. But when he gets close to others he is overwhelmed by the futility of genuine communication and doubts he has anything truly important to say. In the end, he recognizes that his dreams of intimacy and heroic importance will always be shattered by the banal difficulties of real human interactions.

Resources

Viewing and Representing
Fine Art Transparency

The fine art transparency of *The Poet and Painter Adolf Uzarski* by Otto Dix will intrigue students with the extreme caricature of its subject. See *Viewing and Representing*:

- Transparency 13
- Worksheet, p. 52

Ⓐ Elements of Literature

Dramatic Monologue

? Dramatic monologues like "Prufrock" often have complex or multiple settings. What do you know about the setting so far? [It is evening; the mention of half-deserted streets indicates a town or city.]

Answer to Margin Question
Line 3. With an anesthetized patient lying on an operating table.

Reaching All Students

Struggling Readers

This is a tough text and struggling readers will be tempted to tune out and refuse to tackle it. Try using the Read Rate and Reread strategy here. Divide the poem into several manageable sections, perhaps ll. 1–36, 37–69, 70–86, 87–110, 111–131. Then, follow the step-by-step instructions for this strategy, as presented in the *Reading Strategies Handbook*, p. 59 in the *Reading Skills and Strategies* binder.

Advanced Learners

There are many parallels between Dante's *Inferno* and "Prufrock." For instance, Prufrock, like Dante, wanders through a labyrinth of his own fears. He descends into a world of personal torment that is often as rich and intricate as Dante's circles of hell. Both speakers seek answers to ultimate questions. Have students read the section of Dante's *Inferno* from which the epigraph is taken, and take notes on the connections between Dante's work and Eliot's.

Reading Skills and Strategies

Understanding Metaphor

❓ In this famous extended metaphor, what is the fog compared to? [a cat] Why does Prufrock spend so long on this description? [Possible responses: The fog seems to obsess the speaker for a time. Perhaps it suggests Prufrock's isolation; his lack of vision; his "clouded" mind. See if any students are reminded of Sandburg's "Fog."]

B **Reading Skills and Strategies**

Understanding Rhythm

❓ What effect does repeating "there will be time" and "time" have? [The repetition suggests both eternity and hesitation.]

C **Reading Skills and Strategies**

Identifying Main Ideas and Supporting Details

❓ What are the main things you know about Prufrock so far? [Possible responses: He is insecure; he worries about what others will say of him. He doubts that his feelings are important or profound enough to "disturb the universe." He can't decide whether or not to speak to someone.]

Answers to Margin Questions

Line 7. He would take this companion on a tour of run-down streets, hotels, and restaurants—places that Prufrock spends time in or identifies with. He is speaking to a potential friend or lover, the reader, or perhaps another side of himself.

Line 22. Water stands in drains. Soot falls from the chimneys. The fog is compared to a cat.

Line 27. Possible paraphrase: to contrive a mask or an attitude to help you face the people you meet socially.

Line 34. "There will be time," "time," "for a hundred," and "and"

Line 38. Possible answers: honestly express himself to others; talk to a particular person at the gathering.

Line 41. They are people whom Prufrock meets socially, especially women.

Line 42. He is expensively dressed. He is balding and has thin arms and legs; he sounds middle-aged (though Eliot wrote the poem when he was in his mid-twenties).

Of restless nights in one-night cheap hotels
And sawdust restaurants with oyster-shells:
Streets that follow like a tedious argument
Of insidious intent
10 To lead you to an overwhelming question . . .
Oh, do not ask, "What is it?"
Let us go and make our visit.

In the room the women come and go
Talking of Michelangelo.°

15 The yellow fog that rubs its back upon the window-panes,
The yellow smoke that rubs its muzzle on the window-panes,
Licked its tongue into the corners of the evening,
Lingered upon the pools that stand in drains,
Let fall upon its back the soot that falls from chimneys,
20 Slipped by the terrace, made a sudden leap,
And seeing that it was a soft October night,
Curled once about the house, and fell asleep.

And indeed there will be time
For the yellow smoke that slides along the street
25 Rubbing its back upon the window-panes;
There will be time, there will be time
To prepare a face to meet the faces that you meet;
There will be time to murder and create,
And time for all the works and days of hands
30 That lift and drop a question on your plate;
Time for you and time for me,
And time yet for a hundred indecisions,
And for a hundred visions and revisions,
Before the taking of a toast and tea.

35 In the room the women come and go
Talking of Michelangelo.

And indeed there will be time
To wonder, "Do I dare?" and, "Do I dare?"
Time to turn back and descend the stair,
40 With a bald spot in the middle of my hair—
(They will say: "How his hair is growing thin!")
My morning coat, my collar mounting firmly to the chin,
My necktie rich and modest, but asserted by a simple pin—
(They will say: "But how his arms and legs are thin!")
45 Do I dare
Disturb the universe?
In a minute there is time
For decisions and revisions which a minute will reverse.

For I have known them all already, known them all—

664 THE MODERNS

❓ **7.** *Where does the speaker want to take his companion? Whom could he be talking to?*

14. Michelangelo: Michelangelo Buonarroti (1475–1564), a great artist of the Italian Renaissance.

❓ **22.** *What details are you given about this setting? What is the fog compared to?*

❓ **27.** *How would you paraphrase this line?*

❓ **34.** *What words are repeated in this stanza for poetic effect?*

❓ **38.** *What could he want to dare to do?*

❓ **41.** *Who are "they"?*

❓ **42.** *A morning coat is formal daytime dress for men. What does Prufrock look like? Is he young, middle-aged, or elderly?*

Using Students' Strengths

Visual Learners

Eliot's poem is intensely visual. Suggest that students keep a list of all the images in the poem that help them see something. (The first three might be the evening sky, a patient on an operating table, and half-deserted streets.) When they complete the poem, they could make a "J. Alfred Prufrock" collage.

Intrapersonal Learners

Have students consider Prufrock's opinion of himself, how it has shaped his life, what he may have done in the past, and what may be in store for him in the future. Students can then write three prose "diary entries" for Prufrock: one from his boyhood, one for the time of the poem, and one from his future. How does he feel about himself at each stage?

50 Have known the evenings, mornings, afternoons,
I have measured out my life with coffee spoons;
I know the voices dying with a dying fall°
Beneath the music from a farther room.
      So how should I presume?

55 And I have known the eyes already, known them all—
The eyes that fix you in a formulated° phrase,
And when I am formulated, sprawling on a pin,
When I am pinned and wriggling on the wall,
Then how should I begin
60 To spit out all the butt-ends of my days and ways?
      And how should I presume?

And I have known the arms already, known them all—
Arms that are braceleted and white and bare
(But in the lamplight, downed with light brown hair!)
65 Is it perfume from a dress
That makes me so digress?
Arms that lie along a table, or wrap about a shawl.
      And should I then presume?
      And how should I begin?
            .   .   .   .   .

70 Shall I say, I have gone at dusk through narrow streets
And watched the smoke that rises from the pipes
Of lonely men in shirt-sleeves, leaning out of windows? . . .

I should have been a pair of ragged claws
Scuttling across the floors of silent seas.
            .   .   .   .   .

75 And the afternoon, the evening, sleeps so peacefully!
Smoothed by long fingers,
Asleep . . . tired . . . or it malingers,
Stretched on the floor, here beside you and me.
Should I, after tea and cakes and ices,
80 Have the strength to force the moment to its crisis?
But though I have wept and fasted, wept and prayed,
Though I have seen my head (grown slightly bald) brought in
      upon a platter,°
I am no prophet—and here's no great matter;
I have seen the moment of my greatness flicker,
And I have seen the eternal Footman hold my coat, and
85   snicker,
And in short, I was afraid.

And would it have been worth it, after all,
After the cups, the marmalade, the tea,
Among the porcelain, among some talk of you and me,
90 Would it have been worth while,

T. S. ELIOT 665

? 51. *Has a life that is measured in coffee spoons been very exciting or heroic?*

52. dying fall: in music, notes that fade away.

56. formulated: reduced to a formula and made insignificant.

? 58. *What do you see here?*

? 60. *What are his days compared to? Is this a positive or a negative image?*

? 72. *What has Prufrock done in early evening?*

? 74. *What is the speaker comparing himself to here?*

? 77. Malingers *means "pretends to be sick." How is this image of the evening connected to the one that opens the poem?*

82. my head . . . a platter: allusion to the execution of John the Baptist (Mark 6:17–28 and Matthew 14:3–11). The dancing of Salome so pleased Herod Antipas, ruler of ancient Galilee, that he offered her any reward she desired. Goaded by her mother, who hated John, Salome asked for John's head. Herod ordered the prophet beheaded and his head delivered on a serving plate.

? 85. *The "eternal Footman" is death. What does this line tell you about Prufrock's confidence?*

D ## Appreciating Language
Word Choice
Ask students why they think Eliot chooses to repeat the word "formulated" here. Have them check a dictionary for a precise definition. [Possible response: Eliot emphasizes this word because it captures Prufrock's experience of failed communication. The precise denotation is to reduce to or express in a formula.] In what context is this word usually used, and why does Prufrock use it to refer to the way other people see him? [The term comes from mathematics, and suggests Prufrock's feeling of being reduced to a "type" or formula by his social contacts.]

E ## Critical Thinking
Interpreting
? Does Prufrock really consider recounting these memories to someone, in order to "begin," or is he asking a rhetorical question? [He is asking a rhetorical question, because he fears he won't be able to communicate anything more important than these ordinary scenes.]

F ## Struggling Readers
Reading Elliptical Constructions
? What does the word "here" refer to and how does the word "matter" relate to Prufrock's claim that he isn't a prophet? [With "here," Prufrock refers to himself. He doubts that he has the inner substance to make pronouncements—like a prophet—about the world or about himself.]

G ## Appreciating Language
Tense
Point out the shift in verb tense here (from "Should I" to "would it have been"). Ask students what this shift in tense conveys. [Prufrock seems to give up on taking action and instead wonders what his life *would* have been like had he been less timid.]

Answers to Margin Questions
Line 51. No, it suggests a life of small, cautious decisions.
Line 58. an insect pinned to a board
Line 60. cigarette or cigar butts; this image is negative—one of waste
Line 72. He has walked the streets and seen lonely men smoking pipes.
Line 74. to a crab or other crustacean
Line 77. Both link evening to sickness and oblivion.
Line 85. Prufrock lacks confidence; he expects even death to mock him.

Skill Link

Creating an Oral Interpretation
After analyzing Prufrock's ideas about himself and the world around him, ask students how they think he speaks. Does he sigh? whine? whisper? What mannerisms does Prufrock have as he talks? Does he look directly into his companion's eyes? Explain that an oral interpretation is similar to a theatrical performance. Discuss facial expressions, gestures, and movements that can indicate specific feelings.

Activities
1. Allow individual students to choose passages to memorize and recite to the class in the way they think Prufrock would speak them.
2. Have small groups choose passages to enact. One student could recite Prufrock's lines while others play the women discussing Michelangelo, the yellow fog, the tea parties. You may wish to have groups write original lines for the other characters.

T665

A Elements of Literature
Dramatic Monologue

? How would you characterize the woman who speaks in ll. 109–110? What does she think of Prufrock? [Possible responses: She is bored or embarrassed by Prufrock's conversation; she is frustrated at being misunderstood.]

B Advanced Learners
Understanding Allusions

? Have students share what they know about *Hamlet*. Then ask the following: How are Hamlet and Prufrock alike? How are they different? Do you agree that Prufrock is no Hamlet? [Possible answers: Both are indecisive and ponder an important question. But Hamlet has a mandate to avenge his father's murder; he is a prince and a tragic figure. Prufrock seems rather ordinary and has no clear aim in life.]

C Literary Connections

Prufrock's reference to singing mermaids may be an allusion to the Sirens in Homer's *Odyssey*. The Sirens are mythical creatures who sing to passing sailors and lure them to their deaths. Odysseus is warned that he and his crew will find the Sirens' song irresistible. He saves his crew by having them plug their ears.

Answers to Margin Questions
Line 94. Guido does not expect anyone to return to earth from the dead; but Jesus enables Lazarus to do so. Prufrock wonders what it would be like to be Lazarus.

Line 98. He fears his ideas might seem irrelevant and alienate his companion.

Line 110. It is the woman to whom his observations are addressed. The repetition of "settling a pillow" suggests that she might be the same woman.

Line 111. He denies the temptation to feel that he is a tragic hero with profound thoughts.

Line 119. He feels he can be useful on occasion, but that he often looks foolish, like the pompous old man Polonius in *Hamlet*.

Line 121. Prufrock is thinking about making a feeble attempt to look young and dashing.

Line 125. He will miss real intimacy, self-expression, and love.

Line 128. He sees the mermaids riding out to sea and his hopes for change fading.

Line 131. Human voices break the spell. "Drown" could mean "lose hope."

T666

To have bitten off the matter with a smile,
To have squeezed the universe into a ball
To roll it towards some overwhelming question,
To say: "I am Lazarus, come from the dead,
95 Come back to tell you all, I shall tell you all"—
If one, settling a pillow by her head,
    Should say: "That is not what I meant at all.
    That is not it, at all."

And would it have been worth it, after all,
100 Would it have been worth while,
After the sunsets and the dooryards and the sprinkled streets,
After the novels, after the teacups, after the skirts that trail
        along the floor—
And this, and so much more?—
It is impossible to say just what I mean!
But as if a magic lantern° threw the nerves in patterns on a
105   screen:
Would it have been worth while
If one, settling a pillow or throwing off a shawl,
And turning toward the window, should say:
    "That is not it at all,
A 110   That is not what I meant, at all."
          .   .   .   .   .   .

B No! I am not Prince Hamlet, nor was meant to be;
Am an attendant lord, one that will do
To swell a progress,° start a scene or two,
Advise the prince; no doubt, an easy tool,
115 Deferential, glad to be of use,
Politic, cautious, and meticulous;
Full of high sentence,° but a bit obtuse;
At times, indeed, almost ridiculous—
Almost, at times, the Fool.

120 I grow old . . . I grow old . . .
I shall wear the bottoms of my trousers rolled.

Shall I part my hair behind? Do I dare to eat a peach?
I shall wear white flannel trousers, and walk upon the beach.
I have heard the mermaids singing, each to each.

C 125 I do not think that they will sing to me.

I have seen them riding seaward on the waves
Combing the white hair of the waves blown back
When the wind blows the water white and black.

We have lingered in the chambers of the sea
130 By sea-girls wreathed with seaweed red and brown
Till human voices wake us, and we drown.

666 THE MODERNS

? **94.** *In the Bible, a man named Lazarus is raised from the dead by Jesus (John 11:38-44). How do these lines connect with the opening quote from Dante?*

? **98.** *What is he afraid would happen if he "squeezed the universe into a ball"?*

105. magic lantern: early type of projector that could magnify and project opaque photographs or book pages as well as transparent slides.

? **110.** *Who do you think might say this to Prufrock? Is it the same person as in lines 97–98?*

? **111.** *Hamlet is the hero of Shakespeare's tragedy about a prince of Denmark. What is Prufrock saying "No!" to?*

113. swell a progress: fill out a scene in a play or pageant by serving as an extra.

117. high sentence: pompous talk.

? **119.** *How does Prufrock feel about himself?*

? **121.** *The style of the time called for fashionable young men to turn up the cuffs of their trousers. What is Prufrock hoping for here?*

? **125.** *If the mermaids do not sing to him, what will he miss in life?*

? **128.** *What does he see here?*

? **131.** *What breaks the romantic spell cast by the sight of the mermaids? What could "drown" mean here?*

Skill Link

Modifying Reading Strategies: Rereading

Readers can't always understand everything the first time they read a work. Rereading can make puzzling things clear and reveal nuances of word choice and other details that a reader might have missed the first time around.

Activities

1. Have students read "Prufrock" and "Miniver Cheevy" in class or at home. Tell them to read slowly, and out loud. After their first reading, students should write two or three paragraphs, responding to each poem's "story," its main character, or its language.

2. Have students reread the two poems every day for a week. At week's end students should write another response. They can compare their two responses to see how their understanding of the poems changed simply by rereading.

The Oddest Love Song

Of all the love songs ever written, this must be one of the oddest and most pathetic. The man who "sings" it has feelings but no one to share them with and ideas that are realized nowhere but in his own mind. Sensitive emotions and sophisticated thoughts do nothing to help him come to grips with the real world of the streets. He knows that life is "out there," but he also knows that he will never join it, and so he takes refuge in self-dramatization and heroic fantasy. Yet the man himself is not pitiful. He has sufficient knowledge of himself to control his longings and enough of a sense of humor to portray himself as a victim without being victimized.

"I am not Prince Hamlet," he says; and yet, he shares with Hamlet a breadth of vision to see two sides or more of every issue and the inability to act decisively upon any of his insights. If, in the jargon of today, we'd ask, "What's his problem?" the answer might be "self-consciousness—the egocentric trap that keeps an extraordinarily sophisticated man from enjoying the pleasures of this world that simpler men and women pursue and embrace without a thought."

One way to read the poem is to think of it as a movie—scenes follow one another immediately, without the connections or transitions that a conventional writer would provide. Consequently, the poem is demanding. What it demands is that, in the absence of logical connections, the reader must make the *psychological* connections that underlie the poem's structure and content.

"Let us go then," says the speaker, and so invites us (or someone) to join him on a "visit." But, instead of going wherever it is he has in mind, we soon find ourselves observers in the course of the man's search. Our companion seems to be looking for answers to the meaning of life and the nature of romantic love. He tries, without success, to find some place for himself even in the world he knows well. In line 10, we read that he has an "overwhelming question." But he impatiently brushes us aside before we can ask what it is.

Quick as a flash, we're confronted with something unexpected: women passing back and forth in a room and discussing Michelangelo, one of the greatest artists of all time. This little glimpse from the corner of the eye, so to speak, introduces an aspect of Prufrock's character that we'll find illustrated time and again. Focusing on one thing, he can't help thinking of something else. Everything actual has its counterpart in an image or a metaphor or a situation, by means of which Eliot can dramatize the dilemma of a man suffering a kind of emotional paralysis. As for the women who "come and go," they may be in an art gallery or in a museum or at a party or someplace else. The importance of their early and sudden appearance is to prepare us for the *method* of the poem. It is made up of a sequence of disjointed scenes that are psychologically related to the speaker's half-formed thoughts.

Time is a motif that recurs throughout the poem. Prufrock is conscious of time, and toward the end of his "love song," he makes his preoccupation clear: "I grow old . . . I grow old. . . ." Oppressed by time, he makes fun of his own obsession with it when he says, "There will be time . . . for a hundred visions." This statement might make us think of a religious revelation and the promise of salvation. But only for a moment. Prufrock soon drops us back into reality by the workaday word *revisions*—as if he is suggesting that the grandeur of imagination could be edited with a blue pencil, and that this would all take place before teatime.

T. S. ELIOT 667

This commentary was written by John Malcolm Brinnin—the poetry editor for this anthology and an acquaintance of T. S. Eliot. Brinnin helps us understand Prufrock as a man paralyzed by his own intelligence and self-consciousness—a man who struggles with profound questions about life and love, and yet cannot escape these questions long enough to spontaneously enjoy his own life.

D Reading Skills and Strategies
Responding to the Text
? Do you agree that Prufrock is not pitiful? Does he have a sense of humor? [Possible answers: He wins respect for his intelligence and self-awareness; his humor is self-mocking and bitter.]

E Reading Skills and Strategies
Connecting with the Text
? The method of the poem—a sequence of "*psychological* connections"—conveys Prufrock's pivotal lack of self-confidence and his "emotional paralysis." As time ticks by, the speaker remains trapped by his own self-awareness, having "visions" but then making "revisions." Do you know anyone who, like Prufrock, seems paralyzed by shyness and indecision? [Accept all serious responses.]

F Critical Thinking
Discerning the Author's Purpose
This is a reference to one of Eliot's theories about how poetry works—the objective correlative—and how he uses it in "Prufrock." Eliot explains the idea as a set of objects, a chain of events, or a single situation that evokes a certain emotion when it is stated or written.

Making the Connections

Connecting to the Theme:
"No Time for Heroes"
After students have finished reading the poem, discuss the collection theme. Prufrock was for many generations the very embodiment of an antiheroic era. Ask students to compare and contrast Prufrock with Cory, Cheevy, and Krebs. [Students may feel that Prufrock resembles Miniver Cheevy, for although both seem to despise their present circumstances, both remain paralyzed, unable to move beyond the realm of thought to effect any change in their worlds. Miniver Cheevy, however, drinks and calls it fate, while Prufrock only wonders whether he dares. Students may also suggest that Prufrock is similar to Krebs, since both experience inertia. Krebs, however, has a specific reason for his paralysis while the causes of Prufrock's vacillations are more ambiguous.]

Professional Notes

Critical Comment: Moral Cowardice?
The poet Stephen Spender sternly criticizes Prufrock: "His failure, for which he despises himself, is failure to relate either with another person or with the Absolute. He is isolated, he cannot communicate. Although the fact that he is *conditioned* by the society in which he lives may account for his spiritual and sexual enervation, this does not excuse his moral cowardice."

Connections

In this biographical study, John Malcolm Brinnin recalls T. S. Eliot's reading in New York City in 1950. Brinnin describes the fanfare surrounding the reading, and emphasizes Eliot's modesty, directness, and candor—in spite of his celebrity.

Ⓐ Historical Connections

This title plays on the famous understatement made by Dr. Stanley when, in 1871, he finally found the explorer Dr. Livingstone in the middle of a Central African jungle. In true British fashion, the explorer greeted the man everyone was searching for with the greeting: "Dr. Livingstone, I presume." The use of the word *presume* here also echoes its use in Eliot's poem.

Ⓑ Cultural Connections

Thurber's Cartoons

❓ Look back at the Thurber cartoons used to illustrate "Walter Mitty" (pp. 624 and 631). How does seeing the cartoons clarify the simile comparing a policeman's face to that of a Thurber dog? [They clarify the policeman's annoyance and disdain—and the comic aspect of the situation.]

BROWSING IN THE FILES

Writers on Writing. As this essay shows, Eliot's words have special meaning for many readers. About his use of allusions in his poetry, Eliot wrote, "[I]t was my intention that the reader should recognize them . . . [V]ery often it is possible to increase the effect for the reader by letting him know a reference or meaning; but if the reader knew more, the poetic effect would actually be diminished. [A] good poem should have a potentiality of evoking feelings and associations in the reader of which the author is wholly ignorant. [M]y best poems are possibly those which evoke the greatest number and variety of interpretations surprising to myself." (See p. 670 for more on allusions.)

For a number of years, John Malcolm Brinnin was the director of the noted Poetry Center of the 92nd Street YM-YWHA, in New York City. The center features public readings by leading poets.

Ⓐ *from* Mr. Eliot, I Presume
from **Sextet** *by* **John Malcolm Brinnin**

This late in his life (he was sixty-one) Eliot had given less than a handful of readings in the United States and, I believe, had read only once before in New York. The response to our announcement of the event suggested that many people thought his reading at the Poetry Center might well be his last. On the morning after we had named his date in *The New York Times*, fifteen or twenty requests were made for every seat available. Pursued and badgered to use my influence to produce tickets, I found that people who'd never read a sonnet since the seventh grade were suddenly lovers of poetry whose devotion I was implored not to dismiss. Whatever else he might have been in the eyes of the world, T. S. Eliot in 1950 was for New Yorkers a hot ticket....

On the appointed evening early in December, I got to the Poetry Center an hour before the reading and found myself barred from even entering the building. Crowds on the sidewalk were being kept in check by uniformed policemen, one of whom, as I attempted to identify myself, looked at me like a Thurber dog confronted by an insect. Rescued by an usher, I was finally able to muscle my way to the Green Room, where Eliot was chatting with a man of cherubic countenance who turned out to be his American editor, Robert Giroux.

Eliot's face seemed weighted with weariness, and when he stood up, I thought he was even more deeply bent than he'd been in London. But his sad, lingering hint of a smile suggested he was at ease with the circumstance. "Do you suppose I might read 'Prufrock'?" he asked. "Or would that be altogether too familiar to a sophisticated audience?"

As far as I was concerned, I told him, to hear him read "Prufrock" would be a very special pleasure.

"I want to make a good appearance," he said. The directness and humility of this left me with nothing to say.

When I presented him with his check, he gave it a glance. "Are you entirely sure you can afford as much as this?"

Since the figure was the one agreed upon, I took his question as a form of solicitude, or an indication of embarrassment. In any case, the check went into his pocket and in a few minutes he was onstage, not quite smiling into the waves of an ovation that kept him standing, bowing, unable to speak.

In the wings, entranced by the particular nuances he gave to words I'd long ago memorized, I felt again what had occurred to me in the course of our talk in London: He was a man trapped, condemned to live up to an image he could not live down. By all accounts I'd read or heard, he was masked and Parnassian[1]—an oracle who spoke in many voices, all his own. In actuality I had found him to be gentle and open, with a slow-fused kind of humor and a slightly wicked sense of conspiracy he seemed to want to share. Had he, in life as in poetry, carried his conviction about the self-effacement of the artist too far?

1. Parnassian: of the mountain Parnassus, seen by the ancient Greeks as the seat of poetry and music; here, forbidding and mysterious.

MAKING MEANINGS

First Thoughts

1. What words would you use to describe Prufrock's emotional difficulty in the poem?

Shaping Interpretations

2. What hints does the name "J. Alfred Prufrock" give us about the **character** of the "hero"?

3. How could the famous **simile** in lines 2–3 reveal that the speaker's mind or will is paralyzed?

4. What is the speaker inviting someone to do in lines 1–12? What is suggested by the **images** of the place they are going to travel through?

5. What does the name Michelangelo contribute in lines 13–14? What would be the effect if, for instance, the women were "talking of Joe DiMaggio" or "discussing detergents"?

6. In lines 15–25, we have one of the most famous **extended metaphors** in modern poetry. What is being indirectly compared to what? How many details extend the metaphor?

7. The self-consciousness of the speaker is nowhere more evident than in lines 37–44.

What do you think he is self-conscious and worried about in these lines?

8. What does line 51 imply about the way Prufrock has lived? What other measuring devices would suggest a different kind of life?

9. What references to women does Prufrock make in the poem? How do you think he feels about women and his attractiveness to them?

10. How are the **setting** and people described in lines 70–72 different from those familiar to Prufrock? What might this experience with another segment of city life tell us about Prufrock?

11. In lines 73–74, the speaker creates a **metaphor** to pointedly dramatize his alienation from the rest of the world. Can you explain why Prufrock thinks he should have been a clawed creature on the floor of the sea?

12. Lines 87–98 echo the widely heard complaint that a "lack of communication" between people is the cause of misunderstanding. What do you think Prufrock would like to tell people?

13. In lines 99–104, Prufrock considers summarizing his life to another person and reaches a point of exasperation that seems close to surrender: "It is impossible to say just what I mean!" Why does Prufrock find it so difficult to express himself to others?

I SHOULD HAVE BEEN A PAIR OF RAGGED CLAWS SCUTTLING ACROSS THE FLOORS OF SILENT SEAS.

Drawing by C. Barsotti. © 1987
The New Yorker Magazine, Inc.

T. S. ELIOT 669

6. The fog or smoke is being compared to a cat. It rubs its back and muzzle on the windowpanes, licks the evening with its tongue, lingers on pools in drains, allows soot to fall on it, leaps, slips by the terrace, observes the night, curls up, and falls asleep.

7. He is embarrassed about his thinning hair and his sticklike arms and legs. He does not think he is attractive.

8. Coffee spoons suggest a life of tiny, cautious movements, rather than the grand gestures one might associate with gallon jugs or barrels of oil.

9. Prufrock refers to the women "talking of Michelangelo"; to women's arms and their perfume; to Salome's request for John the Baptist's head; to women's "skirts that trail along the floor"; to a woman saying "That is not what I meant at all." He also refers to hearing the mermaids singing, but not to him. He feels ambivalent about women; he desires their company, yet can't connect with them. He does not understand what they are thinking, but he is afraid it is critical and cruel. He has no confidence in his ability to attract women.

10. Prufrock usually spends his time in richer and more comfortable settings than this one. However, his repeated descriptions of this poorer part of town may suggest he feels some kind of identification with its squalor.

11. He feels insignificant, exposed, and lonely. "Ragged claws" implies that he must snatch what he wants from life, but doing so tears at him.

12. He seems to want to claim a grander sense of purpose and meaning in his life, but also to express his loneliness and fear.

13. Possible response: He seems to doubt whether communication is ever possible without dishonesty and reduction. Or he may just be too insecure and indecisive to really want to connect with others.

MAKING MEANINGS

First Thoughts [Respond]

1. Possible responses: fear, self-consciousness, insecurity, shyness.

Shaping Interpretations [Interpret]

2. Possible responses: The use of the initial and the middle name sounds formal and pompous. "Prufrock" sounds like "prude" or "prudent," and "frock," like the garment a priest (or a little girl) would wear.

3. A patient under ether is unconscious and cannot move or feel anything.

4. He is inviting someone to take a walk with him. The images suggest a tour through the run-down section of a city.

5. It suggests that the women are sophisticated or wish to impress one another. DiMaggio or detergents would suggest a lack of sophistication or a concern with everyday matters rather than intellectual ones.

14. Prufrock is certain that others are criticizing him. Like Prufrock, Eliot's desire to make a good impression reflects a certain self-consciousness.

15. The metaphor compares the lantern's projections to the possibility of completely revealing emotions and "nerves" to others. But like the whole poem, it can only figure communication as a humiliating, painful self-distortion.

16. The speaker sees himself as an aging man trying to cling to youth and the chance to connect with others—but he does not expect to succeed.

17. Possible answers: fussy, nervous, insecure, overanxious.

18. The singing mermaids suggest a vision of beauty, harmony, and peace—qualities that Prufrock longs for. They may also symbolize women who are forever out of reach. He considers himself unlovable and unworthy of their company.

19. Possible response: We cling to the illusion that true intimacy, beauty, and joy are within our grasp. Yet real human interaction destroys this illusion, and we find ourselves drowning in a harsh reality of isolation and miscommunication.

Connecting with the Text [Analyze]

20. The journey leads to realism and resignation. Or the reader experiences the despair of one man.

Extending the Text [Evaluate]

21. Possible response: In any age, people can feel alienated and isolated.

Challenging the Text [Analyze]

22. The title is ironic; the poem is about a lack of love. "The Requiem" and "The Complaint" are other possibilities.

---

14. In *Sextet* (see **Connections**, page 668), John Malcolm Brinnin says that at a poetry reading in 1950, Eliot asked him whether it would be all right to read "Prufrock." " 'I want to make a good appearance,' " Eliot said. Do you think Eliot's concern was Prufrockian, or would appearances not have troubled Prufrock? Cite evidence from the poem to back up your interpretation.

15. Identify the brilliant visual **metaphor** in line 105. How does it relate to the rest of the poem? How does the speaker think people will respond to his "exposure"?

16. Read lines 120–125 closely. Explain how the speaker sees his role in life. Do you think he has overcome his doubts?

17. How would you characterize someone who worries about the part in his hair and about what he should dare to eat (line 122)?

18. In lines 125–128, the speaker thinks that the mermaids are indifferent to him, yet he is held by this romantic vision. Why do you think he is so fascinated by these mythological creatures, and what might they represent for him? Why does he believe they will not sing to him?

19. By means of **paraphrase,** can you restate the meaning of lines 129–131? When "human voices wake us," what do we "drown" in?

Connecting with the Text

20. Think about this poem as a journey, a quest that begins with an invitation to join the man who makes it. What do you think the journey has finally led us to? Or do you think that the point of the poem is not so much an answer arrived at as an experience lived? Explain.

Extending the Text

21. Review the notes you made in your second reading, about how Prufrock's thoughts reflect the times he lived in. Explain why this poem—one of the most famous poems of the twentieth century—has been described as a reflection of spiritual emptiness and emotional paralysis. Do you think its depiction of life in Eliot's day or our own is accurate? Why or why not?

Challenging the Text

22. Why do you think Eliot called this a "love song"? How is it different from the usual love song? If you were titling it, would you keep "love song" or use some other phrase?

READING SKILLS AND STRATEGIES

Understanding Rhythm, Rhymes, Metaphors, and Allusions

"No *vers* [verse] is *libre* [free] for the man who wants to do a good job," Eliot once remarked. Though Eliot's poem is written in free verse (page 355), it makes use of rhythm, rhyme, and, of course, figurative language.

1. Reread the first stanza, and identify the lines that conform to a particular **metrical pattern.**

2. How does repetition in the first thirty-six lines help create **rhythm** in the poem?

3. How many **end rhymes** can you find in the poem? How many **internal rhymes**?

4. Make a list of at least five **metaphors** in the poem that you think are particularly original and memorable.

5. Note the terms of comparison in the metaphors. Has Eliot based his comparison on "things" from modern life? Or has he used comparisons based mostly on elements from the world of nature?

It is characteristic of many poets who are highly educated and intimately aware of the history of their art to make use of **allusions.** Eliot expects that his readers will identify his references and see their relationship to the poem. Here is a list of a few of the allusions in "Prufrock." What do you think each one means in the **context** of the poem?

1. Dante's *Inferno,* a section of *The Divine Comedy* (opening quotation)

2. Michelangelo (line 14)

3. Salome and John the Baptist (line 82)

4. Jesus's raising of Lazarus from the dead (line 94)

5. Hamlet, Prince of Denmark, in Shakespeare's play (line 111)

READING SKILLS AND STRATEGIES

Understanding Rhythm, Rhymes, Metaphors, and Allusions

1. Lines 6 and 7 are iambic pentameter; l. 12 is iambic tetrameter.

2. Repetition sustains the beat in the stanzas.

3. End rhymes occur in almost every line. Example: *dare/stair/hair* and *chin/pin/thin* in Stanza 6. Internal rhymes include: *visions/revisions* (l. 33), and *days/ways* (l. 60).

4. Possible choices include "butt-ends of my days," "I am formulated, sprawling on a pin," "measured out my life with coffee spoons," "I should have been a pair of ragged claws."

5. both: "cigarette butts, coffee spoons" and "fog, cat, crab."

Allusions

1. Prufrock is living in his own hell and is afraid to bare his soul to others.

2. Prufrock moves in sophisticated circles where women talk about Michelangelo's heroic figures, not about men like Prufrock.

3. Prufrock feels that the people he meets mock and humiliate him, figuratively beheading him before he can speak.

4. Prufrock sees his attempts at self-expression as a possible resurrection.

5. Hamlet is a tragic hero, whose stature Prufrock feels he cannot emulate.

CHOICES: Building Your Portfolio

Writer's Notebook

1. Collecting Ideas for an Analysis of Causes and Effects

What is the matter with J. Alfred Prufrock? Join the critics who have been debating this question for years. Write down thoughts of your own about the possible causes of Prufrock's isolation and his difficulty acting on or committing himself to anything. You could collect your ideas in a cluster diagram or other graphic organizer. Be sure to cite lines from the poem that support your interpretation. Save your notes for possible use in the Writer's Workshop on page 685.

Comparing Poems

2. Soul Searching

Write a short essay in which you compare "the explorer" in Gwendolyn Brooks's poem (page 643) with Prufrock. Consider how the explorer's search differs from Prufrock's, the fears each of them has, and the discoveries they each make. What does each poem have to say about the difficulty of making choices in today's world?

Responding to a Review of the Poem

3. Triumph or Tragedy?

Ezra Pound made the following comments about "Prufrock" in a personal letter to Harriet Monroe, the editor of *Poetry* magazine. Pound defends the ending of Eliot's poem against Monroe's objection that it goes "off at the end" (that it lacks a strong, triumphant **resolution**). In a brief essay, respond to Pound's comments.

> Now as to Eliot: "Mr. Prufrock" does not "go off at the end." It is a portrait of failure, or of a character which fails, and it would be false art to make it end on a note of triumph. I dislike the paragraph about Hamlet, but it is an early and cherished bit and T. E. won't give it up, and as it is the only portion of the poem that most readers will like at first reading, I don't see that it will do much harm. . . .
>
> —Ezra Pound

Art

4. Prufrock in Cartoons

Draw a cartoon based on a line or two from the poem. You will probably get best results if you focus on a figure of speech, as the artist of the cartoon on page 669 did.

Creative Writing

5. "Let Us Go Then . . ."

Write a **dramatic monologue** spoken by someone who wants to invite another person to do something. Let your monologue reflect the random process of the speaker's thoughts. Try to find **images** that suggest your speaker's feeling and state of mind. Open with Eliot's words: "Let us go then, you and I."

Comparing Characters

6. A Modern Trio

Is J. Alfred Prufrock like Walter Mitty in James Thurber's story (page 625)? Is he like Miniver Cheevy in Edwin Arlington Robinson's poem (page 646)? In a brief essay, compare these three characters. In what ways are they different? In what ways are they all types of the modern antihero?

Creative Writing/ Performance

7. Talking It Through

Write a dialogue between Prufrock and another person. Include references to topics in the poem that concern Prufrock. You might even imagine the conversation as being with Ralph Waldo Emerson (page 216), with references to Emerson's advice in the essay "Self-Reliance" (page 224). With another student, present your dialogue to the class.

T. S. ELIOT **671**

 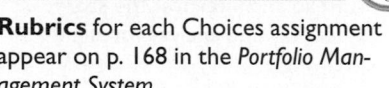
Rubrics for each Choices assignment appear on p. 168 in the *Portfolio Management System*.

CHOICES: Building Your Portfolio

1. **Writer's Notebook** Students might wish to take this exercise one step further and ask themselves whether Prufrock can change.

2. **Comparing Poems** Students should consider what each character is searching for, what problems each encounters, and whether each is successful.

3. **Responding to a Review** Recommend that students speculate about other possible endings to the poem. Doing so will help them evaluate Pound's comments.

4. **Art** Remind students that their cartoons need not be silly or hilarious. They can be satirical, dramatic, or merely illustrative. Remind students to caption their cartoons with the lines that inspired them.

5. **Creative Writing** Assure students that their monologues need not be as profound as Eliot's. Suggest that they decide on plot, characters, setting, and theme before they begin writing.

6. **Comparing Characters** Students might want to use a Venn diagram to organize shared and unique traits before they begin writing.

7. **Creative Writing/Performance** Emily Dickinson (pp. 371–393) is another possible dialogue partner for Prufrock. Before they write, students should list possible topics of conversation.

1. Read and interpret the story
2. Identify and analyze foreshadowing
3. Identify and distinguish among the four modes of fiction
4. Make predictions about a story
5. Express understanding through writing, discussion, and art
6. Demonstrate understanding of new words

SKILLS

Literary
- Analyze foreshadowing
- Identify four modes of fiction

Reading
- Make predictions

Writing
- Collect ideas about the absence of the hero in modern literature.
- Analyze the story's ironic commentary on romance.
- Write a creative sequel to the story
- Design a bumper sticker

Speaking/Listening
- Lead a discussion

Vocabulary
- Use new words

Viewing/Representing
- Evaluate two paintings as story illustrations (ATE)

Planning

- **Traditional Schedule**
  Lesson Plans Including Strategies for English-Language Learners
- **One-Stop Planner**
  CD-ROM with Test Generator

Flannery O'Connor

(1925–1964)

The Bettmann Archive.

Flannery O'Connor with self-portrait.

Flannery O'Connor was born in Savannah, Georgia, and spent her short life almost entirely in nearby Milledgeville, where her family had lived since before the Civil War. Although she limited herself to a rural, Southern literary terrain and the body of her work was small, her place in American literature is secure.

O'Connor wrote steadily from 1948 until her death sixteen years later. For fourteen of those sixteen years, she was plagued by lupus, a painful, wasting disease that she had inherited from her father and that kept her ever more confined and immobile. "I have never been anywhere but sick," she wrote. "In a sense sickness is a place, more instructive than a long trip to Europe, and it's always a place where there's no company, and where nobody can follow. Sickness before death is a very appropriate thing and I think those who don't have it miss one of God's mercies."

O'Connor graduated from the Women's College of Georgia in 1945. She then went to the Writers' Workshop at the University of Iowa. Her first novel, *Wise Blood,* was published in 1952. She followed that novel with a short-story collection, *A Good Man Is Hard to Find,* in 1955; a second novel, *The Violent Bear It Away,* in 1960; and a second set of stories, *Everything That Rises Must Converge,* in 1965 (posthumous).

Always disciplined as a writer, O'Connor forced herself to sit at her desk without conscious distraction of any sort at the same time every day for two hours, even if no inspiration came. "Sometimes I work for months and have to throw everything away," she commented, "but I don't think any of that was time wasted." While her central concern in her fiction was the abstract idea of good and evil, she felt compelled to confine herself to the concrete. She noted that the short-story writer has "only a short space" to "reveal as much of the mystery of existence as possible" and must therefore "do it by showing, not by saying, and by showing the concrete. . . ."

From the first, O'Connor was recognized as a satirist of astonishing originality and vigor, whose targets were smugness, optimism, and self-righteousness. However, the essential element of O'Connor's life and work is that she remained a Roman Catholic without the slightest wavering of faith throughout her thirty-nine years. A thunder-and-lightning Christian belief pervades every story and novel she wrote. Her attraction to the grotesque and the violent puts off many critics and readers. They fail to appreciate that the violent motifs in her fiction grow from her passionate, Christian vision of our secular times.

What O'Connor wants to tell us is that, in our rationality, we have lost the one essential—a spiritual center for our lives. "Redemption is meaningless," O'Connor wrote, "unless there is cause for it in the actual life we live, and for the last few centuries there has been operating in our culture the secular belief that there is no such cause."

In her works, O'Connor seems to be saying that we have become so accustomed to the lack of God in our lives that a writer must use violent means to make a point. Just as we are made to feel comfortable, enjoying O'Connor's carnival show, the comedy is miraculously transcended, and we realize that the situation has a philosophical meaning. All the freaks and clowns have taken on God's meaning. God is here, and the devil is, too.

 go.hrw.com
LEO 11-13

 Resources: Print and Media

Reading
- *Reading Skills and Strategies*
  MiniRead Skill Lesson, p. 93
  Selection Skill Lesson, p. 99
- *Graphic Organizers for Active Reading,* p. 67
- *Words to Own,* p. 40
- *Audio CD Library,*
  Disc 18, Track 5

Elements of Literature
- *Literary Elements*
  Transparency 22
  Worksheet, p. 67

Writing and Language
- *Daily Oral Grammar*
  Transparency 43
- *Grammar and Language Links*
  Worksheet, p. 59

Viewing and Representing
- *Visual Connections*
  Videocassette B, Segment 8

Assessment
- *Formal Assessment,* p. 132
- *Portfolio Management System,* p. 170
- *Preparation for College Admission Exams,* p. 47
- *Test Generator (One-Stop Planner CD-ROM)*

Internet
- go.hrw.com (keyword: LE0 11-13)

Before You Read
THE LIFE YOU SAVE MAY BE YOUR OWN

Make the Connection
Truth in the Grotesque
The characters in this story act out a classic **theme**—that of innocence beset by evil. But, from the very beginning, we are confronted with dark hints that this is no comforting fairy tale or noble heroic epic. In this exquisite piece of storytelling, ideals of romance and heroism are turned upside down.

There are three vivid characters here, each one a masterful portrait from the rural South. With all their peculiarities, O'Connor's characters are disturbingly familiar. They are homespun figures, as real as any Georgia barnyard or roadside cafe, drawn with a kind of humor that balances on the edge of terror. They find themselves in a situation that is both tragic and comic, an odd mixture that O'Connor often used in order to communicate her points.

Reading Skills and Strategies
Making Predictions
You won't have to read very far to discover that this story is both disturbing and funny. Pay special attention to the way the characters speak, but don't let their casual, down-home voices fool you.

As you read, fill in a prediction chart like the one below. Record events or details from the story, along with your predictions about what these events or details suggest might happen later in the story. As you continue reading, write down what actually happens.

Detail or Event in Story	My Prediction	Actual Outcome

Elements of Literature
Foreshadowing
Writers often **foreshadow** what will happen later on in a story by giving hints or clues. These hints, which often create **suspense** and arouse curiosity, can carry potentially ominous or menacing undertones, so subtle sometimes as to escape notice on a first reading.

> **F**oreshadowing is the use of hints and clues to suggest what will happen later in a plot.
>
> *For more on Foreshadowing, see the Handbook of Literary Terms.*

Summary ■■

Tom Shiftlet, a cunning drifter, arrives at the desolate homestead of Mrs. Crater and her deaf, mentally disabled daughter, Lucynell. Shiftlet and the old woman bargain; he agrees to do work for meals and a place to sleep. Mrs. Crater, as crafty as Shiftlet, ultimately suggests that Shiftlet marry the unfortunate Lucynell. With his eye on Mrs. Crater's car, Shiftlet agrees. He departs on the "honeymoon," but abandons Lucynell at a diner. Soon after, he picks up a boy hitchhiker, whom he hypocritically lectures for leaving his mother. The boy curses Shiftlet and jumps from the car. Shocked, but certain of his own moral superiority, Shiftlet drives on, racing a storm to Mobile.

BROWSING IN THE FILES

Writers on Writing. O'Connor commented: "I have very little to say about short-story writing. It's one thing to write short stories and another thing to talk about writing them, and I hope you realize that your asking me to talk about story-writing is just like asking a fish to lecture on swimming. The more stories I write, the more mysterious I find the process and the less I find myself capable of analyzing it. Before I started writing stories, I suppose I could have given you a pretty good lecture on the subject, but nothing produces silence like experience, and at this point I have very little to say about how stories are written."

Preteaching Vocabulary

Words to Own
Have students read the Words to Own and definitions at the bottom of the selection pages. Then have them choose partners. One partner selects a Word to Own at random, and then acts out its definition. His or her partner must guess the word. Partners alternate roles until they use all the words. Then, have students complete the following activity, matching each word on the left with its synonym on the right.

1. irked [b]
2. amble [i]
3. guffawing [h]
4. listed [c]
5. rued [j]
6. morose [a]
7. ravenous [d]
8. gaunt [e]
9. sultry [f]
10. volley [g]

a. gloomy
b. annoyed
c. tilted
d. starving
e. thin
f. muggy
g. barrage
h. laughing
i. walk
j. regretted

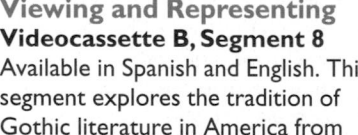

Resources

Viewing and Representing
Videocassette B, Segment 8
Available in Spanish and English. This segment explores the tradition of Gothic literature in America from Edgar Allan Poe to recent Southern writers. For full lesson plans, see *Visual Connections Teacher's Manual.*

Ⓐ Elements of Literature

Foreshadowing
? What might Mr. Shiftlet's name suggest about his role in the story that follows? [It suggests he may turn out to be shifty or shiftless.]

Lilacs (1924–1927) by Charles Burchfield.
Oil on board.

The Life You Save May Be Your Own

Flannery O'Connor

Ⓐ The old woman and her daughter were sitting on their porch when Mr. Shiftlet came up their road for the first time. The old woman slid to the edge of her chair and leaned forward, shading her eyes from the piercing sunset with her hand. The daughter could not see far in front of her and continued to play with her fingers. Although the old woman lived in this desolate spot with only her daughter and she had never seen Mr. Shiftlet before, she could tell, even from a distance, that he was a tramp and no one to be afraid of. His left coat sleeve was folded up to show there was only half an arm in it and his gaunt figure listed slightly to the side as if the breeze were pushing him. He

had on a black town suit and a brown felt hat that was turned up in the front and down in the back and he carried a tin toolbox by a handle. He came on, at an amble, up her road, his face turned toward the sun which appeared to be balancing itself on the peak of a small mountain.

The old woman didn't change her position until he was almost into her yard; then she rose

---

WORDS TO OWN
gaunt (gônt) *adj.:* very thin.
listed (list'id) *v.:* tilted.
amble (am'bəl) *n.:* leisurely pace.

---

674 THE MODERNS

with one hand fisted on her hip. The daughter, a large girl in a short blue organdy dress, saw him all at once and jumped up and began to stamp and point and make excited speechless sounds.

Mr. Shiftlet stopped just inside the yard and set his box on the ground and tipped his hat at her as if she were not in the least afflicted; then he turned toward the old woman and swung the hat all the way off. He had long black slick hair that hung flat from a part in the middle to beyond the tips of his ears on either side. His face descended in forehead for more than half its length and ended suddenly with his features just balanced over a jutting steel-trap jaw. He seemed to be a young man but he had a look of composed dissatisfaction as if he understood life thoroughly.

"Good evening," the old woman said. She was about the size of a cedar fence post and she had a man's gray hat pulled down low over her head.

The tramp stood looking at her and didn't answer. He turned his back and faced the sunset. He swung both his whole and his short arm up slowly so that they indicated an expanse of sky and his figure formed a crooked cross. The old woman watched him with her arms folded across her chest as if she were the owner of the sun, and the daughter watched, her head thrust forward and her fat helpless hands hanging at the wrists. She had long pink-gold hair and eyes as blue as a peacock's neck.

He held the pose for almost fifty seconds and then he picked up his box and came on to the porch and dropped down on the bottom step. "Lady," he said in a firm nasal voice, "I'd give a fortune to live where I could see me a sun do that every evening."

"Does it every evening," the old woman said and sat back down. The daughter sat down too and watched him with a cautious sly look as if he were a bird that had come up very close. He leaned to one side, rooting in his pants pocket, and in a second he brought out a package of chewing gum and offered her a piece. She took it and unpeeled it and began to chew without taking her eyes off him. He offered the old woman a piece but she only raised her upper lip to indicate she had no teeth.

Mr. Shiftlet's pale sharp glance had already passed over everything in the yard—the pump near the corner of the house and the big fig tree that three or four chickens were preparing to

roost in—and had moved to a shed where he saw the square rusted back of an automobile. "You ladies drive?" he asked.

"That car ain't run in fifteen year," the old woman said. "The day my husband died, it quit running."

"Nothing is like it used to be, lady," he said. "The world is almost rotten."

"That's right," the old woman said. "You from around here?"

"Name Tom T. Shiftlet," he murmured, looking at the tires.

"I'm pleased to meet you," the old woman said. "Name Lucynell Crater and daughter Lucynell Crater. What you doing around here, Mr. Shiftlet?"

He judged the car to be about a 1928 or '29 Ford. "Lady," he said, and turned and gave her his full attention, "lemme tell you something. There's one of these doctors in Atlanta that's taken a knife and cut the human heart—the human heart," he repeated, leaning forward, "out of a man's chest and held it in his hand," and he held his hand out, palm up, as if it were slightly weighted with the human heart, "and studied it like it was a day-old chicken, and lady," he said, allowing a long significant pause in which his head slid forward and his clay-colored eyes brightened, "he don't know no more about it than you or me."

"That's right," the old woman said.

"Why, if he was to take that knife and cut into every corner of it, he still wouldn't know no more than you or me. What you want to bet?"

"Nothing," the old woman said wisely. "Where you come from, Mr. Shiftlet?"

He didn't answer. He reached into his pocket and brought out a sack of tobacco and a package of cigarette papers and rolled himself a cigarette, expertly with one hand, and attached it in a hanging position to his upper lip. Then he took a box of wooden matches from his pocket and struck one on his shoe. He held the burning match as if he were studying the mystery of flame while it traveled dangerously toward his skin. The daughter began to make loud noises and to point to his hand and shake her finger at him, but when the flame was just before touching him, he leaned down with his hand cupped over it as if he were going to set fire to his nose and lit the cigarette.

He flipped away the dead match and blew a stream of gray into the evening. A sly look came

FLANNERY O'CONNOR 675

B Elements of Literature
Description

❓ How does O'Connor use descriptive language to enable the reader to visualize her characters? [O'Connor compares the old woman to "a cedar fence post" to suggest her withered, yet strong presence; students may select other evocative descriptions of young Lucynell and Mr. Shiftlet.]

C Elements of Literature
Imagery

❓ What might the image of the crooked cross suggest? [Possible responses: "Crooked" suggests that Shiftlet may be a crook or thief. "Crooked cross" might suggest a contrast and/or comparison between Shiftlet and Jesus, who died on the cross.]

D Reading Skills and Strategies

Making Predictions

Ask students to predict whether Shiftlet will get his wish. [Possible answers: no, because the old woman does not seem welcoming; yes, because he seems very sure of himself.]

E English Language Learners
Understanding Dialect

Students may be puzzled by the missing verbs ("What [are] you doing around here") and words like "lemme," meaning "let me." Explain that the characters speak in a rural Southern dialect. Have English language learners work with more English-proficient partners to interpret unfamiliar words or expressions.

F Critical Thinking
Analyzing Motivation

❓ Why does Shiftlet make this speech to Mrs. Crater? [Possible responses: to avoid answering her question about what he's doing there; to flatter Mrs. Crater by comparing her knowledge to that of a doctor; to make her think he is intelligent and sensitive.]

Using Students' Strengths

Visual Learners
O'Connor brings her characters to life with a few deft descriptive words. At the start of the story, ask students to close their eyes and create mental pictures of the three main characters. Then have them sketch the characters as they see them. They should collect other descriptive details as they read. Once students have finished the story, they can finalize their sketches.

Kinesthetic Learners
Have a group of students silently act out the first scene of the story while another student reads it aloud. Let the class discuss how the physical presence of Mrs. Crater, Lucynell, and Shiftlet affects their experience of the story.

A Critical Thinking

Analyzing Motivation

❓ Why does Shiftlet suggest to Mrs. Crater that he may be lying? [Possible responses: He wants her to realize it is useless to question him; or he may be trying to prove how honest he is by pointing out how easily he could lie.]

B Reading Skills and Strategies

Responding to the Text

❓ Do you believe what Shiftlet says about his past? [Sample responses: No, Shiftlet is a con artist. He says he has been to every foreign land, which isn't likely. Some of what he says may be true: He could have lost his arm working for the railroad.]

C Elements of Literature

Character

❓ Why is Mrs. Crater trying to convince Shiftlet that her "afflicted" daughter is "smart"? What does it tell you about her character? [Possible responses: She's a con artist too. She wants Shiftlet to stay and work for her; she wants to lure Shiftlet into marrying her daughter. Mrs. Crater is willing to selfishly bargain over her daughter's future.]

D Vocabulary Note

Multiple Meanings

Ask students to define *casket* in this sentence. [treasure box] Then ask if anyone knows another meaning of *casket*. [coffin] Why might O'Connor have used this word? [Possible answer: The suggestion of death enhances the menacing and threatening atmosphere of the story.]

E Elements of Literature

Foreshadowing

❓ What do Mrs. Crater's questions about Shiftlet's marital status, her comments about Lucynell, and Shiftlet's glance at the car suggest will happen next? [She wants him to marry Lucynell so she will have a man around the place; he wants the car. Perhaps the two will strike a bargain.]

---

over his face. "Lady," he said, "nowadays, people'll do anything anyways. I can tell you my name is Tom T. Shiftlet, and I come from Tarwater, Tennessee, but you never have seen me before: How you know I ain't lying? How you know my name ain't Aaron Sparks, lady, and I come from Singleberry, Georgia, or how you know it's not George Speeds and I come from Lucy, Alabama, or how you know I ain't Thompson Bright from Toolafalls, Mississippi?"

"I don't know nothing about you," the old woman muttered, irked.

"Lady," he said, "people don't care how they lie. Maybe the best I can tell you is, I'm a man; but listen lady," he said and paused and made his tone more ominous still, "what is a man?"

The old woman began to gum a seed. "What you carry in that tin box, Mr. Shiftlet?" she asked.

"Tools," he said, put back. "I'm a carpenter."

"Well, if you come out here to work, I'll be able to feed you and give you a place to sleep but I can't pay. I'll tell you that before you begin," she said.

There was no answer at once and no particular expression on his face. He leaned back against the two-by-four that helped support the porch roof. "Lady," he said slowly, "there's some men that some things mean more to them than money." The old woman rocked without comment and the daughter watched the trigger that moved up and down in his neck. He told the old woman then that all most people were interested in was money, but he asked what a man was made for. He asked her if a man was made for money, or what. He asked her what she thought she was made for but she didn't answer, she only sat rocking and wondered if a one-armed man could put a new roof on her garden house. He asked a lot of questions that she didn't answer. He told her that he was twenty-eight years old and had lived a varied life. He had been a gospel singer, a foreman on the railroad, an assistant in an undertaking parlor, and he come over the radio for three months with Uncle Roy and his Red Creek Wranglers. He said he had fought and bled in the Arm Service of his country and visited every foreign land and that everywhere he had seen people that didn't care if they did a thing one way or another. He said he hadn't been raised thataway.

A fat yellow moon appeared in the branches of the fig tree as if it were going to roost there with the chickens. He said that a man had to escape to the country to see the world whole and that he wished he lived in a desolate place like this where he could see the sun go down every evening like God made it to do.

"Are you married or are you single?" the old woman asked.

There was a long silence. "Lady," he asked finally, "where would you find you an innocent woman today? I wouldn't have any of this trash I could just pick up."

The daughter was leaning very far down, hanging her head almost between her knees watching him through a triangular door she had made in her overturned hair; and she suddenly fell in a heap on the floor and began to whimper. Mr. Shiftlet straightened her out and helped her get back in the chair.

"Is she your baby girl?" he asked.

"My only," the old woman said, "and she's the sweetest girl in the world. I would give her up for nothing on earth. She's smart too. She can sweep the floor, cook, wash, feed the chickens, and hoe. I wouldn't give her up for a casket of jewels."

"No," he said kindly, "don't ever let any man take her away from you."

"Any man come after her," the old woman said, "'ll have to stay around the place."

Mr. Shiftlet's eye in the darkness was focused on a part of the automobile bumper that glittered in the distance. "Lady," he said, jerking his short arm up as if he could point with it to her house and yard and pump, "there ain't a broken thing on this plantation that I couldn't fix for you, one-arm jackleg[1] or not. I'm a man," he said with a sullen dignity, "even if I ain't a whole one. I got," he said, tapping his knuckles on the floor to emphasize the immensity of what he was going to say, "a moral intelligence!" and his face pierced out of the darkness into a shaft of doorlight and he stared at her as if he were astonished himself at this impossible truth.

The old woman was not impressed with the

---

1. **jackleg:** not properly trained; amateur. O'Connor is possibly playing on the word's other meaning: "dishonest."

- -

WORDS TO OWN

irked (ʉrkt) v. used as *adj.*: annoyed; irritated.

- -

Professional Notes

Literature of the Grotesque

In literature, a grotesque character is one whose psyche is distorted because he or she develops an obsession or latches on to only one idea. The characters' appearance may reflect these psychic obsessions. Mention to students that a strain of the grotesque runs throughout the works of such Southern writers as William Faulkner, Eudora Welty, Erskine Caldwell, and Flannery O'Connor.

In "The Life You Save May Be Your Own," the daughter and Shiftlet both have disabilities, but only Shiftlet fits the definition of a grotesque. After students have finished reading the story, have them consider this quotation from O'Connor: "I am interested in making up a good case for distortion, as I am coming to believe it is the only way to make people see."

phrase. "I told you you could hang around and work for food," she said, "if you don't mind sleeping in that car yonder."

"Why listen, lady," he said with a grin of delight, "the monks of old slept in their coffins!"

"They wasn't as advanced as we are," the old woman said.

The next morning he began on the roof of the garden house while Lucynell, the daughter, sat on a rock and watched him work. He had not been around a week before the change he had made in the place was apparent. He had patched the front and back steps, built a new hog pen, restored a fence, and taught Lucynell, who was completely deaf and had never said a word in her life, to say the word "bird." The big rosy-faced girl followed him everywhere, saying "Burrttddt ddbirrrttdt," and clapping her hands. The old woman watched from a distance, secretly pleased. She was <u>ravenous</u> for a son-in-law.

In the evenings he sat on the steps and talked while the old woman and Lucynell rocked violently in their chairs on either side of him.

Mr. Shiftlet slept on the hard narrow back seat of the car with his feet out the side window. He had his razor and a can of water on a crate that served him as a bedside table and he put up a piece of mirror against the back glass and kept his coat neatly on a hanger that he hung over one of the windows.

In the evenings he sat on the steps and talked while the old woman and Lucynell rocked violently in their chairs on either side of him. The old woman's three mountains were black against the dark blue sky and were visited off and on by vari-

ous planets and by the moon after it had left the chickens. Mr. Shiftlet pointed out that the reason he had improved this plantation was because he had taken a personal interest in it. He said he was even going to make the automobile run.

He had raised the hood and studied the mechanism and he said he could tell that the car had been built in the days when cars were really built. You take now, he said, one man puts in one bolt and another man puts in another bolt and another man puts in another bolt so that it's a man for a bolt. That's why you have to pay so much for a car: you're paying all those men. Now if you didn't have to pay but one man, you could get you a cheaper car and one that had had a personal interest taken in it, and it would be a better car. The old woman agreed with him that this was so.

Mr. Shiftlet said that the trouble with the world was that nobody cared, or stopped and took any trouble. He said he never would have been able to teach Lucynell to say a word if he hadn't cared and stopped long enough.

"Teach her to say something else," the old woman said.

"What you want her to say next?" Mr. Shiftlet asked.

The old woman's smile was broad and toothless and suggestive. "Teach her to say 'sugarpie,'" she said.

Mr. Shiftlet already knew what was on her mind.

The next day he began to tinker with the automobile and that evening he told her that if she would buy a fan belt, he would be able to make the car run.

The old woman said she would give him the money. "You see that girl yonder?" she asked, pointing to Lucynell who was sitting on the floor a foot away, watching him, her eyes blue even in the dark. "If it was ever a man wanted to take her away, I would say, 'No man on earth is going to take that sweet girl of mine away from me!' but if he was to say, 'Lady, I don't want to take her away, I want her right here,' I would say, 'Mister, I don't blame you none. I wouldn't pass up a chance to live in a permanent place and get the sweetest girl

- -

WORDS TO OWN

ravenous (rav'ə·nəs) *adj.*: very eager; hungry.

- -

FLANNERY O'CONNOR 677

F **Elements of Literature**

Analogies

? What does Shiftlet's analogy suggest about him? [Possible response: It highlights his disturbing faith in his unique "moral intelligence."]

G **Reading Skills and Strategies**

Making Predictions

? Do you think Mrs. Crater will get her wish? [Possible responses: Yes, because Shiftlet seems kind to Lucynell and content to stay. No, because Shiftlet seems too self-interested and conniving to be talked into a marriage with Lucynell.]

H **Appreciating Language**

Word Choice

? Why do you think O'Connor uses the word "violently" in this sentence? [Possible answers: to underline Mrs. Crater's obsession with marrying off Lucynell; to foreshadow a violent conclusion to the story.]

I **Critical Thinking**

Responding to the Text

? Could it be possible that Shiftlet cares for Lucynell? Why or why not? [A savvy reader will say no, seeing all of Shiftlet's machinations as efforts to get that car.]

J **Critical Thinking**

Making Inferences

? Why does the old woman suggest that Shiftlet teach Lucynell to say *sugarpie*? [Possible answer: She offers this term of endearment to hint that she wants Shiftlet to marry her daughter.]

Skill Link

Determining Connotations

Throughout this story, O'Connor builds a sense of menace and corruption by choosing words with ominous or negative connotations. Remind students that connotations are the emotional overtones attached to words (they exist along with strict denotations, or dictionary definitions).

Activity

Have students discuss the connotations of the following italicized words from the story:

1. "His face . . . ended suddenly with his features just balanced over a jutting, *steel-trap* jaw." [violent, hard]

2. ". . . the daughter watched the *trigger* that moved up and down in his neck." [associated with a gun]

3. "She was *ravenous* for a son-in-law." [animal-like hunger]

4. "The old woman's smile was broad and toothless and *suggestive*." [lewdly alluring]

A Elements of Literature
Simile
? To whom is Shiftlet being compared? [Jesus, who raised Lazarus from the dead] Why is this a particularly ironic comparison? [Possible answers: because Shiftlet is raising up a car, not a person, and he is doing this for his own purposes; because Shiftlet does not resemble Christ.]

B Struggling Readers
Summarizing
Ask students to summarize in their own words what is happening between Shiftlet and the old woman in this scene. [They are bargaining about what Shiftlet will get for marrying Lucynell.]

C Historical Connections
Shiftlet is referring to Wallis Simpson, an American divorcée for whom King Edward VIII of England gave up his throne in 1936. The Duke and Duchess of Windsor were one of the most wealthy and stylish couples in the world. The fact that the repellent Shiftlet would imagine himself escorting the elegant Duchess of Windsor to a hotel to give her "something good to eat" is hilarious.

D Appreciating Language
Descriptive Words
? What is the effect of this harsh string of adjectives on Shiftlet? [He feels insulted and angry.] Why does Mrs. Crater risk alienating him this way? [She is getting more and more desperate to bring about the marriage.]

E Elements of Literature
Foreshadowing
? What does this simile suggest Shiftlet may be planning? [Snakes usually symbolize deception; he may intend to pacify Mrs. Crater with the marriage and then steal the car.]

---

in the world myself. You ain't no fool,' I would say."

"How old is she?" Mr. Shiftlet asked casually.

"Fifteen, sixteen," the old woman said. The girl was nearly thirty but because of her innocence it was impossible to guess.

"It would be a good idea to paint it too," Mr. Shiftlet remarked. "You don't want it to rust out."

"We'll see about that later," the old woman said.

The next day he walked into town and returned with the parts he needed and a can of gasoline. Late in the afternoon, terrible noises

In the darkness, Mr. Shiftlet's smile stretched like a weary snake waking up by a fire.

issued from the shed and the old woman rushed out of the house, thinking Lucynell was somewhere having a fit. Lucynell was sitting on a chicken crate, stamping her feet and screaming, "Burrddttt! bddurrddtttt!" but her fuss was drowned out by the car. With a volley of blasts it emerged from the shed, moving in a fierce and stately way. Mr. Shiftlet was in the driver's seat, sitting very erect. He had an expression of serious modesty on his face as if he had just raised the dead.

That night, rocking on the porch, the old woman began her business, at once. "You want you an innocent woman, don't you?" she asked sympathetically. "You don't want none of this trash."

"No'm, I don't," Mr. Shiftlet said.

"One that can't talk," she continued, "can't sass you back or use foul language. That's the kind for you to have. Right there," and she pointed to Lucynell sitting cross-legged in her chair, holding both feet in her hands.

"That's right," he admitted. "She wouldn't give me any trouble."

"Saturday," the old woman said, "you and her and me can drive into town and get married."

678 THE MODERNS

Mr. Shiftlet eased his position on the steps.

"I can't get married right now," he said. "Everything you want to do takes money and I ain't got any."

"What you need with money?" she asked.

"It takes money," he said. "Some people'll do anything anyhow these days, but the way I think, I wouldn't marry no woman that I couldn't take on a trip like she was somebody. I mean take her to a hotel and treat her. I wouldn't marry the Duchesser Windsor," he said firmly, "unless I could take her to a hotel and giver something good to eat.

"I was raised thataway and there ain't a thing I can do about it. My old mother taught me how to do."

"Lucynell don't even know what a hotel is," the old woman muttered. "Listen here, Mr. Shiftlet," she said, sliding forward in her chair, "you'd be getting a permanent house and a deep well and the most innocent girl in the world. You don't need no money. Lemme tell you something: there ain't any place in the world for a poor disabled friendless drifting man."

The ugly words settled in Mr. Shiftlet's head like a group of buzzards in the top of a tree. He didn't answer at once. He rolled himself a cigarette and lit it and then he said in an even voice, "Lady, a man is divided into two parts, body and spirit."

The old woman clamped her gums together.

"A body and a spirit," he repeated. "The body, lady, is like a house: it don't go anywhere; but the spirit, lady, is like a automobile: always on the move, always . . ."

"Listen, Mr. Shiftlet," she said, "my well never goes dry and my house is always warm in the winter and there's no mortgage on a thing about this place. You can go to the courthouse and see for yourself. And yonder under that shed is a fine automobile." She laid the bait carefully. "You can have it painted by Saturday. I'll pay for the paint."

In the darkness, Mr. Shiftlet's smile stretched like a weary snake waking up by a fire. After a second he recalled himself and said, "I'm only saying

---

WORDS TO OWN
volley (väl'ē) n.: firing of many shots at once.

Taking a Second Look

Review: Making Inferences About Character
Review with students how to make inferences about characters in a story. Students should note descriptions, compare what characters say with what they do and think, and notice how the characters react to one another.

Activity
1. Have students choose one of the main characters from the story: Mrs. Crater, Lucynell, or Shiftlet. As they read the story, they should gather details about this character and make inferences based on those details. Students might find a graphic organizer helpful. One column of the chart should list specific pieces of textual evidence, while the other column should list the inferences based on them.
2. After they have finished reading and making notes, organize students into three groups, one for each character. Have these small groups summarize the inferences they've made about the characters.

a man's spirit means more to him than anything else. I would have to take my wife off for the weekend without no regards at all for cost. I got to follow where my spirit says to go."

"I'll give you fifteen dollars for a weekend trip," the old woman said in a crabbed voice. "That's the best I can do."

"That wouldn't hardly pay for more than the gas and the hotel," he said. "It wouldn't feed her."

"Seventeen-fifty," the old woman said. "That's all I got so it isn't any use you trying to milk me. You can take a lunch."

Mr. Shiftlet was deeply hurt by the word "milk." He didn't doubt that she had more money sewed up in her mattress but he had already told her he was not interested in her money. "I'll make that do," he said and rose and walked off without treating[2] with her further.

On Saturday the three of them drove into town in the car that the paint had barely dried on and Mr. Shiftlet and Lucynell were married in the Ordinary's[3] office while the old woman witnessed. As they came out of the courthouse, Mr. Shiftlet began twisting his neck in his collar. He looked <u>morose</u> and bitter as if he had been insulted while someone held him. "That didn't satisfy me none," he said. "That was just something a woman in an office did, nothing but paperwork and blood

Occasionally he stopped his thoughts long enough to look at Lucynell in the seat beside him.

tests. What do they know about my blood? If they was to take my heart and cut it out," he said, "they wouldn't know a thing about me. It didn't satisfy me at all."

"It satisfied the law," the old woman said sharply.

"The law," Mr. Shiftlet said and spit. "It's the law that don't satisfy me."

He had painted the car dark green with a yellow band around it just under the windows. The three of them climbed in the front seat and the

old woman said, "Don't Lucynell look pretty? Looks like a baby doll." Lucynell was dressed up in a white dress that her mother had uprooted from a trunk and there was a Panama hat on her head with a bunch of red wooden cherries on the brim. Every now and then her placid expression was changed by a sly isolated little thought like a shoot of green in the desert. "You got a prize!" the old woman said.

Mr. Shiftlet didn't even look at her.

They drove back to the house to let the old woman off and pick up the lunch. When they were ready to leave, she stood staring in the window of the car, with her fingers clenched around the glass. Tears began to seep sideways out of her eyes and run along the dirty creases in her face. "I ain't ever been parted with her for two days before," she said.

Mr. Shiftlet started the motor.

"And I wouldn't let no man have her but you because I seen you would do right. Good-bye, Sugarbaby," she said, clutching at the sleeve of the white dress. Lucynell looked straight at her and didn't seem to see her there at all. Mr. Shiftlet eased the car forward so that she had to move her hands.

The early afternoon was clear and open and surrounded by pale blue sky. Although the car would go only thirty miles an hour, Mr. Shiftlet imagined a terrific climb and dip and swerve that went entirely to his head so that he forgot his morning bitterness. He had always wanted an automobile but he had never been able to afford one before. He drove very fast because he wanted to make Mobile by nightfall.

Occasionally he stopped his thoughts long enough to look at Lucynell in the seat beside him. She had eaten the lunch as soon as they were out

----

WORDS TO OWN
morose (mə·rōs′) *adj.*: gloomy.

----

2. **treating:** dealing; negotiating.
3. **Ordinary's:** judge's.

F **Vocabulary Note**
Multiple Meanings
? Define the word *milk*. [a drink; to extract milk from an animal] **What does "milk" mean in this sentence?** [to extract money from Mrs. Crater] **Why is this an effective word to use?** [Mrs. Crater is showing Shiftlet that she knows he is trying to manipulate her.]

G **Critical Thinking**
Analyzing Motivation
? Why does Shiftlet react this way to the wedding ceremony? [Possible responses: The civil ceremony didn't satisfy his pretension to moral grandeur. He wants to make sure he gets away on the weekend trip.]

H **Critical Thinking**
Analyzing Character
? Do you think Lucynell is as innocent now as she was at the beginning of the story? If not, what has made the change? [Possible responses: Yes, the word *sly* is used to describe her on p. 675; no, the mention of sly thoughts suggests that she has lost a little of her innocence. O'Connor may be suggesting that the presence of Shiftlet has corrupted her.]

I **Reading Skills and Strategies**
Making Predictions
? What does this detail lead you to predict for the honeymoon? [Possible answers: Shiftlet may treat her cruelly; he may desert Lucynell; he may send her back home.]

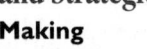

Getting Students Involved

Cooperative Learning

Readers' Theater. Have students work in groups of three or four to adapt a scene from the story as a script. (The scene at the Hot Spot and the final scene in the car are both challenging and interesting.) Students can divide up the responsibilities of writing the script, playing the roles, finding costumes and props, creating sound effects, and directing.

Debate. After students have finished reading the story, stage a debate on the question, "Is Shiftlet an evil character?" Six or eight students can be organized into two teams, to take up opposing positions. Team members on both sides should prepare their arguments beforehand, taking notes of story details that will support their position. After each side has presented its argument, it should rebut the argument of the other side.

T679

of the yard and now she was pulling the cherries off the hat one by one and throwing them out the window. He became depressed in spite of the car. He had driven about a hundred miles when he decided that she must be hungry again and at the next small town they came to, he stopped in front of an aluminum-painted eating place called The Hot Spot and took her in and ordered her a plate of ham and grits. The ride had made her sleepy and as soon as she got up on the stool, she rested her head on the counter and shut her eyes. There

set directly in front of the automobile. It was a reddening ball that through his windshield was slightly flat on the bottom and top. He saw a boy in overalls and a gray hat standing on the edge of the road and he slowed the car down and stopped in front of him. The boy didn't have his hand raised to thumb the ride, he was only standing there, but he had a small cardboard suitcase and his hat was set on his head in a way to indicate that he had left somewhere for good. "Son," Mr. Shiftlet said, "I see you want a ride."

Occasionally he saw a sign that warned: "Drive carefully. The life you save may be your own."

was no one in The Hot Spot but Mr. Shiftlet and the boy behind the counter, a pale youth with a greasy rag hung over his shoulder. Before he could dish up the food, she was snoring gently.

"Give it to her when she wakes up," Mr. Shiftlet said. "I'll pay for it now."

The boy bent over her and stared at the long pink-gold hair and the half-shut sleeping eyes. Then he looked up and stared at Mr. Shiftlet. "She looks like an angel of Gawd," he murmured.

"Hitchhiker," Mr. Shiftlet explained. "I can't wait. I got to make Tuscaloosa."

A The boy bent over again and very carefully touched his finger to a strand of the golden hair and Mr. Shiftlet left.

He was more depressed than ever as he drove on by himself. The late afternoon had grown hot and <u>sultry</u> and the country had flattened out. Deep in the sky a storm was preparing very slowly and without thunder as if it meant to drain every drop of air from the earth before it broke. **B** There were times when Mr. Shiftlet preferred not to be alone. He felt too that a man with a car had a responsibility to others and he kept his eye out for a hitchhiker. Occasionally he saw a sign that **C** warned: "Drive carefully. The life you save may be your own."

The narrow road dropped off on either side into dry fields and here and there a shack or a filling station stood in a clearing. The sun began to

The boy didn't say he did or he didn't but he opened the door of the car and got in, and Mr. Shiftlet started driving again. The child held the suitcase on his lap and folded his arms on top of it. He turned his head and looked out the window away from Mr. Shiftlet. Mr. Shiftlet felt oppressed. "Son," he said after a minute, "I got the best old mother in the world so I reckon you only got the second best."

The boy gave him a quick dark glance and then turned his face back out the window.

"It's nothing so sweet," Mr. Shiftlet continued, "as a boy's mother. She taught him his first prayers at her knee, she give him love when no other would, she told him what was right and what wasn't, and she seen that he done the right thing. Son," he said, "I never <u>rued</u> a day in my life like the one I rued when I left that old mother of mine."

The boy shifted in his seat but he didn't look at Mr. Shiftlet. He unfolded his arms and put one hand on the door handle.

D "My mother was a angel of Gawd," Mr. Shiftlet said in a very strained voice. "He took her from heaven and giver to me and I left her." His eyes

---

WORDS TO OWN
sultry (sul′trē) *adj.*: humid and still.
rued (ro̅o̅d) *v.*: regretted.

Making the Connections

Connecting to the Theme: "No Time for Heroes"

After students have finished reading the story, discuss the collection theme. How does Shiftlet compare to Prufrock, Cory, Cheevy, and Krebs? Is Shiftlet in any way heroic in his hypocritical disdain for the "slime" of the earth?

Professional Notes

Critical Comment: Valiant Foes

According to the critic Michael D. True, "The paradox of keeping Christ alive by making heroes of His most formidable antagonists lies in the center of Miss O'Connor's fiction." In her stories, "the weak in spirit, the vulgar in speech, the superficial and even insipid in moral and religious values, the demonic characters often stand out clearly as the ones to be pre- ferred. . . . In a chaotic world, plagued by casual violence and meaningless pursuits, she finds much to admire in those valiant foes who take the devil's part knowingly and enthusiastically, bent on the annihilation of a world without meaning. . . ." Discuss this commentary with the class. Be sure to encourage dissent.

Williams College Museum of Art, Gift of Cole Porter (47.1.3). © Estate of Grant Wood/Licensed by VAGA, New York, NY.

Death on Ridge Road (1935) by Grant Wood.
Oil on masonite (39″ x 46 1/16″).

were instantly clouded over with a mist of tears. The car was barely moving.

The boy turned angrily in the seat. "You go to the devil!" he cried. "My old woman is a fleabag and yours is a stinking polecat!" and with that he flung the door open and jumped out with his suitcase into the ditch.

Mr. Shiftlet was so shocked that for about a hundred feet he drove along slowly with the door still open. A cloud, the exact color of the boy's hat and shaped like a turnip, had descended over the sun, and another, worse looking, crouched behind the car. Mr. Shiftlet felt that the rottenness of the world was about to engulf him. He raised his arm and let it fall again to his breast. "Oh Lord!"

he prayed. "Break forth and wash the slime from this earth!"

The turnip continued slowly to descend. After a few minutes there was a guffawing peal of thunder from behind and fantastic raindrops, like tin-can tops, crashed over the rear of Mr. Shiftlet's car. Very quickly he stepped on the gas and with his stump sticking out the window he raced the galloping shower into Mobile.

(E) WORDS TO OWN

guffawing (gu·fô′iŋ) v. used as *adj.*: like a loud burst of laughter. "Guffaw" is an echoic word—one that imitates the sound it stands for.

FLANNERY O'CONNOR 681

RESPONDING TO THE ART

Grant Wood (1892–1942) died at the peak of his fame, on the eve of his 51st birthday. He is best remembered as the painter of *American Gothic,* an image of a man, a woman, and a pitchfork, in front of a white farmhouse, that is as recognizable as the *Mona Lisa. Death on Ridge Road* is typical of Wood's stylized landscapes and eccentric views of everyday scenes. (See also pp. 550 and 647.)

Activities

1. Ask students what makes this painting an appropriate illustration for the story. [Possible responses: The telephone poles echo the "crooked cross" image. The odd angles of the cars and truck, together with the title, suggest menace and violence, like the mood at the end of the story.]

2. Ask students to identify where the viewer is in relation to the scene [high above, off-center] and why Wood showed the scene from this standpoint. [Possible response: The viewer is caught up in the impending crash, but too far away to prevent it.]

(E) Elements of Literature

Foreshadowing

? What do these clouds suggest will happen next? [Possible responses: They suggest the arrival of a bad storm or tornado; they suggest that some kind of punishment may be in store for Mr. Shiftlet.]

(F) Reading Skills and Strategies

Making Predictions

? Did you predict a conclusion like this at any point in your reading? Why or why not? [Possible answers: No, various details hinted Shiftlet would be defeated. Yes, Shiftlet seemed very sly, clever and likely to get away with anything.]

Assessing Learning

Check Test: True-False

1. Tom Shiftlet is interested in Mrs. Crater's car. [True]
2. Young Lucynell loves someone else. [False]
3. Mrs. Crater opposes Shiftlet marrying her daughter. [False]
4. Shiftlet marries Lucynell. [True]
5. Shiftlet abandons Lucynell in an eating place. [True]

Informal Assessment

Observation Assessment. As students discuss the story, use the following checklist to evaluate their reading skills.

1 = Rarely   2 = Sometimes   3 = Always

_____ Attends to multiple levels of meaning.
_____ Uses the text to verify and clarify ideas.
_____ Connects the text to other works.
_____ Makes personal connections.
_____ Challenges the text.

In these witty, ironic letters, O'Connor describes her amusement and horror as her work is taken up (and usually distorted) by popular culture. In the first letter (written before a television interview in New York), she worries about being "corrupted" and satirizes the assumption that she is an inarticulate hillbilly. In the next two letters, she jokes about the bizarre process by which "The Life You Save May Be Your Own" was twisted for television into a sentimental "backwoods love story."

Ⓐ Cultural Connections

Gene Kelly (1912–1997) was the star of a number of Hollywood musicals, and is probably best remembered for his singing and dancing in *An American in Paris* (1951) and *Singin' in the Rain* (1952). It is understandable why O'Connor found it hard to picture this graceful and charming star playing the role of a grotesque and manipulative drifter like Shiftlet.

Ⓑ Critical Thinking

Challenging the Text

❓ Why didn't O'Connor end her story with the next-to-last paragraph? Do you agree with her choice? Why or why not? [Possible responses: Yes, she needs to show that Shiftlet sticks to his plan in spite of his last words. No, the last paragraph detracts from the power of Shiftlet's prayer.]

BROWSING IN THE FILES

Writers on Writing. O'Connor was never able to convince her aunt that "The Life You Save" was complete. The aunt always wanted "to know what happened to the idiot daughter after that." As O'Connor had anticipated, the teleplay was not faithful to her work—it ends with Shiftlet returning to the diner and driving away with Lucynell. "My aunt believes the story is complete at last," wrote O'Connor, "but I have other sentiments about it—which are not suitable for public utterance. [T]here will always be people who will refuse to read the story you have written."

The Adventures of Mr. Shiftlet

The following comments are from The Habit of Being *(1979), a collection of O'Connor's letters.*

I am going to New York on the 30th to be, if you please, interviewed by Mr. Harvey Breit (on the 31st) on a program he is starting over at NBC-TV [called *Galley-Proof*]. They are also going to dramatize the opening scene from "The Life You Save" etc. Do you reckon this is going to corrupt me? I already feel like a combination of Msgr. Sheen[1] and Gorgeous George [a wrestler]. Everybody who has read *Wise Blood* thinks I'm a hillbilly nihilist, whereas I would like to create the impression over the television that I'm a hillbilly Thomist,[2] but I will probably not be able to think of anything to say to Mr. Harvey Breit but "Huh?" and "Ah dunno." When I come back I'll probably have to spend three months day and night in the chicken pen to counteract these evil influences.

. . .

I have just sold the television rights to "The Life You Save May Be Your Own" to what I understand is called the General Electric Playhouse. All I know about television is hearsay but somebody told me that this was a production conducted by Ronald Regan (?). I don't know if this means RR will be Mr. Shiftlet or not. A staggering thought. Mr. Shiftlet and the idiot daughter will no doubt go off in a Chrysler and live happily ever after. Anyway, on account of this, I am buying my mother a new refrigerator. While they make hash out of my story, she and me will make ice in the new refrigerator.

. . .

I have just learned via one of those gossip columns that the story I sold for a TV play is going to be put on in the spring and that a *tap-dancer* by the name of Gene Kelly is going to make his tellyvision debut in it. The punishment always fits the crime. They must be going to make a musical out of it.

. . .

A letter from my agent today announces that "The Life You Save" will be presented February 1 on the Schlitz Playhouse at 9:30 New York time. My eager beaver friend in NY keeps sending me clippings of gossip columns, one announcing that Kelly will star in Flannery O'Connor's "backwoods love story." Another saying Kelly says "It's a kind of hillbilly thing in which I play a guy who *befriends* a deaf-mute girl in the hills of Kentucky. It gives me a great chance to do some straight acting, something I really have no opportunity to do in movies." See? He ain't had the opportunity before. There'll be no singing & dancing, Kelly says. I think it's channel 5 and people tell me you can't get it very good here, so I hope you will absolutely be in front of your set this time at the correct hour, as I must have some representative there to give Kelly a good leer every now and then for me. I don't know who his leading lady will be, but doubtless my NY friend will be providing that information before long. She thinks this is all hilariously funny and keeps writing me, "Has dignity no value for you?" etc. It will probably be appropriate to smoke a corncob pipe while watching this. All my kinfolks are going to think that it is a great improvement over the original story.

. . .

Someone has just called my attention to the fact that this . . . text which has "The Life You Save" in it has it with the last paragraph omitted. I would be much obliged if you would call Harcourt [O'Connor's publisher] and tell them. I think some kind of protest ought to be lodged. I suppose there is nothing that can be done about it now but I certainly don't like the idea of my story being in a textbook and the last paragraph omitted. . . ."

—Flannery O'Connor

1. **Msgr. Sheen:** Monsignor Fulton J. Sheen, a Catholic priest who had a popular TV show in the 1950s.
2. **Thomist** (tō′mist): someone who follows the thinking of the thirteenth-century philosopher Thomas Aquinas.

Crossing the Curriculum

Economics

Have students think about the business side of producing a television program. What artistic elements of a production might a producer have to consider? Why does TV often soften a harsh or unpleasant story? Should considerations of profit outweigh artistic considerations? Have students debate these issues.

First Thoughts

1. Were you surprised at the way the story ended? Review your prediction chart, and describe how the story's outcome affected you.

Shaping Interpretations

2. In the opening pages of the story, what details of setting, of characterization, and of dialogue carry menacing undertones and seem to **foreshadow** later events? (Look back over your prediction chart.)

3. What is the significance of the remarks made by the hitchhiker just before he leaps from the moving car?

4. What are we to make of the fact that Mr. Shiftlet feels that "the rottenness of the world [is] about to engulf him"? What **irony** do you sense in Mr. Shiftlet's realization?

5. Find four **figures of speech** and several words with strong **connotations** that reveal the narrator's attitude toward Mr. Shiftlet. Consider, for example, why the narrator says that Shiftlet's "figure formed a crooked cross" (page 675) and describes his eyes as "clay-colored" (page 675). How does the narrator want us to regard Mr. Shiftlet? Is he a prophet or a demon or both?

6. What do you think is the significance of the peculiar clouds and storm that pursue Mr. Shiftlet toward Mobile at the end of the story?

7. Do you sense **irony** in the story's title? How would you state the story's **theme,** based on the warning implied in the title?

> ### Reading Check
> a. Describe the improvements Mr. Shiftlet makes in the Craters' place during his first week there.
> b. Explain how Mr. Shiftlet seems to want to exploit the Craters.
> c. How does the older Lucynell want to exploit Mr. Shiftlet?
> d. What has become of young Lucynell and Mr. Shiftlet by story's end?

8. Are there any heroes in this story? Do you think it is a story about innocence versus evil, or is it a story about a world in which everyone is morally questionable? Explain.

ELEMENTS OF LITERATURE

The Four "Modes" of Fiction

According to some critics, all narrative literature can be more or less described in terms of four basic "modes," or story patterns. These modes are tragedy, comedy, romance, and irony. Tragedy and comedy are opposites, as are romance and irony.

In a typical **tragedy,** the hero is a noble, admirable character who falls from a position of some prominence to disaster or even death. This tragic hero is overcome by evil, but in the course of the struggle, he or she gains self-knowledge and wisdom. Watching a tragedy, we feel exhilarated, for we have seen the best that human beings are capable of in the face of overwhelming adversity. Greek tragedies such as *Antigone* and Shakespearean plays such as *Hamlet* best exemplify the tragic mode.

In a **comedy,** on the other hand, the central characters are often two lovers who want to marry despite parental and societal obstacles. By the end of a comedy, the young lovers have triumphed over the forces blocking them and are to be married. Many comedies end with a wedding, suggesting the renewal of life and love. Shakespeare's comedies, such as *Much Ado About Nothing* and *A Midsummer Night's Dream,* are perfect examples of comedy.

In the typical **romance** story, a hero undertakes a quest, during which his or her heroic qualities are put to the test. The hero is usually successful and returns having learned something of value. In such a story, beauty, innocence, and goodness prevail over evil, often with the help of magic or supernatural intervention. If you've ever read a fairy tale or a superhero comic, watched *Star Wars* or *Star Trek,* or gotten caught up in an adventure like *Raiders of the Lost Ark,* you've encountered the world of romance.

In the world of **irony,** as opposed to romance, there are no heroes and no triumphs. The world is a place where injustice, crime, and general foolishness prevail. The characters who triumph in such a

FLANNERY O'CONNOR 683

ELEMENTS OF LITERATURE

Make copies of a chart with four columns and the four modes of literature as column heads. With the class, discuss some of the works you have read during the year and place them in the appropriate categories. You might wish to fill in one or two titles ahead of time.

> ### Reading Check
> a. He works on the roof, patches the steps, and fixes the hog pen.
> b. He has his eye on the Craters' car. He wants to repair it, apparently so he can steal it.
> c. She does not pay him for his work, and wants him to become her daughter's caretaker.
> d. Lucynell is deserted, asleep in a diner. Shiftlet is driving to Mobile.

MAKING MEANINGS

First Thoughts [Respond]

1. Possible responses: Shiftlet's desertion of Lucynell is not surprising. His riding off in the storm, unpunished, is shocking.

Shaping Interpretations [Interpret]

2. Setting: The house is isolated and run-down. Characterization: Mrs. Crater's first reaction is to decide whether the stranger is safe. Dialogue: Characters mention death, coffins, and the cutting out of a heart.

3. The boy is the first person to openly reject Shiftlet's hypocrisy and to tell him to go to the devil.

4. Shiftlet's realization is ironic because the story chronicles his own significant contribution to the rottenness of the world.

5. Possible choices: "long black slick hair," "jutting steel-trap jaw," "pale sharp glance," "smile stretched like a weary snake." The narrator includes allusions to Jesus ("crooked cross," "three mountains," "I'm a carpenter") for irony and paradox. Shiftlet understands moral corruption like a prophet, yet thrives on it like a demon.

6. The first cloud is shaped like a turnip. It resembles a tornado and the hat of the boy who was the only one to denounce Shiftlet as a liar. The clouds and storm might symbolize the wrath of God pursuing Shiftlet.

7. Possible responses: The title, which derives from the road sign in the story, evokes people's selfish concerns for their own safety. It can be read as an ironic comment and warning in a world where self-serving people like Shiftlet succeed all too often. One statement of O'Connor's theme might run as follows: Most people, whatever they say, are motivated by self-interest.

8. Possible responses: There are no heroes. It is a story where most characters are morally questionable, and where innocence is only possible in extreme ignorance. The boy in the diner seems kind, but he might also take advantage of Lucynell.

Rubrics for each Choices assignment appear on p. 170 in the *Portfolio Management System*.

CHOICES: Building Your Portfolio

1. **Writer's Notebook** Suggest that students use their knowledge of twentieth-century history as they consider this question.

2. **Analyzing a Story** Students should be able to easily identify O'Connor's versions of these four elements of a romance. Then discuss what point O'Connor is trying to make through her ironic reversals.

3. **Critical Thinking/Speaking and Listening** Suggest that students consider how they might dramatize this story. What difficulties does it present? Might it, for example, need more dialogue?

4. **Creative Writing** Remind students that Lucynell and Shiftlet's future actions should be consistent with details in the story. Students may want to consider what role Mrs. Crater might play in either or both characters' futures.

5. **Creative Writing/Art** Encourage students not to pick up a phrase from the story. They can either write a motto in their own words, or perhaps look back through previous selections in *Elements of Literature* for an appropriate phrase.

---

world are often crafty rascals and even con artists—people who learn how to manipulate the world for their own gain. In other forms of irony, the characters are ordinary human beings like ourselves and are caught in a world that offers little opportunity for heroism. Walter Mitty (page 625) is an example of this type of character, one who longs for heroism but is limited to shopping for puppy biscuits in Waterbury, Connecticut. The characters in ironic fiction often find themselves in settings that are confining, that offer no opportunities for free choice: prisons, totalitarian societies, or even madhouses.

What modes are used in the stories you have read in the modern literature collections thus far?

CHOICES: Building Your Portfolio

Writer's Notebook

1. Collecting Ideas for an Analysis of Causes and Effects

The dominant mode in today's stories, novels, and plays is irony. In Arthur Miller's famous play *The Death of a Salesman,* for example, the characters and their problems are very ordinary. No longer do we find larger-than-life heroes struggling admirably against some malign fate, emerging with increased self-knowledge, even if the conflict ends in death. In Miller's play, the main character is an antihero named, appropriately, Loman. He is not a king or superman, but a failed salesman. His troubles are not caused by the gods or by fate, but by a boss who wants to make more money. Think of other ironic stories or novels you've read or ironic movies or plays you've seen. Then, write down some ideas about why the dominant mode in literature today is irony. In other words, why do we rarely write about great heroes anymore? Save your ideas for possible use in the Writer's Workshop on page 685.

Analyzing a Story

2. Romantic Reversal

In a brief essay, analyze O'Connor's story as an **ironic** commentary on a **romance.** (See *Elements of Literature,* page 683.) Account for the ironic reversals of these typical elements of a romance story: (a) the nurturing mother; (b) the beautiful, innocent young woman; (c) the hero who rescues the young woman; and (d) the romantic setting in a fairy-tale kingdom.

Critical Thinking / Speaking and Listening

3. Have Things Changed?

Lead a discussion in class analyzing O'Connor's comments about this story in Primary Sources (page 682). Consider (a) why TV producers would change the story, (b) whether the story would be popular if it were dramatized on TV today or made into a movie, and (c) why a textbook might omit the last paragraph (which is not omitted in this text).

Creative Writing

4. What Fate Awaits?

What becomes of Lucynell, asleep in The Hot Spot, and Mr. Shiftlet, driving on toward Mobile? In the form of a screenplay, story, magazine interview, or newspaper article, relate what their futures hold.

Creative Writing / Art

5. Mr. Shiftlet's Motto

Design a bumper sticker for Mr. Shiftlet that, in a very few words, expresses his philosophy of life. Include a logo or graphic device appropriate to his saying. Here's an example:

"The world is almost rotten."

The history
of the written
word is rich a

Page 1

EXPOSITORY WRITING

ANALYZING CAUSES AND EFFECTS

In our everyday lives we frequently think about what caused an event to occur, or we predict the effects of an event or a situation that has already occurred. Whether we're discussing why the basketball team lost last week's game, deciding what electives will most benefit us in our school careers, or determining why there's been an increase in crime in our neighborhood, we are thinking about causes and effects. In fact, the world would make almost no sense to us unless we made connections between causes and effects. Thus, when you write a cause-and-effect essay, you're simply doing in a more formal and careful way what you informally or even unconsciously do most of the time.

A cause-and-effect essay is one in which the writer analyzes either the causes or the effects of an event, a situation, or a trend. (An *event* is a specific occurrence, such as an automobile accident; a *situation* is a continuing state of affairs, such as the lack of genuine heroes in movies today; and a *trend* is a pattern that changes over time, such as the increasing use of home computers.) To write an effective cause-and-effect essay, you must present reasons, evidence, and examples to convince your readers that your argument is correct. One way to think of the cause-and-effect essay is as an analysis that answers the questions *Why?* (by identifying causes) and *What's the result?* (by describing or predicting effects).

Prewriting

1. **Choosing a topic.** Changes often give rise to thinking about causes and effects: Perhaps there has been a change in the number of homeless people in a city park and we want to determine the cause or causes. Change is also involved when we predict the effects or results of an event, a situation, or a trend. For instance, we might want to predict the effects of a school's new policy on locker searches.

Puzzling issues also lend themselves to weighing causes or effects. Literary works, for example, can suggest many possible topics for contemplation: Why does Richard Cory take his own life? Why is J. Alfred Prufrock so indecisive? What if Walter Mitty accomplished a heroic feat in real life?

Your Writer's Notebook jottings from Collections 11–13 probably contain ideas for a cause or an effect essay about a literary topic. If you lack ideas for an essay topic, try listing events, situations, and trends you would

Technology HELP

See Writer's Workshop 2 CD-ROM. *Assignment: Cause and Effect.*

ASSIGNMENT
Write an essay analyzing the causes and/or the effects of an event, a situation, or a trend.

AIM
To explain or inform; to persuade; to explore.

AUDIENCE
Your teacher, classmates, and perhaps the readers of a particular magazine or newspaper.

MAIN OBJECTIVE
Write an essay analyzing the causes and/or the effects of an event, a situation, or a trend

PROCESS OBJECTIVES
1. Use appropriate prewriting techniques to identify and develop a topic
2. Create a first draft
3. Use Evaluation Criteria as a basis for determining revision strategies
4. Revise the first draft incorporating suggestions generated by self- or peer evaluation
5. Proofread and correct errors
6. Create a final draft
7. Choose an appropriate method of publication
8. Reflect on writing progress

Planning

- **Block Schedule**
  Block Scheduling Lesson Plans with Pacing Guide
- **One-Stop Planner**
  CD-ROM with Test Generator

 *Resources: Print and Media*

Writing and Language
- *Portfolio Management System*
  Prewriting, p. 172
  Peer Editing, p. 173
  Assessment Rubric, p. 174
- *Workshop Resources*
  Revision Strategy Teaching Notes, p. 27
  Revision Strategy Transparencies 14 and 15

- *Writer's Workshop 2 CD-ROM*
  Cause and Effect

Introducing the Writer's Workshop

- Write on the chalkboard several headlines from a recent local or school newspaper.
- Ask students to suggest reasons (or causes) for the events mentioned in the headlines. Jot down their responses underneath the headlines.
- Read aloud one or two of the articles to determine whether the students' speculations are affirmed by the news writer's account.
- Use the discussion to demonstrate to students that they already have many of the necessary skills to write an analysis of a cause and effect relationship.

Teaching the Writer's Workshop

Prewriting

Remind students that a cause may have many effects and an effect may have many causes. Encourage students to focus on the most significant causes and/or effects of their topics.

Using the Model

Point out to students that the information offered under Possible Explanations does not, under normal circumstances, have to be verified scientifically. The explanations do, however, have to be logical and reasonable.

Try It Out

Students should specify the causal *mechanism* in each case, and should attempt to spell out *exactly* how each cause produced its effect. For example, if students wish to assert that the hiring of a new principal caused a reduction in student absences, they should specify how the new principal's policies caused this effect.

Try It Out

When you brainstorm topics, it is useful to consider different categories. You can analyze causes and effects, for example, in the physical, social, economic, ecological, political, cultural, educational, and technological spheres.

Choose two topics from the above categories. For each topic, explore possible causes and effects by completing these sentence beginnings:

- This (event, situation, trend) occurred because _____
- As a result of this (event, situation, trend), _____.

enjoy analyzing. If you are not really interested in your topic, you'll probably have trouble engaging your reader.

After you list five or more topics, participate in a classwide brainstorming session led by your teacher or a classmate. The group should write as many topics as possible on the chalkboard, where everyone can see them. Seeing the ideas of others may prompt you to come up with additional topics. For each topic, make sure you can ask either *Why?* (for causes) or *What's the result?* (for effects). Look at your list, and choose the topic that you find most interesting. Decide whether you are going to address causes, effects, or both.

2. **Charting causes and effects.** Depending on your topic, organize your information using a table, cluster diagram, or other graphic organizer (see models).

Model

Topic: *What are the causes of decreasing voter turnout in local elections?*

Causes	Possible Explanations
People are not interested in local issues.	The issues have become so complicated that people are confused.
	People don't have time to watch local news programs or read newspaper articles on local issues.
Polling places are not conveniently located.	Working people often must vote during a lunch hour or short break; if it takes too long to reach a polling place, many people may not want to expend the time or energy.
	The downtown polling places often have long lines, while the polling places near people's homes are hardly used.
People don't trust local politicians.	The media have portrayed politicians as dishonest.
	The city is so large that few people have a chance to meet politicians.
People are apathetic.	People hear the results of opinion polls and figure their vote won't matter.
	People feel powerless to bring about desired changes; this becomes a self-fulfilling prophecy.
People are not interested in candidates' ideas.	People feel there is no real choice among candidates because all the candidates' ideas are virtually the same.

Study your graphic organizer, and select the elements you want to include in your essay. Make an outline of the major structure of your essay. If possible, meet with one or two classmates and exchange outlines. Briefly discuss each other's outlines, pointing out major causes or effects that may have been overlooked.

Reaching All Students

Struggling Writers

For additional help with the cause and/or effect essay, have students do one of the following:

- Keep a "Wonder" journal, filling in blanks for "I wonder what would happen if. . . ." (focus on effects), or "I wonder why. . . ." (focus on causes).
- List recent changes in the school or community with direct impact upon students. List reasons why the change occured (causes) or results of the change (effects).

Advanced Writers

Have students select a recent shift in local school or community policy, and interview the persons responsible for the changes. Ask why the changes are necessary (the causes), and what are the desired results (the effects). Obtain permission from parents or guardians of interviewers and from the interviewees before giving the assignment.

A Chain of Causes and Effects in "The Secret Life of Walter Mitty"

Cause
Henpecked Walter Mitty feels inadequate.

Effect/Cause
While driving, Mitty daydreams of being a daring airplane pilot.

Effect/Cause
Wife nags distracted Mitty about driving too fast; orders him to buy overshoes, wear gloves.

Effect/Cause
After driving by hospital, Mitty daydreams of being a famous physician.

Effect
Distracted, Mitty positions car incorrectly in parking lot.

3. **Swaying the crowd.** If you are examining a social issue, will your audience be citizens of your town? members of the student body? readers of a particular magazine or newspaper in which the essay might appear? If you are analyzing the causes of a character's actions in a literary work, will your audience be other students who have read the work? Once you have identified your audience, think about background information you may need to provide. You will also need to use sound reasoning.

Inductive Thinking: Drawing Conclusions

Analyzing causes and effects requires that you use a critical-thinking process called **induction.** When you use induction to figure out something, you begin with a specific set of facts or observations, study them carefully, and then draw a general conclusion from them. In other words, induction is a kind of thinking in which you reason from the specific to the general. Here's a model:

Evidence:	A local defense plant with 10,000 employees has closed down in our city.
Evidence:	The local jobless rate has risen by 2 percent.
Evidence:	Local retail sales are off significantly from the same time last year. Retailers are worried.
Generalization:	The closing of a defense plant has had a noticeably negative effect on our local economy.

You need to be sure of the validity of the generalization you've made. Here are some questions to ask yourself in order to test the validity of your conclusion:

1. Do I have enough evidence to support my generalization? Is the sample I have selected truly representative of a larger population?
2. Is the source of my evidence trustworthy? Have I used a mixture of sound research sources—published statistics, opinions of authorities, eyewitness testimonies—and not just personal observations?
3. Does all my evidence lead to the generalization, or does some evidence refute it? What can I make of such discrepancies?

With a partner, study the inductive statements below, and brainstorm possible sources of evidence to support or refute each generalization.

1. Traffic fatalities will increase if the speed limit is raised to 70 miles per hour.
2. A law allowing people to carry concealed weapons will reduce crime.
3. Students who have above-average aptitude in mathematics will have higher earning potential in their future careers.

Questions for Gathering Data

Causes
- What are the obvious causes?
- Are there any hidden causes?
- Is there a most important cause?
- What is the most recent cause?
- Did any causes occur much earlier?

Effects
- What are the obvious effects?
- Are there any hidden effects?
- What was (or will be) the first effect?
- What effect(s) might occur much later?

Evidence
- What constitutes sufficient evidence?
- Do experts support my analysis?

Strategies for Elaboration

- Supply historical evidence, statistics, analogous cases, or other facts to underpin your analysis.
- Cite experts in order to support your conclusions.
- Apply observations or anecdotes from your own experience.
- In writing about a literary work, quote relevant passages.
- Include less obvious causes and effects.

Using the Model

After the students have completed their own graphic organizers, they might benefit from a second look at the models on pp. 686 and 687. Have them answer questions such as these:

❓ What is the purpose of listing an effect for every cause?

❓ Can an effect also be a cause? Why or why not?

❓ How could the model be changed if one cause had many effects? If one effect had many causes?

After reviewing the models, have students adjust or revise their own organizers.

Drafting

- If students are having trouble writing attention-grabbing lead sentences, suggest that they skip ahead to the introductions, bodies, and conclusions of their essays. Drafting most of their essays might give them ideas for stronger beginnings.
- Remind students to double-space their drafts, leaving wide right margins for comments and editing.

Using Students' Strengths

Kinesthetic/Spatial Learners

Students can use index cards to organize their essays. Ask students to write causes and effects on separate cards and to color-code them by highlighting the causes in one color and the effects in another. They should highlight topics that function as both causes and effects in a third color. Ask students to arrange the index cards in various patterns until the order reflects the chain or web of causes and effects as they understand them.

Interpersonal Learners

Divide students into groups, assigning each group one topic to discuss. Instruct students to subdivide the topic so that each person is responsible for coming up with one cause and one effect for the topic. Then, have students rank the causes and effects in order of importance and present these rankings to the class as they discuss their topics.

Evaluating and Revising

- Have students use the Evaluation Criteria provided here to review their drafts and determine needed revisions.
- As students revise their work, encourage them to use subordinating conjunctions to show the relationships between points and to make the organization of the paper clear to readers. If students are having difficulty, you may wish to have them complete the Language Workshop on p. 689 before they revise their papers.

Proofreading

- Have students proofread their own papers first and then exchange with other students. For this assignment, remind students to be particularly careful to use coordinating and subordinating conjunctions correctly, to indicate clear cause and effect relationships.
- If time permits, the final copy should be put aside for at least a day before it is proofread for the final time by the author.

Publishing

Students may want to submit their final drafts for possible publication in school papers, class anthologies, and local newspapers. If students intend to publish on the Internet, caution them to first determine the nature and purpose of all possible Internet sites.

Reflecting

Ask students what steps they followed in composing their essays. Chart on the chalkboard the steps followed by those who wrote about causes, those who wrote about effects and those who wrote about both. Work with students to compare the three columns and to note similarities and differences in the composition process.

Resources ───────

Peer Editing Forms and Rubrics
- *Portfolio Management System*, p. 173

Revision Transparencies
- *Workshop Resources*, p. 27

Language Handbook HELP

See The Subordinate Clause, pages 1231–1232; Combining by Subordinating Ideas, page 1238.

Communications Handbook HELP

See Taking Notes and Documenting Sources; Proofreading.

Revision STRATEGIES

Review the body of the essay to make sure all of it is directly related to the thesis statement.

▌*Evaluation Criteria*

A good cause-and-effect essay has
1. *a clear thesis statement*
2. *clear explanations of plausible and logical causes and/or effects*
3. *appropriate evidence and examples*
4. *acknowledgment of potential counterarguments, with rebuttals*
5. *clear, coherent organization and appropriate transitions*
6. *an attention-getting introduction and an engaging conclusion*

---

688 THE MODERNS

Drafting

With your audience firmly in mind, begin drafting your essay.

1. **Lead.** Begin by grabbing your reader's attention. You might open with a startling observation, an anecdote, an interesting situation, a telling quotation, or a vivid what-if scenario.

2. **Introduction.** State the event, situation, or trend that you will analyze. Include sufficient—but not too much—background information. Then, briefly state your topic as a **thesis statement.** In your statement, be sure you say whether you will discuss causes, effects, or both.

3. **Body.** In the body of your paper, present your analysis of causes or effects or both. For each cause or effect, you should elaborate by explaining the cause or effect and providing logical and convincing evidence of connections. You may organize your arguments in order of importance or in chronological order. Use separate paragraphs to make your method of organization clear to the reader. It is also helpful to use **subordinating conjunctions** when discussing causes and effects. (For more on subordinating conjunctions, see the Language Workshop on page 689.)

4. **Conclusion.** Conclude your essay by summarizing your main points. Perhaps end with a thought-provoking comment or a prediction of future effects.

Evaluating and Revising

1. **Peer review.** Share your draft with a classmate, and have him or her act as a critical reader by answering these questions:
   - Is the event, situation, or trend well-defined? Has the writer provided enough elaboration to convince the reader?
   - Are the essay's statements clear and unambiguous? Are they presented in a logical order?
   - Has the writer provided several causes or effects or both? Are there too many elements? too few?
   - Has the writer overlooked important matters?
   - Are the introduction and conclusion original and engaging?

2. **Self-evaluation.** Review your critical-reader's comments, and make needed revisions. Consult the list above to evaluate your own work.

Grading Timesaver 🕐

Rubrics for this Writer's Workshop assignment appear on p. 174 of the *Portfolio Management System.*

Language Workshop

The history of the written word is rich and

OBJECTIVES
1. Recognize the functions of subordinating conjunctions
2. Use subordinating conjunctions to show the relationships between ideas

SHOWING RELATIONSHIPS: USING SUBORDINATING CONJUNCTIONS

When you write, part of your job is to sort out and define for your readers the relationships between the ideas you present. In the following sentence, two clauses are joined with the conjunction *and*. As you will see, this conjunction fails to indicate the relationship between the two clauses.

EXAMPLE   Flannery O'Connor was sick for fourteen years, and she wrote critically acclaimed novels and short stories.

By using a subordinating conjunction instead, you can join the same clauses above in a way that more clearly conveys the relationship between the ideas expressed:

EXAMPLE   *Although* Flannery O'Connor was sick for fourteen years, she wrote critically acclaimed novels and short stories.

A **subordinating conjunction** begins a subordinate clause and indicates the relationship of this clause to an independent clause in the same sentence. A subordinating conjunction may come between two clauses, or it may appear at the beginning of a sentence.

EXAMPLES   Lucynell was sitting on the porch *when* Mr. Shiftlet arrived.

                    When Mr. Shiftlet arrived, Lucynell was sitting on the porch.

The chart below shows some subordinating conjunctions.

Subordinating Conjunctions		
although	in order that	until
as	since	when
because	so that	whereas
before	that	while

Writer's Workshop Follow-Up: Revising

In writing about causes and/or effects for the Writer's Workshop on page 685, you analyzed the relationships among events, situations, or trends. Now, review your essay to see whether you can better pinpoint the connections by using subordinating conjunctions in your sentences.

Technology HELP

See Language Workshop CD-ROM. *Key word entry: subordinating conjunctions.*

Language Handbook HELP

Subordinating ideas: pages 1235 and 1238.

Try It Out

Rewrite these sentences, replacing *and* with a subordinating conjunction that more precisely explains the relationship between the two clauses.
1. Mr. Shiftlet claimed to be honest, and he betrayed the old woman and her daughter.
2. The old woman gave Mr. Shiftlet her car, and he married her daughter.
3. Mr. Shiftlet worked hard at fixing up the old woman's place, and he planned to con her.

LANGUAGE WORKSHOP 689

Resources

Workshop Resources
- Worksheet, p. 58

Language Workshop CD-ROM
- Subordinating Conjunctions

Try It Out
Possible Answers
1. Although Mr. Shiftlet claimed to be honest, he betrayed the old woman and her daughter.
2. The old woman gave Mr. Shiftlet her car so that he would marry her daughter.
3. Mr. Shiftlet worked hard at fixing up the old woman's place because he planned to con her.

Assessing Learning

Quick Check: Using Subordinating Conjunctions

In the sentences below, replace the simple conjunction *and* with a subordinating conjunction that more clearly expresses the relationship.
1. People think well of Richard Cory, and he shoots himself. [Although people think well of Richard Cory, he shoots himself.]
2. Krebs suffers from shell shock, and he does nothing all day. [Since Krebs suffers from shell shock, he does nothing all day.]
3. Lucynell falls asleep in the diner, and Mr. Shiftlet leaves her [When Lucynell falls asleep in the diner, Mr. Shiftlet leaves her.]
4. Prufrock worries about his appearance, and he avoids talking to women. [Prufrock avoids talking to women because he worries about his appearance.]

Reading for Life

Interpreting and Constructing a Graphic Organizer

Teaching the Lesson

Explain to students that using graphic organizers makes information easy to access by separating and highlighting important pieces of information. To help students understand the graphics being described here, draw examples of each and discuss their strengths.

Using the Strategies

1. Members of the American Indian, Inuit, and Aleut groups, and members of the Asian and Pacific Island groups
2. African Americans and Hispanics
3. Either a pie graph or a bar chart could be used.

Situation

You and a classmate want to settle an argument about the range of ethnic diversity in the United States. You've compiled information about America's major ethnic groups (see box) and want to display that information in graphic form. You need to learn how to interpret and construct a graphic organizer.

Strategies

Recognize the different kinds of graphic organizers.

• A **line graph** charts a pattern over time, such as the yearly increase in immigration of a certain group over a ten-year period.

• A **pie graph** (it looks like a pie cut into wedge-shaped pieces) shows percentages of elements that make up a whole, such as the percentages of earnings from a farm's various crops.

• A **bar graph** uses parallel bars to compare two or more kinds of information in relation to time and quantity. A bar graph might compare student enrollment by ethnic group for a given year.

Examine your information and decide which kind of graph would best illustrate your data.

• In creating your own graphic organizer, use appropriate measurements and labels. For example, to make a bar graph, you

---

1998 Population Estimate

Total United States population: 270,733,000.

• White Americans constituted 233,401,000, or 82.5 percent.

• African Americans constituted 34,489,000, or 12.7 percent.

• Persons of Hispanic origin constituted 30,680,000 or 11.3 percent.

• Members of the American Indian, Eskimo, and Aleut groups constituted 2,366,000, or 0.9 percent.

• Members of Asian and Pacific Island groups constituted 10,476,000, or 3.9 percent.

Note: The groups listed above total 311,412,000, or 111.3 percent, because persons may belong in more than one category.
Source: U.S. Bureau of the Census.

e pluribus Unum

---

will need to show a scale divided into numerical units (such as "thousands," or "millions") that encompasses the range of data you are comparing. To make a pie graph, you'll need to create wedge-shaped segments that are scaled to the percentages that they represent.

Using the Strategies

1. Based on the data on this page, which two groups made up the smallest percentage of the U.S. population?

2. Which two groups had about the same percentage of the total population?

3. Which of the three kinds of graphs described above would you use to illustrate this data? On a separate

sheet of paper, sketch the graph using appropriate labels.

Extending the Strategies

• Using the Internet or printed materials, research information about a selected aspect of your community, city, or school (population makeup, income, growth, voting patterns, reading scores, etc.). Display the information on a graph.

• Be aware of the different kinds of graphic organizers used in print and electronic media. Bring in examples of graphic organizers for a permanent classroom exhibit. Note that newsmagazines often use elaborate pictorial graphics. Be sure to find some of these for your exhibit.

690 THE MODERNS

Crossing the Curriculum

Math

Assign groups of students to collect statistical information over the past several years for each of the school's men's and women's athletic teams. Include win/loss records, individual achievements, and team records. Ask the groups to organize and graph the data they have collected and present their findings to the class.

Computer Science

Ask an expert (teacher or community representative) to demonstrate how computer software can be used to organize data into different kinds of charts, tables, and graphs. If time and equipment are available, have students create a graphic organizer from the information they have collected in the Extending the Strategies section on this page.

Collection 14

Shadows of the Past

Theme

Inner Voices *At this point in our literary history, many writers began to experiment with narrative style and imitated a stream-of-consciousness technique, in which the characters' inner lives are revealed through an imitation of their thought processes. Faulker is the major writer here.*

Reading the Anthology

Reaching Struggling Readers

The *Reading Skills and Strategies: Reaching Struggling Readers* binder includes a Reading Strategies Handbook that offers concrete suggestions to help students who have difficulty reading and comprehending text, or students who are reluctant readers. When a specific strategy is most appropriate for a selection, a correlation to the Handbook is provided at the bottom of the teacher's page under the head Reaching Struggling Readers. This head may also be used to introduce additional ideas for helping students read challenging texts.

Reading Beyond the Anthology

Read On At the end of The Moderns collections, the grade eleven book includes an annotated bibliography of books suitable for extended reading. The suggested books are related to works in these collections by theme, by author, or by subject. To preview the Read On for The Moderns period, please turn to p. T800.

Collection 14 Shadows of the Past

Resources for this Collection

Note: All resources for this collection are available for preview on the *One-Stop Planner CD-ROM 2 with Test Generator.* All worksheets and blackline masters may be printed from the CD-ROM.

Internet Resources
go.hrw.com LE0 11-14

Selection or Feature	Reading and Literary Skills	Vocabulary, Language, and Grammar
• **Richard Bone** (p. 692) **Primary Sources: The Genesis of Spoon River** (p. 693) Edgar Lee Masters • **"Butch" Weldy** (p. 694) • **Fiddler Jones** (p. 694) • **Petit, the Poet** (p. 695) • **Mrs. George Reece** (p. 695) Edgar Lee Masters	• *Graphic Organizers for Active Reading,* Worksheet pp. 68, 69	
Recuerdo (p. 698) Edna St. Vincent Millay **Primary Sources: "The brawny male sends his picture"** (p. 700) Edna St. Vincent Millay	• *Graphic Organizers for Active Reading,* Worksheet p. 70	
The Jilting of Granny Weatherall (p. 703) Katherine Anne Porter **Connections:** *from* **"Discordants"** (p. 711) Conrad Aiken	• *Graphic Organizers for Active Reading,* Worksheet p. 71	• *Words to Own,* Worksheet p. 41 • *Grammar and Language Links:* Stream of Consciousness, Worksheet p. 61 • *Daily Oral Grammar,* Transparency 44
A Rose for Emily (p. 715) William Faulkner **Primary Sources: Nobel Prize Acceptance Speech, 1950** (p. 723) William Faulkner	• *Graphic Organizers for Active Reading,* Worksheet p. 72	• *Words to Own,* Worksheet p. 42 • *Daily Oral Grammar,* Transparency 45
Literature of the Americas: Uruguay **The Feather Pillow** (p. 728) Horacio Quiroga *translated by* Margaret Sayers Peden	The Literature of the Americas feature offers selections from a variety of American cultures representing North, Central, and South America. These selections connect to the collection theme, and students explore the thematic links through structured group discussions called Finding Common Ground.	

Collection Planner

Other Resources for this Collection

- *Cross-Curricular Activities,* p. 14
- *Portfolio Management System,* Introduction to Portfolio Assessment, p. 1
- *Test Generator,* Collection Test

Writing	Listening and Speaking / Viewing and Representing	Assessment
• *Portfolio Management System,* Rubrics for Choices, p. 175	• *Audio CD Library,* Disc 19, Tracks 2, 3, 4, 5, 6 • *Portfolio Management System,* Rubrics for Choices, p. 175	• *Formal Assessment,* Selection Tests, pp. 134, 135 • *Test Generator (One-Stop Planner CD-ROM)*
• *Portfolio Management System,* Rubrics for Choices, p. 176	• *Audio CD Library,* Disc 19, Track 7 • *Portfolio Management System,* Rubrics for Choices, p. 176	• *Formal Assessment,* Selection Test, p. 136 • *Test Generator (One-Stop Planner CD-ROM)*
• *Portfolio Management System,* Rubrics for Choices, p. 177	• *Audio CD Library,* Disc 19, Track 8 • *Viewing and Representing:* Fine Art Transparency 14 Worksheet p. 56 • *Portfolio Management System,* Rubrics for Choices, p. 177	• *Formal Assessment,* Selection Test, p. 137 • *Test Generator (One-Stop Planner CD-ROM)*
• *Portfolio Management System,* Rubrics for Choices, p. 178	• *Audio CD Library,* Disc 20, Tracks 2, 3 • *Portfolio Management System,* Rubrics for Choices, p. 178	• *Formal Assessment,* Selection Test, p. 139 • *Test Generator (One-Stop Planner CD-ROM)* • *Preparation for College Admission Exams,* p. 49
	• *Audio CD Library,* Disc 20, Track 4	• *Preparation for College Admission Exams,* p. 51

 Transparency   CD-ROM    Video   Audio CD

Collection Planner

Collection 14 Shadows of the Past

Skills Focus

Selection or Feature	Reading Skills and Strategies	Elements of Literature and Language	Writing	Listening and Speaking	Viewing and Representing
• **Richard Bone** (p. 692) • **"Butch" Weldy** (p. 694) • **Fiddler Jones** (p. 694) • **Petit, the Poet** (p. 695) • **Mrs. George Reece** (p. 695) Edgar Lee Masters	Oral Interpretations, pp. 692, 696	Epitaph, p. 692 Tone, p. 696 Metaphor, p. 696 Theme, p. 696	Identify the Author's Attitude Toward His Subjects, p. 692 Write an Essay Analyzing the Poems as a Reflection of American Life, p. 696	Stage a Performance of *Spoon River Anthology,* p. 696	
Recuerdo (p. 698) Edna St. Vincent Millay	Appreciate Imagery, p. 701 Connotation, p. 701	Metaphor, p. 701 Meter, p. 701 Rhyme Scheme, p. 701 Tone, p. 701 Message, p. 701 Imagery, p. 701 Rhyme, p. 701 Rhythm, p. 701 Image, p. 701	Evaluate the Work of an Author, p. 701 Write an Essay Comparing and Contrasting the Poems of Two Authors, p. 701 Write a Poem Based on a Quickwrite, p. 701		
The Jilting of Granny Weatherall (p. 703) Katherine Anne Porter	Read Closely, pp. 703, 712	Stream of Consciousness, pp. 703, 712 Tenses of Verbs, p. 703 Quotation Marks, p. 703 Irony, p. 712 Ambiguity, p. 712 Point of View, p. 712	Identify Ambiguities in the Story, p. 712 Write an Essay Reconstructing Granny Weatherall's Life, p. 712 Write a Monologue Using Stream of Consciousness from the Point of View of George, p. 712		Use a Graphic to Organize Information, p. 712
A Rose for Emily (p. 715) William Faulkner	Take Notes on a Character, pp. 715, 725 Identify Key Events and List Them in Chronological Order, p. 725	Setting, pp. 715, 724–725 Foreshadowing, p. 724 Conflict, p. 724 Narrator, p. 724 Symbol, p. 724 Character, p. 725 Chronological Order, p. 725 Plot Sequence, p. 725 Atmosphere, p. 725	Analyze a Character, p. 725 Write an Essay Analyzing Plot Sequence, p. 725	Organize a Literary Debate, p. 725	Use a Graphic to Organize Information, p. 725
Reading Skills and Strategies: Semantic Features Analysis (p. 726)	Synonyms, p. 726 Connotation, p. 726 Thesaurus, p. 726 Denotation, p. 726				Make a Semantic Features Analysis Chart, p. 726
Literature of the Americas: Uruguay The Feather Pillow (p. 728) Horacio Quiroga *translated by* Margaret Sayers Peden	Dialogue with the Text, pp. 728, 732	The Literature of the Americas feature offers selections from a variety of American cultures representing North, Central, and South America. These selections connect to the collection theme, and students explore the thematic links through structured group discussions called Finding Common Ground.			

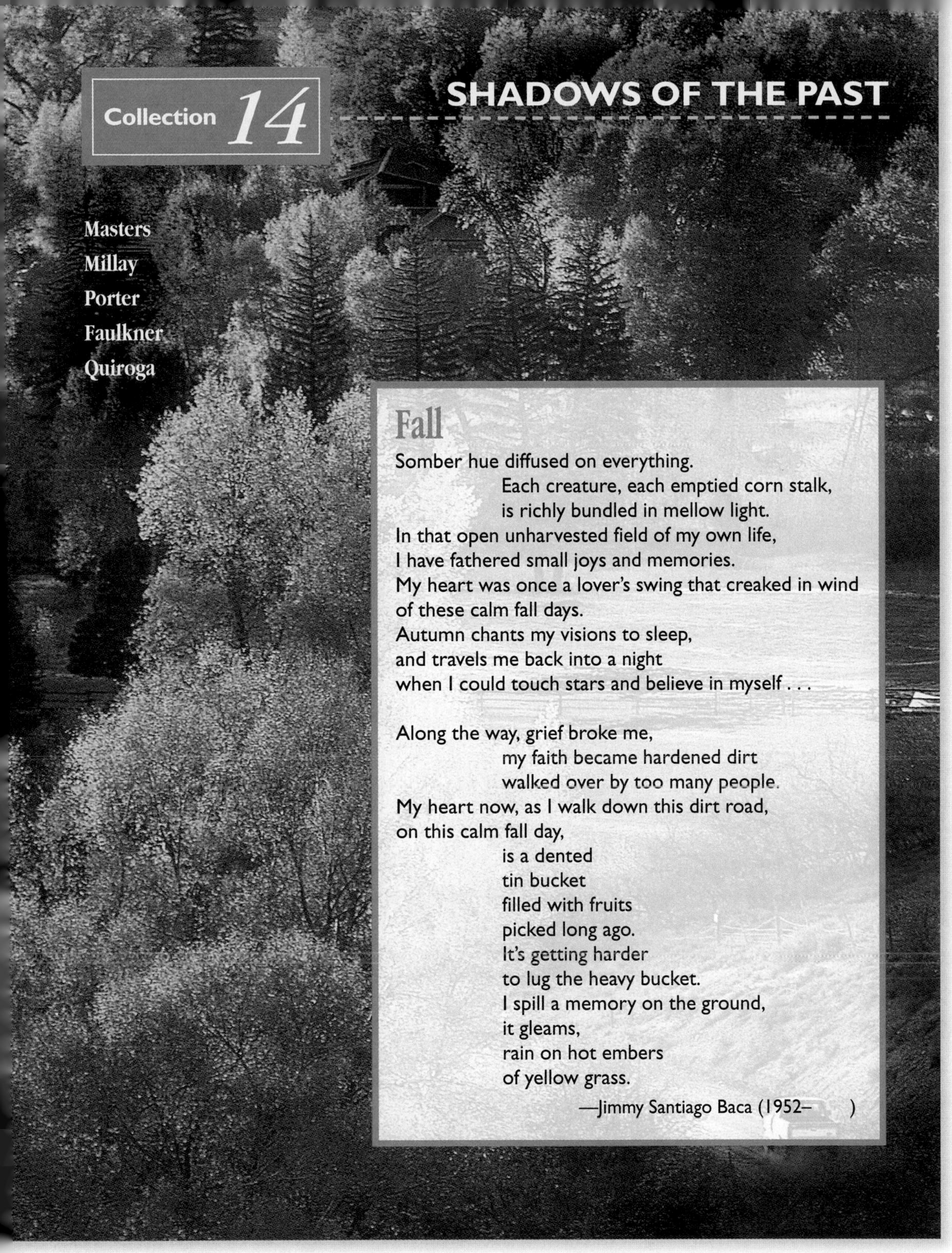

Masters
Millay
Porter
Faulkner
Quiroga

Fall

Somber hue diffused on everything.
      Each creature, each emptied corn stalk,
      is richly bundled in mellow light.
In that open unharvested field of my own life,
I have fathered small joys and memories.
My heart was once a lover's swing that creaked in wind
of these calm fall days.
Autumn chants my visions to sleep,
and travels me back into a night
when I could touch stars and believe in myself . . .

Along the way, grief broke me,
      my faith became hardened dirt
      walked over by too many people.
My heart now, as I walk down this dirt road,
on this calm fall day,
      is a dented
      tin bucket
      filled with fruits
      picked long ago.
      It's getting harder
      to lug the heavy bucket.
      I spill a memory on the ground,
      it gleams,
      rain on hot embers
      of yellow grass.

—Jimmy Santiago Baca (1952—   )

Responding to the Poem

? **Where is this speaker? What is he doing?** [Possible response: The speaker is walking down a dirt road during the fall, thinking about his life.] **How does the speaker feel about his own "shadows of the past"?** [Possible response: The speaker feels haunted by the small joys he has experienced and the hurts he has suffered in the past. His memories are getting heavy for him to carry. He is trying to inspire himself by remembering the hopes and confidence he once had.] **What is the tone of poem?** [meditative, sad, nostalgic]

RESPONDING TO THE ART

Ask students whether the photograph captures the mood and meaning of the poem. Discuss the brilliant fall colors and the country scene. Ask them what they would have chosen to illustrate the poem.

Resources

Viewing and Representing
Videocassette A, Segment 2
Available in English and Spanish. This segment explores the American dream through our literary heritage. For full lesson plans and worksheets, see *Visual Connections Teacher's Manual.*

Writing Focus: Interpretive Essay

The following **Work in Progress** assignments in this collection build to a culminating **Writer's Workshop** at the end of Collection 16.

OBJECTIVES

Richard Bone / "Butch" Weldy / Fiddler Jones / Petit, the Poet / Mrs. George Reece

1. Read and interpret the poems
2. Make an oral interpretation
3. Express understanding through writing and performance

SKILLS

Reading
• Make an oral interpretation

Writing
• Collect ideas for an interpretive essay
• Explain what makes characters uniquely American

Speaking/Listening
• Perform poems aloud

Planning

• **Block Schedule**
Block Scheduling Lesson Plans with Pacing Guide

• **Traditional Schedule**
Lesson Plans Including Strategies for English-Language Learners

• **One-Stop Planner**
CD-ROM with Test Generator

BROWSING IN THE FILES

Writers on Writing. Masters described *Spoon River Anthology* as "nineteen stories developed by interrelated portraits. . . ." where "the fools, the drunkards, and the failures came first, the people of one-birth minds got second place, and the heroes and the enlightened spirits came last, a sort of *Divine Comedy*. . . ."

Edgar Lee Masters

(1869–1950)

Edgar Lee Masters was born in Garnett, Kansas. Like Carl Sandburg (page 792), he was a product of that part of the Middle West known as the Corn Belt or Bible Belt. Also like Sandburg, he found his voice in the free verse that characterized the second decade of the twentieth century. But unlike Sandburg, Masters produced just one book in a spare style that served his homely subject matter. After that he reverted to a more conventional poetic style: pretty, romantic, and wordy.

Yet this one book, *Spoon River Anthology* (1915), was a landmark in American literature, and it made Masters famous. It is a collection of some 250 epitaphs—memorial inscriptions on gravestones—spoken by the inhabitants of a cemetery in the fictional town of Spoon River: drunkards, bankers, judges, poets, atheists, preachers, gamblers, druggists, and housewives.

The dramatic device of having dead people speak their own epitaphs served Masters brilliantly. Drawing upon his memories of Petersburg and Lewistown—the Illinois towns he knew during his first twenty years—he used these epitaphs to show the hidden underside of American life. Victims of that life, freed by death to speak without fear of consequences, tell their stories. Bit by bit, they fill in a picture of small-town life that is vastly different from the folksy, sentimental magazine cover images of the time. Masters's speakers from beyond the grave bring buried truth into the daylight.

Spoon River Anthology became one of the most widely read books of an age that was fascinated by psychology. Better than any scientific study, it revealed how the conventions of society warred with people's real needs and beliefs. By turning psychological "case histories" into lyric poems, Masters gave speech to the inarticulate and, at the same time, brought a new kind of realism to poetry.

APWide World Photos.

Before You Read

FROM SPOON RIVER ANTHOLOGY

Make the Connection

Having Their Say
Have you ever stood in a graveyard and thought of all the hundreds of stories that lie buried there—all the secrets, the loves, the angers, the disappointments, all the unfinished business of lives that have ended? Have you ever thought of how the people in that graveyard were connected in life—by family, by occupation, by feuds, even by scandal?

Reading Skills and Strategies

Oral Interpretations
In *Spoon River Anthology*, Masters captures the sounds and rhythms of American English spoken by ordinary people from a small Midwestern town. Read each poem aloud in order to appreciate how Masters imitates real speech and conveys a sense of the person who is speaking. Can you interpret the poems in different ways by using different tones of voice?

go.hrw.com
LE0 11-14

692 THE MODERNS

Resources: Print and Media

Reading
• *Graphic Organizers for Active Reading,* p. 68, 69
• *Audio CD Library*
   Disc 19, Tracks 2, 3, 4, 5, 6

Assessment
• *Formal Assessment,* pp. 134, 135
• *Portfolio Management System,* p. 175
• *Test Generator (One-Stop Planner CD-ROM)*

Internet
• go.hrw.com (keyword: LE0 11–14)

Masters often gives his speakers names that are clues to their character. As a stonecutter, Bone engraved words that identified skeletons. As a spokesman for his own conscience, he speaks words that cut to the bone.

Richard Bone

Edgar Lee Masters

When I first came to Spoon River
I did not know whether what they told me
Was true or false.
They would bring me the epitaph
5 And stand around the shop while I worked
And say "He was so kind," "He was wonderful,"
"She was the sweetest woman," "He was a consistent Christian."
And I chiseled for them whatever they wished,
All in ignorance of its truth.
10 But later, as I lived among the people here,
I knew how near to the life
Were the epitaphs that were ordered for them as they died.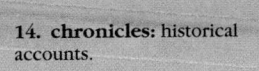
But still I chiseled whatever they paid me to chisel
And made myself party to the false chronicles°

14. **chronicles:** historical accounts.

15 Of the stones,
Even as the historian does who writes
Without knowing the truth,
Or because he is influenced to hide it.

PRIMARY **Sources**   AN **AUTOBIOGRAPHY**

The Genesis of Spoon River [1914]

About the 20th of May my mother came to visit us, and we had many long talks. . . . In our talks now we went over the whole past of Lewistown and Petersburg, bringing up characters and events that had passed from my mind. We traced these persons to their final fates, to the positions in life that they were then in. We had many sessions at this recalling of old days. . . .

The psychological experience of this was truly wonderful. Finally on the morning she was leaving for Springfield we had a last and a rather sobering talk. It was Sunday, too, and after putting her on the train at 53rd Street I walked back home full of strange pensiveness. The little church bell was ringing, but spring was in the air. I went to my room and immediately wrote "The Hill," and two or three of the portraits of *Spoon River Anthology.* Almost at once the idea came to me: Why not make this book the book I had thought about in 1906, in which I should draw the macrocosm by portraying the microcosm? Why not put side by side the stories of two characters interlocked in fate, thus giving both misunderstood souls a chance to be justly weighed? . . .

—Edgar Lee Masters, *from Across Spoon River: An Autobiography*

EDGAR LEE MASTERS 693

Reaching All Students

Struggling Readers
After students have read and discussed "Richard Bone," model the Most Important Word strategy for them, demonstrating how the word you have chosen is a key to the overall message or meaning of the poem. For information on applying this strategy, see the *Reading Strategies Handbook*, p. 45 in the *Reading Skills and Strategies* binder.

Advanced Learners
Encourage students to read the entire *Spoon River Anthology.* Have them pay particular attention to the characters mentioned in the epitaphs on the next two pages, such as Old Rhodes and Jack the Fiddler, and share the stories of these characters with the class.

Summary ■

These dramatic monologues are spoken by the dead in the Spoon River cemetery. Richard Bone spent his days chiseling words of tribute on tombstones but comes to doubt the truth of these epitaphs. "Butch" Weldy recalls the accident that blinded him. Fiddler Jones looks back on a life of music, natural beauty, and no regrets. Petit the Poet regrets his life of "little iambics," blind to the epic poetic material around him. Mrs. George Reece takes pride in having raised her children alone after her husband was unjustly imprisoned.

Ⓐ **Reading Skills and Strategies**
Making an Oral Interpretation
❓ How might Bone speak these lines? Why? [Possible answers: with bitter irony, because he feels he perpetuated lies; matter-of-factly, because he feels he was only doing his job.]

Ⓑ **Elements of Literature**
Metaphor
❓ How are epitaphs like historical chronicles? [Possible answers: Both tell a story, usually from a limited point of view; both are meant to be authoritative; both concern past generations.]

Primary Sources

In this excerpt from his autobiography, Masters traces the origin of his *Spoon River Anthology* to conversations he had with his mother. They recalled the inhabitants of two towns in which Masters was raised and what became of these people in later life. These life stories prompted Masters to begin work on the ambitious poetic project that would become *Spoon River Anthology.*

Ⓒ **Vocabulary Note**
Greek Roots
Introduce students to the Greek roots *makros* ("great"), *mikros* ("small"), and *kosmos* ("world"). Then, ask someone to explain what Masters means by "drawing the macrocosm by portraying the microcosm." [The voices of this particular small town speak for the human condition in general.]

T693

Many of the stories from *Spoon River* are interlocking. The villain of the whole book is Deacon Thomas Rhodes, who "ran the church as well as the store and the bank." We hear about Rhodes from a number of his victims, including "Butch" Weldy. "Butch" refers to Jack the Fiddler, a blind man also buried in the cemetery. Jack was killed when "Butch," who had been drinking, drove a carriage into a ditch.

"Butch" Weldy

Edgar Lee Masters

After I got religion and steadied down
They gave me a job in the canning works,
And every morning I had to fill
The tank in the yard with gasoline,
5 That fed the blow-fires in the sheds
To heat the soldering irons.
And I mounted a rickety ladder to do it,
Carrying buckets full of the stuff.
One morning, as I stood there pouring,
10 The air grew still and seemed to heave,
And I shot up as the tank exploded,
And down I came with both legs broken
And my eyes burned crisp as a couple of eggs,
For someone left a blow-fire going,
15 And something sucked the flame in the tank.
The Circuit Judge said whoever did it
Was a fellow-servant of mine, and so
Old Rhodes' son didn't have to pay me.
And I sat on the witness stand as blind
20 As Jack the Fiddler, saying over and over,
"I didn't know him at all."

694 THE MODERNS

Like many characters in *Spoon River Anthology*, Fiddler Jones is based on a real person, a Petersburg-area fiddler named John Jones. Cooney Potter was a hard-working farmer, and Red-Head Sammy Watkins was a local musician.

Fiddler Jones

Edgar Lee Masters

The earth keeps some vibration going
There in your heart, and that is you.
And if the people find you can fiddle,
Why, fiddle you must, for all your life.
5 What do you see, a harvest of clover?
Or a meadow to walk through to the river?
The wind's in the corn; you rub your hands
For beeves° hereafter ready for market;
Or else you hear the rustle of skirts
10 Like the girls when dancing at Little Grove.
To Cooney Potter a pillar of dust
Or whirling leaves meant ruinous drouth;°
They looked to me like Red-Head Sammy
Stepping it off, to "Toor-a-Loor."
15 How could I till my forty acres
Not to speak of getting more,
With a medley of horns, bassoons and piccolos
Stirred in my brain by crows and robins
And the creak of a wind-mill—only these?
20 And I never started to plow in my life
That someone did not stop in the road
And take me away to a dance or picnic.
I ended up with forty acres;
I ended up with a broken fiddle—
25 And a broken laugh, and a thousand memories,
And not a single regret.

8. beeves: alternative plural of *beef;* here, the meaning is "cattle."
12. drouth: archaic spelling of *drought.*

Crossing the Curriculum

Petit, the Poet

Edgar Lee Masters

Seeds in a dry pod, tick, tick, tick,
Tick, tick, tick, like mites in a quarrel—
Faint iambics that the full breeze wakens—
But the pine tree makes a symphony thereof.
5 Triolets, villanelles, rondels, rondeaus,
Ballades° by the score with the same old
  thought:
The snows and the roses of yesterday are
  vanished;
And what is love but a rose that fades?
Life all around me here in the village:
10 Tragedy, comedy, valor and truth,
Courage, constancy, heroism, failure—
All in the loom, and oh what patterns!
Woodlands, meadows, streams and rivers—
Blind to all of it all my life long.
15 Triolets, villanelles, rondels, rondeaus,
Seeds in a dry pod, tick, tick, tick,
Tick, tick, tick, what little iambics,
While Homer and Whitman roared in the
  pines.

6. Triolets . . . Ballades: various complicated forms of poetry.

Mrs. George Reece

Edgar Lee Masters

To this generation I would say:
Memorize some bit of verse of truth or
  beauty.
It may serve a turn in your life.
My husband had nothing to do
5 With the fall of the bank—he was only
  cashier.
The wreck was due to the president, Thomas
  Rhodes,
And his vain, unscrupulous son.
Yet my husband was sent to prison,
And I was left with the children,
10 To feed and clothe and school them.
And I did it, and sent them forth
Into the world all clean and strong,
And all through the wisdom of Pope, the
  poet:°
"Act well your part, there all the honor lies."

13. Pope, the poet: The English poet Alexander Pope (1688–1744), whose wise sayings are often quoted.

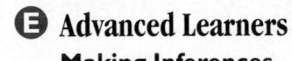

JOE M'LANE. BLACKS

E Advanced Learners
Making Inferences
❓ After students read Petit's epitaph, point out the footnote. Then, have them look up these verse forms in a handbook of literary terms. What is significant about Petit's list? [All are French lyric forms with rigid rhyme schemes. Petit considers himself a failure for writing these types of poems instead of spontaneous, unrhymed verse of epic proportions, like that of Homer and Whitman.]

F Literary Connections
Students should recall Walt Whitman's poems from Collection 7 (p. 347). Tell them that Homer was the blind bard of ancient Greece who composed the *Iliad* and the *Odyssey*. Homer's epics are peopled with gods and goddesses, warriors, kings and queens. His characters suffer the same human problems as Masters's: temptation, lost love, anger, bitterness, regret, and the whims of fate.

G Elements of Literature
Character
❓ After students read this epitaph, point out that this speaker is referred to as "Mrs. George Reece" in the title and never mentions her own given name. What does this say about her? [Possible answers: She is proud of being married; she is loyal to her husband because she knows he is innocent; she believes that one should "Act well your part" and thus follows the customs of her time.]

H Critical Thinking
Drawing Conclusions
❓ What kind of person do you think Mrs. Reece is? Why? [Possible answers: She is strong, proud, honest, and sensible; she wastes little time weeping over her husband's imprisonment but instead does the work necessary for her family's survival.]

Making the Connections

Connecting to the Theme: "Shadows of the Past"
After students have read the poems, discuss the collection theme. How are these voices from Spoon River "shadows" from the town's past? Why do you think Masters chose to evoke the Spoon River of memory and history rather than the present? What might he be trying to say about this past era in midwestern America? What might he be trying to say about memory in general?

Listening to Music 🎵

"Turkey in the Straw" (Traditional), performed by Vassar Clements
Though the terms *violin* and *fiddle* are virtually synonymous, we associate a violin with classical music, while a fiddle evokes a far more folksy affair. In the era before radio and musical recordings, dancing to live music was a popular form of recreation. A proficient fiddler was all that was needed for a lively barnyard dance.

Activity
As students read the poem "Fiddler Jones," play "Turkey in the Straw" in the background. Then, have them discuss how the music enhances appreciation of the poem.

MAKING MEANINGS

First Thoughts [Respond]

1. Students will probably find the characters realistic because of their familiar experiences of nostalgia, bitterness, pride, and happiness.

Shaping Interpretations [Interpret]

2. He realizes that the epitaphs people request often misrepresent their subjects and that he is making a living by perpetuating comforting lies.

3. Possible answers: He seems resigned about the accident, bitter toward old Rhodes's son, bewildered in his suffering.

4. Jones feels his life, filled with "a thousand memories," was well spent. He says he has "not a single regret" over leaving the plowing to play music.

5. Petit compares his own poetry to insignificant things: dried-up seeds and mites. He feels that his work was trite because it was based on calculated clichés. Petit now realizes that material for great poetry (like Homer's and Whitman's) was all around him, and he missed it.

6. Mrs. Reece suggests that people should take comfort in doing their duty. Given Mr. Reece's unjust conviction, he might not agree that personal honor is all the comfort one needs.

7. Masters gave names that help define the characters. "Butch" implies careless or aggressive behavior. "Weldy," which sounds like *welding*, reflects his job soldering at the cannery. "Fiddler" is named for his avocation. "Petit" means "small" in French and echoes his insignificance as a poet.

8. Possible responses: Mrs. Reece and Fiddler look back on their lives with satisfaction and seem to generally accept their fates. Bone and Petit feel more shame and regret about their lives and rebel against their fates. They also seem less accepting of others.

Connecting with the Texts

[Respond]

9. Students might praise Fiddler Jones and Mrs. Reece and console the others.

MAKING MEANINGS

First Thoughts

1. Think of the people you know in your own town or neighborhood. Compared with them, do these Spoon River characters sound real to you? Cite reasons to support your responses.

Shaping Interpretations

2. What does Richard Bone, the stone carver, come to realize about the people of Spoon River? What does he come to realize about himself?

3. How does Butch Weldy feel about the accident that ruined his life? What is the **tone** of his epitaph?

4. How does Fiddler Jones feel about his life? Cite passages from the poem to support your interpretation.

5. Appropriately, Petit, the poet, uses **metaphors** to talk about his experiences. In lines 1–3, what is he comparing his own poetry to? How does this small-town poet feel about his work—and why does he mention Homer and Whitman at the end of his epitaph?

6. Summarize Mrs. George Reece's advice. Do you think her husband would have agreed with her? Explain.

7. What significance can you find in some of the names that Masters gave his characters?

8. Compare the ways any two of these Spoon River speakers feel about life. Consider their feelings about their own work, their attitudes toward other people, and their responses to chance or fate.

Connecting with the Texts

9. If you had the chance, how would you reply to these speakers of *Spoon River Anthology*?

Extending the Texts

10. In what ways do the speakers' feelings—such as Bone's remorse or Petit's regrets—suggest universal **themes**? What experiences in today's world might produce a contemporary Butch Weldy, Fiddler Jones, or Mrs. George Reece?

Extending the Text [Evaluate]

10. "Richard Bone" expresses a universal theme about the untruths that we depend on to make our lives and our memories more secure. "Mrs. George Reece" suggests that reliance on duty and simple directives is often the only thing that will pull us through life's difficulties. Today's Americans still have ample experience with industrial accidents, corporate irresponsibility, the joys of music and nature, and the struggles of single motherhood.

CHOICES:
Building Your Portfolio

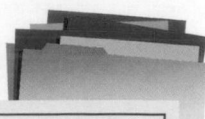

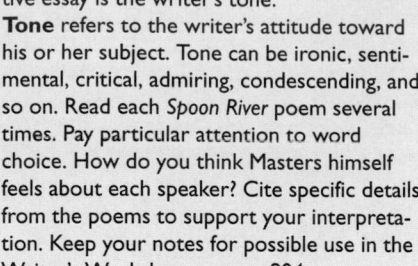

Writer's Notebook

1. Collecting Ideas for an Interpretive Essay

A good focus for an interpretive essay is the writer's tone.

Tone refers to the writer's attitude toward his or her subject. Tone can be ironic, sentimental, critical, admiring, condescending, and so on. Read each *Spoon River* poem several times. Pay particular attention to word choice. How do you think Masters himself feels about each speaker? Cite specific details from the poems to support your interpretation. Keep your notes for possible use in the Writer's Workshop on page 804.

Analyzing the Poems

2. The American Way

In a brief essay, tell what the five *Spoon River* poems in this text say about life in a Midwestern American town in the early twentieth century. Consider the values of the people, their hopes and dreams, their problems, and their sense of community. What beliefs and experiences, in your opinion, make Masters's characters especially American? (You might want to read more *Spoon River* poems before writing.)

Speaking and Listening

3. *Spoon River* in Performance

The entire *Spoon River Anthology* has been performed onstage, with several actors taking the parts of the speakers. Prepare these five poems for a performance of your own. The performers' first task is to analyze each character: What is this person's attitude toward life? What tone of voice would he or she speak in? You might wish to include music in your performance and to dress your speakers in some kind of costume (perhaps they could all dress in black). You might also add other Spoon Riverites to your performance. Ask your listeners to evaluate your performance.

Grading Timesaver

Rubrics for each Choices assignment appear on p. 175 in the *Portfolio Management System.*

Edna St. Vincent Millay

(1892–1950)

Like Edwin Arlington Robinson (page 644), Edna St. Vincent Millay was born on the granite coast of Maine and established her poetic reputation in New York. Also like Robinson, she lived to see the day when, despite

AP/Wide World Photos.

many honors and the devotion of a wide audience, she had to realize that her reputation had barely withstood the onslaught of modernism.

Millay achieved fame even before she graduated from Vassar College, with the publication of her first collection of verse, *Renascence and Other Poems* (1917). After World War I, she moved to Greenwich Village. This was an era when that section of New York City was not only a haven for artists, but also a place where women were as free as men to speak their minds, to live by their own rules, and to pursue careers—activities that most Americans still considered improper for women. Taking advantage of this liberated atmosphere, Millay became one of its leading voices—a free spirit who wrote saucy and slightly scandalous lyrics in a style that occasionally evoked Elizabethan verse. Millay's philosophy might best be described in her own words:

First Fig

My candle burns at both ends;
    It will not last the night;
But ah, my foes, and oh, my friends—
    It gives a lovely light!

Millay also became caught up in the radical dissent of the time, and she worked passionately, if vainly, to save the anarchists Sacco and Vanzetti, who were executed in Massachusetts in 1927 after a celebrated trial.

"Vincent," as she was familiarly known, was a skilled actress and speaker with the flair of a seasoned performer. She gave recitals during long, nationwide tours in which she won a degree of celebrity seldom associated with poets.

Both shocking and fascinating to her audiences, Millay grew in popularity even as her poetic achievements began to decline. Her most productive period was between the two world wars, when she published seven collections of poetry, as well as a series of dramas written for the Provincetown Players in New York. In 1923, she became the first woman to win the Pulitzer Prize in poetry.

During World War II, Millay determined to write "public" poetry to contribute to the Allied cause. She produced scores of poems which, although widely read, proved that outrage and passion could not substitute for the verbal artistry that poetry demands. The lyricist had been overtaken by the propagandist.

One of the brightest literary stars of a generation was all but faded from sight when, in her fifty-eighth year, Edna St. Vincent Millay died alone at her home, Steepletop.

go.hrw.com
LEO 11-14

EDNA ST. VINCENT MILLAY **697**

Resources: Print and Media

Reading
- *Graphic Organizers for Active Reading*, p. 70
- Audio CD Library
  Disc 19, Track 7

Assessment
- *Formal Assessment*, p. 136
- *Portfolio Management System*, p. 176
- *Test Generator (One-Stop Planner CD-ROM)*

Internet
- go.hrw.com (keyword: LEO 11–14)

OBJECTIVES
1. Read and interpret the poem
2. Analyze imagery
3. Express understanding through critical and creative writing

SKILLS
Reading
- Identify and use imagery

Writing
- Collect ideas for an interpretive essay
- Compare two poems
- Write a poem about a happy memory

Viewing/Representing
- Compare a work of art to a poem (ATE)

Planning

- **Traditional Schedule**
  Lesson Plans Including Strategies for English-Language Learners
- **One-Stop Planner**
  CD-ROM with Test Generator

BROWSING IN THE FILES

About the Author. Millay graduated from high school with no idea what she would do in the future. Few Americans had made careers for themselves as poets, and Millay did not even consider the possibility. However, she continued writing, and in 1912 her poem "Renascence" (see Primary Sources feature, p. 700) put her firmly in the spotlight. Caroline Dow, head of the National YWCA Training School, heard Millay recite "Renascence" and arranged for her to receive a scholarship to Vassar College.

Summary ■

In this rhymed narrative poem, which uses repetition, highly connotative diction, and subtle metaphors, the speaker recalls a happy night spent riding back and forth on the ferry with a friend. In the morning, on their way to the subway, the two give money and a gift of fruit to an old woman selling newspapers.

RESPONDING TO THE ART

Reginald Marsh (1898–1954) studied painting with John Sloan, a member of the artistic circle known as The Eight (see p. 523). Marsh painted realistic, lively scenes of New York City life, capturing both the squalor and the energy of urban living. His subjects included street scenes, subways, cheap Bowery hotels, and crowds on the Coney Island boardwalk. Marsh later taught at the Art Students' League in New York City for more than twenty years and also worked as a magazine illustrator.

Activity. After students read Millay's poem, ask them how the painting reflects its mood and tone. [Possible response: The swirling lines and red and gold splashes of light suggest the poem's celebration of movement, life, warmth, and merriment.]

Before You Read
RECUERDO

Make the Connection
Happy Memories
Remembering a happy event can cast a sudden glow over our lives. The title of this poem is a Spanish word meaning "remembrance" or "souvenir." Here the poet evokes a happy memory of time past—a carefree night spent riding one of the ferry boats that connect the island of Manhattan with other parts of New York City.

Quickwrite
Without pausing for critical thought, freewrite a list of three or four memories of happy times that pop into your mind.

The Normandie (1938)
by Reginald Marsh.
Watercolor (30″ × 50″).
The Butler Institute of American
Art, Youngstown, Ohio.
Purchased 1962.

Reaching All Students

Struggling Readers
Point out to students that the first two lines of each stanza form a refrain. Ask students why this repetition would be appropriate to a poem about a ferry ride. [Like a refrain, a ferry ride repeats its journey over and over again.] Then, have students focus on the last four lines of each stanza and visualize the scenes Millay describes. What mood do these scenes create? [a warm, joyous mood]

English Language Learners
Have students create a classroom chart of this poem's title in various languages, such as the following: Spanish, "Recuerdo"; English, "Remembrance"; French, "Souvenir." Then, direct students to write their own poems of remembrance, narrating events from their own lives and choosing the title in the language they are most comfortable with. Students can then share their poems with the class.

Recuerdo

Edna St. Vincent Millay

We were very tired, we were very merry— Ⓐ
We had gone back and forth all night on the ferry.
It was bare and bright, and smelled like a stable—
But we looked into a fire, we leaned across a table, Ⓑ
5 We lay on a hill-top underneath the moon;
And the whistles kept blowing, and the dawn came soon.

We were very tired, we were very merry— Ⓒ
We had gone back and forth all night on the ferry;
And you ate an apple, and I ate a pear,
10 From a dozen of each we had bought somewhere;
And the sky went wan, and the wind came cold,
And the sun rose dripping, a bucketful of gold.

We were very tired, we were very merry,
We had gone back and forth all night on the ferry.
15 We hailed, "Good morrow, mother!" to a shawl-covered head,
And bought a morning paper, which neither of us read; Ⓓ
And she wept, "God bless you!" for the apples and pears,
And we gave her all our money but our subway fares.

EDNA ST. VINCENT MILLAY **699**

Ⓐ Historical Connections

New York Ferries

Explain to students that until the Brooklyn Bridge was completed in 1883, ferries were the only way to travel to and from New York's Manhattan Island. Today, Manhattan is connected to other islands and to the mainland by bridges and tunnels. However, ferries still run to Ellis Island and Staten Island, as well as New Jersey.

Ⓑ Reading Skills and Strategies

Appreciating Imagery

❓ How does the description of the actual ferry as "bare and bright" and smelling "like a stable" contrast with the mood of the two friends? [The ferry is a cavernous, functional vessel, probably old, harshly lit, and smelly, but the friends are so happy in each other's company that it seems warm, cozy, and wondrous.]

Ⓒ Elements of Literature

Refrain

❓ Point out that a refrain usually comes at the end of a stanza. What is the effect of placing the refrain at the beginning of each stanza? [Possible response: It functions like a topic sentence, emphasizing that the two do nothing but ride back and forth all night; what matters is each other's company.]

Ⓓ Critical Thinking

Analyzing Author's Purpose

❓ Why do you think Millay includes the detail that neither character reads the paper? [Possible answers: to emphasize their absorption in each other; to show that they buy the paper simply to please the old woman.]

Using Students' Strengths

Verbal Learners

Students may enjoy contrasting "Recuerdo" with Walt Whitman's poem "Crossing Brooklyn Ferry." Have them read Whitman's poem and write brief essays comparing the two speakers. Volunteers could give dramatic readings of sections of "Crossing Brooklyn Ferry."

Visual Learners

Have students get together for a small-group discussion of the visual impact of "Recuerdo." You might start them off with the following questions: How does Millay use words to create a picture in the reader's mind? How does she convey an impression of color and light? What colors, contrasts, and images do students see in the poem? Ask each group to provide their own illustrations of the poem.

Making the Connections

Connecting to the Theme: "Shadows of the Past"

After students have finished reading the poem, discuss the collection theme. Why has this particular memory remained with the speaker as a "shadow" of her past? How is it different from the memories that Spoon River's inhabitants recall? Can a fleeting, happy memory like the one in "Recuerdo" have the same impact as the more dramatic, life-changing memories of "Butch" Weldy and Mrs. George Reece?

Primary Sources

In this lighthearted letter, Millay addresses two young male poets who, after the publication of her poem "Renascence," assumed it was written by a middle-aged man. She corrects their error, questions the sexist assumptions that it seems to be based on, and directs them to a review of another poem she has written.

Background

The poetry contest that Millay sent "Renascence" to offered three prizes and publication for the one hundred best submissions; Millay's poem was judged fourth-best of ten thousand entries. However, the three prize winners and many readers insisted that "Renascence" was clearly the best poem.

RESPONDING TO THE ART

Charles Ellis met Millay in 1917, when they were both associated with the Provincetown Players. Ellis designed sets and costumes for Millay's play *Aria da Capo*. His portrait emphasizes Millay's career as a writer by depicting her surrounded by books.

Activity. Ask students to compare and contrast Ellis's portrait with the photograph on p. 697. Which image better catches the humor of the woman who wrote the letter shown on this page? [Possible responses: In the photo, Millay wears a suit and stands working at a desk, like a businesswoman. In the portrait, she sits, wearing a loose, white gown that makes her look more "poetic." The faint smile in both images hints at her sense of humor.]

Ⓐ Reading Skills and Strategies
Making Inferences

❓ Ask students what *Esq.* means. [It stands for *Esquire* and often identifies a lawyer.] In 1912, few lawyers were women. Did Millay want to be mistaken for a man? [Possible answer: She may have felt a man would have a better chance of winning the contest or of being judged fairly.]

T700

Ⓐ In 1912, two talented young poets wrote a letter to the editor of a poetry anthology saying that "Renascence," the poem submitted by E. St. Vincent Millay, Esq., must surely be the work of a forty-five-year-old brawny male. When she heard of the letter, Millay replied as follows.

"The brawny male sends his picture"

[December 5, 1912]

To Mr. Ficke and Mr. Bynner:

Mr. Earle has acquainted me with your wild surmises. Gentlemen: I must convince you of your error; my reputation is at stake. I simply will not be a "brawny male." Not that I have an aversion to brawny males; *au contraire, au contraire.* But I cling to my femininity!

Is it that you consider brain and brawn so inseparable?—I have thought otherwise. Still, that is all a matter of personal opinion. But, gentlemen: When a woman insists that she is twenty, you must not, must not call her forty-five. That is more than wicked; it is indiscreet.

Mr. Ficke, you are a lawyer. I am very much afraid of lawyers. Spare me, kind sir! Take into consideration my youth—for I am indeed but twenty—and my fragility—for "I do protest I am a maid"—and—sleuth me no sleuths!

Seriously: I thank you also for the compliment you have unwittingly given me. For tho I do not yet aspire to be forty-five and brawny, if my verse so represents me, I am more gratified than I can say. When I was a little girl, this is what I thought and wrote:

> Let me not shout into the world's great ear
> Ere I have something for the world to hear.
> Then let my message like an arrow dart
> And pierce a way into the world's great heart.

You cannot know how much I appreciate what you have said about my *Renascence.*

If you should care to look up the April, 1907, number of *Current Literature,* you

Portrait of Edna St. Vincent Millay (1934) by Charles Ellis.
National Portrait Gallery, Washington, D.C./Courtesy Art Resource.

would find a review of my *Land of Romance* (near a review of Mr. Bynner's *Fair of My Fancy*). And you might be interested in Mr. Edward Wheeler's comment: "The poem which follows (by E. St. Vincent Millay) seems to me to be phenomenal. The author, whether boy or girl we do not know, is just fourteen years of age."

E. St. V. M.

P. S. The brawny male sends his picture. I *have* to laugh.

Taking a Second Look

Review: Identifying Main Idea and Details

Review the technique of outlining a text by identifying its main idea and supporting details. This can serve as preparation for the first Choices activity on p. 701.

Activities

1. Have students identify the main idea of Millay's poem. Then, have them list the details that develop the idea in each stanza.

2. Have students identify the main idea of another poem or story. Then, have them list the details in a simple graphic like this one.

Main Idea	hit first home run
Detail	top of the tenth inning
Detail	fans screaming my name
Detail	

MAKING MEANINGS

First Thoughts

1. Do you recognize the feelings described in this poem? When have you ever had similar feelings?

Shaping Interpretations

2. Whom do you think the "we" in the poem refers to? What do lines 4–5 suggest about their feelings for each other?

3. Why do you think the people in the poem gave their money to the "shawl-covered head"? What does this action say about the power of love?

4. Identify the **metaphor** in line 12. What does this image reveal about the speaker's feelings?

5. Describe the poem's **meter** and **rhyme scheme**.

6. How would you describe the **tone** of "Recuerdo"? (You may find it easier to answer this question if you first read the poem aloud.)

READING SKILLS AND STRATEGIES

Appreciating Imagery

Imagery in poetry is more than decoration. It helps express the poet's feelings, and it evokes feelings in the reader. Imagery depends a great deal on the **connotations** of words—their suggestive power. For example, "smelled like a stable" in line 3 of Millay's "Recuerdo" might create a feeling of distaste in someone who despises the odor of stables. But for other readers, the image might evoke something pleasant—earthiness, the warmth of animals, the coziness of a place protected from the out-of-doors. The image would have been quite different if the poet had said "smelled of manure."

Try your hand at changing the effect Millay created with her words and images in the poem "Recuerdo."

a. In line 6, replace "blowing" with a word that creates a negative or unpleasant feeling.

b. In line 12, think of an image to replace "a bucketful of gold" that would make the rising sun seem unpleasant.

---

c. Think of the image suggested by the phrase "shawl-covered head." Replace that image with one suggesting that the woman is threatening or dangerous.

CHOICES: Building Your Portfolio

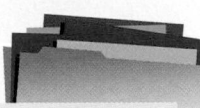

Writer's Notebook

1. Collecting Ideas for an Interpretive Essay

Nowadays, Millay's name is better known than her work. Some critics see her as lacking depth and complexity, in spite of her knack for simple, evocative descriptions of nature and human emotions. Jot down your own assessment of Millay's abilities, based on "Recuerdo." Save your notes for possible use in the Writer's Workshop on page 804.

Comparing Poems

2. Art and Life

The contrasts between America's most famous early-twentieth-century female poet (Millay) and America's most famous nineteenth-century female poet (Emily Dickinson) are interesting. Dickinson—quiet, reserved, and a social hermit—was an experimenter in poetry, a true original. Millay—socially unconventional and adventuresome—was more imitative and conservative as a poet. In a brief essay, contrast "Recuerdo" with at least one of Dickinson's poems (perhaps "Heart! We will forget him!" on page 374). Consider differences in **message, imagery, rhyme, meter,** and **tone.** Which poem do you prefer?

Creative Writing

3. Merry Memory

Review the Quickwrite you wrote before reading "Recuerdo," and use it as a springboard for a poem about a happy memory in your life. Your poem can be written as you like, rhymed or unrhymed, but it should have a **tone** and **rhythm** that convey joy and lightheartedness.

EDNA ST. VINCENT MILLAY **701**

MAKING MEANINGS

First Thoughts [Respond]

1. All students have probably experienced nostalgia for a happy moment. They may mention such occasions as an athletic victory, a birthday spent with friends, or a day at the beach.

Shaping Interpretations [Interpret]

2. "We" refers to the speaker and a friend. Lines 4–5 suggest a close emotional relationship—a deep friendship or a romance.

3. They are so happy that they want to share their feelings with others. The scene implies that love inspires generosity.

4. The sun is compared to a bucketful of gold, as if the speaker sees riches everywhere.

5. The meter is strong and lilting, although slightly irregular; the feet are principally iambic and anapestic. The rhyme scheme is *aabbcc aaddee aaffgg*.

6. The tone is ecstatic, passionate, and warm.

READING SKILLS AND STRATEGIES

Possible Answers

a. shrieking; howling; cutting

b. The sun rose like a spreading fire.

c. a shrouded, glowering face

Grading Timesaver

Rubrics for each Choices assignment appear on p. 176 in the *Portfolio Management System*.

CHOICES: Building Your Portfolio

1–3. As you complete these writing assignments, consider not only Millay's poetic form but also her message. What attitude or philosophy of life does this poem seem to embody?

T701

Planning

- **Block Schedule**
  Block Scheduling Lesson Plans with Pacing Guide

- **Traditional Schedule**
  Lesson Plans Including Strategies for English-Language Learners

- **One-Stop Planner**
  CD-ROM with Test Generator

BROWSING IN THE FILES

Writers on Writing. Katherine Anne Porter offered the following advice to her fellow writers: "First, have faith in your theme, then get so well acquainted with your characters that they live and grow in your imagination exactly as if you saw them in the flesh . . . tell their story with all the truth and sensitivity and tenderness you are capable of. . . . Add a little something, even if it is the merest fraction of an atom, to the sum of human achievement."

© Rollie McKenna.

Katherine Anne Porter

(1890–1980)

Katherine Anne Porter was born in a Texas log cabin. She was raised, mostly by her grandmother, as a member of a sprawling family on close terms with hardship and deprivation. Her schooling was fragmentary. In later life, Porter tended to embroider these plain origins with a certain romantic opulence, as though her past could be revised like a novel in progress.

The first of Porter's four marriages took place when she was sixteen. She was consistently impatient with lasting marital relationships, and yet she disliked being alone. Her early years were a struggle to define herself as an individual, as a Southern woman, and as the writer that, so very slowly, she was becoming.

After her Texas youth, Porter traveled widely, living at various times in the West, New York City's Greenwich Village, New England, Washington, Mexico, Paris, and Berlin. She supported herself as a newspaper reporter and editor and as a translator of French and Spanish literature.

As a creative writer, Porter was largely self-taught. She became well read and had a natural talent for clear, flowing language. She could tell a seemingly effortless story, combining a searching intelligence, honesty, sound psychology, a flawless memory, and a vivid sense of scene. The grace of her objective style concealed the labor that went into it. Porter worked slowly and painstakingly, and she did not begin publishing until she was over thirty. Her first book of stories, *Flowering Judas* (1930), grew out of her recollections of her experiences in Mexico immediately after World War I. This collection won her a critical reputation as a stylist.

Much of Porter's work presents Southern women caught up in a web of custom and obligation. Her main themes include the burden of past evil and the strain with which that evil holds us captive in the present. Miranda, the clearly autobiographical central figure of so many of her stories, is forever trying to separate the fictions of family legend from objective truth. She knows that people do not always tell the truth, and she is skeptical of the romantic sheen with which they disguise the realities of poverty and sexuality.

With the publication of her finest story collection, *Pale Horse, Pale Rider* (1939), Porter's growing audience eagerly awaited a promised novel. In 1941, Porter began her novel, titled *Ship of Fools*. The novel takes place during the early days of Hitler's rise to power and chronicles the passage of a steamer ship whose passengers, in escaping their loneliness, search for fantasy rather than friendship or love. *Ship of Fools* is really about the seeds of World War II—a bitter portrait of the Nazi state and the human race's capacity for cruelty. When it finally appeared in 1962, the novel enjoyed a wide popular success. It was followed by the many awards and tributes (including the National Book Award and the Pulitzer Prize) that embellished the final years of Porter's long life.

go.hrw.com
LEO 11-14

 Resources: Print and Media

Reading
- *Graphic Organizers for Active Reading*, p. 71
- *Words to Own*, p. 41
- *Audio CD Library*
  Disc 19, Track 8

Writing and Language
- *Daily Oral Grammar*
  Transparency 44
- *Grammar and Language Links*
  Worksheet, p. 61

Viewing and Representing
- *Viewing and Representing*
  Fine Art Transparency 14
  Fine Art Worksheet, p. 56

Assessment
- *Formal Assessment*, p. 137
- *Portfolio Management System*, p. 177
- *Test Generator (One-Stop Planner CD-ROM)*

Internet
- go.hrw.com (keyword: LEO 11–14)

Before You Read
THE JILTING OF GRANNY WEATHERALL

Make the Connection

Alive in Memory

Most of the people we know and come across in the course of a day are looking ahead. Even for those in middle or old age, much of life seems to lie before them. What's the weather going to be next Sunday? Where shall we go on vacation?

Often, older persons can vividly recall events of long ago but have more difficulty remembering the recent past. That is surely true of Ellen Weatherall. Ellen is nearly eighty years old, and she has little interest in the future, which she knows is over for her. But the past! Now *there's* something to think about.

The point of this story is what Granny Weatherall recalls most vividly of all. It happened sixty years ago, Granny tells us, and the memory still hurts.

Reading Skills and Strategies

Reading Closely

You will need to be a good detective as you sift clues to learn who all the people in Granny's mind are. As you meet them, take notes on their relationship to Granny and note whether they are living or dead.

Here are some suggestions: Pay careful attention to **tenses of verbs,** since they help distinguish past from present. Also, pay attention to the use of **quotation marks**. They enclose words actually spoken as opposed to unspoken thoughts. Finally, be patient. If a character is mentioned but not immediately identified, wait until more clues are given.

Elements of Literature

Stream of Consciousness

Although this story uses some dialogue, it mostly employs a modernist narrative technique called **stream of consciousness.** This technique allows the reader to overhear Granny's thoughts and memories. These occur to her in no special order, her mind switching back and forth from what is going on around her to what happened long ago, including the central episode of the story.

> **S**tream of consciousness is a style of writing that conveys the inner—and sometimes chaotic—workings of a character's mind.
>
> *For more on Stream of Consciousness, see the Handbook of Literary Terms.*

KATHERINE ANNE PORTER **703**

Summary ■■■

In this stream-of-consciousness narrative, an eighty-year-old grandmother, Ellen Weatherall, lies dying. As she passes in and out of consciousness, she interacts with her doctor and her daughter Cornelia and thinks back on her long life. Although many memories are pleasant, she also recalls being jilted by a man named George on their wedding day. Weatherall tells herself that she was "given back everything he took away and more" by the man she ultimately married and her children, but this memory actually reflects a deep inner hurt. As death nears, a priest gives Granny the last rites and Porter evokes a "tiny point in the center of her brain" surrounded by blackness as a metaphor for Granny's life. Out of this blackness, Granny seeks a sign from God, the divine bridegroom, but at the story's climax, no sign appears. In her last thought, Granny decides that she will never forgive this final "jilting," and she herself blows out the light of her life.

BROWSING IN THE FILES

About the Author. Katherine Anne Porter is widely regarded as one of this century's greatest American writers of short fiction. In her work, she often draws from her personal experience of growing up in the South. Porter's fiction often centers on an epiphany, or sudden internal realization, rather than on external action.

Preteaching Vocabulary

Words to Own

Have students read the Words to Own and their definitions listed at the bottom of the selection pages. Then, have students write imaginative sentences using one new vocabulary word in each sentence. When they finish writing their sentences, ask students to match each word on the left with its synonym on the right.

1. disputed [f] **a.** frills
2. plague [h] **b.** pride
3. tactful [d] **c.** damp
4. vanity [b] **d.** polite
5. dwindled [j] **e.** halo
6. margin [i] **f.** argued
7. jilted [g] **g.** rejected
8. clammy [c] **h.** annoy
9. frippery [a] **i.** excess
10. nimbus [e] **j.** shrank

Resources

Viewing and Representing
Fine Art Transparency
Use the fine art transparency of Maria Brito's *Meanderings* to pique students' curiosity and raise questions about the stream of consciousness technique. See the *Viewing and Representing Transparencies and Worksheets:*
- Transparency 14
- Worksheet, p. 56

A Vocabulary Note
Multiple Meanings
Ask students to define the word *weather.* [noun: "temperature and precipitation"; verb: "to endure"] Then, ask what Granny's last name implies about her character and about the story. [that she is strong; that she has triumphed over a lot of trouble or suffering]

B Reading Skills and Strategies
Reading Closely
? What is happening to Granny at this point? [Granny is so ill that her sight and sensations are affected. In her distorted perceptions, both her own bones and Dr. Harry seem to float.]

The Jilting of
Ⓐ Granny Weatherall

Katherine Anne Porter

She flicked her wrist neatly out of Doctor Harry's pudgy careful fingers and pulled the sheet up to her chin. The brat ought to be in knee breeches. Doctoring around the country with spectacles on his nose! "Get along now, take your schoolbooks and go. There's nothing wrong with me."

Doctor Harry spread a warm paw like a cushion on her forehead where the forked green vein danced and made her eyelids twitch. "Now, now, be a good girl, and we'll have you up in no time."

"That's no way to speak to a woman nearly eighty years old just because she's down. I'd have you respect your elders, young man."

"Well, Missy, excuse me." Doctor Harry patted her cheek. "But I've got to warn you, haven't I? You're a marvel, but you must be careful or you're going to be good and sorry."

"Don't tell me what I'm going to be. I'm on my feet now, morally speaking. It's Cornelia. I had to go to bed to get rid of her."

Ⓑ Her bones felt loose, and floated around in her skin, and Doctor Harry floated like a balloon around the foot of the bed. He floated and pulled down his waistcoat and swung his glasses on a cord. "Well, stay where you are, it certainly can't hurt you."

704 THE MODERNS

Reaching All Students

Struggling Readers
In order to help struggling readers follow the course of Ellen Weatherall's stream of consciousness, have them read carefully to see what she thinks of the various people she has been close to. Students can make charts showing each character, his or her relationship to Granny Weatherall, and Granny Weatherall's feelings about this person. By examining the quoted dialogue, students can also discover how each character feels about the dying woman.

English Language Learners
Make sure students have a clear understanding of what it means to be *jilted* (rejected; dropped by a lover), since the concept plays a central role in the story. Then, help students understand some of Granny's rural expressions, such as "Get along now" (p. 704) and "Don't let good things rot for want of using" (p. 707).

Advanced Learners
As students read, have them jot down images of darkness and light, such as "it was like a dark curtain drawn around the bed" (p. 706). After reading, students can discuss the overall significance of this motif. What does darkness symbolize? What does light symbolize? How do these images contribute to the story's theme? Once students have concluded their small-group discussion, they can share their ideas with the class.

New England Woman (1895) by Cecilia Beaux. Oil on canvas (43″ × 24¼″).

The Pennsylvania Academy of the Fine Arts, Philadelphia. Joseph E. Temple Fund.

Using Students' Strengths

Intrapersonal Learners

Have students recall times when they have been ill and had to spend whole days in bed. Does physical confinement make their thoughts wander? Do they often doze off? Does the time pass slowly or quickly? Students should collect these memories in a brief journal entry or piece of creative fiction. Remind them to consider how their experiences compare with Granny Weatherall's and not to include any details they wouldn't feel comfortable sharing with others.

Visual Learners

Have students work in groups of four or five to make a time line of key events in the story. Students should first cooperate to list the events in chronological order, distinguishing between events that happened in the past and those that happen in the present of the story. Then, each student can use a large piece of poster board to draw in the logical and associative connections that link these events. Students can use different colored markers to distinguish cause-and-effect connections from those links that are more thematic or metaphorical. Students should explain their charts to the class.

"Get along and doctor your sick," said Granny Weatherall. "Leave a well woman alone. I'll call for you when I want you. . . . Where were you forty years ago when I pulled through milk leg[1] and double pneumonia? You weren't even born. Don't let Cornelia lead you on," she shouted, because Doctor Harry appeared to float up to the ceiling and out. "I pay my own bills, and I don't throw my money away on nonsense!"

She meant to wave goodbye, but it was too much trouble. Her eyes closed of themselves, it was like a dark curtain drawn around the bed. The pillow rose and floated under her, pleasant as a hammock in a light wind. She listened to the leaves rustling outside the window. No, somebody was swishing newspapers: No, Cornelia and Doctor Harry were whispering together. She leaped broad awake, thinking they whispered in her ear.

"She was never like this, *never* like this!" "Well, what can we expect?" "Yes, eighty years old. . . ."

Well, and what if she was? She still had ears. It was like Cornelia to whisper around doors. She always kept things secret in such a public way. She was always being tactful and kind. Cornelia was dutiful; that was the trouble with her. Dutiful and good: "So good and dutiful," said Granny, "that I'd like to spank her." She saw herself spanking Cornelia and making a fine job of it.

"What'd you say, Mother?"

Granny felt her face tying up in hard knots.

"Can't a body think, I'd like to know?"

"I thought you might want something."

"I do. I want a lot of things. First off, go away and don't whisper."

She lay and drowsed, hoping in her sleep that the children would keep out and let her rest a minute. It had been a long day. Not that she was tired. It was always pleasant to snatch a minute now and then. There was always so much to be done, let me see: tomorrow.

Tomorrow was far away and there was nothing to trouble about. Things were finished somehow when the time came; thank God there was always a little margin over for peace: Then a person could spread out the plan of life and tuck in the edges orderly. It was good to have everything clean and folded away, with the hairbrushes and tonic bottles sitting straight on the white embroidered linen: the day started without fuss and the pantry shelves laid out with rows of jelly glasses and brown jugs and white stone-china jars with blue whirligigs and words painted on them: coffee, tea, sugar, ginger, cinnamon, allspice: and the bronze clock with the lion on top nicely dusted off. The dust that lion could collect in twenty-four hours! The box in the attic with all those letters tied up, well, she'd have to go through that tomorrow. All those letters—George's letters and John's letters and her letters to them both—lying around for the children to find afterward made her uneasy. Yes, that would be tomorrow's business. No use to let them know how silly she had been once.

While she was rummaging around she found death in her mind and it felt clammy and unfamiliar. She had spent so much time preparing for death there was no need for bringing it up again. Let it take care of itself now. When she was sixty she had felt very old, finished, and went around making farewell trips to see her children and grandchildren, with a secret in her mind: This is the very last of your mother, children! Then she made her will and came down with a long fever. That was all just a notion like a lot of other things, but it was lucky too, for she had once for all got over the idea of dying for a long time. Now she couldn't be worried. She hoped she had better sense now. Her father had lived to be one hundred and two years old and had drunk a noggin[2] of strong hot toddy[3] on his last birthday. He told the reporters it was his daily habit, and he owed his long life to that. He had made quite a scandal and was very pleased about it. She believed she'd just plague Cornelia a little.

"Cornelia! Cornelia!" No footsteps, but a sudden hand on her cheek. "Bless you, where have you been?"

---

1. **milk leg:** painful swelling of the leg, usually as a result of an infection during childbirth.
2. **noggin:** mug.
3. **hot toddy:** drink made of liquor mixed with hot water, sugar, and spices.

- -

WORDS TO OWN

tactful (takt′fəl) *adj.:* skilled in saying the right thing.
margin (mär′jən) *n.:* extra amount.
clammy (klam′ē) *adj.:* cold and damp.
plague (plāg) *v.:* annoy.

- -

706 THE MODERNS

"Here, Mother."

"Well, Cornelia, I want a noggin of hot toddy."

"Are you cold, darling?"

"I'm chilly, Cornelia. Lying in bed stops the circulation. I must have told you that a thousand times."

Well, she could just hear Cornelia telling her husband that Mother was getting a little childish and they'd have to humor her. The thing that most annoyed her was that Cornelia thought she was deaf, dumb, and blind. Little hasty glances and tiny gestures tossed around her and over her head saying, "Don't cross her, let her have her way, she's eighty years old," and she sitting there as if she lived in a thin glass cage. Sometimes Granny almost made up her mind to pack up and move back to her own house where nobody could remind her every minute that she was old. Wait, wait, Cornelia, till your own children whisper behind your back!

In her day she had kept a better house and had got more work done. She wasn't too old yet for Lydia to be driving eighty miles for advice when one of the children jumped the track, and Jimmy still dropped in and talked things over: "Now, Mammy, you've a good business head, I want to know what you think of this? . . ." Old. Cornelia couldn't change the furniture around without asking. Little things, little things! They had been so sweet when they were little. Granny wished the old days were back again with the children young and everything to be done over. It had been a hard pull, but not too much for her. When she thought of all the food she had cooked, and all the clothes she had cut and sewed, and all the gardens she had made—well, the children showed it. There they were, made out of her, and they couldn't get away from that. Sometimes she wanted to see John again and point to them and say, Well, I didn't do so badly, did I? But that would have to wait. That was for tomorrow. She used to think of him as a man, but now all the children were older than their father, and he would be a child beside her if she saw him now. It seemed strange and there was something wrong in the idea. Why, he couldn't possibly recognize her. She had fenced in a hundred acres once, digging the postholes herself and clamping the wires with just a Negro boy to help. That changed a woman. John would be looking for a young woman with the peaked Spanish comb in her hair and the painted fan. Digging postholes changed a woman. Riding country roads in the winter when women had their babies was another thing: sitting up nights with sick horses and sick Negroes and sick children and hardly ever losing one. John, I hardly ever lost one of them! John would see that in a minute, that would be something he could understand, she wouldn't have to explain anything!

It made her feel like rolling up her sleeves and putting the whole place to rights again. No matter if Cornelia was determined to be everywhere at once, there were a great many things left undone on this place. She would start tomorrow and do them. It was good to be strong enough for everything, even if all you made melted and changed and slipped under your hands, so that by the time you finished you almost forgot what you were working for. What was it I set out to do? she asked herself intently, but she could not remember. A fog rose over the valley, she saw it marching across the creek swallowing the trees and moving up the hill like an army of ghosts. Soon it would be at the near edge of the orchard, and then it was time to go in and light the lamps. Come in, children, don't stay out in the night air.

Lighting the lamps had been beautiful. The children huddled up to her and breathed like little calves waiting at the bars in the twilight. Their eyes followed the match and watched the flame rise and settle in a blue curve, then they moved away from her. The lamp was lit, they didn't have to be scared and hang on to mother any more. Never, never, never more. God, for all my life I thank Thee. Without Thee, my God, I could never have done it. Hail, Mary, full of grace.

I want you to pick all the fruit this year and see that nothing is wasted. There's always someone who can use it. Don't let good things rot for want of using. You waste life when you waste good food. Don't let things get lost. It's bitter to lose things. Now, don't let me get to thinking, not when I am tired and taking a little nap before supper. . . .

The pillow rose about her shoulders and pressed against her heart and the memory was being squeezed out of it: Oh, push down the pillow, somebody: It would smother her if she tried to hold it. Such a fresh breeze blowing and such a green day with no threats in it. But he had not

KATHERINE ANNE PORTER 707

F Elements of Literature
Character

? What do these details add to your knowledge of Granny's character? [She has been capable, intelligent, and reliable; her grown children have still come to her for advice. She is proud of her home and the way her children have depended on her.]

G Reading Skills and Strategies
Reading Closely

Ask students why Granny Weatherall feels her husband, John, will be like "a child beside her." [Granny's husband, John, died long ago, before their children were grown. Now that she is much older than he lived to be, he would seem like a child to her.]

H Elements of Literature
Stream of Consciousness

? How does the memory of the encroaching fog relate to Granny's thoughts? Where does it lead her? [The fog is like the growing darkness of death; Granny's sense of purpose seems clouded by this fog. The "army of ghosts" might be people from her past; this thought carries her to a fond memory, the lighting of the lamps at twilight, surrounded by her children.]

I Elements of Literature
Symbol

? What do you think the lamp symbolizes for Granny Weatherall? Whom and what does it prompt her to think about next? Why? Whom is she addressing in the next paragraph? [Possible answers: It seems to symbolize a deeply religious sense of security, love, and gratitude—a sense that she and her children shared God's grace. It prompts her to think of advice she gave to her children, not to waste or lose God's gifts, to be grateful for their lives. She seems to address this advice now to herself and to her remaining children.]

Getting Students Involved

Extending Dialogues

To give students further insight into the characters in the story, have them work in groups of four on Speaking-Thinking Dialogues. Each group should choose a piece of dialogue from the selection. One student reads what the first character is saying, and the second student gives an interpretation of what the character is thinking. The other two students present what the second character is saying and may be thinking. The group should then discuss what they learned.

? What happened to Granny Weatherall sixty years ago, when she "put on the white veil"? [Her fiancé, George, failed to show up for their wedding.] **How has it affected her?** [She tried hard to forget him but had to pray for forgetfulness every day. Remembering him now feels like slipping into damnation, and the thought of him fills her mind like "a smoky cloud from hell."]

B Advanced Learners

Noting Significant Details

? After students have read the story, have them return to this line of text. Why are the names listed in this order? Which names are missing, and why? [The names seem to occur in order of their importance to Granny, Hapsy being the dearest. The absence of John and Cornelia from the list suggests that she has less interest in seeing either of them again.]

C Critical Thinking

Interpreting

? Who is Hapsy and where is she? [Possible answers: Hapsy is one of Granny's daughters who lives far away, or who may be dead. Granny loves Hapsy dearly and longs for her presence here at her deathbed—or perhaps Hapsy is welcoming her mother into death.]

D Critical Thinking

Evaluating

? Can you accept Granny's statement about George at face value? If not, what do you think she means? [Possible answer: If she has really forgotten George, she would not need to send him this message. Instead she seems to want to strike back at him—to tell him he meant nothing to her and she had a good life without him. Even then, she wonders if there was something missing in this good life.]

A come, just the same. What does a woman do when she has put on the white veil and set out the white cake for a man and he doesn't come? She tried to remember. No, I swear he never harmed me but in that. He never harmed me but in that . . . and what if he did? There was the day, the day, but a whirl of dark smoke rose and covered it, crept up and over into the bright field where everything was planted so carefully in orderly rows. That was hell, she knew hell when she saw it. For sixty years she had prayed against remembering him and against losing her soul in the deep pit of hell, and now the two things were mingled in one and the thought of him was a smoky cloud from hell that moved and crept in her head when she had just got rid of Doctor Harry and was trying to rest a minute. Wounded <u>vanity</u>, Ellen, said a sharp voice in the top of her mind. Don't let your wounded vanity get the upper hand of you. Plenty of girls get <u>jilted</u>. You were jilted, weren't you? Then stand up to it. Her eyelids wavered and let in streamers of blue-gray light like tissue paper over her eyes. She must get up and pull the shades down or she'd never sleep. She was in bed again and the shades were not down. How could that happen? Better turn over, hide from the light, sleeping in the light gave you nightmares. "Mother, how do you feel now?" and a stinging wetness on her forehead. But I don't like having my face washed in cold water!

B Hapsy? George? Lydia? Jimmy? No, Cornelia, and her features were swollen and full of little puddles. "They're coming, darling, they'll all be here soon." Go wash your face, child, you look funny.

Instead of obeying, Cornelia knelt down and put her head on the pillow. She seemed to be talking but there was no sound. "Well, are you tongue-tied? Whose birthday is it? Are you going to give a party?"

Cornelia's mouth moved urgently in strange shapes. "Don't do that, you bother me, daughter."

"Oh, no, Mother. Oh, no . . ."

Nonsense. It was strange about children. They <u>disputed</u> your every word. "No what, Cornelia?"

"Here's Doctor Harry."

"I won't see that boy again. He just left five minutes ago."

"That was this morning, Mother. It's night now. Here's the nurse."

"This is Doctor Harry, Mrs. Weatherall. I never saw you look so young and happy!"

"Ah, I'll never be young again—but I'd be happy if they'd let me lie in peace and get rested."

She thought she spoke up loudly, but no one answered. A warm weight on her forehead, a warm bracelet on her wrist, and a breeze went on whispering, trying to tell her something. A shuffle of leaves in the everlasting hand of God, He blew on them and they danced and rattled. "Mother, don't mind, we're going to give you a little hypodermic."[4] "Look here, daughter, how do ants get in this bed? I saw sugar ants yesterday." Did you send for Hapsy too?

C It was Hapsy she really wanted. She had to go a long way back through a great many rooms to find Hapsy standing with a baby on her arm. She seemed to herself to be Hapsy also, and the baby on Hapsy's arm was Hapsy and himself and herself, all at once, and there was no surprise in the meeting. Then Hapsy melted from within and turned flimsy as gray gauze and the baby was a gauzy shadow, and Hapsy came up close and said, "I thought you'd never come," and looked at her very searchingly and said, "You haven't changed a bit!" They leaned forward to kiss, when Cornelia began whispering from a long way off, "Oh, is there anything you want to tell me? Is there anything I can do for you?"

D Yes, she had changed her mind after sixty years and she would like to see George. I want you to find George. Find him and be sure to tell him I forgot him. I want him to know I had my husband just the same and my children and my house like any other woman. A good house too and a good husband that I loved and fine children out of him. Better than I hoped for even. Tell him I was given back everything he took away and more. Oh, no, oh, God, no, there was something else besides the house and the man and the children. Oh, surely they were not all? What was it? Something not given back. . . . Her breath crowded down under

---

4. **hypodermic:** injection of medicine.

WORDS TO OWN

vanity (van′ə·tē) *n.:* excessive pride.
jilted (jilt′id) *v.:* rejected (as a lover).
disputed (di·spyoot′id) *v.:* contested.

Crossing the Curriculum

Social Studies

Respect Your Elders. Have students explore attitudes toward older people in their own and other cultures. Are the elderly respected? What are the advantages and disadvantages of multigenerational households? What are the causes and implications of the recent expansion of "senior housing"? When the elderly need care, are their children obliged to provide it themselves? Why might people choose to seek other options for housing their older relatives?

Health

Medical Advances. Granny Weatherall is almost eighty when she dies, but her husband and at least one of her children died at a much younger age. Have students research and report on life expectancy, death rates, and infant mortality rates in the United States in the late 1800s. They can then compare the statistics with birth and death rates in today's society. Students can graph or chart their findings and discuss them with the class.

Evening Light (1908) by Frank Benson. Oil on canvas (25¼″ × 30½″).

her ribs and grew into a monstrous frightening shape with cutting edges; it bored up into her head, and the agony was unbelievable: Yes, John, get the Doctor now, no more talk, my time has come.

When this one was born it should be the last. The last. It should have been born first, for it was the one she had truly wanted. Everything came in good time. Nothing left out, left over. She was strong, in three days she would be as well as ever. Better. A woman needed milk in her to have her full health.

"Mother, do you hear me?"

"I've been telling you—"

"Mother, Father Connolly's here."

"I went to Holy Communion only last week. Tell him I'm not so sinful as all that."

"Father just wants to speak to you."

He could speak as much as he pleased. It was like him to drop in and inquire about her soul as if it were a teething baby, and then stay on for a cup of tea and a round of cards and gossip. He always had a funny story of some sort, usually about an Irishman who made his little mistakes and confessed them, and the point lay in some absurd thing he would blurt out in the confessional showing his struggles between native piety and original sin.[5] Granny felt easy about her soul. Cornelia, where are your manners? Give Father Connolly a chair. She had her secret comfortable understanding with a few favorite saints who cleared a straight road to God for her. All as surely signed and sealed as the papers for the new Forty Acres. Forever . . . heirs and assigns forever. Since the day the wedding cake was not cut, but thrown

5. **original sin:** in Christian theology, the sin of disobedience committed by Adam and Eve, the first man and woman, which is passed on to all persons.

KATHERINE ANNE PORTER 709

RESPONDING TO THE ART

Frank Weston Benson (1862–1951) was an American painter known for his portrayals of women and children in brilliantly lighted pastoral settings. Born in Salem, Massachusetts, Benson taught at the Museum of Fine Arts in Boston from 1889 to 1912. (See also p. 578.)
Activity. Why might this painting have been chosen to illustrate this story? [Its rural setting, with children coming to their mother at twilight, echoes Granny Weatherall's recollections.]

E **Appreciating Language**
Idioms
? Tell students that "my time has come" is an old-fashioned expression that indicates a woman is about to give birth. How does the memory of this phrase have a double meaning in this context? [Possible answer: Granny's time to die has come; she experiences the pangs of death through the memory of another excruciating experience, childbirth.]

F **Reading Skills and Strategies**

Reading Closely
Have students explain what Granny is remembering. (If students have difficulty, point out clue words, such as *born, milk,* and *last.*) [the birth of her last child] Once students have finished the story, they may surmise this child is Hapsy.

Professional Notes

Critical Comment: Interior Worlds
Eudora Welty (see p. 633) greatly admired Porter's work. In an essay titled "Katherine Anne Porter: The Eye of the Story," Welty wrote: "Most good stories are about the interior of our lives, but Katherine Anne Porter's stories take place there; they show surface only at her own choosing. Her use of the physical world is enough to meet her needs and no more; she is not wasteful with anything. This artist, writing her stories with a power that stamps them to their last detail on the memory, does so to an extraordinary degree without sensory imagery." Ask students if they agree or disagree with this assessment. Have them support their opinions with specific details from the text.

A Critical Thinking

Speculating

? Who is "he"? Explain your view. [Possible answers: John, Ellen Weatherall's future husband, or perhaps her father. His fury suggests that he is someone very close to her.]

B Reading Skills and Strategies

Reading Closely

? Who is the man and what is the situation? [Granny might be recalling a long-past drive in the country with George; the birds could be singing her wedding mass. The driver, however, might also symbolize death, with the birds singing a funeral mass. In Granny's mind, the two occasions—her missed wedding and her death—are inextricably joined.]

C Elements of Literature

Stream of Consciousness

? Have students explain the associations in this passage. [The birds sound like a church choir, which reminds Granny of her rosary and of the presence of a priest. The touch of hands on her feet—the priest giving her the last rites—makes her think for a moment that he is flirting with her. Granny's comparison of her husband to St. Michael brings her attention to the fact that she is dying.] Point out that Weatherall's repeated, unconvincing protests that George means nothing to her ("with a thank you in the bargain") betray her long-held pain.

---

out and wasted. The whole bottom dropped out of the world, and there she was blind and sweating with nothing under her feet and the walls falling away. His hand had caught her under the breast, she had not fallen, there was the freshly polished floor with the green rug on it, just as before. He had cursed like a sailor's parrot and said, "I'll kill him for you." Don't lay a hand on him, for my sake leave something to God. "Now, Ellen, you must believe what I tell you. . . ."

So there was nothing, nothing to worry about any more, except sometimes in the night one of the children screamed in a nightmare, and they both hustled out shaking and hunting for the matches and calling, "There, wait a minute, here we are!" John, get the doctor now, Hapsy's time has come. But there was Hapsy standing by the bed in a white cap. "Cornelia, tell Hapsy to take off her cap. I can't see her plain."

Her eyes opened very wide and the room stood out like a picture she had seen somewhere. Dark colors with the shadows rising toward the ceiling in long angles. The tall black dresser gleamed with nothing on it but John's picture, enlarged from a little one, with John's eyes very black when they should have been blue. You never saw him, so how do you know how he looked? But the man insisted the copy was perfect, it was very rich and handsome. For a picture, yes, but it's not my husband. The table by the bed had a linen cover and a candle and a crucifix. The light was blue from Cornelia's silk lampshades. No sort of light at all, just <u>frippery</u>. You had to live forty years with kerosene lamps to appreciate honest electricity. She felt very strong and she saw Doctor Harry with a rosy <u>nimbus</u> around him.

"You look like a saint, Doctor Harry, and I vow that's as near as you'll ever come to it."

"She's saying something."

"I heard you, Cornelia. What's all this carrying-on?"

"Father Connolly's saying—"

Cornelia's voice staggered and bumped like a cart in a bad road. It rounded corners and turned back again and arrived nowhere. Granny stepped up in the cart very lightly and reached for the reins, but a man sat beside her and she knew him by his hands, driving the cart. She did not look in his face, for she knew without seeing, but looked instead down the road where the trees leaned over and

bowed to each other and a thousand birds were singing a Mass. She felt like singing too, but she put her hand in the bosom of her dress and pulled out a rosary, and Father Connolly murmured Latin in a very solemn voice and tickled her feet.[6] My God, will you stop that nonsense? I'm a married woman. What if he did run away and leave me to face the priest by myself? I found another a whole world better. I wouldn't have exchanged my husband for anybody except St. Michael[7] himself, and you may tell him that for me with a thank you in the bargain.

Light flashed on her closed eyelids, and a deep roaring shook her. Cornelia, is that lightning? I hear thunder. There's going to be a storm. Close all the windows. Call the children in. . . . "Mother, here we are, all of us." "Is that you, Hapsy?" "Oh, no, I'm Lydia. We drove as fast as we could." Their faces drifted above her, drifted away. The rosary fell out of her hands and Lydia put it back. Jimmy tried to help, their hands fumbled together, and Granny closed two fingers around Jimmy's thumb. Beads wouldn't do, it must be something alive. She was so amazed her thoughts ran round and round. So, my dear Lord, this is my death and I wasn't even thinking about it. My children have come to see me die. But I can't, it's not time. Oh, I always hated surprises. I wanted to give Cornelia the amethyst[8] set—Cornelia, you're to have the amethyst set, but Hapsy's to wear it when she wants, and, Doctor Harry, do shut up. Nobody sent for you. Oh, my dear Lord, do wait a minute. I meant to do something about the Forty Acres, Jimmy doesn't need it and Lydia will later on, with that worthless husband of hers. I meant to finish the altar cloth and send six bottles of wine to Sister Borgia for her dyspepsia.[9] I want to send six

6. **murmured . . . feet:** The priest is performing the sacramental last rites of the Roman Catholic Church, which include anointing the dying person's feet with oil.
7. **Michael:** most powerful of the four archangels in Jewish and Christian doctrine. In Christian art, he is usually depicted as a handsome knight in white armor.
8. **amethyst** (am'i·thist): purple or violet quartz gemstone, used in jewelry.
9. **dyspepsia** (dis·pep'sē·ə): indigestion.

WORDS TO OWN

frippery (frip'ər·ē) n.: something showy, frivolous, or unnecessary.
nimbus (nim'bəs) n.: aura; halo.

Making the Connections

**Connecting to the Theme:
"Shadows of the Past"**

After students have finished reading the story, discuss the collection theme. What are the shadows from Granny's past that haunt her? How has she responded to those shadows? Can shadows from the past ever really be eliminated or conquered? Have students consider these questions as they read "A Rose for Emily."

Assessing Learning

Check Test: Multiple Choice

1. Who is taking care of Granny? (a) Hapsy (b) Cornelia (c) John [b]
2. What is the main event in the story? (a) a wedding (b) a birth (c) a death [c]
3. Who jilted young Ellen? (a) John (b) George (c) Hapsy [b]
4. Which religion does Granny follow? (a) Catholic (b) Jewish (c) Mormon [a]
5. Whom did Ellen marry? (a) John (b) George (c) Jimmy [a]

Informal Assessment

Self-Assessment. Ask students to use the following prompts to evaluate their understanding of the story:

1. One strategy that helped me understand new words was _____.
2. One strategy that helped me keep track of events and characters was _____.
3. One way I can improve my reading comprehension is _____.

bottles of wine to Sister Borgia, Father Connolly, now don't let me forget.

Cornelia's voice made short turns and tilted over and crashed. "Oh, Mother, oh, Mother, oh, Mother . . ."

"I'm not going, Cornelia. I'm taken by surprise. I can't go."

You'll see Hapsy again. What about her? "I thought you'd never come." Granny made a long journey outward, looking for Hapsy. What if I don't find her? What then? Her heart sank down and down, there was no bottom to death, she couldn't come to the end of it. The blue light from Cornelia's lampshade drew into a tiny point in the center of her brain, it flickered and winked like an eye, quietly it fluttered and <u>dwindled</u>. Granny lay curled down within herself, amazed and watchful, staring at the point of light that was herself; her body was now only a deeper mass of shadow in an endless darkness and this darkness would curl around the light and swallow it up. God, give a sign!

For the second time there was no sign. Again no bridegroom and the priest in the house. She could not remember any other sorrow because this grief wiped them all away. Oh, no, there's nothing more cruel than this—I'll never forgive it. She stretched herself with a deep breath and blew out the light.

A

B

WORDS TO OWN
dwindled (dwin′dəld) *v.*: diminished.

Connections   A POEM

Conrad Aiken (1889–1973), an influential American writer, was concerned with how we construct a personal identity. He was a friend of T.S. Eliot's, and in the 1920s he helped establish Emily Dickinson's reputation as a major poet. Aiken often wrote poetry that mimicked a musical form or referred to music. The following lines are taken from a longer poem in which the speaker tries to come to terms with the loss of a person he loved dearly.

from **Discordants**

Conrad Aiken

Music I heard with you was more than music,
And bread I broke with you was more than bread;
Now that I am without you, all is desolate;
All that was once so beautiful is dead.

5 Your hands once touched this table and this silver,
And I have seen your fingers hold this glass.
These things do not remember you, beloved,—
And yet your touch upon them will not pass.

For it was in my heart you moved among them,
10 And blessed them with your hands and with your eyes;
And in my heart they will remember always,—
They knew you once, O beautiful and wise.

C

D

The Green Blouse (1919) by Pierre Bonnard (1867–1947), French. Oil on canvas (40⅛″ × 26⅛″).

The Metropolitan Museum of Art, Mr. and Mrs. Henry Ittleson, Jr., Fund, 1963 (63.64). Photograph © 1993 The Metropolitan Museum of Art.

KATHERINE ANNE PORTER   711

A Critical Thinking
Challenging the Text
? Why does Porter end the story as she does? [Possible answers: She wants to suggest that we are all "jilted" in death—that we die alone and that this solitude is greater than any loss we know in life. She wants to show Weatherall's strength—accepting her own death in the face of this ultimate jilting.]

B Elements of Literature
Symbol
? How do you interpret this final sentence? What does the light stand for? [Possible answers: Granny gives herself up to death. The light represents the last flicker of her consciousness; she gives up this consciousness and her life.]

Connections

In this excerpt from Aiken's "Discordants," the speaker mourns a lost love, noting the way in which his beloved enhanced and enlivened the music, bread, and miscellaneous objects they shared together. Now that these things are "dead," he insists that, at some level, they "remember" the touch of his beloved.

C Elements of Literature
Character
? How does Aiken characterize the speaker? [He uses the words "desolate" and "dead" to show that the speaker is suffering deeply.]

D Reading Skills and Strategies
Reading Closely
? Why do you think the speaker is alone? [Although the poem is ambiguous, most students will say the speaker's beloved has died.]

Connecting Across Texts

Connecting with "The Jilting of Granny Weatherall"

1. Have students imagine a conversation between Granny Weatherall and the speaker of "Discordants." What would they say to each other? What advice might Granny give the speaker of the poem? Students might want to choose partners to work out their ideas with. One pair can enact the conversation for the class as a springboard to a class discussion about the two characters.

2. Explore with students other works they have read in which characters express bittersweet satisfaction with life, as Granny and the speaker in the Aiken poem do. Consider the speaker in "Fall" (p. 691) or "Mrs. George Reece" (p. 695). Note, too, the similarity between Granny's image of death as a driver (p. 710) and Emily Dickinson's "Because I could not stop for Death" (p. 391).

Skill Link

Analyzing Sentence Fragments
Ask groups of four or five students to look at the way Porter uses sentence fragments to manipulate language to her own ends. Have them read the eleven-sentence paragraph on p. 710 that begins "Her eyes opened very wide. . . ." Ask students to individually find and make a note of the sentence fragments. [sentences 2, 6, and 9] Then, ask them to decide why Porter has used this unusual syntax in the paragraph. [to mirror the path of Granny's wandering thoughts]

First Thoughts [Respond]

1. Possible answers: Yes, rejection is deeply painful and lasting. No, too much time has passed.

Shaping Interpretations [Interpret]

2. Ellen Weatherall never forgot George. Her experience with him made her strong but also seems to have made it impossible for her to be completely happy with John and her children.

3. Possible answers: Granny never regained a sense of wholeness—she feels that she irrevocably lost something, perhaps her pride or self-esteem. Other ambiguities include the question of whether her married life was happy and satisfying and whether Hapsy is dead or alive. The stream-of-consciousness technique presents one person's associative train of thought, which is subjective, indirect, and often contradictory.

4. The story is told from Granny's point of view (third-person limited or first-person). If Porter had included the views of the other characters, the story might have had less ambiguity—but also less impact.

5. She means that George caused her terrible pain and suffering and also that thinking of him seems like a sin to her. She expects to see her loved ones again in heaven.

6. Granny looks in vain for a sign from God. She is heartbroken and bitter at this final betrayal—so much so that she releases her fierce grasp on life.

7. Granny remembers George with bitterness and humiliation. The speaker of Aiken's poem remembers his beloved with tenderness alone.

Grading Timesaver

Rubrics for each Choices assignment appear on p. 177 in the *Portfolio Management System*.

MAKING MEANINGS

First Thoughts

1. Granny's last thoughts revolve around a rejection that occurred six decades before. Do you find this believable? Why or why not?

Shaping Interpretations

2. When Granny recalls George, she thinks, "Find him and be sure to tell him I forgot him" (page 708). What is **ironic** in Granny's thought? How did George really affect her life?

3. **Ambiguity** is a technique by which a writer deliberately suggests two or more different, and possibly conflicting, meanings in a work. Granny feels that she was "given back everything" that was taken away by the jilting. Yet, she then says that something was "not given back." Identify what that something might be. What other ambiguities do you find in the story? How does Porter's use of **stream of consciousness** contribute to these ambiguities?

4. From what **point of view** is this story told? How would the effect of the story have been different if another point of view had been used?

5. What does Granny mean when she thinks, "That was hell, she knew hell when she saw it" (page 708)? How does she feel about heaven?

6. The end of the story suggests that Granny is jilted again. Who jilts her this time? How does Granny feel at this moment of revelation?

7. Read Conrad Aiken's lines from "Discordants" (see *Connections,* page 711). How would you compare the speaker's feelings toward the lost loved one with Granny's feelings about George?

Reading Check

a. Review the notes you made as you read the story. When the story opens, who is with Granny?

b. What are the names of Granny's children?

c. Which child was Granny's favorite? Is she still alive—or did she even exist at all?

d. What incident does the **title** of the story refer to?

Reading Check

a. Doctor Harry and Granny's daughter Cornelia are with her.

b. Cornelia, Lydia, Jimmy, and Hapsy

c. Hapsy is Granny's favorite. She appears to be dead or to live far away.

d. The title refers to two incidents. When Ellen was twenty, her fiancé, George, did not show up at their planned wedding. Now, at the end of the story, she looks in vain for a sign from God in the nothingness of death.

CHOICES:
Building Your Portfolio

Writer's Notebook

1. Collecting Ideas for an Interpretive Essay

Porter's story contains enough **ambiguities** to give a reader plenty of food for thought. Jot down some questions you have about the meanings of this story. Keep your notes for possible use in the Writer's Workshop on page 804.

Describing a Character

2. Portrait of Granny

Write an essay that tells Granny Weatherall's life story, based on the information in Porter's story. Include a description of her personality. Before you write, organize the information about Granny in a chart like the following one.

1. Key events in Granny's life	
2. Kind of life she led	
3. Attitude toward other people	
4. Feelings about death	

Creative Writing

3. Too Late the Bridegroom

George, now eighty years old, has returned just in time to visit Ellen at her bedside. Write a brief **monologue** in which you reproduce George's thoughts as he looks at the woman he jilted sixty years earlier. Use **stream of consciousness** to show George's flow of thoughts.

William Faulkner

(1897–1962)

Yoknapatawpha County, Mississippi, is surely the hardest of American literary place names to pronounce. Still, it is wise to learn how (yäk′nə·pə·tô′fə), for it is famous as the imagined world of William Faulkner, the scene of his most celebrated novels and stories. Imaginary Yoknapatawpha is similar in many ways to the actual impoverished farmland, with its red clay hills, that rings Oxford, Mississippi, home of the state's main university. It was there that William's father, Murry Falkner (William added the *u* to the family name), ran a livery stable and later became the university's business manager. William Faulkner lived and wrote there throughout most of his life.

The South Provides a Theme

Faulkner was a mediocre student and quit high school in the tenth grade, but he read widely and he wrote poetry. At the outbreak of World War I, the United States Army rejected him because he failed to meet their height and weight requirements. However, he enlisted in the Royal Air Force of Canada and trained for flight duty, only to see the war end before he was commissioned. Returning to Oxford after the war, he took some courses at the university and did poorly in English. With neither profession nor skill, and a marked distaste for regular employment, he seemed a moody and puzzling young man to his neighbors.

Faulkner took several short-lived jobs, among them that of postmaster for the university. Resigning from this job, he wrote, "I will be damned if I propose to be at the beck and call of every itinerant scoundrel who has two cents to invest in a postage stamp."

Brown Brothers.

In 1924, Faulkner left Oxford for New Orleans, where he met Sherwood Anderson, who had attracted much attention with the publication of *Winesburg, Ohio* (1919), his study of small-town life. Impressed and encouraged by Anderson, Faulkner tried his hand at fiction. In five months, he completed a first novel, *Soldier's Pay,* a self-conscious story about the lost generation. Thereafter, Faulkner wrote with a tireless energy.

Within the next three years, Faulkner found his great theme: the American South as a microcosm for the universal themes of time, the passions of the human heart, and the destruction of the wilderness. Faulkner saw the South as a nation unto itself, with a strong sense of its noble past and an array of myths by which it clung to its pride, despite the humiliating defeat of the Civil War and the acceptance of the distasteful values of an industrial North. Faulkner started to explore these themes in *Sartoris* (the first story set in mythical Yoknapatawpha) and *The Sound and the Fury,* two novels published within months of each other in 1929. *The Sound and the Fury* was a milestone in American literature, owing to Faulkner's bold manipulation of point of view and its stream-of-consciousness narrative technique.

In the decade that followed, Faulkner produced a succession of dazzling books: *As I Lay Dying* (1930), *Sanctuary* (1931), *Light in August* (1932), *Absalom, Absalom!* (1936)—considered by many readers to be his finest work—*The Unvanquished* (1938), and *The Hamlet* (1940). These works reveal Faulkner as equally skillful in the tragic or comic mode. He portrayed the South accurately, perceptively, and with a poignant ambivalence—on the one hand affectionate, on the other critical. He once said of the South, "Well, I love it and I hate it."

go.hrw.com
LEO 11-14

OBJECTIVES

1. Read and interpret the story
2. Identify and analyze setting
3. Take notes on character
4. Analyze semantic features of synonyms
5. Express understanding through critical and creative writing and oral argument
6. Understand and use new words

SKILLS

Literary
- Identify and analyze setting

Reading
- Take notes on character
- Analyze semantic features of synonyms

Writing
- Collect ideas for an interpretive essay
- Analyze the story line
- Write a short story

Speaking/Listening
- Defend conclusions about literary works

Vocabulary
- Use new words

Viewing/Representing
- Compare a painting to the story (ATE)

Planning

- **Block Schedule**
  Block Scheduling Lesson Plans with Pacing Guide

- **Traditional Schedule**
  Lesson Plans Including Strategies for English-Language Learners

- **One-Stop Planner**
  CD-ROM with Test Generator

— *Resources: Print and Media* —

Reading
- *Graphic Organizers for Active Reading,* p. 72
- *Words to Own,* p. 42
- *Audio CD Library*
  Disc 20, Tracks 2, 3

Writing and Language
- *Daily Oral Grammar*
  Transparency 45

Viewing and Representing
- *Visual Connections*
  Videocassette B, Segment 8

Assessment
- *Formal Assessment,* p. 139
- *Portfolio Management System,* p. 178
- *Preparation for College Admission Exams,* p. 49
- *Test Generator (One-Stop Planner CD-ROM)*

Internet
- go.hrw.com (keyword: LEO 11–14)

About the Author. Looking back over his career in 1953, Faulkner wrote: "And now, at last, I have some perspective on all I have done. I mean, the work apart from me, the work which I did, apart from what I am. . . . And now I realize for the first time what an amazing gift I had: uneducated in every formal sense, without even very literate, let alone literary, companions, yet to have made the things I made. I don't know where it came from. I don't know why God or gods, or whoever it was, selected me to be the vessel. Believe me, this is not humility, false modesty; it is simply amazement."

Writers on Writing. About being a Southern writer, Faulkner had this to say: "[In the South, we] need to talk, to tell, since oratory is our heritage. We seem to try in the simple furious breathing (or writing) span of the individual to draw a savage indictment of the contemporary scene or to escape from it into a make-believe region of swords and magnolias and mockingbirds which perhaps never existed anywhere. Both of the courses are rooted in sentiment. . . . That cold intellect which can write with calm and complete detachment and gusto of its contemporary scene is not among us; I do not believe there lives the Southern writer who can say without lying that writing is any fun to him. Perhaps we do not want it to be."

Faulkner's Fictional Families

Faulkner described his South through fictional families who often reappear from novel to novel. They resemble trees, attaining grandeur, casting much shade, and then growing old and dry, crumbling as the seedlings of social change grow up around their fallen limbs and stumps.

There are the aristocratic Sartorises, who resemble Faulkner's own ancestors. Colonel John Sartoris, for example, was patterned after Faulkner's great-grandfather, who rose from rural poverty to command the Second Mississippi Regiment, built a railroad, wrote a best-selling novel, and was murdered on the street by his business partner.

There are also the Compsons, who incorporate some characteristics of the author's immediate family. They form the centerpiece of *The Sound and the Fury,* which records the decline of a once great clan, and with it the passing of a traditionally Southern world.

As I Lay Dying tells of the poor-white Bundren family and its efforts to bring the body of its matriarch, Addie, back to the town of Jefferson for burial. The novel reveals these humble people as more enduring than their social betters. *Light in August* concerns other Southern families and explores the problem of racism through the character of the protagonist, Joe Christmas. Although he appears white, Joe's racial heritage is mixed. His failure to find a place in either white or black society leads to his murder.

And, finally, there is Faulkner's unforgettable portrayal of the Snopeses—a sprawling clan of irresponsible, depraved, socially ambitious varmints who rise from the dust and cheat their way to respectability and wealth, destroying the old values of aristocracy and peasantry alike.

Faulkner often forces the reader to piece together events from a seemingly random and fragmentary series of impressions experienced by a variety of narrators. Faulkner's style often strains conventional syntax; he might pile up clause upon clause in an effort to capture the complexity of thought. In *The Sound and the Fury,* for example, he entrusts part of the narra-

> Moral dilemmas are the perennial mysteries of human existence.

tive to the chaotic intelligence of one of the sons, Benjy Compson. But the efforts of patient readers are richly repaid, as they discover in book after book a mythical universe in which the moral dilemmas are the perennial mysteries of human existence.

"The Dream of Perfection"

By the time he received the Nobel Prize in literature in 1950, Faulkner's best work was behind him. After his richly productive period (1929–1942), he wrote many more stories and novels, including *Intruder in the Dust* (1948), *Requiem for a Nun* (1951), *A Fable* (1954), *The Town* (1957), *The Mansion* (1959), and *The Reivers* (1962). These works displayed his virtuosity and willingness to experiment, but his powers were clearly diminished.

Faulkner's writing surely diverged from that of his realist contemporaries—notably Ernest Hemingway, whom he put at the bottom of his own list of the best American contemporary writers. "I said we were all failures. All of us had failed to match the dream of perfection. . . . I rated Hemingway last because he stayed within what he knew. He did it fine, but he didn't try for the impossible."

Faulkner had this to say about the qualities of a novel: "The only mistake with any novel is if it fails to create pleasure. That it is not true is irrelevant; a novel is to be enjoyed. A book that fails to create enjoyment is not a good one."

Debate will always rage about the position of figures in our literary pantheon, but critics are now unanimous in their opinion that Faulkner is one of the greatest of all American novelists. There is certainly no argument over William Faulkner's preeminence among Southern writers. As Flannery O'Connor once put it: "The presence alone of Faulkner in our midst makes a great difference in what the writer can and cannot permit himself to do. Nobody wants his mule and wagon stalled on the same track the Dixie Limited is roaring down."

Before You Read
A ROSE FOR EMILY

Make the Connection
Skeletons in the Closet
Faulkner, the master of the Southern Gothic tale, knew first-hand the old American South and its powerful social traditions. It's all here in "A Rose for Emily"—the small-town social castes, the changing social values, the politeness with which people go about the routine of life, and the struggles they undergo to find joy in it.

The facts of this story tell a lurid tale, as sensational as any you will see headlined in those scandal sheets displayed at the supermarket checkouts. But what primarily turns this account of outrageous human behavior into literature is the relationship between the event and its setting. As the story of one eccentric woman unfolds, we learn some important truths about the rest of her community: its loyalty to family and the past, its pride, its faithfulness to old values, its fierce independence, and its scorn for all that is new and widely accepted.

Reading Skills and Strategies

Taking Notes on a Character
Miss Emily has a quality we all share to some degree: a tendency to retreat from a reality we don't like into a fantasy world where we can have things our own way. But is her bizarre behavior merely madness, or an extension of qualities admired in her community? As you read the story, take notes on Miss Emily's characteristics. Include your ideas about the motives for her strange actions.

Elements of Literature
Setting
Setting is the time and location in which a story takes place. Setting also includes the customs and social conditions of a time—including, in this case, such things as racial stereotyping. If parts of this story give off an offensive odor, it comes only in part from Miss Emily's house and her horrible deed: It comes also from the racial slurs used by some of the characters. Although we find this language offensive, we must remember that Faulkner used it to portray as realistically as possible a racially segregated town of the rural South in the early part of the twentieth century.

> **S**etting is the time and location in which a story takes place.
>
> *For more on Setting, see the Handbook of Literary Terms.*

WILLIAM FAULKNER 715

Summary ■■■

Faulkner's story is set in Jefferson, Mississippi, at the turn of the twentieth century and is narrated from the first-person plural perspective of its watchful citizens. The story uses a series of flashbacks to explore an external conflict between the increasingly obsessive, insular world of an aging spinster and the community around her. The story opens in the present, with the death of Emily Grierson. As a young woman, she lived with her possessive father, who drove off all her suitors. When her father died, however, she initially refused to give up his body for burial. After she recovered from his death, she eventually began going out on drives with Homer Barron, a Yankee construction worker. When he disappeared, she became even more reclusive and eccentric. After her death, the neighbors break open a locked door in the house. Under layers of dust, they discover a bedroom decorated for a wedding night. Barron's poisoned, decomposing corpse lies in the bed, while the imprint of Emily's head and a strand of her iron-gray hair are visible on the pillow beside him.

FROM THE EDITOR'S DESK
We have paired "A Rose for Emily" with Faulkner's Nobel Prize acceptance speech so that students can get a sense of his career as a whole. "A Rose for Emily" was the first of Faulkner's short stories to be nationally published. He was awarded a Nobel Prize in literature near the end of his career.

Preteaching Vocabulary

Words to Own
Have students read the Words to Own and their definitions listed at the bottom of the selection pages. Then, have them choose partners and practice pronouncing each word correctly. Partners can take turns quizzing each other on the words until both can define all the words. Then, have students complete the following exercise by filling in the word that best completes each sentence.

1. The founders of the town were members of the club in _____. [perpetuity]
2. The anxious lady became _____ when the foreman arrived on time. [tranquil]
3. After spending every penny he had, he became a _____. [pauper]
4. In the attic she found a case containing _____ clothing. [archaic]
5. The _____ old man's hands shook as he opened the gate. [doddering]
6. The thick, _____ smoke irritated her eyes. [acrid]
7. The fringed _____ dressed up the window. [valance]
8. Don't think you can _____ the rules. [circumvent]
9. The _____ tone of her remarks showed how much she hated the townspeople. [virulent]
10. The journalist was _____ when the source confirmed her horrifying story. [vindicated]

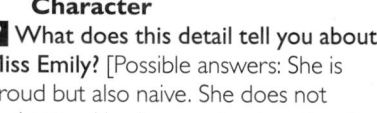
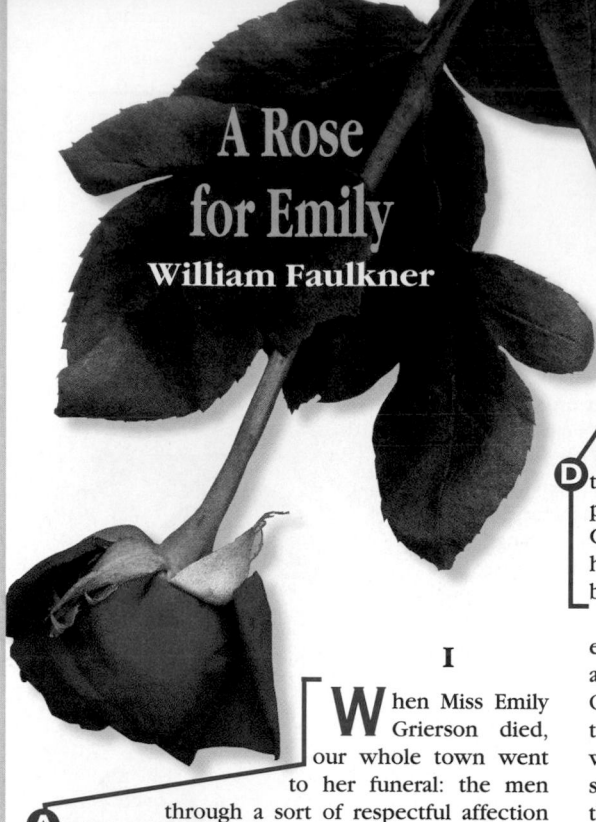

A Rose for Emily
William Faulkner

I

Ⓐ **W**hen Miss Emily Grierson died, our whole town went to her funeral: the men through a sort of respectful affection for a fallen monument, the women mostly out of curiosity to see the inside of her house, which no one save an old manservant—a combined gardener and cook—had seen in at least ten years.

Ⓑ It was a big, squarish frame house that had once been white, decorated with cupolas[1] and spires and scrolled balconies in the heavily lightsome style of the seventies,[2] set on what had once been our most select street. But garages and cotton gins had encroached and obliterated even the august names of that neighborhood; only Miss Emily's house was left, lifting its stubborn and coquettish decay above the cotton wagons and the gasoline pumps—an eyesore among eyesores. And now Miss Emily had gone to join the representatives of those august names where they lay in the cedar-bemused cemetery among the ranked and anonymous graves of Union and Confederate soldiers who fell at the battle of Jefferson.

Ⓒ Alive, Miss Emily had been a tradition, a duty, and a care; a sort of hereditary obligation upon the town, dating from that day in 1894 when Colonel Sartoris, the mayor—he who fathered the edict that no Negro woman should appear on the streets without an apron—remitted[3] her taxes, the dispensation dating from the death of her father on into perpetuity. Not that Miss Emily would have accepted charity. Colonel Sartoris invented an involved tale to the effect Ⓓ that Miss Emily's father had loaned money to the town, which the town, as a matter of business, preferred this way of repaying. Only a man of Colonel Sartoris' generation and thought could have invented it, and only a woman could have believed it.

When the next generation, with its more modern ideas, became mayors and aldermen, this arrangement created some little dissatisfaction. On the first of the year they mailed her a tax notice. February came, and there was no reply. They wrote her a formal letter, asking her to call at the sheriff's office at her convenience. A week later the mayor wrote her himself, offering to call or to send his car for her and received in reply a note on paper of an archaic shape in a thin, flowing calligraphy in faded ink, to the effect that she no longer went out at all. The tax notice was also enclosed, without comment.

They called a special meeting of the Board of Aldermen. A deputation waited upon her, knocked at the door through which no visitor had passed since she ceased giving china-painting lessons eight or ten years earlier. They were admitted by the old Negro into a dim hall from which a stairway mounted into still more shadow. It smelled of dust and disuse—a close, dank smell. The Negro led them into the parlor. It was furnished in heavy, leather-covered furniture. When

---

3. remitted: refrained from enforcing payment of.

WORDS TO OWN
perpetuity (pʉr′pə·tōō′ə·tē) *n.:* eternity.
archaic (är·kā′ik) *adj.:* old-fashioned.

---

1. **cupolas** (kyōō′pə·ləz): small, dome-shaped structures built on a roof.
2. **the seventies:** the 1870s.

716 THE MODERNS

Reaching All Students

My Mother (1921) by George Wesley Bellows. American (1882–1925). Oil on canvas (210.9 cm × 124.5 cm).

Frank Russell Wadsworth Memorial, 1923.975. Photograph © 1998, The Art Institute of Chicago. All Rights Reserved.

RESPONDING TO THE ART

George Bellows (1882–1925) was a member of the group of innovative American painters known as the Eight or the Ashcan School (see p. T523). Born in Columbus, Ohio, Bellows studied painting at the New York School of Art under Robert Henri. Bellows painted New York City in all its vigor and vitality; his best-known works are *Cliff Dwellers* (1913), a Manhattan slum scene, and *Stag at Sharkey's* (1909), a depiction of a brutal saloon prize-fight. Bellows's works were included in the landmark Armory Show of 1913, an exhibit of new paintings that marked a great turning point in American art. After 1914 Bellows concentrated on portraits that combine close observation with sympathetic treatment of the subject.

Activity. After students have read the story, have them compare the mood of this painting to the atmosphere of the story. How are they alike? How are they different? [Possible answers: Alike: The painting shows a dark, shadowy room, lace curtains, and a sedentary figure, all of which are featured in the story. The dominant color, black, suggests death. Different: The painting is generally warm and sympathetic; Miss Emily and her house are more sinister and foreboding.]

Using Students' Strengths

Visual Learners

Point out that Faulkner describes Miss Emily's appearance at several points during the story. Have students work in pairs to create illustrations showing how Faulkner uses these descriptions to characterize his protagonist. For each description, students should ask themselves:

- How old is Miss Emily at this point?
- How has her appearance changed since the previous description?
- What has happened during this time?

Verbal Learners

Ask a small group of students to work as the staff of the Jefferson newspaper on a special edition reporting the death of Miss Emily and the discovery of her crime. Ask the group to choose an editor and to decide on reporting assignments. The journalists should cover not only the main stories but also related features, such as official and community reaction. The articles could be presented in newspaper format on a piece of poster board and displayed in the classroom.

? What do you learn about the house from this description? What feeling does this setting convey? What does the condition of the house suggest about Miss Emily? [The house has not been cleaned in a long time; worn furniture has not been replaced. There is a feeling of decay and decrepitude. Miss Emily may be indifferent to her surroundings or reluctant to make any changes.]

B **Reading Skills and Strategies**

Taking Notes on a Character

? What does this detail about Colonel Sartoris suggest about Miss Emily? [Possible answers: She has no friends to tell her the news of the town; she does not read the paper or stay in touch with what is going on in the town; she has lost touch with reality and so chooses to believe that Sartoris is alive because it comforts her.]

C **English Language Learners**

Understanding Idioms

? Explain that *horse and foot* is an idiom derived from battle. *Horse* refers to cavalry, and *foot* to infantry. Why do you think Faulkner uses this idiom? [Possible answers: to underline the hostility Emily feels toward this deputation of officials; to emphasize the strength of her will.]

D **Reading Skills and Strategies**

Analyzing Synonyms

Point out Faulkner's shift from *ladies* above to *woman* here. Explain that in the context of this story, the words are not synonyms. Ladies were members of the Southern aristocracy; women were ordinary people crass enough to complain publicly about a member of the aristocracy.

A the Negro opened the blinds of one window they could see that the leather was cracked; and when they sat down, a faint dust rose sluggishly about their thighs spinning with slow motes in the single sun-ray. On a tarnished gilt easel before the fireplace stood a crayon portrait of Miss Emily's father.

They rose when she entered—a small, fat woman in black, with a thin gold chain descending to her waist and vanishing into her belt, leaning on an ebony cane with a tarnished gold head. Her skeleton was small and spare; perhaps that was why what would have been merely plumpness in another was obesity in her. She looked bloated, like a body long submerged in motionless water, and of that pallid hue. Her eyes, lost in the fatty ridges of her face, looked like two small pieces of coal pressed into a lump of dough as they moved from one face to another while the visitors stated their errand.

She did not ask them to sit. She just stood in the door and listened quietly until the spokesman came to a stumbling halt. Then they could hear the invisible watch ticking at the end of the gold chain.

Her voice was dry and cold. "I have no taxes in Jefferson. Colonel Sartoris explained it to me. Perhaps one of you can gain access to the city records and satisfy yourselves."

"But we have. We are the city authorities, Miss Emily. Didn't you get a notice from the sheriff, signed by him?"

"I received a paper, yes," Miss Emily said. "Perhaps he considers himself the sheriff . . . I have no taxes in Jefferson."

"But there is nothing on the books to show that, you see. We must go by the—"

B "See Colonel Sartoris. I have no taxes in Jefferson."

"But, Miss Emily—"

"See Colonel Sartoris." (Colonel Sartoris had been dead almost ten years.) "I have no taxes in Jefferson. Tobe!" The Negro appeared. "Show these gentlemen out."

II

C So she vanquished them, horse and foot, just as she had vanquished their fathers thirty years before about the smell. That was two years after her

father's death and a short time after her sweetheart—the one we believed would marry her—had deserted her. After her father's death she went out very little; after her sweetheart went away, people hardly saw her at all. A few of the ladies had the temerity[4] to call, but were not received, and the only sign of life about the place was the Negro man—a young man then—going in and out with a market basket.

"Just as if a man—any man—could keep a kitchen properly," the ladies said; so they were not surprised when the smell developed. It was another link between the gross, teeming world and the high and mighty Griersons.

D A neighbor, a woman, complained to the mayor, Judge Stevens, eighty years old.

"But what will you have me do about it, madam?" he said.

"Why, send her word to stop it," the woman said. "Isn't there a law?"

"I'm sure that won't be necessary," Judge Stevens said. "It's probably just a snake or a rat that nigger of hers killed in the yard. I'll speak to him about it."

The next day he received two more complaints, one from a man who came in diffident deprecation.[5] "We really must do something about it, Judge. I'd be the last one in the world to bother Miss Emily, but we've got to do something." That night the Board of Aldermen met—three graybeards and one younger man, a member of the rising generation.

"It's simple enough," he said. "Send her word to have her place cleaned up. Give her a certain time to do it in, and if she don't . . ."

"Dammit, sir," Judge Stevens said, "will you accuse a lady to her face of smelling bad?"

So the next night, after midnight, four men crossed Miss Emily's lawn and slunk about the house like burglars, sniffing along the base of the brickwork and at the cellar openings while one of them performed a regular sowing motion with his hand out of a sack slung from his shoulder. They broke open the cellar door and sprinkled lime there, and in all the outbuildings. As they recrossed the lawn, a window that had been dark was lighted and Miss Emily sat in it, the light

---

4. **temerity:** foolish boldness; rashness.
5. **diffident deprecation:** timid disapproval.

Taking a Second Look

Review: Drawing Conclusions
Review the strategy of drawing conclusions. A writer may not immediately reveal every detail about the plot, setting, or characters; instead, the writer often drops hints along the way. It is up to the reader to put that information together and infer its meaning. For instance, Faulkner tells the reader about a foul odor coming from Miss Emily's house, but he does not directly explain what causes it.

Activities
1. As students read "A Rose for Emily," have them keep notes of significant details, such as the smell coming from Miss Emily's house and her purchase of the rat poison. Encourage students to think about what each unexplained detail might mean.
2. Have students pause at the end of each of the story's five sections. What conclusions can they draw at each point?

behind her, and her upright torso motionless as that of an idol. They crept quietly across the lawn and into the shadow of the locusts that lined the street. After a week or two the smell went away.

That was when people had begun to feel really sorry for her. People in our town, remembering how old lady Wyatt, her great-aunt, had gone completely crazy at last, believed that the Griersons held themselves a little too high for what they really were. None of the young men were quite good enough for Miss Emily and such. We had long thought of them as a tableau,[6] Miss Emily a slender figure in white in the background, her father a spraddled silhouette in the foreground, his back to her and clutching a horsewhip, the two of them framed by the back-flung front door. So when she got to be thirty and was still single, we were not pleased exactly, but <u>vindicated</u>; even with insanity in the family she wouldn't have turned down all of her chances if they had really materialized.

When her father died, it got about that the house was all that was left to her; and in a way, people were glad. At last they could pity Miss Emily. Being left alone, and a <u>pauper</u>, she had become humanized. Now she too would know the old thrill and the old despair of a penny more or less.

The day after his death all the ladies prepared to call at the house and offer condolence and aid, as is our custom. Miss Emily met them at the door, dressed as usual and with no trace of grief on her face. She told them that her father was not dead. She did that for three days, with the ministers calling on her, and the doctors, trying to persuade her to let them dispose of the body. Just as they were about to resort to law and force, she broke down, and they buried her father quickly.

We did not say she was crazy then. We believed she had to do that. We remembered all the young men her father had driven away, and we knew that with nothing left, she would have to cling to that which had robbed her, as people will.

III

She was sick for a long time. When we saw her again, her hair was cut short, making her look like

6. **tableau:** set scene, as in the theater.

---

a girl, with a vague resemblance to those angels in colored church windows—sort of tragic and serene.

The town had just let the contracts for paving the sidewalks, and in the summer after her father's death they began the work. The construction company came with niggers and mules and machinery, and a foreman named Homer Barron, a Yankee—a big, dark, ready man, with a big voice and eyes lighter than his face. The little boys would follow in groups to hear him cuss the niggers, and the niggers singing in time to the rise and fall of picks. Pretty soon he knew everybody in town. Whenever you heard a lot of laughing anywhere about the square, Homer Barron would be in the center of the group. Presently we began to see him and Miss Emily on Sunday afternoons driving in the yellow-wheeled buggy and the matched team of bays from the livery stable.

At first we were glad that Miss Emily would have an interest, because the ladies all said, "Of course a Grierson would not think seriously of a Northerner, a day laborer." But there were still others, older people, who said that even grief could not cause a real lady to forget *noblesse oblige*[7]—without calling it *noblesse oblige*. They just said, "Poor Emily. Her kinsfolk should come to her." She had some kin in Alabama; but years ago her father had fallen out with them over the estate of old lady Wyatt, the crazy woman, and there was no communication between the two families. They had not even been represented at the funeral.

And as soon as the old people said, "Poor Emily," the whispering began. "Do you suppose it's really so?" they said to one another. "Of course it is. What else could . . ." This behind their hands; rustling of craned[8] silk and satin behind jalousies[9]

---

7. **noblesse oblige** (nō·bles′ ô·blēzh′): French for "nobility obliges"; that is, the supposed obligation of the upper classes to act nobly or kindly toward the lower classes.
8. **craned:** stretched.
9. **jalousies** (jal′ə·sēz′): windows, shades, or doors made of overlapping, adjustable slats.

WORDS TO OWN

vindicated (vin′də·kāt′id) *v.* used as *adj.:* proved correct.
pauper (pô′pər) *n.:* extremely poor person.

WILLIAM FAULKNER 719

E **Struggling Readers**
Finding Details
? What do these two sentences suggest about the Grierson family's place in the community? [The townspeople do not quite agree with the Griersons' high opinion of themselves and their social standing.]

F **Critical Thinking**
Interpreting
? Why is the community's reaction to the death of Miss Emily's father one of satisfaction? [Sample response: They feel more comfortable being able to pity Miss Emily in her impoverished solitude than being looked down upon by the haughty father and daughter.]

G **Reading Skills and Strategies**
Taking Notes on a Character
? Do you agree with the narrator's assessment of Emily's actions? [Possible answers: Yes; she was afraid to face the future alone. No; she was showing signs of mental illness.]

H **Critical Thinking**
Hypothesizing
? How do you think Homer and Miss Emily met? [Possible answer: He might have been working on the sidewalk on her block.]

I **Elements of Literature**
Setting
? What do the attitudes of the town reveal about the time and place? [In this paragraph the townspeople reveal the intense class consciousness, generational differences, and prejudice against Northerners characteristic of the deep South at that time.]

Skill Link

Understanding Literary Concepts: The Narrator

Remind students that the **narrator** of a work of literature is the voice that tells the story. Sometimes a narrator is a character in the work, like J. Alfred Prufrock or the speaker of "Recuerdo." At other times, the narrator takes no part in the story. "Miniver Cheevy" and "Soldier's Home" are told from an anonymous, third-person point of view.

Activities

1. As students read "A Rose for Emily," have them pay close attention to the narrator's voice and consider that the narrator speaks as a plural "we" rather than as a singular "I."

2. After students have read the story, have a class discussion about the narrating voice. You may want to use the following questions to start off the discussion.

- What is the narrator's attitude toward Miss Emily?
- What is the narrator's tone?
- What is the relationship between Miss Emily and the narrator?
- Who do you think the narrator is?
- How does the narrator shape our reactions to Miss Emily and the events in her life?

A Vocabulary Note

Multiple Meanings

Ask students to define *fallen* in this context. [The neighbors suspect Homer has become Emily's lover.]

B Reading Skills and Strategies

Taking Notes on a Character

? Why doesn't Miss Emily answer the pharmacist's question? [She is too arrogant to allow clerks to question her motives. Or, she has an illicit purpose in mind and is too naive to try to cover it up with an excuse.] **Why is her face compared to "a lighthouse-keeper's" and "a strained flag"?** [These attributes help convey her inner strain, her strange isolation, and her inscrutable desires.]

C Elements of Literature

Setting

? How do you explain the community's response to Miss Emily's purchase? [Possible responses: Community members are enthralled with her life, as with a soap opera; they don't care whether Miss Emily kills herself or not; they believe that death is preferable to public humiliation; perhaps they are a little frightened of Miss Emily.]

That Which I Should Have Done I Did Not Do (1931–1941) by Ivan Le Lorraine Albright (1897–1983). American. Oil on canvas (246.5 cm × 91.5 cm).

720 THE MODERNS

closed upon the sun of Sunday afternoon as the thin, swift, clop-clop-clop of the matched team passed: "Poor Emily."

A She carried her head high enough—even when we believed that she was fallen. It was as if she demanded more than ever the recognition of her dignity as the last Grierson; as if it had wanted that touch of earthiness to reaffirm her imperviousness. Like when she bought the rat poison, the arsenic. That was over a year after they had begun to say "Poor Emily," and while the two female cousins were visiting her.

"I want some poison," she said to the druggist. She was over thirty then, still a slight woman, though thinner than usual, with cold, haughty black eyes in a face the flesh of which was strained across the temples and about the eye-sockets as you imagine a lighthouse-keeper's face ought to look. "I want some poison," she said.

"Yes, Miss Emily. What kind? For rats and such? I'd recom—"

"I want the best you have. I don't care what kind."

The druggist named several. "They'll kill anything up to an elephant. But what you want is—"

B "Arsenic," Miss Emily said. "Is that a good one?"

"Is . . . arsenic? Yes, ma'am. But what you want—"

"I want arsenic."

The druggist looked down at her. She looked back at him, erect, her face like a strained flag. "Why, of course," the druggist said. "If that's what you want. But the law requires you to tell what you are going to use it for."

Miss Emily just stared at him, her head tilted back in order to look him eye for eye, until he looked away and went and got the arsenic and wrapped it up. The Negro delivery boy brought her the package; the druggist didn't come back. When she opened the package at home there was written on the box, under the skull and bones: "For rats."

IV

C So the next day we all said, "She will kill herself"; and we said it would be the best thing. When she had first begun to be seen with Homer Barron, we had said, "She will marry him." Then we said, "She will persuade him yet," because Homer himself

Crossing the Curriculum

Science

Have students look up *arsenic* in an encyclopedia or a science book. Where does it come from? What is it used for? Is death by arsenic slow or instantaneous? Have students design a warning label for a container of this deadly substance.

History

"A Rose for Emily" is full of references to racial prejudice. Have students do some research into the South's reaction to its defeat in the Civil War. How did white Southerners react to the new freedom of African Americans? What steps did whites take to restrict these new freedoms? Have interested students work together on a time line of important dates in race relations in the South between the time of the Emancipation Proclamation and 1930. Post the time line, and discuss with students how this historical context might affect the plot, character, and narrative voice of the story.

had remarked—he liked men, and it was known that he drank with the younger men in the Elks' Club—that he was not a marrying man. Later we said, "Poor Emily," behind the jalousies as they passed on Sunday afternoon in the glittering buggy, Miss Emily with her head high and Homer Barron with his hat cocked and a cigar in his teeth, reins and whip in a yellow glove.

Then some of the ladies began to say that it was a disgrace to the town and a bad example to the young people. The men did not want to interfere, but at last the ladies forced the Baptist minister—Miss Emily's people were Episcopal—to call upon her. He would never divulge what happened during that interview, but he refused to go back again. The next Sunday they again drove about the streets, and the following day the minister's wife wrote to Miss Emily's relations in Alabama.

So she had blood-kin under her roof again and we sat back to watch developments. At first nothing happened. Then we were sure that they were to be married. We learned that Miss Emily had been to the jeweler's and ordered a man's toilet set[10] in silver, with the letters H. B. on each piece. Two days later we learned that she had bought a complete outfit of men's clothing, including a nightshirt, and we said, "They are married." We were really glad. We were glad because the two female cousins were even more Grierson than Miss Emily had ever been.

So we were not surprised when Homer Barron—the streets had been finished some time since—was gone. We were a little disappointed that there was not a public blowing-off, but we believed that he had gone on to prepare for Miss Emily's coming, or to give her a chance to get rid of the cousins. (By that time it was a cabal,[11] and we were all Miss Emily's allies to help <u>circumvent</u> the cousins.) Sure enough, after another week they departed. And, as we had expected all along, within three days Homer Barron was back in town. A neighbor saw the Negro man admit him at the kitchen door at dusk one evening.

And that was the last we saw of Homer Barron. And of Miss Emily for some time. The Negro man went in and out with the market basket, but the

front door remained closed. Now and then we would see her at a window for a moment, as the men did that night when they sprinkled the lime, but for almost six months she did not appear on the streets. Then we knew that this was to be expected too; as if that quality of her father which had thwarted her woman's life so many times had been too <u>virulent</u> and too furious to die.

When we next saw Miss Emily, she had grown fat and her hair was turning gray. During the next few years it grew grayer and grayer until it attained an even pepper-and-salt iron-gray, when it ceased turning. Up to the day of her death at seventy-four it was still that vigorous iron-gray, like the hair of an active man.

From that time on her front door remained closed, save for a period of six or seven years, when she was about forty, during which she gave lessons in china-painting. She fitted up a studio in one of the downstairs rooms, where the daughters and granddaughters of Colonel Sartoris' contemporaries were sent to her with the same regularity and in the same spirit that they were sent to church on Sundays with a twenty-five-cent piece for the collection plate. Meanwhile her taxes had been remitted.

Then the newer generation became the backbone and the spirit of the town, and the painting pupils grew up and fell away and did not send their children to her with boxes of color and tedious brushes and pictures cut from the ladies' magazines. The front door closed upon the last one and remained closed for good. When the town got free postal delivery, Miss Emily alone refused to let them fasten the metal numbers above her door and attach a mailbox to it. She would not listen to them.

Daily, monthly, yearly we watched the Negro grow grayer and more stooped, going in and out with the market basket. Each December we sent her a tax notice, which would be returned by the post office a week later, unclaimed. Now and then we would see her in one of the downstairs windows—she had evidently shut up the top floor of

---

WORDS TO OWN

circumvent (sʉr′kəm·vent′) v.: to get the better of by craft or ingenuity.
virulent (vir′yo͞o·lənt) adj.: full of hate; venomous.

---

10. **toilet set:** set of grooming aids, such as a hand mirror, hairbrush, and comb.
11. **cabal** (kə·bäl′): small group involved in a secret intrigue.

D Elements of Literature
Setting
❓ What does this detail about the Baptist preacher and the local ladies tell you about the time and place of the story? [It suggests the insularity of the town and its class divisions. Note that the old aristocracy is probably Episcopalian, while it is the middle-class Baptists who do not accept Miss Emily's behavior and want to impose a stricter morality on her.]

E Critical Thinking
Interpreting
❓ Why does Emily want to get rid of her cousins? [She wants privacy; she wants to be with Homer.] Why are the townspeople her allies here? [They are critical of anyone who, like the cousins, strikes them as arrogant or haughty.]

F Critical Thinking
Interpreting
❓ Why does Faulkner compare sending pupils to Miss Emily to donating money in church? [to emphasize that the town helps her out of pity and a sense of duty, not out of love or friendship]

G Reading Skills and Strategies
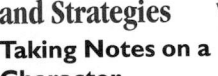
Taking Notes on a Character
❓ Why does Emily refuse a mailbox? How does this compare with her other actions? [Throughout the story, Emily refuses to acknowledge the passage of time. She ignores the fact that Sartoris is dead; she denies the death of her father; she wants no change in her way of life, not even a mailbox. She also refuses to be part of the community.]

Getting Students Involved

A Confrontation
Have a small group of students imagine and stage the conversation between Miss Emily and the Baptist minister. To prepare, students should read through the story on their own for any clues to what the characters might have said in this interaction. They can then discuss their findings with the rest of the group. One student can incorporate those ideas into a script, two can play the roles of Emily and the minister, one can direct the scene, and one can plan and provide costumes and props.

Dramatic Reading
Have several students collaborate on a dramatic reading of the story. Some students can play specific characters, such as Miss Emily and the druggist; the narrator will be played by several different students. Students should reread the story carefully to decide which citizen of Jefferson might speak which lines of the narration. One student can direct rehearsals, and one can serve as his or her assistant.

A Elements of Literature

Atmosphere

? How would you describe the atmosphere of this room? How might it have looked forty years earlier? [Possible responses: haunted; creepy; tragic; neglected; gloomy. Forty years earlier, it might have been warm, inviting, and romantic.]

B Reading Skills and Strategies

Taking Notes on a Character

? What is the implication in the last paragraph? What might have been the motivations for this action? [Emily has been sleeping in this bed with the corpse—years after the murder. This may be an extension of her refusal to accept the deaths of her father and Colonel Sartoris. It may reflect a pathological determination that no one, especially Barron, would leave her again.]

---

the house—like the carven torso of an idol in a niche, looking or not looking at us, we could never tell which. Thus she passed from generation to generation—dear, inescapable, impervious, tranquil, and perverse.

And so she died. Fell ill in the house filled with dust and shadows, with only a doddering Negro man to wait on her. We did not even know she was sick; we had long since given up trying to get any information from the Negro. He talked to no one, probably not even to her, for his voice had grown harsh and rusty, as if from disuse.

She died in one of the downstairs rooms, in a heavy walnut bed with a curtain, her gray head propped on a pillow yellow and moldy with age and lack of sunlight.

V

The Negro met the first of the ladies at the front door and let them in, with their hushed, sibilant[12] voices and their quick, curious glances, and then he disappeared. He walked right through the house and out the back and was not seen again.

The two female cousins came at once. They held the funeral on the second day, with the town coming to look at Miss Emily beneath a mass of bought flowers, with the crayon face of her father musing profoundly above the bier[13] and the ladies sibilant and macabre;[14] and the very old men—some in their brushed Confederate uniforms—on the porch and the lawn, talking of Miss Emily as if she had been a contemporary of theirs, believing that they had danced with her and courted her perhaps, confusing time with its mathematical progression, as the old do, to whom all the past is not a diminishing road but, instead, a huge meadow which no winter ever quite touches, divided from them now by the narrow bottle-neck of the most recent decade of years.

Already we knew that there was one room in that region above stairs which no one had seen in forty years, and which would have to be forced. They waited until Miss Emily was decently in the ground before they opened it.

The violence of breaking down the door

12. **sibilant** (sib'əl·ənt): hissing.
13. **bier** (bir): coffin and its supporting platform.
14. **macabre** (mə·käb'rə): focused on the gruesome; horrible.

---

seemed to fill this room with pervading dust. A thin, acrid pall as of the tomb seemed to lie everywhere upon this room decked and furnished as for a bridal: upon the valance curtains of faded rose color, upon the rose-shaded lights, upon the dressing table, upon the delicate array of crystal and the man's toilet things backed with tarnished silver, silver so tarnished that the monogram was obscured. Among them lay a collar and tie, as if they had just been removed, which, lifted, left upon the surface a pale crescent in the dust. Upon a chair hung the suit, carefully folded; beneath it the two mute shoes and the discarded socks.

The man himself lay in the bed.

For a long while we just stood there, looking down at the profound and fleshless grin. The body had apparently once lain in the attitude of an embrace, but now the long sleep that outlasts love, that conquers even the grimace of love, had cuckolded[15] him. What was left of him, rotted beneath what was left of the nightshirt, had become inextricable from the bed in which he lay; and upon him and upon the pillow beside him lay that even coating of the patient and biding dust.

Then we noticed that in the second pillow was the indentation of a head. One of us lifted something from it, and leaning forward, that faint and invisible dust dry and acrid in the nostrils, we saw a long strand of iron-gray hair.

15. **cuckolded** (kuk'əld·id): betrayed, as in the sense of a husband whose wife has been unfaithful.

WORDS TO OWN

tranquil (tran'kwil) adj.: calm; quiet.
doddering (däd'ər·iŋ) adj.: shaky; trembling from old age.
acrid (ak'rid) adj.: bitter; irritating.
valance (val'əns) n. used as adj.: short decorative drapery.

Assessing Learning

Check Test: True-False

1. Miss Emily refuses to tell the druggist why she wants the arsenic. [True]
2. When the aldermen come to ask her to pay her taxes, Miss Emily sends them away empty-handed. [True]
3. When Homer Barron comes calling, Emily's father threatens him with a whip, as he did all of Emily's other suitors. [False]

4. Townspeople find Homer Barron's body behind a locked door that has to be forced open. [True]

Informal Assessment

Self-Assessment. To check students' reading comprehension and to encourage them to reflect on what they have read, have them respond to the following questions:

- Did you like this story? Why or why not?
- What do you feel is the most important scene, conversation, or passage in this story? Explain your choice.
- What literary elements did you find most difficult to understand? Why?

Nobel Prize Acceptance Speech, 1950

I feel that this award was not made to me as a man, but to my work—a life's work in the agony and sweat of the human spirit, not for glory and least of all for profit, but to create out of the materials of the human spirit something which did not exist before. So this award is only mine in trust. It will not be difficult to find a dedication for the money part of it commensurate with the purpose and significance of its origin. But I would like to do the same with the acclaim too, by using this moment as a pinnacle from which I might be listened to by the young men and women already dedicated to the same anguish and travail, among whom is already that one who will someday stand here where I am standing.

Our tragedy today is a general and universal physical fear so long sustained by now that we can even bear it. There are no longer problems of the spirit. There is only the question: When will I be blown up? Because of this, the young man or woman writing today has forgotten the problems of the human heart in conflict with itself which alone can make good writing because only that is worth writing about, worth the agony and the sweat.

He must learn them again. He must teach himself that the basest of all things is to be afraid; and, teaching himself that, forget it forever, leaving no room in his workshop for anything but the old verities and truths of the heart, the old universal truths lacking which any story is ephemeral and doomed—love and honor and pity and pride and compassion and sacrifice. Until he does so, he labors under a curse. He writes not of love but of lust, of defeats in which nobody loses anything of value, of victories without hope and, worst of all, without pity or compassion. His griefs grieve on no universal bones, leaving no scars. He writes not of the heart but of the glands.

William Faulkner (right) receiving the Nobel Prize in literature (1950). AP/Wide World Photos.

Until he relearns these things, he will write as though he stood among and watched the end of man. I decline to accept the end of man. It is easy enough to say that man is immortal simply because he will endure: that when the last dingdong of doom has clanged and faded from the last worthless rock hanging tideless in the last red and dying evening, that even then there will still be one more sound: that of his puny inexhaustible voice, still talking. I refuse to accept this. I believe that man will not merely endure: he will prevail. He is immortal, not because he alone among creatures has an inexhaustible voice, but because he has a soul, a spirit capable of compassion and sacrifice and endurance. The poet's, the writer's, duty is to write about these things. It is his privilege to help man endure by lifting his heart, by reminding him of the courage and honor and hope and pride and compassion and pity and sacrifice which have been the glory of his past. The poet's voice need not merely be the record of man, it can be one of the props, the pillars to help him endure and prevail.

—William Faulkner

WILLIAM FAULKNER 723

Primary Sources

In this eloquent acceptance speech, Faulkner insists that the Nobel Prize is his only "in trust" and that he must use it to give something back to his fellow writers. He thus warns them against a literature based on "physical fear," which might, under the threat of nuclear annihilation, abandon the eternal questions of the human heart "in conflict with itself" for a superficial literature "of the glands." He goes on to champion the redemptive power of literature, its ability to connect human beings to the "compassion and sacrifice and endurance" of our souls. Literature, in his view, will help us not merely endure but prevail.

Background

Faulkner had to be convinced to travel to Stockholm to accept the Nobel Prize. He did not even own a white tie and tails; his wife, Estelle, rented him a suit for the occasion. Faulkner had never spoken in public before, and his inexperience led him to stand too far from the microphone and to speak too quickly. Most of his audience did not know what he had said until the papers came out the next morning. In later years, however, it was recalled as the finest speech ever given at a Nobel Prize awards dinner.

Ⓐ Historical Connections

Explain to students that Faulkner is expressing an anxiety that was widely felt at this time. Beginning with the Japanese invasion of Manchuria in 1931 and continuing through World War II, millions of people died. The Cold War began soon after the end of World War II, as the U.S.S.R. and the United States competed for global dominance. In 1949 the Soviet Union became the second nuclear power, renewing memories of the bombing of Hiroshima and Nagasaki and awakening fears of global nuclear war.

Ⓑ Critical Thinking
Synthesizing

❓ Does "A Rose for Emily" illustrate this belief in the compassion, sacrifice, and endurance of the human soul? If so, how? [Possible answers: Yes; the story itself grants Miss Emily a kind of subtle compassion and pity, examining her history and her madness with patience and perhaps even a certain admiration for her twisted pride.]

Making the Connections

Connecting to the Theme: "Shadows of the Past"
Thwarted love shadows the past of both Miss Emily and Granny Weatherall. Have students compare how each deals with the experience. Then, have students compare the points of view of each story: Miss Emily's, told from the outside perspective of a community narrator; and Granny Weatherall's, in an interior monologue. Ask students how each point of view affects the narration of the story.

Connecting Across Texts

Connecting with "Richard Cory"
Have students look back at "Richard Cory" (p. 645). What similarities do students see between the poem and this story? Suggest that they concentrate on the following elements:
• The protagonist (Cory/Emily)
• The narrator
• The protagonist's place in the community
• The theme
Students can write brief essays in response.

First Thoughts [Respond]

1. Students may feel the ending is foreshadowed by clues in the story but may also be shocked by the implications raised by the hair on the pillow.

Shaping Interpretations [Interpret]

2. Emily's father apparently used the horsewhip to threaten the young men who came to call on her. The conflict is also internal, between Emily's duty to obey her father and her desire for love.

3. Colonel Sartoris wants to help Emily financially without hurting her pride or her standing as a "lady." Later, rather than tell Miss Emily about the neighbors' complaints, Judge Stevens has lime strewn around the house. As the South becomes more industrialized, the old aristocracy loses its privileges.

4. Emily's hair begins to turn gray after she kills Barron. It is as if she withdraws from the living. Her hair is compared to that of an active man because she has committed the decisive act of murder.

5. The hair indicates that Emily has slept beside Barron's corpse—and that, at some level, she has refused to understand that he is dead and that they are not married.

6. Tobe never betrays Emily's secret to the town. However, because of the difference in class and race, he cannot be Emily's friend. He only emphasizes her isolation and the social divisions of the old South.

7. The narrator, most likely a man, often speaks for all the white citizens of Jefferson. The narrator refers to the townspeople as "we," implying that he represents the group. The narrator shows pity, horror, admiration, and curiosity with regard to Emily.

8. Possible responses: Yes, Emily's sense of superiority isolates her from the community and allows her pathology to grow. Yet the community itself seems "warped" in certain respects, and it is hard to say how much acceptance it could ever have granted Miss Emily.

9. Themes of the story include the strength and decay of antebellum Southern values, the tragic consequences of isolation and loneliness, and the deep and twisted human

First Thoughts

1. Did the ending of this story surprise you, or were you prepared for it? Explain.

Shaping Interpretations

2. The community thought of Emily and her father "as a tableau"—a kind of dramatic picture. This tableau suggests conflict. What **conflicts** do you think existed between Emily and her father? (For whom or what was that horsewhip intended?)

3. How is Colonel Sartoris's white lie to Miss Emily about her taxes an attempt to spare her any embarrassment? Explain how Judge Stevens has also taken steps to avoid embarrassing her. How do the later changes in attitude toward Miss Emily's taxes reflect wider social and economic changes in the South?

4. Why do you think Faulkner emphasizes the way Miss Emily's hair turned gray—and what do you think is significant about the time it started to happen?

5. What significance do you see in the long strand of iron-gray hair found on the second pillow?

6. What part do you think Tobe, the manservant, plays in Miss Emily's history?

7. What sort of person do you think the **narrator** of this story is? Is it a man or a woman? Does the narrator pity Miss Emily? admire her? hold her in contempt?

8. The critics Cleanth Brooks, R. W. B. Lewis, and Robert Penn Warren noted of this story: "The community is nearly everywhere in Faulkner's

> **Reading Check**
>
> a. What do people think is causing Miss Emily's house to smell? What really causes the odor?
>
> b. How does Miss Emily's odd behavior when her father dies **foreshadow** the end of the story?
>
> c. Why does the minister's wife send for Miss Emily's relations?
>
> d. Who is Homer Barron? What makes him disappear?

work as an important force and, diffused and anonymous though it be, it becomes one of the most important elements in the story. . . . Miss Emily Grierson is one of the numerous characters in Faulkner's work who are warped by their inheritance from the past and who are cut off from the community—sometimes by their own will—to their detriment." Do you agree with these critics? Why or why not?

9. Another observation made by the same critics is that Faulkner's story has significance far beyond its horror-story ending: "To read 'A Rose for Emily' as merely a piece of cheap Southern Gothicism, an attempt to shock and horrify, would be to miss the point." Do you agree or disagree with these critics? What is the point of the story, in your opinion?

Extending the Text

10. Historical details in this story reveal a great deal about its **setting**. What do you learn about the times from the townspeople's attitude toward the African Americans who live in Jefferson? In our time, have such attitudes changed or stayed much the same? Discuss how Faulkner might have changed his story if he'd written it today.

Challenging the Text

11. Faulkner once explained the title "A Rose for Emily" this way:

> "Oh, it's simply the poor woman had had no life at all. Her father had kept her more or less locked up and then she had a lover who was about to quit her, she had to murder him. It was just 'A Rose for Emily'—that's all."

Faulkner's answer is not very helpful. Consider what roses usually **symbolize.** Then defend the title of the story, or propose a more appropriate title.

need for love. The convincing portrait of the community and the sympathy many readers feel for Emily show that shock value is not the main point of the story.

Extending the Text [Synthesize]

10. The white people of Jefferson take for granted a social order in which African Americans are treated as fundamentally inferior to and separate from whites. While this belief in the inferiority of African Americans is now considered unacceptable in

both the South and the North, blacks and whites still tend to live in separate (and often unequal) Americas. If Faulkner had set his story today, he might have included the views of black characters.

Challenging the Text [Evaluate]

11. Roses are associated with love but also with death and funerals. Students may suggest that it aptly conveys the story's combined focus on love and morbid tragedy. The rose may be Faulkner's tribute to Miss Emily.

CHOICES: Building Your Portfolio

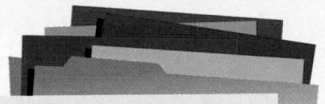

Writer's Notebook

1. Collecting Ideas for an Interpretive Essay

See if you can better understand Miss Emily by analyzing her **character.** Review the places in this story where the narrator directly describes what the townspeople thought of Miss Emily. For example, in part IV, the narrator says they thought of her as "dear, inescapable, impervious, tranquil, and perverse" (page 722). Use these descriptions, together with the notes you made while reading, to make a chart (see below). When you have finished your chart, write a few sentences summarizing your insights into Miss Emily. Save your work for possible use in the Writer's Workshop on page 804.

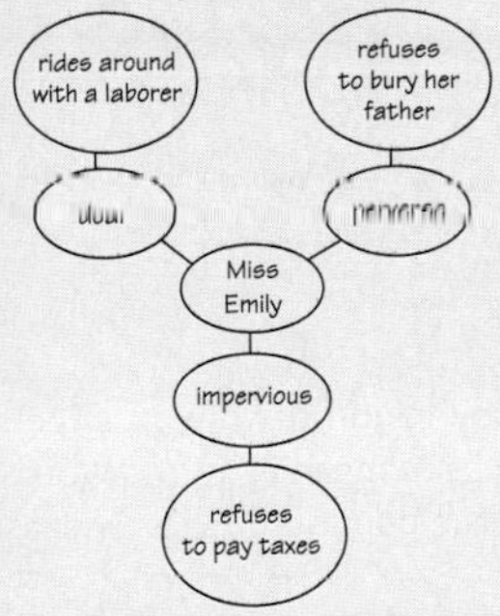
rides around with a laborer
refuses to bury her father
Miss Emily
impervious
refuses to pay taxes

Analyzing a Story Line

2. Sequencing the Plot

The order in which the narrator *mentions* events in this story differs from the order in which they occurred. Go through the story, listing the key events as they are mentioned: Homer's arriving in town, Emily's buying the poison, the death of Emily's father, and so on. Then, rearrange your list in **chronological order.** Compare the lists, and write a brief essay in which you analyze Faulkner's **plot sequence.** Try to explain Faulkner's purpose in fragmenting time (presenting events out of order).

Creative Writing

3. Nightmare on *Your* Street

Write a short-short story (no more than 1,200 words) about a fictional solitary person who lives in your neighborhood. A shocking secret should lie hidden in this person's past. Before you begin writing, decide what the secret is and what events occur in the plot of your story. Include vivid, descriptive details that create a mysterious **atmosphere** and a believable **setting.** Save the startling truth for the last sentences, as Faulkner does in "A Rose for Emily."

Speaking and Listening

4. Literary Likenesses

With a small group, choose one of the statements below. Divide your group in half, and decide which side will argue in support of and which in opposition to each statement. Do whatever research is needed (using this book, a library, or the Internet) before deciding which side you can argue most convincingly.

a. Miss Emily's house is like Roderick Usher's house in "The Fall of the House of Usher" by Edgar Allan Poe (page 263). (You could also compare it with Julio Cortázar's "House Taken Over" on page 291.)

b. Miss Emily and Richard Cory in the poem by Edwin Arlington Robinson (page 645) are both victims of their extreme isolation from their communities.

c. Miss Emily is haunted by a lost love in much the same way that Granny Weatherall in Katherine Anne Porter's story (page 704) turns out to be haunted by the memory of the man who jilted her.

d. Miss Emily and Miss Havisham, in the novel *Great Expectations* by Charles Dickens, react to losing a lover in similar ways.

Grading Timesaver

Rubrics for each Choices assignment appear on p. 178 in the *Portfolio Management System.*

CHOICES: Building Your Portfolio

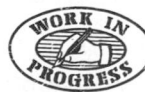

1. Writer's Notebook Have students consider Miss Emily's actions and words, as well as what other characters say about her. Students should also consider who those characters are and whether their opinions are reliable.

2. Analyzing a Story Line Have students consider the effect that the time scheme had on them while they were reading. How would the story's impact have changed if the events had been presented in the order in which they occurred?

3. Creative Writing Encourage students to outline their stories before they begin writing. Have them brainstorm more than one possible sequence of events. How would a different order alter the story's effect? They may enjoy sharing their finished stories with classmates.

4. Speaking and Listening You might assign each of the four groups a different statement. Groups can stage their debates in class so that all students can share in the experience of comparing works of literature. Each debate can conclude with a question-and-answer period.

Reading Check

a. Judge Stevens suspects a dead rat or snake; neighbors think it is a dirty kitchen. It is really Barron's corpse.

b. She refuses to surrender his body for burial, just as she later keeps Barron's body in the house.

c. She is aware of the gossip and feels Emily should be chaperoned.

d. Barron is a Yankee, the foreman of a construction crew, and Emily's love. He disappears when Emily poisons him and keeps his corpse in the house.

Assessing Learning

Standardized Test Preparation

For practice with ACT and SAT formats, see

- *Preparation for College Admission Exams,* p. 49

For practice in proofreading and editing, see

- *Daily Oral Grammar,* Transparency 45

Reading Skills and Strategies

This feature focuses on semantic features analysis, which is applied to "A Rose for Emily."

Mini-Lesson: Distinguishing Connotations of Synonyms

As a fun way of getting students to think about the importance of word choice in writing, share Mark Twain's rules for good writing: "The author shall: 1. *Say* what he is proposing to say, not merely come near it. 2. Use the right word, not its second cousin." Have students think about Twain's rules as they look at the table of synonyms. Then, students can reread the beginning of the story and discuss how this exercise has enriched their understanding of the relationship between Miss Emily and the people of Jefferson. As an extension, you might draw students' attention to the synonym pair *lady/woman,* highlighted on p. T718.

Try It Out

If students have trouble finding synonyms for this exercise, you might suggest *pity/compassion* and *spirit/soul* from Faulkner's speech (p. 723) or *tactful/kind, dutiful/good,* and *flimsy/gauzy* from "The Jilting of Granny Weatherall" (pp. 706, 708). Encourage students to look at the subtle differences between synonyms and to think about what precise description can do to make writing more powerful and interesting.

Possible Answers

Answers will vary. For the first example given, students should see that *pity* implies a feeling of superiority to the sufferer, while *compassion* suggests equality and fellow feeling.

Reading Skills and Strategies

VOCABULARY: SEMANTIC FEATURES ANALYSIS

Semantic features analysis is a way of analyzing related words, or **synonyms**—words having nearly the same meaning—to highlight their similarities and differences. A good way to see distinctions between terms that have overlapping meanings or subtle differences in **connotation** is to analyze their semantic features.

Here's an example of an occasion when you might want to use this technique. Near the beginning of "A Rose for Emily," William Faulkner writes, "Alive, Miss Emily had been a tradition, a duty, and a care; a sort of hereditary obligation upon the town. . . ." You can be sure that Faulkner precisely chose the words *tradition, duty, care,* and *obligation* and made a considered decision to use all four to describe Miss Emily. Why? A semantic features analysis might help you understand why.

To make a semantic features chart, list the words being analyzed down the left-hand side. From a thesaurus and a dictionary, gather various meanings and connotations of the words to list along the top. (A **thesaurus** is a compilation of synonyms and antonyms.)

If a word has or suggests a particular meaning or connotation, mark +. If the word does *not* have that meaning or connotation, mark –. If a word potentially, but not necessarily, has a specific connotation, you may want to mark it ∗.

For the four words from "A Rose for Emily," you might need to begin with a dictionary definition to be sure you know the exact meaning—or **denotation**—of each word. Then you would choose connotations, and you might create a chart like the one below.

The analysis done in the chart shows that each word listed emphasizes a different aspect of responsibility. *Tradition* is the only word that suggests something that is necessarily passed along over generations. *Duty* emphasizes requirement. *Care* implies a burden. *Obligation* emphasizes the contractual nature of the responsibility. Thus, it could be argued, Faulkner has used these four words together to build a composite, or combined, meaning that is richer than the meaning of any one or two of the words alone.

	felt as burdensome	something long-established	something that is required	suggests a social obligation	has aspects of a law or contract
tradition	∗	+	∗	+	∗
duty	+	∗	+	∗	+
care	+	∗	–	∗	–
obligation	+	∗	+	∗	+

Try It Out

Choose words with similar meanings from a selection in this collection to form an appropriate group for a semantic features analysis. Make a chart, and use a thesaurus and a dictionary to help you identify definitions and connotations. Then, fill in the chart.

Finally, try to describe in your own words the similarities and differences in meaning of the words you chose. Think about the connotations as well as the denotations.

Getting Students Involved

Synonym Jeopardy

Before class, prepare fifteen index cards, each with a useful vocabulary word on one side and three standard synonyms from a thesaurus on the other. To set up the game, divide the class into teams of four or five students, each equipped with a dictionary. To begin play, select an index card and read the three synonyms aloud. Give the teams five to ten minutes to 1) guess the original word and 2) construct a semantic features analysis of the three synonyms. When time is up, each team should select a representative to present the team's guess and its synonym analysis. Each team gets one point for guessing the original word correctly and two points for a thorough semantic features analysis. Repeat this process until all the index cards have been used. The team with the most points wins the game.

LITERATURE OF THE AMERICAS
URUGUAY

Horacio Quiroga
(1878–1937)

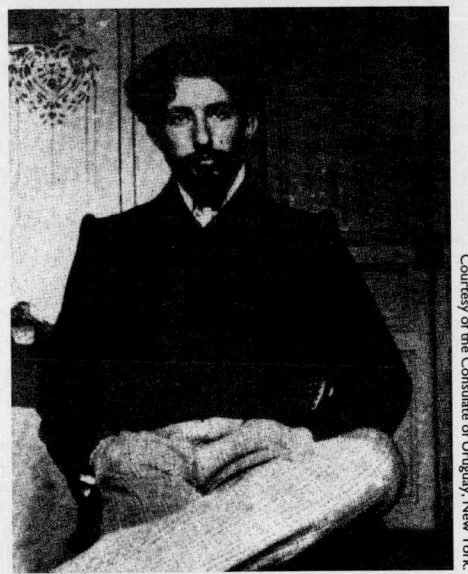

Courtesy of the Consulate of Uruguay, New York.

Horacio Quiroga (kē·rō'gä) was one of Latin America's finest and most celebrated short-story writers, a master of the taut, suspenseful, well-crafted tale. Born in Salto, Uruguay, Quiroga was an avid admirer of Edgar Allan Poe's fiction. Like Poe, Quiroga wrote stories that blend horror with psychological suspense. Also like Poe, Quiroga developed a philosophy of short-story writing. In his essay "Manual of the Perfect Short Story Writer," Quiroga presents an approach to writing not unlike Poe's theory of the "single effect": the idea that every word and detail in a story should build to a single, unified emotional effect. Quiroga warns writers to avoid unnecessary words and details and never to begin a story without knowing exactly where it is heading. He felt that in the perfect short story the first few sentences are as important as the last few, and inevitably lead to them. In his best stories—among which is "The Feather Pillow" (first published in 1907)—Quiroga achieves a compressed, sustained effect with every word and sentence. By the time of his death, he had written about two hundred works of fiction, including the classic story collections *Jungle Tales* (1918) and *The Decapitated Chicken and Other Stories* (1925).

A master of dramatic technique, Quiroga was also superb at creating setting. In his stories, as in the stories of William Faulkner and other American writers who explore in depth certain real or fictionalized regions, Quiroga makes setting almost a character in itself. He spent a good portion of his life in San Ignacio, a jungle province in Misiones (in northern Argentina) that provided inspiration for his settings. In many of his stories, he deals with fundamental conflicts between human beings and the world of nature—conflicts in which nature is invariably the victor. Many of his jungle stories illustrate his uncompromising vision of life as an eternal, often brutal, struggle for survival, not unlike some of the tales of Jack London, to whom Quiroga has also been compared.

Quiroga's Poe-like obsession with death and the grotesque is not surprising, given that his life was a patchwork of nightmares as disturbing as the tales he crafted. Quiroga came face to face with gruesome death early in his life. First, his father accidentally killed himself with a shotgun. When he was twenty-three, Quiroga accidentally shot to death one of his closest friends. There were more personal tragedies: Quiroga's attempts to start a business in the rugged and dangerous Argentine jungle failed; his first wife, in despair over their living conditions in the jungle, took her own life; and his second marriage ended unhappily in separation. Quiroga ended his own tragic life in 1937, after discovering that he was dying of cancer.

OBJECTIVES

1. Read and interpret the story
2. Generate relevant, interesting, and researchable questions
3. Recognize distinctive and shared characteristics of cultures
4. Express understanding through discussion
5. Recognize and discuss themes and connections that cross cultures

Planning

- **Traditional Schedule**
  Lesson Plans Including Strategies for English-Language Learners
- **One-Stop Planner**
  CD-ROM with Test Generator

BROWSING IN THE FILES

About the Author. Quiroga grew up in Uruguay but made his home in the jungles of northern Argentina. His fables of the jungle were written for an audience of both adults and children. Like Aesop's fables, Quiroga's *cuentos* (tales) often feature animal characters. *Anaconda,* one of his best-known works, tells of the struggle between the anaconda and the viper, two fierce jungle snakes. Like most of Quiroga's work, *Anaconda* can be read on many different levels.

Resources: Print and Media

Reading
- *Audio CD Library*
  Disc 20, Track 4

Assessment
- *Preparation for College Admission Exams,* p. 51

Internet
- go.hrw.com (keyword: LE0 11–14)

Summary ▪▪

This suspense story is set in the home of a newly married couple. Alicia and Jordan love each other deeply, but the timid Alicia is unsettled by Jordan's reserved manner and his cold, silent, white house. One day she comes down with what seems like the flu, which later turns into acute anemia. The doctors cannot account for her illness or cure her. Alicia begins to have nightmare visions, grows paler and weaker every day, and eventually dies. Stripping Alicia's bed, the servant backs away from her impossibly heavy pillow. In the story's chilling climax, the cause of Alicia's death is revealed when Jordan rips open the pillow to find a parasite—bloated with Alicia's blood—living inside.

Before You Read
THE FEATHER PILLOW

Background

The Gothic tale has been well represented in literature of the United States, starting with Edgar Allan Poe, moving to Southern Gothic writers like William Faulkner and Flannery O'Connor, and continuing into the present with best-selling writers like Stephen King and Anne Rice.

Like their counterparts in the United States, many Latin American writers have used Gothic conventions to craft unsettling tales of the fantastic. One of the most successful of these writers is Horacio Quiroga, who used his fascination with the dark side of the human mind to craft a number of powerful stories with Gothic-horror overtones. A typical Quiroga story quickly reaches its terrible conclusion with not a word or detail wasted.

Be warned: The story you are about to read is one you won't soon forget. After you come to the stunning conclusion of this tale, you may never look at feather pillows the same way again.

Reading Skills and Strategies

Dialogue with the Text
As you read this story, pause to jot down

- questions that occur to you
- emotional reactions to the story
- predictions of where the story is heading
- thoughts about characters, details of the plot, or issues the story raises

The Lovers (1928) by René Magritte. Oil on canvas (21⅜″ × 28⅞″).

Richard S. Zeisler Collection, New York. © 1998 C. Herscovici, Brussels/Artists Rights Society (ARS), New York.

728 THE MODERNS

Getting Students Involved

LITERATURE OF THE AMERICAS
URUGUAY

Horacio Quiroga
(1878–1937)

Horacio Quiroga (kē·rō′gä) was one of Latin America's finest and most celebrated short-story writers, a master of the taut, suspenseful, well-crafted tale. Born in Salto, Uruguay, Quiroga was an avid admirer of Edgar Allan Poe's fiction. Like Poe, Quiroga wrote stories that blend horror with psychological suspense. Also like Poe, Quiroga developed a philosophy of short-story writing. In his essay "Manual of the Perfect Short Story Writer," Quiroga presents an approach to writing not unlike Poe's theory of the "single effect": the idea that every word and detail in a story should build to a single, unified emotional effect. Quiroga warns writers to avoid unnecessary words and details and never to begin a story without knowing exactly where it is heading. He felt that in the perfect short story the first few sentences are as important as the last few, and inevitably lead to them. In his best stories—among which is "The Feather Pillow" (first published in 1907)—Quiroga achieves a compressed, sustained effect with every word and sentence. By the time of his death, he had written about two hundred works of fiction, including the classic story collections *Jungle Tales* (1918) and *The Decapitated Chicken and Other Stories* (1925).

A master of dramatic technique, Quiroga was also superb at creating setting. In his stories, as in the stories of William Faulkner and other American writers who explore in depth certain real or fictionalized regions, Quiroga makes setting almost a character in itself. He spent a good portion of his life in San Ignacio, a jungle province in Misiones (in northern Argentina) that provided inspiration for his settings. In many of his stories, he deals with fundamental conflicts between human beings and the world of nature—conflicts in which nature is invariably the victor. Many of his jungle stories illustrate his uncompromising vision of life as an eternal, often brutal, struggle for survival, not unlike some of the tales of Jack London, to whom Quiroga has also been compared.

Quiroga's Poe-like obsession with death and the grotesque is not surprising, given that his life was a patchwork of nightmares as disturbing as the tales he crafted. Quiroga came face to face with gruesome death early in his life. First, his father accidentally killed himself with a shotgun. When he was twenty-three, Quiroga accidentally shot to death one of his closest friends. There were more personal tragedies: Quiroga's attempts to start a business in the rugged and dangerous Argentine jungle failed; his first wife, in despair over their living conditions in the jungle, took her own life; and his second marriage ended unhappily in separation. Quiroga ended his own tragic life in 1937, after discovering that he was dying of cancer.

OBJECTIVES

1. Read and interpret the story
2. Generate relevant, interesting, and researchable questions
3. Recognize distinctive and shared characteristics of cultures
4. Express understanding through discussion
5. Recognize and discuss themes and connections that cross cultures

Planning

- **Traditional Schedule**
  Lesson Plans Including Strategies for English-Language Learners
- **One-Stop Planner**
  CD-ROM with Test Generator

BROWSING IN THE FILES

About the Author. Quiroga grew up in Uruguay but made his home in the jungles of northern Argentina. His fables of the jungle were written for an audience of both adults and children. Like Aesop's fables, Quiroga's *cuentos* (tales) often feature animal characters. *Anaconda,* one of his best-known works, tells of the struggle between the anaconda and the viper, two fierce jungle snakes. Like most of Quiroga's work, *Anaconda* can be read on many different levels.

  — *Resources: Print and Media* —

Reading
- *Audio CD Library*
  Disc 20, Track 4

Assessment
- *Preparation for College Admission Exams,* p. 51

Internet
- go.hrw.com (keyword: LE0 11–14)

Summary ▪▪

This suspense story is set in the home of a newly married couple. Alicia and Jordan love each other deeply, but the timid Alicia is unsettled by Jordan's reserved manner and his cold, silent, white house. One day she comes down with what seems like the flu, which later turns into acute anemia. The doctors cannot account for her illness or cure her. Alicia begins to have nightmare visions, grows paler and weaker every day, and eventually dies. Stripping Alicia's bed, the servant backs away from her impossibly heavy pillow. In the story's chilling climax, the cause of Alicia's death is revealed when Jordan rips open the pillow to find a parasite—bloated with Alicia's blood—living inside.

Before You Read
THE FEATHER PILLOW

Background

The Gothic tale has been well represented in literature of the United States, starting with Edgar Allan Poe, moving to Southern Gothic writers like William Faulkner and Flannery O'Connor, and continuing into the present with best-selling writers like Stephen King and Anne Rice.

Like their counterparts in the United States, many Latin American writers have used Gothic conventions to craft unsettling tales of the fantastic. One of the most successful of these writers is Horacio Quiroga, who used his fascination with the dark side of the human mind to craft a number of powerful stories with Gothic-horror overtones. A typical Quiroga story quickly reaches its terrible conclusion with not a word or detail wasted.

Be warned: The story you are about to read is one you won't soon forget. After you come to the stunning conclusion of this tale, you may never look at feather pillows the same way again.

Reading Skills and Strategies

Dialogue with the Text
As you read this story, pause to jot down

• questions that occur to you
• emotional reactions to the story
• predictions of where the story is heading
• thoughts about characters, details of the plot, or issues the story raises

The Lovers (1928) by René Magritte. Oil on canvas (21⅜″ × 28⅞″).

Richard S. Zeisler Collection, New York. © 1998 C. Herscovici, Brussels/Artists Rights Society (ARS), New York.

728 THE MODERNS

Getting Students Involved

Cooperative Learning
Staging a Story. Have an interested group of students adapt Quiroga's short story into a one-act play. Group members can collaborate on writing the play, following the original story as closely as possible, and then divide up roles, such as those of actors, director, and stage manager. Encourage students to focus on capturing the mood and symbolic overtones of the story, not just its horrifying details.

The Feather Pillow

Horacio Quiroga

translated from the Spanish by **Margaret Sayers Peden**

Her entire honeymoon gave her hot and cold shivers. A blond, angelic, and timid young girl, the childish fancies she had dreamed about being a bride had been chilled by her husband's rough character. She loved him very much, nonetheless, although sometimes she gave a light shudder when, as they returned home through the streets together at night, she cast a furtive glance at the impressive stature of her Jordan, who had been silent for an hour. He, for his part, loved her profoundly but never let it be seen.

For three months—they had been married in April—they lived in a special kind of bliss. Doubtless she would have wished less severity in the rigorous sky of love, more expansive and less cautious tenderness, but her husband's impassive manner always restrained her.

The house in which they lived influenced her chills and shuddering to no small degree. The whiteness of the silent patio—friezes,[1] columns, and marble statues—produced the wintry impression of an enchanted palace. Inside, the glacial brilliance of stucco, the completely bare walls, affirmed the sensation of unpleasant coldness. As one crossed from one room to another, the echo of his steps reverberated throughout the house, as if long abandonment had sensitized its resonance.

Alicia passed the autumn in this strange love nest. She had determined, however, to cast a veil over her former dreams and live like a sleeping beauty in the hostile house, trying not to think about anything until her husband arrived each evening.

It is not strange that she grew thin. She had a light attack of influenza that dragged on insidiously for days and days: After that Alicia's health never returned. Finally one afternoon she was able to go into the garden, supported on her husband's arm. She looked around listlessly. Suddenly Jordan, with deep tenderness, ran his hand very slowly over her head, and Alicia instantly burst into sobs, throwing her arms around his neck. For a long time she cried out all the fears she had kept silent, redoubling her weeping at Jordan's

---

1. **friezes** (frēz'iz): decorative, ornamental bands around a room or along a wall.

HORACIO QUIROGA 729

A **Reading Skills and Strategies**
Dialogue with the Text
❓ Ask students to offer their reactions to the opening sentence. Where may the story be headed? [Possible answers: The story may be about a passionate marriage; it may be about an abused wife.]

B **Struggling Readers**
Related Word Forms
❓ Students may have difficulty with the story's sophisticated vocabulary. Help students figure out the meaning of unfamiliar words by directing them to identify related word forms. Demonstrate for the class how one can figure out the meaning of *severity* (harshness) by relating it to the word *severe* (harsh). Ask students what word is hidden in the word *expansive*. [*expand*] What might "more expansive . . . tenderness" mean? [more visible, active affection]

C **Elements of Literature**
Setting
❓ What is the setting of the story? [a cold, silent, white house with an ominous atmosphere] What kind of place does the house suggest? [Possible answers: It seems like a tomb, a mausoleum, or a museum.]

D **English Language Learners**
Identifying Antecedents of Pronouns
❓ Whom does the pronoun *his* refer to? Explain what the sentence means. [It refers to *one*, the second word in the sentence. It means that everyone's steps echo throughout the house.]

Reaching All Students

Struggling Readers
You may want to get struggling readers engaged with this text by giving them the key words and concepts they need to write a Story Impression. For step-by-step instructions on how to apply this strategy, see the *Reading Strategies Handbook*, p. 119 in the *Reading Skills and Strategies* binder.

English Language Learners
Ask Spanish-speaking students to provide additional information on Quiroga's native country, Uruguay, perhaps via Internet research. For additional strategies to engage English language learners, see
• *Lesson Plans Including Strategies for English-Language Learners*

Advanced Learners
Advanced learners may find it interesting to compare Alicia and Jordan's relationship to that of Roderick and Madeline Usher in "The Fall of the House of Usher" (p. 263). You might suggest that they reread Poe's story after they read "The Feather Pillow." They can then note similarities and differences between the elements of plot, character, setting, and theme. Students should share their discoveries during class discussion.

A Reading Skills and Strategies

Dialogue with the Text

Ask students what they think has caused Alicia's illness. [Possible answers: Her fear and nervousness have made her sick; Jordan is a villain who is secretly hurting her in some way.]

B Appreciating Language

Diction

❓ What is the effect of the author's use of the word *swallowed* in this sentence? [The word gives the carpet (and the house) the attributes of a living, hungry creature; the effect of this personification is sinister and unnerving.]

C Critical Thinking

Interpreting

❓ What is the significance of this hallucination? [Possible answer: Jordan's reserve and the chilling atmosphere make Alicia see him as a monster. The anthropoid stands on the carpet and looks at her, just as Jordan does. This crouching animal may also foreshadow the appearance of the bloated, hairy creature in Alicia's pillow.]

D Advanced Learners

Word Choice

❓ Why do you think Quiroga narrates this *cuento* with such precise, formal diction? [Possible answers: The diction reflects the influence of Poe, whom Quiroga admired. It gives the tale the analytical, detached tone of a medical case history, which heightens the air of visceral horror.]

E Vocabulary Note

Greek and Latin Roots

Point out the footnoted words on pp. 730–731. Have students look up the Latin and Greek roots that they are derived from and list related words with the same roots. [Possible words: *anthropology; delirious.*]

---

slightest caress. Then her sobs subsided, and she stood a long while, her face hidden in the hollow of his neck, not moving or speaking a word.

This was the last day Alicia was well enough to be up. On the following day she awakened feeling faint. Jordan's doctor examined her with minute attention, prescribing calm and absolute rest.

A "I don't know," he said to Jordan at the street door. "She has a great weakness that I am unable to explain. And with no vomiting, nothing . . . if she wakes tomorrow as she did today, call me at once."

When she awakened the following day, Alicia was worse. There was consultation. It was agreed there was an anemia of incredible progression, completely inexplicable. Alicia had no more fainting spells, but she was visibly moving toward death. The lights were lighted all day long in her bedroom, and there was complete silence. Hours went by without the slightest sound. Alicia dozed. Jordan virtually lived in the drawing room, which was also always lighted. With tireless persistence he paced ceaselessly from one **B** end of the room to the other. The carpet swallowed his steps. At times he entered the bedroom and continued his silent pacing back and forth alongside the bed, stopping for an instant at each end to regard his wife.

Suddenly Alicia began to have hallucinations, vague images, at first seeming to float in the air, then descending to floor level. Her eyes excessively wide, she stared continuously at the carpet on either side of the head of her bed. One night she suddenly focused on one spot. Then she opened her mouth to scream, and pearls of sweat suddenly beaded her nose and lips.

"Jordan! Jordan!" she clamored, rigid with fright, still staring at the carpet.

Jordan ran to the bedroom, and, when she saw him appear, Alicia screamed with terror.

"It's I, Alicia, it's I!"

Alicia looked at him confusedly; she looked at the carpet; she looked at him once again; and after a long moment of stupefied confrontation, she regained her senses. She smiled and took her husband's hand in hers, caressing it, trembling, for half an hour.

C Among her most persistent hallucinations was that of an anthropoid[2] poised on his fingertips on the carpet, staring at her.

The doctors returned, but to no avail. They saw before them a diminishing life, a life bleeding away day by day, hour by hour, absolutely without their knowing why. During their last consultation Alicia lay in a stupor while they took her pulse, passing her inert wrist from one to another. They observed her a long time in silence and then moved into the dining room.

"Phew . . ." The discouraged chief physician shrugged his shoulders. "It is an inexplicable case. There is little we can do . . ."

"That's my last hope!" Jordan groaned. And he staggered blindly against the table.

D Alicia's life was fading away in the subdelirium[3] of anemia, a delirium which grew worse throughout the evening hours but which let up somewhat after dawn. The illness never worsened during the daytime, but

E 2. **anthropoid** (an'thrə·poid'): humanlike creature, such as an ape.
3. **subdelirium** (sub·di·lir'ē·əm): restless, feverish state in which a person hallucinates.

Skill Link

Using a Dictionary

Because "The Feather Pillow" contains relatively sophisticated vocabulary, the story provides a good opportunity for students to enhance their dictionary skills. Review the importance of using guide words—usually located at the top of each dictionary page—to find new words quickly. Also suggest that students utilize the pronunciation guide—usually located at the front or back of the dictionary—to figure out how to pronounce specific words.

Then, ask students to complete the following exercises:

Activities

1. Have students choose partners. Each student should read the story individually and keep a list of any new or unfamiliar words. After they finish reading, partners can compare lists.

2. Partners can look up their listed words together in a dictionary. Encourage them to use guide words and to look at word origins and pronunciations, as well as definitions.

3. Partners can quiz each other on their new words until both students have learned all of them. They can then go back and reread the story to see how their understanding is enriched by a more precise understanding of the vocabulary.

each morning she awakened pale as death, almost in a swoon. It seemed only at night that her life drained out of her in new waves of blood. Always when she awakened she had the sensation of lying collapsed in the bed with a million-pound weight on top of her. Following the third day of this relapse she never left her bed again. She could scarcely move her head. She did not want her bed to be touched, not even to have her bedcovers arranged. Her crepuscular[4] terrors advanced now in the form of monsters that dragged themselves toward the bed and laboriously climbed upon the bedspread.

Then she lost consciousness. The final two days she raved ceaselessly in a weak voice. The lights funereally illuminated the bedroom and drawing room. In the deathly silence of the house the only sound was the monotonous delirium from the bedroom and the dull echoes of Jordan's eternal pacing.

Finally, Alicia died. The servant, when she came in afterward to strip the now empty bed, stared wonderingly for a moment at the pillow.

"Sir!" she called Jordan in a low voice. "There are stains on the pillow that look like blood."

Jordan approached rapidly and bent over the pillow. Truly, on the case, on both sides of the hollow left by Alicia's head, were two small, dark spots.

"They look like punctures," the servant murmured after a moment of motionless observation.

"Hold it up to the light," Jordan told her.

The servant raised the pillow but immediately dropped it and stood staring at it, livid and trembling. Without knowing why, Jordan felt the hair rise on the back of his neck.

"What is it?" he murmured in a hoarse voice.

"It's very heavy," the servant whispered, still trembling.

Jordan picked it up; it was extraordinarily heavy. He carried it out of the room, and on the dining room table he ripped open the case and the ticking with a slash. The top feathers floated away, and the servant, her mouth opened wide, gave a scream of horror and covered her face with her clenched fists: In the bottom of the pillowcase, among the feathers, slowly moving its hairy legs, was a monstrous animal, a living, viscous ball. It was so swollen one could scarcely make out its mouth.

Night after night, since Alicia had taken to her bed, this abomination had stealthily applied its mouth—its proboscis[5] one might better say—to the girl's temples, sucking her blood. The puncture was scarcely perceptible. The daily plumping of the pillow had doubtlessly at first impeded its progress, but as soon as the girl could no longer move, the suction became vertiginous.[6] In five days, in five nights, the monster had drained Alicia's life away.

These parasites of feathered creatures, diminutive in their habitual environment, reach enormous proportions under certain conditions. Human blood seems particularly favorable to them, and it is not rare to encounter them in feather pillows.

4. **crepuscular** (kri·pus′kyo͞o·lər): happening at or related to twilight.
5. **proboscis** (prō·bäs′is): tubular mouthpart used by parasites to attach to a host and withdraw blood.
6. **vertiginous** (vər·tij′ə·nəs): causing vertigo; dizzying.

HORACIO QUIROGA 731

Ⓕ Critical Thinking
Speculating

❓ What is happening to Alicia? [Possible answers: Her blood is being drained nightly; there is something in the night that is killing her slowly; something sneaks into her bedroom in the darkness and harms her. The title suggests that the pillow might be related to her affliction.]

Ⓖ Elements of Literature
Imagery

Discuss how the image of the lighted lamps, the ominous silence, and Jordan's pacing might represent Alicia's losing struggle for life. (Students may also wish to examine the images in the third full paragraph of p. 730.) [Possible answer: The lighted lamps and the silence might suggest a funeral wake, while Jordan's constant pacing might represent the slow, step-by-step depletion of Alicia's vitality.]

Ⓗ Critical Thinking
Evaluating the Ending

❓ Ask students why Quiroga did not end his story with the previous paragraph or the one before it. Is the last paragraph effective? [Possible answers: Quiroga may be trying to raise the horror of the last scene to a more symbolic level by emphasizing those "certain conditions" under which parasites grow. Yes; the clinical, matter-of-fact tone of this last paragraph makes the grotesque ending more convincing and powerful.]

Making the Connections

Connecting to the Theme: "Shadows of the Past"

After students have read the story, discuss the collection theme. Ask if they think the creature that "haunts" Alicia might represent something deeper about Alicia, Jordan, or the events and expectations of the past. Does Alicia have anything in common with Miss Emily or the young Ellen Weatherall? What do you think Alicia's ghost might say to Jordan?

Assessing Learning

Check Test: True-False

1. Alicia feels a sudden calm after her marriage. [False]
2. Alicia is disturbed by the house's strange noises. [False]
3. Jordan frequently expresses his love for Alicia. [False]
4. Alicia's health begins to slip after she and her husband fight. [False]
5. The creature that kills Alicia is an overgrown parasite. [True]

Self-Assessment

Have students use the following rubric to judge their own reading skills:

Always=4   Usually=3   Seldom=2   Never=1

____ I understand most of the reading assignment.

____ I use strategies to find the meanings of unfamiliar words.

____ I remember information I have read.

____ I take organized notes on what I read.

____ I review my notes frequently.

FINDING COMMON GROUND

As its name suggests, this feature helps students discover commonalities or shared qualities between different works of literature and between different literary and cultural contexts. You may want to divide students into two groups. One can compare Quiroga with Faulkner, and the other can discuss Quiroga and Poe. Students may want to focus on Faulkner's and Poe's stories as representative of a distinct Southern American literary culture and Quiroga's as emblematic of a distinctly Uruguayan and Latin American literary culture. They may also notice the ways in which Gothic and modernist themes and techniques seem to cross these cultural lines. Any students who completed the Advanced Learners activity on p. 729 of this teacher's edition can share their work with the Poe group.

LITERATURE AND POPULAR CULTURE

Probably the most famous of all scary stories about blood-sucking parasites is Bram Stoker's novel *Dracula,* which was published in 1897. Like Quiroga's parasite, Dracula sleeps during the day and sucks the blood of his victims at night. Like Alicia, Dracula's victims seem to regain some strength during the day, but each night they grow mysteriously weaker. Stoker's novel has been filmed and staged many times, and his tale of the ravenous Transylvanian vampire has spawned so many imitations that vampires have become a perpetual theme in popular culture.

FINDING COMMON GROUND

Now that you've finished the story, meet in small groups, and share the questions and comments you noted while reading.

- Read aloud your notes, or pass the notes around so that everyone can read the comments.
- Identify and discuss three or four issues, comments, or reactions that seem most interesting or widely shared within your group.
- Compare the effect of this story to that of "A Rose for Emily." For example, both stories end on a shocking note. But Faulkner does not spell out what happens to Miss Emily and Homer Barron; Quiroga, on the other hand, reveals Alicia's fate in graphic detail. In what other ways are Faulkner's and Quiroga's stories alike and different?
- Quiroga also has much in common with Edgar Allan Poe. Like Poe, he was fascinated by madness and obsession, and he mastered the short-story format, creating a single sustained effect in each story. What does "The Feather Pillow" have in common with "The Fall of the House of Usher" and other Poe stories you have read?
- Reconvene as a class, and share the results of your discussion.

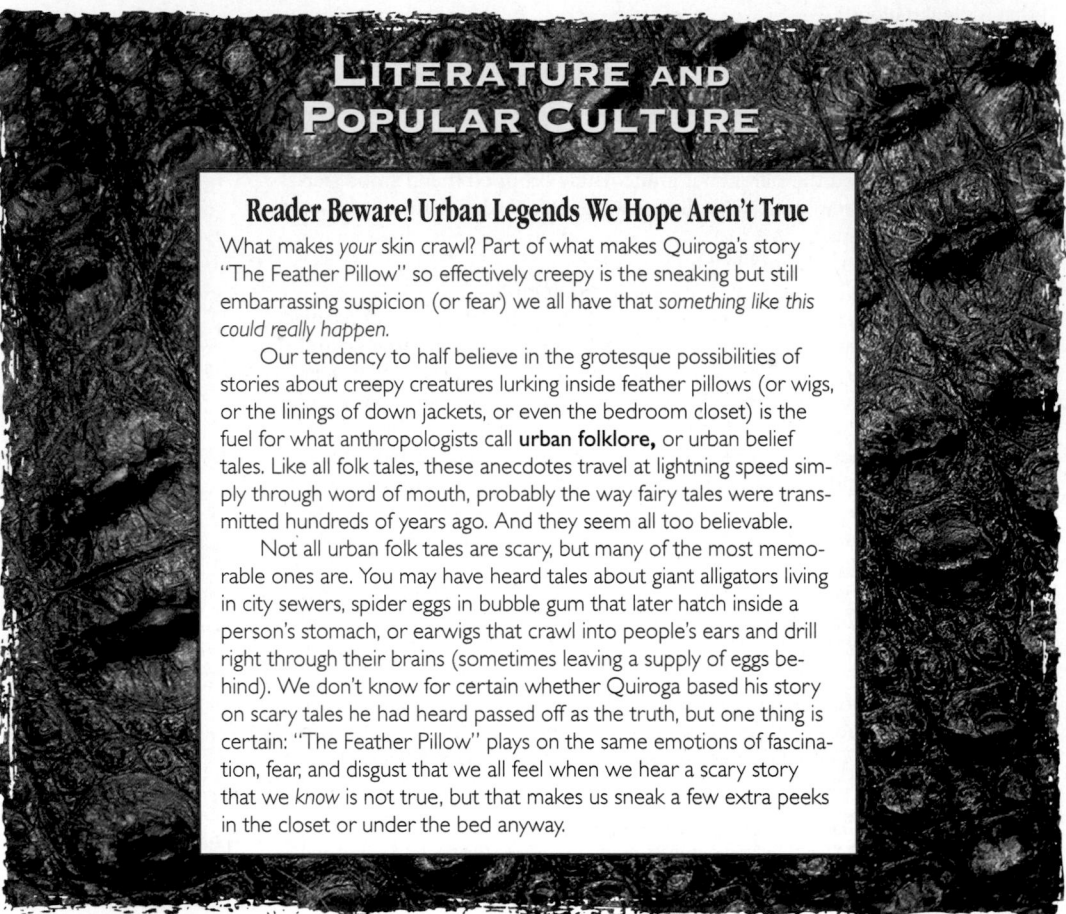

LITERATURE AND POPULAR CULTURE

Reader Beware! Urban Legends We Hope Aren't True

What makes *your* skin crawl? Part of what makes Quiroga's story "The Feather Pillow" so effectively creepy is the sneaking but still embarrassing suspicion (or fear) we all have that *something like this could really happen.*

Our tendency to half believe in the grotesque possibilities of stories about creepy creatures lurking inside feather pillows (or wigs, or the linings of down jackets, or even the bedroom closet) is the fuel for what anthropologists call **urban folklore,** or urban belief tales. Like all folk tales, these anecdotes travel at lightning speed simply through word of mouth, probably the way fairy tales were transmitted hundreds of years ago. And they seem all too believable.

Not all urban folk tales are scary, but many of the most memorable ones are. You may have heard tales about giant alligators living in city sewers, spider eggs in bubble gum that later hatch inside a person's stomach, or earwigs that crawl into people's ears and drill right through their brains (sometimes leaving a supply of eggs behind). We don't know for certain whether Quiroga based his story on scary tales he had heard passed off as the truth, but one thing is certain: "The Feather Pillow" plays on the same emotions of fascination, fear, and disgust that we all feel when we hear a scary story that we *know* is not true, but that makes us sneak a few extra peeks in the closet or under the bed anyway.

732 THE MODERNS

Crossing the Curriculum

Film
Students may enjoy viewing one of the films based on *Dracula.* You might suggest the classic version with Bela Lugosi. After seeing the film, students can compare and contrast it with Quiroga's story for mood, symbolism, and atmosphere.

Science
Have students find out as much as they can about anemia. What causes this disease? What are the symptoms? What is the cure? Is the disease ever fatal? Does the doctor's diagnosis of Alicia make sense under the circumstances? Students can share the results of their research with the class.

Standardized Test Preparation
For practice with ACT and SAT formats, see
- *Preparation for College Admissions Exams,* p. 51

I, Too, Sing America: The Harlem Renaissance

Theme

The Harlem Renaissance *In the early 1920s a burst of creativity came from Harlem, a section of New York City. There, African American writers, painters, and musicians flourished, and their art reflected the struggle of African Americans to obtain the rights promised to all American citizens.*

Reading the Anthology

Reaching Struggling Readers The *Reading Skills and Strategies: Reaching Struggling Readers* binder includes a Reading Strategies Handbook that offers concrete suggestions to help students who have difficulty reading and comprehending text, or students who are reluctant readers. When a specific strategy is most appropriate for a selection, a correlation to the Handbook is provided at the bottom of the teacher's page under the head Reaching Struggling Readers. This head may also be used to introduce additional ideas for helping students read challenging texts.

Reading Beyond the Anthology

Read On At the end of The Moderns collections, the grade eleven book includes an annotated bibliography of books suitable for extended reading. The suggested books are related to works in these collections by theme, by author, or by subject. To preview the Read On for The Moderns period, please turn to p. T800.

HRW Library The *HRW Library* offers novels, plays, nonfiction, and short-story collections for extended reading. Each book in the Library includes one or more major works and thematically related Connections. The Connections are magazine articles, poems, or other pieces of literature. Each book in the *HRW Library* is also accompanied by a Study Guide that provides teaching suggestions and worksheets. For Collection 15, the following title is recommended.

THE FIRE NEXT TIME
James Baldwin
Baldwin's ground-breaking book, which includes a letter to his nephew on the hundredth anniversary of the Emancipation Proclamation, was published in 1962, but its themes reflect the themes of the Harlem Renaissance artists. Baldwin's eloquent—and angry—book has made millions of Americans think differently about race.

Resources for this Collection

Internet Resources
go.hrw.com LE0 11-15

Note: All resources for this collection are available for preview on the *One-Stop Planner CD-ROM 2 with Test Generator.* All worksheets and blackline masters may be printed from the CD-ROM.

Collection Planner

Selection or Feature	Reading and Literary Skills	Vocabulary, Language, and Grammar
Go Down, Death (p. 737) James Weldon Johnson **Primary Sources: God's Trombones** (p. 740) James Weldon Johnson **Connections: of DeWitt Williams on his way to Lincoln Cemetery** (p. 741) Gwendolyn Brooks	• *Graphic Organizers for Active Reading,* Worksheet p. 73	• *Daily Oral Grammar,* Transparency 46
America (p. 744) Claude McKay	• *Graphic Organizers for Active Reading,* Worksheet p. 74	
• **Tableau** (p. 747) • **Incident** (p. 748) Countee Cullen	• *Graphic Organizers for Active Reading,* Worksheet pp. 75, 76	
from **Dust Tracks on a Road** (p. 751) Zora Neale Hurston **Primary Sources: In Search of a Story** (p. 758) Zora Neale Hurston	• *Graphic Organizers for Active Reading,* Worksheet p. 77	• *Words to Own,* Worksheet p. 44 • *Grammar and Language Links:* Using Commas, Worksheet p. 63 • *Language Workshop CD-ROM,* Punctuation • *Daily Oral Grammar,* Transparency 47
• **The Weary Blues** (p. 761) • **Harlem** (p. 764) Langston Hughes **Primary Sources: Heyday in Harlem** (p. 766) Langston Hughes	• *Graphic Organizers for Active Reading,* Worksheet pp. 78, 79 • *Literary Elements:* Transparencies 23, 24 Worksheet pp. 70, 73	• *Grammar and Language Links:* End Punctuation Marks, Worksheet p. 65 • *Language Workshop CD-ROM,* Punctuation

Other Resources for this Collection

- *Cross-Curricular Activities*, p. 15
- *Portfolio Management System*, Introduction to Portfolio Assessment, p. 1
- *Test Generator*, Collection Test

Writing	Listening and Speaking Viewing and Representing	Assessment
• *Portfolio Management System*, Rubrics for Choices, p. 179	• *Audio CD Library*, Disc 21, Track 2  • *Viewing and Representing:* Fine Art Transparency 15  Worksheet p. 60 • *Portfolio Management System*, Rubrics for Choices, p. 179	• *Formal Assessment*, Selection Test, p. 141 • *Test Generator (One-Stop Planner CD-ROM)* 
• *Portfolio Management System*, Rubrics for Choices, p. 180	• *Audio CD Library*, Disc 21, Track 3  • *Portfolio Management System*, Rubrics for Choices, p. 180	• *Formal Assessment*, Selection Test, p. 141 • *Test Generator (One-Stop Planner CD-ROM)* 
• *Portfolio Management System*, Rubrics for Choices, p. 181	• *Audio CD Library*, Disc 21, Tracks 4, 5  • *Portfolio Management System*, Rubrics for Choices, p. 181	• *Formal Assessment*, Selection Test, p. 143 • *Test Generator (One-Stop Planner CD-ROM)* 
• *Portfolio Management System*, Rubrics for Choices, p. 182	• *Audio CD Library*, Disc 21, Track 6  • *Portfolio Management System*, Rubrics for Choices, p. 182	• *Formal Assessment*, Selection Test, p. 145 • *Test Generator (One-Stop Planner CD-ROM)*  • *Preparation for College Admission Exams*, p. 53
• *Portfolio Management System*, Rubrics for Choices, p. 183	• *Audio CD Library*, Disc 21, Tracks 7, 8  • *Portfolio Management System*, Rubrics for Choices, p. 183	• *Formal Assessment*, Selection Test, p. 147 • *Test Generator (One-Stop Planner CD-ROM)* 

 Transparency  CD-ROM  Video  Audio CD

Collection Planner

Collection 15 I, Too, Sing America:
The Harlem Renaissance
Skills Focus

Selection or Feature	Reading Skills and Strategies	Elements of Literature and Language	Writing	Listening and Speaking	Viewing and Representing
Go Down, Death (p. 737) James Weldon Johnson	Tracking Your Responses, pp. 737, 742 Identify Details Supporting an Interpretation, p. 742	Personification, pp. 737, 742 Simile, p. 742 Symbol, p. 742 Free Verse and the Orator's Style, p. 742 Repetition, p. 742 Parallel Structure, p. 742 Cadence, p. 742 Sound Effects, p. 742	Compare and Contrast Attitudes Toward Death in Two Poems, p. 742 Compare and Contrast Two Sermons, p. 742		Use a Comparison-Contrast Chart to Organize Information, p. 742
America (p. 744) Claude McKay		Personification, p. 745 Image, p. 745 Paradox, p. 745 Form, p. 745 Subject, p. 745 Point of View, p. 745 Tone, p. 745	Compare Two Poems, p. 745		Use a Venn Diagram, p. 745 Design a Poster or Bumper Sticker That Expresses the Main Idea of the Poem, p. 745
• **Tableau** (p. 747) • **Incident** (p. 748) Countee Cullen		Tableau Vivant, p. 747 Metaphor, p. 749 Topic, p. 749 Message, p. 749	Compare and Contrast the Diction and Sentence Structure in Two Poems, p. 749 Write a Conversation Among Three Characters, p. 749		Write a Film Treatment, p. 749
from **Dust Tracks on a Road** (p. 751) Zora Neale Hurston	Analyze an Autobiography, pp. 751, 759	Characterize, p. 759 Title, p. 759	Speculate About the Author's Choice of a Title, p. 759 Write an Essay Comparing Two Autobiographies, p. 759	Dramatize and Perform an Excerpt from *Dust Tracks on a Road,* p. 759	
• **The Weary Blues** (p. 761) • **Harlem** (p. 764) Langston Hughes		Rhythm, pp. 761, 768 Tone, pp. 764, 768 Image, p. 768 Simile, p. 768 Message, p. 768 Mood, p. 768 Alliteration, p. 768 Onomatopoeia, p. 768	Compare and Contrast the Attitudes of the Speakers in Two Poems, p. 768 Write an Essay Comparing and Contrasting Two Poems by Different Authors, p. 768 Write the Opening Paragraph for a Newspaper Article About Harlem, p. 768 Research and Write the Liner Notes for a Blues Album, p. 768	Set a Poem to Music, p. 768	

I, TOO, SING AMERICA
THE HARLEM RENAISSANCE

Johnson
McKay
Cullen
Hurston
Hughes

OBJECTIVES
1. Read literature of the modern period on the theme of "I, Too, Sing America"
2. Identify literary elements used in the selections
3. Apply a variety of reading strategies
4. Respond to literature in a variety of modes
5. Learn and use new words

I, Too

I, too, sing America.

I am the darker brother.
They send me to eat in the kitchen
When company comes,
But I laugh,
And eat well,
And grow strong.

Tomorrow,
I'll be at the table
When company comes.
Nobody'll dare
Say to me,
"Eat in the kitchen,"
Then.

Besides,
They'll see how beautiful I am
And be ashamed—

I, too, am America.

—Langston Hughes (1902–1967)

Responding to the Poem

❓ Hughes's famous poem alludes to an equally famous poem by another American poet, Walt Whitman (see p. 352). What do people feel when they experience exclusion—such as being omitted from group activities or being forbidden membership in an organization? [Possible responses: loneliness, unworthiness, shame, depression.] **What does "I, Too" suggest about people who are excluded?** [Possible responses: They all have voices and wish to be heard. They feel frustration when their important contributions go unrecognized. They look forward to the day when they will be recognized as valuable American citizens.] **Hughes uses metaphors to describe his feelings and hopes. What are the metaphors?** [His feelings of being regarded as an outsider and looked down on are compared with being sent to eat in the kitchen when company comes—he's excluded from the dining room. His hopes for tomorrow—when he'll be accepted—are compared with sitting at that better table.] **What warnings are contained in the poem?** [ll. 5–7, 11–14] **How would you paraphrase the title? How would the meaning change if a comma were added after "sing"?** [Hughes seems to be saying that he sings "about" America. If a comma were added, he would be addressing America and telling her that he sings also.]

For a biography of Hughes and more writings by Hughes, see pp. 760–768.

Writing Focus: Interpretive Essay

The following **Work in Progress** assignments in this collection build to a culminating **Writer's Workshop** at the end of Collection 16.

- Go Down, Death   Compare and contrast two poems (p. 742)
- America   Compare and contrast two poems using a Venn diagram (p. 745)

- Tableau; Incident   Compare and contrast diction and sentence structure in two poems (p. 749)

- Dust Tracks on a Road   Write down reactions to a title (p. 759)
- The Weary Blues; Harlem   Analyze speakers in two poems (p. 768)

Writer's Workshop: Expository Writing / Interpretive Essay (p. 804)

A Cultural Connections

Harlem Renaissance

The word *renaissance,* meaning "rebirth or revival," usually designates the Renaissance that flourished in Europe between 1300 and 1600, an era characterized by its spirit of innovation, curiosity, and adventure in fields ranging from architecture to science to fine art. The European Renaissance was considered a rebirth of the Golden Age of classical culture in ancient Greece and Rome. The upsurge in African American cultural expression that took place in Harlem, New York, in the 1920s occurred with such compelling force and had so much influence that it became known as the Harlem Renaissance.

B Historical Connections

Marcus Garvey

Marcus Garvey (1887–1940) was a Jamaican-born American who exhorted African Americans to view Africa as their primary homeland and urged them to emigrate there in large numbers.

C Humanities Connections

Jazz

Jazz, a truly original American art form, evolved from African American folk music. Its roots lie in African rhythms, European harmonies, American gospel sounds, and work songs that flourished during and after slavery among plantation workers. These last two forms, along with "sorrow songs," influenced the rise of the blues, which in turn contributed to jazz. Ragtime and Dixieland, both arising in New Orleans in the 1890s, were the earliest jazz styles. Jazz spread to Chicago, Kansas City, and other cities after 1917, and developed rapidly into an improvisational music, played by big bands and small groups, that remains popular around the world.

D Historical Connections

Bessie Smith

Bessie Smith (1894–1937) was born in Chattanooga, Tennessee, and began her music career around 1910. In the 1920s, in New York, she made the bold, powerful recordings that earned her the nickname "Empress of the Blues."

A The Harlem Renaissance

In the early 1920s, African American artists, writers, musicians, and performers were part of a great cultural movement known as the Harlem Renaissance. The huge migration to the north after World War I brought African Americans of all ages and walks of life to the thriving New York City neighborhood called Harlem. Doctors, singers, students, musicians, shopkeepers, painters, and writers congregated, forming a vibrant mecca of cultural affirmation and inspiration.

B As Langston Hughes wrote, "It was the period when the Negro was in vogue." Marcus Garvey's "Back to
C Africa" movement was in full swing. The blues were vibrantly alive; jazz was just beginning. An all-black show, *Shuffle Along,* opened on Broadway with the performers Josephine Baker and Florence Mills, music composed by Eubie Blake, and lyrics by Noble Sissle. And mainstream America was developing a new respect for African art and culture, thanks in part to its reflection in the work of the modernist artists Pablo Picasso and Georges Braque.

Against this backdrop, Harlem Renaissance artists insisted that the African American be accepted as "a collaborator and participant in American civilization," in the words of the educator and critic Alain Locke. Writers such as Jean Toomer and Zora Neale Hurston (page 750) wrote about the African American experience. Artists such as Aaron Douglas and William H. Johnson painted it. The photographer James Van Der Zee recorded it with his camera. The trumpeter Louis Armstrong and the pianist Fletcher Henderson set it to music, and vocalists Bessie Smith and Ma Rainey sang it.

Harlem newspapers and journals, such as *Crisis* and *Opportunity,* published the work of both new and established African American writers. To promote and support intellectually gifted young people, the journals sponsored literary contests that encouraged creative writing and rewarded it with cash prizes and social introductions to the top writers of the time.

In autobiographies, poetry, short stories, novels, and folklore, African American writers affirmed the role of black talent in American culture and focused on different aspects of black life in Harlem, the South, Europe, the

D Bessie Smith.
Brown Brothers.

Researching on the HRW Site

Before you begin this collection, guide your students to Harlem Renaissance resources on the Internet. After they have explored the links at the HRW site, have them conduct further research using an Internet search engine. Because any Internet resources can sometimes be public forums, their content may be unpredictable.

The Migration of the Negro, Panel No. 1 (1940–1941) by Jacob Lawrence. Tempera on masonite (12″ × 18″).

The Phillips Collection, Washington, D.C. Acquired 1942. Courtesy of the artist and the Francine Seders Gallery, Seattle, WA.

Caribbean, and even Russia. They addressed issues of race, class, religion, and gender. Some writers focused entirely on black characters, while others addressed relationships among people of different races. Some writers attacked racism; others addressed issues within black communities. A by-product of African American writing was the affirmation that black dialects were as legitimate as standard English.

Unfortunately, by the early 1930s, the Great Depression had depleted many of the funds that had provided financial support to individual African American writers, institutions, and publications. Nevertheless, Harlem and African American culture were forever changed. The foundation was laid for Ralph Ellison, James Baldwin, Gwendolyn Brooks, Alice Walker, Toni Morrison, Maya Angelou, Terry McMillan, Rita Dove, and thousands of other African American writers, painters, composers, and singers to make their feelings and experiences part of American artistic expression: "I, too, sing America."

Louis Armstrong. **E**
Brown Brothers.

(See more Lawrence works on pp. 427, 428, 480, and 765.)

RESPONDING TO THE ART

Jacob Lawrence (1917–   ) carefully researched the history behind his sixty-panel *Migration Series*. He was the first artist to recognize the magnitude of what was the biggest internal migration in American history: the odyssey of as many as a million African Americans from the rural South to the industrial North in the early decades of the twentieth century. (See more Lawrence works on pp. 427, 428, 480, and 765.) **Activity.** What details suggest the goals of migrating African Americans? [The signs over the gates suggest they sought opportunities in large cities.] Note the impression of urgency, of mobs surging onto those trains.

E Historical Connections

Louis Armstrong

Louis Armstrong (1901–1971) was born in New Orleans and raised by his mother in extreme poverty. At the age of eleven, he was sent to reform school (for firing a gun in the air on New Year's Eve). It was there that he learned to play cornet. He gained prominence in the 1920s as a member of King Oliver's band, and then as leader of his own Hot Five and Hot Seven bands. His brilliant trumpet and cornet playing brought the role of the Dixieland soloist to greater prominence. He also pioneered the improvisational singing style known as "scat," in which sound syllables replace words.

Skill Link

Researching on the Internet

Encourage students to browse the HRW site and to conduct an Internet search on the Harlem Renaissance. Direct students to generate three relevant, interesting questions about the Harlem Renaissance, jazz, blues, an African American writer, artist, or musician, or the social scene in Harlem in the 1920s. Have individual students or groups choose one of these questions, research it further via the Internet or other sources, and present a brief written report. Have students supplement their reports with an illustration, poster, graph, time line, audio- or videotape. If class time is limited, direct students to provide a one-paragraph summary or a one-minute oral statement of their findings.

James Weldon Johnson (c. 1925) by Winold Reiss.
Pastel on artist board (30 1/16″ × 21 9/16″).

National Portrait Gallery, Washington, D.C. Courtesy Art Resource, NY.

James Weldon Johnson

(1871–1938)

James Weldon Johnson—poet, teacher, and lawyer—was born in Jacksonville, Florida. Educated at Atlanta University in Georgia and Columbia University in New York City, he was the first African American to be admitted to the Florida bar after Reconstruction. Throughout his career, Johnson was an energetic exponent of civil rights, and in his writing he constantly sought recognition for the contributions that African Americans had made to American culture.

After serving as U.S. consul in Venezuela and then in Nicaragua (1907–1913), Johnson worked as field secretary of the National Association for the Advancement of Colored People (NAACP) for four years and then served as the association's general secretary for the following ten years. In 1931, he was appointed professor of creative literature at Fisk University. Seven years later, he died in an automobile accident.

Although some of Johnson's early poems are in dialect, he soon abandoned that style for standard English, which he felt was capable of greater variety and power. His principal theme was black pride, which he celebrated in such poems as "Fifty Years," written on the fiftieth anniversary of the Emancipation Proclamation, and "O Black and Unknown Bards," a tribute to the anonymous authors of African American spirituals. With his brother, the composer John Rosamond Johnson, he wrote a number of very successful light operas and songs for Tin Pan Alley, and the brothers collaborated in editing two collections of spirituals.

Johnson was an important leader of the first phase of the Harlem Renaissance. His anthology, *The Book of American Negro Poetry* (1922), was one of the significant early collections of poems by African Americans. In addition to poetry, Johnson wrote fiction (most notably *The Autobiography of an Ex-Colored Man,* published in 1912), nonfiction studies of black life, and an autobiography, *Along This Way* (1933).

It was Johnson's extensive research for one collection, *The Book of American Negro Spirituals* (1925), that inspired his poem "Go Down, Death." Describing this experience, he said: "The research which I did in collecting the spirituals and gathering the data for my introductory essay had an effect on me similar to what I received from hearing the Negro evangelist preach. . . . I was in touch with the deepest revelation of the Negro's soul that has yet been made, and I felt myself attuned to it. I made an outline of the second poem that I wrote of this series. It was to be a 'funeral sermon.' I decided to call it 'Go Down, Death.'

"On Thanksgiving Day, 1926, I was at home. After breakfast I went to my desk and began work in earnest on the poem. As I worked, my own spirit rose till it reached a degree almost of ecstasy. The poem shaped itself easily and before the hour for dinner I had written it as it stands published."

go.hrw.com
LEO 11-15

— *Resources: Print and Media* —

Before You Read

GO DOWN, DEATH

Make the Connection

Death at the Doorstep

Every religion has its own view of what happens when we die, and countless storytellers, philosophers, and writers have added their views to the sum of our understanding of the great mystery we call death. Is death a source of pain and sorrow, or is it a comfort—perhaps even a joyous affirmation of life?

Reading Skills and Strategies

Tracking Your Responses

This poem is one of seven "sermons" written by Johnson in the style of the old-time African American preachers. He collected the sermons in a book called *God's Trombones*—the trombone being "of just the tone and timbre to represent the old-time Negro preacher's voice."

Johnson tells us that the person reading "Go Down, Death" would intone, moan, plead, blare, crash, and thunder. As you read, jot down the words, lines, or stanzas that have the strongest emotional effect on you.

Elements of Literature

Personification

Personification is a figure of speech in which an animal, object, or abstract concept is portrayed with human qualities. In this poem, Johnson invites readers to see and understand Death as a character rather than as an abstract concept.

Go Down, Death

A Funeral Sermon

James Weldon Johnson

Weep not, weep not,
She is not dead;
She's resting in the bosom of Jesus.
Heart-broken husband—weep no more;
5 Grief-stricken son—weep no more;
Left-lonesome daughter—weep no more;
She's only just gone home.

Day before yesterday morning,
God was looking down from his great, high heaven,
10 Looking down on all his children,
And his eye fell on Sister Caroline,
Tossing on her bed of pain.
And God's big heart was touched with pity,
With the everlasting pity.

15 And God sat back on his throne,
And he commanded that tall, bright angel standing at his right
   hand:
Call me Death!
And that tall, bright angel cried in a voice
That broke like a clap of thunder:
20 Call Death!—Call Death!
And the echo sounded down the streets of heaven
Till it reached away back to that shadowy place,
Where Death waits with his pale, white horses.°

And Death heard the summons,
25 And he leaped on his fastest horse,
Pale as a sheet in the moonlight.
Up the golden street Death galloped,
And the hoofs of his horse struck fire from the gold,
But they didn't make no sound.
30 Up Death rode to the Great White Throne,
And waited for God's command.

And God said: Go down, Death, go down,
Go down to Savannah, Georgia,
Down in Yamacraw,

23. Death waits . . . horses: allusion to Revelation 6:8, "And I looked, and behold a pale horse: and his name that sat on him was Death."

A

B

JAMES WELDON JOHNSON 737

Summary ■

The poem is a funeral sermon written in free verse. God sees Sister Caroline in mortal pain and calls Death to release her. The personified figure of Death rides down to earth, gently takes up the ailing woman, and places her on the breast of Jesus.

Resources

Viewing and Representing
Fine Art Transparency
The transparency to accompany "Go Down, Death" is *The Passing of Eloise* by Jonathan Green. See the *Viewing and Representing Transparencies and Worksheets:*
- Transparency 15
- Worksheet, p. 60

FROM THE EDITOR'S DESK
We believe that if any poem exemplifies poetic voice, and begs to be read aloud, this one does.

A **Reading Skills and Strategies**
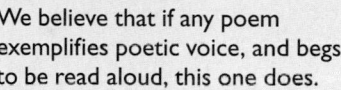
Tracking Your Responses
❓ How does the first stanza solicit the reader's emotional response? [It directly addresses the reader as one of the weeping mourners.]

B **Elements of Literature**
Personification
❓ What specific details personify Death? [He hears the summons; he rides a pale, white horse; he leaps at God's command.]

Reaching All Students

Struggling Readers
After students have read the poem, have them form small groups to discuss their choice for the Most Important Word. Model this process for the class if you have not already done so. For specific, step-by-step instructions, see the *Reading Strategies Handbook*, p. 45 in the *Reading Skills and Strategies* binder.

English Language Learners
Use oral reading and the audio CD recording to help students understand regional African American speech patterns, such as *a-saying* (l. 75), and the two meanings of *she's* ("she has," ll. 36–39, and "she is," l. 79). Also point out the places where the poem contains dialogue that is not in quotation marks, as in l. 17.

Collection of Professor and Mrs. David Driskell, Hyattsville, Maryland.

Go Down Death (1927) by Aaron Douglas. Oil on masonite.

738 THE MODERNS

Using Students' Strengths

Visual Learners

Using Douglas's painting as a point of departure, have a group of students compose a series of drawings or paintings which represent the later stanzas of the poem. Suggest that the students try to get at the main idea or most meaningful phrase of each stanza as they work. Then have them present their art to the class while one student reads the poem aloud.

35 And find Sister Caroline.
    She's borne the burden and heat of the day,
    She's labored long in my vineyard,
    And she's tired—
    She's weary—
40 Go down, Death, and bring her to me.

    And Death didn't say a word,
    But he loosed the reins on his pale, white horse,
    And he clamped the spurs to his bloodless sides,
    And out and down he rode,
45 Through heaven's pearly gates,
    Past suns and moons and stars;
    On Death rode,
    And the foam from his horse was like a comet in the sky;
    On Death rode,
50 Leaving the lightning's flash behind;
    Straight on down he came.

    While we were watching round her bed,
    She turned her eyes and looked away,
    She saw what we couldn't see;
55 She saw Old Death. She saw Old Death
    Coming like a falling star.
    But Death didn't frighten Sister Caroline;
    He looked to her like a welcome friend.
    And she whispered to us: I'm going home,
60 And she smiled and closed her eyes.

    And Death took her up like a baby,
    And she lay in his icy arms,
    But she didn't feel no chill.
    And Death began to ride again—
65 Up beyond the evening star,
    Out beyond the morning star,°
    Into the glittering light of glory,
    On to the Great White Throne.
    And there he laid Sister Caroline
70 On the loving breast of Jesus.

    And Jesus took his own hand and wiped away her tears,
    And he smoothed the furrows from her face,
    And the angels sang a little song,
    And Jesus rocked her in his arms,
75 And kept a-saying: Take your rest,
    Take your rest, take your rest.

    Weep not—weep not,
    She is not dead;
    She's resting in the bosom of Jesus.

66. evening star . . . morning
star: the planet Venus, which is traditionally referred to as both the morning star and the evening star. Its
orbital path makes it visible for no
more than about three hours after
sunset and three hours before
sunrise.

JAMES WELDON JOHNSON **739**

Making the Connections

Connecting to the Theme: "I, Too, Sing America"

In "Go Down, Death," Johnson employs a distinctively African American religious language that had traditionally been excluded from mainstream American poetry and theology. Ask students what someone unfamiliar with this African American preaching style might gain from the poem. [Possible responses: greater appreciation of African American culture; greater insight into the richness of the English language.]

Assessing Learning

Informal Assessment

Have pairs of students discuss the poem and assess each other's understanding of it. Have students select three difficult passages in the poem and reread them aloud. The partners will then work together to paraphrase these passages in their own words and share them with the class.

A **Struggling Readers**

Breaking Down Difficult Text

Point out that l. 40 ends God's speech, which began on l. 32. On l. 41, the preacher resumes his narration. Invite volunteers to read ll. 32–51 aloud, marking the change in speakers with appropriate changes in tone of voice.

B **Elements of Literature**

Personification

❓ What details in ll. 61–70 portray Death in a sympathetic light? [Death carries Sister Caroline gently in his arms; Death presents Sister Caroline to Jesus.]

C **Critical Thinking**

Evaluating

❓ What impact is created by repeating the poem's first three lines at its ending? [Possible answers: It emphasizes the theme of the poem, as expressed at the beginning; the repetition is intended to comfort the mourners; it underscores the preacher's faith.]

D **Reading Skills and Strategies**

Tracking Your Responses

❓ How do you feel about death after reading the whole poem? [Possible responses: Death can bring relief to people who are suffering; death hurts the living who feel the loss of a loved one; religious people may find hope in death, because it may unite the deceased with God.]

Appreciating Language

Free Verse and Oratorical Style

Have the class reread Johnson's poem along with Walt Whitman's "A Sight in Camp in the Daybreak Gray and Dim" (p. 362). Then have students discuss the thematic connection between the two poems and look for the stylistic similarities listed in the Elements of Literature feature on p. 742. [Possible response: Students might point out that both poems focus on death as a state of beauty and union with Christ. They might also notice the use of direct address and parallel structure in both poems.]

In this excerpt from the preface to *God's Trombones*, James Weldon Johnson describes the pivotal role of the old-time African American preacher. With their keen intelligence and stunning oratorical powers, these men were not only powerful moral and religious leaders, but also the unofficial poets laureate of their communities.

Background

In his 1922 anthology, *The Book of American Negro Poetry*, Johnson wrote, "What the colored poet in the United States needs to do is . . . find a form that will express the racial spirit by symbols from within rather than symbols from without, such as the mere mutilation of English spelling and pronunciation. He needs a form that is freer and larger than dialect . . . a form expressing the imagery, the idioms . . . of the Negro, but which will also be capable of voicing the deepest and highest emotions and aspirations, and allow for the widest range of subjects and the widest scope of treatment." Have students discuss ways in which Johnson's poem voices "the deepest and highest emotions and aspirations." You might also play students recordings of speeches by African American ministers, such as Martin Luther King, Jr., or Jesse Jackson, and compare their styles with that of Johnson's speaker.

RESPONDING TO THE ART

Samella Sanders Lewis (1924–   ) is a prominent painter, sculptor, author, and director, whose work often focuses on the social and political struggles of African Americans. In this painting, she depicts an African American church service. The central figure might resemble the "old-time preacher" described in Johnson's preface to *God's Trombones*.

Activity. Have students compare and contrast the setting and tone of the painting with those of "Go Down, Death." [Both are set in African American churches, but the tone of the painting is subdued, while that of the poem is vibrant and impassioned.]

PRIMARY Sources A PREFACE

God's Trombones

In his preface to *God's Trombones*, from which "Go Down, Death" is taken, Johnson describes the origin of his idea for his collection of poems.

The old-time preacher was generally a man far above the average in intelligence; he was, not infrequently, a man of positive genius. The earliest of these preachers must have virtually committed many parts of the Bible to memory through hearing the scriptures read or preached from in the white churches which the slaves attended. They were the first of the slaves to learn to read, and their reading was confined to the Bible, and specifically to the more dramatic passages of the Old Testament. A text served mainly as a starting point and often had no relation to the development of the sermon. Nor would the old-time preacher balk at any text within the lids of the Bible. There is the story of one who after reading a rather cryptic passage took off his spectacles, closed the Bible with a bang and by way of preface said, "Brothers and sisters, this morning—I intend to explain the unexplainable—find out the undefinable—ponder over the imponderable—and unscrew the inscrutable."

The old-time Negro preacher of parts was above all an orator, and in good measure an actor. He knew the secret of oratory, that at bottom it is a progression of rhythmic words more than it is anything else. Indeed, I have witnessed congregations moved to ecstasy by the rhythmic intoning of sheer incoherencies. He was a master of all the modes of eloquence. He often possessed a voice that was a marvelous instrument, a voice he could modulate from a sepulchral whisper to a crashing thunder clap. His discourse was generally kept at a high pitch of fervency, but occasionally he dropped into colloquialisms and, less often, into humor. He preached a personal and anthropomorphic God, a sure-enough heaven and a red-hot hell. His imagination was bold and unfettered. He had the power to sweep his hearers before him; and so himself was often swept away. At such times his language was not prose but poetry. It was from memories of such preachers there grew the idea of this book of poems.

—James Weldon Johnson

Prayer Meeting (1951) by Samella Sanders Lewis. Watercolor (17" × 14¾").
Hampton University Museum, Hampton, Virginia.

Skill Link

Interpreting Historical Context

Jonathan Edwards, in "Sinners in the Hands of an Angry God" (pp. 79–81), delivers a very different sermon from the one called "Go Down, Death." Ask students to work in pairs to explore how the historical and cultural context of each minister affects his purpose, message, tone, and imagery. Students' analyses might focus on these points: Each preacher makes a strong appeal to the emotions of his congregation. Edwards seeks to terrify his audience into upholding Puritan strictures in a strange new land. The preacher in Johnson's poem, on the other hand, seeks to comfort an audience that has inherited the legacies of slavery and discrimination. Edwards's tone is harsh and judgmental; the preacher's is sympathetic and understanding. By implication, Edwards's image of death is terrible—a prelude to damnation. Johnson's is warm; death is a deliverance from hardship.

Borrowing from the spiritual "Swing Low, Sweet Chariot," the African American poet Gwendolyn Brooks (1917–   ) creates a poem that also has the rhythm of a song. (For more on spirituals, see page 432.) Lincoln Cemetery is in Chicago.

of De Witt Williams on his way to Lincoln Cemetery

Gwendolyn Brooks

He was born in Alabama.
He was bred in Illinois.
He was nothing but a
Plain black boy.

5   Swing low swing low sweet sweet chariot.
Nothing but a plain black boy.

Drive him past the Pool Hall.
Drive him past the Show.
Blind within his casket,
10 But maybe he will know.

Down through Forty-seventh Street:
Underneath the L,
And—Northwest Corner, Prairie,
That he loved so well.

15 Don't forget the Dance Halls—
Warwick and Savoy,
Where he picked his women, where
He drank his liquid joy.

Born in Alabama.
20 Bred in Illinois.
He was nothing but a
Plain black boy.

Swing low swing low sweet sweet chariot.
Nothing but a plain black boy.

Haitian Funeral Procession (c. 1950s) by Ellis Wilson. Oil on canvas (30 ½″ × 29 ¼″).
Aaron Douglas Collection, Amistad Research Center, Tulane University, New Orleans, Louisiana.

Connections

This poem describes the funeral procession of "a plain black boy." Brooks takes the reader on a "tour" of the places that the dead man spent his days—thereby communicating a rich impression of his character and his lifestyle.

A **Elements of Literature**
Tone
❓ What is the tone of the title, and how does it relate to the rest of the poem? [Possible response: The tone is ironic, since it suggests the grand funeral procession of a respected gentleman. The body of the poem, however, describes an anonymous man and his ordinary pleasures.]

B **Historical Connections**
Spiritual
Line 5 refers to the spiritual "Swing Low, Sweet Chariot," in which a chariot and a band of angels arrive to take a dying person to heaven. African Americans often sang this song to express their desire for freedom from bondage.

C **Cultural Connections**
Chicago
The L, usually spelled *el*, is Chicago's *el*evated railway. Forty-Seventh Street, Northwest Corner, and Prairie are locations on the city's economically depressed South Side.

D **Elements of Literature**
Refrain
❓ What is the effect of ending the poem with the repetition of the opening? [Possible responses: It emphasizes the ordinariness of the man's life; the effect is ironic and suggests that the man's life meant more than this.]

RESPONDING TO THE ART

Ellis Wilson (1899–1977) was an early leader in the African American art movement. His paintings are distinguished by their bold colors, expressionistic distortion of forms, and his frequent focus on Haiti and the Caribbean.
Activity. Have students describe the mood of this painting. [Possible answers: dignified, religious, solemn.]

Connecting Across Texts

Connecting with "Go Down, Death"
Have students discuss the specific ways in which "of De Witt Williams on his way to Lincoln Cemetery" resembles "Go Down, Death." For example, both poems focus on the death of an individual; both have a songlike free-verse rhythm that might have been influenced by Whitman; both use repetition, parallel structure, and colloquial vocabulary; and both alternate long and short lines for effect. You might also have students discuss how these poems reflect both the richness and the hardships of African American experience in the first half of the twentieth century.

MAKING MEANINGS

First Thoughts [Respond]

1. Students might choose the opening three lines, the description of Death's ride, or the speeches of God.

Shaping Interpretations [Interpret]

2. God is in heaven; Death is in a "shadowy place" (l. 22). Sister Caroline is in Savannah, Georgia; she welcomes Death as a friend.

3. The comparison of the angel's voice to a clap of thunder (l. 19), the comparison of foam from Death's horse to a comet (l. 48), and the comparison of Death himself to a falling star (l. 56)

4. Most students will agree that the portrait of God and Jesus stresses mercy and gentleness. Supporting details include the pity that touches God's heart (ll. 13–14), God's compassion for Sister Caroline's weariness (ll. 36–39), and the description of Jesus rocking Sister Caroline in his arms (ll. 71–76).

5. Possible responses: The horse's pallor may indicate a chilling absence of life or a kind of purity. Melville uses the white whale to represent the blankness of evil in *Moby Dick* (pp. 313–327).

Extending the Text [Synthesize]

6. Possible response: Johnson and Dickinson both portray Death as "kind," but Dickinson's Death figure, for all his civility, is disturbing and cool. Johnson's Death is a loving, humanized figure.

ELEMENTS OF LITERATURE

1. Sample response: In stanza 1, "weep not" and "Weep no more" are repeated; in stanza 4, "Death galloped" and "Death rode" are parallel.

2. Sample response: "Straight on down" (l. 51) and "she didn't feel no chill" (l. 63) are examples of informal language.

3. Sample response: ll. 16 (long) and 17 (short); ll. 70 (short) and 71 (long).

4. Sample response: "clap of thunder" (l. 19) and "clamped the spurs" (l. 43) are examples of onomatopoeia.

Grading Timesaver

Rubrics for each Choices assignment appear on p. 179 in the *Portfolio Management System*.

T742

MAKING MEANINGS

First Thoughts

1. Review the notes you made as you read "Go Down, Death." Which words, lines, or stanzas had the strongest effect on you? Why?

Shaping Interpretations

2. Identify where God is in stanza 2, and where Death is in stanza 3. According to stanza 5, where is Sister Caroline? How does Sister Caroline respond to Death's arrival in stanza 7?

3. Find three **similes** that help to suggest the magnificence of the workings of heaven.

4. Does the speaker portray God and Jesus as distant, forbidding figures, or as familiar, gentle ones? Point out at least four **details** that support your interpretation.

5. Why do you think Death rides a "pale, white horse"? Where else have you seen the color white used in a similar **symbolic** way?

Extending the Text

6. While many of the traditional representations of death are fearful, the one in this poem is not. Discuss the ways Johnson **personifies** death in this poem. Then compare Johnson's image with images you have encountered in literature (see especially Emily Dickinson's "Because I could not stop for Death" on page 391) or on film.

ELEMENTS OF LITERATURE

Free Verse and the Orator's Style

When Johnson was working on the poems that would eventually become *God's Trombones,* he talked with the African American poet Paul Laurence Dunbar (1872–1906).

> I showed Paul the things I had done under the sudden influence of Whitman. He read them through and, looking at me with a queer smile, said, "I don't like them, and I don't see what you are driving at." He may have been

742 THE MODERNS

> justified, but I was taken aback. I got out my copy of *Leaves of Grass* and read him some of the things I admired most. There was, at least, some personal consolation in the fact that his verdict was the same on Whitman himself.
>
> —James Weldon Johnson

Examine "Go Down, Death," and see if you can identify the influence of Whitman (page 348). Look for these elements of Whitman's style: (1) **repetition** and **parallel structure** to create rhythm; (2) the simple language of everyday conversation, including slang; (3) variation of line length, from very long to very short, to create a rolling **cadence;** (4) other **sound effects.**

CHOICES: Building Your Portfolio

Writer's Notebook

1. Collecting Ideas for an Interpretive Essay

Explore the similarities and differences in the attitudes toward death in Johnson's "Go Down, Death" and Gwendolyn Brooks's "of De Witt Williams on his way to Lincoln Cemetery" (see *Connections* on page 741). Take notes in a double-column comparison-contrast chart. Save your notes for possible use in the Writer's Workshop on page 804.

Comparing Sermons

2. Sermons Side by Side

Extracts from another famous sermon in American literature are on page 79—Jonathan Edwards's "Sinners in the Hands of an Angry God." In a brief essay, compare and contrast Johnson's sermon with Edwards's. Consider these elements of each sermon: (a) imagery, (b) figures of speech, (c) message, (d) tone, (e) audience, and (f) purpose.

CHOICES: Building Your Portfolio

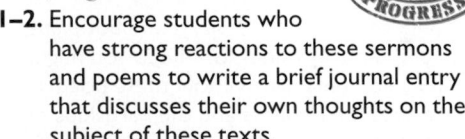

1–2. Encourage students who have strong reactions to these sermons and poems to write a brief journal entry that discusses their own thoughts on the subject of these texts.

Claude McKay (1941) by Carl Van Vechten.

The Beinecke Rare Book and Manuscript Library, Yale University, New Haven, Connecticut. Estate of Carl Van Vechten, Joseph Solomon, Executor.

Claude McKay

(1890–1948)

Claude McKay was born and raised on the Caribbean island of Jamaica, the eighth child of farmers. When he was nine, he went to live with his eldest brother, who was a schoolmaster, and his early education came chiefly from his brother's classroom and library. McKay apprenticed as a wheelwright and cabinetmaker, then worked as a constable. All the while, he was writing poems in a Jamaican dialect of English. In 1912, with the help of an English friend, he published his first two collections of verse, *Songs of Jamaica* and *Constab Ballads,* then traveled to the United States to study agriculture. After briefly enrolling at Tuskegee Institute in Alabama, McKay transferred to Kansas State College, where he studied for two years.

In 1914, McKay moved to Harlem and opened a restaurant with a friend. When this venture failed, he supported himself with a variety of jobs, from janitor to butler, while he continued to refine his craft and publish poems in periodicals. In 1920, his third book, *Spring in New Hampshire,* was published. His most important book of poetry, *Harlem Shadows,* appeared in 1922.

By this time, McKay was a major figure in the Harlem Renaissance. He had served as an editor of the radical newspapers the *Liberator* and *The Masses.* Like many writers of the period, he was drawn to the "noble experiment" of communism. In 1922, he signed on as a stoker for a merchant ship and toured Russia for a year.

McKay lived abroad, principally in France, until 1934. During this time he concentrated on writing fiction and essays rather than poetry, and he published four novels, including the best-selling *Home to Harlem* (1928). Disillusioned with communism, in 1942 he converted to Roman Catholicism. McKay spent the rest of his life teaching in Catholic schools in Chicago.

Despite the use of Jamaican dialect early in his career, much of McKay's poetry shows the influence of the English Romantic poets, especially Wordsworth, Keats, and Shelley. In subject matter, however, the Romantics and McKay diverge widely: McKay's sonnets voice his ambivalent and often defiant feelings about African American life in the United States.

 go.hrw.com
LEO 11-15

CLAUDE MCKAY 743

OBJECTIVES

1. Read and interpret the poem
2. Express understanding through creative writing and art

SKILLS

Writing
- Collect ideas for an interpretive essay

Writing/Art
- Design a poster or bumper sticker

Viewing/Representing
- Identify details in a painting (ATE)

Planning

- **Traditional Schedule**
  Lesson Plans Including Strategies for English-Language Learners
- **One-Stop Planner**
  CD-ROM with Test Generator

BROWSING IN THE FILES

Writers on Writing. In his autobiography, *A Long Way from Home,* McKay wrote, "I thought that if a Negro writer were sincere in creating a plausible Negro tale . . . he would obtain some recognition and appreciation. For Negro writers are not alone in competing with heavy handicaps. They have allies among some of the white writers and artists, who are fighting formalism and classicism, crusading for new forms and ideas against the dead weight of the old."

Resources: Print and Media

Reading
- *Graphic Organizers for Active Reading,* p. 74
- Audio CD Library
  Disc 21, Track 3

Assessment
- *Portfolio Management System,* p. 180
- *Test Generator (One-Stop Planner CD-ROM)*

Internet
- go.hrw.com (keyword: LE0 11–15)

Summary ■

Through simile, metaphor, imagery, and personification, the speaker of this sonnet expresses his bitterness at America's social, racial, and economic injustice. Yet he is awed and revitalized by her vigor and size. He regards America without fear, ill-will, or mockery, but foresees her decline.

RESPONDING TO THE ART

Kindred McLeary (1901–   ) was famous for his populist murals, many commissioned by the Works Projects Administration in the 1940s. This mural evokes the lives of poor people living on the Lower East Side of New York City.

Activity. Ask students to identify the images within the mural. [people at a produce stand, reading, looking into a baby carriage, all against a background of high-rise buildings] Ask students to find phrases in the poem that might correspond to the mural. [Possible responses: "bread of bitterness," "I love this cultured hell," "her might and granite wonders."]

Ⓐ Critical Thinking
Allusions

Ask students what the speaker sees sinking into the sand. [America's "might and granite wonders"] You may wish to point out that these lines are reminiscent of Shelley's "Ozymandias," in their emphasis on the way time destroys civilizations, leaving "the low and level sands stretching far away."

Make the Connection
America the Beautiful?
By expressing defiance as well as love, McKay reveals the complexity of the African American experience in the United States—an experience that requires a large measure of strength and courage.

Quickwrite
Write down four or five adjectives that you feel describe the heart of today's American society. Then, in two or three sentences, tell how you see yourself in relation to that society.

National Museum of American Art, Washington, D.C. Courtesy Art Resource, NY.

Lower East Side from *Scenes of New York* (Mural study, Madison Square Postal Station, New York City) by Kindred McLeary. Tempera on fiberboard (23¾" × 20").

America

Claude McKay

Although she feeds me bread of bitterness,°
And sinks into my throat her tiger's tooth,
Stealing my breath of life, I will confess
I love this cultured hell that tests my youth!
5   Her vigor flows like tides into my blood,
Giving me strength erect against her hate.
Her bigness sweeps my being like a flood.
Yet as a rebel fronts° a king in state,
I stand within her walls with not a shred
10 Of terror, malice, not a word of jeer.
Darkly I gaze into the days ahead,
And see her might and granite wonders there,
Beneath the touch of Time's unerring hand,
Like priceless treasures sinking in the sand.

1. **bread of bitterness:** allusion to Psalm 80:5, "Thou feedest them with the bread of tears; and givest them tears to drink in great measure."
8. **fronts:** confronts.

Reaching All Students

Struggling Readers
Show the class drawings that you or students have created using the Sketch to Stretch strategy with this poem. For specific instructions, see the *Reading Strategies Handbook,* p. 101 in the *Reading Skills and Strategies* binder. Make sure students understand that these drawings are not simple, literal renderings of the metaphors in the poem, but *interpretations* of the whole poem.

English Language Learners
Help students read phrases and clauses rather than word by word. Encourage them to find the meaningful units for themselves by locating commas, periods, and other punctuation marks that signal the ends of ideas. For other strategies for engaging English language learners with literature, see
• *Lesson Plans Including Strategies for English-Language Learners*

First Thoughts

1. Review your Quickwrite. Then, compare your views of America, and your place in it, with McKay's.

Shaping Interpretations

2. In lines 1–3, what treatment does the poem's speaker say he receives from America? What qualities of America cause the speaker to love the country anyway?

3. America is **personified** in this poem as an entity both cruel and powerful. What **images** suggest America's cruelty and injustice? What images convey its power?

4. A rebel with "not a shred / Of terror, malice, not a word of jeer" might seem to be a rebel who does not really rebel. How does the poem resolve this **paradox,** or apparent contradiction?

Extending the Text

5. What does this speaker see happening to America as he gazes into "the days ahead"? What messages about America's future do you hear today in various sources—films, TV shows, news programs, magazines, and other media?

Street vendors in Harlem in the 1920s.
UPI/Bettmann.

CHOICES:
Building Your Portfolio

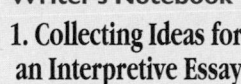

Writer's Notebook

1. Collecting Ideas for an Interpretive Essay

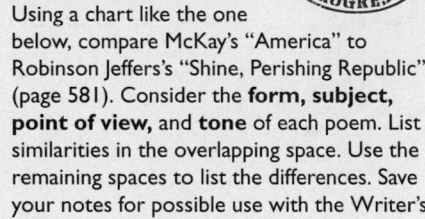

Using a chart like the one below, compare McKay's "America" to Robinson Jeffers's "Shine, Perishing Republic" (page 581). Consider the **form, subject, point of view,** and **tone** of each poem. List similarities in the overlapping space. Use the remaining spaces to list the differences. Save your notes for possible use with the Writer's Workshop on page 804.

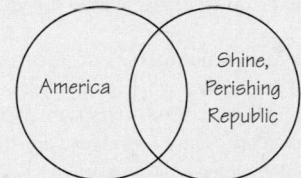

America | Shine, Perishing Republic

Creative Writing / Art

2. Get the Message

Design a poster or write a bumper sticker that the speaker in "America" might display. Try to capture in a phrase or two the main idea expressed in the poem.

CLAUDE MCKAY 745

First Thoughts [Respond]

1. Responses will depend on students' personal experiences as Americans. Accept all responses that draw specific comparisons with McKay's poem.

Shaping Interpretations [Interpret]

2. The speaker indicates that the country not only makes him bitter but threatens his life and his well-being. However, he loves America's culture, vigor, and magnitude.

3. Images of cruelty: "bread of bitterness" (l. 1), "tiger's tooth" (l. 2), "her hate" (l. 6). Images of power: "Tides" of vigor (l. 5), bigness sweeping "like a flood" (l. 7), "king in state" (l. 8).

4. The speaker might be seen as a patriotic rebel, who resists injustice and cruelty in the hope of ultimately changing his society for the better.

Extending the Text [Synthesize]

5. He sees the country and "her might and granite wonders" decaying or destroyed by time. Students may cite present-day authorities who see America in danger because of internal fragmentation and external competition as well as those who are optimistic because of the country's technological and social advances.

Grading Timesaver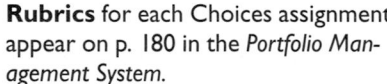

Rubrics for each Choices assignment appear on p. 180 in the *Portfolio Management System.*

CHOICES:
Building Your Portfolio

1. **Writer's Notebook**
   Encourage students to draw a large Venn diagram with plenty of writing room. Have them include direct quotes from each poem, along with their interpretations.

2. **Creative Writing/Art** Students might enjoy working in pairs on this project. They could begin by brainstorming orally, or freewriting individually and then discussing

their ideas together. They should jot down words and short phrases that might make catchy slogans, especially those that employ alliteration, onomatopoeia, or other sound effects. Emphasize that the key to a successful slogan is finding vivid, concrete words or phrases with wide implications. Students should make a rough sketch rather than a finished model of their poster or bumper sticker.

OBJECTIVES
Tableau/Incident
1. Read and interpret the poems
2. Express understanding through writing and music

SKILLS
Writing
- Compare and contrast diction and sentence structure in two poems
- Write a conversation between two characters
- Plan a film version of a poem, complete with camera shots and music

Viewing/Representing
- Compare a painting with a poem (ATE)

Planning

- **Block Schedule**
  Block Scheduling Lesson Plans with Pacing Guide
- **Traditional Schedule**
  Lesson Plans Including Strategies for English-Language Learners
- **One-Stop Planner**
  CD-ROM with Test Generator

BROWSING IN THE FILES

Writers on Writing. Countee Cullen once said that "good poetry is a lofty thought beautifully expressed," a thing that "should not be too intellectual" but should "deal more . . . with the emotions." While Cullen aimed to transcend the issue of race, his poems never abandoned the predicaments faced by African Americans.

Countee Cullen

(1903–1946)

Countee Cullen grew up in New York City as the adopted son of Rev. and Mrs. Frederick Cullen. He was a brilliant student, and during high school he was already writing accomplished poems in traditional forms. He graduated Phi Beta Kappa from New York University in 1925. While in college, Cullen won the Witter Bynner Poetry Prize; that same year, *Color,* his first volume of poetry, was published. This collection won a gold medal from the Harmon Foundation and established the young poet's reputation.

After earning his master's degree from Harvard in 1926, Cullen worked as an assistant editor of the important African American magazine *Opportunity.* His poems were published in such influential periodicals as *Harper's, Poetry,* and *Crisis.* In 1927, he published *Copper Sun,* a collection of poems, and *Caroling Dusk,* an anthology of poetry by African Americans. *Caroling Dusk* was a significant contribution to the Harlem Renaissance, but the introduction Cullen wrote for the book was controversial. He called for black poets to write traditional verse and to avoid the restrictions of solely racial themes.

At the peak of his career, Cullen married the daughter of the famous black writer W.E.B. Du Bois and published a third collection of poems, *The Ballad of the Brown Girl.* In 1929, he published a fourth volume, *The Black Christ.* Although he continued to write prose until the end of his life, this was his last collection of poetry. During the Great Depression of the 1930s, unable to make a living solely from writing, he began teaching in Harlem public schools, a job that he held until his early death.

Countee Porter Cullen (c. 1925) by Winold Reiss. Pastel on artist board (30 1/16" × 21 1/2").

Cullen's verse was heavily influenced by the poetry of the English Romantics, especially John Keats. He thought of himself primarily as a lyric poet in the Romantic tradition, not as a black poet writing about social and racial themes. Nevertheless, Cullen found himself repeatedly drawn to such themes: "Somehow or other I find my poetry of itself treating of the Negro, of his joys and his sorrows—mostly of the latter—and of the heights and depths of emotion which I feel as a Negro."

National Portrait Gallery, Smithsonian Institution, Washington, D.C. Gift of Lawrence A. Fleischman and Howard Garfinkle with a matching grant from the National Endowment for the Arts. Courtesy Art Resource, NY.

 go.hrw.com
LEO 11-15

 Resources: Print and Media

Reading
- *Graphic Organizers for Active Reading,* pp. 75, 76
- *Audio CD Library*
    Disc 21, Tracks 4, 5

Assessment
- *Formal Assessment,* p. 143
- *Portfolio Management System,* p. 181
- *Test Generator (One-Stop Planner CD-ROM)*

Internet
- go.hrw.com (keyword: LE0 11–15)

Make the Connection
Still Life

Usually, *tableau* means a scene or an action stopped cold, like a still picture in a reel of film. Here we have a *tableau vivant;* that is, a little scene in which figures silently pose, a significant moment caught and preserved. This preserved moment is a disarmingly simple glimpse of a friendship—a friendship that speaks silently but forcefully of a much larger issue.

Quickwrite

If you were sure you were behaving correctly, how would you deal with critics of your actions? Write down your thoughts in a few sentences.

Tableau
(For Donald Duff)
Countee Cullen

Locked arm in arm they cross the way,
  The black boy and the white,
The golden splendor of the day,
  The sable pride of night.

5 From lowered blinds the dark folk stare,
  And here the fair folk talk,
Indignant that these two should dare
  In unison to walk.

Oblivious to look and word
10 They pass, and see no wonder
That lightning brilliant as a sword
  Should blaze the path of thunder.

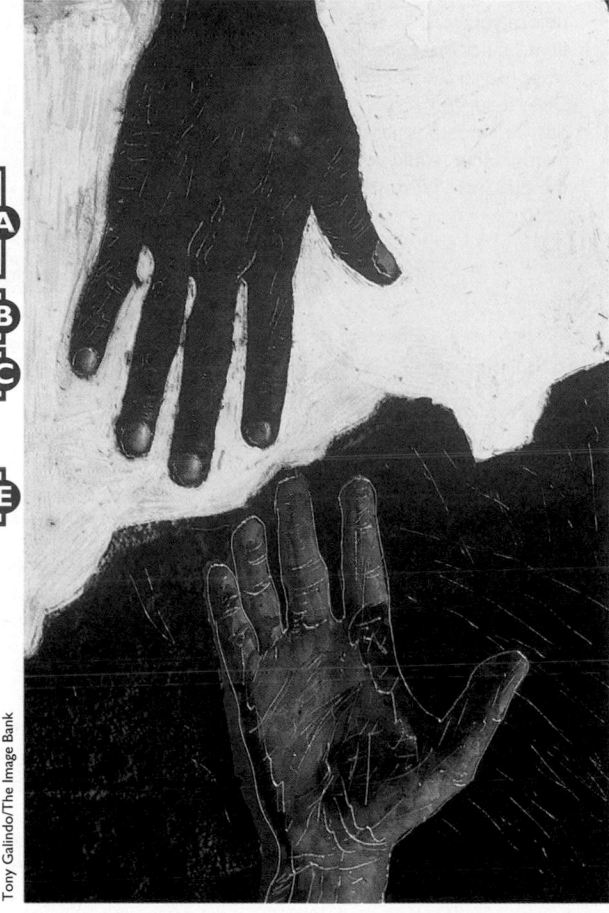

Tony Galindo/The Image Bank

COUNTEE CULLEN 747

Summary ■

A black boy and a white boy walk arm in arm down a street, oblivious to stares and comments from the people watching them.

Ⓐ Reading Skills and Strategies
Visualizing
? What do the first two lines describe? [A black boy and a white boy are crossing a street arm in arm.] What metaphors does the poet use to show that he sees the two boys as equal? [He uses the parallel metaphors of "Golden splendor of the day" and "sable pride of the night."]

Ⓑ Critical Thinking
Interpreting
? What point is being made in the description of the onlookers? [Possible response: Both communities are suspicious, nosy, and perturbed by this interracial friendship.]

Ⓒ Struggling Readers
Reading Inverted Sentences
Ask a volunteer to rearrange "should dare in unison to walk" in everyday word order and to paraphrase it. ["should dare to walk in unison"; "should dare to walk together"] Why might Cullen have inverted this phrase? [Possible responses: to produce the rhyme "talk/walk"; to emphasize the word "unison."]

Ⓓ Vocabulary Note
Connotation
Discuss the connotations of the word *unison.* [Unison means "as one"; it connotes a closer relationship than "together."] Encourage students to use reference material such as a dictionary or thesaurus to determine the meaning of *oblivious.* [unaware, unmindful]

Ⓔ Advanced Learners
Figures of Speech
Point out that "lightning brilliant as a sword" contains a simile within a metaphor. "Lightning" and "thunder" are also symbols of the boys' unconventional friendship, the explosive emotions it stirs up, and the dramatic changes it might cause.

Reaching All Students

Struggling Readers
After students have read the poem once, they can extend their comprehension by using a strategy called Text Reformulation. Read students a reformulated version of the poem. See the *Reading Strategies Handbook,* p. 127 in the *Reading Skills and Strategies* binder, for step-by-step instructions for using this strategy.

English Language Learners
Interpreting Idioms. Some of the more difficult idiomatic expressions in the poem can be pantomimed, such as "Locked arm in arm" (l. 1) and "in unison to walk" (l. 8). In other cases, have students use a dictionary, thesaurus and other reference materials to research the meaning of words and phrases such as *sable* ("black") and *blaze the path* ("mark or carve out the path").

Summary ■

The speaker recounts a childhood incident that left an indelible mark in his mind: being taunted with a cruel racial epithet by a white boy, while riding public transportation in Baltimore.

RESPONDING TO THE ART

Raphael Soyer (1899–1987) came to New York City from Russia in 1913. He became famous for his sensitive portraits of urban life in America.

Activity. Ask students how Soyer's scene resembles and differs from that in Cullen's poem. [Both depict whites and blacks riding public transportation together, but while Cullen focuses on two children interacting, Soyer focuses on the discomfort of a mother and child.]

Ⓐ Reading Skills and Strategies

Visualizing

❓ Encourage students to picture this scene in their minds. What feeling or mood does this scene evoke? [Possible response: It evokes both the innocent joy of a child on a trip and a mature sadness about racial prejudice.]

Ⓑ Critical Thinking

Analyzing

❓ Ask students to notice the singsong meter and regular rhyme scheme of the poem. Each stanza is composed of alternating lines of iambic tetrameter and iambic trimeter. The second and fourth lines of each stanza rhyme and thus follow the pattern *abcb*. What tone or mood does this formal structure evoke? [Possible response: an ironic lightheartedness or humor, as in a nursery rhyme.] What effect is created by rhyming the innocent-sounding *bigger* with the epithet *nigger*? [an ironic reversal and a shift in tone from the whimsical to the tragic]

Ⓒ Elements of Literature

Theme

❓ What is the poem's message? [Possible response: For many African American children, an early experience of racism can indelibly tarnish the innocent joys of childhood.]

Before You Read
INCIDENT

Make the Connection
A Word Remembered
The power of a word to taunt, to criticize, to dehumanize can't be underestimated. You might be shaken by the offensive word in this poem—imagine how it would affect a child.

Quickwrite

Before you read "Incident," quickwrite your response to the poem's title. Does it suggest something serious, or something relatively minor? How would you react if the title were "Catastrophe"?

Passengers (1953) by Raphael Soyer. Oil on canvas.
© Estate of Raphael Soyer, Forum Gallery, New York.

Incident

Countee Cullen

Ⓐ
Once, riding in old Baltimore,
    Heart-filled, head-filled with glee,
I saw a Baltimorean
    Keep looking straight at me.

5 Now I was eight and very small,
    And he was no whit bigger,
And so I smiled, but he poked out
    His tongue, and called me "Nigger."

I saw the whole of Baltimore
10   From May until December;
Of all the things that happened there
    That's all that I remember.

Ⓑ Ⓒ

Using Students' Strengths

Visual Learners

Invite students to draw the incident so as to convey its emotional impact on the speaker or on them. They may use any available, practical medium, such as pen and ink, charcoal, or pencil. Encourage them to use any style they find effective, including abstract symbolism or a comic-book style with speech and thought balloons. Suggest that students add a title that summarizes their interpretation of the poem.

Crossing the Curriculum

Social Sciences

Both of Cullen's poems were written during a period in American history when the races were largely segregated. The Civil Rights movement that began in the 1950s was aimed at ending segregation and racial discrimination. Have students research and report on one of the following:
• Montgomery bus boycott
• "I Have A Dream" speech
• Civil Rights Act of 1964
• Registration of African American voters

MAKING MEANINGS

Tableau

First Thoughts

1. Review your Quickwrite. Do the boys in "Tableau" act toward their critics as you would act toward yours?

Shaping Interpretations

2. What **metaphors** describe the two boys in the first stanza?

3. In the third stanza, who or what is "lightning brilliant as a sword"? Who or what is the "path of thunder"?

4. Why should such a commonplace thing as the friendship between two boys evoke such a dramatic response? What larger **topic** do you think the poem is really about?

Incident

First Thoughts

1. Look at your Quickwrite notes. Does the poem describe a mere incident or something much larger? Explain.

Shaping Interpretations

2. What might lead a child to insult an eight-year-old boy in the way described here? In what ways is a child's prejudice even more disturbing than an adult's?

3. Review your response to First Thoughts. What **ironic** overtones does the title have?

4. The speaker never directly states his emotional response to the experience. How does the last stanza indirectly make clear the impact the event had on him?

Extending the Text

5. Do you think that the content and **message** of "Tableau" and "Incident" are outdated, or are the scenes described in these poems still occurring today? Explain.

CHOICES:
Building Your Portfolio

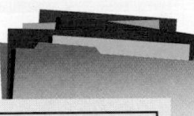

Writer's Notebook

1. Collecting Ideas for an Interpretive Essay

Compare and contrast the **diction** and **sentence structure** in "Tableau" and "Incident." Take notes that show how Cullen uses language to create two different effects in poems that are about very similar subjects. Save your notes for possible use in the Writer's Workshop on page 804.

Creative Writing

2. Kindred Spirits

Write a conversation in which the two boys who appear in "Tableau" discuss what happens in "Incident" with the eight-year-old boy who was the victim of the incident.

Creative Writing / Music

3. A Film Version

Suppose you were going to make a short film based on the poem "Incident." To convince a producer that you have a good idea, write a list of planned camera shots, in the order in which they would appear on screen. Then write a treatment, or summary, of your vision of the film. If you wish, find or compose music that you would use as an appropriate soundtrack for your film, and include a recording of that music with your film treatment.

PROD. NO.			
SCENE	TAKE	ROLL	
DATE		SOUND	
PROD. CO.			
DIRECTOR			
CAMERAMAN			

Incident

First Thoughts [Respond]

1. Possible responses: It was much more than an incident: it was a critical, traumatic event in the speaker's childhood. Students may point out that it could well have been a mere "incident" for the white boy, but that the title is ironic for the speaker.

Shaping Interpretations [Interpret]

2. Possible responses: Parental influence, meanness, as well as cultural and educational background, might prompt such an insult. A child's prejudice suggests that racism is learned at home.

3. To call the event an "incident" is ironic since that word understates the trauma the speaker suffered. The dictionary defines *incident* as "a minor event."

4. By telling us that this event remains his only memory from a long stay in Baltimore, the speaker dramatizes the profound impact of this painful moment.

Extending the Text [Synthesize]

5. Possible response: The poems capture the persistence of racial prejudice; sadly, neither the details nor the messages are dated.

Grading Timesaver

Rubrics for each Choices assignment appear on p. 181 in the *Portfolio Management System*.

CHOICES:
Building Your Portfolio

1–3. Have students try to imaginatively enter the setting of the poem before they begin their activities.

MAKING MEANINGS

Tableau

First Thoughts [Respond]

1. Possible responses: Some students may approve of the disregard that the boys show their disapproving neighbors. Others may feel that a direct and outspoken response would be more appropriate.

Shaping Interpretations [Interpret]

2. The white boy is compared to "the golden splendor of the day," and the black boy to "the sable pride of the night."

3. Possible responses: "Lightning" might refer to the boys' courage in pursuing their friendship, and "thunder" might suggest the rumbling of social change.

4. Their friendship transgresses the customs of their time and place. The larger focus of the poem includes race relations and social nonconformity in general.

Zora Neale Hurston

(c. 1903–1960)

Zora Neale Hurston was born in the all-black town of Eatonville, Florida. Her father was a preacher, and her mother, a schoolteacher, urged her talented daughter to "jump at the sun."

In her autobiography, Hurston recalls that as a young girl, "I used to climb to the top of one of the huge chinaberry trees which guarded our front gate and look out over the world. The most interesting thing that I saw was the horizon. . . . It grew upon me that I ought to walk out to the horizon and see what the end of the world was like."

When Hurston was about nine, her mother died, and Zora was passed among relatives and family friends, supporting herself from her early teens on. Eventually, she enrolled at Howard University in Washington, D.C., where she published her first story in 1921.

Four years later, she set out for New York City to attend Barnard College, arriving with a dollar and a half in her pocket. Hurston was soon in the midst of the Harlem Renaissance, writing stories and plays that celebrated her African American heritage. She wore big hats and turbans, danced, gave parties, and sometimes shocked other African American artists, especially male writers like James Weldon Johnson and Langston Hughes.

Enrolling at prestigious Barnard College, Hurston met the famous anthropologist Franz Boas. Boas believed that Hurston's interest was really in his field, the study of human social and cultural behavior. Indeed, Hurston, who became his protégé, did eventually make her reputation not just as a fiction writer, but also as a folklorist. She traveled through Alabama, Florida, and Louisiana to gather folklore material, using

Zora Neale Hurston (1935) by Carl Van Vechten.

a scholar's eye to evaluate oral tales, many of which were familiar to her from earliest childhood. Eventually, she gathered enough folklore to fill two groundbreaking collections, *Mules and Men* (1935) and *Tell My Horse* (1938). Alice Walker (page 1101) says that the stories in *Mules and Men* gave back to her own relatives in the South all the stories they'd forgotten or grown ashamed of.

Hurston also wrote musical revues portraying black folk-culture, and these brought her initial success. But it was *Story* magazine's publication of her short story "The Gilded Six Bits" that launched her literary career. When the Philadelphia publisher J. B. Lippincott asked if she had a novel, Hurston promptly sat down and wrote *Jonah's Gourd Vine*, published in 1934. Three years later, Hurston published her best novel, *Their Eyes Were Watching God*, the story of a young African American woman who strikes out for a life beyond a conventional marriage, much as Hurston herself had done.

Throughout the last twenty years of her life, Hurston continued to produce fiction and nonfiction, including her autobiography, *Dust Tracks on a Road*. But she began to have difficulty finding a market for her work, some of which was criticized in the African American community for celebrating the life of black people in the United States rather than confronting the white community for its discrimination.

In the late 1940s, Hurston left New York and returned to Florida. In 1960, she died, broke, in a Florida welfare home. A collection had to be taken up to pay for her funeral. Ironically, in the years since her death, much of her work has been brought back into print, and Hurston is now recognized as the forerunner of such celebrated contemporary writers as Toni Morrison and Alice Walker.

go.hrw.com
LE0 11-15

Before You Read

FROM **DUST TRACKS ON A ROAD**

Make the Connection

Looking for the Threads

It's no surprise that the auto-biographies of writers often include lovingly detailed memories of childhood interests and discoveries that paved the way for the adult writer. In her autobiography, *One Writer's Beginnings,* Eudora Welty (page 633) notes, "Writing fiction has developed in me an abiding respect for the unknown in a human lifetime and a sense of where to look for the threads, how to follow, how to connect, find in the thick of the tangle what clear line persists. The strands are all there: To the memory nothing is ever really lost." Here, Zora Neale Hurston connects some of her own threads by recounting what is surely every writer's first experience of falling in love: the passion for hearing and reading stories.

Reading Skills and Strategies

Analyzing an Autobiography

As you read, write down what you learn about Hurston's character from her thoughts and actions, as well as any details that suggest Hurston's early interest in people, her fascination with storytelling, and her later devotion to anthropology and folklore research.

Background

Zora Neale Hurston's *Dust Tracks on a Road* is rich with cultural and historical meaning, as well as personal insight and data. Woven through these recollections of Hurston's childhood are her impressions of racial segregation, economic conditions, education, social customs, and family, as well as general attitudes of Southerners around 1900.

> *I used to take a seat on top of the gatepost and watch the world go by.*

Her World (1948) by Philip Evergood. Oil on canvas (48″ × 35⅝″).

The Metropolitan Museum of Art, Arthur Hoppock Hearn Fund, 1950 (50.29). Photograph ©1982 The Metropolitan Museum of Art.

ZORA NEALE HURSTON **751**

Summary ■

Hurston describes her first encounters with white people from outside her community, and her earliest exposures to literature. As a child, she waves to travelers who drive past her house, talking with them and hitching rides. At school, she is introduced to two visiting white women from Minnesota. Impressed by Hurston's reading, they give her gifts—most importantly, books.

BROWSING IN THE FILES

About the Author. Forced to earn her own living after her mother's death, Hurston dropped out of high school and worked as a maid, then as a wardrobe girl in a traveling variety show. She worked as a manicurist while attending Howard University on a part-time basis for six years. After arriving in New York in 1925, however, she was quickly taken up by influential people. Hurston had fallings-out with Langston Hughes and several other prominent literary figures who criticized Hurston's writings for not being political. Her books, though well-received by the critics, did not sell well. She published only one book in the last eighteen years of her life. In 1950 she was working as a hotel maid for thirty dollars a week. Her reputation was revived in the 1970s. See Alice Walker's essays "Zora Hurston: A Cautionary Tale and a Partisan View" and "Looking for Zora" in *In Search of Our Mother's Gardens* (1983).

RESPONDING TO THE ART

Philip Evergood (1901–1973) was born in New York City and educated in England. Returning to the U.S. in 1923, he produced a series of lyrical paintings on social and racial themes.

Activity. Ask students to find parallels between Evergood's painting and Hurston's autobiography. [Both Hurston and this young girl lean on fences in front of their houses, watching "the world go by."]

Preteaching Vocabulary

Words to Own

Have small groups of students take turns reading each word and its definition aloud. On the second round, have each student in turn choose one definition from the list and read it aloud. Volunteers from the group should raise their hands to provide the defined word. After students have shown a good grasp of the words, have them complete the following exercise. For each word in the numbered list, find its synonym in the lettered list.

1. deeply [f]
2. kingdom [d]
3. stunt [h]
4. uplifted [i]
5. boldness [a]
6. step [c]
7. decided [g]
8. greet [j]
9. imagine [b]
10. greed [e]

a. brazenness
b. conceive
c. tread
d. realm
e. avarice
f. profoundly
g. resolved
h. caper
i. exalted
j. hail

from **Dust Tracks on a Road**

Zora Neale Hurston

RESPONDING TO THE ART

The photograph shown in various details on pp. 752–753, 755, and 756 was taken at Hurston's school in Quincy, Florida. **Activity.** You might have students select a caption for this photograph from one of the poems in this collection. The flags, for example, suggest the title of Hughes's poem "I, Too, Sing America." Another poem that could accompany this photograph is Alice Walker's "Women" (in *Elements of Literature, Third Course*).

Background

Hurston once said that the folk tradition she was born into was so familiar it fit her "like a tight chemise" she could not see because she was wearing it. "It was only when I was off in college," she said, "away from my native surroundings, that I could see myself like somebody else and stand off and look at my garment. Then I had to have the spy-glass of Anthropology to look through at that."

Dunbar High School, Quincy, Florida (pages 752–753, 755, 756).
Florida State Archives.

752 THE MODERNS

Reaching All Students

Struggling Readers
Read a selected passage from the autobiography aloud to the class. Then model the Say Something strategy with another teacher or with a prepared dialogue. For specific instructions on how to apply this strategy see the *Reading Strategies Handbook,* p. 85 in the *Reading Skills and Strategies* binder.

Advanced Learners
Encourage students to focus on what they learn about Hurston's character from the myths, heroes, and stories that she especially loved.

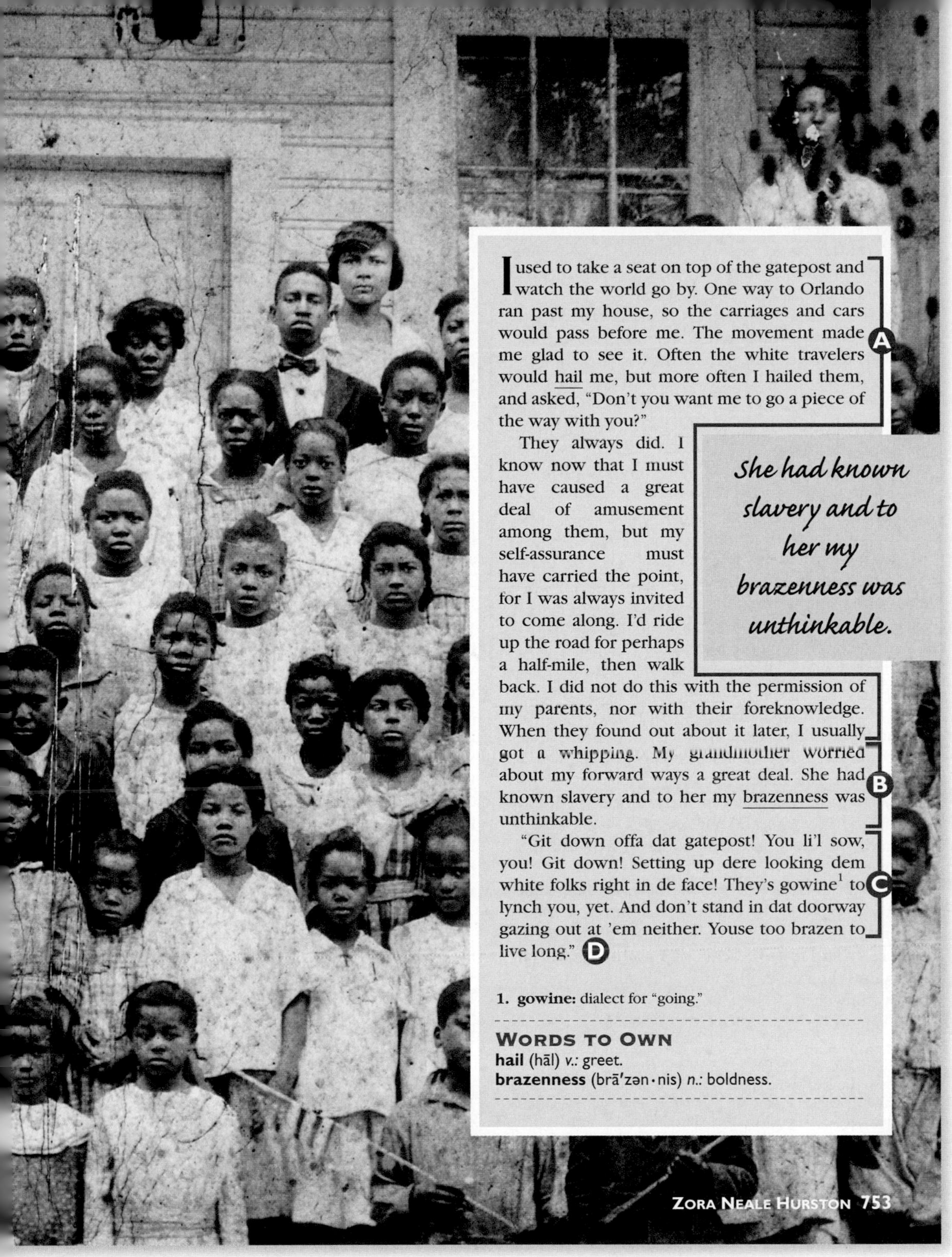

I used to take a seat on top of the gatepost and watch the world go by. One way to Orlando ran past my house, so the carriages and cars would pass before me. The movement made me glad to see it. Often the white travelers would hail me, but more often I hailed them, and asked, "Don't you want me to go a piece of the way with you?" **A**

They always did. I know now that I must have caused a great deal of amusement among them, but my self-assurance must have carried the point, for I was always invited to come along. I'd ride up the road for perhaps a half-mile, then walk back. I did not do this with the permission of my parents, nor with their foreknowledge. When they found out about it later, I usually got a whipping. My grandmother worried about my forward ways a great deal. She had known slavery and to her my brazenness was unthinkable. **B**

She had known slavery and to her my brazenness was unthinkable.

"Git down offa dat gatepost! You li'l sow, you! Git down! Setting up dere looking dem white folks right in de face! They's gowine[1] to lynch you, yet. And don't stand in dat doorway gazing out at 'em neither. Youse too brazen to live long." **C** **D**

1. **gowine:** dialect for "going."

Words to Own
hail (hāl) *v.:* greet.
brazenness (brā′zən·nis) *n.:* boldness.

Using Students' Strengths

Intrapersonal Learners

To supplement the Reading Skills and Strategies activity, have students freewrite their responses to Hurston and her experiences as they read. They should then go back and circle or highlight any notes that give them insight into Hurston's character or connect them emotionally to her narrative. Students may then wish to condense these thoughts into a more personal, creative format, such as a journal entry, a letter to Hurston, or a poem.

Verbal Learners

Ask students to write a two- or three-paragraph account of one of their own childhood memories, at first informally, in their own words, and then in formal prose. Have students form small groups and read their two accounts aloud. The other group members can then offer comments, connections, and constructive suggestions for change.

A Reading Skills and Strategies

Analyzing an Autobiography

Have students write down as many details about Hurston as they can find in or infer from the first two paragraphs. Suggest that they divide their findings into those details that demonstrate Hurston's character as a young girl and those details that suggest what Hurston is like as the grown woman writing her autobiography. Encourage students to share their ideas with the class. [Possible responses: As a girl she is innocently, boldly friendly; as a woman she seems reflective, amused by her youthful self. The phrase *self-assurance* seems applicable to her at both times.]

B Critical Thinking

Extending the Text

? Why might Hurston's parents and grandmother have reacted as they did to her "brazenness"? [Possible responses: They feared that she might be harmed by a passerby; they did not want her to become fearless toward white people, because they did not trust whites themselves.]

C English Language Learners

Understanding Dialect

Transfer this paragraph of dialect into standard colloquial English for students, or ask a volunteer to do so. ["Get off that gatepost! You little sow, you! Get down! Sitting up there looking those white folks in the face! They're going to lynch you yet. And don't stand in that doorway looking out at them either. You're too bold to live long."] Clarify any words that still need to be explained, such as *sow* [female pig] and *lynch* [murder by mob action].

D Critical Thinking

Evaluating

? Hurston used dialect to reproduce the African American pattern of speech she grew up with in the South. Writer Richard Wright resented her use of dialect, believing that it perpetuated a comic, minstrel-show stereotype of African Americans and promoted racism. Do you agree with Wright or Hurston?

A Literary Connections

Walden

Ask students if they see any parallel between Hurston's metaphor here and Thoreau's famous words in *Walden*: "If a man does not keep pace with his companions, perhaps it is because he hears a different drummer. Let him step to the music which he hears, however measured or far away." (pp. 243–244)

B Historical Connections

Segregated Schools

Hurston grew up in a time when schools and most other public facilities were segregated by race in the American South. Her childhood also predated much of the great migration of African Americans from the South to the North. Thus, the whites who came down from the North were curious about Hurston's all-black school.

C Appreciating Language

Idiom

? How do the expression *cut a caper* and other idiomatic expressions throughout the story contribute to the overall effect? [Possible responses: They give an authentic voice to the narrative; they make the writing personal and unique.]

D Reading Skills and Strategies

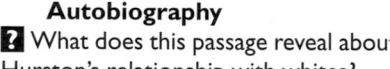

Analyzing an Autobiography

? What does this passage reveal about Hurston's relationship with whites? [Possible response: Her fascination with the visitors' hands and hair suggests that she has seen few white people and thus finds them strange and exotic.]

Nevertheless, I kept right on gazing at them, and "going a piece of the way" whenever I could make it. The village seemed dull to me most of the time. If the village was singing a chorus, I must have missed the tune.

Perhaps a year before the old man[2] died, I came to know two other white people for myself. They were women.

It came about this way. The whites who came down from the North were often brought by their friends to visit the village school. A Negro school was something strange to them, and while they were always sympathetic and kind, curiosity must have been present, also. They came and went, came and went. Always, the room was hurriedly put in order, and we were threatened with a prompt and bloody death if we cut one caper while the visitors were present. We always sang a spiritual, led by Mr. Calhoun himself. Mrs. Calhoun always stood in the back, with a palmetto switch[3] in her hand as a squelcher. We were all little angels for the duration, because we'd better be. She would cut her eyes[4] and give us a glare that meant trouble, then turn her face toward the visitors and beam as much as to say it was a great privilege and pleasure to teach lovely children like us. They couldn't see that palmetto hickory in her hand behind all those benches, but we knew where our angelic behavior was coming from.

Usually, the visitors gave warning a day ahead and we would be cautioned to put on shoes, comb our heads, and see to ears and fingernails. There was a close inspection of every one of us before we marched in that morning. Knotty heads, dirty ears, and fingernails got hauled out of line, strapped, and sent home to lick the calf[5] over again.

This particular afternoon, the two young ladies just popped in. Mr. Calhoun was flustered, but he put on the best show he could. He dismissed the class that he was teaching up at the front of the room, then called the fifth grade in reading. That was my class.

---

2. **old man:** a white farmer who knew Hurston's family, took her fishing, and gave her advice.
3. **palmetto switch:** whip made from the stem of a large, fanlike leaf of a kind of palm tree. Teachers sometimes used these switches to discipline students.
4. **cut her eyes:** slang for "look scornfully."
5. **lick the calf:** slang for "wash up."

754 THE MODERNS

So we took our readers and went up front. We stood up in the usual line, and opened to the lesson. It was the story of Pluto and Persephone.[6] It was new and hard to the class in general, and Mr. Calhoun was very uncomfortable as the readers stumbled along, spelling out words with their lips, and in mumbling undertones before they exposed them experimentally to the teacher's ears.

Then it came to me. I was fifth or sixth down the line. The story was not new to me, because I had read my reader through from lid to lid, the first week that Papa had bought it for me.

That is how it was that my eyes were not in the book, working out the paragraph which I knew would be mine by counting the children ahead of me. I was observing our visitors, who held a book between them, following the lesson. They had shiny hair, mostly brownish. One had a looping gold chain around her neck. The other one was dressed all over in black and white with a pretty finger ring on her left hand. But the thing that held my eyes were their fingers. They were long and thin, and very white, except up near the tips. There they were baby pink. I had never seen such hands. It was a fascinating discovery for me. I wondered how they felt. I would have given those hands more attention, but the child before me was almost through. My turn next, so I got on my mark, bringing my eyes back to the book and made sure of my place. Some of the stories I had reread several times, and this Greco-Roman myth was one of my favorites. I was exalted by it, and that is the way I read my paragraph.

"Yes, Jupiter[7] had seen her (Persephone). He had seen the maiden picking flowers in the field. He had seen the chariot of the dark monarch pause by the maiden's side. He had seen him when he seized Persephone. He had seen the

---

6. **Pluto and Persephone** (pər·sef'ə·nē): In classical mythology, Pluto, or Hades, is the god who rules the underworld; Persephone, also known as Proserpina, is his wife, queen of the underworld. In this version of the origin of the seasons, Hurston uses the names of Roman and Greek gods interchangeably.
7. **Jupiter:** in Roman mythology, king of the gods.

WORDS TO OWN

caper (kā'pər) *n.:* foolish prank.
exalted (eg·zôlt'id) *v.:* lifted up.

Skill Link

Understanding Idioms

Explain to students how Hurston skillfully uses idioms—unique expressions that arise in a given language or dialect—to give her autobiography the flavor of her personality and her environment. For example, *lick the calf* is a regional Southern idiom meaning "wash up" (which is itself a widely used American idiom). Encourage students to note idioms in the narrative and to figure out their meaning by reading footnotes and using context clues. Ask students to "translate" the following idioms from this page.

1. "going a piece of the way" ["going partway down the road"]
2. "if we cut one caper" ["if we played any pranks"]
3. "the two young ladies just popped in" ["the two young ladies visited the school without warning"]
4. "I got on my mark" ["I got ready"]

Now invite students to use a book like *A Hog on Ice and Other Curious Expressions* by Charles Earle Funk to create a poster of interesting idioms centered on a particular word—such as *go*, whose idioms include *go about, go at, go in for, go over*, and *on the go*. Students could also include idioms from other languages, such as *lécher les vitrines*, French for "to go window shopping," though it literally means "to lick the windows." (Of course, *window shopping* is itself an idiom.)

black horses leap down Mount Aetna's[8] fiery throat. Persephone was now in Pluto's dark <u>realm</u> and he had made her his wife."

The two women looked at each other and then back to me. Mr. Calhoun broke out with a proud smile beneath his bristly moustache, and instead of the next child taking up where I had ended, he nodded to me to go on. So I read the story to the end, where flying Mercury, the messenger of the Gods, brought Persephone back to the sunlit earth and restored her to the arms of Dame Ceres, her mother, that the world might have springtime and summer flowers, autumn and harvest. But because she had bitten the pomegranate while in Pluto's kingdom, she must return to him for three months of each year, and be his queen. Then the world had winter, until she returned to earth.

The class was dismissed and the visitors smiled us away and went into a low-voiced conversation with Mr. Calhoun for a few minutes. They glanced my way once or twice and I began to worry. Not only was I barefooted, but my feet and legs were dusty. My hair was more uncombed than usual, and my nails were not shiny clean. Oh, I'm going to catch it now. Those ladies saw me, too. Mr. Calhoun is promising to 'tend to me. So I thought.

Then Mr. Calhoun called me. I went up thinking how awful it was to get a whipping before company. Furthermore, I heard a snicker run over the room. Hennie Clark and Stell Brazzle did it out loud, so I would be sure to hear them. The smart aleck was going to get it. I slipped one hand behind me and switched my dress tail at them, indicating scorn.

"Come here, Zora Neale," Mr. Calhoun cooed as I reached the desk. He put his hand on my shoulder and gave me little pats. The ladies smiled and

The ladies smiled and held out those flower-looking fingers toward me.

held out those flower-looking fingers toward me. I seized the opportunity for a good look.

"Shake hands with the ladies, Zora Neale," Mr. Calhoun prompted and they took my hand one after the other and smiled. They asked me if I loved school, and I lied that I did. There was *some* truth in it, because I liked geography and reading, and I liked to play at recess time. Whoever it was invented writing and arithmetic got no thanks from me. Neither did I like the arrangement where the teacher could sit up there with a palmetto stem and lick me whenever he saw fit. I hated things I couldn't do anything about. But I knew better than to bring that up right there, so I said yes, I *loved* school.

"I can tell you do," Brown Taffeta gleamed. She patted my head, and was lucky enough not to get sandspurs in her hand. Children who roll and tumble in the grass in Florida are apt to get sandspurs in their hair. They shook hands with me again and I went back to my seat.

When school let out at three o'clock, Mr. Calhoun told me to wait. When everybody had gone, he told me I was to go to the Park House, that was the hotel in Maitland, the next afternoon to call upon Mrs. Johnstone and Miss Hurd. I must tell Mama to see that I was clean and brushed from head to feet, and I must wear shoes and stockings. The ladies liked me, he said, and I must be on my best behavior.

The next day I was let out of school an hour early, and went home to be stood up in a tub of suds and be scrubbed and have my ears dug into. My sandy hair sported a red ribbon to match my red and white checked gingham dress, starched until it could stand alone. Mama saw to it that my shoes were on the right feet, since I was

----

WORDS TO OWN

realm (relm) *n.*: kingdom.

---

8. Mount Aetna's: Mount Aetna (also spelled Etna) is a volcanic mountain in eastern Sicily.

E **Advanced Learners**

Making Inferences

❓ Why do you think the myth of Persephone was a favorite of Hurston's? [Possible responses: She may have identified with Persephone, a young maiden who travels between two different worlds; she may have found the story romantic.]

F **Reading Skills and Strategies**

Analyzing an Autobiography

❓ How might the fact that Hurston is recalling the incident after many years affect the way she recounts it? [Possible response: She knows now what she didn't know at that moment—that she was going to be praised and rewarded for her intelligence, not punished for her grooming—so she recounts it with subtle irony.]

G **Elements of Literature**

Characterization

❓ What does this passage reveal about Hurston's character? [It shows her to be strategic and perceptive, for she understands this is not the moment to talk about what she doesn't like in school; it shows that she has strong opinions; it shows that she knows herself and her social surroundings.]

H **Elements of Literature**

Metonymy

❓ Remind students that metonymy is a figure of speech in which the part represents the whole. What is the effect of equating this woman with her "brown taffeta"? [It shows that Hurston does not know the woman personally; it shows that the woman's dress is made of fine fabric—underscoring the difference in their economic situations since Hurston's best dress is made out of inexpensive gingham.]

Taking a Second Look

Review:
Monitoring Reading Strategies
Remind students that one important reading skill consists of checking how well they understand what they are reading. When their understanding breaks down, they should modify their reading strategy: reread a passage more slowly, use resources such as an encyclopedia or a dictionary, or ask questions about the text.

Activity
1. Choose a passage and demonstrate how students could apply the three strategies.
2. Have students independently select a personal trouble spot in the narrative and jot down a list of specific questions they have about it, such as "What does this sentence mean?" or "Why did such and such happen?"

Have students reread the passage slowly, keeping their questions in mind. Then have them rate their understanding on a scale of 1 to 10. Repeat this process, following the Read Rate Reread model found in the *Reading Strategies Handbook,* p. 59 in the *Reading Skills and Strategies* binder.

careless about left and right. Last thing, I was given a handkerchief to carry, warned again about my behavior, and sent off, with my big brother John to go as far as the hotel gate with me.

A First thing, the ladies gave me strange things, like stuffed dates and preserved ginger, and encouraged me to eat all that I wanted. Then they showed me their Japanese dolls and just talked. I was then handed a copy of *Scribner's Magazine,* and asked to read a place that was pointed out to me. After a paragraph or two, I was told with smiles, that that would do.

I was led out on the grounds and they took my picture under a palm tree. They handed me what was to me then a heavy cylinder done up in fancy paper, tied with a ribbon, and they told me goodbye, asking me not to open it until I got home.

My brother was waiting for me down by the lake, and we hurried home, eager to see what was in the thing. It was too heavy to be candy or anything like that. John insisted on toting it for me.

B My mother made John give it back to me and let me open it. Perhaps, I shall never experience such joy again. The nearest thing to that moment was the telegram accepting my first book. One hundred goldy-new pennies rolled out of the cylinder. Their gleam lit up the world. It was not avarice that moved me. It was the beauty of the thing. I stood on the mountain. Mama let me play with my pennies for a while, then put them away for me to keep.

C That was only the beginning. The next day I received an Episcopal hymnbook bound in white leather with a golden cross stamped into the front cover, a copy of *The Swiss Family Robinson,* and a book of fairy tales.

I set about to commit the song words to memory. There was no music written there, just the words. But there was to my consciousness music in between them just the same. "When I survey the Wondrous Cross" seemed the most beautiful to me, so I committed that to memory first of all.

D Some of them seemed dull and without life, and I pretended they were not there. If white people liked trashy singing like that, there must be something funny about them that I had not noticed before. I stuck to the pretty ones where the words marched to a throb I could feel.

Of the Greeks, Hercules moved me most.

WORDS TO OWN
avarice (av′ə·ris) *n.:* greed.

Crossing the Curriculum

Social Studies

In *Plessy v. Ferguson* in 1896, the Supreme Court affirmed racial segregation that provided "separate but equal" public facilities. Yet this was rarely the case in practice. African American schools were generally given inferior facilities, staff, and educational resources—and their textbooks were usually the castoffs from white schools. African Americans received similarly *unequal* treatment in the dirty, overcrowded "colored" theaters and restaurants, and were forced to sit at the back of most trains and buses. In 1954, in the famous case of *Brown v. the Board of Education of Topeka,* the Supreme Court ruled unanimously that segregated schools are unconstitutional because they are inherently unequal and thus violate the Fourteenth Amendment, which guarantees equal protection of the law to all citizens. Students should be encouraged to pursue these issues further.

A month or so after the two young ladies returned to Minnesota, they sent me a huge box packed with clothes and books. The red coat with a wide circular collar and the red tam pleased me more than any of the other things. My chums pretended not to like anything that I had, but even then I knew that they were jealous. Old Smarty had gotten by them again. The clothes were not new, but they were very good. I shone like the morning sun.

But the books gave me more pleasure than the clothes. I had never been too keen on dressing up. It called for hard scrubbings with Octagon soap suds getting in my eyes, and none too gentle fingers scrubbing my neck and gouging in my ears.

In that box were *Gulliver's Travels, Grimm's Fairy Tales, Dick Whittington, Greek and Roman Myths,* and best of all, *Norse Tales.* Why did the Norse tales strike so deeply into my soul? I do not know, but they did. I seemed to remember seeing Thor swing his mighty short-handled hammer as he sped across the sky in rumbling thunder, lightning flashing from the <u>tread</u> of his steeds and the wheels of his chariot. The great and good Odin, who went down to the well of knowledge to drink, and was told that the price of a drink from that fountain was an eye. Odin drank deeply, then plucked out one eye without a murmur and handed it to the grizzly keeper, and walked away. That held majesty for me.

Of the Greeks, Hercules moved me most. I followed him eagerly on his tasks. The story of the choice of Hercules as a boy when he met Pleasure and Duty, and put his hand in that of Duty and followed her steep way to the blue hills of fame and glory, which she pointed out at the end, moved me <u>profoundly</u>. I <u>resolved</u> to be like him. The tricks and turns of the other gods and goddesses left me cold. There were other thin books about this and that sweet and gentle little girl who gave up her heart to Christ and good works. Almost always they died from it, preaching as they passed. I was utterly indifferent to their deaths. In the first place I could not <u>conceive</u> of death, and in the next place they never had any funerals that amounted to a hill of beans, so I didn't care how soon they rolled up their big, soulful, blue eyes and kicked the bucket. They had no meat on their bones.

But I also met Hans Andersen[9] and Robert Louis Stevenson.[10] They seemed to know what I wanted to hear and said it in a way that tingled me. Just a little below these friends was Rudyard Kipling in his Jungle Books.[11] I loved his talking snakes as much as I did the hero.

I came to start reading the Bible through my mother. She gave me a licking one afternoon for repeating something I had overheard a neighbor telling her. She locked me in her room after the whipping, and the Bible was the only thing in there for me to read. I happened to open to the place where David was doing some mighty smiting, and I got interested. David went here and he went there, and no matter where he went, he smote 'em hip and thigh. Then he sung songs to his harp awhile, and went out and smote some more. Not one time did David stop and preach about sins and things. All David wanted to know from God was who to kill and when. He took care of the other details himself. Never a quiet moment. I liked him a lot. So I read a great deal more in the Bible, hunting for some more active people like David. Except for the beautiful language of Luke and Paul, the New Testament still plays a poor second to the Old Testament for me. The Jews had a God who laid about Him[12] when they needed Him. I could see no use waiting till Judgment Day to see a man who was just crying for a good killing, to be told to go and roast.[13] My idea was to give him a good killing first, and then if he got roasted later on, so much the better.

9. Hans Andersen: Hans Christian Andersen (1805–1875), Danish writer known primarily for his fairy tales.
10. Robert Louis Stevenson (1850–1894): Scottish writer of adventure stories such as *Kidnapped* and *Treasure Island.*
11. Rudyard Kipling . . . Books: Kipling (1865–1936) was an English writer born in India. His *Jungle Book* and *Second Jungle Book* contain stories of the adventures of Mowgli, a boy raised by animals in the jungles of India.
12. laid about Him: slang for "struck blows in every direction."
13. roast: slang for "burn in hell."

WORDS TO OWN

tread (tred) *n.*: stepping.
profoundly (prō·found'lē) *adv.*: deeply.
resolved (rē·zälvd') *v.*: made a decision; determined.
conceive (kən·sēv') *v.*: think; imagine.

ZORA NEALE HURSTON 757

Making the Connections

Connecting to the Theme: "I, Too, Sing America"

Hurston was a passionate and confident person whose voice naturally made itself heard; but that voice was muted at times, both because of the social conditions for blacks and because of her own stubborn individualism, which sometimes caused conflicts with her colleagues. Only since the 1970s has Hurston's voice and work received the recognition they deserve.

Assessing Learning

Check Test: Questions and Answers

1. What does Zora do when she sits on the gatepost? [She greets travelers and takes rides with them.]
2. What does Zora find most fascinating about the two white women who visit the school? [their hands]
3. Why does she come to the attention of the women? [She reads fluently from a difficult text.]
4. What is inside the cylinder that the two women give Zora? [a hundred new pennies]
5. Why does Zora like the stories about David? [He is an active person who takes care of things himself.]

In these two excerpts from her autobiography, Hurston speaks of her fascination with the folk stories and oral traditions of African American culture. In the first, she recalls her childhood thrill at hearing men tell tall tales on the store porch. In the second, she explains how her formal, collegiate approach to research initially prevented her from making contact with the people whose oral traditions she hoped to record.

Background

Hurston's love of anthropological research was so great that, according to Langston Hughes (see p. 760), she would sometimes stop passersby on the streets of Harlem and ask to measure their heads. She was once initiated into a voodoo cult in order to facilitate her research. Her collections of folklore were not always well received by African American intellectuals of the time, who felt that she soft-pedaled the evils of segregation. Today, her collections of tales are generally viewed as a cultural treasure.

Activity. Have each student collect a piece of folklore from his or her community by asking friends, neighbors, relatives, or local experts. Encourage students to use an audiotape recorder. Invite them to share their stories at a class storytelling session. Students can also transcribe the stories and write introductions explaining how they gathered the material and whom it came from. The class can then publish the stories and give copies to the school library.

RESPONDING TO THE ART

Romare Bearden (1914–1988) is celebrated for his colorful collages of African American life. (See also p. 762.)

Activity. Have students speculate about the story behind the painting. [Possible response: A family sits on its front porch telling stories.]

PRIMARY Sources — AN AUTOBIOGRAPHY

In Search of a Story

- In another section of *Dust Tracks on a Road*, Zora Neale Hurston tells of her passion, as a child, for hearing stories from the African American tradition.

For me, the store porch was the most interesting place that I could think of. I was not allowed to sit around there, naturally. But, I could and did drag my feet going in and out, whenever I was sent there for something, to allow whatever was being said to hang in my ear. I would hear an occasional scrap of gossip in what to me was adult double talk, but which I understood at times. . . .

But what I really loved to hear was the menfolks holding a "lying" session. That is, straining against each other in telling folks tales. God, Devil, Brer Rabbit, Brer Fox, Sis Cat, Brer Bear, Lion, Tiger, Buzzard, and all the wood folk walked and talked like natural men. The wives of the storytellers might yell from back yards for them to come and tote some water, or chop wood for the cookstove and never get a move out of the men. The usual rejoinder was, "Oh, she's got enough to go on. No matter how much wood you chop, a woman will burn it all up to get a meal. If she got a couple of pieces, she will make it do. If you chop up a whole boxful, she will burn every stick of it. Pay her no mind." So the storytelling would go right on.

• • •

- This passion for listening to stories from the oral tradition led Hurston to collect folklore as a field researcher. In this section of her autobiography, Hurston tells of studying anthropology at Barnard College in New York City and of how she went out among African Americans to gather their folk tales. In her first attempts as a folklore collector, she did not succeed. She had to learn the hard way that a folklorist must use just the right approach with his or her sources.

Mecklenburg Evening (1984) by Romare Bearden. Collage and watercolor on board.
© Romare Bearden Foundation/Licensed by VAGA, New York, NY.

Research is formalized curiosity. It is poking and prying with a purpose. It is a seeking that he who wishes may know the cosmic secrets of the world and they that dwell therein. . . .

My first six months were disappointing. I found out later that it was not because I had no talents for research, but because I did not have the right approach. The glamour of Barnard College was still upon me. I dwelt in marble halls. I knew where the material was all right. But, I went about asking, in carefully accented Barnardese, "Pardon me, but do you know any folk tales or folk songs?" The men and women who had whole treasuries of material just seeping through their pores looked at me and shook their heads. No, they had never heard of anything like that around there. Maybe it was over in the next county. Why didn't I try over there? I did, and got the selfsame answer. Oh, I got a few little items. But compared with what I did later, not enough to make a flea a waltzing jacket.

—Zora Neale Hurston

Crossing the Curriculum

Art

Have students create identity collages for Hurston as a child. Ask them to gather pictures, words, and letters from magazines and newspapers that describe or embody Hurston's character—her personality, appearance, likes and dislikes, interests, etc. Display the collages in the classroom and invite each student to discuss the one he or she made.

Mythology

Have small groups of students prepare short presentations on one or more of the mythological figures Hurston mentions in the excerpt: Pluto, Persephone, Ceres, Odin, or Hercules. Have each group explain the relationship between the figures and Hurston's autobiography and use drawings, illustrations, or fine art in their presentation.

First Thoughts

1. Did you iden-
tify with
Hurston's love
of books?
What were
your feelings
about books
when you
were younger?
Have your feel-
ings changed?

Reading Check

a. Why is Hurston's
grandmother afraid
of Zora's boldness?

b. Why do white
Northerners visit the
school?

c. What do the two
young ladies send
from Minnesota?

d. What are the narra-
tor's favorite books?

Shaping Interpretations

2. Consulting the notes you took while
reading, **characterize** the narrator.
Find examples from the text to support your
view of Hurston.

3. What qualities does the young Hurston exhibit
when she reads aloud in class?

4. What does Hurston think about the two women
who visit? How do you know?

5. Why do you think the visitors invite Hurston to
their hotel?

6. Why does the young Hurston treasure the
books the ladies from Minnesota send her?

Challenging the Text

7. Hurston was criticized by some of her contemporaries because they felt she did not place
enough emphasis on the racial oppression of
African Americans by the white community.
Using references from this autobiographical excerpt, explain whether you agree or disagree
with this criticism.

CHOICES: Building Your Portfolio

Writer's Notebook

1. Collecting Ideas for an Interpretive Essay

The **title** of an autobiography
can tell you a great deal about how a writer
views his or her life. Write down your reactions to the title *Dust Tracks on a Road*. Based
on what you learned about Hurston in the biography on page 750 and in this excerpt, why
do you think she chose this title? What does
it reveal about her life experiences? Keep
your notes for possible use in the Writer's
Workshop on page 804.

Comparing Autobiographies

2. Real-Life Stories

In a brief essay, compare this passage from
Hurston's autobiography with the selection
from Benjamin Franklin's *Autobiography* (page
86). You might compare (a) the narrators'
actions and motives; (b) the narrators' relationships with other people; (c) the incidents
described and why the narrators might have
chosen to write about them.

Creative Writing / Performance

3. *Dust Tracks* Onstage

Autobiographies are often successfully
adapted and dramatized for the stage. Working with a group, prepare this excerpt from
Dust Tracks on a Road for performance. You
will have to assign scriptwriters, a director,
actors, costume designers, and set designers.
You might also need a narrator to tell the
parts of the story that are not told directly in
dialogue. Consider using music (such as
orchestral, rock, folk, blues, jazz, or rap) to
emphasize important moments.

ZORA NEALE HURSTON **759**

Reading Check

a. Her memories from the days of slavery
make her worry that Zora will be
harmed by whites.

b. They are curious to see an all-black
school.

c. a box packed with books and clothes

d. *Norse Tales, Greek and Roman Myths,*
Kipling's *Jungle Books,* the Bible, and
books by Robert Louis Stevenson and
Hans Christian Andersen

First Thoughts [Respond]

1. Possible responses: Students may or
may not identify with Hurston's
youthful love of books. Accept all
reasonable responses.

Shaping Interpretations [Interpret]

2. Self-assured, bright, strong-willed.
Supporting examples: Her independence in hitching rides in spite of
her parents' wishes, her reading
ability, her mischievous attitude
toward Bible stories.

3. Possible responses: Self-assurance,
dramatic flair, and intelligence—
demonstrated by her passionate
reading and deep understanding of
the text.

4. She is fascinated by their difference,
but worried about her appearance
and about being whipped in front of
them.

5. They notice how gifted she is and
wish to help and reward her. It also
seems possible that they like the
idea of doing a "good deed" more
than they actually want to get to
know Hurston.

6. She treasures the books because
they speak profoundly to her and
she didn't have many.

Challenging the Text [Evaluate]

7. She is recounting a time when she
was secure in her own community
and did not feel the sting of racial
oppression. Or she does show
the poverty and lost potential of
a segregated society, but only indirectly.

Grading Timesaver

Rubrics for each Choices assignment
appear on p. 182 in the *Portfolio Management System*.

CHOICES: Building Your Portfolio

1. **Writer's Notebook**   Ask students to speculate on how Hurston
might have viewed the legacy of her
writing. Be sure students save their
work for the Writer's Workshop
on p. 804.

2. **Writing**   You might have students
focus on the characteristics of self-
assurance and gentle self-mockery

3. **Performance**   Be sure to tell students to use all of Hurston's dialogue before creating their own.

Portrait of Langston Hughes by Winold Reiss. National Portrait Gallery, Washington, D.C., U.S.A.

Langston Hughes
(1902–1967)

One evening toward the end of 1925, the poet Vachel Lindsay was eating dinner in the Wardman Park Hotel in Washington, D.C. The busboy, a twenty-three-year-old African American, left three poems near Lindsay's plate. Lindsay was so impressed by the poems that he presented them in his reading that night, telling the audience that he had discovered a true poet—a young black man who was working as a busboy in the hotel restaurant. Over the next few days, articles about the "busboy poet" appeared in newspapers up and down the East Coast.

The busboy, Langston Hughes, was no beginning writer. In fact, when he shyly approached Lindsay, Hughes's first book of poetry, *The Weary Blues,* was about to be published by a prestigious New York company, and individual poems had appeared in numerous places. Lindsay warned the young poet about literary "lionizers" who might exploit him for their own purpose: "Hide and write and study and think. I know what factions do. Beware of them. I know what lionizers do. Beware of them." In response to Lindsay, Hughes wrote back: "If anything is important, it is my poetry, not me. I do not want folks to know me, but if they know and like some of my poems I am glad. Perhaps the mission of an artist is to interpret beauty to the people—the beauty within themselves. That is what I want to do, if I consciously want to do anything with poetry."

Before this encounter, Hughes had attended Columbia University and worked his way to Africa and back as a crew member on an ocean freighter. Ambitious and energetic, Hughes had learned early to rely on himself. He spoke German and Spanish; he had lived in Mexico, France, and Italy. In the years that followed his "overnight" celebrity, he earned his degree at Lincoln University, wrote fifteen volumes of poetry, six novels, three books of short stories, eleven plays, and a variety of nonfiction works.

Born in Joplin, Missouri, Hughes spent most of his childhood in Lawrence, Kansas, with his grandmother. When he was thirteen, she died, and he moved to Lincoln, Illinois, and then to Cleveland, Ohio, to live with his mother and stepfather.

Hughes began writing poems in the eighth grade, and he began publishing his work as a high school student in his school literary magazine. He read voraciously and greatly admired the work of Edgar Lee Masters, Vachel Lindsay, Amy Lowell, Carl Sandburg, and Walt Whitman.

The most important influences on Hughes's poetry were Walt Whitman and Carl Sandburg. Both poets broke from traditional poetic forms and used free verse to express the humanity of all people regardless of their age, gender, race, and class. Encouraged by the examples of Whitman and Sandburg, Hughes celebrated the experiences of African Americans, often using jazz rhythms and the repetitive structure of the blues in his poems. Toward the end of his life, he wrote poems specifically for jazz accompaniment. He was also responsible for the founding of several black theater companies, and he wrote and translated a number of dramatic works. His work, he said, was an attempt to "explain and illuminate the Negro condition in America." It succeeded in doing that with both vigor and compassion.

go.hrw.com
LEO 11-15

Before You Read
THE WEARY BLUES

Make the Connection
Sweet Blues
Among the great contributions of American culture to the world is the music produced by African Americans: orchestral, blues, ragtime, jazz, rap, and new musical expressions that you can hear every day.

The kind of music known as the blues started to attract attention at the turn of the century, eventually becoming widely popular in the United States and abroad and making stars out of such blues singers as Bessie Smith and Ethel Waters. In this poem, Hughes tries both to report the experience of a "sad raggy tune" and to capture some of its rhythms in words.

Quickwrite
Blues music has influenced all kinds of popular music, from rock and soul to country, folk, and jazz. Jot down any associations you have with the word *blues*. What do you already know about blues music? Is there any blues influence in the kinds of music you like?

Elements of Literature
Rhythm
Rhythm in poetry is the rise and fall of the voice, produced by the alternation of stressed and unstressed syllables. Langston Hughes uses several different kinds of rhythms in "The Weary Blues." As he says in the first line, he uses the "syncopated tune" of a piano. He also uses the rhythm

of everyday speech, the soulful rhythm of the blues, and even the formal meter of traditional poetry. His poems are true originals.

Background
On a March night in 1922, Langston Hughes sat in a small Harlem cabaret and wrote "The Weary Blues." In this poem, Hughes incorporated the many elements of his life—the music of

Southern black speech, the lyrics of the first blues he ever heard, and conventional poetic forms he learned in school. While the body of the poem took shape quickly, it took the poet two years to get the ending right: "I could not achieve an ending I liked, although I worked and worked on it." When he at last completed the poem, "The Weary Blues" marked the beginning of his literary career.

The Weary Blues

Langston Hughes

Droning a drowsy syncopated tune,°
Rocking back and forth to a mellow croon,
   I heard a Negro play.
Down on Lenox Avenue° the other night
5 By the pale dull pallor of an old gas light
      He did a lazy sway . . .
      He did a lazy sway . . .
To the tune o' those Weary Blues.
With his ebony hands on each ivory key
10 He made that poor piano moan with melody.
      O Blues!
Swaying to and fro on his rickety stool
He played that sad raggy tune like a musical fool.
      Sweet Blues!

A

B

1. **syncopated tune:** melody in which accents are placed on normally unaccented beats.
4. **Lenox Avenue:** street in Harlem.

Summary ■

The poem is written in rhymed couplets, with significant variations. It evokes feeling through use of alliteration, onomatopoeia, and simile.

The speaker re-creates the sounds and emotions he experiences while listening to an African American piano player singing the blues in a Harlem cafe. He suggests that even after the musician has gone to bed, the blues will keep playing in the player's mind.

Ⓐ Elements of Literature
Rhythm
❓ How would you describe the rhythm of this poem? [Possible responses: bluesy, syncopated, slowly rocking.] **What techniques does Hughes use to create this rhythm?** [Possible responses: alternation of accented and unaccented syllables ("the tune o' those Weary Blues"); alternation of long and short lines (ll. 2–3); repetition ("He did a lazy sway"); alliteration ("droning"/"drowsy"); assonance ("lazy sway"); onomatopoeia ("drowsy").]

Ⓑ English Language Learners
Connotation
Assist English language learners by asking volunteers to explain the connotations of *rickety* [unsteady], *raggy* [in a ragtime rhythm; tattered like a rag], and *fool* [used affectionately here]. Then discuss what connotations these colloquial words have in common and what general impression they leave of the piano player. [They all link the musician with poverty, uncertainty, and fatigue.]

Reaching All Students

Struggling Readers
After students have read and begun to discuss the poem, model a Save the Last Word for Me discussion with them based on your own favorite line from the poem. For specific instructions on how to apply this strategy, see the *Reading Strategies Handbook,* p. 77 in the *Reading Skills and Strategies* binder.

English Language Learners
Idioms such as "to and fro" (l. 12) and dialect such as "ma salf" (l. 20) are likely to be confusing. Some, such as "to and fro," can be pantomimed. Reading aloud should resolve any problems students encounter with this poem.

Advanced Learners
Like many other first-rate poems, "The Weary Blues" is carefully and subtly crafted to seem simple. Encourage students to find details and "touches" that mark the hand of a master. Examples include the syncopation of the line in which the word *syncopation* appears (l. 1); the slow, flexible beat that resembles the bass line of a blues piano; and the startling simile in the last line.

Out Chorus by Romare Bearden. Silkscreen (12⅜″ × 16½″).

RESPONDING TO THE ART

Romare Bearden (1914–1988) was a prominent African American painter, collagist, and illustrator. He trained in New York City in the 1930s and at the Sorbonne in Paris after army service during World War II. The young Bearden sharply criticized other black visual artists for failing to develop an artistic technique with as much originality as jazz music or the spiritual—but he later became an outspoken advocate for African American artists. The title of this work, *Out Chorus,* refers to the final chorus of a jazz piece.

Activity. Ask students how the painting relates to "The Weary Blues." [The musicians are probably playing jazz or blues. The painting includes a pianist, who might be like the one in the poem.] Then have them identify the instruments in the collage. [double bass, percussion, guitar, saxophones, trumpet, piano]

A **Elements of Literature**
Lyric Poetry
? This lyric poem contains a song lyric within it. Where is the song-within-the-poem? [ll. 19–22, 25–30] How does the language of the song lyrics differ from the rest of the poem? [The song is written in dialect. Its double negatives and mournful refrain emphasize the singer's unhappiness.]

B **Reading Skills and Strategies**
Making Inferences
? What troubles might the pianist be experiencing? [Possible response: He seems to carry a lifetime of burdens—which might have included poverty, loneliness, discrimination, heartache, or loss of a loved one.]

C **Critical Thinking**
Evaluating
? According to the Background headnote, Hughes spent two years on this ending. Do you think his final version is effective? Why? [Most students will praise the stark drama of the ending.]

15 Coming from a black man's soul.
        O Blues!
     In a deep song voice with a melancholy tone
     I heard that Negro sing, that old piano moan—
A   "Ain't got nobody in all this world,
20   Ain't got nobody but ma salf.
         I's gwine to quit ma frownin'
         And put ma troubles on the shelf."
     Thump, thump, thump, went his foot on the floor.
     He played a few chords then he sang some more—
25   "I got the Weary Blues
         And I can't be satisfied.
B   Got the Weary Blues
         And can't be satisfied—
         I ain't happy no mo'
30   And I wish that I had died."
     And far into the night he crooned that tune.
     The stars went out and so did the moon.
     The singer stopped playing and went to bed
     While the Weary Blues echoed through his head.
C 35 He slept like a rock or a man that's dead.

762 THE MODERNS

Listening to Music

"St. Louis Blues" by W. C. Handy, performed by Bessie Smith

Composer and bandmaster William Christopher Handy (1873–1958) helped make the blues successful as popular music. Perhaps the best known version of Handy's famous "St. Louis Blues" is the one by the "Empress of the Blues," Bessie Smith, whose music was said to be capable of causing mass hypnosis.

Activity
At the beginning of class play students the recording of Bessie Smith's "St. Louis Blues." Then have them reread the poem, focusing especially on its use of rhythm, repetition, and musical sound effects. Volunteers may want to try writing their own blues music to accompany Hughes's poem.

Birth of the Blues

When asked about the origins of the blues, a veteran New Orleans fiddler once said: "The blues? Ain't no first blues! The blues always been." The first form of blues, country blues, developed in several parts of the United States, most notably the Mississippi Delta, around 1900. Country blues tunes were typically sung by men—usually sharecroppers. The subject was often the relationship between men and women. As the contemporary blues singer B. B. King once said, the blues is about a man losing his woman.

From the start, blues music was improvisational—it changed with every singer and performance. Parts of lyrics were freely borrowed from other songs or based on folk songs or figures of speech. Lines might be repeated two or three times, with different accents and emphases, then answered or completed by a rhyming line:

> Black cat on my doorstep, black cat on my window sill. (repeat)
> If some black cat don't cross me, some other black cat will.
>
> —Ma Rainey

The blues catch on. The earliest blues singers, among them Charley Patton, Robert Johnson, and Blind Lemon Jefferson, played at country stores, at Friday- and Saturday-night dances, at cafes, and at picnics. The first popular blues recordings, made in the 1920s, featured female singers such as Ma Rainey and Bessie Smith backed by a piano or a jazz band.

When rural Southern African Americans migrated after World War I to cities like Chicago, New York, Detroit, St. Louis, and Memphis, the blues sound evolved further. Musicians sang about their experiences in the city, adding the electric guitar, amplified harmonica, bass, and drums to blues ensembles. Musicians such as Sunnyland Slim, T-Bone Walker, and Memphis Minnie pioneered the urban blues sound in the 1930s and 1940s; the next generation included the blues greats Muddy Waters, Howlin' Wolf, and B. B. King. Since then, blues music has influenced virtually every genre of music, including folk, country and western, and—most profoundly—rock. Elvis Presley, Bob Dylan, the Rolling Stones, Eric Clapton, and Bonnie Raitt have all borrowed freely from the blues tradition. Today, blues music is still being played and created by such artists as Buddy Guy, Etta James, Otis Rush, Koko Taylor, Keb' Mo', and Robert Cray. They are carrying on a musical tradition that was invented at a particular time and place—the American South in the early 1900s—to express the African American experience. The genius of the blues is that it has honored its origins even as it expresses universal hopes, fears, and sorrows.

LANGSTON HUGHES 763

Ⓓ Literary Connections
Blues Brother

Harlem Renaissance scholar Edward E. Waldron writes, "Many writers/poets have attempted for years to incorporate the essence of the blues into works outside the reference of music—i.e., into stories and poetry. One of the most successful in this endeavor was Langston Hughes, the 'Poet Laureate' of Black America. In his blues poetry Langston Hughes captures the mood, the feel, and the spirit of the blues; his poems have the rhythm and the impact of the musical form they incorporate. Indeed, the blues poems of Langston Hughes are blues as well as poetry."

Historical Connections
House Parties

Since discrimination and poverty often prevented African Americans from accessing large concert halls and other public venues, many early blues performers got their start at informal, private gatherings called house parties. These parties often featured dancing, bootleg liquor, and the fast, upbeat form of blues known as "jump blues." In the first half of this century, there was even a house party "circuit" across the South, an entertainment network in which legendary figures such as Robert Johnson and Howlin' Wolf began their careers.

Making the Connections

Cultural Connections

While blues songs often feature informal language and off-color subject matter, they usually follow a tight formal structure, much like a sonnet or a haiku. The blues stanza has a pattern of one long line, a second line that repeats the first or varies it slightly, and a third line that resolves the problem posed in the first two. An instrumental part then echoes the voice. In Hughes's poem, the speaker's descriptions take the instrumental part.

Getting Students Involved

Making a Classic Anthology

A classic work of the Harlem Renaissance was Alain Locke's anthology *The New Negro,* published in 1925. In this anthology writers struggled to convey the African American experience, expressing their pride in their heritage, their anger at the discrimination they faced, and their hope for the future. Ask students to imagine an anthology about themselves entitled *The New Teenager.* What articles, stories, and poems might they include to establish their identity? Ask students to work together to create a prospective table of contents.

Summary ∎

The speaker employs irony, figurative language, and free verse to evoke the economic and emotional distress of African Americans "on the edge of hell" in Depression-era Harlem.

Ⓐ Elements of Literature
Tone

Ask students to select words and phrases from each stanza that suggest the speaker's attitude or tone. Have students create a three-column chart, listing the words and phrases in the first column, their literal meanings in the second column, and their implicit meaning and tone in the third column. [Sample response: The phrase "edge of hell" literally means "the border of a place of punishment after death" and implies an attitude of despair about a life of poverty and oppression.]

Ⓑ Elements of Literature
Repetition

❓ How does the repeated use of both "remember" and "never" in this stanza develop the main idea or message of the poem? [Possible response: This repetition suggests that for these residents of Harlem, to remember is only to recall a series of obstacles and refusals.]

Ⓒ Critical Thinking
Interpreting

❓ What does the speaker imply when he says he looks "out on the world"? [Possible response: He implies that Harlem is excluded from the larger economic and social world.]

Before You Read
HARLEM

Make the Connection
Feeling Trapped

The Harlem Renaissance writers created many poems that were responses to the feeling of oppression that pervaded the lives of Harlem residents. Hughes himself wrote several poems called "Harlem." This poem is set during the Great Depression, a time when even a one-cent increase in the price of bread could be disastrous, when being black and poor meant that there were limited opportunities.

Quickwrite

How would it feel to be the victim of discrimination? List some adjectives describing a victim's emotions.

Elements of Literature
Tone

Tone is the attitude a writer takes toward the subject of a literary work, the characters or events in it, or the audience that it is directed to. Some early African American writers conveyed their real emotions under masks of carefully shaped observations, images, and thoughts. In "Harlem," Langston Hughes manipulates the poem's tone to both hide and reveal his feelings.

Harlem
Langston Hughes

Ⓐ Here on the edge of hell
Stands Harlem—
Remembering the old lies,
The old kicks in the back,
5 The old "Be patient"
They told us before.

Ⓑ Sure, we remember.
Now when the man at the corner store
Says sugar's gone up another two cents,
10 And bread one,
And there's a new tax on cigarettes—
We remember the job we never had,
Never could get,
And can't have now
15 Because we're colored.

Ⓒ So we stand here
On the edge of hell
In Harlem
And look out on the world
20 And wonder
What we're gonna do
In the face of what
We remember.

Making the Connections

Connecting to the Theme:
"I, Too, Sing America"

"Harlem" is a poem about the African American experience in the United States. Have students compare "Harlem" with Cullen's poems "Tableau" and "Incident." Ask students to compare and contrast the different ways in which each poem speaks out against oppression.

Crossing the Curriculum

Music

Rap is one of the most popular forms of African American music. Ask students to comment on the differences and similarities between rap and the poems "Harlem" and "The Weary Blues."

Harlem Street Scene (1975) by Jacob Lawrence. Serigraph (27″ × 24″).

RESPONDING TO THE ART

Jacob Lawrence (1917–)
usually paints in tempera, but
Harlem Street Scene is a serigraph,
or silk-screen print. The process
involves printing flat colors
through a piece of silk or fine
cloth. A stencil is cut for the areas
to be printed in one specific color,
another stencil is cut for each
additional color, and the print is
made one color at a time. (Other
works by Lawrence appear on
pp. 427, 428, 480, and 735.)
Activity. Have students contrast
the mood of Lawrence's print
with the mood of Hughes's poem
"Harlem." [Possible response: The
poem presents disturbing aspects
of Harlem life; the painting seems
more cheerful, perhaps because of
the musician, the children at play,
and the hint of a smile on the face
of the gentleman with the cane.]

BROWSING IN THE FILES

Writers on Writing. In his
autobiography, Hughes wrote
about his early work, "I had been
. . . a writer who wrote mostly
because, when I felt bad, writing
kept me from feeling worse; it put
my inner emotions into exterior
form, and gave me an outlet for
words that never came in conversation."

Getting Students Involved

Cooperative Learning

Multimedia. Have students work together in
groups of four to prepare a multimedia presentation that interprets one of Hughes's poems.
One group member should be chosen to direct
the group's progress and coordinate the final
presentation. Each of the other three members
will focus on a particular medium—art, photography, music, dance, video, or theater—to

interpret the poem. Students may create their
own drawings, paintings, photographs, musical
composition, dances, videotapes, or scenes, or
they may use works by established artists. The
final presentation should include a reading of
the poem, along with the audio and/or visual
interpretation.

Primary Sources

In this excerpt from his autobiographical memoir *The Big Sea,* Langston Hughes describes the ironies, contradictions, and pleasures of the years when African American culture in Harlem became fashionable among the white elite of New York. He recalls the vogue for Harlem's Cotton Club, which refused admission to African Americans, as well as the sudden appearance of famous white New Yorkers in his social circle. By contrast, he describes the spontaneous pleasure in African American culture which took place at private "rent" parties.

RESPONDING TO THE ART

Archibald John Motley, Jr.
(1891–1981) often painted gritty urban settings and declined to glorify or idealize his subjects. His favorite topics included high-energy scenes of Prohibition-era gambling and drinking in Harlem, and colorful glimpses of Paris night life. Over time, his style evolved from academic realism to the stylized distortions of works such as *Jockey Club.*

Activity. Ask students how the composition and content of Motley's scene mirror Hughes's description of Harlem in the 1920s. [Possible response: The contrast of the brightly lit club against the surrounding darkness, the approaching car, the woman with the poodle, and the other well-dressed people suggest the kind of club and clientele Hughes describes.]

PRIMARY Sources — AN ESSAY

Heyday in Harlem

Langston Hughes describes the vigor and excitement of Harlem in the 1920s and 1930s.

White people began to come to Harlem in droves. For several years they packed the expensive Cotton Club on Lenox Avenue. But I was never there, because the Cotton Club was a Jim Crow club[1] for gangsters and monied whites. They were not cordial to Negro patronage, unless you were a celebrity like Bojangles.[2] So Harlem Negroes did not like the Cotton Club and never appreciated its Jim Crow policy in the very heart of their dark community....

It was a period when, at almost every Harlem upper-crust dance or party, one would be introduced to various distinguished white

1. **Jim Crow club:** segregated nightclub.

2. **Bojangles:** Bill "Bojangles" Robinson (1879–1949), star of black musical comedies and vaudeville.

Jockey Club (1929) by Archibald John Motley, Jr. Oil on canvas.
Schomburg Center for Research in Black Culture. Art and Artifacts Division. The New York Public Library, Astor, Lenox and Tilden Foundations.

766 THE MODERNS

Taking a Second Look

Review: Taking Notes

Remind students that note-taking involves writing down the important points of a text, usually using words and phrases instead of complete sentences. Effective note-takers recognize main ideas and supporting details, then record them in their own words. They may also construct graphic organizers as part of their notes.

Activities

1. Have students form three groups to take notes on the lives of Langston Hughes, Zora Neale Hurston, and James Weldon Johnson, using the author biographies and Primary Sources essays. In each group, students should take notes individually, noting at least one main idea and three supporting details. They should then read their notes aloud and discuss why they chose to include specific pieces of information.

2. Have each group design and fill in two graphic organizers using their notes. Possible types of graphic organizers include a chart showing a writer's works and his or her subjects and themes, a cluster diagram showing a character profile of the writer, an outline indicating the central themes of a writer's life and work, or a timeline of the writer's life and career. Ask each group to present its graphic organizer to the class.

celebrities there as guests. It was a period when almost any Harlem Negro of any social importance at all would be likely to say casually: "As I was remarking the other day to Heywood—," meaning Heywood Broun.[3] Or: "As I said to George—," referring to George Gershwin.[4] It was a period when local and visiting royalty were not at all uncommon in Harlem. And when the parties of A'Lelia Walker, the Negro heiress, were filled with guests whose names would turn any Nordic[5] social climber green with envy. . . . It was a period when every season there was at least one hit play on Broadway acted by a Negro cast. And when books by Negro authors were being published with much greater frequency and much more publicity than ever before or since in history. It was a period when white writers wrote about Negroes more successfully (commercially speaking) than Negroes did about themselves. It was the period (God help us!) when Ethel Barrymore[6] appeared in blackface in *Scarlet Sister Mary*! It was the period when the Negro was in vogue. . . .

Then it was that house-rent parties began to flourish—and not always to raise the rent either. But, as often as not, to have a get-together of one's own, where you could do the black-bottom[7] with no stranger behind you trying to do it, too. Nontheatrical, nonintellectual Harlem was an unwilling victim of its own vogue. It didn't like to be stared at by white folks. But perhaps the downtowners never knew this—for the cabaret owners, the entertainers, and the speakeasy[8] proprietors treated them fine—as long as they paid.

3. **Heywood Broun** (1888–1939): American journalist during the 1920s and 1930s.
4. **George Gershwin** (1898–1937): great American composer of both popular and serious music.
5. **Nordic:** white.
6. **Ethel Barrymore** (1879–1959): American stage and movie actress.
7. **black-bottom:** popular dance of the late 1920s.
8. **speakeasy:** club where alcoholic drinks were sold illegally during Prohibition.

The Saturday night rent parties that I attended were often more amusing than any night club, in small apartments where God knows who lived—because the guests seldom did—but where the piano would often be augmented by a guitar, or an odd cornet, or somebody with a pair of drums walking in off the street. And where awful bootleg whiskey and good fried fish or steaming chitterling[9] were sold at very low prices. And the dancing and singing and impromptu entertaining went on until dawn came in at the windows.

These parties, often termed whist[10] parties or dances, were usually announced by brightly colored cards stuck in the grille of apartment house elevators. Some of the cards were highly entertaining in themselves:

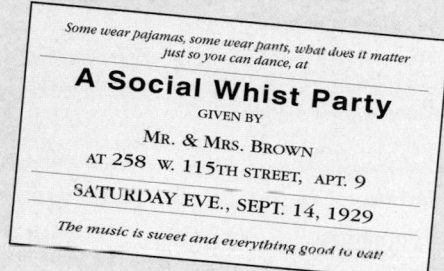

Some wear pajamas, some wear pants, what does it matter just so you can dance, at

A Social Whist Party

GIVEN BY

MR. & MRS. BROWN

AT 258 W. 115TH STREET, APT. 9

SATURDAY EVE., SEPT. 14, 1929

The music is sweet and everything good to eat!

Almost every Saturday night when I was in Harlem I went to a house-rent party. I wrote lots of poems about house-rent parties, and ate thereat many a fried fish and pig's foot—with liquid refreshments on the side. I met ladies' maids and truck drivers, laundry workers and shoeshine boys, seamstresses and porters. I can still hear their laughter in my ears, hear the soft slow music, and feel the floor shaking as the dancers danced.

—Langston Hughes,
from "When the Negro Was in Vogue,"
from The Big Sea

9. **chitterling** (chit′lin): food made from small intestines of pigs, deep-fried in hot oil.
10. **whist:** card game.

Background

According to historian David Levering Lewis, the leading lights of the Harlem Renaissance took part in "a moveable feast to which the anointed were invited" in Harlem apartments, where the guests might include British poet Sir Osbert Sitwell, the Crown Prince of Sweden, singer-actor Paul Robeson, novelist Sinclair Lewis, journalist H. L. Mencken, and composer George Gershwin at the piano.

Conditions for the average Harlem resident were not nearly so glamorous, however, and they became worse with the Depression. The repeal of Prohibition in 1933 brought a sharp downturn to the Harlem entertainment business, with many of the clubs either closing or moving downtown. As the Depression deepened, African Americans were typically faced with much worse living conditions than whites. Median family income in Harlem was cut almost in half. Harlemites lived with a tuberculosis rate five times that of white Manhattanites, and rates of pneumonia and typhoid were double those of the rest of the borough. African American rates of infant mortality and maternal death were also double those of whites. Apartment rent for Harlem residents took double the percentage of family income that it did for whites.

This was the backdrop against which house-rent parties, also called rent parties, became customary both as a boost to the partygivers' income and as a psychological relief from economic and social stress. Have students do further research and report on African Americans in Harlem and in other parts of the country during the Great Depression.

Skill Link

Researching Word Origins
Point out that most English words are derived from older words in English and words from other languages. Idioms, colloquialisms, slang terms, and regional or ethnic vocabulary often have especially interesting derivations. Have students find the derivations of the following words and phrases. Students may wish to use specialized resources, such as a dictionary of word origins and a dictionary of Black English.

1. Jim Crow
2. Negro
3. upper-crust
4. cabaret
5. speakeasy
6. guitar
7. cornet
8. bootleg
9. chitterling
10. whist

The Weary Blues

First Thoughts [Respond]

1. Possible response: The image of the musician sleeping like a rock or a dead man may strike many students as most powerful, because it dramatizes his despair and exhaustion.

Shaping Interpretations [Interpret]

2. In the first verse the speaker says that despite his isolation, he will put aside his troubles. But in the second, he despairs, and indicates that *nothing* could free him from his troubles.

3. They include "droning" (l. 1), "drowsy" (l. 1), "pale dull pallor" (l. 5), "Weary Blues" (l. 8), "moan" (ll. 10 and 18), "melancholy" (l. 17), "troubles" (l. 22).

4. The repetition of words and phrases and the syncopation of longer lines when combined with shorter lines contribute to the rhythmic effect. Examples include "droning a drowsy" (l. 1), "Pale dull pallor of an old gas light" (l. 5), "lazy sway" (l. 6), "poor piano moan with melody" (l. 10), "sad raggy tune like a musical fool" (l. 13), "thump, thump, thump" (l. 23).

5. Possible response: ominous and foreboding; the extinction of the stars and moon and the loss of light suggest quiet despair and possibly death.

6. The singer sleeps "like a rock" or like "a man that's dead." Possible responses: The singer has given up hope; sleep is the only place he finds relief from his troubles; his spirit is dead.

Harlem

First Thoughts [Respond]

1. Possible responses: angry, bitter, frustrated.

Shaping Interpretations [Interpret]

2. The poem suggests that many remember the lies they were told, physical abuse, poverty, and employment discrimination.

3. Possible response: It suggests that while the community is perched on the precipice of even greater hardship, nevertheless it "stands" as a testament to its people.

4. Possible responses: The repetition emphasizes the anger, frustration, and bitterness they feel.

MAKING MEANINGS

The Weary Blues

First Thoughts

1. What would you say is the most powerful **image** in "The Weary Blues"? Why?

Shaping Interpretations

2. How does the **message** of the blues singer's first verse contrast with that of his second?

3. What are some of the words in the poem that help to create a slow, weary, melancholy **mood**?

4. Review your Quickwrite to see how well this poem fits your concept of blues music. Describe how the poem's structure suggests the **rhythms** of blues music. Point out examples of **alliteration** and **onomatopoeia** that also add to the poem's wailing, musical effect.

5. How would you describe the emotional effect of the **image** in line 32?

6. What **similes** in the poem's last line describe how the singer sleeps? What do you think the last five words suggest?

Harlem

First Thoughts

1. Did any of the adjectives in your Quickwrite describe the feelings of the speaker in this poem? If not, what adjective would best describe the speaker's **tone**?

Shaping Interpretations

2. Name the specific hardships and injustices that the people of Harlem remember, according to the speaker in the poem.

3. In "Harlem," what does the speaker suggest when he says "Here on the edge of hell / Stands Harlem—"?

4. What is the effect of the repetition of "remember"?

5. Do you interpret the poem's final stanza as an expression of powerlessness, or as a threat? Defend your opinion.

6. How would you read this poem and "The Weary Blues" aloud to express the **tones** you hear in them?

5. Possible response: powerlessness, for knowing the past, they have little hope for the future. It might also indicate a stubborn resolve to do something, *anything*, to redress past wrongs.

6. Possible responses: angrily, sadly, defiantly.

Grading Timesaver

Rubrics for each Choices assignment appear on p. 183 of the *Portfolio Management System*.

CHOICES:
Building Your Portfolio

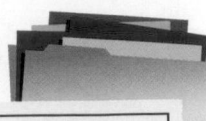

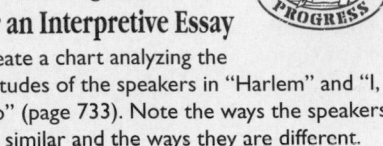

Writer's Notebook

1. Collecting Ideas for an Interpretive Essay

Create a chart analyzing the attitudes of the speakers in "Harlem" and "I, Too" (page 733). Note the ways the speakers are similar and the ways they are different. Save your notes for possible use in the Writer's Workshop on page 804.

Comparing Poems

2. Echoes of Whitman

In a brief essay, compare and contrast Walt Whitman's "I celebrate myself, and sing myself" (page 347) with Hughes's "I, Too" (page 733).

Creative Writing

3. The Harlem Beat

Write the opening paragraph for a newspaper article about the Harlem described in "Harlem." Include a portion of an interview with an imagined resident of Hughes's Harlem.

Describing Blues Music / Research

4. Liner Notes

Write brief liner notes (400 to 800 words) for a recording of classic blues songs. Your notes should briefly explain what the blues are and how they developed, as well as tell a bit about each of the blues artists (your choice) represented in the anthology.

Music / Performance

5. Blues Riff

Choose any passage in "The Weary Blues," and set it to a rhythmic or other musical accompaniment. Or adapt an existing blues melody to the poem. When you've brought music to Hughes's verse, perform your work for the class.

Make It New!

Theme

Experimentation and a New Poetry *Poets begin to experiment with symbolism and imagism. Pound's call "Make it new! Art is a joyful thing" also resulted in poems written in free verse, and on a range of subjects that could include a trash can as well as a Chinese porcelain vase.*

Reading the Anthology

Reaching Struggling Readers

The *Reading Skills and Strategies: Reaching Struggling Readers* binder includes a Reading Strategies Handbook that offers concrete suggestions to help students who have difficulty reading and comprehending text, or students who are reluctant readers. When a specific strategy is most appropriate for a selection, a correlation to the Handbook is provided at the bottom of the teacher's page under the head Reaching Struggling Readers. This head may also be used to introduce additional ideas for helping students read challenging texts.

Reading Beyond the Anthology

Read On At the end of The Moderns collections, the grade eleven book includes an annotated bibliography of books suitable for extended reading. The suggested books are related to works in these collections by theme, by author, or by subject. To preview the Read On for The Moderns period, please turn to p. T800.

Collection 16 Make It New!

Resources for this Collection

Note: All resources for this collection are available for preview on the *One-Stop Planner CD-ROM 2 with Test Generator.* All worksheets and blackline masters may be printed from the CD-ROM.

Internet Resources
go.hrw.com LE0 11-16

Selection or Feature	Reading and Literary Skills	Vocabulary, Language, and Grammar
The River-Merchant's Wife: A Letter (p. 774) Ezra Pound **Primary Sources: A Few Don'ts by an Imagiste** (p. 776) Ezra Pound	• *Graphic Organizers for Active Reading,* Worksheet p. 80 • *Literary Elements:* Transparency 25 Worksheet p. 76	
• **The Red Wheelbarrow** (p. 779) • **The Great Figure** (p. 780) **Critical Comment: So Much Depends** (p. 780) **Primary Sources: Williams Talks About Poetry** (p. 780) William Carlos Williams • **Spring and All** (p. 781) William Carlos Williams	• *Graphic Organizers for Active Reading,* Worksheet p. 81	• *Grammar and Language Links:* Run-on Sentences, Worksheet p. 67 • *Language Workshop CD-ROM,* Run-on Sentences
• **Anecdote of the Jar** (p. 784) • **Disillusionment of Ten O'Clock** (p. 784) Wallace Stevens **Critical Comment: Taking Dominion, Catching Tigers** (p. 785) **Primary Sources: Notebooks** (p. 786) Wallace Stevens	• *Graphic Organizers for Active Reading,* Worksheet p. 82	• *Daily Oral Grammar,* Transparency 48
Poetry (p. 787) Marianne Moore **Connections: Ars Poetica** (p. 789) Archibald MacLeish **Connections: Of Modern Poetry** (p. 790) Wallace Stevens	• *Graphic Organizers for Active Reading,* Worksheet p. 83	• *Daily Oral Grammar,* Transparency 49
Chicago (p. 792) Carl Sandburg	• *Graphic Organizers for Active Reading,* Worksheet p. 84 • *Literary Elements:* Transparency 26 Worksheet p. 79	
• **what if a much of a which of a wind** (p. 797) **Primary Sources: "Miracles are to come"** (p. 797) E. E. Cummings • **somewhere i have never travelled, gladly beyond** (p. 798) E. E. Cummings	• *Graphic Organizers for Active Reading,* Worksheet p. 85	
The American Language: American Slang (p. 801) Gary Q. Arpin		
Writer's Workshop: Interpretive Essay (p. 804)		
Language Workshop: Using the Literary Present (p. 807)		• *Workshop Resources,* p. 59
Learning for Life: Planning for the Future (p. 809)		

Other Resources for this Collection

- *Cross-Curricular Activities*, p. 16
- *Portfolio Management System*, Introduction to Portfolio Assessment, p. 1
- *Formal Assessment:* Literary Period Test, p. 160; Literary Elements Test, p. 158
- *Words to Own*, Worksheet p. 45
- *Test Generator*, Collection Test

Writing	Listening and Speaking Viewing and Representing	Assessment
• *Portfolio Management System*, Rubrics for Choices, p. 185	• *Audio CD Library*, Disc 21, Track 10 • *Portfolio Management System*, Rubrics for Choices, p. 185	• *Formal Assessment*, Selection Test, p. 149 • *Test Generator (One-Stop Planner CD-ROM)*
• *Portfolio Management System*, Rubrics for Choices, p. 186	• *Audio CD Library*, Disc 21, Tracks 11, 12, 13 • *Portfolio Management System*, Rubrics for Choices, p. 186	• *Formal Assessment*, Selection Test, p. 150 • *Test Generator (One-Stop Planner CD-ROM)*
• *Portfolio Management System*, Rubrics for Choices, p. 187	• *Audio CD Library*, Disc 21, Tracks 14, 15 • *Portfolio Management System*, Rubrics for Choices, p. 187	• *Formal Assessment*, Selection Test, p. 152 • *Test Generator (One-Stop Planner CD-ROM)*
• *Portfolio Management System*, Rubrics for Choices, p. 188	• *Audio CD Library*, Disc 21, Tracks 16, 17 • *Portfolio Management System*, Rubrics for Choices, p. 188	• *Formal Assessment*, Selection Test, p. 153 • *Test Generator (One-Stop Planner CD-ROM)*
• *Portfolio Management System*, Rubrics for Choices, p. 190	• *Audio CD Library*, Disc 21, Track 18 • *Viewing and Representing:* Fine Art Transparency 16; Worksheet p. 64 • *Portfolio Management System*, Rubrics for Choices, p. 190	• *Formal Assessment*, Selection Test, p. 154 • *Test Generator (One-Stop Planner CD-ROM)*
• *Portfolio Management System*, Rubrics for Choices, p. 191	• *Audio CD Library*, Disc 21, Tracks 19, 20 • *Portfolio Management System*, Rubrics for Choices, p. 191	• *Formal Assessment*, Selection Test, p. 154 • *Test Generator (One-Stop Planner CD-ROM)*
		• *Formal Assessment*, The American Language Test, p. 156
• *Workshop Resources*, p. 31 • *Writer's Workshop 2 CD-ROM*, Interpretation	• *Viewing and Representing*, HRW Multimedia Presentation Maker	• *Portfolio Management System*, p. 192
		• *Portfolio Management System*, Rubrics, p. 195

 Transparency  CD-ROM  Video  Audio CD

Collection 16 **Make It New!**

Skills Focus

Selection or Feature	Reading Skills and Strategies	Elements of Literature and Language	Writing	Listening and Speaking	Viewing and Representing
The River Merchant's Wife: A Letter (p. 774) Ezra Pound	Identify Images, pp. 774, 777	Imagism, p. 771 Free Verse, p. 772 Turning Point, p. 777 Image, p. 777 Mood, p. 777 The Objective Correlative, p. 777	Compare Two Poems, p. 777 Explain the Use of Three Images as Objective Correlatives, p. 777 Write a Paragraph Using a Single Concrete Image to Suggest a Feeling, p. 777		
• **The Red Wheelbarrow** (p. 779) • **The Great Figure** (p. 780) • **Spring and All** (p. 781) William Carlos Williams		Title, p. 782 Paradox, p. 782	Identify Concrete Objects Used as Images by Williams, p. 782 Write an Imagist Poem, p. 782 Write a Poem Based on Images in a Painting or Photograph, p. 782	Write a Critique of a Poetry Reading, p. 782	
• **Anecdote of the Jar** (p. 784) • **Disillusionment of Ten O'Clock** (p. 784) Wallace Stevens	Analyze a Metaphor, pp. 784, 785	Metaphor, pp. 784, 785 Title, pp. 785–786 Subject, p. 786 Tone, p. 786 Image, p. 786 Figures of Speech, p. 786 Symbols, p. 786 Rhyme, Meter, and Sound Effects, p. 786 Theme, p. 786	Freewrite an Explanation of How the Elements of Literature Work Together in a Particular Poem, p. 786 Write an Essay Analyzing a Poem, p. 786 Write an Analytical Essay, p. 786		
Poetry (p. 787) Marianne Moore	Paraphrase, p. 791	End Rhyme, p. 791 Exact Rhyme, p. 791 Slant Rhyme, p. 791	Compare Ideas About Poetry, p. 791 Write a Letter to a Poet, p. 791 Write a "Poetry Is . . ." List, p. 791 Write a Poem Based on a Nature Article, p. 791	Prepare and Present a Poetry Reading, p. 791	
Chicago (p. 792) Carl Sandburg		Image, pp. 792, 795 Apostrophe, pp. 792, 795 Epithets, p. 795	Compare and Contrast Two Poems by Different Authors, p. 795 Write an Apostrophe Including Five Epithets, p. 795	Prepare and Present an Oral Performance of the Poem, p. 795	Use a Graphic to Organize Information, p. 795 Create a Collage, p. 795
• **what if a much of a which of a wind** (p. 797) • **somewhere i have never travelled,gladly beyond** (p. 798) E. E. Cummings	Paraphrase a Stanza of a Poem, p. 799	Image, p. 799 Rhyme Scheme, p. 799 Slant Rhyme, p. 799 Figures of Speech, p. 799 Synesthesia, p. 799 Paradox, p. 799 Syntax, p. 799 Theme, p. 799 Tone, p. 799 Structure, p. 799	Paraphrase a Poem by Cummings, p. 799 Write an Essay Evaluating a Poet's Ideas in Relation to His Work, p. 799 Write an Essay Comparing Poems by Two Authors, p. 799	Create a Melody to Accompany a Poem, and Perform the Song, p. 799	
The American Language: American Slang (p. 801) Gary Q. Arpin		Slang, p. 801 Standard English, p. 802	Identify the Full-Form of Clipped Slang, p. 803 Explain Local Slang Terms, p. 803	Compile a List of Slang Terms, and Discuss the Base Metaphors, p. 803	
Writer's Workshop: Interpretive Essay (p. 804)	Use a Double-Entry Journal, p. 805		Write an Essay Interpreting a Work of Literature, a Movie, or a Work of Visual Art, pp. 804–806		
Language Workshop: Using the Literary Present (p. 807)	Correct Verb Tense, p. 807	Literary Present, p. 807	Revise Sentences to Make Verb Tenses Consistent, p. 807		
Reading for Life: Obtaining Information from an Internet Database (p. 808)	Conduct an Internet Search, p. 808 Evaluate a Database, p. 808		Research a Topic on the Internet, and Write a Report, p. 808		
Learning for Life: Planning for the Future (p. 809)			Research Contemporary Issues Related to Aging, p. 809		Design a Brochure, p. 809 Create a Documentary, p. 809 Create a Visual Display, p. 809

MAKE IT NEW!

Pound
Williams
Stevens
Moore
Sandburg
Cummings

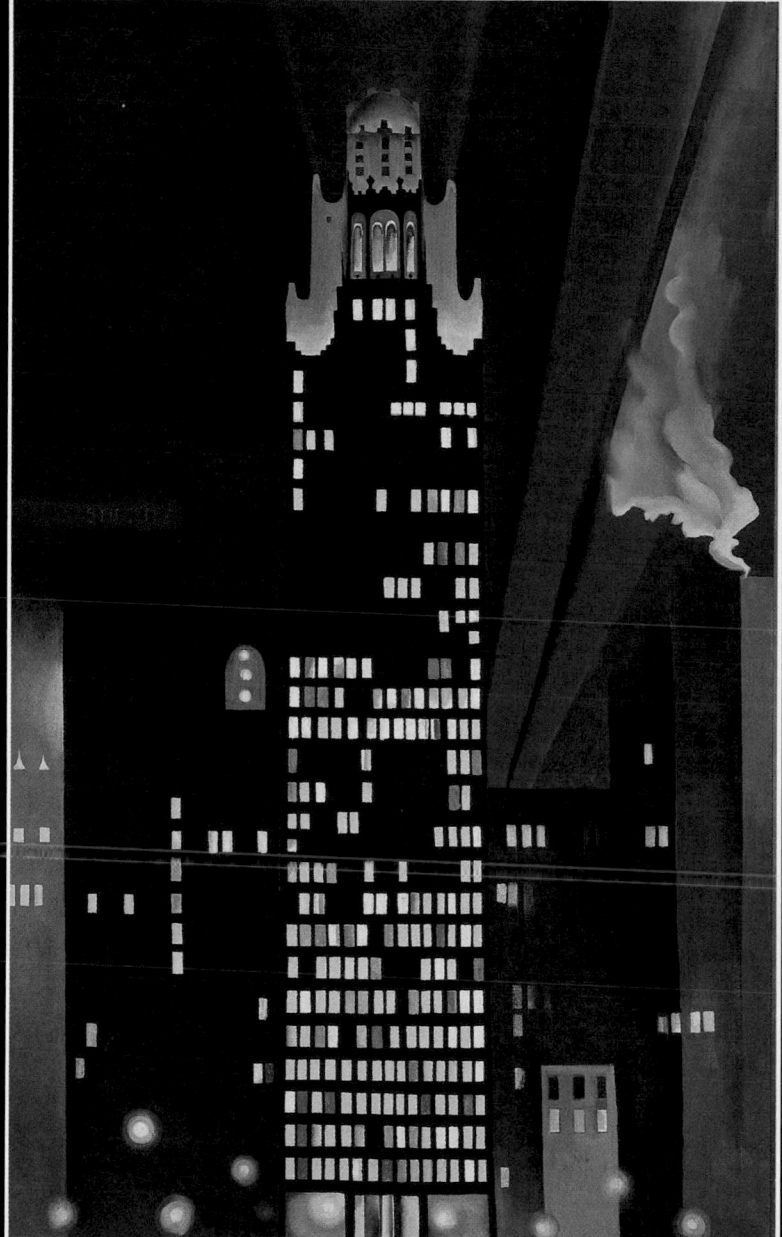

Make it new! Art is a joyous thing.

—Ezra Pound

The Radiator Building— Night, New York, 1927 (1927) by Georgia O'Keeffe. Oil on canvas (48″ × 30″).

Collection of Fisk University, Nashville, Tennessee. ©1998 The Georgia O'Keeffe Foundation/Artists Rights Society (ARS), New York.

Responding to the Quotation

Have students read Pound's challenge and then write a brief interpretation of it. What might Pound mean by "new" art? Why does he emphasize the "joyous" quality of artistic creation? [Possible response: Pound feels that art should reflect a spontaneous joy in creation, which constantly demands new forms and new artistic strategies.]

RESPONDING TO THE ART

One of the most influential figures in twentieth-century American art, **Georgia O'Keeffe** (1887–1986) used clear, strong colors to capture the sensuous and abstract qualities of her subjects—especially the natural world with its flowers, bones, shells, rocks, and mountains.

Activity. Have students discuss how this painting might represent Pound's sense of newness and joy in art. [Possible response: O'Keeffe's building is both stylized and functional, modern and beautiful. As architecture and art, it represents a joy in innovation and industry.]

Writing Focus: Interpretive Essay

The following **Work in Progress** assignments in this collection build to a culminating **Writer's Workshop** at the end of Collection 16.

Writer's Workshop: Expository Writing / Interpretive Essay (p. 804)

Symbolism, Imagism, and Beyond
by John Malcolm Brinnin

Left margin column

A Literary Connections
Charles Baudelaire
An important forerunner of both the Symbolists and the Imagists, French poet Charles Baudelaire (1821–1867) was strongly influenced by the writings of Edgar Allan Poe, who emphasized the conscious choice of sounds, images, and atmosphere to create an overall emotional effect.

B Cultural Connections
Symbols
❓ What are some of the religious, national, and psychological symbols that most people are familiar with? [Possible responses: cross, star of David, crescent; eagle, buffalo, rising sun; snow (for purity), red (for passion).] Why might the Symbolists have sought to avoid such symbols? [Possible response: because they have predictable, clichéd associations and fail to bring out the freshness and immediacy of experience.]

C Literary Connections
Romanticism
Briefly review the definition of Romanticism. Ask students to skim the table of contents for the names of some of the authors and major works in the American Romantic tradition.

D Literary Connections
Poète Maudit
French Symbolist poet Paul Verlaine used the term *poète maudit* (French for "accursed poet") to characterize the poet as an outcast of modern society, feared and reviled by those in power because the poet sees the spiritual malaise of the times.

Resources ▭

Viewing and Representing
Videocassette B, Segment 6
Available in Spanish and English. This *Visual Connections* segment explores the working of modern American poets.

Crossing the Curriculum

Art
Have students do research on French Symbolist painters, who shared a theoretical foundation with the Symbolist writers. They might look up Odilon Redon, Pierre Bonnard, Edouard Vuillard, and Paul Gauguin. Ask them to bring to class copies of paintings by these artists and to explain what they have in common with the Symbolist poets.

T770

Main body

Sometime in the early twentieth century, Americans awoke to a sense that their own national culture had come of age. This was true in poetry and in painting, in music and in dance, even in the new architecture of the skyscraper. Ironically, American poets found their new inspiration in Paris rather than their homeland. Learning from the French Symbolist poets, who dominated French literature from about 1875 to 1895, Americans were able to produce a new type of poetry through which the true American genius could speak.

Symbolism: The Search for a New Reality

Symbolism is a form of expression in which the world of appearances is violently rearranged by artists who seek a different and more truthful version of reality. The Symbolist poets did not merely describe objects; they tried to portray the emotional effects that objects can suggest. But don't be misled by the term *symbolism*. It has nothing to do with the religious, national, or psychological symbols we are all familiar with. In fact, the Symbolists were concerned with getting rid of such symbols, which they saw as having become dull and meaningless through overuse. The Symbolists stressed instead the need for a trust in the nonrational. Imagination is more reliable than reason, the Symbolists argued, and just as precise. With their emphasis on the mysterious and the intuitive, Symbolists hoped to bring revelation—self-discovery—to the reader through poems that lead the imagination to discover truths.

Symbolism was a new manifestation of the **Romanticism** that had swept over Europe and the United States in the nineteenth century. The Romantics had stressed the importance of feeling and the independence of the individual, and they had made a great stand against the mechanization of human life. In the natural world, the Romantics found messages that spoke to the soul and gave it strength.

The Symbolists, however, could find neither solace nor spiritual renewal in nature. By the start of the twentieth century, nature had been subjected to so much scientific classification and interpretation that it had been stripped of much of its mystery. Artists now faced the onslaught of the modern world, which in spite of advances in science and technology suffered increased poverty, violence, and conflict. The Symbolist poets saw this new world as spiritually debased, and they faced it with a distaste amounting to outrage. They knew they could not transform or erase the modern world, though, so their revolt was spiritual. They tried to redefine what it meant to be human in a time when individualism was succumbing to the power of mass culture.

770 THE MODERNS

 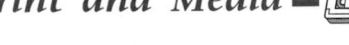 

Resources: Print and Media

Reading
• *Words to Own*, p. 45
Viewing and Representing
• *Visual Connections* Videocassette B, Segment 6

Assessment
• *Preparation for College Admission Exams*, p. 55
• *Test Generator (One-Stop Planner CD-ROM)*
Internet
• go.hrw.com (keyword: LE0 11-16)

Night Fires (c. 1919) by Joseph Stella. Pastel on paper (22 ½″ × 29″).
Milwaukee Art Museum, Gift of Friends of Art.

Imagism: "The *Exact* Word"

The two Americans who first came into close contact with Symbolism and introduced the techniques of the movement to the United States were Ezra Pound (page 773) and T. S. Eliot (page 661). With the help of several British poets, a group of Americans led by Pound founded a school perhaps better known and understood in the United States than Symbolism itself. This was **Imagism,** which flourished in the years 1912–1917. **E**

Like the Symbolists, Imagists believed that poetry can be made purer by concentration on the precise, clear, unqualified image. Imagery alone, the Imagists believed, could carry a poem's emotion and message. It could do this almost instantly, without all the elaborate metrics and

SYMBOLISM, IMAGISM, AND BEYOND **771**

E **Historical Connections**
1912–1917
Remind students that in the United States, the years 1912–1917 marked a time of great industrial and economic growth, peak immigration, and a world war.

Reaching All Students

Struggling Readers

Give students the outline below. Filling it in as they read will help them identify the main ideas and facts in this complex essay. Have students extend the outline with their own categories as they read later sections.

I. French Symbolist Movement
  A. Dates:
  B. Main idea:
  C. Differences from Romanticism:
  D. Relation to modern, industrial society:

II. Imagism
  A. Dates:
  B. Important poets:
  C. Main idea:
  D. One source of inspiration:
  E. Definition of the poetic image:

Advanced Learners

A prose writer who "made it new" was Upton Sinclair (1878–1968), whose best known novel is *The Jungle* (1906). Sinclair ironically acknowledged that "I aimed at the public's heart [in the story of ill-treated immigrant workers] and by accident I hit it in the stomach [in the depiction of the dreadful, unsanitary conditions in the Chicago stockyards]." Have students read and report on *The Jungle* and on the food inspection laws it generated.

A Literary Connections
H. D.

Hilda Doolittle (1886–1961) is admired for the precise visual image in her poetry. Ezra Pound, with whom she had a college love affair, gave her *Hilda's Book* when their affair ended. It is a hand-bound set of poems which was kept private until her memoir of Pound was published in 1979.

B Literary Connections
Amy Lowell

Amy Lowell (1874–1925) was a member of a distinguished Boston family and a relative of poets James Russell Lowell (1819–1891) and Robert Lowell (1917–1977). When she replaced Ezra Pound as the de facto leader of the Imagists, he nicknamed the group the "Amygists" in recognition of her outspoken, dominant personality. A celebrated eccentric, Lowell kept numerous dogs and smoked large, black cigars.

C Literary Connections
Haiku

The most popular poetic form in Japan, haiku shares with Imagism an emphasis on the precise image to suggest emotion. It differs from most Imagist poems, however, in its adherence to a rigid form: seventeen syllables arranged in three lines of five, seven, and five syllables each.

D Background
Revise, Revise, Revise

Ezra Pound recalled the inspiration for this poem: "Three years ago in Paris I got out of a 'metro' train at La Concorde, and saw suddenly a beautiful face, and then another and another, and then a beautiful child's face, and then another beautiful woman, and I tried all that day to find words for what this had meant to me, and I could not find any words that seemed to me worthy, or as lovely as that sudden emotion." This extremely short poem took a long time to write. Pound's first attempt contained thirty lines; his second, fifteen. A year after that subway ride he settled on this two-line poem.

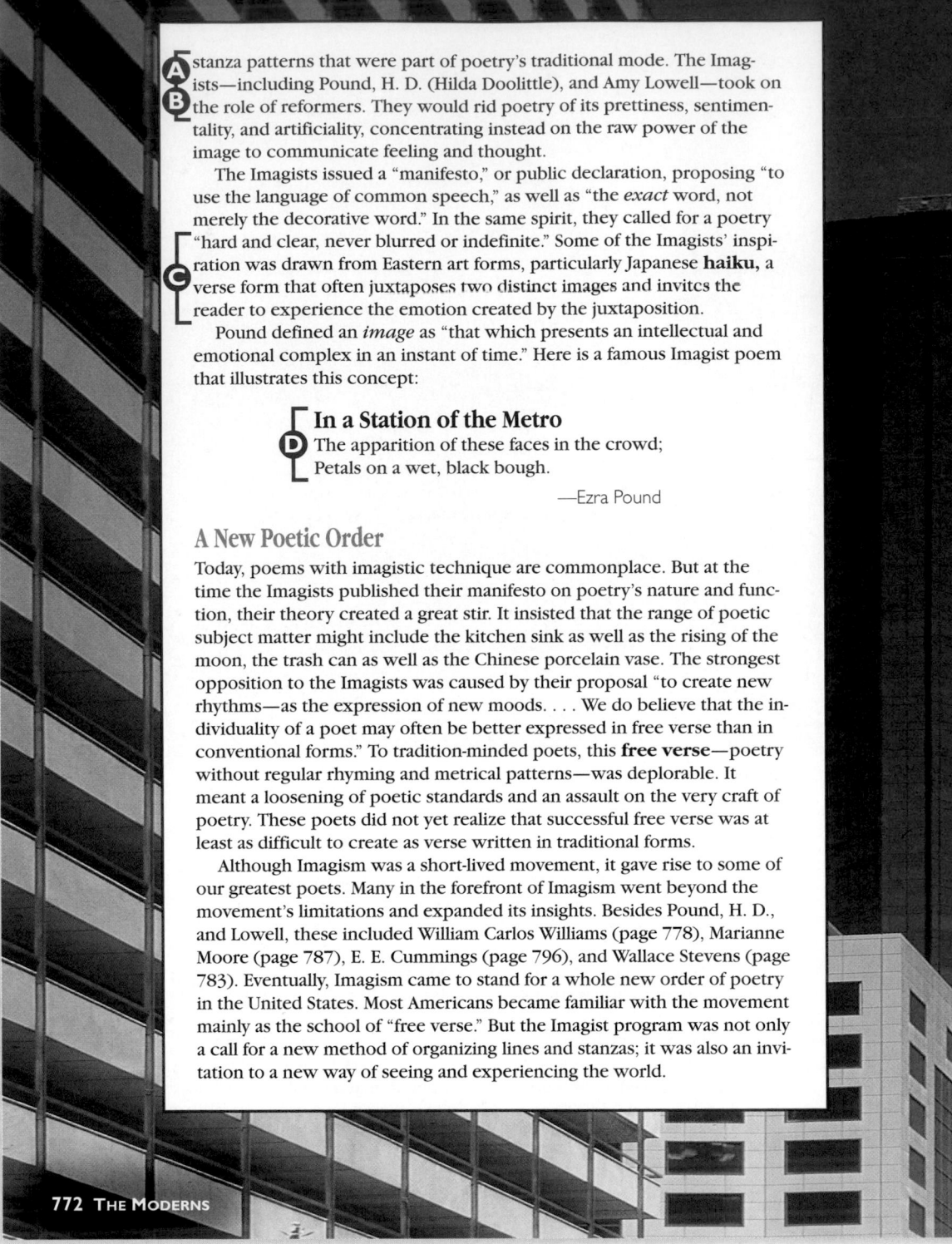

stanza patterns that were part of poetry's traditional mode. The Imagists—including Pound, H. D. (Hilda Doolittle), and Amy Lowell—took on the role of reformers. They would rid poetry of its prettiness, sentimentality, and artificiality, concentrating instead on the raw power of the image to communicate feeling and thought.

The Imagists issued a "manifesto," or public declaration, proposing "to use the language of common speech," as well as "the *exact* word, not merely the decorative word." In the same spirit, they called for a poetry "hard and clear, never blurred or indefinite." Some of the Imagists' inspiration was drawn from Eastern art forms, particularly Japanese **haiku,** a verse form that often juxtaposes two distinct images and invites the reader to experience the emotion created by the juxtaposition.

Pound defined an *image* as "that which presents an intellectual and emotional complex in an instant of time." Here is a famous Imagist poem that illustrates this concept:

In a Station of the Metro
The apparition of these faces in the crowd;
Petals on a wet, black bough.

—Ezra Pound

A New Poetic Order

Today, poems with imagistic technique are commonplace. But at the time the Imagists published their manifesto on poetry's nature and function, their theory created a great stir. It insisted that the range of poetic subject matter might include the kitchen sink as well as the rising of the moon, the trash can as well as the Chinese porcelain vase. The strongest opposition to the Imagists was caused by their proposal "to create new rhythms—as the expression of new moods. . . . We do believe that the individuality of a poet may often be better expressed in free verse than in conventional forms." To tradition-minded poets, this **free verse**—poetry without regular rhyming and metrical patterns—was deplorable. It meant a loosening of poetic standards and an assault on the very craft of poetry. These poets did not yet realize that successful free verse was at least as difficult to create as verse written in traditional forms.

Although Imagism was a short-lived movement, it gave rise to some of our greatest poets. Many in the forefront of Imagism went beyond the movement's limitations and expanded its insights. Besides Pound, H. D., and Lowell, these included William Carlos Williams (page 778), Marianne Moore (page 787), E. E. Cummings (page 796), and Wallace Stevens (page 783). Eventually, Imagism came to stand for a whole new order of poetry in the United States. Most Americans became familiar with the movement mainly as the school of "free verse." But the Imagist program was not only a call for a new method of organizing lines and stanzas; it was also an invitation to a new way of seeing and experiencing the world.

772 THE MODERNS

Using Students' Strengths

Musical Learners

The Symbolists and Imagists were poetic innovators distinguished by the striking originality and immediacy of their images. Ask students to think of musical groups that have an innovative approach to composition, technique, or performance and to list these groups' innovative qualities. Students may then compile a tape of innovative music and another of more conventional music and play them both for the class, comparing and contrasting the two.

Visual Learners

Ask students to design visual symbols to represent issues important to them. Students may redesign a symbol to replace a well-known symbol (like the peace sign), or they may make up their own symbols for new issues. Ask students to explain each element of their symbol to the class, emphasizing how color, line, form, and texture each contribute to the central idea.

Ezra Pound

(1885–1972)

Boris De Rachewiltz/New Directions Publishing.

Ezra Pound is remembered by many people as the man who was charged with treason during World War II and who spent many years in a psychiatric hospital. This notoriety has tended to obscure Pound's impact on American poetry. But his influence is still apparent everywhere; the generations of poets who have come after Pound have kept alive a complex memory of a man whose career wavered between brilliance and episodic madness.

Pound was born in Hailey, Idaho, and grew up in Pennsylvania. He taught at a conservative religious college for a while but his bohemian lifestyle was out of tune with his surroundings.

In search of greater personal freedom and contacts with European poets, Pound settled in London in 1908. There he became a self-appointed spokesperson for the new poetic movement known as Imagism. He also became a self-exiled critic of American life and torchbearer for any art that challenged the complacent middle class.

Pound—whose slogan was "Make it new!"—was a born teacher whose advice was sought by the most brilliant writers of the period. T. S. Eliot acknowledged Pound's valuable advice when he dedicated his great poem *The Waste Land* (1922) to Pound.

After World War I, Pound felt the need for even broader horizons than London offered him. He moved to Paris in 1921, and to Italy three years later, where he continued to write poetry and criticism. And now came a tragic turning point in Pound's life. His interest in economics and social theory led him to support Benito Mussolini, the Fascist dictator of Italy.

When World War II broke out, Pound stayed in Italy and turned propagandist for Mussolini's policies. In his radio broadcasts from Italy, Pound denounced the struggle of the United States and its allies against Germany, Italy, and Japan. Many of these broadcasts were viciously antisemitic.

When the American army advanced northward up the Italian peninsula in 1945, Pound was taken prisoner. He was confined to a cage on an airstrip near Pisa and eventually returned to the United States to be tried for treason. But psychiatrists judged him to be mentally incompetent, and in 1946 the poet was committed to St. Elizabeth's, at the time designated as a hospital for the criminally insane, in Washington, D.C.

Twelve years later, he was released through the intercession of writers, including Archibald MacLeish and Robert Frost, who argued that his literary contributions outweighed his disastrous lack of judgment and his notorious bigotry. Pound returned to Italy, where he lived the rest of his life. During these last years of exile, a reporter once asked Pound where he was living. "In hell," Pound answered. "Which hell?" the reporter asked. "Here," said Pound, pressing his heart. "Here."

When he died in Venice, Pound left behind a body of work extending from the delicate lyrics he wrote at the turn of the century to *The Cantos*, an enormous epic he did not complete until well over fifty years later. He also left a public record that still uncomfortably involves scholars and historians in "The Case of Ezra Pound."

go.hrw.com
LE0 11-16

EZRA POUND **773**

OBJECTIVES
1. Read and interpret the poem
2. Identify images
3. Analyze objective correlatives
4. Express understanding through critical and creative writing

SKILLS
Literary
- Analyze objective correlatives

Reading
- Identify images

Writing
- Collect ideas for an interpretive essay
- Analyze three objective correlatives
- Use an image to express feelings

Viewing/Representing (ATE)
- Compare the tone of an artwork with the tone of a poem

Planning

- **Block Schedule**
  Block Scheduling Lesson Plans with Pacing Guide
- **Traditional Schedule**
  Lesson Plans Including Strategies for English-Language Learners
- **One-Stop Planner**
  CD-ROM with Test Generator

Resources: Print and Media

Reading
- *Graphic Organizers for Active Reading*, p. 80
- *Audio CD Library*
  Disc 21, Track 10

Elements of Literature
- *Literary Elements*
  Transparency 25
  Worksheet, p. 76

Assessment
- *Formal Assessment*, p. 149
- *Portfolio Management System*, p. 185
- *Test Generator (One-Stop Planner CD-ROM)*

Internet
- go.hrw.com (keyword: LE0 11-16)

Summary ■

Through a series of imagistic flash-backs, the speaker evokes various stages of her life and how she felt about her husband at those times: during their childhood, at her marriage when she was fourteen, and now when she is sixteen and he has gone away. The final images reveal how the beauty of the natural world aggravates the pain she now feels over her husband's long absence. She closes her "letter" by asking that he inform her when he will be returning so she can come out to meet him.

FROM THE EDITOR'S DESK
We thought students would be interested in this poem by Pound because, although the speaker is roughly the same age as readers of this text, she has a sharply different perspective on male/female relationships that is rooted in her culture and historical period.

Ⓐ Reading Skills and Strategies

Identifying Images

❓ What emotions and character traits do the images in these lines suggest? [Possible response: The images convey the creativity and self-sufficiency of both children, as well as the speaker's nostalgia for these days of innocent indifference.] **How might these images provide a meaningful contrast with the later stanzas of the poem?** [In this stanza, the speaker is indifferent to her future husband's comings and goings, absorbed in her game. Later, she mourns his absence terribly.]

Ⓑ Critical Thinking

Speculating

❓ What do these lines allow you to infer about the circumstances of the speaker's marriage and how she feels about it for the first year? Cite specific details to support your answer. [The speaker's mistrustful silence before her husband and her reference to him as "My Lord" suggest that it was a formal, arranged marriage and that for the first year the speaker was uncertain of her feelings for her husband.]

THE RIVER-MERCHANT'S WIFE: A LETTER

Make the Connection

Missing You
Have you ever been moved to write a letter to someone you loved and missed? In this letter-poem, Pound assumes the voice of a river merchant's wife as she contemplates her life, love, and longing. This poem is a tribute to Li Po (701–762), one of the greatest Chinese poets. Though Pound crosses generations, cultures, continents, and gender, the intimate tone of the poem creates a bridge for the reader, inviting understanding and even identification with the eighth-century Chinese speaker.

Reading Skills and Strategies

Identifying Images
This poem is not a word-for-word translation of Li's poem but an adaptation based on the feelings and images that Pound experienced when reading translations of the original poem. As you read, note **images** that seem to suggest specific emotions.

Handscroll: *Wang Hsi-chih Watching Geese* (detail) (c. 1235–before 1307) by Ch'ien Hsüan. Ink and color on paper (9⅛″ × 36½″).

The River-Merchant's Wife: A Letter

Li T'ai Po

Ezra Pound

　　While my hair was still cut straight across my forehead
　　Played I about the front gate, pulling flowers.
　　You came by on bamboo stilts, playing horse,
　　You walked about my seat, playing with blue plums.
5　And we went on living in the village of Chokan:
　　Two small people, without dislike or suspicion.

　　At fourteen I married My Lord you.
　　I never laughed, being bashful.
　　Lowering my head, I looked at the wall.
10　Called to, a thousand times, I never looked back.

　　At fifteen I stopped scowling,
　　I desired my dust to be mingled with yours

Reaching All Students

Struggling Readers
Have students read the title of the poem. Then read them the first six lines and ask students to identify the *I* and the *you*. As they read the rest of the poem, have students construct a two-column graphic organizer. In one column, students should list details, characteristics, and inferences about the speaker, "I." In the second column they should list the same information for the absent "you."

English Language Learners
Remind students that poets sometimes use unusual word order to emphasize a word or to create a rhythm. Point out two instances of unusual word order. [in l. 2: "Played I" and in l. 7: "I married My Lord you."] Have students explain how these lines would be written in normal word order.

The Metropolitan Museum of Art, Gift of The Dillon Fund, 1973 (1973.120.6). Photograph © 1981 The Metropolitan Museum of Art.

Forever and forever and forever.
Why should I climb the lookout?

15 At sixteen you departed,
You went into far Ku-to-yen, by the river of swirling eddies,
And you have been gone five months.
The monkeys make sorrowful noise overhead.

You dragged your feet when you went out.
20 By the gate now, the moss is grown, the different mosses,
Too deep to clear them away!
The leaves fall early this autumn, in wind.
The paired butterflies are already yellow with August
Over the grass in the West garden;
25 They hurt me. I grow older.
If you are coming down through the narrows of the river Kiang,
Please let me know beforehand.
And I will come out to meet you
          As far as Cho-fu-Sa.

EZRA POUND 775

Using Students' Strengths

Verbal Learners

Have students compose a return letter from the speaker's husband that parallels the form of her letter. In other words, they should use images to convey his feelings about each stage of their relationship.

Visual Learners

Ask students to create their own visual interpretation of the poem, incorporating Pound's images in a four-panel work.

This excerpt from Pound's article in the March 1913 issue of *Poetry* contains a wide range of advice and criticism directed at Pound's fellow poets and includes some of the founding propositions of Pound's Imagism. These include the Imagist emphasis on the use of concrete objects rather than figurative or abstract language to convey emotion and ideas, and the Imagist exploration of irregular line lengths and meters. Pound also offers more general advice to beginning poets.

Ⓐ Background

Poetry magazine was founded in Chicago by Harriet Monroe, a descendant of President James Monroe. In 1912, she wrote to Pound in England, asking him to contribute to the magazine. Pound proposed that he be the magazine's European editor and used the magazine to promote his ideas about poetry and the poems of his friends.

Ⓑ Appreciating Language
Style

American essayist E. B. White (1899–1985) gave similar advice in his addition to William Strunk, Jr.'s famous little book *Elements of Style*: "Write with nouns and verbs, not with adjectives and adverbs. The adjective hasn't been built that can pull a weak or inaccurate noun out of a tight place."

Ⓒ Appreciating Language
The Craft of Poetry

Pound also had a critical perspective on the writing of free verse: "[Free verse] has brought faults of its own. The actual language and phrasing is often as bad as that of our elders without even the excuse that the words are shoveled in to fill a metric pattern or to complete the noise of a rhyme sound."

PRIMARY Sources | AN ARTICLE

Ⓐ Ezra Pound wrote the following "rules" for poets in an article in the March 1913 issue of *Poetry* magazine. Many of them are useful to all writers.

A Few Don'ts by an Imagiste

It is better to present one Image in a lifetime than to produce voluminous works. . . .

Pay no attention to the criticism of men who have never themselves written a notable work. Consider the discrepancies between the actual writing of the Greek poets and dramatists, and the theories of the Greco-Roman grammarians, concocted to explain their meters.

Language

Ⓑ Use no superfluous word, no adjective, which does not reveal something.

Don't use such an expression as "dim lands of peace." It dulls the image. It mixes an abstraction with the concrete. It comes from the writer's not realizing that the natural object is always the *adequate* symbol.

Go in fear of abstractions. Don't retell in mediocre verse what has already been done in good prose. Don't think any intelligent person is going to be deceived when you try to shirk all the difficulties of the unspeakably difficult art of good prose by chopping your composition into line lengths. . . .

Don't imagine that the art of poetry is any simpler than the art of music, or that you can please the expert before you have spent at least as much effort on the art of verse as the average piano teacher spends on the art of music.

Be influenced by as many great artists as you can, but have the decency either to acknowledge the debt outright, or to try to conceal it. . . .

Rhythm and Rhyme

. . . Let the neophyte know assonance and alliteration, rhyme immediate and delayed, simple and polyphonic, as a musician would expect to know harmony and counterpoint and all the minutiae of his craft. No time is too great to give to these matters or to any one of them, even if the artist seldom have need of them. . . .

Consider the way of the scientists rather than the way of an advertising agent for a new soap.

The scientist does not expect to be acclaimed as a great scientist until he has *discovered* something. He begins by learning what has been discovered already. He goes from that point onward. He does not bank on being a charming fellow personally. He does not expect his friends to applaud the results of his freshman classwork. Freshmen in poetry are unfortunately not confined to a definite and recognizable classroom. They are "all over the shop." Is it any wonder "the public is indifferent to poetry"?

Ⓒ Don't chop your stuff into separate *iambs*. Don't make each line stop dead at the end, and then begin every next line with a heave. Let the beginning of the next line catch the rise of the rhythm wave, unless you want a definite longish pause. . . .

If you are using a symmetrical form, don't put in what you want to say and then fill up the remaining vacuums with slush.

—Ezra Pound

Making the Connections

Connecting to the Theme: "Make It New!"

The title of this collection is from a quotation by Ezra Pound: "Make it new! Art is a joyous thing." The poem, however, is an adaptation of one by an eighth-century Chinese poet. Explore with students how an adaptation of another poet's work can "make it new."

Assessing Learning

Check Test: True-False

1. The speaker and her husband did not know each other as children. [False]
2. The speaker married at the age of fourteen. [True]
3. The husband deserted his wife. [False]
4. Nature provides comfort to the speaker. [False]
5. The speaker offers to meet her husband. [True]

MAKING MEANINGS

First Thoughts

1. Which line or image in this poem do you think is most important or most vivid? Compare your choices in class.

Shaping Interpretations

2. What events are referred to in the first four stanzas?

3. How is the third stanza a **turning point** in the poem? What do you think the wife expresses in line 14?

4. What **image** suggests that the husband was reluctant to leave home?

5. How is the season appropriate to the **mood** of the poem?

6. What hurts the young wife in line 25, and why? In the same line, why does she say, after only five months, that she grows "older"?

7. What does the wife promise to do?

8. Think of possible reasons why the husband left. Do you think he will ever return? What may have delayed him?

ELEMENTS OF LITERATURE

The Objective Correlative

Throughout Pound's poem, the letter writer's feelings are expressed more often by references to objects and activities than by direct statements. This is a method often practiced by Pound and identified by T. S. Eliot as the **objective correlative.** Eliot defined this term as "a set of objects, a situation, a chain of events which shall be the formula of [a] *particular* emotion." According to Eliot, the only valid way to express an emotion in art is to find such an objective correlative.

The term *objective correlative* soon became a permanent part of the vocabulary of poetic analysis. Several years earlier, however, Pound had anticipated the essence of the term, when he referred to poetry as "a sort of inspired mathematics" that gives us "equations for the human emotions."

Both Eliot and Pound believed that poetry is a means of expressing emotions *indirectly* but

precisely. Poetry does this by finding the images and actions that best embody a feeling. (An example in Pound's poem might be the "river of swirling eddies.") This kind of poetic shorthand leaves the reader without the connections that usually join the parts of an argument, a story, or even most poems. Readers are forced to supply these connections and find the logic of a poem by themselves.

Not every poem deals in objective correlatives. Most poems have a logical or narrative sequence that is easy to recognize. But other poems are organized, not by a logical sequence, but by a *psychological* one. Such poems will make no logical sense until you supply the connecting links. These are the poems that can be analyzed according to Eliot's definition of the objective correlative.

CHOICES: Building Your Portfolio

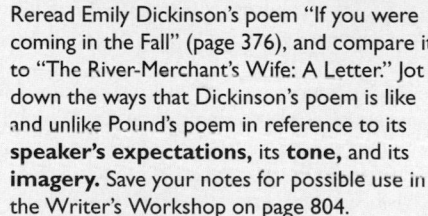

Writer's Notebook

1. Collecting Ideas for an Interpretive Essay

Reread Emily Dickinson's poem "If you were coming in the Fall" (page 376), and compare it to "The River-Merchant's Wife: A Letter." Jot down the ways that Dickinson's poem is like and unlike Pound's poem in reference to its **speaker's expectations,** its **tone,** and its **imagery.** Save your notes for possible use in the Writer's Workshop on page 804.

Analyzing Imagery

2. Indirect Expression

Choose at least three **images** from the poem, and, in a paragraph, explain how each image is used as an **objective correlative** to convey emotion indirectly.

Creative Writing

3. Tell It Slant

Choose a topic you feel strongly about. Then, think of a single concrete **image** that suggests your feelings. In a paragraph, include your image in a way that communicates your feelings but doesn't express them directly.

MAKING MEANINGS

First Thoughts [Respond]

1. Possible responses: "I desired my dust to be mingled with yours" because it shows the depth of the speaker's passion; "The paired butterflies" because it gracefully evokes her sense of loss.

Shaping Interpretations [Interpret]

2. (1) The girl and boy play together as children. (2) The girl marries the boy. (3) The wife stops scowling. (4) The husband leaves on a long journey.

3. It reveals her change from shy wariness to deep commitment. She expresses her acceptance of and contentment with a life she initially resisted.

4. He drags his feet as he leaves.

5. The fall season, a time associated with dying and loss, contributes to the mood of sadness and longing.

6. The "paired butterflies" contrast with her own sense of separation. The separation makes her more conscious of the passage of time.

7. If her husband sends advance notice of his return, she will come to meet him along the way.

8. The husband may have left for business. He might have been delayed (or perhaps even killed) by unforeseen circumstances.

Grading Timesaver

Rubrics for each Choices assignment appear on p. 185 in the *Portfolio Management System.*

CHOICES: Building Your Portfolio

1. **Writer's Notebook** Have students fill out a graphic organizer like the following for each poem, and then have them compare and contrast the two charts.

Image	Tone	Expectation

2. **Analyzing Imagery** Remind students that images are concrete while emotions are abstract. Struggling readers may benefit from a small-group brainstorming session to list the images in the poem.

3. **Creative Writing** Allow students to write a poem instead of a paragraph, as long as the poem contains a single concrete image that conveys a strong feeling.

William Carlos Williams

(1883–1963)

Pach/Bettmann.

William Carlos Williams was born in Rutherford, New Jersey, where he lived and practiced medicine as a pediatrician and obstetrician for most of his adult life. While studying medicine at the University of Pennsylvania, he came in contact with Ezra Pound (page 773). Pound's theories of Imagism had a considerable influence on Williams's early verse, which was published in *Poems* (1909) and *The Tempers* (1913). During the next two decades, however, Williams went on to evolve his own distinctive poetic style, which he called *objectivism*.

Williams defined the source of his poetry as "the local," by which he meant a strict focus on the reality of individual life and its surroundings. Williams looked for a return to the barest essentials in poetry. In this respect, he opposed such contemporaries as T. S. Eliot (page 661) and, to a certain extent, Pound himself, in their frequent use of allusions to art, history, religion, and foreign cultures. (Williams and Eliot, in fact, made no secret of their dislike of each other's work.)

In addition to poetry, Williams produced novels, plays, essays, and several autobiographical memoirs. His influence on twentieth-century American poetry, especially since World War II, has been considerable, and he was awarded a Pulitzer Prize in 1963. His masterpiece is the long epic *Paterson,* a poem that appeared in five volumes over a twelve-year span (1946–1958). In this partly autobiographical epic, a poet wanders the neighborhoods of Paterson, New Jersey, an industrial town near Williams's home, and meditates on the variegated experiences of urban life.

In his insistence on local topics and colloquial speech, Williams was allying himself with the kind of poetic revolution championed by the English Romantics a century earlier. William Wordsworth, in his preface to the third edition of *Lyrical Ballads* (1802), had written that poetry should treat "incidents and situations from common life . . . in a selection of language really used by men."

Williams deliberately wrote in a spare, detached style about commonplace subjects, the very opposite of what many nineteenth-century American writers had thought of as poetic material. Using as his slogan "No ideas but in things," Williams wrote of such sights and events as animals at the zoo, schoolgirls walking down a street, a piece of paper blowing down a street, or a raid on the refrigerator. As Marianne Moore, an admirer, pointed out, Williams's topics are "American"—crowds at the movies, turkey nests, mushrooms among fir trees, mist rising from a duck pond, a ballgame.

 go.hrw.com
LEO 11-16

  —  — *Resources: Print and Media* —

Make the Connection

A Recovery from Stodginess

The Imagists wanted to describe commonplace subjects, just as they are. These new poets were very different from many popular poets of the nineteenth century, who believed that poetry should be "about" certain poetic subjects. Do you think there is any limitation on subject matter?

Quickwrite

Make a list of at least six subjects from your ordinary world that might be subjects for a poem.

The Red Wheelbarrow

William Carlos Williams

so much depends
upon   **A**

a red wheel
barrow   **B**

glazed with rain
water

beside the white
chickens.

Critical Comment

So Much Depends

Williams's "The Red Wheelbarrow" at first glance seems to be very slight. But it has proved to have the leverage power that the ancient Greek inventor and mathematician Archimedes spoke of when he said, "Give me a place to stand, and I will move the world." Where William Carlos Williams stood was a place where ordinary things were *not* used as symbols or metaphors; they were simply ordinary things. The world he moved was the world of poetry. Before Williams, poets saw things not as things in themselves, but as objects to be used (to be compared, to be endowed with alien meaning, or to be played with); in themselves, things meant nothing.

How do we talk about this poem? When we consider analyzing it, where do we begin? Trying to answer these questions leads only to frustration. This poem is a composition of words so complete and simple that it denies all attempts to treat it as a poem.

And yet, there is the temptation to ask what happens in the brief course of the poem that has made it so durable. It was, after all, not a typographical accident; it was composed, and as such it can be analyzed. But our analysis must be concerned with the modest premises of the poem; we must not attempt to give it meanings that it does not claim.

The first line contains a vague but enormously suggestive phrase that leads the reader to expect an answer. (*What* depends on *what*?) But, except for the metaphorical lift of the word *glazed* in line 5, what the reader gets is only bare, flat reality—a moment captured as permanently as if it had been photographed. If the poem can be said to have some movement, some progress, from its first word to its last, it would be in what we call "reverse action." Our yearning toward what might be implicit in "so much depends" is quietly checked by the homely beauty of what *is*.   **C**

Do you like or dislike this poem? Why?

Reaching All Students

Struggling Readers

The first two poems by Williams are so simply stated that they may leave students asking "What's the big deal?" especially since the sight of a wheelbarrow or of a fire engine is not likely to cause a deep emotional response in young people today. Ask students what everyday sights or sounds produce strong feelings in them and why a wheelbarrow or a fire engine might cause an emotional response in someone.

English Language Learners

In "Spring and All," the speaker describes the arrival of spring in an unspecified geographic location. Suggest that students describe a change in season specific to a geographic area they know. Invite them to include the names of specific plants, insects, and other natural objects.

Summary ■ ■ ■

"The Red Wheelbarrow" opens with the suggestive and dramatic assertion that "so much depends/upon" . . . whatever follows. Yet these two lines—which hint that what follows will represent an important idea or phenomenon—are followed by a simple, concrete description of white chickens next to a wet, red wheelbarrow. With this reversal of expectations, Williams captures the poetic power of this ordinary, concrete image—not as a symbolic substitute for an abstract idea, but as a powerful moment of reality-in-itself.

In "The Great Figure," Williams again raises his readers' expectations, this time with the title's ironic hint that the poem will concern a great leader or idol. What follows is a powerful, luminous, but again decidedly concrete and pragmatic image of a gold number "5" painted on a fire truck that rumbles through a dark city.

A Critical Thinking

Speculating

❓ What might depend on a red wheelbarrow? [A wheelbarrow is essential to the work of a farm; a family's livelihood could depend on that. Williams might also be stressing the importance of noticing the vividness and poetic power of everyday scenes and objects.]

B Elements of Literature

Imagery

❓ In a poem this short, diction, or word choice, becomes especially important. Which words are crucial to the imagery? [Possible responses: *red, white, glazed,* and *beside.*]

Critical Comment

This feature discusses the powerful effect that Williams's poem had on the world of poetry. It suggests that this poem is a work that refused traditional assumptions about what a poem is and how it should be read. Instead of using the central image as a symbol or metaphor, Williams uses it to communicate the "homely beauty of what *is.*"

C Reading Skills and Strategies

Responding to the Text

❓ Do you agree with this assessment of the reader's experience with this poem? [Some students may indicate that they became preoccupied with the question "What depends on what?"]

The Metropolitan Museum of Art, Alfred Stieglitz Collection, 1949 (49.59.1). Photograph © 1986 The Metropolitan Museum of Art.

Ⓐ Critical Thinking
Making Connections

? If you look at both "The Red Wheelbarrow" and this poem, which is the more purely Imagist poem? Why? [Possible responses: This poem is, because the speaker presents an image without comment; in "The Red Wheelbarrow," the words "so much depends" color the image. "The Red Wheelbarrow" is, because the poem is completely descriptive; in this poem, he personifies the fire truck as "tense and unheeded."]

Primary Sources

This feature contains two excerpts from Williams's *Autobiography,* which concern his pride and doubt about the poetic revolution that he helped produce. The first describes a dream in which his recently deceased father reappears only to dismiss his son's poetry. In the second, Williams considers the ambiguous goals and achievements of the "movement" he helped inaugurate. After linking this movement to the Impressionist, Dadaist, and Surrealist movements in painting and to the literary austerity of Pound's Imagism, Williams concludes that the overriding goal was the "recovery" of the poetic line "from stodginess"—to make it evoke experience itself, unmediated by literary interpretation.

T780

The Great Figure

William Carlos Williams

Among the rain
and lights
I saw the figure 5
in gold
5 on a red
  Ⓐ fire truck
moving
tense
unheeded
10 to gong clangs
siren howls
and wheels rumbling
through the dark city.

The Figure 5 in Gold (1928) by Charles Henry Demuth. Oil on composition board (36″ × 29¾″).

Williams Talks About Poetry

I'll never forget the dream I had a few days after he [Williams's father] died, after a wasting illness, on Christmas Day, 1918. I saw him coming down a peculiar flight of exposed steps, steps I have since identified as those before the dais of Pontius Pilate in some well-known painting. But this was in a New York office building, Pop's office. He was bare-headed and had some business letters in his hand on which he was concentrating as he descended. I noticed him and with joy cried out, "Pop! So, you're *not* dead!" But he only looked up at me over his right shoulder and commented severely, "You know all that poetry you're writing. Well, it's no good." I was left speechless and woke trembling.

. . .

What were we seeking? No one knew consistently enough to formulate a "movement." We were restless and constrained, closely allied with the painters. Impressionism, dadaism, surrealism applied to both painting and the poem.

What a battle we made of it merely getting rid of capitals at the beginning of every line! The immediate image, which was impressionistic, sure enough, fascinated us all. We had followed Pound's instructions, his famous "Don'ts," eschewing inversions of the phrase. . . . Literary allusions, save in very attenuated form, were unknown to us. Few had the necessary reading.

We were looked at askance by scholars and those who turned to scholarship for their norm. To my mind the thing that gave us most a semblance of a cause was not Imagism, as some thought, but the line: the poetic line and our hopes for its recovery from stodginess. I say recovery in the sense that one recovers a salt from solution by chemical action. We were destroyers, vulgarians, obscurantists to most who read; though occasionally a witty line, an unusual reference, or a wrench of the simile to force it into approximation with experience rather than reading—bringing a whole proximate "material" into view—found some response from the alert.

—William Carlos Williams,
from The Autobiography

Skill Link

Comparing and Contrasting

Remind students that critics often gain insight about a poet's work by finding similarities and differences among various poems. Use these questions to help students pinpoint the striking similarities and noticeable differences in "The Red Wheelbarrow" and "The Great Figure."

1. How do the two poems compare with respect to the use of sensory images? [Both poems use vivid color, but in "The Red Wheelbarrow" the image is frozen as if it were a photograph, while in "The Great Figure" the image seems blurred with speed.]
2. What contrast is there between the subjects of the two poems? [The wheelbarrow and the chickens are small, quiet subjects, while the fire truck is a large, loud one. The first scene is rural, while the second is urban.]
3. How do the moods of the two poems compare? ["The Red Wheelbarrow" is more peaceful than "The Great Figure."]

Make the Connection

Becoming Spring

Like many other poems by Williams, this one is about a process—a development, a transformation, or a condition at the point of change. Here the subject is the coming of spring, examined as seen under a magnifying glass. The poet also examines the feeling of spring, in which changes in nature are reflected in someone who observes them.

Quickwrite

Try to picture the look of nature as spring begins. Then, write down several visual images you associate with this turning point in the earth's yearly cycle. Be sure to mention the main colors of the images. Note also the feelings the images arouse in you.

Spring and All

William Carlos Williams

By the road to the contagious hospital°
under the surge of the blue
mottled clouds driven from the
northeast—a cold wind. Beyond, the
5   waste of broad, muddy fields
brown with dried weeds, standing and fallen

patches of standing water
the scattering of tall trees

All along the road the reddish
10 purplish, forked, upstanding, twiggy
stuff of bushes and small trees
with dead, brown leaves under them
leafless vines—

Lifeless in appearance, sluggish
15 dazed spring approaches—

They enter the new world naked,
cold, uncertain of all
save that they enter. All about them
the cold, familiar wind—

20 Now the grass, tomorrow
the stiff curl of wildcarrot leaf
One by one objects are defined—
It quickens:° clarity, outline of leaf

But now the stark dignity of
25 entrance—Still, the profound change
has come upon them: rooted, they
grip down and begin to awaken

23. **quickens:** enlivens; revives. The speaker may also be referring to a less common meaning: "enters the stage of pregnancy when the fetus's movement can be felt."

1. **contagious hospital:** hospital for people with contagious diseases.

WILLIAM CARLOS WILLIAMS **781**

Summary ■■

With concrete images, the speaker paints a picture of "lifeless" nature at the end of winter. He then traces the arrival of spring through the awakening of vegetation from its blind and senseless winter sleep—a description that subtly parallels human birth.

Ⓑ Struggling Readers
Reading Elliptical Constructions

❓ There are no verbs in the first fourteen lines of the poem. To aid comprehension, what verbs might be inserted, and where? [*Are* might be inserted before "driven." *Is* might be inserted after "Beyond" and after "All along the road."]

Ⓒ Background

This setting is a logical one for Williams, who was a practicing physician for most of his adult life. In the Foreword to his autobiography, Williams discussed the tension between his medical and poetic careers:

"I had my typewriter in my office desk. All I needed to do was to pull up the leaf to which it was fastened and I was ready to go. I worked at top speed. If a patient came in at the door while I was in the middle of a sentence, bang would go the machine—I was a physician. When the patient left, up would come the machine."

Ask students to discuss what two contradictory attitudes toward his writing are revealed in these excerpts. [Possible response: self-doubt and pride.]

Ⓓ Advanced Learners
Identifying Pronoun Antecedents

❓ The pronoun *They* in l. 16 comes as a surprise, as does the pronoun *It* in l. 23. What is the antecedent of each pronoun? [The antecedents of *They* come after the pronoun: *grass* and *curl*. *It* may refer to one of the *objects* or to *outline* or to life-giving spring itself.

Ⓔ Appreciating Language
Diction

❓ As explained in the footnote, the word *quickens* has several meanings. It also calls to mind the adjective *quick*. What point about spring does the speaker's choice of this word make? [Possible response: The word contrasts with the words *sluggish* and *dazed* in ll. 14 and 15. It suggests that spring has an element of sudden surprise.]

Getting Students Involved

Cooperative Learning

Homage to William Carlos Williams. The painting reproduced on p. 780 was a direct response to William Carlos Williams's poem "The Great Figure." Divide students into small groups based on their interests and/or strengths: visual, auditory, dramatic, or scientific. Ask each group to plan a homage to

William Carlos Williams using a mode of expression other than poetry. The homage might be visual, musical, dramatic, or factual. Remind groups to make use of each member's skills in the planning, drafting, and revising stages of their project.

First Thoughts [Respond]

1. Some students may say that both a fire engine speeding through a city and the rebirth of spring are ordinary. To others, the drama of a fire may seem out of the ordinary, and spring and human birth like mysteries of nature.

Shaping Interpretations [Interpret]

2. Possible responses: Diagonal lines create a sense of movement in the painting, as does the figure 5, which seems to speed toward the viewer. In the poem, the reader "hears" gong clangs, siren howls, and wheels rumbling.

3. Students may say that the red creates a feeling of excitement and the gold a sense of importance. Darker colors might make the poem ominous.

4. Possible response: The poem presents images of the awakening of vegetation in early spring. The "and All" of the title may refer to the speaker's experience of spring or to the human birth that the poem parallels.

5. It might refer to any creatures that grow and live.

6. *Still* may mean "quiet, unmoving," and it may also mean "nevertheless, even so." The paradox is that new growth could be quiet and immobile while it undergoes profound changes.

7. The words *naked, enter, quickens,* and *awaken* could refer to human birth as well as to the arrival of spring.

8. The speaker would probably not agree. The images of birth and the "dignity of entrance" suggest hope rather than cruelty.

Extending the Texts [Apply]

9. Some students may say they would use the simple images and colors mentioned in the texts. Others may say they would try to re-create the feeling of rustic usefulness in "The Red Wheelbarrow," of excitement and energy in "The Great Figure," and of quiet growth in "Spring and All."

MAKING MEANINGS

The Great Figure

Spring and All

First Thoughts

1. In "The Red Wheelbarrow" Williams says "so much depends" on an ordinary, workaday wheelbarrow. Do "The Great Figure" and "Spring and All" also focus on the very ordinary things in life? Explain.

Shaping Interpretations

2. The painter Charles Henry Demuth (1883–1935) was so moved by the dynamic imagery in "The Great Figure" that he painted *The Figure Five in Gold* (see page 780). What movement do you *see* in the painting? What do you *hear* in the poem itself?

3. How would the feeling of "The Great Figure" change if the colors were different? Try it.

4. What significance can you find in the **title** "Spring and All"?

5. The first three stanzas of "Spring and All" are about plants. The pronoun in line 16, however, may refer to more than plants. What broader meaning might the word *they* have?

6. Reread the last stanza of "Spring and All." Which two meanings of the word *still* make line 25 a **paradox**? (A paradox is a statement that appears self-contradictory but that reveals a kind of truth.)

7. As a physician, Williams delivered thousands of babies. Can you see any connections between that fact and the last three stanzas of "Spring and All"? What references would apply equally to the coming of spring and the birth of an infant?

8. The famous opening of *The Waste Land,* by T. S. Eliot, declares that "April is the cruelest month." Would the speaker of "Spring and All" agree with this view of the start of spring? Explain.

Extending the Texts

9. If you were an artist and wanted to paint what you see and feel in any of these poems by Williams, what images and feelings would you focus on? What colors would you use?

CHOICES: Building Your Portfolio

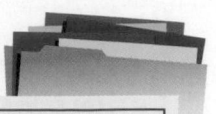

Writer's Notebook

1. Collecting Ideas for an Interpretive Essay

Jot down some notes about Williams's use of concrete objects to make you think in new ways about people, art, or life in general. Save your notes for possible use in the Writer's Workshop on page 804.

Creative Writing

2. An Imagist Poem

Write a brief imagist poem describing some subject from your everyday life. Before you write, reread what Williams says in his comments on poetry on page 780. Strive to capture a thing and a moment as precisely as you can. Your Quickwrite notes might help you find a subject.

Creative Writing

3. Picture Poem

Find a painting or photograph that interests you (perhaps one from this book). Write a six-line poem describing the **images** you see in the picture. Try to record details exactly as they are, without using them as symbols or ascribing any significance to them beyond the fact that they simply are what they are.

Reviewing a Performance

4. Springs to Life?

Along with a group of three or four classmates, listen to the performance of "Spring and All" on the HRW Audio CD or have a group member read the poem aloud. Then, each student (except the student reader, if any) should write a short review of the performance. Did the performer catch the poem's meaning and rhythm? Was the pronunciation clear, with the correct words emphasized? Exchange reviews, and discuss the similarities and differences of your critiques.

Grading Timesaver

Rubrics for each Choices assignment appear on p. 186 in the *Portfolio Management System.*

Wallace Stevens

(1879–1955)

The Bettmann Archive.

Americans are often surprised to learn that one of their greatest poets was a business executive who walked to his downtown office, sat on boards of directors, served as a vice president of a major insurance company, and became one of the pillars of a local society dedicated to the collection, investment, and distribution of money. Wallace Stevens was all of these and, almost incidentally, a genius of such magnitude that his place in American literature is still being reassessed and the depth of his vision ever more closely examined. Yet Stevens's life was a remarkably quiet, undramatic, and private one.

Stevens was born in Reading, Pennsylvania. He was educated at Harvard College and the New York Law School. Married in 1909 (to a woman who modeled for the image on the liberty-head dime), he and his wife had one child, Holly, who after his death assumed the editorship of his letters and other posthumously published works.

When he was thirty-six, Stevens moved to Hartford, Connecticut, where he entered the insurance business. He kept his creative life completely apart from his preoccupations as a business executive and maintained his literary friendships almost exclusively by correspondence. Happy with routine, a connoisseur of wines and French painting, and a lover of music, Stevens traveled to Cuba and often to Key West. Unlike most of his equally eminent contemporaries, he refused all invitations (until the last years of his life) to give interviews or to recite his poetry in public.

Almost forty-four when he published his first book of verse, *Harmonium* (1923)—a volume that sold a meager few hundred copies—Stevens came late and very quietly onto a scene already occupied by two quite different kinds of poetic expression: the colloquial rhythms and down-to-earth concerns of Carl Sandburg and Edgar Lee Masters, and the intellectual style exemplified by Ezra Pound and T. S. Eliot. Stevens shared the aspirations of both movements; yet he made his way along a path that avoided the extreme practices of either. His sense of place and American character kept him firmly rooted on native ground, but his grasp of metaphysical precision allowed him to soar into realms of "pure" poetry. Stevens went beyond where any other American poet had gone before.

Stevens admired the work of many contemporary American poets with whom he would seem to have little in common. Long before critics or the reading public were aware of William Carlos Williams's common speech and of his flat, almost casual rendering of everyday experience, Stevens knew exactly what his friend was up to. His respect and affection for Marianne Moore, his beloved "Marianna," was lifelong, as was his admiration for the precisely intricate structures that were the hallmark of her poetry. Toward Robert Frost, his attitude was one of friendly rivalry. "The trouble with you, Robert," Stevens once remarked in the course of one of their meetings, "is that [all of your poems] have *subjects*." That statement contains a clue to the originality of Stevens's work: For him, objects are important only as touchstones for the play of the imagination.

In 1955, Stevens's *Collected Poems* won the Pulitzer Prize in poetry. In a poem called "Of Modern Poetry" (printed in full on page 790), Stevens said this of his craft:

> It has to be living, to learn the speech of the
> place.
> It has to face the men of the time and to
> meet
> The women of the time. It has to think about
> war
> And it has to find what will suffice. It has
> To construct a new stage.

go.hrw.com
LE0 11-16

OBJECTIVES
Anecdote of the Jar/Disillusionment of Ten O'Clock
1. Read and interpret the poems
2. Analyze metaphor
3. Express understanding through critical writing

SKILLS
Reading
• Analyze metaphor

Writing
• Collect ideas for an interpretive essay
• Analyze poetry
• Write an analytical essay

Planning

• **Traditional Schedule**
  Lesson Plans Including Strategies for English-Language Learners

• **One-Stop Planner**
  CD-ROM with Test Generator

BROWSING IN THE FILES

Writers on Writing. In 1953, Stevens wrote to a friend: "It is a queer thing that so few reviewers seem to realize that one writes poetry because one must. Most of them seem to think that one writes poetry in order to imitate Mallarmé, or in order to be a member of this or that school. It is quite possible to have a feeling about the world which creates a need that nothing satisfies except poetry and this has nothing to do with other poets or with anything else."

Resources: Print and Media

Reading
• *Graphic Organizers for Active Reading,* p. 82
• *Audio CD Library*
  Disc 21, Tracks 14, 15

Writing and Language
• *Daily Oral Grammar*
  Transparency 48

Assessment
• *Formal Assessment,* p. 152
• *Portfolio Management System,* p. 187
• *Test Generator (One-Stop Planner CD-ROM)*

Internet
• go.hrw.com (keyword: LE0 11-16)

Summary ■■■

In "Anecdote of the Jar," the speaker places a jar on a hill in Tennessee. The "slovenly wilderness" rises up around it, "no longer wild."

In "Disillusionment of Ten O'Clock," the speaker presents an image of houses "haunted by white night-gowns" and contrasts the mundane dreams of the people in these houses with the exotic reveries of a drunken sailor.

Ⓐ Critical Thinking
Analyzing

❓ Why does the speaker repeatedly emphasize the roundness of the jar in ll. 2 and 7, rather than some other aspect? [Possible response: This geometrical, symmetrical quality is mostly a product of the human mind and does not often occur in nature. It also suggests the power of the human imagination to focus and give meaning to nature.]

Ⓑ Reading Skills and Strategies

Analyzing Metaphor

❓ What is the jar compared to through this implied metaphor? [to a king or a ruler] What idea is being expressed through this comparison? How is it possible for the jar to take dominion? [Possible response: As a product and symbol of the human imagination, the jar is the focal point that renders the chaotic wilderness intelligible and meaningful.]

Ⓒ Elements of Literature
Imagery

❓ Unlike the images of Ezra Pound and William Carlos Williams, which come from the concrete world, those of Wallace Stevens come from his imagination. What do the contrasting images of white and colorful nightgowns suggest about the people in the houses? [Possible responses: They are bland, uninteresting, undifferentiated; in a way, they are also dead (white is traditionally associated with ghosts).]

Ⓓ Critical Thinking
Speculating

❓ What kinds of things are they going to dream about? [Possible responses: realistic, everyday events; objects and events from the human-dominated world, rather than any aspect of the human or natural world that might disrupt the boundaries of normal life.]

T784

Before You Read
ANECDOTE OF THE JAR
DISILLUSIONMENT OF TEN O'CLOCK

Make the Connection
The World in Our Hands
People often say, "Life is what we make of it." Wallace Stevens developed that idea into a full-fledged philosophy of life and art. He built his poetry on the belief that our imaginations are always interacting with the world around us, with both engaged in a vital creative partnership. The result of this dynamic interplay of imagination and reality is our ever-changing experience of life.

Quickwrite

Do you think that most people you know have active and creative imaginations? Write down your thoughts in a few sentences.

Reading Skills and Strategies
Analyzing Metaphor
A **metaphor** is a figure of speech that makes a comparison between two unlike things. When you sense that a writer is using an **implied metaphor**—one that does not state explicitly the two things being compared—how do you determine the comparison being made?

For example, suppose a poem described a jar. You sense that the jar is more than a jar—but what? Start by listing the jar's qualities: It's made by skilled craftspeople; it comes in various sizes and shapes; it is useful; it often contains things; you can usually see through it. Now, use your imagination: Why didn't the poet describe a building or a statue or a stone? Why the *jar*?

Anecdote of the Jar
Wallace Stevens

    Ⓐ I placed a jar in Tennessee,
    And round it was, upon a hill.
    It made the slovenly wilderness
    Surround that hill.

5   The wilderness rose up to it,
    And sprawled around, no longer wild.
    The jar was round upon the ground
    And tall and of a port in air.

    Ⓑ It took dominion everywhere.
10   The jar was gray and bare.
    It did not give of bird or bush,
    Like nothing else in Tennessee.

784 THE MODERNS

Disillusionment of Ten O'Clock
Wallace Stevens

    The houses are haunted
    By white night-gowns.
    None are green,
    Or purple with green rings,
  Ⓒ 5 Or green with yellow rings,
    Or yellow with blue rings.
    None of them are strange,
    With socks of lace
    And beaded ceintures.°
 Ⓓ 10 People are not going
    To dream of baboons and periwinkles.°
    Only, here and there, an old sailor,
    Drunk and asleep in his boots,
    Catches tigers
15   In red weather.

9. ceintures (san'tyo͞orz): belts.
11. periwinkles (per'i·wiŋ'kəlz): saltwater snails.

Reaching All Students

Struggling Readers
To understand the implied metaphor in "Anecdote of the Jar," students have to know that one definition of art is that it orders the experiences of the world according to the artist's point of view. Discuss with students how a jar does the same thing; that is, it contains, limits, and gives shape to things.

English Language Learners
Two idioms in "Anecdote of the Jar" may need to be explained: in l. 8, *of a port* means "like a port," and in l. 11, *give of* means "produce" or "create."

Advanced Learners
Have students compare the images of nature expressed in both poems and the way in which nature images are used to develop the theme of each poem.

ritical Comment

Taking Dominion, Catching Tigers

Wallace Stevens's great subject—reality and the imagination—appears in virtually every poem he wrote. He knew of course that we live in the physical world that he called "things as they are." However, he knew too that we shape that world into something else, an imagined world that is the place where our deepest and truest experiences occur. The key to happiness is balancing those worlds. Too much reality leaves us dull, passive, overwhelmed by the ordinary. Too much imagina-

tion makes us creatures of fantasy, lightweight, out of touch with the actual.

In "Anecdote of the Jar," the jar creates an ordered world out of the chaos of nature. It is a work of art standing at the center of a universe that it has organized. It can't actually create a living bird or a bush, but without it all the birds and bushes have no meaning. In "Disillusionment of Ten O'Clock," the sailor's spectacular dream invigorates the environment around him. For Stevens, the jar and the dream accomplish the same purpose—creating a new, ordered, heroic world out of the real and the imagined.

MAKING MEANINGS

First Thoughts

1. Read "Anecdote of the Jar" and "Disillusionment of Ten O'Clock" at least twice. After each reading, write down what you think each poem is about. Exchange your ideas with a partner. How similar are your statements about the poems?

Anecdote of the Jar

Shaping Interpretations

2. Describe what the speaker does in the first stanza. What adjective does the speaker use to describe the jar? How does he describe the wilderness in which he places the jar?
3. In the second stanza, what effect does the jar have on the wilderness?
4. What does the jar "not give" in the last stanza?
5. Some critics say that the jar is a **metaphor** for the poet's act of imagination in creating this poem, or for the poem itself. Do you agree with either interpretation? Why or why not? What else could the jar stand for?
6. If the jar stands for the poet's art (or for any kind of art), what is the "wilderness" that the jar has "dominion" or control over?

7. Some other critics think the jar is a **metaphor** for human interference with nature. Reread the poem and see if you could justify this interpretation.

Disillusionment of Ten O'Clock

Shaping Interpretations

1. Describe the nightgowns that do *not* haunt the houses.
2. What *won't* the people in these houses dream about?
3. Why do you suppose the poet says that the houses are "haunted" by white nightgowns?
4. What is the speaker implying about the old sailor, based on the sailor's dream? How does the sailor contrast with the other people?
5. What could the "disillusionment" of the **title** refer to? (What does the speaker expect? What does he discover?)
6. List other fantastic things that these people will never dream about.

Critical Comment

This feature analyzes both Stevens poems as products of his philosophy of reality and imagination. For Stevens, human experience is a complex blend of reality's overwhelming, brute being and the imagination's meaningful transformation of that being. Thus, both the jar and the sailor's dream take the meaningless and banal chaos of reality and create a rich human world

MAKING MEANINGS

First Thoughts [Respond]

1. Students may say that "Anecdote of the Jar" is about poetry or art and that "Disillusionment of Ten O'Clock" is about imagination.

Anecdote of the Jar

Shaping Interpretations [Interpret]

2. The speaker places a jar on a hill in Tennessee. The jar is "round"; the wilderness is "slovenly."
3. The jar tames and gathers in the wilderness.
4. It does not "give" any living thing.
5. Students who agree may say that a poem gives shape to human experience, just as a jar gives shape to what is put in it. Those who do not agree may say that a jar is not a work of art and that it stands for human intervention in nature.
6. Possible response: The "wilderness" represents the world before it is given shape by human art and human perception.
7. Possible responses: The interpretation can be justified because the jar is described as "gray and bare," making it sound like a modern machine, or because there are repeated images of the jar's aggressive dominance.

Disillusionment of Ten O'Clock

Shaping Interpretations [Interpret]

1. They are colorful and patterned or ornate.
2. They won't dream about baboons, periwinkles, tigers, or red weather.
3. Possible response: "Haunted" implies a curse, a tragedy, an undesirable situation. The speaker implies the people's lack of imagination is a curse.
4. The speaker is implying that the sailor has a vivid imagination. The sailor's mind is colorful and unpredictable, while those of the others are dull and unimaginative.
5. Possible response: The "disillusionment" refers to the speaker's disappointment that a failure of imagination constrains people even in their dreams.
6. Possible responses: kangaroos, orange whales, baobab trees.

Rubrics for each Choices assignment appear on p. 187 in the *Portfolio Management System*.

CHOICES:
Building Your Portfolio

1. **Writer's Notebook** Suggest that students who have chosen the same poem compare and discuss their notes on the questions before individually writing their paragraphs.
2. **Analyzing Poetry** As a first step, students might paraphrase the aphorism they choose. Remind them to make reference to specific elements of the poem in support of their argument.
3. **Writing an Analytical Essay** Encourage students to develop multiple, concrete examples of where imagination is needed and how it is developed.

Primary Sources

This section contains a small sample of Wallace Stevens's aphorisms, particularly those that focus on the definition and purpose of poetry.

Ⓐ Background

Stevens's name for the notebooks in which he collected his thoughts about poetry, *Adagia*, comes from the same root as the word *adage*, an old saying accepted as truth. It may have been with tongue in cheek that he labeled his original thinking "adages." Have students choose the aphorism they like best and apply it to any poem they have read.

CHOICES: Building Your Portfolio

Writer's Notebook
1. Collecting Ideas for an Interpretive Essay

Use the following questions to analyze any poem in this collection. Then, freewrite a paragraph explaining how literary elements work together to help create the poem's meaning. Save your notes for possible use in the Writer's Workshop on page 804.

1. What is the **subject** of the poem?
2. What is the **tone** of the poem?
3. What **images** does the poet use?
4. What **figures of speech** does the poem contain?
5. What **symbols** does the poem contain?
6. How does the poet use **rhyme, meter,** and other **sound effects**?
7. Which elements are most important in the poem? Which are least important?
8. What does the poem's **title** mean?
9. What is the poem's **theme**?
10. What is your emotional response to the text?

Analyzing Poetry
2. A Poem's World

Choose one of Stevens's aphorisms in Primary Sources (see below), and in a short essay, apply it to either "Anecdote of the Jar" or "Disillusionment of Ten O'Clock." Explain the ways in which the poem reflects—or doesn't reflect—the aphorism.

Writing an Analytical Essay
3. Imagination: Necessary?

Refer to your Quickwrite notes, and write an essay about people's imaginative lives today. Where is imagination needed? How can imagination be nourished? How do children lose their imagination? If you wish, refer to Stevens's poems to make your point.

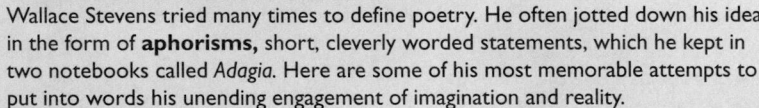

Ⓐ Wallace Stevens tried many times to define poetry. He often jotted down his ideas in the form of **aphorisms**, short, cleverly worded statements, which he kept in two notebooks called *Adagia*. Here are some of his most memorable attempts to put into words his unending engagement of imagination and reality.

- Poetry is a response to the daily necessity of getting the world right.
- Poetry is a renovation of experience.
- Poetry is the expression of the experience of poetry.
- Poetry must resist the intelligence almost successfully.
- Poetry is the statement of a relation between a man and the world.

- Every poem is a poem within a poem: the poem of the idea within the poem of the words.
- The theory of poetry is the theory of life.
- The poem is a nature created by the poet.
- The purpose of poetry is to contribute to man's happiness.
- The purpose of poetry is to make life complete in itself.

—Wallace Stevens

Assessing Learning

Check Test: Sentence Completion

1. In "Anecdote of the Jar," the speaker places a jar in [Tennessee].
2. The jar tames the [wilderness].
3. In "Disillusionment of Ten O'Clock," the houses are haunted by [white night-gowns].
4. Some things that people are not going to dream about are [baboons, periwinkles].
5. The only person having interesting dreams is [a drunk sailor].

Self-Assessment

Ask students to think about which aspects of the lesson best helped them appreciate the poems.

Marianne Moore

(1887–1972)

Esther Bubley/Life Magazine
© Time, Inc.

Marianne Moore is remembered by many people as the woman who wrote a poem in 1955 celebrating the only World Series the Brooklyn Dodgers ever won. Moore spent almost half her life in Brooklyn, where she became one of the most famous supporters of the local baseball team.

She was born in Kirkwood, a suburb of St. Louis, Missouri. After graduating from Bryn Mawr College outside Philadelphia, Moore worked as a teacher and a librarian, and later served as the editor of *The Dial,* a magazine that encouraged young writers. She spent a good part of her life caring for her brother and mother. When her mother died, Moore lost her best friend—and her toughest critic.

All the while, Moore was writing and publishing her poems in the prestigious journals of the time. By 1921, she was living in New York City and had just published her first collection of poetry, *Poems.* Among the literary celebrities in New York, she was easily identifiable by her antique capes and other nineteenth-century touches in costume.

Behind the costume, however, Moore was a serious poet of meticulous detail, clarity, and humor. Mixing with the *literati* did not mean that she endorsed their tolerance in matters of personal behavior or their embrace of anything in the arts that seemed new, or bold, or simply amusing.

In fact, the only thing "modern" about Moore was her poetry. Like a bird building an intricate nest, she carefully pieced together her poems by combining her own writing with quotations and excerpts from social science and natural history journals. It has been said of her that no one was ever more indebted to other writers for material and, at the same time, more original. Her poetry reflects some of the influence of the Imagists, and it also makes constant use of the concrete in the tradition of William Carlos Williams. Williams himself assessed his colleague's achievement when he said, "The magic name, Marianne Moore . . . I don't think there is a better poet writing in America today or one who touches so deftly a great range of our thought."

Like the visual artists of the twentieth century, Moore was able to join apparently unrelated elements of what she observed and bring them into a "picture" with a single focus. In some of her poems, Moore works like a painter whose nervous strokes and jagged edges capture a hundred details in one moment stopped in time. What she says in one famous poem, "The Steeple-Jack," might apply to readers approaching her work for the first time: "[i]t is a privilege to see so much confusion."

Before You Read

POETRY

Make the Connection

Beyond This Fiddle

Without even really knowing why, many people say, "I hate poetry! I never understand it." In the following poem, Moore directly and humorously explains the usefulness and the characteristics of good poetry. She takes the role of the critic explaining her own work, as well as the critic confronting the entire genre.

Quickwrite

Before you read, jot down your thoughts about poetry. Be honest: What do you like about poetry, and what don't you like? What, to you, should a poem be?

go.hrw.com
LEO 11-16

Planning

- **Traditional Schedule**
  Lesson Plans Including Strategies for English-Language Learners

- **One-Stop Planner**
  CD-ROM with Test Generator

Summary ■ ■

The speaker meditates on the purpose of poetry and the characteristics of good poetry. She starts with the ironic admission that she dislikes the "fiddle" of poetry. On second thought, however, she insists that it is "useful" because it expresses "genuine" human experience. She criticizes "derivative" and "unintelligible" poetry and champions a poetry that we always already "know": a poetry that presents "imaginary gardens with real toads in them," a poetry that combines the rawness of the literal and the authenticity of the imagination.

Resources: Print and Media

Reading
- *Graphic Organizers for Active Reading,* p. 83
- *Audio CD Library*
  Disc 21, Tracks 16, 17

Writing and Language
- *Daily Oral Grammar*
  Transparency 49

Assessment
- *Formal Assessment,* p. 153
- *Portfolio Management System,* p. 188
- *Test Generator (One-Stop Planner CD-ROM)*

Internet
- go.hrw.com (keyword: LEO 11-16)

A Critical Thinking

Challenging the Text

? Do you think the speaker really dislikes poetry? [Possible responses: No, she is probably just saying that poetry is not as important as life; or yes, she may dislike most of the poetry that she reads.]

B Elements of Literature

Imagery

? In the middle of a poem that explores the abstract idea of what poetry should be, Moore lists a series of concrete images. How do they illustrate a crucial point in Moore's poem? [They illustrate the speaker's insistence that poetry be useful and intelligible to its audience; in listing these images, she seems to be saying that the subject matter of poetry should be all-inclusive but treated with originality.]

C Literary Connections

Diary of Tolstoy

Moore alludes to a quotation from the *Diary of Tolstoy,* in which Tolstoy writes that "poetry is everything with the exception of business documents and school books."

D Struggling Readers

Paraphrasing

? What does Moore finally tell the person who dislikes poetry? [Possible response: If you are interested in life itself and what is genuine, poetry has something to offer you.]

Poetry

Marianne Moore

A I, too, dislike it: there are things that are important beyond all this fiddle.°
    Reading it, however, with a perfect contempt for it, one discovers in
    it after all, a place for the genuine.
        Hands that can grasp, eyes
5   that can dilate, hair that can rise
            if it must, these things are important not because a

high-sounding interpretation can be put upon them but because they are
    useful. When they become so derivative° as to become unintelligible,
    the same thing may be said for all of us, that we
10   do not admire what
        we cannot understand: the bat
            holding on upside down or in quest of something to

B eat, elephants pushing, a wild horse taking a roll, a tireless wolf under
    a tree, the immovable critic twitching his skin like a horse that feels a flea, the base-
    ball fan, the statistician—
15   nor is it valid
            to discriminate against "business documents and

school-books"; all these phenomena are important. One must make a distinction
    however: when dragged into prominence by half poets, the result is not poetry,
    nor till the poets among us can be
20   'literalists of
        the imagination'—above
            insolence and triviality and can present

for inspection, "imaginary gardens with real toads in them," shall we have
    it. In the meantime, if you demand on the one hand,
25   the raw material of poetry in
        all its rawness and
        that which is on the other hand
            genuine, then you are interested in poetry.

1. fiddle: slang for "nonsense."
8. derivative: based on the work of others; unoriginal.

Netsuke carved in the shape of a frog. Japanese (18th century).
Victoria & Albert Museum, London.

788 THE MODERNS

Reaching All Students

Struggling Readers

Tell students that to make sense of this poem, they have to pay attention to the punctuation and not stop at the ends of lines or even stanzas. Read the poem aloud once. Then, go over it again, helping students identify the subject and verb in each sentence. In ll. 11–24, some of the punctuation does not follow standard usage, but it can be used as a guide to pauses and thought groupings.

English Language Learners

Pronoun referents may cause some difficulty for English language learners. Read the poem aloud once. Then read it a second time, stopping to ask students to identify the referents of *it* in l. 1 [poetry], *they* in l. 8 ["these things," hands, eyes, hair], and *it* in l. 25 [poetry].

Advanced Learners

The biographical material on p. 787 mentions that Marianne Moore's poetry shows the influence of the Imagists but also makes use of the concrete, as did William Carlos Williams. Have students analyze this poem in the light of these observations.

Archibald MacLeish (1892–1982), an American poet and Moore's contemporary, reflects on the means and ends of poetry in the following poem. *Ars poetica* translates from Latin as "the art of poetry." It is also the title of a work by the Roman poet Horace (65 B.C.–8 B.C.).

Ars Poetica

Archibald MacLeish

A poem should be palpable and mute
As a globed fruit,

Dumb
As old medallions to the thumb,

5 Silent as the sleeve-worn stone
Of casement ledges where the moss has grown—

A poem should be wordless
As the flight of birds.

          •

A poem should be motionless in time
10 As the moon climbs,

Leaving, as the moon releases
Twig by twig the night-entangled trees,

Leaving, as the moon behind the winter leaves,
Memory by memory the mind—

15 A poem should be motionless in time
As the moon climbs.

          •

A poem should be equal to:
Not true.

For all the history of grief
20 An empty doorway and a maple leaf.

For love
The leaning grasses and two lights above the sea—

A poem should not mean
But be.

MARIANNE MOORE **789**

Connections

The speaker insists, following Pound and Williams, that a good poem should make a powerful and immediate appeal to our experience. The speaker warns against making poetry factual, autobiographical, or "true" and says that instead it should be composed of images "equal to" life's powerful emotions and experiences.

Ⓐ Elements of Literature
Paradox
❓ A **paradox** is a statement that appears self-contradictory but reveals a kind of truth. In stanza 1, the speaker develops the paradoxical statement that a poem should be wordless. What truth lies behind that seeming contradiction? [Possible response: A reader should be more aware of a poem's immediate impact than of the words the poet uses.]

Ⓑ Critical Thinking
Interpreting
❓ In what sense must a poem be "not true"? [Possible response: It must convey emotion and experience through parallel images and ideas, rather than any direct statement of facts.]

Ⓒ Elements of Literature
Metaphor
❓ How might these two images be seen as metaphors for grief? [Possible response: The empty doorway suggests separation or absence; it suggests that someone should be there waiting but isn't. The maple leaf may have fallen from a tree, suggesting autumn, a time when things in nature are dying.]

Taking a Second Look

Review: Analyzing Text Structures (Inversion)
Inversion occurs when words are written in reversed or nonconventional order. In earlier times, poets used inversion to accommodate meter and rhyme scheme. Modern poets may use inversion for the same reasons or for emphasis. In ll. 13–14 of *Ars Poetica*, MacLeish uses inverted word order to achieve the assonance of *mind* and *time,* to create symmetry, and to get the word *leaves* closer to the next line.

Activity
Have students find another example of inversion in the poem and restate it in normal word order. [lines 11 and 12: as the moon releases the night-entangled trees twig by twig] Now ask students why the poet might have used inversion in this case. [Possible responses: for assonance; to emphasize the slowness of the moon's progression.]

Connecting Across Texts

Connecting with "Poetry"
Poetics, the aesthetic theory of poetry, is extremely important to both Moore and MacLeish, who have definite ideas about what poetry should be. Ask the class how MacLeish's requirement that a poem be "palpable and mute" is like Moore's urging for "imaginary gardens with real toads in them." Have the class brainstorm images from the poems that are similar or that recall each other in some way, while you make cluster diagrams for the images on the board.

Connections

In this poem, Stevens makes the point that poetry must accurately address relevant, significant issues in an original way. It must "construct a new stage" in order to ring true and strike an emotional chord with the reader/listener.

Ⓐ Elements of Literature
Extended Metaphor

❓ What two things are being compared in this extended metaphor? [poetry and theater] How does the poet use it to make a distinction between modern poetry and what came earlier? [Earlier poetry had a "script"—conventions that it followed. Modern poetry has to "learn the speech of the place," that is, find new ways of speaking to its audience.]

Ⓑ Critical Thinking
Analyzing

❓ What is the speaker suggesting about the new relationship between poetry and its audience? Why does the speaker say that the audience doesn't listen "to the play, but to itself"? [Possible response: The speaker is suggesting that modern poetry, freed from past conventions, acts as a facilitator for audiences to explore their own emotions.]

Ⓒ Struggling Readers
Summarizing

❓ Bearing the previous twenty-three lines in mind, how would you summarize the final stanza of the poem? [Possible response: The "subject" of modern poetry must be the heightened activity of the reader's mind, finding satisfaction in the "sudden rightnesses" of its images and phrases.]

Wallace Stevens (see page 783) was, like MacLeish, a contemporary of Marianne Moore. In the following *ars poetica*, Stevens is particularly concerned with the raw material a poem draws on and how a poem works in the mind of the reader or listener. Above all, a poem must be fresh—it must avoid outdated concerns and forms.

Of Modern Poetry

Wallace Stevens

The poem of the mind in the act of finding
What will suffice. It has not always had
To find: the scene was set; it repeated what
Was in the script.
            Then the theatre was changed
5   To something else. Its past was a souvenir.

It has to be living, to learn the speech of the place.
It has to face the men of the time and to meet
The women of the time. It has to think about war
And it has to find what will suffice. It has
10   To construct a new stage. It has to be on that stage
And, like an insatiable° actor, slowly and
With meditation, speak words that in the ear,
In the delicatest ear of the mind, repeat,
Exactly, that which it wants to hear, at the sound
15   Of which, an invisible audience listens,
Not to the play, but to itself, expressed
In an emotion as of two people, as of two
Emotions becoming one. The actor is
A metaphysician° in the dark, twanging
20   An instrument, twanging a wiry string that gives
Sounds passing through sudden rightnesses, wholly
Containing the mind, below which it cannot descend
Beyond which it has no will to rise.
                    It must
25   Be the finding of a satisfaction, and may
Be of a man skating, a woman dancing, a woman
Combing. The poem of the act of the mind.

12. insatiable (in·sā′shə·bəl): incapable of being satisfied.
20. metaphysician (met′ə·fə·zish′ən): philosopher who studies the nature of being or reality.

Connecting Across Texts

Connecting with "Poetry"

1. Have students discuss whether Wallace Stevens would agree with Marianne Moore that poetry is a place for the "genuine" and that genuine things are "useful." Remind them to cite lines from "Of Modern Poetry" to support their opinions. [Possible responses: Students who would agree with Moore may say that ll. 6–9 and 25–27 correspond to Moore's use of the word "genuine" and that the repetition of the phrase "what will suffice" corresponds to Moore's insistence on what is useful or relevant. Others might say that, while Stevens might not disagree with Moore, his concerns about poetry are different. The first and last lines of the poem emphasize the mind, whereas Moore focuses on "phenomena," or "real toads."]

2. Like Moore and MacLeish, Stevens is also concerned with poetics, the aesthetic theory of poetry. Divide students into groups of three, and ask them to imagine a meeting among the three poets. What would each one say about the others' poems and theories of poetics? Have each group write and act out a dialogue that might occur among the three poets.

MAKING MEANINGS

First Thoughts

1. How do *you* feel about poetry? Do you agree with Moore about what "real" poetry is? Review the notes you made in your Quickwrite.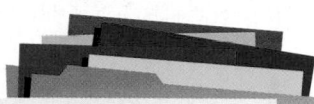

Shaping Interpretations

2. Whom do you think Moore is addressing in this poem?

3. What kind of poetry does Moore dislike?

4. What elements does Moore think useful poetry should contain?

5. Moore says "literalists of the imagination" are necessary for true poetry. What do you think she means? How is this idea related to those "imaginary gardens with real toads in them"?

6. Identify the **end rhymes** of the fourth and fifth lines of stanzas 1, 2, 4, and 5. Which are **exact rhymes,** and which are **slant rhymes**?

Connecting with the Text

7. List five experiences from your life that Moore would consider the "raw material of poetry."

CHOICES: Building Your Portfolio

Writer's Notebook

1. Collecting Ideas for an Interpretive Essay

In your own words, **paraphrase** Moore's criteria for good poetry as stated in her poem. Which of these criteria would you apply to your own interpretation of a poem? Which of the criteria would you change or expand? Keep your notes for possible use in the Writer's Workshop on page 804.

Comparing Literary Theories

2. Poems About Poetry

In a brief essay, compare Marianne Moore's ideas about poetry with Archibald MacLeish's ideas in "Ars Poetica" (see *Connections,* page 789) or with Wallace Stevens's in "Of Modern Poetry" (*Connections,* page 790). What does each poet require in a poem? What do their descriptions of poetry have in common? For another poem on poetry, try Dickinson's "Tell all the Truth. . ." on page 386.

Evaluating a Poem

3. Letter to a Poet

Write a letter to Marianne Moore, describing your response to "Poetry." Cite specific passages from her poem.

Creative Writing

4. Poetry Is . . .

The most famous line in this poem is the one that says that poetry should show us " 'imaginary gardens with real toads in them.' " Write your own list of what poetry is. Start with the words "Poetry is."

Creative Writing

5. Moore's Method

Marianne Moore often used information that she took from science and nature publications. Look through nature magazines or journals, and find an article that includes illustrations of animals, insects, birds, or fish that interest you. Write a poem about your chosen subject. Incorporate quotations from the article into your poem.

Performance

6. "Poetry" Reading

With a partner, take turns reading "Poetry" aloud. Pay attention to line and stanza breaks and to the alternation of long and short lines. Note also the punctuation: Where would you read quickly, and where would you slow down for emphasis? Record or perform two or three renditions for your class, and discuss how responses and interpretations differ for each reading.

MARIANNE MOORE 791

MAKING MEANINGS

First Thoughts [Respond]

1. Possible responses: Poetry is important. It touches the emotions and makes readers think about human experience in all its variety; or poetry is less important than other human activities like earning a living or developing and nurturing relationships.

Shaping Interpretations [Interpret]

2. She addresses readers who think they dislike poetry.

3. She dislikes derivative and unintelligible poetry.

4. Moore thinks useful poetry should include elements of rawness and genuineness.

5. Moore means that the imagined symbols or images of poetry must be so concretely described that readers can see the toad's warts, toe pads, and sticky tongue.

6. Stanza 1: *eyes/rise* (exact); stanza 2: *what/bat* (slant); stanza 4: *of/above* (exact); stanza 5: *and/hand* (exact).

Connecting with the Text [Apply]

7. Students may mention a loss, a success or a failure, conflicts with family or friends, a pet, or a special event in their lives.

Grading Timesaver

Rubrics for each Choices assignment appear on p. 188 in the *Portfolio Management System.*

CHOICES:
Building Your Portfolio

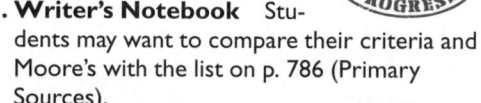

1. **Writer's Notebook** Students may want to compare their criteria and Moore's with the list on p. 786 (Primary Sources).

2. **Comparing Literary Theories** The Connecting Across Texts activity on pp. 789 and 790 is a good starting point.

3. **Evaluating a Poem** Suggest that students pick out passages that they had strong responses to, both positive and negative, and have them explain their responses.

4. **Creative Writing** Spark informal discussion by posting students' lists around the classroom.

5. **Creative Writing** Suggest to students that they look for various articles on nature on the Internet.

6. **Performance** Remind students that longer lines lend themselves to a faster reading pace than do shorter lines.

T791

Carl Sandburg

(1878–1967)

When he died in his nine-tieth year, Carl Sandburg was already an American myth. Sandburg's deeply lined, leathery face and his boyish shock of hair had been familiar to the American public for more than five decades. As the author of two of the most popular poems of the first half of the century—"Chicago" (1914) and "Fog" (1916)—and a six-volume biography of Abraham Lincoln, Sandburg had carved a place for himself in modern literature. As a poetic spokesperson for the American laborer, he had become part of the folklore from which he drew his inspiration. While he seemed on the page to be the roughest of American poets, Sandburg was actually a gentle and contemplative man. He found his most characteristic voice in the vernacular—in slang, street talk, and the common speech of clichés and plain expressions.

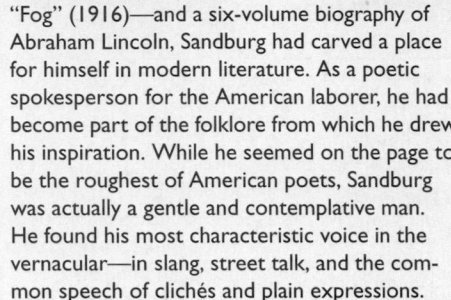

Brown Brothers.

A descendant of Swedes who had settled in Galesburg, Illinois, where he was born, Sandburg was not so much schooled in a classroom as in the proverbial "school of hard knocks." Before he was twenty, he had ranged the Middle West from Illinois to Nebraska. He thus came in contact with workers in the fields and factories that would one day provide his own poetic landscape. Sandburg volunteered, more from restlessness than from patriotism, to fight in the Spanish-American War that broke out in 1898, and he served in the first Puerto Rican campaign. When the war ended, he was finally ready to go back to school. He attended Lombard College in his hometown, where he was captain of the basketball team and editor of the college newspaper. It was at Lombard that Sandburg first began to think of himself as a writer. But his first professional writing was in advertising, politics, and journalism.

After a succession of jobs, Sandburg became nationally known as a poet at the age of thirty-six when *Poetry* magazine published some of his shorter poems, including "Chicago." Sandburg's daring use of colloquialism and free verse (suggesting the influence of Walt Whitman) involved him in critical controversy and established his reputation as a major literary figure.

Sandburg's affirmation of American democracy and of the inherent nobility of labor and the working person culminated in one of his best-known collections of poems, *The People, Yes* (1936), a Whitmanesque panorama of American life that expressed a profound faith in his country. One of Sandburg's many enterprises was compiling a sort of folk-song history of America, consisting of songs collected coast to coast.

Before You Read

CHICAGO

Make the Connection

Echoes of Whitman
Free verse with a ring of oratory in its cadences is characteristic of Sandburg's poetry. Be sure to read the following poem aloud to hear the echoes of Whitman.

792 THE MODERNS

Quickwrite

Sandburg uses vivid words and **images** to portray a city of enormous energy. Jot down words or phrases that might capture a city's energy. What key image would best describe a city you are familiar with? (Be sure to name the city.)

Elements of Literature

Apostrophe
Apostrophe is a technique in which a writer addresses an inanimate object, an idea, or a person who is either dead or absent. In this poem, Sandburg addresses an entire city as though it were a kind of intelligent being, capable of understanding what he says.

go.hrw.com
LE0 11-16

Chicago (1923) by Louis Lozowick. Oil on canvas.

Private Collection, Washington, D.C.

Chicago

Carl Sandburg

Hog Butcher for the World,
Tool Maker, Stacker of Wheat,
Player with Railroads and the Nation's Freight Handler;
Stormy, husky, brawling,
5   City of the Big Shoulders:

Ⓐ

CARL SANDBURG 793

Reaching All Students

Struggling Readers
To help students remain focused on the poem, have them create a cluster diagram describing the sights and sounds of Chicago as they listen to you read the poem aloud.

English Language Learners
To help students comprehend that the city of Chicago is being compared to a person, point out that all of the words used to characterize Chicago in the first three lines end in the suffix *-er*, which means "a person who."

Advanced Learners
The speaker characterizes Chicago as a city where physical labor predominates, and in l. 12, he contrasts Chicago with "the little soft cities," which presumably are more devoted to commercial, financial, academic, literary, and artistic pursuits. Challenge students to write some epithets that could be used to glorify a "little soft city" they are familiar with.

Summary ■■

This apostrophe opens with a series of epithets emphasizing Chicago's industrial and Midwestern character. While the speaker admits that Chicago may be wicked, philistine, and brutal, he asks rhetorically if the listener can name another city so proud, strong, and cunning. Through use of verbal irony and emotional ambiguity, Sandburg, like Whitman before him, creates a triumphant, ambivalent, and original portrait of urban America.

Resources

Viewing and Representing
Fine Art Transparency
A fine art transparency of Rafael Lopez's *Endangered Species,* with its startling juxtaposition of animal aggression and city life, can be used with this lesson as a springboard for a postreading discussion. See the *Viewing and Representing Transparencies and Worksheets:*
- Transparency 16
- Worksheet, p. 64

RESPONDING TO THE ART
Russian-born **Louis Lozowick** (1892–1973) studied in Europe before coming to the United States. His early work focused on structure and line in architectural and industrial scenes.
Activity. Ask students what the shapes, lines, and colors suggest about the city that the photograph on p. 794 does not. [Possible response: The half-completed structure in the upper right of the painting emphasizes the ongoing industrial development of Chicago, while the geometric forms and sweeping lines of perspective suggest the motion and rough pragmatism of the city.]

Ⓐ **Appreciating Language**
Epithet
? An **epithet** is a descriptive word or phrase used to characterize a person or thing. What do these epithets reveal about Chicago? [It is an industrial, transportation, and agricultural processing center.]

A **Reading Skills and Strategies**

Making Inferences

❓ What clue does the poem give about its time setting? [the reference to "gas lamps," a kind of street lighting that preceded electricity] Note that the poem first appeared in 1914; the speaker is describing Chicago at that time.

B **Elements of Literature**

Apostrophe

❓ How does the speaker personify the city? [He uses an apostrophe, addressing the city directly as "you."] Ask students to jot down the words the speaker uses to describe this "you" as they read the poem.

C **Critical Thinking**

Interpreting

❓ What do you think the poet really thinks about Chicago? [Possible responses: He recognizes that the city has flaws, but its strengths and vitality far outweigh any deficiencies; or he admires it as the embodiment of a young, raw American city.]

D **Elements of Literature**

Metaphor

❓ Why might the speaker compare Chicago to a "Youth" rather than to an adult or older person? [Possible responses: Chicago, located in the Midwest, developed later than cities on the two coasts; the spontaneity and vigor (as well as the recklessness and violence) that the speaker sees in the city are all qualities associated with youth.]

They tell me you are wicked and I believe them, for I have
    seen your painted women under the gas lamps luring the
    farm boys.
And they tell me you are crooked and I answer: Yes, it is true I
    have seen the gunman kill and go free to kill again.
And they tell me you are brutal and my reply is: On the faces
    of women and children I have seen the marks of wanton
    hunger.
And having answered so I turn once more to those who sneer
    at this my city, and I give them back the sneer and say to
    them:
10 Come and show me another city with lifted head singing so
    proud to be alive and coarse and strong and cunning.
Flinging magnetic curses amid the toil of piling job on job,
    here is a tall bold slugger set vivid against the little soft
    cities;
Fierce as a dog with tongue lapping for action, cunning as a
    savage pitted against the wilderness,
       Bareheaded,
       Shoveling,
15   Wrecking,
       Planning,
       Building, breaking, rebuilding.
Under the smoke, dust all over his mouth, laughing with white
    teeth,
Under the terrible burden of destiny laughing as a young man
    laughs,
Laughing even as an ignorant fighter laughs who has never lost
20   a battle,
Bragging and laughing that under his wrist is the pulse, and
    under his ribs the heart of the people,
        Laughing!
Laughing the stormy, husky, brawling laughter of Youth, half-
    naked, sweating, proud to be Hog Butcher, Tool Maker,
    Stacker of Wheat, Player with Railroads and Freight Handler
    to the Nation.

Crossing the Curriculum

Music

Have students locate a recording of the song "Chicago" or a musical tribute to your city or one near you. Ask students to analyze the song using these questions as a starting point: What about the city does the song honor? Is the song an example of free verse, or does it have a definite rhyme and/or rhythm? Which offers a more complex, sophisticated picture, Sandburg's poem or the selected song?

Economics

Sandburg's poem can be read as an economic portrait of Chicago in the first quarter of the twentieth century. Ask students to conduct research to discover what dominated the economy of your state or area in the same period. Was it agriculture, industry, commerce, or some combination? Was your area continuing in a similar pattern to its nineteenth-century history, or was change afoot? What did people do for a living?

Social Studies

Have students update Sandburg's vision of Chicago by researching and delivering oral presentations about an aspect of Chicago mentioned in the poem. Suggested topics: stockyards, railroads, construction, urban development, poverty, crime. Students with a naturalist bent could report on Chicago's parklands, remnant prairies, or environmental problems and solutions.

First Thoughts

1. How does Sandburg make you feel about the city he describes?

Shaping Interpretations

2. Sandburg opens with a series of **epithets,** or descriptive phrases, about Chicago. What does each of these epithets reveal about the city and the various activities that make up its economy?

3. What do "they" tell the speaker about Chicago? What is the speaker's answer to each of these comments about the city?

4. Many different **images** contribute to this portrait of Chicago, but its central image is never named. To what is Chicago really being compared? How is this image introduced and extended?

5. What are the city's main strengths and main weaknesses, according to Sandburg? What seems to be the poet's attitude toward the city?

Extending the Text

6. Which features of Chicago do you think have changed since this poem was written in 1914?

Challenging the Text

7. What would you say to those critics who have claimed that Sandburg's poetry is full of bluster and proclamation at the expense of thought?

CHOICES:
Building Your Portfolio

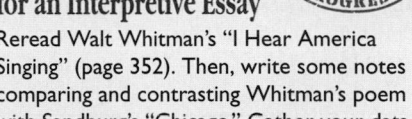

Writer's Notebook

1. Collecting Ideas for an Interpretive Essay

Reread Walt Whitman's "I Hear America Singing" (page 352). Then, write some notes comparing and contrasting Whitman's poem with Sandburg's "Chicago." Gather your data in a chart like the following one.

Save your notes for possible use in the Writer's Workshop on page 804.

	Whitman	Sandburg
Subject		
Imagery		
Figures of speech		
Rhythm		
Catalogs of details		
Slang and colloquial language		
Tone		

Creative Writing

2. Apt Epithets

Review the **epithets** Sandburg uses in addressing Chicago in the opening stanza. Then, choose a city, town, or other area you know well. Write an **apostrophe**— a direct address to an inanimate object—using at least five epithets about the place you have chosen. Be sure to refer to your Quickwrite notes.

Performance

3. Sing It Out

Prepare this famous poem for a group performance. Your first task will be to decide how many speakers you will need and whether you will use a group of voices to recite some passages. You will also want to decide whether you will use sound effects, even music. Perform the poem for your class.

Art

4. Chicago Illustrated

Using pictures from magazines and newspapers, create a collage to illustrate Sandburg's "Chicago." Look for references to specific images in the poem as you select drawings and photographs for the collage.

CARL SANDBURG 795

CHOICES:
Building Your Portfolio

1. **Writer's Notebook** You could also use this chart for a class discussion, recording student responses on the board.

2. **Creative Writing** Encourage students to brainstorm to create a list of characteristics of the place they chose. Tell them that the epithets they use may relate to the place's past or present and may be either particular to the place or general.

3. **Performance** After different groups have performed for the class, have students vote on the performance that best captures the spirit of the poem.

4. **Art** Suggest that students reread the poem carefully, circling the images that Sandburg uses.

MAKING MEANINGS

First Thoughts [Respond]

1. Students may say that Sandburg arouses their interest in the city or makes them proud of its energy.

Shaping Interpretations [Interpret]

2. Chicago is a center of meat-packing, heavy industry, grain processing, and train lines.

3. People say the city is wicked, crooked, and brutal. The speaker agrees, mentioning prostitutes, murderers, and hungry children.

4. The central image of a strong, exuberant young man is introduced in the opening lines and extended with other dynamic images, like "tall bold slugger" in l. 11 and "laughing as a young man laughs" in l. 19.

5. The city's main strengths are vitality, industry, pride, joy, and endurance. Its weaknesses include wickedness, crookedness, and brutality. Sandburg loves and admires the city despite its flaws.

Extending the Text [Evaluate]

6. Possible responses: The stockyards are now an industrial park. Financing and wholesaling are important now. Heavy industry is less important. The gas lamps are gone.

Challenging the Text [Evaluate]

7. Possible response: In his attempt to capture the spontaneous and reckless energy of his subject, Sandburg abandons the precise, restrained language of conventional poetry. But, like Whitman's, Sandburg's exuberant, unrestrained poetic voice is backed up by serious thought and a unique perspective on ethics, philosophy, and American culture.

Grading Timesaver

Rubrics for each Choices assignment appear on p. 190 in the *Portfolio Management System.*

SKILLS

Writing
- Collect ideas for an interpretive essay
- Evaluate ideas
- Compare poems

Speaking/Listening
- Perform a song

Music
- Create a melody

Planning

- **Block Schedule**
  Block Scheduling Lesson Plans with Pacing Guide
- **Traditional Schedule**
  Lesson Plans Including Strategies for English-Language Learners
- **One-Stop Planner**
  CD-ROM with Test Generator

BROWSING IN THE FILES

About the Author. Cummings's unusual typography may appear arbitrary to some students, just as it did to some early critics. In fact the punctuation was intentional, precise, and extremely important to Cummings.

Self-Portrait by E. E. Cummings.

Berg Collection of English and American Literature, The New York Public Library. © Astor, Lenox, and Tilden Foundations. Photograph by John Lei.

E. E. Cummings

(1894–1962)

Edward Estlin (E. E.) Cummings was born in Cambridge, Massachusetts, the son of a Unitarian minister. After a childhood spent within walking distance of Harvard, he attended the university at a time when French Symbolism and free verse were major new influences on American poetry. Like other poets, Cummings found in the Imagist manifesto guidelines that allowed him to experiment and to break old rules.

If there is such a thing as "rugged individualism" in poetry, Cummings may be its prime example. All by himself, he altered conventional English syntax and made typography and the division of words part of the shape and meaning of a poem. And—in the age of celebration of the common person—he went against the grain by championing the virtues of elitism. "So far as I am concerned," he wrote, "poetry and every other art was and is and forever will be strictly and distinctly a question of individuality. . . . Poetry is being, not doing. If you wish to follow, even at a distance, the poet's calling . . . you've got to come out of the measurable doing universe into the immeasurable house of being. . . . Nobody else can be alive for you; nor can you be alive for anybody else."

Graduating from college in the midst of World War I, Cummings became part of the conflict well before American soldiers appeared on European battlefields in 1917. He volunteered for an ambulance corps privately financed by Americans and staffed by young men like himself. Crossing to Bordeaux on a French troop ship threatened by German U-boats, Cummings had hardly begun his duties when a French censor, intercepting one of his typographically odd letters, imprisoned him on suspicion of espionage. Released within three months, Cummings drew on the experience to produce his first important book of prose, *The Enormous Room* (1922).

After World War I, Cummings returned to France. He was one of the American literary expatriates who found in Paris the freedom and inspiration they felt were denied them by the restrictive Puritan climate of their own country. During this period, Cummings refined the eccentric shifts of syntax and typography that would become his trademark. In 1923, he published his first collection of verse, *Tulips and Chimneys,* which was followed by & (1925), *XLI Poems* (1925), and *is 5* (1926). His poetry is often marked by jubilant lyricism, as he celebrates love, nature's beauty, and an almost Transcendentalist affirmation of the individual. He reserved his mischievous wit for the satire of the "unman," by which he meant the unthinking, unfeeling temperament of urban "humans."

Back in the United States, Cummings split his time between an apartment in Greenwich Village in New York City and a house in Silver Lake, New Hampshire. He died still believing that "when skies are hanged and oceans drowned, / the single secret will still be man."

go.hrw.com
LE0 11-16

Resources: Print and Media

Reading
- *Graphic Organizers for Active Reading,* p. 85
- *Audio CD Library*
  Disc 21, Tracks 19, 20

Assessment
- *Portfolio Management System,* p. 191
- *Test Generator (One-Stop Planner CD-ROM)*

Internet
- go.hrw.com (keyword: LE0 11-16)

Make the Connection

The Prevailing Spirit
Modern literature is full of bleak
images of destruction and the
wane of civilization. At the same
time, an extraordinary number
of writers explore the determination of the human spirit to
prevail in spite of hardship and
even devastation. What tone
about the future of this planet do
you hear in Cummings's poem?

Quickwrite

Before you read this
poem, jot down some of
your predictions about the future
of the planet. You could focus
your thoughts on "What if . . . ?"

what if a much of a which of a wind

E. E. Cummings

what if a much of a which of a wind
gives the truth to summer's lie; **(A)**
bloodies with dizzying leaves the sun
and yanks immortal stars awry?°
5 Blow king to beggar and queen to seem
(blow friend to fiend:blow space to time)
—when skies are hanged and oceans drowned,
the single secret will still be man

what if a keen of a lean wind flays°
10 screaming hills with sleet and snow:
strangles valleys by ropes of thing
and stifles forests in white ago?
Blow hope to terror;blow seeing to blind
(blow pity to envy and soul to mind)
15 —whose hearts are mountains,roots are trees,
it's they shall cry hello to the spring **(B)**

what if a dawn of a doom of a dream
bites this universe in two,
peels forever out of his grave
20 and sprinkles nowhere with me and you? **(C)**
Blow soon to never and never to twice
(blow life to isn't:blow death to was)
—all nothing's only our hugest home;
the most who die,the more we live

4. **awry** (ə·rī'):
out of place.

9. **flays:** here,
whips; lashes.

PRIMARY Sources — — AN INTRODUCTION

"Miracles are to come"

The poems to come are for you and for me and
are not for mostpeople—it's no use trying to
pretend that mostpeople and ourselves are alike.
Mostpeople have less in common with ourselves
than the squarerootofminusone. You and I are
human beings;mostpeople are snobs. . . .

you and I are not snobs. We can never be
born enough. We are human beings;for whom
birth is a supremely welcome mystery,the mystery of growing:the mystery which happens
only and whenever we are faithful to ourselves.
You and I wear the dangerous looseness of

doom and find it becoming. Life,for eternal us,is
now;and now is much too busy being a little
more than everything to seem anything,
catastrophic included. . . .

Miracles are to come. With you I leave a
remembrance of miracles:they are by somebody
who can love and who shall be continually reborn,a human being;somebody who said to
those near him,when his fingers would not hold
a brush "tie it into my hand"—

—E. E. Cummings,
from New Poems

E. E. CUMMINGS **797**

Summary ■■

The speaker insists that in spite of
every destruction physical forces could
inflict upon the earth, "the single
secret will still be man." Indeed, the
speaker continues, the spirit of human
beings, "whose hearts are mountains,
roots are trees," remains immune to
all natural powers. Extending the
hyperbolic language, the speaker concludes that even the apocalyptic "isn't"
of a barren universe is "only our
hugest home."

(A) Critical Thinking
Interpreting
? What might "summer's lie" be?
[Possible responses: that a rich, thriving
life will go on indefinitely; that all is well
in the world.]

(B) Appreciating Language
Diction
? E. E. Cummings is noted for using
verbs, adjectives, and adverbs as
nouns. What examples can you find?
[l. 9, *keen*; l. 12, *ago*; l. 21, *soon, never,
twice*; l. 22, *isn't, was*]

(C) Elements of Literature
Paradox
? How do you explain the paradox
developed in the third stanza—in
which the universe is reduced to a
colossal nothing, yet the "we" of
humankind lives on? [Possible response:
The meaning and emotion that human
beings invest in existence is not a physical entity—therefore, this meaningful
essence of the human spirit will survive
when the last human has disappeared
into the void.]

Primary Sources

In this ironic, jubilant excerpt from
New Poems, Cummings addresses his
reader, using the irregular punctuation,
neologisms, and unconventional sentence structure that characterize his
poetry. With tongue firmly in cheek,
Cummings flatters his reader, as part
of an exclusive club of "human beings,"
who are not snobs, who welcome life's
mystery, and who are faithful to themselves. On a more serious note, he
claims that he and his reader concern
themselves more with "being" than
with how they present themselves, or
"seem." He insists that "miracles" are
in store and that his poems are memories of such miracles, written by a
human being, capable of love, constant
renewal, and artistic dedication.

Reaching All Students

Struggling Readers
Tell students that in the first seven lines of each
stanza Cummings sets up a scene of destruction
and upheaval. Ask them to point out some of
the images of violence and destruction. Then
ask them what message of hope the last two
lines in each stanza give.

English Language Learners
Remind students that Cummings is playing with
language and that, as a result, the sentences
don't necessarily make sense in a logical way.
Tell them it is more important to enjoy the flow
of the words and get the gist of the poem than
to understand the syntax of each sentence.
Read aloud the first stanza with appropriate
intonation and then ask for volunteers to read
the last two stanzas with feeling.

Summary ■■

In this love poem, the speaker uses synesthesia, paradoxes, and similes to describe the effect his beloved has on him. The presence of his love has the capacity to "unclose" the speaker, opening him to emotions and experiences just as Spring skillfully opens the first rose of the season. Similarly, his love can neatly shut down this metaphorical bloom, just as snow closes a flower. The speaker concludes by expressing his awe and ignorance at this subtle yet overwhelming power and compares his beloved's touch to the "small hands" of the rain.

Ⓐ Elements of Literature

Paradox

❓ A **paradox** is a seemingly self-contradictory statement that actually reveals a truth. What truth might Cummings be hinting at when he refers to things that cannot be touched "because they are too near"? [Possible responses: Sometimes people are frightened of emotional closeness and retreat when another person gets too close; or sometimes it's hard to "see," or comprehend, something that you are very close to.]

Ⓑ Critical Thinking

Interpreting

❓ In your own words, what effect does the speaker's loved one have on him? [Possible responses: She makes him open to experiencing life; or she helps him reveal his feelings.]

Ⓒ Elements of Literature

Simile

❓ A **simile** is a comparison between two essentially unlike things using the word *like* or *as*. In the simile developed in these two stanzas, who is compared to a rose? [the speaker] To what is the person he loves compared? [forces of nature—spring, snow]

Ⓓ Critical Thinking

Interpreting

❓ In what way could the rain be said to have small hands? [Possible responses: Hands touch things, and when the rain falls gently, each individual raindrop might be seen as a "small hand."] What is the speaker saying about his love through this metaphor? [Possible response: He is commenting on the delicacy and sensitivity of his beloved's touch.]

Before You Read

SOMEWHERE I . . .

Make the Connection

Searching for Words

Have you ever been at a loss for words, unable to find the right way to express a deep feeling or a complex thought? Poets, too, search for ways of using language that will at least approximate their complicated feelings and thoughts. In a sense, therefore, a poem is an attempt to put on paper what cannot quite be expressed in words.

Quickwrite

Maybe love is the hardest feeling of all to put into words. Poets often use figures of speech to try to express how they feel when they love someone very much. What comparisons would you use to describe that feeling of being in love—or of longing for a loved person?

---

somewhere i have never travelled, gladly beyond

E. E. Cummings

somewhere i have never travelled,gladly beyond
any experience,your eyes have their silence:
 in your most frail gesture are things which enclose me,
or which i cannot touch because they are too near

5 your slightest look easily will unclose me
though i have closed myself as fingers,
you open always petal by petal myself as Spring opens
(touching skilfully,mysteriously)her first rose

or if your wish be to close me,i and
10 my life will shut very beautifully,suddenly,
as when the heart of this flower imagines
the snow carefully everywhere descending;

nothing which we are to perceive in this world equals
the power of your intense fragility:whose texture
15 compels me with the colour of its countries,
rendering death and forever with each breathing

(i do not know what it is about you that closes
and opens;only something in me understands
the voice of your eyes is deeper than all roses)
Ⓓ 20 nobody,not even the rain,has such small hands

The Kiss (Der Kuss) (1907–1908) by Gustav Klimt.
Oesterreichische Galerie, Vienna, Austria.

798 THE MODERNS

---

what if a much of a which of a wind

First Thoughts

1. How did you react to the poem's message? Did the message differ from the predictions you made in your Quickwrite?

Shaping Interpretations

2. If the world is destroyed, what will still survive?

3. What **images** describe the seasons of the year in the first two stanzas?

4. Describe the **rhyme scheme** of the poem. How is **slant rhyme** used?

5. What common human fears does Cummings refer to in the first six lines of each stanza? How does he comment on those fears in the last two lines of each stanza?

6. What do you think Cummings means by the last two lines? Is he celebrating life or death?

somewhere i have never travelled,gladly beyond

First Thoughts

1. Which line or **image** in the poem made the strongest impression on you? Explain.

Shaping Interpretations

2. What **figures of speech** does Cummings use to talk about his love? (How do they compare with your Quickwrite notes?)

3. The poem rises in intensity in stanza 4. **Paraphrase** this stanza, making clear what you think the speaker means by "death and forever."

4. In line 2 the phrase "your eyes have their silence" is an example of **synesthesia**—the juxtaposition of one sensory image with another image that appeals to a different sense. Where else does Cummings use synesthesia?

5. A **paradox** is a statement that appears contradictory but that reveals a kind of truth. Find at least two paradoxes in the poem and explain what you think they mean.

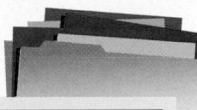

Writer's Notebook

1. Collecting Ideas for an Interpretive Essay

Cummings's style can be challenging because he uses a difficult **syntax** consisting of thought groupings that often don't have any punctuation or that use unusual punctuation. He also often uses verbs, adjectives, and adverbs as nouns. Go back over one of the two poems by Cummings, and determine where thought groupings begin and end. Paraphrase these thought groupings in a brief paragraph. Save your notes for possible use in the Writer's Workshop on page 804.

Evaluating Ideas

2. Snobs, Look Elsewhere

In Primary Sources (page 797), taken from the introduction to his collection *New Poems* (1938), Cummings makes several statements about poetry and his audience, and at the same time reveals an attitude toward life itself. In a brief essay, tell whether you find that any of these statements relate to the messages In "what if a much of a which of a wind" or "somewhere i have never travelled,gladly beyond." Use specific lines to support your opinions.

Comparing Poems

3. That Which Survives

In a brief essay, compare "what if a much of a which of a wind" with Robert Frost's "Once by the Pacific" (page 564). Consider in your essay the **theme** or **message, imagery, tone,** and **structure** of the poems.

Music / Performance

4. A Poem Is a Song

Create a melody to accompany either poem by Cummings. Then, with two or three classmates, perform the song for your class.

E. E. CUMMINGS **799**

6. Possible response: He celebrates human consciousness and meaning as a mystery that is only intensified by a total material annihilation and that cannot be reduced to either life or death.

somewhere i have never travelled,gladly beyond

First Thoughts [Respond]

1. Some students may mention the image of the rose opening and closing in response to the seasons; others may say the last line stands out because it is the only one that describes something specific about the speaker's beloved.

Shaping Interpretations [Interpret]

2. He compares his love to spring, snow, and the rain. Students may have used images of nature or perhaps even images from the modern electronic age.

3. Possible response: Your delicacy is more powerful than anything else in the world and draws me to you. With each breath you make me feel both death and eternal life.

4. Lines 14–15: "whose texture compels me with the color of its countries"; l. 19: "the voice of your eyes."

5. Line 3: "in your most frail gesture are things which enclose me" may mean that a gesture that seems weak actually has such strong emotional power that it makes me a captive in your world. Line 14: "the power of your intense fragility" may mean that someone who appears physically fragile can be strong in other ways.

Grading Timesaver

Rubrics for each Choices assignment appear on p. 191 in the *Portfolio Management System*.

what if a much ...

First Thoughts [Respond]

1. Students may judge the poem either negative or life-affirming. Some may have predicted a dire future for the planet; others may have a more rosy outlook.

Shaping Interpretations [Interpret]

2. The mystery of human existence and human consciousness will survive.

3. Summer is seen as a lie, winter as a violent killer, spring as a survivor of winter's wrath.

4. The rhyme scheme of each stanza is *abcbddac*. Examples of slant rhyme include ll. 3 and 8 and ll. 5 and 6, among others.

5. Cummings refers to fears of loss, disappointment, death, and oblivion but counters the fears with a positive image.

READ ON

Lifestyles of the Rich and Famous

He's rich, he's handsome, he throws great parties—so why does Jay Gatsby stand outside his opulent Long Island mansion, gazing longingly at a light across the water? The narrator Nick Carraway tries to unlock the puzzle in *The Great Gatsby,* F. Scott Fitzgerald's novel of American dreams and disappointments during the Jazz Age. This title is available in the HRW Library. A movie adaptation (1974) is also available on video.

Small-Town Americana

Like Edwin Arlington Robinson's Tilbury Town and Edgar Lee Masters' Spoon River, Sherwood Anderson's Winesburg is a typical American small town. In *Winesburg, Ohio* (Viking), Anderson explores the splendid hopes and stifled dreams of Winesburg's inhabitants in a series of interconnected stories set in the early decades of the twentieth century. For another view of a small town, read Thornton Wilder's classic play *Our Town.*

Wounds of War

Ernest Hemingway is famous for his realistic, almost journalistic accounts of the triumphs and tragedies of warfare. In *A Farewell to Arms* (Scribner's), he sets a tragic romance against the backdrop of World War I Italy. In *For Whom the Bell Tolls* (Scribner's), the backdrop changes to the Spanish civil war. Both novels have been adapted as films.

Take the "A" Train

From about 1919 to 1932, New York City experienced a blossoming of African American culture known as the Harlem Renaissance (see page 734). Langston Hughes, Zora Neale Hurston, and James Weldon Johnson are just three of the many creative talents featured in *When Harlem Was in Vogue* (Random House), a highly readable social history by David Levering Lewis.

Two Sisters Have Their Say

The Delany sisters, Sarah Louise and Annie Elizabeth, were 104 and 102 in 1993 when they wrote *Having Our Say* (Dell). Their father was born into slavery; the sisters lived through the northern migration of African Americans, the Harlem Renaissance, and the civil rights movement of the 1960s. Their story gives a unique perspective of life in the United States over the last hundred years. This nonfiction best-seller has been adapted as a stage play. In 1997, after the death of her younger sister, Sarah Louise Delaney published *On My Own at 107: Reflections on Life Without Bessie* (HarperCollins).

800 THE MODERNS

The American Language

American Slang

by Gary Q. Arpin

OBJECTIVES

1. Understand the origins of American slang
2. Recognize jargon
3. Appreciate the role of usage in the transition of a word from slang to standard English
4. Compile slang terms

Many people think of slang as a kind of corrupt English, the product of ignorance and laziness. They see slang as a sort of linguistic disease that flourishes in the poorest and worst-maintained neighborhoods of the language. Slang, they feel, should be stamped out for the health and well-being of the general public.

But slang is as old as language itself. In fact, many words that at one time were considered slang later entered the language and are now used by all speakers. Perhaps Carl Sandburg (page 792) sized up the appeal of slang best: "Slang is language that rolls up its sleeves, spits on its hands, and goes to work."

Before the middle of the eighteenth century, slang as we know it today was called *cant* and *argot*. *Cant* referred to the secret language of thieves and beggars. *Argot* referred to the specialized vocabulary of occupations (sailors and farmers, for example). Gradually, the word *slang* came to refer to any informal, nonstandard, specialized language. Today, slang specifically refers to a kind of colorful, irreverent, lively language that quickly becomes popular and often just as quickly drops out of use. It has always been popular among the young.

Why Do We Use Slang?

Why do people use slang? Not usually out of ignorance, despite widespread misconceptions. Most slang terms are substitutes for fairly common words or phrases. A waitress who calls out the food order "Adam and Eve on a raft—wreck 'em," knows how to say "two scrambled eggs on toast." She is just using the **jargon,** or specialized vocabulary, of her occupation.

We ordinarily think of language only as a means of communication. But anthropologists point out that it has a more subtle function as well—marking relatedness. Members of a family or other group reinforce their connections by their language. If you think about it for a moment, you will probably realize that your family or group of friends does the same thing by using key words or unusual pronunciations. This is the most important function of slang: It marks members of a group and asserts the group's relatedness, thereby helping to keep it together.

The group can be of any size and come from any social class. It can be a single family or a large and widespread profession. Teenagers, athletes, actors, truck drivers, doctors, criminals, filmmakers, and soldiers all have their own slang. People outside the group who try to use its slang often appear ridiculous.

Walt Whitman (page 348) claimed that slang produced poets and poetry. This is an exaggeration, but it might point to another explanation for the persistence of slang. Slang may be used for the sheer pleasure of making sounds. It may also be a way to create new metaphors, sometimes just for the fun of it, sometimes to capture attention. Perhaps slang is used because as humans, we have an impulse to be wordsmiths. Certainly, people have persisted in making up new slang terms for concepts that already have more than enough terms to name them. Even some forty-five years ago, there were 180 slang terms for "having no money," 400 slang terms for "failing," and 200 slang terms for "getting angry." By now, who can tell how many new slang terms have been added to those lists?

People who do not speak a particular slang often are highly critical of it. This can be because some slang is vulgar or is a pointless corruption of standard

> Walt Whitman claimed that slang produced poets and poetry.

A Background

Both Walt Whitman and Carl Sandburg wrote poetry that celebrated the common man and woman. Slang is the language of the common people; it is no wonder that these two poets admired that speech as much as they honored their fellow citizens who spoke it. Had they not used slang words and expressions in their verse, both men's poetry would have been robbed of much of its color, life, and authenticity.

B Elements of Literature
Metaphor

Remind students that a metaphor is a comparison between two unlike things. Many slang expressions are lively metaphors that draw on aspects of everyday life.

Ask students to define *jackknife* as a verb and to give examples of its use. [to bend sharply; trucks *jackknife* in accidents, baseball players *jackknife* away from inside pitches to avoid being hit.] Because jackknives are common pocket tools, this metaphorical use of *jackknife* as a verb creates a clear picture in the listener's mind of the truck or batter bending at a sharp angle, like that of the knife as it unfolds from the handle.

Ⓐ Background

Perhaps because it is a uniquely American game, baseball has contributed numerous slang words and phrases to the American vocabulary. "I'll take a rain check," "out in left field," "batting a thousand," "three strikes and you're out"—these and many other common everyday phrases of American speech were born on the baseball field. These phrases and expressions became familiar because of baseball's vast popularity in the first half of the century. They have endured because most American children learn to play the game at an early age and because the professional leagues still draw millions of fans. The expression "out in left field" is meaningful because most people understand the comparison to the great distance between the left fielder and home plate.

speech with no apparent justification other than novelty. Some slang can also be criticized for being imprecise. Often, however, naysayers are simply annoyed at not being part of the in-group associated with the slang they are criticizing.

Origins of American Slang

America has always been a fertile ground for the development of slang, especially since the 1830s, when informality began to be considered an almost essential aspect of democracy. The country's cowboys, railroad workers, politicians, and members of hundreds of new occupations introduced many slang terms, often to name things for which there were no existing words. The media then helped to popularize the new terms.

Slang words and phrases develop in the same ways as other additions to standard English.

1. Existing words may be given a new meaning. *Sack,* during World War II, became the almost universal slang word for "bed." It helped to create countless new phrases for "sleep": *hit the sack, sack out,* *sack time, sack duty,* and *sack drill.*

2. Two or more words may be combined to form a new expression. Americans' love affair with cars, for example, gave us the marvelously inventive *rattletrap* and the more recent *gas guzzler.* One witty compound verb, *to rubberneck,* meaning to stretch one's neck to see an accident or traffic tie-up, was once said to be the best slang term ever coined.

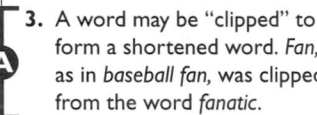

3. A word may be "clipped" to form a shortened word. *Fan,* as in *baseball fan,* was clipped from the word *fanatic.*

4. Words may also be borrowed from other languages. (These are often called *loanwords.*) During the westward expansion, for example, *bronco* was borrowed from the Spanish for "rough" and *mustang* from the Spanish for "stray."

5. Some slang words are simply invented. Among American backwoodsmen of the nineteenth century, the wilder the invention, the better. If

you were *puckerstoppled,* you were embarrassed; confusion was *conbobberation;* and a heavy blow, in a fight or from the weather, was a *sockdologer.* Those words have disappeared, but other invented words have remained. *Blizzard,* for example, was first defined as a violent blow, perhaps from the German word *blitz,* for "lightning." In 1870, *blizzard* was applied by newspapers to violent snowstorms and was found to be so useful that it became standard English.

From Slang to Standard English

Most slang terms die quickly. There is a constant turnover, especially among "in" words. *Lounge lizard, hootchie-kootchie,* and *goo-goo eyes* came and went as fast as *cool cat, squaresville,* and *hep.* (*Hep's* offspring, *hip,* is still with us, however.) Terms that fill a need in standard English sometimes make the transition from slang to standard. *Plunder, fix, all right,* and *rough-*

"Luann" reprinted by permission of United Feature Syndicate, Inc.

Crossing the Curriculum

Music

Since the days of George M. Cohan, Broadway shows have often told life stories of Americans, usually ordinary people in contemporary situations. Broadway songwriters are notable for their slangy lyrics. Have students listen to recordings of the Broadway shows *Gypsy* (Styne/Sondheim) and *West Side Story* (Bernstein/ Sondheim). Have them compare and contrast the slang vocabularies of the characters. Which lyrics seem dated? Which seem completely up-to-date? Were there expressions, words, or idioms students did not understand? How did this impact their enjoyment of the songs?

neck all started as slang and were once condemned by one *highbrow* or another.

Who decides what is slang and what is standard usage? The answer to this is that we all do. Native speakers of a language have a finely tuned sense of the distinction between formal and informal language. As some slang words achieve wide popular usage, though, that distinction may blur. For example, which of these words would you say are slang, and which are standard: *corny, scrumptious, pinhead*? You might say, "Look it up in the dictionary." But the answer depends on which dictionary you use. Dictionaries whose primary purpose is to *describe* the language are apt to provide fewer usage distinctions than dictionaries prepared by lexicographers who feel that it is important to *prescribe* usage. The chart below shows the verdicts of three popular American dictionaries on whether or not our three test words are slang.

Obviously, lexicographers disagree on when a word becomes widely enough used to qualify as "standard." Some words, in fact, never make the jump at all. Terms that fill a real informal need often remain as slang for generations. Terms like *rubberneck, to squeal, baloney,* and *nifty* have endured, although regarded as slang for years. These words seem so informal that they resist incorporation into standard English, but they survive to remind us of our capacity for making poetry out of the commonplace.

Harbaugh/Rothco.

"Failure to do your homework on proper grammatical usage will result in a final grade of zero, zip, zilch . . ."

Try It Out

1. **Listing slang terms.**
   There are hundreds of slang terms for some common experiences or things. With two or three other students, list as many slang terms as you can for the following.

   a. an automobile
   b. failing a test
   c. getting angry
   d. stealing

   Once you've completed the lists, talk about the **metaphors** on which some of the slang terms may be based.

2. **Identifying full-word forms.** Here are some clipped forms of words in current use. Identify their full forms, referring to a dictionary if necessary.

ad lib	flu	pep
bus	gas	prom
cello	gym	prop

3. **Compiling local slang.** Join with the rest of the class in compiling a list of slang words that you believe are used only in your particular school or community. Try to explain the origin of each word.

Are They Slang? Three Verdicts			
Dictionary	Word		
	Corny	Scrumptious	Pinhead
Webster's Second International	No	Yes	No
Webster's Third International	No	No	No
American Heritage Dictionary	No	No	Yes

B ## Elements of Literature
Slang
Ask students to identify the slang expression in these sentences. ["make the jump"] Have them rewrite the sentence in more formal English. [Possible answer: Some words, in fact, never qualify as standard.] Ask what the sentence loses or gains by this change. [Loses: "make the jump" is a vivid expression that creates a clear picture in the reader's mind. Gains: "qualify as standard" is more in keeping with the tone of the essay and still makes the meaning clear.]

Try It Out
Possible Answers
1. a. wheels, chariot
   b. crashing and burning, bombing
   c. getting one's back up, getting sore, having a hissy fit, seeing red
   d. swiping, ripping off, lifting
2. *ad libitum,* omnibus, violoncello, influenza, gasoline, gymnasium, pepper, promenade, property
3. Students may suggest slang phrases associated with local hangouts or gathering places on the school grounds, local sports teams, or prominent individuals.

Resources
Assessment
Formal Assessment
• The American Language Test, p. 156

Assessing Learning

Check Test: True-False
1. The term *slang* refers to colorful, irreverent, lively language that quickly becomes popular and often quickly disappears. [True]
2. The main function of slang is to show membership in a group. [True]
3. Americans began using slang in the 1960s. [False]
4. The term *fan,* as in baseball fan, is a shortened version of the word *fanatic* and was once a "clipped" slang word. [True]
5. Editors of dictionaries always agree on whether or not a word is slang. [False]

Writer's Workshop

MAIN OBJECTIVE
Write an interpretive essay

PROCESS OBJECTIVES
1. Use appropriate prewriting techniques to identify and develop a topic
2. Create a first draft
3. Use Evaluation Criteria as a basis for determining revision strategies
4. Revise the first draft incorporating suggestions generated by self- or peer evaluation
5. Proofread and correct errors
6. Create a final draft
7. Choose an appropriate method of publication
8. Reflect on progress as a writer

Planning

- **Block Schedule**
  Block Scheduling Lesson Plans with Pacing Guide

- **One-Stop Planner**
  CD-ROM with Test Generator

Try It Out
Be sure to remind students to support their interpretive claims with specific examples from the work. For textual works, make sure they quote the relevant passages accurately and include the page numbers and bibliographic information. For film or video works, students should try to obtain film stills that show the relevant scenes or sequences. For other visual art, students should try to obtain a reproduction of the work to point out specific details.

Technology HELP

See Writer's Workshop 2 CD-ROM. *Assignment: Interpretation.*

ASSIGNMENT
Write an essay interpreting a work of literature, a movie, or a work of visual art.

AIM
To inform; to explain; to persuade.

AUDIENCE
Your teacher; your classmates; members of a literature, film, or art appreciation group.

Try It Out

With a partner or a small group, choose a poem, story, film, or work of visual art. Identify two or three of the most important elements in the work, and discuss how they relate to the work's meaning. Then, develop three or four interpretive claims you can make about the work.

EXPOSITORY WRITING
INTERPRETIVE ESSAY

Every day you interpret information you receive from your environment and arrive at conclusions based on evidence presented to you. You might see dark clouds and infer that it's going to rain, or notice how shy a classmate is and infer that he may have difficulty making friends. Interpreting a literary work, a movie, or a painting isn't as straightforward as inferring the meaning of an ordinary event. However, it can be fascinating and satisfying to make sense of a work of verbal or visual art and to share your interpretation with others.

Prewriting

1. **What hooks your interest?** When you write an interpretation, it's important to feel strongly about the work you're interpreting. Perhaps one poem or story in this book or in your outside reading moved you in a way no other literary work has. Perhaps you have had a similar response to a favorite painting or film. Be sure to review your Writer's Notebook entries for Collections 14–16; you may have already made a head start on prewriting for an interpretive essay.

2. **Ask yourself about the work.** "What does this mean to me?" is perhaps the most productive question to ask yourself about a literary work or a work of visual art. Spend time developing a thorough answer. Remember—this question can take you anywhere: into your own life experience; into the society around you; into historical events; into other subject areas; into other literary works, films, and other works of art; or into an examination of the life and personality of a writer, a director, or an artist.

3. **Use a double-entry journal.** A double-entry journal is one of the simplest and best response tools you can use. Divide a sheet of paper into two columns. In the left column, include quotations from the work you're analyzing (literature), descriptions of significant dialogue or images (film or video), or notes on visual elements such as color and composition (fine art). In the right column, write your response to each quotation or description. Then, select those entries in the left column that you sense are crucial to the work's meaning. Think of the double-entry journal as a written dialogue with yourself, full of questions and unexpected discoveries.

804 THE MODERNS

 Resources: Print and Media

Writing and Language
- *Portfolio Management System*
  - Prewriting, p. 192
  - Peer Editing, p. 193
  - Assessment Rubric, p. 194
- *Workshop Resources*
  - Revision Strategy Teaching Notes, p. 31
  - Revision Strategy Transparencies 16, 17, 18
- *Writer's Workshop 2 CD-ROM*
  - Interpretation

The history of the written word is rich and... Once upon a time...

Model: A Double-Entry Journal

"A Rose for Emily" by William Faulkner

title: "A Rose for Emily"	The title seems kind of romantic, maybe sentimental and nostalgic.
her house: "stubborn and coquettish decay"; "an eyesore among eyesores" (p. 716)	I had to look up the word "coquettish." It comes from the word coquette, a vain girl or woman who tries to get the attention of admirers. A clue to Miss Emily's personality? The house reminds me of the house in Poe's "Fall of the House of Usher." It's creepy.
"Miss Emily had been a tradition, a duty, and a care; a sort of hereditary obligation upon the town." (p. 716)	She sounds like a burden. I wonder if anyone really liked her? Sounds like they probably didn't.

4. **Make interpretive claims.** An **interpretive claim** is a general statement about what the work means. You might make several interpretive claims in one essay, especially if you focus on several key elements in the work. To make your interpretive claims, begin thinking in general terms about what the work means. For stories and novels, think about character, plot, setting, point of view, and theme. For poems, think about diction, imagery, symbolism, figurative language, and sound. For the visual arts, think about subject matter, colors, shapes, tone, and overall effect. Try to make at least one generalization for each element that is important to the work. For Faulkner's "A Rose for Emily," for example, you might write, "Events in the story are presented out of sequence so that Faulkner can explore the effects of the past on the present" (plot). (Unsupportable opinions such as "I like this poem" or "I have mixed feelings about this painting" are not interpretive claims.)

5. **Focus on a thesis.** Choose the interpretive claim that you feel is the strongest or most interesting, and make it your thesis: the central idea that will unify your essay. A thesis statement might be, "At first glance 'A Rose for Emily' seems to be merely a shocking horror story, but it has a serious theme: it explores the risks of clinging obstinately to the past and tradition."

6. **Support your claims.** Types of supporting evidence include quotations and paraphrases from the text, details from related works, and your own knowledge and experience. You might also wish to support your interpretive claim with quotations from critics. Be sure all quoted material is carefully documented.

Strategies for Elaboration

To ensure that your essay reads well:
- Use transitional words and phrases.
- Use definite, specific, concrete language instead of vague generalities.
- Use the literary present tense when appropriate (see page 807).
- Use a relatively formal tone, avoiding slang and colloquialisms.

Have students interpret the following scene, using the clues provided. Give the clues one at a time, and let students respond after each.

Basic situation: You are home alone.
1. It is a rainy fall night, and the lights in the house have been flickering off and on.
2. The dog, who has been sleeping at your feet, suddenly sits up and begins to look intently at the front door of the house.
3. From outside in the street, you hear a muffled shriek.
4. The date is October 31.
   How does our interpretation change with clue #4? Suppose you didn't know that October 31 was Halloween; would the date make a difference in your interpretation of the situation?

Summarize with students by pointing out that we constantly interpret the meaning of events, friends' actions, even natural occurrences, but our interpretations are necessarily limited by what we know or what we have experienced.

Teaching the Writer's Workshop

Prewriting
Discuss all the suggested Prewriting steps with students, but in particular encourage them to try the double-entry journal. As students work on these journals, encourage them to ask the question "why" and to speculate on the reasons behind events and characters' decisions. The answers to these "why" questions may provide valuable insight that could lead to the development of a thesis statement.

Reaching All Students

English Language Learners
Encourage students learning English to choose a piece of literature written in their native tongue to interpret. They should find an English translation of a small but important piece of their selection and focus their interpretation on the importance of this passage to the complete work.

Advanced Learners
Have advanced students research and read professional critiques of the works about which they intend to write. Students can use these secondary sources to enhance or support their own thesis ideas. Refer students to the information about documenting sources and creating a "works cited" page in the Communications Handbook.

Drafting

- Before students begin their drafts, provide a model of an interpretive essay. You may wish to share one you have written yourself or possibly one written by a previous student.
- Before beginning to write, students should have read the material on pp. 806–807. Encourage them to review this information periodically as a way to keep on track.
- Remind students to use only every other line when they write their drafts. They should also leave extra space in the right margin. These blank spaces will be used for comments and editing marks.

Evaluating and Revising

Have students use the Evaluation Criteria provided here to review their drafts and determine needed revisions.

Proofreading

Have students proofread their own papers first and then exchange them with other students. For this assignment, remind students to be particularly careful to use the literary present tense correctly.

Publishing

Students might want to submit their essays for publication in the school literary magazine or in an appropriate journal.

Reflecting

If students are adding their interpretive essays to their portfolios, they should also include answers to the following questions:

1. How did my writing increase my understanding of the work I selected?
2. What problems did I have understanding the literary work, and how did I solve them?
3. What, if anything, will I do differently the next time I write an interpretive essay?

Resources

Peer Editing Forms and Rubrics
- *Portfolio Management System*, p. 193

Revision Transparencies
- *Workshop Resources*, p. 31

Language Handbook HELP

See *Quotation Marks*, page 1246.

Revision STRATEGIES

Reread your conclusion to see if it wraps up your essay satisfactorily. If your essay leaves any loose ends, go back and focus your argument to make sure that every step supports your thesis.

▍ Evaluation Criteria

A good interpretive essay
1. *focuses on a central thesis*
2. *presents a coherent series of interpretive claims that are relevant to the thesis*
3. *provides specific support for each claim with evidence from the text or authoritative sources*
4. *properly documents all sources*
5. *is clearly organized and remains on topic*
6. *has a conclusion that reinforces the thesis*

Communications Handbook HELP

See *Taking Notes and Documenting Sources; List of Sources Cited; Proofreading.*

806 THE MODERNS

Drafting

1. **Getting Started.** At the beginning of your essay, identify the work you are writing about (by title and author, artist, or director), and provide necessary background information (perhaps a *very* brief summary of the work). You also need to give your readers a sense of where the essay as a whole is going. You might do that by stating your thesis directly in your opening paragraph.

2. **Organizing your thoughts.** Choose a sensible order for presenting your ideas. An interpretive essay may be organized in one of several ways.

   - **Chronological order.** Show the order in which certain details occur in the work (such as changes in a character).

   - **Order of importance.** Move from your least important point to your most important point, or vice versa.

   - **Logical order.** Group related ideas together. If, for example, you're focusing on plot and setting, present all your points about plot in one section and all your points about setting in another section. If you've chosen to compare and contrast two works, you can either treat the elements of one work before turning to elements of the other work (block method) or alternate between the works as you discuss each element in turn (point-by-point organization).

3. **Presenting and developing your interpretive claims.** The heart of your essay is an organized presentation of your claim about the work. Stating your generalizations may only require a sentence or two. Many more sentences will be needed to support these claims, including evidence from the text and related works. You'll need to document your sources in two places—in parenthetical citations and in the list of Works Cited.

4. **Staying on topic.** Keep your thesis in mind at all times; never lose the thread of your analysis; include only relevant points; be specific and concrete. Conclude your essay with an insight that sums up your thesis or leads to intriguing new questions.

Evaluating and Revising

1. **Peer review.** Exchange papers with one or more classmates, and answer the following questions about the paper you read:

   - Can you clearly identify the writer's thesis? Does the writer provide sufficient background information about the work?

   - Does the writer present enough evidence to support his or her interpretive claims? Were you convinced of the writer's position?

   - Does the essay come to a conclusion that ties all the writer's ideas together and reinforces the thesis?

2. **Self-evaluation.** Read your peers' comments; then, reread your own essay as if you were not the author. Decide if your essay needs more of something (more supporting evidence, more focus) or less of something (less padding, less personal opinion). Then, make appropriate revisions.

Grading Timesaver

Rubrics for this Writer's Workshop assignment appear on p. 194 of the *Portfolio Management System*.

Language Workshop

THE RIGHT TENSE FOR SENSE: USING THE LITERARY PRESENT

When you write, you can help your readers to understand the order in which things occur by using verb tenses correctly—and consistently. Each of the six basic verb tenses—present, past, future, present perfect, past perfect, and future perfect—has its own applications. The present tense, for example, is used to express an action or state of being that is current, that is happening right now.

When you write about literature, you'll want to use a form of present tense called the **literary present.** You may write, for example, "'A Rose for Emily' *is* a story about a solitary individual with a shocking secret." You use the literary present because a work of literature Is continually alive, re-created each time someone reads it. "A Rose for Emily" will *always* be a story about an individual with a shocking secret.

Strategies for Using the Literary Present

1. Use the present tense when analyzing a story or paraphrasing the author's ideas. Use the past tense when the characters themselves use the past tense. In other words, when you're quoting directly from a work, use the same tense the author uses. Otherwise, keep your essay in the literary present.

2. Sometimes, using the literary present and the past tense can create awkward situations. When your tenses sound awkward, try rewriting. For example, this sentence is awkward even though it correctly uses past and present tenses: "In 'A Rose for Emily,' William Faulkner, who *was* a Southerner, *shows* his understanding of the traditions of the American South." This could be rewritten in the following way: "In 'A Rose for Emily,' William Faulkner, a Southerner, *shows* his understanding of the traditions of the American South."

3. When you **summarize** the plot of a story or a poem, you can use the present or past tense, but you must be consistent. If you use the literary present and refer to an action that took place in the past, you must use the past tense. Thus you would say "After Miss Emily dies, the ladies go to her house and are met by the Negro servant who had worked for Miss Emily for years."

Writer's Workshop Follow-Up: Revising

Reread the interpretive essay you wrote for the Writer's Workshop on page 804, and make sure you use the literary present correctly. If you have summarized a plot, be sure your verb tenses are consistent.

Technology HELP

See Language Workshop CD-ROM. *Key word entry: consistency of tense.*

Language Handbook HELP

See Tenses and Their Uses, pages 1224–1225.

Try It Out

Revise the paragraph below so that it consistently uses the literary present.

"A Rose for Emily" was a complex story that could be interpreted on several levels. On one level the story was about the conflict between the individual and the community. It was also about the conflicts between tradition and modern life. Faulkner, a modernist, contrasted the "New South" with the "Old South," which was symbolized by Miss Emily's old-style, crumbling house.

Resources

Workshop Resources
• Worksheet, p. 59
Language Workshop CD-ROM
• Consistency of Tense

Try It Out
Possible Answers
(Verbs that have been changed to the present tense are underlined.)
"A Rose for Emily" <u>is</u> a complex story that <u>can</u> be interpreted on several levels. On one level the story <u>is</u> about the conflict between the individual and the community. It <u>is</u> also about the conflicts between tradition and modern life. Faulkner, a modernist, <u>contrasts</u> the "New South" with the "Old South," which <u>is</u> symbolized by Miss Emily's old-style, crumbling house.

Assessing Learning

Quick Check:
Using the Literary Present Tense
Change the verbs in the following sentences to the literary present. If a sentence is already in the literary present, write "correct."

1. William Faulkner, the author of "A Rose for Emily," <u>wrote</u> about a wide variety of people in his works. [writes]

2. For example, in his novel *As I Lay Dying,* Faulkner <u>shows</u> the tribulations of a poor family. [correct]

3. In another novel, *The Sound and the Fury,* he <u>presented</u> the saga of an aristocratic family, the Compsons. [presents]

4. Many readers and critics believe that Faulkner <u>captured</u> the whole spectrum of Southern life in his writings. [captures]

OBJECTIVES

1. Obtain information from an Internet database
2. Focus an Internet search
3. Evaluate a database
4. Cite the source of data obtained from the Internet

Teaching the Lesson

Explain to students that the Internet is in a constant state of change and that finding a particular Web site may require searching through a number of different key words to find the right site. For instance, if the key word search for "Rangers statistics" failed to bring up the appropriate site, a good strategy might be to broaden the search by looking for "Rangers baseball." Remember that content on the Internet is unpredictable, and be prepared to handle the appearance of inappropriate or irrelevant material in the course of students' Internet searches.

Using the Strategies
Possible Answers

1. Roberto Kelly (.323)
2. Juan Gonzalez (606)
3. Juan Gonzalez (110), R. Greer (107), Tom Goodwin (102)
4. Royce Clayton, Todd Zeile
5. on base percentage
6. compare players' productivity; determine strikeout to at-bat ratio
7. Official Website of Major League Baseball
8. Stats, Inc.

Situation

Like Marianne Moore, you're a sports fan and you want to research data on a baseball team in the American League. You have access to a commercial on-line service or to the Internet.

Strategies

When using an electronic database, apply the following strategies:

Focus on the data you need.

- Formulate a clear idea of the data you want to find and how you intend to use it. This will help you focus your search.

Search the Internet.

- Use the search feature of your on-line service provider or an Internet portal. You may need to enter the category of information you're looking for, such as "baseball statistics." You can also enter a specific Uniform Resource Locator (URL) for a Web site. See also the Communications Handbook.

Evaluate the database.

- Once you've found some data, scan through it to make sure it's what you want.
- Evaluate the source of the data. Is it a reputable source? Is the data current and updated regularly? Does the data agree with data from at least one other source?
- Cite the source of any data you use. For example, give the

Web site or the name of the on-line service.

Using the Strategies

Examine the database on this page. Then, answer the following questions.

1. Which Texas Rangers player had the highest batting average?
2. Which player had the most official at-bats?
3. Which three players scored the most runs?
4. Who played for more than one team in 1998?
5. What does OBP mean?
6. What are two possible uses you might have for this data?
7. What resources might you use to corroborate the data?
8. Where did this data come from?

Extending the Strategies

Using the strategies you've learned, research data on another sports team or on a different subject that interests you. Focus on a specific topic, and in a paragraph or two report the information you found and the problems you encountered. If you like, suggest ways in which the database could be improved.

TEXAS RANGERS

1998 TEXAS RANGERS REGULAR SEASON BATTING STATISTICS

PLAYER	G	AB	R	H	2B	3B	HR	RBI	BB	SO	OBP	SLG	AVG
Roberto Kelly	75	257	48	83	7	3	16	46	8	46	.349	.560	.323
Ivan Rodriguez	145	579	88	186	40	4	21	91	32	88	.358	.513	.321
Juan Gonzalez	154	606	110	193	50	2	45	157	46	126	.366	.630	.318
Rusty Greer	155	598	107	183	31	5	16	108	80	93	.386	.455	.306
Will Clark	149	554	98	169	41	1	23	102	72	97	.384	.507	.305
Mike Simms	86	186	36	55	11	0	16	46	24	47	.381	.613	.296
Tom Goodwin	154	520	102	151	13	3	2	33	73	90	.378	.338	.290
Luis Alecea	101	259	51	71	15	3	6	33	37	40	.372	.425	.274
Todd Zeile	158	572	85	155	32	3	19	94	69	90	.350	.437	.271
...Tex	52	180	26	47	14	1	6	28	28	32	.358	.450	.261
...La	40	158	22	40	6	1	7	27	10	24	.300	.437	.253
...Fla	66	234	37	68	12	1	6	39	31	34	.374	.427	.291
Lee Stevens	120	344	52	91	17	4	20	59	31	93	.324	.512	.265
Domingo Cedeno	61	141	19	37	9	1	2	21	10	32	.309	.383	.262
Royce Clayton	142	541	89	136	31	2	9	53	53	83	.319	.366	.251
...Tex	52	186	30	53	12	1	5	24	13	32	.330	.441	.285
...StL	90	355	59	83	19	1	4	29	40	51	.313	.327	.234
Mark McLemore	126	461	79	114	15	1	5	53	89	64	.369	.317	.247
Kevin Elster	84	297	33	69	10	1	8	37	33	66	.311	.354	.232
Totals (including players not listed)	162	5672	940	1637	314	32	201	894	595	1045	.375	.462	.289

Data Source: Stats, Inc. Copyright © by STATS™ Inc. All rights reserved. Commercial distribution without the express written consent of Stats is prohibited.

Reaching All Students

English Language Learners

Some students, especially those from countries where baseball is not a popular sport, might not be familiar with specialized terms, such as *home runs, switch hits,* and *at bats.* So that these students are not completely baffled by the chart in this lesson, briefly explain, or have another student explain, these terms.

Learning for Life

Planning for the Future

OBJECTIVES
1. Research issues pertaining to aging
2. Present the research in an appropriate format

Problem

Many of the stories and poems in the collections you have just read are told from the perspective of people looking back on their lives from the vantage point of old age. How do people in our society make fulfilling lives for themselves as they grow older? How can you plan for your later years so that life is meaningful and enjoyable?

Project

Research contemporary issues pertaining to aging: geriatric health care, the future of Social Security and retirement benefits, increases in life expectancy, older employees returning to the work force, changing perspectives of older adults, and so on.

Preparation

1. With a group, brainstorm a list of questions you have about the topic of aging.
2. Make a list of current books, periodicals, and other sources for information on aging.

Procedure

1. You might want to interview an older relative or friend about individual perspectives on aging and retirement. You might also choose to
   - interview a geriatric doctor or nurse about the medical aspects of aging

   - investigate retirement options by contacting the American Association of Retired Persons (AARP)
   - examine retirement financing with a planning expert
   - discuss social and emotional aspects of aging with a social worker or psychologist

   Set a time for your interview, and prepare questions.

2. Study current social views of aging and the elderly by paying attention to media representations. You might take notes on news programs devoted to the topic of the elderly, keep track of the number of elderly characters on TV shows and note how they are portrayed, and watch popular films such as *The Trip to Bountiful* and *Driving Miss Daisy*. What positive and negative messages about aging is society giving us?

Presentation

Present your information on aging in one of the following formats (or another that your teacher approves):

1. **Retirement Brochure**
   Write and design a brochure describing the ideal retirement plan for you. Be sure to include the following:
   - whether you plan to continue working part time, perform community service, and so on

   - a description of the living situation you would prefer
   - recreational activities you hope to participate in

2. **In Praise of Old Age**
   Put together a video documentary or a photo-essay of interviews with older adults. Show as many sides of the realities of aging as you can. If you wish, include interviews with people who work with the aged or who live with or know the particular persons you have interviewed.

3. **Graphic Communication**
   Share your findings about aging (what happens to the body as it ages, life expectancy in the twenty-first century, media depictions of the elderly, economic trends among retired people, and so on) in a visual display that combines two or more types of graphic communication: charts, graphs, diagrams, illustrations, and so on. Set up your graphic display in your school.

Processing

What did you learn about aging by completing this project? What can people do to develop more realistic ideas of what growing older entails? What can you do now to make sure that your own later years are meaningful and enjoyable? Write a reflection for your portfolio.

Resources

Viewing and Representing
HRW Multimedia Presentation Maker

Students may wish to use the *HRW Multimedia Presentation Maker* to create visuals for their displays.

Grading Timesaver

Rubrics for this Learning for Life project appear on p. 195 of the *Portfolio Management System*.

Developing Workplace Competencies

Preparation	Procedure	Presentation
• Makes decisions	• Acquires data	• Thinks creatively
• Works on teams	• Evaluates data	• Teaches others
• Demonstrates individual responsibility	• Applies technology to specific tasks	• Selects equipment
• Works with people from diverse backgrounds	• Improves systems	• Communicates ideas and information

OBJECTIVES

1. Read a modern American drama on the theme "The Breaking of Charity"
2. Interpret literary elements with special emphasis on character motivation
3. Apply a variety of reading strategies to the literature, including interpreting a text
4. Respond to the literature in a variety of modes
5. Learn and use new words
6. Learn about the development of modern American drama
7. Plan, revise, draft, and edit an autobiographical essay
8. Develop sentence combining skills
9. Demonstrate the ability to read a film review
10. Evaluate dramatic choices

RESPONDING TO THE ART

Carousel, like many Broadway musicals, has an intriguing dark side. It was adapted from Hungarian playwright Ferenc Molnár's grim *Liliom,* which seemed an unlikely source for a Rodgers and Hammerstein musical. In the musical, shadowy Budapest becomes a small New England town where carnival barker Billy Bigelow catches the eye of wholesome Julie Jordan. Their marriage settles him a bit, until Julie becomes pregnant and Billy gets involved in a robbery scheme that costs him his life. *Liliom* ends tragically, but *Carousel* ends hopefully. Julie's love for her husband goes beyond the grave, and Billy, in death, comes to realize his mistakes.

Activity. Ask students how this photograph reflects *Carousel's* bittersweet tone, as well as its use of fantastical and nonrealistic dramatic elements. [Students might note the wistful expression of the woman at left as she looks into the night sky, along with the exaggerated and simplified forms of the moon and the church.]

American Drama

Selection Readability

This Annotated Teacher's Edition provides a summary of each selection in the student book. Following each Summary heading, you will find one, two, or three small icons. These icons indicate, in an approximate sense, the reading level of the selection.

- One icon indicates that the selection is easy.
- ■ ■ Two icons indicate that the selection is on an intermediate reading level.
- ■ ■ ■ Three icons indicate that the selection is challenging.

Cultural Connections

Probably the most successful American composer-librettist duo ever, Richard Rodgers (1902–1979) and Oscar Hammerstein II (1895–1960) helped to transform American musical comedy into true musical theater. They earned a Pulitzer Prize with their very first collaboration, *Oklahoma!* (1943). Other smash hits included *South Pacific* (1949; Pulitzer Prize, 1950), *Carousel* (1945), *The King and I* (1951), and *The Sound of Music* (1959). Altogether, they collaborated on ten Broadway musicals. In dramatic terms, one of their greatest accomplishments was uniting music and drama so that songs were no longer interludes or interruptions, but rather ways of advancing the plot and revealing character.

Scene from Rodgers and Hammerstein's *Carousel*. Lincoln Center, New York City, 1994. **A**

811

Resources: Print and Media

Viewing and Representing
- *Visual Connections*
  Videocassette A, Segment 1

Assessment
- *Formal Assessment, p. 164*
- *Preparation for College Admission Exams, p. 57*
- *Test Generator (One-Stop Planner CD-ROM)*

Internet
- go.hrw.com (keyword: LE0 11-17)

OBJECTIVES
1. Learn about the development of modern American drama
2. Write notes predicting trends in American drama in the next decade

Responding to the Quotation

? Even if you have never seen professional theater, you probably have enjoyed school, community, and other live performances. Why do you think the performance of a story through dialogue and action affects our emotions so powerfully? How is it that live theater "touches our inner core"? [Possible responses: The dialogue and action of theatrical performance removes the intellectual mediation and distance that the narrator of a novel or the speaker of a poem can impose. Live theater helps us understand ourselves and the world around us by lending immediacy to the written word.]

Resources

Viewing and Representing
Videocassette: Drama: The Live Connection
This videotape segment explores how theater is alive today.
• Videocassette A, Segment 1
Formal Assessment
• Literary Period Introduction Test, p. 164

American Drama

by **Robert Anderson**

Theater is one of the most emotionally satisfying experiences imaginable. It touches our inner core, and gives insight into who we are.

—*Theodore Mann*

812 AMERICAN DRAMA

Reaching All Students

Struggling Readers
On a flow chart or other linear graphic organizer, have students note each step in the process of producing a play, from the first readings through local or regional tryouts to a full-fledged production (locally, regionally, or on Broadway). As students read the second half of this essay, have them create a time line to track the development of modern American drama, from Eugene O'Neill to Arthur Miller, Tennessee Williams, and Edward Albee.

English Language Learners
The technical theater terms used in this essay, such as *exposition, agent, director,* and *producer,* may confuse students unfamiliar with the conventions of live performance. As they read, have students create a personal glossary of new terms they encounter. Then have pairs of students use context clues to define each word. If they cannot figure out the word from context clues, have students use a dictionary or the glossary in the back of the book.

Advanced Students
Explain to students that Robert Anderson, the author of this essay, is an outstanding dramatist in his own right. Invite students to find out more about Anderson's career, including his Broadway hit *Tea and Sympathy* (1953). Students can share their findings with the class in a brief oral or written report.

Drama is probably the most difficult form of writing; it certainly seems to take the longest to learn. According to a saying, young poets are eighteen, young novelists are twenty-four, and young playwrights are thirty.

George S. Kaufman, a noted American writer of comedies during the 1920s and 1930s, said that writing plays was not an art but a trick. Art or trick, it is difficult, possibly because when a play is written, it is not finished in the same way that a poem or novel is. There remains the painful and pleasurable process of bringing the play to life on stage, with the help of a director, actors, set designer, costume designer, lighting technician, stagehands, musicians—and a responsive audience. Producing a play is a team effort, and much can go wrong. A beautifully written and acted scene, for example, can be ruined if the lighting technician dims the lights too rapidly.

Another difference between drama and other literary forms is that movement and gesture are essential elements in drama. Some of the high points in a play may even be nonverbal. In *The Diary of Anne Frank*, for example, Mr. Frank realizes that the Nazis are downstairs and that the family's hiding place is about to be discovered. He turns to his family and friends and spreads his hands in resignation. This heartbreaking moment is conceived by the playwright, but its achievement on the stage—the exact gesture—requires the close and creative cooperation of actor and director.

Young writers are often drawn to the stage by the theatrical trappings: the gestures, the colorful sets, and the magical effects that drama can achieve. But playwrights soon learn that theatrical effects are rarely enough in themselves. The effects and gestures are there only to serve a story, and it must be a story that engages the passions of the collaborators—the director, the actors, and dozens of others who work to produce a play. Stage technicians may dazzle our senses with intricate and fascinating effects, but if a play doesn't have a significant story, we find nothing moving in the end, because our emotions have not been touched.

> . . . [W]hile I am working I toss papers right and left; at the end of each day I gather them helter-skelter and pile them together. So that the ultimate arrangement is a colossal job, which I do with actual groans and muttered curses, sitting on the floor with papers all about me, gradually going into little separate stacks, some order finally emerging, but not till I have died a thousand deaths. . . . Writing is not a happy profession.
> —Tennessee Williams

PLAYBILL®

THE MUSIC BOX

THE DIARY OF ANNE FRANK

THE DIARY OF ANNE FRANK

PLAYBILL® is a registered trademark of Playbill Incorporated, N.Y.C. All rights reserved. Used by permission.

go.hrw.com
LEO 11-Drama

AMERICAN DRAMA **813**

A Critical Thinking
Speculating
? What difficulties does drama impose on a writer that a novel or a poem does not? What is unique about this genre that might make it so challenging to write? [Possible response: Drama requires that all information about characters' emotions, thoughts, and development be communicated *externally,* through speech, gesture, facial expression, and so on. It is also limited by the two- or three-hour attention span of most audiences, by technical challenges involved in lighting and set design, and by the essentially collaborative character of the final product.]

B Literary Connections
The Diary of Anne Frank
The Diary of Anne Frank, written by Frances Goodrich and Albert Hackett, is based on the diary kept by Anne Frank, a teenage Jewish girl, as she hid with her family in an Amsterdam attic during the Nazi occupation of Holland. The play won many awards, and its first production ran for seven hundred seventeen performances. Despite its successful run, the play was not universally applauded; Arthur Miller, for example, found it powerful but thought that it lacked a far-reaching vision.

C Reading Skills and Strategies
Summarizing
? According to the writer, what makes a play successful? Summarize his point in your own words. [Possible responses: A play is successful only when the plot touches the theatergoer's feelings. No matter how technically proficient and dazzling a play may be, it is ultimately a failure unless it presents a story with some larger meaning and purpose.]

Crossing the Curriculum

Architecture/Mechanical Drawing
Invite students to select a play that they have never seen performed and "stage" it by designing sets for each act. If resources are available, some students may want to create scale models of their sets. Students can include sketches of costumes as well, if they wish.

History/Musical Theater
Have students read a play or work of fiction from which a musical has been adapted and then watch a video of the musical. Possibilities include *Romeo and Juliet* / *West Side Story*, *Pygmalion* / *My Fair Lady*, and *The Matchmaker* / *Hello, Dolly!* Students can also compare a musical and its original work of literature, such as *Oliver Twist* / *Oliver*, *The Once and Future King* / *Camelot*, or *Tales of Sholom Aleichem* / *Fiddler on the Roof*. In an oral report to the class, have students draw comparisons between the play or novel and the musical. Which form tells a more effective story? Why? How does the writer adapt the original work to the unique requirements of musical theater?

Structure: Organizing Our Emotions

When a play goes wrong, it is almost always because the writer has failed to conceive the story in dramatic terms. There are, of course, some plays (such as Thornton Wilder's *Our Town*) that work in the theater even though they ignore the usual principles of drama. But over the centuries certain principles have developed, and they are usually observed by playwrights who want to catch, hold, and reward the attention of an audience.

The analogy is slightly oversimplified, but we respond to a play in very much the way we respond to a sports event. Let's assume that one summer evening you go to a professional baseball game. For some reason, you take a liking to one of the pitchers. Then someone sitting next to you says that the pitcher has been out for several weeks with an injured elbow and is trying to make a comeback. If he fails in this game, he is finished. You start rooting for him. He gets some bad calls from the plate umpire, and you boo or whistle. Then your neighbor tells you that the pitcher is not pitching his best. Unless he stops protecting his injured elbow and starts putting more speed in his pitches, he will not win.

Most plays have more psychological complexity than this situation does. With a little imagination, however, we can add to the pitcher's problems. Suppose, for instance, that the pitcher's wife is afraid that if he throws too hard, he will ruin his elbow and be unable to play. She tells him that if he damages his elbow further, she will leave him; but, to him, the glory of winning transcends practical matters. To his wife, he is a ball-playing "boy," careless and immature. And so forth. . . . What has happened in this scenario is what happens in almost every play. Early on, the playwright organizes our emotions behind some character or group of characters: We are "for" them. The playwright has placed these characters in a situation involving **conflict** and then has made us understand that it is not just any conflict: The character or characters have something vital at stake. They want to win, and they need to win in order to survive. In the baseball game, the situation is made difficult for the pitcher, who is the **protagonist** (the major character who wants something and who drives the action forward). The pitcher struggles against

> You have to hit the public when it is not looking . . . you have to make it real to them the way the subway is real. You can't depend on their embracing your work because it is art, but only because it somehow reaches into the part of them that is still alive and questing.
>
> —Arthur Miller

Using Students' Strengths

Kinesthetic Learners

To help students apply the central concept that a play is formed from the interaction between actors and audience, have several students work together to present a scene from a play, such as The Crucible (pp. 829–887). When the performance is over, have the actors and the audience describe how the performers responded to each other and to the audience. Have students discuss specific examples from the performance.

Interpersonal Learners

Invite students to imagine that they are producing a new play. In a whole-class or small-group discussion, have them explain what their tasks would be, how they could establish good working relationships among all the people involved, and how they would produce the play efficiently without sacrificing creativity. Then, have them discuss what they would do if the play had poor ticket sales and received mixed or unfavorable reviews.

both **external conflict** (the opposing side) and **internal conflict** (his fears of damaging his arm, his feelings about the pressure from his wife). The fan sitting next to you has given us the background information, or **exposition** (who the pitcher is, what he wants to do, and what he has at stake). The story of a character who, against the odds, wants something meaningful has been set in motion. The tension mounts as the innings pass; we are witnessing, or participating in and enjoying, a drama.

> . . . I would say that the whole notion of going into a theater and sitting with a lot of other people and watching a spectacle, especially now when you can watch television or the movies with greater convenience, tells me that, apart from the fact that it's a little more exciting to see a live actor on the stage, it's also exciting to sit next to human beings.
> —Arthur Miller

The word *participation* is important. We have all heard ballplayers say how encouraged they are by the response of the spectators. Actors, too, may say as they come offstage after a scene, "That's a wonderful audience out there tonight!" And because of the audience, performances often rise to a higher level. It has often been said that a play exists halfway between the stage and the audience. What an audience gets from a performance is directly related to what it brings to the performance, not only in the way of understanding and feeling but also in enthusiasm. In successful dramatic performances, a note is sounded onstage, and a chord of recognition or responsiveness echoes back from the audience. A play performed in an empty theater is not a play.

Ⓓ

The basic elements of drama include exposition, which gives us information, and a protagonist, the major character who struggles against internal conflict and external conflict.

How a Play Is Produced (It's a Miracle!)

The English plays of the late Middle Ages were called miracle plays because they often dealt with stories of miracles from the Bible or the lives of the saints. Any modern-day American play might also be called a miracle play, because it is a miracle that it was written and even more of a miracle that it was produced. In the United States today, drama is dependent on money. Only a few institutional theaters are able to present plays with little or no regard for profit. Most of the plays that are produced (and that therefore stand a chance of becoming part of our dramatic literature) are put on with the idea that they will make money.

To produce any writer's new play on Broadway costs a minimum of half a million dollars (at this writing). The **producers** (people who advance the money) willing to take such a risk are rare, although such risks *are* taken every season. Even though it operates in a very costly manner, the professional Broadway theater, to its credit, has been the launching pad for most of the distinguished plays in American dramatic literature.

Ⓔ

Ⓓ Exploring the Culture
Drama in a Prison

The power of a dramatic performance can often be measured by its ability to transcend the audience's background. For example, there was great concern about the reception that *Waiting for Godot* would receive when it was performed at San Quentin penitentiary in November 1957, by the San Francisco's Actors' Workshop. The prison newspaper reported the response as follows: "[The] San Francisco company had its audience of captives in its collective hand . . . . Those that had felt a less controversial vehicle should be attempted as a first play here had their fears allayed a short five minutes after the Samuel Beckett piece began to unfold. . . . We're still waiting for Godot, and shall continue to wait. When the scenery gets too drab and the action too slow, we'll call each other names and swear to part forever—but then, there's no place to go!" For some time afterward, names and phrases from the play remained a part of the private language of San Quentin.

Ⓔ Reading Skills and Strategies
Drawing Conclusions

? The *producer* finds investors willing to fund a show, hires the director and the production staff, and establishes a budget. The *director* is responsible for creating a team that will work to put on the play. The director deals with the day-to-day staging of the production. Which of the two do you think gets more credit if the play is a success—or more blame if it isn't? [Possible response: Since directors have control of the artistic side of a production, they are usually credited with the play's success or failure.]

Getting Students Involved

Cooperative Learning

Your Number Is Up. Help students summarize the main points presented in this introduction by using a "Numbers Up" approach. Divide the class into heterogeneous groups and have students number off within each group, so that each student has a number. Ask questions on the following topics and have students consult to make sure that everyone knows the answer.

Then call a number: Every student with that number answers. Topics include:
- introduction and structure
- how a play is produced
- the history of American drama
- O'Neill, Miller, Williams
- the "revolt against realism"

Enrichment Activity

Invite students to supplement the discussion in the text by researching and reporting on one or more of the following topics:
- the history of comedy on the American stage
- the history of Broadway musicals
- today's best-known American playwrights
- stock and repertory companies
- regional theater
- drama in the students' community

Explain these terms:
Broadway: A group of New York theaters (more than 30 theaters, each seating more than 800 people), on or near Broadway in Manhattan.
Off-Broadway: A group of New York theaters, seating less than 300 people each, that was established in the 1950s beyond the Broadway theater district. Off-Broadway theaters feature more experimental, less expensive productions than do Broadway theaters.
Off-Off-Broadway: An even more experimental and often not-for-profit group of about 125 theaters.
Regional theater: Dramatic productions—especially, year-round professional drama—staged outside New York City.

B Critical Thinking
Analyzing

? Why can't a producer guarantee that a play will be produced, even if the producer is very interested in the play? [Possible responses: There are too many factors outside the producer's control: the availability of an appropriate theater, financial backing, and the most suitable actors. Timing and the public's current taste are also factors. That's why a producer will often negotiate for an *option*—the exclusive right to produce a play within a given time if he or she decides to do so.]

C Exploring the Culture
Slings and Arrows

Sometimes frustrations over the production or individual differences spill over into the performance. In Paul Rudnick's 1991 production of *I Hate Hamlet,* actor Evan Handler walked off after Nicol Williamson deliberately whacked him with a sword. Williamson was following in a long tradition: When he played Hamlet at the turn of the century, John Barrymore often terrified actors playing Laertes with his all-too-realistic swordplay.

A Recently, regional theaters throughout the country have been presenting new plays by both new and established playwrights. The Broadway producers often visit, look, and take whatever they want for production. For the most part, only a successful Broadway production gives a playwright enough income to plunge in and take the years necessary to write the next play. For that reason, Broadway remains the goal of most playwrights.

There are many stops on the way to New York, some of which become full stops. Over ten thousand plays are copyrighted every year; this probably represents only half of the plays that are actually written. Perhaps several hundred new plays are produced onstage *somewhere* around the country; maybe ten appear on Broadway.

Producers could not hope to cope with reading thousands and thousands of plays, so playwrights must generally find an **agent** who will handle their work. The agent is the producer's first line of defense. Knowing their various tastes, the agent submits a play to likely producers, who **B** may take three months to a year to read it. They may admire the play but still be unwilling to produce it. One playwright used to say, "If they take you to lunch, they're not going to invest in your play." A good lunch is a consolation prize, and many playwrights have eaten very well off plays that were never produced.

A manuscript page of *The Glass Menagerie,* by Tennessee Williams, with alterations in the playwright's hand.

But if the producer should decide to finance the play, he or she then sits down with the playwright to go over changes suggested for the script or ideas for directors and actors. Authors maintain control over their scripts, and the playwright is very much involved in the selection of the director and the actors. Of course, since theater is a collaborative medium, the playwright tries to get along with the producer. But if the playwright and producer discover during these preliminary talks that they have incompatible ideas, they can shake hands and part.

The director becomes the playwright's surrogate at rehearsals. In a sense, the director takes the play away from the playwright, and, finally, the actors take it away from both of them.

Rehearsals involve both pleasure and tension. Many temperaments must mesh as the actors move forward to the climactic moment of opening night. (Note that all the elements of drama itself are also **C** present at play rehearsals: striving for a goal, having something at stake, dealing with internal and external conflicts, etc.)

To a certain extent I imagine a play is completely finished in my mind—in my case, at any rate—without my knowing it, before I sit down to write. So in that sense, I suppose, writing a play is *finding out* what the play is.
—Edward Albee

Using Students' Strengths

Verbal Learners
Invite groups of students to write a letter to a fictional agent to attract his or her interest in an original play. The letter should include a summary of the play as well as a persuasive appeal describing why the play would be successful. After students have presented their letters, have the class discuss and vote on which play they think would interest the agent the most.

Kinesthetic Learners
After students read the discussion of O'Neill's experimental theater on p. 820, have small groups of students improvise scenes that show how masks might be used to distinguish between a character's social and private sides, how asides may reveal inner feelings, and how two actors may portray the same character. Students' improvised scenes could involve anything from applying for a job to asking for a date. Follow each skit with a class discussion.

Scenes from 1989 production
of *A Raisin in the Sun* by Lorraine Hansberry.

© Mitzi Trumbo for PBS
American Playhouse,
KCET Los Angeles.

The play opens in a smaller city for a tryout run or in New York for previews. Sometimes all goes well, and the production needs only some refining and sharpening. More often, the play needs work—rewriting, new sets, new costumes, sometimes a new director or a new star. Chaos reigns until opening night, when all the cast will suddenly come down with laryngitis, intestinal upsets, sinus trouble, or splitting headaches. Somehow, the curtain rises, and the show goes on.

The day after the opening, there may or may not be a line of eager theatergoers at the box office. If there is, the playwright has created what may later be called an American classic, which will be performed around the world and will find its way into the anthologies you study in school. If there isn't a line, the playwright will quickly look around for a way to make a living while writing the next play—if he or she has the courage. The second instance is the more usual. The theater has been called the "fabulous invalid," always teetering on the edge of extinction. If so, playwrights themselves might be called the walking wounded—working, barely surviving, but finally enduring to try once again.

The production of a play depends on a successful working relationship between the playwright, the producer, the director, and the actors.

> . . . [T]he final evaluation of a play has nothing to do with immediate audience or critical response. The playwright, along with any writer, composer, painter in this society, has got to have a terribly private view of his own value, of his own work. He's got to listen to his own voice primarily.
> —Edward Albee

D Literary Connections

A Raisin in the Sun
Lorraine Hansberry's *A Raisin in the Sun* opened on Broadway on March 11, 1959. A smash hit, it starred Ruby Dee, Sidney Poitier, and Claudia McNeil and earned the new playwright the Drama Critics' Circle Award for 1958–1959—over Eugene O'Neill's *A Touch of the Poet* and Tennessee Williams's *Sweet Bird of Youth.* The photos on this page are from the 1989 production starring Esther Rolle and Danny Glover.

E Critical Thinking

Speculating
❓ How would you explain these sudden opening-night illnesses? [Possible responses: They may be caused by opening-night jitters or the build up of stress and fatigue over the weeks and months of intensive rehearsal.]

F Reading Skills and Strategies

Responding to the Text
❓ Mark Twain satirically called a classic "a book that everyone talks about but no one reads." How do you define a classic play? [Possible responses: A classic play is one that everyone feels compelled to read or see because it has universal power and appeal; it is a play that people talk about but don't feel the need to see.]

Taking a Second Look

Review: Outlining

Explore with the class how outlining a text can help them improve their reading comprehension. Discuss how outlining requires two tasks: understanding the text itself and then condensing the material into logical notes. Review the format of an outline and then use this page to demonstrate how to find the main idea and supporting details in a passage.

Activities

1. Have students outline pp. 813–817. First, students should skim these pages to find the main idea, supporting details, and examples. Then, students should create their outlines, using Roman numerals, capital letters, and Arabic numerals correctly.
2. Students can outline each section of the introduction as they read it.

B Literary Connections

Eugene O'Neill

Eugene O'Neill's intense psychological plays marked a radical departure from the romantic convention of theater as entertainment. With no uniquely American tradition to guide him, O'Neill introduced or revived many techniques that have since become staples of the theater: repetition of actions or phrases to underscore dramatic intent; use of symbolic masks or costumes; use of archetypal themes from classical religion and myth; and revival of the Elizabethan devices of soliloquy and aside to reveal a character's inner state.

Like Walt Whitman and Mark Twain, O'Neill gained material for his plays from the many odd jobs he held as he moved around the country before he began his career as a playwright. He looked deeply into all his characters, producing searing portraits of desire and frustration, delusion and failure. Although several Americans have won the Nobel Prize in literature, O'Neill is the only American playwright to have done so, in 1936.

C Literary Connections

The Piano Lesson

The Piano Lesson, which opened on Broadway in April of 1990, won August Wilson the New York Drama Critics' Circle Award, the Drama Desk Award, and the Pulitzer Prize (Wilson's second). The play revolves around an African American family that is haunted by its roots in slavery.

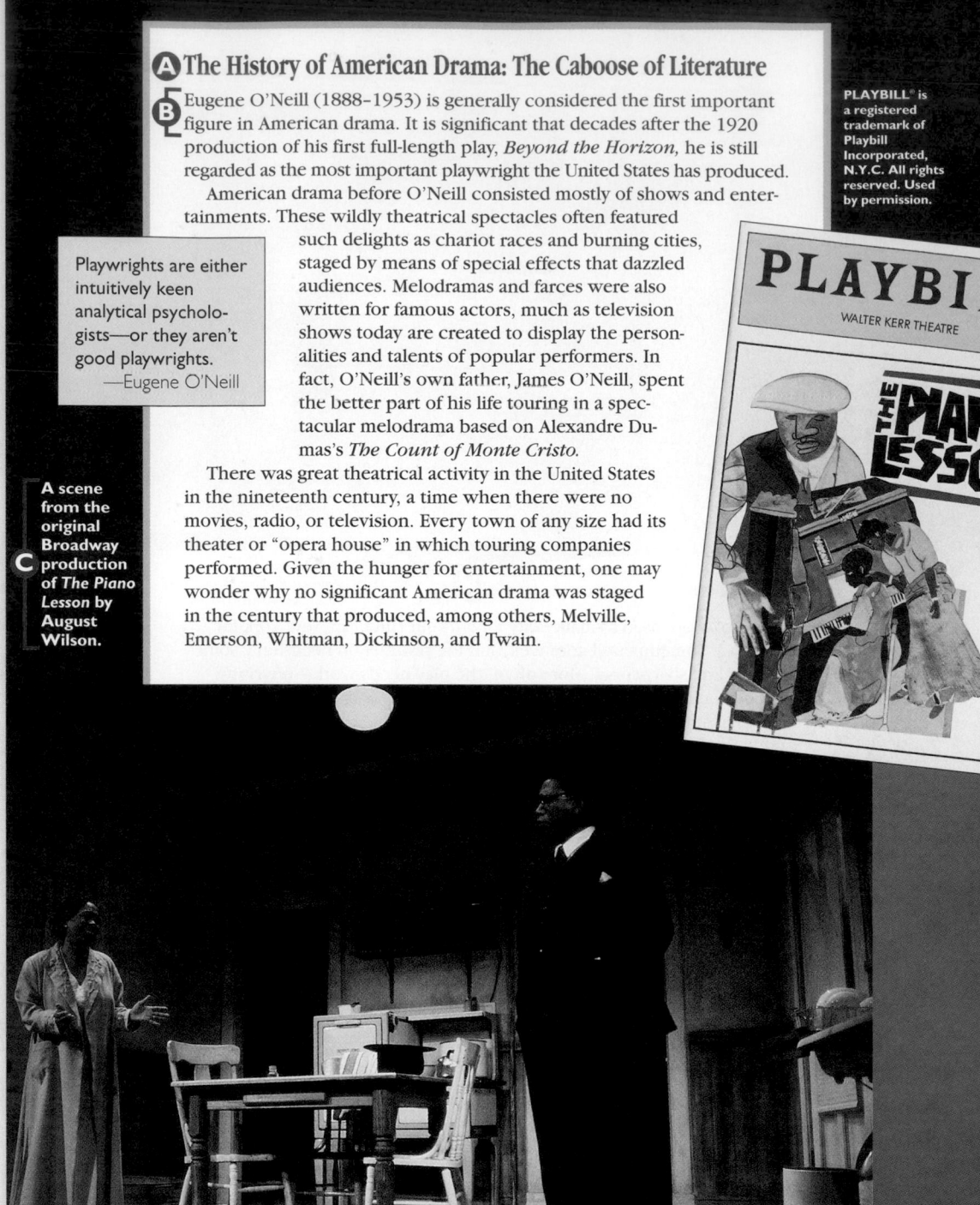

A The History of American Drama: The Caboose of Literature

B Eugene O'Neill (1888–1953) is generally considered the first important figure in American drama. It is significant that decades after the 1920 production of his first full-length play, *Beyond the Horizon,* he is still regarded as the most important playwright the United States has produced.

American drama before O'Neill consisted mostly of shows and entertainments. These wildly theatrical spectacles often featured such delights as chariot races and burning cities, staged by means of special effects that dazzled audiences. Melodramas and farces were also written for famous actors, much as television shows today are created to display the personalities and talents of popular performers. In fact, O'Neill's own father, James O'Neill, spent the better part of his life touring in a spectacular melodrama based on Alexandre Dumas's *The Count of Monte Cristo.*

There was great theatrical activity in the United States in the nineteenth century, a time when there were no movies, radio, or television. Every town of any size had its theater or "opera house" in which touring companies performed. Given the hunger for entertainment, one may wonder why no significant American drama was staged in the century that produced, among others, Melville, Emerson, Whitman, Dickinson, and Twain.

> Playwrights are either intuitively keen analytical psychologists—or they aren't good playwrights.
> —Eugene O'Neill

C A scene from the original Broadway production of *The Piano Lesson* by August Wilson.

Crossing the Curriculum

Art

Throughout history, masks have been an important element of the theater. Greek masks, for example, had highly stylized features that enabled the actors to be seen (and heard) from a distance. The various characters in Italian commedia dell'arte were identified by their masks; Japanese Kabuki masks are a focal point of the performance. Invite students to select a character from a favorite play and create a mask that symbolizes that character.

Math

Invite students to prepare the budget for a school play. The budget must include the cost of advertising, printing, and purchase or rental of costumes, equipment, and props. Students should consider anticipated income from ticket sales, patrons or sponsors, and program advertising. After students prepare their budget, challenge them to come up with ways to make up any shortfall without impairing the production.

One explanation is that theater has usually followed the other arts, rather than pointing the way toward new directions. Robert Sherwood, one of a group of notable American playwrights between 1920 and 1940, once said, "Drama travels in the caboose of literature." Theater seems to take up new attitudes, subject matter, and forms only after they have been explored in the other arts. For the most part, theater tends to dramatize accepted attitudes and values.

The reason for this is that theater is a social art, one we attend as part of a large group; we seem to respond to something new much more slowly as a group than we do as individuals. When you laugh or cry in the theater, your response is noticed. You are, in a sense, giving your approval, and this approval may be subject to criticism or condemnation by those sitting around you who are not laughing or crying. Furthermore, you may not be shocked to *read* about your secret thoughts, dreams, and desires; but if you *see* them shown on stage as you sit among a thousand people, you may refuse to respond, refuse to acknowledge them. You may even rise up and stalk out of the theater.

Thus, the novel and, to some extent, the poetry of the nineteenth and early twentieth centuries were more daring than the theater in giving us a record of experience, in showing us life as it *is* lived rather than as it *should be* lived.

During the period before Eugene O'Neill, American drama tended to be mild and sentimental, rarely questioning the life and attitudes it depicted, almost never challenging the accepted traditions of its times.

The Influence of Europe: Psychology and Taboo Subjects

European drama, which was to influence modern American drama profoundly, matured in the last third of the nineteenth century with the achievements of three playwrights: the Norwegian Henrik Ibsen, the Swede August Strindberg, and the Russian Anton Chekhov. Ibsen deliberately tackled subjects such as guilt, sexuality, and mental illness—subjects that had never before been so realistically and disturbingly portrayed on stage. Strindberg brought to his characterizations an unprecedented level of psychological complexity. And Chekhov, along with Ibsen and Strindberg, shifted the subject matter of drama from wildly theatrical displays of external action to inner action and emotions and the concerns of everyday life. Chekhov once remarked, "People don't go to the North Pole and fall off icebergs. They go to the office and quarrel with their wives and eat cabbage soup."

Ibsen, Strindberg, and Chekhov bequeathed to their American heirs plays about life as it is actually lived. They presented characters and situations more or less realistically, in what has been called the "slice-of-life" dramatic technique.

D Literary Connections
Robert Sherwood
Wounded in World War I, Robert Sherwood (1896–1955) vowed to lend his efforts to stop future wars—an attitude evident in his first play, *The Road to Rome* (1927), and his Pulitzer Prize-winning play *Idiot's Delight* (1936). He won his second Pulitzer Prize in 1941 for *There Shall Be No Night,* a play about the Soviet Union's invasion of Finland. Extremely vocal in warning of the dangers of European totalitarianism, Sherwood also served at times as a special assistant in the War Department (now the Department of Defense) and was a speechwriter for President Franklin D. Roosevelt.

E Vocabulary Note
Word Origins
? *Taboo* comes from a Polynesian word that means "set apart, forbidden." How do we use this word today? [Today, the word is used to mean "improper and unacceptable."]

F Literary Connections
Some European Masterpieces
Notable plays by these authors include the following. Henrik Ibsen: *Peer Gynt* (1867), *A Doll's House* (1879), *Ghosts* (1881), *An Enemy of the People* (1882), *The Wild Duck* (1884), *Hedda Gabler* (1890), *The Master Builder* (1892). August Strindberg: *The Father* (1887), *The Dance of Death* (1901), *Easter* (1901), *A Dream Play* (1902). Anton Chekhov: *The Seagull* (1896), *Uncle Vanya* (1899), *The Three Sisters* (1901), *The Cherry Orchard* (1904).

G Reading Skills and Strategies
Responding to the Text
? Do you agree with Chekhov's vision of the appropriate subject matter for the theater? Why or why not? [Some students are likely to prefer spectacles with plenty of music and special effects, as in *Cats* or *The Phantom of the Opera.* Others may appreciate more subtle explorations of everyday life found in such plays as *A Raisin in the Sun* or *Death of a Salesman.*]

Using Students' Strengths

Verbal/Kinesthetic Learners
Invite students to select a monologue from an American play to present to the class. Possibilities include excerpts from *The Piano Lesson, Fences, A Raisin in the Sun, Death of a Salesman, The Glass Menagerie, The Diary of Anne Frank,* and *Barefoot in the Park.* After students deliver their monologue, have them explain how they decided on the interpretation they used.

Visual Learners
Light and color add emotional overtones that can support or detract from a play's overall dramatic effect. Have small groups of students discuss the colors and lighting effects they would use to create the moods for these scenes:
- the reunion of a parent and child after a twenty-year separation
- a strained family holiday
- the office of an aged salesman who is about to be fired

Realism and Eugene O'Neill: Putting American Drama on the Map

Realistic drama is based on the illusion that when we watch a play, we are looking at life through a "fourth wall" that has been removed so that we can see the action. Soon after the beginning of the twentieth century, realism became the dominant mode of American drama.

As with all theatrical revolutions, the movement toward realism began apart from the commercial theater. But very soon after the new drama succeeded in the little theaters off Broadway (about 1916), the commercial theater adopted realism, too.

In 1916 and 1917, two small theater groups in New York—the Provincetown Players and the Washington Square Players—began to produce new American plays. They provided a congenial home for new American playwrights, notably Eugene O'Neill, whose first one-act plays about the sea were produced by the Provincetown Players in Greenwich Village in 1916. (New movements in the theater have often begun with one-act plays. In addition to O'Neill, Tennessee Williams, Clifford Odets, and Edward Albee all started with short plays.)

These theater groups seemed to have no program. They were not sure what they were for, but they were sure what they were against: the established commercial theater. They would produce any play, in any style, that commercial theater would not touch.

O'Neill gravitated there naturally. Well aware of Sigmund Freud and his new theories about the complex self, O'Neill tried especially hard to reveal more than realism—or Naturalism—could normally reveal. "The old naturalism," he wrote, "no longer applies. We have taken too many snapshots of each other in every graceless position; we have endured too much from the banality of surfaces."

In *The Great God Brown* (1926), O'Neill experimented with using masks to differentiate between two sides of a personality. In *Days Without End* (1934), he had two actors play one character to achieve the same end. And in *Strange Interlude* (1928), characters spoke in asides to the audience, revealing thoughts and feelings that could not be expressed in dialogue to other characters.

> Sure, I'll write about happiness if I ever happen to meet up with that luxury and find it sufficiently dramatic and in harmony with any deep rhythm of life. But happiness is a word. What does it mean? Exaltation, an intensified feeling of the significant worth of man's being and becoming? Well, if it means that—and not a mere smirking contentment with one's lot—I know that there is more of it in one real tragedy than in all the happy ending plays ever written.
> —Eugene O'Neill

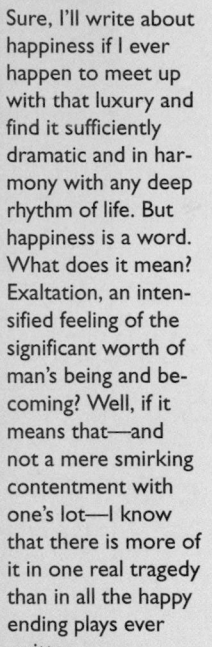
Goodspeed Opera House, East Haddam, Connecticut.
Inge Morath/Magnum.

Taking a Second Look

Review: Using Graphic Aids
Remind students that graphic aids can help them clarify a text by consolidating information and providing a pictorial representation of the text. As a result, graphic aids offer a way to help readers visualize important facts and concepts. Review the basic graphic aids often used in texts: *illustrations, photographs, charts, graphs, maps, diagrams, tables, lists,* and *time lines.*

Activities
1. Have students analyze the photographs on pp. 820 and 821. What information do the pictures provide? How do they help students understand the reading?
2. Remind students that the captions for graphic aids also add key information. Have students discuss what facts they learn from the captions throughout this introductory essay.
3. Invite students to make predictions about the text based on the content of the graphic aids in this essay.

Scene from *Death of a Salesman* by Arthur Miller.

Americans fancy themselves . . . to be openhanded, on the side of justice, a little bit careless about what they buy, wasteful, but essentially good guys, optimistic. But under that level of awareness there is another one, which gets expressed in very few movies and very few plays, but in more plays in proportion than in the movies: the level which confronts our bewilderment, our lonely naïveté, our hunger for purpose.
—Arthur Miller

Arthur Miller: Playwright of Our Social Conscience

The post–World War II years brought two important figures to prominence in American drama: Arthur Miller (1915–   ) and Tennessee Williams (1911–1983). Although other playwrights, such as William Inge (1913–1973), have contributed striking and effective plays, Miller and Williams remain the dominant figures of the second half of the century. Miller and Williams represent the two principal movements in modern American drama: realism, and realism combined with an attempt at something more imaginative. From the beginning, American playwrights have tried to break away from realism or to blend it with more poetic expression, as in Miller's *Death of a Salesman* (1949), Williams's *The Glass Menagerie* (1944), and Thornton Wilder's *Our Town* (1938) and *The Skin of Our Teeth* (1942).

○ English Language Learners
Figurative Expressions
? Have students analyze the figurative expression "put it on the map" to determine its meaning. What is the operative metaphor in the expression? [Possible response: The expression means to make something stand out as important, just as a landmark or major city stands out on a map. The central metaphor compares society or culture to a map.] What, specifically, might the "map" represent in this context? [It might represent world culture and theater.]

RESPONDING TO THE ART
This photograph depicts a scene from the original Broadway production of *Death of a Salesman*. The 1984 revival, starring Dustin Hoffman in the title role of Willy Loman, was a startling revision. Critics and audiences alike were stunned by Hoffman's portrayal of Willy as a "little man," a sharp contrast with Lee J. Cobb's commanding bluster.

○ Critical Thinking
Making Judgments
? Do you agree with Arthur Miller's assessment of the American character? Why or why not? [Possible response: Students may not be willing to accept the level of dependency and loss that Miller sees in the American psyche, preferring instead to embrace the view of Americans as sturdy and self-sufficient individuals.]

Crossing the Curriculum

Social Studies/History
Have a small group of students present an oral report about a play that has been a milestone in its dramatization of pressing social issues. Some plays to consider are Ibsen's *A Doll's House* (which concerns many of the issues taken up by the women's movement) and Ionesco's *Rhinoceros* (dealing with the rise of fascism). Teams should read and analyze the play and consult critical reviews.

Psychology
After undergoing psychoanalysis in 1927, Eugene O'Neill wrote a number of plays that reflect the revolutionary ideas of Sigmund Freud. O'Neill was influenced not only by Freud but also by Carl Jung, who defined character-splitting—a phenomenon in which a person deceives others about his or her true character. O'Neill used actual masks to symbolize this splitting. Invite students to research the influence of one of the seminal figures in the history of psychology.

A Literary Connections

Henrik Ibsen (1828–1906) was not only a master of realistic drama but also a courageous and perceptive social critic. During the middle period of Ibsen's career, in the 1880s, he wrote a series of social dramas that explored the individual's fate in conflict with society's norms. The most famous of these plays is *A Doll's House* (1879), in which Ibsen's protagonist, Nora Helmer, is forced to break free from a marriage and a motherhood that infantilizes her and stifles her humanity. Like Miller's protagonists in *The Crucible,* Nora is an individual who aspires to a morality higher than societal convention. As she says toward the end of the play: "I will have to find out who is right, society or myself." Other classic plays of this period in Ibsen's career include *Ghosts* (1881), *An Enemy of the People* (1882), *The Wild Duck* (1884), and *Hedda Gabler* (1890). In all, Ibsen, like Miller after him, confronts the tension between the order of society and the freedoms of the individual. As Ibsen wrote, concerning *Hedda Gabler:* "My main goal has been to depict people, human moods and human fates, on the basis of certain predominant social conditions and perceptions."

B Exploring the Culture

A Streetcar Named Desire

The celebrated 1951 film version of *A Streetcar Named Desire,* starring Marlon Brando, Vivien Leigh, Kim Hunter, and Karl Malden, earned a shelf of Oscars and established Brando as the unrivaled interpreter of one of the play's central roles, Stanley Kowalski.

Arthur Miller's best work, *Death of a Salesman,* is one of the most successful in fusing the realistic and the imaginative; in all of his other plays, however, Miller is the master of realism. He is a true disciple of Henrik Ibsen, not only in his realistic technique but also in his concern about society's impact on his characters' lives.

In Miller's plays, the course of the action and the development of characters depend not only on the characters' psychological makeup but also on the social, philosophical, and economic atmosphere of their times. Miller's most notable character, Willy Loman in *Death of a Salesman,* is a self-deluded man; but he is also a product of the American dream of success and a victim of the American business machine, which disposes of him when he has outlived his usefulness.

Miller is a writer of high moral seriousness, whether he is dealing with personal versus social responsibility, as in *All My Sons* (1947), or with witch hunts past and present, as in *The Crucible* (1953), which you are about to read. Miller writes a plain and muscular prose that under the force of emotion often becomes eloquent, as in Linda Loman's famous speech in *Death of a Salesman,* in which she talks to her two sons about their father:

> I don't say he's a great man. Willy Loman never made a lot of money. His name was never in the paper. He's not the finest character that ever lived. But he's a human being, and a terrible thing is happening to him. So attention must be paid. He's not to be allowed to fall into his grave like an old dog. Attention, attention must finally be paid to such a person.

—Arthur Miller,
from Death of a Salesman

PLAYBILL® covers printed by permission of PLAYBILL Incorporated. PLAYBILL® is a registered Trademark of PLAYBILL Incorporated, New York, New York.

Tennessee Williams: Playwright of Our Souls

Although Tennessee Williams was Miller's contemporary, his concern was not with social matters, but with personal ones. If Miller was often the playwright of our social conscience, then Williams was the playwright of our souls. In play after play, he probed the psychological complexities of his characters, especially of his female characters: Amanda and Laura in *The Glass Menagerie* (1944), Blanche in *A Streetcar Named Desire* (1947), and Alma in *Summer and Smoke* (1948).

In contrast to Miller's spare, plain language, Williams's writing is delicate and sensuous; it is often colored with lush imagery and evocative rhythms. Miller's characters are, by and large, ordinary people with whom we identify because they are caught up in the social tensions of our times. Williams's characters are often women who are lost ladies, drowning in their own neuroses, but somehow mirroring a part of our own complex psychological selves.

Assessing Learning

Check Test: Questions and Answers

1. Why is it desirable for an audience to respond actively to a play? [Actors respond better to an involved audience, resulting in a more expressive performance. Also, the audience gains a better understanding of the production if it is involved.]

2. What control do playwrights have over their plays? [They usually control the scripts and are often involved in the selection of the director and actors.]

3. How did Eugene O'Neill change American drama? [by focusing on psychology and challenging the conventions of realistic drama]

4. How are Arthur Miller's dramatic concerns different from Tennessee Williams's? [Miller focuses on social issues; Williams, on more personal ones.]

5. How is the Theater of the Absurd unique? [Experimental and expressionistic, it communicates meaning through poetic images.]

The actual scenes in Williams's plays are usually purely realistic, even though these scenes may deal with colorful and extreme characters. But Williams usually theatricalized the realism with "music in the wings" or symbolic props, such as Laura's unicorn in *The Glass Menagerie* or the looming statue of Eternity in *Summer and Smoke*. He always conceived his plays in visually arresting, colorful, theatrical environments—an effort in which he was aided **C** by the imaginative designer Jo Mielziner, who designed the sets for many of his plays.

In the works of Arthur Miller and Tennessee Williams, we see the two strongest strands in American drama: pure realism, and realism blended with an imaginative, poetic sensibility.

The Revolt Against Realism: Theater of Fragmentation

In the mid-nineteenth century, realism in drama was conceived as a revolt against crude theatricalism. Currently, there is a revolt against realism itself in American drama. Naturally, the movement is toward theatricalism again, with its emphasis on stage effects and imaginative settings. This revolt does not confine itself to a particular manner of staging; instead, it extends to the texture of language and plot in the scripts themselves.

The moral and religious certainties that once bound people together exert little or no force on many modern audiences. Some people believe that survival itself depends on a willingness to accept life as formless or meaningless.

Some American playwrights found this new outlook on life impossible to express in the orderly "beginning, middle, end" format of realism. They borrowed, again from Europe, a theater of fragmentation, impressions, and stream of consciousness that was called "expressionist." **Expressionist drama** aimed at the revelation of characters' interior consciousness without reference to a logical sequence of surface actions. Many writers who used expressionist techniques in drama came to be called playwrights of the Theater of the Absurd. Samuel Beckett (1906–1989) and Eugene Ionesco (1912–1994) were among the founders of the Theater of the Absurd. The drama critic Martin Esslin has written this about the Absurdists:

The action of a play of the Theater of the Absurd is not intended to tell a story but to communicate a pattern of poetic images. To give but one example: Things happen in [Samuel Beckett's] *Waiting*

Scene from *The Glass Menagerie* by Tennessee Williams. Long Wharf Theater, New Haven, Connecticut, 1986.

C ## Humanities Connection
Seeing Through Walls
Describing Tennessee Williams and *The Glass Menagerie,* the innovative Broadway stage designer Jo Mielziner noted, "My use of translucent and transparent scenic interior walls was not just another trick. It was a true reflection of the contemporary playwright's interest in—and at times obsession with—the exploration of the inner man."

D ## Critical Thinking
Analyzing
? Why might realist drama thrive in a society with broadly shared moral and religious certainties, yet be displaced in a society where those certainties are in jeopardy? [Possible response: Realism depends on the idea that art can capture and communicate the truths of "real life" and may be undermined in a society where it is difficult for an audience to agree about what those truths are.]

E ## Literary Connections
Beckett and Ionesco
Samuel Beckett's best-known plays are *Waiting for Godot* (1952), *Endgame* (1957), and *Krapp's Last Tape* (1958). In 1969, Beckett was awarded the Nobel Prize. Eugene Ionesco is best remembered for his first play, *The Bald Soprano* (1950), and *Rhinoceros* (1959).

F ## Exploring the Culture
Absurdly Comic
As the word *absurd* suggests, some aspects of this movement stress comedy. For example, the first New York production of *Waiting for Godot* featured the film comedian Bert Lahr (best known as the Cowardly Lion in *The Wizard of Oz*). The 1988 revival at Lincoln Center starred Steve Martin and Robin Williams.

Professional Notes

Tennessee Williams: Reflections on Work

In 1947, four days before the opening of *A Streetcar Named Desire,* Tennessee Williams published the following observations: "I was snatched out of virtual oblivion and thrust into sudden prominence, and from that precarious tenancy of furnished rooms about the country I was removed to a suite in a first-class Manhattan hotel. . . . I sat down and looked about me and was suddenly very depressed. . . . I no longer felt any pride in the play itself but began to dislike it, probably because I felt too lifeless inside ever to create another."

For Williams, the antidote to this malaise was work: "It is only in his work that an artist can find reality and satisfaction, for the actual world is less intense than the world of his invention and consequently his life, without recourse to violent disorder, does not seem very substantial."

T823

B Literary Connections

Some Contemporaries

Today's most exciting American playwrights include Ntozake Shange (*for colored girls who have considered suicide/when the rainbow is enuf*), Sam Shepard (*Buried Child, Fool for Love*), Wendy Wasserstein (*The Heidi Chronicles, An American Daughter*), Marsha Norman ('*Night, Mother; Getting Out; The Secret Garden*), August Wilson (*Fences, Ma Rainey's Black Bottom*), David Henry Hwang (*M. Butterfly*), David Mamet (*Glengarry Glen Ross, Oleanna*), and Tony Kushner (*Angels in America*).

So, I would say, our main tradition from O'Neill to the present revolves around the question of integrity—not moral integrity alone, but the integrity of the personality. The difficulty is to locate the forces of disintegration. I have to believe they exist and can be unveiled.

—Arthur Miller

---

for *Godot,* but these things do not constitute a plot or a story; they are an image of Beckett's intuition that *nothing really ever happens* in man's existence.

—Martin Esslin

The trouble with a static play that mirrors a static life is that it is static. It is an image, a picture; and a picture can absorb our interest for only so long because it lacks the progression and development of a dramatic story. We can observe a situation without development for about the length of a one-act play. Perhaps this is why so many of the Absurdist plays *are* only one act, such as Beckett's *Krapp's Last Tape* and Ionesco's *The Bald Soprano.*

The most significant Absurdist in the United States has been Edward Albee (1928–). Albee is not a pure Absurdist, since, like all innovative playwrights, he experiments with many forms. From 1959 to 1970, Albee produced a play a year. These works ranged from his startling one-act debut, *The Zoo Story* (1959), through the Absurdist play *The American Dream* (1961), to the savage and electrifying domestic drama *Who's Afraid of Virginia Woolf?* (1962), which made Albee world famous.

Experimental drama has increased the options that are open to playwrights. There are practically no conventions in the theater anymore; there is simply a stage and an audience. Playwrights are free to load the stage with scenery, lights, and special effects; but they are equally free—as the playwright was in the age of Shakespeare—to have an actor gesture toward one side of an utterly bare stage and say, "This is the Forest of Arden."

Scene from *Happy Days* by Samuel Beckett. The entire play takes place while the actors are half buried in a pile of sand.

Dramatists now have the freedom to express their deepest feelings in almost any form they choose—provided that their approach can be made comprehensible to an audience and touch their emotions.

Quickwrite What do you predict will happen to American drama in the next ten years? Consider subject matter, sets and costume design, popularity, and competition with movies, television, and the Internet. Jot down your thoughts, and then compare notes with your classmates.

Taking a Second Look

Review: Justify Interpretations

Remind students that **pantomime** is the art of acting without words. Often called the "art of silence," pantomime uses facial expressions, gestures, and body language to communicate meaning. Verbal performance, in contrast, involves such factors as pitch, volume, rate, diction, inflection, and pronunciation.

Activity. Have students select any one of the dramatic selections, short stories, or poems in their textbook, analyze the text, and decide which verbal and nonverbal techniques to use to interpret it most effectively. Have students perform their interpretation for the class and then discuss why they chose these particular performance techniques and how they relate to the overall theme or message of the work.

The Breaking of Charity

Theme

A City on a Hill? *Arthur Miller's most frequently produced play is set in seventeenth-century Salem, where, for many months, suspicion and jealousy tore asunder the fabric of a small community. Echoes of that witch hunt have been heard throughout American history.*

Reading the Anthology

Reaching Struggling Readers

The *Reading Skills and Strategies: Reaching Struggling Readers* binder includes a Reading Strategies Handbook that offers concrete suggestions to help students who have difficulty reading and comprehending text, or students who are reluctant readers. When a specific strategy is most appropriate for a selection, a correlation to the Handbook is provided at the bottom of the teacher's page under the head Reaching Struggling Readers. This head may also be used to introduce additional ideas for helping students read challenging texts.

Reading Beyond the Anthology

Read On Collection 17 includes an annotated bibliography of books suitable for extended reading. The suggested books are related to works in this collection by theme, by author, or by subject. To preview the Read On for Collection 17, please turn to p. T891.

Collection Planner

Resources for this Collection

Note: All resources for this collection are available for preview on the *One-Stop Planner CD-ROM 2 with Test Generator.* All worksheets and blackline masters may be printed from the CD-ROM.

Internet Resources
go.hrw.com LE0 11-17

Selection or Feature	Reading and Literary Skills	Vocabulary, Language, and Grammar
The Crucible (p. 828) Arthur Miller	• *Graphic Organizers for Active Reading,* Worksheet pp. 86, 87, 88, 89 • *Literary Elements:* Transparency 27 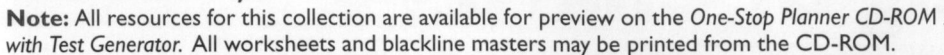 Worksheet p. 82	• *Grammar and Language Links:* Revision Worksheet p. 69 • *Daily Oral Grammar,* Transparencies 50, 51
The American Language: Euphemisms (p. 892) Gary Q. Arpin		
Writer's Workshop: Problem-Solution Essay (p. 895)		
Language Workshop: Using Transitional Expressions (p. 899)		• *Workshop Resources,* p. 61 • *Language Workshop CD-ROM,* Transitional Expressions
Learning for Life: Evaluating Play Choices (p. 901)		

Other Resources for this Collection

- *Cross-Curricular Activities*, p. 17
- *Portfolio Management System*, Introduction to Portfolio Assessment, p. 1

- *Formal Assessment:*
  Literary Period Introduction Test, p. 164;
  Literary Period Test, p. 178;
  Literary Elements Test, p. 176
- *Test Generator*, Collection Test

Writing	Listening and Speaking / Viewing and Representing	Assessment
• *Portfolio Management System*, Rubrics for Choices, p. 196	• *Viewing and Representing:* Fine Art Transparency 17  Worksheet p. 68 • *Portfolio Management System*, Rubrics for Choices, p. 196	• *Formal Assessment*, Selection Tests, pp. 166, 168, 170, 172 • *Test Generator (One-Stop Planner CD-ROM)* 
		• *Formal Assessment*, The American Language Test, p. 174
• *Workshop Resources*, p. 37 • *Writer's Workshop 2 CD-ROM*, Controversial Issue	• *Viewing and Representing*, HRW Multimedia Presentation Maker	• *Portfolio Management System* • Prewriting, p. 198 • Peer Editing, p. 199 • Assessment Rubric, p. 200
		• *Portfolio Management System*, Rubrics, p. 201

 Transparency    CD-ROM   Video   Audio CD

T824C

Skills Focus

Selection or Feature	Reading Skills and Strategies	Elements of Literature and Language	Writing	Listening and Speaking	Viewing and Representing
The Crucible (p. 828) Arthur Miller	Interpreting a Text, pp. 828, 849, 862, 877, 888 • Organize by Time Line • Organize by Character	Motivation, pp. 828, 849, 862, 877, 888 Static Character, p. 849 Dynamic Character, pp. 849, 877 Metaphor, p. 862 Irony, pp. 862, 888 Protagonist, p. 862 Antagonist, p. 862 External Conflict, pp. 862, 888 Internal Conflict, pp. 862, 888 Comic Relief, p. 877 Climax, p. 888 Title, p. 888	Identify a Social or Political Problem Suggested by *The Crucible*, p. 889 Write an Essay Responding to a Quote from the Author, p. 889 Write an Essay Analyzing a Character from the Play, p. 889 Write an Essay Comparing the Real Salem Witch Trials with *The Crucible*, p. 889 Research the Historical Context of the Play's Creation, p. 889		
Reading Skills and Strategies: Vocabulary— Doing Analogies (p. 890)	Analogy, p. 890 Types of Analogy Relationships, p. 890		Write an Example for Each of the Analogy Relationships, p. 890		
The American Language: Euphemisms (p. 892) Gary Q. Arpin	Interpret Connotations, p. 894	Euphemisms, p. 892	Identify Word Origins, p. 894 Replace Euphemisms, p. 894		
Writer's Workshop: Problem-Solution Essay (p. 895)			Write a Problem-Solution Essay, pp. 895–898		Use a Graphic to Organize Information, p. 896
Language Workshop: Using Transitional Expressions (p. 899)		Transitional Expressions, p. 899	Revise Sentences to Improve Coherence, p. 899		
Reading for Life: Reading a Film Review (p. 900)	Identify the Critic's Criteria, p. 900 Evaluate the Criteria, p. 900 Identify Bias, p. 900		Compare Reviews, p. 900		
Learning for Life: Evaluating Play Choices (p. 901)			Write a Letter to the Drama Teacher, p. 901	Prepare and Present Oral Reviews, p. 901	Create an Informational Display, p. 901

THE BREAKING OF CHARITY

Miller

In a sense I went naked to Salem, still unable to accept the most common experience of humanity, the shifts of interests that turned loving husbands and wives into stony enemies, loving parents into indifferent supervisors or even exploiters of their children, and so forth. As I already knew from my reading, that was the real story of ancient Salem Village, what they called then the breaking of charity with one another. The gray rain on my windshield was falling into my soul.

—Arthur Miller,
from *Timebends: A Life*

Responding to the Quotation

? What do you think it means to "break charity"? Do you agree with Arthur Miller that it is "the most common experience of humanity"? Why or why not? [Possible responses: To break charity may mean to betray someone, or to refuse him or her basic human generosity and respect. On a personal level, many students may disagree with Miller's assessment of human relationships; but other students may point to partisan politics, tolerance of poverty, and other social problems as examples of our willingness to break charity with our fellow citizens.]

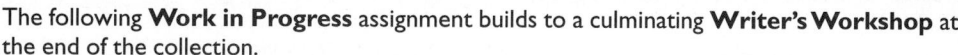

Writing Focus: Problem-Solution Essay

WORK IN PROGRESS

The following **Work in Progress** assignment builds to a culminating **Writer's Workshop** at the end of the collection.

• The Crucible

Take notes to analyze a social or political problem in play (p. 889)

Writer's Workshop: Persuasive Writing / Problem-Solution Essay (p. 895)

Planning

- **Block Schedule**
  Block Scheduling Lesson Plans with Pacing Guide

- **Traditional Schedule**
  Lesson Plans Including Strategies for English-Language Learners

- **One-Stop Planner**
  CD-ROM with Test Generator

Arthur Miller
(1915–   )
by Robert Anderson

Arthur Miller, considered by many to be the pre-eminent American playwright of the second half of the twentieth century, was born in New York City. His father manufactured women's coats, and his mother was a schoolteacher. In high school, Arthur was more involved with sports than with literature. "Until the age of seventeen," Miller said, "I can safely say that I never read a book weightier than *Tom Swift* and *The Rover Boys,* and only verged on literature with some Dickens."

On graduation from high school, Miller applied to the University of Michigan, but his grades were not good enough for a scholarship, and the Depression left his father unable to finance his tuition. To earn money for college, Miller worked for two years in an automobile parts plant, where, incidentally, he read Tolstoy's *War and Peace.* The experience in the parts plant later supplied him with the material for his 1955 play *A Memory of Two Mondays.*

Miller eventually enrolled in the University of Michigan. To help finance his education, he took on various jobs. First, he was a mouse tender in the university science laboratory. Later, he moved on (and up) to become the night editor of the *Michigan Daily.* More important, he started to write plays.

After graduation, Miller returned to New York and, like many of us "playwrights-in-waiting," earned a living by writing radio scripts for such programs as *Cavalcade of America,* the *Columbia Workshop,* and *The Theatre Guild of the Air.*

Miller's first Broadway success, *All My Sons,* was produced in 1947 and won The New York Drama Critic's award for Best Play. That play struck a note that was to become familiar in Miller's work: the need for moral responsibility in families and society.

In 1949, with the production of his masterpiece, *Death of a Salesman* (written in a small studio he built with his own hands on his prop-erty in northwestern Connecticut), all promises were fulfilled. Miller instantly joined the pantheon of the great American playwrights.

It was totally in character that Miller's next play, produced in 1953, should be *The Crucible*—about a witch hunt that took place in 1692 in Salem, Massachusetts. In that witch-hunt, Miller found parallels to the "Red hunt" being conducted in the 1950s in Washington, D.C., by Senator Joseph McCarthy. Writers, actors, politicians—and all kinds of other people—were summoned to appear before McCarthy to answer the question: "Are you now or were you ever a Communist?" Those summoned were required to inform on neighbors and friends or be sent to jail.

Three years after the production of *The Crucible* in New York, Miller was summoned before a congressional committee. He spoke freely about himself and his occasional attendance, years before, as a guest at Communist meetings; but he refused to name names of other people in attendance. Miller was found in contempt of Congress, but his conviction was later overturned by the Supreme Court.

The Crucible was not successful in its first production. Some critics questioned the comparison between the old witch-hunts and the contemporary hunt for Communists in government. In a later production, supervised by Miller himself, the play ran for over six hundred performances. It is now Miller's most produced play.

go.hrw.com
LE0 11-17

 —◉— *Resources: Print and Media* —▭—

Why I Wrote *The Crucible*
An artist's answer to politics

by Arthur Miller

As I watched *The Crucible* taking shape as a movie over much of the past year, the sheer depth of time that it represents for me kept returning to mind. As those powerful actors blossomed on the screen, and the children and the horses, and the crowds and the wagons, I thought again about how I came to cook all this up nearly fifty years ago, in an America almost nobody I know seems to remember clearly. . . .

I remember those years—they formed *The Crucible's* skeleton—but I have lost the dead weight of the fear I had then. Fear doesn't travel well; just as it can warp judgment, its absence can diminish memory's truth. What terrifies one generation is likely to bring only a puzzled smile to the next. . . .

[Senator] McCarthy's power to stir fears of creeping Communism was not entirely based on illusion, of course. . . . From being our wartime ally, the Soviet Union rapidly became an expanding empire. In 1949, Mao Zedong took power in China. Western Europe also seemed ready to become Red, especially Italy, where the Communist Party was the largest outside Russia, and was growing. . . . McCarthy—brash and ill-mannered but to many authentic and true—boiled it all down to what anyone could understand: We had "lost China" and would soon lose Europe as well, because the State Department—staffed, of course, under Democratic presidents—was full of treasonous pro-Soviet intellectuals. It was as simple as that. . . .

The Crucible was an act of desperation. . . . By 1950 when I began to think of writing about the hunt for Reds in America, I was motivated in some great part by the paralysis that had set in among many liberals who, despite their discomfort with the inquisitors' violations of civil rights, were fearful, and with good reason, of being identified as covert Communists if they should protest too strongly. . . .

I visited Salem for the first time on a dismal spring day in 1952. . . . In the gloomy courthouse there I read the transcripts of the witchcraft trials of 1692, as taken down in a primitive shorthand by ministers who were spelling each other. But there was one entry in Upham° in which the thousands of pieces I had come across were jogged into place. It was from a report written by the Reverend Samuel Parris, who was one of the chief instigators of the witch-hunt. "During the examination of Elizabeth Proctor, Abigail Williams, and Ann Putnam"—the two were "afflicted" teen-age accusers, and Abigail was Parris's niece—"both made offer to strike at said Proctor; but when Abigail's hand came near, it opened, whereas it was made up, into a fist before, and came down exceeding lightly as it drew near to said Proctor, and at length, with open and extended fingers, touched Proctor's hood very lightly. Immediately Abigail cried out her fingers, her fingers, her fingers burned. . . ."

In this remarkably observed gesture of a troubled young girl, I believed, a play became possible. Elizabeth Proctor had been the orphaned Abigail's mistress, and they had lived together in the same small house until Elizabeth fired the girl. By this time, I was sure, John Proctor had bedded Abigail, who had to be dismissed most likely to appease Elizabeth. There was bad blood between the two women now. That Abigail started, in effect, to condemn Elizabeth to death with her touch, then stopped her hand, then went through with it, was quite suddenly the human center of all this turmoil.

All this I understood. I had not approached the witchcraft out of nowhere or from purely social and political considerations. My own marriage of twelve years was teetering and I knew more than I wished to know about where the blame lay. That John Proctor the sinner might overturn his paralyzing personal guilt and become the most forthright voice against the madness around him was a reassurance to me, and, I suppose, an inspiration: It demonstrated that a clear moral outcry could still spring even from an ambiguously unblemished soul. Moving crabwise across the profusion of evidence, I sensed that I had at last found something of myself in it, and a play began to accumulate around this man.

—*from The New Yorker,*
October 21 and 28, 1996

°Charles W. Upham, a mayor of Salem, published a two-volume study of the trials in 1867.

A Cultural Connections
The McCarthy Hearings
Joseph R. McCarthy, U.S. senator from Wisconsin from 1946 to his death in 1957, burst on the public scene in February 1950 with his claim that Communists had infiltrated the Department of State. Even though his accusations were never proved, during the next three years McCarthy charged many government officials, members of the media, and other prominent figures with engaging in subversive activities and having Communist sympathies. The "witch hunt" climaxed in April of 1954, when McCarthy accused the secretary of the Navy of sheltering Communist spies. The secretary mounted a vigorous and effective defense, which exposed McCarthy's ruthless tactics and questionable motives. As a result, McCarthy was censured by the Senate and his influence declined.

B Historical Connections
On January 20, 1692, Elizabeth Parris, daughter of Reverend Samuel Parris, and Abigail Williams, his niece, started acting strangely. They shook uncontrollably, crawled under tables, uttered strange sounds, and screamed that they were being tortured. Since doctors could not determine a medical cause for the bizarre behavior, they concluded the girls were bewitched. Soon, other girls exhibited the same symptoms. They cried out the names of Tituba, Sarah Good, and Sarah Osburn, sparking the witch hunt. During the next eight months of terror, more than one hundred fifty people were imprisoned for witchcraft. By the time the court was dismissed, twenty-seven people had been convicted, nineteen hanged, one pressed to death, fifty had confessed, and more than one hundred were imprisoned awaiting trial.

Professional Notes

Critical Comment
In his 1957 introduction to *Collected Plays*, Miller offered another perspective on the atmosphere that inspired *The Crucible*: "If the reception of *All My Sons* and *Death of a Salesman* made the world a friendly place for me, events of the early fifties quickly turned that warmth into an illusion. It was not only the rise of 'McCarthyism' that moved me, but something that seemed much more weird and mysterious. It was the fact that a political, objective, knowledgeable campaign from the far Right was capable of creating not only a terror, but a new subjective reality, a veritable mystique which was gradually assuming even a holy resonance. The wonder of it all struck me that so practical and picayune a cause, carried forward by such manifestly ridiculous men, should be capable of paralyzing thought itself, and worse, causing to billow up such pervasive clouds of 'mysterious' feelings within people."

Summary
Act One ▪▪

The setting is the village of Salem, Massachusetts, in the spring of 1692. The village minister, Reverend Samuel Parris, waits in terror at the bedside of his daughter, Betty, who has been apparently unconscious since the previous night, when Parris caught her with his niece, Abigail, other girls, and Parris's slave, Tituba, dancing wildly in the forest. Parris berates his niece for participating in what he thinks may have been an occult ritual, complete with incantations and nudity—and becomes paranoid that his "enemies" in the village will find out about it. Abigail denies witchcraft and insists she is a virtuous girl, even though she has been fired under suspicious circumstances from the household of John and Elizabeth Proctor. Thomas Putnam, an acquisitive landowner, arrives with his wife, Ann. Ann admits she sent her daughter, Ruth, to the forest, to ask Tituba's occult intervention in Ann's loss of seven newborn babies, but now Ruth, too, is sick, and Ann charges witchcraft. Alone briefly, Abigail, the Putnams' servant, Mercy Lewis, and the Proctors' servant, Mary Warren, worry about how much more they should admit. Abby is threatening them to keep quiet when John Proctor, a local farmer, enters, and all the girls except Abigail leave. John questions Abigail about the witchcraft scare and refuses her plea that he resume their affair—the reason for Abigail's dismissal from his house. The two begin to argue when Betty starts screaming in response to the singing of a psalm downstairs, and a crowd rushes into the room. After Betty is calmed by Rebecca Nurse, a pious and well-respected matriarch, the villagers begin to quarrel about the witchcraft question. Reverend Hale, a witchcraft specialist summoned by Parris, enters and sets to work interrogating Tituba. Terrified for her life, the slave names two poor and disreputable Salem women as consorting with the devil. As the act closes, Abigail and Betty also "confess," screaming out more accusations and more names.

Before You Read
THE CRUCIBLE

cru·ci·ble (krōō′sə bəl) *n.* [ML *crucibulum,* lamp, crucible, prob. < Gmc, as in OE *cruce,* pot, jug, MHG *kruse,* earthen pot (see CRUSE) a+ L suffix *-ibulum* (as in *thuribulum,* censer), but assoc. by folk etym. with L *crux,* CROSS, as if lamp burning before cross] **1** a container made of a substance that can resist great heat, for melting, fusing, or calcining ores, metals, etc. **2** the hollow at the bottom of an ore furnace, where the molten metal collects **3** a severe test or trial

Make the Connection

Public Voices, Private Lives
Most of us recognize and live with the difference between our public self and our private self. Sometimes, however, those selves—with all their convictions, passions, and values—come into conflict. Then, we must make a choice. Which self will triumph and which self must be sacrificed? Can we find a compromise? These choices are sometimes simply matters of avoiding embarrassment or preventing hurt feelings or confessing dishonesty. Sometimes they are matters of life and death.

Quickwrite

How do you think most people try to resolve conflicts between their public and their private lives?

How can people be true to their values? What situations might challenge their honesty and integrity? How can people sometimes slip into hypocrisy or conflicts of interest? Jot down your thoughts on these issues.

Reading Skills and Strategies

Interpreting a Text
To read a complex dramatic work like *The Crucible,* you need to **interpret** it—you need to offer your own explanations of who the characters really are, why they behave the way they do, and what the larger meaning of their tragedy is.

As you read *The Crucible,* take notes. (You might also want to start a **time line** to organize the events that lead up to the tragedy.) You can organize your notes by **character.** Jot down your interpretation of what the dialogue and the action reveal about the characters' values, emotions, motivations, and personal histories. Feel free to include your own views of what the characters look like, how they speak, and how they perform the actions called for in the stage directions. If you become confused about any aspect of a particular character, don't be afraid to adjust your reading. Go back and reread sections of the play simply to find out information that will clarify what makes the character tick.

Elements of Literature

Motivation
Motivation is the reason for a character's behavior. Just as in life, character motivations are often complex, and a particular action is often produced by several motivating factors. Motivation provides the driving force of *The Crucible.*

Miller demonstrates that the residents of Salem were not simply a hysterical mob; every person had at least one reason for acting the way he or she did— psychological, sexual, financial, theological, or political.

In an essay about Nathaniel Hawthorne, a critic describes Salem and the past that still hung over the town when Hawthorne lived there in the early 1800s. Hawthorne's ancestor is Judge Hathorne, and he is in the play.

Salem bristled with old wives' tales and old men's legends. One heard of locked closets in haunted houses where skeletons had been found. One heard of walls that resounded with knocks where there had once been doorways, now bricked up. One heard of poisonous houses and blood-stained houses. . . .

—from "Hawthorne in Salem," Van Wyck Brooks

The Crucible
Arthur Miller

They believed that they held in their steady hands the candle that would light the world.

The photographs that illustrate this play are from the 1996 film adaptation starring Daniel Day-Lewis, Joan Allen, and Winona Ryder.

Reaching All Students

Struggling Readers

Guide struggling readers to question each character's motives. Partners can hold question and answer sessions, taking turns asking questions and scanning the text to find the answers. For example, if the first partner questions why Elizabeth Proctor fired Abigail, the second partner can infer the answer from the information on pp. 838–839 when we learn that Abigail and John had an affair, which John ended.

English Language Learners

Miller's re-creation of seventeenth-century colonial diction is apt to challenge nonnative speakers, especially his use of archaic words and idioms. Since plays are meant to be seen rather than read, have students act out key scenes or conversations. Guide student actors to use gestures, facial expressions, and other means of nonverbal communication to clarify the dialogue and to compensate for language difficulties.

Advanced Students

Miller believes that *The Crucible's* "paranoid center is still pumping out the same darkly attractive warning that it did in the fifties." Invite advanced students to read the play as a contemporary allegory rather than as a parable about McCarthyism. What is today's "witchcraft hysteria"? How might it mirror the play's mixture of illicit sexuality, fear of the supernatural, and lust for power?

Elements of Literature
Motivation

For additional instruction on motivation, see *Literary Elements:*
• Transparency 27
• Worksheet p. 82

A Historical Connections

The City of God

Salem is a shortened version of *Jerusalem*. This name reflects the Pilgrims' conviction that they were the chosen people sent on a holy mission to establish a New Jerusalem in the North American wilderness.

B Elements of Literature

Motivation

? Why do you think Miller begins with this background rather than immediately plunging into the action? [Possible responses: It allows Miller both to establish the historical authenticity of the material and to explain the instances where he departs from it. This particular commentary clarifies Parris's motivation for not halting the witch hunt, even though he knows his niece may have iniated the hunt to shift the blame away from her own sins.]

C Reading Skills and Strategies

Interpreting a Text

Point out that sometimes an author will state clearly an essential belief or provide a fundamental clue for interpreting a text. Explain in your own words what Miller means by this statement. [Possible responses: This play will explore depths of the Puritans' lives that are essentially mysterious. We may never fully understand the Salem experience.]

The Crucible was first presented by Kermit Bloomgarden at the Martin Beck Theatre, New York City, January 22, 1953, with the following cast.

(in order of appearance)

Reverend Parris . . . . .Fred Stewart
Betty Parris . . . . .Janet Alexander
Tituba . . . . .Jacqueline Andre
Abigail Williams . . . . . . .Madeleine Sherwood
Susanna Walcott . . . . .Barbara Stanton
Mrs. Ann Putnam . . . . .Jane Hoffman
Thomas Putnam . . . . .Raymond Bramley
Mercy Lewis . . . . .Dorothy Joliffe
Mary Warren . . . . .Jennie Egan
John Proctor . . . . .Arthur Kennedy
Rebecca Nurse . . . . .Jean Adair
Giles Corey . . . . .Joseph Sweeney
Reverend John Hale . . . . .E. G. Marshall
Elizabeth Proctor . . . . .Beatrice Straight
Francis Nurse . . . . .Graham Velsey
Ezekiel Cheever . . . . .Don McHenry
Marshal Herrick . . . . .George Mitchell
Judge Hathorne . . . . .Philip Coolidge
Deputy Governor Danforth . . .Walter Hampden
Sarah Good . . . . .Adele Fortin
Hopkins . . . . .Donald Marye

Staged by Jed Harris

Settings by Boris Aronson

Costumes made and designed by Edith Lutyens

The play is set in Salem, Massachusetts, in 1692.

Act One (An Overture)
   Home of Rev. Samuel Parris.

Act Two
   John Proctor's house, eight days later.

Act Three
   Salem meeting house, serving as the General Court.

Act Four
   A cell in Salem jail, fall 1692.

Act One

(An Overture)

A small upper bedroom in the home of REVEREND SAMUEL PARRIS, *Salem, Massachusetts, in the spring of the year 1692.*

   There is a narrow window at the left. Through its leaded panes the morning sunlight streams. A candle still burns near the bed, which is at the right. A chest, a chair, and a small table are the other furnishings. At the back a door opens on the landing of the stairway to the ground floor. The room gives off an air of clean spareness. The roof rafters are exposed, and the wood colors are raw and unmellowed.

   As the curtain rises, REVEREND PARRIS *is discovered kneeling beside the bed, evidently in prayer. His daughter,* BETTY PARRIS, *aged ten, is lying on the bed, inert.*

At the time of these events Parris was in his middle forties. In history he cut a villainous path, and there is very little good to be said for him. He believed he was being persecuted wherever he went, despite his best efforts to win people and God to his side. In meeting, he felt insulted if someone rose to shut the door without first asking his permission. He was a widower with no interest in children, or talent with them. He regarded them as young adults, and until this strange crisis he, like the rest of Salem, never conceived that the children were anything but thankful for being permitted to walk straight, eyes slightly lowered, arms at the sides, and mouths shut until bidden to speak.

   His house stood in the "town"—but we today would hardly call it a village. The meeting house was nearby, and from this point outward—toward the bay or inland—there were a few small-windowed, dark houses snuggling against the raw Massachusetts winter. Salem had been established hardly forty years before. To the European world the whole province was a barbaric frontier inhabited by a sect of fanatics who, nevertheless, were shipping out products of slowly increasing quantity and value.

   No one can really know what their lives were like. They had no novelists—and would not have

830 AMERICAN DRAMA

Using Students' Strengths

Intrapersonal Learners

Probing the Puritan psyche, Miller finds much to admire—and much to condemn. He praises the Puritans for their determination, discipline, and sense of community, but criticizes their harsh treatment of children, their autocratic control over private and spiritual life, as well as their self-righteous and condescending approach to Native Americans and other settlers. Have students make up a profile of the ideal settler. What character traits would enable this person not only to survive the demands of pioneering but also to flourish? Would students themselves be good settlers? Why or why not?

permitted anyone to read a novel if one were handy. Their creed forbade anything resembling a theater or "vain enjoyment." They did not celebrate Christmas, and a holiday from work meant only that they must concentrate even more upon prayer.

Which is not to say that nothing broke into this strict and somber way of life. When a new farmhouse was built, friends assembled to "raise the roof," and there would be special foods cooked and probably some potent cider passed around. There was a good supply of ne'er-do-wells in Salem, who dallied at the shovelboard in Bridget Bishop's tavern. Probably more than the creed, hard work kept the morals of the place from spoiling, for the people were forced to fight the land like heroes for every grain of corn, and no man had very much time for fooling around.

That there were some jokers, however, is indicated by the practice of appointing a two-man patrol whose duty was to "walk forth in the time of God's worship to take notice of such as either lye about the meeting house, without attending to the word and ordinances, or that lye at home or in the fields without giving good account thereof, and to take the names of such persons, and to present them to the magistrates, whereby they may be accordingly proceeded against." This predilection for minding other people's business was time-honored among the people of Salem, and it undoubtedly created many of the suspicions which were to feed the coming madness. It was also, in my opinion, one of the things that a John Proctor would rebel against, for the time of the armed camp had almost passed, and since the country was reasonably—although not wholly— safe, the old disciplines were beginning to rankle. But, as in all such matters, the issue was not clearcut, for danger was still a possibility, and in unity still lay the best promise of safety.

The edge of the wilderness was close by. The American continent stretched endlessly west, and it was full of mystery for them. It stood, dark and threatening, over their shoulders night and day, for out of it Indian tribes marauded from time to time, and Reverend Parris had parishioners who had lost relatives to these heathen.

The parochial snobbery of these people was partly responsible for their failure to convert the Indians. Probably they also preferred to take land from heathens rather than from fellow Christians. At any rate, very few Indians were converted, and the Salem folk believed that the virgin forest was the Devil's last preserve, his home base and the citadel of his final stand. To the best of their knowledge the American forest was the last place on earth that was not paying homage to God.

For these reasons, among others, they carried about an air of innate resistance, even of persecution. Their fathers had, of course, been persecuted in England. So now they and their church found it necessary to deny any other sect its freedom, lest their New Jerusalem[2] be defiled and corrupted by wrong ways and deceitful ideas.

They believed, in short, that they held in their steady hands the candle that would light the world. We have inherited this belief, and it has helped and hurt us. It helped them with the discipline it gave them. They were a dedicated folk, by and large, and they had to be to survive the life they had chosen or been born into in this country.

The proof of their belief's value to them may be taken from the opposite character of the first Jamestown settlement, farther south, in Virginia. The Englishmen who landed there were motivated mainly by a hunt for profit. They had thought to pick off the wealth of the new country and then return rich to England. They were a band of individualists, and a much more ingratiating group than the Massachusetts men. But Virginia destroyed them. Massachusetts tried to kill off the Puritans, but they combined; they set up a communal society which, in the beginning, was little more than an armed camp with an autocratic and very devoted leadership. It was, however, an autocracy by consent, for they were united from top to bottom by a commonly held ideology whose perpetuation was the reason and justification for all their sufferings. So their self-denial, their purposefulness, their suspicion of all vain pursuits, their hard-handed justice were altogether perfect instruments for the conquest of this space so antagonistic to man.

But the people of Salem in 1692 were not quite the dedicated folk that arrived on the *Mayflower.*

2. **New Jerusalem:** in the Bible (Revelations 21), the holy city of heaven.

D ⬤ **Reading Skills and Strategies**
Making Predictions
❓ "Ne'er-do-well" is a contraction for "never-do-well," a term used to describe lazy or disreputable people who don't amount to much. Why do you think Miller brings up those who hang around the tavern playing games? What prediction can you make, based on this reference? [Possible response: Miller foreshadows the path the witch hunt will take: The ne'er-do-wells will likely be the first accused of witchcraft since they have already earned society's disfavor.] You may want to point out that Bridget Bishop, the proprietress of the tavern, was later executed as a witch.

E ⬤ **English Language Learners**
Breaking Down Difficult Text
Since this passage contains elevated vocabulary as well as complex ideas, have students divide the text into main clauses and paraphrase each sentence before moving on.

F ⬤ **Reading Skills and Strategies**
Connecting with the Text
❓ What does it mean to believe one holds the candle that lights the world? [It means that one believes one has the single truth or the way of life that all people should ultimately embrace.] Do you agree that contemporary Americans have inherited this belief from the Puritans? If so, give examples of how you think this belief has "helped and hurt us." [Many students will agree that contemporary Americans feel entitled to lead the world with the "light" of democracy and capitalism. Some will mention the U.S. victories in World War II and the Gulf War as examples of how this belief helps, while some might mention the Vietnam War and the Bay of Pigs invasion as examples of this belief's drawbacks.]

G ⬤ **Historical Connections**
Roanoke
The Southeastern region "destroyed" the settlers not only in Jamestown, but also in the ill-fated Roanoke Colony. In 1585 and 1587, Sir Walter Raleigh attempted to settle this island off the coast of what is now North Carolina. In fact, the first English child to be born in the New World, Virginia Dare, was born there in 1587. However, when her grandfather returned with supplies in 1590, he found the colony deserted. The colonists' fate remains a mystery.

Using Students' Strengths

Naturalist/Logical Learners
Establishing a colony in the New World was a daunting undertaking, fraught with danger. Invite students to plan an expedition to found a settlement in New England in the early seventeenth century, traveling with their friends, family, and classmates. Students should decide whom to take and why, list the supplies they need, and draft the constitution and laws the community will need in order to operate smoothly.

A Critical Thinking
Speculating

❓ Miller quotes Shakespeare's *Hamlet* ("The time is out of joint. O cursèd spite / That ever I was born to set it right!" Act 1, Scene 5) to refer to society in the 1690s *and* the 1950s. What else might have made society seem "insoluble and complicated" in both eras? [Possible responses: religious strife and the threat of Native American attack in the 1690s; the Cold War and the Red Scare in the 1950s.]

B Critical Thinking
Synthesizing

❓ What is the "paradox" which Miller explores here? Do you agree that all social organization must be founded on "exclusion and prohibition"? [Possible response: Strong and secure social organization depends on the prohibition and exclusion of some individual freedoms, yet these repressions in turn often undermine the social fabric when taken to their logical conclusions. Students will probably agree that some prohibitions (such as those against murder, revolution, etc.) are necessary for any society to function.]

C Vocabulary Note
Greek Roots

❓ *Theo* is a root meaning "God"; *cracy,* a root meaning "government." How can you use this information to define the word *theocracy*? What other words use this root? [Possible response: A theocracy is a form of government in which God or a deity is regarded as the supreme authority. Other uses include *atheism, monotheism, pantheism, theology, apotheosis*.]

D Reading Skills and Strategies
Interpreting a Text

❓ How do you interpret Miller's main idea here? [The witchcraft trials gave people an excuse to act out their petty grievances about their relative success or personal property under the guise of a moral and religious crusade.]

E Critical Thinking
Interpreting

❓ What does this information suggest about Parris's character? [Possible response: He is mercenary and profit-oriented and condones slavery—not traits people expect to find in a minister.]

T832

A vast differentiation had taken place, and in their own time a revolution had unseated the royal government and substituted a junta which was at this moment in power. The times, to their eyes, must have been out of joint, and to the common folk must have seemed as insoluble and complicated as do ours today. It is not hard to see how easily many could have been led to believe that the time of confusion had been brought upon them by deep and darkling forces. No hint of such speculation appears on the court record, but social disorder in any age breeds such mystical suspicions, and, when, as in Salem, wonders are brought forth from below the social surface, it is too much to expect people to hold back very long from laying on the victims with all the force of their frustrations.

The Salem tragedy, which is about to begin in these pages, developed from a paradox. It is a paradox in whose grip we still live, and there is no prospect yet that we will discover its resolution. Simply, it was this: for good purposes, even high purposes, the people of Salem developed a theocracy, a combine of state and religious power whose function was to keep the community together, and to prevent any kind of disunity that might open it to destruction by material or ideological enemies. It was forged for a necessary purpose and accomplished that purpose. But all organization is and must be grounded on the idea of exclusion and prohibition, just as two objects cannot occupy the same space. Evidently the time came in New England when the repressions of order were heavier than seemed warranted by the dangers against which the order was organized. The witch-hunt was a perverse manifestation of the panic which set in among all classes when the balance began to turn toward greater individual freedom.

When one rises above the individual villainy displayed, one can only pity them all, just as we shall be pitied someday. It is still impossible for man to organize his social life without repressions, and the balance has yet to be struck between order and freedom.

The witch-hunt was not, however, a mere repression. It was also, and as importantly, a long overdue opportunity for everyone so inclined to express publicly his guilt and sins, under the cover of accusations against the victims. It suddenly became possible—and patriotic and holy—for a man to say that Martha Corey had come into his bedroom at night, and that, while his wife was sleeping at his side, Martha laid herself down on his chest and "nearly suffocated him." Of course it was her spirit only, but his satisfaction at confessing himself was no lighter than if it had been Martha herself. One could not ordinarily speak such things in public.

Long-held hatreds of neighbors could now be openly expressed, and vengeance taken, despite the Bible's charitable injunctions. Land-lust, which had been expressed by constant bickering over boundaries and deeds, could now be elevated to the arena of morality; one could cry witch against one's neighbor and feel perfectly justified in the bargain. Old scores could be settled on a plane of heavenly combat between Lucifer and the Lord; suspicions and the envy of the miserable toward the happy could and did burst out in the general revenge.

REVEREND PARRIS is praying now, and, though we cannot hear his words, a sense of his confusion hangs about him. He mumbles, then seems about to weep; then he weeps, then prays again; but his daughter does not stir on the bed.

The door opens, and his Negro slave enters. TITUBA *is in her forties.* PARRIS *brought her with him from Barbados, where he spent some years as a merchant before entering the ministry. She enters as one does who can no longer bear to be barred from the sight of her beloved, but she is also very frightened because her slave sense has warned her that, as always, trouble in this house eventually lands on her back.*

Tituba, *already taking a step backward:* My Betty be hearty soon?
Parris: Out of here!
Tituba, *backing to the door:* My Betty not goin' die . . .
Parris, *scrambling to his feet in a fury:* Out of my sight! She is gone. Out of my— He is overcome with sobs. He clamps his teeth against them and closes the door and leans against it, exhausted. Oh, my God! God help me! Quaking with fear, mumbling to himself through his sobs, he goes to the bed and gently takes BETTY's hand.

832 **AMERICAN DRAMA**

Crossing the Curriculum

Architecture

The first homes built by the Pilgrims had only one room, with an overhead loft for sleeping. The roofs were thatched with rushes and the chimneys were made of sticks of wood daubed with clay. The tiny windows were covered with oilpaper and were heavily draped with cloth to keep out the cold. By 1640, wealthy colonists built larger homes with central brick chimneys and wooden roofs. The new houses also had a parlor, often used as a bedroom. Upstairs, there were two more bedrooms with fireplaces. Most of the oil-paper windows had been replaced by diamond-paned glass casements; however, these still did not let in much light. Inside and out, the walls were made of cedar.

Invite students to make a blueprint, model, or scale drawing of a typical house in colonial New England, based on the information found here and in *The Crucible*.

Betty. Child. Dear child. Will you wake, will you open up your eyes! Betty, little one . . .

He is bending to kneel again when his niece, ABIGAIL WILLIAMS, *seventeen, enters—a strikingly beautiful girl, an orphan, with an endless capacity for dissembling. Now she is all worry and apprehension and propriety.*

Abigail: Uncle? *He looks to her.* Susanna Walcott's here from Doctor Griggs.
Parris: Oh? Let her come, let her come.
Abigail, *leaning out the door to call to* SUSANNA, *who is down the hall a few steps:* Come in, Susanna.

SUSANNA WALCOTT, *a little younger than* ABIGAIL, *a nervous, hurried girl, enters.*

Parris, *eagerly:* What does the doctor say, child?
Susanna, *craning around* PARRIS *to get a look at* BETTY: He bid me come and tell you, reverend sir, that he cannot discover no medicine for it in his books.
Parris: Then he must search on.
Susanna: Aye, sir, he have been searchin' his books since he left you, sir. But he bid me tell you, that you might look to unnatural things for the cause of it.
Parris, *his eyes going wide:* No—no. There be no unnatural cause here. Tell him I have sent for Reverend Hale of Beverly, and Mr. Hale will surely confirm that. Let him look to medicine and put out all thought of unnatural causes here. There be none.
Susanna: Aye, sir. He bid me tell you. *She turns to go.*
Abigail: Speak nothin' of it in the village, Susanna.
Parris: Go directly home and speak nothing of unnatural causes.
Susanna: Aye, sir. I pray for her. *She goes out.*
Abigail: Uncle, the rumor of witchcraft is all about; I think you'd best go down and deny it yourself. The parlor's packed with people, sir. I'll sit with her.
Parris, *pressed, turns on her:* And what shall I say to them? That my daughter and my niece I discovered dancing like heathen in the forest?
Abigail: Uncle, we did dance; let you tell them I confessed it—and I'll be whipped if I must be. But they're speakin' of witchcraft. Betty's not witched.

Parris: Abigail, I cannot go before the congregation when I know you have not opened with me. What did you do with her in the forest?
Abigail: We did dance, uncle, and when you leaped out of the bush so suddenly, Betty was frightened and then she fainted. And there's the whole of it.
Parris: Child. Sit you down.
Abigail, *quavering, as she sits:* I would never hurt Betty. I love her dearly.
Parris: Now look you, child, your punishment will come in its time. But if you trafficked with spirits in the forest I must know it now, for surely my enemies will, and they will ruin me with it.
Abigail: But we never conjured spirits.
Parris: Then why can she not move herself since midnight? This child is desperate! ABIGAIL *lowers her eyes.* It must come out—my enemies will bring it out. Let me know what you done there. Abigail, do you understand that I have many enemies?
Abigail: I have heard of it, uncle.
Parris: There is a faction that is sworn to drive me from my pulpit. Do you understand that?
Abigail: I think so, sir.
Parris: Now then, in the midst of such disruption, my own household is discovered to be the very center of some obscene practice. Abominations are done in the forest—
Abigail: It were sport, uncle!
Parris, *pointing at* BETTY: You call this sport? *She lowers her eyes. He pleads:* Abigail, if you know something that may help the doctor, for God's sake tell it to me. *She is silent.* I saw Tituba waving her arms over the fire when I came on you. Why was she doing that? And I heard a screeching and gibberish coming from her mouth. She were swaying like a dumb beast over that fire!
Abigail: She always sings her Barbados songs, and we dance.
Parris: I cannot blink what I saw, Abigail, for my enemies will not blink it. I saw a dress lying on the grass.
Abigail, *innocently:* A dress?
Parris—*it is very hard to say:* Aye, a dress. And I thought I saw—someone naked running through the trees!
Abigail, *in terror:* No one was naked! You mistake yourself, uncle!

F Elements of Literature
Motivation
? The real Abigail Williams was twelve or thirteen years old in 1692. How does Miller attempt to establish Abigail's motives, by changing her age and emphasizing that she is an orphan? [Possible response: By changing her age, Miller makes it more credible for her to be motivated by romantic love or sexual jealousy; by depicting her as an orphan, Miller implies that Abigail has had to learn to depend on, and, at times, manipulate, adults for her survival.]

G Reading Skills and Strategies
Making Inferences
? What can you infer about Puritan beliefs from what Parris says here? [Students might infer that the Puritans regarded dancing as sinful and Native Americans as infidels and were terrified of public opinion.]

H Reading Skills and Strategies
Interpreting a Text
? What does this passage reveal about Parris's character? [Possible responses: It suggests that he is far more concerned about himself than about his daughter's well-being; he is suspicious, distrustful and perhaps even paranoid.]

Taking a Second Look

Review: Making Predictions
Review how active readers use story details to make predictions about what's going to happen next. Ask students what predictions they could make if the temperature dropped below freezing and thick white clouds rolled in. [It is likely to snow.]

Activities
1. Have students make predictions. For example, will Betty wake from her strange trance?

Will we discover what the girls were really doing in the forest?
2. Have students set up a KWL chart or other graphic organizer to track their predictions.
3. Guide students to revise their predictions as they read, based on the new information they gather.

Parris, *with anger:* I saw it! *He moves from her. Then, resolved:* Now tell me true, Abigail. And I pray you feel the weight of truth upon you, for now my ministry's at stake, my ministry and perhaps your cousin's life. Whatever abomination you have done, give me all of it now, for I dare not be taken unaware when I go before them down there.

Abigail: There is nothin' more. I swear it, uncle.

Parris, *studies her, then nods, half convinced:* Abigail, I have fought here three long years to bend these stiff-necked people to me, and now, just now when some good respect is rising for me in the parish, you compromise my very character. I have given you a home, child, I have put clothes upon your back—now give me upright answer. Your name in the town—it is entirely white, is it not?

Abigail, *with an edge of resentment:* Why, I am sure it is, sir. There be no blush about my name.

Parris, *to the point:* Abigail, is there any other cause than you have told me, for your being discharged from Goody[3] Proctor's service? I have

---

3. **Goody:** formerly a title (short for *goodwife*) for a woman, especially a housewife or older woman.

---

heard it said, and I tell you as I heard it, that she comes so rarely to the church this year for she will not sit so close to something soiled. What signified that remark?

Abigail: She hates me, uncle, she must, for I would not be her slave. It's a bitter woman, a lying, cold, sniveling woman, and I will not work for such a woman!

Parris: She may be. And yet it has troubled me that you are now seven month out of their house, and in all this time no other family has ever called for your service.

Abigail: They want slaves, not such as I. Let them send to Barbados for that. I will not black my face for any of them! *With ill-concealed resentment at him:* Do you begrudge my bed, uncle?

Parris: No—no.

Abigail, *in a temper:* My name is good in the village! I will not have it said my name is soiled! Goody Proctor is a gossiping liar!

Enter MRS. ANN PUTNAM. *She is a twisted soul of forty-five, a death-ridden woman, haunted by dreams.*

Parris, *as soon as the door begins to open:* No—no, I cannot have anyone. *He sees her, and a certain deference springs into him, although his*

Thomas Putnam was a man with many grievances.

Crossing the Curriculum

Art

The Puritans were haunted by imagined terrors of the night: appearances by the devil and his subordinates, such as demons, imps, incubi, and succubi. These were horribly gruesome figures, as real to the Puritans as their friends and neighbors. But most sinister of all was the figure of the witch—an ordinary citizen, usually a woman, who had given her- or himself over to occult powers. The harm witches were thought to do ranged from the merely annoying to the totally destructive. They kept beer from fermenting and butter from hardening; they prevented conception and caused miscarriage. They were thought to boil infants, eat their flesh, and drink their blood, as well as cast spells on animals and humans, causing sickness and death.

Have students create a picture of a witch, as imagined by the Puritans, using available materials.

worry remains. Why, Goody Putnam, come in.

Mrs. Putnam, *full of breath, shiny-eyed:* It is a marvel. It is surely a stroke of hell upon you.

Parris: No, Goody Putnam, it is—

Mrs. Putnam, *glancing at* BETTY: How high did she fly, how high?

Parris: No, no, she never flew—

Mrs. Putnam, *very pleased with it:* Why, it's sure she did. Mr. Collins saw her goin' over Ingersoll's barn, and come down light as bird, he says!

Parris: Now, look you, Goody Putnam, she never— *Enter* THOMAS PUTNAM, *a well-to-do, hard-handed landowner, near fifty.* Oh, good morning, Mr. Putnam.

Putnam: It is a providence the thing is out now! It is a providence. *He goes directly to the bed.*

Parris: What's out, sir, what's—?

MRS. PUTNAM *goes to the bed.*

Putnam, *looking down at* BETTY: Why, *her* eyes is closed! Look you, Ann.

Mrs. Putnam: Why, that's strange. *To* PARRIS: Ours is open.

Parris, *shocked:* Your Ruth is sick?

Mrs. Putnam, *with vicious certainty:* I'd not call it sick; the Devil's touch is heavier than sick. It's death, y'know, it's death drivin' into them, forked and hoofed.

Parris: Oh, pray not! Why, how does Ruth ail?

Mrs. Putnam: She ails as she must—she never waked this morning, but her eyes open and she walks, and hears naught, sees naught, and cannot eat. Her soul is taken, surely.

PARRIS *is struck.*

Putnam, *as though for further details:* They say you've sent for Reverend Hale of Beverly?

Parris, *with dwindling conviction now:* A precaution only. He has much experience in all demonic arts, and I—

Mrs. Putnam: He has indeed; and found a witch in Beverly last year, and let you remember that.

Parris: Now, Goody Ann, they only thought that were a witch, and I am certain there be no element of witchcraft here.

Putnam: No witchcraft! Now look you, Mr. Parris—

Parris: Thomas, Thomas, I pray you, leap not to witchcraft. I know that you—you least of all, Thomas, would ever wish so disastrous a charge laid upon me. We cannot leap to witchcraft. They will howl me out of Salem for such corruption in my house.

A word about Thomas Putnam. He was a man with many grievances, at least one of which appears justified. Some time before, his wife's brother-in-law, James Bayley, had been turned down as minister of Salem. Bayley had all the qualifications, and a two-thirds vote into the bargain, but a faction stopped his acceptance, for reasons that are not clear.

Thomas Putnam was the eldest son of the richest man in the village. He had fought the Indians at Narragansett, and was deeply interested in parish affairs. He undoubtedly felt it poor payment that the village should so blatantly disregard his candidate for one of its more important offices, especially since he regarded himself as the intellectual superior of most of the people around him.

His vindictive nature was demonstrated long before the witchcraft began. A former Salem minister, George Burroughs, had had to borrow money to pay for his wife's funeral, and, since the parish was remiss in his salary, he was soon bankrupt. Thomas and his brother John had Burroughs jailed for debts the man did not owe. The incident is important only in that Burroughs succeeded in becoming minister where Bayley, Thomas Putnam's brother-in-law, had been rejected; the motif of resentment is clear here. Thomas Putnam felt that his own name and the honor of his family had been smirched by the village, and he meant to right matters however he could.

Another reason to believe him a deeply embittered man was his attempt to break his father's will, which left a disproportionate amount to a stepbrother. As with every other public cause in which he tried to force his way, he failed in this.

So it is not surprising to find that so many accusations against people are in the handwriting of Thomas Putnam, or that his name is so often found as a witness corroborating the supernatural testimony, or that his daughter led the crying-out at the most opportune junctures of the trials, especially when—But we'll speak of that when we come to it.

THE CRUCIBLE, ACT ONE 835

C Critical Thinking

Speculating

❓ Why is Mrs. Putnam convinced that Betty flew over Ingersoll's barn? Why is she so ready to believe that witchcraft is the cause of the girls' condition? [Possible response: The community shares a common set of assumptions about witchcraft and what it involves, and thus any mysterious phenomena lead to such rumors. As a "twisted" and "death-ridden woman," Ann Putnam seems to take pleasure in the misfortune of others, and is thus eager to believe in this "stroke of hell" upon her minister.]

D Struggling Readers

Interpreting Archaic Diction

❓ What does *naught* mean? According to Mrs. Putnam, what are Ruth's symptoms? [*Naught* means "nothing." Ruth seems to be in a trance-like state; her eyes are open and she can walk, but she is not responsive. She does not eat.]

E Elements of Literature

Motivation

Have students summarize this passage and explain how it might relate to Putnam's motivation in the witch hunt. [Possible response: Putnam wants the high public standing he feels he deserves and wants revenge for the rejection of his candidate for minister—to the point of having the successful candidate jailed. He may see the witch hunt as a way to punish his rivals and to increase his influence over the religious and political life of the village.]

Getting Students Involved

Cooperative Learning

A Helping Hand. In Puritan villages, it was common for families to hire young, single women as live-in servants. In return for their work, these girls were given room and board. The practice continues today with "au pairs." Have students work in groups to design a booklet that today's nannies and au pairs could use. The booklet should address such topics as child care, food, safety, payment, and legal issues.

Crossing the Curriculum

Mental Health

What is really wrong with Betty and Ruth? Have students consult health care workers, their parents, and psychology textbooks to see if they can pin a label on their condition. Based on their diagnosis, how would they treat the girls' condition? Mercy suggests a good beating is in order; Abigail uses threats. Students can present their conclusions in the form of a case study.

A Reading Skills
and Strategies

Interpreting a Text

❓ What is the "abyss" that Putnam is trying to get Parris to move toward? Why? [Possible response: By getting Parris to lay the blame for the girls' condition on witchcraft, Putnam will have a lever to use against his enemies. Putnam is manipulating Parris for his own ends.]

B Reading Skills and Strategies

Responding to the Text

❓ What is Mrs. Putnam's fundamental motivation for seeking solace in the idea of occult phenomena? Does this explanation make you feel more compassion for Mrs. Putnam? [Possible response: She feels guilty and shameful about her inability to keep her sick infants alive and seeks to find some outside explanation. Most students will say that this information increases their understanding of and compassion for Mrs. Putnam.]

C Elements of Literature

Motivation

❓ What other reason might Ruth have for not speaking? [Possible responses: She is terrified that she will be punished severely if the full extent of the girls' actions in the woods is discovered. By staying mute, she gets sympathy while the others take the blame.]

D Critical Thinking

Evaluating

❓ What is your opinion of Parris? What evidence did you use? [Possible responses: He is concerned only for himself, focusing on saving his reputation and job. He shows little concern for his daughter's condition or for reassuring and calming the town.]

E Reading Skills and Strategies

Making Inferences

❓ What can you infer about Abigail from this action? [Possible response: She is forceful and decisive and seems to doubt that any witchcraft is involved in Betty's affliction.]

A **Putnam**—*at the moment he is intent upon getting* PARRIS, *for whom he has only contempt, to move toward the abyss:* Mr. Parris, I have taken your part in all contention here, and I would continue; but I cannot if you hold back in this. There are hurtful, vengeful spirits layin' hands on these children.

Parris: But, Thomas, you cannot—

Putnam: Ann! Tell Mr. Parris what you have done.

B **Mrs. Putnam:** Reverend Parris, I have laid seven babies unbaptized in the earth. Believe me, sir, you never saw more hearty babies born. And yet, each would wither in my arms the very night of their birth. I have spoke nothin', but my heart has clamored intimations. And now, this year, my Ruth, my only— I see her turning strange. A secret child she has become this year, and shrivels like a sucking mouth were pullin' on her life too. And so I thought to send her to your Tituba—

Parris: To Tituba! What may Tituba—?

Mrs. Putnam: Tituba knows how to speak to the dead, Mr. Parris.

Parris: Goody Ann, it is a formidable sin to conjure up the dead!

Mrs. Putnam: I take it on my soul, but who else may surely tell us what person murdered my babies?

Parris, *horrified:* Woman!

C **Mrs. Putnam:** They were murdered, Mr. Parris! And mark this proof! Mark it! Last night my Ruth were ever so close to their little spirits; I know it, sir. For how else is she struck dumb now except some power of darkness would stop her mouth? It is a marvelous sign, Mr. Parris!

Putnam: Don't you understand it, sir? There is a murdering witch among us, bound to keep herself in the dark. PARRIS *turns to* BETTY, *a frantic terror rising in him.* Let your enemies make of it what they will, you cannot blink it more.

Parris, *to* ABIGAIL: Then you were conjuring spirits last night.

Abigail, *whispering:* Not I, sir—Tituba and Ruth.

D **Parris,** *turns now, with new fear, and goes to* BETTY, *looks down at her, and then, gazing off:* Oh, Abigail, what proper payment for my charity! Now I am undone.

Putnam: You are not undone! Let you take hold here. Wait for no one to charge you—declare it yourself. You have discovered witchcraft—

Parris: In my house? In my house, Thomas? They will topple me with this! They will make of it a—

Enter MERCY LEWIS, *the* PUTNAMS' *servant, a fat, sly, merciless girl of eighteen.*

Mercy: Your pardons. I only thought to see how Betty is.

Putnam: Why aren't you home? Who's with Ruth?

Mercy: Her grandma come. She's improved a little, I think—she give a powerful sneeze before.

Mrs. Putnam: Ah, there's a sign of life!

Mercy: I'd fear no more, Goody Putnam. It were a grand sneeze; another like it will shake her wits together, I'm sure. *She goes to the bed to look.*

Parris: Will you leave me now, Thomas? I would pray a while alone.

Abigail: Uncle, you've prayed since midnight. Why do you not go down and—

Parris: No—no. *To* PUTNAM: I have no answer for that crowd. I'll wait till Mr. Hale arrives. *To get* MRS. PUTNAM *to leave:* If you will, Goody Ann . . .

Putnam: Now look you, sir. Let you strike out against the Devil, and the village will bless you for it! Come down, speak to them—pray with them. They're thirsting for your word, Mister! Surely you'll pray with them.

Parris, *swayed:* I'll lead them in a psalm, but let you say nothing of witchcraft yet. I will not discuss it. The cause is yet unknown. I have had enough contention since I came; I want no more.

Mrs. Putnam: Mercy, you go home to Ruth, d'y'hear?

Mercy: Aye, mum.

MRS. PUTNAM *goes out.*

Parris, *to* ABIGAIL: If she starts for the window, cry for me at once.

Abigail: I will, uncle.

Parris, *to* PUTNAM: There is a terrible power in her arms today. *He goes out with* PUTNAM.

Abigail, *with hushed trepidation:* How is Ruth sick?

Mercy: It's weirdish, I know not—she seems to walk like a dead one since last night.

E **Abigail,** *turns at once and goes to* BETTY, *and now, with fear in her voice:* Betty? BETTY *doesn't move. She shakes her.* Now stop this! Betty! Sit up now!

836 AMERICAN DRAMA

Crossing the Curriculum

Geography

Parris's slave, Tituba, and her husband, John, came from Barbados, an island in the West Indies. Probably named by Portuguese sailors for its bearded fig trees, the uninhabited island was settled by the British in 1627. Slaves were brought from Africa to work on plantations until slavery in the colonies was abolished by Parliament in 1834. Have students research the island's geography and climate to find out why it was a desirable site for colonization.

Public Health/History

Miller finds the root of the witchcraft hysteria in social, political, religious, and economic issues. However, some historians have proposed quite a different explanation for the madness: ergot poisoning (hallucinations caused by eating moldy wheat). Have students research this theory and then decide whether or not it seems valid. Which explanation do they think best explains the girls' strange behavior? Why?

BETTY *doesn't stir.* MERCY *comes over.*

Mercy: Have you tried beatin' her? I gave Ruth a good one and it waked her for a minute. Here, let me have her.

Abigail, *holding* MERCY *back:* No, he'll be comin' up. Listen, now; if they be questioning us, tell them we danced—I told him as much already.

Mercy: Aye. And what more?

Abigail: He knows Tituba conjured Ruth's sisters to come out of the grave.

Mercy: And what more?

Abigail: He saw you naked.

Mercy, *clapping her hands together with a frightened laugh:* Oh, Jesus!

Enter MARY WARREN, *breathless. She is seventeen, a subservient, naïve, lonely girl.*

Mary Warren: What'll we do? The village is out! I just come from the farm; the whole country's talkin' witchcraft! They'll be callin' us witches, Abby!

Mercy, *pointing and looking at* MARY WARREN: She means to tell, I know it.

Mary Warren: Abby, we've got to tell. Witchery's a hangin' error, a hangin' like they done in Boston two year ago! We must tell the truth, Abby! You'll only be whipped for dancin', and the other things!

Abigail: Oh, *we'll* be whipped!

Mary Warren: I never done none of it, Abby. I only looked!

Mercy, *moving menacingly toward* MARY: Oh, you're a great one for lookin', aren't you, Mary Warren? What a grand peeping courage you have!

BETTY, *on the bed, whimpers.* ABIGAIL *turns to her at once.*

Abigail: Betty? *She goes to* BETTY. Now, Betty, dear, wake up now. It's Abigail. *She sits* BETTY *up and furiously shakes her.* I'll beat you, Betty! BETTY *whimpers.* My, you seem improving. I talked to your papa and I told him everything. So there's nothing to—

Betty, *darts off the bed, frightened of* ABIGAIL, *and flattens herself against the wall:* I want my mama!

Abigail, *with alarm, as she cautiously approaches* BETTY: What ails you, Betty? Your mama's dead and buried.

Betty: I'll fly to Mama. Let me fly! *She raises her arms as though to fly, and streaks for the window, gets one leg out.*

Abigail, *pulling her away from the window:* I told him everything; he knows now, he knows everything we—

Betty: You drank blood, Abby! You didn't tell him that!

Abigail: Betty, you never say that again! You will never—

Betty: You did, you did! You drank a charm to kill John Proctor's wife! You drank a charm to kill Goody Proctor!

Abigail, *smashes her across the face:* Shut it! Now shut it!

Betty, *collapsing on the bed:* Mama, Mama! *She dissolves into sobs.*

Abigail: Now look you. All of you. We danced. And Tituba conjured Ruth Putnam's dead sisters. And that is all. And mark this. Let either of you breathe a word, or the edge of a word, about the other things, and I will come to you in the black of some terrible night and I will bring a pointy reckoning that will shudder you. And you know I can do it; I saw Indians smash my dear parents' heads on the pillow next to mine, and I have seen some reddish work done at night, and I can make you wish you had never seen the sun go down! *She goes to* BETTY *and roughly sits her up.* Now, you—sit up and stop this!

But BETTY *collapses in her hands and lies inert on the bed.*

F Critical Thinking
Interpreting

? What does this scene reveal about the girls and their relationship to each other? [Possible responses: Abigail emerges as the leader, coolly laying out the story and giving orders. When Mary Warren, the weakest child, attempts to extricate herself, Abigail quickly pulls her back in line with a threat. Mercy functions as Abigail's lieutenant.]

G Reading Skills and Strategies
Interpreting a Text

? Why did Abigail drink a charm to kill Goody Proctor? What does this action reveal about Abigail's character? [Possible responses: Abigail may want to kill Elizabeth Proctor simply because she fired her and lowered her standing in the town; or, given Betty's reference to "John Proctor's wife," it may be that Abigail is interested in John Proctor and wants his wife out of the way. Drinking blood reveals the extraordinary lengths to which she will go to achieve her goals. She emerges as totally ruthless.]

H Struggling Readers
Interpreting Metaphorical Language

? What is a "pointy reckoning"? Why do you think Miller used this phrase rather than more direct language? [Possible responses: It seems to refer to a knife or dagger. The phrase captures the rich, evocative diction of the time and intensifies the ominous mood.]

Crossing the Curriculum

Music

The Whole Booke of Psalmes Faithfully Translated into English Meter came off the press in Massachusetts in 1640. A slender leather-bound book with sturdy brass clasps, it was the first book printed in the New World. Today it is known as the *Bay Psalm Book* because it was immediately adopted as a hymnal by the churches in the Massachusetts Bay Colony. The book, which sold for twenty pence a copy, was a colonial best seller. Although we rarely associate the Puritans with music, the singing of the Psalms was an integral part of their worship. The translation sacrificed rhythm and graceful expression for accuracy. Here's an excerpt from their translation of the Twenty-third Psalm:

The Lord to mee a shepheard is.
  want therefore shall not I.
Hee in the folds of tender grasse,
doth cause mee downe to lie:
To waters calme me gently leads
  Restore my soule doth hee:
He doth in paths of righteousness:
  for his names sake leade mee.

Have groups of students set this lyric to music they think the Puritans might have used. Guide students to explain their choices.

? What similarities can you find between Proctor and the protagonists of other works in this book? In what ways does he share the characteristics of a classical tragic hero? (See pp. 683 and 1203.) [Possible response: Proctor resembles Hemingway's protagonist Krebs in his intolerance for hypocrisy; like Hawthorne's Mr. Hooper, Proctor is an honest, decent man who is haunted by his failure to uphold his own values. Like the classical tragic hero, Proctor is a prominent figure, a leader in his community, who has a "tragic flaw" that may lead to his downfall.]

B Cultural Connections
Theology

By pointing out that the Puritans had no "ritual for the washing away of sins," Miller emphasizes their Protestant departure from Catholicism and Anglicanism, which both retained rituals such as confession, which are designed, among other things, to cleanse the penitent of sin. For the Puritans, with their Calvinist legacy of predestination to heaven or hell, these options were not available. Have students decide whether they agree that twentieth-century Americans have no ritual for washing away sin.

C English Language Learners
Using Context Clues

? What is Mary claiming here? What does the context indicate she is hiding? [She wants Proctor to think she was merely curious about the witchcraft crisis in Salem. She conceals her personal stake in the witchcraft issue and her participation in the forest dancing.]

D Elements of Literature
Tone

? What is the tone of Abigail's comment? What does it imply? [The tone is familiar, flirtatious, and daring. It suggests that Abigail and Proctor have had some kind of intimate relationship.]

E Elements of Literature
Motivation

? What does Abigail want from John Proctor? [Possible responses: She wants to rekindle their affair; she still loves him and hopes to displace Elizabeth and marry him.]

Mary Warren, *with hysterical fright:* What's got her? ABIGAIL *stares in fright at* BETTY. Abby, she's going to die! It's a sin to conjure, and we—
Abigail, *starting for* MARY: I say shut it, Mary Warren!
Enter JOHN PROCTOR. *On seeing him,* MARY WARREN *leaps in fright.*

Proctor was a farmer in his middle thirties. He need not have been a partisan of any faction in the town, but there is evidence to suggest that he had a sharp and biting way with hypocrites. He was the kind of man—powerful of body, even-tempered, and not easily led—who cannot refuse support to partisans without drawing their deepest resentment. In Proctor's presence a fool felt his foolishness instantly—and a Proctor is always marked for calumny therefore.

But as we shall see, the steady manner he displays does not spring from an untroubled soul. He is a sinner, a sinner not only against the moral fashion of the time, but against his own vision of decent conduct. These people had no ritual for the washing away of sins. It is another trait we inherited from them, and it has helped to discipline us as well as to breed hypocrisy among us. Proctor, respected and even feared in Salem, has come to regard himself as a kind of fraud. But no hint of this has yet appeared on the surface, and as he enters from the crowded parlor below it is a man in his prime we see, with a quiet confidence and an unexpressed, hidden force. Mary Warren, his servant, can barely speak for embarrassment and fear.

Mary Warren: Oh! I'm just going home, Mr. Proctor.
Proctor: Be you foolish, Mary Warren? Be you deaf? I forbid you leave the house, did I not? Why shall I pay you? I am looking for you more often than my cows!
Mary Warren: I only come to see the great doings in the world.
Proctor: I'll show you a great doin' on your arse one of these days. Now get you home; my wife is waitin' with your work! *Trying to retain a shred of dignity, she goes slowly out.*
Mercy Lewis, *both afraid of him and strangely titillated:* I'd best be off. I have my Ruth to watch. Good morning, Mr. Proctor.

MERCY *sidles out. Since* PROCTOR's *entrance,* ABIGAIL *has stood as though on tiptoe, absorbing his presence, wide-eyed. He glances at her, then goes to* BETTY *on the bed.*

Abigail: Gah! I'd almost forgot how strong you are, John Proctor!
Proctor, *looking at* ABIGAIL *now, the faintest suggestion of a knowing smile on his face:* What's this mischief here?
Abigail, *with a nervous laugh:* Oh, she's only gone silly somehow.
Proctor: The road past my house is a pilgrimage to Salem all morning. The town's mumbling witchcraft.
Abigail: Oh, posh! *Winningly she comes a little closer, with a confidential, wicked air.* We were dancin' in the woods last night, and my uncle leaped in on us. She took fright, is all.
Proctor, *his smile widening:* Ah, you're wicked yet, aren't y'! *A trill of expectant laughter escapes her, and she dares come closer, feverishly looking into his eyes.* You'll be clapped in the stocks before you're twenty.

He takes a step to go, and she springs into his path.

Abigail: Give me a word, John. A soft word. *Her concentrated desire destroys his smile.*
Proctor: No, no, Abby. That's done with.
Abigail, *tauntingly:* You come five mile to see a silly girl fly? I know you better.
Proctor, *setting her firmly out of his path:* I come to see what mischief your uncle's brewin' now. *With final emphasis:* Put it out of mind, Abby.
Abigail, *grasping his hand before he can release her:* John—I am waitin' for you every night.
Proctor: Abby, I never give you hope to wait for me.
Abigail, *now beginning to anger—she can't believe it:* I have something better than hope, I think!
Proctor: Abby, you'll put it out of mind. I'll not be comin' for you more.
Abigail: You're surely sportin' with me.
Proctor: You know me better.
Abigail: I know how you clutched my back behind your house and sweated like a stallion when

Skill Link

Tell students that the characters in *The Crucible* speak colonial American English, as Miller has re-created it. This style of speech includes archaic words and expressions, inverted syntax, and unfamiliar allusions.

Activity

Call on volunteers to read some of the dialogue aloud and translate it into today's conversational English. Here are some examples from this page:

1. "Be you foolish, Mary Warren?"
2. "Now get you home; my wife is waitin' with your work!"
3. "I have my Ruth to watch."
4. "Oh, she's only gone silly somehow."
5. "I'll not be comin' for you more."

Encourage students to try several variations of their "translations" until they find the ones that best capture the rhythms of contemporary speech.

ever I come near! Or did I dream that? It's she put me out, you cannot pretend it were you. I saw your face when she put me out, and you loved me then and you do now!

Proctor: Abby, that's a wild thing to say—

Abigail: A wild thing may say wild things. But not so wild, I think. I have seen you since she put me out; I have seen you nights.

Proctor: I have hardly stepped off my farm this sevenmonth.

Abigail: I have a sense for heat, John, and yours has drawn me to my window, and I have seen you looking up, burning in your loneliness. Do you tell me you've never looked up at my window?

Proctor: I may have looked up.

Abigail, *now softening:* And you must. You are no wintry man. I know you, John. I *know* you. *She is weeping.* I cannot sleep for dreamin'; I cannot dream but I wake and walk about the house as though I'd find you comin' through some door. *She clutches him desperately.*

Proctor, *gently pressing her from him, with great sympathy but firmly:* Child—

Abigail, *with a flash of anger:* How do you call me child!

Proctor: Abby, I may think of you softly from time to time. But I will cut off my hand before I'll ever reach for you again. Wipe it out of mind. We never touched, Abby.

Abigail: Aye, but we did.

Proctor: Aye, but we did not.

Abigail, *with a bitter anger:* Oh, I marvel how such a strong man may let such a sickly wife be—

Proctor, *angered—at himself as well:* You'll speak nothin' of Elizabeth!

Abigail: She is blackening my name in the village! She is telling lies about me! She is a cold, sniveling woman, and you bend to her! Let her turn you like a—

Proctor, *shaking her:* Do you look for whippin'?

A psalm is heard being sung below.

Abigail, *in tears:* I look for John Proctor that took me from my sleep and put knowledge in my heart! I never knew what pretense Salem was, I never knew the lying lessons I was taught by all these Christian women and their covenanted men! And now you bid me tear the light out of my eyes? I will not, I cannot! You loved me, John Proctor,

"We never touched, Abby."

and whatever sin it is, you love me yet! *He turns abruptly to go out. She rushes to him.* John, pity me, pity me!

The words "going up to Jesus" are heard in the psalm, and BETTY *claps her ears suddenly and whines loudly.*

Abigail: Betty? *She hurries to* BETTY, *who is now sitting up and screaming.* PROCTOR *goes to* BETTY *as* ABIGAIL *is trying to pull her hands down, calling "Betty!"*

Proctor, *growing unnerved:* What's she doing? Girl, what ails you? Stop that wailing!

The singing has stopped in the midst of this, and now PARRIS *rushes in.*

Parris: What happened? What are you doing to her? Betty! *He rushes to the bed, crying, "Betty, Betty!"* MRS. PUTNAM *enters, feverish with curiosity, and with her* THOMAS PUTNAM *and* MERCY LEWIS. PARRIS, *at the bed, keeps lightly slapping* BETTY's *face, while she moans and tries to get up.*

Abigail: She heard you singin' and suddenly she's up and screamin'.

Mrs. Putnam: The psalm! The psalm! She cannot bear to hear the Lord's name!

Parris: No, God forbid. Mercy, run to the doctor! Tell him what's happened here! MERCY LEWIS *rushes out.*

Mrs. Putnam: Mark it for a sign, mark it!

REBECCA NURSE, *seventy-two, enters. She is white-haired, leaning upon her walking-stick.*

THE CRUCIBLE, ACT ONE **839**

F **Reading Skills and Strategies**
Interpreting a Text

? What is Abigail hoping to achieve with this assertion? Does she really know Proctor? [Possible response: Abigail wants to believe that she alone knows Proctor's true feelings and motivations. She may also be reminding Proctor that she *knows* him in the Biblical sense of the word—that is, sexually—as a subtle threat. Nevertheless, Abigail seems to misunderstand Proctor on many fundamental levels, especially his love and respect for his wife.]

G **Elements of Literature**
Motivation

? Why is Abigail so angry when John Proctor calls her "child"? [Possible responses: She is angry because it is Proctor that has, in some sense, taken her childhood from her, by bringing her into the world of adult sexuality, jealousy, and power. She also resents this statement because it suggests that she is not Proctor's equal and will never be his partner in romance or marriage.]

H **Elements of Literature**
Characterization

? What does this speech tell you about Abigail's view of society? What is the "light" that she claims Proctor showed her? [Possible responses: Abby views society as built on hypocrisy and pretense, in which people pretend to act according to principles but really live according to their own selfish desires and whims. She claims that Proctor showed her the "light" of this sinful life beneath Salem's "lying lessons."]

I **Vocabulary Note**
Word Origins
The word *psalm* refers to a sacred song or hymn, most often those found in Jewish and Christian sacred texts. The word, however, comes from the Greek verb *psallein,* which means "to play the harp."

Putnam, *pointing at the whimpering* BETTY: That is a notorious sign of witchcraft afoot, Goody Nurse, a prodigious sign!

Mrs. Putnam: My mother told me that! When they cannot bear to hear the name of—

Parris, *trembling:* Rebecca, Rebecca, go to her, we're lost. She suddenly cannot bear to hear the Lord's—

GILES COREY, *eighty-three, enters. He is knotted with muscle, canny, inquisitive, and still powerful.*

Rebecca: There is hard sickness here, Giles Corey, so please to keep the quiet.

A **Giles:** I've not said a word. No one here can testify I've said a word. Is she going to fly again? I hear she flies.

Putnam: Man, be quiet now!

Everything is quiet. REBECCA *walks across the room to the bed. Gentleness exudes from her.* BETTY *is quietly whimpering, eyes shut.* REBECCA *simply stands over the child, who gradually quiets.*

And while they are so absorbed, we may put a word in for Rebecca. Rebecca was the wife of Francis Nurse, who, from all accounts, was one of those men for whom both sides of the argument had to have respect. He was called upon to arbitrate disputes as though he were an unofficial judge, and Rebecca also enjoyed the high opinion most people had for him. By the time of the delusion, they had three hundred acres, and their children were settled in separate homesteads within the same estate. However, Francis had originally rented the land, and one theory has it that, as he gradually paid for it and raised his social status, there were those who resented his rise.

Another suggestion to explain the systematic campaign against Rebecca, and inferentially against Francis, is the land war he fought with his neighbors, one of whom was a Putnam. This squabble grew to the proportions of a battle in the woods between partisans of both sides, and it is **B** said to have lasted for two days. As for Rebecca herself, the general opinion of her character was so high that to explain how anyone dared cry her out for a witch—and more, how adults could bring themselves to lay hands on her—we must look to the fields and boundaries of that time.

As we have seen, Thomas Putnam's man for the Salem ministry was Bayley. The Nurse clan had been in the faction that prevented Bayley's taking office. In addition, certain families allied to the Nurses by blood or friendship, and whose farms were contiguous with the Nurse farm or close to it, combined to break away from the Salem town authority and set up Topsfield, a new and independent entity whose existence was resented by old Salemites.

That the guiding hand behind the outcry was Putnam's is indicated by the fact that, as soon as it began, this Topsfield-Nurse faction absented themselves from church in protest and disbelief. It was Edward and Jonathan Putnam who signed the first complaint against Rebecca; and Thomas Putnam's little daughter was the one who fell into a fit at the hearing and pointed to Rebecca as her attacker. To top it all, Mrs. Putnam—who is now staring at the bewitched child on the bed—soon **C** accused Rebecca's spirit of "tempting her to iniquity," a charge that had more truth in it than Mrs. Putnam could know.

Mrs. Putnam, *astonished:* What have you done?

REBECCA, *in thought, now leaves the bedside and sits.*

Parris, *wondrous and relieved:* What do you make of it, Rebecca?

Putnam, *eagerly:* Goody Nurse, will you go to my Ruth and see if you can wake her?

Rebecca, *sitting:* I think she'll wake in time. Pray calm yourselves. I have eleven children, and I am twenty-six times a grandma, and I have seen them all through their silly seasons, and when it come on them they will run the Devil bowlegged keeping up with their mischief. I think she'll wake **D** when she tires of it. A child's spirit is like a child, you can never catch it by running after it; you must stand still, and, for love, it will soon itself come back.

Proctor: Aye, that's the truth of it, Rebecca.

Mrs. Putnam: This is no silly season, Rebecca. My Ruth is bewildered, Rebecca; she cannot eat.

E **Rebecca:** Perhaps she is not hungered yet. *To* PARRIS: I hope you are not decided to go in search of loose spirits, Mr. Parris. I've heard promise of that outside.

Parris: A wide opinion's running in the parish that the Devil may be among us, and I would satisfy them that they are wrong.

Proctor: Then let you come out and call them wrong. Did you consult the wardens before you called this minister to look for devils?

Parris: He is not coming to look for devils!

Proctor: Then what's he coming for?

Putnam: There be children dyin' in the village, Mister!

Proctor: I seen none dyin'. This society will not be a bag to swing around your head, Mr. Putnam. *To* PARRIS: Did you call a meeting before you—?

Putnam: I am sick of meetings; cannot the man turn his head without he have a meeting?

Proctor: He may turn his head, but not to Hell!

Rebecca: Pray, John, be calm. *Pause. He defers to her.* Mr. Parris, I think you'd best send Reverend Hale back as soon as he come. This will set us all to arguin' again in the society, and we thought to have peace this year. I think we ought rely on the doctor now, and good prayer.

Mrs. Putnam: Rebecca, the doctor's baffled!

Rebecca: If so he is, then let us go to God for the cause of it. There is prodigious danger in the seeking of loose spirits. I fear it, I fear it. Let us rather blame ourselves and—

Putnam: How may we blame ourselves? I am one of nine sons; the Putnam seed have peopled this province. And yet I have but one child left of eight—and now she shrivels!

Rebecca: I cannot fathom that.

Mrs. Putnam, *with a growing edge of sarcasm:* But I must! You think it God's work you should never lose a child, nor grandchild either, and I bury all but one? There are wheels within wheels in this village, and fires within fires!

Putnam, *to* PARRIS: When Reverend Hale comes, you will proceed to look for signs of witchcraft here.

Proctor, *to* PUTNAM: You cannot command Mr. Parris. We vote by name in this society, not by acreage.

Putnam: I never heard you worried so on this society, Mr. Proctor. I do not think I saw you at Sabbath meeting since snow flew.

Proctor: I have trouble enough without I come five mile to hear him preach only hellfire and bloody damnation. Take it to heart, Mr. Parris.

There are many others who stay away from church these days because you hardly ever mention God any more.

Parris, *now aroused:* Why, that's a drastic charge!

Rebecca: It's somewhat true; there are many that quail to bring their children—

Parris: I do not preach for children, Rebecca. It is not the children who are unmindful of their obligations toward this ministry.

Rebecca: Are there really those unmindful?

Parris: I should say the better half of Salem village—

Putnam: And more than that!

Parris: Where is my wood? My contract provides I be supplied with all my firewood. I am waiting since November for a stick, and even in November I had to show my frostbitten hands like some London beggar!

Giles: You are allowed six pound a year to buy your wood, Mr. Parris.

Parris: I regard that six pound as part of my salary. I am paid little enough without I spend six pound on firewood.

Proctor: Sixty, plus six for firewood—

Parris: The salary is sixty-six pound, Mr. Proctor!  I am not some preaching farmer with a book under my arm; I am a graduate of Harvard College.

Giles: Aye, and well instructed in arithmetic!

Parris: Mr. Corey, you will look far for a man of my kind at sixty pound a year! I am not used to this poverty; I left a thrifty business in the Barbados to serve the Lord. I do not fathom it, why am I persecuted here? I cannot offer one proposition but there be a howling riot of argument. I have often wondered if the Devil be in it somewhere; I cannot understand you people otherwise.

Proctor: Mr. Parris, you are the first minister ever did demand the deed to this house—

Parris: Man! Don't a minister deserve a house to live in?

Proctor: To live in, yes. But to ask ownership is like you shall own the meeting house itself; the last meeting I were at you spoke so long on deeds and mortgages I thought it were an auction.

Parris: I want a mark of confidence, is all! I am your third preacher in seven years. I do not wish to be put out like the cat whenever some majority feels the whim. You people seem not to comprehend that a minister is the Lord's man in the

Taking a Second Look

parish; a minister is not to be so lightly crossed and contradicted—

Putnam: Aye!

Parris: There is either obedience or the church will burn like Hell is burning!

Proctor: Can you speak one minute without we land in Hell again? I am sick of Hell!

Parris: It is not for you to say what is good for you to hear!

Proctor: I may speak my heart, I think!

Parris, *in a fury:* What, are we Quakers?[4] We are not Quakers here yet, Mr. Proctor. And you may tell that to your followers!

Proctor: My followers!

Parris—*now he's out with it:* There is a party in this church. I am not blind; there is a faction and a party.

Proctor: Against you?

Putnam: Against him and all authority!

Proctor: Why, then I must find it and join it.

There is shock among the others.

Rebecca: He does not mean that.

Putnam: He confessed it now!

Proctor: I mean it solemnly, Rebecca; I like not the smell of this "authority."

Rebecca: No, you cannot break charity with your minister. You are another kind, John. Clasp his hand, make your peace.

Proctor: I have a crop to sow and lumber to drag home. *He goes angrily to the door and turns to* COREY *with a smile.* What say you, Giles, let's find the party. He says there's a party.

Giles: I've changed my opinion of this man, John. Mr. Parris, I beg your pardon. I never thought you had so much iron in you.

Parris, *surprised:* Why, thank you, Giles!

Giles: It suggests to the mind what the trouble be among us all these years. *To all:* Think on it. Wherefore is everybody suing everybody else? Think on it now, it's a deep thing, and dark as a pit. I have been six time in court this year—

Proctor, *familiarly, with warmth, although he knows he is approaching the edge of* GILES' *tolerance with this:* Is it the Devil's fault that a man

4. **Quakers:** Most Quakers believe that no rite or formally trained priest is needed to commune with God; instead, divine truth can be found in one's "inner light."

cannot say you good morning without you clap him for defamation? You're old, Giles, and you're not hearin' so well as you did.

Giles—*he cannot be crossed:* John Proctor, I have only last month collected four pound damages for you publicly sayin' I burned the roof off your house, and I—

Proctor, *laughing:* I never said no such thing, but I've paid you for it, so I hope I can call you deaf without charge. Now come along, Giles, and help me drag my lumber home.

Putnam: A moment, Mr. Proctor. What lumber is that you're draggin', if I may ask you?

Proctor: My lumber. From out my forest by the riverside.

Putnam: Why, we are surely gone wild this year. What anarchy is this? That tract is in my bounds, it's in my bounds, Mr. Proctor.

Proctor: In your bounds! *Indicating* REBECCA: I bought that tract from Goody Nurse's husband five months ago.

Putnam: He had no right to sell it. It stands clear in my grandfather's will that all the land between the river and—

Proctor: Your grandfather had a habit of willing land that never belonged to him, if I may say it plain.

Giles: That's God's truth; he nearly willed away my north pasture but he knew I'd break his fingers before he'd set his name to it. Let's get your lumber home, John. I feel a sudden will to work coming on.

Putnam: You load one oak of mine and you'll fight to drag it home!

Giles: Aye, and we'll win too, Putnam—this fool and I. Come on! *He turns to* PROCTOR *and starts out.*

Putnam: I'll have my men on you, Corey! I'll clap a writ on you!

Enter REVEREND JOHN HALE *of Beverly.*

Mr. Hale is nearing forty, a tight-skinned, eager-eyed intellectual. This is a beloved errand for him; on being called here to ascertain witchcraft he felt the pride of the specialist whose unique knowledge has at last been publicly called for. Like almost all men of learning, he spent a good deal of his time pondering the invisible world, especially

842 AMERICAN DRAMA

Crossing the Curriculum

History

Witchcraft. Many of today's scholars believe that witchcraft was the remnant of a fertility cult that ancient Europeans followed before the introduction of Christianity. As Christianity became the dominant belief system, people came to see the gods of the fertility cult as devils. But not everyone was persuaded to follow Christianity; those people unwilling to give up the old ways became witches in the eyes of devout Christians. Matters came to a head at

the end of the fifteenth century, when Pope Innocent VIII (1432–1492) issued a papal document against witchcraft, *Summis Desiderantes*. To ferret out the remaining witches, the Pope established a cadre of witch hunters who traveled from region to region. As a result of this clash of cultures, the witch-hunting hysteria tore through Europe from about 1050 to the late 1600s. Husbands turned in their wives; children informed against their parents.

How could you tell if your wife, mother, sister, or other female relative was a witch? Conveniently, there were many "tests" to determine a witch's guilt: For example, it was plain that a woman was a witch if she could not cry and had additional breasts (to nurse her devilish "familiars"). The ultimate test involved water: If a woman stayed afloat when thrown into a body of water, she was clearly guilty; if she sank, she was considered innocent.

since he had himself encountered a witch in his parish not long before. That woman, however, turned into a mere pest under his searching scrutiny, and the child she had allegedly been afflicting recovered her normal behavior after Hale had given her his kindness and a few days of rest in his own house. However, that experience never raised a doubt in his mind as to the reality of the underworld or the existence of Lucifer's many-faced lieutenants. And his belief is not to his discredit. Better minds than Hale's were—and still are—convinced that there is a society of spirits beyond our ken. One cannot help noting that one of his lines has never yet raised a laugh in any audience that has seen this play; it is his assurance that "We cannot look to superstition in this. The Devil is precise." Evidently we are not quite certain even now whether diabolism is holy and not to be scoffed at. And it is no accident that we should be so bemused.

Like Reverend Hale and the others on this stage, we conceive the Devil as a necessary part of a respectable view of cosmology. Ours is a divided empire in which certain ideas and emotions and actions are of God, and their opposites are of Lucifer. It is as impossible for most men to conceive of a morality without sin as of an earth without "sky." Since 1692 a great but superficial change has wiped out God's beard and the Devil's horns, but the world is still gripped between two diametrically opposed absolutes. The concept of unity, in which positive and negative are attributes of the same force, in which good and evil are relative, ever-changing, and always joined to the same phenomenon—such a concept is still reserved to the physical sciences and to the few who have grasped the history of ideas. When it is recalled that until the Christian era the underworld was never regarded as a hostile area, that all gods were useful and essentially friendly to man despite occasional lapses; when we see the steady and methodical inculcation into humanity of the idea of man's worthlessness—until redeemed—the necessity of the Devil may become evident as a weapon, a weapon designed and used time and time again in every age to whip men into a surrender to a particular church or church-state.

Our difficulty in believing the—for want of a better word—political inspiration of the Devil is due in great part to the fact that he is called up and damned not only by our social antagonists but by our own side, whatever it may be. The Catholic Church, through its Inquisition,[5] is famous for cultivating Lucifer as the arch-fiend, but the Church's enemies relied no less upon the Old Boy to keep the human mind enthralled. Luther[6] was himself accused of alliance with Hell, and he in turn accused his enemies. To complicate matters further, he believed that he had had contact with the Devil, and had argued theology with him. I am not surprised at this, for at my own university a professor of history—a Lutheran, by the way—used to assemble his graduate students, draw the shades, and commune in the classroom with Erasmus.[7] He was never, to my knowledge, officially scoffed at for this, the reason being that the university officials, like most of us, are the children of a history which still sucks at the Devil's teats. At this writing, only England has held back before the temptations of contemporary diabolism. In the countries of the Communist ideology, all resistance of any import is linked to the totally malign capitalist succubi,[8] and in America any man who is not reactionary in his views is open to the charge of alliance with the Red hell. Political opposition, thereby, is given an inhumane overlay which then justifies the abrogation of all normally applied customs of civilized intercourse. A political policy is equated with moral right, and opposition to it with diabolical malevolence. Once such an equation is effectively made, society becomes a congerie of plots and counterplots, and the main role of government changes from that of the arbiter to that of the scourge of God.

The results of this process are no different now from what they ever were, except sometimes in the degree of cruelty inflicted, and not always

5. **Inquisition:** suppression and punishment, begun in the thirteenth century, by the Roman Catholic Church of people thought to hold heretical beliefs.
6. **Luther:** Martin Luther (1483–1546), a German theologian and leader of the Protestant Reformation.
7. **Erasmus** (i·raz′məs) (c. 1466–1536): Dutch scholar and humanist, who came into conflict with Luther over predestination. (Erasmus believed in free will.)
8. **succubi** (suk′yōō·bī): plural of *succubus,* a female evil spirit or demon thought in medieval times to have sexual intercourse with sleeping men.

THE CRUCIBLE, ACT ONE **843**

A Critical Thinking
Synthesizing
? What is Miller's underlying point in this paragraph? Why is it beside the point that there were practicing witches as well as Communist and capitalist spies? [Possible response: Miller's point is that in all three cases, authorities employed the theory of diabolism as a tool to persecute people not for what they had done, but for what they thought and felt—what their intentions were.]

B Historical Connections
Spies like Us
The 1950s saw a number of famous and controversial espionage cases. In 1950, Alger Hiss, a Department of State official, was sentenced to four years in prison for allegedly transmitting government documents to the Soviets. In 1992, Russian officials said they found no evidence in the Kremlin archives to indicate that Hiss was guilty. In 1953, New York electrical engineer Julius Rosenberg and his wife, Ethel, were found guilty and executed for allegedly transmitting top-secret information on nuclear weapons to the Soviets. While most observers ultimately concluded that the Rosenbergs were probably guilty of espionage, the case has sparked controversy for decades, due to questions about the role the "Red Scare" political climate and anti-Semitism might have played in the couple's death sentence.

C Reading Skills and Strategies

Interpreting a Text
? What is implied in the statement "Our opposites are always robed in sexual sin"? [It implies that we tend to see or portray our opponents as sinful or deviant in sexual matters.]

D Vocabulary Note
Using Context Clues
? Who is the "Old Boy"? How can you figure this out? [Possible response: It is the devil. Students can infer this from the fact that the Reverend Hale has come to investigate the possibility of witchcraft.] **What are some other nicknames for the devil?** [Possible responses: Beelzebub, Old Scratch, Lord of the Flies.]

---

even in that department. Normally the actions and deeds of a man were all that society felt comfortable in judging. The secret intent of an action was left to the ministers, priests, and rabbis to deal with. When diabolism rises, however, actions are the least important manifests of the true nature of a man. The Devil, as Reverend Hale said, is a wily one, and, until an hour before he fell, even God thought him beautiful in Heaven.

The analogy, however, seems to falter when one considers that, while there were no witches then, there are Communists and capitalists now, and in each camp there is certain proof that spies of each side are at work undermining the other. But this is a snobbish objection and not at all warranted by the facts. I have no doubt that people *were* communing with, and even worshiping, the Devil in Salem, and if the whole truth could be known in this case, as it is in others, we should discover a regular and conventionalized propitiation of the dark spirit. One certain evidence of this is the confession of Tituba, the slave of Reverend Parris, and another is the behavior of the children who were known to have indulged in sorceries with her.

There are accounts of similar *klatches* in Europe, where the daughters of the towns would assemble at night and, sometimes with fetishes, sometimes with a selected young man, give themselves to love, with some bastardly results. The Church, sharp-eyed as it must be when gods long dead are brought to life, condemned these orgies as witchcraft and interpreted them rightly, as a resurgence of the Dionysiac[9] forces it had crushed long before. Sex, sin, and the Devil were early linked, and so they continued to be in Salem, and are today. From all accounts there are no more puritanical mores in the world than those enforced by the Communists in Russia, where women's fashions, for instance, are as prudent and all-covering as any American Baptist would desire. The divorce laws lay a tremendous responsibility on the father for the care of his children. Even the laxity of divorce regulations in the early years of the revolution was undoubtedly a revulsion from the nineteenth-century Victorian immobility of

9. **Dionysiac** (dī'ə·nis'ē·ak): like Dionysius (dī'ə·nish'əs), the ancient Greek god of wine and revelry.

marriage and the consequent hypocrisy that developed from it. If for no other reasons, a state so powerful, so jealous of the uniformity of its citizens, cannot long tolerate the atomization of the family. And yet, in American eyes at least, there remains the conviction that the Russian attitude toward women is lascivious. It is the Devil working again, just as he is working within the Slav who is shocked at the very idea of a woman's disrobing herself in a burlesque show. Our opposites are always robed in sexual sin, and it is from this unconscious conviction that demonology gains both its attractive sensuality and its capacity to infuriate and frighten.

Coming into Salem now, Reverend Hale conceives of himself much as a young doctor on his first call. His painfully acquired armory of symptoms, catchwords, and diagnostic procedures is now to be put to use at last. The road from Beverly is unusually busy this morning, and he has passed a hundred rumors that make him smile at the ignorance of the yeomanry in this most precise science. He feels himself allied with the best minds of Europe—kings, philosophers, scientists, and ecclesiasts of all churches. His goal is light, goodness and its preservation, and he knows the exaltation of the blessed whose intelligence, sharpened by minute examinations of enormous tracts, is finally called upon to face what may be a bloody fight with the Fiend himself.

He appears loaded down with half a dozen heavy books.

Hale: Pray you, someone take these!
Parris, *delighted:* Mr. Hale! Oh! it's good to see you again! *Taking some books:* My, they're heavy!
Hale, *setting down his books:* They must be; they are weighted with authority.
Parris, *a little scared:* Well, you do come prepared!
Hale: We shall need hard study if it comes to tracking down the Old Boy. *Noticing* REBECCA: You cannot be Rebecca Nurse?
Rebecca: I am, sir. Do you know me?
Hale: It's strange how I knew you, but I suppose you look as such a good soul should. We have all heard of your great charities in Beverly.
Parris: Do you know this gentleman? Mr. Thomas Putnam. And his good wife Ann.

844 AMERICAN DRAMA

Using Students' Strengths

Interpersonal Learners
Since he is a noted authority on witchcraft, the Reverend Hale is an important visitor to Salem. As a result, the inhabitants of Salem respect him, admire him—and fear him. Have small groups of students enact this scene, showing how each character might greet Reverend Hale. Which characters want to make the strongest first impression and why? Which characters are less concerned with impressing Hale? Students can perform their scenes for the class.

Logical/Mathematical Learners
Have students compare and contrast the Puritan philosophy of Reverend Hale with the ideas of one or more of the leading European philosophers of the seventeenth and early eighteenth centuries, such as René Descartes, Thomas Hobbes, Baruch Spinoza, John Locke, and G. W. Leibniz.

Hale: Putnam! I had not expected such distinguished company, sir.

Putnam, *pleased:* It does not seem to help us today, Mr. Hale. We look to you to come to our house and save our child.

Hale: Your child ails too?

Mrs. Putnam: Her soul, her soul seems flown away. She sleeps and yet she walks . . .

Putnam: She cannot eat.

Hale: Cannot eat! *Thinks on it. Then, to* PROCTOR *and* GILES COREY: Do you men have afflicted children?

Parris: No, no, these are farmers. John Proctor—

Giles Corey: He don't believe in witches.

Proctor, *to* HALE: I never spoke on witches one way or the other. Will you come, Giles?

Giles: No—no, John, I think not. I have some few queer questions of my own to ask this fellow.

Proctor: I've heard you to be a sensible man, Mr. Hale. I hope you'll leave some of it in Salem.

PROCTOR *goes.* HALE *stands embarrassed for an instant.*

Parris, *quickly:* Will you look at my daughter, sir? *Leads* HALE *to the bed.* She has tried to leap out the window; we discovered her this morning on the highroad, waving her arms as though she'd fly.

Hale, *narrowing his eyes:* Trics to fly.

Putnam: She cannot bear to hear the Lord's name, Mr. Hale; that's a sure sign of witchcraft afloat.

Hale, *holding up his hands:* No, no. Now let me instruct you. We cannot look to superstition in this. The Devil is precise; the marks of his presence are definite as stone, and I must tell you all that I shall not proceed unless you are prepared to believe me if I should find no bruise of Hell upon her.

Parris: It is agreed, sir, it is agreed—we will abide by your judgment.

Hale: Good then. *He goes to the bed, looks down at* BETTY. *To* PARRIS: Now, sir, what were your first warning of this strangeness?

Parris: Why, sir—I discovered her—*indicating* ABIGAIL—and my niece and ten or twelve of the other girls, dancing in the forest last night.

Hale, *surprised:* You permit dancing?

Parris: No, no, it were secret—

Mrs. Putnam, *unable to wait:* Mr. Parris's slave has knowledge of conjurin', sir.

Parris, *to* MRS. PUTNAM: We cannot be sure of that, Goody Ann—

Mrs. Putnam, *frightened, very softly:* I know it, sir. I sent my child—she should learn from Tituba who murdered her sisters.

Rebecca, *horrified:* Goody Ann! You sent a child to conjure up the dead?

Mrs. Putnam: Let God blame me, not you, not you, Rebecca! I'll not have you judging me any more! *To* HALE: Is it a natural work to lose seven children before they live a day?

Parris: Sssh!

REBECCA, *with great pain, turns her face away. There is a pause.*

Hale: Seven dead in childbirth.

Mrs. Putnam, *softly:* Aye. *Her voice breaks; she looks up at him. Silence.* HALE *is impressed.* PARRIS *looks to him. He goes to his books, opens one, turns pages, then reads. All wait, avidly.*

Parris, *hushed:* What book is that?

Mrs. Putnam: What's there, sir?

Hale, *with a tasty love of intellectual pursuit:* Here is all the invisible world, caught, defined, and calculated. In these books the Devil stands stripped of all his brute disguises. Here are all your familiar spirits—your incubi and succubi; your witches that go by land, by air, and by sea; your wizards of the night and of the day. Have no fear now—we shall find him out if he has come among us, and I mean to crush him utterly if he has shown his face! *He starts for the bed.*

Rebecca: Will it hurt the child, sir?

Hale: I cannot tell. If she is truly in the Devil's grip we may have to rip and tear to get her free.

Rebecca: I think I'll go, then. I am too old for this. *She rises.*

Parris, *striving for conviction:* Why, Rebecca, we may open up the boil of all our troubles today!

Rebecca: Let us hope for that. I go to God for you, sir.

"I mean to crush him utterly . . ."

THE CRUCIBLE, ACT ONE **845**

E Elements of Literature
Motivation

? Why is the Reverend Hale embarrassed at John Proctor's comment? [Possible responses: Hale may be embarrassed because the witchcraft accusations which he investigated in his native Beverly turned out to be groundless, or he may feel worried that he has let a desire for notoriety and influence cloud his judgment again. He might also feel embarrassed because it is true that in "Proctor's presence a fool felt his foolishness instantly" (p. 838).]

F Reading Skills and Strategies
Making Predictions

? Hale says he will not go on with his investigation unless everyone agrees to accept his results, whether he finds the girls to be bewitched or not. What do you think he will find? Why? [Possible responses: Some students may believe Hale is absolutely determined to find evidence of witchcraft. Others, in contrast, may argue that Hale will discover the truth underlying the accusations—the desire for vengeance and personal gain—and have the courage to admit it.]

G Critical Thinking
Analyzing

? How does Hale see himself? What role does he think he will play in Salem village? [Possible responses: Hale sees himself as someone who can rescue Salem from either the grip of witchcraft or mass delusion. He has great moral certainty.]

Professional Notes

The Political and the Personal

Although most people read many of Miller's plays, especially *All My Sons* and *A View from the Bridge,* as political allegories, he denies this was his primary intention in *The Crucible.* Rather, he asserts, "I am not pressing a historical allegory here, and I have even eliminated certain striking similarities from *The Crucible* which may have started the audience to drawing such an allegory. For instance, the Salemites believed that the surrounding Indians, who had never been converted to Christianity, were in alliance with the witches, who were acting as a Fifth Column for them within the town. It was even thought that the outbreak of witchcraft was the last attack by the devil, who was being pressed into the wilderness by the expanding colony. Some might have equated the Indians with the Russians and the local witches with Communists.

My intent and interest is wider and I think deeper than this. From my first acquaintance with the story I was struck hard by the breathtaking heroism of certain of the victims who displayed an almost frightening personal integrity. It seemed to me that the best part of the country was made of such stuff, and I had a strong desire to celebrate them and to raise them out of historic dust."

T845

A Elements of Literature
Characterization

❓ Why do you think Parris responds this way to Rebecca's comment? What does it demonstrate about his character and his philosophy? [Possible responses: It echoes Parris's insecurity about his family's close connection to the forest ritual and also demonstrates his vision of good and evil as opposite, mutually exclusive forces.]

B Reading Skills and Strategies
Making Predictions

❓ What might be the result of Giles's comments in this passage? Were his remarks wise? Why or why not? [Possible responses: Giles could be laying the seeds for Martha's being accused of witchcraft, since he has suggested that there is something strange about her. His claim about her ability to stop his prayer is especially damning.]

C Critical Thinking
Evaluating

❓ What do you make of Hale's "deep" logic in this explanation? Does it lead to any contradictory or illogical conclusions? [It would seem to lead to the conclusion that those who are most afflicted by the devil (e.g., witches) are the most virtuous, since they most attract the devil's hunger for a challenge.]

D Critical Thinking
Making Judgments

❓ Do you think Hale's questions are fair? Why or why not? [Possible responses: His questions are leading, since he could be planting ideas about witchcraft in Betty's mind. His unfair tactics in this scene foreshadow the actual witchcraft trial, which is completely corrupt.]

Parris, *with trepidation—and resentment:* I hope you do not mean we go to Satan here! *Slight pause.*

Rebecca: I wish I knew. *She goes out; they feel resentful of her note of moral superiority.*

Putnam, *abruptly:* Come, Mr. Hale, let's get on. Sit you here.

Giles: Mr. Hale, I have always wanted to ask a learned man—what signifies the readin' of strange books?

Hale: What books?

Giles: I cannot tell; she hides them.

Hale: Who does this?

Giles: Martha, my wife. I have waked at night many a time and found her in a corner, readin' of a book. Now what do you make of that?

Hale: Why, that's not necessarily—

Giles: It discomfits me! Last night—mark this—I tried and tried and could not say my prayers. And then she close her book and walks out of the house, and suddenly—mark this—I could pray again!

Old Giles must be spoken for, if only because his fate was to be so remarkable and so different from that of all the others. He was in his early eighties at this time, and was the most comical hero in the history. No man has ever been blamed for so much. If a cow was missed, the first thought was to look for her around Corey's house; a fire blazing up at night brought suspicion of arson to his door. He didn't give a hoot for public opinion, and only in his last years—after he had married Martha—did he bother much with the church. That she stopped his prayer is very probable, but he forgot to say that he'd only recently learned any prayers and it didn't take much to make him stumble over them. He was a crank and a nuisance, but withal a deeply innocent and brave man. In court, once, he was asked if it were true that he had been frightened by the strange behavior of a hog and had then said he knew it to be the Devil in an animal's shape. "What frighted you?" he was asked. He forgot everything but the word "frighted," and instantly replied, "I do not know that I ever spoke that word in my life."

Hale: Ah! The stoppage of prayer—that is strange. I'll speak further on that with you.

Giles: I'm not sayin' she's touched the Devil, now, but I'd admire to know what books she reads and why she hides them. She'll not answer me, y' see.

Hale: Aye, we'll discuss it. *To all:* Now mark me, if the Devil is in her you will witness some frightful wonders in this room, so please to keep your wits about you. Mr. Putnam, stand close in case she flies. Now, Betty, dear, will you sit up? PUTNAM *comes in closer, ready-handed.* HALE *sits* BETTY *up, but she hangs limp in his hands.* Hmmm. *He observes her carefully. The others watch breathlessly.* Can you hear me? I am John Hale, minister of Beverly. I have come to help you, dear. Do you remember my two little girls in Beverly? *She does not stir in his hands.*

Parris, *in fright:* How can it be the Devil? Why would he choose my house to strike? We have all manner of licentious people in the village!

Hale: What victory would the Devil have to win a soul already bad? It is the best the Devil wants, and who is better than the minister?

Giles: That's deep, Mr. Parris, deep, deep!

Parris, *with resolution now:* Betty! Answer Mr. Hale! Betty!

Hale: Does someone afflict you, child? It need not be a woman, mind you, or a man. Perhaps some bird invisible to others comes to you—perhaps a pig, a mouse, or any beast at all. Is there some figure bids you fly? *The child remains limp in his hands. In silence he lays her back on the pillow. Now, holding out his hands toward her, he intones:* In nomine Domini Sabaoth sui filiique ite ad infernos.[10] *She does not stir. He turns to* ABIGAIL, *his eyes narrowing.* Abigail, what sort of dancing were you doing with her in the forest?

Abigail: Why—common dancing is all.

Parris: I think I ought to say that I—I saw a kettle in the grass where they were dancing.

Abigail: That were only soup.

Hale: What sort of soup were in this kettle, Abigail?

Abigail: Why, it were beans—and lentils, I think, and—

Hale: Mr. Parris, you did not notice, did you, any living thing in the kettle? A mouse, perhaps, a spider, a frog—?

10. In nomine Domini Sabaoth sui filiique ite ad infernos: Latin for "In the name of the Lord of Hosts and his son, get thee to hell."

Crossing the Curriculum

Social Studies/History

The Puritans were deeply superstitious, looking for signs and portents in even the most commonplace events. Are people superstitious today? Have students list today's common superstitions and provide possible explanations for any two of them. Challenge students to research factual information or cite other evidence that might support a superstition.

Science

Death—not divorce—was the great Puritan homebreaker. Its preferred victims were infants and children: If infants were lucky to survive the perils of birth, they still faced infectious diseases, malnutrition, and a host of other terrors. As a result, infant mortality topped fifty percent. Have students find out what diseases common in Puritan times have been conquered today. Students should research which inoculations people should get and when.

Parris, *fearfully:* I—do believe there were some movement—in the soup.

Abigail: That jumped in, we never put it in!

Hale, *quickly:* What jumped in?

Abigail: Why, a very little frog jumped—

Parris: A frog, Abby!

Hale, *grasping* ABIGAIL: Abigail, it may be your cousin is dying. Did you call the Devil last night?

Abigail: I never called him? Tituba, Tituba . . .

Parris, *blanched:* She called the Devil?

Hale: I should like to speak with Tituba.

Parris: Goody Ann, will you bring her up? MRS. PUTNAM *exits.*

Hale: How did she call him?

Abigail: I know not—she spoke Barbados.

Hale: Did you feel any strangeness when she called him? A sudden cold wind, perhaps? A trembling below the ground?

Abigail: I didn't see no Devil! *Shaking* BETTY: Betty, wake up. Betty! Betty!

Hale: You cannot evade me, Abigail. Did your cousin drink any of the brew in that kettle?

Abigail: She never drank it!

Hale: Did you drink it?

Abigail: No, sir!

Hale: Did Tituba ask you to drink it?

Abigail: She tried, but I refused.

Hale: Why are you concealing? Have you sold yourself to Lucifer?

Abigail: I never sold myself! I'm a good girl! I'm a proper girl!

MRS. PUTNAM *enters with* TITUBA, *and instantly* ABIGAIL *points at* TITUBA.

E **Abigail:** She made me do it! She made Betty do it!

Tituba, *shocked and angry:* Abby!

Abigail: She makes me drink blood!

Parris: Blood!!

Mrs. Putnam: My baby's blood?

Tituba: No, no, chicken blood. I give she chicken blood!

Hale: Woman, have you enlisted these children for the Devil?

Tituba: No, no, sir, I don't truck with no Devil!

Hale: Why can she not wake? Are you silencing this child?

F **Tituba:** I love me Betty!

Hale: You have sent your spirit out upon this child, have you not? Are you gathering souls for the Devil?

Abigail: She sends her spirit on me in church; she makes me laugh at prayer! **G**

Parris: She have often laughed at prayer!

Abigail: She comes to me every night to go and drink blood!

Tituba: You beg *me* to conjure! She beg *me* make charm—

Abigail: Don't lie! *To* HALE: She comes to me while I sleep; she's always making me dream corruptions!

Tituba: Why you say that, Abby?

Abigail: Sometimes I wake and find myself standing in the open doorway and not a stitch on my body! I always hear her laughing in my sleep. I hear her singing her Barbados songs and tempting me with—

Tituba: Mister Reverend, I never—

Hale, *resolved now:* Tituba, I want you to wake this child.

Tituba: I have no power on this child, sir.

Hale: You most certainly do, and you will free her from it now! When did you compact with the Devil?

Tituba: I don't compact with no Devil!

Parris: You will confess yourself or I will take you out and whip you to your death, Tituba!

Putnam: This woman must be hanged! She must be taken and hanged!

Tituba, *terrified, falls to her knees:* No, no, don't hang Tituba! I tell him I don't desire to work for him, sir.

Parris: The Devil?

Hale: Then you saw him! TITUBA *weeps.* Now Tituba, I know that when we bind ourselves to Hell it is very hard to break with it. We are going to help you tear yourself free— **H**

Tituba, *frightened by the coming process:* Mister Reverend, I do believe somebody else be witchin' these children.

Hale: Who?

Tituba: I don't know, sir, but the Devil got him numerous witches.

Hale: Does he! *It is a clue.* Tituba, look into my eyes. Come, look into me. *She raises her eyes to his fearfully.* You would be a good Christian woman, would you not, Tituba?

Tituba: Aye, sir, a good Christian woman.

THE CRUCIBLE, ACT ONE **847**

E **Elements of Literature**

Motivation

? Why do you think Abigail places the blame on Tituba? [Possible responses: As a slave, Tituba would be a logical scapegoat since she is already an outsider deprived of her rights; Hale has already paved the way for Tituba to assume the blame.]

F **Critical Thinking**

Evaluating

? What do you think of Miller's portrayal of Tituba thus far? Do you think she is a credible representation of the speech, behavior, and emotions of a seventeenth-century African slave? Or do you think her broken English, strong, simple emotions, and cowardice amount to a familiar and/or distasteful stereotype? You might want to compare this depiction of Tituba with Olaudah Equiano's narrative of his life, pp. 56–65. [Many students will feel that while Miller is attuned to the injustice of Tituba's situation, he doesn't really humanize her beyond stereotype.]

G **Reading Skills and Strategies**

Interpreting a Text

? What do you think makes Abigail laugh at church? [Possible response: She is laughing at the hypocrisy and pretense which, as a result of her affair with Proctor, she now believes to underlie any pretense to moral stature or responsibility.]

H **Elements of Literature**

Motivation

? Why does Tituba suddenly change her story? What does this suggest will happen later in the play? [Possible response: She suddenly grasps the logic of the witch hunt process, in which accused people must relent in their protestations of innocence and then, in turn, accuse someone else as proof of their commitment to the process.]

Assessing Learning

Check Test: True-False

Act One

1. The play is set in Salem, Massachusetts, in 1692. [True]

2. As the play opens, Betty Parris's mother, Tituba, weeps to see her daughter in a coma. [False]

3. Abigail Williams is deeply in love with Giles Corey, but he won't leave his wife, Martha. [False]

4. Mrs. Putnam sent her daughter Ruth into the forest to conjure the spirits of her dead siblings. [True]

5. John Proctor firmly supports Parris in his quest to get the deed to the church. [False]

Standardized Test Preparation

For practice with proofreading and editing, see

• *Daily Oral Grammar,* Transparency 50

A Historical Connections

The historical record shows that Tituba made herself a likely target for witchcraft accusations when, right after Betty began having strange fits, she made a "witchcake," a mixture of rye and Betty's urine, cooked and fed to a dog, in the belief that the dog would then reveal the identity of the person responsible for Betty's affliction. Parris was enraged when he found out about the cake, and, soon after, the afflicted girls named Tituba as a witch. Parris is reported to have beaten her until she confessed.

B Critical Thinking

Making Judgments

? Do you think Tituba should trust Reverend Hale? Why or why not? [Possible responses: Yes, because Hale simply wants to discover the truth and rid Salem of witches and has no personal ax to grind; no, because we don't know enough about Hale yet to understand his true motivation.]

C Reading Skills and Strategies

Interpreting a Text

? What does Tituba's "confession" here suggest about her life in Parris's household? [Possible responses: It suggests that she was bitterly unhappy, that Parris was cruel, and that she dreamed of returning to her homeland and freedom.]

D Elements of Literature

Motivation

? What motivates Abigail to "confess"? Is this a wise move on her part? Why or why not? [Possible responses: Abigail is motivated by a desire to shift the blame for her activities to someone else and thus save her neck. It is a very wise move because she will escape being hanged by confessing to being "afflicted" by witchcraft.]

T848

Hale: And you love these little children?

Tituba: Oh, yes, sir, I don't desire to hurt little children.

Hale: And you love God, Tituba?

Tituba: I love God with all my bein'.

Hale: Now, in God's holy name—

Tituba: Bless Him. Bless Him. *She is rocking on her knees, sobbing in terror.*

Hale: And to His glory—

Tituba: Eternal glory. Bless Him—bless God . . .

Hale: Open yourself, Tituba—open yourself and let God's holy light shine on you.

Tituba: Oh, bless the Lord.

A **Hale:** When the Devil comes to you does he ever come—with another person? *She stares up into his face.* Perhaps another person in the village? Someone you know.

Parris: Who came with him?

Putnam: Sarah Good? Did you ever see Sarah Good with him? Or Osburn?

Parris: Was it man or woman came with him?

Tituba: Man or woman. Was—was woman.

Parris: What woman? A woman, you said. What woman?

Tituba: It was black dark, and I—

Parris: You could see him, why could you not see her?

Tituba: Well, they was always talking; they was always runnin' round and carryin' on—

Parris: You mean out of Salem? Salem witches?

Tituba: I believe so, yes, sir.

Now HALE *takes her hand. She is surprised.*

B **Hale:** Tituba. You must have no fear to tell us who they are, do you understand? We will protect you. The Devil can never overcome a minister. You know that, do you not?

Tituba—*she kisses* HALE's *hand:* Aye, sir, oh, I do.

Hale: You have confessed yourself to witchcraft, and that speaks a wish to come to Heaven's side. And we will bless you, Tituba.

Tituba, *deeply relieved:* Oh, God bless you, Mr. Hale!

Hale, *with rising exaltation:* You are God's instrument put in our hands to discover the Devil's agents among us. You are selected, Tituba, you are chosen to help us cleanse our village. So speak utterly, Tituba, turn your back on him and face God—face God, Tituba, and God will protect you.

Tituba, *joining with him:* Oh, God, protect Tituba!

Hale, *kindly:* Who came to you with the Devil? Two? Three? Four? How many?

TITUBA *pants and begins rocking back and forth again, staring ahead.*

Tituba: There was four. There was four.

Parris, *pressing in on her:* Who? Who? Their names, their names!

Tituba, *suddenly bursting out:* Oh, how many times he bid me kill you, Mr. Parris!

Parris: Kill me!

C **Tituba,** *in a fury:* He say Mr. Parris must be kill! Mr. Parris no goodly man, Mr. Parris mean man and no gentle man, and he bid me rise out of my bed and cut your throat! *They gasp.* But I tell him "No! I don't hate that man. I don't want kill that man." But he say, "You work for me, Tituba, and I make you free! I give you pretty dress to wear, and put you way high up in the air, and you gone fly back to Barbados!" And I say, "You lie, Devil, you lie!" And then he come one stormy night to me, and he say, "Look! I have *white* people belong to me." And I look—and there was Goody Good.

Parris: Sarah Good!

Tituba, *rocking and weeping:* Aye, sir, and Goody Osburn.

Mrs. Putnam: I knew it! Goody Osburn were midwife to me three times. I begged you, Thomas, did I not? I begged him not to call Osburn because I feared her. My babies always shriveled in her hands!

Hale: Take courage, you must give us all their names. How can you bear to see this child suffering? Look at her, Tituba. *He is indicating* BETTY *on the bed.* Look at her God-given innocence; her soul is so tender; we must protect her, Tituba; the Devil is out and preying on her like a beast upon the flesh of the pure lamb. God will bless you for your help.

D ABIGAIL *rises, staring as though inspired, and cries out.*

Abigail: I want to open myself! *They turn to her, startled. She is enraptured, as though in a pearly light.* I want the light of God, I want the sweet love of Jesus! I danced for the Devil; I saw him; I wrote in his book; I go back to Jesus; I kiss His

Making the Connections

Connecting to the Theme: "The Breaking of Charity"

After students have read Act One, have them develop the full implications of the collection theme. For instance, what does it mean to "keep charity" with someone? How does one need to view and treat a person in order to keep charity with him or her? Can one criticize or disagree with people and still keep charity with them, as long as one doesn't betray them or hurt them for selfish gain? Write these criteria up on the board. Then have students analyze each relationship in the play, and decide who has kept (and broken) charity with whom. For example, has Rebecca kept charity with Parris, even though she criticizes his behavior? Has Proctor kept charity with Abigail? Does Giles break charity with his wife when he complains about her suspicious behavior?

hand. I saw Sarah Good with the Devil! I saw Goody Osburn with the Devil! I saw Bridget Bishop with the Devil!

As she is speaking, BETTY *is rising from the bed, a fever in her eyes, and picks up the chant.*

Betty, *staring too:* I saw George Jacobs with the Devil! I saw Goody Howe with the Devil!
Parris: She speaks! *He rushes to embrace* BETTY. She speaks!
Hale: Glory to God! It is broken, they are free!
Betty, *calling out hysterically and with great relief:* I saw Martha Bellows with the Devil!
Abigail: I saw Goody Sibber with the Devil! *It is rising to a great glee.*

Putnam: The marshal, I'll call the marshal!

PARRIS *is shouting a prayer of thanksgiving.*

Betty: I saw Alice Barrow with the Devil!

The curtain begins to fall.

Hale, *as* PUTNAM *goes out:* Let the marshal bring irons!
Abigail: I saw Goody Hawkins with the Devil!
Betty: I saw Goody Bibber with the Devil!
Abigail: I saw Goody Booth with the Devil!

On their ecstatic cries

The curtain falls

MAKING MEANINGS

Act One

First Thoughts

1. What do you think of Abigail, and what would you have said to her if you had been present at the end of Act One?

Reading Check
a. When Abigail is alone with Proctor, what claim does she make?
b. Whom has Parris invited to Salem?
c. Why are both Mrs. Putnam and Abigail interested in Tituba's "conjuring"?

Shaping Interpretations

2. Why is Reverend Parris so terrified by the events in Salem? What possible result does he fear?
3. How would you explain the "illnesses" of Betty and Ruth?
4. Using your reading notes as a guide, reread the background information that Miller provides about the history of Salem, in order to find out when important events occurred. Then make a **time line** that places in rough **chronological order** events such as the murder of Abigail's parents, the dispute over the election of the minister, the battle over Francis Nurse's land, and the death of Mrs. Putnam's babies.

5. How would you interpret Abigail's relationship to the other girls and her relationship to Proctor? Be sure to check your reading notes.
6. Summarize Hale's view of his mission in Salem. What does he mean when he says the Devil is "precise"?
7. At the beginning of the act, Tituba enters Betty's bedroom in fright because she knows "trouble in this house eventually lands on her back." Are her fears justified? To what extent is Tituba a scapegoat for Abigail and the other girls, and to what extent does she share responsibility for the witch hunt?
8. At the end of the act, what do you think is Abigail's **motivation** to "open" herself and begin naming names?
9. A **static character** changes little or not at all during a story. A **dynamic character** changes in an important way as a result of the story's action. Among the characters introduced in Act One, which do you think have potential for change as the play progresses?

Connecting with the Text

10. When someone is accused of a crime today, do people still have a tendency to "jump on the bandwagon" with the accusers? Explain your answer.

THE CRUCIBLE, ACT ONE **849**

Reading Check
a. Abigail claims that John still loves and wants her.
b. Parris has invited the Reverend Hale, a well-respected witch hunter, to come to Salem.
c. Mrs. Putnam wants to know the fate of her dead babies; Abigail wants to make a charm to kill Mrs. Proctor.

MAKING MEANINGS

Act One

First Thoughts [Respond]

1. Students are likely to see Abigail as cruel, dishonest, and opportunistic. They might have asked her to tell the truth to halt the growing hysteria.

E Elements of Literature
Motivation
? Why do Hale, Parris, Putnam, and the other adults believe the children's accusations without proof? [Possible responses: The accusations fit with their belief systems and fulfill individual desires for scapegoating and vengeance.]

Shaping Interpretations [Interpret]

2. Parris fears that he will lose his reputation and livelihood.
3. Possible response: The girls are overwhelmed by the emotional trauma of being discovered by Parris and withdraw into themselves to avoid facing the consequences of their actions.
4. The dispute over the minister's election, the land battles, the murder of Abigail's parents, and the death of Mrs. Putnam's babies all took place in the distant past. In 1691, a witch hunt took place in Beverly; in the fall of 1691, Mrs. Proctor fired Abigail; early in the spring of 1692, the girls are caught dancing in the forest.
5. Abigail controls the girls through fear and intimidation, threatening them with a "pointy reckoning" if they reveal the conjuring. She is flirtatious and warm with Proctor, and is clearly attached to him; yet she is furious and spiteful when he refuses her advances.
6. Summoned to find evidence of witchcraft, Hale sees himself on a holy mission, bringing light to the ignorant. He believes there are exact, verifiable signs of satanic activity.
7. Tituba's fears are justified because she was a scapegoat. However, she does give the girls access to West Indian witchcraft, preparing the potions and leading the incantations.
8. Now, Abigail wants only to save her life. Later, she will seek revenge.
9. Possible response: Hale, Corey, and Proctor are likely to prove to be dynamic characters.

Connecting with the Text

[Evaluate]

10. Yes. Some people are afraid to stand alone; others are just easily swayed.

The setting is the farmhouse of John and Elizabeth Proctor, eight days later, and already the witch hunt is in full gear. A court has been convened, with Abigail and the other girls as star witnesses, presenting new symptoms (and new accusations) daily. Elizabeth Proctor wants John to expose Abigail as a fraud, but he hesitates because of his past relationship with Abigail. Hale arrives to question the Proctors about their religious observance, but before he can finish, Elizabeth is arrested and jailed for the attempted murder of Abigail. The principal "evidence" is a doll with a needle in it, which Mary Warren has planted in the Proctor home on the same evening that Abigail has been discovered screaming, with a needle stuck in her belly. On this same evening, Rebecca Nurse is arrested, and Hale begins to doubt his mission.

Ⓐ Critical Thinking
Determining the Author's Purpose
❓ Why do you think Miller includes this detail? What does it suggest about Proctor? [Possible response: It suggests his tendency to conceal information from Elizabeth that he fears might hurt her or aggravate the tensions between them.]

Ⓑ Elements of Literature
Motivation
❓ Why does John feel "a certain disappointment"? [Possible responses: Elizabeth *receives* John's kiss; she does not *return* it. This suggests their marriage is still strained and that Elizabeth is preoccupied with suspicion and worry.]

Ⓒ Elements of Literature
Symbolism
❓ How can John's comments be interpreted symbolically? What is the "winter" to which he refers? [Possible responses: John suggests the flowers as a hopeful symbol for the rejuvenation of his marriage. The "winter" might symbolize the coldness in the marriage, the estrangement since John's affair with Abigail. While the couple is clearly making an effort to repair the damage caused by John's infidelity, they are still distrustful and uneasy.]

Act Two

The common room of PROCTOR's *house, eight days later.*

At the right is a door opening on the fields outside. A fireplace is at the left, and behind it a stairway leading upstairs. It is the low, dark, and rather long living room of the time. As the curtain rises, the room is empty. From above, ELIZABETH *is heard softly singing to the children. Presently the door opens and* JOHN PROCTOR *enters, carrying his gun. He glances about the room as he comes toward the fireplace, then halts for an instant as he hears her singing. He continues on to the fireplace, leans the gun against the wall as he swings a pot out of the fire and smells it. Then he lifts out the ladle and tastes. He is not quite pleased. He reaches to a cupboard, takes a pinch of salt, and drops it into the pot. As he is tasting again, her footsteps are heard on the stair. He swings the pot into the fireplace and goes to a basin and washes his hands and face.* ELIZABETH *enters.*

Elizabeth: What keeps you so late? It's almost dark.
Proctor: I were planting far out to the forest edge.
Elizabeth: Oh, you're done then.
Proctor: Aye, the farm is seeded. The boys asleep?
Elizabeth: They will be soon. *And she goes to the fireplace, proceeds to ladle up stew in a dish.*
Proctor: Pray now for a fair summer.
Elizabeth: Aye.
Proctor: Are you well today?
Elizabeth: I am. *She brings the plate to the table, and, indicating the food:* It is a rabbit.
Proctor, *going to the table:* Oh, is it! In Jonathan's trap?
Elizabeth: No, she walked into the house this afternoon; I found her sittin' in the corner like she come to visit.
Proctor: Oh, that's a good sign walkin' in.
Elizabeth: Pray God. It hurt my heart to strip her, poor rabbit. *She sits and watches him taste it.*
Proctor: It's well seasoned.
Elizabeth, *blushing with pleasure:* I took great care. She's tender?
Proctor: Aye. *He eats. She watches him.* I think

we'll see green fields soon. It's warm as blood beneath the clods.
Elizabeth: That's well.

PROCTOR *eats, then looks up.*

Proctor: If the crop is good I'll buy George Jacobs' heifer. How would that please you?
Elizabeth: Aye, it would.
Proctor, *with a grin:* I mean to please you, Elizabeth.
Elizabeth—*it is hard to say:* I know it, John.

He gets up, goes to her, kisses her. She receives it. With a certain disappointment, he returns to the table.

Proctor, *as gently as he can:* Cider?
Elizabeth, *with a sense of reprimanding herself for having forgot:* Aye! *She gets up and goes and pours a glass for him. He now arches his back.*
Proctor: This farm's a continent when you go foot by foot droppin' seeds in it.
Elizabeth, *coming with the cider:* It must be.
Proctor, *he drinks a long draught, then, putting the glass down:* You ought to bring some flowers in the house.
Elizabeth: Oh! I forgot! I will tomorrow.
Proctor: It's winter in here yet. On Sunday let you come with me, and we'll walk the farm together; I never see such a load of flowers on the earth. *With good feeling he goes and looks up at the sky through the open doorway.* Lilacs have a purple smell. Lilac is the smell of nightfall, I think. Massachusetts is a beauty in the spring!
Elizabeth: Aye, it is.

There is a pause. She is watching him from the table as he stands there absorbing the night. It is as though she would speak but cannot. Instead, now, she takes up his plate and glass and fork and goes with them to the basin. Her back is turned to him. He turns to her and watches her. A sense of their separation rises.

Proctor: I think you're sad again. Are you?
Elizabeth—*she doesn't want friction, and yet she must:* You come so late I thought you'd gone to Salem this afternoon.
Proctor: Why? I have no business in Salem.
Elizabeth: You did speak of going, earlier this week.

Getting Students Involved

Cooperative Learning
Hard Times. Running a farm and household in Puritan New England required hard work and dedication. Suggest that students form small groups to identify and investigate major tasks facing a Puritan couple such as the Proctors. (Students can find clues in the play itself.) Dif-

ferent members of the group can assume responsibility for reporting one aspect or more of running a farm and managing a household—namely, daily and seasonal tasks. Then, group members can share their information and make a group presentation to the class.

"The town's gone wild . . ."

Proctor—*he knows what she means:* I thought better of it since.

Elizabeth: Mary Warren's there today.

Proctor: Why'd you let her? You heard me forbid her to go to Salem any more!

Elizabeth: I couldn't stop her.

Proctor, *holding back a full condemnation of her:* It is a fault, it is a fault, Elizabeth—you're the mistress here, not Mary Warren.

Elizabeth: She frightened all my strength away.

Proctor: How may that mouse frighten you, Elizabeth? You—

Elizabeth: It is a mouse no more. I forbid her go, and she raises up her chin like the daughter of a prince and says to me, "I must go to Salem, Goody Proctor; I am an official of the court!"

Proctor: Court! What court?

Elizabeth: Aye, it is a proper court they have now. They've sent four judges out of Boston, she says, weighty magistrates of the General Court, and at the head sits the Deputy Governor of the Province.

Proctor, *astonished:* Why, she's mad.

Elizabeth: I would to God she were. There be fourteen people in the jail now, she says. PROCTOR *simply looks at her, unable to grasp it.* And they'll be tried, and the court have power to hang them too, she says.

Proctor, *scoffing, but without conviction:* Ah, they'd never hang—

Elizabeth: The Deputy Governor promise hangin' if they'll not confess, John. The town's gone wild, I think. She speak of Abigail, and I thought she were a saint, to hear her. Abigail brings the other girls into the court, and where she walks the crowd will part like the sea for Israel. And folks are brought before them, and if they scream and howl and fall to the floor—the person's clapped in the jail for bewitchin' them.

Proctor, *wide-eyed:* Oh, it is a black mischief.

Elizabeth: I think you must go to Salem, John. *He turns to her.* I think so. You must tell them it is a fraud.

Proctor, *thinking beyond this:* Aye, it is, it is surely.

Elizabeth: Let you go to Ezekiel Cheever—he knows you well. And tell him what she said to you last week in her uncle's house. She said it had naught to do with witchcraft, did she not?

Proctor, *in thought:* Aye, she did, she did. *Now a pause.*

Elizabeth, *quietly, fearing to anger him by prodding:* God forbid you keep that from the court, John. I think they must be told.

Proctor, *quietly, struggling with his thought:* Aye, they must, they must. It is a wonder they do believe her.

Elizabeth: I would go to Salem now, John—let you go tonight.

Proctor: I'll think on it.

Elizabeth, *with her courage now:* You cannot keep it, John.

Proctor, *angering:* I know I cannot keep it. I say I will think on it!

Elizabeth, *hurt, and very coldly:* Good, then, let you think on it. *She stands and starts to walk out of the room.*

Proctor: I am only wondering how I may prove what she told me, Elizabeth. If the girl's a saint now, I think it is not easy to prove she's fraud, and the town gone so silly. She told it to me in a room alone—I have no proof for it.

Elizabeth: You were alone with her?

Proctor, *stubbornly:* For a moment alone, aye.

Elizabeth: Why, then, it is not as you told me.

Proctor, *his anger rising:* For a moment, I say. The others come in soon after.

Elizabeth, *quietly—she has suddenly lost all faith in him:* Do as you wish, then. *She starts to turn.*

Proctor: Woman. *She turns to him.* I'll not have your suspicion any more.

Elizabeth, *a little loftily:* I have no—

Proctor: I'll not have it!

Elizabeth: Then let you not earn it.

Proctor, *with a violent undertone:* You doubt me yet?

Elizabeth, *with a smile, to keep her dignity:* John, if it were not Abigail that you must go to hurt, would you falter now? I think not.

Proctor: Now look you—

Elizabeth: I see what I see, John.

D **Reading Skills and Strategies**

Interpreting a Text

? Why does everyone follow Abigail as if she were a "saint"? [Possible responses: Abigail has discovered that in the logic of the witch hunt, the accuser is holy, worshiped as the revealer of truth. In part, this is a result of Abigail's self-assured manner. It is also due to her ability to give the crowd the drama and moral certainty they want.]

E **Critical Thinking**

Making Judgments

? Do you think Elizabeth's suspicion and pain are warranted at this point? Are her questions justified, or should she not ask Proctor about Abigail at all? [Students may be sharply divided on this issue, but most will agree that there is still chemistry between Abigail and Proctor and that the kind of betrayal of trust that Elizabeth has suffered inevitably takes a long time to get over.]

F **Elements of Literature**

Motivation

? Do you agree with Elizabeth's assessment? What *is* motivating John to hold back? [Possible responses: John does not have any proof and the town seems solidly behind Abigail; he does not want to risk revealing his affair with Abigail to the court and so to the entire town.]

Getting Students Involved

Enrichment Activity

Just the Facts, Ma'am. In researching *The Crucible*, Arthur Miller read the original court reports from Salem. Relevant excerpts from the original documents can be found in George Lincoln Burr's *Narratives of the Witchcraft Cases, 1648–1706* and Charles W. Upham's *Salem Witchcraft*. Have students work in teams to select a character from *The Crucible* accused of witchcraft, read that person's real testimony, and analyze the testimony in relation to the person's fate in court. Students wishing further information can also consult Marion Starkey's *The Devil in Massachusetts* and Chadwick Hansen's *Witchcraft at Salem*.

A Reading Skills and Strategies
Comparing and Contrasting

[?] Is John right to imply that Elizabeth has "broken charity" with him? How does this compare with John's betrayal of Elizabeth or the frenzy of mutual betrayal that is tearing Salem apart? [Many students will feel that Elizabeth's lapse of charity is much less grave than John's or Salem's, given her wounded trust and pride—but will feel that it would be best for John *and her* if she works to forgive and trust him again.]

B Reading Skills and Strategies

Interpreting a Text

[?] How do you interpret Proctor's bitter response regarding Elizabeth's coldness? Is Proctor's response appropriate, or does his anger indicate that he knows she is actually right—that it is his own heart that judges him most harshly? [Possible response: Elizabeth is correct—Proctor's conscience torments him more than Elizabeth ever has; yet Proctor is correct as well—Elizabeth has nursed her grievance for too long.]

C Critical Thinking
Analyzing

[?] Mary's gift is unusual; as in today's world, grown women were normally not given dolls in the seventeenth century. Why, then, might Mary Warren give Elizabeth a doll? [Possible responses: She wants to show her remorse for her disobedience; she was put up to it by someone else and the doll will turn out to have a sinister purpose.]

D Elements of Literature
Motivation

[?] How is the punishment ironic? What does this suggest about the court's true motivation? [Possible responses: People who confess to being guilty and implicate others are released, while those who maintain their innocence are hanged. This suggests that the court is more interested in affirming its own authority and in targeting specific people than determining truth.]

Proctor, *with solemn warning:* You will not judge me more, Elizabeth. I have good reason to think before I charge fraud on Abigail, and I will think on it. Let you look to your own improvement before you go to judge your husband any more. I have forgot Abigail, and—

Elizabeth: And I.

A **Proctor:** Spare me! You forget nothin' and forgive nothin.' Learn charity, woman. I have gone tiptoe in this house all seven month since she is gone. I have not moved from there to there without I think to please you, and still an everlasting funeral marches round your heart. I cannot speak but I am doubted, every moment judged for lies, as though I come into a court when I come into this house!

Elizabeth: John, you are not open with me. You saw her with a crowd, you said. Now you—

Proctor: I'll plead my honesty no more, Elizabeth.

Elizabeth—*now she would justify herself:* John, I am only—

Proctor: No more! I should have roared you down when first you told me your suspicion. But I wilted, and, like a Christian, I confessed. Confessed! Some dream I had must have mistaken you for God that day. But you're not, you're not, and let you remember it! Let you look sometimes for the goodness in me, and judge me not.

B **Elizabeth:** I do not judge you. The magistrate sits in your heart that judges you. I never thought you but a good man, John—*with a smile*—only somewhat bewildered.

Proctor, *laughing bitterly:* Oh, Elizabeth, your justice would freeze beer! *He turns suddenly toward a sound outside. He starts for the door as* MARY WARREN *enters. As soon as he sees her, he goes directly to her and grabs her by her cloak, furious.* How do you go to Salem when I forbid it? Do you mock me? *Shaking her:* I'll whip you if you dare leave this house again!

Strangely, she doesn't resist him but hangs limply by his grip.

Mary Warren: I am sick, I am sick, Mr. Proctor. Pray, pray, hurt me not. *Her strangeness throws him off, and her evident pallor and weakness. He frees her.* My insides are all shuddery; I am in the proceedings all day, sir.

Proctor, *with draining anger—his curiosity is draining it:* And what of these proceedings here?

When will you proceed to keep this house, as you are paid nine pound a year to do—and my wife not wholly well?

As though to compensate, MARY WARREN *goes to* ELIZABETH *with a small rag doll.*

C **Mary Warren:** I made a gift for you today, Goody Proctor. I had to sit long hours in a chair, and passed the time with sewing.

Elizabeth, *perplexed, looking at the doll:* Why, thank you, it's a fair poppet.[1]

Mary Warren, *with a trembling, decayed voice:* We must all love each other now, Goody Proctor.

Elizabeth, *amazed at her strangeness:* Aye, indeed, we must.

Mary Warren, *glancing at the room:* I'll get up early in the morning and clean the house. I must sleep now. *She turns and starts off.*

Proctor: Mary. *She halts.* Is it true? There be fourteen women arrested?

Mary Warren: No, sir. There be thirty-nine now— *She suddenly breaks off and sobs and sits down, exhausted.*

Elizabeth: Why, she's weepin'! What ails you, child?

Mary Warren: Goody Osburn—will hang! *There is a shocked pause, while she sobs.*

Proctor: Hang! *He calls into her face.* Hang, y'say?

Mary Warren, *through her weeping:* Aye.

Proctor: The Deputy Governor will permit it?

Mary Warren: He sentenced her. He must. *To ameliorate it:* But not Sarah Good. For Sarah Good confessed, y'see.

D **Proctor:** Confessed! To what?

Mary Warren: That she—*in horror at the memory*—she sometimes made a compact with Lucifer, and wrote her name in his black book—with her blood—and bound herself to torment Christians till God's thrown down—and we all must worship Hell forevermore.

Pause.

Proctor: But—surely you know what a jabberer she is. Did you tell them that?

Mary Warren: Mr. Proctor, in open court she near to choked us all to death.

Proctor: How, choked you?

Mary Warren: She sent her spirit out.

---

1. **poppet:** doll; puppet.

Taking a Second Look

Review: Making Generalizations

Explain that a *generalization* is a specific kind of conclusion, a broad statement or rule that applies to many examples. Point out that we make generalizations after thinking about what a number of examples or facts have in common. Discuss how a *valid generalization* is adequately supported by facts and logic, while an *invalid generalization* is not. Provide examples of valid and invalid generalizations.

Activities

1. Discuss how clue words, such as *all, none, most, many, always, everyone, never, sometimes, seldom, few, generally,* and *overall,* can signal a generalization. Have students find three generalizations in Act II that use these clue words.

2. Have students make generalizations about Salem and its people, based on what they have read thus far.

The girls of Salem "scream and howl and fall to the floor . . ."

Elizabeth: Oh, Mary, Mary, surely you—

Mary Warren, *with an indignant edge:* She tried to kill me many times, Goody Proctor!

Elizabeth: Why, I never heard you mention that before.

Mary Warren: I never knew it before. I never knew anything before. When she come into the court I say to myself, I must not accuse this woman, for she sleep in ditches, and so very old and poor. But then—then she sit there, denying and denying, and I feel a misty coldness climbin' up my back, and the skin on my skull begin to creep, and I feel a clamp around my neck and I cannot breathe air; and then—*entranced*—I hear a voice, a screamin' voice, and it were my voice—and all at once I remember everything she done to me!

Proctor: Why? What did she do to you?

Mary Warren, *like one awakened to a marvelous secret insight:* So many time, Mr. Proctor, she come to this very door, beggin' bread and a cup of cider—and mark this: whenever I turned her away empty, she *mumbled.*

Elizabeth: Mumbled! She may mumble if she's hungry.

Mary Warren: But *what* does she mumble? You must remember, Goody Proctor. Last month—a Monday, I think—she walked away, and I thought my guts would burst for two days after. Do you remember it?

Elizabeth: Why—I do, I think, but—

Mary Warren: And so I told that to Judge Hathorne, and he asks her so. "Goody Osburn," says he, "what curse do you mumble that this girl must fall sick after turning you away?" And then she replies—*mimicking an old crone*—"Why, your excellence, no curse at all. I only say my commandments; I hope I may say my commandments," says she!

Elizabeth: And that's an upright answer.

Mary Warren: Aye, but then Judge Hathorne say, "Recite for us your commandments!"—*leaning avidly toward them*—and of all the ten she could not say a single one. She never knew no commandments, and they had her in a flat lie!

Proctor: And so condemned her?

THE CRUCIBLE, ACT TWO 853

E Elements of Literature
Motivation

? Why does Mary Warren accuse Goody Osburn? How can you explain her sudden belief that she has been a victim of Osburn's witchcraft? [Possible response: Mary is overcome by the drama of the courtroom and by her own prejudices. Goody Osburn is uncouth, unpleasant, and habitually dishonest, and Mary is impressionable enough to let these qualities overwhelm her and feel that Osburn has personally injured her.]

F Cultural Connections

The Ten Commandments (also called the Decalogue) are the precepts that God gave to Moses on Mount Sinai. According to Exodus 31:18, they were inscribed by God on two stone tablets. Moses later destroyed the tablets and was commanded by God to create new ones, which were deposited in the Ark of the Covenant. In the Protestant division, the commandments are:

1. Thou shalt have no other gods before me.
2. Thou shalt not make thee any graven image.
3. Thou shalt not take the name of the Lord thy God in vain.
4. Keep the Sabbath day to sanctify it.
5. Honor thy father and thy mother.
6. Thou shalt not kill.
7. Neither shalt thou commit adultery.
8. Neither shalt thou steal.
9. Neither shalt thou bear false witness against thy neighbor.
10. Neither shalt thou desire thy neighbor's wife, neither shalt thou covet thy neighbor's house, his field, or his manservant . . . or anything that is thy neighbor's.

(Deuteronomy 5:6–12)

Ask students which commandments John Proctor has broken. [He has broken #4 and #7.]

Crossing the Curriculum

Art

There are no firsthand pictures, photographs, or art depicting the actual Salem witchcraft trials. Invite students to imagine that they are court artists present for Goody Osburn's testimony. Have students sketch the scene, capturing the mood as well as the participants. Students can add captions and display their sketches.

Science

Today, we might administer a *polygraph* or "lie detector" test to help determine innocence or guilt. A polygraph measures changes in blood pressure, pulse, respiration, and muscle movement. Have students find out more about these tests and then devise a set of questions they would ask Mary Warren, Goody Osburn, or any of the other characters in this scene to help determine their honesty.

Mary Warren, *now a little strained, seeing his stubborn doubt:* Why, they must when she condemned herself.

Proctor: But the proof, the proof!

Mary Warren, *with greater impatience with him:* I told you the proof. It's hard proof, hard as rock, the judges said.

Proctor—*he pauses an instant, then:* You will not go to court again, Mary Warren.

Mary Warren: I must tell you, sir, I will be gone every day now. I am amazed you do not see what weighty work we do.

Proctor: What work you do! It's strange work for a Christian girl to hang old women!

Mary Warren: But, Mr. Proctor, they will not hang them if they confess. Sarah Good will only sit in jail some time—*recalling*—and here's a wonder for you; think on this. Goody Good is pregnant!

Elizabeth: Pregnant! Are they mad? The woman's near to sixty!

Mary Warren: They had Doctor Griggs examine her, and she's full to the brim. And smokin' a pipe all these years, and no husband either! But she's safe, thank God, for they'll not hurt the innocent child. But be that not a marvel? You must see it, sir, it's God's work we do. So I'll be gone every day for some time. I'm—I am an official of the court, they say, and I— *She has been edging toward offstage.*

Proctor: I'll official you! *He strides to the mantel, takes down the whip hanging there.*

Mary Warren, *terrified, but coming erect, striving for her authority:* I'll not stand whipping any more!

Elizabeth, *hurriedly, as* PROCTOR *approaches:* Mary, promise now you'll stay at home—

Mary Warren, *backing from him, but keeping her erect posture, striving, striving for her way:* The Devil's loose in Salem, Mr. Proctor; we must discover where he's hiding!

Proctor: I'll whip the Devil out of you! *With whip raised he reaches out for her, and she streaks away and yells.*

Mary Warren, *pointing at* ELIZABETH: I saved her life today!

Silence. His whip comes down.

Elizabeth, *softly:* I am accused?

Mary Warren, *quaking:* Somewhat mentioned. But I said I never see no sign you ever sent your spirit out to hurt no one, and seeing I do live so closely with you, they dismissed it.

Elizabeth: Who accused me?

Mary Warren: I am bound by law, I cannot tell it. *To* PROCTOR: I only hope you'll not be so sarcastical no more. Four judges and the King's deputy sat to dinner with us but an hour ago. I—I would have you speak civilly to me, from this out.

Proctor, *in horror, muttering in disgust at her:* Go to bed.

Mary Warren, *with a stamp of her foot:* I'll not be ordered to bed no more, Mr. Proctor! I am eighteen and a woman, however single!

Proctor: Do you wish to sit up? Then sit up.

Mary Warren: I wish to go to bed!

Proctor, *in anger:* Good night, then!

Mary Warren: Good night. *Dissatisfied, uncertain of herself, she goes out. Wide-eyed, both* PROCTOR *and* ELIZABETH *stand staring.*

Elizabeth, *quietly:* Oh, the noose, the noose is up!

Proctor: There'll be no noose.

Elizabeth: She wants me dead. I knew all week it would come to this!

Proctor, *without conviction:* They dismissed it. You heard her say—

Elizabeth: And what of tomorrow? She will cry me out until they take me!

Proctor: Sit you down.

Elizabeth: She wants me dead, John, you know it!

Proctor: I say sit down! *She sits, trembling. He speaks quietly, trying to keep his wits.* Now we must be wise, Elizabeth.

Elizabeth, *with sarcasm, and a sense of being lost:* Oh, indeed, indeed!

Proctor: Fear nothing. I'll find Ezekiel Cheever. I'll tell him she said it were all sport.

Elizabeth: John, with so many in the jail, more than Cheever's help is needed now, I think. Would you favor me with this? Go to Abigail.

Proctor, *his soul hardening as he senses . . . :* What have I to say to Abigail?

Elizabeth, *delicately:* John—grant me this. You have a faulty understanding of young girls. There is a promise made in any bed—

Proctor, *striving against his anger:* What promise!

Elizabeth: Spoke or silent, a promise is surely made. And she may dote on it now—I am sure she

854 AMERICAN DRAMA

does—and thinks to kill me, then to take my place.

PROCTOR*'s anger is rising; he cannot speak.*

Elizabeth: It is her dearest hope, John, I know it. There be a thousand names; why does she call mine? There be a certain danger in calling such a name—I am no Goody Good that sleeps in ditches, nor Osburn, drunk and half-witted. She'd dare not call out such a farmer's wife but there be monstrous profit in it. She thinks to take my place, John.

Proctor: She cannot think it! *He knows it is true.*

Elizabeth, *"reasonably":* John, have you ever shown her somewhat of contempt? She cannot pass you in the church but you will blush—

Proctor: I may blush for my sin.

Elizabeth: I think she sees another meaning in that blush.

Proctor: And what see you? What see you, Elizabeth?

Elizabeth, *"conceding":* I think you be somewhat ashamed, for I am there, and she so close.

Proctor: When will you know me, woman? Were I stone I would have cracked for shame this seven month!

Elizabeth: Then go and tell her she's a whore. Whatever promise she may sense—break it, John, break it.

Proctor, *between his teeth:* Good, then. I'll go. *He starts for his rifle.*

Elizabeth, *trembling, fearfully:* Oh, how unwillingly!

Proctor, *turning on her, rifle in hand:* I will curse her hotter than the oldest cinder in hell. But pray, begrudge me not my anger!

Elizabeth: Your anger! I only ask you—

Proctor: Woman, am I so base? Do you truly think me base?

Elizabeth: I never called you base.

Proctor: Then how do you charge me with such a promise? The promise that a stallion gives a mare I gave that girl!

Elizabeth: Then why do you anger with me when I bid you break it?

Proctor: Because it speaks deceit, and I am honest! But I'll plead no more! I see now your spirit twists around the single error of my life, and I will never tear it free!

Elizabeth, *crying out:* You'll tear it free—when

you come to know that I will be your only wife, or no wife at all! She has an arrow in you yet, John Proctor, and you know it well!

Quite suddenly, as though from the air, a figure appears in the doorway. They start slightly. It is MR. HALE. *He is different now—drawn a little, and there is a quality of deference, even of guilt, about his manner now.*

Hale: Good evening.

Proctor, *still in his shock:* Why, Mr. Hale! Good evening to you, sir. Come in, come in.

Hale, *to* ELIZABETH: I hope I do not startle you.

Elizabeth: No, no, it's only that I heard no horse—

Hale: You are Goodwife Proctor.

Proctor: Aye; Elizabeth.

Hale, *nods, then:* I hope you're not off to bed yet.

Proctor, *setting down his gun:* No, no. HALE *comes further into the room. And* PROCTOR, *to explain his nervousness:* We are not used to visitors after dark, but you're welcome here. Will you sit you down, sir?

Hale: I will. *He sits.* Let you sit, Goodwife Proctor.

She does, never letting him out of her sight. There is a pause as HALE *looks about the room.*

Proctor, *to break the silence:* Will you drink cider, Mr. Hale?

Hale: No, it rebels my stomach; I have some further traveling yet tonight. Sit you down, sir. PROCTOR *sits.* I will not keep you long, but I have some business with you.

Proctor: Business of the court?

Hale: No—no, I come of my own, without the court's authority. Hear me. *He wets his lips.* I know not if you are aware, but your wife's name is—mentioned in the court.

Proctor: We know it, sir. Our Mary Warren told us. We are entirely amazed.

Hale: I am a stranger here, as you know. And in my ignorance I find it hard to draw a clear opinion of them that come accused before the court. And so this afternoon, and now tonight, I go from house to house—I come now from Rebecca Nurse's house and—

Elizabeth, *shocked:* Rebecca's charged!

Hale: God forbid such a one be charged. She is, however—mentioned somewhat.

E Elements of Literature
Motivation
? Why does John blush when he passes Abigail in church? What meaning might Abigail see in John's blush? [Possible response: John blushes from shame at the memory of his sin; Abigail takes his blush as a sign that he is still interested in her.]

F Appreciating Language
Figures of Speech
? What does this metaphor suggest about the relationship between John and Abigail? [Possible responses: It suggests that their affair was based on animal passion, not love. It indicates that mutual respect and devotion were not part of their relationship.]

G Reading Skills and Strategies

Interpreting a Text
? How has the Reverend Hale changed? [Possible responses: Hale is no longer the self-confident, even brash, bloodhound on the devil's trail. He may be starting to realize that hunting for witches is less clear cut than he imagined, that his zeal in finding evidence of witchery is helping to destroy innocent people and shatter families.]

H Critical Thinking
Speculating
? Why do you think Hale has come to visit the Proctors? [Possible responses: He wants to see for himself how they live, in order to determine the validity of Abigail's charges; he is trying to be as fair as possible and so gathers his own impressions and conducts his own investigation.]

Making the Connections

Connecting with the Film
In 1996, the eighty-one-year-old Miller wrote the screenplay for a film version of *The Crucible* (see pp. 829, 839). Like the play, the movie is a fictionalized version of the events of Salem in 1692, but there are some significant differences between the movie and the play. For example, the movie opens with a scene of the girls sneaking into the woods and dancing with Tituba, until they are all caught by Parris. In the play, this scene is only referred to, not performed.

Although the movie was praised by some critics, it was not as well received as the play has been. Invite students to work in teams to compare and contrast the written version of the play with the filmed version, focusing on plot, characters, and mood. Students should then evaluate each element to decide whether the play or movie version is more successful and why. They can present their findings in a comparison/contrast essay or critical review.

Analyzing and Comparing Reviews
Ask students who have seen movies and any stage performances of *The Crucible* to locate professional critical reviews. (Such reviews are available on the Internet and in library files.) Students should analyze the critics' main points and compare them with their own responses.

> # "The powers of the dark are gathered in monstrous attack upon this village."

Elizabeth, *with an attempt at a laugh:* You will never believe, I hope, that Rebecca trafficked with the Devil.

Hale: Woman, it is possible.

Proctor, *taken aback:* Surely you cannot think so.

Hale: This is a strange time, Mister. No man may longer doubt the powers of the dark are gathered in monstrous attack upon this village. There is too much evidence now to deny it. You will agree, sir?

Proctor, *evading:* I—I have no knowledge in that line. But it's hard to think so pious a woman be secretly a Devil's bitch after seventy year of such good prayer.

Hale: Aye. But the Devil is a wily one, you cannot deny it. However, she is far from accused, and I know she will not be. *Pause.* I thought, sir, to put some questions as to the Christian character of this house, if you'll permit me.

Proctor, *coldly, resentful:* Why, we—have no fear of questions, sir.

Hale: Good, then. *He makes himself more comfortable.* In the book of record that Mr. Parris keeps, I note that you are rarely in the church on Sabbath Day.

Proctor: No, sir, you are mistaken.

Hale: Twenty-six time in seventeen month, sir. I must call that rare. Will you tell me why you are so absent?

Proctor: Mr. Hale, I never knew I must account to that man for I come to church or stay at home. My wife were sick this winter.

Hale: So I am told. But you, Mister, why could you not come alone?

Proctor: I surely did come when I could, and when I could not I prayed in this house.

Hale: Mr. Proctor, your house is not a church; your theology must tell you that.

Proctor: It does, sir, it does; and it tells me that a minister may pray to God without he have golden candlesticks upon the altar.

Hale: What golden candlesticks?

Proctor: Since we built the church there were pewter candlesticks upon the altar; Francis Nurse made them, y'know, and a sweeter hand never touched the metal. But Parris came, and for twenty week he preach nothin' but golden candlesticks until he had them. I labor the earth from dawn of day to blink of night, and I tell you true, when I look to heaven and see my money glaring at his elbows—it hurt my prayer, sir, it hurt my prayer. I think, sometimes, the man dreams cathedrals, not clapboard meetin' houses.

Hale, *thinks, then:* And yet, Mister, a Christian on Sabbath Day must be in church. *Pause.* Tell me—you have three children?

Proctor: Aye. Boys.

Hale: How comes it that only two are baptized?

Proctor, *starts to speak, then stops, then, as though unable to restrain this:* I like it not that Mr. Parris should lay his hand upon my baby. I see no light of God in that man. I'll not conceal it.

Hale: I must say it, Mr. Proctor; that is not for you to decide. The man's ordained, therefore the light of God is in him.

Proctor, *flushed with resentment but trying to smile:* What's your suspicion, Mr. Hale?

Hale: No, no, I have no—

Proctor: I nailed the roof upon the church, I hung the door—

Hale: Oh, did you! That's a good sign, then.

Proctor: It may be I have been too quick to bring the man to book, but you cannot think we ever desired the destruction of religion. I think that's in your mind, is it not?

Hale, *not altogether giving way:* I—have—there is a softness in your record, sir, a softness.

Elizabeth: I think, maybe, we have been too hard with Mr. Parris. I think so. But sure we never loved the Devil here.

Hale, *nods, deliberating this. Then, with the voice of one administering a secret test:* Do you know your Commandments, Elizabeth?

Elizabeth, *without hesitation, even eagerly:* I surely do. There be no mark of blame upon my life, Mr. Hale. I am a covenanted Christian woman.

Hale: And you, Mister?

Professional Notes

The Covenant and Cotton Mather

When Elizabeth refers to herself as "a covenanted Christian woman," she alludes to one of the most significant of Puritan concepts. The idea of the covenant was at the core of the Puritan experience—a certainty that God and the Puritans shared an agreement to establish the rule of heaven on earth. Through right belief and right action, the Puritans fulfilled a divine contract which guaranteed their salvation. Thus, witchcraft meant not only the destruc-

tion of the covenant but also the community. It was both a religious and political act, a kind of spiritual treason. Cotton Mather was not alone in predicting such global consequences when he wrote in *The Wonders of the Invisible World* (1692):

". . . The New Englanders are a people of God settled in those which were once the devil's territories. . . . The devil, thus irritated, immediately tried all sorts of methods

to overturn this poor plantation, and so much of the church as was fled into this wilderness. . . . If the devils now can strike the minds of men with any poisons of so fine a composition and operation that scores of innocent people shall unite in confessions of a crime which we see actually committed, it is a thing prodigious, beyond the wonders of the former ages, and it threatens no less than a sort of dissolution upon the world. . . ."

Proctor, *a trifle unsteadily:* I—am sure I do, sir.
Hale, *glances at her open face, then at* JOHN, *then:* Let you repeat them, if you will.
Proctor: The Commandments.
Hale: Aye.
Proctor, *looking off, beginning to sweat:* Thou shalt not kill.
Hale: Aye.
Proctor, *counting on his fingers:* Thou shalt not steal. Thou shalt not covet thy neighbor's goods, nor make unto thee any graven image. Thou shalt not take the name of the Lord in vain; thou shalt have no other gods before me. *With some hesitation:* Thou shalt remember the Sabbath Day and keep it holy. *Pause. Then:* Thou shalt honor thy father and mother. Thou shalt not bear false witness. *He is stuck. He counts back on his fingers, knowing one is missing.* Thou shalt not make unto thee any graven image.
Hale: You have said that twice, sir.
Proctor, *lost:* Aye. *He is flailing for it.*
Elizabeth, *delicately:* Adultery, John.
Proctor, *as though a secret arrow had pained his heart:* Aye. *Trying to grin it away—to* HALE: You see, sir, between the two of us we do know them all. HALE *only looks at* PROCTOR, *deep in his attempt to define this man.* PROCTOR *grows more uneasy.* I think it be a small fault.
Hale: Theology, sir, is a fortress; no crack in a fortress may be accounted small. *He rises; he seems worried now. He paces a little, in deep thought.*
Proctor: There be no love for Satan in this house, Mister.
Hale: I pray it, I pray it dearly. *He looks to both of them, an attempt at a smile on his face, but his misgivings are clear.* Well, then—I'll bid you good night.
Elizabeth, *unable to restrain herself:* Mr. Hale. *He turns.* I do think you are suspecting me somewhat? Are you not?
Hale, *obviously disturbed—and evasive:* Goody Proctor, I do not judge you. My duty is to add what I may to the godly wisdom of the court. I pray you both good health and good fortune. *To* JOHN: Good night, sir. *He starts out.*
Elizabeth, *with a note of desperation:* I think you must tell him, John.
Hale: What's that?

Elizabeth, *restraining a call:* Will you tell him?

Slight pause. HALE *looks questioningly at* JOHN.

Proctor, *with difficulty:* I—I have no witness and cannot prove it, except my word be taken. But I know the children's sickness had naught to do with witchcraft.
Hale, *stopped, struck:* Naught to do—?
Proctor: Mr. Parris discovered them sportin' in the woods. They were startled and took sick.

Pause.

Hale: Who told you this?
Proctor, *hesitates, then:* Abigail Williams.
Hale: Abigail!
Proctor: Aye.
Hale, *his eyes wide:* Abigail Williams told you it had naught to do with witchcraft!
Proctor: She told me the day you came, sir.
Hale, *suspiciously:* Why—why did you keep this?
Proctor: I never knew until tonight that the world is gone daft with this nonsense.
Hale: Nonsense! Mister, I have myself examined Tituba, Sarah Good, and numerous others that have confessed to dealing with the Devil. They have *confessed* it.
Proctor: And why not, if they must hang for denyin' it? There are them that will swear to anything before they'll hang; have you never thought of that?
Hale: I have. I—I have indeed. *It is his own suspicion, but he resists it. He glances at* ELIZABETH, *then at* JOHN. And you—would you testify to this in court?
Proctor: I—had not reckoned with goin' into court. But if I must I will.
Hale: Do you falter here?
Proctor: I falter nothing, but I may wonder if my story will be credited in such a court. I do wonder on it, when such a steady-minded minister as you will suspicion such a woman that never lied, and cannot, and the world knows she cannot! I may falter somewhat, Mister; I am no fool.
Hale, *quietly—it has impressed him:* Proctor, let you open with me now, for I have a rumor that troubles me. It's said you hold no belief that there may even be witches in the world. Is that true, sir?
Proctor—he knows this is critical, and is

Using Students' Strengths

Logical/Mathematical Learners
Since colonial Salem was a theocracy, it was logical to test character based on a knowledge of the Bible. How could we test or measure character today in America? Have students devise a character test, assess its reliability, and administer it by random sampling. Students should tabulate their results and see what conclusions they can draw about the validity of the test.

E **Elements of Literature**
Irony
? What is ironic about Proctor's forgetting this particular commandment? [Possible response: Ironically, he forgets the commandment he has broken, the one that has helped unleash the witchcraft hysteria.]

F **Critical Thinking**
Interpreting
? What does Hale's remark suggest about the Puritan character? [Possible responses: Hale's inability to ignore even the smallest omission conveys a rigidity and intolerance in the Puritan character that Miller described in the beginning of the play. It also hints that the Salem court is unlikely to swerve from its path, even to accommodate new evidence.]

G **Elements of Literature**
Motivation
? Do you think the courts will accept Proctor's testimony? Why or why not? [Possible responses: It seems highly unlikely that the courts will accept Proctor's testimony, since they have no motivation to do so—just the opposite. The court is making its reputation and settling old scores, so the judges have a stake in keeping it on course.]

H **Elements of Literature**
Character
? What does this exchange suggest about Hale's character? Why might he want to deny the explanation that Proctor offers for the court's "confessions." [Possible response: Hale emerges as a deeply divided character, torn between his intelligence and conscience on the one hand and his pride and self-righteousness on the other. He would seek to repress his suspicion of Proctor's explanation because it could mean that all of the court's "facts" are fraudulent.]

I **Reading Skills and Strategies**
Interpreting a Text
? Why do you think Proctor makes the point that his wife cannot lie? [Possible responses: It establishes her credibility; it will be a crucial element later in the play.]

A Humanities Connections

Witches are indeed mentioned in the Book of Exodus, 22:18, "Thou shalt not suffer a witch to live," and in Deuteronomy 18:10, "There shall not be found among you . . . a witch."

B Elements of Literature
Character

❓ Why do you think Elizabeth speaks so boldly to Hale? How does this highlight a contrast between her character and Proctor's? [Possible response: Elizabeth has suffered deeply after John's infidelity and her illness, and she may feel her honor and honesty are all she has left. She seems to have greater faith than John in the imperative to speak and act on her conscience.]

C Appreciating Language
Figures of Speech

❓ What impression of Rebecca does Francis convey with this metaphor? [Possible response: The metaphor suggests her solidity and uprightness.]

D Historical Connections

The court record shows that the magistrate doubted Rebecca's guilt because of her age, character, appearance, and claims of innocence. However, each time he wavered on the issue, someone would accuse her, or the afflicted girls would break into fits and claim Nurse was tormenting them. When the jury returned a verdict of "not guilty," the afflicted girls and the spectators set up a huge outcry. The magistrates urged reconsideration; the second time, the verdict was "guilty." Governor Phips granted a reprieve, but the accusers had renewed fits, and so Rebecca was executed on July 19. Public outrage at her execution generated the first vocal opposition to the trials.

E Elements of Literature
Motivation

❓ What parallels can you see in the motivation behind the accusation of Rebecca and this accusation of Martha Corey? [Mrs. Putnam accuses Rebecca because she has lost her children and envies Rebecca's large, healthy family. Walcott accuses Martha because his pig has died, and he envies her success with pigs.]

---

striving against his disgust with HALE *and with himself for even answering:* I know not what I have said, I may have said it. I have wondered if there be witches in the world—although I cannot believe they come among us now.

Hale: Then you do not believe—

A Proctor: I have no knowledge of it; the Bible speaks of witches, and I will not deny them.

Hale: And you, woman?

Elizabeth: I—I cannot believe it.

Hale, *shocked:* You cannot!

Proctor: Elizabeth, you bewilder him!

Elizabeth, *to* HALE: I cannot think the Devil may own a woman's soul, Mr. Hale, when she keeps an upright way, as I have. I am a good woman, I know it; and if you believe I may do only good work in the world, and yet be secretly bound to Satan, then I must tell you, sir, I do not believe it.

B Hale: But, woman, you do believe there are witches in—

Elizabeth: If you think that I am one, then I say there are none.

Hale: You surely do not fly against the Gospel, the Gospel—

Proctor: She believe in the Gospel, every word!

Elizabeth: Question Abigail Williams about the Gospel, not myself!

HALE *stares at her.*

Proctor: She do not mean to doubt the Gospel, sir, you cannot think it. This be a Christian house, sir, a Christian house.

Hale: God keep you both; let the third child be quickly baptized, and go you without fail each Sunday in to Sabbath prayer; and keep a solemn, quiet way among you. I think—

GILES COREY *appears in doorway.*

Giles: John!

Proctor: Giles! What's the matter?

Giles: They take my wife.

FRANCIS NURSE *enters.*

Giles: And his Rebecca!

Proctor, *to* FRANCIS: Rebecca's in the *jail!*

Francis: Aye, Cheever come and take her in his wagon. We've only now come from the jail, and they'll not even let us in to see them.

Elizabeth: They've surely gone wild now, Mr. Hale!

Francis, *going to* HALE: Reverend Hale! Can you not speak to the Deputy Governor? I'm sure he mistakes these people—

Hale: Pray calm yourself, Mr. Nurse.

C Francis: My wife is the very brick and mortar of the church, Mr. Hale—*indicating* GILES—and Martha Corey, there cannot be a woman closer yet to God than Martha.

Hale: How is Rebecca charged, Mr. Nurse?

Francis, *with a mocking, half-hearted laugh:* For murder, she's charged! *Mockingly quoting the warrant:* "For the marvelous and supernatural murder of Goody Putnam's babies." What am I to do, Mr. Hale?

D Hale, *turns from* FRANCIS, *deeply troubled, then:* Believe me, Mr. Nurse, if Rebecca Nurse be tainted, then nothing's left to stop the whole green world from burning. Let you rest upon the justice of the court; the court will send her home, I know it.

Francis: You cannot mean she will be tried in court!

Hale, *pleading:* Nurse, though our hearts break, we cannot flinch; these are new times, sir. There is a misty plot afoot so subtle we should be criminal to cling to old respects and ancient friendships. I have seen too many frightful proofs in court—the Devil is alive in Salem, and we dare not quail to follow wherever the accusing finger points!

Proctor, *angered:* How may such a woman murder children?

Hale, *in great pain:* Man, remember, until an hour before the Devil fell, God thought him beautiful in Heaven.

Giles: I never said my wife were a witch, Mr. Hale; I only said she were reading books!

Hale: Mr. Corey, exactly what complaint were made on your wife?

E Giles: That bloody mongrel Walcott charge her. Y'see, he buy a pig of my wife four or five year ago, and the pig died soon after. So he come dancin' in for his money back. So my Martha, she says to him, "Walcott, if you haven't the wit to feed a pig properly, you'll not live to own many," she says. Now he goes to court and claims that from that day to this he cannot keep a pig alive for

Crossing the Curriculum

Social Studies/History

Suggest that interested students investigate and report on the system of civil law by which the Salem trials were conducted. Student reports should include description of the trial process, including the nature and role of the jury, witnesses, evidence, proof, confession, and punishment.

more than four weeks because my Martha bewitch them with her books!

Enter EZEKIEL CHEEVER. *A shocked silence.*

Cheever: Good evening to you, Proctor.
Proctor: Why, Mr. Cheever. Good evening.
Cheever: Good evening, all. Good evening, Mr. Hale.
Proctor: I hope you come not on business of the court.
Cheever: I do, Proctor, aye. I am clerk of the court now, y'know.

Enter MARSHAL HERRICK, *a man in his early thirties, who is somewhat shamefaced at the moment.*

Giles: It's a pity, Ezekiel, that an honest tailor might have gone to Heaven must burn in Hell. You'll burn for this, do you know it?
Cheever: You know yourself I must do as I'm told. You surely know that, Giles. And I'd as lief[2] you'd not be sending me to Hell. I like not the sound of it, I tell you; I like not the sound of it. *He fears* PROCTOR, *but starts to reach inside his coat.* Now believe me, Proctor, how heavy be the law, all its tonnage I do carry on my back tonight. *He takes out a warrant.* I have a warrant for your wife.
Proctor, *to* HALE: You said she were not charged!
Hale: I know nothin' of it. *To* CHEEVER: When were she charged?
Cheever: I am given sixteen warrant tonight, sir, and she is one.
Proctor: Who charged her?
Cheever: Why, Abigail Williams charge her.
Proctor: On what proof, what proof?
Cheever, *looking about the room:* Mr. Proctor, I have little time. The court bid me search your house, but I like not to search a house. So will you hand me any poppets that your wife may keep here?
Proctor: Poppets?
Elizabeth: I never kept no poppets, not since I were a girl.
Cheever, *embarrassed, glancing toward the mantel where sits* MARY WARREN'S *poppet:* I spy a poppet, Goody Proctor.
Elizabeth: Oh! *Going for it:* Why, this is Mary's.

2. **lief:** gladly.

> ## "The Devil is alive in Salem, and we dare not quail to follow wherever the accusing finger points!"

Cheever, *shyly:* Would you please to give it to me?
Elizabeth, *handing it to him, asks* HALE: Has the court discovered a text in poppets now?
Cheever, *carefully holding the poppet:* Do you keep any others in this house?
Proctor: No, not this one either till tonight. What signifies a poppet?
Cheever: Why, a poppet—*he gingerly turns the poppet over*—a poppet may signify— Now, woman, will you please to come with me?
Proctor: She will not! *To* ELIZABETH: Fetch Mary here.
Cheever, *ineptly reaching toward* ELIZABETH: No, no, I am forbid to leave her from my sight.
Proctor, *pushing his arm away:* You'll leave her out of sight and out of mind, Mister. Fetch Mary, Elizabeth. ELIZABETH *goes upstairs.*
Hale: What signifies a poppet, Mr. Cheever?
Cheever, *turning the poppet over in his hands:* Why, they say it may signify that she— *He has lifted the poppet's skirt, and his eyes widen in astonished fear.* Why, this, this—
Proctor, *reaching for the poppet:* What's there?
Cheever: Why—*he draws out a long needle from the poppet*—it is a needle! Herrick, Herrick, it is a needle!

HERRICK *comes toward him.*

Proctor, *angrily, bewildered:* And what signifies a needle!
Cheever, *his hands shaking:* Why, this go hard with her, Proctor, this—I had my doubts, Proctor, I had my doubts, but here's calamity. *To* HALE, *showing the needle:* You see it, sir, it is a needle!
Hale: Why? What meanin' has it?
Cheever, *wide-eyed, trembling:* The girl, the Williams girl, Abigail Williams, sir. She sat to dinner in Reverend Parris's house tonight, and

F Elements of Literature
Motivation
? How does Cheever feel about being a clerk of the court? What motivates him to do his job? [Possible responses: Cheever enjoys the status and power his job confers on him, but regrets he has to do unpopular deeds. He is motivated by a need for self-esteem and respectability.]

G Critical Thinking
Analyzing
? How do you think the court knew that Elizabeth had a poppet? What does this suggest about Abigail? [Possible responses: Abigail told them, which suggests that she had Mary plant the doll so she could use it as evidence against Elizabeth. This suggests that Abigail has a chillingly diabolical mind.]

H Reading Skills and Strategies
Interpreting a Text
? Puritans believed that witches could inflict harm on their victims from a distance by injuring a doll that represented the victim. What do you think the doll and needle represent here? [Possible response: The judge and jury will likely take them as evidence that Elizabeth stabbed Abigail, by sticking a pin into an occult effigy of the girl.]

Professional Notes

Original Document
Here is the text of the arrest warrant issued for Elizabeth Proctor:

> "There Being Complaint this day made (Before us) by capt Jonat Walcott, and Lt Natheniell Ingersull both of Salem Village, in Behalfe of theire Majesties for themselfes and also for severall of their Neighbours Against Sarah Cloyce the wife of peter Cloyce of Salem Village; and Elizabeth Proctor the wife of John Proctor of Salem farmes for high Suspition of Sundry acts of Witchcraft donne or
>
> Committed by them upon the bodys of Abigail Williams, and John Indian both of Mr Sam parris his family of Salem Village and mary Walcott daughter of the abovesaid Complainants, And Ann Putnam and Marcy Lewis of the famyly of Thomas Putnam of Salem Village whereby great hurt and dammage hath beene donne to the Bodys of s'd persons above named therefore Craved Justice.
>
> You are therefore in theire Majest's names hereby required to apprehend and bring before us Sarah Cloyce the wife of peter Cloyce of Salem Village and Elizabeth proctor the wife of John Procter of Salem farmes; on Munday Morneing Next being the Eleventh day of this Instant Aprill aboute Eleven of the Clock, at the publike Meeting house in the Towne, in order to theire Examination Relateing to the premesis aboves'd and here of you are not to faile Dated Salem Aprill 8'th 1692
>
> John Hathorne
>
> Jonathan Corwin   Assists"

A without word nor warnin' she falls to the floor. Like a struck beast, he says, and screamed a scream that a bull would weep to hear. And he goes to save her, and, stuck two inches in the flesh of her belly, he draw a needle out. And demandin' of her how she come to be so stabbed, she—*to* PROCTOR *now*—testify it were your wife's familiar spirit pushed it in.

Proctor: Why, she done it herself! *To* HALE: I hope you're not takin' this for proof, Mister!

HALE, *struck by the proof, is silent.*

Cheever: 'Tis hard proof! *To* HALE: I find her a poppet Goody Proctor keeps. I have found it, sir. And in the belly of the poppet a needle's stuck. I tell you true, Proctor, I never warranted to see such proof of Hell, and I bid you obstruct me not, for I—

Enter ELIZABETH *with* MARY WARREN. PROCTOR, *seeing* MARY WARREN, *draws her by the arm to* HALE.

Proctor: Here now! Mary, how did this poppet come into my house?

Mary Warren, *frightened for herself, her voice very small:* What poppet's that, sir?

Proctor, *impatiently, pointing at the doll in* CHEEVER'*s hand:* This poppet, this poppet.

Mary Warren, *evasively, looking at it:* Why, I—I think it is mine.

Proctor: It is your poppet, is it not?

Mary Warren, *not understanding the direction of this:* It—is, sir.

Proctor: And how did it come into this house?

Mary Warren, *glancing about at the avid faces:* Why—I made it in the court, sir, and—give it to Goody Proctor tonight.

Proctor, *to* HALE: Now, sir—do you have it?

Hale: Mary Warren, a needle have been found inside this poppet.

Mary Warren, *bewildered:* Why, I meant no harm by it, sir.

Proctor, *quickly:* You stuck that needle in yourself?

Mary Warren: I—I believe I did, sir, I—

Proctor, *to* HALE: What say you now?

Hale, *watching* MARY WARREN *closely:* Child, you are certain this be your natural memory? May it be, perhaps, that someone conjures you even now to say this?

Mary Warren: Conjures me? Why, no, sir, I am entirely myself, I think. Let you ask Susanna Walcott—she saw me sewin' it in court. Or better still: Ask Abby, Abby sat beside me when I made it.

Proctor, *to* HALE, *of* CHEEVER: Bid him begone. Your mind is surely settled now. Bid him out, Mr. Hale.

Elizabeth: What signifies a needle?

Hale: Mary—you charge a cold and cruel murder on Abigail.

Mary Warren: Murder! I charge no—

Hale: Abigail were stabbed tonight; a needle were found stuck into her belly—

Elizabeth: And she charges me?

Hale: Aye.

B **Elizabeth,** *her breath knocked out:* Why—! The girl is murder! She must be ripped out of the world!

Cheever, *pointing at* ELIZABETH: You've heard that, sir! Ripped out of the world! Herrick, you heard it!

Proctor, *suddenly snatching the warrant out of* CHEEVER'*s hands:* Out with you.

Cheever: Proctor, you dare not touch the warrant.

Proctor, *ripping the warrant:* Out with you!

Cheever: You've ripped the Deputy Governor's warrant, man!

Proctor: Damn the Deputy Governor! Out of my house!

Hale: Now, Proctor, Proctor!

C **Proctor:** Get y'gone with them! You are a broken minister.

Hale: Proctor, if she is innocent, the court—

D **Proctor:** If *she* is innocent! Why do you never wonder if Parris be innocent, or Abigail? Is the accuser always holy now? Were they born this morning as clean as God's fingers? I'll tell you what's walking Salem—vengeance is walking Salem. We are what we always were in Salem, but now the little crazy children are jangling the keys of the kingdom, and common vengeance writes the law! This warrant's vengeance! I'll not give my wife to vengeance!

Elizabeth: I'll go, John—

Proctor: You will not go!

Herrick: I have nine men outside. You cannot keep her. The law binds me, John, I cannot budge.

Proctor, *to* HALE, *ready to break him:* Will you see her taken?

Hale: Proctor, the court is just—

Proctor: Pontius Pilate![3] God will not let you wash your hands of this!

Elizabeth: John—I think I must go with them. *He cannot bear to look at her.* Mary, there is bread enough for the morning; you will bake, in the afternoon. Help Mr. Proctor as you were his daughter—you owe me that, and much more. *She is fighting her weeping. To* PROCTOR: When the children wake, speak nothing of witchcraft—it will frighten them. *She cannot go on.*

Proctor: I will bring you home. I will bring you soon.

Elizabeth: Oh, John, bring me soon!

Proctor: I will fall like an ocean on that court! Fear nothing, Elizabeth.

Elizabeth, *with great fear:* I will fear nothing. *She looks about the room, as though to fix it in her mind.* Tell the children I have gone to visit someone sick.

She walks out the door, HERRICK *and* CHEEVER *behind her. For a moment,* PROCTOR *watches from the doorway. The clank of chain is heard.*

Proctor: Herrick! Herrick, don't chain her! *He rushes out the door. From outside:* Damn you, man, you will not chain her! Off with them! I'll not have it! I will not have her chained!

There are other men's voices against his. HALE, *in a fever of guilt and uncertainty, turns from the door to avoid the sight;* MARY WARREN *bursts into tears and sits weeping.* GILES COREY *calls to* HALE.

Giles: And yet silent, minister? It is fraud, you know it is fraud! What keeps you, man?

PROCTOR *is half braced, half pushed into the room by two deputies and* HERRICK.

Proctor: I'll pay you, Herrick, I will surely pay you!

Herrick, *panting:* In God's name, John, I cannot help myself. I must chain them all. Now let you keep inside this house till I am gone! *He goes out with his deputies.*

PROCTOR *stands there, gulping air. Horses and a wagon creaking are heard.*

3. **Pontius Pilate** (pun'chəs pī'lət) (1st century A.D.): Roman official who unwillingly condemned Christ to death. Pilate is said to have declared, "I am innocent of the blood of this just man" (Matthew 27:24).

Hale, *in great uncertainty:* Mr. Proctor—

Proctor: Out of my sight!

Hale: Charity, Proctor, charity. What I have heard in her favor, I will not fear to testify in court. God help me, I cannot judge her guilty or innocent—I know not. Only this consider: the world goes mad, and it profit nothing you should lay the cause to the vengeance of a little girl.

Proctor: You are a coward! Though you be ordained in God's own tears, you are a coward now!

Hale: Proctor, I cannot think God be provoked so grandly by such a petty cause. The jails are packed—our greatest judges sit in Salem now—and hangin's promised. Man, we must look to cause proportionate. Were there murder done, perhaps, and never brought to light? Abomination? Some secret blasphemy that stinks to Heaven? Think on cause, man, and let you help me to discover it. For there's your way, believe it, there is your only way, when such confusion strikes upon the world. *He goes to* GILES *and* FRANCIS. Let you counsel among yourselves; think on your village and what may have drawn from heaven such thundering wrath upon you all. I shall pray God open up our eyes.

HALE *goes out.*

Francis, *struck by* HALE's *mood:* I never heard no murder done in Salem.

Proctor—*he has been reached by* HALE's *words:* Leave me, Francis, leave me.

Giles, *shaken:* John—tell me, are we lost?

Proctor: Go home now, Giles. We'll speak on it tomorrow.

Giles: Let you think on it. We'll come early, eh?

Proctor: Aye. Go now, Giles.

Giles: Good night, then.

GILES COREY *and* FRANCIS NURSE *go out. After a moment:*

Mary Warren, *in a fearful squeak of a voice:* Mr. Proctor, very likely they'll let her come home once they're given proper evidence.

Proctor: You're coming to the court with me, Mary. You will tell it in the court.

Mary Warren: I cannot charge murder on Abigail.

Proctor, *moving menacingly toward her:* You will tell the court how that poppet come here and who stuck the needle in.

E **Reading Skills and Strategies**

Interpreting a Text

? Why do you think Proctor *"cannot bear to look"* at Elizabeth now? What emotions is he experiencing? [Possible response: Proctor is feeling overwhelmed by horror and guilt, realizing that his affair with Abigail has caused his wife's imprisonment and possible execution.]

F **Elements of Literature**

Characterization

? What does Elizabeth's behavior here reveal about her character? [Possible responses: Her self-control and concern for her family convey her nobility of character, underscoring the injustice of the charges against her.]

G **English Language Learners**

Figurative Language

? What does Proctor mean when he says that he will "pay" Herrick? [Possible response: Proctor means that he will get revenge for Herrick's arresting and chaining Elizabeth.]

H **Reading Skills and Strategies**

Making Predictions

? Do you think John, Giles, and Francis will prevail and free their wives? Why or why not? [Possible responses: Some students will argue yes, because the courts will not dare execute such pious and respectable women. Other students will take a more pessimistic view, citing the lack of resistance to Abigail and the other girls.]

Making the Connections

Connecting to the Theme: "The Breaking of Charity"

When students have finished reading Act Two, remind them of the collection theme. Then, divide the class in half to debate how to reconcile the Puritans' desire for conformity and cohesion within their community with the presence of betrayal, accusations, and injustice as they hunted and persecuted people believed to be witches. Are there any instances in which it is morally or socially permissible to harm others for the sake of the greater good? If so, describe the circumstances.

A Reading Skills and Strategies

Interpreting a Text

? What does Proctor mean when he says that "We are only what we always were, but naked now"? [He means that facing the lies of the witch hunt will require that *all* the truth be exposed, including his affair with Abigail.]

MAKING MEANINGS

Act Two

First Thoughts [Respond]

1. Possible responses: He could reveal his affair with Abigail, gather signatures in support of his wife, or beg Abigail for mercy.

Shaping Interpretations [Interpret]

2. John's affair has left the couple emotionally estranged. While they are both trying to renew their marriage, Elizabeth still feels pain and mistrust.

3. Abigail used Mary to frame Elizabeth.

4. Weak and insecure, Mary is motivated by a desire to belong to the crowd, to please Abigail, and to feel a power and superiority usually denied to a serving girl.

5. Hale is suspicious of the Proctors' doubts about Reverend Parris and the witchcraft question itself. The irony is that charity is precisely what Hale and the court refuse the Proctors.

6. John, the protagonist, is a good man, briefly gone astray; Abigail, the antagonist, cruelly and deliberately sets out to shatter his family.

7. External: Elizabeth vs. the court, John vs. Parris, and Abigail vs. Elizabeth. John must decide whether to reveal his affair with Abigail and save his wife but lose his reputation. This reflects a wider conflict between personal truth and conformity with public behavior.

Extending the Text [Evaluate]

8. *The Crucible* opens a window into the souls of the participants, showing their hopes and fears. Historical truth demands the review of primary source documents in light of new facts and interpretations.

Mary Warren: She'll kill me for sayin' that! PROCTOR *continues toward her.* Abby'll charge lechery on you, Mr. Proctor!

Proctor, *halting:* She's told you!

Mary Warren: I have known it, sir. She'll ruin you with it, I know she will.

Proctor, *hesitating, and with deep hatred of himself:* Good. Then her saintliness is done with. MARY *backs from him.* We will slide together into our pit; you will tell the court what you know.

Mary Warren, *in terror:* I cannot, they'll turn on me—

PROCTOR *strides and catches her, and she is repeating, "I cannot, I cannot!"*

Proctor: My wife will never die for me! I will bring your guts into your mouth but that goodness will not die for me!

Mary Warren, *struggling to escape him:* I cannot do it, I cannot!

Proctor, *grasping her by the throat as though he would strangle her:* Make your peace with it! Now Hell and Heaven grapple on our backs, and all our old pretense is ripped away—make your peace! He throws her to the floor, where she sobs, "I cannot, I cannot . . ." And now, half to himself, staring, and turning to the open door: Peace. It is a providence, and no great change; we are only what we always were, but naked now. He walks as though toward a great horror, facing the open sky. Aye, naked! And the wind, God's icy wind, will blow!

And she is over and over again sobbing, "I cannot, I cannot, I cannot," as

The curtain falls

MAKING MEANINGS

Act Two

First Thoughts

1. At this point in the play, what would you do if you were John Proctor?

Shaping Interpretations

2. Describe the relationship between John and Elizabeth. In your own words, explain the **metaphor** of the "everlasting funeral" that John sees in Elizabeth's heart.

3. Based on Mary's statements, what do you infer is the real reason Mary gives Elizabeth the gift?

4. Using your reading notes as a starting point, how do you interpret Mary's

> ### Reading Check
> a. At the beginning of the act, why does Elizabeth want John to go to Salem?
> b. What gift does Mary Warren give to Elizabeth?
> c. According to Elizabeth, what is Abigail's true objective in court?
> d. Why has Rebecca Nurse been jailed?
> e. What does John Proctor want Mary to testify?

visions and accusations? What clues does Miller give us about her **motivation**?

5. Why does Hale become suspicious of the Proctors? What is the **irony** in Hale's urging Proctor to show "charity"?

6. The **protagonist** of a story is the central character who drives the action, and is usually considered the hero or heroine. The **antagonist** is the character who struggles against the protagonist, often with cruel or destructive intent. By the end of Act Two, which character seems to have emerged as the protagonist? Which character is most clearly the antagonist? Support your answer with specific evidence from the text.

7. Identify at least three **external conflicts** in the play. Then describe the **internal conflict** that Proctor faces. How could Proctor's conflict relate to a broader conflict in the play—between public appearance and private reality?

Extending the Text

8. What insights about the Puritans do you gain from reading *The Crucible*—insights that you don't usually find in a history textbook? What dangers would there be in relying only on later literature for historical truth?

Reading Check
a. She wants John to share Abigail's admission that the girls were not afflicted by witchcraft.
b. Mary gives Elizabeth a poppet, a doll.
c. Abigail wants to eliminate Elizabeth so that she can have John for herself.
d. Rebecca is charged with killing the Putnams' babies.
e. He wants her to say how Elizabeth got the poppet and who stuck the needle in it.

Act Three

The vestry room of the Salem meeting house, now serving as the anteroom of the General Court.

As the curtain rises, the room is empty, but for sunlight pouring through two high windows in the back wall. The room is solemn, even forbidding. Heavy beams jut out, boards of random widths make up the walls. At the right are two doors leading into the meeting house proper, where the court is being held. At the left another door leads outside.

There is a plain bench at the left, and another at the right. In the center a rather long meeting table, with stools and a considerable armchair snugged up to it.

Through the partitioning wall at the right we hear a prosecutor's voice, JUDGE HATHORNE's, asking a question; then a woman's voice, MARTHA COREY's, replying.

Hathorne's Voice: Now, Martha Corey, there is abundant evidence in our hands to show that you have given yourself to the reading of fortunes. Do you deny it?

Martha Corey's Voice: I am innocent to a witch. I know not what a witch is.

Hathorne's Voice: How do you know, then, that you are not a witch?

Martha Corey's Voice: If I were, I would know it.

Hathorne's Voice: Why do you hurt these children?

Martha Corey's Voice: I do not hurt them. I scorn it!

Giles' Voice, *roaring:* I have evidence for the court!

Voices of townspeople rise in excitement.

Danforth's Voice: You will keep your seat!

Giles' Voice: Thomas Putnam is reaching out for land!

Danforth's Voice: Remove that man, Marshal!

Giles' Voice: You're hearing lies, lies!

A roaring goes up from the people.

Hathorne's Voice: Arrest him, Excellency!

Giles' Voice: I have evidence. Why will you not hear my evidence?

The door opens and GILES *is half carried into the vestry room by* HERRICK. FRANCIS NURSE *enters, trailing anxiously behind* GILES.

Giles: Hands off, damn you, let me go!

Herrick: Giles, Giles!

Giles: Out of my way, Herrick! I bring evidence—

Herrick: You cannot go in there, Giles; it's a court!

Enter HALE *from the court.*

Hale: Pray be calm a moment.

Giles: You, Mr. Hale, go in there and demand I speak.

Hale: A moment, sir, a moment.

Giles: They'll be hangin' my wife!

JUDGE HATHORNE enters. He is in his sixties, a bitter, remorseless Salem judge.

Hathorne: How do you dare come roarin' into this court! Are you gone daft, Corey?

Giles: You're not a Boston judge yet, Hathorne. You'll not call me daft!

Enter DEPUTY GOVERNOR DANFORTH *and, behind him,* EZEKIEL CHEEVER *and* PARRIS. *On his appearance, silence falls.* DANFORTH *is a grave man in his sixties, of some humor and sophistication that do not, however, interfere with an exact loyalty to his position and his cause. He comes down to* GILES, *who awaits his wrath.*

Danforth, *looking directly at* GILES: Who is this man?

Parris: Giles Corey, sir, and a more contentious—

Giles, *to* PARRIS: I am asked the question, and I am old enough to answer it! *To* DANFORTH, *who impresses him and to whom he smiles through his strain:* My name is Corey, sir, Giles Corey. I have six hundred acres, and timber in addition. It is my wife you be condemning now. *He indicates the courtroom.*

Danforth: And how do you imagine to help her cause with such contemptuous riot? Now be gone. Your old age alone keeps you out of jail for this.

Giles, *beginning to plead:* They be tellin' lies about my wife, sir, I—

Danforth: Do you take it upon yourself to determine what this court shall believe and what it shall set aside?

THE CRUCIBLE, ACT THREE **863**

The setting is the Salem meeting house. Giles, Francis Nurse, and John attempt to present a petition to exacting, arrogant Judge Danforth, which testifies to the pious character of Rebecca Nurse, Martha Corey, and Elizabeth Proctor. From the beginning, this plan begins to go astray as Parris and Judge Hathorne accuse the men of coming to overthrow the court and seek to call in the signers of their petition. Danforth, however, is interested in the claim that Proctor's servant, Mary Warren, has recanted her testimony and now swears the girls were feigning the effects of witchcraft. When Abigail haughtily denies this charge and begins to shrink from Mary's "spell," Proctor confesses his affair with Abigail. Danforth sends for the ever-truthful Elizabeth to corroborate John's claim, but insists that she be warned of nothing. Recognizing a trap of some kind and hoping to save her husband's life and reputation, Elizabeth denies the affair, destroying the last shreds of Proctor's case. As Abigail and the girls fall into another witchcraft trance, Mary Warren is overwhelmed and accuses John himself of witchcraft.

Ⓐ Elements of Literature
Motivation

❓ How do the judge's statement and questions reveal his attitude toward Martha Corey? [Possible response: He already assumes she is guilty by saying he has seen "evidence" that she is a witch. Further, he asks a leading question, implying her guilt: "Why do you hurt these children?"]

Ⓑ Reading Skills and Strategies
Interpreting a Text

❓ How have the charges against Martha Corey escalated since Act II? How do you interpret the "evidence" of fortune-telling and Martha's response to it? [Possible responses: The charges have shifted from bewitching animals (see pp. 858–859) to telling human fortunes and mysteriously hurting children. The reference to "evidence" and Martha's response indicate that Martha probably did, like many people today, believe in and practice fortune-telling, and is now being tried for this innocent superstition.]

Giles: Your Excellency, we mean no disrespect for—

Danforth: Disrespect indeed! It is disruption, Mister. This is the highest court of the supreme government of this province, do you know it?

Giles, *beginning to weep:* Your Excellency, I only said she were readin' books, sir, and they come and take her out of my house for—

Danforth, *mystified:* Books! What books?

Giles, *through helpless sobs:* It is my third wife, sir; I never had no wife that be so taken with books, and I thought to find the cause of it, d'y'see, but it were no witch I blamed her for. *He is openly weeping.* I have broke charity with the woman, I have broke charity with her. *He covers his face, ashamed.* DANFORTH *is respectfully silent.*

Hale: Excellency, he claims hard evidence for his wife's defense. I think that in all justice you must—

Danforth: Then let him submit his evidence in proper affidavit.[1] You are certainly aware of our procedure here, Mr. Hale. *To* HERRICK: Clear this room.

Herrick: Come now, Giles. *He gently pushes* COREY *out.*

Francis: We are desperate, sir; we come here three days now and cannot be heard.

Danforth: Who is this man?

Francis: Francis Nurse, Your Excellency.

Hale: His wife's Rebecca that were condemned this morning.

Danforth: Indeed! I am amazed to find you in such uproar. I have only good report of your character, Mr. Nurse.

Hathorne: I think they must both be arrested in contempt, sir.

Danforth, *to* FRANCIS: Let you write your plea, and in due time I will—

Francis: Excellency, we have proof for your eyes; God forbid you shut them to it. The girls, sir, the girls are frauds.

Danforth: What's that?

Francis: We have proof of it, sir. They are all deceiving you.

DANFORTH *is shocked, but studying* FRANCIS.

---

1. **affidavit** (af′ə·dā′vit): written statement made under oath before a legal authority.

Hathorne: This is contempt, sir, contempt!

Danforth: Peace, Judge Hathorne. Do you know who I am, Mr. Nurse?

Francis: I surely do, sir, and I think you must be a wise judge to be what you are.

Danforth: And do you know that near to four hundred are in the jails from Marblehead to Lynn, and upon my signature?

Francis: I—

Danforth: And seventy-two condemned to hang by that signature?

Francis: Excellency, I never thought to say it to such a weighty judge, but you are deceived.

Enter GILES COREY *from left. All turn to see as he beckons in* MARY WARREN *with* PROCTOR. MARY *is keeping her eyes to the ground;* PROCTOR *has her elbow as though she were near collapse.*

Parris, *on seeing her, in shock:* Mary Warren! *He goes directly to bend close to her face.* What are you about here?

Proctor, *pressing* PARRIS *away from her with a gentle but firm motion of protectiveness:* She would speak with the Deputy Governor.

Danforth, *shocked by this, turns to* HERRICK: Did you not tell me Mary Warren were sick in bed?

Herrick: She were, Your Honor. When I go to fetch her to the court last week, she said she were sick.

Giles: She has been strivin' with her soul all week, Your Honor; she comes now to tell the truth of this to you.

Danforth: Who is this?

Proctor: John Proctor, sir. Elizabeth Proctor is my wife.

Parris: Beware this man, Your Excellency, this man is mischief.

Hale, *excitedly:* I think you must hear the girl, sir, she—

Danforth, *who has become very interested in* MARY WARREN *and only raises a hand toward* HALE: Peace. What would you tell us, Mary Warren?

PROCTOR *looks at her, but she cannot speak.*

Proctor: She never saw no spirits, sir.

Danforth, *with great alarm and surprise, to* MARY: Never saw no spirits!

Giles, *eagerly:* Never.

Crossing the Curriculum

History

In 1692, the Puritans in colonial Salem were consumed with their witch hunt. Meanwhile, what was going on in the rest of the world? Have students research one or more important political, economic, scientific, or cultural events around the world at the end of the seventeenth century. Possibilities include the opening of China's ports, the "Glorious Revolution" in England, and the invention of the mercury thermometer. Have students display their findings on a time line.

Art

Many years after the witchcraft trials, compensation was offered to the victims. Many years after that, a monument was erected to their memory. Invite students to design a suitable memorial to the victims of the witchcraft trials. The monument can take any form, such as a memorial garden, statue, or plaque.

Proctor, *reaching into his jacket:* She has signed a deposition, sir—

Danforth, *instantly:* No, no, I accept no depositions. *He is rapidly calculating this; he turns from her to* PROCTOR. Tell me, Mr. Proctor, have you given out this story in the village?

Proctor: We have not.

Parris: They've come to overthrow the court, sir! This man is—

Danforth: I pray you, Mr. Parris. Do you know, Mr. Proctor, that the entire contention of the state in these trials is that the voice of Heaven is speaking through the children?

Proctor: I know that, sir.

Danforth, *thinks, staring at* PROCTOR, *then turns to* MARY WARREN: And you, Mary Warren, how came you to cry out people for sending their spirits against you?

Mary Warren: It were pretense, sir.

Danforth: I cannot hear you.

Proctor: It were pretense, she says.

Danforth: Ah? And the other girls? Susanna Walcott, and—the others? They are also pretending?

Mary Warren: Aye, sir.

Danforth, *wide-eyed:* Indeed. *Pause. He is baffled by this. He turns to study* PROCTOR'*s face.*

Parris, *in a sweat:* Excellency, you surely cannot think to let so vile a lie be spread in open court!

Danforth: Indeed not, but it strike hard upon me that she will dare come here with such a tale. Now, Mr. Proctor, before I decide whether I shall hear you or not, it is my duty to tell you this. We burn a hot fire here; it melts down all concealment.

Proctor: I know that, sir.

Danforth: Let me continue. I understand well, a husband's tenderness may drive him to extravagance in defense of a wife. Are you certain in your conscience, Mister, that your evidence is the truth?

Proctor: It is. And you will surely know it.

Danforth: And you thought to declare this revelation in the open court before the public?

Proctor: I thought I would, aye—with your permission.

Danforth, *his eyes narrowing:* Now, sir, what is your purpose in so doing?

Proctor: Why, I—I would free my wife, sir.

Danforth: There lurks nowhere in your heart, nor hidden in your spirit, any desire to undermine this court?

Proctor, *with the faintest faltering:* Why, no, sir.

Cheever, *clears his throat, awakening:* I— Your Excellency.

Danforth: Mr. Cheever.

Cheever: I think it be my duty, sir—*Kindly, to* PROCTOR: You'll not deny it, John. *To* DANFORTH: When we come to take his wife, he damned the court and ripped your warrant.

Parris: Now you have it!

Danforth: He did that, Mr. Hale?

Hale, *takes a breath:* Aye, he did.

Proctor: It were a temper, sir. I knew not what I did.

Danforth, *studying him:* Mr. Proctor.

Proctor: Aye, sir.

Danforth, *straight into his eyes:* Have you ever seen the Devil?

Proctor: No, sir.

Danforth: You are in all respects a Gospel Christian?

Proctor: I am, sir.

Parris: Such a Christian that will not come to church but once in a month!

Danforth, *restrained—he is curious:* Not come to church?

Proctor: I—I have no love for Mr. Parris. It is no secret. But God I surely love.

Cheever: He plow on Sunday, sir.

Danforth: Plow on Sunday!

Cheever, *apologetically:* I think it be evidence, John. I am an official of the court, I cannot keep it.

Proctor: I—I have once or twice plowed on Sunday. I have three children, sir, and until last year my land give little.

Giles: You'll find other Christians that do plow on Sunday if the truth be known.

Hale: Your Honor, I cannot think you may judge the man on such evidence.

Danforth: I judge nothing. *Pause. He keeps watching* PROCTOR, *who tries to meet his gaze.* I tell you straight, Mister—I have seen marvels in this court. I have seen people choked before my eyes by spirits; I have seen them stuck by pins and slashed by daggers. I have until this moment not the slightest reason to suspect that the children may be deceiving me. Do you understand my meaning?

E Elements of Literature
Motivation

? Why won't Judge Danforth accept Proctor's deposition? Why is he concerned that Proctor might have spread the story through the village? [Possible response: It may be that he wants to avoid a potentially coerced deposition, but more likely that he will do anything to make sure his theatrical testimony-driven inquisition will continue unimpeded. Danforth is worried that Proctor and his supporters might be able to undermine the authority of court.]

F Reading Skills and Strategies
Interpreting a Text

? How does this passage reinforce the play's theme, as suggested in the title? [A *crucible* is a container used in heating and melting metals. When subjected to great heat in a crucible, valuable metals are separated from baser ones. Figuratively, a *crucible* is a severe test, such as the trial Danforth alludes to here. By the end of the play, the Proctors, Rebecca, and Giles choose death rather than betrayal of others and themselves, proving that they cannot be corrupted or "melted."]

G Elements of Literature
Motivation

? Why do you think Hale tries to intervene? What is he feeling at this point in the proceedings? [Possible response: Hale is overwhelmed by the illogic and injustice of the court, as well as by guilt for his own active role in setting it up.]

Using Students' Strengths

Verbal/Interpersonal Learners

Share this excerpt from the actual examination of Sarah Good with students:

"(Hathorne) Sarah Good what evil spirit have you familiarity with

(Sarah Good) None

(H) Have you made no contract with the devil?

(G) Good answered no

(H) Why doe you hurt these children?

(G) I doe not hurt them. I scorn it.

(H) Who doe you imploy then to doe it?

(G) No creature but I am falsely accused.

(H) Why did you go away muttering from mr Parris his house?

(G) I did not mutter but I thanked him for what he gave my child.

(H) Have you made no contract with the devil?

(G) No.

(H) [The judge] desired the children all of them to look upon her, and see, if this were the person that had hurt them and so they all did looke upon her and said this was one of the persons that did torment them—presently they were all tormented. Sarah good doe you not see now what you have done why doe you not tell us the truth, why doe you thus torment these poor children?"

Have pairs of students write and enact for the class a similar scene between any of the judges and any of the citizens from Act Three. Characters should be consistent with those in the play.

T865

A Elements of Literature
Motivation

? Why is it important to the plot that Elizabeth is pregnant? [Possible response: As established earlier in the play, a pregnant woman would not be executed. Since Elizabeth is therefore safe for several months, her pregnancy removes a large part of John's motivation for giving testimony against Abigail. It also gives Danforth the wedge he needs to remove John from court.]

B Critical Thinking
Determining the Author's Purpose

? Why might Miller keep stressing Elizabeth's truthfulness? [Possible responses: It establishes her exemplary character; it is a pivotal plot element, because she will lie in a crucial, tragic moment in the play.]

C Extending the Text

? Do you agree with Danforth's assertion? Do people on trial need lawyers? Why or why not? [Possible responses: The witchcraft trials were corrupt. The chained defendants had no legal advice and no chance to prove they weren't conspiring with Satan. They could only plead guilty and be released, or plead innocent and be hanged. But even today, most people need lawyers to help them navigate complex legal systems and ensure their rights.]

D Reading Skills and Strategies

Interpreting a Text

? Why does Parris begin to sweat? [Possible response: He realizes that the petition may carry considerable weight and so fears that the court might be dismissed. As a result, he would lose status and his household might be exposed as the true source of occult practices in Salem.]

T866

Proctor: Excellency, does it not strike upon you that so many of these women have lived so long with such upright reputation, and—

Parris: Do you read the Gospel, Mr. Proctor?

Proctor: I read the Gospel.

Parris: I think not, or you should surely know that Cain were an upright man, and yet he did kill Abel.[2]

Proctor: Aye, God tells us that. *To* DANFORTH: But who tells us Rebecca Nurse murdered seven babies by sending out her spirit on them? It is the children only, and this one will swear she lied to you.

DANFORTH *considers, then beckons* HATHORNE *to him.* HATHORNE *leans in, and he speaks in his ear.* HATHORNE *nods.*

Hathorne: Aye, she's the one.

Danforth: Mr. Proctor, this morning, your wife send me a claim in which she states that she is pregnant now.

Proctor: My wife pregnant!

Danforth: There be no sign of it—we have examined her body.

Proctor: But if she say she is pregnant, then she must be! That woman will never lie, Mr. Danforth.

Danforth: She will not?

Proctor: Never, sir, never.

Danforth: We have thought it too convenient to be credited. However, if I should tell you now that I will let her be kept another month; and if she begin to show her natural signs, you shall have her living yet another year until she is delivered—what say you to that? JOHN PROCTOR *is struck silent.* Come now. You say your only purpose is to save your wife. Good, then, she is saved at least this year, and a year is long. What say you, sir? It is done now. *In conflict,* PROCTOR *glances at* FRANCIS *and* GILES. Will you drop this charge?

Proctor: I—I think I cannot.

Danforth, *now an almost imperceptible hardness in his voice:* Then your purpose is somewhat larger.

Parris: He's come to overthrow this court, Your Honor!

---

2. **Cain...Abel:** according to the Book of Genesis, Cain, the oldest son of Adam and Eve, killed his brother Abel.

866 AMERICAN DRAMA

Proctor: These are my friends. Their wives are also accused—

Danforth, *with a sudden briskness of manner:* I judge you not, sir. I am ready to hear your evidence.

Proctor: I come not to hurt the court; I only—

Danforth, *cutting him off:* Marshal, go into the court and bid Judge Stoughton and Judge Sewall declare recess for one hour. And let them go to the tavern, if they will. All witnesses and prisoners are to be kept in the building.

Herrick: Aye, sir. *Very deferentially:* If I may say it, sir, I know this man all my life. It is a good man, sir.

Danforth—*it is the reflection on himself he resents:* I am sure of it, Marshal. HERRICK *nods, then goes out.* Now, what deposition do you have for us, Mr. Proctor? And I beg you be clear, open as the sky, and honest.

Proctor, *as he takes out several papers:* I am no lawyer, so I'll—

Danforth: The pure in heart need no lawyers. Proceed as you will.

Proctor, *handing* DANFORTH *a paper:* Will you read this first, sir? It's a sort of testament. The people signing it declare their good opinion of Rebecca, and my wife, and Martha Corey. DANFORTH *looks down at the paper.*

Parris, *to enlist* DANFORTH*'s sarcasm:* Their good opinion! *But* DANFORTH *goes on reading, and* PROCTOR *is heartened.*

Proctor: These are all landholding farmers, members of the church. *Delicately, trying to point out a paragraph:* If you'll notice, sir—they've known the women many years and never saw no sign they had dealings with the Devil.

PARRIS *nervously moves over and reads over* DANFORTH*'s shoulder.*

Danforth, *glancing down a long list:* How many names are here?

Francis: Ninety-one, Your Excellency.

Parris, *sweating:* These people should be summoned. DANFORTH *looks up at him questioningly.* For questioning.

Francis, *trembling with anger:* Mr. Danforth, I gave them all my word no harm would come to them for signing this.

Parris: This is a clear attack upon the court!

Skill Link

How relevant is the setting to *The Crucible's* meaning? Remind students that the *setting* of a work of literature is the time and place where the events take place. The setting may be stated outright, or readers may have to infer it from details.

Activities

1. What details of the setting does Miller use to advance his theme?

2. How would *The Crucible* be different if it were set in the present?

3. How do the play's allegorical overtones depend on the colonial setting?

Hale, *to* PARRIS, *trying to contain himself:* Is every defense an attack upon the court? Can no one—?

Parris: All innocent and Christian people are happy for the courts in Salem! These people are gloomy for it. *To* DANFORTH *directly:* And I think you will want to know, from each and every one of them, what discontents them with you!

Hathorne: I think they ought to be examined, sir.

Danforth: It is not necessarily an attack, I think. Yet—

Francis: These are all covenanted Christians, sir.

Danforth: Then I am sure they may have nothing to fear. *Hands* CHEEVER *the paper.* Mr. Cheever, have warrants drawn for all of these—arrest for examination. *To* PROCTOR: Now, Mister, what other information do you have for us? FRANCIS *is still standing, horrified.* You may sit, Mr. Nurse.

Francis: I have brought trouble on these people; I have—

Danforth: No, old man, you have not hurt these people if they are of good conscience. But you must understand, sir, that a person is either with this court or he must be counted against it, there be no road between. This is a sharp time, now, a precise time—we live no longer in the dusky afternoon when evil mixed itself with good and befuddled the world. Now, by God's grace, the shining sun is up, and them that fear not light will surely praise it. I hope you will be one of those. MARY WARREN *suddenly sobs.* She's not hearty, I see.

Proctor: No, she's not, sir. *To* MARY, *bending to her, holding her hand, quietly:* Now remember what the angel Raphael said to the boy Tobias.[3] Remember it.

Mary Warren, *hardly audible:* Aye.

Proctor: "Do that which is good, and no harm shall come to thee."

Mary Warren: Aye.

Danforth: Come, man, we wait you.

MARSHAL HERRICK *returns, and takes his post at the door.*

Giles: John, my deposition, give him mine.

Proctor: Aye. *He hands* DANFORTH *another paper.* This is Mr. Corey's deposition.

Danforth: Oh? *He looks down at it.* Now

---

3. **Raphael...Tobias:** in the Old Testament Apocrypha, the archangel Raphael guides Tobias, an exiled Jew.

HATHORNE *comes behind him and reads with him.*

Hathorne, *suspiciously:* What lawyer drew this, Corey?

Giles: You know I never hired a lawyer in my life, Hathorne.

Danforth, *finishing the reading:* It is very well phrased. My compliments. Mr. Parris, if Mr. Putnam is in the court, will you bring him in? HATHORNE *takes the deposition, and walks to the window with it.* PARRIS *goes into the court.* You have no legal training, Mr. Corey?

Giles, *very pleased:* I have the best, sir—I am thirty-three time in court in my life. And always plaintiff, too.

Danforth: Oh, then you're much put-upon.

Giles: I am never put-upon; I know my rights, sir, and I will have them. You know, your father tried a case of mine—might be thirty-five year ago, I think.

Danforth: Indeed.

Giles: He never spoke to you of it?

Danforth: No, I cannot recall it.

Giles: That's strange, he give me nine pound damages. He were a fair judge, your father. Y'see, I had a white mare that time, and this fellow come to borrow the mare— *Enter* PARRIS *with* THOMAS PUTNAM. *When he sees* PUTNAM, GILES' *ease goes; he is hard.* Aye, there he is.

Danforth: Mr. Putnam, I have here an accusation by Mr. Corey against you. He states that you coldly prompted your daughter to cry witchery upon George Jacobs that is now in jail.

Putnam: It is a lie.

Danforth, *turning to* GILES: Mr. Putnam states your charge is a lie. What say you to that?

Giles, *furious, his fists clenched:* A fart on Thomas Putnam, that is what I say to that!

Danforth: What proof do you submit for your charge, sir?

Giles: My proof is there! *Pointing to the paper.* If Jacobs hangs for a witch he forfeit up his property—that's law! And there is none but Putnam with the coin to buy so great a piece. This man is killing his neighbors for their land!

Danforth: But proof, sir, proof.

Giles, *pointing at his deposition:* The proof is there! I have it from an honest man who heard Putnam say it! The day his daughter cried out on Jacobs, he said she'd given him a fair gift of land.

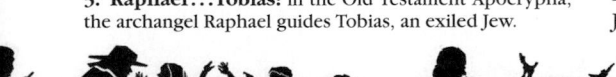

THE CRUCIBLE, ACT THREE **867**

E Elements of Literature
Motivation
? What is the flaw in Parris's assertion? Why does he make this statement? [Possible responses: Since the court is completely biased, even innocent people have reason to fear it. Parris is doing whatever he can to implicate Proctor.]

F Humanities Connections
This instruction, from the Apocryphal Book of Tobit 12:77, can also be translated as "Do good and evil will not overtake you." What do you think it means? Do you think it is good advice to give Mary? [Possible response: If the instruction literally means that no harm will come to those who do the right thing, it may not be the best advice for Mary—since it is important to do the right thing even if a situation starts to look bad. On the other hand, if the instruction is read more figuratively, as a call to maintain one's soul against moral corruption, it is good advice for everyone in the play.]

G Critical Thinking
Determining the Author's Purpose
? What purpose does Giles Corey serve in the play? [Possible responses: As this scene shows, Giles adds comic relief to a somber drama. Eccentric and slightly dotty, Giles is proud of his many bouts with the law. Giles's plight shows the absurd pretexts used to charge harmless people, once the fear of witchcraft has been roused. Under normal circumstances, no one would have taken his complaints about his wife's reading seriously. Finally, he emerges as a man of integrity and courage, dedicated to the rule of law. He will endure an agonizing death in silence in order to protect the rights of his children.]

Getting Students Involved

Cooperative Learning
Arthur Miller's plays are often considered "social dramas" since they deal with issues affecting contemporary society. Eugene O'Neill and Clifford Odets were among the American playwrights before Miller who took up various social questions.

Have students work in a "think-pair-share" to determine how *The Crucible* takes up the question of social responsibility. Students should evaluate the motivation of those who support the witchcraft persecutions, including Abigail, Parris, Putnam, and the judges, and those who do not, including John Proctor, Elizabeth Proctor, Rebecca Nurse, and Giles Corey. Have students summarize their work by deciding what social message *The Crucible* has for us today.

A Historical Connections

This section parallels the tactics used during the McCarthy era; people called before the House Un-American Activities Committee were threatened and browbeaten into revealing "fellow travelers," friends or acquaintances who might also have had Socialist or Communist sympathies. Arthur Miller himself refused to "name names" when called to testify.

B Elements of Literature
Motivation

❓ Why does Danforth try to force Giles to give the name of the man from whom he got the information? [Possible responses: Danforth's court thrives on the ability to intimidate witnesses, to make them confess, capitulate, and pass the blame on to someone else—until everyone has given in to the authority of the court. Anonymous witnesses frustrate this project. Danforth may also honestly want to try to substantiate Corey's claim against Putnam.]

C Struggling Readers
Paraphrasing

❓ What does Hale mean? How would you rephrase this comment in your own words? [Possible responses: "People are afraid of the court; we cannot ignore it any longer."]

D Reading Skills and Strategies

Interpreting a Text

❓ Is Giles correct in his assessment of Danforth? Why or why not? [Possible response: Unlike Parris, Danforth seems to have no ulterior motive to find people guilty, and his disregard for some of Parris's suggestions confirms this. Instead, he seems to be motivated by his own authoritarian vision of law and justice—a vision that makes it extremely difficult, but perhaps not impossible, for an accused person to go free.]

Hathorne: And the name of this man?
Giles, *taken aback:* What name?
Hathorne: The man that give you this information.
A Giles, *hesitates, then:* Why, I—I cannot give you his name.
Hathorne: And why not?
Giles, *hesitates, then bursts out:* You know well why not! He'll lay in jail if I give his name!
Hathorne: This is contempt of the court, Mr. Danforth!
Danforth, *to avoid that:* You will surely tell us the name.
Giles: I will not give you no name. I mentioned my wife's name once and I'll burn in hell long enough for that. I stand mute.
Danforth: In that case, I have no choice but to arrest you for contempt of this court, do you know that?
Giles: This is a hearing; you cannot clap me for contempt of a hearing.
B Danforth: Oh, it is a proper lawyer! Do you wish me to declare the court in full session here? Or will you give me good reply?
Giles, *faltering:* I cannot give you no name, sir, I cannot.
Danforth: You are a foolish old man. Mr. Cheever, begin the record. The court is now in session. I ask you, Mr. Corey—
Proctor, *breaking in:* Your Honor—he has the story in confidence, sir, and he—
Parris: The Devil lives on such confidences! *To* DANFORTH: Without confidences there could be no conspiracy, Your Honor!
Hathorne: I think it must be broken, sir.
Danforth, *to* GILES: Old man, if your informant tells the truth let him come here openly like a decent man. But if he hide in anonymity I must know why. Now sir, the government and central church demand of you the name of him who reported Mr. Thomas Putnam a common murderer.
Hale: Excellency—
Danforth: Mr. Hale.
C Hale: We cannot blink it more. There is a prodigious fear of this court in the country—
Danforth: Then there is a prodigious guilt in the country. Are *you* afraid to be questioned here?
Hale: I may only fear the Lord, sir, but there is fear in the country nevertheless.

Danforth, *angered now:* Reproach me not with the fear in the country; there is fear in the country because there is a moving plot to topple Christ in the country!
Hale: But it does not follow that everyone accused is part of it.
Danforth: No uncorrupted man may fear this court, Mr. Hale! None! *To* GILES. You are under arrest in contempt of this court. Now sit you down and take counsel with yourself, or you will be set in the jail until you decide to answer all questions.

GILES COREY *makes a rush for* PUTNAM. PROCTOR *lunges and holds him.*

Proctor: No, Giles!
Giles, *over* PROCTOR'*s shoulder at* PUTNAM: I'll cut your throat, Putnam, I'll kill you yet!
Proctor, *forcing him into a chair:* Peace, Giles, peace. *Releasing him.* We'll prove ourselves. Now we will. *He starts to turn to* DANFORTH.
D Giles: Say nothin' more, John. *Pointing at* DANFORTH: He's only playin' you! He means to hang us all!

MARY WARREN *bursts into sobs.*

Danforth: This is a court of law, Mister. I'll have no effrontery here!
Proctor: Forgive him, sir, for his old age. Peace, Giles, we'll prove it all now. *He lifts up* MARY'*s chin.* You cannot weep, Mary. Remember the angel, what he say to the boy. Hold to it, now; there is your rock. MARY *quiets. He takes out a paper, and turns to* DANFORTH. This is Mary Warren's deposition. I—I would ask you remember, sir, while you read it, that until two week ago she were no different than the other children are today. *He is speaking reasonably, restraining all his fears, his anger, his anxiety.* You saw her scream, she howled, she swore familiar spirits choked her; she even testified that Satan, in the form of women now in jail, tried to win her soul away, and then when she refused—
Danforth: We know all this.
Proctor: Aye, sir. She swears now that she never saw Satan; not any spirit, vague or clear, that Satan may have sent to hurt her. And she declares her friends are lying now.

PROCTOR *starts to hand* DANFORTH *the deposition,*

868 AMERICAN DRAMA

Using Students' Strengths

Auditory/Musical Learners

Remind students that a **ballad** is a story told in song form. Since traditional ballads were passed down by word of mouth from person to person, the words are simple and have a strong beat. Ballads often tell stories about important local events. Invite students to create a ballad summarizing the life and death of one of the main characters in *The Crucible*. Have students skim the play to find key events to include. Invite volunteers to perform their ballads for the class.

and HALE *comes up to* DANFORTH *in a trembling state.*

Hale: Excellency, a moment. I think this goes to the heart of the matter.

Danforth, *with deep misgivings:* It surely does.

Hale: I cannot say he is an honest man; I know him little. But in all justice, sir, a claim so weighty cannot be argued by a farmer. In God's name, sir, stop here; send him home and let him come again with a lawyer—

Danforth, *patiently:* Now look you, Mr. Hale—

Hale: Excellency, I have signed seventy-two death warrants; I am a minister of the Lord, and I dare not take a life without there be a proof so immaculate no slightest qualm of conscience may doubt it.

Danforth: Mr. Hale, you surely do not doubt my justice.

Hale: I have this morning signed away the soul of Rebecca Nurse, Your Honor. I'll not conceal it, my hand shakes yet as with a wound! I pray you, sir, *this* argument let lawyers present to you.

Danforth: Mr. Hale, believe me; for a man of such terrible learning you are most bewildered—I hope you will forgive me. I have been thirty-two year at the bar, sir, and I should be confounded were I called upon to defend these people. Let you consider, now— *To* PROCTOR *and the others:* And I bid you all do likewise. In an ordinary crime, how does one defend the accused? One calls up witnesses to prove his innocence. But witchcraft is *ipso facto,*[4] on its face and by its nature, an invisible crime, is it not? Therefore, who may possibly be witness to it? The witch and the victim. None other. Now we cannot hope the witch will accuse herself; granted? Therefore, we must rely upon her victims—and they do testify, the children certainly do testify. As for the witches, none will deny that we are most eager for all their confessions. Therefore, what is left for a lawyer to bring out? I think I have made my point. Have I not?

Hale: But this child claims the girls are not truthful, and if they are not—

Danforth: That is precisely what I am about to consider, sir. What more may you ask of me? Unless you doubt my probity?[5]

4. **ipso facto:** by that very fact.
5. **probity:** integrity.

Hale, *defeated:* I surely do not, sir. Let you consider it, then.

Danforth: And let you put your heart to rest. Her deposition, Mr. Proctor.

PROCTOR *hands it to him.* HATHORNE *rises, goes beside* DANFORTH, *and starts reading.* PARRIS *comes to his other side.* DANFORTH *looks at* JOHN PROCTOR, *then proceeds to read.* HALE *gets up, finds position near the judge, reads too.* PROCTOR *glances at* GILES. FRANCIS *prays silently, hands pressed together.* CHEEVER *waits placidly, the sublime official, dutiful.* MARY WARREN *sobs once.* JOHN PROCTOR *touches her head reassuringly. Presently* DANFORTH *lifts his eyes, stands up, takes out a kerchief and blows his nose. The others stand aside as he moves in thought toward the window.*

Parris, *hardly able to contain his anger and fear:* I should like to question—

Danforth—*his first real outburst, in which his contempt for* PARRIS *is clear:* Mr. Parris, I bid you be silent! *He stands in silence, looking out the window. Now, having established that he will set the gait:* Mr. Cheever, will you go into the court and bring the children here? CHEEVER *gets up and goes out upstage.* DANFORTH *now turns to* MARY. Mary Warren, how came you to this turnabout? Has Mr. Proctor threatened you for this deposition?

Mary Warren: No, sir.

Danforth: Has he ever threatened you?

Mary Warren, *weaker:* No, sir.

Danforth, *sensing a weakening:* Has he threatened you?

Mary Warren: No, sir.

Danforth: Then you tell me that you sat in my court, callously lying, when you knew that people would hang by your evidence? *She does not answer.* Answer me!

Mary Warren, *almost inaudibly:* I did, sir.

Danforth: How were you instructed in your life? Do you not know that God damns all liars? *She cannot speak.* Or is it now that you lie?

Mary Warren: No, sir—I am with God now.

Danforth: You are with God now.

Mary Warren: Aye, sir.

Danforth, *containing himself:* I will tell you this—you are either lying now, or you were lying in the court, and in either case you have commit-

A Reading Skills and Strategies

Interpreting a Text

❓ What does Mary mean by "I am with God"? Do you think the pressure will cause Mary to recant her story? Why or why not? [Possible responses: She means that she is now telling the truth and that God will protect her. Mary is weak, so it is possible she will crumble under the pressure, but she might cling to the truth and stay strong.]

B Elements of Literature

Motivation

❓ Why is Danforth being so deliberate and careful in his questioning of Abigail and her followers? [Possible response: The entire trial hinges on Mary's testimony, for it has the power to discredit Abigail. If Abigail is revealed to be a liar, the court's entire case against the "witches" will collapse.] What assumption does Danforth make here about the faith of Abigail and the girls? Why is this a mistake? [Danforth assumes that the girls have a deep fear of and faith in God, and that by highlighting the sin of false witness, he will shake them into admitting any dishonesty. This is a mistake because the girls seem to view faith as an abstraction that has little to do with their own behavior; Abigail in particular seems to view religion as little more than a tool to manipulate others with—a lack of faith that the murder of her parents and her affair with Proctor may have instilled in her.]

C Critical Thinking

Analyzing

❓ What does this passage reveal about Abigail's character? [Possible response: She comes across as brazen, ruthless, and amoral.]

D Reading Skills and Strategies

Making Predictions

❓ How far do you think John Proctor will go to save his wife? What reason will he give to explain his accusation that Abigail wants to murder Elizabeth? [Possible response: John will tell the court the truth about his affair with Abigail, even though it will disgrace him.]

---

ted perjury and you will go to jail for it. You cannot lightly say you lied, Mary. Do you know that?

Mary Warren: I cannot lie no more. I am with God, I am with God.

But she breaks into sobs at the thought of it, and the right door opens, and enter SUSANNA WALCOTT, MERCY LEWIS, BETTY PARRIS, *and finally* ABIGAIL. CHEEVER *comes to* DANFORTH.

Cheever: Ruth Putnam's not in the court, sir, nor the other children.

Danforth: These will be sufficient. Sit you down, children. *Silently they sit.* Your friend, Mary Warren, has given us a deposition. In which she swears that she never saw familiar spirits, apparitions, nor any manifest of the Devil. She claims as well that none of you have seen these things either. *Slight pause.* Now, children, this is a court of law. The law, based upon the Bible, and the Bible, writ by Almighty God, forbid the practice of witchcraft, and describe death as the penalty thereof. But likewise, children, the law and Bible damn all bearers of false witness. *Slight pause.* Now then. It does not escape me that this deposition may be devised to blind us; it may well be that Mary Warren has been conquered by Satan, who sends her here to distract our sacred purpose. If so, her neck will break for it. But if she speak true, I bid you now drop your guile and confess your pretense, for a quick confession will go easier with you. *Pause.* Abigail Williams, rise. ABIGAIL *slowly rises.* Is there any truth in this?

Abigail: No, sir.

Danforth, *thinks, glances at* MARY, *then back to* ABIGAIL: Children, a very augur bit[6] will now be turned into your souls until your honesty is proved. Will either of you change your positions now, or do you force me to hard questioning?

Abigail: I have naught to change, sir. She lies.

Danforth, *to* MARY: You would still go on with this?

Mary Warren, *faintly:* Aye, sir.

Danforth, *turning to* ABIGAIL: A poppet were discovered in Mr. Proctor's house, stabbed by a needle. Mary Warren claims that you sat beside her in the court when she made it, and that you saw her make it and witnessed how she herself stuck her

6. **augur bit:** drilling tool with pointed end and spiral grooves. (The conventional spelling is *auger*.)

---

needle into it for safe-keeping. What say you to that?

Abigail, *with a slight note of indignation:* It is a lie, sir.

Danforth, *after a slight pause:* While you worked for Mr. Proctor, did you see poppets in that house?

Abigail: Goody Proctor always kept poppets.

Proctor: Your Honor, my wife never kept no poppets. Mary Warren confesses it was her poppet.

Cheever: Your Excellency.

Danforth: Mr. Cheever.

Cheever: When I spoke with Goody Proctor in that house, she said she never kept no poppets. But she said she did keep poppets when she were a girl.

Proctor: She has not been a girl these fifteen years, Your Honor.

Hathorne: But a poppet will keep fifteen years, will it not?

Proctor: It will keep if it is kept, but Mary Warren swears she never saw no poppets in my house, nor anyone else.

Parris: Why could there not have been poppets hid where no one ever saw them?

Proctor, *furious:* There might also be a dragon with five legs in my house, but no one has ever seen it.

Parris: We are here, Your Honor, precisely to discover what no one has ever seen.

Proctor: Mr. Danforth, what profit this girl to turn herself about? What may Mary Warren gain but hard questioning and worse?

Danforth: You are charging Abigail Williams with a marvelous cool plot to murder, do you understand that?

Proctor: I do, sir. I believe she means to murder.

Danforth, *pointing at* ABIGAIL, *incredulously:* This child would murder your wife?

Proctor: It is not a child. Now hear me, sir. In the sight of the congregation she were twice this year put out of this meetin' house for laughter during prayer.

Danforth, *shocked, turning to* ABIGAIL: What's this? Laughter during—!

Parris: Excellency, she were under Tituba's power at that time, but she is solemn now.

Giles: Aye, now she is solemn and goes to hang people!

Crossing the Curriculum

Geography

To help his audience visualize colonial New England, Miller mentions a number of important towns. Have students use a map of the northeast United States to locate each of the following towns: Salem, Beverly, Narrangansett, Andover, Marblehead, Lynn. Students should then use the map to show how the witchcraft hysteria spread down the New England coast.

Media

Since its debut on January 22, 1953, *The Crucible* has rarely been off the stage. The paperback editions have sold more than six million copies. Nonetheless, there have been only two filmed versions of the play. Invite students to select a cast of twenty-one actors for a third film version. After the name of each actor, have students write a brief paragraph explaining why that performer would be a good choice for the role.

Danforth: Quiet, man.

Hathorne: Surely it have no bearing on the question, sir. He charges contemplation of murder.

Danforth: Aye. *He studies* ABIGAIL *for a moment, then:* Continue, Mr. Proctor.

Proctor: Mary. Now tell the Governor how you danced in the woods.

Parris, *instantly:* Excellency, since I come to Salem this man is blackening my name. He—

Danforth: In a moment, sir. *To* MARY WARREN, *sternly, and surprised:* What is this dancing?

Mary Warren: I— *She glances at* ABIGAIL, *who is staring down at her remorselessly. Then, appealing to* PROCTOR: Mr. Proctor—

Proctor, *taking it right up:* Abigail leads the girls to the woods, Your Honor, and they have danced there naked—

Parris: Your Honor, this—

Proctor, *at once:* Mr. Parris discovered them himself in the dead of night! There's the "child" she is!

Danforth—*it is growing into a nightmare, and he turns, astonished, to* PARRIS: Mr. Parris—

Parris: I can only say, sir, that I never found any of them naked, and this man is—

Danforth: But you discovered them dancing in the woods? *Eyes on* PARRIS, *he points at* ABIGAIL. Abigail?

Hale: Excellency, when I first arrived from Beverly, Mr. Parris told me that.

Danforth: Do you deny it, Mr. Parris?

Parris: I do not, sir, but I never saw any of them naked.

Danforth: But she have *danced?*

Parris, *unwillingly:* Aye, sir.

DANFORTH, *as though with new eyes, looks at* ABIGAIL.

Hathorne: Excellency, will you permit me? *He points at* MARY WARREN.

Danforth, *with great worry:* Pray, proceed.

Hathorne: You say you never saw no spirits, Mary, were never threatened or afflicted by any manifest of the Devil or the Devil's agents.

Mary Warren, *very faintly:* No, sir.

Hathorne, *with a gleam of victory:* And yet, when people accused of witchery confronted you in court, you would faint, saying their spirits came out of their bodies and choked you—

Mary Warren: That were pretense, sir.

Danforth: I cannot hear you.

Mary Warren: Pretense, sir.

Parris: But you did turn cold, did you not? I myself picked you up many times, and your skin were icy. Mr. Danforth, you—

Danforth: I saw that many times.

Proctor: She only pretended to faint, Your Excellency. They're all marvelous pretenders.

Hathorne: Then can she pretend to faint now?

Proctor: Now?

Parris: Why not? Now there are no spirits attacking her, for none in this room is accused of witchcraft. So let her turn herself cold now, let her pretend she is attacked now, let her faint. *He turns to* MARY WARREN. Faint!

Mary Warren: Faint?

Parris: Aye, faint. Prove to us how you pretended in the court so many times.

Mary Warren, *looking to* PROCTOR: I—cannot faint now, sir.

Proctor, *alarmed, quietly:* Can you not pretend it?

Mary Warren: I— *She looks about as though searching for the passion to faint.* I—have no *sense* of it now, I—

Danforth: Why? What is lacking now?

Mary Warren: I—cannot tell, sir, I—

Danforth: Might it be that here we have no afflicting spirit loose, but in the court there were some?

Mary Warren: I never saw no spirits.

Parris: Then see no spirits now, and prove to us that you can faint by your own will, as you claim.

Mary Warren, *stares, searching for the emotion of it, and then shakes her head:* I—cannot do it.

Parris: Then you will confess, will you not? It were attacking spirits made you faint!

Mary Warren: No, sir, I—

Parris: Your Excellency, this is a trick to blind the court!

Mary Warren: It's not a trick! *She stands.* I—I used to faint because I—I thought I saw spirits.

Danforth: *Thought* you saw them!

Mary Warren: But I did not, Your Honor.

Hathorne: How could you think you saw them unless you saw them?

Mary Warren: I—I cannot tell how, but I did. I—I heard the other girls screaming, and you, Your Honor, you seemed to believe them, and I— It

THE CRUCIBLE, ACT THREE **871**

E **Elements of Literature**
Motivation
? Why does Parris keep interrupting the court proceedings? [Possible response: He knows that the girls are lying and he wants to make sure their story doesn't crumble under investigation. He is trying to make sure that Proctor and his supporters will be found guilty.]

F **Reading Skills and Strategies**
Interpreting a Text
? At first, the judges presented a united front: stern, forbidding, and prejudiced. Now, however, it becomes apparent they are not all assessing the situation the same way. What differences in attitude do you see between Hathorne and Danforth here? [Possible response: Danforth has serious doubts about the girls' story and realizes that Parris knows much more than he has admitted. Hathorne, in contrast, seems determined to support Abigail and discredit Mary and John, despite evidence that supports their story.]

G **Elements of Literature**
Motivation
? Why can't Mary Warren faint now? What *is* lacking? [Possible response: Mary fainted each time because she was caught up in the frenzied, terror-stricken mood of the other girls. Now, she does not feel the same emotions.] **What is wrong with Danforth's understanding of how Mary has "pretended"?** [Possible response: Danforth has a legalistic understanding of pretending as a deliberate, calculated attempt to deceive—which misses the spontaneous power of group psychology that was at the root of Mary's fainting.]

Skill Link

Dramatic Power

The Crucible is an effective drama on the stage for several reasons. First, point out the strong conflict, a basis for good theater. Then, discuss the play's suspense and how it is maintained: Will Mary Warren's testimony be accepted? Will Elizabeth confirm Proctor's confession? Will Hale be able to postpone the executions? Thirdly, the characters, from cranky Giles Corey to heroic John Proctor, are complex and fascinating.

Activities

1. Have students decide which conflicts in *The Crucible* are the most exciting and why. Students should consider how Proctor and Corey align themselves against Putnam and Parris, the conflicts between John and Elizabeth, and the trial confrontations.

2. Since the penalty for conviction in the trials is death, the stakes throughout are high. Have students trace how Miller builds suspense to the play's climax.

3. A play becomes more interesting if the audience cares about the characters. As *The Crucible* proceeds, we find ourselves concerned with the fate of the men and women whose lives are so unjustly jeopardized. Have students decide which characters they care for most and why.

? How is Abigail's attitude toward the judges different from the attitude the other witnesses show? How can you explain this difference? [Possible responses: Abigail is brash and fearless; the other characters, in contrast, are deferential and fearful. Abigail knows she has the upper hand and is determined to exercise her power to the fullest.]

B Historical Connections

The famous "crying out" scene has been compared to Senator Joseph McCarthy's attack on the Army, which brought the Communist "witch hunt" trials to their climax. Invite interested students to do appropriate research and create a comparison-contrast chart of the 1692 Salem witch hunt as portrayed in *The Crucible* and the 1950s Communist investigations. Students should consider similarities and differences among characters, events, and settings.

---

were only sport in the beginning, sir, but then the whole world cried spirits, spirits, and I—I promise you, Mr. Danforth, I only thought I saw them but I did not.

DANFORTH *peers at her.*

Parris, *smiling, but nervous because* DANFORTH *seems to be struck by* MARY WARREN'*s story:* Surely Your Excellency is not taken by this simple lie.

Danforth, *turning worriedly to* ABIGAIL: Abigail. I bid you now search your heart and tell me this—and beware of it, child, to God every soul is precious and His vengeance is terrible on them that take life without cause. Is it possible, child, that the spirits you have seen are illusion only, some deception that may cross your mind when—

Abigail: Why, this—this—is a base question, sir.

Danforth: Child, I would have you consider it—

Abigail: I have been hurt, Mr. Danforth; I have seen my blood runnin' out! I have been near to murdered every day because I done my duty pointing out the Devil's people—and this is my reward? To be mistrusted, denied, questioned like a—

Danforth, *weakening:* Child, I do not mistrust you—

Abigail, *in an open threat:* Let *you* beware, Mr. Danforth. Think you to be so mighty that the power of Hell may not turn *your* wits? Beware of it! There is— *Suddenly, from an accusatory attitude, her face turns, looking into the air above—it is truly frightened.*

Danforth, *apprehensively:* What is it, child?

Abigail, *looking about in the air, clasping her arms about her as though cold:* I—I know not. A wind, a cold wind, has come. *Her eyes fall on* MARY WARREN.

Mary Warren, *terrified, pleading:* Abby!

Mercy Lewis, *shivering:* Your Honor, I freeze!

Proctor: They're pretending!

Hathorne, *touching* ABIGAIL'*s hand:* She is cold, Your Honor, touch her!

Mercy Lewis, *through chattering teeth:* Mary, do you send this shadow on me?

Mary Warren: Lord, save me!

Susanna Walcott: I freeze, I freeze!

Abigail, *shivering visibly:* It is a wind, a wind!

Mary Warren: Abby, don't do that!

"Do you witch her?"

Taking a Second Look

Review: Interpreting a Play

Remind students that the *theme* of a literary work is its main idea, a general statement about life. The theme can be stated outright in the work, or readers may infer it from details about plot, characters, and setting. Point out that many works of literature have more than one theme.

Activity

Present the following four themes from *The Crucible:*

- Fear and suspicion can destroy society.

- People can use the ideas of virtue and piety to advance a selfish or malevolent agenda.
- People who claim to be good may be hypocrites.
- It may be better to die with integrity than to compromise your honor, decency, and faith in order to live.

Have students find one or more passages from *The Crucible* that illustrate each of these themes. Students should copy the passage and explain in their own words how it expresses the play's theme.

Danforth, *himself engaged and entered by* ABI-GAIL: Mary Warren, do you witch her? I say to you, do you send your spirit out?

With a hysterical cry MARY WARREN *starts to run.* PROCTOR *catches her.*

Mary Warren, *almost collapsing:* Let me go, Mr. Proctor, I cannot, I cannot—
Abigail, *crying to Heaven:* Oh, Heavenly Father, take away this shadow!

Without warning or hesitation, PROCTOR *leaps at* ABIGAIL *and, grabbing her by the hair, pulls her to her feet. She screams in pain.* DANFORTH, *astonished, cries, "What are you about?" and* HATHORNE *and* PARRIS *call, "Take your hands off her!" and out of it all comes* PROCTOR'S *roaring voice.*

Proctor: How do you call Heaven! Whore! Whore!

HERRICK *breaks* PROCTOR *from her.*

Herrick: John!
Danforth: Man! Man, what do you—
Proctor, *breathless and in agony:* It is a whore!
Danforth, *dumfounded:* You charge—?
Abigail: Mr. Danforth, he is lying!
Proctor: Mark her! Now she'll suck a scream to stab me with, but—
Danforth: You will prove this! This will not pass!
Proctor, *trembling, his life collapsing about him:* I have known her, sir. I have known her.
Danforth: You—you are a lecher?
Francis, *horrified:* John, you cannot say such a—
Proctor: Oh, Francis, I wish you had some evil in you that you might know me! *To* DANFORTH: A man will not cast away his good name. You surely know that.
Danforth, *dumfounded:* In—in what time? In what place?
Proctor, *his voice about to break, and his shame great:* In the proper place—where my beasts are bedded. On the last night of my joy, some eight months past. She used to serve me in my house, sir. *He has to clamp his jaw to keep from weeping.* A man may think God sleeps, but God sees everything, I know it now. I beg you, sir, I beg you—see her what she is. My wife, my dear good wife, took this girl soon after, sir, and put her

out on the highroad. And being what she is, a lump of vanity, sir— *He is being overcome.* Excellency, forgive me, forgive me. *Angrily against himself, he turns away from the Governor for a moment. Then, as though to cry out is his only means of speech left:* She thinks to dance with me on my wife's grave! And well she might, for I thought of her softly. God help me, I lusted, and there *is* a promise in such sweat. But it is a whore's vengeance, and you must see it; I set myself entirely in your hands. I know you must see it now.

Danforth, *blanched, in horror, turning to* ABIGAIL: You deny every scrap and tittle of this?
Abigail: If I must answer that, I will leave and I will not come back again!

DANFORTH *seems unsteady.*

Proctor: I have made a bell of my honor! I have rung the doom of my good name—you will believe me, Mr. Danforth! My wife is innocent, except she knew a whore when she saw one!
Abigail, *stepping up to* DANFORTH: What look do you give me? DANFORTH *cannot speak.* I'll not have such looks! *She turns and starts for the door.*
Danforth: You will remain where you are! HERRICK *steps into her path. She comes up short, fire in her eyes.* Mr. Parris, go into the court and bring Goodwife Proctor out.
Parris, *objecting:* Your Honor, this is all a—
Danforth, *sharply to* PARRIS: Bring her out! And tell her not one word of what's been spoken here. And let you knock before you enter. PARRIS *goes out.* Now we shall touch the bottom of this swamp. *To* PROCTOR: Your wife, you say, is an honest woman.
Proctor: In her life, sir, she have never lied. There are them that cannot sing, and them that cannot weep—my wife cannot lie. I have paid much to learn it, sir.
Danforth: And when she put this girl out of your house, she put her out for a harlot?
Proctor: Aye, sir.
Danforth: And knew her for a harlot?
Proctor: Aye, sir, she knew her for a harlot.
Danforth: Good then. *To* ABIGAIL: And if she tell me, child, it were for harlotry, may God spread His mercy on you! *There is a knock. He calls to the door.* Hold! *To* ABIGAIL: Turn your back. Turn your

THE CRUCIBLE, ACT THREE 873

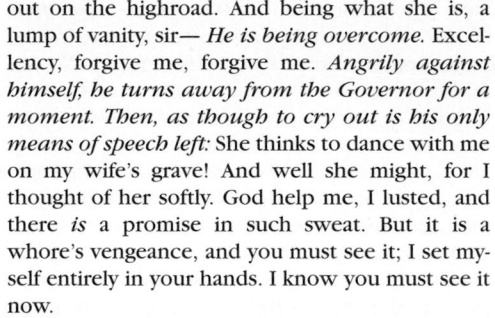

C Critical Thinking
Identifying Author's Purpose
? Why does Miller have John admit his guilt this way rather than through a letter or petition, for example? What does this scene accomplish? [Possible responses: By presenting the truth this way, Miller builds the rising action closer to the climax and creates great drama and excitement.]

D Elements of Literature
Motivation
? Why does John reveal his affair with Abigail? [Possible responses: John has no other choice if he wishes to save Elizabeth (as well as the wives of his friends). The hysteria has built to such a fever pitch that only revealing Abigail as a fraud can possibly reverse the tide.]

E Struggling Readers
Paraphrasing
? What does Proctor mean by "the last night of my joy"? What is he saying about the past eight months? [Proctor means that the night he became involved with Abigail, he destroyed his happiness and has not been able to recover it since then.]

F Appreciating Language
Figures of Speech
? What does this metaphor mean? How does it capture Proctor's situation? [Possible responses: It means that he is announcing his own destruction, the end of his reputation and respect in the community. The name Proctor will now be a synonym for lechery and deceit.]

Using Students' Strengths

Verbal Learners
At the beginning of the witch hunt, Elizabeth warned John that Abigail wanted her dead so that she could marry John. Divide the class in half to debate whether John could have prevented the witch hunt if he had revealed Abigail as a fraud when Elizabeth asked. To what extent is John to blame for the tragedy? Guide students to cite specific details from the text to support their contention.

Interpersonal Learners
John correctly states that his confession has tarnished his good name, perhaps irreparably, given the nature of his crime in his time and place. Yet many people do rebound from setbacks such as this one. If given the chance, how could John restore his reputation and good standing in the community? Make a list of at least five methods he could use.

A Reading Skills and Strategies

Interpreting a Text

❓ Why does Danforth have John and Abigail turn their backs on Elizabeth? What is the problem with this strategy? [Danforth hopes to prevent Elizabeth's testimony from being influenced by any signal or body language from John or Abigail, so that her honesty will settle the question. The problem with this idea is that it will indicate to Elizabeth that *something* monumental hinges on her answer—perhaps the life or death of her husband—and will make it more likely that she will lie to protect him.]

B Critical Thinking

Analyzing

❓ Is Elizabeth's assessment of John as a "good and righteous man" correct? Why or why not? [Possible response: Yes, because at root, John is a strong, ethical man struggling to find the courage and discipline to consistently live up to what he knows is right.]

C Elements of Literature

Motivation

❓ Earlier, we learned that Elizabeth never lies. Why, then, does she lie here? How is her action ironic? [Possible responses: She loves her husband and will perjure herself to save his life. Ironically, in trying to save her husband, Elizabeth condemns him.]

D Critical Thinking

Making Connections

❓ When Hale identifies "private vengeance" as the source of the testimony, whose words does he echo? From where in the play? [He echoes Proctor himself, after his wife's arrest in Act Two, p. 860.]

---

back. *To* PROCTOR: Do likewise. *Both turn their backs—* ABIGAIL *with indignant slowness.* Now let neither of you turn to face Goody Proctor. No one in this room is to speak one word, or raise a gesture aye or nay. *He turns toward the door, calls:* Enter! *The door opens.* ELIZABETH *enters with* PARRIS. PARRIS *leaves her. She stands alone, her eyes looking for* PROCTOR. Mr. Cheever, report this testimony in all exactness. Are you ready?

Cheever: Ready, sir.

Danforth: Come here, woman. ELIZABETH *comes to him, glancing at* PROCTOR'S *back.* Look at me only, not at your husband. In my eyes only.

Elizabeth, *faintly:* Good, sir.

Danforth: We are given to understand that at one time you dismissed your servant, Abigail Williams.

Elizabeth: That is true, sir.

Danforth: For what cause did you dismiss her? *Slight pause. Then* ELIZABETH *tries to glance at* PROCTOR. You will look in my eyes only and not at your husband. The answer is in your memory and you need no help to give it to me. Why did you dismiss Abigail Williams?

Elizabeth, *not knowing what to say, sensing a situation, wetting her lips to stall for time:* She—dissatisfied me. *Pause.* And my husband.

Danforth: In what way dissatisfied you?

Elizabeth: She were— *She glances at* PROCTOR *for a cue.*

Danforth: Woman, look at me! ELIZABETH *does.* Were she slovenly? Lazy? What disturbance did she cause?

Elizabeth: Your Honor, I—in that time I were sick. And I—My husband is a good and righteous man. He is never drunk as some are, nor wastin' his time at the shovelboard, but always at his work. But in my sickness—you see, sir. I were a long time sick after my last baby, and I thought I saw my husband somewhat turning from me. And this girl— *She turns to* ABIGAIL.

Danforth: Look at me.

Elizabeth: Aye, sir. Abigail Williams— *She breaks off.*

Danforth: What of Abigail Williams?

Elizabeth: I came to think he fancied her. And so one night I lost my wits, I think, and put her out on the highroad.

Danforth: Your husband—did he indeed turn from you?

Elizabeth, *in agony:* My husband—is a goodly man, sir.

Danforth: Then he did not turn from you.

Elizabeth, *starting to glance at* PROCTOR: He—

Danforth, *reaches out and holds her face, then:* Look at me! To your own knowledge, has John Proctor ever committed the crime of lechery? *In a crisis of indecision she cannot speak.* Answer my question! Is your husband a lecher!

Elizabeth, *faintly:* No, sir.

Danforth: Remove her, Marshal.

Proctor: Elizabeth, tell the truth!

Danforth: She has spoken. Remove her!

Proctor, *crying out:* Elizabeth, I have confessed it!

Elizabeth: Oh, God! *The door closes behind her.*

Proctor: She only thought to save my name!

Hale: Excellency, it is a natural lie to tell; I beg you, stop now before another is condemned! I may shut my conscience to it no more—private vengeance is working through this testimony! From the beginning this man has struck me true. By my oath to Heaven, I believe him now, and I pray you call back his wife before we—

Danforth: She spoke nothing of lechery, and this man has lied!

Hale: I believe him! *Pointing at* ABIGAIL: This girl has always struck me false! She has—

ABIGAIL, *with a weird, wild, chilling cry, screams up to the ceiling.*

Abigail: You will not! Begone! Begone, I say!

Danforth: What is it, child? *But* ABIGAIL, *pointing with fear, is now raising up her frightened eyes, her awed face, toward the ceiling—the girls are doing the same—and now* HATHORNE, HALE, PUTNAM, CHEEVER, HERRICK, *and* DANFORTH *do the same.* What's there? *He lowers his eyes from the ceiling, and now he is frightened; there is real tension in his voice.* Child! *She is transfixed—with all the girls, she is whimpering open-mouthed, agape at the ceiling.* Girls! Why do you—?

Mercy Lewis, *pointing:* It's on the beam! Behind the rafter!

Danforth, *looking up:* Where!

Abigail: Why—? *She gulps.* Why do you come, yellow bird?

Proctor: Where's a bird? I see no bird!

Abigail, *to the ceiling:* My face? My face?

874 AMERICAN DRAMA

Assessing Learning

Proctor: Mr. Hale—

Danforth: Be quiet!

Proctor, *to* HALE: Do you see a bird?

Danforth: Be quiet!!

Abigail, *to the ceiling, in a genuine conversation with the "bird," as though trying to talk it out of attacking her:* But God made my face; you cannot want to tear my face. Envy is a deadly sin, Mary.

Mary Warren, *on her feet with a spring, and horrified, pleading:* Abby!

Abigail, *unperturbed, continuing to the "bird":* Oh, Mary, this is a black art to change your shape. No, I cannot, I cannot stop my mouth; it's God's work I do.

Mary Warren: Abby, I'm *here!*

Proctor, *frantically:* They're pretending, Mr. Danforth!

Abigail—*now she takes a backward step, as though in fear the bird will swoop down momentarily:* Oh, please, Mary! Don't come down.

Susanna Walcott: Her claws, she's stretching her claws!

Proctor: Lies, lies.

Abigail, *backing further, eyes still fixed above:* Mary, please don't hurt me!

Mary Warren, *to* DANFORTH: I'm not hurting her!

Danforth, *to* MARY WARREN: Why does she see this vision?

Mary Warren: She sees nothin'!

Abigail, *now staring full front as though hypnotized, and mimicking the exact tone of* MARY WARREN's *cry:* She sees nothin'!

Mary Warren, *pleading:* Abby, you mustn't!

Abigail and All the Girls, *all transfixed:* Abby, you mustn't!

Mary Warren, *to all the girls:* I'm here, I'm here!

Girls: I'm here, I'm here!

Danforth, *horrified:* Mary Warren! Draw back your spirit out of them!

Mary Warren: Mr. Danforth!

Girls, *cutting her off:* Mr. Danforth!

Danforth: Have you compacted with the Devil? Have you?

Mary Warren: Never, never!

Girls: Never, never!

Danforth, *growing hysterical:* Why can they only repeat you?

Proctor: Give me a whip—I'll stop it!

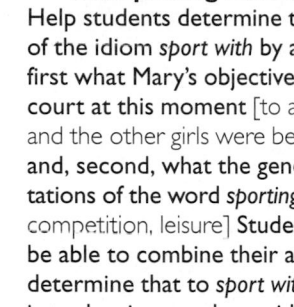

Mary Warren: They're sporting. They—!

Girls: They're sporting!

Mary Warren, *turning on them all hysterically and stamping her feet:* Abby, stop it!

Girls, *stamping their feet:* Abby, stop it!

Mary Warren: Stop it!

Girls: Stop it!

Mary Warren, *screaming it out at the top of her lungs, and raising her fists:* Stop it!!

Girls, *raising their fists:* Stop it!!

MARY WARREN, *utterly confounded, and becoming overwhelmed by* ABIGAIL's—*and the girls'—utter conviction, starts to whimper, hands half raised, powerless, and all the girls begin whimpering exactly as she does.*

Danforth: A little while ago you were afflicted. Now it seems you afflict others; where did you find this power?

Mary Warren, *staring at* ABIGAIL: I—have no power.

Girls: I have no power.

Proctor: They're gulling you, Mister!

Danforth: Why did you turn about this past two weeks? You have seen the Devil, have you not?

Hale, *indicating* ABIGAIL *and the girls:* You cannot believe them!

Mary Warren: I—

Proctor, *sensing her weakening:* Mary, God damns all liars!

Danforth, *pounding it into her:* You have seen the Devil, you have made compact with Lucifer, have you not?

Proctor: God damns liars, Mary!

MARY *utters something unintelligible, staring at* ABIGAIL, *who keeps watching the "bird" above.*

Danforth: I cannot hear you. What do you say? MARY *utters again unintelligibly.* You will confess yourself or you will hang! *He turns her roughly to face him.* Do you know who I am? I say you will hang if you do not open with me!

Proctor: Mary, remember the angel Raphael—do that which is good and—

Abigail, *pointing upward:* The wings! Her wings are spreading! Mary, please, don't, don't—!

Hale: I see nothing, Your Honor!

Danforth: Do you confess this power! *He is an inch from her face.* Speak!

Crossing the Curriculum

Theater

One of the values in reading a work like *The Crucible* is that in any given year you might be able to see a live performance of the play. Seeing a play after reading its script provides a unique perspective. For one thing we know how the plot is resolved. We also know the significance of all the clues: If a gun is left in a drawer in Act 1, we know how that gun will be used in Act 3. As a result, some of the suspense will be missing. However, we will also see new things in the play. We will notice movements and facial expressions that clarify motives. We will see how the characters dress and how the people onstage relate to one another.

Encourage students to attend a performance of *The Crucible* at some time during the year. Have them meet in groups later and list facets of the performance that surprised them or confused them or clarified a situation for them. Finally, have them read reviews of the performance and analyze the critics' observations and compare them with their own.

Abigail: She's going to come down! She's walking the beam!

Danforth: Will you speak!

A **Mary Warren,** *staring in horror:* I cannot!

Girls: I cannot!

Parris: Cast the Devil out! Look him in the face! Trample him! We'll save you, Mary, only stand fast against him and—

Abigail, *looking up:* Look out! She's coming down!

She and all the girls run to one wall, shielding their eyes. And now, as though cornered, they let out a gigantic scream, and MARY, *as though infected, opens her mouth and screams with them. Gradually* ABIGAIL *and the girls leave off, until only* MARY *is left there, staring up at the "bird," screaming madly. All watch her, horrified by this evident fit.* PROCTOR *strides to her.*

Proctor: Mary, tell the Governor what they— *He has hardly got a word out, when, seeing him coming for her, she rushes out of his reach, screaming in horror.*

B **Mary Warren:** Don't touch me—don't touch me! *At which the girls halt at the door.*

Proctor, *astonished:* Mary!

Mary Warren, *pointing at* PROCTOR: You're the Devil's man!

He is stopped in his tracks.

Parris: Praise God!

Girls: Praise God!

C **Proctor,** *numbed:* Mary, how—?

Mary Warren: I'll not hang with you! I love God, I love God.

Danforth, *to* MARY: He bid you do the Devil's work?

Mary Warren, *hysterically, indicating* PROCTOR: He come at me by night and every day to sign, to sign, to—

Danforth: Sign what?

Parris: The Devil's book? He come with a book?

Mary Warren, *hysterically, pointing at* PROCTOR, *fearful of him:* My name, he want my name. "I'll murder you," he says, "if my wife hangs! We must go and overthrow the court," he says!

DANFORTH's *head jerks toward* PROCTOR, *shock and horror in his face.*

Proctor, *turning, appealing to* HALE: Mr. Hale!

Mary Warren, *her sobs beginning:* He wake me every night, his eyes were like coals and his fingers claw my neck, and I sign, I sign . . .

Hale: Excellency, this child's gone wild!

Proctor, *as* DANFORTH's *wide eyes pour on him:* Mary, Mary!

Mary Warren, *screaming at him:* No, I love God; I go your way no more. I love God, I bless God. *Sobbing, she rushes to* ABIGAIL. Abby, Abby, I'll never hurt you more! *They all watch, as* ABIGAIL, *out of her infinite charity, reaches out and draws the sobbing* MARY *to her, and then looks up to* DANFORTH.

Danforth, *to* PROCTOR: What are you? PROCTOR *is beyond speech in his anger.* You are combined with anti-Christ,[7] are you not? I have seen your power; you will not deny it! What say you, Mister?

Hale: Excellency—

Danforth: I will have nothing from you, Mr. Hale! *To* PROCTOR: Will you confess yourself befouled with Hell, or do you keep that black allegiance yet? What say you?

D **Proctor,** *his mind wild, breathless:* I say—I say— God is dead!

Parris: Hear it, hear it!

Proctor, *laughs insanely, then:* A fire, a fire is burning! I hear the boot of Lucifer, I see his filthy face! And it is my face, and yours, Danforth! For them that quail to bring men out of ignorance, as I have quailed, and as you quail now when you know in all your black hearts that this be fraud— God damns our kind especially, and we will burn, we will burn together!

Danforth: Marshal! Take him and Corey with him to the jail!

Hale, *starting across to the door:* I denounce these proceedings!

Proctor: You are pulling Heaven down and raising up a whore!

Hale: I denounce these proceedings, I quit this court! *He slams the door to the outside behind*

E *him.*

Danforth, *calling to him in a fury:* Mr. Hale! Mr. Hale!

The curtain falls

7. **anti-Christ:** in the Bible, Christ's great enemy, expected to spread evil before Christ conquers him and the world ends (1 John 2:18).

Making the Connections

Connecting to the Theme: "The Breaking of Charity"

Now that students have read Acts One, Two, and Three, ask them to recall the "shifts in interest" that have created the breaking of charity within the Puritan community. What—if anything—could the characters do at this point to repair the situation? Is it even possible, after what the townspeople have undergone, to return to their ideal of a "New Eden"? Why or why not?

MAKING MEANINGS

Act Three

First Thoughts

1. Identify one phrase or expression in Act Three that made a strong impression on you. Tell why the phrase affected you.

Shaping Interpretations

2. Danforth believes that he is living in a "sharp time" in which good and evil are not "mixed" in people, but are easily distinguishable. Do you agree with his viewpoint? Why or why not?

Reading Check

a. How does Mary respond when Danforth asks her to explain the "crying out"?

b. What does Danforth do with the list of people supporting Rebecca and Martha?

c. What test does Danforth devise to determine why Abigail was put out of the Proctor house?

d. What is Abigail's "vision"?

3. Serious dramatic works often include **comic relief**—the inclusion of a comic episode or element to relieve emotional tension. In Shakespeare's tragedies, comic relief is often provided by the absurd wisdom of a clown or fool (such as the gravedigger in *Hamlet*). Do you think Giles Corey's eccentric and earthy dialogue provides **comic relief** in *The Crucible*? Support your answer with specific examples from the play.

4. What does Hale mean when he asks if every defense is an attack upon the court? How has Hale changed by the end of this act? Use your reading notes to help explain the transformation of this **dynamic** character.

5. When John reveals his true relationship to Abigail, what do you think he also reveals about his character and his **motivation**?

Extending the Text

6. In sports, in politics, and in war, people often *demonize* their opponents—that is, they portray their enemies as incarnations of evil. Can you think of examples? Why do you think people do this? What effect do you think such behavior has on society as a whole?

Reading Check

a. Mary explains that she "cannot tell how," but she "thought" she saw the spirits.

b. He plans to call all ninety-one signers in for questioning.

c. Danforth asks Elizabeth to testify without consulting her husband.

d. Abigail envisions Mary's spirit as a yellow bird.

Act Three

First Thoughts [Respond]

1. Possibilities include Elizabeth's "My husband is a good and righteous man" (p. 874) or John's "I say—I say—God is dead!" (p. 876). Elizabeth is grappling with morality and conscience; John, with the nature of good and evil. Students should select a phrase that expresses one of the play's themes or shows the character wrestling with major life decisions.

Shaping Interpretations [Interpret]

2. The Puritans saw the world in black and white, but even in colonial Salem, good and evil were not that sharply delineated. For example, there is some "evil" in Proctor, the hero; and no doubt Betty Parris could find some sympathetic qualities in her otherwise despicable father, Reverend Parris.

3. Corey's senile pursuit of lawsuits, his cantankerous complaints about his wife and neighbors, and his blunt one-liners like "a fart on Thomas Putnam" all offer comic relief—without sacrificing Corey's essential nobility and depth.

4. Hale now sees that the court is more concerned with the preservation of its own authority than with justice. At the end, Hale is less sure of his erudition and his moral compass and quits the courtroom in an attempt to escape the legacy of his own actions.

5. John's confession reveals that he places his wife and their love above his reputation, that he is willing to suffer the loss of his good name to save his wife.

Extending the Text [Evaluate]

6. People demonize their opponents to make it easier to attack and destroy them without considering them to be complex human beings. (Students might cite examples from contemporary politics or from sports such as boxing and pro wrestling.) Many students will say that such behavior degrades society, making it more cruel and violent.

Summary
Act Four ▪▪

The setting is a cell in the Salem jail, three months later. The town is rife with misery. Tituba and Sarah Good have descended into near-madness, waiting for the devil. Abigail and Mercy Lewis have stolen Parris's money and fled Salem. A broken man, Parris pleads that the executions of Proctor and Rebecca be postponed, but the judges refuse. Giles has been tortured to death, since he refused to disinherit his sons by entering a plea. Hale is trying to persuade the prisoners to falsely confess, rather than throw away the life God gave them. He arranges for Elizabeth to see John, in the hope that she will convince him to confess. She does not try to influence him either way—trusting that his conscience will tell him what to do. At first Proctor decides he doesn't have the virtue to be a martyr and signs a confession. But when he is asked to implicate others, he rips up the confession and is led out to his execution.

Ⓐ Cultural Connections

Notice how in Tituba's reference to the religion of Barbados, Miller again recalls his discussion of the pre-Christian pantheon of gods who were "useful and essentially friendly . . . despite occasional lapses" and an underworld that "was never regarded as a hostile area" (p. 843).

Ⓑ Critical Thinking

Evaluating

❓ What do you think of Tituba's routine in this scene? Is it ironic and amusing or more predictable and stereotyped? [While students should note the irony of Tituba's joyful anticipation of the devil after such ideas have caused so much misery, most will also find this portrayal rather caricatured and cartoonish.]

Ⓒ Elements of Literature

Motivation

❓ Do you think Hale is simply performing the traditional role of minister to the condemned, or is he himself seeking absolution? [Most students will feel that Hale seeks absolution for his role in the tragedy.]

Act Four

A cell in Salem jail, that fall.

At the back is a high barred window; near it, a great, heavy door. Along the walls are two benches.

The place is in darkness but for the moonlight seeping through the bars. It appears empty. Presently footsteps are heard coming down a corridor beyond the wall, keys rattle, and the door swings open. MARSHAL HERRICK *enters with a lantern.*

He is nearly drunk, and heavy-footed. He goes to a bench and nudges a bundle of rags lying on it.

Herrick: Sarah, wake up! Sarah Good! *He then crosses to the other bench.*

Sarah Good, *rising in her rags:* Oh, Majesty! Comin', comin'! Tituba, he's here, His Majesty's come!

Herrick: Go to the north cell; this place is wanted now. *He hangs his lantern on the wall.* TITUBA *sits up.*

Tituba: That don't look to me like His Majesty; look to me like the marshal.

Herrick, *taking out a flask:* Get along with you now, clear this place. *He drinks, and* SARAH GOOD *comes and peers up into his face.*

Sarah Good: Oh, is it you, Marshal! I thought sure you be the Devil comin' for us. Could I have a sip of cider for me goin'-away?

Herrick, *handing her the flask:* And where are you off to, Sarah?

Tituba, *as* SARAH *drinks:* We goin' to Barbados, soon the Devil gits here with the feathers and the wings.

Herrick: Oh? A happy voyage to you.

Sarah Good: A pair of bluebirds wingin' southerly, the two of us! Oh, it be a grand transformation, Marshal! *She raises the flask to drink again.*

Herrick, *taking the flask from her lips:* You'd best give me that or you'll never rise off the ground. Come along now.

Tituba: I'll speak to him for you, if you desires to come along, Marshal.

Herrick: I'd not refuse it, Tituba; it's the proper morning to fly into Hell.

Tituba: Oh, it be no Hell in Barbados. Devil, him be pleasureman in Barbados, him be singin' and dancin' in Barbados. It's you folks—you riles him up 'round here; it be too cold 'round here for that Old Boy. He freeze his soul in Massachusetts, but in Barbados he just as sweet and— *A bellowing cow is heard, and* TITUBA *leaps up and calls to the window:* Aye, sir! That's him, Sarah!

Sarah Good: I'm here, Majesty! *They hurriedly pick up their rags as* HOPKINS, *a guard, enters.*

Hopkins: The Deputy Governor's arrived.

Herrick, *grabbing* TITUBA: Come along, come along.

Tituba, *resisting him:* No, he comin' for me. I goin' home!

Herrick, *pulling her to the door:* That's not Satan, just a poor old cow with a hatful of milk. Come along now, out with you!

Tituba, *calling to the window:* Take me home, Devil! Take me home!

Sarah Good, *following the shouting* TITUBA *out:* Tell him I'm goin', Tituba! Now you tell him Sarah Good is goin' too!

In the corridor outside TITUBA *calls on—"Take me home, Devil; Devil take me home!" and* HOPKINS' *voice orders her to move on.* HERRICK *returns and begins to push old rags and straw into a corner. Hearing footsteps, he turns, and enter* DANFORTH *and* JUDGE HATHORNE. *They are in greatcoats and wear hats against the bitter cold. They are followed in by* CHEEVER, *who carries a dispatch case and a flat wooden box containing his writing materials.*

Herrick: Good morning, Excellency.

Danforth: Where is Mr. Parris?

Herrick: I'll fetch him. *He starts for the door.*

Danforth: Marshal. HERRICK *stops.* When did Reverend Hale arrive?

Herrick: It were toward midnight, I think.

Danforth, *suspiciously:* What is he about here?

Herrick: He goes among them that will hang, sir. And he prays with them. He sits with Goody Nurse now. And Mr. Parris with him.

Danforth: Indeed. That man have no authority to enter here, Marshal. Why have you let him in?

Herrick: Why, Mr. Parris command me, sir. I cannot deny him.

Danforth: Are you drunk, Marshal?

878 AMERICAN DRAMA

Professional Notes

Tituba's History

Tituba was the first witch to confess in Salem, her haste to unburden herself no doubt sparked by the severe beatings she had received. In her statement, Tituba claimed she never wanted to hurt Betty and professed her love for the child. She also recounted wild tales of witchcraft in Salem, naming Sarah Good and Sarah Osburn as witches. By confessing at the start of the hysteria, Tituba avoided being tried in court.

When public sentiment toward the accusers and the trials began to change, however, Tituba recanted her confession. Enraged, Parris refused to pay the jailers' fee to get her out of prison. As a result, she languished in jail for more than a year until an anonymous donor paid for her release and bought her. History has not recorded Tituba's fate after the witch hunt ended.

Herrick: No, sir; it is a bitter night, and I have no fire here.

Danforth, *containing his anger:* Fetch Mr. Parris.

Herrick: Aye, sir.

Danforth: There is a prodigious stench in this place.

Herrick: I have only now cleared the people out for you.

Danforth: Beware hard drink, Marshal.

Herrick: Aye, sir. *He waits an instant for further orders. But* DANFORTH, *in dissatisfaction, turns his back on him, and* HERRICK *goes out. There is a pause.* DANFORTH *stands in thought.*

Hathorne: Let you question Hale, Excellency; I should not be surprised he have been preaching in Andover lately.

Danforth: We'll come to that; speak nothing of Andover. Parris prays with him. That's strange. *He blows on his hands, moves toward the window, and looks out.*

Hathorne: Excellency, I wonder if it be wise to let Mr. Parris so continuously with the prisoners. DANFORTH *turns to him, interested.* I think, sometimes, the man has a mad look these days.

Danforth: Mad?

Hathorne: I met him yesterday coming out of his house, and I bid him good morning—and he wept and went his way. I think it is not well the village sees him so unsteady.

Danforth: Perhaps he have some sorrow.

Cheever, *stamping his feet against the cold:* I think it be the cows, sir.

Danforth: Cows?

Cheever: There be so many cows wanderin' the highroads, now their masters are in the jails, and much disagreement who they will belong to now. I know Mr. Parris be arguin' with farmers all yesterday—there is great contention, sir, about the cows. Contention make him weep, sir; it were always a man that weep for contention. *He turns, as do* HATHORNE *and* DANFORTH, *hearing someone coming up the corridor.* DANFORTH *raises his head as* PARRIS *enters. He is gaunt, frightened, and sweating in his greatcoat.*

Parris, *to* DANFORTH, *instantly:* Oh, good morning, sir, thank you for coming, I beg your pardon wakin' you so early. Good morning, Judge Hathorne.

Danforth: Reverend Hale have no right to enter this—

Parris: Excellency, a moment. *He hurries back and shuts the door.*

Hathorne: Do you leave him alone with the prisoners?

Danforth: What's his business here?

Parris, *prayerfully holding up his hands:* Excellency, hear me. It is a providence. Reverend Hale has returned to bring Rebecca Nurse to God.

Danforth, *surprised:* He bids her confess?

Parris, *sitting:* Hear me. Rebecca have not given me a word this three month since she came. Now she sits with him, and her sister and Martha Corey and two or three others, and he pleads with them, confess their crimes and save their lives.

Danforth: Why—this is indeed a providence. And they soften, they soften?

Parris: Not yet, not yet. But I thought to summon you, sir, that we might think on whether it be not wise, to— *He dares not say it.* I had thought to put a question, sir, and I hope you will not—

Danforth: Mr. Parris, be plain, what troubles you?

Parris: There is news, sir, that the court—the court must reckon with. My niece, sir, my niece— I believe she has vanished.

Danforth: Vanished!

Parris: I had thought to advise you of it earlier in the week, but—

Danforth: Why? How long is she gone?

Parris: This be the third night. You see, sir, she told me she would stay a night with Mercy Lewis. And next day, when she does not return, I send to Mr. Lewis to inquire. Mercy told him she would sleep in *my* house for a night.

Danforth: They are both gone?!

Parris, *in fear of him:* They are, sir.

Danforth, *alarmed:* I will send a party for them. Where may they be?

Parris: Excellency, I think they be aboard a ship. DANFORTH *stands agape.* My daughter tells me how she heard them speaking of ships last week, and tonight I discover my—my strongbox is broke into. *He presses his fingers against his eyes to keep back tears.*

Hathorne, *astonished:* She have robbed you?

Parris: Thirty-one pound is gone. I am penniless. *He covers his face and sobs.*

Danforth: Mr. Parris, you are a brainless man! *He walks in thought, deeply worried.*

Parris: Excellency, it profit nothing you should

D Elements of Literature

Irony

? What is ironic about Cheever's characterization of Parris here? [Possible response: Cheever's insistence that Parris can't stand "contention" is ironic because Parris has been responsible for so much strife and bad blood in Salem.]

E Elements of Literature

Motivation

? What outcome does Parris hope for at this point? Why? [Possible response: It seems likely that Parris, too, is troubled by the deadly consequences of his crusade and now hopes that the remaining prisoners will confess—an outcome that would preserve both their lives and his standing as their just accuser.]

F Critical Thinking

Speculating

? Why might Abigail and Mercy have run away at this point? [Possible responses: They sense that the tide of public opinion is turning against them; Abigail has lost all hope of anything more than vengeance on Proctor and has nothing to gain by staying in Salem.]

Taking a Second Look

Review:
Interpreting the Influences of Historical Context

Remind students that *The Crucible* is rooted in the actual events of the Salem witchcraft trials of the 1690s, as Miller explains in his narrative interludes. In addition, *The Crucible* serves as an allegory for the Communist "witch hunt" of the 1950s.

Activities

1. Have students identify important aspects of the historical context that influence the events in the play—for example, Salem's relative geographic isolation in the late seventeenth century.

2. Have students explain why Miller used the events in Salem to help explore the events of the 1950s.

3. Have students explain what relevance the play's historical context has for readers today.

T879

A Elements of Literature
Characterization

❓ How does this discussion of the rebellion in Andover highlight a significant difference in the characters of Danforth and Parris? How do their goals and philosophies in the witchcraft inquiry differ sharply? [Possible response: Parris is, at root, a self-serving coward and pragmatist, out to preserve his wealth, pride, and community standing. Therefore, he takes the Andover rebellion seriously, as a threat to his mercenary goals. Danforth, on the other hand, is a committed and, in a sense, more "idealistic" authoritarian, bent on carrying out his harsh "justice" no matter how it affects his standing or his person.]

B Critical Thinking
Analyzing

❓ How is public opinion changing in Salem? What has caused this change of heart? [Possible response: Most people accepted—and even embraced—the witchcraft trials when disreputable citizens were being accused and killed, but they are uneasy now that the town's most honorable people are on the scaffold. People now realize that no one is safe and so wish to halt the proceedings.]

C Elements of Literature
Motivation

❓ What message do you think the dagger was meant to convey to Parris? What other explanation could there be for the dagger? [Possible responses: It is likely the dagger was meant as a warning, a death threat from the relatives of someone condemned to be executed. Students might also suggest that he imagined seeing the dagger, a hallucination caused by his increasing paranoia and guilt. This may also be an allusion to Shakespeare's *Macbeth,* Act II, scene 1, where the guilty central character is afflicted by a "dagger of the mind."]

D Reading Skills and Strategies

Interpreting a Text

❓ Why is Danforth's comment ironic? [Possible responses: Killing the first twelve people was not just. Adding injustice to injustice does not create justice, and equality before the law in death doesn't count for much.]

blame me. I cannot think they would run off except they fear to keep in Salem any more. *He is pleading.* Mark it, sir, Abigail had close knowledge of the town, and since the news of Andover has broken here—

Danforth: Andover is remedied. The court returns there on Friday, and will resume examinations.

Parris: I am sure of it, sir. But the rumor here speaks rebellion in Andover, and it— ⒶＡ

Danforth: There is no rebellion in Andover!

Parris: I tell you what is said here, sir. Andover has thrown out the court, they say, and will have no part of witchcraft. There be a faction here, feeding on that news, and I tell you true, sir, I fear there will be riot here.

Hathorne: Riot! Why at every execution I have seen naught but high satisfaction in the town.

Parris: Judge Hathorne—it were another sort that hanged till now. Rebecca Nurse is no Bridget that lived three year with Bishop before she married him. John Proctor is not Isaac Ward that drank his family to ruin. *To* DANFORTH: I would to God it were not so, Excellency, but these people have great weight yet in the town. Let Rebecca stand upon the gibbet[1] and send up some righteous prayer, and I fear she'll wake a vengeance on you. Ⓑ

Hathorne: Excellency, she is condemned a witch. The court have—

Danforth, *in deep concern, raising a hand to* HATHORNE: Pray you. *To* PARRIS: How do you propose, then?

Parris: Excellency, I would postpone these hangin's for a time.

Danforth: There will be no postponement.

Parris: Now Mr. Hale's returned, there is hope, I think—for if he bring even one of these to God, that confession surely damns the others in the public eye, and none may doubt more that they are all linked to Hell. This way, unconfessed and claiming innocence, doubts are multiplied, many honest people will weep for them, and our good purpose is lost in their tears.

Danforth, *after thinking a moment, then going to* CHEEVER: Give me the list.

---

1. **gibbet** (jib′it): gallows, or structure from which a person is executed by hanging.

CHEEVER *opens the dispatch case, searches.*

Parris: It cannot be forgot, sir, that when I summoned the congregation for John Proctor's excommunication there were hardly thirty people come to hear it. That speak a discontent, I think, and—

Danforth, *studying the list:* There will be no postponement.

Parris: Excellency—

Danforth: Now, sir—which of these in your opinion may be brought to God? I will myself strive with him till dawn. *He hands the list to* PARRIS, *who merely glances at it.*

Parris: There is not sufficient time till dawn.

Danforth: I shall do my utmost. Which of them do you have hope for?

Parris, *not even glancing at the list now, and in a quavering voice, quietly:* Excellency—a dagger— *He chokes up.*

Danforth: What do you say?

Parris: Tonight, when I open my door to leave my house—a dagger clattered to the ground. *Silence.* DANFORTH *absorbs this. Now* PARRIS *cries out:* You cannot hang this sort. There is danger for me. I dare not step outside at night! ⒸＣ

REVEREND HALE *enters. They look at him for an instant in silence. He is steeped in sorrow, exhausted, and more direct than he ever was.*

Danforth: Accept my congratulations, Reverend Hale; we are gladdened to see you returned to your good work.

Hale, *coming to* DANFORTH *now:* You must pardon them. They will not budge.

HERRICK *enters, waits.*

Danforth, *conciliatory:* You misunderstand, sir; I cannot pardon these when twelve are already hanged for the same crime. It is not just. ⒹＤ

Parris, *with failing heart:* Rebecca will not confess?

Hale: The sun will rise in a few minutes. Excellency, I must have more time.

Danforth: Now hear me, and beguile yourselves no more. I will not receive a single plea for pardon or postponement. Them that will not confess will hang. Twelve are already executed; the names of

880 AMERICAN DRAMA

Professional Notes

New Court, New Cases

As this scene shows, the jails were full and Salem teetered on the edge of chaos. When Governor Phips returned from England, he created a new court to hear the witchcraft cases. Judges also decided to allow the "touching test," in which the accused were asked to touch afflicted persons because it was believed that a witch's touch could stop their shaking. In addition, the judges examined the accused for evidence of "witches' marks," such as moles.

these seven are given out, and the village expects to see them die this morning. Postponement now speaks a floundering on my part; reprieve or pardon must cast doubt upon the guilt of them that died till now. While I speak God's law, I will not crack its voice with whimpering. If retaliation is your fear, know this—I should hang ten thousand that dared to rise against the law, and an ocean of salt tears could not melt the resolution of the statutes. Now draw yourselves up like men and help me, as you are bound by Heaven to do. Have you spoken with them all, Mr. Hale?

Hale: All but Proctor. He is in the dungeon.

Danforth, *to* HERRICK: What's Proctor's way now?

Herrick: He sits like some great bird; you'd not know he lived except he will take food from time to time.

Danforth, *after thinking a moment:* His wife—his wife must be well on with child now.

Herrick: She is, sir.

Danforth: What think you, Mr. Parris? You have closer knowledge of this man; might her presence soften him?

Parris: It is possible, sir. He have not laid eyes on her these three months. I should summon her.

Danforth, *to* HERRICK: Is he yet adamant? Has he struck at you again?

Herrick: He cannot, sir, he is chained to the wall now.

Danforth, *after thinking on it:* Fetch Goody Proctor to me. Then let you bring him up.

Herrick: Aye, sir. HERRICK *goes. There is silence.*

Hale: Excellency, if you postpone a week and publish to the town that you are striving for their confessions, that speak mercy on your part, not faltering.

Danforth: Mr. Hale, as God have not empowered me like Joshua to stop this sun from rising,[2] so I cannot withhold from them the perfection of their punishment.

Hale, *harder now:* If you think God wills you to raise rebellion, Mr. Danforth, you are mistaken!

Danforth, *instantly:* You have heard rebellion spoken in the town?

2. **Joshua...rising:** in the Bible, Joshua, the successor of Moses, commands the sun and moon to stand still while his people take vengeance on their enemies.

Hale: Excellency, there are orphans wandering from house to house; abandoned cattle bellow on the highroads, the stink of rotting crops hangs everywhere, and no man knows when the harlots' cry will end his life—and you wonder yet if rebellion's spoke? Better you should marvel how they do not burn your province!

Danforth: Mr. Hale, have you preached in Andover this month?

Hale: Thank God they have no need of me in Andover.

Danforth: You baffle me, sir. Why have you returned here?

Hale: Why, it is all simple. I come to do the Devil's work. I come to counsel Christians they should belie themselves. *His sarcasm collapses.* There is blood on my head! Can you not see the blood on my head!!

Parris: Hush! *For he has heard footsteps. They all face the door.* HERRICK *enters with* ELIZABETH. *Her wrists are linked by heavy chain, which* HERRICK *now removes. Her clothes are dirty; her face is pale and gaunt.* HERRICK *goes out.*

Danforth, *very politely:* Goody Proctor. *She is silent.* I hope you are hearty?

Elizabeth, *as a warning reminder:* I am yet six month before my time.

Danforth: Pray be at your ease, we come not for your life. We—*uncertain how to plead, for he is not accustomed to it.* Mr. Hale, will you speak with the woman?

Hale: Goody Proctor, your husband is marked to hang this morning.

Pause.

Elizabeth, *quietly:* I have heard it.

Hale: You know, do you not, that I have no connection with the court? *She seems to doubt it.* I come of my own, Goody Proctor. I would save your husband's life, for if he is taken I count myself his murderer. Do you understand me?

Elizabeth: What do you want of me?

Hale: Goody Proctor, I have gone this three month like our Lord into the wilderness. I have sought a Christian way, for damnation's doubled on a minister who counsels men to lie.

Hathorne: It is no lie, you cannot speak of lies.

Hale: It is a lie! They are innocent!

Danforth: I'll hear no more of that!

E Elements of Literature
Motivation
? How does this passage highlight Danforth's fundamental motivations in the trials? How are they different from those of other accusers? [Possible response: While Parris, Hathorne, Putnam, and even Hale are all, to varying degrees, motivated by self-interest, Danforth seems to be moved primarily by a fanatical, even sadistic, dedication to the power of law over the will of the individual.]

F Reading Skills and Strategies
Making Predictions
? Do you think Elizabeth will try to convince John to confess? Why or why not? [Possible responses: Given Elizabeth's love of the truth and the fact that she herself has not confessed, it seems unlikely that she will actively advise John to confess; but given her willingness to lie to save her husband's life in court, she may support him if he chooses to lie now; she may not advise him either way, out of the belief that he must make his decision based on his own conscience, just as she has made hers.]

G Critical Thinking
Analyzing
? How does this speech help explain why Abigail and Mercy have fled Salem? What does it imply about Proctor's efforts in court? [Hale indicates that Proctor's challenge to the credibility of Abigail and the girls has had considerable influence on the community, if not the court. It suggests that Proctor's efforts were not in vain, even if they didn't win freedom for his wife.]

H Elements of Literature
Motivation
? What does Hale's sarcastic tone reveal about his state of mind? [Possible response: Hale's sarcasm reveals the depth of his despair and the lengths to which he is willing to go to redress the miscarriage of justice.]

Getting Students Involved

Enrichment Activity
Biblical Allusions. *The Crucible* contains many allusions to the Bible, the constitution of the Puritan theocracy as well as its religious authority. Have students research and explain each of the following Biblical allusions from the play: Cain, Abel, "the angel Raphael said to the boy Tobias," Joshua, Pontius Pilate, Lucifer. Then, ask students to describe what each allusion adds to the play's mood, setting, or theme.

T881

Hale, *continuing to* ELIZABETH: Let you not mistake your duty as I mistook my own. I came into this village like a bridegroom to his beloved, bearing gifts of high religion; the very crowns of holy law I brought, and what I touched with my bright confidence, it died; and where I turned the eye of my great faith, blood flowed up. Beware, Goody Proctor—cleave to no faith when faith brings blood. It is mistaken law that leads you to sacrifice. Life, woman, life is God's most precious gift; no principle, however glorious, may justify the taking of it. I beg you, woman, prevail upon your husband to confess. Let him give his lie. Quail not before God's judgment in this, for it may well be God damns a liar less than he that throws his life away for pride. Will you plead with him? I cannot think he will listen to another.

Elizabeth, *quietly:* I think that be the Devil's argument.

Hale, *with a climactic desperation:* Woman, before the laws of God we are as swine! We cannot read His will!

Elizabeth: I cannot dispute with you, sir; I lack learning for it.

Danforth, *going to her:* Goody Proctor, you are not summoned here for disputation. Be there no wifely tenderness within you? He will die with the sunrise. Your husband. Do you understand it? *She only looks at him.* What say you? Will you contend with him? *She is silent.* Are you stone? I tell you true, woman, had I no other proof of your unnatural life, your dry eyes now would be sufficient evidence that you delivered up your soul to Hell! A very ape would weep at such calamity! Have the Devil dried up any tear of pity in you? *She is silent.* Take her out. It profit nothing she should speak to him!

Elizabeth, *quietly:* Let me speak with him, Excellency.

Parris, *with hope:* You'll strive with him? *She hesitates.*

Danforth: Will you plead for his confession or will you not?

Elizabeth: I promise nothing. Let me speak with him.

A sound—the sibilance of dragging feet on stone. They turn. A pause. HERRICK *enters with* JOHN PROCTOR. *His wrists are chained. He is another man, bearded, filthy, his eyes misty as though webs had overgrown them. He halts inside the doorway, his eye caught by the sight of* ELIZABETH. *The emotion flowing between them prevents anyone from speaking for an instant. Now* HALE, *visibly affected, goes to* DANFORTH *and speaks quietly.*

Hale: Pray, leave them, Excellency.

Danforth, *pressing* HALE *impatiently aside:* Mr. Proctor, you have been notified, have you not? PROCTOR *is silent, staring at* ELIZABETH. I see light in the sky, Mister; let you counsel with your wife, and may God help you turn your back on Hell. PROCTOR *is silent, staring at* ELIZABETH.

Hale, *quietly:* Excellency, let—

DANFORTH *brushes past* HALE *and walks out.* HALE *follows.* CHEEVER *stands and follows,* HATHORNE *behind.* HERRICK *goes.* PARRIS, *from a safe distance, offers:*

Parris: If you desire a cup of cider, Mr. Proctor, I am sure I— PROCTOR *turns an icy stare at him, and he breaks off.* PARRIS *raises his palms toward* PROCTOR. God lead you now. PARRIS *goes out.*

Alone. PROCTOR *walks to her, halts. It is as though they stood in a spinning world. It is beyond sorrow, above it. He reaches out his hand as though toward an embodiment not quite real, and as he touches her, a strange soft sound, half laughter, half amazement, comes from his throat. He pats her hand. She covers his hand with hers. And then, weak, he sits. Then she sits, facing him.*

Proctor: The child?

Elizabeth: It grows.

Proctor: There is no word of the boys?

Elizabeth: They're well. Rebecca's Samuel keeps them.

Proctor: You have not seen them?

Elizabeth: I have not. *She catches a weakening in herself and downs it.*

Proctor: You are a—marvel, Elizabeth.

Elizabeth: You—have been tortured?

Proctor: Aye. *Pause.* She will not let herself be drowned in the sea that threatens her. They come for my life now.

Elizabeth: I know it.

Pause.

Getting Students Involved

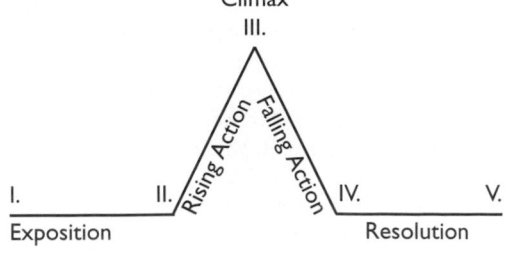

Proctor: None—have yet confessed?

Elizabeth: There be many confessed.

Proctor: Who are they?

Elizabeth: There be a hundred or more, they say. Goody Ballard is one; Isaiah Goodkind is one. There be many.

Proctor: Rebecca?

Elizabeth: Not Rebecca. She is one foot in Heaven now; naught may hurt her more.

Proctor: And Giles?

Elizabeth: You have not heard of it?

Proctor: I hear nothin', where I am kept.

Elizabeth: Giles is dead.

He looks at her incredulously.

Proctor: When were he hanged?

Elizabeth, *quietly, factually:* He were not hanged. He would not answer aye or nay to his indictment; for if he denied the charge they'd hang him surely, and auction out his property. So he stand mute, and died Christian under the law. And so his sons will have his farm. It is the law, for he could not be condemned a wizard without he answer the indictment, aye or nay.

Proctor: Then how does he die?

Elizabeth, *gently:* They press him, John.

Proctor: Press?

Elizabeth: Great stones they lay upon his chest until he plead aye or nay. *With a tender smile for the old man:* They say he give them but two words. "More weight," he says. And died.

Proctor, *numbed—a thread to weave into his agony:* "More weight."

Elizabeth: Aye. It were a fearsome man, Giles Corey.

Pause.

Proctor, *with great force of will, but not quite looking at her:* I have been thinking I would confess to them, Elizabeth. *She shows nothing.* What say you? If I give them that?

Elizabeth: I cannot judge you, John.

Pause.

Proctor, *simply—a pure question:* What would you have me do?

Elizabeth: As you will, I would have it. *Slight pause.* I want you living, John. That's sure.

Proctor—*he pauses, then with a flailing of hope:* Giles' wife? Have she confessed?

Elizabeth: She will not.

Pause.

Proctor: It is a pretense, Elizabeth.

Elizabeth: What is?

Proctor: I cannot mount the gibbet like a saint. It is a fraud. I am not that man. *She is silent.* My honesty is broke, Elizabeth; I am no good man. Nothing's spoiled by giving them this lie that were not rotten long before.

Elizabeth: And yet you've not confessed till now. That speak goodness in you.

Proctor: Spite only keeps me silent. It is hard to give a lie to dogs. *Pause, for the first time he turns directly to her.* I would have your forgiveness, Elizabeth.

Elizabeth: It is not for me to give, John, I am—

Proctor: I'd have you see some honesty in it. Let them that never lied die now to keep their souls. It is pretense for me, a vanity that will not blind God nor keep my children out of the wind. *Pause.* What say you?

Elizabeth, *upon a heaving sob that always threatens:* John, it come to naught that I should forgive you, if you'll not forgive yourself. *Now he turns away a little, in great agony.* It is not my soul, John, it is yours. *He stands, as though in physical pain, slowly rising to his feet with a great immortal longing to find his answer. It is difficult to say, and she is on the verge of tears.* Only be sure of this, for I know it now: Whatever you will do, it is a good man does it. *He turns his doubting, searching gaze upon her.* I have read my heart this three month, John. *Pause.* I have sins of my own to count. It needs a cold wife to prompt lechery.

> "Only be sure of this:
> Whatever you will do,
> it is a good man does it."

THE CRUCIBLE, ACT FOUR **883**

Taking a Second Look

Review: Conflict

Remind students that a *conflict* in literature is a struggle or fight. Explore how conflict makes a story interesting because readers want to find out the outcome. Explain that in an *external conflict*, characters struggle against a force outside themselves, such as nature or other people; in an *internal conflict*, characters struggle with opposing forces within themselves. Be sure students understand that many works of literature contain both external and internal conflicts.

Activities

1. Miller explains that an internal conflict arises when there is a "conflict between a man's raw deeds and his concept of himself." Have students identify Proctor's "raw deeds" and his "concept of himself" and explain how Proctor grapples with this internal conflict.

2. Have students describe the external conflict in the play between traditional authority and the individual conscience.

D **Elements of Literature**
Motivation

? What motivated Giles to die without confessing? How does his decision compare with John Proctor's decisions thus far? [Possible responses: Giles decided to die mute to preserve his property for his family; so far, John's motivation for not confessing seems to be pride.]

E **Historical Connections**

The historical record suggests that after spending five months in chains in the Salem jail, Giles Corey saw the futility of a trial. The penalty for such a refusal was *peine et fort,* or pressing to death. On September 19, Corey was stripped naked, a board was placed upon his chest, and then heavy stones and rocks were piled on the board while his neighbors watched. The pressing lasted for two days until Corey finally died. Three days after Corey's death, his wife Martha was hanged.

F **Reading Skills and Strategies**
Interpreting a Text

? How does the relationship between John and Elizabeth change throughout the play? [Possible responses: In the first scene with Abigail, John announces that he would never again be unfaithful to Elizabeth, but he does not deny Abby's charge that Elizabeth is cold. In Act Two, John tries to reconcile with Elizabeth, but she remains wounded and resentful. As a result, he becomes angry and protests harshly that she will never let him forget his infidelity. Once Hale arrives, however, John and Elizabeth are united in their efforts to convince the minister of their solid Christian convictions. When she is arrested, John tears up the warrant and tries in vain to prevent the arrest. At the trial, he makes every effort to save Elizabeth, confessing his shame to secure her release. She, in turn, lies to try to save his reputation. By Act Four, their renewed love and mutual respect are obvious to the audience.]

T883

A Elements of Literature
Motivation

? According to Elizabeth, why was she always suspicious of John's love? Do you think her feelings are understandable? Why or why not? [Elizabeth says she felt that she was unattractive and that no man could truly love her. Her feelings are understandable because many people—probably even more in contemporary culture—experience these debilitating feelings.]

B Critical Thinking
Analyzing

? What is Proctor trying to make himself believe here? [He wants to believe that he is a sinner and a fraud with no principles left and thus should not die for any principle.]

C Literary Connections

In the aesthetic tradition we inherit from Aristotle, tragedy is a dramatic representation of an "action of high importance" featuring a well-born hero with a tragic flaw that brings about his or her downfall. The downfall leads to new moral awareness, which moves the audience to fear and pity. Arthur Miller has argued that an ordinary person can be a tragic hero, if he or she believes in something intensely enough to give up everything else. Miller's tragic figures (like Willy Loman in *Death of a Salesman*) are often confused, yet they are still capable of making a tragic commitment. John Proctor is a common man, rather than a traditional ruler. He does not want to be heroic—he is willing to admit to a lie to save his life. But he will go only so far. He will not sign his name to a lie that betrays Rebecca and his community. He goes to his death with new self-respect and awareness of the truth, and he is thus a tragic hero.

Proctor, *in great pain:* Enough, enough—
Elizabeth, *now pouring out her heart:* Better you should know me!
Proctor: I will not hear it! I know you!
Elizabeth: You take my sins upon you, John—
Proctor, *in agony:* No, I take my own, my own!
Elizabeth: John, I counted myself so plain, so poorly made, no honest love could come to me! Suspicion kissed you when I did; I never knew how I should say my love. It were a cold house I kept! *In fright, she swerves, as* HATHORNE *enters.*
Hathorne: What say you, Proctor? The sun is soon up.

PROCTOR, *his chest heaving, stares, turns to* ELIZA-BETH. *She comes to him as though to plead, her voice quaking.*

Elizabeth: Do what you will. But let none be your judge. There be no higher judge under Heaven than Proctor is! Forgive me, forgive me, John—I never knew such goodness in the world! *She covers her face, weeping.*

PROCTOR *turns from her to* HATHORNE; *he is off the earth, his voice hollow.*

Proctor: I want my life.
Hathorne, *electrified, surprised:* You'll confess yourself?
Proctor: I will have my life.
Hathorne, *with a mystical tone:* God be praised! It is a providence! *He rushes out the door, and his voice is heard calling down the corridor:* He will confess! Proctor will confess!
Proctor, *with a cry, as he strides to the door:* Why do you cry it? *In great pain he turns back to her:* It is evil, is it not? It is evil.
Elizabeth, *in terror, weeping:* I cannot judge you, John, I cannot!
Proctor: Then who will judge me? *Suddenly clasping his hands:* God in Heaven, what is John Proctor, what is John Proctor? *He moves as an animal, and a fury is riding in him, a tantalized search.* I think it is honest, I think so; I am no saint. *As though she had denied this he calls angrily at her:* Let Rebecca go like a saint; for me it is fraud!

Voices are heard in the hall, speaking together in suppressed excitement.

Elizabeth: I am not your judge, I cannot be. *As though giving him release:* Do as you will, do as you will!
Proctor: Would you give them such a lie? Say it. Would you ever give them this? *She cannot answer.* You would not; if tongs of fire were singeing you you would not! It is evil. Good, then—it is evil, and I do it!

HATHORNE *enters with* DANFORTH, *and, with them,* CHEEVER, PARRIS, *and* HALE. *It is a businesslike, rapid entrance, as though the ice had been broken.*

Danforth, *with great relief and gratitude:* Praise to God, man, praise to God; you shall be blessed in Heaven for this. CHEEVER *has hurried to the bench with pen, ink, and paper.* PROCTOR *watches him.* Now then, let us have it. Are you ready, Mr. Cheever?
Proctor, *with a cold, cold horror at their efficiency:* Why must it be written?
Danforth: Why, for the good instruction of the village, Mister; this we shall post upon the church door! *To* PARRIS, *urgently:* Where is the marshal?
Parris, *runs to the door and calls down the corridor:* Marshal! Hurry!
Danforth: Now, then, Mister, will you speak slowly, and directly to the point, for Mr. Cheever's sake. *He is on record now, and is really dictating to* CHEEVER, *who writes.* Mr. Proctor, have you seen the Devil in your life? PROCTOR's *jaws lock.* Come, man, there is light in the sky; the town waits at the scaffold; I would give out this news. Did you see the Devil?
Proctor: I did.
Parris: Praise God!
Danforth: And when he come to you, what were his demand? PROCTOR *is silent.* DANFORTH *helps.* Did he bid you to do his work upon the earth?
Proctor: He did.
Danforth: And you bound yourself to his service? DANFORTH *turns, as* REBECCA NURSE *enters, with* HERRICK *helping to support her. She is barely able to walk.* Come in, come in, woman!
Rebecca, *brightening as she sees* PROCTOR: Ah, John! You are well, then, eh?

PROCTOR *turns his face to the wall.*

Professional Notes

John Proctor and George Burroughs

The real John Proctor was an opinionated tavern owner who openly denounced the witch hunt. Ann Putnam, Abigail Williams, Indian John (Tituba's husband), and Elizabeth Booth testified against Proctor, the latter claiming that ghosts told her that Proctor was a serial murderer. Proctor fought back vigorously, accusing confessed witches of lying, complaining of torture, and demanding that his trial be moved to Boston. His efforts were in vain, and he was hanged.

Although Proctor is the focus of *The Crucible*, the execution of the former minister George Burroughs was the epicenter of the real-life tragedy. Mercy Lewis, the most vicious of the young accusers, told the court that Burroughs flew her to the top of a mountain and, pointing toward the surrounding land, promised her all the kingdoms if only she would sign his book. At his execution, the former minister insisted on his innocence and recited the Lord's Prayer

perfectly (something witches were thought not to be able to do). The crowd was so swayed that the judges stepped in to remind everyone that Burroughs had had his day in court and lost. The execution went forward as scheduled.

Danforth: Courage, man, courage—let her witness your good example that she may come to God herself. Now hear it, Goody Nurse! Say on, Mr. Proctor. Did you bind yourself to the Devil's service?

Rebecca, *astonished:* Why, John!

Proctor, *through his teeth, his face turned from* REBECCA: I did.

Danforth: Now, woman, you surely see it profit nothin' to keep this conspiracy any further. Will you confess yourself with him?

Rebecca: Oh, John—God send his mercy on you!

Danforth: I say, will you confess yourself, Goody Nurse?

Rebecca: Why, it is a lie, it is a lie; how may I damn myself? I cannot, I cannot.

Danforth: Mr. Proctor. When the Devil came to you did you see Rebecca Nurse in his company? PROCTOR *is silent.* Come, man, take courage—did you ever see her with the Devil?

Proctor, *almost inaudibly:* No.

DANFORTH, *now sensing trouble, glances at* JOHN *and goes to the table, and picks up a sheet—the list of condemned.*

Danforth: Did you ever see her sister, Mary Easty, with the Devil?

Proctor: No, I did not.

Danforth, *his eyes narrow on* PROCTOR: Did you ever see Martha Corey with the Devil?

Proctor: I did not.

Danforth, *realizing, slowly putting the sheet down:* Did you ever see anyone with the Devil?

Proctor: I did not.

Danforth: Proctor, you mistake me. I am not empowered to trade your life for a lie. You have most certainly seen some person with the Devil. PROCTOR *is silent.* Mr. Proctor, a score of people have already testified they saw this woman with the Devil.

Proctor: Then it is proved. Why must I say it?

Danforth: Why "must" you say it! Why, you should rejoice to say it if your soul is truly purged of any love for Hell!

Proctor: They think to go like saints. I like not to spoil their names.

Danforth, *inquiring, incredulous:* Mr. Proctor, do you think they go like saints?

Proctor, *evading:* This woman never thought she done the Devil's work.

Danforth: Look you, sir. I think you mistake your duty here. It matters nothing what she thought—she is convicted of the unnatural murder of children, and you for sending your spirit out upon Mary Warren. Your soul alone is the issue here, Mister, and you will prove its whiteness or you cannot live in a Christian country. Will you tell me now what persons conspired with you in the Devil's company? PROCTOR *is silent.* To your knowledge was Rebecca Nurse ever—

Proctor: I speak my own sins; I cannot judge another. *Crying out, with hatred:* I have no tongue for it.

Hale, *quickly to* DANFORTH: Excellency, it is enough he confess himself. Let him sign it, let him sign it.

Parris, *feverishly:* It is a great service, sir. It is a weighty name; it will strike the village that Proctor confess. I beg you, let him sign it. The sun is up, Excellency!

Danforth, *considers; then with dissatisfaction:* Come, then, sign your testimony. *To* CHEEVER: Give it to him. CHEEVER *goes to* PROCTOR, *the confession and a pen in hand.* PROCTOR *does not look at it.* Come, man, sign it.

Proctor, *after glancing at the confession:* You have all witnessed it—it is enough.

Danforth: You will not sign it?

Proctor: You have all witnessed it; what more is needed?

Danforth: Do you sport with me? You will sign your name or it is no confession, Mister! *His breast heaving with agonized breathing,* PROCTOR *now lays the paper down and signs his name.*

Parris: Praise be to the Lord!

PROCTOR *has just finished signing when* DANFORTH *reaches for the paper. But* PROCTOR *snatches it up, and now a wild terror is rising in him, and a boundless anger.*

Danforth, *perplexed, but politely extending his hand:* If you please, sir.

Proctor: No.

Danforth, *as though* PROCTOR *did not understand:* Mr. Proctor, I must have—

THE CRUCIBLE, ACT FOUR **885**

Crossing the Curriculum

Social Studies

In our time, people are sometimes "tried in the media" before they are tried in a court of law. Invite students to examine print and electronic media to find a current example of a trial by media, including tough-questioning talk shows, newspaper editorials, opinion polls, and Internet chat. Students should compare and contrast the role of the media in current events with the role of public opinion described in *The Crucible*.

Music

Invite students to find a musical selection they think captures the mood of the play's climax. The music should not have lyrics. Students should play the selection for the class as volunteers read these final pages. Then, have students explain how the music fits the play's theme and tone here.

? What does John Proctor mean when he refers to his *name?* Why is his name so important to him? [Possible responses: Proctor may be referring to his public reputation and honor—even though he compromised his soul by accepting the lie, he does not want his name (in history, in the public record) to indicate nothing but capitulation before the court. His name might also represent the ultimate mark of his will in the world, and he wants his *will,* if not the actual deeds of his soul, to show resistance to this injustice.]

B Critical Thinking

Synthesizing

? Why does this act, which some (such as Hale) can only see as suicidal, represent for Proctor some "shred of goodness" in him? [Possible responses: On an immediate level, it represents Proctor's refusal to cooperate in the executions of Rebecca and Martha and to soil his own name. On a more fundamental level, it represents his final resistance to the "breaking of charity" that made the witch hunt possible in the first place: the process by which each person in the community became willing to sacrifice his or her principles, honor, friends, and loved ones in order to save him- or herself.]

C Critical Thinking

Analyzing

? Rebecca's solid faith in God's judgment helps her find courage to face the court's judgment. How might Salem's crisis during the witch hunt be seen as a crisis of *faith?* [Possible response: One by one, most community members let fear, paranoia, and self-interest outweigh their faith in God and in each other. Thus, they disregard what they know is ultimately right in order to help themselves in the present.]

"How may I live without my name? I have given you my soul; leave me my name!"

Proctor: No, no. I have signed it. You have seen me. It is done! You have no need for this.

Parris: Proctor, the village must have proof that—

Proctor: Damn the village! I confess to God, and God has seen my name on this! It is enough!

Danforth: No, sir, it is—

Proctor: You came to save my soul, did you not? Here! I have confessed myself; it is enough!

Danforth: You have not con—

Proctor: I have confessed myself! Is there no good penitence but it be public? God does not need my name nailed upon the church! God sees my name; God knows how black my sins are! It is enough!

Danforth: Mr. Proctor—

Proctor: You will not use me! I am no Sarah Good or Tituba, I am John Proctor! You will not use me! It is no part of salvation that you should use me!

Danforth: I do not wish to—

Proctor: I have three children—how may I teach them to walk like men in the world, and I sold my friends?

Danforth: You have not sold your friends—

Proctor: Beguile me not! I blacken all of them when this is nailed to the church the very day they hang for silence!

Danforth: Mr. Proctor, I must have good and legal proof that you—

Proctor: You are the high court, your word is good enough! Tell them I confessed myself; say Proctor broke his knees and wept like a woman; say what you will, but my name cannot—

Danforth, *with suspicion:* It is the same, is it not? If I report it or you sign to it?

Proctor—*he knows it is insane:* No, it is not the same! What others say and what I sign to is not the same!

Danforth: Why? Do you mean to deny this confession when you are free?

Proctor: I mean to deny nothing!

Danforth: Then explain to me, Mr. Proctor, why you will not let—

A **Proctor,** *with a cry of his whole soul:* Because it is my name! Because I cannot have another in my life! Because I lie and sign myself to lies! Because I am not worth the dust on the feet of them that hang! How may I live without my name? I have given you my soul; leave me my name!

Danforth, *pointing at the confession in* PROCTOR's *hand:* Is that document a lie? If it is a lie I will not accept it! What say you? I will not deal in lies, Mister! PROCTOR *is motionless.* You will give me your honest confession in my hand, or I cannot keep you from the rope. PROCTOR *does not reply.* Which way do you go, Mister?

His breast heaving, his eyes staring, PROCTOR *tears the paper and crumples it, and he is weeping in fury, but erect.*

Danforth: Marshal!

Parris, *hysterically, as though the tearing paper were his life:* Proctor, Proctor!

Hale: Man, you will hang! You cannot!

B **Proctor,** *his eyes full of tears:* I can. And there's your first marvel, that I can. You have made your magic now, for now I do think I see some shred of goodness in John Proctor. Not enough to weave a banner with, but white enough to keep it from such dogs. ELIZABETH, *in a burst of terror, rushes to him and weeps against his hand.* Give them no tear! Tears pleasure them! Show honor now, show a stony heart and sink them with it! *He has lifted her, and kisses her now with great passion.*

C **Rebecca:** Let you fear nothing! Another judgment waits us all!

Danforth: Hang them high over the town! Who weeps for these, weeps for corruption! *He sweeps out past them.* HERRICK *starts to lead* REBECCA, *who*

886 AMERICAN DRAMA

Assessing Learning

Check Test: True-False

Act Four

1. Salem is in great turmoil, with livestock wandering the roads and farms falling apart. [True]

2. Abigail and Mercy Lewis have run away, taking Parris's money with them. [True]

3. At Hale's urging, Rebecca Nurse confesses to witchcraft. [False]

4. Elizabeth refuses to visit John in jail because she is pregnant. [False]

5. John rips up his confession and is hanged. [True]

Standardized Test Preparation

For practice with proofreading and editing, see
- *Daily Oral Grammar,* Transparency 51

almost collapses, but PROCTOR catches her, and she glances up at him apologetically.

Rebecca: I've had no breakfast.

Herrick: Come, man.

HERRICK *escorts them out,* HATHORNE *and* CHEEVER *behind them.* ELIZABETH *stands staring at the empty doorway.*

Parris, *in deadly fear, to* ELIZABETH: Go to him, Goody Proctor! There is yet time!

From outside a drumroll strikes the air. PARRIS *is startled.* ELIZABETH *jerks about toward the window.*

Parris: Go to him! *He rushes out the door, as though to hold back his fate.* Proctor! Proctor!

Again, a short burst of drums.

"He have his goodness now."

Hale: Woman, plead with him! *He starts to rush out the door, and then goes back to her.* Woman! It is pride, it is vanity. *She avoids his eyes, and moves to the window. He drops to his knees.* Be his helper! What profit him to bleed? Shall the dust praise him? Shall the worms declare his truth? Go to him, take his shame away!

Elizabeth, *supporting herself against collapse, grips the bars of the window, and with a cry:* He have his goodness now. God forbid I take it from him!

The final drumroll crashes, then heightens violently. HALE *weeps in frantic prayer, and the new sun is pouring in upon her face, and the drums rattle like bones in the morning air.*

The curtain falls

THE CRUCIBLE, ACT FOUR **887**

Making the Connections

Connecting to the Theme: "The Breaking of Charity"

When students are finished reading the entire play, remind them of the collection theme. Have students identify various instances when charity was broken. Discuss whether or not students think this was the "real story" of Salem. Why or why not?

MAKING MEANINGS

Act Four

First Thoughts [Respond]

1. Students may identify with John Proctor's flawed heroism, Elizabeth's stoic endurance, or Giles's sturdy individualism. As Miller indicates in his essay on p. 827, he identifies most with Proctor.

Shaping Interpretations [Interpret]

2. Hale feels he has betrayed the people he tried to help by advising them to lie. He is motivated by a desire to save their lives and to assuage his own guilt.

3. When prominent citizens are accused, the tide begins to turn and both girls become vulnerable. Realizing that she will not win John and that her treachery may be exposed, Abigail flees with her friend.

4. Parris fears that the revolt in Andover will spread to Salem.

5. Hale wants John to accept the witchcraft charges to save his life. Students may agree that no principle is worth dying for or feel that life without principles has no purpose.

6. The couple has lost everything but their love and their values, which lie beyond pain.

7. He wants to confess because he *does* feel guilty and because he wants to live. But he also knows a cowardly embrace of the witchcraft lie would, ironically, be his greatest sin.

8. He recognizes that he cannot sign his name to a lie that others will innocently hang for—and that his moral legacy matters to himself, his wife, his children, and God.

The Play as a Whole

Shaping Interpretations [Interpret]

1. Each of the characters undergoes a severe crisis in the crucible of the witchcraft trials. This crucible separates the precious metal (morality, faith, dignity) from the dross (cowardice, betrayal, cruelty).

2. In spite of the immediate tragedy, most students will agree that it is in the conscience of Rebecca, Corey, Elizabeth, and John that the best spirit of Puritan society will live on. It is they who ultimately "keep charity" for future generations.

T888

MAKING MEANINGS

Act Four

First Thoughts

1. Which character do you most identify with? Why? Whom did Miller identify with? (Check his comments on page 827.)

Shaping Interpretations

2. Why does Hale say he has come "to do the Devil's work"? What **motivates** his actions?

3. What events precede the sudden disappearance of Abigail and Mercy?

4. What does Parris fear about the response of the people in Andover?

5. Why does Hale counsel Elizabeth to persuade John Proctor to lie? Do you think he is right to do so?

6. How do you interpret Arthur Miller's statement that John and Elizabeth inhabit a world "beyond sorrow, above it"?

7. What **motivations** does Proctor have for confessing? At the same time, why does he see his confession as deeply **ironic**?

8. In the play's **climax**, Proctor destroys his own confession. Review your reading notes interpreting Proctor's character: Why does he ultimately choose his "goodness"?

The Play as a Whole

Shaping Interpretations

1. Refer back to the dictionary definition of *crucible* on page 828, and explain the **title** of the play.

2. Miller has said he wrote *The Crucible* with the

> ### Reading Check
> a. Why has Reverend Hale returned to Salem?
> b. What news about Abigail does Parris give Danforth?
> c. What two things does Elizabeth say she is unable to do for John?
> d. Why does Danforth want a written confession from Proctor?

conviction that "there were moments when an individual conscience was all that could keep the world from falling apart." Do you agree with his conviction? Do you think the play actually demonstrates a triumph of individual conscience? Explain your answers.

3. What, in your opinion, is the difference between the ways Proctor and Hale resolve the **conflicts** between their public and their private lives? Whose solution is better? Could their conflicts be found in people today? Support your answers with examples from the text and from life.

Extending the Text

4. In Act One, after the introduction of Proctor, Miller writes that modern Americans have "inherited" the Puritan idea that sin cannot be washed away—an idea that has disciplined us, but has also bred hypocrisy. Explain why you agree or disagree with Miller's assessment of American culture.

Challenging the Text

5. The writer of a literary work may have responsibilities not only to readers and publishers but also to the people he or she chooses to write about. Do you think Arthur Miller had a responsibility to portray the Salem witchcraft trials accurately? Is his use of "artistic license" with respect to some of the historical facts justifiable? To what extent do you think a writer, artist, or filmmaker should be accurate when basing a work of fiction on historical events? Explain your opinion.

6. Miller has called *The Crucible* a tragedy. Do you think it is a tragedy? Why or why not?

7. Some critics have claimed that Miller's play is really only a vehicle for his own political viewpoints. How do you feel about these criticisms of the play? Miller's lengthy comments on his characters, on their problems, and on history in general are certainly unusual in a play. How do you respond to Miller's commentary throughout the play? Be specific in your answers.

---

3. Proctor ultimately makes a bold declaration of private truth and private conscience, in spite of the adverse public consequences. Hale lets public injustice dominate private conscience, a process made complete by his insistence that the victims stifle their own consciences in order to live. Most students will feel that Proctor's solution is, in general, the only way to handle such conflict and should find numerous examples of this approach (and Hale's) in contemporary society.

Extending the Text [Evaluate]

4. Many students will agree with Miller's assessment, citing hypocritical attitudes toward violence and sex, for example. Others may believe that cases of hypocrisy do not undermine the moral foundation of American culture.

Challenging the Text [Synthesize]

5. Possible response: Artists creating fiction are not bound by fact. Additionally, artists are justified in using historical facts to portray a larger truth and convey their themes.

CHOICES: Building Your Portfolio

Writer's Notebook

1. Collecting Ideas for a Problem-Solution Essay

Think of a social or political problem suggested by *The Crucible*. To analyze the problem, answer as many of the following questions as you can.

Description:
What is the problem? How widespread is it?

Narration:
What is the problem's history? What are its causes? What are its effects?

Classification:
What are the major parts of the problem? How is the problem similar to other problems? How is it unique?

Evaluation:
Why is the problem important? What solutions have been tried? Which solution is most practical? Which does the most good for the most people? Which has moral and ethical justification?

Keep your notes for possible use in the Writer's Workshop on page 895.

Interpreting Theme

2. The Breaking of Charity

In his autobiography, *Timebends*, Arthur Miller writes that "the real story" of the Salem witch trials is to be found in "the breaking of charity" within a human community. Write a brief essay explaining what you think Miller means by this interesting statement, and support your opinion with evidence from the text. Conclude your essay with your reflection on whether "the breaking of charity" could destroy a community today.

Analyzing Character

3. Private Lives

In an essay, analyze one of the characters in *The Crucible*. (You can use the notes you took on an interesting character as you read the play.) Some possible characters are John Proctor, Elizabeth Proctor, Judge Danforth, and Abigail Williams. In your essay, focus on these aspects of the character:

- conflicts
- motivation
- significant actions or decisions
- changes or discoveries

Include at the end of the essay your response to the character: Did you find the character believable? Did he or she do the right thing? Did you admire this person? Were your feelings negative? Or was your response mixed or complex?

Comparing Text and History

4. Is It True?

Compare details of the actual Salem witchcraft trials with details presented in *The Crucible*. You'll find information on the trials on pages 10–11 of this book. Use this feature and other resources, including the Internet, to gather data on the trials. Before looking further, formulate questions that will guide your research. Present your findings in an essay.

Researching Historical Context

5. Naming Names

Research the 1950s Congressional hearings into "un-American activities," and analyze the relationship of Miller's play to this painful American event. Examine Miller's own comments about his intentions (see the playwright's essay "Why I Wrote *The Crucible*," on page 827), as well as the reactions of contemporary literary and social critics. Include your own assessment of how effectively a work of fiction can comment on a real-life political or social situation.

Grading Timesaver

Rubrics for each Choices assignment appear on p. 196 in the *Portfolio Management System*.

CHOICES: Building Your Portfolio

1. **Collecting Ideas for a Problem-Solution Essay** Remind students, as they answer the questions, that some questions may have more than one possible answer. Encourage students to be as flexible as possible in their thinking, considering multiple causes, effects, parts of the problem, and possible solutions.

2. **Interpreting Theme** Before students consider present-day examples of "the breaking of charity," encourage them to define *charity* in detail. Help them move beyond the practical definition of giving alms to the poor and consider *charity* as a social, religious, and philosophical idea. You might also ask them how they think *charity* is related to *justice* and *mercy*.

3. **Analyzing Character** Remind students that, although this assignment is headed "Private Lives," no individual character is completely private. That is, every character is influenced in some way by other characters. Students might include in their essays an analysis of how one character was affected or changed by another character: for example, how John was affected by Elizabeth or by Abigail; how Abigail was affected by John or by Elizabeth.

4–5. **Critical Writing** As students work on their research-based essays, remind them to cite all their sources carefully and to consider the reliability and biases of their sources.

6. *The Crucible* is a tragedy because John Proctor, its hero, makes a tragic commitment. Proctor does not want to be heroic, but since he will not sign his name to a lie, he goes to his death with self-respect and new moral awareness.

7. Some students will feel that the passages of historical interpretation and references to contemporary politics detract from the play's artistic power. Others will feel these passages only add to the dramatic effect and that the play succeeds with or without its allegorical element.

Reading Check

a. He counsels people to confess to witchcraft to save their lives.

b. Abigail and Mercy Lewis have run off with Parris's money.

c. Elizabeth cannot judge John or forgive him (because he cannot forgive himself).

d. Proctor's confession will carry great weight in Salem. It will show the power of the court and help persuade others to confess.

OBJECTIVES

1. Recognize the structure of an analogy
2. Identify types of analogy relationships
3. Create examples of a formal analogy

Reading Skills and Strategies

Mini-Lesson: Analogies

This feature focuses on the strategy of solving the word and logic problems called analogies, a task students will often find on standardized tests.

One of the pitfalls of solving analogies is focusing solely on the word which the correct answer is related to. Offer this example:

HOUSE: SHELTER :: sweater : _____

Explain that focusing on *sweater* might lead to *wool* or *heavy* rather than to *warmth,* a far better response in relation to the entire analogy.

Try It Out
Possible Answers

Classification
BAGEL : BREAD :: pork : [meat]
Agent and related object
BRICK : MASON :: pipe: [plumber]
Characteristic quality
FURRY : KITTEN :: scaly : [fish]
Cause and effect
BLEACH : WHITENESS :: dye : [color]
Part and whole
DROPLET : SEA :: grains : [desert]
Synonym
ROUND : CIRCULAR :: smart : [intelligent]
Antonym
PATRIOT : TRAITOR :: loyalty : [unfaithfulness]
Function
DESK : STUDY :: bed : [sleep]
Degree
COLOSSAL : LARGE :: microscopic : [small]
Agent and related action
AUTHOR : WRITE :: violinist : [play]

VOCABULARY: DOING ANALOGIES

A kind of comparison called an **analogy** often appears as a logic problem in standardized tests. An analogy begins with a related pair of words or phrases. The goal is to create or identify a second pair that has a similar relationship.

Analogies appearing on tests are always written in a set form. Often the last word is omitted, and you must supply it.

TREE : FLORA :: mammal : _____

The colon (:) stands for the phrase "is related to." The double colon (::) between the capitalized word pair and the first word of the incomplete pair can be read as "in the same way that." Thus, you'd read the above analogy like this: "Tree is related to flora in the same way that mammal is related to . . ."

Now you have to do two things: Identify the relationship between the first two elements as precisely as possible, and choose a word that will make the final pair have a parallel relationship. In this case, you could say TREE **is a type of** FLORA. **Is a type of** is the relationship. Now read the first word of the second pair, supplying the same relationship: "mammal **is a type of** _____." The only word that fits this blank adequately is "fauna," a term often paired with "flora."

TREE : FLORA :: mammal : fauna

The chart in the next column shows the relationships that are most frequently used in formal analogies. In reading an analogy, you can substitute the phrasing of the relationship—"is a type of," for example, or "is similar in meaning to"—for the colon.

Sometimes only the first pair of an analogy will be presented, and you have to come up with a parallel second pair. If you are doing this type of analogy exercise, keep the following guidelines in mind:

1. Look for a second pair with a clear, precise relationship.
2. Compare the relationship, not the words.
3. Knowing the precise denotation (dictionary definition) of words will help. Consult a dictionary frequently.

4. Don't be tricked by choices in which the order is reversed. For example, if the first pair has first the part and then the whole, the second pair must appear in the same order.

TYPES OF ANALOGY RELATIONSHIPS		
TYPE	RELATIONSHIP	EXAMPLE
Classification	. . . is a type of . . .	TREE : FLORA
Performer and related object	. . . is the tool of . . .	BATON : CONDUCTOR
Characteristic quality	. . . is characteristic of . . .	SURLINESS : CURMUDGEON
Cause and effect	. . . is a cause (or effect) of . . .	FIRE : SMOKE
Part and whole	. . . is a part of . . .	STOMACH : DIGESTIVE TRACT
Synonym	. . . is similar in meaning to . . .	DRY : ARID
Antonym	. . . is opposite in meaning to . . .	KIND : CRUEL
Function	. . . is used to . . .	PEN : WRITE
Degree	. . . is a small (or large) . . .	CHUCKLE : LAUGH
Performer and related action	. . . does/performs . . .	CHEF : COOKS

Try It Out

Write an analogy exercise for each of the ten relationships defined above. Leave out the last word in each analogy, and trade papers with a partner. See if you can complete his or her exercises. Then, discuss the answers and any differences between the responses expected and those given.

Using Students' Strengths

Visual Learners

Have students who demonstrate an ability to grasp the abstract relationships in analogies work together to prepare a visual representation of each of the types of relationships outlined above. Encourage them to share their work with the class.

Auditory/Musical Learners

Invite students to create a series of rhymes, jingles, or poems to help everyone remember each of the analogy relationships. Suggest that students start with well-known songs and fit their words to the rhythm. Students should incorporate examples of the analogies in their songs.

READ ON

More from Miller

Arthur Miller has produced a great body of work. Some of his notable plays, besides *The Crucible* and *Death of a Salesman,* include *A View from the Bridge* (1955), about longshoremen without immigration papers; *Incident At Vichy* (1965), about French citizens arrested by the Nazis in 1942; and *The Price* (1968), about two adult brothers comparing their lives. He also wrote the screenplay for *The Misfits* (1961), a drama starring Clark Gable and Miller's then-wife Marilyn Monroe.

The Beginning of Black Theater

When *A Raisin in the Sun,* by Lorraine Hansberry, opened in 1959, it was an instant success. This play about an African American family in Chicago marked the beginning of a vigorous black theater movement, which became one of the most vital forces in the modern American theater. Lloyd Richards directed a superb cast, which included Sidney Poitier, Claudia McNeil, Diana Sands, Ruby Dee, and Louis Gossett. The play was translated into thirty languages and won the New York Drama Critics' Circle Award. At twenty-nine, Hansberry became the youngest person—and the first African American playwright—ever to win this award. The play is available in the HRW Library. A 1961 film adaptation starring Sidney Poitier and Ruby Dee is available on videotape, as is a 1989 American Playhouse television production.

Lessons and Legacies

Would you part with a cherished family heirloom if you thought that by selling it you could make a better life for your family? This is the question the Charles family must answer in August Wilson's 1990 Pulitzer Prize-winning play *The Piano Lesson.* An antique piano thus becomes the catalyst for the discovery of the family's African American heritage.

A Long Drive Together

For twenty-five years in midcentury Atlanta, Hoke Coleburn, an African American, works as the chauffeur for Daisy Werthan, an elderly white woman. Their evolving relationship is traced in *Driving Miss Daisy* (Theatre Communications), a gentle depiction of prejudice and aging that won the playwright Alfred Uhry a Pulitzer Prize in 1988. The Academy Award-winning film adaptation (1989) is available on videotape.

Dreams vs. Reality

Shy Laura Wingfield finds it easier to talk to her collection of glass animals than to people, but her mother insists that Laura prepare for "gentleman callers." Their poignant story is recounted in Tennessee Williams's *The Glass Menagerie* (1944), one of the best-loved dramas of the American Stage. Another Williams classic, *A Streetcar Named Desire* (1947), depicts a monumental clash of dream and reality in New Orleans. Both plays were made into notable films, available on videotape.

READ ON **891**

The American Language

Euphemisms

by Gary Q. Arpin

One day in 1837, Captain Frederick Marryat, a British naval officer visiting the United States, was escorting a young lady in Niagara Falls, New York. She slipped and grazed her shin, and Marryat asked, "Did you hurt your leg much?" What he said seemed to offend her.

"She turned from me," Marryat wrote, "evidently much shocked." Puzzled, he asked her what he had done wrong. The word *leg*, she told him, was never used in the presence of ladies. What word was used for "such articles," the captain asked her. "Her reply," he wrote, "was that the word *limb* was used."

Victorian Prudery

Ⓐ The young lady did not invent the delicacy that had caused a leg to become a limb. The year 1837 marked the beginning of the long reign of Queen Victoria in England. One of the meanings of the adjective formed from her name—*Victorian*—is "having excessively severe standards of respectability." The Victorian Age became known for its prudery, an attitude that was as common in some American social circles as it was in England.

During this period in America, the only polite word for women's stockings was *hose*, and undergarments were referred to as *unmentionables*. Even the word *woman* was considered vulgar; *female* and *lady* became its acceptable substitutes.

Victorians were so offended by the names of body parts that they developed a new vocabulary for meals. A chicken or turkey leg became a *drumstick* or a *first joint;* the *thigh* became the *second joint;* chicken or turkey breast came to be called simply *white meat.*

Euphemisms for Taboo Words

A **euphemism** is a word or phrase that is substituted for another word or phrase considered offensive or upsetting. The word *euphemism* comes from a Greek term meaning "to use words of good omen." People use euphemisms in an attempt to hide a reality they find unpleasant, or to politely communicate something that another person might find offensive.

Why do certain words become taboo or forbidden, while other words with the same meaning are acceptable? There is no simple answer, because the role that language plays in our lives is so complex. One thing is certain, though. There is nothing inherent in any word that makes it good or bad. Words become acceptable or offensive only because people give them those qualities.

Some words become taboo because they refer to experiences we find psychologically overwhelming. The more terrifying the experience, the more euphemisms we are likely to devise for it. For example, we have dozens of ways of talking about death without using that word. Some of our euphemisms for death are respectful, such as *departed, breathed her last, went to her final reward,* and *met his Maker.* Some are neutral, like *passed on, passed away,* and *deceased.* Others are humorous: *kicked the bucket, went West, bought the farm,* and *cashed in his chips* are flippant ways of reducing the horror of death.

Euphemisms and "Civilized Behavior"

For a number of reasons, Americans have been especially prone to using euphemisms. The early Puritans were concerned with

> Ⓑ People use euphemisms in an attempt to hide a reality they find unpleasant, or to politely communicate something that another person might find offensive.

go.hrw.com
LEO 11-American Language

purifying language as well as religious practice. While they did not completely eradicate profanity, they certainly created an atmosphere hostile to vulgar speech. Though Americans who later moved westward were not averse to using profanity, it was in the pioneer communities that linguistic delicacy often was most prevalent. "The essentially English word *bull*," William Bartlett wrote, "is refined beyond the mountains . . . into *cow-creature, male-cow,* and even *gentleman-cow!*"

"The Language of Anticipation"

Another aspect of the need to provide a kind of instant civilization through gentility in language is what the historian Daniel Boorstin has called "the language of anticipation." This form of "good speaking" described things as they were to be in the future, rather than as they actually were at the time. Wealthy City, Kansas, which never fulfilled the promise of its name and dwindled into extinction, is an example of this kind of positive thinking. This linguistic optimism was a common phenomenon in a country where someone confronting a muddy, stump-filled plain might imagine a prosperous farm in its place. As Boorstin points out, even the country's name, "United States of America," which appears in the Constitution, was anticipatory. "It expressed hope that the new nation be *united,* that the components really be *states,* and that somehow they could be identified with the whole of *America.*" (*State,* until that time, referred only to sovereign nations.)

Examples of this kind of anticipatory euphemism abound in American history. Americans needed to talk "big." For instance, *city* was preferred over the more modest (if more accurate) *town* or *village.* Many cities boasted an *opera house,* even if it usually was only a tiny auditorium that presented troupes of traveling jugglers. "The elegant *hotel,*" Boorstin writes, "was widely applied to ramshackle, flea-bitten inns and taverns. Americans thought they were not exaggerating but only anticipating—describing things which had not quite yet 'gone through the formality of taking place.'"

Euphemisms and Democracy

A love of inflated descriptive terms has a long history in America. Relentlessly democratic, Americans declared every man a "gentleman," while the British restricted the term to men of a particular social standing. Proud of being a nation with no inherited titles, Americans almost immediately began to generate countless acquired titles.

A British traveler in New York in 1744 remarked on the great many colonels he encountered. "It is a common saying here," he wrote, "that a man has no right to that dignity unless he has killed a rattlesnake." Governors of states were later empowered to bestow the title (along with *captain* and *major*) on virtually anyone they wished, and many did so with great zeal, notably in Kentucky.

Americans applied a similar principle to occupations. Any occupation that was in danger of falling below a certain level of acceptability was usually yanked up by its linguistic bootstraps. This relentless linguistic upgrading of occupational titles is especially popular today. At times, this upgrading is very subtle; at other times, very obvious.

What is the difference, for example, between a *teacher* and an *educator?* Most people would agree that *educator* has a slightly more prestigious ring to it. This can be accounted for by taking a look at where English words come from.

English is composed primarily of Anglo-Saxon and Latin-based words. Historically, the Anglo-Saxon words have been the property of the common people, while the Latinate words have filtered down from the upper classes. This was especially the case following the Norman conquest of England in 1066. After that invasion, French (which is derived ultimately from Latin) was the official language of England for generations. Most people in England, however, continued to speak their own Anglo-Saxon language. During this bilingual period, the language was further enriched with synonyms. In most cases, the French word became the genteel word, while the Anglo-Saxon word became the common word. This explains the difference between the Latin *educare* (to educate) and the Anglo-Saxon word *taecan* (to teach).

C Critical Thinking
Analyzing
? What does the pioneer emphasis on "linguistic delicacy" suggest about our attitudes toward how we speak and write? [Possible responses: It suggests that we link language with culture, social standing, and success. We tend to judge people initially on their language rather than on their accomplishments.]

D Vocabulary Note
Word Origins
Have students look at a map of their state (or the United States) and find at least five place names they consider to be examples of anticipatory naming. For example, Columbia Cross Roads, a tiny community in northern Pennsylvania, did not become the hub of the nation that its name suggests.

E Reading Skills and Strategies
Making Connections
Students might want to review the Declaration of Independence (pp. 115–125), where the transitional name "United Colonies" is in use. Have students research the shift away from this colonial name in the Articles of Confederation (the first U.S. constitution).

F Exploring the Culture
British Titles
? What are some of the inherited titles in Great Britain? [king, queen, prince, princess, duke, duchess, marquis, earl, viscount, viscountess, baron, baroness]

Using Students' Strengths

Visual Learners
Have students make a visual representation of the development of American English from its roots in Anglo-Saxon and Latin-based words. Students can show the formation of the language in any form they wish, such as a tree, flow chart, or time line. Display the visuals for the entire class to study.

A Elements of Literature
Diction

❓ What is a shorter, easier word for each of the following Latinate words: *acrimonious, homicide, iniquitous, velocity, veracity?* Check a dictionary to see if the shorter word has an Old English origin (OE). [Possible responses: *bitter, murder, evil, speed, truth.* Every word has an Old English origin.]

B Exploring the Culture
Fighting Words

In the twentieth century, war has been one of the primary sources of euphemistic language, from "collateral damage" (civilian casualties) to "redeployment" (withdrawal or retreat). When the United States entered World War I, German words and place names suddenly seemed unpatriotic. As a result, *sauerkraut* became *liberty cabbage,* and *Brandenberg,* Texas, became *Old Glory.*

C Critical Thinking
Speculating

❓ Why do you think euphemisms are as prevalent today as they were more than a century ago? [Possible responses: Time may have passed, but human nature has not changed. As a result, we still have a need to soften harsh realities. Though we live in a realistic age, it is as important as ever to soften the cruel edges of everyday life.]

Try It Out
Possible Answers

1. Answers will vary. Possible responses include "disposal service" for *garbage collector,* "funeral director" for *undertaker,* "previously owned vehicles" for *used cars.*
2. Plain words: *eat, spit, love, cheap, win, cow, pig, work, calf, father*—all classified as Anglo-Saxon (AS). Fancy words: *dine, expectorate, cherish, inexpensive, achieve, beef, pork, career, veal, parent*—classified as Latin (L), except for *achieve,* Old French (OF).
3. More direct words and phrases are a. *toilet* or *bathroom,* b. *died,* c. *poor,* d. *elderly people,* e. *janitor,* f. *garbage collectors,* g. *strike,* h. *pregnant,* i. *graves.*

T894

A Latinate words usually have more syllables than Anglo-Saxon words. Hence, a greater number of syllables often indicates a slide up the scale of acceptability. A *profession* (Latinate) somehow seems more important than a *job* (Anglo-Saxon). American job titles (or "career designations") have undergone frequent upgradings as a result of this tendency toward linguistic respectability. Thus, *mortician* (Latinate) was coined in the 1890s as a more dignified term than *undertaker* (Anglo-Saxon) for a person who manages a funeral home.

Euphemism and Distortion

Euphemisms can demonstrate sensitivity to the feelings of others. But euphemisms can also obscure meaning. Language can provide a veil to hide behind.

A boss would rather "excess" an employee than "fire" her, not because it makes the employee feel any better but because it makes the boss feel better. A government does not like to think of itself as "invading" another country, for example. It will make an *incursion,* or *liberate* **B** the country instead. It is wrong to be the aggressor in a war, and *invasion* is a very aggressive word.

Many people have attacked the bureaucratic tendency to use long Latinate words where a short Anglo-Saxon word would serve just as well. The state and federal governments are particularly creative in generating euphemisms: prison guards have become "correctional officers," budget deficits are "negative growth," and taxes are sometimes called "revenue enhancement." This tendency has also spilled over to the general public in the language of advertising. Secondhand clothes are now sold as "vintage clothing," and used cars are called "previously owned" or "pre-driven." Even in **C** this so-called modern age, softening blunt or distasteful names for things sometimes seems as prevalent now as in those prudish Victorian times.

Try It Out

1. **Interpreting connotations.** With another student, look through the local Yellow Pages or another business directory. Find at least three examples of euphemistic titles for occupations or businesses. Write the titles on a sheet of paper, and next to each write the ordinary word it is replacing. (For example, "resale boutique" is a euphemism that sometimes replaces "thrift shop.")

2. **Researching word origins.** Make two columns on a sheet of paper. Write the column titles *Plain* and *Fancy* at the top of the page. Decide which word in each of the following pairs belongs in each column. Then find each word in a dictionary. Write *L* next to the word if it is derived from Latin. Write *OE* if it is derived from Old English—that is, if it has Anglo-Saxon roots. What patterns do you notice?
   eat / dine
   spit / expectorate
   love / cherish
   cheap / inexpensive
   achieve / win
   beef / cow
   pig / pork
   work / career
   veal / calf
   father / parent

3. **Replacing euphemisms.** The following words are commonly used euphemisms. See if you can come up with a word or phrase that is a more direct way of saying the same thing.
   a. restroom
   b. passed on
   c. underprivileged
   d. senior citizens
   e. custodian
   f. sanitation engineers
   g. work stoppage
   h. expecting
   i. resting places

Assessing Learning

Check Test: True-False

1. During the Victorian age, the word *woman* was considered vulgar. [True]
2. The word *euphemism* comes from an Anglo-Saxon term meaning "good saying." [False]
3. In pioneer communities, the language spoken was often surprisingly delicate. [True]
4. The United States has a long tradition of using euphemisms. [True]
5. For generations, French was the official language of England. [True]

Writer's Workshop

The history of the writt... word is rich
Page 1

PERSUASIVE WRITING
PROBLEM-SOLUTION ESSAY

If you've ever tried to work out a problem or dilemma by writing about it in a diary, journal, or letter, you know how the simple act of writing can help you think through problems and possible solutions. When you write a **problem-solution essay,** you thoroughly explore a problem and its possible solutions in a formal, methodical way. In a problem-solution essay, you identify and describe a problem and then propose one or more solutions to that problem.

Prewriting

1. **Looking for problems.** The problems you think about in a given day may range from how to save enough money for a new bicycle to how to implement world peace. The problem of saving money is probably going to be too personal and specific to be of interest to a general audience. The problem of world peace is, on the other hand, far too broad for an essay. In selecting a topic for a problem-solution essay, think of a problem that is interesting to other people and manageable in a short paper.

You might already have an idea for a problem to explore if you completed the Writer's Notebook assignment on page 889. If you are starting from scratch, you might begin by thinking of problems that affect the everyday life of yourself, your family, and your friends. Think about problems you have observed firsthand in your school or community. Are students having a problem getting access to computers? Does your community need to do more to respond to the needs of people with disabilities by improving wheelchair access and increasing handicapped parking? Are families failing to participate fully in your local recycling program? Quickwrite a list of problems you would like to write about.

You might focus on the theme of this collection, "the breaking of charity." How is "charity" broken in the world today? How does the breaking of charity cause problems in families, in communities, and in the wider society?

In selecting a problem to write about, consider these questions:

• Which problem do I care most about solving?

• Which problem do I most want to learn about?

• Which problem could I, or others, act on?

Technology
HELP

See Writer's Workshop 2 CD-ROM. *Assignment: Controversial Issue.*

ASSIGNMENT
Describe a problem, and then propose and defend the solution or solutions you believe are best.

AIM
To explore; to explain; to persuade.

AUDIENCE
People who are affected by the problem; people who can carry out your suggested solution; your teacher and classmates.

WRITER'S WORKSHOP 895

MAIN OBJECTIVE
Write a problem-solution essay which identifies and describes a problem and then proposes one or more solutions

PROCESS OBJECTIVES
1. Use appropriate prewriting techniques to identify and develop a topic
2. Create a first draft
3. Use Evaluation Criteria as a basis for determining revision strategies
4. Revise the first draft, incorporating suggestions generated by self- or peer evaluation
5. Proofread and correct errors (ATE)
6. Create a final draft
7. Choose an appropriate method of publication (ATE)
8. Reflect on progress as a writer (ATE)

Planning

• **Block Schedule**
Block Scheduling Lesson Plans with Pacing Guide

• **One-Stop Planner**
CD-ROM with Test Generator

— *Resources: Print and Media* —

Writing and Language
• *Portfolio Management System*
    Prewriting, p. 198
    Peer Editing, p. 199
    Assessment Rubric, p. 200

• *Workshop Resources*
    Revision Strategy Teaching Notes, p. 37
    Revision Strategy Transparencies 19, 20
• *Writer's Workshop 2 CD-ROM*
    Controversial Issue

Introducing the Writer's Workshop

- Bring copies of recent local newspapers to class, and ask each student to read at least one editorial or column dealing with a local problem.
- After students have read the piece they selected, ask volunteers to outline briefly the problems addressed and the solutions proposed in the editorial or article.
- Then, ask students whether or not they found the writers convincing. Was the problem real? Was it serious? Were the solutions proposed adequate to resolve the problem? If one solution was recommended, did the writer seem to be making an objective judgment?
- After several volunteers have reported, point out that we encounter problem-solution writing in almost every issue of a newspaper. We see it in headlines, editorials, even on the sports page.

Teaching the Writer's Workshop

Prewriting
Encourage students to choose problems they have observed firsthand. Students should also consider whether information on the problem can be readily obtained. The school environment is a good place to begin because students are probably most familiar with school problems. An added benefit is that they can discuss the problems and solutions with other students and with school personnel.

2. **Defining the problem.** Once you've chosen a problem to write about, you need to define it: You can't solve a problem that you don't understand. To define the problem you want to write about, ask yourself these questions:

- Why is it a problem?
- What causes this problem?
- What or whom does the problem affect?
- How does it affect them?

If you don't have the answers to all these questions, you'll want to do some research, which will probably involve reading, interviewing, viewing, or listening. For example, if you are interested in the effectiveness of neighborhood crime-prevention efforts in your community, you might want to interview local police officers.

3. **Brainstorming solutions.** Once you have thoroughly investigated your problem, you can move on to finding some answers. Remember, don't censor yourself. Often, good solutions come from seemingly improbable ideas.

One way to thoroughly explore multiple solutions is to make a chart in which you list the advantages and disadvantages of each solution. Don't forget to include solutions that have already been tried, perhaps in other schools or communities, and to note how effective these solutions have been. The chart below explores the topic of community recycling.

Model

Problem: *Families in the community do not recycle cans, glass, and newspapers.*

Possible Solutions	Advantages	Disadvantages
Give an award to one family each week, on the basis of that family's recycling	Encourages family participation; enhances public awareness of problem	Cost of awards; people who don't promptly win awards may lose interest
Provide recycling containers and pickup service	Makes participation easier; can use existing volunteer groups	Expense of containers and pickup service; requires long-term management
Fine people who do not recycle	Provides incentive to recycle	Requires regulatory staff; may foster negative feelings

Try It Out
Together with one or more classmates, choose a problem from the Quickwrite list you made while prewriting, and use a cluster diagram, map, double-entry journal, or other graphic organizer to list possible solutions.

Review your chart, and ask these questions to help you evaluate all possible solutions and select the best one:

- What are possible objections to these solutions?
- What are the counterarguments to these objections?
- Which solutions seem better than others?
- Is one solution more practical than the others?
- Does one solution do the most good for the most people?

4. **Outlining.** Once you have decided on a solution, pull all the information you've gathered together, and plan your essay. Outline the following items:

- the problem
- your proposed solution
- the steps necessary to implement your solution

Reaching All Students

Struggling Writers
If students have difficulty arriving at a topic that is appropriate for the assignment, encourage them to brainstorm with other students to generate a list of possibilities. Then, have them classify the problems on their list, using a chart like the following.

School	Local	National	International

After students have filled out the chart, encourage them to consider the problems listed in the first and second columns as possible topics. They can then use the Brainstorming Solutions chart (p. 896) to generate further ideas.

- evidence to support your solution, including reasons, facts, examples, and statistics (If you need more support, now is the time to gather it.)
- possible objections to your solution
- other possible solutions and the reasons you rejected them

5. Targeting your audience. When you write a problem-solution essay, it's crucial to know who your audience is: Remember, you are trying to convince people that (a) your problem is serious and (b) your proposed solution is the best one. To convince your readers, you have to know what point of view and what concerns they bring to your essay.

After you decide who your audience is, ask these questions: Are your target readers aware that there is a problem? If so, what do they already know about it? In other words, what background information do you need to provide?

Drafting

A problem-solution essay can take many different forms. One effective pattern is as follows:

1. Introducing the problem. Think about how you can best engage your readers' interest. If you're confident that your readers share your interest in the problem, you might simply introduce it directly, together with a statement of its importance. Or, you might start with an anecdote or attention-getting fact. For example, in an essay about recycling, you may open with this detail: "Every day, thousands of pounds of newspapers, glass jars, and aluminum cans are needlessly thrown into our town dump."

2. Stating the problem. State the problem clearly. In an essay about recycling, you might write, "Most of the families in our community are simply not recycling their newspapers, glass jars, and cans." In describing the problem, you might want to use anecdotes or testimonies from interviews to engage the readers' interest. You might also want to use **connotative language**—words and phrases that create a specific emotional response.

3. Discussing the solutions. Use your chart as a guide to touch briefly on two or three solutions that have been suggested or tried. You might choose the solutions you think your audience is inclined to favor. Discuss the disadvantages of these solutions in a balanced, fair way, being as thorough and persuasive as you can.

Devote about a paragraph to describing your solution and how it would be implemented. Be sure to outline the steps involved in implementing your solution. Remember that one purpose of your essay is to persuade your reader that, having considered all factors, you have chosen the best solution. Think of arguments you might make for your solution based on, for example, its practicality, feasibility, low cost, easy implementation, or other benefits.

4. Producing the evidence. Use the most persuasive reasoning and information you've collected to show your readers that your solution is the best. Bolster your argument, if possible, with evidence from some other community or school that has tried this solution. You may even be able to locate statistics that back up your claim that this is an effective solution.

Strategies for Elaboration

The evidence you plan to use in your essay should be evaluated against these standards, or **criteria:**

1. Is the evidence **trustworthy?** Is it from a reliable source or from an expert?

2. Is the evidence **accurate?** If it seems suspect, check it against other sources.

3. Is the evidence **useful?** Is it logically connected to your problem or your solution?

Communications Handbook HELP

See Taking Notes and Documenting Sources; List of Sources Cited; Proofreading.

Proofreading Tips HELP

Double-check all statistics against your sources. Be sure you have used quotation marks when quoting from your sources and experts.

Drafting

- Students will benefit from studying additional models of problem-solution essays. Models of these are widely available in newspapers and magazines, or you may wish to write one yourself for students to study. Ask students to bring in examples of problem-solution articles in the publications they read, and you can help them evaluate these examples.
- Remind students that opening paragraphs are important in catching the reader's attention. If students have difficulty developing good paragraphs at the start of the drafting phase, suggest they postpone writing the introductory paragraph until they have written the rest of the essay.
- Remind students to use anecdotes, testimonies, statistics, and evidence as elaboration. Their elaboration will be most effective if they evaluate it using the criteria listed in the Strategies for Elaboration box.

Using Students' Strengths

Spatial/Kinesthetic Learners
Some of the solutions that students recommend might lend themselves to model building. For example, if a student tackles the problem of how to ease the parking situation at school, it might be helpful to create a model of how the parking lot could be laid out differently. Students will use the models to think through their solutions. Having a concrete model available to consult will help students express their solutions more clearly and concisely.

Linguistic/Interpersonal Learners
Some students may find it useful to conduct interviews with people who can provide information about the problems or react to proposed solutions. Have students prepare an interview protocol that contains the planned questions and a place to write responses. Each interview should be recorded on a separate protocol sheet. Ask students to practice by interviewing one another. If possible, videotape practice sessions and have students review their tapes to spot places where their interview techniques could be improved. *Obtain permission from parents or guardians and from the parties students will contact before work begins on this activity.*

Evaluating and Revising

Have students use the Evaluation Criteria provided here to review their drafts and determine needed revisions.

Proofreading

Have students proofread their own papers first and then exchange them with other students. For this assignment, remind students to be particularly careful of the use of quotation marks and transitional expressions.

If time permits, the final copy should be put aside for at least a day before it is proofread for the final time by the author.

Publishing

Have students compile their essays in a class book with a title such as "Building a Better World" or "Creative Problem Solving." You might also suggest that some students submit their essays to the school or local newspaper for publication as expanded letters to the editor or as guest editorials.

Reflecting

Help students reflect on their writing by answering questions such as these:
1. Did you enjoy the problem-solving process?
2. Did you find that you came up with more solutions than you thought you would?
3. Did the problems discourage you, or did you feel hopeful about finding workable solutions?
4. Do you feel that writing about problems can be a significant part of developing solutions?
5. Do you think sharing your essay will help get your solution enacted?

Resources

Peer Editing Forms and Rubrics
• *Portfolio Management System,* p. 199
Revision Transparencies
• *Workshop Resources,* p. 37

Revision STRATEGIES

Reread your essay from the viewpoint of your readers. Ask yourself: Have I presented the problem in a compelling way? How strong a case have I made for my solution? Have I responded to all likely objections? Have I addressed alternative solutions?

Language Handbook HELP

See Revising to Reduce Wordiness, page 1237.

■ Evaluation Criteria

A good problem-solution essay
1. *has a strong opening that elicits interest in the topic*
2. *clearly states the problem and its importance*
3. *addresses solutions other than your own and explains their disadvantages*
4. *clearly explains your solution and supports it with evidence*
5. *addresses possible objections to your proposed solution*
6. *takes into account the reader's point of view*
7. *has an objective, authoritative tone that reflects your commitment to your solution*
8. *leaves the reader feeling convinced of the soundness of the solution*

Remember that you will want to credit your sources with full documentation. In your essay, you'll credit sources in two places—in parenthetical citations and in the list of Works Cited at the end of your essay. (For more information on documenting sources, see page 518.)

5. **Answering possible objections.** In presenting your solution, you will have to respond to the logical arguments your readers may raise against it. What concerns and objections to your solution might your audience raise? Your paper will be most persuasive if you directly address all possible disadvantages to your solution that you can think of. Explain why you consider these disadvantages negligible compared to the advantages.

6. **Concluding.** Conclude by again stating your solution and briefly restating its advantages. You might conclude your essay with your personal conviction that this solution should be implemented, or end with a clear call to action—advice about what readers themselves can do.

Evaluating and Revising

1. **Peer review.** After you have a rough draft, ask one or more classmates who are interested in the problem to read your essay. Then, ask them the following questions.

   • Did I help you to understand the problem, and did I convince you that it is a significant one? If not, how can I persuade you to care about this problem as I do?
   • Do you think I clearly and fully described my proposed solution? Did I provide sound reasons for adopting my solution? If not, what reasons should I add?
   • Which solution is the most convincing? the least convincing? Should any proposed solutions be omitted?
   • Do you feel I have overlooked a potential solution? If so, how can I address this other solution while still showing why I think my solution is preferable?
   • Are my tone and approach appropriate for the subject?
   • What is the strongest aspect of my essay? What parts of the essay need more work?

2. **Self-evaluation.** Revise your essay according to the feedback that you find most helpful. Then, do your own critique using the same list of questions. Eliminate any unnecessary words in your essay so that your arguments are forceful and easy to grasp.

Grading Timesaver

Rubrics for this Writer's Workshop assignment appear on p. 200 of the *Portfolio Management System.*

Language Workshop

OBJECTIVES
1. Use transitional words and phrases to connect ideas
2. Understand the meaning and use of particular transitions

FITTING IT ALL TOGETHER: USING TRANSITIONAL EXPRESSIONS

Transitional expressions are words or phrases that provide a transition between ideas, making writing more coherent. Often these expressions show chronological or spatial relationships. They may also show relationships of cause and effect, definition, or contrast.

EXAMPLE Arthur Miller was worried about a climate of fear in the United States in the early 1950s. **Therefore,** he wrote *The Crucible,* about a similar period of public anxiety in Colonial America. (**Therefore** indicates a cause-and-effect relationship.)

TRANSITIONAL WORDS AND PHRASES

Comparing Ideas / Classification and Definition		
also	another	similarly
and	moreover	too

Contrasting Ideas / Classification and Definition		
although	in spite of	on the other hand
but	instead	still
however	nevertheless	yet

Showing Cause and Effect / Narration		
as a result	consequently	so that
because	since	therefore

Showing Time / Narration		
after	eventually	next
at last	finally	then
at once	first	thereafter
before	meanwhile	when

Showing Place / Description		
above	down	next
across	here	over
around	in	there
before	inside	to
beyond	into	under

Showing Importance / Evaluation		
first	mainly	then
last	more important	to begin with

Writer's Workshop Follow-Up: Revising

Reread the problem-solution essay you wrote for the Writer's Workshop (page 895). If some of your ideas seem disconnected, or if cause-and-effect and other relationships are unclear, revise your essay by adding transitions for coherence.

Technology HELP

See Language Workshop CD-ROM. *Key word entry: transitional expressions.*

Language Handbook HELP

See Commas, pages 1243-1244.

Try It Out
Use transitional words or phrases to combine sentences as you rewrite the following paragraph about *The Crucible.*

Reverend Parris's daughter Betty engages in some type of ritual with Tituba, Parris's slave. Betty becomes very ill. Tituba is forced to admit she practices witchcraft, with the power to harm other people. Leading citizens of Salem, including John Proctor, are accused of doing the devil's work. Proctor is sentenced to hang.

LANGUAGE WORKSHOP 899

Resources
Workshop Resources
• Worksheet, p. 61
Language Workshop CD-ROM
• Transitional Expressions
Try It Out
Possible Answer
Reverend Parris's daughter Betty becomes very ill *after* she engages in some type of ritual with Tituba, Parris's slave. *Consequently,* Tituba is forced to admit she practices witchcraft, with the power to harm other people. *Eventually,* leading citizens of Salem, including John Proctor, are accused of doing the devil's work. *As a result,* Proctor is sentenced to hang.

Assessing Learning

Quick Check: Transitional Expressions
Fill in the blanks with appropriate transitional expressions. Possible answers are provided in brackets.

1. Growing up during the Depression gave Arthur Miller a sense of social awareness. _____ his plays have strong social themes [As a result,]

2. _____ he graduated from high school, he worked in a warehouse to earn money for college. [After]

3. He attended the University of Michigan; _____ he began to write plays. [there]

4. _____ his plays, he has written novels, nonfiction, a screenplay, and an autobiography. [In addition to]

OBJECTIVES

1. Identify a critic's criteria for judgment
2. Recognize bias
3. Identify one's own evaluation criteria
4. Clarify or defend views different from those of a critic

Using the Strategies
Possible Answers

1. Maslin focuses on the adaptation of a classic—the setting, theme, visual style, and acting.
2. Her criteria are as follows: an interesting setting that works with the story, straightforward directing, "realistic" visual style, successful expression of a universal theme, and clear acting by subtle actors.
3. She has a favorable view of the film. She likes the way the director has adapted the play, which she supports by saying ". . . Hytner's vibrant screen version succeeds so well in transcending time and place." She also thinks that the theme is communicated well, pointing out that the film suggests a range of themes "without losing track of its central concern, the murderous power of lies." Maslin also thinks that the look of the film and the acting are successful: She says the film's "museum realism" has a way of "heightening its drama," and she mentions that the actors "speak quaintly" while remaining "resoundingly clear."
4. Answers will vary.

Alternative Strategy
Analyzing and Comparing Reviews
Students may also read reviews of live performances and compare their responses with those of the critics. Features peculiar to live performance include **sets**, which can range from realistic (see p. 817) to symbolic (see pp. 810–811); **lighting; voice projection; movements onstage** (the camera can zoom in for close-ups, but the actors are always "onstage"—the perspective doesn't change the way it can in a film); and the **effects of an enthusiastic or indifferent audience** on the performances.

Situation
Suppose you've seen the film adaptation (available on videotape) of Arthur Miller's play *The Crucible*, and you want to compare your opinions with those of a film critic. An excerpt from a critic's review appears in the box to the right. Here are strategies you can follow in comparing your response to that of the critic.

Strategies
Recognize the critic's criteria.
- Note which elements of the film the critic focuses on. What elements, if any, does the critic ignore?
- What seem to be the critic's criteria for a good film?

Compare the criteria with those elements you look for in a good film.
- Your criteria might include an original **plot**; believable **dialogue** and **characters**; skillful **directing**; an interesting **setting**; realistic **acting**; good camera **work, costume design,** and **pacing.** Which of these are most important to you?

Be aware of bias.
- Does the reviewer seem biased against anyone involved in the film?
- Does the reviewer seem biased against the film's topic? Are any loaded words used?

The Crucible
JANET MASLIN

We've grown so accustomed to seeing classic works transposed to jazzier settings that it's startling to see what Nicholas Hytner has done to *The Crucible*: played it straight. Yet it is precisely by leaving Arthur Miller's 1953 play so emphatically in the Salem, Mass., of 1692 that Hytner's vibrant screen version succeeds so well in transcending time and place. . . .

As adapted gamely by the playwright into a screenplay that takes advantage of scenic backgrounds and photogenic stars, *The Crucible* now speaks to subtler forms of dishonesty and opportunism than it did before.

This agile film is so simply, abstractly rooted in Salem's soil that it becomes free to suggest anything from the impact of religious fundamentalism on politics to the hysterical excess of tabloid television. Along the way, this *Crucible* heats up its dramatic tale of marital betrayal and redemption without losing track of its central concern, the murderous power of lies.

Hytner . . . is particularly adept at balancing the film's look of museum realism with its frankly theatrical ways of heightening its drama. . . . The actors speak quaintly ("Are the accusers always holy now, were they born this morning pure as God's fingers?") without ever making their meaning less than resoundingly clear. Especially impressive here is Ms. Allen, whose look of luminous simplicity suits the film's visual style and whose immensely dignified performance captures the essence of Miller's concerns.

—*The New York Times,* November 27, 1996

- What evidence does the critic provide to support his or her opinions? Is the evidence credible, even if you disagree with the critic's opinions?
- Note the **tone** of the review and how it affects your reading.

Using the Strategies

1. In this excerpt from her review of *The Crucible*, what elements does critic Janet Maslin focus on?
2. What are her criteria for a good film (insofar as you can tell from this excerpt)?
3. What are the critic's opinions of this film? Does she support her opinions effectively? Cite specific examples.
4. Decide if you agree or disagree with the critic's main opinions, and why.

Extending the Strategies
- Make a list of what *you* look for in a good film.
- Look for two different reviews of the same film. Do you find one review more convincing than the other? (Note: The Internet is a good source.)
- Read the reviews in several different newspapers and magazines. Which publication publishes the best reviews, in your opinion?

Crossing the Curriculum

Music
Ask students to apply the strategies in this lesson to evaluate the work of a music critic. Have students find reviews of music that they are familiar with in newspapers or magazines. Have them evaluate the reviews and then write their own critical evaluations.

History
Find reviews of other productions of *The Crucible* or reviews by other critics of the same film. Compare these critics' views with those of Janet Maslin. Determine whether the critics use the same evaluation criteria. If not, what are the differences? What criteria do they use? Do styles of criticism change, just as methods of acting or filming do?

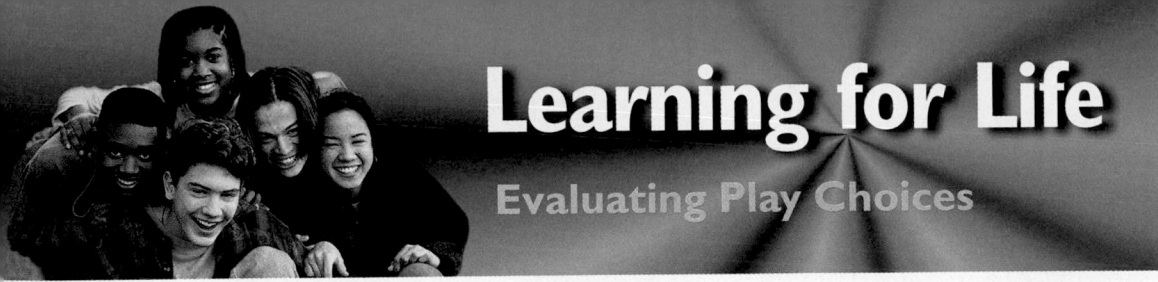

Learning for Life

Evaluating Play Choices

OBJECTIVES
1. Conduct research
2. Evaluate a play
3. Work cooperatively to reach a consensus
4. Create and evaluate a persuasive presentation

Problem

Evaluating a drama means more than just saying "I liked that play" or "It stinks." Sometimes we may need to evaluate a play's suitability for a specific purpose or its appropriateness for a certain audience, setting, or physical location. A play that addresses adult themes would be suitable for a professional theater but inappropriate in a middle school. One that calls for elaborate costumes, special effects, and a huge stage belongs on Broadway—not in a small community playhouse. How can we evaluate a play's suitability for a particular situation, purpose, and audience?

Project

Collect and evaluate information on a number of plays in order to recommend one to be performed next year by your school.

Preparation

1. Form a team of evaluators.
2. In your school or community library, research eight to ten plays to evaluate. You can consult with a librarian, your English teacher, or the school drama teacher. Start with plays commonly taught and/or performed in high schools.
3. Decide the role each team member will play in evaluating the eight to ten plays.
4. Come to a consensus on the criteria you will use to evaluate the plays. Some criteria you might use are
   - general quality and value
   - number and types of roles
   - staging requirements
   - subject matter and language suitability for high school

   Include any other criteria you think are important in making your recommendation.
5. Prepare an evaluation form that each team member will fill out for each play that is being considered. Your form should list the various criteria your team agreed upon.

Procedure

1. Read the plays and any critical literature you can find about them. Fill out your evaluation forms.
2. As a group, convene to discuss the plays and your evaluations.
3. Reach consensus on one play you will recommend as being suitable for your school to perform next year.

Presentation

Present your drama evaluations and recommendations in one of the following formats (or another your teacher approves):

1. **Letter to the Drama Teacher**
   Working as a group, compose a detailed, persuasive letter to a drama or English teacher in your school, describing your project and the evaluation process, listing the plays you examined, and justifying your recommendation.

2. **Informational Display**
   As a group, create an informational display about the plays. Include excerpts from your evaluations, dialogue from the plays, photographs of the playwrights or performances of the plays, and any other elements that will make your display attractive and informative. Exhibit your display in your school or your community library.

3. **Critics' Corner**
   Prepare a "Sneak Previews"–style presentation of your reviews. Each member of your group should orally present his or her evaluation of a play. If individuals from different groups evaluated the same play, you could pair reviewers from the different groups and have them present a spirited discussion of the play.

Processing

What did this project teach you about evaluating drama? How could you apply techniques you used to make decisions and choose from various alternatives in your everyday life? Write a reflection for your portfolio.

Resources

Viewing and Representing
HRW Multimedia Presentation Maker
Students may wish to use the *Multimedia Presentation Maker* to create their informational displays.

Teaching the Lesson

One of the uses of reviews, of course, is that they can help us make personal choices. Have students choose a play from their collection of reviews and attend a live performance. (This might not be as difficult as it sounds. Regional theaters abound; encourage students to research regional theaters in their area. They could select plays for this project based on plays currently "on the boards" in a theater near them.) They themselves should act as reviewers during the performance. They should go equipped with a small notepad and pen or pencil (many reviewers take notes on the program; some even stay in their seats during intermission and use laptops). Before students attend the performance, suggest that they review the basic elements of drama (see the comments by playwright Robert Anderson on pp. 813–815). When they return from the play, they should immediately organize their responses. Then, in a group, have them compare their responses to the play with the review they read. What are the points on which they agree, and disagree, with the critic?

Grading Timesaver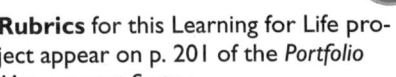

Rubrics for this Learning for Life project appear on p. 201 of the *Portfolio Management System*.

Developing Workplace Competencies

Preparation	Procedure	Presentation
• Uses resources well • Makes decisions • Works on teams • Evaluates data	• Communicates ideas and information • Works well with people from diverse backgrounds • Reasons	• Thinks creatively • Demonstrates individual responsibility • Exhibits self-esteem

1. Read literature of the contemporary period (1950 to the present) on the themes "The Wages of War," "Discoveries and Awakenings," "From Generation to Generation," and "The Created Self"
2. Interpret literary elements used in the literature with special emphasis on satire
3. Apply a variety of reading strategies to contemporary American literature
4. Respond to literature in a variety of modes
5. Learn and use new words
6. Learn about the influence of technology on the American language
7. Plan, draft, revise, edit, proof, and publish an evaluation
8. Write sentences using effective diction
9. Demonstrate the ability to read a memorandum
10. Explore ways to promote appreciation of culturally diverse contemporary arts

Swing Landscape
(1938) by Stuart Davis.
Oil on canvas
(86¾″ x 172⅛″)
(220.3 cm x 437.2 cm).

© Indiana University Art Museum, Bloomington. Photograph by Michael Cavanagh and Kevin Montague, Copyright 1998: Indiana University Art Museum. © Estate of Stuart Davis/ Licensed by VAGA, New York, NY.

Selection Readability

This Annotated Teacher's Edition provides a summary of each selection in the student book. Following each Summary heading, you will find one, two, or three small icons. These icons indicate, in an approximate sense, the reading level of the selection.

■ One icon indicates that the selection is easy.

■ ■ Two icons indicate that the selection is on an intermediate reading level.

■ ■ ■ Three icons indicate that the selection is challenging.

Contemporary Literature
1950 to Present

903

RESPONDING TO THE ART

Stuart Davis (1894–1964), an American painter, was associated early in his career with the Ashcan School of artists, also known as The Eight. (For more information on this group, see pp. T523 and T525.) Davis's later paintings typically employ forms found in nature and in everyday American life, composed in flat patterns that resemble posters. Davis is recognized as the finest American Cubist and an artist of originality, wit, and energy. He was a devoted fan of jazz and American music, and *Swing Landscape* reflects the verve and spontaneity of jazz rhythms.

Activity. Stuart Davis claimed that even his most abstract forms were based on shapes and objects observed in reality. Ask students what they see in this painting. [Possible responses: buildings, bricks, rooftops, a city scene.] How would you describe the painting's mood? [Possible answers: jazzy, energetic, lively, exciting.] Have students look through the book to find paintings that evoke a similar mood.

Resources

Viewing and Representing
Videocassette
Use the videocassette to explore stories and ways of storytelling.
• Videocassette B, Segment 10

Responding to the Quotation

❓ What does this description of Catch-22 say about life in combat? Do you think the catch applies to other aspects of contemporary life? Explain. [Possible responses: Catch-22 embodies the senseless contradictions of life during wartime. In everyday life, Catch-22 suggests a wide variety of absurd and inescapable circumstances, which are sometimes called "lose-lose situations." In such situations, no matter what you do, you lose. Like Joseph Heller, people often use humor to mask the desperation of such conditions. As a contemporary bumper sticker puts it, "In today's rat race, even if you win, you're still a rat."]

Contemporary Literature

by **John Leggett, Susan Allen Toth,**

John Malcolm Brinnin, *and* **Thomas Hernacki**

"You mean there's a catch?"

"Sure there's a catch," Doc Daneeka replied. "Catch-22. Anyone who wants to get out of combat duty isn't really crazy."

There was only one catch and that was Catch-22, which specified that a concern for one's own safety in the face of dangers that were real and immediate was the process of a rational mind. Orr was crazy and could be grounded. All he had to do was ask; and as soon as he did, he would no longer be crazy and would have to fly more missions. Orr would be crazy to fly more missions and sane if he didn't, but if he was sane he had to fly them. If he flew them he was crazy and didn't have to; but if he didn't want to he was sane and had to. Yossarian was moved very deeply by the absolute simplicity of this clause of Catch-22 and let out a respectful whistle.

"That's some catch, that Catch-22," he observed.

"It's the best there is," Doc Daneeka agreed.

—Joseph Heller, from Catch-22

Reaching All Students

Struggling Readers

Have students use a chart such as Transparency 11: Analysis Chart in the Transparency Package to record supporting information for inferences they make as they read this introduction. Encourage students to make at least three inferences based on the information in the essay. After students have finished reading, have them explain the thought process they used in making each inference.

English Language Learners

Have students create a glossary of words relating to contemporary literature and culture. As they read this introduction, have them record words that give them difficulty or words that define some aspect of contemporary arts, using a college or unabridged dictionary when necessary. When they have finished reading the introduction, ask them to review the words and make sure all the definitions make sense to them.

Advanced Learners

Have students research and report on one contemporary literary technique or cultural movement. Students might consider Feminist Criticism, Cultural Literacy, Semiotics, or New Historicism. Skimming an encyclopedia of contemporary culture will increase students' awareness of possible movements or techniques to research. *The Columbia Dictionary of Modern Literary and Cultural Criticism* is a good place to start.

On August 6, 1945, at 8:15 A.M., an atomic bomb was dropped on the Japanese city of Hiroshima from the U.S. airplane *Enola Gay.* Within seconds, the center of Hiroshima had disappeared. The bomb, in effect, ended World War II, and its mushroom cloud has cast a shadow over each generation since.

Although many Americans disapproved of the use of the atomic bomb to end World War II, most Americans agreed with the purpose of the war itself. They were fighting against tyranny, against regimes that would destroy the American way of life. Only twenty years later, however, the United States became deeply involved in another overseas war—this time in Vietnam—that would sharply divide the nation. In the 1960s, demonstrations, both peaceful and violent, became commonplace. To some writers, such as Kurt Vonnegut, Jr., the madness of the war-torn world was an inescapable condition of modern life, and the only appropriate response was hard-edged laughter at life's tragic ironies. The term *gallows humor*—ironic humor arising from an acknowledgment of the absurd or grotesque—was often used to describe Vonnegut's work, as well as that of Joseph Heller, Terry Southern, and others. Heller's novel *Catch-22* (1961) is set in World War II, but the absurdities it describes belong to postwar life. In *Catch-22,* madness and war are inextricably mixed, not because madness is a result of war but because war is the result of our madness.

Whaam!
(1963) by Roy Lichtenstein. Acrylic on canvas (172.7cm × 406.4cm).

© Copyright Contemporary Art Services, New York. Tate Gallery, London. Courtesy Art Resource, NY.

> At all times, an old world is collapsing and a new world arising; we have better eyes for the collapse than the rise, for the old one is the world we know. The artist, in focusing on his own creation, finds, and offers, relief from the tension and sadness of being burdened not just with consciousness but with historical consciousness. . . .
>
> —John Updike, *from Hugging the Shore*

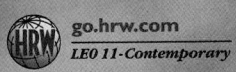
go.hrw.com
LE0 11-Contemporary

CONTEMPORARY LITERATURE 905

Taking a Second Look

Time Line

• 1950–1959

Lorraine Hansberry died from cancer in 1965 at the age of thirty-four, six years after she had won the New York Drama Critics Circle Award for her first completed play, *A Raisin in the Sun* (see p. T817). Two other Hansberry plays, *The Sign in Sidney Brustein's Window* and *Les Blancs,* were published, and most of Hansberry's unpublished writings and letters later appeared in the book *To Be Young, Gifted and Black.*

• 1960–1964

Dr. Martin Luther King, Jr.'s "I Have a Dream" speech reached an audience of more than two hundred thousand people gathered in Washington, D.C. —and millions more watching on television—in a passionate demonstration for civil rights and racial justice. Standing on the steps of the Lincoln Memorial, King proclaimed the need for change through nonviolent political action and peaceful demonstration. He said: "I have a dream that one day this nation will rise up and live out the true meaning of its creed: 'We hold these truths to be self-evident; that all men are created equal.'" King's efforts helped lead to the passage of the Civil Rights Act of 1964 and the Voting Rights Act of 1965, two landmark pieces of legislation that were designed to guarantee all Americans, regardless of color or creed, equal access to the political process.

• 1965–1969

Bernard Malamud (p. 980) wrote primarily about Jews in America, creating memorable characters through humor, pathos, and a sensitivity to human suffering. He published several collections of short stories, including *The Magic Barrel* and *Idiots First,* plus the novels *Dubin's Lives, The Assistant,* and *The Fixer.*

• 1970–1974

To this day, Americans remain emotionally torn about the U.S. involvement in Vietnam. About 57,000 U.S. soldiers, 254,000 South Vietnamese soldiers, and 1,027,000 North Vietnamese and Viet Cong troops were killed between 1957 and 1975.

Contemporary Literature 1950–Present

LITERARY EVENTS

1950–1959

A Raisin in the Sun, a play by Lorraine Hansberry, opens, 1959

•

Ralph Ellison publishes his novel *Invisible Man,* 1952

•

J. D. Salinger publishes his novel *The Catcher in the Rye,* 1951

1960–1964

The Autobiography of Malcolm X published, 1965

•

Edward Albee's play *Who's Afraid of Virginia Woolf?* opens, 1962

•

John Steinbeck wins the Nobel Prize for Literature, 1962

•

Harper Lee publishes her novel *To Kill a Mockingbird,* 1960

1965–1969

Colombian **Gabriel García Márquez** publishes *One Hundred Years of Solitude,* 1967

•

Bernard Malamud publishes *The Fixer,* a novel about Jewish life in czarist Russia, 1966

•

Truman Capote publishes his "nonfiction novel" *In Cold Blood,* 1966

1970–1974

Aleksandr Solzhenitsyn publishes the first volume of *The Gulag Archipelago,* documenting oppression in the Soviet Union, 1973

•

James Dickey publishes *Deliverance,* a novel about a violent canoe trip in Georgia, 1970

| 1950–1959 | 1960–1964 | 1965–1969 | 1970–1974 |

CULTURAL/HISTORICAL EVENTS

1950–1959

Senator Joseph McCarthy charges that 205 Communists infiltrated the State Department, February 1950

•

Korean War ends, 1953

•

U.S. Supreme Court rules that segregation in public schools is unconstitutional, 1954

•

Soviet Union launches first artificial satellite, *Sputnik I,* thereby beginning the "space race" with the U.S., 1957

•

Federal troops enforce the integration of Central High School in Little Rock, Arkansas, 1957

Arkansas student heckled during enforced integration, September 4, 1957.

1960–1964

U.S. population is about 179 million, 1960

•

Many African countries, including Nigeria and Senegal, achieve independence, 1960

•

Bay of Pigs invasion of Cuba fails, 1961

•

Rev. Martin Luther King, Jr., delivers "I Have a Dream" speech during the March on Washington, 1963

•

President John F. Kennedy is assassinated, 1963

1965–1969

U.S. escalates involvement in Vietnam War, 1965

•

Israel occupies nearby territory as a result of Six-Day War with Arab countries, 1967

•

Rev. Martin Luther King, Jr., and Senator Robert F. Kennedy are assassinated, 1968

•

Two U.S. astronauts become first humans to walk on the moon, 1969

•

Woodstock music festival takes place in Bethel, NY, August 1969

1970–1974

Peace treaty provides for cease-fire in Vietnam and withdrawal of U.S. forces, 1973

•

World economy is jolted by a sharp rise in petroleum prices, 1973

•

Watergate scandal forces Richard M. Nixon to resign as U.S. president, 1974

President John F. Kennedy's funeral procession, November 25, 1963.

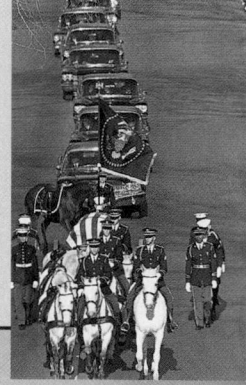

Using the Time Line

Arrange students in small groups and instruct each group to choose one of the following categories (political, economic, sociocultural, geographical, scientific, or artistic) and then to classify all events from the lower half of the time line that fall into their category. Have groups share their classifications with the whole class.

Ask each group to choose two events and collaborate to write a paragraph answering the following question for each event: How would the world be different today if this event had never happened? Have groups share their paragraphs and discuss them in class.

Toni Morrison.

Alex Haley publishes *Roots*, a history of his family from its origins in Africa, 1976

•

Saul Bellow publishes his novel *Humboldt's Gift*, 1975

•

E. L. Doctorow publishes *Ragtime*, a novel mixing fictional and real characters, 1975

Raymond Carver publishes *Cathedral*, a collection of his stories, 1983

•

Alice Walker publishes her novel *The Color Purple*, 1982

•

John Updike publishes his novel *Rabbit Is Rich*, 1981

Amy Tan publishes her novel *The Joy Luck Club*, 1989

•

Richard Wilbur publishes *New and Collected Poems*, 1988

•

Anne Tyler publishes her novel *Breathing Lessons*, 1988

•

Larry McMurtry publishes his novel *Lonesome Dove*, 1985

Garrett Hongo publishes *Volcano: A Memoir of Hawaii*, 1995

•

Steven Spielberg directs the film *Schindler's List*, based on the novel (1982) by Australia's Thomas Keneally, 1993

•

Toni Morrison wins the Nobel Prize for Literature, 1993

•

Tim O'Brien publishes *The Things They Carried*, 1990

1975–1979	1980–1984	1985–1989	1990–

Israel and Egypt agree to a landmark peace treaty, 1978–1979

•

Iranian militants seize the U.S. embassy in Tehran and take 52 Americans hostage, thus beginning 444-day "hostage crisis," 1979

•

Soviet Union invades Afghanistan, 1979

Eight-year war between Iran and Iraq begins, 1980

•

Sandra Day O'Connor becomes the first female justice on U.S. Supreme Court, 1981

•

United States invades Grenada after a military coup there, 1983

Era of great change in Soviet Union begins as Mikhail Gorbachev rises to power, 1985

•

U.S. space shuttle *Challenger* explodes soon after liftoff, 1986

•

U.S. stock market crashes, 1987

•

United States and Soviet Union sign treaty reducing medium-range nuclear weapons, 1987

•

Berlin Wall comes down, 1989

•

Pro-democracy demonstrations crushed in Tiananmen Square, Beijing, 1989

U.S. population is about 249 million, 1990

•

Iraq invades Kuwait but is forced to retreat by Operation Desert Storm, led by the United States, 1990–1991

•

West Germany and East Germany unite, 1990

•

Soviet Union is dissolved, 1991

•

British transfer sovereignty over Hong Kong to China, 1997

•

Internet becomes major form of communication, late 1990s

View of the shuttle *Atlantis* docked to the *Kristall* module of the Russian space agency's MIR space station.

CONTEMPORARY LITERATURE **907**

Using Students' Strengths

Visual Learners

To help students understand cultural changes that occurred from 1950 to 2000, gather popular periodicals (such as *Life* and *Time*) from each decade so that students can study the American way of life as revealed (and concealed) in ads and articles. Ask the class to try to form generalizations that capture the essence of each decade (for example, "In the 1980s the 'Me Generation' focused on personal wealth and social status").

Musical Learners

Have students compare a number of popular songs from different eras. Students can look up old singles charts or ask their older relatives and friends to suggest songs from the times. Play a few examples in class and challenge students to make inferences about the time periods based on their music.

• **1975–1979**

In 1979, the Ayatollah Ruholla Khomeini led Islamic fundamentalists to overthrow the shah of Iran because of the shah's secular, pro-Western policies, and his government's abuse of human rights (most infamously in the shah's Savak secret police). While the shah's thirty-eight years in power were hardly democratic, his regime was characterized by an expansion of women's rights (in politics and work), and considerable technological advances. After the successful revolution, Ayatollah Khomeini declared Iran an Islamic state with laws based on the teachings of Islam, and largely reversed these changes. When the shah fled, the Ayatollah's forces seized the U.S. Embassy in Tehran and took a group of U.S. citizens hostage, refusing to release them until the United States returned the shah for trial. When the United States refused, a hostage crisis ensued, lasting more than fourteen months. Six months after the shah died of cancer the hostages were freed.

• **1990–**

The United States is not only a growing nation, but also a nation of people growing older. Census figures in 1990 showed the median age to be 32.9 years, up 2.9 years from 1980. The percentage of the population over 65 increased from 11 percent in 1980 to 13 percent in 1990, partly due to the increasing number of young adults delaying marriage and having children. In 1970, the median age at first marriage was 23.2 years for males and 20.8 for females; in 1990, it was 26.1 for males and 23.9 for females. In 1970, the marriage rate was 10.6 percent and the divorce rate 3.5 percent; in 1990 the marriage rate was 9.8 percent and the divorce rate 4.7 percent. In 1990, a survey showed 77 percent of those between 18 and 24 were not married, with 66 percent still living with their parents.

In 1998, former U.S. Senator John Glenn, at the age of 77, blasted off with six crewmates aboard the space shuttle *Discovery*. Senator/Astronaut Glenn participated in age-related experiments in space (such as those calculating bone loss and monitoring sleep patterns), as well as experiments in astronomy and solar physics. In 1962, Glenn was the first American to orbit the earth.

A Vocabulary Note

Atomic Language

Point out to students that, since the invention of the atomic bomb, nuclear technology has contributed many new words and expressions to our language. Some of these words have become common expressions, and many have taken on multiple meanings, including meanings in contexts far removed from science and technology. Discuss with students the following words, exploring their meanings in various contexts:

- nuclear
- fallout
- chain reaction
- proving ground
- ground zero
- countdown
- fail-safe

B Historical Connections

Watergate's Aftermath

President Richard M. Nixon resigned from the presidency on August 9, 1974, after the House Judiciary Committee voted to recommend three articles of impeachment against him. The recommendations were based on evidence from the Watergate scandal, which began with the arrest and conviction of several of Nixon's 1972 campaign employees for a burglary at the Democratic Party Headquarters in the Watergate office-apartment-hotel complex in Washington, D.C. Nixon was charged with obstructing justice, abusing presidential powers, and disobeying subpoenas. Vice President Gerald Ford was sworn in as his successor. Later in 1974, Bob Woodward and Carl Bernstein, the two reporters for the *Washington Post* who had uncovered most of the facts that led to Nixon's resignation, published a narrative of the scandal called *All the President's Men.* A film of the book, starring Robert Redford and Dustin Hoffman, came out in 1976.

A CLOSER LOOK

ATOMIC ANXIETY

Things are probably going to look different when you get outside.
—from *How to Survive an Atomic Bomb* (1950)

A At the end of World War II, Americans confronted two unsettling new facts of life: the atomic bomb and the cold war with the Soviet Union. U.S. scientists published chilling calculations of what would happen if atomic (and later, hydrogen) bombs were dropped on American cities. Meanwhile, a vivid image of a malignant Soviet leadership with its collective finger poised over the red button that would launch a nuclear attack was created in the American psyche—an image memorably evoked in the 1963 film *Dr. Strangelove: or, How I Learned to Stop Worrying and Love the Bomb.* Politicians warned that war would come, in the words of New York Governor Thomas E. Dewey, "whenever the fourteen evil men in Moscow decide to have it break out." It was high time, experts of various stripes agreed, to devise a new national civil defense plan.

The possible responses to nuclear attack were succinctly described by one U.S. government official as "dig, die, or get out." The second option aside, "getting out" meant leaving big cities, which presumably would be targets of Soviet bombs. Some policymakers urged that major cities be relocated under mountain ranges or in 30-foot strips alongside highways. Government officials ultimately rejected these and other relocation schemes. Even the less ambitious idea of evacuating cities drove planners to despair as they pondered maps of New York City and Los Angeles.

What was left but to dig? The notion of burrowing underground took root, partly because it allowed every citizen a personal response to nuclear war: Build a bomb shelter. Companies selling shelters proliferated in the 1950s, and marketing creativity soared. Using fictitious "protection factor" ratings, shelter ads boasted blastproof rooms; one ad featured a decontamination room for latecomers to the shelter. Aesthetic considerations came into play in one prefab shelter that featured a window with a woodland view painted on one wall. Ingenious designs and vigorous advertising

By permission of the artist. National Museum of American Art, Washington, D.C.

B The 1970s saw the winding down of the Vietnam War, but another focus of disillusion filled the news: the Watergate scandal that in 1974 forced the only resignation of an American president. On the other hand, the celebration in 1976 of the bicentennial of the Declaration of Independence witnessed a prideful restatement of fundamental American values.

Then came the 1980s, which many Americans now regard as the time of the Me Generation, when individual enjoyment and material success seemed to overshadow other concerns.

Miss Liberty (1987) by Malcah Zeldis. Oil on corrugated cardboard.

908 CONTEMPORARY LITERATURE

Getting Students Involved

Cooperative Learning

Who We Are. How do students characterize their own generation? Have students divide into groups of four to discuss this question and to try to come up with a name that fits their generation (e.g., the "Me generation" of the 1980s). As the discussions proceed, each student in the group should be responsible for keeping a record of one of the following topics:
- What our generation likes

- What our generation dislikes
- What our generation thinks of the previous generation
- Our generation's goals for the future

After the discussions, have each group make a brief oral presentation to the class in which each member summarizes the discussion of his or her topic.

were essential, because bomb shelters were a considerable investment: Models typically cost several hundred dollars (a large sum in those days), and that didn't include the requisite first-aid kit, flashlights, sandbags, periscope, supply of water and canned food, and pliers (in case of toothache). Economy-minded citizens were encouraged to improvise a shelter in their homes by stacking brick-filled dresser drawers on a table, and to crawl underneath in the event of a nuclear strike. (Helpful instructions warned the builder to "be careful not to overload the table to the point where it will collapse.") Bomb shelters generated so much enthusiasm that, by the end of 1960, industrious Americans had constructed about one million of them.

Although shelters and other civil defense schemes of the fifties sound far-fetched today, the fears that inspired them were entirely justified. In

Bomb shelter in New York, 1952.

fact, interest in civil defense waned in the early 1960s partly because people began to understand just how disastrous nuclear war could be. Antiradiation suits and community loudspeaker systems began to seem ridiculous in light of dangerously high and long-lived radiation levels. Moreover, weapons delivery systems had been improved so that bombs could reach the United States in minutes—hardly time to alert entire communities. The final blow to civil defense programs, however, was a positive development: The signing of the Limited Test Ban Treaty in 1963 officially ended aboveground nuclear testing—and thus the fallout that had aroused so much alarm. The bomb shelters of the fifties have long since been converted into toolsheds and wine cellars—or storage spaces for the home Geiger counters and antiradiation pills of another era.

As the 1980s ended, so did the cold war, the struggle between the United States and the Soviet Union that had dominated international politics since shortly after the end of World War II. The Soviet Union collapsed as its republics and satellite nations declared independence. The end of the cold war reduced but did not end the threat of nuclear warfare.

In many ways, the nuclear bomb is the dramatic symbol of the last half of the twentieth century. Its infamous mushroom cloud represents the proliferation of science and technology, the purpose of which was, ironically enough, to benefit humankind, to make life richer and easier for all.

In some ways, science and technology have fulfilled their promise. They have increased the life spans of many and have fed and housed many people better. They have moved us faster from place to place—even allowing a few of us to stroll on the surface of the moon.

But at the same time, poverty and crime have increased, not diminished. Science and technology have standardized and "assembly-lined" our lives and displaced countless workers. The era of the computer chip has **D**

Neil Armstrong on the moon, 1969.

C

Peace Today by Rube Goldberg.

The Granger Collection, New York.

Crossing the Curriculum

Science
Interested students can research and report on ways in which nuclear power is being used to benefit humanity. Students might especially consider researching advances in using nuclear energy to provide electricity for entire communities and ways in which nuclear medicine can save people's lives.

Space Science
Encourage students to learn more about the extraordinary accomplishments of NASA (The National Aeronautics and Space Administration) since the 1969 landing on the moon. They might explore such topics as other moon landings, the Hubble Telescope, the space shuttle program, communications satellites, and deep-space probes.

C Historical Connections
The Threat Continues
Changing political conditions around the world have changed the nature of the nuclear threat. Nuclear capability is no longer limited to two superpowers. Now, other nations, such as India and Pakistan, have tested nuclear weapons, greatly complicating international relations and the burdens of diplomacy. With the proliferation of nuclear weapons, the possibility that terrorist organizations may also gain access to them continues to grow.

D Literary Connections
Computer Poetry
Although the computer era sometimes seems to have diminished the power of the individual, the computer has also enhanced the power of average citizens to acquire and even to create information. In fact, computers have attempted one of the most private and individual of human tasks—writing poetry. In *Virtual Muse* (1996), Charles O. Hartman describes experiments in designing computer poetry programs and provides examples of computer-generated poems.

RESPONDING TO THE ART
Rube Goldberg (1883–1970) was a popular American cartoonist and satirist. He was famous for drawing incredibly complicated mechanical devices that achieved simple results, such as a fifteen-step contraption for cracking an egg. His name became synonymous with absurd, complex schemes. In *Peace Today*, he takes the opposite approach, reducing the world situation to a single effective image of a house atop a teetering atomic bomb. The title of the cartoon increases its ironic effect, suggesting the extent to which peace rests on the threat of destruction.
Activity. Ask students if they think this cartoon is still relevant today. You might have them work in small groups to think about how they would visually represent a threat to the world today, using a single image to convey their message. Ask each group to draw one or more cartoons.

Ⓐ Literary Connections

Ralph Waldo Emerson's idea of the individual is grounded in a transcendentalist philosophy that privileges human individuality over social authority. In his essay "Self-Reliance," he writes: "Nothing is at last sacred but the integrity of your own mind."

Ⓑ Humanities Connections

Many scholars point out that postmodern movements have appeared in other fields besides the visual and literary arts, including politics, philosophy, and theology. Rather than defining it as a style, some critics think of postmodernism as a sensibility defined by a set of tastes and attitudes. In the visual arts, postmodernism has four basic and interrelated characteristics: *pluralism* (a profusion of style and modes); *eclecticism* (consisting of borrowed fragments); *self-consciousness* (emphasis on the codes used to transmit content rather than on the content itself); and *contextualism* (awareness of the historical and cultural context of any given truth).

Lucy (1992) by Nam June Paik.

Courtesy Carl Solway Gallery, Cincinnatz, Ohio. Photo by Michael Tropea.

Bernard Malamud writing.

Photograph © 1977 by Jill Krementz.

Ⓐ diminished Emerson's rugged individual. Many people often feel they are only a number on a computer disk or credit card. Even our thoughts seem to be shaped or controlled by mass advertising, mass journalism, and mass entertainment. Some people even predict that our new technologies will deliver the planet itself back to lower organisms—to the cockroaches and ants, perhaps—who may survive the nuclear holocaust that might one day engulf us.

The aftermath of World War II ushered in an age of rapid developments in science and technology. The postwar years have offered many Americans increased opportunities for economic and cultural growth, but the individual person often seems lost in the fast-paced, computerized world.

Contemporary Fiction: Diversity and Vitality

Ⓑ Probably the most common word used to describe American culture at the end of the twentieth century is **postmodern,** a term that, like our age, is still in the process of being defined. Postmodernism sees contemporary culture as a change—a development or a departure—from

Getting Students Involved

Enrichment Activity

Nothing but the Best. In 1998, Random House, an American publisher, assembled a list of the "One Hundred Best" twentieth-century novels written in English. The list sparked much discussion and controversy over which books were on it, which authors were not represented, and how the editorial board of selectors was constituted. Have students research the list and identify the American works on it. (F. Scott Fitzgerald's *The Great Gatsby* was ranked second, after James Joyce's *Ulysses*.) Interested students might also research some of the alternative lists that sprang up during the controversy. Encourage interested students to create their own lists of the "Top Ten" American novels and accompany each work with a few sentences justifying its selection.

modernism, the dominant movement in the arts from about 1890 to 1945. In literature, the great American modernists, notably Ezra Pound, T. S. Eliot, Willa Cather, William Carlos Williams, Marianne Moore, Wallace Stevens, Katherine Anne Porter, William Faulkner, and Ernest Hemingway, forged new styles and new forms to express the sensibility of the twentieth century. Postmodern writers build with many of the tools provided by the modernists, and they are now constructing a body of literature that is strikingly different from that of the first half of the century.

New perspectives in postmodern fiction.

Postmodern fiction writers allow for multiple meanings and multiple worlds in their works. Realistic and literal worlds, future worlds, and dreamlike metaphorical worlds may merge, as they do in Thomas Pynchon's dazzling novel *Gravity's Rainbow* (1973). Narrators and characters may tell different versions of a story, or a story may deliberately accommodate several valid interpretations, as in *Pale Fire* (1962), by the Russian American novelist Vladimir Nabokov. The postmodernist asks, Why choose only one version? Why limit ourselves?

Writers of our time often structure their works in a variety of nontraditional forms and do not abide by conventional rules of shaping fiction. Sometimes these forms are quite arbitrary. Donald Barthelme's story "Sentence," for example, is a nine-page tale that consists entirely of one sentence. In Walter Abish's novel *Alphabetical Africa* (1974), every word in the first chapter begins with the letter *a;* every word in the second chapter begins with *a* or *b,* and so on through the alphabet to *z* and then, in reverse, all the way back to *a.*

Some postmodern works are also intensely self-conscious: They comment upon themselves, criticize themselves, take themselves apart, and encourage us to put

I am an invisible man. No, I am not a spook, like those who haunted Edgar Allan Poe; nor am I one of your Hollywood-movie ectoplasms. I am a man of substance, of flesh and bone, fiber and liquids, —and I might even be said to possess a mind. I am invisible, understand, simply because people refuse to see me. Like the bodiless heads you see sometimes in circus sideshows, it is as though I have been surrounded by mirrors of hard, distorted glass. When they approach me they see only themselves or figments of their imagination—indeed, everything and anything except me. Nor is my invisibility exactly a matter of a biochemical accident to my epidermis. That is

Untitled (Ralph Ellison) (1994) by Glenn Ligon. Oil stick on paper (32″ x 15⅝″).
Collection of Whitney Museum of American Art. Gift of the artist (94.140).
Photograph © 1998 Whitney Museum of American Art.

C Literary Connections
Postmodern Narrative

Narrative forms of traditional fiction are usually driven by content, such as the events in a character's life. In contrast, narrative forms of postmodern fiction are often driven by elements of form itself—the conventions associated with the act of storytelling. Traditional realistic narratives depend for coherence on the created illusion of a character's life. This illusion of a real life is created by portraying events and emotional responses to events as they unfold in that life. Postmodern narratives, on the other hand, consciously call attention to, comment on, and manipulate the very techniques the writer uses to create those illusions. Instead of writing to paint a picture of reality, the postmodern storyteller may write to paint a picture of himself or herself painting a picture.

D Humanities Connections
Pastiche

Pastiche is a term used to describe the postmodern tendency to appropriate ideas and forms from the past and use them again in new creations. Although this process may sound like plagiarism, pastiche involves stripping ideas and forms from their original contexts and replacing them in surprising new contexts. It is this contextual upheaval that distinguishes pastiche from plagiarism. The postmodern artist's object is the effect created by placing the image into a different context, rather than the effect created by the image itself. For example, putting Leonardo da Vinci's painting *Mona Lisa* on a necktie might be seen as a playful example of postmodern pastiche.

Taking a Second Look

Review: Summarizing

Remind students that stopping to summarize a section of a long essay is an effective reading and study strategy. The task of summarizing is made easier when an essay, like this one, is divided into sections with descriptive headings.

Activities

1. Have students read the boldface summaries at the end of each of the essay's sections. Ask them to add at least one idea or example to each summary.

2. Have students find and read a review of a contemporary novel and then summarize the review. Each summary should be one paragraph long, contain a clear statement of the main idea of the review, and give several supporting ideas or examples.

Ⓐ Literary Connections

Hispanic American Writers

The contemporary period in America enjoys an extraordinary flowering of writing by Hispanic Americans. These writers use both old and new forms to explore, in American contexts, the cultural inheritances of Mexico, Puerto Rico, Cuba, and other Hispanic countries. Here are some of the most recent notable literary works by Hispanic Americans:

The Mambo Kings Play Songs of Love by Oscar Hijuelos (1989, Pulitzer Prize 1990)

How the Garcia Girls Lost Their Accents by Julia Alvarez (1991)

Loose Woman by Sandra Cisneros (1994)

My Father Was a Toltec and Selected Poems by Ana Castillo (1995)

Something to Declare by Julia Alvarez (1998)

Ⓑ Literary Connections

Native American Writers

With poems, novels, and nonfiction memoirs, Native American writers play a major role in contemporary American literature. These writers often focus on issues of cultural survival, on remaking inherited customs in a changing world, on the uses of the oral tradition, and on coming to grips with a turbulent and painful history. They offer all readers opportunities to witness a uniquely American blending of the old with the new. Here are some of the most recent notable literary works by Native Americans:

Lakota Woman by Mary Brave Bird (1990, American Book Award 1991)

Dawn Land by Joseph Bruchac (1993)

The Woman Who Fell From the Sky by Joy Harjo (1994)

Tales of Burning Love by Louise Erdrich (1996)

Blue Horses Rush In by Luci Tapahonso (1997)

---

them together again. In his novel *Operation Shylock* (1993), the author Philip Roth meets a character named Philip Roth and wonders which one of them is "real." In other words, postmodern literature is aware of itself as literature and encourages the reader's self-awareness as well.

Ⓐ Ⓑ The vitality of contemporary fiction lies in its cultural diversity, in its enthusiasm for blending fiction with nonfiction, and in its extraordinary sense of play. It also demonstrates a typically American ability to invigorate the old with the new.

Contemporary fiction allows for multiple meanings and multiple worlds, uses nontraditional forms, and comments upon itself. But it embraces traditional storytellers as well as postmodern risk-takers. It features cultural diversity, crisscrosses the boundaries between fiction and nonfiction, and uses subjects, images, and themes from the past fearlessly.

Contemporary Nonfiction: Breaking the Barriers

Until fairly recently, "nonfiction" meant whatever was *not* fiction—suggesting that nonfiction was a nonliterary form and a nonart. Nonfiction writers were lumped together with journalists, who were in turn defined as nonliterary folk whose work was quickly written, read, and discarded. Critics tended to concentrate on the search for the elusive Great American Novel, which was thought to be more important than anything a nonfiction writer could produce.

Since the 1970s, however, nonfiction has come into its own. Featured reviews now discuss the art (not just the factual content) of books on computers, architecture, travel, history, film, and other subjects. Bestseller lists, which have always included self-help books, cookbooks, and exercise manuals, now also regularly feature memoirs, biographies, and histories.

> . . . [N]onfiction is the place where much of the best writing of the day is being done. Yet many writers and teachers of writing continue to feel vaguely guilty if they prefer it to fiction—nonfiction is the slightly disreputable younger brother in the royal house of literature. No such guilt is necessary. While the keepers of the temple weren't looking, nonfiction crept in and occupied the throne.
> —William Zinsser

"*On the Internet, nobody knows you're a dog.*"

Getting Students Involved

Enrichment Activity

Interactive Fiction. One new development in contemporary fiction has been made possible by the computer. Hyperfiction is a new, interactive way of writing and reading that presents stories, novels, and plays as computer "documents." Hyperfictions are not read in the usual linear progression, page after page. Instead, they are fields of linked characters and events that can be navigated or explored by the reader. With a mouse or keyboard, the reader chooses which parts of the story to read next, which characters to follow, or which themes to explore. Encourage interested students to research and report on this new and exciting method of storytelling.

Questions of terminology and accuracy.

Critics, however, are still uncertain about the terminology we should apply to nonfiction. For instance, when discussing fiction, we can talk about point of view, character, plot, theme, and setting; with more complex fiction, we can analyze irony, metaphors, symbols, and levels of meaning. But these traditional literary terms don't always apply to nonfiction.

More troubling is the problem of accuracy. No one expects a novel to be true, although it may be based on verifiable facts. But truth or accuracy is often a test applied to nonfiction, with frequently unsatisfactory results. A class recently read Peter Matthiessen's *The Snow Leopard* (1978), a travel memoir about wildlife in the Himalayas and the writer's search for the meaning of life. The class praised the book for its penetrating observations, philosophical depth, and narrative technique. Students were then asked if they would like it just as much if they learned that it was fiction, that Matthiessen had done extensive library research but had never gone to the Himalayas at all. (This is, of course, *not* the case.) No, many students said, they would not like the book as well. It would no longer be true. Wasn't truth what distinguished nonfiction from fiction?

The New Journalism.

This question was often raised in the 1960s when the New Journalism (also called Literary Journalism) began to appear. Truman Capote, Tom Wolfe, Joan Didion, Norman Mailer, and others attracted attention by describing contemporary culture and actual events in strongly individual voices. They employed many of the devices of fiction, including complex characterization, plot, suspense, setting, symbolism, and irony.

A New Journalist did not feel obliged to keep personal opinion and his or her presence out of the writing; in fact, presence and participation were often crucial. Joan Didion bought a dress for a defendant in a trial she was covering as a journalist. Truman Capote befriended the murderers he was writing about in his book *In Cold Blood*, which he called a nonfiction novel—a perfect example of the overlapping of genres. Readers wanted to know just what the writer was thinking or feeling about the subject, and so the tone of a book became nearly as important as its facts.

If facts alone do not distinguish nonfiction from fiction, what does? No one is sure. What readers *are* sure about is their interest in nonfiction that uses the traditional attractions of accomplished fiction:

Don't Buy (1988) by Phoebe Beasley. Collage (36″ × 28″).
Courtesy of the artist.

Characteristics of Postmodern Literature

- Allows for multiple meanings and multiple worlds
- Structures works in nontraditional forms
- Comments upon itself
- Features cultural diversity
- Blends and overlaps fiction and non-fiction
- Uses the past fearlessly

Fact vs. Fiction in the Media

The contemporary tendency to blur the lines between fact and fiction may be much more than an aesthetic or a literary matter. It may affect interpretations of the news and politics, and it may have serious legal and ethical ramifications. In order to capture viewers' attention, prime-time television news journalists sometimes find themselves using techniques that are borrowed from Hollywood. For example:

- Newsmagazine shows may dramatize or re-create scenes so that the audience can visualize an accident, a trial, or a crime.
- Gossip, rumor, speculation, or sensational details may be emphasized in order to grab the attention of passing channel-surfers.
- Background music may be used to enhance the "drama" of a news story or an interview.

For journalists, accurate information has traditionally been more important than entertainment. However, during the 1990s, the airwaves began to carry a hybrid that is a serious challenge to authentic journalists—"infotainment."

Professional Notes

Critical Comment: Story Webs

In her 1997 book, *Hamlet on the Holodeck: The Future of Narrative in Cyberspace,* Janet H. Murray describes the basics of hyperfiction, a new way of reading and writing stories:

"The accessibility of the World Wide Web has introduced a growing audience to hypertext fiction. Hypertext is a set of documents of any kind (images, text, charts, tables, video clips) connected to one another by links. Stories written in hypertext . . . are best thought of as segmented into generic chunks of information called 'lexias' (or reading units). . . . [They] occupy a virtual space in which they can be preceded by, followed by, and placed next to an infinite number of other lexias. . . . The existence of hypertext has given writers a new means of experimenting with segmentation, juxtaposition, and connectedness. Stories written in hypertext generally have more than one entry point, many internal branches, and no clear ending. Like the multiform life stories imagined by [Jorge Luis] Borges and [Alan] Lightman, hypertext narratives are intricate, many-threaded webs."

characters to care about, suspense, and compelling use of language. Many readers, eager for literature that will illuminate their lives, enrich their knowledge, and entertain them, have become as willing to pursue those goals in nonfiction as they are in fiction. They find what they are looking for in the works of the writers mentioned above and many others, including Annie Dillard, Lewis Thomas, Paul Theroux, Alice Walker, and Barry Lopez.

Contemporary nonfiction has become a field equal to fiction, though questions about terminology and accuracy still give rise to controversy. New Journalism (or Literary Journalism) has added personal and fictional elements to nonfiction, enhancing its popularity with today's readers.

Contemporary Poetry: Varied and Intensely Personal

It is difficult to describe the course of American poetry since 1945, because recent trends are still too close to be viewed objectively. Moreover, in recent years, unprecedented numbers of Americans have been writing poetry, so it is a special challenge to determine which poets and which movements will last.

The decline of modernism. There are a number of clear, significant differences between American poetry written before 1945 and the poetry written in the decades since. The twenty years between World War I and World War II marked the flowering and near monopoly of modernist poetry. This was the kind of poetry defined, by and large, by the theory and practice of T. S. Eliot, Ezra Pound, and, somewhat later, W. H. Auden.

In 1917, Eliot had called for an impersonal, objective poetry that would transcend the subjective emotions of the poet. The poem, said Eliot, should be impersonal, allusive (it should make references, or allusions, to other works), and intellectually challenging. Modernist writers followed Ezra Pound's insistence that the image was all-important and that all unnecessary words should be omitted; but in doing this, they often eliminated material that could have made their poetry more accessible to readers.

By the early 1950s, though, there was a growing sense that modernism was somehow becoming played out, that it was no longer appropriate for the times. The era itself may have had something to do with the shift away from modernism. A generation had returned from war to a country where conformity and material success were predominant values. The Soviet Union and the atomic bomb worried Americans in the late

Maya Angelou reciting her poem "On the Pulse of Morning" at the presidential inauguration in 1993.

914 **CONTEMPORARY LITERATURE**

Skill Link

Speaking/Listening

Despite the charge that much modernist poetry requires classroom study to overcome its challenges, many modernist poems can have a powerful effect when read aloud to a live audience. Modernist poets adapted and reinterpreted rhythm and rhyme to create a new twentieth-century sound—especially through *vers libre* (free verse) and the "unit" of meter that William Carlos Williams called the "variable foot."

Activities

1. Have students choose and recite one favorite modernist American poem. Students should give a brief introduction, explaining why it is a modernist poem and why they like it.
2. Have students use the library or the Internet to listen to a recorded reading of a contemporary poem of their choice. Have students evaluate the interpretations and suggest different ways to read the poems.

1940s and early 1950s, but acquiring a house and a car and making money were generally of more immediate importance. "These are the tranquilized *Fifties*," Robert Lowell wrote in a poem toward the end of that decade, as he ironically described the complacent scene around him:

> I hog a whole house on Boston's
> "hardly passionate Marlborough Street,"
> where even the man
> scavenging filth in the back alley trash cans,
> has two children, a beach wagon, a helpmate,
> and is a "young Republican."

> —Robert Lowell, *from*
> "Memories of West Street and Lepke"

By the early 1950s, many writers and readers felt that modernist poetry—impersonal, allusive, difficult—was no longer appropriate. The times called for a more personal and accessible approach that challenged complacency and convention. **D**

The Beat poets. In 1956, a long poem called *Howl* was published by **E** Allen Ginsberg, who could by no stretch of the imagination be described as dull. A cry of outrage against the conformity of the 1950s, *Howl* was as far removed from the safe confines of modernism as could be imagined. It begins, "I saw the best minds of my generation destroyed by madness, starving hysterical naked," and it continues at the same intense pitch for hundreds of lines.

Student reading at the 1995 Dodge Poetry Festival.

D **Literary Connections**
Projective Verse
During the 1950s, not all poets believed that greater accessibility was the only new track to follow after modernism. Charles Olson, Robert Duncan, and Robert Creeley—(now collectively referred to as the "Black Mountain School" after the North Carolina college at which they taught)—produced volumes of "projective verse." Influenced strongly by Ezra Pound and William Carlos Williams, projective verse favored "open form," considering each poem an individual organic entity, creating its own form spontaneously as it proceeded. Open-form poems denied the strict rules and sense of closure required by the modernist New Criticism, avoided regular meter and rhyme, and refused to impose prefabricated forms on the poet's immediate thoughts and feelings. Led by Olson, whose major work is *The Maximus Poems,* open-form poets created "fields" that imitated the spontaneity and complexity of reality itself. Other open-form poets included Denise Levertov, Paul Blackburn, Ed Dorn, and Louis Zukofsky.

E **Cultural Connections**
The Beats
The Beat movement of the 1950s maintained a critical stance toward mainstream American culture. Also known as beatniks, the Beats were seen by many as praising individuality while speaking out against social injustice and conventional middle-class conformity. The Beats declared mainstream America morally bankrupt and, in their literature, planted seeds of protest that germinated in the rebellious youth culture of the 1960s.

Professional Notes

Critical Comment:
American Poetry Today
In an essay called "State of the Art" from his 1992 book *A Poetics,* poet and teacher Charles Bernstein sets forth the sense of diversity, possibility, and creative conflict that characterizes American poetry at the millennium:

"There is of course no state of American poetry, but states, moods, agitations, dissipations, renunciations, depressions, acquiescences, elations, angers, ecstasies; no music to our verse but vastly incompatible musics; no single sentiment but clashes of sentience: the magnificent cacophany of different bodies making different sounds, as different as the hum of Hester Street from the gush of Grand Coulee, the buzz of Central Park on August afternoons from the shrieks of oil-coated birds in Prince William Sound.

The state of American poetry can be characterized by the sharp ideological disagreements that lacerate our communal field of action, making it volatile, dynamic, engaging.

What I hear, then, in the poetries of this New American fin de siècle is an implicit refusal of unity that is the result of our prodigious and magnanimous outpouring of words."

Ⓐ Cultural Connections

Bohemians

The word *bohemian*—meaning "an unconventional and nonconforming person, often an artist"—originated from the fact that wandering gypsies passed through Bohemia (a region of Czechoslovakia) to reach western Europe. The term's popular use increased when Italian composer Giacomo Puccini created the opera *La Bohème* in 1896. This story of struggling artists in the Latin Quarter of Paris was drawn from a novel by Henri Murger, *Scènes de la vie de Bohème*. Students may know that *Rent*, the 1997 rock opera hit, is an updated version of *La Bohème*.

Ⓑ Literary Connections

The Confessional School

The Confessional poets listed all won the Pulitzer Prize in poetry, an annual award given for a distinguished book of verse by an American author. The prize was awarded to John Berryman (1965, *77 Dream Songs*); Anne Sexton (1967, *Live or Die*); and Sylvia Plath (1982, *The Collected Poems*).

American Flag: A Mosaic of Faces is part of an exhibit at the Ellis Island Immigration Museum. From 1891 to 1954 this New York Harbor island processed over 16 million immigrants.

Together with *On the Road* (1957), Jack Kerouac's novel celebrating the bohemian life, *Howl* quickly became a kind of bible for young nonconformists known as the Beat Generation. Beat poetry and the Beat lifestyle of poetry readings, jazz, and late-night coffeehouses in San Francisco and New York's Greenwich Village had an immediate impact on American popular culture. *Life* magazine even ran illustrated Ⓐ stories about the new bohemians.

> One judges an age, just as one judges a poet, by its best poems.
>
> —Randall Jarrell

Howl provided the first clear alternative to academic poetry—intellectual poetry that seemed to be written for analysis in the classroom rather than poetry that addressed the real concerns of contemporary life. Many of Ginsberg's concerns—the injustices of modern life, the importance of the imagination—would become the principal themes of poetry a decade later.

Poetry and personal experience. In 1959, Robert Lowell published *Life Studies,* one of the most important and influential volumes of verse to appear since World War II. These poems are about personal experiences that modernist poets had avoided dealing with directly: emotional problems, alcoholism, illness, and depression. In *Life Studies,* Lowell clearly and decisively broke with Eliot's theory that poetry should be impersonal; in doing so, he helped to reunite, both for himself and for other writers, "the man who suffers and the mind which creates."

Shortly after *Life Studies* appeared, a critic described Lowell's poems as "confessional." The label stuck, and the **Confessional School** of poets, Ⓑ mostly friends or students of Lowell, was officially born. These poets—including Sylvia Plath, Anne Sexton, and John Berryman—wrote frank,

Taking a Second Look

Review: Making Generalizations

A generalization is a type of inference in which readers combine information in a text with information that they already know to make a judgment that extends beyond a specific text to the general world. Remind students that when they include generalizations in an essay, they should support each generalization with evidence from the text or examples from their own experience.

Activities

1. Have students identify one generalization in this essay. Do students agree with it? Do they think it is supported sufficiently? Why or why not?

2. Have students make one generalization about the literature of their own time. Each generalization should be adequately supported with facts or examples.

sometimes brutal poems about their private lives. Nothing could have been further from Eliot's model.

By the mid-1970s, many of the first generation of major postwar poets were dead, as were some of the second generation. William Carlos Williams, Theodore Roethke, and Plath all died in 1963. The 1970s saw the deaths of Berryman, Sexton, and Lowell. With Lowell's death, the American literary world was again without a major poet to provide it with definition and a common sense of direction.

Landmarks in the revolt against modernist poetry include Allen Ginsberg's Howl *(1956) and Robert Lowell's* Life Studies *(1959), both of which deal vividly with the poets' personal experience. The Confessional School of poets, which included Lowell, Sylvia Plath, and Anne Sexton, wrote frank and revealing poems about their private lives.*

A time of diversity. Since the 1970s, American poetry has been characterized by diversity. Extraordinary variety in style and attitude has attracted large new audiences to poetry. Oral performance of poetry has increased, with live poetry "slams" **C** at such places as the Nuyorican Poets Cafe in New York City. Technology has made available thousands of readings on audiotape and videotape, and even some television broadcasts devoted to poetry.

Much contemporary poetry reflects a democratic quality, often influenced by the works of Walt Whitman and William Carlos Williams. Poetry lives in the people, contemporary poets seem to say, and any walk of life, any everyday experience, any style of expression can result in authentic poetry. These poets often write in the vernacular, the language of common speech, and do not hesitate to surprise or even shock with their language, attitudes, and details of their private lives.

Poetry today is anything but impersonal. **D E**

There are good reasons for suggesting that the modern age has ended. Many things indicate that we are going through a transitional period, when it seems that something is on the way out and something else is painfully being born. It is as if something were crumbling, decaying, and exhausting itself, while something else, still indistinct, were arising from the rubble.

The distinguishing features of transitional periods are a mixing and blending of cultures and a plurality or parallelism of intellectual and spiritual worlds. These are periods when all consistent value systems collapse, when cultures distant in time and space are discovered or rediscovered. New meaning is gradually born from the encounter, or the intersection, of many different elements.

Today, this state of mind, or of the human world, is called postmodernism. For me, a symbol of that state is a Bedouin mounted on a camel and clad in traditional robes under which he is wearing jeans, with a transistor radio in his hands and an ad for Coca-Cola on the camel's back.

—Vaclav Havel, political leader of the Czech Republic, on receiving the Philadelphia Liberty Medal, July 4, 1994

917

C Cultural Connections

Poetry Slams

Poetry "slams" are popular in many American cities. They usually occur in coffeehouses where avant-garde self-expression is the norm. The slam format is often "open mike," meaning anyone can take the floor and read. Poets may read with great verve and passion. Often, the tone is not that of a gentle offering of poems for the pleasure of a polite, mannered audience, but rather a deeply moved, impassioned voice "slamming" poems with a force and boldness intended to provoke strong responses from the audience.

D Literary Connections

John Ashbery

One of the most honored and influential American poets at the end of the twentieth century is John Ashbery. Ashbery's *Self-Portrait in a Convex Mirror* won the National Book Award, the National Book Critics Circle Award, and the Pulitzer Prize in 1976. He writes poems that are both deeply personal and revelatory of the act of creation itself. To many readers, Ashbery embodies postmodernism: self-conscious, playful, and open to worlds of possibilities. His recent collections include *And the Stars Were Shining* (1994), *Can You Hear, Bird* (1995), and *Wakefulness* (1998).

E Literary Connections

Jorie Graham

The powerful and challenging lyrics of Jorie Graham are among the finest creations of the current generation of American poets. Like Emily Dickinson, to whom she has been compared, Graham lifts the local into the universal, finding the sublime in the surfaces of everyday reality. Her books include *The Dream of the Unified Field: Selected Poems 1974–1994* (Pulitzer Prize, 1996) and *The Errancy* (1997).

Ⓐ Literary Connections

American Memoirists

The search for values in the contemporary period may be illuminated by the current outpouring of memoirs. Here are some notable recent American memoirs:

The Woman Warrior: Memoirs of a Girlhood Among Ghosts by Maxine Hong Kingston (1976)

Facts of Life by Maureen Howard (1980)

Growing Up by Russell Baker (1982)

Clear Pictures by Reynolds Price (1989)

Having Our Say: The Delany Sisters' First 100 Years by Sarah and A. Elizabeth Delany with Amy Hill Hearth (1993)

Modern American Memoirs edited by Annie Dillard and Cort Conley (1995)

Something to Declare by Julia Alvarez (1998)

Where the Present Meets the Past on the Way to the Future

The literature that captures a wide audience often does so by offering a fresh voice and a new attitude, for these are the powerful needs of each new generation. Yet much of contemporary American literature still deals with the same themes that concerned our greatest writers of the nineteenth century: Poe, Hawthorne, Whitman, Dickinson, Melville, Emerson, and Thoreau. The characters of the novelist John Updike, for example, seek spiritual revelations in ordinary life. "The invariable mark of wisdom," Emerson wrote, "is to find the miraculous in the common." But it is more difficult to find transcendent Ⓐ spiritual values in the cheap clutter of modern life than it was in the woods around Emerson's Concord. Still, Updike's characters continue the search. "I find myself . . . circling back to man's religious nature," Updike has written of his own work, "and the real loss to man and art alike when that nature has nowhere to plug itself in. . . ." These words could serve to describe the work of a great number of contemporary writers whose intellectual roots can be traced to the Transcendentalists of the nineteenth century, and even further back to those hardy, practical Puritans who braved that two-month voyage in a small wooden boat.

> Everything is connected in the end.
> —Don DeLillo from *Underworld*

> Today, this state of mind, or of the human world, is called postmodernism.

Untitled, 1980 by Keith Haring. Black ink on Bristol board (20″ x 25¾″).
© The Estate of Keith Haring

Quickwrite

Read the quote about postmodernism by Vaclav Havel at the bottom of page 917. How do you think contemporary literature bears out his assertion that new meanings arise from the meeting of a variety of old and new elements? What striking image—like Havel's camel-riding, jeans-clad Bedouin listening to a radio—can you think of that would symbolize the qualities of contemporary American culture?

Assessing Learning

Check Test: Questions and Answers

1. What does the phrase "dig, die, or get out" refer to? [possible responses to nuclear attack]

2. What are two characteristics of postmodern literature. [Possible responses: multiple meanings/multiple words; nontraditional forms; self-reflexivity; cultural diversity; blending of fiction and nonfiction; borrowing or manipulating ideas from the past.]

3. What is the New Journalism? [an approach to writing nonfiction that employs many of fiction's techniques]

4. What was the long poem that launched the Beat Generation? Who wrote it? [*Howl;* Allen Ginsberg]

5. What school of poets was influenced by Robert Lowell's *Life Studies*? [the Confessional School]

The Wages of War

Theme

The Horror *The twentieth century saw two world wars and the development of weapons that could destroy all life on earth. In the face of questions posed by the carnage of war, writers still search for meaning. The genre of the "nonfiction novel" is introduced, in which the techniques of the novel are used in factual journalism. The absurd point of view is also introduced, as a way of dealing with a world that seems to offer no answers.*

Reading the Anthology

Reaching Struggling Readers
The *Reading Skills and Strategies: Reaching Struggling Readers* binder includes a Reading Strategies Handbook that offers concrete suggestions to help students who have difficulty reading and comprehending text, or students who are reluctant readers. When a specific strategy is most appropriate for a selection, a correlation to the Handbook is provided at the bottom of the teacher's page under the head Reaching Struggling Readers. This head may also be used to introduce additional ideas for helping students read challenging texts.

Reading Beyond the Anthology

Read On
At the end of the Contemporary Literature collections, the grade eleven book includes an annotated bibliography of books suitable for extended reading. The suggested books are related to works in these collections by theme, by author, or by subject. To preview the Read On for the Contemporary Literature period, please turn to p. T1177.

HRW Library
The *HRW Library* offers novels, plays, nonfiction, and short-story collections for extended reading. Each book in the Library includes one or more major works and thematically related Connections. The Connections are magazine articles, poems, or other pieces of literature. Each book in the *HRW Library* is also accompanied by a Study Guide that provides teaching suggestions and worksheets. For Collection 18, the following titles are recommended.

NIGHT
Elie Wiesel
The Romanian-born writer's personal memories of the Holocaust are a best-selling testament to hope and a tribute to his beloved family, who perished at the hands of the Nazis.

SCHINDLER'S LIST
Thomas Keneally
This true story is about the triumph of pragmatic good over senseless evil. The hero is an Austrian businessman who decides to save Jews from almost certain death in Nazi concentration camps.

Collection Planner *(vertical sidebar)*

Resources for this Collection

Note: All resources for this collection are available for preview on the *One-Stop Planner CD-ROM 2 with Test Generator.* All worksheets and blackline masters may be printed from the CD-ROM.

Internet Resources
go.hrw.com LE0 11-18

Selection or Feature	Reading and Literary Skills	Vocabulary, Language, and Grammar
from **Night** (p. 921) Elie Wiesel	• *Graphic Organizers for Active Reading,* Worksheet p. 90	• *Words to Own,* Worksheet p. 47 • *Daily Oral Grammar,* Transparency 52
The Death of the Ball Turret Gunner (p. 932) Randall Jarrell **Primary Sources: The Ball Turret** (p. 933) Randall Jarrell	• *Graphic Organizers for Active Reading,* Worksheet p. 91	
A Noiseless Flash *from* **Hiroshima** (p. 936) John Hersey	• *Graphic Organizers for Active Reading,* Worksheet p. 92 • *Literary Elements:* Transparency 28 Worksheet p. 85	• *Words to Own,* Worksheet p. 48 • *Daily Oral Grammar,* Transparency 53
For the Union Dead (p. 949) Robert Lowell **Critical Comment: A Vision of Blacks and Whites United** (p. 953)	• *Graphic Organizers for Active Reading,* Worksheet p. 93	
Game (p. 956) Donald Barthelme **Critical Comment: Absurd World** (p. 961) **Elements of Literature: Satire** (p. 962)	• *Graphic Organizers for Active Reading,* Worksheet p. 94 • *Literary Elements:* Transparency 29 Worksheet p. 88	• *Words to Own,* Worksheet p. 49 • *Daily Oral Grammar,* Transparency 54
Speaking of Courage (p. 965) Tim O'Brien	• *Graphic Organizers for Active Reading,* Worksheet p. 95	• *Words to Own,* Worksheet p. 50 • *Grammar and Language Links:* Punctuating Dialogue, Worksheet p. 71 • *Language Workshop CD-ROM,* Punctuating Quotations • *Daily Oral Grammar,* Transparency 55
Monsoon Season (p. 975) Yusef Komunyakaa **Connections: Poetry Emotion** Anna Quindlen (p. 977)	• *Graphic Organizers for Active Reading,* Worksheet p. 96	

Other Resources for this Collection

- *Cross-Curricular Activities*, p. 18
- *Portfolio Management System*, Introduction to Portfolio Assessment, p. 1
- *Formal Assessment:* Literary Period Introduction Test, p. 184

- *Test Generator,* Collection Test

Writing	Listening and Speaking Viewing and Representing	Assessment
• *Portfolio Management System*, Rubrics for Choices, p. 202	• *Audio CD Library,* Disc 23, Track 2 • *Portfolio Management System*, Rubrics for Choices, p. 202	• *Formal Assessment*, Selection Test, p. 186 • *Test Generator (One-Stop Planner CD-ROM)*
• *Portfolio Management System*, Rubrics for Choices, p. 203	• *Audio CD Library,* Disc 23, Track 3 • *Portfolio Management System*, Rubrics for Choices, p. 203	• *Formal Assessment*, Selection Test, p. 188 • *Test Generator (One-Stop Planner CD-ROM)*
• *Portfolio Management System*, Rubrics for Choices, p. 204	• *Audio CD Library,* Disc 24, Track 2 • *Viewing and Representing:* Fine Art Transparency 18 Worksheet p. 72 • *Portfolio Management System*, Rubrics for Choices, p. 204	• *Formal Assessment*, Selection Test, p. 188 • *Test Generator (One-Stop Planner CD-ROM)* • *Preparation for College Admission Exams*, p. 59
• *Portfolio Management System*, Rubrics for Choices, p. 205	• *Audio CD Library,* Disc 24, Track 3 • *Portfolio Management System*, Rubrics for Choices, p. 205	• *Formal Assessment*, Selection Test, p. 190 • *Test Generator (One-Stop Planner CD-ROM)*
• *Portfolio Management System*, Rubrics for Choices, p. 206	• *Portfolio Management System*, Rubrics for Choices, p. 206	• *Formal Assessment*, Selection Test, p. 190 • *Test Generator (One-Stop Planner CD-ROM)*
• *Portfolio Management System*, Rubrics for Choices, p. 207	• *Audio CD Library,* Disc 24, Track 4 • *Portfolio Management System*, Rubrics for Choices, p. 207	• *Formal Assessment*, Selection Test, p. 192 • *Test Generator (One-Stop Planner CD-ROM)* • *Preparation for College Admission Exams*, p. 61
• *Portfolio Management System*, Rubrics for Choices, p. 208	• *Audio CD Library,* Disc 24, Track 5 • *Portfolio Management System*, Rubrics for Choices, p. 208	• *Formal Assessment*, Selection Test, p. 194 • *Test Generator (One-Stop Planner CD-ROM)*

 Transparency    CD-ROM    Video    Audio CD

Collection Planner

Collection 18 The Wages of War

Skills Focus

Selection or Feature	Reading Skills and Strategies	Elements of Literature and Language	Writing	Listening and Speaking	Viewing and Representing
from **Night** (p. 921) Elie Wiesel	Identify the Main Point, p. 931	Atmosphere, pp. 921, 931 Irony, p. 930 Metaphor, p. 931 Symbol, p. 931 Objective Reporting, p. 931 Tone, p. 931 Foreshadow, p. 931 Main Point, p. 931	Make a Judgment and Support It with Evidence from the Text, p. 931 Write an Essay Connecting Texts, p. 931		
The Death of the Ball Turret Gunner (p. 932) Randall Jarrell	Identify Levels of Meaning, p. 934	Extended Metaphor, p. 934 Irony, p. 934	Determine the Real-World Context of a Poem, p. 934 Write an Essay Interpreting an Extended Metaphor, p. 934 Write a Paragraph or a Poem from a Specific Point of View, p. 934	Compare Oral Interpretations of the Poem, p. 934	
A Noiseless Flash *from* **Hiroshima** (p. 936) John Hersey	Reading Closely for Details, pp. 936, 946 Context Clues, p. 947	Subjective Reporting, pp. 936, 946–947 Objective Reporting, pp. 936, 946–947 Image, p. 946 Irony, p. 946 Suspense, p. 947	Identify Examples of Subjective and Objective Reporting, p. 947 Write an Essay Explaining Hersey's Techniques for Creating Suspense, p. 947 Research and Report on the Decision to Use the Atomic Bomb, p. 947 Write an Essay Discussing Hersey's Techniques, p. 947		
For the Union Dead (p. 949) Robert Lowell	Gaining Understanding Through Questioning, pp. 949, 954	Imagery, pp. 949, 954 Message, p. 954 Title, p. 954 Irony, p. 954 Tone, p. 954	Adjust Content for Audience, p. 954 Write an Essay Comparing and Contrasting Two Poems by Different Authors, p. 954		
Game (p. 956) Donald Barthelme	Interpret Word Meanings and Connotations, p. 956	Narrator, p. 961 Setting, p. 961 Resolution, p. 961 Repetition, p. 961 Characterization, p. 961 Theme, p. 961 Satire, p. 962 • Irony • Hyperbole • Incongruity • Fantasy Theme, p. 963	State the Theme of a Story, and Describe Your Responses, p. 963 Write an Essay Comparing Texts, p. 963		
Speaking of Courage (p. 965) Tim O'Brien	Make Predictions, p. 973	Conflict, pp. 965, 973 • Internal • External Setting, p. 973 Symbolic Meaning, p. 973 Irony, p. 973 Characterization, p. 973 Tone, p. 973	Identify Criteria for a Well-Conceived Character, p. 973 Write an Essay Analyzing Contrasted Elements, p. 973 Write an Essay Comparing and Contrasting Stories, p. 973	Write and Direct a Television Interview with a Character, p. 973	
Monsoon Season (p. 975) Yusef Komunyakaa	Cite Passages to Support an Opinion, p. 978	Imagery, pp. 975, 978 Symbols, p. 978	Evaluate Images from the Poem, p. 978 Write an Essay Evaluating the Use of Symbols, p. 978	Respond Orally to a Statement by an Author, p. 978	

THE WAGES OF WAR

Wiesel

Jarrell

Hersey

Lowell

Barthelme

O'Brien

Komunyakaa

At the Bomb Testing Site

At noon in the desert a panting lizard
waited for history, its elbows tense,
watching the curve of a particular road
as if something might happen.

It was looking at something farther off
than people could see, an important scene
acted in stone for little selves
at the flute end of consequences.

There was just a continent without much on it
under a sky that never cared less.
Ready for a change, the elbows waited.
The hands gripped hard on the desert.

—William Stafford
(1914–1993)

Responding to the Poem

? Discuss with students the point of view of the poem. What does it say about warfare and nature? [Possible responses: The poem presents the development of the atomic bomb from the point of view of nature. It emphasizes both the pettiness and the danger of human history against the backdrop of nature's fragile neutrality. With the splitting of the atom, nature braces itself, and waits in its beauty and its indifference for the "consequences" (l. 8).] **What might be the "something farther off / than people could see"?** [Possible response: The lizard might sense the consequences of the unique natural and historical phenomenon of atomic explosion; it might have a sense of nature's neutral continuity, even in the face of this catastrophic threat.]

Writing Focus: Evaluation

The following **Work in Progress** assignments in this collection build to a culminating **Writer's Workshop** at the end of Collection 21.

Writer's Workshop: Persuasive Writing / Evaluation (p. 1181)

OBJECTIVES

1. Read and interpret the memoir
2. Identify and interpret atmosphere
3. Express understanding through writing
4. Understand and use new words

SKILLS

Literary
- Identify and interpret atmosphere

Writing
- Evaluate use of objective reporting
- Compare narratives of captivity
- Identify the main point of a brief testimonial and connect it with the memoir

Vocabulary
- Understand and use new words

Viewing/Representing
- Relate fine art to the memoir (ATE)

Planning

- **Block Schedule**
  Block Scheduling Lesson Plans with Pacing Guide
- **Traditional Schedule**
  Lesson Plans Including Strategies for English-Language Learners
- **One-Stop Planner**
  CD-ROM with Test Generator

Elie Wiesel

(1928–   )

In March of 1944, when Elie Wiesel (el´ē wi·zel´) was fifteen, his life changed forever. At the time, Wiesel was living in the little town where he was born—Sighet, a remote village in the Carpathian Mountains of Hungary (now Romania). Raised in the Jewish mystical tradition of Hasidism, Wiesel had spent his childhood years immersed in the heritage of his extended family and in intense religious study. But in March 1944, the German army invaded Hungary. Soon Wiesel, his family, and some fifteen thousand other Jews from his region were rounded up and deported to extermination camps in Nazi-occupied Poland.

What Wiesel experienced in the camps was an unremitting horror. He saw his mother and youngest sister sent to die in a gas chamber, he saw his father succumb to dysentery and senseless violence, and he saw great numbers of fellow prisoners, many of them children, tortured and murdered by the Nazis.

After Wiesel was liberated from Buchenwald concentration camp in April 1945, he could not bring himself to write of the Holocaust for a decade, for fear "that words might betray it." Yet he also remembered the promise he had made to himself: "If, by some miracle, I survive, I will devote my life to testifying on behalf of all those whose shadows will be bound to mine forever." The result of this promise was *Night,* Wiesel's devastating memoir of his experiences under the Nazi terror, originally published in Yiddish as *Un di Velt Hot geshvigen (And the World Kept Silent)* in 1956. In the same year, he came to the United States to cover the United Nations as a reporter. He became a U.S. citizen in 1963 and is now a professor at Boston University.

For over four decades, Wiesel has continued to be a powerful advocate for human dignity—as a novelist, dramatist, journalist, religious scholar, and international activist. Seeking to maintain global awareness of the Nazi atrocities, and to prevent similar crimes against humanity, he has spoken out against human rights abuses in Cambodia, the former Soviet Union, Bosnia and Herzegovina, and South Africa under the Apartheid regime. Such work earned Wiesel a Nobel Peace Prize in 1986. In his acceptance speech, he reflected on his past and his purpose in life.

"This is what I say to the young Jewish boy wondering what I have done with his years. It is in his name that I speak to you and that I express to you my deepest gratitude. No one is as capable of gratitude as one who has emerged from the Kingdom of Night. We know that every moment is a moment of grace, every hour an offering; not to share them would mean to betray them. Our lives no longer belong to us alone; they belong to all those who need us desperately."

go.hrw.com
LEO 11-18

Preteaching Vocabulary

Words to Own

After students have studied the Words to Own listed at the bottom of selection pages, ask them to study the sentence in which each word appears, and write a sentence of their own using the word. Then ask them to complete a chart like the one at the right, listing a synonym and an antonym for each word. Allow students who need help to use a dictionary or a thesaurus to complete the exercise.

Words to Own	Synonym	Antonym
abyss	[chasm]	[peak]
scouring	[foraging]	[squandering]
encumbrance	[burden]	[alleviation]
semblance	[pretense]	[reality]
conscientiously	[scrupulously]	[carelessly]

Before You Read

FROM NIGHT

Make the Connection

Part of the power of Wiesel's memoir lies in its ability to make us feel both enormous empathy and deep fear. How can these feelings change a person? When a writer fulfills his responsibility as a witness, what is your responsibility as a reader?

Quickwrite

Think about a difficult time in your life, one in which you felt afraid, hopeless, or helpless. Jot down your thoughts on how you responded and how you feel you ought to have responded (or how you would respond now).

Elements of Literature

Atmosphere: Witnessing the Scene
As you read these sections of *Night*, notice how Wiesel evokes

the terrifying and brutal **atmosphere** of the Nazi extermination camps without using elaborate figures of speech or ornamentation. How does Wiesel's unadorned style make this atmosphere all the more powerful and disturbing?

Background

World War II forced people to face not only battlefield atrocities, but also the grim reality that an industrialized, civilized society was capable of profound evil. In the Holocaust, or Shoah, the German Nazis and their collaborators made a systematic attempt to destroy all of Europe's Jewish people, who were deemed "racially inferior" by Nazi ideology. By the war's end in 1945, the Nazis had killed over 6 million Jews in what their leaders termed "The

Final Solution." In all, the Nazis murdered more than 11 million civilians—among whom were gypsies, homosexuals, "non-Aryans," political opponents, and captured resistance fighters.

This was an appalling evil: the deliberate torture, starvation, and murder of millions of men, women, and children—without even the pretense that they posed a military threat. But it happened.

On the following pages, you will find three excerpts from Wiesel's memoir. The first excerpt occurs on a train headed for Auschwitz (oush'vits'), the most infamous of the "concentration camps." The account opens after Wiesel and his family have been forced into a railroad car with eighty other Hungarian Jews. They are only beginning to comprehend the horror that awaits them.

Arriving at Auschwitz from Hungary in Spring, 1944.

from Night

Elie Wiesel

translated from the French by **Stella Rodway**

The train stopped at Kaschau,[1] a little town on the Czechoslovak frontier. We realized then that we were not going to stay in Hungary. Our eyes were opened, but too late.

The door of the car slid open. A German officer, accompanied by a Hungarian lieutenant-interpreter, came up and introduced himself.

"From this moment, you come under the authority of the German army. Those of you who

1. **Kaschau** (käsh'ou'): Polish; Košice (kô'shē·tse).

ELIE WIESEL 921

Resources: Print and Media

Reading
- *Graphic Organizers for Active Reading*, p. 90
- *Words to Own*, p. 47
- Audio CD Library
  Disc 23, Track 2

Writing and Language
- *Daily Oral Grammar*
  Transparency 52

Assessment
- *Formal Assessment*, p. 186
- *Portfolio Management System*, p. 202
- *Test Generator (One-Stop Planner CD-ROM)*

Internet
- go.hrw.com (keyword: LE0 11-18)

Summary ■■

In the first excerpt from his memoir, Wiesel describes the forced transport of his family and other Jews to Poland, after they were deported from their community in Hungary. Packed in a cattle car without water, food, or sanitation, they are forced to travel for days as the claustrophobia and terror rises. Madame Schächter, separated from her husband and older son, loses control and screams for hours about a nightmarish vision of a fiery furnace. Her cries so unnerve the other prisoners that they gag her and later beat her. Wiesel takes the episode as a grim omen of the cremation furnace at Auschwitz—the train's destination—and a sign of the captives' progressive dehumanization.

The second excerpt describes the death-selection process at Buna, after Wiesel has lost his mother and little sister to the Auschwitz gas chamber, and has been moved with his father to this new camp. Wiesel makes it through the selection, but his father is marked down for death, and gives Elie a spoon and knife as a tragic "inheritance." Wiesel spends a day in terror of losing this last surviving member of his family. While his father narrowly escapes death the next day, Wiesel describes the death-sentence of Akiba Drumer—a respected man from the community who has begun to lose faith—and mourns how quickly he is forgotten by others in the nightmare of the camps.

The third excerpt describes a grisly death march from the Buna camp to Gleiwitz. The Nazi guards have indiscriminately shot prisoners who slow the pace, and Rabbi Eliahou becomes terrified when he can't find his son. With horror, Wiesel remembers that he has seen Eliahou's son—pushing to the front of the march in order to escape responsibility for his weak, elderly father. The next night, the prisoners arrive at the murderously overcrowded barracks of Gleiwitz, and are pushed inside into a sea of dead and dying human bodies. Suffocating, Wiesel claws his way to the top of the heap, and recognizes the weak voice of Juliek, a violin player he has met earlier. In the darkness, Juliek plays part of a Beethoven concerto for this audience of dead and dying prisoners. But in the morning, Wiesel finds Juliek dead, beside his crushed violin.

A Historical Connections

Annexation of Eastern Europe

Three countries are referred to in the opening paragraphs: Czechoslovakia, Hungary, and Germany. Locate them for the class on a map, and explain that at this point in 1944 Hitler still controlled most of Eastern Europe.

B Elements of Literature

Characterization

❓ What do these details reveal about the character of Madame Schächter? [Possible response: She was once an intense but capable middle-aged woman whose mind has now become unhinged by the deportation and her separation from her husband and older sons.]

C Reading Skills and Strategies

Identifying Cause and Effect

❓ How does Madame Schächter's screaming intensify the others' fear? [Possible response: Powerless and trapped in a horrifying nightmare, it is hard for the captives to dismiss Madame Schächter's vision as crazy; instead these screams in the night strike them as ominous and terrifying.]

D Critical Thinking

Interpreting

❓ Why would the image of the boy calming his mother disturb the narrator more than her screaming? [Possible response: For the young Wiesel, this image of a ten-year-old boy trying to comfort and stabilize his mother is emblematic of the nightmarish experience they are all entering—one in which even the adults are suddenly as powerless and frightened as children.]

still have gold, silver, or watches in your possession must give them up now. Anyone who is later found to have kept anything will be shot on the spot. Secondly, anyone who feels ill may go to the hospital car. That's all."

The Hungarian lieutenant went among us with a basket and collected the last possessions from those who no longer wished to taste the bitterness of terror.

"There are eighty of you in this wagon," added the German officer. "If anyone is missing, you'll all be shot, like dogs. . . ."

They disappeared. The doors were closed. We were caught in a trap, right up to our necks. The doors were nailed up; the way back was finally cut off. The world was a cattle wagon hermetically sealed.[2]

We had a woman with us named Madame Schächter.[3] She was about fifty; her ten-year-old son was with her, crouched in a corner. Her husband and two eldest sons had been deported with the first transport by mistake. The separation had completely broken her.

I knew her well. A quiet woman with tense, burning eyes, she had often been to our house. Her husband, who was a pious man, spent his days and nights in study, and it was she who worked to support the family.

Madame Schächter had gone out of her mind. On the first day of the journey she had already begun to moan and to keep asking why she had been separated from her family. As time went on, her cries grew hysterical.

On the third night, while we slept, some of us sitting one against the other and some standing, a piercing cry split the silence:

"Fire! I can see a fire! I can see a fire!"

There was a moment's panic. Who was it who had cried out? It was Madame Schächter. Standing in the middle of the wagon, in the pale light from the windows, she looked like a withered tree in a cornfield. She pointed her arm toward the window, screaming:

"Look! Look at it! Fire! A terrible fire! Mercy! *Oh, that fire!*"

Some of the men pressed up against the bars. There was nothing there; only the darkness.

2. **hermetically** (hər·met′ik·lē) **sealed:** airtight.
3. **Schächter** (shekh′tər).

The shock of this terrible awakening stayed with us for a long time. We still trembled from it. With every groan of the wheels on the rail, we felt that an abyss was about to open beneath our bodies. Powerless to still our own anguish, we tried to console ourselves:

"She's mad, poor soul. . . ."

Someone had put a damp cloth on her brow, to calm her, but still her screams went on:

"Fire! Fire!"

Her little boy was crying, hanging onto her skirt, trying to take hold of her hands. "It's all right, Mummy! There's nothing there. . . . Sit down. . . ." This shook me even more than his mother's screams had done.

Some women tried to calm her. "You'll find your husband and your sons again. . . . in a few days. . . ."

She continued to scream, breathless, her voice broken by sobs. "Jews, listen to me! I can see a fire! There are huge flames! It is a furnace!"

It was as though she were possessed by an evil spirit which spoke from the depths of her being.

We tried to explain it away, more to calm ourselves and to recover our own breath than to comfort her. "She must be very thirsty, poor thing! That's why she keeps talking about a fire devouring her."

But it was in vain. Our terror was about to burst the sides of the train. Our nerves were at breaking point. Our flesh was creeping. It was as though madness were taking possession of us all. We could stand it no longer. Some of the young men forced her to sit down, tied her up, and put a gag in her mouth.

Silence again. The little boy sat down by his mother, crying. I had begun to breathe normally again. We could hear the wheels churning out that monotonous rhythm of a train traveling through the night. We could begin to doze, to rest, to dream. . . .

An hour or two went by like this. Then another scream took our breath away. The woman had broken loose from her bonds and was crying out more loudly than ever:

WORDS TO OWN
abyss (ə·bis′) *n.*: gulf or void too deep for measurement.

922 CONTEMPORARY LITERATURE

Reaching All Students

Struggling Readers

Have students make predictions about the meaning of Madame Schächter's vision to compare them later with actual outcomes. Suggest that they create a two-column chart, and write their predictions in the first column. After students have read the selection, ask them to complete the second column by inserting actual events. Encourage volunteers to share their entries with the class.

English Language Learners

To help students stay focused while reading, first have them create a glossary of the German and English terms defined in footnotes throughout the selection. Have them write each term and its page number on a separate 3" x 5" card. Review pronunciations and help students write on their cards a brief definition of each term. Then, have them arrange the cards by page number, for easy reference as they read.

Advanced Learners

Assign a small group of students to research and map the advance and retreat of the German army through Eastern Europe, with emphasis on Czechoslovakia, Hungary, and Poland. Ask visual learners in the group to draw a map that is large enough to display in the classroom. The map should plot the army's path and give all locations mentioned in the excerpts from Wiesel's memoir: Kaschau, Birkenau, Auschwitz, Buna, and Gleiwitz.

"Look at the fire! Flames, flames everywhere. . . ."

Once more the young men tied her up and gagged her. They even struck her. People encouraged them:

"Make her be quiet! She's mad! Shut her up! She's not the only one. She can keep her mouth shut. . . ."

They struck her several times on the head—blows that might have killed her. Her little boy clung to her; he did not cry out; he did not say a word. He was not even weeping now.

An endless night. Toward dawn, Madame Schächter calmed down. Crouched in her corner, her bewildered gaze scouring the emptiness, she could no longer see us.

She stayed like that all through the day, dumb, absent, isolated among us. As soon as night fell, she began to scream: "There's a fire over there!" She would point at a spot in space, always the same one. They were tired of hitting her. The heat, the thirst, the pestilential[4] stench, the suffocating lack of air—these were as nothing compared with these screams which tore us to shreds. A few days more and we should all have started to scream too.

But we had reached a station. Those who were next to the windows told us its name:

"Auschwitz."

No one had ever heard that name.

The train did not start up again. The afternoon passed slowly. Then the wagon doors slid open. Two men were allowed to get down to fetch water.

When they came back, they told us that, in exchange for a gold watch, they had discovered that this was the last stop. We would be getting out here. There was a labor camp. Conditions were good. Families would not be split up. Only the young people would go to work in the factories. The old men and invalids would be kept occupied in the fields.

The barometer of confidence soared. Here was a sudden release from the terrors of the previous nights. We gave thanks to God.

Madame Schächter stayed in her corner, wilted, dumb, indifferent to the general confidence. Her little boy stroked her hand.

4. **pestilential** (pes′tə·len′shəl): like a pestilence or deadly infection; dangerous and harmful.

As dusk fell, darkness gathered inside the wagon. We started to eat our last provisions. At ten in the evening, everyone was looking for a convenient position in which to sleep for a while, and soon we were all asleep. Suddenly:

"The fire! The furnace! Look, over there! . . ."

Waking with a start, we rushed to the window. Yet again we had believed her, even if only for a moment. But there was nothing outside save the darkness of night. With shame in our souls, we went back to our places, gnawed by fear, in spite of ourselves. As she continued to scream, they began to hit her again, and it was with the greatest difficulty that they silenced her.

The man in charge of our wagon called a German officer who was walking about on the platform, and asked him if Madame Schächter could be taken to the hospital car.

"You must be patient," the German replied. "She'll be taken there soon."

Toward eleven o'clock, the train began to move. We pressed against the windows. The convoy was moving slowly. A quarter of an hour later, it slowed down again. Through the windows we could see barbed wire; we realized that this must be the camp.

We had forgotten the existence of Madame Schächter. Suddenly, we heard terrible screams:

"Jews, look! Look through the window! Flames! Look!"

And as the train stopped, we saw this time that flames were gushing out of a tall chimney into the black sky.

Madame Schächter was silent herself. Once more she had become dumb, indifferent, absent, and had gone back to her corner.

We looked at the flames in the darkness. There was an abominable odor floating in the air. Suddenly, our doors opened. Some odd-looking characters, dressed in striped shirts and black trousers, leapt into the wagon. They held electric torches[5] and truncheons.[6] They began to strike out to right and left, shouting:

5. **electric torches:** flashlights.
6. **truncheons** (trun′chənz): short, thick clubs.

WORDS TO OWN

scouring (skour′iŋ) v.: roaming about, searching.

E Critical Thinking
Analyzing
? What do the reactions of the young men and Madame Schächter's son imply about the mental and spiritual condition of the prisoners? [Possible responses: The confinement and terror are making them behave like caged animals, emptied of compassion and tears.]

F Elements of Literature
Dramatic Irony
? How does the stark simplicity of this passage heighten the atmosphere through dramatic irony? [Possible response: The captives have simply never heard the name of this obscure Polish town, which the reader associates with the greatest acts of human evil in the twentieth century.]

G Critical Thinking
Making Judgments
? Have students discuss how and why the Nazis were able to affect this tone of calm, perhaps even polite, efficiency, given their knowledge of where they were taking the Jews? How does it make their actions and their ideology all the more horrifying? [Possible response: Their tone demonstrates how antisemitism and Nazi ideology allowed them to dehumanize their victims to such an extent that many could send Jews to their deaths calmly, without expressions of anger or guilt.]

Using Students' Strengths

Intrapersonal Learners
Students may have seen movies like *Schindler's List,* read *The Diary of a Young Girl* by Anne Frank, or heard about family experiences in the concentration camps—or maybe this is the first time they've been taken inside the horror of the Holocaust. As students read Wiesel's memoir, ask them to freewrite about the thoughts and feelings it triggers. What is the relevance of the memoir to their lives now?

Verbal/Linguistic Learners
Ask students to locate a copy of Mark Helprin's story, "Tamar," which begins in London just before the outbreak of World War II. The story presumes that the reader is aware of the Holocaust. Ask students to read the story and to write about how it connects with Wiesel's memoir. Alternatively, students who have never read *The Diary of a Young Girl* by Anne Frank (1947) may wish to read and write about that work.

Visual Learners
Provide visual learners with supplies for creating paintings or other artworks that evoke the atmosphere of the crowded deportation train, the march to Gleiwitz in the snow, or events at the barracks in the final scenes from the excerpt. Encourage them to use colors that evoke the mood, and to include symbols (such as broken branches or a shattered violin). Ask students to caption their work with a line from the memoir, and post it for the class.

"Everybody get out! Everyone out of the wagon! Quickly!"

We jumped out. I threw a last glance toward Madame Schächter. Her little boy was holding her hand.

A In front of us flames. In the air that smell of burning flesh. It must have been about midnight. We had arrived—at Birkenau,[7] reception center for Auschwitz. . . .

7. **Birkenau** (bir′kə·nou).

B *The following section of* Night *takes place in Buna* (boo′nə), *another camp in Poland, where Wiesel and his father were sent from Auschwitz. It documents the horrifying process of selection, by which the Nazis separated those prisoners judged fit to perform slave labor from those who were to be killed immediately. It was after just such a selection that Wiesel's mother and sister were murdered in the Auschwitz gas chamber.*

The head of our block had never been outside concentration camps since 1933. He had already been through all the slaughterhouses, all the factories of death. At about nine o'clock, he took up his position in our midst:

"Achtung!"[8]

There was instant silence.

"Listen carefully to what I am going to say." (For the first time, I heard his voice quiver.) "In a few moments the selection will begin. You must get completely undressed. Then one by one you go before the SS[9] doctors. I hope you will all succeed in getting through. But you must help your own chances. Before you go into the next room, move about in some way so that you give yourselves a little color. Don't walk slowly, run! Run as if the devil were after you! Don't look at the SS. Run, straight in front of you!"

He broke off for a moment, then added:

"And, the essential thing, don't be afraid!"

Here was a piece of advice we should have liked very much to be able to follow.

I got undressed, leaving my clothes on the bed. There was no danger of anyone stealing them this evening.

Tibi and Yossi, who had changed their unit at the same time as I had, came up to me and said:

"Let's keep together. We shall be stronger."

Yossi was murmuring something between his teeth. He must have been praying. I had never realized that Yossi was a believer. I had even always

thought the reverse. Tibi was silent, very pale. All the prisoners in the block stood naked between the beds. This must be how one stands at the last judgment.

"They're coming!"

C There were three SS officers standing round the notorious Dr. Mengele,[10] who had received us at Birkenau. The head of the block, with an attempt at a smile, asked us:

"Ready?"

Yes, we were ready. So were the SS doctors. Dr. Mengele was holding a list in his hand: our numbers.[11] He made a sign to the head of the block: "We can begin!" As if this were a game!

The first to go by were the "officials" of the block: *Stubenaelteste*,[12] Kapos,[13] foremen, all in perfect physical condition of course! Then came the ordinary prisoners' turn. Dr. Mengele took stock of them from head to foot. Every now and then, he wrote a number down. One single thought filled my mind: not to let my number be taken; not to show my left arm.

There were only Tibi and Yossi in front of me. They passed. I had time to notice that Mengele had not written their numbers down. Someone pushed me. It was my turn. I ran without looking

8. **Achtung** (əkh′toon): German for "attention."
9. **SS:** Abbreviation for the German *Schutzstaffel* (shoots′shtə′fəl), meaning "protection squad," the elite Nazi guards who oversaw the operation of the concentration camps.

10. **Dr. Mengele:** Josef Mengele (yō′zef′ men′ə·lə) (1911–1979) was a Nazi doctor and SS officer infamous for torturing camp prisoners, often children, sometimes in pseudoscientific experiments.
11. **our numbers:** Concentration camp prisoners were identified by a number, which was usually tattooed on the left arm shortly after arrival.
12. *Stubenaelteste* (shtoob′ən·el′təst·ə): German for "barracks leaders" or "room leaders."
13. **Kapos** (kä′pōz): prisoners appointed by the Nazis to head work gangs, often in exchange for better treatment.

Crossing the Curriculum

back. My head was spinning: you're too thin, you're weak, you're too thin, you're good for the furnace. . . . The race seemed interminable. I thought I had been running for years. . . . You're too thin, you're too weak. . . . At last I had arrived exhausted. When I regained my breath, I questioned Yossi and Tibi:

"Was I written down?"

"No," said Yossi. He added, smiling: "In any case, he couldn't have written you down, you were running too fast. . . ." **D**

I began to laugh. I was glad. I would have liked to kiss him. At that moment, what did the others matter! I hadn't been written down.

Those whose numbers had been noted stood apart, abandoned by the whole world. Some were weeping in silence. . . .

Several days had elapsed. We no longer thought about the selection. We went to work as usual, loading heavy stones into railway wagons. Rations had become more meager: this was the only change.

We had risen before dawn, as on every day. We had received the black coffee, the ration of bread. We were about to set out for the yard as usual. The head of the block arrived, running.

"Silence for a moment. I have a list of numbers here. I'm going to read them to you. Those whose numbers I call won't be going to work this morning; they'll stay behind in the camp."

And, in a soft voice, he read out about ten numbers. We had understood. These were numbers chosen at the selection. Dr. Mengele had not forgotten. **E**

The head of the block went toward his room. Ten prisoners surrounded him, hanging onto his clothes:

"Save us! You promised . . . ! We want to go to the yard. We're strong enough to work. We're good workers. We can . . . we will. . . ."

He tried to calm them, to reassure them about their fate, to explain to them that the fact that they were staying behind in the camp did not mean much, had no tragic significance.

"After all, I stay here myself every day," he added.

It was a somewhat feeble argument. He realized it, and without another word went and shut himself up in his room.

The bell had just rung.

"Form up!"

It scarcely mattered now that the work was hard. The essential thing was to be as far away as possible from the block, from the crucible of death, from the center of hell. **F**

I saw my father running toward me. I became frightened all of a sudden.

"What's the matter?"

Out of breath, he could hardly open his mouth.

"Me, too . . . me, too . . . ! They told me to stay behind in the camp."

They had written down his number without his being aware of it.

"What will happen?" I asked in anguish.

But it was he who tried to reassure me.

"It isn't certain yet. There's still a chance of escape. They're going to do another selection today . . . a decisive selection." **G**

I was silent.

He felt that his time was short. He spoke quickly. He would have liked to say so many

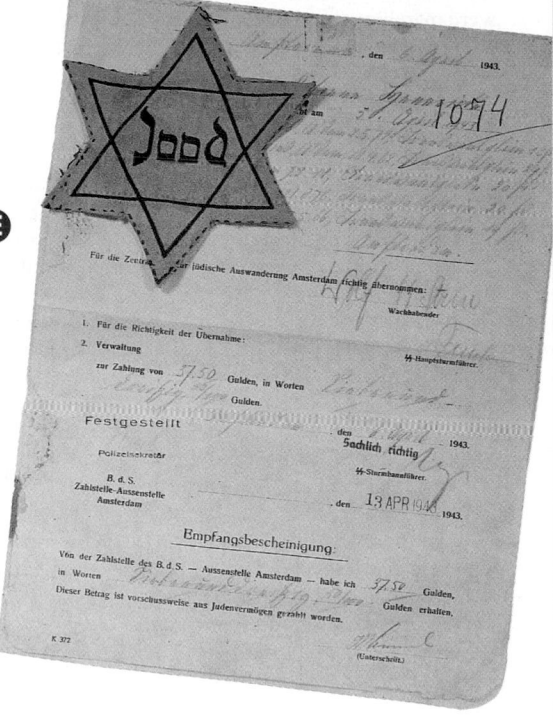

Identity card and yellow star for a Jew living in Amsterdam in 1943.

ELIE WIESEL 925

D **Reading Skills and Strategies**
Making Inferences
? Explain to students how people in oppressive situations often take on or *internalize* the objectives of the people who oppress them. How might this passage suggest that Wiesel has internalized, in spite of himself, some of the camp's structure and ideology? [Possible response: He finds himself valuing strength and survival alone, accepting that the thin and the weak are "good for the furnace," and feeling momentary indifference and aversion to those selected and "abandoned by the whole world."]

E **Struggling Readers**
Noting Details
? Why, after his shouting of orders, does the cell block head read out the numbers "in a soft voice"? [because he knows that the people whose numbers have been selected are almost certain to be killed]

F **Elements of Literature**
Appositive Phrases
? An appositive phrase consists of a noun or pronoun and its modifiers— which is placed beside (usually after) another noun or pronoun to identify or explain it (see p. 1231). How do the two appositive phrases that follow "from the block," evoke a powerful sense of setting and atmosphere? [They make it clear that the cell barracks have become indelibly associated with death and torment for Wiesel.]

G **Reading Skills and Strategies**
Making Predictions
Have students pause here to predict what will happen to the narrator's father. After students have read the next page, have them check the accuracy of their predictions.

Getting Students Involved

Cooperative Learning
Panels. Divide the class into three groups, one for each of the following topics. Have each group discuss its topic and prepare a panel discussion to present to the class. Each group must support its points with examples. Panels may be free-flowing discussions, or formal presentations led by a moderator, but should be no more than ten minutes long. Some members of each group may serve as research and resource personnel, while others may present the actual panel discussions. After each presentation, ask the rest of the class to evaluate its effectiveness in persuading the audience to adopt its point of view.

• Examine films or television programs you have seen that confront troubling, tragic events like the Holocaust. Are these depictions usually realistic or do they sensationalize or trivialize real human suffering. How do they compare with Elie Wiesel's *Night*?

• How would you define *evil*? Why are memoirs like Wiesel's—firsthand accounts of shocking events of human history—important to us? What is their application to our lives?

• After his experiences in the camps, Wiesel vowed never to be silent in the face of human suffering. Who speaks out against human misery today? What forms do such protests take? How can students become involved?

? How does the gift from father to son make you feel? What does it reveal about their relationship? [Sample response: The gift of the knife and spoon is heart-rending because it is so little, but it is all Wiesel's father has. Elie and his father managed to retain love and loyalty despite their dehumanizing situation.]

B Elements of Literature
Internal Conflict

? Notice the narrator's frantic, conflicting thoughts. Why would it be good to die before returning to camp? [Possible response: so he would not have to face his father's death—if it has occurred.] Moments later, why does he want to run to camp? [to find out what really has happened to his father]

C Reading Skills and Strategies
Comparing Predictions

? What outcome did most members of the class predict when the narrator's father said that he had to stay behind? [Responses will vary.] How do you feel about the actual outcome? [Most students will feel relief, even though they may recall from the author's biography on p. 920 that Wiesel's father ultimately died in the camps.]

D Cultural Connections
The Talmud

The Talmud is a huge compendium of Jewish law and tradition, usually thought to include the *Mishna,* the first definitive codification of Jewish oral laws (completed during the third century), and the *Gemara,* the commentary on those laws (with two versions, completed in Palestine in approximately A.D. 400, and in Babylonia in approximately A.D. 500). It is this commentary on religion and on law, comprised of arguments, debates, and questions among the early rabbis, that is generally most associated with Talmudic scholarship.

E Cultural Connections
The Kaddish

The Kaddish is one of the most solemn liturgies in Judaism. It is important that the Kaddish be said, especially by children for their deceased parents. The Kaddish never mentions death but calls for the coming of God's kingdom on Earth.

---

things. His speech grew confused; his voice choked. He knew that I would have to go in a few moments. He would have to stay behind alone, so very alone.

"Look, take this knife," he said to me. "I don't need it any longer. It might be useful to you. And take this spoon as well. Don't sell them. Quickly! Go on. Take what I'm giving you!"

The inheritance.

"Don't talk like that, Father." (I felt that I would break into sobs.) "I don't want you to say that. Keep the spoon and knife. You need them as much as I do. We shall see each other again this evening, after work."

He looked at me with his tired eyes, veiled with despair. He went on:

"I'm asking this of you. . . . Take them. Do as I ask, my son. We have no time. . . . Do as your father asks."

Our Kapo yelled that we should start.

The unit set out toward the camp gate. Left, right! I bit my lips. My father had stayed by the block, leaning against the wall. Then he began to run, to catch up with us. Perhaps he had forgotten something he wanted to say to me. . . . But we were marching too quickly . . . Left, right!

We were already at the gate. They counted us, to the din of military music. We were outside.

The whole day, I wandered about as if sleepwalking. Now and then Tibi and Yossi would throw me a brotherly word. The Kapo, too, tried to reassure me. He had given me easier work today. I felt sick at heart. How well they were treating me! Like an orphan! I thought: even now, my father is still helping me.

I did not know myself what I wanted—for the day to pass quickly or not. I was afraid of finding myself alone that night. How good it would be to die here!

At last we began the return journey. How I longed for orders to run!

The military march. The gate. The camp.

I ran to Block 36.

Were there still miracles on this earth? He was alive. He had escaped the second selection. He had been able to prove that he was still useful. . . . I gave him back his knife and spoon.

Akiba Drumer left us, a victim of the selection. Lately, he had wandered among us, his eyes glazed, telling everyone of his weakness: "I can't go on . . . It's all over. . . ." It was impossible to raise his morale. He didn't listen to what we told him. He could only repeat that all was over for him, that he could no longer keep up the struggle, that he had no strength left, nor faith. Suddenly his eyes would become blank, nothing but two open wounds, two pits of terror.

He was not the only one to lose his faith during those selection days. I knew a rabbi from a little town in Poland, a bent old man, whose lips were always trembling. He used to pray all the time, in the block, in the yard, in the ranks. He would recite whole pages of the Talmud from memory, argue with himself, ask himself questions and answer himself. And one day he said to me: "It's the end. God is no longer with us."

And, as though he had repented of having spoken such words, so clipped, so cold, he added in his faint voice:

"I know. One has no right to say things like that. I know. Man is too small, too humble and inconsiderable to seek to understand the mysterious ways of God. But what can I do? I'm not a sage, one of the elect, nor a saint. I'm just an ordinary creature of flesh and blood. I've got eyes, too, and I can see what they're doing here. Where is the divine Mercy? Where is God? How can I believe, how could anyone believe, in this merciful God?"

Poor Akiba Drumer, if he could have gone on believing in God, if he could have seen a proof of God in this Calvary,[14] he would not have been taken by the selection. But as soon as he felt the first cracks forming in his faith, he had lost his reason for struggling and had begun to die.

When the selection came, he was condemned in advance, offering his own neck to the executioner. All he asked of us was:

"In three days I shall no longer be here. . . . Say the Kaddish[15] for me."

---

14. **Calvary:** Wiesel compares Drumer's tragedy to the crucifixion of Jesus, which took place at the site near Jerusalem called Golgotha, or Calvary.
15. **Kaddish** (käd′ish): Jewish prayer in praise of God, one form of which is recited to mourn a death.

Crossing the Curriculum

Music

Above, Wiesel writes, "They counted us, to the din of military music." Who played the music? Have students research the use of music in German concentration camps, the formation of orchestras staffed by prisoners, and the privileges (if any) granted to musicians. As a starting point, students might seek information on the "showplace" camp, Theresienstadt, or contact the Holocaust Memorial Museum in Washington, D.C.

We promised him. In three days' time, when we saw the smoke rising from the chimney, we would think of him. Ten of us would gather together and hold a special service. All his friends would say the Kaddish.

Then he went off toward the hospital, his step steadier, not looking back. An ambulance was waiting to take him to Birkenau.

These were terrible days. We received more blows than food; we were crushed with work. And three days after he had gone we forgot to say the Kaddish. . . .

Concentration Camp (1944) by Ben Shahn. Tempera (24″ x 24″).
©Estate of Ben Shahn/Licensed by VAGA, New York, NY. Courtesy Sotheby's N.Y.

ELIE WIESEL 927

Professional Notes

Critical Comments: Wiesel's Universality

Have students consider the following assessments, all of which touch on the universality of Wiesel's message. In a class discussion, examine each opinion and debate its validity.

- Wiesel "touches universal chords" because "in writing about the Jewish condition, he thereby writes about the human condition. For the human condition is not generalized existence; it is a huge, crazy-quilt sum of particularized existences all woven together." —Robert McAfee Brown, *The Christian Century*
- "Wiesel has taken the Jew as his metaphor—and his reality—in order to unite a moral and aesthetic vision in terms of all men." —Daniel Stern, *The Washington Post Book World*
- "Wiesel is one of the few writers who . . . has succeeded in revealing in the Jewish tragedy those features by which it has become again and again a paradigm of the human condition." —Manes Sperber, *The New York Times Book Review*
- "Wiesel is a messenger to mankind. . . . His message is one of peace, atonement and human dignity." —Egil Aarvik, chairman of the Nobel Prize committee.

? Why might a rabbi's words of comfort provoke rebellion? How might people's experiences in the Holocaust make it difficult, if not impossible and offensive, to claim comfort in seeing God's will at work in the world? [Possible response: The extreme inhumanity and apocalyptic horror of the Holocaust made it hard for anyone to claim that it was in any way a result of "God's will"—and a rabbi who advanced such traditional theology might deeply hurt and offend his congregation.] Advanced students may want to research the deep impact of the Holocaust on modern theology and philosophy.

B Critical Thinking

Interpreting Motivation

? Why is Wiesel glad that Rabbi Eliahou will continue to search for his "beloved son"? How does Wiesel maintain a moral outlook in the face of the immoral world of the Holocaust? [Possible response: He hopes Rabbi Eliahou will live with the idea of his loving and devoted son, and feels he should not be forced to face his son's betrayal—borne of the most immoral and abominable circumstances imaginable. Wiesel claims no fundamental superiority to Eliahou's son, but only prays for the strength to resist the same dehumanizing impulses.]

C Reading Skills and Strategies

Making Generalizations

? What does it mean to pray to a God in whom one no longer believes? Has Wiesel lost his faith? What has he retained? [Possible response: Wiesel may be praying to the God of morality and faith, while he has lost his faith in the God of intervention and reward in the world—for he believes that such a God could not have allowed the Holocaust to happen.]

D Background

In an intervening section, the narrator's right foot became infected and his sole has been surgically drained. Although his foot has not yet healed, when Russian troops press westward into Poland he prefers to join his father and other prisoners on the evacuation march towards Germany described here, rather than risk being selected for death.

The next section of Night *occurs toward the end of Wiesel's eleven months in the concentration camps. It opens during a brutal march toward a new camp, Gleiwitz (glī′vits). The Nazi guards have forced the prisoners to run for miles in the snow without adequate rest or clothing. As a result, hundreds will die before they reach the dangerously overcrowded barracks.*

The door of the shed opened. An old man appeared, his moustache covered with frost, his lips blue with cold. It was Rabbi Eliahou,[16] the rabbi of a small Polish community. He was a very good man, well loved by everyone in the camp, even by the Kapos and the heads of the blocks. Despite the trials and privations, his face still shone with his inner purity. He was the only rabbi who was always addressed as "Rabbi" at Buna. He was like one of the old prophets, always in the midst of his people to comfort them. And, strangely, his words of comfort never provoked rebellion; they really brought peace.

He came into the shed and his eyes, brighter than ever, seemed to be looking for someone:

"Perhaps someone has seen my son somewhere?"

He had lost his son in the crowd. He had looked in vain among the dying. Then he had scratched up the snow to find his corpse. Without result.

For three years they had stuck together. Always near each other, for suffering, for blows, for the ration of bread, for prayer. Three years, from camp to camp, from selection to selection. And now—when the end seemed near—fate had separated them. Finding himself near me, Rabbi Eliahou whispered:

"It happened on the road. We lost sight of one another during the journey. I had stayed a little to the rear of the column. I hadn't any strength left for running. And my son didn't notice. That's all I know. Where has he disappeared? Where can I find him? Perhaps you've seen him somewhere?"

"No, Rabbi Eliahou, I haven't seen him."

He left then as he had come: like a wind-swept shadow.

He had already passed through the door when I suddenly remembered seeing his son running by my side. I had forgotten that, and I didn't tell Rabbi Eliahou!

16. **Eliahou** (el·ē·ä′hoo′).

Then I remembered something else: his son had seen him losing ground, limping, staggering back to the rear of the column. He had seen him. And he had continued to run on in front, letting the distance between them grow greater.

A terrible thought loomed up in my mind: he had wanted to get rid of his father! He had felt that his father was growing weak, he had believed that the end was near and had sought this separation in order to get rid of the burden, to free himself from an encumbrance which could lessen his own chances of survival.

I had done well to forget that. And I was glad that Rabbi Eliahou should continue to look for his beloved son.

And, in spite of myself, a prayer rose in my heart, to that God in whom I no longer believed.

My God, Lord of the Universe, give me strength never to do what Rabbi Eliahou's son has done.

Shouts rose outside in the yard, where darkness had fallen. The SS ordered the ranks to form up.

The march began again. The dead stayed in the yard under the snow, like faithful guards assassinated, without burial. No one had said the prayer for the dead over them. Sons abandoned their fathers' remains without a tear.

On the way it snowed, snowed, snowed endlessly. We were marching more slowly. The guards themselves seemed tired. My wounded foot no longer hurt me. It must have been completely frozen. The foot was lost to me. It had detached itself from my body like the wheel of a car. Too bad. I should have to resign myself; I could live with only one leg. The main thing was not to think about it. Above all, not at this moment. Leave thoughts for later.

Our march had lost all semblance of discipline.

WORDS TO OWN
encumbrance (en·kum′brəns) *n.*: hindrance; burden.
semblance (sem′bləns) *n.*: appearance, resemblance.

Making the Connections

Cultural Connections

Remind students that the Holocaust is, tragically, but one example of genocidal mass murder in recent centuries. Other examples include the European and American killing of millions of African slaves from the sixteenth through the nineteenth centuries; the deaths of millions of Native Americans due to disease and forced relocation during the same period; the Turkish deportation and slaughter of hundreds of thousands of Armenians in 1915; the extermination of a million fellow Cambodians by the Khmer Rouge during the 1970s; the 1994 killing of hundreds of thousands of the Tutsi people of Rwanda by the Hutu; and the "ethnic cleansing" practiced by the Bosnian Serbs and others during the civil war of the 1990s. Discuss the continuing need for works like Wiesel's *Night* as a response to the recurrence of such horrors.

We went as we wanted, as we could. We heard no more shots. Our guards must have been tired.

But death scarcely needed any help from them. The cold was <u>conscientiously</u> doing its work. At every step someone fell and suffered no more.

From time to time, SS officers on motorcycles would go down the length of the column to try and shake us out of our growing apathy:

"Keep going! We are getting there!"

"Courage! Only a few more hours!"

"We're reaching Gleiwitz."

These words of encouragement, even though they came from the mouths of our assassins, did us a great deal of good. No one wanted to give up now, just before the end, so near to the goal. Our eyes searched the horizon for the barbed wire of Gleiwitz. Our only desire was to reach it as quickly as possible.

The night had now set in. The snow had ceased to fall. We walked for several more hours before arriving.

We did not notice the camp until we were just in front of the gate.

Some Kapos rapidly installed us in the barracks. We pushed and jostled one another as if this were the supreme refuge, the gateway to life. We walked over pain-racked bodies. We trod on wounded faces. No cries. A few groans. My father and I were ourselves thrown to the ground by this rolling tide. Beneath our feet someone let out a rattling cry:

"You're crushing me . . . mercy!"

A voice that was not unknown to me.

"You're crushing me . . . mercy! mercy!"

The same faint voice, the same rattle, heard somewhere before. That voice had spoken to me one day. Where? When? Years ago? No, it could only have been at the camp.

"Mercy!"

I felt that I was crushing him. I was stopping his breath. I wanted to get up. I struggled to disengage myself, so that he could breathe. But I was crushed myself beneath the weight of other bodies. I could hardly breathe. I dug my nails into unknown faces. I was biting all round me, in order to get air. No one cried out.

Suddenly I remembered. Juliek![17] The boy from

17. **Juliek** (yoo′lē·ek).

Warsaw who played the violin in the band at Buna. . . .

"Juliek, is it you?"

"Eliezer[18]. . . the twenty-five strokes of the whip. Yes . . . I remember."

He was silent. A long moment elapsed.

"Juliek! Can you hear me, Juliek?"

"Yes . . . ," he said, in a feeble voice. "What do you want?"

He was not dead.

"How do you feel, Juliek?" I asked, less to know the answer than to hear that he could speak, that he was alive.

"All right, Eliezer. . . . I'm getting on all right . . . hardly any air . . . worn out. My feet are swollen. It's good to rest, but my violin . . ."

I thought he had gone out of his mind. What use was the violin here?

"What, your violin?"

He gasped.

"I'm afraid . . . I'm afraid . . . that they'll break my violin. . . . I've brought it with me."

I could not answer him. Someone was lying full length on top of me, covering my face. I was unable to breathe, through either mouth or nose. Sweat beaded my brow, ran down my spine. This was the end—the end of the road. A silent death, suffocation. No way of crying out, of calling for help.

I tried to get rid of my invisible assassin. My whole will to live was centered in my nails. I scratched. I battled for a mouthful of air. I tore at decaying flesh which did not respond. I could not free myself from this mass weighing down my chest. Was it a dead man I was struggling against? Who knows?

I shall never know. All I can say is that I won. I succeeded in digging a hole through this wall of dying people, a little hole through which I could drink in a small quantity of air.

"Father, how are you?" I asked, as soon as I could utter a word.

I knew he could not be far from me.

18. **Eliezer** (ā·lē·ā′zər).

- -

WORDS TO OWN

conscientiously (kän′shē·en′shəs·lē) *adv.*: diligently; thoroughly.

- -

ELIE WIESEL **929**

Assessing Learning

Check Test: Questions and Answers

1. On the train to Auschwitz, what horrifying visions cause Madame Schächter repeatedly to cry out? [visions of fire and a furnace]

2. What do Madame Schächter's visions foresee? [the crematorium at Auschwitz]

3. Why do prisoners run during a medical examination observed by Dr. Mengele? [to appear strong and healthy; to avoid selection for death]

4. On the march to Gleiwitz, what happens to those who lag behind? [They are shot or left behind to die in the snow.]

5. What instance of beauty touches the narrator during the night, in the closing scene from the memoir? [the violin playing of another prisoner]

E **Elements of Literature**

Personification

? Identify the personification in this passage and describe how it affects the atmosphere. How does it relate to the information above it? [Possible response: Wiesel personifies the cold, which, like the German officers discussed above, carries out the work of death with a careful and ruthless efficiency.]

F **Reading Skills and Strategies**

Determining the Author's Purpose

? After his liberation from the concentration camp in 1945, Wiesel struggled for years to find a language, a style of writing that could approach the horror of his Holocaust experiences. Why do you think he ultimately chose this spare, declarative style? Where does its power lie? What, for instance, is the effect of Wiesel's repeated simple observation that "No one cried out"? [Most students will recognize that the power of Wiesel's style lies in what he chooses *not* to say, because to do so might trivialize or reduce its intensity. The immense terror, guilt, and dismay involved in this passage, for instance, doesn't require that Wiesel speak directly of his emotions. Instead, the sad refrain "No one cried out" eloquently mourns the dehumanization, brutality, and utter despair of the prisoners.]

G **Background**

Juliek uses Elie's full first name, Eliezer (Hebrew for "my God is help"), and refers to an earlier incident at Buna, during which Elie received twenty-five lashes after he witnessed a Kapo's sexual encounter with a young Polish girl.

H **Elements of Literature**

Symbol

? What use *is* a violin in such a place? What could it represent for Juliek? [Possible response: The violin could symbolize civilization, beauty, joy, and hope for return to a normal life.]

I **Elements of Literature**

Atmosphere

? What feelings does this passage arouse in you? [Possible response: Horror, revulsion, terror.] Which words or phrases especially contribute to that effect? [Possible response: *suffocation, invisible assassin, tore, decaying, dying.*]

Ⓐ **Elements of Literature**

Metaphor

❓ What does Wiesel mean when he says that Juliek is "playing his life"?
[Juliek is using the concerto to express all he feels about his life and his imminent death.] What kinds of metaphors are used to describe the state of Juliek's existence? [fire metaphors]

MAKING MEANINGS

First Thoughts [Respond]

1. Students might speculate that an experience like Wiesel's would make them more serious, make them feel more gratitude for every day of life, or make them struggle like Wiesel, against other sources of injustice and human suffering.

Shaping Interpretations [Interpret]

2. She has been separated from her husband and elder sons during the deportation, and has "gone out of her mind." She also may have a premonition of the terrible fate that awaits her, a fear borne out in the very real crematory of Auschwitz.

3. Possible response: Drumer loses his sense of divine purpose and meaning in life, and becomes visibly resigned to the deadly logic of the camps—a condition that marks him for death in the Nazi selection. Wiesel clings to his love for his father and his prayers to a god in whom he "no longer believed."

4. Rabbi Eliahou's search is painfully ironic because we know from Wiesel that his "beloved son" has abandoned his father to increase his own chances of survival. Wiesel is glad that the Rabbi isn't forced to understand what the camps have done to his son, and can live with his fond memories of their strong relationship.

"Well!" answered a distant voice, which seemed to come from another world. I tried to sleep.

He tried to sleep. Was he right or wrong? Could one sleep here? Was it not dangerous to allow your vigilance to fail, even for a moment, when at any minute death could pounce upon you?

I was thinking of this when I heard the sound of a violin. The sound of a violin, in this dark shed, where the dead were heaped on the living. What madman could be playing the violin here, at the brink of his own grave? Or was it really an hallucination?

It must have been Juliek.

He played a fragment from Beethoven's concerto. I had never heard sounds so pure. In such a silence.

How had he managed to free himself? To draw his body from under mine without my being aware of it?

It was pitch-dark. I could hear only the violin, and it was as though Juliek's soul were the bow. Ⓐ He was playing his life. The whole of his life was gliding on the strings—his lost hopes, his charred past, his extinguished future. He played as he would never play again.

I shall never forget Juliek. How could I forget that concert, given to an audience of dying and dead men! To this day, whenever I hear Beethoven played my eyes close and out of the dark rises the sad, pale face of my Polish friend, as he said farewell on his violin to an audience of dying men.

I do not know for how long he played. I was overcome by sleep. When I awoke, in the daylight, I could see Juliek, opposite me, slumped over, dead. Near him lay his violin, smashed, trampled, a strange overwhelming little corpse.

MAKING MEANINGS

First Thoughts

1. Wiesel was just fifteen years old when he arrived at Auschwitz. Imagine what it would have been like to experience what he experienced at that age. How might it have changed you? Look over your Quickwrite notes as you formulate your answer.

Shaping Interpretations

2. In the first excerpt, what do you think is the cause of Madame Schächter's terrible vision?

3. In the second excerpt, how has Akiba Drumer "begun to die" when he starts to lose his faith in God? What do you think kept Wiesel from giving up?

4. In the third excerpt, why is it **ironic** that Rabbi Eliahou will "continue to look for his beloved son"? Why is Wiesel glad that he will keep looking?

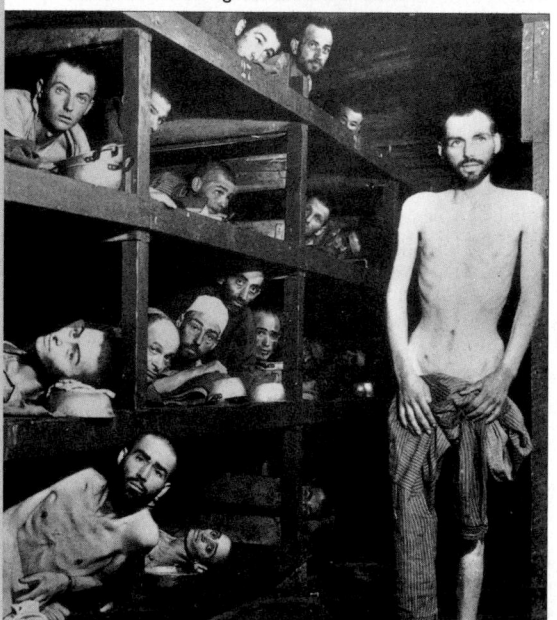

Slave laborers in the barracks of Buchenwald concentration camp, April 16, 1945. Elie Wiesel is the man whose face can be seen on the far right of the center bunk.

Reading Check

a. What does Madame Schächter see on the journey? What effects do her cries have on her fellow prisoners?

b. When they arrive at Auschwitz, what do the prisoners find that shows Madame Schächter's vision was tragically accurate?

c. In the second excerpt, what does the head of Wiesel's block advise the prisoners to do before the selection process? Why?

d. What is Akiba Drumer's last request?

e. In the third excerpt, what does Juliek play at Gleiwitz? Who is his audience?

Reading Check

a. She sees herself and the Jews around her headed towards a flaming furnace. Her cries terrify the others, who react by attempting to silence her.

b. The prisoners see the flames and smoke of the Auschwitz crematory, and smell the odor of burning flesh.

c. He advises them to jump around to bring color into their bodies and to run by the S.S. doctors, who will mark them for death if they look weak or unhealthy.

d. He asks that his friends recite the Kaddish for him after his corpse has been sent to Buna crematory, but they forget.

e. Juliek plays a fragment of a Beethoven concerto for the dead and the dying prisoners, who are being crushed in the barracks.

5. At the end of the third excerpt, why do you think Wiesel uses the **metaphor** of "a strange overwhelming little corpse" to describe Juliek's violin? What might the violin **symbolize** for Wiesel?

6. Select at least two passages from this text that create, for you, the dreadful **atmosphere** of the camps where Wiesel was held prisoner. Which specific words help create that atmosphere? Be sure to share your passages in class.

Connecting with the Text

7. When Wiesel accepted the Nobel Peace Prize, he said that "[i]ndifference is the greatest source of evil and danger in the world." He also sug-gested that if humanity ever forgets the Holo-caust, "we are guilty, we are accomplices." What do you think Wiesel meant? Do you agree? What actions could people take to help combat such indifference to human suffering?

Extending the Text

8. In his humanitarian work, Wiesel struggles against what he calls "selective sensitivity," in which "people are sensitive only to one category of victims and not to the others." He demands instead that "[i]f one is sensitive to one injustice, one must be sensitive to all injustice." Discuss situations in the world today where you find this "selective sensitivity" at work.

5. He may describe it as a corpse because its owner has been crushed to death in the barracks. The crushed violin may also symbolize for Wiesel a more general death of culture and beauty in the Holocaust.

6. Sample choices include: the para-graphs on p. 924 beginning "Listen carefully" and "The first to go by"; the scene between Elie and his father on pp. 925–926; the paragraph on p. 928 beginning "The march began again"; the description on p. 930 of Juliek's violin playing.

Connecting with the Text [Apply]

7. Students should understand Wiesel's conviction that to remain indifferent to the memory of the Holocaust is to participate, however remotely, in the same indifference and self-interest that allowed it to be carried out. Students will agree or disagree whether this amounts to complicity in the Nazi crimes. Ask students to be specific in nam-ing ways to combat indifference— everything from writing letters to working in shelters for victims of abuse.

Extending the Text [Synthesize]

8. Students may point to a wide variety of political and social issues: the "ethnic cleansing" of civilian war vic-tims in Bosnia and Herzegovina, the stigmatization of people with AIDS as opposed to people with cancer, the actions of extremists who are willing to terrorize some people in order to ensure the rights of others.

CHOICES: Building Your Portfolio

Writer's Notebook

1. Collecting Ideas for an Evaluation

Wiesel and other sur-vivors of the Holocaust are living exam-ples of how the human spirit and its best impulses can endure in the worst, most immoral circumstances. Yet Wiesel also chooses not to ignore how cruelly some of his fellow prisoners treated one another in their terror and desperation. Do you approve of his decision? Is such **objective reporting** always necessary? Jot down some points in support of your position, using specific examples from the text. Save your notes for possible use in the Writer's Work-shop on page 1181.

Comparing Texts

2. Journeys into Night

Write a brief essay in which you compare Wiesel's nar-ration of his journey to Auschwitz with Olaudah Equiano's narration of his middle-passage journey in a slave ship (page 57). What **tone** does each narrator take when describing the conditions under which the captives are forced to live? How does each narrator feel about his captors? How does each narrator use **foreshadowing** to prepare readers for what lies ahead?

Comparing Texts

3. No One Left

The following tale was told by a German pastor named Martin Niemöller, who found the courage to resist the Nazis during World War II. Read Niemöller's cautionary tale carefully. In a brief essay, explain the **main point** of the tale and tell how it connects with Wiesel's experience. Is there any connection with world events today?

> In Germany, the Nazis first came for the Communists and I didn't speak up because I wasn't a Communist. Then they came for the Jews and I did not speak up because I was not a Jew. Then they came for the trade unionists and I didn't speak up because I was not a trade unionist. Then they came for the Catholics and I was a Protestant so I didn't speak up. Then they came for me: by that time there was no one left to speak up.
>
> —Martin Niemöller

ELIE WIESEL **931**

Grading Timesaver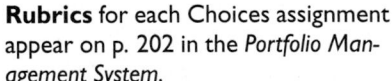

Rubrics for each Choices assignment appear on p. 202 in the *Portfolio Man-agement System.*

CHOICES: Building Your Portfolio

1. Writer's Notebook
Remind students to save their work.

2. Comparing Texts Students may find it helpful to organize their review of the texts in chart form. Their charts should provide space to list details used by each author to make a horrifying situation real, and specific phrases that help establish tone.

3. Comparing Texts Encourage students to rephrase Niemöller's testimonial in the form of a moral, such as "All people are intercon-nected" or "No one is an island."

T931

Randall Jarrell

(1914–1965)

Elliott Erwitt/Magnum.

One of the most careful and erudite readers of contemporary poetry, Randall Jarrell was, at the same time, both an abrasive critic and a generous promoter of the art of poetry.

Born in Nashville, Tennessee, Jarrell was brought up in California. His childhood experiences included close observation of the gaudy remnants of the old Hollywood, a personal acquaintance with the MGM lion, and an appreciation of the difference between fantasy and fact—between life and myths about life—that would provide him with themes for poetry for years to come.

After graduating from Vanderbilt University in his native city, Jarrell began a career that led to positions in the English departments of many colleges and universities from Texas to New York. In 1942, he joined the Army Air Corps and served for a time as a pilot and then, for a longer time, as Celestial Navigation Trainer of pilots assigned to fly the famous B-29 bombers of World War II. Out of this experience came two notable books of poetry, *Little Friend, Little Friend* (1945) and *Losses* (1948). Many critics say these books rank among the best American contributions to the literature of World War II.

A man of extraordinary wit, Jarrell gave full play to his gifts in his often caustic and devastating critical articles and essays, particularly in the collection *A Sad Heart at the Supermarket* (1962). In poetry, however, his faculty for contemptuous criticism is kept under wraps: His wit shows itself only in mellow good humor ("I feel like the first men who read Wordsworth. / It's so simple I can't understand it.") and in a resigned toleration of the more absurd aspects of American life.

Jarrell died when struck by a car while walking on a North Carolina highway in 1965. His tragic death raised a question: Was it actually a suicide? But of his loss to American letters and to the poets who had counted upon him to explain, judge, and celebrate their art, there was no question at all.

go.hrw.com
LE0 11-18

Before You Read

THE DEATH OF THE BALL TURRET GUNNER

Make the Connection

Five Famous Lines
These five lines, written in 1945, make up the most famous poem to come out of World War II.

Quickwrite

Write your thoughts on these questions: What attitude toward war do you expect to find in most literature and films produced today? Is war literature today more cynical than it used to be?

The Death of the Ball Turret Gunner

Randall Jarrell

From my mother's sleep I fell into the State,
And I hunched in its belly till my wet fur froze.
Six miles from earth, loosed from its dream of life,
I woke to black flak and the nightmare fighters.
When I died they washed me out of the turret with a hose.

The Ball Turret

A ball turret was a plexiglass sphere set into the belly of a B-17 or B-24, and inhabited by two .50 caliber machine guns and one man, a short, small man. When this gunner tracked with his machine guns a fighter attacking his bomber from below, he revolved with the turret; hunched upside down in his little sphere, he looked like the fetus in the womb. The fighters which attacked him were armed with cannon firing explosive shells. The hose was a steam hose.

—Randall Jarrell

RANDALL JARRELL 933

Summary ■■

The speaker tells the story of his own life and death in war, as if the poem were an epitaph on a gravestone. He says that he was taken into the army by the State before he became fully alive; metaphorically, he was an infant who went directly from womb to war. The ball turret of his plane became a second womb. Hunched in the turret's bubble, he was separated from the common life of earth, which seemed as unreal as a dream. The brutal reality of war awakened him, and, ironically, he woke to life at the moment of death. The remains of his bullet-riddled body were washed out of the turret with a hose.

A Elements of Literature
Imagery
❓ What do you associate with the image of "my mother's sleep"? [Possible responses: time before birth, safety, comfort, innocence.]

B Reading Skills and Strategies
Comparing/Contrasting
❓ The phrases "dream of life" and "nightmare fighters" are in contrast. What do these phrases suggest? [Possible responses: The first phrase suggests the naive innocence and stability the young soldier felt at home; the second implies his harsh initiation into the brutal realities of war.]

C Critical Thinking
Challenging the Text
❓ Do you think the last line has a meaning beyond shock value? Why or why not? [Possible responses: The line moves beyond shock because it emphasizes the degradation of war; the line shocks but doesn't add any new ideas to the poem.]

Primary Sources

Here Jarrell provides some technical background information about his poem—which helps explain his metaphors and emphasizes the harsh reality of the event he describes.

Reaching All Students

Advanced Learners
You might have these students find and read another of Jarrell's war poems, "Gunner." It consists largely of questions the speaker asks about his life during peacetime. Ask students to compare the two poems, find similarities between the speakers, and explain which poem they prefer and why.

Using Students' Strengths

Visual Learners
Have students draw a political cartoon in which they express the same attitude toward war as the speaker in this poem. Students can choose any situation and image that convey a similar message. Display the cartoons in class.

First Thoughts [Respond]

1. Possible responses: No, because war is always disillusioning and gruesome; yes, because its tone is so detached.

Shaping Interpretations [Interpret]

2. He refers to both the protection of a mother's womb and the isolation of the ball turret.
3. "I fell" implies he was drafted or enlisted thoughtlessly.
4. Possible responses: The "wet fur" could be his fleece-lined flight suit, sweat-soaked from fear. Fear reduces the gunner to an animal frozen in the gun sight of the enemy.
5. Possible responses: Yes, because he dies for his country; no, because he does not choose any part of his fate.
6. If students decide that the poem is about dissent, they should summarize its protest. If they think it focuses on mechanization, they should contrast the human with the machine. If they think the poem concerns the destruction of innocence, they should state what that loss means.

Extending the Text [Synthesize]

7. Students should note a variety of war movies, and specify the attitudes of each. Help students go beyond the simple "war is wrong" theme by discussing each film in the context of the time in which it was made.

Grading Timesaver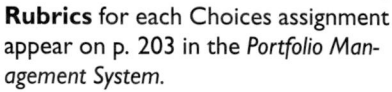

Rubrics for each Choices assignment appear on p. 203 in the *Portfolio Management System*.

MAKING MEANINGS

First Thoughts

1. Do you find this poem shocking? Why or why not?

Shaping Interpretations

2. "Belly" here can be read on two levels. What two bellies is the speaker talking about?
3. How do you know that the speaker didn't enter the army on the basis of a rational decision?
4. What is the speaker's "wet fur"? Why do you think he compares himself to an animal?
5. Do you think the speaker is a hero? Explain.
6. What, in the long run, do you think this poem is about? Is it about political dissent? Is it a statement about the way things in the world are regimented and mechanized? Is it about the destruction of the innocent? Explain your views.

Extending the Text

7. Hollywood has produced hundreds of movies about war. These movies reflect a wide spectrum of attitudes. Some show soldiers as heroes, some as victims; some evoke pride in one's country, some hatred of another country; some summon nostalgia for a past era. Think of some war movies you have seen, and analyze their attitudes toward war. (Be sure to check your Quickwrite notes.)

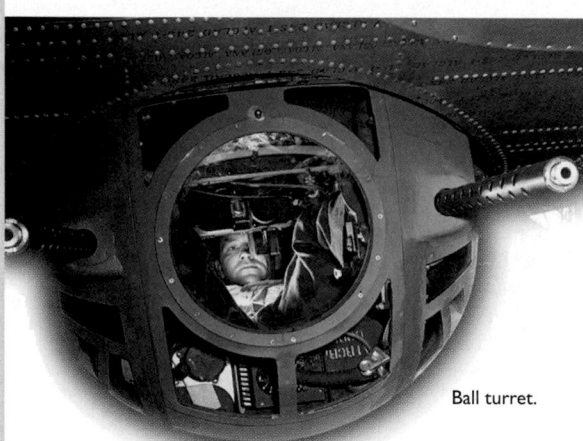

Ball turret.

934 CONTEMPORARY LITERATURE

CHOICES: Building Your Portfolio

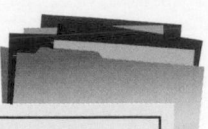

Writer's Notebook

1. Collecting Ideas for an Evaluation

If you were writing an evaluation of "The Death of the Ball Turret Gunner," what facts would a general audience need to know? Write down aspects of the real-world context of the poem—relevant information about World War II, the ball turret, and Jarrell's experiences. Keep your notes for possible use in the Writer's Workshop on page 1181.

Interpreting an Extended Metaphor

2. Hunched in the Belly

In a brief essay, explain the **extended metaphor** that runs through the poem. Is there something **ironic** about the metaphor? Explain your interpretation.

Creative Writing

3. Speaking Out

Find a newspaper article about someone who has died. Write a paragraph or a short poem from the point of view of that person as you imagine him or her. Imitate the style of "The Death of the Ball Turret Gunner." Speak as "I."

Speaking and Listening

4. Whose Emphasis?

Poems are musical. They are meant to be read aloud or recited from memory. When performing a poem aloud, each of us tends to emphasize different words as we give our particular spin to the poem. Together with another student, perform "The Death of the Ball Turret Gunner" before the class. The class should try to spot differences, even small differences, between the performances, and discuss how different interpretations affect the meaning of the poem.

CHOICES: Building Your Portfolio

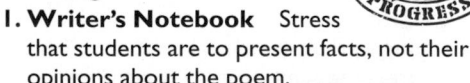

1. **Writer's Notebook** Stress that students are to present facts, not their opinions about the poem.
2. **Interpreting an Extended Metaphor** Students should understand that the extended metaphor is that the gunner is being born (coming to awareness) in his ball turret. The irony is that he dies at the same moment.
3. **Creative Writing** Before students write, you might read aloud one of the epitaph poems from *Spoon River Anthology* by Edgar Lee Masters (pp. 693–695). Students might want to write about a famous person, even someone long dead.
4. **Speaking and Listening** When students perform the poem, encourage them to use gestures, body language, and expressions to enhance their readings. Remind them to vary the rhythm, volume, and speed of their voices.

John Hersey

(1914–1993)

Brown Brothers.

What book was considered so extraordinary that the great scientist Albert Einstein ordered one thousand copies? What book was thought so compelling that the Book-of-the-Month Club distributed free copies because no book "could be of more importance at this moment to the human race"? The book is *Hiroshima,* by John Hersey.

Hersey was born in China, where he lived until he was ten. He later graduated from Yale and studied at Cambridge University in England, served as private secretary to the American novelist Sinclair Lewis, and reported from the South Pacific and the Mediterranean during World War II for *Time* and *Life* magazines.

But journalism (if that means objective, factual reporting) could not contain Hersey's passionate concern about contemporary events. In 1945, he won a Pulitzer Prize for his novel *A Bell for Adano,* based on what he had seen of American military government in Italy. Some critics saw this novel as a troubling examination of democracy and its ideals, and the difficulties of putting it into practice.

In 1946, Hersey published *Hiroshima.* Combining techniques of a novel and the factual air of journalism to describe a real event, *Hiroshima* began what some critics call the genre of the "nonfiction novel." (Other examples include Truman Capote's *In Cold Blood* [1966] and Norman Mailer's *The Executioner's Song* [1979].) Hersey took an almost incomprehensible act, the dropping of an atomic bomb on a civilian population, and showed how it affected the lives of six survivors. Through their eyes, Americans could experience this catastrophe as if it were happening to them and to their friends and neighbors. Through Hersey's vivid narrative and his gift for characterization, the unimaginable became horrifyingly real.

Hiroshima became a national event, a precursor of the kind of celebrity status that best-sellers often enjoy today, with attention paid to the authors on talk shows and in interviews in magazines and newspapers. *Hiroshima* first appeared in *The New Yorker,* which devoted an entire issue to the book—a startling commitment for a magazine. The American Broadcasting Company had the book read aloud on its radio stations. *Hiroshima* has since been called the most significant piece of reportage in modern times.

After *Hiroshima,* Hersey became famous as a writer who could make history understandable. While serving as a teacher and mentor at Yale, he continued to dramatize issues and events, dealing with the Holocaust, racism, fascism, and other evils of modern life. He called his type of fiction "the novel of contemporary history" and wrote that "this kind of novel should make anyone who reads it better able to meet life in his generation—whenever that generation may be." He produced books in a steady stream from the 1940s to the 1990s, sending his publisher a manuscript of new short stories, *Key West Tales,* six weeks before his death. His books include the highly acclaimed novel *The Wall* (1950), about the annihilation of Polish Jews in the Warsaw ghetto, and *Blues* (1987), a brilliant meditation on Hersey's favorite sport, fishing, (The book, of course, turns out to be about much more than fly-casting and trolling).

None of Hersey's other works achieved the impact of *Hiroshima.* The book continues to force readers to face the horrifying realities of nuclear war. In half a century, no book on nuclear warfare has come close to *Hiroshima's* impact on our moral and ethical sensibilities.

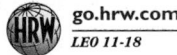 go.hrw.com
LEO 11-18

OBJECTIVES

1. Read and interpret the story
2. Identify and analyze subjective and objective reporting
3. Read closely for details
4. Express understanding through critical writing
5. Demonstrate understanding of new words

SKILLS

Literary
- Identify and analyze subjective and objective reporting

Reading
- Read closely for details

Writing
- Collect ideas for an evaluation
- Write an essay analyzing suspense
- Write an essay based on historical research and reflecting on the decision to use the atomic bomb
- Write an essay about Hersey's use of Japanese terms

Vocabulary
- Demonstrate understanding of new words

Viewing/Representing
- Reflect on a painting by an eyewitness (ATE)

Planning

- **Block Schedule**
  Block Scheduling Lesson Plans with Pacing Guide
- **Traditional Schedule**
  Lesson Plans Including Strategies for English-Language Learners
- **One-Stop Planner**
  CD-ROM with Test Generator

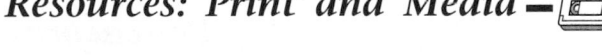 *Resources: Print and Media*

Reading
- *Graphic Organizers for Active Reading,* p. 92
- *Words to Own,* p. 48
- *Audio CD Library*
  Disc 24, Track 2

Elements of Literature
- *Literary Elements*
  Transparency 28
  Worksheet, p. 85

Writing and Language
- *Daily Oral Grammar*
  Transparency 53

Viewing and Representing
- *Viewing and Representing*
  Fine Art Transparency 18
  Fine Art Worksheet, p. 72

Assessment
- *Portfolio Management System,* p. 204
- *Preparation for College Admission Exams,* p. 59
- *Test Generator (One-Stop Planner CD-ROM)*

Internet
- go.hrw.com (keyword: LEO 11-18)

Summary ■ ■

Hersey describes the experiences of six survivors of the atomic blast in Hiroshima on August 6, 1945. Using foreshadowing, chilling imagery, and an objective tone, Hersey creates a powerful yet restrained "nonfiction novel." At the moment of the blast, Reverend Tanimoto, a Methodist pastor, is moving a cabinet to a suburb two miles away. Mrs. Hatsuyo Nakamura, a tailor's widow, is looking out the window when the blast throws her across the room and buries her children alive. Dr. Fujii is reading when the blast throws him—and his hospital—into the river. Father Kleinsorge, a German Jesuit, is on the third floor of the mission when the blast hits; the next moment he finds himself wandering the ruins of the mission garden, dazed and bleeding. Dr. Sasaki is walking along a corridor at the moment of the explosion; he is the only unwounded hospital doctor available to care for the multitude of victims. Toshiko Sasaki, a clerk, is at her desk when the blast hits and is buried under an avalanche of books.

Background

Since the firebombing of Tokyo in March 1945, Japanese cities had been repeatedly devastated by U.S. bombing raids. Because Hiroshima was one of the few cities to escape bombing, its citizens expected a massive attack with conventional weapons, but no one anticipated the magnitude of nuclear destruction. The Hiroshima bomb killed more than 100,000 people, leveled four square miles, and effectively destroyed the entire Japanese Second Army.

Before You Read
A NOISELESS FLASH

Make the Connection

The Human Element
Modern war, waged with highly sophisticated weaponry, is often described in *numerical* terms: how many missiles fired, how many targets annihilated, how many people killed. In the face of such abstraction, writers and artists force us to confront the personal element in war. By telling us about the details of other people's lives, writers remind us that, even in war, we are all—friend and foe—human beings first and foremost.

Reading Skills and Strategies

Reading Closely for Details
As you read this account of the effects of the atomic bomb explosion on six people in Hiroshima, note the many precise details Hersey uses to lend his account authenticity. Skim the account before you start reading. Note the six sections, each set off by extra space. Locate the name of the person Hersey is focusing on in each section. Then, pick one of the six people, and, as you read, take notes on the key details Hersey gives you about that person.

Elements of Literature

Subjectivity and Objectivity
In **subjective reporting,** the writer openly expresses personal emotions and attitudes toward the events and characters he or she is writing about. In **objective reporting,** such as John Hersey's, the writer presents mainly observable, verifiable facts and keeps his or her own feelings at a distance. At times, the only way we can discover how such a writer feels about an event is by analyzing the details specifically chosen for inclusion or omission.

> In **subjective reporting,** the writer openly expresses emotions and attitudes toward events and characters. In **objective reporting,** the writer keeps his or her feelings at a distance.

Background

War between the United States and Japan began on December 7, 1941, when the Japanese suddenly attacked the U.S. naval base at Pearl Harbor, in Hawaii. By mid-1945, after many costly battles, the United States and its allies were nearing the final victory in World War II as they pressed toward an invasion of the main Japanese islands. As part of the endgame against Japan, the United States used its newest and most powerful weapon, the atomic bomb, twice—first to destroy Hiroshima, and then, three days later, to devastate another Japanese city, Nagasaki.

First photo taken of Hiroshima after the atomic explosion, August 6, 1945.
Matsushige/Sygma.

Preteaching Vocabulary

Words to Own

Have students read the Words to Own and their definitions listed at the bottom of the selection pages. Then have students match each of the words with one of the following definitions:

1. gifts to the needy [philanthropies]
2. dreamer; not a realist [idealist]
3. broken pieces [debris]

4. causing fires [incendiary]
5. thinking always about one thing [obsessed]
6. meeting [rendezvous]
7. friendly [convivial]
8. pursuing pleasure [hedonistic]
9. staying away [abstinence]
10. prolonged [sustained]

A Noiseless Flash

from Hiroshima

John Hersey

Resources

Viewing and Representing
Fine Art Transparency
A fine art transparency of Herb Tauss's *East Meets West* can be used to complement John Hersey's "A Noiseless Flash." See the *Viewing and Representing Transparencies and Worksheets:*
- Transparency 18
- Worksheet, p. 72

Ⓐ Reading Skills and Strategies

Reading Closely for Details

Point out to students that the first sentence demonstrates Hersey's skillful use of details. What new information does Hersey add to the well-known facts about the atomic bomb? [Possible response: He relates a personal detail that only a few people in Hiroshima could know. He juxtaposes a fact of unthinkable scope and destruction with a tiny, mundane detail.]

Ⓑ Reading Skills and Strategies

Making Predictions

❓ Based on the first two sentences, what do you expect the selection will be like? [Possible responses: The selection will focus closely on details of the lives of these six people. Perhaps it will try to identify a common thread in their actions or experiences. The selection reads like a newspaper article and may not have the drama or excitement of a novel.]

Ⓐt exactly fifteen minutes past eight in the morning, on August 6, 1945, Japanese time, at the moment when the atomic bomb flashed above Hiroshima, Miss Toshiko Sasaki, a clerk in the personnel department of the East Asia Tin Works, had just sat down at her place in the plant office and was turning her head to speak to the girl at the next desk. At that same moment, Dr. Masakazu Fujii was settling down cross-legged to read the Osaka *Asahi*[1] on the porch of his private Ⓑ hospital, overhanging one of the seven deltaic rivers which divide Hiroshima; Mrs. Hatsuyo Nakamura, a tailor's widow, stood by the window of her kitchen, watching a neighbor tearing down

his house because it lay in the path of an air-raid-defense fire lane; Father Wilhelm Kleinsorge, a German priest of the Society of Jesus,[2] reclined in his underwear on a cot on the top floor of his order's three-story mission house, reading a Jesuit magazine, *Stimmen der Zeit;*[3] Dr. Terufumi Sasaki, a young member of the surgical staff of the city's large, modern Red Cross Hospital, walked along one of the hospital corridors with a blood specimen for a Wassermann test[4] in his hand; and the

1. **Asahi:** Japanese for "morning sun." The Osaka *Asahi* is the city newspaper.

2. **Society of Jesus:** Roman Catholic religious order of priests and brothers, also known as the Jesuit (jezh'ōō·it) order.

3. ***Stimmen der Zeit*** (shtim'ən der tsīt): German for "Voices of the Times."

4. **Wassermann test:** blood test used to diagnose syphilis.

JOHN HERSEY 937

Reaching All Students

Struggling Readers
You might read aloud the first section, which ends on p. 938. Because Hersey uses numerous compound and compound-complex sentences, encourage struggling readers to work in pairs, breaking the longer sentences into smaller parts as they read. For example, have them insert a full stop at every semicolon. They might also identify the separate ideas in long compound sentences joined by *and*.

English Language Learners
Have students concentrate on the details of the survivors' experiences. Ask pairs of students to choose one survivor and make a chart listing the details they find. Charts should have columns labeled *who, what, why, when,* and *where,* with the details listed in rows underneath. Students who have chosen the same person might compare their charts.

Advanced Learners
Tell students that John Hersey returned to Japan forty years after the events he described here. He then wrote an additional chapter for the 1985 edition of *Hiroshima,* telling what eventually happened to each of the six survivors in this selection. Have advanced learners read the chapter ("The Aftermath") and report to the class on the post-war lives of these six people.

A Reading Skills and Strategies

Reading Closely for Details

This selection is unusual in that the author specifically tells the reader that details are at the heart of the story, that the lives of the people concerned hinge on "many small items of chance or volition." As they read the selection, have students search for the details that determine each person's fate.

B Background

In a way, the entire population of Hiroshima was a victim of chance detail. When the *Enola Gay*—the B-29 that dropped the first atomic bomb (code name Little Boy)—headed for Japan on August 6, 1945, its destination was not yet determined. Weather reports it received while airborne dictated its course. Of its three possible targets, Hiroshima, Kokura, and Nagasaki, Hiroshima had the best weather.

C Cultural Connections

❓ In the Japanese language, the suffix *-san* is attached to a noun as a way of showing respect. Why is it ironic that the people would attach this suffix to the B-29? [Possible response: While this word formation indicates the grave respect civilians developed for the plane and its destructive power, it is also bitterly ironic, for it personifies the plane that brought death to thousands of Japanese.]

D Critical Thinking

Analyzing Character

❓ What inferences can you draw about Mr. Tanimoto, based on the details given here? [Possible responses: He is an intelligent and sensitive man, prudent but full of anxiety, friendly but growing increasingly paranoid.]

Reverend Mr. Kiyoshi Tanimoto, pastor of the Hiroshima Methodist Church, paused at the door of a rich man's house in Koi, the city's western suburb, and prepared to unload a handcart full of things he had evacuated from town in fear of the massive B-29 raid which everyone expected Hiroshima to suffer. A hundred thousand people were killed by the atomic bomb, and these six were among the survivors. They still wonder why they lived when so many others died. Each of them counts many small items of chance or volition—a step taken in time, a decision to go indoors, catching one streetcar instead of the next—that spared him. And now each knows that in the act of survival he lived a dozen lives and saw more death than he ever thought he would see. At the time, none of them knew anything.

The Reverend Mr. Tanimoto got up at five o'clock that morning. He was alone in the parsonage, because for some time his wife had been commuting with their year-old baby to spend nights with a friend in Ushida, a suburb to the north. Of all the important cities of Japan, only two, Kyoto[5] and Hiroshima, had not been visited in strength by *B-san,* or Mr. B, as the Japanese, with a mixture of respect and unhappy familiarity, called the B-29; and Mr. Tanimoto, like all his neighbors and friends, was almost sick with anxiety. He had heard uncomfortably detailed accounts of mass raids on Kure, Iwakuni, Tokuyama, and other nearby towns; he was sure Hiroshima's turn would come soon. He had slept badly the night before, because there had been several air-raid warnings. Hiroshima had been getting such warnings almost every night for weeks, for at that time the B-29s were using Lake Biwa, northeast of Hiroshima, as a rendezvous point, and no matter what city the Americans planned to hit, the Superfortresses streamed in over the coast near Hiroshima. The frequency of the warnings and the continued abstinence of Mr. B with respect to Hiroshima had made its citizens jittery; a rumor was going around that the Americans were saving something special for the city.

Mr. Tanimoto is a small man, quick to talk, laugh, and cry. He wears his black hair parted in the middle and rather long; the prominence of the frontal bones just above his eyebrows and the smallness of his moustache, mouth, and chin give him a strange, old-young look, boyish and yet wise, weak and yet fiery. He moves nervously and fast, but with a restraint which suggests that he is a cautious, thoughtful man. He showed, indeed, just those qualities in the uneasy days before the bomb fell. Besides having his wife spend the nights in Ushida, Mr. Tanimoto had been carrying all the portable things from his church, in the close-packed residential district called Nagaragawa, to a house that belonged to a rayon manufacturer in Koi, two miles from the center of town. The rayon man, a Mr. Matsui, had opened his then unoccupied estate to a large number of his friends and acquaintances, so that they might evacuate whatever they wished to a safe distance from the probable target area. Mr. Tanimoto had had no difficulty in moving chairs, hymnals, Bibles, altar gear, and church records by pushcart himself, but the organ console and an upright piano required some aid. A friend of his named Matsuo had, the day before, helped him get the piano out to Koi; in return, he had promised this day to assist Mr. Matsui in hauling out a daughter's belongings. That is why he had risen so early.

Mr. Tanimoto cooked his own breakfast. He felt awfully tired. The effort of moving the piano the day before, a sleepless night, weeks of worry and unbalanced diet, the cares of his parish—all combined to make him feel hardly adequate to the new day's work. There was another thing, too: Mr. Tanimoto had studied theology at Emory College, in Atlanta, Georgia; he had graduated in 1940; he spoke excellent English; he dressed in American clothes; he had corresponded with many American friends right up to the time the war began; and among a people obsessed with a fear of being spied upon—perhaps almost obsessed himself—he found himself growing increasingly uneasy. The police had questioned him several times, and just a few days before, he had heard that an influential acquaintance, a Mr. Tanaka, a retired

---

5. **Kyoto:** city some 200 miles east of Hiroshima.

938 CONTEMPORARY LITERATURE

WORDS TO OWN

rendezvous (rän'dā·vōō') *adj.:* meeting.
abstinence (ab'stə·nəns') *n.:* staying away.
obsessed (əb·sest') *v.* used as *adj.:* preoccupied; haunted.

Skill Link

Appositives and Appositive Phrases

Remind students that an appositive is a noun or pronoun that identifies a preceding noun or pronoun. An appositive phrase contains an appositive and all its modifiers. Throughout his report, Hersey uses appositives to add details and to define Japanese words and phrases. Ask students to find four examples of appositive phrases in the first section (through the top of p. 938).

[Possible answers: "a clerk in the personnel department of the East Asia Tin Works"; "a tailor's widow"; "a German Priest of the Society of Jesus"; "a young member of the surgical staff of the city's large, modern, Red Cross Hospital"; "pastor of the Hiroshima Methodist Church."]

Using the Internet

Students can research information related to the selection by entering the keyword "Hiroshima" into a Web search engine. One site that includes excerpts from and references to literature, film, and works of art related to the atomic bomb is called the Hiroshima Project. *You may want to preview any Internet activity that you suggest to students. Because these resources are sometimes public forums, their content can be unpredictable.*

officer of the Toyo Kisen Kaisha steamship line, an anti-Christian, a man famous in Hiroshima for his showy philanthropies and notorious for his personal tyrannies, had been telling people that Tanimoto should not be trusted. In compensation, to show himself publicly a good Japanese, Mr. Tanimoto had taken on the chairmanship of his local *tonarigumi*, or Neighborhood Association, and to his other duties and concerns this position had added the business of organizing air-raid defense for about twenty families.

Before six o'clock that morning, Mr. Tanimoto started for Mr. Matsuo's house. There he found that their burden was to be a *tansu*, a large Japanese cabinet, full of clothing and household goods. The two men set out. The morning was perfectly clear and so warm that the day promised to be uncomfortable. A few minutes after they started, the air-raid siren went off—a minute-long blast that warned of approaching planes but indicated to the people of Hiroshima only a slight degree of danger, since it sounded every morning at this time, when an American weather plane came over. The two men pulled and pushed the handcart through the city streets. Hiroshima was a fan-shaped city, lying mostly on the six islands formed by the seven estuarial[6] rivers that branch out from the Ota River; its main commercial and residential districts, covering about four square miles in the center of the city, contained three-quarters of its population, which had been reduced by several evacuation programs from a wartime peak of 380,000 to about 245,000. Factories and other residential districts, or suburbs, lay compactly around the edges of the city. To the south were the docks, an airport, and the island-studded Inland Sea. A rim of mountains runs around the other three sides of the delta. Mr. Tanimoto and Mr. Matsuo took their way through the shopping center, already full of people, and across two of the rivers to the sloping streets of Koi, and up them to the outskirts and foothills. As they started up a valley away from the tight-ranked houses, the all-clear sounded. (The Japanese radar operators, detecting only three planes, supposed that they comprised a reconnaissance.)[7] Pushing the hand-

cart up to the rayon man's house was tiring, and the men, after they had maneuvered their load into the driveway and to the front steps, paused to rest awhile. They stood with a wing of the house between them and the city. Like most homes in this part of Japan, the house consisted of a wooden frame and wooden walls supporting a heavy tile roof. Its front hall, packed with rolls of bedding and clothing, looked like a cool cave full of fat cushions. Opposite the house, to the right of the front door, there was a large, finicky rock garden. There was no sound of planes. The morning was still; the place was cool and pleasant.

Then a tremendous flash of light cut across the sky. Mr. Tanimoto has a distinct recollection that it traveled from east to west, from the city toward the hills. It seemed a sheet of sun. Both he and Mr. Matsuo reacted in terror—and both had time to react (for they were 3,500 yards, or two miles, from the center of the explosion). Mr. Matsuo dashed up the front steps into the house and dived among the bedrolls and buried himself there. Mr. Tanimoto took four or five steps and threw himself between two big rocks in the garden. He bellied up very hard against one of them. As his face was against the stone, he did not see what happened. He felt a sudden pressure, and then splinters and pieces of board and fragments of tile fell on him. He heard no roar. (Almost no one in Hiroshima recalls hearing any noise of the bomb. But a fisherman in his *sampan*[8] on the Inland Sea near Tsuzu, the man with whom Mr. Tanimoto's mother-in-law and sister-in-law were living, saw the flash and heard a tremendous explosion; he was nearly twenty miles from Hiroshima, but the thunder was greater than when the B-29s hit Iwakuni, only five miles away.)

When he dared, Mr. Tanimoto raised his head and saw that the rayon man's house had collapsed. He thought a bomb had fallen directly on it. Such clouds of dust had risen that there was a sort of twilight around. In panic, not thinking for the moment of Mr. Matsuo under the ruins, he dashed out into the street. He noticed as he ran that the

8. **sampan:** small, flat-bottomed boat.

WORDS TO OWN

philanthropies (fə·lan'thrə·pēz) *n. pl.:* charitable gifts.

---

6. **estuarial** (es'tyōō·er'ē·əl): on the estuary, or mouth of a river, where freshwater meets saltwater.
7. **reconnaissance** (ri·kän'ə·səns): exploratory mission.

JOHN HERSEY 939

E **Vocabulary Note**
Context Clues
? Hersey uses many Japanese words. How can you figure out what they mean? [He almost always uses restatement—giving the English meaning right after the Japanese word or expression. You can also make a good guess based on other context clues.]

F **Elements of Literature**
Subjectivity and Objectivity
? What do these objective descriptions and statistics add to the overall description of the scene? [Possible responses: The precise, objective reporting helps the reader get an overview of the city and its inhabitants. The bare facts help set the scene for the more subjective descriptions of the personal lives of the individuals.]

G **Elements of Literature**
Irony
? What is ironic about the sounding of the all-clear? [Possible response: The radar operators think they are safe because there are only three planes; the reader knows that these three planes are more dangerous than hundreds of bombers with conventional explosives.]

H **Elements of Literature**
Subjectivity and Objectivity
? What are some elements of subjectivity in the description? What do these subjective elements add? [Possible responses: the description of the garden as "finicky"; the place as "cool and pleasant." They make the scene more vivid and immediate.]

Using Students' Strengths

Verbal Learners
Have students list the Japanese words they find as they read, along with their English translations. Discuss with students the effect of these Japanese words. Why do they think Hersey includes them? Would the narrative be more or less effective if Hersey had simply translated these Japanese words? Have students discuss this question of cultural "translation" with respect to other works and media.

Visual Learners
Ask students to turn to the map on p. 945 to note the survivors' locations in relation to the blast center. The inset locator map shows where Hiroshima is located (on the island of Honshu) in relation to other major Japanese cities. Students may research and bring to class photos of Hiroshima after the atomic blast, Hiroshima today, and other visuals related to the topic.

Naturalist Learners
Have students research the short- and long-term effects of the atomic bomb and of subsequent atomic testing. They might consider the effects on food and water supplies, animal populations, and human beings. Students might prepare a display (perhaps with a model and a poster) to explain their findings to the class.

The picture by **Yasuko Yamagata** appears in a collection called *Unforgettable Fire: Pictures Drawn by Atomic Bomb Survivors,* edited by the Japan Broadcasting Corporation (NHK). John Hersey himself commented on the book: "*Unforgettable Fire* is tremendously moving—more moving than any book of photographs of the horror could be, because what is registered is what has been burned into the minds of the survivors."

One day in 1974, a 77-year-old man named Iwakichi Kobayashi came to the NHK television studio in Hiroshima and showed the directors a picture he had drawn of the aftermath of the atomic bomb explosion. His picture made such an impression that the company launched a television appeal called "Let Us Leave for Posterity Pictures About the Atomic Bomb Drawn by Citizens." About one thousand pictures were collected, all by amateur artists, and exhibited in the Peace Memorial Museum in Hiroshima.

Some of the pictures were hand-delivered to the studio's offices by old people who were barely able to walk. The pictures were drawn with pencils, crayons, and markers on a wide variety of paper, including the backs of calendars, paper used for covering sliding doors, and the backs of children's scribbled-on scrap paper. Almost all of the pictures include a written explanation, and many of the explanations end with the words *gashoo,* or *gashoonembutsu,* "praying hands" or "folded hands in prayer for the dead."

Activity. Have students draw an important event they remember vividly and include a brief written explanation on the back of their pictures. The event may be one of worldwide or national significance or a personal event that they recall vividly. Ask them to try to include many visual details. Display these memory pictures in class.

Yasuko Yamagata, age 49.

From *Unforgettable Fire,* edited by The Japan Broadcasting Association. Copyright © 1977 by NHK. Reprinted by permission of Pantheon Books, a division of Random House, Inc.

Some thirty years later, the horror of the bombing of Hiroshima remained etched in the mind of Yasuko Yamagata, a survivor. She explains her painting:

"About 8:00 A.M., August 7, on the street in front of the former Hiroshima Broadcasting Station.

"Since I was at school in Ujina I had been exposed to radiation separately from my parents. The next morning at 7:30 I started from school toward the ruins of my house in Nobori-cho. I passed by Hijiyama. There were few people to be seen in the scorched field. I saw for the first time a pile of burned bodies in a water tank by the entrance to the broadcasting station. Then I was suddenly frightened by a terrible sight on the street 40 to 50 meters from Shukkeien Garden. There was a charred body of a woman standing frozen in a running position with one leg lifted and her baby tightly clutched in her arms. Who on earth could she be? This cruel sight still vividly remains in my mind."

Professional Notes

Critical Comment: Hersey's Legacy

In the July 31, 1995, issue of *The New Yorker* magazine, Roger Angell tries to assess the impact of this piece that was published in its entirety in the magazine almost fifty years before. "John Hersey's 'Hiroshima,'" he writes, ". . . is a work of sustained silence. Its appearance . . . offered one of the first detailed accounts of the effects of nuclear warfare on its survivors, in a prose so stripped of mannerism, sentimentality, and even minimal emphasis as to place each reader alone within scenes laid bare of all but pain." Angell points out that Hersey's words "abstain from the smallest judgment or moral positioning, and leave the reader to deal with the consequences and the questions." Hersey's work had tremendous impact, for as soon as people understood the horror of atomic bombs, many began to try to ensure they could never be used again.

concrete wall of the estate had fallen over—toward the house rather than away from it. In the street, the first thing he saw was a squad of soldiers who had been burrowing into the hillside opposite, making one of the thousands of dugouts in which the Japanese apparently intended to resist invasion, hill by hill, life for life; the soldiers were coming out of the hole, where they should have been safe, and blood was running from their heads, chests, and backs. They were silent and dazed.

Under what seemed to be a local dust cloud, the day grew darker and darker.

At nearly midnight, the night before the bomb was dropped, an announcer on the city's radio station said that about two hundred B-29s were approaching southern Honshu[9] and advised the population of Hiroshima to evacuate to their designated "safe areas." Mrs. Hatsuyo Nakamura, the tailor's widow, who lived in the section called Noboricho and who had long had a habit of doing as she was told, got her three children—a ten-year-old boy, Toshio, an eight-year-old girl, Yaeko, and a five-year-old girl, Myeko—out of bed and dressed them and walked with them to the military area known as the East Parade Ground, on the northeast edge of the city. There she unrolled some mats and the children lay down on them. They slept until about two, when they were awakened by the roar of the planes going over Hiroshima.

As soon as the planes had passed, Mrs. Nakamura started back with her children. They reached home a little after two-thirty and she immediately turned on the radio, which, to her distress, was just then broadcasting a fresh warning. When she looked at the children and saw how tired they were, and when she thought of the number of trips they had made in past weeks, all to no purpose, to the East Parade Ground, she decided that in spite of the instructions on the radio, she simply could not face starting out all over again. She put the children in their bedrolls on the floor, lay down herself at three o'clock, and fell asleep at once, so soundly that when the planes passed over later, she did not waken to their sound.

9. **Honshu:** largest island of Japan. Hiroshima is in southern Honshu.

The siren jarred her awake at about seven. She arose, dressed quickly, and hurried to the house of Mr. Nakamoto, the head of her Neighborhood Association, and asked him what she should do. He said that she should remain at home unless an urgent warning—a series of intermittent blasts of the siren—was sounded. She returned home, lit the stove in the kitchen, set some rice to cook, and sat down to read that morning's Hiroshima *Chugoku.*[10] To her relief, the all-clear sounded at eight o'clock. She heard the children stirring, so she went and gave each of them a handful of peanuts and told them to stay on their bedrolls, because they were tired from the night's walk. She had hoped that they would go back to sleep, but the man in the house directly to the south began to make a terrible hullabaloo of hammering, wedging, ripping, and splitting. The prefectural government,[11] convinced, as everyone in Hiroshima was, that the city would be attacked soon, had begun to press with threats and warnings for the completion of wide fire lanes, which, it was hoped, might act in conjunction with the rivers to localize any fires started by an incendiary raid; and the neighbor was reluctantly sacrificing his home to the city's safety. Just the day before, the prefecture had ordered all able-bodied girls from the secondary schools to spend a few days helping to clear these lanes, and they started work soon after the all-clear sounded.

Mrs. Nakamura went back to the kitchen, looked at the rice, and began watching the man next door. At first, she was annoyed with him for making so much noise, but then she was moved almost to tears by pity. Her emotion was specifically directed toward her neighbor, tearing down his home, board by board, at a time when there was so much unavoidable destruction, but undoubtedly she also felt a generalized, community pity, to say nothing of self-pity. She had not had an easy time. Her husband, Isawa, had gone into the

10. *Chugoku:* newspaper named for the region where Hiroshima is located.
11. **prefectural government:** the regional administration of each Japanese district, called a prefecture.

WORDS TO OWN
incendiary (in·sen′dē·er′ē) *adj.*: designed to cause fires.

Ⓐ Critical Thinking
Interpreting
❓ Hersey avoids literary language and overt symbolism. However, this sentence may be read symbolically. What might the darkness stand for in terms of the world's history? [Possible responses: the world's blindness; anxiety over nuclear destruction.]

Ⓑ Elements of Literature
Irony
❓ What is ironic about this reference to the "safe areas"? [There are no clearly safe areas when an atomic bomb is dropped.]

Ⓒ Reading Skills and Strategies
Reading Closely for Details
❓ What details reveal Mrs. Nakamura's devotion to her children? [Her work to provide food (rice and peanuts) for her children, as well as her sensitivity to their fatigue after the long walk, highlights her devotion to them, along with her fundamental concern for their well-being in these dangerous times.]

Ⓓ Reading Skills and Strategies
Making Inferences
❓ Why does her neighbor's dismantling of his house almost move Mrs. Nakamura to tears? What might it represent for her? How does it relate to her sense of "generalized, community pity." [Her neighbor's action might seem to mirror the slow, stubborn dismantling of imperial Japanese society in the face of almost certain defeat, or it might evoke a more personal identification with her neighbor's persistent attempt to control his life in the face of increasing chaos.]

Getting Students Involved

Cooperative Learning
Front Page Mock-Up. Have students work in groups of four or five to design the front page of an American newspaper dated August 7, 1945. Students should research statistics and general information about the bombing of Hiroshima, then write an appropriate banner headline, headlines of related stories that might appear, and captions for photos and other graphics. Students should appoint a managing editor to oversee the project, a layout artist to provide art to accompany the stories, and reporters to research and write the stories. Have the groups display their work.

Enrichment Activity
Interview. Have students work in groups of four or five to interview older relatives or acquaintances, both American and Japanese, who remember or have family stories about the bombing of Hiroshima. *You may want to obtain permission from parents and from the interviewees before students begin work on this activity.* Encourage students to tape-record or videotape their interviews. Then, have each group present its findings to the class in the form of an eyewitness account or an oral report.

Army just after Myeko was born, and she had heard nothing from or of him for a long time, until, on March 5, 1942, she received a seven-word telegram: "Isawa died an honorable death at Singapore." She learned later that he had died on February 15th, the day Singapore fell, and that he had been a corporal. Isawa had been a not particularly prosperous tailor, and his only capital was a Sankoku sewing machine. After his death, when his allotments stopped coming, Mrs. Nakamura got out the machine and began to take in piece-work[12] herself, and since then had supported the children, but poorly, by sewing.

As Mrs. Nakamura stood watching her neighbor, everything flashed whiter than any white she had ever seen. She did not notice what happened to the man next door; the reflex of a mother set her in motion toward her children. She had taken a single step (the house was 1,350 yards, or three-quarters of a mile, from the center of the explosion) when something picked her up and she seemed to fly into the next room over the raised sleeping platform, pursued by parts of her house.

Timbers fell around her as she landed, and a shower of tiles pummeled her; everything became dark, for she was buried. The debris did not cover her deeply. She rose up and freed herself. She heard a child cry, "Mother, help me!," and saw her youngest—Myeko, the five-year-old—buried up to her breast and unable to move. As Mrs. Nakamura started frantically to claw her way toward the baby, she could see or hear nothing of her other children.

In the days right before the bombing, Dr. Masakazu Fujii, being prosperous, hedonistic, and at the time not too busy, had been allowing himself the luxury of sleeping until nine or nine-thirty, but fortunately he had to get up early the morning the bomb was dropped to see a house guest off on a train. He rose at six, and half an hour later walked with his friend to the station, not far away, across two of the rivers. He was back home by seven, just as the siren sounded its sustained warning. He ate breakfast and then, because the morning was already hot, undressed down to his underwear and went out on the porch to read the paper. This porch—in fact, the whole building—was curiously constructed. Dr. Fujii was the proprietor of a peculiarly Japanese institution: a private, single-doctor hospital. This building, perched beside and over the water of the Kyo River, and next to the bridge of the same name, contained thirty rooms for thirty patients and their kinfolk—for, according to Japanese custom, when a person falls sick and goes to a hospital, one or more members of his family go and live there with him, to cook for him, bathe, massage, and read to him, and to offer incessant familial sympathy, without which a Japanese patient would be miserable indeed. Dr. Fujii had no beds—only straw mats—for his patients. He did, however, have all sorts of modern equipment: an X-ray machine, diathermy[13] apparatus, and a fine tiled laboratory. The structure rested two-thirds on the land, one-third on piles over the tidal waters of the Kyo. This overhang, the part of the building where Dr. Fujii lived, was queer-looking, but it was cool in summer and from the porch, which faced away from the center of the city, the prospect of the river, with pleasure boats drifting up and down it, was always refreshing. Dr. Fujii had occasionally had anxious moments when the Ota and its mouth branches rose to flood, but the piling was apparently firm enough and the house had always held.

Dr. Fujii had been relatively idle for about a month because in July, as the number of untouched cities in Japan dwindled and as Hiroshima seemed more and more inevitably a target, he began turning patients away, on the ground that in case of a fire raid he would not be able to evacuate them. Now he had only two patients left—a woman from Yano, injured in the shoulder, and a young man of twenty-five recovering from burns he had suffered when the steel factory near Hiroshima in which he worked had been hit. Dr. Fujii had six nurses to tend his patients. His wife and children were safe; his wife

---

13. **diathermy:** heat treatment.

WORDS TO OWN

debris (də·brē′) *n.:* rubble; broken pieces.
hedonistic (hē′də·nis′tik) *adj.:* pleasure-loving; self-indulgent.
sustained (sə·stānd′) *v.* used as *adj.:* prolonged.

---

12. **piecework:** work paid at a fixed rate for each piece completed.

Crossing the Curriculum

and one son were living outside Osaka, and another son and two daughters were in the country on Kyushu.[14] A niece was living with him, and a maid and a manservant. He had little to do and did not mind, for he had saved some money. At fifty, he was healthy, convivial, and calm, and he was pleased to pass the evenings drinking whiskey with friends, always sensibly and for the sake of conversation. Before the war, he had affected brands imported from Scotland and America; now he was perfectly satisfied with the best Japanese brand, Suntory.

Dr. Fujii sat down cross-legged in his underwear on the spotless matting of the porch, put on his glasses, and started reading the Osaka *Asahi*. He liked to read the Osaka news because his wife was there. He saw the flash. To him—faced away from the center and looking at his paper—it seemed a brilliant yellow. Startled, he began to rise to his feet. In that moment (he was 1,550 yards from the center), the hospital leaned behind his rising and, with a terrible ripping noise, toppled into the river. The doctor, still in the act of getting to his feet, was thrown forward and around and over; he was buffeted and gripped; he lost track of everything, because things were so speeded up; he felt the water.

Dr. Fujii hardly had time to think that he was dying before he realized that he was alive, squeezed tightly by two long timbers in a V across his chest, like a morsel suspended between two huge chopsticks—held upright, so that he could not move, with his head miraculously above water and his torso and legs in it. The remains of his hospital were all around him in a mad assortment of splintered lumber and materials for the relief of pain. His left shoulder hurt terribly. His glasses were gone.

Father Wilhelm Kleinsorge, of the Society of Jesus, was, on the morning of the explosion, in rather frail condition. The Japanese wartime diet had not sustained him, and he felt the strain of being a foreigner in an increasingly xenophobic[15] Japan; even a German, since the defeat of the

Fatherland,[16] was unpopular. Father Kleinsorge had, at thirty-eight, the look of a boy growing too fast—thin in the face, with a prominent Adam's apple, a hollow chest, dangling hands, big feet. He walked clumsily, leaning forward a little. He was tired all the time. To make matters worse, he had suffered for two days, along with Father Cieslik, a fellow-priest, from a rather painful and urgent diarrhea, which they blamed on the beans and black ration bread they were obliged to eat. Two other priests then living in the mission compound, which was in the Noboricho section—Father Superior LaSalle and Father Schiffer—had happily escaped this affliction.

Father Kleinsorge woke up about six the morning the bomb was dropped, and half an hour later—he was a bit tardy because of his sickness—he began to read Mass in the mission chapel, a small Japanese-style wooden building which was without pews, since its worshipers knelt on the usual Japanese matted floor, facing an altar graced with splendid silks, brass, silver, and heavy embroideries. This morning, a Monday, the only worshipers were Mr. Takemoto, a theological student living in the mission house; Mr. Fukai, the secretary of the diocese;[17] Mrs. Murata, the mission's devoutly Christian housekeeper; and his fellow-priests. After Mass, while Father Kleinsorge was reading the Prayers of Thanksgiving, the siren sounded. He stopped the service and the missionaries retired across the compound to the bigger building. There, in his room on the ground floor, to the right of the front door, Father Kleinsorge changed into a military uniform which he had acquired when he was teaching at the Rokko Middle School in Kobe and which he wore during air-raid alerts.

After an alarm, Father Kleinsorge always went out and scanned the sky, and in this instance, when he stepped outside, he was glad to see only the single weather plane that flew over Hiroshima each day about this time. Satisfied that nothing

16. **defeat of the Fatherland:** Germany surrendered to the Allies on May 7, 1945, approximately three months before the bombing of Hiroshima.
17. **diocese** (dī′ə·sis): church district administered by a bishop.

WORDS TO OWN
convivial (kən·viv′ē·əl) *adj.:* jovial; sociable.

JOHN HERSEY **943**

14. **Kyushu** (kyōō′shōō′): southernmost of the principal islands of Japan.
15. **xenophobic** (zen′ō·fō′bik): fearing or disliking foreigners.

E Struggling Readers
Finding the Main Idea
Note how this single sentence combines four main ideas separated by semicolons. Have students use context clues to paraphrase what happens to the doctor. [Dr. Fujii tries to get up when he sees the flash of the bomb, but as he does so the blast hits him, flipping him forward and down. As he falls, he is hit by timbers from the hospital and gripped by them. He then feels the river water on his skin.]

F Elements of Literature
Imagery
? Why is the description of Dr. Fujii's being pinned by the timbers a particularly strange or ironic image? [Possible response: The image compares his position to the common Japanese experience of eating with chopsticks, only this time he finds himself dangling between the "chopsticks."]

G Cultural Connections
Religions in Japan
There were not very many Christians in Japan at the time of the bombing (1945). The majority of Japanese practiced Buddhism, which was introduced from China in about the sixth century. Many Japanese also practiced Shintoism, a religion closely related to Buddhism; it was the ancient Japanese and former state religion. Confucianism, which was introduced to Japan during the fourth century, also had many followers.

Crossing the Curriculum

Film
Students might view and report on *Rhapsody in August,* a 1990 film by the great Japanese filmmaker Akira Kurosawa (1910–1998). This powerful film deals directly with personal reactions—both Japanese and American—to the atomic bombing. Starring Richard Gere as an American visiting Japan, the movie is available on videotape.

Music
One of the most famous and unusual musical responses to the bombing is *Threnody to the Victims of Hiroshima* by the Polish composer Krzysztof Penderecki (1933–   ). This 1961 avant-garde work for 52 strings is full of eerie effects and strange clusters of tones that suggest the sounds of falling objects, sirens, and blasts of wind. This short piece is available on several recordings.

A Elements of Literature
Subjectivity and Objectivity

One of the elements that contributes to Hersey's objective style and tone is his straightforward naming of events in chronological order, using primarily declarative sentences. Help students recognize this technique by recapping each separate event in this passage about Father Kleinsorge. For example:

- He went in.
- He breakfasted.
- The Fathers sat and talked.
- They heard the all-clear.
- They went to various parts of the building.
- The atomic blast hit them.

Point out to students that by the time the reader reaches the last item on the list, the event has acquired a powerfully neutral matter-of-factness.

B Historical Connections
Tsingtao

Tsingtao (chin′dou′), now spelled Qingdao, is a large city on the Yellow Sea in China. It was occupied by Japan at the time Dr. Sasaki trained there.

C Reading Skills and Strategies

Reading Closely for Details

? What is the significance of the detail in parentheses? [It demonstrates the extensive role that chance plays in life and death.]

---

would happen, he went in and breakfasted with the other Fathers on substitute coffee and ration bread, which, under the circumstances, was especially repugnant to him. The Fathers sat and talked awhile, until, at eight, they heard the all-clear. They went then to various parts of the building. Father Schiffer retired to his room to do some writing. Father Cieslik sat in his room in a straight chair with a pillow over his stomach to ease his pain, and read. Father Superior LaSalle stood at the window of his room, thinking. Father Kleinsorge went up to a room on the third floor, took off all his clothes except his underwear, and stretched out on his right side on a cot and began reading his *Stimmen der Zeit.*

After the terrible flash—which, Father Kleinsorge later realized, reminded him of something he had read as a boy about a large meteor colliding with the earth—he had time (since he was 1,400 yards from the center) for one thought: A bomb has fallen directly on us. Then, for a few seconds or minutes, he went out of his mind.

Father Kleinsorge never knew how he got out of the house. The next things he was conscious of were that he was wandering around in the mission's vegetable garden in his underwear, bleeding slightly from small cuts along his left flank; that all the buildings round about had fallen down except the Jesuits' mission house, which had long before been braced and double-braced by a priest named Gropper, who was terrified of earthquakes; that the day had turned dark; and that Murata-*san*, the housekeeper, was nearby, crying over and over, "*Shu Jesusu, awaremi tamai!* Our Lord Jesus, have pity on us!"

On the train on the way into Hiroshima from the country, where he lived with his mother, Dr. Terufumi Sasaki, the Red Cross Hospital surgeon, thought over an unpleasant nightmare he had had the night before. His mother's home was in Mukai-hara, thirty miles from the city, and it took him two hours by train and tram to reach the hospital. He had slept uneasily all night and had wakened an hour earlier than usual, and, feeling sluggish and slightly feverish, had debated whether to go to the hospital at all; his sense of duty finally forced him to go, and he had started out on an earlier train than he took most mornings. The dream had particularly frightened him

because it was so closely associated, on the surface at least, with a disturbing actuality. He was only twenty-five years old and had just completed his training at the Eastern Medical University, in Tsingtao, China. He was something of an <u>idealist</u> and was much distressed by the inadequacy of medical facilities in the country town where his mother lived. Quite on his own, and without a permit, he had begun visiting a few sick people out there in the evenings, after his eight hours at the hospital and four hours' commuting. He had recently learned that the penalty for practicing without a permit was severe; a fellow-doctor whom he had asked about it had given him a serious scolding. Nevertheless, he had continued to practice. In his dream, he had been at the bedside of a country patient when the police and the doctor he had consulted burst into the room, seized him, dragged him outside, and beat him up cruelly. On the train, he just about decided to give up the work in Mukai-hara, since he felt it would be impossible to get a permit, because the authorities would hold that it would conflict with his duties at the Red Cross Hospital.

At the terminus, he caught a streetcar at once. (He later calculated that if he had taken his customary train that morning, and if he had had to wait a few minutes for the streetcar, as often happened, he would have been close to the center at the time of the explosion and would surely have perished.) He arrived at the hospital at seven-forty and reported to the chief surgeon. A few minutes later, he went to a room on the first floor and drew blood from the arm of a man in order to perform a Wassermann test. The laboratory containing the incubators[18] for the test was on the third floor. With the blood specimen in his left hand, walking in a kind of distraction he had felt all morning, probably because of the dream and his restless night, he started along the main corridor on his way toward the stairs. He was one step beyond an open window when the light of the bomb was reflected, like a gigantic photographic

18. **incubators:** equipment providing a favorable environment for the growth of cell cultures.

WORDS TO OWN

idealist (ī·dē′əl·ist) *n.:* one who believes in noble, though often impractical, goals; dreamer.

Taking a Second Look

Review: Drawing Conclusions

Remind students that drawing conclusions involves research, logic, and common sense. Solid conclusions are based on an unbiased analysis of accurate and complete evidence.

Activities

1. Have students summarize Dr. Sasaki's thought process in the last paragraph on p. 944. What information did he consider when he "calculated"? What did he conclude?

2. Ask students what conclusions, if any, Hersey reaches in his narrative. What types of information (technological, political, social, cultural, psychological, personal) contribute to his conclusions?

3. Have students organize a panel discussion on the question "What conclusions have people around the world drawn from the bombing of Hiroshima?"

Making the Connections

Connecting to the Theme: "The Wages of War"

Ask students to list words that come to mind when they think about war (*battles, casualties, destruction, death,* etc.). Then, discuss with students how Hersey's presentation of the effects war has on specific civilians brings a new perspective to the traditional images of war that students have come to expect.

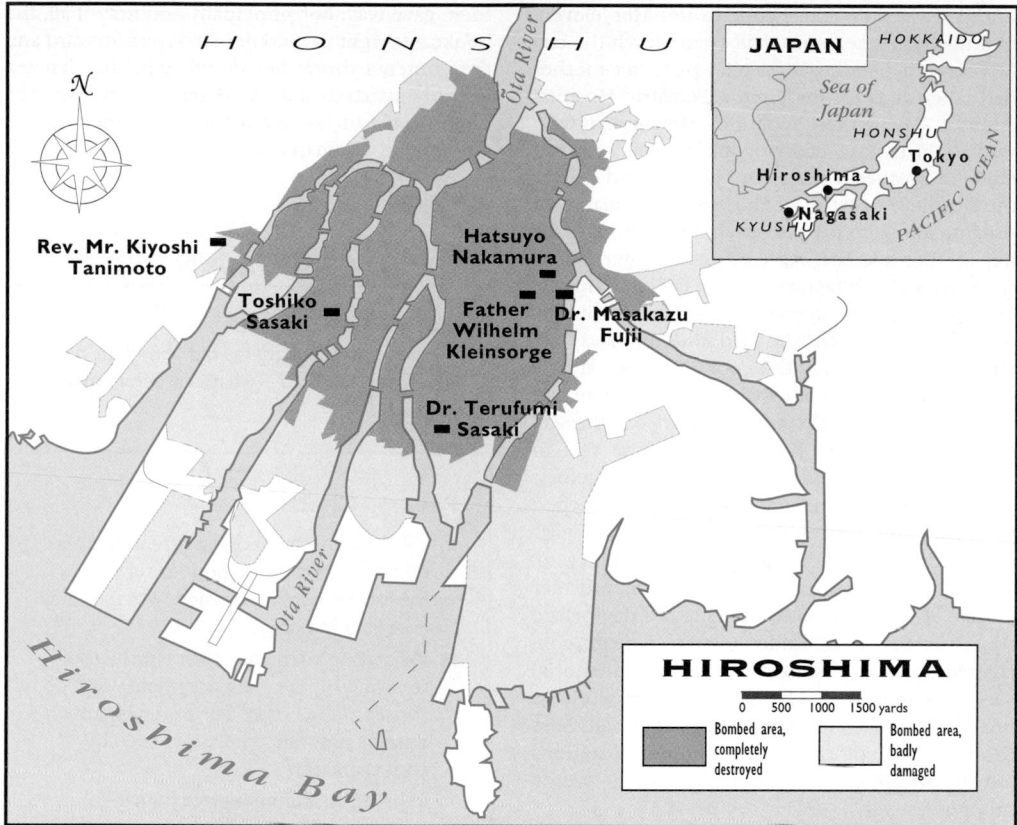

Map labels:
HONSHU
Ota River
JAPAN
HOKKAIDO
Sea of Japan
HONSHU
Hiroshima • • Tokyo
Nagasaki •
KYUSHU
PACIFIC OCEAN

Rev. Mr. Kiyoshi Tanimoto
Hatsuyo Nakamura
Toshiko Sasaki
Father Wilhelm Kleinsorge
Dr. Masakazu Fujii
Dr. Terufumi Sasaki
Ota River
Hiroshima Bay

HIROSHIMA
0   500   1000   1500 yards
Bombed area, completely destroyed
Bombed area, badly damaged

RESPONDING TO THE ART
Activity. You might use this map to sharpen students' map-reading skills. Ask questions such as these:
- Which survivor was in an area that wasn't completely destroyed?
- About how far away from each other were Dr. Fujii and Dr. Sasaki?
- What river runs through the city?
- Name three Japanese islands.

flash, in the corridor. He ducked down on one knee and said to himself, as only a Japanese would, "Sasaki, *gambare!* Be brave!" Just then (the building was 1,650 yards from the center), the blast ripped through the hospital. The glasses he was wearing flew off his face; the bottle of blood crashed against one wall; his Japanese slippers zipped out from under his feet—but otherwise, thanks to where he stood, he was untouched.

Dr. Sasaki shouted the name of the chief surgeon and rushed around to the man's office and found him terribly cut by glass. The hospital was in horrible confusion: Heavy partitions and ceilings had fallen on patients, beds had overturned, windows had blown in and cut people, blood was spattered on the walls and floors, instruments were everywhere, many of the patients were running about screaming, many more lay dead. (A

colleague working in the laboratory to which Dr. Sasaki had been walking was dead; Dr. Sasaki's patient, whom he had just left and who a few moments before had been dreadfully afraid of syphilis, was also dead.) Dr. Sasaki found himself the only doctor in the hospital who was unhurt.

Dr. Sasaki, who believed that the enemy had hit only the building he was in, got bandages and began to bind the wounds of those inside the hospital; while outside, all over Hiroshima, maimed and dying citizens turned their unsteady steps toward the Red Cross Hospital to begin an invasion that was to make Dr. Sasaki forget his private nightmare for a long, long time.

Miss Toshiko Sasaki, the East Asia Tin Works clerk, who is not related to Dr. Sasaki, got up at three o'clock in the morning on the day the bomb fell.

JOHN HERSEY 945

Ⓓ Cultural Connections
? Why do you think Hersey uses the phrase "as only a Japanese would" in describing Dr. Sasaki's behavior? [Possible response: Honor is traditionally very important to the Japanese, and Dr. Sasaki might feel his honor to be jeopardized by cowardly behavior, even though no one was there to witness it.]

Ⓔ Appreciating Language
Multiple Meanings
? At many points in his report, Hersey uses common words that take on additional meanings when viewed in the context of the historical event of the bombing. Here, for example, Dr. Sasaki deals with an *invasion* of maimed and dying citizens. What is ironic about the word *invasion*? [The Japanese expected an invasion of American troops.]

Ⓕ Critical Thinking
Analyzing Narrative Structure
? The narration again shifts to focus on another person. What provides the link between the two strangers' experiences? [Possible response: They were both mentioned at the beginning as survivors of the bombing.]

Assessing Learning

Check Test: True-False
1. Dr. Sasaki and Miss Toshiko Sasaki are brother and sister. [False]
2. Hiroshima was relatively unharmed by conventional warfare. [True]
3. Mrs. Nakamura hears only one of her three children after the blast. [True]
4. Father Kleinsorge is a German priest. [True]
5. Dr. Sasaki is the only doctor in his hospital who is unhurt. [True]

Observation Assessment
Use the following points to assess how well each student interacts with others in cooperative learning situations.
  1=Rarely   2=Sometimes   3=Often
___ Participates willingly
___ Takes a leadership role
___ Listens attentively to others' ideas
___ Easily grasps the task or problem
___ Offers innovative approach to the task
___ Accepts and works with group decisions

Standardized Test Preparation
For practice with ACT and SAT formats see
- *Preparation for College Admission Exams,* p. 59
For practice in proofreading and editing, see
- *Daily Oral Grammar,* Transparency 53

 **Reading Skills and Strategies**

Making Predictions

❓ What do you think will happen to Miss Sasaki, given her distance from center of the blast? [Possible response: She will be severely injured by the explosion, since it is so close.]

 **Reading Skills and Strategies**

Reading Closely for Details

❓ What is the ironic detail in this sentence? [Possible responses: The detail is ironic because books are symbols and tools of civilization, while the atomic bomb is the ultimate threat to civilization.]

MAKING MEANINGS

First Thoughts [Respond]

1. Possible response: Mrs. Nakamura, because she struggles alone to protect her children.

Shaping Interpretations [Interpret]

2. Possible responses: Mr. Tanimoto's anxiety about his American connections is ironic, given that the American bomb is about to render all those issues irrelevant; Mrs. Nakamura's pity for her neighbor's lost home is ironic, since her home is about to be destroyed; it is ironic that Dr. Fujii finds himself wounded by the blast, yet surrounded by his hospital's "materials for the relief of pain"; it is ironic that the Jesuit mission house remains standing, since it was reinforced by a priest who was "terrified of earthquakes"; Dr. Sasaki's patient's fear of syphilis is bitterly ironic, since he is killed by the bomb soon after expressing his worry; it is ironic that books become an instrument of violence, since they are generally associated with calm and gentility.

3. He presents the horrors of war, not the glories; he reports the bomb's effects on ordinary, innocent people. Hersey seems sympathetic toward the Japanese victims, but neither justifies nor condemns the American attack.

4. Students should give reasons to support their own responses. Students may say that a 1946 audience may have been shocked or offended by Hersey's sympathetic treatment of the Japanese so soon after the war.

There was extra housework to do. Her eleven-month-old brother, Akio, had come down the day before with a serious stomach upset; her mother had taken him to the Tamura Pediatric Hospital and was staying there with him. Miss Sasaki, who was about twenty, had to cook breakfast for her father, a brother, a sister, and herself, and—since the hospital, because of the war, was unable to provide food—to prepare a whole day's meals for her mother and the baby, in time for her father, who worked in a factory making rubber earplugs for artillery crews, to take the food by on his way to the plant. When she had finished and had cleaned and put away the cooking things, it was nearly seven. The family lived in Koi, and she had a forty-five-minute trip to the tin works, in the section of town called Kannon-machi. She was in charge of the personnel records in the factory. She left Koi at seven, and as soon as she reached the plant, she went with some of the other girls from the personnel department to the factory auditorium. A prominent local Navy man, a former employee, had committed suicide the day before by throwing himself under a train—a death considered honorable enough to warrant a memorial service, which was to be held at the tin works at ten o'clock that morning. In the large hall, Miss Sasaki and the others made suitable preparations for the meeting. This work took about twenty minutes.

Miss Sasaki went back to her office and sat down at her desk. She was quite far from the windows, which were off to her left, and behind her were a couple of tall bookcases containing all the books of the factory library, which the personnel department had organized. She settled herself at her desk, put some things in a drawer, and shifted papers. She thought that before she began to make entries in her lists of new employees, discharges, and departures for the Army, she would chat for a moment with the girl at her right. Just as she turned her head away from the windows, the room was filled with a blinding light. She was paralyzed by fear, fixed still in her chair for a long moment (the plant was 1,600 yards from the center).

Everything fell, and Miss Sasaki lost consciousness. The ceiling dropped suddenly and the wooden floor above collapsed in splinters and the people up there came down and the roof above

946 CONTEMPORARY LITERATURE

them gave way; but principally and first of all, the bookcases right behind her swooped forward and the contents threw her down, with her left leg horribly twisted and breaking underneath her. There, in the tin factory, in the first moment of the atomic age, a human being was crushed by books.

MAKING MEANINGS

First Thoughts

1. What aspect of *Hiroshima* did you focus on most intently as you read—what character, image, or idea?

> **Reading Check**
>
> a. Who are the six people presented in this section of *Hiroshima*? Besides surviving the atomic bomb explosion, what do they have in common?
>
> b. What simple **images** does Hersey use to help us imagine the actual physical impact of the bomb? For example, how does he describe the flash as seen by each character?
>
> c. What small, commonplace human-interest details does Hersey give about his characters so that they come alive and seem like people we might know?
>
> d. How does Hersey explain the **ironic** fact that an all-clear signal sounded just before the bomb was dropped?

Shaping Interpretations

2. What **ironies** can you find in each character's story—including the irony of the last image?

3. While mostly recounting facts **objectively,** Hersey communicates a **subjective** attitude toward war. How does he accomplish that? How would you describe his attitude toward the Japanese? toward the Americans?

4. During World War II, most Americans felt that the Japanese, like the Germans, were enemies to be destroyed no matter what the cost. How do

Reading Check

a. Miss Sasaki, Dr. Fujii, Mrs. Nakamura, Father Kleinsorge, Dr. Sasaki, and the Rev. Mr. Tanimoto all owe their lives to chance.

b. All the images are a variation of a flash: Mr. Tanimoto (a "sheet of sun"), Mrs. Nakamura (a flash "whiter than any white she had ever seen"), Dr. Fujii (a brilliant yellow), Father Kleinsorge (a meteor colliding with the earth), Dr. Sasaki (a gigantic photographic flash), Miss Sasaki (a "blinding light").

c. Possible responses: Miss Sasaki had just turned to talk to the girl next to her. Father Kleinsorge was in his underwear reading a magazine.

d. Japanese radar operators, detecting only three planes, concluded it was a reconnaissance flight.

you respond to Hersey's treatment of the Japanese in this account? How do you think readers in 1946—one year after the war had ended—would have responded?

Extending the Text

5. From what you know of history and from what you have read here, tell why, in human and political terms, the explosion at Hiroshima was a central event in the twentieth century. How has this distant event affected our lives even today? How did it affect the poet William Stafford, whose "At the Bomb Testing Site" appears on the Collection 18 opener (page 919)?

Challenging the Text

6. What other methods might a historian or journalist have used to tell this story? What do you think of Hersey's method? Cite passages from the text to support your evaluation.

CHOICES: Building Your Portfolio

Writer's Notebook

1. Collecting Ideas for an Evaluation

Write down some of the facts and events in this excerpt from *Hiroshima* that are striking examples of **objective reporting**. Then, choose examples of vivid **subjective reporting** and personal involvement by the author. Which type of reporting dominates, and how effective is it? Keep your notes for possible use in the Writer's Workshop on page 1181.

Analyzing Suspense

2. Page Turner

Readers of Hersey's *Hiroshima* know the outcome of the narrative before they open the book. In a brief essay, show how in this excerpt Hersey manages, nevertheless, to create **suspense**. What questions does he plant in your mind? When does he answer them?

Crossing the Curriculum: History

3. Enormous Decision

Research the decision by U.S. President Harry S Truman to use the atomic bomb against Japan. You will find facts and opinions in biographies and memoirs of Truman and other U.S. and British government officials, in government reports, and in a wide variety of additional works by historians and journalists. In an essay, describe how the decision was made and what factors were considered. End the essay with your own reflections about whether Truman made the correct decision.

Critical Writing

4. Telling Words

Hersey notes that the Japanese had a nickname for the B-29 bomber planes that regularly damaged their cities: "*B-san*, or Mr. B" (page 938). The appositive (which is a context clue that directly defines the word) also gives us an idea of what *—san* means when attached to a noun. Hersey almost always helps his readers by including strong **context clues** with Japanese terms. In a brief essay, describe how Hersey's use of Japanese terms helps to establish the authenticity of his report, and explain the insight these terms provide into the people, the culture, or the events described. (For example, the information about the Japanese nickname "B-san" for the B-29 bomber might tell you something about how some Japanese were coping psychologically with the frequent bombings.)

Extending the Text [Evaluate]

5. Possible response: Hiroshima demonstrated the first use of the ultimate weapon of mass destruction. Technology showed its ability to destroy the world. It raised the question of whether there were limits to the human capacity for violence and destruction. Students' responses will vary on how the event affects their own lives. Stafford focuses on the fragility of life and the natural world.

Challenging the Text [Evaluate]

6. Possible responses: Many historians or journalists might have focused on reporting the facts and numbers. Students' opinions may vary from approval of Hersey's method of personalizing history by making us see the real people involved to a wish for a more fictionalized approach. Ask them to support their responses and offer alternative approaches.

Grading Timesaver

Rubrics for each Choices assignment appear on p. 204 in the *Portfolio Management System*.

CHOICES: Building Your Portfolio

1. **Writer's Notebook** Suggest that students create a two-column chart headed *Subjective* and *Objective*.
2. **Analyzing Suspense** Pair students. Have them list the suspense strategies they find and use their lists to write their essays individually.
3. **Crossing the Curriculum: History** Small groups can pool their findings, discuss their opinions and reasons, then write their essays individually.
4. **Critical Writing** Students might begin by examining each Japanese word in context. Remind them to deal with two issues in their essays: authenticity and insights.

T947

UPI/Bettmann.

Robert Lowell

(1917–1977)

From virtually the beginning of his career, Robert Lowell was a major presence in American poetry. He was born into an aristocratic Boston family whose ancestors went back to the *Mayflower*. The nineteenth-century poet James Russell Lowell (1819–1891) was his great-uncle; the early-twentieth-century poet Amy Lowell (1874–1925), a promoter of Imagism, was his cousin. Lowell felt he had to rebel against his family's conservative, traditional background in order to carve out his own identity as an individual and as a poet.

Lowell left Harvard after two years to attend Kenyon College in Ohio, where the poet John Crowe Ransom was teaching. The summer before enrolling at Kenyon, Lowell lived in a tent on the poet Allen Tate's lawn in Nashville, Tennessee, soaking up all he could learn from Tate about writing poetry. Ransom and Tate were both supporters of what is called the New Criticism. They admired densely packed, "formal, difficult poems," as Lowell later put it, and Lowell began writing poems in this style.

Lowell graduated from Kenyon in 1940, married the novelist Jean Stafford, and started what would be a distinguished career of teaching and writing. Shortly thereafter, in what was at least partly another rebellious act against his family's Protestant roots, he converted to Roman Catholicism.

In the early days of World War II, Lowell tried several times to enlist in the Navy, but was rejected for his poor eyesight. By 1943, appalled at the destruction caused by American bombing in Europe, he refused induction into the Army and served a five-month prison sentence. His poems of this period—in the collections *Land of Unlikeness* (1944), *Lord Weary's Castle* (1946) (which won a Pulitzer Prize), and *The Mills of the Kavanaughs* (1951)—were tight, formal, and intellectually challenging. Most poems presented a grim vision of a world about to end.

In the 1950s, Lowell's style and subject matter gradually changed. At poetry readings with Allen Ginsberg, whose loose and free-wheeling style immediately touched audiences, Lowell, an endless reviser, would sometimes simplify some of his own poems as he read them. He began writing a looser, freer verse, with more natural rhythms and more personal subject matter.

All his life, Lowell suffered great bouts of mental instability. In 1959, he published *Life Studies,* in which he wrote frankly about his condition. His tone was neither self-pitying nor self-indulgent. Instead, he described his suffering with a light irony.

Life Studies became one of the most influential works of poetry written after World War II. It helped to make acceptable the highly personal poetry being written by Sylvia Plath (page 1148), Anne Sexton (page 1088), and John Berryman (1914–1972)—the group now referred to as the Confessional School of poets.

In the 1960s, Lowell became more and more of a public figure. Like many writers of the time, he expressed opposition to the war in Vietnam. His poetry remained deeply personal, however, and he wrote a great many unrhymed sonnets, first published as *Notebooks* in 1969 and then revised as *History* in 1973. He also wrote several well-received plays, notably *The Old Glory* (1965), based on stories by Herman Melville and Nathaniel Hawthorne.

In 1977, returning to New York from London, Robert Lowell died of a heart attack in a taxi taking him home from the airport.

go.hrw.com
LE0 11-18

 Resources: Print and Media

Before You Read

FOR THE UNION DEAD

Make the Connection

What Have We Gained?
After all the wars that Americans have fought, after all the suffering and loss and sacrifice, what kind of a world have we created? Poets and politicians, sages and students ask this question in different ways every day: Are we satisfied with our world?

Reading Skills and Strategies

Gaining Understanding Through Questioning
As you read "For the Union

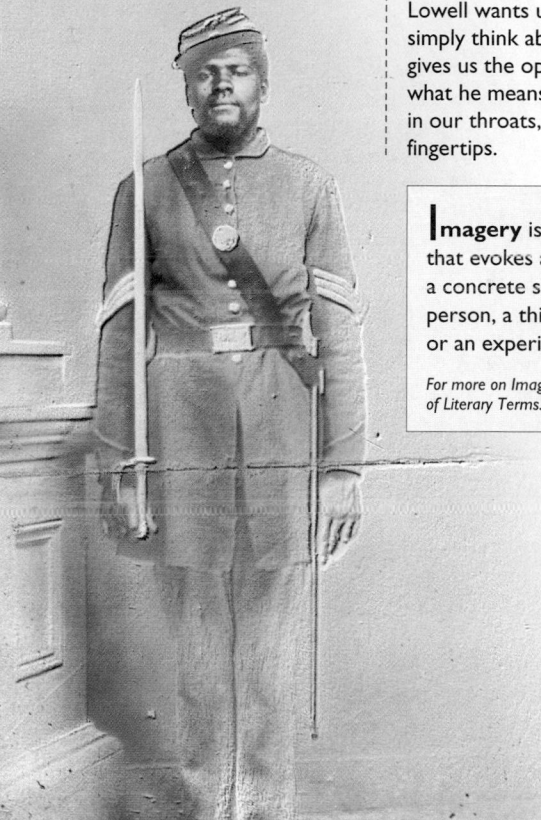

Henry Steward, Sergeant, Fifty-fourth Massachusetts Infantry Regiment, Company E.

Massachusetts Historical Society, Boston.

Dead," keep a record of your questions and uncertainties about the poem. If a passage seems confusing or obscure, try to write down exactly what you need to learn in order to understand the passage. Remember, no great work of art gives up all its secrets upon first acquaintance.

Elements of Literature

Imagery
"For the Union Dead" resonates with powerful **imagery**—language that evokes a picture or a concrete sensation of a person, a thing, a place, or an experience. Lowell wants us to do more than simply think about his ideas; he gives us the opportunity to *feel* what he means—in our noses, in our throats, and on our fingertips.

> **I**magery is language that evokes a picture or a concrete sensation of a person, a thing, a place, or an experience.
>
> *For more on Imagery, see the Handbook of Literary Terms.*

Background

"They give up everything to serve the Republic," says the Latin inscription preceding this poem. "They" are all the Union soldiers who served during the Civil War. But, more specifically, "they" are the members of the first regiment of African American soldiers from a free state, in this case Massachusetts. Under a white commander, Robert Gould Shaw, this regiment stormed Fort Wagner, South Carolina, in an assault resulting in many deaths, including that of the commander himself. The event is dramatized in the award-winning film *Glory*.

The subject of the poem is not that event, however, but its memorial—the bronze monument by the great sculptor Augustus Saint-Gaudens, which stands in Boston Common, the park directly across from the State House.

Today, Boston has a new aquarium that is a major tourist attraction. In 1960, when "For the Union Dead" was written, an older aquarium in South Boston—empty, deserted, and dilapidated—provided just the right image to set up the relationship between past and present.

Because this is a complex poem, you should read it at least twice. A comment follows the poem.

ROBERT LOWELL 949

Summary ■ ■ ■

The speaker meditates on the boarded-up ruins of the old South Boston Aquarium, remembering his visits there as a child. Now, Boston Common is being torn up to build an underground parking lot. Near the construction site is the Civil War Monument to Colonel Robert Gould Shaw and his African American regiment—a commemoration of patriotic sacrifice and a heroic past event. The speaker hints at the continuing irony of such a statue in a society that has not achieved racial equality. With luxury cars replacing the gliding fish of the old aquarium, the speaker reluctantly, even bitterly, admits the triumph of the modern world. He can locate no heroism or nobility in its commercialism, servility to technology, and relentless pursuit of "progress."

Background

On one level, Lowell's poem compares the social and racial ideals of the Union in 1863 with those of American society nearly one hundred years later. In order to better grasp the poet's shock and dismay, students should be aware of some of the social, political, cultural, and technological phenomena in America during the 1950s and early 1960s:

- "Red scare" terror of the Communism and the abuses of the McCarthy hearings
- fear of nuclear war (U.S. and Russia stockpile enough atomic bombs to kill every person on earth several times)
- rampant consumerism
- large "gas-guzzling" cars
- environmental protection movement in its infancy
- rapid development of television
- civil rights protests and marches
- John F. Kennedy's election (1960) and assassination (1963)

Reaching All Students

Struggling Readers

Have students follow in their books as they listen to the poem being read aloud. Then, have them make a chart to help them recognize and respond to the poem's imagery. Students should write the names of the five senses at the tops of the columns, list the images according to sense, and then try to express the thoughts and feelings each image suggests to them.

English Language Learners

Encourage English language learners to read beyond the literal meaning of important terms and images. For example, have students focus on such words as *aquarium, weathervane, cage, compass needle, graveyards,* and *statues.* Ask them to define the words literally and also to explore how each word has connotations that convey the poet's thought or feeling.

William Johnson/Stock Boston.

Civil War monument by Augustus Saint-Gaudens honoring the Fifty-fourth Regiment of Black Soldiers, led by Col. Robert Gould Shaw, Boston Common.

For the Union Dead

"Relinquunt Omnia Servare Rem Publicam."°

subtitle: They give up everything to serve the Republic.

Robert Lowell

Ⓐ
The old South Boston Aquarium stands
in a Sahara of snow now. Its broken windows are boarded.
The bronze weathervane cod has lost half its scales.
The airy tanks are dry.

Ⓑ 5 Once my nose crawled like a snail on the glass;
my hand tingled
to burst the bubbles
drifting from the noses of the cowed, compliant fish.

My hand draws back. I often sigh still
10 for the dark downward and vegetating kingdom
of the fish and reptile. One morning last March,
I pressed against the new barbed and galvanized

fence on the Boston Common. Behind their cage,
yellow dinosaur steamshovels were grunting

950 CONTEMPORARY LITERATURE

Crossing the Curriculum

History

Have the class form several groups and allow each group to choose one American war for consideration (the Revolutionary War, the Civil War, the Vietnam War, etc.). Ask each group to list the reasons why the United States became involved in the conflict. Then, have them explain how the world (or the country) did, or did not, change as a result. Groups should present their conclusions to the entire class.

Social Science

Have small groups explore specific aspects of race relations in the United States between the Civil War and the early 1960s. Students may research a single topic such as a Supreme Court ruling or a civil rights leader. Each group can present its research findings in an oral report to the rest of the class.

15 as they cropped up tons of mush and grass
    to gouge their underworld garage.

    Parking spaces luxuriate like civic
    sandpiles in the heart of Boston.
    A girdle of orange, Puritan-pumpkin colored girders
20 braces the tingling Statehouse,

    shaking over the excavations, as it faces Colonel Shaw
    and his bell-cheeked Negro infantry
    on St. Gaudens' shaking Civil War relief,   **C**
    propped by a plank splint against the garage's earthquake.

25 Two months after marching through Boston,
    half the regiment was dead;
    at the dedication,
    William James° could almost hear the bronze Negroes breathe.

    Their monument sticks like a fishbone   **D**
30 in the city's throat.
    Its Colonel is as lean
    as a compass-needle.   **E**

    He has an angry wrenlike vigilance,
    a greyhound's gentle tautness;
35 he seems to wince at pleasure,
    and suffocate for privacy.

    He is out of bounds now. He rejoices in man's lovely,   **F**
    peculiar power to choose life and die—
    when he leads his black soldiers to death,
40 he cannot bend his back.

    On a thousand small town New England greens,
    the old white churches hold their air
    of sparse, sincere rebellion; frayed flags
    quilt the graveyards of the Grand Army of the Republic.

45 The stone statues of the abstract Union Soldier
    grow slimmer and younger each year—
    wasp-wasted, they doze over muskets
    and muse through their sideburns . . .

    Shaw's father wanted no monument
50 except the ditch,
    where his son's body was thrown
    and lost with his "niggers."   **G**

    The ditch is nearer.
    There are no statues for the last war° here;

28. William James (1842–1910): American philosopher and psychologist who taught at Harvard University, which is adjacent to Boston.

54. the last war: World War II.

ROBERT LOWELL 951

C Literary Connections

Robert Lowell's great uncle, the American poet James Russell Lowell, was grief-stricken at the death of Colonel Robert Gould Shaw, his nephew-in-law. He wrote a poem to commemorate the twenty-five-year-old colonel's heroism, "Memoriae Positum" (1863). The Saint-Gaudens monument bears an inscription written by James Russell Lowell.

D Reading Skills and Strategies

Gaining Understanding Through Questioning

❓ Why is the monument "a fishbone / In the city's throat"? [Possible response: The monument commemorates an ideal of racial equality that the city is ashamed of not having fulfilled, or does not feel comfortable fulfilling.]

E Elements of Literature

Imagery

❓ Why is the image of the compass-needle especially appropriate for the heroic colonel? [Possible responses: The compass-needle (thin, straight, made of metal, and pointing the true direction) suggests not only Shaw's physical appearance but also his inner strength and moral leadership. Both Shaw and the compass-needle "point the way" for others to follow.]

F Appreciating Language

Multiple Meanings

Point out to students that *peculiar* has several dictionary meanings and that Lowell suggests more than one meaning here. The power to choose to die for a higher purpose is both *unique* to humans and *strange*.

G Reading Skills and Strategies

Gaining Understanding Through Questioning

❓ Why is this word in quotation marks and what does Shaw's father's conclusion indicate? [Possible response: The epithet is spoken by Shaw's father, who seems to have had difficulty viewing his son's African American comrades as full human beings. He may refuse a monument because he is bitter about his son's association with the regiment or because he thinks the heroism of his son's death speaks for itself.]

Making the Connections

Connecting to the Theme: "The Wages of War"

Have students consider the connections between Lowell's view of the Civil War through Colonel Shaw, and Wiesel and Hersey's view of World War II through other unique individuals. Unlike the other wars covered in this collection, the war in which Colonel Shaw fought was not an international, twentieth-century conflict. Nevertheless, the experience of war itself is presented as having universal, timeless qualities. The horrors of death and destruction, and the act of courage and heroism are a part of every war. Lowell's poem also relates to contemporary society. He is deeply moved by the "urban warfare": the destruction of what is old and beautiful by the new and advanced technology. In a time of racial turmoil, he brings us face to face with the "war" throughout America for a just, truly equal, and civil society.

ⓐ Reading Skills and Strategies

Responding to the Text

❓ What is your reaction to the commercial use of a photograph of the bombed Hiroshima to advertise a brand of safe? [Possible responses: Using the sufferings of war victims to sell a product demonstrates insensitivity and a desire for profit at any cost. The mass media can turn any atrocity into a money-making enterprise.]

ⓑ Reading Skills and Strategies

Gaining Understanding Through Questioning

❓ Why do you think the word *is* is emphasized in the sentence? [Possible response: The emphasis establishes conclusively that the Aquarium has been razed, that the poet is not dreaming, and that the past is not recoverable.]

ⓒ Critical Thinking

Analyzing Structure

❓ How do the last four lines of the poem balance and contrast with the first eight lines of the poem? [Possible response: In the last four lines, the Aquarium is mentioned again, although now it has been totally destroyed. The fish have been replaced by finned cars, and the bubbling water has been replaced by grease. The last four lines bring the poem full circle, returning us to the opening scene, but now with a deeper understanding of all that is lost in the march of social expediency and technological "progress."]

ⓓ Critical Thinking

Challenging the Text

❓ The last two lines of the poem are famous as a grim depiction of the modern world. Do you agree that the contemporary world is a scene of "savage servility"? Explain your response. [Possible responses: Yes, people today treat other people with contempt and are willing to do anything in order to make money. No, Lowell is exaggerating; people are still compassionate and altruistic.]

---

55   on Boylston Street, a commercial photograph
      shows Hiroshima boiling

      over a Mosler Safe, the "Rock of Ages"
      that survived the blast. Space is nearer.
      When I crouch to my television set,
60   the drained faces of Negro school-children rise like balloons.

      Colonel Shaw
      is riding on his bubble,
      he waits
      for the blesséd break.

65   The Aquarium *is* gone. Everywhere,
      giant finned cars nose forward like fish;
      a savage servility
      slides by on grease.

Courtesy of the Bostonian Society, Old State House.

Aerial view of excavation site for Boston Common garage. Lowell's poem was inspired by the scene of this razing—a deep scar on a landscape that once boasted the old South Boston Aquarium.

952 CONTEMPORARY LITERATURE

Assessing Learning

Check Test: Questions and Answers

1. What is the setting of the poem? [Boston during winter in 1960]

2. What is the monument on which the poet meditates? [a monument to Colonel Shaw and his African American infantry in the Civil War]

3. What building is important in the poem? [the old South Boston Aquarium]

4. What object does the speaker notice that is now called the "Rock of Ages"? [a safe]

5. To what are cars compared in the last stanza? [fish]

Critical Comment

A Vision of Blacks and Whites United

A good poem can withstand anything said about it. Understanding "For the Union Dead" depends on the knowledge and experiences you bring to it as much as it depends upon what the poem itself offers. After you read the poem, try to paraphrase it in order to clarify some of its references and to open possibilities of interpretation.

Looking at the ruined aquarium in its desert of snow, the poet remembers how, as a child, he used to press his nose right up against the glass of the great fish tanks; he recalls how his hand itched to get inside the tanks and play with the rising bubbles and all the marvelous sea creatures. But he is no longer a child. He draws back his hand, even though something in his nature still hungers to explore another order of life—that subconscious region where all beings in the "vegetating kingdom" had their beginnings.

The grown man presses himself against the fence that makes a "cage" in which steamshovels are gouging out space for an underground parking garage. The tremors of excavation work are so thunderous that both the State House and the bronze monument facing it have to be braced for protection. The jeopardy in which "progress" has placed both State House and monument brings the poet's central subject—the black regiment—into focus.

Having paraded through Boston as heroes on their way to the battlefield, half of these soldiers were dead within two months. When the monument to them was dedicated in 1897, the memory of these men was so much alive, and their faces and figures so faithfully rendered in bronze, that the great American psychologist William James felt that they almost breathed.

But now the poet observes that the monument "sticks like a fishbone / in the city's throat," meaning that it is an irritant. Ironically, Boston is not only one of the cities where the abolitionist movement was strongest; it is also, like many places in the United States, a place where racism has persisted. The poet compares Colonel Shaw, the regiment's leader, to the needle on a compass; this characterization suggests that Shaw pointed the way—a way in which whites and blacks united might become part of a nation's most honorable history. But Shaw is now "out of bounds" in a time and place where his special kind of vision and integrity are conspicuously lacking.

Then, instantaneously, like a change of scene in a movie, the poet's eye suddenly "pans" over the New England landscape (lines 41–48). Churches on village greens remind him of the Revolutionary War; cemeteries with their "quilt" of ragged flags recall the Civil War; the young soldiers of the Union, "stone statues" all alike, remain young and slim as their nation grows older and fatter.

Colonel Shaw's father, we learn, felt that the monument to his son was unnecessary; people had only to remember the ditch where the young commander's body was thrown with those of his soldiers. "The ditch," that common boneyard of blacks and whites, "is nearer." Why? Because nuclear holocaust threatens a world more preoccupied with sales and profits than with its own survival.

The bubbles that rose in the fish tanks of the old aquarium return at the end of the poem. They are now "balloons" that are compared to the "drained faces" of young African Americans. They also appear as the buried dream of Colonel Shaw that, like a bubble, may burst forth when idealism explodes into reality.

The old aquarium and everything it stood for in the speaker's childhood imagination no longer exist. "Finned" luxury cars now "slide by," just as the marvelous fish once glided through the bubbly depths of their tanks. To the speaker, the chrome-laden automobiles represent a "savage servility." They move "on grease," the by-product of the oil that supplies the modern world's energy, and the end product and sludgy residue of the world's great power.

Critical Comment

This feature offers a sustained paraphrase of Lowell's poem, highlighting the thematic contrast between a lost vision of social harmony and a contemporary reality of divisive materialism and looming apocalypse.

Ⓐ Reading Skills and Strategies
Responding to the Text

❓ How do the strategies the author mentions help a reader understand a poem? Can you think of other useful strategies? [Possible responses: Paraphrasing a literary work helps a reader understand its main points, and making interpretations allows a reader to make sense of ambiguities or subtle, easily overlooked points. Another strategy is applying prior knowledge, using one's own information and experiences in order to understand a poem's references or context. Asking questions is also a useful strategy; sometimes merely stating a question goes a long way toward finding an answer.]

Ⓑ Critical Thinking
Evaluating an Interpretation

❓ Do you think this interpretation of l. 53 of the poem is valid? Explain. [Possible responses: The interpretation is valid because it is a logical conclusion based on the poem's references to Hiroshima and the hedonism of modern society. The interpretation is shaky because the poem concerns itself more with social intolerance and racial injustice.]

Ⓒ Critical Thinking
Challenging the Text

❓ Do you agree with the way the critic has united the imagery of the poem into a central message? Explain. [Possible responses: Yes, the unity of the images makes sense because it shows how the poem, which displays a wide range of ideas, actually has a tight thematic focus: the difference between an idealistic view of race and society and the more sordid reality of cutthroat materialism. No, the unity of the images seems forced because it confuses two separate issues—racial conflict and technological progress.]

Reaching All Students

Struggling Readers
Students may be confused by the different connections the critic makes between the ideas in the poem. Remind them that the critic attempts to deal logically with material that the poet deals with in images and associations. Encourage students to keep track of the connections by using a graphic organizer such as a cluster diagram. As they read, students can periodically compare organizers.

Advanced Learners
Encourage advanced learners to read more about Robert Lowell's view of history, one of his favorite subjects. Students might read some of the poems in Lowell's collection *History,* or they might read an essay by one of the critics who has dealt with this topic, such as David Kalstone or Frances Ferguson. Have students summarize their findings for the class.

First Thoughts [Respond]

1. Possible responses: American ideals have decayed; greed and materialism dominate our culture; racism remains a serious problem.

Shaping Interpretations [Interpret]

2. Lowell suggests that only humans have the ability to choose to risk life for their consciences or for important values.

3. He may refer to events which occurred during the struggle for school desegregation resulting from the Supreme Court decision on *Brown v. Board of Education of Topeka* (1954).

4. "Savage servility" suggests a greedy materialism in contrast to Colonel Shaw's idealism.

5. "Union" as an adjective and "dead" as a noun refers to soldiers who died for the Union. "Union" as a noun with "dead" as its adjective implies that the Union and its ideals are now dead. The subtitle seems like a serious commendation of Shaw's regiment, with the ironic twist that society now makes their sacrifices seem to be in vain.

6. Possible responses: The tone is mixed—nostalgic, ironic, meditative, and disillusioned.

Grading Timesaver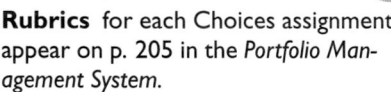

Rubrics for each Choices assignment appear on p. 205 in the *Portfolio Management System.*

CHOICES:
Building Your Portfolio

1. **Writer's Notebook** Have students review the poem to see if their notes contain all the references they would need to support their evaluation.

2. **Comparing Poems** Urge students to use questioning skills as they compare the poems.

First Thoughts

1. What basic **message** does this poem suggest to you? Explain it briefly.

Shaping Interpretations

2. What do you think the poet means by saying Colonel Shaw "rejoices in man's lovely, / peculiar power to choose life and die" (lines 37–38)?

3. What historical events in Boston and other American cities might the poet be referring to with the mention of the "drained faces" of African American children on television (line 60)?

4. What do you think is the "savage servility" (line 67) mentioned in the last stanza?

5. Explain how the **title** of the poem could have at least two meanings. Does Lowell use the Latin subtitle **ironically,** or seriously? Explain.

6. How would you describe the poem's **tone**?

Reading Check

a. What **images** describe the old South Boston Aquarium?

b. What **images** describe what the speaker saw on Boston Common?

c. What **images** describe the Saint-Gaudens monument? How many things is the colonel compared with?

d. What details tell you what happened to Colonel Shaw and his men?

CHOICES:
Building Your Portfolio

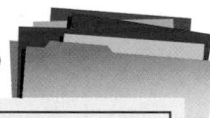

Writer's Notebook

1. Collecting Ideas for an Evaluation

When you write an evaluation, you need to be aware of your readers—the knowledge and experience they bring to a reading of the text. Review the notes you

---

made as you read Lowell's poem. Then, make a list of the historical information, allusions, vocabulary, and other data you would need to include in an evaluation of this poem written for students your own age who are not in your class. Save your notes for possible use in the Writer's Workshop on page 1181.

Comparing Poems

2. Monuments and Messages

In an essay, explain how the following poem by Henry Timrod (1828–1867) is like or unlike Lowell's poem in terms of (a) theme, (b) tone, (c) diction, and (d) form.

Ode on the Confederate Dead

Sung on the Occasion of Decorating the Graves of the Confederate Dead, at Magnolia Cemetery, Charleston, S.C., 1867

> Sleep sweetly in your humble graves,
>   Sleep, martyrs of a fallen cause;
> Though yet no marble column craves
>   The pilgrim here to pause.
>
> 5 In seeds of laurel in the earth
>   The blossom of your fame is blown,
> And somewhere, waiting for its birth,
>   The shaft is in the stone!°
>
> Meanwhile, behalf the tardy years
> 10 Which keep in trust your storied tombs,
> Behold! your sisters bring their tears,
>   And these memorial blooms.
>
> Small tributes! but your shades will smile
>   More proudly on these wreaths today,
> 15 Than when some cannon-molded pile
>   Shall overlook this bay.
>
> Stoop, angels, hither from the skies!
>   There is no holier spot of ground
> Than where defeated valor lies,
> 20 By mourning beauty crowned!

8. shaft . . . stone: allusion to Arthurian legend. Arthur proved he was the rightful king by pulling a sword out of a stone.

Reading Check

a. The aquarium stands in a Sahara of snow; it has broken and boarded windows; its tanks are dry.

b. The speaker sees yellow steam shovels that look like dinosaurs gouging the earth.

c. The monument is shaking (l. 23); the Negro infantrymen are bell-cheeked (l. 22). Shaw is compared with a compass-needle (l. 32), an angry wren (l. 33), and a taut greyhound (l. 34).

d. Half the regiment was dead two months after marching through Boston (ll. 25–26); their bodies ended up in a ditch (ll. 50–52).

Donald Barthelme
(1931–1989)

© Nancy Crampton.

Donald Barthelme (bär′thəl·mē) was an experimenter in fiction and a true member of the avant-garde. Sometimes known as a postmodernist, he is widely regarded as one of the ablest and most versatile American stylists—witty, adventurous, and profound.

In broad terms, Barthelme believed that while literature of the past functioned to revitalize the imagination, storytelling had largely lost the power to inspire, persuade, or even entertain us. He felt that our language had gone bankrupt. Since words no longer effectively communicated feelings, he said, they had lost the power to move us. Contemporary language, Barthelme asserted, is thick with sludge and stuffing. Its use of clichés and its verbosity obscure truth rather than reveal it. As Snow White, the title character of Barthelme's 1967 novel, says, "Oh I wish there were some words in the world that were not the words I always hear!"

Barthelme saw the problems with language as a reflection of a society so dehumanized, so lacking in quality, that it could no longer sustain the kinds of myths that once gave us our identity. Thus, he felt, the whole point of storytelling was lost.

In his fiction, Barthelme set out to create a banal world that fails to make distinctions of quality in people, things, and ideas. Then, since he felt it was no longer possible to write about real life or the real world, he took writing itself for his subject—the art of making art out of language. His interest lay in the form and sound of language, and he tended to play with words,

to make art out of fragments, much as some contemporary sculptors fashion works out of everyday objects and some pop artists transform cartoons into art.

Barthelme's plots are also unconventional. They are episodic, a clutter of styles, absurdities, and slapstick. "Fragments are the only forms I trust," says one of his narrators. His characters are types rather than fully developed individuals.

In Barthelme's hands, myth may turn into realism and realism into absurdity; readers can lose their way as they try to identify with the proceedings and wonder about the writer's point. Barthelme explained to the puzzled: "Art is not difficult because it wishes to be difficult, rather because it wishes to be art. However much the writer might long to be, in his work, simple, honest, straightforward, these virtues are no longer available to him. He discovers that in being simple, honest, straightforward, nothing much happens. . . . We are looking for the as yet unspeakable, the as yet unspoken."

Barthelme was born in Philadelphia, the son of an avant-garde architect, and was raised and educated in Texas. After serving with the U.S. Army, he worked as a reporter for the *Houston Post*, as a museum director, as the editor of an art and literature review, as a professor of English at the City University of New York, and as a teacher of creative writing at the University of Houston. He was a regular contributor to *The New Yorker* magazine. Collections of his stories include *Come Back, Dr. Caligari* (1964), *Unspeakable Practices, Unnatural Acts* (1968), in which "Game" appears, *Sixty Stories* (1981), and *Overnight to Many Distant Cities* (1983).

go.hrw.com
LEO 11-18

DONALD BARTHELME 955

Summary ▪ ▪

The first-person narrator and his co-worker Shotwell are responsible for a nuclear weapon they may be ordered to launch by simultaneously turning their control keys. The men have been locked underground for 133 days and don't know why they haven't been relieved. Each is supposed to shoot the other if he acts strangely. But as the story opens, both have slipped into infantile behavior such as writing on the walls and playing jacks. As we travel deeper into the repetitive and surreal psyche of the narrator, we learn he suspects that Shotwell wants him to help launch the missile and indicates that he may do it, but only if Shotwell lets him play with his jacks.

Ⓐ Element of Literature
Satire

The narrator describes the tiniest actions, since he is reduced to finding meaning in the only "data" he has. Here he focuses on the jacks, the attaché case, and the tone of Shotwell's voice. As they read, have students note how the incongruity between nuclear war and the narrator's trivial concerns emerges as a major source of disturbing satire.

Ⓑ Reading Skills and Strategies
Interpreting Word Meanings and Connotations

❓ What connotation of *sated* throws light on the narrator's attitude toward Shotwell? [Possible response: *Sated* suggests the satisfaction of a primitive appetite, as if Shotwell were uncivilized or even an animal. The narrator seems disgusted but also fascinated by Shotwell's habits.]

Before You Read
GAME

Make the Connection
Games People Play
We are all part of the physical and social world around us. How we view that world determines in large measure how we live our lives. The following story offers a rather quirky view of our times. "Game" won't give you a clear picture of your world, but it may start you thinking.

Reading Skills and Strategies
Interpreting Word Meanings and Connotations
How many distinct meanings can you think of for the word *game*? What does it mean to a child? to a professional athlete? to a hunter? Does the word connote, or suggest, something serious or something frivolous? Jot down the meanings of the word that occur to you as you read the story.

And don't forget: Barthelme said that art is difficult, and "Game" is no exception. Read the story slowly, and don't expect everything to be immediately understandable.

If I behave strangely Shotwell is supposed to shoot me.

Game

Donald Barthelme

Ⓐ **S**hotwell keeps the jacks and the rubber ball in his attaché case and will not allow me to play with them. He plays with them, alone, sitting on the floor near the console hour after hour, chanting "onesies, twosies, threesies, foursies" in a precise, well-modulated voice, not so loud as to be annoying, not so soft as to allow me to forget. I point out to Shotwell that two can derive more enjoyment from playing jacks than one, but he is not interested. I have asked repeatedly to be allowed to play by myself, but he simply shakes his head. "Why?" I ask. "They're mine," he says. And Ⓑ when he has finished, when he has sated himself, back they go into the attaché case.

- -

WORDS TO OWN
console (kän′sōl′) *n.:* desklike control panel.
sated (sāt′id) *v.:* satisfied.

- -

Preteaching Vocabulary

Words to Own
Have students use the Words to Own to complete the following sentences.

1. Neither side made any _____ of peace. [overtures]
2. The _____ detected intruders. [sensors]
3. If the disguise is realistic, the _____ will definitely work. [ruse]
4. The ancients referred to the underworld as the _____ regions. [nether]
5. The phone and doorbell rang _____. [simultaneously]
6. After the accident, they argued _____. [acrimoniously]
7. We hope to imitate his _____ behavior. [exemplary]
8. Safety always takes _____. [precedence]
9. He ate until he was _____. [sated]
10. She directed the operation from the central _____. [console]

DONALD BARTHELME **957**

RESPONDING TO THE ART

Book illustrators strive to reflect the atmosphere, or mood, of the literary work they are illustrating. Any two illustrators will differ in the ways they think a text should be illustrated. However, whether an artist is illustrating *The Three Little Pigs* or *Moby-Dick,* the images should be consistent in some way with the atmosphere of the story. **Activity.** What mood does this image create? [Possible responses: ominous, mysterious, confined, lonely.] What expectations do you have of the story, based on this image? [Possible answer: that the story will be scary or perhaps a work of science fiction.] What questions does the image raise about the story? [Possible responses: Why is the chair empty? What or who broke through the wall?] When students have finished reading the story, ask them to describe how they would illustrate it. You might also ask students what kinds of illustrations they like best and have them refer to specific illustrations in this book.

Reaching All Students

Struggling Readers
Students may have trouble identifying the conflicts in the story and differentiating between the narrator and Shotwell. Have students keep notes in a two-column chart as they read. In one column, students can list details about the narrator, and in the other column students can describe Shotwell. Have students identify the two characters' similarities and differences.

English Language Learners
Students may have difficulty identifying the narrator's tone in this story. Help them to recognize that at different times he speaks like a spoiled child, a sensitive and suffering man, a mental patient, and a military man. Point out that Barthelme deliberately creates an ambiguity, an uncertainty, that keeps readers off balance. Have them look for the use of repetition.

Advanced Learners
Encourage these students to read another of Barthelme's strange, unsettling stories and to compare it to "Game." You might have them focus on such typical Barthelme themes and devices as ambiguity, paranoia, humor, wordplay, the unreliable narrator, or the self-conscious act of fiction-making. Students might also discuss ways in which all of Barthelme's stories are "games."

Ⓐ Appreciating Language

Jargon

? What does "the bird flies" mean? Where are the two men? [The phrase seems to be military jargon or private code for the launching of a missile. The two men are in an underground bunker connected to a missile silo.]

Ⓑ Reading Skills and Strategies

Making Inferences

? What does the repetition in these lines suggest about the speaker's state of mind? [Possible responses: The obsessive repetition of key words indicates that he is nervous or paranoid, or that he distrusts language and feels awkward speaking.]

Ⓒ Elements of Literature

Ambiguity

? Responsibility—both personal and national—is one of the story's themes. Point out that responsibility for the narrator's situation is left ambiguous by the use of the passive voice ("an error had been made") and by an impersonal euphemism ("Owing to an oversight"). What do such expressions suggest about the government? [Possible responses: It is distant, bureaucratic, irresponsible, and uncaring.]

Ⓓ Reading Skills and Strategies

Interpreting Word Meanings and Connotations

? What are the connotations of the capitalized phrase "The Agreement"? [Possible responses: The term suggests a formal treaty between nations or a legal contract between opposing parties.]

Ⓔ Elements of Literature

Satire

? Incongruity, a common satiric device, is evident here. What is so shocking about the attitudes the narrator reveals? [Possible responses: Neither he nor Shotwell seems to fully understand or care about their awesome responsibility; the reader realizes that millions of lives depend upon two men who are losing their minds.]

It is unfair but there is nothing I can do about it. I am aching to get my hands on them.

Shotwell and I watch the console. Shotwell and I live under the ground and watch the console. If certain events take place upon the console, we are to insert our keys in the appropriate locks and turn our keys. Shotwell has a key and I have a key. Ⓐ If we turn our keys simultaneously the bird flies, certain switches are activated and the bird flies. But the bird never flies. In one hundred thirty-three days the bird has not flown. Meanwhile Shotwell and I watch each other. We each wear a .45 and if Shotwell behaves strangely I am supposed to shoot him. If I behave strangely Shotwell is supposed to shoot me. We watch the console and think about shooting each other and think about the bird. Shotwell's behavior with the jacks is strange. Is it strange? I do not know. Perhaps he is merely selfish . . . perhaps his character is flawed, perhaps his childhood was twisted. I do not know.

Each of us wears a .45 and each of us is supposed to shoot the other if the other is behaving strangely. How strangely is strangely? I do not know. In addition to the .45 I have a .38 which Shotwell does not know about concealed in my attaché case, and Shotwell has a .25 caliber Beretta which I do not know about strapped to his right calf. Sometimes instead of watching the console I pointedly watch Shotwell's .45, but this is simply a <u>ruse</u>, simply a maneuver, in reality I am watching his hand when it dangles in the vicinity of his right calf. If he decides I am behaving strangely he will shoot me not with the .45 but with the Beretta. Similarly, Shotwell pretends to watch my .45 but he is really watching my hand Ⓑ resting idly atop my attaché case, my hand resting idly atop my attaché case, my hand. My hand resting idly atop my attaché case.

In the beginning I took care to behave normally. So did Shotwell. Our behavior was painfully normal. Norms of politeness, consideration, speech, and personal habits were scrupulously observed. But then it became apparent that an Ⓒ error had been made, that our relief was not going to arrive. Owing to an oversight. Owing to an oversight we have been here for one hundred thirty-three days. When it became clear that an error had been made, that we were not to be relieved, the norms were relaxed. Definitions of normality were redrawn in the agreement of Janu-Ⓓ ary 1, called by us, The Agreement. Uniform regulations were relaxed, and mealtimes are no longer rigorously scheduled. We eat when we are hungry and sleep when we are tired. Considerations of rank and <u>precedence</u> were temporarily put aside, a handsome concession on the part of Shotwell, who is a captain, whereas I am only a first lieutenant. One of us watches the console at all times rather than two of us watching the console at all times, except when we are both on our feet. One of us watches the console at all times and if the bird flies then that one wakes the other and we turn our keys in the locks <u>simultaneously</u> and the Ⓔ bird flies. Our system involves a delay of perhaps twelve seconds but I do not care because I am not well, and Shotwell does not care because he is not himself. After the agreement was signed Shotwell produced the jacks and the rubber ball from his attaché case, and I began to write a series of descriptions of forms occurring in nature, such as a shell, a leaf, a stone, an animal. On the walls.

Shotwell plays jacks and I write descriptions of natural forms on the walls.

Shotwell is enrolled in a USAFI[1] course which leads to a master's degree in business administration from the University of Wisconsin (although we are not in Wisconsin, we are in Utah, Montana or Idaho). When we went down it was in either Utah, Montana or Idaho, I don't remember. We have been here for one hundred thirty-three days owing to an oversight. The pale green reinforced concrete walls sweat and the air conditioning zips on and off erratically and Shotwell reads *Introduction to Marketing* by Lassiter and Munk, making notes with a blue ballpoint pen. Shotwell is not himself but I do not know it, he presents a calm

---

1. **USAFI:** United States Armed Forces Information, an organization that supervises courses taken by service members.

WORDS TO OWN

ruse (ro͞oz) *n.:* trick; deception.
precedence (pres'ə·dəns) *n.:* order.
simultaneously (sī'məl·tā'nē·əs·lē) *adv.:* at the same time.

Using Students' Strengths

Verbal Learners

Have students read the story aloud with a partner. Encourage partners to comment on the ways the speaker's paranoia and obsessiveness come through in the patterns of his speech. Students can take notes on specific examples and share them with the class after they have read the story.

Kinesthetic Learners

Encourage students to imagine how they would feel trapped for more than four months in an underground bunker less than a quarter the size of the classroom. How does such confinement affect people? Students can use their responses to help them understand the "games" that go on in the story.

aspect and reads *Introduction to Marketing* and makes his <u>exemplary</u> notes with a blue ballpoint pen, meanwhile controlling the .38 in my attaché case with one-third of his attention. I am not well.

We have been here one hundred thirty-three days owing to an oversight. Although now we are not sure what is oversight, what is plan. Perhaps the plan is for us to stay here permanently, or if not permanently at least for a year, for three hundred sixty-five days. Or if not for a year for some number of days known to them and not known to us, such as two hundred days. Or perhaps they are observing our behavior in some way, <u>sensors</u> of some kind, perhaps our behavior determines the number of days. It may be that they are pleased with us, with our behavior, not in every detail but in sum. Perhaps the whole thing is very successful, perhaps the whole thing is an experiment and the experiment is very successful. I do not know. But I suspect that the only way they can persuade sun-loving creatures into their pale green sweating reinforced concrete rooms under the ground is to say that the system is twelve hours on, twelve hours off. And then lock us below for some number of days known to them and not known to us. We eat well although the frozen enchiladas are damp when defrosted and the frozen devil's food cake is sour and untasty. We sleep uneasily and <u>acrimoniously</u>. I hear Shotwell shouting in his sleep, objecting, denouncing, cursing sometimes, weeping sometimes, in his sleep. When Shotwell sleeps I try to pick the lock on his attaché case, so as to get at the jacks. Thus far I have been unsuccessful. Nor has Shotwell been successful in picking the locks on my attaché case so as to get at the .38. I have seen the marks on the shiny surface. I laughed, in the latrine, pale green walls sweating and the air conditioning whispering, in the latrine.

I write descriptions of natural forms on the walls, scratching them on the tile surface with a diamond. The diamond is a two and one-half carat solitaire I had in my attaché case when we went down. It was for Lucy. The south wall of the room containing the console is already covered. I have described a shell, a leaf, a stone, animals, a baseball bat. I am aware that the baseball bat is not a natural form. Yet I described it. "The baseball bat," I said, "is typically made of wood. It is typically one meter in length or a little longer, fat at one end, tapering to afford a comfortable grip at the other. The end with the handhold typically offers a slight rim, or lip, at the <u>nether</u> extremity, to prevent slippage." My description of the baseball bat ran to 4500 words, all scratched with a diamond on the south wall. Does Shotwell read what I have written? I do not know. I am aware that Shotwell regards my writing-behavior as a little strange. Yet it is no stranger than his jacks-behavior, or the day he appeared in black bathing trunks with the .25 caliber Beretta strapped to his right calf and stood over the console, trying to span with his two arms outstretched the distance between the locks. He could not do it, I had already tried, standing over

WORDS TO OWN

exemplary (eg·zem′plə·rē) *adj.*: serving as a model.
sensors (sen′sərz) *n. pl.*: detecting devices.
acrimoniously (ak′ri·mō′nē·əs·lē) *adv.*: bitterly; harshly.
nether (neth′ər) *adj.*: lower.

DONALD BARTHELME **959**

Taking a Second Look

Review: Making Predictions
Remind students that the best predictions are supported with solid textual evidence and backed up by the reader's own experience. Predicting what a character will do is a way of participating actively in the drama and suspense of fiction.

Activities
1. Have students predict what happens after the story's ending. Ask them to provide a quotation from the story and a personal

observation for support. Most important, will the missile be fired and, if so, what will be the result?

2. Ask students to predict what this story would be like if it were written by John Hersey instead of Donald Barthelme. Be sure that students draw on their observations about Hersey's style, based on their reading "A Noiseless Flash" (p. 937).

F Elements of Literature
Irony
? One of Barthelme's central themes is control. What message about the ironies of control do you find in this paragraph? [Possible responses: The narrator and Shotwell are obviously losing control of themselves, even though they have control over a weapon of mass destruction. The narrator and Shotwell, who are fighting for control over each other, may be part of a controlled behavior experiment, or they may not. A government that controls nuclear weapons still cannot control the irrational thoughts and emotions of two men.]

G Reading Skills and Strategies
Interpreting Word Meanings and Connotations
Interpreting the word *strange* is essential to the story—both for the characters and for the reader. Point out to students that *strange* comes from a Latin word that means "on the outside." Have students consider how the meaning of the word *strange* changes depending on the circumstances. How does the insularity and paranoia of the narrator's and Shotwell's circumstances change the meaning of *strange*? [Possible response: *Strange* becomes relative to whatever the two men "inside" agree is acceptable behavior—that is *not* "on the outside" (and that will *not* induce one to shoot the other); at the same time, their very instructions inspire a level of paranoia and boredom that cannot help but make both lose touch with reality.] Have students give their own definitions of *strange*. [Possible response: any behavior that is not normal or usual.]

H Reading Skills and Strategies
Making Inferences
? Why does Shotwell try to reach both locks at once? [Possible responses: He does not trust the narrator and wants to know if he can launch the missile on his own; out of boredom and morbid curiosity he is testing the parameters of his situation.]

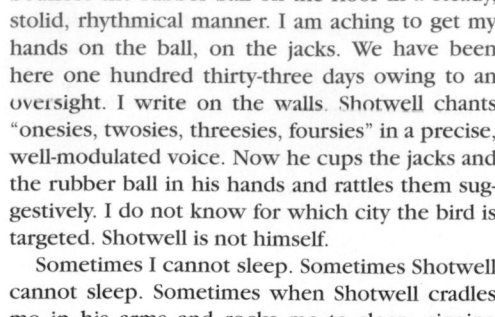

Ⓐ Reading Skills and Strategies

Interpreting Word Meanings and Connotations

❓ Sometimes the most common words carry a heavy burden of meaning. Who are "they"? [Possible responses: scientists, military leaders, government officials.] Who or what are "they" being ironically compared to here, and what might this suggest about the story's larger implications? [Possible response: "They" are being compared to God, who, too, can be seen to have planned the universe, set up the rules of the "game," and then abandoned us to try to figure out the ultimate purpose.]

Ⓑ Critical Thinking

Interpreting

❓ What do you think each man "has in mind"? [Possible response: Each man may be thinking of launching the missile simply to end their prisonlike confinement.]

Ⓒ Reading Skills and Strategies

Responding to the Text

❓ What do you think of the story's ending? [Possible responses: It's a good ending because it suggests that the men will launch the missile and take the rules of the game to their logical conclusion. It's a weak ending because it circles back to the beginning; nothing has happened and nothing will.]

---

the console with my two arms outstretched, the distance is too great. I was moved to comment but did not comment, comment would have provoked counter-comment, comment would have led God knows where. They had in their infinite patience, in their infinite foresight, in their infinite wisdom already imagined a man standing over the console with his two arms outstretched, trying to span with his two arms outstretched the distance between the locks.

Shotwell is not himself. He has made certain overtures. The burden of his message is not clear. It has something to do with the keys, with the locks. Shotwell is a strange person. He appears to be less affected by our situation than I. He goes about his business stolidly, watching the console, studying *Introduction to Marketing*, bouncing his rubber ball on the floor in a steady, rhythmical, conscientious manner. He appears to be less affected by our situation than I am. He is stolid. He says nothing. But he has made certain overtures, certain overtures have been made. I am not sure that I understand them. They have something to do with the keys, with the locks. Shotwell has something in mind. Stolidly he shucks the shiny silver paper from the frozen enchiladas, stolidly he stuffs them into the electric oven. But he has something in mind. But there must be a quid pro quo.[2] I insist on a quid pro quo. I have something in mind.

I am not well. I do not know our target. They do not tell us for which city the bird is targeted. I do not know. That is planning. That is not my responsibility. My responsibility is to watch the console and when certain events take place upon the console, turn my key in the lock. Shotwell

2. quid pro quo: Latin for "something for something." The phrase is used here to mean an even exchange.

bounces the rubber ball on the floor in a steady, stolid, rhythmical manner. I am aching to get my hands on the ball, on the jacks. We have been here one hundred thirty-three days owing to an oversight. I write on the walls. Shotwell chants "onesies, twosies, threesies, foursies" in a precise, well-modulated voice. Now he cups the jacks and the rubber ball in his hands and rattles them suggestively. I do not know for which city the bird is targeted. Shotwell is not himself.

Sometimes I cannot sleep. Sometimes Shotwell cannot sleep. Sometimes when Shotwell cradles me in his arms and rocks me to sleep, singing Brahms' "Guten Abend, gute Nacht,"[3] or I cradle Shotwell in my arms and rock him to sleep, singing, I understand what it is Shotwell wishes me to do. At such moments we are very close. But only if he will give me the jacks. That is fair. There is something he wants me to do with my key, while he does something with his key. But only if he will give me my turn. That is fair. I am not well.

3. Guten Abend, gute Nacht (go͞ot''n ä'bənt go͞ot'ə näkht): German for "good evening, good night." This line is from the musical composition popularly known as "Brahms' Lullaby" by Johannes Brahms (1833–1897).

WORDS TO OWN

overtures (ō'vər·chərz) *n. pl.:* approaches; offers.

Crossing the Curriculum

Social Sciences

Ask students to research the topic of nuclear weapons and nuclear weapon agreements. How many American nuclear weapons are there today? How can they be launched? What other countries have nuclear weapons? Organize students into groups of four, with each member responsible for researching a distinct question. Have the groups share their findings with the class.

Assessing Learning

Check Test: True-False

1. Each of the men has a hidden weapon. [True]
2. Each of the men has tried to reach both locks at once. [True]
3. The narrator writes poetry on the walls. [False]
4. The men are ordered to launch the missile. [False]

Standardized Test Preparation

For practice in proofreading and editing, see
• *Daily Oral Grammar*, Transparency 54

Critical Comment

Absurd World

Almost every element of Barthelme's story contributes to its satirical, absurdist tone. As in the plays of the Theater of the Absurd, such as those composed by Samuel Beckett and Eugene Ionesco, statements either do not follow each other logically, or they are connected by pseudologic. The narrator's constant repetition suggests the mind of someone on the brink of a precipice, desperately trying to hold on to words as symbols of reality and sanity.

The two characters, Shotwell and the unnamed narrator, are confined underground for an indefinite period. We never learn the exact details of the mission they may be called to carry out, but it seems to involve nuclear warfare and so could result in world destruction.

The first-person narration underscores the horror, as we know only what the speaker can tell us about his situation. Both he and Shotwell have been reduced to infantilism as they wait for the terrible contingency on the console: Childlike pastimes alternate with petty jealousies and disturbing nightmares. The two men's gradual dehumanization is relieved only when they rock each other to sleep. The men's eccentric behavior is portrayed as a desperate attempt to blot out the horror of their circumstances, but the story makes it clear that they are on the edge of madness: Note that Shotwell seems determined to destroy them by activating the two locks that apparently will launch a destructive event.

As you read Barthelme's vignette of life in the nuclear age, it may be easy to dismiss the particulars of his vision as exaggerated or surrealistic. But consider that a serious theme may underlie this apparently absurdist story. Our modern methods of warfare, Barthelme seems to be suggesting, are horrible not only because of their potential for physical destruction, but also because of the way their very existence corrodes and perverts humanity.

MAKING MEANINGS

First Thoughts

1. What was your emotional reaction to "Game"?

Shaping Interpretations

2. Which details in the first three paragraphs suggest the state of Shotwell's and the narrator's minds?

3. How would you explain the strange behavior of the men? What do you think happened before the story begins?

Reading Check

a. Despite his experimentation, Barthelme still uses essential elements of fiction. Who is the **narrator** of this story? What is the **setting**?

b. What is the narrator's problem, or **conflict**? Is there a **resolution** to it? If so, describe it.

4. How would you explain what the "bird" is?

5. What might be the "oversight" that has led to the men's confinement?

6. The narrator is apprehensive that Shotwell "has something in mind." What might that something be? How can you tell?

7. Barthelme uses a great deal of **repetition** in this story. What phrases are most often repeated? How does the repetition contribute to the **characterization**?

8. What meanings and connotations does the word *game* have in the story? How does the word *game* point to the story's **theme**?

Challenging the Text

9. Is the world as absurd as Barthelme describes it? Describe your response to the world Barthelme has created.

DONALD BARTHELME 961

Reading Check

a. The narrator is a lieutenant in the U.S. armed forces on duty in a missile silo. The setting of the story is the underground silo.

b. The narrator does not know how much longer he will be in the bunker; he does not trust his partner, Shotwell; he does not feel well; and he wants to play with Shotwell's jacks. The story does not resolve these problems.

Professional Notes

Critical Comments: Waiting Game

Critic Lois Gordon says that "Game" resembles Samuel Beckett's absurdist play *Waiting for Godot:* ". . . Barthelme adds his own twists. Products of the perfect bureaucracy, the two men accept their uncertain fate, and in mock-Beckettian form, they utter the existential problems of waiting: 'Perhaps the whole thing is . . . [a] very successful . . . experiment. . . I do not know.'"

Critical Comment

This feature examines the story as a "vignette of life in the nuclear age," where the threat of mutual betrayal and destruction robs us of our sanity and humanity.

MAKING MEANINGS

First Thoughts [Respond]

1. Students may be amused by the story's irony and satire, moved by its portrait of human pathos, or possibly annoyed by its repetition and ambiguity.

Shaping Interpretations [Interpret]

2. The dispute over the jacks, the paranoia about the weapons, and the narrator's repetitions suggest that they are both descending into infantilism and madness.

3. Possible response: The men suffer from isolation, constant fear, and lack of knowledge. Their sanity probably broke down slowly, before the story began.

4. The "bird" is the missile the two men apparently command.

5. The "oversight" is never clarified; but it is implied that the men have been forgotten or intentionally confined as an experiment.

6. Shotwell wants to launch the missile. His plan is suggested by his desire to turn both keys in the console.

7. The narrator's repetition ("owing to an oversight"; "I am not well") underscores his mental distress.

8. The word *game* refers literally to jacks. However, it also connotes the stockpiling of nuclear weapons and the maneuvers Shotwell and the narrator employ to trick each other. The word *game* reinforces the theme of manipulative strategizing that can only end in destruction.

Challenging the Text

9. Possible responses: The world is not as absurd as the one Barthelme describes. Students may respond to Barthelme's vision with horror, amazement, amusement, or disgust.

Resources

ELEMENTS OF LITERATURE

Satire

Satire—ridiculing human foolishness or wrong-doing—ultimately holds a moral. The sting of satire is meant to cure us of our pretensions and blindness. While a realistic, ironic writer wants us to come to terms with the world as it is, the satirist wants to reform that world. The satirist's premise is that when an unacceptable situation is exposed to ridicule and laughter, it cannot last very long.

The tools of satire. Satire requires two ingredients to be successful: (1) either wit, humor based on fantasy, or humor based on a sense of the absurd and (2) a target.

The humor of the satirist almost always involves some use of **irony**—that is, it involves a discrepancy between what is said and what is actually meant, or between what we expect to happen and what actually happens. Satirists also use **hyperbole,** or exaggeration, for effect, and **incongruity,** a kind of irony that brings together two ideas (or events or people) that do not belong together (*incongruous* means "not fitting together"). Donald Barthelme uses all three devices in "Game."

A famous satirist: Jonathan Swift. One of the greatest satirists of all time was the Irish-born writer Jonathan Swift. In *Gulliver's Travels* (1726), Swift took as his target the narrow-minded, hypocritical, and cruel English society of his time. Swift mocked his fellow citizens' pretensions to superiority by describing, among other wonders, a race of noble horses who are unquestionably superior to the English in intellect and in morals. In 1729, Swift published a satiric essay called *A Modest Proposal,* in which his fictional narrator suggests that the English could solve their vexing "Irish problem" (and also their food shortages) by serving poor Irish children up as food for the rich landlords, "who, as they have already devoured most of the parents, seem to have the best title to the children."

Fantasy and the collapse of common sense. One of the greatest weapons of a certain type of satire is **fantasy,** the creation of a world where common sense has collapsed. Two of the most famous fantasies in the English language are Lewis Carroll's *Alice's Adventures in Wonderland* (1865) and

Through the Looking-Glass (1871). In these books, the whole world is turned on its head. Even language itself no longer means what we think it means. "When *I* use a word," proclaims Humpty Dumpty, "it means just what I choose it to mean—neither more nor less." This world of satiric fantasy is also found in *Gulliver's Travels.* There, for example, the horses not only speak, but also govern themselves in a way far superior to human governments.

Satire and the absurd. At times, a satirist's fantasy will turn to the absurd or grotesque, and we can get what is known as *gallows humor,* an Americanism that means "morbid or cynical humor" (literally, humor when facing the executioner). Swift's *A Modest Proposal* becomes grotesque when the narrator dares to suggest cannibalism as a solution to an economic problem.

Satire in American literature. Satire has a long history in American literature. The shrewd counsels of prudence we hear from Benjamin Franklin's Poor Richard (page 95) are a kind of satire, in which the writer suggests practical ways to succeed in a world that is less than ideal. Mark Twain (page 450) was more of a satirist than he generally receives credit for; his Mr. Bixby in *Life on the Mississippi* is part of a long line of boasters and rogues in literature who use wit and verbal exuberance to survive in an imperfect world. James Thurber created in Walter Mitty (page 625) an American version of the man bullied by a woman, an archetypal character popular in satire at least from the days of ancient Rome. And, of course, the daily newspapers are filled with biting editorial cartoons built on satire.

What elements of satire do you find in Barthelme's story?

The Mad Hatter at the tea party, after Sir John Tenniel's design for the first edition of Lewis Carroll's *Alice's Adventures in Wonderland* (1865).

The Granger Collection, New York.

CHOICES: Building Your Portfolio

Writer's Notebook

1. Collecting Ideas for an Evaluation

Suppose you want to evaluate the **theme** of "Game." Take notes now that you might use later in an essay of evaluation. First, try to state the theme as accurately as you can. Then, describe your responses to the theme. Here are some questions you can cover: Is the theme clearly presented, or is it ambiguous? Do I agree with the theme? Is the theme popular in contemporary literature and film? How does its presentation in "Game" compare with its presentation in other texts? What does the theme reveal about the writer's view of the world? Jot down evidence to support your responses. Save your work for possible use in the Writer's Workshop on page 1181.

Comparing Texts

2. The World According to Barthelme, Auden, and You

In the following famous poem, W. H. Auden (1907–1973) describes a citizen of the modern world. In a brief essay, tell whether you think Barthelme's characters and Auden's citizen live in the same world. Has society taken away their freedom and ignored their humanity? Do you agree with these views of the world?

The Unknown Citizen

To JS/07/M/378
This Marble Monument Is Erected by the State

He was found by the Bureau of Statistics to be
One against whom there was no official complaint,
And all the reports on his conduct agree
That, in the modern sense of an old-fashioned word,
    he was a saint,
5 For in everything he did he served the Greater Community.
Except for the War till the day he retired
He worked in a factory and never got fired,
But satisfied his employers, Fudge Motors Inc.
Yet he wasn't a scab or odd in his views,
10 For his Union reports that he paid his dues,
(Our report on his Union shows it was sound)
And our Social Psychology workers found
That he was popular with his mates and liked a drink.
The Press are convinced that he bought a paper every day
And that his reactions to advertisements were normal in
15   every way.
Policies taken out in his name prove that he was fully insured,
And his Health-card shows he was once in hospital but
    left it cured.
Both Producers Research and High-Grade Living declare
He was fully sensible to the advantages of the Installment Plan
20 And had everything necessary to the Modern Man,
A gramophone, a radio, a car, and a frigidaire.
Our researchers into Public Opinion are content
That he held the proper opinions for the time of year;
When there was peace, he was for peace; when there
    was war, he went.
25 He was married and added five children to the population,
Which our Eugenist says was the right number for a parent of
    his generation,
And our teachers report that he never interfered with
    their education.
Was he free? Was he happy? The question is absurd:
Had anything been wrong, we should certainly have heard.

              —W. H. Auden

Grading Timesaver

Rubrics for each Choices assignment appear on p. 206 in the *Portfolio Management System*.

CHOICES
Building Your Portfolio

1. **Writer's Notebook** Before students begin, review the discussion of theme on pp. 634 and 1202. Students will benefit from working in small groups to discuss the theme of the story. Ask those who are having difficulty expressing the theme to imagine themselves describing the story to a friend. How would they explain the story's basic idea?

2. **Comparing Texts** Tell students to freewrite a response to the poem as soon as they have read it. Remind them to consider emotional responses, questions, associated ideas, and challenges to the text. Direct students to use their initial responses to compare the effects of the two texts on the reader. Students might use a graphic organizer to compare and contrast the two works. They can use a Venn diagram such as the one on Transparency 5 in the Transparency Package. Have students compare their graphic organizers in small groups before they write their essays.

Making the Connections

Connecting to the Theme:
"The Wages of War"

Barthelme's story focuses on the emotional and psychological damage inflicted by war, rather than on the physical destruction. The sacrifices made by Shotwell and the narrator are involuntary (they did not volunteer to lose their minds), increasing the irony of the story. Have students discuss the nature of the physical, mental, and emotional "wages" that war or the threat of war inflicts on individuals.

OBJECTIVES

1. Read and interpret the story
2. Identify and analyze internal and external conflicts
3. Express understanding through writing or performance
4. Understand and use new words

SKILLS

Literary
- Identify and analyze internal and external conflicts

Writing
- Collect ideas for an evaluation
- Write an essay analyzing the use of contrast in a story
- Write an essay comparing stories

Speaking/Listening
- Write and perform a dialogue for a television interview

Vocabulary
- Understand and use new words

Viewing/Representing
- Describe a work of art to someone who cannot see it (ATE)
- Design, sketch, or model a war memorial (ATE)

Planning

- **Traditional Schedule**
  Lesson Plans Including Strategies for English-Language Learners

- **One-Stop Planner**
  CD-ROM with Test Generator

BROWSING IN THE FILES

Writers on Writing. O'Brien aspires to follow Joseph Conrad's simple dictum: "Every day I go to my room religiously and sit down to write." In fact, O'Brien organizes his life around writing. "Everything else is peripheral to it. Books I may read, newspapers I may read, friends I may see, golf I may play. I make decisions about when to do those other things around how the writing is going."

Tim O'Brien

(1946–   )

© Jerry Bauer.

"All my work has been somewhat political in that it's been directed at big issues," Tim O'Brien once said. "My concerns have to do with the abstractions: What's courage and how do you get it? What's justice and how do you achieve it? How does one do right in an evil situation?" O'Brien turned those questions into powerful artistic tools in his gripping war novel *Going After Cacciato* (1978).

O'Brien was born in Austin, Minnesota, and graduated from Macalester College. In 1968, he was drafted and served with the U.S. Army in Vietnam, where he attained the rank of sergeant. Returning from the war, he went to Harvard for graduate work in English. A summer internship on the *Washington Post* led to a job as national affairs reporter for that newspaper.

O'Brien had been writing stories since childhood, and even in the midst of his academic work, he knew he wanted to write full time. It was his military experience in Vietnam that provided much of the material for his fiction and personal narratives. *If I Die in a Combat Zone, Box Me Up and Ship Me Home* (1973) is a collection of anecdotes and observations of his duty in Vietnam. The book drew widespread praise, particularly from veterans, as an authentic re-creation of the foot soldier's experience in an unpopular war.

O'Brien's first novel, *Northern Lights*, appeared in 1974 and dealt with a veteran returned to civilian life. *Going After Cacciato,* his second novel, followed four years later. This novel returned to the jungle war and depicted a soldier's fantasy of quitting the battle and walking off across the mountains to find Paris. *Cacciato* was acclaimed as one of the few novels to have captured the essence of the Vietnam experience, and it won a prestigious National Book Award in 1979.

O'Brien has said of his novel, "It's not really Vietnam that I was concerned about when I wrote *Cacciato;* rather it was to have readers care about what's right and wrong and about the difficulty of doing right, the difficulty of saying no to a war."

In 1990, O'Brien published *The Things They Carried,* another remarkable book dealing with the Vietnam War and its human effects. At publication, he told an interviewer:

My life is storytelling. I believe in stories, in their incredible power to keep people alive, to keep the living alive, and the dead. And if I have started now to play with the stories, inside the stories themselves, well, that's what people do all the time.

Storytelling is the essential human activity. The harder the situation, the more essential it is. In Vietnam men were constantly telling one another stories about the war. Our unit lost a lot of guys around My Lai, but the stories they told stay around after them. I would be mad not to tell the stories I know.

O'Brien keeps the Vietnam experience at the core of his psychological thriller *In the Lake of the Woods* (1994). This is a novel about a politician who attempts to conceal his past involvement in the massacre of Vietnamese civilians by American soldiers at My Lai in 1968.

go.hrw.com
LEO 11-18

Resources: Print and Media

Reading
- *Graphic Organizers for Active Reading,* p. 95
- *Words to Own,* p. 50
- *Audio CD Library*
  Disc 24, Track 4

Writing and Language
- *Daily Oral Grammar,* Transparency 55
- *Grammar and Language Links*
  Worksheet, p. 71
- *Language Workshop CD-ROM*

Assessment
- *Formal Assessment,* p. 192
- *Portfolio Management System,* p. 207
- *Preparation for College Admission Exams,* p. 61
- *Test Generator (One-Stop Planner CD-ROM)*

Internet
- go.hrw.com (keyword: LEO 11-18)

Three Flags (1958) by Jasper Johns. Encaustic on canvas (30⅞″ × 45½″ × 5″).

Collection of Whitney Museum of American Art. Fiftieth Anniversary Gift of the Gilman Foundation, Inc., The Lauder Foundation, A. Alfred Taubman, an anonymous donor, and purchase. 80.32. Photograph ©1998: Whitney Museum of American Art, ©Jasper Johns/Licensed by VAGA, New York, NY.

Before You Read
SPEAKING OF COURAGE

Make the Connection

Courage and Common Sense

What is courage? At what point does it become foolhardiness? In retrospect, Paul Berlin wishes he had been *really* courageous in war, especially during a particular incident. Maybe he was following good common sense, however, in acting as he did.

Quickwrite

Why might it be difficult for a young soldier to speak with a parent about a difficult experience in war? Write down some reasons why such a communication might be strained.

Elements of Literature

Conflict

A **conflict** is a struggle between opposing forces or characters. An **external conflict** can involve two people, a person and nature, a person and a machine, and many other situations. An **internal conflict** involves opposing forces within a person's mind. "Speaking of Courage" is largely about an internal conflict in Paul Berlin's mind.

> **A conflict** is a struggle between opposing forces or characters.
>
> *For more on Conflict, see page 607 and the Handbook of Literary Terms.*

Background

Before he published the full novel *Going After Cacciato,* O'Brien published portions of it as short stories in magazines. This story, which appeared in a different form in the novel, was named one of the O. Henry Prize Stories of 1978.

The novel about Cacciato is told through the eyes and sensibilities of a young soldier from Iowa named Paul Berlin. In this story, Paul has recently returned from battle duty in Vietnam. Like many veterans of that war, he is confused over the meaning of his experience. He is also vaguely dissatisfied with his performance in the war.

TIM O'BRIEN 965

Summary ■■

On Independence Day, Paul Berlin, a Vietnam veteran, drives repeatedly around a small lake in his hometown and imagines a conversation he longs to have with his father. The conversation concerns an incident that haunts Paul from his service in Vietnam, where he believes he had an opportunity to win a Silver Star for valor, but his courage failed him. In this incident Paul passed out in a Vietcong tunnel after a fellow soldier had been killed there. In the imaginary conversation, his father reassures him of his bravery, but Paul knows the exchange will never happen. Preoccupied with the soldier's death and his own sense of failure, Paul stops for a meal at a drive-in, and, as the day ends, watches the holiday fireworks display—numb, detached, and isolated.

RESPONDING TO THE ART

Jasper Johns (1930–   ) has exerted a powerful influence on twentieth-century art by raising fundamental questions about the nature of art and of perception. He helps viewers look at seemingly ordinary objects (flags, targets, cups, numbers) as bold aesthetic compositions.

Activity. Encourage students to describe *Three Flags* to someone who cannot see it. Have them focus solely on their perceptions and describe precisely what they see in the painting.

Preteaching Vocabulary

Words to Own

Have students read the Words to Own and their definitions listed at the bottom of the selection pages. Then, have them match each of the following words with its definition.

1. mortars [h]
2. valor [f]
3. tepid [b]
4. affluent [a]
5. recede [e]
6. profundity [i]
7. municipal [g]
8. mesmerizing [c]
9. tactile [j]
10. drone [d]

a. wealthy people
b. lukewarm
c. hypnotic
d. constant hum
e. fade
f. bravery
g. of a city
h. cannons
i. depth of thought
j. can be touched

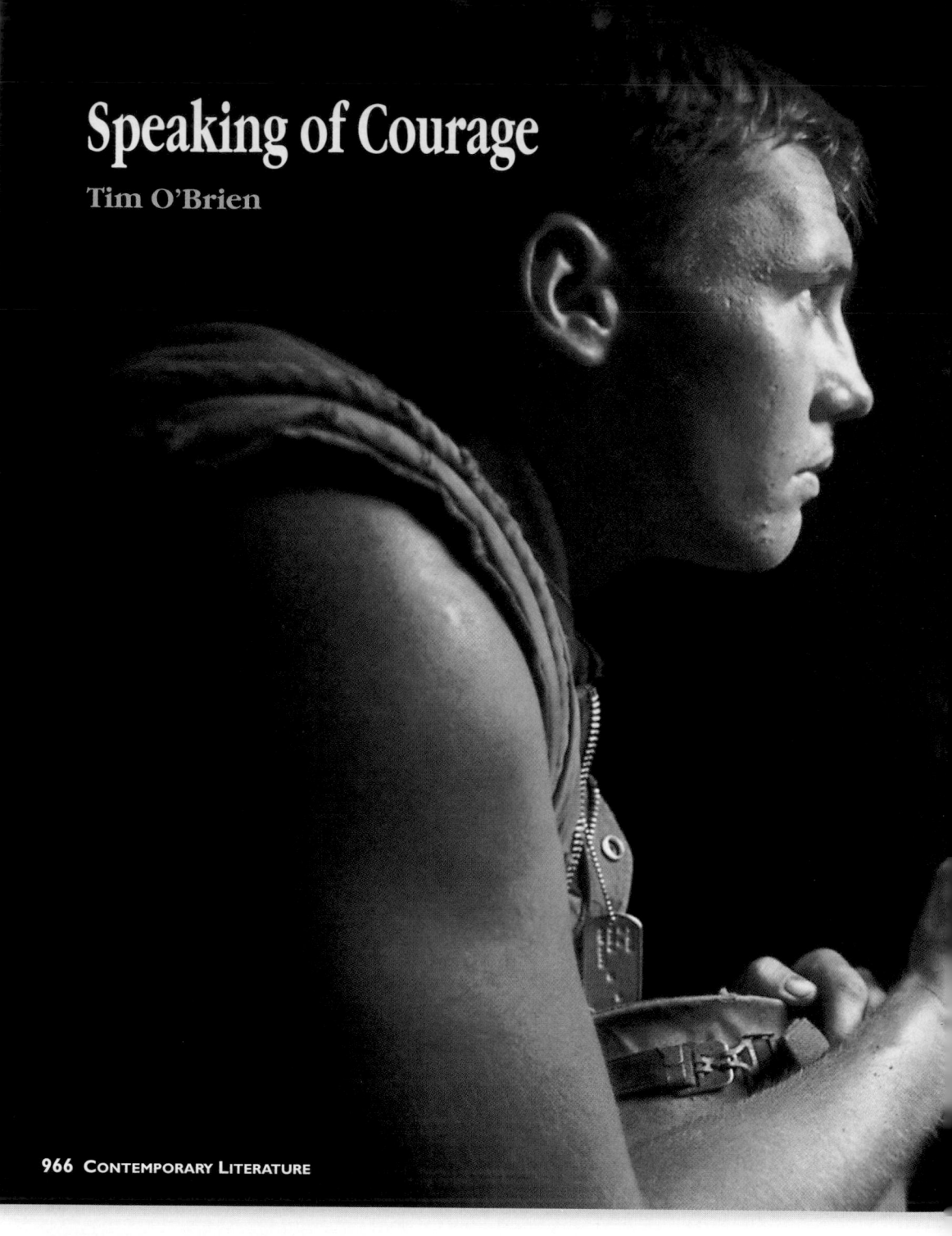

Speaking of Courage

Tim O'Brien

Reaching All Students

Struggling Readers
To help students develop a description of the main character, pair struggling readers with more advanced readers. Ask pairs to review the story and mark with adhesive notes anything in the text that provides information about Paul Berlin. Then, the pairs can summarize what they have marked in a single word or phrase. After they have finished, partners can combine their words and phrases to form a unified character description.

English Language Learners
Help students investigate the significance of repeated ideas in the story. Have each student choose a repeated word or phrase and use a cluster diagram to record ideas and images associated with it. For example, students can write "no place in particular to go" in a central circle and then include in surrounding circles repetitions or elaborations of the idea. Students can compare diagrams with a partner.

Advanced Learners
Have each student write a letter from Paul to his father that expresses everything he wants to say in the story. Students should review the story and take notes on Paul's imaginary conversations with his father. Then, students can brainstorm a list of emotions Paul might feel toward his father. Students should use their notes to write their letters. Volunteers can share their work with the class.

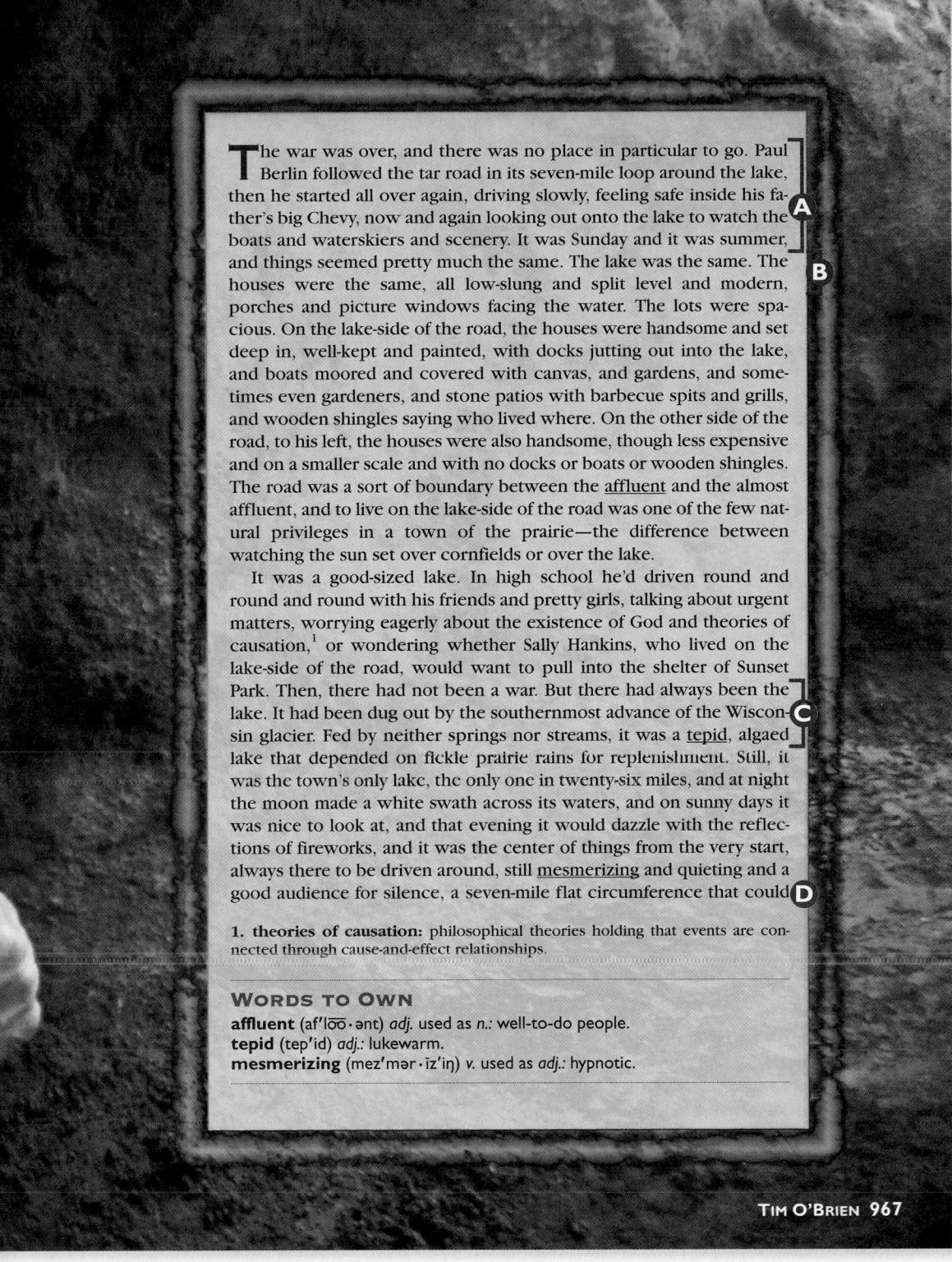

The war was over, and there was no place in particular to go. Paul Berlin followed the tar road in its seven-mile loop around the lake, then he started all over again, driving slowly, feeling safe inside his father's big Chevy, now and again looking out onto the lake to watch the boats and waterskiers and scenery. It was Sunday and it was summer, and things seemed pretty much the same. The lake was the same. The houses were the same, all low-slung and split level and modern, porches and picture windows facing the water. The lots were spacious. On the lake-side of the road, the houses were handsome and set deep in, well-kept and painted, with docks jutting out into the lake, and boats moored and covered with canvas, and gardens, and sometimes even gardeners, and stone patios with barbecue spits and grills, and wooden shingles saying who lived where. On the other side of the road, to his left, the houses were also handsome, though less expensive and on a smaller scale and with no docks or boats or wooden shingles. The road was a sort of boundary between the <u>affluent</u> and the almost affluent, and to live on the lake-side of the road was one of the few natural privileges in a town of the prairie—the difference between watching the sun set over cornfields or over the lake.

It was a good-sized lake. In high school he'd driven round and round and round with his friends and pretty girls, talking about urgent matters, worrying eagerly about the existence of God and theories of causation,[1] or wondering whether Sally Hankins, who lived on the lake-side of the road, would want to pull into the shelter of Sunset Park. Then, there had not been a war. But there had always been the lake. It had been dug out by the southernmost advance of the Wisconsin glacier. Fed by neither springs nor streams, it was a <u>tepid</u>, algaed lake that depended on fickle prairie rains for replenishment. Still, it was the town's only lake, the only one in twenty-six miles, and at night the moon made a white swath across its waters, and on sunny days it was nice to look at, and that evening it would dazzle with the reflections of fireworks, and it was the center of things from the very start, always there to be driven around, still <u>mesmerizing</u> and quieting and a good audience for silence, a seven-mile flat circumference that could

1. **theories of causation:** philosophical theories holding that events are connected through cause-and-effect relationships.

WORDS TO OWN

affluent (af′lōō·ənt) *adj.* used as *n.:* well-to-do people.
tepid (tep′id) *adj.:* lukewarm.
mesmerizing (mez′mər·īz′iŋ) *v.* used as *adj.:* hypnotic.

TIM O'BRIEN **967**

Using Students' Strengths

? What is "the truth" that Paul's father knows but will not talk about? [Possible responses: Paul's father knows that war is a shameful, humiliating horror that cannot be expressed in words. The truth is a general one about the absurdity of human life, especially as revealed by the senseless destruction of war.]

B ### Elements of Literature
Imagery

? Why is this an appropriate image for Paul to encounter on his drive? How does it reflect his internal state? [Possible response: The image is one of stasis, frustration, and dysfunction. Like the man with his motorboat, Paul finds himself "stalled," confused, and frustrated.]

C ### Struggling Readers
Finding Details

? What does the word *might* reveal about the conversation? [Possible response: The conversation is imagined.]

D ### Elements of Literature
Conflict

Point out to students that external and internal conflicts are often closely interrelated. External conflicts can generate a wide array of conflicting emotions, ideas, and behaviors. Similarly, internal conflicts can lead to arguments, fights, and battles of many kinds. As they read the rest of the story, ask students to try to describe in their own words the conflict or conflicts Paul Berlin is experiencing. [Possible response: For Paul, the external conflict of the war has created an internal conflict about courage and self-worth.]

E ### Advanced Learners
Military Medals and Honors

? Ask advanced learners to research and report to the class on the variety of medals and honors bestowed by the armed forces. What criteria are applied in deciding who will be awarded a medal? What procedures are followed?

---

be traveled by slow car in twenty-five minutes. It was not such a good lake for swimming. After college, he'd caught an ear infection that had almost kept him out of the war. And the lake had drowned Max Arnold, keeping him out of the war entirely. Max had been one who liked to talk about the existence of God. "No, I'm not saying *that*," he would say carefully against the <u>drone</u> of the engine. "I'm saying it is possible as an idea, even necessary as an idea, a final cause in the whole structure of causation." Now he knew, perhaps. Before the war, they'd driven around the lake as friends, but now Max was dead and most of the others were living in Des Moines or Sioux City, or going to school somewhere, or holding down jobs. None of the girls was left. Sally Hankins was married. His father would not talk. His father had been in another war, so he knew the truth already, and he would not talk about it, and there was no one left to talk with.

He turned on the radio. The car's big engine fired machinery that blew cold air all over him. Clockwise, like an electron spinning forever around its nucleus, the big Chevy circled the lake, and he had little to do but sit in the air-conditioning, both hands on the wheel, letting the car carry him in orbit. It was a lazy Sunday. The town was small. Out on the lake, a man's motorboat had stalled, and the fellow was bent over the silver motor with a wrench and a frown, and beyond him there were waterskiers and smooth July waters and two mud hens.

The road curved west. The sun was low in front of him, and he figured it was close to five o'clock. Twenty after, he guessed. The war had taught him to figure time. Even without the sun, waking from sleep, he could usually place it within fifteen minutes either way. He wished his father were there beside him, so he could say, "Well, looks about five-twenty," and his father would look at his watch and say, "Hey! How'd you do that?" "One of those things you learn in the war," he would say. "I know exactly what you mean," his father would then say, and the ice would be broken, and then they would be able to talk about it as they circled the lake.

He drove past Slater Park and across the causeway and past Sunset Park. The radio announcer sounded tired. He said it was five-thirty. The temperature in Des Moines was eighty-one degrees,

and "All you on the road, drive carefully now, you hear, on this fine Fourth of July." Along the road, kicking stones in front of them, two young boys were hiking with knapsacks and toy rifles and canteens. He honked going by, but neither boy looked up. Already he'd passed them six times, forty-two miles, nearly three hours. He watched the boys <u>recede</u> in his rearview mirror. They turned purply colored, like clotted blood, before finally disappearing.

"How many medals did you win?" his father might have asked.

"Seven," he would have said, "though none of them were for <u>valor</u>."

"That's all right," his father would have answered, knowing full well that many brave men did not win medals for their bravery, and that others won medals for doing nothing. "What are the medals you won?"

And he would have listed them, as a kind of starting place for talking about the war: the Combat Infantryman's Badge, the Air Medal, the Bronze Star (without a V-device for valor), the Army Commendation Medal, the Vietnam Campaign Medal, the Good Conduct Medal, and the Purple Heart, though it wasn't much of a wound, and there was no scar, and it didn't hurt and never had. While none of them was for valor, the decorations still looked good on the uniform in his closet, and if anyone were to ask, he would have explained what each signified, and eventually he would have talked about the medals he did not win, and why he did not win them, and how afraid he had been.

"Well," his father might have said, "that's an impressive list of medals, all right."

"But none were for valor."

"I understand."

And that would have been the time for telling his father that he'd almost won the Silver Star, or maybe even the Medal of Honor.

"I almost won the Silver Star," he would have said.

"How's that?"

WORDS TO OWN

drone *n.*: monotonous hum.
recede (ri·sēd′) *v.*: become more distant and indistinct.
valor (val′ər) *n.*: great courage.

Connecting Across Texts

Connecting with "Game"

Tim O'Brien's "Speaking of Courage" and Donald Barthelme's "Game" (p. 956) both focus on the mental states of men deeply affected by their military experiences. Ask students to compare and contrast the two stories. You might ask the following questions:

- Who has been damaged more by war—Paul Berlin or Barthelme's narrator?
- Which story is more sympathetic toward its protagonist? Explain.

- Which story's setting has a stronger effect on you? Why?
- Which story is more optimistic about the future? How can you tell?
- Which author—Barthelme or O'Brien—do you think has a better perspective on the meaning of war? Explain your opinion.
- Which story do you prefer, and why?

"Oh, it's just a war story."

"What's wrong with war stories?" his father would have said.

"Nothing, except I guess nobody wants to hear them."

"Tell me," his father would have said.

And then, circling the lake, he would have started the story by saying what a crazy hot day it had been when Frenchie Tucker crawled like a snake into the clay tunnel and got shot in the neck, going on with the story in great detail, telling how it smelled and what the sounds had been, everything, then going on to say how he'd almost won the Silver Star for valor.

"Well," his father would have said, "that's not a very pretty story."

"I wasn't very brave."

"You have seven medals."

"True, true," he would have said, "but I might have had eight," but even so, seven medals was pretty good, hinting at courage with their bright colors and heavy metals. "But I wasn't brave," he would have admitted.

"You weren't a coward, either," his father would have said.

"I might have been a hero."

"But you weren't a coward," his father would have insisted.

"No," Paul Berlin would have said, holding the wheel slightly right of center to produce the constant clockwise motion, "no, I wasn't a coward, and I wasn't brave, but I had the chance." He would have explained, if anyone were there to listen, that his most precious medal, except for the one he did not win, was the Combat Infantryman's Badge. While not strictly speaking a genuine medal—more an insignia of soldierdom—the CIB meant that he had seen the war as a real soldier, on the ground. It meant he'd had the opportunity to be brave, it meant that. It meant, too, that he'd . . . seen Frenchie Tucker crawl into the tunnel so that just his feet were left showing, and heard the sound when he got shot in the neck. With its crossed rifles and silver and blue colors, the CIB was really not such a bad decoration, not as good as the Silver Star or Medal of Honor, but still evidence that he'd once been there with the chance to be very brave. "I wasn't brave," he would have said, "but I might have been."

The road descended into the outskirts of town, turning northwest past the junior college and tennis courts, then past the city park where tables were spread with sheets of colored plastic as picnickers listened to the high school band, then past the municipal docks where a fat woman stood in pedal-pushers and white socks, fishing for bullheads.[2] There were no other fish in the lake, excepting some perch and a few worthless carp. It was a bad lake for swimming and fishing both.

He was in no great hurry. There was no place in particular to go. The day was very hot, but inside the Chevy the air was cold and oily and secure, and he liked the sound of the big engine and the radio and the air-conditioning. Through the windows, as though seen through one-way glass, the town shined like a stop-motion photograph, or a memory. The town could not talk, and it would not listen, and it was really a very small town anyway. "How'd you like to hear about the time I almost won the Silver Star for valor?" he might have said. The Chevy seemed to know its way around the lake.

It was late afternoon. Along an unused railway spur, four men were erecting steel launchers for the evening fireworks. They were dressed alike in khaki trousers, work shirts, visored caps and black boots. They were sweating. Two of them were unloading crates of explosives from a city truck, stacking the crates near the steel launchers. They were talking. One of them was laughing. "How'd you like to hear about it?" he might have murmured, but the men did not look up. Later they would blow color into the sky. The lake would be like a mirror, and the picnickers would sigh. The colors would open wide. "Well, it was this crazy hot day," he would have said to anyone who asked, "and Frenchie Tucker took off his helmet and pack and crawled into the tunnel with a forty-five and a knife, and the whole platoon stood in a circle around the mouth of the tunnel to watch him go down. 'Don't get blowed away,' said Stink Harris, but Frenchie was already inside and he didn't hear. You could see his feet wiggling,

2. **bullheads:** A bullhead is a type of freshwater catfish with hornlike growths near its mouth.

WORDS TO OWN

municipal (my$\overline{oo}$·nis′ə·pəl) *adj.*: belonging to a city or town.

TIM O'BRIEN **969**

Skill Link

and you could smell the dirt and clay, and then, when he got shot through the neck, you could smell the gunpowder and you could see Frenchie's feet jerk, and that was the day I could have won the Silver Star for valor."

The Chevy rolled smoothly across the old railroad spur. To his right, there was only the open lake. To his left, the lawns were scorched dry like October corn. Hopelessly, round and round, a rotating sprinkler scattered water into Doctor Mason's vegetable garden. In August it would get worse. The lake would turn green, thick with bacteria and decay, and the golf course would dry up, and dragonflies would crack open for lack of good water. The summer seemed permanent.

The big Chevy curled past the A&W[3] and Centennial Beach, and he started his seventh revolution around the lake.

He followed the road past the handsome low-slung houses. Back to Slater Park, across the causeway, around to Sunset Park, as though riding on tracks.

Out on the lake, the man with the stalled motorboat was still fiddling with the engine.

The two boys were still trudging on their hike. They did not look up when he honked.

The pair of mud hens floated like wooden decoys. The waterskiers looked tan and happy, and the spray behind them looked clean.

It was all distant and pretty.

Facing the sun again, he figured it was nearly six o'clock. Not much later the tired announcer in Des Moines confirmed it, his voice seeming to rock itself into a Sunday afternoon snooze.

Too bad, he thought. If Max were there, he would say something meaningful about the announcer's fatigue, and relate it to the sun low and red now over the lake, and the war, and courage. Too bad that all the girls had gone away. And his father, who already knew the difficulties of being brave, and who preferred silence.

Circling the lake, with time to talk, he would have told the truth. He would not have faked it. Starting with the admission that he had not been truly brave, he would have next said he hadn't been a coward, either. "I almost won the Silver Star for valor," he would have said, and, even so, he'd learned many important things in the war.

3. **A&W:** chain of drive-in, fast-food restaurants.

970 CONTEMPORARY LITERATURE

Like telling time without a watch. He had learned to step lightly. He knew, just by the sound, the difference between friendly and enemy mortars, and with time to talk and with an audience, he could explain the difference in great detail. He could tell people that the enemy fired 82-millimeter mortar rounds, while we fired 81's, and that this was a real advantage to the enemy since they could steal our rounds and shoot them from their own weapons. He knew many lies. Simple, unprofound things. He knew it is a lie that only stupid men are brave. He knew that a man can die of fright, literally, because it had happened just that way to Billy Boy Watkins after his foot had been blown off. Billy Boy had been scared to death. Dead of a heart attack caused by fright, according to Doc Peret, who would know. He knew, too, that it is a lie, the old saying that you never hear the shot that gets you, because Frenchie Tucker was shot in the neck, and after they dragged him out of the tunnel he lay there and told everyone his great discovery; he'd heard it coming the whole way, he said excitedly; and then he raised his thumb and bled through his mouth, grinning at the great discovery. So the old saying was surely a lie, or else Frenchie Tucker was lying himself, which under the circumstances was hard to believe. He knew a lot of things. They were not new or profound, but they were true. He knew that he might have won a Silver Star, like Frenchie, if he'd been able to finish what Frenchie started in the foul tunnel. He knew many war stories, a thousand details, smells and the confusion of the senses, but nobody was there to listen, and nobody knew a damn about the war because nobody believed it was really a war at all. It was not a war for war stories, or talk of valor, and nobody asked questions about the details, such as how afraid you can be, or what the particular sounds were, or whether it hurts to be shot, or what you think about and hear and see on ambush, or whether you can really tell in a firefight which way to shoot, which you can't, or how you become brave enough to win the Silver Star, or how it smells of sulfur against your cheek after firing

WORDS TO OWN
mortars (môrt′ərz) *n. pl.*: cannons used to fire explosive shells.

Crossing the Curriculum

T970

eighteen fast rounds, or how you crawl on hands and knees without knowing direction, and how, after crawling into the red-mouthed tunnel, you close your eyes like a mole and follow the tunnel walls and smell Frenchie's fresh blood and know a bullet cannot miss in there, and how there is nowhere to go but forward or backward, eyes closed, and how you can't go forward, and lose all sense, and are dragged out by the heels, losing the Silver Star. All the details,

Vietnam Veterans Memorial (detail), Washington, D.C.

Bill Hickey/The Image Bank.

without profundity, simple and age old, but nobody wants to hear war stories because they are age old and not new and not profound, and because everyone knows already that it hadn't been a war like other wars. If Max or his father were ever to ask, or anybody, he would say, "Well, first off, it was a war the same as any war," which would not sound profound at all, but which **D** would be the truth. Then he would explain what he meant in great detail, explaining that, right or wrong or win or lose, at root it had been a real war, regardless of corruption in high places or politics or sociology or the existence of God. His father knew it already, though. Which was why he didn't ask. And Max could not ask. It was a small town, but it wasn't the town's fault, either.

He passed the sprawling ranch-style homes. He lit a cigarette. He had learned to smoke in the war. He opened the window a crack but kept the air-conditioner going full, and again he circled the lake. His thoughts were the same. Out on the **E** lake, the man was frantically yanking the cord to his stalled outboard motor. Along the causeway, the two boys marched on. The pair of mud hens sought sludge at the bottom of the lake, heads under water and tails bobbing.

Six-thirty, he thought. The lake had divided into two halves. One half still glistened. The other was caught in shadow. Soon it would be dark. The

crew of workers would shoot the sky full of color, for the war was over, and the town would celebrate independence. He passed Sunset Park once again, and more houses, and the junior college and tennis courts, and the picnickers and the high school band, and the municipal docks where the fat woman patiently waited for fish.

Already, though it wasn't quite dusk, the A&W was awash in neon lights.

He maneuvered his father's Chevy into one of the parking slots, let the engine idle, and waited. The place was doing a good holiday business. Mostly kids in their fathers' cars, a few farmers in for the day, a few faces he thought he remembered, but no names. He sat still. With the sound of the engine and air-conditioning and radio, he could not hear the kids laughing, or the cars coming and going and burning rubber. But it didn't matter, it seemed proper, and he sat patiently and watched while mosquitoes and June bugs swarmed off the lake to attack the orange-colored lighting. A slim, hipless, deft young blonde delivered trays of food, passing him by as if the big Chevy were invisible, but he waited. The tired announcer in Des Moines gave the time, seven

---

WORDS TO OWN

profundity (prō·fun′də·tē) n.: intellectual depth.

TIM O'BRIEN **971**

D **Reading Skills and Strategies**
Finding the Main Idea

? What is the truth that Paul desperately wants to communicate and why is it "not profound"? [He wants to work through the simple, but overwhelming truth of his day-by-day experiences in Vietnam. By "not profound," he means that he cannot portray them as part of a righteous cause, ideological quest, or philosophical journey.]

E **English Language Learners**
Syntax

Discuss O'Brien's use of short, simple sentences. Draw attention to the paragraph on p. 971 that begins "He passed the sprawling . . ." and ask students how many simple sentences they can find. [Seven; the fourth sentence is a compound sentence.] Challenge students to relate the style to Paul's character and to the story's theme. [Possible responses: The simple sentences reflect the honesty of Paul's search for answers. The style's simplicity mirrors the elemental problem of the theme—how to go on with life when faced with the simple, but devastating weight of memory and regret.]

Getting Students Involved

Enrichment Activity

A TV Talk Show. Have students work in groups of four or five to present a television literary review talk show focusing on the O'Brien story. Groups should consist of a host asking questions and guests expressing their opinions, which they support with specific details from the text. Encourage groups to begin by drawing up a list of questions for the show. The host's

questions might focus on the story's theme, the author's style, and the main character. Talk show guests can analyze these elements, express their opinions, and make connections with other works. Each group should then practice their discussions and take notes to use when presenting their literary review to the class.

Interpreting

? How does Paul think going forward in the tunnel would have helped him go forward with his life? [Possible response: He imagines that the concrete presence of the Silver Star would give his experiences in Vietnam a sense of profundity and purpose, and erase the ambiguity and fear that his memory of the tunnel inspires.]

B **Elements of Literature**

Irony

? Note that the interval at the drive-in is Paul's only real human contact in this story. What is ironic about it? [Possible responses: The carhop refuses to take his order because it must be done impersonally through an intercom; the dialogue over the speaker mimics a military exchange.]

C **Critical Thinking**

Challenging the Text

? How do you feel about the ending of the story? Is it effective? [Possible responses: The ending is good because it provides a note of hope that Paul can come to appreciate and live in the present. The ending is ironic because Paul is viewing a patriotic celebration from a distance, as a "pretty good show," which he has no real connection to. The ending fails to provide the reader with a clear sense of Paul's state of mind, and leaves his future too ambiguous.]

---

o'clock. He could trace the fall of dusk in the orange lights which grew brighter and sharper. It was a bad war for medals. But the Silver Star would have been nice. Nice to have been brave. **A** The tactile, certain substance of the Silver Star, and how he could have rubbed his fingers over it, remembering the tunnel and the smell of clay in his nose, going forward and not backward in simple bravery. He waited patiently. The mosquitoes **B** were electrocuting themselves against a Pest-Rid machine. The slim young carhop ignored him, chatting with four boys in a Firebird, her legs in nylons even in mid-summer.

He honked once, a little embarrassed, but she did not turn. The four boys were laughing. He could not hear them, or the joke, but he could see their bright eyes and the way their heads moved. She patted the cheek of the driver.

He honked again, twice. He could not hear the sound. The girl did not hear, either.

He honked again, this time leaning on the horn. His ears buzzed. The air-conditioning shot cold air into his lap. The girl turned slowly, as though hearing something very distant, not at all sure. She said something to the boys, and they laughed, then she moved reluctantly toward him. EAT MAMA BURGERS said the orange and brown button on her chest. "How'd you like to hear about the war," he whispered, feeling vengeful. "The time I almost won the Silver Star."

She stood at the window, straight up so he could not see her face, only the button that said, EAT MAMA BURGERS. "Papa Burger, root beer, and french fries," he said, but the girl did not move or answer. She rapped on the window.

"Papa Burger, root beer, and french fries," he said, rolling it down.

She leaned down. She shook her head dumbly. Her eyes were as lovely and fuzzy as cotton candy.

"Papa Burger, root beer, and french fries," he said slowly, pronouncing the words separately and distinctly for her.

She stared at him with her strange eyes. "You blind?" she chirped suddenly. She gestured toward an intercom attached to a steel post. "You blind or something?"

"Papa Burger, root beer, and french fries."

"Push the button," she said, "and place your order." Then, first punching the button for him, she returned to her friends in the Firebird.

972 CONTEMPORARY LITERATURE

"Order," commanded a tinny voice.

"Papa Burger, root beer, and french fries."

"Roger-dodger," the voice said. "Repeat: one Papa, one beer, one fries. Stand by. That's it?"

"Roger," said Paul Berlin.

"Out," said the voice, and the intercom squeaked and went dead.

"Out," said Paul Berlin.

When the slim carhop brought him his tray, he ate quickly, without looking up, then punched the intercom button.

"Order," said the tinny voice.

"I'm done."

"That's it?"

"Yes, all done."

"Roger-dodger, over n' out," said the voice.

"Out."

On his ninth revolution around the lake he passed the hiking boys for the last time. The man with the stalled motorboat was paddling toward shore. The mud hens were gone. The fat woman was reeling in her line. The sun had left a smudge of watercolor on the horizon, and the bandshell[4] was empty, and Doctor Mason's sprinkler went round and round.

On his tenth revolution, he switched off the air-conditioning, cranked open a window, and rested his elbow comfortably on the sill, driving with one hand. He could trace the contours of the tunnel. He could talk about the scrambling sense of being lost, though he could not describe it even in his thoughts. He could talk about the terror, but he could not describe it or even feel it anymore. He could talk about emerging to see sunlight, but he could not feel the warmth, or see the faces of the men who looked away, or talk about his shame. There was no one to talk to, and nothing to say.

On his eleventh revolution, the sky went crazy with color.

C He pulled into Sunset Park and stopped in the shadow of a picnic shelter. After a time, he got out and walked down to the beach and stood with his arms folded and watched the fireworks. For a small town, it was a pretty good show.

4. **bandshell:** open-air stage with a rear sounding board shaped like the shell of a scallop.

- -

WORDS TO OWN

tactile (tak′tǝl) *adj.*: able to be perceived by touch.

- -

Making the Connections

Connecting to the Theme: "The Wages of War"

Ask students to try to express the story's theme in one or two sentences. Then, discuss with students how the story reveals different interpretations of the "wages" of war. For example, does the country owe Paul a "debt"? How will that debt be paid? Has Paul been "paid" in a currency that he does not want or that he does not deserve?

Assessing Learning

Check Test: True-False

1. Paul is amazed at how much everything has changed in his hometown. [False]
2. Paul receives seven medals, but none of them is for valor. [True]
3. Paul believes he could have won the Silver Star the day Frenchie Tucker died. [True]
4. In Vietnam, Paul learned that a man can die from fright. [True]
5. The man whose motorboat stalls finally gets the engine going. [False]

Standardized Test Preparation

For practice with ACT and SAT formats see
• *Preparation for College Admissions Exams*, p. 61
For practice in proofreading and editing, see
• *Daily Oral Grammar*, Transparency 55

First Thoughts

1. How would you have felt if you had been in Paul Berlin's shoes?

Shaping Interpretations

2. Explain why it is so difficult for Paul and his father to talk. What do you think Paul means when he says that his father "knew the truth already"? What truth does his father know, and how does he know it?

3. Discuss the **symbolic** meaning of the repeated circular action in the story and of the repeated references to time.

4. What is the **symbolic** meaning of the date in the story's context?

5. Given his experiences, what is **ironic** about the military language in Paul's conversation with the disembodied voice on the drive-in restaurant's intercom system?

6. Find the passages in which Paul mentions conversations about God. What purpose do you think these passages serve?

7. Do you think Paul's **internal conflict** has been resolved by the end of the story? Explain.

8. Do you think Paul is or is not a courageous person? Explain your answer.

Extending the Text

9. What will happen to Paul next? Share your predictions about Paul's future, and explain your reasons.

Reading Check

a. Describe the story's **setting.** In contrast, what sights, sounds, and smells does Paul remember from his time in Vietnam?

b. What does Paul wish his father would do?

c. List the things Paul has learned as a result of the war. According to Paul, why don't people want to hear about the war?

d. What does Paul wish he had done in Vietnam? What does he want to tell his father?

Writer's Notebook

1. Collecting Ideas for an Evaluation

What are your criteria for judging whether a writer has been successful in creating a character? List some qualities you expect to find in a well-conceived character. Then, note whether Paul Berlin meets those criteria. Save your notes for possible use in the Writer's Workshop on page 1181.

Analyzing Contrast

2. War and Peace, Peace and War

"Speaking of Courage" deals indirectly with the horror of warfare. In a brief essay, explain how the story uses **contrast** to deal with this subject. In planning your essay, consider how contrast is evident in the story's **setting, characterization,** and **tone.**

Comparing Stories

3. Soldiers' Homes

In a brief essay, compare and contrast the situation and character of Paul Berlin with that of Harold Krebs in Ernest Hemingway's "Soldier's Home" (page 653). What can you infer about the similarities and differences in the experiences of soldiers returning from World War I and soldiers returning from Vietnam?

Creative Writing / Performance

4. "What Did You Do in the War?"

Write the dialogue for a television interview about Vietnam with Paul Berlin to be broadcast on a July 4 newscast. Then, ask two students to perform the dialogue, with you as director. Instruct them in how to speak and how to incorporate gestures and facial expressions. Allow them to ad-lib a little as well.

TIM O'BRIEN 973

First Thoughts [Respond]

1. Possible response: I would have felt bad but would not have continued to blame myself.

Shaping Interpretations [Interpret]

2. Possible response: Due to his own war experience, Paul's father knows that war is filled with harsh, devastating, and meaningless moments that cannot be easily communicated.

3. Paul's revolutions around the lake and his repeated estimations of the hour both symbolize his inertia, and suggest that time and the past lock him in a repetitive loop, instead of moving him forward in his life.

4. The Fourth of July celebrates national pride and freedom. No one acknowledges Paul's contribution to this ideal.

5. Nobody wants to hear Paul's war stories, yet people use the language of war in peaceful contexts.

6. The second paragraph juxtaposes the ephemeral conversations about God with the inescapable reality of war and Max's death.

7. Paul's conflict over courage remains unresolved, but he may have found some sort of numbness or distraction that lets his memory fade.

8. Most will agree he is courageous. He fought, survived, and now struggles to make sense of his experience and go on.

Extending the Text [Synthesize]

9. Students may point to his inertia and predict no change or even a decline. Those who read the last paragraph as being hopeful may predict that his internal wounds will heal.

Grading Timesaver

Rubrics for each Choices assignment appear on p. 207 in the *Portfolio Management System*.

Reading Check

a. The story takes place on a Sunday, the Fourth of July, around the lake in Paul's hometown near Des Moines, Iowa, after his tour of duty in Vietnam. Paul remembers the blackness of a tunnel and his comrade bleeding; he remembers the sounds of enemy mortars and shots, the smells of sulfur, dirt, clay, gunpowder, and blood.

b. Paul wishes his father would talk to him about the war and courage.

c. Possible answers: He learned how to tell time without a watch; he learned to step lightly; he learned to differentiate between sounds of friendly and enemy fire. He also learned that some things that people say are true are lies. Nobody believes it was a war like other wars.

d. Paul wishes he had won a medal for valor. He wants to tell his father how he almost won the Silver Star and how he feels about the war and himself.

© Nancy Crampton

Yusef Komunyakaa

(1947–   )

" Vietnam helped me to look at the horror and terror in the hearts of people and realize how we can't aim guns and set booby traps for people we have never spoken a word to. That kind of impersonal violence mystifies me." These are the heartfelt reflections of one of the finest poets to emerge from the Vietnam conflict, Yusef Komunyakaa (kō·mun·yä′kə), the soldier-writer-teacher who was awarded a Pulitzer Prize in 1994 for his poetry collection *Neon Vernacular.*

A poet of both unflinching honesty and emotional restraint, Komunyakaa was born and raised in Bogalusa, Louisiana. His impulse to write, he recalls, first came when he was sixteen and read a copy of James Baldwin's *Nobody Knows My Name,* which he had found in a tiny church library. After high school, he served as a soldier in Vietnam and was awarded the Bronze Star. He then worked as a military "information specialist," corresponding from the front for a service newspaper. After the war, Komunyakaa earned advanced degrees: a master's from Colorado State University in 1979 and a master's in creative writing from the University of California, Irvine, in 1980.

Like so many American poets, Komunyakaa has made his living as a teacher. He has taught at the University of New Orleans and Indiana University, and he has given special poetry classes to elementary school students. Essentially a private and even shy man, Komunyakaa once said, "I'm happier talking about the process of writing, yes. . . . I'm even happier to have people read my work. I'm uncomfortable with the focus on the poet and not on the poem." Nevertheless, he gives poetry readings across America and in other countries. One critic, Kirkland C. Jones, points out the close connection for Komunyakaa between the written and the spoken word:

> In his Vietnam verse he keeps before the world what it meant and still means to be American, black, and a soldier, and what the painful inequities of this combination add up to. His poetry is as rhythmic and fluid as his speaking voice, and just as mellow and introspective.

Komunyakaa's collections include *Lost in the Bonewheel Factory* (1979); *Copacetic* (1984), in which critics have noted jazzlike poems that recall the verse of Langston Hughes and Jean Toomer; *I Apologize for the Eyes in My Head* (1986); *Magic City* (1992), and *Thieves of Paradise* (1998). His poems cluster around themes of violent conflict and loss, of family and racial identity, of survival and memory, and of facing up to the harsh facts of life and death. In 1988, Komunyakaa published a powerful volume devoted entirely to his Vietnam experience, *Dien Cai Dau.* Kirkland Jones ranks this among the most highly accomplished books generated by the war because Komunyakaa

focuses on the mental horrors of war—the anguish shared by the soldiers, those left at home to keep watch, and other observers, participants, objectors, who are all part of the "psychological terrain," as he has termed it, "that makes us all victims" and rages behind the eyes long after the actual fighting has ceased.

go.hrw.com
LE0 11-18

 —  — *Resources: Print and Media* —

Reading
- *Graphic Organizers for Active Reading,* p. 96
- *Audio CD Library*
  Disc 24, Track 5

Assessment
- *Formal Assessment,* p. 194
- *Portfolio Management System,* p. 208
- *Test Generator (One-Stop Planner CD-ROM)*

Internet
- go.hrw.com (keyword: LE0 11-18)

Before You Read

MONSOON SEASON

Make the Connection

Living with Dying

Memories of violence last far longer than the physical pain. Sometimes the most common things—a leaf, a breeze, a drop of rain—can trigger those memories and bring seemingly forgotten experiences back to life.

Elements of Literature

Imagery

Images in literature use language to evoke a picture or a sensation of a person or thing. Poetry is closely related to music, so it is not surprising that many poems contain **images** of sound. "Monsoon Season" includes several. Try to spot them as you read. It will probably help to read the poem aloud.

Quickwrite

Write down some **images** that you might find in a poem set during the Vietnam War in a heavy rainstorm. For ideas, you might look at the photographs on these pages.

Background

U.S. soldiers fighting the ground war during the Vietnam conflict had to contend with conditions completely alien to them. The moist, hot, tropical climate of Vietnam, its extensive jungles and mountains, and the ever-present threat of an often invisible enemy made fighting conditions unusually hazardous and frightening. And then there were the monsoons—year-round winds bringing torrents of seemingly unending rain in the hot summer and lighter but still frequent showers in the somewhat cooler winter.

Monsoon Season

Yusef Komunyakaa

A river shines in the jungle's
wet leaves. The rain's finally
let up but whenever wind shakes
the foliage it starts to fall.

5　The monsoon uncovers troubled
seasons we tried to forget.
Dead men slip through bad weather,
stamping their muddy boots to wake us,
their curses coming easier.
10　There's a bend in everything,
in elephant grass & flame trees,
raindrops pelting the sand-bagged
bunker like a muted gong.

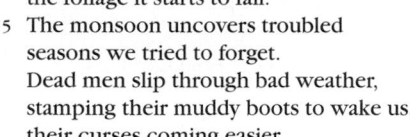

YUSEF KOMUNYAKAA 975

Summary ■■

The speaker is a soldier in the Vietnam War. He waits in the jungle during a monsoon and describes what he sees, hears, and feels. The physical effects of the rain, wind, and mud—coupled with the soldier's fear and fatigue—bring horrifying thoughts to his mind. The men around him seem already dead, like living ghosts. The entire landscape seems distorted, and he feels reduced to a mere rotting element of the earth. The helicopters are grounded by the monsoon and unable to fly out the wounded. He occupies himself by listening to a frog and counting raindrops. His poncho feels like a body bag—that is, he feels like a living dead man—and the swirling leaves recall dead men being unearthed by the monsoon.

Ⓐ Elements of Literature
Imagery

❓ Which senses are involved in the imagery of the first sentence? [Possible response: sight (the shine of the river and of the wet leaves); touch (the wetness of the river and the leaves).]

Ⓑ Critical Thinking
Interpreting

❓ How can the monsoon bring back "troubled seasons"? [Possible responses: The rain may remind the speaker of unpleasant memories; the rain may force a hiatus in activity and movement that allows time for troubling experiences to come back and haunt the speaker.]

Ⓒ Reading Skills and Strategies
Drawing Conclusions

❓ How can "dead men . . . . wake us"? [Possible responses: The speaker is remembering men who have died. The speaker is looking at soldiers who will not last long in the war—in a way, they are dead already.]

Reaching All Students

Struggling Readers

Have students read the poem in pairs, taking turns reading aloud and discussing the layers of meaning in the work. After a first reading, partners can discuss the setting, characters, and events in the poem. After a second reading, partners can discuss the literary elements, including imagery. Then, after a third reading, partners can discuss the theme and ideas. The partners should take notes on their discussions.

English Language Learners

Discuss with English language learners the idiomatic expression "down to earth" in l. 17 of the poem. Point out that this is a casual way of saying that someone is unpretentious, unaffected, plain, and honest. It also suggests that a person is beaten down, defeated, reduced to lying on the ground covered with mud—perhaps even dead and buried in the earth.

A Reading Skills and Strategies
Visualizing

Ask students to name all the colors they can imagine in the scene evoked by the speaker. [Possible responses: the white of chemicals in the air, the violet and green of the foliage, the black of the shadows, the brownish green of the water and of soldiers' camouflage, the red of blood.]

B Critical Thinking
Making the Connections

? Remind students of Randall Jarrell's similar image in "The Death of the Ball Turret Gunner." Having "fallen" down into the "State," the gunner is "hunched" like an animal with "wet fur." What emotions do both of these images evoke in you? [Possible responses: fear; the feeling of falling down and being trampled in the mud; feeling like an animal.]

C Elements of Literature
Imagery

? How might this image be symbolic? How does it reflect the speaker's feelings about death and nature? [Possible response: The image of the frog begging a snake for mercy (or perhaps, through its very existence, begging the snake to eat it), might symbolize the speaker's sense of mortality and vulnerability when faced by an enemy attack and by nature itself.]

D Critical Thinking
Interpreting

? How is the monsoon "unburying the dead"? [Possible responses: The soldiers' pause in activity caused by the monsoon leads inevitably to thoughts about dead comrades. It is only when the fighting pauses that the men realize the extent of war's destruction. The strong winds and rain might also uncover dead soldiers lost in the jungle.]

White phosphorus° washed from the air,
15 wind sways with violet myrtle,°
      beating it naked. Soaked to the bone,
      jungle rot brings us down to earth.
      We sit in our hooches°
20 with too much time,
      where grounded choppers
      can't fly out the wounded.
      Somewhere nearby a frog
      begs a snake.
      I try counting droplets,
25 stars that aren't in the sky.
      My poncho feels like a body bag.
      I lose count. Red leaves
      whirl by, the monsoon
      unburying the dead.

14. white phosphorus: poisonous, highly flammable chemical element used in weapons during the Vietnam War.
15. myrtle: type of evergreen shrub.
18. hooches: U.S. military slang for huts and other simple buildings in which soldiers lived while at base camps.

U.S. soldier of the Second Battalion in Mekong Delta, Vietnam, 1967.
Larry Burrows © 1967 Time, Inc.

976 CONTEMPORARY LITERATURE

Making the Connections

Connecting to the Theme: "The Wages of War"

With his use of powerful imagery, Komunyakaa brings home for the reader the horror and futility of slaughter as experienced by an American soldier in the jungles of Vietnam. Does the soldier's vivid experience bring a new perspective to the images that students have come to expect of contemporary warfare? If so, how?

Using Students' Strengths

Visual Learners

Have students draw some of the images in the poem. Students can do sketches to clarify the text as they read, or they can choose a significant scene from the poem and illustrate it for display in the classroom. Encourage students to include lines from the poem as captions for their drawings.

Assessing Learning

Check Test: True-False

1. The setting of the poem is a jungle during a lull in a monsoon. [True]
2. White phosphorus is a natural coating on jungle plants. [False]
3. The speaker feels at peace in the setting. [False]
4. The speaker compares his poncho to a body bag. [True]
5. The speaker watches a snake swallow a frog. [False]

T976

Poetry Emotion

ANNA QUINDLEN

Yusef Komunyakaa won the Pulitzer Prize this week, but he does not expect to become a household name, and not because his name itself, phonetically simple once parsed out bit by bit, looks at first glance so unpronounceable. Mr. Komunyakaa won the prize for poetry, and there is little premium in poetry in a world that thinks of Pound and Whitman as a weight and sampler, not an Ezra, a Walt, a thing of beauty, a joy forever.

It's hard to figure out why this should be true, why poetry has been shunted onto a siding at a time, a place, so in need of brevity and truth. We still use the word as a synonym for a kind of lovely perfection, for an inspired figure skater, an accomplished ballet dancer. Many of the finest books children read when young are poetry: "The Cat in the Hat," "Goodnight Moon," the free verse of "Where the Wild Things Are."

And then suddenly, just as their faces lose the soft curves of babyhood, the children harden into prose, and leave verse behind, or reject it entirely. Their summer reading lists rarely include poetry, only stories; *The Red Badge of Courage,* not Mr. Komunyakaa's spare and evocative poems about his hitch in Vietnam:

He danced with tall grass
for a moment, like he was
*   swaying*
with a woman. Our gun barrels
glowed white-hot.
When I got to him,
a blue halo
of flies had already claimed
*   him.*

For some of those children who once were lulled to sleep by the rhythms of Seuss and Sendak, poetry comes now set to music: Nirvana and Arrested Development, Tori Amos and the Indigo Girls. Many readers are scared off young, put off by the belief that poetry is difficult and demanding. We complain that it doesn't sound like the way we talk, but if it sounds like the way we talk, we complain that it doesn't rhyme.

A poet who teaches in the schools tells of how one boy told him he couldn't, wouldn't write poetry. Then one day in class he heard Hayden Carruth's "Cows at Night" and cried, "I didn't know we were allowed to write poems about cows."

Or to write a poem about two women talking in the kitchen:

Crazy as a bessy bug.
Jack wasn't cold
In his grave before
She done up & gave all
The insurance money
To some young pigeon
Who never hit a lick
At work in his life.
He cleaned her out & left
With Donna Faye's girl.
Honey, hush. You don't
Say . . .

That's Mr. Komunyakaa, from the collection, *Neon Vernacular,* that won the Pulitzer. His publisher originally printed 2,500 copies, which is fairly large for poetry but a joke to the folks who stock those racks at the airport. Few are the parents who leap up with soundless joy when a son or daughter announces, "Mom, Dad, I've decided to become a poet."

People who are knowledgeable about poetry sometimes discuss it in that knowing, rather hateful way in which enophiles talk about wine: robust, delicate, muscular. This has nothing to do with how most of us experience it, the heart coming around the corner and unexpectedly running into the mind. Of all the words that have stuck to the ribs of my soul, poetry has been the most filling. Robert Frost, Robert Lowell, Elizabeth Bishop, Emily Dickinson, the divine W. B. Yeats. April is the cruellest month. O World, I cannot hold thee close enough! After the first death, there is no other. A terrible beauty is born.

Poems are now appearing on posters in subway trains; one commuter said of a Langston Hughes poem, "I can't express it, but I get it." Now rolling through the soot-black dark of the tunnels and the surprising sunshine where the subways suddenly shoot aboveground: Marianne Moore, William Carlos Williams, Audre Lorde, May Swenson, Rita Dove, and Gwendolyn Brooks, who wrote that exquisite evocation of *carpe diem,* and perhaps of poetry too:

Exhaust the little moment.
*   Soon it dies.*
And be it gash or gold it will
*   not come*
Again in this identical
*   disguise.*

Says Mr. Komunyakaa, who teaches, "I never really approached it from the perspective of making a living. It was simply a need." Maybe it's a need for us all and we just forget it, as we move past bedtime-story rhythms and into a world without rhyme or reason.

—*The New York Times,*
April 16, 1994

Connecting Across Texts

Connecting with "Monsoon Season"
After students have read the column, ask them to review "Monsoon Season" and discuss how Quindlen's views affect their rereading. Do they appreciate Komunyakaa's skill more? Do they find new meanings in the poem?

You might also suggest that students find other poems about war and bring them to class to read aloud.

Discuss Quindlen's description of the way she experiences poetry: "the heart coming around the corner and unexpectedly running into the mind." Challenge students to recite lines from other poems that they have found stirring and inspirational.

Connections

In this article, novelist and journalist Anna Quindlen celebrates the awarding of the Pulitzer Prize to Yusef Komunyakaa and wonders why poetry isn't popular with American readers. She points out that our times demand poetry's concentrated truths and that poetry is still the foundation of children's books. Yet, she speculates that Americans are intimidated by poetry and its critical reception. For Quindlen, poetry strikes the heart and mind without need of criticism, and she takes Komunyakaa's as a winning example.

Ⓐ Literary Connections
Allusion
Ask students if they can identify this allusion. ["A thing of beauty is a joy forever," John Keats, "Endymion"]

Ⓑ Connecting with the Text
Have students bring in their favorite childhood books and rhymes and analyze them using the interpretive strategies employed in this textbook.

Ⓒ Elements of Literature
Figures of Speech
❓ Ask students to read this poem without its powerful simile and metaphor. What do these figures of speech add? [Possible responses: They make the poem more vivid and ironic—that a wounded man dances on a battlefield; that flies on a dead body can form a halo.]

Ⓓ Literary Connections
This passage contains the following allusions:
- "April is the cruellest month," T. S. Eliot, *The Waste Land*
- "O World, I cannot hold thee close enough!" Edna St. Vincent Millay, "God's World"
- "After the first death, there is no other," Dylan Thomas, "A Refusal to Mourn the Death, by Fire, of a Child in London"
- "A terrible beauty is born," William Butler Yeats, "Easter 1916"

Ⓔ Critical Thinking
Challenging the Text
❓ Do you agree that poetry is a "need" for everyone? Why or why not? [Possible responses: No, people can live a full, complete life without poetry. Yes, people need the awareness of beauty and the insights that poetry provides.]

MAKING MEANINGS

First Thoughts [Respond]

1. Possible responses: apprehensive, depressed, disheartened, disillusioned. Make sure students cite supporting lines.

Shaping Interpretations [Interpret]

2. He's in a Vietnam jungle during the war. The "troubled / seasons" may be memories of battle and dead comrades.

3. Possible response: Milder weather would likely lighten his mood, and the rain allows time to brood.

4. The monsoon (the rain, wind and leaves) triggers this.

5. Possible responses: The sound is muffled and heavy; the sound is metallic and suggests that it is announcing something far away. The image is surprising because the rain is neither refreshing nor frightening, merely loud and dull, suggesting that nature is somehow out of joint.

6. Possible response: He says he is counting raindrops or imaginary stars, but hints he may be really counting dead bodies or wasted moments.

7. Students' responses will vary. Their Quickwrite images might include rain, wind, mud, leaves, and trees. Students might have been surprised by the images of the gong, jungle rot, and the frog.

Extending the Text [Evaluate]

8. Possible response: Quindlen describes a feeling put into words so that readers are able to see something in a new way. Some may feel that this observation is too romantic or carefree for "Monsoon Season."

Grading Timesaver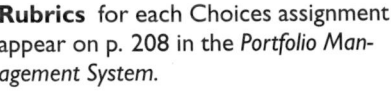

Rubrics for each Choices assignment appear on p. 208 in the *Portfolio Management System*.

MAKING MEANINGS

First Thoughts

1. How would you characterize the speaker's mood? Cite passages to support your opinion.

Shaping Interpretations

2. Where is the poem's speaker? What are the "troubled / seasons we tried to forget" (lines 5–6)?

3. How might the rainy weather have influenced the speaker's thoughts and feelings?

4. What specifically triggers the speaker's memory of past experiences?

5. In an **image** of sound, the speaker of "Monsoon Season" says the raindrops pelted the bunker "like a muted gong" (line 13). In your own words, tell what the sound of the raindrops was like to the speaker. Why is the image surprising?

6. When the speaker says "I lose count" (line 27), what does he *explicitly* say he is counting? What does he *imply* he has been counting?

7. Review your Quickwrite. In what ways were the **images** in the poem similar to or different from the ones you wrote down?

Extending the Text

8. In *Connections* on page 977, Anna Quindlen describes most people's experience of poetry as "the heart coming around the corner and unexpectedly running into the mind." Choose this or another observation of Quindlen's, and tell what you think it means and whether it seems to fit your experience of "Monsoon Season."

U.S. Army helmet, Vietnam.
Henri Bureau/Sygma.

978 CONTEMPORARY LITERATURE

CHOICES:
Building Your Portfolio

1–2. Before students write, encourage them to get together in small groups or with a partner to discuss their ideas.

3. Suggest that students begin their statement by defining what they mean by the term hero.

CHOICES:
Building Your Portfolio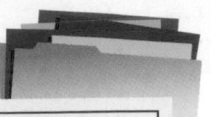

Writer's Notebook
1. Collecting Ideas for an Evaluation

One criterion for evaluating a poem is the success with which it uses **imagery.** Review Komunyakaa's poem. Then, list some of the visual images in "Monsoon Season," and jot down notes evaluating whether the poet uses them effectively. Save your notes for possible use in the Writer's Workshop on page 1181.

Analyzing Symbolism
2. Frogs and Snakes

Poets frequently use **symbols**—persons, places, things, or events that have meaning in themselves but also stand for something more. In the passage "Somewhere nearby a frog / begs a snake," what might the frog and the snake symbolize? Do you think the poet has chosen his symbols wisely? Present your answers in a short essay.

Analyzing Our Culture / Speaking and Listening
3. "I have a real problem with that."

Komunyakaa struggles to understand the contemporary legacy of violence. He once said in an interview, "In our culture we celebrate violence. All of our heroes have blood on their hands. I have a real problem with that." Imagine that you are present at the interview in which Komunyakaa delivers this opinion. In a brief statement of your own, with no wasted words, tell him—and your class—why you agree or disagree with his statement.

Discoveries and Awakenings

Theme

Who Are We? *A theme that is as old as literature itself is given new focus. In the world of irony, which is the dominant mode in modern literature, the discoveries and awakenings are not always positive, and the endings of stories are often ambiguous. One selection here picks up the archetypal American quest for adventure and meaning "on the road."*

Reading the Anthology

Reaching Struggling Readers

The *Reading Skills and Strategies: Reaching Struggling Readers* binder includes a Reading Strategies Handbook that offers concrete suggestions to help students who have difficulty reading and comprehending text, or students who are reluctant readers. When a specific strategy is most appropriate for a selection, a correlation to the Handbook is provided at the bottom of the teacher's page under the head Reaching Struggling Readers. This head may also be used to introduce additional ideas for helping students read challenging texts.

Reading Beyond the Anthology

Read On
At the end of the Contemporary Literature collections, the grade eleven book includes an annotated bibliography of books suitable for extended reading. The suggested books are related to works in these collections by theme, by author, or by subject. To preview the Read On for the Contemporary Literature period, please turn to p. T1177.

HRW Library
The *HRW Library* offers novels, plays, and short-story collections for extended reading. Each book in the Library includes one or more major works and thematically related Connections. The Connections are magazine articles, poems, or other pieces of literature. Each book in the *HRW Library* is also accompanied by a Study Guide that provides teaching suggestions and worksheets. For Collection 19, the following title is recommended.

A SEPARATE PEACE
John Knowles
A prep school boy discovers his own capacity for cruelty, even evil, in this best-selling novel set in the summer before the outbreak of World War II.

Resources for this Collection

Note: All resources for this collection are available for preview on the *One-Stop Planner CD-ROM 2 with Test Generator.* All worksheets and blackline masters may be printed from the CD-ROM.

Internet Resources
go.hrw.com LE0 11-19

Collection Planner (side tab)

Selection or Feature	Reading and Literary Skills	Vocabulary, Language, and Grammar
The Magic Barrel (p. 981) Bernard Malamud **Critical Comment: A Tale of Self-Discovery** (p. 993)	• *Graphic Organizers for Active Reading,* Worksheet p. 97 • *Literary Elements:* Transparency 30; Worksheet p. 91	• *Words to Own,* Worksheet p. 51 • *Grammar and Language Links:* Semicolons and Colons, Worksheet p. 73 • *Language Workshop CD-ROM,* Common Uses of Punctuation Marks • *Daily Oral Grammar,* Transparency 56
Literature of the Americas: Colombia **The Handsomest Drowned Man in the World** (p. 996) Gabriel García Márquez	The Literature of the Americas feature offers selections from a variety of American cultures representing North, Central, and South America. These selections connect to the collection theme, and students explore the thematic links through structured group discussions called Finding Common Ground.	
• **Elegy for Jane** (p. 1002) • **Night Journey** (p. 1003) Theodore Roethke	• *Graphic Organizers for Active Reading,* Worksheet p. 98	
• **The Beautiful Changes** (p. 1006) • **Boy at the Window** (p. 1007) Richard Wilbur	• *Graphic Organizers for Active Reading,* Worksheet p. 99	
Auto Wreck (p. 1010) Karl Shapiro	• *Graphic Organizers for Active Reading,* Worksheet p. 100	
from **Black Boy** (p. 1013) Richard Wright	• *Graphic Organizers for Active Reading,* Worksheet p. 101 • *Literary Elements:* Transparency 31; Worksheet p. 94	• *Words to Own,* Worksheet p. 52 • *Grammar and Language Links:* Varying Sentence Length, Worksheet p. 75 • *Daily Oral Grammar,* Transparency 57
Everything Stuck to Him (p. 1027) Raymond Carver **Primary Sources: "Paddlewheel of Days"** (p. 1032) Raymond Carver	• *Graphic Organizers for Active Reading,* Worksheet p. 102	• *Words to Own,* Worksheet p. 53 • *Daily Oral Grammar,* Transparency 58
The Fish (p. 1035) Elizabeth Bishop	• *Graphic Organizers for Active Reading,* Worksheet p. 103	• *Daily Oral Grammar,* Transparency 59
Remember (p. 1040) Joy Harjo	• *Graphic Organizers for Active Reading,* Worksheet p. 104	
The Girl Who Wouldn't Talk *from* **The Woman Warrior** (p. 1044) Maxine Hong Kingston	• *Graphic Organizers for Active Reading,* Worksheet p. 105	• *Words to Own,* Worksheet p. 54 • *Daily Oral Grammar,* Transparency 60
from **Blue Highways** (p. 1054) William Least Heat-Moon **Connections:** *from* **Let Us Now Praise Famous Men** (p. 1064) James Agee	• *Graphic Organizers for Active Reading,* Worksheet p. 106	• *Words to Own,* Worksheet p. 55 • *Daily Oral Grammar,* Transparency 61

Other Resources for this Collection

- *Cross-Curricular Activities*, p. 19
- *Portfolio Management System*, Introduction to Portfolio Assessment, p. 1
- *Test Generator*, Collection Test ⊚

Writing	Listening and Speaking Viewing and Representing	Assessment
• *Portfolio Management System*, Rubrics for Choices, p. 209	• *Audio CD Library*, Disc 25, Track 2 🎧 • *Viewing and Representing:* Fine Art Transparency 19 📠 Worksheet p. 76 • *Portfolio Management System*, Rubrics for Choices, p. 209	• *Formal Assessment*, Selection Test, p. 195 • *Test Generator (One-Stop Planner CD-ROM)* ⊚
• *Portfolio Management System*, Rubrics for Choices, p. 210	• *Audio CD Library*, Disc 25, Tracks 3, 4 🎧 • *Portfolio Management System*, Rubrics for Choices, p. 210	• *Formal Assessment*, Selection Test, p. 197 • *Test Generator (One-Stop Planner CD-ROM)* ⊚
• *Portfolio Management System*, Rubrics for Choices, p. 211	• *Audio CD Library*, Disc 25, Tracks 5, 6 🎧 • *Portfolio Management System*, Rubrics for Choices, p. 211	• *Formal Assessment*, Selection Test, p. 197 • *Test Generator (One-Stop Planner CD-ROM)* ⊚
• *Portfolio Management System*, Rubrics for Choices, p. 212	• *Audio CD Library*, Disc 25, Track 7 🎧 • *Portfolio Management System*, Rubrics for Choices, p. 212	• *Formal Assessment*, Selection Test, p. 199 • *Test Generator (One-Stop Planner CD-ROM)* ⊚
• *Portfolio Management System*, Rubrics for Choices, p. 213	• *Audio CD Library*, Disc 26, Track 2 🎧 • *Portfolio Management System*, Rubrics for Choices, p. 213	• *Formal Assessment*, Selection Test, p. 200 • *Test Generator (One-Stop Planner CD-ROM)* ⊚
• *Portfolio Management System*, Rubrics for Choices, p. 214	• *Audio CD Library*, Disc 26, Track 3 🎧 • *Portfolio Management System*, Rubrics for Choices, p. 214	• *Formal Assessment*, Selection Test, p. 202 • *Test Generator (One-Stop Planner CD-ROM)* ⊚
• *Portfolio Management System*, Rubrics for Choices, p. 215	• *Audio CD Library*, Disc 26, Track 4 🎧 • *Portfolio Management System*, Rubrics for Choices, p. 215	• *Formal Assessment*, Selection Test, p. 204 • *Test Generator (One-Stop Planner CD-ROM)* ⊚
• *Portfolio Management System*, Rubrics for Choices, p. 216	• *Audio CD Library*, Disc 26, Track 5 🎧 • *Portfolio Management System*, Rubrics for Choices, p. 216	• *Formal Assessment*, Selection Test, p. 204 • *Test Generator (One-Stop Planner CD-ROM)* ⊚
• *Portfolio Management System*, Rubrics for Choices, p. 218	• *Audio CD Library*, Disc 27, Track 2 🎧 • *Portfolio Management System*, Rubrics for Choices, p. 218	• *Formal Assessment*, Selection Test, p. 206 • *Test Generator (One-Stop Planner CD-ROM)* ⊚ • *Preparation for College Admission Exams*, p. 63
• *Portfolio Management System*, Rubrics for Choices, p. 219	• *Audio CD Library*, Disc 27, Track 3 🎧 • *Portfolio Management System*, Rubrics for Choices, p. 219	• *Formal Assessment*, Selection Test, p. 208 • *Test Generator (One-Stop Planner CD-ROM)* ⊚ • *Preparation for College Admission Exams*, p. 65

 Transparency    CD-ROM   Video    Audio CD

Collection Planner

Collection 19 Discoveries and Awakenings
Skills Focus

Skills Focus

Selection or Feature	Reading Skills and Strategies	Elements of Literature and Language	Writing	Listening and Speaking	Viewing and Representing
The Magic Barrel (p. 981) Bernard Malamud	Summarize, p. 994	Character, pp. 981, 994 Protagonist, p. 994 Paradox, p. 994 Plot, p. 994 Theme, p. 994	Identify Criteria for Skillful Characterization, and Evaluate Two Characters, p. 994 Write an Essay Responding to a Critical Comment, p. 994	Prepare and Tell an Extension of the Story, p. 994	
Literature of the Americas: Colombia **The Handsomest Drowned Man in the World** (p. 996) Gabriel García Márquez	Dialogue with the Text, pp. 996, 1000	Magic Realism, p. 996 Myth, p. 996 Legend, p. 996 Folk Tale, p. 996	The Literature of the Americas feature offers selections from a variety of American cultures representing North, Central, and South America. These selections connect to the collection theme, and students explore the thematic links through structured group discussions called Finding Common Ground.		
• **Elegy for Jane** (p. 1002) • **Night Journey** (p. 1003) Theodore Roethke		Simile, p. 1002 Metaphor, p. 1002 Personification, p. 1002 Elegy, p. 1004 Image, p. 1004 Rhythm, p. 1004 Tone, p. 1004 Mood, p. 1004	Make an Informal Outline for an Evaluation of a Poem, p. 1004 Write an Essay Comparing and Contrasting Two Poems by Different Authors, p. 1004		Evaluate the Appropriateness of a Painting to Illustrate a Poem, p. 1004 Draw or Paint the Landscape of a Poem, p. 1004
• **The Beautiful Changes** (p. 1006) • **Boy at the Window** (p. 1007) Richard Wilbur	Paraphrase a Stanza of a Poem, p. 1008	Ambiguity, pp. 1006, 1008 Personify, pp. 1007, 1008 Title, p. 1008 Allusion, p. 1008 Lyric Poems, p. 1008	Establish Criteria for an Effective Lyric Poem, and Make an Evaluation, p. 1008 Write an Essay in Response to an Author's Comment, p. 1008 Write an Essay Explaining the "motive for metaphor," p. 1008		
Auto Wreck (p. 1010) Karl Shapiro	Summarize, p. 1011	Synesthesia, p. 1010 Image, p. 1010	Agree or Disagree with a Critical Assessment of an Author, p. 1011 Write About a Disaster, p. 1011		
from **Black Boy** (p. 1013) Richard Wright	Interpret Details, pp. 1013, 1025	Dialogue, p. 1013 Image, p. 1025 Character, p. 1025	Identify Key Passages that Support an Opinion, p. 1025 Write an Essay Analyzing a Character, p. 1025	Present an Oral Reading of a Passage, p. 1025	
Everything Stuck to Him (p. 1027) Raymond Carver	Learning Through Questioning, p. 1027	Style, pp. 1027, 1033 Setting, p. 1033 Character, p. 1033 Frame Story, p. 1033 Inner Story, p. 1033 Conflict, p. 1033 Theme, p. 1033 Understatement, p. 1033	Write an Essay Stating and Defending an Opinion, p. 1033 Write a Monologue from the Point of View of a Character, p. 1033	Interview Class Members and Record Their Opinions, p. 1033	
The Fish (p. 1035) Elizabeth Bishop	Make Predictions, pp. 1035, 1038	Figures of Speech, pp. 1035, 1038 Symbol, p. 1038 Theme, p. 1038 Image, p. 1038	Identify Common Elements in Stories, p. 1038 Write an Essay Identifying a Critical Moment, p. 1038 Write a Short Poem from the Fish's Point of View, p. 1038		
Remember (p. 1040) Joy Harjo		Speaker, p. 1042 Theme, p. 1042 Personification, p. 1042 Refrain, p. 1042	Identify Related Experiences, p. 1042 Compare and Contrast Texts, p. 1042 Write a "Remember" Poem, p. 1042	Prepare and Present an Oral Interpretation of the Poem, p. 1042	
The Girl Who Wouldn't Talk *from* **The Woman Warrior** (p. 1044) Maxine Hong Kingston	Draw Inferences About Characters, p. 1044	Conflict, pp. 1044, 1053 Title, p. 1053 Image, p. 1053 Tone, p. 1053 Character, p. 1053	Evaluate Imagery, p. 1053 Write an Essay Discussing the Character of the Narrator, p. 1053 Write a Story Explaining Unexplained Events, p. 1053		
from **Blue Highways** (p. 1054) William Least Heat-Moon	Analyze Metaphors, p. 1066	Dialect, pp. 1055, 1066 Character, p. 1066 Image, p. 1066 Expressions, p. 1066 Proverbs, p. 1066 Grammar, p. 1066 Tone, p. 1066 Style, p. 1066	Compare and Contrast Texts, p. 1066 Write an Essay Describing Your Neighborhood or Community, p. 1066 Write an Essay About Place Names in Your State, p. 1066		Use a Map, p. 1066

Pine Tree Tops

In the blue night
frost haze, the sky glows
with the moon
pine tree tops
bend snow-blue, fade
into sky, frost, starlight.
The creak of boots.
Rabbit tracks, deer tracks,
what do we know.

—Gary Snyder (1930–   )

Responding to the Poem

Gary Snyder is one of the Beat poets, who first made their mark in the 1950s. A student of Zen Buddhism, he has been influenced by Chinese and Japanese poetry and is a respected environmentalist.

Ask more than one volunteer to read the poem aloud. Encourage them to read it slowly to allow its images time to make an impact. Ask students to discuss what the poem describes. Ask what kinds of things the speaker discovers. What does the scene awaken in him? [The speaker discovers the color of the night sky, the presence of frost, the glow of the moon, the moonlight on the snow-covered pine tree, starlight, the sound of boots in the snow, and the tracks of animals. It awakens in him a new sense of humility, possibility, and wonder.]

Writing Focus: Evaluation

The following **Work in Progress** assignments in this collection build to a culminating **Writer's Workshop** at the end of Collection 21.

• The Magic Barrel	Create a chart to evaluate characters (p. 994)
• Elegy for Jane; Night Journey	Make an informal outline (p. 1004)
• The Beautiful Changes; Boy at the Window	List criteria for a good lyric poem (p. 1008)
• Auto Wreck	Write thoughts on poem's tone (p. 1011)
• Black Boy	Note two details to support an evaluation (p. 1025)
• Everything Stuck to Him	Interview other readers for their opinions (p. 1033)
• The Fish	Compare poem to another work (p. 1038)
• Remember	Note personal experiences that support an evaluation (p. 1042)
• The Girl Who Wouldn't Talk	Evaluate the use of imagery (p. 1053)
• Blue Highways	Use a chart to compare works (p. 1066)

Writer's Workshop: Persuasive Writing / Evaluation (p. 1181)

OBJECTIVES

1. Read and interpret the story
2. Identify static and dynamic characters
3. Express understanding through critical and creative writing
4. Demonstrate an understanding of new words

SKILLS

Literary
- Identify static and dynamic characters

Writing
- Collect ideas for an evaluation
- Interpret a story
- Write dialogue

Vocabulary
- Use new words

Viewing/Representing
- Create a character profile for the subject of a portrait (ATE)
- Express opinions about the figures in a painting (ATE)
- Compare the subject of a painting with a character in a story (ATE)

Planning

- **Block Schedule**
  Block Scheduling with Pacing Guide

- **Traditional Schedule**
  Lesson Plans Including Strategies for English-Language Learners

- **One-Stop Planner**
  CD-ROM with Test Generator

Bernard Malamud

(1914–1986)

© Nancy Crampton.

Bernard Malamud is a principal figure in the group of Jewish writers whose work has enriched contemporary American literature. Yet Malamud preferred not to be easily pigeonholed. He did write *about* Jews, but he wrote *for* all people.

Malamud's characters usually live at a level of bare physical subsistence. Though we may feel compassion for them, they do not display the least self-pity. If their plight is sad, it is also triumphant, because they survive in heroic fashion against the odds all humans face.

"As you are grooved, so you are grieved," Malamud once wrote as preamble to an account of his own bleak upbringing. He was the older of two sons of a Russian immigrant storekeeper. His mother died when he was fourteen. He grew up in Brooklyn in a household without books, music, or pictures on the walls. During the Great Depression, he worked at a census office and a yarn factory to help support his family, but he felt these experiences were important to him as a writer. Getting down to essential needs and "turning inward," Malamud believed, are the best preparation for writing.

It was the suffering of European Jews during World War II that convinced Malamud he had something to say as a writer. "I for one believe that not enough has been made of the tragedy of the destruction of six million Jews," he said. "Somebody has to cry—even if it's just a writer, twenty years later."

Malamud's unique drama is spun out of the commonplace, the tragicomedy of survival in a brutal world. But his stories are always informed by love, and, indeed, his characters are largely redeemed by love. Philip Roth, whose own notable writing covers some of the same ground as Malamud's, wrote the following analysis:

"Malamud wrote of a meager world of pain in a language all his own. [It was] an English that often appeared, even outside the idiosyncratic dialogue, to have in large part been clipped together from out of what one might have thought to be the least promising stockpile, most unmagical barrel, around: the locutions, inversions, and diction of Jewish immigrant speech, a heap of broken verbal bones that looked, until he came along in those early stories to make them dance to his sad tune, to be of no use to anyone any longer other than the Borscht Belt comic and the professional nostalgia-monger."

Malamud taught English in New York City high schools and fiction at Oregon State University and Bennington College in Vermont. His first novel, *The Natural* (1952), whose central character is a baseball player, was made into a popular film in 1984. His other books include *The Assistant* (1957), a novel set in Brooklyn, considered by some critics to be his best work; the short-story collections *The Magic Barrel* (1958; National Book Award) and *Idiots First* (1963); and the novels *The Fixer* (1966; National Book Award and Pulitzer Prize), set in czarist Russia, and *The Tenants* (1971).

Malamud was a firm believer in the power of story. "The story will be with us as long as man is," he once said. "You know that, in part because of its effect on children. It's through story they realize that mystery won't kill them. Through story they learn they have a future."

(HRW) go.hrw.com
LE0 11-19

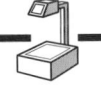

Resources: Print and Media

Reading
- *Graphic Organizers for Active Reading,* p. 97
- *Words to Own,* p. 51
- *Audio CD Library*
  Disc 25, Track 2

Elements of Literature
- *Literary Elements*
  Transparency 30
  Worksheet, p. 91

Writing and Language
- *Daily Oral Grammar*
  Transparency 56
- *Grammar and Language Links*
  Worksheet 73
- *Language Workshop CD-ROM*

Viewing and Representing
- *Viewing and Representing*
  Fine Art Transparency 19
  Fine Art Worksheet, p. 76

Assessment
- *Formal Assessment,* p. 195
- *Portfolio Management System,* p. 209
- *Test Generator (One-Stop Planner CD-ROM)*

Internet
- go.hrw.com (keyword: LE0 11-19)

Before You Read
THE MAGIC BARREL

Make the Connection
"When I fall in love . . ."
"Unbelievable!" "You're kidding!"
Many of us react with exclamations like these when we hear of two seemingly mismatched people falling in love. After all, what do they have in common? A great deal, apparently. It may happen to friends or people in our families, to a famous actress who marries a quiet intellectual, to a king who gives up his throne for a commoner—to ourselves, even. Suddenly, deep emotional connections are made between people who, on the surface, inhabit different worlds.

Quickwrite
Why do people fall in love? Poets, philosophers, playwrights, and just about everybody else have been offering answers to that question for thousands of years. Yet we are still not sure about the answer. Is love purely emotional? Does it involve the mind as well as the heart? Write down some of your ideas on the subject.

Elements of Literature
Static and Dynamic Characters
A **static character** does not change much over the course of a story. A **dynamic character,** on the other hand, changes in an important way as the story unfolds. As you read, ask yourself: Which type of character is Leo Finkle? Which type is Pinye Salzman?

> **A** **static character** does not change much over the course of a story. A **dynamic character** changes in an important way as a result of the story's action.
>
> For more on Character, see the Handbook of Literary Terms.

Phyllis Seated (1952) by Moses Soyer. Oil on canvas (42″ × 36″).

Courtesy ACA Galleries, NY/Munich.

BERNARD MALAMUD 981

Summary ■■

Leo Finkle, a twenty-seven-year-old rabbinical student, consults Pinye Salzman, a matchmaker, to help him find a wife. Leo is soon disappointed with Salzman's selection of prospects and with his tendency to overstate their charms. He fires Salzman, but Salzman returns, recommending Lily Hirschorn, whom Leo has already rejected as being too old. Salzman insists that Lily is only twenty-nine. When Leo meets Lily, he realizes that not only has Salzman lied about her youth, but he has given Lily a hyperbolic account of Leo's religious fervor. Under questioning by Lily, Leo confesses that he was drawn to rabbinical study out of a *lack* of love for God. Later, he realizes he has never felt love for anyone except his parents, and experiences a severe crisis of faith and purpose. Leo rejects Lily and again fires Salzman, who gives him a packet with photographs of six more prospective brides. There, Leo finds a sad but beautiful face that moves him deeply. Salzman, however, insists that the photo was included by mistake and that the woman is too wild and unsuitable. Pressed by Leo, Salzman admits that the woman is his own daughter, Stella, whom he has disowned. Finally, Salzman agrees to let Leo meet Stella. In the story's denouement, Leo meets Stella with flowers in his hand while Salzman, around the corner, chants prayers for the dead.

Preteaching Vocabulary

Words to Own
Have students read the words and definitions at the bottom of the selection pages. Then, use these questions to reinforce understanding:

1. If you were a man getting married, would you hope for a meager dowry? [Sample answer: No, I would hope the bride's family had a lot of money.]
2. Do you hope to have a traditional nuptial ceremony someday? [Sample answer: Yes, I want a big "white wedding."]
3. If someone were an ascetic, what might he or she suppress? [Sample response: his or her appetite for food.]
4. Who might you be, and what might you be doing, if you upbraided your clientele? [Sample response: You might be a doctor scolding patients who did not take their medicine.]
5. What machinations are evident in this vocabulary exercise? [Sample response: cramming two Words to Own into every question.]

Vertical credit text: The Museum of Modern Art, New York. Acquired through the Lillie P. Bliss Bequest. Photograph © 1998 The Museum of Modern Art, New York. © 1998 Artists Rights Society (ARS), New York/ADAGP, Paris.

Birthday (L'Anniversaire) (1915) by Marc Chagall. Oil on cardboard.

The Magic Barrel

Bernard Malamud

"Love comes with the right person, not before."

Reaching All Students

Struggling Readers

Use Anticipation Guides to help students make predictions. For help, see the *Reading Strategies Handbook*, p. 17 in the *Reading Skills and Strategies* binder. Possible Anticipation Guide statements: Agree or Disagree

- Choosing a marriage partner involves more than falling in love.
- People pick marriage partners that remind them of some characteristic in themselves.
- Opposites attract.

English Language Learners

The Yiddish-influenced English of the immigrant Pinye Salzman may need standardizing. Model an example, such as "You wouldn't believe me how much cards I got in my office" (p. 984). ("You wouldn't believe how many cards I've got in my office.") Help students paraphrase later examples. For additional strategies for English language learners, see

- *Lesson Plans Including Strategies for English-Language Learners*

Not long ago there lived in uptown New York, in a small, almost meager room, though crowded with books, Leo Finkle, a rabbinical student in the Yeshivah University.[1] Finkle, after six years of study, was to be ordained in June and had been advised by an acquaintance that he might find it easier to win himself a congregation if he were married. Since he had no present prospects of marriage, after two tormented days of turning it over in his mind, he called in Pinye Salzman, a marriage broker whose two-line advertisement he had read in the *Forward*.[2]

The matchmaker appeared one night out of the dark fourth-floor hallway of the graystone rooming house where Finkle lived, grasping a black, strapped portfolio that had been worn thin with use. Salzman, who had been long in the business, was of slight but dignified build, wearing an old hat, and an overcoat too short and tight for him. He smelled frankly of fish, which he loved to eat, and although he was missing a few teeth, his presence was not displeasing, because of an amiable manner curiously contrasted with mournful eyes. His voice, his lips, his wisp of beard, his bony fingers were animated, but give him a moment of repose and his mild blue eyes revealed a depth of sadness, a characteristic that put Leo a little at ease although the situation, for him, was inherently tense.

He at once informed Salzman why he had asked him to come, explaining that his home was in Cleveland, and that but for his parents, who had married comparatively late in life, he was alone in the world. He had for six years devoted himself almost entirely to his studies, as a result of which, understandably, he had found himself without time for a social life and the company of young women. Therefore he thought it the better part of trial and error—of embarrassing fumbling—to call in an experienced person to advise him on these matters. He remarked in passing that the function of the marriage broker was ancient and honorable, highly approved in the Jewish community, because it made practical the necessary without hindering joy. Moreover, his own parents had been brought together by a matchmaker. They had made, if not a financially profitable marriage—since neither had possessed any worldly goods to speak of—at least a successful one in the sense of their everlasting devotion to each other. Salzman listened in embarrassed surprise, sensing a sort of apology. Later, however, he experienced a glow of pride in his work, an emotion that had left him years ago, and he heartily approved of Finkle.

The two went to their business. Leo had led Salzman to the only clear place in the room, a table near a window that overlooked the lamp-lit city. He seated himself at the matchmaker's side but facing him, attempting by an act of will to suppress the unpleasant tickle in his throat. Salzman eagerly unstrapped his portfolio and removed a loose rubber band from a thin packet of much-handled cards. As he flipped through them, a gesture and sound that physically hurt Leo, the student pretended not to see and gazed steadfastly out the window. Although it was still February, winter was on its last legs, signs of which he had for the first time in years begun to notice. He now observed the round white moon, moving high in the sky through a cloud menagerie, and watched with half-open mouth as it penetrated a huge hen, and dropped out of her like an egg laying itself. Salzman, though pretending through eyeglasses he had just slipped on, to be engaged in scanning the writing on the cards, stole occasional glances at the young man's distinguished face, noting with pleasure the long, severe scholar's nose, brown eyes heavy with learning, sensitive yet ascetic lips, and a certain, almost hollow quality of the dark cheeks. He gazed around at shelves upon shelves of books and let out a soft, contented sigh.

When Leo's eyes fell upon the cards, he counted six spread out in Salzman's hand.

WORDS TO OWN

meager (mē′gər) *adj.:* poor; inadequate.
suppress (sə·pres′) *v.:* to restrain; to hold back.
ascetic (ə·set′ik) *adj.:* severe; stern.

---

1. **Yeshivah** (ye·shē′və) **University:** prominent New York City school serving both as a general college and as a seminary for Orthodox Jewish rabbis.
2. *Forward:* formerly the *Jewish Daily Forward*, a newspaper published in New York City.

Ⓐ Historical Connections

This story was published in 1954. "Not long ago" probably refers to the post–World War II period after 1945, a time of sorrow for Jews mourning the colossal tragedy of the Holocaust. However, the vague phrase "Not long ago" also implies a timeless folkloric setting, similar to that evoked by the words "Once upon a time."

Ⓑ Elements of Literature

Static and Dynamic Characters

Ask students to describe Leo Finkle and Pinye Salzman based on the detailed information on this page. As students read on, have them use graphic organizers like the following to note change, or lack of it, in the appearance, thoughts, actions, and words of the characters as the story progresses.

Finkle

	Beginning	Middle	End
Appearance			
Thoughts			
Actions			
Words			

Salzman

	Beginning	Middle	End
Appearance			
Thoughts			
Actions			
Words			

Ⓒ Elements of Literature

Static and Dynamic Characters

❓ What do Finkle's thoughts reveal about him? [Possible responses: He is highly imaginative; he is sensitive to nature.] What traits does Salzman see in Finkle? [Possible responses: Salzman feels the student is distinguished, scholarly, sensitive, and disciplined.]

Reaching All Students

Advanced Learners

Malamud achieves a highly personal style by mixing lyrical descriptions, richly idiosyncratic dialogue, and unexpected juxtapositions and images. Ask students to locate passages of the following kinds: (1) where description builds characterization, (2) where dialogue builds characterization, (3) where character is revealed in unlikely ways or in an unlikely setting. [Possible responses: (1) Description builds characterization in the introductory descriptions of Leo and Salzman on p. 983; (2) dialogue builds characterization on p. 984, where Leo and Salzman spar verbally over prospective matches; (3) the unlikely image of Salzman as Pan on p. 987 richly evokes his character.] Ask students to share favorite examples with the class.

"So few?" he asked in disappointment.

"You wouldn't believe me how much cards I got in my office," Salzman replied. "The drawers are already filled to the top, so I keep them now in a barrel, but is every girl good for a new rabbi?"

Leo blushed at this, regretting all he had revealed of himself in a curriculum vitae[3] he had sent to Salzman. He had thought it best to acquaint him with his strict standards and specifications, but in having done so, felt he had told the marriage broker more than was absolutely necessary.

He hesitantly inquired, "Do you keep photographs of your clients on file?"

"First comes family, amount of <u>dowry</u>, also what kind promises," Salzman replied, unbuttoning his tight coat and settling himself in the chair. "After comes pictures, rabbi."

"Call me Mr. Finkle. I'm not yet a rabbi."

Salzman said he would, but instead called him doctor, which he changed to rabbi when Leo was not listening too attentively.

Salzman adjusted his horn-rimmed spectacles, gently cleared his throat and read in an eager voice the contents of the top card:

"Sophie P. Twenty four year. Widow one year. No children. Educated high school and two years college. Father promises eight thousand dollars. Has wonderful wholesale business. Also real estate. On the mother's side comes teachers, also one actor. Well known on Second Avenue."

Leo gazed up in surprise. "Did you say a widow?"

"A widow don't mean spoiled, rabbi. She lived with her husband maybe four months. He was a sick boy she made a mistake to marry him."

"Marrying a widow has never entered my mind."

"This is because you have no experience. A widow, especially if she is young and healthy like this girl, is a wonderful person to marry. She will be thankful to you the rest of her life. Believe me, if I was looking now for a bride, I would marry a widow."

Leo reflected, then shook his head.

3. *curriculum vitae* (kə·rik′yōō·ləm vīt′ē): Latin for "course of life"; that is, a résumé or summary of one's career and qualifications.

Salzman hunched his shoulders in an almost imperceptible gesture of disappointment. He placed the card down on the wooden table and began to read another:

"Lily H. High school teacher. Regular. Not a substitute. Has savings and new Dodge car. Lived in Paris one year. Father is successful dentist thirty-five years. Interested in professional man. Well Americanized family. Wonderful opportunity.

"I knew her personally," said Salzman. "I wish you could see this girl. She is a doll. Also very intelligent. All day you could talk to her about books and theyater and what not. She also knows current events."

"I don't believe you mentioned her age?"

"Her age?" Salzman said, raising his brows. "Her age is thirty-two years."

Leo said after a while, "I'm afraid that seems a little too old."

Salzman let out a laugh. "So how old are you, rabbi?"

"Twenty-seven."

"So what is the difference, tell me, between twenty-seven and thirty-two? My own wife is seven years older than me. So what did I suffer?—Nothing. If a Rothschild's[4] daughter wants to marry you, would you say on account her age, no?"

"Yes," Leo said dryly.

Salzman shook off the no in the yes. "Five years don't mean a thing. I give you my word that when you will live with her for one week you will forget her age. What does it mean five years—that she lived more and knows more than somebody who is younger? On this girl, God bless her, years are not wasted. Each one that it comes makes better the bargain."

"What subject does she teach in high school?"

"Languages. If you heard the way she speaks French, you will think it is music. I am in the business twenty-five years, and I recommend her

4. **Rothschild's:** The Rothschilds are a wealthy banking family.

WORDS TO OWN

dowry (dou′rē) *n.:* money or goods a bride brings with her in a marriage.

Making the Connections

Cultural Connections: Wedding Customs

Courtship and betrothal customs vary, although there are patterns that recur in widely diverse cultures. For example, matchmaking for a young couple who have never seen each other was (and to some extent is still) practiced not only in many Jewish cultures, but also in Chinese, Indian, African, Arab, and Japanese cultures. Payment by one family to the other upon mar-

riage is widespread in traditional cultures around the world.

Ask students the following questions:

1. What courtship and marriage customs are common in cultures you know personally?

2. What might be the advantages and disadvantages of an arranged marriage?

3. What might be the advantages and disadvantages of marrying independently for love?

with my whole heart. Believe me, I know what I'm talking, rabbi."

"What's on the next card?" Leo said abruptly.

Salzman reluctantly turned up the third card:

"Ruth K. Nineteen years. Honor student. Father offers thirteen thousand cash to the right bridegroom. He is a medical doctor. Stomach specialist with marvelous practice. Brother-in-law owns own garment business. Particular people."

Salzman looked as if he had read his trump card.

"Did you say nineteen?" Leo asked with interest.

"On the dot."

"Is she attractive?" He blushed. "Pretty?"

Salzman kissed his finger tips. "A little doll. On this I give you my word. Let me call the father tonight and you will see what means pretty."

But Leo was troubled. "You're sure she's that young?"

"This I am positive. The father will show you the birth certificate."

"Are you positive there isn't something wrong with her?" Leo insisted.

"Who says there is wrong?"

"I don't understand why an American girl her age should go to a marriage broker."

A smile spread over Salzman's face.

"So for the same reason you went, she comes."

Leo flushed. "I am pressed for time."

Salzman, realizing he had been tactless, quickly explained. "The father came, not her. He wants she should have the best, so he looks around himself. When we will locate the right boy he will introduce him and encourage. This makes a better marriage than if a young girl without experience takes for herself. I don't have to tell you this."

"But don't you think this young girl believes in love?" Leo spoke uneasily.

Salzman was about to guffaw but caught himself and said soberly, "Love comes with the right person, not before."

Leo parted dry lips but did not speak. Noticing that Salzman had snatched a glance at the next card, he cleverly asked, "How is her health?"

"Perfect," Salzman said, breathing with diffi-

culty. "Of course, she is a little lame on her right foot from an auto accident that it happened to her when she was twelve years, but nobody notices on account she is so brilliant and also beautiful."

Leo got up heavily and went to the window. He felt curiously bitter and upbraided himself for having called in the marriage broker. Finally, he shook his head.

"Why not?" Salzman persisted, the pitch of his voice rising.

"Because I detest stomach specialists."

"So what do you care what is his business? After you marry her do you need him? Who says he must come every Friday night in your house?"

Ashamed of the way the talk was going, Leo dismissed Salzman, who went home with heavy, melancholy eyes.

Though he had felt only relief at the marriage broker's departure, Leo was in low spirits the next day. He explained it as arising from Salzman's failure to produce a suitable bride for him. He did not care for his type of clientele. But when Leo found himself hesitating whether to seek out another matchmaker, one more polished than Pinye, he wondered if it could be—his protestations to the contrary, and although he honored his father and mother—that he did not, in essence, care for the matchmaking institution? This thought he quickly put out of mind yet found himself still upset. All day he ran around in the woods—missed an important appointment, forgot to give out his laundry, walked out of a Broadway cafeteria without paying and had to run back with the ticket in his hand; had even not recognized his landlady in the street when she passed with a friend and courteously called out, "A good evening to you, Doctor Finkle." By nightfall, however, he had regained sufficient calm to sink his nose into a book and there found peace from his thoughts.

Almost at once there came a knock on the door. Before Leo could say enter, Salzman, commercial cupid, was standing in the room. His face was gray and meager, his expression hungry, and

---

WORDS TO OWN

upbraided (up·brād'id) v.: severely criticized.
clientele (klī'ən·tel') n.: customers.

G English Language Learners
Understanding Dialect
❓ How would you say, "I know what I'm talking" in standard English? ["I know what I'm talking about."]

H Critical Thinking
Interpreting
❓ Why does Leo think that a young American girl would not go to a matchmaker? [Possible answers: She would want to marry for love, and would already be able to choose from a variety of suitors.]

I Elements of Literature
Static and Dynamic Characters
❓ What does this question reveal about Finkle's character? How is he conflicted? What does Salzman's response reveal about his character? [Possible response: Finkle doubts his own ability to find or feel love and suspects anyone who, like him, must find it through a matchmaker. Salzman's view of love is much more stable and static—he believes it must come *after* one accepts a reasonable match.]

J Critical Thinking
Interpreting
❓ What does Leo really mean when he says, "Because I detest stomach specialists"? [Possible responses: He is probably implying tactfully that he doesn't want to marry a woman with a limp; he has become embarrassed and frustrated by the whole process.]

K Cultural Connections
Leo obeys the Mosaic commandment to honor one's father and mother (Exodus 20:12) and thus may feel duty-bound to find a spouse as his parents did, through a matchmaker—although he is clearly uneasy about the process.

Crossing the Curriculum

Social Studies
To help students understand the historical and cultural context of the story, assign two groups to research and make oral presentations on (1) the post–World War II history of Jewish culture in New York City, and (2) the major branches of Judaism: Orthodox, Conservative, Reform, and Hasidic. (The characters in this story are most likely Orthodox.) Each group should report on one of the topics.

Social Studies
Have students research aspects of Jewish life and history by accessing an on-line encyclopedia or database. They may also do keyword searches on the Internet. *You may want to preview any Internet activity that you suggest to students. Because these resources are often public forums, their content can be unpredictable.* If possible, invite a rabbi or Jewish scholar in to discuss Judaism and Jewish culture. If possible, video tape the session for use with other classes.

Static and Dynamic Characters

? What details suggest continuity and stasis in Salzman's character and approach to life? [Possible answers: his dialect; his intrusiveness; his upbeat promises; his flattering of Leo.]

B Cultural Connections

The Matchmaker

Tell students that the matchmaker or *shadkhen* is a stereotypical Yiddish figure who is partly comic, partly tragic, and usually teetering at the edge of destitution. The matchmaker is often a sufferer nursing a secret sorrow. Have students discuss the figure of Salzman in light of this tradition.

C Critical Thinking

Interpreting/Recognizing Humor

? What's the joke in Leo's question "Reduced from thirty-two?" [He implies that Salzman views Lily as an item of unwanted merchandise that has been marked down for a discount.]

D Reading Skills and Strategies

Understanding Motivation

? Groucho Marx was once quoted as saying he wouldn't want to belong to any club that would accept him as a member. How might this joke help explain Finkle's motivation in this passage? How does Salzman attempt to change his perspective? [Possible response: Finkle sees *his own* (and thus, Lily's) visit to Salzman as a sign of pathos and desperation and thus expects to find something wrong in her, as he finds it in himself. Salzman attempts to recast Lily (and thus Finkle) as motivated by high standards alone.]

---

he looked as if he would expire on his feet. Yet the marriage broker managed, by some trick of the muscles, to display a broad smile.

A "So good evening. I am invited?"

Leo nodded, disturbed to see him again, yet unwilling to ask the man to leave.

Beaming still, Salzman laid his portfolio on the table. "Rabbi, I got for you tonight good news."

"I've asked you not to call me rabbi. I'm still a student."

"Your worries are finished. I have for you a first-class bride."

"Leave me in peace concerning this subject." Leo pretended lack of interest.

"The world will dance at your wedding."

"Please, Mr. Salzman, no more."

B "But first must come back my strength," Salzman said weakly. He fumbled with the portfolio straps and took out of the leather case an oily paper bag, from which he extracted a hard, seeded roll and a small, smoked whitefish. With a quick motion of his hand he stripped the fish out of its skin and began ravenously to chew. "All day in a rush," he muttered.

Leo watched him eat.

"A sliced tomato you have maybe?" Salzman hesitantly inquired.

"No."

The marriage broker shut his eyes and ate. When he had finished he carefully cleaned up the crumbs and rolled up the remains of the fish, in the paper bag. His spectacled eyes roamed the room until he discovered, amid some piles of books, a one-burner gas stove. Lifting his hat he humbly asked, "A glass tea you got, rabbi?"

Conscience-striken, Leo rose and brewed the tea. He served it with a chunk of lemon and two cubes of lump sugar, delighting Salzman.

After he had drunk his tea, Salzman's strength and good spirits were restored.

"So tell me, rabbi," he said amiably, "you considered some more the three clients I mentioned yesterday?"

"There was no need to consider."

"Why not?"

"None of them suits me."

"What then suits you?"

Leo let it pass because he could give only a confused answer.

Without waiting for a reply, Salzman asked, "You remember this girl I talked to you—the high school teacher?"

"Age thirty-two?"

But, surprisingly, Salzman's face lit in a smile. "Age twenty-nine."

C Leo shot him a look. "Reduced from thirty-two?"

"A mistake," Salzman avowed. "I talked today with the dentist. He took me to his safety deposit box and showed me the birth certificate. She was twenty-nine years last August. They made her a party in the mountains where she went for her vacation. When her father spoke to me the first time I forgot to write the age and I told you thirty-two, but now I remember this was a different client, a widow."

"The same one you told me about? I thought she was twenty-four?"

"A different. Am I responsible that the world is filled with widows?"

"No, but I'm not interested in them, nor for that matter, in school teachers."

Salzman pulled his clasped hands to his breast. Looking at the ceiling he devoutly exclaimed, "Yiddishe kinder,[5] what can I say to somebody that he is not interested in high school teachers? So what then you are interested?"

Leo flushed but controlled himself.

"In what else will you be interested," Salzman went on, "if you not interested in this fine girl that she speaks four languages and has personally in the bank ten thousand dollars? Also her father guarantees further twelve thousand. Also she has a new car, wonderful clothes, talks on all subjects, and she will give you a first-class home and children. How near do we come in our life to paradise?"

D "If she's so wonderful, why wasn't she married ten years ago?"

"Why?" said Salzman with a heavy laugh. "—Why? Because she is *partikiler*. This is why. She wants the *best*."

Leo was silent, amused at how he had entangled himself. But Salzman had aroused his interest in Lily H., and he began seriously to consider

5. Yiddishe kinder: Yiddish for "Jewish children."

Getting Students Involved

Cooperative Learning

Duologue. To help students understand the conflict between the main characters, pair students, having one in each pair role-play Leo and the other role-play Salzman. Have "Leo" ask "Salzman" for advice based upon a conflict in the story. Have "Salzman" offer counsel. Then, have the students switch roles. They should

then complete the following statements for each character.

My problem is _____.

I was advised to _____.

I will/won't take the advice because

_____.

Enrichment Activity

Writing Film Scripts. Have groups create film scripts for the story, with each student writing one scene—for example, the scene in which Leo and Salzman meet or the scene in which Leo and Lily talk. Have groups enact and, if possible, videotape their scenes.

calling on her. When the marriage broker observed how intently Leo's mind was at work on the facts he had supplied, he felt certain they would soon come to an agreement.

Late Saturday afternoon, conscious of Salzman, Leo Finkle walked with Lily Hirschorn along Riverside Drive. He walked briskly and erectly, wearing with distinction the black fedora he had that morning taken with trepidation out of the dusty hat box on his closet shelf, and the heavy black Saturday coat he had thoroughly whisked clean. Leo also owned a walking stick, a present from a distant relative, but quickly put temptation aside and did not use it. Lily, petite and not unpretty, had on something signifying the approach of spring. She was au courant,[6] animatedly, with all sorts of subjects, and he weighed her words and found her surprisingly sound—score another for Salzman, whom he uneasily sensed to be somewhere around, hiding perhaps high in a tree along the street, flashing the lady signals with a pocket mirror; or perhaps a cloven-hoofed Pan,[7] piping nuptial ditties as he danced his invisible way before them, strewing wild buds on the walk and purple grapes in their path, symbolizing fruit of a union, though there was of course still none.

Lily startled Leo by remarking, "I was thinking of Mr. Salzman, a curious figure, wouldn't you say?"

Not certain what to answer, he nodded.

She bravely went on, blushing, "I for one am grateful for his introducing us. Aren't you?"

He courteously replied, "I am."

"I mean," she said with a little laugh—and it was all in good taste, or at least gave the effect of being not in bad—"do you mind that we came together so?"

He was not displeased with her honesty, recognizing that she meant to set the relationship aright, and understanding that it took a certain amount of experience in life, and courage, to want to do it quite that way. One had to have some sort of past to make that kind of beginning.

He said that he did not mind. Salzman's function was traditional and honorable—valuable for what it might achieve, which, he pointed out, was frequently nothing.

Lily agreed with a sigh. They walked on for a while and she said after a long silence, again with a nervous laugh, "Would you mind if I asked you something a little bit personal? Frankly, I find the subject fascinating." Although Leo shrugged, she went on half embarrassedly, "How was it that you came to your calling? I mean was it a sudden passionate inspiration?"

Leo, after a time, slowly replied, "I was always interested in the Law."[8]

"You saw revealed in it the presence of the Highest?"

He nodded and changed the subject. "I understand that you spent a little time in Paris, Miss Hirschorn?"

"Oh, did Mr. Salzman tell you, Rabbi Finkle?" Leo winced but she went on, "It was ages ago and almost forgotten. I remember I had to return for my sister's wedding."

And Lily would not be put off. "When," she asked in a trembly voice, "did you become enamored of God?"

He stared at her. Then it came to him that she was talking not about Leo Finkle, but of a total stranger, some mystical figure, perhaps even passionate prophet that Salzman had dreamed up for her—no relation to the living or dead. Leo trembled with rage and weakness. The trickster had obviously sold her a bill of goods, just as he had him, who'd expected to become acquainted with a young lady of twenty-nine, only to behold, the moment he laid eyes upon her strained

---

8. Law: first five books of the Bible, the most sacred texts of Judaism. These books are also called the Torah or the Five Books of Moses.

WORDS TO OWN

nuptial (nup′shəl) adj.: related to weddings or marriage.

traditional (trə·dish′ə·nel) adj.: established; customary.

---

6. au courant (ō kōō·rän′): French for "in the current," that is, up-to-date on news or events.
7. Pan: in Greek mythology, a god associated with forests, pastures, flocks, and shepherds. Pan is usually pictured as having the legs, horns, and ears of a goat, and the head and upper body of a man. He plays music on reed pipes.

BERNARD MALAMUD **987**

E Critical Thinking
Determining Author's Purpose
❓ What is Malamud's purpose in having Leo suspect that Salzman is up in a tree watching him or having Leo imagine that Salzman is Pan? [Possible response: Malamud is emphasizing Salzman's role as a magical trickster, who may or may not be pulling the wool over Finkle's eyes from the start.]

F Elements of Literature
Static and Dynamic Characters
❓ As this line indicates, Lily has arrived at a point where she chooses to speak her feelings honestly, without games or distortions. What does this suggest about her? Can the same be said of Finkle? If not, do you think he will change or remain static? [Possible responses: It suggests that Lily is mature, self-confident, and is not, like Finkle, dominated by insecurity and pride. She has suffered in love, while Finkle isn't sure that he *can* love. Most students will predict that something will shock this dynamic character out of his emotional retreat.]

G Struggling Readers
Using Context Clues
Have students use the religious context of this dialogue and the capitalization of the term "the Highest" in order to guess its meaning. [God]

H Critical Thinking
Interpreting
❓ What uncomfortable realization has just struck Leo? [Salzman has treated him as merchandise to be sold to a customer through trickery, the same way Salzman presented Lily to Leo.]

Using Students' Strengths

Musical/Auditory Learners
Playing the audio recording of this story will greatly help students hear the characters' personalities and cultural context in a way that reveals Malamud's humor and compassion. This additional sensory input should also help students grasp the content of dialect passages. See *Audio CD Library*, Disc 25, Track 2.

Kinesthetic Learners
Suggest that pairs of students act out a scene between Leo and Salzman, using the author's descriptions of movements and gestures. In addition, encourage students to add movements and gestures in keeping with their understanding of the characters and the situation.

A Advanced Learners
Making Judgments

? Should Leo's modest disclaimer of religious gifts be taken at face value, or is he a potentially gifted religious person who might someday become a good rabbi? [Possible responses: The mature insight he expresses in this paragraph seems like that of someone capable of religious leadership. On the other hand, he may know his own limitations.]

B Critical Thinking
Interpreting

? How would you intepret Leo's vision of the winged loaves? [Possible responses: This surreal image is similar to Leo's vision of Salzman as Pan; the bread with wings might symbolize Leo's elusive hopes for a bride, his longing for the bounty of love.]

C Cultural Connections
The Pentateuch

By the "Five Books," Leo refers to the first five books of the Hebrew Bible, also called the Pentateuch, the Torah, or the Law. These five books are usually ascribed to Moses, and thus seen as records of the original revelation from God on Mt. Sinai.

D Elements of Literature
Static and Dynamic Characters

? What important change occurs in Leo's character at this point? [Possible responses: He matures as a result of his conversation with Lily and his awareness that he had never loved God because he had never loved anyone except his parents; he comes to glimpse the possibility of real love and personal autonomy.]

E Appreciating Language
Archaisms

Withal, a word often seen in Shakespeare, is rarely used by contemporary American writers. It means "besides," "in addition," or "nevertheless."

---

and anxious face, a woman past thirty-five and aging rapidly. Only his self-control had kept him this long in her presence.

"I am not," he said gravely, "a talented religious person," and in seeking words to go on, found himself possessed by shame and fear. "I think," he said in a strained manner, "that I came to God not because I loved Him, but because I did not."

This confession he spoke harshly because its unexpectedness shook him.

Lily wilted. Leo saw a profusion of loaves of bread go flying like ducks high over his head, not unlike the winged loaves by which he had counted himself to sleep last night. Mercifully, then, it snowed, which he would not put past Salzman's <u>machinations</u>.

He was infuriated with the marriage broker and swore he would throw him out of the room the minute he reappeared. But Salzman did not come that night, and when Leo's anger had subsided, an unaccountable despair grew in its place. At first he thought this was caused by his disappointment in Lily, but before long it became <u>evident</u> that he had involved himself with Salzman without a true knowledge of his own intent. He gradually realized—with an emptiness that seized him with six hands—that he had called in the broker to find him a bride because he was incapable of doing it himself. This terrifying insight he had derived as a result of his meeting and conversation with Lily Hirschorn. Her probing questions had somehow irritated him into revealing—to himself more than her—the true nature of his relationship to God, and from that it had come upon him, with shocking force, that apart from his parents, he had never loved anyone. Or perhaps it went the other way, that he did not love God so well as he might, because he had not loved man. It seemed to Leo that his whole life stood starkly revealed and he saw himself for the first time as he truly was—unloved and loveless. This bitter but somehow not fully unexpected revelation brought him to a point of panic, controlled only by extraordinary effort. He covered his face with his hands and cried.

The week that followed was the worst of his life. He did not eat and lost weight. His beard darkened and grew ragged. He stopped attending seminars and almost never opened a book. He seriously considered leaving the Yeshivah, although he was deeply troubled at the thought of the loss of all his years of study—saw them like pages torn from a book, strewn over the city—and at the devastating effect of this decision upon his parents. But he had lived without knowledge of himself, and never in the Five Books and all the Commentaries—mea culpa[9]—had the truth been revealed to him. He did not know where to turn, and in all this desolating loneliness there was no *to whom,* although he often thought of Lily but not once could bring himself to go downstairs and make the call. He became touchy and irritable, especially with his landlady, who asked him all manner of personal questions; on the other hand, sensing his own disagreeableness, he waylaid her on the stairs and apologized abjectly, until mortified, she ran from him. Out of this, however, he drew the consolation that he was a Jew and that a Jew suffered. But gradually, as the long and terrible week drew to a close, he regained his composure and some idea of purpose in life: to go on as planned. Although he was imperfect, the ideal was not. As for his quest of a bride, the thought of continuing afflicted him with anxiety and heartburn, yet perhaps with this new knowledge of himself he would be more successful than in the past. Perhaps love would now come to him and a bride to that love. And for this sanctified seeking who needed a Salzman?

The marriage broker, a skeleton with haunted eyes, returned that very night. He looked, withal, the picture of frustrated expectancy—as if he had steadfastly waited the week at Miss Lily Hirschorn's side for a telephone call that never came.

Casually coughing, Salzman came immediately to the point: "So how did you like her?"

9. *mea culpa* (māʹä ko͞olʹpä): Latin for "by my fault."

WORDS TO OWN
machinations (makʹə·nāʹshənz) *n. pl.*: plots; schemes.
evident (evʹə·dənt) *adj.*: clear; obvious.

---

988 CONTEMPORARY LITERATURE

Professional Notes

Critical Comment:
The Sorrow of a Generation

Mark Schechner, reviewing *The Stories of Bernard Malamud* (1983), emphasizes Malamud's attention to the "sad music of humanity": "It is a commonplace of criticism that [Malamud's characters] are ruined by circumstance, but it is less often observed that those circumstances are helped along by their own narrowness and rigidity.

"So deeply ingrained is this woe that it seems virtually biological. . . . But in the first postwar decade, it had the full sanction of the times and was well-nigh universal among Jewish writers and intellectuals. The sorrow that penetrates to the bone in Malamud was the mood of a generation of Jewish writers who had been raised on immigrant poverty and worldwide depression and brought abruptly to adulthood by the holocaust. Low spirits came as naturally to them as hunger or ambition or breath."

Readers familiar with matchmaker Pinye Salzman, however, know that Malamud's ingrained sadness is leavened by comedy. Two other great writers who were the sons of poor storekeepers and whose comedy has a pessimistic tinge are Mark Twain (p. 450) and Anton Chekhov.

The Rabbi by Marc Chagall.

Kunstmuseum, Basel. Courtesy Scala/Art Resource, N.Y. © 1998 Artists Rights Society (A.R.S.), New York/ADAGP, Paris.

BERNARD MALAMUD **989**

RESPONDING TO THE ART

Marc Chagall was born into a Hasidic Jewish family. (For a more detailed biography of Chagall, see p. T982.) In paintings such as *The Rabbi,* he calls up images from his religious and cultural heritage. These figures are often rendered with a dreamlike, almost Surrealistic style and often carry pictorial symbolism, as in the Star of David and the religious text here.

Activity. Lead students in discussing how the picture might resemble Leo Finkle and, equally important, how it might not.

Leo's anger rose and he could not refrain from chiding the matchmaker: "Why did you lie to me, Salzman?"

Salzman's pale face went dead white, the world had snowed on him.

"Did you not state that she was twenty-nine?" Leo insisted.

"I give you my word—"

"She was thirty-five, if a day. *At least* thirty-five."

"Of this don't be too sure. Her father told me—"

"Never mind. The worst of it was that you lied to her."

"How did I lie to her, tell me?"

A "You told her things about me that weren't true. You made me out to be more, consequently less than I am. She had in mind a totally different person, a sort of semi-mystical Wonder Rabbi."

"All I said, you was a religious man."

"I can imagine."

Salzman sighed. "This is my weakness that I have," he confessed. "My wife says to me I shouldn't be a salesman, but when I have two fine people that they would be wonderful to be married, I am so happy that I talk too much." He smiled wanly. "This is why Salzman is a poor man."

Leo's anger left him. "Well, Salzman, I'm afraid that's all."

The marriage broker fastened hungry eyes on him.

"You don't want any more a bride?"

"I do," said Leo, "but I have decided to seek her in a different way. I am no longer interested in an arranged marriage. To be frank, I now admit the necessity of premarital love. That is, I want to be in love with the one I marry."

"Love?" said Salzman, astounded. After a moment he remarked, "For us, our love is our life, not for the ladies. In the ghetto they—"

B "I know, I know," said Leo. "I've thought of it often. Love, I have said to myself, should be a by-product of living and worship rather than its own end. Yet for myself I find it necessary to establish the level of my need and fulfill it."

Salzman shrugged but answered, "Listen, rabbi, if you want love, this I can find for you also. I have such beautiful clients that you will love them the minute your eyes will see them."

Leo smiled unhappily. "I'm afraid you don't understand."

But Salzman hastily unstrapped his portfolio and withdrew a manila packet from it.

"Pictures," he said, quickly laying the envelope on the table.

Leo called after him to take the pictures away, but as if on the wings of the wind, Salzman had disappeared.

C March came. Leo had returned to his regular routine. Although he felt not quite himself yet—lacked energy—he was making plans for a more active social life. Of course it would cost something, but he was an expert in cutting corners; and when there were no corners left he would make circles rounder. All the while Salzman's pictures had lain on the table, gathering dust. Occasionally as Leo sat studying, or enjoying a cup of tea, his eyes fell on the manila envelope, but he never opened it.

The days went by and no social life to speak of developed with a member of the opposite sex—it was difficult, given the circumstances of his situation. One morning Leo toiled up the stairs to his room and stared out the window at the city. Although the day was bright his view of it was dark. For some time he watched the people in the street below hurrying along and then turned with a heavy heart to his little room. On the table was the packet. With a sudden relentless gesture he tore it open. For a half-hour he stood by the table in a state of excitement, examining the photographs of the ladies Salzman had included. Finally, with a deep sigh he put them down. There were six, of varying degrees of attractiveness, but look at them long enough and they all became Lily Hirschorn: all past their prime, all starved behind bright smiles, not a true personality in the lot. Life, despite their frantic yoohooings, had passed them by; they were pictures in a briefcase that stank of fish.

D After a while, however, as Leo attempted to return the photographs into the envelope, he found in it another, a snapshot of the type taken by a machine for a quarter. He gazed at it a moment and let out a cry.

Her face deeply moved him. Why, he could at first not say. It gave him the impression of youth—spring flowers, yet age—a sense of

Skill Link

Understanding Denotation and Connotation

Remind students that a word may have both a *denotative* meaning (its dictionary meaning) and *connotative* meanings (its associations and emotional overtones). Likewise, a word may have a *literal* meaning and a *figurative* meaning: The word may be used to mean exactly what it says or it can be used in an imaginative comparison, to describe something completely different from what it literally refers to. Malamud often

uses simple words in a richly connotative or figurative way, which adds emotional and thematic depth to his writing.

Activity

For each underlined word, have students state both the denotative meaning and the shades of meaning the word acquires in the story. All the passages appear on this page.

1. "the world had <u>snowed</u> on him"
2. "fastened <u>hungry</u> eyes on him"
3. "With a sudden <u>relentless</u> gesture he tore it open."
4. "Leo <u>toiled</u> up the stairs"
5. "despite their frantic <u>yoohooings</u>"

having been used to the bone, wasted; this came from the eyes, which were hauntingly familiar, yet absolutely strange. He had a vivid impression that he had met her before, but try as he might he could not place her although he could almost recall her name, as if he had read it in her own handwriting. No, this couldn't be; he would have remembered her. It was not, he affirmed, that she had an extraordinary beauty—no, though her face was attractive enough; it was that *something* about her moved him. Feature for feature, even some of the ladies of the photographs could do better; but she leaped forth to his heart—had *lived,* or wanted to—more than just wanted, perhaps regretted how she had lived—had somehow deeply suffered: It could be seen in the depths of those reluctant eyes, and from the way the light enclosed and shone from her, and within her, opening realms of possibility: This was her own. Her he desired. His head ached and eyes narrowed with the intensity of his gazing, then as if an obscure fog had blown up in the mind, he experienced fear of her and was aware that he had received an impression, somehow, of evil. He shuddered, saying softly, it is thus with us all. Leo brewed some tea in a small pot and sat sipping it without sugar, to calm himself. But before he had finished drinking, again with excitement he examined the face and found it good: good for Leo Finkle. Only such a one could understand him and help him seek whatever he was seeking. She might, perhaps, love him. How she had happened to be among the discards in Salzman's barrel he could never guess, but he knew he must urgently go find her.

Leo rushed downstairs, grabbed up the Bronx[10] telephone book, and searched for Salzman's home address. He was not listed, nor was his office. Neither was he in the Manhattan[11] book. But Leo remembered having written down the address on a slip of paper after he had read Salzman's advertisement in the "personals" column of the *Forward.* He ran up to his room and tore through his papers, without luck. It was

10. **Bronx:** borough of New York City.
11. **Manhattan:** borough of New York City, south of the Bronx.

exasperating. Just when he needed the matchmaker he was nowhere to be found. Fortunately Leo remembered to look in his wallet. There on a card he found his name written and a Bronx address. No phone number was listed, the reason—Leo now recalled—he had originally communicated with Salzman by letter. He got on his coat, put a hat on over his skullcap and hurried to the subway station. All the way to the far end of the Bronx he sat on the edge of his seat. He was more than once tempted to take out the picture and see if the girl's face was as he remembered it, but he refrained, allowing the snapshot to remain in his inside coat pocket, content to have her so close. When the train pulled into the station he was waiting at the door and bolted out. He quickly located the street Salzman had advertised.

The building he sought was less than a block from the subway, but it was not an office building, nor even a loft, nor a store in which one could rent office space. It was a very old tenement house. Leo found Salzman's name in pencil on a soiled tag under the bell and climbed three dark flights to his apartment. When he knocked, the door was opened by a thin, asthmatic, gray-haired woman, in felt slippers.

"Yes?" she said, expecting nothing. She listened without listening. He could have sworn he had seen her, too, before but knew it was an illusion.

"Salzman—does he live here? Pinye Salzman," he said, "the matchmaker?"

She stared at him a long minute. "Of course."

He felt embarrassed. "Is he in?"

"No." Her mouth, though left open, offered nothing more.

"The matter is urgent. Can you tell me where his office is?"

"In the air." She pointed upward.

"You mean he has no office?" Leo asked.

"In his socks."

He peered into the apartment. It was sunless and dingy, one large room divided by a half-open curtain, beyond which he could see a sagging metal bed. The near side of the room was crowded with rickety chairs, old bureaus, a three-legged table, racks of cooking utensils, and all the apparatus of a kitchen. But there was no

---

E. Critical Thinking
Speculating
? Based on previous events in the story, where do you think Leo might have seen the woman in the photograph or someone resembling her? [Possible responses: She might be Lily when she was younger; she might be related to Salzman.]

F. Elements of Literature
Static and Dynamic Characters
? This is a moment of dynamic change for Leo. What is he experiencing? [Possible responses: He is falling in love at first sight; he is losing his pride and insecurity and is experiencing an overwhelming emotion.] Why does he think this change is somehow evil? [Possible responses: He is afraid of the new; he has long suppressed spontaneous emotions.]

G. Critical Thinking
Making Judgments
? Does the change in Leo give him a more realistic or a less realistic view of life? Why? [Possible responses: more realistic, because he is free to seek the things he really wants; less realistic, because he has not even met this woman and is already half in love with her.]

H. Critical Thinking
Interpreting
? What does Mrs. Salzman mean when she says her husband's office is "in the air" and "in his socks"? [He has no office; his is an intangible and somewhat mysterious business.]

BROWSING IN THE FILES
About the Author. Malamud was not fond of explaining his own fiction: "I don't like questions of explication. What did I mean by this or that? I want the books to speak for themselves." Yet as an English teacher and professor of creative writing, he undoubtedly asked students to explicate many works of fiction. His reticence about his own work may have been a sign of personal modesty or a desire to allow others to have their own interpretations.

Taking a Second Look

Review:
Producing Summaries of Texts
Remind students that a summary is a short restatement of the main idea and essential details of a text. A summary of a work of fiction tells about the most important characters and events; it describes causes and effects and other connections among events. It is written in a logical order and in the summarizer's own words. A good summary helps a student remember and share a story.

Activity
1. Divide students into groups, and have each student write a one-paragraph summary of "The Magic Barrel."
2. Then, have students read their summaries aloud within their group.
3. Have groups come to a consensus on which points should be included and which points should be omitted.

A Elements of Literature

Static and Dynamic Characters

? Salzman tries to steer Leo away from the woman in the photo. Has Salzman changed, or is this just a new twist on his former salesmanlike character? [Possible responses: He is acting against his own professional interests, so a change must have come over him; he is using a new tactic, but his goal is the same—to hook Leo.]

B Cultural Connections

Traditionally, Orthodox Jews might disown (and say the prayer for the dead for) offspring who rejected their religious heritage, dishonored their parents, married a Gentile, or committed some other grave violation of the *halacha,* or traditional Jewish law.

C Elements of Literature

Static and Dynamic Characters

? The ambiguity of Salzman's motives is deliberate on the author's part. Did Salzman leave Stella's picture with Finkle on purpose or by accident? Is the deep emotion Salzman shows here real or an act? [Possible responses: Yes, Leo's infatuation with Stella has forced Salzman to think about his daughter and her suffering; no, his emotional behavior is also an act, designed to pique Leo's interest.]

D Critical Thinking

Connecting with the Text

? As far as you know, whose view of life is closer to the truth, Leo's or Salzman's? Why? [Sample responses: Leo's, because love happens in all kinds of unexpected ways; Salzman's, because what Leo is feeling is not real love, but infatuation (even though it may ultimately become love).]

---

sign of Salzman or his magic barrel, probably also a figment of the imagination. An odor of frying fish made Leo weak to the knees.

"Where is he?" he insisted. "I've got to see your husband."

At length she answered, "So who knows where he is? Every time he thinks a new thought he runs to a different place. Go home, he will find you."

"Tell him Leo Finkle."

She gave no sign she had heard.

He walked downstairs, depressed.

But Salzman, breathless, stood waiting at his door.

Leo was astounded and overjoyed. "How did you get here before me?"

"I rushed."

"Come inside."

They entered. Leo fixed tea, and a sardine sandwich for Salzman. As they were drinking he reached behind him for the packet of pictures and handed them to the marriage broker.

Salzman put down his glass and said expectantly, "You found somebody you like?"

"Not among these."

The marriage broker turned away.

"Here is the one I want." Leo held forth the snapshot.

Salzman slipped on his glasses and took the picture into his trembling hand. He turned ghastly and let out a groan.

"What's the matter?" cried Leo.

A "Excuse me. Was an accident this picture. She isn't for you."

Salzman frantically shoved the manila packet into his portfolio. He thrust the snapshot into his pocket and fled down the stairs.

Leo, after momentary paralysis, gave chase and cornered the marriage broker in the vestibule. The landlady made hysterical outcries but neither of them listened.

"Give me back the picture, Salzman."

"No." The pain in his eyes was terrible.

"Tell me who she is then."

"This I can't tell you. Excuse me."

He made to depart, but Leo, forgetting himself, seized the matchmaker by his tight coat and shook him frenziedly.

"Please," sighed Salzman. "*Please.*"

Leo ashamedly let him go. "Tell me who she is," he begged. "It's very important for me to know."

"She is not for you. She is a wild one—wild, without shame. This is not a bride for a rabbi."

"What do you mean wild?"

B "Like an animal. Like a dog. For her to be poor was a sin. This is why to me she is dead now."

"In God's name, what do you mean?"

"Her I can't introduce to you," Salzman cried.

"Why are you so excited?"

C "Why, he asks," Salzman said, bursting into tears. "This is my baby, my Stella, she should burn in hell."

Leo hurried up to bed and hid under the covers. Under the covers he thought his life through. Although he soon fell asleep he could not sleep her out of his mind. He woke, beating his breast. Though he prayed to be rid of her, his prayers went unanswered. Through days of torment he endlessly struggled not to love her; fearing success, he escaped it. He then concluded to convert her to goodness, himself to God. The idea alternately nauseated and exalted him.

He perhaps did not know that he had come to a final decision until he encountered Salzman in a Broadway cafeteria. He was sitting alone at a rear table, sucking the bony remains of a fish. The marriage broker appeared haggard, and transparent to the point of vanishing.

Salzman looked up at first without recognizing him. Leo had grown a pointed beard and his eyes were weighted with wisdom.

"Salzman," he said, "love has at last come to my heart."

D "Who can love from a picture?" mocked the marriage broker.

"It is not impossible."

"If you can love her, then you can love anybody. Let me show you some new clients that they just sent me their photographs. One is a little doll."

"Just her I want," Leo murmured.

"Don't be a fool, doctor. Don't bother with her."

"Put me in touch with her, Salzman," Leo said humbly. "Perhaps I can be of service."

Salzman had stopped eating and Leo understood with emotion that it was now arranged.

Assessing Learning

Check Test: Fill-in-the-Blank

1. Pinye Salzman's favorite food is _____. [fish]

2. Leo does not want to be called _____. [rabbi]

3. At first Leo is not interested in Lily, because she is _____. [too old]

4. Leo says that he decided to study religion because he did not love _____. [God]

5. At the very end of the story, Salzman chants prayers for _____. [the dead]

Informal Assessment

After using the Enrichment Activity on p. T986, Getting Students Involved, have groups exchange papers and rate their peers' scripts on a scale of one to five (five being the highest) for the following criteria:

- action and dialogue that are faithful to the story
- believable characters with convincing motivations

- stage and camera directions that enhance the dialogue

Ask groups to write additional comments about the scripts based on these criteria and to return the evaluations to the script writers. Have groups revise their scripts after receiving the evaluations.

Leaving the cafeteria, he was, however, afflicted by a tormenting suspicion that Salzman had planned it all to happen this way.

Leo was informed by letter that she would meet him on a certain corner, and she was there one spring night, waiting under a street lamp. He appeared, carrying a small bouquet of violets and rosebuds. Stella stood by the lamppost, smoking. She wore white with red shoes, which fitted his expectations, although in a troubled moment he had imagined the dress red, and only the shoes white. She waited uneasily and shyly. From afar he saw that her eyes—clearly her father's—were filled with desperate innocence. He pictured, in her, his own redemption. Violins and lit candles revolved in the sky. Leo ran forward with flowers outthrust.

Around the corner, Salzman, leaning against a wall, chanted prayers for the dead.

A Tale of Self-Discovery

At the opening of this story, a lonely young rabbinical student decides to contact a marriage broker through a newspaper ad. Leo Finkle has been immersed in his studies for six years, he is painfully shy, and he can think of no other way to meet suitable young women. (If the custom seems strange, think of the thousands of people today who use dating services.)

Finkle's attitudes have been shaped by years of study and theological debate. It is not surprising that he has had very little time to think about his social life. The tradition of the marriage broker, seemingly exotic in America, was familiar to European Jews in the early part of this century. Brokers fulfilled a genuine social function by negotiating between families and easing embarrassment. It was inevitable that, in some of these arranged marriages, the chief feature was not the partners' mutual devotion but the financial or social advantages to the families involved.

Finkle is portrayed as wavering between two worlds. In the old world of his parents (who owed their marriage to a broker), social criteria for marriage were more important than love. Leo himself is originally impelled to look for a wife by an acquaintance's suggestion that "he might find it easier to win himself a congregation if he were married." In his first conversations with Salzman, Finkle is preoccupied by external, superficial criteria. But a profound change is at work in Leo, and he reaches a turning point when he suddenly finds himself admitting to the pleasant but superficial Lily that "I came to God not because I loved Him, but because I did not." The story then shows him dramatically, even transcendentally, caught up in love at first sight. As you think about the story, consider the possibility that Malamud's real interest is not in the probability—or even the future consequences—of Leo's change of heart. Perhaps the writer wants us to witness Leo Finkle's process of self-discovery: his initiation into a new world, where he can exist as an authentic person, capable of love.

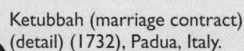

Ketubbah (marriage contract) (detail) (1732), Padua, Italy.
Collection Israel Museum, Jerusalem. Photo Israel Museum.

BERNARD MALAMUD 993

Making the Connections

Connecting to the Theme: "Discoveries and Awakenings"
Leo Finkle awakens to—or discovers both within himself and in the world around him— the possibility of a changed way of life, a changed attitude toward love and toward what he perceives as his obligations. There is some loss connected with this: a weakening of old values, such as marrying to please one's parents. However, from a contemporary American standpoint, the gain of personal fulfillment outweighs this loss. Continuity is shown in the fact that Leo does, after all, find love through the services of a matchmaker. Invite students to discuss their own ideas about what they think Leo and the other characters have discovered or awakened to and what students themselves have discovered in the story.

E **Elements of Literature**
Static and Dynamic Characters
? Do you think Salzman hopes that his daughter, if married to a rabbi, will return to the fold of her family and religion? [Possible responses: Since Leo says he may be "of service" and Salzman agrees, this is likely; on the other hand, the plural *prayers* may imply that Salzman now regards Leo, too, as dead.]

Critical Comment
This commentary on "The Magic Barrel" puts Leo Finkle's quest for a spouse in the context of both Old World European Judaism and the modern quest for self-identity and authenticity. The fulfillment of this quest, the author suggests, outweighs the actual results of Leo's feelings for Stella.

F **Cultural Connections**
Study and debate in Jewish theological law revolve around the Talmud, a massive set of commentaries upon the Torah. The Talmud was compiled by groups of scholar-teachers in the first six centuries of the Christian era. The Talmud includes both accepted opinions and dissenting opinions on such subjects as the keeping of ceremonial observances, civil and criminal law, marriage and divorce, the role of women, dietary laws, and ritual slaughter. It also includes stories, such as legends, anecdotes, and parables, with commentaries.

G **Cultural Connections**
? In what other professions has it traditionally been considered an asset for a man to be well married? [Possible responses: politics; the Protestant clergy; executive-level corporate jobs; corporate law.]

H **Critical Thinking**
Analyzing
? How might Leo be seen to be "inauthentic" before his passionate pursuit of Stella? [Possible response: He has gone through the motions in life, trying to compensate for a lack of spontaneous religious feeling with his studies, and trying to compensate for a lack of feeling for others by seeking the broker.]

MAKING MEANINGS

First Thoughts [Respond]

1. Possible responses: She somehow brought disgrace upon her family, perhaps by refusing to observe the Sabbath, by smoking, drinking, and socializing with a secular crowd, or by getting involved with a Gentile or someone who was married.

Shaping Interpretations [Interpret]

2. Possible responses: Doubt can be a stimulus to soul-searching and thus to deep faith; true faith, like true love, requires honesty; he may have thought he could come to love God by devoting himself to religious studies.

3. He glimpses in her the possibility of love. He wants to be redeemed from an existence devoid of spontaneity, true feeling, and true companionship.

4. He learns his search for a spouse is, in fact, a search for authentic feeling in all aspects of his life—and he learns to give up pride and propriety as he follows such a feeling for Stella.

5. Possible responses: Salzman has orchestrated the entire chain of events, as a magical solution to Leo's woes and his own. Salzman is genuinely resistant to Leo's interest in his daughter, but gives in.

6. Positive: Leo has been emotionally reborn, and Stella might share his feelings. Negative: Some part of the Old World is dying, and Salzman cannot accept this loss in Leo or Stella.

7. Possible responses: The barrel that supposedly contains pictures of Salzman's clients is indeed magical because it brings love to Leo in a strange, unexpected way.

Extending the Text [Synthesize]

8. Possible responses: They will stay together, because both have been lonely enough in the past to welcome love; they will drift apart, because they are incompatible.

MAKING MEANINGS

First Thoughts

1. What do you think caused Stella's father to regard her as dead?

Shaping Interpretations

2. Finkle confesses to Lily "…I came to God not because I loved Him, but because I did not." How would you explain this **paradox,** or seeming contradiction?

3. Why do you think Finkle pictures in Stella his own redemption? What does he want to be redeemed *from?*

4. **Summarize** what you think Finkle has learned about love and about himself by the end of the story. Has he changed in an important way?

5. What do you think of the scene with Finkle and Stella near the end of the story? Do you think Salzman arranged a marriage for Finkle after all?

6. Does Malamud end the story on a positive or a negative note? How would you explain the last sentence of the story: "Around the corner, Salzman, leaning against a wall, chanted prayers for the dead"?

7. Explain the story's **title.**

Reading Check

a. According to the first paragraph, who is the story's **protagonist,** and what does he want?

b. Another character—Pinye Salzman—is introduced in the second paragraph. Find the descriptive details that hint of something tragic in his past.

c. Explain what Finkle discovers about himself after the experience with Lily.

d. Why does Finkle fall in love with the woman in the photograph?

Extending the Text

8. What do you think will happen to Leo and Stella once they learn more about each other? Will they marry? Will they drift apart? Consult your Quickwrite notes for ideas.

994 CONTEMPORARY LITERATURE

CHOICES:
Building Your Portfolio

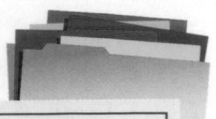

Writer's Notebook

1. Collecting Ideas for an Evaluation

What makes for skillful characterization? Create a chart to organize the criteria you'd use to evaluate the characters Leo Finkle and Pinye Salzman in "The Magic Barrel." In column one, enter five or six qualities that make for skillful characterization. (Two criteria might be that a character be **believable** and **dynamic.**) In columns two and three (headed "Leo" and "Pinye"), list specific examples from the text that show how each character meets (or does not meet) each criterion. Save your notes for possible use in the Writer's Workshop on page 1181.

Interpreting a Story

2. What's at the Heart of Malamud?

Select one of the following comments about Bernard Malamud's fiction, and write a brief essay responding to it. Tell whether or not the comment has to do with the **plot, characters,** or **theme** of "The Magic Barrel."

a. "Malamud has always had a fondness for telling tales arranged for the purpose of a specific moral lesson." (Alan Lelchuk)

b. "What it is to be human, and to be humane, is his [Malamud's] deepest concern." (Philip Roth)

Telling a Story

3. Stella by Starlight

One spring night, Leo runs toward Stella "with flowers outthrust." That's about where "The Magic Barrel" ends. Tell a story to the class that extends Malamud's story. Include the dialogue that might take place as Leo and Stella meet. Bring your story to an ambiguous conclusion, in Malamud's style.

CHOICES:
Building Your Portfolio

1. Students may use this as prewriting for the Writer's Workshop on p. 1181.
2. Both quotes can be applied to all three elements.
3. Some students may enjoy improvising dialogue aloud with partners before writing.

Grading Timesaver

Rubrics for each assignment appear on p. 209 in the *Portfolio Management System.*

Reading Check

a. A young rabbinical student named Leo Finkle, who lives in New York City, wants to find a wife.

b. He appears suddenly in the dark; his hat is old; his overcoat fits badly; he smells of fish; his eyes are sad.

c. He realizes that he has never loved God or any person, except for his parents.

d. He feels that she has suffered and that she might understand and love him.

Gabriel García Márquez
(1928 –   )

Gabriel García Márquez (gä′brē·el′ gär·sē′ä mär′kes) was born in Aracataca, Colombia, the town that became the model for the fictional village of Macondo in his popular novel *One Hundred Years of Solitude* (1967). He spent his early years with his maternal grandparents, whom he regards as "wonderful beings." According to García Márquez, "They had an enormous house, full of ghosts. They were people of great imagination and superstitions. In every corner there were dead people and memories, and after six o'clock in the [evening] the house was untraversable. It was a world prodigious with terror. There were conversations in code."

After attending universities in Bogotá and Cartagena, García Márquez worked as a journalist in Colombia and in Rome, Paris, Barcelona, Caracas, and New York. Newspaper work helped García Márquez (like Ernest Hemingway) develop a style of writing fiction. Even after ending his newspaper career in 1965, García Márquez considered himself to be at heart a journalist, which is one reason for the factual or realistic basis for his fiction. It also accounts for his occasional nonfiction books, such as *News of a Kidnapping* (1997). Because of serious political differences with the Colombian government, he lives in Mexico City.

García Márquez has achieved international renown mainly for his fiction, which includes, besides *One Hundred Years of Solitude, The Autumn of the Patriarch* (1976), *Love in the Time of Cholera* (1988), *Strange Pilgrims* (1993), and *Of Love and Other Demons* (1995). He was awarded the Nobel Prize in literature in 1982.

Gabriel García Márquez signing autographs in the streets of Cartagena.

Carlos Angel/Gamma Liaison.

GABRIEL GARCÍA MÁRQUEZ 995

Summary ▪▪

Children in a seaside village discover a drowned man on the beach. The conflict and central themes of the story derive from the villagers' attempts to identify the drowned man and to make sense of his life and death. First, they find that the drowned man is a stranger, not only to their village but to all neighboring villages. As the women clean the corpse, they are stunned by its beauty, strength, and enormous size, and they begin to imagine his life. They envision not only his prowess but also his awkwardness and embarrassment due to his size. The oldest declares that the drowned man has the face of someone named Esteban. He becomes for them "the most destitute, most peaceful, and most obliging man on earth." At first the men are irritated, but they too decide that the man *is* Esteban and hold a lavish funeral for him. They throw the body out to sea without an anchor, so that he can return to the village as he pleases. Afterwards the villagers realize that the drowned man has made them reevaluate their lives, that they will cherish his memory in their community to ensure that he will never again feel awkward or lonely. They imagine passing sailors calling their village Esteban's village.

Background

"The Handsomest Drowned Man in the World" was originally collected in García Márquez's 1972 book of seven stories, *The Incredible and Sad Tale of Innocent Erendira and Her Heartless Grandmother*. In addition to the title tale and "The Handsomest Drowned Man in the World," the volume is known for "A Very Old Man with Enormous Wings," which, like this one, was labeled a children's story.

Before You Read
THE HANDSOMEST DROWNED MAN IN THE WORLD

Background

Gabriel García Márquez blends **realism** with playful imagination to create a type of literature known as **magic realism.** Developed in Latin America around the middle of the twentieth century, the genre has proved popular and influential in much of the world. You can see echoes of magic (also called marvelous) realism in works by such noted U.S. authors as Donald Barthelme (page 955), Thomas Pynchon, and Kurt Vonnegut, Jr., and in the writing of Günter Grass of Germany and John Fowles of England. A key novel of magic realism is García Márquez's best-selling *Cien años de soledad* (1967), translated into English as *One Hundred Years of Solitude* (1970).

Art on pages 996, 997, 999 by Sergio Bustamente/Photo by Clint Clemens.

According to a perceptive analysis by the literary critic David Young, "One way to understand magic realism is as a kind of pleasant joke on realism, suggesting as it does a new kind of fiction, produced in reaction to the confining assumptions of realism. [Magic realism is] a hybrid that somehow manages to combine the truthful and verifiable aspects of realism with the magical effects we associate with myth, folk tale, tall story, and that being in all of us—our childhood self, perhaps—who loves the spell that narrative casts even when it is perfectly implausible." The critic James Park Sloan observes that an essential element of García Márquez's magic realism is "a steadily toneless background in which everyday events become marvelous and marvelous events are assimilated without comment into everyday life."

García Márquez identifies an additional important aspect of his writing: "There's no doubt nostalgia is one of the important ingredients of my books and life. I make decisions, basic decisions, out of sheer nostalgia. Nostalgia gives my books the distance they bear from reality."

Reading Skills and Strategies

Dialogue with the Text
As you read this story by García Márquez, write down your responses to the following questions. Where appropriate, back up your responses by quoting passages from the story.

- The author subtitles the story "A Tale for Children." In what ways do you need to become childlike again in order to really enjoy this work?
- Which passages remind you in general of a **myth, legend,** or **folk tale**? Are you reminded at any point of a specific myth or tale?
- How does the villagers' attitude toward the drowned man change over the course of the story?
- What ultimate effect does the arrival of the drowned man have on the villagers' lives?
  - What did you find puzzling or difficult to understand about this story?

Reaching All Students

Struggling Readers
Some students may have difficulty with the shifts between third-person omniscient and first-person points of view in the story. Alert students to this issue before they begin reading. Have them note, in writing or mentally, places where shifts occur. Encourage them to raise and discuss questions they have about this technique.

English Language Learners
Spanish-speaking students will appreciate reading this story in two languages; García Márquez's works are available in any library or bookstore that stocks books in Spanish. For strategies for engaging English language learners with the literature, see
- *Lesson Plans Including Strategies for English-Language Learners*

Advanced Learners
To deepen their understanding of magic realism, students may want to read or reread some of the works of the following Latin American writers: Jorge Luis Borges (see p. 1152), Julio Cortázar (p. 290), Alejo Carpenter, Carlos Fuentes, Jose Donoso, and Mario Vargas Llosa. Interested students may wish to write papers analyzing the history of the Magic Realist movement and the similarities and differences among its major writers.

The Handsomest Drowned Man in the World

Gabriel García Márquez

translated by Gregory Rabassa

A Tale for Children

The first children who saw the dark and slinky bulge approaching through the sea let themselves think it was an enemy ship. Then they saw it had no flags or masts and they thought it was a whale. But when it was washed up on the beach, they removed the clumps of seaweed, the jellyfish tentacles, and the remains of fish and flotsam, and only then did they see that it was a drowned man.

They had been playing with him all afternoon, burying him in the sand and digging him up again, when someone chanced to see them and spread the alarm in the village. The men who carried him to the nearest house noticed that he weighed more than any dead man they had ever known, almost as much as a horse, and they said to each other that maybe he'd been floating too long and the water had got into his bones. When they laid him on the floor they said he'd been taller than all other men because there was barely enough room for him in the house, but they thought that maybe the ability to keep on growing after death was part of the nature of certain drowned men. He had the smell of the sea about him and only his shape gave one to suppose that it was the corpse of a human being, because the skin was covered with a crust of mud and scales.

They did not even have to clean off his face to know that the dead man was a stranger. The village was made up of only twenty-odd wooden houses that had stone courtyards with no flowers and which were spread about on the end of a desertlike cape. There was so little land that mothers always went about with the fear that the wind would carry off their children and the few dead that the years had caused among them had to be thrown off the cliffs. But the sea was calm and bountiful and all the men fit into seven boats. So when they found the drowned man they simply had to look at one another to see that they were all there.

That night they did not go out to work at sea. While the men went to find out if anyone was missing in neighboring villages, the women stayed behind to care for the drowned man. They took the mud off with grass swabs, they removed the underwater stones entangled in his hair, and they scraped the crust off with tools used for scaling fish. As they were doing that they noticed that the vegetation on him came from faraway oceans and deep water and that his clothes were in tatters, as if he had sailed through labyrinths of coral. They noticed too that he bore his death with pride, for he did not have the lonely look of other drowned men who came out of the sea or that haggard, needy look of men who drowned in rivers. But only when they finished cleaning him off did they become aware of the kind of man he

GABRIEL GARCÍA MÁRQUEZ **997**

Ⓐ Reading Skills and Strategies
Responding to the Text
? What would your response be to finding a drowned man on the shore? [Sample responses: Some students might call 911; others might be too scared to go near him.]

Ⓑ Elements of Literature
Magic Realism
Point out examples of exaggeration or ambiguity that enhance the atmosphere of magic realism. The dead man's enormous weight is an exaggeration; his encrustation with scales is ambiguous, for it makes him seem like some magical sea creature, yet there is nothing supernatural in the description. Encourage students to point out other magic realist touches as they come across them.

Ⓒ Elements of Literature
Humor
? What is humorous about the description of the men looking at one another? [Ordinarily, people would look at the corpse, rather than at each other, to see whether the dead man was a member of the community.]

Ⓓ Reading Skills and Strategies
Dialogue with the Text
? How is the dead man described in traditional heroic terms? [Like Greek heroes, he crosses "faraway oceans," makes it through "labyrinths," and like other traditional heroes he is endowed with a certain pride and self-sufficiency.] **Why are these terms ironic?** [He has all these qualities in death, he is a posthumous hero.]

Using Students' Strengths

Logical/Mathematical Learners
To help students conceptualize the drowned man's physical dimensions, assign individual students one section of the story apiece to scrutinize for details that refer to his size. When students finish, have them compile their results on the chalkboard and work together to determine the drowned man's approximate height, weight, and shoe size.

Spatial Learners
Using the dimensions determined by the logical/mathematical learners, have a student draw a life-size outline of the drowned man on large art paper. (The artist may wish to tape several sheets of paper together.) Ask students to stand around it in a circle to get a sense of his size.

Naturalist Learners
Invite students to research the flora and fauna of coastal Colombia. Encourage students to pick out places in the story where plants or animals are mentioned (such as a macaw or a sperm whale), and to bring in pictures of, and information about, those species. Where the author's descriptions are generic (such as "flowers"), have students suggest possible local species based on their research.

was and it left them breathless. Not only was he the tallest, strongest, most virile, and best-built man they had ever seen, but even though they were looking at him there was no room for him in their imagination.

They could not find a bed in the village large enough to lay him on nor was there a table solid enough to use for his wake. The tallest men's holiday pants would not fit him, not the fattest ones' Sunday shirts, nor the shoes of the one with the biggest feet. Fascinated by his huge size and his beauty, the women then decided to make him some pants from a large piece of sail and a shirt from some bridal brabant linen[1] so that he could continue through his death with dignity. As they sewed, sitting in a circle and gazing at the corpse between stitches, it seemed to them that the wind had never been so steady nor the sea so restless as on that night and they supposed that the change had something to do with the dead man. They thought that if that magnificent man had lived in the village, his house would have had the widest doors, the highest ceiling, and the strongest floor, his bedstead would have been made from a midship frame held together by iron bolts, and his wife would have been the happiest woman. They thought that he would have had so much authority that he could have drawn fish out of the sea simply by calling their names and that he would have put so much work into his land that springs would have burst forth from among the rocks so that he would have been able to plant flowers on the cliffs. They secretly compared him to their own men, thinking that for all their lives theirs were incapable of doing what he could do in one night, and they ended up dismissing them deep in their hearts as the weakest, meanest, and most useless creatures on earth. They were wandering through that maze of fantasy when the oldest woman, who as the oldest had looked upon the drowned man with more compassion than passion, sighed:

"He has the face of someone called Esteban."[2]

It was true. Most of them had only to take another look at him to see that he could not have any other name. The more stubborn among them, who were the youngest, still lived for a few hours with the illusion that when they put his clothes on and he lay among the flowers in patent leather shoes his name might be Lautaro.[3] But it was a vain illusion. There had not been enough canvas, the poorly cut and worse sewn pants were too tight, and the hidden strength of his heart popped the buttons on his shirt. After midnight the whistling of the wind died down and the sea fell into its Wednesday drowsiness.[4] The silence put an end to any last doubts: he was Esteban. The women who had dressed him, who had combed his hair, had cut his nails and shaved him were unable to hold back a shudder of pity when they had to resign themselves to his being dragged along the ground. It was then that they understood how unhappy he must have been with that huge body since it bothered him even after death. They could see him in life, condemned to going through doors sideways, cracking his head on crossbeams, remaining on his feet during visits, not knowing what to do with his soft, pink, sea lion hands while the lady of the house looked for her most resistant chair and begged him, frightened to death, sit here, Esteban, please, and he, leaning against the wall, smiling, don't bother, ma'am, I'm fine where I am, his heels raw and his back roasted from having done the same thing so many times whenever he paid a visit, don't bother, ma'am, I'm fine where I am, just to avoid the embarrassment of breaking up the chair, and never knowing perhaps that the ones who said don't go, Esteban, at least wait till the coffee's ready, were the ones who later on would whisper the big boob finally left, how nice, the handsome fool has gone. That was what the women were thinking beside the body a little before dawn. Later, when they covered his face with a handkerchief so that the light would not bother him, he looked so forever dead, so defenseless, so much

---

1. **brabant** (brə·bant′) **linen:** linen from Brabant, a province of Belgium known for its fine lace and cloth.
2. **Esteban** (es·te′bän): Spanish equivalent for "Stephen." In Christian tradition, Stephen was the first martyr. He was stoned to death because of his beliefs.

3. **Lautaro** (lou·tä′rô): leader of Araucanian Indian people who resisted the Spanish conquistadors entering their land, in what is now Chile, during the sixteenth century. Lautaro is now seen as a Chilean national hero.
4. **Wednesday drowsiness** (and later **Wednesday meat** and **Wednesday dead body**): *Wednesday* is a colloquial expression for "tiresome." In many fishing villages, fishers returned from the sea on Thursday, so by Wednesday, people began running out of food and were generally weary and bored.

998 CONTEMPORARY LITERATURE

blind and divers die of nostalgia, and bad currents would not bring him back to shore, as had happened with other bodies. But the more they hurried, the more the women thought of ways to waste time. They walked about like startled hens, pecking with the sea charms[6] on their breasts, some interfering on one side to put a scapular[7] of the good wind on the drowned man, some on the other side to put a wrist compass on him, and after a great deal of *get away from there, woman, stay out of the way, look, you almost made me fall on top of the dead man,* the men began to feel mistrust in their livers and started grumbling about why so many main-altar decorations for a stranger, because no matter how many nails and holy-water jars he had on him, the sharks would chew him all the same, but the women kept piling on their junk relics, running back and forth, stumbling, while they released in sighs what they did not in tears, so that the men finally exploded with *since when has there ever been such a fuss over a drifting corpse, a drowned nobody, a piece of cold Wednesday meat.* One of the women, mortified by so much lack of care, then removed the handkerchief from the dead man's face and the men were left breathless too.

He was Esteban. It was not necessary to repeat it for them to recognize him. If they had been told Sir Walter Raleigh, even they might have been impressed with his gringo accent, the macaw[8] on his shoulder, his cannibal-killing blunderbuss,[9] but there could be only one Esteban in the world and there he was, stretched out like a sperm whale, shoeless, wearing the pants of an undersized child, and with those stony nails that had to be cut with a knife. They only had to take the handkerchief off his face to see that he was ashamed, that it was not his fault that he was so big or so heavy or so handsome, and if he had known that this

---

like their men that the first furrows of tears opened in their hearts. It was one of the younger ones who began the weeping. The others, coming to, went from sighs to wails, and the more they sobbed the more they felt like weeping, because the drowned man was becoming all the more Esteban for them, and so they wept so much, for he was the most destitute, most peaceful, and most obliging man on earth, poor Esteban. So when the men returned with the news that the drowned man was not from the neighboring villages either, the women felt an opening of jubilation in the midst of their tears.

"Praise the Lord," they sighed, "he's ours!"

The men thought the fuss was only womanish frivolity. Fatigued because of the difficult nighttime inquiries, all they wanted was to get rid of the bother of the newcomer once and for all before the sun grew strong on that arid, windless day. They improvised a litter with the remains of foremasts and gaffs,[5] tying it together with rigging so that it would bear the weight of the body until they reached the cliffs. They wanted to tie the anchor from a cargo ship to him so that he would sink easily into the deepest waves, where fish are

---

5. **gaffs:** poles used on a boat to support a sail.

6. **sea charms:** magic charms worn to protect the wearer from dangers at sea.

7. **scapular** (skap′yə·lər): pair of small cloth squares with images of saints, joined by string and worn under clothing by some Roman Catholics as a symbol of religious devotion.

8. **macaw:** large, brightly colored parrot.

9. **blunderbuss:** now-obsolete gun with a short, flaring muzzle.

GABRIEL GARCÍA MÁRQUEZ 999

E Reading Skills and Strategies
Comparing and Contrasting
? How do the men's reactions differ from the women's? [Possible answer: The women create a past for him and imagine how he might have felt; they feel sorry for him and worship him. The men see the body as an inconvenience that creates more work for them; they do not attribute a past to him.]

F Elements of Literature
Magic Realism
? The phrase "where . . . divers die of nostalgia" is a beautiful example of magic-realist imagery. In what sense is the description fantastic, and in what sense is it realistic? [Possible response: It is fantastic in that divers do not literally die of nostalgia; it is realistic in that divers do die because they stray too far from their home, the land, and surely feel a kind of desperate "nostalgia" for it.]

G Critical Thinking
Determining Author's Purpose
? Why might García Márquez run the men's words together and write them in italics and without quotation marks? [Possible responses: He might run them together to show the conformity of the group's thinking; he might use italics to signal that these are the characters' words, but not worth differentiating, since they are knee-jerk reactions.]

H Historical Connections
Sir Walter Raleigh (1554?–1618) was the archetypal Renaissance man of Elizabethan England: a soldier, privateer, explorer, courtier, poet, historian, and member of Parliament. He helped defend England against Spain in 1588. His ventures into the New World included two expeditions on the Orinoco River in South America and the organizing of the famous "lost colony" of Roanoke Island, North Carolina. He was executed for treason in 1618. By mentioning Sir Walter Raleigh and then overshadowing him with Esteban, the author evokes colonial history in South America.

Assessing Learning

was going to happen, he would have looked for a more discreet place to drown in, seriously, I even would have tied the anchor off a galleon around my neck and staggered off a cliff like someone who doesn't like things in order not to be upsetting people now with this Wednesday dead body, as you people say, in order not to be bothering anyone with this filthy piece of cold meat that doesn't have anything to do with me. There was so much truth in his manner that even the most mistrustful men, the ones who felt the bitterness of endless nights at sea fearing that their women would tire of dreaming about them and begin to dream of drowned men, even they and others who were harder still shuddered in the marrow of their bones at Esteban's sincerity.

That was how they came to hold the most splendid funeral they could conceive of for an abandoned drowned man. Some women who had gone to get flowers in the neighboring villages returned with other women who could not believe what they had been told, and those women went back for more flowers when they saw the dead man, and they brought more and more until there were so many flowers and so many people that it was hard to walk about. At the final moment it pained them to return him to the waters as an orphan and they chose a father and mother from among the best people, and aunts and uncles and cousins, so that through him all the inhabitants of the village became kinsmen. Some sailors who heard the weeping from a distance went off course and people heard of one who had himself tied to the mainmast, remembering ancient fables about sirens.[10] While they fought for the privilege of carrying him on their shoulders along the steep escarpment by the cliffs, men and women became aware for the first time of the desolation of their streets, the dryness of their courtyards, the narrowness of their dreams as they faced the splendor and beauty of their drowned man. They let him go without an anchor so that he could come back if he wished and whenever he wished, and they all held their breath for the fraction of centuries the body took to fall into the abyss. They did not need to look at one another to realize that they were no longer all present, that they would never be. But they also knew that everything would be different from then on, that their houses would have wider doors, higher ceilings, and stronger floors so that Esteban's memory could go everywhere without bumping into beams and so that no one in the future would dare whisper the big boob finally died, too bad, the handsome fool has finally died, because they were going to paint their house fronts gay colors to make Esteban's memory eternal and they were going to break their backs digging for springs among the stones and planting flowers on the cliffs so that in future years at dawn the passengers on great liners would awaken, suffocated by the smell of gardens on the high seas, and the captain would have to come down from the bridge in his dress uniform, with his astrolabe,[11] his polestar, and his row of war medals and, pointing to the promontory of roses on the horizon, he would say in fourteen languages, look there, where the wind is so peaceful now that it's gone to sleep beneath the beds, over there, where the sun's so bright that the sunflowers don't know which way to turn, yes, over there, that's Esteban's village.

---

10. **sirens:** In Greek mythology, the sirens are sea maidens whose seductive singing lures men to wreck their boats on coastal rocks. Odysseus, hero of Homer's *Odyssey,* fills his crew's ears with wax so that they can pass the sirens safely. Odysseus, however, has his crew tie him to the ship's mast so that he can listen to the sirens' songs without plunging into the sea.

11. **astrolabe** (as′trō·lāb′): instrument used to find a star's altitude and to help navigators determine their position at sea.

FINDING COMMON GROUND

Meet in small groups to discuss "The Handsomest Drowned Man in the World." As you talk about the story, refer to the notes you made while reading.

- First, decide how to run your discussion group. If you want a moderator, choose a group member to fill that role.

- Second, draw up an agenda of topics for consideration. (Refer to your reading notes for some ideas.) It will be helpful for a group member to act as a recorder, writing down the agenda as well as the main points brought up in the discussion.

UPI/Bettmann.

Theodore Roethke

(1908–1963)

"Everything that lives is holy: I call upon these holy forms of life." These words of Theodore Roethke (retʹkē), which sound like the words of a religious ceremony, are at the core of his intense vision. For Roethke, the function of poetry is to represent in words the sanctified forms and experiences of life.

A native of Saginaw, Michigan, Roethke grew up in a family situation that had an enormous influence on his poetry. His father owned the largest greenhouse complex in the state, and Roethke's childhood was spent close to nature, nurturing cuttings and small plants and walking in the vast acres of woodlands owned by his family. This childhood world provided the foundation for much of his poetry, which often looks at the smallest aspects of nature—worms, snails, tiny seedlings—through the eyes of a child. "I have a genuine love of nature," he

wrote when he was a sophomore in college. "When I get alone under an open sky where man isn't too evident—then I'm tremendously exalted and a thousand vivid ideas and sweet visions flood my consciousness."

Roethke studied law and worked in public relations for some time after graduating from college, but his desire to become a writer finally led him to graduate school. He began a teaching career at Lafayette College in Easton, Pennsylvania (where he also coached the tennis team); taught at Pennsylvania State University; and, from 1947 until his death, taught at the University of Washington.

A passionate and dedicated teacher, Roethke brought the same energy to the classroom that he brought to poetry. In teaching, he sought the same rewards he searched for in his writing: transcendence and illumination. "Most teaching is visceral," he wrote, "and the genial uproar that constitutes a verse class, especially so. It is as ephemeral as the dance. . . . [Teaching] is what is left after all the reading and thinking and reciting: the residue, the illumination."

The search for illumination and ecstasy was a fundamental concern for Roethke in life as well as in poetry. This search brought with it a psychological imbalance that he tried to face openly and employ honestly in his verse. "My heart keeps open house," he wrote in an early poem.

> My truths are all foreknown,
> This anguish self-revealed.
> I'm naked to the bone,
> With nakedness my shield.
>
> —from "Open House"

Between 1947 and 1958, Roethke published four volumes of poetry and received a number of honors, including a Pulitzer Prize, a National Book Award, and a Bollingen Prize. A poet of both pain and joy, the dark and the light, Roethke tried to find in both extremes the same transcendent moment, "a consciousness beyond the mundane," as he once put it, "a purity, a final innocence."

go.hrw.com
LEO 11-19

THEODORE ROETHKE **1001**

Planning

- **Traditional Schedule**
  Lesson Plans Including Strategies for English-Language Learners
- **One-Stop Planner**
  CD-ROM with Test Generator

BROWSING IN THE FILES

About the Author. Roethke struggled all his life with self-doubt. Even as an adult, he felt he could do nothing to win his father's approval. In high school, he craved acceptance by his peers, who thought his love of reading unmanly. When he began to write poetry in college, he did so in secret. He began to drink while at the University of Michigan and drank heavily for the rest of his life, most likely to ease the pain of his depression and anxiety. He was hospitalized for alcohol-related health problems several times before his death.

Summary ▪▪

Elegy for Jane
The speaker lovingly remembers Jane, a student of his who was thrown by a horse. He evokes her quick intelligence and grace, comparing her to a wren, a sparrow, and a pigeon—and asserting her harmony with nature. Now, however, nature provides no consolation as he tries to make sense of her death and his place in her life.

Night Journey
The speaker lies in a train berth, staring into the night while "others take their rest." He describes his view of bridges, trees, and mountains in increasingly figurative language, and then begins to depict himself in terms of the train's attributes. Now it is the speaker who strains "at a curve" and whose muscles "move with steel." As the train rushes on, the speaker is exhilarated, and stays up all night to see the land he loves.

Ⓐ Elements of Literature
Figures of Speech
❓ How do the figures of speech in these first lines characterize Jane? [Possible responses: Roethke's simile comparing Jane's hair to plant tendrils, along with the metaphors of the darting "pickerel smile," and the balancing of a happy wren—all characterize her as delicate, intelligent, energetic, and shy.]

Ⓑ Elements of Literature
Figures of Speech
❓ When Roethke says the "wet stones" and "moss" cannot console him for Jane's loss, what figure of speech is he using? [personification] Where else does he use this technique? [l. 7, "[t]he shade sang"; l. 8, "the leaves, their whispers turn to kissing"]

Before You Read

ELEGY FOR JANE

Make the Connection

In Moments of Intensity
At the most intense and concentrated moments of our lives, we often focus on the tiniest things. Like one of Shakespeare's great tragic kings musing on a straw or a worm, people in crisis seem to search for a comforting balance between the infinite and the infinitesimal. On the one hand, we face love and death and grief and fate; on the other hand, we take note of a bird, a smile, a leaf, a strand of hair.

Quickwrite
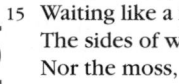
Think of a person you hold dear. Then, write down five of his or her special characteristics.

Elements of Literature

Figures of Speech
A **figure of speech** is a word or phrase that describes one thing in terms of another and that is not meant to be taken literally. It always involves a comparison of two things that are very dissimilar. Many such figures of speech have been identified by scholars. Among the most common are the **simile,** which makes an explicit comparison, using *like, as, than, resembles,* or another connective; **metaphor,** which (in contrast to a simile) makes a comparison without using a connective; and **personification,** which ascribes to an object or animal human feelings, thoughts, or attitudes. Watch for all three figures of speech in "Elegy for Jane."

Elegy for Jane
My Student, Thrown by a Horse

Theodore Roethke

> I remember the neckcurls, limp and damp as tendrils,°
> And her quick look, a sidelong pickerel° smile;
> And how, once startled into talk, the light syllables leaped for her,
> And she balanced in the delight of her thought,
> 5 A wren, happy, tail into the wind,
> Her song trembling the twigs and small branches.
> The shade sang with her;
> The leaves, their whispers turned to kissing;
> And the mold sang in the bleached valleys under the rose.
>
> Oh, when she was sad, she cast herself down into such a
> 10 pure depth,
> Even a father could not find her:
> Scraping her cheek against straw;
> Stirring the clearest water.
>
> My sparrow, you are not here,
> 15 Waiting like a fern, making a spiny shadow.
> The sides of wet stones cannot console me,
> Nor the moss, wound with the last light.
>
> If only I could nudge you from this sleep,
> My maimed darling, my skittery pigeon.
> 20 Over this damp grave I speak the words of my love:
> I, with no rights in this matter,
> Neither father nor lover.

1. **tendrils:** coiled strands, as of a climbing plant.
2. **pickerel:** small, North American pike fish.

Reaching All Students

Struggling Readers
"Elegy for Jane" was written by a teacher after the sudden death of a student. Tell students to reread ll. 5–9, in which the speaker describes Jane's personality by comparing her to a bird. Ask students to choose five adjectives based on this metaphor that might illustrate the personality of this student. Work with students to arrange the five words as a poem, beginning and ending with the name Jane.

English Language Learners
Help students understand the figures of speech in "Night Journey" on p. 1003. Then, ask them to describe the landscape of the poem in their own words. For strategies for engaging English language learners with the literature, see
• *Lesson Plans Including Strategies for English-Language Learners*

Make the Connection
The Land I Love

The crack trains that once were the fastest way to cross America found their way into the works of poets and painters. Today, most of those trains have been replaced by airplanes. What do we miss when we cannot see the prairies, the lighted windows in small towns, the mountains, and the cities that those trains used to roar past? A cross-country train ride was once a real journey; on a plane, that journey becomes a mere trip.

Quickwrite

Recall a trip that you have made in a plane, train, bus, or car—whether it was a short one (like the trip to school) or a long one (like a journey to another state or country). Write down your memories and impressions of what you saw and felt along the way.

Night Journey
Theodore Roethke

Now as the train bears west,
Its rhythm rocks the earth,
And from my pullman berth
I stare into the night
5   While others take their rest.
Bridges of iron lace,
A suddenness of trees,
A lap of mountain mist
All cross my line of sight,
10   Then a bleak wasted place,
And a lake below my knees.
Full on my neck I feel
The straining at the curve;
My muscles move with steel,
15   I wake in every nerve.
I watch a beacon swing
From dark to blazing bright;
We thunder through ravines
And gullies washed with light.
20   Beyond the mountain pass
Mist deepens on the pane;
We rush into the rain
That rattles double glass.
Wheels shake the roadbed stone,
25   The pistons jerk and shove.
I stay up half the night
To see the land I love.

Railroad Sunset
(1929) by
Edward Hopper.
Oil on canvas
(28¼" × 47¾");
(71.8 cm ×
121.3 cm).

Collection of
Whitney Museum
of American Art,
Josephine N.
Hopper Bequest
(Acq. 70.1170).
Photograph ©1998
by Whitney
Museum of
American Art.

1003

C Elements of Literature
Sound Effects

❓ What poetic sound effects does Roethke use in "Night Journey"? Give examples. [meter (iambic trimeter); rhyme, as in *earth/berth,* ll. 2–3; internal rhyme, as in *bears/stare,* ll. 1 and 4; alliteration, as in "*rhythm rocks,*" l. 2; assonance, as in "*I* stare into the n*i*ght," l. 4; consonance, as in "Bridges of iron," l. 6]

D Reading Skills and Strategies
Responding to the Text

❓ What mood, feelings, or thoughts did the poem arouse in you? [Possible responses: It made me feel the excitement of travel and the sublime power of the American wilderness. It evoked important train and plane journeys I have taken.]

Using Students' Strengths

Linguistic Learners
Encourage students to analyze the poem's rhyme scheme, which is a flexible one in which the sound *ight* is inserted periodically within groups of other repeated sounds (ll. 4, 9, 17, 19, and 26). The repeated sounds are sometimes placed in adjacent lines (*r*'s in ll. 22–23), sometimes separated by one line (*m*'s and *e*'s in ll. 12 and 14), and sometimes separated by several lines (*est* in ll. 1 and 5; *ees* in ll. 7 and 11).

Musical/Auditory Learners
Have one or more volunteers from this group read the poem aloud to the class. Encourage them to read in a natural but expressive way, conveying but not exaggerating the mood of the speaker and the rhythms and sound effects of the words. Invite students to point out passages that are enhanced for them by oral reading and to explain the enhanced effect.

Crossing the Curriculum

Social Studies
The railroad played a major role in the settling of the American West and in the expansion of the nation. Railroads still play an important part in transporting freight and a secondary role in personal transportation. Invite an interested student or students to research and report on the history of the American railroad system, its impact on our society, and the continuing romance of the rails.

MAKING MEANINGS

Elegy for Jane

First Thoughts [Respond]

1. Sample response: She is basically happy and hopeful but has moments of pure sadness, like the person I wrote about.

Shaping Interpretations [Interpret]

2. She is compared to a wren, making her seem happy and energetic; a sparrow, making her seem tiny and delicate; and a pigeon, making her seem excitable and nervous.

3. The focus of the elegy is on Jane, her relation to the speaker, and the relation of both to the natural world.

4. Possible response: His grief has no clear social sanction, since he has only the professional relationship to Jane of professor to student. Most students will feel that, as someone who cared about her, he still has a right to grieve.

Night Journey

First Thoughts [Respond]

1. Sample responses: the train rocking; the dark land washed with light; the "Bridges of iron lace"; the train and the speaker almost merging into one figure. Reasons will vary.

Shaping Interpretations [Interpret]

2. Possible responses: "A lap of mountain mist" (l. 8); "a lake below my knees" (l. 11); "Full on my neck I feel / The straining at the curve" (ll. 12–13); "My muscles move with steel" (l. 14); "We thunder through ravines" (l. 18); "We rush into the rain" (l. 22).

3. The short lines in iambic trimeter have a rocking but flowing rhythm, similar to that of a speeding train.

4. He expresses love for both the train and the land, explicitly in l. 27 and implicitly throughout the poem. Students may or may not have expressed similar feelings.

MAKING MEANINGS

Elegy for Jane

First Thoughts

1. Describe Jane's personality. Has Roethke focused on characteristics that you might focus on in a person you love? Explain. (Review your Quickwrite notes.)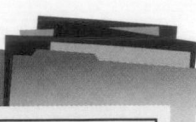

Shaping Interpretations

2. In the poem, Jane is compared to three birds. Name them, and tell how the comparisons help build an overall impression of the young woman.

3. An **elegy** is a poem of mourning. Some elegies concentrate fully on the person who has died; others extend their subject to reflect on general matters, such as life, death, beauty, even politics. Which type of elegy is Roethke's poem? Explain.

4. The poem's speaker says he has "no rights in this matter" (line 21). In your own words, explain what he means. Do you think he is correct? Why or why not?

Night Journey

First Thoughts

1. What **image** in the poem strikes you as especially powerful or memorable? Explain.

Shaping Interpretations

2. Roethke uses **figurative language** to convey the physical intensity of the journey. Which lines suggest a kind of fusion between the speaker, the speeding train, and the countryside?

3. Read "Night Journey" aloud, emphasizing its **rhythm.** How does the rhythm give you the feeling of being on a train?

4. What are the speaker's attitudes toward the train and toward the land? Are his feelings similar to those you noted in your Quickwrite?

CHOICES:
Building Your Portfolio

Writer's Notebook

1. Collecting Ideas for an Evaluation

A well-written evaluation of a work of literature includes an *orientation* for the audience, a clearly stated *judgment,* identification of the *criteria* used in judging, and *evidence* to back up the judgment. Make an informal outline for an evaluation of "Elegy for Jane" or "Night Journey." What would your readers need to know? What specific aspects of the poem would you evaluate—**figures of speech, theme, form, emotional effect, sounds,** some other element? What criteria would you apply? What evidence (examples, experiences, authorities) would you cite? Save your notes for possible use in the Writer's Workshop on page 1181.

Comparing Poems

2. Two Young Women

Write a brief essay comparing and contrasting "Elegy for Jane" with John Crowe Ransom's "Bells for John Whiteside's Daughter" (page 578). Consider especially the **figures of speech** and **tone** used in each elegy.

Responding to Art

3. Does It Fit?

In a brief essay tell whether or not you feel that the Edward Hopper painting used with "Night Journey" fits the **mood** of the poem. To support your response, refer to at least one specific detail in the painting.

Art

4. Painting a Poem

Draw or paint the landscape of Roethke's "Night Journey." Before you start, list all the specific **images** you'll want to consider including, starting with the "bridges of iron lace." Select a phrase from the poem as your title.

Grading Timesaver

Rubrics for each Choices assignment appear on p. 210 in the *Portfolio Management System.*

CHOICES:
Building Your Portfolio

1. **Writer's Notebook**
   Remind students to save their work. They may use it as prewriting for the Writer's Workshop on p. 1181.

2–3. **Comparing Poems/Responding to Art**
   Comparison and contrast is a promising mode for either of these essays.

4. **Art** Students may enjoy completing this project at home.

Richard Wilbur

(1921–   )

© Nancy Crampton.

"No poetry can have any strength unless it continually bashes itself against the reality of things." This poetic credo of Richard Wilbur has given us some of the strongest poems of our time—rock hard at the center, subtle and delicate on the edges.

From the time of his first book, *The Beautiful Changes and Other Poems* (1947), Wilbur was recognized as one of the most graceful and technically adept poets in the generation then coming of age. His poetry reminds us of the meters and natural speech of Robert Frost and of the metaphysical elegance and emotional reticence of Wallace Stevens.

But the influences of Frost and Stevens are merely overtones. Wilbur's poetic character is forged of his own unassertive religious devotion, his political liberalism, and his irrepressible delight in "the things of this world." Wilbur writes at a time when poetry has often been marked by self-promotion and seeming formlessness, as well as by uneasy borrowings from the paintings of minimalists and surrealists. But Wilbur has continued to write lyrics demanding scrupulous care and skill. His inward vision of delight finds expression in measured speech and indelible metaphor.

Wilbur was born in New York City but grew up in suburban New Jersey. He attended Amherst College in Massachusetts, served with combat troops in Europe during World War II, and went to graduate school at Harvard. There he prepared for the illustrious teaching career that has taken him to long-term appointments at Wellesley, Wesleyan (Connecticut), and Smith. During 1987–1988, Wilbur served as poet laureate of the United States.

When Wilbur is not embarked on reading tours that take him across the breadth of the continent, he divides his time between Cummington, Massachusetts, the Berkshire village where he lives within a stone's throw of the homestead where William Cullen Bryant (page 169) lived, and Key West, Florida.

In addition to poetry, Wilbur has produced sparkling translations of the plays of Molière, including *The Misanthrope* (1955) and *Tartuffe* (1963). These rhymed-verse versions of the seventeenth-century French playwright's work are both elegant and earthy, as well as practical enough to be successfully produced on stage.

Two of Wilbur's poetry collections, *Things of This World: Poems* (1956) and *New and Collected Poems* (1988), won Pulitzer Prizes. He has also published several noted books for children, including *A Bestiary* (1955), illustrated by Alexander Calder. Wilbur's fondness for wordplay is evident in his book *Pedestrian Flight: Twenty-one Clerihews for the Telephone* (1981). A *clerihew* is a humorous poem made up of two rhymed couplets that give some real and some imagined biographical information about a famous person.

go.hrw.com
LE0 11-19

RICHARD WILBUR 1005

OBJECTIVES
The Beautiful Changes / Boy at the Window
1. Read and interpret the poems
2. Explain ambiguity
3. Express understanding through writing

SKILLS
Literary
- Explain ambiguity

Writing
- Collect ideas for an evaluation
- Interpret a poem
- Write a reflective essay

Viewing/Representing
- Compare and contrast a picture with one's own visualization of a poem (ATE)

Planning

- **Block Schedule**
  Block Scheduling Lesson Plan with Pacing Guide
- **Traditional Schedule**
  Lesson Plans Including Strategies for English-Language Learners
- **One-Stop Planner**
  CD-ROM with Test Generator

BROWSING IN THE FILES
About the Author. Richard Wilbur began writing poetry in earnest as a soldier in World War II. The war took him to Monte Cassino and Anzio, in Italy, and to the Siegfried Line across northern France and Belgium. He turned to poetry to make sense out of the destruction and chaos he witnessed.

Resources: Print and Media

Reading
- *Graphic Organizers for Active Reading,* p. 99
- *Audio CD Library*
  Disc 25, Tracks 5, 6

Assessment
- *Portfolio Management System,* p. 211
- *Test Generator (One-Stop Planner CD-ROM)*

Internet
- go.hrw.com (keyword: LE0 11-19)

The Beautiful Changes

The poem's theme is the ambiguous phrase, "the beautiful changes"—where 'beautiful' can be both noun and adjective, and "changes" both verb and noun. Thus the beautiful Queen Anne's Lace changes a dry meadow into a lake, just as the thought of the speaker's beloved "valleys" the mind, and the camouflage of a praying mantis makes a leaf seem greener. Ultimately, the speaker focuses on the "second finding" of the world that the beautiful allows for, exemplified by the hands of a lover, which touch roses "back to wonder," beyond customary meanings.

Boy at the Window

The speaker describes a young boy, crying with pity for a snowman alone in the cold. But while the boy views the snowman as an outcast from Paradise, the snowman, in fact, feels a kind of pity for the boy. In his inanimate purity and contentment, he mourns the vulnerability of human life, susceptible to comfort, love, and fear.

Ⓐ Elements of Literature

Ambiguity

Make sure students see both ways of reading the title phrase: (1) as a sentence in which "beautiful" is the subject and "changes" is the verb, and (2) as a phrase in which "beautiful" is an adjective modifying the plural noun "changes."

Ⓑ Struggling Readers

Breaking Down Difficult Text

❓ Who is "One," and what is One doing? [One is anyone who is wading (that is, walking) through a meadow of wildflowers in autumn.]

Ⓒ Critical Thinking

Analyzing

❓ How can a chameleon and a praying mantis change a forest? [Possible response: Their camouflaged harmony with their environment creates a subtly deeper range of natural color.]

Ⓓ Critical Thinking

Interpreting

❓ How does the person addressed hold the roses? [He or she holds them in a way that preserves their wildness and surprise, and strips them of clichéd meaning.]

Before You Read

THE BEAUTIFUL CHANGES

Make the Connection

The Eye of the Beholder

Beauty often seems to have something magical about it. "Now you see it, now you don't" is a magician's cliché that could just as easily be a poet's catch phrase. The poet, like the magician, knows that beauty can be ever-shifting, forged in a fleeting moment by combining everyday people and things with the artist's creative eye.

Quickwrite

Think about a person or a thing you consider beautiful. Then, write down some of the special characteristics of this person or thing. For instance, a beautiful person might radiate an aura of kindness.

Elements of Literature

Ambiguity

The title of Wilbur's poem presents us with an **ambiguity**—an expression that deliberately suggests two or more different, and sometimes conflicting, meanings. Does "the beautiful changes" mean that our idea of the beautiful changes? Or is the poem about beautiful transformations? Do both meanings apply?

Background

Queen Anne's lace (or wild carrot) is a common weed. Its flower looks like a crocheted doily with a tiny ruby at its center. "Lucernes" (loō·sʉrnz′) is a reference to the glacier-fed Lake of Lucerne in Switzerland.

1006 CONTEMPORARY LITERATURE

Bonnie Sue/Photo Researchers.

The Beautiful Changes

Richard Wilbur

One wading a Fall meadow finds on all sides
The Queen Anne's Lace lying like lilies
On water; it glides
So from the walker, it turns
5 Dry grass to a lake, as the slightest shade of you
Valleys my mind in fabulous blue Lucernes.

The beautiful changes as a forest is changed
By a chameleon's tuning his skin to it;
As a mantis, arranged
10 On a green leaf, grows
Into it, makes the leaf leafier, and proves
Any greenness is deeper than anyone knows.

Your hands hold roses always in a way that says
They are not only yours; the beautiful changes
15 In such kind ways,
Wishing ever to sunder
Things and things' selves for a second finding, to lose
For a moment all that it touches back to wonder.

Reaching All Students

Struggling Readers

Have students work with more advanced partners to recast the poem into written prose. After the recasting is completed, have students respond individually to the process and the product in their journals. Have them state whether the recasting created new meaning for them or took away from the poem's meaning and explain why.

Spring by
Donald C. Martin.
Private Collection.

**RESPONDING TO
THE ART**

Activity. After students have
read "Boy at the Window," invite
them to discuss the ways in which
the picture does and does not
match their personal visualiza-
tions of the poem's scenario and
theme.

ⓔ Critical Thinking

Interpreting

❓ How does the "contentment" of
the snowman undermine the boy's personification of him? How is his tear different from the boy's—why is it pure?
[Possible response: The inanimate snowman feels none of the vulnerability and
fear the boy ascribes to him, he is content in his pure elemental being. Thus
the only feeling his "tear" represents is
the inhuman condition of being without
consciousness and emotion.]

ⓕ Critical Thinking

Hypothesizing

❓ What fears might the snowman and
the speaker perceive in the child's
world? [Possible responses: fear of the
dark; fear of storms; fear of illness and
death; fear of the adult world.]

Before You Read
BOY AT THE WINDOW

Make the Connection

Inside and Outside

Indoors is warm, bright, and protected
from harsh weather. Outdoors is cold,
dark, and lashed by snow and rain.
Indoors and outdoors are very different—but there can be connections.
There may be, for instance, danger in
both places. Have you ever felt that outdoors was just an extension of indoors?

Quickwrite

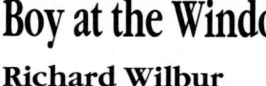

At times, some
people feel that
inanimate objects—trees, clouds, snowmen—are almost human. Write down
some notes explaining why people might
personify such things in the natural
world.

Boy at the Window

Richard Wilbur

Seeing the snowman standing all alone
In dusk and cold is more than he can bear.
The small boy weeps to hear the wind prepare
A night of gnashings° and enormous moan.
His tearful sight can hardly reach to where   5
The pale-faced figure with bitumen° eyes
Returns him such a god-forsaken stare
As outcast Adam gave to Paradise.

The man of snow is, nonetheless, content,
Having no wish to go inside and die.   10
Still, he is moved to see the youngster cry.
Though frozen water is his element,
He melts enough to drop from one soft eye
A trickle of the purest rain, a tear
For the child at the bright pane surrounded by   15
Such warmth, such light, such love, and so much fear. **ⓕ**

ⓔ

4. gnashings (nash′iŋz): grinding of teeth, as in anger.
6. bitumen (bi·too′mən): thick, coal-like substance.

RICHARD WILBUR 1007

Using Students' Strengths

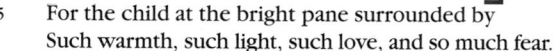

Logical/Mathematical Learners

Ask students to copy down, on one side of a
sheet of paper, any passages in "The Beautiful
Changes" that they think do not make literal
sense; for example, "makes the leaf leafier"
(l. 11). On the other side of the paper, have students explain what they think the poet means.
Discuss whether students find the poetic meaning valid and why or why not.

Visual Learners

Invite students to create their own illustration
of "Boy at the Window." Their illustration may
be representative of the boy, the snowman, the
window, and so on; or students may create an
abstract illustration evoking the emotions in the
poem and its effect on them.

Intrapersonal Learners

Ask students to write an interior monologue in
which the boy, having turned away from the
window, expresses the thoughts and feelings the
snowman prompted in him.

The Beautiful Changes

First Thoughts [Respond]

1. Students might reference their changing experience of a beautiful song in different emotional contexts, or recall the unexpected beauty of ordinary surroundings and objects.

Shaping Interpretations [Interpret]

2. It causes a meadow of dry grass to resemble a lake.

3. Possible responses: a loved one, or the reader, or both. Both "you" and Queen Anne's lace inspire an expanse of beautiful images and heightened perceptions.

4. The beautiful both inspires and *is* a renewal of perception, which lets us rediscover the world with fresh meaning and wonder.

5. Beautiful things and people change, as does our perception of them. Changes in nature and human perception are beautiful. The poem supports both meanings.

6. Possible responses: References to "you" (ll. 5, 13–14) suggest a specific beloved person. References to "the beautiful" (ll. 7, 14) indicate a general love of beauty.

Boy at the Window

First Thoughts [Respond]

1. Possible response: The boy's human fears indoors may be as harmful to him as he thinks the weather is to the snowman outside.

Shaping Interpretations [Interpret]

2. Adam was banished from the harmony and peace of Eden. The boy projects his fear of nature and the cold on the snowman, and thus sees him as banished "outside." Yet it is the boy who, inside his anxiety and vulnerability, is cut-off from nature's pure contentment and peace.

3. Possible responses: He may have built the snowman and so may feel connected to it; this lone figure comes to represent the boy's own fear of abandonment and exposure to the elements.

4. Possible response: The inanimate snowman has no use for fear or comfort, but exists as a natural element among elements. Thus the speaker suggests that, in his neutrality, he feels a kind of pity for the boy's alienation from nature.

The Beautiful Changes

First Thoughts

1. Is anything in the poem similar to your own experience? Can you make a connection between the poem and anything you noted in your Quickwrite?

Shaping Interpretations

2. According to the poem's speaker, in what way does Queen Anne's lace change a meadow?

3. Who is "you"? In what way is the effect of "you" similar to the effect of Queen Anne's lace?

4. The third stanza makes a strong statement. Paraphrase that statement and tell what you think the "second finding" might be.

5. In your own words, explain the **ambiguity** of the **title.** Does the poem as a whole support one meaning or the other, or both?

6. Is this a love poem? If so, who or what does the speaker love? Pick out the lines that support your answer.

Boy at the Window

First Thoughts

1. What do you think the poem is suggesting about the boy and his fears? (How is the boy's indoor "weather" like the outdoors?)

Shaping Interpretations

2. Explain the **allusion** at the end of the first stanza. Could it apply to both the snowman and the boy? Why or why not?

3. Why do you think the boy feels a connection with the snowman?

4. Why does the snowman feel sympathy for the boy?

5. Who is more comfortable in his situation—the boy or the snowman? Do you think this indicates something about the difference between the human world and the world of nature?

5. The snowman is "content" (l. 9), while the boy stares out the window in discomfort. The poem emphasizes the self-sufficiency and harmony of the natural world—and the vulnerability and isolation of human consciousness in it. Thus, like the boy, we seek relief by projecting human meaning onto nature.

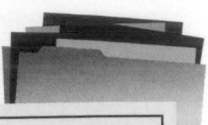

Writer's Notebook

1. Collecting Ideas for an Evaluation

"The Beautiful Changes" and "Boy at the Window" are **lyric poems,** or poems that express the personal feelings and thoughts of a speaker. In your opinion, what makes such a poem effective? Consider elements like **message, language, form,** and **tone.** Then, note how either of Wilbur's poems meets or does not meet each of your criteria. Save your notes for possible use in the Writer's Workshop on page 1181.

Interpreting a Poem
2. "Glorious Energy"

In an interview, Wilbur made this statement: "To put it simply, I feel that the universe is full of glorious energy, that the energy tends to take pattern and shape, and that the ultimate character of things is comely and good." In a brief essay, discuss how "The Beautiful Changes" demonstrates what Wilbur means in this statement. Do you agree or disagree with the poet?

A Reflection
3. The Motive for Metaphor

Why do you think we humans imagine that snowmen can feel the cold or that a storm can gnash its teeth? Get together with a partner and exchange some ideas about this question. Don't worry about a definite answer; philosophers still don't know the answer to that question, but that doesn't mean they stop asking. When you have some ideas about "the motive for metaphor," write them up in a brief essay. In your essay, refer to the little boy in the poem. Try to explain *why* the boy **personifies** the snowman—when he knows very well that the snowman cannot feel the cold. Be sure to refer to your Quickwrite notes.

Karl Shapiro

(1913–   )

© Rollie McKenna.

Karl Shapiro has made a career out of defying literary classification. As a poet, novelist, and literary critic, he has a self-acknowledged determination to "take the other side of almost any argument" and to pursue "the anti-poem" that cuts through "traditional poetic faking."

Shapiro's resistance to doctrine has led him to reject contemporary wisdom about how a poem should be written and to take up forms and styles that are either radically new or unfashionably old. As the critic Michael True observes, "[i]f he were asked to speak at the White House, he would probably arrive dressed in a Hawaiian shirt, orange trousers, and sneakers; at a rock concert he would be the one in white tie and tails." In spite of—perhaps because of—this fierce independence, Shapiro's poetry reflects the conflicts and contradictions of a crucial transition period in American history and American literature.

Born in Baltimore, Maryland, in 1913, Shapiro was raised in a Jewish household in an urban environment, a world that was both inside and outside the centers of traditional American culture. While he was determined to become a poet from an early age, Shapiro had to be "coaxed and cajoled through grade after grade," and he dropped out of the University of Virginia after one unhappy semester. It was only after he was inducted into the Army Medical Corps and served for five years in the South Pacific that Shapiro began to achieve academic and literary success. During World War II, he wrote the hard-edged, tightly metered poems that would establish his literary reputation, culminating in the collection *V-Letter and Other Poems,* which won the Pulitzer Prize in 1945.

As one of the first young literary figures to emerge from the devastation of World War II, Shapiro was often seen as the voice of a new generation. Members of this literary group rejected the formalism, abstract subject matter, and occasional obscurity of modernist poets like T. S. Eliot and Ezra Pound. At the same time, they anticipated the rougher forms and nontraditional subject matter that characterized the Beat poetry of the 1950s and '60s. Indeed, Shapiro seems to speak for the Beats and their literary forefathers, William Carlos Williams and Walt Whitman, with the credo: "Between the poetry of language or symbol and that of situation, I choose situation." Yet, Shapiro's frequent use of traditional metric forms distinguishes him from Beat poets like Allen Ginsberg and Lawrence Ferlinghetti.

Shapiro's later disillusionment with the artistic standards of the 1960s "counterculture" and with what he termed "the intellectual infantilism of the American radical" further established his stubborn independence as an artist and cultural critic. This mistrust of popular movements in poetry and politics has remained a constant in Shapiro's long and varied career. It is also reflected in his searching, moving poems about his Jewish identity, his flirtations with both communism and Catholicism, and his service in World War II.

Shapiro said of "Elegy for a Dead Soldier," his celebrated war poem, "It was not a flag-waving poem, and it was not an anti-flag-waving poem, a hard balance which [I] always tried for." It is this kind of balance that has established Shapiro as one of America's most innovative poets, one whose work consistently challenges conventional assumptions about what constitutes good politics, good culture, and good art.

KARL SHAPIRO 1009

Planning

Summary ■ ■

This unrhymed, carefully metered poem moves from an impersonal account of an ambulance's arrival at a crash scene to a reflection on the witnesses' collective "wound" in the accident's aftermath. The first stanza narrates the arrival and departure of the ambulance; the second maintains a detached, almost clinical tone as the police clean up and the witnesses wander the site "deranged." In the third stanza, it is the spectators who metaphorically take on the wounds of the accident, making small-talk and trying in vain to make meaning out of the unpredictability and randomness of sudden death.

Ⓐ Elements of Literature
Synesthesia

❓ What is the synesthesia in l. 1? [The sound of a bell is described in terms of vision ("silver") and touch ("soft").]

Ⓑ Elements of Literature
Diction

❓ What is the effect of Shapiro's word choice in this stanza, especially in words such as "floating," "dips," "emptying," "stowed," "cargo," and so on? [Possible responses: It suggests the smooth, almost casual efficiency of the ambulance workers; It reflects the numb, dreamlike horror of the speaker and other witnesses.]

Ⓒ Critical Thinking
Interpreting

❓ Whom do "We" and "Our" refer to? [Possible responses: The words refer to the spectators; however, the spectators and the crash victims are identified with one another through imagery, such as "We are deranged," "Our throats were tight as tourniquets," and "Our feet were bound with splints."]

Before You Read
AUTO WRECK

Make the Connection
Lack of Control
Most of us live under the assumption that we can control or at least understand events that happen to us and around us. Yet we often encounter accidents, mysterious events, and random tragedies that mock this sense of order. How have you dealt with unexpected and unexplained events in your own life?

Quickwrite
Shapiro's poem has the simple and powerful title "Auto Wreck." Before you read, think of a time that you witnessed or learned about an accident or a natural disaster. Jot down some of your responses at the time—sorrow, fear, curiosity, even guilt or shame.

Elements of Literature
Synesthesia
The first line of "Auto Wreck" contains a striking example of **synesthesia,** the juxtaposition of images that appeal to different kinds of sensory experience. As a literary technique, synesthesia is often an attempt to capture the complex blend of sensory data that helps make up human experience.

Auto Wreck

Karl Shapiro

Ⓐ Its quick soft silver bell beating, beating,
And down the dark one ruby flare
Pulsing out red light like an artery,
The ambulance at top speed floating down
5 Past beacons and illuminated clocks
Wings in a heavy curve, dips down,
And brakes speed, entering the crowd.
Ⓑ The doors leap open, emptying light;
Stretchers are laid out, the mangled lifted
10 And stowed into the little hospital.
Then the bell, breaking the hush, tolls once,
And the ambulance with its terrible cargo
Rocking, slightly rocking, moves away,
As the doors, an afterthought, are closed.

15 We are deranged, walking among the cops
Who sweep glass and are large and
    composed.
One is still making notes under the light.
Ⓒ One with a bucket douches° ponds of blood
Into the street and gutter.
20 One hangs lanterns on the wrecks that cling,
Empty husks of locusts, to iron poles.

Our throats were tight as tourniquets,
Our feet were bound with splints, but now,

18. **douches** (do͞osh′iz): splashes or flushes with water to clean; washes.

Reaching All Students

Struggling Readers
Focus students' attention on the physical description of the accident and its aftermath, having students point out specific lines and phrases that evoke the scene for them. Be sure that students know that *tourniquets* are "bands twisted tight to control the flow of blood" and *splints* are "thin strips of wood or metal used to keep a part of the body in place."

English Language Learners
Help students write a summary of the poem that includes the significant events and the conclusions the speaker draws from them. Then, have them analyze how the speaker communicates these events and conclusions through condensed, often figurative language. For strategies for engaging English language learners with the literature, see
• *Lesson Plans Including Strategies for English-Language Learners*

Advanced Learners
Have students discuss the thematic material in ll. 29–39. Ask questions based on this passage, such as "What is 'our richest horror'?" and "Who is innocent?" Then, have students compare this poem's view of death with those of other poems, such as Walt Whitman's "Out of the Cradle Endlessly Rocking" and John Donne's "Death, Be Not Proud."

	Like convalescents intimate and gauche,°
25	We speak through sickly smiles and warn
	With the stubborn saw of common sense, 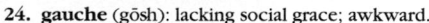
	The grim joke and the banal resolution.
	The traffic moves around with care,
	But we remain, touching a wound
30	That opens to our richest horror.
	Already old, the question Who shall die?
	Becomes unspoken Who is innocent?

24. gauche (gōsh): lacking social grace; awkward.

For death in war is done by hands;
Suicide has cause and stillbirth, logic;
35 And cancer, simple as a flower, blooms.
But this invites the occult mind,
Cancels our physics with a sneer,
And spatters all we knew of
    denouement°
Across the expedient and wicked stones.

38. denouement (dā′noo·män′): outcome of a drama or story.

MAKING MEANINGS

First Thoughts

1. How do you think the speaker in "Auto Wreck" is changed by this experience of human tragedy?

Shaping Interpretations

2. In your own words, **summarize** very briefly what happens in each stanza.

3. Describe what you *see* and *hear* in the first two stanzas. Which details in the poem evoke those sensations?

4. What details in lines 22–27 tell you how the spectators are feeling and what they are saying to one another?

5. Which **images** in the poem are based on medical terminology? Why do you think the poet decided to choose these images?

6. According to the speaker, how are deaths by war, suicide, and stillbirth different from the kind of accidental death described in the poem? What do you think the speaker is really so disturbed about in the last lines?

7. What might the speaker mean by saying that his questions can be answered only by an "occult" mind? What verb in line 38 reminds you again of the auto wreck?

Extending the Text

8. Do you think someone the speaker knew was in the auto wreck, or is he just a bystander? Do you think it is important to know the answer to this question? Explain your response.

CHOICES:
Building Your Portfolio

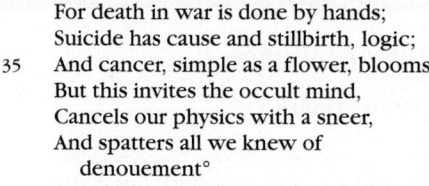

Writer's Notebook

1. Collecting Ideas for an Evaluation

Shapiro's poetry is admired for its technical and intellectual brilliance, but some critics say his tone is too harsh and short on compassion. Based on your reading of "Auto Wreck," do you agree with this assessment? Does the speaker's focus on the witnesses make him seem indifferent to the victims? Write down some thoughts and cite details from the poem to support your ideas. Save your notes for possible use in the Writer's Workshop on page 1181.

Creative Writing

2. A Witness

Refer to your Quickwrite notes, and use them to write a brief essay about your own experience with an accident or disaster. The event need not be tragic, or even significant to anyone else. It should be something that affected you in some way, perhaps by raising some of the questions Shapiro raises in the poem. A broken arm, for example, might have made you think for the first time about how fragile our bodies really are and how we should take care of them. Be sure to write about something you don't mind sharing.

KARL SHAPIRO 1011

D **English Language Learners**
Multiple Meanings of Words
A *saw* in this context is an adage or an old, familiar saying. A *saw* is also a toothed cutting tool.

E **Critical Thinking**
Interpreting
? What wound is the poet referring to? [Possible responses: mortality; fear of death; sin.]

5. "Artery" (l. 3), "tourniquets" (l. 22), "splints" (l. 23), "convalescents" (l. 24), "sickly" (l. 25), "wound" (l. 29), "stillbirth" (l. 34), and "cancer" (l. 35) are medical images; they reinforce the coldly clinical description of the accident and of death in general.

6. Death in war, suicide, and stillbirth can be explained in human terms; cancer develops slowly and predictably; this accident, on the other hand, resists human meaning in its random violence. The speaker may be disturbed by this sudden destruction of meaning and order.

7. The speaker suggests that the inexplicable horror of the accident invites speculation about such things as divine retribution, mystical curses, and unlucky omens; the verb "spatters" reminds us of the wreck.

Extending the Text [Synthesize]

8. Possible responses: Answers will vary. Since the poem is ambiguous, it may not be important.

Grading Timesaver

Rubrics for each Choices Assignment appear on p. 212 in the *Portfolio Management System*.

MAKING MEANINGS

First Thoughts [Respond]

1. Sample response: The accident jolts the speaker into thinking about sudden, random death and death in general.

Shaping Interpretations [Interpret]

2. Stanza one (ll. 1–14): Ambulance arrives and departs with victims; stanza two (ll. 15–21): Police clean up scene as spectators watch; stanza three (ll. 22–39): Spectators make grim jokes and reflect on death.

3. Possible details include the sound and sight of the ambulance, the crowd, the emergency workers lifting the victims onto stretchers, and the police cleaning up.

4. Constriction of the spectators' throats and limbs, and their "sickly smiles," suggest that they feel horrified, shaken, and afraid. The "common sense," "grim joke," and "banal resolution" suggest that their conversation is a half-hearted attempt at reassurance.

Richard Wright

(1908–1960)

Richard Wright by Carl Van Vechten.

"It had been only through books—at best, no more than vicarious cultural transfusions—that I had managed to keep myself alive. . . ." Richard Wright *did* keep himself alive, and he became a writer with a gift for conveying the intensity of his struggle. He is typically described as the first African American writer to expose American racism to a large white audience. But this cool academic assessment fails to capture the angry, relentless drive of his most famous novel, *Native Son* (1940), or of his autobiography, *Black Boy* (1945).

Critics have labored to justify Wright's twelve-year membership in the Communist Party and explain his self-exile in Paris for the last fourteen years of his life. Full of contradictions, Wright is hard to label, yet it is clear that African American writers who have followed him have had to emerge from his shadow.

When the University of Mississippi organized a symposium on Wright in 1985, it was front-page news. Part of the poignancy of such posthumous recognition comes from the fact that Wright had remembered his home state of Mississippi with "ambivalence." We can only speculate on how Wright might have reacted to an authority on Southern culture who told *The New York Times:* "Faulkner is considered the top Mississippi writer, but I would put Wright with Eudora Welty and Tennessee Williams in their international reputation."

Wright's life began in poverty. His father, a Mississippi sharecropper, abandoned his family when Wright was five; when the boy was twelve, his mother could no longer support the family. Raised by various relatives, Wright early learned the bitter lessons of survival on ghetto streets. He remembered living with "the sustained expectation of violence." By borrowing a white man's library card, he was finally able to gain access to books.

Before he was twenty, Wright fled the South forever, moving to Chicago and then to New York. He joined the WPA Federal Writers Project, a Depression-era government organization that provided a livelihood for unemployed writers. He began to explore Marxism and eventually joined the Communist Party at a time when many people thought it offered hope for a more equitable reorganization of society (and before the horrors of the Stalinist purges of the 1930s became public). Eventually disillusioned, Wright left the party in 1944.

Wright achieved his first real recognition with *Native Son,* a tale of a victimized black man, Bigger Thomas, who accidentally kills once, then murders again to avoid betrayal. *Black Boy* secured Wright's fame and became a best-seller. But in the fifteen years between its publication and his death, Wright wrote no other book that equaled its success. He struggled to understand the historical and cultural place of African Americans in modern life, visiting Africa and recording his observations in *Black Power* (1954) and *White Man, Listen!* (1957). But he felt as much an alien in Africa as anywhere else. He died in Paris, where he had found as much of a home as he could.

 **go.hrw.com**
LE0 11-19

Resources: Print and Media

Reading
• *Graphic Organizers for Active Reading,* p. 101
• *Words to Own,* p. 52
• *Audio CD Library*
    Disc 26, Track 2

Elements of Literature
• *Literary Elements*
    Transparency 31
    Worksheet, p. 94

Writing and Language
• *Daily Oral Grammar*
    Transparency 57
• *Grammar and Language Links*
    Worksheet, p. 75

Assessment
• *Formal Assessment,* p. 200
• *Portfolio Management System,* p. 213
• *Test Generator (One-Stop Planner CD-ROM)*

Internet
• go.hrw.com (keyword: LE0 11-19)

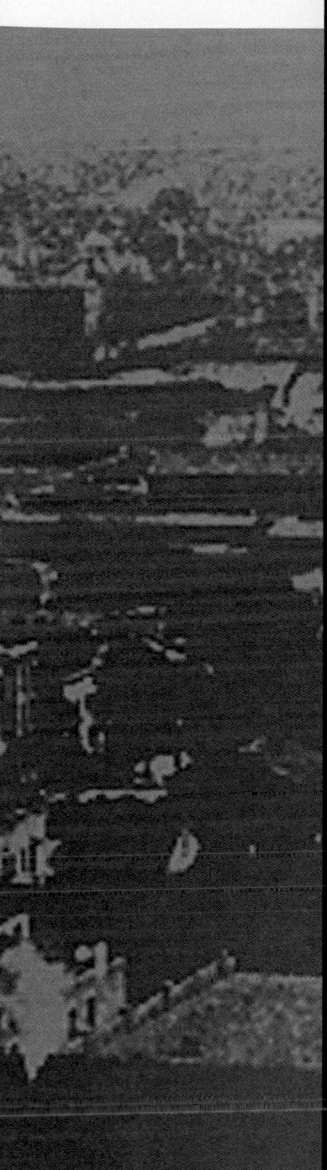

Before You Read

FROM **BLACK BOY**

Make the Connection

The Child Is Father to the Man

What does it mean to grow up, to put away our toys, and to participate in the world as mature and responsible adults? What elements of childhood do we carry with us forever? The discoveries we make as children, awakening to what the world is really like, can be harsh or sweet, shocking or gradual, depending on the specific circumstances of our lives. Yet in one way or another, we are all deeply affected by our childhood awakenings.

Reading Skills and Strategies

Interpreting Details

In this excerpt, images of "home" are associated mainly with physical and emotional hunger. As you read, make note of details that express the two kinds of hunger the young Wright feels—physical, gnawing hunger and another, emotional kind of hunger. Which hunger do you think Wright feels most acutely?

Elements of Literature

Dialogue

We often think of **dialogue**, or the directly quoted words of conversation between two or more people, as the property of drama and fiction. But dialogue can also play a significant role in nonfiction.

In nonfiction, though, dialogue can be controversial. Reporters and biographers are often challenged in court to prove that the conversations they put in quotation marks really occurred. In this excerpt from Wright's autobiography, most scenes are dramatized through dialogue. By presenting conversations, Wright *shows*, rather than describes, his own thoughts and feelings. With dialogue, he creates vivid pictures of the people in his life.

> **D**ialogue is the directly quoted words of conversation between two or more people.

Summary ■ ■

In this selection from his autobiography, Wright describes events from his childhood in Memphis, Tennessee, using a neutral, objective tone—even as he details the extreme hardships of his formative years. After his father abandons the family, Richard, his mother, and his brother face malnutrition and crushing poverty. Richard bitterly associates his father with his constant hunger pangs. His mother tells her sons to be self-reliant and responsible, but they are filled with a vague dread of the future. In order to buy groceries without being robbed on the way, Richard learns, at his mother's insistence, to beat the local bullies with a stick. Later, he is brought to his parents' alimony trial and watches his father con a judge into believing that he can't support the family (despite his comfortable lifestyle). Unable to support her sons on her income as a cook, Wright's mother puts them in an orphanage, where conditions are harsh and bleak. After Wright tries to flee, he accompanies his mother to beg his father again for money but is so disgusted by the condescension of his father and his father's mistress that he refuses the paltry sum they offer. Twenty-five years later, Wright again sees his father, now a sharecropper in Mississippi. This time, Wright forgives and pities him but realizes that there is an unbridgeable gap between them.

RICHARD WRIGHT 1013

Preteaching Vocabulary

Words to Own

All ten Words to Own for this selection can be acted out or pantomimed by students with only a modicum of performance skill. Divide students into groups, and have them take turns acting out a word of their choice. The rest of the group must guess the word. One or two additional clues may be given; after two clues, the actor should tell the group the word. Then, have the class work on the following activity.

Do steps 1–3 for each Word to Own. (If less time is available, use fewer words.)

1. Locate the sentence in which the Word to Own is first used.
2. Write a new sentence using the Word to Own and using the same structure as Wright's sentence but changing all other words.
3. Read your sentence aloud to the class.

Hughie Lee-Smith (1915–   ) was born in Eustis, Florida, to parents who supported his passion for art. As a young child, he moved to Cleveland, where he studied at Karamu House, a community center known for its art program. Later, he taught for nearly two decades at the Art Students League in New York, where students select the faculty. He chose to paint the urban ghetto, and his paintings address the contradictions of loneliness and community, poverty and wealth. Many show young people in scenes of isolation or alienation, with urban decay around them. Although basically realistic, the paintings convey a mystery, an almost surreal quality, that unsettles some viewers. His figures often have their backs to the viewer, yet they also seem alert and poised for action; and they are treated with sympathy but not sentimentality. *Boy with Tire* is one of Lee-Smith's most famous works. Critics have called it "allegorical" for the symbolic implications of the boy, tire, buildings, and shadows.

Activity. Ask students to discuss what elements of the painting are realistic, what elements of the painting seem stylized or abstract, and how the painting makes them feel.

Boy with Tire (1952) by Hughie Lee-Smith. Oil on prestwood panel (60.3 cm × 82.6 cm).

1014 CONTEMPORARY LITERATURE

Getting Students Involved

Using the Internet

You may want to suggest that students conduct Internet research on African American writers or painters. On-line sources include encyclopedias and databases, as well as search engines. *You may want to preview any Internet activity that you suggest to students. Because these resources are sometimes public forums, their content can be unpredictable.*

The Detroit Institute of Arts, Gift of Dr. S. B. Milton, Dr. James A. Owen, Dr. B. F. Seabrooks, and Dr. A. E. Thomas, Jr. © Hughie Lee-Smith/Licensed by VAGA, New York, NY.

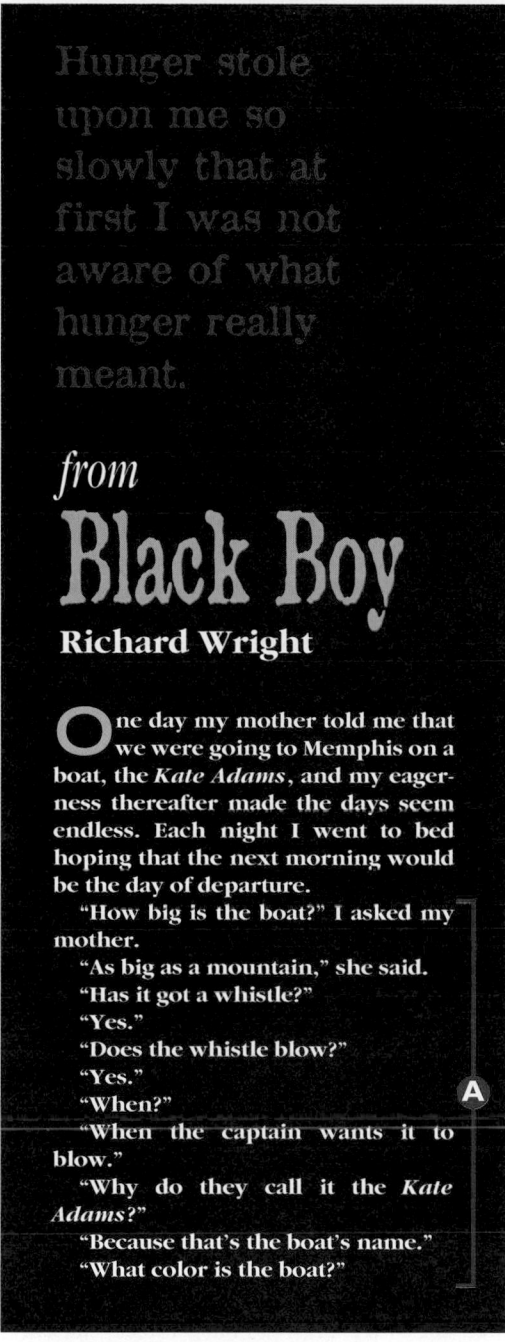

Hunger stole upon me so slowly that at first I was not aware of what hunger really meant.

from

Black Boy

Richard Wright

One day my mother told me that we were going to Memphis on a boat, the *Kate Adams*, and my eagerness thereafter made the days seem endless. Each night I went to bed hoping that the next morning would be the day of departure.

"How big is the boat?" I asked my mother.

"As big as a mountain," she said.

"Has it got a whistle?"

"Yes."

"Does the whistle blow?"

"Yes."

"When?"

"When the captain wants it to blow."

"Why do they call it the *Kate Adams*?"

"Because that's the boat's name."

"What color is the boat?"

RICHARD WRIGHT 1015

"White."

"How long will we be on the boat?"

"All day and all night."

"Will we sleep on the boat?"

"Yes, when we get sleepy, we'll sleep. Now, hush."

For days I had dreamed about a huge white boat floating on a vast body of water, but when my mother took me down to the levee on the day of leaving, I saw a tiny, dirty boat that was not at all like the boat I had imagined. I was disappointed and when time came to go on board I cried and my mother thought that I did not want to go with her to Memphis, and I could not tell her what the trouble was. Solace came when I wandered about the boat and gazed at Negroes throwing dice, drinking whiskey, playing cards, lolling on boxes, eating, talking, and singing. My father took me down into the engine room and the throbbing machines enthralled me for hours.

In Memphis we lived in a one-story brick tenement. The stone buildings and the concrete pavements looked bleak and hostile to me. The absence of green, growing things made the city seem dead. Living space for the four of us—my mother, my brother, my father, and me—was a kitchen and a bedroom. In the front and rear were paved areas in which my brother and I could play, but for days I was afraid to go into the strange city streets alone.

It was in this tenement that the personality of my father first came fully into the orbit of my concern. He worked as a night porter in a Beale Street drugstore and he became important and forbidding to me only when I learned that I could not make noise when he was asleep in the daytime. He was the lawgiver in our family and I never laughed in his presence. I used to lurk timidly in the kitchen doorway and watch his huge body sitting slumped at the table. I stared at him with awe as he gulped his beer from a tin bucket, as he ate long and heavily, sighed, belched, closed his eyes to nod on a stuffed belly. He was quite fat and his bloated stomach always lapped over his belt. He was always a stranger to me, always somehow alien and remote. . . .

Hunger stole upon me so slowly that at first I was not aware of what hunger really meant. Hunger had always been more or less at my elbow when I played, but now I began to wake up at night to find hunger standing at my bedside, staring at me gauntly. The hunger I had known before this had been no grim, hostile stranger; it had been a normal hunger that had made me beg constantly for bread, and when I ate a crust or two I was satisfied. But this new hunger baffled me, scared me, made me angry and insistent. Whenever I begged for food now my mother would pour me a cup of tea which would still the clamor in my stomach for a moment or two; but a little later I would feel hunger nudging my ribs, twisting my empty guts until they ached. I would grow dizzy and my vision would dim. I became less active in my play, and for the first time in my life I had to pause and think of what was happening to me.

"Mama, I'm hungry," I complained one afternoon.

"Jump up and catch a kungry," she said, trying to make me laugh and forget.

"What's a *kungry*?"

"It's what little boys eat when they get hungry," she said.

"What does it taste like?"

"I don't know."

"Then why do you tell me to catch one?"

"Because you said that you were hungry," she said, smiling.

I sensed that she was teasing me and it made me angry.

"But I'm hungry. I want to eat."

"You'll have to wait."

"But I want to eat now."

"But there's nothing to eat," she told me.

"Why?"

"Just because there's none," she explained.

"But I want to eat," I said, beginning to cry.

"You'll just have to wait," she said again.

"But why?"

"For God to send some food."

"When is He going to send it?"

"I don't know."

"But I'm hungry!"

WORDS TO OWN
enthralled (en·thrôld′) *v.*: fascinated.
lurk (lurk) *v.*: to hide unnoticed.
clamor (klam′ər) *n.*: loud noise; uproar.

Listening to Music

First Movement of the *Afro-American Symphony* by William Grant Still, Performed by the Cincinnati Philharmonia Orchestra
William Grant Still (1895–1978) was the first African American composer ever to have a symphony performed by a major American orchestra. The work was Still's *Afro-American Symphony,* which premiered in 1931 with the Eastman Rochester Philharmonic. At its core was a standard blues theme—like the ones Still had arranged for blues composer W. C. Handy before branching out on his own.

Activity
Before students read the selection from *Black Boy,* play the First Movement of Still's *Afro-American Symphony*. Ask students to pick out the basic blues theme at its core. Then, ask them to try interpreting in words the expression of African American identity that Still conveys with music.

She was ironing and she paused and looked at me with tears in her eyes.

"Where's your father?" she asked me.

I stared in bewilderment. Yes, it was true that my father had not come home to sleep for many days now and I could make as much noise as I wanted. Though I had not known why he was absent, I had been glad that he was not there to shout his restrictions at me. But it had never occurred to me that his absence would mean that there would be no food.

"I don't know," I said.

"Who brings food into the house?" my mother asked me.

"Papa," I said. "He always brought food."

"Well, your father isn't here now," she said.

"Where is he?"

"I don't know," she said.

"But I'm hungry," I whimpered, stomping my feet.

"You'll have to wait until I get a job and buy food," she said.

As the days slid past, the image of my father became associated with my pangs of hunger, and whenever I felt hunger I thought of him with a deep biological bitterness.

My mother finally went to work as a cook and left me and my brother alone in the flat each day with a loaf of bread and a pot of tea. When she returned at evening she would be tired and <u>dispirited</u> and would cry a lot. Sometimes, when she was in despair, she would call us to her and talk to us for hours, telling us that we now had no father, that our lives would be different from those of other children, that we must learn as soon as possible to take care of ourselves, to dress ourselves, to prepare our own food; that we must take upon ourselves the responsibility of the flat while she worked. Half frightened, we would promise solemnly. We did not understand what had happened between our father and our mother and the most that these long talks did to us was to make us feel a vague dread. Whenever we asked why father had left, she would tell us that we were too young to know.

One evening my mother told me that thereafter I would have to do the shopping for food. She took me to the corner store to show me the way. I was proud; I felt like a grownup. The next afternoon I looped the basket over my arm and went down the pavement toward the store. When I reached the corner, a gang of boys grabbed me, knocked me down, snatched the basket, took the money, and sent me running home in panic. That evening I told my mother what had happened, but she made no comment; she sat down at once, wrote another note, gave me more money, and sent me out to the grocery again. I crept down the steps and saw the same gang of boys playing down the street. I ran back into the house.

"What's the matter?" my mother asked.

"It's those same boys," I said. "They'll beat me."

"You've got to get over that," she said. "Now, go on."

"I'm scared," I said.

"Go on and don't pay any attention to them," she said.

I went out of the door and walked briskly down the sidewalk, praying that the gang would not molest me. But when I came abreast of them someone shouted.

"There he is!"

They came toward me and I broke into a wild run toward home. They overtook me and flung me to the pavement. I yelled, pleaded, kicked, but they wrenched the money out of my hand. They yanked me to my feet, gave me a few slaps, and sent me home sobbing. My mother met me at the door.

"They b-beat m-me," I gasped. "They t-t-took the m-money."

I started up the steps, seeking the shelter of the house.

"Don't you come in here," my mother warned me.

I froze in my tracks and stared at her.

"But they're coming after me," I said.

"You just stay right where you are," she said in a deadly tone. "I'm going to teach you this night to stand up and fight for yourself."

She went into the house and I waited, terrified, wondering what she was about. Presently she returned with more money and another note, she also had a long heavy stick.

"Take this money, this note, and this stick," she said. "Go to the store and buy those groceries. If those boys bother you, then fight."

WORDS TO OWN

dispirited (di·spir'it·id) *adj.:* discouraged.

ⓔ Reading Skills and Strategies
Interpreting Details

❓ What did Wright come to associate his father with? [hunger and "a deep biological bitterness"] **Why?** [Possible responses: His father's absence was a major cause of his hunger; he resented that his father did not return with food for the family.]

ⓕ Reading Skills and Strategies
Predicting

Ask students to predict how Wright's life will change now that his father has left. [Possible repsonses: He will have little time for play; he will have to look out for his brother; he will be hungry.]

ⓖ Critical Thinking
Speculating

❓ Why might Wright's father have left the family? [Possible responses: He is an irresponsible person who resents the demands of family life; he has fallen in love with another woman.]

ⓗ Elements of Literature
Dialogue

❓ From the dialogue, what can you gather about the mother's character and motivations? [Possible responses: She is stern; she wants to train her son to stand up for himself.] **What does the dialogue *not* tell you about her?** [Possible responses: her inner feelings; her past experiences.]

Reaching All Students

Interpersonal Learners

Wright had a difficult childhood that left him bitter and frustrated. However, he was eventually able to succeed as a writer. Ask students to discuss the personal strengths Wright developed as a child that enabled him to succeed in spite of the difficulties he faced. Ask groups of three to develop lists of skills people need to succeed today. You may wish to specify different contexts: for example, success in school, success in personal relationships, economic success, and social success.

Intrapersonal Learners

To help students identify with the material, ask them to close their eyes for a minute or two and imagine that they are Richard Wright. (Students may imagine the impoverished youth, the successful author, or both.) Have students freewrite their interpretation of Wright's feelings about his struggles. Then, ask students to reread their freewriting and circle the most powerful ideas for possible later use.

A **Critical Thinking**

Interpreting

? What can you infer about Wright's mother from the fact that she never told her son to fight before? [Possible response: Wright's mother wants to instill a firm sense of decency and propriety in her sons, but she also knows that they will have to adapt to the difficult circumstances in Memphis in order for the family to survive.]

B **Struggling Readers**

Understanding Details

Be sure students understand that "I let the stick fly" in this context means that Richard swung the stick, not that he threw it. Encourage students to notice other vivid words that describe the action of the fight. [Possible responses: *lamming, flayed, frenzy, panting.*]

C **English Language Learners**

Colloquialisms

Explain that *egging someone on* means "prodding or taunting into action." *To tear out* means "to run," and *to give them the same* means "to do the same thing to them," which, in this case, means to fight them.

D **Critical Thinking**

Extending the Text

Having to fight for one's right to walk down a street or a hallway is an experience many children—but not all—have had. Invite students to discuss whether or not they identify with Wright's experience and what impact they feel this kind of childhood trauma has on a young person.

E **Reading Skills and Strategies**

Interpreting Details

? What details remain in your memory from this passage? [Possible responses: the huge platter of crispy, golden chicken; the smiling, gluttonous preacher; Wright's inability to eat the soup.] What do you see as the main idea of this passage? [Possible response: The passage emphasizes Wright's frustration and helplessness before an adult world that provides few easy breaks for him.]

A I was baffled. My mother was telling me to fight, a thing that she had never done before.

"But I'm scared," I said.

"Don't you come into this house until you've gotten those groceries," she said.

"They'll beat me; they'll beat me," I said.

"Then stay in the streets; don't come back here!"

I ran up the steps and tried to force my way past her into the house. A stinging slap came on my jaw. I stood on the sidewalk, crying.

"Please, let me wait until tomorrow," I begged.

"No," she said. "Go now! If you come back into this house without those groceries, I'll whip you!"

She slammed the door and I heard the key turn in the lock. I shook with fright. I was alone upon the dark, hostile streets and gangs were after me. I had the choice of being beaten at home or away from home. I clutched the stick, crying, trying to reason. If I were beaten at home, there was absolutely nothing that I could do about it; but if I were beaten in the streets, I had a chance to fight and defend myself. I walked slowly down the sidewalk, coming closer to the gang of boys, holding the stick tightly. I was so full of fear that I could scarcely breathe. I was almost upon them now.

"There he is again!" the cry went up.

They surrounded me quickly and began to grab for my hand.

"I'll kill you!" I threatened.

B They closed in. In blind fear I let the stick fly, feeling it crack against a boy's skull. I swung again, lamming another skull, then another. Realizing that they would retaliate if I let up for but a second, I fought to lay them low, to knock them cold, to kill them so that they could not strike back at me. I flayed with tears in my eyes, teeth clenched, stark fear making me throw every ounce of my strength behind each blow. I hit again and again, dropping the money and the grocery list. The boys scattered, yelling, nursing their heads, staring at me in utter disbelief. They had never seen such <u>frenzy</u>. I stood panting, egging them on, taunting them to come on and fight. When they refused, I ran after them and they tore **C** out for their homes, screaming. The parents of the boys rushed into the streets and threatened me, and for the first time in my life I shouted at grownups, telling them that I would give them the same if they bothered me. I finally found my grocery list and the money and went to the store. On my way back I kept my stick poised for instant **D** use, but there was not a single boy in sight. That night I won the right to the streets of Memphis....

After my father's desertion, my mother's ar-<u>dently</u> religious disposition dominated the household and I was often taken to Sunday school where I met God's representative in the guise of a tall, black preacher. One Sunday my mother invited the tall, black preacher to a dinner of fried chicken. I was happy, not because the preacher was coming but because of the chicken. One or two neighbors also were invited. But no sooner had the preacher arrived than I began to resent him, for I learned at once that he, like my father, was used to having his own way. The hour for dinner came and I was wedged at the table between talking and laughing adults. In the center of the table was a huge platter of golden-brown fried chicken. I compared the bowl of soup that sat before me with the crispy chicken and decided in favor of the chicken. The others began to eat their soup, but I could not touch mine.

"Eat your soup," my mother said.

"I don't want any," I said.

"You won't get anything else until you've eaten your soup," she said.

The preacher had finished his soup and had asked that the platter of chicken be passed to him. It <u>galled</u> me. He smiled, cocked his head this way **E** and that, picking out choice pieces. I forced a spoonful of soup down my throat and looked to see if my speed matched that of the preacher. It did not. There were already bare chicken bones on his plate, and he was reaching for more. I tried eating my soup faster, but it was no use; the other people were now serving themselves chicken and the platter was more than half empty. I gave up and sat staring in despair at the vanishing pieces of fried chicken.

"Eat your soup or you won't get anything," my mother warned.

I looked at her appealingly and could not answer. As piece after piece of chicken was eaten, I

WORDS TO OWN

frenzy (fren′zē) *n.:* frantic behavior; wildness.
ardently (ärd′'nt·lē) *adv.:* intensely; eagerly.
galled (gôld) *v.:* irritated; angered.

1018 CONTEMPORARY LITERATURE

Getting Students Involved

Cooperative Learning

Time Line. Have groups research poverty and hunger in the United States from 1910 to 2000, assigning each group one decade. Have group members assume responsibilities, such as lead researcher, information organizer, speaker, and time-line designer. For each time period, students should look into the number of poor people, the percentage of the national population living in poverty, the dollar level of the poverty line, the available relief services and solutions, and important changes within the decade. After each group has researched its time period, have volunteers draw a time line on the chalkboard or on large art paper. Proceeding from the earliest to the latest decades, have a member from each group write the information on the time line as another member from that group explains the information to the class.

My Brother (1942) by John Wilson. Oil on panel (12″ × 10⅝″).

Smith College Museum of Art, Northampton, Massachusetts.

RESPONDING TO THE ART

John Wilson (1922–   ) is a socially conscious painter, print-maker, illustrator, and teacher. In the 1940s, Wilson's teacher at the Boston Art Museum encouraged him to use social art as a means of fighting racism. *My Brother* is an intimate portrait that reveals a deep bond of sympathy between the artist and the subject. The background works as an interesting surface in itself while setting the finely rendered portrait against a sketchy urban landscape.

Activity. Ask students to discuss what qualities of the person the artist is trying to convey and why this portrait seems appropriate—or not appropriate—to the character described in *Black Boy*.

F **Elements of Literature**

Dialogue

? How did you respond to this line of dialogue and its aftermath? [Sample responses: Some students may laugh; most will feel sorry for Wright.] **What impression of Wright does it give you?** [Sample responses: He is a bright but frustrated child who doesn't know how to get what he wants yet. When he tries to speak up for himself, he is punished.]

was unable to eat my soup at all. I grew hot with anger. The preacher was laughing and joking and the grownups were hanging on his words. My growing hate of the preacher finally became more important than God or religion and I could no longer contain myself. I leaped up from the table, knowing that I should be ashamed of what I was doing, but unable to stop, and screamed, running blindly from the room.

"That preacher's going to eat *all* the chicken!" I bawled.

The preacher tossed back his head and roared with laughter, but my mother was angry and told me that I was to have no dinner because of my bad manners.

When I awakened one morning my mother told me that we were going to see a judge who

RICHARD WRIGHT **1019**

Crossing the Curriculum

Economics/Mathematics

Have students research what five cents could buy in 1917 in order to determine what Wright was refusing when he did not take his father's nickel (p. 1022). Have them chart the change in what that sum could buy over the years on a time line. In addition, have students research the cost of three bus tickets (for an adult and two children) from Memphis to Little Rock,

Arkansas. Have students calculate how much the tickets would have cost in 1917 in order to guess how much money Wright's mother wanted from his father.

Social Studies

It was not uncommon, in the late nineteenth and early twentieth centuries, for poverty-stricken parents to seek placement of their children outside the family as a matter of sheer

survival. Have students research the orphanage as an institution in the United States in the 1910s and 1920s. Students should consider the administration of orphanages, the conditions in orphanages, the population of children in them, and the rate of adoption. Have students report their findings to the class and relate them to the selection.

A Reading Skills and Strategies

Interpreting Details

? How has Wright's attitude toward his hunger and his father changed at this point? [He no longer wants his father to feed him.] **Why does he feel that way?** [Sample responses: He is too disillusioned with his father to hope for help from him; he is too proud to ask for help from someone who has deserted him; he is so hungry that he no longer cares.]

B Elements of Literature

Dialogue

? Why does the judge accept the father's word? [Possible responses: The judge is a fool; the judge doesn't care about the case; the judge takes a man's word over a woman's; the judge's prejudices about African Americans blind him to the reality of the case.]

C Advanced Learners

Discussing Character and Theme

Point out that as a boy, Wright preferred the simplicity of action to the complexities of words. What experiences might have influenced Wright? [Possible responses: his success in fighting off the gang of older boys; his lack of success when asking for food or money.] **Point out that as an adult, Wright lived by words. Invite students to discuss how such a change might occur in a person.** [Possible responses: Education and adult experience can awaken an appreciation of the power of words; Wright was inherently a verbally gifted person but did not discover it till later in his life.]

D Struggling Readers

Finding Sequence of Events

Have students list in chronological order the major changes in Richard Wright's life that have occurred in this passage and previously on this page. [His mother lost her child-support case in court; his mother fell ill, and the family was increasingly hard-pressed; the possibility of living with Wright's grandmother was raised and rejected; there was no longer enough money to pay the rent; Wright's mother searched for and found an orphanage; Wright and his brother went to live there.]

T1020

would make my father support me and my brother. An hour later all three of us were sitting in a huge crowded room. I was overwhelmed by the many faces and the voices which I could not understand. High above me was a white face which my mother told me was the face of the judge. Across the huge room sat my father, smiling confidently, looking at us. My mother warned me not to be fooled by my father's friendly manner; she told me that the judge might ask me questions, and if he did I must tell him the truth. I agreed, yet I hoped that the judge would not ask me anything.

A For some reason the entire thing struck me as being useless; I felt that if my father were going to feed me, then he would have done so regardless of what a judge said to him. And I did not want my father to feed me; I was hungry, but my thoughts of food did not now center about him. I waited, growing restless, hungry. My mother gave me a dry sandwich and I munched and stared, longing to go home. Finally I heard my mother's name called; she rose and began weeping so copiously that she could not talk for a few moments; at last she managed to say that her husband had deserted her and two children, that her children were hungry, that they stayed hungry, that she worked, that she was trying to raise them alone. Then my father was called; he came forward jauntily, smiling. He tried to kiss my mother, but she turned away from him. I only heard one sentence of what he said.

B "I'm doing all I can, Your Honor," he mumbled, grinning.

It had been painful to sit and watch my mother crying and my father laughing and I was glad when we were outside in the sunny streets. Back at home my mother wept again and talked complainingly about the unfairness of the judge who had accepted my father's word. After the court scene, I tried to forget my father; I did not hate him; I simply did not want to think of him. Often when we were hungry my mother would beg me to go to my father's job and ask him for a dollar, a dime, a nickel . . . But I would never consent to go. I did not want to see him.

My mother fell ill and the problem of food became an acute, daily agony. Hunger was with us always. Sometimes the neighbors would feed us or a dollar bill would come in the mail from my grandmother. It was winter and I would buy a

dime's worth of coal each morning from the corner coalyard and lug it home in paper bags. For a time I remained out of school to wait upon my mother, then Granny came to visit us and I returned to school.

At night there were long, halting discussions about our going to live with Granny, but nothing came of it. Perhaps there was not enough money for railroad fare. Angered by having been hauled into court, my father now spurned us completely. I heard long, angrily whispered conversations between my mother and grandmother to the effect that "that woman ought to be killed for breaking up a home." What irked me was the ceaseless talk and no action. If someone had suggested that my father be killed, I would perhaps have become interested; if someone had suggested that his name never be mentioned, I would no doubt have **C** agreed; if someone had suggested that we move to another city, I would have been glad. But there was only endless talk that led nowhere and I began to keep away from home as much as possible, preferring the simplicity of the streets to the worried, <u>futile</u> talk at home.

Finally we could no longer pay the rent for our dingy flat; the few dollars that Granny had left us before she went home were gone. Half sick and in despair, my mother made the rounds of the charitable institutions, seeking help. She found an orphan home that agreed to assume the guidance of **D** me and my brother provided my mother worked and made small payments. My mother hated to be separated from us, but she had no choice.

The orphan home was a two-story frame building set amid trees in a wide, green field. My mother ushered me and my brother one morning into the building and into the presence of a tall, gaunt, mulatto woman who called herself Miss Simon. At once she took a fancy to me and I was frightened speechless; I was afraid of her the moment I saw her and my fear lasted during my entire stay in the home.

The house was crowded with children and there was always a storm of noise. The daily routine was blurred to me and I never quite grasped it. The most abiding feeling I had each day was

---

WORDS TO OWN

futile (fyōōt′'l) *adj.:* useless; pointless.

Professional Notes

Critical Comment: The Wright Stuff

Orville Prescott wrote, in his review of *Black Boy:* "Mr. Wright in this explosive autobiography does not suggest any constructive means for improving the lot of the Negro in this country. . . . [H]e can only display suffering and cruelty with harsh dramatic power, he can only arouse anger and sympathy. If enough such books are written, if enough millions of people read them, maybe, some day, in the fullness of time, there

will be a greater understanding and a more true democracy." In a class discussion, ask students to evaluate Prescott's statements. Begin by asking these questions: What "greater understanding" was he referring to, and on whose part? Has that understanding been generally achieved in the United States? Have "enough such books" been written? Have "enough millions of people" read them?

hunger and fear. The meals were skimpy and there were only two of them. Just before we went to bed each night we were given a slice of bread smeared with molasses. The children were silent, hostile, vindictive, continuously complaining of hunger. There was an overall atmosphere of nervousness and intrigue, of children telling tales upon others, of children being deprived of food to punish them.

The home did not have the money to check the growth of the wide stretches of grass by having it mown, so it had to be pulled by hand. Each morning after we had eaten a breakfast that seemed like no breakfast at all, an older child would lead a herd of us to the vast lawn and we would get to our knees and wrench the grass loose from the dirt with our fingers. At intervals Miss Simon would make a tour of inspection, examining the pile of pulled grass beside each child, scolding or praising according to the size of the pile. Many mornings I was too weak from hunger to pull the grass; I would grow dizzy and my mind would become blank and I would find myself, after an interval of unconsciousness, upon my hands and knees, my head whirling, my eyes staring in bleak astonishment at the green grass, wondering where I was, feeling that I was emerging from a dream . . .

During the first days my mother came each night to visit me and my brother, then her visits stopped. I began to wonder if she, too, like my father, had disappeared into the unknown. I was rapidly learning to distrust everything and everybody. When my mother did come, I asked her why had she remained away so long and she told me that Miss Simon had forbidden her to visit us, that Miss Simon had said that she was spoiling us with too much attention. I begged my mother to take me away; she wept and told me to wait, that soon she would take us to Arkansas. She left and my heart sank.

Miss Simon tried to win my confidence; she asked me if I would like to be adopted by her if my mother consented and I said no. She would take me into her apartment and talk to me, but her words had no effect. Dread and mistrust had already become a daily part of my being and my memory grew sharp, my senses more impressionable; I began to be aware of myself as a distinct personality striving against others. I held myself

in, afraid to act or speak until I was sure of my surroundings, feeling most of the time that I was suspended over a void. My imagination soared; I dreamed of running away. Each morning I vowed that I would leave the next morning, but the next morning always found me afraid.

One day Miss Simon told me that thereafter I was to help her in the office. I ate lunch with her and, strangely, when I sat facing her at the table, my hunger vanished. The woman killed something in me. Next she called me to her desk where she sat addressing envelopes.

"Step up close to the desk," she said. "Don't be afraid."

I went and stood at her elbow. There was a wart on her chin and I stared at it.

"Now, take a blotter from over there and blot each envelope after I'm through writing on it," she instructed me, pointing to a blotter that stood about a foot from my hand.

I stared and did not move or answer.

"Take the blotter," she said.

I wanted to reach for the blotter and succeeded only in twitching my arm.

"Here," she said sharply, reaching for the blotter and shoving it into my fingers.

She wrote in ink on an envelope and pushed it toward me. Holding the blotter in my hand, I stared at the envelope and could not move.

"Blot it," she said.

I could not lift my hand. I knew what she had said; I knew what she wanted me to do; and I had heard her correctly. I wanted to look at her and say something, tell her why I could not move; but my eyes were fixed upon the floor. I could not summon enough courage while she sat there looking at me to reach over the yawning space of twelve inches and blot the wet ink on the envelope.

"Blot it!" she spoke sharply.

Still I could not move or answer.

"Look at me!"

I could not lift my eyes. She reached her hand to my face and I twisted away.

"What's wrong with you?" she demanded.

I began to cry and she drove me from the room. I decided that as soon as night came I would run away. The dinner bell rang and I did not go to the table, but hid in a corner of the hallway. When I heard the dishes rattling at the table, I opened the door and ran down the walk to the street. Dusk

RICHARD WRIGHT 1021

E Reading Skills and Strategies

Interpreting Details

? From these details, how would you characterize the care of the children by the orphanage? [Possible responses: Most students will say the children are neglected; some may say they are abused because they are deprived of food as a punishment.]

F Struggling Readers

Multiple Meanings of Words
Make sure students understand that *check,* in this context, means "to stop," not the more common "to take a look at."

G Reading Skills and Strategies

Interpreting Details

? Compare and contrast this description of hunger's effects with the description on p. 1016 that begins, "Hunger stole upon me so slowly. . . ." How are they alike? How are they different? [Both describe the subjective effects of hunger, but here it is at a more advanced stage. Before, hunger caused Wright pain, dizziness, and blurry vision. Now the hunger is so intense that he actually blacks out.]

H Elements of Literature

Dialogue
? What are Miss Simon's emotions as she keeps telling him to blot the envelope? [Possible responses: increasing anger; frustration; irritation; incomprehension.] **What are Wright's emotions?** [Possible responses: terror; numbness; confusion.]

Making the Connections

Cultural Connections

In some cultures, frequent change of residence is an accepted part of life; nomads, such as Plains Indians, Eskimos, or Bushmen, traditionally moved to follow the game they hunted. In other cultures, moves are rare: An English farm laborer in the nineteenth century might live in the same village all his life. In many pastoral cultures, change of residence follows a seasonal cycle as a community leads its herds from summer to winter feeding grounds. Westward expansion and immigration were causes of moves for millions of Americans in the past. In our own time, many Americans have become used to moving as a result of job changes. Refugees are often forced to move because of political or economic turmoil. Ask groups of students to discuss the possible effects of frequent moving on young people. Does it affect the development of an identity within a culture? After groups have discussed the topic, open discussion to the whole class.

A Reading Skills and Strategies

Interpreting Details

❓ What is the crucial thing the policemen do for Wright that wins his trust? [They feed him.]

B Reading Skills and Strategies

Understanding Quotation Marks

❓ What is the point of the repeated use of *white* in quotation marks in this paragraph? [This usage emphasizes that Wright sees the police as belonging to a threatening and radically different social category.] What does "he was not 'white' any more" mean? [Wright has come to see the officer as an individual human being, not just a member of an alien group.]

C Reading Skills and Strategies

Summarizing

Help students to summarize the events that have taken place since Wright entered the orphanage. [Possible response: The children are made to pull grass by hand; they are inadequately fed; Wright is repelled by Miss Simon; Wright runs away from the orphanage and is picked up by the police and fed a meal. He is returned to the orphanage where Miss Simon beats him.]

D Elements of Literature

Setting

❓ What does this setting indicate about the truthfulness of Wright's father in court? Why? [Possible response: Wright's father and his girl-friend live in a frame house (as opposed to the crumbling tenement he leaves his wife in) and can afford to have a fire. All these things indicate he was lying in court when he convinced the judge he could do no more to support his children.]

was falling. Doubt made me stop. Ought I go back? No; hunger was back there, and fear. I went on, coming to concrete sidewalks. People passed me. Where was I going? I did not know. The farther I walked the more frantic I became. In a confused and vague way I knew that I was doing more running *away* from than running *toward* something. I stopped. The streets seemed dangerous. The buildings were massive and dark. The moon shone and the trees loomed frighteningly. No, I could not go on. I would go back. But I had walked so far and had turned too many corners and had not kept track of the direction. Which way led back to the orphan home? I did not know. I was lost.

I stood in the middle of the sidewalk and cried. A "white" policeman came to me and I wondered if he was going to beat me. He asked me what was the matter and I told him that I was trying to find my mother. His "white" face created a new fear in me. I was remembering the tale of the "white" man who had beaten the "black" boy. A crowd gathered and I was urged to tell where I lived. Curiously, I was too full of fear to cry now. I wanted to tell the "white" face that I had run off from an orphan home and that Miss Simon ran it, but I was afraid. Finally I was taken to the police station where I was fed. I felt better. I sat in a big chair where I was surrounded by "white" policemen, but they seemed to ignore me. Through the window I could see that night had completely fallen and that lights now gleamed in the streets. I grew sleepy and dozed. My shoulder was shaken gently and I opened my eyes and looked into a "white" face of another policeman who was sitting beside me. He asked me questions in a quiet, confidential tone, and quite before I knew it he was not "white" any more. I told him that I had run away from an orphan home and that Miss Simon ran it.

It was but a matter of minutes before I was walking alongside a policeman, heading toward the home. The policeman led me to the front gate and I saw Miss Simon waiting for me on the steps. She identified me and I was left in her charge. I begged her not to beat me, but she yanked me up-stairs into an empty room and lashed me thoroughly. Sobbing, I slunk off to bed, resolved to run away again. But I was watched closely after that.

My mother was informed upon her next visit that I had tried to run away and she was terribly upset.

1022 **Contemporary Literature**

"Why did you do it?" she asked.

"I don't want to stay here," I told her.

"But you must," she said. "How can I work if I'm to worry about you? You must remember that you have no father. I'm doing all I can."

"I don't want to stay here," I repeated.

"Then, if I take you to your father . . ."

"I don't want to stay with him either," I said.

"But I want you to ask him for enough money for us to go to my sister's in Arkansas," she said.

Again I was faced with choices I did not like, but I finally agreed. After all, my hate for my father was not so great and urgent as my hate for the orphan home. My mother held to her idea and one night a week or so later I found myself standing in a room in a frame house. My father and a strange woman were sitting before a bright fire that blazed in a grate. My mother and I were standing about six feet away, as though we were afraid to approach them any closer.

"It's not for me," my mother was saying. "It's for your children that I'm asking you for money."

"I ain't got nothing," my father said, laughing.

"Come here, boy," the strange woman called to me.

I looked at her and did not move.

"Give him a nickel," the woman said. "He's cute."

"Come here, Richard," my father said, stretching out his hand.

I backed away, shaking my head, keeping my eyes on the fire.

"He is a cute child," the strange woman said.

"You ought to be ashamed," my mother said to the strange woman. "You're starving my children."

"Now, don't you-all fight," my father said, laughing.

"I'll take that poker and hit you!" I blurted at my father.

He looked at my mother and laughed louder.

"You told him to say that," he said.

"Don't say such things, Richard," my mother said.

"You ought to be dead," I said to the strange woman.

The woman laughed and threw her arms about my father's neck. I grew ashamed and wanted to leave.

"How can you starve your children?" my mother asked.

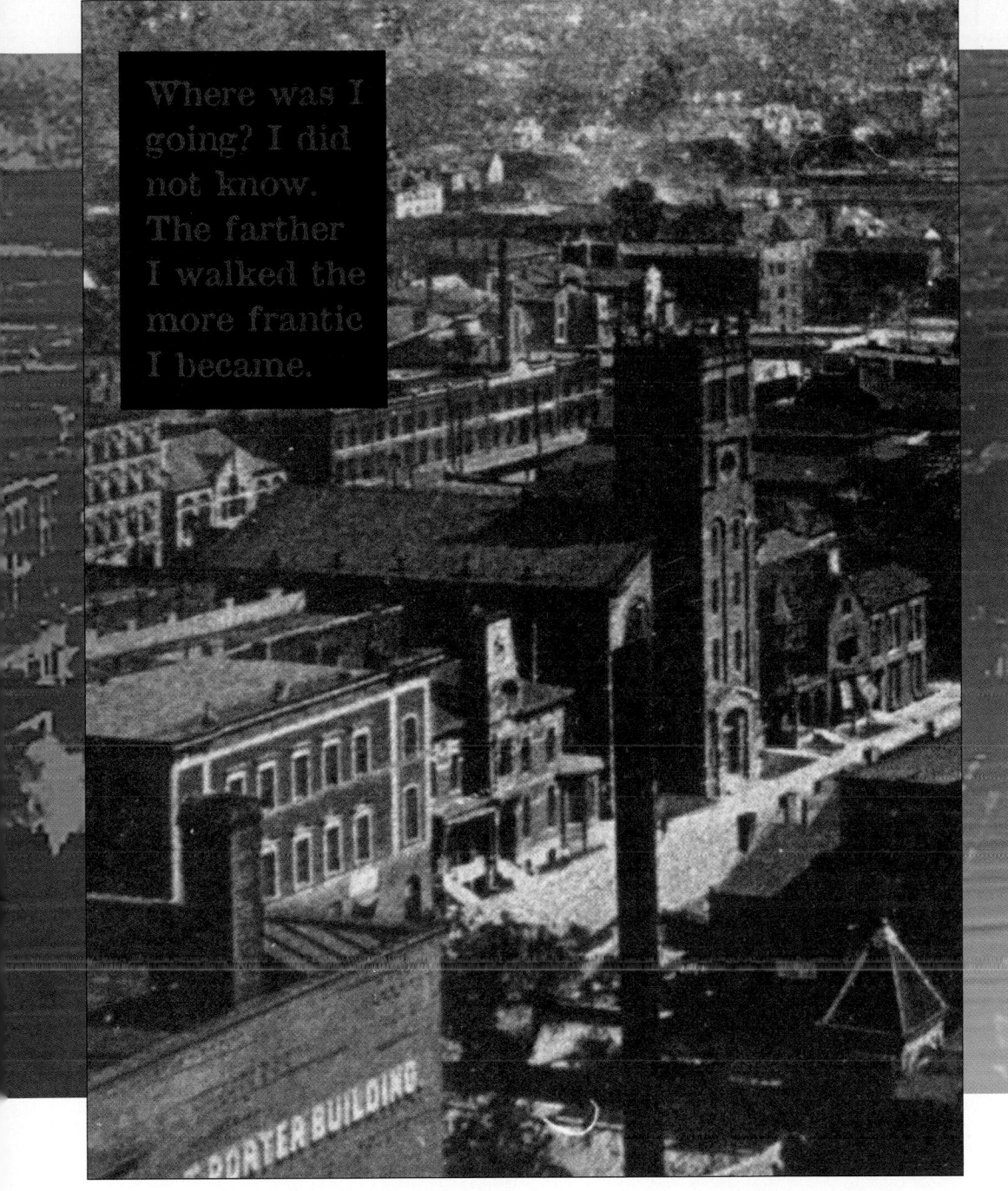

Where was I going? I did not know. The farther I walked the more frantic I became.

RICHARD WRIGHT 1023

RESPONDING TO THE ART

In this photograph of an urban landscape, the mazelike mass of densely packed brick buildings and smokestacks and the absence of people make for a scene some viewers might find desolate or uninviting. The dark windows and the many shadows, especially at the lower right, add to this impression. Other viewers, however, might find this to be an exciting city block, full of hidden places to explore, historically interesting, and ripe for renovation!

Activity. Ask students to give their impressions of the photograph and of urban landscapes in general. Ask them to explain why they like or dislike cities. Then, have students compare the photograph's tone with that of the excerpt from *Black Boy*.

Assessing Learning

Check Test: True-False

1. This autobiography takes place in Atlanta, Georgia. [False]

2. Wright's mother would not let him back in the house until he faced down the bullies. [True]

3. The judge ordered Wright's father to contribute money to his family's support. [False]

4. As a bedtime snack, the orphanage children were given bread and molasses. [True]

5. Richard's mother told him not to take the nickel his father offered him. [True]

Dialogue

? What opinions of the main characters did you form during this conversation, and what specific lines of dialogue helped shape those opinions? [Possible responses: I disliked Wright's father because of his hollow, taunting laugh and his unconvincing claims of poverty; I respected the mother for challenging him but questioned her judgment about refusing the nickel; I admired Richard Wright for sounding so strong at such a young age.]

B **Critical Thinking**

Synthesizing

? What changes happened to Wright's father since they last met? [His father became aged and destitute; he no longer is frightening.] What changes happened to Wright since he last saw his father? [He became an educated, sophisticated, modern writer and urban resident.]

C **Reading Skills and Strategies**

Identifying the Main Idea

? What is Wright's final assessment of his father? [His father was a black peasant who had gone to the city and failed. He endured without regrets or hopes.]

D **Critical Thinking**

Synthesizing

? What else is Wright's description of his father about, in addition to being about this one individual? [Possible response: He sees his father as a representative of rural southern African Americans whose personal (and interpersonal) horizons have been limited by the oppressive experiences of racism and poverty.]

"Let Richard stay with me," my father said.

"Do you want to stay with your father, Richard?" my mother asked.

"No," I said.

"You'll get plenty to eat," he said.

"I'm hungry now," I told him. "But I won't stay with you."

"Aw, give the boy a nickel," the woman said.

My father ran his hand into his pocket and pulled out a nickel.

"Here, Richard," he said.

"Don't take it," my mother said.

"Don't teach him to be a fool," my father said. "Here, Richard, take it."

I looked at my mother, at the strange woman, at my father, then into the fire. I wanted to take the nickel, but I did not want to take it from my father.

"You ought to be ashamed," my mother said, weeping. "Giving your son a nickel when he's hungry. If there's a God, He'll pay you back."

"That's all I got," my father said, laughing again and returning the nickel to his pocket.

We left. I had the feeling that I had had to do with something unclean. Many times in the years after that the image of my father and the strange woman, their faces lit by the dancing flames, would surge up in my imagination so vivid and strong that I felt I could reach out and touch it; I would stare at it, feeling that it possessed some vital meaning which always eluded me.

A quarter of a century was to elapse between the time when I saw my father sitting with the strange woman and the time when I was to see him again, standing alone upon the red clay of a Mississippi plantation, a sharecropper,[1] clad in ragged overalls, holding a muddy hoe in his gnarled, veined hands—a quarter of a century during which my mind and consciousness had become so greatly and violently altered that when I tried to talk to him I realized that, though ties of blood made us kin, though I could see a shadow of my face in his face, though there was

---

1. **sharecropper:** farmer who works a piece of land for its owner and gets a small portion of the crop in return.

---

an echo of my voice in his voice, we were forever strangers, speaking a different language, living on vastly distant planes of reality. That day a quarter of a century later when I visited him on the plantation—he was standing against the sky, smiling toothlessly, his hair whitened, his body bent, his eyes glazed with dim recollection, his fearsome aspect of twenty-five years ago gone forever from him—I was overwhelmed to realize that he could never understand me or the scalding experiences that had swept me beyond his life and into an area of living that he could never know. I stood before him, poised, my mind aching as it embraced the simple nakedness of his life, feeling how completely his soul was imprisoned by the slow flow of the seasons, by wind and rain and sun, how fastened were his memories to a crude and raw past, how chained were his actions and emotions to the direct, animalistic impulses of his withering body . . .

From the white landowners above him there had not been handed to him a chance to learn the meaning of loyalty, of sentiment, of tradition. Joy was as unknown to him as was despair. As a creature of the earth, he endured, hearty, whole, seemingly indestructible, with no regrets and no hope. He asked easy, drawling questions about me, his other son, his wife, and he laughed, amused, when I informed him of their destinies. I forgave him and pitied him as my eyes looked past him to the unpainted wooden shack. From far beyond the horizons that bound this bleak plantation there had come to me through my living the knowledge that my father was a black peasant who had gone to the city seeking life, but who had failed in the city; a black peasant whose life had been hopelessly snarled in the city, and who had at last fled the city—that same city which had lifted me in its burning arms and borne me toward alien and undreamed-of shores of knowing.

WORDS TO OWN

elapse (ē·laps') v.: to pass by; to slip away.
withering (with'ər·in) v. used as adj.: drying up; weakening.

Making the Connections

Connecting to the Theme:
"Discoveries and Awakenings"
By enduring many hardships and "scalding" experiences, Wright awakened to an awareness of his inner strengths and to a new appreciation of the limitations that made his father who he was. Invite students to discuss the following questions:

1. If you had grown up in Richard Wright's circumstances, what do you think would have become of you? What lasting feelings would you have about your childhood?

2. How might you have felt about your father?

3. What have you discovered, or awakened to, in writing an autobiography?

MAKING MEANINGS

First Thoughts

1. Wright works in swift strokes to draw sharp **images** of his life. Which images stand out most clearly in your mind?

Shaping Interpretations

2. When his mother gives Richard a stick and sends him back to confront the bullies, what lesson is she trying to teach? Was there anything else she could have done?

3. Why can't Richard eat his soup when the preacher is devouring the chicken? What does this incident reveal about the boy's **character**?

4. Remembering his father and the strange woman, "their faces lit by the dancing flames," Wright says this **image** "possessed some vital meaning which always eluded me" (page 1024). What do you think he means?

Connecting with the Text

5. The **image** of the boy pulling grass at the orphanage is a powerful one, although Wright makes no comment on it. Do you wish he had commented, or do you think it wasn't necessary? How does this scene make you feel?

Reading Check

a. What details does Wright use to make the reader feel the physical and emotional hunger he experienced as a boy? (Check your reading notes.)

b. How did Richard win the right to the streets of Memphis?

c. How does Wright's father behave in the courtroom scene and in the meeting with Richard, his mother, and the strange woman?

d. How is the city's effect on his father different from its effect on Wright?

CHOICES:
Building Your Portfolio

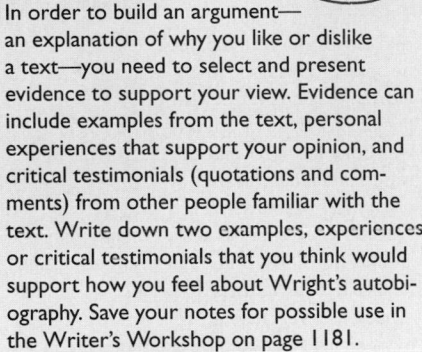

Writer's Notebook
1. Collecting Ideas for an Evaluation

In order to build an argument—an explanation of why you like or dislike a text—you need to select and present evidence to support your view. Evidence can include examples from the text, personal experiences that support your opinion, and critical testimonials (quotations and comments) from other people familiar with the text. Write down two examples, experiences, or critical testimonials that you think would support how you feel about Wright's autobiography. Save your notes for possible use in the Writer's Workshop on page 1181.

Analyzing a Character
2. "The simple nakedness of his life . . ."

The father changes tremendously in this excerpt from *Black Boy*. In a short essay, analyze the **character** of the father as Wright presents him. Consider the father when he lives in Memphis and, twenty-five years later, when he lives as a sharecropper. Why does he change? Does he see his son in a different light? What assessment does Wright make of his father at the end?

Speaking and Listening/ Oral Interpretation
3. Interpreting Wright Aloud

Select a section of *Black Boy*, and present your interpretation of the text in an oral reading. (Be sure to choose a passage with dialogue.) In preparing for your performance, consider the following: Who is your audience? How many speakers will you use? Will you include sound or visual effects, such as music or dramatic lighting? What different tones of voice will you use to present your interpretation of different parts of the text?

RICHARD WRIGHT 1025

Reading Check

a. He details his waking up at night, the clamor in his stomach, and his dizziness and listlessness.

b. He fights back with a stick against the boys who attack him.

c. He is offhand and irresponsible. He says he is doing what he can and laughs.

d. Whereas his father failed there, the city has ultimately given Wright knowledge and self-assurance.

CHOICES:
Building Your Portfolio

1. **Writer's Notebook**
   Remind students to save their work. They may use it as prewriting for the Writer's Workshop on p. 1181.

2. **Analyzing a Character** Encourage students to link personal change in Wright's father's life to social change in his era.

3. **Speaking and Listening/Performance**
   This activity may be done either by individual students or by groups of up to four.

Making Meanings [Respond]

1. Possible responses: his descriptions of hunger or of the orphanage; the fight scene.

Shaping Interpretations [Interpret]

2. She is trying to teach him to stand up for himself and be self-sufficient at a time when she can do little to help him. She could, of course, have confronted the boys, called the police, or spoken to the boy's parents, but these are all unlikely and somewhat risky solutions for a woman in dire economic and social circumstances.

3. In his family's desperate circumstances, Wright resents the preacher's buoyant spirits, huge appetite, and claim on the center of attention. Wright is stubborn and determined, but also somewhat bitter and self-destructive.

4. Possible response: He may mean that he was trying to find in that image a clue as to why and how his father was so callous and cruel to his family, or why so many people in general were cruel. The answer he ultimately finds comes through better understanding his father's personal history.

Connecting with the Text

[Synthesize]

5. Possible responses: The image is powerful as it is and needs no elaboration; a brief comment would have given the scene more emphasis; the scene may make readers realize how poor the orphanage is or how harsh Miss Simon is.

Grading Timesaver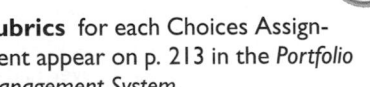

Rubrics for each Choices Assignment appear on p. 213 in the *Portfolio Management System*.

Raymond Carver

(1938–1988)

AP/Wide World Photos.

"We didn't have any youth," Raymond Carver remembered in a 1983 interview. He was thinking of the tough days he spent growing up in a working-class family in the Pacific Northwest. Carver was born in Oregon and raised in Yakima, Washington, where his father worked in a lumber mill and his mother worked periodically as a waitress and a clerk. Carver married soon after graduating from high school, and by the time he turned twenty he and his wife were raising two children. To support his family, he worked at a variety of blue-collar jobs: pumping gas, sweeping hospital corridors, picking tulips.

Given Carver's experiences, it is no surprise that in his stories—as the critic Thomas R. Edwards has commented—"people worry about whether their old cars will start, [and] unemployment or personal bankruptcy are present dangers." Carver's characters typically work as mechanics, factory workers, waitresses, or door-to-door salespeople in an America where making a living can be difficult and uncertain. Characters often survive their difficulties, however, and there is a sense of hope in many Carver stories. "I have a great deal of sympathy with [characters in my stories]," Carver once said. "They're my people. I know them. I could never write down to them."

In the late 1950s, the Carvers moved to California, where Raymond enrolled in college, taking a course in fiction writing with the novelist John Gardner. In 1963, he earned a college degree and then attended the University of Iowa's highly regarded Writers' Workshop.

In the 1960s and early 1970s, Carver published stories and poems, some dealing with favorite topics like hunting and fishing. A breakthrough came in 1976 with the publication of a collection of his stories, *Will You Please Be Quiet, Please?* The lavish praise bestowed upon this book earned Carver wide recognition as a hugely talented writer. The critic Margo Johnson noted that the stories "are filled with glass-sharp details, images and conversations, meticulously arranged." In 1977, Carver won a prestigious Guggenheim fellowship. Yet as he succeeded professionally, his personal life deteriorated, and his marriage ended.

In 1981, Carver published another collection of stories, *What We Talk About When We Talk About Love*, and in 1983, his story collection *Cathedral* enjoyed enormous critical and popular success. By now critics were talking of Carver's permanent place in American literature. The critic Irving Howe compared his work to that of Stephen Crane and Ernest Hemingway. The *Washington Post* book reviewer Jonathan Yardley called Carver "a writer of astonishing compassion and honesty, utterly free of pretense and affectation, his eye set only on describing and revealing the world as he sees it. His eye is so clear, it almost breaks your heart."

Carver's personal life brightened in the years before his early death from lung cancer. He formed a close relationship with the poet and short-story writer Tess Gallagher, who eventually became his wife. Since his death, and despite recent revelations about the significant role one editor played in shaping his stories, Carver's reputation as an important poet and short-story writer has remained firm. His work has been translated into more than twenty languages.

go.hrw.com
LE0 11-19

L. (1986) by Mike & Doug Starn. Toned silver print on polyester, tape, wood (48″ × 48″).

Leo Castelli Photo Archives. © 1998 Mike & Doug Starn/Artists Rights Society (ARS), New York.

Before You Read

EVERYTHING STUCK TO HIM

Make the Connection

Life's Give-and-Take

If we think in simple terms about human feelings, reducing them to clear-cut patterns and easy definitions, we may be tricked into believing that feelings themselves are simple. Great fiction, no matter how simple on the surface, enables us to discover the depths of feelings. We respond to such fiction because we recognize in it the give-and-take of real experience, the gains and the losses, the complex interactions of people who defy stereotyping.

Reading Skills and Strategies

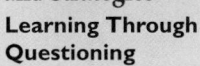

Learning Through Questioning

As you read "Everything Stuck to Him," make a list of questions that occur to you about the characters. You might ask, for instance, about their feelings and what they are *not* saying to each other.

Elements of Literature

Style

One of the most striking elements of Raymond Carver's writing is its **style,** the unique way in which he uses language. Carver's prose has a chiseled quality, as if he has chipped away every unnecessary word. There are some oddities, however. No quotation marks surround dialogue. Most characters aren't given names. You need to read carefully to catch every turn of Carver's meticulously crafted prose.

> **S**tyle is the unique way in which a writer uses language.
>
> *For more on Style, see the Handbook of Literary Terms.*

Summary ▪

The story begins with a frame story, told from a third-person limited point of view, in which a father and daughter meet in Milan, and she asks to hear about her childhood. In the inner story, the father recalls the early years of his marriage, using a third-person perspective, as if describing an anonymous "boy" and "girl." The conflict of the inner story, and ultimately of the frame story as well, begins with the young father's plan to go ahead with a hunting trip, leaving his wife alone with their sick baby girl. They argue, the wife insisting that her husband choose whether or not his family comes first. The husband returns, makes up with his wife, and accidentally spills his breakfast, which comically sticks to his long underwear. But the frame story suggests that this happiness was transient. The title becomes ironic as it becomes clear that in the long run, the man refused to let marriage, family, and his other emotional obligations "stick" to him at all.

RESPONDING TO THE ART

Mike and Doug Starn taped a photograph of a woman's face onto a forty-nine-square grid with a wood frame to make a mixed-media portrait.

Activity. The title *L* is a pun: *Elle* is French for "she." Ask students what this information adds to the photo's meaning for them. Have students make up their own stories about "*L.*"

Preteaching Vocabulary

Words to Own

Divide students into groups of four or five, and have them locate the Words to Own and definitions at the bottom of pp. 1028 and 1030. Have group members take turns reading aloud one word and definition at a time. Have groups discuss any remaining uncertainty about the meanings of the words until all members are confident they understand the words. Then, have groups conduct the following activity: Brainstorm an idea for a short story that would contain the words *coincide, correspondence, striking, overcast,* and *fitfully.* (It might contain a character of striking appearance, a baby crying fitfully, an overcast sky, some correspondence, and two events coinciding.) They don't have to plot the story completely or use the words in sentences. A sketchy preliminary idea is enough. Have them explain their idea to the class and explain how the Words to Own fit into it.

A Reading Skills and Strategies

Learning Through Questioning

? What question might you ask about "she," based on this sentence? [Possible responses: What is she a survivor of? How old is she?]

B Reading Skills and Strategies

Learning Through Questioning

? What is the connection between the frame story and the inner story? [The man in the frame story tells the woman the inner story as an incident from her childhood.] Who are the "he" and "she" in Milan, and who are the boy, girl, and baby daughter in the inner story? ["He" and "she" in the frame story (in Milan) are father and daughter. In the inner story, "he" is the frame-story father, "she" is his wife at the time, and the baby is "she" in the frame story.]

C Critical Thinking

Speculating

? Why might the father ask these questions? What is the picture that he wants to make sure his daughter gets? [Possible responses: He may feel that his daughter has a narrow or insufficient sense of her parents' marriage, and wishes to convey their ordinariness, their hard work, their hope, or some other quality.]

D Elements of Literature

Style

? So far, what would you say are the hallmarks of Carver's style? [Possible responses: extreme conciseness; ordinary language; no quotation marks for dialogue; unnamed characters.]

Everything Stuck to Him

Raymond Carver

They were kids themselves, but they were crazy in love.

She's in Milan[1] for Christmas and wants to know what it was like when she was a kid.

Tell me, she says. Tell me what it was like when I was a kid. She sips Strega, waits, eyes him closely.

She is a cool, slim, attractive girl, a survivor from top to bottom.

That was a long time ago. That was twenty years ago, he says.

You can remember, she says. Go on.

What do you want to hear? he says. What else can I tell you? I could tell you about something that happened when you were a baby. It involves you, he says. But only in a minor way.

Tell me, she says. But first fix us another so you won't have to stop in the middle.

He comes back from the kitchen with drinks, settles into his chair, begins.

They were kids themselves, but they were crazy in love, this eighteen-year-old boy and this seventeen-year-old girl when they married. Not all that long afterwards they had a daughter.

---

1. **Milan** (mi·lan'): city in northwestern Italy.

The baby came along in late November during a cold spell that just happened to coincide with the peak of the waterfowl season. The boy loved to hunt, you see. That's part of it.

The boy and girl, husband and wife, father and mother, they lived in a little apartment under a dentist's office. Each night they cleaned the dentist's place upstairs in exchange for rent and utilities. In summer they were expected to maintain the lawn and the flowers. In winter the boy shoveled snow and spread rock salt on the walks. Are you still with me? Are you getting the picture?

I am, she says.

That's good, he says. So one day the dentist finds out they were using his letterhead for their personal correspondence. But that's another story.

He gets up from his chair and looks out the window. He sees the tile rooftops and the snow that is falling steadily on them.

Tell the story, she says.

WORDS TO OWN

coincide (kō'in·sīd') v.: to occur at the same time.
correspondence (kôr'ə·spän'dəns) n.: communication by letters.

Reaching All Students

Struggling Readers
Learning Through Questioning was introduced on p. 1027. A good strategy to use with questioning is Think-Aloud. For information on using this strategy, see the *Reading Strategies Handbook*, p. 135 in the *Reading Skills and Strategies* binder.

English Language Learners
Explain the title word *stuck,* meaning both "physically attached to something" (like glue) and, in personal relationships, "committed," such as being married. Some students' first languages may contain words with parallel double meanings. For strategies for engaging English language learners with the literature, see
- *Lesson Plans Including Strategies for English-Language Learners*

Advanced Learners
Carver's work makes an ideal point of departure for studying the modern short story, in which theme is usually implied ironically rather than stated. Encourage students to discover the influences of Hemingway (p. 650) and Katherine Mansfield on Carver. Also, steer them to Carver's fellow 1980s minimalists, such as Ann Beattie and Mary Robison, and contrasting "maximalists," such as Alice Munro.

Couple in Open Doorway (1977) by George Segal. Painted plaster, wood, and metal (96" × 69" × 52").

Courtesy Sidney Janis Gallery, New York. © George Segal, Licensed by VAGA, New York, NY.

George Segal (1924–) began his career as a painter but gained recognition for his life-size experimental sculptures in the late 1950s. These sculptures are made of white plaster, chicken wire, burlap, and molds taken from living models—friends, relatives, even himself—and are placed in bare, lonely "environments" defined by a few common objects, such as chairs, tables, and beds. Later, Segal also cast in plaster of Paris directly from human forms, producing mummylike molds that look as though they might still contain bodies. Segal's figures usually have a rough finish, and their individual features are not clearly defined. They seldom communicate with each other, and they often appear disaffected. Segal is sometimes considered a Pop artist, but the overall effect of his works is somber rather than ironic or exuberant.

Activity. After students have read "Everything Stuck to Him," have them compare the styles of Carver's work and Segal's, as well as the implied commentary on contemporary American life in both. [Students might note the mutual use of sparse representations with little ornament, as well as the mutual focus on couples, on miscommunication, and on people who seem trapped in static postures—all of which might be taken to comprise a commentary on the state of intimacy in American life.]

Using Students' Strengths

Visual Learners
Despite, or even because of, its spareness of detail, Carver's work is highly visual. (Several of his stories were adapted by director Robert Altman for the movie *Short Cuts*.) Invite students to sketch a storyboard or comic strip for "Everything Stuck to Him," either while they read or after they read, expanding on the few visual details of setting and character that Carver provides.

Verbal Learners
As students read, have them take notes on the daughter's and the father's possible feelings. Then, have students form pairs, and have one partner write a letter from the daughter to her father, responding to the story he has told and perhaps to related issues in her mind. Have the other partner read the letter and respond in a letter from the father. Have pairs read their two letters aloud to the class.

Interpersonal Learners
Divide students into groups of three, and have them act out the story in separate scenes. (Each scene will use only two of the three characters.) Afterward, invite each group, remaining in character, to discuss the family members' history and their feelings about one another. Then, have students (out of character) discuss the insights they gained from this dramatization.

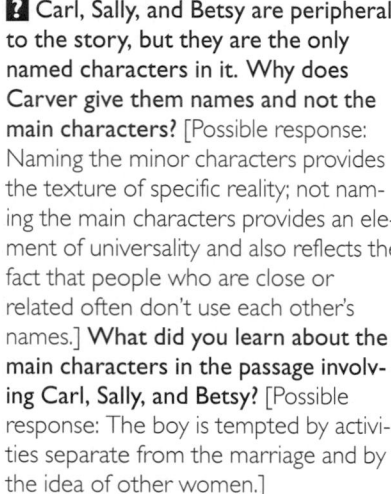

A The two kids were very much in love. On top of this they had great ambitions. They were always talking about the things they were going to do and the places they were going to go.

Now the boy and girl slept in the bedroom, and the baby slept in the living room. Let's say the baby was about three months old and had only just begun to sleep through the night.

On this one Saturday night after finishing his work upstairs, the boy stayed in the dentist's office and called an old hunting friend of his father's.

Carl, he said when the man picked up the receiver, believe it or not, I'm a father.

Congratulations, Carl said. How is the wife?

She's fine, Carl. Everybody's fine.

That's good, Carl said, I'm glad to hear it. But if you called about going hunting, I'll tell you something. The geese are flying to beat the band. I don't think I've ever seen so many. Got five today. Going back in the morning, so come along if you want to.

I want to, the boy said.

The boy hung up the telephone and went downstairs to tell the girl. She watched while he laid out his things. Hunting coat, shell bag, boots, socks, hunting cap, long underwear, pump gun.

B What time will you be back? the girl said.

Probably around noon, the boy said. But maybe as late as six o'clock. Would that be too late?

It's fine, she said. The baby and I will get along fine. You go and have some fun. When you get back, we'll dress the baby up and go visit Sally.

The boy said, Sounds like a good idea.

Sally was the girl's sister. She was striking. I don't know if you've seen pictures of her. The boy was a little in love with Sally, just as he was a little in love with Betsy, who was another sister the girl had. The boy used to say to the girl, If we weren't married, I could go for Sally.

What about Betsy? the girl used to say. I hate to admit it, but I truly feel she's better looking than Sally and me. What about Betsy?

Betsy too, the boy used to say.

After dinner he turned up the furnace and helped her bathe the baby. He marveled again at the infant who had half his features and half the girl's. He powdered the tiny body. He powdered between fingers and toes.

He emptied the bath into the sink and went upstairs to check the air. It was overcast and cold. The grass, what there was of it, looked like canvas, stiff and gray under the street light.

Snow lay in piles beside the walk. A car went by. He heard sand under the tires. He let himself imagine what it might be like tomorrow, geese beating the air over his head, shotgun plunging against his shoulder.

Then he locked the door and went downstairs.

In bed they tried to read. But both of them fell asleep, she first, letting the magazine sink to the quilt.

It was the baby's cries that woke him up.

The light was on out there, and the girl was standing next to the crib rocking the baby in her arms. She put the baby down, turned out the light, and came back to the bed.

He heard the baby cry. This time the girl stayed where she was. The baby cried fitfully and stopped. The boy listened, then dozed. But the baby's cries woke him again. The living-room light was burning. He sat up and turned on the lamp.

C I don't know what's wrong, the girl said, walking back and forth with the baby. I've changed her and fed her, but she keeps on crying. I'm so tired I'm afraid I might drop her.

You come back to bed, the boy said. I'll hold her for a while.

He got up and took the baby, and the girl went to lie down again.

Just rock her for a few minutes, the girl said from the bedroom. Maybe she'll go back to sleep.

The boy sat on the sofa and held the baby. He jiggled it in his lap until he got its eyes to close, his own eyes closing right along. He rose carefully and put the baby back in the crib.

It was a quarter to four, which gave him forty-five minutes. He crawled into bed and dropped off. But a few minutes later the baby was crying again, and this time they both got up.

WORDS TO OWN

striking *adj.*: impressive; attractive.
overcast *adj.*: cloudy; gloomy.
fitfully *adv.*: irregularly; in stops and starts.

1030 CONTEMPORARY LITERATURE

Crossing the Curriculum

Health

Have students research some of the difficulties facing new, young parents. In addition to library and Internet research, suggest that students talk with obstetricians, midwives, pediatricians, nurses, and social workers specializing in these fields. Have students present their findings as though they were talking to couples preparing for their first child. *You may want to obtain permission from parents or guardians and from the parties the students will contact before they begin work on this activity.*

Art

Have students illustrate the concept of love in an abstract fashion—with colors, shapes, forms, objects, and symbols, but not with images of people or scenes. Invite students to choose a visual medium they feel comfortable with, such as drawing, painting, photography, or collage. Have them write a caption explaining what their work of art says about love. Display their illustrations in the classroom.

The boy did a terrible thing. He swore.

For God's sake, what's the matter with you? the girl said to the boy. Maybe she's sick or something. Maybe we shouldn't have given her the bath.

The boy picked up the baby. The baby kicked its feet and smiled.

Look, the boy said, I really don't think there's anything wrong with her.

How do you know that? the girl said. Here, let me have her. I know I ought to give her something, but I don't know what it's supposed to be.

The girl put the baby down again. The boy and the girl looked at the baby, and the baby began to cry.

The girl took the baby. Baby, baby, the girl said with tears in her eyes.

Probably it's something on her stomach, the boy said.

The girl didn't answer. She went on rocking the baby, paying no attention to the boy.

The boy waited. He went to the kitchen and put on water for coffee. He drew his woolen underwear on over his shorts and T-shirt, buttoned up, then got into his clothes.

What are you doing? the girl said.

Going hunting, the boy said.

I don't think you should, she said. I don't want to be left alone with her like this.

Carl's planning on me going, the boy said. We've planned it.

I don't care about what you and Carl planned, she said. And I don't care about Carl, either. I don't even know Carl.

You've met Carl before. You know him, the boy said. What do you mean you don't know him?

That's not the point and you know it, the girl said.

What is the point? the boy said. The point is we planned it.

The girl said, I'm your wife. This is your baby. She's sick or something. Look at her. Why else is she crying?

I know you're my wife, the boy said.

The girl began to cry. She put the baby back in the crib. But the baby started up again. The girl dried her eyes on the sleeve of her nightgown and picked the baby up.

The boy laced up his boots. He put on his shirt, his sweater, his coat. The kettle whistled on the stove in the kitchen.

You're going to have to choose, the girl said. Carl or us. I mean it.

What do you mean? the boy said.

You heard what I said, the girl said. If you want a family, you're going to have to choose.

They stared at each other. Then the boy took up his hunting gear and went outside. He started the car. He went around to the car windows and, making a job of it, scraped away the ice.

He turned off the motor and sat awhile. And then he got out and went back inside.

The living-room light was on. The girl was asleep on the bed. The baby was asleep beside her.

The boy took off his boots. Then he took off everything else. In his socks and his long underwear, he sat on the sofa and read the Sunday paper.

The girl and the baby slept on. After a while, the boy went to the kitchen and started frying bacon.

The girl came out in her robe and put her arms around the boy.

Hey, the boy said.

I'm sorry, the girl said.

It's all right, the boy said.

I didn't mean to snap like that.

It was my fault, he said.

You sit down, the girl said. How does a waffle sound with bacon?

Sounds great, the boy said.

She took the bacon out of the pan and made waffle batter. He sat at the table and watched her move around the kitchen.

She put a plate in front of him with bacon, a waffle. He spread butter and poured syrup. But when he started to cut, he turned the plate into his lap.

I don't believe it, he said, jumping up from the table.

If you could see yourself, the girl said.

The boy looked down at himself, at everything stuck to his underwear.

I was starved, he said, shaking his head.

You were starved, she said, laughing.

He peeled off the woolen underwear and threw it at the bathroom door. Then he opened his arms and the girl moved into them.

RAYMOND CARVER 1031

ⓓ English Language Learners

Interpreting Idioms

Have students use the context of this conversation to determine what the boy means by the idiom "it's something on her stomach." [He means that the baby has eaten something that has upset her stomach.]

ⓔ Critical Thinking

Interpreting

❓ What is the immediate choice that the boy faces? [whether or not to go hunting with Carl] What is the larger, more dramatic choice that his wife is asking him to make? [whether or not he is willing to sacrifice his personal goals and desires for his new family]

ⓕ Elements of Literature

Dialogue

❓ Notice how, unlike Wright, for example, Carver rarely uses any other word than "said" to narrate dialogue. Why do you think he avoids words like "explained," "whispered," "sighed," or "complained" in his dialogue? [Possible response: He wants to let the dialogue speak for itself—descriptive words would detract from the immediacy and simplicity of the story.]

ⓖ Reading Skills and Strategies

Learning Through Questioning

❓ The breakfast falling in the boy's lap is a key event in the story, providing its title. Is this just a slapstick moment, or does it have deeper implications, and if so, what are they? [Possible responses: On the surface, the incident breaks the ice and helps the couple laugh off their recent dispute. Deeper down, it may imply that the boy is not fully comfortable with his decision not to go, and that he has gotten himself "stuck" in something (a family) that he will ultimately want to escape.]

Assessing Learning

Check Test: Fill-in-the-Blank

1. The opening conversation takes place between a man and _____. [his daughter]
2. The husband wants to go _____. [hunting]
3. He is awakened by _____. [the baby's crying]
4. The husband decides _____. [to stay with his wife and child]
5. The couple agrees to _____. [never argue again]

? What do you think happened to the boy and girl? [Possible responses: The boy left, the marriage broke up, and the wife took custody of their daughter; the wife died.]

? What else might be included in "everything else"? [Possible responses: conflict in the marriage; the boy's desire to stray; the couple's poor skills in dealing with problems; the adult daughter's bitterness or sense of loss.] **What was "the cold, and where he'd go in it?"** [Possible response: The cold was the tempting but loveless world outside the family, commitment, and intimacy.]

Primary Sources

In this interview Carver talks about how his writing flows in fits and starts and how much he enjoys the process of revising. Inform students that the literary journal *The Paris Review* has for decades run a series of highly regarded long interviews with prominent writers.

C Background

John Ashbery is a major contemporary American poet noted for the difficulty and originality of his work. (For more on Ashbery, see p. T917.)

D Background

Leo Tolstoy, the nineteenth-century Russian author of *War and Peace* and *Anna Karenina,* is considered one of the greatest of all novelists.

We won't fight anymore, she said.

The boy said, We won't.

He gets up from his chair and refills their glasses.

That's it, he says. End of story. I admit it's not much of a story.

I was interested, she says.

He shrugs and carries his drink over to the window. It's dark now but still snowing.

Things change, he says. I don't know how they **A** do. But they do without your realizing it or wanting them to.

Yes, that's true, only——But she does not finish what she started.

She drops the subject. In the window's reflection he sees her study her nails. Then she raises her head. Speaking brightly, she asks if he is going to show her the city, after all.

He says, Put your boots on and let's go.

But he stays by the window, remembering. They had laughed. They had leaned on each other and laughed until the tears had come, while **B** everything else—the cold, and where he'd go in it—was outside, for a while anyway.

PRIMARY **Sources** — AN INTERVIEW

When Raymond Carver was interviewed by *The Paris Review* in 1983, he was asked, "What are your writing habits like? Are you always working on a story?" This was his reply.

"Paddlewheel of Days"

When I'm writing, I write every day. It's lovely when that's happening. One day dovetailing into the next. Sometimes I don't even know what day of the week it is. The "paddlewheel **C** of days," John Ashbery has called it. When I'm not writing, like now, when I'm tied up with teaching duties as I have been the last while, it's as if I've never written a word or had any desire to write. I fall into bad habits. I stay up too late and sleep in too long. But it's okay. I've learned to be patient and to bide my time. I had to learn that a long time ago. Patience. If I believed in signs, I suppose my sign would be the sign of the turtle. I write in fits and starts. But when I'm writing, I put in a lot of hours at the desk, ten or twelve or fifteen hours at a stretch, day after day. I love that, when that's happening. Much of this work time, understand, is given over to revising and rewriting. There's not much that I like better than to take a story that I've had around the house for a while and

work it over again. It's the same with the poems I write. I'm in no hurry to send something off just after I write it, and I sometimes keep it around the house for months doing this or that to it, taking this out and putting that in. It doesn't take that long to do the first draft of the story, that usually happens in one sitting, but it does take a while to do the various versions of the story. I've done as many as twenty or thirty drafts of a story. Never less than ten or twelve drafts. It's instructive, and heartening both, to look at the early drafts of great writers. I'm thinking of the photographs of galleys be- **D** longing to Tolstoy, to name one writer who loved to revise. I mean, I don't know if he loved it or not, but he did a great deal of it. He was always revising, right down to the time of page proofs. He went through and rewrote *War and Peace* eight times and was still making corrections in the galleys. Things like this should hearten every writer whose first drafts are dreadful, like mine are.

—Raymond Carver

Making the Connections

Connecting to the Theme: "Discoveries and Awakenings"

Like much else in this story, the discoveries and awakenings in it must be discerned between the lines, but they are very real. Invite students to reimagine the story first from the point of view of "she," the grown daughter, and then from the point of view of "he," the middle-aged father, who was once the young husband. What did "she" discover about life between the time of the inner story and the time of the frame story? What did hearing the inner story awaken her to? What did "he" discover during the events of the inner story? What did he awaken to by telling the story to his grown daughter? Invite a variety of hypotheses based on students' knowledge of life and of the things characters learn in fiction.

First Thoughts

1. What was your emotional reaction to "Everything Stuck to Him"?

Shaping Interpretations

2. What is the effect of not giving names to the main characters? Why do you think Carver uses the terms *boy* and *girl* rather than *man* and *woman* or *father* and *mother*?

3. How would you describe the main **conflict** between the husband and wife in the inner story?

4. What thoughts and emotions do you think the boy experienced as he "sat awhile" in the car?

5. The man, having told the tale of the boy and the girl, says that "things change." What has changed since the time of the inner story? What has the man discovered?

6. Near the end of the story, after the man offers statements about change, the woman replies "Yes, that's true, only——" She does not finish. What do you think she intended to say, and why did she stop?

7. The story's **title** refers to an incident in the inner story. Explain how the title also refers to something much more important to the man.

Challenging the Text

8. As Carver says in Primary Sources on page 1032, his **style** is the result of much revising. What scenes, speeches, or com-

---

Reading Check

a. What is the **setting** and who are the **characters** in the **frame story**—the introductory narrative within which a character proceeds to tell a story (the **inner story**)?

b. What is the **setting** and who are the main **characters** in the inner story? Which characters appear in both stories?

c. What happened during the night when the baby kept crying?

d. What promise did the couple make on Sunday morning?

---

ments do you think might have been deleted from earlier drafts of this story? Do you think Carver should have provided more details? For ideas, refer to the notes you made while reading.

CHOICES: Building Your Portfolio

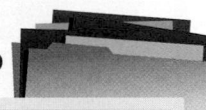

Writer's Notebook

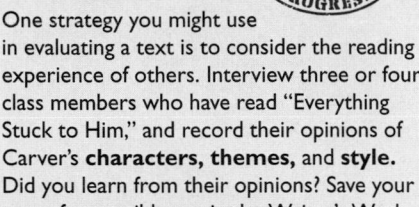

1. Collecting Ideas for an Evaluation

One strategy you might use in evaluating a text is to consider the reading experience of others. Interview three or four class members who have read "Everything Stuck to Him," and record their opinions of Carver's **characters, themes,** and **style.** Did you learn from their opinions? Save your notes for possible use in the Writer's Workshop on page 1181.

Interpreting a Story

2. Major or Minor?

Early on, the man says the inner story involves the woman, "but only in a minor way." Do you take this comment at face value, or is it an **understatement,** a statement that downplays the importance or magnitude of something? Explain your opinion in a short essay, defending it with evidence from the text.

Creative Writing

3. Words Unspoken

Write a **monologue** revealing the unspoken thoughts and feelings of one of the characters in "Everything Stuck to Him." Use the personal pronoun *I*. Choose one of the following scenes in the story to step into the character's mind: (a) the girl sitting up alone with the crying baby, (b) the boy sitting alone in the car, or (c) the woman looking at her fingernails after hearing the story.

First Thoughts [Respond]

1. Sample responses: I was chilled by its view of love; I felt sorry for all the characters.

Shaping Interpretations [Interpret]

2. The absence of names makes the characters seem universal. *Boy* and *girl* convey immaturity.

3. Possible response: They seem to have conflicting ideas about the level of commitment and self-sacrifice that being part of a family requires.

4. Possible responses: guilt; understanding that his family's well-being was more important than his recreation.

5. Possible response: The man has matured and understands the depth of his loss in regard to his family.

6. Possible responses: Things change, but we are responsible for our actions; things change, but you wanted to leave all along; things change, but you and my mother could have tried harder to stay together. She doesn't want to hurt her father or spark conflict.

7. Possible answers: The boy wanted to be free of his family, but family needs "stuck" to him temporarily; the pain and guilt about his past choices have "stuck" to him up to the present.

Challenging the Text [Synthesize]

8. Possible deletions: what the daughter said at the end of the story; what became of the man's wife; the "other story" in the dentist's office; more about Sally and Betsy. Some students may wish for more details to enhance their comprehension; others may find the need to infer details a welcome challenge.

Grading Timesaver

Rubrics for each Choices Assignment appear on p. 214 in the *Portfolio Management System.*

Reading Check

a. setting: Milan, Italy, at Christmas; characters: a father and his grown daughter

b. setting: November, a generation before, in an apartment under a dentist's office; characters: a husband and wife and their baby. The husband is the father in the frame story, and the baby is the daughter.

c. The husband and wife took turns rocking the baby; they argued.

d. They promise not to fight anymore.

CHOICES: Building Your Portfolio

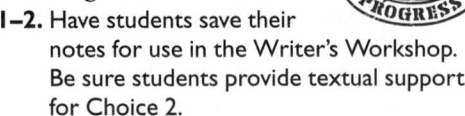

1–2. Have students save their notes for use in the Writer's Workshop. Be sure students provide textual support for Choice 2.

3. Suggest that students imagine the monologue inwardly for a few minutes, write a quick draft without stopping, and revise later.

UPI/Bettmann.

Elizabeth Bishop

(1911–1979)

A "poet's poet," Elizabeth Bishop has been, for many important poets of our time, an acknowledged master of the highest art and most meticulous craft. She has also been an unacknowledged inspiration for many others still trying to solve the mystery of her impenetrable simplicity. Her poetry has won wide formal recognition, including a Pulitzer Prize for *Poems: North and South—A Cold Spring* (1955) and a National Book Award for *Complete Poems* (1969).

Born in Worcester, Massachusetts, Bishop spent her early years in a Nova Scotia village—a childhood marked by the early death of her father and darkened by the long illness of her mother. These circumstances, in effect, made her an orphan whose upbringing was entrusted to relatives.

At the time of her mother's death in a psychiatric hospital, Bishop was a student at Vassar College. After graduation, she embarked on a career quietly devoted to poetry and, by means of a private income, to travels. During these travels, she discovered two places congenial enough to detain her for years—Key West, Florida, and Rio de Janeiro. *Questions of Travel* (1965), the title she gave to one of her books, might serve as an index to the story of a life told in poems that are always "letters from abroad." In these poems, places—near or far—provide temporary settings for an endless inquiry into the nature of perception and reality.

In the final years of her life, Bishop lived in a condominium on a Boston Harbor wharf and spent her summers on an island off the coast of Maine. These changes of scene came about when her close friend Robert Lowell (page 948) became ill, and Harvard University invited her to take over the classes he had been scheduled to teach. She continued to teach at Harvard until her death.

A shy woman with a taste for the exotic as well as a love of the ordinary, Bishop surrounded herself with artifacts acquired in the course of her travels. She conducted herself with a scrupulous conventionality much at odds with the audacity and profundity of her imagination. Her poems most truly reveal her character: a combination of the conservatism and moral rectitude many associate with "the North" and the casual sensuousness and cheerfully untidy sprawl many associate with nature and the everyday outdoor life of "the South." For Elizabeth Bishop, geography was less a matter of maps and place names than of states of mind and areas of feeling.

go.hrw.com
LE0 11-19

 Resources: Print and Media

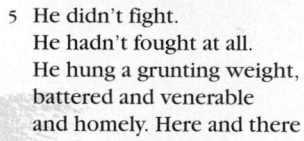

Make the Connection
Creature Teachers

Since ancient times, writers and storytellers have used creatures from the natural world to illustrate all aspects of human behavior, from the wisest to the most absurd. Ancient Greek myths, Aesop's fables, and Grimms' fairy tales contain famous examples. American literature also includes many notable examples, such as "The Chambered Nautilus" by Oliver Wendell Holmes (page 189) and *Moby-Dick; or The Whale* by Herman Melville (page 313).

Quickwrite

Read the first nine lines of the poem, and then stop: Write what you predict the poem's speaker will do with the fish.

Elements of Literature
Personification

A metaphor is a comparison between two unlike things. **Personification** is a kind of metaphor in which a nonhuman thing or quality is talked about as if it were human. It may be given human feelings, thoughts, or attitudes. In the poem that follows, the speaker uses many metaphors and similes to describe the fish. Watch for instances of personification.

The Fish
Elizabeth Bishop

I caught a tremendous fish
and held him beside the boat
half out of water, with my hook
fast in a corner of his mouth.
5   He didn't fight.
He hadn't fought at all.
He hung a grunting weight,
battered and venerable
and homely. Here and there
10 his brown skin hung in strips
like ancient wall-paper,
and its pattern of darker brown
was like wall-paper:
shapes like full-blown roses
15 stained and lost through age.
He was speckled with barnacles,
fine rosettes of lime,
and infested
with tiny white sea-lice,
20 and underneath two or three
rags of green weed hung down.
While his gills were breathing in
the terrible oxygen
—the frightening gills
25 fresh and crisp with blood,
that can cut so badly—
I thought of the coarse white flesh
packed in like feathers,
the big bones and the little bones,
30 the dramatic reds and blacks
of his shiny entrails,
and the pink swim-bladder
like a big peony.
I looked into his eyes
35 which were far larger than mine
but shallower, and yellowed,
the irises backed and packed
with tarnished tinfoil
seen through the lenses
40 of old scratched isinglass.°
They shifted a little, but not
to return my stare.

40. **isinglass** (ī′zin·glas′): mica, glasslike mineral that crystallizes in thin layers.

Summary ■■

The first-person speaker recalls catching a large, old, battered fish. In the first half of the poem she describes the fish in detail, using a variety of similes and metaphors that emphasize its impersonal, almost mechanical strangeness. Yet in the second half of the poem she expresses increasing admiration for the fish and its "sullen face." She views the hooks and lines as medals and ribbons won in combat. Staring at the fish and at the rainbow pattern of oil in the bottom of the boat, she is overwhelmed by a sense of the fish's victory and releases it into the water.

Ⓐ Advanced Learners
Rhythm

❓ What is the poem's rhythm? [It is a flexible rhythm with two or three accented beats per line, neither free verse nor strict meter.]

Ⓑ Elements of Literature
Metaphor

❓ Later in the poem, the fish will be personified. Here, however, the fish is compared to inorganic things. What are some of those things? [wallpaper; tinfoil; isinglass]

Reaching All Students

Struggling Readers

After students have read "The Fish" once, have them divide the poem into sentences and paraphrase each sentence in order to grasp the major points. Then use Choice 2 (p. 1038) to guide students through the events of the poem and to glimpse the possibility of deeper meaning beneath the deceptively simple surface action.

English Language Learners

Focus on concrete nouns, such as *wall-paper* and *weed;* adjectives, such as *battered* and *sullen;* and verbs, such as *admired* and *shifted.* After students comprehend the words in context, ask students to use the words in different everyday contexts. For strategies to engage English language learners with the literature, see
• *Lesson Plans Including Strategies for English-Language Learners*

Winslow Homer (1836–1910) first established himself as a realistic illustrator of the Civil War. At the same time, he had begun to paint oils of country life. He took up watercolors in 1873 and eventually became America's greatest watercolorist. The two years he spent in the early 1880s in a North Sea fishing village near Tynemouth, England, were the turning point of his life. There, he painted nature, especially the sea, and not only developed a mature technique but also found his central subject: the relationship between human beings and the natural world. He settled in Prout's Neck, Maine, in 1883, and his sea painting and wilderness scenes brought him recognition and great financial success. *Leaping Trout,* one of Homer's later watercolors, embodies his use of transparent washes of color that convey a sense of light and drama.

Activity. Have students look for specific lines in Bishop's poem that might fit the image of Homer's leaping trout. Also, invite students to describe their own responses to the fish. [Possible responses: "his gills were breathing in / the terrible oxygen" (ll. 22–23), "rainbow, rainbow, rainbow!" (l. 75), "And I let the fish go" (l. 76). Student responses to the fish will vary.]

Using Students' Strengths

Intrapersonal Learners
Have students do a freewrite about a living thing that symbolizes, or represents, survival in the face of adversity, such as a neglected plant or an endangered animal. Then, have them read or reread the poem to find possible symbolic significance in the fish Bishop describes.

Visual Learners
Before students read the poem, hand out pictures of a variety of different types of fish. Work with students to develop similes and metaphors to describe these fish. Then, have students read the poem and identify the similes and metaphors Bishop uses to describe her fish. Some students may wish to draw a fish based on Bishop's verbal description.

—It was more like the tipping
of an object toward the light.
45 I admired his sullen face,
the mechanism of his jaw,
and then I saw
that from his lower lip
—if you could call it a lip—
50 grim, wet, and weapon-like,
hung five old pieces of fish-line,
or four and a wire leader
with the swivel still attached,
with all their five big hooks
55 grown firmly in his mouth.
A green line, frayed at the end
where he broke it, two heavier lines,
and a fine black thread
still crimped from the strain and snap
60 when it broke and he got away.
Like medals with their ribbons
frayed and wavering,
a five-haired beard of wisdom
trailing from his aching jaw.
65 I stared and stared
and victory filled up
the little rented boat,
from the pool of bilge
where oil had spread a rainbow
70 around the rusted engine
to the bailer rusted orange,
the sun-cracked thwarts,
the oarlocks on their strings,
the gunnels—until everything
75 was rainbow, rainbow, rainbow!
And I let the fish go.

Leaping Trout (1889) by Winslow Homer.
Watercolor on paper (14″ × 19¾″).

Portland Museum of Art, Portland, Maine. Bequest of Charles Shipman
Payson (1988.55.7). Photo by Melville McLean.

ELIZABETH BISHOP 1037

Ⓐ Struggling Readers
Questioning
❓ What do these pieces of line and leader reveal about the fish's history? [It has been caught and gotten away at least five times before; it is a survivor.]

Ⓑ Elements of Literature
Personification
❓ What is the effect of personifying the fish at this point? [Possible responses: It conveys the speaker's admiration for the fish; it makes the fish seem more like a decorated war veteran who has had many victories over anglers.]

Ⓒ Critical Thinking
Interpreting
❓ What does Bishop mean by "rainbow, rainbow, rainbow!"? [Possible responses: The repetition expresses her sudden overwhelming sense of the fish's triumph and her wish to participate in it; it conveys an almost religious ecstasy about nature and the world.]

Ⓓ Critical Thinking
Responding to the Text
❓ What was your response to the last line? [Sample responses: I thought she was right to let the fish go because of its nobility; I thought she was sentimental to let the fish go; I thought the line was an exciting summation; I thought the line was flat and anticlimactic.]

Crossing the Curriculum

Social Studies/Environmental Science
Ask students to research and report on wildlife management programs, such as the catch-and-release programs that help preserve the populations of fish in many of our nation's streams, and the arguments for and against managing fish species. If possible, invite a park ranger or wildlife specialist to augment students' research.

Art
From John James Audubon to the present, numerous visual artists have made it their life's work to depict natural species in a way that combines scientific accuracy with emotional appeal. Ask interested students to locate art books in the library that feature nature illustrators and to show their favorite illustrations to the class, giving a brief talk about the artist and subject.

Making the Connections

Connecting to the Theme: "Discoveries and Awakenings"
During a seemingly mundane activity, the catching of a fish, the speaker awakens to the symbolic implications of nature around her: a discovery of the triumph of life over death, hinting at religious faith. Remind students that one traditional symbol of Christianity is the fish.

First Thoughts [Respond]

1. Sample responses: No, I predicted the speaker would let it go; yes, I thought the fish would make a good prize.

Shaping Interpretations [Interpret]

2. Simile: ll. 10–11, the fish's skin hung like strips of wallpaper; ll. 14–15, the pattern of the skin like old roses; ll. 27–28, flesh packed like feathers; ll. 32–33, the fish's bladder like a peony. Metaphor: l. 7, the fish compared to a weight; ll. 37–38, the fish's eyes compared to tinfoil, and ll. 39–40, to isinglass.

3. The simile in l. 61, refering to wearing medals, and the metaphoric references to a beard and jaw in ll. 63–64 compare the fish to an old war hero.

4. Possible responses: The speaker realizes that letting the fish go would be a victory. The speaker is the victor for catching the fish, but the fish is the victor for surviving and for rekindling the speaker's respect for natural life. Death or human destruction of nature might be the enemy.

5. The rainbow and the personification of the fish suggest symbolism; the fish might symbolize the triumph of life or spirit over death.

6. Possible response: The fish's longevity and victory make her reevaluate her dilapidated rental boat, and see her surroundings in the light of the fish's triumph. This renewed sense of purpose and faith makes the capture of the fish seem unnecessary and wrong—so she releases it.

Connecting with the Text

[Synthesize]

7. Sample responses: I felt similarly when I had a deer in my sights but didn't shoot; I felt a similar sense of majesty while camping in the Tetons.

8. Sample responses: I agree with the decision, since the fish has "paid its dues" and deserves to live; I would have kept the fish as a trophy to remind me of its strength.

First Thoughts

1. Did the ending of "The Fish" surprise you? (Review the prediction you made in your Quickwrite notes.) Explain.

Shaping Interpretations

2. As the speaker examines the fish, a series of **similes** and **metaphors** are used to describe it. Find at least six figures of speech in lines 1–40 that help you see the fish.

3. Identify the two figures of speech in lines 61–64 that **personify** the fish. How would you characterize the type of person these comparisons suggest?

4. As the speaker stares at the fish, "victory filled up" the boat. What does this mean? Whose "victory" is it, and who or what was the enemy?

5. What clues suggest that the fish might have **symbolic** meaning? What might it symbolize?

6. As the speaker thinks "rainbow, rainbow, rainbow," she sees the pool of oil, the "rusted engine," and the "sun-cracked thwarts" in a totally new way. Why do you think she lets the fish go?

Connecting with the Text

7. Have you ever experienced a moment when the ordinary suddenly seemed full of beauty and wonder? Describe your experience.

8. What do you think of the speaker's decision to let the old fish go? What would you have done?

CHOICES:
Building Your Portfolio

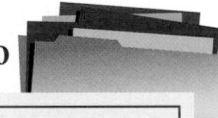

Writer's Notebook

1. Collecting Ideas for an Evaluation

Comparing "The Fish" to another literary work could be an effective strategy for arriving at an evaluation of this

poem. List several American works that center around the conflict between a main character and an animal, such as Ernest Hemingway's *The Old Man and the Sea* or William Faulkner's "The Bear." Jot down your thoughts on **themes, plots, characters,** or **images** that each work might have in common with Bishop's "The Fish," or tell how each work might be different. Keep your notes for possible use in the Writer's Workshop on page 1181.

Analyzing a Poem
2. What Happened?

The first line of "The Fish" is a simple statement: "I caught a tremendous fish." So is the last line: "And I let the fish go." Between the moment the speaker announces the catch and the moment the fish is let go, something important happens, and that is what the poem is all about. Make a list of the speaker's actions in the poem. Then, in a brief essay, recount these actions in chronological order. At the conclusion of your essay, identify the moment when something happens that makes the speaker give up what most other fishers would be only too happy to keep. Explain this moment of discovery in a few sentences.

Creative Writing
3. A Fish's Story

Write a short poem telling the poem's story from the fish's point of view. You might begin with the line "I was caught," and end with the line "I was let go." How does the fish feel about being caught? about being set free? What does the fish think of the speaker? Try to imitate the style of "The Fish."

Grading Timesaver

Rubrics for each Choices assignment appear on p. 215 in the *Portfolio Management System.*

CHOICES:
Building Your Portfolio

1. **Writer's Workshop**
   Remind students to save their work. They may use it as prewriting for the Writer's Workshop on p. 1181.

2. **Analyzing a Poem** Listing the actions should lead students to see meaning in the interaction between the speaker and the fish.

3. **Creative Writing** Suggest that students use short lines of free verse.

Joy Harjo
(1951–   )

And I write it to you
at this moment
never being able to get
the essence
   the true breath
in words, because we exist
not in words, but in the motion
set off by them. . . .

—*from "Motion"*

© Paul Abdoo.

Joy Harjo is a poet who puts words in their place, who doesn't let them take over life itself. Stymied, she says, by the limitations of language, she has written that "all poets / understand the final uselessness of words." Nevertheless, she produces vibrant poetry and screenplays, teaches Native American literature and creative writing, edits poetry journals, and holds a master's degree from the University of Iowa Writers' Workshop.

Harjo is mostly of mixed Muscogee Creek and Cherokee descent. She grew up in Oklahoma in difficult circumstances, as her divorced mother struggled to feed and clothe four children. Partly in response to the poverty and frustration of her mother's life, Harjo has said, she "wanted something different" for herself and for her son and her daughter. "I obtained two degrees as a single mother. I wrote poetry, screenplays, became a professor, and tried to live a life that would be a positive influence for both of my children." In addition to being a poet, the multitalented Harjo is an editor, filmmaker, painter, and jazz saxophonist.

Harjo's first collection of poems, *The Last Song,* appeared in 1975, when she was still a student at the University of New Mexico. Her 1983 volume, *She Had Some Horses,* met with particular acclaim, and she issued another poetry collection, *In Mad Love and War,* in 1990. Her ability to invest the contemporary scene with American Indian myths is evident in *The Woman Who Fell from the Sky* (1994), a book accompanied by an audiocassette of Harjo reading her words.

Harjo's work is rooted in the past and the present of her fellow Native Americans. She has written that "my work in this life has to do with reclaiming the memory stolen from our peoples when we were dispossessed from our lands east of the Mississippi; it has to do with restoring us. I am proud of our history." As she asks in her poem "Anchorage,"

   who would believe
the fantastic and terrible story of all of our
   survival
those who were never meant to survive?

As an American Indian and as a contemporary woman, Harjo uses poetry as a vehicle for moving beyond survival to success. She writes, she tells us, because "if Indian people, Indian women, keep silent, then we will disappear."

go.hrw.com
LE0 11-19

OBJECTIVES
1. Read and interpret the poem
2. Express understanding through critical and creative writing

SKILLS
Writing
- Collect ideas for an evaluation
- Compare two texts
- Write a poem

Speaking and Listening
- Read a poem aloud

Viewing/Representing
- Compare the effects of a poem and a painting (ATE)
- Suggest another literary selection to connect to the painting (ATE)

Planning

- **Traditional Schedule**
  Lesson Plans Including Strategies for English-Language Learners
- **One-Stop Planner**
  CD-ROM with Test Generator

Resources: Print and Media

Reading
- *Graphic Organizers for Active Reading,* p. 104
- *Audio CD Library*
    Disc 26, Track 5

Assessment
- *Portfolio Management System,* p. 216
- *Test Generator (One-Stop Planner CD-ROM)*

Internet
- go.hrw.com (keyword: LE0 11-19)

Summary ∎

Harjo's poem echoes traditional Native American songs, and features a wide array of natural images, as well as a refrain of "remember" at the start of most lines. The speaker implores an anonymous collective audience to remember the moon and sun, personified with a "birth" and character traits. Similarly, the collective "you" the speaker addresses are called upon to remember their own births, and their mothers and fathers, whose lives are bound up in their children's. The earth, with all its different shades, must also be remembered as part of this "you." The speaker goes on to insist that plants and animals must be remembered as well, for they are "alive poems." Ultimately, the speaker identifies her audience with all the universe, and like Whitman, links that universe to language. In the end, both language and life are figured as a kind of "dance."

Ⓐ Elements of Literature
Metaphor

❓ What does the speaker mean when she says that we are the skin of the earth? [People are part of the earth—the outside, visible part.]

Ⓑ Humanities Connections

The ideas of the unity of humanity and its oneness with the universe can be found in the literature of many cultures. Examples include Walt Whitman's poetry (see pp. 347–359), the Hindu Vedas, and the Taoist *Tao Te Ching*.

Ⓒ Elements of Literature
Refrain

❓ Why does Harjo repeat the word "Remember" at the beginning of each line? [Possible responses: Repetition makes the poem resemble a chant or a prayer and emphasizes the theme.]

Before You Read
REMEMBER

Make the Connection
Connected

In this age of isolated computer modems, the impersonal information superhighway, and lonely flickering TV screens, it is easy to overlook the many ways we can connect with fellow humans and with the world around us. One of the main functions of poets through the ages has been to re-mind us of connections we have forgotten or take for granted and to show us new connections.

Quickwrite

Freewrite all the associations you make with the word *connection*. How many possible connections can human beings make with one another and with the world around them?

Remember

Joy Harjo

Remember the sky that you were born under,
know each of the stars' stories.
Remember the moon, know who she is.
Remember the sun's birth at dawn, that is the
5 strongest point of time. Remember sundown
and the giving away to night.
Remember your birth, how your mother struggled
to give you form and breath. You are evidence of
her life, and her mother's, and hers.
10 Remember your father. He is your life, also.
Remember the earth whose skin you are:
red earth, black earth, yellow earth, white earth
brown earth, we are earth.
Remember the plants, trees, animal life who all have their
15 tribes, their families, their histories, too. Talk to them,
listen to them. They are alive poems.
Remember the wind. Remember her voice. She knows the
origin of this universe.
Remember that you are all people and that all people
20 are you.
Remember that you are this universe and that this
universe is you.
Remember that all is in motion, is growing, is you.
Remember that language comes from this.
25 Remember the dance that language is, that life is.
Remember.

1040 CONTEMPORARY LITERATURE

Reaching All Students

Struggling Readers

Many of the songs and poems students have read in this book have refrains. To help students identify Harjo's refrain and understand its pur-pose, share examples of refrains from familiar songs. Ask students to bring in other examples and to explain why they think Harjo decided to use the refrain.

English Language Learners

The simple vocabulary and refrain of the poem make it ideal for students to memorize—in part or as a whole—and to practice reciting aloud in order to improve their English pronun-ciation and cadence. For strategies to engage English language learners with the literature, see
• *Lesson Plans Including Strategies for English-Language Learners*

Sun (1943) by Arthur G. Dove. Wax emulsion on canvas (24″ × 32″).

National Museum of American Art, Washington, D.C. Bequest of Suzanne M. Smith.
By permission of D. Mullett Smith Trust. © 1976 by Suzanne Mullett Smith. Courtesy Art Resource, NY.

Using Students' Strengths

Musical/Auditory Learners
Have students research American Indian music and choose selections to play as background for an oral reading of the poem.

Kinesthetic Learners
In conjunction with the activity for Musical/Auditory Learners, ask students to choreograph or improvise a dance to accompany the oral reading of the poem to music.

Logical/Mathematical Learners
Invite students to search for paradoxes or contradictions in the poem. For example, how can a plant be a poem? How can the wind remember the origin of the universe? How can one person be all people? How is language a dance? Invite students to discuss possible resolutions of these paradoxes.

Making the Connections

Connecting to the Theme: "Discoveries and Awakenings"
In telling the reader to remember, the speaker is, in a sense, urging the reader to awaken: to discover the unity and harmony of the whole natural world—indeed, the whole universe—rather than go through life feeling isolated.

First Thoughts [Respond]

1. Sample responses: ll. 7–9 on birth, because of the tradition of passing on life; ll. 21–22 because it is intriguing to think we are one with the universe.

Shaping Interpretations

[Synthesize]

2. Possible responses: The speaker might be Harjo addressing the reader, or an American Indian elder addressing younger people, or someone facing death and addressing his or her family.

3. Possible response: the importance of remembering the connection people have to one another, to the earth, and to the universe.

4. Each star is personified in l. 2; the moon in l. 3; the sun in l. 4; the earth in l. 11; plants, trees, and animals in ll. 14–16; the wind in ll. 17–18. By personifying them, the poet honors nonhuman things and may endow them with a religious quality.

5. "Remember"; it suggests that this advice is something that the audience already knows on some primal level—they must simply recall it.

Connecting with the Text

[Synthesize]

6. Sample responses: Yes, if we listen to plants, trees, and animals, we will learn things we didn't know before. No, only people can communicate philosophical ideas; plants and animals can only serve as human-made symbols.

Grading Timesaver

Rubrics for each Choices assignment appear on p. 216 in the *Portfolio Management System*.

First Thoughts

1. Which passage in the poem had the strongest effect on you? Why?

Shaping Interpretations

2. Who do you think is the **speaker** of "Remember"? Whom is the speaker addressing?

3. How would you state the main **theme** of the poem in your own words?

4. "Remember" includes several instances of **personification** (a figure of speech in which an object or animal is given human attributes). Identify two such instances, and explain what they add to the poem.

5. Identify the **refrain** of the poem. What does it contribute to the poem's message?

Connecting with the Text

6. The speaker asks the reader to talk to and listen to plants, trees, and animal life. Does this request make sense to you? Explain, referring to your Quickwrite notes.

David L. Brown/The Stock Market

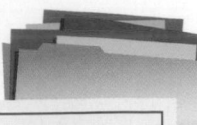

Writer's Notebook

1. Collecting Ideas for an Evaluation

When writing an evaluation, you can cite your own experience to support your judgment of a text. Jot down experiences you can recall that relate to Harjo's "Remember." Do any match the speaker's? Based on your own experience, which of the speaker's requests could you follow easily? Which would be more difficult or even impossible to follow? Save your notes for possible use in the Writer's Workshop on page 1181.

Comparing Texts

2. The American Tradition

Ralph Waldo Emerson, born in a very different era, almost 150 years before Joy Harjo, shares with her a keen appreciation of the natural world. In a short essay, compare the messages of Harjo's "Remember" and the excerpt from Emerson's *Nature* (page 219). How are they similar and different?

Creative Writing / Speaking and Listening

3. All Your Yesterdays

Write a "Remember" poem in which you relate some of your own memories and experiences. Start each line or stanza with "Remember" or "I remember."

Oral Interpretation

4. Joy's Dance

Prepare the poem for an oral reading. You will have to decide if you will read the poem alone, or use solo voices and a chorus. Decide how you will pace your reading and how you will vary the tone of your voice. Be sure to ask your audience for evaluations.

1. **Writer's Notebook**
   Remind students to save their work. They may use it as prewriting for the Writer's Workshop on p. 1181. Also, remind students to choose an experience they would not mind sharing with others. Some students may prefer to recall experiences other than their own.

2. **Critical Writing** Before students turn to Emerson's *Nature,* invite those who choose this activity to brainstorm what they recall of the essay from memory. Then, have them check their understanding by reviewing the text.

3. **Creative Writing** Students may put a new spin on their poems by writing a "Remember" poem in the voice of a famous real or fictional person and having classmates guess the speaker's identity.

4. **Oral Interpretation** Allow plenty of time for practice.

Maxine Hong Kingston

(1940–)

© Nancy Crampton.

Maxine Hong Kingston burst onto the literary scene in 1976 with an extraordinary and innovative book—*The Woman Warrior: Memoirs of a Girlhood Among Ghosts.* Kingston, who was born in California of Chinese immigrant parents, uses a mixture of autobiography, myth, poetic meditation, and fiction to convey her memories and feelings about growing up in a strange world (the United States) populated by what she and her family thought of as white-skinned "ghosts."

The book received immediate acclaim. William McPherson of the *Washington Post* wrote: "*The Woman Warrior* is a strange, sometimes savagely terrifying and, in the literal sense, wonderful story about growing up caught between two highly sophisticated and utterly alien cultures, both vivid, often menacing, and equally mysterious." Paul Gray said in *Time:* "Exiles and refugees tell sad stories of the life they left behind. Even sadder, sometimes, is the muteness of their children. They are likely to find the old ways and old language excess baggage, especially if their adopted homeland is the United States, where the race is to the swift and the adaptable. Thus a heritage of centuries can die in a generation of embarrassed silence. *The Woman Warrior* gives that silence a voice."

When *The Woman Warrior* won the National Book Critics Circle Award for general nonfiction in 1976, Kingston gained national attention. The suddenness of her appearance as an important literary figure was startling.

Where had Kingston been until the age of thirty-six? Named for an American woman in the gambling house where her father worked for a time, Maxine Hong grew up in the Chinatown of Stockton, California. She earned a B.A. from the University of California at Berkeley in 1962 and married the actor Earll Kingston. After their son was born, the Kingstons lived in Hawaii for a time, where Maxine taught English at the high school and college levels, before returning to California.

In 1980, Kingston published a companion piece to *The Woman Warrior,* a kind of ancestral history called *China Men.* The critic Susan Currier has described this book as "a sort of vindication of all the Chinese who helped build America but who were rewarded with abuse and neglect." In 1988, Kingston published an extravagant novel called *Tripmaster Monkey: His Fake Book,* blending Chinese history and myth and vivid storytelling in the adventures of a young Chinese American named Wittman Ah Sing. The noted novelist Anne Tyler called *Tripmaster Monkey* "a novel of satisfying complexity and bite and verve." In the 1990s, Kingston taught creative writing at the University of California at Berkeley and worked on a book of nonfiction.

Despite the attention given to her books, Kingston has remained relatively private. She seldom gives interviews or appears at public readings. In her two memoirs, she does not answer all of the personal questions raised by her writing. In the selection that follows, even a careful reader will not be able to decide what is truth, what is fiction, and what is simply left unsaid. This ambiguity gives Kingston's work much of its haunting quality.

go.hrw.com
LE0 11-19

MAXINE HONG KINGSTON 1043

 *Resources: Print and Media*

Reading
- *Graphic Organizers for Active Reading,* p. 105
- *Words to Own,* p. 54
- *Audio CD Library*
  Disc 27, Track 2

Writing and Language
- *Daily Oral Grammar*
  Transparency 60

Assessment
- *Formal Assessment,* p. 206
- *Portfolio Management System,* p. 218
- *Preparation for College Admission Exams,* p. 63
- *Test Generator (One-Stop Planner CD-ROM)*

Internet
- go.hrw.com (keyword: LE0 11-19)

OBJECTIVES
1. Read and interpret the memoir
2. Analyze internal and external conflict
3. Draw inferences about characters
4. Demonstrate understanding through critical and creative writing
5. Demonstrate understanding of new words

SKILLS
Literary
- Analyze internal and external conflict

Reading
- Draw inferences about characters

Writing
- Collect ideas for an evaluation
- Interpret character
- Write a story

Planning

- **Block Schedule**
  Block Scheduling Lesson Plan with Pacing Guide
- **Traditional Schedule**
  Lesson Plans Including Strategies for English-Language Learners
- **One-Stop Planner**
  CD-ROM with Test Generator

BROWSING IN THE FILES

About the Author. Kingston's parents married in China. Her father emigrated to New York City and worked in a laundry for fifteen years to send his wife money to study for certifications in medicine and midwifery in China. She established a practice in China but gave it up when her husband sent for her to come to the United States. In the United States, she worked as a laundress and a field hand. Kingston may have found in her parents a model for some of the Chinese immigrants in her writing.

Summary ∎

At the beginning of this excerpt from Kingston's memoir *The Woman Warrior,* the Chinese American narrator describes her attempt to create a soft, "American-feminine speaking personality" to compensate for what she sees as her "strong and bossy" Chinese voice. This issue of speaking is a focal point for Kingston's thematic examination of assimilation and cultural difference. The narrator describes a Chinese American girl in her class who refuses to speak unless reading aloud. The narrator remarks that she and the "quiet girl" are very similar but explains that she has a largely irrational hatred for the girl, who seems to represent the narrator's internal conflicts over her own awkward assimilation into American life. One day in sixth grade, the narrator and the quiet girl are alone in the lavatory. The narrator tries to force the girl to speak, harassing her, hurting her and even bribing her. The girl cries but will not speak, and the narrator ends up crying, too, out of frustration and sorrow. After this external conflict, the narrator is kept out of school for eighteen months by a "mysterious illness." When she returns, she finds the girl hasn't changed: She remains strangely immune to social pressures, sheltered by her family and her culture.

Before You Read
THE GIRL WHO WOULDN'T TALK

Make the Connection
Things Left Unspoken
It happens just about every day to all of us: For one reason or another, we don't tell others about something important we know or feel. Out of self-doubt, politeness, love, fear, or many other reasons, we don't express in conversation certain thoughts or feelings that are near to us. Instead, we sometimes express them in writing, painting, dance, song, or some other art form.

Reading Skills and Strategies
Drawing Inferences About Characters
As you read "The Girl Who Wouldn't Talk," take notes on the author's **characterization** of the silent girl and the narrator. Then, stop near the end of page 1049, and write down what you think the silent girl is not saying—that is, what her unexpressed thoughts and feelings are. You might also jot down what you think the *narrator* is not saying.

Elements of Literature
Conflict
Conflict—the struggle between opposing forces or characters in a story—can be either external or internal. **External conflict** can take many forms. For example, it can involve two people, a person and a force of nature, a person and a machine, or a person and a society or community. **Internal conflict** involves opposing forces within a person's mind. Kingston's story presents both external and internal conflicts centering around childhood cruelty, a problem that knows no cultural or linguistic barriers.

> **C**onflict is the struggle between opposing forces or characters in a story.
>
> *For more on Conflict, see page 607 and the Handbook of Literary Terms.*

Background
The Chinese American family in this extract from *The Woman Warrior* lives in Stockton, California. Just before the episode starts, the narrator talks about speech and Chinese voices, which she says are louder than American voices. Describing her own voice, the narrator says: "You could hear splinters in my voice, bones rubbing jagged against one another. I was loud, though. I was glad I didn't whisper."

The "ghosts" mentioned by the narrator are white Americans, who seemed so strange to this Chinese family.

Preteaching Vocabulary

Words to Own
Ask a volunteer to write the Words to Own on the board in four columns, grouping them by parts of speech (noun, verb, adjective, adverb). Ask what the two nouns, *nape* and *temples,* have in common. [They name parts of the head or neck.] **Ask what the other three words have in** common. [They describe kinds of behavior or speech.]

Then, divide students into groups of two or three, and have them compose sentences using the vocabulary words as follows:
1. Compose a sentence using both nouns.
2. Compose a sentence using one of the nouns and one of the other words.
3. Compose a sentence using two of the words that are not nouns.

In the passages surrounding this excerpt in *The Woman Warrior*, Kingston elaborates on the mutual difficulties in communication between Chinese immigrants and native-born Americans. According to the narrator's father, American speech and music were too soft for the Chinese to enjoy hearing, while Americans found Chinese speech too loud and its sharply varying tones unfamiliar. Chinese children's desire to fit in was one reason for their adoption of a quiet persona; another was the need they felt to keep family secrets. Fear of the immigration authorities was an important motive for secrecy, since some immigrants had arrived as stowaways or with improper papers. Simple shame was another reason for secrecy: As the narrator reports on the first page of *The Woman Warrior*, her family kept secret the story of an aunt's suicide in China.

The Girl Who Wouldn't Talk

from The Woman Warrior

Maxine Hong Kingston

Reaching All Students

Struggling Readers
Drawing Inferences About Characters was introduced on p. 1044. A good strategy to use with drawing inferences is It Says . . . I Say. Have students use an It Says . . . I Say chart to help them answer the questions on p. 1053. For information on using this strategy, see the *Reading Strategies Handbook*, p. 25 in the *Reading Skills and Strategies* binder.

English Language Learners
Some words and phrases in the selection may be unfamiliar to students raised in other cultures. Provide explanations of *easy out, automatic walk, tetherball, Korean War* (1950–1953), *air raid drill, did a flip, permanents, throw fists,* and *Baby Ruth*. For strategies to engage English language learners with the literature, see
* *Lesson Plans Including Strategies for English-Language Learners*

Advanced Learners
Invite students to read more of *Woman Warrior*. Pose a question that critics are still asking about the book: "Is it a novel or a memoir?" Although published as nonfiction, it contains passages that are admittedly folk tales and other passages that seem embellished. Meanwhile, many books published as novels seem equally autobiographical. Ask students to present evidence for placing the book in each genre.

Normal Chinese women's voices are strong and bossy. We American-Chinese girls had to whisper to make ourselves American-feminine. Apparently we whispered even more softly than the Americans. Once a year the teachers referred my sister and me to speech therapy, but our voices would straighten out, unpredictably normal, for the therapists. Some of us gave up, shook our heads, and said nothing, not one word. Some of us could not even shake our heads. At times shaking my head no is more self-assertion than I can manage. Most of us eventually found some voice, however faltering. We invented an American-feminine speaking personality, except for that one girl who could not speak up even in Chinese school.

She was a year older than I and was in my class for twelve years. During all those years she read aloud but would not talk. Her older sister was usually beside her; their parents kept the older daughter back to protect the younger one. They were six and seven years old when they began school. Although I had flunked kindergarten, I was the same age as most other students in our class; my parents had probably lied about my age, so I had had a head start and came out even. My younger sister was in the class below me; we were normal ages and normally separated. The parents of the quiet girl, on the other hand, protected both daughters. When it sprinkled, they kept them home from school. The girls did not work for a living the way we did. But in other ways we were the same.

We were similar in sports. We held the bat on our shoulders until we walked to first base. (You got a strike only when you actually struck at the ball.) Sometimes the pitcher wouldn't bother to throw to us. "Automatic walk," the other children would call, sending us on our way. By fourth or fifth grade, though, some of us would try to hit the ball. "Easy out," the other kids would say. I hit the ball a couple of times. Baseball was nice in that there was a definite spot to run to after hitting the ball. Basketball confused me because when I caught the ball I didn't know whom to throw it to. "Me. Me," the

kids would be yelling. "Over here." Suddenly it would occur to me I hadn't memorized which ghosts were on my team and which were on the other. When the kids said, "Automatic walk," the girl who was quieter than I kneeled with one end of the bat in each hand and placed it carefully on the plate. Then she dusted her hands as she walked to first base, where she rubbed her hands softly, fingers spread. She always got tagged out before second base. She would whisper-read but not talk. Her whisper was as soft as if she had no muscles. She seemed to be breathing from a distance. I heard no anger or tension.

I joined in at lunchtime when the other students, the Chinese too, talked about whether or not she was mute, although obviously she was not if she could read aloud. People told how *they* had tried *their* best to be friendly. *They* said hello, but if she refused to answer, well, they didn't see why they had to say hello anymore. She had no friends of her own but followed her sister everywhere, although people and she herself probably thought I was her friend. I also followed her sister about, who was fairly normal. She was almost two years older and read more than anyone else.

I hated the younger sister, the quiet one. I hated her when she was the last chosen for her team and I, the last chosen for my team. I hated her for her China doll hair cut. I hated her at music time for the wheezes that came out of her plastic flute.

One afternoon in the sixth grade (that year I was arrogant with talk, not knowing there were going to be high school dances and college seminars to set me back), I and my little sister and the quiet girl and her big sister stayed late after school for some reason. The cement was cooling, and the tetherball poles made shadows across the gravel. The hooks at the rope ends were clinking against the poles. We shouldn't have been so late; there was laundry work to do and Chinese school to get to by 5:00. The last time we had stayed late, my mother had phoned the police and told them we had been kidnapped by bandits. The radio stations broadcast our descriptions. I had to get home before she did that again. But sometimes if you <u>loitered</u> long enough in the schoolyard, the other children would have gone home and you could play with the equipment before the office took it away. We were chasing one another through the playground and in and out of the basement, where the playroom and lavatory were. During air raid drills (it was during the Korean War, which you knew about because every day the front page of the newspaper printed a map of Korea with the top part red and going up and down like a window shade), we curled up in this basement. Now everyone was gone. The playroom was army green and had nothing in it but a long trough with drinking spigots in rows. Pipes across the ceiling led to the drinking fountains and to the toilets in the next room. When someone flushed you could hear the water and other matter, which the children named, running inside the big pipe above the drinking spigots. There was one playroom for girls next to the girls' lavatory and one playroom for boys next to the boys' lavatory. The stalls were open and the toilets had no lids, by which we knew that ghosts have no sense of shame or privacy.

Inside the playroom the lightbulbs in cages had already been turned off. Daylight came in x-patterns through the caging at the windows. I looked out and, seeing no one in the schoolyard, ran outside to climb the fire escape upside down, hanging on to the metal stairs with fingers and toes.

I did a flip off the fire escape and ran across the schoolyard. The day was a great eye, and it was not paying much attention to me now. I could disappear with the sun; I could turn quickly sideways and slip into a different world. It seemed I could run faster at this time, and by evening I would be able to fly. As the afternoon wore on we could run into the forbidden places—the boys' big yard, the boys' playroom. We could go into the boys' lavatory and look at the urinals. The only time during school hours I had

crossed the boys' yard was when a flatbed truck with a giant thing covered with canvas and tied down with ropes had parked across the street. The children had told one another that it was a gorilla in captivity; we couldn't decide whether the sign said "Trail of the Gorilla" or "Trial of the Gorilla." The thing was as big as a house. The teachers couldn't stop us from hysterically rushing to the fence and clinging to the wire mesh. Now I ran across the boys' yard clear to the Cyclone fence and thought about the hair that I had seen sticking out of the canvas. It was going to be summer soon, so you could feel that freedom coming on too.

I ran back into the girls' yard, and there was the quiet sister all by herself. I ran past her, and she followed me into the girls' lavatory. My footsteps rang hard against cement and tile because of the taps I had nailed into my shoes. Her footsteps were soft, padding after me. There was no one in the lavatory but the two of us. I ran all around the rows of twenty-five open stalls to make sure of that. No sisters. I think we must have been playing hide-and-go-seek. She was not good at hiding by herself and usually followed her sister; they'd hide in the same place. They must have gotten separated. In this growing twilight, a child could hide and never be found.

I stopped abruptly in front of the sinks, and she came running toward me before she could stop herself, so that she almost collided with me. I walked closer. She backed away, puzzlement, then alarm in her eyes.

"You're going to talk," I said, my voice steady and normal, as it is when talking to the familiar, the weak, and the small. "I am going to make you talk, you sissy-girl." She stopped backing away and stood fixed.

I looked into her face so I could hate it close up. She wore black bangs, and her cheeks were pink and white. She was baby-soft. I thought that I could put my thumb on

---

WORDS TO OWN

loitered (loit'ərd) v.: spent time; hung around.

The Korean War, an undeclared war in which the United States and 15 other United Nations members were allied against Communist nations, was begun on June 25, 1950, in order to stop the invasion of South Korea by North Korea. After difficult truce negotiations that broke down several times, an armistice agreement was signed on July 27, 1953, with neither side victorious and the post–World War II division at the 38th parallel still in effect. The newspaper map that the narrator refers to showed the ups and downs of Allied fortunes during the war: At first, the North Koreans occupied most of South Korea; then, they were driven back almost to the Chinese border; then, Chinese troops entered the war on the North Korean side, and the South Korean and U.N. forces were pushed back again.

F Elements of Literature

Metaphor and Personification

? What does the narrator compare the day to? [a great eye] How does she personify the day? [She says it "was not paying much attention" to her.]

G Cultural Connections

? Explain that taps on the soles of shoes, to make loud, metallic footsteps, were popular among teens and some children in the 1950s. How does her use of taps show that the narrator is different from the quiet girl? [Possible responses: Taps were a sign of Americanization; taps make noise and draw attention to the wearer.]

H Reading Skills and Strategies

Drawing Inferences About Characters

? What do you infer about the narrator from her statement that she had a steady voice when talking to "the familiar, the weak, and the small"? [Possible responses: She is confident only when she is talking to people lower in the social pecking-order; she feels less sure of herself when talking to authorities or "larger" people.]

Getting Students Involved

Cooperative Learning

Jigsaw Reading. Have students work in groups for ten minutes. Each member should concentrate on a different one of the following literary elements, cite examples of the element, and explain how the element is important in the story: tone, motivation, external conflict, and internal conflict. After ten minutes, ask students who worked on the same element to form new groups to discuss their findings. Recommend that students take notes on new ideas they hear in these cross-group discussions. After five minutes, ask students to return to their original groups to share their information with the other members.

A **Critical Thinking**

Hypothesizing

? What motivates people to hate weakness in others and to bully them? [Possible responses: They fear weakness in themselves and, by defeating a weaker person, hope to feel strong; they may have picked up this attitude from an older person or from the mass media.]

B **Elements of Literature**

Conflict

? What is the external conflict in this passage, and what is the internal conflict? [Possible response: The external conflict is between the narrator and the quiet girl; the internal conflict is between the narrator's desire to be tough and her fear that, like the quiet girl, she is weak.]

C **Elements of Literature**

Figures of Speech

? What unpleasant comparisons suggest how distasteful the narrator finds the quiet girl? [Possible responses: The narrator compares the girl's cheek to dough and then meat; she compares her skin to boned squid.]

D **Critical Thinking**

Extending the Text

? How should the teacher have acted in this situation? [Possible responses: She should have avoided sarcasm; she should have privately asked another teacher or a different Chinese American student to explain the boy's confusion.] How should the boy's classmates have acted? [Possible responses: They should have explained the boy's confusion to the teacher; they should not have laughed.]

A her nose and push it bonelessly in, indent her face. I could poke dimples into her cheeks. I could work her face around like dough. She stood still, and I did not want to look at her face anymore; I hated fragility. I walked around her, looked her up and down the way the Mexican and Negro girls did when they fought, so tough. I hated her weak neck, the way it did not support her **B** head but let it droop; her head would fall backward. I stared at the curve of her <u>nape</u>. I wished I was able to see what my own neck looked like from the back and sides. I hoped it did not look like hers; I wanted a stout neck. I grew my hair long to hide it in case it was a flower-stem neck. I walked around to the front of her to hate her face some more.

C I reached up and took the fatty part of her cheek, not dough, but meat, between my thumb and finger. This close, and I saw no pores. "Talk," I said. "Are you going to talk?" Her skin was fleshy, like squid out of which the glassy blades of bones had been pulled. I wanted tough skin, hard brown skin. I had callused my hands; I had scratched dirt to blacken the nails, which I cut straight across to make stubby fingers. I gave her face a squeeze. "Talk." When I let go, the pink rushed back into my white thumbprint on her skin. I walked around to her side. "Talk!" I shouted into the side of her head. Her straight hair hung, the same all these years, no ringlets or braids or permanents. I squeezed her other cheek. "Are you? Huh? Are you going to talk?" She tried to shake her head, but I had hold of her face. She had no muscles to jerk away. Her skin seemed to stretch. I let go in horror. What if it came away in my hand? "No, huh?" I said, rubbing the touch of her off my fingers. "Say 'No,' then," I said. I gave her another pinch and a twist. "Say 'No.'" She shook her head, her straight hair turning with her head, not swinging side to side like the pretty girls'. She was so neat. Her neatness bothered me. I hated the way she folded the wax paper from her lunch; she did not wad her brown paper bag and her school papers. I hated her clothes—the blue pastel cardigan, the white

blouse with the collar that lay flat over the cardigan, the homemade flat, cotton skirt she wore when everybody else was wearing flared skirts. I hated pastels; I would wear black always. I squeezed again, harder, even though her cheek had a weak rubbery feeling I did not like. I squeezed one cheek, then the other, back and forth until the tears ran out of her eyes as if I had pulled them out. "Stop crying," I said, but although she <u>habitually</u> followed me around, she did not obey. Her eyes dripped; her nose dripped. She wiped her eyes with her papery fingers. The skin on her hands and arms seemed powdery-dry, like tracing paper, onion paper. I hated her fingers. I could snap them like breadsticks. I pushed her hands down. "Say 'Hi,'" I said. "'Hi.' Like that. Say your name. Go ahead. Say it. Or are you stupid? You're so stupid, you don't know your own name, is that it? When I say, 'What's your name?' you just blurt it out, O.K.? What's **D** your name?" Last year the whole class had laughed at a boy who couldn't fill out a form because he didn't know his father's name. The teacher sighed, exasperated and was very <u>sarcastic</u>, "Don't you notice things? What does your mother call him?" she said. The class laughed at how dumb he was not to notice things. "She calls him father of me," he said. Even we laughed although we knew that his mother did not call his father by name, and a son does not know his father's name. We laughed and were relieved that our parents had had the foresight to tell us some names we could give the teachers. "If you're not stupid," I said to the quiet girl, "what's your name?" She shook her head, and some hair caught in the tears; wet black hair stuck to the side of the pink and white face. I reached up (she was taller than I) and took a strand of hair. I pulled it. "Well, then,

---

WORDS TO OWN

nape (nāp) *n.*: back of the neck.
habitually (hə·bich′o͞o·əl·lē) *adv.*: usually; by habit.
sarcastic (sär·kas′tik) *adj.*: scornful; mocking.

Making the Connections

Cultural Connections:
The Power of Names

Names and naming practices differ widely from culture to culture and therefore can prove to be sticking points for emigrants from one country to another. For example, in both Chinese and Japanese usages, the family name is given first, and then the personal name; this tends to confuse Americans, with the result that many immi-grants from those two countries switch the order of their names upon arrival. Asian immi-grants have also faced the dilemma of whether to give their children Asian first names or Eng-lish first names: The former preserves tradition, but the latter is seen as a cultural advantage in the United States. Many immigrants from coun-tries such as Russia, Poland, Italy, and Ireland had the spellings of their family names changed upon arrival at Ellis Island, often because immigration officials could not spell long names properly. Ask students to find out whether their family names have changed over time, how, and why. Invite students to report briefly to the class.

let's honk your hair," I said. "Honk. Honk." Then I pulled the other side—"ho-o-n-nk"— a long pull; "ho-o-n-n-nk"—a longer pull. I could see her little white ears, like white cutworms curled underneath the hair. "Talk!" I yelled into each cutworm.

I looked right at her. "I know you talk," I said. "I've heard you." Her eyebrows flew up. Something in those black eyes was startled, and I pursued it. "I was walking past your house when you didn't know I was there. I heard you yell in English and in Chinese. You weren't just talking. You were shouting. I heard you shout. You were saying, 'Where are you?' Say that again. Go ahead, just the way you did at home." I yanked harder on the hair, but steadily, not jerking. I did not want to pull it out. "Go ahead. Say, 'Where are you?' Say it loud enough for your sister to come. Call her. Make her come help you. Call her name. I'll stop if she comes. So call. Go ahead."

She shook her head, her mouth curved down, crying. I could see her tiny white teeth, baby teeth. I wanted to grow big strong yellow teeth. "You do have a tongue," I said. "So use it." I pulled the hair at her <u>temples</u>, pulled the tears out of her eyes. "Say, 'Ow'" I said. "Just 'Ow.' Say, 'Let go.' Go ahead. Say it. I'll honk you again if you don't say, 'Let me alone.' Say, 'Leave me alone,' and I'll let you go. I will. I'll let go if you say it. You can stop this anytime you want to, you know. All you have to do is tell me to stop. Just say, 'Stop.' You're just asking for it, aren't you? You're just asking for another honk. Well then, I'll have to give you another honk. Say, 'Stop.'" But she didn't. I had to pull again and again.

Sounds did come out of her mouth, sobs, chokes, noises that were almost words. Snot ran out of her nose. She tried to wipe it on her hands, but there was too much of it. She used her sleeve. "You're disgusting," I told her. "Look at you, snot streaming down your nose, and you won't say a word to stop it. You're such a nothing." I moved behind her and pulled the hair growing out of her weak neck. I let go. I stood silent for a long time.

Then I screamed, "Talk!" I would scare the words out of her. If she had had little bound feet, the toes twisted under the balls, I would have jumped up and landed on them—crunch!—stomped on them with my iron shoes. She cried hard, sobbing aloud. "Cry, 'Mama,'" I said. "Come on. Cry, 'Mama.' Say, 'Stop it.'"

I put my finger on her pointed chin. "I don't like you. I don't like the weak little toots you make on your flute. Wheeze. Wheeze. I don't like the way you don't swing at the ball. I don't like the way you're the last one chosen. I don't like the way you can't make a fist for tetherball. Why don't you make a fist? Come on. Get tough. Come on. Throw fists." I pushed at her long hands; they swung limply at her sides. Her fingers were so long, I thought maybe they had an extra joint. They couldn't possibly make fists like other people's. "Make a fist," I said. "Come on. Just fold those fingers up; fingers on the inside, thumbs on the outside. Say something. Honk me back. You're so tall, and you let me pick on you.

"Would you like a hanky? I can't get you one with embroidery on it or crocheting along the edges, but I'll get you some toilet paper if you tell me to. Go ahead. Ask me. I'll get it for you if you ask." She did not stop crying. "Why don't you scream, 'Help'?" I suggested. "Say, 'Help.' Go ahead." She cried on. "O.K. O.K. Don't talk. Just scream, and I'll let you go. Won't that feel good? Go ahead. Like this." I screamed not too loudly. My voice hit the tile and rang it as if I had thrown a rock at it. The stalls opened wider and the toilets wider and darker. Shadows leaned at angles I had not seen before. It was very late. Maybe a janitor had locked me in with this **girl** for the night. Her black eyes blinked and stared, blinked and stared. I felt dizzy from hunger. We had been in this lavatory together forever. My mother would call

----

WORDS TO OWN
temples (tem′pəlz) *n. pl.*: sides of the forehead, just above and in front of the ears.

E

F

G

H

E ### Reading Skills and Strategies

Drawing Inferences About Characters

? What do you infer about the quiet girl based on what the narrator heard when walking past the girl's house? [Possible responses: She is able to talk and assert herself in situations where she feels comfortable; she is very frightened at school.]

F ### Reading Skills and Strategies

Drawing Inferences About Characters

? What do you think makes the quiet girl so unresponsive? [Possible responses: She is afraid of the narrator; she has made a firm decision never to talk in the school building except for reading aloud; for her, unresponsiveness is a form of strength.]

G ### Cultural Connections
Bound Feet

The narrator is referring to the ancient Chinese custom of binding the feet of girls and women, supposedly to achieve a more "feminine" walking gait, a practice that permanently crippled generations of upper class Chinese women. This custom was the object of protests and is no longer practiced.

H ### Critical Thinking
Interpreting

? Even though the narrator is scared to be in the building this late and is weak with hunger, she continues to torment the silent girl. Why does this struggle mean so much to her? [Possible response: Forcing the girl to talk has become an attempt to prove to herself that she herself can survive in America without withdrawing into a shell—it feels like a matter of life or death to her.]

Getting Students Involved

Writing Activity
Assessing Characters. Have students work in pairs to write one-sentence character assessments of the narrator and the quiet girl. Students may refer to the information on Character in the Handbook of Literary Terms. After five minutes, ask partners to read their sentences aloud. Have a volunteer record the sentences at the board in two columns, one for the narrator and one for the quiet girl. After all partners have read their sentences, review the list of sentences for the narrator and for the quiet girl, and invite the class to discuss any additions or changes they would like to make or any questions they would like to ask for clarification. The result should be two thorough character descriptions, one for the narrator and one for the quiet girl.

Have student groups research and report in detail on a particular Chinese custom or facet of Chinese culture. The report could focus on one custom mentioned here, such as reverence toward ancestors or the Chinese New Year, or it could focus on a subject of the group's own choosing, such as Confucianism, calligraphy, Chinese characters, Taoism, or the Cultural Revolution. Be sure each group chooses a different subject. Have the groups hold "Chinese school," where they teach the class about Chinese life and customs.

Ⓐ Critical Thinking
Hypothesizing

❓ What effect do you think the narrator's long verbal assault is having on the quiet girl? [Possible responses: It is terrifying her; it is making her problem worse by reinforcing a view of herself as weak; it has shocked her into numbness.] What effect do you think it is having on the narrator? [Possible responses: It is making her feel powerful at the moment but will make her feel ashamed and sorrowful later; it is bringing out her own inner conflicts about such subjects as popularity, personal strength, and being Chinese American.]

Ⓑ Reading Skills and Strategies
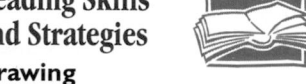

Drawing Inferences About Characters

❓ The narrator makes a distinction between how the girl might act in front of a group and how she might act in front of one person. What in her own life might have led the narrator to understand this distinction? [Possible responses: She herself might feel more comfortable speaking to one person than to many; she might know other people who feel similarly.]

The Chinese American Family

In her story, Maxine Hong Kingston mentions that the girl who wouldn't talk was supported and protected by her family. This isn't surprising, given the importance of family relationships in Chinese culture. As the Chinese American writer Leslie Li notes, solitude is not a coveted state among most Chinese people. "They love their family and friends and want them around, along with the *renao* they bring, the heat and noise of human relationships."

Family ties. In Chinese culture, "name" does not so much signify individual identity as relationship to others, such as daughter, son, aunt, uncle, and so on. In Chinese tradition, the family name is given first—for example, "Chung Connie," not the Americanized "Connie Chung"—and family members are often introduced not by their names but by their family relationships. Children may address family members not by name but as Aunt, Second Older Brother, Grandfather, and so on. In Kingston's story, a boy is

laughed at in class because he doesn't know his father's name; at home, he says, his father is called only "father of me." In the story "Rules of the Game" by the Chinese American writer Amy Tan (page 1110), the character Waverly is called "Waverly" for the benefit of outsiders, but at home she is "Meimei" (Little Sister).

Bridging two worlds. Ultimately, many Chinese Americans choose to integrate the cultures of both China and the United States in their family life. They embrace some traditional beliefs of their immigrant parents or grandparents, but they also take part in mainstream American traditions. They may celebrate both Chinese and American holidays, for example, or enjoy traditional Chinese foods one day, grilled steak the next. They may use American names with outsiders but their Chinese middle names at home. In addition to attending regular public or private school all day, some Chinese American children spend three or four hours at Chinese school (often held on Saturdays), where their

the police again if I didn't bring my sister home soon. "I'll let you go if you say just one word," I said. "You can even say 'a' or 'the,' and I'll let you go. Come on. Please." She didn't shake her head anymore, only cried steadily, so much water coming out of her. I could see the two duct holes where the tears welled out. Quarts of tears but no words. I grabbed her by the shoulder. I could feel bones. The light was coming in queerly through the frosted glass with the chicken wire embedded in it. Her crying was like an animal's—a seal's—and it echoed around the basement. "Do you want to stay here all night?" I asked. "Your mother is wondering what happened to her baby. You

wouldn't want to have her mad at you. You'd better say something." I shook her shoulder. I pulled her hair again. I squeezed her face. "Come on! Talk! Talk! Talk!" She didn't seem to feel it anymore when I pulled her hair. "There's nobody here but you and me. This isn't a classroom or a playground or a crowd. I'm just one person. You can talk in front of one person. Don't make me pull harder and harder until you talk." But her hair seemed to stretch; she did not say a word. "I'm going to pull harder. Don't make me pull anymore, or your hair will come out and you're going to be bald. Do you want to be bald? You don't want to be bald, do you?"

Far away, coming from the edge of town, I

1050 CONTEMPORARY LITERATURE

Crossing the Curriculum

History
Suggest that some students research and report on the role of Chinese workers in building the western branches of the American railroad system in the 1860s. Other students may research and report on the establishment and growth of Chinese communities in the United States in the early twentieth century.

Journalism
Have pairs of students research and write newspaper articles that might have appeared in a U.S. newspaper during the Korean War. Possible topics include reports from the war, other national and international news, sports, and features on the rise of the suburbs and the beginnings of 1950s "youth culture." Post the articles, with illustrations if possible, on bulletin boards in the classroom.

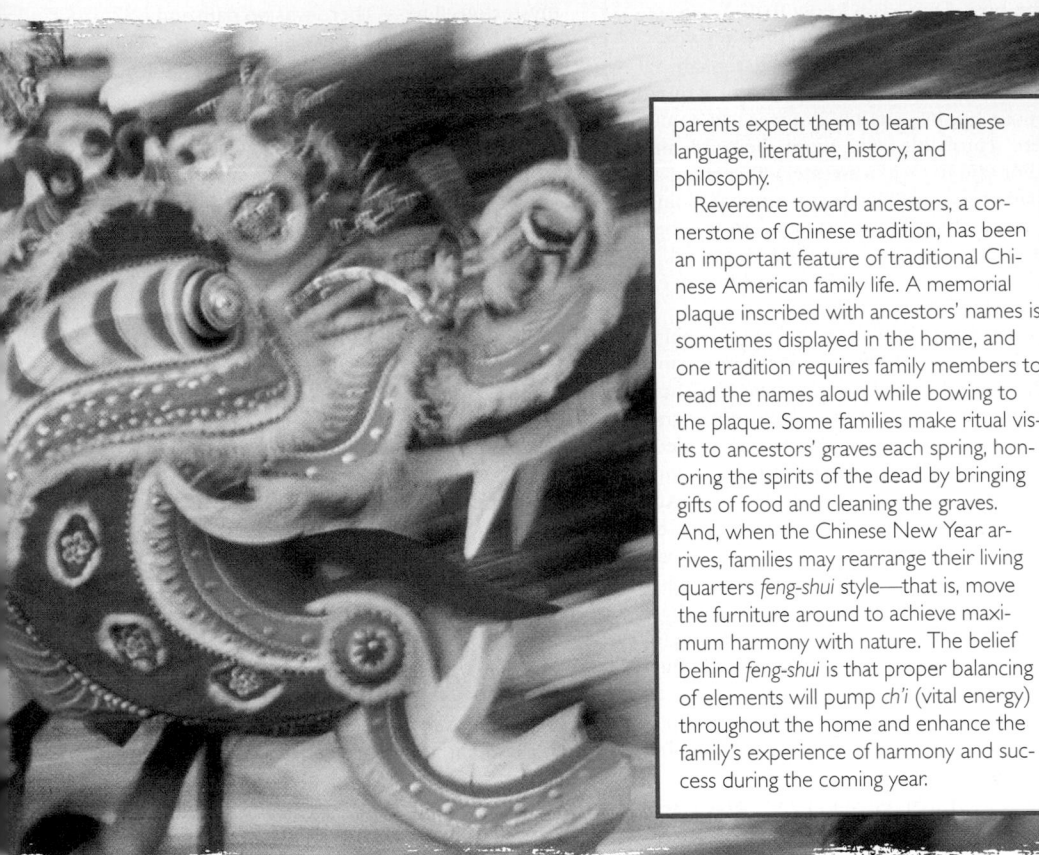

parents expect them to learn Chinese language, literature, history, and philosophy.

Reverence toward ancestors, a cornerstone of Chinese tradition, has been an important feature of traditional Chinese American family life. A memorial plaque inscribed with ancestors' names is sometimes displayed in the home, and one tradition requires family members to read the names aloud while bowing to the plaque. Some families make ritual visits to ancestors' graves each spring, honoring the spirits of the dead by bringing gifts of food and cleaning the graves. And, when the Chinese New Year arrives, families may rearrange their living quarters *feng-shui* style—that is, move the furniture around to achieve maximum harmony with nature. The belief behind *feng-shui* is that proper balancing of elements will pump *ch'i* (vital energy) throughout the home and enhance the family's experience of harmony and success during the coming year.

heard whistles blow. The cannery was changing shifts, letting out the afternoon people, and still we were here at school. It was a sad sound—work done. The air was lonelier after the sound died.

"Why won't you talk?" I started to cry. What if I couldn't stop, and everyone would want to know what happened? "Now look what you've done," I scolded. "You're going to pay for this. I want to know why. And you're going to tell me why. You don't see I'm trying to help you out, do you? Do you want to be like this, dumb (do you know what dumb means?), your whole life? Don't you ever want to be a cheerleader? Or a pompom girl? What are you going to do for a **C**

living? Yeah, you're going to have to work because you can't be a housewife. Somebody has to marry you before you can be a housewife. And you, you are a plant. Do you know that? That's all you are if you don't talk. If you don't talk, you can't have a personality. You'll have no personality and no hair. You've got to let people know you have a personality and a brain. You think somebody is going to take care of you all your stupid life? You think you'll always have your big sister? You think somebody's going to marry you, is that it? Well, you're not the type that gets dates, let alone gets married. Nobody's going to notice you. And you have to talk for interviews, speak right up in front

MAXINE HONG KINGSTON 1051

Professional Notes

Critical Comment: Finding a Voice
Scholar Amy Ling writes: "A major theme in Kingston's *Woman Warrior* is the importance of articulateness. Finding one's voice and telling one's stories represents power, just as having one's stories buried is powerlessness." Have students discuss how this quotation relates to "The Girl Who Wouldn't Talk."

Making the Connections

Connecting to the Theme: "Discoveries and Awakenings"
The narrator not only learns about the character of the quiet girl but also awakens to her own character. Later in life, recalling these events, she may have awakened even more to her inner conflicts and to the power of culture over society in general and over individuals, including herself. Have students list what the

narrator discovers. Ask them to meet in groups and to discuss their lists. Then, have them compare the discoveries and awakenings in this memoir with those in the other selections in this collection. Ask group members what they have discovered in the process.

of the boss. Don't you know that? You're so dumb. Why do I waste my time on you?" Sniffling and snorting, I couldn't stop crying and talking at the same time. I kept wiping my nose on my arm, my sweater lost somewhere (probably not worn because my mother said to wear a sweater). It seemed as if I had spent my life in that basement, doing the worst thing I had yet done to another person. "I'm doing this for your own good," I said. "Don't you dare tell anyone I've been bad to you. Talk. Please talk."

I was getting dizzy from the air I was gulping. Her sobs and my sobs were bouncing wildly off the tile, sometimes together, sometimes alternating. "I don't understand why you won't say just one word," I cried, clenching my teeth. My knees were shaking, and I hung on to her hair to stand up. Another time I'd stayed too late, I had had to walk around two Negro kids who were bonking each other's head on the concrete. I went back later to see if the concrete had cracks in it. "Look. I'll give you something if you talk. I'll give you my pencil box. I'll buy you some candy. O.K.? What do you want? Tell me. Just say it, and I'll give it to you. Just say, 'yes,' or, 'O.K.,' or, 'Baby Ruth.'" But she didn't want anything.

I had stopped pinching her cheek because I did not like the feel of her skin. I would go crazy if it came away in my hands. "I skinned her," I would have to confess.

Suddenly I heard footsteps hurrying through the basement, and her sister ran into the lavatory calling her name. "Oh, there you are," I said. "We've been waiting for you. I was only trying to teach her to talk. She wouldn't cooperate, though." Her sister went into one of the stalls and got handfuls of toilet paper and wiped her off. Then we found my sister, and we walked home together. "Your family really ought to force her to speak," I advised all the way home. "You mustn't pamper her."

The world is sometimes just, and I spent the next eighteen months sick in bed with a mysterious illness. There was no pain and no symptoms, though the middle line in my left palm broke in two. Instead of starting junior high school, I lived like the Victorian recluses[1] I read about. I had a rented hospital bed in the living room, where I watched soap operas on TV, and my family cranked me up and down. I saw no one but my family, who took good care of me. I could have no visitors, no other relatives, no villagers. My bed was against the west window, and I watched the seasons change the peach tree. I had a bell to ring for help. I used a bedpan. It was the best year and a half of my life. Nothing happened.

But one day my mother, the doctor, said, "You're ready to get up today. It's time to get up and go to school." I walked about outside to get my legs working, leaning on a staff I cut from the peach tree. The sky and trees, the sun were immense—no longer framed by a window, no longer grayed with a fly screen. I sat down on the sidewalk in amazement—the night, the stars. But at school I had to figure out again how to talk. I met again the poor girl I had tormented. She had not changed. She wore the same clothes, hair cut, and manner as when we were in elementary school, no make-up on the pink and white face, while the other Asian girls were starting to tape their eyelids. She continued to be able to read aloud. But there was hardly any reading aloud anymore, less and less as we got into high school.

I was wrong about nobody taking care of her. Her sister became a clerk-typist and stayed unmarried. They lived with their mother and father. She did not have to leave the house except to go to the movies. She was supported. She was protected by her family, as they would normally have done in China if they could have afforded it, not sent off to school with strangers, ghosts, boys.

---

1. **Victorian recluses:** like characters in Victorian novels who, because of some illness or incapacity, lived shut away from the world.

Assessing Learning

Check Test: True-False

1. The girl who wouldn't talk does use her voice when she reads aloud. [True]
2. The quiet girl and the narrator are different in every way. [False]
3. One day the narrator catches the quiet girl in the school lavatory. [True]
4. The narrator torments the girl by pinching her and trying to make her talk. [True]
5. Soon after the incident with the narrator, the quiet girl becomes ill with a mysterious paralysis. [False]

First Thoughts

1. What is your reaction to the silent girl? How do you feel about the narrator?

Shaping Interpretations

2. The narrator's deep undercurrent of anger seems directed solely at the silent girl. What else do you think the narrator could be angry about? Is she affected by an **internal conflict**? Explain.

3. The silent girl is obviously able to speak. Review the notes you made while reading. Why do you think the girl does *not* speak? What **external** or **internal conflicts** might cause her to remain silent?

4. What inference do you draw from the fact that the narrator says that her time in bed "was the best year and a half of my life"? What discoveries about herself or about the silent girl might she have made during this time?

5. This episode comes from a chapter called "A Song for a Barbarian Reed Pipe." What could be the significance of that **title**? How is this story of the silent girl related to that title?

6. At times, Kingston's **images** can evoke powerful responses from us and can reveal the narrator's strong feelings as well. Find the images describing the silent girl's skin, her fingers, the skin of her hands and arms, her ears, and her crying. What feelings about the girl do these images reveal? How do they make you respond to the girl and to her tormentor, the narrator?

Reading Check

a. What reasons does the narrator give for hating the silent girl?

b. What do the other students think of the silent girl?

c. How does the narrator try to make the silent girl talk? (Note the physical and the psychological torments she applies.) What is the girl's response?

d. What happens to the narrator to make her say that "the world is sometimes just"?

Connecting with the Text

7. Why do you think the narrator cares so intensely about making the silent girl talk? Do her feelings strike you as believable—have you experienced or observed feelings like these?

CHOICES:
Building Your Portfolio

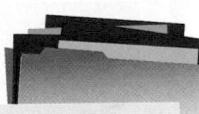

Writer's Notebook

1. Collecting Ideas for an Evaluation

A well-written evaluation maintains a consistent and confident **tone**. Whether stating your judgment or offering evidence, express your thoughts clearly and with confidence. As practice, write several sentences evaluating the use of **imagery** in Kingston's work. Make sure your tone is crystal clear and consistent. Save your sentences for possible use in the Writer's Workshop on page 1181.

Interpreting Character

2. Tortured Tormentor

In a short essay, discuss the **character** of the narrator. As a first step, review your reading notes. Then, write about these basic elements of characterization: (a) appearance, (b) speech, (c) actions, (d) private thoughts and feelings, and (e) responses of other people to the character. Conclude by discussing your own response to the narrator.

Creative Writing

3. Time Out

The narrator says that "nothing happened" during her time sick in bed. Yet something must have happened, because one day her mother said that she was "ready" to return to school. In a brief story, reveal what you think happened to prepare the narrator to rejoin the world.

Reading Check

a. She regards her as weak, fragile, delicate, and too "Chinese."

b. They say that they try to be friendly but get no response.

c. She pushes, pinches, and shakes her, pulls her hair, taunts her, shouts at her, calls her stupid and disgusting, tells her she will never get a husband, and offers to give her things. The silent girl is alarmed and puzzled but endures the torments silently.

d. She falls ill and spends a year and a half at home in bed.

First Thoughts [Respond]

1. Possible response: I feel frustrated by the silent girl; however, the narrator is cruel.

Shaping Interpretations [Interpret]

2. She seems angry at her own family, at American society, at herself, and at the conflict between assimilation and tradition. Her internal conflict consists of wrestling with herself about whether or not she will be accepted by American society.

3. Possible responses: The girl is probably terrified but also may view her silence as a vow of cultural integrity requiring resolve. External conflict is posed by her peer group and the American world around her, which pressure her to speak; the girl's internal conflicts might concern her shyness, her obligations to her family and culture, and her desire not to be persecuted.

4. Possible responses: At home, she is spared the stress of growing up between two cultures; she is cared for and protected. She recognizes her own cruelty and perhaps her similarities to the quiet girl.

5. The narrator says she hates the wheezing of the quiet girl's flute in school.

6. The silent girl's cheeks are pink and white, her fingers "papery," her eyes and nose dripping, her ears like cutworms; her hands and arms limp. Her crying is "like an animal's." The images make her seem weak and pathetic. They might evoke revulsion, compassion, or both for the girl and anger, understanding or both for the narrator.

Connecting with the Text
[Synthesize]

7. Sample response: The girl represents an image of Chinese submissiveness and passivity, which the narrator has rejected. I have not experienced such hatred, but the feeling is believable.

OBJECTIVES

1. Read and interpret the excerpt
2. Identify examples of dialect
3. Express understanding through writing
4. Demonstrate an understanding of new words

SKILLS

Literary
- Identify dialect

Writing
- Collect ideas for an evaluation
- Write personal essays

Viewing/Representing
- Compose a dialogue to accompany a painting (ATE)
- Comment on a painting from the viewpoint of one or more authors (ATE)
- Find photographs to illustrate a selection (ATE)

Planning

- **Block Schedule**
  Block Scheduling Lesson Plan with Pacing Guide
- **Traditional Schedule**
  Lesson Plans Including Strategies for English-Language Learners
- **One-Stop Planner**
  CD-ROM with Test Generator

BROWSING IN THE FILES

About the Author. One of Heat-Moon's ancestors, an Englishman, emigrated to North Carolina and was killed by Tories for giving food to rebel colonists during the American Revolution. The first leg of Heat-Moon's journey, from Missouri to North Carolina, retraced in reverse the journey other forebears of his had made.

© Robert M. Lindholm.

William Least Heat-Moon

(1939–   )

Some of the finest insights into American ways of life have appeared in the nonfiction accounts of travelers. As early as 1835, Alexis de Tocqueville, a visiting Frenchman, wrote *Democracy in America,* still treasured as a profound commentary on the American character.

Traveling Americans turned their journals into such classics as Henry David Thoreau's *The Maine Woods* (1864), Mark Twain's *Roughing It* (1872) and *Life on the Mississippi* (1883), and Henry James's *The American Scene* (1907). Modern writers have explored America—Jack Kerouac, in *On the Road* (1957); John Steinbeck, in *Travels with Charley* (1962); and Robert Pirsig, in *Zen and the Art of Motorcycle Maintenance* (1974). William Least Heat-Moon's *Blue Highways: A Journey into America* (1982) thus takes its place in a vital American literary tradition. In fact, the writer says that Steinbeck's *Charley* inspired him to embark on the journey described in *Blue Highways*.

William Least Heat-Moon is the pen name of William Trogdon, who is descended mainly from the Osage people in Missouri. His given name, he explains, comes from an immigrant English ancestor eight generations back, and the name Heat-Moon comes from his Osage father (William added the hyphen). "My father calls himself Heat Moon"—the name for the seventh month in the Osage calendar—"[and] my elder brother Little Heat Moon. I, coming last, am therefore Least. It has been a long lesson of a name to learn."

When Heat-Moon was thirty-eight, his first marriage was ending, and he was laid off from a teaching job. So he left Missouri in a converted van that became both transport and home. He called his van *Ghost Dancing,* after the name the Plains Indians gave to ceremonies of the 1890s

go.hrw.com
LE0 11-19

Resources: Print and Media

Reading
- *Graphic Organizers for Active Reading,* p. 106
- *Words to Own,* p. 55
- *Audio CD Library*
  Disc 27, Track 3

Writing and Language
- *Daily Oral Grammar*
  Transparency 61

Assessment
- *Formal Assessment,* p. 208
- *Portfolio Management System,* p. 219
- *Preparation for College Admission Exams,* p. 65
- *Test Generator (One-Stop Planner CD-ROM)*

Internet
- go.hrw.com (keyword: LE0 11-19)

in which they prayed for the return of their old life. And in a sense, Heat-Moon's trip was such a ceremony. "I took to the open road in search of places where change did not mean ruin and where time and men and deeds connected." At the start of the trip, he decided to use his Osage last name rather than Trogdon.

Blue Highways, the edited journal of his travels, shows that Heat-Moon found what he sought. He stayed on the back roads, the ones printed in blue on old highway maps, not the main routes printed in red. His quest took him east from Missouri to North Carolina, south to Louisiana, then west across Texas to New Mexico, north through Utah and California to Washington State, back across the northernmost boundary of the United States all the way to Maine, south again to New Jersey, and finally west back to Missouri. The roughly circular trip, he thought, "would give a purpose—to come around again."

Some contemporary travelers have found a sad, petty-minded, and materialistic America. But Heat-Moon usually liked the people he met in such places as Lookingglass and Simplicity, New Hope and New Freedom, Cutthroat Gulch and Calamity River, Why and Whynot. He found the inhabitants as vigorous, imaginative, and astonishing as the names of their towns. His journal celebrates these people— their struggles, their poverty, their spiritual wealth, and their dignity. They treated him well, and he admired them.

In 1991, Heat-Moon continued that celebration with *PrairyErth (a deep map).* Instead of offering a wide-ranging view of America, *PrairyErth* delves into the landscape and the people of one Kansas county.

Heat-Moon returned to a broader view of the United States in 1995, when he undertook an approximately 5,200-mile coast-to-coast journey of North America's inland waterways, almost all on a 22-foot cruiser named *Nikawa.* The four-month voyage began in New York and ended in Oregon. Perhaps we can look forward to a Heat-Moon celebration of America's "blue waterways" and the people who live along them.

Before You Read
FROM **BLUE HIGHWAYS**

Make the Connection
Discovering Harmony
"Where are you going?" We hear that question often, and the answer is usually something like "the gym" or "shopping" or "Omaha." Heat-Moon goes out to discover *harmony.* In music, harmony is the sounding of separate tones in a satisfying combination. In human experience, its definition is much more elusive. We search for harmony in our individual lives, families, communities, and nations. Perhaps the real discovery is that harmony has to be created, not found.

Quickwrite
Think about the community where you live. What's unusual or quirky about it? List some of the unconventional people, places, or things that make your community special.

Elements of Literature
Dialect
As he travels across America, Heat-Moon *listens* to the people he meets. By accurately transferring their dialects to the printed page, he lets us hear them too. **Dialect** is a way of speaking that is characteristic of a certain social group or of the inhabitants of a certain geographical area. It is an authentic link between people and the places they have made their own.

> **D**ialect is a way of speaking that is characteristic of a certain social group or of the inhabitants of a certain geographical area.
>
> *For more on Dialect, see page 512 and the Handbook of Literary Terms.*

WILLIAM LEAST HEAT-MOON 1055

Summary ■

The excerpt opens in the middle of Heat-Moon's back-road journey and chronicles his search for the town of Nameless, Tennessee. After he picks Nameless out of his atlas, he goes in search of directions to the town. He wittily describes his strategy for finding cheap, delicious food in small-town cafes: The more calendars there are on the wall, the better the home-style cooking promises to be. When he finally reaches Nameless, he talks with Thurmond and Virginia Watts, owners of an old-fashioned general store that is now closing after thirty-five years. They tell him how Nameless got its name and reminisce about life in the town. Heat-Moon meets their daughter, Hilda, and is treated to buttermilk pie while Thurmond plays music on an old Edison phonograph. It is for this revelatory moment of old-fashioned life that the narrator knows he has come. His hosts feed him lunch and bring out Mrs. Watts's *Deathbook,* a record of local obituaries that she has kept for twenty years. As Heat-Moon leaves, the Watts family wishes him well and invites him back.

Preteaching Vocabulary

Words to Own
First, have students find the words and definitions at the bottom of the excerpt pages or in the Glossary. To deepen students' acquaintance with these words, have students look up the words in a dictionary and compare the dictionary definitions with the Glossary definitions. If your students have access to several different dictionaries, ask volunteers to read definitions from each one aloud. This exercise will enhance students' appreciation of varied reference sources, as well as the specific meanings of the Words to Own. Finally, you might challenge students to become dictionary writers and compose their own definitions for the Words to Own.

Ralph Goings (1928–   ) is an American Photo-realist painter. Photo-realism is a style of painting, most popular in the 1970s, that attempts to imitate the flat, intensely detailed look of still photographs. It is concerned with the visual perception of things rather than with their underlying meanings, though the viewer may wish to create his or her own meanings from the viewing experience. Photo-realists emphasize the play of light in windows, mirrors, automobile surfaces, coffee cups, metal strips, and other reflective or refractive objects. The artists' interest in optical effects links them to the Op art artists of the 1960s, while their interest in contemporary American culture links them to Pop art artists. Photo-realists also represent a reaction against the abandonment of subject matter by earlier abstract painters. Goings, like Heat-Moon in *Blue Highways*, pays close attention to every object that appears in the setting. His meticulous, accurate depictions of everyday things and ordinary people invite the viewer to discover and delight in the pleasures of ordinary reality.

Activity. Ask groups of two or three students to create a brief dialogue for the two people in the painting. In addition, invite students to think about and discuss what a writer might find interesting in Pee Wee's Diner and its two inhabitants.

Courtesy OK Harris Gallery, New York.

Pee Wee's Diner, Warnerville, N.Y. (1977) by Ralph Goings. Oil on canvas (48″ × 48″).

1056 CONTEMPORARY LITERATURE

Reaching All Students

Struggling Readers
Heat-Moon uses a rating system to evaluate cafes as he travels. Have students use a rating system for the excerpt, using symbols of books instead of calendars. Five books is the highest rating, and one book the lowest. Have students read p. 1057 and the end of the paragraph at the top of p. 1058. Then, have them rate the passage, and state their reasons for the rating, referring to specific aspects of the text. Repeat this process at regular intervals.

English Language Learners
Provide standard English paraphrases for unfamiliar expressions both in the dialogue (for example, "*You from the North?*") and in the narration (for example, *cracker, cowhand*). For strategies to engage students with the literature, see
• *Lesson Plans Including Strategies for English-Language Learners*

Advanced Learners
Although Heat-Moon does not provide much direct detail about himself, he does offer tantalizing glimpses in occasional comments, such as the one about losing the right road in 1965 (p. 1059). Encourage students to make inferences and hypotheses about the author as they read. They may wish to read more of *Blue Highways* in order to deepen their understanding.

from Blue Highways

William Least Heat-Moon

Had it not been raining hard that morning on the Livingston square, I never would have learned of Nameless, Tennessee. Waiting for the rain to ease, I lay on my bunk and read the atlas to pass time rather than to see where I might go. In Kentucky were towns with fine names like Boreing, Bear Wallow, Decoy, Subtle, Mud Lick, Mummie, Neon; Belcher was just down the road from Mouthcard, and Minnie only ten miles from Mousie.

I looked at Tennessee. Turtletown eight miles from Ducktown. And also: Peavine, Wheel, Milky Way, Love Joy, Dull, Weakly, Fly, Spot, Miser Station, Only, McBurg, Peeled Chestnut, Clouds, Topsy, Isoline. And the best of all, Nameless. The logic! I was heading east, and Nameless lay forty-five miles west. I decided to go anyway.

The rain stopped, but things looked saturated, even bricks. In Gainesboro, a hill town with a square of businesses around the Jackson County Courthouse, I stopped for directions and breakfast. There is one almost infallible way to find honest food at just prices in blue-highway America: Count the wall calendars in a cafe.

No calendar: Same as an interstate pit stop.
One calendar: Preprocessed food assembled in
    New Jersey.
Two calendars: Only if fish trophies present.
Three calendars: Can't miss on the farm-boy
    breakfasts.
Four calendars: Try the ho-made pie too.
Five calendars: Keep it under your hat, or
    they'll franchise.

One time I found a six-calendar cafe in the Ozarks, which served fried chicken, peach pie, and chocolate malts, that left me searching for another ever since. I've never seen a seven-calendar place. But old-time travelers—road men in a day when cars had running

---

WORDS TO OWN

saturated (sach′ə·rāt′id) *adj.*: completely soaked.
infallible (in·fal′ə·bəl) *adj.*: sure; never wrong.

WILLIAM LEAST HEAT-MOON 1057

A Critical Thinking
Drawing Inferences
? The title *Blue Highways* comes from the fact that Heat-Moon was driving on small roads colored blue on the map, but what else might it imply? [Possible responses: Blue is associated with sadness and may refer both to the author's mood and to his impression of small-town America.]

B Background
There is also a Nameless, Texas. It is in the hill country of south-central Texas, about 19 miles (30 kilometers) northwest of Austin.

C Critical Thinking
Hypothesizing
? Why would people give their towns names like these? [Possible responses: Names such as Boreing, Dull, and Only show a self-deprecating sense of humor on the part of the people who built those small towns. Among the other names, Miser Station may poke fun at a specific early settler; Bear Wallow seems to immortalize a part of local natural history; Neon may refer to an early neon sign in the town.]

D English Language Learners
Cultural Concepts/Idioms
To help students understand the humor of this passage, provide explanations of the following terms: *pit stop* (an ordinary roadside restaurant, usually serving truckers); *assembled in New Jersey* (in this case implying something remote, mass-produced, and characterless); *fish trophies* (a caught fish preserved and displayed to indicate the catcher's skill) *ho-made* (dialectal spelling of *home-made*); *franchise* (to open up a chain of establishments based on an original model).

Using Students' Strengths

Logical/Mathematical Learners
Ask students to list factors to consider when deciding which route to take to a given destination. Sample criteria might include travel time, road conditions, weather conditions, and the purpose of the trip (for example, to attend a business meeting, to sightsee, or to visit relatives along the way). Then, invite students to describe Heat-Moon's purpose and to suggest travel choices they would make to achieve it.

Auditory Learners
Invite students to share oral recollections of interesting or unusual places they have visited and of cultural variations they have encountered. You might begin by providing a recollection from your own experience. Remind students to choose an experience they would not mind sharing with others.

Naturalist Learners
Although Heat-Moon's emphasis is on the social landscape, encourage students to spot evidence in the text about the natural surroundings on his travels. There are mentions of huckleberries, tree stumps, and oaks, for example. Encourage students to deepen their mental picture of the natural world in this selection by consulting field guides to Tennessee and Kentucky.

Describe, in your own words, the kinds of people Heat-Moon describes as eating in restaurants on interstate highways. [Possible response: people who stop to fill their gas tank; people who need to go to the bathroom; people whose children are restless; truckers with CB radios.]

B **Appreciating Language**

Jargon

? The special vocabulary of short-order cooks is widely enjoyed in the United States. What are *two eggs up*? [two eggs sunny side up: two fried eggs with the yolks facing up and unbroken]

C **Cultural Connections**

Historically, the state of Missouri has been considered the midpoint of the United States, the state where the North, South, East, and West meet. St. Louis, in the nineteenth century, was considered the gateway to the West.

D **Elements of Literature**

Dialect

? A common characteristic of everyday American speech is the omission of one or more words at the beginning of a statement or question. What words would precede "Time I" in standard English? ["By the . . ."] Encourage students to cite other examples of omitted sentence beginnings in this selection and in their own speech.

---

boards and lunchroom windows said AIR COOLED in blue letters with icicles dripping from the tops—those travelers have told me the golden legends of seven-calendar cafes.

To the rider of back roads, nothing shows the tone, the voice of a small town more quickly than the breakfast grill or the five-thirty tavern. Much of what the people do and believe and share is evident then. The City Cafe in Gainesboro had three calendars that I could see from the walk. Inside were no interstate refugees with full bladders and empty tanks, no wild-eyed children just released from the glassy cell of a station-wagon backseat, no long-haul truckers talking in CB numbers.[1] There were only townspeople wearing overalls, or catalog-order suits with five-and-dime ties, or uniforms. That is, here were farmers and mill hands, bank clerks, the dry goods merchant, a policeman, and chiropractor's receptionist. Because it was Saturday, there were also mothers and children.

I ordered my standard on-the-road breakfast: two eggs up, hash browns, tomato juice. The waitress, whose pale, almost translucent skin shifted hue in the gray light like a thin slice of mother of pearl, brought the food. Next to the eggs was a biscuit with a little yellow Smiley button stuck in it. She said, "You from the North?"

"I guess I am." A Missourian gets used to Southerners thinking him a Yankee, a Northerner considering him a cracker, a Westerner sneering at his effete Easternness, and the Easterner taking him for a cowhand.

"So whata you doin' in the mountains?"

"Talking to people. Taking some pictures. Looking mostly."

"Lookin' for what?"

"A three-calendar cafe that serves Smiley buttons on the biscuits."

"You needed a smile. Tell me really."

"I don't know. Actually, I'm looking for some jam to put on this biscuit now that you've brought one."

1. **CB numbers:** Users of CB (citizens' band) shortwave radios substitute numbers for simple messages (such as "10–4" for "message received").

She came back with grape jelly. In a land of quince jelly, apple butter, apricot jam, blueberry preserves, pear conserves, and lemon marmalade, you always get grape jelly.

"Whata you lookin' for?"

Like anyone else, I'm embarrassed to eat in front of a watcher, particularly if I'm getting interviewed. "Why don't you have a cup of coffee?"

"Cain't right now. You gonna tell me?"

"I don't know how to describe it to you. Call it harmony."

She waited for something more. "Is that it?" Someone called her to the kitchen. I had managed almost to finish by the time she came back. She sat on the edge of the booth. "I started out in life not likin' anything, but then it grew on me. Maybe that'll happen to you." She watched me spread the jelly. "Saw your van." She watched me eat the biscuit. "You sleep in there?" I told her I did. "I'd love to do that, but I'd be scared spitless."

"I don't mind being scared spitless. Sometimes."

"I'd love to take off cross country. I like to look at different license plates. But I'd take a dog. You carry a dog?"

"No dogs, no cats, no budgie birds. It's a one-man campaign to show Americans a person can travel alone without a pet."

"Cain't travel without a dog!"

"I like to do things the hard way."

"Shoot! I'd take me a dog to talk to. And for protection."

"It isn't traveling to cross the country and talk to your pug instead of people along the way. Besides, being alone on the road makes you ready to meet someone when you stop. You get sociable traveling alone."

She looked out toward the van again. "Time I get the nerve to take a trip, gas'll cost five dollars a gallon."

"Could be. My rig might go the way of the

WORDS TO OWN

translucent (trans·lōō′sənt) *adj.*: allowing light to pass through.

Professional Notes

Cultural Criticism

The search for the authentic national culture has been a frequent theme in American writing, including the excerpts from Heat-Moon in this selection and James Agee in the Connection, the "road" novels of Jack Kerouac, the experimental novels of John Dos Passos, and John Steinbeck's *Travels with Charley.* Heat-Moon thinks that he finds the authentic America on back roads, far from the interstate highways and the fast-food restaurants. A case could be

made, however, that this is nostalgic thinking and that the real America today is found precisely in the places that Heat-Moon disdains. Have students discuss whether they incline more to Heat-Moon's quest for back-road America or to the view that America today is in the chain stores and on the superhighways. Prompt discussion by asking a question, such as the following: "Imagine there are two restaurants on the same block. One is a little old

place owned by a local couple, where they serve home-cooked meals. The other is a popular chain restaurant. What kind of people and experience do you think you would find in each? Which do you think represents the real America, and why?" [Possible response: Both do, because the people eating in each restaurant are in some ways representative of America.]

steamboat." I remembered why I'd come to Gainesboro. "You know the way to Nameless?"

"Nameless? I've heard of Nameless. Better ask the amlance driver in the corner booth." She pinned the Smiley on my jacket. "Maybe I'll see you on the road somewhere. His name's Bob, by the way."

"The ambulance driver?"

"The Smiley. I always name my Smileys—otherwise they all look alike. I'd talk to him before you go."

"The Smiley?"

"The amlance driver."

And so I went looking for Nameless, Tennessee, with a Smiley button named Bob.

"I don't know if I got directions for where you're goin'," the ambulance driver said. "I *think* there's a Nameless down the Shepardsville Road."

"When I get to Shepardsville, will I have gone too far?"

"Ain't no Shepardsville."

"How will I know when I'm there?"

"Cain't say for certain."

"What's Nameless look like?"

"Don't recollect."

"Is the road paved?"

"It's possible."

Those were the directions. I was looking for an unnumbered road named after a nonexistent town that would take me to a place called Nameless that nobody was sure existed.

Clumps of wild garlic lined the county highway that I hoped was the Shepardsville Road. It scrimmaged with the mountain as it tried to stay on top of the ridges; the hillsides were so steep and thick with oak, I felt as if I were following a trail through the misty treetops. Chickens, doing more work with their necks than legs, ran across the road, and, with a battering of wings, half leapt and half flew into the lower branches of oaks. A vicious

pair of mixed-breed German shepherds raced along trying to eat the tires. After miles, I decided I'd missed the town—assuming there truly *was* a Nameless, Tennessee. It wouldn't be the first time I'd qualified for the Ponce de Leon[2] Believe Anything Award.

I stopped beside a big man loading tools in a pickup. "I may be lost."

"Where'd you lose the right road?"

"I don't know. Somewhere around nineteen sixty-five."

"Highway fifty-six, you mean?"

"I came down fifty-six. I think I should've turned at the last junction."

"Only thing down that road's stumps and huckleberries, and the berries ain't there in March. Where you tryin' to get to?"

"Nameless. If there is such a place."

"You might not know Thurmond Watts, but he's got him a store down the road. That's Nameless at his store. Still there all right, but I might not vouch you that tomorrow." He came up to the van. "In my army days, I wrote Nameless, Tennessee, for my place of birth on all the papers, even though I lived on this end of the ridge. All these ridges and hollers got names of their own. That's Steam Mill Holler over yonder. Named after the steam engine in the gristmill. Miller had him just one arm but done a good business."

"What business you in?"

"I've always farmed, but I work in Cookeville now in a heatin' element factory. Bad back made me go to town to work." He pointed to a wooden building not much bigger than his truck. By the slanting porch, a faded Double Cola sign said J M WHEELER STORE. "That used to be my business. That's me—Madison Wheeler. Feller came by one day. From Detroit. He wanted to buy the sign because he carried my name too. But I didn't sell. Want to keep my name up." He gave a cigarette a good slow smoking. "Had a decent business for

2. **Ponce de Leon:** Juan Ponce de Leon, Spanish explorer and discoverer of Florida. According to legend, he searched for a fountain said to have the power to restore youth.

WORDS TO OWN
recollect (rek'ə·lekt') v.: remember.
vouch (vouch) v.: guarantee.

WILLIAM LEAST HEAT-MOON 1059

Getting Students Involved

RESPONDING TO THE ART

Allan D'Arcangelo (1930–   ) is an American painter and printmaker in the Pop art movement, which includes Roy Lichtenstein (p. 905) and Jasper Johns (p. 965). D'Arcangelo has often painted industrial landscapes and highways in a flat style, using generalized forms and familiar shapes such as highway signs. His highway paintings, such as *Highway US 1, Panel 3,* create an illusion of space while always reminding the viewer that the picture is just a picture.

Activity. Ask students what Heat-Moon might think of the picture. Then, invite them to comment on the picture from the possible viewpoints of other authors, such as Elie Wiesel, Zora Neal Hurston, and Ernest Hemingway.

Highway US 1, Panel 3 (1963) by Allan D'Arcangelo. Acrylic on canvas (69½" × 81").

Ⓐ Elements of Literature

Dialect

❓ A *briar blade* is a scythe—a farm tool with a long, curved blade attached to a long handle, used for cutting wheat or tall grass. How does Wheeler's dialect reveal his character? [Possible response: The terms and expressions he uses show the importance of the region in shaping his life experience and outlook. His nonstandard pronunciations of words and his nonstandard grammar might also suggest a limited formal education.]

five years, but too much of it was in credit. Then them supermarkets down in Cookeville opened, and I was buyin' higher than they was sellin'. With these hard roads now, everybody gets out of the hollers to shop or work. Don't stay up in here anymore. This tar road under my shoes done my business in, and it's likely to do Nameless in."

"Do you wish it was still the old way?"

"I got no debts now. I got two boys raised, and they never been in trouble. I got a brick house and some corn and tobacco and a few Hampshire hogs and Herefords. A good bull. Bull's pumpin' better blood than I do. Real generous man in town let me put my cow in with his stud. I couldna paid the fee on that specimen otherwise." He took an-

other long, meditative pull on his filter tip. "If you're satisfied, that's all they are to it. I'll tell you, people from all over the nation—Florida, Mississippi—are comin' in here to retire because it's good country. But our young ones don't stay on. Not much way to make a livin' in here anymore. Take me. I been beatin' on these stumps all my life, tryin' to farm these hills. They don't give much up to you. Fightin' rocks and briars all the time. One of the first things I recollect is swingin' a briar blade—filed out of an old saw it was. Now they come in with them crawlers and push out a pasture in a day. Still, it's a grudgin' land—like the gourd. Got to hard cuss gourd seed, they say, to get it up out of the ground."

1060 CONTEMPORARY LITERATURE

Getting Students Involved

Cooperative Learning

Travel Book Proposal. Have students fill out interest surveys about which regions of North America they would most like to travel in. Based on their answers, divide students into groups of four or five to plan a hypothetical road trip during which they will be looking for material for a travel memoir. Group members should assume responsibility for brainstorming and planning the trip, for research, and for writ-

ing and revising their proposal. Have teams use the library and Internet to obtain information for their region: maps, guidebooks, Chamber of Commerce materials, automobile club literature, lists of important sites, and previous travel memoirs. Then, have students write a book proposal—at least one page long—in which they try to "sell" prospective publishers on the idea of their book. The proposal should include

a brief summary of the travel route, attractions to be seen along the way, and an explanation of what the authors will be looking for during the trip. Finally, the proposal should state why the book will be appealing to readers: what is original and thought-provoking about it. Have students submit written proposals to the class, and have the class vote on which proposals it would want to publish.

The whole time, my rig sat in the middle of the right lane while we stood talking next to it and wiped at the mist. No one else came or went. Wheeler said, "Factory work's easier on the back, and I don't mind it, understand, but a man becomes what he does. Got to watch that. That's why I keep at farmin', although the crops haven't ever throve. It's the doin' that's important." He looked up suddenly. "My apologies. I didn't ask what you do that gets you into these hollers."

I told him. I'd been gone only six days, but my account of the trip already had taken on some polish.

He nodded. "Satisfaction is doin' what's important to yourself. A man ought to honor other people, but he's got to honor what he believes in too."

As I started the engine, Wheeler said, "If you get back this way, stop in and see me. Always got beans and taters and a little piece of meat."

Down along the ridge, I wondered why it's always those who live on little who are the ones to ask you to dinner.

Nameless, Tennessee, was a town of maybe ninety people if you pushed it, a dozen houses along the road, a couple of barns, same number of churches, a general merchandise store selling Fire Chief gasoline, and a community center with a lighted volleyball court. Behind the center was an open-roof, rusting metal privy with PAINT ME on the door; in the hollow of a nearby oak lay a full pint of Jack Daniel's Black Label. From the houses, the odor of coal smoke.

Next to a red tobacco barn stood the general merchandise with a poster of Senator Albert Gore, Jr.,[3] smiling from the window. I knocked. The door opened partway. A tall, thin man said, "Closed up. For good," and started to shut the door.

"Don't want to buy anything. Just a question for Mr. Thurmond Watts."

The man peered through the slight opening.

---

3. **Senator Albert Gore, Jr.** (1948–   ): United States senator from Tennessee, 1985–1992; elected vice president of the United States in 1992 and 1996.

He looked me over. "What question would that be?"

"If this is Nameless, Tennessee, could he tell me how it got that name?"

The man turned back into the store and called out, "Miss Ginny! Somebody here wants to know how Nameless come to be Nameless."

Miss Ginny edged to the door and looked me and my truck over. Clearly, she didn't approve. She said, "You know as well as I do, Thurmond. Don't keep him on the stoop in the damp to tell him." Miss Ginny, I found out, was Mrs. Virginia Watts, Thurmond's wife.

I stepped in and they both began telling the story, adding a detail here, the other correcting a fact there, both smiling at the foolishness of it all. It seems the hilltop settlement went for years without a name. Then one day the Post Office Department told the people if they wanted mail up on the mountain they would have to give the place a name you could properly address a letter to. The community met; there were only a handful, but they commenced debating. Some wanted patriotic names, some names from nature, one man recommended in all seriousness his own name. They couldn't agree, and they ran out of names to argue about. Finally, a fellow tired of the talk; he didn't like the mail he received anyway. "Forget the durn Post Office," he said. "This here's a nameless place if I ever seen one, so leave it be." And that's just what they did.

Watts pointed out the window. "We used to have signs on the road, but the Halloween boys keep tearin' them down."

"You think Nameless is a funny name," Miss Ginny said. "I see it plain in your eyes. Well, you take yourself up north a piece to Difficult or Defeated or Shake Rag. Now them are silly names."

The old store, lighted only by three fifty-watt bulbs, smelled of coal oil and baking bread. In the middle of the rectangular room, where the oak floor sagged a little, stood an iron stove. To the right was a wooden table with an unfinished

---

WORDS TO OWN

commenced (kə·menst') v.: started.

WILLIAM LEAST HEAT-MOON 1061

B Elements of Literature

Dialect

? What does *throve* mean? [It is a variant of *thrived* and means "succeeded."]

C Critical Thinking

Connecting to the Text

? How would you explain the purpose of your trip if you were Heat-Moon? [Possible responses: I'd say I was a writer working on a travel book; I'd say I was on vacation.]

D Critical Thinking

Extending the Text

? Which do you think comes first, honoring others' needs or honoring your own beliefs? Why? [Possible responses: honoring others, because the other choice is unfair; honoring oneself, because an unfulfilled person can't help others effectively.]

E Elements of Literature

Dialect

? What are *taters*? [potatoes]

F English Language Learners

Colloquialisms

? This is an example of Heat-Moon's adaptation of colloquialisms to narrative. What does "maybe ninety people if you pushed it" mean? [a little less than ninety people]

G Elements of Literature

Dialect

? What is the standard way of saying "Them are silly names"? ["Those are silly names".]

Crossing the Curriculum

Social Studies

Have students, individually or in pairs, interview an older person from their community—someone who has lived in the community a long time and can discuss how it has changed. After students have written several questions that would be appropriate to ask, have them record the interview on audiotape or videotape, if possible, or on paper. If students do not videotape the interview, ask them to take photographs if

the interviewee permits it. After students report on their interviews and play portions of the tapes, collect the reports and tapes into an archive of oral histories. The local library or historical society may wish to house the materials, as may the high school and local college libraries. *You may want to obtain permission from parents or guardians and from the parties students will contact before they begin work on this activity.*

Architecture

Ask students to create a photo essay featuring local architecture. They should focus on both residential and business architecture. Have them conduct library research, take photographs, and, if possible, examine local buildings. Students should accompany their photographs with written descriptions of buildings, including dates of construction, architects, and descriptions of styles.

T1061

A Elements of Literature
Dialect
? What would most Americans say instead of *deliver a woman?* [*deliver a baby; deliver a woman's baby*]

B Elements of Literature
Dialect
? What is *the drop edge of yonder?* [the brink of death] What does *unless you want to get shut of me* mean? [unless you want to get rid of me; unless you want me to die]

C Elements of Literature
Irony
? What does *I studied on it* mean? [I thought about it.] How is Mr. Watts's statement ironic? [He's only pretending he had to think about it for a long time; actually, he called the doctor immediately, as Mrs. Watts points out in the next paragraph.]

D Cultural Connections
You might point out that traditional medicines from North America and Asia have become increasingly popular since *Blue Highways* was published. Herbal remedies and acupuncture, for example, are increasingly used in tandem with Western medicine for some illnesses.

E Elements of Literature
Dialect
? Watts's question about the clam highlights a crucial aspect of traditional colloquial speech: its creativity, which can be seen in countless figurative expressions, proverbs, adages, and regional or slang terms. Where do colorful new terms usually come from in American English today? [Possible responses: urban styles, such as hip-hop; the first languages of immigrants; technology; show business; sports.]

game of checkers and a stool made from an apple-tree stump. On shelves around the walls sat earthen jugs with corncob stoppers, a few canned goods, and some of the two thousand old clocks and clockworks Thurmond Watts owned. Only one was ticking; the others he just looked at. I asked how long he'd been in the store.

"Thirty-five years, but we closed the first day of the year. We're hopin' to sell it to a churchly couple. Upright people. No athians."[4]

"Did you build this store?"

"I built this one, but it's the third general store on the ground. I fear it'll be the last. I take no pleasure in that. Once you could come in here for a gallon of paint, a pickle, a pair of shoes, and a can of corn."

"Or horehound candy," Miss Ginny said. "Or corsets and salves. We had cough syrups and all that for the body. In season, we'd buy and sell blackberries and walnuts and chestnuts, before the blight got them. And outside, Thurmond milled corn and sharpened plows. Even shoed a horse sometimes."

"We could fix up a horse or a man or a baby," Watts said.

"Thurmond, tell him we had a doctor on the ridge in them days."

"We had a doctor on the ridge in them days. As good as any doctor alivin'. He'd cut a crooked toenail **(A)** or deliver a woman. Dead these last years."

"I got some bad ham meat one day," Miss Ginny said, "and took to vomitin'. All day, all night. Hangin' on **(B)** the drop edge of yonder. I said to Thurmond, 'Thurmond, unless you want shut of me, call the doctor.'"

(C) "I studied on it," Watts said.

"You never did. You got him right now. He come over and put three drops of iodeen in half a glass of well water. I drank it down and the vomitin' stopped with the last swallow. Would you think iodeen could do that?"

4. **athians:** Mr. Watts means "atheists," people who deny the existence of God.

"He put Miss Ginny on one teaspoon of spirits of ammonia in well water for her nerves. Ain't nothin' works better for her to this day."

"Calms me like the hand of the Lord."

Hilda, the Wattses' daughter, came out of the backroom. "I remember him," she said. "I was just a baby. Y'all were talkin' to him, and he lifted me up on the counter and gave me a stick of Juicy Fruit and a piece of cheese."

(D) "Knew the old medicines," Watts said. "Only drugstore he needed was a good kitchen cabinet. None of them antee-beeotics that hit you worsen your ailment. Forgotten <u>lore</u> now, the old medicines, because they ain't profit in iodeen."

Miss Ginny started back to the side room where she and her sister Marilyn were taking apart a duck-down mattress to make bolsters. She stopped at the window for another look at *Ghost Dancing.*[5] "How do you sleep in that thing? Ain't you all cramped and cold?"

(E) "How does the clam sleep in the shell?" Watts said in my defense.

"Thurmond, get the boy a piece of buttermilk pie afore he goes on."

"Hilda, get him some buttermilk pie." He looked at me. "You like good music?" I said I did. He cranked up an old Edison phonograph, the kind with the big morning-glory blossom for a speaker, and put on a wax cylinder. "This will be 'My Mother's Prayer,'" he said.

While I ate buttermilk pie, Watts served as disc jockey of Nameless, Tennessee. "Here's 'Mountain Rose.'" It was one of those moments that you know at the time will stay with you to the grave: the sweet pie, the

5. **Ghost Dancing:** Least Heat-Moon's van, named for the Plains Indian ceremony performed for the restoration of the buffalo and old ways of life.

WORDS TO OWN
lore (lôr) *n.:* traditional knowledge or teachings.

Making the Connections

Connecting to the Theme: "Discoveries and Awakenings"
Remind students of the collection theme, and ask how this selection fits the theme. Divide the class into groups to discuss the following questions:

1. What did Heat-Moon discover or awaken to on his travels?
2. What did you discover or awaken to in reading his account?
3. What would you like to learn about Heat-Moon and about his subject that this excerpt didn't show you?
4. On the whole, does this selection fit the collection theme or not? Why?

gaunt man playing the old music, the coals in the stove glowing orange, the scent of kerosene and hot bread. "Here's 'Evening Rhapsody.'" The music was so heavily romantic we both laughed. I thought: It is for this I have come.

Feathered over and giggling, Miss Ginny stepped from the side room. She knew she was a sight. "Thurmond, give him some lunch. Still looks hungry."

Hilda pulled food off the woodstove in the backroom: home-butchered and canned whole-hog sausage, home-canned June apples, turnip greens, coleslaw, potatoes, stuffing, hot cornbread. All delicious.

Watts and Hilda sat and talked while I ate. "Wish you would join me."

"We've ate," Watts said. "Cain't beat a woodstove for flavorful cookin'."

He told me he was raised in a one-hundred-fifty-year-old cabin still standing in one of the hollows. "How many's left," he said, "that grew up in a log cabin? I ain't the last surely, but I must be climbin' on the list."

Hilda cleared the table. "You Watts ladies know how to cook."

"She's in nursin' school at Tennessee Tech. I went over for one of them football games last year there at Coevul." To say *Cookeville,* you let the word collapse in upon itself so that it comes out "Coevul."

"Do you like football?" I asked.

"Don't know. I was so high up in that stadium, I never opened my eyes."

Watts went to the back and returned with a fat spiral notebook that he set on the table. His expression had changed. "Miss Ginny's *Deathbook.*"

The thing startled me. Was it something I was supposed to sign? He opened it but said nothing. There were scads of names written in a tidy hand over pages <u>incised</u> to crinkliness by a ballpoint. <u>Chronologically</u>, the names had piled up: wives, grandparents, a stillborn infant, relatives, friends close and distant. Names, names. After each, the date of *the* unknown finally known and <u>transcribed</u>. The last entry bore yesterday's date.

"She's wrote out twenty years' worth. Ever day she listens to the hospital report on the radio and puts the names in. Folks come by to check a date. Or they just turn through the books. Read them like a scrapbook."

Hilda said, "Like Saint Peter at the gates inscribin' the names."

Watts took my arm. "Come along." He led me to the fruit cellar under the store. As we went down, he said, "Always take a newborn baby upstairs afore you take him downstairs, otherwise you'll incline him downwards."

The cellar was dry and full of cobwebs and jar after jar of home-canned food, the bottles organized as a shopkeeper would: sausage, pumpkin, sweet pickles, tomatoes, corn relish, blackberries, peppers, squash, jellies. He held a hand toward the dusty bottles. "Our tomorrows."

Upstairs again, he said, "Hope to sell the store to the right folk. I see now, though, it'll be somebody offen the ridge. I've studied on it, and maybe it's the end of our place." He stirred the coals. "This store could give a comfortable livin', but not likely get you rich. But just gettin' by is dice rollin' to people nowadays. I never did see my day guaranteed."

When it was time to go, Watts said, "If you find anyone along your way wants a good store—on the road to Cordell Hull Lake—tell them about us."

I said I would. Miss Ginny and Hilda and Marilyn came out to say goodbye. It was cold and drizzling again. "Weather to give a man the weary dismals," Watts grumbled. "Where you headed from here?"

"I don't know."

"Cain't get lost then." **ⓘ**

Miss Ginny looked again at my rig. It had worried her from the first as it had my mother. "I hope you don't get yourself kilt in that durn thing gallivantin' around the country."

"Come back when the hills dry off," Watts said. "We'll go lookin' for some of them round rocks all sparkly inside."

I thought a moment. "Geodes?"[6]

"Them's the ones. The county's properly full of them."

---

6. **geodes** (jē′ōdz′): stones having cavities lined with crystals or minerals.

WORDS TO OWN

ⓗ incised (in·sīzd′): *v.* used as *adj.*: deeply marked.
chronologically (krän′ō·läj′i·kə·lē) *adv.*: arranged in order of occurrence.
transcribed (tran·skrībd′) *v.* used as *adj.*: written down.

WILLIAM LEAST HEAT-MOON 1063

ⓕ Critical Thinking

Connecting with the Text

? Sausage, apples, greens, coleslaw, potatoes, stuffing, and cornbread are all available in supermarkets throughout the United States. What is different about these foods in the Wattses' home? [Possible answers: They are raised and processed (the fruits and vegetables canned, the meat butchered) on the Wattses' farm and cooked on a wood stove; their taste is probably better than that of store-bought equivalents.]

ⓖ Critical Thinking

Making Judgments

? Is Mr. Watts serious about his experience at the football game? [No, he seems to be making fun of himself.]

ⓗ Elements of Literature

Dialect

? What is the standard way of saying "She's wrote out"? ["She has (or She's) written out."]

ⓘ Elements of Literature

Paradox

? How is this statement contradictory yet true? [Possible response: On the one hand, if you don't know where you're going, you're lost; on the other, you can be lost only if you have a specific destination and don't know how to get there. Since Heat-Moon is on a quest to discover the unknown, he will probably find something worthwhile wherever he goes.]

Assessing Learning

Check Test: Multiple Choice

1. The author says that the best way to find a good cafe is to (a) count the trucks in the lot; (b) count the wall calendars; (c) see if the cook is fat or skinny. [b]

2. What town is the author trying to find? (a) Peavine, Kentucky; (b) Bear Wallow, North Carolina; (c) Nameless, Tennessee [c]

3. The author feels that those most likely to invite a traveler to supper are (a) those who have plenty to spare; (b) those who are superstitious; (c) those who have little. [c]

4. Thurmond Watts (a) has just bought his store; (b) is trying to sell his store; (c) has built another store. [b]

5. Ginny Watts keeps (a) a wedding book; (b) a death book; (c) a wish book. [b]

This excerpt describes the author's encounter with the hospitality of poor sharecroppers in the 1930s.

Ⓐ Elements of Literature
Dialect

? In the midst of his long, almost stream-of-consciousness sentences, Agee includes snatches of speech that contain dialect expressions. What are some of these expressions? [*making you enough bother; awful sorry; 'tain't*]

Ⓑ Cultural Connections
Forms of Etiquette

Invite students to point out examples of the emphasis on good manners that was prevalent in the rural South in the 1930s. [Possible responses: Agee's refraining from offering to help; Mrs. Gudger's staying up with Agee but sitting a little away from the table; her serving a plentiful meal despite her poverty; and Agee's eating a generous portion even though he is full.]

Connections — AN ESSAY

James Agee (1909–1955) was a Tennessee-born author who is now remembered primarily for his Pulitzer Prize–winning autobiographical novel, *A Death in the Family* (1957). He also wrote poetry, much-admired movie criticism for *The Nation* and *Time* magazines, and several screenplays, including adaptations of two of Stephen Crane's short stories.

In 1936, during the Great Depression, *Fortune* magazine assigned Agee to write about sharecroppers in the South. The result was too passionate for the magazine, but was eventually published as a book, *Let Us Now Praise Famous Men* (1941), one of the lesser-known masterpieces of American literature. Like Heat-Moon, Agee wrote about the people he discovered along back roads in rural America. Issued with photographs by Walker Evans, *Let Us Now Praise Famous Men* is Agee's dignified and heart-rending portrait of three Alabama families.

In the following passage, the young journalist shares a meal with a family he calls the Gudgers. As you read, notice how Agee's meditative style adds a layer of personal interpretation over the spare reality he is observing. He avoids quotation marks, and his long sentences and stream of thoughts are reminiscent of the modernist style of William Faulkner (page 713).

from Let Us Now Praise Famous Men

James Agee

So it was there was neither any fake warmth and heartiness nor any coldness in his saying, Sure, come on in, to my asking could he put me up for the night after all, and he added, Better eat some supper. I was in fact very hungry, but I did all I was able to stop this, finally trying to compromise it to a piece of bread and some milk, that needn't be prepared; I'm making you enough bother already; but no; Can't go to bed without no supper; you just hold on a second or two; and he leans his head through the bedroom door and speaks to his wife, explaining, and lights the lamp for her. After a few moments, during which I hear her breathing and a weary shuffling of her heels, she comes out **Ⓐ** barefooted carrying the lamp, frankly and profoundly sleepy as a child; feeling disgusted to wake her further with so many words I say, Hello, Mrs. Gudger: say I want to tell you I'm *aw*ful sorry to give you all this bother: you just, honest I don't need much of anything, if you'd just tell me where a piece of bread is, it'll be *plenty*, I'd hate for you to bother to cook anything up for me: but she answers me while passing, looking at me, trying to get me into focus from between her sticky eyelashes, that 'tain't no bother at all, and for me not to worry over that, and goes on into the kitchen; and how quickly I don't understand, for I am too much occupied to see, with Gudger, and with **Ⓑ** holding myself from the cardinal error of hovering around her, or of offering to help her, she has built a pine fire and set in front of me, on the table in the hall, warmed-over biscuit and butter and blackberry jam and a jelly-glass full of buttermilk, and warmed field peas, fried pork, and four fried eggs, and she sits a little away from the table out of courtesy, trying to hold her head up and her eyes open, until I shall have finished eating, saying at one time how it's an awful poor sort of supper and at another how it's awful plain, mean food; I tell her different, and eat as rapidly as possible and a good deal more than I can hold, in fact, all the eggs, a second large plateful of peas, most of the biscuit, feeling it is better to keep them awake and to eat too much than in the least to let them continue to believe I am what they

Connecting Across Texts

Connecting with *Blue Highways*
Both Heat-Moon and Agee recount their experiences of meeting strangers in small towns. Have students list what each writer discovers about people on a chart like the one at the right. Have students compare what the two writers discovered. Then, ask students to discuss what differences they have found and to account for those differences.

People's Characteristics	Heat-Moon	Agee	Similar	Different
[Friendly to strangers]	[The Wattses invite him to dinner.]	[Mr. Gudger gets his wife up to serve Agee dinner.]	[Both couples trouble themselves to serve a stranger.]	[The Gudgers probably go to more trouble and are poorer.]

assume I must be: 'superior' to them or to their food, eating only so much as I need to be 'polite'; and I see that they are, in fact, quietly surprised and gratified in my appetite.

But somehow I have lost hold of the reality of all this, I scarcely can understand how; a loss of the reality of simple actions upon the specific surface of the earth. This country, these roads, these odors and noises, the action of walking the dark in mud, the approach, just what a slow succession of certain trees past your walking can implant in you, can mean to you, the house as it stands there dark in darkness, the indecisiveness and the bellowing dog, the conversations of questioning, defense, assurance, acceptance, the subtle yet strong distinctions of attitude, the walking between the walls of wood and the sitting and eating, the tastes of the several foods, the weights of our bodies in our chairs, the look of us in the lamplight in the presence of the walls of the house and of the country night, the beauty and the stress of our tiredness, how we held quietness, gentleness, and care toward one another like three mild lanterns held each at the met heads of strangers in darkness: such things, and these are just a few, I have not managed to give their truth in words, which are a soft, plain-featured, and

Depression-era photo of living room by Walker Evans.
Library of Congress.

noble music, each part in the experience of it and in the memory so cleanly and so simply defined in its own terms, striking so many chords and relationships at once, which I can but have blurred in the telling at all.

WILLIAM LEAST HEAT-MOON 1065

© Advanced Learners

Crossing the Curriculum

Photography

Have students encounter the great twentieth-century tradition of American documentary photography by looking in the library for books containing the works of Evans, Dorothea Lange, Eudora Welty, Gordon Parks, Margaret Bourke-White, and others who took pictures under public auspices during the 1930s. Students might also look at more recent examples of documentary photography by such artists as Robert Frank and Helen Levitt. After students have looked at a variety of photographs and chosen personal favorites, have them brainstorm a list of answers to the questions "What makes a great photograph?" and "What does a great photograph do for the viewer?"

MAKING MEANINGS

First Thoughts [Respond]

1. Sample responses: What was your favorite moment of the journey? your least favorite? Were you ever worried about your safety, and if so, when?

Shaping Interpretations [Interpret]

2. The sharing of food tells us that the Wattses are generous, open-hearted people.

3. Numerous passages describe poverty, such as the description of the three bulbs that light the store. The Wattses' cheerfulness, humor, and generosity keep the story from being depressing.

4. Possible responses: image: "Like Saint Peter at the gates inscribin' names"; expression: "I ain't the last surely, but I must be climbin' on the list"; proverb: "Always take a new-born baby upstairs before you take him downstairs, otherwise you'll incline him downwards"; uncommon grammar: "We've ate."

5. He has found tranquillity in sharing the evening with the Wattses; he has found the harmony he was seeking; he has found his ideal image of America.

6. Agee is hungry; in addition, he does not want to insult the Gudgers by eating sparingly. Heat-Moon feels that sharing food is a good way to understand people.

Reading Check

a. The author says you can learn the "tone" or "voice" of a small town, much of "what the people do and believe and share."

b. harmony

c. The Post Office Department insisted that the community have a name so that mail could be delivered. The inhabitants could not agree on a name, so the place was called Nameless.

d. food and local lore

MAKING MEANINGS

First Thoughts

1. What would you most like to ask Heat-Moon about his travels?

Shaping Interpretations

2. Heat-Moon knows that food tells a lot about the people who serve and eat it. Where in this excerpt does food tell us about **character**?

3. What concrete details help paint a vivid picture of the Wattses' home? What details keep the Wattses' story from being a depressing one?

4. Heat-Moon captures the flavor of the country in re-creating the **dialect** of Madison Wheeler and the Watts family. Find examples of **images, expressions, proverbs,** and uncommon **grammar** that tell us who and what these people are.

5. Heat-Moon eats buttermilk pie while an old man plays music on a hand-cranked phonograph. Heat-Moon thinks, "It is for this I have come." What does he mean?

6. In *Let Us Now Praise Famous Men* (see **Connections** on page 1064), James Agee spends the night with the Gudger family in Alabama. Why does Agee eat so heartily there? Does Heat-Moon eat a huge meal at the Wattses' for the same reasons? Explain.

Reading Check

a. What can you learn about a small town by observing people eating breakfast at a restaurant?

b. According to what he tells the waitress, what is Heat-Moon searching for?

c. Explain how Nameless, Tennessee, got its name.

d. What does the Watts family share with the narrator?

READING SKILLS AND STRATEGIES

Analyzing Metaphors

When a man asks Heat-Moon, "Where'd you lose the right road?" his reply is "Somewhere around nineteen sixty-five" (page 1059). This befuddles the

1066 CONTEMPORARY LITERATURE

---

man, because he doesn't grasp that Heat-Moon is using a **metaphor**, a figure of speech in which one thing is compared to another thing, as in "the voyage of life."

1. In the metaphor of "the right road," what two things is Heat-Moon comparing?

2. Explain what is meant by these metaphors:

   a. "Hangin' on the drop edge of yonder" (page 1062)

   b. "How does the clam sleep in the shell?" (page 1062)

CHOICES: Building Your Portfolio

Writer's Notebook

1. Collecting Ideas for an Evaluation

Comparing and contrasting are effective methods of evaluation. Try comparing or contrasting Heat-Moon's narrative with the excerpt from Thoreau's *Walden* (page 233). Make a chart in which you compare the two works in terms of **topics, tone, style,** and each narrator's **quest.** Save your notes for possible use in the Writer's Workshop on page 1181.

Creative Writing

2. My Neighborhood

In a brief essay, describe your own neighborhood or community. Imitate Heat-Moon and pick up all the small, seemingly insignificant details about where you live. Think of things like where people eat, what they eat, what they hang on their wall, what they talk about, how they talk, how they feel about strangers. Be sure to check your Quickwrite notes.

Crossing the Curriculum: Geography

3. What's in a Name?

Heat-Moon delights in American place names. Find a detailed map of your state, and write an essay about the place names that amuse or please you, telling why they do so. What do the names suggest about your state's geography or history?

READING SKILLS AND STRATEGIES

1. the actual road he missed and the course his life has taken

2. a. near death

   b. A creature is comfortable in its own environment.

CHOICES: Building Your Portfolio

1. **Writer's Notebook** Remind students to save their work as prewriting for the Writer's Workshop on p. 1181.

2. **Creative Writing** Have students from the same neighborhood or community brainstorm ideas in a group but write their essays individually.

3. **Crossing the Curriculum: Geography** Urge students to notice a variety of name origins, including Native American words and European geography.

From Generation to Generation

Theme

Passing It On *Postmodern writers still explore issues involving generations—conflicts within families, questions about values, changes in society. Cultural diversity has become a characteristic of American writing, and the boundaries between fiction and nonfiction continue to be blurred.*

Reading the Anthology

Reaching Struggling Readers

The *Reading Skills and Strategies: Reaching Struggling Readers* binder includes a Reading Strategies Handbook that offers concrete suggestions to help students who have difficulty reading and comprehending text, or students who are reluctant readers. When a specific strategy is most appropriate for a selection, a correlation to the Handbook is provided at the bottom of the teacher's page under the head Reaching Struggling Readers. This head may also be used to introduce additional ideas for helping students read challenging texts.

Reading Beyond the Anthology

Read On At the end of the Contemporary Literature collections, the grade eleven book includes an annotated bibliography of books suitable for extended reading. The suggested books are related to works in these collections by theme, by author, or by subject. To preview the Read On for the Contemporary Literature period, please turn to p. T1177.

HRW Library The *HRW Library* offers novels, plays, and short-story collections for extended reading. Each book in the Library includes one or more major works and thematically related Connections. The Connections are magazine articles, poems, or other pieces of literature. Each book in the *HRW Library* is also accompanied by a Study Guide that provides teaching suggestions and worksheets. For Collection 20, the following title is recommended.

THE CHOSEN
Chaim Potok
Potok's novel takes a look at two fathers and their sons. Despite the disapproval of one father, the boys, from two different worlds, forge a friendship and make choices about their future.

Resources for this Collection

Note: All resources for this collection are available for preview on the *One-Stop Planner CD-ROM 2 with Test Generator.* All worksheets and blackline masters may be printed from the CD-ROM.

Internet Resources
go.hrw.com LE0 11-20

Collection Planner

Selection or Feature	Reading and Literary Skills	Vocabulary, Language, and Grammar
Son (p. 1069) John Updike **Connections:** *from "Still Just Writing"* (p. 1074) Anne Tyler	• *Graphic Organizers for Active Reading,* Worksheet p. 107	• *Words to Own,* Worksheet p. 56 • *Daily Oral Grammar,* Transparency 62
Daughter of Invention (p. 1077) Julia Alvarez	• *Graphic Organizers for Active Reading,* Worksheet p. 108	• *Words to Own,* Worksheet p. 57 • *Daily Oral Grammar,* Transparency 63
• **The Bells** (p. 1089) • **Young** (p. 1090) Anne Sexton	• *Graphic Organizers for Active Reading,* Worksheet p. 109	
from **The Way to Rainy Mountain** (p. 1093) N. Scott Momaday	• *Graphic Organizers for Active Reading,* Worksheet p. 110	• *Words to Own,* Worksheet p. 58 • *Daily Oral Grammar,* Transparency 64
from **In Search of Our Mothers' Gardens** (p. 1102) Alice Walker	• *Graphic Organizers for Active Reading,* Worksheet p. 111 • *Literary Elements:* Transparency 32 Worksheet p. 97	• *Words to Own,* Worksheet p. 59 • *Daily Oral Grammar,* Transparency 65
from **Rules of the Game** *from* **The Joy Luck Club** (p. 1110) Amy Tan **Primary Sources: An Interview with Amy Tan** (p. 1118) Joan Chatfield Taylor	• *Graphic Organizers for Active Reading,* Worksheet p. 112	• *Words to Own,* Worksheet p. 60 • *Grammar and Language Links:* Irregular Verbs, Worksheet p. 77 • *Language Workshop CD-ROM,* Verb Forms • *Daily Oral Grammar,* Transparency 66
What For (p. 1122) Garrett Hongo **Primary Sources: A Different Story** (p. 1125) Garrett Hongo	• *Graphic Organizers for Active Reading,* Worksheet p. 113	

Other Resources for this Collection

- *Cross-Curricular Activities*, p. 20
- *Portfolio Management System*, Introduction to Portfolio Assessment, p. 1
- *Test Generator*, Collection Test

Writing	Listening and Speaking Viewing and Representing	Assessment
• *Portfolio Management System*, Rubrics for Choices, p. 220	• *Audio CD Library*, Disc 28, Track 3 • *Viewing and Representing:* Fine Art Transparency 20 Worksheet p. 80 • *Portfolio Management System*, Rubrics for Choices, p. 220	• *Formal Assessment*, Selection Test, p. 210 • *Test Generator (One-Stop Planner CD-ROM)*
• *Portfolio Management System*, Rubrics for Choices, p. 221	• *Portfolio Management System*, Rubrics for Choices, p. 221	• *Formal Assessment*, Selection Test, p. 212 • *Test Generator (One-Stop Planner CD-ROM)*
• *Portfolio Management System*, Rubrics for Choices, p. 222	• *Audio CD Library*, Disc 28, Tracks 4, 5 • *Portfolio Management System*, Rubrics for Choices, p. 222	• *Formal Assessment*, Selection Test, p. 214 • *Test Generator (One-Stop Planner CD-ROM)*
• *Portfolio Management System*, Rubrics for Choices, p. 223	• *Audio CD Library*, Disc 29, Track 2 • *Portfolio Management System*, Rubrics for Choices, p. 223	• *Formal Assessment*, Selection Test, p. 215 • *Test Generator (One-Stop Planner CD-ROM)*
• *Portfolio Management System*, Rubrics for Choices, p. 224	• *Audio CD Library*, Disc 29, Track 3 • *Portfolio Management System*, Rubrics for Choices, p. 224	• *Formal Assessment*, Selection Test, p. 217 • *Test Generator (One-Stop Planner CD-ROM)* • *Preparation for College Admission Exams*, p. 67
• *Portfolio Management System*, Rubrics for Choices, p. 226	• *Audio CD Library*, Disc 29, Track 4 • *Portfolio Management System*, Rubrics for Choices, p. 226	• *Formal Assessment*, Selection Test, p. 219 • *Test Generator (One-Stop Planner CD-ROM)* • *Preparation for College Admission Exams*, p. 69
• *Portfolio Management System*, Rubrics for Choices, p. 227	• *Audio CD Library*, Disc 29, Track 5 • *Portfolio Management System*, Rubrics for Choices, p. 227	• *Formal Assessment*, Selection Test, p. 219 • *Test Generator (One-Stop Planner CD-ROM)*

 Transparency    CD-ROM   Video    Audio CD

Collection Planner

Collection 20 From Generation to Generation

Skills Focus

Selection or Feature	Reading Skills and Strategies	Elements of Literature and Language	Writing	Listening and Speaking	Viewing and Representing
Son (p. 1069) John Updike	Analyze Text Structures: Non-chrono-logical Order, pp. 1069, 1075	Theme, p. 1075 Tone, p. 1075	Identify the Theme of a Story, p. 1075 Write an Essay Interpreting the Theme of a Story, p. 1075 Write Episodes of a "Daughter" Story, p. 1075		Use a Graphic to Organize Information, p. 1075
Daughter of Invention (p. 1077) Julia Alvarez	Draw Infer-ences About Characters, pp. 1077, 1087	Conflict: External and Internal, pp. 1077, 1087 Aphorisms, p. 1087 Theme, p. 1087 Climax, p. 1087 Title, p. 1087	Identify Conflicts in a Story, p. 1087 Write an Essay Interpreting the Title of the Story, p. 1087	Write and Deliver a Speech from the Point of View of the Narrator, p. 1087	
• **The Bells** (p. 1089) • **Young** (p. 1090) Anne Sexton		Imagery, pp. 1089, 1091 Synesthesia, p. 1091 Theme, p. 1091 Metaphor, p. 1091 Tone, p. 1091 Approximate Rhyme, p. 1091 Alliteration, p. 1091	Establish Criteria for Effective Images, and Evaluate Sexton's Images, p. 1091 Write an Essay Analyzing the Sound Struc-ture of Sexton's Poems, p. 1091		Draw or Paint an Image from the Poem, p. 1091
from **The Way to Rainy Mountain** (p. 1093) N. Scott Momaday	Identify Main Ideas and Supporting Details, pp. 1093, 1100	Setting, pp. 1093, 1100 Flashback, p. 1093 Image, p. 1100 Symbolize, p. 1100 Mood, p. 1100 Figures of Speech, p. 1100 Elegy, p. 1100	Evaluate Momaday's Success in Describing a Setting, p. 1100 Write an Essay Responding to an Author's Comment, p. 1100 Write a Description of a Childhood Refuge, p. 1100		
from **In Search of Our Mothers' Gardens** (p. 1102) Alice Walker	Identify the Main Idea, pp. 1102, 1108 Identify Key Passages, p. 1102	Personal Essay, pp. 1102, 1108 Metaphor, p. 1108 Simile, p. 1108 Paradox, p. 1108 Character Sketch, p. 1108	Evaluate a Personal Essay, p. 1108 State the Main Idea and Summarize Support-ing Details, p. 1108 Write a Character Sketch, p. 1108		Write an Essay Analyzing Bear-den's Collages, p. 1108
from **Rules of the Game** from **The Joy Luck Club** (p. 1110) Amy Tan		Motivation, pp. 1110, 1119 Conflict, p. 1119 Title, p. 1119	Write a Response to a Critical Evaluation, p. 1119 Write an Essay Predicting Characters' Inter-actions, p. 1119	Deliver Oral Reports on the Etiquette of a Specific Game, p. 1119	
Reading Skills and Strategies: Base Words, Roots, and Word Families (p. 1120)	Base Words, p. 1120 Roots, p. 1120 Word Fami-lies, p. 1120 Prefixes and Suffixes, p. 1120				
What For (p. 1122) Garrett Hongo	Identify Spe-cific Details, p. 1122	Refrain, pp. 1122, 1126 Image, p. 1126	Establish Criteria, and Evaluate the Emotional Impact of a Poem, p. 1126 Write an Essay Discussing the Impact of Details, p. 1126 Compare the Styles of Two Poets, p. 1126 Write a Poem from the Point of View of the Father, p. 1126		

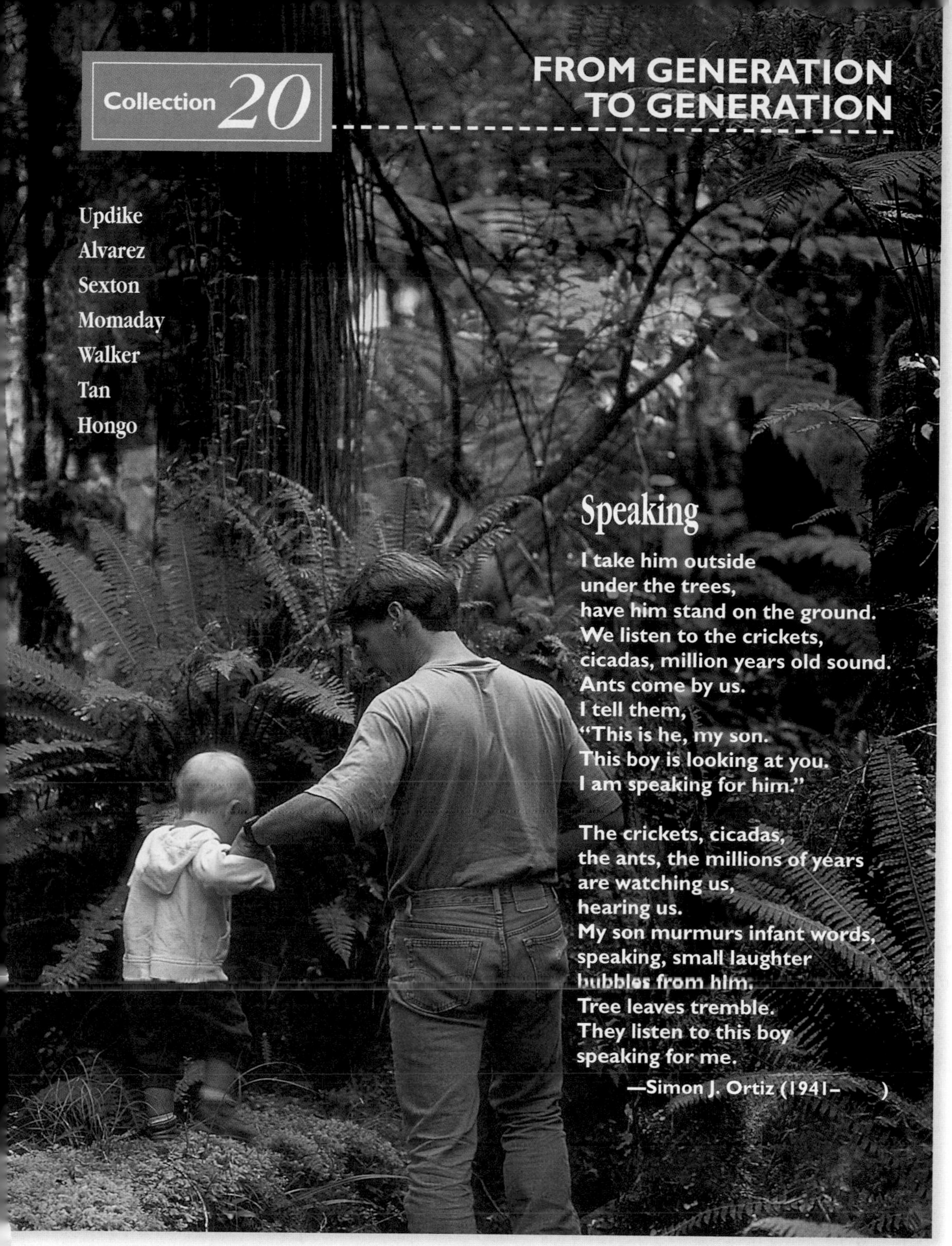

Collection 20

FROM GENERATION TO GENERATION

Updike
Alvarez
Sexton
Momaday
Walker
Tan
Hongo

Speaking

I take him outside
under the trees,
have him stand on the ground.
We listen to the crickets,
cicadas, million years old sound.
Ants come by us.
I tell them,
"This is he, my son.
This boy is looking at you.
I am speaking for him."

The crickets, cicadas,
the ants, the millions of years
are watching us,
hearing us.
My son murmurs infant words,
speaking, small laughter
bubbles from him.
Tree leaves tremble.
They listen to this boy
speaking for me.

—Simon J. Ortiz (1941–)

Objectives

1. Read contemporary literature on the theme "From Generation to Generation"
2. Interpret literary elements used in the literature
3. Apply a variety of reading strategies
4. Respond to the literature in a variety of modes

Responding to the Poem

? How does this poem relate to the theme of this collection—"From Generation to Generation"? [Possible responses: The poem is about two generations, a father and his infant son, each of whom speaks to nature in his own way; the poem is about a father passing on his appreciation of nature to his son.]

Responding to the Art

In this photograph, father and young son, hand in hand, take a walk in the woods. Point out that it is not entirely clear who is leading whom.

Activity. Ask students how this ambiguous image reflects the meaning of the poem. [Possible response: At the end of the first stanza, the speaker says he is speaking for his son, while at the end of the poem, he says his son is speaking for him. Both the poem and the photograph suggest that sometimes the older generation leads the younger, and sometimes the younger leads the older.]

Writing Focus: Evaluation

WORK IN PROGRESS

The following **Work in Progress** assignments in this collection build to a culminating **Writer's Workshop** at the end of Collection 21.

Planning

- **Block Schedule**
  Block Scheduling Lesson Plans with Pacing Guide
- **Traditional Schedule**
  Lesson Plans Including Strategies for English-Language Learners
- **One-Stop Planner**
  CD-ROM with Test Generator

BROWSING IN THE FILES

Writers on Writing. On writing, Updike says, ". . . I distrust prolific writers. I think that if they'd write half as much, they might be twice as good. I think of myself as writing at a stately pace—a few pages a day. That's really less than a thousand words—a very modest quota compared with that which many writers have set for themselves."

John Updike
(1932–   )

Accepting the National Book Award in 1982, John Updike offered this advice to young writers: "Have faith. May you surround yourselves with parents, editors, mates, and children as supportive as mine have been. But the essential support and encouragement of course come from within, arising out of the mad notion that your society needs to know what only you can tell it." That "mad notion" has generated some of our finest contemporary short stories.

© Nancy Crampton.

John Updike spent his youth in the small town of Shillington in rural Pennsylvania. Gifted with what seems like total recall of growing up in the American middle class, Updike also displays a skill with language that can evoke responses to the most ordinary and familiar events, endowing them with importance.

In his memoir, "The Dogwood Tree: A Boyhood" (published in *Assorted Prose* in 1965), Updike crafts an image of his youthful artistic ambition: ". . . riding a thin pencil line out of Shillington, out of time altogether, into an infinity of unseen and even unborn hearts." As a mature and successful writer, he confronts that image and senses disappointment: "Like some phantom conjured by this child from a glue bottle, I have executed his commands; acquired pencils, paper, and an office. Now I wait apprehensively for his next command, or at least a nod of appreciation, and he smiles through me as if I am already transparent with failure."

After graduating *summa cum laude* from Harvard University in 1954, Updike studied drawing in England for a year, and on his return to the United States went to work for *The New Yorker*

magazine. After two years, he made the courageous decision to support his young family entirely by writing. He left New York for Massachusetts and has since produced a long shelf of impressive novels, stories, poems, memoirs, and critical essays.

Although critics are a cantankerous lot, nearly all agree with Rachael C. Burchard that Updike's "style is superb. His work is worth reading if for no reason other than to enjoy the piquant phrase, the lyric vision, the fluent rhetoric." Among his successful novels have been the tales in the Rabbit series—*Rabbit, Run* (1960), *Rabbit Redux* (1971), *Rabbit Is Rich* (1981; Pulitzer Prize), and *Rabbit at Rest* (1990).

The Rabbit novels mark the ends of four consecutive decades and embody the concerns of their time. They chronicle the life of Harry "Rabbit" Angstrom, who lives, as his creator might have, an outwardly conventional life in a small Pennsylvania town. In revealing Rabbit's yearnings and disappointments and the fluctuations of his relationships, Updike gives us a portrait of forty years of American social behavior. As always with an Updike novel, readers enjoy the feel of life—the sights, smells, and sounds that bring life into focus.

Among Updike's other novels are *The Centaur* (1963; National Book Award) and a trilogy, *A Month of Sundays* (1975), *Roger's Version* (1986), and *S.* (1988), which make up a modern version of Nathaniel Hawthorne's *The Scarlet Letter*. In 1996 he published *In the Beauty of the Lilies*, a novel that spans the twentieth century and focuses, in Updike's characteristic way, on generations of a family and on the mysteries of faith—and, as something new, on the American love affair with the movies.

go.hrw.com
LE0 11-20

Resources: Print and Media

Eli (1963) by Alex Katz. Oil on canvas (72″ × 86″).

Before You Read
SON

Make the Connection
Fathers and Sons
"Fathers and sons"—simple words that hide complex, mystifying, and aching relationships. Why do a father's good intentions and thoughts go astray? Why does a son feel antagonized and trapped by a well-meaning father? These are age-old questions that always intrigue us and never seem to receive satisfactory answers.

Reading Skills and Strategies

Analyzing Text Structures: Non-chronological Order
Updike has used an unusual narrative structure for this story about generations. As you read, or after you read, you will want to organize these events into chronological order. One way to do this is to create a time line.

On the time line, plot the story's important time periods and information concerning the son whose life is described in that period. Here is an example:

late 1880s	1913	1949	1973
narrator's grandfather			narrator's son

JOHN UPDIKE 1069

Summary ■■

Updike's story examines the complex and painful relationships among four successive generations of fathers and sons. As the narrative moves back and forth in time among the four generations, the conflict between the youthful ambitions of sons and the "balance of compromises" that they, like their fathers, ultimately accept, remains a thematic emphasis. Repeatedly, parents and children seem unable to appreciate each other's accomplishments or each other's love and find true connection only in rare moments—before their generational roles in the "wrathful pantomime of power" divide them again.

RESPONDING TO THE ART
Alex Katz (1927–), an American painter, sculptor, and printmaker, does not fit neatly into any one school or movement. His work consists mainly of representational portraits, cityscapes, and landscapes that emphasize a flat picture plane. Always straightforward and economical, Katz has painted many portraits of ordinary people—such as *Eli* (1963)—in a smooth, almost impersonal style.
Activity. What do the clothes and background details reveal about this boy? [The boy is white, well dressed in sports clothes, and set against a background suggesting suburbia. His clothes are "correct" for this setting.] Katz's picture matches Updike's characters and settings, which are usually people living in American suburban towns of the northeast.

Preteaching Vocabulary

Words to Own
Have students read the definitions of the Words to Own listed at the bottom of the selection pages. Then, have volunteers use the words in context. When you are sure that students understand the correct way to use each word, have them complete the following phrases.

1. tried to finish the _____ task [irksome]
2. invited her _____ to a family reunion [siblings]
3. children parading _____ in their dress-up clothes [mincingly]
4. amused by the _____ remarks [jocular]
5. a cap set at a _____ angle [jaunty]
6. graduated from the _____ [seminary]
7. surprisingly _____ tigers [docile]
8. a vase with a _____ design [symmetrical]
9. beaten by his _____ [antagonists]
10. established rigid rules to prevent _____ [anarchy]

SON

John Updike

He is often upstairs, when he has to be home. He prefers to be elsewhere. He is almost sixteen, though beardless still, a man's mind indignantly captive in the frame of a child. I love touching him, but don't often dare. The other day, he had the flu, and a fever, and I gave him a back rub, marvelling at the <u>symmetrical</u> knit of muscle, the organic tension. He is high-strung. Yet his sleep is so solid he sweats like a stone in the wall of a well. He wishes for perfection. He would like to destroy us, for we are, variously, too fat, too <u>jocular</u>, too sloppy, too affectionate, too grotesque and heedless in our ways. His mother smokes too much. His younger brother chews with his mouth open. His older sister leaves unbuttoned the top button of her blouses. His younger sister tussles with the dogs, getting them overexcited, avoiding doing her homework. Everyone in the house talks nonsense. He would be a better father than his father. But time has tricked him, has made him a son. After a quarrel, if he cannot go outside and kick a ball, he retreats to a corner of the house and reclines on the beanbag chair in an attitude of strange—infantile or leonine—torpor.[1] We exhaust him, without meaning to. He takes an interest in the newspaper now, the front page as well as the sports, in this tiring year of 1973.

Ⓐ He is upstairs, writing a musical comedy. It is a Sunday in 1949. He has volunteered to prepare a high-school assembly program; people will sing. Ⓑ Songs of the time go through his head, as he scribbles new words. *Up in de mornin', down at de school, work like a debil for my grades.* Below him, <u>irksome</u> voices grind on, like machines working their way through tunnels. His parents each want something from the other. "Marion, you don't understand that man like I do; he has a heart of gold." His father's charade is very complex: the

world, which he fears, is used as a flail[2] on his wife. But from his cringing attitude he would seem to an outsider the one being flailed. With burning red face, the woman accepts the role of aggressor as penance for the fact, the incessant shameful fact, that *he* has to wrestle with the world while she hides here, in solitude, at home. This is normal, but does not seem to them to be so. Only by convolution[3] have they arrived at the dominant/submissive relationship society has assigned them. For the man is maternally kind and with a smile hugs to himself his jewel, his certainty of being victimized; it is the mother whose tongue is sharp, who sometimes strikes. "Well, he gets you out of the house, and I guess that's gold to you." His answer is "Duty calls," pronounced <u>mincingly</u>. "The social contract is a balance of compromises." This will infuriate her, the son knows; as his heart thickens, the downstairs overflows with her hot voice. "*Don't* wear that smile at me! And *take* your hands off your hips; you look like a sissy!" Their son tries not to listen. When he does, visual details of the downstairs flood his mind: the two <u>antagonists</u>, circling with their coffee cups; the shabby mismatched furniture; the hopeful books; the <u>docile</u> framed photographs of the dead, docile and still like cowed Ⓒ students. This matrix of pain that bore him—he

---

2. **flail:** a kind of whip.
3. **convolution:** twisting together until distinctions are obscured.

WORDS TO OWN
symmetrical (si·me′tri·kəl) *adj.*: equally balanced.
jocular (jäk′yōō·lər) *adj.*: joking; comical.
irksome (ʉrk′səm) *adj.*: irritating.
mincingly (mins′iŋ·lē) *adv.*: in an affectedly dainty manner.
antagonists (an·tag′ə·nists) *n. pl.*: adversaries; opponents.
docile (däs′əl) *adj.*: passive.

----

1. **torpor** (tôr′pər): sluggishness; dormancy.

Reaching All Students

Laurence Typing (1952) by Fairfield Porter. Oil on canvas (40″ × 30⅛″).

The Parrish Art Museum, Southampton, New York. Gift of the Estate of Fairfield Porter. Photo by Noel Rowe.

JOHN UPDIKE 1071

RESPONDING TO THE ART

Laurence Typing displays one of the most common motifs of **Fairfield Porter** (1907–1975), an American painter and art critic who specialized in quiet, domestic scenes. Although mainly self-taught, Porter also studied under Thomas Hart Benton (see p. 7) and was heavily influenced by the French painters Édouard Vuillard (1868–1940) and Pierre Bonnard (1867–1947). Basically realist and representational, his style has been described by the Australian art critic Robert Hughes as modernist, "but classically so." Porter focused on the ordinary and became a master of color and subtle tones. He succeeded best in conveying the "presences" of places—landscapes, houses, and rooms that seem to radiate personality as if they were human characters.

Activity. Ask students which son in the Updike story this painting might represent and why they think so. [Possible response: the son writing the musical comedy in 1949 because the boy is typing and the painting is dated 1952.] Students might compare this painting to the drawing of Edgar Allan Poe at work (p. 289)

Using Students' Strengths

Interpersonal Learners
Divide the class into pairs, and ask students to read or reread the story with their partners, one section at a time. (Sections are delineated by extra space.) Have students stop reading at the end of each section to discuss the events with their partners and to write a one- to three-sentence summary before reading the next section.

Visual Learners
Before the class reads the story, ask small groups of students to find or to create illustrations of men in the four stages of life covered in the story: a teenage boy, a father, a grandfather, and a great-grandfather. Suggest that students use original sketches, computer clip art, photographs, or magazine clippings for their illustrations. Ask them to write original captions for each illustration.

Kinesthetic Learners
Have individual students or groups of students pantomime the actions or scenes depicted in each section with an emphasis on revealing the emotions of the characters.

Ⓐ English Language Learners

Finding Details

❓ This is a different "he" from the one in the previous paragraph. What detail reveals who this is? [The fact that the year is 1913 reveals that this character must be the father of the previous "he."]

Ⓑ Advanced Learners

Making Connections

❓ What pattern seems to be unfolding from one vignette to the next? [Possible response: The sons and fathers have similar feelings of dissatisfaction. The narrator's father feels trapped as a paperboy and later as a teacher. The narrator's grandfather knows he is preparing for the wrong vocation.]

Ⓒ Critical Thinking

Interpreting

❓ Why is the narrator's father so depressed by his visit to the seminary town of his father? [Possible responses: Perhaps by visiting the scene, he is reminded of his own dissatisfaction in life; he may feel angry about the choices his father made or about his passivity.]

Ⓓ Reading Skills and Strategies

Analyzing Text Structures: Non-chronological Order

❓ This is the first paragraph in which a year is not mentioned. Who is the son in this paragraph? [the narrator's son, the boy described in the first paragraph]

---

feels he is floating above it, sprawled on the bed as on a cloud, stealing songs as they come into his head (*Across the hallway from the guidance room / Lives a French instructor called Mrs. Blum*), contemplating the view from the upstairs window (last summer's burdock[4] stalks like the beginnings of an alphabet, an apple tree holding three rotten apples as if pondering why they failed to fall), yearning for Monday, for the ride to school with his father, for the bell that calls him to homeroom, for the excitements of class, for Broadway, for fame, for the cloud that will carry him away, out of this, out.

Ⓐ He returns from his paper-delivery route and finds a few Christmas presents for him on the kitchen table. I must guess at the year. 1913? Without opening them, he knocks them to the floor, puts his head on the table, and falls asleep. He must have been consciously dramatizing his plight: His father was sick, money was scarce, he had to work, to win food for the family when he was still a child. In his dismissal of Christmas, he touched a nerve: his love of <u>anarchy</u>, his distrust of the social contract. He treasured this moment of revolt; else why remember it, hoard a memory so bitter, and confide it to his son many Christmases later? He had a teaching instinct, though he claimed that life miscast him as a schoolteacher. I suffered in his classes, feeling the confusion as a persecution of him, but now wonder if his rebellious heart did not court confusion, not as Communists do, to intrude their own order, but, more radical still, as an end pleasurable in itself, as truth's very body. Yet his handwriting (an old pink permission slip recently fluttered from a book where it had been marking a page for twenty years) was always considerably legible, and he was sitting up doing arithmetic the morning of the day he died.

And letters survive from that yet prior son, written in brown ink, in a tidy tame hand, home to his mother from the Missouri <u>seminary</u> where he was preparing for his vocation. The dates are 1887, 1888, 1889. Nothing much happened: He missed New Jersey, and was teased at a church social for escorting a widow. He wanted to do the right

4. **burdock:** coarse, hairy weed with thick stalks, heart-shaped leaves, and prickly purple flowers.

thing, but the little sheets of faded penscript ex-Ⓑ hale a dispirited calm, as if his heart already knew he would not make a successful minister, or live to be old. His son, my father, when old, drove hundreds of miles out of his way to visit the Missouri town from which those letters had been sent. Strangely, the town had not changed; it looked just as he had imagined, from his father's descriptions: tall wooden houses, rain-soaked, stacked on a bluff. The town was a sepia[5] postcard mailed homesick home and preserved in an attic. My father cursed: His father's old sorrow Ⓒ bore him down into depression, into hatred of life. My mother claims his decline in health began at that moment.

Ⓓ He is wonderful to watch, playing soccer. Smaller than the others, my son leaps, heads, dribbles, feints, passes. When a big boy knocks him down, he tumbles on the mud, in his green-and-black school uniform, in an ecstasy of falling. I am envious. Never for me the <u>jaunty</u> pride of the school uniform, the solemn ritual of the coach's pep talk, the camaraderie of shook hands and slapped backsides, the shadow-striped hush of late afternoon and last quarter, the solemn vaulted universe of official combat, with its cheering mothers and referees exotic as zebras and the bespectacled timekeeper alert with his claxon.[6] When the boy scores a goal, he runs into the arms of his teammates with upraised arms and his face alight as if blinded by triumph. They lift him from the earth in a union of muddy hugs. What spirit! What valor! What skill! His father, watching from the sidelines, inwardly registers only one complaint: He feels the boy, with his talent, should be more aggressive.

5. **sepia** (sē′pē·ə): brownish ink used in artwork and photography.
6. **claxon** (klaks′ən): more correctly, Klaxon, the trademark for a type of electric horn with a distinctively loud, shrill sound. Such a horn is often used to mark the end of a time period in sporting events.

WORDS TO OWN

anarchy (an′ər·kē) *n.*: complete disorder.
seminary (sem′ə·ner′ē) *n.*: school for training ministers, priests, or rabbis.
jaunty (jônt′ē) *adj.*: confident; carefree.

Professional Notes

Critical Comment

In 1963, the literary critic Norman Podhoretz wrote of Updike, "His short stories . . . strike me as all windup and no delivery, and I am alternately bored and exasperated by the verbal pyrotechnics they specialize in. . . ." In 1967, critic Richard H. Rupp wrote, "At worst . . . [his] style leaves an empty husk. At best, it reveals characters only potentially interesting. One does not remember them by name, only collectively."

"Son" was published in 1973. Ask students to respond to Podhoretz's and Rupp's criticisms by writing a short evaluation of the characterization and style in "Son." Ask students to state whether "Son" has the faults the critics saw in Updike's earlier writing and to include specific examples from the story to support their opinions.

They drove across the Commonwealth of Pennsylvania to hear their son read in Pittsburgh. But when their presence was announced to the audience, they did not stand; the applause groped for them and died. My mother said afterwards she was afraid she might fall into the next row if she tried to stand in the dark. Next morning was sunny, and the three of us searched for the house where once they had lived. They had been happy there; I imagined, indeed, that I had been conceived there, just before the slope of the Depression steepened and fear gripped my family. We found the library where she used to read Turgenev,[7] and the little park where the bums slept close as paving stones in the summer night; but their street kept eluding us, though we circled in the car. On foot, my mother found the tree. She claimed she recognized it, the sooty linden tree she would gaze into from their apartment windows. The branches, though thicker, had held their pattern. But the house itself, and the entire block, was gone. Stray bricks and rods of iron in the grass suggested that the demolition had been recent. We stood on the empty spot and laughed. They knew it was right, because the railroad tracks were the right distance away. In confirmation, a long freight train pulled itself east around the curve, its great weight gliding as if on a river current; then a silver passenger train came gliding as effortlessly in the other direction. The curve of the tracks tipped the cars slightly toward us. The Golden Triangle,[8] gray and hazed, was off to our left, beyond a forest of bridges. We stood on the grassy rubble that morning, where something once had been, beside the tree still there, and were intensely happy. Why? We knew.

"'No,' Dad said to me, 'the Christian ministry isn't a job you choose, it's a vocation for which you got to receive a call.' I could tell he wanted me to ask him. We never talked much, but we understood each other, we were both scared devils, not like you and the kid. I asked him, Had he ever received the call? He said No. He said No, he never had. Received the call. That was a terrible thing, for him to admit. And I was the one he told. As far as I knew he never admitted it to anybody, but he admitted it to me. He felt like hell about it, I could tell. That was all we ever said about it. That was enough."

He has made his younger brother cry, and justice must be done. A father enforces justice. I corner the rat in our bedroom; he is holding a cardboard mailing tube like a sword. The challenge flares white-hot; I roll my weight toward him like a rock down a mountain, and knock the weapon from his hand. He smiles. Smiles! Because my facial expression is silly? Because he is glad that he can still be overpowered, and hence is still protected? Why? I do not hit him. We stand a second, father and son, and then as nimbly as on the soccer field he steps around me and out the door. He slams the door. He shouts obscenities in the hall, slams all the doors he can find on the way to his room. Our moment of smilingly shared silence was the moment of compression; now the explosion. The whole house rocks with it. Downstairs, his siblings and mother come to me and offer advice and psychological analysis. I was too aggressive. He is spoiled. What they can never know, my grief alone to treasure, was that lucid many-sided second of his smiling and my relenting, before the world's wrathful pantomime of power resumed.

As we huddle whispering about him, my son takes his revenge. In his room, he plays his guitar. He has greatly improved this winter; his hands getting bigger is the least of it. He has found in the guitar an escape. He plays the Romanza[9] wherein repeated notes, with a sliding like the heart's valves, let themselves fall along the scale:

The notes fall, so gently he bombs us, drops feathery notes down upon us, our visitor, our prisoner.

9. **Romanza** (rō·män′zə): musical term. Italian for "romance."

7. **Turgenev** (toor·gän′əf): Ivan Turgenev (1818–1883), Russian writer.
8. **The Golden Triangle:** wedge-shaped piece of land formed by the junction of the Allegheny and Monongahela Rivers in Pittsburgh, Pennsylvania. The two rivers join to form the Ohio River at this point.

WORDS TO OWN
siblings (sib′liŋz) n. pl.: brothers or sisters.

JOHN UPDIKE 1073

Skill Link

Connections

In this essay, Anne Tyler talks about her life as a writer. She says she keeps thinking that eventually she will run out of ideas and then be free to get on with her "real life." However, as fast as she empties out the ideas from her head, new ideas crowd in. She ends her essay by recalling her debt to Eudora Welty, whose stories taught her that you could write about ordinary people—people you know.

Ⓐ Reading Skills and Strategies
Responding to the Text
❓ What do you think it would be like to make your living as a writer? [Possible responses: It would be a good job because the hours would be flexible and you could work at home; it would be stressful because you might run out of ideas or not know where your next paycheck is coming from.]

Ⓑ Elements of Literature
Simile
❓ The whimsical tone of this passage results from the fact that a simile compares two essentially unlike things. How is a writer's job *not* like that of a dentist? [It might be physically possible to eliminate tooth decay, but the human brain can generate an infinite number of ideas.]

Ⓒ Literary Connections
Edna Earle
The character of Edna Earle also turns up in Welty's comic novella *The Ponder Heart.*

Connections — AN ESSAY

One of contemporary America's best fiction writers, Anne Tyler (1941–) has written several widely read novels, including *Dinner at the Homesick Restaurant* (1982), *The Accidental Tourist* (1985), which was made into a popular film, and *A Patchwork Planet* (1998). In the following passage, Tyler talks about writing as a craft and about how she discovered that one can write interestingly about ordinary people. "Even the most ordinary person, in real life," she says, "will turn out to have something unusual at his center."

from "Still Just Writing"
Anne Tyler

I was standing in the schoolyard waiting for a child when another mother came up to me. "Have you found work yet?" she asked "Or are you still just writing?"

Now, how am I supposed to answer that?

Ⓐ I could take offense, come to think of it. Maybe the reason I didn't is that I halfway share her attitude. They're *paying* me for this? For just writing down untruthful stories? I'd better look around for more permanent employment. For I do consider writing to be a finite job. I expect that any day now, I will have said all I have to say; I'll have used up all my characters, and then I'll be free to get on with my real life. When I make a note of new ideas on index cards, I imagine I'm clearing out my head, and that soon it will be empty and spacious. I file the cards in a little blue box, and I can picture myself using the final card one day—ah! through at last!—and throwing the blue box away. I'm like a dentist who continually fights Ⓑ tooth decay, working toward the time when he's conquered it altogether and done himself out of a job. But my head keeps loading up again; the little blue box stays crowded and messy. Even when I feel I have no ideas at all, and can't possibly start the next chapter, I have a sense of something still bottled in me, trying to get out. . . .

Walker/Gamma Liaison.

I spent my adolescence planning to be an artist, not a writer. After all, books had to be about major events, and none had ever happened to me. All I knew were tobacco workers, stringing the leaves I handed them and talking up a storm. Then I found a book of Ⓒ Eudora Welty's short stories in the high school library. She was writing about Edna Earle, who was so slow-witted she could sit all day just pondering how the tail of the *C* got through the loop of the *L* on the Coca-Cola sign. Why, I knew Edna Earle. You mean you could *write* about such people? I have always meant to send Eudora Welty a thank-you note, but I imagine she would find it a little strange.

Assessing Learning

Check Test: Fill in the Blank
1. This story covers events in the lives of _____ sons. [four]
2. The son in 1949 is disturbed when his mother and father _____. [argue]
3. One father enters the _____ in the late 1880s. [seminary]
4. During Christmas in or around the year _____, a son must work to help his family. [1913]
5. A father is watching his son play _____ in one of the sections of the story. [soccer]

Connecting Across Texts

Connecting with "Son"
Discuss with students the ways in which the characters in "Son" are similar to Tyler's tobacco workers and Welty's Edna Earle? [They are ordinary people without "great events" in their lives.] Then, ask them if they think that Updike would agree with Tyler's and Welty's approach to fiction writing. [Possible response: Yes, because his characters are like theirs.]

First Thoughts

1. What thoughts about parents and children did you have as you read "Son"?

Shaping Interpretations

2. This story includes a variety of incidents that range over several different time periods. What **thematic** thread unifies the story? How does the time frame relate to the story's meaning?

3. In the long line of the generations, hope keeps reappearing. In what ways are the characters' hopes for each other disappointed? How are they fulfilled?

4. In the context of the story, what do you think Updike means by the phrase "the social contract"? Would he say that this contract is or is not honored between fathers and sons? Explain.

5. At the end of the story, why does the narrator refer to his son as "our visitor, our prisoner"?

6. Why do you think Updike gave the story the title "Son" instead of "Father"? Would you read the story differently if it had been called "Father"?

7. How would you describe the narrator's **tone** in telling this story? How does he feel about the people in this family?

8. Updike is known as a great wordsmith. Describe some aspects of "Son" that show him to be a skilled practitioner of the writer's craft.

Extending the Text

9. What discovery about writing, described by Anne Tyler in "Still Just Writing" (see *Connections* on page 1074), is also apparent in "Son"? Explain.

Reading Check

a. For each of the story's eight sections, identify the time period and the characters. Refer to your time line as necessary.

b. Find passages in each section in which the narrator reveals private thoughts of the characters.

c. What test does the father-narrator face in the last section?

d. How does the son respond to the father's discipline?

CHOICES:
Building Your Portfolio

Writer's Notebook

1. Collecting Ideas for an Evaluation

When you evaluate a short story, you need to show how separate elements work (or do not work) together. Use a graphic organizer, such as a cluster diagram, to demonstrate how the eight sections of Updike's "Son" contribute to the story's main theme. Write the theme in the center of the cluster, and, in each of the eight bubbles, identify the words, images, characters, or ideas that help convey the theme. Save your notes for possible use in the Writer's Workshop on page 1181.

Interpreting Theme

2. "A contact barely reached"

Analyzing Updike's book *Problems and Other Stories* (1979), in which "Son" appears, the critic Donald J. Greiner wrote:

> The stories were written from 1971 to 1978, a period of unsettling family conditions for Updike himself. Although the tales are not autobiography, the specter of domestic loss, of love moving forward from all sides toward a contact barely reached, hovers around most of them. It is not that love is denied but that it is difficult to sustain.

Write a brief essay applying Greiner's statement to "Son." What does this story say about loss, love, and "a contact barely reached"?

Creative Writing

3. "Daughter"

Imitating the structure of "Son," write some episodes of a story called "Daughter." Let your narrator reveal the thoughts and feelings of at least three generations of one family.

JOHN UPDIKE 1075

First Thoughts [Respond]

1. Students may say they understood the dynamics between children and their parents better after reading the story.

Shaping Interpretations [Interpret]

2. The thematic thread is the relationship between fathers and sons. The time frame spans almost a century, yet all of the sons experience conflicts with their fathers.

3. Disappointed hopes: The narrator's grandfather becomes a minister even though he knows he will be unsuccessful; the narrator's father dislikes his career as a teacher. Fulfilled hopes: The narrator has a satisfying career; he admires his son's athletic accomplishments.

4. Possible response: the responsibilities that people have toward one another. He might say it is honored only when sons and fathers try to balance their needs for power, love, and independence.

5. Possible responses: because the son will soon leave home; because he resents the family arrangement that he has started to outgrow.

6. Possible response: Updike wanted readers to focus on the sons' points of view. If it were called "Father," readers would focus on the fathers.

7. The tone is nostalgic or bittersweet. The narrator loves them, yet he sees their flaws.

8. Students may refer to such descriptive phrases as "the symmetrical knit of muscle."

Extending the Text [Synthesize]

9. Possible response: that ordinary people can be the subjects of interesting stories.

Grading Timesaver

Rubrics for each Choices assignment appear on p. 220 in the *Portfolio Management System*.

Reading Check

a. (1) Narrator's teenage son is described (1973). (2) Narrator appears as a teen dreaming of becoming a playwright (1949). (3) Narrator's father appears as a young paperboy (around 1913). (4) Narrator's grandfather speaks through old letters (1887–1889). (5) Narrator's teenage son appears again (1973). (6) Narrator's parents hear their grown son read from his work (probably after 1960). (7) Narrator's father tells him about a talk he had with his own father (no date). (8) Narrator again describes his son (1973).

b. Students may identify a variety of passages.

c. The narrator tries to discipline his son but is stopped by his affection for the boy.

d. Son and father share a smile; then the son rushes out, slams the door, shouts, and goes off to play his guitar in revenge.

Planning

- **Block Schedule**
  Block Scheduling Lesson Plans with Pacing Guide

- **Traditional Schedule**
  Lesson Plans Including Strategies for English-Language Learners

- **One-Stop Planner**
  CD-ROM with Test Generator

Julia Alvarez

(1950–   )

"**A**ll my childhood I had dressed like an American, eaten American foods, and befriended American children. I had gone to an American school and spent most of the day speaking and reading English. At night, my prayers were full of blond hair and blue eyes and snow. . . . All my childhood I had longed for this moment of arrival. And here I was, an American girl, coming home at last."

With these words, Julia (pronounced hōō′lē·ä) Alvarez describes stepping back into America. Although born in New York City, Alvarez spent her early childhood in the Dominican Republic. In 1960, just before her father was to be arrested for his involvement in a secret plot to overthrow the dictator Rafael Trujillo Molina, Alvarez and her family were tipped off by an American agent and escaped to the United States.

Paradoxically, her homecoming was filled with all the difficulties of adjusting to a brand-new life. Learning contemporary American English was only part of the adjustment. Alvarez also had to learn to compromise in order to resolve conflicts between American customs and her parents' more traditional views. This theme is at the heart of her fiction—particularly her short stories and her best-known work, the novel *How the Garcia Girls Lost Their Accents* (1991).

Before concentrating on writing fiction, Alvarez taught courses in poetry for twelve years in schools in Kentucky, California, Vermont, Illinois, and Washington, D.C. Her first collection of poems, appropriately titled *Homecoming*, was published in 1984. Alvarez has also won the American Academy of Poetry Prize, but it is as a novelist that she has received the most notice.

How the Garcia Girls Lost Their Accents is a novel of fifteen interlocking stories with engaging and memorable characters. The Garcia family, with its four daughters, struggles to overcome a variety of cultural and generational conflicts, and comparisons with Alvarez's own family make it clear that the novel is highly autobiographical. Her 1994 novel, *In the Time of the Butterflies,* is a fictionalized account of the lives and deaths of three sisters, Patria, Minerva, and María Teresa Mirabal, the wives of political prisoners in the Dominican Republic. The women, who had been visiting their husbands, were murdered in 1960 by thugs connected to the Trujillo regime. Alvarez's 1997 novel *Yo!* is populated by some of the *Garcia Girls* characters.

It is clear that Alvarez has forged, out of memory and imagination, a novelist's sensibility. As one critic said about *Garcia Girls,* Alvarez has "beautifully captured the threshold experience of the new immigrant, where the past is not yet a memory and the future remains an anxious dream."

Theo Westenberger/Gamma Liaison.

 go.hrw.com
LE0 11-20

Resources: Print and Media

Reading
- *Graphic Organizers for Active Reading,* p. 108
- *Words to Own,* p. 57

Writing and Language
- *Daily Oral Grammar*
  Transparency 63

Assessment
- *Formal Assessment,* p. 212
- *Portfolio Management System,* p. 221
- *Test Generator (One-Stop Planner CD-ROM)*

Internet
- go.hrw.com (keyword: LE0 11-20)

Before You Read

DAUGHTER OF INVENTION

Make the Connection

Generations

From the Biblical parable of the prodigal son to a short story written this morning, literature will probably never end its chronicle of children and parents struggling to understand and make peace with each other. "Experience is the greatest teacher, so trust us," says the older generation. "We want to live our own lives, not yours," say the children. Both have valid points, of course, and the search for equilibrium goes on.

Reading Skills and Strategies

Drawing Inferences About Characters

It is fascinating to see how the three characters in the following story have adapted so differently to the liberty the family enjoys in its new country. As you read, jot down notes on how Cukita, Mami, and Papi adjust to the United States.

"Daughters of Invention" is one of the fifteen interlocking stories in *How the Garcia Girls Lost Their Accents*.

Elements of Literature

Conflict

Do you doubt that a story runs on **conflict**? Here is a splendid example that takes its strength and much of its fun from the clash between the anxious values of Latin American parents and the liberated ones of their New York–raised daughter. Each major character in this story experiences both **external conflict** (with other people, a government, or society in general) and **internal conflict** (within his or her own mind).

> **E**xternal conflict exists between two people, between a person and a thing, or between a person and society. **Internal conflict** involves opposing forces within a person's mind.
>
> *For more on Conflict, see the Handbook of Literary Terms.*

JULIA ALVAREZ 1077

Summary ▪▪

The story, told from the first-person point of view, focuses on the narrator's immigrant family from the Dominican Republic. The story reveals several interrelated conflicts that arise out of the family's Dominican heritage, the pressure to assimilate into American culture, and the creative ambitions of both the narrator and her mother. The story opens with the narrator's recollections of her mother's nightly "inventing" of time- and labor-saving gadgets and of how the rest of the family scoffed at them. When the narrator is asked to deliver a speech at school, she puts off the writing for weeks. Finally, some lines by Whitman inspire a passionate and personal speech. Although her mother approves, her father is infuriated by the speech, which he sees as dangerously disrespectful of authority. In the story's climax, he tears up the manuscript. The narrator's mother intervenes and helps her daughter construct a new speech saying all the "right" things. The next day, the narrator's revised speech is a success, but this resolution marks the end of her mother's inventing. That night the narrator's contrite father brings home an electric typewriter, which the narrator will use to become a writer, following in her mother's creative tradition.

WRITERS ON WRITING

During her migratory days, Alvarez wrote mostly poetry. She says, "It used to turn me off, the idea of writing something bigger than a poem. But you grow as a writer and you start to imagine other possibilities."

Preteaching Vocabulary

Words to Own

Have students read the Words to Own listed at the bottom of the selection pages. Then, have volunteers act out the meaning of *vengeful* and *reconcile* and illustrate the meaning of *labyrinth* and *misnomers*. After this exercise, have students complete each of the following analogies with the correct Word to Own.

1. cars : convertibles :: errors : [misnomers]
2. jubilant : depressed :: forgiving : [vengeful]
3. ancient : contemporary :: individual : [communal]
4. basement : cellar :: maze : [labyrinth]
5. tragic : comic :: physical : [disembodied]
6. early : preview :: final : [ultimatum]
7. cautious : daring :: subdued : [florid]
8. patients : heal :: enemies : [reconcile]
9. responsibility : negligence :: connection : [disclaimer]
10. poem : haiku :: speech : [eulogy]

RESPONDING TO THE ART

Oscar Pardo uses predominantly dark tones with expressive application, producing a strong feeling of bittersweet love between mother and daughter.

Activity. Point out to students that *Madre e hija* is Spanish for "mother and daughter." Then, have them discuss what the placement of the two figures might suggest about their attitude toward one another. [Possible response: They are not facing each other, so it may indicate that the two of them are not communicating.] Why might this painting have been chosen to illustrate the upcoming story? [Possible response: The girl is looking at her mother, who is not looking at her. It could be hinting that the story will have a daughter who needs more attention from her mother.]

Reaching All Students

Struggling Readers

The motivation for Papi's violent reaction to the narrator's speech (p. 1083) may not be clear to some students. Prepare them for this climax by discussing Papi's experiences in the Dominican Republic, which led the family to immigrate to the United States. One way to do this is to read aloud the paragraph that begins on p. 1080 and ends on p. 1081, and discuss what it is like to live in a politically repressive country.

English Language Learners

Mami struggles with idioms and aphorisms, sometimes mixing parts of two different sayings. (See English Language Learners, p. T1079.) Help students sort out these sayings of Mami's. Then, ask them to watch for other "mixed-up sayings" in the story.

1. "You'll be safely sorry."
2. "Sticks and stones don't break bones."
3. "It takes two to tangle."
4. "He didn't put all his pokers on a back burner."
5. "Necessity is the daughter of invention."

Advanced Learners

As they read, have these students take notes for psychological profiles of Mami and Papi, focusing on this question: What in their experiences and/or personalities causes the two to react very differently to the narrator's speech?

Daughter of Invention

Julia Alvarez

She wanted to invent something, my mother. There was a period after we arrived in this country, until five or so years later, when my mother was inventing. They were never pressing, global needs she was addressing with her pencil and pad. She would have said that was for men to do, rockets and engines that ran on gasoline and turned the wheels of the world. She was just fussing with little house things, don't mind her.

She always invented at night, after settling her house down. On his side of the bed my father would be conked out for an hour already, his Spanish newspaper draped over his chest, his glasses, propped up on his bedside table, looking out eerily at the darkened room like a disembodied guard. But in her lighted corner, like some devoted scholar burning the midnight oil, my mother was inventing, sheets pulled to her lap, pillows propped up behind her, her reading glasses riding the bridge of her nose like a schoolmarm's. On her lap lay one of those innumerable pads of paper my father always brought home from his office, compliments of some pharmaceutical company, advertising tranquilizers or antibiotics or skin cream; in her other hand, my mother held a pencil that looked like a pen with a little cylinder of lead inside. She would work on a sketch of something familiar, but drawn at such close range so she could attach a special nozzle or handier handle, the thing looked peculiar. Once, I mistook the spiral of a corkscrew for a nautilus shell, but it could just as well have been a galaxy forming.

It was the only time all day we'd catch her sitting down, for she herself was living proof of the *perpetuum mobile*[1] machine so many inventors had sought over the ages. My sisters and I would seek her out now when she seemed to have a moment to talk to us: We were having trouble at

1. *perpetuum mobile* (per·pe′too·əm mo′bi·le): Latin for "perpetual motion."

Madre e hija (1995) by Oscar Pardo. Pastel on paper (19″ × 12½″). Courtesy of the artist.

school or we wanted her to persuade my father to give us permission to go into the city or to a shopping mall or a movie—in broad daylight! My mother would wave us out of her room. "The problem with you girls . . ." I can tell you right now what the problem always boiled down to: We wanted to become Americans and my father—and my mother, at first—would have none of it.

"You girls are going to drive me crazy!" She always threatened if we kept nagging. "When I end up in Bellevue,[2] you'll be safely sorry!"

She spoke in English when she argued with us, even though, in a matter of months, her daughters were the fluent ones. Her English was much better than my father's, but it was still a mishmash of mixed-up idioms and sayings that showed she was "green behind the ears," as she called it.

If my sisters and I tried to get her to talk in Spanish, she'd snap, "When in Rome, do unto the Romans . . ."

I had become the spokesman for my sisters, and I would stand my ground in that bedroom. "We're not going to that school anymore, Mami!"

"You have to." Her eyes would widen with worry. "In this country, it is against the law not to go to school. You want us to get thrown out?"

"You want us to get killed? Those kids were throwing stones today!"

"Sticks and stones don't break bones . . ." she chanted. I could tell, though, by the look on her face, it was as if one of those stones the kids had aimed at us had hit her. But she always pretended we were at fault. "What did you do to provoke them? It takes two to tangle, you know."

"Thanks, thanks a lot, Mom!" I'd storm out of that room and into mine. I never called her *Mom* except when I wanted her to feel how much she had failed us in this country. She was a good enough Mami, fussing and scolding and giving advice, but a terrible girlfriend parent, a real failure of a Mom.

Back she'd go to her pencil and pad, scribbling and tsking and tearing off paper, finally giving up,

2. **Bellevue:** large New York City hospital known for its psychiatric department.

WORDS TO OWN

disembodied (dis′im·bäd′ēd) v. used as *adj.*: separated from the body.

A Reading Skills and Strategies

Drawing Inferences About Characters

? What inferences can you make about the narrator's mother from this paragraph? [She has a traditional view of male/female roles in the world, yet she has a longing to achieve something of lasting value.]

B English Language Learners

Idioms

? What idioms or sayings does the narrator's mother mangle or combine in these paragraphs? ["You'll be sorry" combined with "Better safe than sorry"; "green" (meaning inexperienced) with "Wet behind the ears"; "When in Rome, do as the Romans do" with "Do unto others as you would have them do unto you."]

C Elements of Literature

Conflict

? What internal conflict is Mami faced with? [She loves her daughters and is hurt by the hostility they face, but she feels she must "teach" them to get along because she cannot control how others treat them.]

D English Language Learners

Idioms

Explain that Mami's expression "It takes two to tangle" is a mixed-up version of "It takes two to tango," meaning that both people usually contribute to a conflict.

E Reading Skills and Strategies

Comparing and Contrasting

? What does the narrator say is the difference between a Mami and a Mom? [A Mami is a traditional mother who corrects her children and gives them guidance, but a Mom is more like a friend who offers support.]

Using Students' Strengths

Verbal Learners

Provide these students with a dictionary of aphorisms or clichés. Ask them to choose a few and create fractured versions of them, as Mami does unintentionally. Suggest that students change key words or substitute rhyming words for one or more words. Have students explain how the changes affect the meanings of the sayings.

Logical/Mathematical Learners

Ask students to work independently to come up with an idea for an original invention that might be used to solve a household problem that exists today. Have them present their ideas to the class, using scale drawings or other visual aids. After students have read the story, review the narrator's descriptions of Mami's invention ideas, and ask students to compare them with their own ideas.

Intrapersonal Learners

Ask students to imagine themselves as the narrator and to chart their emotional responses at key moments in the story. For example, how would they feel when Mami says, "It takes two to tangle"? Or, how would they feel if they were chosen to give a speech in appreciation of teachers?

Ⓐ English Language Learners
Idioms

❓ To "butter up someone" is to say nice things to put that person in a good mood. Why does Mami butter up the narrator? [Mami wants the narrator to like her invention.]

Ⓑ Reading Skills and Strategies
Responding to the Text

❓ What do you think of Mami's inventions? [Possible responses: They are clever, impractical, unimportant.] What do you think of her daughters' responses to them? [Possible responses: It's typical for children to disparage their parents' ideas; they should have been more careful of their mother's feelings.] Be sure students know that Thomas Edison invented the light bulb and Benjamin Franklin discovered that lightning is electricity.

Ⓒ Reading Skills and Strategies
Drawing Inferences About Characters

❓ What does Mami's reaction to the narrator's lack of enthusiasm tell you about Mami? [She does not have as much self-confidence as she seems to on the surface.]

Ⓓ Elements of Literature
Conflict

❓ How do the mother's and the daughters' needs come into conflict? [Possible response: The mother has a need to create. Creating takes time, which the daughters feel she should spend helping them adjust to their new life.]

and taking up her *New York Times.* Some nights, though, she'd get a good idea, and she'd rush into my room, a flushed look on her face, her tablet of paper in her hand, a cursory knock on the door she'd just thrown open: "Do I have something to show you, Cukita!"

This was my time to myself, after I'd finished my homework, while my sisters were still downstairs watching TV in the basement. Hunched over my small desk, the overhead light turned off, my lamp shining poignantly on my paper, the rest of the room in warm, soft, uncreated darkness, I wrote my secret poems in my new language.

"You're going to ruin your eyes!" My mother would storm into my room, turning on the overly bright overhead light, scaring off whatever shy passion I had just begun coaxing out of a <u>labyrinth</u> of feelings with the blue thread of my writing.

"Oh Mami!" I'd cry out, my eyes blinking up at her. "I'm writing."

"Ay, Cukita." That was her <u>communal</u> pet name for whoever was in her favor. "Cukita, when I make a million, I'll buy you your very own typewriter." (I'd been nagging my mother for one just like the one father had bought her to do his order forms at home.) "Gravy on the turkey" was what she called it when someone was buttering her up. She'd butter and pour. "I'll hire you your very own typist."

Down she'd plop on my bed and hold out her pad to me. "Take a guess, Cukita?" I'd study her rough sketch a moment: soap sprayed from the nozzle head of a shower when you turned the knob a certain way? Coffee with creamer already mixed in? Time-released water capsules for your plants when you were away? A key chain with a timer that would go off when your parking meter was about to expire? (The ticking would help you find your keys easily if you mislaid them.) The famous one, famous only in hindsight, was the stick person dragging a square by a rope—a suitcase with wheels? "Oh, of course," we'd humor her. "What every household needs: a shower like a car wash, keys ticking like a bomb, luggage on a leash!" By now, as you can see, it'd become something of a family joke, our Thomas Edison Mami, our Benjamin Franklin Mom.

Her face would fall. "Come on now! Use your head." One more wrong guess, and she'd tell me,

pressing with her pencil point the different highlights of this incredible new wonder. "Remember that time we took the car to Bear Mountain, and we re-ah-lized that we had forgotten to pack an opener with our pick-a-nick?" (We kept correcting her, but she insisted this is how it should be said.) "When we were ready to eat we didn't have any way to open the refreshments cans?" (This before fliptop lids, which she claimed had crossed her mind.) "You know what this is now?" A shake of my head. "Is a car bumper, but see this part is a removable can opener. So simple and yet so necessary, no?"

"Yeah, Mami. You should patent it." I'd shrug. She'd tear off the scratch paper and fold it, carefully, corner to corner, as if she were going to save it. But then, she'd toss it in the wastebasket on her way out of the room and give a little laugh like a <u>disclaimer</u>. "It's half of one or two dozen of another . . ."

I suppose none of her daughters was very encouraging. We resented her spending time on those dumb inventions. Here, we were trying to fit in America among Americans; we needed help figuring out who we were, why these Irish kids whose grandparents were micks two generations ago, why they were calling us spics. Why had we come to the country in the first place? Important, crucial, final things, you see, and here was our own mother, who didn't have a second to help us puzzle any of this out, inventing gadgets to make life easier for American moms. Why, it seemed as if she were arming our own enemy against us!

One time, she did have a moment of triumph. Every night, she liked to read *The New York Times* in bed before turning off her light, to see what the Americans were up to. One night, she let out a yelp to wake up my father beside her, bolt upright, reaching for his glasses which, in his haste, he knocked across the room. *"Que pasa? Que pasa?"*³ What is wrong? There was terror in

---

3. *Que pasa?* (kā pä'sä): Spanish for "What's going on?"

- -

WORDS TO OWN

labyrinth (lab'ə·rinth') *n.*: place full of intricate passageways; maze.

communal (kə·myōō'nəl) *adj.*: belonging to an entire group (in this case, Mami's daughters).

disclaimer (dis·klām'ər) *n.*: a giving up of a claim or connection.

- -

Getting Students Involved

Cooperative Learning

Student Counselors. Ask groups of four to six students to think about the issues that Mami's daughters face as immigrants. What advice would they give the girls? Have each group first draw up a list of questions and issues taken both from the story and from their own experiences in new situations. Then, ask each

group to write the script of a conversation between one or more of the characters. Some members of the group can act out the conversation for the class. Remind students to take into account the interests and skills of group members when deciding who will do what.

Exchanging Letters. After students have read the story, ask them to write a letter that the narrator might send to a relative or friend in the Dominican Republic. The letter should briefly describe the conflict the narrator has with her father about her speech. Then, have students assume the persona of the letter's recipient and write back to the narrator with advice.

his voice, fear she'd seen in his eyes in the Dominican Republic before we left. We were being watched there; he was being followed; he and mother had often exchanged those looks. They could not talk, of course, though they must have whispered to each other in fear at night in the dark bed. Now in America, he was safe, a success even; his Centro Medico in Brooklyn was thronged with the sick and the homesick. But in dreams, he went back to those awful days and long nights, and my mother's screams confirmed his secret fear: We had not gotten away after all; they had come for us at last.

"Ay, Papi, I'm sorry. Go back to sleep, Cukito. It's nothing, nothing really." My mother held up the *Times* for him to squint at the small print, back page headline, one hand tapping all over the top of the bedside table for his glasses, the other rubbing his eyes to wakefulness.

"Remember, remember how I showed you that suitcase with little wheels so we would not have to carry those heavy bags when we traveled? Someone stole my idea and made a million!" She shook the paper in his face. She shook the paper in all our faces that night. "See! See! This man was no *bobo*![4] He didn't put all his pokers on a back burner. I kept telling you, one of these days my ship would pass me by in the night!" She wagged her finger at my sisters and my father and me, laughing all the while, one of those eerie laughs crazy people in movies laugh. We had congregated in her room to hear the good news she'd been yelling down the stairs, and now we eyed her and each other. I suppose we were all thinking the same thing: Wouldn't it be weird and sad if Mami did end up in Bellevue as she'd always threatened she might?

"*Ya, ya*! Enough!" She waved us out of her room at last. "There is no use trying to drink spilt milk, that's for sure."

It was the suitcase rollers that stopped my mother's hand; she had weather vaned a minor brainstorm. She would have to start taking herself seriously. That blocked the free play of her ingenuity. Besides, she had also begun working at my father's office, and at night, she was too tired and busy filling in columns with how much money they had made that day to be fooling with gadgets!

4. *bobo*: Spanish for "fool."

She did take up her pencil and pad one last time to help me out. In ninth grade, I was chosen by my English teacher, Sister Mary Joseph, to deliver the teacher's day address at the school assembly. Back in the Dominican Republic, I was a terrible student. No one could ever get me to sit down to a book. But in New York, I needed to settle somewhere, and the natives were unfriendly, the country inhospitable, so I took root in the language. By high school, the nuns were reading my stories and compositions out loud to my classmates as examples of imagination at work.

This time my imagination jammed. At first I didn't want and then I couldn't seem to write that speech. I suppose I should have thought of it as a "great honor," as my father called it. But I was mortified. I still had a pronounced lilt to my accent, and I did not like to speak in public, subjecting myself to my classmates' ridicule. Recently, they had begun to warm toward my sisters and me, and it took no great figuring to see that to deliver a eulogy for a convent full of crazy, old overweight nuns was no way to endear myself to the members of my class.

But I didn't know how to get out of it. Week after week, I'd sit down, hoping to polish off some quick, noncommittal little speech. I couldn't get anything down.

The weekend before our Monday morning assembly I went into a panic. My mother would just have to call in and say I was in the hospital, in a coma. I was in the Dominican Republic. Yeah, that was it! Recently, my father had been talking about going back home to live.

My mother tried to calm me down. "Just remember how Mister Lincoln couldn't think of anything to say at the Gettysburg, but then, Bang! 'Four score and once upon a time ago,'" she began reciting. Her version of history was half invention and half truths and whatever else she needed to prove a point. "Something is going to come if you just relax. You'll see, like the Americans say, 'Necessity is the daughter of invention.' I'll help you."

All weekend, she kept coming into my room with help. "Please, Mami, just leave me alone, please," I pleaded with her. But I'd get rid of the

---

WORDS TO OWN

eulogy (yoo′lə·jē) *n.*: public speech of praise.

E **Critical Thinking**

E **Critical Thinking**
Speculating
? Who might have been watching and following Papi in the Dominican Republic and why? [Possible response: Government agents or the police might have been watching Papi because he was suspected of anti-government opinions.]

F **English Language Learners**
Idioms/Figurative Language
Discuss the meanings of the words *weather vaned* and *brainstorm*. Tell students that *weather vaned* is a verb created by the author from the noun *weather vane* to form an image that aptly describes what Mami did: She pointed her attention in the direction in which a *brainstorm*, or idea, was brewing. In this context a *brainstorm* means a "good new idea."

G **Struggling Readers**
Summarizing
? Why does Mami stop inventing? [Possible response: The fact that she actually had thought of a marketable idea frightens her, and her work at her husband's office takes up too much time.]

H **Vocabulary Note**
The Prefix *non-*
The prefix *non-* comes from the Latin word for "not." What kind of speech would a noncommittal one be? [Possible answers: A speech that does not contain a strong commitment to any idea or course of action; a speech lacking passion or emotional involvement on the part of the speaker.]

Taking a Second Look

Review: Cause and Effect

A cause makes something happen. An effect is what happens as a result of the cause. Remind students that sometimes an author states a cause without showing the effect, and sometimes an author states an effect without explaining the cause. Readers must infer the probable cause or effect. Doing so may help them understand the story more fully.

Activities

1. Sometimes cause-and-effect relationships are self-perpetuating: one event causes another, which causes the first to happen again. Have students draw a circular diagram that shows how the narrator's interest in the English language stems from her isolation and could lead to more isolation.

2. Have students discuss what role fear plays as a cause in the story.

goose only to have to contend with the gander. My father kept poking his head in the door just to see if I had "fulfilled my obligations," a phrase he'd used when we were a little younger, and he'd check to see whether we had gone to the bathroom before a car trip. Several times that weekend around the supper table, he'd recite his valedictorian speech from when he graduated from high school. He'd give me pointers on delivery, on the great orators and their tricks. (Humbleness and praise and falling silent with great emotion were his favorites.)

My mother sat across the table, the only one who seemed to be listening to him. My sisters and I were forgetting a lot of our Spanish, and my father's formal, <u>florid</u> diction was even harder to understand. But my mother smiled softly to herself, and turned the Lazy Susan at the center of the table around and around as if it were the prime mover,[5] the first gear of attention.

That Sunday evening, I was reading some poetry to get myself inspired: Whitman in an old book with an engraved cover my father had picked up in a thrift shop next to his office a few weeks back. "I celebrate myself and sing myself . . ." "He most honors my style who learns under it to destroy the teacher." The poet's words shocked and thrilled me. I had gotten used to the nuns, a literature of appropriate sentiments, poems with a message, expurgated texts. But here was a flesh and blood man, belching and laughing and sweating in poems. "Who touches this book touches a man."

That night, at last, I started to write, recklessly, three, five pages, looking up once only to see my father passing by the hall on tiptoe. When I was done, I read over my words, and my eyes filled. I finally sounded like myself in English!

As soon as I had finished that first draft, I called my mother to my room. She listened attentively, as she had to my father's speech, and in the end, her eyes were glistening too. Her face was soft and warm and proud. "That is a beautiful, beautiful speech, Cukita. I want for your father to hear it before he goes to sleep. Then I will type it for you, all right?"

Down the hall we went, the two of us, faces

5. **prime mover:** in philosophy, the self-moved being that is the source of all motion; in machinery, the source of power, such as a windmill or an engine.

1082 CONTEMPORARY LITERATURE

flushed with accomplishment. Into the master bedroom where my father was propped up on his pillows, still awake, reading the Dominican papers, already days old. He had become interested in his country's fate again. The dictatorship had been toppled. The interim government was going to hold the first free elections in thirty years. There was still some question in his mind whether or not we might want to move back. History was in the making, freedom and hope were in the air again! But my mother had gotten used to the life here. She did not want to go back to the old country where she was only a wife and a mother (and a failed one at that, since she had never had the required son). She did not come straight out and disagree with my father's plans. Instead, she fussed with him about reading the papers in bed, soiling those sheets with those poorly printed, foreign tabloids. "*The Times* is not that bad!" she'd claim if my father tried to humor her by saying they shared the same dirty habit.

The minute my father saw my mother and me, filing in, he put his paper down, and his face brightened as if at long last his wife had delivered a son, and that was the news we were bringing him. His teeth were already grinning from the glass of water next to his bedside lamp, so he lisped when he said, "Eh-speech, eh-speech!"

"It is so beautiful, Papi," my mother previewed him, turning the sound off on his TV. She sat down at the foot of the bed. I stood before both of them, blocking their view of the soldiers in helicopters landing amid silenced gun reports and explosions. A few weeks ago it had been the shores of the Dominican Republic. Now it was the jungles of Southeast Asia they were saving. My mother gave me the nod to begin reading.

I didn't need much encouragement. I put my nose to the fire, as my mother would have said, and read from start to finish without looking up. When I was done, I was a little embarrassed at my pride in my own words. I pretended to quibble with a phrase or two I was sure I'd be talked out of changing. I looked questioningly to my mother. Her face was radiant. She turned to share her pride with my father.

WORDS TO OWN
florid (flôr′id) *adj.*: showy.

Skill Link

Uno (1920) by Alejandro Xul Solar. Watercolor and pencil on paper on card (5⁹⁄₃₂″ × 7½″).

But the expression on his face shocked us both. His toothless mouth had collapsed into a dark zero. His eyes glared at me, then shifted to my mother, accusingly. In barely audible Spanish, as if secret microphones or informers were all about, he whispered, "You will permit her to read *that*?"

My mother's eyebrows shot up, her mouth fell open. In the old country, any whisper of a challenge to authority could bring the secret police in their black V.W.'s. But this was America. People could say what they thought. "What is wrong with her speech?" my mother questioned him.

"What ees wrrrong with her eh-speech?" My father wagged his head at her. His anger was always more frightening in his broken English. As if he had mutilated the language in his fury—and now there was nothing to stand between us and his raw, dumb anger. "What is wrong? I will tell you what is wrong. It shows no gratitude. It is boastful. 'I celebrate myself'? 'The best student learns to destroy the teacher'?" He mocked my plagiarized words. "That is insubordinate. It is improper. It is

disrespecting of her teachers—" In his anger he had forgotten his fear of lurking spies: Each wrong he voiced was a decibel higher than the last outrage. Finally, he was yelling at me, "As your father, I forbid you to say that eh-speech!"

My mother leapt to her feet, a sign always that she was about to make a speech or deliver an <u>ultimatum</u>. She was a small woman, and she spoke all her pronouncements standing up, either for more protection or as a carry-over from her girlhood in convent schools where one asked for, and literally took, the floor in order to speak. She stood by my side, shoulder to shoulder; we looked down at my father. "That is no tone of voice, Eduardo—" she began.

By now, my father was truly furious. I suppose it was bad enough I was rebelling, but here was

<hr>

WORDS TO OWN
ultimatum (ul′tə·māt′əm) *n.:* last offer; final proposition.

<hr>

JULIA ALVAREZ **1083**

RESPONDING TO THE ART
Alejandro Xul Solar (1888–1963), an Argentine painter, was a highly unconventional and imaginative artist who helped to introduce the avant-garde in Argentina. In works like *Uno,* Xul Solar made use of extravagant colors and fantastic, often mystical, forms to reveal the spiritual side of human nature and to picture heightened states of awareness.
Activity. Ask students what they see in the picture. [Possible responses: a human figure or a robot; candles; abstract shapes.] **What emotion or idea is the human figure meant to suggest?** [Possible responses: solitude, assertiveness, isolation, hope.] **Which character in the story does the figure suggest?** [Possible response: The father or the daughter because the figure stands alone raising its arms, perhaps in protest.]

D Reading Skills and Strategies
Connecting with the Text
❓ What experiences have you had with people who responded differently from what you expected to something you did or said? [Students may mention someone taking offense at an innocent remark or getting unexpected praise for work they didn't think was very good.]

E Elements of Literature
Conflict
❓ What internal conflict of Papi's is evident here? [He came to the United States to escape from a repressive, authoritarian political regime, but he has internalized some of the attitudes of such a regime.]

Crossing the Curriculum

Geography/History
Ask students to do independent research on the Dominican Republic, especially the history of the country just before and after the time in which "Daughter of Invention" is set (probably 1961 or 1962). Discuss as a class the information students collect, and ask them to write a short paragraph describing what effect the political events could have had on the narrator's father. Follow up by asking students to find out about recent events in that country.

Spanish
Ask students who speak or have studied Spanish to come up with a list of proverbs and folk sayings in Spanish and to provide translations for students who do not understand the language. Students might have some fun imagining how a Spanish language learner might mix up some of these sayings, as Mami mixes up English sayings.

LITERATURE AND TECHNOLOGY

Patently American Inventions

Have an invention of your own you'd like to protect? Consider patenting it. A U.S. patent gives you the right to exclude all others from making, using, or selling your invention within the United States for a limited number of years. To start, put your idea in writing, illustrate your device or process, and sign and date the document (use indelible ink). But before you reach for pad and pen, you might want to learn a little more about patents and inventions.

Patents are granted by the U.S. Patent and Trademark Office, in Arlington, Virginia. The Patent Office is flooded with over 150,000 applications a year, each of which takes about two years to process. If you can convince the patent officer that your invention is (1) new, (2) useful, and (3) original, a patent is yours. But be warned: You'll need deep pockets, since patent fees typically exceed $1,000.

Patented inventions we haven't seen in stores. Anyone wanting an afternoon's—or a lifetime's—entertainment could do worse than browse through the five million patents on record at the Patent Office. Ideas on record include these:

- eye protectors for chickens
- suspenders that convert into ropes in case the wearer needs to escape a burning building
- a device combining a plow and a gun
- a locket for storing used chewing gum
- a wake-up device consisting of suspended wood blocks that fall on the sleeper's face
- a device to create or maintain dimples
- balloons powered by large birds
- farms that rest on giant saucers floating in the sea

my mother joining forces with me. Soon he would be surrounded by a house full of independent American women. He too leapt from his bed, throwing off his covers. The Spanish newspapers flew across the room. He snatched my speech out of my hands, held it before my panicked eyes, a <u>vengeful</u>, mad look in his own, and then once, twice, three, four, countless times, he tore my prize into shreds.

"Are you crazy?" My mother lunged at him. "Have you gone mad? That is her speech for tomorrow you have torn up!"

"Have *you* gone mad?" He shook her away. "You were going to let her read that . . . that insult to her teachers?"

"Insult to her teachers!" My mother's face had

crumpled up like a piece of paper. On it was written a love note to my father. Ever since they had come to this country, their life together was a constant war. "This is America, Papi, America!" she reminded him now. "You are not in a savage country any more!"

I was on my knees, weeping wildly, collecting all the little pieces of my speech, hoping that I could put it back together before the assembly tomorrow morning. But not even a sibyl[6] could

6. **sibyl** (sib′əl): in ancient Greece and Rome, a woman who foretold the future.

WORDS TO OWN
vengeful (venj′fəl) *adj.*: intent on revenge.

Making the Connections

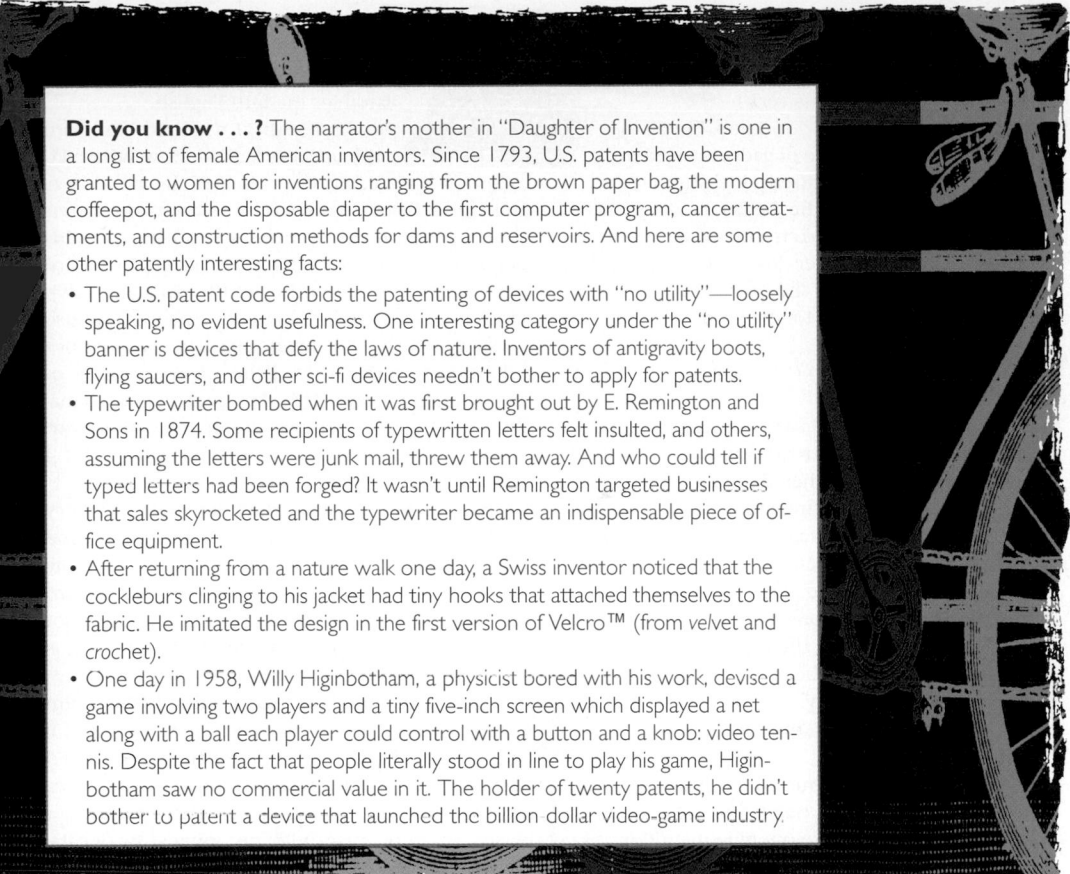

Did you know . . . ? The narrator's mother in "Daughter of Invention" is one in a long list of female American inventors. Since 1793, U.S. patents have been granted to women for inventions ranging from the brown paper bag, the modern coffeepot, and the disposable diaper to the first computer program, cancer treatments, and construction methods for dams and reservoirs. And here are some other patently interesting facts:

• The U.S. patent code forbids the patenting of devices with "no utility"—loosely speaking, no evident usefulness. One interesting category under the "no utility" banner is devices that defy the laws of nature. Inventors of antigravity boots, flying saucers, and other sci-fi devices needn't bother to apply for patents.

• The typewriter bombed when it was first brought out by E. Remington and Sons in 1874. Some recipients of typewritten letters felt insulted, and others, assuming the letters were junk mail, threw them away. And who could tell if typed letters had been forged? It wasn't until Remington targeted businesses that sales skyrocketed and the typewriter became an indispensable piece of office equipment.

• After returning from a nature walk one day, a Swiss inventor noticed that the cockleburs clinging to his jacket had tiny hooks that attached themselves to the fabric. He imitated the design in the first version of Velcro™ (from *velvet* and *crochet*).

• One day in 1958, Willy Higinbotham, a physicist bored with his work, devised a game involving two players and a tiny five-inch screen which displayed a net along with a ball each player could control with a button and a knob: video tennis. Despite the fact that people literally stood in line to play his game, Higinbotham saw no commercial value in it. The holder of twenty patents, he didn't bother to patent a device that launched the billion-dollar video-game industry.

B Humanities Connections
Francisco Goya
Though Goya (1746–1828) painted portraits of the Spanish royal family, he sympathized with the ideals of the French Revolution. One of his greatest paintings, *The Third of May,* showing the execution of a group of Madrid citizens, makes a dramatic statement about political oppression. It is not surprising that this artist would be a favorite of Papi's.

C Historical Connections
Life Under Trujillo
During Trujillo's regime, the people of the Dominican Republic had virtually no civil or political freedom—dissent and even suspected opposition were dealt with harshly. The mention of Trujillo's nickname probably evokes memories of oppression, terror, and brutality in the narrator's father.

have made sense of all those scattered pieces of paper. All hope was lost. "He broke it, he broke it," I moaned as I picked up a handful of pieces.

Probably, if I had thought a moment about it, I would not have done what I did next. I would have realized my father had lost brothers and comrades to the dictator Trujillo.[7] For the rest of his life, he would be haunted by blood in the streets and late night disappearances. Even after he had been in the states for years, he jumped if a black Volkswagen passed him on the street. He feared anyone in uniform: the meter maid giving out parking tickets, a museum guard approaching to tell him not to touch his favorite Goya at the Metropolitan.[8] **B**

I took a handful of the scraps I had gathered, stood up, and hurled them in his face. "Chapita!" I said in a low, ugly whisper. "You're just another Chapita!"

It took my father only a moment to register the hated nickname of our dictator, and he was after me. Down the halls we raced, but I was quicker than he and made it to my room just in time to lock the door as my father threw his weight **C**

---

7. **Trujillo** (trōō·hē′yō): Rafael Leonidas Trujillo Molina, general who took over as president of the Dominican Republic and ruled oppressively from 1930 to 1938 and from 1942 until he was assassinated in 1961.

8. **Goya . . . Metropolitan:** a painting by the Spanish artist Francisco José de Goya y Lucientes at the Metropolitan Museum of Art in New York City.

JULIA ALVAREZ 1085

Assessing Learning

Check Test: Multiple Choice
1. The narrator's family emigrated from (a) Puerto Rico. (b) Colombia. (c) Mexico. (d) the Dominican Republic. [d]
2. The narrator's father runs (a) a large law office. (b) an elementary school. (c) a medical center. (d) a small restaurant. [c]
3. The narrator and her sister attend a (a) public school. (b) parochial school. (c) small school in the country. (d) prep school. [b]

4. The narrator's mother designs her inventions (a) at the kitchen table. (b) using the computer. (c) with pencil and paper. (d) at a drafting table. [c]
5. The narrator's mother is continually getting (a) clichés wrong. (b) people's names wrong. (c) inventions confused. (d) countries mixed up. [a]

Informal Assessment
Self Assessment. Ask students to assess their own understanding of the story by considering these questions:
• Why do you think this story was included in this collection?
• Why was this story used to discuss the literary element of conflict?
• Do you understand all the vocabulary words underlined in this story?

A Elements of Literature
Conflict

? What conflict between the narrator and her mother is resolved here? [Possible response: The narrator and her mother, who was once too absorbed in her own invention ideas to notice when her daughter needed her support, are brought closer together when Papi destroys the speech.]

B Struggling Readers
Using Graphic Aids

Have students make a three-column chart to show the conflicts explored in this story. The first column should list all the conflicts. The second should state whether a conflict is external or internal. The third column should state briefly the resolution.

C Reading Skills and Strategies
Drawing Inferences About Characters

? What does Papi's gift suggest about his new attitude toward his daughter? [Possible responses: The gift is his way of showing that he knows the speech he destroyed was very important to her; it shows that although he was appalled by the disrespectful tone he perceived in the speech, he also recognizes her talent and wants to nurture it with the typewriter.]

D Critical Thinking
Interpreting

? What does the narrator's mother pass on to her? What does the narrator do with her gift? [Possible responses: Her mother passes on her creativity or inventiveness. The narrator uses her gift to create ideas for the stories, such as this one, that she writes.]

against it. He called down curses on my head, ordered me on his authority as my father to open that door this very instant! He throttled that doorknob, but all to no avail. My mother's love of gadgets saved my hide that night. She had hired a locksmith to install good locks on all the bedroom doors after our house had been broken into while we were away the previous summer. In case burglars broke in again, and we were in the house, they'd have a second round of locks to contend with before they got to us.

"Eduardo," she tried to calm him down. "Don't you ruin my new locks."

He finally did calm down, his anger spent. I heard their footsteps retreating down the hall. I heard their door close, the clicking of their lock. Then, muffled voices, my mother's peaking in anger, in persuasion, my father's deep murmurs of explanation and of self-defense. At last, the house fell silent, before I heard, far off, the gun blasts and explosions, the serious, self-important voices of newscasters reporting their TV war.

A little while later, there was a quiet knock at my door, followed by a tentative attempt at the doorknob. "Cukita?" my mother whispered. "Open up, Cukita."

"Go away," I wailed, but we both knew I was glad she was there, and I needed only a moment's protest to save face before opening that door.

What we ended up doing that night was putting together a speech at the last moment. Two brief pages of stale compliments and the polite commonplaces on teachers, wrought by necessity without much invention by mother for daughter late into the night in the basement on the pad of paper and with the same pencil she had once used for her own inventions, for I was too upset to compose the speech myself. After it was drafted, she typed it up while I stood by, correcting her <u>misnomers</u> and mis-sayings.

She was so very proud of herself when I came home the next day with the success story of the assembly. The nuns had been flattered, the audience had stood up and given "our devoted teachers a standing ovation," what my mother had suggested they do at the end of my speech.

She clapped her hands together as I recreated the moment for her. "I stole that from your father's speech, remember? Remember how he put that in at the end?" She quoted him in Spanish, then translated for me into English.

That night, I watched him from the upstairs hall window where I'd retreated the minute I heard his car pull up in front of our house. Slowly, my father came up the driveway, a grim expression on his face as he grappled with a large, heavy cardboard box. At the front door, he set the package down carefully and patted all his pockets for his house keys—precisely why my mother had invented her ticking key chain. I heard the snapping open of the locks downstairs. Heard as he struggled to maneuver the box through the narrow doorway. Then, he called my name several times. But I would not answer him.

"My daughter, your father, he love you very much," he explained from the bottom of the stairs. "He just want to protect you." Finally, my mother came up and pleaded with me to go down and <u>reconcile</u> with him. "Your father did not mean to harm. You must pardon him. Always it is better to let bygones be forgotten, no?"

I guess she was right. Downstairs, I found him setting up a brand new electric typewriter on the kitchen table. It was even better than the one I'd been begging to get like my mother's. My father had outdone himself with all the extra features: a plastic carrying case with my initials, in decals, below the handle, a brace to lift the paper upright while I typed, an erase cartridge, an automatic margin tab, a plastic hood like a toaster cover to keep the dust away. Not even my mother, I think, could have invented such a machine!

But her inventing days were over just as mine were starting up with my schoolwide success. That's why I've always thought of that speech my mother wrote for me as her last invention rather than the suitcase rollers everyone else in the family remembers. It was as if she had passed on to me her pencil and pad and said, "Okay, Cukita, here's the buck. You give it a shot."

WORDS TO OWN

misnomers (mis·nō'merz) *n. pl.:* wrong terms or names.
reconcile (rek'ən·sīl') *v.:* to make peace.

1086 CONTEMPORARY LITERATURE

MAKING MEANINGS

First Thoughts

1. Did your feelings about any of the characters change as you read the story? Explain.

Shaping Interpretations

2. The narrator wants to use Whitman's words: "He most honors my style who learns under it to destroy the teacher" (page 1082). How does the girl's father interpret the words? What do you think Whitman was really saying?

3. The narrator says, "She was a good enough Mami, fussing and scolding and giving advice, but a terrible girlfriend parent, a real failure of a Mom" (page 1079). What does the narrator mean?

4. What **conflicts** does the father face in this story? How does the narrator address the conflicts?

5. Review the notes you made while reading, and **compare** and **contrast** how Cukita, Mami, and Papi have adjusted to life in the United States. What adjustments occur over the course of the story?

Extending the Text

6. In this story, the father's experience of politics in his country of origin clearly influences his behavior in the United States. Can you identify other contemporary or past immigrants who have vivid memories of politics in their native lands?

Reading Check

a. Which of the mother's ideas for an invention is a huge success for somebody else?

b. Why did the daughters resent the time the mother spent on inventions?

c. The narrator's mother is fond of English-language **aphorisms** (brief, wise sayings), but she gets them slightly wrong. Provide corrected versions of some of her sayings.

d. How does the daughter insult her father after he destroys her speech?

CHOICES:
Building Your Portfolio

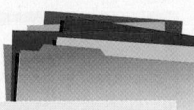

Writer's Notebook
1. Collecting Ideas for an Evaluation

Readers often evaluate a story according to the power of its conflicts. "Daughter of Invention" offers a variety of **external** and **internal conflicts**. Make a four-column chart to help organize your thoughts about them. In the first column, list all the conflicts you can identify, such as interpersonal, social, cultural, and political conflicts. In the second column, tell who is involved in each conflict: for example, mother/daughter, father/daughter, husband/wife. In the third column, describe the resolution—if any—of each conflict in the story. In the fourth column, evaluate each conflict's power to hold your interest and to evoke emotions and thoughts. Save your chart for possible use in the Writer's Workshop on page 1181.

Interpreting a Title
2. Resonance

A good **title** often has what might be called resonance—it echoes with meaning. In an essay, explain how Alvarez's title touches on (a) a humorous detail of the story, (b) a **theme** of the story, and (c) the **climax** of the story.

Creative Writing /
Speaking and Listening
3. "All these I feel or am"

The narrator's Walt Whitman–inspired speech ends up as little pieces of paper on the floor. Reread the Whitman selections in this book (beginning on page 352), and then write the first page of the speech the narrator might have written. You can use the lines she uses or any other appropriate Whitman lines. If you like, read the opening of your speech to the class.

JULIA ALVAREZ 1087

CHOICES:
Building Your Portfolio

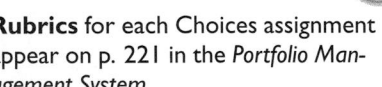

1. Writer's Notebook
Remind students to use their work as prewriting for the Writer's Workshop on p. 1181.

2. Interpreting a Title Discuss the substitution of *daughter* in the expression "Necessity is the mother of invention" and the fact that Cukita feels she has inherited her creativity from Mami.

3. Creative Writing/Speaking and Listening Remind students to consider the intended audience for the speech.

Reading Check

a. luggage with wheels

b. They think she cares more about inventions than about helping them adjust.

c. Sample responses: "It's half of one or two dozen of another"—Six of one, half-dozen of another; "There is no use trying to drink spilt milk"—There is no use crying over spilt milk.

d. She throws the paper scraps in his face and calls him "Chapita," the nickname of the dictator Trujillo.

MAKING MEANINGS

First Thoughts [Respond]

1. Possible responses: At first, Mami seems selfish and unconcerned, but in the end, she shows concern by helping her daughter and husband understand one another and by helping her daughter write the speech.

Shaping Interpretations [Interpret]

2. Papi thinks the words insult teachers by expressing contempt for them. Whitman may have been saying that a good teacher gives students the skills to think independently.

3. Possible response: that her mother was fine as a traditional, stern Mami in the Dominican Republic but was unable to be the helpful, supportive Mom they needed in the United States.

4. His traditional values conflict with his daughter's need to express her own ideas; his family's desire to remain in the United States conflicts with his own yearnings to return to the Dominican Republic. She relies on her mother to be a go-between.

5. Cukita is accepted at school, develops an appreciation for Whitman's poetry, and gains a better understanding of her parents; Mami becomes more of a "Mom" for her daughter; Papi learns to acknowledge and support his daughter's dreams.

Extending the Text [Synthesize]

6. Students may cite immigrants from countries that have experienced turmoil, including Vietnam, Cambodia, Bosnia.

Grading Timesaver

Rubrics for each Choices assignment appear on p. 221 in the *Portfolio Management System*.

T1087

Planning

- **Traditional Schedule**
  Lesson Plans Including Strategies for English-Language Learners
- **One-Stop Planner**
  CD-ROM with Test Generator

Anne Sexton

(1928–1974)

From the very beginning of her literary career, Anne Sexton was recognized as a spirit in turmoil. The writer James Dickey (page 1155) put it this way: "Anne Sexton's poems so obviously come out of deep, painful sections of the author's life that one's literary opinions scarcely seem to matter; one feels tempted to drop them furtively into the nearest ashcan, rather than be caught with them in the presence of so much naked suffering."

© Rollie McKenna.

Sexton's poetry was an eruption into art of her stormy emotional life. The titles of her most gripping volumes indicate a preoccupation with bouts of mental illness and anxiety and with the need to confront ultimate questions: *To Bedlam and Part Way Back* (1960), *Live or Die* (1966), *The Death Notebooks* (1974), and *The Awful Rowing Toward God* (1975).

Anne Gray Harvey was born in Newton, Massachusetts, and attended the public schools in nearby Wellesley. In 1947, she enrolled in the Garland School, a finishing school for women, and in 1948 married Alfred Sexton. Anne Sexton worked for a time as a fashion model, gave birth to two daughters, and then, at age 28, began writing poetry.

Sexton studied with Robert Lowell (page 948) in his graduate writing seminar at Boston University, and developed friendships with other important poets, including Sylvia Plath (page 1148), Maxine Kumin, and George Starbuck. One of the strongest influences on her was the work of her friend W. D. Snodgrass, whose volume of poetry, *Heart's Needle* (1959), traced the emotional consequences of a difficult midlife divorce.

Sexton traveled to Europe and Africa, taught at Boston University, gave readings, and earned several honorary doctorates and numerous poetry prizes, including a Pulitzer Prize for *Live or Die*. In 1968, she formed a rock music group called Anne Sexton and Her Kind. In performance, Sexton read her poems while musicians accompanied her on guitar, flute, saxophone, drums, bass, and keyboards. She believed, she said, that the music "opens up my poems in a new way, by involving them in the sound of rock music."

Sexton's poetry was intended to be, as she said, "a shock to the senses." In her second book, *All My Pretty Ones* (1962), she quoted Franz Kafka: ". . . the books we need are the kind that act upon us like a misfortune, that make us suffer like the death of someone we love more than ourselves . . . [A] book should serve as the ax for the frozen sea within us." Her books were personal axes, but they also opened up a wider vision of contemporary women. Many of her poems are dramatic monologues that portray women in moments of crisis.

The general public as well as other poets responded enthusiastically to Sexton's poems. But artistic success did not strengthen her fragile personality. As her close friend Robert Lowell remembered: "At a time when poetry readings were expected to be boring, no one ever fell asleep at Anne's. I see her as having the large, transparent, breakable, and increasingly ragged wings of a dragonfly—her poor, shy, driven life, the blind terror behind her bravado, her deadly increasing pace . . . her bravery while she lasted."

go.hrw.com
LEO 11-20

 —  *Resources: Print and Media* —

Reading
- *Graphic Organizers for Active Reading,* p. 109
- *Audio CD Library*
  Disc 28, Tracks 4, 5

Assessment
- *Formal Assessment,* p. 214
- *Portfolio Management System,* p. 222
- *Test Generator (One-Stop Planner CD-ROM)*

Internet
- go.hrw.com (keyword: LEO 11-20)

"The Bells"
Sexton depicts a relationship between a father and child through the powerful memory of a trip to the circus. The speaker mentions her father's patient explanations of the circus, his kindness, and their love for one another. The "sound where it began," the speaker tells us, is the sound of the bells for the "flying man," whose identity seems to merge with that of her father. She closes the poem by rejoicing in the time when "all the trembling bells" of her father belonged to her.
"Young"
The speaker describes herself as a "lonely kid," lying on the grass outside her parents' big house on a summer night, looking at her parents' bedroom windows, asking the stars questions, and believing that God watches over all.

Before You Read

THE BELLS

YOUNG

Make the Connection

Remembrance of Things Past

Some events, major or minor at the time, stick in our minds many years later. A parade, a kiss, a summer night—it could be anything that brings back the past for us, reminding us of our younger selves.

Quickwrite

Jot down an experience from the past that makes you feel joy. What image or sound prompts your memory of the experience?

Elements of Literature

Imagery

Imagery is the use of language to evoke a picture or a concrete sensation of a person, place, thing, or experience. Most images in literature appeal to our sense of sight. An image can, however, also appeal to our senses of taste, smell, hearing, and touch. In the following poems, look for images of sight, hearing, and touch.

The Bells

Anne Sexton

Today the circus poster
is scabbing off the concrete wall
and the children have forgotten
if they knew at all.
5 Father, do you remember?
Only the sound remains,
the distant thump of the good elephants,
the voice of the ancient lions
and how the bells
10 trembled for the flying man. **Ⓐ**
I, laughing,
lifted to your high shoulder
or small at the rough legs of strangers,
was not afraid.
15 You held my hand
and were instant to explain
the three rings of danger.
Oh see the naughty clown
and the wild parade
20 while love love
love grew rings around me.
This was the sound where it began;
our breath pounding up to see
the flying man breast out
25 across the boarded sky
and climb the air.
I remember the color of music
and how forever
all the trembling bells of you **Ⓑ**
30 were mine.

ANNE SEXTON 1089

Ⓐ Elements of Literature

Imagery

Point out the verb *trembled* in this line. Discuss some of the connotations of the word and ask students why the poet might have chosen it. Call on students to name other verbs the poet might have used here in place of *trembled*. [Possible responses: *shook, rang, jingled, shuddered.*]

Ⓑ Critical Thinking

Interpreting

❓ Why might the speaker use the phrase "all the trembling bells of you" to describe her father? [Possible responses: to convey her excitement at being with him; to convey the joy he brought her.]

Reaching All Students

Struggling Readers

In both poems, Sexton describes a moment in childhood as a way of capturing the feelings attached to those moments. While "The Bells" is fairly straightforward, struggling readers may need some help with "Young." Read it aloud to them. Then, ask them to imagine what the speaker's life was like at the time she describes. Does she seem content, happy, sad, angry, confused? What outlook do the last four lines suggest?

English Language Learners

The "three rings of danger" may not mean anything to students unfamiliar with a three-ring circus. Tell them that large circuses often have three circles with three different acts going on at the same time. Ask them why the speaker might call them "rings of danger"? You might also introduce the expression "like a three-ring circus," which is used to suggest a busy, chaotic scene.

Advanced Learners

Ask students to compare and contrast the view of the father in each poem. Could the speaker in each poem be the same person at different ages? If so, what seems to have changed in the second poem?

Imagery

? What effect do these two images of the natural world have on the tone of the poem? [Possible responses: They create the impression that the speaker is safely enveloped by a benevolent natural world; because they suggest that the speaker is at peace but also isolated from other people, they contribute to a bittersweet tone.]

B Reading Skills and Strategies

Making Inferences

? Does the speaker still believe this? **Explain.** [Possible responses: No, because she mentions that it was something she believed in the past; she may still believe in God but not believe that God pays attention to her personal concerns.]

RESPONDING TO THE ART

Arthur G. Dove (1880–1946) was one of the first American abstract artists. He began as a magazine illustrator, but he soon left his job to study art in Paris. By 1910, his works had become abstract, reflecting his belief that an artist must use color and form to capture a reality beneath the physical exterior of things. Though nonrepresentational, his paintings often call to mind the forms of nature. This can be seen in *Me and the Moon,* which suggests a moon embraced by the landscape of Earth.

Activity. Ask students to discuss how the colors and shapes of the painting correspond to the mood of "Young." [Possible response: The dark mass might correspond to the loneliness of the speaker, while the bright moon could suggest the hopeful, peaceful tone of most of the poem.]

‖ Anne Sexton said that "Young" should be "said in *one breath*" and was composed of only one sentence in order to better capture a single moment of time.

Young

Anne Sexton

A thousand doors ago
when I was a lonely kid
in a big house with four
garages and it was summer
5 as long as I could remember,
I lay on the lawn at night,
clover wrinkling under me,
the wise stars bedding over me,
my mother's window a funnel
10 of yellow heat running out,
my father's window, half shut,
an eye where sleepers pass,

and the boards of the house
were smooth and white as wax
15 and probably a million leaves
sailed on their strange stalks
as the crickets ticked together
and I, in my brand new body,
which was not a woman's yet,
20 told the stars my questions
and thought God could really see
the heat and the painted light,
elbows, knees, dreams, goodnight.

Me and the Moon (1937) by Arthur G. Dove. Graphite on paper (7″ x 10″; 17.9 cm x 25.5 cm).

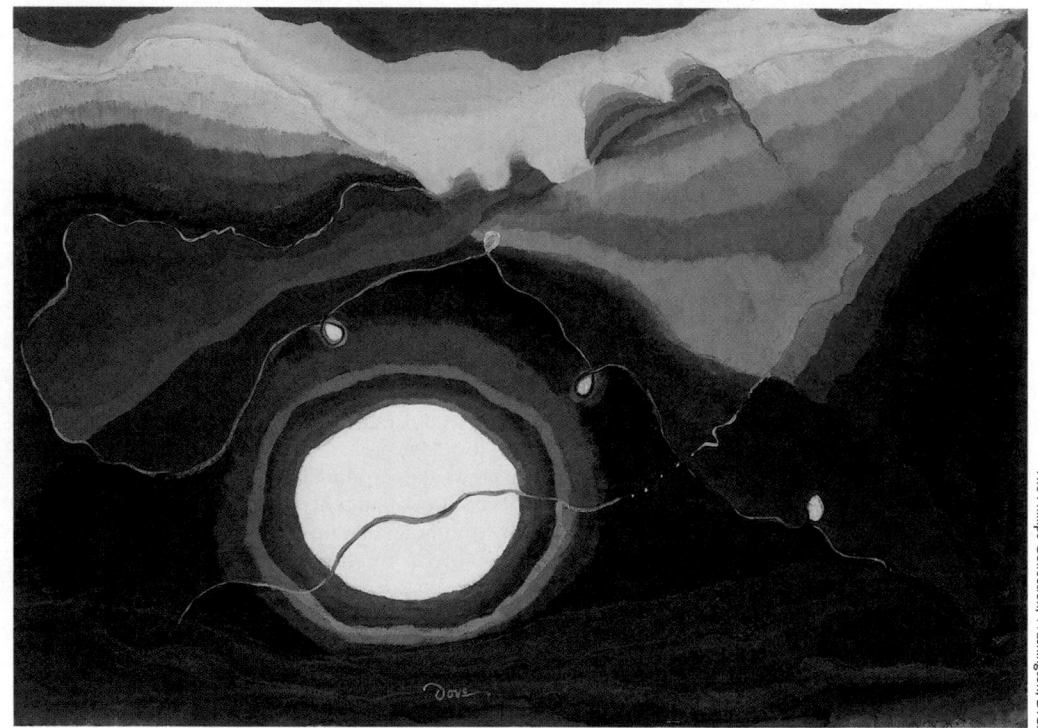

The Phillips Collection, Washington, D.C.

MAKING MEANINGS

The Bells

First Thoughts [Respond]

1. Possible responses: happiness, nostalgia, sadness.

Shaping Interpretations [Interpret]

2. She sees an old circus poster. Students will probably say their memories have a lot in common with those of Sexton.
3. Sounds of the circus remain in her memory; because the loud sounds may have seemed overwhelming to a small child.
4. She remembers being happy and excited. Students may describe the poem's tone as nostalgic or wistful.
5. Love transforms the "rings of danger" into rings that protect and envelop.
6. She mixes sight and sound.
7. The intensity of the experience of the circus and the loving presence of her father are linked forever in her memory.

The Bells

First Thoughts

1. What emotions did you feel as you read "The Bells"?

Shaping Interpretations

2. What prompts the speaker to remember the scene from her past? (How do her memories compare with your own, as recorded in your Quickwrite notes?)

3. According to line 6, what "remains"? Where does it remain, and why do you think it does so?

4. What feelings does the poem's speaker remember? How would you describe the poem's **tone**?

5. "Rings" are mentioned twice in the poem. At first they are "rings of danger." What do they become, and what is it that transforms them?

6. Describing a perception of one sense in terms of another sense is called **synesthesia**. What senses does Sexton mix in line 27?

7. One **theme** of the poem is conveyed with childlike simplicity in the last two lines. How would you paraphrase this message?

Young

First Thoughts

1. Is this a happy memory for the speaker? Compare it with the memory you described in the Quickwrite.

Shaping Interpretations

2. Why do you think the speaker says her youth took place "a thousand doors ago"?

3. Identify the **metaphors** used to describe the windows. Do you think the metaphors reflect the speaker's feelings about her mother and father? Explain your responses.

4. Describe the **tone** of the poem, as you "hear" it. Which words in the poem convey this tone?

5. Read the poem aloud, which Sexton recommended. Where would you pause slightly for breath and emphasis? Do you think the poem sounds like a young girl speaking?

CHOICES:
Building Your Portfolio

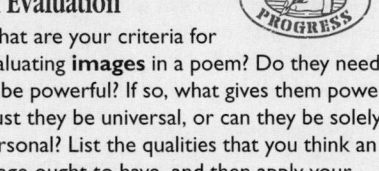

Writer's Notebook

1. Collecting Ideas for an Evaluation

What are your criteria for evaluating **images** in a poem? Do they need to be powerful? If so, what gives them power? Must they be universal, or can they be solely personal? List the qualities that you think an image ought to have, and then apply your criteria to Sexton's images in either poem. Save your notes for possible use in the Writer's Workshop on page 1181.

Analyzing Sounds

2. The Poet's Craft

Sexton uses **rhymes** very subtly and very skillfully. Many are **approximate rhymes** (words that have some correspondence in sound but not an exact one), and therefore they may not be apparent at first. (Reading the poems aloud should help reveal these "hidden" rhymes.) In a short essay, identify some of the rhymes and other sound effects, such as **alliteration,** in "The Bells" and "Young." In your essay, answer these questions about the use of sound in the poems:

- What are the effects of the sounds in the poem? Are the sounds harsh, discordant, pleasing, harmonious?
- How do the sounds affect the tone of the poem? How do they reinforce its sense?
- Do the rhymes and other sound effects call attention to certain key words or ideas?

Viewing and Representing

3. A Poem's Pictures

"Young" overflows with visual **imagery.** Draw or paint the speaker, her family's house and its surroundings, or whatever else interests you. You might want to focus on a detail, such as one of those windows. (As a starting point, you may wish to respond visually to the painting on page 1090.)

ANNE SEXTON 1091

Young

First Thoughts [Respond]

1. Possible responses: Yes, because she recalls a peaceful time; no, it is a bittersweet memory because she was at peace but lonely. Some students may say that the memory they described was a similarly peaceful moment, while others may have described a more exuberant moment.

Shaping Interpretations [Interpret]

2. It suggests she has been through many "doors," or stages, in her life.

3. Her mother's window is a funnel sending out heat and light. Her father's is a half-shut eye. Possible response: The metaphors may suggest that the speaker feels her mother is open to her, but her father is more closed off.

4. Possible response: The tone could be described as bittersweet, peaceful, or nostalgic. Students might mention the words *lonely, wise, yellow, heat, half-shut, smooth, white, sailed,* and *together.*

5. Possible response: Pause at the end of ll. 5, 12, 17. Most students will say the poem has the breathless quality of a young girl speaking since the whole poem is all one sentence.

Grading Timesaver

Rubrics for each Choices assignment appear on p. 222 in the *Portfolio Management System.*

CHOICES:
Building Your Portfolio

1. **Writer's Notebook** Remind students that they may use their work as prewriting for the Writer's Workshop on p. 1181.

2. **Analyzing Sounds** Have small groups of students work together to locate and discuss the rhymes in the poem. Remind students that they may want to compare this poem to the work of another poet, such as Emily Dickinson, who uses approximate, or "slant," rhymes.

3. **Viewing and Representing** Remind students that they can use different media, colors, and brush strokes to help convey the mood of the poem.

Planning

- **Block Schedule**
  Block Scheduling Lesson Plans with Pacing Guide

- **Traditional Schedule**
  Lesson Plans Including Strategies for English-Language Learners

- **One-Stop Planner**
  CD-ROM with Test Generator

BROWSING IN THE FILES

About the Author. When N. Scott Momaday was a youngster, his family lived at various times on the Navajo reservation, two Apache reservations, and at the Pueblo of Jemez. Thus, Momaday had "a Pan-Indian experience before [he] knew what that term meant."

Writers on Writing. "I can take credit for setting down those Kiowa stories in English, in *The Way to Rainy Mountain,* but I didn't invent them. The imagination that informs those stories is really not mine, though it exists, I think in my blood. It's an ancestral imagination."

N. Scott Momaday

(1934–   )

Courtesy N. Scott Momaday.

Among American voices, one of the most poignant and powerful to make itself heard at long last has been that of the Native American. In the past, the American Indian appeared in literature and the other arts mostly in the baldest of stereotypes, either as a noble, primitive warrior or as a fearsome, ignorant savage. One has only to look at Western movies from the 1940s and 1950s to see how blatant the stereotypes were. Even American history textbooks seldom questioned the popular view that the white settlers' gradual "winning" of the West was a virtuous struggle against the unwarranted resistance of American Indians. Few Americans gave much thought either to the moral basis on which the United States expanded or to the history of the American Indians.

When the civil rights movement of the 1950s and 1960s brought discrimination against African Americans to the forefront of public discussion, other minority groups began to demand a fairer social and political standing for themselves. Native Americans spoke loudly and clearly of loss, injustice, and prejudice. Among the notable books on the Native American experience are Vine Deloria, Jr.'s novel *Custer Died for Your Sins* (1969), the historian Dee Brown's *Bury My Heart at Wounded Knee* (1970), Louise Erdrich's novel *Love Medicine* (1984), and the works of N. Scott Momaday.

Navarre Scott Momaday was born in Lawton, Oklahoma, of Kiowa ancestry on his father's side, and some Cherokee on his mother's. After receiving an undergraduate degree from the University of New Mexico in 1958, Momaday studied creative writing at Stanford University, where he earned a Ph.D. in 1963.

But Momaday broke loose from the standard academic mold with three works grounded in his knowledge of American Indian life: a Pulitzer Prize–winning novel, *House Made of Dawn* (1968), and two memoirs, *The Way to Rainy Mountain* (1969) and *The Names* (1976).

The Way to Rainy Mountain is part legend, part history, and part poetry, with an artistic addition of striking illustrations by Momaday's father, Alfred Momaday. Following the introduction, Momaday describes Kiowa history in a form that is associative and imagistic; it works on the reader's imagination in subtle ways that do not depend on a straightforward narrative. On one page, he sets down a Kiowa myth or legend; on the facing page, he places a short excerpt from a traditional history and then a personal memory of his own. In the mind of the reader, the inner truth blends with the outer; emotion mixes with fact.

The Kiowas' journey to Rainy Mountain begins in the hidden mists of time, when a tribe of unknown origin descends from the headwaters of the Yellowstone River eastward to the Black Hills (in present-day South Dakota) and south to the Wichita Mountains. It ends in a cemetery where many of Momaday's Kiowa relatives are buried. Momaday says that "the journey is an evocation of three things in particular: a landscape that is incomparable, a time that is gone forever, and the human spirit, which endures."

The incomparable landscape is the Great Plains, wind-swept and lonely, in turn brilliant with summer sun and buried in winter snows. Momaday's love of the land where he grew up suffuses everything he writes. He reminds us of both the spiritual richness and the rigors of living close to the land, under a wide, open sky, in harmony with the changing seasons. In his work, Momaday has looked at his own particular landscape from so many angles that his pictures often shimmer like prisms.

go.hrw.com
LEO 11-20

 — *Resources: Print and Media* —

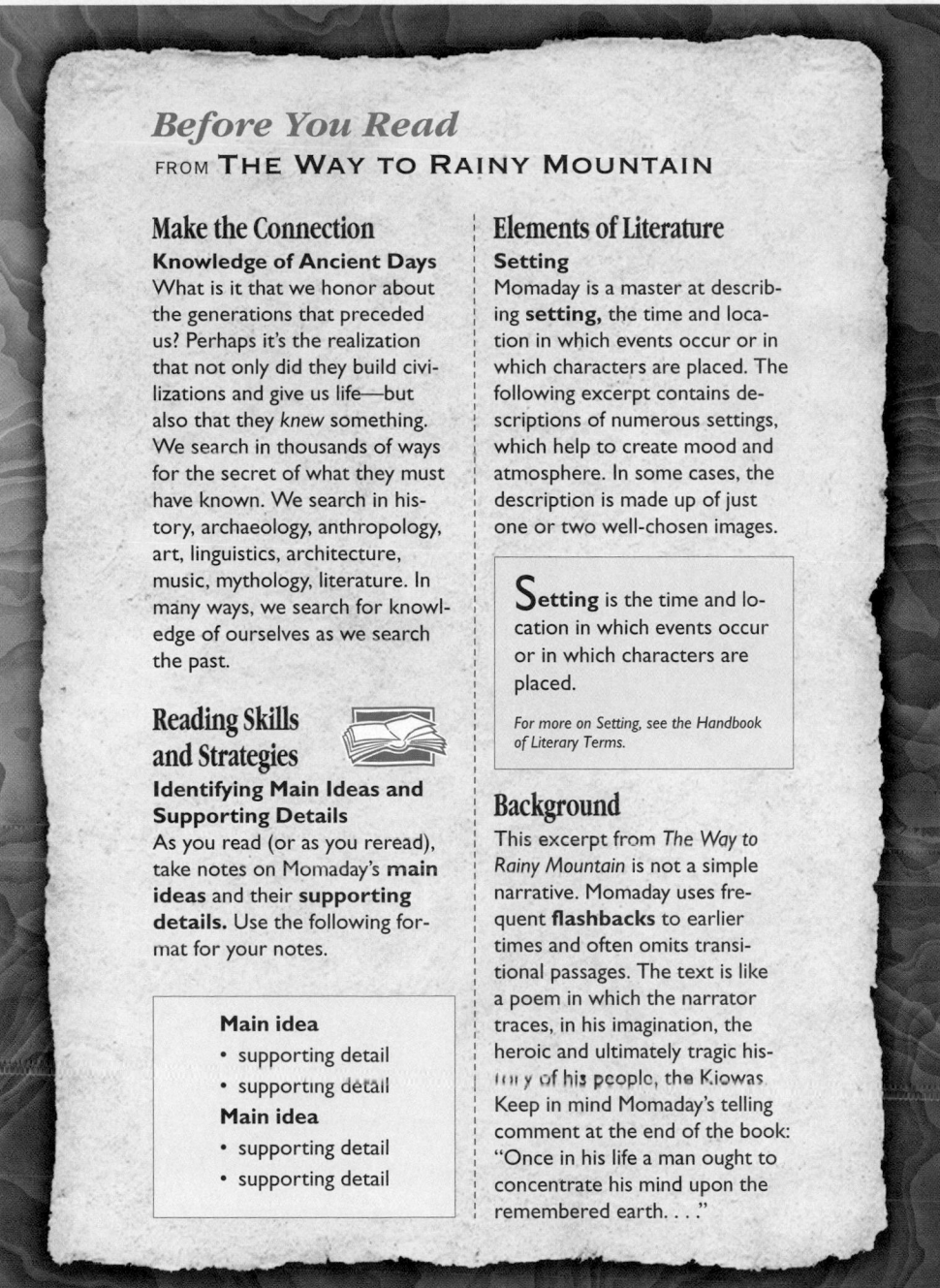

Before You Read

FROM **THE WAY TO RAINY MOUNTAIN**

Make the Connection

Knowledge of Ancient Days

What is it that we honor about the generations that preceded us? Perhaps it's the realization that not only did they build civilizations and give us life—but also that they *knew* something. We search in thousands of ways for the secret of what they must have known. We search in history, archaeology, anthropology, art, linguistics, architecture, music, mythology, literature. In many ways, we search for knowledge of ourselves as we search the past.

Reading Skills and Strategies

Identifying Main Ideas and Supporting Details

As you read (or as you reread), take notes on Momaday's **main ideas** and their **supporting details.** Use the following format for your notes.

> **Main idea**
> • supporting detail
> • supporting detail
> **Main idea**
> • supporting detail
> • supporting detail

Elements of Literature

Setting

Momaday is a master at describing **setting,** the time and location in which events occur or in which characters are placed. The following excerpt contains descriptions of numerous settings, which help to create mood and atmosphere. In some cases, the description is made up of just one or two well-chosen images.

> **S**etting is the time and location in which events occur or in which characters are placed.
>
> *For more on Setting, see the Handbook of Literary Terms.*

Background

This excerpt from *The Way to Rainy Mountain* is not a simple narrative. Momaday uses frequent **flashbacks** to earlier times and often omits transitional passages. The text is like a poem in which the narrator traces, in his imagination, the heroic and ultimately tragic history of his people, the Kiowas. Keep in mind Momaday's telling comment at the end of the book: "Once in his life a man ought to concentrate his mind upon the remembered earth. . . ."

N. SCOTT MOMADAY **1093**

Summary ■■

After his grandmother's death, the narrator returns to her Oklahoma home, which is near Rainy Mountain, an important site in the religion and history of his Kiowa ancestors. He evokes the birth of his grandmother, just after the Kiowa were forced to surrender their land to the U.S. government, and then he sets out to recount an ancestral event from a much earlier time: the Kiowa's migration from what is now western Montana, south and east to the plains. He decides to retrace the steps of that migration. On his journey, he encounters numerous natural wonders, including Devils Tower. He recounts the Kiowa legend associated with it— the tale of a boy who is transformed into a bear and whose sisters become the stars of the Big Dipper. The narrator recalls his grandmother's reverence for the sun and her bustling house, filled with prayer meetings and great feasts. When he returns to her home, however, he finds the house silent and small. Early in the morning, he visits his grandmother's grave. He then looks once more at the mountain and leaves.

Background

Until approximately the middle of the seventeenth century, the Kiowas lived in the rugged mountains of western Montana, at the headwaters of the Yellowstone River. For undetermined reasons, they migrated from that terrain onto the plains, where they took up a new way of life, becoming expert horse riders, buffalo hunters, and warriors. This plains culture, the period of Kiowa predominance, lasted only a century. By the mid-nineteenth century, they had to face another transformation, adapting to the rapid encroachment of European American settlers.

Preteaching Vocabulary

Words to Own

Have students meet in groups to read the Words to Own and their definitions at the bottom of the selection pages. Ask them to study the context of each word by reading the sentence in the story in which it appears. Then, have each group compose sentences using the words in context. When you are sure students understand the words, assign this exercise.

Write the vocabulary word that is an antonym for each of these words.

1. substantial [tenuous]
2. deny [indulge]
3. secondarily [preeminently]
4. transparent [opaque]
5. strong [infirm]
6. friendships [enmities]
7. recklessness [wariness]
8. gather [disperse]
9. sparse [luxuriant]
10. lifeless [vital]

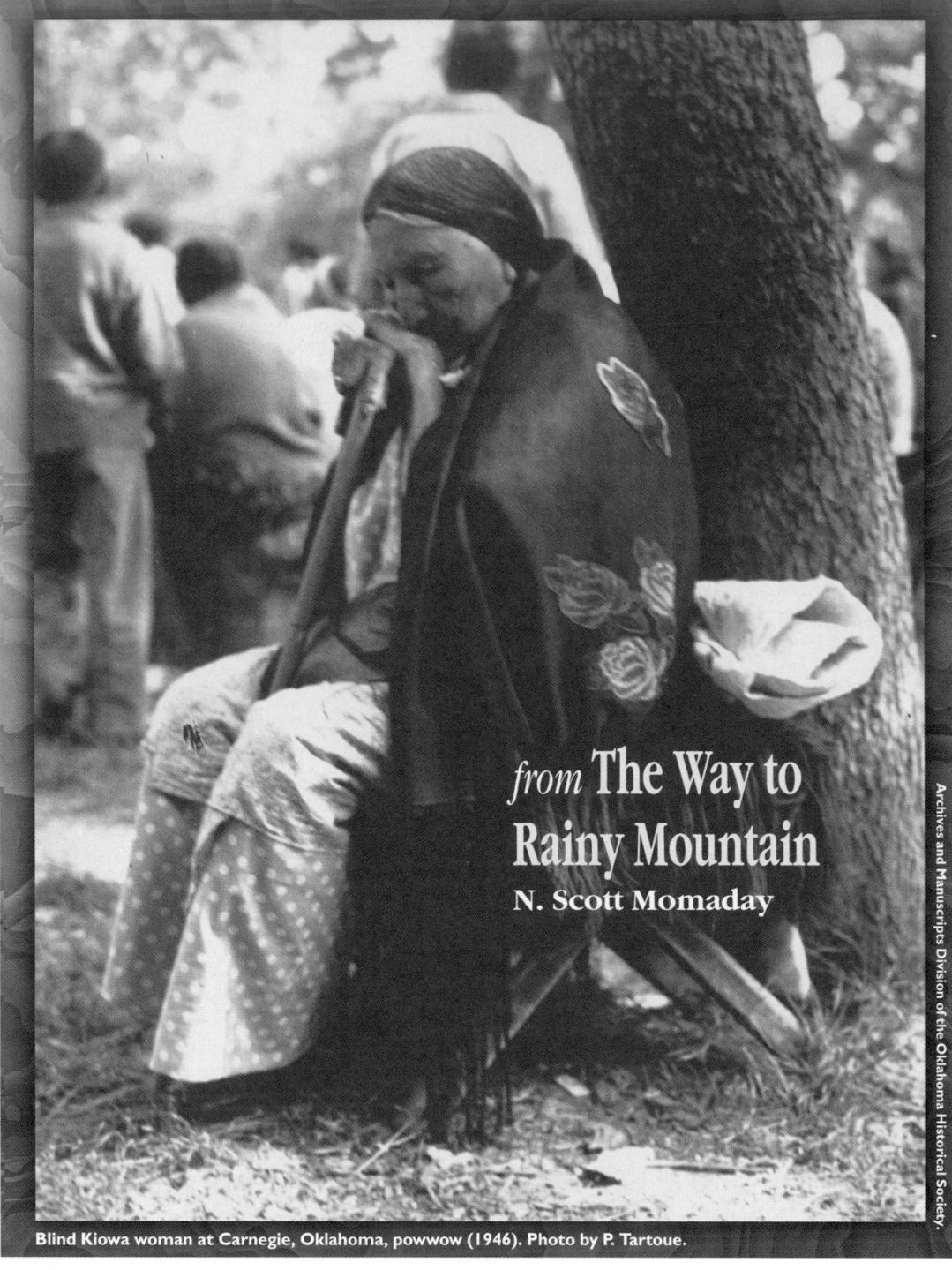

from **The Way to Rainy Mountain**

N. Scott Momaday

Archives and Manuscripts Division of the Oklahoma Historical Society.

Blind Kiowa woman at Carnegie, Oklahoma, powwow (1946). Photo by P. Tartoue.

Reaching All Students

Devils Tower, Wyoming.

A single knoll rises out of the plain in Oklahoma north and west of the Wichita Range. For my people, the Kiowas, it is an old landmark, and they gave it the name Rainy Mountain. The hardest weather in the world is there. Winter brings blizzards, hot tornadic winds arise in the spring, and in summer the prairie is an anvil's edge. The grass turns brittle and brown, and it cracks beneath your feet. There are green belts along the rivers and creeks, linear groves of hickory and pecan, willow and witch hazel. At a distance in July or August the steaming foliage seems almost to writhe in fire. Great green and yellow grasshoppers are everywhere in the tall grass, popping up like corn to sting the flesh, and tortoises crawl about on the red earth, going nowhere in the plenty of time. Loneliness is an aspect of the land. All things in the plain are isolate; there is no confusion of objects in the eye, but *one* hill or *one* tree or *one* man. To look upon that landscape in the early morning, with the sun at your back, is to lose the sense of proportion. Your imagination comes to life, and this, you think, is where Creation was begun.

I returned to Rainy Mountain in July. My grandmother had died in the spring, and I wanted to be at her grave. She had lived to be very old and at last infirm. Her only living daughter was with her when she died, and I was told that in death her face was that of a child.

I like to think of her as a child. When she was born, the Kiowas were living that last great moment of their history. For more than a hundred years they had controlled the open range from the Smoky Hill River to the Red, from the headwaters of the Canadian to the fork of the Arkansas and Cimarron. In alliance with the Comanches, they had ruled the whole of the southern Plains. War was their sacred business, and they were among the finest horsemen the world has ever known. But warfare for the Kiowas was preeminently a matter of disposition rather than of survival, and they never understood the grim, unrelenting advance of the U.S. Cavalry. When at last, divided

and ill-provisioned, they were driven onto the Staked Plains in the cold rains of autumn, they fell into panic. In Palo Duro Canyon they abandoned their crucial stores to pillage and had nothing then but their lives. In order to save themselves, they surrendered to the soldiers at Fort Sill and were imprisoned in the old stone corral that now stands as a military museum. My grandmother was spared the humiliation of those high gray walls by eight or ten years, but she must have known from birth the affliction of defeat, the dark brooding of old warriors.

Her name was Aho, and she belonged to the last culture to evolve in North America. Her forebears came down from the high country in western Montana nearly three centuries ago. They were a mountain people, a mysterious tribe of hunters whose language has never been positively classified in any major group. In the late seventeenth century they began a long migration to the south and east. It was a journey toward the dawn, and it led to a golden age. Along the way the Kiowas were befriended by the Crows, who gave them the culture and religion of the Plains. They acquired horses, and their ancient nomadic spirit was suddenly free of the ground. They acquired Tai-me, the sacred Sun Dance doll, from that moment the object and symbol of their worship, and so shared in the divinity of the sun. Not least, they acquired the sense of destiny, therefore courage and pride. When they entered upon the southern Plains they had been transformed. No longer were they slaves to the simple necessity of survival; they were a lordly and dangerous society of fighters and thieves, hunters and priests of the sun. According to their origin myth, they entered the world through a hollow log. From one point of view, their migration was the fruit of an old prophecy, for indeed they emerged from a sunless world.

Although my grandmother lived out her long life in the shadow of Rainy Mountain, the immense landscape of the continental interior lay like memory in her blood. She could tell of the Crows, whom she had never seen, and of the

---

WORDS TO OWN

infirm (in·furm′) *adj.*: physically weak.
preeminently (prē·em′ə·nənt·lē) *adv.*: above all else.

N. SCOTT MOMADAY 1095

A **Reading Skills and Strategies**
Identifying Main Ideas and Supporting Details
❓ What main idea is stated and what details does the narrator provide to support it? [Main idea: Rainy Mountain has the hardest weather in the world. Details: winter blizzards; hot tornadic winds in spring; hot, dry summers.]

B **Elements of Literature**
Setting
❓ What word would you use to describe the setting the author portrays in this paragraph? [Possible responses: rugged; harsh; desolate; lonely.]

C **Critical Thinking**
Speculating
❓ In the past, why had warfare not been a matter of survival? [Possible response: In the past, the Kiowas and their opponents had had similar weapons and had operated with an understanding of each other's rules of warfare; there was enough land and food for all.]

D **Struggling Readers**
Summarizing
❓ According to the author, in what ways did the Kiowas' journey change them? [Possible response: He says that the journey gave them a new culture, religion, and sense of pride.]

Crossing the Curriculum

History
In this excerpt, Momaday refers to the destructive role that the United States Cavalry played in the history of the Kiowas. Ask students to do independent research on the part the Cavalry played in the wars against the Indians throughout the West between 1850 and 1890. After students have completed their research, ask them to report to the class, using informational handouts and charts, maps, photographs, or other visual aids.

Geography
Show the class the map on p. 1098, and ask students to use the scale to measure the distance the Kiowas traveled on their journey from western Montana to Rainy Mountain in southern Oklahoma. Point out that although the Kiowa migration was gradual, it was significant. To give students a sense of the difficulty of the journey, ask them to calculate roughly how long it would take to travel the distance on foot.

Art
Have students find photographs of landscapes in western Montana and southern Oklahoma. Then, ask them to make two drawings that show the contrast between the Kiowas' original homeland and the place where they settled at the end of their migration.

Black Hills, where she had never been. I wanted to see in reality what she had seen more perfectly in the mind's eye, and traveled fifteen hundred miles to begin my pilgrimage.

Yellowstone, it seemed to me, was the top of the world, a region of deep lakes and dark timber, canyons and waterfalls. But, beautiful as it is, one might have the sense of confinement there. The skyline in all directions is close at hand, the high wall of the woods and deep cleavages of shade. There is a perfect freedom in the mountains, but it belongs to the eagle and the elk, the badger and the bear. The Kiowas reckoned their stature by the distance they could see, and they were bent and blind in the wilderness.

Descending eastward, the highland meadows are a stairway to the plain. In July the inland slope of the Rockies is luxuriant with flax and buckwheat, stonecrop and larkspur. The earth unfolds and the limit of the land recedes. Clusters of trees, and animals grazing far in the distance, cause the vision to reach away and wonder to build upon the mind. The sun follows a longer course in the day, and the sky is immense beyond all comparison. The great billowing clouds that sail upon it are shadows that move upon the grain like water, dividing light. Farther down, in the land of the Crows and Blackfeet, the plain is yellow. Sweet clover takes hold of the hills and bends upon itself to cover and seal the soil. There the Kiowas paused on their way; they had come to the place where they must change their lives. The sun is at home on the plains. Precisely there does it have the certain character of a god. When the Kiowas came to the land of the Crows, they could see the dark lees of the hills at dawn across the Bighorn River, the profusion of light on the grain shelves, the oldest deity ranging after the solstices.[1] Not yet would they veer southward to the caldron of the land that lay below; they must

wean their blood from the northern winter and hold the mountains a while longer in their view. They bore Tai-me in procession to the east.

A dark mist lay over the Black Hills, and the land was like iron. At the top of a ridge I caught sight of Devils Tower upthrust against the gray sky as if in the birth of time the core of the earth had broken through its crust and the motion of the world was begun. There are things in nature that engender an awful quiet in the heart of man; Devils Tower is one of them. Two centuries ago, because they could not do otherwise, the Kiowas made a legend at the base of the rock. My grandmother said:

Eight children were there at play, seven sisters and their brother. Suddenly the boy was struck dumb; he trembled and began to run upon his hands and feet. His fingers became claws, and his body was covered with fur. Directly there was a bear where the boy had been. The sisters were terrified; they ran, and the bear after them. They came to the stump of a great tree, and the tree spoke to them. It bade them climb upon it, and as they did so it began to rise into the air. The bear came to kill them, but they were just beyond its reach. It reared against the tree and scored the bark all around with its claws. The seven sisters were borne into the sky, and they became the stars of the Big Dipper.

From that moment, and so long as the legend lives, the Kiowas have kinsmen in the night sky. Whatever they were in the mountains, they could be no more. However tenuous their well-being, however much they had suffered and would suffer again, they had found a way out of the wilderness.

My grandmother had a reverence for the sun, a holy regard that now is all but gone out of mankind. There was a wariness in her, and an an-

1. solstices: The solstices are the points where the sun is farthest north and farthest south of the celestial equator, creating the longest day (June 21) and the shortest day (December 21) of sunlight in the Northern Hemisphere.

WORDS TO OWN

luxuriant (lug·zhoor′ē·ənt) *adj.*: rich; abundant.
tenuous (ten′yōō·əs) *adj.*: slight; insubstantial; not firm.
wariness (wer′ē·nis) *n.*: caution; carefulness.

Getting Students Involved

Cooperative Learning

Video Teams. Have students work in groups of three to draft a film script based on the selection. Ask students to include three quotations from the selection as voice-overs. Since the selection contains no dialogue, ask students to use camera directions to indicate what details viewers would see and from what angles scenes would be shot. Encourage students to

suggest music and sound effects that would be appropriate to the author's tone and to the atmosphere of the selection. Ask students to divide the tasks according to their interests and skills. For example, one student could be responsible for choosing the quotations, another for planning the visual shots and angles, and a third for thinking about the music and sound effects.

Writing a Legend

Legends for Our Times. Discuss the legend of the seven sisters and the Big Dipper. Then, ask students to write their own legends based on natural phenomena. They should try to create a legend that might help a certain group of people give meaning to something in their world that is otherwise inexplicable. Point out that many legends involve metamorphosis, and encourage students to include such transformations in their legends.

John Stevens/The Stock Solution.

F **Reading Skills and Strategies**
Identifying Cause and Effect
? Why was the Sun Dance so important to the Kiowas, and why would the government have sent soldiers to stop it? [Possible responses: The Sun Dance brought the Kiowas together and reaffirmed their pride in themselves as a people; perhaps the government feared the power of a people strong in their religion.]

G **Reading Skills and Strategies**
Identifying Main Ideas and Supporting Details
? A main idea may be expressed after the details that support it. What details support this idea? [White settlers had killed off the buffalo, which were integral to the Kiowas' worship of their deity; the soldiers forcibly prevented the Kiowa from worshipping.]

H **Vocabulary Note**
The Root *dei*
? Tell students that the root *dei* in *deicide* comes from the Latin word *deus*, meaning "god." What other word has the same root? [*deity*, meaning "god"]

cient awe. She was a Christian in her later years, but she had come a long way about, and she never forgot her birthright. As a child she had been to the Sun Dances; she had taken part in those annual rites, and by them she had learned the restoration of her people in the presence of Tai-me. She was about seven when the last Kiowa Sun Dance was held in 1887 on the Washita River above Rainy Mountain Creek. The buffalo were gone. In order to consummate the ancient sacrifice—to impale the head of a buffalo bull upon the medicine tree—a delegation of old men journeyed into Texas, there to beg and barter for an animal from the Goodnight herd. She was ten when the Kiowas came together for the last time as a living Sun Dance culture. They could find no buffalo; they had to hang an old hide from the sacred tree. Before the dance could begin, a company of soldiers rode out from Fort Sill under orders to disperse the tribe. Forbidden without cause the essential act of their faith, having seen the wild herds slaughtered and left to rot upon the ground, the Kiowas backed away forever from the medicine tree. That was July 20, 1890, at the great bend of the Washita. My grandmother was there. Without bitterness, and for as long as she lived, she bore a vision of deicide.[2]   **F**

G H

2. **deicide** (dē′ə·sīd′): murder of a god.

WORDS TO OWN
disperse (di·spʉrs′) *v.*: to scatter.

N. SCOTT MOMADAY 1097

RESPONDING TO THE ART
To the Kiowa, the buffalo provided both material and spiritual essentials for living. By 1885, however, the buffalo were gone.
Activity. Rsearch ways in which the Kiowa used the various parts of the buffalo.

Taking a Second Look

Review: Analyzing Text Structures
Comparison/Contrast. Point out to students that Momaday uses comparison and contrast throughout this excerpt to show the changes experienced over time by the Kiowa in general and by his family in particular. Rather than state the comparisons and contrasts directly, however, he relies on readers to make the connections between various sections of the text.

Activities
1. On pp. 1095 and 1096, Momaday describes three different homes of the Kiowas. Have students make a chart that shows the similarities and differences among the Kiowas' original home in Montana, their interim home in Wyoming and South Dakota, and their final home in Oklahoma.
2. Have students locate passages in which Momaday contrasts his grandmother's house when she was alive with the house after her death.
3. Discuss the contrast between the Kiowas' life before and after the arrival of whites.
4. Finally, have students choose one of the above topics to explore in a paragraph of comparison/contrast. Or, have them write a paragraph, analyzing and evaluating the structure that Momaday uses for his comparison/contrasts.

Point out the shift in narrative time that this paragraph marks. Remind students that at the beginning of this piece, the author says that he has returned to Rainy Mountain to visit his grandmother's grave; then, he shifts the focus to a description of the Kiowa people and the values that shaped his grandmother's life. Now, he begins a more personal description of her.

B Advanced Learners

Elegy

? What images in this paragraph contribute to an elegiac tone? [Possible responses: the grandmother standing by her bed alone to pray; the sound of her prayer; the shadows in the room.]

RESPONDING TO THE ART

The map shows the approximate course of the Kiowa migrations that took place from about 1700 to 1830. It shows the boundaries of states that did not exist at that time.

Activity. Have students look for other maps that show the area of the migration route as it was in about 1800. Discuss with them what such maps suggest about the rightful ownership of the land. Some students might also research the earliest written description of the Kiowas— found in the journal of the Lewis and Clark expedition.

A Now that I can have her only in memory, I see my grandmother in the several postures that were peculiar to her: standing at the wood stove on a winter morning and turning meat in a great iron skillet; sitting at the south window, bent above her beadwork, and afterwards, when her vision failed, looking down for a long time into the fold of her hands; going out upon a cane, very slowly as she did when the weight of age came upon her; praying. I remember her most often at prayer. She made long, rambling prayers out of suffering and hope, having seen many things. I was never sure that I had the right to hear, so exclusive were they **B** of all mere custom and company. The last time I saw her she prayed standing by the side of her bed at night, naked to the waist, the light of a kerosene lamp moving upon her dark skin. Her long, black hair, always drawn and braided in the day, lay upon her shoulders and against her breasts like a shawl. I do not speak Kiowa, and I never understood her prayers, but there was something inherently sad in the sound, some merest hesitation upon the syllables of sorrow. She began in a high and descending pitch, exhausting her breath to silence; then again and again—and always the same intensity of effort, of something that is, and is not, like urgency in the human voice. Transported so in the dancing light among the shadows of her room, she seemed beyond the reach of time. But that was illusion; I think I knew then that I should not see her again.

Houses are like sentinels in the plain, old keepers of the weather watch. There, in a very little while, wood takes on the appearance of great age. All colors wear soon away in the wind and rain, and then the wood is burned gray and the grain appears

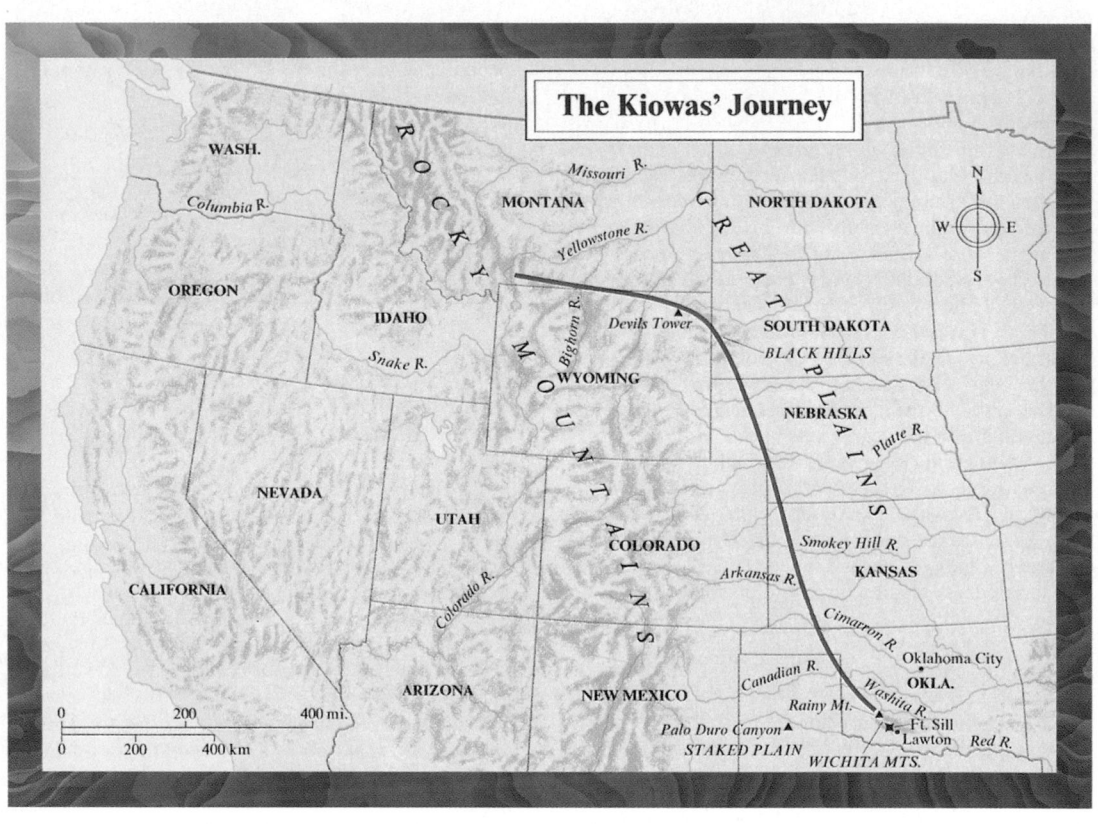

Making the Connections

Connecting to the Theme: "From Generation to Generation"
After students have finished reading the selection, talk about the theme. Point out that the narrator's affection for his grandmother is based not only on his memories of a happy childhood at her home but also on the fact that she is a major connection to his cultural heritage. Have them speculate about why the narrator does not mention his parents in this excerpt. Then, have them discuss whether most grandparents today provide a connection to a child's cultural heritage.

Cultural Connections
The narrator writes: "My grandmother had a reverence for the sun. . . ." There is a common perception that less technologically advanced cultures have a deeper, more spiritual connection to nature than technologically advanced cultures. Some Native Americans see this as a romanticized view of their culture and suggest that all humans have a longing for a deep connection with nature. Ask students to discuss what they think of these two views.

and the nails turn red with rust. The window-panes are black and opaque; you imagine there is nothing within, and indeed there are many ghosts, bones given up to the land. They stand here and there against the sky, and you approach them for a longer time than you expect. They belong in the distance; it is their domain.

Once there was a lot of sound in my grandmother's house, a lot of coming and going, feasting and talk. The summers there were full of excitement and reunion. The Kiowas are a summer people; they abide the cold and keep to themselves, but when the season turns and the land becomes warm and vital they cannot hold still; an old love of going returns upon them. The aged visitors who came to my grandmother's house when I was a child were made of lean and leather, and they bore themselves upright. They wore great black hats and bright ample shirts that shook in the wind. They rubbed fat upon their hair and wound their braids with strips of colored cloth. Some of them painted their faces and carried the scars of old and cherished enmities. They were an old council of warlords, come to remind and be reminded of who they were. Their wives and daughters served them well. The women might indulge themselves; gossip was at once the mark and compensation of their servitude. They made loud and elaborate talk among themselves, full of jest and gesture, fright and false alarm. They went abroad in fringed and flowered shawls, bright beadwork and German silver. They were at home in the kitchen, and they prepared meals that were banquets.

There were frequent prayer meetings, and great nocturnal feasts. When I was a child I played with my cousins outside, where the lamplight fell upon the ground and the singing of the old people rose up around us and carried away into the darkness. There were a lot of good things to eat, a lot of laughter and surprise. And afterwards, when the quiet returned, I lay down with my grandmother and could hear the frogs away by the river and feel the motion of the air.

Now there is a funeral silence in the rooms, the endless wake of some final word. The walls have closed in upon my grandmother's house. When I returned to it in mourning, I saw for the first time in my life how small it was. It was late at night, and there was a white moon, nearly full. I sat for a long time on the stone steps by the kitchen door. From there I could see out across the land; I could see the long row of trees by the creek, the low light upon the rolling plains, and the stars of the Big Dipper. Once I looked at the moon and caught sight of a strange thing. A cricket had perched upon the handrail, only a few inches away from me. My line of vision was such that the creature filled the moon like a fossil.[3] It had gone there, I thought, to live and die, for there, of all places, was its small definition made whole and eternal. A warm wind rose up and purled[4] like the longing within me.

The next morning I awoke at dawn and went out on the dirt road to Rainy Mountain. It was already hot, and the grasshoppers began to fill the air. Still, it was early in the morning, and the birds sang out of the shadows. The long yellow grass on the mountain shone in the bright light, and a scissortail[5] hied above the land. There, where it ought to be, at the end of a long and legendary way, was my grandmother's grave. Here and there on the dark stones were ancestral names. Looking back once, I saw the mountain and came away.

3. **fossil:** hardened remains of plant or animal life from a previous geological time period.
4. **purled** (purld): moved in ripples.
5. **scissortail:** a species of flycatcher bird. The bird's distinctive tail is an average of thirteen inches long and is divided like scissors near its end.

WORDS TO OWN

opaque (ō·pāk') *adj.:* not transparent; not letting light pass through.
vital (vīt'l) *adj.:* filled with life.
enmities (en'mə·tēz) *n. pl.:* hatreds.
indulge (in·dulj') *v.:* to satisfy; to please; to humor.

N. SCOTT MOMADAY 1099

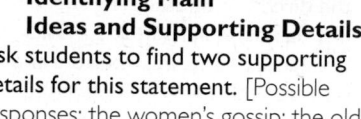

C Appreciating Language

Description
Point out the similarities between the descriptive language the author uses to portray houses on the plain and the language used in the first paragraph of the selection to describe the plain itself.

D Reading Skills and Strategies

Identifying Main Ideas and Supporting Details
Ask students to find two supporting details for this statement. [Possible responses: the women's gossip; the old peoples' singing.]

E Elements of Literature

Imagery
❓ How is this image of a cricket filling the moon connected to the narrator's view of his grandmother? [Possible response: Because of her connection to nature, she seemed to fill the emotional landscape of his life.]

F Elements of Literature

Setting
❓ How is the author's tone here appropriate to the setting he describes? [Possible response: He is describing a place of natural beauty where his ancestors triumphed and he had a happy childhood, but also a place where his grandmother—along with the heritage she represents—is buried. Accordingly, the tone is at once optimistic (bird song, bright light, bird flight) and somber (shadows, grave, dark stones).]

Reading Check
The Reading Check is on p. 1100.
a. to visit his grandmother's grave
b. After acquiring a sacred Sun Dance doll, the Kiowas worshipped the sun.
c. To escape their brother, who had become a bear, seven sisters climbed a tree and were lifted into the sky to form the Big Dipper. Devils Tower looks like a tree trunk scored with claw marks.
d. Their culture is forever changed when they can no longer practice the Sun Dance.

Assessing Learning

Check Test: True–False

1. The American Indians described in the essay are Sioux. [False]
2. The narrator recalls a legend about a fire god. [False]
3. The sacred animal associated with the Sun Dance is the buffalo. [True]
4. The Kiowas are described as excellent horse trainers. [True]
5. At the end, the narrator climbs Rainy Mountain. [False]

Informal Assessment

Use this assessment scale to record the progress of students as you observe them working in groups or individually on assignments for this selection.

1 = Never   2 = Sometimes   3 = Always
_____ Asks appropriate questions
_____ Stays on task unreminded
_____ Completes work on time
_____ Maintains positive attitude
_____ Participates actively

First Thoughts [Respond]

1. Possible response: Devils Tower, because it combines elements of myth, magic, geology, and history.

Shaping Interpretations [Interpret]

2. Possible response: The journey led to a "golden age" for the Kiowas and was also an eastward journey, the direction of the rising sun.

3. She had dark skin and long, black braided hair and was sociable and devout, with a reverence for the sun. Momaday loves and respects her.

4. Possible response: Momaday's grandmother, who lived and died on the same land that gave her life meaning.

5. Possible responses: light and life—sun, sky, yellow plain; darkness and death—dark mist, night, stones of the cemetery. Images of darkness and light are fairly balanced; the overall mood is somewhat dark.

6. "Meadows are a stairway" (metaphor); "shadows moving like water" (simile); "clover taking hold of the hills" (personification). The images make the setting more vivid.

7. Momaday praises the Kiowas' pride, fighting abilities, and sense of freedom. He mourns the assault on their religion and the loss of many of their cultural traditions.

8. Yes, the Kiowas read a lesson in the Big Dipper and probably look to nature for other truths and explanations. In his description of the cricket, Momaday also reads a lesson in nature.

9. Possible responses: Main idea—the Kiowa migration was a journey out of the wilderness into a golden age. Details—there was a sense of confinement in the mountains, and for one hundred years, they ruled the southern plains; main idea—the narrator's grandmother provided an important connection to his heritage. Details—her home was a place of reunion, and she attended the last Sun Dance.

First Thoughts

1. What single visual **image** in Momaday's text strikes you as the most memorable? Why?

Shaping Interpretations

2. What do you think Momaday means when he calls the Kiowa migration "a journey toward the dawn"?

> ### Reading Check
>
> a. Why does the narrator return to Rainy Mountain?
>
> b. What does this memoir tell about the Kiowa religion and the role of the sun in their rituals?
>
> c. According to Kiowa legend, what is the origin of the Big Dipper? How does this myth explain the peculiar formation called Devils Tower?
>
> d. What eventually happens to the Kiowa?

3. Describe Momaday's grandmother Aho, noting her physical appearance and her thoughts. What is Momaday's attitude toward her?

4. When Momaday tells of a cricket near the end of the excerpt, he says: "It had gone there, I thought, to live and die, for there, of all places, was its small definition made whole and eternal." How do you interpret this comment? What do you think the cricket might **symbolize**?

5. List **images** that Momaday uses to convey strongly contrasting feelings of light and life versus darkness and death. Is the overall **mood** of this essay light or dark? Explain your answer.

6. Momaday writes in gracefully evocative poetic prose. On page 1096, reread the paragraph that begins "Descending eastward . . .". Then, identify at least three figures of speech (**metaphor, simile, personification**) in the paragraph that refer to the **setting**. How do they contribute to the overall effect of the writing?

7. *The Way to Rainy Mountain* is in part an **elegy,** a song or poem contemplating a dead person—or, by extension, a way of life that has been destroyed. What does Momaday praise about the Kiowas? What loss does he mourn?

---

8. Do you think Momaday and the Kiowas, like earlier Puritans and Romantics, read lessons in nature? Explain.

9. Referring to your reading notes, **summarize** the **main ideas** in Momaday's piece. Include at least two **details** that support each main idea.

CHOICES:
Building Your Portfolio

Writer's Notebook

1. Collecting Ideas for an Evaluation

Just about every work of literature has at least one **setting.** One criterion for evaluating a work is the skill with which setting is evoked. In a few sentences, evaluate Momaday's success in describing setting, giving specific reasons for your judgment. Consider these uses of setting:

- creates an impression or mood
- tells about society's manners, beliefs, values, customs, etc.
- helps reveal character

Save your notes for possible use in the Writer's Workshop on page 1181.

Interpreting a Statement

2. "An awful quiet"

Momaday writes "There are things in nature that engender an awful quiet in the heart of man" (page 1096). In a two-paragraph essay, explain in your own words what the writer means by this statement. Then, tell whether you agree with him, and why.

Creative Writing

3. The Remembered Earth

For Momaday, the land around Rainy Mountain is associated with childhood and ancestral traditions. Think of a place you associate with your own childhood—a store, a park, a play area. Write a description of this place, using vivid imagery to describe what it looked like and to suggest what it meant to you.

Grading Timesaver

Rubrics for each Choices assignment appear on p. 223 in the *Portfolio Management System.*

CHOICES:
Building Your Portfolio

1 and 3. Urge students to look for fresh figures of speech.

2. Remind students that Momaday is referring to Devils Tower. If possible, show them a larger photograph of the tower.

Alice Walker

(1944–)

© Jeff Reinking.

In her poetry, essays, and novels, Alice Walker has celebrated the endurance, the strength, and the creativity of African American women like her mother—unsung women who carried immense familial and social burdens even as they struggled against low status and a complete lack of recognition.

Walker was born in Eatonton, Georgia, and grew up on a succession of farms in the area. Her father was a sharecropper, and her mother labored side-by-side with him in the fields, cared for their eight children, and still never failed, wherever they were living, to cultivate a large and beautiful flower garden. Her mother's hard work and determination to enrich her own life have served as an inspiration to Walker throughout her career.

A childhood accident that blinded Walker in one eye made her feel for a time disfigured and outcast. Seeking solace, she turned to writing poetry and reading, and also to closely observing people around her. Walker later attended Spelman College in Atlanta for two and a half years, before transferring to Sarah Lawrence College, near New York City. There she studied with the noted poet Muriel Rukeyser (1913–1980) before graduating in 1965.

During her college years, Walker was active in the civil rights movement in Georgia and Mississippi, and she traveled in Africa. Many of the poems in her first published collection, *Once: Poems* (1968), were inspired by these activities. The poems were written in a burst of creativity while Walker was at Sarah Lawrence. As quickly as she completed a poem, she would rush over to Muriel Rukeyser's classroom (a converted gardener's cottage in the center of the campus) and shove it under the door, then go back to her own room and write some more. This immense outpouring of creative energy continued night and day for the short period it lasted, but

Walker didn't even care what Rukeyser did with the poems—the point was the creative surge of expression, not the end goal of publication. But the result was that Rukeyser gave the poems to her agent, and *Once: Poems* was published a few years later.

After graduating from college, Walker began a career of teaching and writing. She was among the first to teach university courses on the work of African American women writers, and she has since brought an understanding of their work to a wider audience. For example, Walker edited a collection of the writing of Zora Neale Hurston (page 750) called *I Love Myself When I Am Laughing . . .* (1979). In addition to poetry, short stories, and essays, Walker has written a number of well-received novels, including *Meridian* (1976), the Pulitzer Prize–winning *The Color Purple* (1982), *The Temple of My Familiar* (1989), and *Possessing the Secret of Joy* (1992).

According to the critic Donna Haisty Winchell, Walker "comes across in her writing from the 1980s and 1990s as a woman at peace with herself and with the universe. Some of the anger of her youth remains, but it is more tempered and more focused." This mellowing is evident in her 1983 collection of essays, *In Search of Our Mothers' Gardens*. In 1996, Walker published *The Same River Twice*, a memoir about the filming of her novel *The Color Purple*.

  **go.hrw.com**
LE0 11-20

OBJECTIVES

1. Read and interpret the personal essay
2. Analyze and evaluate a personal essay
3. Identify the main idea through outlining
4. Express understanding through writing
5. Demonstrate an understanding of new words

SKILLS

Literary
- Analyze and evaluate a personal essay

Reading
- Identify the main idea

Writing
- Apply evaluation criteria to the essay
- Summarize a text
- Write a character sketch
- Analyze art

Art
- Draw a portrait

Vocabulary
- Use new words

Viewing/Representing
- Analyze collages (ATE)

Planning

- **Block Schedule**
  Block Scheduling Lesson Plans with Pacing Guide

- **Traditional Schedule**
  Lesson Plans Including Strategies for English-Language Learners

- **One-Stop Planner**
  CD-ROM with Test Generator

BROWSING IN THE FILES

Writers on Writing. In answer to an interviewer who asked her why she wrote, Alice Walker said, "I'm really paying homage to people I love, the people who are thought to be dumb and backward but who were the ones who first taught me to see beauty."

 *Resources: Print and Media*

Reading
- *Graphic Organizers for Active Reading,* p. 111
- *Words to Own,* p. 59
- *Audio CD Library*
  Disc 29, Track 3

Elements of Literature
- *Literary Elements*
  Transparency 32
  Worksheet, p. 97

Writing and Language
- *Daily Oral Grammar*
  Transparency 65

Assessment
- *Formal Assessment,* p. 217
- *Portfolio Management System,* p. 224
- *Preparation for College Admission Exams,* p. 67
- *Test Generator (One-Stop Planner CD-ROM)*

Internet
- go.hrw.com (keyword: LE0 11-20)

Summary ▪▪

In this excerpt from her essay, Walker outlines the life of her mother—marriage at seventeen, unceasing work, devotion to her many children—and wonders when this woman had the time or energy to "feed the creative spirit." Looking for the answer, Walker recalls a magnificent quilt in a museum made by an "anonymous Black woman . . . ." In such anonymous, practical objects, the narrator finds the genius of many generations of African American women. Her mother's creative spark, for example, manifested itself in storytelling and in her ambitious gardens. The narrator offers a poem in tribute to the strong, determined women of her mother's generation. She concludes that in search of her mother's garden, she found her own and suggests this may be true of other African American women in the arts.

Background

In the first part of her essay, not printed here, Walker describes the harsh lives of black women in the South and wonders how the creativity of these women was kept alive century after century in the inhospitable climate of slavery and economic oppression. She recalls Virginia Woolf's dictum that a woman writing fiction must have a room of her own and enough money to support herself. In light of this, she wonders what we are to make of Phillis Wheatley (see p. 113), whose life she describes in detail. Walker then suggests that in looking for the source of black women's creativity, she found the answer to be very close to her.

from
In Search of Our Mothers' Gardens

Alice Walker

In the late 1920s my mother ran away from home to marry my father. Marriage, if not running away, was expected of seventeen-year-old girls. By the time she was twenty, she had two children and was pregnant with a third. Five children later, I was born. And this is how I came to know my mother: She seemed a large, soft, loving-eyed woman who was rarely impatient in our home. Her quick, violent temper was on view only a few times a year, when she battled with the white landlord who had the misfortune to suggest to her that her children did not need to go to school. **A**

She made all the clothes we wore, even my brothers' overalls. She made all the towels and sheets we used. She spent the summers canning vegetables and fruits. She spent the winter evenings making quilts enough to cover all our beds. **B**

During the "working" day, she labored beside—not behind—my father in the fields. Her day began before sunup, and did not end until late at night. There was never a moment for her to sit down, undisturbed, to unravel her own private thoughts; never a time free from interruption—by work or the noisy inquiries of her many children. And yet, it is to my mother—and all our mothers who were not famous—that I went in search of the secret of what has fed that muzzled and often mutilated, but vibrant, creative spirit that the black woman has inherited, and that pops out in wild and unlikely places to this day. **C**

But when, you will ask, did my overworked mother have time to know or care about feeding the creative spirit?

The answer is so simple that many of us have spent years discovering it. We have constantly looked high, when we should have looked high—and low.

For example: In the Smithsonian Institution in Washington, D.C., there hangs a quilt unlike any other in the world. In fanciful, inspired, and yet simple and identifiable figures, it portrays the story of the Crucifixion. It is considered rare, beyond price. Though it follows no known pattern of quilt-making, and though it is made of bits and pieces of worthless rags, it is obviously the work of a person of powerful imagination and deep spiritual feeling. Below this quilt I saw a note that says it was made by "an anonymous Black woman in Alabama, a hundred years ago." **D**

If we could locate this "anonymous" black woman from Alabama, she would turn out to be one of our grandmothers—an artist who left her mark in the

---

WORDS TO OWN

vibrant (vī′brənt) *adj.:* full of energy.

Ⓐ Critical Thinking

Making Connections

? What fictional characters in books or movies does Walker's mother remind you of? [Possible responses: Phoenix Jackson in Eudora Welty's short story "A Worn Path" or Mama in *A Raisin in the Sun.*]

Ⓑ Reading Skills and Strategies

Responding to the Text

? What is your first impression of the author's mother? [Possible responses: She had a difficult life; she must have cared a lot about raising her children well.]

Ⓒ Elements of Literature

Personal Essay

? What purpose for her essay does the author reveal here? [Possible response: She suggests that the essay will explore the secret of African American women's "creative spirit," and she implies that she wants to understand the force that enables that spirit to survive.]

Ⓓ Reading Skills and Strategies

Identifying the Main Idea: Outlining

? What main idea does this example support? [It supports the idea that the creative expression of African American women is found in "unlikely places."]

Reaching All Students

Struggling Readers

Help students determine their purpose for reading by having them state in their own words the question that Walker sets out to answer in this portion of her essay. First, read them the Background on p. T1102. Then, have them read the first three paragraphs on p. 1103. Ask them to express in their own words the question Walker wants to answer. Remind them to look for her answer in the rest of the essay.

English Language Learners

Walker emphasizes the extravagance of her mother's garden by naming some of the kinds of flowers it contained—zinnias, sunflowers, petunias, roses, dahlias, forsythia, spirea, delphiniums, verbena. Help students appreciate this image by showing them photographs of these different types of flowers and guiding them to match each name with a picture.

Advanced Learners

Have students find a copy of the complete essay from which this excerpt is taken, and ask them to read all of it. Then, have them write a paragraph explaining the significance of the ending of the essay in light of the earlier part. Students might also read Walker's short story "Everyday Use" and compare its theme to that of the essay.

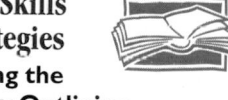

A Struggling Readers

Paraphrasing

The many cultural references and Walker's bracketed substitutions make this passage dense. Help students paraphrase it so they understand Virginia Woolf's main idea and the reason Alice Walker makes the bracketed substitutions.

B Vocabulary Note

The Prefix sup-

Point out that the prefix *sup-*, or *sub-*, means "under." Ask students how that can help them understand the meaning of *suppressed*. [The word means "pressed down."]

C Elements of Literature

Personal Essay

❓ Walker has already given one detailed example of an anonymous black woman's creative achievement. Why do you think she gives this additional example? [Possible responses: to make her case stronger; because this example had a very direct effect on her.]

D Reading Skills and Strategies

Identifying the Main Idea: Outlining

❓ What previously stated main idea does this information support? [Black women of an earlier time had to create beauty from materials they could afford and in ways their position in society allowed them to.]

---

only materials she could afford, and in the only medium her position in society allowed her to use.

As Virginia Woolf[1] wrote further, in *A Room of One's Own:*

A **B** Yet genius of a sort must have existed among women as it must have existed among the working class. [Change this to "slaves" and "the wives and daughters of sharecroppers."] Now and again an Emily Brontë[2] or a Robert Burns[3] [change this to "a Zora Hurston or a Richard Wright"] blazes out and proves its presence. But certainly it never got itself on to paper. When, however, one reads of a witch being ducked, of a woman possessed by devils [or "Sainthood"[4]], of a wise woman selling herbs [our root workers], or even a very remarkable man who had a mother, then I think we are on the track of a lost novelist, a suppressed poet, of some mute and inglorious Jane Austen. . . .[5] Indeed, I would venture to guess that Anon, who wrote so many poems without signing them, was often a woman. . . .

And so our mothers and grandmothers have, more often than not anonymously, handed on the creative spark, the seed of the flower they themselves never hoped to see: or like a sealed letter they could not plainly read.

And so it is, certainly, with my own mother. Unlike "Ma" Rainey's[6] songs, which retained their creator's name even while blasting forth from Bessie Smith's[7] mouth, no song or poem will bear my mother's name. Yet so many of the stories that I write, that we all write, are my mother's stories. **C** Only recently did I fully realize this: that through years of listening to my mother's stories of her life, I have absorbed not only the stories themselves, but something of the manner in which she spoke, something of the urgency that involves the knowledge that her stories—like her life—must be recorded. It is probably for this reason that so much of what I have written is about characters whose counterparts in real life are so much older than I am.

But the telling of these stories, which came from my mother's lips as naturally as breathing, was not the only way my mother showed herself as an artist. For stories, too, were subject to being distracted, to dying without conclusion. Dinners must be started, and cotton must be gathered before the big rains. The artist that was and is my mother showed itself to me only after many years. This is what I finally noticed:

D Like Mem, a character in *The Third Life of Grange Copeland,*[8] my mother adorned with flowers whatever shabby house we were forced to live in. And not just your typical straggly country stand of zinnias, either. She planted ambitious gardens—and still does—with over fifty different varieties of plants that bloom profusely from early March until late November. Before she left home for the fields, she watered her flowers, chopped up the grass, and laid out new beds. When she returned from the fields she might divide clumps of bulbs, dig a cold pit,[9] uproot and replant roses, or prune branches from her taller bushes or trees—until night came and it was too dark to see.

---

1. **Virginia Woolf:** English novelist and critic. In *A Room of One's Own* (1929), Woolf says that, in order to write, a woman must have a room of her own (privacy) and the means to support herself (money).
2. **Emily Brontë:** English novelist and poet, best known for her novel *Wuthering Heights* (1847).
3. **Robert Burns:** eighteenth-century Scottish poet.
4. **"Sainthood":** In the early part of this essay, Walker talks about certain black women in the South called Saints. Intensely spiritual, these women were driven to madness by their creativity, for which they could find no release.
5. **Jane Austen:** English novelist, best known for *Pride and Prejudice* (1813).
6. **"Ma" Rainey:** nickname of Gertrude Malissa Nix Pridgett Rainey. She was the first great African American professional blues vocalist and is considered to be the mother of the blues.

7. **Bessie Smith:** One of the greatest of blues singers, Smith was helped to professional status by Ma Rainey. She became known in her lifetime as "Empress of the Blues."
8. *The Third Life of Grange Copeland:* Alice Walker's first novel, published in 1970.
9. **cold pit:** shallow pit, usually covered with glass, that is used for rooting plants or sheltering young plants from temperature variations in the spring.

WORDS TO OWN

medium (mē′dē·əm) *n.:* material for an artist.
profusely (prō·fyo͞os′lē) *adv.:* in great quantities.

Skill Link

Understanding Analogies

Remind students that an analogy is a comparison between two things to show how they are alike. Analogies are often used in persuasive writing to make a point. In the quotation from Virginia Woolf's writing, Walker inserts several analogies to make the point that the experiences of black women are similar to those of the white women that Virginia Woolf described.

Ask students to explain each analogy.
1. women/slaves
2. working class/wives and daughters of sharecroppers
3. Emily Brontë/Zora Neale Hurston
4. Robert Burns/Richard Wright
5. woman possessed by devils/"Sainthood"
6. wise women selling herbs/root workers

Courtesy ACA Gallery, New York. © Romare Bearden Foundation/Licensed by VAGA, New York, NY.

Sunset and Moonrise with Maudell Sleet (1978) by Romare Bearden. From the *Profile/Part 1: The Twenties* series (Mecklenburg County). Collage on board (41″ × 29″).

ALICE WALKER 1105

Using Students' Strengths

Interpersonal Learners
Working in small groups, have students take turns reading aloud sections of the essay. After a reader has finished a section, each student in the group should write a one-sentence summary of the section; then, another student should read aloud the next section. After the whole essay has been read aloud, students should review it in their groups by comparing and discussing their one-sentence summaries for each section.

Spatial Learners
After students have read the essay, have them plan a garden that would do well in the local climate. Suggest that they consult flower catalogs to get an idea of the different flowers available. Students can represent their ideal gardens either by making a diagram that shows where each kind of flower would be planted or by making a drawing or collage that shows what the garden would look like in bloom.

Verbal/Linguistic Learners
After students have read the essay, read aloud the poem on p. 1107. Ask students to choose, as the subject for a poem, a person or group that has made an important but overlooked contribution to the world. Give the class time to record a few notes. Then, ask students to use Walker's poem as a model and write their own poetic tributes to the people or groups they chose. Encourage students to read their poems to the class.

While **Romare Bearden** worked in a wide variety of media, his greatest achievements were made in collage, the technique of pasting paper, cloth, or other material onto a background. The nature of the medium makes it especially effective for conveying the fragmentation and jazzlike improvisation of contemporary urban life. In fact, Bearden, a passionate jazz fan, thought of his works as acts of improvisation, like the letting loose of a jazz musician. He often enlarged photographs of human faces or masks and then cut them to fit into a collage, blending elements of the real world with elements of pure imagination.

Activity. Have students compare and contrast this collage with the one on the previous page. How are they alike, and how are they different? [Possible response: Students might mention that the titles suggest this is the same person, but in this collage, she and her environment are on the same scale.] **Do the two collages comment on each other?** [Possible responses: Because she works until moonrise, Maudell Sleet has a "magic garden"; the first collage shows her in harmony with the larger universe (sun, moon, and stars), while the second shows her in harmony with her more immediate surroundings.]

Maudell Sleet's Magic Garden (1978) by Romare Bearden. From the *Profile/Part 1: The Twenties* series (Mecklenburg County). Collage on board (10⅛″ × 7″).

Making the Connections

Connecting to the Theme: "From Generation to Generation"

After students have finished reading the essay, discuss the theme with them. Do they agree that examples set by parents are important in determining a young person's expectations and achievements? What do they think was Walker's mother's most important contribution to her daughter's development as a writer?

In addition to this selection, have them think about earlier selections in the collection. Which ones seem to support the idea that parents' attitudes make a difference? Then, ask them to think about children who achieve despite lack of parental interest and children who do not live up to their parents' ambitions and expectations. What might be the causes of these phenomena?

Whatever she planted grew as if by magic, and her fame as a grower of flowers spread over three counties. Because of her creativity with her flowers, even my memories of poverty are seen through a screen of blooms—sunflowers, petunias, roses, dahlias, forsythia, spirea, delphiniums, verbena . . . and on and on.

And I remember people coming to my mother's yard to be given cuttings from her flowers; I hear again the praise showered on her because whatever rocky soil she landed on, she turned into a garden. A garden so brilliant with colors, so original in its design, so magnificent with life and creativity, that to this day people drive by our house in Georgia—perfect strangers and imperfect strangers—and ask to stand or walk among my mother's art.

I notice that it is only when my mother is working in her flowers that she is radiant, almost to the point of being invisible—except as Creator: hand and eye. She is involved in work her soul must have. Ordering the universe in the image of her personal <u>conception</u> of Beauty.

Her face, as she prepares the Art that is her gift, is a legacy of respect she leaves to me, for all that illuminates and cherishes life. She has handed down respect for the possibilities—and the will to grasp them.

For her, so hindered and intruded upon in so many ways, being an artist has still been a daily part of her life. This ability to hold on, even in very simple ways, is work black women have done for a very long time.

This poem is not enough, but it is something, for the woman who literally covered the holes in our walls with sunflowers:

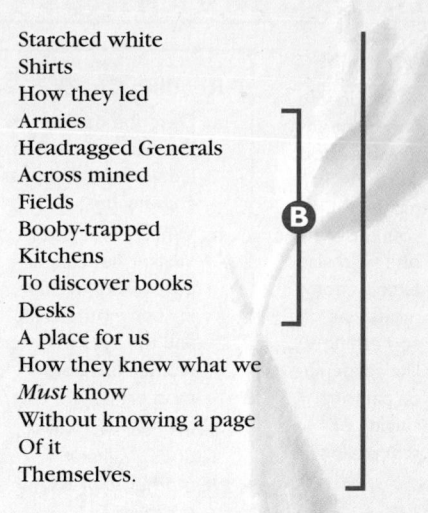

> They were women then
> My mama's generation
> Husky of voice—Stout of
> Step
> With fists as well as
> Hands
> How they battered down
> Doors
> And ironed

Ⓐ

> Starched white
> Shirts
> How they led
> Armies
> Headragged Generals
> Across mined
> Fields
> Booby-trapped
> Kitchens
> To discover books
> Desks
> A place for us
> How they knew what we
> *Must* know
> Without knowing a page
> Of it
> Themselves.

Ⓑ

Guided by my heritage of a love of beauty and a respect for strength—in search of my mother's garden, I found my own.

And perhaps in Africa over two hundred years ago, there was just such a mother; perhaps she painted vivid and daring decorations in oranges and yellows and greens on the walls of her hut; perhaps she sang—in a voice like Roberta Flack's[10]—*sweetly* over the compounds of her village; perhaps she wove the most stunning mats or told the most <u>ingenious</u> stories of all the village storytellers. Perhaps she was herself a poet—though only her daughter's name is signed to the poems that we know.

Perhaps Phillis Wheatley's mother was also an artist.

Perhaps in more than Phillis Wheatley's biological life is her mother's signature made clear.

Ⓒ

Ⓓ

10. **Roberta Flack's:** Roberta Flack is a popular African American singer-songwriter.

WORDS TO OWN

conception (kən·sep′shən) n.: mental formation of ideas.
ingenious (in·jēn′yəs) adj.: clever.

ALICE WALKER **1107**

First Thoughts [Respond]

1. Possible responses: She never became bitter or discouraged; she brought beauty into the world; she passed on her creative spirit. Students may mention a friend or relative with creative talent.

Shaping Interpretations [Interpret]

2. by both its content and its style

3. Metaphor: the seed of a flower; simile: like a sealed letter. Possible response: yeast in dough (metaphor); like a safe-deposit box (simile).

4. Possible response: that whatever one does in life should be done with love, passion, and respect for beauty and order.

5. Possible response: Even though the mothers were uneducated, they knew that educating their children was important.

6. Possible response: In searching to understand the force that drove her mother to create her gardens, she discovered the same creative spirit motivating her own work.

Challenging the Text [Evaluate]

7. Possible responses: Yes, the essay is a tribute to Walker's mother and might have been stronger if Walker let her speak for herself; no, quotations from Walker's mother might have altered the tone of the essay and made her mother a less universal figure.

Grading Timesaver

Rubrics for each Choices assignment appear on p. 224 in the *Portfolio Management System.*

First Thoughts

1. What do you find most admirable about Alice Walker's mother? Do you know anyone who also excels anonymously at something—like gardening or painting, singing or storytelling?

Shaping Interpretations

2. As a writer, how does Walker feel she has been enriched by her mother's storytelling?

3. On page 1104, in a key passage, Walker uses a **metaphor** and a **simile** to describe how African American women handed down this "creative spark" over the generations. What are these figures of speech? (Can you think of others that could be used?)

4. What do you think Walker the writer has learned from her mother the gardener?

5. In the last five lines of the poem Walker uses in the essay, she presents a **paradox,** or apparent contradiction. State the paradox in your own words, and tell what kinds of knowledge you think Walker is talking about.

6. What do you think Walker means when she says that she found her own "garden" in the process of searching for her mother's?

Challenging the Text

7. Walker describes her mother's life and feelings but never allows her mother to speak for herself. Would the essay be improved if it included quotations from Walker's mother? Explain.

> #### Reading Check
>
> a. Describe the kind of life Walker's mother led while Walker was growing up.
>
> b. What secret does Walker hope to discover from examining her mother's life and the lives of other women like her mother?
>
> c. In what two ways does Walker's mother express her creativity?
>
> d. What happens to Walker's mother when she works in her garden?

CHOICES:
Building Your Portfolio

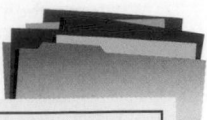

Writer's Notebook
1. Collecting Ideas for an Evaluation

When you evaluate a **personal essay,** you might want to consider such criteria as interest of topic, clarity of theme, and emotional effect. Apply such criteria to Walker's essay, citing specific passages to support your evaluation. Save your notes for possible use in the workshop on page 1181.

Summarizing a Text
2. Creativity in Everyday Places

Refer to your reading notes and the outline you made of Walker's essay. Then, in three or four paragraphs, state the main ideas of the essay and summarize the details Walker uses to support and illuminate them. Conclude with your response to Walker's ideas.

Creative Writing / Art
3. Quiet Strengths

Write a **character sketch** of someone you admire who is not at all famous. Indicate exactly what you admire about this person. Try to include the person's occupation and a description of what he or she looks like. If you wish, include a picture or photograph.

Viewing and Representing
4. Bearden's Heroines

Pages 1105 and 1106 each feature a collage by American artist Romare Bearden (1914–1988). Look up *collage* in an encyclopedia or dictionary and try to figure out what bits of materials Bearden used in these works. Then, in a brief essay, analyze these collages and tell if you think they are appropriate for Walker's essay. Open your analysis by describing exactly what you see in each work.

CHOICES:
Building Your Portfolio

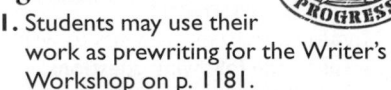

1. Students may use their work as prewriting for the Writer's Workshop on p. 1181.

2. Remind students not to summarize paragraph by paragraph but rather to identify the main idea and the details.

3 and 4. Ask students to use cluster diagrams to list details about the subjects they depict.

> #### Reading Check
>
> a. It was a hard life. She worked in the fields all day, made all of her family's clothes, raised eight children, and battled prejudice to send her children to school.
>
> b. the source of their creative spirit
>
> c. through her stories and her flower gardens
>
> d. She becomes radiantly creative as she brings order and beauty to her garden.

Amy Tan
(1952–   )

Amy Tan had not planned to become a fiction writer. In fact, for years she worked as a freelance writer for high-technology companies, a career in which flights of imagination are not permitted. To ease the pressures of her job, she decided to take jazz piano lessons—and she began writing fiction. The result was the release of a dazzling new storyteller.

Tan's parents had fled Communist China and had come to the United States shortly before she was born in Oakland, California. Her mother, a nurse, was originally from Shanghai; her father, an engineer and a Baptist minister, came from Beijing.

After her father and young brother both died of brain tumors when Amy Tan was just fifteen, her mother took her away from the "diseased" house to Switzerland, where she finished high school. Her mother expected her talented daughter to become a neurosurgeon, as well as a pianist, in her spare time. When

they returned to the United States, Tan enrolled as a premed student at Linfield College, a Baptist school in Oregon, which had been selected by her mother. But she defied her mother by leaving Linfield to join her boyfriend at San Jose State University, where she changed her major from premed to English. Tan's mother took this defiance as a sort of death between them, and mother and daughter did not speak for six months.

Tan was well aware of her mother's narrative gift (she says her mother can talk for three hours straight), and perhaps it was this which eventually prompted her own desire to write. However, she was thirty-three before she wrote her first story. Called "Endgame" (retitled "Rules of the Game") and written for a Squaw Valley writers' conference, it was the first of many Tan stories that would explore the dynamic relationship between daughters and their mothers.

These stories were collected in 1989 in one volume, the now widely known best-seller *The Joy Luck Club* (also made into a popular movie). In it, stories about Chinese American daughters are interwoven with stories of their four Chinese mothers, who are members of a mah-jongg club in San Francisco.

Tan's 1991 novel, *The Kitchen God's Wife*, was hailed by some critics as even more artistically successful than *The Joy Luck Club*. In this second book, a mother tells her grown daughter what life was like in China during World War II—and the daughter begins to see both her mother and herself with enlightened eyes. A third novel, *The Hundred Secret Senses* (1995), also explores a familial relationship—this time between two sisters whose lives are transformed during a visit to a small village in China.

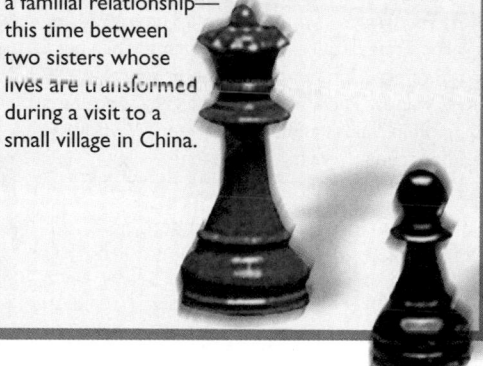

go.hrw.com
LE0 11-20

— Resources: Print and Media —

Reading
- *Graphic Organizers for Active Reading*, p. 112
- *Words to Own*, p. 60
- *Audio CD Library*
  Disc 29, Track 4

Writing and Language
- *Daily Oral Grammar*
  Transparency 66
- *Grammar and Language Links*
  Worksheet, p. 77

- *Language Workshop CD-ROM*

Assessment
- *Portfolio Management System*, p. 226
- *Preparation for College Admission Exams*, p. 69
- *Test Generator (One-Stop Planner CD-ROM)*

Internet
- go.hrw.com (keyword: LE0 11-20)

Summary ▪▪

In this excerpt from *The Joy Luck Club*, young Waverly Jong narrates her story of generational conflict. When Waverly's brothers learn to play chess, her interest is piqued. She succeeds in learning the game so well that her brothers eventually refuse to play with her. Waverly studies chess strategy with Lau Po, an older man she meets in the park. By the end of the summer, she is defeating all opponents in chess exhibitions. She competes in local tournaments and becomes a national chess champion at the age of nine. Waverly's mother proudly watches over her daughter, encourages her, and shows her off—a habit that irritates Waverly more and more. One day, Waverly expresses her displeasure at her mother's bragging, then runs off and doesn't return for two hours. When she gets home, her mother says that the family is no longer to be concerned with "this girl." Waverly goes to her room and imagines an allegorical chess game, with an opponent resembling her mother. As the opponent triumphs, Waverly imagines herself flying away from her house and her neighborhood to a place where she can ponder "her next move."

Background

This story is set in San Francisco's Chinatown district in the 1950s. This district has many small alleys crowded with shops.

Before You Read
FROM RULES OF THE GAME

Make the Connection
Parents and Children

At first, the following story appears to be about a Chinese American girl who stumbles into the forbidding world of championship chess and becomes an absolute whiz at it. But presently we come to understand that the story is about a matter far more familiar to us: the clash between a mother's authority over her children and her ambition for them, and a child's need to find his or her own way.

Quickwrite

Think about the rules of chess or another game you know. Then, write down some ways a game's rules might be similar to rules of human relations, especially between parents and children. What do you think the title of this story might mean? (Might it have more than one meaning?)

Elements of Literature
Motivation

Motivation refers to the reasons for a character's behavior. A writer can reveal motivation directly by telling us what makes a character tick. In many works, however, the writer shows us characters talking and acting but does not tell us the reasons for their behavior: We must sift through the details and then infer motivation. Tan's story fits into this second category. Pay particular attention to how the beat-up chess set arrives in the Jong family, how Waverly becomes interested in the game while her brothers play, and how her interest grows as theirs wanes. Then, ask yourself: What's really going on in that final match between Waverly and her true adversary and coach?

> **M**otivation refers to the underlying reasons for a character's behavior.
>
> *For more on Motivation, see the Handbook of Literary Terms.*

1110 CONTEMPORARY LITERATURE

---

from
Rules of the Game
from The Joy Luck Club
Amy Tan

Preteaching Vocabulary

Words to Own

Put students in small groups to read the definitions of the Words to Own listed at the bottom of the selection pages. Then, have volunteers draw visual images on the board to represent each of the following words: *intricate, ancestral, obscured, touted, prodigy, malodorous, careened,* and *successive.* When you are sure students understand the meanings of the words, have them do the following exercise by matching each vocabulary word with its synonym.

1. ____ intricate [d]		**a.** genius
2. ____ ancestral [i]		**b.** reply
3. ____ obscured [j]		**c.** consecutive
4. ____ retort [b]		**d.** complicated
5. ____ touted [e]		**e.** praised
6. ____ prodigy [a]		**f.** compromises
7. ____ malodorous [g]		**g.** smelly
8. ____ concessions [f]		**h.** lurched
9. ____ careened [h]		**i.** inherited
10. ____ successive [c]		**j.** concealed

My older brother Vincent was the one who actually got the chess set. We had gone to the annual Christmas party held at the First Chinese Baptist Church at the end of the alley. The missionary ladies had put together a Santa bag of gifts donated by members of another church. None of the gifts had names on them. There were separate sacks for boys and girls of different ages.

One of the Chinese parishioners had donned a Santa Claus costume and a stiff paper beard with cotton balls glued to it. I think the only children who thought he was the real thing were too young to know that Santa Claus was not Chinese. When my turn came up, the Santa man asked me how old I was. I thought it was a trick question; I was seven according to the American formula and

A **Reading Skills and Strategies**
Making Inferences
❓ This is an excerpt from a novel. The narrator seems to jump into the middle of a story. What topic do you think was covered just before this first sentence of the excerpt? [Possible response: The narrator might have introduced the topic of chess.]

B **Critical Thinking**
Extending the Text
❓ The spread of Christianity and European culture around the world has introduced Santa Claus to many cultures. Do you think this is a positive or a negative development? [Possible responses: It is positive because it promotes the spirit of giving; it is negative because it detracts from other cultural traditions.]

RESPONDING TO THE ART
Tell students that the game of chess is played on a square board with 64 smaller squares that alternate between red and black or black and white. Each player has 16 men: 1 king, 1 queen, 2 bishops, 2 knights, 2 castles or rooks, and 8 pawns.
Activity. Ask students who play chess to identify the pieces they see in the illustration.

Reaching All Students

Struggling Readers
For students to understand the connection between a chess game and the mother-daughter struggle portrayed in this story, they must understand the basics of chess. Tell them that the chess board is a miniature battlefield with opposing armies facing each other. The object of the game is to put the enemy king in a position where its capture is unavoidable. Ask students how a game of chess might be symbolic of a parent-child relationship.

English Language Learners
Tan has captured the rhythms of the immigrant mother's speech. Have these students look at the mother's speech patterns and notice where they depart from standard English. Be sure to point out that it makes sense for English language learners to achieve basic communication before making their speech conform to standard English. Read them the passage in the middle of the first column on p. 1113 and then translate it into standard English.

Advanced Learners
Ask students to infer what they can about traditional Chinese manners from this story and then to use their inferences to write an etiquette booklet for Americans traveling in China.

eight by the Chinese calendar. I said I was born on March 17, 1951. That seemed to satisfy him. He then solemnly asked if I had been a very, very good girl this year and did I believe in Jesus Christ and obey my parents. I knew the only answer to that. I nodded back with equal solemnity.

Having watched the other children opening their gifts, I already knew that the big gifts were not necessarily the nicest ones. One girl my age got a large coloring book of biblical characters, while a less greedy girl who selected a smaller box received a glass vial of lavender toilet water.[1] The sound of the box was also important. A ten-year-old boy had chosen a box that jangled when he shook it. It was a tin globe of the world with a slit for inserting money. He must have thought it was full of dimes and nickels, because when he saw that it had just ten pennies, his face fell with such undisguised disappointment that his mother slapped the side of his head and led him out of the church hall, apologizing to the crowd for her son who had such bad manners he couldn't appreciate such a fine gift.

As I peered into the sack, I quickly fingered the remaining presents, testing their weight, imagining what they contained. I chose a heavy, compact one that was wrapped in shiny silver foil and a red satin ribbon. It was a twelve-pack of Life Savers and I spent the rest of the party arranging and rearranging the candy tubes in the order of my favorites. My brother Winston chose wisely as well. His present turned out to be a box of intricate plastic parts; the instructions on the box proclaimed that when they were properly assembled he would have an authentic miniature replica of a World War II submarine.

Vincent got the chess set, which would have been a very decent present to get at a church Christmas party, except it was obviously used and, as we discovered later, it was missing a black pawn and a white knight. My mother graciously thanked the unknown benefactor, saying, "Too good. Cost too much." At which point, an old lady with fine white, wispy hair nodded toward our family and said with a whistling whisper, "Merry, merry Christmas."

When we got home, my mother told Vincent to throw the chess set away. "She not want it. We

1. **toilet water:** perfumed after-bath skin freshener.

A little knowledge withheld is a great advantage one should store for future use. That is the power of chess. It is a game of secrets in which one must show and never tell.

not want it," she said, tossing her head stiffly to the side with a tight, proud smile. My brothers had deaf ears. They were already lining up the chess pieces and reading from the dog-eared instruction book.

I watched Vincent and Winston play during Christmas week. The chess board seemed to hold elaborate secrets waiting to be untangled. The chessmen were more powerful than Old Li's magic herbs that cured ancestral curses. And my brothers wore such serious faces that I was sure something was at stake that was greater than avoiding the tradesmen's door to Hong Sing's.

"Let me! Let me!" I begged between games when one brother or the other would sit back with a deep sigh of relief and victory, the other annoyed, unable to let go of the outcome. Vincent at first refused to let me play, but when I offered my Life Savers as replacements for the buttons that filled in for the missing pieces, he relented. He chose the flavors: wild cherry for the black pawn and peppermint for the white knight. Winner could eat both.

As our mother sprinkled flour and rolled out small doughy circles for the steamed dumplings that would be our dinner that night, Vincent explained the rules, pointing to each piece. "You

WORDS TO OWN
intricate (in′tri·kit) *adj.*: complicated.
ancestral (an·ses′trəl) *adj.*: inherited.

Using Students' Strengths

Mathematical/Logical

Discuss as a class the rules of chess. Ask one student volunteer to describe the permitted moves of the various pieces, and ask another to explain briefly how computer programs are created to compete against highly skilled players. Also ask the volunteers to describe the thought processes that occur during a chess game. Finally, call on them to define chess terms used in the text, like *endgame* and *check*.

Spatial

Ask students to locate or create a photograph, drawing, or other illustration that represents for them the conflict that takes place between the narrator and her mother in the selection. Call on students to display their illustrations for the class and to explain their connection to the story. Encourage students to use slides or computer presentation programs to display their images.

Interpersonal

Help students monitor their own reading by demonstrating how you would read the selection. Read aloud the first paragraph, and talk about any images it suggests. Remark on confusing language, and explain how you adjust your thinking as you read. Then, ask pairs to take turns reading the selection. Each student should read a paragraph, pause, and talk to the other student, using the strategies you demonstrated.

have sixteen pieces and so do I. One king and queen, two bishops, two knights, two castles, and eight pawns. The pawns can only move forward one step, except on the first move. Then they can move two. But they can only take men by moving crossways like this, except in the beginning, when you can move ahead and take another pawn."

"Why?" I asked as I moved my pawn. "Why can't they move more steps?"

"Because they're pawns," he said.

"But why do they go crossways to take other men. Why aren't there any women and children?"

"Why is the sky blue? Why must you always ask stupid questions?" asked Vincent. "This is a game. These are the rules. I didn't make them up. See. Here. In the book." He jabbed a page with a pawn in his hand. "Pawn. P-A-W-N. Pawn. Read it yourself."

My mother patted the flour off her hands. "Let me see book," she said quietly. She scanned the pages quickly, not reading the foreign English symbols, seeming to search deliberately for nothing in particular.

"This American rules," she concluded at last. "Every time people come out from foreign country, must know rules. You not know, judge say, Too bad, go back. They not telling you why so you can use their way go forward. They say, Don't know why, you find out yourself. But they knowing all the time. Better you take it, find out why yourself." She tossed her head back with a satisfied smile.

I found out about all the whys later. I read the rules and looked up all the big words in a dictionary. I borrowed books from the Chinatown library. I studied each chess piece, trying to absorb the power each contained.

I learned about opening moves and why it's important to control the center early on; the shortest distance between two points is straight down the middle. I learned about the middle game and why tactics between two adversaries are like clashing ideas; the one who plays better has the clearest plans for both attacking and getting out of traps. I learned why it is essential in the endgame to have foresight, a mathematical understanding of all possible moves, and patience; all weaknesses and advantages become evident to a strong adversary and are <u>obscured</u> to a tiring opponent. I discovered that for the whole game one must

gather invisible strengths and see the endgame before the game begins.

I also found out why I should never reveal "why" to others. A little knowledge withheld is a great advantage one should store for future use. That is the power of chess. It is a game of secrets in which one must show and never tell.

I loved the secrets I found within the sixty-four black and white squares. I carefully drew a hand-made chessboard and pinned it to the wall next to my bed, where at night I would stare for hours at imaginary battles. Soon I no longer lost any games or Life Savers, but I lost my adversaries. Winston and Vincent decided they were more interested in roaming the streets after school in their Hopalong Cassidy[2] cowboy hats.

On a cold spring afternoon, while walking home from school, I detoured through the playground at the end of our alley. I saw a group of old men, two seated across a folding table playing a game of chess, others smoking pipes, eating peanuts, and watching. I ran home and grabbed Vincent's chess set, which was bound in a cardboard box with rubber bands. I also carefully selected two prized rolls of Life Savers. I came back to the park and approached a man who was observing the game.

"Want to play?" I asked him. His face widened with surprise and he grinned as he looked at the box under my arm.

"Little sister, been a long time since I play with dolls," he said, smiling benevolently. I quickly put the box down next to him on the bench and displayed my <u>retort</u>.

Lau Po, as he allowed me to call him, turned out to be a much better player than my brothers. I lost many games and many Life Savers. But over the weeks, with each diminishing roll of candies, I added new secrets. Lau Po gave me the names. The Double Attack from the East and West Shores. Throwing Stones on the Drowning Man. The Sudden Meeting of the Clan. The Surprise from

---

2. Hopalong Cassidy: cowboy hero of movies and television from the 1930s through the early 1950s.

WORDS TO OWN

obscured (əb·skyoord′) v.: concealed.
retort (ri·tôrt′) n.: quick answer.

AMY TAN **1113**

E Struggling Readers
Paraphrasing
Read this passage to students. Then, ask them to paraphrase what the mother is saying. [Possible response: Immigrants to the United States are expected to know the rules. No one gives them a helping hand, so it's best for immigrants to take charge and figure things out for themselves.]

F Reading Skills and Strategies
Making Generalizations
? How might the narrator's comments about chess strategy apply to life as well? [Possible responses: To be successful, a person needs to make long-term plans—to anticipate success before it comes; the people with the clearest plans for the future are the ones who have the best chance for success.]

G Critical Thinking
Making Connections
? Which of the narrator's earlier comments about chess is echoed in her unspoken retort to the man's taunt? [Possible response: The narrator said earlier that chess is a game of showing, not telling. Here, she does not answer the man in words but instead attempts to show him her skill.]

Skill Link

Generating Study-Guide Questions

Tell students they can begin their study of a story by generating generic study-guide questions and then answering them.

Activities

1. Ask students to list questions that they frequently ask themselves as they are reading a short story. You might have them consider these categories: title, motivation, cause and effect, conflict, resolution, author's intent.

2. Compile a class list of questions on these elements, and have the class edit the list.

3. Have students answer the questions as they are reading and share their answers at the end.

4. Then, have the class evaluate the study-guide questions they used. Were they helpful in getting at the heart of the story? Why or why not? How should the guide questions be changed?

RESPONDING TO THE ART

The film version of *The Joy Luck Club* (1993), directed by Wayne Wang, with a screenplay by Amy Tan and Ronald Bass, portrays a shortened and somewhat different version of the events related in "Rules of the Game." In the film version, Waverly, after arguing fiercely with her mother, vows to give up chess. When, after a few months, she returns to the game, she performs badly at a tournament and simply never plays chess again. She says (in a voiceover by the adult Waverly) that she knew she had an "amazing gift," but she felt all her powers drained from her. In the movie still shown here, Young Waverly (played by Yu Mai) faces her opponent.

Activity. After students have read the story, have them invent a few lines of dialogue to give their impressions of what Waverly might be thinking at the chess board.

Crossing the Curriculum

Art

Games and competition have been a common subject of art for centuries. Have students do independent research to locate drawings, paintings, photographs, or other works that depict competition or games. Ask them to bring in copies of the works and to share the pictures with the rest of the class. Call on students to compare the works and to point out common elements.

History

Ask students to research and prepare a news report on the career of chess prodigy Bobby Fischer, based on encyclopedia articles and news stories or information from other news media. Suggest that students include a discussion about how Fischer's personal conflicts may have affected his chess playing. If copies of photographs or illustrations are available, encourage students to include them with their reports.

Foreign Languages

Have interested students research and report on the Chinese language. Suggest that they look into such topics as dialects, the written language, and the basic syntax of Chinese. They might try to figure out if the English speech patterns of the narrator's mother bear any relationship to the syntax of her native language.

As I began to play, the boy disappeared, the color ran out of the room, and I saw only my white pieces and his black ones waiting on the other side. A light wind began blowing past my ears. It whispered secrets only I could hear.

the Sleeping Guard. The Humble Servant Who Kills the King. Sand in the Eyes of Advancing Forces. A Double Killing Without Blood. **(A)**

There were also the fine points of chess etiquette. Keep captured men in neat rows, as well-tended prisoners. Never announce "Check" with vanity, lest someone with an unseen sword slit your throat. Never hurl pieces into the sandbox after you have lost a game, because then you must find them again, by yourself, after apologizing to all around you. By the end of the summer, Lau Po had taught me all he knew, and I had become a better chess player.

A small weekend crowd of Chinese people and tourists would gather as I played and defeated my opponents one by one. My mother would join the crowds during these outdoor exhibition games. She sat proudly on the bench, telling my admirers with proper Chinese humility, "Is luck."

A man who watched me play in the park suggested that my mother allow me to play in local chess tournaments. My mother smiled graciously, an answer that meant nothing. I desperately wanted to go, but I bit back my tongue. I knew she would not let me play among strangers. So as we walked home I said in a small voice that I didn't want to play in the local tournament. They would have American rules. If I lost, I would bring shame on my family. **(B)**

"Is shame you fall down nobody push you," said my mother.

During my first tournament, my mother sat with me in the front row as I waited for my turn. I frequently bounced my legs to unstick them from the cold metal seat of the folding chair. When my name was called, I leapt up. My mother unwrapped something in her lap. It was her *chang,* a small tablet of red jade which held the sun's fire. "Is luck," she whispered, and tucked it into my dress pocket. I turned to my opponent, a fifteen-year-old boy from Oakland. He looked at me, wrinkling his nose. **(C)**

As I began to play, the boy disappeared, the color ran out of the room, and I saw only my white pieces and his black ones waiting on the other side. A light wind began blowing past my ears. It whispered secrets only I could hear. **(D)**

Scene from the movie *The Joy Luck Club.*
©Buena Vista Pictures Distribution, Inc.

AMY TAN 1115

Skill Link

A Reading Skills and Strategies

Drawing Conclusions

? What might the wind represent to the narrator? [Possible responses: quiet strength; silent strategy.] How does the wind's advice echo the narrator's earlier comments about chess? [Possible responses: She keeps her opponent guessing; avoids his traps; and effectively distracts him.]

B Historical Connections

Bobby Fischer

Bobby Fischer (1943–   ), also a child prodigy, at the age of fifteen became the youngest chess player ever ranked as an international grand master. He won the first of many United States championships at age fourteen. When Fischer won the world championship in 1972, he generated enormous worldwide interest in chess. Fischer would have made his remark about a woman never becoming a grand master in the late 1950s, a time when gender stereotyping was virtually uncontested. Ask students why Fischer might have assumed this about females. [Possible response: Chess is a game of warlike strategy. At the time, most females were assumed to be uninterested in conflict or competition.]

C Vocabulary Note

The Prefix mal-

Ask students to infer the meaning of the prefix from the definition. [bad] Then, ask them to think of other words formed from the same prefix. [Possible responses: malicious; malevolent; malfunction; malice; malignant.]

D Elements of Literature

Characterization

? What does the mother's attention to Waverly's clothes and mannerisms reveal about her? [Possible response: She is concerned with how things look.]

A "Blow from the South," it murmured. "The wind leaves no trail." I saw a clear path, the traps to avoid. The crowd rustled. "Shhh! Shhh!" said the corners of the room. The wind blew stronger. "Throw sand from the East to distract him." The knight came forward ready for the sacrifice. The wind hissed, louder and louder. "Blow, blow, blow. He cannot see. He is blind now. Make him lean away from the wind so he is easier to knock down."

"Check," I said, as the wind roared with laughter. The wind died down to little puffs, my own breath.

My mother placed my first trophy next to a new plastic chess set that the neighborhood Tao society had given to me. As she wiped each piece with a soft cloth, she said, "Next time win more, lose less."

"Ma, it's not how many pieces you lose," I said. "Sometimes you need to lose pieces to get ahead."

"Better to lose less, see if you really need."

At the next tournament, I won again, but it was my mother who wore the triumphant grin.

"Lost eight piece this time. Last time was eleven. What I tell you? Better off lose less!" I was annoyed, but I couldn't say anything.

I attended more tournaments, each one farther away from home. I won all games, in all divisions. The Chinese bakery downstairs from our flat displayed my growing collection of trophies in its window, amidst the dust-covered cakes that were never picked up. The day after I won an important regional tournament, the window encased a fresh sheet cake with whipped-cream frosting and red script saying, "Congratulations, Waverly Jong, Chinatown Chess Champion." Soon after that, a flower shop, headstone engraver, and funeral parlor offered to sponsor me in national tournaments. That's when my mother decided I no longer had to do the dishes. Winston and Vincent had to do my chores.

"Why does she get to play and we do all the work," complained Vincent.

"Is new American rules," said my mother. "Meimei[3] play, squeeze all her brains out for win chess. You play, worth squeeze towel."

By my ninth birthday, I was a national chess

---

3. **Meimei** (mā′mā′): Chinese for "little sister."

1116 CONTEMPORARY LITERATURE

---

champion. I was still some 429 points away from grand-master status,[4] but I was touted as the Great American Hope, a child prodigy and a girl to boot. **B** They ran a photo of me in *Life* magazine next to a quote in which Bobby Fischer said, "There will never be a woman grand master." "Your move, Bobby," said the caption.

The day they took the magazine picture I wore neatly plaited braids clipped with plastic barrettes trimmed with rhinestones. I was playing in a large high school auditorium that echoed with phlegmy coughs and the squeaky rubber knobs of chair legs sliding across freshly waxed wooden floors. Seated across from me was an American man, about the same age as Lau Po, maybe fifty. I remember that his sweaty brow seemed to weep at **C** my every move. He wore a dark, malodorous suit. One of his pockets was stuffed with a great white kerchief on which he wiped his palm before sweeping his hand over the chosen chess piece with great flourish.

In my crisp pink-and-white dress with scratchy lace at the neck, one of two my mother had sewn for these special occasions, I would clasp my hands under my chin, the delicate points of my elbows poised lightly on the table in the manner my mother had shown me for posing for the press. I **D** would swing my patent leather shoes back and forth like an impatient child riding on a school bus. Then I would pause, suck in my lips, twirl my chosen piece in midair as if undecided, and then firmly plant it in its new threatening place, with a triumphant smile thrown back at my opponent for good measure.

I no longer played in the alley of Waverly Place. I never visited the playground where the pigeons and old men gathered. I went to school, then directly home to learn new chess secrets, cleverly concealed advantages, more escape routes.

But I found it difficult to concentrate at home. My mother had a habit of standing over me while

---

4. **grand-master status:** top rank in international chess competition.

WORDS TO OWN
touted (tout′id) *v.*: highly praised.
prodigy (präd′ə·jē) *n.*: extremely gifted person.
malodorous (mal·ō′dər·əs) *adj.*: bad-smelling.

Getting Students Involved

Cooperative Learning

Group Sketches. Ask students to work in groups of four to prepare dramatic sketches based on scenes from the story. Allow students to base their sketches on dialogue or on action. Suggest that the groups select one member to act as a narrator who introduces and explains the sketch. Encourage students to include sound effects and background music when they perform. Remind the class that the sketches

may be interpretations based only loosely on events in the story. Encourage students to divide up the work based on members' skills and interests. A few students might work together on a script or the music. Still others might do the acting. One person might pull it all together as producer/director.

Speaking and Listening

Hot Seat. Place students in pairs and ask each one to portray either the narrator or her mother. Ask both students to create a short list of their character's attributes. Then, ask them to give their partners two minutes on the Hot Seat to respond in character to questions about the story's conflicts.

I plotted out my games. I think she thought of herself as my protective ally. Her lips would be sealed tight, and after each move I made, a soft "Hmmmmph" would escape from her nose.

"Ma, I can't practice when you stand there like that," I said one day. She retreated to the kitchen and made loud noises with the pots and pans. When the crashing stopped, I could see out of the corner of my eye that she was standing in the doorway. "Hmmmph!" Only this one came out of her tight throat.

My parents made many concessions to allow me to practice. One time I complained that the bedroom I shared was so noisy that I couldn't think. Thereafter, my brothers slept in a bed in the living room facing the street. I said I couldn't finish my rice; my head didn't work right when my stomach was too full. I left the table with half-finished bowls and nobody complained. But there was one duty I couldn't avoid. I had to accompany my mother on Saturday market days when I had no tournament to play. My mother would proudly walk with me, visiting many shops, buying very little. "This my daughter Wave-ly Jong," she said to whoever looked her way.

One day, after we left a shop I said under my breath, "I wish you wouldn't do that, telling everybody I'm your daughter." My mother stopped walking. Crowds of people with heavy bags pushed past us on the sidewalk, bumping into first one shoulder, then another.

"Aii-ya. So shame be with mother?" She grasped my hand even tighter as she glared at me.

I looked down. "It's not that, it's just so obvious. It's just so embarrassing."

"Embarrass you be my daughter?" Her voice was cracking with anger.

"That's not what I meant. That's not what I said."

"What you say?"

I knew it was a mistake to say anything more, but I heard my voice speaking. "Why do you have to use me to show off? If you want to show off, then why don't you learn to play chess."

My mother's eyes turned into dangerous black slits. She had no words for me, just sharp silence.

I felt the wind rushing around my hot ears. I jerked my hand out of my mother's tight grasp and spun around, knocking into an old woman. Her bag of groceries spilled to the ground.

"Aii-ya! Stupid girl!" my mother and the woman cried. Oranges and tin cans careened down the sidewalk. As my mother stooped to help the old woman pick up the escaping food, I took off.

I raced down the street, dashing between people, not looking back as my mother screamed shrilly, "Meimei! Meimei!" I fled down an alley, past dark curtained shops and merchants washing the grime off their windows. I sped into the sunlight, into a large street crowded with tourists examining trinkets and souvenirs. I ducked into another dark alley, down another street, up another alley. I ran until it hurt and I realized I had nowhere to go, that I was not running from anything. The alleys contained no escape routes.

My breath came out like angry smoke. It was cold. I sat down on an upturned plastic pail next to a stack of empty boxes, cupping my chin with my hands, thinking hard. I imagined my mother, first walking briskly down one street or another looking for me, then giving up and returning home to await my arrival. After two hours, I stood up on creaking legs and slowly walked home.

The alley was quiet and I could see the yellow lights shining from our flat like two tiger's eyes in the night. I climbed the sixteen steps to the door, advancing quietly up each so as not to make any warning sounds. I turned the knob; the door was locked. I heard a chair moving, quick steps, the locks turning—click! click! click!—and then the door opened.

"About time you got home," said Vincent. "Boy, are you in trouble."

He slid back to the dinner table. On a platter were the remains of a large fish, its fleshy head still connected to bones swimming upstream in vain escape. Standing there waiting for my punishment, I heard my mother speak in a dry voice.

"We are not concerning this girl. This girl not have concerning for us."

Nobody looked at me. Bone chopsticks clinked against the insides of bowls being emptied into hungry mouths.

I walked into my room, closed the door, and lay down on my bed. The room was dark, the ceiling

---

WORDS TO OWN

concessions (kən·sesh′ənz) *n. pl.*: acts of giving in.
careened (kə·rēnd′) *v.*: lurched sideways.

AMY TAN 1117

E Critical Thinking
Extending the Text
? How can parents be close to their children without smothering them or trying to control their lives? [Possible responses: They can wait for the children to ask for help; they can let children teach them things.]

F Elements of Literature
Motivation
? What does this passage suggest about the difference between the motivations of the narrator and those of her mother? [Possible response: While the narrator simply enjoys excelling at a challenging task, the narrator's mother enjoys that success because of the attention and respect it brings to the family.]

G Reading Skills and Strategies
Making Inferences
? What does this comment reveal about the mother's feelings? [Possible responses: The comment shows that she was hurt by the way the narrator spoke to her earlier; she thinks the narrator is not concerned about her feelings.]

Professional Notes

Critical Comment: Tan's Characters
About *The Joy Luck Club,* reviewer Orville Schell wrote: "In the hands of a less talented writer . . . the characters might have seemed like cutouts from a Chinese-American knockoff of *Roots.* But in the hands of Amy Tan, who has a wonderful eye for what is telling, a fine ear for dialogue, a deep empathy for her subject matter, and a guilelessly straightforward way of writing, they sing with a rare fidelity and beauty." Other reviewers were less enthusiastic. Rhoda Koenig wrote: "*The Joy Luck Club* is lively but not terribly deep. The stories resolve themselves too neatly and cozily, and are often burdened with symbols that flatten them out." Ask students which of these observations they agree with, and have them give their reasons.

? Tan uses the imagery of a chessboard to represent the conflict between daughter and mother. What does the image suggest about the probable resolution of the conflict between Waverly and her mother? [Possible response: Waverly will feel defeated, and she will cope with the sense of defeat by becoming emotionally distant from her mother.]

Primary Sources

In this interview, Tan urges writers to develop their own voices. She also notes that her stories appeal to many Chinese Americans, even though they are very personal. Her mother, Tan says, continues to have high expectations of her.

---

filled with shadows from the dinnertime lights of neighboring flats.

In my head, I saw a chessboard with sixty-four black and white squares. Opposite me was my opponent, two angry black slits. She wore a triumphant smile. "Strongest wind cannot be seen," she said.

A Her black men advanced across the plane, slowly marching to each <u>successive</u> level as a single unit. My white pieces screamed as they scurried and fell off the board one by one. As her men drew closer to my edge, I felt myself growing light. I rose up into the air and flew out the window. Higher and higher, above the alley, over the tops of tiled roofs, where I was gathered up by the wind and pushed up toward the night sky until everything below me disappeared and I was alone.

I closed my eyes and pondered my next move.

WORDS TO OWN
successive (sək·ses′iv) *adj.*: consecutive.

PRIMARY Sources — AN INTERVIEW

An Interview with Amy Tan

In a magazine interview, Amy Tan answered questions about her stories of mothers and daughters in *The Joy Luck Club*. Here are some of her responses:

Q: Do you have advice to offer aspiring novelists?

A: You have to develop a discipline, and you have to learn that you can't always wait for inspiration. Also, I think young writers try to imitate the people they admire, and that's dangerous. No matter how well you imitate Tama Janowitz or Jay McInerney, it doesn't work. You have to find your own voice.

Q: How do Chinese Americans like your book?

A: My feelings were so personal; I didn't think anyone else felt that way. The surprise is how many Chinese people have said, "Your stories are so much like my family." They thought I had been eavesdropping in their living rooms.

Q: How does your mother feel about your success?

A: The day the book was number four on *The New York Times* Best Seller List, I showed the list to my mother. She looked at it, laid her finger across the line, and asked, "Who's number three? And two? And one?" She's very proud, but none of this impresses her too much, and she doesn't think that I should be impressed either. But she was also saying, "I think you should be number one."

—Joan Chatfield Taylor,
"Cosmo Talks to Amy Tan"

Archive Photos.

Making the Connections

Connecting to the Theme:
"From Generation to Generation"
This story portrays intergenerational conflict in a Chinese immigrant family. Ask students to compare the main conflicts in this story with those in "Son" and "Daughter of Invention." Which aspects of intergenerational conflicts seem to cross all cultures, and which seem specific to particular cultures?

Assessing Learning

Check Test: True–False
1. The narrator receives a new chess set at a Christmas party. [False]
2. The narrator's first chess games were with her brothers. [True]
3. Other players are intimidated by the narrator and her appearance. [False]
4. Her brothers willingly help with chores so that Waverly may practice chess. [False]
5. The conflict in the story is about the mother's jealousy of her daughter. [False]

Standardized Test Preparation
For practice with ACT and SAT formats, see
• *Preparation for College Admission Exams*, p. 69
For practice in proofreading and editing, see
• *Daily Oral Grammar*, Transparency 66

First Thoughts

1. Did you find the relationship between mother and daughter believable? Why or why not?

Shaping Interpretations

2. What does Waverly's mother mean when she says, on page 1112, "She not want it. We not want it"? How do the boys' actions show cultural and generational **conflicts** between the mother and her children?

3. Review your Quickwrite notes. How does the "power of chess" relate to the relationship between Waverly and her mother?

4. What do you think is Mrs. Jong's **motivation** for showing off Waverly? Why does Waverly resent her mother's actions?

5. Near the end of the story, Waverly's imaginary opponent says, "Strongest wind cannot be seen." Where else in the story is that statement used? Explain what you think it means.

6. What do you think is the meaning of Waverly's fantasy at the story's end? What do you predict will be her "next move"?

7. Find passages in the story where rules of various sorts are talked about. What multiple meanings might the **title** have?

> **Reading Check**
>
> a. How did the Jongs get their first chess set?
> b. Explain how young Waverly came to be allowed to play with her brothers.
> c. Point out some of the ways in which Waverly's mother shows she is ambitious for her daughter and proud of her accomplishments.
> d. As a result of Waverly's success at chess, what **conflicts** arise between her and her mother?

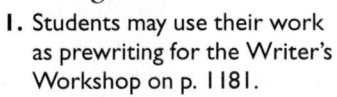
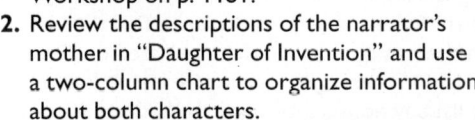

CHOICES:
Building Your Portfolio

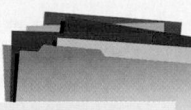

> **Writer's Notebook**
>
> **1. Collecting Ideas for an Evaluation**
>
> In a review of *The Joy Luck Club,* the critic Susan Dooley wrote: "These women from China find trying to talk to their daughters like trying to plug a foreign appliance into an American outlet. The current won't work. Impulses collide and nothing flows through the wires except anger and exasperation." Write your thoughts on how well this critical evaluation applies to "Rules of the Game." Use specific examples from the story as well as your personal comments. Save your notes for possible use in the Writer's Workshop on page 1181.
>
> **Interpreting Characters**
>
> **2. Visitors from Other Stories**
>
> In a brief essay, tell what you think would happen if Mrs. Jong and Cukita's mother (from Julia Alvarez's "Daughter of Invention" on page 1079) were to enter each other's story. If Mrs. Jong could be brought into Alvarez's story, whose side would she take—the mother's or the father's? If Cukita's mother could be introduced to Mrs. Jong, what advice would she give Mrs. Jong? Write one paragraph about each character. Be sure to explain *why* you think each character would behave in a particular way if she were inserted into another situation.
>
> **Speaking and Listening**
>
> **3. Rules of the Games**
>
> Choose a sport or game familiar to you and other class members. Working in groups, prepare oral reports on the etiquette of the game—its unwritten rules, examples of gamesmanship, and the terms used to describe its special maneuvers or plays. Before you begin, review Tan's discussion of the essence of chess on page 1113.

AMY TAN 1119

CHOICES:
Building Your Portfolio

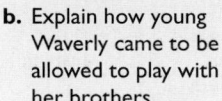

1. Students may use their work as prewriting for the Writer's Workshop on p. 1181.
2. Review the descriptions of the narrator's mother in "Daughter of Invention" and use a two-column chart to organize information about both characters.
3. With students brainstorm a list of games and their rules, including computer games and television quiz shows.

> **Reading Check**
>
> a. Vincent receives one at a church Christmas party.
> b. She offers them candy.
> c. She tells her to lose fewer pieces, excuses her from chores so that she can practice, and introduces her proudly to strangers.
> d. Her mother's uninformed advice annoys Waverly. Waverly just wants to enjoy chess, while her mother wants to show off Waverly's success.

First Thoughts [Respond]

1. Possible response: Yes, because it shows both positive and negative interactions between the mother and daughter.

Shaping Interpretations [Interpret]

2. She means that she does not want anything that someone else would not value. Her children do not share her view—the boys ignore her order to throw the chess set away.
3. Waverly tricks her mother into letting her play in the tournament by using a chesslike strategy.
4. Possible response: Her motivation stems from pride in Waverly's accomplishments and a desire to share in her victories. Waverly resents this because she wonders if she is valued only for her accomplishments.
5. The wind uses a similar expression when giving advice to Waverly during her first tournament (p. 1116). Possible response: It refers to the importance of hiding strategies or feelings from an opponent.
6. Possible response: Waverly may be trying to understand her conflict with her mother by comparing it to chess. Her fantasy of flight may reflect her desire to escape her mother's influence. Her next move may be to appear contrite while establishing emotional distance from her mother.
7. Possible response: the rules implied by the Santa Claus about being a good girl (p. 1112), the rules of chess (p. 1113), the American rules and procedures (p. 1113), the rules of chess etiquette (p. 1115). The title could refer to chess, to family relationships, or to life.

Grading Timesaver

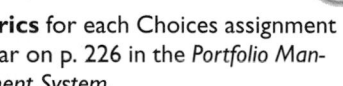

Rubrics for each Choices assignment appear on p. 226 in the *Portfolio Management System.*

Reading Skills and Strategies

Mini-Lesson:
Vocabulary—Base Words, Roots, and Word Families
Remind the class that not all roots come from Greek or Latin. Point out that learning the meanings of roots, prefixes, and suffixes is one of the best ways to prepare to read more challenging materials and to study for standardized tests. Emphasize to students that every time they learn a new prefix, suffix, or root word, they are acquiring a key that will help them unlock the meanings of many words.

Try It Out
1. -bene-; benefit, benign
2. -audi-; audience, audible
3. -ver-; invert, vertex
4. -pon-, -pos-; component, oppose
5. -sacr-, -sanc-; sacrament, sanctify

VOCABULARY: BASE WORDS, ROOTS, AND WORD FAMILIES

Amy Tan opens "Rules of the Game" with a Christmas party at which the narrator receives a gift after satisfactorily answering a set of questions.

> He then *solemnly* asked if I had been a very, very good girl this year and did I believe in Jesus Christ and obey my parents. I knew the only answer to that. I nodded back with equal *solemnity*.

Notice the appropriateness of the narrator's answer. Tan uses a noun to describe the manner of the answer (*solemnity*) that is nearly identical to the adverb used to describe the tone of the question (*solemnly*). The two words, *solemnly* and *solemnity*, belong to the same word family.

In general, there are two broad categories of words in English: those that can be divided into smaller parts (*unkind, repackage*) and those that cannot (*proud, high*). Words that stand alone and are complete by themselves are called **base words:** *solemn, answer, equal.* Words that can be divided (*solemnity, equality*) are made up of two or more of these three word parts: **roots, prefixes, suffixes.** Roots are word parts that carry the core meaning of a word, but usually do not stand alone (the root *graph* is an exception). Most often, they are combined with a prefix and/or suffix to form a word. Words that share the same root or base word can be considered word families.

In the English language, many words are formed from Greek and Latin roots. To the right are some examples of common word roots.

Common Word Roots		
Root	**Meaning**	**Examples**
GREEK		
–anthrop–	human	anthropology
–chrom–	color	monochrome
–dem–	people	demagogue, democrat
–derm–	skin	dermatology
–log–, –logy–	study, word	logic, theology
–ortho–	straight	orthodox, orthography
–phil–	like, love	philanthropy
LATIN		
–audi–	hear	audio, auditorium
–ben–, –bene–	good	benign, beneficial
–cogn–	know	recognize
–duc–, –duct–	draw, lead	induce, deduct
–loc–	place	locality, locate
–magn–	large, grand	magnify, magnitude
–mor–, –mort–	death	moribund, mortal
–omni–	all	omniscient
–pon–, –pos–	place	impose, postpone
–prim–	early	primeval, primitive
–sacr–, –sanc–	sacred, holy	sacrilege, sanctify
–spir–	breath	expire, inspire
–uni–	one	unify, universe
–ver–	turn	reverse, aversion

Try It Out

At right are some other words from "Rules of the Game." Identify the word roots. Then, find at least two other words that belong to the same word family, using a dictionary if necessary. Do not include forms whose only difference is an **inflectional suffix**—a suffix that changes person, number, or tense (*–s, –ed, –ing*).

1. benefactor
2. auditorium
3. adversaries
4. opponent
5. sacrifice

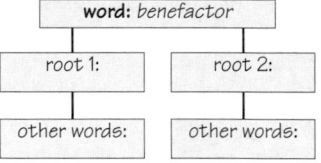

Reaching All Students

Advanced Learners
Ask students to use the list of roots above and prefixes or suffixes of their own choice to build neologisms, or new words, that make creative use of the word parts' meanings or connotations. Encourage students to create puns or other humorous words, but remind them to develop only words that would be appropriate to share aloud in class.

Crossing the Curriculum

Science
Assign pairs of students to review different pages from a science textbook or dictionary of scientific terms. Ask each pair to find the words on their assigned page that are based on Greek or Latin roots, prefixes, or suffixes. Ask them to list any nonscientific words that use the same word parts. Then, with students, create a class master list of the terms students find.

Garrett Hongo

(1951–)

Charles Wright.

"For me, one voice among so many others, a voice I've tried to train as much out of a passion for English and American poetry as out of my loyalties to the Japanese American past of four generations and to the landscape of Hawaii, the place of my birth, it has been a *feeling* for language and its beauty that has brought me to poetry and kept me at it."

In this one long sentence, Garrett Hongo seems to unite all the most vital elements that characterize his work: a distinctive voice, a passion for poetry, loyalty to past generations, a sense of place, and a love of language itself.

Garrett Hongo was born in Volcano, Hawaii, and grew up on the North Shore of Oahu and in the Los Angeles area. He graduated from Pomona College in 1973 and earned a Master of Fine Arts degree from the University of California, Irvine, in 1980. His first poetry collection, *Yellow Light,* was published in 1982. But it was his second collection, *The River of Heaven* (1988), that made a strong impression on literary critics. The book was chosen as the Lamont Poetry Selection of the Academy of American Poets and was a finalist for a Pulitzer Prize. While writing, Hongo taught at the University of Missouri and the University of Houston before becoming professor of English at the University of Oregon. In 1995, he published a well-received prose work, *Volcano: A Memoir of Hawaii.*

Garrett Hongo's poems often center on the complexities facing Americans of Asian descent as they labor to establish a personal identity, interact with people of other backgrounds, and express themselves artistically. His poems also overflow with the common details of contemporary American popular culture, such as television shows and pop music, all delivered in a language and style that blends passion and delicacy.

Hongo says that he strives for "emotional nobility of some kind, the idea that poems might help produce and reveal our 'better nature.'" He reaches for "the *jen* of Confucianism which was a notion of the innate moral and spiritual 'good' in people that impressed Ezra Pound as one of the highest poetic values; and the idea of *samadhi,* or sensate and sentient calm, that we get from Buddhism."

Hongo's wife, his friends, his fellow poets, all those who share his ideals—these are his audience, he tells us. Yet he adds with pride, "I think I must say that I write for my father, Albert Kazuyoshi Hongo, in a very personal way. I want to be his witness, to testify to his great and noble life, in struggle against anger, in struggle against his own loneliness and isolation for being a Hawaiian Japanese who emigrated to Los Angeles without much family or community. He was a great example to me of a man who refused to hate, or, being different himself, to be afraid of difference, who accepted the friendship of all the strange and underprivileged ostracized by the rest of 'normal' society—Vietnamese, Mexicans, Southern blacks, reservation Indians relocated to the city—and I want my poems to be equal to his heart." The following poem certainly is devoted to that goal.

go.hrw.com
LE0 11-20

GARRETT HONGO 1121

Summary ■■

The speaker recalls a childhood in which the mystical power of spoken words fascinated him and made him long to master their secrets. The second half of the poem is devoted to the speaker's father, who came home tired and sore from his construction job. The speaker describes wanting to become a "doctor of pure magic," chanting magical healing words for his father. Hongo's emphasis on verbal magic suggests that his own work may be a fulfillment of the speaker's dream.

Ⓐ Struggling Readers
Paraphrasing
Tell students that these five lines discuss the power of the Buddhist mantras. Ask students to paraphrase these lines. [The Amida's ballads get money from the poor and give them prayers that banish desire.]

Ⓑ Historical Connections
Point out that in the early 1900s, many Japanese citizens came to Hawaii to work on sugar cane plantations, where they endured difficult living and working conditions. The war referred to here is World War II, which the United States entered after its naval base at Pearl Harbor, Hawaii, was bombed by Japan.

Make the Connection
Language Matters
Sometimes we forget that language matters—it affects us in many important ways, whether it is spoken or written. The poem that follows zeroes in on spoken language—old Hawaiian chants, Buddhist mantras, the stories and songs of grandparents. We learn from language, the poem's speaker tells us, and we try to change the world with spoken words and syllables passed from generation to generation.

Reading Skills and Strategies

Identifying Specific Details
As you read the poem a second time, write down details that you feel are particularly vivid or interesting.

Elements of Literature
Refrain
A **refrain** is a word, phrase, line, or group of lines that is repeated several times in a poem. A poet may use a refrain to help establish rhythm, to emphasize a point, or to achieve some other effect. Short refrains typically appear at the ends of lines, but in the following poem they appear at the beginnings of lines.

What For

Garrett Hongo

At six I lived for spells:
how a few Hawaiian words could call
up the rain, could hymn like the sea
in the long swirl of chambers
5   curling in the nautilus of a shell,
how Amida's° ballads of the Buddhaland
in the drone of the priest's liturgy
could conjure money from the poor
and give them nothing but mantras,°
10   the strange syllables that healed desire.

I lived for stories about the war
my grandfather told over *hana* cards,°
slapping them down on the mats
with a sharp Japanese *kiai*.°

6. Amida's: *Amida* is Japanese for "Amitābha," Sanskrit for "infinite light." Amida is the great savior worshiped by members of the Pure Land sect, one of the most popular forms of Buddhism in eastern Asia.
9. mantras: hymns or other portions of sacred Hindu text, chanted or intoned as incantations or prayers.
12. *hana* cards: cards used in a Japanese game in which players attempt to match pairs of flower patterns. *Hana* is Japanese for "flower."
14. *kiai*: a Japanese onomatopoeic word for the sound made by slapping down *hana* cards.

1122 CONTEMPORARY LITERATURE

Reaching All Students

Struggling Readers
This poem has several side glosses to explain terms from the poet's culture that will not be familiar to most students. Struggling readers will benefit from a thorough discussion of the glosses before they attempt to read the poem.

English Language Learners
Before students read, give them this list of words from the poem: *liturgy* (l. 7), *conjure* (l. 8), *calligraphy* (l. 17), and *fragrant* (ll. 55 and 56). Read aloud the phrases from the poem in which the words occur. Ask students to use context clues to write definitions for the words. Then, ask them to look up the definitions and to compare them to their predictions.

Advanced Learners
After students have read the poem, ask them to use "What For," as a model for an original poem in which the speaker is a youth of today, looking back from the perspective of an adult on his or her feelings about a parent. They might use the same two refrains—"I lived for" and "I wanted to."

15 I lived for songs my grandmother sang
   stirring curry into a thick stew,
   weaving a calligraphy of Kannon's° love  **C**
   into grass mats and straw sandals.

   I lived for the red volcano dirt
20 staining my toes, the salt residue
   of surf and sea wind in my hair,
   the arc of a flat stone skipping
   in the hollow trough of a wave.

   I lived a child's world, waited **D**
25 for my father to drag himself home,
   dusted with blasts of sand, powdered rock,
   and the strange ash of raw cement, **E**
   his deafness made worse by the clang
   of pneumatic drills, sore in his bones

17. Kannon's: In Japanese Buddhism, Kannon is the bodhisattva ("Buddha to be") of infinite compassion and mercy.

GARRETT HONGO 1123

C **Reading Skills and Strategies**
Identifying Specific Details
? What specific details in this and the previous stanza reveal the speaker's attitude toward his grandparents? [He lived for his grandfather's stories and his grandmother's songs, revealing his respect and affection for them.]

D **Elements of Literature**
Refrain
Ask students to locate the words of the refrain in the first line of the first five stanzas. How does the refrain differ in the fifth stanza. [Instead of "I lived for . . . ," it becomes "I lived a child's world," summarizing everything that came before it.]

E **Reading Skills and Strategies**
Comparing/Contrasting
? How does the speaker's image of his father returning from work contrast with the description of his own life given in the first four stanzas? [The child's life is easy, magical, filled with interesting events and the beauty of the natural world. His father's world is hard and filled with exhausting work that is damaging to his health.]

Crossing the Curriculum

Geography
In this poem, the speaker evokes the beauty of the Hawaiian Islands by mentioning such traditional flora as papaya trees, plumeria, and *pikake* flowers. Have students research the native trees and flowers of the islands and present their findings in a pictorial report.

History
Although many Japanese Americans were treated as potential enemies to their chosen homeland during World War II, some were allowed to serve in the U.S. Army, but only in Europe. Have students find out about the Japanese American troops that fought in Europe during the war and report to the class.

Using Students' Strengths

Auditory/Musical Learners
The speaker uses a number of sound images, such as crystal chimes and the clang of drills. Have students put together a tape of music and/or sound effects that could be used as background for a reading of the poem.

A Reading Skills and Strategies

Identifying Specific Details

? What details in this stanza suggest the importance of language in the speaker's relationship with his father? [Possible response: He invents names for his father and tells them to him when he comes home.]

B Elements of Literature

Refrain

? A new refrain is taken up in the first lines of the last three stanzas. How are the poem's two refrains connected? [Possible response: The speaker uses what he "lived for" to accomplish what he "wanted to."]

C Critical Thinking

Making Judgments

? How well did the speaker do what he "wanted to"? [Possible responses: Quite well, because he has succeeded in using words to make a tribute to his father, which could heal some of his father's pain; not very well, because nothing could take away his father's pain or restore his hearing.]

> 30   from the buckings of a jackhammer.
> He'd hand me a scarred lunchpail,
> let me unlace the hightop G.I. boots,
> call him the new name I'd invented
> that day in school, write it for him
> 35   on his newspaper. He'd rub my face
> with hands that felt like gravel roads,
> tell me to move, go play, and then he'd
> walk to the laundry sink to scrub,
> rinse the dirt of his long day
> 40   from a face brown and grained as koa° wood.

40. **koa:** Hawaiian mimosa tree valued for its wood and bark.

> I wanted to take away the pain
> in his legs, the swelling in his joints,
> give him back his hearing,
> clear and rare as crystal chimes,
> 45   the fins of glass that wrinkled
> and sparked the air with their sound.
>
> I wanted to heal the sores that work
> and war had sent to him,
> let him play catch in the backyard
> 50   with me, tossing a tennis ball
> past papaya trees without the shoulders
> of pain shrugging back his arms.
>
> I wanted to become a doctor of pure magic,
> to string a necklace of sweet words
> 55   fragrant as pine needles and plumeria,°
> fragrant as the bread my mother baked,
> place it like a lei of cowrie shells
> and *pikake*° flowers around my father's neck,
> and chant him a blessing, a sutra.°

55. **plumeria:** classification of fragrant, flowering, tropical American trees.
58. *pikake:* Hawaiian for "Arabian jasmine."
59. **sutra:** in general, one of the sacred scriptures of Buddhism.

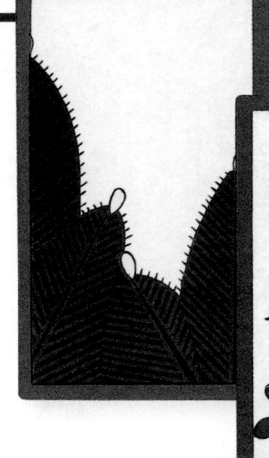

Getting Students Involved

Cooperative Learning

Collaborative Reading. Divide the class into groups of four and ask them to perform a collaborative reading of the poem for the class. Let students determine how the poem will be read, deciding who will read which lines and how the readers will communicate ideas and feelings. Emphasize that everyone in the group must participate in the reading and in the decision-making process.

Connecting Across Texts

Connecting with "Young"

Have students compare and contrast the tone of this poem with that of Anne Sexton's "Young" (p. 1090). How are the speakers' recollections of childhood similar and how are they different? What attitude do the two speakers have toward their fathers?

A Different Story

In this excerpt from a personal essay, Garrett Hongo remembers his maternal grandfather, who was known by his last name, Kubota. During most of Hongo's childhood and adolescence, Kubota lived with the poet's family near Los Angeles, California. The grandfather is also remembered in "What For."

I was a teenager and, though I was bored listening to stories I'd heard often enough before at holiday dinners, I was dutiful. I took my spot on the couch next to Kubota and heard him out. Usually, he'd tell me about his schooling in Japan where he learned judo along with mathematics and literature. He'd learned the *soroban* there— the abacus, which was the original pocket calculator of the Far East—and that, along with his strong, judo-trained back, got him his first job in Hawaii. This was the moral. "Study *ha-ahd*," he'd say with pidgin emphasis. "Learn read good. Learn speak da kine *good* English." The message is the familiar one taught to any children of immigrants: succeed through education. And imitation. But this time, Kubota reached down into his past and told me a different story. I was thirteen by then, and I suppose he thought me ready for it. He told me about Pearl Harbor, how the planes flew in wing after wing of formations over his old house in La'ie in Hawaii, and how, the next day, after Roosevelt had made his famous "Day of Infamy" speech about the treachery of the Japanese, the FBI agents had come to his door and taken him in, hauled him off to Honolulu for questioning, and held him without charge for several days. I thought he was lying. I thought he was making up a kind of horror story to shock me and give his moral that much more starch. But it was true. I asked around. I brought it up during history class in junior high school, and my teacher, after silencing me and stepping me off to the back of the room, told me that it was indeed so. I asked my mother and she said it was true. I asked my schoolmates, who laughed and ridiculed me

for being so ignorant. We lived in a Japanese-American community, and the parents of most of my classmates were the *nisei* who had been interned as teenagers all through the war. . . .

I was not made yet, and [Kubota] was determined that his stories be part of my making. He spoke quietly at first, mildly, but once into his narrative and after his drink was down, his voice would rise and quaver with resentment and he'd make his accusations. He gave his testimony to me and I held it at first cautiously in my conscience like it was an heirloom too delicate to expose to strangers and anyone outside of the world Kubota made with his words. "I give you story now," he once said, "and you learn speak good, eh?" It was my job, as the disciple of his preaching I had then become, Ananda to his Buddha, to reassure him with a promise. "You learn speak good like the Dillingham," he'd say another time, referring to the wealthy scion of the grower family who had once run, unsuccessfully, for one of Hawaii's first senatorial seats. Or he'd then invoke a magical name, the name of one of his heroes, a man he thought particularly exemplary and righteous. "Learn speak dah good Ing-rish like *Mistah Inouye*," Kubota shouted. "He *lick* dah Dillingham even in debate. I saw on *terre-bision* myself." He was remembering the debates before the first senatorial election just before Hawaii was admitted to the Union as its fiftieth state. "You *tell* story," Kubota would end. And I had my injunction.

—Garrett Hongo
from "Kubota"

Primary Sources

In this excerpt from Hongo's award-winning essay "Kubota," he evokes his grandfather's complex relationship to the United States and his troubled history as a Japanese immigrant. On the one hand, Hongo's grandfather Kubota is a staunch believer in the American dream and urges his grandson to study, assimilate, and grasp the opportunities embodied in a figure like Hawaiian Senator Daniel Inouye. On the other hand, he recalls his harsh and unjust treatment following the bombing of Pearl Harbor—a fact which, like the internment of Japanese Americans during the same period, shocks the young Hongo. Ultimately, he accepts both parts of his grandfather's legacy, and works hard in order to pass on the stories his grandfather has told him.

Ⓐ Humanities Connections

The essay "Kubota," from which this excerpt is taken, appeared in the volume *The Best American Essays 1991*, edited by Joyce Carol Oates. She called Hongo's memoir of his "dispossessed grandfather" "almost too painful to be borne."

After students have read the excerpt, ask them to reread "What For" and to make notes on the lines in which Hongo mentions songs, stories, or other special uses of language. Point out that in both this excerpt and the poem, Hongo writes about how his parents' and grandparents' words and stories have shaped his life and his work. Have them shape their notes into a one-paragraph commentary on this topic.

Making the Connections

Connecting to the Theme: "From Generation to Generation"
After students have read both the poem and the excerpt from the essay, point out to them that the theme "From Generation to Generation" can encompass many different attitudes between members of a family—from anger and hostility to great affection. Ask them to discuss the tone of these two pieces and to point to specific places in the texts where they see that tone reflected.

Cultural Connections
In a part of the essay "Kubota" not reprinted here, Hongo mentions that many of his Japanese American classmates did not want to discuss the wartime internment of their parents. They were "busy trying to forget it ever happened." The same attitude was found among some Holocaust survivors directly after World War II. In more recent years, however, survivors and their children have been more willing to look at those experiences. Why might this be so?

Assessing Learning

Check Test: Fill-in-the-Blank
1. The speaker grew up in _____. [Hawaii]
2. His grandfather told stories about the _____. [the second world war]
3. His father worked in _____. [construction]
4. The father's job affected his _____. [hearing]
5. The speaker wanted to take away his father's pain with _____. [words]

First Thoughts [Respond]

1. Possible responses: the ocean, sea-shells, card games, flowers, and the father's rough hands. They are effective because they appeal to more than one sense.

Shaping Interpretations [Interpret]

2. Possible response: He wants to heal his father's pain with words, perhaps by writing a poem that would express his love for his father.

3. Possible responses: It may refer to the refrain "I lived for"; it may indicate that the speaker is explaining what he, his father, and his grandparents lived for, what was important to them; it's an idiomatic expression explaining why Hongo wrote the poem.

4. The refrain in the first part of the poem is "I lived" and in the second part, "I wanted." Possible response: The "I lived" stanzas introduce a child who passively takes in images and words, and the "I wanted" stanzas show the child wanting to use words to heal his father.

Extending the Text [Evaluate]

5. Possible responses: It comes to us through stories; through legends; through traditions; through prayers.

Grading Timesaver

Rubrics for each Choices assignment appear on p. 227 in the *Portfolio Management System*.

First Thoughts

1. What **images** stood out for you as you read the poem? Why were they so effective?

Shaping Interpretations

2. What do you think the speaker means by saying "I wanted to become a doctor of pure magic" (line 53)?

3. What does the title of the poem mean?

4. Identify the two **refrains** of the poem. What effects do each of them have?

Extending the Text

5. In Primary Sources (page 1125), Garrett Hongo remembers holding his grandfather's "testimony" in his mind "like it was an heirloom." How do you think the testimony of previous generations comes down to us?

Left, A. K. Hongo (Garrett Hongo's father) on the docks of Honolulu Harbor, shipping out to Oakland, then boot camp, then Italy (1944).
Courtesy Garrett Hongo.

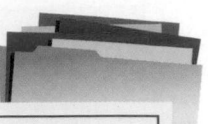

Writer's Notebook

1. Collecting Ideas for an Evaluation

Establishing criteria for evaluating the emotional impact of a poem (or other work of art) is not easy. You might consider the power of the emotional effect, whether it appeals to sentiment or to more complex feelings, or whether it changes you in any way. Establish your own criteria for evaluating emotional impact, and then apply them to Hongo's "What For." Save your notes for possible use in the Writer's Workshop on page 1181.

Analyzing Technique

2. Details Add Up

Hongo includes much concrete detail in "What For." Review the notes you made while reading. Then, write a short essay in which you discuss the effect of supplying so much detail. Which details are especially powerful? Would the poem be as effective if it used only abstract generalizations?

Comparing Poems

3. Walt Whitman Redux?

Some critics say Garrett Hongo's style is similar to Walt Whitman's, partly because both poets repeat words, word order, and phrasing, include catalogs of concrete items, and show empathy for other people. Pick a poem or two by Whitman (pages 352–362), and in a brief essay, compare Whitman's style with Hongo's style in "What For."

Creative Writing

4. The Father's Poem

What might the father in Hongo's poem have thought of his son and his son's attitude toward him? Have the father tell us in a poem the structure and style of which resemble the final three stanzas of "What For."

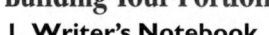

1. **Writer's Notebook**
   Remind students that they may use their work as prewriting for the Writer's Workshop on p. 1181.

2. **Analyzing Technique** Before students begin the activity, ask them to give a few examples of concrete details and abstract generalizations.

3. **Comparing Poems** Briefly review the elements that go into a writer's style: sentence length and complexity, diction, use of figurative language, imagery, repetition, and concrete details.

4. **Creative Writing** If students have difficulty imagining what Hongo's father might have wanted for him, ask them to imagine what they would want for their children.

Collection 21

The Created Self

Theme

New Meanings *Intense self-consciousness, always a hallmark of the American imagination, dates back to those introspective and self-questioning journals of the first Puritans. Postmodern writers continue to explore questions of identity, as cultures clash and blend, as consistent value systems seem to collapse, as new generations challenge old assumptions.*

Reading the Anthology

Reaching Struggling Readers

The *Reading Skills and Strategies: Reaching Struggling Readers* binder includes a Reading Strategies Handbook that offers concrete suggestions to help students who have difficulty reading and comprehending text, or students who are reluctant readers. When a specific strategy is most appropriate for a selection, a correlation to the Handbook is provided at the bottom of the teacher's page under the head Reaching Struggling Readers. This head may also be used to introduce additional ideas for helping students read challenging texts.

Reading Beyond the Anthology

Read On At the end of the Contemporary Literature collections, the grade eleven book includes an annotated bibliography of books suitable for extended reading. The suggested books are related to works in these collections by theme, by author, or by subject. To preview the Read On for the Contemporary Literature period, please turn to p. T1177.

Resources for this Collection

Note: All resources for this collection are available for preview on the *One-Stop Planner CD-ROM 2 with Test Generator.* All worksheets and blackline masters may be printed from the CD-ROM.

Internet Resources
go.hrw.com LE0 11-21

Selection or Feature	Reading and Literary Skills	Vocabulary, Language, and Grammar
New African (p. 1129) Andrea Lee	• *Graphic Organizers for Active Reading,* Worksheet p. 114	• *Words to Own,* Worksheet p. 61
Autobiographical Notes (p. 1142) James Baldwin **Connections:** *from* **On James Baldwin** (p. 1146) Toni Morrison	• *Graphic Organizers for Active Reading,* Worksheet p. 115	• *Words to Own,* Worksheet p. 62 • *Grammar and Language Links:* Weak Words and Clichés, Worksheet p. 79 • *Language Workshop CD-ROM,* Improving Your Writing Style • *Daily Oral Grammar,* Transparency 67
• **Mirror** (p. 1149) • **Mushrooms** (p. 1150) Sylvia Plath	• *Graphic Organizers for Active Reading,* Worksheet p. 116	
Literature of the Americas: Argentina **Borges and Myself** (p. 1152) Jorge Luis Borges *translated by* Norman Thomas de Giovanni *and* Jorge Luis Borges	The Literature of the Americas feature offers selections from a variety of American cultures representing North, Central, and South America. These selections connect to the collection theme, and students explore the thematic links through structured group discussions called Finding Common Ground.	
The Lifeguard (p. 1156) James Dickey	• *Graphic Organizers for Active Reading,* Worksheet p. 117	
Straw Into Gold (p. 1159) Sandra Cisneros	• *Graphic Organizers for Active Reading,* Worksheet p. 118 • *Literary Elements:* Transparency 33 Worksheet p. 100	• *Words to Own,* Worksheet p. 63 • *Daily Oral Grammar,* Transparency 68
The Latin Deli: An Ars Poetica (p. 1167) Judith Ortiz Cofer	• *Graphic Organizers for Active Reading,* Worksheet p. 119	
The Satisfaction Coal Company (p. 1171) Rita Dove	• *Graphic Organizers for Active Reading,* Worksheet p. 120	• *Daily Oral Grammar,* Transparency 69
The American Language: High Tech's Influence (p. 1178) Gary Q. Arpin		

Collection Planner

Other Resources for this Collection

- *Cross-Curricular Activities*, p. 21
- *Portfolio Management System*, Introduction to Portfolio Assessment, p. 1
- *Formal Assessment*: Literary Period Test, p. 235; Literary Elements Test, p. 233
- *Test Generator*, Collection Test

Writing	Listening and Speaking Viewing and Representing	Assessment
• *Portfolio Management System*, Rubrics for Choices, p. 228	• *Audio CD Library*, Disc 30, Track 2  • *Portfolio Management System*, Rubrics for Choices, p. 228	• *Formal Assessment*, Selection Test, p. 221 • *Test Generator (One-Stop Planner CD-ROM)*  • *Preparation for College Admission Exams*, p. 71
• *Portfolio Management System*, Rubrics for Choices, p. 229	• *Audio CD Library*, Disc 30, Track 3  • *Portfolio Management System*, Rubrics for Choices, p. 229	• *Formal Assessment*, Selection Test, p. 223 • *Test Generator (One-Stop Planner CD-ROM)*  • *Preparation for College Admission Exams*, p. 73
• *Portfolio Management System*, Rubrics for Choices, p. 230	• *Audio CD Library*, Disc 31, Tracks 2, 3  • *Viewing and Representing*: Fine Art Transparency 21  Worksheet p. 84 • *Portfolio Management System*, Rubrics for Choices, p. 230	• *Formal Assessment*, Selection Test, p. 225 • *Test Generator (One-Stop Planner CD-ROM)* 
• *Portfolio Management System*, Rubrics for Choices, p. 231	• *Audio CD Library*, Disc 31, Track 4  • *Portfolio Management System*, Rubrics for Choices, p. 231	• *Formal Assessment*, Selection Test, p. 225 • *Test Generator (One-Stop Planner CD-ROM)* 
• *Portfolio Management System*, Rubrics for Choices, p. 232	• *Portfolio Management System*, Rubrics for Choices, p. 232	• *Formal Assessment*, Selection Test, p. 227 • *Test Generator (One-Stop Planner CD-ROM)* 
• *Portfolio Management System*, Rubrics for Choices, p. 233	• *Audio CD Library*, Disc 31, Track 5  • *Portfolio Management System*, Rubrics for Choices, p. 233	• *Formal Assessment*, Selection Test, p. 229 • *Test Generator (One-Stop Planner CD-ROM)* 
• *Portfolio Management System*, Rubrics for Choices, p. 234	• *Audio CD Library*, Disc 31, Track 6  • *Portfolio Management System*, Rubrics for Choices, p. 234	• *Formal Assessment*, Selection Test, p. 229 • *Test Generator (One-Stop Planner CD-ROM)* 
		• *Formal Assessment*, The American Language Test, p. 231

 Transparency    CD-ROM    Video    Audio CD

Resources for this Collection (cont'd)

Note: All resources for this collection are available for preview on the *One-Stop Planner CD-ROM 2 with Test Generator.* All worksheets and blackline masters may be printed from the CD-ROM.

Internet Resources
go.hrw.com LE0 11-21

Collection Planner

Selection or Feature	Reading and Literary Skills	Vocabulary, Language, and Grammar
Writer's Workshop: Evaluation (p. 1181)		
Language Workshop: Using Effective Diction (p. 1185)		• *Workshop Resources,* p. 63
Learning for Life: Celebrating Cultural Diversity (p. 1187)		

Other Resources for this Collection

- *Cross-Curricular Activities*, p. 21
- *Portfolio Management System*, Introduction to Portfolio Assessment, p. 1
- *Formal Assessment:* Literary Period Test, p. 235; Literary Elements Test, p. 233
- *Test Generator,* Collection Test

Writing	Listening and Speaking Viewing and Representing	Assessment
• *Workshop Resources,* p. 41 • *Writer's Workshop 2 CD-ROM,* Evaluation	• *Viewing and Representing,* HRW Multimedia Presentation Maker	• *Portfolio Management System* • Prewriting, p. 235 • Peer Editing, p. 236 • Assessment Rubric, p. 237
		• *Portfolio Management System,* Rubrics, p. 238

 Transparency    CD-ROM    Video    Audio CD

Collection Planner

Skills Focus

Selection or Feature	Reading Skills and Strategies	Elements of Literature and Language	Writing	Listening and Speaking	Viewing and Representing
New African (p. 1129) Andrea Lee	Interpret a Character, p. 1129 Identify and Evaluate Significant Details from the Story, p. 1140	Internal Conflict, pp. 1129, 1140 Resolution, p. 1140 Setting, p. 1140 Characterize, p. 1140 Title, p. 1140 Theme, p. 1140 Point of View, p. 1140 First-Person Narrative, p. 1140	Write an Essay Describing a Character, p. 1140 Write a First-Person Narrative, p. 1140		
Autobiographical Notes (p. 1142) James Baldwin	Use Study Strategies, p. 1142 Identify Important Ideas, p. 1147	Tone, p. 1147 Objectivity, p. 1147	Evaluate Baldwin's Objectivity, p. 1147 Write an Essay Responding to a Quote, p. 1147 Write an Essay Comparing the Diction and Tone of Two Authors, p. 1147 Write and Essay Analyzing Baldwin's Diction, p. 1147		
• **Mirror** (p. 1149) • **Mushrooms** (p. 1149) Sylvia Plath		Personification, pp. 1149, 1151 Tone, pp. 1150, 1151 Image, p. 1151 Speaker, p. 1151	Draft the Opening Paragraph of an Essay, p. 1151 Write an Essay Comparing and Contrasting Texts, p. 1151 Write a Poem from a Specified Point of View, p. 1151		
Literature of the Americas: Argentina **Borges and Myself** (p. 1152) Jorge Luis Borges	The Literature of the Americas feature offers selections from a variety of American cultures representing North, Central, and South America. These selections connect the collection theme, and students explore the thematic links through structured group discussion called Finding Common Ground.				
The Lifeguard (p. 1156) James Dickey		Flashback, p. 1157 Theme, p. 1157 Allusion, p. 1157 Interior Monologue, p. 1157	Write an Evaluation, p. 1157 Write an Evaluation of the Poem, p. 1157 Write an Essay Evaluating an Interior Monologue, p. 1157	Rehearse and Perform an Oral Reading, p. 1157	
Straw Into Gold (p. 1159) Sandra Cisneros	Identify Main Ideas, p. 1159 Identify Key Passage, p. 1159	Theme, p. 1165 Tone, p. 1165 Allusion, p. 1165 Images, p. 1165	Evaluate a Work Based on Personal Criteria, p. 1165 Write an Essay Identifying Key Passages, and Main Ideas, p. 1165		
The Latin Deli: An Ars Poetica (p. 1167) Judith Ortiz Cofer		Concrete and Abstract Language, p. 1169 Images, p. 1169			Make a Painting or Collage, p. 1169
The Satisfaction Coal Company (p. 1171) Rita Dove	Responding to Aesthetic Elements, pp. 1171, 1176	Diction, p. 1176 Image, p. 1176 Theme, p. 1176	Write in Response to an Author's Comment, p. 1176 Write an Essay Interpreting a Poem, p. 1176	Panel Discussion on the Role of the Poet Laureate, p. 1176	
The American Language: High Tech's Influence (p. 1178) Gary Q. Arpin		Acronyms, p. 1179 Computerspeak, p. 1179	Research and Report on Technical Terms, p. 1180 Compile a Glossary of Computer Terms, p. 1180 Identify and Report on Acronyms, p. 1180		
Writer's Workshop: Evaluation (p. 1181)	Logical Fallacies, p. 1184		Write an Essay Evaluating a Short Story, Essay, or Poem, pp. 1181–1184		Chart Information, p. 1182
Language Workshop: Using Effective Diction (p. 1185)		Diction, p. 1185	Revise Sentences to Improve Diction, p. 1185		
Reading for Life: Reading Memoranda (p. 1186)	Identify Key Information, p. 1186 Decide on an Appropriate Response, p. 1186		Write a Memo Using Technical Terms, p. 1186		
Learning for Life: Celebrating Cultural Diversity (p. 1187)			Write a Feature Article on Culturally Diverse Art, p. 1187		Prepare a Multimedia Presentation, p. 1187 Create an Advertising Campaign, p. 1187

Skills Focus

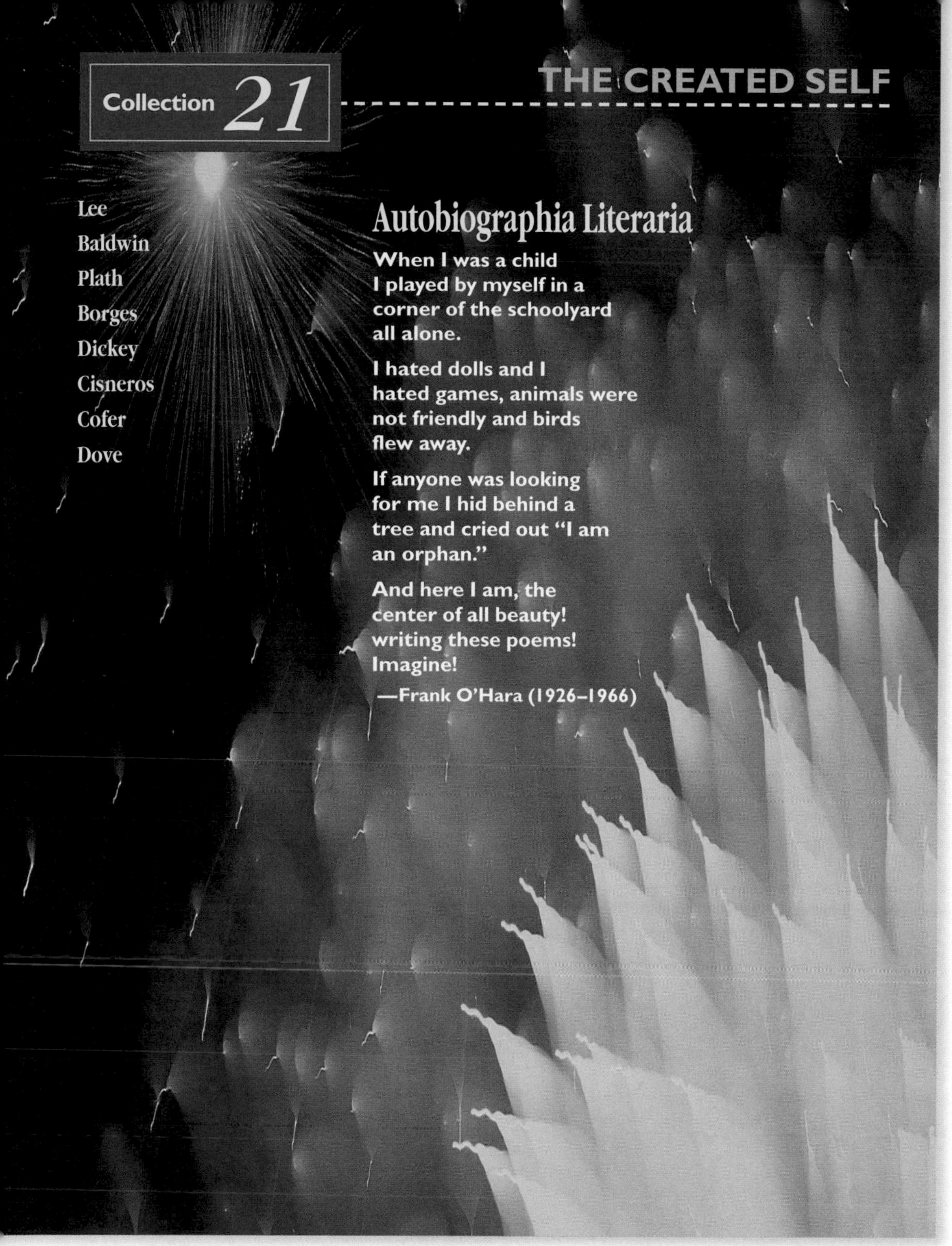

Collection 21 THE CREATED SELF

Lee
Baldwin
Plath
Borges
Dickey
Cisneros
Cofer
Dove

Autobiographia Literaria

When I was a child
I played by myself in a
corner of the schoolyard
all alone.

I hated dolls and I
hated games, animals were
not friendly and birds
flew away.

If anyone was looking
for me I hid behind a
tree and cried out "I am
an orphan."

And here I am, the
center of all beauty!
writing these poems!
Imagine!

—Frank O'Hara (1926–1966)

OBJECTIVES

1. Read literature of the contemporary period on the theme "The Created Self"
2. Interpret literary elements used in the literature
3. Apply a variety of reading strategies
4. Respond to the literature in a variety of modes
5. Learn and use new words

Responding to the Poem

? How does the speaker say he has changed since he was a child? What is the cause of the change? [Possible response: The speaker was a shy, uncertain, and lonely child, but now he is confident and proud because he writes poetry.]

Literary Connections

The title is an allusion to the *Biographia Literaria* (1817) by the English Romantic poet Samuel Taylor Coleridge, which attempted to formulate a theory of literature based on the distinction between "Fancy" and "Imagination."

WORK IN PROGRESS

Writing Focus: Evaluation

The following **Work in Progress** assignments in this collection build to a culminating **Writer's Workshop** at the end of Collection 21.

- New African — Evaluate details and how they contribute to total effect (p. 1140)
- Autobiographical Notes — Examine writer's objectivity (p. 1147)
- Mirror; Mushrooms — Note background information necessary for understanding (p. 1151)
- The Lifeguard — Evaluate how well poem communicates meaning (p. 1157)
- Straw into Gold — List criteria for an effective autobiography (p. 1165)
- The Latin Deli: An Ars Poetica — Compare definitions of poetry (p. 1169)
- The Satisfaction Coal Company — Judge how well poem reflects author's comments (p. 1176)

Writer's Workshop: Persuasive Writing / Evaluation (p. 1181)

Planning

- **Traditional Schedule**
  Lesson Plans Including Strategies for English-Language Learners
- **One-Stop Planner**
  CD-ROM with Test Generator

BROWSING IN THE FILES

About the Author. Lee's quiet, affluent upbringing forms the background of her first novel, *Sarah Phillips,* whose heroine observes the old-fashioned black middle class that "has carried on with cautious pomp for years in eastern cities and suburbs, using its considerable funds to attempt poignant imitations of high society . . . ."

Andrea Lee

(1953–   )

© Jerry Bauer.

Andrea Lee grew up in Yeadon, a prosperous Philadelphia suburb favored by African American professionals. It was a place where grounds were well kept, children were sent off to good schools, and prejudice was something the residents knew only from books and television.

"Yeadon . . . was as solid a repository of American virtues and American flaws as any other close-knit suburban community," Lee wrote in the early 1980s. "It had, and still has, its own peculiar flavor—a lively mixture of materialism, idealism, and ironic humor that prevents the minds of its children from stagnating."

In 1978, Lee went to Russia with her husband, a graduate student in Russian history, for eight months' study at Moscow State University and for another two months in Leningrad (now St. Petersburg). The young Americans stood in lines and rode the subways with ordinary Russians. They absorbed, as Lee wrote, "a view of life in Moscow and Leningrad that was very different from that of the diplomats and journalists we knew." This yearlong trip resulted in a series of articles that were collected in her well-received book *Russian Journal,* nominated for a National Book Award in 1981.

Lee's novel *Sarah Phillips* was published in 1984. The title character shares with the author a prosperous upbringing and a Harvard education. Sarah is the daughter of an African American minister who combines old-fashioned Baptist charisma with a contemporary dedication to the civil rights movement. The reviewer Bruce Van Wyngarden praised *Sarah Phillips* as a "coming-of-age remembrance in which detail and insight are delightfully, and sometimes poignantly, blended." The story that follows is an excerpt from that novel.

A longtime contributor to *The New Yorker,* Lee, who now lives in Italy, has proved herself as both a journalist and a novelist. Her style manifests the craft essential to both nonfiction and fiction. She combines the pinpoint accuracy of observation that we expect of nonfiction with the warmth that gives life to fictional characters. One critic called her writing "luminous," a word that suggests her appealing clarity and grace.

go.hrw.com
LEO 11-21

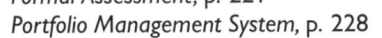

Resources: Print and Media

Reading
- *Graphic Organizers for Active Reading,* p. 114
- *Words to Own,* p. 61
- *Audio CD Library*
    Disc 30, Track 2

Viewing and Representing
- *Visual Connections*
    Videocassette B, Segment 6

Assessment
- *Formal Assessment,* p. 221
- *Portfolio Management System,* p. 228
- *Preparation for College Admission Exams,* p. 71
- *Test Generator (One-Stop Planner CD-ROM)*

Internet
- go.hrw.com (keyword: LEO 11-21)

Before You Read
NEW AFRICAN

Make the Connection
Coming of Age

"New African" is about the love and conflicts in an African American family. The story is in particular about how a girl establishes a place for herself in the family and takes a huge step toward forging her own identity. Watch for the give-and-take as the narrator tries to come to terms with her father and her father's world.

Reading Skills and Strategies

Interpreting a Character

"New African" is in large part a character study of the narrator's father. As you read, write down details that give you insight into Reverend Phillips.

Elements of Literature
Internal Conflict

An **internal conflict** is a struggle between opposing forces within a person's mind. Much of the power and suspense of "New African" derives from several internal conflicts the narrator experiences as she struggles to make her own place in the world.

> **A**n **internal conflict** is a struggle between opposing forces within a person's mind.
>
> *For more on Conflict, see the Handbook of Literary Terms.*

Background

Before you read "New African," you might review the section on Puritan religious beliefs in the "Beginnings" introduction (see page 10). This story, set in Philadelphia in 1963, deals with a Baptist church whose members believe that baptism should be given only to those people who ask for it after receiving a special call from God.

ANDREA LEE 1129

Summary ■ ■

The first person narrator of Lee's story is Sarah, the daughter of a celebrated minister, who has yet to be baptized in her father's church. The story is set in Philadelphia in 1963. It revolves around an external conflict between Sarah and her father's congregation (in which many are scandalized that she has not been baptized) and an inner conflict that Sarah experiences over her own relationship to the church. As the story opens, Sarah sits in church during her father's sermon, dreaming of her treehouse and books and feeling frustrated by her brother's newfound absorption in religious life. After the sermon, Sarah's father begins the baptismal ceremony for several young people, and Sarah is obliged to watch on the lap of Aunt Bessie, a devout family friend. In the story's climax, Aunt Bessie pushes Sarah forward to volunteer for next month's baptism. Sarah refuses, and she and Aunt Bessie struggle until Sarah runs to her mother. Sarah's adamant refusal is a moment of self-definition that both her father and her mother respect by accepting her decision without reproach or question. Years later, in the story's resolution, Sarah thinks back warmly on the gift of religious freedom that her parents granted her.

Preteaching Vocabulary

Words to Own

Have students read the Words to Own and their definitions on the selection pages. Then have students complete the following sentences with the correct words.

1. During the storm, adults tried _____ the children's fears. [dispelling]
2. Calm and _____, Irina answered every question addressed to her. [sedate]
3. He resisted the attack _____. [defiantly]
4. The two were in _____ combat. [mortal]

5. The story had no clear message; we are puzzled by its _____. [ambiguousness]
6. The _____ narrator knows what all the characters think. [omniscient]
7. Lost in his dream of the past, Jack gave in to _____. [wistfulness]
8. A good spy needs to be _____. [discreet]
9. She puts on airs; people can't stand her _____ behavior. [affected]
10. Writing on the Bible is a _____! [sacrilege]

Background

The action of "New African" centers on a stirring religious ceremony and features parts of a sermon by a Baptist minister. Religious orations hold an honored place in the American literary tradition. Review with students the literary qualities and the historical context of the renowned sermon delivered by Jonathan Edwards, "Sinners in the Hands of an Angry God" (p. 79). You might discuss with students what the Reverend Phillips and Jonathan Edwards have in common, how they differ, and how their audiences respond to them.

Using Students' Strengths

Logical/Mathematical Learners
As students read, have them create a chart, listing each example of Sarah's conflicting thoughts or emotions in one column and the subject or cause of the conflict in a second column. After students have finished the story, they may review their chart and analyze connections between the conflicts. Challenge students to find a pattern in the development of the conflicts.

Intrapersonal Learners
After students have finished reading the story, ask them to write a diary entry that Sarah might have written after the climactic scene in the church. Encourage students to explore Sarah's point of view. What are her hopes and fears? What is her understanding of her refusal to be baptized and its consequences? Then, students should review the story and write their diary entries.

New African

Andrea Lee

On a hot Sunday morning in the summer of 1963, I was sitting restlessly with my mother, my brother Matthew, and my aunts Lily, Emma, and May in a central pew of the New African Baptist Church. It was mid-August, and the hum of the big electric fans at the back of the church was almost enough to muffle my father's voice from the pulpit; behind me I could hear Mrs. Gordon, a stout, feeble old woman who always complained of dizziness, remark sharply to her daughter that at the rate the air-conditioning fund was growing, it might as well be for the next century. Facing the congregation, my father—who was Reverend Phillips to the rest of the world—seemed hot himself; he mopped his brow with a handkerchief and drank several glasses of ice water from the heavy pitcher on the table by the pulpit. I looked at him critically. He's still reading the text, I thought. Then he'll do the sermon, then the baptism, and it will be an hour, maybe two.

I rubbed my chin and then idly began to snap the elastic band that held my red straw hat in place. What I would really like to do, I decided, would be to go home, put on my shorts, and climb up into the treehouse I had set up the day before with Matthew. We'd nailed an old bushel basket up in the branches of the big maple that stretched above the sidewalk in front of the house; it made a sort of crow's nest where you could sit comfortably, except for a few splinters, and read, or peer through the dusty leaves at the cars that passed down the quiet suburban road. There was shade and wind and a feeling of high adventure up in the treetop, where the air seemed to vibrate with the dry rhythms of the cicadas; it was as different as possible from church, where the packed congregation sat in a near-visible miasma of emotion and cologne, and trolleys[1] passing in the city street outside set the stained-glass windows rattling.

I slouched between Mama and Aunt Lily and felt myself going limp with lassitude and boredom, as if the heat had melted my bones; the only thing about me with any character seemed to be my firmly starched eyelet dress. Below the scalloped hem, my legs were skinny and wiry,

1. **trolleys:** mass-transit vehicles that run along tracks set into the street.

ANDREA LEE 1131

A Critical Thinking
Speculating
❓ Just from reading the title, what would you speculate this short story will be about? [Possible responses: It could be about a person who has just moved to Africa or a person discovering his or her African roots or an African American trying to redefine himself or herself in a time of social change.]

B Historical Connections
During the summer of 1963, an African American church in Birmingham, Alabama, was bombed, killing four girls. Dr. Martin Luther King, Jr., led the March on Washington that same summer.

C Reading Skills and Strategies

Interpreting a Character
❓ At the beginning of the story, the reader is told that the character of Reverend Phillips has two aspects— the narrator's father and the public figure of the Reverend. What issues do you think might arise for such a character? [Possible responses: The character may have to balance family and professional responsibilities; the character may seem a different person to his family when he acts in his public function. Such a figure may seem to have two distinct personalities.]

D Elements of Literature
Internal Conflict
❓ What do these details reveal about the internal conflict the narrator is experiencing? [Possible responses: She is bored and not paying attention, even though she loves and respects her father. She is respectful of the service, but she is also impatient and likes to daydream.]

Reaching All Students

Struggling Readers
To prepare students to read this selection try having them do a Story Impression. For information on using this strategy, see the *Reading Strategies Handbook*, p. 119 in the *Reading Skills and Strategies* binder. Have students look at the following list of words and phrases from the story. Then, in groups, have them write how they think those words might be related to each other to make a story. They must use the list in the order that it appears (first the left column,

then the right). After students have read the story discuss how their Story Impressions compare to the actual text.

Sunday morning	preacher
church service	baptism
bored child	make a scene
father	refuse

English Language Learners
Ask students what they think *miasma* means, based on the context of the sentence in which it appears. Help them to see that the sentence suggests that it is like a fog or a cloud and rather unhealthy, since it is contrasted with the fresh air outside. For additional strategies to supplement instruction for English language learners, see
• *Lesson Plans Including Strategies for English-Language Learners*

the legs of a ten-year-old amazon,[2] scarred from violent adventures with bicycles and skates. A fingernail tapped my wrist; it was Aunt Emma, reaching across Aunt Lily to press a piece of butterscotch into my hand. When I slipped the candy into my mouth, it tasted faintly of Arpège;[3] my mother and her three sisters were monumental women, ample of bust and slim of ankle, with a weakness for elegant footwear and French perfume. As they leaned back and forth to exchange discreet tidbits of gossip, they fanned themselves and me with fans from the Byron J. Wiggins Funeral Parlor. The fans, which were fluttering throughout the church, bore a depiction of the Good Shepherd: a hollow-eyed blond Christ holding three fat pink-cheeked children. This Christ resembled the Christ who stood among apostles on the stained-glass windows of the church. Deacon Wiggins, a thoughtful man, had also provided New African with a few dozen fans bearing the picture of a black child praying, but I rarely saw those in use.

There was little that was new or very African about the New African Baptist Church. The original congregation had been formed in 1813 by three young men from Philadelphia's large community of free blacks, and before many generations had passed, it had become spiritual home to a collection of prosperous, conservative, generally light-skinned parishioners. The church was a gray Gothic structure, set on the corner of a run-down street in South Philadelphia a dozen blocks below Rittenhouse Square and a few blocks west of the spare, clannish Italian neighborhoods that produced Frankie Avalon[4] and Frank Rizzo.[5] At the turn of the century, the neighborhood had been a tidy collection of brick houses with scrubbed marble steps—the homes of a group of solid citizens whom Booker T. Washington,[6] in a centennial address to the church, described as "the ablest Negro businessmen of our generation." Here my father had grown up aspiring to preach

to the congregation of New African—an ambition encouraged by my grandmother Phillips, a formidable churchwoman. Here, too, my mother and her sisters had walked with linked arms to Sunday services, exchanging affected little catch phrases of French and Latin they had learned at Girls' High.

In the 1950s many of the parishioners, seized by the national urge toward the suburbs, moved to newly integrated towns outside the city, leaving the streets around New African to fill with bottles and papers and loungers. The big church stood suddenly isolated. It had not been abandoned—on Sundays the front steps overflowed with members who had driven in—but there was a tentative feeling in the atmosphere of those Sunday mornings, as if through the muddle of social change, the future of New African had become unclear. Matthew and I, suburban children, felt a mixture of pride and animosity toward the church. On the one hand, it was a marvelous private domain, a richly decorated and infinitely suggestive playground where we were petted by a congregation that adored our father; on the other hand, it seemed a bit like a dreadful old relative in the city, one who forced us into tedious visits and who linked us to a past that came to seem embarrassingly primitive as we grew older.

I slid down in my seat, let my head roll back, and looked up at the blue arches of the church ceiling. Lower than these, in back of the altar, was an enormous gilded cross. Still lower, in a semicircle near the pulpit, sat the choir, flanked by two tall golden files of organ pipes, and below the choir was a somber crescent of dark-suited deacons. In front, at the center of everything, his bald head gleaming under the lights, was Daddy. On summer Sundays he wore white robes, and when he raised his arms, the heavy material fell in curving folds like the ridged petals of an Easter lily. Usually when I came through the crowd to kiss him after the service, his cheek against my lips felt wet and gravelly with sweat and a new growth of beard sprouted since morning. Today, however, was a baptismal Sunday, and I wouldn't have a chance to kiss him until he was freshly shaven and

---

2. **amazon:** strong, athletic woman. The Amazons of Greek mythology were a race of female warriors.
3. **Arpège** (är·pezh′): brand of perfume.
4. **Frankie Avalon** (1940-   ): popular singer and film actor in the 1950s and 1960s.
5. **Frank Rizzo** (1920-1991): Philadelphia's mayor, 1972-1980.
6. **Booker T. Washington** (1856-1915): noted African American author and educator.

WORDS TO OWN

discreet (di·skrēt′) *adj.:* wisely cautious.
affected (a·fekt′id) *v.* used as *adj.:* put on for show.

Getting Students Involved

Cooperative Learning

Presenting a Performance. After students finish the story, arrange them in groups of four or five. Have each group write a short play that dramatizes the climactic scene in the story and adds insight into the characters. The groups might retell the story from another point of view, such as the father's, the brother's, or Aunt Bessie's. Or students may use stage conventions such as soliloquies, or film conventions such as voice-overs, to reveal characters' thoughts and emotions. Each group should present its performance to the class. Each group member should participate in the writing of the play and in its performance, by taking on the role of a character.

cool from the shower he took after the ceremony. The baptismal pool was in an alcove to the left of the altar; it had mirrored walls and red velvet curtains, and above it, swaying on a string, hung a stuffed white dove.

Daddy paused in the invocation and asked the congregation to pray. The choir began to sing softly:

> Blessed assurance,
> Jesus is mine!
> Oh what a foretaste
> Of glory divine!

In the middle of the hymn, I edged my head around my mother's cool, muscular arm (she swam every day of the summer) and peered at Matthew. He was sitting bolt upright holding a hymnal and a pencil, his long legs inside his navy-blue summer suit planted neatly in front of him, his freckled thirteen-year-old face that was so like my father's wearing not the demonic grin it bore when we played alone but a maddeningly composed, attentive expression. "Two hours!" I mouthed at him, and pulled back at a warning pressure from my mother. Then I joined in the singing, feeling disappointed: Matthew had returned me a glance of scorn. Just lately he had started acting very superior and tolerant about tedious Sunday mornings. A month before, he'd been baptized, marching up to the pool in a line of white-robed children as the congregation murmured happily about Reverend Phillips's son. Afterward Mrs. Pinkston, a tiny, yellow-skinned old woman with a blind left eye, had come up to me and given me a painful hug, whispering that she was praying night and day for the pastor's daughter to hear the call as well.

I bit my fingernails whenever I thought about baptism; the subject brought out a deep-rooted balkiness in me. Ever since I could remember, Matthew and I had made a game of dispelling the mysteries of worship with a gleeful secular eye: We knew how the bread and wine were prepared for Communion, and where Daddy bought his robes (Ekhardt Brothers, in North Philadelphia, makers also of robes for choirs, academicians, and judges). Yet there was an unassailable magic about an act as public and dramatic as baptism. I felt toward it the slightly exasperated awe a stagehand might feel on realizing that although he can

identify with professional exactitude the minutest components of a show, there is still something indefinable in the power that makes it a cohesive whole. Though I could not have put it into words, I believed that the decision to make a frightening and embarrassing backward plunge into a pool of sanctified water meant that one had received a summons to Christianity as unmistakable as the blare of an automobile horn. I believed this with the same fervor with which, already, I believed in the power of romance, especially in the miraculous efficacy of a lover's first kiss. I had never been kissed by a lover, nor had I heard the call to baptism.

For a Baptist minister and his wife, my father and mother were unusually relaxed about religion; Matthew and I had never been required to read the Bible, and my father's sermons had been criticized by some older church members for omitting the word "sin." Mama and Daddy never tried to push me toward baptism, but a number of other people did. Often on holidays, when I had retreated from the noise of the family dinner table and sat trying to read in my favorite place (the window seat in Matthew's room, with the curtains drawn to form a tent), Aunt Lily would come and find me. Aunt Lily was the youngest of my mother's sisters, a kindergarten teacher with the fatally overdeveloped air of quaintness that is the infallible mark of an old maid. Aunt Lily hoped and hoped again with various suitors, but even I knew she would never find a husband. I respected her because she gave me wonderful books of fairy tales, inscribed in her neat, loopy hand; when she talked about religion, however, she assumed an anxious, flirtatious air that made me cringe. "Well, Miss Sarah, what are you scared of?" she would ask, tugging gently on one of my braids and bringing her plump face so close to mine that I could see her powder, which was, in accordance with the custom of fashionable colored ladies, several shades lighter than her olive skin. "God isn't anyone to be afraid of!" she'd continue as I looked at her with my best deadpan expression. "He's someone nice, just as nice as your daddy"—I had always suspected Aunt Lily of

---

WORDS TO OWN

dispelling (di·spel'iŋ) v. used as n.: driving away.

E **Elements of Literature**

External Conflict

? Why does Sarah find Matthew's "maddenly composed, attentive expression" annoying? [Possible response: He is behaving in a pious manner that pleases the congregation; Sarah feels he has abandoned her by no longer finding church tedious.]

F **Elements of Literature**

Internal Conflict

? What is Sarah's internal conflict? [Possible responses: She is skeptical about the church's ceremonies, especially baptism, because she knows the mundane details that go into the spectacle; but she also is sensitive to the drama and the magic of the ceremonies. She does not know whether she wants to be baptized or not.]

G **Reading Skills and Strategies**

Interpreting a Character

? How would you describe Aunt Lily? [Possible responses: She is dreamy, religious, eccentric, and a little pretentious.]

Skill Link

Evaluating Effective Diction

Draw students' attention to Lee's precise and vivid diction in the story. Have them consider the following examples from the paragraph on p. 1133 that begins "For a Baptist minister and his wife . . . ." and have them tell why each example is effective.

Activity

1. "Mama and Daddy never tried to push me . . ."
2. ". . . when I had retreated from the noise . . ."
3. ". . . the fatally overdeveloped air of quaintness . . ."
4. "Aunt Lily hoped and hoped again . . ."
5. ". . . an anxious, flirtatious air that made me cringe."

having a crush on my father—"and he loves you, in the same way your daddy does!"

"You would make us all so happy!" I was told at different times by Aunt Lily, Aunt Emma, and Aunt May. The only people who said nothing at all were Mama and Daddy, but I sensed in them a thoughtful, suppressed <u>wistfulness</u> that maddened me.

After the hymn, Daddy read aloud a few verses from the third chapter of Luke, verses I recognized in the almost instinctive way in which I was familiar with all of the well-traveled parts of the Old and New Testaments. "Prepare the way of the Lord, make his paths straight," read my father in a mild voice. "Every valley shall be filled, and every mountain and hill shall be brought low, and the crooked shall be made straight, and the rough paths made smooth, and all flesh shall see the salvation of God."

He had a habit of pausing to fix his gaze on part of the congregation as he read, and that Sunday he seemed to be talking to a small group of strangers who sat in the front row. These visitors were young white men and women, students from Philadelphia colleges, who for the past year had been coming to hear him talk. It was hard to tell them apart: All the men seemed to have beards, and the women wore their hair long and straight. Their informal clothes stood out in that elaborate assembly, and church members whispered angrily that the young women didn't wear hats. I found the students appealing and rather romantic, with their earnest eyes and timid air of being perpetually sorry about something. It was clear that they had good intentions, and I couldn't understand why so many of the adults in the congregation seemed to dislike them so much. After services, they would hover around Daddy. "Never a more beautiful civil rights sermon!" they would say in low, fervent voices. Sometimes they seemed to have tears in their eyes.

I wasn't impressed by their praise of my father; it was only what everyone said. People called him a champion of civil rights; he gave speeches on the radio, and occasionally he appeared on television. (The first time I'd seen him on Channel 5, I'd been gravely disappointed by the way he looked: The bright lights exaggerated the furrows that ran between his nose and mouth, and his narrow eyes gave him a sinister air; he looked like an Oriental villain in a Saturday afternoon thriller.) During the

past year he had organized a boycott that integrated the staff of a huge frozen-food plant in Philadelphia, and he'd been away several times to attend marches and meetings in the South. I was privately embarrassed to have a parent who freely admitted going to jail in Alabama, but the students who visited New African seemed to think it almost miraculous. Their conversations with my father were peppered with references to places I had never seen, towns I imagined as being swathed in a mist of darkness visible: Selma, Macon, Birmingham, Biloxi.[7]

Matthew and I had long ago observed that what Daddy generally did in his sermons was to speak very softly and then surprise everyone with a shout. Of course, I knew that there was more to it than that; even in those days I recognized a genius of personality in my father. He loved crowds, handling them with the expert good humor of a man entirely in his element. At church banquets, at the vast annual picnic that was held beside a lake in New Jersey, or at any gathering in the backyards and living rooms of the town where we lived, the sound I heard most often was the booming of my father's voice followed by shouts of laughter from the people around him. He had a passion for oratory; at home, he infuriated Matthew and me by staging absurd debates at the dinner table, verbal melees[8] that he won quite selfishly, with a loud crow of delight at his own virtuosity. "Is a fruit a vegetable?" he would demand. "Is a zipper a machine?" Matthew and I would plead with him to be quiet as we strained to get our own points across, but it was no use. When the last word had resounded and we sat looking at him in irritated silence, he would clear his throat, settle his collar, and resume eating, his face still glowing with an irrepressible glee.

When he preached, he showed the same private delight. A look of rapt pleasure seemed to broaden and brighten the contours of his angular face until it actually appeared to give off light as

---

7. **Selma . . . Biloxi:** Selma, Alabama; Macon, Georgia; Birmingham, Alabama; and Biloxi, Mississippi: sites of significant civil rights protests during the 1960s.
8. **melees** (mā′lāz′): battles.

WORDS TO OWN
wistfulness (wist′fəl·nis) *n.:* vague longing.

Listening to Music

"We Shall Overcome," performed by the SNCC Freedom Singers

Based on a 1901 Baptist hymn rediscovered and adapted by the civil rights activist and folk singer Pete Seeger, "We Shall Overcome" became the anthem of America's civil rights movement. Its title is virtually synonymous with the movement itself. A favorite song of Dr. Martin Luther King, Jr., it was recorded by African American gospel singers like the great Mahalia Jackson, by choruses like the SNCC Freedom Singers, and by protest singers of the 1960s like Joan Baez and the pop-folk group Peter, Paul & Mary. But most of all, it was the song civil rights activists sang themselves when they marched for racial equality.

Activity
Listen to this recording of "We Shall Overcome," and try to decide why the song was so successful at stirring people to work together for racial justice. What role do you think music plays in social movements? Share your ideas in a class discussion.

F Reading Skills and Strategies

Comparing and Contrasting

? How do the two styles of oratory differ? How are they similar? [Possible responses: The two styles differ in that one is calm, well-argued, and rational, and the other is more passionate and moving. They are similar in that both have an identifiable rhythm and an entrancing musicality.]

G Vocabulary Note

Latin Roots

Have students look up *incantatory* in the dictionary and identify the Latin root of the word—*canto*. Note that the root suggests not only singing but also enchanting—that is, using the human voice to weave a spell and lift the listener into another world or state of consciousness.

H Cultural Connections

Baptists

Roger Williams founded the first American Baptist church in Providence, Rhode Island, in 1639. The membership has spread throughout the United States, with by far the greatest concentration in the Southern Baptist Convention. The African American Baptist churches played a significant role in the civil rights movement in the 1950s and 1960s. Churches were used as meeting places for the Freedom Movement, with Baptist ministers serving as leaders.

he spoke. He could preach in two very different ways. One was the delicate, sonorous idiom of formal oratory, with which he must have won the prizes he held from his seminary days. The second was a hectoring,[9] insinuating, incantatory tone, full of the rhythms of the South he had never lived in, linking him to generations of thun-derous Baptist preachers. When he used this tone, as he was doing now, affectionate laughter rippled through the pews.

"I know," he said, looking out over the congregation and blinking his eyes rapidly, "that there are certain people in this room—oh, I don't have to name names or point a finger—who have ignored that small true voice, the voice that is the voice of Jesus calling out in the shadowy depths

9. **hectoring:** bullying.

ANDREA LEE 1135

Crossing the Curriculum

Social Sciences

Have students locate the cities mentioned on p. 1134, where civil rights struggles were especially intense. Then, ask students to research people and events associated with each city at the time. For instance, students might research the confrontation between "Bull" Connor and Dr. King in Birmingham. Students may meet in small groups to share their findings on the events in the cities and the importance of each event to the civil rights movement of the 1960s.

History

Ask students to research the role of the church in the twentieth-century civil rights movement. For instance, they might find out more about the Southern Christian Leadership Conference or Reverend Ralph Abernathy. Have students create an oral presentation, complete with visuals, describing the role played by religion and the church in the civil rights struggle.

A Appreciating Language
Word Choice

❓ What does the expression *sulky indifference* mean? What insight does the word *sulky* add to the Reverend's depiction of everyone's tendency to ignore the voice of Jesus? [Possible responses: *Sulky* makes the indifference seem immature and temporary. (*Sulky* suggests the actions of a child, pouting in a corner.)] Why do you think Sarah recalls this sermon in particular? [Possible response: because she is grappling with the question of whether her own "indifference" is mere immaturity, or an adult choice of personal philosophy.]

B Reading Skills and Strategies
Interpreting a Character

❓ How does Sarah's father feel about the behavior of the church members? [Possible response: He is disappointed yet amused by their reserved manner, and he privately pokes fun at them.]

C Reading Skills and Strategies
Making Inferences

❓ What can you infer about how the narrator now feels about her mother and aunts' reactions to Miss Middleton? How did she probably feel about her then? [Possible response: In retrospect, the narrator seems more appreciative of Mrs. Middleton and more critical of her mother's and aunts' disdain. At the time, she probably felt a mixture of embarrassment of and curiosity about Miss Middleton.]

D Elements of Literature
Simile

❓ What makes this simile—"like carvings on a scarab"—appropriate? [Possible responses: The creases on Deacon West's brow suggest his age; an Egyptian scarab is an ancient artifact. A scarab is mysterious; Deacon West's age makes him mysterious because he was personally involved in past events that nearly everyone has forgotten.]

E Critical Thinking
Interpreting

❓ Why might Sarah be so affected by this event? [Possible responses: Sarah takes baptism seriously; it awes her, as it does the other children. She is excited by the spectacle but unsure if she wants to be personally involved in its drama.]

T1136

---

of the soul. And while you all are looking around and wondering just who those 'certain people' are, I want to tell you all a secret: They are you and me, and your brother-in-law, and every man, woman, and child in this room this morning. All of us listen to our bellies when they tell us it is time to eat, we pay attention to our eyes when they grow heavy from wanting sleep, but when it comes to the sacred knowledge our hearts can offer, we are deaf, dumb, blind, and senseless. Throw away that blindness, that deafness, that sulky indifference. When all the world lies to you, Jesus will tell you what is right. Listen to him. Call on him. In these times of confusion, when there are a dozen different ways to turn, and Mama and Papa can't help you, trust Jesus to set you straight. Listen to him. The Son of God has the answers. Call on him. Call on him. Call on him."

The sermon was punctuated with an occasional loud "Amen!" from Miss Middleton, an excitable old lady whose eyes flashed <u>defiantly</u> at the reproving faces of those around her. New African was not the kind of Baptist church where shouting was a normal part of the service; I occasionally heard my father mock the staid congregation by calling it Saint African. Whenever Miss Middleton loosed her tongue (sometimes she went off into fits of rapturous shrieks and had to be helped out of the service by the church nurse), my mother and aunts exchanged grimaces and shrugged, as if confronted by incomprehensibly barbarous behavior.

When Daddy had spoken the final words of the sermon, he drank a glass of water and vanished through a set of red velvet curtains to the right of the altar. At the same time, the choir began to sing what was described in the church bulletin as a "selection." These selections were always arenas for the running dispute between the choirmaster and the choir. Jordan Grimes, the choirmaster, was a Curtis[10] graduate who was partial to Handel,[11] but the choir preferred artistic spirituals performed in the lush, heroic style of Paul Robeson.[12] Grimes had triumphed that Sunday. As the

---

10. **Curtis:** Curtis Institute of Music in Philadelphia.
11. **Handel:** George Frideric Handel (1685–1759), German-born composer of religious music, including the oratorio *Messiah.*
12. **Paul Robeson** (1898–1976): African American actor and singer, famous for his interpretations of black spirituals.

1136 CONTEMPORARY LITERATURE

---

choir gave a spirited but unwilling rendition of Agnus Dei,[13] I watched old Deacon West smile in approval. A Spanish-American War veteran, he admitted to being ninety-four but was said to be older; his round yellowish face, otherwise unwrinkled, bore three deep, deliberate-looking horizontal creases on the brow, like carvings on a scarab.[14] "That old man is as flirtatious as a boy of twenty!" my mother often said, watching his stiff, courtly movements among the ladies of the church. Sometimes he gave me a dry kiss and a piece of peppermint candy after the service; I liked his crackling white collars and smell of bay rum.[15]

The selection ended; Jordan Grimes struck two deep chords on the organ, and the lights in the church went low. A subtle stir ran through the congregation, and I moved closer to my mother. This was the moment that fascinated and disturbed me more than anything else at church: the prelude to the ceremony of baptism. Deacon West rose and drew open the draperies that had been closed round the baptismal pool, and there stood my father in water to his waist. The choir began to sing:

> We're marching to Zion,
> Beautiful, beautiful Zion,
> We're marching upward to Zion,
> The beautiful city of God!

Down the aisle, guided by two church mothers, came a procession of eight children and adolescents. They wore white robes, the girls with white ribbons in their hair, and they all had solemn expressions of terror on their faces. I knew each one of them. There was Billy Price, a big, slow-moving boy of thirteen, the son of Deacon Price. There were the Duckery twins. There was Caroline Piggee, whom I hated because of her long, soft black curls, her dimpled pink face, and her lisp that ravished grown-ups. There was

---

13. **Agnus Dei** (äg'noos dā'ē'): Latin for "lamb of God," a very formal prayer for mercy and peace recited in the Catholic Mass.
14. **scarab** (skar'əb): beetle-shaped religious symbol of ancient Egypt.
15. **bay rum:** fragrant after-shave lotion.

WORDS TO OWN
defiantly (dē·fī'ənt·lē) *adv.:* strongly resisting.

Connecting Across Texts

Connecting with Spirituals

Review with students the information about spirituals on pp. 432–434 and have them reread the songs themselves. Ask them to compare the images and symbols in those spirituals with the images and symbols in the spiritual "Wade in the Water" excerpted in Lee's story.

Suggest that students focus particularly on the images of water, children, and deliverance, and then pose the following questions:
- In what ways have the meanings of the images and symbols changed over the years?
- To what extent have the meanings of the images and symbols remained the same?
- Do you think authentic spirituals can be composed today? Why or why not?

Georgie Battis and Sue Anne Ivory, and Wendell and Mabel Cullen.

My mother gave me a nudge. "Run up to the side of the pool!" she whispered. It was the custom for unbaptized children to watch the ceremony from the front of the church. They sat on the knees of the deacons and church mothers, and it was not unusual for a child to volunteer then and there for next month's baptism. I made my way quickly down the dark aisle, feeling the carpet slip under the smooth soles of my patent-leather shoes.

When I reached the side of the pool, I sat down in the bony lap of Bessie Gray, an old woman who often took care of Matthew and me when our parents were away; we called her Aunt Bessie. She was a fanatically devout Christian whose strict ideas on child rearing had evolved over decades of domestic service to a rich white family in Delaware. The link between us, a mixture of hostility and grudging affection, had been forged in hours of pitched battles over bedtimes and proper behavior. Her worshipful respect for my father, whom she called "the Rev," was exceeded only by her pride—the malice-tinged pride of an <u>omniscient</u> family servant—in her "white children," to whom she often unflatteringly compared Matthew and me. It was easy to see why my mother and her circle of fashionable matrons described Bessie Gray as "archaic"—one had only to look at her black straw hat attached with three enormous old-fashioned pins to her knot of frizzy white hair. Her lean, brown-skinned face was dominated by a hawk nose inherited from some Indian ancestor and punctuated by a big black mole; her eyes were small, shrewd, and baleful. She talked in ways that were already passing into history and parody, and she wore a thick orange face powder that smelled like dead leaves.

I leaned against her spare bosom and watched the other children clustered near the pool, their bonnets and hair ribbons and round heads outlined in the dim light. For a minute it was very still. Somewhere in the hot, darkened church a baby gave a fretful murmur; from outside came the sound of cars passing in the street. The candidates for baptism, looking stiff and self-conscious, stood lined up on the short stairway leading to the pool. Sue Anne Ivory fiddled with her sleeve and then put her fingers in her mouth.

Daddy spoke the opening phrases of the ceremony: "In the Baptist Church, we do not baptize infants, but believe that a person must choose salvation for himself." **[F]**

I didn't listen to the words; what I noticed was the music of the whole—how the big voice darkened and lightened in tone, and how the grand architecture of the Biblical sentences ennobled the voice. The story, of course, was about Jesus and John the Baptist. One phrase struck me newly each time: "This is my beloved son, in whom I am well pleased!" Daddy sang out these words in a clear, triumphant tone, and the choir echoed him. Ever since I could understand it, this phrase had made me feel melancholy; it seemed to expose a hard knot of disobedience that had always lain inside me. When I heard it, I thought enviously of Matthew, for whom life seemed to be a <u>sedate</u> and ordered affair: He, not I, was a child in whom a father could be well pleased. **[H] [I] [J]**

Daddy beckoned to Billy Price, the first baptismal candidate in line, and Billy, ungainly in his white robe, descended the steps into the pool. In soft, slow voices the choir began to sing:

> Wade in the water,
> Wade in the water, children,
> Wade in the water,
> God gonna trouble
> The water.

In spite of Jordan Grimes's efforts, the choir swayed like a gospel chorus as it sang this spiritual; the result was to add an eerie jazz beat to the minor chords. The music gave me goose flesh. Daddy had told me that this was the same song that the slaves had sung long ago in the South, when they gathered to be baptized in rivers and streams. Although I cared little about history, and found it hard to picture the slaves as being any ancestors of mine, I could clearly imagine them coming together beside a broad muddy river that wound away between trees drooping with strange vegetation. They walked silently in lines, their faces very black against their white clothes, leading their children. The whole scene was bathed in

---

WORDS TO OWN

omniscient (äm·nish′ənt) *adj.*: all-knowing.
sedate (si·dāt′) *adj.*: calm and composed.

ANDREA LEE **1137**

Skill Link

the heavy golden light that meant age and solemnity, the same light that seemed to weigh down the Israelites in illustrated volumes of Bible stories, and that shone now from the baptismal pool, giving the ceremony the air of a spectacle staged in a dream.

All attention in the darkened auditorium was now focused on the pool, where between the red curtains my father stood holding Billy Price by the shoulders. Daddy stared into Billy's face, and the boy stared back, his lips set and trembling. "And now, by the power invested in me," said Daddy, "I baptize you in the name of the Father, the Son, and the Holy Ghost." As he pronounced these words, he conveyed a tenderness as efficient and impersonal as a physician's professional manner; beneath it, however, I could see a strong private gladness, the same delight that transformed his face when he preached a sermon. He paused to flick a drop of water off his forehead, and then, with a single smooth, powerful motion of his arms, he laid Billy Price back into the water as if he were putting an infant to bed. I caught my breath as the boy went backward. When he came up, sputtering, two church mothers helped him out of the pool and through a doorway into a room where he would be dried and dressed. Daddy shook the water from his hands and gave a slight smile as another child entered the pool.

One by one, the baptismal candidates descended the steps. Sue Anne Ivory began to cry and had to be comforted. Caroline Piggee blushed and looked up at my father with such a coquettish air that I jealously wondered how he could stand it. After a few baptisms my attention wandered, and I began to gnaw the edge of my thumb and to peer at the pale faces of the visiting college students. Then I thought about Matthew, who had punched me in the arm that morning and had shouted, "No punchbacks!" I thought as well about a collection of horse chestnuts I meant to assemble in the fall, and about two books, one whose subject was adults and divorces, and another, by E. Nesbit, that continued the adventures of the Bastable children.

After Wendell Cullen had left the water (glancing uneasily back at the wet robe trailing behind him), Daddy stood alone among the curtains and the mirrors. The moving reflections from the pool

made the stuffed dove hanging over him seem to flutter on its string. "Dear Lord," said Daddy, as Jordan Grimes struck a chord, "bless these children who have chosen to be baptized in accordance with your teaching, and who have been reborn to carry out your work. In each of them, surely, you are well pleased." He paused, staring out into the darkened auditorium. "And if there is anyone out there—man, woman, child—who wishes to be baptized next month, let him come forward now." He glanced around eagerly. "Oh, do come forward and give Christ your heart and give me your hand!"

Just then Aunt Bessie gave me a little shake and whispered sharply, "Go on up and accept Jesus!"

I stiffened and dug my bitten fingernails into my palms. The last clash of wills I had had with Aunt Bessie had been when she, crazily set in her old southern attitudes, had tried to make me wear an enormous straw hat, as her "white children" did, when I played outside in the sun. The old woman had driven me to madness, and I had ended up spanked and sullen, crouching moodily under the dining-room table. But this was different, outrageous, none of her business, I thought. I shook my head violently and she took advantage of the darkness in the church to seize both of my shoulders and jounce me with considerable roughness, whispering, "Now, listen, young lady! Your daddy up there is calling you to Christ. Your big brother has already offered his soul to the Lord. Now Daddy wants his little girl to step forward."

"No, he doesn't." I glanced at the baptismal pool, where my father was clasping the hand of a strange man who had come up to him. I hoped that this would distract Aunt Bessie, but she was tireless.

"Your mama and your aunt Lily and your aunt May all want you to answer the call. You're hurting them when you say no to Jesus."

"No, I'm not!" I spoke out loud and I saw the people nearby turn to look at me. At the sound of my voice, Daddy, who was a few yards away, faltered for a minute in what he was saying and glanced over in my direction.

Aunt Bessie seemed to lose her head. She stood up abruptly, pulling me with her, and, while I was still frozen in a dreadful paralysis, tried to drag me

Making the Connections

Connecting to the Theme: "The Created Self"

Ask students to identify the central event in the story that affected the narrator's life. Then, have them discuss how Sarah's life is changed by the encounter with Aunt Bessie. How could Sarah be said to have created or recreated herself in this moment? How does she define herself through her honest resistance to the congregation's social pressures and her assertion of her own *uncertainty* about the religious commitment of baptism? How might this simple statement of her continuing ambivalence and doubt be seen as an act of courage and self-creation? Students might also discuss the role of such personal choices in the creation of an identity, as well as the role played by other people, and by the culture in general.

down the aisle toward my father. The two of us began a brief struggle that could not have lasted for more than a few seconds but that seemed an endless mortal conflict—my slippery patent-leather shoes braced against the floor, my straw hat sliding cockeyed and lodging against one ear, my right arm twisting and twisting in the iron circle of the old woman's grip, my nostrils full of the dead-leaf smell of her powder and black skirts. In an instant I had wrenched my arm free and darted up the aisle toward Mama, my aunts, and Matthew. As I slipped past the pews in the darkness, I imagined that I could feel eyes fixed on me and hear whispers. "What'd you do, dummy?" whispered Matthew, tugging on my sash as I reached our pew, but I pushed past him without answering. Although it was hot in the church, my teeth were chattering: It was the first time I had won a battle with a grown-up, and the earth seemed to be about to cave in beneath me. I squeezed in between Mama and Aunt Lily just as the lights came back on in the church. In the baptismal pool, Daddy raised his arms for the last time. "The Lord bless you and keep you," came his big voice. "The Lord be gracious unto you, and give you peace."

What was curious was how uncannily subdued my parents were when they heard of my skirmish with Aunt Bessie. Normally they were swift to punish Matthew and me for misbehavior in church and for breaches in politeness toward adults; this episode combined the two, and smacked of sacrilege besides. Yet once I had made an unwilling apology to the old woman (as I kissed her she shot me such a vengeful glare that I realized that forever after it was to be war to the death between the two of us), I was permitted, once we had driven home, to climb up into the green shade of the big maple tree I had dreamed of throughout the service. In those days, more than now, I fell away into a remote dimension whenever I opened a book; that afternoon, as I sat with rings of sunlight and shadow moving over my arms and legs, and winged yellow seeds plopping down on the pages of *The Story of the Treasure Seekers*, I felt a vague uneasiness floating in the back of my mind—a sense of having misplaced something, of being myself misplaced. I was holding myself quite aloof from considering

what had happened, as I did with most serious events, but through the adventures of the Bastables I kept remembering the way my father had looked when he'd heard what had happened. He hadn't looked severe or angry, but merely puzzled, and he had regarded me with the same puzzled expression, as if he'd just discovered that I existed and didn't know what to do with me. "What happened, Sairy?" he asked, using an old baby nickname, and I said, "I didn't want to go up there." I hadn't cried at all, and that was another curious thing.

After that Sunday, through some adjustment in the adult spheres beyond my perception, all pressure on me to accept baptism ceased. I turned twelve, fifteen, then eighteen without being baptized, a fact that scandalized some of the congregation; however, my parents, who openly discussed everything else, never said a word to me. The issue, and the episode that had illuminated it, was surrounded by a clear ring of silence that, for our garrulous[16] family, was something close to supernatural. I continued to go to New African—in fact, continued after Matthew, who dropped out abruptly during his freshman year in college; the ambiguousness in my relations with the old church gave me at times an inflated sense of privilege (I saw myself as a romantically isolated religious heroine, a sort of self-made Baptist martyr) and at other times a feeling of loss that I was too proud ever to acknowledge. I never went up to take my father's hand, and he never commented upon that fact to me. It was an odd pact, one that I could never consider in the light of day; I stored it in the subchambers of my heart and mind. It was only much later, after he died, and I left New African forever, that I began to examine the peculiar gift of freedom my father—whose entire soul was in the church, and in his exuberant, bewitching tongue—had granted me through his silence.

16. **garrulous** (gar′ə·ləs): talkative.

WORDS TO OWN

mortal (môr′təl) *adj.*: life-threatening; extreme.
sacrilege (sak′rə·lij) *n.*: violation of something sacred.
ambiguousness (am·big′yo͞o·əs·nis) *n.*: lack of clarity; uncertainty.

ANDREA LEE 1139

Assessing Learning

T1139

MAKING MEANINGS

First Thoughts [Respond]

1. Possible responses: Yes, her honesty is a mark of maturity and strong character. No, most children lack such a strong sense of spiritual indepence.

Shaping Interpretations [Interpret]

2. Possible response: Sarah's refusal marks an insistence that her religious and cultural identity be spontaneously felt and honestly claimed—an independence that leaves her slightly "misplaced" in the world of social convention and conformity.

3. He is an inspiring preacher, a committed social activist, and a morally sensitive man—who sees faith as a personal blessing to be spontaneously accepted, not a social norm to be publicly enforced.

4. Many of the conflicts center around an older generation of pious, culturally conservative African Americans in the congregation, and those (like Sarah, Miss Middleton, the white students, Jordan Grimes) who offend their sense of religious and cultural propriety.

5. Possible responses: Both the daughter and father are "new" Africans in that each shows a willingness to challenge traditional expectations. Sarah's father fights for civil rights for African Americans, while Sarah claims cultural and spiritual freedom.

6. Lee uses the specific circumstances of the Philadelphia congregation in 1963 to address broader themes of the "ambiguousness" of identity for African Americans—the struggle to reclaim a rich mixture of African and European spirituality and culture, while examining the insidious legacies of racism and slavery.

Grading Timesaver

Rubrics for each Choices assignment appear on p. 228 in the *Portfolio Management System*.

MAKING MEANINGS

First Thoughts

1. Do you find the narrator's attitudes and feelings believable? Why or why not?

Shaping Interpretations

2. In refusing to be baptized, what do you think Sarah is really objecting to? How would you explain the feeling of being misplaced that she experiences at the end of the story?

3. Referring to the notes you made while reading, how would you **characterize** Sarah's father? What does Sarah mean in the tribute she pays to her father in the story's last sentence?

4. What **conflicts** between generations and cultures can you identify in the story?

5. The **title** of a work of art often is a key to its meaning. In what ways is the father a "new" African? In what ways is Sarah?

6. Is Lee's main purpose in this story to present a realistic record of a single experience in 1963, or is she presenting a broader **theme** about coming of age as an African American woman in the early 1960s? Support your answer with specific references to the story.

Reading Check

a. Describe the **setting** as it is presented in the opening of "New African." What details in the first three paragraphs help you feel the summer heat of the city?

b. In what ways does Sarah feel her brother growing away from her? What passages show that she regards him as more "acceptable" than she is?

c. What passages throughout the story reveal Sarah's **inner conflict** about her father's church?

d. Is there a **resolution** to Sarah's conflict by story's end? Explain.

CHOICES:
Building Your Portfolio

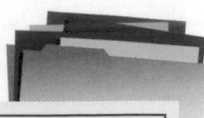

Writer's Notebook

1. Collecting Ideas for an Evaluation

One characteristic of almost all good writing is the inclusion of interesting details. The details should be relevant to the work, not just tossed in for no apparent reason. "New African" contains many details about the setting and characters. Pick out at least three details, and write notes evaluating their contribution to the story's overall effect. Save your notes for possible use in the Writer's Workshop on page 1181.

Interpreting a Character

2. Breaking Free

In a brief essay, describe Sarah—her thoughts, her feelings, her relationships with others. Remember that **character** can be revealed by these methods: (a) describing physical appearance; (b) describing actions; (c) quoting spoken words; (d) showing people's responses to the character; (e) revealing private thoughts and feelings; and (f) direct comments by the author.

Creative Writing

3. A Face in the Crowd

Write a first-person narrative told from the **point of view** of a young person (any young person, including yourself) who is a member of a large audience attending a public function. Imitating Lee's style in the opening paragraphs of this story, have your narrator describe the setting and reveal what he or she sees, hears, and smells—and thinks about the setting and audience. Before you write, decide what tone your narrator will adopt in describing the situation. Then, read your narrative aloud for the class.

Reading Check

a. It is a hot summer day in 1963 in the New African Baptist Church in Philadelphia. The fans, Reverend Phillips's mopping his brow and drinking ice water, and Sarah's wish to put on shorts and go outside all evoke the intense heat.

b. Matthew projects a superior attitude now that he has been baptized. Sarah suspects her father addresses the phrase "This is my beloved son, in whom I am well pleased!" especially to her brother.

c. Sarah is bored and daydreams. She is awed and frightened by the baptism ceremony, but she clearly admires her father and she wants to please him.

d. Most students will agree that there is a resolution. Sarah is grateful that her father granted her spiritual and intellectual freedom.

James Baldwin
(1924–1987)

Y. Coatsaliou/Sygma.

James Baldwin felt compelled to write at length about being an African American "because it was the gate I had to unlock before I could hope to write about anything else." His essays flow from his conviction that a writer's duty is "to examine attitudes, to go beneath the surface, to tap the source."

One of the most controversial and stirring writers of the twentieth century, James Baldwin was born and raised in New York City's Harlem, where his stepfather was the minister of a small evangelical church. As a young man, Baldwin read voraciously and served as a junior minister for a few years at the Fireside Pentecostal Assembly. At the age of twenty-four, he used funds from a fellowship to move to Europe. While living in Paris, he completed his first—and some say best—novel, *Go Tell It on the Mountain* (1953). *Notes of a Native Son,* a collection of autobiographical essays published in 1955, established Baldwin as an American writer of the first rank. The critic Irving Howe said Baldwin was among "the two or three greatest essayists this country has ever produced."

Although he lived much of his life in France, Baldwin never relinquished his U.S. citizenship, and in later years he traveled back to his homeland so often that he considered himself a transatlantic commuter. While abroad, he wrote in a variety of forms, including novels, plays, essays, poetry, and book reviews. Two of Baldwin's plays, *The Amen Corner* (1955) and *Blues for Mister Charlie* (1964), were produced on Broadway.

In the 1950s, the decade that witnessed the early growth of the American civil rights movement, Baldwin's audacious, searing scrutiny of racial injustice played a major role in forcing leaders, black and white, to come to terms with one of the nation's most anguishing problems—the treatment of African Americans. He saw himself as a "disturber of the peace," and some chided him for his unrelenting criticism. For instance, Benjamin DeMott wrote in the *Saturday Review,* "To function as a voice of outrage month after month for a decade and more strains heart and mind, and rhetoric as well; the consequence is a writing style ever on the edge of being winded by too many summonses to intensity."

In the early sixties, Baldwin's reputation grew with the publication of additional essays, *Nobody Knows My Name: More Notes of a Native Son* (1961) and *The Fire Next Time* (1963), a groundbreaking book on race relations that had wide influence. He later published several novels, participated in TV documentaries, and remained a prominent, humane advocate of racial justice in American life.

At the time of his death in France, Baldwin was working on a biography of the Reverend Martin Luther King, Jr. Soon after Baldwin died, two noted African American writers praised his lifework. Orde Coombs wrote, "Because he existed we felt that the racial miasma that swirled around us would not consume us, and it is not too much to say that this man saved our lives." Juan Williams of the *Washington Post* said, "America and the literary world are far richer for [Baldwin's] witness. The proof of a shared humanity across the divides of race, class, and more is the testament that the preacher's son, James Arthur Baldwin, has left us."

 go.hrw.com
LE0 11-21

 — Resources: Print and Media —

Reading
- *Graphic Organizers for Active Reading,* p. 115
- *Words to Own,* p. 62
- *Audio CD Library*
    Disc 30, Track 3

Writing and Language
- *Daily Oral Grammar,* Transparency 67
- *Grammar and Language Links*
    Worksheet, p. 79
- *Language Workshop CD-ROM*

Assessment
- *Formal Assessment,* p. 223
- *Portfolio Management System,* p. 229
- *Preparation for College Admission Exams,* p. 73
- *Test Generator (One-Stop Planner CD-ROM)*

Internet
- go.hrw.com (keyword: LE0 11-21)

OBJECTIVES

1. Read and interpret the autobiographical essay
2. Use study strategies such as outlining
3. Express understanding through writing or speaking/listening
4. Understand and use new words

SKILLS

Reading
- Use study strategies such as outlining

Writing
- Collect ideas for an evaluation
- Write an essay discussing the effects of the past on the present
- Compare the diction and tone of two essays
- Write a letter, poem, article, or dialogue responding to the essay

Vocabulary
- Understand and use new words

Planning

- **Block Schedule**
  Block Scheduling Lesson Plans with Pacing Guide
- **Traditional Schedule**
  Lesson Plan Including Strategies for English-Language Learners
- **One-Stop Planner**
  CD-ROM with Test Generator

BROWSING IN THE FILES

About the Author. After graduating from De Witt Clinton High School in 1942, James Baldwin held a number of jobs in order to support himself while writing book reviews for such national publications as *The New Leader* and *The Nation.* He was befriended by Richard Wright (p. 1012), who helped him obtain a writing fellowship. Like Wright, Baldwin based much of his writing on his own experiences.

Summary ■ ■

These "Notes" offer a compelling portrait of Baldwin's development as a writer and thinker, concluding with a catalogue of his personal precepts. Baldwin's tone is lightly ironic throughout, and he relies on wit, understatement, and literary allusions to express some of his most serious and moving thoughts on writing, personal integrity, and the paradoxes of African American identity. He begins with a dismissive and satirical account of his childhood as "the usual bleak fantasy," in which we nevertheless infer his heavy responsibilities in caring for his mother's younger children under difficult circumstances. We also see his early ambition as a writer and reader. He meditates on what he sees as the strange position of the African American writer—one who must not only first achieve some kind of clarity regarding the "Negro problem" in America, but also establish a stance vis-à-vis Western culture in general, in which he or she is always a kind of "interloper." Baldwin closes with a witty and powerful discussion of his personal principles: his likes and dislikes, his ambivalent love for America, his faith in his own "moral center," and his duties as a writer.

Before You Read
AUTOBIOGRAPHICAL NOTES

Make the Connection
Know Thyself
The ancient Greek philosopher Socrates believed that only an *examined* life is worth living. What exactly does it mean to live an examined life? At the least, it means stepping back from the whirl of daily activities and gaining some perspective on who you are, where you have been, and where you are heading. It means creating new angles of vision, asking questions, proposing answers. It means self-assessment as a part of self-creation. As you will see, James Baldwin certainly took Socrates' dictum to heart. The autobiographical notes that follow first appeared as a preface to Baldwin's acclaimed *Notes of a Native Son*.

Reading Skills and Strategies
Using Study Strategies: Outlining
As you read, begin an **outline** of Baldwin's essay by pausing to identify and write down the **main idea** of each paragraph. When you have finished reading the essay, go back over the text and add the most important **supporting details** for each main idea. If necessary, revise your paraphrases of Baldwin's main ideas so that they accurately reflect the text.

Autobiographical Notes

James Baldwin

1142 CONTEMPORARY LITERATURE

Preteaching Vocabulary

Words to Own
Have students read the Words to Own and their definitions listed at the bottom of the selection pages. Then have students match each of the words listed in column 1 with its synonym in column 2.

1. bleak [c]
2. censored [f]
3. assess [e]

a. take over
b. crushed
c. cheerless

4. conundrum [i]
5. coherent [j]
6. crucial [d]
7. interloper [h]
8. appropriate [a]
9. explicit [g]
10. pulverized [b]

d. critical
e. evaluate
f. changed to remove objectionable material
g. definite
h. intruder
i. riddle
j. logical

I was born in Harlem thirty-one years ago. I began plotting novels at about the time I learned to read. The story of my childhood is the usual bleak fantasy, and we can dismiss it with the restrained observation that I certainly would not consider living it again. In those days my mother was given to the exasperating and mysterious habit of having babies. As they were born, I took them over with one hand and held a book with the other. The children probably suffered, though they have since been kind enough to deny it, and in this way I read *Uncle Tom's Cabin* and *A Tale of Two Cities* over and over and over again; in this way, in fact, I read just about everything I could get my hands on—except the Bible, probably because it was the only book I was encouraged to read. I must also confess that I wrote—a great deal—and my first professional triumph, in any case, the first effort of mine to be seen in print, occurred at the age of twelve or thereabouts, when a short story I had written about the Spanish revolution won some sort of a prize in an extremely short-lived church newspaper. I remember the story was censored by the lady editor, though I don't remember why, and I was outraged.

Also wrote plays, and songs, for one of which I received a letter of congratulations from Mayor La Guardia,[1] and poetry, about which the less said, the better. My mother was delighted by all these goings-on, but my father wasn't; he wanted me to be a preacher. When I was fourteen I became a preacher, and when I was seventeen I stopped. Very shortly thereafter I left home. For God knows how long I struggled with the world of commerce

1. Mayor La Guardia: Fiorello La Guardia, mayor of New York City from 1934 to 1945.

and industry—I guess they would say they struggled with *me*—and when I was about twenty-one I had enough done of a novel to get a Saxton Fellowship. When I was twenty-two the fellowship was over, the novel turned out to be unsalable, and I started waiting on tables in a Village[2] restaurant and writing book reviews—mostly, as it turned out, about the Negro problem, concerning which the color of my skin made me automatically an expert. Did another book, in company with photographer Theodore Pelatowski, about the store-front churches in Harlem. This book met exactly the same fate as my first—fellowship, but no sale. (It was a Rosenwald Fellowship.) By the time I was twenty-four I had decided to stop reviewing books about the Negro problem—which, by this time, was only slightly less horrible in print than it was in life—and I packed my bags and went to France, where I finished, God knows how, *Go Tell It on the Mountain.*

Any writer, I suppose, feels that the world into which he was born is nothing less than a conspiracy against the cultivation of his talent—which attitude certainly has a great deal to support it. On the other hand, it is only because the world looks on his talent with such a frightening indifference that the artist is compelled to make his talent important. So that any writer, looking back over even so short a span of time as I am here forced to assess, finds that the things which hurt him and the things which helped him cannot be divorced from each other; he could be helped in a certain way only because he was hurt in a certain way; and his help is simply to be enabled to move from one conundrum to the next—one is tempted to say that he moves from one disaster to the next. When one begins looking for influences one finds them by the score. I haven't thought much about my own, not enough anyway; I hazard that the King James Bible, the rhetoric of the store-

2. Village: Greenwich Village, a section of Manhattan noted as a center for writers and other artists.

WORDS TO OWN

bleak (blēk) *adj.:* cheerless.
censored (sen′sərd) *v.:* cut or changed to remove material deemed objectionable.
assess (ə·ses′) *v.:* to evaluate; to judge the value of.
conundrum (kə·nun′drəm) *n.:* riddle.

JAMES BALDWIN 1143

A Critical Thinking
Interpreting

❓ What does Baldwin mean by this "truce"? What is he saying about the status of African American identity? [Possible response: He suggests that race-consciousness is so complex and deeply rooted in the American psyche that the most an African American can do is find some acceptance of the self-consiousness and pain that it imposes.]

B Critical Thinking
Hypothesizing

❓ Why might Baldwin be concerned to avoid the impression of "special pleading" in his work? [He wants to make sure that African American writers are judged on their merits alone.]

C Reading Skills and Strategies
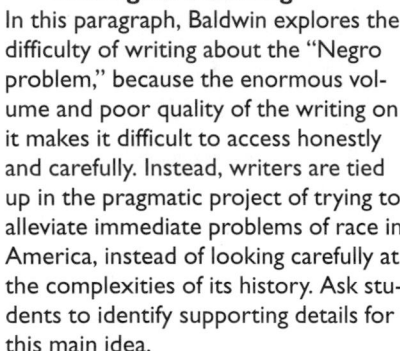
Using Study Strategies: Outlining

In this paragraph, Baldwin explores the difficulty of writing about the "Negro problem," because the enormous volume and poor quality of the writing on it makes it difficult to access honestly and carefully. Instead, writers are tied up in the pragmatic project of trying to alleviate immediate problems of race in America, instead of looking carefully at the complexities of its history. Ask students to identify supporting details for this main idea.

D Critical Thinking
Extending the Text

❓ Do you agree with what Baldwin says about the effect of not facing up to history? Why or why not? [Possible responses: I agree; a society must address the past or it will repeat its mistakes. I disagree because race relations require that people concentrate on common situations and common goals, which can only be done by looking to the future.]

E Reading Skills and Strategies
Using Study Strategies: Outlining

As students outline each paragraph, remind them that asking questions can clarify the main idea and supporting details of a paragraph. For example, a reader might ask: "Why does Baldwin call himself an interloper?" The answer is the main idea of the paragraph, and the causes and consequences of being an interloper are supporting details.

T1144

---

front church, something ironic and violent and perpetually understated in Negro speech—and something of Dickens' love for bravura[3]—have something to do with me today; but I wouldn't stake my life on it. Likewise, innumerable people have helped me in many ways; but finally, I suppose, the most difficult (and most rewarding) thing in my life has been the fact that I was born a Negro and was forced, therefore, to effect some **A** kind of truce with this reality. (Truce, by the way, is the best one can hope for.)

One of the difficulties about being a Negro **B** writer (and this is not special pleading, since I don't mean to suggest that he has it worse than anybody else) is that the Negro problem is written about so widely. The bookshelves groan under the weight of information, and everyone therefore considers himself informed. And this information, furthermore, operates usually (generally, popularly) to reinforce traditional attitudes. Of traditional attitudes there are only two—For or Against—and I, personally, find it difficult to say which attitude has caused me the most pain. I am speaking as a writer; from a social point of view I am perfectly aware that the change from ill-will to good-will, however motivated, however imperfect, however expressed, is better than no change at all.

But it is part of the business of the writer—as I see it—to examine attitudes, to go beneath the surface, to tap the source. From this point of view the Negro problem is nearly inaccessible. It is not only written about so widely; it is written about so badly. It is quite possible to say that the price a Negro pays for becoming articulate is to find himself, at length, with nothing to be articulate about. **C** ("You taught me language," says Caliban to Prospero,[4] "and my profit on't is I know how to curse.") Consider: the tremendous social activity that this problem generates imposes on whites and Negroes alike the necessity of looking forward, of working to bring about a better day. This is fine, it keeps the waters troubled; it is all, indeed, that has made possible the Negro's progress. Nevertheless, social affairs are not generally speaking

---

3. **bravura** (brə·vyoor′ə): florid, brilliant style.
4. **Caliban to Prospero:** Caliban, a rough creature, is Prospero's slave, whom Prospero tries to civilize in *The Tempest* by William Shakespeare. The quotation is from Act I, Scene 2.

1144 CONTEMPORARY LITERATURE

---

the writer's prime concern, whether they ought to be or not; it is absolutely necessary that he establish between himself and these affairs a distance which will allow, at least, for clarity, so that before **D** he can look forward in any meaningful sense, he must first be allowed to take a long look back. In the context of the Negro problem neither whites nor blacks, for excellent reasons of their own, have the faintest desire to look back; but I think that the past is all that makes the present coherent, and further, that the past will remain horrible for exactly as long as we refuse to assess it honestly.

I know, in any case, that the most crucial time in my own development came when I was forced to recognize that I was a kind of bastard of the West; when I followed the line of my past I did not find myself in Europe but in Africa. And this meant that in some subtle way, in a really profound way, I brought to Shakespeare, Bach, Rembrandt, to the stones of Paris, to the cathedral at Chartres, and to the Empire State Building, a special attitude. These were not really my creations, they did not contain my history; I might search in them in vain forever for any reflection of myself. I **E** was an interloper; this was not my heritage. At the same time I had no other heritage which I could possibly hope to use—I had certainly been unfitted for the jungle or the tribe. I would have to appropriate these white centuries, I would have to make them mine—I would have to accept my special attitude, my special place in this scheme—otherwise I would have no place in *any* scheme. What was the most difficult was the fact that I was forced to admit something I had always hidden from myself, which the American Negro has had to hide from himself as the price of his public progress; that I hated and feared white people. This did not mean that I loved black people; on the contrary, I despised them, possibly because they failed to produce Rembrandt. In effect, I hated and feared the world. And this meant, not only that I thus gave the world an altogether mur-

WORDS TO OWN

coherent (kō·hir′ənt) *adj.*: clear, logical, and consistent.
crucial (kroo′shəl) *adj.*: critical; decisive.
interloper (in′tər·lō′pər) *n.*: intruder; meddler.
appropriate (ə·prō′prē·āt) *v.*: to take over.

Using Students' Strengths

Musical Learners
Point out to students that Baldwin, on p. 1145, compares African American prose and music. Ask students to bring in samples of African American styles of music, such as blues, jazz, or rap. Have students listen to the music and then, discuss why Baldwin thought that, in general, African American prose was "pallid and harsh" by contrast.

Visual Learners
Point out that, although he mentions music, Baldwin does not compare African American prose to African American accomplishments in the visual arts. Would his response have been the same? Have students find examples of African American visual art and discuss Baldwin's complaint about "pallid" prose falling short of artistic excellence.

derous power over me, but also that in such a self-destroying limbo[5] I could never hope to write.

One writes out of one thing only—one's own experience. Everything depends on how relentlessly one forces from this experience the last drop, sweet or bitter, it can possibly give. This is the only real concern of the artist, to recreate out of the disorder of life that order which is art. The difficulty then, for me, of being a Negro writer was the fact that I was, in effect, prohibited from examining my own experience too closely by the tremendous demands and the very real dangers of my social situation.

F

I don't think the dilemma outlined above is uncommon. I do think, since writers work in the disastrously <u>explicit</u> medium of language, that it goes a little way toward explaining why, out of the enormous resources of Negro speech and life, and despite the example of Negro music, prose written by Negroes has been generally speaking so pallid and so harsh. I have not written about being a Negro at such length because I expect that to be my only subject, but only because it was the gate I had to unlock before I could hope to write about anything else. I don't think that the Negro problem in America can be even discussed coherently without bearing in mind its context; its context being the history, traditions, customs, the moral assumptions and preoccupations of the country; in short, the general social fabric. Appearances to the contrary, no one in America escapes its effects and everyone in America bears some responsibility for it. I believe this the more firmly because it is the overwhelming tendency to speak of this problem as though it were a thing apart. But in the work of Faulkner, in the general attitude and certain specific passages in Robert Penn Warren, and, most significantly, in the advent of Ralph Ellison, one sees the beginnings—at least—of a more genuinely penetrating

G

H

5. **limbo:** borderland state of uncertainty and oblivion.

search. Mr. Ellison, by the way, is the first Negro novelist I have ever read to utilize in language, and brilliantly, some of the ambiguity and irony of Negro life.

About my interests: I don't know if I have any, unless the morbid desire to own a sixteen millimeter camera and make experimental movies can be so classified. Otherwise, I love to eat and drink—it's my melancholy conviction that I've scarcely ever had enough to eat (this is because it's *impossible* to eat enough if you're worried about the next meal)—and I love to argue with people who do not disagree with me too profoundly, and I love to laugh. I do *not* like bohemia,[6] or bohemians, I do not like people whose principal aim is pleasure, and I do not like people who are *earnest* about anything. I don't like people who like me because I'm a Negro; neither do I like people who find in the same accident grounds for contempt. I love America more than any other country in the world, and, exactly for this reason, I insist on the right to criticize her perpetually. I think all theories are suspect, that the finest principles may have to be modified, or may even be <u>pulverized</u> by the demands of life, and that one must find, therefore, one's own moral center and move through the world hoping that this center will guide one aright. I consider that I have many responsibilities, but none greater than this: to last, as Hemingway says, and get my work done.

I want to be an honest man and a good writer.

I

J

6. **bohemia:** any nonconformist, unconventional community, often made up of writers and other artists.

WORDS TO OWN

explicit (eks·plis′it) *adj.:* clear; definite.
pulverized (pul′vər·īzd′) *v.:* crushed; destroyed.

> **T**HIS IS THE ONLY REAL CONCERN OF THE ARTIST, TO RECREATE OUT OF THE DISORDER OF LIFE THAT ORDER WHICH IS ART.

F **Critical Thinking**

Expressing an Opinion

? Do you agree that art is the making of order out of personal experience? Explain. [Possible responses: Yes, because an artist has to come to some conclusions about personal experiences before he or she can express them in art. No, because art just as easily can reflect life's disorder without organizing it.]

G **English Language Learners**

Breaking Down Difficult Text

Have students read this sentence aloud, with clear-cut pauses at each comma. Then, have them identify the main subject (*I*), verb (*think*), and object (*that it goes toward explaining*). Finally, have them identify the subordinate ideas: writers work in language, Negro speech and life are enormous resources, Negro music is an example, prose written by Negroes has been pallid and harsh.

H **Literary Connections**

In 1949, William Faulkner (p. 713) received the Nobel Prize in literature. Robert Penn Warren was the first poet laureate of the United States. Ralph Ellison wrote about the African American search for identity in his novel *Invisible Man.*

I **Advanced Learners**

Paraphrasing

In this long passage, Baldwin condenses his "notes" on his own character into a series of polished, aphoristic observations. Have students choose two or three of these to paraphrase in their own words. [Possible responses: Baldwin is disturbed by people who patronize and idealize him because of his race as much as by people who are prejudiced against him because of it. Deep patriotism demands that one criticize the country one loves, in the hopes of making it better. Theories and principles have to be modified by the pragmatic project of moving through life with a personal moral compass.]

J **Critical Thinking**

Interpreting

? How might this essay itself be an attempt to reconcile these two goals? [Possible response: In this essay, Baldwin attempts to honestly analyze his own character and motivations, in order to claim this life experience as the foundation of his work.]

Assessing Learning

Check Test: True-False

1. James Baldwin is the youngest in a family of many children. [False]
2. Baldwin was encouraged as a child to read the Bible. [True]
3. As a young man, Baldwin lived for a while in France. [True]
4. Baldwin accuses both blacks and whites of dwelling too much on their past conflicts. [False]
5. Baldwin says that it is important for a writer to get his or her work done. [True]

Connections

Toni Morrison's eulogy for James Baldwin emphasizes his life and work as a mirror that allowed her generation to see itself. For Morrison, Baldwin gave America and African Americans a more honest American English, the courage and mercy necessary to explore the painful complexities of race and oppression in America, as well as a deep tenderness for his readers, friends, and family. Such gifts, she concludes, ensure that his death is no calamity, but a jubilee.

Ⓐ Historical Connections

Memorial Service for Baldwin

In his biography of Baldwin, David Leeming adds these details of the memorial service: "As many have said, it was a 'celebration' of Baldwin's life, attended by several thousand people: friends, relatives, lovers, and admirers—leaders of the old civil rights movement, classmates from De Witt Clinton, friends from France and Turkey. The coffin, draped in black, stood at the cathedral crossing in front of the high altar. The procession of the family and the honorary pallbearers, led by Baldwin's grieving mother in a wheelchair, moved down the long aisle to the African drumbeats of the Babatunde Olatunji Ensemble.

"The cathedral choir, led by the head chorister, brother Wilmer's son Trevor, sang the psalms. The words of the King James Bible provided a strange contrast to the drums and suggested, like the mix of the congregation, Baldwin's role as a prophet to the whole nation, his constant insistence on the blood kinship of American blacks and whites. This was a ceremony conducted in the author's two languages: 'black English' and 'white English.' . . . Perhaps the highlight of the service was Baldwin himself on tape singing 'Precious Lord, take my hand, lead me on.' This part of the service had been announced in the program, but, nevertheless, it startled the listeners. He seemed to be there, still witnessing, and people were moved."

Ⓑ Reading Skills and Strategies

Using Study Strategies: Outlining

Sometimes writers provide an explicit outline. Here Morrison tells how she will proceed—by enumerating Baldwin's three "gifts." Have students identify the "gifts."

Toni Morrison (1931–   ) was awarded the Nobel Prize in literature in 1993 (see page 1174). She is noted for her novels *Song of Solomon* (1977) and *Beloved* (1987). She Ⓐ delivered this eulogy at Baldwin's memorial service at the Cathedral of St. John the Divine in New York City on December 8, 1987.

from On James Baldwin

Toni Morrison

Jimmy, there is too much to think about you, and too much to feel. The difficulty is your life refuses summation—it always did—and invites contemplation instead. Like many of us left here I thought I knew you. Now I discover that in your company it is myself I know. That is the astonishing gift of your art and your friendship: You gave us ourselves to think about, to cherish. We are like Hall Montana[1] watching "with new wonder" his brother saints, knowing the song he sang is us, "He is us."

I never heard a single command from you, yet the demands you made on me, the challenges you issued to me, were nevertheless unmistakable, even if unenforced: that I work and think at the top of my form, that I stand on moral ground but know that ground must be shored up by mercy, that "the world is before [me] and [I] need not take it or leave it as it was when [I] came in."

Ⓑ Well, the season was always Christmas with you there and, like one aspect of that scenario, you did not neglect to bring at least three gifts. You gave me a language to dwell in, a gift so perfect it seems my own invention. I have been thinking your spoken and written thoughts for so long I believed they were mine. I have been seeing the world through your eyes for so long, I believed that clear clear view was my own. Even now, even here, I need you to tell me what I am feeling and how to articulate it. So I have pored again through the 6,895 pages of your published work to acknowledge the debt and thank you for the credit. No one possessed or inhabited language for me the way you did. You made American English honest—genuinely international. . . .

The second gift was your courage, which you let us share: the courage of one who could go as a stranger in the village and transform the distances between people into intimacy with the whole world; courage to understand that experience in ways that made it a personal revelation for each of us. It was you who gave us the courage to appropriate an alien, hostile, all-white geography because you had discovered that "this world [meaning history] is white no longer and it will never be white again." Yours was the courage to live life in and from its belly as well as beyond its edges, to see and say what it was, to recognize and identify evil but never fear or stand in awe of it. It is a courage that came from a ruthless intelligence married to a pity so profound it could convince anyone who cared to know that those who despised us "need the moral authority of their former slaves, who are the only people in the world who know anything about them and who may be indeed, the only people in the world who really care anything about them.". . .

The third gift was hard to fathom and even harder to accept. It was your tenderness—a tenderness so delicate I thought it could not last, but last it did and envelop me it did. In the midst of anger it tapped me lightly like the child in Tish's[2] womb. . . .

You knew, didn't you, how I needed your language and the mind that formed it? How I relied on your fierce courage to tame wildernesses for me? How strengthened I was by the certainty that came from knowing you would never hurt me? You knew, didn't you, how I loved your love? You knew. This then is no calamity. No. This is jubilee. "Our crown," you said, "has already been bought and paid for. All we have to do," you said, "is wear it."

And we do, Jimmy. You crowned us.

1. **Hall Montana:** a character in Baldwin's novel *Just Above My Head.*
2. **Tish's:** Tish is a character in Baldwin's novel *If Beale Street Could Talk.*

Connecting Across Texts

Connecting with "Autobiographical Notes"

Toni Morrison identifies three "gifts" given to her by James Baldwin. Discuss with students how Baldwin was able to acquire these "gifts". How, then, was he able to bestow them on those who knew and read him? How might Baldwin's assessment of his "special attitude" with regard to Western culture have helped Americans—both black and white—come to terms with their own cultural inheritance?

Connecting with "New African"

In "New African," Andrea Lee also remembers with gratitude the "gift" granted to her by her father. In what way is the gift given by Lee's father like the gifts given by Baldwin? How might the tenderness of Reverend Phillips toward his daughter and his parishioners also be seen as "delicate"?

First Thoughts

1. What do you think were James Baldwin's main goals in writing "Autobiographical Notes"? Do you think he achieved his purpose? Explain.

Shaping Interpretations

2. Describe Baldwin's **tone** toward his subject matter. What specific words or details helped you to identify the tone? Do you share his attitude?

3. How do you think Baldwin feels about himself?

4. Baldwin says that Ralph Ellison was the first African American novelist "to utilize in language, and brilliantly, some of the ambiguity and irony of Negro life." What do you think he means?

5. Why does Baldwin say his "social situation" as an African American creates a dilemma for him as a writer?

6. Review your outline of Baldwin's essay. Then, in your own words, state the three most important **ideas** in the text. Explain why you chose them.

Challenging the Text

7. Do you agree with Baldwin's statement that "the world looks on [the artist's] talent with such a frightening indifference"? Back up your opinion with examples of contemporary writers, painters, musicians, or other artists.

Reading Check

a. According to the essay, what was the most crucial time in Baldwin's development? What did he learn about himself then?

b. How does Baldwin describe the business of the writer, and what does this have to do with what he calls "the Negro problem"?

c. According to Baldwin, how does a writer make use of his or her experiences?

d. What does Baldwin say is his greatest responsibility?

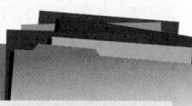

Writer's Notebook

1. Collecting Ideas for an Evaluation

When you evaluate nonfiction, you can focus on the writer's objectivity. That is, you can examine how balanced the writer is, how much evidence the writer uses to support his or her opinions and judgments. Examine Baldwin's essay to see if he offers examples, facts, and reasons for his views. Does he try to be objective in all his statements? Or are some statements purely subjective and emotional, not supported by hard evidence? Take notes on the ways Baldwin presents his views, and save your notes for the Writer's Workshop on page 1181.

Critical Writing

2. The Past Is Prologue

Baldwin believes that "the past is all that makes the present coherent." In a short essay, discuss the implications of this belief. You may want to consider the effects of the past on education, government, the arts, or an individual's intellectual or spiritual growth.

Critical Writing

3. Echoes of Emerson

Reread the excerpt from Ralph Waldo Emerson's "Self-Reliance" (page 224) closely. Then, in a few paragraphs, compare the **diction** and **tone** of Emerson's essay with those of Baldwin's "Autobiographical Notes."

Analyzing Diction

4. Handsome Again

In her eloquent eulogy (see **Connections** on page 1146), Toni Morrison praises Baldwin's use of language. Applying Morrison's criteria, such as honesty and clarity, analyze Baldwin's **diction** in "Autobiographical Notes." Be sure to support your analysis with examples from the text.

JAMES BALDWIN 1147

First Thoughts [Respond]

1. Possible response: His goal is to describe his evolution both as a writer and as a man. He succeeds by exploring his struggle with African American identity and his moral responsibilities as a writer.

Shaping Interpretations [Interpret]

2. His tone may be described as lightly ironic, passionate, direct, creative, and critical. Students may cite various examples, such as "We can dismiss," "exasperating and mysterious habit of having babies," "These goings-on," "I was an interloper." Students may or may not share Baldwin's attitudes.

3. Baldwin sees himself as a man and a writer trying to chart a moral course through the maze of racial identity and personal experience.

4. Students may say that Ellison is able to express in fiction the complex and contradictory reality of life as an African American.

5. The troubled relation of African American identity to Western culture led him to loathe culture itself and often hindered his writing.

6. Writers must view their experience in a social and historical context. African American writers must work from a unique and troubled relation to the social and historical context of Western culture. Yet no political or social theory can guide a writer through such complexities—only the writer's moral center can do so.

Challenging the Text [Evaluate]

7. Answers will vary—make sure that students consider the role of mass media in this indifference.

Grading Timesaver

Rubrics for each Choices assignment appear on p. 229 in the *Portfolio Management System.*

Reading Check

a. The most crucial time in his development was when he realized that he had to approach Western culture with an African American perspective. He learned that he hated and feared the world.

b. The business of the writer is going beneath the surfaces and examining attitudes. The "Negro problem" is inaccessible—written about widely but analyzed badly. An honest assessment of the past may be painful for both blacks and whites, but it is vital.

c. A writer uses personal experience to analyze and utilize the past.

d. His greatest responsibility is to last and to get his work done.

Sylvia Plath

(1932–1963)

Until her death in 1963, Sylvia Plath's life was, to most outward appearances, a model of achievement. This success, however, could not fully mask nor calm a fearsome inner turmoil. Plath was born in Boston and spent her early years in the nearby seaside town of Winthrop. Both her parents were immigrants—her father, a professor of biology, from Poland; her mother,

© Rollie McKenna.

a teacher of office skills, from Austria. Plath later seemed convinced that the reason for her emotional suffering as an adult was her father's death from diabetes when she was only eight.

Plath started writing poems and stories in elementary school, and she first published a poem in a Boston newspaper around the time of her father's death. From an early age, she was persistent in finding a publisher for her work; for instance, she persevered through forty-five rejection slips from *Seventeen* magazine before landing a story there in 1950. Plath was awarded a scholarship to Smith College, where she flourished academically and continued to pursue creative writing. She won a much-coveted fiction prize from *Mademoiselle* magazine in her junior year and spent that summer as a guest editor in the magazine's New York office.

The first serious sign of dangerous turbulence in Plath's emotional life came at the end of that seemingly storybook summer, when she was overcome by depression and attempted suicide, an experience that became the basis for her novel, *The Bell Jar*. After psychiatric treatment and electroshock therapy—"the painful agony of slow rebirth and psychic regeneration," as she called it—she returned to college. But she was ill with manic depression, years before effective drug therapy was available.

After graduating from Smith, Plath attended Cambridge University in England on a Fulbright fellowship. At Cambridge, she met the noted English poet Ted Hughes, whom she married in 1956. They lived in Boston during most of the late 1950s and moved to London at the end of 1959. The following year, Plath's first book of poetry, *The Colossus,* was published, and their daughter Frieda was born; their son Nicholas was born in 1962.

In January 1963, Plath's famous autobiographical novel, *The Bell Jar,* was published. In the few weeks between its publication and her death, Plath wrote poetry at a furious pace—sometimes two or three poems a day. The subject matter and style of these poems, published posthumously in *Ariel* (1965), were different from her earlier work. Most poems in *The Colossus* were relatively restrained and formal, influenced by a number of poetic styles, from the classicism of John Crowe Ransom (page 577) to the exuberance of Theodore Roethke (page 1001). But the *Ariel* poems, especially the bitter poems about her father and her attempts at suicide, showed a violence and a frankness absent from her earlier work. Robert Lowell (page 948) wrote in the book's foreword, "These poems are playing Russian roulette with six cartridges in the cylinder, a game of 'chicken,' the wheels of both cars locked and unable to swerve." The poems were, he said, an "appalling and triumphant fulfillment" of her talents.

In 1963, Plath was separated from her husband and caring for their two young children in an unheated London flat. In February, during a very cold London winter, Plath's depression returned. She attempted suicide again. This time she succeeded.

In 1998, to mark what would have been Plath's sixty-fifth birthday, Hughes published *Birthday Letters,* a series of poems about Plath and their passionate but troubled relationship.

 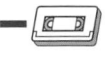
T1148

Before You Read

MIRROR

Make the Connection

Reflections

We all do it: We check our appearance in a mirror, partly to make sure we are appropriately groomed, partly in order to discover and polish our self-image. What might a mirror—"silver and exact"—think of the person peering into it?

Quickwrite

If a mirror could talk, what might it say about the concerns of the people passing before it? Write down a few observations that a "talking" mirror might make.

Elements of Literature

Personification

Personification is a figure of speech in which an object (such as a mirror) or an animal is given human qualities, such as feelings, thoughts, and attitudes. At its heart, personification is a type of metaphor in which two dissimilar things are compared. For instance, if you say "A mirror tells no lies," you are comparing a mirror to a person by giving it a human attribute.

Courtesy Marisa Del Re Gallery, New York.

Mirror IV (1976–1979) by George Tooker. Egg tempera on gesso panel (24″ × 20″).

Mirror

Sylvia Plath

I am silver and exact. I have no preconceptions.
Whatever I see I swallow immediately
Just as it is, unmisted by love or dislike.
I am not cruel, only truthful—
5　The eye of a little god, four-cornered.
Most of the time I meditate on the opposite wall.
It is pink, with speckles. I have looked at it so long
I think it is a part of my heart. But it flickers.
Faces and darkness separate us over and over. **Ⓐ**

10　Now I am a lake. A woman bends over me,
Searching my reaches for what she really is. **Ⓑ**
Then she turns to those liars, the candles or the moon.
I see her back, and reflect it faithfully.
She rewards me with tears and an agitation of hands. **Ⓒ**

15　I am important to her. She comes and goes.
Each morning it is her face that replaces the darkness.
In me she has drowned a young girl, and in me an old woman
Rises toward her day after day, like a terrible fish.

SYLVIA PLATH 1149

Summary ■■

In "Mirror," Plath personifies a mirror as the first person speaker, who witnesses a woman growing old in its "silver and exact" reflection. The speaker's tone is cool, clinical, and merciless. In figurative language, the mirror describes itself as both "a little god" and a "lake" who shows the woman "what she really is." The mirror's "reward" and the measure of its importance is the woman's agitation. In the final two lines, the mirror confronts the woman with her own image, as an old woman, rising "like a terrible fish."

Resources ———

Viewing and Representing
Fine Art Transparency
Students can compare the woman in *Pat Combing Her Hair* by James Valerio with the woman in "Mirror." See *Viewing and Representing:*
• Transparency 21
• Worksheet, p. 84

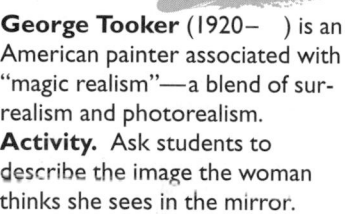

RESPONDING TO THE ART

George Tooker (1920–) is an American painter associated with "magic realism"—a blend of surrealism and photorealism. **Activity.** Ask students to describe the image the woman thinks she sees in the mirror.

Ⓐ Elements of Literature
　　Personification
❓ **How does the mirror describe itself?** [Possible responses: The mirror sees itself as honest and exact, but it also seems to thrive on the godlike power of its cold neutrality.]

Ⓑ Literary Connections
In Greek mythology, Narcissus is a handsome young man so enamored with his own reflection in a pool that he is turned into a flower. Ask students to compare and contrast Narcissus and the woman in the poem.

Ⓒ Reading Skills and Strategies
　　Making Inferences
❓ **How does the woman "reward" the mirror?** [Possible response: She cries over her lost youth, and thus affirms the emotional power of this "god."]

Reaching All Students

Struggling Readers
Have students take notes on the connection between the poem's speaker and the woman. Students may write their notes in two columns. In the right column, students should write the mirror's thoughts and feelings, and in the left column, the thoughts and feelings of the woman. Direct students to connect the notes on both sides and to label each connection. Is it cause and effect? A similarity? A contrast?

English Language Learners
Clarify the idiom of "swallow" (l. 2)—to accept uncritically, without bias. For additional strategies to supplement instruction for these students, see
• *Lesson Plans Including Strategies for English-Language Learners*

Advanced Learners
Have students compare Plath's "terrible fish" to Elizabeth Bishop's "The Fish" (p. 1035).

T1149

Summary ■ ■

In "Mushrooms," Plath personifies the fungi whose sinister growth takes on symbolic overtones. The mushrooms assert themselves through their "bland-mannered," banal, and steady insistence, and proclaim that they will inherit the earth.

Ⓐ Elements of Literature
Tone
❓ How would you describe the tone of the first nine lines of the poem? What elements contribute to the tone? [Possible responses: The tone at the opening of the poem might be described as playful, yet sinister. The effect is created by the use of repetition, rhythm, rhyme and wordplay.]

Ⓑ Elements of Literature
Consonance and Assonance
❓ Identify the consonance and assonance in ll. 1–11. What effect do these devices have on the tone? [Possible responses: Consonance occurs in the *v* and *r* sounds (l. 1), the *t* and *l* sounds (l. 2), the *r* and *s* sounds (l. 4), the *l* sounds (l. 5), the *r* sounds (l. 6), the *s* sounds (ll. 7-8), and the *s* and *m* sounds (l. 9). Assonance occurs in the *e* sounds (l. 2), the *o* sounds (l. 4), the *i* sounds (l. 6), and the *a* sounds (l. 9). The effect of these devices is a musical, sing-song quality that is both comic and sinister.]

Ⓒ Elements of Literature
Tone
❓ How would you describe the tone at the end of the poem? [Possible response: The tone is menacing, with the prophecy of the world taken over by steady banality and petty ambition.]

BROWSING IN THE FILES

About the Author. Though her writing career was relatively short, Sylvia Plath is considered one of the most important American writers of the post-World War II period. Before the posthumous publication of the collection *Ariel,* however, she was known more for her novel *The Bell Jar,* than for her poetry. It was not until 1981, eighteen years after her death, that her *Collected Poems* won a Pulitzer Prize.

Before You Read
MUSHROOMS

Make the Connection
Amazing Nature
Have you ever thought about the power of nature—how flowers can appear out of nowhere after a rainstorm? how plants can slice through a sidewalk? how mushrooms can multiply silently overnight? What do such natural events make you think about? Could your reactions range from awe to horror?

Quickwrite
In a few sentences, describe some natural processes and tell how they make you feel.

Elements of Literature
Tone is the attitude a writer takes toward the subject of a work, the characters in it, or the audience. Tone, which results from the complex interplay of **diction** and **style,** can often be described in a word (for instance, playful, sarcastic, or tragic). As you read "Mushrooms" try to hear its tone.

Mushrooms
Sylvia Plath

Overnight, very
Whitely, discreetly,
Very quietly

Our toes, our noses
5 Take hold on the loam,
Acquire the air.

Nobody sees us,
Stops us, betrays us;
The small grains make room.

10 Soft fists insist on
Heaving the needles,
The leafy bedding,

Even the paving.
Our hammers, our rams,
15 Earless and eyeless,

Perfectly voiceless,
Widen the crannies,
Shoulder through holes. We

Diet on water,
20 On crumbs of shadow,
Bland-mannered, asking

Little or nothing.
So many of us!
So many of us!

25 We are shelves, we are
Tables, we are meek,
We are edible,

Nudgers and shovers
In spite of ourselves.
30 Our kind multiplies:

We shall by morning
Inherit the earth.
Our foot's in the door.

Using Students' Strengths

Naturalist Learners
Encourage students to use prior knowledge and research, if necessary, to describe how mushrooms grow, the speed at which they reproduce, and the environments in which they grow. Students may create a dialogue with the speakers of the poem and respond to the mushrooms' claim that they will take over the world.

MAKING MEANINGS

Mirror

First Thoughts

1. What thoughts or feelings did "Mirror" evoke in you? Did you find the poem surprising? Explain. (Review your Quickwrite.)

Shaping Interpretations

2. Identify the **speaker** of the poem. In what ways does Plath **personify** the speaker?

3. Describe the qualities that the speaker claims to possess. What does the speaker imply by saying "the eye of a little god" (line 5)?

4. The last line of "Mirror" contains the striking **image** of "a terrible fish." How would you explain the significance of this image in the poem? What associations and emotional overtones does the image have for you?

Mushrooms

First Thoughts

1. What do you think this poem is really about?

Shaping Interpretations

2. Who is speaking in the poem?

3. What natural process do the speakers describe? What figures of speech help you to picture parts of that process?

4. "Blessed are the meek, for they shall inherit the earth" is a well known expression from the New Testament of the Bible. What **ironic** twist is given to this scripture at the end of the poem?

5. What **tone** do you hear in the poem? What specific words help create that tone?

6. Both "Mirror" and "Mushrooms" deal with realities that lurk beneath the surface of appearances. What would you say those realities are?

Extending the Text

7. What kind of people are like the mushrooms? Is the story told in the poem a sinister one or a comical one—or is it something else? Compare your interpretation with those of your classmates. How have life experiences affected your interpretations?

CHOICES:
Building Your Portfolio

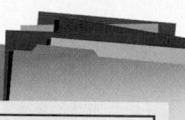

Writer's Notebook

1. Collecting Ideas for an Evaluation

When you evaluate a work of literature, you must decide how much background information you'll need to supply—either on the writer or on the text. Draft the opening paragraph of an evaluation of Plath's "Mirror" or "Mushrooms," in which you present some biographical background information about the poet. (Your essay should be targeted at readers with no familiarity with Plath.) Save your draft for possible use in the Writer's Workshop on page 1181.

Contrasting Texts
2. Visions or Nightmares?

In a brief essay, compare and contrast Plath's attitude toward nature in "Mushrooms" with the attitude expressed toward nature in another text. Try Emerson's *Nature* (page 219), Thoreau's *Walden* (page 233), Dickinson's "Apparently with no surprise" (page 385), Frost's "Design" (page 560), or Bishop's "The Fish" (page 1035). Does each text see nature and the universe as benign or malevolent or indifferent? What does the text say about the relationship between human nature and the natural world? What is the tone of each text? What do you think of "Mushrooms" and the other text you've chosen?

Creative Writing
3. Nature Speaks

Imitate Plath's device in "Mushrooms" of having something in nature speak and describe its growing process. Before you start to write, decide what tone you will give your speaker or speakers. Will your speaker use prose or poetry? Be sure to refer to your Quickwrite notes.

SYLVIA PLATH 1151

4. Possible responses: The image is so monstrous that it suggests the deep distortions of identity and self-worth, brought on by a fear of aging and the cult of beauty.

Mushrooms

First Thoughts [Respond]

1. Possible response: the poem reflects horror of a bland, persistant, and disturbing urge to domination in people, and perhaps in nature itself.

Shaping Interpretations [Interpret]

2. Mushrooms are the speakers.

3. The poem describes the growth of fungi in dark, damp environments. The images are tactile and violent—taking "hold" on the loam, "fists," "acquiring" air, hammering, ramming, and taking over.

4. The irony lies in the fact that these ambassadors of banal, unthinking domination are hardly "meek" (l. 26).

5. Possible responses: The tone is horrified, even paranoid. "Acquire" connotes aggressive possession, without scruples. "Fists" connotes force. "Shadow" connotes darkness. "Nudgers and shovers" suggests a slow but sinister ambition.

6. Both poems meditate on the merciless, unfeeling progress of natural processes—realities which rupture the fragile world of human sensitivity and meaning.

Extending the Text [Synthesize]

7. Possible response: The mushrooms might resemble a steady, blandly ambitious bureaucrat—who slowly acquires power without any guiding vision or ideal.

MAKING MEANINGS

Mirror

First Thoughts [Respond]

1. Possible response: I first thought of human vanity—how much we value physical appearance as a way of confirming who we are—but the horror of the poem's ending surprised me. The poem is not about vanity but its opposite, a kind of overly critical cruelty or self-loathing.

Shaping Interpretations [Interpret]

2. The speaker is the mirror. Plath gives the mirror a speaking voice, the first person pronoun *I*, and human attributes of thought, vision, and intention.

3. Possible responses: The speaker claims to possess the capacity to see and reflect reality without illusions. The speaker claims to have an omniscient, even divine perspective—yet it only sees surface reality.

OBJECTIVES

1. Read and interpret the essay
2. Use a graphic organizer to understand a text
3. Recognize and discuss themes and connections that cross cultures

Planning

- **Traditional Schedule**
  Lesson Plans Including Strategies for English-Language Learners
- **One-Stop Planner**
  CD-ROM with Test Generator

BROWSING IN THE FILES

About the Author. Jorge Luis Borges was one of the primary figures of the *Ultraísta* movement in Spanish and Spanish American literature after World War I. The *Ultraístas* were a group of avant-garde poets who were influenced heavily by the French Symbolists. They were distinguished by their use of free verse and unconventional imagery. Borges's first published work was *Fervor de Buenos Aires* (1923), a collection of poems. His writing has been compared to the mysterious and unsettling work of Franz Kafka. In 1961, he and Samuel Beckett shared the Formentor Prize. Like James Joyce and Vladimir Nabokov, Borges was never awarded the Nobel Prize. However, his influence has been so strong that his last name has frequently been used as an adjective—*Borgesian*, like *Joycean* and *Nabokovian*—to describe a dominant strain of modernist writing. In 1998, his *Collected Fictions* was published in a new English translation.

Jorge Luis Borges
(1899–1986)

Jorge Luis Borges (hôr′hä lōō·ēs′ bôr′hes) was born in Buenos Aires, Argentina. As a youth, Borges spent many hours reading in his father's large collection of Spanish and English books. He later wrote, "If I were asked to name the chief event in my life, I should say my father's library." Borges lived in Europe with his family from 1914 to 1921, attending school for four of those years in Geneva, Switzerland.

Returning to Buenos Aires, the highly educated Borges soon turned to writing and to editing literary journals. Beginning in the late 1930s, he earned a living mostly as a librarian and teacher, serving from 1955 to 1973 as director of Argentina's national library. Borges continued to write, and in the early 1960s he gained wide recognition as one of the world's great contemporary writers. He subsequently taught at leading universities (including Harvard) and was awarded high honors by numerous countries and educational institutions.

Borges's long list of publications (some translated into English) includes the remarkable stories in *Ficciones, 1935–1944* (1944); the

prose and poetry of *El hacedor* (1960); the poetry collection *Elogio de la sombra* (1969); and the subtle stories of *El libro de arena* (1975). Borges also translated into Spanish the writings of Herman Melville, Walt Whitman, Virginia Woolf, William Faulkner, Franz Kafka, and other noted authors. Translations into English of Borges's writing include *Selected Poems, 1923–1967* (1972) and *Borges: A Reader* (1981).

S. Bassouls/Sygma.

Borges began to lose his eyesight in his twenties, and as he grew into total blindness in his fifties, he took to dictating his works. Late in life, when Borges learned he was suffering from cancer, he returned to Switzerland. He married his longtime assistant and collaborator María Kodama just seven weeks before he died.

Before You Read
BORGES AND MYSELF

Background

Few writers create a body of literature so distinctive that its characteristics are immediately recognizable, widely imitated, and ultimately turned into an adjective—for example, *Dantean,*

Shakespearean, Emersonian, Whitmanesque, Kafkaesque. In our time, *Borgesian* is an adjective frequently applied to writing that is mysterious, playful, ambiguous, and profoundly concerned with questions of identity, fate, time, and language.

Perhaps the writer who most fully exemplifies the experimental side of postmodern literature, Jorge Luis Borges has produced fictionlike essays, nonfictionlike stories, essaylike poems, and other hybrid, unclassifiable works. His characters are as

go.hrw.com
LEO 11-21

Reaching All Students

Struggling Readers
Students may easily be confused by the differences between Borges and his alter ego in "Borges and Myself" (p. 1154). Have students read the piece with a partner, and encourage students to pause in their reading to share their observations and questions. Direct students to read the piece two or three times, and then have the partners discuss their notes with the rest of the class.

English Language Learners
Review with students the definition and uses of reflexive pronouns, such as *myself.* For additional strategies to supplement instruction for these students, see
- *Lesson Plans Including Strategies for English-Language Learners*

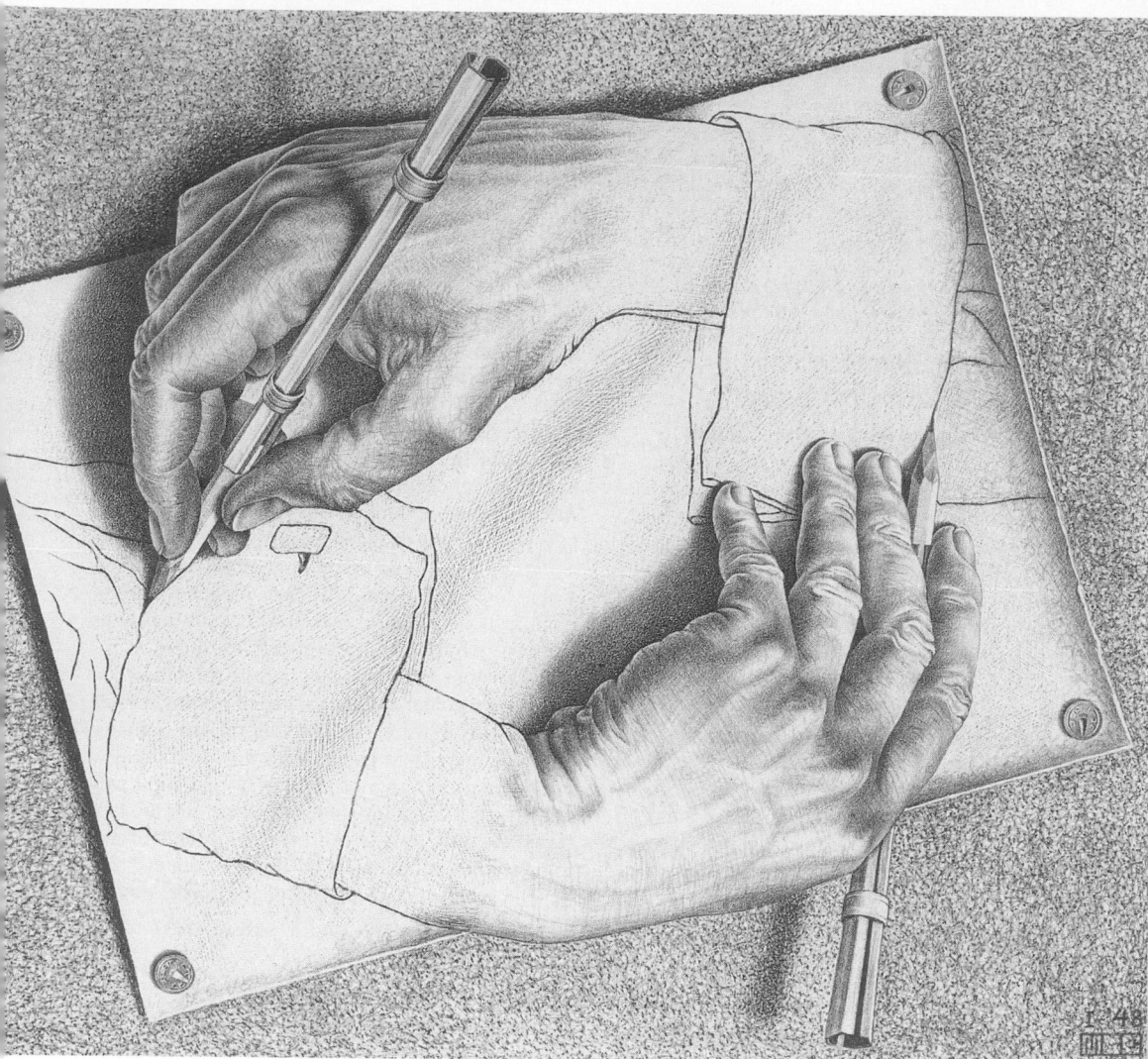

Drawing Hands (1948) by M. C. Escher. Lithograph (11⅛″ × 13⅛″).

hybrid as his forms. People meet their doubles and often don't know whether they are coming or going, literally, in the labyrinth of the universe. Borgesian time can be circular, events can be endlessly repeated, and the boundaries between dream and reality are often erased.

Influenced by Edgar Allan Poe's sense of fantasy and by Walt Whitman's vision of universality, Borges in his turn has had an enormous influence on contemporary literature. His stories-within-stories approach, his concern with personal identity, and his self-conscious literariness have become part of the common literary vocabulary of our age.

JORGE LUIS BORGES 1153

RESPONDING TO THE ART

Maurits Cornelis Escher (1898–1972) was a Dutch print-maker known for lithographs and woodcuts that include optical illusions and intricate geometric patterns. Both playful and serious, Escher's work often contains interlocking designs that baffle the reason but delight the eye. *Drawing Hands* (1948) embodies surrealist ambiguity. Like "Borges and Myself," it poses the chicken-and-egg puzzle: Who is creating whom?

Activity. Ask students to express their initial reactions to the lithograph. Does it make sense? Does it leave them frustrated, or is the image satisfying in some way? Why do people enjoy such visual magic? Students might also create a display of puzzle pictures and optical illusions that trick perception the way Borges plays with narrative and rationality.

Summary ■■

The subject of "Borges and Myself" is the paradox of personal identity faced by writers, artists, and perhaps everyone—caused by the split between an expressive, public life and an inner, private life. The narrator describes his life in relation to someone he calls "the other man," a famous and flamboyant literary creator known as "Borges." The two share the same body, tastes, and experiences, yet they remain separate—if ultimately indistinguishable—from each other. In fact, the narrator says that he lives so that Borges can write his tales and poems. Nevertheless, he believes that some small part of him will survive in the other man after he himself is gone. The narrator says that he has tried to rid himself of Borges but failed, and now his whole life is a futile attempt to escape, for the "other man" will ultimately appropriate everything about the narrator that won't be lost to oblivion. In the startling final sentence, the narrator admits that he does not know whether he or Borges is writing this very piece.

Professional Notes

Critical Comment: Double Trouble

In his critical biography of Borges, literary critic James Woodall analyzes "Borges and Myself":

This was as clear an articulation as Borges ever made about the manner in which texts "wrote him," rather than the other way around. They lived through him, not he through them. He acknowledges an animus, more or less outside his control, as being responsible for work which has made the reputation of a certain "Borges."

He was always modest. Here, the writer takes that virtue to a metaphysical extreme, bowing to the publicly "visible" other—a fiction—and as ever, when in most exquisitely skeptical mood, casting doubt over the existence of a "real" Borges. "Which of us is writing this page I don't know," the text ends. In the most cunning and diverting move of his literary career, Borges had become his double.

After students have completed their two-column charts, have them circle characteristics that seem to belong equally to both the "Narrator" and to "Borges." Based on what they have written in each column, have students decide which side of this person is in charge.

B ## Critical Thinking

Interpreting

? Who is this "other man," Borges, and what is his relation to the narrator? [Possible response: Borges may be the literary persona who lives on the pages of work by Borges, the creative, public voice who exists in literature and the media. The narrator is the ordinary man who makes that voice possible, but who is not identical to it.]

C ## Reading Skills and Strategies

Making Inferences

? How will "some moment" of the narrator "remain" in Borges? Why might he not recognize it? [Moments of his experience and thought will live on in the body of work that is "Borges," but even as it is written it takes on a literary voice of its own—and will even more as it is interpreted, anthologized, and read.]

D ## Advanced Learners

Authenticity

Have students note how this last sentence poses the problem of authentic identity. Is is possible, Borges asks, to write truly as oneself, truly autobiographically—or is one always trapped in a persona, a performance?

FINDING COMMON GROUND

Have each group use its discussion notes to write a paragraph stating and supporting the consensus of the group members. Have groups read their paragraphs aloud. Then, have the groups work together to find common ground in their reactions to Borges's writing.

Reading Skills and Strategies

Using a Graphic Organizer to Understand a Text
The following famous piece by Jorge Luis Borges is a very short investigation of personal identity and personal psychology. Like a great poem, however, it is so packed with subtleties and connections and surprises that you could profitably spend hours—even days—analyzing its contents. In fact, many scholarly essays have been written about the last sentence alone.

Divide a sheet of paper into two columns, one headed "Narrator," the other "Borges." As you read, write down the key characteristics of each in the appropriate column.

Borges and Myself

Jorge Luis Borges
translated by **Norman Thomas di Giovanni** *and* **Jorge Luis Borges**

A It's to the other man, to Borges, that things happen. I walk along the streets of Buenos Aires, stopping now and then—perhaps out of habit—to look at the arch of an old entranceway or a grillwork gate; of Borges I get news through the mail and glimpse his name among a committee of professors or in a dictionary of biography. I have a **B** taste for hourglasses, maps, eighteenth-century typography, the roots of words, the smell of coffee, and Stevenson's[1] prose; the other man shares these likes, but in a showy way that turns them into stagy mannerisms. It would be an exaggeration to say that we are on bad terms; I live, I let myself live, so that Borges can weave his tales and poems, and those tales and poems are my justifica-

tion. It is not hard for me to admit that he has managed to write a few worthwhile pages, but these pages cannot save me, perhaps because what is good no longer belongs to anyone—not even the other man—but rather to speech or tradition. In any case, I am fated to become lost once and for all, and only some moment of myself will survive in the other man. Little by little, I have been surrendering everything to him, even though I have evidence of his stubborn habit of falsification and exaggerating. Spinoza[2] held that all things try to keep on being themselves; a stone **C** wants to be a stone and the tiger, a tiger. I shall remain in Borges, not in myself (if it is so that I am someone), but I recognize myself less in his books than in those of others or than in the laborious tuning of a guitar. Years ago, I tried ridding myself of him and I went from myths of the outlying slums of the city to games with time and infinity, but those games are now part of Borges and I will have to turn to other things. And so, my life is a running away, and I lose everything and everything is left to oblivion or to the other man.

D Which of us is writing this page I don't know.

1. **Stevenson's:** Robert Louis Stevenson (1850-1894), Scottish, author of *Treasure Island* and other adventure stories.

2. **Spinoza** (spi·nō′zə): Baruch Spinoza (1632-1677), Dutch philosopher.

FINDING COMMON GROUND

Form a discussion group with four or five other students, with one student acting as recording secretary. Before you begin discussing Borges's piece, review your reading notes. Then, refer to them as necessary during the exchange of views.

• First, each person should present his or her overall reaction to the work. Then, begin to pin down the main characteristics of the story's narrator and of Borges.

• As the group comes to an agreement on a characteristic, the recording secretary should write it down. The secretary should also note separately whenever group members can't agree on whether a particular characteristic applies.

• Finally, discuss the meaning of the selection's last sentence. Can you determine with some certainty who exactly wrote "Borges and Myself"? What do you think this selection is saying about questions of identity and self-creation?

Making the Connections

Connecting to the Theme:
"The Created Self"
Twentieth-century literature is frequently concerned with the meaning of individual identity, how identity develops, how it breaks down, and how it is perceived by others. What aspect of human identity does Borges explore in his work? [Possible response: He explores the ambiguity of the very concept of identity and the difficulty of capturing one's "authentic" identity in speech or writing.]

Assessing Learning

Check Test: Questions and Answers
1. Who is "the other man" the narrator names? [Borges the writer or public figure]
2. Who is the narrator (at first)? [Borges the ordinary man]
3. How does the narrator feel about Borges's writing? [It is his "justification" but it does not do him much good.]
4. Which writer does the narrator say he admires? [Robert Louis Stevenson]

James Dickey
(1923–1997)

"I came to poetry with no particular qualifications," James Dickey recalled in 1966. "I had begun to suspect, however, that there is a poet—or a kind of poet—buried in every human being . . . and that the people whom we are pleased to call poets are only those who have felt the need and contrived the means to release this spirit from its prison." Dickey's poetic spirit proved to be powerful and original.

James Dickey.

Dickey, who was born in Atlanta, grew up with a greater interest in athletics than in academics, and published his first volume of poetry, *Into the Stone,* at the relatively late age of thirty-seven. He had led a life of action—as a high school football player, a soldier in wartime, and an enthusiastic hunter (sometimes with bow and arrow). Dickey had also been a successful advertising executive, handling major accounts ranging from potato chips to airlines. With the publication of *Into the Stone,* however, Dickey became a full-time poet. Like most poets, he also held teaching posts. For many years Dickey taught at the University of South Carolina.

At his best, Dickey was a poet of personal dilemmas gravely posed, of situations dramatized by moral alternatives or made urgent by haunting questions of guilt and regret. In exploring these situations, his poems often include multiple voices and perspectives—some human, some animal, some that represent mythological or supernatural beings. The result is a quality Dickey called "country surrealism," the often violent confrontation of primitive impulses and civilized values.

The expansive range of Dickey's subject matter is matched by the vigor and skill of his "open" poetic techniques, which include such features as horizontal spacing within lines, inverted syntax, and a bold, often distinctly Southern tone. Paul Zweig, writing in *The New York Times Book Review,* observed that Dickey's poems are "like richly modulated hollers; a sort of rough, American-style bel canto advertising its freedom from the constraints of ordinary language. Dickey's style is so personal, his rhythms so willfully eccentric, that the poems seem to swell up and overflow like that oldest of American art forms, the boast."

One of the most popular and charismatic American poets of his generation, James Dickey not only won a National Book Award for his poetry and an appointment as Poetry Consultant to the Library of Congress, but also established himself as a skillful and entertaining reader of his own work.

Dickey produced fewer poems in his later years, but his visibility as a writer and public figure increased. In 1970, he published an immensely successful novel, *Deliverance,* about the brutal encounter of four suburban men with the Georgia wilderness. Two years later he appeared in a minor role in the very popular motion-picture adaptation of his novel. Dickey's turbulent life at the time is recalled in a poignant and somewhat bitter memoir by his son Christopher Dickey, *Summer of Deliverance* (1998).

go.hrw.com
LE0 11-21

OBJECTIVES
1. Read and interpret the poem
2. Express understanding through writing, speaking, and listening

SKILLS
Writing
- Collect ideas for an evaluation
- Write an essay analyzing a poem

Speaking/Listening
- Perform an oral interpretation of a poem

Planning

- **Traditional Schedule**
  Lesson Plans Including Strategies for English-Language Learners
- **One-Stop Planner**
  CD-ROM with Test Generator

BROWSING IN THE FILES

About the Author. In 1977, James Dickey read a specially commissioned poem, "The Strength of Fields," at the inauguration ceremonies of his friend and fellow Georgian, President Jimmy Carter.

  *Resources: Print and Media*

Reading
- *Graphic Organizers for Active Reading,* p. 117
- *Audio CD Library*
  Disc 31, Track 4

Assessment
- *Portfolio Management System,* p. 231
- *Test Generator (One-Stop Planner CD-ROM)*

Internet
- go.hrw.com (keyword: LE0 11-21)

The first-person speaker is a lifeguard at a summer camp who has failed to save a boy from drowning on his watch. As the poem opens, he lies in the boathouse at night while the children sleep, hiding out of his guilt, grief, and helplessness. As the moon rises though, he imagines the lake as a solid "snowfield" that he can cross to its center. There, he sees himself performing "the miracle," calling to the child and summoning him to the surface. Yet it is not the drowned boy who answers his call, but someone else— perhaps the lifeguard himself as a reflection or symbol. With this recognition, the lifeguard is finally able to grieve beside the illuminated lake ("the grave"), and see that he holds in his arms a child of "water, water, water."

Ⓐ Elements of Literature
Setting and Atmosphere

❓ How would you describe the setting and atmosphere of the poem? [Possible response: The setting is a lake during the day and later at night. The atmosphere is dreamlike, with few details other than the water and the moonlight that seems to mesmerize the lifeguard.]

Ⓑ Critical Thinking
Interpreting

❓ Have students note how the poem shifts toward the language of a prayer or a ritual in these lines. Then have students interpret the scenario of the "savior." Do student see it as an elaborate wish for a different outcome, or as something else? Does saving one who has "already died" represent some step towards healing and acceptance for the lifeguard? [Many students will see the scenario as an elaborate fantasy or hallucination that nevertheless ultimately allows the speaker to come to terms with his actions, and to thus, in some sense, "save" himself.]

Ⓒ Elements of Literature
Repetition

❓ What is the significance of the repeated word in l. 60? What does it mean to the speaker? [Possible response: It signifies the speaker's recognition that the boy is really dead, and that the only child he can revive is one of his own creation, made of water and his own reflection.]

Before You Read
THE LIFEGUARD

Make the Connection
Undoing What's Done
"He wishes to undo what has already been done," James

Dickey once wrote of the speaker in the poem you are about to read. "That's what we all want to be able to do, isn't it?"

Quickwrite
Take a few minutes to respond to Dickey's comment. Do you agree?

The Lifeguard
James Dickey

In a stable of boats I lie still,
From all sleeping children hidden.
The leap of a fish from its shadow
Makes the whole lake instantly tremble.
5 With my foot on the water, I feel
The moon outside

Take on the utmost of its power.
I rise and go out through the boats.
I set my broad sole upon silver,
10 On the skin of the sky, on the moonlight,
Stepping outward from earth onto water
In quest of the miracle

This village of children believed
That I could perform as I dived
15 For one who had sunk from my sight.
I saw his cropped haircut go under.
I leapt, and my steep body flashed
Once, in the sun.

Dark drew all the light from my eyes.
20 Like a man who explores his death
By the pull of his slow-moving shoulders,
I hung head down in the cold,
Wide-eyed, contained, and alone
Among the weeds,

25 And my fingertips turned into stone
From clutching immovable blackness.
Time after time I leapt upward
Exploding in breath, and fell back
From the change in the children's faces
30 At my defeat.

Lake Superior, about 1948, by Lawren Stewart Harris. Oil on canvas (87 cm x 102.8 cm).
Hood Museum of Art, Dartmouth College, Hanover, NH. Gift of the artist, Lawren S. Harris, in memory of his uncle, William Kilborne Stewart, through the Friends of Dartmouth Library.

Beneath them I swam to the boathouse
With only my life in my arms
To wait for the lake to shine back
At the risen moon with such power
35 That my steps on the light of the ripples
Might be sustained.

Beneath me is nothing but brightness
Like the ghost of a snowfield in summer.
As I move toward the center of the lake,
40 Which is also the center of the moon,
I am thinking of how I may be
The savior of one

Reaching All Students

Struggling Readers
To help students follow the narrative line of the poem, ask them to make a list or use a graphic organizer, such as a story map, to identify all the "events" of the poem. Have students pay careful attention to the chronological order of the events and identify which events seem to take place in reality and which take place in the lifeguard's imagination.

English Language Learners
Have students read the poem aloud slowly, summarizing the action of each stanza. For additional strategies to supplement instruction for these students, see
• *Lesson Plans Including Strategies for English-Language Learners*

Advanced Learners
Ask students to compare the experience of the lifeguard with the Greek myth in which Orpheus attempts to rescue Eurydice.

Who has already died in my care.
The dark trees fade from around me.
45 The moon's dust hovers together.
I call softly out, and the child's
Voice answers through blinding water.
Patiently, slowly,

He rises, dilating to break
50 The surface of stone with his forehead.
He is one I do not remember
Having ever seen in his life.
The ground I stand on is trembling
Upon his smile.

55 I wash the black mud from my hands.
On a light given off by the grave
I kneel in the quick of the moon
At the heart of a distant forest
And hold in my arms a child
60 Of water, water, water. **C**

MAKING MEANINGS

First Thoughts

1. Write down one question you have about this poem.

Shaping Interpretations

2. Who is the speaker in "The Lifeguard"? Where is he, according to stanza 1? What are the children doing?

3. In stanza 2, what does the lifeguard do? What is he searching for?

4. According to the **flashback** in stanzas 3–6, what did the lifeguard do to try to save the boy that day? Why did he swim to the boathouse?

5. In stanza 7, we are back in the present. What is the lifeguard hoping to accomplish?

6. What does the lifeguard do in stanza 8? How do you interpret the events in lines 46–54?

7. One of the **themes** of the poem has to do with the miracle that the lifeguard hopes for: to save the boy. In developing that theme, Dickey makes **allusions** to two of Christ's miracles: walking on water and bringing a dead man to life. Which lines of the poem allude to these miracles?

CHOICES:
Building Your Portfolio

Writer's Notebook
1. Collecting Ideas for an Evaluation

Evaluate Dickey's poem in terms of how well it communicates its meaning. If there is any passage in the text that puzzles you, note it and describe the difficulty you have with it. Save your notes for possible use in the Writer's Workshop on page 1181.

Interpreting a Theme
2. Undoing What's Done

In an essay discuss the theme of the poem in light of Dickey's comment on page 1156. Could his **title** be interpreted on several levels? Refer to your Quickwrite notes.

Analyzing a Poem
3. Reality and Fantasy

"The Lifeguard" is written as an **interior monologue**—a narrative technique that records a character's internal flow of thoughts, memories, and fantasies. The poem mixes the speaker's actual experience with his thoughts and fantasies about that experience. In a short essay, describe these two aspects of the monologue. It may be difficult in some cases to differentiate between the real and the imagined, and you might discuss that aspect of the poem.

Speaking and Listening
4. A Verbal Vision

While Dickey avoids traditional patterns of meter and rhyme, he carefully controls **line length, spacing,** and **rhythm.** Rehearse and perform a reading of "The Lifeguard." Ask your listeners to evaluate your performance. Did you make the chronology clear? Did you successfully convey the speaker's emotional state?

JAMES DICKEY 1157

MAKING MEANINGS

First Thoughts [Respond]

1. Possible responses: Why is the drowned boy smiling? Is the boy who "rises" in the lake the same boy who drowned? Did the people on the shore blame the lifeguard for the boy's death?

Shaping Interpretations [Interpret]

2. The speaker is a lifeguard, presumably at a summer camp, who has failed to save a child from drowning in the lake. While before he was a proud example to the children, he now hides from them in the boathouse as they sleep in their cabins.

3. The lifeguard fantasizes about "the miracle"—by which he might step across the moonlit lake, and raise the boy to the surface alive.

4. He dived repeatedly into the cold water, searching with his eyes and with his fingers in the dark. Unable to find the boy, he swam to the boathouse to avoid the eyes of the people and to be alone with his guilt and anguish.

5. He imagines himself walking across the surface of the water, turned solid by the brightness of the moon, calling to the boy, and bringing him to the surface.

6. Possible response: The lifeguard calls out. The child who answers is *not* the drowned boy ("He is one I do not remember / Having ever seen in his life"). Instead, he might represent some aspect of the speaker himself: his childhood, his innocence, or his sense of self-worth. These are all things which, in this moment of crisis, he may need to "resurrect." This fantasy of saving the boy ultimately allows him to acknowledge the lake as the boy's "grave" and accept his own human weakness and grief.

7. The allusion to walking on water occurs in ll. 5, 9–11, and 53. The allusion to bringing a dead man back to life occurs in ll. 12, 41–43, and 46–50.

CHOICES:
Building Your Portfolio

1–4. Remind students to reread the poem a number of times before starting any of these activities.

Sandra Cisneros

(1954–   )

© Rubén Guzmán.

Sandra Cisneros remembers her Chicago childhood as solitary, even though, she says, her parents would be hard pressed to remember it that way. The nine members of her Mexican American family lived in cramped apartments where the only room with any privacy was the bathroom. But as the only female child in a family of six sons, Cisneros often felt as solitary as an only child.

To Cisneros, solitude proved important. If she had had a sister or a best friend, Cisneros thinks, she would not have buried herself in books. She read voraciously—lives of the saints, Horatio Alger's office-boy-makes-good stories, Doctor Doolittle books, Alice in Wonderland, and fairy tales. (She imagined herself as the lone sister in "Six Swans." Coincidentally, her family name is translated as "keepers of swans.")

Cisneros received a bachelor's degree from Loyola University, in Chicago, and then earned a master's at The Writers' Workshop at the University of Iowa. There she found her subject matter in her own life, and she began writing in earnest. Finding her own voice did not come easily or quickly for Cisneros; she did not realize for a long time that her best writer's voice was the voice of the home she grew up in, a voice that was a combination of her mother's South Side Chicago "tough" street English and her father's gentle, lulling Spanish. The result is a style that suggests a unique synthesis of the disparate languages of her childhood. Cisneros writes in English, but it is an English often heavily informed by Spanish diction and grammatical structure.

Cisneros's first book of poetry is called *Bad Boys* (1980); her first novel, *The House on Mango Street* (1983), won the American Book Award of the Before Columbus Foundation. The title of her second book of poetry, *My Wicked Wicked Ways* (1987), alludes to the title of the autobiography of Errol Flynn, a movie star of the 1930s and 1940s. In 1991, she published another prose collection—*Woman Hollering Creek and Other Stories.* As the following selection tells you, Cisneros has lived in many places. In 1995, she was awarded a prestigious long-term fellowship by the John D. and Catherine T. MacArthur Foundation.

Growing up and attending college in Chicago, Cisneros led a circumscribed life and, like many young people (not just writers), desperately yearned to break away. She took comfort from thinking of Emily Dickinson (page 372), who seldom left her house, let alone her hometown, but still managed to create a magnificent legacy of creative work. Dickinson became Cisneros's source of inspiration, the image to which she hitched her dreams of becoming a professional writer. Only years later did Cisneros, all too aware of the struggles of working-class people (especially women), realize that Dickinson lived a uniquely privileged existence in circumstances any aspiring writer would envy: She had money, a fine education, her own room in her own house, and even household help to take care of time-consuming chores. Cisneros, growing up, had none of these advantages. Yet, like Dickinson, Cisneros has been able to take both the possibilities and the constraints of her unique situation and weave them into art.

 go.hrw.com
LEO 11-21

LA NORTEÑA TORTILLERIA
734-5620
RESTAURANT
Cocktails 768-4153

Before You Read
STRAW INTO GOLD

Summary ■

In this autobiographical essay, Cisneros recalls being asked by some friends to make corn tortillas for a Mexican dinner in the south of France. The friends assume she knows how to make them because she is Mexican, but she has never made a corn tortilla in her life. At this point, she alludes to the fairy tale Rumpelstiltskin, in which a woman is given the impossible task of spinning straw into gold. Like the fairy tale heroine, Cisneros succeeds with her impossible task, and makes the tortillas—and she recalls that she has been able to do many other things that she and others first doubted she could do: becoming a writer, traveling, teaching, and earning university degrees. She describes family experiences and other influences that shaped her as a writer. Her whole life, she suggests, is an illustration of how everyday experiences can be imaginatively transformed into art.

Make the Connection

Transforming the Everyday
One of the oldest bits of advice to an aspiring author is simply to "write about what you know." Taking that advice, just about every good writer discovers that personal experience is what gives vitality and authenticity to literature. Some of the best writers have an uncanny ability to discover the essential that is hidden in the everyday, the universal that is hidden in the local. In the following autobiographical essay, Sandra Cisneros tells us about some of the raw material she has transformed into literature.

Reading Skills and Strategies

Identifying Main Ideas
In this essay, Cisneros voices a recurrent **theme** in American culture and literature: the possibility of transforming something very ordinary—even something considered a failure—into something successful, original, or beautiful. Make a cluster diagram and, as you read, fill in the large circles with Cisneros's main ideas and the small circles with her supporting details. Be sure to look for **key passages** (starting with the title) that point to her general theme.

Elements of Literature

Allusion
An **allusion** is a reference to someone or something that is known from history, literature, religion, politics, sports, science, or some other branch of culture. Cisneros builds an allusion into the title of this essay. To what old folk tale is she referring? What do you think she is suggesting through this allusion?

> **A**n **allusion** is a reference to someone or something from history, literature, the arts, politics, or some other branch of culture.
>
> *For more on Allusion, see the Handbook of Literary Terms.*

FROM THE EDITOR'S DESK
One of the joys of assembling an anthology of contemporary literature is finding the great old stories revisited. Cisneros alludes to "Rumpelstiltskin" here, and many other writers find inspiration in traditional tales. An allusion such as this one shows how the past is alive in the present.

SANDRA CISNEROS 1159

Preteaching Vocabulary

Words to Own
Have students read the Words to Own and their definitions listed at the bottom of the selection pages. Then have students complete each of the following sentences with the correct vocabulary word.

1. Wandering tribes lead a _____ life. [nomadic]
2. Which mushrooms are _____! [edible]
3. Avoid that _____ topic! [taboo]
4. It is a _____ school. [prestigious]
5. They survived for five days, _____ only on nuts and grubs. [subsisting]
6. Do you _____ over details? [obsess]
7. During the _____ craze, everyone went to see old movies. [nostalgia]
8. He solved problems _____. [intuitively]
9. Timidly, the mice _____ out. [ventured]
10. Sculpture _____ during the Renaissance. [flourished]

Straw into Gold:
A The Metamorphosis of the Everyday
Sandra Cisneros

When I was living in an artists' colony in the south of France, some fellow Latin-Americans who taught at the university in Aix-en-Provence invited me to share a home-cooked meal with them. I had been living abroad almost a year then on an NEA[1] grant, <u>subsisting</u> mainly on French bread and lentils so that my money could last longer. So when the invitation to dinner arrived, I accepted without hesitation. Especially since they had promised Mexican food.

B What I didn't realize when they made this invitation was that I was supposed to be involved in preparing the meal. I guess they assumed I knew how to cook Mexican food because I am Mexican. They wanted specifically tortillas, though I'd never made a tortilla in my life.

It's true I had witnessed my mother rolling the little armies of dough into perfect circles, but my mother's family is from Guanajuato; they are **C** *provincianos,* country folk. They only know how to make flour tortillas. My father's family, on the other hand, is *chilango*[2] from Mexico City. We ate corn tortillas but we didn't make them. Someone was sent to the corner tortilleria to buy some. I'd never seen anybody make corn tortillas. Ever.

Somehow my Latino hosts had gotten a hold of a packet of corn flour, and this is what they tossed my way with orders to produce tortillas. *Así como sea.* Any ol' way, they said and went back to their cooking.

1. **NEA:** National Endowment for the Arts, a federal agency that grants money to selected organizations and individuals so they may engage in creative pursuits.
2. *chilango:* variation of "*Shilango,*" name used by people of coastal Veracruz for those who live inland, especially the poor people of Mexico.

WORDS TO OWN
subsisting (səb·sist′iŋ) *v.* used as *adj.:* staying alive.

1160 CONTEMPORARY LITERATURE

Diego Rivera.

Reaching All Students

Woman Making Tortillas (1945) by Diego Rivera. Watercolor (12″ × 15¾″).

Courtesy of Mary-Anne Martin/Fine Art, New York. Reproducción autorizada por el Instituto Nacional de Bellas Artes y Literatura.

The art of **Diego Rivera** (1886–1957) is personal and national, intimate and representative of an entire people. Rivera was a major figure in the Mexican muralist movement, embodying in vast wall paintings not only his socialist ideals but also his pride in his heritage. As a young man he studied in Paris, and when he returned to Mexico in the 1920s, the new socialist government began to commission him (and other artists such as David Alfaro Siqueiros and José Clemente Orozco) to celebrate the Mexican people and culture on the walls of huge public buildings. Rivera combined his knowledge of Italian murals with intense study of Mexican (including Mayan and Aztec) folk art. His style is a combination of realism and cubism, with strong allegorical content. Indeed, Rivera's political commitments ran deep, and controversy accompanied him everywhere. On one occasion, he was prevented from continuing with a mural in Rockefeller Center in New York because he refused to remove a portrait of Lenin; later the mural was destroyed. Rivera's style has had a lasting influence on socially committed art around the world.

Woman Making Tortillas shows how Rivera conveyed cultural pride and achieved monumentality even in an intimate watercolor. Although Rivera made much of his money by painting portraits of rich patrons, here he exalts a different kind of value—the unsentimental dignity of simple, honest labor.

Activity. Ask students to interpret the woman's feelings while she is making the tortillas. [Possible response: She seems calm, with a faint smile, intent on her work with efficiency and skill.] How do students think the colors of the painting affect its mood? [Possible response: The colors are muted and earthy, giving the scene simplicity and warmth.]

Using Students' Strengths

Auditory Learners

Read the fairy tale "Rumpelstiltskin" to the class, or summarize its plot. Explain that a miller's daughter is married off to a prince on the promise that she can spin straw into gold. When she cannot, the elf Rumpelstiltskin helps her, but only after she promises him her first-born child. Afterward, discuss the lesson that the tale teaches. Alert students to look for parallels between the story and Cisneros' essay as they read.

Verbal Learners

Challenge students to read the essay for evidence of the "gold in the straw" that the author describes. For example, ask students if there is anything in Cisneros' description of herself as an eleven-year-old that indicates she would make a good writer. Encourage students to focus on a particular passage about the writer's early life. Have students share their findings.

A Elements of Literature

Allusion

? To which fairy tale does Cisneros refer, and why? [Possible responses: She refers to the tale of "Rumpelstiltskin," because she feels as if she has been given a task as impossible as the heroine's. The allusion helps to describe her feeling of being overwhelmed by expectations.]

B Reading Skills and Strategies

Making Inferences

? Why would Cisneros be glad that her mother was not there to see her first tortillas? [Possible responses: Her mother, unlike her hosts, knows how tortillas are supposed to be made. Her mother would not have been impressed by her daughter's tortillas.]

C Cultural Connections

A Quiet War

Discuss with students the taboo that Cisneros broke, and ask students to think of similar taboos in various cultures. You might also ask students to think of how movements to end discrimination against women have caused changes in various cultures. Encourage students to listen to other viewpoints without rushing to judgment.

D Struggling Readers

Summarizing

? What has the writer inherited from her parents? [Possible responses: from her father, a love of wandering and a "sappy heart"; from her mother, a "tough, streetwise voice."]

E English Language Learners

Idioms

? What does Cisneros mean by the expression "odd woman out"? [Possible responses: On the return of his older brother, Kiki transfers his allegiance from Sandra to his brother. The brothers share boys' experiences, and Sandra is left to herself.] Point out that this expression is a play on words on the traditional idiomatic expression "odd man out."

Why did I feel like the woman in the fairy tale who was locked in a room and ordered to spin straw into gold? I had the same sick feeling when I was required to write my critical essay for the MFA[3] exam—the only piece of noncreative writing necessary in order to get my graduate degree. How was I to start? There were rules involved here, unlike writing a poem or story, which I did intuitively. There was a step by step process needed and I had better know it. I felt as if making tortillas—or writing a critical paper, for that matter—were tasks so impossible I wanted to break down into tears.

Somehow though, I managed to make tortillas—crooked and burnt, but edible nonetheless. My hosts were absolutely ignorant when it came to Mexican food; they thought my tortillas were delicious. (I'm glad my mama wasn't there.) Thinking back and looking at an old photograph documenting the three of us consuming those lopsided circles I am amazed. Just as I am amazed I could finish my MFA exam.

I've managed to do a lot of things in my life I didn't think I was capable of and which many others didn't think I was capable of either. Especially because I am a woman, a Latina, an only daughter in a family of six men. My father would've liked to have seen me married long ago. In our culture men and women don't leave their father's house except by way of marriage. I crossed my father's threshold with nothing carrying me but my own two feet. A woman whom no one came for and no one chased away.

To make matters worse, I left before any of my six brothers had ventured away from home. I broke a terrible taboo. Somehow, looking back at photos of myself as a child, I wonder if I was aware of having begun already my own quiet war.

I like to think that somehow my family, my Mexicanness, my poverty, all had something to do with shaping me into a writer. I like to think my parents were preparing me all along for my life as an artist even though they didn't know it. From my father I inherited a love of wandering. He was born in Mexico City but as a young man he traveled into the U.S. vagabonding. He eventually was drafted and thus became a citizen. Some of the stories he has told about his first months in the U.S. with little or no English surface in my stories in *The House on Mango Street* as well as others I have in mind to write in the future. From him I inherited a sappy heart. (He still cries when he watches Mexican soaps—especially if they deal with children who have forsaken their parents.)

My mother was born like me—in Chicago but of Mexican descent. It would be her tough streetwise voice that would haunt all my stories and poems. An amazing woman who loves to draw and read books and can sing an opera. A smart cookie.

When I was a little girl we traveled to Mexico City so much I thought my grandparents' house on La Fortuna, number 12, was home. It was the only constant in our nomadic ramblings from one Chicago flat to another. The house on Destiny Street, number 12, in the colonia Tepeyac would be perhaps the only home I knew, and that nostalgia for a home would be a theme that would obsess me.

My brothers also figured greatly in my art. Especially the older two; I grew up in their shadows. Henry, the second oldest and my favorite, appears often in poems I have written and in stories which at times only borrow his nickname, Kiki. He played a major role in my childhood. We were bunk-bed mates. We were co-conspirators. We were pals. Until my oldest brother came back from studying in Mexico and left me odd woman out for always.

What would my teachers say if they knew I was a writer now? Who would've guessed it? I wasn't a very bright student. I didn't much like school because we moved so much and I was always new and funny looking. In my fifth-grade report card I have nothing but an avalanche of C's and D's, but I don't remember being that stupid. I was good at art and I read plenty of library books and Kiki laughed at all my jokes. At home I was fine, but at

---

WORDS TO OWN

intuitively (in·tŏŏ′i·tiv·lē) *adv.:* without conscious reasoning.
edible (ed′ə·bəl) *adj.:* capable of being eaten.
ventured (ven′chərd) *v.:* dared or risked going.
taboo (ta·bŏŏ′) *n.:* something that is forbidden.
nomadic (nō·mad′ik) *adj.:* wandering.
nostalgia (näs·tal′jə) *n.:* longing.
obsess (əb·ses′) *v.:* take all of one's attention.

---

3. **MFA:** Master of Fine Arts.

Skill Link

Understanding Sentence Variety

Remind students that good writers use a variety of sentence structures and sentence lengths. They build an essay using simple, compound, complex, and compound-complex sentences, and they can create rhythm and emphasis throughout a piece of writing by blending long and short sentences. In the paragraph beginning "My brothers also figured . . ." Cisneros uses a long, detailed sentence to describe how her brother appears in her writing, and later, three short parallel sentences that describe her relationship to her brother.

Activity

Have students find other examples of varied sentence structure in the essay and then describe the effects of these structures. Students should find examples of variety used

• to create interest or emphasis
• to create rhythm
• to imitate natural speech

La Llorona (*The Crying Woman*) by Carmen Lomas Garza. Gouache (18″ × 26″).

school I never opened my mouth except when the teacher called on me.

When I think of how I see myself it would have to be at age eleven. I know I'm thirty-two on the outside, but inside I'm eleven. I'm the girl in the picture with skinny arms and a crumpled skirt and crooked hair. I didn't like school because all they saw was the outside me. School was lots of rules and sitting with your hands folded and being very afraid all the time. I liked looking out the window and thinking. I liked staring at the girl across the way writing her name over and over again in red ink. I wondered why the boy with the dirty collar in front of me didn't have a mama who took better care of him.

I think my mama and papa did the best they could to keep us warm and clean and never hungry. We had birthday and graduation parties and things like that, but there was another hunger that had to be fed. There was a hunger I didn't even have a name for. Was this when I began writing?

In 1966 we moved into a house, a real one, our first real home. This meant we didn't have to change schools and be the new kids on the block every couple of years. We could make friends and not be afraid we'd have to say goodbye to them and start all over. My brothers and the flock of boys they brought home would become important characters eventually for my stories—Louie and his cousins, Meme Ortiz and his dog with two names, one in English and one in Spanish.

My mother <u>flourished</u> in her own home. She took books out of the library and taught herself to garden—to grow flowers so envied we had to put a lock on the gate to keep out the midnight flower thieves. My mother has never quit gardening.

This was the period in my life, that slippery age when you are both child and woman and neither, I was to record in *The House on Mango Street*. I was still shy. I was a girl who couldn't come out of her shell.

WORDS TO OWN
flourished (flʉr′ishd) *v.:* did well; blossomed.

SANDRA CISNEROS 1163

RESPONDING TO THE ART
Carmen Lomas Garza (1948–   ) is one of the most important Chicana artists working in the United States. She captures scenes from her childhood and Mexican American heritage with a variety of media, including paintings, fine art prints, paper cutouts, and video installations.
Activity. Have students write a brief narrative that explains the family scenario in the painting and its title, using a style similar to Cisneros in this selection.

F Reading Skills and Strategies
Drawing Conclusions
? What can you tell about Cisneros from her description of herself? [Possible response: She feels younger than her years and still sees herself as awkward but full of curiosity and interest in fine details.]

G Reading Skills and Strategies

Identifying Main Ideas
? Writers often use unexpected connections between ideas or situations as metaphors to illustrate their arguments. What unexpected connections does Cisneros discover here? [She connects hunger for food and the act of writing; she has already made a similar connection—between the preparation of food and the writing of her M. F. A. essay.

H Reading Skills and Strategies
Identifying Cause and Effect
? What are the effects Cisneros notes of moving into their "first real home"? [Possible responses: not having to change schools; not having to be the "new kids"; not having to leave their old friends. The narrator's mother takes up gardening.]

Making the Connections

Cultural Connections
Like Cisneros, the Mexican American labor leader César Chávez also attended many schools as a young child. He attended over thirty elementary schools because his father was a migrant farm worker. In 1962, he began to organize the United Farm Workers, or UFW, a union to help protect migrant farm workers. In an attempt to stop the grape growers from using pesticides while the pickers were in the vineyards, Chávez organized a national boycott of table grapes. His efforts led to some important steps toward protecting migrant farm workers. Ask students to research and report on other Mexicans or Mexican Americans who have made significant contributions to social change, the arts, or the sciences, noting obstacles that were overcome in achieving success.

A Reading Skills and Strategies

Identifying Main Ideas

Sometimes writers of biographical and autobiographical works provide straightforward statements of their insights into their own or their subjects' characters. Paraphrase the insight Cisneros describes here. [Possible responses: She discovered a power of personality and character that she never suspected. She discovered that it's a mistake to judge one's future possibilities completely in terms of the past.]

B Critical Thinking

Interpreting

❓ What can you tell about Cisneros from the list of things of which she is proud? [Possible responses: She is proud of her accomplishments as a writer and of all the places she has been; she is an active, energetic person. She speaks about the variety of her experience because she appreciates diversity and adventure.]

C Reading Skills and Strategies

Making Inferences

❓ How has Texas brought Mexico back to her? [Possible responses: Texas was formerly a part of Mexico and is still heavily influenced by Mexican culture. By living in Texas, Cisneros has come back to the ideas that influenced her during the time she spent with her grandmother in Mexico.]

D Elements of Literature

Allusion

❓ Cisneros ties the end of the essay back to its beginning by alluding again to the fairy tale. What tool does she say she used to create the metamorphosis? [imagination] What other tools do you think might also be required? [Possible responses: curiosity, hard work, discipline, good teachers.]

How was I to know I would be recording and documenting the women who sat their sadness on an elbow and stared out a window? It would be the city streets of Chicago I would later record, as seen through a child's eyes.

A I've done all kinds of things I didn't think I could do since then. I've gone to a <u>prestigious</u> university, studied with famous writers, and taken an MFA degree. I've taught poetry in schools in Illinois and Texas. I've gotten an NEA grant and run away with it as far as my courage would take me. I've seen the bleached and bitter mountains of the **B** Peloponnesus.[4] I've lived on an island. I've been to Venice twice. I've lived in Yugoslavia. I've been to the famous Nice[5] flower market behind the opera house. I've lived in a village in the pre-Alps and witnessed the daily parade of promenaders.

I've moved since Europe to the strange and wonderful country of Texas, land of polaroid-blue skies and big bugs. I met a mayor with my last name. I met famous Chicana and Chicano artists and writers and *políticos.*

Texas is another chapter in my life. It brought with it the Dobie-Paisano Fellowship, a six-month **C** residency on a 265-acre ranch. But most important, Texas brought Mexico back to me.

In the days when I would sit at my favorite people-watching spot, the snakey Woolworth's counter across the street from the Alamo (the Woolworth's which has since been torn down to make way for progress), I couldn't think of anything else I'd rather be than a writer. I've traveled and lectured from Cape Cod to San Francisco, to Spain, Yugoslavia, Greece, Mexico, France, Italy, and now today to Texas. Along the way there has been straw for the taking. With a little imagina- **D** tion, it can be spun into gold.

---

4. **Peloponnesus** (pel′ə·pə·nē′səs): large peninsula on the mainland of Greece.
5. **Nice** (nēs): port city in southern France.

WORDS TO OWN

prestigious (pres·tij′əs) *adj.:* impressive; having distinction.

Alan Pogue/University of Texas, Austin.

J. Frank Dobie's Paisano Ranch.

1164 CONTEMPORARY LITERATURE

Making the Connections

Connecting to the Theme: "The Created Self"

Several aspects of self-creation connect this selection to the collection theme:

- Early experiences can have a profound effect on shaping your adult self.
- No self is created in isolation from others.
- Humans have an amazing ability to improvise and recreate themselves.

Have students analyze Cisneros' essay from these perspectives.

Assessing Learning

Check Test: Questions and Answers

1. Cisneros is asked to make _____. [tortillas]
2. Cisneros is the only daughter in a family of _____ men. [six]
3. Cisneros was not a successful student and felt _____ at school. [uncomfortable]
4. As an adult, Cisneros studied with _____. [famous writers]
5. Cisneros is proud of her _____. [achievements]

First Thoughts

1. What do you still want to know about Cisneros after reading this essay?

Shaping Interpretations

2. How would you interpret the essay's subtitle, "The Metamorphosis of the Everyday"?

3. It is characteristic of most American writers that they turn to their childhoods for subject matter. How do you explain Cisneros's interest in her childhood experiences?

4. Describe the **tone** of Cisneros's essay. Do you think it is appropriate for the subject matter?

5. Describe in your own words the kind of writer that Cisneros believes she has become. What qualities as a writer has she developed from the raw material of her personal experience?

6. What do you think Cisneros means when she says she found herself "documenting the women who sat their sadness on an elbow and stared out a window" (page 1164)?

7. Identify some fresh **images** and **figures of speech** in the essay that reveal Cisneros as an accomplished writer. How would you describe her style?

8. The title of the essay includes an **allusion** to the folk tale about Rumpelstiltskin. In the essay itself, how does Cisneros use that magical story as a metaphor for her writing? What do you think of the metaphor?

Reading Check

a. How do the writer's feelings about making the tortillas connect to her feelings about writing the MFA essay?

b. Describe Cisneros's experiences at school.

c. Exactly how did her family help shape Cisneros into a writer?

d. Why does Cisneros think nostalgia for a home is a **theme** that obsesses her?

CHOICES:
Building Your Portfolio

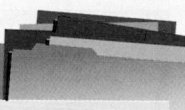

Writer's Notebook

1. Collecting Ideas for an Evaluation

What qualities give life to the story of a life? In other words, what are your criteria for evaluating an autobiographical work? Think of autobiographies you have enjoyed, and make a list of their key characteristics. Among your criteria might be that an autobiography be honest, that it makes times and places come alive, that it reveals the writer's feelings. Save your notes for possible use in the Writer's Workshop on page 1181.

Analyzing Nonfiction

2. To What End?

Cisneros's essay is the revised version of a speech delivered at Texas Lutheran College. In a brief essay, discuss the following questions: What are the **key passages** in her essay? What are her **main ideas**? (Refer to your cluster diagram.) How would you state her general **theme**? If you had been a member of her audience, how would this speech have affected you?

Interpreting Contemporary Culture

3. Multicultural Celebrations

In essays and lectures, Cisneros has told of dual cultural influences on her writing. This mix of cultures is a common feature of the arts in a multicultural society like that of the United States. The writer Bernard Malamud (page 980), for example, often included Yiddish expressions in his English-language texts, thus combining two heritages. In a brief essay, identify and describe two or three specific examples of contemporary arts—writing, dance, music, painting, fashion, or another art form—that fuse elements of two or more cultural heritages. In what ways do such fusions of cultural influences enrich contemporary artistic expressions?

SANDRA CISNEROS 1165

First Thoughts [Respond]

1. Possible response: I want to know more about Cisneros's experiences in high school, and why she felt alienated from her studies.

Shaping Interpretations [Interpret]

2. The subtitle refers to both Cisneros's creative transformation of the everyday experiences of her family and childhood, and her daring, improvisational approach to life in general.

3. Cisneros seems to find in her childhood experiences several keys to her identity as an adult. She is also fascinated by the events that led her to become a writer.

4. Cisneros' tone is heartfelt, sincere, enthusiastic, and full of wonder. It is an appropriate tone for an autobiographical account of unexpected transformations in life and art.

5. Possible responses: Cisneros believes she has become an imaginative, compassionate, and honest writer. She depends on her past experiences for material, but she has also acquired qualities that help her as a writer, such as her strong, personal voice.

6. Possible responses: Cisneros observed the women and wondered about them so much that their worries, dreams, and actions became a source for her writing.

7. Some of Cisneros' figures of speech and images include her description of places she has traveled to ("daily parade of promenaders"), her descriptions of herself as an eleven-year-old schoolgirl ("that slippery age"), and her descriptions of the women "who sat their sadness on an elbow." Her style is direct but graceful and poetic.

8. Possible responses: Cisneros uses the tale in two ways. The task of spinning straw into gold is a metaphor describing Cisneros' feelings when faced with a challenging task. The transformation of the straw into gold is also a metaphor for her belief that all of life's experiences can be raw material for art.

Reading Check

a. Writing the M.F.A. essay is a step-by-step process with rigid rules, just like the procedure for making tortillas. At first, she is overwhelmed by both tasks.

b. Her school experiences were not positive; she moved a lot, and school was geared to seeing a person's outside instead of a person's inside. She obeyed the rules but got average grades, spending much of her time lost in her imagination.

c. From her father, she inherited love for travel, storytelling, and sentimentality. Her mother gave her a streetwise voice.

d. As a child, Cisneros moved around a lot and had a constant home only in her teens.

Judith Ortiz Cofer

(1952–   )

According to Judith Ortiz Cofer, "My family is one of the main topics of my poetry; the ones left behind on the island of Puerto Rico, and the ones who came to the United States. In tracing their lives, I discover more about mine." This impulse toward self-discovery and self-definition emerges in Cofer's stories, essays, and poems. By delving into her past, she clarifies her place in the present; by writing of those who shaped her life, she shapes her own life.

"We lived in Puerto Rico until my brother was born in 1954," Cofer has written. "Soon after, because of economic pressures on our growing family, my father joined the United States Navy. He was assigned to duty on a ship in Brooklyn [Navy] Yard . . . that was to be his home base in the States until his retirement more than twenty years later." Subsequently, Cofer's childhood was divided between a mainland American urban environment and Puerto Rico. She lived mostly in Paterson, New Jersey, but moved temporarily to Puerto Rico with her mother and brother when her father was at sea.

Cofer earned a master's degree in English from Florida Atlantic University in 1977 and then taught at the University of Miami and the University of Georgia, conducting poetry workshops on the side. Her first publication, *Latin Women Pray,* appeared in 1980. Since then she has published several additional volumes of poetry, including *Peregrina* (1986) and *Terms of Survival* (1987). Her semiautobiographical first novel, *The Line of the Sun* (1989), traces a family that moves from Puerto Rico to Paterson and is then caught between two cultural heritages. A reviewer of the novel describes Cofer as "a prose writer of evocatively lyrical authority." She has also published a volume of personal essays called *Silent Dancing: A Partial Remembrance of a Puerto Rican Childhood* (1990); *An Island Like You: Stories from the Barrio* (1995); and *The Year of Our Revolution: Selected and New Stories and Poems* (1998).

Some consider Cofer's *The Latin Deli* (1993), a collection of poetry and prose, her most powerful book. It is a mosaic of responses to cultural differences, an evocation of places past and present, and an engaging blend of poetry and lyrical prose. As Cofer has said, "The place of birth itself becomes a metaphor for the things we all must leave behind; the assimilation of a new culture is the coming into maturity by accepting the terms necessary for survival. My poetry is a study of this process of change, assimilation, and transformation."

Language, of course, plays a major role in such a transformation. In one interview, Cofer summed up what the dynamic force of language has meant to her: "The 'infinite variety' and power of language interest me. I never cease to experiment with it. As a native Puerto Rican, my first language was Spanish. It was a challenge, not only to learn English, but to master it enough to teach it and—the ultimate goal—to write poetry in it."

Arte Público Press/University of Houston.

Before You Read
THE LATIN DELI: AN ARS POETICA

Make the Connection
Native Tongue
Language is our most common tool of self-expression. Hidden in the words we say, beneath the immediate practical meanings, are layers of personal associations, complex social implications, and even cultural histories. This is especially true of immigrants, who try to adjust to a new country but are still drawn to their former homelands. You may know recent immigrants who intermix words of their native language with English.

Quickwrite
On a sheet of paper, write some of the things an immigrant might remember with fondness about his or her native country. Be as precise as possible.

Elements of Literature
Concrete and Abstract Language
In literature, **concrete language** involves the use of well-chosen sensory details to evoke and describe a particular subject. In contrast, **abstract language** deals with a subject in general terms and emphasizes intangible concepts like qualities and values. In abstract language, there are few sensory words, and details do not play a large role. The following poem is a striking example of the effective use of concrete language. (*Ars poetica*, by the way, is Latin for "the art of poetry.")

Summary ■ ■

The poem features metaphor, simile, and powerful concrete imagery to evoke the atmosphere of a small Latino deli: what the deli means to its customers, and what that meaning might suggest about art and poetry in general. The poem evokes the colors, smells, and textures of the items in the store, as well as the sounds of the Spanish language. The owner and her store serve as a touchstone for Puerto Rican, Cuban, and Mexican immigrants who long for the cultures they left behind. The experience of patronizing the store and talking with the woman seems to give the customers much more than familiar foods: the deli provides them with emotional and spiritual comfort, and opens up a figurative "trade" with their hearts, which have become "closed ports." Cofer's subtitle, "An Ars Poetica," suggests that good poetry might function like the deli: offering everyday concrete experiences that nevertheless elicit a strong emotional and philosophical response from readers.

Reaching All Students

Struggling Readers
Have students make a diagram of the details in the poem. Students may use a graphic organizer, such as a cluster diagram. Students may group details with common themes and jot down observations about the details. Encourage students to investigate how the specific details work to support more general or abstract ideas in the poem.

English Language Learners
Have students list the sensory details in the poem according to the senses to which they appeal. Students might also add sensory details of their own, based on their own experience. For additional strategies to supplement instruction for these students, see
• *Lesson Plans Including Strategies for English-Language Learners*

Advanced Learners
Ask students to compile lists of borrowed words—words that English has borrowed from other languages and that have become part of the English vocabulary. Students might also speculate about new words that are currently being borrowed. Encourage students to explore possibilities from several different languages.

The Latin Deli:
An Ars Poetica

Judith Ortiz Cofer

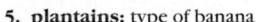

A Presiding over a formica counter,
plastic Mother and Child magnetized
to the top of an ancient register,
the heady mix of smells from the open bins
5 of dried codfish, the green plantains°
hanging in stalks like votive offerings,°
she is the Patroness of Exiles,
a woman of no-age who was never pretty,
B who spends her days selling canned memories
10 while listening to the Puerto Ricans complain
that it would be cheaper to fly to San Juan
than to buy a pound of Bustelo coffee here,
and to Cubans perfecting their speech
C of a "glorious return" to Havana—where no one
15 has been allowed to die and nothing to change until then;
to Mexicans who pass through, talking lyrically
of *dólares* to be made in El Norte—

                all wanting the comfort
of spoken Spanish, to gaze upon the family portrait
20 of her plain wide face, her ample bosom
resting on her plump arms, her look of maternal interest
as they speak to her and each other
of their dreams and their disillusions—
how she smiles understanding,
25 when they walk down the narrow aisles of her store
reading the labels of packages aloud, as if
D they were the names of lost lovers: *Suspiros,*°
Merengues,° the stale candy of everyone's childhood.

                      She spends her days
30 slicing *jamón y queso*° and wrapping it in wax paper
tied with string: plain ham and cheese
that would cost less at the A&P, but it would not satisfy
the hunger of the fragile old man lost in the folds
of his winter coat, who brings her lists of items
E 35 that he reads to her like poetry, or the others,
whose needs she must divine, conjuring up products
from places that now exist only in their hearts—
closed ports she must trade with.

5. plantains: type of banana.
6. votive offerings: sacrifices made to fulfill a vow or offered in
devotion.
27. Suspiros (so͞os·pē′ro͞s): type of small spongecake.
28. Merengues (mā·rān′gās): candy made of meringue (mixture of egg
whites and sugar).
30. jamón y queso (khä·mōn′ ē kä′sō): Spanish for "ham and cheese."

1168 **CONTEMPORARY LITERATURE**

A Elements of Literature
Concrete and Abstract Language
? The poem plunges the reader immediately into the concrete sights, sounds, smells, and textures of the deli. How would you describe the effect of this concrete language? [Possible responses: The concrete language makes it seem as if the reader had just opened the door of the deli and walked right in. The concrete language doesn't *talk* about what the poem will be about; it *shows* what the poem is about.]

B Critical Thinking
Interpreting
? What do you think the "canned memories" consist of? [Possible responses: For the immigrants, just being surrounded by familiar sights and smells brings back preserved or "canned" memories of their homeland. The canned goods recall memories of meals shared in the homeland.]

C Historical Connections
Following Fidel Castro's revolution in 1959, many Cubans left family, homes, and friends to forge a new life in the United States. The speeches of "glorious return" refer to some Cubans' hope for Castro's downfall so that they can return home to a democratic form of government.

D Elements of Literature
Tone
? What tone is produced by the detail that the immigrants read the labels as if "they were the names of lost lovers"? [Possible response: The tone is one of dreamy longing, of being lost in fond memories.]

E Elements of Literature
Concrete and Abstract Language
? The detailed, concrete description of the deli's version of a ham-and-cheese sandwich leads to a more abstract conclusion about the immigrants. What is the conclusion? [Possible response: Far from their homelands and their native tongue, the immigrants are in some sense emotionally shutdown, and the sales at the Latin Deli are first and foremost emotional transactions, giving the customers access to regions of feeling that they have walled off in their new American lives.]

Making the Connections

Cultural Connections
Although Cofer details Latino experience, immigrants from a wide variety of cultures have felt the longings she describes. Ask students to name Asian, African, Caribbean, European, and Latin American countries from which people have emigrated to America. What cultural artifacts or institutions (foods, clothing, ceremonies, traditions, arts and crafts) did these groups bring with them? How did they adapt to life in America?

Connecting to the Theme: "The Created Self"
After students have finished reading the poem, discuss with them the theme of re-creating the self in a new environment. Immigrants are often forced to adapt to new ways of life even while they strive to preserve the best of the old ways. What is notable about the immigrant experience as an act of self-creation?

T1168

First Thoughts

1. What do you think of the woman who runs the deli? What does she do for her customers?

Shaping Interpretations

2. Describe in your own words the feelings of the customers in the deli.

3. Were you surprised that the proprietor of a deli and the things she sells could have so many important associations for the customers? Explain your answer.

4. The poem contains many sensory **images.** Identify at least one image each of sight, hearing, taste, smell, and touch.

5. What **concrete details** help make this poem very specific—and rooted in a particular time and place?

Extending the Text

6. Language is important to the deli's customers. Review your Quickwrite notes, and discuss the various ways immigrants to this country might have a perspective on language and culture that is different from the perspective of Americans who have lived their whole lives here.

Challenging the Text

7. In ancient Rome, the poet Horace (65–8 B.C.) wrote a treatise called *Ars Poetica,* or *The Art of Poetry,* setting forth his own rules for writing poetry. Since Horace's time, many poets have explored ideas about what makes a good poem. Why do you think Cofer subtitles her poem "An Ars Poetica"? In what sense might this poem reflect her ideas about what constitutes good poetry?

CHOICES:
Building Your Portfolio

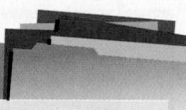

Writer's Notebook

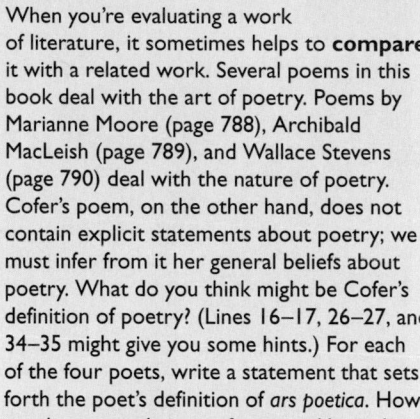

1. Collecting Ideas for an Evaluation

When you're evaluating a work of literature, it sometimes helps to **compare** it with a related work. Several poems in this book deal with the art of poetry. Poems by Marianne Moore (page 788), Archibald MacLeish (page 789), and Wallace Stevens (page 790) deal with the nature of poetry. Cofer's poem, on the other hand, does not contain explicit statements about poetry; we must infer from it her general beliefs about poetry. What do you think might be Cofer's definition of poetry? (Lines 16–17, 26–27, and 34–35 might give you some hints.) For each of the four poets, write a statement that sets forth the poet's definition of *ars poetica.* How are these poets' views of poetry alike and different? Save your notes for possible use in the Writer's Workshop on page 1181.

Analyzing a Poem's Sound/Music

2. The Music of Words

In a brief essay, analyze the musical qualities of Cofer's poem: its **rhythm, assonance, alliteration,** and other sound effects. If this poem were a piece of music, what musical qualities would it have? Describe the kind of music you associate with this poem, and, if possible, accompany your essay with a recording of vocal or instrumental music that "sounds" like the poem.

Art

3. Many Parts to the Whole

Cofer uses many **images** to craft this poem. Transfer her technique to the visual arts by making a collage or painting that unites numerous images in one work. You may want to follow Cofer's lead and use a deli as your subject; you could also assemble images of a restaurant, a ballgame, a city, or another subject.

JUDITH ORTIZ COFER 1169

Grading Timesaver

Rubrics for each Choices assignment appear on p. 233 in the *Portfolio Management System.*

MAKING MEANINGS

First Thoughts [Respond]

1. Possible responses: The woman in the deli is probably an immigrant herself. She provides a kind of spiritual and emotional home for the homesick immigrants.

Shaping Interpretations [Interpret]

2. Possible response: The customers in the deli seem full of longing for the tiny details and the general feelings associated with their homelands.

3. Possible responses: No, I wasn't surprised, because certain sensory experiences can bring back strong memories. Yes, I never really thought of a deli in this way.

4. Possible responses: Sight: "a formica counter, / plastic Mother and Child magnetized"; hearing: "reading the labels of packages aloud . . . Suspiros, / Merengues"; taste: "the stale candy"; smell: "open bins / of dried codfish"; touch: "slicing jamon y queso and wrapping it in wax paper / tied with string."

5. Concrete details that make the setting specific include the description of the woman who runs the deli and names like "A&P."

Extending the Text [Synthesize]

6. Possible responses: An immigrant's experience of language is likely to be more emotional—both positively and negatively—than a native speaker's. Positively, language can provoke a rich store of memories associated with one's native country. Negatively, it can present obstacles to a successful assimilation into the new culture. Native speakers are more likely to take language for granted.

Challenging the Text [Synthesize]

7. Cofer's subtitle suggests that one finds poetry in ordinary, concrete places and images. This concrete language is emotionally charged and rich in figurative meaning that leads the reader to reflection and deep feeling.

Robert Severi/Gamma Liaison.

Rita Dove

(1952–   )

Rita Dove's best-known work, *Thomas and Beulah* (1986), is a sequence of poems (including the following selection) loosely based on the lives of her maternal grandparents. Dove described the poems in an interview:

> I know that when I was writing the poems that went into *Thomas and Beulah* . . . I realized that what I was trying to tell, let's say, was not a narrative as we know narratives but actually the moments that matter most in our lives. I began to think, how do we remember our lives? How do we think of our lives or shape our lives in our own consciousnesses, and I realized that we don't actually think of our lives in very cohesive strands but we remember as beads on a necklace, moments that matter to us, come to us in flashes, and the connections are submerged.

This statement expresses the central concern of much of Dove's poetry: how memory shapes who we are—in other words, how we become ourselves.

In addition to *Thomas and Beulah,* Dove's books of poetry include *The Other Side of the House* (1988), *Grace Notes* (1989), *Selected Poems* (1993), and *Mother Love* (1995), a book largely inspired by the ancient Greek myths of Demeter and Persephone. The esteemed poetry critic Helen Vendler, writing in *The New Yorker,* has praised Dove's "laser glance" and "remarkable objectivity." Dove has also written short stories, a novel, and a verse play, but it is her poetry that has brought her renown. From 1993 to 1995, she served as poet laureate of the United States.

Born and raised in Akron, Ohio, Dove graduated *summa cum laude* from Miami University (in Ohio), studied literature at the University of Tübingen in Germany, and attended the noted Writers' Workshop at the University of Iowa, where she received a master's degree in 1977. After teaching at several universities, Dove became professor of English at the University of Virginia, Charlottesville, in 1989.

The joys and trials of raising a family play as large a part in Dove's life as they do in her writing. Dove says that after her daughter, Aviva, was born, she felt she was living "the story of many women who all have three full-time jobs: You teach, you do parenting, and you try to write, too. I just was tired all the time. I remember days when I came back home and fell asleep over dessert."

Besides writing on personal subjects, Dove interweaves historical themes, including race relations, into her verse. As she told the *Washington Post,* "Obviously, as a black woman, I am concerned with race. But certainly not every poem of mine mentions the fact of being black. They are poems about humanity, and sometimes humanity happens to be black. I cannot run from, I *won't* run from any kind of truth." This honesty, strength, and vision of universality are the very qualities that distinguish Dove's work.

THE SATISFACTION COAL COMPANY

Make the Connection

Moments That Matter

Rita Dove once said, "I think all of us have moments, particularly in our childhood, where we come alive, maybe for the first time. And we go back to those moments and think, 'This is when I became myself.'"

Reading Skills and Strategies

Responding to Aesthetic Elements

Aesthetic simply means "artistic" or "having to do with beauty and art." You can respond aesthetically to many things, including colors, forms, textures, words, and sounds. Before you read this poem, look at the way it is presented. Jot down your initial response to the visuals, including the black background. As you read, note your response to the poem's images and sound.

Background

In Dove's book *Thomas and Beulah,* "The Satisfaction Coal Company" appears as the second-to-last poem in the section on Thomas, a character who represents Rita Dove's maternal grandfather. Thomas found part-time work during the Great Depression of the 1930s as a cleaner at the offices of the Satisfaction Coal Company, in Akron, Ohio. Coal was still widely used to heat homes, which explains the importance of the coal scraps Thomas carries home. The poem that precedes "The Satisfaction Coal Company" in *Thomas and Beulah* tells of the stroke Thomas suffered; the section's next, and final, poem tells of Thomas's death in 1963.

Aaron by Thomas Hart Benton. Oil-tempera on canvas (30¼" × 20¼").

The Pennsylvania Academy of Fine Arts, Philadelphia; Joseph E. Temple Fund. © T.H. Benton and R.P. Benton Testamentary Trusts/Licensed by VAGA, New York, NY.

The Satisfaction Coal Company

Rita Dove

1.

What to do with a day.
Leaf through *Jet.* Watch T.V.
Freezing on the porch
but he goes anyhow, snow too high (A)
5   for a walk, the ice treacherous.
Inside, the gas heater takes care of itself;
he doesn't even notice being warm.

Everyone says he looks great.
Across the street a drunk stands smiling
10   at something carved in a tree.

RITA DOVE   1171

Summary ■ ■

This free verse poem is composed of three sections, which alternate between the present and the Great Depression, circa 1934. Throughout the poem, simile, metaphor, and onomatopoeia evoke the experiences and memories of Thomas, an elderly working man now in retirement. In section 1, Thomas listlessly passes time on a snowy day. Distracted, he watches a drunk across the street and a neighbor getting the mail. Section 2 depicts Thomas's years sweeping up at a coal company during the Depression, watching children and passing trains. In section 3, Thomas thinks back on his poverty and recalls walking home with coal scraps. Now, alone in a comfortable but empty house, he longs to return to work at the coal company, if only to "get warm."

(A) Reading Skills and Strategies

Responding to Aesthetic Elements

? What do the images in the first stanza suggest about Thomas's life and emotional state? [Possible responses: The mundane possibilities of magazines and T.V., which drift through Thomas's mind, along with the harshness of the elements to which he seems oblivious, suggest that he is a tired, lonely man who feels empty, distracted, and numb.]

Reaching All Students

Struggling Readers

Have partners take turns reading the poem aloud. The partners should discuss their interpretations, take notes on their discussions, and review any parts of the poem that confuse them. Ask partners to share the difficulties they had with the poem, the strategies they used to resolve those difficulties, and their final interpretations.

English Language Learners

Note that the narrator describes Thomas's actions and tells what he thinks and feels. For additional strategies to supplement instruction for these students, see

• *Lesson Plans Including Strategies for English-Language Learners*

Advanced Learners

Have students read the rest of *Thomas and Beulah* and then summarize Thomas's character for the class.

A Critical Thinking

Interpreting

? What attitude did Thomas bring to his work? [Possible response: He looked at his work as a reflection of himself and did it with care.]

B Historical Connections

The year 1934 marked the midpoint in the worst economic depression in modern history. The Great Depression started in 1929 as an extended slump in business activity that continued well into the 1930s. Huge numbers of people lost their life savings when the stock market crashed and banks failed. Thousands of Americans lost jobs and homes, and many were forced to live on charity. Unemployment reached epidemic proportions with about thirteen million people in the United States out of work by 1933. During the Great Depression, a job was something highly cherished.

C Reading Skills and Strategies

Responding to Aesthetic Elements

? Onomatopoeia—use of a word whose sound imitates or suggests its meaning—is a reminder that many poems are meant to be read aloud. How would you describe the effect of l. 39? [Possible responses: The sound of the train's engine adds immediacy and power to the experience.]

D Reading Skills and Strategies

Making Inferences

? What can you tell about Thomas from his use of the phrase "I'm listening"? [Possible responses: He doesn't like to have attention drawn to himself, so he avoids voicing his feelings. He enjoys being transported by memories (and perhaps the sounds of memories) and is reluctant to try to articulate them in the present.]

E Critical Thinking

Interpreting

? What do you think is the meaning of "the nights / take care of themselves"? How are they like the gas heater that "takes care of itself"? [Possible response: He experiences both the nights and the heater with a numb, dreamlike passivity—they represent bland, empty experiences that don't require any real work or engagement like the furnace or his night walks did. Consequently, his heater and his nights now drift onward with his days, without meaning or purpose.]

The new neighbor with the floating hips
scoots out to get the mail
and waves once, brightly,
storm door clipping her heel on the way in.

2.

15 Twice a week he had taken the bus down Glendale hill
to the corner of Market. Slipped through
the alley by the canal and let himself in.
Started to sweep
with terrible care, like a woman
20 brushing shine into her hair,
same motion, same lullaby.
No curtains—the cop on the beat
stopped outside once in the hour
to swing his billy club and glare.

25 It was better on Saturdays
when the children came along:
he mopped while they emptied
ashtrays, clang of glass on metal
then a dry scutter. Next they counted
30 nailheads studding the leather cushions.
Thirty-four! they shouted,
that was the year and
they found it mighty amusing.

But during the week he noticed more—
35 lights when they gushed or dimmed
at the Portage Hotel, the 10:32
picking up speed past the B & O switchyard,°
floorboards trembling and the explosive
kachook kachook kachook kachook
40 and the oiled rails ticking underneath.

37. **B & O switchyard:** yard of the Baltimore and Ohio Railroad where train cars are switched from one track to another to make up trains.

3.

They were poor then but everyone had been poor.
He hadn't minded the sweeping,
just the thought of it—like now
when people ask him what he's thinking
45 and he says *I'm listening.*

Those nights walking home alone,
the bucket of coal scraps banging his knee,
he'd hear a roaring furnace
with its dry, familiar heat. Now the nights
50 take care of themselves—as for the days,

Crossing the Curriculum

Social Sciences

Ask students to research one or more personal accounts of life during the Great Depression. Ask students to concentrate on finding out how a specific person survived the era: What strategies did the person use? How did he or she adapt to changes in surroundings? Have volunteers briefly share their findings with the class. Ask students to speculate on how they would have approached the time period.

Art

Ask students to illustrate one or more images from Dove's poem, choosing one that reveals in some way the meaning and feeling of the poem. As an alternative, students might research artworks produced during the Great Depression, especially those commissioned by the New Deal's Works Progress Administration (WPA).

there is the canary's sweet curdled song,
the wino smiling through his dribble.
Past the hill, past the gorge
choked with wild sumac in summer,
55 the corner has been upgraded.
Still, he'd like to go down there someday
to stand for a while, and get warm.

F
G

RITA DOVE 1173

Professional Notes

A Delicate Balance
In an essay on Rita Dove, the eminent literary critic Helen Vendler makes this observation:

Thomas and Beulah represents Dove's rethinking of the lyric poet's relation to the history of blackness. No longer bound to a single lyric moment, she lets the successive raw data of life (perceived over time by a man and by his wife during the same epoch and in the same circumstances) become

pieces for a reader to assemble. The sure hand of structural form supports each life-glimpse: cunningly counter-balancing each other into stability, the tart and touching individual poems add up to a sturdy two-part invention which symbolizes that mysterious third thing, a lifelong marriage—lived, it is true, in blackness but not determined by blackness alone.

Assessing Learning

The following Americans have been awarded the Nobel Prize in Literature:

- 1930 Sinclair Lewis
- 1936 Eugene O'Neill
- 1938 Pearl Buck
- 1948 T. S. Eliot
- 1949 William Faulkner
- 1954 Ernest Hemingway
- 1962 John Steinbeck
- 1976 Saul Bellow
- 1993 Toni Morrison

Nobel laureates in literature who were born in other countries but who made their homes in the United States include Isaac Bashevis Singer (1978) and Joseph Brodsky (1987).

The Pulitzer Prize is awarded for individual works. Many American masterpieces have won the award. Here are some of them:

Fiction
- 1940 *The Grapes of Wrath* by John Steinbeck
- 1953 *The Old Man and the Sea* by Ernest Hemingway
- 1958 *A Death in the Family* by James Agee
- 1961 *To Kill a Mockingbird* by Harper Lee
- 1969 *House Made of Dawn* by N. Scott Momaday

Drama
- 1928 *Strange Interlude* by Eugene O'Neill
- 1938 *Our Town* by Thornton Wilder
- 1948 *A Streetcar Named Desire* by Tennessee Williams
- 1957 *Long Day's Journey into Night* by Eugene O'Neill
- 1976 *A Chorus Line* by Michael Bennet and others

Poetry
- 1924 *New Hampshire* by Robert Frost
- 1947 *Lord Weary's Castle* by Robert Lowell
- 1948 *The Age of Anxiety* by W. H. Auden
- 1950 *Annie Allen* by Gwendolyn Brooks
- 1955 *Collected Poems* by Wallace Stevens
- 1963 *Pictures from Brueghel* by William Carlos Williams
- 1976 *Self-Portrait in a Convex Mirror* by John Ashbery

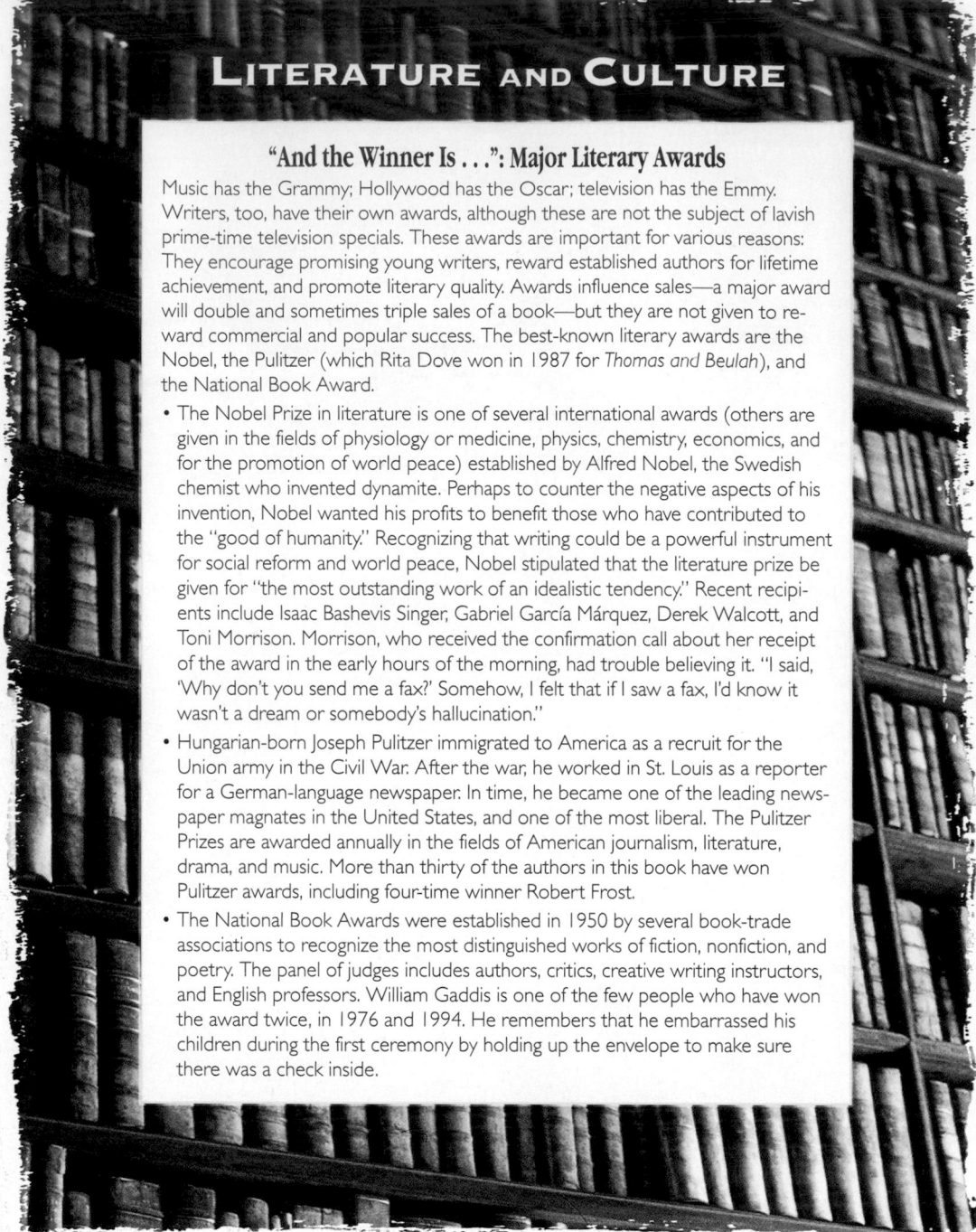

LITERATURE AND CULTURE

"And the Winner Is . . .": Major Literary Awards

Music has the Grammy; Hollywood has the Oscar; television has the Emmy. Writers, too, have their own awards, although these are not the subject of lavish prime-time television specials. These awards are important for various reasons: They encourage promising young writers, reward established authors for lifetime achievement, and promote literary quality. Awards influence sales—a major award will double and sometimes triple sales of a book—but they are not given to reward commercial and popular success. The best-known literary awards are the Nobel, the Pulitzer (which Rita Dove won in 1987 for *Thomas and Beulah*), and the National Book Award.

- The Nobel Prize in literature is one of several international awards (others are given in the fields of physiology or medicine, physics, chemistry, economics, and for the promotion of world peace) established by Alfred Nobel, the Swedish chemist who invented dynamite. Perhaps to counter the negative aspects of his invention, Nobel wanted his profits to benefit those who have contributed to the "good of humanity." Recognizing that writing could be a powerful instrument for social reform and world peace, Nobel stipulated that the literature prize be given for "the most outstanding work of an idealistic tendency." Recent recipients include Isaac Bashevis Singer, Gabriel García Márquez, Derek Walcott, and Toni Morrison. Morrison, who received the confirmation call about her receipt of the award in the early hours of the morning, had trouble believing it. "I said, 'Why don't you send me a fax?' Somehow, I felt that if I saw a fax, I'd know it wasn't a dream or somebody's hallucination."

- Hungarian-born Joseph Pulitzer immigrated to America as a recruit for the Union army in the Civil War. After the war, he worked in St. Louis as a reporter for a German-language newspaper. In time, he became one of the leading newspaper magnates in the United States, and one of the most liberal. The Pulitzer Prizes are awarded annually in the fields of American journalism, literature, drama, and music. More than thirty of the authors in this book have won Pulitzer awards, including four-time winner Robert Frost.

- The National Book Awards were established in 1950 by several book-trade associations to recognize the most distinguished works of fiction, nonfiction, and poetry. The panel of judges includes authors, critics, creative writing instructors, and English professors. William Gaddis is one of the few people who have won the award twice, in 1976 and 1994. He remembers that he embarrassed his children during the first ceremony by holding up the envelope to make sure there was a check inside.

Getting Students Involved

Book Awards
Invite students to nominate books for a class book award. As a class or in small groups, students should propose candidates for the award and present supporting arguments. To vote, students should have read the book. You may want to limit the number of nominees so that interested students have time to read the books.

Research Activity
Award Winners. Ask students to research the most recent recipients of the Nobel Prize in Literature, the Pulitzer Prize in Literature, and the National Book Award. You might want to set aside part of a class period to have students read excerpts from the winners' works.

Student to Student

from An Interview with Rita Dove:
Poet Laureate of the United States (1994)

We stood in a cool, dimly lit room in the Library of Congress with a nervousness to be expected when meeting the poet laureate of the United States. In our minds, we were reviewing possible questions and camera angles and hoping we would not seem immature or unprepared. When Rita Dove appeared, her energy and friendliness—together with her M & M multicolored fingernails—put us in a creative, relaxed frame of mind and led us to a fascinating interview with a remarkable writer.

Heritage: Why do you think it's important for the United States to have a poet laureate?

Rita Dove: Our country thrives on symbolism. Because it's so large and spread out, we get our energy when there are people to focus on. A poet laureate reminds us that the cultural life in this country is necessary. Practically speaking, it gives people someone to write to when they have questions. I can't tell you how many letters I get from people who simply say, "Here I am in Idaho, and I like to write poetry and I don't even know if there's anyone else around me who writes poetry." Then I am able to tell them how they can find someone: where they can go, what community centers there are, and how they can find out about poetry readings.

H: How do you see your appointment as poet laureate in terms of your career?

R. D.: It has given me incredible exposure and publicity that I did not count on at this point in my life. It has changed my life in the sense that I'm not going to have as much private time ever again, probably. But in terms of writing my poems, I'm trying very hard not to let it affect that. When I sit down to write, I don't think, "Well, there are all these people waiting. . . ."

I'm in my room; it's just me and a circle of light and the page. The main difference now is that it is harder to get to the room. Critics and reporters ask, "Won't it just give you pressure to do better on your next work?" I think that's not the point. The point is to write the poem, then let people think of it what they may.

H: Do you feel strongly about writing as an African American woman?

R. D.: It's extremely important for writers to write fully about their own experience and about whatever other experiences strike their fancy. It is important for all the stories to be told. I don't feel a particular obligation to write only about the African American experience or the experience of being a woman. I would not want to limit myself, and I don't think anyone should. But I also feel very, very lucky to be writing in a time when people are beginning to understand, to realize, that the experience of an African American woman could also have relevance to their life.

H: From where do you get your inspiration?

R. D.: I get it from everywhere: from other authors, from just walking down the street. Sometimes I think of myself as a giant sponge; I just keep soaking all this stuff up. I think that anything, *anything* that interests one is worthy of a poem. I don't cut things out by saying, "Well, this is math; there's nothing I can do with poetry and math." You never know.

—Moira Haney and Catherine Nicholas
Heritage, Spring 1994
James Madison High School
Vienna, Virginia

RITA DOVE 1175

Connecting Across Texts

Connecting with "The Satisfaction Coal Company"

Discuss with students whether the interview gives them a different perspective on Rita Dove's "The Satisfaction Coal Company." Ask students if they can find evidence of Dove's methods and ideas in the poem (such as the idea that every subject of interest is worthy of a poem). Encourage students to refer to specific passages for support.

Ask students if other poets they have read would be likely to agree with Dove's answers in this interview. For example, what would Edgar Allan Poe, Walt Whitman, or William Carlos Williams say to the idea that every subject one is interested in is worthy of a poem? Would Ralph Waldo Emerson, Emily Dickinson, or Ezra Pound agree that "our country thrives on symbolism"?

First Thoughts [Respond]

1. Possible responses: I like the presentation, especially the Benton painting, which gives me a way to visualize the character; I dislike all the clutter of notes and pictures; I'd rather just read the poet's words.

Shaping Interpretations [Interpret]

2. Possible responses: "the ice treacherous" (l. 5), "brushing shine" (l. 20), "the canary's sweet curdled song" (l. 51). I was surprised by the unusual phrases, and I think that element of surprise makes the poem worth reading.

3. Possible responses: Line 1: "What to do with a day" suggests the boredom of an aimless season. Line 25: "Saturdays" are a time of pleasure in the active weekly routine. Line 31: *"Thirty-four!"* establishes the year, and highlights the innocence and exuberance of these needy children. Line 36: "the 10:32" emphasizes the long hours and regular rhythms of Thomas's job.

4. Possible responses: Thomas's response seems to be lethargy and numbness, and his reminiscence suggests an urge to escape from daily reality. "What to do with a day" reinforces his aimlessness, as does the ambiguity of his future plans.

5. Possible responses: Dove's theme is that even in difficult circumstances, there is pleasure in active labor and engagement in the intensity and motion of sensory life. The title reinforces the theme by combining "satisfaction" and "coal company," seemingly disparate elements (like happiness and hard times).

Connecting with the Text [Apply]

6. While now free from the burdens of hard work and hunger, Thomas struggles with chains of lethargy, emptiness, and numbness, and strives to recapture the sensory vitality and warmth of his working days.

MAKING MEANINGS

First Thoughts

1. What do you think about the way this poem is presented and illustrated?

Shaping Interpretations

2. One of this poem's strengths is its **diction**—the poet's choice of words. For instance, Dove writes that lights "gushed" rather than "brightened." What other examples of unusual diction can you find in the poem? How did you respond to this poet's use of language?

3. Dove's poem teems with **images** and phrases related to time, like days of the week and seasons of the year. Identify some of these images and explain their significance in the poem.

4. How would you describe Thomas's response to the circumstances of his life? What do his reminiscences tell us about him? Support your interpretation with specific evidence from the poem.

5. State what you think is the central **theme** of Dove's poem. In what ways does part 3 develop this theme? Does the **title** suggest a clue?

Connecting with the Text

6. Dove has said that some individuals in her poems "are struggling to sing in their chains." How do you think this statement applies to Thomas, if at all? How does it describe his response to the circumstances of his life?

1176 CONTEMPORARY LITERATURE

Reading Check

a. In the first and last stanzas of the poem, what seasons of the year are referred to?

b. What actions and events are described in part 2 of the poem? What things does Thomas notice during the week (lines 34–40)?

c. What things do we see other people, aside from Thomas, doing in the poem?

d. In part 3, what are Thomas's feelings about the sweeping? What does he want to do at the end of the poem?

CHOICES:
Building Your Portfolio

Writer's Notebook

1. Collecting Ideas for an Evaluation

One way to make a judgment about a work you're reviewing is by evaluating how it supports—or does not support—a comment made by a critic or by the work's author. Reread the biography of Rita Dove on page 1170, as well as comments Dove made to the student interviewers in Student to Student (page 1175). Using a quotation from Dove as a starting point, make some notes on how well "The Satisfaction Coal Company" reflects or fails to reflect Dove's comments about "moments that matter" and other aspects of poetry. Save your notes for possible use in the Writer's Workshop on page 1181.

Interpreting a Poem

2. Moments of Discovery

One critic has written, "Dove's poems enter the mysterious by opening themselves to the moment of discovery. Usually that discovery is not rational, but emotional or physical." In a brief essay, explain how this statement applies to "The Satisfaction Coal Company."

Research / Speaking and Listening

3. Laurels for a Poet

Rita Dove once commented, "I'm hoping that by the end of my term people will think of a poet laureate as someone who's out there with her sleeves rolled up and working. . . ." With three or four other students, organize a panel discussion on the position of U.S. poet laureate. Panel members should report on (a) how the poet laureate is chosen; (b) the main functions of the post; (c) which poets have held the post in the past and who holds it now; and (d) how it compares with the similarly named post in Great Britain. After the panel discussion, field questions and comments from the class.

Reading Check

a. The first and last stanzas refer to winter. The last stanza also refers to summer.

b. Part 2 describes Thomas's going to work at the coal company building to sweep up. Thomas notices the hotel lights through the window and the sounds of the trains.

c. We see a drunk smiling at a tree; a woman retrieving mail and waving; a cop swinging his billy club and glaring; children cleaning ashtrays and counting nailheads in a leather chair; the drunk smiling through his dribble.

d. He doesn't really mind the sweeping. At the end of the poem, he'd like to stand and listen to the familiar old sounds again and let his memories warm him.

READ ON

Many works of contemporary literature use realistic language and graphic depictions of characters in crises and conflict. Be sure to check with your teacher and parent or guardian before reading any of the following books.

There's Always a Catch

"Orr was crazy and could be grounded. All he had to do was ask; and as soon as he did, he would no longer be crazy." Paradoxical military rules and the madness of war become a metaphor for life's absurdities in Joseph Heller's sharp satire *Catch-22* (Simon and Schuster). *Closing Time* (Simon and Schuster) is Heller's long-awaited sequel.

Yiddish Yarns

If you liked Bernard Malamud's "The Magic Barrel," then you'll probably enjoy Isaac Bashevis Singer's writing, largely rooted in the Polish-Jewish culture of his youth. Singer, whose work is mostly translated from the Yiddish, was awarded the Nobel Prize in literature in 1978 for his novels, memoirs, children's books, and, most notably, his dozens of short stories. *Collected Stories* (Farrar, Straus and Giroux) reveals the range and scope of this master storyteller.

Both Sides of the Story

Another consummate storyteller is Toni Morrison (see page 1146), winner of the 1993 Nobel Prize in literature. Morrison writes of the debilitating effects of oppression against African Americans on victim and perpetrator alike; she also explores the other side of the coin, writing about the richness of African American community and traditions. *Beloved* (Alfred A. Knopf) tells the story of a mother's desperate attempt to save her children from slavery.

Irrational Acts

Into the Wild and *Into Thin Air* (both Villard Books), both by journalist John Krakauer, are examples of nonfiction writing at its best. *Into the Wild* is the tragic story of a young man who, after graduation from college, set off to experience the wilderness, and on his way divested himself of every link to his past life. His adventure ended in an abandoned school bus in Denali National Park in Alaska. *Into Thin Air* is participatory journalism of the highest quality: Krakauer accompanied a guided ascent of Mt. Everest at the request of *Outside* magazine. Krakauer reached the summit but at a terrible cost. As it happened, an IMAX crew was on Everest; their film of the tragedy has been released.

A Nation of Poets

More people are writing poetry than ever before, and, happily, the audience for poetry is also growing—especially for coffeehouse readings. *Contemporary American Poetry,* edited by Donald Hall (Penguin), samples work published through the early 1970s. To explore the more recent work of poets such as Charles Olson, Denise Levertov, and Jimmy Santiago Baca, see *Postmodern American Poetry,* edited by Paul Hoover (Norton).

Background

The word *technology* itself is derived from two Greek roots: *techno-*, meaning "art, craft, or skill" and *-logy,* meaning "science."

B Historical Connections

The growth of railroads meant that people and goods could be carried east and west across the nation at an unprecedented speed. Midwestern cities such as Chicago underwent population booms. Mines and farms in the West became important suppliers of food and of raw materials for factories in the East, and there were expanded markets in the West for manufactured goods.

C Advanced Learners

Have these students research the origins of other technology-related terms that were developed from the names of inventors and innovators: *Geiger counters, diesel engines, shrapnel,* the *Bessemer furnace, pasteurization, Gatling guns, Braille writing,* and the *Ferris wheel.*

D Biographical Connections

In addition to developing the first electric telegraph in the United States and inventing the Morse code, Samuel Morse was a well-known portrait painter. Morse entered work in a competition for four paintings to hang in the rotunda of the Capitol in Washington, D.C. When his entries were not accepted, he started work on the telegraph.

Resources

The American Language

High Tech's Influence

by Gary Q. Arpin

A Before *high tech,* there was just plain *technology.* The nineteenth-century British author Richard Burton used the word *technology* in his book *Travels in Arabia and Africa* (1829) to refer to fairly simple practical arts, such as extracting dye from plants. In 1829, an American, Professor Jacob Bigelow, first used the word in its present meaning of "applied science" when he published *The Elements of Technology* (subtitled *On the Application of the Sciences to the Useful Arts*).

Training for New Vocabulary

B The advanced technology of the early nineteenth century was chiefly steam, and the steam engine entered people's lives in the form of factories, steamboats, and train locomotives. The railroad's impact on American lives was speedy and unprecedented. In 1830, there were just 73 miles of railroad tracks in the United States. By 1850, the number had increased to some 8,900 miles, and by 1860, to about 30,600 miles. "The world has seen nothing like it before," Daniel Webster wrote. "The progress of the age has almost outstripped human belief."

The new application of steam technology required a host of new words. Where did these terms come from? The same processes of word formation applied to railroad terms as had applied to Americanisms in general. Some new words celebrated innovators; for instance, **C** the *Pullman car,* a railroad car with berths for sleeping, was named after George Pullman, who invented it in 1865. Many other terms were formed by combining existing words, such as *redcap* and *whistle-stop.*

A substantial number of railroad terms were borrowed from earlier forms of transportation. Sailing ships and steamboats provided the railroad with terms like *berth, caboose, crew, gondola,* and *all aboard.* The stagecoach provided *car, coach, conductor,* and *station.* This process continues today, as each technology lends its words to its successors.

Most technological terms have a well-defined and specific job to do. Some terms find a broader popularity, usually through metaphor, and enter standard usage. To be *under pressure,* for example, is a phrase borrowed from the steam engine. Most of us use the term only in its metaphoric sense, without thinking about its origin. The train gave people a new way to speak of failure, when a project is *derailed*—and

it also gave rise to a new social designation, *the wrong side of the tracks,* as well as such terms as *right of way* and *sidetrack.*

New Words from *Tele* and *Graph*

About the same time the railroad was crisscrossing the American continent, the telegraph was doing so, too. The word *telegraph* (coined from two Greek terms, *tele,* "afar," and *graphein,* "to write"), had been used in England since the eighteenth century to refer to various forms of semaphores (systems of signaling). However, **D** it became popular only with the invention of the Morse telegraph in the mid–nineteenth century—another example of one technology lending its words to another.

Telegram is a true Americanism, coined in Albany, New York, in 1852. "A friend desires us to give notice," wrote an Albany *Evening Journal* reporter, "that he will ask leave . . . to introduce a new word. It is *telegram,* instead of *telegraphic dispatch.*" The word, so politely brought into the world, encountered some vigorous opposition before being accepted. The reason? It was not a proper combination of Greek words. The proper word, purists argued, would be *telegrapheme.*

Tele and *graph* have been busy root words since the early nineteenth century. *Photograph* appeared in 1839 (*photo* is Greek for "light"). For a number of years, *photographist* fought it out with *photographer* before disappearing. Late in the nineteenth century came the *cinematograph* (*kinema* is Greek for "motion"). It was shortened to *cinema* in England, but changed to *moving picture* in the United States and later shortened to *movie*.

The *telephone* was invented in 1876 and the *phonograph* in 1877 (*phono* is Greek for "sound" or "voice"). The technology for wireless communication led to the *radiotelegraph* in 1903, which was shortened to *radio*.

Television first achieved commercial success in the late 1940s. The British shortened *television* to *telly*, while Americans abbreviated it to *TV*. (As we shall see, initials and acronyms became especially popular during this period in the United States.) **E**

Acronyms: Convenient Abbreviations

One method of forming new words, now so popular that it almost threatens to overwhelm us, is the use of acronyms. The word *acronym* is probably an Americanism, although the practice is ancient. The term comes from the Greek words for "top" and "name," and refers to a word formed from the combina-

tion of the first letters of the words in a phrase. *Radar* was a technological acronym (from "*ra*dio *d*etecting *a*nd *r*anging"), and it quickly knocked out the British candidate, *radiolocator*. *Sonar* ("*so*und *na*vigation and *r*anging") followed, as did *laser* ("*l*ight *a*mplification by *s*timulated *e*mission of *r*adiation").

The acronym device was not the sole property of scientists and technologists. In the twentieth century, the military and other bureaucracies have bred many acronyms, from AWOL ("*a*bsent *w*ithout *leave*"), coined in World War I, to NATO (*N*orth *A*tlantic *T*reaty *O*rganization) to *snafu* (*s*ituation *n*ormal, *a*ll *f*ouled *u*p). World War II saw the development of a great many acronyms, such as WAVES and WAC ("*W*omen *A*ppointed for *V*oluntary *E*mergency *S*ervice" and "*W*omen's *A*rmy *C*orps"), the women's branches of the U.S. Navy and Army.

Airplane Argot

The airplane had an effect on American culture in the twentieth century similar to the effect of the railroad in the nineteenth. When the Wright brothers patented their flying machine in 1906, the word *airplane* was already there, waiting for them. The new technology of *aeronautics* borrowed part of its name from sailing technology (*nautes* is Greek for "sailor"), and it borrowed a number of technical

> One method of forming new words, now so popular that it almost threatens to overwhelm us, is the use of acronyms.

terms from sailing as well. *Cockpit, cabin, steward, rudder,* and many other terms were adapted from the ocean liners that the airplane would eventually make almost obsolete. New words and combinations, like *barnstorm, tailspin,* and *Mayday* (from the French *m'aidez,* "help me"), came into common usage as a result of the airplane.

Nautes, by the way, connects the ancient and the modern worlds in a strikingly direct way. In Greek mythology, the *Argonauts* sailed with Jason in a ship called the *Argo* in search of the Golden Fleece. The U.S. *astronauts* ("star sailors") sail to outer space in the twentieth century, as do the Russian *cosmonauts* ("universe sailors").

Terms like *countdown, blastoff, malfunction,* and *put on hold* are the legacy of jargon, or argot, from the space program. Airplane flyers had long had a number of colorful terms for unexplained malfunctions. The word *gremlin* was commonly used by pilots during World War II, but was later replaced by *bug,* which is still in use. The word today's astronauts probably use most often, though, is *glitch,* a term taken over by computer experts. **F**

Computerspeak

Much of the language associated with computers is highly specific and may never be extended to a noncomputer field. Such computer terms include *RAM, ROM,* and *WYSIWYG,* acronyms for "*r*andom *a*ccess *memory,*" "*r*ead *o*nly *memory,*" and "*w*hat you *s*ee *i*s *w*hat you *g*et." People in

THE AMERICAN LANGUAGE 1179

E Cultural Connections

Television (from *tele,* "afar" and *videre,* "to see") did not become popular in the United States until after World War II. Between 1945 and 1960, the number of television sets in the United States skyrocketed from a few thousand to nearly sixty million. In the second half of the twentieth century, television clearly established itself as a powerful and pervasive force. The year 1960 marked the first televised presidential campaign debates, between Richard Nixon and John F. Kennedy, a significant event that may have given the photogenic J. F. K. his slim victory over Nixon.

F Background

Jargon is any specialized language used by a specific social group. Doctors, sportscasters, sailors, educators, and countless other groups use jargon when communicating with colleagues and other specialists.

Using Students' Strengths

Visual Learners
To help students form a picture of how words with common roots and affixes are related, have students make drawings that show the relationships among words with common elements. Words with a common root such as —*graph* (*telegraph, autograph, biography*) or —*scope* (*telescope, microscope, stethoscope*) can be shown in a graphic organizer as branches on a tree labeled with the root.

Interpersonal Learners
Assign students to small groups, and ask each group to compose a list of jargon with which its members are familiar. Direct members to begin by thinking of their common interests and activities. Encourage the groups to compete with each other to compose the longest list. Each term on the list should be accompanied by its loose definition and area of special interest.

A Reading Skills and Strategies

Connecting with the Text

Students may be more familiar with whimsical computer language associated with e-mail. Have them discuss terms such as *spamming* (inundating someone with "junk" e-mail) and *flaming* (a wave of critical responses from members of a list-serve group addressed to a fellow member with whom they disagree).

Try It Out
Possible Answers

1. **sidetrack** railroad—to divert
   stopover stagecoach—an interruption in the course of a journey
   tune-up automobile—an adjusting, as of an engine, to proper condition.
   tank town railroad—small town
   tailspin aircraft—loss of control
   nose dive aircraft—any sudden, swift downward plunge
2. CAT scan (computerized axial tomography); COBOL (common business oriented language); CAD/CAM (Computer-Aided Design/Computer-Aided Manufacturing); NASA (National Aeronautics and Space Administration); and SCUBA (self-contained underwater breathing apparatus).
3. Glossaries will vary widely. Encourage students to provide the part of speech and possible conjugations for each word.

---

face • mail (fās′māl) Technologically backward means of communication, clearly inferior to voice mail or E-mail. Involves actually walking to someone's office and speaking to him or her face to face. Considered highly inefficient and déclassé.

Definition from *The Microsoft Lexicon.*

the computer industry have adapted many standard English words to technical uses, though, and a number of these terms are edging back into the noncomputer world with slightly different meanings. The most notable are nouns that have been changed to verbs. *Access, format, interface,* and *program* are being used as verbs with some frequency today. *Program* has already produced an offspring, *deprogram,* referring to "reverse brainwashing."

A   Computer language is often lively and whimsical. If a programmer interferes with someone else's program, for example, he or she is said to *bomb the program* (not a nice thing to do). Programs that stop working unexpectedly *hang* or *crash,* sometimes as the result of a *spike,* or a surge in electricity. When we start a computer, we *boot* it. *Boot* is a shortening of *bootstrap,* which comes from the familiar expression "to pull yourself up by your bootstraps," meaning "to succeed on your own without the help of others," or, in computer jargon, "to be self-initiating."

Try It Out

1. **Researching technical terms.** The following terms, once associated only with trains, automobiles, or airplanes, have entered general usage. For each term, (1) identify the technology with which it was originally associated, and (2) give its meaning in general usage. You might want to refer to a dictionary.

   sidetrack
   stopover
   tune-up
   tank town
   tailspin
   nose dive

2. **Identifying acronyms.** Look at some newspapers or newsmagazines to find five acronyms related to technology that are in current usage. Remember that an acronym is an abbreviation that is pronounced like a word, not as separate letters.

3. **Computerspeak: Compiling a glossary.** Prepare a glossary of computer terms that includes definitions and origins of terms. Include pronunciations and illustrations, when visuals will help. You can be humorous. (The definition at the left of *face-mail* is from a lexicon of computer language used by Microsoft.)

"You've learned to respond to verbal commands. Now let's test your computer literacy."

Rothco Cartoons.

Assessing Learning

Check Test: Questions and Answers

1. What is the present meaning of technology? [applied science]
2. What is an acronym? Give an example. [a word formed by the first letters of words in a phrase; Possible example: AWOL (Absent Without Leave)]
3. What does Jason of ancient Greek mythology share with NASA's space exploration program? [Jason and the Argonauts sailed the ship *Argo* in quest of the Golden Fleece; NASA astronauts "sail" through space in quest of knowledge; the root *nautes* means "sailor."]
4. What are two ways words come into existence? [Any two of the following : A word can celebrate an innovator (*Pullman* cars), combine existing words (*whistle-stop*), borrow from related fields (*caboose*), be used metaphorically (*under pressure*), shorten a longer word (*television* to *TV*), be an acronym (*NASA*), or be created as jargon (*computer interface*).]

PERSUASIVE WRITING

EVALUATION

When you evaluate something, you present a well-considered judgment about its worth, offering reasons that support your stance and evidence that those reasons are valid. In English classes, you are often asked to evaluate works of literature; in life, you may need to evaluate anything from the color scheme of a room to a politician's voting record to your own job performance.

Prewriting

1. **Choose a literary work.** Of the stories and poems you have read in the Contemporary Literature collections, which moved you most strongly, either to delight or to distaste? Which seemed to be the most flawless—or most flawed—examples of their art forms? Which stayed in your mind the longest? Quickwrite a list of outstanding works from the Contemporary Literature collections. The ones that first spring to mind may be the ones that left the strongest impression; however, take a few moments to allow less obvious choices to emerge from the back of your mind. Circle two or three titles that seem promising. Then, skim over the circled works, and decide which to write about. If you completed and kept any of the Writer's Notebook activities from these collections, you may already have a head start on a topic for evaluation. Of course, you can always choose to evaluate a literary work you've encountered on your own, outside this textbook.

WORK IN PROGRESS

2. **Reacquaint yourself with the work.** Reread the work, the prereading and postreading materials, and your notes, immersing yourself in the work's content and your own response to it. Take new notes as you go along. You'll continue consulting the work as you move through the writing process.

3. **Explore the work in writing.** Put your thoughts and feelings about the work on paper in a quick paragraph or two. State your opinion of the work, and mention as many specific reasons for your stance as you can. Note passages, scenes, characters, or other literary elements that make strong impressions on you. Include both positive and negative responses to the work.

4. **Decide on your criteria.** To evaluate something, you must apply standards to it. These standards, or **criteria,** are objective rather than personal. Criteria are used to assess whether

Technology HELP

See Writer's Workshop 2 CD-ROM. *Assignment: Evaluation.*

ASSIGNMENT
> Write an essay evaluating a short story, essay, or poem.

AIM
> To inform; to explain; to persuade.

AUDIENCE
> Your classmates and teacher or a specialized audience interested in the subject of your evaluation.

Try It Out

In a small group, come up with as many valid criteria as you can for evaluating any of the following:

1. What are the qualities of a good elective course?
2. What makes a first-rate film?
3. What are the qualities of good conversation?
4. What qualities do you look for in a good teacher?
5. What are the qualities of an excellent radio station?

WRITER'S WORKSHOP 1181

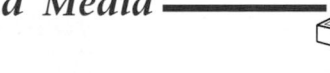
Resources: Print and Media

Have students work in pairs or small groups to identify a favorite movie or album and some reasons why they like it. Ask for reasons beyond the "I just love her voice" category. Have the pairs or groups present their most persuasive reasons to the rest of the class. Ask other students to identify well-supported arguments. Explain that we use this process of choosing and supporting criteria when evaluating a literary work.

Teaching the Workshop

Prewriting

- Note that evaluations can reveal why one didn't like a work as well as why one did; the important point is that writers choose a work to which they have a strong reaction.
- Students who have difficulty choosing a work to write about can review the table of contents of this book and rate each work they have read. Have them choose either their highest rated or lowest rated work.
- Point out that students are not limited to the literary elements used in the model chart on this page. Suggest setting, symbolism, point of view, or other elements listed in the Handbook of Literary Terms at the back of this text.

something is an excellent example of its type or kind. For example, if a car is what you wish to evaluate, you might use criteria like cost, gas mileage, repair record, and structural integrity. Similarly, the criteria you would apply to a literary work should agree, on the whole, with accepted critical standards of what makes a literary work successful or unsuccessful. It's important, of course, to develop criteria that are relevant to the unique characteristics of the subject you are evaluating. You might give a thumbs up to a popular science fiction novel because it is fast-paced, contains innovative ideas, and has interesting, larger-than-life characters. But the criteria you'd use to judge a more reflective, overtly "literary" novel would be quite different.

5. **Make a criterion-assessment-evidence chart.** Make a list of several criteria you think are important in the genre of literature you've chosen to evaluate. Then, make a three-column criteria-evaluation chart. In the left column, list your criteria. In the middle column, assess how you think the work either meets or does not meet each criterion, giving a brief reason for your judgment. In the right column, give text evidence for each assessment. To generate evidence for your chart, you might

- compare and/or contrast two works
- relate the work to your own experience
- cite the evaluations and judgments of experts

Model

	"Rules of the Game"	
Criterion	Assessment	Evidence
language fresh, vivid	very readable; suggests believable narrator's voice	many short, simple sentences; colloquial language; humor (second paragraph, p. 1111)
original treatment of theme	timeless: conflict between generations & cultures	Waverly & her mother have unpredictable responses to her chess victories
believable characterization	individuality of mother & daughter overcomes possible stereotypes	the mother's speeches in dialect are sometimes wise, sometimes not—she's complex (pp. 1113, 1117)
imaginative plot	a success story with a twist	the story is open-ended; ends with a question

Shoe by Jeff MacNelly, reprinted by permission: Tribune Media Services.

Reaching All Students

Struggling Writers

As students review a literary work, allow them to use adhesive notes to mark points in the work that interest, confuse, or even bore them. These passages may provide support for their evaluations. You or another student might help them identify the criterion to which each marked passage relates. Students can then review their adhesive notes and record the location of important passages in one column of a two-column chart. In the other column, students should note how the marked material would support their argument.

6. Choose your final criteria. You may not want to discuss every single one of your criteria when you draft your essay, and within a criterion you may not need to cite every aspect you evaluated or every piece of evidence. Mark or highlight the entries on your chart that seem strongest. Add new elements to your chart as you think of them.

Drafting

1. Present your subject and judgment. Think about how you can capture your reader's attention at the start of your essay—perhaps by opening with an anecdote, a description, a personal observation, or simply an arresting statement of your evaluation. Identify the work of literature you're evaluating, and express your basic judgment of it, if you haven't done so in your opening sentence. Your readers want to know from the start what you're discussing and what your thumbs-up or thumbs-down verdict is.

Make your evaluation statement—your claim—specific and fresh. "'Rules of the Game' is one of the best stories I've ever read" does not give the reader any concrete idea of why you think Amy Tan's story is a good one. Indicate what you see in the literary work and why: "'Rules of the Game' is about a Chinese American girl who becomes a chess champion, but anyone who has ever been a teenager in conflict with a parent can identify with it."

2. Clarify your criteria. Your criteria should become apparent to the reader as you explore the reasons for your judgment. If your reasons for liking a story include its plot, characterization, and theme, for instance, readers who are familiar with literature will recognize those criteria. You might need to state your criteria explicitly, however, if you have omitted some that readers might have expected, if you have included unusual criteria, or if you give a different weight to certain criteria than your readers might.

3. Develop your reasons coherently. Most of your essay will be devoted to your reasons for your overall judgment of the literary work. Evidence to support your reasoning usually comes immediately after, or immediately before, each reason. Use your prewriting chart as a guide, and add details that a chart can't contain. Using transitional words and phrases (*in addition, moreover, likewise*) is one way to create a coherent flow from point to point. Even more important is the placement of your points. For instance, if you discuss plot first, then characterization, then theme, the reader should sense that you ordered those elements thoughtfully rather than just tossing them in the air and seeing which fell first. Their placement should reflect your understanding of the literary work. In evaluating Amy Tan's story, for example, you might show how characterization grows out of plot and how both elements lead to thematic insight.

Strategies for Elaboration

Use these strategies to find evidence from the text to support your literary evaluation:

- Keep rereading the work, and give yourself time to ponder what you've read.
- Go from a general question or issue to specific evidence. You may ask yourself, "Where can I find evidence for the characterization of Mrs. Jong?" and then search the story for any passages that contain her thoughts, spoken words, or vivid actions.
- Move from a specific point or question to an assessment or conclusion. You may wonder, "What does the last paragraph mean?" and then draw a conclusion about Waverly's possible future and her changing attitudes toward her mother and herself.
- Remember that in a strong work of literature, every word and action serves a purpose. Focus not only on the things you understand in the story or poem but also on the things you don't. Ask yourself, "Why did the author put that there?" When you find the answer, you'll have both a reason and the evidence for it.

Language Handbook HELP

See Ways to Achieve Clarity, pages 1235–1236.

Drafting

- Have students begin drafts in class so you can check their evaluation statements and offer advice for improving specificity and clarity.
- Emphasize the need for elaborating on reasons using supporting evidence. Have students review the model on p. 1182 for examples of the kinds of support they might provide.
- Remind students to use only every other line when they write their drafts. They should also leave extra space in the right margin. These blank spaces will be used for comments and editing marks.

Using Students' Strengths

Spatial Learners
Students may use a pyramid-shaped graphic organizer to list ideas for evaluation. Students can place their judgment at the top of the pyramid, their reasons based on evaluation criteria in the middle, and support for those reasons at the bottom of the pyramid. Note that the wide base of the pyramid is where students will list elaborations.

Interpersonal Learners
In small groups, students can discuss their criterion-assessment-evidence charts to determine what makes a good literary work. Each student should offer three ideas and list at least three insights from others that they find useful.

Evaluating and Revising

Have students use the Evaluation Criteria provided here to review their drafts and determine needed revisions. Students should read their papers at least once while pretending they have never seen the essays before. This "cold read" may help them identify places where their arguments are unclear or lack sufficient support.

Proofreading

Have students proofread their own papers first and then exchange them with other students. For this assignment, remind students to be particularly careful of lapses in tone. The tone should be both appropriate and consistent.

If time permits, the final copy should be put aside for at least a day before it is proofread for the final time. Have each author do a final check to be sure that quotations have been handled properly.

Publishing

Final essays might be collected in a single volume for in-class reference. Students could use this collection to deepen their understanding of a particular work. Other publishing options include school or professional literary magazines or Internet options such as literary bulletin boards and homepages concerning the author or the work a student evaluated.

Reflecting

Finally, students should date their essays and reflect on them, using the following statements.

1. As I evaluated this work, I discovered that _____.
2. A writer can make a literary evaluation enjoyable to read by _____.
3. Writing this evaluation will help me to evaluate other things, from extracurricular activities to new restaurants, because _____.

Communications Handbook HELP

See Taking Notes and Documenting Sources; Recognizing Logical Fallacies; Proofreading.

Revision STRATEGIES

When you find a general statement in your evaluation, such as "This is a fine story" or "This is a great poem," be suspicious. Cross out this generalization, and say something specific about a particular aspect of the work.

■ **Evaluation Criteria**

A good evaluative essay
1. identifies the subject of your evaluation
2. presents your criteria explicitly
3. provides factual evidence to support your views
4. makes its points in a coherent order
5. avoids logical fallacies
6. concludes effectively
7. has an authoritative, confident tone

Incorporating Supporting Evidence

In a literary evaluation, your main supporting evidence will be in the form of direct quotations and paraphrases from the work you're evaluating. Here are ways to smoothly incorporate supporting evidence into your evaluation:

1. If you're using a direct quotation, make it a seamless part of your sentence structure. A passage you're quoting directly should match the subject and tense of the sentence it's being woven into. Although you should try to avoid it, you may need to use brackets to indicate slight alterations you've made in the quotation to make it fit smoothly with the rest of your sentence.
2. Enclose a direct quotation in double quotation marks. If part of your quotation includes a character's dialogue, place that in single quotation marks. Be sure that you've copied the quote word-for-word as it appears in the work.
3. Use ellipsis points (. . .) to indicate the omission of any part of the quotation.
4. For both direct quotations and paraphrases, cite the page number from which the quotation is taken. For poetry, cite line numbers.

   EXAMPLE   Waverly, the story's narrator, "learn[s] why it is essential in the endgame to have foresight, a mathematical understanding of all possible moves, and patience . . ." (page 1113).

5. When you're quoting poetry, use a slash (/) with a space before and after it to indicate the end of a line.

---

4. **Avoid logical fallacies.**   To lend credibility to your essay, avoid:
   * *hasty generalizations* (praising or condemning a work without weighing sufficient evidence)
   * *overstatement* (giving the work an artificially high or low rating in order to make your evaluation seem dramatic)
   * *either/or fallacy* (purporting that the work is all good or all bad)
   * *straw-man arguments* (stacking the deck in favor of or against a work by comparing it to something that is clearly inferior or superior to it. A "straw man" is something that can be easily knocked down.)

5. **End decisively.**   You can conclude your essay by restating your judgment, summarizing your reasons, or doing both. Your conclusion should bring the essay to a definite close.

Evaluating and Revising

1. **Peer review.**   Exchange papers with one or more classmates. Address questions such as the following:
   * What are the writer's criteria? Do they seem valid and well chosen?
   * Are the reasons for the evaluation adequate and convincing?
   * Are the reasons backed up by detailed, specific evidence?
   * Does the essay help you understand the literary work better?

2. **Self-evaluation.**   Consider your peers' comments carefully. Act on those you agree with. Try reading the literary work one more time to see what new insights emerge. You'll be revising both for content (to strengthen your reasons and evidence) and for style (to make your essay more readable).

Resources

Peer Editing Forms and Rubrics
* *Portfolio Management System,* p. 236

Revision Transparencies
* *Workshop Resources,* p. 41

Grading Timesaver

Rubrics for this Writer's Workshop assignment appear on p. 237 of the *Portfolio Management System.*

Language Workshop

Language Handbook HELP

See Glossary of Usage, pages 1252-1257.

The history
of the written
word is rich and
Page 1

WORDS TO THE WISE: USING EFFECTIVE DICTION

Consider the difference between these two sentences:

He is almost sixteen, and though he doesn't have a beard yet, he has a man's mind in a boy's body.

He is almost sixteen, **though beardless still,** a man's mind **indignantly captive** in **the frame of a child.**

In the second sentence (from John Updike's story "Son"), the boldface phrases are more imaginative, more rhythmical, and more precise than the phrases in the first sentence. The difference is in **diction,** or word choice. Diction may be plain or ornate, formal or informal, and so on. In this example, from Julia Alvarez's "Daughter of Invention," the informal, colloquial phrases are in boldface:

She was **just fussing** with **little house things, don't mind her.**

To use effective diction in your writing, pay attention to the following:

1. Choose words that are appropriate to your subject. You would use technical words in a science report but informal, colloquial language in a personal essay.

2. Choose words that are appropriate to your audience. Your word choice when addressing third-grade students would differ from diction you would use with a group of high school students.

3. Choose words that are appropriate to your purpose. If you were writing a speech for your high school graduation, you would choose words that are different from those you'd use in writing a humorous letter to a friend.

4. Use precise, vivid words instead of vague ones. (Don't say "The weather was unfavorable." Say "For a week, the sun was hidden by fog.")

5. Use figures of speech when they are fresh and meaningful, but avoid **clichés.**

6. When choosing among synonyms, consider their different connotations.

Writer's Workshop Follow-Up: Revising

Reread the evaluation you wrote for the Writer's Workshop (page 1181). Examine it carefully for vague words and for phrases that don't quite say what you intended. Work to improve your diction, using a dictionary and a thesaurus to help you choose the most precise words.

Try It Out

For each sentence below, write a word or phrase describing the diction. Then state which words or phrases in the sentence led you to that conclusion.

1. For a small town, it was a pretty good show.
   —Tim O'Brien, *from* "Speaking of Courage"

2. It was in this tenement that the personality of my father first came fully into the orbit of my concern.
   —Richard Wright, *from Black Boy*

Resources

Workshop Resources
• Worksheet, p. 63

Try It Out
Possible Answers
1. casual or informal— "pretty good show"
2. formal or poetic—"first came fully," "orbit of my concern"

Assessing Learning

Quick Check:
Common Usage Problems
State a word or phrase that describes the diction of each of the following expressions. Possible answers are set in brackets.
1. her cool car [informal; colloquial]
2. your considerable fortitude in the face of near disaster [formal; ornate]

3. The computer printer spat out my essay. [using a figure of speech—colorful or poetic; informal]
4. What did you say? [informal]
5. I beg your pardon; kindly repeat your statement [formal]

Teaching the Lesson

Have students share any experiences they have had with memoranda. Guide them to consider what purposes memos serve in the workplace, why it is important for a memo to be clear, and what makes a memo easy to understand.

Using the Strategies
Possible Answers

1. *NIC* stands for Network Interface Cards; *specs* is short for specifications.
2. *Server computers* control the computer network, *client computers* are individual stations within the network, and *throughput* is a measure of how much data the interface can transmit between computers.
3. *LAN,* or local area network, is a network confined to one small area, such as an office or building. *CPU,* which stands for central processing unit, is the "brain" of an individual computer. *Bits* (binary digits) are the smallest units of data a computer uses.
4. TO: Dave Davison
   FROM: Jane Employee
   RE: NIC Evaluation
   DATE: June 23, 2000
   CC: Edgar Smith,
          Director of Accounting

The phrase "copy Ed Smith" indicates that a copy of the memo is being sent to Edgar Smith.

Situation

You are a part-time employee at First XYZ Bank, working in its MIS (Management Information Systems) department. This department handles the bank's internal flow of information, which is vital to executives as they make decisions affecting the success of the bank. You receive a memorandum from the director of MIS discussing a purchase. The memo contains technical terms and abbreviations, some new to you. How do you comprehend a difficult memo?

Strategies

Isolate the memo's key information.

- First, read the heading of the memo carefully. You'll see at a glance who sent the memo and when, who is receiving it, and its subject.
- Next, skim over the memo to determine its purpose. Is it intended only to give you information? Does it ask for a reply? If so, determine the deadline for the reply.

Find supporting details.

- Third, read the memo closely. Highlight words or concepts that are unclear to you. Mark important passages. Write marginal notes.
- For anything unclear, first use context clues to determine meaning. If you remain uncertain, consult a colleague or a reference work.

Decide the appropriate response to the memo.

- Once you fully understand the memo, take appropriate action, if any is called for.

Using the Strategies

Read the sample memo on this page very closely.

1. Using context clues, determine what the abbreviations *NIC* and *specs* stand for.
2. Again using context clues, tell what the terms *server computers, client computers,* and *throughput* mean.
3. Explain the abbreviations *LAN* and *CPU* and the term *bits.* (If necessary, consult a person who knows computers or look up the abbreviations in a dictionary.)
4. Write the headings for a memo that replies to this memo. (What action does the phrase "copy Ed Smith" call for?)

Extending the Strategies

Write a short memo containing technical terms concerning computers, automobiles, filmmaking, or another field. The memo should be from a supervisor to an employee in a work situation. Context clues should explain some but not all of the technical terms.

Exchange memos with a classmate. After a half-hour or so, see whether each of you has understood the other's memo. If not, each might suggest ways (1) to write a clearer memo and (2) to get help when it is difficult to understand technical writing.

FIR☆T XYZ Bank

TO: All Staff in MIS Department
FROM: Dave Davison, Director of MIS
RE: Evaluating Network Interface Cards
DATE: June 19, 2000
CC: Edgar Smith, Director of Accounting

In order to improve the Bank's LAN, we are evaluating new NICs manufactured by several vendors. Specs are attached. The NIC we use plays a vital role in transmitting bits of data to and from our server computers and client computers. Please evaluate the NICs in terms of their throughput, CPU utilization, and cost. Please reply to me by 3 p.m. Friday (copy Ed Smith).

Attachments.

1186 CONTEMPORARY LITERATURE

Reaching All Students

Struggling Readers

The memo format, technical terms, and abbreviations may cause difficulty. Let students map out the memo with a partner, first taking apart the format, then substituting definitions for unfamiliar terms. Finally, have them explain the contents in their own words to confirm understanding.

English Language Learners

These students may need several terms defined and the format of the memo explained (*RE:, CC:*) in order to complete this assignment. Keep in mind you may want to modify this activity to first address a more familiar workplace setting, such as a shop or restaurant.

Learning for Life

State of the Arts: Celebrating Cultural Diversity

OBJECTIVES
1. Determine the variety of culturally diverse arts available in a community
2. Work with others to promote awareness of culturally diverse arts

Problem

The vitality and diversity of contemporary American literature is shared by other contemporary American art forms, from the visual arts to theater. How can people be made more aware of the range and richness of the arts relating to the various cultures in their communities?

Project

Recommend ways that your school or community can promote awareness and appreciation of culturally diverse contemporary arts.

Preparation

1. Work with a partner or a small group to brainstorm a list of various art forms available in your community: dance, drama, poetry, storytelling, sculpture, opera, painting, and so on.
2. Formulate a list of *5W-How?* questions (*Who? What? When? Where? Why? How?*) about one or more of these art forms.

Procedure

1. Research local museums, galleries, performing-arts centers, playhouses, writers' groups, poetry readings, storytelling sessions, and other sources of art and culture in your community or city. Collect brochures, advertisements, mission statements, program notes, and the like from your sources.
2. Research local newspapers, magazines, newsletters, and other publications for write-ups or reviews of your local arts scene. Focus especially on arts from specific cultural groups: African American or Russian theater groups; galleries or museums of Latino art; local or visiting troupes who perform traditional Asian or Irish dance; community spaces for poetry readings celebrating ethnic diversity; and so on.
3. Arrange interviews with local museum directors, theater directors, gallery owners, arts reviewers, or any others who make their living from the arts (painters, writers, actors, and so on). Ask the people you interview about cultural diversity in their area, their predictions about where the arts are heading, local audience response to multicultural arts, and other questions relevant to your research.

Presentation

Present your findings in one of the following formats (or another that your teacher approves):

1. **Feature Article**
   Write a feature article on some aspect of culturally diverse art in your community, such as a Latino art gallery, a local American Indian craftsperson, or multicultural poetry readings. Submit your article to your school or local newspaper. Provide quotations from any interviews you've conducted.

2. **Multimedia Presentation**
   Working in a small group, create and present a multimedia exhibit showcasing examples of drama, music, visual art, dance, and other art forms available in your community. Demonstrate the variety of art forms available to the public, with an emphasis on cultural diversity.

3. **Advertising Campaign**
   With a small group, develop and present a "State of the Arts" advertising campaign for your school. Create posters, brochures, slogans, and other advertising tools. Emphasize cultural diversity in the arts, and highlight appropriate examples available in your community.

Processing

What did you learn about the importance of the arts to a community? How are multicultural trends in all the arts changing our cultural climate? In the years to come, what roles do you think the arts will fulfill in both celebrating diversity and uniting people of diverse backgrounds? Write a reflection for your portfolio.

Resources ───────

Viewing and Representing
HRW Multimedia Presentation Maker
Students may wish to use the *Multimedia Presentation Maker* to present images of various art forms as part of the Multimedia Presentation.

Teaching the Lesson

If your students have limited access to community arts resources, you might allow them to gather information about multicultural arts using the Internet. A keyword search for "multicultural arts" or "cultural diversity" will turn up a number of potential sources.

Grading Timesaver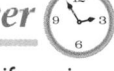

Rubrics for this Learning for Life project appear on p. 238 of the *Portfolio Management System*.

Developing Workplace Competencies

Preparation	Procedure	Presentation
• Thinks creatively	• Uses resources well	• Evaluates data
• Works on teams	• Acquires data	• Interprets information
• Exhibits sociability	• Communicates ideas and information	• Monitors and corrects performance
• Uses self-management skills	• Demonstrates individual responsibility	• Reasons
• Designs systems	• Selects equipment	• Solves problems

RESOURCE CENTER

HANDBOOK OF LITERARY TERMS

You will find more information about the terms in this Handbook on the pages given at the ends of the entries. To learn more about **Allusion,** for example, turn to pages 39, 186, 670, and 1159 in this book.

Cross-references at the ends of some entries refer to other entries in the Handbook containing related information. For instance, at the end of **Antagonist,** you are referred to **Protagonist.**

ALLEGORY   A story or poem in which characters, settings, and events stand for other people or events or for abstract ideas or qualities. An allegory can be read on one level for its literal meaning and on a second level for its symbolic, or allegorical, meaning. The most famous allegory in the English language is *The Pilgrim's Progress* (1678) by the English Puritan writer John Bunyan, in which Christian, on his journey to the Celestial City, meets such personages as Mr. Worldly Wiseman, Hopeful, and Giant Despair and travels to such places as the Slough of Despond, the Valley of Humiliation, and Doubting Castle. Puritans were trained to see their own lives as allegories of Biblical experiences. Nathaniel Hawthorne's and Edgar Allan Poe's fictions are often called allegorical.

See page 280.

ALLITERATION   The repetition of the same or similar consonant sounds in words that are close together. Alliteration is used to create musical effects and to establish mood. In the following line from "The Tide Rises, the Tide Falls" (page 177) by Henry Wadsworth Longfellow, the repetition of the *s* sound is an example of alliteration:

But the sea, the sea in the darkness calls

See pages 288, 355.
See also *Assonance, Onomatopoeia, Rhyme.*

ALLUSION   A reference to someone or something that is known from history, literature, religion, politics, sports, science, or some other branch of culture. T. S. Eliot drew on his knowledge of the Bible when he alluded to the raising of Lazarus from the dead in "The Love Song of J. Alfred Prufrock" (page 666). The title of Sandra Cisneros's essay "Straw into Gold" (page 1160) is an allusion to the folk tale about Rumpelstiltskin.

You won't understand the cartoon to the right unless you recognize the fairy tale it alludes to.

See pages 39, 186, 670, 1159.

AMBIGUITY   A technique by which a writer deliberately suggests two or more different, and sometimes conflicting, meanings in a work. Langston Hughes's poem "Harlem" (page 764) has an ambiguous ending; the title of Richard Wilbur's "The Beautiful Changes" (page 1006) is also deliberately ambiguous.

See page 493.

ANALOGY   A comparison made between two things to show how they are alike. In "The Crisis, No. 1" (page 108), Thomas Paine draws an analogy between a thief breaking into a house and the king of England interfering in the affairs of the American Colonies.

See pages 112, 890.

ANAPEST   A metrical foot that has two unstressed syllables followed by one stressed syllable. The word *coexist* (˘ ˘ ′) is an example of an anapest.
See also *Dactyl, Foot.*

ANECDOTE   A very brief story, told to illustrate a point or serve as an example of something. In Thomas Paine's "The Crisis, No. 1," the tale of the Tory tavern keeper and his child (page 108) is an anecdote.

See page 465.

ANTAGONIST   The opponent who struggles against or blocks the hero, or protagonist, in a story. In *The Narrative of the Life of Frederick Douglass,* Mr. Covey is Douglass's antagonist. In Herman Melville's *Moby-Dick,* the white whale is Ahab's antagonist.

See also *Protagonist.*

"They're offering a deal—you can pay court costs and damages, they drop charges of breaking and entering."
Drawing by Maslin. © 1988 The New Yorker Magazine, Inc.

HANDBOOK OF LITERARY TERMS   1189

Researching and Performing Ballads

There are many American ballads that students could focus on for a research assignment and for performance. A classic general work on American songs is Carl Sandburg's *The American Songbag,* which places American songs in interesting categories, some of them named here: "Dramas and Portraits" (which includes "Foggy, Foggy Dew" and "John Henry"), "The Ould Sod" (which includes "Kevin Barry"), "Frankie and Her Man," "Pioneer Memories" (which includes "Turkey in the Straw" and "Sweet Betsy from Pike"), "Kentucky Blazing Star" (which includes "Liza Jane" and "Down in the Valley"), "The Lincolns and Hankses," "Great Lakes and Erie Canal," "Hobo Songs," "The Big Brutal City," "Prison and Jail Songs," "The Great Open Spaces" (which includes "As I Walked Out in the Streets of Laredo"), "Mexican Border Songs" (which includes "Cielito Lindo"), "Southern Mountains," "Railroad and Work Gangs," "Lumberjacks, Loggers, Shanty-Boys" (which includes "The Jam on Gerry's Rock") and "Bandit Biographies" (which includes "Jesse James").

Students could include literary ballads in their research. One of the most famous American literary ballad is Longfellow's "The Wreck of the Hesperus." A contemporary literary ballad, and a moving one, is Dudley Randall's "Ballad of Birmingham," about the deaths of four young girls in the 1963 bombing of the Sixteenth Street Baptist Church in Birmingham, Alabama. The ballad appears in *Elements of Literature, Third Course.*

Students should also research *corridos,* ballads that are part of Mexican culture. Try "Corrido de Gregorio Cortez."

An interesting focus would be an investigation of the ballad form in contemporary songs.

Results of the students' research could be gathered in a booklet and added to the classroom library.

ANTHROPOMORPHISM Attributing human characteristics to an animal or inanimate object. Writers often anthropomorphize animals or objects in order to achieve humorous or satirical effects.

See also *Personification.*

APHORISM A brief, cleverly worded statement that makes a wise observation about life. Benjamin Franklin's *Poor Richard's Almanack* is a book of aphorisms. Ralph Waldo Emerson's style is **aphoristic**—he incorporates many pithy sayings into his essays (which is why he is so quotable).

See pages 95, 222, 786, 1087.

APOSTROPHE A technique by which a writer addresses an inanimate object, an idea, or a person who is either dead or absent. Sor Juana Inés de la Cruz apostrophizes her critics in "World, in Hounding Me . . ." (page 76). Oliver Wendell Holmes apostrophizes a shell and his soul in "The Chambered Nautilus" (page 189).

See pages 188, 792, 795.

ARGUMENT A form of persuasion that appeals to reason, rather than emotion, to convince an audience to think or act in a certain way. The Declaration of Independence provides some famous examples of argument.

See page 112.
See also *Persuasion.*

ASSONANCE The repetition of similar vowel sounds followed by different consonant sounds, especially in words close together. Notice the repeated sound of *i* in these lines from "The Tide Rises, the Tide Falls" (page 177) by Henry Wadsworth Longfellow. Read the lines aloud to hear the verbal music created by assonance.

The tide rises, the tide falls,
The twilight darkens, the curlew calls

See page 355.
See also *Alliteration, Onomatopoeia, Rhyme.*

ATMOSPHERE The mood or feeling created in a piece of writing. A story's atmosphere might be peaceful, festive, menacing, melancholy, and so on. Edgar Allan Poe's "The Fall of the House of Usher," for example, conveys an atmosphere of gloom.

See page 262.
See also *Setting.*

AUTOBIOGRAPHY An account of the writer's own life. Benjamin Franklin's autobiography (page 86)

is one of the most famous autobiographies in American literature. A selection from Richard Wright's autobiography, *Black Boy,* is on page 1015.

See pages 57, 97.

BALLAD A song or poem that tells a story. The typical ballad tells a tragic story in the form of a monologue or dialogue. Ballads usually have a simple, steady rhythm, a rhyme pattern, and a refrain, all of which make them easy to memorize. Ballads composed by unknown singers and passed on orally from one generation to the next are called **folk ballads.** **Literary ballads** are written to imitate the sounds and subjects of folk ballads. A strong tradition of folk ballads and of literary ballads exists in the United States. Country-and-western music, for example, frequently features songs written to imitate the older ballads. Here's the start of a favorite ballad, telling the story of Betsy and Ike:

Oh don't you remember sweet Betsy from Pike,
Who crossed the big mountains with her lover Ike,
With two yoke of oxen, a big yellow dog,
A tall Shanghai rooster, and one spotted hog?

Chorus:
Singing dang fol dee dido,
  Singing dang fol dee day.

One evening quite early they camped on the Platte.
'Twas near by the road on a green shady flat,
Where Betsy, sore-footed, lay down to repose—
With wonder Ike gazed on that Pike County rose.

BIOGRAPHY An account of someone's life written by another person. One of the most famous biographies in American literature is Carl Sandburg's multivolume life of Abraham Lincoln.

BLANK VERSE Poetry written in unrhymed iambic pentameter. Blank verse has a long history in English literature. It was used notably by such poets as Shakespeare and Milton in the sixteenth and seventeenth centuries and by Robert Frost in the twentieth.

See pages 569, 575.
See also *Iambic Pentameter.*

CADENCE The natural, rhythmic rise and fall of a language as it is normally spoken. Cadence is different from **meter,** in which the stressed and unstressed syllables of a poetic line are carefully counted to conform to a regular pattern. Walt Whitman was a master at imitating the cadences of spoken American English in his free verse.

See page 355.
See also *Free Verse, Meter, Rhythm*

1190 HANDBOOK OF LITERARY TERMS

CAESURA **A pause or break within a line of poetry.** Some pauses are indicated by punctuation; others are suggested by phrasing or meaning. In the lines below, the caesuras are marked by double vertical lines. These pauses are indicated by punctuation.

> Announced by all the trumpets of the sky,
> Arrives the snow, || and, || driving o'er the fields,
> Seems nowhere to alight: || the whited air
> Hides hills and woods . . .

> —Ralph Waldo Emerson,
> *from* "The Snow-Storm"

CATALOG **A list of things, people, or events.** Cataloging was a favorite device of Walt Whitman, who included long, descriptive lists throughout *Leaves of Grass.*

> See page 351.

CHARACTER **An individual in a story or play.** A character always has human traits, even if the character is an animal, as in Aesop's fables, or a god, as in the Greek and Roman myths.

The process by which the writer reveals the personality of a character is called **characterization.** A writer can reveal a character in the following ways:

- by telling us directly what the character is like: sneaky, generous, mean to pets, and so on
- by describing how the character looks and dresses
- by letting us hear the character speak
- by revealing the character's private thoughts and feelings
- by revealing the character's effect on other people—showing how other characters feel or behave toward the character
- by showing the character in action

The first method of revealing a character is called **direct characterization.** When a writer uses this method, we do not have to figure out what a character's personality is like—the writer tells us directly. The other five methods of revealing a character are known as **indirect characterization.** When a writer uses these methods, we have to exercise our own judgment, putting clues together to infer what a character is like—just as we do in real life when we are getting to know someone.

Characters are often classified as static or dynamic. A **static character** is one who does not change much in the course of a story. A **dynamic character,** on the other hand, changes in some important way as a result of the story's action. Characters can also be classified as flat or round. **Flat characters** have few personality traits. They can be summed up by a single phrase: the loyal sidekick, the buffoon, the nosy neighbor. In contrast, **round characters** have more dimensions to their personalities—they are complex, just as real people are.

> See pages 313, 981.
> See also *Motivation, Setting, Stereotype.*

CLICHÉ **A word or phrase, often a figure of speech, that has become lifeless because of overuse.** Some examples of clichés are "green with envy," "quiet as a mouse," and "pretty as a picture."

CLIMAX **That point in a plot that creates the greatest intensity, suspense, or interest.** The climax is usually the point at which the conflict in the story is resolved.

> See also *Plot.*

COMEDY **In general, a story that ends with a happy resolution of the conflicts faced by the main character or characters.** In many comedies, the conflict is provided when a young couple who wish to marry are blocked by adults. In many comedies, the main character at the end has moved into a world of greater freedom; this is the kind of comedy we see in Washington Irving's "Rip Van Winkle" (page 154). In literature, the word *comedy* is not synonymous with *humor.* Some comedies are humorous; some are not.

> See page 683.
> See also *Tragedy.*

CONCEIT **An elaborate metaphor or other figure of speech that compares two things that are startlingly different.** Often a conceit is also a very lengthy comparison. The conceit was a popular figure of speech in seventeenth-century English metaphysical poetry. In American literature, the poems of Edward Taylor (page 72) and Emily Dickinson (page 372) are known for their conceits. T. S. Eliot, in more recent literary history, also used conceits (page 661).

> See page 74.
> See also *Figure of Speech, Metaphor.*

CONCRETE POEM **A poem in which the words are arranged on a page to suggest a visual representation of the subject.** In English poetry in the seventeenth century, poets wrote concrete poems in the shapes of such things as crosses, altars, and wings; today, poets write concrete poems in every conceivable shape: waves, hearts, cats, flowers.

> See page 65.

CONFLICT **The struggle between opposing forces or characters in a story.** A conflict can be **internal,** involving opposing forces within a person's

HANDBOOK OF LITERARY TERMS **1191**

Reading Biographies

For further readings in biography (see the definition on p. 1190), check the Read On pages in the Pupil's Edition. Biographies will supply students with excellent background information on the historical periods. The best biographies provide accurate historical information, at the same time using the elements of fiction—suspense, characterization, setting, climax, irony—to capture interest. Some excellent biographies that can supplement students' work in American literature are the following:

The Most Dangerous Man in America: Scenes from the Life of Benjamin Franklin by Catherine Drinker Bowen

Edgar A. Poe: Mournful and Never-Ending Remembrance by Kenneth Silverman

Walt Whitman: The Making of the Poet by Paul Zweig

The Life of Emily Dickinson by Richard B. Sewall

Zelda: A Biography by Nancy Milford

The Life of Langston Hughes (two volumes: *I, Too, Sing America* and *I Dream a World*) by Arnold Rampersad

No Ordinary Time: Franklin and Eleanor Roosevelt: The Home Front in World War II by Doris Kearns Goodwin (a dual portrait of the president and the first lady)

James Baldwin: A Biography by David Leeming

Several publishers are producing new lines of short paperback biographies of famous people, each one by a well-known writer. These biographies would be well worth students' investigation. Each biography is about 150 to 200 pages. One line is called Penguin Lives; the general editor is James Atlas. In that series, Marshall Frady, for example, has a biography of Martin Luther King, Jr.

mind. In James Thurber's "The Secret Life of Walter Mitty" (page 625), for example, the title character has a comical internal conflict between his desire for heroism and his cowardice in the face of a formidable spouse. **External** conflicts can exist between two people, between a person and nature or a machine, or between a person and a whole society. In one segment of "Son" (page 1070), for example, John Updike shows the narrator in conflict with his son. Many stories have both internal and external conflict.

See pages 607, 965, 1044, 1077, 1129.
See also *Settings*.

CONNOTATION **The associations and emotional overtones that have become attached to a word or phrase, in addition to its strict dictionary definition.** The words *determined, firm, rigid, stubborn,* and *pigheaded* have similar dictionary definitions, but widely varying connotations, or overtones of meaning. *Determined* and *firm* both suggest an admirable kind of resoluteness; *rigid* suggests an inability to bend and a kind of mindless refusal to change. *Stubborn* and *pigheaded,* on the other hand, have even more negative connotations. *Stubborn* has associations with a mule, and *pigheaded* with the pig, which, wrongly or not, is an animal often associated with mindless willfulness. Here are some other words that are more or less synonymous but which have vastly different connotations: *fastidious* and *fussy; daydreamer* and *escapist; scent, odor, smell,* and *stink.* Words with strong connotations are often called **loaded words** or **suggestive words.**

See pages 46, 281, 701, 726.

CONSONANCE **The repetition of the same or similar final consonant sounds on accented syllables or in important words.** The words *ticktock* and *singsong* contain examples of consonance. Some modern poets use consonance in place of rhyme.

COUPLET **Two consecutive rhyming lines of poetry.** If the two rhyming lines express a complete thought, they are called a **closed couplet.** The following lines are from a poem built on a series of closed couplets.

> If ever wife was happy in a man,
> Compare with me, ye women, if you can.
>
> —Anne Bradstreet, *from* "To My
> Dear and Loving Husband"

DACTYL **A metrical foot of three syllables in which the first syllable is stressed and the next two are unstressed.** The word *tendency* (′ ˘ ˘) is a dactyl.

See also *Anapest, Foot.*

DENOUEMENT (dā′noo·män′) **The conclusion (or resolution) of a story.** In French, the word means "unraveling." At this point in a story, all the mysteries are unraveled, the conflicts are resolved, and all the questions raised by the plot are answered. Much modern fiction ends without a denouement, so that the story leaves us with a sense of incompleteness.

See also *Plot, Resolution.*

DESCRIPTION **One of the four major forms of discourse, in which language is used to create a mood or emotion.** Description does this by the use of words that appeal to our senses: sight, hearing, touch, smell, taste. Walt Whitman gives a wonderful description of a Civil War battlefield in *Specimen Days* (page 363).

See page 549.

DIALECT **A way of speaking that is characteristic of a certain social group or of the inhabitants of a certain geographical area.** Dialects may differ from one another in vocabulary, pronunciation, and grammar. One dialect has become dominant in America, and it is known as Standard English. This is the dialect used most often on national radio news and television news broadcasts. Many writers try to capture dialects to give their stories local color, humor, or an air of authenticity. Among the writers in this book who make skilled use of dialect are Mark Twain, Eudora Welty, Flannery O'Connor, William Faulkner, and Langston Hughes.

See pages 512, 1055, 1066.
See also *Vernacular.*

DICTION **A speaker or writer's choice of words.** Diction can be formal, informal, colloquial, full of slang, poetic, ornate, plain, abstract, concrete, and so on. Diction depends on the writer's subject, purpose, and audience. Some words, for example, are suited to informal conversations but are inappropriate in a formal speech. Diction has a powerful effect on the **tone** of a piece of writing.

See pages 107, 1176.
See also *Tone.*

DRAMATIC MONOLOGUE **A poem in which a character speaks to one or more listeners.** The reactions of the listener must be inferred by the reader. From the speaker's words, the reader learns about the setting, the situation, the identity of the other characters, and the personality of the speaker. The outstanding dramatic monologue in American literature is T. S. Eliot's "The Love Song of J. Alfred Prufrock." The poems in Edgar Lee Masters's *Spoon River Anthology* (page 693) are also dramatic monologues.

See page 663.

ELEGY **A poem of mourning, usually about someone who has died.** Most elegies are written to mark a person's death, but some extend their subject to reflect on life, death, and the fleeting nature of beauty. The elegies in this book include William Cullen Bryant's "Thanatopsis" (page 171), John Crowe Ransom's "Bells for John Whiteside's Daughter" (page 578), and Theodore Roethke's "Elegy for Jane" (page 1002).

See pages 1004, 1100.

EPIC **A long narrative poem, written in heightened language, which recounts the deeds of a heroic character who embodies the values of a particular society.** Epics in English include *Beowulf* (c. 700) and John Milton's *Paradise Lost* (1667). Some critics view Walt Whitman's *Leaves of Grass* as an American epic in which the hero is the questing poet.

See pages 328, 350.

EPITHET **A descriptive word or phrase that is frequently used to characterize a person or thing.** The epithet "the father of his country" is often used to characterize George Washington. New York City's popular epithet, "the Big Apple," is frequently used by advertisers. Epics such as Homer's *Odyssey* and *Iliad* frequently use **stock epithets** over and over again to describe certain characters or places: "patient Penelope," "wily Odysseus," and "earthshaker" (for Poseidon).

See page 795.

ESSAY **A short piece of nonfiction prose in which the writer discusses some aspect of a subject.** The word *essay* comes from the French *essai,* meaning "to try," a derivation that suggests that the essay form is not an exhaustive treatment of a subject. Essays are sometimes classified as formal or informal, or as formal or personal (or familiar). The essay form has been especially popular in the twentieth century, particularly among American writers. Some famous American essayists of the past include Thomas Paine (page 106), Ralph Waldo Emerson (page 216), and Henry David Thoreau (page 230). More recent essayists include E. B. White, Alice Walker (page 1101), James Baldwin (page 1141), Annie Dillard, Joan Didion, Lewis Thomas, and Edward Abbey.

See page 1102.

EXPOSITION **One of the four major forms of discourse, in which something is explained or "set forth."** Exposition is most commonly used in nonfiction. The word *exposition* also refers to that part of a plot in which the reader is given important background information on the characters, their setting, and their problems. Such exposition is usually provided at the opening of a story or play. See Washington Irving's "Rip Van Winkle" for an example (page 155, starting second paragraph).

See page 815.
See also *Plot.*

FABLE **A very short story told in prose or poetry that teaches a practical lesson about how to succeed in life.** In many fables, the characters are animals that behave like people. The most ancient fabulist is the Greek Aesop; the most famous American fabulist is James Thurber (page 623), who produced two collections: *Fables for Our Time* and *Further Fables for Our Time.*

FARCE **A type of comedy in which ridiculous and often stereotyped characters are involved in silly, far-fetched situations.** The humor in a farce is often physical and slapstick, with characters being hit in the face with pies or running into closed doors. The American cinema has produced many farces, including those starring Laurel and Hardy, Abbott and Costello, and the Marx brothers.

FIGURE OF SPEECH **A word or phrase that describes one thing in terms of another and that is not meant to be taken literally.** Figures of speech always involve a comparison of two things that are basically very dissimilar. Hundreds of figures of speech have been identified by scholars; the most common ones are **simile, metaphor, personification,** and **symbol.** Figures of speech, also called, more generally, **figurative language,** are basic to everyday speech. Statements like "She is a tower of strength" and "He is a pain in the neck" are figures of speech.

See pages 78, 224, 228, 622, 1002.
See also *Conceit, Metaphor, Personification, Simile, Symbol.*

FLASHBACK **A scene that interrupts the normal chronological sequence of events in a story to depict something that happened at an earlier time.** Although the word was coined to describe a technique used by movie makers, the technique itself is at least as old as ancient Greek literature. Much of Homer's epic poem the *Odyssey* is a flashback. Willa Cather uses frequent flashbacks to reveal the past of Georgiana in "A Wagner Matinée" (page 540).

FOIL **A character who acts as a contrast to another character.** In Herman Melville's *Moby-Dick,* First Mate Starbuck is a foil to Captain Ahab.

HANDBOOK OF LITERARY TERMS 1193

FOOT **A metrical unit of poetry.** A foot always contains at least one stressed syllable and, usually, one or more unstressed syllables. An **iamb** is a common foot in English poetry: It consists of an unstressed syllable followed by a stressed syllable (˘ ').

See also *Anapest, Dactyl, Iamb, Iambic Pentameter, Meter, Spondee, Trochee.*

FORESHADOWING **The use of hints and clues to suggest what will happen later in a plot.** A writer might use foreshadowing to create suspense or to prefigure later events. In "To Build a Fire" (page 496), for example, Jack London foreshadows the conclusion of his story by placing hints throughout the story.

See page 673.

FREE VERSE **Poetry that does not conform to a regular meter or rhyme scheme.** Poets who write in free verse try to reproduce the natural rhythms of the spoken language. Free verse uses the traditional poetic elements of **imagery, figures of speech, repetition, internal rhyme, alliteration, assonance,** and **onomatopoeia.** The first American practitioner of free verse was Walt Whitman (page 348). Some of Whitman's heirs are William Carlos Williams (page 778), Carl Sandburg (page 792), and Allen Ginsberg.

See pages 355, 742, 772.
See also *Cadence, Meter, Rhythm.*

HYPERBOLE **A figure of speech that uses an incredible exaggeration, or overstatement, for effect.** In *Life on the Mississippi* (page 453), Mark Twain uses hyperbole for comic effect. An example is Twain's response when Mr. Bixby tells him he must learn the shape of the Mississippi River throughout its course:

> Have I got to learn the shape of the river according
> to all these five hundred thousand different ways?
> If I tried to carry all that cargo in my head it
> would make me stoop-shouldered.
>
> —Mark Twain, *from Life on the Mississippi*

See pages 463, 622, 962.
See also *Understatement.*

IAMB **A metrical foot in poetry that has an unstressed syllable followed by a stressed syllable, as in the word *protect.*** The iamb (˘ ') is a common foot in poetry written in English.

See page 176.
See also *Foot, Iambic Pentameter, Meter, Spondee, Trochee.*

IAMBIC PENTAMETER **A line of poetry that contains five iambic feet.** The iambic pentameter line is the most common in English and American poetry. Shakespeare and John Milton, among others, used iambic pentameter in their major works. So did such American poets as William Cullen Bryant, Ralph Waldo Emerson, Robert Frost, and Wallace Stevens. Here, for example, is the opening line of a poem by Emerson:

> ˘ ' ˘ ' ˘ ' ˘ ' ˘ '
> In May, when sea-winds pierced our solitudes
>
> —Ralph Waldo Emerson,
> *from* "The Rhodora"

See page 180.
See also *Blank Verse, Foot, Iamb, Meter, Scanning.*

IDIOM **An expression that means something different from the literal definitions of its parts.** "Falling in love" is an idiom, as is "I lost my head."

See also *Figure of Speech.*

IMAGERY **The use of language to evoke a picture or a concrete sensation of a person, a thing, a place, or an experience.** Although most images appeal to the sense of sight, they also sometimes appeal to the senses of taste, smell, hearing, and touch as well.

See pages 218, 355, 701, 949, 1089.

IMAGISM **A twentieth-century movement in European and American poetry that advocated the creation of hard, clear images, concisely expressed in everyday speech.** The leading Imagist poets in America were Ezra Pound (page 773), Amy Lowell, H. D. [Hilda Doolittle], and William Carlos Williams (page 778).

See pages 533, 771.

IMPRESSIONISM **A nineteenth-century movement in literature and art that advocated a recording of the artist's personal impressions of the world, rather than a strict representation of reality.** Some famous American Impressionists in art are Mary Cassatt, Maurice Prendergast, and William Merritt Chase. In fiction, Stephen Crane pioneered a kind of literary impressionism in which he portrayed not objective reality but one character's impressions of reality. Crane's impressionistic technique is best seen in his novel *The Red Badge of Courage.*

See page 484.

INCONGRUITY **The deliberate joining of opposites or of elements that are not appropriate to each other.** T. S. Eliot's famous opening simile in "The Love Song of J. Alfred Prufrock" (page 663) joins two incongruous elements: a sunset and a patient knocked out by ether on an operating table. Incongruity can also be used for humor: We laugh at the sight of an elephant dressed in a pink tutu because the two elements are incongruous. Writers also use incongruity for dramatic effect. In Donald Barthelme's "Game" (page 956), the childish actions of the characters are in sharp contrast with the devastation they can cause by turning a key.

See page 962.

INTERIOR MONOLOGUE   A narrative technique that records a character's internal flow of thoughts, memories, and ideas. Parts of James Joyce's *Ulysses* and William Faulkner's *The Sound and the Fury* are written as interior monologues.

See page 1157.

INTERNAL RHYME   Rhyme that occurs within a line of poetry or within consecutive lines. The first line of the following couplet includes an internal rhyme.

> And so, all the night-*tide*, I lie down by the *side*
> Of my darling—my darling—my life and my bride

—Edgar Allan Poe, *from* "Annabel Lee"

See page 288.
See also *Rhyme*.

INVERSION   The reversal of the normal word order in a sentence or phrase. An English sentence normally is built on subject-verb-complement, in that order. An inverted sentence reverses one or more of those elements. In poetry written many years ago, writers often inverted word order as a matter of course, in order to have the words conform to the meter, or to create rhymes. The poetry of Anne Bradstreet (page 68) contains many inversions, as in the first line of the poem on the burning of her house:

> In silent night when rest I took

In prose, inversion is often used for emphasis, as when Patrick Henry, in his fiery speech to the Virginia Convention (page 102), said "Suffer not yourselves to be betrayed with a kiss" (instead of "Do not suffer [allow] yourselves," etc.).

See pages 69, 174.

IRONY   In general, a discrepancy between appearances and reality. There are three main types of irony:

1. **Verbal irony** occurs when someone says one thing but really means something else. Oliver Wendell Holmes uses irony when, in "Old Ironsides" (page 190), he urges that the warship be destroyed.

2. **Situational irony** takes place when there is a discrepancy between what is expected to happen, or what would be appropriate to happen, and what really does happen. A famous use of situational irony is in Stephen Crane's "A Mystery of Heroism" (page 487), in which a soldier risks his life to get water which is then spilled.

3. **Dramatic irony** is so called because it is often used on stage. In this kind of irony, a character in the play or story thinks one thing is true, but the audience or reader knows better. In Edwin Arlington Robinson's "Miniver Cheevy" (page 646), Miniver thinks he is too refined for his age, but in the reader's eyes, he seems foolish and somewhat pathetic.

See pages 422, 485, 683.

LYRIC POEM   A poem that does not tell a story but expresses the personal feelings or thoughts of a speaker. The many lyric poems in this textbook include the philosophic "Thanatopsis" by William Cullen Bryant (page 171) and the elegiac "Bells for John Whiteside's Daughter" by John Crowe Ransom (page 578).

See page 1008.

MAGIC REALISM   A genre developed in Latin America that juxtaposes the everyday with the marvelous or magical. Myths, folk tales, religious beliefs, and tall tales are the raw material for many magic realist writers. Gabriel García Márquez's work, particularly his novel *One Hundred Years of Solitude* (1970), established him as a master of the genre. Other prominent Latin American magic realists include Jorge Luis Borges, Julio Cortázar, and Isabel Allende. Among American writers, Donald Barthelme and Thomas Pynchon have been influenced by magic realism.

See page 996.

METAPHOR   A figure of speech that makes a comparison between two unlike things without the use of such specific words of comparison as *like, as, than,* or *resembles.* There are several kinds of metaphor:

1. A **directly stated metaphor** states the comparison explicitly: "Fame is a bee" (Emily Dickinson).

2. An **implied metaphor** does not state explicitly the two terms of the comparison: "I like to see it lap the Miles" (Emily Dickinson) is an implied metaphor in which the verb *lap* implies a comparison between "it" (which is a train) and some animal that "laps" up water.

3. An **extended metaphor** is a metaphor that is extended or developed over a number of lines or

HANDBOOK OF LITERARY TERMS   1195

with several examples. Dickinson's poem beginning "Fame is a bee" is an extended metaphor: The comparison of fame to a bee is extended for four lines:

> Fame is a bee.
>   It has a song—
> It has a sting—
>   Ah, too, it has a wing.

4. A **dead metaphor** is a metaphor that has been used so often that the comparison is no longer vivid: "The head of the house," "the seat of government," and "a knotty problem" are all dead metaphors.

5. A **mixed metaphor** is a metaphor that fails to make a logical comparison because its mixed terms are visually or imaginatively incompatible. If you say, "The President is a lame duck who is running out of gas," you've lost control of your metaphor and have produced a statement that is ridiculous (ducks do not run out of gas).

See pages 74, 188, 246, 431, 452, 463, 622, 1002, 1066.
See also *Conceit, Figure of Speech, Simile.*

METER   A pattern of stressed and unstressed syllables in poetry. The meter of a poem is commonly indicated by using the symbol (′) for stressed syllables and the symbol (˘) for unstressed syllables. This is called **scanning** the poem.

Meter is described as **iambic, trochaic, dactylic,** or **anapestic.** These scanned lines from "Richard Cory" are iambic because they are built on iambs—an unstressed syllable followed by a stressed syllable.

˘ ′ ˘ ′ ˘   ′ ˘ ′ ˘ ′
And he was always quietly arrayed

˘ ′ ˘ ′ ˘ ′ ˘   ′ ˘ ′
And he was always human when he talked

See pages 69, 176, 396.
See also *Cadence, Foot, Free Verse, Iamb, Iambic Pentameter, Rhythm, Scanning, Spondee, Trochee.*

METONYMY   A figure of speech in which a person, place, or thing is referred to by something closely associated with it. Referring to a king or queen as "the crown" is an example of metonymy, as is calling a car "wheels."

See also *Synecdoche.*

MODERNISM   A term for the bold new experimental styles and forms that swept the arts during the first third of the twentieth century. Modernism called for changes in subject matter, in fictional styles, in poetic forms, and in attitudes. T. S. Eliot (page 661) and Ezra Pound (page 773) are associated with the modernist movement in poetry. Their aim was to rid poetry of its nineteenth-century "prettiness" and sentimentality.

See pages 525, 533.
See also *Imagism, Symbolism.*

MOTIVATION   The reasons for a character's behavior. In order for us to understand why characters act the way they do, their motivation has to be believable, at least in terms of the story. At times, a writer directly reveals motivation; in subtler fiction, we must use details from the story to infer motivation.

See pages 586, 828, 1110.
See also *Character.*

MYTH   An anonymous traditional story that is basically religious in nature and that usually serves to explain a belief, ritual, or mysterious natural phenomenon. Most myths have grown out of religious rituals, and almost all of them involve the exploits of gods and humans. Works of magic realism often draw on myths or mythlike tales.

See page 996.

NARRATIVE   The form of discourse that tells about a series of events. Narration is used in all kinds of literature: fiction, nonfiction, and poetry. Usually a narrative is told in **chronological order**—in the order in which the events occurred. The other three major forms of discourse are **description, exposition,** and **persuasion.**

NATURALISM   A nineteenth-century literary movement that was an extension of realism and that claimed to portray life exactly as it was. The naturalists relied heavily on the new fields of psychology and sociology, and they tended to dissect human behavior with complete objectivity, the way a scientist would dissect a specimen in the laboratory. The naturalists were also influenced by Darwinian theories of the survival of the fittest. Naturalists believed that human behavior is determined by heredity and environment; they felt that people have no recourse to supernatural forces and that human beings, like animals, are subject to laws of nature beyond their control. The outstanding naturalists among American writers are Theodore Dreiser, Stephen Crane (page 484), and Frank Norris. Some people consider John Steinbeck's *The Grapes of Wrath* a naturalistic novel, in which characters are the pawns of economic conditions.

See pages 421, 484, 496.
See also *Realism.*

OBJECTIVE CORRELATIVE **An object, a situation, or a chain of events that serves as the formula for a specific emotion.** The term was first used in an essay by T. S. Eliot.

See page 777.

OCTAVE **An eight-line poem, or the first eight lines of a Petrarchan, or Italian, sonnet.** In a Petrarchan sonnet, the octave states the subject of the sonnet, or poses a problem or question.

See page 180.
See also *Sestet, Sonnet.*

ODE **A lyric poem, usually long, on a serious subject and written in dignified language.** In ancient Greece and Rome, odes were written to be read in public at ceremonial occasions. In modern literature, odes tend to be more private, informal, and reflective. Robert Lowell's "For the Union Dead" (page 950) and Henry Timrod's "Ode on the Confederate Dead" (page 954) are examples of the personal, meditative ode.

ONOMATOPOEIA **The use of a word whose sound imitates or suggests its meaning.** The word *buzz* is onomatopoeic; it imitates the sound it names.

See pages 288, 355.

OXYMORON **A figure of speech that combines opposite or contradictory terms in a brief phrase.** "Sweet sorrow," "deafening silence," and "living death" are common oxymorons. (Some jokesters claim that phrases like "jumbo shrimp," "congressional leadership," and "limited nuclear war" are also oxymorons.)

See page 622.

PARABLE **A relatively short story that teaches a moral, or lesson, about how to lead a good life.** The most famous parables are those told by Jesus in the Gospels.

See pages 308, 567.

PARADOX **A statement that appears self-contradictory but that reveals a kind of truth.** Many writers like to use paradox because it allows them to express the complexity of life by showing how opposing ideas can be both contradictory and true. Emily Dickinson often used paradoxes, as in this line: "I taste a liquor never brewed" (page 382).

See pages 229, 248, 604, 1108.

PARALLEL STRUCTURE **(also called *parallelism*) The repetition of words or phrases that have similar grammatical structures.** Lincoln, in his Gettysburg Address (page 479), uses several memorable parallel structures, as when he refers to "government of the people, by the people, for the people."

See pages 115, 355.

PARODY **A work that makes fun of another work by imitating some aspect of the writer's style.** Parodies often achieve their effects by humorously exaggerating certain features in the original work.

See pages 289, 320, 624.

PERSONIFICATION **A figure of speech in which an object or animal is given human feelings, thoughts, or attitudes.** Personification is a type of metaphor in which two dissimilar things are compared. In "To the Fringed Gentian," William Cullen Bryant personifies a flower by giving it an eye and eyelashes:

> Then doth thy sweet and quiet eye
> Look through its fringes to the sky.

See pages 622, 737, 1002, 1035, 1042, 1151.
See also *Anthropomorphism, Apostrophe, Figure of speech.*

PERSUASION **One of the four forms of discourse, which uses reason and emotional appeals to convince a reader to think or act in a certain way.** Persuasion is used in the Declaration of Independence (page 116), in Patrick Henry's "Give me liberty, or give me death" speech (page 102), and in Thomas Paine's "The Crisis, No. 1" (page 108). Persuasion is almost exclusively used in nonfiction, particularly in essays and speeches.

See pages 101, 112.
See also *Argument.*

PLAIN STYLE **A way of writing that stresses simplicity and clarity of expression.** The plain style was favored by most Puritan writers, who avoided unnecessary ornamentation in all aspects of their lives, including church ritual. Simple sentences, everyday words from common speech, and clear and direct statements characterize the plain style. The plain style eliminates elaborate figures of speech and imagery. One of the chief exponents of the plain style in recent American literature was Ernest Hemingway (page 650).

See pages 12, 27, 35.
See also *Style.*

PLOT **The series of related events in a story or play, sometimes called the *story line*.** Most short-story plots contain the following elements: **exposition,** which tells us who the characters are and introduces their conflict; **complications,** which arise as the characters take steps to resolve their conflicts; the **climax,** that exciting or suspenseful moment when the outcome of the conflict is imminent; and a **resolution** or **denouement,** when the story's problems are all resolved and the story ends.

The plots of dramas and novels are somewhat more complex because of their length. A schematic representation of a typical dramatic plot follows. It is based on a "pyramid" developed by the nineteenth-century German critic Gustav Freitag. The **rising action** refers to all the actions that take place before the **turning point** (sometimes called the **crisis**). This is the point at which the hero experiences a reversal of fortune: In a comedy, things begin to work out well; in a tragedy, they get worse and worse. (In Shakespeare's plays, the turning point takes place in the third act. In *Romeo and Juliet,* for example, after he kills Tybalt in the third act, Romeo experiences one disaster after another.) All the action after the turning point is called **falling action** because it is leading to the final resolution (happy or unhappy) of the conflict. The major **climax** in most plays and novels takes place just before the ending; in Shakespeare's plays, it takes place in the fifth, or last, act. (In *Romeo and Juliet,* the major climax takes place when the two young people kill themselves.)

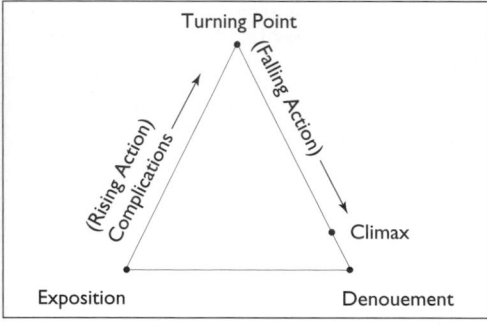

See also *Climax, Denouement, Exposition, Resolution.*

POINT OF VIEW   The vantage point from which the writer tells a story. In broad terms, there are four main points of view: **first-person, third-person limited, omniscient,** and **objective.**

1. In the **first-person point of view,** one of the characters in the story tells the story, using first-person pronouns such as *I* and *we.* With this point of view, we can know only what the narrator knows. Mark Twain's novel *Adventures of Huckleberry Finn* is told from the first-person point of view, by the novel's main character, a boy named Huck Finn. One of the great pleasures of that novel, in fact, is that its point of view allows us to hear Huck's very distinct voice and dialect.

2. In the **third-person limited point of view,** an unknown narrator (usually thought of as the author) tells the story, but this narrator zooms in to focus on the thoughts and feelings of only one character. (This point of view gets its name because the narrator refers to all the characters as *he, she,* and *they;* this narrator does not use the first-person pronoun *I.*) Like the first-person point of view, however, this point of view also limits us to the perceptions of one character, but in this case the narrator can tell us many things about the character, things that the character himself (or herself) might be unaware of. For example, Eudora Welty tells "A Worn Path" (page 634) from the third-person limited point of view of her protagonist, an old woman named Phoenix Jackson. At one point, Welty's narrator tells us that Phoenix was "like an old woman begging a dignified forgiveness."

3. In the **omniscient point of view,** an omniscient, or "all-knowing," narrator tells the story, also using the third-person pronouns. However, this narrator, instead of focusing on one character only, often tells us everything about many characters: their motives, weaknesses, hopes, childhoods, and sometimes even their futures. This narrator can also comment directly on the character's actions. Washington Irving's "Rip Van Winkle" (page 154) is told from the omniscient point of view.

4. In the **objective point of view,** a narrator who is totally impersonal and objective tells the story, with no comment on any characters or events. The objective point of view is like the point of view of a movie camera; it is totally impersonal, and what we know is only what the camera might see. This narrator never gives any direct revelation of the characters' thoughts or motives. Ernest Hemingway (page 650) uses this objective point of view, which is why his stories often seem so puzzling to readers. "What happened?" we ask. The *reader* must infer what happens in Hemingway's stories, just as in real life we have to infer the motives, thoughts, and feelings of people we meet.

See pages 232, 467.

POSTMODERNISM   A term for the dominant trend in the arts since 1945. Postmodern writing typically experiments with nontraditional forms and allows for multiple meanings. The lines between real and imaginary worlds are often blurred, as is the boundary between fiction and nonfiction. Other characteristics of postmodern literature are cultural diversity and an often playful self-consciousness; that is, an acknowledgment that literature is not a mirror that accurately reflects the world, but a created world unto itself.

See page 910.

PROTAGONIST **The central character in a story, the one who initiates or drives the action.** The protagonist might or might not be the story's hero; some protagonists are actually the villains in the story.

See page 814.
See also *Antagonist.*

PROVERB **A short, well-known statement that expresses a common truth or experience.** Many of Benjamin Franklin's sayings have become proverbs in American culture.

See page 465.

PUN **A "play on words" based on the multiple meanings of a single word or on words that sound alike but mean different things.** An example of the first type of pun is a singer explaining her claim that she was locked out of an audition because she couldn't find the right key. The second kind of pun can be found in the opening lines of Shakespeare's *Julius Caesar,* where a man who repairs shoes claims to be a mender of men's souls (soles). Puns are often used for humor, but some puns are a serious element in poetry.

See page 390.

QUATRAIN **A poem consisting of four lines, or four lines of a poem that can be considered as a unit.** The typical ballad stanza, for example, is a quatrain.

REALISM **A style of writing, developed in the nineteenth century, that attempts to depict life accurately without idealizing or romanticizing it.** Instead of writing about the long ago or far away, the realists concentrated on contemporary life and on middle- and lower-class lives in particular. Among the outstanding realistic novelists in America are Stephen Crane (page 484), Willa Cather (page 538), and John Steinbeck (page 606). European playwrights who wrote realistic dramas, including Henrik Ibsen, August Strindberg, and Anton Chekov, discarded artificial plots in favor of themes centering on contemporary society. They also rejected extravagant language in favor of simpler, everyday diction.

See pages 418, 820.
See also *Naturalism, Romanticism.*

REFRAIN **A word, phrase, line, or group of lines that is repeated, for effect, several times in a poem.** Refrains are often used in ballads and other narrative poems. "Nevermore" is a refrain in Poe's "The Raven" (page 282).

See pages 288, 1122.

REGIONALISM **Literature that emphasizes a specific geographic setting and that reproduces the speech, behavior, and attitudes of the people who live in that region.** Among the great regional writers of the twentieth century are Sinclair Lewis (Midwest); John Steinbeck (California); and William Faulkner, Flannery O'Connor, and Eudora Welty (the South).

See page 419.

RESOLUTION **The conclusion of a story, when all or most of the conflicts have been settled.** The resolution is also often called the *denouement.*

See also *Denouement, Plot.*

RHETORICAL QUESTION **A question asked for an effect, not actually requiring an answer.** In his speech to the Virginia Convention, Patrick Henry asks several rhetorical questions. Such questions presume the audience agrees with the speaker on the answers.

See page 105.

RHYME **The repetition of vowel sounds in accented syllables and all succeeding syllables.** *Listen* and *glisten* rhyme, as do *chime* and *sublime.* When words within the same line of poetry have repeated sounds, we have an example of **internal rhyme. End rhyme** refers to rhyming words at the ends of lines.

The pattern of rhymes in a poem is called a **rhyme scheme.** Rhyme scheme is commonly indicated with letters of the alphabet, each rhyming sound represented by a different letter of the alphabet. For example, the rhyme scheme of the following lines is *abab.*

Tell me not, in mournful numbers,	*a*
Life is but an empty dream!—	*b*
For the soul is dead that slumbers,	*a*
And things are not what they seem.	*b*

—Henry Wadsworth Longfellow,
from "A Psalm of Life"

Approximate rhymes (also called **off rhymes, half rhymes, imperfect rhymes,** or **slant rhymes**) are words that have some correspondence in sound but not an exact one. Examples of approximate rhymes are often found in Emily Dickinson's poems. *Flash* and *flesh* are approximate rhymes, as are *stream* and *storm,* and *early* and *barley.* Approximate rhyme has the effect of catching the reader off guard: Where you expect a perfect rhyme, you get only an approximation. The emotional effect is something like that of the sound of a sharp or flat note in music.

See pages 288, 380.
See also *Internal Rhyme, Rhythm, Slant Rhyme.*

HANDBOOK OF LITERARY TERMS **1199**

RHYTHM The alternation of stressed and un-stressed syllables in language. Rhythm occurs natu-rally in all forms of spoken and written language. The most obvious kind of rhythm is produced by **meter**, the regular pattern of stressed and unstressed syllables found in some poetry. Writers can also create less structured rhythms by using rhyme, repetition, pauses, and variations in line length and by balancing long and short words or phrases.

See pages 670, 761.
See also *Cadence, Free Verse, Meter, Rhyme.*

ROMANCE In general, a story in which an ide-alized hero or heroine undertakes a quest and is successful. In a romance, beauty, innocence, and goodness usually prevail over evil. Romances are tradi-tionally set in the distant past and use a great deal of fantasy. The laws of nature are often suspended in a ro-mance, so that the hero often has supernatural powers, as we see in the adventures of King Arthur and his knights. Stories set in the American West are in the ro-mance mode, except that the supernatural elements are eliminated (though the sheriff-hero usually has a nearly magical skill with his gun). Today we also use the word *romance* to refer to a kind of popular escapist love story, which often takes place in an exotic setting.

See page 683.

ROMANTICISM A revolt against rationalism that affected literature and the other arts, beginning in the late eighteenth century and remaining strong throughout most of the nine-teenth century. Romanticism is marked by these char-acteristics: (1) a conviction that intuition, imagination, and emotion are superior to reason; (2) a conviction that poetry is superior to science; (3) a belief that con-templation of the natural world is a means of discovering the truth that lies behind mere reality; (4) a distrust of industry and city life and an idealization of rural life and of the wilderness; (5) an interest in the more "natural" past and in the supernatural. Romanticism affected so many creative people that it was bound to take many dif-ferent forms; the result is that it is difficult to define the word in a way that includes everyone who might be called a Romantic. In the nineteenth century, for exam-ple, Romantics were outspoken in their love of nature and contempt for technology. In this century, however, as nature has been taken over by developers and high-ways, some writers have taken a romantic view of ma-chines, buildings, and other products of technology.

See pages 143, 144, 212, 770.
See also *Realism.*

SATIRE A type of writing that ridicules the shortcomings of people or institutions in an at-tempt to bring about a change. Satire can cover a wide range of tones, from gentle spoofing to savage mockery. In "Rip Van Winkle" (page 154), for example, Washington Irving pokes good-natured fun at the Van Winkles and the townspeople. In Donald Barthelme's "Game" (page 956), the satire is harsher, as it points out the absurdity and illogic of nuclear war games. Satire is always intensely moral in its purpose. Mark Twain, in *Adventures of Huckleberry Finn*, satirizes a whole spec-trum of American life, but the thrust of the novel is moral: Twain is making us see things that should not be permitted to exist (slavery is one of them).

See pages 50, 962.

SCANNING The analysis of a poem to deter-mine its meter. When you scan a poem, you de-scribe the pattern of stressed and unstressed syllables in each line. Stresses or accents are indicated by the symbol (′) and unstressed syllables by the symbol (˘).

> ˘ ′ ˘ ′ ˘ ′ ˘ ′ ˘ ′
> To him who in the love of Nature holds
>
> ˘ ′ ˘ ˘ ˘ ′ ˘ ˘ ′ ˘ ′
> Communion with her visible forms, she speaks
>
> ˘ ′ ˘ ˘ ′ ˘ ˘ ˘ ′ ˘ ′
> A various language: for his gayer hours
>
> ˘ ′ ˘ ′ ˘ ′ ˘ ˘ ˘ ′
> She has a voice of gladness, and a smile

—William Cullen Bryant,
from "Thanatopsis"

See also *Iambic Pentameter, Meter.*

SESTET Six lines of poetry, especially the last six lines of a Petrarchan, or Italian, sonnet. In the Petrarchan sonnet, the sestet offers a comment on the subject or problem presented in the first eight lines (the octave) of the poem.

See page 180.
See also *Octave, Sonnet.*

SETTING The time and location in which a story takes place. Setting can have several functions in fiction:

1. Setting is often used to create **conflict.** In the purest and often simplest form of story, a charac-ter is in conflict with some element of a setting: The narrator in Jack London's "To Build a Fire" (page 497) is in conflict with extreme cold (the cold wins).

2. Often the setting helps to create **atmosphere** or **mood,** as does Edgar Allan Poe's setting of a de-

caying mansion in "The Fall of the House of Usher" (page 263).

3. Setting can also create and delineate **character:** In William Faulkner's "A Rose for Emily" (page 716), Miss Emily Grierson's old-fashioned house with its musty rooms reflects her refusal to live in the present.

See pages 153, 539, 715, 1093.

SIMILE **A figure of speech that makes an explicit comparison between two unlike things, using a word such as *like, as, than,* or *resembles.***

Helen, thy beauty is to me
Like those Nicéan barks of yore

—Edgar Allan Poe, *from* "To Helen"

See pages 622, 1002.
See also *Figure of Speech, Metaphor.*

SLANT RHYME **A rhyming sound that is not exact.** *Follow/fellow* and *mystery/mastery* are examples of slant or approximate rhyme. Emily Dickinson frequently used the subtleties of slant rhyme.

See page 380.
See also *Rhyme.*

SOLILOQUY **A long speech made by a character in a play while no other characters are on stage.** A soliloquy is different from a monologue in that the speaker appears to be thinking aloud, not addressing a listener.

SONNET **A fourteen-line poem, usually written in iambic pentameter, that has one of two basic structures.** The **Petrarchan sonnet,** also called the **Italian sonnet,** is named after the fourteenth-century Italian poet Petrarch. Its first eight lines, called the **octave,** ask a question or pose a problem. These lines have a rhyme scheme of *abba, abba.* The last six lines, called the **sestet,** respond to the question or problem. These lines have a rhyme scheme of *cde, cde.*

The form used to such perfection by William Shakespeare is known as the **English, Elizabethan,** or **Shakespearean sonnet.** It has three four-line units, or **quatrains,** and it concludes with a **couplet.** The most common rhyme scheme for the Shakespearean sonnet is *abab, cdcd, efef, gg.*

Longfellow wrote many sonnets, such as "The Cross of Snow" (page 178), as did Edna St. Vincent Millay (page 697), Robert Frost (page 558), and E. E. Cummings (page 796).

See pages 180, 560.
See also *Octave, Sestet.*

SOUND EFFECTS **The use of sounds to create specific literary effects.** Writers use devices such as **rhythm, rhyme, meter, alliteration, onomatopoeia, assonance, consonance,** and **repetition** to make the sounds of a work convey and enhance its meaning.

See pages 282, 288.

SPONDEE **A metrical foot consisting of two syllables, both of which are stressed.** The words *true-blue* and *nineteen* are made of spondees. When Walt Whitman wrote "Beat! beat! drums," he used spondees. Spondaic feet are rarely used extensively because of their "thump-thump" sound. However, poets sometimes use spondees to provide a brief change from an iambic or trochaic beat or to provide emphasis.

See also *Foot, Meter, Trochee.*

STEREOTYPE **A fixed idea or conception of a character or an idea that does not allow for any individuality, and is often based on religious, social, or racial prejudices.** Some common stereotypes are the unsophisticated farmer, the socially inept honor student, the dumb athlete, and the lazy teenager. Stereotypes, also called **stock characters,** are often deliberately used in comedies and in melodramas, where they receive instant recognition from the audience and make fully fleshed characterization unnecessary. Dame Van Winkle and Rip are stereotypes (page 154), as are Walter and Mrs. Mitty (page 625).

See pages 166, 631.
See also *Character.*

STREAM OF CONSCIOUSNESS **A style of writing that portrays the inner (often chaotic) workings of a character's mind.** The stream-of-consciousness technique usually consists of a recording of the random flow of ideas, memories, associations, images, and emotions, as they arise spontaneously in a character's mind. William Faulkner, in his great novel *The Sound and the Fury,* used a stream-of-consciousness technique. Two of the other great writers that successfully used a stream-of-consciousness technique are the Irish writer James Joyce and the English writer Virginia Woolf.

See pages 530, 703.

STYLE **The distinctive way in which a writer uses language.** Styles can be plain, ornate, metaphorical, spare, descriptive, and so on. Style is determined by such factors as sentence length and complexity, syntax, use of figurative language and imagery, and diction.

See pages 107, 1027.
See also *Plain Style, Stream of Consciousness, Tone.*

HANDBOOK OF LITERARY TERMS **1201**

SURREALISM A movement in art and literature that started in Europe during the 1920s. Surrealists wanted to replace conventional realism with the full expression of the unconscious mind, which they considered to be more real than the "real" world of appearances. Surrealists, influenced by the psychoanalytic theories of Sigmund Freud, tried not to censor the images that came from their dreams or to impose logical connections on these images. This resulted in surprising combinations of "inner" and "outer" reality—a "suprareality." Surrealism affected writers as different as T. S. Eliot (page 661) and Donald Barthelme (page 955). Two famous Surrealist artists are Salvador Dali and Marc Chagall (see art on pages 982 and 989).

SUSPENSE A feeling of uncertainty and curiosity about what will happen next in a story. A key element in fiction and drama, suspense is one of the "hooks" a writer uses to keep the audience interested.

SYMBOL A person, place, thing, or event that has meaning in itself and that also stands for something more than itself. We can distinguish between **public** and **personal symbols.** The dove, for example, is a public symbol of peace—that is, it is widely accepted the world over as such a symbol. Uncle Sam is a public symbol that stands for the United States; a picture of a skull and crossbones is a public symbol of death; two snakes coiled around a staff is a widely accepted symbol of the medical profession.

Most symbols used in literature are personal symbols; even though a symbol may be widely used, a writer will usually adapt it in some imaginative, personal way so that it can suggest not just one, but a myriad of meanings. One of the most commonly used symbols in literature, for example, is the journey, which can stand for a search for truth, for redemption from evil, or for discovery of the self and freedom. The journey of Huck Finn and Jim down the Mississippi River has been interpreted to symbolize all of these concepts, and more.

The writers known as the Dark Romantics—Poe, Hawthorne, and Melville—used symbolism heavily in their works, owing to the allegorical nature of much of what they wrote. One of American literature's most famous symbols is Melville's white whale, Moby-Dick (page 313).

See pages 280, 298.
See also Figure of Speech.

SYMBOLISM A literary movement that originated in late-nineteenth-century France, in which writers rearranged the world of appearances in order to reveal a more truthful version of reality. The Symbolists believed that direct state-

ments of feeling were inadequate; instead, they called for new and striking imaginative images to evoke complexities of meaning and mood. The French Symbolists were influenced by the poetry and critical writings of the American writer Edgar Allan Poe (page 260). The poetry of Ezra Pound (page 773), T. S. Eliot (page 661), and Wallace Stevens (page 783) is in the Symbolist tradition.

See pages 533, 770.

SYNECDOCHE A figure of speech in which a part represents the whole. The capital city of a nation, for example, is often spoken of as though it were the government: "Washington and Tehran are both claiming popular support for their positions." In "The Love Song of J. Alfred Prufrock" (page 663), T. S. Eliot writes, "And I have known the arms already. . . ." *Arms* stands for all the women he has known.

See also Metonymy.

SYNESTHESIA The juxtaposition of one sensory image with another image that appeals to an unrelated sense. In synesthesia, an image of sound might be conveyed in terms of an image of taste, as in "sweet laughter," or an image that appeals to the sense of touch might be combined with an image that appeals to the sense of sight, as in this example from Emily Dickinson: "golden touch."

See page 1091.

TALL TALE An outrageously exaggerated, humorous story that is obviously unbelievable. Tall tales are part of the folk literature of many countries, including America. Perhaps the most famous tall tale in American literature is Mark Twain's "The Celebrated Jumping Frog of Calaveras County."

THEME The insight about human life that is revealed in a literary work. Themes are rarely stated directly in literature. Most often, a reader has to infer the theme of a work after considerable thought. Theme is different from **subject.** A story's subject might be stated as "growing up," "love," "heroism," or "fear." The theme is the statement the writer wants to make about that subject: "For most young people, growing up is a process that involves the pain of achieving self-knowledge." Theme must be stated in at least one sentence; most themes are complex enough to require several sentences, or even an essay.

See page 634.

TONE The attitude a writer takes toward the subject of a work, the characters in it, or the audience. In speaking, we use voice inflections to show how we feel about what we are saying. Writers manipulate language in an attempt to achieve the same effect. For example, John Hersey takes an objective tone in telling about the nuclear explosion in *Hiroshima* (see "A Noiseless Flash," page 937). In contrast, the tone in Patrick Henry's speech to the Virginia Convention (page 102) is subjective, even impassioned. Tone is dependent on **diction** and **style,** and we cannot say we have understood any work of literature until we have sensed the writer's tone. Tone can be described in a single word: objective, solemn, playful, ironic, sarcastic, critical, reverent, irreverent, philosophical, cynical, and so on.

See pages 577, 764.
See also *Diction, Style.*

TRAGEDY **In general, a story in which a heroic character either dies or comes to some other unhappy end.** In most tragedies, the main character is in an enviable, even exalted, position when the story begins (in classical tragedies and in Shakespeare, the tragic hero is of noble origin, often a king or queen, prince or princess). The character's downfall generally occurs because of some combination of fate, an error in judgment, or a personality failure known as a **tragic flaw** (Creon's stubbornness in *Antigone* or Hamlet's indecision, for example). The tragic character has usually gained wisdom at the end of the story, in spite of suffering defeat, or even death. Our feeling on reading or viewing a tragedy is usually exaltation—despite the unhappy ending—because we have witnessed the best that human beings are capable of.

See page 683.
See also *Comedy.*

TRANSCENDENTALISM **A nineteenth-century movement in the Romantic tradition, which held that every individual can reach ultimate truths through spiritual intuition, which transcends reason and sensory experience.** The Tran-scendental movement was centered in Concord, Massachusetts, the home of its leading exponents, Ralph Waldo Emerson (page 216) and Henry David Thoreau (page 230). The basic tenets of the Transcendentalists were (1) a belief that God is present in every aspect of Nature, including every human being; (2) the conviction that everyone is capable of apprehending God through the use of intuition; (3) the belief that all of Nature is symbolic of the spirit. A corollary of these beliefs was an optimistic view of the world as good and evil as nonexistent.

See pages 211, 212.

TROCHEE **A metrical foot made up of an accented syllable followed by an unaccented syllable, as in the word** *taxi.* A trochee, the opposite of an iamb, is sometimes used to vary iambic rhythm.

See also *Foot, Iamb, Meter, Spondee.*

UNDERSTATEMENT **A statement that says less than what is meant.** Understatement, paradoxically, can make us recognize the truth of something by saying that just the opposite is true. If you are sitting down to enjoy a ten-course meal and say, "Ah! A little snack before bedtime," you are using an understatement to emphasize the tremendous amount of food you are about to eat. Understatement is often used to make an ironic point; it can also be used for humor.

See pages 463, 1033.
See also *Hyperbole.*

VERNACULAR **The language spoken by the people who live in a particular locality.** Regionalist writers try to capture the vernacular of their area.

See page 398.
See also *Dialect.*

ACTIVE READING STRATEGIES

Use the following reading strategies to help you discover meaning in what you read and relate that meaning to your life.

PREVIEWING AND SETTING A PURPOSE

Previewing the Text   Preview a reading assignment or a book to get an overview of its organization. Read the title and any information included about the author. Flip through the pages and look at the table of contents, the index, and any illustrations, charts, or diagrams. Note the genre of the text—poem, short story, play, essay—and the difficulty of the vocabulary. Finally, consider what you already know about the reading assignment or book and what you'd like to find out.

Setting a Purpose   Before you begin to read, you should establish a clear purpose for reading. Purposes include (1) to be entertained, (2) to find out specific information, and (3) to learn about the craft of writing. You may have more than one purpose in mind as you read a particular text. Your purpose can dictate how closely you read and whether you take notes or use other study skills.

Activating Prior Knowledge   As you read, you should recall your prior knowledge and experiences in order to look for connections with the text. For example, as you read from Emerson's essay "Self-Reliance" (page 224), you might recall that Benjamin Franklin's autobiography (page 86) also stresses self-reliance. In turn, you may consider the significance of this quality in American culture.

Constructing a KWL Chart   To help you keep track of your prior knowledge and your new learning, make a three-column chart and use it before, as, and after you read a work. In the first column, write what you already know (K) about the work. In the middle column, write what you want (W) to know. In the last column, record what you learned (L) as a result of your reading.

K	W	L
What I **know**	What I **want** to know	What I **learned**

READING ACTIVELY

Making and Confirming Predictions   For some texts, such as short stories and novels, you should occasionally think ahead to predict what will happen next. To start the process of making predictions, ask yourself questions like *Where will the plot lead to next? How will the character act when he begins to lose his struggle with nature?* Your answers will be predictions about what you are going to read. For example, in the first lines of Edgar Allan Poe's "The Fall of the House of Usher" (page 263), the narrator approaches a gloomy building. You predict that the Usher's house will not be a happy home and that the narrator will experience unsettling events there. As you read, adjust your predictions according to what you learn from the story.

Making Inferences   An **inference** is an educated guess. Inferences about a literary work are based on clues in the text and on your own knowledge. For instance, the title of Edgar Allan Poe's "The Fall of the House of Usher" strongly suggests the inference that Roderick Usher and his house are headed for serious trouble. Jack London's title "To Build a Fire" (page 497) will almost automatically lead to the inference that fire will be an important subject of the story.

Conclusions and generalizations are types of inferences. A **conclusion** is a judgment based on evidence in a text. You will probably conclude from the speaker's words in Theodore Roethke's "Elegy for Jane" (page 1002) that he is deeply moved by the death of his student. A **generalization** is a broad statement based on specific examples. You might generalize from the stories by Ernest Hemingway (page 653) and Tim O'Brien (page 966) that soldiers have great difficulty readjusting to civilian life.

Noting Organization   As you read, think about the way the writer presents ideas, people, and events. **Sequential,** or **chronological, order** arranges the events in a historical account or a story in the order in which they occur. You may find words such as *first, then, next, while,* and *finally.* Some great literary works, such as William Faulkner's "A Rose For Emily" (page 716), present events in **nonsequential order,** thereby "fragmenting" time. **Spatial order** tells you where one person or thing is in relation to another. Factual information is usually presented in **order of importance,** either from most to least important, or from least to most important.

Logical order, a type of sequential order, organizes ideas in terms of meaning, so that one idea leads directly to the next. In an essay, an argument is best made in logical order, rather than scattering ideas so that a point in paragraph six is explained in paragraph two.

DEALING WITH DIFFICULT TEXTS

When you're having difficulty understanding a text, try one or more of these strategies:

1. **Rereading.** Stop reading and go back to the last point at which you had a grasp on the text. Reread from there.
2. **Reading on.** Keep reading to see whether context clues and/or new information clarify the text.
3. **Pausing to reflect.** Stop and think about what you've read so far. Perhaps construct a graphic organizer.
4. **Asking questions.** Ask *who, what, where, when, why,* and *how* questions about the text.
5. **Using resources.** Use a dictionary or other reference works to clarify the meaning of a passage.

MAKING SURE YOU UNDERSTAND A TEXT

Paraphrasing, outlining, and summarizing are useful strategies to make sure you understand a text. When you **paraphrase,** you restate an entire work or passage in your own words. Paraphrasing helps you to clarify anything that may have been fuzzy as you read. Here is a paraphrase of the first verse of

Edgar Allan Poe's "The Raven" (page 282):

One midnight, when I was tired and weak, glancing through / A lot of old albums and books, / As I was dozing off, I suddenly heard a tap, / As if a person were knocking at my door. / "There's a visitor knocking at my door," I thought. / "It's only a visitor."

A work of nonfiction, such as Thoreau's *Walden, or Life in the Woods* (page 233), can be **outlined** by showing its **main ideas** and **supporting details,** as below:

I. Main idea
  A. Supporting detail
    1. Supporting detail
    2. Supporting detail

A **summary** is a concise restatement of the principal ideas and details of a text (usually prose). You can do a summary in different ways—for example, in paragraph form or in a story map like the following:

Story Map

Basic situation
Setting
Main character
His or her problem
Main events or complications
Climax
Resolution

STUDY SKILLS

USING A DICTIONARY

Use a dictionary to find the precise meaning (**denotation**) and usage of words. The elements of a typical entry are explained below.

1. **Entry word.** The entry word shows how the word is spelled (capitalizing the first letter if required) and divided into syllables.
2. **Pronunciation.** Phonetic symbols, sometimes with diacritical marks above them, show how to pronounce the entry word. Accent marks indicate which syllables are stressed. A key to symbols usually appears on every other page.

3. **Part-of-speech label.** This label classifies the entry word as noun, adjective, adverb, and so forth. When a word can be used as more than one part of speech, definitions are grouped by part of speech. The sample entry shows four definitions for *derive* as a transitive verb (**vt.**) and one as an intransitive verb (**vi.**)
4. **Other forms.** Some dictionaries show the spellings of plural forms of nouns, principal parts of verbs (like **-rived'** and **-riv'ing** in the sample), and comparative and superlative forms of adjectives and adverbs.
5. **Word origin.** A word's **etymology** (et'ə·mäl'ə·jē) shows its linguistic history. According to the sample entry, the word *derive* comes from the Middle English word

T1205

deriven, which in turn comes from the Old French word *deriver*, which itself comes from the Latin word *derivare*, meaning "to divert." *Derivare* was created by adding the prefix *de-*, meaning "from," to the word *rivus*, meaning "stream." The sample entry shows that additional information on etymology appears in the entry for *rival*.

6. **Definitions.** If a word has more than one meaning, the meanings are numbered or lettered.

7. **Special-usage labels.** These labels identify special meanings or special uses of the word. Here, *Chem.* indicates that the fourth definition is a meaning of *derive* used in chemistry.

8. **Synonyms and antonyms. Synonyms** (words similar in meaning) and **antonyms** (words opposite in meaning) may appear at the end of an entry. Here, **—SYN.** RISE tells you that synonyms for *derive* are given in the entry for *rise*.

9. **Related word forms.** Different forms of the entry word are listed. Usually these are created by the addition of suffixes, such as in *derivable*.

Sample Dictionary Entry

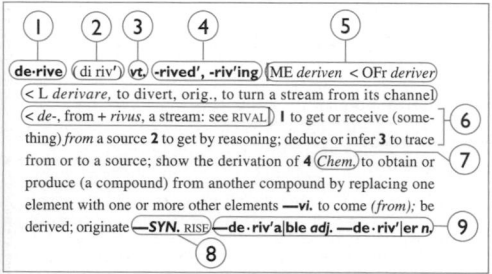

Webster's New World Dictionary of American English, Third College Edition.

USING A THESAURUS

A **thesaurus** is a collection of synonyms. You use a thesaurus to find a word with a specific meaning. There are two basic formats for a thesaurus. The first, developed by Peter Mark Roget (1779–1869), groups words in categories. To use Roget's format, follow these steps:

- In the index, look up the word that expresses the general meaning of the word you are looking for. You may be looking for a synonym of the verb *thin*, for example. Under *thin*, you find the words *dilute, rarefy,* and *weed*.
- Choose the subentry closest to the meaning you have in mind. In this case, suppose you choose *dilute*.
- Note the number that follows the subentry, and find it in the body of the text. There, you will find synonyms of *dilute*.

The second kind of thesaurus presents words in alphabetical order like a dictionary, as in the following example.

Sample Thesaurus Entry

commencement, *n.* **1.** [A beginning] —*Syn.* genesis, start, initiation; see **origin** 1, 2. [Graduation ceremony] —*Syn.* convocation, graduation, commencement exercises, services; see **celebration** 1, 2, **ceremony** 2, **graduation**.

©1997 Webster's New World Thesaurus, Third Edition.

USING STUDY GUIDES

A **study guide** works as a reader's companion by providing help in understanding a text. It can clarify points and stimulate thinking. Study guides often include a biography of the author, critical reaction to the work, and analyses of characters, themes, and other literary elements. Many study guides also include suggestions for further reading and viewing.

A study guide usually examines a text in sections. A play by Eugene O'Neill, for instance, might be examined scene by scene or act by act. Besides giving a summary of the section, a study guide might include commentary, helpful information, and questions to consider.

RECOGNIZING LOGICAL FALLACIES

Writers should argue their points logically in order to convince readers. Sometimes, however, they use incorrect or fallacious reasoning. Be on the lookout for **fallacies.** They appear at first glance to be based on sound reasoning but in fact contain mistakes of logic. Here are six common fallacies; there are many more.

1. **Circular reasoning** or **"begging the question."** The writer restates a point just made as if it were a new conclusion. In the sentence *Alison is lazy because she doesn't like to work,* the clause after *because* just restates the opening clause and doesn't tell you why Alison is lazy. The sentence *Alison is lazy because she enjoys sitting around and daydreaming* gives you a reason for Alison's laziness.

2. **Arguing ad hominem ("to the person").** The writer attacks the person or people presenting the issue rather than dealing logically with the issue itself. In the sentence *People who oppose a lower speed limit don't care about children,* "people" who oppose lower speed limits are attacked—but reasons for lowering the speed limit are not given.

3. **Hasty generalization.** The writer draws a conclusion from insufficient evidence or from exceptional or biased evidence. In the sentence *Today's films are loaded with foul language,* the writer incorrectly categorizes all films, failing to account for the many films that have little or no foul language.

4. **Either-or fallacy** or **false dichotomy.** The writer presents only two alternatives when there are more than two. In the sentence *We have just two choices—either go to the ballgame or sit around the house,* the writer fails to mention additional choices like seeing a movie.
5. **False analogy.** The writer assumes that because two things are alike in some ways, they must be alike in other ways. Notice the false analogy in the sentence *Since player A and player B are the same height and are both fast runners, they must have similar batting averages.* The writer ignores other important reasons for a particular batting average.

6. **False cause.** This fallacy is also known as *post hoc, ergo propter hoc,* meaning "after this, therefore because of this." In this fallacy, the writer argues that because A preceded B, A caused B. For example, *Right after Jim joined the Cardinals as a bench warmer, the team began a ten-game winning streak.* The writer makes a false connection between a winning streak and a player who rarely plays.

(For more on fallacies, see page 1184).

RESEARCH STRATEGIES

When you're looking for information, where should you begin? You might first create a research plan that outlines the topics you want to explore or the questions you want to answer. Then you can begin your search for print and nonprint resources that might be relevant to your plan. When doing research, do not rely solely on one source; instead, consult as many reliable sources as possible. The following research strategies can help you find resources in a library or media center or on a computer linked to the Internet.

USING A LIBRARY OR MEDIA CENTER

Library Catalogs

A library's main resources usually are printed volumes stored on shelves. More and more often, however, libraries (or, as they are sometimes called, media centers) feature holdings stored in electronic form and accessed from a computer terminal or other electronic device. To find information in a library, start by looking in the catalog. Most libraries record their holdings in an **on-line,** or **computer, catalog.**

On-line catalogs vary from library to library. With some, you begin by searching for resources by **title, author,** or **subject.** With others, you simply enter **key words** related to the subject you're researching. With either system, when you enter the relevant information in response to on-screen prompts, a new screen will display a list of materials or subject headings related to your request. When you find an item you want to examine, write down the title, author, and **call number,** the code of numbers and letters that shows you where in the library the item is located.

Some libraries still use **card catalogs.** A card catalog is a collection of index cards containing key information about each library holding. The cards are arranged in alphabetical order

by surname of author, by the first word of title (omitting initial articles), and—for works of nonfiction—by subject.

Other Library Resources

Every library has a **reference section** containing materials you can use only in the library. Reference works include encyclopedias; yearbooks; dictionaries; directories; almanacs; atlases; and **indices,** extensive alphabetical lists (often of books or periodicals). *Books in Print* is a useful index, as is *The Reader's Catalog.* Reference works can appear in electronic or print format. Because many reference books are updated periodically, look for the most recent edition.

Electronic Databases These are large collections of information that you access at a computer terminal. Among the types of information stored on databases are statistics, biographical data, museum holdings, indices, and back issues of magazines.

There are two basic kinds of electronic databases. An **on-line database** is accessed at a computer terminal that is connected to a distant server computer that contains the database. Many computers can access the database at the same time. A **portable database** is available on magnetic tape, disk, CD-ROM, or other electronic medium not connected to a server computer. As a rule, only one person at a time can access the database.

A **CD-ROM** (compact disc–read-only memory) is a portable database stored on a disk that you access via a computer's CD-ROM drive. CD-ROMs can store not only text but also sound, images, and video clips. If you were to look up John Steinbeck in a CD-ROM encyclopedia, you might find a clip from a film version of one of his novels.

Periodicals Most libraries hold a variety of periodicals as well as indices that help you locate information in them. To find up-to-date magazine or newspaper articles on a topic, look in an electronic index such as *InfoTrac, ProQuest,* or *EBSCO.* Some electronic indices provide summaries, or **abstracts,** of articles. Other databases allow you to access the entire text of articles, which you can read on screen or print out. The *Readers' Guide to Periodical Literature* is an excellent index to hundreds of periodicals. Back issues of periodicals may be stored in print form or on **microfilm** (a reel of film), **microfiche** (a sheet of film), CD-ROM, or other information storage-and-retrieval device.

Audiovisual Resources Most libraries hold recordings of actors or authors reading books, videotapes of movies, and CDs and DVDs. These resources are useful when preparing a multimedia project.

USING THE INTERNET

The **Internet,** or **Net,** is a worldwide electronic network that connects millions of personal computers to other personal computers and to server computers containing vast amounts of data, words, and images. On the Net you can find information on almost any topic by accessing libraries, museums, electronic newspapers, government agencies, and many other sources. **E-zines** (often called **zines**) and **e-journals** are periodicals found only on-line. You gain access to the Net via Internet service providers (ISPs). The following are some ways in which the Internet can be used for research.

E-Mail

E-mail is an electronic message sent over a computer network. On the Internet you can use e-mail to contact institutions, businesses, and individuals. This is a quick and inexpensive method of consulting experts (located 1 mile or 10,000 miles away) on a topic you're researching. You can also use e-mail to exchange messages with students around the world.

Electronic Forums

Internet forums, or **newsgroups,** enable you to discuss and debate various subjects. You can post a question in a forum and receive responses from other knowledgeable people. Be careful, however: Responses may be incorrect.

The World Wide Web

The easiest way to conduct Internet research is on the World Wide Web (WWW). On the Web, information is provided on colorful, easy-to-access files called **Web pages.** A Web page may include text, images, sounds, and even video clips.

Using a Web Browser You can view Web pages with a **Web browser,** such as Netscape's *Navigator* or Microsoft's *Internet Explorer.* Every page on the Web has its own address, called a **URL,** or Uniform Resource Locator. If you know the URL of a Web page you want to access, enter it in the *location* field of your browser. See the accompanying illustration.

Web pages are connected by **hyperlinks,** which enable you to quickly reach relevant data by jumping from one page to another. These links are indicated by underlined or colored words or by images on your computer screen. When you click on hyperlink words or images, you are automatically transferred to another Web page.

Using a Web Directory and a Search Engine With many millions of linked Web pages, how do you find the information you want? If you're looking for general information on a topic, go to a **Web directory** (such as Yahoo), a list of topics and subtopics created by experts to help you find an appropriate Web site. A directory is like a book's index. Begin with a broad category, such as Literature. Then, work your way down through the subtopics, from perhaps Native American: Literature to Native American: Authors until you find a Web page that looks promising, such as one on Joy Harjo.

Sample Web-Browser Screen (1998)

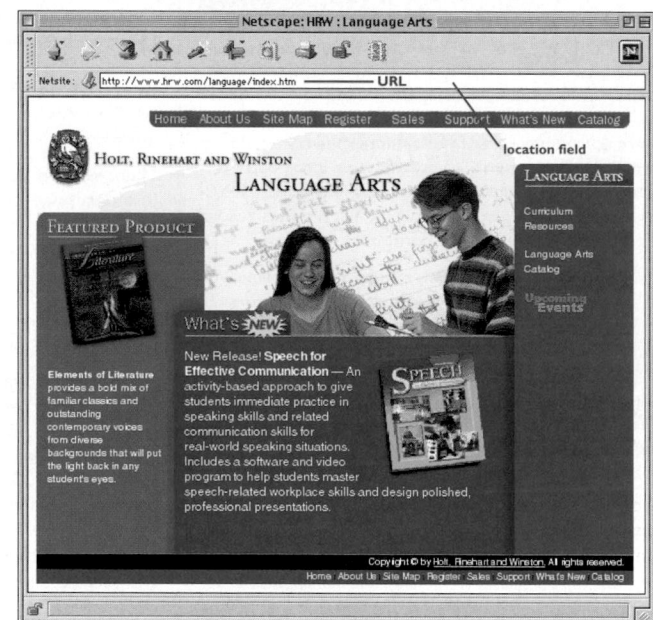

COMMON SEARCH OPERATORS AND WHAT THEY DO	
AND	Demands that both terms appear on the page; narrows search
+	Demands that both terms appear on the page; narrows search
OR	Yields pages that contain either term; widens search
NOT	Excludes a word from consideration; narrows search
–	Excludes a word from consideration; narrows search
NEAR	Demands that two words be in proximity; narrows search
ADJ	Demands that two words be in proximity; narrows search
" "	Demands the exact phrase; narrows search

If you are looking for more specific information, try using a **search engine,** an incredible software tool that indexes millions of Web sites. Some popular search engines are Lycos, AltaVista, and Excite. To use a search engine, enter a **search term,** which is one or more key words. The search engine will then list Web pages that contain your search term along with the first few lines of each page. A search term like the name *Crane* can produce thousands of results, or **hits,** including Web pages dealing with the bird or the heavy equipment. If you're looking for information on the writer Stephen Crane, most hits will be irrelevant. It's important, therefore, to refine, or tailor, your search.

Refining a Key-Word Search   Searches using more than one key word generally provide more focused results. Most search engines allow you to use **search operators** to create a string of key words. Common search operators include the capitalized terms AND, OR, NOT, ADJ (adjacent), and NEAR. Use these operators to focus your search. Here's how the operators work. Let's assume, for example, that you're looking for material on Stephen Crane and his novel *The Red Badge of Courage.* You might use this search term:

Stephen ADJ Crane AND Badge

This search term yields pages that contain the words *Stephen, Crane,* and *badge* but most likely nothing about birds or heavy equipment. Now suppose you want to learn more about Civil War fiction. If your first search turns up words about novels, you can expand your search by using OR:

novels OR stories

Doing a Phrase Search   Exact phrases often produce better results than single words or strings of key words. If you're looking for information on American poetry, for example, a search made with the unlinked key words *American* and *poetry* will yield thousands of pages about Americans and about poetry in general. On the other hand, a search using the exact phrase "American poetry"—signaled by quotation marks—will yield only pages containing that phrase.

Knowing Your Search Engine   Not all search engines operate in the same way. Some have rules about using uppercase and lowercase letters. Some require a plus sign or minus sign between key words, rather than the operator AND or NOT. Some require that you enter exact phrases within quotation marks. Some provide a list of options that enable you to search by exact phrases, individual words, and so on. Because the rules governing search engines differ, read the online Help information before you begin a search.

EVALUATING AND CITING SOURCES

Before you begin taking notes from any source—print or electronic or an interviewee—be sure your source provides information that is current, accurate, and free of strong bias. Evaluate both primary and secondary sources. **Primary** sources, or firsthand accounts, include letters, autobiographies, diaries, historical documents, and interviews. **Secondary sources,** which are derived from primary sources, include encyclopedias, documentary films, biographies, and historical books. To evaluate the usefulness of a source, use this 4R test.

1. **Relevant**   The source must have information *directly* related to your topic. To find out if a book is relevant, you can check its table of contents and index. For some books and for articles, skimming can help. *Book Review Digest* offers, for selected titles, useful summaries and review excerpts; videotapes and audiotapes sometimes provide written summaries of their content; and periodical indices may include summaries of articles.
2. **Reliable**   The source must be accurate. A periodical whose reputation depends on accuracy, such as *Smithsonian* or *National Geographic,* or a well-regarded authority, such as a scholar, generally can be counted on to fact-check rigorously before publication. If in doubt about the reliability of a source, consult an expert, such as a teacher or librarian.
3. **Recent**   For most topics, use sources that are as current as possible. Ongoing research findings can change perceptions, generalizations, and opinions. For example, the discovery of a poet's childhood illness can lead to a new interpretation of her or his poems about childhood. Often, long-ago political events are reinterpreted in light of newly discovered information.
4. **Representative**   If there are opposing viewpoints on your topic, you should consult sources that provide a variety of interpretations. If one interpretation is strongly favored, you should also consult another source with a different slant.

TAKING NOTES AND DOCUMENTING SOURCES

If you use another person's words or ideas without giving credit, you are **plagiarizing,** which is a serious offense. Avoid plagiarizing by acknowledging in your work the source of each quotation, paraphrase, statistic, figure, and idea that you found through research. Careful documentation starts with accurate source cards and notes.

Preparing Source Cards

As you gather information, you can save time and ensure accurate documentation by preparing source cards in the format needed for your report's **sources cited** list (see page 1213). Put each source on a 3-inch × 5-inch card, or record it in a computer file. Follow these guidelines:

1. **Assign each source a different number.**   When taking notes, it will save time to write the number rather than the author and title. Place the number at the top right of the card or computer entry.

2. **Record full publication data.** Data include subtitles, translators, and volume and edition numbers. Use a shortened form of the publisher's name, deleting initial articles and the type of business organization.
3. **Note the call number or location.** This information will help you reaccess the source quickly.

Sample Source Card

3

Williams, Tennessee. <u>Memoirs</u>.
Garden City, New York:
Doubleday, 1975.

Central Performing Arts Library

Taking Notes

After evaluating your sources and preparing source cards, you are ready to read carefully and take notes. Use the following guidelines to prepare note cards that will be easy to use when writing your paper.

GUIDELINES FOR TAKING NOTES

1. Use a 4-inch × 6-inch note card, a half sheet of paper, or a separate computer file. Never put notes from more than one source on the same card or sheet of paper or in the same electronic file.
2. In the upper right, write the number you have assigned to the source.
3. In the upper left, use a word or phrase to identify the topic or main idea.
4. In the lower right, note the page numbers from which the information is taken.
5. Reread the note to be sure it is accurate.

Your notes may be direct quotations, summaries, or paraphrases. A **direct quotation** contains the author's exact words. When quoting directly, copy the statement word for word—including punctuation, capitalization, and spelling—and enclose the passage in quotation marks. A **summary** condenses the author's ideas and facts in your own words. A **paraphrase** restates information in your own words. To summarize or paraphrase, use lists and phrases instead of complete sentences.

Using Quotations

Relevant, interesting quotations add authority and punch to your research paper. The following chart describes several ways to use quotations effectively.

GUIDELINES FOR USING QUOTATIONS

- **Quote a whole sentence, introducing it in your own words.**

  EXAMPLE Williams and Mead describe the author's year at the University of Iowa as very productive. "Tom's preoccupation at Iowa must have been work, and huge amounts of it" (69).

- **Quote part of a sentence within a sentence of your own.**

  EXAMPLE According to his mother, Tennessee Williams changed his name because "Thomas Lanier Williams reminded him of bad poetry" (Williams and Mead 71).

- **Quote just one or a few words within a sentence of your own.**

  EXAMPLE Williams gathered material for dialogue, collecting "colorful idioms of speech" at beaches and hotels (Williams and Mead 71).

- **Use an ellipsis (. . .) to indicate omissions from quotations.** Sometimes you need only a part of a quotation to make your point. Insert an ellipsis where words have been deleted.

  EXAMPLE According to Patricia C. Click, Williams used "glass as an important symbol of impermanence . . . to imply that nothing lasts" (43).

- **Set off longer quotations as extract blocks.** If a quotation will be more than four typed lines, start a new line and indent the entire quotation ten spaces from the left. Double-space, and do not use quotation marks.

Formatting Electronic-Source Citations

Writing electronic-source citations for a list of sources cited can be difficult. On-line sources often change, and many do not provide all the information required. For instance, many Web pages don't identify an author. In such cases, include in your citation whatever relevant information is available.

The format for citing electronic sources depends on (1) whether the source is on-line or portable and (2) whether the source has an identical print version or stands alone.

Listed below are the elements required for the citation of various kinds of electronic sources—in the order in which they should appear. Most elements likely to be included are listed, but many actual citations will not include all possible elements. (Note: If a URL runs onto a second line, divide the address immediately *after* a slash mark or *before* a dot. Never use a hyphen to divide a URL.)

Source from a Computer Network, such as the World Wide Web, with an Identical Print Version

- author's last name, then first name
- title of poem, short story, essay, document, or similar short work, set off by quotation marks
- title of book or periodical, underlined
- name of editor of book, preceded by *Ed.*
- publication data for print version
- title of scholarly project, database, or professional or personal site, underlined; or, for a professional or personal site with no title, a description such as *Home page*
- volume or issue number
- number range, or total number, of any numbered pages or paragraphs
- date of electronic publication or latest revision
- name of any sponsoring institution
- date you accessed the information
- full URL, in angle brackets

EXAMPLE Crane, Stephen. The Red Badge of Courage. New York: Appleton, 1895. Hypertexts. 1 Jan. 1998. U of Virginia. 27 Feb. 1998 <http://xroads.virginia.edu/~HYPER/CRANE/badge.html>.

Source from a Computer Network, such as the World Wide Web, with No Print Version

- author's last name, then first name
- title of poem, short story, essay, document, or similar short work, set off by quotation marks.
- title of scholarly project, database, periodical, or professional or personal site, underlined; or, for a professional or personal site with no title, a description such as *Home page.*
- name of editor of complete work or database, preceded by *Ed.*
- publication date or date of last revision
- number range or total number of any numbered sections
- name of any sponsoring organization
- volume, issue, or version number
- date you accessed the information
- the full URL, in angle brackets

EXAMPLE "Arthur Miller." The Kennedy Center Honors. 1998. The Kennedy Center. 26 Apr. 1998 http://kennedy-center.org/honors/1984/miller.html>.

CD-ROM with a Print Version

- author's last name, then first name
- title of document or article, set off by quotation marks
- title of print version, underlined
- publication data for print version
- database title, underlined
- edition, release, or version number
- publication medium (CD-ROM)
- city of publication
- name of publisher of electronic version
- date of electronic publication

> EXAMPLE   Miller, Arthur. <u>The Crucible.</u> New York: Bantam, 1959. <u>The Crucible.</u> CD-ROM. New York: Penguin, 1996.

CD-ROM with No Print Version

Omit the print information called for above.

> EXAMPLE   "American Renaissance." <u>The History of American Literature.</u> CD-ROM. Chicago: CLEARVUE/eav, 1995.

Citing Sources

Parenthetical Citations   A short **parenthetical citation** gives source information in parentheses in the body of the text. It contains just enough information to lead a reader to the correct full entry in the sources cited list. Parenthetical citations include the author's last name and a page number, with these exceptions:

- a nonprint source such as an interview (Use name only.)
- a print source of only one page (Use name only.)
- a sentence that includes the author's name (Use page number only. See the first and fourth bulleted items in Guidelines for Using Quotations, page 1211.)
- an author with more than one entry on your list of sources cited (Add year of publication—for example: Roberts 1992, 65.)

For more information on specific kinds of parenthetical citations, see the chart below or the most recent edition of the Modern Language Association's *MLA Handbook for Writers of Research Papers.*

PARENTHETICAL CITATIONS

Works by One Author

Author's last name and page(s): (Click 43–44)

Works by More Than One Author

All authors' last names (or first author and *et al.* if more than three) and page(s): (Williams and Mead 71)

Multivolume Works

Author's last name, volume number, and page(s): (Morison 1:175)

Works with No Author Listed on Title Page

Full title (or a shortened version) and page(s): (<u>Merriam-Webster's Biographical Dictionary</u> 1061)

Literary Works Published in Several Editions

Full title and any information that would help readers find the quotation in any edition, such as chapter number or act, scene, and line numbers: (<u>The Crucible</u> 1)

Indirect Sources

Qtd. in ("quoted in") before the source and page(s): (qtd. in Click 43)

More Than One Source in the Same Citation

Relevant information for each source, separated by a semicolon: (Click 43; Williams and Mead 71)

Use the following guidelines for correctly placing parenthetical citations.

Placement of Citations

- Place the citation as close as possible to the material it documents. If possible, place it at the end of a sentence.
- Place a citation after closing quotation marks and before the end punctuation mark.
- For an extensive quotation, set as an extract block (see Guidelines for Using Quotations, page 1211), place the citation *two spaces after* the final punctuation mark.

LIST OF SOURCES CITED

The **sources cited** list, which you should include at the end of your report, contains all the sources, print and nonprint, that you credit in your paper. Other names for this list are *Bibliography* and *Works* or *Literature Cited,* but they are only appropriate if your sources are limited to books and articles.

Formatting To prepare the sources cited list, center the words *Sources Cited* on a blank sheet of paper one inch from the top of the page. Double-space between "Sources Cited" and the first entry, and between all subsequent entries. Double-space within entries as well. Begin each entry on a new line, even with the left margin. If an entry runs more than one line, indent the subsequent line or lines in the entry five spaces.

As a general rule, alphabetize your sources by the author's last name. If there is no author (or editor), alphabetize by title, ignoring *A, An,* and *The* as the first word of the title. For example, *The Cambridge History of the Native Peoples of the Americas* would appear under *C* rather than *T.*

Publication Information When providing publication information, use shortened forms of publishers' names, unless this would lead to confusion. Abbreviate U.S. state names and months of the year (except May, June, and July).

Page Numbers You should include page numbers only for articles in periodicals or for other works that are part of a whole work, such as one essay in a book of essays. However, page and volume numbers aren't needed if entries are alphabetized, as in an encyclopedia.

SOURCES CITED: SAMPLE ENTRIES	
STANDARD REFERENCE WORKS	
Encyclopedia	"Miller, Arthur." Encyclopædia Britannica: Micropædia. 15th ed. 1997.
Biographical Reference	"Williams, Tennessee." Merriam-Webster's Biographical Dictionary. 1995 ed.
BOOKS	
Book with One Author	Miller, Arthur. Focus. New York: Reynal, 1945.
Book with Two or More Authors	Williams, Dakin, and Shepherd Mead. Tennessee Williams: An Intimate Biography. New York: Arbor, 1983.
Book with No Author Listed	American Statistics Index. Washington: Congressional Information Service, 1992.
Book with One Editor	Siebold, Thomas, ed. Readings on Arthur Miller. San Diego: Greenhaven, 1997.
Book with Two or More Editors	Block, Haskell, and Robert G. Shedd, eds. Masters of Modern Drama. New York: Random, 1962.
Translation	Williams, Tennessee. Pethe brau. Trans. Emyr Edwards. Llandysul, Wales: Gwasg, 1963. Trans. of The Glass Menagerie. New York: Random, 1945.

SELECTIONS FROM BOOKS	
Selection from Book of Works by One Author	Gould, Jean R. "Arthur Miller." Modern American Playwrights. New York: Dodd, 1966. 247–263.
Selection from Book of Works by Several Authors	Beaurline, Lester A. "The Director, the Script, and Author's Revisions: A Critical Problem." Papers in Dramatic Theory and Criticism. Ed. David M. Knauf. Iowa City: U of Iowa, 1969. 78–91.
Selection from Collection of Longer Works	Wilder, Thornton. Our Town. Three Plays. New York: Avon, 1957. 1–64.
ARTICLES FROM MAGAZINES, NEWSPAPERS, AND JOURNALS	
Weekly Magazine Article	Miller, Arthur. "Why I Wrote The Crucible." The New Yorker 21 Oct. 1996: 158–160.
Monthly or Quarterly Magazine Article	Berkvist, Robert. "The Big Daddy of Playwrights." After Dark Oct. 1981: 52–53.
Article with No Author Shown	"Tennessee Williams." Life Fall 1990: 78–79.
Daily Newspaper Article, with Byline	Kaufman, Sarah. "A Well-Forged Crucible." Washington Post 15 Nov. 1997: C3.
Daily Newspaper Article, No Byline	"Ever Earnest and Funny, Ever Relevant to Youth." The New York Times 7 Sept. 1997: B8.
Unsigned Daily Newspaper Editorial, No City in Title	"The Last Hurrah." Editorial. Star Ledger [Newark, NJ] 29 Aug. 1991: 30.
Scholarly Journal	Click, Patricia C. "The Uncertain Universe of The Glass Menagerie: The Influence of the New Physics on Tennessee Williams." Journal of American Culture 12 (1989): 41–45.
OTHER SOURCES	
Personal Interview	Wilson, August. Personal interview. 7 Jan. 1987.
Telephone Interview	Miller, Arthur. Telephone interview. 8 Oct. 1990.
Published Interview	Williams, Tennessee. Interview. More Memoirs of an Aesthete. Ed. Harold Acton. London: Methuen. 1970.
Radio or Television Interview	Halberstam, David. Interview. Book Notes. C-SPAN, Washington, DC. 1 July 1993.
Thesis or Dissertation	Fisher, Kerk. "The Front Porch in Modern American Drama: The Promise of Mobility in O'Neill, Williams, and Inge." Diss. U of Georgia, 1989.
Cartoon	Frascino, Edward. Cartoon. The New Yorker 2 Sept. 1991: 46.
Speech or Lecture	Browne, Sally. "Three American Playwrights: Wilder, Miller, and Hansberry." Bookbuilders. Lake Worth, FL. 26 Feb. 1998.
Recording	Robeson, Paul. "Going Home." Rec. 9 May 1958. Live at Carnegie Hall—1958. Vanguard, 1986.
Film or Filmstrip	A Streetcar Named Desire. Dir. John Erman. Perf. Ann-Margret, Treat Williams, Beverly D'Angelo, and Randy Quaid. Worldvision Enterprises, 1983.
Videotape	The Crucible. Dir. Raymond Rouleau. Perf. Simone Signoret, Yves Montand. 1957. Videocassette. Hen's Tooth Video, 1995.

WRITING FOR LIFE

The writing you do now prepares you for the writing you will do in college and in your career. Your ability to write clear and effective memos, business letters, and résumés will be a major factor in your success as a professional. As a student, you will write letters of application for admission to colleges and universities, and you will write résumés to apply for jobs at various companies and organizations. As an employee, you will write interoffice memoranda, or memos, and business letters communicating pertinent information.

When composing documents that others will read, follow the steps listed below. (Note: Computers and software programs make the writing process more efficient.)

- **Prewriting**   Make notes about the key points you want to include in your document, and how to present them.
- **Writing a Draft**   Compose a first draft, or version, of the document.
- **Evaluating and Revising**   Evaluate your draft closely, correcting any errors of spelling, grammar, and punctuation. Review the presentation of information and ideas for clarity and readability, and revise as necessary. Delete repetitive or irrelevant material.
- **Preparing the Final Version**   Fine-tune the revised draft as necessary to prepare a final version. Make sure you proofread the document.

WRITING INTEROFFICE MEMOS

In the business world, writing is structured and functional. One standard form of communication within a company or organization is the **memo** (or memorandum). Memos are concise messages that tell the reader *when, who, what, where, why,* and *how.* Memos contain guide words (*DATE, TO, FROM, SUBJECT*) that immediately identify the date, destination, origin, and purpose of a message. Memos generally cover only one of the following categories.

- **Meeting Notices**   Include the meeting date, time, place, purpose, and any other significant information that relates to the meeting, such as the agenda or the guests who will be attending.
- **Meeting Summaries**   Provide a brief, factual report of discussions and decisions. Include the names and titles of individuals involved.
- **Requests for Action or Information**   Open by making the request, and then follow with details. If you have several requests, list them, phrasing each one similarly. Include a deadline stating when you need a response.

WRITING EFFECTIVE BUSINESS LETTERS

Another essential form of business writing is the business letter. Whether you're writing to request information, make an offer, or register a complaint, your business letters can make a lasting impression on readers. If errors and inaccuracies or a sloppy appearance distract readers from the contents of a letter, you risk giving an impression of inefficiency or even incompetence. Keep these rules in mind:

1. Use formal, standard English.
2. Be clear.
3. Use the correct format.

Types of Business Letters

Request and Order Letters   You write a **request letter** to ask for information about a job, college, product, service, policy, or procedure. You write an **order letter** to order merchandise. When writing a request or order letter, include all important details relating to time, location, size, style, cost, and so on.

Complaint or Adjustment Letters   You write a **complaint** or **adjustment letter** when you are dissatisfied with a person, product, or service. Your letter should explain exactly what is wrong and should request a satisfactory resolution of the problem, such as a replacement of merchandise or a refund of your money. Keep the tone of your letter calm and courteous.

Letters of Application   A **letter of application** introduces you to a selection committee or a potential employer. The letter should provide the reader with enough information to determine whether you are a good candidate for a job, scholarship, college, or university. Keep the following points in mind when writing a letter of application.

1. Identify the job or situation for which you are applying, and mention how you heard about it.
2. Depending on the situation, include

   - your age, grade in school, and grade point average
   - your experience, activities, awards, and honors
   - the personal qualities that make you a good choice
   - the dates or times you are available

3. Provide references—names of two or three responsible adults, other than relatives, who agree to recommend you. Include their addresses and telephone numbers.

COMMUNICATIONS HANDBOOK   1215

Sample Letter of Application, Block Style

Heading
Your address, including city, state, and ZIP code. Your e-mail address. Date you write the letter

Inside Address
Name, title, and address of person you are writing to. Use a title (*Mr., Ms., Mrs., Dr., Esq.,* etc.) with the person's name, and put his or her business title after the name.

Salutation (greeting)
Use *Dear* followed by the person's title and last name and a colon. If the letter isn't addressed to a specific person, use a business title.

Body
Your message. If the body contains more than one paragraph, leave a blank line between paragraphs. Don't indent paragraph starts.

Closing
Use *Yours truly* or *Sincerely yours* followed by a comma.

Signature
Type or print your name, leaving space for your signature. Sign your name in ink.

Use "Enclosure" if you're including something with your letter.

1632 Garden View Drive
Anytown, PA 12345
mmanrique@ISP.com

September 23, 2000

Mr. John Lao
Director of Human Resources
XYZ Insurance Company
10 Central Avenue
Anytown, PA 12346

Dear Mr. Lao:

Are you looking for someone who carries out assignments efficiently and enjoys working with people? I have these qualities and other important business skills to bring to the position of administrative assistant you advertised in Sunday's <u>Herald</u>.

I am a 17-year-old junior at Jefferson High School and have completed courses in business English, word processing, and accounting. I can word-process at a rate of 50 words per minute while transcribing from recordings.

This past summer, as a receptionist at QRS Supply Company, I did filing and billing in addition to my regular duties. I feel at home in an office setting and enjoy taking on responsibility.

My résumé, which is enclosed, lists references who can tell you about my business skills and my personal strengths.

I believe that my background qualifies me for the position of administrative assistant. Please contact me by telephone at 555-1234 or by e-mail at mmanrique@ISP.com to set up an interview.

Yours truly,

Marisol Manrique

Marisol Manrique

Enclosure

WRITING A PERSONAL RÉSUMÉ

Your **résumé** (or **curriculum vitae** [CV]) summarizes who you are, what you have learned, and what you have accomplished. The information in your résumé should include skills and achievements that give a potential employer a positive overview of your qualifications. When you apply for a job, you usually include your résumé with your letter of application to potential employers.

The structure, organization, and overall appearance of your résumé will give the reader an impression of you and your abilities. Print out or type your résumé on white or ivory paper. Proofread it carefully, making sure there are no factual or typographical errors, erasures, correction fluid, or stray marks. Your goal is to get an interview. Try your best to make a good first impression.

The following **model résumé** is written in reverse chronological order; it lists the most recent work experience first.

MARISOL MANRIQUE

1632 Garden View Drive
Anytown, PA 12345
Telephone: (215) 555-1234
E-mail: mmanrique@ISP.com

EDUCATION:
Junior, Jefferson High School
Major studies: Business and foreign language courses
Grade point average: 3.0 (B)

WORK EXPERIENCE:

Summer 2000
Receptionist
QRS Supply Company
Anytown, PA

Summer 1998
Volunteer Office Worker
YWCA
Anytown, PA

SKILLS:

Word processing: 50 wpm

Business machines: Dictating, calculating, and copying machines; personal computers

Other languages: Spanish (fluent)

EXTRACURRICULAR
ACTIVITIES:
Vice president, Future Business Leaders of America
Member, Spanish Club

REFERENCES:

Dr. Robert Robertson, Principal   (215) 555-6789
Jefferson High School
Anytown, PA

Ms. Mary Jackson, English Teacher   (215) 555-4567
Jefferson High School
Anytown, PA

Mr. Juan Ramos, Owner   (215) 555-3456
QRS Supply Company
Anytown, PA

COLLEGE ADMISSIONS

To apply to a college, you will have to complete an application. Most applications have two parts: the form and the essay.

Completing the College Application Form

Application forms usually ask for basic information about you: name, address, birth date, grade point average, extracurricular activities, and the educational background and occupations of your parents. Many colleges have adopted the Common Application form so that you need fill this form out only once and send it to all the schools you are applying to. The form can be downloaded from the Internet. It can also be sent by e-mail to many colleges. (Note: Some schools also require their own forms instead of or in addition to the Common Application form.)

Be sure to ask your high school to send a copy of your **transcript** to the colleges you apply to. A transcript lists all the courses you have taken in high school and the grades you earned.

Writing the Admission Essay

Most colleges and universities ask for an admission essay because it tells them things about you that can't be gleaned from bare facts. An essay reveals how you approach a question, how you think, what is important to you, and how well your education and experience have prepared you to express yourself verbally.

Consider these points as you prepare to write your admissions essay:

1. Read the question carefully. Be sure you are answering what is asked.
2. Be yourself. Admissions staff ask for the essay because they want to get to know you. The essay is an opportunity to introduce yourself to the admissions staff—to tell them what you think is really important about yourself, to express opinions about serious issues, to amuse them with your sense of humor, or, in some other way, to present yourself as a person and not a number. Write about something important to you. Your conviction will come across to the reader. Don't worry about what the reader might expect from you—say something you really want to say.
3. Be neat. Write as many drafts as necessary. Fine-tune until your essay is the best you can make it. Then, check the revised draft carefully for any errors in spelling, grammar, and usage before you produce the final version.

PROOFREADING

Proofreading refines the mechanics of your writing. A dictionary and a style book will serve as helpful reference tools when you proofread. As you review your writing, you might find this list of questions helpful: (1) Are all words spelled correctly? (2) Do subjects and verbs agree? (3) Do pronouns agree with their antecedents? (4) Are verb tenses consistent? (5) Are all proper nouns capitalized? (6) Are sentence fragments eliminated? (7) Are all punctuation marks appropriate?

As you proofread your work, use these standard proofreaders' marks:

PROOFREADERS' MARKS

Symbol	Example	Meaning
≡	Twenty-second street	Capitalize lowercase letter.
/	Sarah's Uncle	Lowercase capital letter.
∧	the capital Maine (of)	Insert.
ℯ	What's the the point?	Delete.
∧∨	a heavy back pack	Close up space.
∿	traegdy	Change order (of letters or words). Transpose.
¶	¶"Help," he yelled.	Begin new paragraph.
⊙	Stay calm	Add period.
∧	Of course you may be wrong.	Add comma.

ANSWERING ESSAY QUESTIONS

Essay tests require you to think critically and to clearly express your understanding of a topic. Your answers to essay questions must be well-organized and include details to support your generalizations. A well-written answer must contain a complete response to a question.

Scan the questions on the test before you start writing. If you have a choice of questions, identify the ones you can answer best. Budget your time so you can give adequate attention to each question. These steps will help you better answer essay questions.

1. Read each essay question carefully, and notice whether a question has several parts.
2. Identify the important terms in the questions. Find the key verbs, and identify the tasks you must accomplish. Identify how much evidence is required for an adequate treatment.
3. Take a few minutes to prewrite. Make notes or a simple outline on scratch paper, organize your material logically, and write a thesis statement. Write one paragraph for each point you wish to make, and end with a paragraph that summarizes or restates your main points.
4. Evaluate and revise as you write. Watch for spelling and grammatical errors. You will not have time to redraft the entire essay, but you can edit to strengthen specific parts. Keep your paper neat.

Essay questions usually ask you to perform specific tasks expressed by the verb in the question. The following chart lists the task required by some key verbs.

ESSAY TEST QUESTIONS

KEY VERB	TASK	SAMPLE QUESTION
analyze	Take something apart to see how it creates meaning.	Analyze the plot of "The Magic Barrel."
argue	Take a stand on an issue, and give reasons supporting your opinion.	Argue whether your school should require students to wear a uniform.
compare/contrast	Discuss likenesses/differences.	Compare and contrast Hawkeye in Cooper's novel *The Last of the Mohicans* with Hawkeye in the 1992 movie of the same name.
define	Give specific details that make something unique.	Define the term *modernism* as it relates to literature.
demonstrate (also **illustrate, present, show**)	Provide examples to support a point.	Demonstrate T. S. Eliot's use of symbolism in his poetry.
discuss	Examine in detail.	Discuss the elements of realism in Tennessee Williams's *The Glass Menagerie*.
explain	Clarify, expound on, or give reasons for or a cause of something.	Explain why setting is important in "To Build a Fire."
interpret	Discuss or explain the meaning or significance of something.	Interpret the symbolism of wilderness in Wallace Stevens's "Anecdote of the Jar."
list (also **outline, trace**)	Give all steps (in order) or all details about a subject.	List the events that lead to the death of Willy Loman in *Death of a Salesman*.
summarize	Give a brief overview of the main points.	Summarize the plot of Amy Tan's *The Joy Luck Club*.

Resources

- *Language Handbook Resources,* pp. 1–4
- *Language Workshop CD-ROM,* Chapter 1: Parts of Speech

1 THE PARTS OF SPEECH

PART OF SPEECH	DEFINITION	EXAMPLES
NOUN	Names person, place, thing, or idea	poet, Sylvia Plath, city, Chicago, awards, Nobel Prize, *Of Mice and Men,* books, crew, herd, Harlem Renaissance, realism
PRONOUN	Takes place of one or more nouns or pronouns	
Personal	Refers to one(s) speaking (first person), spoken to (second person), spoken about (third person)	I, me, my, mine, we, us, our, ours you, your, yours he, him, his, she, her, hers, it, its, they, them, their, theirs
Reflexive	Refers to subject and directs action of verb back to subject	myself, ourselves, yourself, yourselves, himself, herself, itself, themselves
Intensive	Refers to and emphasizes noun or another pronoun	(same as examples for Reflexive)
Demonstrative	Refers to specific one(s) of group	this, that, these, those
Interrogative	Introduces question	what, which, who, whom, whose
Relative	Introduces subordinate clause	that, which, who, whom, whose
Indefinite	Refers to one(s) not specifically named	all, any, anyone, both, each, either, everybody, many, none, nothing, someone
ADJECTIVE	Modifies noun or pronoun by telling *what kind, which one, how many,* or *how much*	**a large black** box, **an able-bodied** worker, **that** one, **the five Iroquois** nations, **enough** time, **less** money, **many** choices
VERB	Shows action or state of being	
Action	Expresses physical or mental activity	write, receive, run, think, imagine, understand
Linking	Connects subject with word identifying or describing it	appear, be, seem, become, feel, look, smell, sound, taste
Helping (Auxiliary)	Assists another verb to express time, voice, or mood	be, have, may, can, shall, will, would
ADVERB	Modifies verb, adjective, or adverb by telling *how, when, where,* or *to what extent*	speaks **clearly, quite** interesting, **rather** calmly, arrived **there late**
PREPOSITION	Relates noun or pronoun to another word	about, at, by, for, of, in, on, through, according to, in front of, out of

(continued)

PART OF SPEECH	DEFINITION	EXAMPLES
CONJUNCTION	Joins words or word groups	
Coordinating	Joins words or word groups used in same way	and, but, for, nor, or, so, yet
Correlative	A pair of conjunctions that joins parallel words or word groups	both . . . and, not only . . . but (also), either . . . or, neither . . . nor
Subordinating	Begins subordinate clause and connects it to independent clause	although, as if, because, since, so that, unless, when, where, while
INTERJECTION	Expresses emotion	hey, oh, ouch, wow, well, hooray

2 AGREEMENT

AGREEMENT OF SUBJECT AND VERB

2a. **A verb should agree in number with its subject. Singular subjects take singular verbs. Plural subjects take plural verbs.**

SINGULAR   The **character lives** on a farm in Yoknapatawpha County.

PLURAL   **Both** of the stories **were written** by William Faulkner.

2b. **The number of the subject is not changed by a phrase or a clause following the subject.**

SINGULAR   **Langston Hughes,** who wrote several books of poetry, **was** a major figure in the Harlem Renaissance.

PLURAL   **The students,** as well as Ms. Ramos, **are** eager to use the new software.

2c. **Indefinite pronouns may be singular, plural, or either.**

(1) The following indefinite pronouns are singular: *anybody, anyone, anything, each, either, one, everybody, everyone, everything, neither, nobody, no one, nothing, somebody, someone,* and *something.*

EXAMPLE
Neither of the books **contains** that story.

(2) The following indefinite pronouns are plural: *both, few, many,* and *several.*

EXAMPLE
Both of the poems **were written** by Claude McKay.

(3) The indefinite pronouns *all, any, most, none,* and *some* are singular when they refer to singular words and are plural when they refer to plural words.

SINGULAR   **Some** of her artwork **is** beautiful.
    [*Some* refers to *artwork.*]

PLURAL   **Some** of her paintings **are** beautiful.
    [*Some* refers to *paintings.*]

2d. **A *compound subject,* which is two or more subjects that have the same verb, may be singular or plural.**

(1) Subjects joined by *and* usually take a plural verb.

EXAMPLE
Hemingway, Steinbeck, and Morrison are Nobel Prize winners.

A compound subject that names only one person or thing takes a singular verb.

EXAMPLE
Roderick Usher's **sister and** sole **companion is** Madeline.

(2) Singular subjects joined by *or* or *nor* take a singular verb.

EXAMPLES
Either Amy or Eric plans to report on William Byrd.
Neither the **rain nor** the **wind has stopped**.

(3) When a singular subject and a plural subject are joined by *or* or *nor*, the verb agrees with the subject nearer the verb.

EXAMPLE
Neither the **performers nor** the **director was** eager to rehearse.

Resources
- *Language Handbook Resources, pp. 5–14*
- *Language Workshop CD-ROM, Chapter 2: Agreement*

NOTE Whenever possible, revise the sentence to avoid this awkward construction.

EXAMPLE

The **director was** not eager to rehearse the scene again, and neither **were** the **performers**.

2e. The verb agrees with its subject even when the verb precedes the subject, such as in sentences beginning with *here, there,* or *where.*

EXAMPLES

Here **is** [*or* here's] a **copy** of the Declaration of Independence.
Here **are** [*not* here's] two **copies** of the Declaration of Independence.

2f. A *collective noun* (such as *class, herd,* or *jury*) is singular in form but names a group of persons or things. A collective noun takes a singular verb when the noun refers to the group as a unit and takes a plural verb when the noun refers to the parts or members of the group.

SINGULAR	The **cast** of *A Raisin in the Sun* **is made** up entirely of juniors. [The cast as a unit is made up of juniors.]
PLURAL	After the play, the **cast are joining** their families for a celebration. [The members of the cast are joining their families.]

2g. An expression of an amount (a length of time, a statistic, or a fraction, for example) is singular when the amount is thought of as a unit or when it refers to a singular word. An amount is plural when it is thought of as many parts or when it refers to a plural word.

SINGULAR	**Twenty years was** a long time for Rip Van Winkle to sleep. [one unit]
PLURAL	**Fifty percent** of the students **have** already **read** *Walden.* [The percentage refers to *students.*]

Expressions of measurement (length, weight, capacity, area) are usually singular.

EXAMPLES

Seventy-five degrees below zero was the air temperature in "To Build a Fire."
Four and a half miles was how far the man walked in an hour.

2h. The title of a creative work (such as a book, song, film, or painting) or the name of an organization, a country, or a city (even if the name is plural in form) takes a singular verb.

EXAMPLES

"**Birches**" **was written** by Robert Frost.
The **United States calls** its flag Old Glory.

2i. A verb agrees with its subject, not with its predicate nominative.

SINGULAR	One **symptom** of flu **is** sore muscles.
PLURAL	Sore **muscles are** one symptom of flu.

AGREEMENT OF PRONOUN AND ANTECEDENT

A pronoun usually refers to a noun or another pronoun. The word to which a pronoun refers is called its *antecedent.*

2j. A pronoun agrees with its antecedent in number and gender. Singular pronouns refer to singular antecedents. Plural pronouns refer to plural antecedents. A few singular pronouns indicate gender (neuter, feminine, masculine).

EXAMPLES

Marianne Moore published **her** first book of poems in 1921. [singular, feminine]
Peyton Farquhar thinks **he** has escaped. [singular, masculine]
Benjamin Franklin wrote, "**Three** may keep a secret if two of **them** are dead." [plural]

2k. Indefinite pronouns may be singular, plural, or either.

(1) Singular pronouns are used to refer to the indefinite pronouns *anybody, anyone, anything, each, either, everybody, everyone, everything, neither, nobody, no one, nothing, one, somebody, someone,* and *something.* The gender of any of these pronouns is often determined by a word in a phrase following the pronoun.

EXAMPLES

Each of the **girls** has already memorized **her** part.
One of the **boys** gave **his** interpretation of "Nothing Gold Can Stay."

If the antecedent may be either masculine or feminine, use both the masculine and feminine pronouns to refer to it.

EXAMPLE

Anyone who is qualified for the job may submit **his** or **her** application.

NOTE Whenever possible, revise the sentence to avoid this awkward construction.

EXAMPLE

Anyone who is qualified for the job may submit an application.

(2) Plural pronouns are used to refer to the indefinite pronouns *both, few, many,* and *several.*

EXAMPLE

Both of the finalists played **their** best.

(3) Singular or plural pronouns may be used to refer to the indefinite pronouns *all, any, most, none,* and *some.* These indefinite pronouns are singular when they refer to singular words and are plural when they refer to plural words.

SINGULAR	**All** of our **planning** achieved **its** purpose.
PLURAL	**All** of your **suggestions** had **their** good points.

2l. **A plural pronoun is used to refer to two or more singular antecedents joined by *and.***

EXAMPLE

Jerry and Francesca read the sonnets **they** wrote about Olaudah Equiano.

2m. **A singular pronoun is used to refer to two or more singular antecedents joined by *or* or *nor.***

EXAMPLE

Neither **Cindy nor Carla** thinks **she** is ready to write the final draft.

2n. **When a singular and a plural antecedent are joined by *or* or *nor,* the pronoun agrees with the nearer antecedent.**

EXAMPLE

Either **Jerry or** the **twins** will bring **their** stereo.

TIPS FOR WRITERS

Revising Misleading Sentences

Sentences with antecedents joined by *or* or *nor* can be misleading when the antecedents are of different genders or numbers. Revise the sentences to avoid such constructions.

MISLEADING	Either Christopher or Tiffany will give her report on Transcendentalism. [The sentence suggests that Christopher may give Tiffany's report.]
REVISED	Either **Christopher** will give **his** report on Transcendentalism, or **Tiffany** will give **hers.**

2o. **A collective noun (such as *audience, family,* or *team*) takes a singular pronoun when the noun refers to the group as a unit and takes a plural pronoun when the noun refers to the parts or members of the group.**

SINGULAR	The **debate club** elected **its** new officers.
PLURAL	The **debate club** will practice **their** speeches in this week's workshop.

2p. **The title of a creative work (such as a book, song, film, or painting) or the name of an organization, a country, or a city (even if it is plural in form) takes a singular pronoun.**

EXAMPLES

The teacher read **"Mushrooms"** and then asked me to interpret **it.**

Anderson Outfitters advertises **itself** as "the first step in getting away from it all."

3 USING VERBS

REGULAR AND IRREGULAR VERBS

Every verb has four basic forms called the **principal parts:** the *base form,* the *present participle,* the *past,* and the *past participle.* A verb is classified as *regular* or *irregular* depending on the way it forms the past and past participle.

3a. **A *regular verb* forms the past and past participle by adding *–d* or *–ed* to the base form. An *irregular verb* forms the past and the past participle in some other way.**

The following examples include *is* and *have* in parentheses to show that helping verbs are used with the present participle and past participle forms.

LANGUAGE HANDBOOK 1223

Resources

- *Language Handbook Resources,* pp. 15–26
- *Language Workshop CD-ROM,* Chapter 3: Using Verbs Correctly

COMMON REGULAR AND IRREGULAR VERBS

BASE FORM	PRESENT PARTICIPLE	PAST	PAST PARTICIPLE
REGULAR			
ask	(is) asking	asked	(have) asked
attack	(is) attacking	attacked	(have) attacked
drown	(is) drowning	drowned	(have) drowned
plan	(is) planning	planned	(have) planned
try	(is) trying	tried	(have) tried
use	(is) using	used	(have) used
IRREGULAR			
be	(is) being	was, were	(have) been
begin	(is) beginning	began	(have) begun
catch	(is) catching	caught	(have) caught
drink	(is) drinking	drank	(have) drunk
drive	(is) driving	drove	(have) driven
go	(is) going	went	(have) gone
lend	(is) lending	lent	(have) lent
shake	(is) shaking	shook	(have) shaken
swim	(is) swimming	swam	(have) swum
tear	(is) tearing	tore	(have) torn
throw	(is) throwing	threw	(have) thrown

TIPS FOR SPELLING

Before adding the suffix –*ing* or –*ed* to form the present participle or the past or past participle of a verb, double the final consonant if the base form satisfies both of these conditions:

(1) It has only one syllable or has the accent on the last syllable.

(2) It ends in a single consonant preceded by a single vowel.

EXAMPLES

grin + -ing = gri**nning**
refer + -ed = refe**rred**

See page 1251 for exceptions.

NOTE If you are not sure about the principal parts of a verb, look in a current dictionary. Entries for irregular verbs give the principal parts. If no principal parts are listed, the verb is a regular verb.

TENSES AND THEIR USES

3b. The *tense* of a verb indicates the time of the action or the state of being expressed by the verb.

(1) The ***present tense*** is used mainly to express an action or a state of being that is occurring now.

EXAMPLE
We **understand** now.

The present tense is also used

- to show a customary or habitual action or state of being
- to convey a general truth—something that is always true
- to make a historical event seem current (such use is called the ***historical present***)
- to summarize the plot or subject matter of a literary work or to refer to an author's relationship to his or her work (such use is called the ***literary present***)
- to express future time

EXAMPLES
For breakfast I **eat** cereal and **drink** orange juice. [customary action]

The earth **revolves** once around the sun each year. [general truth]
Several of the *Mayflower* passengers **die** before the ship **reaches** Plymouth. [historical present]
Moby-Dick **tells** the story of a man who **pursues** a white whale. [literary present]
The workshop **begins** tomorrow. [future time]

(2) The ***past tense*** is used to express an action or a state of being that occurred in the past but did not continue into the present.

EXAMPLES
Pepe **grabbed** his rifle and **crawled** into the brush.

(3) The ***future tense*** (*will* or *shall* + base form) is used to express an action or a state of being that will occur.

EXAMPLES
Elisa **will play** the part of Beneatha Younger.
I **will** [*or* shall] **serve** as her understudy.

(4) The ***present perfect tense*** (*have* or *has* + past participle) is used mainly to express an action or a state of being that occurred at some indefinite time in the past.

EXAMPLE
Have you **read** any stories by Sandra Cisneros?

The present perfect tense is also used to express an action or a state of being that began in the past and continues into the present.

EXAMPLE
My sister **has been** a Girl Scout for two years.

(5) The *past perfect tense* (*had* + past participle) is used to express an action or a state of being that was completed in the past before another action or state of being occurred.

EXAMPLE
Miss Emily returned the tax notice that she **had received.**

 NOTE Use the past perfect tense in "if" clauses that express the earlier of two past actions.

> **EXAMPLE**
> If he **had taken** [*not* would have taken *or* took] more time, he would have won.

(6) The *future perfect tense* (*will have* or *shall have* + past participle) is used to express an action or a state of being that will be completed in the future before some other future occurrence.

EXAMPLE
By the time Rip Van Winkle returns to his village, the Revolutionary War **will have occurred.**

3c. Avoid unnecessary shifts in tense.

INCONSISTENT	Shiftlet marries Lucynell and then abandoned her.
CONSISTENT	Shiftlet **marries** Lucynell and then **abandons** her.
CONSISTENT	Shiftlet **married** Lucynell and then **abandoned** her.

When describing events that occur at different times, use verbs in different tenses to show the order of events.

EXAMPLE
She now **works** for *The New York Times,* but she **worked** for *The Wall Street Journal* last year.

ACTIVE VOICE AND PASSIVE VOICE

3d. *Voice* is the form a verb takes to indicate whether the subject of the verb performs or receives the action.

A verb is in the *active voice* when its subject performs the action.

ACTIVE VOICE	Julia Alvarez **wrote** "Daughter of Invention."

A verb is in the *passive voice* when its subject receives the action. A passive voice verb is always a verb phrase that includes a form of *be* and the past participle of an action verb.

PASSIVE VOICE	"Daughter of Invention" **was written** by Julia Alvarez.

3e. Use the passive voice sparingly.

In general, the passive voice is less direct and less forceful than the active voice. In some cases, the passive voice may sound awkward.

AWKWARD PASSIVE	A memorable speech was delivered by William Faulkner when the Nobel Prize was accepted by him in 1950.
ACTIVE	William Faulkner delivered a memorable speech when he accepted the Nobel Prize in 1950.

The passive voice is useful
1. when you do not know the performer of the action
2. when you do not want to reveal the performer of the action
3. when you want to emphasize the receiver of the action

EXAMPLES
Hemingway **was** severely **wounded** during the war.
Many careless errors **were made** in some of the essays about Amy Tan.
Madeline Usher **had been buried** alive!

4 USING PRONOUNS

CASE

Case is the form that a noun or a pronoun takes to indicate its use in a sentence. In English, there are three cases: *nominative, objective,* and *possessive.*

The form of a noun is the same for both the nominative case and the objective case. A noun changes form only in the possessive case. Unlike nouns, most personal pronouns have one form for each case. The form a pronoun takes depends on its function in a sentence.

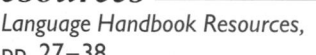

Resources
- *Language Handbook Resources,* pp. 27–38
- *Language Workshop CD-ROM,* Chapter 4: Using Pronouns Correctly

The Nominative Case

4a. A subject of a verb is in the nominative case.

EXAMPLES

They were happy that **he** was home from the war. [*They* is the subject of *were,* and *he* is the subject of *was.*]

4b. A predicate nominative is in the nominative case.

EXAMPLE

The one who jilts Granny Weatherall is **he.** [*He* follows *is* and identifies the subject *one.*]

The Objective Case

4c. An object of a verb is in the objective case.

EXAMPLES

My stepbrother and stepsister don't have driver's licenses yet, so I usually give **them** a ride to school. [*Them* is the direct object of the verb *give.*]

The Jazz Age collage earned **Donna and him** blue ribbons. [*Donna and him* is a compound indirect object of the verb *earned.*]

4d. An object of a preposition is in the objective case.

EXAMPLES

Did you send copies of *Blue Highways* to **her and him**? [*Her and him* is a compound object of the preposition *to.*]

The Possessive Case

4e. A noun or a pronoun preceding a gerund is in the possessive case.

EXAMPLE

Warren did not appreciate **Silas's** [*or* **his**] leaving during haying time. [*Silas's* (or *his*) modifies *leaving,* a gerund used as a direct object telling what Warren did not appreciate.]

SPECIAL PRONOUN PROBLEMS

4f. An appositive is in the same case as the noun or pronoun to which it refers.

EXAMPLES

The Ushers, **Madeline and he,** live in a gloomy mansion. [The appositive, *Madeline and he,* refers to the subject, *Ushers,* which is in the nominative case.]

Tom T. Shiftlet deceives both of them, **Mrs. Crater and her.** [The appositive, *Mrs. Crater and her,* refers to the object of the preposition, *them,* which is in the objective case.]

4g. The pronoun *who* (*whoever*) is in the nominative case. The pronoun *whom* (*whomever*) is in the objective case.

EXAMPLES

Who wrote *Dangling Man*? [*Who* is the subject of *wrote.*]

With **whom** did Moss Hart write the play? [*Whom* is the object of *with.*]

PERSONAL PRONOUNS

SINGULAR

	NOMINATIVE	OBJECTIVE	POSSESSIVE
FIRST PERSON	I	me	my, mine
SECOND PERSON	you	you	your, yours
THIRD PERSON	he, she, it	him, her, it	his, her, hers, its

PLURAL

	NOMINATIVE	OBJECTIVE	POSSESSIVE
FIRST PERSON	we	us	our, ours
SECOND PERSON	you	you	your, yours
THIRD PERSON	they	them	their, theirs

NOTE Notice in the chart that *you* and *it* have the same forms for the nominative and the objective cases. All other personal pronouns have different forms for each case. Notice also that only third-person singular pronouns indicate gender.

☞ For more information about possessive pronouns, see *its, it's* on page 1255, *their, there, they're* on page 1256, and *who's, whose* and *your, you're* on page 1257.

4h. A pronoun ending in *–self* or *–selves* should not be used in place of a personal pronoun.

EXAMPLE
Lupe and **I** [*not* myself] went to the ballet.

4i. A pronoun following *than* or *as* in an elliptical construction is in the same case as it would be if the construction were completed.

An *elliptical construction* is a clause from which words have been omitted. Notice how the meaning of each of the following sentences depends on the pronoun form in the elliptical construction.

NOMINATIVE CASE	I have known Leigh longer **than she.** [I have known Leigh longer than she has known Leigh.]
OBJECTIVE CASE	I have known Leigh longer **than her.** [I have known Leigh longer than I have known her.]

CLEAR PRONOUN REFERENCE

4j. A pronoun should refer clearly to its antecedent. Avoid an ambiguous, a general, a weak, or an indefinite reference by (1) rephrasing the sentence, (2) replacing the pronoun with a noun, or (3) giving the pronoun a clear antecedent.

AMBIGUOUS	Jody talked to Billy Buck while he was working. [*He* refers to either antecedent, *Jody* or *Billy Buck.*]
CLEAR	While Billy Buck was working, Jody talked to him.
CLEAR	While Jody was working, he talked to Billy Buck.
GENERAL	The wind rose, and dark clouds descended on the House of Usher. This seemed to bewilder Roderick. [*This* has no specific antecedent.]
CLEAR	The wind rose, and dark clouds descended on the House of Usher. These ominous conditions seemed to bewilder Roderick.
CLEAR	The rising wind and dark clouds that descended on the House of Usher seemed to bewilder Roderick.
WEAK	He was superstitious. One of these was that walking under a ladder brings bad luck. [The antecedent of *these* is not expressed.]
CLEAR	He was superstitious. One of his superstitions was that walking under a ladder brings bad luck.
CLEAR	He believed in many superstitions, one of which was that walking under a ladder brings bad luck.
INDEFINITE	In this history book, it refers to the American Civil War as the War Between the States. [*It* is unnecessary to the meaning of the sentence.]
CLEAR	This history book refers to the American Civil War as the War Between the States.

5 USING MODIFIERS

WHAT IS A MODIFIER?

A *modifier* is a word or group of words that limits the meaning of another word or group of words. The two kinds of modifiers are *adjectives* and *adverbs*.

COMPARISON OF MODIFIERS

5a. *Comparison* refers to the change in the form of an adjective or an adverb to show increasing or decreasing degrees in the quality the modifier expresses.

The three degrees of comparison are *positive, comparative,* and *superlative.*

(1) Most one-syllable modifiers form the comparative and superlative degrees by adding *–er* (*less*) and *–est* (*least*).

(2) Some two-syllable modifiers form the comparative and superlative degrees by adding *–er* and *–est*; others form the comparative and superlative degrees by using *more* and *most.* All two-syllable modifiers form decreasing comparisons by using *less* and *least.*

(3) Modifiers of more than two syllables form the comparative and superlative degrees by using *more* (*less*) and *most* (*least*).

LANGUAGE HANDBOOK   1227

Resources
- *Language Handbook Resources,* pp. 39–51
- *Language Workshop CD-ROM,* Chapter 5: Using Modifiers Correctly

POSITIVE	COMPARATIVE	SUPERLATIVE
neat	neater	neatest
simple	less simple	least simple
calmly	more calmly	most calmly
optimistic	less optimistic	least optimistic

(4) Some modifiers form the comparative and superlative degrees in other ways.

POSITIVE	COMPARATIVE	SUPERLATIVE
bad	worse	worst
far	farther (further)	farthest (furthest)
good (well)	better	best
little	less	least
many (much)	more	most

5b. Use the comparative degree when comparing two things. Use the superlative degree when comparing more than two.

COMPARATIVE Although both puppies look cute, the **more active** one seems **healthier.**

SUPERLATIVE Of the four plays that we saw, I think *Death of a Salesman* was the **most moving.**

5c. Avoid a double comparison or a double negative. A *double comparison* is the use of two comparative forms (usually –*er* and *more*) or two superlative forms (usually –*est* and *most*) to modify the same word. A *double negative* is the use of two negative words when one is enough.

EXAMPLES
Samuel Clemens is **better** [*not* more better] known as Mark Twain.
She did**n't** say **anything** [*not* nothing].

5d. Include the word *other* or *else* when comparing one member of a group with the rest of the group.

EXAMPLE
Esteban is taller than anyone **else** on the team.

5e. Avoid comparing items that cannot logically be compared.

ILLOGICAL Hemingway's style is perhaps more imitated than any other American

writer. [illogical comparison between a style and a writer]

LOGICAL Hemingway's style is perhaps more imitated than any other American writer's (style). [logical comparison of styles]

PLACEMENT OF MODIFIERS

5f. Avoid using a *misplaced modifier*— a modifying word, phrase, or clause that sounds awkward because it modifies the wrong word or group of words.

To correct a misplaced modifier, place the word, phrase, or clause as close as possible to the word or words you intend it to modify.

MISPLACED Thoreau listened intently to the song of a distant robin looking at the glittering pond. [Was the robin or Thoreau looking at the pond?]

CLEAR **Looking at the glittering pond,** Thoreau listened intently to the song of a distant robin.

For information about phrases, see Part 6: Phrases. For more on clauses, see Part 7: Clauses.

5g. Avoid using a *dangling modifier*— a modifying word, phrase, or clause that does not sensibly modify any word or words in a sentence.

You may correct a dangling modifier by
- adding a word or words that the dangling word, phrase, or clause can sensibly refer to
- adding a word or words to the dangling word, phrase, or clause
- rewording the sentence

DANGLING Alone, the mountain is virtually impossible to climb. [Who or what is alone?]

CLEAR **For a person alone,** the mountain is virtually impossible to climb.

CLEAR The mountain is virtually impossible **for a person** to climb **alone.**

DANGLING After winning the Pulitzer Prize, the novel *Maud Martha* was written. [Who won the Pulitzer Prize?]

CLEAR After winning the Pulitzer Prize, **Gwendolyn Brooks wrote** the novel *Maud Martha.*

CLEAR After **Gwendolyn Brooks won** the Pulitzer Prize, **she wrote** the novel *Maud Martha.*

6 PHRASES

6a. A *phrase* is a group of related words that is used as a single part of speech and that does not contain a verb and its subject.

EXAMPLES
At two o'clock [adverb phrase], the event **of the year** [adjective phrase], the company picnic, **will commence** [verb phrase].

THE PREPOSITIONAL PHRASE

6b. A *prepositional phrase* begins with a preposition and ends with the *object of the preposition,* a word or word group that functions as a noun.

EXAMPLES
On the pillow was a strand **of gray hair.** [The noun *pillow* is the object of the preposition *on.* The noun *hair* is the object of the preposition *of.*]
Brian's Song is an inspiring story **about friendship and courage.** [Both *friendship* and *courage* are objects of the preposition *about.*]

(1) An *adjective phrase* is a prepositional phrase that modifies a noun or a pronoun. An adjective phrase usually follows the word it modifies. That word may be the object of another preposition.

EXAMPLES
Cassie Soldierwolf made a batch **of fry bread,** using a recipe very similar to that **of her ancestors.** [*Of fry bread* modifies the noun *batch. Of her ancestors* modifies the pronoun *that.*]
Sarah Kemble Knight kept a journal **of her trip to New York.** [*Of her trip* modifies the noun *journal. To New York* modifies *trip,* which serves as the object of the preposition *of.*]

More than one adjective phrase may modify the same word.

EXAMPLE
Sarah Kemble Knight's journey **on horseback from Boston to New York** was long and difficult. [*On horseback, from Boston,* and *to New York* modify the noun *journey.*]

(2) An *adverb phrase* is a prepositional phrase that modifies a verb, an adjective, or an adverb. An adverb phrase tells *how, when, where, why,* or *to what extent* (*how long* or *how far*).

More than one adverb phrase can modify the same word. Also, an adverb phrase can precede or follow the word it modifies.

EXAMPLES
During the Civil War, Louisa May Alcott worked **in a hospital as a nurse for six weeks.** [Each phrase modifies the verb *worked. During the Civil War* tells *when, in a hospital* tells *where, as a nurse* tells *how,* and *for six weeks* tells *how long.*]

VERBALS AND VERBAL PHRASES

A *verbal* is a form of a verb used as a noun, an adjective, or an adverb. A *verbal phrase* consists of a verbal and any of its modifiers or complements.

Participles and Participial Phrases

6c. A *participle* is a verb form that is used as an adjective. A *participial phrase* consists of a participle and all words related to the participle.

There are two kinds of participles—the *present participle* and the *past participle.*

(1) **Present participles** end in *–ing.*

EXAMPLES
The explorer could hear something **moving in the brush.** [The participial phrase modifies the pronoun *something. In the brush* is an adverb phrase modifying the present participle *moving.*]
A mountain lion stood there **watching him.** [The participial phrase modifies the noun *mountain lion.* The pronoun *him* is the direct object of the present participle *watching.*]

(2) Most **past participles** end in *–d* or *–ed.* Others are irregularly formed.

EXAMPLES
Obsessed with revenge, Captain Ahab pursued the white whale. [The participial phrase modifies the noun *Captain Ahab.* The adverb phrase *with revenge* modifies the past participle *obsessed.*]
Samuel Clemens, **better known as Mark Twain,** was born in Florida, Missouri, in 1835. [The participial phrase modifies the noun *Samuel Clemens.* The adverb *better* and the adverb phrase *as Mark Twain* modify the past participle *known.*]

Resources
- *Language Handbook Resources,* pp. 52–62
- *Language Workshop CD-ROM,* Chapter 6—Lessons 23–25: Prepositional Phrases, Verbal Phrases, and Appositive Phrases

Do not confuse a participle used as an adjective with a participle used as part of a verb phrase.

ADJECTIVE	The Vietnam Veterans Memorial, **designed** by Maya Ying Lin, is made of black granite.
VERB PHRASE	The Vietnam Veterans Memorial, which **was designed** by Maya Ying Lin, is made of black granite.

 For information about misplaced participial phrases, see page 1228.

Gerunds and Gerund Phrases

6d. A *gerund* is a verb form ending in *–ing* that is used as a noun. A *gerund phrase* consists of a gerund and all words related to the gerund.

EXAMPLES
Exercising regularly is important for maintaining good health. [The gerund phrase is the subject of the verb *is*. The adverb *regularly* modifies the gerund *exercising*.]

Dexter enjoyed **working at the golf club.** [The gerund phrase is the direct object of the verb *enjoyed*. The adverb phrase *at the golf club* modifies the gerund *working*.]

Walter Mitty daydreamed of **being a pilot.** [The gerund phrase is the object of the preposition *of*. The noun *pilot* is a predicate nominative completing the meaning of the gerund *being*.]

One way to build your vocabulary is **reading good literature.** [The gerund phrase is a predicate nominative explaining the subject *way*. *Literature* is the direct object of the gerund *reading*.]

Do not confuse a gerund with a present participle used as an adjective or as part of a verb phrase.

GERUND	I enjoy **reading** at night. [direct object of the verb *enjoy*]
PRESENT PARTICIPLE	I sometimes fall asleep **reading** at night. [adjective modifying the pronoun *I*]
PRESENT PARTICIPLE	Sometimes, I listen to classical music while I am **reading** at night. [part of the verb phrase *am reading*]

 NOTE A noun or pronoun directly before a gerund takes the possessive case.

EXAMPLES
Grandad's cooking tastes great.
The bandleader said that he was pleased with **our** marching.

Infinitives and Infinitive Phrases

6e. An *infinitive* is a verb form that can be used as a noun, an adjective, or an adverb. An infinitive usually begins with *to*. An *infinitive phrase* consists of an infinitive and all words related to the infinitive.

NOUNS
To find Moby-Dick was Ahab's burning ambition. [The infinitive phrase is the subject of *was*. *Moby-Dick* is the direct object of the infinitive *to find*.]

Ahab's burning ambition was **to find Moby-Dick.** [The infinitive phrase is a predicate nominative identifying the subject *ambition*.]

ADJECTIVES
Napoleon's plan **to conquer the world** failed. [The infinitive phrase modifies the noun *plan*. *World* is the direct object of the infinitive *to conquer*.]

The one **to ask** is your guidance counselor. [The infinitive modifies the pronoun *one*.]

ADVERBS
With his dog Wolf, Rip Van Winkle went into the woods **to hunt squirrels.** [The infinitive phrase modifies *went*. *Squirrels* is the direct object of the infinitive *to hunt*.]

Nearly everyone was reluctant **to speak to her.** [The infinitive phrase modifies *reluctant*. The adverb phrase *to her* modifies the infinitive *to speak*.]

The word *to*, the sign of the infinitive, is sometimes omitted.

EXAMPLE
Will you help [to] dry the dishes?

 NOTE Do not confuse an infinitive with a prepositional phrase that begins with *to*.

INFINITIVES	**To have** a friend, you need **to be** a friend.
PREPOSITIONAL PHRASES	Give one sample **to each** of the customers, and return the rest **to Rhonda.**

The Infinitive Clause

6f. Unlike other verbals, an infinitive may have a subject. Such a construction is called an *infinitive clause*.

EXAMPLE
Our teacher asked **us to read "Thanatopsis."** [*Us* is the subject of the infinitive *to read*. The entire infinitive clause is the direct object of *asked*.]

APPOSITIVES AND APPOSITIVE PHRASES

6g. An *appositive* is a noun or a pronoun placed beside (usually after) another noun or pronoun to identify or explain it. An *appositive phrase* consists of an appositive and its modifiers.

An appositive or appositive phrase usually follows the word it identifies or explains.

EXAMPLES

We went to the Navajo Gallery in Taos, New Mexico, to see R. C. Gorman's artwork ***Freeform Lady***. [The appositive *Freeform Lady* identifies the noun *artwork*.]

Can you believe that I **myself** plan to become a **writer**? [The pronoun *myself* refers to the pronoun *I*.]

For emphasis, however, an appositive or appositive phrase may come at the beginning of a sentence.

EXAMPLE

A young painter, Jaune Quick-to-See Smith shows a deep awareness of her French, Shoshone, and Cree heritage.

Appositives are sometimes introduced by a colon or by the expressions *or, namely, such as, for example, i.e.,* or *e.g.*

EXAMPLES

The homeless shelter is accepting donations of the following items**:** canned **foods, blankets,** and winter **coats.**

Beneficial insects, **such as ladybugs** and **praying mantises,** can help control the population of harmful insects in a garden.

 For information on how to punctuate appositives, see pages 1243–1244.

---

7 CLAUSES

7a. A *clause* is a group of words that contains a verb and its subject and that is used as part of a sentence. There are two kinds of clauses: the *independent clause* and the *subordinate clause.*

THE INDEPENDENT CLAUSE

7b. An *independent* (or *main*) *clause* expresses a complete thought and can stand by itself as a sentence.

EXAMPLE

    SUBJECT   VERB
Emily Dickinson wrote nearly eighteen hundred poems.

THE SUBORDINATE CLAUSE

7c. A *subordinate* (or *dependent*) *clause* does not express a complete thought and cannot stand alone as a sentence.

EXAMPLE

    SUBJECT VERB
that   **we**   **read**

The thought expressed by a subordinate clause becomes complete when the clause is combined with an independent clause.

EXAMPLE

The last book **that we read** was *Blue Highways.*

The Adjective Clause

7d. An *adjective clause* is a subordinate clause that modifies a noun or a pronoun.

An adjective clause follows the word or words that it modifies. Usually, an adjective clause begins with a relative pronoun, which (1) relates the adjective clause to the word or words the clause modifies and (2) performs a function within the adjective clause.

EXAMPLE

Li recommends every poem **that Denise Levertov has written.** [The relative pronoun *that* relates the adjective clause to the noun *poem* and serves as the direct object of the verb *has written.*]

An adjective clause may begin with a relative adverb, such as *when* or *where.*

EXAMPLE

From 1914 to 1931, Isak Dinesen lived in Kenya, **where she operated a coffee plantation.**

LANGUAGE HANDBOOK 1231

Resources

- *Language Handbook Resources,* pp. 63–73
- *Language Workshop CD-ROM,* Chapter 6—Lessons 26 and 27: Clauses

Sometimes the relative pronoun or relative adverb is not expressed.

EXAMPLE
The book [that] **I am reading** is a biography.

The Noun Clause

7e. A *noun clause* is a subordinate clause that may be used as a subject, a predicate nominative, a direct object, an indirect object, or an object of a preposition.

Words commonly used to introduce noun clauses include *how, that, what, whether, who,* and *why.*

EXAMPLES
A catchy slogan is **what we will need for this campaign.** [predicate nominative]
Emerson liked **what Whitman wrote.** [direct object]
The director will give **whoever does best in this audition** the lead role. [indirect object]

The word that introduces a noun clause may or may not have another function in the clause.

EXAMPLES
Do any of you know **who wrote *Spoon River Anthology*?** [The word *who* introduces the noun clause and serves as subject of the verb *wrote.*]
She told Walter **that he was driving too fast and should slow down.** [The word *that* introduces the noun clause but does not have any function within the noun clause.]

The word that introduces a noun clause is not always expressed.

EXAMPLE
I think [that] **I've read all of Langston Hughes's poetry.**

The Adverb Clause

7f. An *adverb clause* is a subordinate clause that modifies a verb, an adjective, or an adverb.

An adverb clause, which may come before or after the word or words it modifies, tells *how, when, where, why, to what extent,* or *under what condition.* An adverb clause is introduced by a **subordinating conjunction**—a word or word group that relates the adverb clause to the word or words the clause modifies.

EXAMPLES
William Cullen Bryant wrote the first version of "Thanatopsis" **when he was a teenager.** [The adverb clause modifies the verb *wrote,* telling *when* Bryant wrote the first version.]
Zoë can explain naturalism to you better **than I can.** [The adverb clause modifies the adverb *better,* telling *to what extent* Zoë can better explain naturalism.]

 NOTE An adverb clause that begins a sentence is always set off by a comma.

The Elliptical Clause

7g. Part of a clause may be left out when the meaning can be understood from the context of the sentence. Such a clause is called an *elliptical clause.*

EXAMPLES
Roger knew the rules better **than Elgin [did].**
While [he was] living at Walden Pond, Thoreau wrote his first book.

 For information about using pronouns in elliptical clauses, see page 1227.

Resources
• *Language Handbook Resources,* pp. 74–88
• *Language Workshop CD-ROM,* Chapter 7: Sentences

8 SENTENCE STRUCTURE

SENTENCE OR FRAGMENT?

8a. A *sentence* is a group of words that has a subject and a verb and expresses a complete thought.

EXAMPLE
Benjamin Franklin lived in London and in Paris.

Only a sentence should begin with a capital letter and end with either a period, a question mark, or an exclamation point. A group of words that either does not contain a subject and a verb or does not express a complete thought is called a **sentence fragment.**

| FRAGMENT | Collapses during a storm. |
| SENTENCE | The House of Usher collapses during a storm. |

 For information about how to correct sentence fragments, see page 1236. For information about using end marks with sentences, see page 1242.

1232 LANGUAGE HANDBOOK

SUBJECT AND PREDICATE

8b. A sentence consists of two parts: a subject and a predicate. A *subject* tells *whom* or *what* the sentence is about. A *predicate* tells something about the subject.

In the following examples, all the words labeled *subject* make up the **complete subject,** and all the words labeled *predicate* make up the **complete predicate.**

SUBJECT	PREDICATE
Walt Whitman	wrote *Leaves of Grass.*

PREDICATE	SUBJECT	PREDICATE
Why did	Phoenix	walk to town?

The Simple Subject

8c. A *simple subject* is the main word or group of words that tells *whom* or *what* the sentence is about.

EXAMPLE
Harold Krebs, the protagonist of the story, returns home from the war. [The complete subject is *Harold Krebs, the protagonist of the story.*]

The Simple Predicate

8d. A *simple predicate* is a verb or verb phrase that tells something about the subject.

EXAMPLE
Did Judy **marry** Dexter? [The complete predicate is *did marry Dexter.*]

The Compound Subject and the Compound Verb

8e. A *compound subject* consists of two or more subjects that are joined by a conjunction—usually *and* or *or*—and that have the same verb.

EXAMPLE
Reuben and **I** are preparing a report on "A Wagner Matinée."

8f. A *compound verb* consists of two or more verbs that are joined by a conjunction—usually *and, but,* or *or*—and that have the same subject.

EXAMPLE
Kendra **recognized** the song but **had forgotten** its title.

How to Find the Subject of a Sentence

8g. To find the subject of a sentence, ask *Who?* or *What?* before the verb.

(1) The subject of a sentence is never within a prepositional phrase.

EXAMPLE
On the quarter-deck stood **Captain Ahab.** [Who stood? Captain Ahab stood. *Quarter-deck* is the object of the preposition *on.*]

(2) The subject of a sentence expressing a command or a request is always understood to be *you,* although *you* may not appear in the sentence.

COMMAND   Identify two of the most striking characteristics of E. E. Cummings's poetry. [Who is being told to identify? *You* is understood.]

The subject of a command or a request is *you* even when a sentence contains a **noun of direct address**— a word naming the one or ones spoken to.

REQUEST   Jordan, [you] please read aloud Jimmy Santiago Baca's "Fall."

(3) The subject of a sentence expressing a question usually follows the verb or a part of the verb phrase. Turning the question into a statement will often help you find the subject.

QUESTION   Was Pearl Buck awarded the Nobel Prize in literature in 1938? [Who was awarded?]

STATEMENT   **Pearl Buck** was awarded the Nobel Prize in literature in 1938.

QUESTION   Where is the dog's leash? [Where is what?]

STATEMENT   The dog's **leash** is where.

(4) The word *there* or *here* is never the subject of a sentence.

EXAMPLE
Here are your **gloves.** [What are here? Gloves are.]

COMPLEMENTS

8h. A *complement* is a word or a group of words that completes the meaning of a verb. There are four main kinds of complements: *direct object, indirect object, objective complement,* and *subject complement.*

The Direct Object and the Indirect Object

8i. A *direct object* is a noun, a pronoun, or a word group that functions as a noun and tells *who* or *what* receives the action of a transitive verb.

EXAMPLES
Kerry called **me** at noon. [called whom? me]
Captain Ahab sacrifices his **ship** and almost **all** of his crew. [sacrifices what? ship and all—compound direct object]

8j. An *indirect object* is a word or word group that comes between a transitive verb and a direct object. An indirect object, which may be a noun, a pronoun, or a word group that functions as a noun, tells *to whom* or *to what* or *for whom* or *for what* the action of the verb is done.

EXAMPLES
Emily Dickinson sent **Thomas Wentworth Higginson** four poems. [sent to whom? Thomas Wentworth Higginson]
Ms. Cruz showed **José** and **me** pictures of her trip to Walden Pond. [showed to whom? José and me—compound indirect object]

 NOTE A sentence that has an indirect object must always have a direct object as well.

 For more information about verbs, see Part 3: Using Verbs.

The Objective Complement

8k. An *objective complement* is a word or word group that helps complete the meaning of a transitive verb by identifying or modifying the direct object. An objective complement, which may be a noun, a pronoun, an adjective, or a word group that functions as a noun or adjective, almost always follows the direct object.

EXAMPLES
Everyone considered her **dependable.** [The adjective *dependable* modifies the direct object *her.*]
Many literary historians call Poe **the master of the macabre.** [The word group *the master of the macabre* modifies the direct object *Poe.*]

The Subject Complement

8l. A *subject complement* is a word or word group that completes the meaning of a linking verb and identifies or modifies the subject. There are two kinds of subject complements: the *predicate nominative* and the *predicate adjective.*

(1) A *predicate nominative* is the word or group of words that follows a linking verb and refers to the same person or thing as the subject of the verb.

A predicate nominative may be a noun, a pronoun, or a word group that functions as a noun.

EXAMPLES
Of the three applicants, Carlos is the most competent **one.** [The pronoun *one* refers to the subject *Carlos.*]
The main characters are **Aunt Georgiana** and **Clark.** [The nouns *Aunt Georgiana* and *Clark* refer to the subject *characters.*]

(2) A *predicate adjective* is an adjective that follows a linking verb and modifies the subject of the verb.

EXAMPLES
Eben Flood felt very **lonely.** [The adjective *lonely* modifies the subject *Eben Flood.*]
Shiftlet is **sly** and **scheming.** [The adjectives *sly* and *scheming* modify the subject *Shiftlet.*]

SENTENCES CLASSIFIED ACCORDING TO STRUCTURE

8m. According to structure, sentences are classified as *simple, compound, complex,* and *compound-complex.*

(1) A *simple sentence* has one independent clause and no subordinate clauses.

EXAMPLE
Thornton Wilder's *Our Town* is one of my favorite plays.

(2) A *compound sentence* has two or more independent clauses but no subordinate clauses.

EXAMPLE
Jack London was a prolific writer; he wrote nearly fifty books in less than twenty years. [two independent clauses joined by a semicolon]

 NOTE Do not confuse a simple sentence that has a compound subject or a compound verb with a compound sentence.

(3) A *complex sentence* has one independent clause and at least one subordinate clause.

EXAMPLE
Before we read *The Great Gatsby,* let's talk about the Jazz Age. [The independent clause is *let's talk about the Jazz Age.* The subordinate clause is *before we read* The Great Gatsby.]

(4) A *compound-complex* sentence has two or more independent clauses and at least one subordinate clause.

EXAMPLE
The two eyewitnesses told the police officer what they saw, but their accounts of the accident were quite different. [The two independent clauses are *the two eyewitnesses told the police officer* and *their accounts of the accident were quite different.* The subordinate clause is *what they saw.*]

SENTENCES CLASSIFIED ACCORDING TO PURPOSE

8n. Sentences may be classified according to purpose.

(1) A *declarative sentence* makes a statement. It is followed by a period.

EXAMPLE
Swimming fast toward the ship was the white whale.

(2) An *interrogative sentence* asks a question. It is followed by a question mark.

EXAMPLE
Have you ever read *Blue Highways*?

(3) An *imperative sentence* makes a request or gives a command. It is usually followed by a period. A strong command, however, is followed by an exclamation point.

EXAMPLES
Please give me the dates for the class meetings.
Read Act I of *A Raisin in the Sun* by tomorrow.
Help me!

(4) An *exclamatory sentence* expresses strong feeling or shows excitement. It is followed by an exclamation point.

EXAMPLE
What a noble leader he was!

9 SENTENCE STYLE

WAYS TO ACHIEVE CLARITY

Coordinating Ideas

9a. To *coordinate* two or more ideas, or to give them equal emphasis, link them with a connecting word, an appropriate mark of punctuation, or both.

EXAMPLE
Edgar Allan Poe wrote "The Raven"; Edgar Lee Masters wrote *Spoon River Anthology.*

Subordinating Ideas

9b. To *subordinate* an idea, or to show that one idea is related to but less important than another, use an adverb clause or an adjective clause.

An *adverb clause* begins with a subordinating conjunction, which shows how the adverb clause relates to the main clause. Usually, the relationship is *time, cause or reason, purpose or result,* or *condition.*

EXAMPLES
Whenever I think of Boston, I think of the Lowells. [time]
Janet got a lead role in *Our Town* **because she is one of the best actors in our school.** [cause]
Let's finish now **so that we won't have to come back tomorrow.** [purpose]

An *adjective clause* usually begins with *who, whom, whose, which, that,* or *where.*

EXAMPLE
Tamisha is the one **whose essay won first prize.**

 For more about adjective clauses and adverb clauses, see pages 1231–1232.

Using Parallel Structure

9c. Use the same grammatical form (*parallel structure*) to express ideas of equal weight.

Resources
- *Language Handbook Resources,* pp. 89–112
- *Language Workshop CD-ROM,* Chapter 8—Lessons 31 and 32: Obstacles to Clarity; Lesson 33: Ways to Achieve Clarity; Lesson 39: Revising for Variety; Lesson 40: Revising to Reduce Wordiness

1. Use parallel structure when you link coordinate ideas.

EXAMPLE

The company guaranteed **that salaries would be increased and that working days would be shortened.** [noun clause paired with noun clause]

2. Use parallel structure when you compare or contrast ideas.

EXAMPLE

Thinking logically is as important as **calculating** accurately. [gerund compared with gerund]

3. Use parallel structure when you link ideas with correlative conjunctions (such as *both . . . and, either . . . or, neither . . . nor,* and *not only . . . but also*).

EXAMPLE

With *Ship of Fools,* Katherine Anne Porter proved she was talented not only **as a short-story writer** but also **as a novelist.** [Note that the correlative conjunctions come directly before the parallel terms.]

When you revise for parallel structure, you may need to repeat an article, a preposition, or a pronoun before each of the parallel terms.

UNCLEAR	Through Kate Chopin's stories, we can learn almost as much about the author as the social condition of women in her era.
CLEAR	Through Kate Chopin's stories, we can learn almost as much **about** the author as **about** the social condition of women in her era.

OBSTACLES TO CLARITY

Sentence Fragments

9d. Avoid using a *sentence fragment*— a word or word group that either does not contain a subject and a verb or does not express a complete thought.

Attach the fragment to the sentence that comes before or after it, or add words to or delete words from the fragment to make it a complete sentence.

FRAGMENT	Nina Otero was one of the first Mexican American women. To hold a major public post in New Mexico.
SENTENCE	Nina Otero was one of the first Mexican American women **to hold a major public post in New Mexico.**

 For more information about sentence fragments, see page 1232.

Run-on Sentences

9e. Avoid using a *run-on sentence*—two or more complete thoughts that run together as if they were one complete thought.

There are two kinds of run-on sentences.

- A *fused sentence* has no punctuation at all between the complete thoughts.
- A *comma splice* has just a comma between the complete thoughts.

FUSED SENTENCE	Emerson praised Whitman's poetry most other poets sharply criticized it.
COMMA SPLICE	Emerson praised Whitman's poetry, most other poets sharply criticized it.

You may correct a run-on sentence in one of the following ways. Depending on the relationship you want to show between ideas, facts, and other information, one method will often prove to be more effective than another.

1. Make two sentences.

EXAMPLE

Emerson praised Whitman's poetry**.** **M**ost other poets sharply criticized it.

2. Use a comma and a coordinating conjunction.

EXAMPLE

Emerson praised Whitman's poetry**, but** most other poets sharply criticized it.

3. Change one of the independent clauses to a subordinate clause.

EXAMPLE

Emerson praised Whitman's poetry, **while most other poets sharply criticized it.**

4. Use a semicolon.

EXAMPLE

Emerson praised Whitman's poetry**;** most other poets sharply criticized it.

5. Use a semicolon and a conjunctive adverb followed by a comma.

EXAMPLE

Emerson praised Whitman's poetry**; however,** most other poets sharply criticized it.

Unnecessary Shifts in Sentences

9f. Avoid making unnecessary shifts in subject, in verb tense, and in voice.

AWKWARD Athletes should be at the parking lot by 7:00 so that you can leave by 7:15. [shift in subject]

BETTER **Athletes** should be at the parking lot by 7:00 so that **they** can leave by 7:15.

AWKWARD She walked into the room, and she says, "The lights of the car outside are on." [shift in verb tense]

BETTER She **walked** into the room, and she **said,** "The lights of the car outside are on."

AWKWARD Russell Means starred as Chingachgook in *The Last of the Mohicans,* and an outstanding performance was delivered. [shift in voice]

BETTER Russell Means **starred** as Chingachgook in *The Last of the Mohicans* and **delivered** an outstanding performance.

REVISING FOR VARIETY

9g. Use a variety of sentence beginnings.

The following examples show how a writer can revise sentences to avoid beginning with the subject every time.

SUBJECT FIRST *Billy Budd* was published in 1924 and helped revive an interest in Melville's other works.

PARTICIPIAL PHRASE FIRST **Published in 1924,** *Billy Budd* helped revive an interest in Melville's other works.

PREPOSITIONAL PHRASE FIRST **In 1924,** *Billy Budd* was published and helped revive interest in Melville's other works.

ADVERB CLAUSE FIRST **When** *Billy Budd* **was published in 1924,** it helped revive interest in Melville's other works.

Varying Sentence Structure

9h. Use a mix of simple, compound, complex, and compound-complex sentences in your writing.

The following paragraph shows a mix of sentence structures.

San Francisco is famous for its scenic views. [simple] Because the city sprawls over forty-two hills, driving through San Francisco is like riding a roller coaster. [complex] Atop one of San Francisco's hills is Chinatown; atop another is Coit Tower. [compound] The most popular place to visit is the San Francisco Bay area, where the Golden Gate Bridge and Fisherman's Wharf attract a steady stream of tourists. [complex]

 For information about the four types of sentence structure, see pages 1234–1235.

Revising to Reduce Wordiness

9i. Avoid using unnecessary words in your writing.

The following guidelines suggest some ways to revise wordy sentences.

1. Take out a whole group of unnecessary words.

WORDY After climbing down to the edge of the river, we boarded a small houseboat that was floating there on the surface of the water.

BETTER After climbing down to the edge of the river, we boarded a small houseboat.

2. Replace pretentious words and expressions with straightforward ones.

WORDY The young woman, who was at some indeterminate point in her teenage years, sported through her hair a streak of pink dye that could be considered extremely garish.

BETTER The **teenager** sported a streak of **shocking**-pink dye in her hair.

3. Reduce a clause to a phrase.

WORDY Emily Dickinson fell in love with Charles Wadsworth, who was a Presbyterian minister.

BETTER Emily Dickinson fell in love with Charles Wadsworth, **a Presbyterian minister.**

4. Reduce a phrase or a clause to one word.

WORDY One of the writers from the South was William Faulkner.

BETTER One of the **Southern** writers was William Faulkner.

10 SENTENCE COMBINING

COMBINING SENTENCES FOR VARIETY

Combining by Inserting Words and Phrases

10a. Combine related sentences by taking a key word (or using another form of the word) from one sentence and inserting it into another.

ORIGINAL   Jack London describes the man's attempt to build a fire. The description is vivid.

COMBINED   Jack London **vividly** describes the man's attempt to build a fire. [The adjective *vivid* becomes the adverb *vividly*.]

10b. Combine related sentences by taking (or creating) a phrase from one sentence and inserting it into another.

ORIGINAL   Our class is reading "Everyday Use." It is by Alice Walker.

COMBINED   Our class is reading "Everyday Use" **by Alice Walker.** [prepositional phrase]

Combining by Coordinating Ideas

10c. Combine related sentences whose ideas are equally important by using coordinating conjunctions (*and, but, or, nor, for, yet*) or correlative conjunctions (*both . . . and, either . . . or, neither . . . nor, not only . . . but also*).

The relationship of the ideas determines which connective will work best. When joined, the coordinate ideas form compound elements.

ORIGINAL   Robert Frost did not receive the Nobel Prize. Carl Sandburg never received it, either.

COMBINED   **Neither Robert Frost nor Carl Sandburg** received the Nobel Prize.

You can also form a compound sentence by linking independent clauses with a semicolon and a conjunctive adverb or with just a semicolon.

EXAMPLE
We planned to go swimming**; however,** the weather did not oblige.

Combining by Subordinating Ideas

10d. Combine related sentences whose ideas are not equally important by placing the less important idea in a subordinate clause.

ORIGINAL   The National Air and Space Museum is in Washington, D.C. It contains exhibits on the history of aeronautics.

COMBINED   The National Air and Space Museum, **which contains exhibits on the history of aeronautics,** is in Washington, D.C. [adjective clause]

ORIGINAL   Shiftlet married Lucynell. He wanted her mother's car.

COMBINED   Shiftlet married Lucynell **because he wanted her mother's car.** [adverb clause]

ORIGINAL   Judy Jones was married. Devlin told Dexter this.

COMBINED   Devlin told Dexter **that Judy Jones was married.** [noun clause]

11 CAPITALIZATION

11a. Capitalize the first word in every sentence.

EXAMPLES
The author Leslie Marmon Silko was born in Albuquerque, New Mexico.
Stop!

(1) Capitalize the first word of a sentence following a colon.

EXAMPLE
The police commissioner issued a surprising statement: **In** light of new evidence, the investigation of the Brooks burglary will be reopened.

1238 LANGUAGE HANDBOOK

(2) Capitalize the first word of a direct quotation that is a complete sentence.

EXAMPLE
When he finally surrendered in 1877, Chief Joseph declared, "From where the sun now stands I will fight no more forever."

When quoting from another writer's work, capitalize the first word of the quotation only if the writer has capitalized it in the original work.

EXAMPLE
When he finally surrendered in 1877, Chief Joseph declared that he would "fight no more forever."

 For more information about using capital letters in quotations, see page 1246.

(3) Traditionally, the first word of a line of poetry is capitalized.

EXAMPLES
I placed a jar in Tennessee,
And round it was, upon a hill.
—Wallace Stevens, from "Anecdote of the Jar"

 NOTE Some writers, for reasons of style, do not follow this rule. When you quote from a writer's work, always use capital letters exactly as the writer uses them.

11b. Capitalize the first word in the salutation and the closing of a letter.

EXAMPLES
Dear Maria,   Dear Sir or Madam: Sincerely,

TYPE OF NAME	EXAMPLES	
Countries	Mozambique	Costa Rica
Continents	North America	Asia
Islands	Catalina Island	Isle of Pines
Mountains	Blue Ridge Mountains	Mount McKinley
Other Land Forms and Features	Cape Cod Mojave Desert	Isthmus of Panama Horse Cave
Bodies of Water	Great Lakes Amazon River	Strait of Hormuz Lake Huron
Parks	Mississippi Headwaters State Forest Gates of the Arctic National Park	
Roads, Highways, Streets	Route 30 Interstate 55 Pennsylvania Turnpike	Michigan Avenue Thirty-first Street Morningside Drive

(*continued*)

11c. Capitalize proper nouns and proper adjectives.

A **common noun** is a general name for a person, place, thing, or idea. A **proper noun** is the specific name of a particular person, place, thing, or idea. A **proper adjective** is formed from a proper noun. Common nouns are capitalized only if they begin a sentence (also, in most cases, a line of poetry) or a direct quotation or are part of a title.

COMMON NOUNS	PROPER NOUNS	PROPER ADJECTIVES
poet	Homer	Homeric epithet
country	Russia	Russian diplomat
state	Hawaii	Hawaiian climate

In most proper nouns made up of two or more words, do *not* capitalize articles (*a, an, the*), short prepositions (those with fewer than five letters, such as *at, of, for, to, with*), the mark of the infinitive (*to*), and coordinating conjunctions (*and, but, for, nor, or, so, yet*).

EXAMPLES
Army of the Potomac   "Writing to Persuade"

(1) Capitalize the names of most persons and animals.

GIVEN NAMES	Julia	Richard
SURNAMES	Alvarez	Wright
ANIMALS	Moby-Dick	White Fang

(2) Capitalize geographical names.

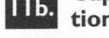 **NOTE** The second word in a hyphenated number begins with a lowercase letter.

EXAMPLES
Forty-second Street
Eighty-ninth District

In addresses, abbreviations such as *St., Ave., Dr.,* and *Blvd.* are capitalized. For more about abbreviations, see pages 1242–1243.

TYPE OF NAME	EXAMPLES	
Towns, Cities	Boston South Bend	Rio de Janeiro St. Petersburg
Counties, Townships, Provinces	Yoknapatawpha County	Lawrence Township
States and Territories	Wisconsin Yukon Territory	Nuevo León The Virgin Islands
Regions	New England the Sunbelt	the West Coast the Southwest

NOTE Words such as *north* and *western* are not capitalized when they indicate direction.

EXAMPLES
east of the river   driving southeast

☞ The abbreviations of names of states are always capitalized. For more about using and punctuating such abbreviations, see pages 1242–1243.

(3) Capitalize the names of organizations, teams, business firms, institutions, buildings and other structures, and government bodies.

TYPE OF NAME	EXAMPLES	
Organizations	National Science Foundation Guide Dog Foundation for the Blind	Future Farmers of America Disabled American Veterans
Teams	Detroit Pistons Harlem Globetrotters	Cedar Hill Bulldogs San Diego Padres
Business Firms	General Electric University Square Mall	Hip-Hop Music, Inc. La Fiesta Restaurant
Institutions	University of California, Los Angeles the Library of Congress	Mayo Clinic Habitat for Humanity
Buildings and Other Structures	Meadowlawn Junior High School the Pyramid of Khufu	the Golden Gate Bridge Rialto Theater
Government Bodies	Atomic Energy Commission Federal Bureau of Investigation	United States Marine Corps House of Representatives

(4) Capitalize the names of historical events and periods, special events, holidays and other calendar items, and time zones.

TYPE OF NAME	EXAMPLES	
Historical Events and Periods	Boston Tea Party Battle of Saratoga Middle Ages	Roaring Twenties French Revolution Mesozoic Era
Special Events	Olympics Earth Summit	Ohio State Fair Sunshine Festival
Holidays and Other Calendar Items	Wednesday September	Fourth of July Hispanic Heritage Month
Time Zones	Mountain Standard Time (MST) Eastern Daylight Time (EDT)	

NOTE Do not capitalize the name of a season unless the season is being personified or unless it is used as part of a proper noun.

EXAMPLES
The winter was unusually warm.
Overnight, Winter crept in, trailing her snowy veil.
We plan to attend the school's Winter Carnival.

(5) Capitalize the brand names of business products.

EXAMPLES

Borden milk   Colonial bread   Zenith television

Notice in these examples that the noun that follows a brand name is not capitalized. Also, over time, some brand names become common nouns. To find out if a name is a brand name, consult a current dictionary.

TYPE OF NAME	EXAMPLES	
Ships	*Cunard Princess*	**U.S.S.** *Forrestal*
Trains	*Orient Express*	*North Coast Limited*
Aircraft	*Spirit of St. Louis*	*Air Force One*
Spacecraft	*Atlantis*	*Apollo 11*
Monuments	Lincoln Memorial	Statue of Liberty
Awards	Academy Award	Pulitzer Prize
Planets, Stars, Constellations	Jupiter Ursa Minor	Orion the Milky Way
Other Particular Things, Places, and Events	Underground Railroad Silk Route Hurricane Andrew	Treaty Oak Valkyries Marshall Plan

(6) Capitalize the names of nationalities, races, and peoples.

EXAMPLES

Chinese   Jewish   Hopi   Caucasian

(7) Capitalize the names of ships, trains, aircraft, spacecraft, monuments, awards, planets, and any other particular places, things, or events.

NOTE Do not capitalize the words *sun* and *moon*. Do not capitalize the word *earth* unless it is used along with the names of other heavenly bodies that are capitalized.

EXAMPLES
This orchid grows wild in only one place on earth.
Venus is closer to the sun than Earth is.

11d. **Do not capitalize the names of school subjects, except for names of languages and course names followed by a number.**

EXAMPLES

Spanish   chemistry   Chemistry II

11e. **Capitalize titles.**

(1) Capitalize a title belonging to a particular person when it comes before the person's name. Also capitalize abbreviations such as *Jr., M.D.,* and *Ph.D.* after a name.

EXAMPLES

General Davis   Ms. Diaz   President Kennedy
Rev. Martin Luther King, Jr.   Dr. Kerry Jones, M.D.

In general, do not capitalize a title used alone or following a name. Some titles, however, are by tradition capitalized. If you are unsure of whether or not to capitalize a title, check in a dictionary.

EXAMPLE
Who is the governor of Kansas?

A title is usually capitalized when it is used alone in direct address.

EXAMPLE
Have you reached your decision, Governor?

(2) Capitalize words showing family relationships except when preceded by a possessive.

EXAMPLES

Aunt Amy   my aunt   Mother   Bill's mother

(3) Capitalize the names of religions and their followers, holy days and celebrations, holy writings, and specific deities and venerated beings.

TYPE OF NAME	EXAMPLES	
Religions and Followers	Islam	Roman Catholic
Holy Days and Celebrations	Epiphany	Rosh Hashanah
Holy Writings	Bible	Upanishads
Specific Deities and Venerated Beings	God the Prophet (Mohammed)	

NOTE The words *god* and *goddess* are not capitalized when they refer to the deities of mythology. The names of specific mythological deities are capitalized, however.

EXAMPLES
The Greek god of war was Ares.

(4) Capitalize the first and last words and all important words in titles of books, periodicals, poems, stories, essays, speeches, plays, historical documents, movies, radio and television programs, works of art, musical compositions, and cartoons.

Unimportant words in a title include articles (*a, an, the*), short prepositions (those with fewer than five letters, such as *of, to, in, for, from, with*), and coordinating conjunctions (*and, but, for, nor, or, so, yet*).

TYPE OF NAME	EXAMPLES
Books	*The Call of the Wild*
Periodicals	*Car and Driver*
Poems	"Once by the Pacific"
Stories	"The Fall of the House of Usher"
Essays and Speeches	"The Lost Worlds of Ancient America" "I Have a Dream"
Plays	*A Raisin in the Sun*
Historical Documents	Declaration of Independence
Movies	*Raiders of the Lost Ark*
Radio and TV Programs	*Star Trek: The Next Generation*
Works of Art	*Double Dutch on the Golden Gate Bridge*
Musical Compositions	"Lift Every Voice and Sing"
Cartoons	*Where I'm Coming From*

 NOTE The article *the* before a title is not capitalized unless it is part of the official title. The official title of a book is found on the title page. The official title of a newspaper or periodical is found on the masthead (usually on the editorial page).

EXAMPLES
the *Odyssey*
the *Boston Herald*

The Wall Street Journal
The Man in the Iron Mask

For information about which titles should be italicized and which should be enclosed in quotation marks, see pages 1245 and 1247.

Resources
- *Language Handbook Resources,* pp. 134–148
- *Language Workshop CD-ROM,* Chapter 9—Lessons 41–45: Punctuating Sentences; Lesson 50: Other Common Uses of Punctuation Marks

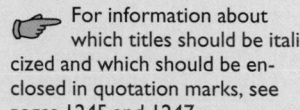
12 PUNCTUATION

END MARKS

For information about how sentences are classified according to purpose, see page 1235.

12a. **A statement (or declarative sentence) is followed by a period.**

EXAMPLE
Felipe asked whether Edgar Allan Poe was primarily a poet, an essayist, or a short-story writer.

12b. **A question (or interrogative sentence) is followed by a question mark.**

EXAMPLE
Have you read any of Edgar Allan Poe's poetry?

12c. **A request or command (or imperative sentence) is followed by either a period or an exclamation point.**

EXAMPLES
Answer the phone, please.
Turn the music down now!

12d. **An exclamation (or exclamatory sentence) is followed by an exclamation point.**

EXAMPLE
What an imagination Edgar Allan Poe had!

 NOTE An exclamation point may be used after a single word (especially an interjection) as well as after a sentence.

EXAMPLE
Hey! Wait for me!

12e. **An abbreviation is usually followed by a period.**

(See the chart at the top of the next page for examples.)

Some common abbreviations, including many for units of measurement, are written without periods.

EXAMPLES
AM/FM, FBI, IOU, MTV, PC, ROTC, SOS, cc, db, ft, lb, kw, ml, psi, rpm [Use a period with the abbreviation *in.* (*inch*) to avoid confusion with the word *in.*]

TYPE OF ABBREVIATION	EXAMPLES
Personal Names	N. Scott Momaday E. A. Robinson
Organizations and Companies	Assn. Co. Corp. Ltd. Inc.
Titles Used with Names	Dr. Jr. Ms. Ph.D.
Times of Day	A.M. (or a.m.) P.M. (or p.m.)
Years	B.C. (written after the date) A.D. (written before the date)
Addresses	Ave. Blvd. Dr. St. P.O. Box
States	Ark. Fla. R.I. N. Mex.

NOTE If an abbreviation has a period, do not place a period after it at the end of a sentence.

NOTE Two-letter state abbreviations without periods are used only when the ZIP Code is included.

EXAMPLE
Springfield, **MA** 01101

COMMAS

12f. Use commas to separate items in a series.

EXAMPLE
The main characters are Huck, Tom, and Jim.

If all the items in a series are linked by *and, or,* or *nor,* do not use commas to separate them.

EXAMPLE
Saul Bellow **and** Isaac Bashevis Singer **and** Toni Morrison won Nobel Prizes.

12g. Use a comma to separate two or more adjectives preceding a noun.

EXAMPLE
Lincoln was a noble, compassionate, wise leader.

12h. Use a comma before *and, but, or, nor, for, so,* and *yet* when they join independent clauses.

EXAMPLE
I read an excerpt from Amy Tan's *The Joy Luck Club,* and now I want to read the entire book.

You may omit the comma before *and, but, or,* or *nor* if the clauses are very short and there is no chance of misunderstanding.

12i. Use commas to set off nonessential clauses and nonessential participial phrases.

A *nonessential* clause or phrase is one that can be left out without changing the meaning of the sentence.

| NONESSENTIAL CLAUSE | Eudora Welty, **who was born in Mississippi,** uses her home state in many of her stories. |
| NONESSENTIAL PHRASE | Lee, **noticing my confusion,** rephrased her question. |

An *essential* clause or phrase is one that can't be left out without changing the meaning of the sentence. Essential clauses and phrases are *not* set off by commas.

| ESSENTIAL CLAUSE | Material **that is quoted verbatim** should be placed in quotation marks. |
| ESSENTIAL PHRASE | The only word **spoken by the raven** is *nevermore.* |

12j. Use a comma after certain introductory elements.

(1) Use a comma after a one-word adverb such as *first, yes,* or *no* and after any mild exclamation such as *well* or *why* at the beginning of a sentence.

EXAMPLE
Yes, Hemingway is my favorite author.

(2) Use a comma after an introductory participial phrase or introductory adverb clause.

EXAMPLES
Standing on the quarter-deck, Captain Ahab spoke to his crew. [participial phrase]
After he had driven around the lake several times, he decided to go to the drive-in restaurant. [adverb clause]

(3) Use a comma after two or more introductory prepositional phrases.

EXAMPLE
At the end of the story, Walter Mitty imagines that he is facing a firing squad.

12k. Use commas to set off elements that interrupt a sentence.

(1) Appositives and appositive phrases are usually set off by commas.

EXAMPLE
My favorite book by Claude McKay, *Banjo,* was first published in 1929.

Sometimes an appositive is so closely related to the word or words it refers to that it should not be set off by commas.

EXAMPLE
The poet **Maya Angelou** read one of her poems on Inauguration Day.

(2) Words used in direct address are set off by commas.

EXAMPLE
Your essay, **Theo,** was well organized.

(3) Parenthetical expressions are set off by commas.

Parenthetical expressions are remarks that add incidental information or that relate ideas to each other.

EXAMPLE
Simón Bolívar liberated much of South America from Spanish rule; he went on, **moreover,** to become the most powerful person on the continent.

12l. Use a comma in certain conventional situations.

(1) Use a comma to separate items in dates and addresses.

EXAMPLES
On Friday, October 23, 1994, my niece Leslie was born.
Please address all further inquiries to 92 Keystone Crossings, Indianapolis, IN 46240. [Notice that a comma is not used between a state abbreviation and a ZIP Code.]

(2) Use a comma after the salutation of a friendly letter and after the closing of any letter.

EXAMPLES
Dear Rosa,   Sincerely yours,

(3) Use a comma to set off an abbreviation such as *Jr., Sr., RN, M.D., Ltd.,* or *Inc.*

EXAMPLE
Is Juan Fuentes, Jr., your cousin?

SEMICOLONS

12m. Use a semicolon between independent clauses that are closely related in thought and are not joined by *and, but, for, nor, or, so,* or *yet.*

EXAMPLE
"Tart words make no friends; a spoonful of honey will catch more flies than a gallon of vinegar."
—Benjamin Franklin, *Poor Richard's Almanack*

12n. Use a semicolon between independent clauses joined by a conjunctive adverb or a transitional expression.

A *conjunctive adverb* (such as *consequently, however,* or *therefore*) or a *transitional expression* (such as *as a result, for example,* or *in other words*) indicates the relationship of the independent clauses that it joins. Notice in the following example that a comma is placed after the conjunctive adverb.

EXAMPLE
Dexter knew that Judy was selfish and insensitive; **nevertheless,** he continued to adore her.

12o. Use a semicolon (rather than a comma) before a coordinating conjunction to join independent clauses that contain commas.

EXAMPLE
During the nineteenth century—the era of such distinguished poets as Longfellow, Whittier, and Holmes—most poetry was written in traditional metrical patterns; but one poet, Walt Whitman, rejected the conventional verse forms.

12p. Use a semicolon between items in a series if the items contain commas.

EXAMPLE
The summer reading list includes *Behind the Trail of Broken Treaties,* by Vine Deloria, Jr.; *House Made of Dawn,* by N. Scott Momaday; and *Blue Highways: A Journey into America,* by William Least Heat-Moon.

COLONS

12q. Use a colon to mean "note what follows."

(1) Use a colon before a list of items, especially after expressions such as *as follows* and *the following.*

EXAMPLE
The magazine article profiles the following famous American authors of the nineteenth century: Edgar Allan Poe, Nathaniel Hawthorne, and Herman Melville.

 NOTE Do not use a colon before a list that directly follows a verb or a preposition.

EXAMPLE
The anthology includes "The Raven," "Richard Cory," and "Thanatopsis." [The list directly follows the verb *includes.*]

(2) Use a colon before a quotation that lacks a speaker tag such as *he said* or *she remarked*.

EXAMPLE
Dad's orders were loud and clear: "Everybody up and at 'em."

(3) Use a colon before a long, formal statement or quotation.

EXAMPLE
Patrick Henry concluded his fiery speech before the Virginia House of Burgesses with these words: "Is life so dear, or peace so sweet, as to be purchased at the price of chains and slavery? Forbid it, Almighty

God! I know not what course others may take; but as for me, give me liberty, or give me death!"

12r. Use a colon in certain conventional situations.

EXAMPLES
5:20 P.M. [between the hour and the minute]
Deuteronomy 5:6–21 [between chapter and verse in referring to passages from the Bible]
Dear Sir or Madam: [after the salutation of a business letter]
"Cold Kills: Hypothermia" [between a title and a subtitle]

13 PUNCTUATION

ITALICS

Italics are printed characters that slant to the right. To indicate italics in handwritten or typewritten work, use underlining.

PRINTED	Who wrote *Black Boy*?
HANDWRITTEN	*Who wrote Black Boy?*

13a. Use italics (underlining) for titles of books, plays, long poems, periodicals, newspapers, works of art, films, television series, long musical compositions, recordings, comic strips, computer software, court cases, trains, ships, aircraft, and spacecraft.

TYPE OF NAME	EXAMPLES	
Books	*The Scarlet Letter*	*Fifth Chinese Daughter*
Plays	*The Crucible*	*West Side Story*
Long Poems	*I Am Joaquín*	the *Epic of Gilgamesh*
Periodicals	*Reader's Digest*	*Newsweek*
Newspapers	*The Wall Street Journal*	the *Austin American-Statesman*
Works of Art	*The Kiss*	*The Starry Night*
Films	*Forrest Gump*	*Stand and Deliver*
TV Series	*Jeopardy!*	*Star Trek: The Next Generation*
Long Musical Compositions	*Liverpool Oratorio*	*Hiawatha's Wedding Feast*
Recordings	*Achtung Baby*	*Sketches of Spain*
Comic Strips	*Peanuts*	*Calvin and Hobbes*
Computer Software	*WordPerfect*	*Paintbrush*
Court Cases	*Plessy v. Ferguson*	*Bailey v. Alabama*
Trains, Ships	*Empire Builder*	*Queen Mary*
Aircraft, Spacecraft	*Solar Challenger*	*Apollo 11*

NOTE The article *the* before the title of a book, periodical, or newspaper is not italicized or capitalized unless it is part of the official title. The official title of a book appears on the title page. The official title of a periodical or newspaper is the name given on the masthead, which usually appears on the editorial page.

EXAMPLES
The article appeared in both the *Philadelphia Inquirer* and *The New York Times*.

For examples of titles that are not italicized but that are enclosed in quotation marks, see page 1247.

Resources

- *Language Handbook Resources,* pp. 149–159
- *Language Workshop CD-ROM,* Chapter 9—Lesson 43: Punctuating Interrupters; Lessons 46 and 47: Punctuating Possessives, Contractions, and Plurals; Lessons 48 and 49: Punctuating Titles and Quotations; Lesson 50: Conventional Uses of Punctuation; Lesson 51: Hyphens; Lesson 52: Ellipsis Points

13b. Use italics (underlining) for words, letters, numerals, and symbols referred to as such and for foreign words that have not been adopted into English.

EXAMPLES

Should the use of *their* for *there* be considered a spelling error or a usage error?

The teacher couldn't tell whether I had written a script *S,* the number *5,* or an *&.*

All U.S. coins are now stamped with the inscription *e pluribus unum.*

QUOTATION MARKS

13c. Use quotation marks to enclose a *direct quotation*—a person's exact words.

EXAMPLE

Chief Joseph said, "The earth is the mother of all people, and all people should have equal rights upon it."

Notice that a direct quotation begins with a capital letter. However, if the quotation is only part of a sentence, it does not begin with a capital letter.

EXAMPLE

Chief Joseph called the earth "the mother of all people."

(1) When the expression identifying the speaker divides a quoted sentence, the second part begins with a lowercase letter.

EXAMPLE

"I really have to leave now," said Gwen, "so that I will be on time." [Notice that each part of a divided quotation is enclosed in quotation marks.]

When the second part of a divided quotation is a new sentence, it begins with a capital letter.

EXAMPLE

"Teddy Roosevelt was the first U.S. president to express concern about the depletion of the nation's natural resources," explained Mr. Fuentes. "He established a conservation program that expanded the national park system."

(2) When used with quotation marks, other marks of punctuation are placed according to the following rules.

- Commas and periods are always placed inside the closing quotation marks.

EXAMPLES

"On the other hand," he said, "your decision may be correct."

- Semicolons and colons are always placed outside the closing quotation marks.

EXAMPLES

My neighbor said, "Sure, I'll buy a subscription"; it was lucky that I asked her on payday.

Edna St. Vincent Millay uses these devices in her poem "Spring": alliteration, slant rhyme, and personification.

- Question marks and exclamation points are placed inside the closing quotation marks if the quotation itself is a question or an exclamation. Otherwise, they are placed outside.

EXAMPLES

Was it you who wrote the poem "Upon Turning Seventeen"?

"What a tortured soul Reverend Dimmesdale is!" said Mr. Klein.

(3) When quoting a passage that consists of more than one paragraph, put quotation marks at the beginning of each paragraph and at the end of only the last paragraph.

EXAMPLE

"As he neared the house, each detail of the scene became vivid to him. He was aware of some bricks of the vanished chimney lying on the sod. There was a door which hung by one hinge.

"Rifle bullets called forth by the insistent skirmishers came from the far-off bank of foliage. They mingled with the shells and the pieces of shells until the air was torn in all directions by hootings, yells, howls. The sky was full of fiends who directed all their wild rage at his head."

—Stephen Crane, "A Mystery of Heroism"

(4) Use single quotation marks to enclose a quotation within a quotation.

EXAMPLES

The teacher requested, "Jorge, please explain what Emerson meant when he said, 'To be great is to be misunderstood.'"

"Have you read 'Rip Van Winkle'?" Jill asked.

(5) When writing *dialogue* (a conversation), begin a new paragraph every time the speaker changes, and enclose the speaker's words in quotation marks.

EXAMPLE

"How far is it to the Owl Creek bridge?" Farquhar asked.

"About thirty miles."

"Is there no force on this side the creek?"

"Only a picket post half a mile out, on the railroad, and a single sentinel at this end of the bridge."

—Ambrose Bierce, "An Occurrence at Owl Creek Bridge"

13d. Use quotation marks to enclose titles of short works, such as short stories, poems, essays, articles, songs, episodes of television series, and chapters and other parts of books.

TYPE OF NAME	EXAMPLES
Short Stories	"The Magic Barrel" "The Tell-Tale Heart"
Poems	"The Latin Deli" "Thanatopsis"
Essays	"On the Mall" "The Creative Process"
Articles	"Old Poetry and Modern Music"
Songs	"On Top of Old Smoky"
TV Episodes	"The Flight of the Condor"
Chapters and Parts of Books	"The World Was New" "The Colonies' Struggle for Freedom"

NOTE Neither italics nor quotation marks are used for titles of major religious works or titles of legal or historical documents.

EXAMPLES
Bible   Bill of Rights

☞ For a list of titles that are italicized rather than placed in quotation marks, see page 1245.

ELLIPSIS POINTS

13e. Use three spaced periods called *ellipsis points* (. . .) to mark omissions from quoted material and pauses in a written passage.

ORIGINAL The second half of the program consisted of four numbers from the *Ring,* and closed with Siegfried's funeral march. My aunt wept quietly, but almost continuously, as a shallow vessel overflows in a rainstorm. From time to time her dim eyes looked up at the lights which studded the ceiling, burning softly under their dull glass globes; doubtless they were stars in truth to her. I was still perplexed as to what measure of musical comprehension was left to her, she who had heard nothing but the singing of gospel hymns at Methodist services in the square frame schoolhouse on Section Thirteen for so many years. I was wholly unable to gauge how much of it had been dissolved in soapsuds, or worked into bread, or milked into the bottom of a pail.
　　　　　　—Willa Cather, "A Wagner Matinée"

(1) If the quoted material that comes before the ellipsis points is not a complete sentence, use three ellipsis points with a space before the first point.

EXAMPLE
The narrator notes, "The second half of the program . . . closed with Siegfried's funeral march."

(2) If the quoted material that comes before or after the ellipsis points is a complete sentence, use an end mark before the ellipsis points.

EXAMPLE
The narrator observes, "My aunt wept quietly. . . . "

(3) If one sentence or more is omitted, ellipsis points follow the end mark that precedes the omitted material.

EXAMPLE
Recalling the experience, the narrator says, "My aunt wept quietly, but almost continuously, as a shallow vessel overflows in a rainstorm. . . . I was still perplexed as to what measure of musical comprehension was left to her, she who had heard nothing but the singing of gospel hymns at Methodist services in the square frame schoolhouse on Section Thirteen for so many years."

(4) To show that a full line or more of poetry has been omitted, use an entire line of spaced periods.

ORIGINAL If you were coming in the Fall,
　　　　I'd brush the Summer by
　　　　With half a smile, and half a spurn,
　　　　As Housewives do, a Fly.
　　　　　—Emily Dickinson, "If you were
　　　　　　coming in the Fall"

WITH OMISSION If you were coming in the Fall,
　　　　I'd brush the Summer by
　　　　. . . . .
　　　　As Housewives do, a Fly.

APOSTROPHES

13f. Use an apostrophe in forming the possessive of nouns and indefinite pronouns.

(1) To form the possessive of a singular noun, add an apostrophe and an *s*.

EXAMPLES
the minister's veil   Ross's opinion

NOTE When forming the possessive of a singular noun ending in an *s* sound, add only an apostrophe if the addition of *'s* will make the noun awkward to pronounce. Otherwise, add *'s*.

EXAMPLES
Douglass's autobiography   Texas' population

(2) To form the possessive of a plural noun ending in *s*, add only the apostrophe. If the plural noun does not end in *s*, add an apostrophe and an *s*.

EXAMPLES
the authors' styles   the Ushers' house
men's fashions   children's toys

(3) To form the possessive of an indefinite pronoun, add an apostrophe and an *s*.

EXAMPLES
each one's time   everybody's opinion

 NOTE In such forms as *anyone else* and *somebody else,* the correct possessives are *anyone else's* and *somebody else's.*

(4) Form the possessive of only the last word in a compound word, in the name of an organization or business firm, or in a word group showing joint possession.

EXAMPLES
father-in-law's gloves   Roz and Denise's idea
Taylor, Sanders, and Weissman's law office

(5) Form the possessive of each noun in a word group showing individual possession of similar items.

EXAMPLE
Baldwin's and Ellison's writings

When a possessive pronoun is part of a word group showing joint possession, each noun in the word group is also possessive.

EXAMPLE
Walter Mitty's and **her** relationship

(6) When used in the possessive form, words that indicate time (such as *hour, week,* and *year*) and words that indicate amounts of money require apostrophes.

EXAMPLES
a week's vacation   five dollars' worth

13g. Use an apostrophe to show where letters, words, or numbers have been omitted in a contraction.

EXAMPLES
they had . . . **they'd**   Kerry is . . . **Kerry's**
let us . . . **let's**   of the clock . . . **o'clock**
where is . . . **where's**   1997 . . . **'97**

The word *not* can be shortened to *–n't* and added to a verb, usually without any change in the spelling of the verb.

EXAMPLES
is not . . . **isn't**   has not . . . **hasn't**
EXCEPTION
will not . . . **won't**

13h. Use an apostrophe and an *s* to form the plurals of all lowercase letters, some uppercase letters, numerals, and some words referred to as words.

EXAMPLES
There are two *r*'s and two *s*'s in *embarrassed.*
Soon after Tom and Lucynell said their *I do*'s, he
      abandoned her.

You may add only an *s* to form the plurals of such items—except lowercase letters—if the plural forms will not cause misreading.

EXAMPLES
Compact discs (**CDs**) were introduced in the
      1980s.
On her report card were three **A's** and three **C's.**

HYPHENS

13i. Use a hyphen to divide a word at the end of a line.

When dividing a word at the end of a line, remember the following rules:

(1) Do not divide a one-syllable word.

EXAMPLE
Peyton Farquhar was captured, and he was finally
hanged from the bridge**.**

(2) Divide a word only between syllables.

EXAMPLE
Ernest Hemingway's *A Farewell to Arms* was **published** in 1929.

(3) Divide an already hyphenated word at the hyphen.

EXAMPLE
Stephen Crane died in Germany at the age of **twenty-
eight.**

(4) Do not divide a word so that one letter stands alone.

EXAMPLE
One fine autumn day, Rip Van Winkle fell fast
asleep in the mountains.

13j. Use a hyphen with compound numbers from twenty-one to ninety-nine and with fractions used as modifiers.

EXAMPLES
six hundred **twenty-five**
a **three-fourths** quorum [*but* three fourths of the audience]

DASHES

13k. Use dashes to set off abrupt breaks in thoughts.

EXAMPLE
The poor condition of this road—it really needs to be paved—makes this route unpopular.

13l. Use dashes to set off an appositive or a parenthetical expression that contains commas.

EXAMPLE
Several of the nineteenth-century American poets—Poe, Dickinson, and Whitman, for example—led remarkable lives.

PARENTHESES

13m. Use parentheses to enclose informative or explanatory material of minor importance.

EXAMPLES
Harriet Tubman (c. 1820–1913) is remembered for her work in the Underground Railroad.
On our vacation we visited Natchitoches (it's pronounced nak′ə·täsh′), Louisiana.
Thoreau lived at Walden Pond for two years. (See the map on page 350.)

BRACKETS

13n. Use brackets to enclose an explanation within quoted or parenthetical material.

EXAMPLE
I think that Hilda Doolittle (more commonly known as H. D. [1886–1961]) is best remembered for her Imagist poetry.

14 SPELLING

UNDERSTANDING WORD STRUCTURE

Many English words are made up of roots and affixes (prefixes and suffixes).

Roots

14a. The *root* of a word is the part that carries the word's core meaning.

ROOTS	MEANINGS	EXAMPLES
–bio–	life	biology, symbiotic
–duc–, –duct–	lead	educate, conductor
–mit–, –miss–	send	remit, emissary
–port–	carry, bear	transport, portable

 NOTE To find the meaning of a root or an affix, look in a dictionary. Most dictionaries have individual entries for word parts.

Prefixes

14b. A *prefix* is one or more letters or syllables added to the beginning of a word or word part to create a new word.

PREFIXES	MEANINGS	EXAMPLES
a–	lacking, without	amorphous, apolitical
dia–	through, across, apart	diagonal, diameter, diagnose
inter–	between, among	intercede, international
mis–	badly, wrongly	misfire, misspell

Resources

- *Language Handbook Resources,* pp. 160–167
- *Language Workshop CD-ROM,* Chapter 10—Lessons 55 and 56: Rules of Spelling; Lesson 57: Words Often Confused

Suffixes

14c. A *suffix* is one or more letters or syllables added to the end of a word or word part to create a new word.

SUFFIXES	MEANINGS	EXAMPLES
–ation, –ition	action, result	repetition, starvation
–er	doer, native of	baker, westerner
–ible	able, likely, fit	edible, possible, divisible
–or	doer, office, action	director, juror, error

SPELLING RULES

ie and *ei*

14d. Write *ie* when the sound is long *e*, except after *c*.

EXAMPLES
believe   field   ceiling   receive
EXCEPTIONS
either   leisure   seize   protein

14e. Write *ei* when the sound is not long *e*.

EXAMPLES
eight   neighbor   weigh   foreign
EXCEPTIONS
ancient   view   friend   efficient

–cede, –ceed, and *–sede*

14f. The only English word ending in *–sede* is *supersede*. The only words ending in *–ceed* are *exceed, proceed,* and *succeed*. Most other words with this sound end in *–cede*.

EXAMPLES
accede   concede   intercede   recede

Adding Prefixes

14g. When adding a prefix, do not change the spelling of the root.

EXAMPLES
mis + spell = **mis**spell
inter + national = **inter**national

Adding Suffixes

14h. When adding the suffix *–ness* or *–ly*, do not change the spelling of the original word.

EXAMPLES
plain + ness = plain**ness**   casual + ly = casual**ly**
EXCEPTIONS
For most words ending in *y*, change the *y* to *i* before adding *-ness* or *-ly*.
empty + ness = empt**iness**   busy + ly = bus**ily**

 NOTE One-syllable adjectives ending in *y* generally follow rule 14h.

EXAMPLES
dry + ness = dry**ness**   shy + ly = shy**ly**

14i. Drop the final silent *e* before a suffix beginning with a vowel.

EXAMPLES
care + ing = car**ing**   dose + age = dos**age**
EXCEPTIONS
Keep the final silent *e*
- in a word ending in *ce* or *ge* before a suffix beginning with *a* or *o*: peac**eable**, courag**eous**
- in *dye* and in *singe* before *–ing*: dy**eing**, sing**eing**
- in *mile* before *–age*: mil**eage**

 NOTE When adding *–ing* to words that end in *ie*, drop the *e* and change the *i* to *y*.

EXAMPLES
die + ing = d**ying**   lie + ing = l**ying**

14j. Keep the final silent *e* before a suffix beginning with a consonant.

EXAMPLES
hope + ful = hope**ful**   love + ly = love**ly**
EXCEPTIONS
awe + ful = aw**ful**   whole + ly = whol**ly**
nine + th = nin**th**   argue + ment = argu**ment**

14k. For words ending in *y* preceded by a consonant, change the *y* to *i* before any suffix that does not begin with *i*.

EXAMPLES
thirsty + est = thirst**iest**   plenty + ful = plent**iful**

14l. For words ending in *y* preceded by a vowel, keep the *y* when adding a suffix.

EXAMPLES
joy + ful = joy**ful**   obey + ing = obey**ing**
EXCEPTIONS
day—da**ily**   lay—la**id**   pay—pa**id**   say—sa**id**

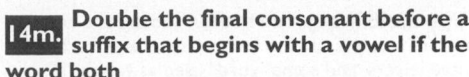
14m. Double the final consonant before a suffix that begins with a vowel if the word both

(1) has only one syllable or has the accent on the last syllable

and

(2) ends in a single consonant preceded by a single vowel.

EXAMPLES
thin + est = thi**nn**est   occur + ed = occu**rr**ed
EXCEPTIONS

● For words ending in *w* or *x*, do not double the final consonant.

new + er = new**er** relax + ing = rela**x**ing

● For words ending in *c*, add *k* before the suffix instead of doubling the *c*.

picnic + k + ed = picnic**ked**

NOTE   The final consonant of some words may or may not be doubled, such as *traveled*/*travelled*. If you are unsure about doubling a final consonant, consult a dictionary.

Forming the Plurals of Nouns

14n. Remembering the following rules will help you spell the plural forms of nouns.

(1) For most nouns, add –s.

EXAMPLES
player**s**   island**s**   Jefferson**s**

(2) For nouns ending in *s*, *x*, *z*, *ch*, or *sh*, add –es.

EXAMPLES
class**es**   match**es**   tax**es**   Cháve**zes**

(3) For nouns ending in *y* preceded by a vowel, add –s.

EXAMPLES
monkey**s**   alloy**s**   McKay**s**

TIPS FOR SPELLING   In some names, diacritical marks (marks that show pronunciation) are as essential to correct spelling as the letters themselves. If you are not sure about the spelling of a name, check with the person whose name it is or consult a reference source.

EXAMPLES
Abolfat'h   Hélène   Bashō   Da 'Shawn

(4) For nouns ending in *y* preceded by a consonant, change the *y* to *i* and add –es.

EXAMPLES
fl**ies**   countr**ies**   troph**ies**
EXCEPTIONS
For proper nouns, add –s: Kennedy**s**

(5) For some nouns ending in *f* or *fe*, add –s. For others, change the *f* or *fe* to *v* and add –es. For proper nouns, add –s.

EXAMPLES
gulf**s**   roof**s**   lea**ves**   kni**ves**   wol**ves**
Tallchief**s**   Wolfe**s**

(6) For nouns ending in *o* preceded by a vowel, add –s.

EXAMPLES
studio**s**   stereo**s**   Ignacio**s**

(7) For nouns ending in *o* preceded by a consonant, add –es.

EXAMPLES
tomato**es**   hero**es**   veto**es**

For some common nouns ending in *o* preceded by a consonant, especially those referring to music, and for proper nouns, add only an –s.

EXAMPLES
taco**s**   piano**s**   alto**s**   Suro**s**

NOTE   For some nouns ending in *o* preceded by a consonant, either –s or –es may be added.

EXAMPLES
zero**s** *or* zero**es**   mosquito**s** *or* mosquito**es**

(8) The plurals of a few nouns are formed in irregular ways.

EXAMPLES
teeth   women   mice   geese

(9) For a few nouns, the singular and the plural forms are the same.

EXAMPLES
sheep   trout   aircraft   Japanese   Sioux

(10) For most compound nouns, form the plural of only the last word of the compound.

EXAMPLES
bookshel**ves**   baby sitter**s**   ten-year-old**s**

(11) For compound nouns in which one of the words is modified by the other word or words, form the plural of the noun modified.

EXAMPLES
sister**s**-in-law   runner**s**-up   mountain goat**s**

LANGUAGE HANDBOOK   1251

(12) For some nouns borrowed from other languages, the plural is formed as in the original languages.

EXAMPLES

alga—algae   hypothesis—hypotheses
ellipsis—ellipses   phenomenon—phenomena

(13) To form the plurals of figures, most uppercase letters, signs, and words used as words, add an *–s* or both an apostrophe and an *–s.*

EXAMPLES

1990—1990s *or* 1990**'s**   *C*—*C*s *or* *C***'s**
and—*and*s *or* *and***'s**   *&*—*&*s *or* *&***'s**

To prevent confusion, add both an apostrophe and an *–s* to form the plural of all lowercase letters, certain uppercase letters, and some words used as words.

EXAMPLES

The word *Mississippi* contains four *s***'s** and four *i***'s.** [Without an apostrophe, the plural of *i* could be confused with *is.*]
Because I mistakenly thought Flannery O'Connor was a man, I used *his***'s** instead of *her***'s** in my paragraph. [Without an apostrophe, the plural of *his* would look like the word *hiss,* and the plural of *her* would look like the pronoun *hers.*]

Resources
• *Language Handbook Resources,* pp. 168–172
• *Language Workshop CD-ROM,* Chapter 11: Usage

15 GLOSSARY OF USAGE

The **Glossary of Usage** is an alphabetical list of words and expressions with definitions, explanations, and examples. Some examples in this list are labeled *standard, nonstandard, formal,* or *informal.* The labels **standard** and **formal** identify usage that is appropriate in serious writing and speaking (such as in compositions and speeches). The label *informal* indicates standard English commonly used in conversation and in everyday writing such as personal letters. The label **nonstandard** identifies usage that does not follow the guidelines of standard English usage.

---

accept, except *Accept* is a verb meaning "to receive." *Except* may be either a verb meaning "to leave out" or a preposition meaning "excluding."

EXAMPLES

I will **accept** another yearbook assignment. [verb]
Should the military services **except** women from combat duty? [verb]
I have read all of Willa Cather's novels **except** *My Ántonia.* [preposition]

affect, effect *Affect* is a verb meaning "to influence." *Effect* may be either a verb meaning "to bring about or accomplish" or a noun meaning "the result [of an action]."

EXAMPLES

How did the House of Usher **affect** the narrator?
Renewed interest in *Moby-Dick* during the 1920s **effected** a change in Melville's reputation.
What **effect** did the war have on Paul Berlin?

all ready, already *All ready* means "all prepared." *Already* means "previously."

EXAMPLES

Are you **all ready** to give your report?
We have **already** read that story.

all the farther, all the faster Avoid using these expressions in formal situations. Use *as far as* or *as fast as.*

EXAMPLE

The first act was **as far as** [*not* all the farther] we had read in *A Raisin in the Sun.*

all together, altogether *All together* means "everyone or everything in the same place." *Altogether* means "entirely."

EXAMPLES

My family will be **all together** for the holidays this year.
The president is **altogether** opposed to the bill.

allusion, illusion An *allusion* is an indirect reference to something. An *illusion* is a mistaken idea or a misleading appearance.

EXAMPLES

In her stories, Flannery O'Connor makes numerous **allusions** to the Bible.
Illusions of success haunt Willy Loman.
Makeup can be used to create an **illusion.**

almost, most Avoid using *most* for *almost* in all writing other than dialogue.

EXAMPLE

Almost [*not* most] everyone in class was surprised by the outcome in Ambrose Bierce's story "An Occurrence at Owl Creek Bridge."

a lot Avoid this expression in formal situations by using *many* or *much.*

already See **all ready, already.**

altogether See **all together, altogether.**

among See **between, among.**

amount, number Use *amount* to refer to a singular word. Use *number* to refer to a plural word.

EXAMPLES
The library has a large **amount** of resource material about the Harlem Renaissance. [*Amount* refers to *material.*]
The library has a large **number** of books about the Harlem Renaissance. [*Number* refers to *books.*]

and, but In general, avoid beginning a sentence with *and* or *but* in formal writing.

and etc. *Etc.* stands for the Latin words *et cetera,* meaning "and others" or "and so forth." Always avoid using *and* before *etc.* In general, avoid using *etc.* in formal situations. Use an unabbreviated English expression instead.

EXAMPLE
We are studying twentieth-century American novelists: Ernest Hemingway, Margaret Walker, Jean Toomer, **and others** [*or* etc., *but not* and etc.].

and/or Avoid using this confusing construction. Decide which alternative, *and* or *or,* expresses what you mean, and use it alone.

any more, anymore The expression *any more* specifies a quantity. *Anymore* means "now; nowadays."

EXAMPLES
Do you know **any more** Caddo folk tales?
Kam doesn't work at the record store **anymore.**

any one, anyone The expression *any one* specifies one member of a group. *Anyone* is a pronoun meaning "one person, no matter which."

EXAMPLES
Any one of you can play the part.
Anyone can try out for the part.

anyways, anywheres Omit the final *s* from these words and others like them (*everywheres, nowheres, somewheres*).

EXAMPLE
I can't go **anywhere** [*not* anywheres] until I finish.

as See **like, as.**

as if See **like, as if.**

at Avoid using *at* after a construction beginning with *where.*

EXAMPLE
Where was Chief Joseph [*not* where was Chief Joseph at] when he delivered his surrender speech?

a while, awhile *A while* means "a period of time." *Awhile* means "for a short time."

EXAMPLES
Let's wait here **awhile.**
Let's sit here for **a while** and listen to the band.

bad, badly *Bad* is an adjective. *Badly* is an adverb. In standard English, *bad* should follow a sense verb, such as *feel, look, sound, taste,* or *smell,* or other linking verb.

NONSTANDARD	If the cole slaw smells badly, don't eat it.
STANDARD	If the cole slaw smells **bad,** don't eat it.

because In formal situations, do not use the construction *reason . . . because.* Instead, use *reason . . . that.*

EXAMPLE
The **reason** for the eclipse is **that** [*not* because] the moon has come between the Earth and the sun.

being as, being that Avoid using either of these expressions in place of *since* or *because.*

EXAMPLE
Because [*not* being as *or* being that] Ms. Ribas is a gemologist, she may know what these stones are.

beside, besides *Beside* is a preposition meaning "by the side of" or "next to." *Besides* may be either a preposition meaning "in addition to" or "other than" or an adverb meaning "moreover."

EXAMPLES
Rip Van Winkle laid his rifle **beside** him on the ground. [preposition]
No one **besides** Lurleen has read all of *Leaves of Grass* [preposition]
I'm not in the mood to go shopping; **besides,** I have an English test tomorrow. [adverb]

between, among Use *between* to refer to only two items or to more than two when comparing each item individually to each of the others.

EXAMPLES
The money from the sale of the property was evenly divided **between** Sasha and Antonio.
Don't you know the difference **between** a simile, a metaphor, and an analogy? [Each figure of speech is compared individually to each of the others.]

Use *among* to refer to more than two items when you are not considering each item in relation to each other item individually.

EXAMPLE
The money from the sale of the property was evenly divided **among** the four relatives.

bring, take *Bring* means "to come carrying something." *Take* means "to go carrying something."

EXAMPLES

I'll **bring** my Wynton Marsalis tapes when I come over.

When he went hunting, Rip Van Winkle **took** his gun and dog.

but See **and, but.**

cannot (can't) help but Avoid using *but* followed by the infinitive form of a verb after the expression *cannot (can't) help*. Instead, use a gerund after the expression.

NONSTANDARD	I can't help but tap my foot whenever I hear mariachi music.
STANDARD	I can't help **tapping** my foot whenever I hear mariachi music.

compare, contrast Used with *to*, *compare* means "to look for similarities between." Used with *with*, *compare* means "to look for similarities and differences between." *Contrast* is always used to point out differences.

EXAMPLES

Write a simile **comparing** a manufactured product **to** something in nature.

How do the haiku of Taniguchi Buson **compare with** those of Matsuo Bashō?

The teacher **contrasted** the writing styles of Walt Whitman and Emily Dickinson.

could of See **of.**

double subject Do not use an unnecessary pronoun after the subject of a sentence.

EXAMPLE

Judy Jones [*not* Judy Jones she] fascinates Dexter Green.

due to Avoid using *due to* for "because of" or "owing to."

EXAMPLE

The game was postponed **because of** [*not* due to] rain.

each and every The expression *each and every* is redundant. Instead, use either *each* or *every* alone.

EXAMPLE

Every [*not* each and every] resident of Jefferson attended Miss Emily Grierson's funeral.

effect See **affect, effect.**

either, neither *Either* usually means "one or the other of two." *Neither* usually means "not one or the other of two." Avoid using *either* or *neither* when referring to more than two.

EXAMPLE

Consider writing about the Jazz Age, the Harlem Renaissance, or the Great Depression; **any one** [*not* either] of those topics would be interesting.

emigrate, immigrate *Emigrate* means "to leave a country or a region to settle elsewhere." *Immigrate* means "to come into a country or a region to settle there."

EXAMPLES

Claude McKay **emigrated** from Jamaica in 1912.

Claude McKay **immigrated** to the United States in 1912.

etc. See **and etc.**

every See **each and every.**

every day, everyday *Every day* means "each day." *Everyday* means "daily" or "usual."

EXAMPLES

Parson Hooper wore the black veil **every day.**

Walking the dog is one of my **everyday** chores.

every one, everyone *Every one* specifies every person or thing of those named. *Everyone* means "every person; everybody."

EXAMPLES

Every one of these poems was written by Anne Sexton.

Has **everyone** read "The Bells"?

except See **accept, except.**

farther, further Use *farther* to express physical distance. Use *further* to express abstract relationships of degree or quantity.

EXAMPLES

We swam **farther** than we usually do.

After discussing "The Road Not Taken" **further**, we agreed with Karl's interpretation of the poem.

fewer, less Use *fewer* to modify a plural noun and *less* to modify a singular noun.

EXAMPLES

Later in life, Emily Dickinson entertained even **fewer** guests.

Later in life, Emily Dickinson spent **less** time entertaining guests.

further See **farther, further.**

good, well Do not use the adjective *good* to modify a verb. Instead, use the adverb *well,* meaning "capably" or "satisfactorily." As an adjective, *well* means "in good health" or "satisfactory in appearance or condition."

EXAMPLES
The school orchestra played **well** [adverb].
He says that he feels quite **well** [adjective].
It's midnight, and all is **well** [adjective].

had of See **of.**

had ought, hadn't ought Do not use *had* or *hadn't* with *ought.*

EXAMPLE
His scores **ought** [*not* had ought] to be back by now.

half Avoid using an indefinite article (*a* or *an*) both before and after *half.*

EXAMPLE
We've waited for **half an hour** [*or* **a half hour**].

if, whether Avoid using *if* for *whether* in indirect questions and in expressions of doubt.

EXAMPLE
Dickinson wanted to know **whether** [*not* if] her poems were "alive."

illusion See **allusion, illusion.**

immigrate See **emigrate, immigrate.**

imply, infer *Imply* means "to suggest indirectly." *Infer* means "to interpret" or "to draw a conclusion."

EXAMPLES
The speaker of "Thanatopsis" **implies** that nature can allay one's fear of death.
I **infer** from the poem that nature can cure many ills.

in, into *In* generally shows location. *Into* generally shows direction.

EXAMPLES
Randall Jarrell was born **in** Nashville, Tennessee.
When Rip walked **into** the village, everybody stared.

irregardless, regardless *Irregardless* is nonstandard. Use *regardless* instead.

EXAMPLE
Regardless [*not* irregardless] of the children's pleas, their father said they had to go to bed.

its, it's *Its* is the possessive form of *it. It's* is the contraction of *it is* or *it has.*

EXAMPLES
The crew prepares for **its** fight with Moby-Dick.
It's [it is] Captain Ahab's obsession.
It's [it has] been many years since Ahab lost his leg.

kind of, sort of In formal situations, avoid using these terms for the adverb *somewhat* or *rather.*

INFORMAL Roderick became kind of agitated.
FORMAL Roderick became **rather** agitated.

kind of a(n), sort of a(n) In formal situations, omit the *a(n).*

INFORMAL What kind of an essay is Baldwin's "The Creative Process"?
FORMAL What **kind of** essay is Baldwin's "The Creative Process"?

kind(s), sort(s), type(s) With the singular form of each of these nouns, use *this* or *that.* With the plural form, use *these* or *those.*

EXAMPLE
This kind of gas is safe, but **those kinds** aren't.

lay, lie See **lie, lay.**

learn, teach *Learn* means "to gain knowledge." *Teach* means "to provide with knowledge."

EXAMPLE
The more you **teach** someone else, the more you **learn** yourself.

less See **fewer, less.**

lie, lay The verb *lie* means "to rest" or "to stay, to recline, or to remain in a certain state or position." Its principal parts are *lie, lying, lay,* and *lain. Lie* never takes an object. The verb *lay* means "to put [something] in a place." Its principal parts are *lay, laying, laid,* and *laid. Lay* usually takes an object.

EXAMPLES
Their land **lay** in the shadow of Rainy Mountain. [no object]
Eduardo **laid** the strips of grilled meat on the tortilla. [*Strips* is the object of *laid.*]

like, as In formal situations, do not use *like* for the conjunction *as* to introduce a subordinate clause.

INFORMAL Plácido Domingo sings like Caruso once did.
FORMAL Plácido Domingo sings **as** Caruso once did.

like, as if In formal situations, avoid using the preposition *like* for the conjunction *as if* or *as though* to introduce a subordinate clause.

INFORMAL The singers sounded like they had not rehearsed.
FORMAL The singers sounded **as if** [*or* **as though**] they had not rehearsed.

might of, must of See **of**.

most See **almost, most**.

neither See **either, neither**.

nor See **or, nor**.

number See **amount, number**.

of *Of* is a preposition. Do not use *of* in place of *have* after verbs such as *could, should, would, might, must,* and *ought* [*to*]. Also, do not use *had of* for *had*.

EXAMPLES
You ought to **have** [*not* of] studied harder.
If he **had** [*not* had of] remembered the name of the author of "Mending Wall," he **would have** [*not* would of] made a perfect score.

Avoid using *of* after other prepositions such as *inside, off,* and *outside*.

EXAMPLE
Chian-Chu dived **off** [*not* off of] the side of the pool into the water.

on to, onto In the expression *on to, on* is an adverb and *to* is a preposition. *Onto* is a preposition.

EXAMPLES
Dexter held **on to** his winter dreams.
The cat leapt gracefully **onto** the windowsill.

or, nor Use *or* with *either;* use *nor* with *neither*.

EXAMPLES
On Tuesdays the school cafeteria offers a choice of **either** a taco salad **or** a pizza.
I wonder why **neither** Ralph Ellison **nor** Robert Frost was given the Nobel Prize in literature.

ought See **had ought, hadn't ought**.

ought to of See **of**.

reason . . . because See **because**.

regardless See **irregardless, regardless**.

rise, raise The verb *rise* means "to go up" or "to get up." Its principal parts are *rise, rising, rose,* and *risen*. *Rise* never takes an object. The verb *raise* means "to cause [something] to rise" or "to lift up." Its principal parts are *raise, raising, raised,* and *raised*. *Raise* usually takes an object.

EXAMPLES
The queen **rose** from her throne. [no object]
The movers **raised** the boxes onto their shoulders. [*Boxes* is the object of *raised*.]

should of See **of**.

sit, set The verb *sit* means "to rest in an upright, seated position." Its principal parts are *sit, sitting, sat,* and *sat*. *Sit* seldom takes an object. The verb *set* means "to put [something] in a place." Its principal parts are *set, setting, set,* and *set*. *Set* usually takes an object.

EXAMPLES
The raven **sat** on the bust of Pallas above the door. [no object]
Eben **set** the jug down. [*Jug* is the object of *set*.]

some, somewhat In formal situations, use *somewhat* instead of *some* to mean "to some extent."

EXAMPLE
My grades have improved **somewhat** [*not* some].

sort(s) See **kind(s), sort(s), type(s)** and **kind of a(n), sort of a(n)**.

sort of See **kind of, sort of**.

take See **bring, take**.

teach See **learn, teach**.

than, then *Than* is a conjunction used in comparisons. *Then* is an adverb meaning "at that time" or "next."

EXAMPLES
Tyrone is more studious **than** I am.
First, mix the wet ingredients; **then,** add the flour and other dry ingredients.

that See **who, which, that**.

their, there, they're *Their* is a possessive form of *they*. As an adverb, *there* means "at that place." *There* can also be used to begin a sentence. *They're* is the contraction of *they are*.

EXAMPLES
The performers are studying **their** lines.
I will be **there** after rehearsal. [adverb]
There will be four acts in the play. [expletive]
They're performing a play by Lorraine Hansberry.

theirs, there's *Theirs* is a possessive form of the pronoun *they*. *There's* is the contraction for *there is* or *there has*.

EXAMPLES
These posters are ours; **theirs** are the ones on the opposite wall.
There's [there is] a biography of W.E.B. DuBois in the library.
There's [there has] been a change in plans.

them Do not use *them* as an adjective. Use *those*.

EXAMPLE
Those [*not* them] lines illustrate Poe's use of internal rhyme.

then See **than, then.**

this here, that there Avoid using *here* or *there* after *this* or *that.*

EXAMPLE
This [*not* this here] magazine has an article about Andrea Lee.

try and, try to Use *try to,* not *try and.*

EXAMPLE
I will **try to** [*not* try and] finish my report on John Updike.

type, type of Avoid using the noun *type* as an adjective. Add *of* after *type.*

EXAMPLE
I prefer this **type of** [*not* type] shirt.

type(s) See **kind(s), sort(s), type(s).**

ways Use *way,* not *ways,* when referring to distance.

EXAMPLE
My home in Wichita is a long **way** [*not* ways] from Tokyo, where my pen pal lives.

well See **good, well.**

when, where Avoid using *when* or *where* to begin a definition.

NONSTANDARD	A predicament is where you are in an embarrassing situation.
STANDARD	A predicament is **an embarrassing situation.**

where Avoid using *where* for *that.*

EXAMPLE
I read **that** [*not* where] the Smithsonian Institution has preserved a great many of William H. Johnson's paintings.

where . . . at See **at.**

whether See **if, whether.**

who, which, that *Who* refers to persons only. *Which* refers to things only. *That* may refer to either persons or things.

EXAMPLES
Wasn't Beethoven the composer **who** [*or that*] continued to write music after he lost his hearing?
First editions of Poe's first book, **which** is titled *Tamerlane and Other Poems,* are worth thousands of dollars.
Is this the only essay **that** James Baldwin wrote?
I've never met or even seen the person **that** delivers our newspaper each morning.

who's, whose *Who's* is the contraction of *who is* or *who has. Whose* is the possessive form of *who.*

EXAMPLES
Who's [who is] going to portray the Navajo detective in the play?
Who's [who has] been using my computer?
Whose artwork is this?

would of See **of.**

your, you're *Your* is a possessive form of *you. You're* is the contraction of *you are.*

EXAMPLES
Is this **your** book?
I hope **you're** able to come to my graduation.

GLOSSARY

The glossary that follows is an alphabetical list of words found in the selections in this book. Use this glossary just as you use a dictionary—to find out the meanings of unfamiliar words. (Some technical, foreign, or more obscure words in this book are not listed here but are defined instead in the footnotes and sidenotes that accompany selections.) Many words in the English language have more than one meaning. This glossary gives the meanings that apply to the words as they are used in the selections in this book. Words closely related in form and meaning are usually listed together in one entry (*irk* and *irksome*); usually the definition is given for the first form only.

The following abbreviations are used:

adj.: adjective	*n.:* noun	*v.:* verb
adv.: adverb	*pl.:* plural form	

Unless a word is very simple to pronounce, its pronunciation is given in parentheses. A guide to the pronunciation symbols appears at the bottom of page 1259.

For more information about the words in this glossary, or about words not listed here, consult a dictionary.

abate (ə·bāt′) *v.:* to lessen.

abdicate (ab′di·kāt′) *v.:* to give up responsibility for.

abhor (ab·hôr′) *v.:* to scorn; hate; disdain.

abominable (ə·bäm′ə·nə·bəl) *adj.:* disgusting; loathsome.

abrasion (ə·brā′zhən) *n.:* scrape.

abstinence (ab′stə·nəns) *n.:* staying away.

abyss (ə·bis′) *n.:* gulf or void too deep for measurement.

acquiesce (ak′wē·es′) *v.:* to agree or accept quietly.

acrid (ak′rid) *adj.:* bitter; irritating.

acrimonious (ak′ri·mō′nē·əs) *adj.:* bitter; harsh. —**acrimoniously** *adv.*

acute (ə·kyo͞ot′) *adj.:* keen; sharp.

admonish (ad·män′ish) *v.:* to warn mildly. —**admonishing** *v. used as adj.*

adversary (ad′vər·ser′ē) *n.:* opponent.

affected (a·fekt′id) *adj.:* put on for show.

affliction (ə·flik′shən) *n.:* pain; hardship.

affluent (af′lo͞o·ənt) *adj.:* rich. —*adj. used as n.:* well-to-do people.

afford (ə·fôrd′) *v.:* to give; provide. —**afforded** *v. used as adj.*

agitated (aj′i·tāt′id) *adj.:* anxious; frantic.

alacrity (ə·lak′rə·tē) *n.:* promptness in responding; eagerness.

allay (a·lā′) *v.:* to lessen; relieve.

alleviate (ə·lē′vē·āt′) *v.:* to relieve; reduce.

alliance (ə·lī′əns) *n.:* close association for a common objective.

ally (al′ī) *n.:* supporter; friend.

ambiguous (am·big′yo͞o·əs) *adj.:* unclear; not certain. —**ambiguousness** *n.*

amble (am′bəl) *n.:* leisurely pace.

amiable (ā′mē·ə·bəl) *adj.:* agreeable; likable.

anarchy (an′ər·kē) *n.:* complete disorder.

ancestral (an·ses′trəl) *adj.:* inherited.

anguish (aŋ′gwish) *n.:* pain and suffering; heartache.

anonymity (an′ə·nim′ə·tē) *n.:* the state of being unnamed or not identified.

antagonist (an·tag′ə·nist) *n.:* adversary; opponent.

antipathy (an·tip′ə·thē) *n.:* strong dislike.

apocryphal (ə·päk′rə·fəl) *adj.:* of questionable authority; false.

appalling (ə·pôl′iŋ) *adj.:* dismaying.

apparition (ap′ə·rish′ən) *n.:* unexpected sight or ghostlike figure that appears suddenly.

appease (ə·pēz′) *v.:* to calm; satisfy.

appoint (ə·point′) *v.:* to assign. —**appointed** *v. used as adj.*

appreciable (ə·prē′shə·bəl) *adj.:* measurable.

appropriate (ə·prō′prē·āt′) *v.:* to take over.

arbitrary (är′bə·trer′ē) *adj.:* based on whims or individual preferences.

archaic (är·kā′ik) *adj.:* old-fashioned.

ardent (ärd′′nt) *adj.:* intense; eager. —**ardently** *adv.*

arduous (är′jo͞o·əs) *adj.:* difficult.

arrogant (ar′ə·gənt) *adj.:* proud and overly confident.

ascetic (ə·set′ik) *adj.:* severe; stern.

ascribe (ə·skrīb′) *v.:* to attribute to a certain cause.

assailant (ə·sāl′ənt) *n.:* attacker.

assert (ə·surt′) *v.:* to declare; claim.

assess (ə·ses′) *v.:* to evaluate; to judge the value of.

atrocity (ə·träs′ə·tē) *n.:* cruelty; brutality.

attribute (ə·trib′yo͞ot) *v.:* to believe to result from.

avarice (av′ə·ris) *n.:* greed.

aversion (ə·vur′zhən) *n.:* intense dislike.

avert (ə·vurt′) *v.:* to prevent; turn away.

bedlam (bed′ləm) *n.:* place or condition of noise and confusion.

benefactor (ben′ə·fak′tər) *n.:* person who helps others.

benevolence (bə·nev′ə·ləns) *n.:* kindness.

bewitch (bē·wich′) *v.:* to entice; fascinate. —**bewitching** *v. used as adj.*

blanch *v.:* to drain of color. —**blanched** *v. used as adj.*

bland *adj.:* mild. —**blandly** *adv.*

bleak (blēk) *adj.:* cheerless.

blithe (blīth) *adj.:* carefree.

brazen (brā′zən) *adj.:* bold. —**brazenness** *n.*

bustle (bus′əl) *v.:* to be busy or energetically active. —**bustling** *v. used as n.*

candid (kan′did) *adj.:* unbiased; fair.

cannonade (kan′ən·ād′) *v.:* to fire artillery. —**cannonading** *v. used as n.*

caper (kā′pər) *n.:* foolish prank.

careen (kə·rēn′) *v.:* to lurch sideways.

celestial (sə·les′chəl) *adj.:* divine; perfect.

censor (sen′sər) *v.:* to cut or change to remove objectionable material.

censure (sen′shər) *n.:* strong, disapproving criticism.

ceremonial (ser′ə·mō′nē·əl) *adj.:* formal.

chafe (chāf) *v.*: to become impatient.

chronological (krän'ō·läj'i·kəl) *adj.*: arranged in order of occurrence. —**chronologically** *adv.*

circumvent (sʉr'kəm·vent') *v.*: to get the better of by craft or ingenuity.

clammy (klam'ē) *adj.*: cold and damp.

clamor (klam'ər) *n.*: loud noise; uproar.

cleft (kleft) *n.*: opening.

clientele (klī'ən·tel') *n.*: customers; clients.

coherent (kō·hir'ənt) *adj.*: connected logically; clear; consistent.

coincide (kō'in·sīd') *v.*: to occur at the same time.

commence (kə·mens') *v.*: to start.

commodious (kə·mō'dē·əs) *adj.*: spacious.

communal (kə·myōōn'əl) *adj.*: belonging to an entire group or community.

complacency (kəm·plā'sən·sē) *n.*: self-satisfaction.

comply (kəm·plī') *v.*: to obey a command; agree to a request.

comprise (kəm·prīz') *v.*: to include.

conceive (kən·sēv') *v.*: to think; imagine.

conception (kən·sep'shən) *n.*: idea; mental formation of ideas.

concession (kən·sesh'ən) *n.*: act of giving in.

confederate (kən·fed'ər·it) *n.*: ally; person who shares a common purpose with another.

confiscation (kän'fis·kā'shən) *n.*: seizure of property by authority.

conflagration (kän'flə·grā'shən) *n.*: huge fire.

conscientious (kän'shē·en'shəs) *adj.*: careful and honest; diligent; thorough. —**conscientiously** *adv.*

consequence (kän'si·kwens') *n.*: result of an action.

consolation (kän'sə·lā'shən) *n.*: comfort.

console (kän'sōl') *n.*: desklike control panel.

conspiracy (kən·spir'ə·sē) *n.*: secret plot with a harmful or illegal purpose.

constitution (kän'stə·tōō'shən) *n.*: physical condition.

constrain (kən·strān') *v.*: to force.

consultation (kän'səl·tā'shən) *n.*: meeting to discuss or plan.

contemptuous (kən·temp'chōō·əs) *adj.*: scornful. —**contemptuously** *adv.*

contrivance (kən·trī'vəns) *n.*: scheme; plan.

conundrum (kə·nun'drəm) *n.*: riddle.

convene (kən·vēn') *v.*: to assemble.

conviction (kən·vik'shən) *n.*: belief.

convivial (kən·viv'ē·əl) *adj.*: jovial; sociable.

copious (kō'pē·əs) *adj.*: great amounts of.

correspondence (kôr'ə·spän'dəns) *n.*: communication by letters.

countenance (koun'tə·nəns) *n.*: face.

craven (krā'vən) *adj.*: very fearful; cowardly.

crucial (krōō'shəl) *adj.*: difficult; decisive.

curry (kʉr'ē) *v.*: to groom.

debris (də·brē') *n.*: rubble; broken pieces.

decrepit (dē·krep'it) *adj.*: run-down; worn out by age or use.

deference (def'ər·əns) *n.*: respect.

defiant (dē·fī'ənt) *adj.*: openly disobedient. —**defiantly** *adv.*: strongly resisting.

dejection (dē·jek'shən) *n.*: discouragement.

deluge (del'yōōj') *n.*: rush; flood.

demeanor (di·mēn'ər) *n.*: behavior; conduct.

derision (di·rizh'ən) *n.*: ridicule; contempt.

discern (di·sʉrn') *v.*: to notice; perceive. —**discernible** (di·sʉrn'ə·bəl) *adj.*

disclaimer (dis·klām'ər) *n.*: refusal of responsibility; giving up of a claim or connection.

disconsolate (dis·kän'sə·lit) *adj.*: unhappy. —**disconsolately** *adv.*

discourse (dis'kôrs') *n.*: conversation.

discreet (di·skrēt') *adj.*: wisely cautious.

disdain (dis·dān') *v.*: to refuse; disapprove; scorn.

disembody (dis'im·bäd'ē) *v.*: to separate from the body. —**disembodied** *v.* used as *adj.*

disheveled (di·shev'əld) *adj.*: rumpled; messed up.

dispel (di·spel') *v.*: to drive away. —**dispelling** *v.* used as *n.*

disperse (di·spʉrs') *v.*: to scatter.

dispirit (di·spir'it) *v.*: to discourage. —**dispirited** *v.* used as *adj.*

dispute (di·spyōōt') *v.*: to contest.

distraction (di·strak'shən) *n.*: mental disturbance or distress.

distraught (di·strôt') *adj.*: troubled.

divergence (dī·vʉr'jəns) *n.*: variance; difference.

docile (däs'əl) *adj.*: passive.

doddering (däd'ər·iŋ) *adj.*: shaky; trembling from old age.

dominant (däm'ə·nənt) *adj.*: prevailing; principal.

dominion (də·min'yən) *n.*: rule.

dowry (dou'rē) *n.*: money or goods the bride brings with her in a marriage.

drily (drī'lē) *adv.*: matter-of-factly; without emotion.

drone (drōn) *n.*: monotonous hum.

dwindle (dwin'dəl) *v.*: to diminish.

edible (ed'ə·bəl) *adj.*: capable of being eaten.

effectual (e·fek'chōō·əl) *adj.*: productive; efficient.

effete (e·fēt') *adj.*: sterile; unproductive.

elaborate (ē·lab'ə·rāt') *v.*: to develop with great care. —**elaborately** *adv.*

elapse (ē·laps') *v.*: to pass by; slip away.

elation (ē·lā'shən) *n.*: celebration.

eloquence (el'ə·kwəns) *n.*: well-articulated, persuasive speech.

elude (ē·lōōd') *v.*: to escape. —**eluding** *v.* used as *adj.*

emaciate (ē·mā'shē·āt') *v.*: to cause to be unusually thin. —**emaciated** *v.* used as *adj.*

---

fat, āpe, cär; ēven; is, bīte; gō, hôrn, look, tōōl; yoo, cure; yōō, use; oil, out; up, fʉr; get; joy; yet; chin; she; thin; then; zh, leisure; ŋ, ring; ə for *a* in *ago*, *e* in *agent*, *i* in *sanity*, *o* in *comply*, *u* in *focus*; ' as in *battle* (bat'l).

---

eminent (em′ə·nənt) *adj.*: well known for excellence; important; outstanding.

encumbrance (en·kum′brəns) *n.*: burden; hindrance.

engagement (en·gāj′mənt) *n.*: battle.

enmity (en′mə·tē) *n.*: hatred.

ensue (en·sōō′) *v.*: to result.

enthrall (en·thrôl′) *v.*: to fascinate.

entreat (en·trēt′) *v.*: to ask sincerely; pray to.

epitaph (ep′ə·taf′) *n.*: memorable or descriptive phrase written on a tombstone or in memory of the dead.

equivocal (ē·kwiv′ə·kəl) *adj.*: having more than one meaning.

eradicate (i·rad′i·kāt′) *v.*: to eliminate.

erudite (er′yōō·dīt′) *adj.*: scholarly; well informed.

ethereal (ē·thir′ē·əl) *adj.*: not earthly; spiritual.

eulogy (yōō′lə·jē) *n.*: public speech of praise.

evident (ev′ə·dənt) *adj.*: clear; obvious.

exaggeration (eg·zaj′ər·ā′·shən) *n.*: overstatement.

exalt (eg·zôlt′) *v.*: to lift up.

excruciating (eks·krōō′shē·āt′iŋ) *adj.*: extreme; intense.

execration (ek′si·krā′shən) *n.*: angry word; curse.

exemplary (eg·zem′plə·rē) *adj.*: serving as a model.

expedient (ek·spē′dē·ənt) *n.*: convenience; means to an end.

expire (ek·spīr′) *v.*: to die. —**expiring** *v.* used as *adj.*

explicit (eks·plis′it) *adj.*: clear; definite.

expunge (ek·spunj′) *v.*: to erase; remove.

extremity (ek·strem′ə·tē) *n.*: limb of the body, especially a hand or foot. —**extremities** *n. pl.*

exuberant (eg·zōō′bər·ənt) *adj.*: intensely happy; visibly enthusiastic.

exult (eg·zult′) *v.*: to rejoice greatly.

facilitate (fə·sil′ə·tāt′) *v.*: to simplify.

fastidious (fas·tid′ē·əs) *adj.*: difficult to please; critical.

ferocity (fə·räs′ə·tē) *n.*: fierce cruelty.

fidelity (fə·del′ə·tē) *n.*: accuracy.

fitful (fit′fəl) *adj.*: restless. —**fitfully** *adv.*: irregularly; in stops and starts.

flippancy (flip′ən·sē) *n.*: impertinence; glibness.

florid (flôr′id) *adj.*: showy.

flourish (flur′ish) *v.*: to do well; blossom.

fraternal (frə·turn′əl) *adj.*: brotherly; friendly.

frenzy (fren′zē) *n.*: frantic behavior; wildness.

frippery (frip′ər·ē) *n.*: something showy, frivolous, or unnecessary.

frugal (frōō′gəl) *adj.*: thrifty; economical.

furrow (fur′ō) *n.*: groove in the land made by a plow.

furtive (fur′tiv) *adj.*: secret; stealthy. —**furtively** *adv.*

futile (fyōōt′′l) *adj.*: useless; pointless.

gait (gāt) *n.*: way of walking; stride.

gall (gôl) *v.*: to irritate; anger.

garnish (gär′nish) *v.*: to top.

gaudy (gôd′ē) *adj.*: showy; lacking in good taste.

gaunt (gônt) *adj.*: very thin.

gesticulate (jes·tik′yōō·lāt′) *v.*: to gesture, especially with the hands and arms, while speaking.

gregarious (grə·ger′ē·əs) *adj.*: sociable. —**gregariousness** *n.*

grope (grōp) *v.*: to search; fumble. —**groping** *v.* used as *adj.*

grotesque (grō·tesk′) *adj.*: strange; absurd.

guffaw (gu·fô′) *v.*: to burst out laughing. —**guffawing** *v.* used as *adj.*

guileless (gīl′lis) *adj.*: innocent or frank; without slyness.

gyration (jī·rā′shən) *n.*: circular movement; whirling.

habitual (hə·bich′ōō·əl) *adj.*: usual. —**habitually** *adv.* usually; by habit.

haggard (hag′ərd) *adj.*: wasted or worn in appearance.

hail *v.*: to greet.

haughty (hôt′ē) *adj.*: proud; disdainful of something or someone.

hedonism (hē′dən·iz′əm) *n.*: self-indulgent pursuit of pleasure. —**hedonistic** *adj.*

hierarchy (hī′ər·är′kē) *n.*: class system of social ranking.

hinder (hin′dər) *v.*: to thwart; impede.

humor (hyōō′mər) *v.*: to indulge.

hysteria (hi·ster′ē·ə) *n.*: uncontrolled excitement.

idealist (ī·dē′əl·ist) *n.*: one who believes in noble, though often impractical, goals; dreamer.

illumine (i·lōō′mən) *v.*: to light up.

immune (im·myōōn′) *adj.*: protected.

impart (im·pärt′) *v.*: to reveal.

imperative (im·per′ə·tiv) *adj.*: absolutely necessary; compulsory.

imperceptible (im′pər·sep′tə·bəl) *adj.*: not easily perceived.

impervious (im·pur′vē·əs) *adj.*: resistant; impenetrable.

impetuous (im·pech′ōō·əs) *adj.*: impulsive.

impious (im′pē·əs) *adj.*: irreverent.

implore (im·plôr′) *v.*: to plead; entreat. —**imploring** *v.* used as *adj.*

imprecation (im′pri·kā′shən) *n.*: curse.

improvident (im·präv′ə·dənt) *adj.*: careless; not providing for the future.

inanimate (in·an′ə·mit) *adj.*: lifeless.

inarticulate (in′är·tik′yōō·lit) *adj.*: not understandable.

incapacitate (in′kə·pas′ə·tāt′) *v.*: to disable. —**incapacitated** *v.* used as *adj.*

incendiary (in·sen′dē·er′ē) *adj.*: designed to cause fires.

incessant (in·ses′ənt) *adj.*: never stopping. —**incessantly** *adv.*

incised (in·sīzd′) *adj.*: deeply marked.

inconceivable (in′kən·sēv′ə·bəl) *adj.*: unimaginable; beyond understanding.

indiscreet (in′di·skrēt′) *adj.*: lack of care in speech or action.

indolent (in′də·lənt) *adj.*: lazy.

indubitable (in·dōō′bi·tə·bəl) *adj.*: that which cannot be doubted. —**indubitably** *adv.*

induce (in·dōōs′) *v.*: to persuade; force; cause.

indulge (in·dulj′) *v.*: to satisfy; please; humor.

inert (in·urt′) *adj.*: inactive; dull.

inevitable (in·ev′i·tə·bəl) *adj.*: not avoidable.

infallible (in·fal′ə·bəl) *adj.*: sure; never wrong.

infirm (in·furm′) *adj.*: physically weak.

ingenious (in·jēn'yəs) *adj.*: clever; original.

inherent (in·hir'ənt) *adj.*: inborn.

iniquity (i·nik'wi·tē) *n.*: wickedness.

inordinate (in·ôr'də·nit) *adj.*: excessive.

inscrutable (in·skrōōt'ə·bəl) *adj.*: mysterious.

insidious (in·sid'ē·əs) *adj.*: sly; sneaky.

insinuate (in·sin'yōō·āt') *v.*: to suggest. —**insinuatingly** *adv.*

insipid (in·sip'id) *adj.*: bland; without flavor.

insolent (in'sə·lənt) *adj.*: arrogant.

insurrection (in'sə·rek'shən) *n.*: rebellion; revolt.

intangible (in·tan'jə·bəl) *adj.*: difficult to define; vague.

integrate (in'tə·grāt') *v.*: to unify.

integrity (in·teg'rə·tē) *n.*: sound moral principles; honesty.

intent (in·tent') *adj.*: purposeful.

interject (in'tər·jekt') *v.*: to interrupt with; insert.

interloper (in'tər·lō'pər) *n.*: intruder; meddler.

interminable (in·tʉr'mi·nə·bəl) *adj.*: endless.

intermittent (in'tər·mit''nt) *adj.*: pausing occasionally.

interpose (in'tər·pōz') *v.*: to put forth in order to intervene.

intersperse (in'tər·spʉrs') *v.*: to place at intervals.

intimate (in'tə·māt') *v.*: to state indirectly; hint.

intricate (in'tri·kit) *adj.*: complicated.

intrigue (in'trēg) *n.*: scheming.

intuitive (in·tōō'i·tiv) *adj.*: known without conscious reasoning. —**intuitively** *adv.*

inviolate (in·vī'ə·lit) *adj.*: uncorrupted; safe.

irk (ʉrk) *v.*: to annoy; irritate. —**irksome** *adj.* —**irked** *v.* used as *adj.*

itinerant (ī·tin'ər·ənt) *adj.*: traveling.

jaunty (jônt'ē) *adj.*: fashionable; confident; carefree.

jilt *v.*: to reject (as a lover).

jocular (jäk'yōō·lər) *adj.*: joking; comical.

judicious (jōō·dish'əs) *adj.*: cautious; wise.

laborious (lə·bôr'ē·əs) *adj.*: difficult; involving much hard work.

labyrinth (lab'ə·rinth') *n.*: puzzling path.

lamentable (lam'ən·tə·bəl) *adj.*: regrettable; distressing.

languid (laŋ'gwid) *adj.*: weak, as from exhaustion.

legacy (leg'ə·sē) *n.*: inheritance.

list *v.*: to tilt.

loiter (loit'ər) *v.*: to spend time; hang around.

lore (lôr) *n.*: traditional knowledge or teachings.

lucidity (lōō·sid'i·tē) *n.*: clarity; rationality.

ludicrous (lōō'di·krəs) *adj.*: laughable; absurd.

lurk (lʉrk) *v.*: to hide unnoticed.

luxuriant (lug·zhoor'ē·ənt) *adj.*: rich; abundant.

machination (mak'ə·nā'shən) *n.*: plot; crafty scheme.

magnanimity (mag'nə·nim'ə·tē) *n.*: nobility of spirit.

malicious (mə·lish'əs) *adj.*: intentionally hurtful.

malign (mə·līn') *adj.*: harmful; evil.

malleable (mal'ē·ə·bəl) *adj.*: capable of being shaped.

malodorous (mal'ō'dər·əs) *adj.*: bad smelling.

manifest (man'ə·fest') *adj.*: plain; clear.

manifold (man'ə·fōld') *adj.*: many and different.

margin (mär'jən) *n.*: extra amount.

marshal (mär'shəl) *v.*: to lead; guide. —**marshaling** *v.* used as *adj.*

martial (mär'shəl) *adj.*: warlike.

meager (mē'gər) *adj.*: poor; inadequate.

meditative (med'ə·tāt'iv) *adj.*: deeply thoughtful; reflective.

medium (mē'dē·əm) *n.*: means of expressing art.

melancholy (mel'ən·käl'ē) *adj.*: sad; sorrowful.

mesmerize (mez'mər·īz') *v.*: to hypnotize. —**mesmerizing** *v.* used as *adj.*

mincing (mins'iŋ) *adj.*: affectedly dainty. —**mincingly** *adv.*

mirth (mʉrth) *n.*: joyfulness.

misgiving (mis·giv'iŋ) *n.*: doubt; worry.

misnomer (mis·nō'mər) *n.*: wrong term or name.

moderate (mäd'ər·it) *adj.*: gentle.

monologue (män'ə·lôg') *n.*: speech given by one person.

morbid (môr'bid) *adj.*: diseased; unhealthy.

morose (mə·rōs') *adj.*: gloomy.

mortal (môr'təl) *adj.*: life-threatening; causing death.

mortar (môrt'ər) *n.*: cannon used to fire explosive shells.

municipal (myōō·nis'ə·pəl) *adj.*: belonging to a city or town.

mutual (myōō'chōō·əl) *adj.*: shared.

myriad (mir'ē·əd) *adj.*: countless.

nape (nāp) *n.*: back of the neck.

nauseate (nô'zhē·āt') *v.*: to cause to feel sickness or discomfort in the stomach. —**nauseated** *v.* used as *adj.*

negotiate (ni·gō'she·āt') *v.*: to make a bargain; come to an agreement.

nether (neth'ər) *adj.*: lower.

nimbus (nim'bəs) *n.*: aura; halo.

nomadic (nō·mad'ik) *adj.*: wandering.

nominal (näm'ə·nəl) *adj.*: very small.

nostalgia (näs·tal'jə) *n.*: longing.

nuptial (nup'shəl) *adj.*: related to weddings or marriage.

oblique (ō·blēk') *adj.*: slanted. —**obliquely** *adv.*

obliterate (ə·blit'ər·āt') *v.*: to destroy.

obscure (əb·skyoor') *v.*: to conceal. —**obscurity** *n.*

obsequious (əb·sē'kwē·əs) *adj.*: overly obedient; submissive.

obsess (əb·ses') *v.*: to preoccupy; haunt. —**obsessed** *v.* used as *adj.*

obstinate (äb'stə·nət) *adj.*: stubborn.

obstruction (əb·struk'shən) *n.*: blockage; hindrance.

occult (ə·kult') *adj.*: hidden.

ominous (äm'ə·nəs) *adj.*: sinister; dangerous; foreboding.

omnipotent (äm·nip'ə·tənt) *adj.*: all-powerful.

omniscient (äm·nish'ənt) *adj.*: all-knowing.

opaque (ō·pāk') *adj.*: not transparent; not letting light pass through.

oppression (ə·presh'ən) *n.*: feeling of being tyrannized.

opulent (äp'yōō·lənt) *adj.*: abundant; plentiful.

oscillation (äs'ə·lā'shən) *n.*: regular back-and-forth movement.

ostentation (äs'tən·tā'shən) *n.*: conspicuous display. —**ostentatious** *adj.*

overcast (ō'vər·kast') *adj.*: cloudy; gloomy.

overture (ō'vər·chər) *n.*: approach; offer.

pallid (pal′id) *adj.*: pale.

palpable (pal′pə·bəl) *adj.*: obvious; perceivable.

pandemonium (pan′də·mō′nē·əm) *n.*: wild confusion.

pauper (pô′pər) *n.*: extremely poor person.

pendulum (pen′dyo͞o·ləm) *n.*: freely swinging weight suspended from a fixed point to regulate a clock's movement.

penitent (pen′i·tənt) *adj.*: sorry for doing wrong.

pensive (pen′siv) *adj.*: thinking deeply or seriously. —**pensively** *adv.*

perennial (pər·en′ē·əl) *adj.*: recurring yearly.

perilous (per′ə·ləs) *adj.*: dangerous.

permeate (pur′mē·āt′) *v.*: to spread through and affect every part of.

perpetual (pər·pech′o͞o·əl) *adj.*: constant; unchanging.

perpetuity (pur′pə·to͞o′ə·tē) *n.*: eternity.

perseverance (pur′sə·vir′əns) *n.*: persistence.

persistent (pər·sist′ənt) *adj.*: continuing.

pertinent (pur′tə·nənt) *adj.*: to the point; applying to the situation.

perturbation (pur′tər·bā′shən) *n.*: feeling of alarm or agitation.

pervade (pər·vād′) *v.*: to spread throughout.

pervert (pər·vurt′) *v.*: to misdirect; corrupt.

petulance (pech′ə·ləns) *n.*: irritability; impatience.

philanthropies (fə·lan′thrə·pēz) *n. pl.*: charitable gifts.

pious (pī′əs) *adj.*: devoted to one's religion.

pivotal (piv′ə·təl) *adj.*: central; acting as a point around which other things turn.

placid (plas′id) *adj.*: calm; quiet.

plague (plāg) *v.*: to annoy.

plaintive (plān′tiv) *adj.*: expressing sadness.

plausibility (plô′zə·bil′i·tē) *n.*: believability.

plunder (plun′dər) *n.*: goods seized, especially during wartime.

poignant (poin′yənt) *adj.*: emotionally moving.

populous (päp′yo͞o·ləs) *adj.*: crowded with people.

portend (pôr·tend′) *v.*: to signify.

posterity (päs·ter′ə·tē) *n.*: generations to come.

potency (pōt′'n·sē) *n.*: strength; power.

precedence (pres′ə·dəns) *n.*: order.

précis (prā·sē′) *n.*: summary.

predominate (prē·däm′ə·nāt′) *v.*: to have influence over. —**predominating** *v.* used as *adj.*

preeminent (prē·em′ə·nənt) *adj.*: above all else. —**preeminently** *adv.*

preposterous (prē·päs′tər·əs) *adj.*: ridiculous.

prestigious (pres·tij′əs) *adj.*: impressive; having an excellent reputation.

pretense (prē·tens′) *n.*: false claim.

procure (prō·kyoor′) *v.*: to gain; obtain; acquire.

prodigal (präd′i·gəl) *adj.*: extremely abundant.

prodigious (prō·dij′əs) *adj.*: of great size and power.

prodigy (präd′ə·jē) *n.*: extremely gifted person.

profane (prō·fān′) *adj.*: irreverent.

profound (prō·found′) *adj.*: deep. —**profoundly** *adv.*

profundity (prō·fun′də·tē) *n.*: intellectual depth.

profuse (prō·fyo͞os′) *adj.*: abundant. —**profusely** *adv.*: in great quantities.

propagate (präp′ə·gāt′) *v.*: to transmit; spread.

proportionate (prō·pôr′shən·it) *adj.*: having a correct relationship between parts; balanced.

prostrate (präs′trāt′) *adj.*: lying flat on the ground.

protrude (prō·tro͞od′) *v.*: to stick out. —**protruding** *v.* used as *adj.*

provisional (prō·vizh′ə·nəl) *adj.*: temporary; for the time being.

provoke (prō·vōk′) *v.*: to enrage; anger.

prudent (pro͞od′'nt) *adj.*: well thought out; cautious.

pulverize (pul′vər·īz′) *v.*: to crush; destroy.

radiation (rā′dē·ā′shən) *n.*: pattern; arrangement.

rakish (rāk′ish) *adj.*: dashing; jaunty. —**rakishly** *adv.*

rancor (raŋ′kər) *n.*: anger.

raucous (rô′kəs) *adj.*: loud; boisterous.

ravage (rav′ij) *n.*: act of violent destruction.

ravenous (rav′ə·nəs) *adj.*: very eager; hungry.

realm (relm) *n.*: kingdom.

recede (ri·sēd′) *v.*: to become more distant and indistinct.

recoil (ri·koil′) *v.*: to shrink away; draw back.

recollect (rek′ə·lekt′) *v.*: to remember.

reconcile (rek′ən·sīl′) *v.*: to make peace.

rectitude (rek′tə·to͞od′) *n.*: correctness.

reflective (ri·flek′tiv) *adj.*: thoughtful; contemplative.

reiterate (rē·it′ə·rāt′) *v.*: to repeat.

rejoinder (ri·join′dər) *n.*: answer.

relent (ri·lent′) *v.*: to soften; to diminish in intensity.

relinquish (ri·liŋ′kwish) *v.*: to give up.

rend *v.*: to rip apart violently. —**rending** *v.* used as *n.*

render (ren′dər) *v.*: to make.

rendezvous (rän′dā·vo͞o′) *n.*: meeting place. —*adj.*: meeting.

renounce (ri·nouns′) *v.*: to give up.

reprobate (rep′rə·bāt′) *n.*: person without any sense of duty or decency.

reprove (ri·pro͞ov′) *v.*: to reprimand.

reserve (ri·zurv′) *n.*: self-restraint.

resignation (rez′ig·nā′shən) *n.*: acquiescence; reluctant acceptance.

resolute (rez′ə·lo͞ot′) *adj.*: determined.

resolve (ri·zälv′) *v.*: to make a decision; determine.

retort (ri·tôrt′) *n.*: quick answer.

retraction (ri·trak′shən) *n.*: withdrawal.

revel (rev′əl) *v.*: to take pleasure.

revelation (rev′ə·lā′shən) *n.*: disclosure; something made known.

reverential (rev′ə·ren′shəl) *adj.*: deeply respectful.

reverie (rev′ər·ē) *n.*: daydream; fantasy; thought; musing.

rue (ro͞o) *v.*: to regret.

ruse (ro͞oz) *n.*: trick; deception.

sacrilege (sak′rə·lij) *n.*: violation of something sacred.

sagacious (sə·gā′shəs) *adj.*: wise; keenly perceptive.

sappy (sap′ē) *adj.*: foolish.

sarcastic (sär·kas′tik) *adj.*: scornful; mocking.

sate (sāt) *v.*: to satisfy.

saturated (sach'ə·rāt'id) *adj.*: completely soaked.

saucy (sô'sē) *adj.*: sassy; impertinent. —**saucily** *adv.*

savory (sā'vər·ē) *adj.*: appetizing; agreeable.

scour (skour) *v.*: to roam about searching.

scrupulous (skrōō'pyə·ləs) *adj.*: careful; painstaking.

scrutinize (skrōōt'n·īz') *v.*: to carefully observe. —**scrutinizing** *v.* used as *adj.*

sedate (si·dāt') *adj.*: calm and composed.

semblance (sem'bləns) *n.*: outward appearance; mere empty show; pretense.

seminary (sem'ə·ner'ē) *n.*: school for training ministers.

sensor (sen'sər) *n.*: detecting device.

sentinel (sen'ti·nəl) *n.*: guard; sentry.

serene (sə·rēn') *adj.*: calm. —**serenely** *adv.*

sibling (sib'liŋ) *n.*: brother or sister.

similitude (sə·mil'ə·tōōd') *n.*: likeness.

simultaneous (sī'məl·tā'nē·əs) *adj.*: at the same time. —**simultaneously** *adv.*

singular (siŋ'gyə·lər) *adj.*: remarkable.

slough (sluf) *n.*: outer layer of snake's skin, shed periodically.

sobriety (sə·brī'ə·tē) *n.*: state or quality of being sober.

sojourn (sō'jurn) *n.*: short stay.

solace (säl'is) *v.*: to comfort.

solemn (säl'əm) *adj.*: serious. —**solemnity** *n.*

solidity (sə·lid'ə·tē) *n.*: firmness; solidness.

somber (säm'bər) *adj.*: gloomy; dark.

specious (spē'shəs) *adj.*: seemingly sound, but not really so.

spurn (spurn) *v.*: to reject with contempt.

squeamish (skwēm'ish) *adj.*: easily offended.

stolid (stäl'id) *adj.*: showing no emotion. —**stolidity** *n.*

striking (strī'kiŋ) *adj.*: impressive; attractive.

stupor (stōō'pər) *n.*: state of mental dullness; loss of the senses.

sublime (sə·blīm') *adj.*: awe-inspiring.

subsequent (sub'si·kwənt) *adj.*: following.

subside (səb·sīd') *v.*: to settle down.

subsist (səb·sist') *v.*: to stay alive. —**subsisting** *v.* used as *adj.*

successive (sək·ses'iv) *adj.*: consecutive.

sultry (sul'trē) *adj.*: humid and still.

sundry (sun'drē) *adj.*: some.

superficial (sōō'pər·fish'əl) *adj.*: obvious; shallow.

superfluous (sə·pur'flōō·əs) *adj.*: unnecessary.

supplication (sup'lə·kā'shən) *n.*: earnest plea.

suppress (sə·pres') *v.*: to restrain; hold back.

surmise (sər·mīz') *n.*: guess.

sustain (sə·stān') *v.*: to prolong. —**sustained** *v.* used as *adj.*

symmetrical (si·me'tri·kəl) *adj.*: equally balanced.

taboo (tə·bōō') *n.*: something that is forbidden.

tacit (tas'it) *adj.*: implied but not expressed openly.

tactful (takt'fəl) *adj.*: skilled in saying the right thing.

tactile (tak'təl) *adj.*: able to be perceived by touch.

taut (tôt) *adj.*: tense; rigid.

tedious (tē'dē·əs) *adj.*: tiring; dreary.

temple (tem'pəl) *n.*: side of the forehead, just above and in front of each ear.

temporal (tem'pə·rəl) *adj.*: worldly.

tenuous (ten'yōō·əs) *adj.*: slight; insubstantial; not firm.

tepid (tep'id) *adj.*: lukewarm.

theologian (thē'ə·lō'jən) *n.*: scholar of religious doctrine.

torpor (tôr'pər) *n.*: inactive period.

tout (tout) *v.*: to praise highly.

traditional (trə·dish'ə·nel) *adj.*: established; customary.

tranquil (traŋ'kwil) *adj.*: calm; quiet.

transcendent (tran·sen'dənt) *adj.*: excelling; surpassing.

transcribe (tran·skrīb') *v.*: to write down.

transient (tran'shənt) *adj.*: temporary; passing.

translucent (trans·lōō'sənt) *adj.*: allowing light to pass through.

tread (tred) *n.*: stepping.

trepidation (trep'ə·dā'shən) *n.*: anxious uncertainty.

tumultuous (tōō·mul'chōō·əs) *adj.*: stormy; turbulent.

turbulence (tur'byōō·ləns) *n.*: wild disorder.

tyranny (tir'ə·nē) *n.*: oppression.

ubiquitous (yōō·bik'wə·təs) *adj.*: everywhere at the same time.

ultimatum (ul'tə·māt'əm) *n.*: last offer; final proposition.

undulation (un'dyōō·lā'shən) *n.*: wavelike motion.

unobtrusive (un·əb·trōō'siv) *adj.*: inconspicuous; quiet. —**unobtrusively** *adv.*

unseemly (un·sēm'lē) *adj.*: improper.

upbraid (up·brād') *v.*: to criticize severely.

valance (val'əns) *n.*: short decorative drapery.

valor (val'ər) *n.*: great courage.

vanity (van'ə·tē) *n.*: excessive pride.

vehement (vē'ə·mənt) *adj.*: emphatic. —**vehemently** *adv.*

venerable (ven'ər·ə·bəl) *adj.*: respected; esteemed for age or distinguished character.

vengeful (venj'fəl) *adj.*: intent on revenge.

venture (ven'chər) *v.*: to dare or risk going.

veritable (ver'i·tə·bəl) *adj.*: genuine; true.

vibrant (vī'brənt) *adj.*: full of energy.

vigilant (vij'ə·lənt) *adj.* used as *n.*: someone who is watchful.

vigor (vig'ər) *n.*: intense strength; vitality.

vindicate (vin'də·kāt') *v.*: to prove correct. —**vindicated** *v.* used as *adj.*

virulent (vir'yōō·lənt) *adj.*: full of hate; venomous.

vista (vis'tə) *n.*: view.

vital (vīt'l) *adj.*: filled with life.

vivacious (vī·vā'shəs) *adj.*: cheerful; lively.

void (void) *adj.*: empty.

volition (vō·lish'ən) *n.*: will.

volley (väl'ē) *n.*: firing of many shots at once.

vouch (vouch) *v.*: to guarantee.

vulnerability (vul'nər·ə·bil'ə·tē) *n.*: state of being open to attack.

wariness (wer'ē·nis) *n.*: caution; carefulness.

wearisome (wir'i·səm) *adj.*: fatiguing; exhausting.

wistfulness (wist'fəl·nis) *n.*: vague longing.

wither (with'ər) *v.*: to dry up; weaken.

wrought (rôt) *v.*: created; made.

ACKNOWLEDGMENTS

For permission to reprint copyrighted material, grateful acknowledgment is made to the following sources:

Agencia Literaria Carmen Balcells, S.A.: "Plenos Poderes" by Pablo Neruda. Copyright © 1958, 1959, 1961, 1962, 1964, 1967 by Pablo Neruda.

The American Scholar: From "An American Childhood in the Dominican Republic" by Julia Alvarez from *The American Scholar*, vol. 56, no. I, Winter 1987. Copyright © 1986 by Julia Alvarez.

Andrews McMeel Universal: "Coyote Finishes His Work" from *Giving Birth to Thunder, Sleeping with His Daughter* by Barry Holstun Lopez. Copyright © 1977 by Barry Holstun Lopez. All rights reserved.

Arte Público Press: From *Silent Dancing* by Judith Ortiz Cofer. Copyright © 1990 by Judith Ortiz Cofer. Published by Arte Público Press—University of Houston, 1990. "The Latin Deli: An Ars Poetica" by Judith Ortiz Cofer from *The Americas Review*, vol. 19, no. I. Copyright © 1991 by Judith Ortiz Cofer. Published by Arte Público Press—University of Houston, 1991. "Now and Then, America" from *Borders* by Pat Mora. Copyright © 1986 by Pat Mora. Published by Arte Público Press—University of Houston, 1986.

Ken Barnes: Definition of "facemail," compiled and edited by Ken Barnes from "The Microsoft Lexicon" from *Jeeem's Cinepad*. Available at http://www.cinepad.com/mslex. htm.

Elizabeth Barnett, Literary Executor: "Recuerdo" from *Collected Poems* by Edna St. Vincent Millay. Copyright © 1922, 1928, 1935, 1950 by Edna St. Vincent Millay and Norma Millay Ellis. Published by HarperCollins.

Beacon Press: "Autobiographical Notes" from *Notes of a Native Son* by James Baldwin. Copyright © 1955 and renewed © 1983 by James Baldwin.

Belles Lettres: Quote by Rita Dove from "Judith Pierce Rosenberg Interviews Our New Poet Laureate" from *Belles Lettres*, Winter 1993/94.

Susan Bergholz Literary Services, New York: "Daughter of Invention" from *How the Garcia Girls Lost Their Accents* by Julia Alvarez. Copyright © 1991 by Julia Alvarez. Published by Plume, a division of Penguin USA Inc. Originally published in hardcover by Algonquin Books of Chapel Hill. All rights reserved. "Straw into Gold" by Sandra Cisneros. Copyright © 1987 by Sandra Cisneros. First published in *The Texas Observer*, September 1987. All rights reserved.

Brandt & Brandt Literary Agents: From "Qualified Homage to Thoreau" by Wallace Stegner from *Heaven Is Under Our Feet*, edited by Don Henley and Dave Marsh. Copyright © 1991 by The Isis Fund.

Gwendolyn Brooks: "Exhaust the little moment," "The Explorer," and "of De Witt Williams on his way to Lincoln Cemetery" from *Blacks* by Gwendolyn Brooks. Copyright © 1991 by Gwendolyn Brooks. Published by Third World Press, Chicago, 60619, 1991.

Grace Cavalieri: From "Rita Dove: An Interview" by Grace Cavalieri from *American Poetry Review*, March/April 1995. Copyright © 1995 by Grace Cavalieri.

Joan Chatfield-Taylor: From "Cosmo Talks to Amy Tan" by Joan Chatfield-Taylor from *Cosmopolitan*, November 1989, pages 178–180. Copyright © 1989 by Joan Chatfield-Taylor.

Lucha Corpi and Catherine Rodríguez-Nieto: "Emily Dickinson" from *Palabras de Mediodía/Noon Words* by Lucha Corpi, translated by Catherine Rodríguez-Nieto. Copyright © 1980 by Lucha Corpi; translation copyright © 1980 by Catherine Rodríguez-Nieto. Published by El Fuego de Aztlán Publications, Berkeley, CA, 1980.

Curbstone Press: "Who Understands Me but Me" from *What's Happening* by Jimmy Santiago Baca. Copyright © 1982 by Jimmy Santiago Baca. Distributed by Consortium.

Delacorte Press/Seymour Lawrence, a division of Bantam Doubleday Dell Publishing Group, Inc.: From *Sextet: T. S. Eliot, Truman Capote and Others* by John Malcolm Brinnin. Copyright © 1981 by John Malcolm Brinnin.

Doubleday, a division of Random House, Inc.: From *The Power of Myth* by Joseph Campbell with Bill Moyers. Copyright © 1988 by Apostrophe S Productions, Inc., and Alfred van der Marck Editions. From "Drowning with Others" by James Dickey from *Self-Interviews*, recorded and edited by Barbara and James Reiss. Published by Doubleday, New York, 1970. From *The Theatre of the Absurd* by Martin Esslin. Copyright © 1961 by Martin Esslin. From "Preface" from *The Open Boat: Poems from Asian America,* edited and with an introduction by Garrett Hongo. Copyright © 1993 by Garrett Hongo. "Elegy for Jane," "Night Journey," and "Open House" from *The Collected Poems of Theodore Roethke* by Theodore Roethke. Copyright 1940, 1941, 1950 by Theodore Roethke.

Rita Dove: "The Satisfaction Coal Company" from *Selected Poems* by Rita Dove. Copyright © 1993 by Rita Dove. Quote by Rita Dove from *Washington Post*, April 17, 1987. Copyright © 1987 by Rita Dove.

Dutton Signet, a division of Penguin Books USA Inc.: "Borges and Myself" from *The Aleph and Other Stories* by Jorge Luis Borges, translated by Norman Thomas di Giovanni. Translation copyright © 1968, 1969, 1970 by Emece Editores, S.A., and Norman Thomas di Giovanni.

Faber and Faber Ltd.: From *The Criterion*, vol. IX, by T. S. Eliot. Copyright © 1967 by Faber and Faber Ltd.

Far Corner Books: "Trying to Name What Doesn't Change" from *Words Under the Words: Selected Poems* by Naomi Shihab Nye. Copyright © 1995 by Naomi Shihab Nye. Published by Far Corner Books, Portland, OR.

Farrar, Straus & Giroux, Inc.: "The Fish" (and excerpts) from *The Complete Poems 1927–1979* by Elizabeth Bishop. Copyright © 1979, 1983 by Alice Helen Methfessel. From "Introduction" and "The Death of the Ball Turret Gunner" from *The Complete Poems* by Randall Jarrell. Copyright © 1969 by Mrs. Randall Jarrell. "For the Union Dead" (and excerpts) from *For the Union Dead* by Robert Lowell. Copyright © 1959 by Robert Lowell; copyright renewed © 1987 by Caroline Lowell, Harriet Lowell, and Sheridan Lowell. From "Memories of West Street and Lepke" from *Life Studies* by Robert Lowell. Copyright © 1959 by Robert Lowell; copyright renewed © 1987 by Caroline Lowell, Sheridan Lowell, and Harriet Lowell. "The Magic Barrel" from *The Magic Barrel* by Bernard Malamud. Copyright © 1950, 1958 and renewed © 1977, 1986 by Bernard Malamud. From "The Murdered Albatross" from *Passions and Impressions* by Pablo Neruda, translated by Margaret Sayers Peden. Translation copyright © 1983 by Farrar, Straus, & Giroux, Inc. From "The Fiction Writer and His Country," from "Some Aspects of the Grotesque in Southern Fiction," and from "Writing Short Stories" from *Mystery and Manners* by Flannery O'Connor, edited by Sally and Robert Fitzgerald. Copyright © 1969 by the Estate of Mary Flannery O'Connor. From *The Habit of Being: Letters of Flannery O'Connor* by Flannery O'Connor, edited by Sally Fitzgerald. Copyright © 1979 by Regina O'Connor. From *The Nobel Lecture* by Isaac Bashevis Singer. Copyright © 1978 by The Nobel Foundation. Yiddish text copyright © 1978 by Isaac Bashevis Singer. "Sea Canes" from *Sea Grapes* by Derek Walcott. Copyright © 1976 by Derek Walcott.

Gerard Flynn: From *Sor Juana Inés de la Cruz* by Gerard Flynn. Copyright © 1971 by Twayne Publishers, Inc. Published in *Twayne's World Authors Series*, edited by John P. Dyson.

Fondo de Cultura Económica: "World, in hounding me, what do you gain?" by Sor Juana Inés de la Cruz from *Obras completas*, edited by Alfonso Méndez Plancarte. Copyright 1952 and © 1955 by Fondo de Cultura Económica.

The Estate of Robert Frost: Quote by Robert Frost from "Robert Frost Relieves His Mind," interviewed by Rose C. Feld, from *The New York Times Book Review*, October 21, 1923. Copyright 1923 by Robert Frost.

Fulcrum Publishing: "The Sky Tree" by

Joseph Bruchac from *Keepers of Life: Discovering Plants Through Native American Stories and Earth Activities for Children* by Michael J. Caduto and Joseph Bruchac. Copyright © 1994 by Fulcrum Publishing.

Gale Research, Inc.: Quote by Judith Ortiz Cofer from *Contemporary Authors, New Revision Series,* vol. 32, edited by James G. Lesniak. Copyright © 1991 by Gale Research, Inc.

Tess Gallagher: "Everything Stuck to Him" (also published as "Distance") from *Fires: Essays, Poems, Stories* by Raymond Carver. Copyright © 1975 by Raymond Carver; copyright © 1989 by Vintage Books; copyright renewed © 1991 by Tess Gallagher.

Paul Gitlin, Administrator of the Estate of Thomas Wolfe: "His Father's Earth" from *The Web and the Rock* by Thomas Wolfe. Copyright 1937, 1938, 1939 by Maxwell Perkins as Executor; copyright renewed © 1967 by Paul Gitlin, C.T.A., Administrator of the Estate of Thomas Wolfe.

Donald J. Greiner: Quote by Donald J. Greiner from *Dictionary of Literary Biography, Volume 143: American Novelists Since World War II,* Third Series, edited by James R. Giles and Wanda H. Giles. Published by Gale Research, Inc., 1994.

GRM Associates, Inc., Agents for the Estate of Ida M. Cullen: "Incident" and "Tableau" (and excerpts) from *Color* by Countee Cullen. Copyright © 1925 by Harper & Brothers; copyright renewed © 1953 by Ida M. Cullen.

Grosset & Dunlap, Inc., a division of Penguin Putnam Inc.: "Knoxville: Summer 1915" from *A Death in the Family* by James Agee. Copyright © 1957 by The James Agee Trust; copyright © renewed 1985 by Mia Agee.

Grove/Atlantic, Inc.: "Full Powers" from *A New Decade (Poems: 1958–1967)* by Pablo Neruda, translated by Alastair Reid. English translation copyright © 1969 by Alastair Reid. "The Journey" from *Dream Work* by Mary Oliver. Copyright © 1986 by Mary Oliver.

Harcourt Brace & Company: "The Life You Save May Be Your Own" from *A Good Man Is Hard to Find and Other Stories* by Flannery O'Connor. Copyright 1953 by Flannery O'Connor; copyright renewed © 1981 by Regina O'Connor. "The Jilting of Granny Weatherall" and excerpt from *Flowering Judas and Other Stories* by Katherine Anne Porter. Copyright 1930 and renewed © 1958 by Katherine Anne Porter. From "In Search of Our Mothers' Gardens" from *In Search of Our Mothers' Gardens: Womanist Prose* by Alice Walker. Copyright © 1974 by Alice Walker. "Women" (as it appears in "In Search of Our Mothers' Gardens") from *Revolutionary Petunias & Other Poems* by Alice Walker. Copyright © 1970 by Alice Walker. "A Worn Path" from *A Curtain of Green and Other Stories* by Eudora Welty. Copyright 1941 and renewed © 1969 by Eudora Welty. "The Beautiful Changes" from *The Beautiful Changes and Other Poems* by Richard Wilbur. Copyright

1947 and renewed © 1975 by Richard Wilbur. "Boy at the Window" from *Things of This World* by Richard Wilbur. Copyright 1952; renewed copyright © 1980 by Richard Wilbur.

Joy Harjo: From "Three Generations of Native American Women's Birth Experience" by Joy Harjo from *Ms.,* vol. II, no. 1, July/August 1991. Copyright © 1991 by Joy Harjo.

HarperCollins Publishers, Inc.: From *Dust Tracks on a Road* by Zora Neale Hurston. Copyright 1942 by Zora Neale Hurston; copyright renewed © 1970 by John C. Hurston. "The Handsomest Drowned Man in the World" from *Leaf Storm and Other Stories* by Gabriel García Márquez. Copyright © 1971 by Gabriel García Márquez. "Mirror" from *Crossing the Water* by Sylvia Plath. Copyright © 1963 by Ted Hughes. Originally appeared in *The New Yorker.* From *Black Boy* by Richard Wright. Copyright 1937, 1942, 1944, 1945 by Richard Wright; copyright renewed © 1973 by Ellen Wright.

Harvard University Press: "World, in hounding me, what do you gain?" #28 from *A Sor Juana Anthology,* translated by Alan S. Trueblood. Copyright © 1988 by the President and Fellows of Harvard College. Published by Harvard University Press, Cambridge, Mass. From *I: Six Nonlectures* by e. e. cummings. Copyright © 1953 by e. e. cummings. Published by Harvard University Press, Cambridge, Mass. From Chapter 10, "The Battle with Mr. Covey" and excerpts from *The Narrative of the Life of Frederick Douglass: An American Slave, Written by Himself,* edited by Benjamin Quarles. Copyright © 1960 by the President and Fellows of Harvard College. Published by Harvard University Press, Cambridge, Mass. From *Sor Juana: Or, The Traps of Faith* by Octavio Paz. Copyright © 1988 by the President and Fellows of Harvard College. Published by Harvard University Press, Cambridge, Mass.

Harvard University Press and the Trustees of Amherst College: "1624: Apparently with no surprise," "712: Because I could not stop for Death," "47: Heart! We will forget him!," "465: I heard a Fly buzz—when I died," "214: I taste a liquor never brewed," "1129: Tell all the Truth but tell it slant—," and from "288: I'm Nobody! Who are you?" from *The Poems of Emily Dickinson,* edited by Thomas H. Johnson. Copyright © 1951, 1955, 1979, 1983 by the President and Fellows of Harvard College. Published by The Belknap Press of Harvard University Press, Cambridge, Mass.

Heritage: "Imagination" by Shelby Pearl from *Heritage,* vol. 31, Spring 1991. Published by James Madison High School, Vienna, VA. From "An Interview with Rita Dove" by Moira Haney and Catherine Nicholas from *Heritage,* vol. 34, Spring 1994. Published by James Madison High School, Vienna, VA.

Hill and Wang, a division of Farrar, Straus & Giroux, Inc.: From "When the Negro Was in Vogue" from *The Big Sea* by Langston

Hughes. Copyright © 1940 by Langston Hughes; copyright renewed © 1968 by Arna Bontemps and George Houston Bass. From *Night* by Elie Wiesel, translated by Stella Rodway. Copyright © 1960 by MacGibbon & Kee; copyright renewed © 1988 by The Collins Publishing Group.

Holocaust Museum & Library: Quote by Martin Niemöller from *Their Brothers' Keepers* by Philip Friedman. Copyright © by Holocaust Museum & Library.

Henry Holt and Company, Inc.: From *Interviews with Robert Frost,* edited by Edward Connery Lathem. Copyright © 1966 by Henry Holt and Company, Inc. "Design," "Neither Out Far Nor in Deep," "Nothing Gold Can Stay," and "Once by the Pacific" from *The Poetry of Robert Frost,* edited by Edward Connery Lathem. Copyright 1923, 1936, © 1956 by Robert Frost; copyright © 1964 by Lesley Frost Ballantine; copyright 1928, © 1969 by Henry Holt and Company, Inc.; copyright © 1997 by Edward Connery Lathem.

John Hopkins University Press: Quote by Tim O'Brien from "Two Interviews: Talks with Tim O'Brien and Robert Stone" by Eric James Schroeder from *Modern Fiction Studies,* 30 Spring 1984. Copyright © 1984 by Eric James Schroeder.

Houghton Mifflin Company: From *Let Us Now Praise Famous Men* by James Agee and Walker Evans. Copyright 1939, 1940 by James Agee; copyright 1941 by James Agee and Walker Evans; copyright renewed © 1969 by Mia Fritsch Agee and Walker Evans. All rights reserved. "Ars Poetica" from *Collected Poems 1917–1982,* by Archibald MacLeish. Copyright © 1985 by The Estate of Archibald MacLeish. All rights reserved. "The Bells" from *To Bedlam and Part Way Back* by Anne Sexton. Copyright © 1960 by Anne Sexton; copyright renewed © 1988 by Linda G. Sexton. All rights reserved. "Young" from *All My Pretty Ones* by Anne Sexton. Copyright © 1962 by Anne Sexton; copyright renewed © 1990 by Linda G. Sexton. All rights reserved.

International Creative Management, Inc.: From "Why I Wrote 'The Crucible'" by Arthur Miller from *The New Yorker,* October 21 & 28, 1996. Copyright © 1996 by Arthur Miller. Quote by Arthur Miller from *Critical Essays on Arthur Miller,* edited by James J. Martine. Copyright © 1960 by Arthur Miller. From "On James Baldwin" by Toni Morrison from *The New York Times Book Review,* December 20, 1987. Copyright © 1987 by Toni Morrison.

Jesse Jackson, Jr., on behalf of Jesse Jackson: From Reverend Jesse Jackson's speech to the Democratic Convention in 1988 from *Vital Speeches of the Day,* vol. LIV, no. 21, August 15, 1988. Copyright © 1988 by Jesse Jackson.

Estate of Kirkland C. Jones: Quotes by Kirkland C. Jones from *Dictionary of Literary Biography®, Volume One Hundred Twenty:*

American Poets Since World War II, Third Series, edited by R. S. Gwynn. Published by Gale Research, Inc., 1992.

The Heirs to the Estate of Martin Luther King, Jr., c/o Writers House, Inc., as agent for the proprietor: From "Letter from Birmingham City Jail" by Martin Luther King, Jr., from *A Testament of Hope,* edited by J. M. Washington. Copyright © 1963 by Martin Luther King, Jr., copyright © 1991 by Coretta Scott King. From "I Have a Dream" by Martin Luther King, Jr. Copyright © 1963 by Martin Luther King, Jr.; copyright renewed © 1991 by Coretta Scott King.

Alfred A. Knopf, Inc.: "A Noiseless Flash" from *Hiroshima* by John Hersey. Copyright 1946 and renewed © 1974 by John Hersey. "Kubota" from *Volcano* by Garrett Hongo. Copyright © 1995 by Garrett Hongo. "Dream Deferred," "Harlem," "I, Too," "The Weary Blues," and from "Let America Be America Again" from *Collected Poems* by Langston Hughes. Copyright © 1994 by the Estate of Langston Hughes. "The Girl Who Wouldn't Talk" from *The Woman Warrior* by Maxine Hong Kingston. Copyright © 1975, 1976 by Maxine Hong Kingston. "Autobiographia Literaria" from *The Collected Poems of Frank O'Hara,* edited by Donald Allen. Copyright © 1971 by Maureen Granville-Smith, Administratrix of the Estate of Frank O'Hara. "Mushrooms" from *The Colossus and Other Poems* by Sylvia Plath. Copyright © 1960 by Sylvia Plath. "Anecdote of the Jar," "Disillusionment of Ten O'Clock," and from "Of Modern Poetry" from *Collected Poems* by Wallace Stevens. Copyright 1923 and renewed 1951, 1954 by Wallace Stevens. "Of Modern Poetry" from *The Palm at The End of the Mind* by Wallace Stevens, edited by Holly Stevens. Copyright © 1967, 1969, 1971 by Holly Stevens. Ten aphorisms from *Opus Posthumous* by Wallace Stevens. Copyright © 1957 by Elsie Stevens and Holly Stevens. "Son" from *Problems and Other Stories* by John Updike. Copyright © 1979 by John Updike.

Yusef Komunyakaa: Quote by Yusef Komunyakaa from "A Man of His Words" by Jeffrey Walker from *Los Angeles Times,* April 13, 1994. "Monsoon Season" from *Toys in a Field* by Yusef Komunyakaa. Copyright © 1986 by Yusef Komunyakaa.

Martin Levin: From "The Dogwood Tree: A Boyhood" from *Five Boyhoods* by John Updike, edited by Martin Levin. Copyright © 1962 and renewed © 1990 by Martin Levin.

Little, Brown and Company: From *Blue Highways* by William Least Heat-Moon. Copyright © 1982 by William Least Heat-Moon.

Liveright Publishing Corporation: "#225: somewhere i have never travelled, gladly beyond" and "what if a much of a which of a wind" (and excerpts) from *Complete Poems: 1904–1962* by E. E. Cummings, edited by George J. Firmage. Copyright 1931, 1944, © 1959, 1972, 1991 by the Trustees for the E. E. Cummings Trust; copyright © 1979 by George James Firmage. From Introduction to *New Poems* (from *Collected Poems: 1904–1962*) by E. E. Cummings, edited by George J. Firmage. Copyright 1938, © 1966, 1991 by the Trustees for the E. E. Cummings Trust.

Macmillan Reference USA: From *Webster's New World™ College Dictionary,* Third Edition. Copyright © 1988, 1991, 1994, 1996, 1997 by Simon & Schuster, Inc.

Ellen C. Masters: From *Across Spoon River* by Edgar Lee Masters. Copyright 1936 by Edgar Lee Masters; copyright renewed © 1964 by Ellen Coyne Masters. Originally published by Farrar & Rinehart.

J. D. McClatchy: Quotes by Robert Lowell and James Dickey from *Anne Sexton: The Artist and Her Critics,* edited by J. D. McClatchy. Copyright © 1978 by J. D. McClatchy.

Merlyn's Pen, Inc.: "The Mirror Girl— stares back at me—" from "Walt and Emily Revisited" by Brigid Spackman from *Merlyn's Pen,* February/March 1993. Copyright © 1993 by Merlyn's Pen, Inc. First appeared in Merlyn's Pen: *The National Magazines of Student Writing.*

Merriam-Webster Inc.: Definition of "proud" from *Webster's Third New International Dictionary,* edited by Philip Babcock Grove, Ph.D. Copyright © 1993 by Merriam-Webster Inc.

William Morris Agency, Inc., on behalf of Edward Albee: From *Conversations with Edward Albee,* edited by Philip C. Kolin. Copyright © 1988 by Edward Albee.

New Directions Publishing Corporation: "Fall" from *Black Mesa Poems* by Jimmy Santiago Baca. Copyright © 1989 by Jimmy Santiago Baca. From "Early Success" from *The Crack-up* by F. Scott Fitzgerald. Copyright © 1945 by New Directions Publishing Corporation. "A Pact," "In a Station of the Metro," and "The River-Merchant's Wife: A Letter" from *Personae: The Collected Poems of Ezra Pound.* Copyright © 1926 by Ezra Pound. From "A Few Dont's by an Imagiste" from *Literary Essays of Ezra Pound.* Copyright © by Faber and Faber Ltd. From letter to Harriet Monroe from *Selected Letters of Ezra Pound.* Copyright © 1950 by Ezra Pound. "Pine Tree Tops" from *Turtle Island* by Gary Snyder. Copyright © 1974 by Gary Snyder. From *The Autobiography of William Carlos Williams.* Copyright © 1951 by William Carlos Williams. "The Great Figure," "The Red Wheelbarrow," and "Spring and All, section I" from *Collected Poems: 1909–1939,* vol. I, by William Carlos Williams. Copyright © 1938 by New Directions Publishing Corporation.

The New York Review of Books: Quote by Thomas R. Edwards from *The New York Review of Books,* November 24, 1983. Copyright © 1983 by NYREV, Inc. From "Fitzgerald Revisited" by Jay McInerney from *The New York Review of Books,* August 15, 1991. Copyright © 1991 by NYREV, Inc.

The New York Times Company: Quote by Carl Sandburg from *The New York Times,* Feb. 13, 1959. Copyright © 1959 by The New York Times Company. Quote by Sugar Ray Leonard from "Durán, Leonard Fit" from *The New York Times,* June 17, 1980. Copyright © 1980 by The New York Times Company. From "Malamud's Dark Fable" by Alan Lelchuk from *The New York Times Book Review,* August 29, 1982. Copyright © 1982 by The New York Times Company. From "Black and Well-to-Do" by Andrea Lee from *The New York Times,* 1984. Copyright © 1984 by the New York Times Company. From "Mississippi Honors a 'Native Son' Who Fled" by Edwin McDowell from *The New York Times,* November 23, 1985. Copyright © 1985 by The New York Times Company. From "Pictures of Malamud" by Philip Roth from *The New York Times Book Review,* April 20, 1986. Copyright © 1986 by The New York Times Company. From "The Promiscuous Cool of Postmodernism" by Denis Donoghue from *The New York Times Book Review,* June 22, 1986. Copyright © 1986 by The New York Times Company. Quote by Raymond Carver from "Grace Has Come into My Life" by Stewart Kellerman from *The New York Times Book Review,* May 15, 1988. Copyright © 1988 by The New York Times Company. Quote by Roberto Márquez from *The New York Times Book Review,* September 24, 1989. Copyright © 1989 by The New York Times Company. "A Poet's Safe Haven in Amherst" by Anne Bernays from *The New York Times Magazine, Part 2: The Sophisticated Traveler,* October 1, 1989. Copyright © 1989 by The New York Times Company. Quote by Tim O'Brien from "A Storyteller for the War That Won't End" by D.J.R. Bruckner from *The New York Times,* April 3, 1990. Copyright © 1990 by The New York Times Company. From a review of *How the Garcia Girls Lost Their Accents* by Julia Alvarez from *The New York Times Book Review,* October 6, 1991. Copyright © 1991 by The New York Times Company. Quote by Toni Morrison from "Toni Morrison Is '93 Winner of Nobel Prize in Literature" by William Grimes from *The New York Times,* October 8, 1993. Copyright © 1993 by The New York Times Company. "An American Story" by Anthony Lewis from *The New York Times,* November 26, 1993. Copyright © 1993 by The New York Times Company. "Poetry Emotion" by Anna Quindlen from *The New York Times,* April 16, 1994. Copyright © 1994 by The New York Times Company. Quote by Yusef Komunyakaa from "A Poet's Values: It's the Words over the Man" by Bruce Weber from *The New York Times,* May 2, 1994. Copyright © 1994 by The New York Times Company. From "The New Measure of Man" by Vaclav Havel from *The New York Times,* July 8, 1994. Copyright © 1994 by The New York Times Company. From Janet Maslin's review of *The Crucible* from *The New York Times,* November

27, 1996. Copyright © 1996 by The New York Times Company.

The New Yorker: From "James Thurber" from *E. B. White: Writings from "The New Yorker," 1927–1976.* Copyright © 1961, 1989 by E. B. White. Published by HarperCollins. Originally appeared in *The New Yorker.*

The Nobel Foundation: Acceptance speeches by William Faulkner, Ernest Hemingway, and John Steinbeck from *Nobel Lectures in Literature: 1901–1967,* edited by Horst Frenz. Copyright 1949, 1954, © 1962 by The Nobel Foundation.

Northern Illinois University Press: From *James Russell Lowell's The Biglow Papers: A Critical Edition* by Thomas Wortham. Copyright © 1977 by Northern Illinois University Press.

W. W. Norton & Company, Inc.: "Emily Dickinson" from *PM/AM: New and Selected Poems* by Linda Pastan. Copyright © 1971 by Linda Pastan. From "Still Just Writing" by Anne Tyler from *The Writer on Her Work,* vol. I, edited by Janet Sternburg. Copyright © 1980 by Janet Sternburg.

Harold Ober Associates Incorporated: From letter to George Freitag (August 27, 1938) from *Letters of Sherwood Anderson,* edited by H. M. Jones and Walter Rideout. Copyright 1953 by Eleanor Anderson. From the James Weldon Johnson Collection: Quotations from "Draft Ideas," December 3, 1964, by Langston Hughes, as they appear in *The Life of Langston Hughes, Volume II: 1941–1967—I Dream a World.* Copyright © 1986 by the Estate of Langston Hughes.

Tim O'Brien, c/o Janklow & Nesbit Associates: Slightly adapted from "Speaking of Courage" by Tim O'Brien from *The Massachusetts Review,* Summer 1976. Copyright © 1976 by Tim O'Brien.

Simon J. Ortiz: "Speaking" by Simon J. Ortiz. Copyright © 1989 by Simon J. Ortiz.

Pantheon Books, a division of Random House, Inc.: "House Taken Over" from *End of the Game and Other Stories* by Julio Cortázar, translated by Paul Blackburn. Copyright © 1967 by Random House, Inc.

The Paris Review: From "The Art of Fiction LXXXIII Julio Cortázar" from *The Paris Review,* vol. 26, no. 93, Fall 1984. Copyright © 1984 by The Paris Review, Inc.

Perspective: Quote by Andrew V. Ettin from *Perspective,* Spring 1967. Copyright © 1967 by Perspective.

Gerald W. Purcell Associates: "My Guilt" from *Just Give Me a Cool Drink of Water 'fore I Diiie* by Maya Angelou. Copyright © 1969 by Hirt Music, Inc.

G. P. Putnam's Sons: From "Rules of the Game" from *The Joy Luck Club* by Amy Tan. Copyright © 1989 by Amy Tan.

Random House, Inc.: "The Unknown Citizen" from *W. H. Auden: Collected Poems.* Copyright © 1940 and copyright renewed © 1968 by W. H. Auden. From *Death Comes for the Archbishop* by Willa Cather. Copyright 1927 by Willa Cather; copyright renewed ©

1955 by the Executors of the Estate of Willa Cather. "A Rose for Emily" (and excerpts) from *A Rose for Emily* by William Faulkner. Copyright © 1930 and renewed © 1958 by William Faulkner. "New African" from *Sarah Phillips* by Andrea Lee. Copyright © 1984 by Andrea Lee. From Appendix from *Hugging the Shore* by John Updike. Copyright © 1983 by John Updike. "Is Phoenix Jackson's Grandson Really Dead?" from *The Eye of the Story* by Eudora Welty. Copyright © 1978 by Eudora Welty.

The Saturday Evening Post Society: From "I Saw Lee Surrender" by Seth M. Flint from *The Saturday Evening Post,* vol. 248, no. 5, July/August 1976. Copyright © 1976 The Saturday Evening Post.

Saturday Review: From "James Baldwin on the Sixties: Acts and Revelations" by Benjamin DeMott from *Saturday Review,* May 27, 1972, pp. 63–64. Copyright © 1972 by SR Publications, Ltd.

Scribner, a division of Simon & Schuster, Inc.: From *The Night Country* by Loren Eiseley. Copyright © 1971 by Loren Eiseley. From letter to Scottie Fitzgerald from *A Life in Letters,* edited by Matthew J. Bruccoli. Copyright © 1994 by The Trustees Under Agreement dated July 3, 1975. From "Absolution" from *The Short Stories of F. Scott Fitzgerald,* edited by Matthew J. Bruccoli. Copyright 1924 by American Mercury, Inc.; copyright renewed 1952 by Frances Scott Fitzgerald Lanahan. "Soldier's Home" from *The Short Stories of Ernest Hemingway.* Copyright 1925 by Charles Scribner's Sons; copyright renewed 1953 by Ernest Hemingway.

Shades Valley Resource Learning Center: "The Sea" by Elizabeth Enloe from *Counterpane,* vol. 18, 1993. Published by Shades Valley Resource Learning Center, Birmingham, AL.

Karl Shapiro, c/o Wieser & Wieser Inc., New York, NY: "Auto Wreck" from *Collected Poems 1940–1978* by Karl Shapiro. Copyright © 1978, 1987 by Karl Shapiro.

Sheaffer-O'Neill Collection, Connecticut College Library: Quote from letter by Eugene O'Neill as it appears in *Selected Letters of Eugene O'Neill,* edited by Travis Bogard and Jackson R. Bryer.

Simon & Schuster, Inc.: From *Catch-22* by Joseph Heller. Copyright © 1955, 1961 by Joseph Heller; copyright renewed © 1989 by Joseph Heller. "Poetry" (and excerpts) from *The Collected Poems of Marianne Moore.* Copyright 1935 by Marianne Moore; copyright renewed © 1963 by Marianne Moore and T. S. Eliot.

Estate of William Stafford: "At the Bomb Testing Site" from *West of Your City* by William Stafford. Copyright © 1960 by William Stafford. Published by Talisman Press.

St. James Press, an imprint of Gale Research, Inc.: Quote by Garrett Hongo and from "Rita Dove" by Julie Miller from *Contem-*

porary Poets, Fifth Edition, edited by Tracy Chevalier. Copyright © 1991 by St. James Press.

The Texas Folklore Society: Song lyrics from "Follow the Drinking Gourd" by H. B. Parks from *Follow de Drinkin' Gou'd,* Publications of the Texas Folklore Society, no. VII, edited by J. Frank Dobie. Copyright 1928 by the Texas Folklore Society.

Texas Rangers Baseball Club: Logo for Texas Rangers baseball team.

Thunder's Mouth Press: From "Anchorage," from "Motion," and "Remember" from *She Had Some Horses* by Joy Harjo. Copyright © 1983 by Joy Harjo.

Rosemary A. Thurber and the Barbara Hogenson Agency, Inc.: "A Biographical Sketch of James Thurber" from *Collecting Himself.* Copyright © 1989 by Rosemary A. Thurber. Originally published by HarperCollins Publishers. "The Secret Life of Walter Mitty" from *My World—and Welcome to It* by James Thurber. Copyright © 1942 by James Thurber; copyright renewed © 1970 by Helen Thurber and Rosemary Thurber. Originally published by Harcourt Brace & Co.

Time Inc.: From "Book of Changes" by Paul Gray from *Time,* December 6, 1976. Copyright © 1976 by Time Inc.

Times Mirror Magazines: From "Winning the Cold War" by Paul G. Gill, Jr., from *Outdoor Life,* vol. 191, February 1993. Copyright © 1993 by Times Mirror Magazines.

Emily Toth: From "Intimate and Untidy Stories" from *Kate Chopin* by Emily Toth. Copyright © 1990 by Emily Toth.

The University of New Mexico Press: From "Introduction" and from *The Way to Rainy Mountain* by N. Scott Momaday. Copyright © 1969 by The University of New Mexico Press. First published in *The Reporter,* January 26, 1967.

University of North Carolina Press: From *The Invasion of America* by Francis Jennings. Copyright © 1975 by the University of North Carolina Press.

University of Oklahoma Press: "For More Than a Hundred Winters Our Nation Was a Powerful, Happy and United People" by Black Hawk and "I Will Fight No More Forever" by Chief Joseph from *Indian Oratory: Famous Speeches by Noted Indian Chieftains,* compiled by W. C. Vanderwerth. Copyright © 1971 by the University of Oklahoma Press. Quote by Robert Frost from *Robert Frost: Life and Talks—Walking* by Louis Mertins. Copyright © 1965 by the University of Oklahoma Press.

University of Texas Press: "The Feather Pillow" from *The Decapitated Chicken and Other Stories* by Horacio Quiroga, translated by Margaret Sayers Peden. Copyright © 1976 by the University of Texas Press.

University Press of New England: "The Lifeguard" from *Poems 1957–1967* by James Dickey. Copyright © 1958, 1959, 1960, 1961, 1962, 1963, 1964, 1965, 1966, 1967 by James Dickey. "What For" from *Yellow Light* by Gar-*

rett Kaoru Hongo. Copyright © 1982 by Garrett Kaoru Hongo. Published by Wesleyan University Press. "We Never Knew" from *Dien Cai Dau* by Yusef Komunyakaa. Copyright © 1988 by Yusef Komunyakaa. "Changes; or, Reveries at a Window Overlooking a Country Road, with Two Women Talking Blues in the Kitchen" from *Neon Vernacular* by Yusef Komunyakaa. Copyright © 1993 by Yusef Komunyakaa. Published by Wesleyan University Press. "A Blessing" from *The Branch Will Not Break* by James Wright. Copyright © 1963 by James Wright. Published by Wesleyan University Press.

Pindar VanArman: "What About Glory" by Pindar VanArman from *Phoenix: The Gonzaga Fine Arts Magazine*, vol. XVI, no. 1, May 1992. Published by Gonzaga College High School, Washington, D.C.

Viking Penguin, a division of Penguin Putnam Inc.: From *Along This Way* by James Weldon Johnson. Copyright 1933 by James Weldon Johnson; copyright renewed © 1961 by Grace Nail Johnson. "Go Down Death—A Funeral Sermon" and "Preface" from *God's Trombones* by James Weldon Johnson. Copyright 1927 by The Viking Press, Inc.; copyright renewed © 1955 by Grace Nail Johnson. *The Crucible* by Arthur Miller. Copyright 1952, 1953, 1954, and renewed © 1980, 1981, 1982 by Arthur Miller. From "The State of the Theater" from *The Theater Essays of Arthur Miller* by Arthur Miller, edited by Robert A. Martin. Copyright © 1960 by Harper's Magazine. From "Raymond Carver" by Mona Simpson and Lewis Buzbee from *Writers at Work, Seventh Series*, edited by George A. Plimpton. Copyright © 1986 by The Paris Review. "The Leader of the People" from *The Red Pony* by John Steinbeck. Copyright 1938, and renewed © 1966 by John Steinbeck.

Villard Books, a division of Random House, Inc.: From *All I Really Need to Know I Learned in Kindergarten* by Robert L. Fulghum. Copyright © 1986, 1988 by Robert L. Fulghum.

Walden Woods Project, an Activity of The Isis Fund: From "Preface" by Don Henley from *Heaven Is Under Our Feet*, edited by Don Henley and Dave Marsh. Copyright © 1991 by The Isis Fund.

Washington Post Book World Service/ Washington Post Writers Group: From William McPherson's review of Maxine Hong Kingston's *The Woman Warrior* from *Washington Post Book World*, October 10, 1976. Copyright © 1976 by Washington Post Book World Service/Washington Post Writers Group. From Jonathan Yardley's review of Raymond Carver's *Cathedral* from *Washington Post Book World*, September 20, 1983. Copyright © 1983 by Washington Post Book World Service/Washington Post Writers

Group. From "Mah-Jongg and The Ladies of the Club" by Susan Dooley from *The Washington Post Book World*, March 5, 1989, p. 7. Copyright © 1989 by Washington Post Book World Service/Washington Post Writers Group.

Washington Post Writers Group: Quote by Juan Williams from *Washington Post*, December 2, 1987. Copyright © 1987 by The Washington Post.

Rhoda Weyr Agency, New York: "The One Who Was Different" from *The Lost World* by Randall Jarrell. Copyright © 1965 by Randall Jarrell. Reprinted in *The Complete Poems of Randall Jarrell*. Published by Farrar, Straus & Giroux, Inc., 1989.

Doretha Williams: "Africa" by Doretha Williams from *Calliope 1993*. Copyright © 1993 by Doretha Williams. Published by Topeka West High School, Topeka, KS.

The H. W. Wilson Company: From "Gabriel García Márquez" from *Spanish American Authors: The Twentieth Century* by Angel Flores. Copyright © 1992 by Angel Flores.

Donald Windham: From *Tennessee Williams' Letters to Donald Windham 1940–1965*, edited by Donald Windham. Copyright © 1976, 1977, 1980 by Donald Windham. Published in paperback by The University of Georgia Press, 1996.

The Wylie Agency, Inc.: "Game" from *Unspeakable Practices, Unnatural Acts* by Donald Barthelme. Copyright © 1968 by Donald Barthelme. From "Not-Knowing" by Donald Barthelme. Copyright © 1985 by Donald Barthelme.

Yale Collection of American Literature, Beinecke Rare Book and Manuscript Library, Yale University: From the James Weldon Johnson Collection: Quotations from "Draft Ideas," December 3, 1964, by Langston Hughes, as they appear in *The Life of Langston Hughes, Volume II: 1941–1967—I Dream a World*.

Yale University Press: From *Selected Letters of Eugene O'Neill*, edited by Travis Bogard and Jackson R. Bryer. Copyright © 1988 by Yale University.

David Young: From Introduction from *Magical Realist Fiction*, edited by David Young and Keith Hollaman. Copyright © 1984 by David Young.

SOURCES CITED

From "Revolutionary Charter" from *Inventing America: Jefferson's Declaration of Independence* by Garry Wills. Published by Doubleday, a division of Bantam Doubleday Dell Publishing Group, Inc., New York, 1978.

Quote by Diarmuid Russell from *Author and Agent: Eudora Welty and Diarmuid Russell* by Michael Kreyling. Published by Farrar, Straus & Giroux, Inc., New York, 1991.

From "Karl Shapiro" from *Contemporary Authors*, vol. 6, edited by Adele Sarkissian. Published by Gale Research Company, New York, 1988.

From "Karl Shapiro" from *American Poets, 1880–1945, Second Series*, edited by Peter Quartermain. Published by Gale Research Company, New York, 1986.

From "Washington Irving: 1783–1859" by William L. Hedges from *Major Writers of America*. Published by Harcourt Brace & Company, Orlando, FL, 1962.

From "The Rookers" from *Shiloh and Other Stories* by Bobbie Ann Mason. Published by HarperCollins Publishers, Inc., New York, 1982.

Quote by William Faulkner from "Preface" from *The Enigma of Thomas Wolfe*, edited by Richard Walser. Published by Harvard University Press, Cambridge, MA, 1953.

From "Interview with Anne Sexton" by Patricia Marx from *The Hudson Review*, vol. XVIII, no. 4, Winter 1965–66. Published by The Hudson Review, Inc., 1966.

From acceptance speech for the American Book Award for fiction, April 27, 1982, from *Hugging the Shore* by John Updike. Published by Alfred A. Knopf, Inc., New York, 1983.

Quote by Eugene O'Neill from *O'Neill: Son and Artist* by Louis Sheaffer. Published by Little, Brown and Company, Boston, MA, 1973.

Quote by Ezra Pound from *Remembering Poets* by Donald Hall. Published by New Directions Publishing Corporation, New York, 1977.

From *Selected Prose 1909–1965* by Ezra Pound, edited by William Cookson. Published by New Directions Publishing Corporation, New York, 1973.

From "The Phantom Dawn" from *The Spirit of Romance* by Ezra Pound. Published by New Directions Publishing Corporation, New York, 1968.

From "10. One True Sentence" from *Ernest Hemingway: A Life Story* by Carlos Baker. Published by Scribner, a division of Simon & Schuster, Inc., New York, 1969.

From "Notes Toward a Biography" by Lois Ames from *Tri-Quarterly*, no. 7, Fall 1966. Published by Tri-Quarterly Books, Northwestern University.

From "Some Self-Analysis" from *On the Poet and His Craft: Selected Prose of Theodore Roethke*, edited by Ralph J. Mills, Jr. Published by University of Washington Press, 1965.

From "Empty Bamboo" by Leslie Li from *American Identities: Contemporary Multicultural Voices*, edited by Robert Pack and Jay Parini. Published by University Press of New England, 1994.

PICTURE CREDITS

Page: 2 (left), Michael S. Yamashita/Woodfin Camp & Associates; 2–3, Kathleen Campbell/Tony Stone Images; 5 (center), Kirchoff/Wohlberg; 6–13 & 16–18 (background), Kirchoff/Wohlberg; 9 (top left), John Carter Brown Library/Brown University, Providence, Rhode Island, (right), Courtesy American Antiquarian Society; 14, Tom Bross/Stock Boston; 14–15 (background), Library of Congress; 15 (left), William Johnson/Stock Boston, (right), Richard Pasley/Stock Boston; 19 (background), Marion Stirrup/Alaska Stock Images; 20–21, Theo Westenberger; 27 (background), John Coletti/Stock Boston; 28–33 (background), Kirchoff/Wohlberg; 35, Haffenreffer Museum of Anthropology/Brown University, Providence, Rhode Island. Photo by Cathy Carver; 42–43 (background), Fred M. Dole—f/Stop Pictures; 48–49, Gene Ahrens/Bruce Coleman, Inc.; 52–53, Wendell Mentzen/Bruce Coleman, Inc; 54, Haffenreffer Museum of Anthropology/Brown University, Providence, Rhode Island; 56–57, 65 (background), Marc & Evelyne Bernheim/Woodfin Camp & Associates; 67, SuperStock; 68–70 (background), Reproduced by kind permission of the vicar and church wardens of St. Botolph's Church, Boston, England; 72–73 (background), 73, FPG International; 90–91 (top background), Telegraph Colour Library/FPG International; 96, B. Timmons/The Image Bank; 99 (upper left), Bruce Mathews/Image Quest, (lower right), Jim Madden/New England Stock Photo; 100–101 (center), John Henley/The Stock Market, (top background), Gene Moore/Phototake, (bottom background), Peter Cole/New England Stock Photo; 106–107 (background), 108 (background), 109 (inset left), 110 (inset top), 112 (background), North Wind Picture Archives; 109, 110, Joe Viesti/Viesti Associates; 120–121, Charlie Ott/Photo Researchers; 135, F. Cruz/SuperStock; 138–150 (background), Kirchoff/Wohlberg; 146, Charles Scribner's Sons, 1925; 151, Robert Maier/Animals, Animals; 154 (top), Neil Meyerhoff/Panoramic Images; 154 (bottom), 164, 165, Ronald F. Thomas/Bruce Coleman, Inc; 155, Courtesy Millport Conservancy, Lititz, Pennsylvania; 160, Robin Jane Solvang/Bruce Coleman, Inc.; 162, Gary Braasch/Tony Stone Images; 167, Photofest; 169–172, Kirchoff/Wohlberg; 173, Hitchcock-Chase Collection of Grass Drawings/Hunt Institute for Botanical Documentation/Carnegie Mellon University, Pittsburgh, Pennsylvania; 173, 182–185 (background), Kirchoff/Wohlberg; 187 (center), Courtesy *The Atlantic Monthly,* (bottom),

Massachusetts Historical Society, Massachusetts; 188, Scott Camazine/Photo Researchers; 189, The Library of the New York Botanical Garden (Bronx, New York); 190, 192, Culver Pictures; 203, F. Cruz/SuperStock; 206–214 (background), Branson Reynolds/Index Stock; 207 (left), Massachusetts Historical Society, Boston, (right), Cooper-Hewitt, National Design Museum, Smithsonian Institution/Art Resource, NY; 208 (right), 208–209 (bottom), 210–211 (bottom), North Wind Picture Archives; 212–213, Kirchoff/Wohlberg; 215, 218–221 (background), William D. Adams/Picture Perfect USA, Inc.; 215 (inset), David Julian/Phototake; 227, Kevin Alexander/Index Stock; 233, 234, 237, 243 © PhotoDisc, Inc. 1998; 249, 251, 254, Robert Essel/The Stock Market; 261, Kirchoff/Wohlberg; 279, Illustration by R. Hoffman; 282, 284–285, 286, Illustrations by Arvis Stewart for "The Raven"; 287, Reprinted by permission of Warner Books, Inc., New York, New York, USA. From *The Illustrated Edgar Allan Poe* by Wilfred Satty and Edgar Allan Poe. Copyright © 1976. All rights reserved; 291, 293–295 (background), Charles A. Mauzy/Tony Stone Images; 298–299, 304, 307, Tom Hopkins Studio; 314–315, Marion Stirrup/Alaska Stock Images; 321, Lon Lauber/Alaska Stock Images; 326, J. Coolidge/The Image Bank; 339, F. Cruz/SuperStock; 340–341, 359, Julie Habel/Woodfin Camp & Associates; 342–346 (background), Maria Stenzel/National Geographic Society Image Collection; 345 (top left), Courtesy of the Trustees of Amherst College/The Emily Dickinson Homestead; 345, Corbis-Bettmann; 345 (right), Courtesy of the Amherst History Museum at the Strong House, Amherst, Massachusetts; 347, University of Virginia Library, Charlottesville, Courtesy NGS; 351, Karen Kasmauski/Woodfin Camp & Associates; 353, From the David T. Vernon Collection of Native American Indian Art, Colter Bay Indian Arts Museum, Grand Teton National Park, Wyoming. Photo by J. Oldenkamp; 360–361 (background), W. Cody/Westlight; 367, AP/Wide World Photos; 368–370 (background), Eastcott & Momatiuk/Woodfin Camp & Associates; 371, Eastcott & Momatiuk/Woodfin Camp & Associates; 377 (background), Stephen P. Parker/Photo Researchers; 380, 384–385, Timothy Eagen/Woodfin Camp & Associates; 380 (bottom), Kirchoff/Wohlberg; 391, Brown Brothers; 405, F. Cruz/SuperStock; 424–425 (background), Lyle Leduc/Index Stock Photography; 425 (inset), 426 (background), Wallace Garrison/Index Stock Photography; 435–443 (background), Kirchoff/Wohlberg; 440 (bottom), Corbis-Bettmann; 448, University of Washington Libraries, Special Collections Division, Seattle, Washington; 449, Gene Ahrens/Bruce

Coleman, Inc.; 452, 454, 460, 461, Corbis-Bettmann; 467 (left), © Erika Klass; 468, Daniel Nichols/Gamma Liaison; 470, Allen Russell/Index Stock; 473, Brett Baunton/Tony Stone Images; 476–483 (background), Kirchoff/Wohlberg; 496–497, Don Pitcher/Alaska Stock Images; 500 (inset), Michael DeYoung/Alaska Stock Images, 500 (background), Alaska Stock Images; 503, Johnny Johnson/Alaska Stock Images; 503 (inset), 507, 508, Jeff Schultz/Alaska Stock Images; 509, Alaska Stock Images; 521, F. Cruz/SuperStock; 524–525 (top), Brown Brothers; 524–525 (bottom), UPI/Corbis-Bettmann; 526 (right), 527 (top right), Corbis-Bettmann, (top left), Archive Photos, (bottom left and bottom center), FPG International, (bottom right), Jeffrey D. Smith/Woodfin Camp & Associates; 528–529 (background), Kirchoff/Wohlberg; 532, Culver Pictures; 533, Courtesy Giraudon/Art Resource, New York; 534, Culver Pictures; 537, Ludovic Molin/Photonica; 539, Archive Photos; 540–541 (background), Kazuya Shimizu/Photonica; 540, Charles Shotwell/Panoramic Images; 545 (bottom), Color Box/FPG International; 559 (background), Royce Blair/The Stock Solution; 563 (inset), Rick Schafer/The Stock Market; 564, 565, © PhotoDisc, Inc. 1998; 566, Barry O'Rourke/The Stock Market; 567–568 (background), Ron Thomas/FPG International; 569–573, Don & Liysa King/The Image Bank; 583, Randy O'Rourke/The Stock Market; 584–587 (background), Kirchoff/Wohlberg; 586, 587, 594, 598–599, 600, 602, Liberty Collection/The Image Bank; 595, 606–607 (background), 616–617 (background), Culver Pictures; 616, Photofest; 624–625 (background), Kirchoff/Wohlberg; 634–635 (background), Marco Polo/Phototake; 643, Susan Stang/Photo Researchers; 652, Kirchoff/Wohlberg; 656–657 (background), Phototone; 688, Robert Brenner/PhotoEdit; 691, Nicholas Devore III/Photographers Aspen; 693, Frederic Stein/FPG International; 694 and 695, © PhotoDisc, Inc. 1998; 703–704 (top and bottom), 714–717, 722, 727, 729–731, Kirchoff/Wohlberg; 704 (left), FPG International; 732, R. A. Clevenger/Westlight; 733, Bonnot/The Image Bank; 734–735 (background), Phototone; 749, Stephen Marks/The Image Bank; 750, The Beinecke Rare Book and Manuscript Library, Yale University, New Haven, Connecticut. Estate of Carl Van Vechten, Joseph Solomon, Executor; 760, National Portrait Gallery, Smithsonian Institution/Art Resource, NY; 763 (top), Javier Romero Design/The Image Bank; 763 (bottom), Ayako Parks/Tony Stone Images; 770–772 (background), Picture Perfect, USA; 781, Index Stock; 788, Bridgeman Art Library, London/New York; 789 (background), Larry West/FPG International; 794, Telegraph Colour Library/FPG International; 798, Erich

INDEX OF SKILLS

LITERARY TERMS

The boldface page numbers indicate an extensive treatment of the topic.

INDEX OF SKILLS 1275

RESEARCH AND STUDY

CROSSING THE CURRICULUM

CRITICAL COMMENTS

CREATIVE PROBLEM SOLVING

INDEX OF ART

FINE ART

INDEX OF AUTHORS AND TITLES

ILLUSTRATIONS

CARTOONS AND CARTOON STRIPS

MAPS